S0-AFI-846

# McGRAW-HILL ENCYCLOPEDIA OF ELECTRONICS AND COMPUTERS

# McGRAW-HILL ENCYCLOPEDIA OF

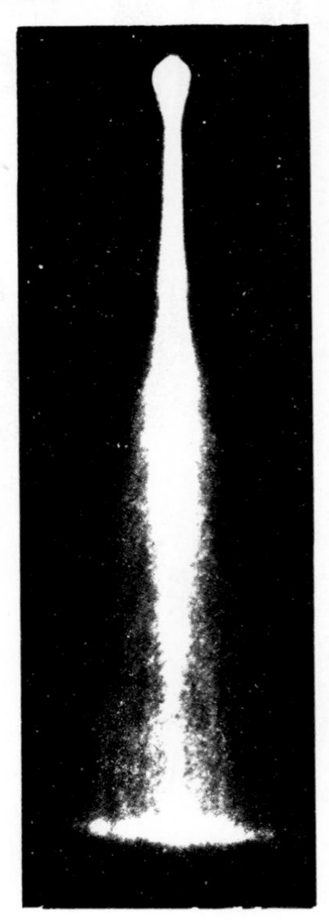

# ELECTRONICS AND COMPUTERS

## Second Edition

**Sybil P. Parker**
EDITOR IN CHIEF

**McGraw-Hill Book Company**

**New York St. Louis San Francisco**
Auckland Bogotá Caracas Colorado Springs
Hamburg Lisbon London Madrid Mexico Milan
Montreal New Delhi Oklahoma City Panama Paris
San Juan São Paulo Singapore Sydney Tokyo Toronto

2 3 4 5 6 7 8 9 0 DOW/DOW 8 9 5 4 3 2 1 0 9 8

ISBN 0-07-045499-X

**Library of Congress Cataloging-in-Publication Data**

McGraw-Hill encyclopedia of electronics and computers / Sybil P. Parker, editor in chief.—2nd ed.
p. cm.
Includes bibliographies and index.
ISBN 0-07-045499-X
1. Electronics—Dictionaries. 2. Computers—Dictionaries.
I. Parker, Sybil P.
TK7804.M43 1988
621.381—dc19 87-37592
CIP

# Editorial Staff

**Sybil P. Parker,** Editor in Chief

**Arthur Biderman,** Senior Editor
**Jonathan Weil,** Editor
**Edward J. Fox,** Art Director
**Joe Faulk,** Editing Manager
**Frank Kotowski, Jr.,** Editing Supervisor
**Patricia W. Albers,** Editorial Administrator

# Consultants

**Robert D. Briskman**
Senior Vice President
Engineering and Operations
Geostar Corporation
Washington, D.C.

**Dr. John K. Galt**
Senior Adviser
Aerospace Corporation
Los Angeles, California

**Dr. David Turnbull**
Gordon McKay Professor of Applied Physics
Division of Applied Sciences
Harvard University

# Contributors

## A

**Adler, Dr. David.** *Department of Electrical Engineering, Massachusetts Institute of Technology.*

**Agerwala, Dr. Tilak.** *Manager, Architecture and System Design, IBM T. J. Watson Research Center, Yorktown Heights, New York.*

**Allan, Roger.** *Senior Editor, "Electronic Design Magazine," Rochelle Park, New Jersey.*

**Alley, Prof. Charles L.** *Department of Electrical Engineering, University of Utah.*

**Altamuro, Vincent M.** *President, VMA, Inc., Toms River, New Jersey.*

**Angelakos, Dr. Diogenes J.** *Department of Electrical Engineering, University of California, Berkeley.*

**Apker, Dr. L.** *General Electric Research Laboratory, Schenectady, New York.*

**Applegate, Charles E.** *Retired; formerly, Consulting Engineer, Weston, Massachusetts.*

**Arbuckle, Earl F., III.** *Engineering Supervisor, WPIX, Inc., New York, New York.*

**Arimura, Kunitaka.** *Consultant in Electronics, Washington, D.C.*

## B

**Bagley, Dr. Brian G.** *Bell Laboratories, Murray Hill, New Jersey.*

**Bailey, Prof. A. E.** *Department of Electrical Engineering, University of Southampton, England.*

**Balabanian, Prof. Norman.** *Department of Electrical and Computer Engineering, Syracuse University.*

**Barbacci, Prof. Mario R.** *Associate Director, Project Engineering, Software Engineering Institute, Carnegie-Mellon University.*

**Barna, Dr. Gabriel G.** *Central Research Laboratories, Texas Instruments Incorporated, Dallas.*

**Bauer, Prof. Charles L.** *Department of Metallurgical Engineering and Materials Science, Carnegie-Mellon University.*

**Beams, Dr. Jesse W.** *Deceased; formerly, Department of Physics, University of Virginia.*

**Belrose, Dr. John S.** *Department of Communications, Communication Research Centre, Ottawa, Ontario, Canada.*

**Berger, Dr. France B.** *Kearfott Division, Singer Company, Little Falls, New Jersey.*

**Bergh, Dr. A. A.** *Bell Telephone Laboratories, Murray Hill, New Jersey.*

**Berglund, C. Neil.** *Manager of Technology Department, Intel Corporation, Aloha, Oregon.*

**Bernstein, Dr. Robert I.** *Professor of Electrical Engineering and Associate Director, Electronics Research Laboratories, Columbia University.*

**Bewley, Dr. Loyal V.** *Retired; formerly, Dean, College of Engineering, Lehigh University.*

**Birkhoff, Prof. Garrett.** *Department of Mathematics, Harvard University.*

**Black, Dr. Harold S.** *Communications Consultant, Summit, New Jersey.*

**Bleiweis, John J.** *COMSAT Labs, Clarksburg, Maryland.*

**Boast, Dr. Warren B.** *Anson Marston Distinguished Professor Emeritus of Electrical Engineering, Iowa State University.*

**Booth, Dr. Grayce M.** *Manager, Business Communication, Honeywell Bull, Inc., Phoenix, Arizona.*

**Borello, Sebastian R.** *Central Research Laboratories, Texas Instruments Inc., Dallas.*

**Boyd, Victor P.** *Deputy Director, International Electronic Message Systems, U.S. Postal Service, Washington, D.C.*

**Brewer, S. Theodore.** *Head, Undersea and Lightwave Engineering Department, Bell Laboratories, Holmdel, New Jersey.*

**Brown, Dr. Glenn H.** *Professor of Chemistry and Director of the Liquid Crystal Institute, Kent State University.*

**Bube, Richard H.** *Professor of Electrical Engineering, Department of Materials Sciences, Stanford University.*

**Burghard, Ron.** *Intel Corporation, Aloha, Oregon.*

**Bursky, David.** *Associate Managing Editor, "Electronic Design," Sunnyvale, California.*

## C

**Callaway, Prof. Joseph.** *Department of Physics and Astronomy, Louisiana State University.*

**Camras, Marvin.** *Senior Scientific Advisor, IIT Research Institute, Chicago, Illinois.*

**Carroll, Dr. John M.** *Associate Professor of Computer Science, University of Western Ontario, London, Canada.*

**Casasent, Prof. David.** *Department of Electrical and Computer Engineering, Carnegie-Mellon University.*

**Casey, Dr. H. C., Jr.,** *Department of Electrical Engineering, Duke University*

**Celler, Dr. George K.** *AT&T Laboratories, Murray Hill, New Jersey.*

**Chaffin, Dr. R. J.** *Solid State Device Physics, Sandia National Laboratories, Albuquerque, New Mexico.*

**Chapman, Dr. Richard A.** *Central Research Laboratory, Texas Instruments, Inc., Dallas.*

**Chaudhari, Praveen.** *Thomas J. Watson Research Center, IBM, Yorktown Heights, New York.*

**Chin, Dr. Gilbert Y.** *Bell Telephone Laboratories, Murray Hill, New Jersey.*

**Christophorou, Dr. L. G.** *Head, Atomic, Molecular and High Voltage Physics Group, Oak Ridge National Laboratory, Oak Ridge, Tennessee.*

**Clark, Richard F.** *Division of Physics, National Research Council of Canada, Ottawa, Ontario.*

**Clarke, John H.** *Engineering Design Consultant, Air Conditioning and Power, Films-Packaging Division, Union Carbide Corporation, Chicago, Illinois.*

**Collier, R. J.** *Bell Telephone Laboratories, Murray Hill, New Jersey.*

**Collins, Dr. Dean R.** *Director, CCD Technology Laboratory, Central Research Laboratories, Texas Instruments Inc., Dallas.*

**Collins, Dr. J. H.** *Professor for Electrical Engineering and Head of Department of Electrical Engineering, University of Edinburgh.*

**Compton, Robert D.** *Electro-Optical Systems Design, Milton S. Kiver Publications, Inc., Chicago, Illinois.*

**Conwell, Dr. Esther M.** *Xerox Webster Research Center, Rochester, New York.*

**Coppersmith, Dr. Don.** *IBM Corporation, Kingston, New York.*

**Cormack, Dr. Gordon V.** *Associate Professor, Department of Computer Science, University of Waterloo, Ontario, Canada.*

**Corson, Almon J.** *Retired; formerly, Consulting Engineer, Instrument Department, General Electric Company, West Lynn, Massachusetts.*

**Curdts, Edward B.** *Retired; formerly, Consultant; Director of Engineering, James G. Biddle Company, Philadelphia, Pennsylvania.*

**Cutler, Prof. C. Chapin.** *Professor of Applied Physics, Stanford University.*

# D

**Dalton, Oliver.** *Retired; formerly, General Manager, Tektronix Portable Instrument Division, Beaverton, Oregon.*

**Date, Prof. H.** *Acoustics Department, Kyusha Institute of Design, Fukuoka, Japan.*

**de Boor, Dr. Carl.** *Mathematical Research Center, University of Wisconsin.*

**Dekker, Dr. Adrianus J.** *Professor of Solid State Physics, University of Groningen, Netherlands.*

**de Neufville, Dr. John P.** *Vice President for Materials Development, Energy Conversion Devices, Inc., North Branch, New Jersey.*

**de Satnick, Steve.** *Vice President, Operations and Engineering, KCET-TV, Los Angeles, California.*

**Dickieson, Alton C.** *Retired; formerly, Vice President, Bell Telephone Laboratories, Sedonia, Arizona.*

**Dix, Dr. Cyril H.** *Bishop Monkton, North Yorkshire, England.*

**Duke, Dr. C. B.** *Senior Research Fellow and Manager, Theoretical Physics and Chemistry Area, Joseph Wilson Center for Technology, Xerox Corporation, Rochester, New York.*

# E

**Eilers, Carl G.** *Manager, Electronics Systems Research and Development, Zenith Radio Corporation, Glenview, Illinois.*

**El-Mansy, Youssef.** *Intel Corporation, Aloha, Oregon.*

**Engen, Glenn F.** *Boulder, Colorado.*

**Engstrom, Dr. Ralph W.** *Electro Optics and Devices, RCA Laboratories, Lancaster, Pennsylvania.*

**Enslow, Prof. Philip H., Jr.** *School of Information and Computer Science, Georgia Institute of Technology.*

**Esaki, Leo.** *Thomas J. Watson Research Center, International Business Machines Corporation, Yorktown Heights, New York.*

**Even, Reed.** *Bell Telephone Laboratories, Whippany, New Jersey.*

**Evenson, Dr. Kenneth M.** *Time and Frequency Division, National Bureau of Standards, Boulder, Colorado.*

# F

**Fan, Prof. Hsu Y.** *Department of Physics, Purdue University.*

**Ferguson, Judith Kagle.** *Planning Engineer, Advanced Technologies, AT&T Communications, Redminster, New Jersey.*

**Fink, Donald G.** *Director Emeritus, IEEE; Editor in Chief, ''Electronics Engineers' Handbook,'' McGraw-Hill Book Company, New York, New York.*

**Frailey, Dr. Dennis J.** *Texas Instruments, Inc., Austin, Texas.*

# G

**Galler, Dr. Bernard A.** *Computing Center, University of Michigan.*

**Galloway, Dr. William J.** *Bolt, Beranek and Newman, Inc., Canoga Park, California.*

**Galt, Dr. J. K.** *Vice President, Sandia Laboratories, Albuquerque, New Mexico.*

**Gannon, J. D.** *Department of Computer Science, University of Maryland.*

**Gewartowski, James W.** *Bell Telephone Laboratories, Murray Hill, New Jersey.*

**Gibbs, Prof. Hyatt M.** *Optical Science Center, University of Arizona.*

**Gilbert, Dr. Edgar N.** *Bell Telephone Laboratories, Murray Hill, New Jersey.*

**Girvin, Dr. S. M.** *National Bureau of Standards, Washington, D.C.*

**Glasford, Prof. Glenn M.** *Department of Electrical Engineering, Syracuse University.*

**Gledhill, Dr. S. J.** *Marconi Instruments, Limited, Longacres, St. Albans, Hertfordshire, England.*

**Golden, F. B.** *Semiconductor Products Department, General Electric Company, Auburn, New York.*

**Gomer, Prof. Robert.** *James Franck Institute, University of Chicago.*

**Gonzalez, Prof. R. C.** *Department of Electrical Engineering and Computer Science, University of Tennessee.*

**Goodheart, Prof. Clarence F.** *Department of Electrical Engineering, Union College.*

**Gordon, Dr. James P.** *Bell Telephone Laboratories, Holmdel, New Jersey.*

**Gränicher, Prof. H.** *Laboratory of Solid State Physics, Swiss Federal Institute of Technology, Zurich.*

**Gregory, Dr. Bob Lee.** *Sandia Laboratories, Albuquerque, New Mexico.*

**Greif, Dr. Jeffrey.** *Inference Corporation, Los Angeles, California.*

**Greiling, Dr. Paul T.** *Hughes Research Laboratories, Malibu, California.*

**Gross, Prof. Jonathan L.** *Department of Mathematics, Columbia University.*

**Grow, Prof. Richard W.** *Department of Electrical Engineering, University of Utah.*

**Gruenberger, Prof. Fred J.** *Department of Computer Science, California State University, Northridge.*

**Grzymala-Busse, Prof. Jerzy W.** *Department of Computer Science, University of Kansas.*

**Guidry, Dr. Mark R.** *Fairchild Camera and Instrument Corporation, Mountain View, California.*

**Gundersen, Prof. Martin.** *Electrical Engineering Department, University of Southern California.*

## H

**Hailpern, Dr. Brent T.** *IBM Research Laboratory, Yorktown Heights, New York.*

**Halkias, Prof. Christos C.** *Chair of Electronics, National Technical University, Athens, Greece.*

**Harris, Dr. Forest K.** *National Bureau of Standards.*

**Harris, Prof. J. Donald.** *U.S. Navy Submarine Medical Laboratory, Groton, Connecticut.*

**Hartson, Prof. H. Rex.** *Department of Computer Science, Virginia Polytechnic Institute and State University.*

**Hayes-Roth, Dr. Frederick.** *Executive Vice President, Technology, Teknowledge, Inc., Palo Alto, California.*

**Helms, Harry L.** *Professional and Reference Book Division, McGraw-Hill Book Company, New York, New York.*

**Henry, Dr. Charles H.** *Bell Laboratories, Murray Hill, New Jersey.*

**Hermach, Dr. F. L.** *National Bureau of Standards, Gaithersburg, Maryland.*

**Herrell, Dr. Dennis J.** *Thomas J. Watson Research Center, Yorktown Heights, New York.*

**Hill, Robert T.** *U.S. Navy, Bowie, Maryland.*

**Hines, Dr. M. E.** *Vice President, Microwave Associates Inc., Burlington, Massachusetts.*

**Hodge, Prof. Bartow.** *Professor, Information Systems, School of Business, Virginia Commonwealth University.*

**Hodgin, David M.** *Spectra Associates Inc., Cedar Rapids, Iowa.*

**Hoffman, Dr. Alan J.** *IBM Corporation, Yorktown Heights, New York.*

**Holdeman, Dr. Louis B.** *National Bureau of Standards.*

**Holmes, Dr. Jack K.** *Holmes Associates, Los Angeles, California.*

**Holst, Per A.** *Foxboro Company, Foxboro, Massachusetts.*

**Horzepa, Joseph J.** *Marketing Director, Visual Communications Services, American Telephone and Telegraph Company, Morristown, New Jersey.*

**Hoxton, Prof. Lewellyn G.** *Deceased; formerly, Professor Emeritus of Physics, University of Virginia.*

**Hubbard, Dr. W. M.** *Central Services Organization, Bell Communications Research, Holmdel, New Jersey.*

**Hunter, Prof. Lloyd P.** *Department of Electrical Engineering, University of Rochester.*

**Huskey, Dr. Velma R.** *Information Sciences, University of California, Santa Cruz.*

## I

**Irene, Dr. Eugene A.** *Department of Chemistry, University of North Carolina.*

## J

**Jacobs, Prof. Stephen F.** *Optical Science Center, University of Arizona.*

**Jarvis, Dr. John F.** *Robotics Systems Research Department, Bell Laboratories, Holmdel, New Jersey.*

**Jen, Dr. C. K.** *Supervisor, Microwave Physics Group, Applied Physics Laboratory, Johns Hopkins University.*

**Joel, Amos E., Jr.** *Bell Laboratories, Holmdel, New Jersey.*

**Johnson, Prof. Walter C.** *Department of Electrical Engineering, Princeton University.*

**Jones, Dr. Edwin C., Jr.** *Department of Electrical and Computer Engineering, Iowa State University.*

**Jory, Howard R.** *Varian Associates, Palo Alto, California.*

**Joseph, Earl C.** *Sperry Univac, St. Paul, Minnesota.*

**Juliussen, Dr. J. Egil.** *Senior Member of Technical Staff, Texas Instruments Inc., Dallas.*

## K

**Kaminow, Ivan P.** *Bell Telephone Laboratories, Holmdel, New Jersey.*

**Kanal, Dr. Laveen N.** *Department of Computer Science, University of Maryland.*

**Kanzig, Prof. Werner.** *Department of Physics, Massachusetts Institute of Technology.*

**Kaufmann, R. H.** *Deceased; formerly, Consultant, Schenectady, New York.*

**Keiser, Bernhard E.** *President, Keiser Engineering, Inc., Vienna, Virginia.*

**Kent, Dr. Ernest W.** *National Bureau of Standards, Gaithersburg, Maryland.*

**Kibble, Dr. Bryan P.** *Division of Electrical Science, National Physical Laboratory, Teddington, Middlesex, England.*

**Kimbark, Dr. Edward W.** *Head, Systems Analysis Group, Bonneville Power Administration, Portland, Oregon.*

**Kinch, Dr. Michael A.** *Central Research Laboratories, Texas Instruments Inc., Dallas.*

**King, Dr. Roger.** *Computer Science Department, University of Colorado.*

**Kinnard, Dr. Isaac F.** *Deceased; formerly, Manager of Engineering, Instrument Department, General Electric Company, Lynn, Massachusetts.*

**Klick, Dr. Clifford C.** *Superintendent, Solid State Division, U.S. Naval Research Laboratory.*

**Klock, Dr. Harold F.** *Department of Electrical Engineering, Ohio University.*

**Kluger, Dr. Leo D.** *American Radio Relay League, Inc., Newington, Connecticut.*

**Knight, Dr. R. B. D.** *Division of Electrical Science, National Physical Laboratory, Teddington, Middlesex, England.*

**Knotek, Dr. M. L.** *Sandia National Laboratories, Albuquerque, New Mexico.*

**Kotter, Dr. F. Ralph.** *National Bureau of Standards.*

**Kreutel, Dr. Randall W.** *COMSAT Laboratories, Clarksburg, Maryland.*

**Land, Dr. Cecil E.** *Sandia National Laboratories, Albuquerque, New Mexico.*

**Landes, Dr. Hugh S.** *Department of Electrical Engineering, University of Virginia.*

**Lanford, Prof. William A.** *Department of Physics, State University of New York, Albany.*

**Langenberg, Dr. D. N.** *Department of Physics, University of Pennsylvania.*

**Laport, Edmund A.** *Director, Communications Engineering, RCA Corp., Princeton, New Jersey.*

**Lathi, Prof. B. P.** *Department of Electrical and Electronic Engineering, California State University, Sacramento.*

**Lea, Dr. Wayne A.** *Director, Speech Science Publications, Apple Valley, Minnesota.*

**Lee, L. K.** *Assistant Director, Product Assurance, TRW Systems, Redondo Beach, California.*

**Lee, Prof. Samuel C.** *Department of Electrical Engineering, University of Oklahoma.*

**Lehmer, Dr. Derrick H.** *Professor Emeritus, Department of Mathematics, University of California, Berkeley.*

**LePage, Dr. Wilbur R.** *Department of Electrical and Computer Engineering, Syracuse University.*

**Lesk, Dr. I. A.** *Vice President, Technical Staff, Motorola Inc., Phoenix, Arizona.*

**Lesso, Dr. William G.** *Department of Mechanical Engineering, University of Texas, Austin.*

**Lewis, Frank D.** *James Millen Manufacturing Company, Malden, Massachusetts.*

**Lewis, Willard D.** *Bell Telephone Laboratories, Murray Hill, New Jersey.*

**Lhermitte, Dr. Roger.** *Professor of Physical Meteorology, University of Miami School of Marine and Atmospheric Science.*

**Lowin, R. J.** *Managing Director, Plessey Microwave Ltd.*

**Lyons, Prof. Walter.** *Consultant in Telecommunications, Flushing, New York.*

## M

**McCarthy, Dr. Dennis D.** *Time Service Division, U.S. Naval Observatory, Washington, D.C.*

**MacCarthy, Donnell D.** *Manager, Voltage Regulator Engineering, Voltage Regulator Product Section, General Electric Company, Pittsfield, Massachusetts.*

**McConnell, Kenneth R.** *Director of Technical Operations, Panafax Corp., Melville, New York.*

**McLeod, John H., Jr.** *Professional Engineer, La Jolla, California.*

**McPherson, Dr. George, Jr.** *Electrical Engineering Department, University of Missouri at Rolla.*

**Maisel, Dr. Herbert.** *Computer Science Program, Georgetown University.*

**Manning, Dr. Kenneth V.** *Professor Emeritus, Pennsylvania State University.*

**Marks, Peter A.** *Director, Product Planning and Development, Milford, Ohio.*

**Markus, John.** *Consultant, Sunnyvale, California.*

**Matyas, Stephen M.** *IBM Systems Communication Division, Kingston, New York.*

**Meade, Prof. M. L.** *Faculty of Technology, Electronics Discipline, The Open University, Milton Keynes, England.*

**Mellichamp, Prof. Duncan A.** *Department of Chemical Engineering, University of California, Santa Barbara.*

**Meyer, Dr. Carl H.** *Advisory Engineer, IBM Systems, Communications Division, Kingston, New York.*

**Meyer, Dr. John F.** *Department of Computer and Communications Sciences, University of Michigan.*

**Miller, Dr. Glenn H.** *Weapons Effects Division, Sandia Laboratories, Albuquerque, New Mexico.*

**Miller, John H.** *Deceased; formerly, Vice President and Chief Engineer, Weston Instrument Division, Dayton, Ohio.*

**Millman, Dr. Jacob.** *Department of Electrical Engineering, Columbia University.*

**Mills, Thomas B.** *National Semiconductor Corporation, Santa Clara, California.*

**Milstein, Prof. Laurence B.** *Department of Electrical Engineering and Computer Science, University of California, San Diego.*

**Mitchell, Dr. Kim W.** *Solar Energy Research Institute, Golden, Colorado.*

**Mitchell, Prof. Larry D.** *Booke and Company, Inc., New York, New York.*

**Mizell, Dr. David W.** *Project Leader, University of Southern California/Information Sciences Institute, Marina del Rey.*

**Moder, Dr. Joseph J.** *Chairperson, Department of Management Science, University of Miami.*

**Morgan, Kelly B.** *AT&T Information Systems, Lincroft, New Jersey.*

**Morrell, A. M.** *Manager, Tube Development, Picture Tube Division, RCA Corporation, Lancaster, Pennsylvania.*

**Moyer, Dr. William W.** *Applied Research Laboratory, Pennsylvania State University.*

**Munn, Prof. R. W.** *Professor of Chemical Physics, Department of Chemistry, University of Manchester Institute of Science and Technology, Manchester, England.*

**Myers, Ware.** *Consultant, Temple City, California.*

**Nelson, Prof. Raymond J.** *Professor of Mathematics and Philosophy, Case Institute of Technology.*

**Nelson, Dr. Richard B.** *Chief Engineer, Varian Associates, Palo Alto, California.*

**Nergaard, Dr. Leon S.** *Director, Microwave Research Laboratory, RCA Laboratories, Princeton, New Jersey.*

**Neuhauser, Robert G.** *Electronic Components, Solid State Division, RCA Corporation, Lancaster, Pennsylvania.*

**Newell, Dr. Allen.** *Department of Computer Science, Carnegie-Mellon University.*

**Nygren, Stephen.** *Bell Telephone Laboratories, Reading, Pennsylvania.*

**Olson, Dr. Harry F.** *Formerly, Staff Vice President, Acoustical and Electromechanical Research, RCA Laboratories, Princeton, New Jersey.*

**Ovshinsky, Stanford R.** *President, Energy Conversion Devices, Inc., Troy, Michigan.*

**Patel, Dr. C. K. N.** *Bell Laboratories, Murray Hill, New Jersey.*

**Patrick, Norman W.** *RCA Corporation, Lancaster, Pennsylvania.*

**Patton, Peter C.** *Minnesota Supercomputer Institute, University of Minnesota.*

**Paul, Prof. Igor.** *Department of Mechanical Engineering, Massachusetts Institute of Technology.*

**Pearce, J. Ralph.** *Solartron Instrumentation Group, Hampshire, England.*

**Pecar, Dr. Joseph A.** *Joseph A. Pecar & Associates, Inc., Potomac, Maryland.*

**Peyghambarian, Nasser.** *Optical Sciences Center and Optical Circuitry Cooperative, University of Arizona.*

**Pfeffer, Dr. Robert A.** *Harry Diamond Laboratories, Woodbridge Research Laboratories,* Woodbridge, Virginia.

**Phister, Montgomery, Jr.** *Consultant, Santa Fe, New Mexico.*

**Picraux, Dr. Samuel T.** *Supervisor, Ion-Solid Interactions, Sandia Laboratories, Albuquerque, New Mexico.*

**Pitchford, Dr. Leanne C.** *Sandia Laboratories, Albuquerque, New Mexico.*

**Plesset, Dr. Michael.** *Aerospace Corporation, Los Angeles, California.*

**Prasad, Ray.** *Senior Staff Engineer, Intel Corporation, Hillsboro, Oregon.*

**Preece, Dr. Carolyn M.** *Bell Laboratories, Murray Hill, New Jersey.*

**Pritchett, Prof. Wilson S.** *Senior Project Engineer, Noller Control Systems Inc., Richmond, California.*

**Pritsker, Prof. A. Alan B.** *School of Industrial Engineering, Purdue University.*

**Pullen, Dr. Keats A., Jr.** *Ballistic Research Laboratories, Aberdeen Proving Ground, Aberdeen, Maryland.*

## R

**Ramberg, Dr. Edward G.** *RCA Laboratories, Princeton, New Jersey.*

**Ramey, Prof. Robert L.** *Department of Electrical Engineering, University of Virginia.*

**Rayner, Dr. G. H.** *Consultant, Teddington, Middlesex, England.*

**Reich, Prof. Herbert J.** *Retired; formerly, Department of Engineering and Applied Science, Yale University.*

**Rickert, Richard M.** *AT&T Consumer Products, Indianapolis, Indiana.*

**Robb, D. D.** *D. D. Robb and Associates, Consulting Engineers, Salina, Kansas.*

**Robertson, Prof. Burtis L.** *Retired; formerly, Professor of Electrical Engineering, University of California, Berkeley.*

**Robinson, W. V.** *Processor Technology Research Group, Bell Laboratories, Whippany, New Jersey.*

**Rochkind, Mark M.** *Bell Laboratories, Holmdel, New Jersey.*

**Rockett, Frank H.** *Engineering Consultant, Charlottesville, Virginia.*

**Rosenbaum, Prof. Fred J.** *Department of Electrical Engineering, Washington University.*

**Ruthroff, Clyde L.** *Consultant, Holmdel, New Jersey.*

## S

**Samek, Michael J.** *Director, Management Services, Celanese Corporation, New York, New York.*

**Scanlan, Prof. J. O.** *Department of Electrical and Electronic Engineering, University College, Dublin, Ireland.*

**Schawlow, Prof. Arthur L.** *Department of Physics, Stanford University.*

**Schelleng, John C.** *Retired; formerly, Bell Telephone Laboratories.*

**Schneidewind, Dr. Norman F.** *Computer Scientist, Computer Research, Pebble Beach, California.*

**Schueler, Dr. Donald G.** *Sandia Laboratories, Albuquerque, New Mexico.*

**Schuller, Dr. Ivan K.** *Solid State Science Division, Argonne National Laboratory, Argonne, Illinois.*

**Schulman, Dr. James H.** *U.S. Naval Research Laboratory.*

**Schwartz, Dr. Bernard.** *IBM Corporation, Thomas J. Watson Research Center, Yorktown Heights, New York.*

**Seager, Dr. C. H.** *Sandia Laboratories, Albuquerque, New Mexico.*

**Seifert, William W.** *Retired; formerly, Professor of Electrical Engineering and Associate Director, Commodity Transportation and Economic Development Laboratory, Massachusetts Institute of Technology.*

**Sessler, Dr. Gerhard M.** *Institut für Elektroakustik, Technische Hochschule, Darmstadt, West Germany.*

**Shaw, Dr. David G.** *Capacitor Products Department, General Electric Company, New York, New York.*

**Sheingold, Daniel H.** *Manager of Technical Marketing, Analog Devices, Incorporated, Norwood, Massachusetts.*

**Shively, R. R.** *Supervisor, Processor Technology Research Group, Bell Laboratories, Whippany, New Jersey.*

**Sibley, Dr. Edgar H.** *Department of Information Systems Management, University of Maryland.*

**Siegman, Dr. A. E.** *Stanford, California.*

**Sinclair, Dr. Malcolm W.** *Procurement Executive, Ministry of Defence, Royal Signals and Radar Establishment, Great Malvern, Worcestershire, England.*

**Singleton, John D.** *Supervisor of Programming, Radio Division, National Broadcasting Company, New York, New York.*

**Sittner, Dr. W. R.** *President, Electro Medical Systems, Inc., Englewood, Colorado.*

**Skilling, Prof. Hugh H.** *Department of Electrical Engineering, Stanford University.*

**Skilling, James K.** *General Radio Company, West Concord, Massachusetts.*

**Slayton, Ransom D.** *Retired; formerly, AT&T Teletype Corporation, Skokie, Illinois.*

**Smith, Carl E.** *Consulting Radio Engineer, Cleveland, Ohio.*

**Smith, Dr. David C.** *Research Center, United Technologies Corporation, East Hartford, Connecticut.*

**Smith, Dr. Warren E.** *Optical Sciences Center, University of Arizona.*

**Snow, William W.** *Consulting Engineer, William W. Snow Associates, Inc., Woodside, New York.*

**Sohon, Dr. Harry.** *Deceased; formerly, Moore School, University of Pennsylvania.*

**Somlo, Dr. Peter I.** *CSIRO Division of Applied Physics, Lindfield, New South Wales, Australia.*

**Sommer, Dr. Alfred H.** *Thermo Electron Corporation, Waltham, Massachusetts.*

**Steen, Dr. Robert F.** *IBM Corporation, Research Triangle Park, North Carolina.*

**Sterzer, Dr. Fred.** *RCA Laboratories, Princeton, New Jersey.*

**Stevenson, Dr. Edward C.** *Department of Electrical Engineering, School of Engineering and Applied Sciences, University of Virginia.*

**Stewart, Dr. John W.** *Department of Physics, University of Virginia.*

**Stillman, Dr. Gregory E.** *Department of Electrical Engineering, University of Illinois, Urbana.*

**Streifer, Dr. William.** *Palo Alto Research Center, Xerox Corporation, Palo Alto, California.*

**Sullivan, John.** *Lee Allan Associates, Sunnyvale, California.*

**Suzuki, Hideo.** *CBS Technology Center, CBS, Inc., Stamford, Connecticut.*

## T

**Tamura, Dr. Masahiko.** *Acoustical Engineering Research Laboratory, Pioneer Electronic Corporation, Saitama, Japan.*

**Tang, Prof. K. Y.** *Deceased; formerly, Department of Electrical Engineering, Ohio State University.*

**Tannas, Lawrence E., Jr.** *Consultant, Orange, California.*

**Tapia, Dr. Richard A.** *Department of Mathematical Sciences, Rice University.*

**Theis, Dr. Douglas J.** *Computer Systems Department, Aerospace Corporation, Los Angeles, California.*

**Thiess, Helmut E.** *Washington, D.C.*

**Thompson, Dr. Richard A.** *Member of Technical Staff, Digital Systems, Research Department, AT&T Bell Laboratories, Murray Hill, New Jersey.*

**Tindell, Larry D.** *Senior Research Engineer, Artificial Intelligence Laboratory, Lockheed Missiles and Space Company, Austin, Texas.*

**Townes, Prof. Charles H.** *Department of Physics, University of California, Berkeley.*

**Trahiotis, Prof. Constantine.** *Department of Speech and Hearing Science, University of Illinois, Urbana-Champaign.*

**Tsaur, Dr. Bor-Yeu.** *Lincoln Laboratories, Lexington, Massachusetts.*

**Tur, Dr. Moshe.** *School of Engineering, Tel-Aviv University, Israel.*

**Tuttle, Dr. W. Norris.** *Consultant, Concord, Massachusetts.*

## U

**Uhlig, Dr. Ronald P.** *Bell Northern Research, Ottawa, Ontario, Canada.*

## V

**Van Valkenburg, Dr. M. E.** *Department of Electrical Engineering, University of Illinois, Urbana.*

**Verma, Dr. Pramode K.** *AT&T Information Systems, Morristown, New Jersey.*

## W

**Waidelich, Dr. Donald L.** *Department of Electrical Engineering, University of Missouri.*

**Waldron, Dr. Robert D.** *Director, Research Enterprises, Scottsdale, Arizona.*

**Walsh, Dr. Walter M.** *Bell Laboratories, Murray Hill, New Jersey.*

**Ward, Jeffrey.** *American Radio, Newington, Connecticut.*

**Ward, John E.** *Electronics Systems Laboratory, Massachusetts Institute of Technology.*

**Warner, Dr. Frank L.** *Royal Signals and Radar Establishment, Malvern, Worcestershire, England.*

**Warwick, Peter S.** *AT&T Information Systems, Lincroft, New Jersey.*

**Watanabe, Dr. K.** *Central Research Laboratory, Daido Steel Company, Nagoya, Japan.*

**Weaver, James L.** *Lockheed Missiles and Space Company, Palo Alto, California.*

**Webber, Bonnie.** *Department of Computer and Information Science, Moore School, University of Pennsylvania.*

**Weil, Robert T., Jr.** *Deceased; formerly, Dean, School of Engineering, Manhattan College.*

**Weiser, M. D.** *Department of Computer Science, University of Maryland.*

**Weisner, Dr. David E.** *VLSI Design Associates, San Jose, California.*

**Weiss, Eric A.** *Consultant, Springfield, Pennsylvania.*

**Wentworth, John W.** *Director, Educational Development Engineering, RCA Corporation, Cherry Hill, New Jersey.*

**White, Donald R. J.** *International Training Centre, Don White Consultants, Inc., Gainesville, Virginia.*

**Williams, Everard M.** *Deceased; formerly, Department of Electrical Engineering, Carnegie-Mellon University.*

**Williams, Dr. Peter.** *Department of Chemistry, Arizona State University.*

**Williams, S. A.** *Department of Physics, Iowa State University.*

**Winch, Prof. Ralph P.** *Department of Physics, Williams College.*

**Wisnosky, Dennis E.** *Group Vice President, Industrial Systems Group, GCA Corporation, Naperville, Illinois.*

**Wolf, Dr. Peter.** *IBM Zurich Research Laboratory, Switzerland.*

**Wolfe, Roger W.** *Plainfield Semiconductor Operation, Burroughs Corporation, Plainfield, New Jersey.*

**Woodall, Dr. Jerry M.** *IBM Watson Research Center, Yorktown Heights, New York.*

**Woodward, Dr. J. Guy.** *David Sarnoff Research Center, RCA Laboratories, Princeton, New Jersey.*

**Wright, Prof. Arthur.** *Department of Electrical and Electronic Engineering, University of Nottingham, England.*

**Wright, James A.** *Strategic Marketing Manager, Motorola, Inc., Boynton Beach, Florida.*

**Wright, Michael E.** *National Semiconductor Corporation, Santa Clara, California.*

**Yamamoto, Dr. Takeo.** *Acoustical Engineering Research Laboratory, Pioneer Electronic Corporation, Saitama, Japan.*

**Yang, Dr. Edward S.** *Department of Electrical Engineering, Columbia University.*

**Yell, Dr. Ralph W.** *National Physical Laboratory, Teddington, Middlesex, England.*

**Yelles, Marvin.** *Formerly, Editor, "McGraw-Hill Encyclopedia of Science and Technology," McGraw-Hill Book Company, New York, New York.*

**Young, W. Rae.** *Retired; formerly, AT&T Bell Laboratories, Holmdel, New Jersey.*

## Z

**Zarbock, William L.** *Staff Manager, Planning and Design, AT&T Communications, Bedminster, New Jersey.*

**Ziegler, Dr. James.** *Watson Research Laboratory, IBM, Yorktown Heights, New York.*

**Zissis, Dr. George J.** *Chief Scientist, Environmental Research Institute of Michigan, Ann Arbor.*

# Preface

Electronics—both the science and the industry—is concerned with the materials, physical processes, design, and applications of various electronic devices, especially semiconductor devices, and to a lesser extent, electron tubes. These devices have a multitude of uses that pervade almost every avenue of human endeavor in the form of computers.

This Encyclopedia explores the diversity of electronics and computers in a comprehensive collection of 520 alphabetically arranged articles which describe everything from the flow of electricity through semiconducting materials; fabrication methods for integrated circuits; types of computer hardware and software; to the use of computers in robotics, data management systems, communications, and consumer products. Specifically, the Encyclopedia includes entries on such topics as artificial intelligence, junction diodes, radar, computer-aided engineering, holes in solids, high-temperature electronics, fault-tolerant systems, negative-resistance circuits, molecular electronics, and computer storage technology.

The second edition of the Encyclopedia is completely revised and updated to present the most current information available. Compared with the first edition, there are a total of 45 new titles and 120 articles have been completely revised. Access to the information is enhanced by the use of cross-references and a detailed analytical index.

Authoritative, up to date, and comprehensive, this Encyclopedia provides both the professional and lay reader with an entrée into the world of electronics and computers. It will become an indispensable source for the writer, librarian, engineer, student, or interested hobbyist or consumer.

**Sybil P. Parker**
Editor in Chief

# McGRAW-HILL ENCYCLOPEDIA OF ELECTRONICS AND COMPUTERS

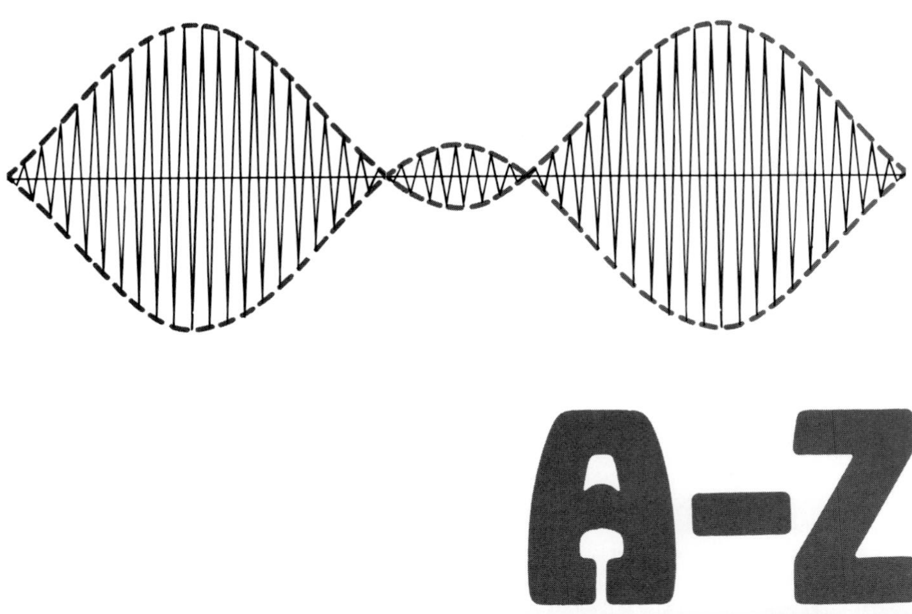

# A-Z

## Abacus

The earliest known computing instrument, consisting of beads (counters) strung on wires mounted in a frame (**Fig. 1**); technically the term also covers the earlier counting tables and the grooved tablets of the Romans. The abacus is still used in parts of the world.

The Latin word *abacus* means simply ''a flat surface'' and is derived from the Greek word *abax*. The ancient Hebrew word *abaq* means ''dust,'' and there are references in the literature which indicate that sanded surfaces were used for reckoning. Stones were probably used as counters on the first counting tables, and the Latin word *calculus* means ''little stone.'' The Romans also had counters of ivory, metal, and glass, while in the Orient pieces of bamboo were used.

The earliest known example of a counting board is the Greek Salamis marble tablet. Its exact date is unknown, but the Greek historian Herodotus (485–425 B.C.) gave examples of mathematical problems, and these have been worked out by using an abacus of the Salamis type.

The Romans also had a hand abacus, examples of which survive. This was a bronze tablet with grooves in which small spherical counters could slide, remarkably like the abacus which came into use later in the Middle and Far East. Although this type of abacus is described in the Chinese literature of the second century, it was not until the thirteenth century that its use became widespread in China. The Chinese abacus had one more counter in each section than the Roman hand abacus, and the counters were mounted on wires in a frame rather than in grooves. It was introduced into Japan in the fifteenth century, and by the nineteenth century a modified version had come into wide use there. In China the abacus is called the *suan-pan*, and in Japan the *soroban* (**Fig. 2**). The Chinese character *suan* means ''to calculate'' and is formed by the characters for two hands holding a counting board made of bamboo. In the Middle East, still another version of the abacus is used, which in the Soviet Union is called the *schoty*.

Fig. 1. Type of abacus now in use.

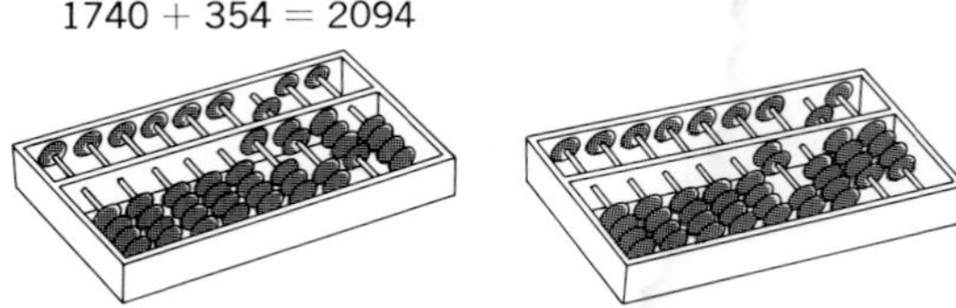


Fig. 2. Addition with a *soroban*.

By the nineteenth century the counting-table type of abacus had essentially gone out of use in the Western world, and there the beads-on-shaft type had never been widely used. Conversely, the nineteenth and twentieth centuries, with their economic development, brought an upsurge in the use of the latter type of abacus in the Middle and Far East. By the end of World War II, abacus operation was included in the curriculum of the fourth and upper grades in Japan, and licenses were issued for proficiency in its use. Teachers preferred it over the pocket electronic calculator as it forced students to grasp fundamental mathematical concepts. In the Soviet Union and China, as in Japan, the abacus is still used, but it remains to be seen whether it will survive competition from the pocket electronic calculator. *SEE CALCULATORS.*

*Velma R. Huskey*

**Bibliography.** N.S. Kagisho, *Soroban, the Japanese Abacus, Its Use and Practice*, 1967; K. Menninger, *Number Words and Number Symbols*, 1969; J. M. Pullan, *The History of the Abacus*, 1968.

## Abstract data types

Mathematical models which may be used to capture the essentials of a problem domain in order to translate it into a computer program.

**Motivation.** It is generally understood that people join a line by standing at the end of the line and are serviced from its front. Stepping into the middle of a line violates the rules of line etiquette, as does servicing someone from the middle of the line.

To describe a particular line of people, it suffices to keep track of the first and last person as the line moves. Then, it will always be far behind whom a new person must stand and who must be served next. Such a description of a line is an example of an abstract data type (ADT). It is a model for representing some sort of structure, with rules for making changes to that structure. The rules may be expressed as operators that perform specific functions.

In the field of computer programming, lines are usually called queues. For a person to enter a queue would be to perform an insertion; to leave the front of a queue would be a deletion. When the rules of line etiquette are broken, that is, an individual enters into or is serviced from the middle, the queue becomes a list. A list is a queue where insertions and deletions may be made at any point.

There are many examples of abstract data types, but this formalism is rarely useful in everyday life. However, an ADT queue would be quite helpful in representing a customer line as a computer program. The queue could be used to express certain business operations in terms of a well-understood model for representing information. This would allow the programmer to simplify the problem to that of implementing the queue in a computer language and then using the queue to represent a business function. Techniques for implementing queues are readily available.

Abstract data types allow the use of previously discovered programming techniques. Another benefit of ADTs is that they allow a programmer to encapsulate the rules for altering a model within a set of procedures, and ignore these details when using the given ADT. In other words, the programmer concerned with modeling a business function could forget exactly how an insertion or deletion is made when procedures that perform these functions are used. *SEE DIGITAL COMPUTER PROGRAMMING.*

**ADTs and data structures.** An ADT is indeed abstract, in that it must be translated into a programming language. This is done by using program data structures, which are formed from the primitive abstract data types supported directly by the given language. The programmer must also implement operators (for example, insert and delete in the queue example) that follow the rules for manipulating the ADT. In essence, then, ADTs are conceptualizations built of simple data structures and augmented with

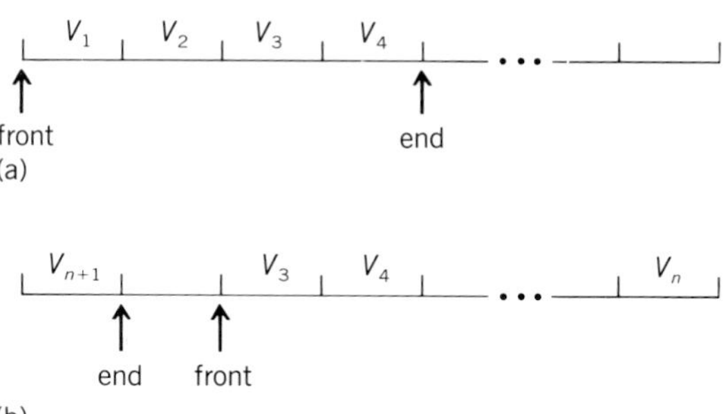


**Fig. 1. A queue (*a*) with four values entered, and markers for the front and end of the queue, and (*b*) with values 1 and 2 removed from the front, and the queue wrapped around so that value *n* + 1, the last value, is situated where value 1 used to be.**

high-level operators. When an ADT is used as the model of information in a specific application, an instance of the ADT is said to be defined. *SEE PROGRAMMING LANGUAGES.*

For example, an instance of a queue used to model a business function could be implemented as a sequential set of text strings in main memory. This implementation is illustrated in **Fig. 1**. Each text string contains the name of a person in line. The rules for manipulating the queue could be implemented by keeping track (in two variables) of the location of the first and last position in the queue. In Fig. 1*a*, the queue is shown with four values entered, and markers for the front and end of the queue. If insertions and deletions cause the first position in the queue to migrate to the end of the allocated queue space, the queue will wrap around on itself. When the last position in the queue is used, the next new value will be inserted in the first position. In Fig. 1*b*, values 1 and 2 have been removed from the front, and value 3 is now first. The queue has wrapped around, and value $n + 1$, the last value, is situated where value 1 used to be.

**Classification of data types.** Abstract data types may be grouped according to the ways they arrange information. Typical abstract data types are discussed below; with each one, particular classes of problems that are best solved using the given ADT are discussed. First, linearly organized data types represent information as a one-dimensional series of elements. Second, nonlinear modeling techniques arrange this information so that one element may be logically followed by more than one other element. (This corresponds to a customer line where there is more than one person directly behind any specific person.) Third, an unordered data type assumes no specific order of the elements of the type. (This corresponds to customers waiting in a chaotic group.) The first three data types are examples of models used to represent information in the fast-access, main memory of a computer. Other data types are oriented toward mass storage devices like magnetic tapes and disks.

Before more interesting ADTs may be considered, however, it is necessary to discuss the primitive ADTs that are typically used to form more complicated data types.

**Primitive ADTs.** There are a number of simple abstract types that are typically implemented directly in a high-level programming language. These include integers and real numbers (with appropriate arithmetic operators), booleans (with appropriate logical operators), text strings (often a programming language provides no special operators for manipulating strings), and pointers. An instance of a pointer data type has as its value a logical address of the instance of another ADT. The ADT pointer is usually implemented as an integer containing the main memory address of some data item. The primitive ADTs generally serve as implementations of the elements of a more sophisticated data type. For example, in the queue example, the data type text string was suggested as a model of the underlying implementation.

**Queues, lists, and stacks.** Queues, lists, and stacks are one-dimensional; what varies are the operators used to manipulate each ADT. A queue needs only two operators: one to insert and one to delete. To use a list, it is also necessary to have operators that may delete any element within the list or insert an element anywhere in the list. This may be done by an operator that steps through the list, locating the elements to insert or delete one by one, or by an operator that locates an element to insert or delete in the list according to some means of identification. A list is a useful ADT for keeping track of sorted information in a situation where insertions and deletions in the middle are common. As an example, a personal telephone directory could be viewed as a list.

A list is clearly a queue with somewhat more generalized data operations. Varying the accessing methods of an ADT usually implies a change in the underlying data structure as well; for example, in a list it is necessary to be able to make insertions and deletions in the middle, not just at the ends. Thus, a list could be represented as a data structure which consists of a set of variables arranged in pairs. These variables would be instances of two different primitive ADTs of the programming language. In each pair, one variable, of type text string, would describe the value of an element (for example, in the telephone directory, a person's name and phone number) and the other, of type pointer, would indicate the next element pair in the queue (**Fig. 2**).

A stack is essentially a queue in which insertions and deletions are both made at the front. Thus, the last element inserted is the first deleted. An insertion is commonly called a push and a deletion is called a pop. Stacks are used when modeling tasks that must be interrupted and then completed. An uncompleted task is pushed onto the stack when it is interrupted, and popped off when it is resumed. Several tasks may be pushed on top of each other; they are popped in reverse order.

**Trees and graphs.** A tree is an ADT where each element may be logically followed by two or more other elements. These are called its children. Each element in a tree may, as always, be of some other abstract data type and is called a node. The element that points to a node is called its parent. A tree may typically be accessed at any node; thus a tree in which each node has at most one child is a list.

A search of, an addition to, or a deletion from a tree is usually based upon an assigned order within the tree. For example, suppose that the tree consists of a number of nodes, each of which may point to two others. (This structure is called binary tree.) Besides the two pointers, each node would contain a value or set of values. The tree may be ordered such that the left child of any node has a value less than the parent that points to it, and the right child has a larger one (**Fig. 3**). Trees are often used to model complex decision spaces; each node represents a process with some number of possible outcomes. SEE DECISION THEORY.

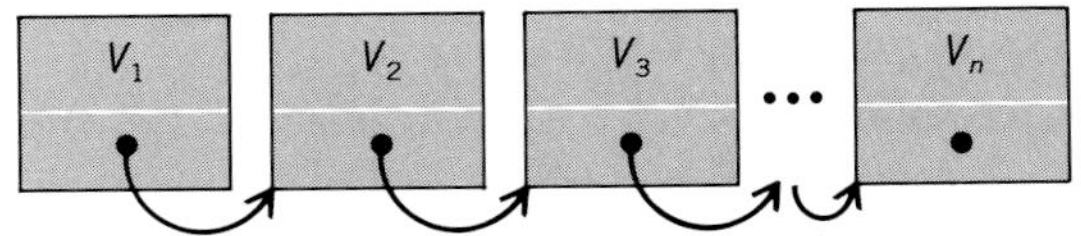


Fig. 2. Implementation of a list; arrows are used to indicate pointer variables.

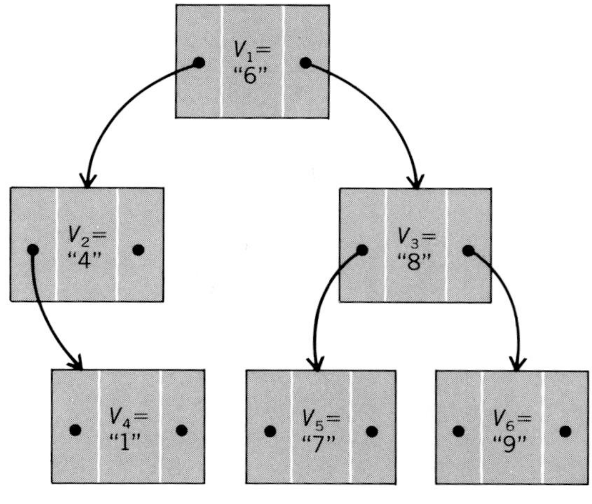


Fig. 3. Implementation of a sorted binary tree. The values $V_1$, $V_2$, and so forth are keys that are used to order the tree.

A graph (**Fig. 4**) is in essence a generalized tree: each node may have more than one parent. In some graphs, there is no parent/child dominance; a path between two nodes (called a link) may be traversed in either direction. Further, in many graphs there may be any number of links emanating from a given node. Graphs are often used to model communication and transportation networks. For example, a graph could represent the American road network, with each node representing a city and each link representing a road. Common operations on a graph are to add a link of a specified weight between two nodes or to find the shortest path between two nodes. SEE GRAPH THEORY.

**Sets.** A set is a data structure that models some group of related concepts. Just as with mathematical sets, the elements of the ADT set are not ordered. For example, an ADT set called colors may consist of the various colors of the rainbow. The set may be represented within a program as the set of character strings: red, yellow, and so forth.

Set operators usually perform insertions and deletions, form set unions and intersections, compare two sets for equality, test to see if an element is in a set, and so forth. Sets are commonly used to solve algebraic problems. For example, a compiler typically contains a module called a lexical analyzer which breaks the input program into identifiable pieces. One of the primary tasks of a lexical analyzer is to judge the legality of each character. For example, when the analyzer encounters a "[" or an "a" it might check to see if the character is an element of a set that contains all the legal characters of the language.

**Files and data bases.** A file is collection of identically formatted records, each containing some number of fields. Each field value is an atomic value, consisting of an integer, character string, real number, and so forth. Unlike the previously mentioned abstract data types, files model data stored on an exter-

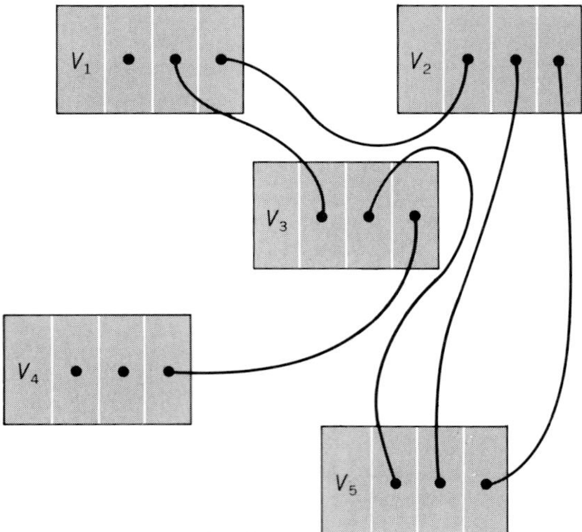


Fig. 4. ADT graph.

nal medium (magnetic disk, tape, and so forth).

Files are accessed either sequentially or randomly, meaning either that one is forced to step sequentially through the file until the desired record is located (for example, a tape file) or that a given record may be located with one logical search operation (for example, a disk). Operators on sequential files usually locate the first record in the file and then step to the next sequential record. Random files also provide operators for locating a record or set of records, given some value or set of values for one or more of the fields. (There is a clear parallel between queues and lists as main memory models and sequential and random files as mass storage models.)

Files are the backbone of external storage structures. They are used whenever main memory is insufficient in size to contain all the information required to solve a programming problem. Often, a file is constructed to consist of a series of records where each one will be transformed into an element in another data structure as the file is read into main memory. Thus, a number of records in a file may be read in and placed in a queue for processing, and when the queue is empty another group of records is read in.

A data base is an extension of the ADT file. The difference between a data base and a file is that a data base is a complex system containing many files and rules for interrelating the data on various files. For example, a typical data base operator is MERGE, which takes two files that share a common field format and forms one file containing the elements of both, sorting them in some manner. *SEE DATA-BASE MANAGEMENT SYSTEMS*.

**Relation to algorithms.** Abstract data types have been discussed as conceptualizations of typical program data structures. Algorithms are techniques for solving programming problems which use the data structures and programs that implement ADTs. A sound knowledge of ADTs and a familiarity with common implementation techniques provide the background necessary to simplify the derivation of many algorithms. *SEE ALGORITHMS*.

*Roger King*

***Bibliography.*** A. V. Aho, J. E. Hopcroft, and J. D. Ullman, *Data Structures and Algorithms,* 1983; T. A. Standish, *Data Structure Techniques,* 1980.

## Acceptor atom

An impurity atom in a semiconductor which can accept or take up one or more electrons from the crystal and become negatively charged. An atom which substitutes for a regular atom of the material but has one less valence electron may be expected to be an acceptor atom. For example, atoms of aluminum, gallium, or indium are acceptors in germanium and silicon, and atoms of antimony and bismuth are acceptors in tellurium crystals. Acceptor atoms tend to increase the number of holes (positive charge carriers) in the semiconductor. The energy gained when an electron is taken up by an acceptor atom from the valance band of the crystal is the ionization energy of the atom. *SEE DONOR ATOM; SEMICONDUCTOR*.

*H. Y. Fan*

## Admittance

The ratio of the current to the voltage in an alternating-current circuit.

In terms of complex current $I$ and voltage $V$, the admittance of a circuit is given by Eq. (1), and is related to the impedance of the circuit $Z$ by Eq. (2).

$$Y = \frac{I}{V} \tag{1}$$

$$Y = \frac{1}{Z} \tag{2}$$

$Y$ is a complex number given by Eq. (3). $G$, the

$$Y = G + jB \tag{3}$$

real part of the admittance, is the conductance of the circuit, and $B$, the imaginary part of the admittance, is the susceptance of the circuit. The units of admittance are called siemens or mhos (reciprocal ohms). *SEE CONDUCTANCE; SUSCEPTANCE*.

The modulus of the admittance is given by Eq. (4),

$$|Y| = \sqrt{G^2 + B^2} \tag{4}$$

which is the ratio of the maximum current to the maximum voltage. The phase angle $\psi$ of the admittance is given by Eq. (5) and is the angle by which the

$$\psi = \tan^{-1}\frac{B}{G} \tag{5}$$

current leads the voltage. The power factor of the circuit is cos $\psi$, given by Eq. (6).

$$\cos\psi = \frac{G}{\sqrt{G^2 + B^2}} \tag{6}$$

From Eq. (2) it follows that Eqs. (7), (8), and (9)

$$|Y| = \frac{1}{|Z|} \tag{7}$$

$$G = \frac{R}{R^2 + X^2} \tag{8}$$

$$B = \frac{-X}{R^2 + X^2} \tag{9}$$

are valid, where $R$, the resistance, and $X$, the reactance, are the real and imaginary parts of the circuit impedance. *SEE ALTERNATING-CURRENT CIRCUIT THEORY; ELECTRICAL RESISTANCE; REACTANCE*.

*J. O. Scanlan*

## Algorithm

A precise formulation of a method for doing something. In computers, an algorithm is usually a collection of procedural steps or instructions organized and designed so that computer processing results in the solution of a specific problem.

Algorithms play an important role in computers. Donald Knuth has suggested that science may be defined as knowledge which is understood well enough to be taught to a computer. In this view, the concept of an algorithm or computer program furnishes an extremely useful test for the depth of knowledge about any particular subject, and the process of going from an art to a science involves learning how to construct an algorithm.

Algorithms are employed to accomplish specific tasks using data and instructions when applying computers. The task may be well definable in either mathematical or nonmathematical terms; it may be either logical or heuristic, and either simple or complex; and it may be either computational or data-processable, or involve sensing and control. In any case, the task must be definable. Then an algorithm can be devised and specified for a computer to perform the required task.

**Properties.** Algorithms are further characterized by several properties. Either the data set over which the algorithm will operate or the process of how the computer is to get access to the data must be specifiable. The process required to be performed can be defined with a finite set of operations or actions together with a unique starting point. The sequence of steps, the tree, the list, or the network describing the process is mappable. This, however, does not imply that the path through these steps is known, since in some cases the data or prior process steps will dictate the actual path. That is, for classical computers it must be possible to "program" the algorithm. The algorithm process must terminate, either with the task completed or with some kind of indication that the task (problem) is unsolvable.

Algorithms define the method of operation for performing a task. However, for each task to be performed, there usually are many different mappable methods for the computer to execute it—but they are not of equal desirability. From the above definitions and characterizations it follows that any computer program that does its intended task is also an algorithm. But to be practical an algorithm must perform its task within the time and memory capacity constraints of the system.

**Hardware implementation.** The so-called silicon revolution has spawned the emergence and growth of smart machines. These devices have embedded microcomputerlike logic which gives them some degree of adaptability to their environment and functionality well beyond that of their dumb forerunners. In such a role, and others, the microcomputer logic becomes an algorithm, the hardware embodiment of a task process. *See Embedded systems; Microprocessor.*

As each generation of computers has emerged, a growing amount of software (programs and algorithms) has been cast in hardware, resulting in so-called hard software. Most computers in the pre-first generation (the late 1940s) did not have sequenceable and combinational primitive instructions, such as multiply and divide, wired in. In the first generation of computers (the early 1950s) these primitives were wired into the hardware. The second computer generation (the 1960s) saw the hardware implementation of computational algorithms, such as hardware algorithms for indexing, floating point, and trigonometric and square root functions. With the third computer generation (the 1970s) came hard software language/control algorithms, such as executive control, I/O (input/output), HLL (High Level Language), microprocessor, and system hardware algorithms. Fourth-generation computers (the 1980s) have hard software application algorithms, such as hardware in the form of peopleware primitives, profession (for example, management) algorithms, accounting primitives (for example, payroll), and MIS and courseware primitives. General-system hardware algorithms, are being developed, and institutional, inference, artificial intelligence, and robotic hardware algorithms are expected in the 1990s.

Most future algorithms for hard software will either (1) be incorporated as part of the hardware architecture of computers or "calculator" devices; (2) be cast as an optional adjunct for attachment to a computer system, memory, calculator, or information appliance to make it smarter; or (3) become a standalone, special-purpose machine—for example, a "payroll machine" or an "electronic file cabinet." Smart people/information appliances could well become the major interface to computers, data bases, information bases, and knowledge-based systems driven by hardware algorithms. *See Computer; Digital computer; Digital computer programming.*

*Earl C. Joseph*

***Bibliography.*** *Collected Algorithms from ACM*, vols. 1–3, and updates.

## Alternating current

Electric current that reverses direction periodically, usually many times per second. Electrical energy is ordinarily generated by a public or a private utility organization and provided to a customer, whether industrial or domestic, as alternating current.

One complete period, with current flow first in one direction and then in the other, is called a cycle, and 60 cycles per second (60 Hz) is the customary frequency of alternation in the United States and in all of North America. In Europe and in many other parts of the world, 50 Hz is the standard frequency. On aircraft a higher frequency, often 400 Hz, is used to make possible lighter electrical machines.

When the term alternating current is used as an adjective, it is commonly abbreviated to ac, as in ac motor. Similarly, direct current as an adjective is abbreviated dc.

**Advantages.** The voltage of an alternating current can be changed by a transformer. This simple, inexpensive, static device permits generation of electric power at moderate voltage, efficient transmission for many miles at high voltage, and distribution and consumption at a conveniently low voltage. With direct (unidirectional) current it is not possible to use a transformer to change voltage. On a few power lines, electric energy is transmitted for great distances as direct current, but the electric energy is generated as alternating current, transformed to a high voltage, then rectified to direct current and transmitted, then changed back to alternating current by an inverter, to be transformed down to a lower voltage for distribution and use.

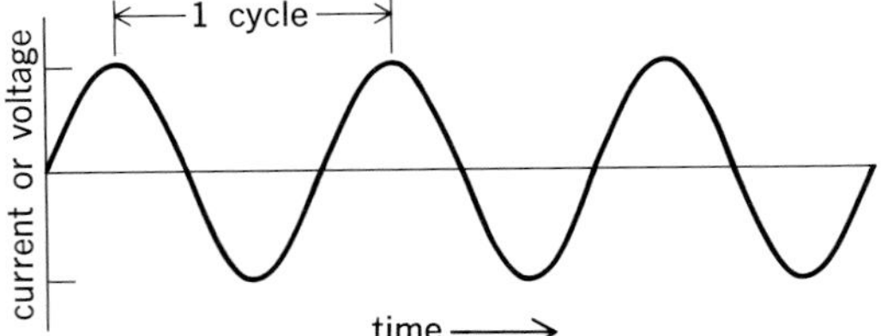


Fig. 1. Diagram of sinusoidal alternating current.

In addition to permitting efficient transmission of energy, alternating current provides advantages in the design of generators and motors, and for some purposes gives better operating characteristics. Certain devices involving chokes and transformers could be operated only with difficulty, if at all, on direct current. Also, the operation of large switches (called circuit breakers) is facilitated because the instantaneous value of alternating current automatically becomes zero twice in each cycle and an opening circuit breaker need not interrupt the current but only prevent current from starting again after its instant of zero value.

**Sinusoidal form.** Alternating current is shown diagrammatically in **Fig. 1**. Time is measured horizontally (beginning at any arbitrary moment) and the current at each instant is measured vertically. In this diagram it is assumed that the current is alternating sinusoidally; that is, the current $i$ is described by Eq. (1), where $I_m$ is the maximum instantaneous current,

$$i = I_m \sin 2\pi ft \tag{1}$$

$f$ is the frequency in cycles per second (hertz), and $t$ is the time in seconds.

A sinusoidal form of current, or voltage, is usually approximated on practical power systems because the sinusoidal form results in less expensive construction and greater efficiency of operation of electric generators, transformers, motors, and other machines.

**Measurement.** Quantities commonly measured by ac meters and instruments are energy, power, voltage, and current. Other quantities less commonly measured are reactive volt-amperes, power factor, frequency, and demand (of energy during a given interval such as 15 min).

Energy is measured on a watt-hour meter. There is usually such a meter where an electric line enters a customer's premises. The meter may be single-phase (usual in residences) or three-phase (customary in industrial installations), and it displays on a register of dials the energy that has passed, to date, to the system beyond the meter. The customer frequently pays for energy consumed according to the reading of such a meter.

Power is measured on a wattmeter. Since power is the rate of consumption of energy, the reading of the wattmeter is proportional to the rate of increase of the reading of a watt-hour meter. The same relation is expressed by saying that the reading of the watt-hour meter, which measures energy, is the integral (through time) of the reading of the wattmeter, which measures power. A wattmeter usually measures power in a single-phase circuit, although three-phase wattmeters are sometimes used.

Current is measured by an ammeter. Current is one component of power, the others being voltage and power factor, as in Eq. (5). With unidirectional (direct) current, the amount of current is the rate of flow of electricity; it is proportional to the number of electrons passing a specified cross section of a wire per second. This is likewise the definition of current at each instant of an alternating-current cycle, as current varies from a maximum in one direction to zero and then to a maximum in the other direction (Fig. 1). An oscilloscope will indicate instantaneous current, but instantaneous current is not often useful. A dc (d'Arsonval-type) ammeter will measure average current, but this is useless in an ac circuit, for the average of sinusoidal current is zero. A useful measure of alternating current is found in the ability of the current to do work, and the amount of current is correspondingly defined as the square root of the average of the square of instantaneous current, the average being taken over an integer number of cycles. This value is known as the root-mean-square (rms) or effective current. It is measured in amperes. It is a useful measure for current of any frequency. The rms value of direct current is identical with its dc value. The rms value of sinusoidally alternating current is $I_m/\sqrt{2}$, where $I_m$ is the maximum instantaneous current. See Fig. 1 and Eq. (1). SEE AMMETER; OSCILLOSCOPE.

Voltage is measured by a voltmeter. Voltage is the electrical pressure. It is measured between one point and another in an electric circuit, often between the two wires of the circuit. As with current, instantaneous voltage in an ac circuit reverses each half cycle and the average of sinusoidal voltage is zero. Therefore the root-mean-square (rms) or effective value of voltage is used in ac systems. The rms value of sinusoidally alternating voltage is $V_m/\sqrt{2}$, where $V_m$ is the maximum instantaneous voltage. This rms voltage, together with rms current and the circuit power factor, is used to compute electrical power, as in Eqs. (4) and (5). SEE VOLTMETER.

The ordinary voltmeter is connected by wires to the two points between which voltage is to be measured, and voltage is proportional to the current that results through a very high electrical resistance within the voltmeter itself. The voltmeter, actuated by this current, is calibrated in volts.

**Phase difference.** Phase difference is a measure of the fraction of a cycle by which one sinusoidally alternating quantity leads or lags another. **Figure 2** shows a voltage $v$ which is described in Eq. (2) and a current $i$ which is described in Eq. (3). The angle $\varphi$

$$v = V_m \sin 2\pi ft \tag{2}$$

$$i = I_m \sin (2\pi ft - \varphi) \tag{3}$$

is called the phase difference between the voltage and the current; this current is said to lag (behind this voltage) by the angle $\varphi$. It would be equally correct to say that the voltage leads the current by the phase angle $\varphi$. Phase difference can be expressed as a fraction of a cycle or in degrees of angle, or as in Eq.

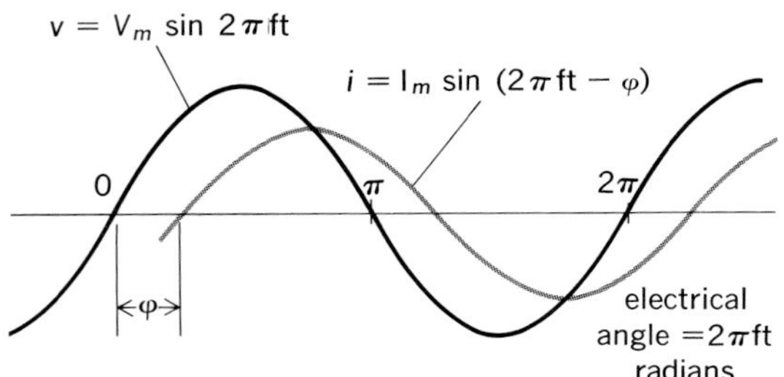


Fig. 2. Phase angle $\varphi$.

(3), in radians of angle, with corresponding minor changes in the equations.

If there is no phase difference, and $\varphi = 0$, voltage and current are in phase. If the phase difference is a quarter cycle, and $\varphi = \pm 90$ degrees, the quantities are in quadrature.

**Power factor.** Power factor is defined in terms of the phase angle. If the rms value of sinusoidal current from a power source to a load is $I$ and the rms value of sinusoidal voltage between the two wires connecting the power source to the load is $V$, the average power $P$ passing from the source to the load is shown as Eq. (4). The cosine of the phase angle, $\cos \varphi$, is

$$P = VI \cos \varphi \quad (4)$$

called the power factor. Thus the rms voltage, the rms current, and the power factor are the components of power.

The foregoing definition of power factor has meaning only if voltage and current are sinusoidal. Whether they are sinusoidal or not, average power, rms voltage, and rms current can be measured, and a value for power factor is implicit in Eq. (5). This

$$P = VI \text{ (power factor)} \quad (5)$$

gives a definition of power factor when $V$ and $I$ are not sinusoidal, but such a value for power factor has limited use.

If voltage and current are in phase (and of the same waveform), power factor equals 1. If voltage and current are out of phase, power factor is less than 1. If voltage and current are sinusoidal and in quadrature, power factor equals zero.

The phase angle and power factor of voltage and current in a circuit that supplies a load are determined by the load. Thus a load of pure resistance, as an electric heater, has unity power factor. An inductive load, such as an induction motor, has a power factor less than 1 and the current lags behind the applied voltage. A capacitive load, such as a bank of capacitors, also has a power factor less than 1, but the current leads the voltage, and the phase angle $\varphi$ is a negative angle.

If a load that draws lagging current (such as an induction motor) and a load that draws leading current (such as a bank of capacitors) are both connected to a source of electric power, the power factor of the two loads together can be higher than that of either one alone, and the current to the combined loads may have a smaller phase angle from the applied voltage than would currents to either of the two loads individually. Although power to the combined loads is equal to the arithmetic sum of power to the two individual loads, the total current will be less than the arithmetic sum of the two individual currents (and may, indeed, actually be less than either of the two individual currents alone). It is often practical to reduce the total incoming current by installing a bank of capacitors near an inductive load, and thus to reduce power lost in the incoming distribution lines and transformers, thereby improving efficiency.

**Three-phase system.** Three-phase systems are commonly used for generation, transmission, and distribution of electric power. A customer may be supplied with three-phase power, particularly if a large amount of power is needed or if the customer wishes to use three-phase loads. Small domestic customers are usually supplied with single-phase power.

A three-phase system is essentially the same as

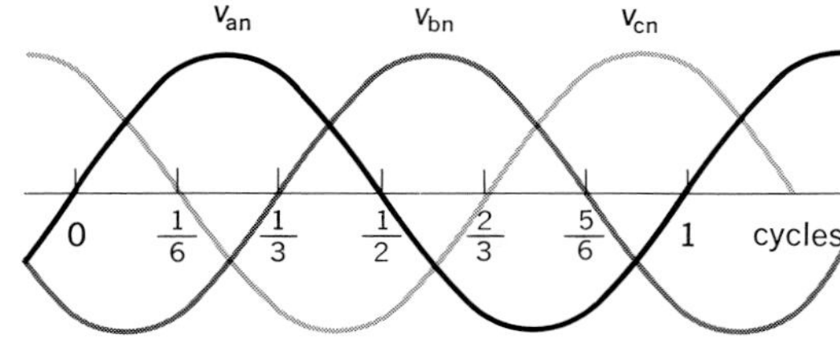


**Fig. 3. Voltages of a balanced three-phase system.**

three ordinary single-phase systems (as in Fig. 2, for instance) with the three voltages of the three single-phase systems out of phase with each other by one-third of a cycle (120 degrees) as shown in **Fig. 3**. The three voltages may be written as Eqs. (6), (7), and (8), where $V_{an(\max)}$ is the maximum value of voltage in

$$v_{an} = V_{an(\max)} \sin 2\pi ft \quad (6)$$

$$v_{bn} = V_{bn(\max)} \sin 2\pi(ft - 1/3) \quad (7)$$

$$v_{cn} = V_{cn(\max)} \sin 2\pi(ft - 2/3) \quad (8)$$

phase $an$, and so on. The three-phase system is balanced if relation (9) holds, and if the three phase an-

$$V_{an(\max} = V_{bn(\max)} = V_{cn(\max)} \quad (9)$$

gles are equal, ⅓ cycle each as shown.

If a three-phase system were actually three separate single-phase systems, there would be two wires between the generator and the load of each system, requiring a total of six wires. In fact, however, a single wire can be common to all three systems, so that it is only necessary to have three wires for a three-phase system ($a$, $b$, and $c$ of **Fig. 4**) plus a fourth wire $n$ to serve as a common return or neutral conductor. On some systems the earth is used as the common or neutral conductor.

Each phase of a three-phase system carries current and conveys power and energy. If the three loads on the three phases of the three-phase system are equal and the voltages are balanced, then the currents are balanced also. Figure 2 can then apply to any one of the three phases. It will be recognized that the three currents in a balanced system are equal in rms (or maximum) value and that they are separated one from the other by phase angles of ⅓ cycle and ⅔ cycle. Thus the currents (in a balanced system) are themselves symmetrical, and Fig. 3 could be applied to line currents $i_a$, $i_b$, and $i_c$ as well as to the three voltages indicated in the figure. Note, however, that the three currents will not necessarily be in phase with their respective voltages; the corresponding voltages and currents will be in phase with each other only if the load is pure resistance and the phase angle between voltage and current is zero. Otherwise some such relation as that of Fig. 2 will apply to each phase.

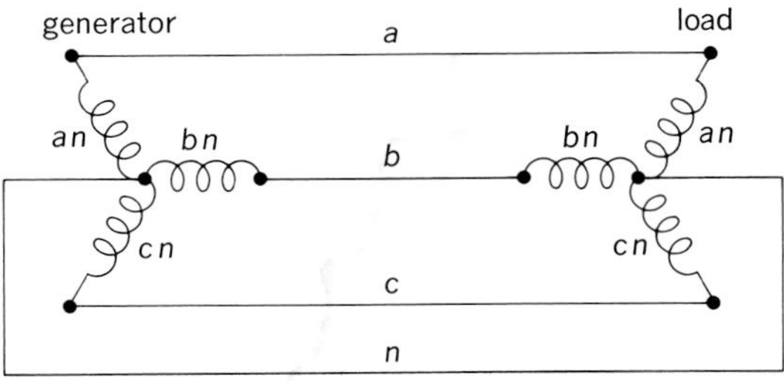


**Fig. 4. Connections of a simple three-phase system.**

It is significant that, if the three currents of a three-phase system are balanced, the sum of the three currents is zero at every instant. Thus if the three curves of Fig. 3 are taken to be the currents of a balanced system, it may be seen that the sum of the three curves at every instant is zero. This means that if the three currents are accurately balanced, current in the common conductor ($n$ of Fig. 4) is always zero, and that conductor could theoretically be omitted entirely. In practice, the three currents are not usually exactly balanced, and either of two situations obtains. Either the common neutral wire $n$ is used, in which case it carries little current (and may be of high resistance compared to the other three line wires), or else the common neutral wire $n$ is not used, only three line wires being installed, and the three phase currents are thereby forced to add to zero even though this requirement results in some inbalance of phase voltages at the load.

It is also significant that the total instantaneous power from generator to load is constant (does not vary with time) in a balanced, sinusoidal, three-phase system. Power in a single-phase system that has current in phase with voltage is maximum when voltage and current are maximum and it is instantaneously zero when voltage and current are zero; if the current of the single-phase system is not in phase with the voltage, the power will reverse its direction of flow during part of each half cycle. However, in a balanced three-phase system, regardless of the phase angle, the flow of power is unvarying from instant to instant. This results in smoother operation and less vibration of motors and other ac devices.

Three-phase systems are almost universally used for large amounts of power. In addition to providing smooth flow of power, three-phase motors and generators are more economical than single-phase machines. Polyphase systems with two, four, or other numbers of phases are possible, but they are little used except when a large number of phases, such as 12, is desired for economical operation of a rectifier.

**Power and information.** Although this article has emphasized electric power, ac circuits are also used to convey information. An information curcuit, such as telephone, radio, or control, employs varying voltage, current, waveform, frequency, and phase. Efficiency is often low, the chief requirement being to convey accurate information even though little of the transmitted power reaches the receiving end. For further consideration of the transmission of information *See Electrical communications; Radio; Telephone; Waveform.*

An ideal power circuit should provide the customer with electric energy always available at unchanging voltage of constant waveform and frequency, the amount of current being determined by the customer's load. High efficiency is greatly desired. *See Alternating-current circuit theory; Capacitance; Circuit (electricity); Electric current; Electric filter; Electrical impedance; Electrical resistance; Inductance; Joule's law; Network theory; Ohm's law; Resonance (alternating-current circuits).*

*H. H. Skilling*

## Alternating-current circuit theory

The mathematical theory for the analysis of electric circuits when the currents and voltages are alternating functions of time.

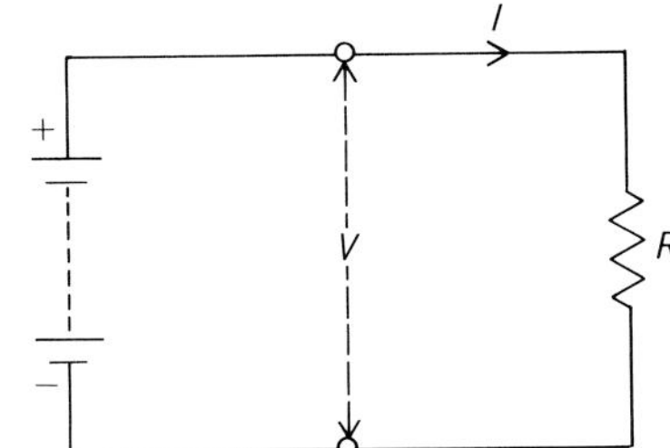


**Fig. 1. Direct-current circuit.**

In an electric circuit carrying direct current only (**Fig. 1**), the current $I$ (amperes) flowing through a circuit of total resistance $R$ (ohms) when a steady voltage $V$ (volts) is applied is given by Ohm's law; Eq. (1).

$$I = V/R \tag{1}$$

*See Circuit (electricity); Direct-current circuit theory; Ohm's law.*

In many practical situations, electrical energy is generated, transmitted, and distributed in a form in which the currents and voltages are not steady but are sinusoidally varying or "alternating" functions of time (**Fig. 2**). Public electricity supply systems are of this type, and many telecommunications systems use electrical signals of sinusoidal form as carriers of information. It is necessary to have a comprehensive theory to analyze such systems and to provide the basis for their design.

This is the object of alternating-current circuit theory. It differs from direct-current theory in that there are circuit elements other than resistors (particularly inductors and capacitors) which impede the flow of current: these are known generally as impedances.

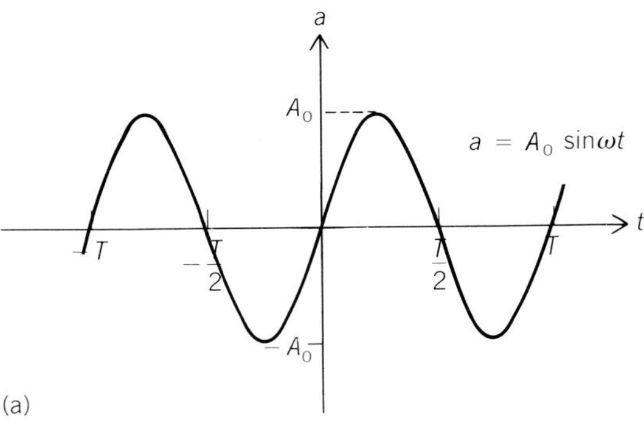


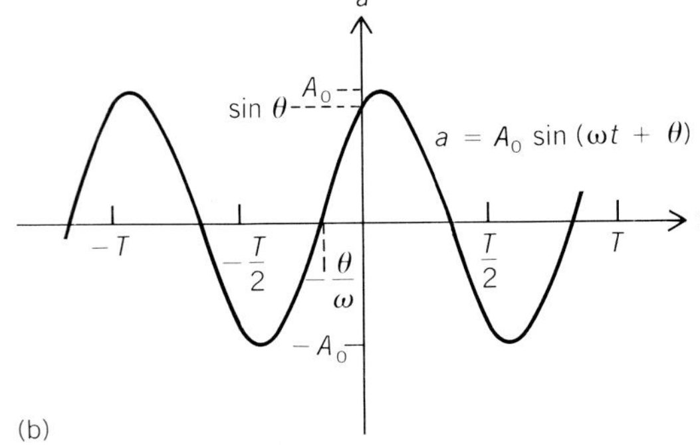


**Fig. 2. Sinusoidal waveforms. (*a*) Simple sinusoid without phase shift. (*b*) Sinusoid with phase shift.**

Also, it is possible to couple energy from one circuit to another by means of mutual inductances or transformers without the need for a linking conductor. Whereas in the dc case the sizes of voltages, currents, and resistors can all be described by single numbers, in the ac case pairs of numbers are needed to describe amplitude and phase or, for an impedance, amplitude ratio and phase shift. Mathematically, the properties and interrelations of pairs of numbers can be dealt with very succinctly by the use of complex algebra. It will be shown how ac circuit theory can be set out by using simple time-domain analysis of waveforms, illustrated by phasor diagrams, and then how the use of complex algebra provides a much more powerful and elegant theory.

**Waveforms.** A sinusoidal (or alternating) function $a$ of time $t$ is shown in Fig. 2*a*. It is described by Eq. (2), where $A_0$ is the maximum value (or amplitude) of

$$a(t) = A_0 \sin \omega t \tag{2}$$

$a$ and $\omega$ is known as the angular or radian frequency. The period $T$ of the function is the time after which the function repeats itself. During one period the function takes on all its possible values and is said to go through one cycle. The frequency $f$ of the sinusoid as usually defined (for example, 60 Hz) is the number of cycles which occur in 1 second, so $f = 1/T$. Since $\sin (x + 2\pi) = \sin x$, $\omega T = 2\pi$, and hence $\omega = 2\pi f$.

It is necessary to consider waveforms which do not cross the zero level at $t = 0$ but which include a phase shift. Figure 2*b* shows the waveform of Eq. (3), which is a waveform identical in shape with the

$$a(t) = A_0 \sin (\omega t + \theta) \tag{3}$$

waveform described by Eq. (2) but shifted in time so that it crosses the zero level at a time $\theta/\omega$ before $t = 0$. This is referred to as a phase advance: the corresponding waveform with $\theta$ negative would illustrate a phase delay.

Since $\sin (x + \pi/2) = \cos x$, Eq. (3) could equally well be written as Eq. (4), where the phase angle is

$$\begin{aligned} a &= A_0 \sin \left( \omega t + \frac{\pi}{2} + \theta - \frac{\pi}{2} \right) \\ &= A_0 \cos (\omega t + \psi) \end{aligned} \tag{4}$$

now $\psi = \theta - \pi/2$ radians. Henceforth, either of the forms in Eqs. (3) and (4) will be used, as convenient, to represent an alternating quantity. An alternating voltage is written as Eq. (5), and an alternating current as Eq. (6), where $v$ and $i$ represent the instantaneous values, and $V_0$ and $I_0$ the maximum values or amplitudes, of voltage and current respectively. SEE ALTERNATING CURRENT.

$$v = V_0 \sin (\omega t + \theta) \text{ or } v = V_0 \cos (\omega t + \psi) \tag{5}$$

$$i = I_0 \sin (\omega t + \theta) \text{ or } i = I_0 \cos (\omega t + \psi) \tag{6}$$

**Phasor diagrams.** It is sometimes helpful to visualize an alternating waveform as the projection of a rotating vector. This may be considered as corresponding in some sense to the generation of an alternating current by the rotation of a coil in a magnetic field.

In **Fig. 3***a*, $OR$ is a vector of length $A_0$ rotating in the anticlockwise direction about the origin of the $x$-$y$ plane with angular velocity $\omega$ radians per second. Then the projection of the vector $OR$ on the $x$ axis is $OX = A_0 \cos \omega t$, and the projection on the $y$ axis is $OY = A_0 \sin \omega t$. The rotating vector can thus be thought of as generating a sinusoidal waveform.

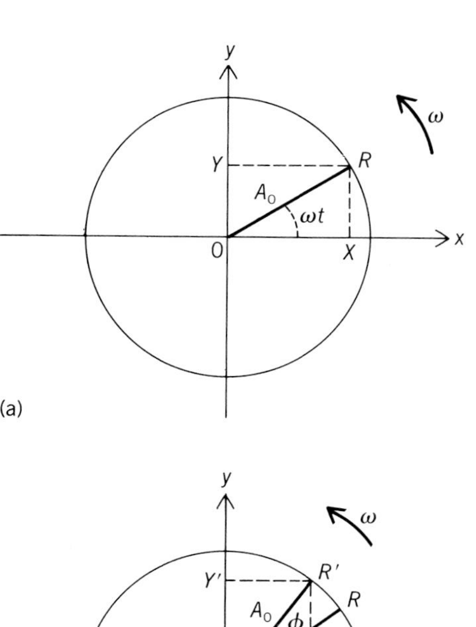


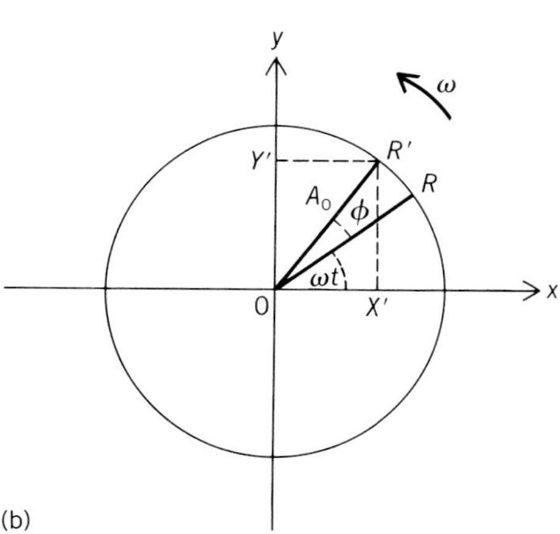


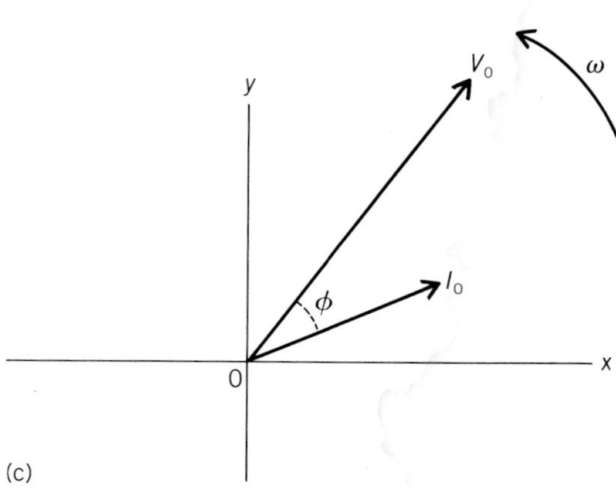


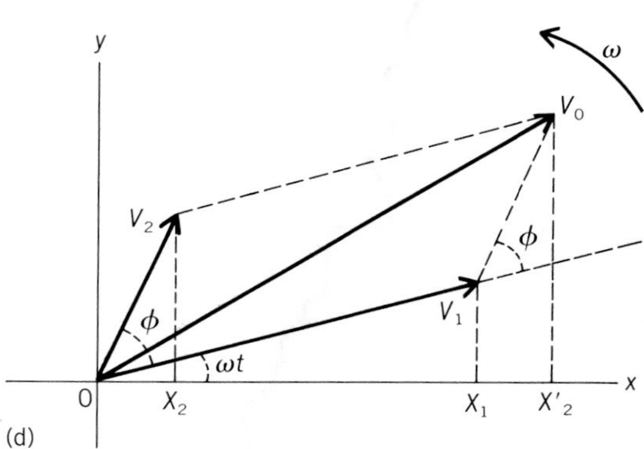


**Fig. 3.** Phasors. **(*a*)** Simple phasor. **(*b*)** Phasor with phase shift. **(c)** Voltage and current phasors. **(*d*)** Phasor for the sum of two voltages.

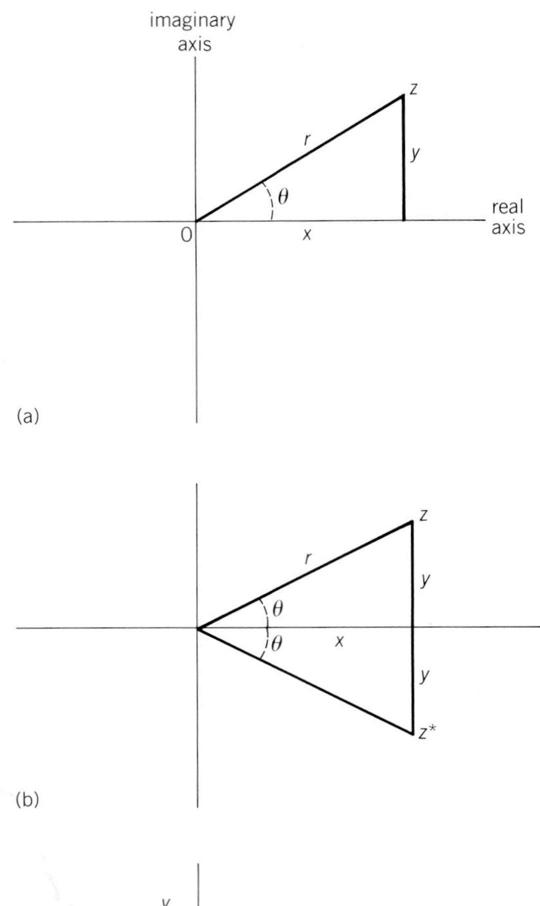


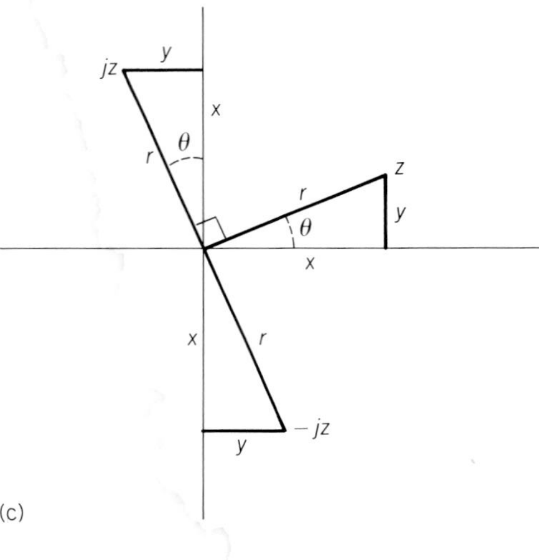


**Fig. 4. Complex numbers. (a) The number $z = x + jy = re^{j\theta}$. (b) Its complex conjugate $z^* = x - jy = re^{-j\theta}$. (c) Multiplication of z by $\pm j$, equivalent to rotation through 90°.**

If, instead of the vector $OR$, the vector $OR'$ in Fig. 3*b* is considered, displaced from $OR$ by an angle $\phi$ and rotating with it, then $OX' = \cos(\omega t + \phi)$ and $OY' = \sin(\omega t + \phi)$, so that rotation of the phasor (the name given to the vector in this type of diagram) corresponds to a phase shift in the waveform.

In a linear circuit, the voltage and current waveforms have related amplitudes and often a phase shift between them, but both are of the same frequency. They can thus be represented, as in Fig. 3*c*, as the projections of phasors of amplitudes $V_0$ and $I_0$ with an angle $\phi$ between them, rotating together in the $x$-$y$ plane. Circuit theory enables the ratio $V_0/I_0$ and the phase shift $\phi$ to be calculated from the circuit parameters.

If there are two voltages (or two currents) of different amplitudes and with a phase shift between them, say $v_1$ and $V_1 \cos \omega t$ and $v_2 = V_2 \cos(\omega t + \phi)$, represented as the projection on the $x$-axis of two phasors of amplitudes $V_1$ and $V_2$, it is easy to see from Fig. 3*d* that their sum can be represented as the projection of the resultant phasor $V_0$, the vector sum of $V_1$ and $V_2$. For $OX_1 = v_1$, $X_1X_2' = OX_2 = v_2$, and therefore $OX_2' = v_1 + v_2$.

**Complex representation.** While a phasor diagram helps to visualize the relationship between current and voltage in an ac circuit, it does little to help with the mathematical calculations. These are greatly simplified if complex algebra is used to describe the current, voltage, and circuit parameters. Only the formulas of complex algebra essential for circuit theory are reviewed here.

A complex number $z$ is defined by a pair of ordinary numbers. It can be written as in Eq. (7), where

$$z = x + jy \tag{7}$$

$x$ and $y$ are real numbers and $j = \sqrt{-1}$. (Mathematicians often use $i$ for this quantity, but in electrical work the symbol $i$ is reserved for electric current.) Here $x$ is called the real part of $z$, written $\mathfrak{Re}\,(z)$, and $y$ the imaginary part, written $\mathfrak{Im}\,(z)$. If $x$ and $y$ are regarded as coordinates in a (complex) plane, $z$ defines a point in the plane, as in **Fig. 4*a***. The distance from the origin $O$ to $z$, shown as $r$ in the diagram, is known as the modulus of $z$ written $|z|$; and the angle $\theta$ between the line from $O$ to $z$ and the real ($x$) axis is known as the argument of $z$. It is clear from the diagram that these quantities are given by Eqs. (8) and (9), and $x$ and $y$ are expressed in terms of them by Eqs. (10).

$$|z| = r = \sqrt{x^2 + y^2} \tag{8}$$

$$\theta = \tan^{-1} y/x \tag{9}$$

$$\begin{aligned} x &= r \cos\theta \\ y &= r \sin\theta \end{aligned} \tag{10}$$

De Moivre's theorem states that Eq. (11) is valid,

$$e^{j\theta} = \cos\theta + j \sin\theta \tag{11}$$

so an alternative way of writing $z$ is Eq. (12), and in

$$z = re^{j\theta} \tag{12}$$

giving numerical values it is often convenient to write Eq. (13).

$$z = r\angle\theta \tag{13}$$

The complex conjugate of $z$, $z^*$, is defined by Eq. (14). This is illustrated in Fig. 4*b*.

$$z^* = x - jy = re^{-j\theta} \tag{14}$$

Multiplication by $j$ is equivalent to rotation through $\pi/2$ radians, or 90°, as Fig. 4*c* illustrates, for Eq. (15)

$$jz = j(x + jy) = -y + jx \tag{15}$$

is valid since $j^2 = -1$, and the real and imaginary parts of the number interchange as shown. Similarly, multiplication by $-j$ corresponds to rotation through 90° in the opposite (clockwise) direction. From this it is apparent that $j = e^{j\pi/2}$.

In circuit analysis it is necessary to combine complex numbers in various ways. The rules of complex algebra for combining the numbers $z_1 = x_1 + jy_1$ and $z_2 = z_2 + jy_2$ are as follows:

The rule for addition is given by Eq. (16). This can

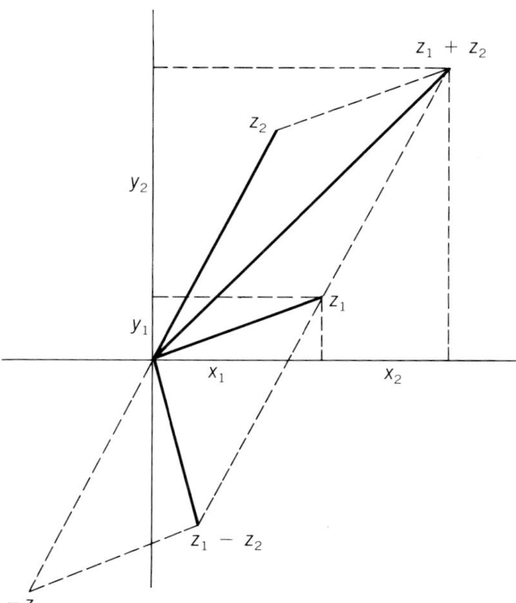


**Fig. 5. Addition and subtraction of complex numbers.**

$$z_1 + z_2 = (x_1 + x_2) + j(y_1 + y_2) \quad (16)$$

be interpreted geometrically by saying that $z_1 + z_2$ is represented by the vector sum of the two vectors $Oz_1$ and $Oz_2$, as shown in **Fig. 5**.

The rule for subtraction is given by Eq. (17). Similarly, $z_1 - z_2$ can be represented as the vector sum of the two vectors $Oz_1$ and $O(-z_2)$, as in Fig. 5.

$$z_1 - z_2 = (x_1 - x_2) + j(y_1 - y_2) \quad (17)$$

The rule for multiplication is given by Eq. (18), and that for division by Eq. (19). The process illustrated in Eq. (19) for converting the quotient of two complex numbers into a number of form $a + jb$ by multiplying both numerator and denominator by the complex conjugate of the denominator is known as rationalization.

$$\begin{aligned} z_1 z_2 &= (x_1 + jy_1)(x_2 + jy_2) \\ &= (x_1x_2 - y_1y_2) + j(x_1y_2 + x_2y_1) \\ &= r_1r_2e^{j(\theta_1 + \theta_2)} \end{aligned} \quad (18)$$

$$\begin{aligned} \frac{z_1}{z_2} &= \frac{x_1 + jy_1}{x_2 + jy_2} \\ &= \frac{(x_1 + jy_1)(x_2 - jy_2)}{(x_2 + jy_2)(x_2 - jy_2)} \\ &= \frac{x_1x_2 + y_1y_2}{x_2^2 + y_2^2} + j\frac{x_2y_1 - x_1y_2}{x_2^2 + y_2^2} \\ &= (r_1/r_2)\, e^{j(\theta_1 - \theta_2)} \end{aligned} \quad (19)$$

A comparison of Figs. 3*a* and 4*a* shows that alternating waveforms can be represented by the real or imaginary parts of complex numbers of argument $\omega t$, as in Eqs. (20).

$$\begin{aligned} A_0 \cos \omega t &= A_0\, \mathcal{R}e\, e^{j\omega t} \\ A_0 \sin \omega t &= A_0\, \mathcal{I}m\, e^{j\omega t} \end{aligned} \quad (20)$$

A sinusoid of arbitrary phase may be written as in Eq. (21), where $B$ is given by Eq. (22) [by De Moivre's theorem]. $B$ contains all the information needed in circuit analysis, since $A_0$ and $\theta$ can be calculated from $B$, and the frequency is given by $\omega$. It is therefore possible to formulate a circuit analysis in which the driving waveforms are of the form given by Eqs. (23), where $V$ and $I$ are complex quantities.

$$\begin{aligned} A_0 \cos(\omega t + \theta) &= {}^1\!/\!_2 A_0\, e^{j(\omega t + \theta)} + {}^1\!/\!_2 A_0\, e^{-j(\omega t + \theta)} \\ &= Be^{j\omega t} + B^* e^{-j\omega t} \end{aligned} \quad (21)$$

$$B = {}^1\!/\!_2 A_0 e^{j\theta} \quad (22)$$

$$\begin{aligned} v &= Ve^{j\omega t} = V_0 e^{j\theta} e^{j\omega t} \\ i &= Ie^{j\omega t} = I_0 e^{j\theta} e^{j\omega t} \end{aligned} \quad (23)$$

The circuit parameters are also in complex form, and from these a response in similar form can be calculated which can be directly interpreted as a sinusoidal waveform.

**Circuit elements.** With steady currents, the only circuit element of significance is resistance. Voltage, current, and resistance are related by Ohm's law: circuit theory is needed to calculate the effective resistance of various series and parallel combinations of individual resistors. With alternating currents, inductance and capacitance have also to be taken into account. In these elements the rate of change of current or voltage is important. The relation between alternating current and voltage in the various types of circuit elements will be discussed. For purposes of theory, these are regarded as ideal elements of one kind only. In practice it is impossible to make an inductor, for example, without some residual resistance, but this will be ignored in the discussion below.

***Resistance.*** As in the dc case, the instantaneous voltage $v$ across a resistance $R$ and the current $i$ through it are related by Ohm's law, Eq. (24). If $v$ is given by Eq. (25), then $i$ is given by Eq. (26). Cur-

$$v = iR \quad (24)$$

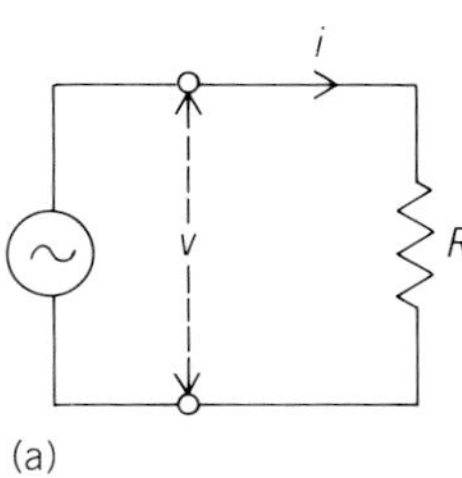


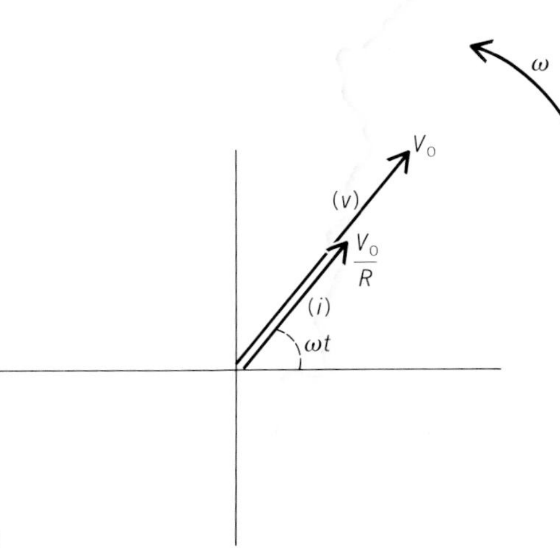


**Fig. 6. Resistance. (*a*) Circuit diagram of resistor and source of alternating voltage. (*b*) Phasor diagram of voltage and current through a resistance.**

$$v = V_0 \cos \omega t \qquad (25)$$

$$i = \left(\frac{V_0}{R}\right) \cos \omega t \qquad (26)$$

rent and voltage are in phase and can be represented in a phasor diagram as in **Fig. 6**, which also shows the conventional circuit representation of a resistor and a source of alternating voltage. SEE ELECTRICAL RESISTANCE; RESISTOR.

***Self-inductance.*** An inductor typically takes the form of a coil of wire, with or without a core of high-permeability magnetic material depending on the value of inductance required and the frequency of operation. The essential property of a single, or self-, inductance (so called to distinguish it from mutual inductance involving two coils, discussed below) is that the voltage across its terminals is related to the rate of change of current through it by Eq. (27). The

$$v = L\left(\frac{di}{dt}\right) \qquad (27)$$

inductance $L$ is measured in henrys when the voltage and current are in volts and amperes.

If the current is alternating and given by Eq. (28), the voltage is then given by Eq. (29). Thus the ratio

$$i = I_0 \cos \omega t \qquad (28)$$

$$v = LI_0(-\omega \sin \omega t) = \omega L I_0 \cos\left(\omega t + \frac{\pi}{2}\right) \qquad (29)$$

of the amplitudes of voltage and current is $\omega L$ and the voltage waveform is in advance of the current by a phase shift of $\pi/2$, or 90° (**Fig. 7**).

If the current is instead represented by a complex quantity as in Eq. (30), then Eq. (31) is obtained.

$$i = Ie^{j\omega t} \qquad (30)$$

$$v = j\omega L I e^{j\omega t} \qquad (31)$$

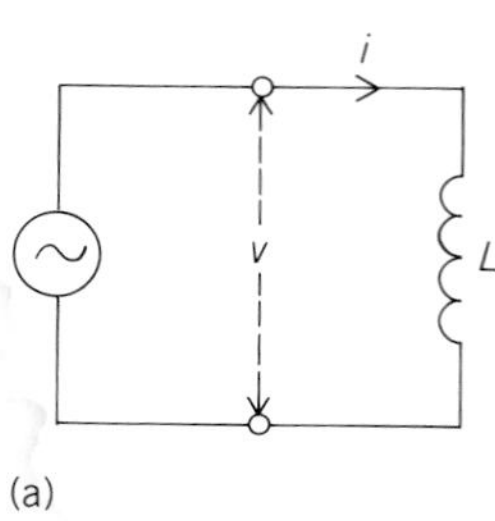


(a)

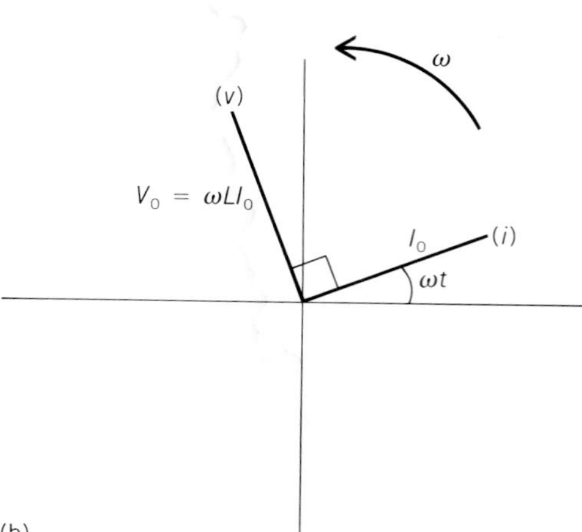


(b)

**Fig. 7. Inductance. (*a*) Circuit diagram of inductor and source of alternating voltage. (*b*) Phasor diagram of voltage and current through an inductance.**

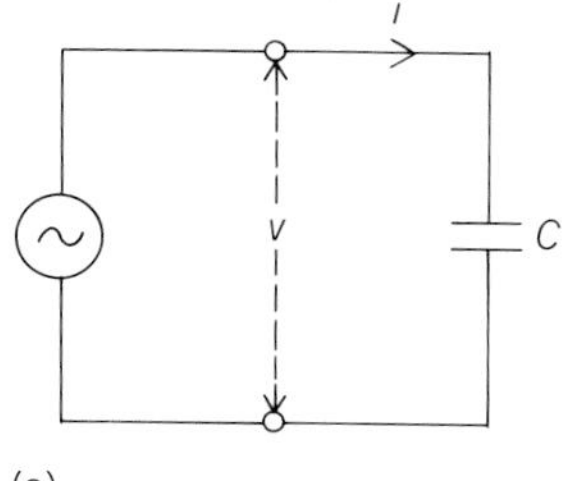


(a)

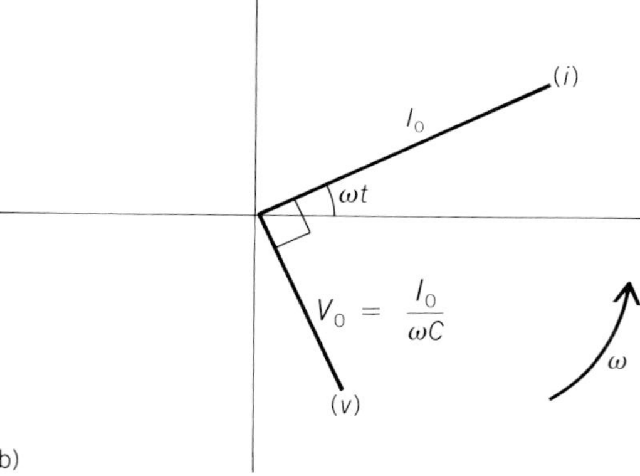


(b)

**Fig. 8. Capacitance. (*a*) Circuit diagram of capacitor and source of alternating voltage. (*b*) Phasor diagram of voltage and current through a capacitance.**

This represents the same result, since multiplying by $j$ is equivalent to a positive (anticlockwise) rotation through a right angle. SEE INDUCTANCE; INDUCTOR.

***Capacitance.*** An inductor stores energy in the magnetic field associated with an electric current. A capacitance stores energy in the electric field produced by the separation of charge in a dielectric medium. Typically a capacitor consists of two conducting plates separated by a dielectric. The current flowing in is related to the rate of change of voltage across the capacitor by Eq. (32), where $C$ is the capacitance in farads.

$$i = C\frac{dv}{dt} \qquad (32)$$

If the voltage is given by Eq. (33), then the current is given by Eq. (34). So in this case the ratio of volt-

$$v = V_0 \cos \omega t \qquad (33)$$

$$i = CV_0(-\omega \sin \omega t) = \omega C V_0 \cos\left(\omega t + \frac{\pi}{2}\right) \qquad (34)$$

age to current amplitudes is $1/\omega C$, and the voltage waveform lags behind the current by $\pi/2$ (**Fig. 8**).

In complex form, if the voltage is given by Eq. (35), the current is given by Eq. (36), representing

$$v = Ve^{j\omega t} \qquad (35)$$

$$i = j\omega C V e^{j\omega t} \qquad (36)$$

the same result. SEE CAPACITANCE; CAPACITOR.

***Mutual inductance.*** If two coils are linked by a common magnetic flux, the voltage $v_2$ across the second coil is related to the rate of change of current $i_1$ in the first coil by Eq. (37), where $M$ is the mutual induc-

$$v_2 = M\frac{di_1}{dt} \qquad (37)$$

tance, measured in henrys. If $i_1$ is given by Eq. (38), then $v_2$ is given by Eq. (39), and the voltage is 90° out of phase with the primary current.

$$i_1 = I_1 e^{j\omega t} \tag{38}$$

$$v_2 = j\omega L I_1 e^{j\omega t} \tag{39}$$

For further discussion of mutual inductance SEE COUPLED CIRCUITS.

**Circuit analysis.** The main problem of ac circuit theory is the calculation of the relationships between currents and voltages in circuits containing various combinations of the circuit elements described above.

In order to analyze any physical electric circuit, it is necessary to construct a mathematical model. Such a model is an idealization of the real circuit, but the behavior of the model may be made to approximate that of the real circuit sufficiently closely so that analysis of the model yields results which may be applied with confidence to the real circuit. In the vast majority of cases the circuits to be analyzed are linear. In a linear circuit the most important property is that if the amplitude of the source voltages or currents is changed then the amplitudes of all other currents and voltages are changed in the same proportion. Further, in the case of sinusoidal currents and voltages every current and voltage in the circuit has the same frequency, ω. In the remainder of this article only linear circuits will be discussed.

In an electric circuit the elements are connected together in some given fashion. Sources (or generators) of external current or voltage are applied to the circuit, and the problem is to calculate the resulting current and voltage associated with each circuit element. **Figure 9***a* and *b* illustrates the symbols used for voltage and current sources respectively. Although voltage and current change direction every half-cycle, it is necessary to have a sign convention to relate voltage and direction of current flow, compatible of course with that used in dc circuits. This is illustrated in Fig. 9*c* which is to be understood in the sense that, during the half-cycle in which the upper terminal of the source in the diagram carries the positive voltage, current flows through the resistor in the direction shown, from top to bottom of the diagram. In the next half-cycle both voltage and current reverse. The power dissipated in the resistor is *vi*, so the convention ensures that the power is positive in each half-cycle.

The analysis of any circuit is based on Kirchhoff's laws, which state that:

1. The sum of the instantaneous currents entering the junction of two or more circuit elements is zero.
2. The sum of the instantaneous voltages around any closed loop formed by two or more circuit elements is zero.

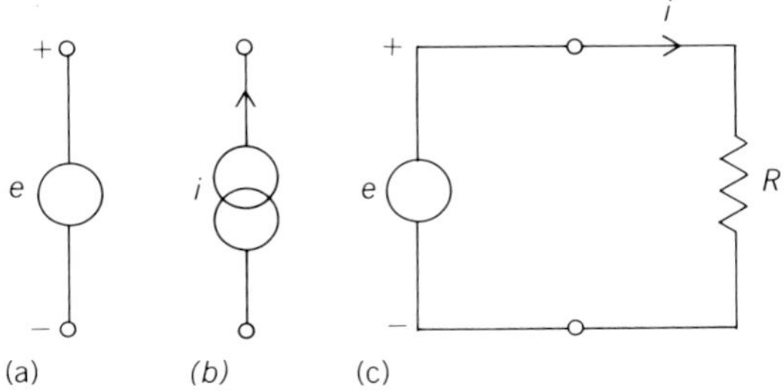


**Fig. 9. Sources and signs. (*a*) Voltage source. (*b*) Current source. (*c*) Sign convention.**

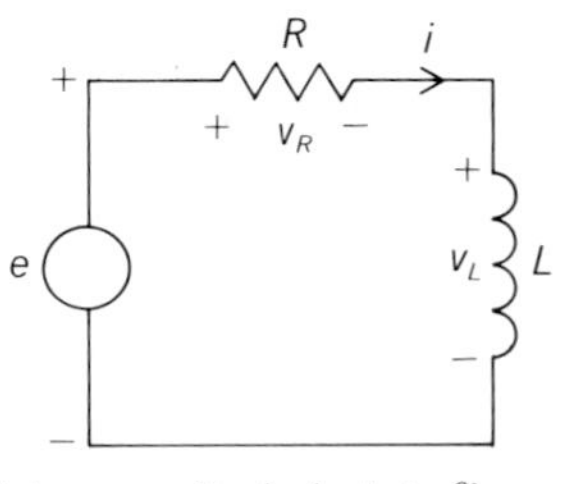


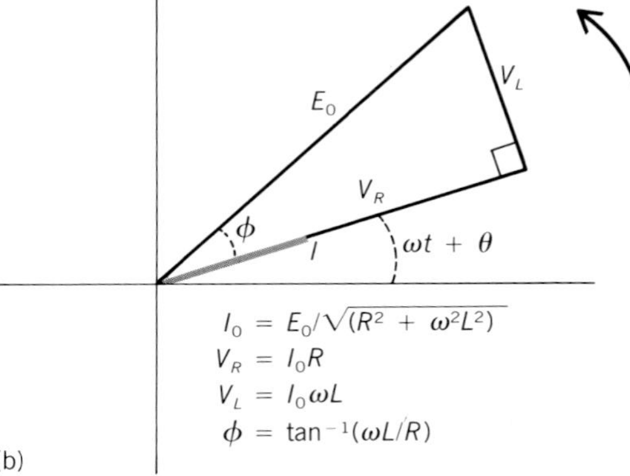


**Fig. 10. Circuit with resistance and inductance. (*a*) Circuit diagram. (*b*) Phasor diagram.**

In both cases, proper account must be taken of the convention regarding positive and negative quantities. SEE KIRCHHOFF'S LAWS OF ELECTRIC CIRCUITS.

***Analysis in the time domain.*** Consider the simple circuit shown in **Fig. 10** which consists of a voltage source, a resistor, and an inductor connected in series. (Components are in series when the same current flows through each.) Kirchhoff's law indicates that the sum of the voltages around the loop is zero; that is, Eq. (40) holds. Now the voltage source $e$ is $E_0$

$$v_R + v_L - e = 0 \tag{40}$$

$\sin(\omega t + \theta)$, and the (unknown) current is assumed to be $I_0 \sin(\omega t + \beta)$, so that Eq. (41) is valid, and

$$RI_0 \sin(\omega t + \beta) + L\omega I_0 \cos(\omega t + \beta) - E_0 \sin(\omega t + \theta) = 0 \tag{41}$$

must be solved to find $I_0$ and β.

When $\omega t + \theta = 0$, Eq. (41) reduces to Eq. (42) or Eq. (43).

$$R \sin(\beta - \theta) + L\omega \cos(\beta - \theta) = 0 \tag{42}$$

$$\tan(\beta - \theta) = -\frac{L\omega}{R} \tag{43}$$

When $\omega t + \theta = \pi/2$, Eq. (41) reduces to Eq. (44) or (45). Substituting from Eq. (43) for $\sin(\beta - \theta)$

$$RI_0 \sin\left(\frac{\pi}{2} + \beta - \theta\right) + L\omega I_0 \cos\left(\frac{\pi}{2} + \beta - \theta\right) = E_0 \tag{44}$$

$$I_0 [R \cos(\beta - \theta) - L\omega \sin(\beta - \theta)] = E_0 \tag{45}$$

and $\cos(\beta - \theta)$ yields Eqs. (46) or (47).

$$I_0 \left(\frac{R^2}{\sqrt{R^2 + L^2\omega^2}} + \frac{L^2\omega^2}{\sqrt{R^2 + L^2\omega^2}}\right) = E_0 \tag{46}$$

$$I_0 = \frac{E_0}{\sqrt{R^2 + L^2\omega^2}} \tag{47}$$

Hence the voltages across the resistor and the inductor are given by Eqs. (48) and (49). The phasor

$$v_R = \frac{E_0 R}{\sqrt{R^2 + \omega^2 L^2}} \cdot \sin\left(\omega t + \theta - \tan^{-1}\frac{\omega L}{R}\right) \tag{48}$$

$$v_L = \frac{E_0 \omega L}{\sqrt{R^2 + \omega^2 L^2}} \cdot \sin\left(\omega t + \theta - \tan^{-1}\frac{\omega L}{R} + \frac{\pi}{2}\right) \tag{49}$$

diagram for this circuit is given in Fig. 10*b*. The voltages across the resistor and the inductor are $\pi/2$ radians out of phase, and the voltage across the circuit leads the current through it by the phase angle $\tan^{-1}(\omega L/R)$.

The analysis of any other circuit proceeds in the same way. The necessary equations are written by using Kirchhoff's laws and the relationships of Eqs. (24), (29), and (34) as appropriate. The solutions for the unknown currents or voltages are sinusoids with the same frequency as the applied voltages and currents but unknown amplitudes and phase angles. By evaluating the equations at particular values of time, as in the above examples, the unknown amplitudes and phase angles are then determined. The phase angles are found as differences relative to the phase angle of the applied generator. In the above example, $\beta - \theta$ is found, but not $\beta$ as such. This is because one phase angle (here $\theta$) must be taken as a reference angle, and the only important quantity is the value of other phase angles relative to this. Another way of looking at this is to note that the choice of origin on the time axis is quite arbitrary since all voltages and currents extend from $t = -\infty$ to $t = \infty$, which is an idealization of the real situation where the generator must start at some definite time. The choice of the reference phase angle corresponds to a particular choice of time origin.

While this method can, in principle, be used to analyze any circuit, it becomes extremely cumbersome for a circuit of even moderate complexity. Simplification of the analysis by the use of complex algebra will be discussed, but first the dissipation of power in an ac circuit must be considered.

***Power.*** Consider the current and voltage associated with an arbitrary circuit (**Fig. 11**). The instantaneous power $p$ is equal to $vi$. Let the voltage and current be given by Eqs. (50) and (51). Then the instantaneous power is given by Eq. (52), which is the sum of a

$$v = V_0 \sin(\omega t + \theta) \tag{50}$$

$$i = I_0 \sin(\omega t + \beta) \tag{51}$$

$$\begin{aligned} p &= V_0 I_0 \sin(\omega t + \theta)\sin(\omega t + \theta) \\ &= {}^1\!/\!{}_2 V_0 I_0[\cos(2\omega t + \theta + \beta) \\ &\qquad + \cos(\beta - \theta)] \end{aligned} \tag{52}$$

sinusoid at radian frequency $2\omega$ and a constant independent of $t$. The instantaneous power is generally of much less interest than the average power $P$. The average value of a sinusoid is zero so that the average power is given by Eq. (53), where $\hat{V} = V/\sqrt{2}$ and

$$\begin{aligned} P &= {}^1\!/\!{}_2 V_0 I_0 \cos(\beta - \theta) \\ &= \hat{V}\hat{I}\cos(\beta - \theta) \end{aligned} \tag{53}$$

$\hat{I} = I/\sqrt{2}$ are called the root-mean-square (rms) values of $v$ and $i$ respectively, and $\cos(\beta - \theta)$ is called the power factor of the circuit. Thus the power depends not only on the amplitudes of the current and voltage but also on the phase angle between them. This is illustrated by the cases of the resistor, given by Eqs. (54); the inductor, given by Eqs. (55); and the capacitor, given by Eqs. (56). For both the inductor and the capacitor the average power is zero.

$$\left.\begin{aligned} V_0 &= RI_0,\ \beta - \theta = 0 \\ P &= \hat{V}\hat{I} = R\hat{I}^2 = \hat{V}^2/R \end{aligned}\right\}\text{resistor} \tag{54}$$

$$\left.\begin{aligned} V_0 &= L\omega\, I_0,\ \beta - \theta = -\frac{\pi}{2} \\ P &= 0 \end{aligned}\right\}\text{inductor} \tag{55}$$

$$\left.\begin{aligned} I_0 &= C\omega V_0,\ \beta - \theta = \frac{\pi}{2} \\ P &= 0 \end{aligned}\right\}\text{capacitor} \tag{56}$$

It follows therefore that in an ac circuit, power is dissipated only in resistive elements, not in inductors or capacitors. The voltage across these latter elements is 90° out of phase with the current through them. The total voltage across a series circuit is made up of the vector sum of the phasors representing the individual element voltages. It is common to speak of in-phase components of the voltage (having the same phase as the current) and out-of-phase or quadrature components with a 90° phase difference. Because no power is dissipated in these components, the current through an inductor or capacitor is sometimes referred to as a wattless current.

In electric power systems the values quoted for current and voltage are usually the rms values since the power available is related directly to these quantities. However, it must be borne in mind that they must be multipled by $\sqrt{2}$ to obtain the actual amplitudes of current and voltage.

***Analysis using complex impedances.*** The method of time domain analysis described above is quite general, and any circuit may be solved with those techniques. However, the method is cumbersome and does not give much insight into circuit behavior. Further, and perhaps more important, there are a wide variety of circuit theorems developed for use in dc circuit analysis which can both simplify analysis and provide considerable insight, but which cannot be used in ac circuits if one is restricted to the methods of time domain analysis. These considerations led to the development of a method of analysis based on complex notation which makes these techniques available in ac circuit analysis.

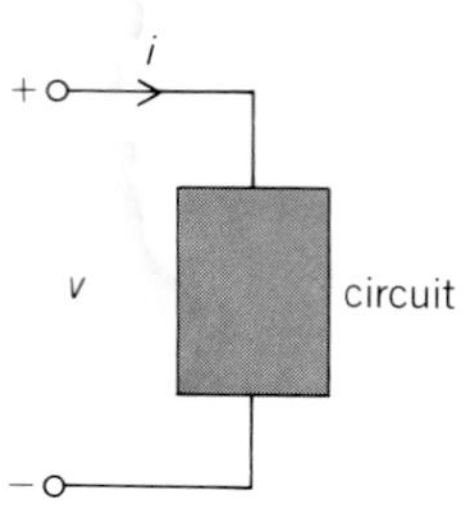


**Fig. 11. Generalized circuit.**

In an ac circuit every current and voltage is a sinusoid of the same frequency $\omega$, and each is characterized by two quantities, namely the amplitude and the phase angle relative to some reference angle. Thus two independent qualities are needed to describe each current and voltage. As discussed above, an alternating current or voltage can be represented by an expression of the form $Ie^{j\omega t}$ or $Ve^{j\omega t}$, and this representation can be applied to circuit analysis.

In the previous example of Fig. 10, Eq. (40) leads to Eq. (57) or (58), from which the modulus and argument of $I$ are given by Eqs. (59) and (60). Thus if

$$RIe^{j\omega t} + jL\omega Ie^{j\omega t} - Ee^{j\omega t} = 0 \qquad (57)$$

$$I = \frac{E}{R + jL\omega} \qquad (58)$$

$$|I| = \frac{E}{\sqrt{R^2 + L^2\omega^2}} \qquad (59)$$

$$\text{Argument } I = \text{Argument } E - \tan^{-1}\frac{L\omega}{R} = \beta \qquad (60)$$

the voltage source is given by Eq. (61), then the current is given by Eq. (62), which is the result previously found. However, now the analysis is very simple by using the complex quantities.

$$e = E_0 \sin(\omega t + \theta) \qquad (61)$$

$$i = |I| \sin\left(\omega t + \theta - \tan^{-1}\frac{L\omega}{R}\right) \qquad (62)$$

In the case of the resistor, inductor, and capacitor and in the example, equations are obtained where every term is multiplied by $e^{j\omega t}$, and this is true in general. Thus, this multiplier could just as well be omitted in every case and equations could be written involving only the complex quantitites $V$ and $I$. Once $V$ and $I$ are found, the answer for sinusoidal generators can be found immediately. Thus, for a resistor, $V = RI$; for an inductor, $V = j\omega LI$ and for a capacitor, $V = I/jC\omega$. For the complex voltages and currents corresponding to a frequency $\omega$, an inductor behaves as if it were a resistor of value $j\omega L$, and a capacitor behaves as if it were a resistor of value $1/j\omega C$. The problem of analysis is thereby reduced to the analysis of dc circuits, except that all currents and voltages are complex numbers and some ''resistors'' are real while others are imaginary. *See* NETWORK THEORY.

When these complex currents and voltages are used, the ratio $V/I$ in a circuit is called the (complex) impedance of the circuit (usually written $Z$; **Fig. 12**), and the ratio $I/V$ is called the (complex) admittance of the circuit (usually written $Y$). The units of impedance are ohms, and of admittance are siemens (mhos). The impedance and admittance are expressed in terms of their real and imaginary parts by Eqs. (63) and (64)

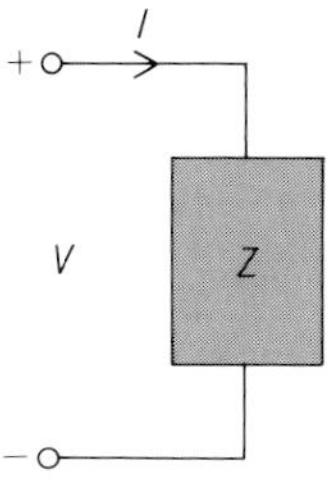


**Fig. 12. General impedance.**

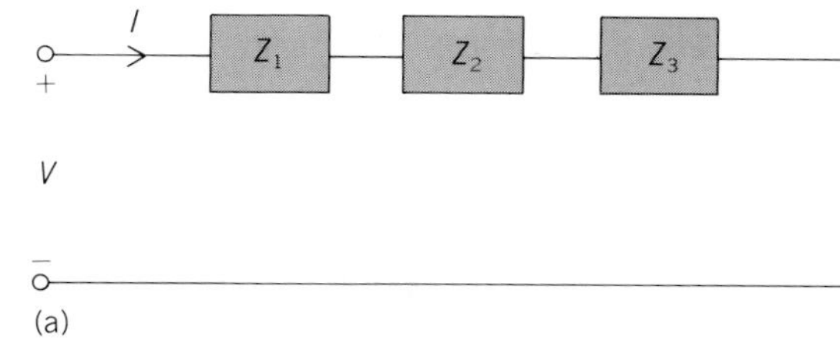


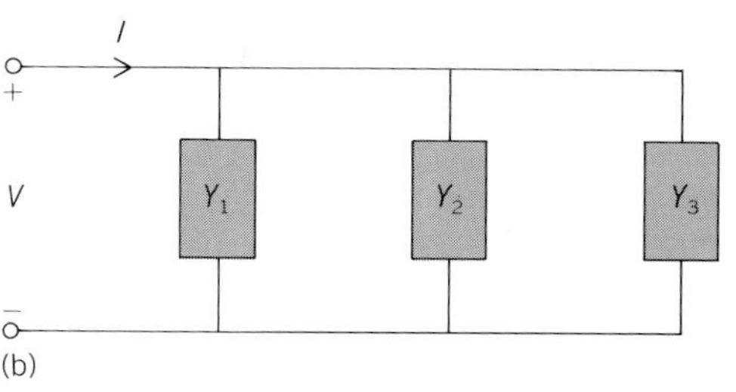


**Fig. 13. Combination of impedances and admittances. (*a*) Impedances in series. (*b*) Admittances in parallel.**

$$\frac{V}{I} = Z = R + jX \qquad (63)$$

$$\frac{I}{V} = Y = G + jB \qquad (64)$$

and are related to each other by Eq. (65) or (66). Similarly, Eq. (67) is valid.

$$Y = \frac{1}{Z} \qquad (65)$$

$$G + jB = \frac{1}{R + jX} = \frac{R}{R^2 + X^2} - j\frac{X}{R^2 + X^2} \qquad (66)$$

$$R + jX = \frac{1}{G + jB} = \frac{G}{G^2 + B^2} - j\frac{B}{G^2 + B^2} \qquad (67)$$

Impedances, like resistances, can be combined in series and parallel. **Figure 13*a*** shows three impedances in series. By definition the voltage across each impedance is $ZI$, and application of Kirchhoff's law to the loop yields Eq. (68) or (69), so the equivalent impedance $Z_{eq}$ is the sum of the impedances in series.

$$Z_1I + Z_2I + Z_3I - V = 0 \qquad (68)$$

$$\frac{V}{I} = Z_1 + Z_2 + Z_3 = Z_{eq} \qquad (69)$$

Figure 13*b* shows three admittances in parallel. By definition the current in each admittance is $YV$, and application of Kirchoff's law yields Eq. (70) or Eq. (71). Thus the reciprocal of the equivalent impedance $Z_{eq}$ is the sum of the admittances in parallel.

$$Y_1V + Y_2V + Y_3V - I = 0 \qquad (70)$$

$$\frac{V}{I} = \frac{1}{Y_1 + Y_2 + Y_3} = Z_{eq} \qquad (71)$$

The real and imaginary components of impedance and admittance are given special names. For impedance, $Z = R + jX$, the real part $R$ is resistance in the usual way; the imaginary part $X$ ($\omega L$ for an inductor or $-1/\omega C$ for a capacitor) is known as reactance.

For admittance, $Y = G + jB$, the real part $G$ is

called conductance, and the imaginary part, $B$, susceptance.

In a series circuit having resistance $R$ and reactance $X$, the conductance is not simply the reciprocal of the resistance but, from Eq. (66), a quantity involving both the resistance and the reactance, namely $R/(R^2 + X^2)$.

Occasionally, it is useful to be able to refer to either impedance or admittance without specifying which in particular is meant. The general term immittance is used to cover both. For obvious reasons it is not possible to specify units for it. SEE ADMITTANCE; CONDUCTANCE; ELECTRICAL IMPEDANCE; IMMITANCE; REACTANCE; SUSCEPTANCE.

***Power dissipated.*** As discussed above, the power entering a circuit, such as Fig. 11, is given by Eq. (72), where $V_0$ and $I_0$ are the amplitudes of the voltage and current sinusoids, and $\theta - \beta$ is the angular phase difference between them. This power can also be expressed in terms of the complex quantities $V$ and $I$.

$$P = \tfrac{1}{2}V_0 I_0 \cos(\theta - \beta) \tag{72}$$

If $V$ and $I$ are written as in Eqs. (73) and (74), then Eqs. (75) and (76) are valid. Thus, the power is given by Eq. (77).

$$V = V_0 e^{j\theta} \tag{73}$$

$$I = I_0 e^{j\beta} \tag{74}$$

$$\begin{aligned} VI^* &= V_0 I_0 e^{j(\theta-\beta)} \\ &= V_0 I_0 [\cos(\theta - \beta) + j\sin(\theta - \beta)] \end{aligned} \tag{75}$$

$$V^*I = V_0 I_0 [\cos(\theta - \beta) - j\sin(\theta - \beta)] \tag{76}$$

$$P = \tfrac{1}{4}(VI^* + V^*I) = \tfrac{1}{2}V_0 I_0 \cos(\theta - \beta) \tag{77}$$

If $V = ZI$, then the power is also given by Eq. (78), and if $I = YV$, then it is also given by Eq. (79).

$$P = \tfrac{1}{4}(ZII^* + Z^*II^*) = \tfrac{1}{4}I_0^2(Z + Z^*) \tag{78}$$

$$P = \tfrac{1}{4}(YVV^* + Y^*VV^*) = \tfrac{1}{4}V_0^2(Y + Y^*) \tag{79}$$

These equations give alternative ways of calculating the power from the voltage or current and circuit parameters.

**Resonant circuit.** Consider the circuit of **Fig. 14*a*** with a voltage generator driving a capacitor in parallel with an inductor and resistance in series. The generator produces a voltage $e = E_0 \sin(\omega t + \theta)$. Suppose it is necessary to calculate the currents in the capacitor, resistor, and inductor, and the power dissipated in the circuit.

The circuit can be redrawn as in Fig. 14*b*. $Y_1$ is the admittance of the capacitor and $Y_2 = 1/Z_2$, where $Z_2$ is the impedance of the resistor and inductor in series. Now $Z_2$ is given by Eq. (80), so $Y_2$ is given by Eq. (81) and $Y_1$ is given by Eq. (82). The equivalent impedance of the circuit, $Z_{eq}$, is given by Eq. (83),

$$Z_2 = R + jL\omega \tag{80}$$

$$\begin{aligned} Y_2 &= \frac{1}{R + jL\omega} \\ &= \frac{R}{R^2 + L^2\omega^2} - j\frac{L\omega}{R^2 + L^2\omega^2} \end{aligned} \tag{81}$$

$$Y_1 = jC\omega \tag{82}$$

$$Z_{eq} = \frac{1}{Y_1 + Y_2} \tag{83}$$

and the generator voltage is related to the total current by Eq. (84) or Eq. (85) so that the total current is given by Eq. (86).

$$E = Z_{eq}I \tag{84}$$

$$I = E/Z_{eq} \tag{85}$$

$$\begin{aligned} I &= E(Y_1 + Y_2) \\ &= E\left[\frac{R}{R^2 + L^2\omega^2} + j\left(C\omega - \frac{L\omega}{R^2 + L^2\omega^2}\right)\right] \end{aligned} \tag{86}$$

The current through the capacitor is $Y_1E = j\omega CE$, while the current through the series combination of the resistor and inductor is $Y_2E$, given by Eq. (87).

$$Y_2E = E\left(\frac{R}{R^2 + L^2\omega^2} - j\frac{L\omega}{R^2 + L^2\omega^2}\right) \tag{87}$$

The power dissipated in the circuit is found, by using Eq. (79), to be given by Eq. (88).

$$\begin{aligned} P &= \tfrac{1}{4}E_0^2(Y_{eq} + Y_{eq}^*) \\ &= \tfrac{1}{4}E_0^2(Y_1 + Y_2 + Y_1^* + Y_2^*) \\ &= \tfrac{1}{2}E_0^2\frac{R}{R^2 + L^2\omega^2} \end{aligned} \tag{88}$$

This circuit exhibits the phenomenon of resonance. Suppose the frequency $\omega$ is varied. Then in Eq. (86) the imaginary part becomes zero when Eq. (89) is satisfied, which gives Eq. (90) for $\omega^2$. This is called the resonant frequency, and at this value of $\omega$ the power dissipated is given by Eq. (91). The quantity $L\omega_0/R$ is called the quality factor or $Q$-factor of the circuit and is given by Eq. (92). Since $Q$ is often very

$$C\omega = \frac{L\omega}{R^2 + L^2\omega^2} \tag{89}$$

$$\omega^2 = \frac{1}{LC} - \left(\frac{R}{L}\right)^2 = \omega_0^2 \tag{90}$$

$$P_0 = \tfrac{1}{2}E_0^2\frac{RC}{L} \tag{91}$$

$$Q = \sqrt{\frac{L}{R^2C} - 1} \tag{92}$$

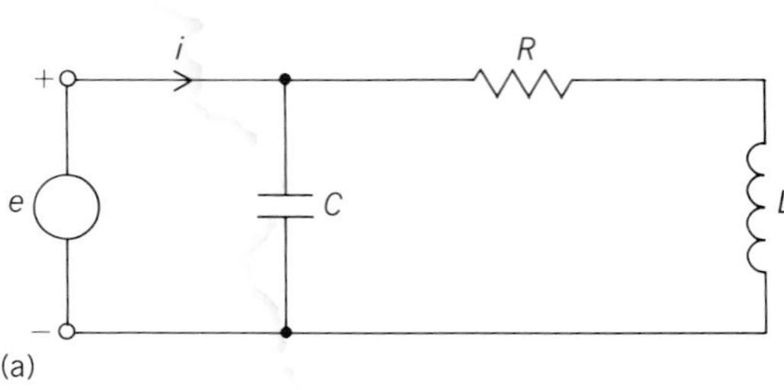


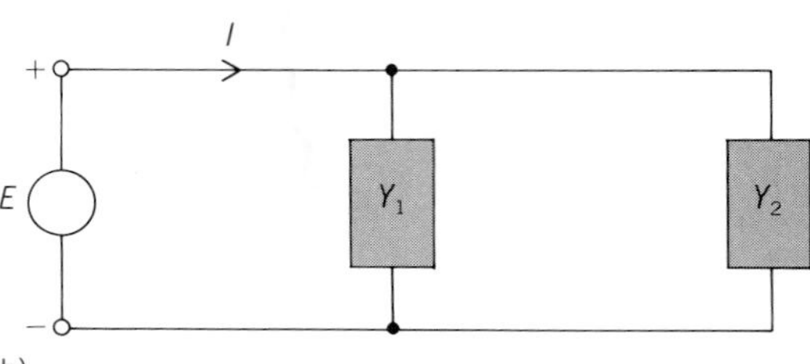


**Fig. 14. Resonant circuit. (*a*) Diagram showing components. (*b*) Diagram showing admittances.**

large, it is usually approximated by Eq. (93).

$$Q = \frac{1}{R}\sqrt{\frac{L}{C}} \tag{93}$$

Having found these various complex voltages and currents, the corresponding sinusoidal quantities could be written immediately, but this is rarely done in practice since all the information is already contained in the complex quantities. SEE RESONANCE (ALTERNATING-CURRENT CIRCUITS).

**Numerical examples.** The following examples illustrate the application of alternating-current circuit theory to power frequency circuits. The first concerns elements in series and division of voltage; the second concerns elements in series and parallel, division of current, and computation of power.

Phasors are used to illustrate the behavior of current and voltage. But a slight change is made from the earlier notation: in practice ac voltages are usually referred to by their rms values, as in "a 115-volt supply." It is convenient to use rms values on phasor diagrams, instead of amplitudes as was done above. To avoid confusion, bold type will be used to indicate complex voltages and currents labeled in this way; so, for example, a 115-volt 60-Hz wave of zero phase will be written as in Eq. (94). When it is necessary

$$\mathbf{V} = 115\underline{/0^\circ} \tag{94}$$

to calculate the amplitude, as in Fig. 16*b*, the rms value must be multiplied by $\sqrt{2}$. For convenience, in this section bold type is also used to indicate complex impedance or admittance.

***Example 1.*** An incoming electric line provides power at 115 volts, 60 Hz. This is the amount of ac voltage as read on an ordinary voltmeter, and is therefore the rms value. Both voltage and frequency are essentially independent of the amount of current received from this line by the load that is about to be considered. The voltage, known to be alternating, is assumed to be sinusoidal.

Onto this line is connected a motor with 60-Hz impedance (at standstill) of $\mathbf{Z}_m = 1 + j5$ ohms in series, with a starting resistance of $\mathbf{Z}_s = 11$ ohms. The motor does not turn, being too heavily loaded. Compute the current that will flow steadily. Also, find voltage across the motor alone with this starting resistance in the circuit.

***Solution.*** Draw **Fig. 15** and start **Fig. 16.** Take voltage to be the reference phasor with zero angle, $\mathbf{V} = 115\underline{/0^\circ}$. Obtain the total impedance $\mathbf{Z}$ by adding, as shown in Eq. (95a). The complex number

$$\mathbf{Z} = \mathbf{Z}_s + \mathbf{Z}_m = 11 + 1 + j5 = 12 + j5 \tag{95a}$$

$$\mathbf{Z} = 12 + j5 = 13\underline{/22.6^\circ} \tag{95b}$$

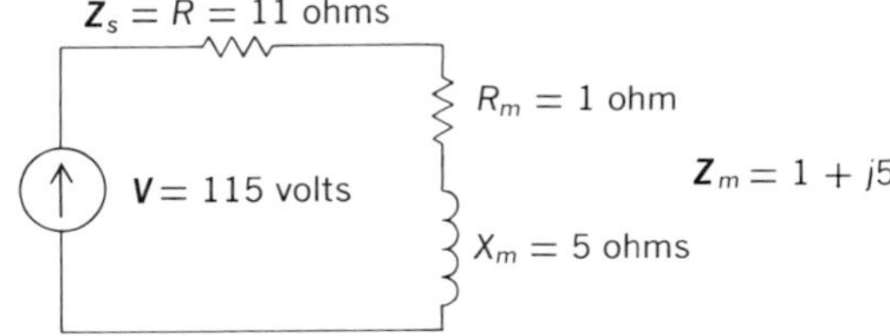


**Fig. 15. Impedances in series: $Z_s$ is starter resistance; $R_m$ and $X_m$ are model of motor with stalled rotor.**

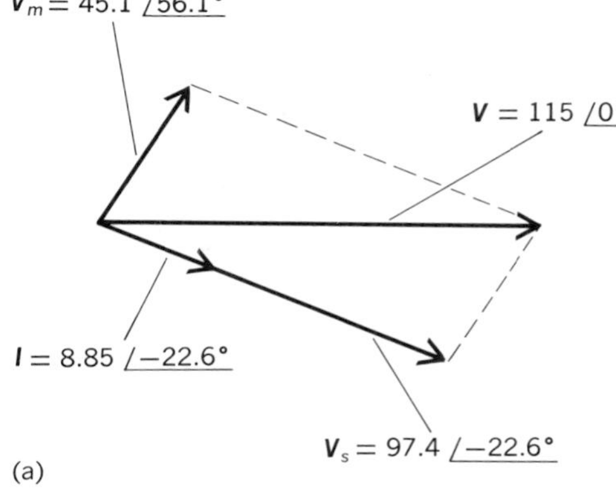


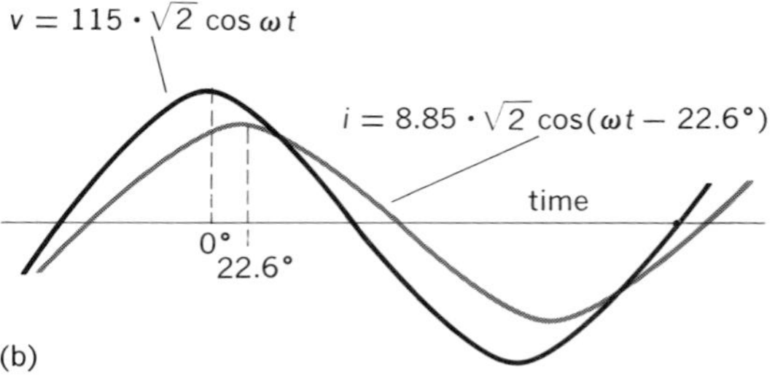


**Fig. 16. Phasors and waves for circuit of Fig. 15.**

$$\mathbf{I} = \frac{\mathbf{V}}{\mathbf{Z}} = \frac{115\underline{/0^\circ}}{13\underline{/22.6^\circ}} = 8.85\underline{/-22.6^\circ} \tag{95c}$$

$12 + j5$ can also be written in polar form, as shown by Eq. (95*b*). By using this polar form and dividing, it is found, as shown in Eq. (95*c*), that the steady current has an rms value of 8.85 amperes, and that the sinusoidal wave of current lags (is delayed behind) the sinusoidal wave of voltage by 22.6°. Voltage and current phasors are shown in Fig. 16*a*, and the corresponding waves are shown in Fig. 16*b*. Usually, phasors are shown but not waves (time functions of voltage and current); this is consistent with the usual practice of calling the phasor a current and leaving the reader to understand that the magnitude is the rms value of current and the angle is phase relative to an assumed reference.

In the present example, it is also required to find voltage across the motor with the starting resistance in the circuit. This voltage $\mathbf{V}_m$ is shown by Eq. (96).

$$\begin{aligned} \mathbf{V}_m &= \mathbf{Z}_m\mathbf{I} \\ &= (1 + j5)(8.85\underline{/-22.6^\circ}) \\ &= (5.10\underline{/78.7^\circ})(8.85\underline{/-22.6^\circ}) = 45.1\underline{/56.1^\circ} \end{aligned} \tag{96}$$

The phasor representing motor voltage is included in Fig. 12*a*.

***Check.*** As a check on the accuracy of the solution, if the voltage across the starting resistor is computed and then added to the motor voltage, the resultant sum should be the line voltage. This computation is shown in Eqs. (97). The sum of the voltage phasors

$$\begin{aligned} \mathbf{V}_s &= \mathbf{Z}_s\mathbf{I} = 11(8.85\underline{/-22.6^\circ}) = 97.4\underline{/-22.6^\circ} \\ &= 89.9 - j37.4 \\ \mathbf{V}_m &= 25.1 + j37.4 \\ \mathbf{V} &= 115.0 + j0 \end{aligned} \tag{97}$$

is $115.0 + j0$, which is the correct line voltage. Graphical addition is illustrated in Fig. 16*a*.

***Example 2.*** An electric furnace of the induction type

has impedance $Z = 360 + j150$ ohms at its rated frequency of 60 Hz. It is connected to an incoming line that provides 2300 volts at this frequency. A purely resistive electric heater is also connected at the line (Fig. 17), and draws 10 amperes at this voltage. To improve the power factor, management has connected to the incoming line a capacitor with 7.5 microfarads capacitance. Find the current supplied from the incoming line; also find total power supplied and power to each load.

***Solution.*** Draw **Fig. 17** and start **Fig. 18.** Take the voltage of the incoming line as the reference phasor, $2300\underline{/0°}$. Compute the admittance of each element of the network and add. Computations are shown in Eqs. (68).

For the capacitor, admittance is given by Eq. (98*a*). For the resistor, admittance is given by Eq. (98*b*). For the furnace, admittance is given by Eq (98*c*). Total line current is then given by Eq. (98*d*).

$$\begin{aligned} Y_C &= j\omega C = j2\pi(60)(7.5)10^{-6} \\ &= j(2.83)10^{-3} \text{ mho} \end{aligned} \tag{98a}$$

$$Y_R = \frac{10}{2300} = (4.35)10^{-3} \text{ mho} \tag{98b}$$

$$\begin{aligned} Y_F &= \frac{1}{360 + j150} = \frac{1}{390\underline{/22.6°}} \\ &= (2.57)10^{-3}\underline{/-22.6°} \\ \text{or } Y_F &= \frac{360 - j150}{(360)^2 + (150)^2} \\ &= (2.37 - j0.986)10^{-3} \text{ mho} \end{aligned} \tag{98c}$$

$$\begin{aligned} I &= VY \\ &= 2300(j2.83 + 4.35 + 2.37 - j0.986)10^{-3} \\ &= 2.30(6.72 + j1.84) = 16.02\underline{/15.3°} \end{aligned} \tag{98d}$$

Power computations shown in Eqs. (99)–(101) are derived from earlier equations as indicated. Power from line, by Eq. (53), is given by Eq. (99). Power

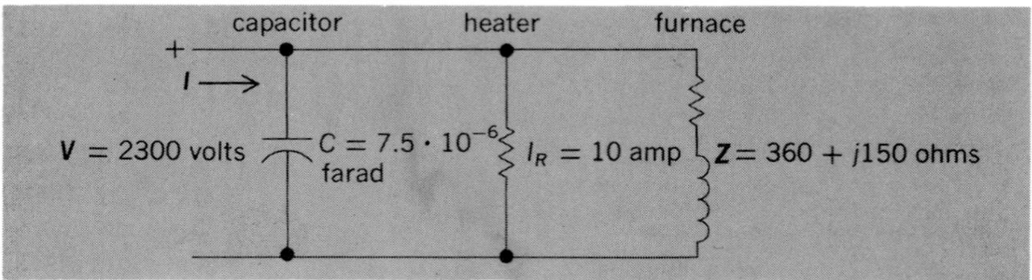


**Fig. 17. Capacitor, heater, and furnace connected in parallel.**

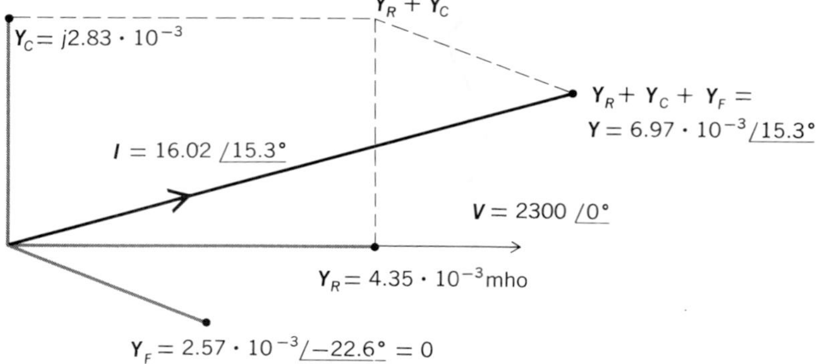


**Fig. 18. Phasors for circuit of Fig. 17.**

$$\begin{aligned} P &= VI \cos \varphi = (2300)(16.02) \cos 15.3° \\ &= 35{,}520 \text{ watts} \end{aligned} \tag{99}$$

to resistor, by Eq. (52), is given by Eq. (100). Power

$$P_R = (2300)(10) = 23{,}000 \text{ watts} \tag{100}$$

to impedance of furnace by Eq. (54) is given by Eq. (101).

$$P_F = I^2R = \left(\frac{2300}{390}\right)^2 360 = 12{,}520 \text{ watts} \tag{101}$$

As a check, no power is supplied to the capacitor, and the sum of power to the resistor, 23.0 kilowatts, and power to the furnace, 12.52 kW, equals the incoming line power, 35.52 kW, which is correct.

**Practical circuit elements.** The two examples in the previous section were of power frequency applications. Alternating-current circuit theory is, of course, applicable also at higher, radio frequencies so long as the circuit elements can be considered as "lumped," that is, so long as their dimensions are small compared with a wavelength of the current and its phase is the same at all points in the component. But particularly at the higher frequencies, the idealized representations of circuit elements which were given earlier need to be replaced by representations which more accurately reflect the properties of actual components.

An inductor, for example, in the form of a wire-wound coil, will have resistance as well as inductance, so it should be shown as a resistance and inductance in series (**Fig. 19***a*), with impedance $R + j\omega L$. For a well-designed coil, $R$ is much smaller than $\omega L$ at the frequency of use. There will also be capacitance between the turns of the coil which becomes important at the higher frequencies, and the effective circuit of the coil can be approximated by Fig. 19*b*. As discussed above in connection with Fig. 14, this is a resonant circuit, and there is for any coil a frequency at which it is self-resonant; above this frequency its effective impedance is capacitative rather than inductive.

A capacitor will generally suffer some power loss in the dielectric medium, which can be represented by a parallel high resistance ($R_2$ in Fig. 19*c*), and the connecting leads will have low resistance and inductance which may be significant at very high frequencies ($R_1$ and $L$).

Other stray impedances may also have to be taken into account. At high frequencies it is particularly important to remember that even lengths of connecting wire may have significant inductance and capacitance to ground.

**Microwave circuits.** At microwave frequencies the assumption of lumped components whose size is small compared with the wavelength breaks down. The basic principles of ac circuit theory can still be applied, but is necessary to assume that the properties of resistance, inductance, and capacitance are no longer localized but distributed throughout the circuits, and to take account of the finite time of travel of a wave from one part of the circuit to another. The concept of impedance then has to be generalized. *See* *Microwave*; *Scattering parameters*; *Transmission lines*.

**Active circuits.** In addition to the passive circuits discussed in this article, circuit theory can be ex-

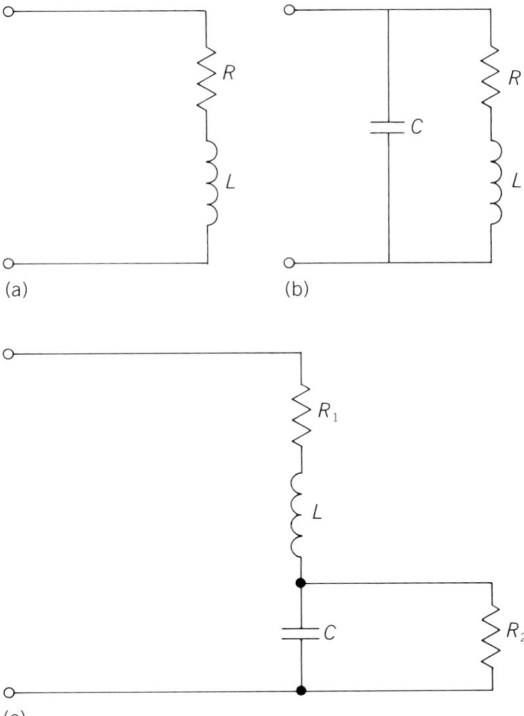


**Fig. 19.** Diagrams of actual circuit elements. (*a*) Inductor with finite wire resistance. (*b*) Inductor with wire resistance and interturn capacitance. (*c*) Capacitance with dielectric loss and connecting lead with finite resistance and inductance.

tended to cover the cases of amplification and feedback. Again the concept of impedance may have to be extended: it is possible, for example, to produce circuits whose effective impedance is that of a negative capacitor, or which do not correspond to any possible combination of simple circuit elements. *See* AMPLIFIER; FEEDBACK CIRCUIT.

**Nonsinusoidal waveforms.** The above analysis of circuits has been entirely in terms of the response to single-frequency sinusoidal waveforms. There are many cases where it is necessary to deal with other waveforms. Two methods are available:

1. When it is necessary to find the response to a repetitive waveform or perhaps a single pulse whose Fourier transform can easily be calculated as $F(\omega)$, the impedance or transfer function (circuit property relating input and output voltage or current) can be calculated in the usual way as $Z(\omega)$, and then the inverse transform of $F(\omega)\cdot Z(\omega)$ can be extracted to give the response waveform as a function of time. *See* FOURIER SERIES AND INTEGRALS.

2. An alternative method, particularly useful in dealing with transient waveforms, is (for example) to take the Laplace transform of the input waveform, $L(s)$, and to multiply it by $Z'(s)$, given by the impedance or transfer function calculated in the usual way but with $j\omega$ replaced by $s$. The output is then the inverse Laplace transform of $L(s)\cdot Z'(s)$.

*J. D. Scanlan; A. E. Bailey*

**Bibliography.** N. Balabanian, *Fundamentals of Circuit Theory*, 1961, W. H. Hayt, Jr., and J. E. Kemmerly, *Engineering Circuit Analysis*, 1982; J. O. Scanlan and R. Levy, *Circuit Theory*, vol. 1, 1970; H. H. Skilling, *Electric Networks*, 1974.

## Amateur radio

Two-way radio communications by private individuals as a leisure-time activity. Amateur, or "ham," radio is defined in international treaty as a "service of self-training, intercommunications, and technical investigations carried on by amateurs; that is, by duly authorized persons interested in radio technique solely with a personal aim and without pecuniary interest."

More than 1,000,000 amateur operators throughout the world (over 430,000 in the United States alone) translate these words into public service and private pleasure. With radio equipment in their homes and cars they set up warning and relief networks during the hurricane season; handle communications when disasters produced by nature or human activity damage phone lines; experiment at the leading edge of communications technology; and communicate by means of very high- and ultrahigh-frequency (VHF and UHF) signals bounced off the Moon or relayed through amateur-built earth satellites called OSCAR (orbiting satellites carrying amateur radio). Amateurs also communicate on a casual basis, becoming radio friends and getting acquainted with people around the world. By reflection of high-frequency (HF) signals (below 30 MHz) from the Kennelly-Heaviside ionosphere layers, international communication between amateurs is common.

**Requirements.** In the United States, five levels of license class are issued by the Federal Communications Commission. These follow a ladderlike progression; each class requires a more stringent examination, but also grants more frequencies and greater privileges. All license classes require a knowledge of international Morse code. The first license level is the Novice Class, requiring the ability to send and receive Morse code at the rate of five words per minute (WPM); the Novice test covers basic radio theory and regulations. Other amateur licenses, in order of increasing privileges, are the Technician Class, General Class, Advanced Class, and Amateur Extra Class. General and Advanced Class licenses must be able to copy Morse code at 13 WPM, while Amateur Extras must have a proficiency of 20 WPM.

**Privileges.** Novice Class licensees can communicate worldwide by Morse code on a range of radio frequencies between 3 and 30 megahertz with a power level of 200 watts peak envelope power (PEP) output; higher classes are permitted 1500 W peak envelope power output. Higher-class licenses may use any of the following modes: code (CW); amplitude-modulated and single-sideband suppressed-carrier voice (AM and SSB); frequency modulation (FM); radioteletype (RTTY), using either the Baudot, ASCII, or AMTOR (amateur teletype over radio) digital codes; facsimile; television; or pulse modulation. *See* AMPLITUDE-MODULATION RADIO; FACSIMILE; FREQUENCY-MODULATION RADIO; PULSE MODULATION; SINGLE SIDEBAND; TELETYPEWRITER; TELEVISION.

Amateur operators with General Class and higher licenses can communicate on portions of or all the following frequency bands (expressed in MHz), depending on their specific license level:

| | | |
|---|---|---|
| 1.8–2.0 MHz | 28.0–29.7 MHz | 3300–3500 MHz |
| 3.5–4.0 | 50.0–54.0 | 5650–5925 |
| 7.0–7.3 | 144.0–148.0 | 10,000–10,500 |
| 10.10–10.15 | 220–225 | 24,000–24,250 |
| 14.00–14.35 | 420–450 | 47,000–47,200 |
| 18.068–18.168* | 902–928* | 75,500–81,000 |
| 21.000–21.450 | 1240–1300 | Others above |
| 24.890–24.990* | 2300–2450 | 119,980 MHz |

The bands marked with an asterisk were allocated to the Amateur Radio Service at the 1979 World Administrative Radio Conference (WARC). The bands 18.068–18.168 and 24.890–24.990 MHz will be released for amateur use no later than 1989. All or part of the band 902–928 MHz is expected to be released for amateur use eventually.

**Regulations.** In addition to the international treaty, United States amateurs are governed by Part 97, Rules of the Federal Communications Commission (FCC). Unlike most radio services, amateurs may design and build their equipment, as long as it meets FCC requirements for spectral purity and bandwidth, may assemble it from kits, or may purchase it ready to go.

**Technical developments.** This open policy toward amateur radio by the government has made it possible for amateurs to pioneer in several areas. In 1923, for instance, amateurs led the way to the short waves after an amateur in Connecticut talked with a ham in France on the previously ignored wavelength of 110 m (360 ft). Until that achievement the accepted theory had been that only wavelengths above 200 m (660 ft) were really useful.

By the early 1930s communications between points on opposite sides of the globe had become commonplace on wavelengths of 80 through 20 m (264 through 66 ft; frequencies of 3.5 through 14.4 MHz). Many hams then turned their attention to higher frequencies. Again amateurs shattered previous conceptions, especially those concerning "line-of-sight" limitations on communications at 56 MHz and above. These pioneers discovered and used means of radio propagation which reached far beyond the usual horizon: reflections from the aurora borealis, from meteor trails, from sporadic *E* layers (patches of ionized particles about 70 mi or 110 km above the Earth), and recently from the Moon; bending of radio waves through layers of stable air; and a phenomenon called transequatorial scatter, by which stations on one side of the equator may communicate with stations on the other over distances of more than 1000 mi (1600 km) at times when such work would not otherwise be expected to succeed. This mode and several of the others were subjects of an International Geophysical Year study undertaken by amateurs through the American Radio Relay League.

Other technical accomplishments and experimentation by amateurs include asynchronous computer multiplexing on common radio channels, or Packet radio; computer station control and interfacing as a result of the popularity and availability of personal computers; and spread spectrum techniques, enabling hundreds of simultaneous conversations to occur on the same frequency without any mutual interference. Amateurs have installed relay repeater stations on mountaintops in many areas, and use them to extend the range of communication on the VHF bands from the tens to hundreds of miles. Under the direction of the Radio Amateur Satellite Corporation (AMSAT), amateurs have built and launched as secondary payloads on scheduled space shots a series of highly advanced satellites, some into low earth orbit and others into high elliptical orbits and containing a refirable hydrazine engine, master on-board computer, and high-power UHF-UHF (ultrahigh-frequency) transponders. *See Spread spectrum communication.*

**Associations.** The developments just described required a clearinghouse, an information exchange, which is embodied in the amateurs' organization, the American Radio Relay League. The league, founded in 1914 by Hiram Percy Maxim, is a nonprofit, nonstock assocation of radio amateurs in North America with headquarters at 225 Main Street, Newington, Connecticut 06111. It publishes *QST* magazine each month (the name comes from an operating signal meaning "calling all radio amateurs"), an annual *Radio Amateur's Handbook,* and 34 other publications and operator aids covering various aspects of the hobby, ranging from beginner material to complex subjects. The league, which has about 130,000 members, serves as spokesman for amateurs in regulatory matters; it presents new technical developments and conducts operating contests and other activities to increase the hams' enjoyment of, and skill in, the hobby; it organizes networks to handle messages described earlier and coordinates emergency communications training. The league is also headquarters for the International Amateur Radio Union, composed of some 119 similar national radio societies around the world. *See Radio.*

*Leo D. Kluger*

***Bibliography.*** American Radio Relay League, *Radio Amateurs Handbook*, annually; *Radio Amateurs License Manual*, 78th ed., 1983; *Tune in the World With Ham Radio*, 1983; *Understanding Amateur Radio*, 1977.

## Ammeter

An electrical instrument for the measurement of electric current. In the usual indicating ammeter, an electromechanical system causes a pointer to traverse a calibrated scale, its position on the scale indicating the value of the current.

Several kinds of ammeter mechanism are used for different kinds of current, different applications, and differing degrees of accuracy.

**Permanent-magnet movable-coil type.** This type of ammeter is used universally for the measurement of direct currents. It is developed from the d'Arsonval movement. **Figure 1***a* shows the general arrangment of the mechanism; Fig. 1*b* is a typical instrument. In the mechanism an external permanent magnet produces a uniform radial magnetic field across the air gap through which the coil rotates. With an air-gap flux density of $B$ tesla, the torque produced by a current of $I$ amperes through $N$ turns in the rotating coil is shown in the equation below, where $L$ is the length

$$T = B2RLIN = BAIN \text{ N-m}$$

of the active conductor in meters, $R$ is the radius of action of those conductors in meters, and $A$ is the effective area of the moving coil in square meters; N-m represents newton-meters.

It is important that the magnetic system be of such

materials and proportions that a constant flux density is maintained in the air gap. For the older tungsten steel magnets, the ratio of the magnet length to air-gap length times the ratio of the air-gap cross section to magnet cross section should be more than 100 for a permanent magnetic system. For the Alnico permanent-magnet alloys with their high coercive force, however, this product can be as low as 10 for a stable system. The resulting short magnet can then be placed inside the rotating coil, as in the core-magnet system of **Fig. 2**. Flux densities typically range from 0.15 T (1500 gauss) in small instruments to 0.5 T (5000 gauss) in larger systems for special uses.

In Fig. 1 the coil is usually wound on a metal form and swung on highly polished steel or hard-alloy pivots between V-cup jewels or bearings of sapphire or hard glass. Bronze springs serve to carry the current in and out of the coil as well as to oppose the electrical torque, resulting in a deflection proportional to the coil current. The coil turns may vary from as few as 15 to as many as 5000; wire size, in turn, may be as small as 0.0006 in. (15 micrometers) in diameter for coils of 1000 turns or more.

Obviously, very weak control springs would allow for a normal deflection on the low torque produced by only a few microamperes in the coil. But the lower limit of useful torque is that which will overcome the residual bearing friction by a factor of several times the expected accuracy in terms of deflection. This sets a definite lower limit to a pivoted instrument, which is usually in the order of 10–20 μA full scale in a coil of several thousand ohms resistance.

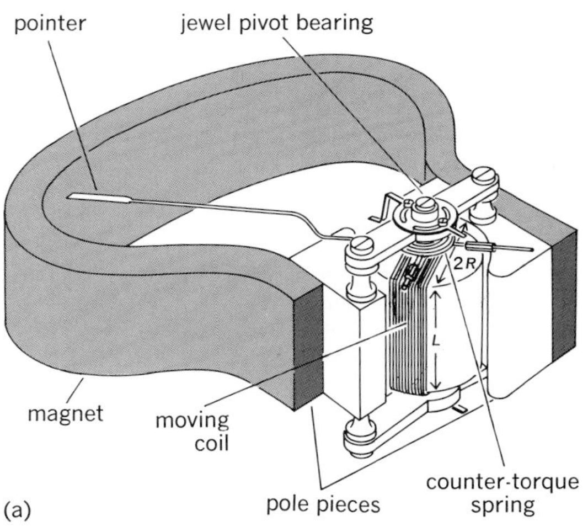

**Fig. 1. Ammeter. (*a*) Permanent-magnetic movable-coil mechanism. (*b*) Typical instrument. (*Weston Instruments, Inc.*)**

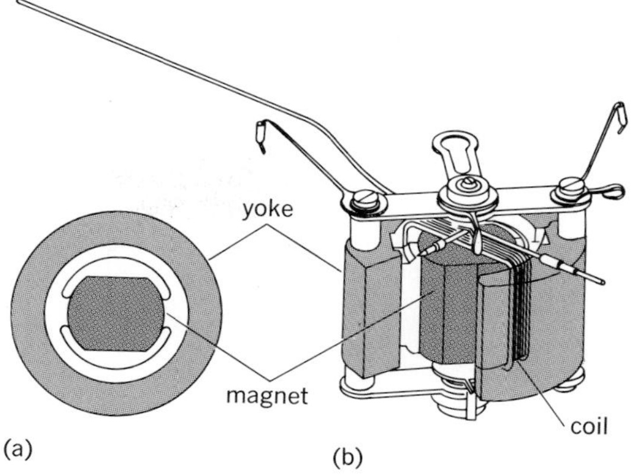


**Fig. 2. Core-magnet version of permanent-magnet movable-coil mechanism. (*a*) Magnetic system. (*b*) Cut-away view. (*Weston Instruments, Inc.*)**

The high limit of current through the coil is set by thermal limits; about 0.03 A is the maximum current in a moving coil. For higher values the instrument is shunted; that is, the bulk of the current is bypassed around the moving coil through a shunt, with only a definite fraction of the current passing through the moving coil itself.

Within the limits given, the permanent-magnet movable-coil ammeter for direct current has high torque and good accuracy, and is made in models varying from a 2-in.-diameter (5-cm) panel type to the large laboratory standards accurate within 0.1%.

**Taut-band type.** In a modification of ammeter design, the jeweled bearings and control springs are replaced by a taut metallic band rigidly held at the ends. The coil is firmly attached to the band. As the coil rotates in the magnetic field under the influence of the current which is being measured, the restoring torque is supplied by the twisting of the band. Thus, bearing friction is completely eliminated, and the resolution of the instrument thereby improved. This type of coil mounting is coming into wide use in applications where high resolution and sensitivity are desired.

**Polarized-vane type.** This instrument, shown in **Fig. 3**, is of only moderate accuracy. It is used in large numbers in battery chargers and automobiles because of its low cost. Current through the small coil distorts the field of the circular permanent magnet; the iron vane aligns itself with the axis of the distorted field, the deflection being roughly proportional to the current. Reversed electrical polarity reverses the direction of motion; the instrument thus indicates current flowing into or out of a battery.

**Electrodynamic type.** This is also a movable-coil instrument, but the coil rotates in the magnetic field produced by a fixed coil. The instrument responds to alternating as well as direct current, and is thus a transfer instrument. Such instruments are precise and may be calibrated accurately and used for secondary standards, but the magnetic field of the fixed-coil system is relatively weak, 60 gauss (6 millitesla) being a common value. The controlling forces are thus much lower than in other types, and the electrodynamic ammeter is mainly used in the laboratory for calibrating the more rugged types.

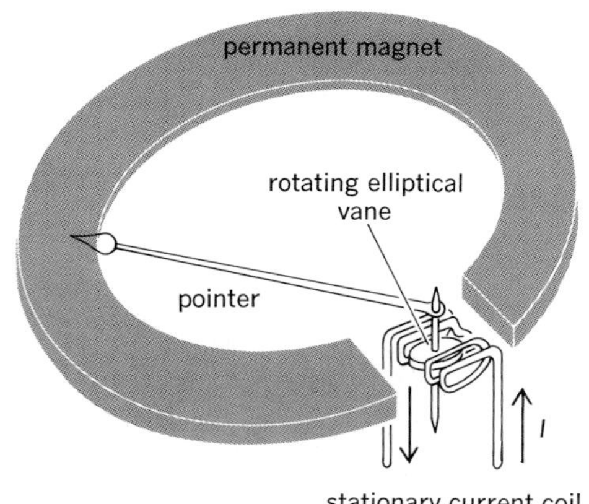


Fig. 3. Polarized-vane ammeter mechanism. (*Weston Instruments, Inc.*)

**Soft-iron type.** These are widely used for alternating-current measurements. **Figure 4** shows a repulsion-vane type with pointer, control spring, and damping vane on the moving element.

Requiring about 300 ampere-turns for full-scale deflection in the larger sizes, the common 5-A range will have a 60-turn coil of 0.06-in.-diameter (1.5-mm) copper wire, ample to carry even considerable overloads. The iron vanes tend to saturate magnetically on overload and thereby act as further overload protection. Actuating forces are high, and only the limitations in the iron vanes in responding exactly to the coil current limit the accuracy. The most accurate instruments of this type are accurate to within 0.25%.

On direct current, iron-vane instruments tend to read low on increasing current and high on decreasing current because of hysteresis in the vanes. Iron-vane instruments should therefore always be calibrated on alternating current using an electrodynamometer standard.

**Thermal type.** Such ammeters function through the medium of the heat generated by the passage of electric current through a resistance element. Early hot-wire ammeters contained a platinum alloy or other resistance wire, heated by the current in question. The rise in temperature of the platinum caused it to expand, and its linear increase was amplified by a mechanical lever system to cause a pointer to travel across a scale calibrated in amperes. Although useful up to very high frequencies, hot-wire ammeters had high electrical losses, were difficult to compensate for variations in ambient temperature, and tended to burn out on moderate overloads. They are now completely obsolete, having been replaced by the thermocouple type developed about 1920.

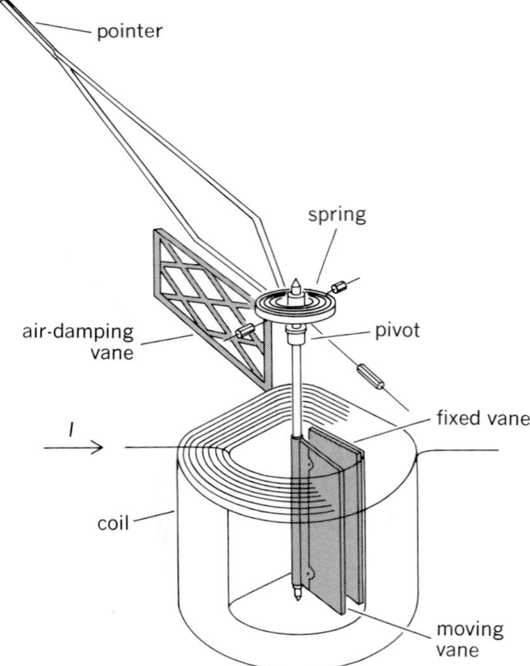


Fig. 4. Repulsion-vane or book-type ammeter mechanism. (*Weston Instruments, Inc.*)

Modern thermal ammeters consist of a thermal converter and a sensitive direct-current (dc) millivoltmeter. **Figure 5** shows such a thermal converter mounted on the instrument terminals. The short and efficient heater is a platinum alloy wire or tube, to which is welded a thermocouple of two dissimilar metals. When the junction of the thermocouple is heated, a small voltage is generated which is proportional to the temperature rise; this in turn is applied to the millivolt mechanism to deflect its pointer. Typically, the heater is so proportioned as to have a temperature rise of 360°F (200°C) on the desired full-scale current; about 10 mV is then available for the dc mechanism. Losses are represented by a potential drop through the heater of 200 mV at full-scale current.

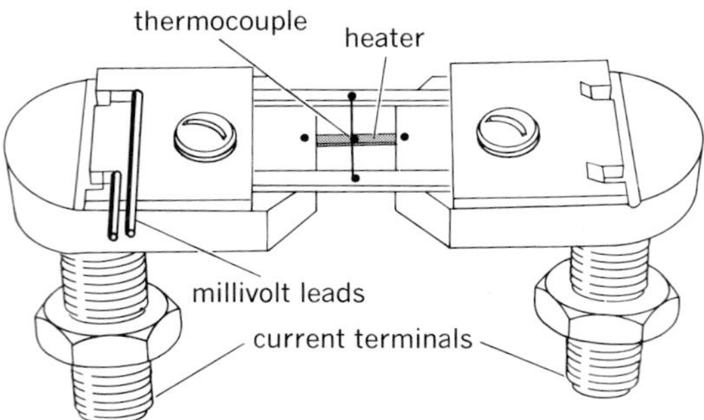


Fig. 5. Thermal converter of thermocouple ammeter. (*Weston Instruments, Inc.*)

The temperature rise of the heater is a function of the square of the current; thus the instrument scale follows a square law, compressed at the start and expanded at full scale.

Using a 1-mil (25-μm) heater wire, full scale represents about 1 A. Higher rangers are made with heavier heaters; losses increase correspondingly, with 60 A representing a practical top limit. For measuring currents under 1 A, the thermoelement is placed in vacuum to reduce heat losses; these are now useful as low as 1 mA. A special bridge form of open thermoelement is also used in the 100-mA range.

Calibration of thermoammeters should be made on a low-frequency (such as 60 Hz) alternating current using appropriate standards. The instruments will then be within 2%, their typical accuracy, on frequencies as high as 50 MHz. On still higher frequencies they tend to read high because of excessive skin-effect losses in the heater.

In addition to the several kinds of ammeter described, there are several composite types used in communications and electronics for low values of

**Kinds of ammeters**

| Type of mechanism | Kind of current | Application and accuracy* |
|---|---|---|
| Permanent-magnet movable-coil (d'Arsonval) | Direct | Very general: panel, switchboard, portable, laboratory instruments; accuracy 0.1–2% |
| Taut band | Direct | General, requiring high resolution and sensitivity; accuracy better than 0.1% |
| Polarized-iron vane | Direct | Battery charging, automobiles; accuracy only moderate |
| Electrodynamic† | Direct and alternating | Laboratory; high accuracy, 0.1%; portable testing, 0.25% |
| Soft-iron vane, repulsion, attraction, inclined-vane types | Alternating, low-frequency | Panel, switchboard, portable; accuracy 0.25–2% |
| Thermoelectric‡ | Alternating, frequencies up to 100 MHz | Panel, switchboard, general testing; accuracy 0.5–3% |
| Miscellaneous composite types | Usually alternating | Communications, electronic circuit testing; accuracy 0.5–5% |

*Accuracy stated as % maximum error of full-scale reading.
†Important as a transfer instrument from basic direct-current standards to use on alternating current.
‡Also may be used as a transfer standard, although usually from low-frequency alternating current via an electrodynamic ammeter to radio frequency.

current. Iron-vane instruments take considerable energy, about 1 W for full scale; low-range thermal instruments are expensive and easily burned out. A rectifier-type alternating-current (ac) milliammeter consisting of a small copper oxide of germanium bridge rectifier feeding a conventional dc milliammeter has low losses, good overload capacity, and adequate accuracy. It is used to monitor voice-frequency currents, with ranges available as low as 100 μA full scale. Similarly, vacuum-tube and transistor amplifying and rectifying systems used with sensitive dc microammeters further expand the coverage in range, frequency, and sensitivity to make available ammeters for most applications. Commercial ammeters are available with range $10^{-10}$ A full scale to $10^{-3}$ A with 14 overlapping ranges. The **table** summarizes the common types of ammeters. *See* CURRENT MEASUREMENT.

*John H. Miller/Jesse Beams*

***Bibliography.*** E. Frank, *Electrical Measurement Analysis*, 1959, reprint 1977; S. Geczy, *Basic Electrical Measurements*, 1984; F. K. Harris, *Electrical Measurements*, 1952; reprint 1975; R. L. Heiserman, *Electrical and Electronic Measuring Instruments*, 1983; J. D. Lenk, *Handbook of Electronic Meters: Theory and Application*, rev. ed., 1981.

## Amorphous solid

A rigid material whose structure lacks crystalline periodicity; that is, the pattern of its constituent atoms or molecules does not repeat periodically in three dimensions. In the present terminology amorphous and noncrystalline are synonymous. A solid is distinguished from its other amorphous counterparts (liquids and gases) by its viscosity: a material is considered solid (rigid) if its shear viscosity exceeds $10^{14.6}$ poise ($10^{13.6}$ pascal·second). *See* CRYSTAL; SOLID-STATE PHYSICS; VISCOSITY.

**Preparation.** Techniques commonly used to prepare amorphous solids include vapor deposition, electrodeposition, anodization, evaporation of a solvent (gel, glue), and chemical reaction (often oxidation) of a crystalline solid. None of these techniques involves the liquid state of the material. A distinctive class of amorphous solids consists of glasses, which are defined as amorphous solids obtained by cooling of the melt. Upon continued cooling below the crystalline melting point, a liquid either crystallizes with a discontinuous change in volume, viscosity, entropy, and internal energy, or (if the crystallization kinetics are slow enough and the quenching rate is fast enough) forms a glass with a continuous change in these properties. The glass transition temperature is defined as the temperature at which the fluid becomes solid (that is, the viscosity = $10^{14.6}$ poise = $10^{13.6}$ Pa·s) and is generally marked by a change in the thermal expansion coefficient and heat capacity. [Silicon dioxide ($SiO_2$) and germanium dioxide ($GeO_2$) are exceptions.] It is intuitively appealing to consider a glass to be both structurally and thermodynamically related to its liquid; such a connection is more tenuous for amorphous solids prepared by the other techniques.

**Types of solids.** Oxide glasses, generally the silicates, are the most familiar amorphous solids. However, as a state of matter, amorphous solids are much more widespread than just the oxide glasses. There are both organic (for example, polyethylene and some hard candies) and inorganic (for example, the silicates) amorphous solids. Examples of glass formers exist for each of the bonding types: covalent [$As_2S_3$], ionic [$KNO_3-Ca(NO_3)_2$], metallic [$Pd_4Si$], van der Waals [*o*-terphenyl], and hydrogen [$KHSO_4$]. Glasses can be prepared which span a broad range of physical properties. Dielectrics (for example, $SiO_2$) have very low electrical conductivity and are optically transparent, hard, and brittle. Semiconductors (for example, $As_2SeTe_2$) have intermediate electrical conductivities and are optically opaque and brittle. Metallic glasses (for example, $Pd_4Si$) have high electrical and thermal conductivities, have metallic luster, and are ductile and strong.

**Uses.** The obvious uses for amorphous solids are as window glass, container glass, and the glassy polymers (plastics). Less widely recognized but nevertheless established technological uses include the dielectrics and protective coatings used in integrated circuits, and the active element in photocopying by xerography, which depends for its action upon photoconduction in an amorphous semiconductor. In optical communications a highly transparent dielectric glass in the form of a fiber is used as the transmission medium. In addition, metallic amorphous solids have been considered for uses that take advantage of their high strength, excellent corrosion resistance, extreme hardness and wear resistance, and unique magnetic properties. *See* OPTICAL COMMUNICATIONS.

**Semiconductors.** It is the changes in short-range order (on the scale of a localized electron), rather than

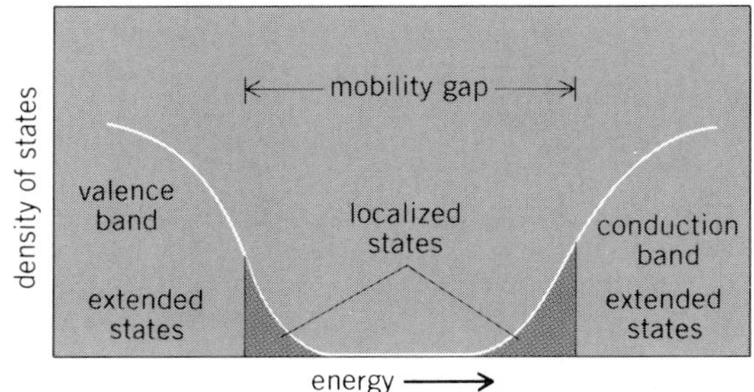


**Fig. 1. Density of states versus energy for an amorphous semiconductor.**

the loss of long-range order alone, that have a profound effect on the properties of amorphous semiconductors. For example, the difference in resistivity between the crystalline and amorphous states for dielectrics and metals is always less than an order of magnitude and is generally less than a factor of 3. For semiconductors, however, resistivity changes of 10 orders of magnitude between the crystalline and amorphous states are not uncommon, and accompanying changes in optical properties can also be large.

***Electronic structure.*** The model that has evolved for the electronic structure of an amorphous semiconductor is that the forbidden energy gap characteristic of the electronic states of a crystalline material is replaced in an amorphous semiconductor by a pseudogap. Within this pseudogap the density of states of the valence and conduction bands is sharply lower but tails off gradually and remains finite due to structural disorder (**Fig. 1**). The states in the tail region are localized; that is, their wave functions extend over small distances in contrast to the extended states that exist elsewhere in the energy spectrum. Because the localized states have low mobility (velocity per unit electric field), the extended states are separated by a mobility gap (Fig. 1) within which charge transport is markedly impeded. In each band, the energy at which the extended states meet the localized states is called the mobility edge. *SEE BAND THEORY OF SOLIDS*.

An ideal amorphous solid can be conceptually defined as having no unsatisfied bonds, a minimum of bond distortions (bond angles and lengths), and no internal surfaces associated with voids. Deviations from this ideality introduce localized states in the gap in addition to those in the band edge tails due to disorder alone. One important defect is called an unsatisfied, broken, or dangling bond. These dangling bonds create states deep in the gap which can act as recombination centers and markedly limit carrier lifetime and mobility. A large number of such states introduced, for example, during the deposition process will dominate the electrical properties.

Charge transport can occur by two mechanisms. The first is conduction of mobile extended-state carriers (analogous to that which occurs in crystalline semiconductors), for which the conductivity is proportional to exp $(-E_g/2kT)$, where $E_g$ is the gap width, $T$ is the absolute temperature, and $k$ is Boltzmann's constant. The second mechanism is hopping of the localized carriers, for which the conductivity is proportional to exp $[-(T_0/T)^{1/4}]$, where $T_0$ is a constant (Mott's law). At low temperatures carriers hop from one localized trap to another, whereas at high temperatures they can be excited to the mobility edge.

***Glassy chalcogenides.*** One class of amorphous semiconductors is the glassy chalcogenides, which contain one (or more) of the chalcogens sulfur, selenium, or tellurium as major constituents. These amorphous solids behave like intrinsic semiconductors, show no detectable unpaired spin states, and exhibit no doping effects. It is thought that essentially all atoms in these glasses assume a bonding configuration such that bonding requirements are satisfied; that is, the structure accommodates the coordination of any atom. These materials have application in switching and memory devices. *SEE GLASS SWITCH*.

***Tetrahedrally bonded solids.*** Another group is the tetrahedrally bonded amorphous solids, such as amorphous silicon and germanium. These materials cannot be easily formed by quenching from the melt (that is, as glasses) but can be prepared by one of the deposition techniques mentioned above.

When amorphous silicon (or germanium) is prepared by evaporation, not all bonding requirements are satisfied, so a large number of dangling bonds are introduced into the material. These dangling bonds are easily detected by spin resonance or low-temperature magnetic susceptibility and create states deep in the gap which limit the transport properties. The number of dangling bonds can be reduced by a thermal anneal below the crystallization temperature, but the number cannot be reduced sufficiently to permit doping.

Amorphous silicon prepared by the decomposition of silane ($SiH_4$) in a plasma has been found to have a significantly lower density of defect states within the gap, and consequently the carrier lifetimes are expected to be longer. This material can be doped *p*- or *n*-type with boron or phosphorus (as examples) by the addition of $B_2H_6$ or $PH_3$ to the $SiH_4$ during deposition. This permits exploration of possible devices based on doping, which are analogous to devices based on doping of crystalline silicon.

One reason plasma-deposited silicon has a significantly lower density of defect states within the gap is that the process codeposits large amounts of hydrogen typically 5–30% of the atoms, depending upon deposition conditions), and this hydrogen is very effective at terminating dangling bonds (**Fig. 2**). Other possible dangling-bond terminators (for example, fluorine) have been explored.

The ability to reduce the number of states deep in the gap and to dope amorphous silicon led directly to the development of an amorphous silicon photovoltaic solar cell. Solar conversion efficiencies of 10% have been achieved in the laboratory, leading to a devel-

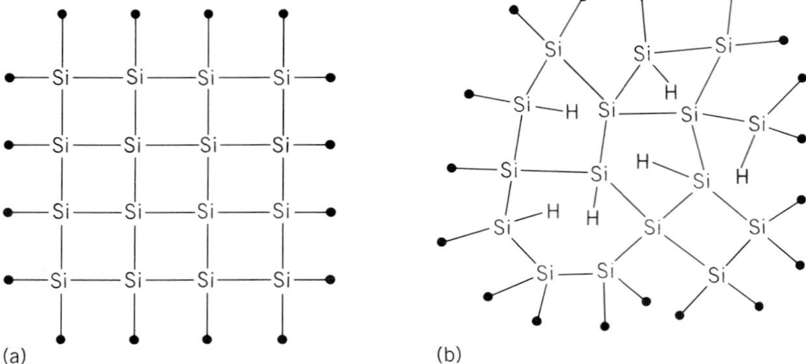


**Fig. 2. Bonding of silicon. Bonds which continue the network are shown terminated by a dot. (*a*) Crystalline arrangement. (*b*) Amorphous structure with dangling bonds terminated by hydrogen.**

opment effort aimed at large-scale power applications. The appeal of amorphous silicon is that it holds promise for low-cost, easily fabricated, large-area cells.

Amorphous silicon solar cells have been constructed in heterojunction, *pin*-junction, and Schottky-barrier device configurations, and are widely used in consumer products such as calculators and watches. The optical properties of amorphous silicon provide a better match to the solar spectrum than do those for crystalline silicon, but the transport properties of the crystalline material are better. Experiments indicate that hole transport in the amorphous material is the limiting factor in the conversion efficiency. *See Semiconductor; Semiconductor diode; Semiconductor heterostructures; Solar cell.*

*Brian G. Bagley*

**Bibliography.** N. F. Mott and E. A. Davis, *Electronic Processes in Non-Crystalline Materials*, 2d ed., 1979; J Tauc (ed.), *Amorphous and Liquid Semiconductors*, 1974; F. Yonezawa (ed.), *Fundamental Physics of Amorphous Semiconductors*, 1981; R. Zallen, *The Physics of Amorphous Solids*, 1983.

## Amplifier

A device capable of increasing the magnitude or power level of a physical quantity that is varying with time, without distorting the wave shape of the quantity. The great majority of amplifiers are electronic and depend upon transistors or vacuum tubes for their operation; such amplifiers will be discussed in this article. A small number of electronic amplifiers are magnetic amplifiers, while others take the form of rotating electrical machinery, such as the Amplidyne. A common nonelectrical amplifier is the hydraulic actuator, which is an amplifier of mechanical forces.

### Transistor Amplifiers

The transistor, since its discovery in 1947, has played an extremely important role as an active circuit element in amplifiers. The great majority of amplifiers employ transistors because of their low cost, long life, high reliability, better overall characteristics, and small size and because the physical nature of the transistor makes possible circuits that are not possible with vacuum tubes.

**Basic principles.** A junction transistor consists of a silicon (or germanium) crystal in which a layer of *n*-type silicon is sandwiched between two layers of *p*-type silicon. Alternatively, a transistor may consist of a layer of *p*-type between two layers of *n*-type material. In the former case, the transistor is referred to as a *pnp* transistor, and in the latter case as an *npn* transistor. The semiconductor sandwich is extremely small and hermetically sealed against moisture inside a metal or plastic case. *See Transistor.*

The two types of transistor are represented in **Fig. 1***a*. The representations employed when transistors are used as circuit elements are shown in Fig. 1*b*. The three portions of a transistor are known as emitter, base, and collector. The arrow on the emitter lead specifies the direction of current flow when the emitter-base junction is biased in the forward direction. In both cases, however, the emitter, base, and collector currents, $I_E$, $I_B$, and $I_C$, respectively, are assumed positive when the currents flow into the transistor. The symbols $V_{EB}$, $V_{CB}$, and $V_{CE}$ are the emitter-base, collector-base, and collector-emitter voltages, respectively. (More specifically, $V_{EB}$ represents the voltage drop from emitter to base.)

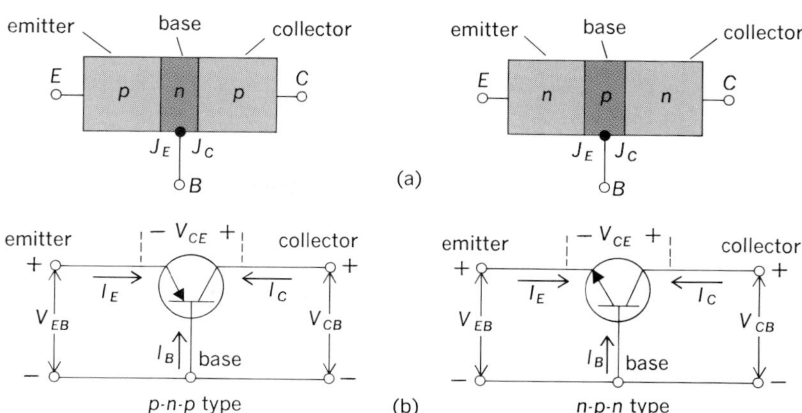


**Fig. 1. Two types of transistor. (*a*) The *p-n-p* and *n-p-n* types. The emitter (collector) junctions is $J_E(J_C)$. (*b*) Circuit representation of the two types.**

**Potential distribution.** The essential features of a transistor as an active circuit element are depicted in **Fig. 2***a*. Here a *pnp* transistor is shown with voltage sources which serve to bias the emitter-base junction in the forward direction and the collector-base junction in the reverse direction. The variation of potential through an unbiased (open-circuited) transistor is shown in Fig. 2*b*. The potential variation through the biased transistor is indicated in Fig. 2*c*. The dashed curve applies to the case before the application of external biasing voltages, and the solid curve to the case after the application of biasing voltages. In the absence of applied voltage, the potential barriers at the junctions adjust themselves to the contact potential $V_o$ (a few tenths of a volt) required so that no current flows across each junction. If now external potentials are applied, these voltages appear essentially across the junctions. Hence the forward biasing of the emitter-base junction lowers the emitter-base potential barrier by $|V_{EB}|$, whereas the reverse biasing of the collector-base junction increases the collector-base potential barrier by $|V_{CB}|$. The lowering of the emitter-base barrier permits the emitter current to increase, and holes are injected into the base region. The potential is constant across the base region (except for the small ohmic drop), and the injected holes diffuse across the *n*-type material to the collector-base junction. The holes which reach this junction fall down the potential barrier, and are therefore collected by the collector. *See Semiconductor.*

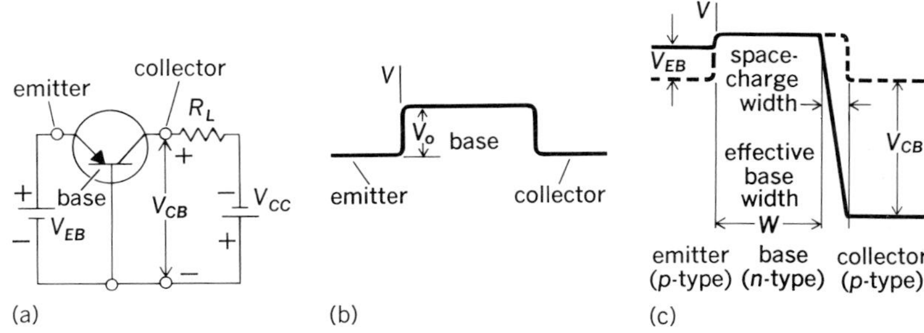


**Fig. 2. A *pnp* transistor with biasing voltages. (*a*) Circuit diagram. (*b*) Potential barriers at the junction of the unbiased transistor. (*c*) Potential variation through the biased transistor.**

A load resistor $R_L$ is in series with the collector supply voltage $V_{CC}$ of Fig. 2*a*. A small voltage change $\Delta V_i$ between emitter and base causes a relatively large emitter-current change $\Delta I_E$. The symbol $\alpha$ defines that fraction of this current change which is collected and passes through $R_L$. The change in output voltage across the load resistor $\Delta V_o = \alpha R_L \Delta I_E$ may be many times the change in input voltage $\Delta V_i$. Under these circumstances, the voltage amplification $A \equiv \Delta V_o/\Delta V_i$ will be greater than unity, and the transistor acts as an amplifier. If the dynamic resistance of the emitter junction is $r_e$, then $\Delta V_i = r_e\,\Delta I_E$, and Eq. (1) exists.

$$A \equiv \frac{\alpha R_L \Delta I_E}{r_e \Delta I_E} = \frac{\alpha R_L}{r_e} \tag{1}$$

For example, if $r_e = 25\ \Omega$, $\alpha = 0.99$, and $R_L = 3000\ \Omega$, $A = 118$. This calculation is oversimplified, but in essence it is correct and gives a physical explanation of why the transistor acts as an amplifier. The transistor provides power gain as well as voltage amplification. From the foregoing explanation it is clear that current in the low-resistance input circuit is transferred to the high-resistance output circuit. The word transistor, which originated as a contraction of "transfer resistor," is based upon the preceding physical picture of the device.

Current amplification as well as voltage amplification may be provided by the transistor if the emitter is used as a common, or grounded, terminal as shown in **Fig. 3**. In this configuration, the input signal voltage is applied between the base and emitter electrodes, as it is in the common-base arrangement of Fig. 2*a*, but the signal source needs only provide the base current $\Delta i_b$, which is small in comparison with the emitter signal current $\Delta i_E$. In order to show the relationship between the output signal current $\Delta i_C$ and the input signal current $\Delta i_B$, one begins with the relationship for the common base amplifier, Eq. (2),

$$\Delta i_C = -\alpha \Delta i_E \tag{2}$$

where $\alpha$ is defined as the ratio of $\Delta i_C$ to $\Delta i_E$ and the negative sign indicates that the current flows into one terminal while flowing out of the other terminal. Then, using Kirchhoff's current law, that the total current flowing into a junction is zero, or $\Delta i_B + \Delta i_C + \Delta i_E = 0$, Eq. (3) is obtained. Substituting this

$$\Delta i_E = -\Delta i_B - \Delta i_C \tag{3}$$

value for $\Delta i_E$ into Eq. (2) results in Eq. (4). Finally,

$$\Delta i_C = \alpha(\Delta i_B + \Delta i_C) \tag{4}$$

the explicity solution of Eq. (4) for $\Delta i_C$ as a function of $\Delta i_B$ is given by Eq. (5). Equation (5) shows that

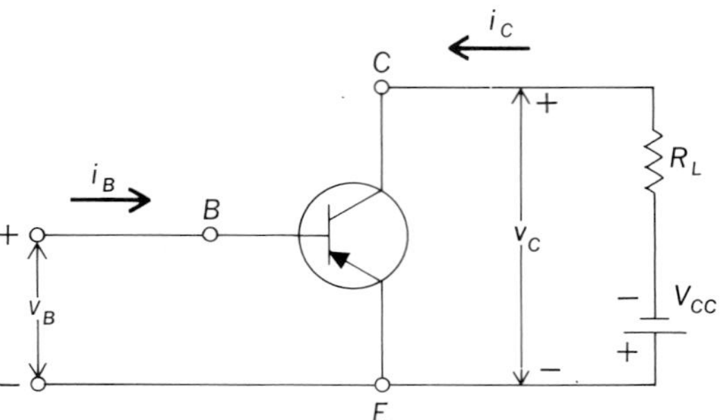


Fig. 3. Transistor common-emitter connection.

$$\Delta i_C = \frac{\alpha}{1-\alpha} \Delta i_B \tag{5}$$

$\alpha/(1 - \alpha)$ is the ratio of collector signal current to the base signal current. This ratio, or current amplification factor, is commonly known as either $\beta$ or $h_{fe}$. Since values of $\alpha$ range from about 0.9 to 0.999, values of $\beta$ range from about 10 to 1000. *See* Kirchhoff's laws of electric circuits.

The small input current of the common-emitter amplifier leads to a higher input resistance as compared with the common-base amplifier. In fact, the input resistance is increased by the factor $\beta + 1$, so the voltage amplification of the common-emitter amplifier is about the same as that of the common-base amplifier.

### Field-Effect Transistor Amplifiers

The field-effect transistor (FET) is a semiconductor electronic device which differs significantly from the ordinary bipolar transistor and depends in its operation on the control of current by an electric field. There are two types of field-effect transistors (each of which is available in two polarities, *n*-channel and *p*-channel), the junction field-effect transistor (JFET, or simply FET) and the insulated-gate or metal-oxide-semiconductor FET (MOSFET). The field-effect transistor differs from the bipolar transistor in the following important characteristics: it is simpler to fabricate and occupies less space in integrated form; the control electrode (the gate) draws essentially no current, resulting in a high input impedance, which can exceed $10^{14}\Omega$; it is less noisy than a bipolar transistor; it exhibits no offset voltage at zero drain current; and the recent availability of high-current FETs (10 nanometers or more) makes possible the replacement of bipolar transistors in many applications, often yielding simpler circuits with better performance. *See* Integrated circuits.

**Junction field-effect transistor.** **Figure 4***a* shows the structure of an *n*-channel junction FET. Ohmic contacts are made to the two ends of a semiconductor bar of *n*-type material (if *p*-type silicon is used, the device is referred to as a *p*-channel FET). Current is caused to flow along the length of the bar because of the voltage supply connected between the ends. This current consists of majority carriers which in this case are electrons. The source $S$ is the terminal through which the majority carriers enter the bar. Conventional current entering the bar at $S$ is designated $I_S$. The drain $D$ is the terminal through which the majority carriers leave the bar. Conventional current entering the bar at $D$ is designated by $I_D$. On both sides of the *n*-type bar of Fig. 4*a*, heavily doped ($p^+$) regions of acceptor impurities have been formed by diffusion or any other procedure available for creating *pn* junctions. These regions are called the gate $G$. Between the gate and source a voltage $V_{GS}$ is applied in the direction to reverse-bias the *pn* junction. Conventional current entering the gate is designated $I_G$. The structure shown in Fig. 4*a* is not practical because of the difficulties involved in diffusing impurities into both sides of a semiconductor wafer. The practical structure has a single-ended geometry where diffusion is from one side only. The region in Fig. 4*a* of *n*-type material between the two gate regions is the channel through which the majority carriers move from source to drain. The circuit symbol with current and voltage polarities marked is given in Fig. 4*b*.

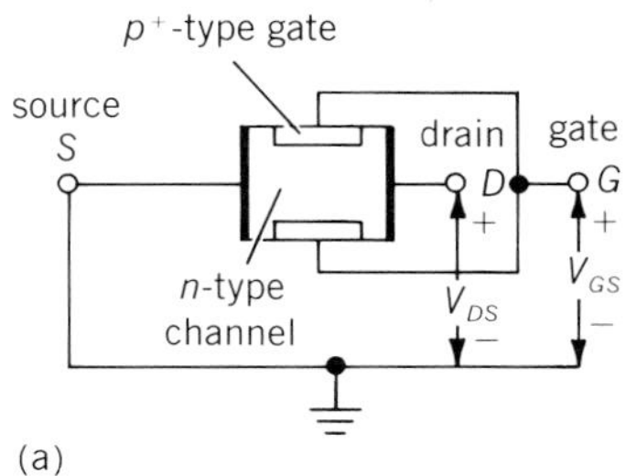


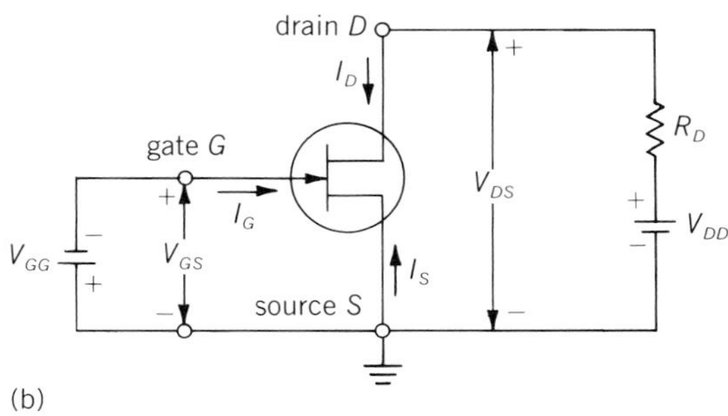


**Fig. 4. An *n*-channel field-effect transistor (FET). (*a*) Basic structure. (*b*) Circuit symbol. (*After J. Millman, Microelectronics, McGraw-Hill, 1979*)**

As discussed above, there are space-charge regions on the two sides of a reverse-biased *pn* junction with uncovered positive ions on the *n* side and negative ions on the *p* side. The electric lines of field intensity originate on the positive ions and terminate, across the junction, on the negative ions. As the reverse bias across the junction increases, so does the thickness of the region of immobile uncovered charges. The conductivity of this region is nominally zero because there are no available charge carriers. Thus, the effective width of the channel in Fig. 4*a* will become progressively decreased with increasing reverse bias. Accordingly, for a fixed drain-to-source voltage, the drain current will be a function of the reverse-biasing voltage across the gate junction. The term ''field effect'' is used to describe this device because the mechanism of current control is the effect of the extension, with increasing reverse bias, of the field associated with the region of uncovered charges. The gate reversed voltage $V_P$ that removes all the free charge from the channel is called the pinch-off voltage $V_P$.

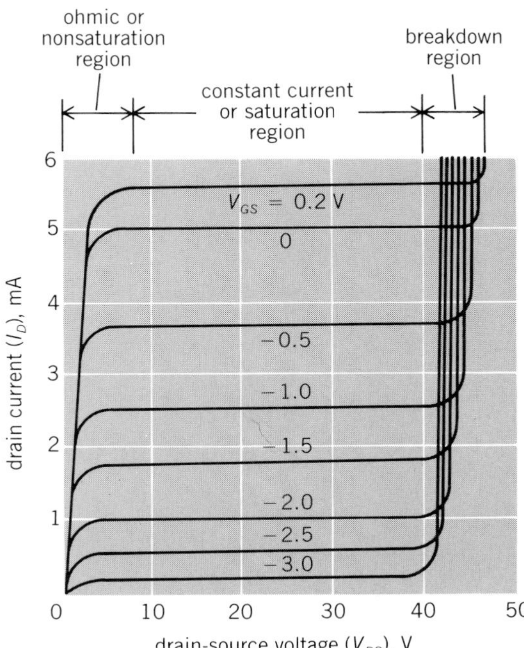


**Fig. 5. Common-source drain characteristics of an *n*-channel field-effect transistor. (*Siliconix Inc., Siliconix Semiconductor Devices, 1972*)**

The common-source drain characteristics for a typical *n*-channel FET (**Fig. 5**) give $I_D$ against $V_{DS}$ with $V_{GS}$ as a parameter. To see qualitatively why the characteristics have the form shown, consider the case for $V_{GS} = 0$. For $I_D = 0$ the channel is entirely open. In response to small applied voltage $V_{DS}$, the *n*-type bar acts as a simple semiconductor resistor, and the current $I_D$ increases linearly with $V_{DS}$.

With increasing current the ohmic voltage drop between the source and channel begins to constrict. Because of the ohmic drop along the length of the channel itself, the construction is not uniform, but is more pronounced at distances further from the source. Eventually a voltage is reached at which the channel is pinched off. This is the voltage not too sharply defined in Fig. 5, where the current $I_D$ begins to level off and approach a constant value. It is not possible for the channel to close completely and thereby reduce the current $I_D$ to zero, because if this happened the current would be reduced to zero and the required ohmic voltage drop which provides the reverse bias would be zero. It is found that in the constant current or saturation region, the mobility of electrons is approximately inversely proportional to the electric field, the drift velocity of the electrons remains constant, and thus the current remains constant (Fig. 5). If a gate voltage $V_{GS}$ is applied in the direction to provide additional reverse bias, pinch-off will occur for smaller values of $|V_{DS}|$, and the maximum drain current will be smaller. The maximum voltage that can be applied between any two terminals of the FET is the lowest voltage that will cause breakdown across the gate junction. From Fig. 5 it is seen that breakdown occurs at lower values of $V_{DS}$ when the gate is reverse-biased than for $V_{GS} = 0$. This is caused by the fact that the reverse-bias gate voltage adds to the drain voltage and hence increases the effective voltage across the gate junction. It is seen from Fig. 5 that the *n*-channel FET requires zero or negative gate bias and positive drain voltage. The *p*-channel FET requires opposite voltage polarities. As $V_{GS}$ is increased in the direction to reverse-bias the gate junction, the conduction channel will narrow, and when $V_{GS} = V_P$ the channel width is reduced to zero and the drain current is cut off.

**MOSFET.** The *p*-channel metal-oxide-semiconductor FET (MOSFET) consists of a lightly doped *n*-type substrate into which two highly doped $p^+$ regions are diffused. A thin (100 to 200 nm) layer of insulating silicon dioxide (glass) is grown over the surface of the structure and holes are cut into the oxide layer, allowing contact with the source and drain (**Fig. 6**). Then the gate-metal area is overlaid on the oxide, covering the entire channel region. Simultaneously, metal contacts are made to the drain and source. The contact to the metal over the channel area is the gate terminal. The chip area of a MOSFET is only about 5% of that required for a bipolar transistor. **Figure 7**

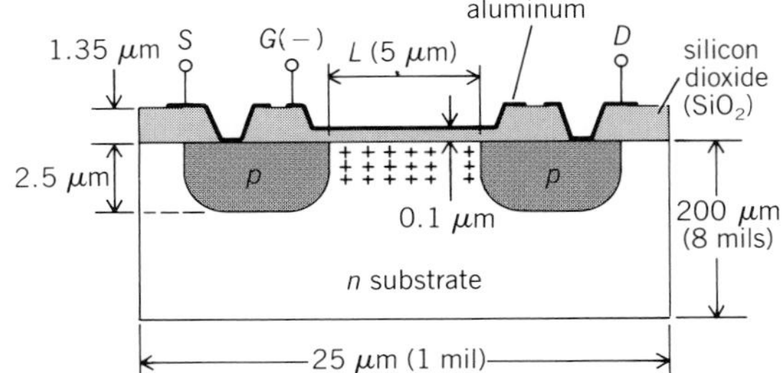


**Fig. 6. Enhancement-type *p*-channel MOSFET. (*After J. Millman, Microelectronics, McGraw-Hill, 1979*)**

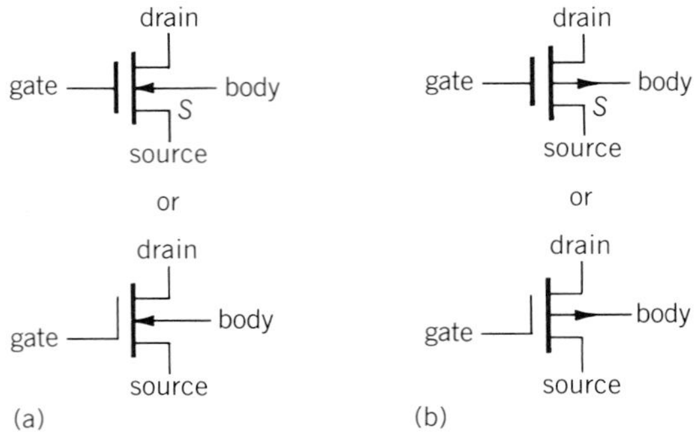

**Fig. 7. Circuit symbols for (*a*) *n*-channel and (*b*) *p*-channel MOSFETs. (*After P. Horowitz and W. Hill, The Art of Electronics, Cambridge University Press, 1980*)**

shows two circuit symbols for a *p*-channel and an *n*-channel MOSFET. If the substrate is grounded and a negative voltage is applied at the gate, an electric field will be directed perpendicularly through the oxide. The field will end on induced positive charges on the semiconductor substrate. The positive charges which are minority carriers in the *n*-type substrate form an inversion layer. As the magnitude of the negative voltage on the gate increases, the induced positive charge in the semiconductor increases. The region beneath the oxide now has *p*-type carriers, the conductivity increases, and current flows from source to drain through the induced channel. Thus the drain current is enhanced by the negative gate voltage, and such a device is called an enhancement *p*-type MOSFET.

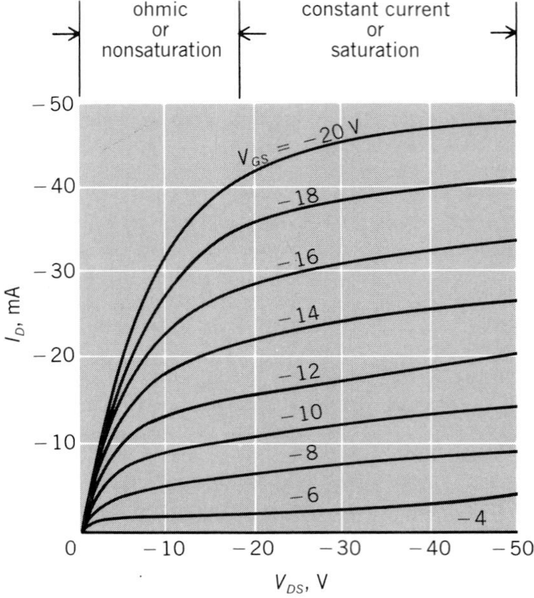


**Fig. 8. Drain characteristics of a *p*-channel enhancement-type MOSFET. (*After J. Millman, Microelectronics, McGraw-Hill, 1979*)**

The volt-ampere drain characteristics of a *p*-channel enhancement mode MOSFET are given in **Fig. 8**. The threshold voltage $V_T$ is the gate-to-source voltage at which drain current begins to flow. The values of $V_T$ for the *p*-channel MOSFET is in the range of $-0.5$ to $-5$ volts. A second type of MOSFET can be made if, to the basic structure of Fig. 6, a channel is diffused between the source and the drain with the same type of impurity as used for the source and the drain diffusion (**Fig. 9**). With this device an appreciable drain current flows for zero gate-to-source voltage $V_{GS} = 0$. If the gate voltage is made negative, positive charges are induced in the channel and these recombine with the free electrons to reduce the majority carriers; thus the channel becomes less conductive and the drain current drops as $V_{GS}$ is made more negative. The reduction in majority carriers causes an effective depletion of majority carriers, which accounts for the designation ''depletion'' MOSFET. This type of device may also be operated in an enhancement mode. It is only necessary to apply a positive gate voltage so that negative charges are induced into the *n*-type channel. In this manner the conductivity of the channel increases and the drain current also increases. For the *n*-type MOSFET a negative gate voltage called gate-source cutoff voltage $V_{GS(\mathrm{OFF})}$ will reduce the drain current $I_D$ to some specified negligible value at a recommended $V_{DS}$. This gate voltage corresponds to the pinch-off voltage $V_P$ of JFET.

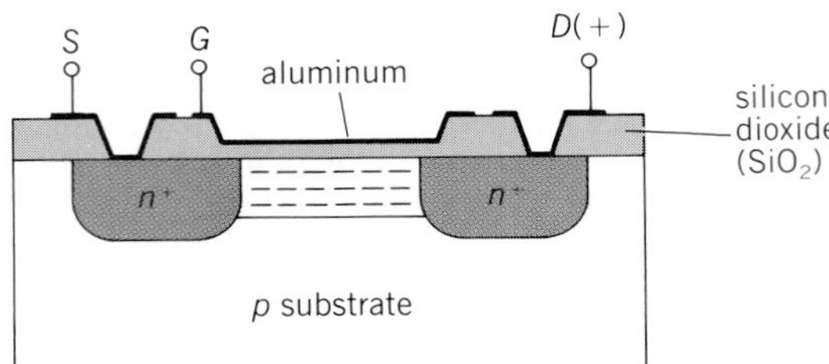


**Fig. 9. Structure of an *n*-channel depletion MOSFET (nMOS). (*After J. Millman, Microelectronics, McGraw-Hill, 1979*).**

**Amplifier application.** FETs and MOSFETs are used as amplifiers by biasing the device to operate in the linear region (constant current region) of its drain characteristics. From these characteristics, the total drain current $i_D$ can be expressed as a function of the gate voltage $V_{GS}$ and the drain voltage $V_{DS}$, Eq. (6).

$$i_D = f(V_{GS}, V_{DS}) \tag{6}$$

If both the drain and gate voltage are varied, the change in drain current is given approximately by the first two terms in the Taylor's series expansion of Eq. (6), that is, by Eq. (7). In the small signal notation

$$\Delta i_D = \left.\frac{\partial i_D}{\partial V_{GS}}\right|_{V_{DS}} \cdot \Delta V_{GS} + \left.\frac{\partial i_D}{\partial V_{DS}}\right|_{V_{GS}} \cdot \Delta V_{DS} \tag{7}$$

$\Delta i_D = i_d$, $\Delta V_{GS} = v_{gs}$, and $\Delta V_{Ds} = v_{ds}$, so that Eq. (7) becomes Eq. (8), where the notation of Eqs. (9)

$$i_d = g_m v_{gs} + \frac{1}{r_d} v_{ds} \tag{8}$$

$$g_m \equiv \left.\frac{\partial i_D}{\partial V_{GS}}\right|_{V_{DS}} \qquad r_d \equiv \left.\frac{\partial V_{DS}}{\partial i_D}\right|_{V_{GS}} \tag{9}$$

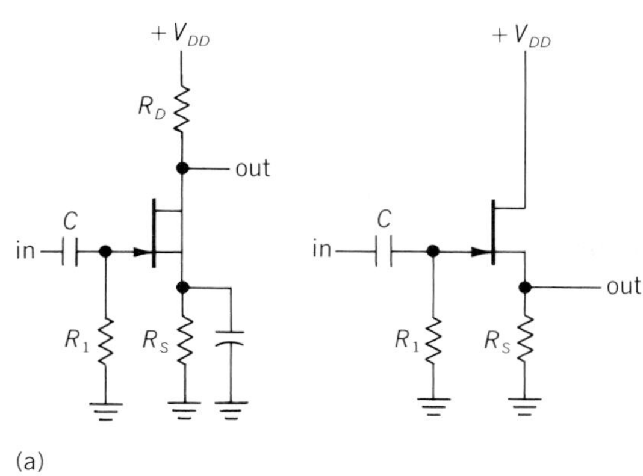


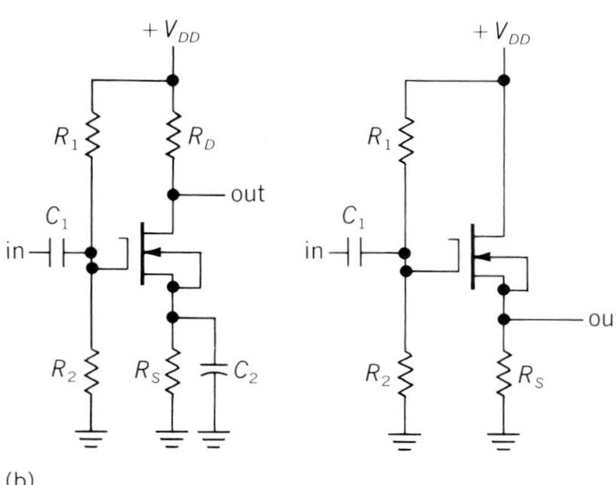


**Fig. 10. Amplifier stages. (*a*) Depletion-mode FET stages. (*b*) Enhancement-mode MOSFET stages. (*After P. Horowitz and W. Hill, The Art of Electronics, Cambridge University Press, 1980*)**

is used. The mutual transconductance $g_m$ for FETS and MOSFETs is of the order of a few thousand microsiemens (micromhos) at a few milliamperes, operating drain current. A major drawback of the amplifier using FETs is that its transconductance is much lower than of an ordinary bipolar transistor operating at the same drain current; however, FETs are used as amplifiers because of the low input current and extremely high input impedance. SEE BIAS OF TRANSISTORS.

**Figure 10*a*** shows common-source and common-drain (source follower) depletion-mode FET amplifier stages, and Fig. 10*b* shows the same circuits using enhancement-mode MOSFETs. The linear equivalent circuit for all FETs and MOSFETs described by Eq. (8) is given in **Fig. 11**.

The equivalent circuit of Fig. 11*a* is used to calculate the voltage gain $A_V$ for the common-source FET or MOSFET amplifier, Eq. (10), and for the common-drain (source follower), Eq. (11).

$$A_V = -g_m \frac{r_d R_D}{r_d + R_D} \tag{10}$$

$$A_V = \frac{g_m R_s}{1 + g_m R_s} \tag{11}$$

FETs are often used as source followers because of their very high input impedance, especially in the input stages of oscilloscopes and measuring instru-

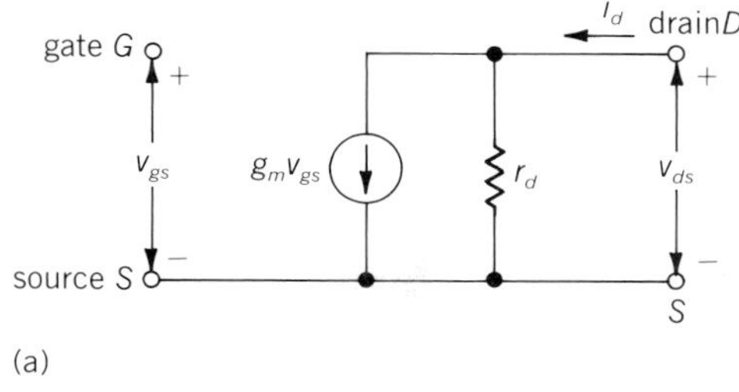


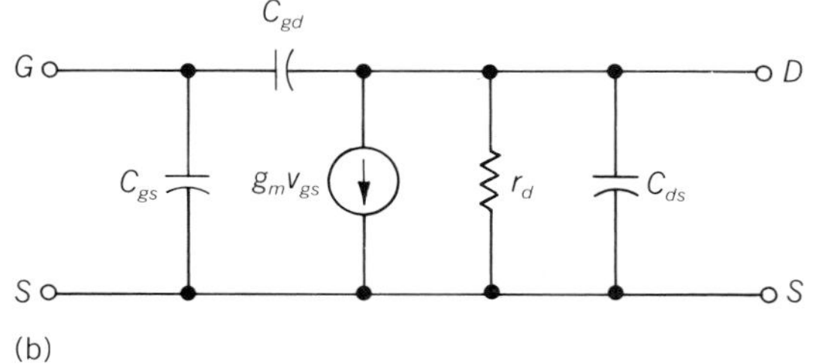


**Fig. 11. Linear equivalent circuits for FETs and MOSFETs. (*a*) Low-frequency, small-signal, equivalent circuit (*after J. Millman, Microelectronics, McGraw-Hill, 1979*). (*b*) High-frequency model, taking node capacitances into account (*after J. Millman and C. C. Halkias, Integrated Electronics, McGraw-Hill, 1972*).**

ments. In other applications, matched FETs are used as an input pair follower, with voltage gain less than unity, followed by an operational amplifier. Also, a matched FET pair is used as a common-source differential amplifier. SEE OSCILLOSCOPE.

### Vacuum-Tube Amplifiers

The basic electron-tube amplifier consists of a vacuum triode tube and associated circuitry, as shown in **Fig. 12**. The signal voltage to be amplified is applied to the input, or grid, circuit and the amplified signal appears across the load resistor $R_L$ in the anode (plate), or output, circuit. A gain in voltage $v$, and power is thereby provided. By selection of tubes and associated circuitry, these gains may be maximized.

In normal operation a small negative voltage called a bias voltage, $V_{GG}$, is applied to the grid of the tube. This voltage establishes a definite plate-to-cathode current through the tube for a fixed load resistor $R_L$ and high-potential plate-supply voltage $V_{PP}$. This plate current $I_P$ is called the quiescent current since it is the zero-signal current. A dc voltage drop $I_P R_L$ appears across the output terminals because of the flow of the quiescent current through the load resistor. In the vacuum tube, electrons are emitted by the cathode and pass through the grid to the plate. The direction

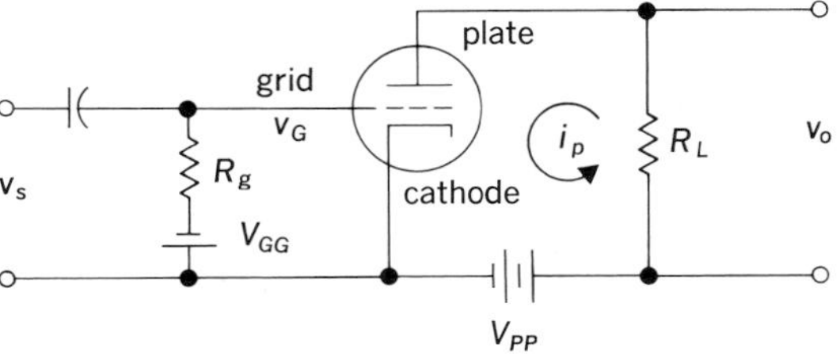


**Fig. 12. Diagram of a basic vacuum-tube amplifier.**

of "conventional" current is opposite to that of the electron, and so the plate current (conventional notation) flows from plate to cathode. SEE VACUUM TUBE.

If a small signal voltage is added to the grid bias voltage, the instantaneous grid voltage $v_G$ is the algebraic sum of the bias voltage $V_{GG}$ and the signal voltage $v_G$. As the instantaneous grid voltage changes, the plate current $i_P$ changes in proportion to the grid voltage changes. The result is a net plate current $i_P$ that is the algebraic sum of the quiescent plate current $I_P$ and a varying or signal component of plate current.

The passage of signal current $i_p$ through the load resistor results in an output voltage $v_p$ that is the product $i_pR_L$. The ratio of $v_p$ to the grid signal voltage $v_s$ is the voltage gain $A$ of the amplifier.

If the root-mean-square (rms) value of signal current is $I_o$, the signal power delivered to the load is $I_oR_L$ watts. For the typical voltage-amplifier vacuum tube the output power may be as high as 1 watt. Large power amplifiers used in broadcasting and commercial rf heating generators range up to 50 kW in power rating. Larger tubes are occasionally used.

## CLASSIFICATIONS

Amplifiers of either the transistor, FET, or tube variety may be classified in any one of several ways. One is by means of the coupling circuitry, such as an $RC$-coupled (resistance-capacitance-coupled) amplifier. Other categories include classification by purpose, such as hi-fi (high-fidelity audio amplifier), and mode of operation, such as class A. Some of the more common methods of classification follow with a brief description of the operating properties.

**Classification by coupling methods.** A great deal of information about an amplifier is conveyed by merely stating the interstage coupling method used. The more common types are listed here.

***RC-coupled amplifier.*** This amplifier (**Fig. 13**) is so named because of the coupling capacitor $C_b$ from the load resistor of stage $A_1$ to the input of the following stage, $A_2$. This capacitor blocks the dc collector drain or plate voltage from reaching the base gate or grid of the next stage. It is by far the commonest form of audio amplifier because of its simplicity and because it can be designed with nearly constant amplification over a wide frequency range. It is essentially an audio amplifier, although with high-frequency compensation the upper half-power frequency can be extended to several megahertz. The lower half-power frequency may be on the order of 20 Hz, and can be extended to lower frequencies by using low-frequency compensation.

***Transformer-coupled amplifier.*** This amplifier is so named because two stages are coupled through a transformer. The dc collector, drain or plate voltage of the transistor, FET, or tube is blocked from reaching the base, gate, or grid of the following stage by the transformer. Transformer coupling finds wide application in tuned amplifiers, such as rf and i-f amplifiers, where tuned air-core transformers or transformers with a core of powdered iron are used.

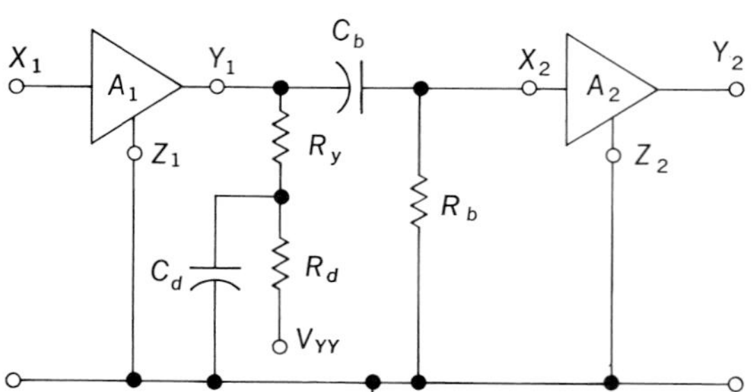


**Fig. 13. Diagram illustrating the use of the decoupling filter $R_d$ and $C_d$ for compensation.**

***Direct-coupled amplifier.*** This form of amplifier, usually called a dc amplifier, allows the amplification of dc as well as ac signals. It has special circuitry, either in the coupling network or in the type of amplifier stages, which eliminates the need for the coupling capacitor. In direct-coupled amplifiers problems arise with drift produced by changes in temperature or aging of components. Therefore, special techniques must be employed to reduce the undesirable signals in the output to negligible values. This type of amplifier finds extensive application whenever very low-frequency signals must be amplified, such as in certain medical instruments and servomechanisms. It also finds extensive application in the electronic differential analyzer (analog computer). SEE ANALOG COMPUTER.

**Classification by selectivity.** An important feature of some amplifiers is their ability to amplify only those signals lying within a certain band of frequencies and to reject signals outside this band. Other amplifiers are designed to amplify an extremely wide range of frequencies.

***Tuned amplifiers.*** A tuned amplifier is one which is designed to amplify signals in a frequency band that is centered on a chosen carrier frequency and not to amplify signals which lie outside this band. Tuned amplifiers form an important part of radio and television receivers in the rf and i-f amplifier sections. The signal picked up by the antenna and appearing at the terminals of the receiver is composed of the desired signal along with signals from other stations. The receiver is tuned to the carrier frequency of the desired signal, and the tuned amplifiers amplify the desired signal. A tuned amplifier is formed by using a collector, drain, or plate load impedance which is a resonant circuit. The gain is normally maximum at the resonant frequency and decreases for frequencies on either side of the resonant frequency. The resonant frequency of the amplifier (the frequency of maximum gain) may be selected by varying either the inductance or capacitance in the circuit. For an i-f amplifier, where the resonant frequency is constant at the intermediate frequency, the tuning for maximum gain is done at the time that the receiver is aligned and remains fixed, except for adjustments made necessary by aging of the components or replacement of the transistors, FETS, or tubes. On the other hand, the tuning of an rf amplifier in a radio receiver must be variable in order to receive stations transmitting at different carrier frequencies. The tuning is usually done with a variable capacitor. Cascaded amplifiers sometimes have different resonant frequencies for each stage in order to produce the required frequency response. Such amplifiers are called stagger-tuned amplifiers. SEE CAPACITOR; RESONANCE (ALTERNATING-CURRENT CIRCUITS); TUNING.

***Untuned amplifiers.*** An untuned amplifier is one in which the coupling circuitry is not a tuned circuit. The audio amplifier and the direct-coupled amplifier are the most important of this type.

**Classification by operating mode.** The operating modes of vacuum tubes are prescribed by the designations class A, class B, and class C, with certain divisions among the classes. The distinction between the various classes is determined for a sinusoidal signal voltage applied to the input. The position of the quiescent point and the extent of the characteristic that is being used determine the method of operation. Whether the transistor or tube is operated as a class A, B, AB, or C amplifier is determined from the following definitions.

***Class A.*** In this amplifier the operating point and the input signal are such that the current in the output circuit (in the collector, drain, or plate) flows at all times. A class A amplifier operates essentially over a linear portion of its characteristic.

***Class B.*** This amplifier has the operating point at an extreme end of its characteristic, so that the quiescent power is very small. Hence either the quiescent current or the quiescent voltage is approximately zero. If the signal voltage is sinusoidal, amplification takes place for only one-half cycle. For example, if the quiescent output-circuit current is zero, this current will remain zero for one-half cycle.

***Class AB.*** This amplifier operates between the two extremes defined for class A and class B. Hence the output signal is zero for part, but less than one-half, of an input sinusoidal signal cycle.

***Class C.*** In this amplifier the operating point is chosen so that the output current (or voltage) is zero for more than one-half of an input sinusoidal signal cycle.

In the case of a vacuum-tube amplifier the suffix 1 may be added to the letter, or letters, of the class identification to denote that grid current does not flow during any part of the input cycle. The suffix 2 may be added to denote that grid current does flow during some part of the input cycle.

**Classification by application.** Amplifiers may be classified by the use for which they are designed.

***Audio-frequency (af) amplifiers.*** These are intended to operate over the general range of about 20–20,000 Hz. Those capable of operating over this full range with a minimum of distortion are often referred to as high-fidelity (hi-fi) amplifiers if they are used with sound-reproducing equipment. Special-purpose amplifiers, such as those used in automatic control equipment, often operate in the audio-frequency range. *See Disk recording.*

***Radio-frequency (rf) amplifiers.*** These are used to amplify signals in the range of about 100–1,000,000 kHz. They are usually used as the first amplifier stage in selective radio receivers, including automobile receivers. Because of the additional cost they are usually not used in the average home receiver designed for local reception.

***Intermediate-frequency (i-f) amplifiers.*** These are used in radio, radar, and television receivers. The majority of broadcast radio receivers employ i-f amplifiers operating at 445 kHz; some automobile receivers use 262 kHz. Communication receivers commonly use 1600-kHz i-f transformers. In frequency-modulated (FM) receivers an i-f of 10.7 MHz is used. Television receivers use 26- or 46-MHz i-f frequencies. Radar receivers commonly use 30- or 60-MHz i-f amplifiers. *See Radar; Radio receiver; Television receiver.*

### Cascade Amplifier

Since, in most applications, one stage of amplification does not provide enough gain, two or more stages are connected together (cascaded) to provide the required gain. For example, many radio receivers have two i-f amplifiers, and the more sensitive receivers have three stages. Similarly, there may be two stages of amplification, and possibly a preamplifier, preceding the power amplifier in an audio amplifier.

The gain of an amplifier is defined as the ratio of the output voltage to the input voltage for a sinusoidal input voltage. Under the usual method for analyzing ac circuits, the gain is a complex number indicating the magnitude of the gain and the phase angle by which the output voltage lags the input voltage in time. Since the gain is a function of frequency, because of the reactive circuit elements, the figure for the gain should be accompanied by the frequency at which it was determined. The practice is to quote the gain for the mid-band region of an audio amplifier or the gain at the resonant frequency for a tuned amplifier. The terms gain and amplification are synonymous, the former being more commonly used. The gain of a cascaded amplifier at any frequency is equal to the product of the gain of each stage. The gain of each stage must be measured or calculated when the stages are connected together, if the frequency at which the gain is being measured is above the mid-band range for an audio amplifier, or if the amplifier is a tuned amplifier. This is necessary because the input impedance of the following stage causes the gain of a stage to be different from what it would be if the following stage were not connected. This is important at high frequencies because the dominant component of the input is a shunt capacitor. If the frequency at which the measurement is made is in the midband range or lower for an audio amplifier, the reactance of the input capacitance is sufficiently high to allow it to be neglected, and the gain is the product of the gain of each stage, where the stage gain is measured before cascading.

### Signal Response

An amplifier cannot exactly reproduce the waveform or frequency spectrum of its input signal. The amplifier's ability to faithfully reproduce a signal is measured by either its frequency response or its time response.

**High-frequency compensation.** As the frequency is increased above the upper limit of the mid-band region, the gain decreases because the reactance of the shunt capacitance is decreasing. High-frequency compensation is employed to increase the upper half-power frequency. One technique is to place a small inductance in series with the load resistor. The reactance of the inductance, and hence the effective amplifier load, increases with increasing frequency. This increased load tends to offset the effect of the decrease in reactance of the shunt capacitance as the frequency increases. The result is that the value for the inductance can be chosen to extend the mid-band region of the compensated amplifier without introducing undesirable characteristics into the frequency response. *See Alternating-current circuit theory; Reactance.*

**Low-frequency compensation.** As the frequency is decreased below the lower limit of the mid-band region, the gain of an *RC*-coupled amplifier decreases because the reactance of the coupling capacitor is increasing.

The decrease in gain can be compensated for by using the compensation network shown in Fig. 13. Devices $A_1$ and $A_2$ may be transistors, FETs, or vacuum tubes. A high resistance $R_d$ in series with the

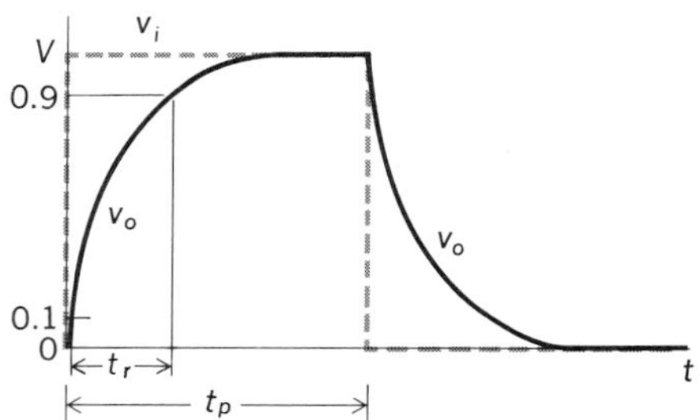


**Fig. 14. The output waveform $v_o$ resulting when a pulse $v_i$ is applied to an amplifier.**

collector, drain, or plate resistance $R_y$ connects to the supply voltage. A large capacitance $C_d$ is used to bypass $R_d$ to ground. The components $R_d$ and $C_d$ are often used with a multistage amplifier as a decoupling filter to minimize the interactions between stages which result from the use of a common power supply. This same decoupling network compensates for the low-frequency distortion introduced by $C_b$. Thus, at high frequencies (in the mid-band region) $C_d$ acts as a short circuit across $R_d$, and the gain of the amplifier is determined by $R_y$. At low frequencies, however, $C_d$ becomes a large reactance, and the effective output-circuit resistance increases toward $R_y + R_d$. This increase in amplification tends to compensate for the loss in output due to the attenuation caused by the reactance of $C_b$, which increases as the frequency is reduced. *See* ELECTRIC FILTER.

**Pulse rise time.** An amplifier may be called upon to increase the size of a signal whose wave shape is that of a narrow pulse. The definition for pulse rise time is the time required for the pulse to increase from 10% of its maximum value (assuming no overshoot) to 90% of its maximum value (see **Fig. 14**). The rise time of the pulse is a function of the frequency response of the amplifier. The rise time $t_r$ is inversely proportional to bandwidth $B$; the constant of proportionality is taken as 0.35. Thus $\Delta\tau = 0.35/B$.

Bandwidth is inversely proportional to equivalent load resistance $R_{eq}$ and shunt capacitance $C_0$ of an amplifier stage; thus the expression for pulse rise time may be written at $t_r = 2.2R_{eq}C_0$.

### Undesirable Conditions

There are a number of undesirable conditions that may occur in amplifiers, produced by improper circuit design and by inherent limitations in the physical operation of the devices. In general, good circuit design can reduce all of the undesirable conditions, including those caused by physical limitations, to the point where they are not noticeable.

**Distortion.** If the output signal from an amplifier is not an exact replica of the input signal, distortion has occurred. In theory it is impossible for an amplifier to avoid introducing distortion. On the other hand, amplifiers have been designed in which the distortion is extremely small. Distortion is introduced by two factors in the amplifier. One factor is a nonlinear relation of the device between the input signal and the output signal. If the input signal is a sinusoidal signal, the output will be composed of harmonics of the input. The second factor is the frequency response of the amplifier. Since the gain of the amplifier is not the same for all frequencies, the amplification of each harmonic component of an input signal is not necessarily the same as that of the others. The output signal, since it is a superposition of the harmonic components, differs from the input signal. Distortion caused by nonlinearities in the amplifier and by the frequency response of the amplifier can be reduced by the proper use of feedback. *See* DISTORTION (ELECTRONIC CIRCUITS); FEEDBACK CIRCUIT; NONSINUSOIDAL WAVEFORM.

**Noise.** The noise encountered in amplifiers may, in general, be classified into thermal noise and shot noise. Thermal noise is caused by the random motion of electrons inside resistors, conductors, tubes, and transistors. It has the characteristic of having uniform power per unit bandwidth. Furthermore, the noise power is directly proportional to the temperature when expressed in Kelvins. Shot noise is the name given to the noise generated in transistors or vacuum tubes by the random emission of holes or electrons from the emitter or cathode. The random emission produces minute fluctuations in the average value of collector or plate current. These fluctuations produce a small noise voltage of the same order of magnitude as thermal noise (a few microvolts).

To analyze the effect of these noise sources upon the circuit and to design the optimum circuit, noise generators are used, and the analysis proceeds in a straightforward manner. Although noise voltages can become bothersome in audio amplifiers, the most common situation where they must be considered is in the design of rf amplifiers, where quite often the signal to be amplified is not much larger than the rms value of the noise voltage. *See* ELECTRICAL NOISE.

**Degeneration.** This undesirable condition is the loss of gain through unintentional negative feedback. Three common sources of degeneration are improperly bypassed emitter, source, or cathode resistors. Ideally the emitter, source, or cathode voltages should be constant with respect to the signal voltage. However, if the emitter bypassing is not effective, that is, if the signal current flowing through the emitter-to-ground impedance produces a varying voltage across the impedance, then the base-to-emitter voltage is less than the signal voltage by the amount of the voltage from emitter to ground. This is equivalent to reducing the gain of the amplifier stage. Degeneration can be reduced to a negligible value by having a bypass capacitor with sufficiently small reactance at the signal frequency.

**Regeneration.** This undesirable condition is an increase in gain through unintentional positive feedback. In its worst form, the amplifier becomes an oscillator. Regeneration can be caused by unwanted capacitive feedback coupling between certain stages. If the regeneration is just less than the amount necessary to cause oscillation, the frequency-response characteristic for the amplifier contains a region where the amplification is much greater than that in the mid-band region. This causes excessive phase and amplitude distortion of the signal and the possibility of lightly damped transient oscillations. *See* OSCILLATOR.

### Differential Amplifiers

Amplifiers that use a single active device such as a FET, vacuum tube, or transistor cannot usually achieve high dc gain, good bias stability, and low noise simultaneously, because large emitter resistors must be used for high bias stability. These resistors restrict the dc gain but may be bypassed for high ac gain. The differential amplifier uses two active devices in an arrangement that overcomes this problem, as illustrated in the balanced transistor amplifier of

**Fig. 15**. As the base of one is driven positive, the other is driven negative. If the transistors are matched and operate in their linear regions, the emitter-current increase of one transistor is equal to the emitter-current decrease of the other. Therefore, the current through the emitter resistor $R_E$ and the voltage drop across $R_E$ remain constant. Thus, $R_E$ causes no degeneration and needs no bypassing. On the other hand, when signals having the same magnitude and polarity are applied to the two bases, the current change through both transistors must flow through $R_E$, and the resulting voltage change across $R_E$ opposes the input voltage, causing degeneration. This is the same effect observed with an unbypassed emitter resistor in a conventional amplifier. This equal-polarity signal is known as a common-mode signal, and the voltage amplification of a differential transistor amplifier with a common-mode input signal is approximately $R_C/R_E$. Voltage or current changes due to temperature changes are common-mode signals. Therefore, best thermal stability is achieved when the common-mode voltage gain is very low. A figure of merit for the differential amplifier is the ratio of differential voltage gain to the common-mode voltage gain. This ratio is known as the common-mode rejection ratio (CMRR). Since the differential gain is the same as that of a single amplifier using the same amplifying device and the same load resistance while the common-mode gain is inversely proportional to the emitter resistor $R_E$, the CMRR improves as $R_E$ is increased. However, the value of $R_E$ in Fig. 15 should not appreciably exceed the value of $R_C$ in order to maintain suitable dynamic range for the amplifier.

The input signal of the differential amplifier may be single-ended, or referenced to ground, and the output signal may be either differential or single-ended, as shown in **Fig. 16**. Besides being unbalanced, an additional transistor $T_3$ is included in the emitter circuit of this differential amplifier. This transistor accurately controls the bias currents in the differential amplifier and therefore acts as a current source, or very high resistance, in the emitter circuit, thus providing a very high CMMR. In this circuit, the voltage across $R_E$ is the same as the voltage across $R_1$. Therefore, the value of $R_E$ controls the bias value of emitter current in all three transistors. The diode $D$ provides temperature compensation. As the input signal goes positive, the forward bias, and hence the emitter current, of transistor $T_1$ is increased. This current increase cannot pass through transistor $T_3$ but opposes the emitter bias current of transistor $T_2$. Thus, the currents in transistor $T_2$ decrease by the same amount as the currents in transistor $T_1$ increase, as they did in the balanced amplifier.

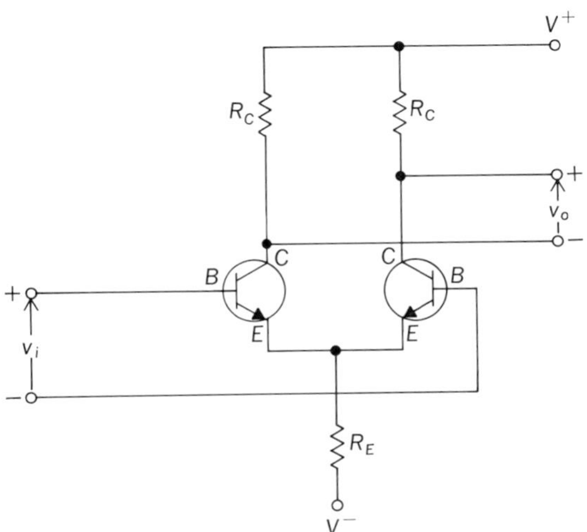


**Fig. 15. A balanced differential transistor amplifier.**

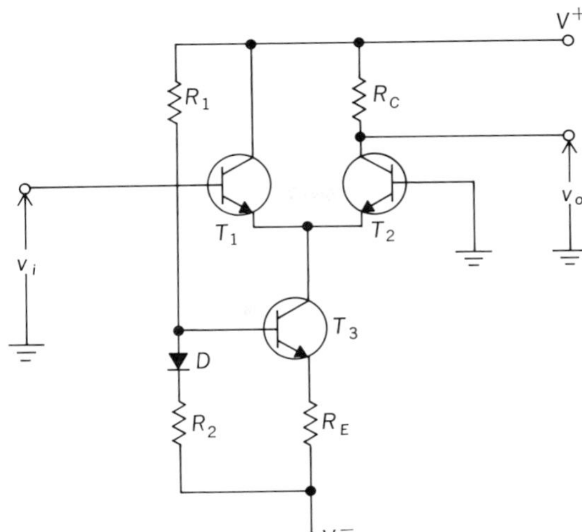


**Fig. 16. An unbalanced differential, or emitter-coupled, amplifier.**

When the desired output from the differential amplifier is unbalanced, as shown in Fig. 16, there is no need to include a load resistor in the collector circuit of both transistors. In fact, the omission of the load resistance from the collector circuit of $T_1$ increases the bandwidth of the amplifier considerably, because the amplifier then appears as an emitter-follower amplifier coupled to a common-base amplifier and both of these configurations may have much wider bandwidth than the common-emitter configuration. The arrangement shown in Fig. 16 is commonly known as an emitter-coupled amplifier. The bandwidth increase actually results from the reduction of the effective capacitance, known as Miller capacitance, in transistor $T_1$.

### Operational Amplifiers

The term "operational amplifier" was coined by people in the analog computer field and was used to designate an amplifier with very high voltage gain, high input impedance, and low output impedance. This type of amplifier is used as the basic element in the performance of the basic mathematical operations such as addition, subtraction, multiplication, integration, differentiation, and logarithms. These operations can be performed with high accuracy, providing the amplifier has a voltage gain of the order of 100,000, an input impedance of the order of 1 megohm or higher, and an output impedance no greater than a few hundred ohms. Thus, the operational amplifier is a special type of cascade amplifier having these characteristics.

Operational amplifiers, called op amps, are used extensively in the areas of electronic instrumentation and communication in addition to analog computing devices. These amplifiers are available in integrated-circuit, or solid-state-chip, form and come in a variety of bandwidths. The op amp is normally direct-coupled, so it may be used for either dc or ac applications and its gain may be accurately controlled by negative feedback. Thus, the op amp has become a universal amplifying device. The following applications illustrate the operating principles as well as some uses of the op amp.

**Voltage amplifier.** A voltage amplifier simply multiplies the input voltage by a constant, the voltage gain of the amplifier, which may be controlled by negative feedback as illustrated in **Fig. 17***a*. The op amp, represented by the triangular symbol, is assumed to have very high voltage amplification $a_v$ so the input voltage $v_a$ to the amplifier is negligibly small, since $v_a = v_o/a_v$. Then, the current $i$ provided by the driving source $v_s$ is essentially given by Eq. (12). Since the amplifier input voltage $v_a$ is very small

$$i = \frac{v_s}{R_s} \tag{12}$$

and the input resistance of the amplifier is very high, the amplifier input current is negligible compared with the source current $i$. Therefore, essentially all of the current $i$ must flow through the feedback resistor $R_f$. Then, since $v_a$ is negligible compared with $v_o$, Eq. (13) follows. Substituting Eq. (12) into Eq. (13) and

$$v_o = -iR_f \tag{13}$$

rearranging, Eq. (14) is obtained. But the voltage

$$\frac{v_o}{v_s} = -\frac{R_f}{R_s} \tag{14}$$

gain of the amplifier with feedback is $A_v = v_o/v_s$. Therefore Eq. (15) is valid. Thus the voltage ampli-

$$A_v = -\frac{R_f}{R_s} \tag{15}$$

fication is controlled by the ratio of the feedback resistance $R_s$. The resistance $R_s$ may be the actual internal resistance of the driving source or it may include resistance external to the driving source, such as resistance needed to reduce the loading on the driving source. *See* Voltage amplifier.

Most operational amplifiers may have their dc input and output voltages referenced to ground when the power supply provides balanced voltages $V^+$ and $V^-$ with respect to ground, as indicated in Fig. 17*a*. However, when the op amp uses a transistor differential amplifier as the input stage, the base currents of the two input transistors must flow from ground through the external circuit resistances to both the inverting and noninverting inputs of the amplifier. When the *iR* drop to the inverting input differs from the *iR* drop to the noninverting input, a dc offset voltage appears between the input terminals. This voltage is amplified by the gain $A_v$ of the amplifier and appears as a magnified dc voltage in the output. This unwanted voltage may be largely eliminated by placing a resistor $R_1$ between the noninverting input and ground, as shown in Fig. 17*b*. This resistance should have a value equal to the parallel combination of $R_s$ and $R_f$, assuming the two bias currents are equal. On the other hand, the value of $R_1$ may be adjusted to compensate for any difference, or offset, in the bias currents.

It can be seen from Fig. 17*a* that a voltage polarity reversal occurs between the input and output of the amplifier since the input voltage is applied to the inverting input terminal. Thus, the input is multiplied by a negative constant. When the voltage gain of such an amplifier is adjusted to one, or unity, the amplifier becomes a sign changer or simply an inverter.

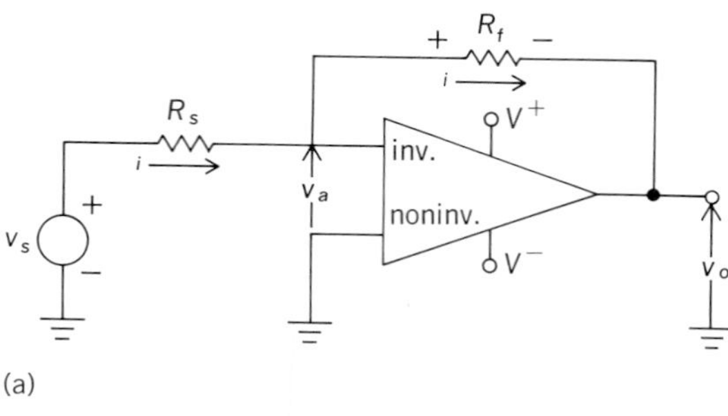


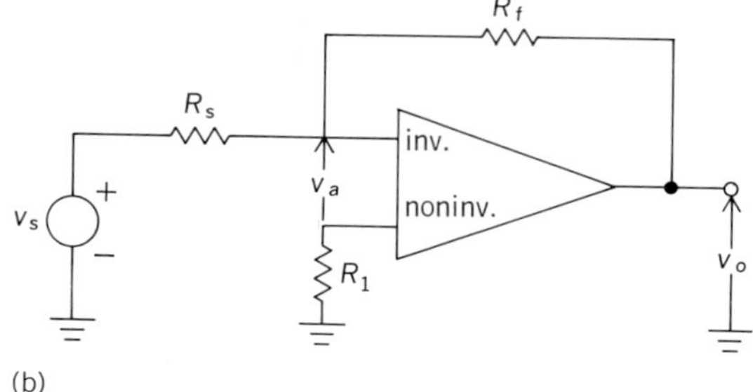


**Fig. 17. An operational amplifier with feedback gain control. (*a*) With input referenced to ground. (*b*) With equalized resistances between the inputs and ground to reduce the input offset voltage.**

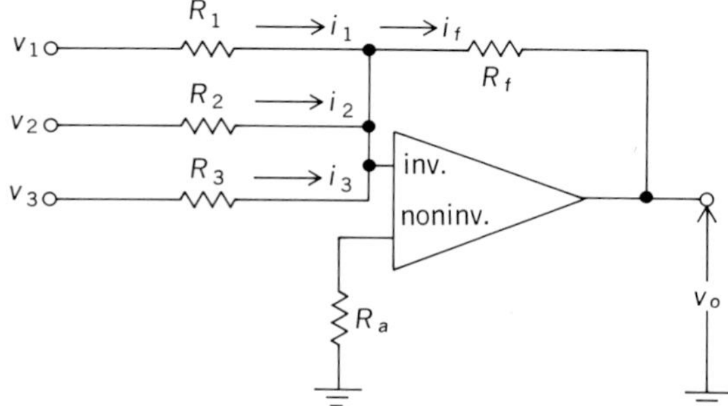


**Fig. 18. A summing amplifier, or summer.**

**Summing amplifier.** Several different voltage sources may be connected to the input of an op amp, as shown in **Fig. 18**. Since both the input voltage and the input current of the amplifier are negligible, $i_f$ is given by Eq. (16). Also, $i_1 = v_1/R_1$, $i_2 = v_2/R_2$,

$$i_1 + i_2 + i_3 = i_f \tag{16}$$

$i_3 = v_3/R_3$, and $i_f = -v_o/R_f$. Therefore, Eq. (17) follows.

$$\frac{v_1}{R_1} + \frac{v_2}{R_2} + \frac{v_3}{R_3} = -\frac{v_o}{R_f} \tag{17}$$

lows. Solving Eq. (17) for $v_o$ explicitly, Eq. (18) is

$$v_o = -\left(\frac{R_f}{R_1}v_1 + \frac{R_f}{R_2}v_2 + \frac{R_f}{R_3}v_3\right) \tag{18}$$

obtained. When $R_f = R_1 = R_2 = R_3$, $v_o = -(v_1 + v_2 + v_3)$ and the output voltage is simply the sum of the input voltages. However, as Eq. (18) shows, multiplication may be performed as well as addition when the resistance values are not equal. Again, the negative sum is obtained unless an inverter is used to restore the initial polarities. On the other hand, an inverter may be placed in an input lead to perform subtraction on that input.

**Integrator.** When the feedback resistor $R_f$ is replaced by a capacitor $C$, as shown in **Fig. 19**, the op amp circuit becomes an integrator. Again $i_i = v_i/R$

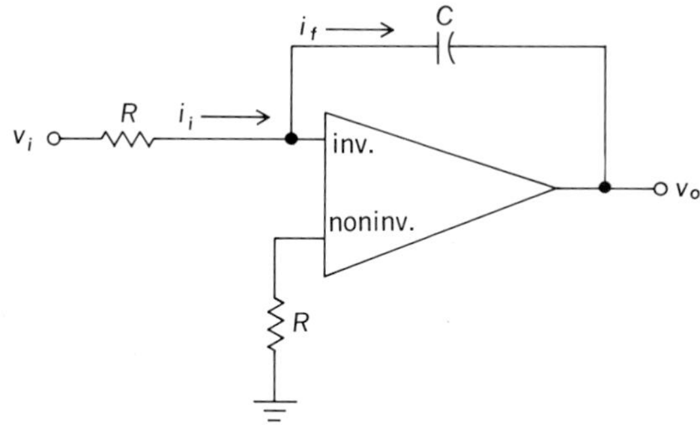


**Fig. 19. An integrating amplifier, or integrator.**

and $i_i = i_f$. However, the current through a capacitor is proportional to the rate of change of voltage across it, as shown in Eq. (19). By solving this equation

$$i_f = -C\frac{dv_o}{dt} \tag{19}$$

explicitly for $v_o$, Eq. (20) is obtained, where $k$ is the

$$v_o = -\frac{1}{C}\int i_f\,dt + k \tag{20}$$

constant of integration or initial output voltage. When this initial voltage is assumed to be zero and the relationship $i_f = i_1 = v_i/R$ is substituted into Eq. (20), this equation becomes Eq. (21). Thus, the circuit is

$$v_o = -\frac{1}{RC}\int v_i\,dt \tag{21}$$

an integrator having a multiplying factor $1/RC$ which may be made equal to unity if desired.

The positions of $R$ and $C$ could be exchanged in the circuit of Fig. 19 to produce a differentiating amplifier, or differentiator. However, the differentiator is seldom used because of its inherent high noise level.

*Christos C. Halkias; Charles L. Alley*

**Bibliography.** C. L. Alley and K. W. Atwood, *Electronic Engineering,* 3d ed., 1973; D. J. Comer, *Modern Electronic Circuit Design,* 1976; C. A. Holt, *Electronic Circuits: Digital and Analog,* 1978; P. Horowitz and W. Hill, *The Art of Electronics,* 1980; D. L. Schilling and C. Belove, *Electronic Circuits: Discrete and Integrated,* 2d ed., 1979; J. Millman, *Microelectronics,* 1979.

## Amplitude (wave motion)

The maximum magnitude (value without regard to sign) of the disturbance of a wave. The term "disturbance" refers to that property of a wave which perturbs or alters its surroundings. It may mean, for example, the displacement of mechanical waves, the pressure variations of a sound wave, or the electric or magnetic field of light waves. Sometimes in older texts the word "amplitude" is used for the disturbance itself; in that case, amplitude as meant there is called peak amplitude. This is no longer common usage.

As an example, consider one-dimensional traveling waves in a linear, homogeneous medium. The wave disturbance $y$ is a function of both a space coordinate $x$ and time $t$. Frequently the disturbance may be expressed as $y(x,t) = f(x \pm vt)$, where $v$ denotes the wave velocity. The plus or minus sign indicates the direction in which the wave moves, and the shape of the wave dictates the functonal form symbolized by $f$. Then, the amplitude of the disturbance at some point $x_0$ is the maximum magnitude (that is, the maximum absolute value) achieved by $f$ as time changes over the duration required for the wave to pass point $x_0$. A special case of this is the one-dimensional, simple harmonic wave $y(x,t) = A \sin [k(x \pm vt)]$, where $k$ is a constant. The amplitude is $A$ since the absolute maximum of the sine function is $+1$. The amplitude for such a wave is a constant.

If the medium which a wave disturbs dissipates the wave by some nonlinear behavior or other means, then the amplitude will, in general, depend upon position.

*S. A. Williams*

## Amplitude modulation

The process or result of the process whereby the amplitude of a carrier wave is changed in accordance with a modulating wave. This broad definition includes applications using sinusoidal carriers, pulse carriers, or any other form of carrier, the amplitude factor of which changes in accordance with the modulating wave in any unique manner. SEE MODULATION.

Amplitude modulation (AM) is also defined in a more restrictive sense to mean modulation in which the amplitude factor of a sine-wave carrier is linearly proportional to the modulating wave. AM radio broadcasting is a familiar example. At the radio transmitter the modulating wave is the audio-frequency program signal to be communicated; the modulated wave that is broadcast is a radio-frequency, amplitude-modulated sinusoid.

In AM the modulated wave is composed of the transmitted carrier, which conveys no information, plus the upper and lower sidebands, which (assuming the carrier frequency exceeds twice the top audio frequency) convey identical and therefore mutually redundant information. J. R. Carson in 1915 was the first to recognize that, under these conditions and assuming adequate knowledge of the carrier, either sideband alone would uniquely define the message. Apart from a scale factor, the spectrum of the upper sideband and lower sideband is the spectrum of the modulating wave displaced, respectively, without and with inversion by an amount equal to the carrier frequency.

For example, suppose the audio-frequency signal is a single-frequency tone, such as 1000 Hz, and the carrier frequency is 1,000,000 Hz; then the lower and upper sidebands will be a pair of single-frequency waves. The lower-sideband frequency will be 999,000 Hz, corresponding to the difference between the carrier and audio-signal frequencies; and the upper-sideband frequency will be 1,001,000 Hz, corresponding to the sum of the carrier and audio-signal frequencies. The amplitude of the signal appears in the amplitude of the sidebands. In practice, the modulating waveform will be more complex. A typical program signal might occupy a frequency band range of perhaps 100 Hz to 5000 Hz.

An important characteristic of AM, as illustrated by **Fig. 1**, is that, apart from a scale factor and constant term, either the upper or lower envelope of the modulated wave is an exact replica of the modulating

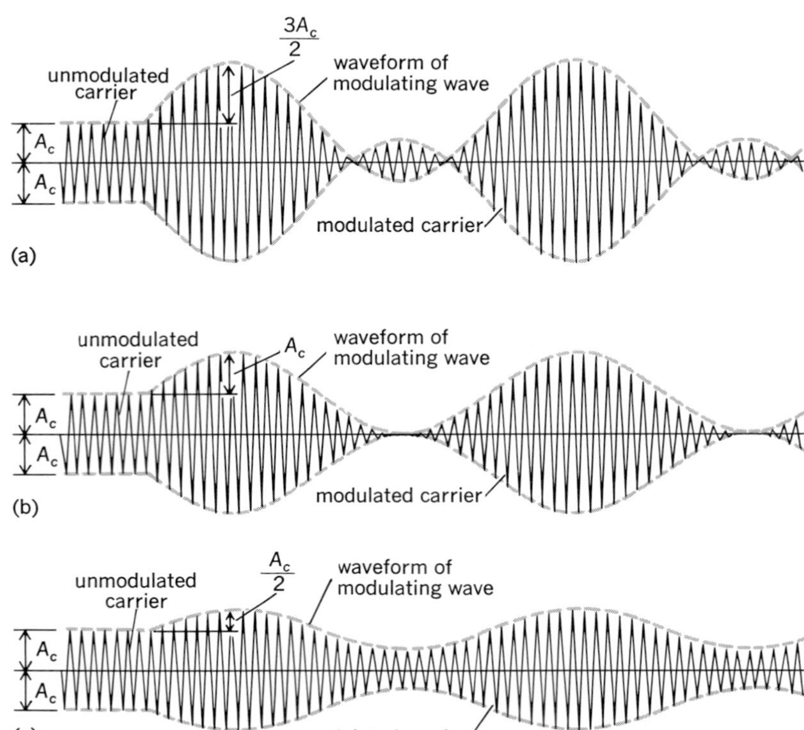


**Fig. 1. Amplitude modulation of a sine-wave carrier by a sine-wave signal, with (*a*) 50% overmodulation, (*b*) 100% modulation, and (c) 50% modulation. (*After H. S. Black, Modulation Theory, Van Nostrand, 1953*)**

wave, provided two conditions are satisfied: first, that the carrier frequency exceeds twice the highest speech frequency to be transmitted; and second, that the carrier is not overmodulated.

*Harold S. Black*

**Single-sideband (SSB) modulation.** This is a form of linear modulation that takes advantage of the fact that in an AM signal the carrier conveys no information and each of the two sidebands (that is, the upper sideband and the lower sideband) contains the same information. Hence it is not necessary to transmit both of them, and it is possible to achieve a 50% savings in bandwidth relative to normal AM or double-sideband (DSB) modulation.

The price for this bandwidth efficiency is increased complexity. The generation of SSB is typically accomplished either by filtering out the unwanted sideband of a DSB signal or by using a phase-shift modulator. This latter system involves use of a Hilbert transformer to shift the phase of the frequency components of the message by $-90°$. Specifically, if the message is denoted by $m(t)$, the transmitted waveform $s(t)$ is given by the equation below, where $\omega_0$ is the

$$s(t) = m(t) \cos \omega_0 t \pm \hat{m}(t) \sin \omega_0 t$$

angular frequency of the carrier and $\hat{m}(t)$ is the Hilbert transform of $m(t)$. If the plus sign is used in the above equation, the lower sideband is retained, whereas if the minus sign is used, the upper sideband is retained.

Either a coherent demodulator or a carrier reinsertion receiver can be used to demodulate an SSB signal. In either case, there are certain limits on phase and frequency errors that can be tolerated. Also of concern in SSB transmission are linearity requirements, since the envelope of an SSB signal can undergo significant variations.

SSB signaling is extensively used in voice transmission. Indeed, for applications such as telephone transmission over satellite links, one of the most common forms of modulation is the use of SSB subcarriers, which in turn frequency-modulate a carrier. The technique works as follows: Each voice message occupies roughly a 3-kHz bandwidth. The various voice messages are SSB-modulated onto individual subcarriers spaced 4 kHz apart. This composite baseband signal then frequency-modulates a carrier which is transmitted over the radio channel.

SSB modulation is also used for voice transmission in radio relay systems and coaxial cable systems. Indeed, this type of transmission has become so well accepted on a worldwide basis that standard frequency allocation plans have been set up by the Consultative Committee in International Telegraphy and Telephony (CCITT).

The choice of whether or not to use SSB depends upon the particular conditions under which the system is operating. SSB requires both less power and less bandwidth than does AM, but requires a more complex transmitter and receiver. Also, SSB systems have been shown to be less sensitive to the effects of selective fading than are both AM and DSB. *See Single sideband.*

*Laurence B. Milstein*

**Vestigial-sideband (VSB) modulation.** This is modulation whereby in effect the modulated wave to be transmitted is composed of one sideband plus a portion of the other adjoining the carrier. The carrier may or may not be transmitted. VSB is like SSB except in a restricted region around the carrier. The overall frequency response to the wanted sideband and to the vestigial sideband is so proportioned by networks that upon demodulation, preferably but not necessarily by a product demodulator, the original modulating wave will be recovered with adequate accuracy.

By thus transmitting a linearly distorted copy of both sidebands in a restricted frequency region above and below the carrier, the original modulating wave can now be permitted to contain significant components at extremely low frequencies, even approaching zero in the limit. By this means, at the cost of a modest increase in bandwidth occupancy, network requirements are greatly simplified. Furthermore, the low-frequency limitation and the inherent delay associated with SSB are avoided.

In standard television broadcasting in the continental United States the carrier is transmitted, envelope detection is used, and the vestigial sideband possesses a bandwidth one-sixth that of a full sideband. *See Television.*

**Uses of AM in multiplexing.** Multiplexing is the process of transmitting a number of independent messages over a common medium simultaneously. To multiplex, it is necessary to modulate. Two or more communicating channels sharing a common propagation path may be multiplexed by arranging them along the frequency scale as in frequency division, by arranging them in time sequence as in time division, or by a process known as phase discrimination, in which there need be no separation of channels in either frequency or time.

***Frequency-division multiplexing.*** When communication channels are multiplexed by frequency division, a different frequency band is allocated to each channel. Single-sideband carrier telephone systems are a good example. At the sending end, the spectrum of each channel input is translated by SSB to a different frequency band. For example, speech signals occupying a band of 300–3300 Hz might be translated to occupy a band range of 12,300–15,300 Hz corresponding to the upper sideband of a sinusoidal carrier, the frequency of which is 12,000 Hz. Another message channel might be transmitted as the upper sideband of a different carrier, the frequency of which might be 16,000 Hz.

At the receiving end, individual channels are separated by electric networks called filters, and each original message is recovered by demodulation. The modulated wave produced by SSB at the sending end becomes the modulating wave applied to the receiving demodulator.

When communication channels are multiplexed by frequency division, all channels may be busy simultaneously and continuously, but each uses only its allocated fraction of the total available frequency range.

***Time-division multiplexing.*** When communication channels are multiplexed by time division, a number of messages is propagated over a common transmitting medium by allocating different time intervals in sequence for the transmission of each message. **Figure 2** depicts a particularly simple example of a two-channel, time-division system. Ordinarily, the number of channels to be multiplexed would be considerably greater. Transmitting and receiving switches must be synchronized; time is of the essence in this system, and the problem is to switch at the right time.

On the theoretical side there is a certain basic, fundamental question which must always be answered about any time-division system. The question is: At what rate must each communication channel be connected to its common transmitting path? Today it is known from the sampling principle that for successful communication each channel must be momentarily connected to the common path at a rate that is in excess of twice the highest message frequency conveyed by that channel. *See* Pulse modulation.

Viewed broadly, amplitude modulation of pulse carriers generates the desired amplitude and phase relationships essential to time-division multiplexing. In addition, whereas each communication channel may use the entire available frequency band for transmitting its message, it may transmit only during its allocated fraction of the total time.

***Phase-discrimination multiplexing.*** This type of multiplexing, like SSB, saves bandwidth, may save signal power, and, like AM and VSB, has the important advantage of freely transmitting extremely low mod-

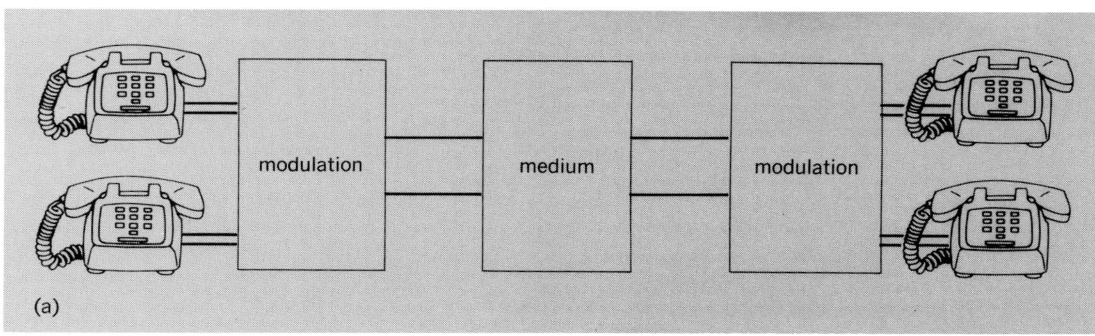


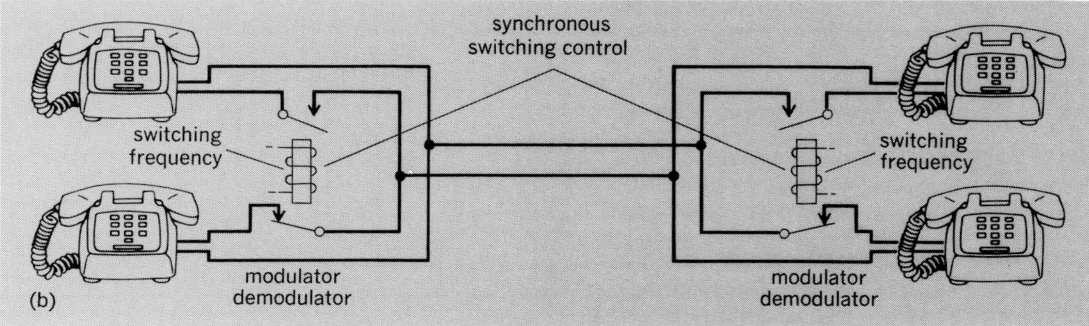


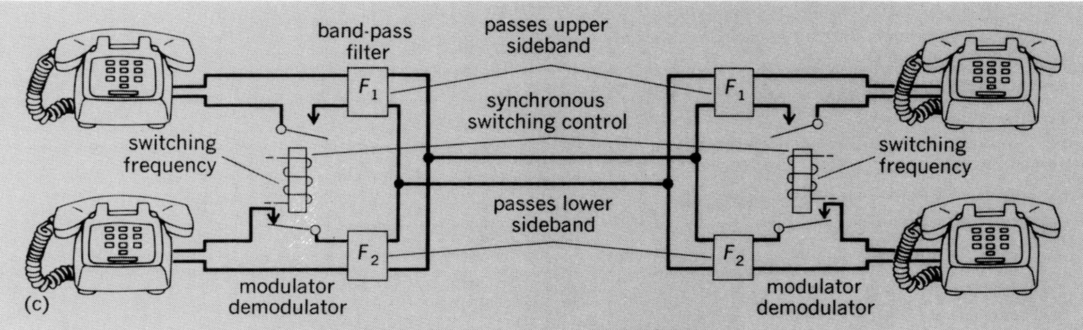


**Fig. 2.** Two-channel, time-division carrier system and two-channel, frequency-division carrier system. (*a*) General diagram of two-channel carrier system. (*b*) Amplitude modulation, time division. (c) Single-sideband modulation, frequency division. (*After H. S. Black, Modulation Theory, Van Nostrand, 1953*)

ulating frequencies. Furthermore, each communication channel may utilize all of the available frequency range all of the time.

When $n$ channels are multiplexed by phase discrimination, the modulating wave associated with each channel simultaneously amplitude-modulates $n/2$ carriers, with a different set of carrier phases provided for each channel. All sidebands are transmitted; $n/2$ carriers may or may not be transmitted. At the receiving end, with the aid of locally supplied carriers and an appropriate demodulation process, the $n$ channels can be separated, assuming distortionless transmission, ideal modulators, and so on. Systems with odd numbers of channels can also be devised. Equality of sidebands and their exact phases account for the suppression of interchannel interference.

***Day's system.*** This is a simple example of phase-discrimination multiplexing. Two sine-wave carriers of the same frequency but differing in phase by 90° are amplitude-modulated, each by a different message wave. The spectrum of each modulated sinusoid occupies the same frequency band. These modulated sinusoids are then added and propagated without distortion to a pair of demodulators. Quadrature carriers of correct frequency and phase are applied locally, one to each demodulator. Theoretically, a faithful copy of each message can be recovered.

Within the continental United States, for purposes of saving bandwidth, Day's system is used for multiplexing the two so-called color components associated with color tv broadcasting.

**Modulator and demodulator.** Many methods of modulating and demodulating are possible, and many kinds of modulators and demodulators are available for each method. *SEE MODULATOR.*

Fundamentally, since the sidebands of an amplitude-modulated sinusoid are generated by a multiplication of wave components which produces frequency components corresponding to the products, it is natural to envisage a product modulator having an output proportional to the product of two inputs: modulating wave and carrier. An ideal product modulator suppresses both modulating wave and carrier, transmitting only upper and lower sidebands. *SEE AMPLITUDE MODULATOR.*

At the receiving end, the original message may be recovered from either sideband or from both sidebands by a repetition of the original modulating process using a product modulator, commonly referred to as a product demodulator, followed by a low-pass filter. Perfect recovery requires a locally applied demodulator carrier of the correct frequency and phase. For example, a reduced carrier system creates its correct demodulator carrier supply by transmitting only enough carrier to control the frequency and phase of a strong, locally generated carrier at the receiver. *SEE AMPLITUDE-MODULATION DETECTOR.*

SSB systems commonly generate their modulator and demodulator carriers locally with independent oscillators. For the high-quality reproduction of music, the permissible frequency difference between modulator and demodulator carriers associated with a particular channel is limited to about 1–2 Hz. For monaural telephony, frequency differences approaching 10 Hz are permissible.

Unbalanced square-law demodulators, rectifier-type demodulators, and envelope detectors are often used to demodulate AM. However, even though overmodulation (Fig. 1) is avoided, significant distortion may be introduced. In general, the amount of distortion introduced in this manner will depend upon the kind of demodulator or detector used, the amount of noise and distorsion introduced prior to reception, and the percentage modulation.

*Harold S. Black*

***Bibliography.*** L. W. Couch, *Digital and Analog Communication Systems,* 1983; M. Schwartz, *Information, Transmission, Modulation and Noise,* 3d ed., 1980; F. G. Stremler, *Introduction to Communication Systems,* 1982; H. Taub and D. L. Schilling, *Principles of Communication Systems,* 1971; R. E. Ziemer and W. H. Tranter, *Principles of Communications,* 1976.

## Amplitude-modulation detector

A device for the recovery of the modulating signal from an amplitude-modulated carrier. A detector, like a modulator, must employ a nonlinear device and therefore usually includes either a diode or a nonlinear amplifier. Detectors are sometimes known as demodulators. Several types of detector circuits are discussed in this article. *SEE MODULATION.*

**Diode detectors.** A simple diode detector circuit (**Fig. 1**) was frequently used as an entire receiver in the early days of radio; it was known as a crystal set. Its radio-frequency (rf) input signal, which was obtained by attaching an antenna and a ground to the input terminals, induced a voltage in a secondary coil $L_2$ by magnetic induction. Capacitor $C_t$ was adjusted to resonate with inductance $L_2$ at the desired input frequency. Because of the high resonant impedance of the tuned circuit, a voltage was induced in a narrow band of frequencies about the resonant frequency to a high enough level for satisfactory operation of the diode. The desired radio station was thus selected. *SEE RADIO.*

Modern diode detectors operate similarly. The average value of the modulated input voltage is zero because the negative half cycles have the same amplitude as the positive half cycles. Only high, or radio, frequencies, consisting of the carrier plus sideband frequencies, are present in this input signal; the original modulating frequency appears as the modulation envelope. The diode or rectifier recovers this envelope by allowing current to flow primarily in only one direction, thereby eliminating either the positive or negative half cycles (**Fig. 2**). Average current through the diode is not zero, but has a component which varies with the amplitude of the input signal and thus contains the original modulating frequencies. Theoretically, nonlinearity produces sum and difference frequencies, as well as harmonics, of the input

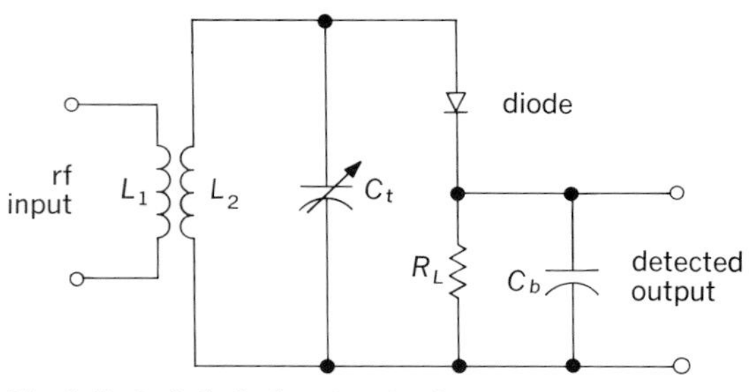


**Fig. 1. Typical diode detector circuit.**

frequencies. The difference between the carrier frequency and a sideband frequency is the modulating frequency that produced the sideband frequency during modulation. Thus amplitude modulation and detection are basically the same process. *See* Rectifier.

The diode current contains the carrier frequency and harmonics as well as the original modulating frequencies and a dc component produced by the rectification.

***Conditions for high efficiency.*** Load resistor $R_L$ is placed in series with the diode to produce an output voltage. Without capacitor $C_b$ the voltage across the load resistor would have the same wave form as the current through the diode. However, capacitor $C_b$ greatly reduces the magnitude of the high-frequency components and increases the desired modulating frequency components if the circuit components have the proper relationships. High-detection efficiency can be obtained if the following conditions are met:

1. Load resistance should be large in comparison with forward resistance of the diode so the peak voltage across the load will be almost equal to the peak voltage applied from the secondary of the coupling coil.
2. Reactance of bypass capacitor $C_b$ should be small compared with the load resistance at the carrier frequency, but large compared with the load resistance at the highest modulating frequency.
3. The diode is fast enough so its charge storage time is short compared with the period of the input carrier frequency.

Under these conditions bypass capacitor $C_b$ will charge quickly through the small forward resistance of the diode, and the capacitor voltage will closely follow the input voltage while the diode is conducting. However, the capacitor cannot discharge through the diode because of its unilateral characteristics and therefore must discharge through the load resistor. Because under the above conditions time constant $R_LC_b$ is long compared with the period of the carrier, the capacitor voltage almost follows the peaks of the input voltage (Fig. 2*b*). In most applications the ratios of carrier frequency to modulator frequency are much higher than that illustrated in Fig. 2. Therefore, the high-frequency sawtoothlike variations in output voltage are much smaller than those shown in Fig. 2*b*.

Typical values of load resistance and bypass capacitance for broadcast-frequency radio receivers are $R_L$ = 2000–10,000 ohms for semiconductor diodes, and 0.1–0.5 megohm for vacuum diodes; $C_b$ = .002–.01 microfarad for semiconductor diodes, and 100–500 picofarads for vacuum diodes.

***Special features.*** A diode detector in a modern radio receiver usually includes additional features and refinements (**Fig. 3**). The tuning capacitor usually appears on the primary side of the coupling coil in transistor-type receivers. The dc component of voltage across diode load resistor $R_d$ is blocked by the ac coupling (or dc blocking) capacitor $C_c$, because this dc component would otherwise upset the dc operating potentials of the amplifier that normally follows the detector. The input resistance of this amplifier is represented by resistor $R_i$. The reactance of coupling capacitor $C_c$ should be small in comparison with $R_i$ at the lowest desired output frequency in order to avoid reduction of the output voltage.

The dc component of voltage across $R_d$ is often used to automatically control the gain of the amplifiers that precede the detector in a radio receiver, thus making the output voltage relatively independent of the strength of the input signal to the receiver. This automatic gain control (AGC) voltage, which is proportional to the carrier voltage into the detector, must have proper polarity to reduce the gain of the controlled amplifiers. Because this polarity can be reversed by reversing the direction of the diode, the proper polarity is easily obtained. The modulating frequencies as well as the carrier frequencies are filtered from the AGC voltage by capacitor $C_A$ and resistor $R_A$ combination. *See* Automatic gain control (AGC).

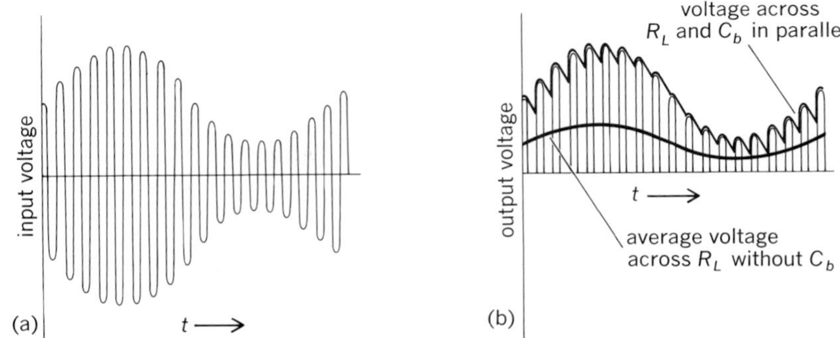

**Fig. 2. Input and output waveforms of a detector. (*a*) Modulated rf input. (*b*) Detected output, with modulation envelope recovered by rectification and filtering.**

***Requirements for linearity.*** The diode detector just described is linear, the output voltage being linearly related to the waveform of the modulation envelope. This linearity is based on the requirement that the load resistance be large in comparison with the average forward resistance of the diode. Another requirement for linearity is that the ac load resistance be almost as large as the dc load resistance. In Fig. 3 the dc load resistance is $R_d$ only if no direct current flows through AGC resistor $R_A$. However, ac or signal currents flow through $R_A$ and $R_i$ as well as $R_d$, so these three resistors in parallel constitute the ac load resistance $R_L$ for the diode. Of course the high-frequency bypass $C_b$ is in parallel with $R_L$ and lowers the ac load impedance $Z_L$ at high modulating frequencies. Therefore, the ac load impedance can be nearly as large as the dc load resistance only if $R_i$ and $R_A$ are both large in comparison with $R_d$, and if the reactance of bypass capacitor $C_b$ is greater than $R_d$ at the highest modulating frequency component of interest.

When the ac load resistance is much lower than the dc load resistance, distortion results (**Fig. 4**). This phenomenon, called negative clipping, is caused by the fact that the diode is kept from conducting for a number of carrier cycles. The load voltage then cannot follow the modulating voltage. Let $I_D$ be the av-

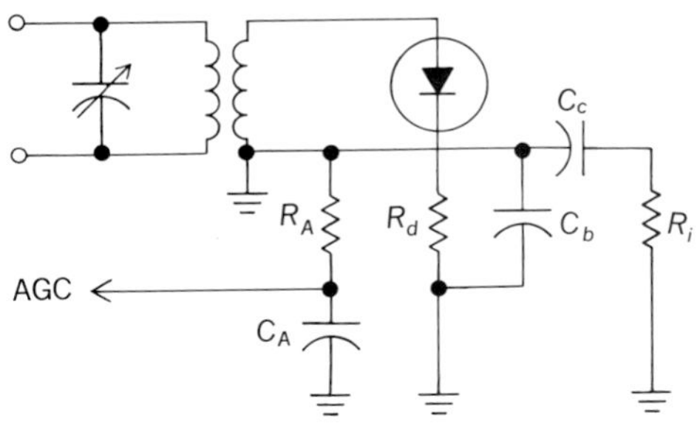

**Fig. 3. Diode detector circuit with features usually found in a radio receiver.**

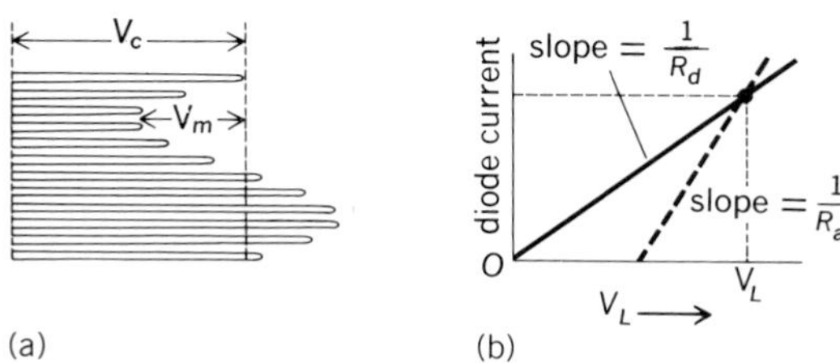


**Fig. 4. Distortion. (*a*) Sinusoidal modulation of the carrier. (*b*) Graphical construction showing that distortion results when ac load resistance is much smaller than dc load resistance.**

erage diode current, which is also the average current through dc load resistance $R_d$. Bypass capacitor $C_b$ (Fig. 3) causes voltage $V_L$ across the load to follow the peaks of the carrier input, neglecting the forward voltage drop across the diode. The average, or dc, voltage $V_L$ across the load is shown in Eq. (1). This

$$V_L = I_D R_L \tag{1}$$

voltage is also equal to peak carrier voltage $V_c$, by using the approximations given above.

Assume that the carrier is sinusoidally modulated with a peak voltage variation $V_m$ (Fig. 4*a*). Then this varying component is coupled through the coupling capacitors and appears across the total ac load resistance $r_{ac}$ to produce a peak current variation as shown in Eq. (2).

$$I_p = V_m / r_{ac} \quad \text{or} \quad V_m = I_p r_{ac} \tag{2}$$

But the largest possible decrease in diode current from the average value is the average current $I_D$. Then the maximum permissible voltage variation is as shown in Eq. (3). If the peak variation given by Eq.

$$V_{m(\max)} = I_D r_{ac} \tag{3}$$

(2) exceeds the value given by Eq. (3), diode current remains zero for part of the modulation cycle, and the voltage across the load cannot follow the modulation voltage.

This is the negative clipping phenomenon, mentioned above. It is shown by Fig. 4*b*, in which average load voltage $V_L$ and average diode current $I_D$ are given by the solid line with slope $1/R_d$, known as the dc load line. Similarly, the relationship between the varying, or modulation, voltage $V_m$ and the change in load current is given by the dashed line, with slope $1/r_{ac}$, known as the ac load line. Clipping begins where the ac load line intersects the $I_D = 0$ axis. SEE CLIPPING CIRCUIT.

A simple relationship exists between the maximum modulation index that will not produce clipping and the ratio of ac load resistance to dc load resistance. Because the modulation index is defined as $M = V_m/V_c$, Eq. (2) can be divided by Eq. (3) to obtain Eq. (4). Thus, if the modulation index is 90%, distortion-

$$M_{(\max)} = \frac{V_{m(\max)}}{V_c} = \frac{I_D r_{ac}}{I_D R_d} = \frac{r_{ac}}{R_d} \tag{4}$$

less detection or demodulation can be obtained only if $r_{ac} \geq 0.9\ R_d$.

**Square-law detectors.** Another important detector is the square-law detector. This device has an output current proportional to the square of the input voltage (**Fig. 5**). Almost all diodes and electronic amplifying devices have this type of characteristic, basically, and linear operation is obtained only by careful selection of the combination of operating point, signal level, driving source resistance, and load resistance. For example, the diode provides linear detection only when the load resistance is large in comparison with the average forward resistance of the diode, as previously mentioned. On the other hand, the diode is a square-law detector if the load resistance is small in comparison with diode resistance. Amplification can be obtained in addition to square-law detection if an amplifying device, such as a transistor or vacuum tube, is used with bias such that the quiescent operating point is near zero current. This condition is obtained with zero bias in an enhancement-mode insulated-gate transistor circuit (Fig. 5).

The square-law detector distorts or changes the waveform of the modulation envelope, as shown in Fig. 5*b*. This distortion is sometimes desirable, as in single-sideband transmission, where one sideband has been eliminated. Single-frequency modulation then produces a nonsinusoidal modulation envelope, but the square-law detector produces a sinusoidal or single-frequency output. In other words, as can be shown mathematically, a square-law detector is necessary for distortionless single-sideband transmission. Square-law detectors are sometimes used for convenience in other applications where preservation of the modulation envelope waveform is not necessary or desirable. SEE DISTORTION (ELECTRONIC CIRCUITS).

**Regenerative detectors.** A high-gain narrow-band radio receiver can be achieved with a single amplifying detector by providing positive or regenerative feedback from the output to the input (**Fig. 6**). This arrangement is known as a regenerative detector. The feedback adjustment is critical and distortion is high because the feedback must maintain operation on the verge of oscillation.

The feedback adjustment can be made less critical and the gain increased if a signal from an oscillator is injected into the detector to periodically squelch its oscillations, which tend to build up slowly. This type of detector is known as a super regenerative detector.

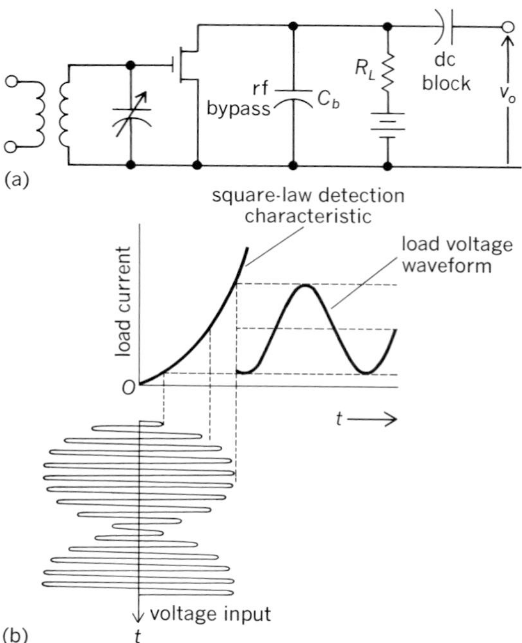


**Fig. 5. Square-law detector and its operation. (*a*) Typical circuit. (*b*) Characteristics and operation.**

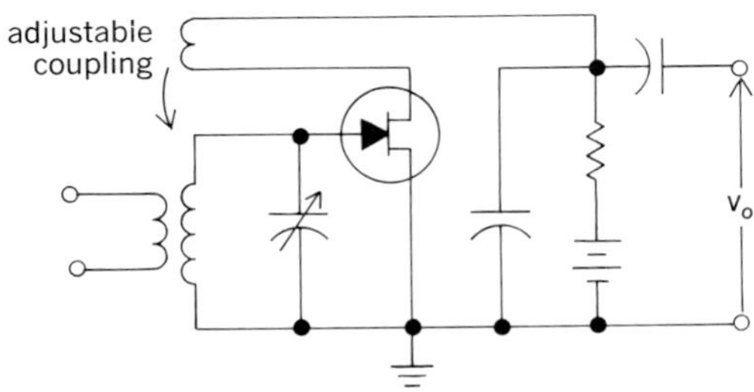


**Fig. 6. Elementary regenerative detector.**

The oscillator frequently must be above the audible range, but much lower than the carrier frequency. *SEE DETECTOR; OSCILLATOR.*

**Synchronous detectors.** A four-quadrant multiplier, available as an integrated circuit, may be used as a demodulator or detector, as shown by the trigonometric identity in Eq. (5), where $\omega_c$ is the angular

$$A \cos \omega_c t[\cos (\omega_c + \omega_m)t + \cos (\omega_c - \omega_m)t] = A[\cos \omega_m t + {}^1/_2 \cos (2\omega_c + \omega_m)t + {}^1/_2 \cos (2\omega_c - \omega_m)t] \quad (5)$$

carrier frequency and $\omega_m$ is the angular modulating frequency. A filter in the output of the multiplier will eliminate the high-frequency terms on the right-hand side of the equation and leave only the modulating-frequency term $\cos \omega_m t$. This type of detector is known as a synchronous detector because the original carrier, without modulation, must be reinserted into the detector. In the multiplication above, the carrier multiplied only the upper and lower sidebands with no carrier, so suppressed carrier transmission was assumed. The multiplier performs equally well when the carrier is not suppressed. Then there is a carrier frequency term at each of the multiplier input terminals, but their product is a double carrier frequency term $2\omega_c$ and a dc, or constant, term, both of which are removed by the output filter. The unmodulated carrier frequency $\omega_c$ is usually generated in the receiver by either a local oscillator or a phase-locked loop. When double sideband transmission is used, these devices must be synchronized with the original carrier. *SEE AMPLITUDE MODULATION; AMPLITUDE MODULATOR; PHASE-LOCKED LOOPS.*

*Charles L. Alley*

***Bibliography.*** C. Alley and K. Atwood, *Electronic Engineering,* 3d ed., 1973; D. J. Comer, *Modern Electronic Circuit Design,* 1976; J. Millman, *Microelectronics,* 1979; D. Schilling and C. Belove, *Electronic Circuits: Discrete and Integrated,* 1979.

## Amplitude-modulation radio

Radio communication employing amplitude modulation of a radio-frequency carrier wave as the means of conveying the desired intelligence. In amplitude modulation the amplitude of the carrier wave is made to vary corresponding to the fluctuations of a sound wave, television image, or other information to be conveyed. *SEE AMPLITUDE MODULATION; RADIO.*

Amplitude modulation (AM), the oldest and simplest form of modulation, is widely used for radio services. The most familiar of these is broadcasting; others include radiotelephony and radiotelegraphy, television picture transmission, and navigational aids. The essentials of these radio systems are discussed in this article.

**Low frequency (long wave).** European and Asian countries use frequencies in the range 150–255 kHz for some broadcast services. An advantage of these frequencies is stable and relatively low-attenuation wave propagation. When not limited by atmospheric noise, large areas may be served by one station. In the United States these frequencies are reserved for navigational systems and so are not available for broadcasting.

Low-frequency (lf) broadcast antennas are omnidirective and radiate vertically polarized waves. Unless special means are used to reduce antenna selectivity, the highest program frequencies transmitted are substantially below 10,000 Hz.

**Medium frequency.** The frequencies in the range from 535 to 1605 kHz are reserved all over the world for AM (standard) broadcasting. In the Western Hemisphere this band is divided into channels at 10-kHz intervals, certain channels being designated as clear, regional, and local, according to the licensed coverage and class of service. The local channels are occupied by stations, usually of 250-W output, servicing smaller localities. Many stations occupy a channel, but they are separated far enough to permit interference-free coverage in the local area. Fewer stations of higher power, but with greater distances between them, share the regional channels. A few clear channels are occupied by high-power stations (50,000-W maximum output in the United States). These stations may have exclusive use of a channel, or may share it with another distant station.

Interference between co-channel regional stations and clear-channel stations is minimized by use of directive antennas, which suppress radiation toward other stations and direct it to main populated areas from a properly located station.

European medium-frequency (mf) broadcasting channels are assigned at 9-kHz intervals rather than the 10-kHz intervals used in the Western Hemisphere. This reduced spacing provides more channels within the mf band. The technique of directive antennas, which also provides more channels within a band by minimizing interference between stations, has not been used extensively in Europe.

Vertically polarized radiation is used at medium and low frequencies propagated over the Earth's surface. There is also propagation of high-angle radiation via reflection from the ionosphere, a phenomenon that predominates at night but is relatively absent during daylight. This sky-wave propagation accounts for the familiar long-distance reception at night. At distances where the downcoming sky waves overlap the ground wave, fading and distortion of the signal occurs. Receivers in the ground-wave zone get stable signals day and night. In the overlap zone, daylight reception may be stable but night reception disturbed by fading. In the sky-wave zone at night, assuming no interference from other stations, satisfactory service may be received over long distances. Reception in this zone depends on atmospheric noise, which varies seasonally, and the state of the ionosphere, which varies greatly from night to night depending upon astronomical conditions that affect the upper atmosphere.

Individual AM broadcast stations transmit program frequencies ranging from 30 to 10,000 Hz with excellent fidelity. To obtain suitable tuning selectivity between channels, AM broadcast receivers may reproduce program frequencies only up to 4000 Hz, or even less, according to make, cost, and condition of the receiver.

**High frequency (shortwave).** Small bands of frequencies between 3000 and 5000 kHz are used in tropical areas of high atmospheric noise for regional broadcasting. This takes advantage of the lower atmospheric noise at these frequencies and permits service under conditions where medium frequencies have only severely limited coverage. Wave propagation day and night is by sky wave. Ground-wave coverage from such stations is usually negligible, since high-angle horizontally polarized radiation is used. Short-distance coverage by this mode is by ionospheric reflection of waves radiated almost vertically.

Long-distance international broadcasting uses high-power transmitters and directive (beam) antennas operating in the bands 5950–6200 kHz, 9500–9775 kHz, 11,700–11,975 kHz, 15,100–15,450 kHz, 17,700–17,900 kHz, 21,450–21,750 kHz, and 25,600–26,100 kHz. These bands are allocated throughout the world for this purpose, and the band used for any path depends upon ionospheric conditions which vary with direction, distance, hour, season, and the phase of the 11-year sunspot cycle. Typically, waves are propagated in low-angle beams by multiple reflections between ionosphere and Earth to cover transoceanic distances, and signals are often distorted during transmission. These bands are so crowded that a signal is seldom received without interference for any prolonged period. Reception from particular stations can be improved by the use of special directive receiving antennas.

The technical performance of high-frequency (hf) broadcast transmission systems is usually to the same standards employed for mf broadcasting, although propagation and interference conditions seldom make this evident to a listener.

**AM telephony and telegraphy.** The first radiotelephony was by means of amplitude modulation, and its use has continued with increasing importance. Radiotelephony refers to two-way voice communication. Amplitude modulation and a modified form called single-sideband are used almost exclusively for radiotelephony on frequencies below 30 MHz. Above 30 MHz, frequency or phase modulation is used almost exclusively, a notable exception being 118–132 MHz, where amplitude modulation is used for all two-way vhf radiotelephony in aviation operations.

The least expensive method known for communicating by telephony over distances longer than a few tens of miles is by using the high frequencies of 3–30 MHz. Furthermore, since radio is the only way to communicate with ships and aircraft, hf AM radiotelephony has remained essential to these operations, except for short distances that can be covered from land stations using the very high frequencies. Therefore, hf radiotelephony has become established for a great variety of pioneering and exploration enterprises and private, public, and government services needing telephone communication, fixed or mobile, over substantial distances where there are no other ways to telephone. Because AM techniques are simple and inexpensive, this form of modulation has predominated. The economic development of distant hinterland areas depends greatly on hf AM radio telephony to the outside world.

Widespread use has led to serious crowding of the hf band. All governments are suspending the use of the hf band wherever it is technically and economically feasible to employ frequencies above 30 MHz using either direct transmission or radio repeater stations. The trend to single-sideband modulation also alleviates the pressure of congestion in the hf band.

Many of the radiotelephone systems in use operate two ways on one frequency in simplex fashion, that is, all stations on the frequency are normally in a receiving status. Transmission, by press-to-talk (manual) or voice-operated carrier (automatic) switching from reception to transmission, occurs only while the sender is talking. Many stations can thus occupy one frequency provided the volume of traffic by each of the stations is small. Two-way telephony must be strictly sequential. This system is not adapted for connection to a normal two-wire telephone.

Full duplex radiotelephony, for interconnection with wire telephone systems, is essential for most public correspondence. This requires two frequencies, each available full time in one direction. Even so, typical fading of signals during propagation requires that voice-operated antiregeneration devices be used to maintain circuit stability. Talking must be sequential between speakers as there can be no interrupting, but the system will interconnect with conventional business or home telephones.

Amplitude-modulated telegraphy consists of interrupting a carrier wave in accordance with the Morse dot-dash code or codes used for the printing telegraph. Much of the radiotelegraphic traffic of the world uses AM telegraphy, although there has been extensive conversion to frequency-shift (frequency-modulation) telegraphy since 1944, the latter being better adapted to automatic teleprinting operations. Radiotelegraph operations have been refined, speeded, and mechanized, but, under adverse noise and fading conditions, AM manual telegraphy between experienced operators is still more reliable. Most aviation and marine radiotelegraphy uses AM manual methods.

**Single-sideband (SSB) hf telephony.** This is a modified form of amplitude modulation in which only one of the modulation sidebands is transmitted. In some systems the carrier is transmitted at a low level to act as a pilot frequency for the regeneration of a replacement carrier at the receiver. Where other means are available for this purpose, the carrier may be completely suppressed. Where intercommunication between AM and SSB systems is desired, the full carrier may be transmitted with one sideband.

Since 1933 most transoceanic and intercontinental telephony has been by single-sideband reduced-carrier radio transmission on frequencies between 4000 and 27,000 kHz. Since 1954 the use of SSB has expanded rapidly in replacing common AM telephony for military and many nonpublic radio services. In time, SSB will gradually displace AM radiotelephony to reduce serious interference due to overcrowding of the radio spectrum. SSB transmission also is less affected by selective fading in propagation.

Multiplexing, both multiple-voice channels or teleprinter channels included with voice, is applied to SSB transmission. Teleprinting and data transmission by frequency multiplex using SSB radiotelephone equipment is increasing and displacing older methods of radiotelegraphy for fixed point-to-point government and common-carrier services. *See Single sideband.*

**Aviation and marine navigation aids.** Amplitude-modulated radio has a dominant role in guidance and position location, especially in aviation, which is almost wholly under radio guidance. Radio is used in traffic control from point to point, in holding a position in a traffic pattern, and in approach and landing at airports. Distance measuring from a known point, radio position markers, runway localizers, and glide-path directors all use AM in some form, if only for coded identification of a facility.

Marine operations are not so dependent on radio facilities as are those of aviation, but almost every oceangoing ship makes use of direction finding, at least to determine its bearing from a radio station of known location. Special marine coastal beacon stations emit identified signals solely for direction-finding purposes. Certain navigational systems (Decca, loran) for aviation are also used by ships for continuous position indication and guidance.

**Television broadcasting.** Amplitude modulation is used everywhere for the broadcasting of the picture (video) portion of television. In England, France, and a few other places amplitude modulation is also used for the sound channel associated with the television picture, but frequency modulation is more commonly used for sound.

Countries of the Western Hemisphere, Japan, Philippines, Thailand, and Iran broadcast television video in an emission band of 4.25 MHz; the English video bandwidth is 3 MHz; the French system, 10 MHz. The rest of continental Europe (except the Soviet Union) use a bandwidth of 5.25 MHz. The carrier frequencies employed are between 40 and 216 MHz, and 470 to 890 MHz. A channel allocation includes the spectrum needed for both sound and picture. Japan and Australia also use 88–108 MHz for television broadcasting.

The English and French systems employ positive video modulation, in which white corresponds to higher amplitudes of the modulation envelope and black corresponds to lower amplitudes. All other established video broadcasting uses negative modulation, working in the opposite sense. Synchronizing pulses in the negative system are at maximum carrier amplitude. The dynamic range from black to white in the picture varies from 75 to 25% of maximum amplitude.

The upper-frequency portion of one video sideband is suppressed by filters so that its remaining vestige, together with the other complete sideband, is transmitted. This is called vestigial sideband transmission and avoids unnecessary spectrum usage. SEE TELEVISION TRANSMITTER.

*Edmund A. Laport*

## Amplitude modulator

A device for amplitude-modulating a carrier signal. The carrier is usually the radio frequency (rf) in a communications system, but it may also be a carrier signal in a multichannel cable communication system, a telemetering system, a control system, or a data-collecting system. The modulator is usually a vacuum tube or semiconductor amplifier, the output power of which controls the output level of another amplifier which modulates the carrier. SEE AMPLITUDE MODULATION; MODULATION.

**Basic requirements.** The goal of a modulator is to vary the amplitude of a carrier in proportion to the modulating voltage. Departure from this linear relation results in modulation distortion. If the carrier being modulated is at a high power level, such as the rf in the final stage of a radio transmitter, the power output capability and efficiency of the modulator and the efficiency of the carrier amplifier become important.

The process of amplitude modulation produces new frequencies known as side frequencies or sidebands; they are the sum and difference of the carrier and modulating frequencies. Because new frequencies are produced only in nonlinear devices, the carrier amplifier in which modulation is to take place must be nonlinear, insofar as the carrier signal is concerned, and must therefore be either a class B or class C amplifier. This requirement will be discussed further when different types of modulators are considered.

The carrier frequency must not be changed by the modulating voltage. This type of change is known as frequency modulation (FM) and occurs when the modulating voltage is coupled into the oscillator that generates the carrier frequency. Frequency modulation is avoided in high-quality transmitters by including an amplifier known as a buffer between the oscillator and the amplifier being modulated. However, in some transmitters, such as very high-frequency transmitters where amplification is difficult, the oscillator is actually modulated.

**High-level modulation.** The most frequently used method of amplitude modulation employed in radio communications is known as plate or collector modulation. As this name implies, the modulator varies the plate or collector voltage in order to accomplish the modulation (**Fig. 1**).

The vacuum-tube circuit in Fig. 1 will be used to illustrate the operating principles of the modulator and the modulated amplifier. The carrier signal is a medium-level signal obtained from an oscillator, usually through a buffer amplifier. The tuned input coupling coil eliminates dc and undesired harmonics from the carrier and also provides impedance transformation from the previous stage.

Capacitor $C_1$ and resistor $R$ provide self-bias, usually class C, for the grid. This bias is obtained because the input signal drives the grid positive with respect to the cathode on positive peaks of the carrier. During these peaks the resulting grid current charges the grid side of $C_1$ negatively. During the remainder of the input cycle the grid is negative with respect to the cathode, and so the charge on $C_1$ can only leak off through $R$. But resistance $R$ is so large that time constant $RC_1$ is long in comparison with the period of the input cycle, so that the charge on $C_1$ remains substantially constant. Also, the resistance $R$ is large in comparison with the resistance between grid and cathode while the grid is forward-biased. The magnitude of bias voltage $I_gR$, where $I_g$ is the average value of grid current, can be controlled by the choice of $R$. The rf choke $L$ has high reactance at the carrier frequency and therefore reduces the signal currents through $R$ and consequently reduces signal power loss.

The plate current flows only during about one-third of the carrier input cycle because of the high class C bias. The peak amplitude of each partial cycle of plate current depends on the instantaneous applied plate voltage. As shown by the schematic (Fig. 1*a*), the voltage is the sum of the plate supply voltage $+V_{pp}$ and the voltage developed by the modulator across the secondary of its output transformer. If the modulation

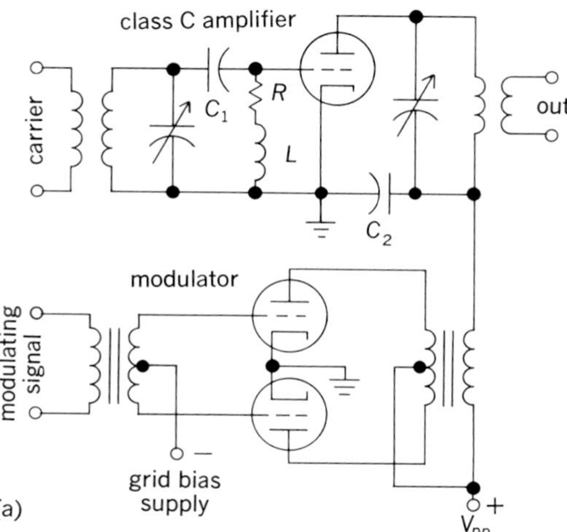


Fig. 1. Schematics of basic high-level modulators. (a) Plate-modulated vacuum-tube amplifier with a vacuum-tube modulator. (b) Collector-modulated transistor amplifier with a solid-state modulator.

signal is sinusoidal, the resulting plate current $i_p$ is as shown in **Fig. 2**. Plate voltage $v_p$ varies in a continuous and nearly sinusoidal manner, because the parallel tuned plate circuit filters out harmonics in the nonsinusoidal plate-current pulses. Also, the plate current flows only during the part of the cycle when plate voltage is low. Because plate dissipation, or power lost at the plate, equals the product of plate current and plate voltage at any instant, plate dissipation is low compared with power output; therefore, plate circuit efficiency is usually about 85%. Plate voltage $v_p$ varies almost sinusoidally about modulated plate supply voltage $v_{pp}$, as shown.

The tuned coupling circuit transfers the modulated rf which consists of the carrier and the side frequencies into the output, but eliminates the dc and the modulating frequencies. Therefore the output voltage $v_o$ varies almost sinusoidally about the zero axis. The rf cycles are not quite sinusoidal because of the amplitude modulation, all harmonics of the carrier frequency are eliminated, but the carrier and the first-order sideband frequencies remain. SEE RADIO.

Carrier harmonics are most effectively removed by a high $Q$ coupling circuit. However the coupling efficiency, which is the ratio of power output to plate circuit power, is high only when the coil $Q$ is high compared with the circuit $Q$. Therefore typical coupling circuits are designed to have values of circuit $Q$ around 12 to 15, whereas the coil $Q$ may be in the order of 100 to 200. Then high efficiency is attained and the harmonics are not excessive.

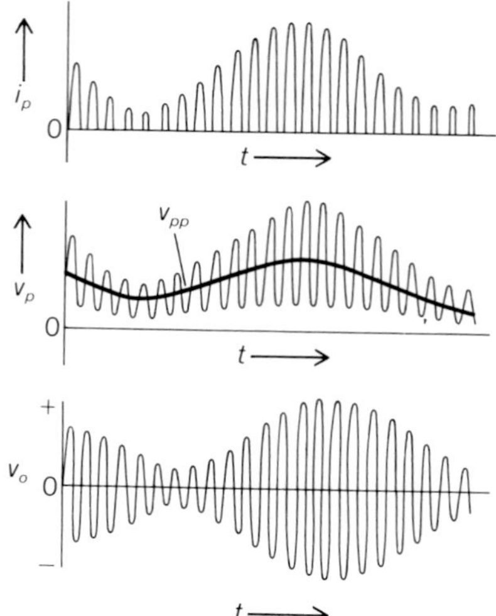


Fig. 2. Current and voltage waveforms in plate circuit of a plate-modulated amplifier.

Low-distortion modulation is easily attained by plate modulation, and high efficiency is attained in the modulated amplifier. However, the power output required from the modulator is high, being for 100% sinusoidal modulation one-half the power provided by the power supply to the rf or carrier power amplifier. This power relationship arises because the voltage induced into the secondary of the modulation transformer alternately adds to and subtracts from power supply voltage $V_{pp}$; therefore the peak modulating voltage must equal power supply voltage $V_{pp}$ in order to cancel this voltage and provide 100% modulation. Also, current $I_p$, which flows from the power supply through the modulation transformer secondary to the rf amplifier, must vary between zero and twice the average value for 100% modulation. Therefore the ac modulator power in the secondary of the modulation transformer is $P = V_{pp}I_p/2$, where the factor 2 is required to reduce peak values to root-mean-square (rms) values. Product $V_{pp}I_p$ is the power delivered by the power supply to the rf (or carrier) power amplifier.

The value of load resistance $R_L$ which the rf amplifier presents to the secondary of the modulation transformer is calculated from the ratio of the peak voltage to peak current; it is $R_L = V_{pp}/I_p$.

As an example of plate modulation, consider a transmitter capable of radiating 1000 W of carrier power. If the rf amplifier and coupling circuit combined are 80% efficient, the rf plate power input is 1250 W, and the power output from the modulator must be 625 W for 100% modulation. This additional power goes into the sidebands and increases the radiated power. If $V_{pp} = 1250$ V and $I_p = 1.0$ A, the load resistance presented to the modulator is 1250 ohms. High-power modulators are usually push-pull class B.

Collector modulation for a transistor amplifier is almost identical to plate modulation. The principal difference is in the comparatively low impedances of the transistor circuit resulting from the low voltages and high currents. Also class B and class C biases are more easily obtained because a transistor is biased beyond cutoff at zero bias; therefore, little or no additional bias is needed for class C operation. A few tenths of a volt forward bias is required for class B

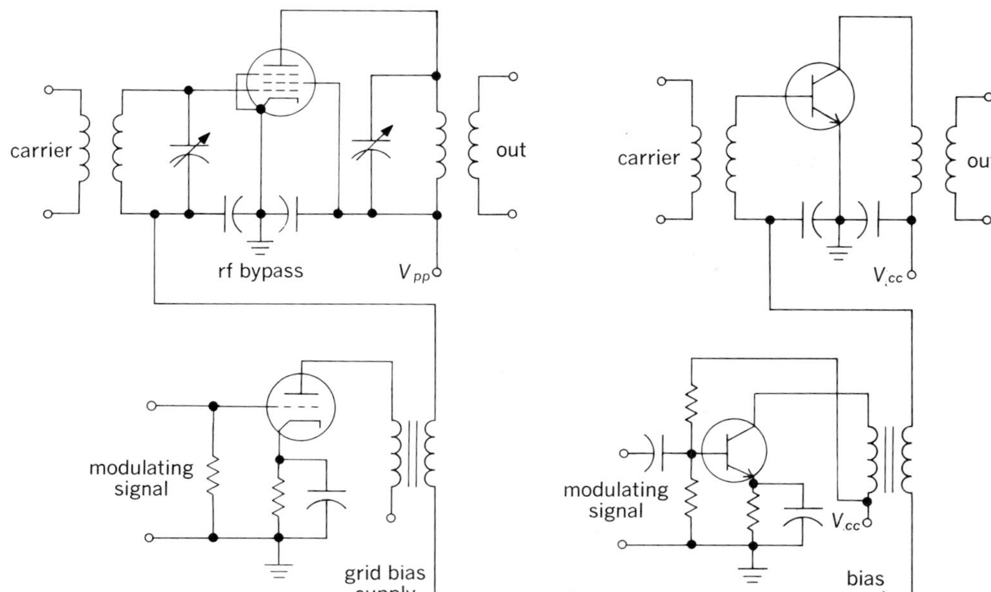


**Fig. 3.** Schematics of basic low-level modulators. (*a*) Grid-modulated vacuum-tube amplifier with a vacuum-tube modulator. (*b*) Base-modulated transistor amplifier with a solid-state modulator.

operation; diode $D$ in Fig. 1 provides this bias in the modulator; without this bias crossover distortion occurs.

**Low-level modulation.** Amplitude modulation can be produced by applying the modulating voltage to one of the grids of a vacuum tube or to the base of a transistor rf or carrier amplifier (**Fig. 3**). Modulation is accomplished by varying the bias of the grid or base (**Fig. 4**). The tube or transistor must be operated class B or class C, as in the plate-modulated amplifier. For the tube amplifier, grid bias, without modulation, is usually class C, or about twice cutoff. The rf or carrier signal amplitude is adjusted until signal peaks are half way between the maximum normally used for class C operation and cutoff. These points are shown as $B$, $A$, and $C$, respectively, in Fig. 4. The modulating voltage in the secondary of the modulation transformer alternately adds to and subtracts from the bias supply voltage, causing the carrier signal peaks to vary between the maximum permissible value $V_A$ and cutoff $V_C$. The peak modulating voltage must therefore be $(V_A - V_C)/2$.

Power required for grid modulation is small compared with that required for plate modulation. However, the power output of the grid-modulated amplifier is only about one-fourth as great as that of a plate-modulated amplifier of the same type, because the amplifier only reaches its full power potential at the peaks of the modulation cycle; average power output is only one-fourth this value. Also, linear modulation is not easily achieved because the grid circuit appears as a high impedance to the modulator over that portion of the modulation cycle during which no grid current flows, but the impedance drops markedly at the positive peaks of the modulation cycle when grid current flows. Distortion can be made small by employing a modulator with a low output impedance compared with the minimum impedance presented by the modulated amplifier. The grid-modulated amplifier also has a much lower efficiency than the plate-modulated amplifier.

The base-modulated transistor amplifier (Fig. 3*b*) operates much like the grid-modulated vacuum-tube amplifier. Power output at the peak of the modulation cycle may be limited by either the peak signal or the average power dissipation capabilities of the transistor, depending upon (1) the transistor used, (2) the potentials applied, and (3) the effectiveness of the heat sink. Linearity of the modulation can be controlled to a large extent by the source impedance of the driver and the modulator.

A transformer is not required to couple the modulator to the modulated amplifier. Resistance coupling can be used (**Fig. 5**). Other coupling systems can also be devised.

The screen grid, suppressor grid, or cathode of a vacuum tube can also be modulated, as can the emitter of a transistor, but the power required from the modulator is somewhat higher than for grid or base modulation. Many different circuits can be devised to modulate these elements. Field-effect transistors can also be modulated in a manner very similar to a triode tube.

**Figure 6** shows that a linear class A amplifier cannot be modulated. In such an amplifier the plate or collector current must flow at all times. Therefore the amplitude of the carrier does not change. The signal intended to modulate is only mixed with the carrier signal, and a tuned output circuit will pass only an unmodulated carrier. Thus cross modulation and other

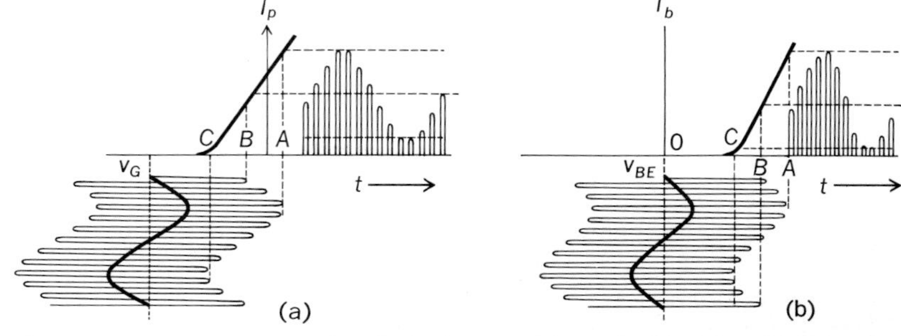


**Fig. 4.** Voltage-current relationships in low-level modulators for (*a*) grid-modulated and (*b*) base-modulated amplifiers.

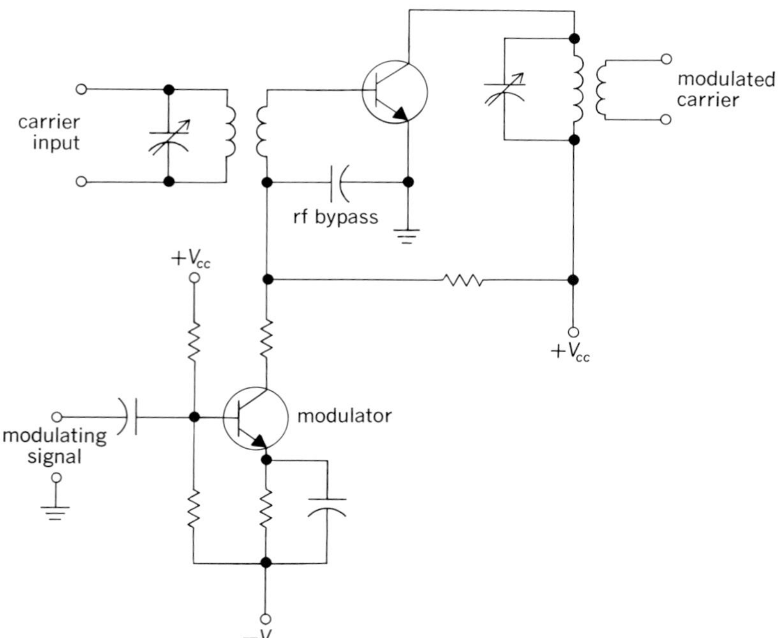


Fig. 5. Schematic of a typical resistance-coupled base modulator.

undesirable modulation effects can be avoided in a radio receiver by the use of linear or low-distortion amplifiers in stages where modulation or detection is not wanted.

**Multiplier modulators.** Low-level modulation can be accomplished by a four-quadrant multiplier, as shown by the trigonometric identity in Eq. (1), where

$$(A_m \cos \omega_m t)\,(A_c \cos \omega_c t) = \frac{A_m A_c}{2}\left[\cos(\omega_c + \omega_m)t + \cos(\omega_c - \omega_m)t\right] \quad (1)$$

$A_m$ is the peak amplitude and $\omega_m$ is the radian frequency of a sinusoidal modulating signal, and $A_c$ is the peak amplitude and $\omega_c$ the radian frequency of a sinusoidal carrier. Observe that the multiplication of these two signals produces the two sidebands having frequencies $\omega_c + \omega_m$ and $\omega_c - \omega_m$. The output of the multiplier modulator contains neither the modulating frequency nor the carrier frequency but only the sidebands. This type of modulator is known as a suppressed carrier or balanced modulator. A four-quadrant multiplier which will handle either positive or negative voltages on both inputs is available as an inexpensive integrated circuit. The linearity of the modulator depends only on the accuracy of the multiplier. Distortion of 1% or less is typical. *See Integrated circuits.*

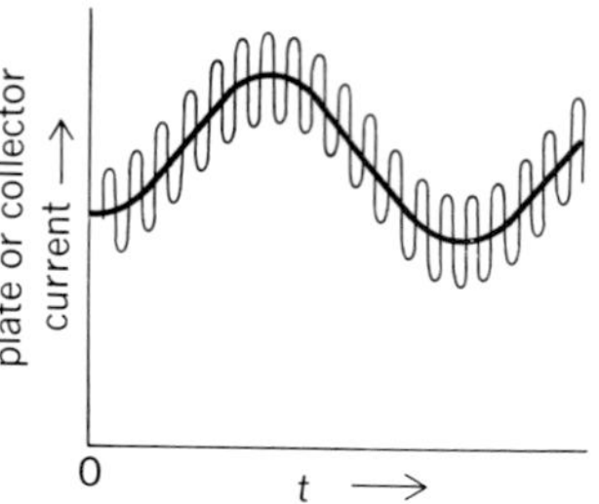


Fig. 6. Current in a linear class A amplifier, showing the absence of modulation.

Regular amplitude modulation, without carrier suppression, may be produced by adding an offset bias voltage to the modulating input of the four-quadrant multiplier, as shown by Eq. (2). This bias offset

$$(1 + A_m \cos \omega_m t)\,(A_c \cos \omega_c t) = A_c \cos \omega_c t + \frac{A_c A_m}{2}\left[\cos(\omega_c + \omega_m)t + \cos(\omega_c - \omega_m)t\right] \quad (2)$$

voltage may be obtained by merely adjusting the input offset adjustment, which is normally included in the multiplier, until the carrier voltage output without modulation is one-half of the peak value obtained when the maximum modulating voltage is applied. The maximum modulation is then 100%. On the other hand, the multiplier acts as a balanced modulator when the input offset adjustment is such that no carrier signal appears in the output when the modulating input voltage is zero.

*Charles L. Alley*

**Bibliography.** C. Alley and K. Atwood, *Electronic Engineering,* 3d ed., 1973; D. J. Comer, *Modern Electronic Circuit Design,* 1976; J. Millman, *Microelectronics,* 1979; D. Schilling and C. Belove, *Electronic Circuits: Discrete and Integrated,* 1979.

## Analog computer

A computer or computational device in which the problem variables are represented as continuous, varying physical quantities. An analog computer implements a model of the system being studied. The physical form of the analog may be functionally similar to that of the system, but more often the analogy is based solely upon the mathematical equivalence of the interdependence of the computer variables and the variables in the physical system. *See Simulation.*

### Computer Types

Analog computers can be classified in two ways: in accordance with their use, and in accordance with the type of components used to assemble them. In terms of use, there are general-purpose and special-purpose analog computers. The general-purpose computer is designed so that it can be programmed to solve many kinds of problems or permit the development of different simulated models as needed (**Fig. 1**). The special-purpose computer has a fixed program with a few or no permitted adjustments; it is generally built into or appended to the physical system it serves (**Fig. 2**).

In terms of the components with which computers are made, there are mechanical, hydraulic, pneumatic, optical, electrical, and electronic analog computers serving in various applications. Because of its ease of programming, flexibility of operation, and repeatable results, the general-purpose electronic analog computer has come into wide use. Therefore this article deals specifically with features and applications of electronic analog computers. The flexibility of the electronic analog computer has allowed it to be augmented with interface channels to the electronic digital computer, so that during the 1960s a third type of general computer, the hybrid computer, came into being. The characteristics of this computer are also described in this article.

**Digital equivalents.** Because of the practical difficulties of scaling, interconnecting, and operating an electronic analog computer, the equivalent of its powerful problem-solving capability has been sought and realized in other forms. Many digital computer programs have been developed which essentially duplicate the functions of analog computers via digital algorithms. Such programs as CSMP, DARE, SIMSCRIPT, CSSL, or CPSS are available for almost all widely used digital computers; these programs approximate the parallel, continuous-time operation of the electronic analog computer by stepwise-incrementing a solution "time" and repeatedly solving the programmed dynamic equations. Digital equivalents to the electronic analog computer are free from scaling requirements and are convenient to run; on the other hand, no interaction within the dynamic response is possible, the solution speed is slower by a factor of a hundred times or more, and little or no online model building and exploring is possible.

**Digital multiprocessor analog system.** Another type of analog computer is the digital multiprocessor analog system (**Fig. 3**), in which the relatively slow speeds of sequential digital increment calculations have been radically boosted through parallel processing. In this type of analog computer it is possible to retain the programming convenience and data storage of the digital computer while approximating the speed, interaction potential, and parallel computations of the traditional electronic analogs.

The digital multiprocessor analog computer typically utilizes several specially designed high-speed processors for the numerical integration functions, the data (or variable) memory distributions, the arithmetic functions, and the decision (logic and control) functions. All variables remain as fixed or floating-point digital data, accessible at all times for computational and operational needs.

The digital multiprocessor analog computer achieves an overall problem-solving efficiency comparable to the very best continuous electronic analog computers, at a substantially lower price. An example of such a computer, the model AD10 (Fig. 3*a*), can solve large, complex, and multivariate problems at very high speeds and with the advantages of all-digital hardware. Its computation system (Fig. 3*b*) is based on five parallel processors working in a special computer architecture designed for high-speed operation. The various elements are interconnected by means of a data bus (MULTIBUS). A highly interleaved data memory of up to $10^6$ words serves the data and program storage functions. The five processors working in parallel are: the control processor (COP), which controls all operations; the arithmetic processor (ARP), which runs the numerical calculations; the decision processor (DEP), which executes the logic parts of the program; the memory address processor (MAP), which makes sure that all data are fetched and stored efficiently; and the numerical integration processor (NIP), which carries out the integration functions that are crucially important in an analog computer.

### History

The slide rule, which originated in the 17th century, represents the first analog computing aid to become a common engineering tool. In it a mechanical position represents the problem variable, and the computations take the form of adding or subtracting linear positional displacements. *See Slide rule.*

Beginning approximately in 1825, several mechanical integrating devices were developed for measuring the area under a curve, and in 1876 William Thomson (later Lord Kelvin) presented a complete description of a process for solving a general ordinary differential equation by analog means. In 1881 the integraph was introduced by C. V. Boys and Abdank-Abakanowicz for drawing the integral curve of a given curve. The mechanical analog computer was greatly improved during World War I; in the succeeding years it was applied primarily to naval gunfire systems.

**Fig. 1. General-purpose electronic analog computer, model EA1-2000. (*Electronic Associates, Inc.*)**

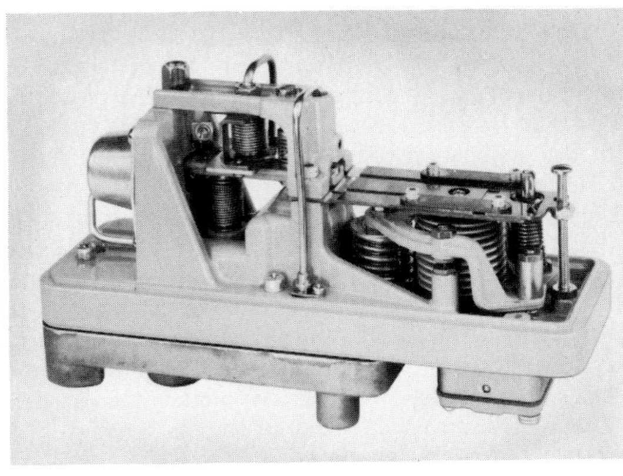

**Fig. 2. Special-purpose pneumatic analog computer, model Foxboro 556. (*Foxboro Co.*)**

(a)

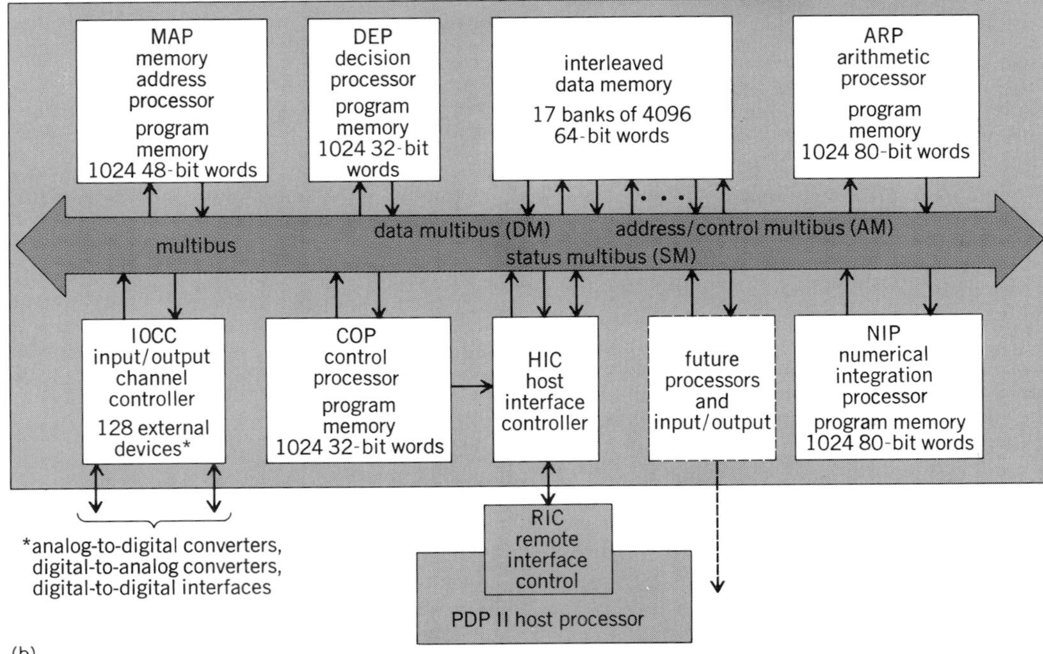


(b)

**Fig. 3. Multiprocessor analog computer, model AD10. (*a*) Exterior. (*b*) Organization. (*Applied Dynamics International*)**

Significant advancements were made by Vannevar Bush and his colleagues at the Massachusetts Institute of Technology when they developed the first large-scale general-purpose mechanical differential analyzer in the early 1930s. The success of this machine led to the construction of similar machines in the United States and other countries and prompted the MIT group to construct a more elaborate machine, placed in operation in 1942.

The electronic analog computer had its origin in the dc network analyzer developed about 1925 by General Electric Company and Westinghouse Corporation; the dc network analyzer was followed in 1929 by the more versatile ac analyzer. The electronic differential analyzer, as it was called, had its fastest growth during World War II and soon displaced mechanical computers except for some special-purpose applications, such as jet-engine fuel controllers. C. A. Lovell and D. B. Parkinson of Bell Telephone Laboratories were responsible for the first published use of operational amplifiers as computer components. They used operational amplifiers in the real-time computer of the M9 antiaircraft-gun director built by Western Electric Company. J. B. Russell of Columbia University brought the circuits used in the M9 computer to the attention of J. R. Ragazzini, R. H. Randall, and F. A. Russell, who then built the first general-purpose electronic analog computer under contract with the National Defense Research Committee. This work led to the publication of the first article, in May 1947, describing the operational amplifier as a computer component. Meanwhile G. A. Philbrick had independently pioneered the use of high-gain direct-coupled amplifiers as components of fast-time electronic analog computers. The invention of the chopper-stabilized direct-coupled amplifier was primarily due to E. Goldberg of RCA Laboratories; it essentially eliminates the problem of drift in dc computation. In 1947 Reeves Instrument Corporation, under a Navy contract, developed a computer which was the forerunner of the present-day electronic analog computer.

## Description and Uses

The typical modern general-purpose analog computer consists of a console containing a collection of operational amplifiers; computing elements, such as summing networks, integrator networks, attenuators, multipliers, and function generators; logic and interface units; control circuits; power supplies; a patch bay; and various meters and display devices. The patch bay is arranged to bring input and output terminals of all programmable devices to one location, where they can be conveniently interconnected by various patch cords and plugs to meet the requirements of a given problem. Prewired problem boards can be exchanged at the patch bay in a few seconds and new coefficients set up typically in less than a half hour. Extensive automatic electronic patching systems have been developed to permit fast setup, as well as remote and time-shared operation.

The analog computer basically represents an instrumentation of calculus, in that it is designed to solve ordinary differential equations. This capability lends itself to the implementation of simulated models of dynamic systems. The computer operates by generating voltages that behave like the physical or mathematical variables in the system under study. Each variable is represented as a continuously varying (or steady) voltage signal at the output of a programmed computational unit. Specific to the analog computer is the fact that individual circuits are used for each feature or equation being represented, so that all variables are generated simultaneously. Thus the analog computer is a parallel computer in which the configuration of the computational units allows direct interactions of the computed variables at all times during the solution of a problem.

An example of a general-purpose electronic analog computer, the model EAI-2000, is shown in Fig. 1. This analog/hybrid computer is controlled by digital means, and operator input/output is through a keyboard-equipped cathode-ray tube. Plug-in analog/digital converters and digital/analog multipliers quickly convert the computer for complete hybrid operation, discussed below. Computational speed is equivalent to 15,000 operations per second, or more.

**Applications.** The analog computer or its equivalent, the continuous system simulation by a digital computer, is employed in every area of science and technology. The range of applications is constantly increasing, from the social sciences, to economics, human relations, political problems and policy/decision-making, to ecology and environmental studies, medicine, health and welfare, up to the more traditional analog computer application areas: science, technology, and hardware and systems development and engineering.

The analog computer is used to gain better insight into research topics, to develop and test methods and equipment, to carry out the design of new processes, or to predict by trial-and-error methods the model responses of system applications beyond known boundaries as well as to improve the behavior of systems already in operation. Special-purpose analog computers are directly connected to or built into physical systems to serve such on-line tasks as immediate and continuous computation or data reduction, or as part of dynamic control. An example of this type is the pneumatic computer shown in Fig. 2. This computer uses standard (3–15 psi or 20–100 kilopascals) air-pressure signals, a mechanical flexure construction, and a readily interchangeable switch plate to perform any one of the following functions: multiplication, division, squaring, and square-root extraction.

The analog computer serves especially well in two categories of systems engineering. In the first, the inductive process of model building, an analytical relation between variables is hypothesized to describe the physical system of interest. Forcing functions identical to those in the physical system can then be applied to the hypothetical model, enabling a comparison of the response of the model with that of the actual physical system. This will often indicate improvements and extensions that should be made in the model to fit it to the system better and thus make it more valid. Because of the ease with which parameter variations and model changes can be accomplished, the analog computer is useful in conducting many trial-and-error experiments on the model to obtain the best fit to the physical system.

In the second category, the deductive process of systems analysis, mathematical statements describing the physical system to be studied are necessary. These mathematical statements (equations) are often supplemented by graphical information as well as by logic statements. Also, validity ranges for parameters are established for the study. Experiments are then performed, varying the inputs and parameters that describe the system, to obtain (finally) a set of optimum responses for the system, to develop a better understanding of the intrinsic nature of the system by studying input-output relations, or to lay a foundation for further investigations into the system.

**Unique features.** The unique features of the analog computer which are of value in science and technology are as follows:

1. Within the useful frequency bandwidth of the computational units and components, all programmed computations take place in parallel and are for practical purposes instantaneous. That is, there is no finite execution time associated with each mathematical operation, as is encountered with digital computer methods.

2. The dynamics of an analog model can be programmed for time expansion (slower than real system time), synchronous time (real time), or time compression (faster than real time).

3. The computer has a flexible addressing system so that almost every computed variable can be measured, viewed with vivid display instruments, and recorded at will.

4. One control mode of the computer, usually called HOLD, can freeze the dynamic response of a model to allow detailed examination of interrelationships at that instant in time, and then, after such study, the computing can be made to resume as though no stop had occurred.

5. By means of patch cords, plugs, switches, and adjustment knobs the analog computer program or model can be directly manipulated, especially during dynamic computation, and the resultant changes in responses observed and interpreted.

6. Because of the fast dynamic response of the analog computer, it is easy to implement implicit computation through the use of problem feedback. (This important and powerful mathematical quality of the analog computer is discussed more fully below.)

7. The computer can be used for on-line model building; that is, a computer model can be constructed in a step-by-step fashion directly at the console by interconnecting computational units on the basis of one-for-one analog representation of the real system elements. Then, by adjusting signal gains and attenuation parameters, dynamic behavior can be generated that corresponds to the desired response or is recognizable as that of the real system. This method allows a skillful person to create models when no rigorous mathematical equations for a system exist.

8. For those applications to which it is well suited, the analog computer operates at relatively low cost, thus affording the analyst ample opportunity to investigate, develop, and experiment within a broad range of parameters and functions.

## Components

Manipulations of the signals (voltages) in the analog computer are based upon the fundamental electri-

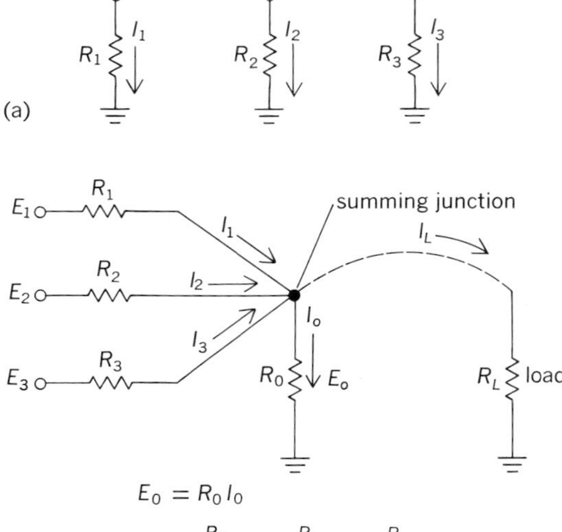


**Fig. 4.** Addition of electric currents by using a passive network of resistors. (*a*) Individual voltages and resistors. (*b*) Voltages and corresponding currents summed into a common resistor.

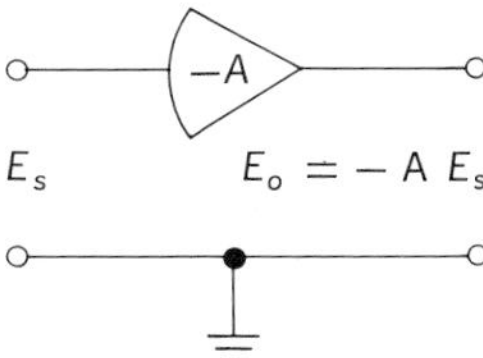


**Fig. 5.** Symbol for a high-gain direct-current amplifier, with one inverting input referenced to ground.

cal properties associated with circuit components. The interrelation of voltages for representing mathematical functions is derived by combining currents at circuit nodes or junctions. SEE KIRCHHOFF'S LAWS OF ELECTRIC CIRCUITS; OHM'S LAW.

**Linear computing units.** The simplest arrangement of components for executing addition would be to impress the voltages to be added across individual resistors (**Fig. 4**$a$). The resistors would then be joined (Fig. 4$b$) to allow the currents to combine and to develop the output voltage across a final resistor. Use of this simple configuration of elements for computation is impractical, because of the undesirable interaction between inputs. A change in one input signal (voltage) causes a change in the current that flows through the input resistor; this changes the voltage at the input resistor junction, and the change secondarily causes a different current to flow in the other input resistors. The situation gets more interactive when another computing circuit is attached so that part of the summing current flows away from the summing junction. This interaction effect also prevents exact computing. If, in some way, each voltage to be summed could be made independent of the other voltages connected to the summing junction, and if the required current fed to other circuits could be obtained without loading the summing junction, then precise computation would be possible. SEE DIRECT-CURRENT CIRCUIT THEORY.

***Function of operational amplifier.*** The electronic analog computer satisfies these needs by using high-gain (high-amplification) dc operational amplifiers. A symbol to represent a dc direct-coupled amplifier is shown in **Fig. 5**. According to convention, the rounded side represents the input to the amplifier, and the pointed end represents the amplifier output. A common reference level or ground exists between the amplifier input and output, and all voltages are measured with respect to it. The ground reference line is understood and is usually omitted from the symbol. The signal input network (consisting of summing resistors) connects to the inverting (or negative) amplifier input terminal. The noninverting (or positive) amplifier input terminal is normally connected to the reference ground. Generally the inverting input is called the summing junction (SJ) of the amplifier. Internal design of the amplifier is such that, if the signal at the summing junction is positive with respect to ground, the amplifier output voltage is negative with respect to ground. The amplifier has an open-loop voltage gain of $-A$; therefore an input voltage of $E_s$ results in an output voltage of $-AE_s$. Gain of a commercial computing amplifier is typically $10^8$; thus, an input voltage of less than 1 μV can produce several volts at the amplifier output. SEE AMPLIFIER; DIRECT-COUPLED AMPLIFIER.

Because the operational amplifier thus inverts the signal (changes its sign or polarity), it lends itself to the use of negative feedback, whereby a portion of the output signal is returned to the input. This arrangement has the effect of lowering the net gain of the amplifier signal channel and of improving overall signal-to-noise ratio and increasing computational accuracy.

Circuit operation (**Fig. 6**) can be viewed in the following manner. A dc voltage $E_{in}$ applied to input resistor $R_{in}$ produces a summing junction voltage $E_s$. The voltage is amplified and appears at the amplifier output as voltage $E_o$, (equal to $-AE_s$, where $A$ is voltage gain of the amplifier). Part of output voltage $E_o$ returns through feedback resistor $R_f$ to the summing junction. Because the returned or feedback voltage is of opposite (negative) polarity to the initial voltage at the summing junction, it tends to reduce the magnitude of $E_s$, resulting in an overall input-output relationship that may be expressed as Eq. (1). In

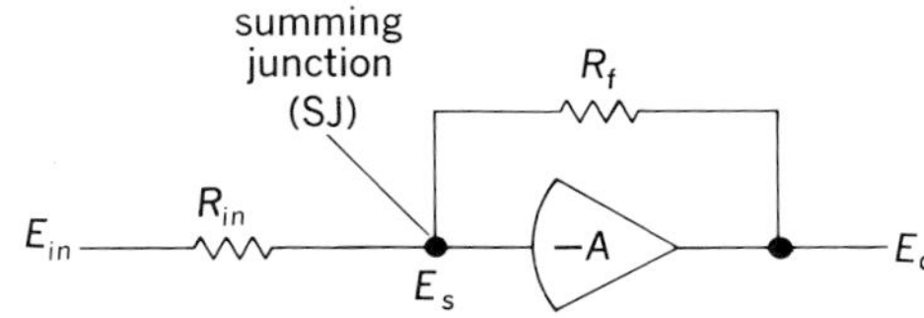


**Fig. 6.** High-gain amplifier which has been made into an operational amplifier through the inclusion of an input resistor and a feedback resistor tied together at the amplifier's summing junction (SJ).

$$\frac{E_o}{E_{in}} = \frac{-A}{A+1} = \frac{-1}{1+1/A} \simeq -1 \qquad A > 10^8 \qquad (1)$$

fact, the summing junction voltage $E_s$ is so small that it is considered to be at practically zero, a condition called virtual ground.

To illustrate how the operational amplifier serves the needs of the computing network, consider the currents that flow and the corresponding algebraic expressions (**Fig. 7**). The operational amplifier is designed to have high input impedance (high resistance to the flow of current into or out of its input terminal); consequently the amplifier input current $I_s$ can then be considered to be practically zero. The resulting cur-

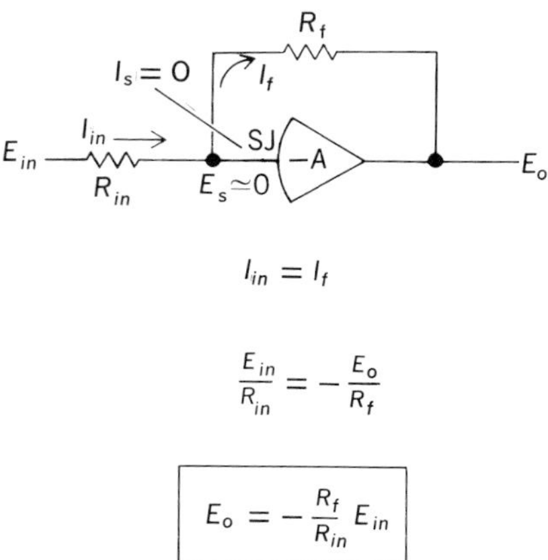


**Fig. 7.** Summing junction currents into an operational amplifier create the fixed gain function, determined by resistor values, as indicated in the box.

rent equation states that input current $I_{in}$ is equal to feedback current $I_f$. Since the amplifier has a very high gain, the summing junction voltage is virtually zero. Voltage drop across $R_{in}$ is thus equal to $E_{in}$; voltage drop across $R_f$ is $E_o$. The equation in the box is the fundamental relationship for the amplifier. As long as the amplifier has such a high gain and requires a negligible current from the summing junction, the amplifier input and output voltages are related by the ratio of the two resistors and are thus not affected by the actual electronic construction of the amplifier. If several input resistors are connected to the same summing junction and voltages are applied to them (**Fig. 8**), then because the summing junction remains at practically zero potential, none of the inputs will interfere with the other inputs. Thus all inputs will exert independent and additive effects on the output.

Because amplifier gain has a negative sign, output voltage equals the negative sum of the input voltages, weighted according to the values of the individual resistors in relation to the feedback resistor, as shown in the box in Fig. 8.

When a computing circuit is connected to the amplifier output, a demand for load current is introduced. Such a required output load current must be supplied by the amplifier without a measurable change in its output voltage. That is, the operational amplifier must act as a voltage controller, supplying whatever current is required within limits, while maintaining the net voltage gain established by the mathematical ratio of its input and feedback elements. The operational amplifier and network is a linear network because once the input-feedback ratios are adjusted, signal channel gains remain constant (a straight-line function) during computation.

***Accessories with operational amplifier.*** The input and feedback elements that can be used with an operational amplifier are not restricted to resistors alone. A reactive feedback component such as a capacitor may also be used, resulting in mathematical operations analogous to integration with respect to time. The capacitor is a device that accumulates electric charge. The voltage that exists across it is related to its electrical size (capacitance in farads) and the quantity of charge (in coulombs) it contains. Should more charge flow into it (an electric current is actually equivalent to charge per unit time), the voltage across the capacitor would rise. To state this concept mathematically: the capacitor integrates electric current (flow of charge) with respect to time. An operational amplifier with a feedback capacitor (**Fig. 9**) will thus generate an output voltage that is the time integral of its input voltage. SEE CAPACITANCE.

To solve equations with specific numerical values, many different circuit gains are needed. Although it is possible to provide almost any desired gain by selecting appropriate resistances for the input-feedback ratio of operational amplifier channels, each one usually remains fixed once it has been established. In practice the choice of gain is limited to a few integer values (amplifier gains such as 1, 5, 10) which are obtained with high accuracy, using matched resistors, on the general-purpose analog computer.

Another linear computing element, called the attenuator, also known as the potentiometer or pot, is used to adjust signal gains to desired fractional values. It thus allows parameters (coefficients in the problems) to be adjusted either manually or automatically, between or during computations. Traditionally, the attenuator is a three-terminal potentiometer consisting of a multiturn, resistive winding with a movable wiper (**Fig. 10***a*). Output voltage is a fraction of the input, depending upon the position of the wiper (Fig. 10*b*). For manually adjusted potentiometers, a dial is mounted on the wiper shaft so that the actual pot position can be read out (Fig. 10*c*). Servo-set potentiometers are adjusted automatically, using individual dc motors in a measurement and control loop fashion; a desired attenuation coefficient value is entered via the console keyboard, and the corresponding potentiometer is set to that value in less than a second. The

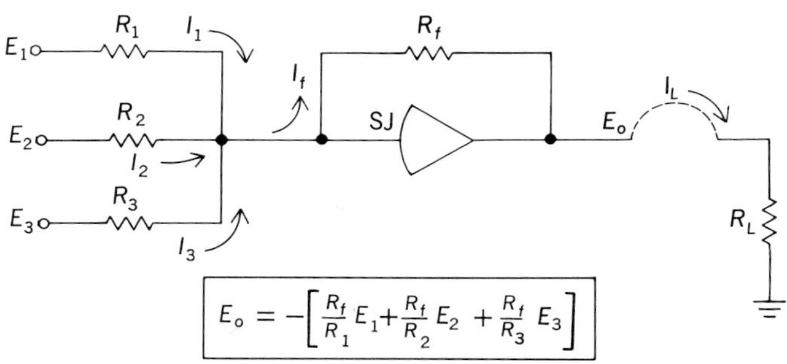


**Fig. 8. Operational amplifier which has been made into a summer through the use of several input resistors connected to the summing junction. Output is equal to the inverted weighted sum of the inputs.**

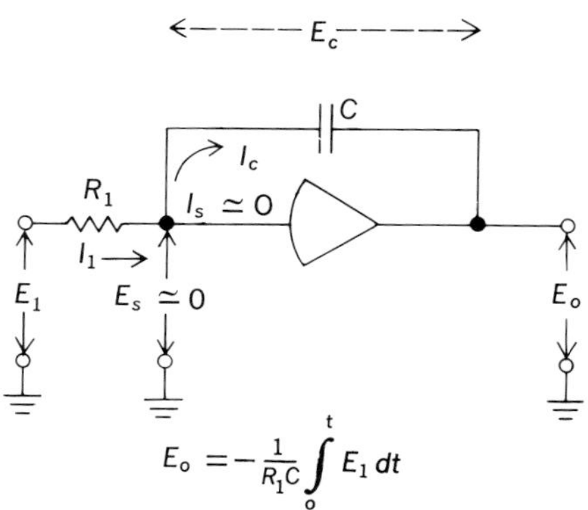


**Fig. 9. Use of a capacitor as a feedback element to turn a high-gain amplifier into an integrator, with a time scale determined by the *RC* time constant.**

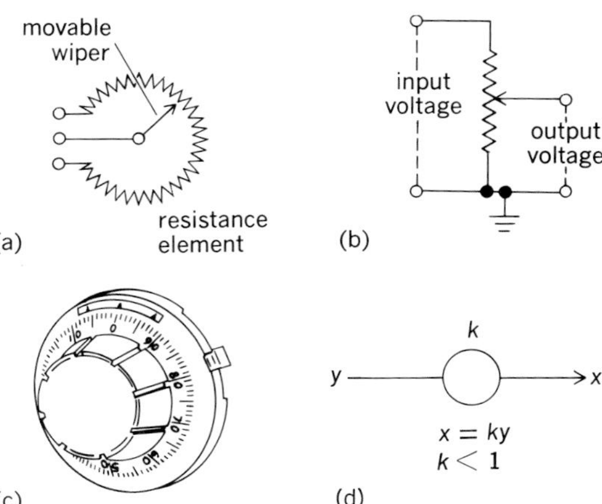


**Fig. 10. Attenuators. (*a*) Traditional potentiometer voltage divider. (*b*) Circuit used in analog computers. (*c*) Typical manually adjusted dial with indication of mechanical position of wiper in 10-turn potentiometer. (*d*) Circuit symbol for attenuator with coefficient *k*.**

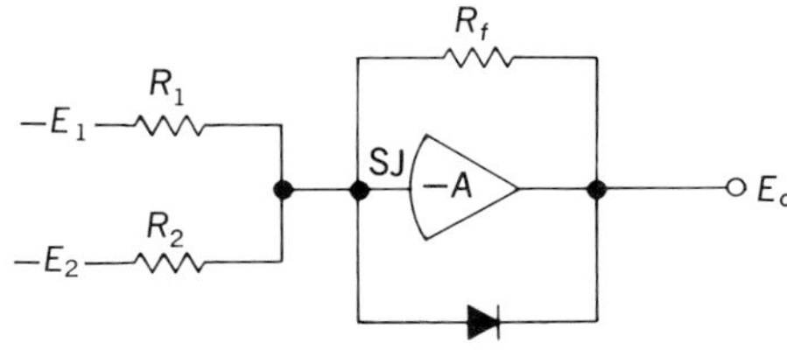


$R_1 = R_2 = R_f$

$E_0 = E_1 + E_2$ when $E_1 + E_2 > 0$

$E_0 = 0$ when $E_1 + E_2 \leq 0$

**Fig. 11. Circuit containing one-way conducting diode that limits the output of an amplifier to positive signals (since a negative output would draw a short-circuit current from the summing junction through the diode).**

most modern attenuator is the digitally set one, in which the coefficient value is established via electronic multiplication techniques, making it possible for a digital computer (in a hybrid setup) to control at high speed the coefficients used in the analog computer program. An in-line circle symbol is used to represent the attenuator in analog circuit diagrams (Fig. 10*d*). *See* POTENTIOMETER (VARIABLE RESISTOR).

Because the classical potentiometer type is a passive element rather than an active one like the operational amplifier, it can only provide signal attenuations of less than unity. When it is connected to other circuits, including amplifier inputs, some current is drawn through its wiper arm. Therefore, for greatest accuracy in setting, the attenuator must be adjusted while measuring the voltage at the wiper arm when it is under load and with a steady, known reference voltage applied to the potentiometer input. This procedure compensates for such slight loading voltage drops as occur when input resistors of value commensurable with the potentiometer resistance are connected to the wiper. Otherwise the result is a dial reading that is higher than the electrical attenuation. As will be described below, attenuators in conjunction with other elements allow the computer to be set up for any required problem value or analog model scale factor.

**Nonlinear computing elements.** In nature nearly all systems or processes exhibit nonlinear features in the form of constraints, discontinuities, and variable gains. If an analog computer is to be programmed and operated as a realistic system model, it must include devices with programmable nonlinear characteristics. The most versatile computing element for this service is the diode function generator. *See* SEMICONDUCTOR DIODE.

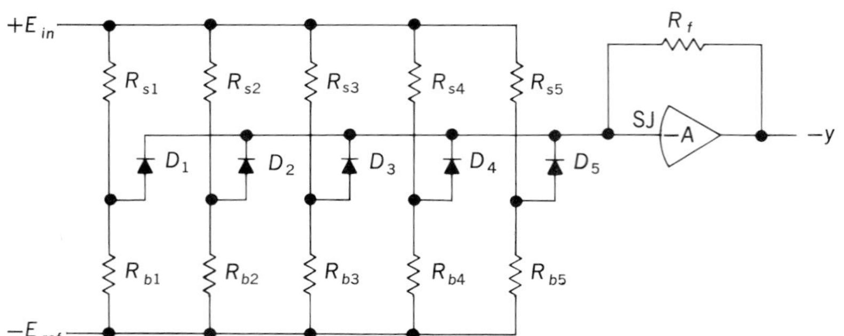


**Fig. 12. Diode function generator with five diodes, each biased to a different voltage and contributing a specified current to the summing amplifier, to generate a desired function of the input signal.**

The diode operates as an electrical one-way check valve, allowing current to flow one way but not the other. Electrically, a diode has two states or conditions: the ON or conducting condition and the OFF or nonconducting condition. Due consideration should be given to the fact that a diode operates solely according to the voltage across it. A diode will assume the ON condition whenever the anode (the positive terminal) is more positive than the cathode. For example, if the anode is at −6 V and the cathode is at −8 V, the diode is in a conducting (ON) condition; if the anode is at +9 V and the cathode is at +15 V, the diode will be in a nonconducting (OFF) condition.

Within various limitations, the diode may be used in the input, feedback, and output circuits of operational amplifiers to simulate nonlinear features that are functions of the variable voltages being computed. To illustrate diode action, the output of an amplifier (**Fig. 11**) might represent the computer altitude of a

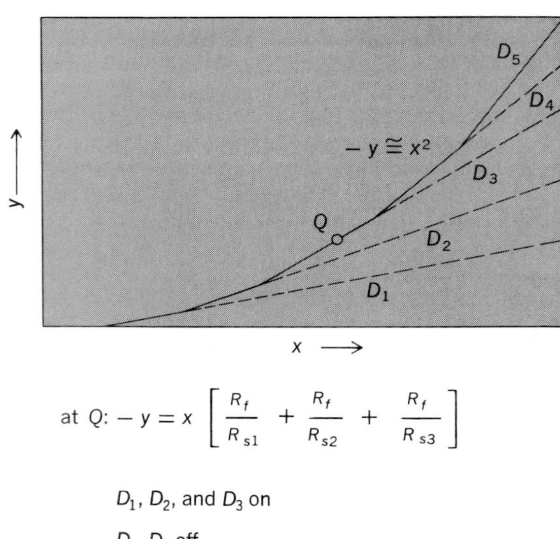


$$\text{at } Q\text{: } -y = x \left[ \frac{R_f}{R_{s1}} + \frac{R_f}{R_{s2}} + \frac{R_f}{R_{s3}} \right]$$

$D_1$, $D_2$, and $D_3$ on

$D_4$, $D_5$ off

**Fig. 13. Resultant function of diode function generator, made up of the sum of currents from the individual diodes; the desired function is approximated by a number of straight-line segments.**

space vehicle above the lunar surface. Upon descent, the constraint is encountered at touchdown that no negative signal (and thus no negative altitude, meaning "flying underground") be allowed to occur, because such conditions obviously make the system equations invalid. Should the amplifier output signal attempt to go negative, the cathode of the diode would assume a lower potential than the anode at the summing junction's virtual ground, placing the diode in the ON condition. The result is to shunt the feedback resistor so that the effective $R_f$ becomes nearly zero. When the amplifier output signal once again goes positive, the diode switches to its OFF condition and no further limiting occurs.

Diodes, in addition to being used to implement simulations of unique nonlinearities such as limits, backlash, and deadzones, can be combined with a network of resistors to produce particular nonlinear functions. A diode function generator (DFG) uses the one-way conducting property of diodes to selectively alter the resultant gain of an operational amplifier in accordance with a desired function of the input voltage. The amplifier input circuit of **Fig. 12** is adjusted so that the breakpoint resistors $R_b$ permit individual diodes to conduct at successively higher values of the input signal $E_{in}$. The resultant input-output gain is determined by the sum of the ratios of feedback resistor $R_f$ and output increment (or slope) resistors $R_s$, as illustrated by the equation for point $Q$ on the curvature in **Fig. 13**. Specific resistor values for the set of $R_b$'s and $R_s$'s can be calculated to generate many mathematical functions, such as $x$, $x^2$, log $x$, $e^x$, cos $x$, or sin $x$. The DFG can be arranged to operate on either positive or negative input signals by choosing the orientation of diodes and reference voltage polarity. Further, by utilizing fully adjustable potentiometers for breakpoint and slope resistances, a variable diode function generator (VDFG) is established, permitting the programming of most analytic, arbitrary, and empirical functions, including functions with one or more inflections.

**Multipliers.** The principal device for multiplication of one variable by another (to yield a product of variables) is the electronic quarter-square multiplier. The mathematical function "multiplication" corresponds to a nonlinearity in which one signal input is acted on through a second input, such as a variable gain. Traditionally, an electromechanical device, the servo-multiplier, accomplished this by dynamically positioning the wiper arm of a potentiometer through a motor drive that responded to the second input signal. Servo-multipliers are now infrequently used in electronic analog computers. However, they represent a type of computing unit having relatively low cost, great versatility, and low signal bandwidth.

The all-electronic quarter-square multiplier achieves the multiplication function to frequencies of several thousand hertz by implementing an algebraic identity (**Fig. 14**). The squaring operations are accomplished with high accuracy by two DFG circuits, as described earlier. Typically, 80 or more properly oriented diodes are employed to permit the accurate generation of the square-law terms of all polarity combinations required for complete four-quadrant multiplication. The simplified symbols which are used in the circuit diagram are more fully discussed below.

**Signal-controlled programming.** An electronic comparator–analog switch combination provides the analog computer with decision-making and preprogrammed automatic signal-rerouting capabilities (**Fig. 15**). These are nonlinear functions preset to take place at some particular point in a calculation run and to cause a change in coefficients or signals, that is, a branching in mathematical procedure or a change in the control of the run. The technique consists of using a comparator with two or three inputs, generating a logic output signal (TRUE-FALSE) which depends on whether or not the sum of the input signals is greater than zero. Basically the comparator responds to its input analog signals and abruptly shifts its output from one logic level (FALSE) to the other (TRUE) whenever there is a polarity change to positive at its summing junction, that is, whenever the sum of the input voltage goes through zero. The comparator must switch its output rapidly because there is no intermediate value assumed in the transition. The comparator output signal $m$ may be used in logic units (AND gates, OR gates, flip-flops, and counters) to achieve complex logic functions and automatic (programmed) control of computations. *See Logic circuits.*

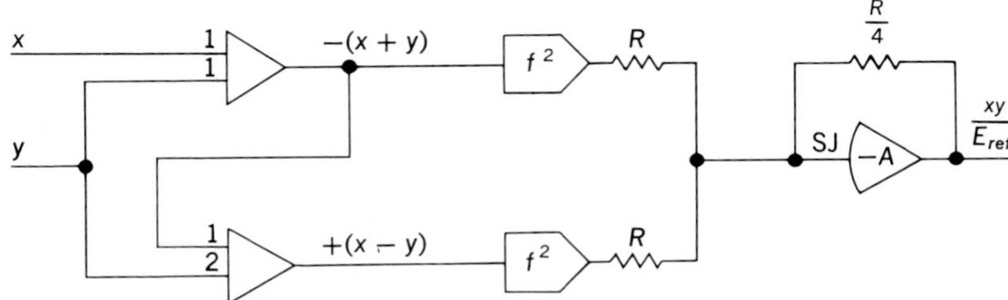


$$xy = 1/4[(x+y)^2 - (x-y)^2]$$
$$= 1/4(x^2 + 2xy + y^2 - x^2 + 2xy - y^2)$$
$$= 1/4(4xy) = xy$$

**Fig. 14. Electronic quarter-square multiplier, which uses an algebraic identity to achieve the multiplication of variables.**

The electronic analog switch is an ON-OFF input network used in connection with an operational amplifier. The network is ON, permitting an analog input signal to propagate through it to the associated amplifier when, and only when, a logic high (TRUE) signal is applied to its command input. If the command input is logic low (FALSE) or absent, the signal switch network remains in its disconnected or shut-off mode, and no analog input signal will be conducted through it.

One or more of the comparator inputs can be dynamically variable inputs, so that the comparison function itself is a function of the analog computation. The analog signal switch can be used to alter the configuration of computing circuits or to change signal gains by switching between pairs of attenuator potentiometers set to different coefficient values. In modern computers, each comparator also applies power to its indicator light bulb on the console front panel to indicate the state of the comparison function.

## Programming

To solve a problem using an analog computer, the problem solver goes through a procedure of general analysis, data preparation, analog circuit development, and patchboard programming. He or she may also make test runs of subprograms to examine partial-system dynamic responses before eventually running the full program to derive specific and final answers. The problem-solving procedure typically

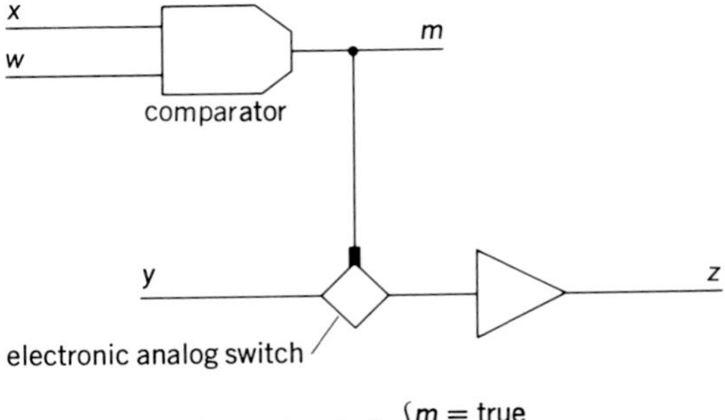


when $x + w > 0$ $\begin{cases} m = \text{true} \\ z = -y \end{cases}$

when $x + w \le 0$ $\begin{cases} m = \text{false} \\ z = 0 \end{cases}$

**Fig. 15. Comparator and electronic analog switch, combined to give signal and coefficient changes in the analog circuits based on the comparison results.**

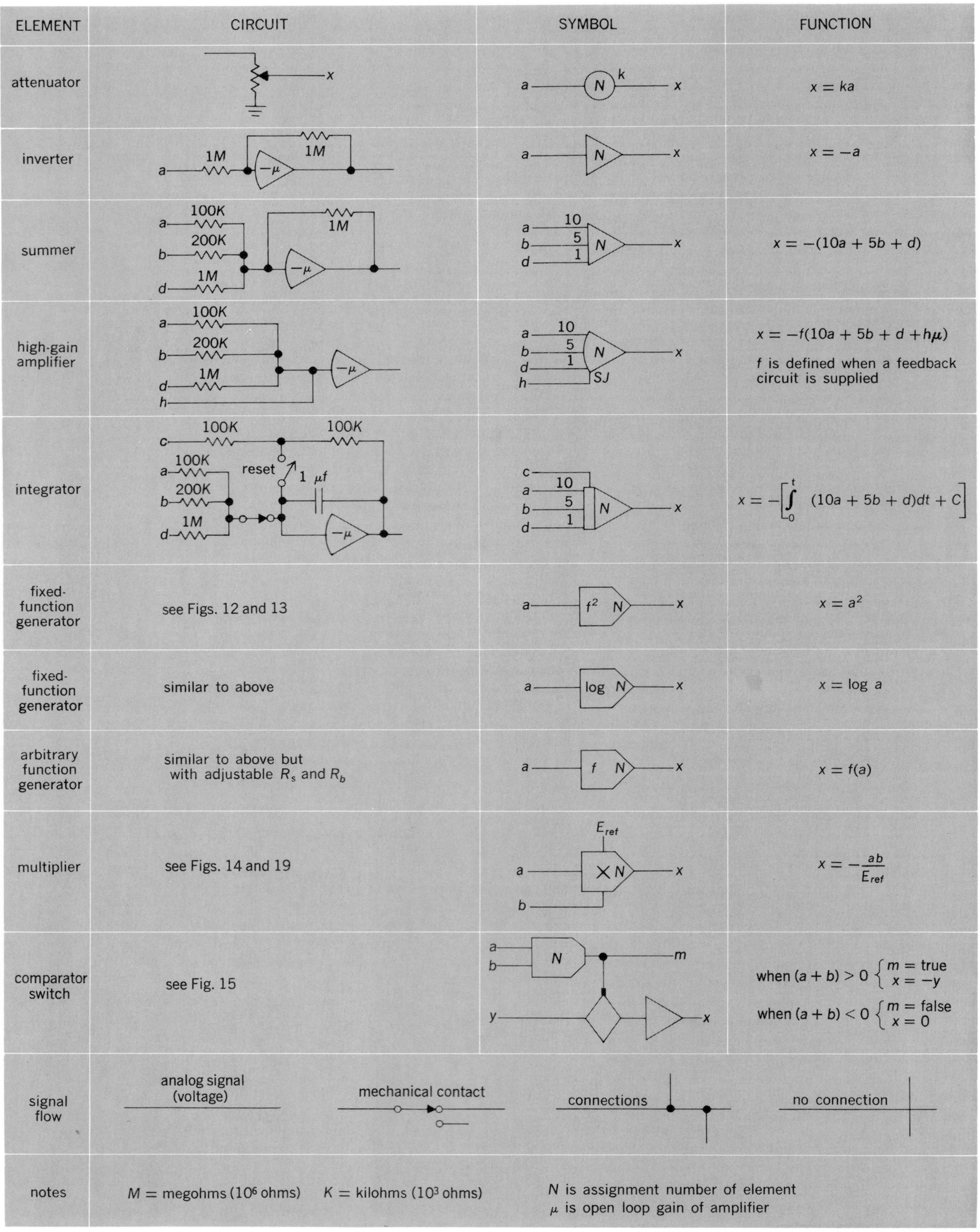

| ELEMENT | CIRCUIT | SYMBOL | FUNCTION |
|---|---|---|---|
| attenuator | | | $x = ka$ |
| inverter | | | $x = -a$ |
| summer | | | $x = -(10a + 5b + d)$ |
| high-gain amplifier | | | $x = -f(10a + 5b + d + h\mu)$<br>$f$ is defined when a feedback circuit is supplied |
| integrator | | | $x = -\left[\int_0^t (10a + 5b + d)dt + C\right]$ |
| fixed-function generator | see Figs. 12 and 13 | | $x = a^2$ |
| fixed-function generator | similar to above | | $x = \log a$ |
| arbitrary function generator | similar to above but with adjustable $R_s$ and $R_b$ | | $x = f(a)$ |
| multiplier | see Figs. 14 and 19 | | $x = -\frac{ab}{E_{ref}}$ |
| comparator switch | see Fig. 15 | | when $(a + b) > 0$ $\begin{cases} m = \text{true} \\ x = -y \end{cases}$<br>when $(a + b) < 0$ $\begin{cases} m = \text{false} \\ x = 0 \end{cases}$ |
| signal flow | analog signal (voltage) | mechanical contact | connections / no connection |
| notes | $M$ = megohms ($10^6$ ohms) $K$ = kilohms ($10^3$ ohms) | $N$ is assignment number of element<br>$\mu$ is open loop gain of amplifier | |

Fig. 16. Symbols used in the programming of analog circuit diagrams.

involves eight major steps, listed below:

1. The problem under study is described with a set of mathematical equations or, when that is not possible, the system configuration and the interrelations of component influences are defined in block-diagram form, with each block described in terms of black-box input-output relationships.

2. Where necessary, the description of the system (equations or system block diagram) is rearranged in a form that may better suit the capabilities of the computer, that is, avoiding duplications or excessive numbers of computational units, or avoiding algebraic (nonintegrational) loops.

3. The assembled information is used to sketch out an analog circuit diagram which shows in detail how the computer could be programmed to handle the problem and achieve the objectives of the study.

4. System variables and parameters are then scaled to fall within the operational ranges of the computer. This may require revisions of the analog circuit diagram and choice of computational units.

5. The finalized circuit arrangement is patched on the computer problem board.

6. Numerical values are set up on the attenuators, the initial conditions of the entire system model established, and test values checked.

7. The computer is run to solve the equations or simulate the black boxes so that the resultant values or system responses can be obtained. This gives the initial answers and the "feel" for the system.

8. Multiple runs are made to check the responses for specific sets of parameters and to explore the influences of problem (system) changes, as well as the behavior which results when the system configuration is driven with different forcing functions.

**Symbols.** A number of concepts and techniques are used to ease the process of programming an analog computer. For example, it usually is too tedious and cumbersome to show all of the wiring associated with the computing devices used in a program; therefore, simplified symbols are used to represent the various computer components (**Fig. 16**). These symbols are easy to draw, and they allow a complex program to be designed quickly, yet with sufficient clarity for unambiguous patching.

When an amplifier symbol is shown with a straight front, it is understood to have a standard feedback resistor; but when the front is curved, the feedback circuit is not included and must be explicitly programmed in the computer diagram. In the integrator, the constant of integration $C$ is applied to a separate, special input terminal through a mode switching network of the integrator to provide for establishment of initial conditions. Function-generating networks as such do not show a polarity reversal because they represent characterized impedances (resistor-diode arrays), but they are usually permanently connected to one or two summing amplifiers. The multiplier normally comes with an output amplifier; thus it provides an inverted output.

**Representation of variables.** When equations are to be solved or a system is to be modeled on the analog computer, all individual parameters and variables must be fitted (scaled) to the available three dimensions of the computer: voltage range, input gains, and computing time. The voltage range spans from negative reference voltage, through zero (ground), to positive voltage reference. The range on large multiconsole analog computers often extends from $-100$ to

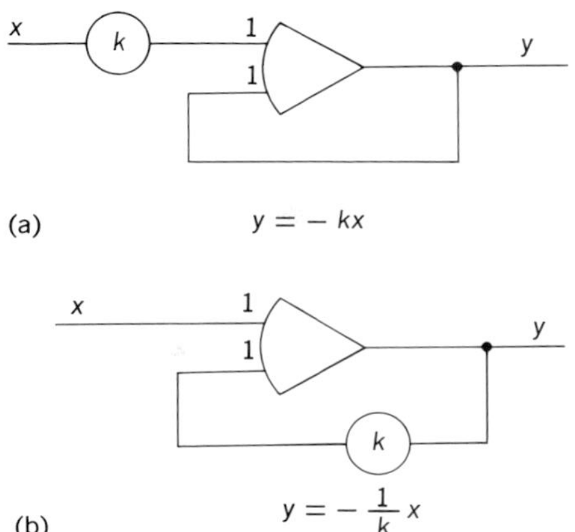


**Fig. 17. Movement of an attenuator from the input to the feedback network of an operational amplifier to create the inverse function: the coefficient changes from *k* in *a* to the inverse, 1/*k* in *b*.**

$+100$ V; on most small desktop or single-console-type computers the range is $-10$ to $+10$ V. Reference voltages are carefully established and rigidly regulated to provide a means of generating accurate input signals and to ensure a reliable base against which computed variables can be measured.

The zero point is usually referred to as high-quality ground; it is wired separately from the standard electronic chassis ground and power return ground. All computing signals are referenced to the high-quality ground. The precision of the computing gain of an amplifier is dependent on carefully matching its input and feedback resistors to provide the desired ratio with great accuracy. To avoid errors due to ambient temperature variations, these resistors as well as the feedback capacitors used in the integrators are either specially compensated against thermal errors, or they are physically maintained at a constant temperature in an oven mounted immediately behind the patch bay. By using multiturn potentiometers as attenuators, excellent resolution is obtained for coefficient adjustment. The maximum range of such coefficient adjustment, using the available input gains (including the combination of a potentiometer and an amplifier), may span approximately six decades (0.0001 to 100).

The time duration required for the dynamic response of a system model determines how long the computer must be programmed to run. A single run can be as short as 1 ms or as long as hours. The precision of the computational results is determined by how accurately all the computer circuits function and how well the operational amplifiers are stabilized against drift.

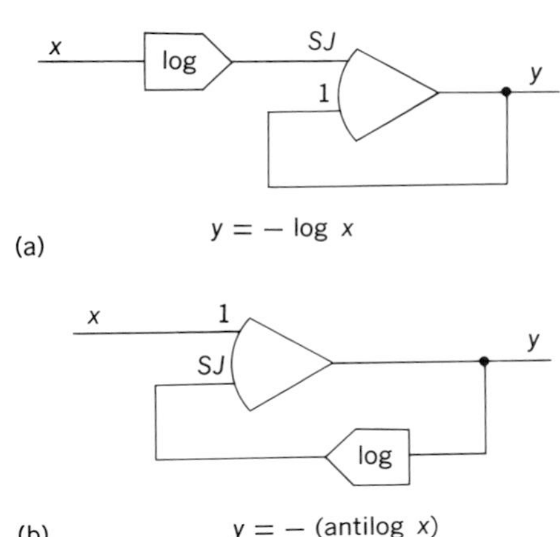


**Fig. 18. Movement of a logarithm function generator from the input to the feedback network of an operational amplifier to change the amplifier function from (*a*) log x to (*b*) antilog x (exp x).**

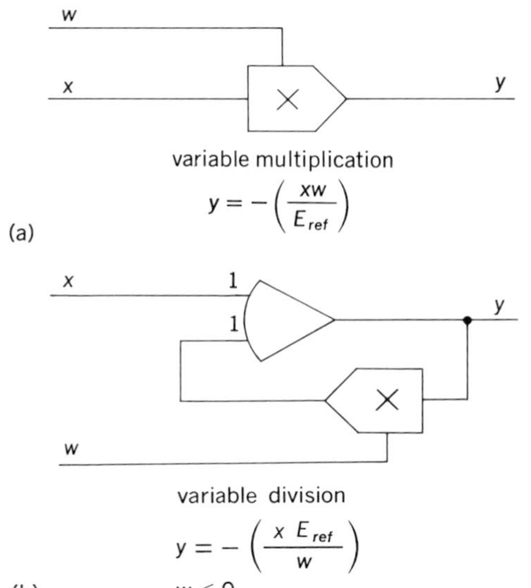


**Fig. 19. Use of multiplier (*a*) to create the variable multiplication function, and (*b*) in the feedback path of an amplifier to create the variable division function.**

Just as the analog voltage range can be scaled to represent the range of any real system variable, so the analog time dimension can be used to represent a system dimension other than time. For example, the problem to be programmed might be the calculation of the temperature profile of a metal rod heated at one end and cooled at the other. The analog computer could be programmed to sweep continuously in time along the length of the rod, developing a varying analog voltage scaled to represent the temperature. Thus, the computer time dimension would correspond to the rod length dimension.

**Inverse operations.** The complementary nature of the input and feedback networks of the operational amplifier gives it one of its most flexible properties. If, for example, a squaring module in an amplifier input circuit is moved to the amplifier feedback circuit, the amplifier will compute the square root. In general, when a function is exchanged between the input and feedback positions of an operational amplifier, the inverse function is obtained. For example, the constant $k$ in **Fig. 17*a*** becomes the reciprocal $1/k$ when relocated in the feedback circuit of Fig. 17*b*. Similarly, the log function exchange (**Fig. 18*a*** and *b*) provides the exponential function.

No special device is needed in an analog computer to divide one variable by another. Division is achieved by placing a multiplier in the feedback path of an amplifier, as shown in **Fig. 19**. (For the division to be stable, the denominator $W$ in Fig. 19*b* must always be negative and larger than zero, so that there is no positive feedback loop around the amplifier.) Similarly, the derivative of a function can be obtained by using this same principle. Since differentiation is the inverse mathematical operation of integration, the feedback circuit in **Fig. 20** incorporates an integrator to satisfy the requirement. The function of differentiation, due to its nature, exhibits higher gain at higher signal frequencies, a characteristic which may often lead to excessive amplification of high-frequency circuit noise; therefore, the addition of a feedback attenuator, indicated with a broken line in Fig. 20, is often useful to reduce the gain above a selected high-frequency roll-off corner. *See* Electric filter.

**Solution of algebraic equations.** Programming an analog computer to solve an equation such as Eq. (2)

$$y = x^2 + 4x - 50 \qquad (2)$$

can be described by referring to **Fig. 21**. Basically, a circuit is devised to generate each term of the equation; the output of each is then summed algebraically by the final amplifier.

The first term results from a squaring function generator in the input circuit of amplifier 6 as defined previously in Fig. 12. The arithmetic for the second term is programmed by dividing the forward gain of amplifier 5 by its feedback gain, 20/5, to yield a net gain of 4. The third term derives from the reference voltage by an adjustment of attenuator 2. Each circuit of the program operates in parallel with all others and instantaneously, so that $y$ is explicitly and immediately developed; thus the circuit will handle either varying or steady-state values of the input signal $x$.

Because the analog computer has a limited operational range and therefore resolution, the desired practical ranges of the various terms in a problem must be scaled to fit the analog voltage range. This requirement corresponds somewhat to that of keeping track of the decimal point when using the slide rule. The circuit of Fig. 21*b* is scaled for a specific range such that a signal voltage $V$ is related to the numerical value $N$ by a scale factor $\alpha$. The maximum value of 80 for $x$ can be directly accommodated within the 100-V range of the computer. Accordingly, its scale factor $\alpha_1$ is set at unity. But the corresponding maximum value for $y$ would exceed the unscaled computer range, necessitating an assignment of 0.01 for $\alpha_9$ (meaning the $y$ signal will not rise above 66.70 V). All the signals collected at the summing junction of amplifier 3 must have scales that are compatible with the output variables; therefore $\alpha_2$, $\alpha_5$, and $\alpha_8$ are matched to $\alpha_9$. Taking into consideration the reference voltage and the choice of slope resistors used to establish the square function generator, a scale of 0.01 at amplifier 6 seems practical when a feedback gain of 10 is used. This scale factor relates directly with $\alpha_1^2$ to yield the desired $\alpha_2$ factor. To adjust the second-term circuit for $\alpha_5$, the forward gain of amplifier 5 must be lowered by a decade to set $\alpha_3$, and attenuator 8 was added to insert $\alpha_4$ so that the product of $\alpha_3$ and $\alpha_4$ would produce the proper scale factor $\alpha_5$. The necessary $\alpha_8$ in the third circuit arises from the $\alpha_6$ associated with a 100-V reference and a readjustment of attenuator 2, taking into account $\alpha_7$ ($10^2 \times 10^{-4} = 10^{-2}$).

**Use with calculus.** Because of its fundamental ability to perform continuous integration, the analog computer is particularly well suited to solve ordinary

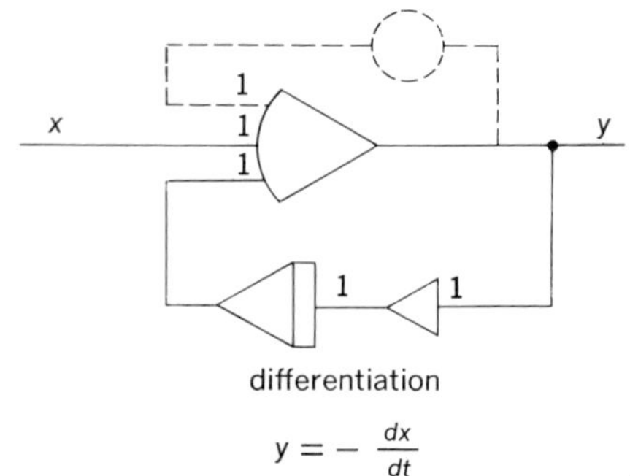


**Fig. 20. Use of an integrator in the feedback path of an operational amplifier to achieve differentiation with respect to time, *dx/dt*.**

differential equations, typically arising in the problems of calculus. Because of this ability, the analog computer has at times been referred to as the electronic differential analyzer. Significantly, the analog computer integrator will respond correctly to any simple or complex signal waveform presented at its input; it is not restricted to applications involving conventional classes of functions defined by analytic calculus.

The analog program for a third-order, nonlinear differential equation is illustrated in **Fig. 22** The equation is nonlinear because the third term has a variable coefficient, $7x$, operating on the first derivative. As a result, this equation has no known analytic solution in closed form. Nevertheless, the analog computer does generate the solution for $x$ by virtue of its instantaneous, parallel structure, its inherent capability to carry out continuous integrations, its ability to multiply variables, and its feature of problem feedback permitting implicit computation. The first step in the programming procedure is to algebraically rearrange the equation so that the highest-order derivative stands alone on the left side, as shown in the second expression in Fig. 22. The second step in the programming is to assume that a condition of signals representing the highest time derivative exists in the form of the summed inputs of an integrator (this condition is justified below). Then, by integration, the next lower time derivative will appear at the output of this integrator. By using a cascade of integrators (composed of three integrators in this case), each derivative is developed in turn until the dependent variable finally is generated. Next, each term on the right side of the expression may now be assembled through separate analog components and circuits and then gathered at the input of the first integrator. Now, when the circuits are activated electronically, the signals that the expression equates as the highest derivative will exist in fact at the integrator, justifying the original assumption. The circuit configuration involves the feedback of problem variables; therefore it is said that an implicit rather than an explicit solution of the equation is being made.

The analog computer can only represent the independent variable as time (clock time or real time). That is, regardless of the nature of the independent dimension in the simulated system, all derivatives in the computer representation are taken with respect to time. Because the computer accommodates a practical but finite time span, time ranges must be scaled in a fashion similar to that for voltage amplitudes discussed earlier. Computer time $T$ is related to real system time $t$ by a scale factor $\beta$. Also, an integrator operates on a voltage with respect to time, so that the gain of an integrator is determined by the ratio $\alpha/\beta$. When $\beta$ is one, the computer calculates in real time; when $\beta$ is greater than one, computer time is expanded (responses take place at speeds slower than real time); and when $\beta$ is less than one, computer time is compressed (and responses occur faster than in real time). In arranging the time scales, it is mandatory that the $\beta$ value be identical for all integrators within one interdependent system program. The potentiometer shown at the top of each integrator is used to preset the integrator to its proper initial condition (also called the constant of integration), as will be discussed later.

**Use as simulator.** The dynamic system in **Fig. 23*a*** is presented to illustrate how an analog computation

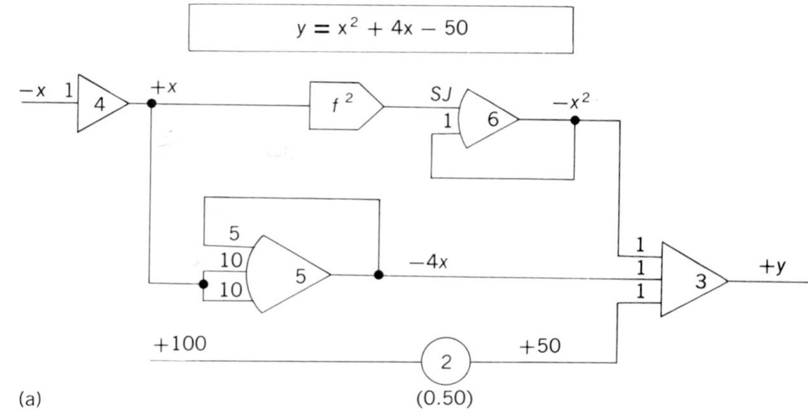


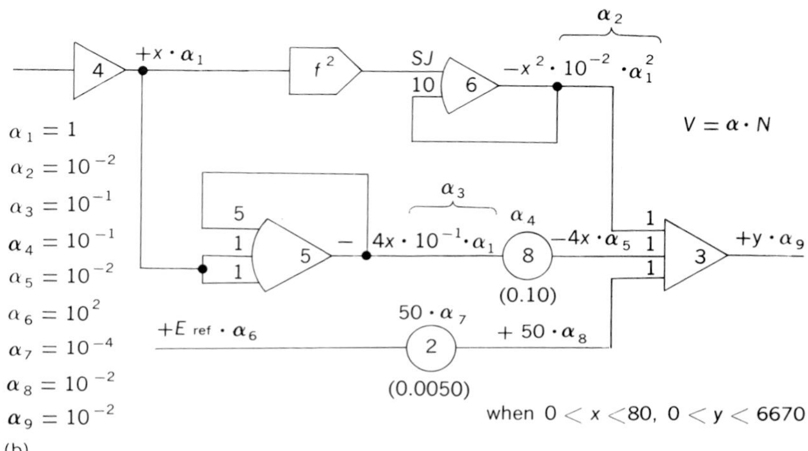


**Fig. 21. Analog computer circuits for solving a problem in algebra. (*a*) Unscaled circuit reflecting the equation given in box. (*b*) Circuit scaled for computation in computer with 100-V range, with appropriate scale factors $\alpha_1$-$\alpha_9$.**

$$4\frac{d^3x}{dt^3} + 5\frac{d^2x}{dt^2} + 7x\frac{dx}{dt} - 3x + 36 = 0$$

$$-\frac{d^3x}{dt^3} = \frac{5}{4}\frac{d^2x}{dt^2} + \frac{7}{4}x\frac{dx}{dt} - \frac{3}{4}x + 9$$

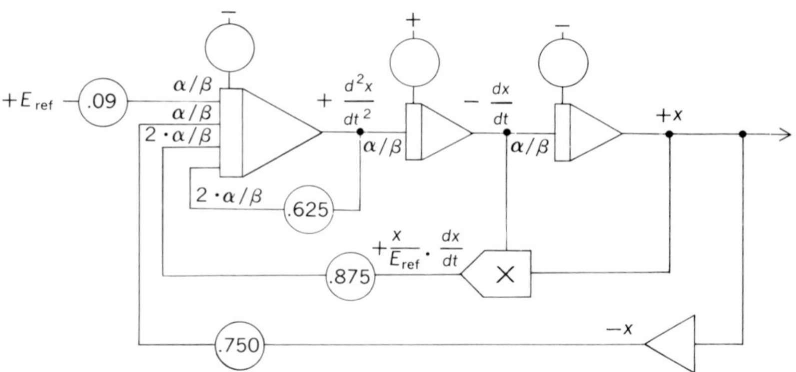


**Fig. 22. Analog computer circuit for solving a problem in calculus, with third-order differential equation shown in box.**

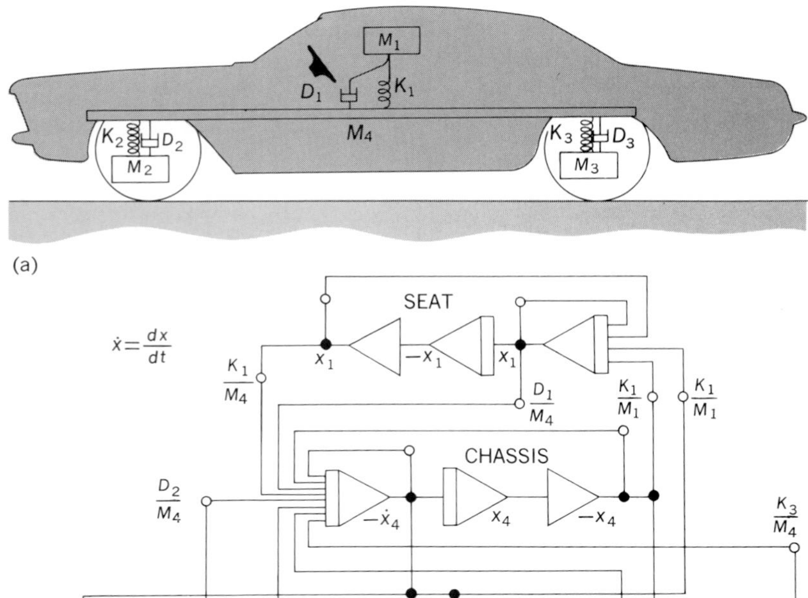


**Fig. 23. Construction of an analog computer model. (*a*) Approximation of the suspension system of an automobile with damped second-order systems. (*b*) Diagram of corresponding analog computer model. (*After T. H. Truitt and A. E. Rogers, Basics of Analog Computers, John F. Rider, 1960*)**

can be built up block by block directly from the characteristics of a system. Each part of the automobile suspension system is treated as a black box containing a second-order response mechanism. These boxes are then strongly intercoupled to the main chassis member. The design objective would be to adjust the masses $M_i$, the spring constants $K_i$, and the dampers $D_i$ to minimize $x_1$, the seat displacement that the driver experiences under various road conditions. Figure 23*b* shows the assembled analog computer model, with its variables labeled.

Finding a single combination of parameter settings is difficult, because at different road speeds the forcing functions at the front and rear wheels, $F_2$ and $F_3$, reflect a shift in frequency content and a difference in the excitation delay time from front to back. Once the building block model has been assembled, it is possible to see that a set of four simultaneous differential equations could be extracted from the analog circuit configuration to represent the system mathematically.

### Operation

After a program has been connected up on the patchboard in accordance with the foregoing programming procedures, the problem patchboard inserted in the patch bay, and the attenuators adjusted to their proper values, the analog computer is ready for a solution run. The mode of operation of the computer is governed by integrator controls, as shown in **Fig. 24**. The input to an integrator amplifier is connected to one of the four possible points: potset (PS) for adjusting potentiometers, in which the integrator is effectively short-circuited; the reset or initial condition (IC) mode, in which the capacitor is charged up to the initial value $E_{IC}$; hold (HD), which is a stop and freeze mode mainly for readout purposes; and operate (OP) mode, in which the intended continuous integration with respect to time takes place. The switching between these modes is done with high-speed electronic analog signal switches (older computers use relay contacts) controlled from the computer console or via logic command signals connected on the patchboard. At the beginning of a run, the computer is put in the reset or initial condition mode, energizing a bus circuit so that the integrators assume their initial conditions. Next, the computer is switched to the operate mode, removing the initial condition inputs and connecting the integrand inputs to the integrators. The generated and connected input signals are now integrated by the integrator according to its programmed time scale.

A study of the recorded responses in **Fig. 25** for the *x*, *y*, and *w* integrators reveals how each linear ramp function develops by the integration of its particular constant-voltage input signal. As the computer modes are exercised, each integrator behaves in accordance with its initial condition and the polarities and amplitudes of input signals imposed upon it. During the normal problem run, the integrators respond to rapidly varying, interacting signals, and many different dynamic results are generated.

In operating the computer, the user must be prepared to deal with many practical circumstances and to diagnose the troubles or errors that arise from the analog computer program. Mistakes in circuit patching, incorrect attenuator settings, wrong reference polarities, misapplication of ranges of computer units and display devices, and inappropriate time scale factor assignments may occur, as well as a host of details associated with the electronic properties of the computer. A smooth-running program, however, returns an extremely large amount of problem insight and experience, well worth the effort required to get the problem running.

### Hybrid Computers

The accuracy of the calculations on a digital computer can often be increased through double precision

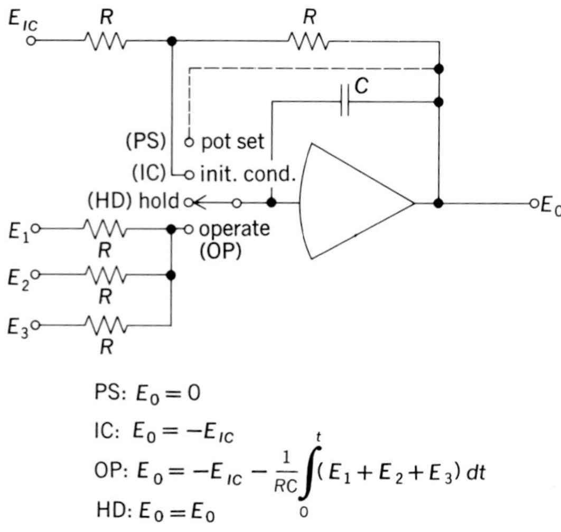


**Fig. 24. Integrator controls.**

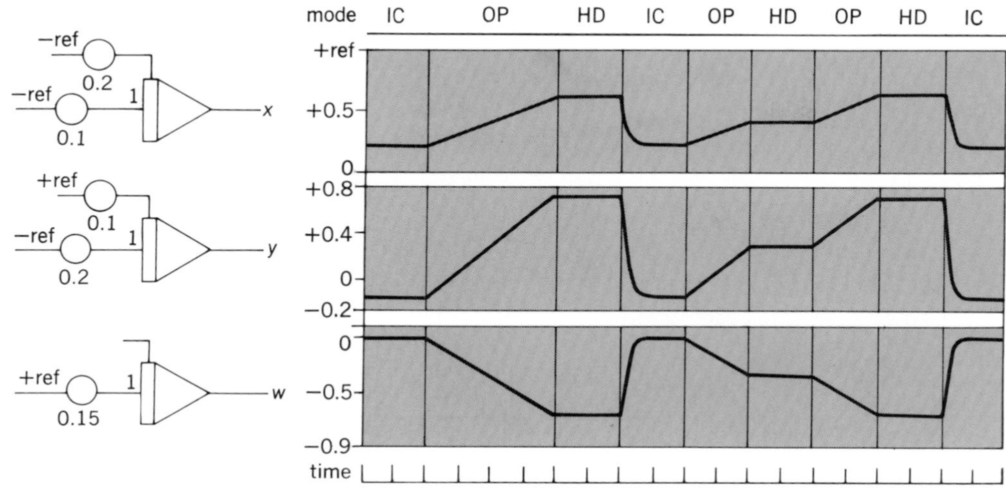


**Fig. 25. Integrator control: outputs from three integrators are recorded with respect to time, showing how they depend on the computer control modes, integration initial conditions, and integrand inputs.**

techniques and more precise algorithms, but at the expense of extended solution time, due to the computer's serial nature of operation. Also, the more computational steps there are to be done, the longer the digital computer will take to do them. On the other hand, the basic solution speed is very rapid on the analog computer because of its parallel nature, but increasing problem complexity demands larger computer size. Thus, for the analog computer the time remains the same regardless of the complexity of the problem, but the size of the computer required grows with the problem.

Interaction between the user and the computer during the course of any calculation, with the ability to vary parameters during computer runs, is a highly desirable and insight-generating part of computer usage. This hands-on interaction with the computed responses is simple to achieve with analog computers. For digital computers, interaction usually takes place through a computer keyboard terminal, between runs, or in an on-line stop-go mode. An often-utilized system combines the speed and interaction possibilities of an analog computer with the accuracy and programming flexibility of a digital computer. This combination is specifically designed into the hybrid computer.

A modern analog-hybrid console is depicted in **Fig. 26**. It contains the typical analog components plus a second patchboard area to include programmable, parallel logic circuits using high-speed gates for the functions of AND, NAND, OR, and NOR, as well as flip-flops, registers, and counters. The mode switches in the integrators are interfaced with the digital computer to permit fast iterations of dynamic runs under digital computer control. As shown in **Fig. 27**, data flow in many ways and formats between the analog computer with its fast, parallel circuits and the digital computer with its sequential, logic-controlled program. Special high-speed analog-to-digital and digital-to-analog converters translate between the continuous signal

**Fig. 26. Analog-hybrid laboratory equipped with a HYSHARE 600 system. This system can include up to six analog computer consoles and one or more digital processors for multiuser, multitask applications. (*Electronic Associates, Inc.*)**

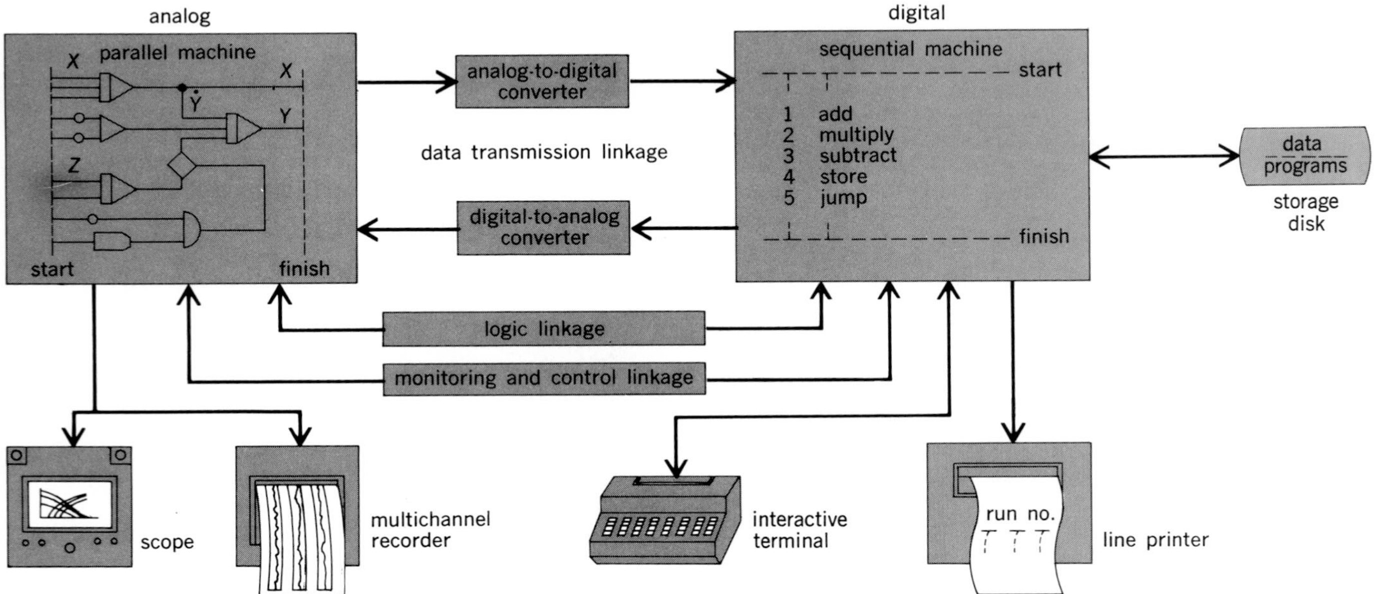


**Fig. 27. Block diagram representation of a hybrid analog-to-digital computer.**

representations of variables in the analog domain and the numerical representations of the digital computer. Control and logic signals are more directly compatible and require only level and timing compatibility. *See* ANALOG-TO-DIGITAL CONVERTER; BOOLEAN ALGEBRA; DIGITAL-TO-ANALOG CONVERTER.

The programming of hybrid models is a more complex challenge than described above, requiring the user to consider the parallel action of the analog computer interlaced with the step-by-step computations progression in the digital computer. For example, in simulating the mission of a space vehicle, the capsule control dynamics will typically be handled on the analog computer in continuous form, but interfaced with the digital computer, where the navigational trajectory is calculated. *See* COMPUTER.

*Per A. Holst*

## Analog-to-digital converter

A device for converting the information contained in the value or magnitude of some characteristics of an input signal, compared to a standard or reference, to information in the form of discrete states of a signal, usually with numerical values assigned to the various combinations of discrete states of the signal.

Analog-to-digital (A/D) converters are used to transform analog information, such as audio signals or measurements of physical variables (for example, temperature, force, or shaft rotation) into a form suitable for digital handling, which might involve any of these operations: (1) processing by a computer or by logic circuits, including arithmetical operations, comparison, sorting, ordering, and code conversion, (2) storage until ready for further handling, (3) display in numerical or graphical form, and (4) transmission.

If a wide-range analog signal can be converted, with adequate frequency, to an appropriate number of two-level digits, or bits, the digital representation of the signal can be transmitted through a noisy medium without relative degradation of the fine structure of the original signal. *See* COMPUTER GRAPHICS; DATA COMMUNICATIONS; DIGITAL COMPUTER.

**Concepts and structure.** Conversion involves quantizing and encoding. Quantizing means partitioning the analog signal range into a number of discrete quanta and determining to which quantum the input signal belongs. Encoding means assigning a unique digital code to each quantum and determining the code that corresponds to the input signal. The most common system is binary, in which there are $2^n$ quanta (where $n$ is some whole number), numbered consecutively; the code is a set of $n$ physical two-valued levels or bits (1 or 0) corresponding to the binary number associated with the signal quantum. *See* BIT.

**Figure 1** shows a typical three-bit binary representation of a range of input signals, partitioned into eight quanta. For example, a signal in the vicinity of 3/8 full scale (between 5/16 and 7/16 will be coded 011 (binary 3). *See* NUMBER SYSTEMS.

Conceptually, the conversion can be made to take place in any kind of medium: electrical, mechanical, fluid, optical, and so on (for example, shaft-rotation-to-optical); but by far the most commonly employed form of A/D converters comprises those devices that convert electrical voltages or currents to coded sets of binary electrical levels (for example, +5 V or 0 V) is simultaneous (parallel) or pulse-train (serial) form, as shown in **Fig. 2**. The serial output is not always made available.

The converter depicted in Fig. 2 converts the analog input to a five-digit "word." If the coding is bi-

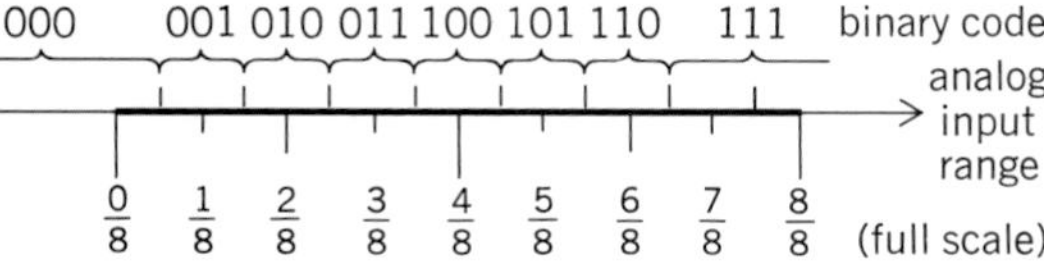


**Fig. 1. A three-bit binary representation of a range of input signals.**

nary, the first digit (most significant bit, abbreviated MSB) has a weight of 1/2 full scale, the second 1/4 full scale, and so on, down to the $n$th digit (least-significant bit, abbreviated LSB), which has a weight of $2^{-n}$ of full scale (1/32 in this example). Thus, for the output word shown, the analog input must be given approximately by the equation shown. The

$$\frac{16}{32}+\frac{0}{32}+\frac{4}{32}+\frac{2}{32}+\frac{0}{32} = \frac{22}{32} = \frac{11}{16}\text{ FS (full scale)}$$

number of bits, $n$, characterizes the resolution of a converter. The **table** translates bits into other conventional measures of resolution in a binary system.

Figure 2 also shows a commonly used configuration of connections to an A/D converter: the analog signal and reference inputs; the parallel and serial digital outputs; the leads from the power supply, which provides the required energy for operation; and two control leads—a start-conversion input and a status-indicating output (busy) that indicates when a conversion is in progress. The reference voltage or current is often developed within the converter.

Second in importance to the binary code and its many variations is the binary-coded decimal (BCD), which is used rather widely, especially when the encoded material is to be displayed in numerical form. In BCD, each digit of a radix-10 number is represented by a four-digit binary subgroup. For example, the BCD code for 379 is 0011 0111 1001. The output of the A/D converter used in digital panel meters is usually BCD.

**Techniques.** There are many techniques used for A/D conversion, ranging from simple voltage-level comparators to sophisticated closed-loop systems, depending on the input level, output format, control features, and the desired speed, resolution, and accuracy. The two most popular techniques are dual-slope conversion and successive-approximations conversion.

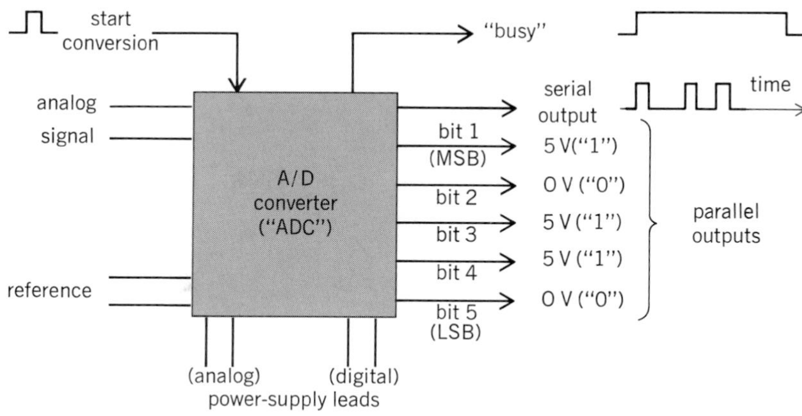


**Fig. 2. Basic diagram of an analog-to-digital converter, showing parallel and serial (return-to-zero) output formats for code 10110.**

***Dual slope.*** Dual-slope converters have high resolution and low noise sensitivity; they operate at relatively low speeds—usually a few conversions per second. They are primarily used for direct dc measurements requiring digital readout; the technique is the basis of the most widely used approach to the design of digital panel meters.

**Figure 3*a*** is a simplified block diagram of a dual-slope converter. The input is integrated for a period of time determined by a clock-pulse generator and counter (Fig. 3*b*). The final value of the signal integral becomes the initial condition for integration of the reference in the opposite sense, while the clock output is counted. When the net integral is zero, the count stops. Since the integral "up" of the input over a fixed time ($N_0$ counts) is equal to the integral "down" of the fixed reference, the ratio of the number of counts of the variable period to that of the fixed period is equal to the ratio of the average value of the signal to the reference.

***Successive approximations.*** Successive-approximations conversion is a high-speed technique used prin-

**Binary resolution equivalents***

| Bit | $2^{-n}$ | $1/2^n$ (fraction) | dB (decibels) | $1/2^n$ (decimal) | % | Parts per million |
|---|---|---|---|---|---|---|
| FS† | $2^0$ | 1 | 0 | 1.0 | 100 | 1,000,000 |
| MSB‡ | $2^{-1}$ | 1/2 | −6 | 0.5 | 50 | 500,000 |
| 2 | $2^{-2}$ | 1/4 | −12 | 0.25 | 25 | 250,000 |
| 3 | $2^{-3}$ | 1/8 | −18.1 | 0.125 | 12.5 | 125,000 |
| 4 | $2^{-4}$ | 1/16 | −24.1 | 0.0625 | 6.2 | 62,500 |
| 5 | $2^{-5}$ | 1/32 | −30.1 | 0.03125 | 3.1 | 31,250 |
| 6 | $2^{-6}$ | 1/64 | −36.1 | 0.015625 | 1.6 | 15,625 |
| 7 | $2^{-7}$ | 1/128 | −42.1 | 0.007812 | 0.8 | 7,812 |
| 8 | $2^{-8}$ | 1/256 | −48.2 | 0.003906 | 0.4 | 3,906 |
| 9 | $2^{-9}$ | 1/512 | −54.2 | 0.001953 | 0.2 | 1,953 |
| 10 | $2^{-10}$ | 1/1024 | −60.2 | 0.0009766 | 0.1 | 977 |
| 11 | $2^{-11}$ | 1/2048 | −66.2 | 0.00048828 | 0.05 | 488 |
| 12 | $2^{-12}$ | 1/4096 | −72.2 | 0.00024414 | 0.024 | 244 |
| 13 | $2^{-13}$ | 1/8192 | −78.3 | 0.00012207 | 0.012 | 122 |
| 14 | $2^{-14}$ | 1/16,384 | −84.3 | 0.000061035 | 0.06 | 61 |
| 15 | $2^{-15}$ | 1/32,768 | −90.3 | 0.0000305176 | 0.003 | 31 |
| 16 | $2^{-16}$ | 1/65,536 | −96.3 | 0.0000152588 | 0.0015 | 15 |
| 17 | $2^{-17}$ | 1/131,072 | −102.3 | 0.00000762939 | 0.0008 | 7.6 |
| 18 | $2^{-18}$ | 1/262,144 | −108.4 | 0.000003814697 | 0.0004 | 3.8 |
| 19 | $2^{-19}$ | 1/524,288 | −114.4 | 0.000001907349 | 0.0002 | 1.9 |
| 20 | $2^{-20}$ | 1/1,048,576 | −120.4 | 0.0000009536743 | 0.0001 | 0.95 |

*From D. H. Sheingold (ed.), *Analog-Digital Conversion Handbook,* Analog Devices, Inc., 1972.
†Full scale.
‡Most significant bit.

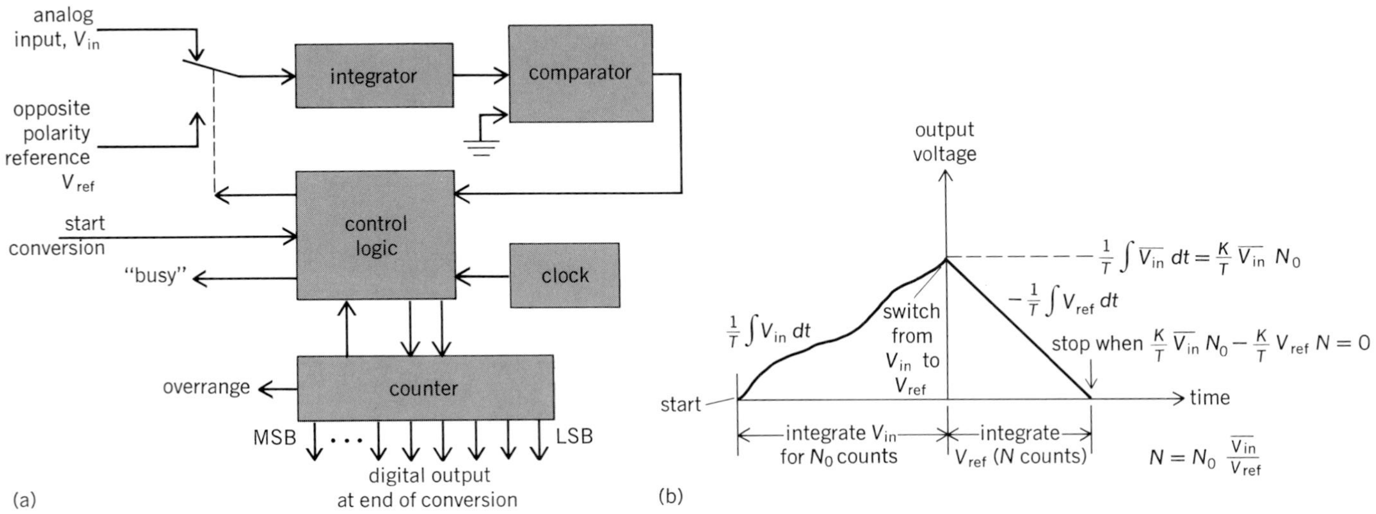


**Fig. 3. Example of a dual-slope conversion. (*a*) Block diagram of converter. (*b*) Integrator output. Here, *k* is a constant, and *T* is the *RC* (resistor-capacitor) time constant of the integrator.**

cipally in data-acquisition and computer-interface systems. **Figure 4*a*** is a simplified block diagram of a successive-approximations converter. In a manner analogous to the operation of an apothecary's scale with a set of binary weights, the input is ''weighed'' against a set of successively smaller fractions of the reference, produced by a digital-to-analog (D/A) converter that reflects the number in the output register. *See* Digital-to-analog converter.

First, the MSB is tried (1/2 full scale). If the signal is less than the MSB, the MSB code is returned to zero; if the signal is equal to or greater than the MSB, the MSB code is latched in the output register (Fig. 4*b*). The second bit is tried (1/4 full scale). If the signal is less than 1/4 or 3/4, depending on the previous choice, bit 2 is set to zero; if the signal is equal to or greater than 1/4 or 3/4, bit 2 is retained in the output register. The third bit is tried (1/8 full scale). If the signal is less than 1/8, 3/8, 5/8, or 7/8, depending on previous choices, bit 2 is set to zero; otherwise, it is accepted. The trial continues until the contribution of the least-significant bit has been weighed and either accepted or rejected. The conversion is then complete. The digital code latched in the output register is the digital equivalent of the analog input signal.

**Physical electronics.** The earliest A/D converters were large rack-panel chassis-type modules using vacuum tubes, requiring about 1.4 $ft^3$ (1/25 $m^3$) of space and many watts of power. Since then, they have become smaller in size and cost, evolving through circuit-board, encapsulated-module, and hybrid construction, with improved speed and resolution. Single-chip 12-bit A/D converters with the abil-

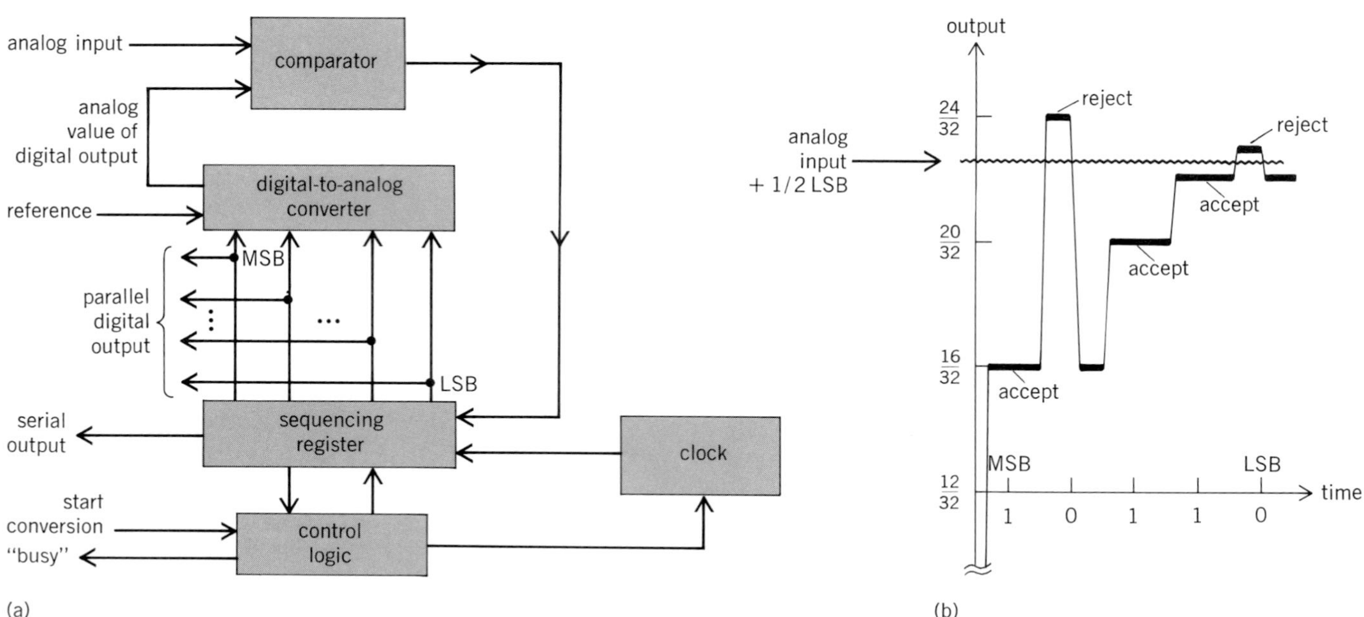


**Fig. 4. Successive-approximations conversion. (*a*) Block diagram of converter. (*b*) Digital-to-analog converter output for the example in Fig. 2.**

ity to interface with microprocessors are now available in small integrated-circuit packages. Integrated-circuit A/D converters, with 6-bit and better resolution and conversion rates to beyond 50 MHz, are also commercially available. *SEE MICROPROCESSOR.*

*Daniel H. Sheingold*

***Bibliography.*** D. J. Dooley (ed.), *Data Conversion Integrated Circuits*, 1980; B. M. Gordon et al., *Data-Conversion Systems Digest*, 1977; *IEEE Transactions on Circuits and Systems*, special issue on analog/digital conversion, AS-25, July 1978; D. Sheingold (ed.), *Analog-Digital Conversion Notes*, 1977; E. Zuch (ed.), *Data Acquisition and Conversion Handbook,* 1979.

## Angle modulation

Modulation in which the instantaneous angle varies in proportion to the modulating waveform. When used in an analog manner, it is referred to as either frequency modulation (FM) or phase modulation (PM), depending upon whether the instantaneous frequency or instantaneous phase varies with the modulation. When used in a digital modulation format, it is referred to as either frequency-shift keying (FSK) or phase-shift keying (PSK). Both FSK and PSK can be used with either a binary or an $M$-ary alphabet, where $M$ is an integer greater than 2. Indeed, the most common forms of PSK correspond to an input alphabet size of either 2 or 4, while for FSK alphabets of two, four, or eight symbols are typically employed. *SEE FREQUENCY MODULATION; MODULATION; PHASE MODULATION.*

*Laurence B. Milstein*

***Bibliography.*** M. Schwartz, *Information Transmission, Modulation and Noise*, 3d ed., 1980; H. Taub and D. L. Schilling, *Principles of Communication Systems*, 1971; R. E. Ziemer and W. H. Tranter, *Principles of Communications*, 1976.

## Antenna

A portion of a radio system especially designed to couple electromagnetic energy between free space and transmission lines. At a radio transmitter the antenna couples energy from the transmitter circuits into free space, thus serving to radiate the transmitter's output as radio waves. At the radio receiver the antenna couples energy from the radio waves into the receiver's circuits. The same antenna structure functions equally well for transmission or reception. Because of this reciprocity, all antennas can serve for either transmission or reception; however, in describing antenna operation it is often more direct to describe the radiation action, with the understanding that reception is the reciprocal. *SEE RECIPROCITY PRINCIPLE.*

Despite this reciprocity antennas used for transmission may differ significantly from those used for reception because of the power levels at which they operate. An antenna for transmitting to a major portion of the world or to a space vehicle must handle large powers; the antenna for receiving from radar reflections or from communication satellites handles negligible power. For these reasons antennas are classified by use; they may also be classified by operating frequency. Antennas for very low frequencies may be a mile long, whereas antennas for very high frequencies may be only a few feet long. More basically, if antenna size is measured in units of the wavelength of the frequency at which the antenna operates, structures that differ greatly in size can be described in similar terms. In describing antennas here, their principal dimensions in wavelengths will be given.

**Mechanism of radiation.** For an antenna to radiate, it must contain charges that oscillate. Such a charge is the electron. Because no other nearby charges oscillate to counteract the effect of the electron, its field extends infinitely into space. This field contains two components: an electric field $E$ and a magnetic field $H$. Energy stored in the electric field when the electron is stationary equals energy in the magnetic field when the electron is moving most rapidly. Basically, the changing electric field induces an adjacent magnetic field, and the changing magnetic field induces an adjacent electric field. The result of this continuing energy exchange is radiation.

**Figure 1** is an elementary graphical representation of the radiating electric field while a single electron oscillates on a short, thin conductor. At the top of the figure, one line of the electric field terminates at the

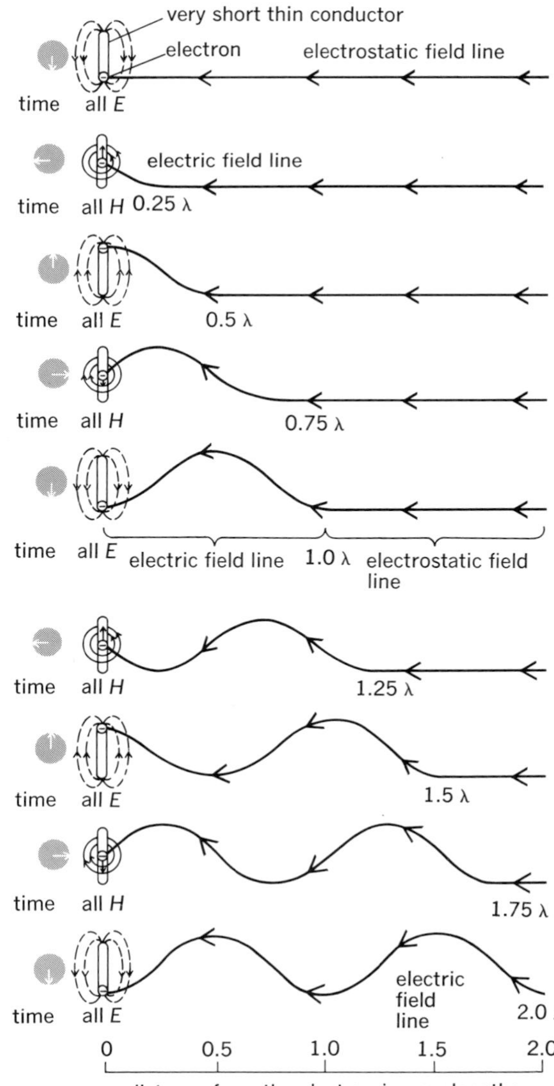


**Fig. 1. Electric *E* and magnetic *H* fields of an oscillating electron.**

electron. Successive drawings down the figure show this field line as the electron oscillates on the conductor. Motion of the electron displaces the line. This displacement travels along the field line, moving in the figure to the right, with the velocity of light. After the electron has completed one cycle of oscillation on its conductor, the initial displacement has traveled one wavelength λ from the conductor.

More rigorously, the oscillating electron has an induction field which decreases rapidly with distance (**Fig. 2**). Energy in this field flows alternately away from and toward the electron and never escapes into space. The magnetic component of this field is a maximum when the electric component is zero. In the radiation field, which extends indefinitely into space, energy flows only outward at all instants of time and all locations in space; magnetic and electric components of this field pass through zero together (**Fig. 3**).

Along with the oscillating negative charge, whose fields are shown in Figs. 1–3, is a positive charge. If all oscillating charges on a short, thin conductor, called a doublet, are considered, the total electromagnetic field is found to contain terms that decrease with distance in the ratios $1/r^3$ and $1/r^2$ in the induction field and $1/r$ in the radiation field. The real part of the resultant field near the doublet is shown in **Fig. 4**. The $1/r$ decrease in radiation field as it spreads out into space from the doublet is due to the greater area of the sphere that bounds it. *SEE ELECTROMAGNETIC WAVE TRANSMISSION.*

The elemental radiator can be either a short electric device or a small current device. If infinitesimally small, their far fields are as given in **Fig. 5**. Even if

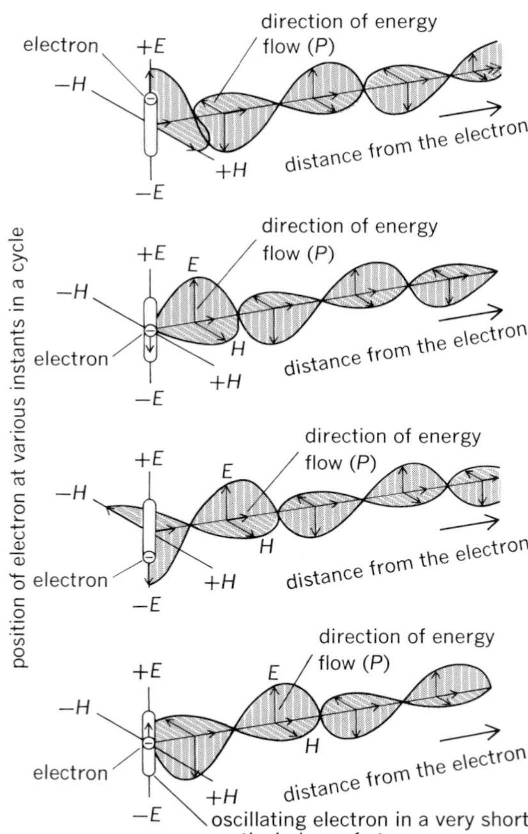

**Fig. 3. Radiation field of an oscillating electron.**

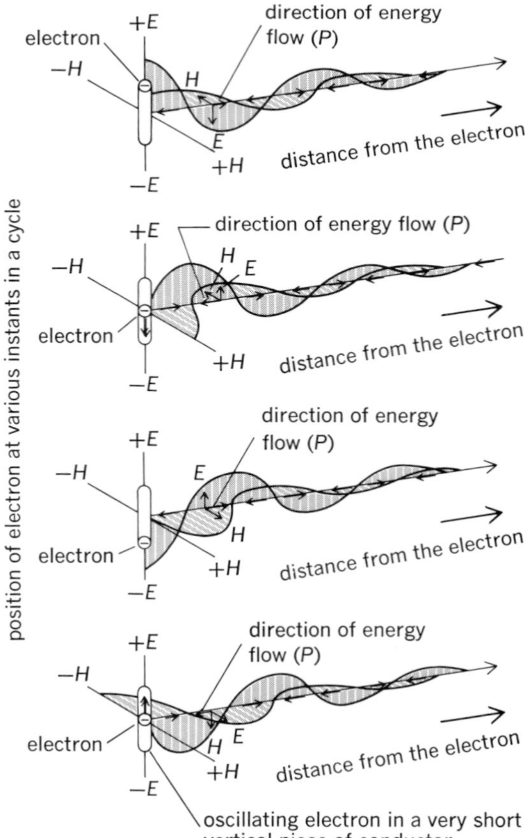

**Fig. 2. Induction field of an oscillating electron.**

the radiators have maximum dimensions of 0.1 λ, the equations are useful approximations for short electric conductors and small current loops.

**Pattern shape.** As Fig. 5 shows, a small electric or magnetic dipole radiates no energy along its axis, the contour of constant energy being a toroid. This contour in space, called the radiation pattern, is usually the most basic requirement of an antenna. The purpose of a transmitting antenna is to direct power into a specified region; whereas the purpose of a receiving antenna is to accept signals from a specified direction. In the case of a vehicle, such as an automobile with a car radio, the receiving antenna needs a nondirectional pattern so that it can accept signals from variously located stations, and from any one station, as the automobile moves. The antenna of a broadcast station may be directional; for example, a station in a coastal city would have an antenna that concentrated most of the power over the populated land. The antenna for transmission to or from a communication satellite should have a narrow radiation pattern directed toward the satellite for efficient operation, preferably radiating essentially zero power in other directions to avoid interference. Each special application of radio waves has its unique requirements for radiation patterns. *SEE RADAR.*

For highly directional beam-type patterns, the concept of directivity is useful in the description of pattern shape. A simple approximation is based on beam area $B$ at the half-power beam width of the pattern, that is, at the angles to the sides of the central beam axis where the radiated power is half the power radiated along the beam axis. Beam area $B$ is defined

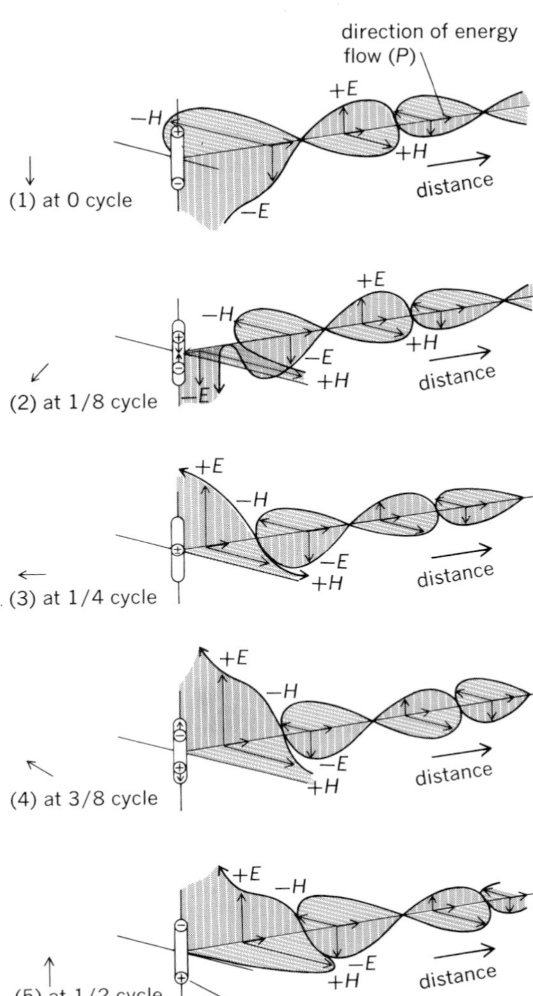


**Fig. 4. Electromagnetic field near an oscillating doublet.**

as the solid angle through which all power would be radiated if the power were constant over the complete solid angle and at maximum level. For these hypothetical conditions directivity $D$ is defined as the surface of the sphere ($4\pi$ radians) divided by beam area $B$ in radians, as shown in Eq. (1). If the beam is

$$D = \frac{4\pi}{B} \tag{1}$$

described as its width in degrees in two orthogonal directions, $D = 41{,}253/\theta\phi$, where $\theta$ and $\phi$ are the two beam widths. These approximations neglect power in secondary lobes and losses in the antenna.

Total radiated power $P_r$ from an antenna can be computed by integrating the energy flow outward through an imaginary sphere surrounding the antenna system. For a hypothetical spherical radiation pattern surface which has a radius of $r$, the radiated power $P_r$ is given by Eq. (2), where $E_s$ is the field strength of

$$P_r = 4\pi\, E_s^2 r^2 / R_c \tag{2}$$

the radiated electric field at the surface of the imaginary sphere, and $R_c$ is the characteristic resistance of free space. If radiated power is 1 kW, field strength $E_s$ at the surface of the imaginary sphere 1 mi (1.609 km) in radius is 107.6 mV/m. This uniform spherical radiator has no directivity and hence no gain with a lossless antenna system. It is referred to as an isotropic radiator and is used as the standard for comparison of the gain of directional antennas.

By analogy one can think of a sphere of given volume as representing the total radiated energy. Field strength at every point on the surface of the sphere is the same as represented by the constant radius. If the sphere is deformed with its volume held constant, the distance from the origin to the surface is longer in some directions and shorter in others. These distances represent field strengths at their various locations on the surface. By the deformation, field strength is gained in a desired direction, although it is decreased in another direction. This antenna gain can be defined as the ratio of maximum field strength from the antenna of interest relative to the field strength that would be radiated from a lossless isotropic antenna fed with the same input power. In relation to directivity $D$, gain $G$ can be expressed as in Eq. (3), where $\eta$ is antenna efficiency.

$$G = \eta D \tag{3}$$

**Efficiency.** Antenna efficiency $\eta$ is defined as the radiated power divided by the input power to the antenna. Input power $P_i$ supplies antenna system losses $P_l$ and the radiated power $P_r$. This is shown by Eq. (4). Losses in an antenna system take place in the

$$\eta = \frac{P_r}{P_l + P_r} \tag{4}$$

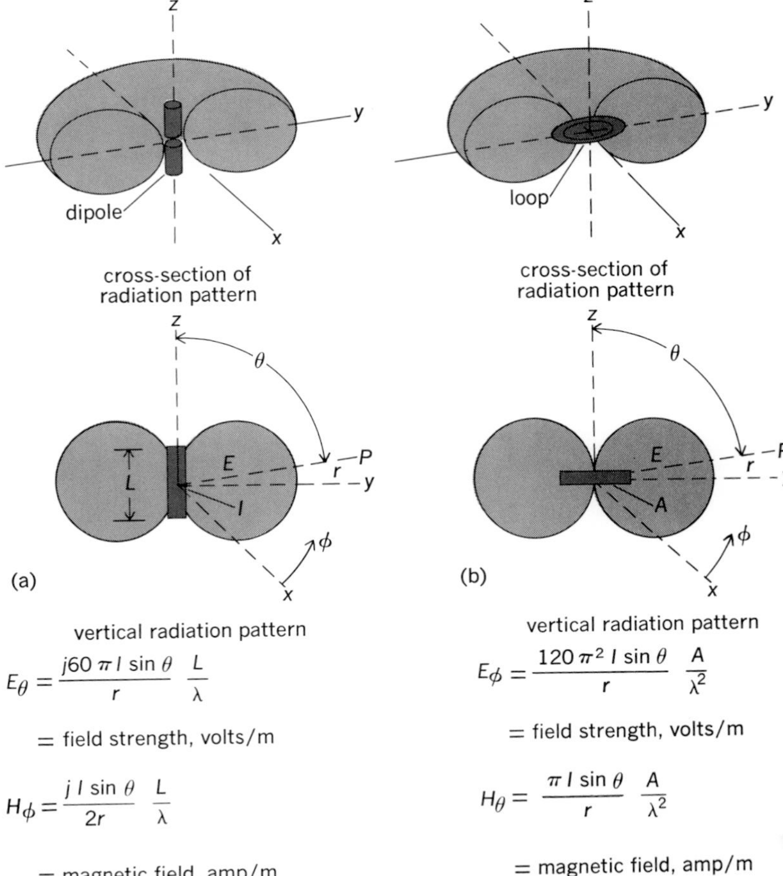


**Fig. 5. Far-field patterns. (*a*) Small electric dipole. (*b*) Small magnetic dipole.**

resistance of the transmission line to the antenna, the coupling network between line and antenna, antenna conductors, insulators, and the ground system. For electrically small antennas even small loss resistances can significantly reduce the efficiency. In the design of transmitting antennas, the heating effect of losses must also be considered together with losses due to corona.

**Polarization.** As shown in Fig. 4, the plane of the electric field depends on the direction in which the electric charge moves on the antenna. The electric field is in a plane orthogonal to the axis of a magnetic dipole (Fig. 5). This dependence of the plane of the radiated electromagnetic wave on the orientation and type of antenna is termed polarization. By combining fields from electric and magnetic dipoles that have a common center, the radiated field can be elliptically polarized; by control of the contribution from each dipole, any ellipticity from plane polarization to circular polarization can be produced. A receiving antenna requires the same polarization as the wave that it is to intercept.

**Impedance.** The input impedance to an antenna is the ratio at its terminals, where the transmission line and transmitter or receiver are connected, of voltage to current. If the antenna is tuned to resonance at the operating frequency, the input impedance will be a pure resistance; otherwise it will also have a reactance component. For simple antennas, input or self-impedance can be computed from a knowledge of radiation pattern and current distribution. For more complicated radiating structures, input impedance is usually measured, computing values serving only as a guide.

To visualize antenna impedance, consider a thin conductor transmission line with sinusoidal current distribution, as shown in **Fig. 6**; the lines can be opened out to form an antenna. Input impedance of the quarter-wave line in Fig. 6*a* will be a low resistance, because the transmission line is resonant and because the opposing currents prevent radiation. SEE TRANSMISSION LINES.

However, as the conductors are partially opened out in Fig. 6*b*, current distribution will remain substantially the same; the input impedance will still be resistive because of resonance, but its value will be larger because the opposing currents are farther apart and there is now an inphase component. Finally, when the transmission line is completely opened out in Fig. 6*c*, input impedance is pure resistance because of resonance and a maximum of 73 ohms, because only the inphase component of current remains. The result is a very practical free-space half-wave antenna often used as a standard reference antenna. If one-half of this antenna is operated above ground (Fig. 6*d*), one has the practical quarter-wave antenna, which is also used as a reference standard with 36.5 ohms of input resistance.

If the input terminals of the half-wave antenna (Fig. 6*c*) are moved from the center toward the end of the resonant antenna, the input impedance remains a pure resistance but can be increased from 73 ohms at the center to a high value near the end.

From Fig. 6*d* the electrical phenomena can be visualized. At the base of the antenna, current $I$ is high while voltage $E$ is low. Because impedance $Z_{in}$ is the complex ratio of $E/I$, at the base of the antenna $Z_{in}$ is low. If the feed point is moved up the antenna where current $I$ is lower and voltage $E$ is higher, the driving-point impedance becomes appreciably higher.

In addition to this effect on input impedance by the standing wave on the antenna, the power radiated into space affects input impedance. Although power radiates from the whole antenna, this radiated power enters at the feed point. Here, radiated power, like all electrical power, can be expressed as the product of in-phase components of voltage $E_r$ and current $I_r$. The ratio $E_r/I_r$ of these values defines a resistance $R_r$, which is termed radiation resistance. For a linear conductor in free space carrying uniform current over its length $s$, which is very short compared to the operating wavelength $\lambda$, resistance $R$ in ohms is shown by Eq. (5).

$$R = 80\pi^2 s^2/\lambda^2 \tag{5}$$

As a component of a receiving circuit, the antenna may be represented by Thévenin's or Norton's equivalence theorems. In the former the representation is a simple series circuit containing impedance, and also containing voltage induced from the incoming wave. Useful power is calculated in terms of the resulting current in the resistance of the load circuit. SEE NETWORK THEORY; THÉVENIN'S THEOREM (ELECTRIC NETWORKS).

If a current element of length $s$ is placed in a field $E$ parallel to it, the root-mean-square voltage induced is $E_s$. If the element is tuned, the available power $P$ which it captures is shown by Eq. (6), and is independent of $s$. The average power per square meter $P_{av}$ in the plane wave is shown in Eq. (7), which indi-

$$P = \frac{E^2\lambda^2}{320\pi^2} \tag{6}$$

$$P_{av} = \frac{E^2}{120\pi} \tag{7}$$

cates that the effective area of the element is $3\lambda^2/8\pi$.

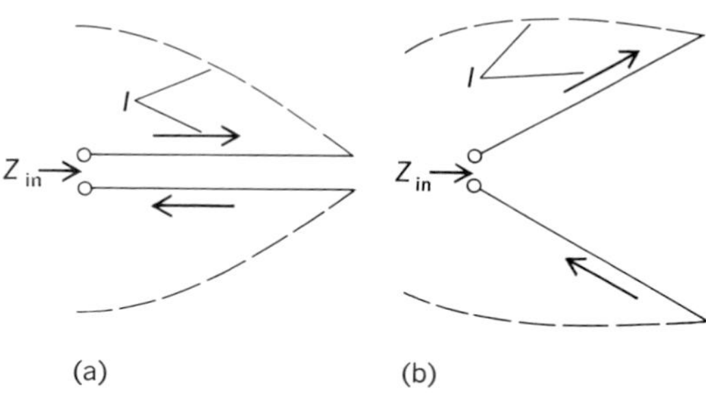


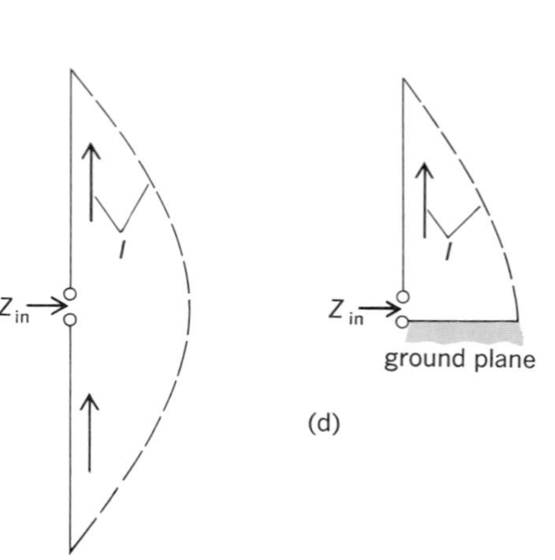


**Fig. 6. Antenna as an opened-out transmission line. (*a*) Standing wave on quarter-wave open circuit transmission line. (*b*) Standing wave on partially opened-out transmission line. (*c*) Standing wave on half-wave antenna. (*d*) Standing wave on quarter-wave antenna.**

If the reactive component of antenna impedance is appreciable, techniques similar to those used in other transmission circuits are required to obtain maximum power; that is, the impedance of the connected circuit must be conjugate to that of the antenna. Reflections caused by a mismatched antenna can cause trouble at a distant point in receiving circuitry. The solution may be to obtain a better match or to employ a nonreciprocal device which discriminates against backward-traveling waves.

When more than one antenna is used in an array, input impedance is called a driving-point impedance because it contains self-impedance plus mutual-impedance terms due to current in other elements of the array. In an array of $n$ elements, the driving-point impedance $Z_k$ of the $k$th element can be written as in Eq. (8), where $I_n$ is current in the $n$th element, $Z_{kn}$ is

$$Z_k = \frac{V_k}{I_k} = \frac{I_1}{I_k} Z_{k1} + \frac{I_2}{I_k} Z_{k2} + \cdots + Z_{kk} + \cdots + \frac{I_n}{I_k} Z_{kn} \qquad (8)$$

mutual impedance between the $k$th element and the $n$th element, and $V_k$ is the input voltage to the $k$th element. From a family of such equations it is possible, with a knowledge of impedances and currents, to solve a set of mesh circuit equations for all of the driving-point impedances. This information is necessary for proper design of a directional-antenna feeder system, such as is commonly used in the standard broadcast band.

Because of interaction between elements of an array, a distinction is made between a driven element to which a transmission line directly connects and a parasitic element that couples into the array only through its mutual electromagnetic coupling to driven elements. Driving-point impedance and radiation pattern are controlled by the tuning and spacing of parasitic elements relative to driven elements. If a parasitic element reduces radiation in its direction from a driven element, it is called a reflector; if it enhances radiation in its direction, it is called a director. SEE YAGI-UDA ANTENNA.

Any conductor, such as a guy wire, in the vicinity of a primary or driven antenna element may act as a parasitic element and affect antenna impedance and radiation pattern.

**Bandwidth.** Bandwidth of an antenna is related to its input impedance characteristics. Bandwidth may be limited by pattern shape, polarization characteristics, and impedance performance. Bandwidth is critically dependent on the value of $Q$; hence the larger the amount of stored reactive energy relative to radiated resistive energy, the less will be the bandwidth. SEE Q (ELECTRICITY).

For efficient operation of low standing-wave ratio at the antenna input terminals is necessary over the operating frequency range. Usually the input impedance will vary in both resistance and reactance over the desired frequency interval. It is, therefore, of interest to determine the bandwidth that can be achieved for a given standing-wave ratio. For a particular antenna the bandwidth that can be obtained by compensating networks has a theoretical limit; therefore, if a wider band is required, it becomes necessary to select antenna types with the inherent characteristic of wider bandwidth.

There are two principal approaches to frequency-independent antennas. The first is to shape the antenna so that it can be specified entirely by angles; hence when dimensions are expressed in wavelengths, they are the same at every frequency. Planar and conical equiangular spiral antennas adhere to this principle. The second principle depends upon complementary shapes so that if, for example, an antenna that is cut from a flat conducting sheet is exactly the same shape as the part removed, its input impedance will be frequency-independent. Many log-periodic anten-

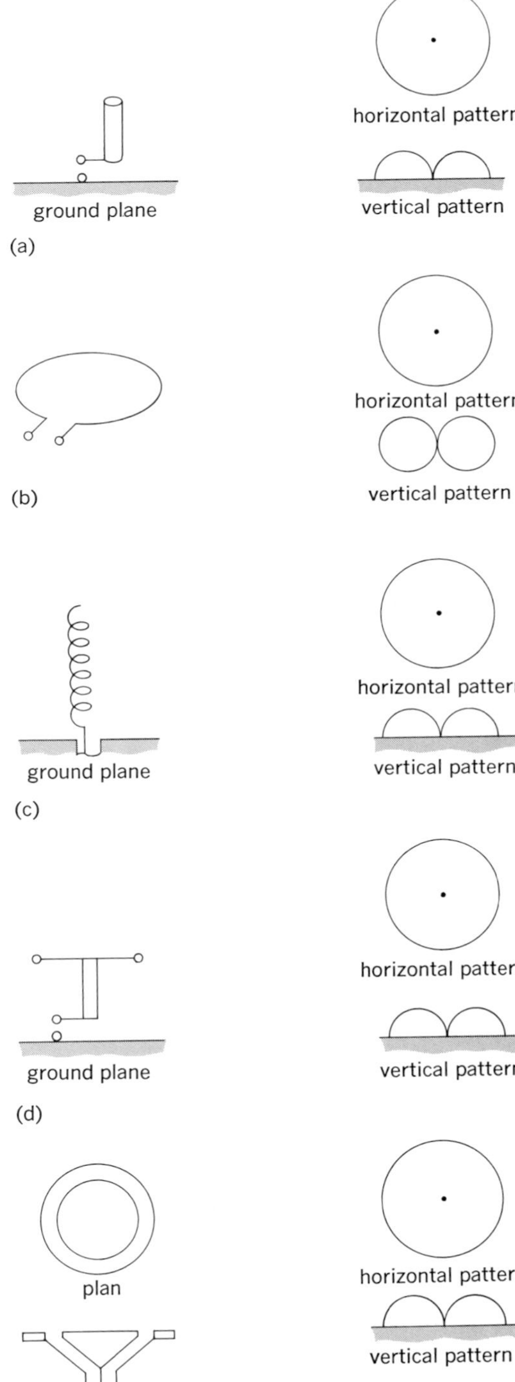


**Fig. 7.** Typical electrically small antennas. (*a*) Monopole. (*b*) Small loop. (*c*) Helical monopole. (*d*) Top loaded monopole. (*e*) Annular slot.

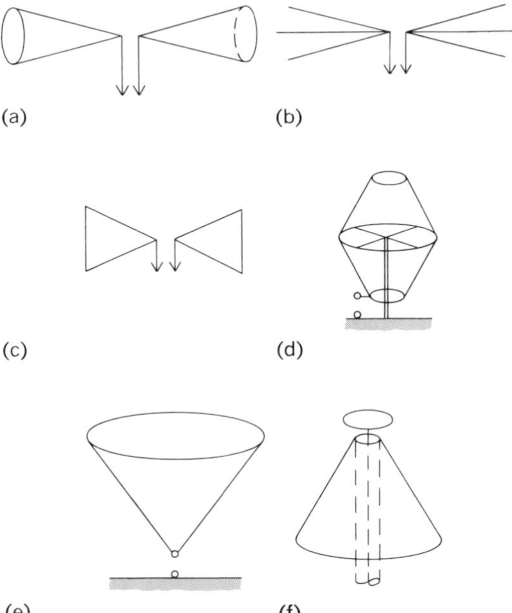

**Fig. 8.** Broadband dipole and monopole antennas. (*a*) Conical broadband dipole. (*b*) UHF-TV broadband dipole, built of fanned wires. (c) UHF-TV broadband dipole, built of flat sheet metal. (*d*) Conical monopole. (e) Inverted discone. (*f*) HF discone.

nas employ this second principle, and before the structure shape changes very much, when measured in wavelengths, the structure repeats itself. By combining periodicity and angle concepts, antenna structures of very large bandwidths become feasible.

**Electrically small antennas.** Antennas whose mechanical dimensions are short compared to their operating wave-lengths are usually characterized by low radiation resistance and large reactance. This combination results in a high $Q$ and consequently a narrow bandwidth. Current distribution on a short conductor is sinusoidal with zero current at the free end, but because the conductor is so short electrically, typically less than 30° of a sine wave, current distribution will be essentially linear. By end loading to give a constant current distribution, the radiation resistance is increased by 4 times, thus greatly improving the efficiency but not noticeably altering the pattern.

An end-fed monopole antenna (**Fig. 7***a*) is common at very low frequencies for long-range communication, commercial broadcasting, and mobile use. The small loop antenna is used extensively for direction finding and navigation (Fig. 7*b*). Where height is a limiting factor at higher frequencies, the monopole height can be reduced by forming the conductor into a helical whip (Fig. 7*c*) or by top loading (Fig. 7*d*).

Where no height is permitted, a slot is used. Just as the magnetic loop is related to the electric dipole, so a slot in a conductive surface is related to a conductive wire in space. The conductive surface is usually the outside surface of a wave guide within which the radio energy travels. A slot in the wave guide allows the energy to radiate. Typically the slot is narrow and half a wavelength long. Configuration of the electric field radiated from the slot is the same as the magnetic field from a wire of like dimensions; thus one is the dual of the other (Fig. 7*e*). The slot may be fed by a transmission line connected across its narrow dimension, by a resonant cavity behind it, or (as mentioned above) from a wave guide. Because it is flush with a metallic surface, a slot antenna is advantageous in aircraft.

**Resonant antennas.** Dipoles and monopoles illustrate resonant antennas which have an approximate sinusoidal current distribution and a pure resistance at their input terminals. However, when the ratio of diameter to length is small, the input impedance varies rapidly and precludes their use as broadband antennas. The impedance bandwidth limitation can be mitigated by increasing the diameter to form a cylinder or by using conical conductors (**Fig. 8**).

Input resistance of a horizontal dipole varies as the antenna height increases. However, as the dipole is moved farther from the ground toward free space, its impedance tends toward 73 ohms. By folding the dipole this impedance can be increased by $n^2$, where $n$ is the number of conductors; hence by using two conductors a 300-ohm line can be used to feed the antenna, or by using three conductors a 600-ohm line can be used.

**Nonresonant antennas.** Long-wire antennas, or traveling-wave antennas, are usually one or more wavelengths long and are untuned or nonresonant.

***Horizontal single-conductor type.*** The radiation pattern of a long conductor in free space depends upon its length in wavelengths. A 0.5-λ conductor will radiate broadside, but as it is made longer the pattern splits, the major lobe coming closer to, but never reaching, the direction of the conductor. A cross section of the pattern is a figure of revolution around the conductor as an axis.

When a horizontal unterminated line with standing electric current waves of uniform amplitude is placed above perfect ground (**Fig. 9***a*), it has a radiation pattern symmetrical about the center with its major lobes

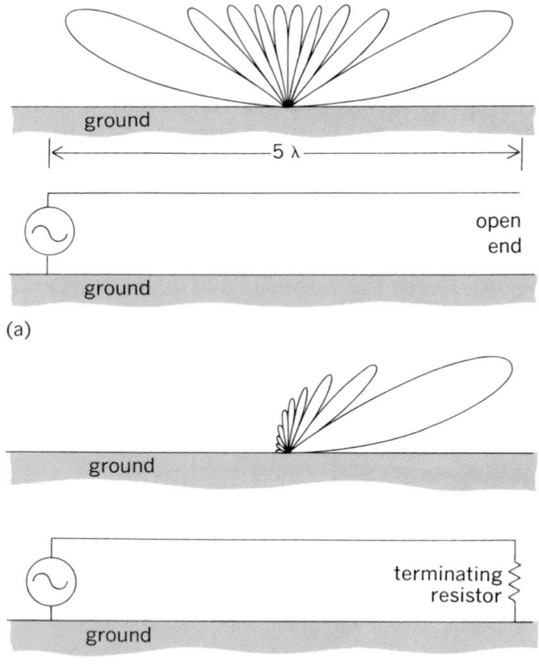

**Fig. 9.** Long single-conductor antennas produce multiple-lobed patterns. (*a*) Unterminated conductor and pattern. (*b*) Terminated conductor and pattern.

closest to the line in both directions. In the practical case with constant phase velocity and exponential variation in amplitude, the pattern lobes will be unsymmetrical with larger lobes toward the open end. The total number of lobes is the same as the number of 0.5 λ lengths of the conductor.

If the far end of the line is terminated (Fig. 9*b*), the antenna radiates only one major lobe in the direction the wave travels down the line to the termination.

***Arrays of long-conductor type.*** Because a single long-conductor terminated antenna has rather high side lobes and a major lobe at an angle to the axis of the conductor, two long terminated conductors can be combined into a horizontal V array (**Fig. 10***a*). The angle between the V array is determined by the length of the conductors and is usually chosen so that major lobes will add in phase.

The commonest type of long-conductor array is the rhombic antenna (Fig. 10*b*). Major lobes of four legs add in phase to form the resultant major lobe, while major lobes at right angles tend to cancel leaving only smaller side lobes. Because of its simplicity, low cost, and wide bandwidth, the rhombic array is widely used for both transmission and reception where the side lobes can be tolerated and the real estate dimensions permit.

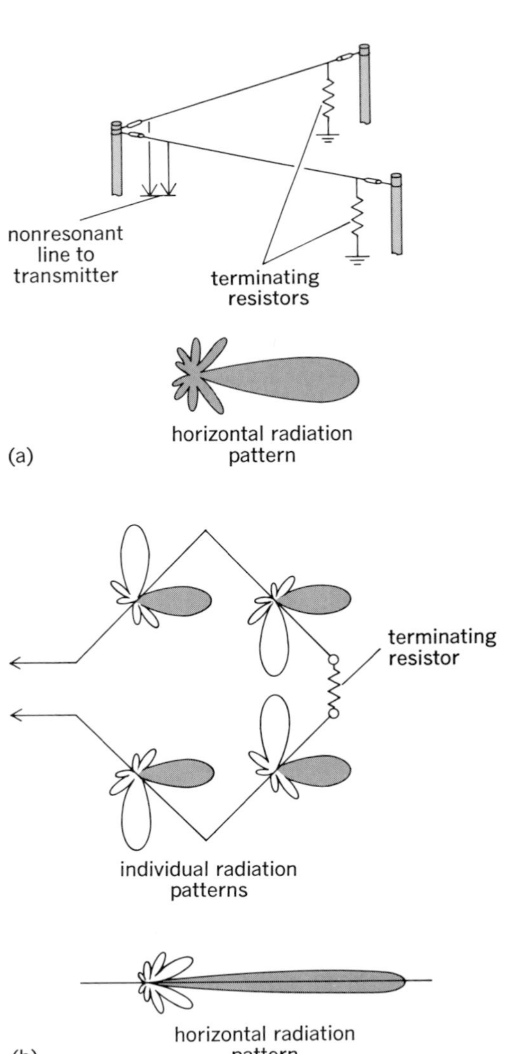


**Fig. 10. Arrays of long-conductor antennas. (*a*) Horizontal terminated V. (*b*) Horizontal terminated rhombic.**

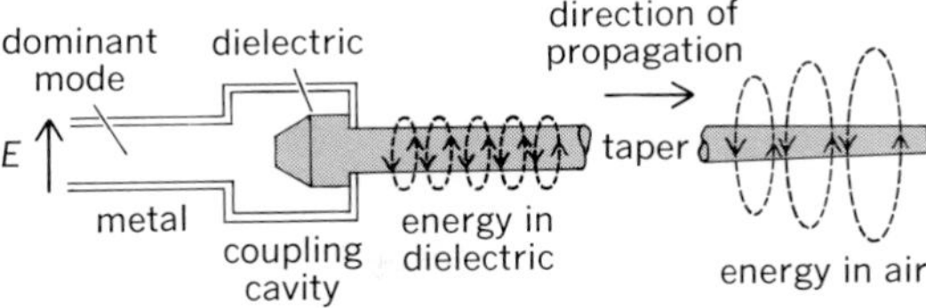


**Fig. 11. Dielectric-rod antenna.**

***Dielectric type.*** Dielectric material, either as a solid rod or as a cylinder, is a wave guide. The wavelength inside a large, solid dielectric rod is less than the free-space wavelength; rather, the wavelength is this free-space length divided by the square root of the dielectric constant of the rod. If rod diameter is large compared to the wavelength inside it, most of the energy in the wave travels inside the dielectric. Even if the rod diameter is somewhat less than the wavelength inside the dielectric, the wave travels along the rod, some inside the dielectric and some outside. However, if the diameter is reduced below a half wavelength, the velocity increases to that of free space and the wave continues beyond the end of the rod into free space (**Fig. 11**). The major lobe is then in the direction of the rod. *See Wave guide.*

**Frequency-independent type.** Equiangular and log-periodic structures conform to both the angle condition and repetitive condition, hence should expand from a zero center out toward infinity. Actually, it is practical to start the structure at a radius corresponding to the shortest wavelength and to end at one representing the longest.

The antenna structure is fed at the inner radius with a coupling network that will not unduly influence the pattern shape or impedance over the operating frequency range. One method is to run a transmission line into the rear of the antenna, or long-wavelength end, then along one of the radiating elements to the feed point at the short-wavelength end, or within the transmission line that feeds the log-periodic elements.

The log-periodic dipole antenna can be used as a free-space antenna, or it can be placed over ground to produce either horizontal or vertical polarization. A diversely polarized log-periodic antenna is obtained by using two coaxial transmission line feeds; it can generate orthogonal patterns independently, or by proper combination can produce any desired elliptically polarized pattern.

**Direct-aperture type.** When they are to be used at short wavelengths, antennas can be built as horns, mirrors, or lenses. Such antennas use conductors and dielectrics as surfaces or solids in contrast to the antennas described thus far, in which the conductors were used basically as discrete lines. *See Microwave optics.*

***Horn radiators.*** Directivity of a horn increases with the size of the mouth of the horn; however, tolerances must be held close if the variations in magnitude and phase distribution are to be low enough to maintain high gain over a broad band. Conical and pyramidal horns are commonly used for high gain beams (**Fig. 12***a* and *b*). Biconical horns (Fig. 12*c*) have an omnidirectional pattern with either vertical or horizontal polarization.

***Luneberg lens.*** If in a dielectric sphere the index of refraction varies with distance from the center of the

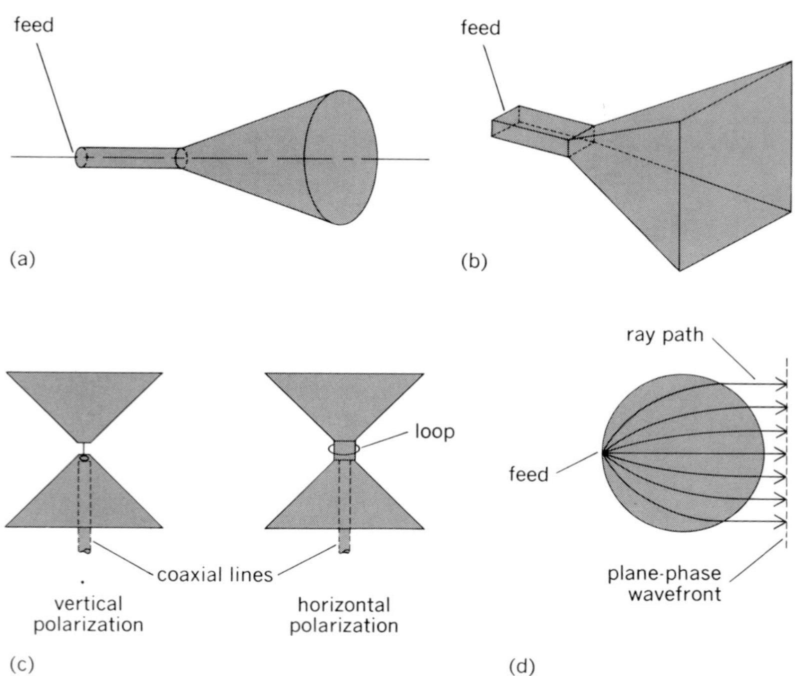


**Fig. 12. Direct-aperture antennas. (*a*) Conical horn. (*b*) Pyramidal horn. (c) Biconical horns, electrically fed for vertical polarization or magnetically fed for horizontal polarization. (*d*) Luneberg lens with dielectric sphere between feed and plane-phase wavefront.**

sphere, a plane wave falling on the surface of one hemisphere is focused at the center of the opposite hemisphere. Such an arrangement is called a Luneberg lens (Fig. 12*d*). By reciprocity, energy is fed into the lens at the focal point for transmitting; energy is removed from the lens at this point for receiving. Only the feed point need be moved around the lens to steer the pencil beam.

For high frequencies a horizontal conducting grid structure serves as a Luneberg lens antenna. Because it will focus rays from any azimuth direction, several high-frequency beams can be generated in different azimuth directions at the same time.

**Reflector type.** By using reflectors one can achieve high gain, modify patterns, and eliminate backward radiation. A low-gain dipole, a slot, or a horn, called the primary aperture, radiates toward a larger reflector called the secondary aperture. The large reflector further shapes the radiated wave to produce the desired pattern.

***Plane sheet reflectors.*** One common plane reflector antenna consists of a dipole parallel to a flat conducting sheet (**Fig. 13***a*). The perfectly conducting screen creates an image, and the forward pattern is the same as that of a two-element dipole array. If the screen is large enough, it prevents all back radiation. Usually the screen is limited in size and some radiation exists to the rear. Gain depends on spacing and can exceed 6 dB above a free-space dipole.

***Corner reflectors.*** If two flat conducting sheets intersect along the *y* axis at an angle $\alpha$, as shown in Fig. 13*b*, an effective directional antenna results when a dipole is placed a distance *S* from the corner. Gain depends on corner angle $\alpha$, dipole spacing *S*, and antenna losses; gain can exceed 12 dB for $\alpha = 45°$. *See* Corner reflector antenna.

***Parabolic reflectors.*** By placing an isotropic source at the focus of a parabola, the radiated wave will be reflected from the parabolic surface as a plane wave at the aperture plane (Fig. 13*c*). The physical size of the parabola determines the size of the aperture plane.

If the parabolic reflector is a surface of translation (Fig. 13*d*), an in-phase line source serves as the pri-

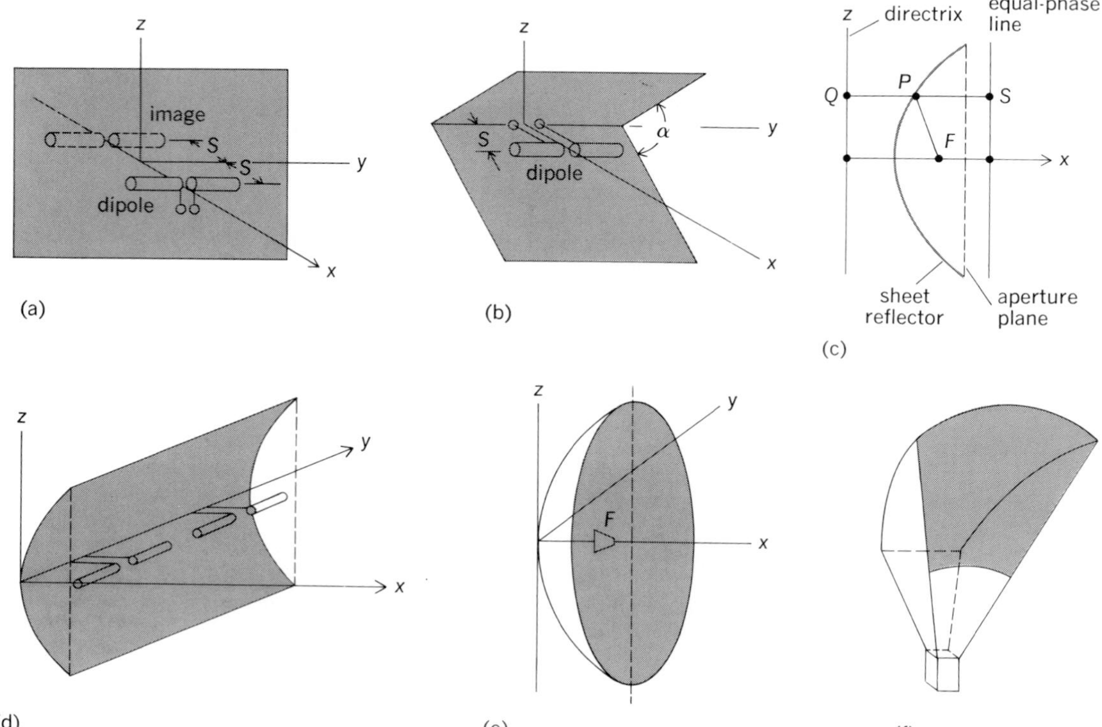


**Fig. 13. Reflector antennas. (*a*) Plane sheet reflector. (*b*) Corner reflector. (c) Parabolic reflector. (*d*) Cylindrical parabolic reflector. (e) (*f*) Paraboloidal reflector. (*f*) Horn paraboloid reflector.**

mary aperture, such as the two dipoles in the illustration. Beam width in the vertical, $z$ direction is controlled by the parabola aperture, while the azimuth beam width, in the $y$ direction, is controlled by the length of the cylindrical parabola.

If the parabolic reflector is a surface of rotation, it converts a spherical wave from an isotropic source at its focus to a uniform plane wave at its aperture. The presence of the primary antenna in the path of the reflected wave has two disadvantages: (1) The reflected wave modifies the primary radiator input impedance. (2) The primary radiator obstructs the reflected wave over the central portion of the aperture (Fig. 13*e*).

To avoid both of these disadvantages, only a portion of the paraboloid can be used; the focus, where the primary aperture must be placed, is then to one side of the secondary aperture. For example, a primary aperture horn placed at one side illuminates the parabolic reflector, as shown in Fig. 13*f*. This type of antenna is commonly used in point-to-point microwave systems, because it is broad-band and has a very low noise level. Because of its high front-to-back ratio, the horn paraboloid reflector is used at the ground station for satellite communication.

**Two-reflector antennas.** A beam can be formed in limited space by a two-reflector system. The commonest two-reflector antenna, the Cassegrain system, consists of a large paraboloidal reflector. It is illuminated by a hyperbolic reflector, which in turn is illuminated by the primary feed (**Fig. 14***a*). The Gregorian system (Fig. 14*b*) is similar, except that an elliptical reflector replaces the hyperbolic reflector and consequently must be placed farther out than the focal point of the paraboloid. This system is less compact than the Cassegrain system and for this reason is less popular.

In microwave relay systems one common practice is to place the paraboloid at ground level (Fig. 14*c*). The feed system is readily accessible, and long lengths of transmission line are not required. A flat sheet at the top of a tall tower redirects the beam over obstacles to the next antenna.

By using a portion of a hemisphere (Fig. 14*d*) illuminated by a feed located at focus $F$, the spherical reflecting surface causes the wave to be reflected off the ground to form a beam at an elevation angle $\theta$. With this arrangement it is possible to steer the beam both in elevation $\theta$ and in azimuth $\phi$. **Figure 15** shows such a shortwave multiplex steerable antenna system. **Figure 16** shows the Arecibo instrument, a 1000-ft (300-m) radio telescope antenna.

**Array antennas.** An array of antennas is an arrangement of several individual antennas so spaced and phased that their individual contributions add in the preferred direction and cancel in other directions. One practical objective is to increase the signal-to-noise ratio in the desired direction. Another objective may be to protect the service area of other radio stations, such as broadcast stations.

The simplest array consists of two antennas. The azimuth pattern is given by Eq. (9), where $E$ is field

$$E = E_1 \underline{/0^\circ} + E_2 \underline{/S_2 \cos\phi + \psi_2} \tag{9}$$

strength for unit distance at azimuth angle $\phi$, $E_1$ and $E_2$ are individual antenna nondirectional values of field strength, $S_2$ is electrical spacing from antenna 1 to antenna 2, and $\psi_2$ is electrical phasing of antenna 2 with respect to antenna 1.

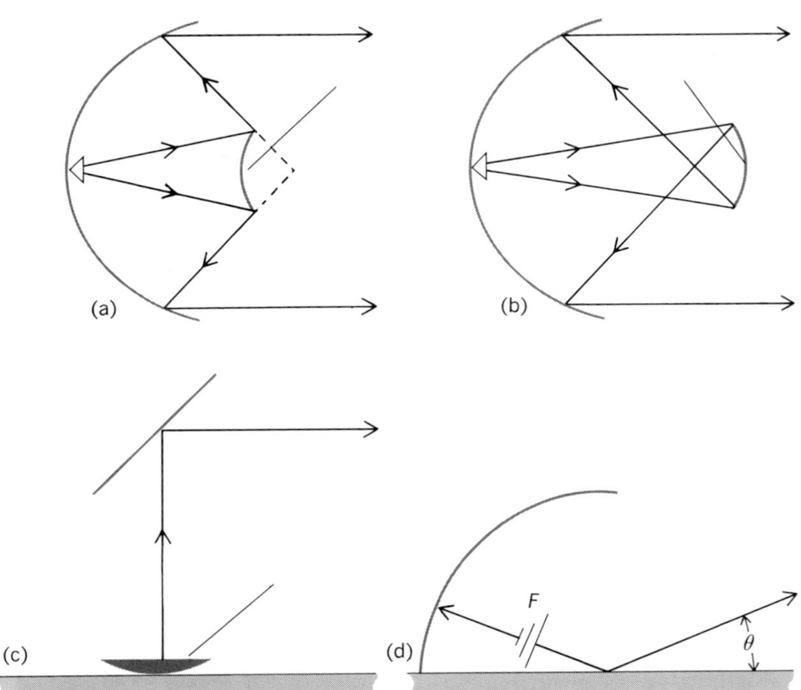


**Fig. 14.** Two-reflector systems. (*a*) Cassegrain. (*b*) Gregorian. (*c*) Periscope. (*d*) Spherical steerable system.

The four variables that the simple two-antenna array provides make possible a wide variety of radiation patterns, from nearly uniform radiation in azimuth to a concentration of most of the energy into one hemisphere, or from energy in two or more equal lobes to radiation into symmetrical but unequal lobes.

In a directional antenna a feeder system is required for proper division of power and control of phase of the radiated fields. The feeder system is also called upon to match impedances between transmitter or transmission line and antenna.

For further control over the radiation pattern a preferred arrangement is the broadside array. In this array, antennas are placed in a line perpendicular to the bidirectional beam. Individual antenna currents are identical in magnitude and phase. The array can be made unidirectional by placing an identical array 90° to the rear and holding its phase at 90°.

The directivity of such a box array increases with the length or aperture of the array. Individual pairs of antennas in the broadside array must be spaced 217° for maximum gain with two pairs; spacing increases as more pairs as used.

Another popular arrangement is the in-line array, in which the current in each antenna is equal but the phase varies progressively to give an end-fire unidirectional pattern. The end-fire array, for a given number of elements, does not have as much gain as the broadside box array.

If antennas are stacked vertically in line to form a collinear array with the currents of each antenna in phase, a symmetrical pattern results in the azimuth plane. This type of array is used for commercial broadcasting to increase the nondirectional ground coverage for a given transmitter power.

Where more than two antennas are required to give the desired pattern shape, it is possible to use more antennas in the array. If a symmetrical pattern is sat-

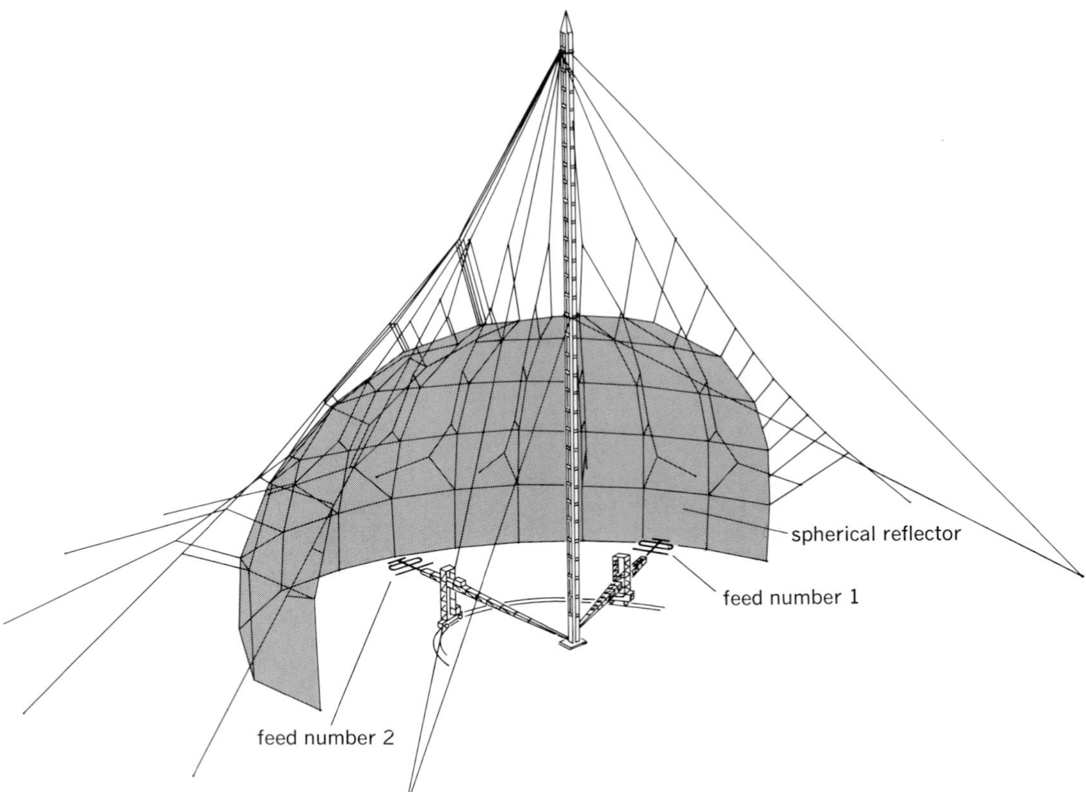


**Fig. 15.** Superpower multiplex steerable shortwave antenna system with two feeds. Each feed is independently positionable to steer its beam and a spherical reflector of wire mesh which is accurately suspended in position from a tower.

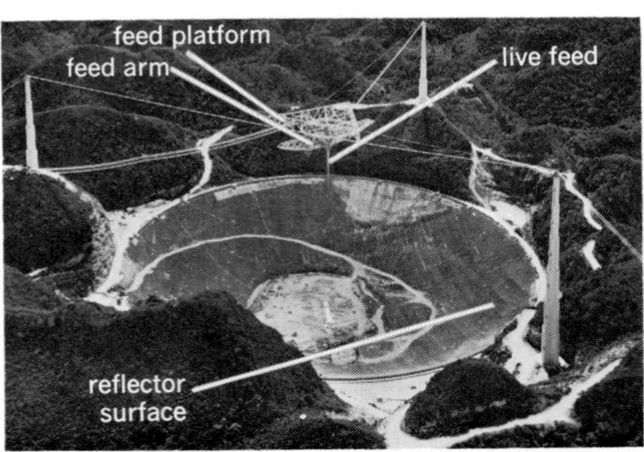


**Fig. 16.** Arecibo Radio Observatory antenna. Reflector is supported on a valley floor that has feed suspended from cables. Rotation of Earth serves to scan the reflector across the sky; reflector has 870-ft (265-m) radius of curvature and circular aperture with 1000-ft (305-m) diameter. Line feed is moved along feed arm to steer beam.

isfactory, antennas can be in line. If the arrays are not in line, the protection directions can be specified by the nulls of the individual pairs of antennas used in the array. When necessary the number of pairs of antennas can be increased to provide further control of the pattern shape.

*Carl E. Smith*

**Bibliography.** American Radio Relay League, *ARRL Antenna Anthology*, 1979; American Radio Relay League, *ARRL Antenna Book*, 2d ed., 1980; C. A. Balanis, *Antenna Theory: Analysis and Design*, 1982; H. Jasik and R. C. Johnson, *Antenna Engineering Handbook*, 2d ed., 1984; M. T. Ma, *Theory and Application of Antenna Arrays*, 1974; W. V. Rusch and P. D. Potter, *Analysis of Reflector Antennas*, 1970; C. E. Smith, *Directional Antenna Patterns*, 2d ed., 1958; C. E. Smith, *Theory and Design of Directional Antennas*, 1959; C. E. Smith et al., *Log Periodic Antenna Design Handbook*, 1966; C. E. Smith and D. B. Hutton, *Standard Broadcast Antenna Systems*, 1968; W. L. Stutzman and G. A. Thiele, *Antenna Theory and Design*, 1981; C. H. Walter, *Traveling Wave Antennas*, 1970.

## Antiresonance

The condition for which the impedance of a given electric, acoustic, or dynamic system is very high, approaching infinity. In an electric circuit consisting of a capacitor and a coil in parallel, antiresonance occurs when the alternating-current line voltage and the resultant current are in phase. Under these conditions the line current is very small because of the high impedance of the parallel circuit at antiresonance. The branch currents are almost equal in magnitude and opposite in phase.

The principle of antiresonance is used in wave traps, which are sometimes inserted in series with antennas of radio receivers to block the flow of alternating current at the frequency of an interfering station, while allowing other frequencies to pass. SEE ANTENNA; RESONANCE (ALTERNATING-CURRENT CIRCUITS).

*John Markus*

## Arc discharge

A type of electrical conduction in gases characterized by high current density and low potential drop. It is closely related to the glow discharge but has a much lower potential drop in the cathode region, as well as greater current density. *SEE GLOW DISCHARGE.*

There are many arc devices, and they operate under a wide range of conditions. For example, an arc discharge may be sustained at either high pressure (of the order of atmospheres) or low pressure. The cathode may or may not be heated from an external source. Furthermore, the applied potential difference may be either direct or alternating. Numerous applications have been made of such devices, some having large commercial value. A few of these applications are illuminating devices, high-current rectifiers, high-current switches, welding devices, and ion sources of nuclear accelators and thermonuclear devices.

**Arc production.** Although an arc may be initiated in several ways, it is instructive to consider the transition from a cold-cathode glow discharge (see **illus.**).

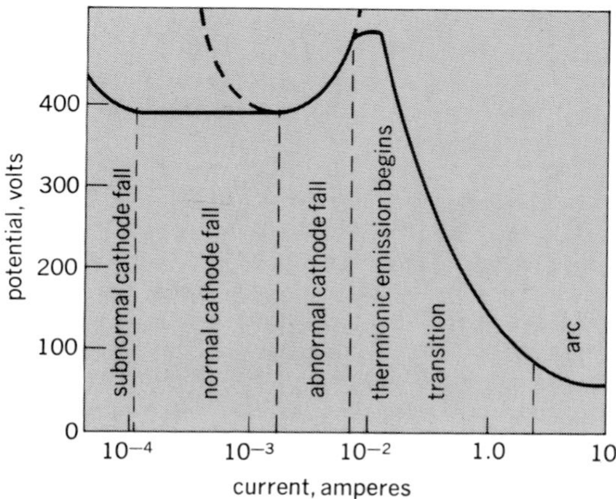


**Transition from glow discharge to arc with increase of current. (*After L. B. Loeb, Basic Processes of Gaseous Electronics, University of Caliornia Press, 1955*)**

In the normal condition, the glow partially covers the cathode, and the voltage drop remains nearly constant as the current is increased. In this condition, the ionization is produced primarily by electron impact. As the current is increased, the cathode glow spreads out, eventually covering the cathode completely. Further increase in current can now be obtained only by an increase in the potential drop across the discharge. The cathode temperature increases in this process, resulting in the abnormal glow region. As the cathode temperature is increased further, thermionic emission becomes an important factor. At this point the discharge characteristic may acquire a negative slope; that is, a further increase in current may increase the cathode temperature, and the resulting thermionic emission, enough actually to reduce the potential drop. Unless the external resistance is sufficiently great to make the overall resistance positive, the discharge will change suddenly to the arc mode. Typical values in this region are a potential drop of a few tens of volts and a current ranging from amperes to thousands of amperes. For a more detailed discussion of the foregoing *SEE ELECTRICAL CONDUCTION IN GASES.*

**Regions of an arc.** There are three geometrical regions in an arc. These are the cathode fall, the anode rise, and the arc body.

***Cathode fall.*** The cathode region is characterized by a high potential gradient. There will be a large positive ion current to the cathode, but the electron current from the cathode may be greater than this. It is not difficult to understand the large thermionic emission for a cathode of refractory metal having a very high melting temperature. However, for a metal with a low melting temperature, such as copper, the situation is not quite so clear. The best explanation appears to be that advanced first by J. J. Thomson and later by L. B. Loeb, who pointed out that the cathode must be viewed on a microscopic basis, and that the local temperature may be vastly greater than the macroscopic cathode temperature. Under these conditions it is not unreasonable to believe that there may be extensive thermionic emission. As in the glow discharge, the cathode is surrounded by a positive ion sheath, resulting in a large space charge.

***Anode rise.*** The anode region requires considerable explanation. To this electrode flows a large electron current which may raise the anode to a temperature even greater than that of the cathode. Thus the anode is also a thermionic emitter, although the electrons are returned to it. Hence there is a large negative space charge and a resulting anode rise. Cooling the anode may result in a reduction in anode rise, indicating a decrease in thermionic emission. Again it is necessary to use the microscopic viewpoint.

***Arc body.*** The main body of the arc is characterized by secondary ionization. This is predominantly a temperature effect. The electrons produce very little ionization by impact, because the electron energy is generally low. However, energy can be imparted to the gas molecules in the form of atomic and molecular excitation. With the many intermolecular collisions that occur, this energy is readily degraded to thermal energy of the gas. Thus a high temperature may be achieved and ionization occur by virtue of intermolecular collisions. This is expressed quantitatively by the equation, shown below, derived by M. N. Saha. Here

$$\log_{10}\left(\frac{n_i^2}{n_0}\right) = -5040\frac{v_i}{T} + {}^{5}\!/\!_{2}\log_{10}(T) + 15.385$$

$n_i$ and $n_0$ are the ionic and neutral densities, respectively, $v_i$ the ionization potential in volts, and $T$ the Kelvin temperature. This equation refers to the equilibrium condition.

It is difficult to make accurate and meaningful measurements because of the high temperature and large current. Thus there is much that is not understood or substantiated.

An interesting situation obtains in connection with an externally heated cathode. Here may exist an arc in which the potential drop is less than the ionization potential of the gas. Several factors are important in this case. First, a positive space charge in the arc body results in a maximum potential there, and a potential drop actually occurs from that point to the anode. Second, there may be many excited or metastable atoms or molecules in the discharge. It seems likely that ionization may take place in several steps rather than one. The most important mechanism, however, appears to involve removal of electrons that have lost so much energy by inelastic collisions that they are trapped near the potential maximum. A fast electron may give up enough energy by coulomb interaction with one of these so that both electrons may reach the anode. If this were not so, neutralization would occur and the arc would be quenched.

In any arc there will be vaporization of the electrodes, and the gas will have in it molecules of the electrode material. For this reason the electrode material may have a profound effect on the arc characteristics.

*Glenn H. Miller*

**Bibliography.** P. Llewellyn-Jones, *The Glow Discharge and an Introduction to Plasma Physics,* 1966; L. B. Loeb, *Basic Processes of Gaseous Electronics*, 1955; F. A. Maxfield and R. R. Benedict, *Theory of Gaseous Conduction and Electronics*, 1941; J. Millman and S. Seely, *Electronics*, 2d ed., 1951.

## Artificial intelligence

The subfield of computer science concerned with understanding the nature of intelligent action and constructing computer systems capable of such action. It embodies the dual motives of furthering basic scientific understanding and making computers more sophisticated in the service of humanity.

Many activities involve intelligent action—problem solving, perception, learning, symbolic activity, creativity, language, and so forth—and therein lie an immense diversity of phenomena. Scientific concern for these phenomena is shared by many fields, for example, psychology, linguistics, and philosophy of mind, in addition to artificial intelligence. This implies no contradiction, the phenomena being rich enough to support many starting points and diverse perspectives. The starting point for artificial intelligence is the capability of the computer to manipulate symbolic expressions that can represent all manner of things, including the programs of action of the computer itself.

The approach of artificial intelligence is largely experimental, although it contains some general principles and small patches of mathematical theory. The unit of experimental investigation is the computer program. New programs are created to explore and test new ideas about how intelligent action might be attained. Artificial intelligence lives in a world of throw-away programs; once a program has yielded its bit of scientific evidence, it is often of little further interest.

**Foundations.** The foundations of artificial intelligence are divided into representation, problem-solving methods, architecture, and knowledge. The four together are necessary ingredients of any intelligent agent.

***Representation.*** To work on a task, a computer must have an internal representation in its memory, for example, the symbolic description of a room for a moving robot, or a set of algebraic expressions for a program integrating mathematical functions. The representation also includes all the basic programs for testing and measuring the structure, plus all the programs for transforming the structure into another one in ways appropriate to the task.

Many representations may be used. The task may pass through a sequence of representations with successive processing, or through alternative representations to find a good one. The representation used for a task can make an immense amount of difference, turning a problem from impossible to trivial.

***Problem-solving methods.*** Given the representation of a task, a method must be adopted that has some chance of accomplishing the task. Artificial intelligence has gradually built up a stock of relevant problem-solving methods (the so-called weak methods) that apply extremely generally: generate-and-test (a sequence of candidates is generated, each being tested for solutionhood); heuristic search (sequences of operations are tried to construct a path from an initial situation to the desired one); hill climbing (a measure of progress is used to guide each step); means-ends analysis (the difference between the desired situation and the present one is used to select the next step); operator subgoaling (the inability to take the desired next step leads to a subgoal of making the step feasible); planning by abstraction (the task is simplified, solved, and the solution used as a guide); and matching (the present situation is represented as a schema to be mapped into the desired situation by putting the two in correspondence). An important feature of all the weak methods is that they involve search. One of the most important generalizations to arise in artificial intelligence is the ubiquity of search. It appears to underlie all intelligent action.

***Architecture.*** A general intelligent agent has multiple means for representing tasks and dealing with them. Also required is an operating frame within which to select and carry out these activities. Often called the executive or control structure, it is best viewed as a total architecture (as in computer architecture), that is, a machine that provides data structures, operations on those data structures, memory for holding data structures, accessing operations for retrieving data structures from memory, a programming language for expressing integrated patterns of conditional operations, and an interpreter for carrying out programs. Any digital computer provides an architecture, as does any programming language. Architectures are not all equivalent, and the scientific question is what architecture is appropriate for a general intelligent agent.

In artificial intelligence, this question has taken the form of determining what language is good for programming artificial intelligence systems. Although the question is seemingly about research tools, in reality its investigation has been a search for the properties that make intelligence possible. The main development has been the list-processing languages, which embody a general homogeneous and flexible notion of symbols and symbolic structure. LISP, one of the early list-processing languages, has evolved until it functions as the common language for artificial intelligence programs. Work on high-level artificial intelligence languages has added to the architecture four notions that previously had existed only separately: (1) the goal, a data structure to be an associative focus for knowledge relevant to obtaining the desired situation; (2) a uniform data base to hold all knowledge, avoiding ad hoc encodings for each type of data; (3) pattern-directed invocation, or finding what method or process to use by matching rather than having to know its name; and (4) the incorporation of search into the fabric of the programming language, so that search can be used anywhere. SEE PROGRAMMING LANGUAGES.

***Knowledge.*** The basic paradigm of intelligent action is that of search through a space of partial solutions (called the problem space) for a goal situation. The search is combinatorial, each step offering several possibilities, leading to a cascading of possibilities in a branching tree. What keeps the search under control is knowledge, which tells how to choose or narrow the options at each step. Thus the fourth fundamental ingredient is how to represent knowledge in the memory of the system so it can be brought to bear on the search when relevant.

A general intelligent system will have immense amounts of knowledge. This implies a major problem, that of discovering the relevant knowledge as the solution attempt progresses. This is the second problem of search that inevitably attends an intelligent system. Unlike the combinatorial explosion characteristic of the problem space search, this one involves a fixed, though large, data base, whose structure can be carefully tailored by the architecture to make the search efficient. This problem of encoding and access constitutes the final ingredient of an intelligent system.

**Examples.** Three examples will provide some flavor of research in artificial intelligence.

***Games.*** Games form a classical arena for artificial intelligence. They provide easily defined, isolated worlds which still permit the indefinite play of reason.

All the ingredients of an artificial intelligence program can be seen in game programs. A chess program must have a representation of the current chess position. Besides the bits that describe the position, there must be procedures for analyzing the position and for making the moves to create new legal positions. All these capabilities constitute the representation. Their efficiency is important; some special computing hardware has even been designed to make them faster.

The basic method used for chess is to generate the moves and test their worth. The test is a form of heuristic search that explores the consequences of a candidate move many potential moves into the future. This search is combinatorial and much too big to accomplish without the aid of knowedge. The main technique for bringing knowledge to bear is the evaluation function, which can be applied to a position to estimate directly its chance of being on a winning path. Many features of the position are calculated, each representing a bit of chess knowledge (for instance, queens are better than pawns). Such value functions are heuristic, only approximating a correct analysis. Evaluation turns the search into hill climbing. Not all the knowledge stems from the evaluation functions; many subtleties of the search allow great improvement.

The Northwestern chess program searches about $10^6$ positions per move in tournament play (about 2.5 min per move). It has played in many official tournaments against human competition and has an official U.S. Chess Federation rating of a low expert. At fast play (5 min per game) it has beaten several grand masters. The program's large search compared with that of humans (estimated at a few hundred positions at most) illustrates that exploiting the speed and reliability of computers can produce a distinctive style of problem solving.

A program for another game, backgammon, illustrates further the role of knowledge. In 1979 a program developed at Carnegie-Mellon University played an exhibition match with the world backgammon champion Luigi Villa, winning 7 points to 1. Since backgammon involves chance as well as skill, the program in fact is not the superior player, but it is definitely formidable.

The interest in the feat from an artificial intelligence point of view is twofold. First is the calibration against human talent under real conditions. Second is the mechanisms that enabled such play; these are the basic scientific contribution. In backgammon, the number of moves from a single position is so large that search is almost totally ineffective. Instead, the evaluation function must contain an immense amount of knowledge of the game. The success of the program rests in part on using separate evaluation functions during different regions of play and, moreover, adjusting the transitions between these different views so that they are smooth and continuous. Analysis reveals a general principle: discontinuous jumps in value (in crossing a boundary of two evaluation regions) inevitably lead to serious errors. The discovery of this principle, its testing by being embodied in a program, and its tentative support by the program's success form a typical example of scientific activity and progress in artificial intelligence.

***Perception.*** Perception is the formation, from a sensory signal, of an internal representation suitable for intelligent processing. Though there are many types of sensory signals, computer perception has focused on vision and speech. Perception might seem to be distinct from intelligence, since it involves incident time-varying continuous energy distributions prior to interpretation in symbolic terms. However, all the same ingredients occur: representation, search, architecture, and knowledge. Thus, perception by computers is a part of artificial intelligence.

Speech perception starts with the acoustic wave of a human utterance and proceeds to an internal representation of what the speech is about. A sequence of representations is used: the digitization of the acoustic wave into an array of intensities; the formation of a small set of parametric quantities that vary continuously with time (such as the intensities and frequencies of the formants, bands of resonant energy characteristic of speech); a sequence of phones (members of a finite alphabet of labels for characteristic sounds, analogous to letters); a sequence of words; a parsed sequence of words reflecting grammatical structure; and finally a semantic data structure representing the final meaning.

Speech perception is difficult, because the encoding of the intended utterance by the speaker is extremely convoluted, the acoustic wave at any point being influenced in complex ways by substantial context on either side. Added to this are multiple sources of noise and variability (for example, speakers differ and vary over time). To unravel this requires search, generating hypotheses about the identity of some element in the representation (for example, a phone or a word) and then testing how well it fits with the other hypothesized elements. Several possibilities can be hypothesized at each point (and at each level of representation), the whole becoming combinatorial. Thus, knowledge about the encoding and noise at each level must be brought to bear to control the search: knowledge of speech articulation, phonological regularities, lexical restrictions, grammar, the task, and so forth.

There are speech recognition programs that recognize continuous speech with high accuracy (a few percent utterance error) from several speakers with vocabularies of about 1000 words in environments that are not too noisy, within restricted grammatical and task contexts. These higher-level restrictions are extremely important. Recent work indicates that humans are several magnitudes better than current computer systems in extracting the phonetic codes directly from the speech signal, without use of higher-level knowledge. Discovering how that happens is an active area of research. *See Speech recognition*.

***Expert systems.*** Extensive experience enables humans to exhibit expert performance in many tasks, even though no firm scientific or calculational base exists and the knowledge does not exist in any explicit form. So-called expert artificial intelligence systems attempt to exhibit equivalent performance by acquiring and incorporating the same knowledge that the human expert has. Many attempts to apply artificial intelligence to socially significant tasks take the form of expert programs. Even though the emphasis is on knowledge, all the standard ingredients are present: representation of the task, methods of manipulating the representation, an architecture to make processing easy, as well as the knowledge.

An example is MYCIN, developed at Stanford University, which makes judgments on the diagnosis of bacterial infection in patients and proposes courses of therapy with antibiotics. MYCIN operates as a consultant by interacting with a physician who knows the history of the patient. The knowledge of the program is encoded in a large number of if-then rules, for example, "If the site of the culture is blood, and the identity of the organisms may be pseudomonas, and the patient has ecthyma gangrenosum skin lesions, then there is strongly suggestive evidence (.8) that the identity of the organism is pseudomonas." There are several hundred such rules, which jointly encode what expert physicians know about the signs, symptoms, and causes of disease and the effects of drugs. The program uses these rules to search for a diagnosis, letting them guide what specific knowledge it must seek from the physician about the patient.

Obtaining and codifying such hitherto implicit expert knowledge is a critical aspect of developing artificial intelligence expert programs. That entire bodies of knowledge could be embodied as sets of active if-then rules, even though they did not yet form a coherent scientific theory, has been an important discovery.

A number of expert systems (including MYCIN) have shown performance at levels of quality equivalent to average practicing professionals (for example, average practicing physicians) on the restricted domains over which they operate, as shown by careful tests. Incorporation into ongoing practice, which has not yet generally occurred, depends on many other aspects besides the intrinsic intellectual quality (for example, ease of interacting, system costs). From a scientific viewpoint, the lessons in understanding the nature of knowledge and its organization are already apparent. These expert systems illustrate that there is no hard separation between pure and applied artificial intelligence; finding what is required for intelligent action in a complex applied area makes a significant contribution to basic knowledge. *See Expert system.*

**Scope and implications.** Research in artificial intelligence spreads out to explore the full range of intellectual tasks. The three areas above—games, speech, and medical diagnosis—are only a sample. Significant work has been done on puzzles and reasoning tasks, induction and concept identification, symbolic mathematics, theorem-proving in formal logic, natural language understanding, vision, robotics, chemistry, engineering analysis, and computer-program synthesis and verification, to name only the most prominent. As in any developing science, there occurs both a recurrence of the basic ideas (about representation, search, architecture, and knowledge) and the discovery of new mechanisms; both extend existing ideas and reveal limits.

Artificial intelligence has close ties with several surrounding fields. As part of computer science, it plays the role of expanding the intellectual sophistication of the tasks to which computers can be applied. Various subfields, once viewed as part of artificial intelligence, have become autonomous fields, most notably symbolic mathematics and program verification. The work on vision and speech shares its concern with signal processing with the field of pattern recognition in electrical engineering.

The relation of artificial intelligence to the study of cognitive and linguistic processes in humans is especially important. Human experimental psychology and linguistics underwent a transformation in the late 1950s, coincident with the birth of artificial intelligence, to an essentially symbolic and information-processing viewpoint. The sources were much broader than artificial intelligence, especially in linguistics, but the history of these three fields has been intertwined ever since. The relations with linguistics have been marked with controversy, but the relations with cognitive psychology (as human experimental psychology has come to be called) have been mostly symbiotic. The psychological theories of problem solving, long-term memory structure, and the organization of knowledge are essentially the theories from artificial intelligence. In fact, a new interdiscipline, cognitive science, has emerged to encompass artificial intelligence, cognitive psychology, linguistics, philosophy of mind, and cognitive anthropology.

Fascination with accomplishing mental activities by mechanical means has a long history; it became channeled into cybernetics, which had its advent in the 1940s. Cybernetics focused on the role of feedback mechanisms and on the analysis of purpose they made possible in mechanical terms. Artificial intelligence did not really begin until the emergence of the digital computer. This added to the notions of cybernetics the notions of symbolic systems and programmability; it shifted concern from the construction of simple adaptive circuits to experimentation with programs, which is still the hallmark of artificial intelligence. Many of the pioneers of digital computers and operational mathematics played some part in the prehistory of artificial intelligence: Claude Shannon, John von Neumann, Norbert Wiener, and above all Alan Turing. However, the start of the field is usually located in the last half of the 1950s, when a large amount of important work was done, associated with the names of John McCarthy, Marvin Minsky, Oliver Selfridge, Herbert Simon, and Allen Newell.

The major centers for artificial intelligence research are in the United States (primarily at Stanford, the Massachusetts Institute of Technology, and Carnegie-Mellon), but research exists in all major countries. The success in expert systems, even though only a few applications are yet in routine use, has precipitated substantial commercial activity, including the formation of many small venture firms. Noteworthy in this regard has been the coordinated effort by the Japanese government and industry to develop a fifth-generation computer, which is to be a supercomputer designed for artificial intelligence applications. The specific design objectives for this system are extremely ambitious along multiple dimensions of computer architecture and technology, as well as artificial intelligence. However, in the light of Japan's success in capturing major industrial markets, this effort has been taken seriously by other industrial nations, such as Britain and the United States, and an increase in activity in artificial intelligence around the world has occurred. *SEE AUTOMATA THEORY; COMPUTER; DIGITAL COMPUTER; DIGITAL COMPUTER PROGRAMMING; INTELLIGENT MACHINE; ROBOTICS.*

*Allen Newell*

***Bibliography.*** E. A. Feigenbaum and P. McCorduck, *The Fifth Generation: Artificial Intelligence and Japan's Challenge to the World,* 1983; N. Nilsson, *Principles of Artificial Intelligence,* 1980; A. Newell and H. A. Simon, *Human Problem Solving,* 1972; E. Shortliffe, *Computer Based Medical Consultations: MYCIN,* 1976; P. Winston, *Artificial Intelligence,* 2d ed., 1983.

## Artificially layered structures

Manufactured, reproducibly layered structures with layer thicknesses approaching interatomic distances. Modern thin-film techniques are at a stage at which it is possible to fabricate these structures, also known as artificial crystals or superlattices, opening up the possibility of engineering new desirable properties into materials. In addition, a variety of solid-state physics problems can be studied which are otherwise inaccessible. The various possibilities include: the application of negative pressure, that is, stretching of the crystalline lattice; the study of dimensional crossover, that is, the transition from a situation in which the layers are isolated and two-dimensional in character to where the layers couple together to form a three-dimensional material; the study of collective behavior, that is, properties which depend on the cooperative behavior of the whole superlattice; and the effect and physics of multiple interfaces and surfaces. A variety of applications have also been proposed or discovered. Of course, one of the most exciting prospects is the discovery of new, yet unpredicted phenomena. For a discussion of semiconductor superlattices *SEE SEMICONDUCTOR HETEROSTRUCTURES.*

**Preparation.** Artificially layered structures have been prepared since the beginning of the century, using mostly chemical methods for deposition. With the advent of sophisticated high-vacuum preparation techniques, there has been a significant increase in activities in this field since the early 1970s. The preparation techniques can be conveniently classified into two groups: evaporation and sputtering. In evaporation system, two or more particle sources (thermal or electron beam gun) are aimed at a heated substrate where the artificially layered structure is grown. The rates are precisely controlled by using rate monitors, and the various beams are chopped by using shutters in various configurations. The ultrahigh-vacuum (UHV) version has been commonly designated as a molecular beam epitaxy (MBE) apparatus. The sputtering method relies on bombarding targets of the proper materials with an inert gas, such as argon, thus producing the beams of the various elements. Commonly, in this case, the substrate is held against a rotating, heated table and so moved from one beam to the next. *SEE SPUTTERING.*

**Structure.** Once the artificially layered structure is prepared, it is necessary to characterize whether the layer structure is stable at the growth temperature. This is of considerable importance, since the interdiffusion of the constituents in many cases eliminates the layered growth. A direct image of the layers in gallium arsenide–aluminum arsenide superlattices, using electron micrography, is shown in **Fig. 1**. One of the most successful methods of characterizing layered growth has been x-ray diffraction. In this method the intensity of x-rays elastically reflected from a sample is measured as a function of incidence angle. The layered growth is indicated by the existence of many superlattice peaks, which are due to the Bragg reflection by the superlattice planes. The spacing of these peaks is related to the thickness of the layers, whereas the amplitude is related to the admixture of one constituent into the other and the amount of strain present.

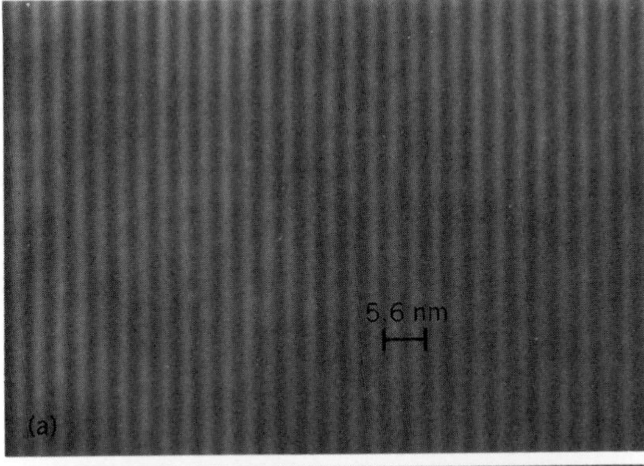


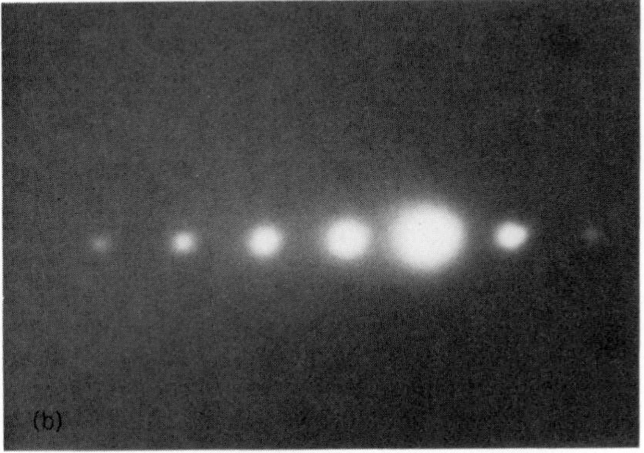


**Fig. 1. Ordered superlattice consisting of alternating layers of gallium arsenide (GaAs) and aluminum arsenide (AlAs), each four atomic layers thick, deposited by molecular beam epitaxy. (*a*) Transmission electron micrograph of the superlattice. (*b*) Electron diffraction pattern of the superlattice. (*From P. M. Petroff et al., Crystal growth kinetics in* $(GaAs)_n$*-*$(AlAs)_m$ *superlattices deposited by molecular beam epitaxy, J. Cryst. Growth, 44:5–13, 1978*)**

**Physical properties.** The normal-state properties of non-lattice-matched metallic superlattices show anomalies at small thicknesses of the order of 2.0 nanometers periodicity (that is, repeat distance; **Fig. 2**). The lattice expands slightly (approximately 2%) in the direction perpendicular to the layers, the shear elastic constant decreases markedly (approximately 35%), and the temperature coefficient of resistivity changes sign, as in a metal–nonmetal transition.

The superconducting properties exhibit dimensional crossover, as is shown (**Fig. 3**) beautifully by the temperature dependence of the superconducting critical field. When the superconducting layers are thin and well separated, the critical field shows a characteristic square-rootlike behavior, as is expected for two-dimensional superconductors. If the superconducting layers are close together, the layers are strongly coupled and show a linear temperature de-

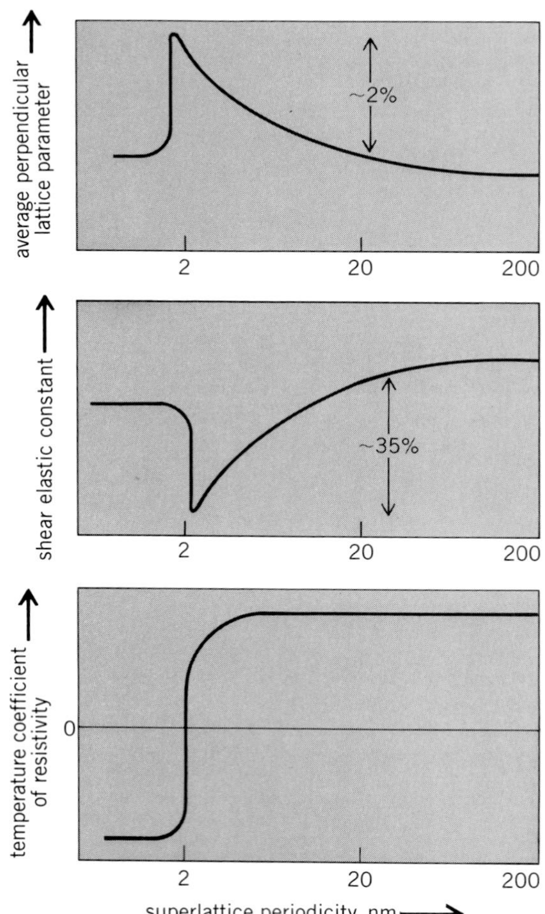


**Fig. 2. Average perpendicular lattice parameter, shear elastic constant, and temperature coefficient of resistivity versus superlattice periodicity.** ***(After M. R. Khan et al., Structural, elastic and transport anomalies in molybdenum-nickel superlattices, Phys. Rev., B27:7186–7193, 1983)***

pendence typical of a three-dimensional material. At intermediate separation the behavior can change from three-dimensional at high temperatures to two-dimensional at low temperatures, a phenomenon known as dimensional crossover. *See Superconductivity.*

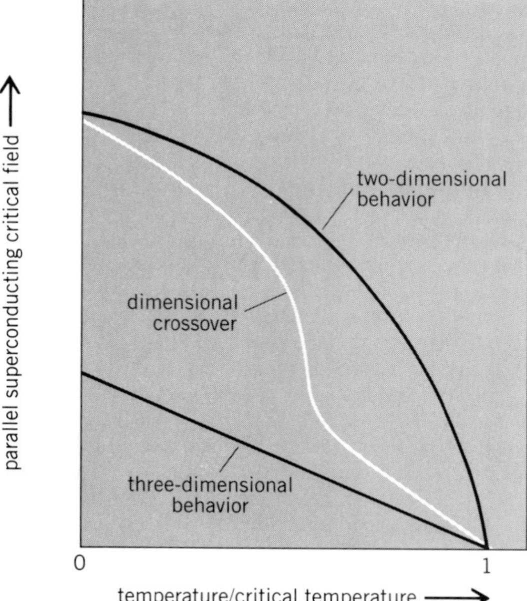


**Fig. 3. Parallel superconducting critical field versus temperature at various layer thicknesses.** ***(After S. T. Ruggiero, T. W. Barbee, and M. R. Beasley, Superconductivity in quasi-two-dimensional layered deposits, Phys. Rev. Lett., 45:1299–1302, 1980)***

Although much effort has gone into the fabrication of magnetic superlattices, their behavior is simply what is expected from thin layers of magnetic materials. A notable exception to this is the existence of collective spin waves in molybdenum–nickel superlattices.

**Applications.** Artificially layered structures are especially useful for the construction of mirrors for soft x-rays since there are no suitable, naturally occurring crystals for this purpose. This application was one of the main motivations for research on artificially layered structures. Mirrors and polarizers for neutrons have also been manufactured and are currently used in the United States and Europe. Superlattices with zero temperature coefficient of resistivity are useful as resistor material, and high-critical-field-magnet tapes using superconducting–insulator superlattices have been proposed.

*Ivan K. Schuller*

***Bibliography.*** M. Bartusiak, Architects in the laboratory, *Discover*, 2:60–61, 1981; L. Chang and B. B. Giessen (eds.), *Synthetic Modulated Structure Materials*, 1984; N. G. Einspruch (ed.), *VLSI Electronics: Microstructure Science*, vol.4, 1982. K. N. Tu and R. Rosenberg (eds.), *Thin Films: Preparation and Properties*, 1983.

## Attenuation (electricity)

The exponential decrease with distance in the amplitude of an electrical signal traveling along a very long uniform transmission line, due to conductor and dielectric losses. If the peak voltage at the sending end of the transmission line is denoted by $V_0$, the peak voltage at a distance $x$ from the sending end is given by Eq. (1), where $\alpha$ is the attenuation constant of the line.

$$V_x = V_0 e^{-\alpha x} \tag{1}$$

**Characteristic impedance.** Transmission-line theory shows that the input impedance of such a line has a purely resistive value $Z_0$ at high frequencies, where $Z_0$ is the characteristic impedance of the line. If the line is terminated at any point by a resistance of value $Z_0$, all of the power that reaches the termination will be dissipated and the line is said to be matched. If the line is terminated by any other impedance $Z_t$, part of the incident voltage will be reflected and the reflection coefficient $\Gamma$ of the termination is defined as the ratio of the reflected voltage to the incident voltage. The value of $\Gamma$ is shown by Eq. (2). Thus, when $Z_t = 0$,

$$\Gamma = \frac{Z_t - Z_0}{Z_t + Z_0} \tag{2}$$

$\Gamma = -1$; when $Z_t = 3Z_0$, $\Gamma = 0.5$; and when $Z_t$ approaches infinity, $\Gamma$ approaches $+1$. *See Electrical impedance; Impedance matching.*

**Neper and decibel.** Electronic engineers usually express power ratios in a logarithmic manner, using either nepers or decibels (dB) as in Eqs. (3) and (4),

$$\text{Power ratio in nepers} = {}^1\!/_2 \log_e \frac{P_1}{P_2} \tag{3}$$

$$\text{Power ratio in decibels} = 10 \log_{10} \frac{P_1}{P_2} \tag{4}$$

where $P_1$ and $P_2$ are the power levels to be compared. The advantages of using the decibel or neper, instead of just $P_1/P_2$, are that very large power ratios can be expressed by conveniently small numbers, and the overall gain or loss of a cascade of matched networks can be found by addition and subtraction instead of multiplication. SEE NEPER.

The well-known relationship between neperian and common logarithms yields Eq. (5).

$$\text{Power ratio in decibels} = 8.686 \times \text{power ratio in nepers} \quad (5)$$

**Insertion loss.** When a generator with a reflection coefficient $\Gamma_G$ is connected directly to a load with a reflection coefficient $\Gamma_L$, let the power dissipated in the load be denoted by $P_3$. Suppose now that a network, with two connectors called ports, is inserted between the generator and the load, and let this reduce the power dissipated in the load to $P_4$. Then, the insertion loss of this two-port network is given in decibels by Eq. (6).

$$L = 10 \log_{10} \frac{P_3}{P_4} \quad (6)$$

**Definition of attenuation.** The attenuation of the two-port network is defined as the insertion loss when both the source and load are perfectly matched, that is, when $\Gamma_G = 0$ and $\Gamma_L = 0$. Insertion loss depends on the values of $\Gamma_G$ and $\Gamma_L$ as well as on the characteristics of the two-port network, whereas attenuation is a property only of the two-port network.

Returning now to the situation depicted by Eq. (1), the power entering the line is $(V_0)^2/2Z_0$, and the power at a distance $x$ from the sending end is $(V_x)^2/2Z_0$; so, using Eq. (3), the attenuation in nepers over the distance $x$ is seen to be given by Eq. (7). Thus, $\alpha$ gives

$$A = {}^1\!/_2 \log_e \frac{(V_0)^2/2Z_0}{(V_x)^2/2Z_0} = {}^1\!/_2 \log_e (e^{2\alpha x}) = \alpha x \quad (7)$$

the attenuation of the line in nepers per unit length; and the attenuation in decibels per unit length is seen from Eq. (5) to be $8.686\alpha$.

**Types of attenuators.** Attenuators find numerous applications, typical examples being: in a signal generator, to vary the amplitude of the output signal; and in the input line to a television receiver that is very close to a television transmitter, so that overloading can be avoided. SEE SIGNAL GENERATOR; TELEVISION RECEIVER.

Attenuators for the dc (steady voltage) to very high-frequency (VHF) range (frequencies from 0 to 300 MHz) often contain resistors arranged in $T$ or $\pi$ configurations. **Figure 1*a*** shows a one-section $T$-type attenuator that can be switched in or out of a circuit between a matched generator and a matched load. The resistor values are chosen so that the required attenuation is obtained without changing the matching conditions. When a single $T$ section is required to give an attenuation of $A_t$ decibels and be matched to input and output lines of characteristic impedance $Z_0$, the design equations are Eqs. (8) and (9), where $k$ is given by Eq. (10). Thus, when $Z_0 = 50\ \Omega$ and an

$$R_1 = Z_0 \frac{1-k}{1+k} \quad (8)$$

$$R_2 = 2Z_0 \frac{k}{1-k^2} \quad (9)$$

$$k = 10^{-A_t/20} \quad (10)$$

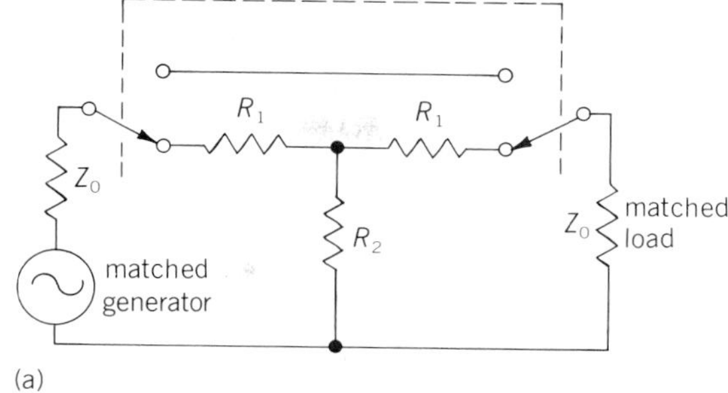


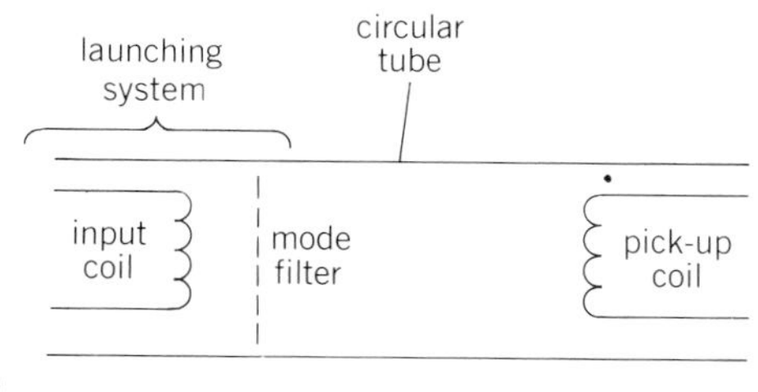


**Fig. 1. Types of attenuators. *(a)* One-section T-type attenuator. *(b)* Piston attenuator.**

attenuation of 10 dB is needed, $R_1 = 25.975\ \Omega$ and $R_2 = 35.136\ \Omega$.

Fixed coaxial attenuators can be designed to operate from dc to frequencies of more than 20 GHz. Various constructional techniques are used; for example, a thin resistive film can be deposited on the inner conductor, or a resistive film can be deposited on a substrate that is furnished with suitable launching, receiving, and earth electrodes.

Piston attenuators (sometimes called waveguide-beyond-cutoff attenuators) are used at both intermediate and microwave frequencies (Fig. 1*b*). The attenuation is varied by altering the separation between the two coils. The circular tube acts as a waveguide beyond cutoff, and the launching system is designed so that only one mode is excited in it. An increase in the coil separation from $x_1$ to $x_2$ produces an attenuation change in decibels given by Eq. (11), where $r$ is the

$$A_p = 8.686 \times 2\pi(x_2 - x_1) \cdot \left[\left(\frac{S_{nm}}{2\pi r}\right)^2 - \frac{1}{\lambda^2}\right]^{1/2} \quad (11)$$

radius of the cylinder, $\lambda$ is the free-space wavelength of the applied signal, and $S_{nm}$ is a constant which depends upon the mode that is excited. The $TE_{11}$ mode is usually employed, and in this case $S_{nm} = 1.84118$. A piston attenuator has a very high dynamic range and a linear decibel scale. When great care is taken in the design and manufacture, an accuracy as high as 0.0002 dB per 10 dB can be achieved over a 120-dB range. SEE WAVEGUIDE.

A variable waveguide attenuator can be produced by moving a lossy vane either sideways across the waveguide or into the waveguide through a longitudinal slot.

The rotary vane attenuator is a very popular instrument. At the input end, there is a rectangular-to-circular waveguide taper containing a fixed lossy vane perpendicular to the incident electric vector. The central section contains a lossy vane diametrically across a circular waveguide that can be rotated, and the output section is a mirror image of the input section.

When the central vane is at an angle θ relative to the two fixed end vanes, the total attenuation in decibels is given by Eq. (12), where $A_0$ is the residual atten-

$$A_{rva} = 40 \log_{10} (\sec \theta) + A_0 \qquad (12)$$

uation when all three vanes lie in the same plane.

**Measurement of attenuation.** Many different techniques for measuring attenuation have been devised. The power-ratio method is widely used. The simplest configuration requires only a stable well-matched filtered source and a well-matched low-drift power meter. Let the measured power be $P_5$ when the source is connected directly to the power meter and $P_6$ when the device under test is inserted between them. Then the attenuation of the device under test in decibels is given by Eq. (13). Insensitivity to source power

$$A_{dut} = 10 \log_{10} \frac{P_5}{P_6} \qquad (13)$$

variations can be achieved by using two power meters as shown in **Fig. 2**. The Kelvin-Varley voltage divider is adjusted to settings $D_1$ and $D_2$ that give nulls before and after inserting the device under test. Then the attenuation of the device under test is given by Eq. (14). If sufficient care is taken, this configuration

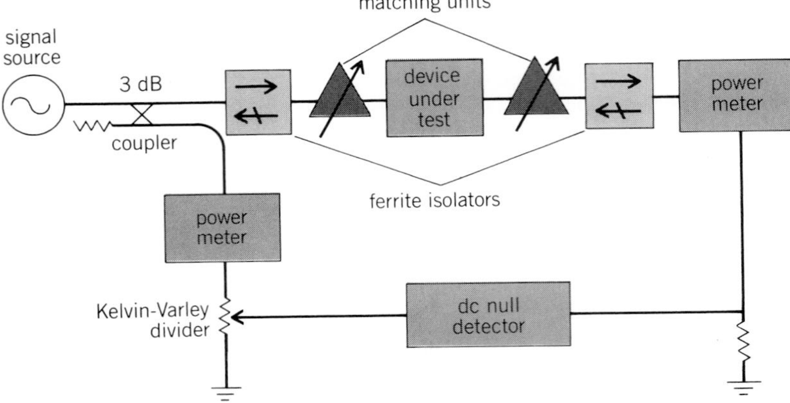


**Fig. 2. Dual-channel power ratio system for attenuation measurement.**

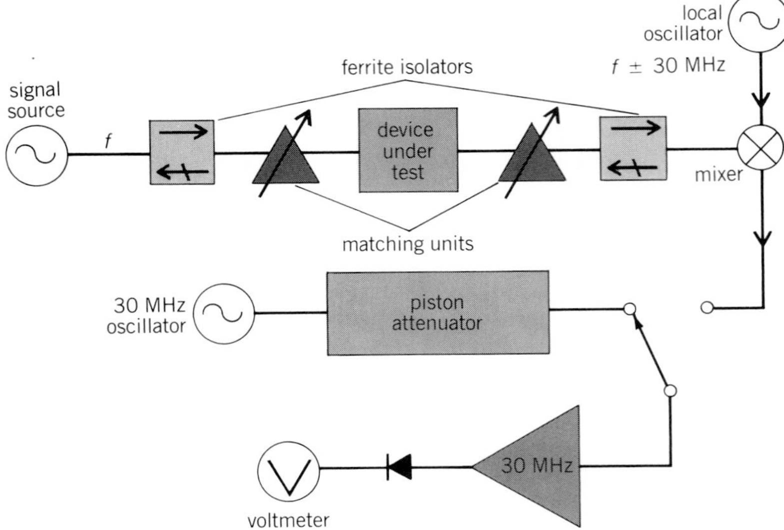


**Fig. 3. Parallel i-f substitution system for attenuation measurement.**

$$A'_{dut} = 10 \log_{10} \frac{D_1}{D_2} \qquad (14)$$

will yield very accurate results over a 30-dB range.

Substitution methods of attenuation measurement are very popular, and the following techniques can be used: (1) radio-frequency (rf) substitution, for example, comparison with an accurate rotary vane attenuator; (2) intermediate-frequency substitution, for example, comparison with an i-f piston attenuator; (3) audio-frequency substitution, for example, comparison with an inductive voltage divider; and (4) dc substitution, for example, comparison with a Kelvin-Varley voltage divider.

The device under test can be connected either in series or in parallel with the reference standard. A manually switched parallel i-f substitution system is shown in **Fig. 3**. The device under test is inserted between matched isolators, and a continuous-wave signal at the required measurement frequency $f$ is passed through it. This signal then has its frequency changed to 30 MHz by a linear mixer that is driven by a local oscillator operating at a frequency of $f \pm 30$ MHz. A stable 30-MHz continuous-wave oscillator energizes the piston attenuator and, at each setting of the device under test, the piston is adjusted until the reading on the output voltmeter is the same in both positions of the switch. A system of this type has a dynamic range of about 100 dB.

Low values of attenuation can be determined accurately by making reflection coefficient measurements on the device under test with a sliding short behind it. Several bridge techniques for measuring attenuation have been devised. Attenuation changes of less than $10^{-4}$ dB can be readily seen on a magic T bridge with a superheterodyne null detector. *SEE MICROWAVE IMPEDANCE MEASUREMENT*.

The attenuation in a waveguide can be found by making $Q$ measurements on resonant sections of different lengths. A shuttle-pulse method has been used widely for measuring the attenuation in long lengths of low-loss circular waveguide for millimeter wave communication systems. A short millimeter wave pulse is bounced back and forth many times in the waveguide under test, and the attenuation is deduced from the amplitudes of the echoes. *SEE CAVITY RESONATOR; Q (ELECTRICITY)*.

The microwave reflection coefficient of a superconducting ring closed by a Josephson junction varies periodically as the current through an adjacent wire is increased. By using this effect (by connecting the device under test in series with the adjacent wire), discrete values of attenuation can be found very accurately by simply counting the number of zero crossovers and making use of a table of Bessel function roots. *SEE JOSEPHSON EFFECT; SUPERCONDUCTIVITY*.

When only moderate accuracy (on the order of ± 0.5 dB) is required over a wide frequency range, a leveled swept source can be connected to the device under test, and the emerging signal can be fed to a diode detector that is followed by a logarithmic amplifier and oscilloscope. With this technique, resonances which can easily be missed using point-by-point methods are clearly revealed, and the effects of adjustments to the device under test can be seen immediately over a wide band. *SEE AMPLITUDE-MODULATION DETECTOR*.

Network analyzers became very popular after 1967. These instruments yield both the magnitude and phase angle of the transmission and reflection coefficients of the device under test over a wide frequency range. By using ingenious calibration and computer-correction techniques, high accuracy can be achieved. To obtain the phase information, a second channel is needed to provide a reference signal. In most network analyzers, mixers are employed. However, considerable effort has been devoted since 1972 to six-port network analyzers in which the phase information is deduced solely from power measurements. SEE MICROWAVE TRANSMISSION LINES; TRANSMISSION LINES.

Frank L. Warner

**Bibliography.** H. M. Barlow and A. L. Cullen, *Microwave Measurements,* 1950; E. L. Ginzton, *Microwave Measurements,* 1957; T. S. Laverghetta, *Microwave Measurements and Techniques,* 1976; C. G. Montgomery (ed.), *Technique of Microwave Measurements,* 1947; M. Sucher and J. Fox, *Handbook of Microwave Measurements,* vol. 1, 1963; F. L. Warner, *Microwave Attenuation Measurement,* 1977.

## Audio amplifier

An electronic circuit for amplification of signals within, and in some cases above, the audible range. The term may mean either the complete amplifier, consisting of the voltage-amplifier and power-amplifier stages, or it may mean just one stage. In the usual case, the term implies that the amplifier is not capable of amplifying a direct-current signal; such an amplifier would more likely be called a direct-coupled (dc) amplifier. SEE DIRECT-COUPLED AMPLIFIER.

The function of an audio amplifier is to amplify a weak electrical signal, such as from a microphone or a phono pickup, to a level capable of driving a loudspeaker at the desired output sound level. The sound power level may be small in such applications as a hearing aid.

Audio amplifiers may be constructed with vacuum tubes, but current technology favors transistors and integrated circuits. Transistor amplifiers generally use *RC* (resistance-capacitance) coupling between stages because of its simplicity, good frequency response, and low cost. When integrated circuits are used, the complete voltage-amplifying portion of the circuit may consist of one chip (containing several stages of amplification) and a few external resistors and capacitors. The voltage amplifier drives the power-amplifier section, composed of transistors that must be capable of supplying the desired power to the loudspeaker. For low-power applications there are integrated circuits that provide the necessary power gain and connect directly to the loudspeaker. SEE INTEGRATED CIRCUITS; TRANSISTOR; VOLTAGE AMPLIFIER.

The amplifier can be designed with a frequency response that is adequate to produce nearly distortionless amplification, particularly when negative feedback is used. Proper feedback can overcome most of the distortion introduced by the nonlinearities in the amplifier transistors or vacuum tubes, the power output transformer, and the loudspeaker, and the lack of a uniform frequency response of the amplifier and loudspeaker. High-fidelity amplifiers use feedback. SEE DISTORTION (ELECTRONIC CIRCUITS).

Audio amplifiers are capable of a power output ranging from a few watts to a few hundred watts, depending on the application.

The term af (audio-frequency) amplifier is occasionally used in place of audio amplifier. This is consistent with the designations of rf (radio-frequency) and i-f (intermediate-frequency) amplifiers. SEE AMPLIFIER.

Harold F. Klock

**Bibliography.** J. Lenk, *Manual for Integrated Circuit Users,* 1973; J. Millman, *Microelectronics,* 1979; D. Schilling and C. Belove, *Electronic Circuits: Discrete and Integrated,* 1979.

## Audion

The name given in 1906 to the electronic amplifying tube by its inventor, Lee DeForest. Although initially copyrighted by DeForest as a trade name, the term was used generically to describe grid-controlled amplifier tubes until the 1920s, when the appearance of multigrid tubes led to an expanded terminology (for example, triode, tetrode, pentode, hexode). SEE ELECTRON TUBE; VACUUM TUBE.

Although the term audion is merely of historical interest in modern electronics, the circumstances surrounding its invention are of continuing interest. The fact that electric current can be carried between a heated filament and a nearby metal plate, when both are enclosed in a rarefied gas or vacuum, had been discovered in 1883 by Thomas Edison, but the mechanism of the transfer of charge was a mystery at that time.

By 1900 J. J. Thompson had advanced the electron theory, which identified the quantified nature of electric current. It was then realized that the Edison effect could be explained by the emission of electrons from the hot filament and their subsequent collection by the metal plate. The current would not travel in the reverse direction since the cold plate was incapable of emitting electrons. This one-way passage gave rise to the use of a device, first developed in 1897 by J. Ambrose Fleming, which rectified alternating current, and acted as a detector of radio waves. At this stage the Fleming "valve" occupied the same position held by the semiconductor diode in the early 1940s, prior to the invention of the transistor. Neither device could amplify, and without amplification, the vast potential of electronic and semiconductor technology could not be realized at the time. SEE TRANSISTOR.

It was DeForest's seminal concept that a third electrode might be inserted into the Fleming valve and that changes in voltage applied to the third electrode would produce corresponding changes in the current passing between the heated filament and the metal plate. This changing current, passed through a resistance external to the device, would generate a magnified copy of the voltage applied to the device; that is, amplification would take place.

DeForest applied for his patent on the three electrode amplifier on October 25, 1906, and the following day presented his paper "The Audion—A New Receiver for Wireless Telegraphy" to the American Institute of Electrical Engineers. The patent (no. 841,387) was issued on January 15, 1907. In one form shown in the first patent (see **illus.**) the signal to be amplified is applied between the heated filament and one plate, and the output is taken from the filament and another plate, which is at the opposite side of the filament, a procedure not favorable to amplifying action in a highly evacuated device. However, reference is made in the patent to a "gaseous me-

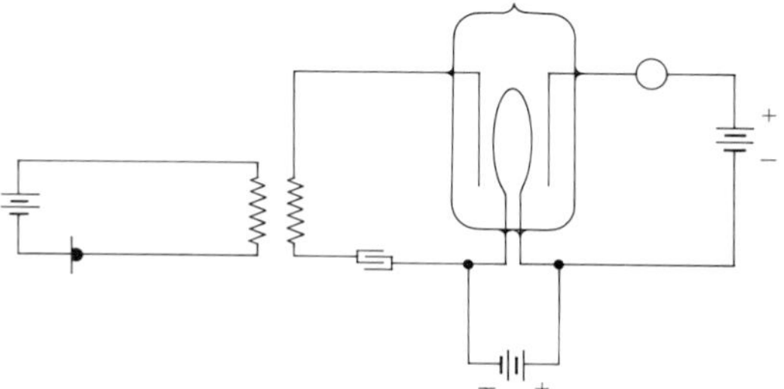

The DeForest audion circuit, as shown in DeForest's patent application. (*U.S. Patent no. 841,387, 1907*)

dium'' within the tube, maintained in a conduction of ''molecular activity.'' It thus appears that the observed amplification resulted from changes in ionization, rather than from attraction and repulsion of the flow of electrons. In fact, the early audions were subject to wide variations of performance arising from uncontrolled factors in their design and construction (particularly the amount and nature of the gas content). Such tubes were known as ''soft tubes'' because of their relatively high gas content. It remained for others, notably Irving Langmuir, to understand the importance of high vacuum in obtaining reproducible characteristics in audions, which later became known as ''hard tubes.'' A similar situation occurred in the early development of transistors, which exhibited erratic behavior and had short life-spans until the importance of hermetically sealing the transistor against intrusion of moisture was understood. SEE ELECTRONICS.

*Donald G. Fink*

**Bibliography.** L. DeForest, The audion: A new receiver for wireless telegraphy, *Trans. A.I.E.E.*, 25:735, 1907; U.S. Patents no. 841, 387 (1907) and no. 879, 532 (1908), issued to L. DeForest.

## Automata theory

A theory concerned with models (automata) used to simulate objects and processes such as computers, digital circuits, nervous systems, cellular growth, and reproduction. Automata theory helps engineers design and analyze digital circuits which are parts of computers, telephone systems, or control systems. It uses ideas and methods of discrete mathematics to determine the limits of computational power for models of existing and future computers. Among many known applications of finite automata are lexical analyzers and hardware controllers.

The concept now known as the automaton was first examined by A. M. Turing in 1936 for the study of limits of human ability to solve mathematical problems in formal ways. His automaton has become known as a Turing machine. The Turing machine is too powerful for simulation of many systems. Therefore, some more appropriate models were introduced, such as the finite-state machine. There exist some intermediate automata between Turing machines and finite-state machines, such as linear bounded automata and push-down automata.

**Turing machines and intermediate automata.** The Turing machine is a suitable model for the computational power of a computer. Its usefulness follows from the thesis of A. Church which may be reformulated as: The computational power of the Turing machine represents a limit for any realizable computer. SEE COMPUTER.

A Turing machine has two main parts: a finite-state machine with a head, and a tape (**Fig. 1**). The tape is infinite in both directions and is divided into squares. The head sees at any moment of time one square of the tape and is able to read the content of the square as well as to write on the square. The finite-state machine is in one of its states. Each square of the tape holds exactly one of the symbols, also called input symbols or machine characters. It is assumed that one of the input symbols is a special one, the blank, denoted by $B$.

At any moment of time, the machine, being in one of its states and looking at one of the input symbols in some square, may act or halt. The action means that, in the next moment of time, the machine erases the old input symbol and writes a new input symbol on the same square (it may be the same symbol as before, or a new symbol; if the old one was not $B$ and the new one is $B$, the machine is said to erase the old symbol), changes the state to a new one (again, it is possible that the new state will be equal to the old one), and finally moves the head one square to the left, or one square to the right, or stays on the same square as before.

For some pairs of states and input symbols the action is not specified in the description of a Turing machine; thus the machine halts. In this case, symbols remaining on the tape form the output, corresponding to the original input, or more precisely, to the input string (or sequence) of input symbols. A sequence of actions, followed by a halt, is called a computation. A Turing machine accepts some input string if it halts on it. The set of all accepted strings over all the input symbols is called a language accepted by the Turing machine. Such languages are called recursively enumerable sets.

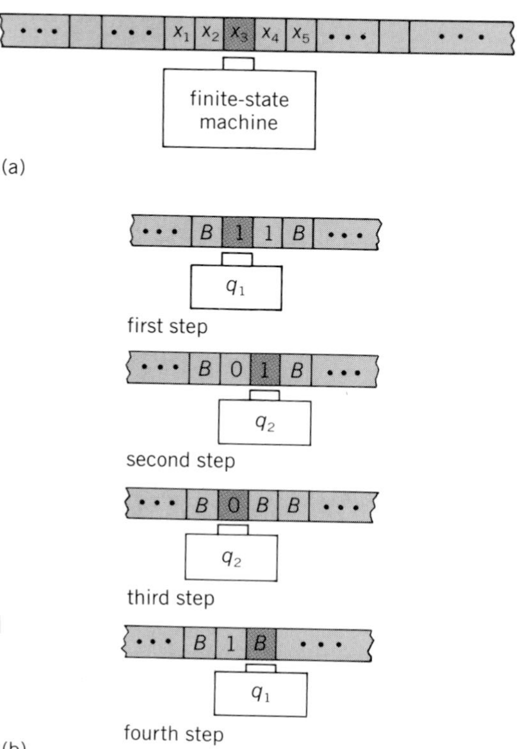


**Fig. 1. Turing machine.** ***(a)*** **General idea.** ***(b)*** **An example of a computation.**

For example, a Turing machine with three input symbols, 0, 1, and $B$, and three states, $q_1$, $q_2$, and $q_3$, is given by the table below. $R$, $L$, and $S$ mean move

| | 0 | 1 | $B$ |
|---|---|---|---|
| $q_1$ | $1\ q_3\ S$ | $0\ q_2\ R$ | |
| $q_2$ | $1\ q_1\ R$ | $B\ q_2\ L$ | |
| $q_3$ | | | |

the head one step to the right, to the left, or stay on the same square, respectively. The entry $1\ q_3\ S$ in row $q_1$ and column 0 of the table means that if the Turing machine reads 0 in the state $q_1$, then, in the next moment of time, it will print 1 on the same square, the next stage will be $q_3$, and the head will stay on the same square. The blank entry in row $q_1$ and column $B$ means that if the machine reads blank $B$ in the state $q_1$, it will halt. It is assumed that the Turing machine always starts the computation in its initial state $q_1$. An example of a computation for input string 11 is given in Fig. 1*b*. The output is 1. This Turing machine will convert the input string 1010 into the output string 0101.

Another automaton is a nondeterministic Turing machine. It differs from an ordinary, deterministic Turing machine in that for a given state and input symbol, the machine has a finite number of choices for the next move. Each choice means a new input symbol, a new state, and a new direction to move its head. The computational power of a nondeterministic Turing machine is the same as a deterministic one, suitably constructed.

A linear bounded automaton is a nondeterministic Turing machine which is restricted to the portion of the tape containing the input. The restriction of the Turing machine to a portion of the tape which is bounded by some linear function of the length of input results in the same computational power as the restriction of the Turing machine to the portion of the tape containing just the input—hence the name.

The capability of the linear bounded automaton is smaller than that of a Turing machine. The languages accepted by linear bounded automata are called context-sensitive. The class of all context-sensitive languages is a proper subclass of the class of recursively enumerable sets.

A computational device with yet smaller capability than that of a linear bounded automaton is a push-down automaton. It consists of a finite-state machine that reads an input symbol from a tape and controls a stack. The stack is a list in which insertions and deletions are possible, both operations taking place at one end, called the top. The intuitive model of a stack is a pile of books on a floor or dishes on a shelf. Symbols from some alphabet are inserted to the top of the stack by a "push" operation. The topmost element may be deleted from the stack by a "pop" operation. The device is nondeterministic, so it has a number of choices for each next move. Two types of moves are possible. In the first type, a choice depends on the input symbol, the top element of the stack, and the state of the finite-state machine. The choice consists of selecting a next state of the finite-state machine, removing the top element, leaving the stack without the top element, or replacing the top element by a sequence of symbols. After performing a choice, the input head reads the next input symbol. The other type is similar to the first one, but now the input symbol is not used and the head is not moved, so the automaton controls the stack without reading input symbols. SEE ABSTRACT DATA TYPES.

A push-down automaton accepts the set of all input strings for which there exists a sequence of moves causing it to empty its stack. Any such set is called a context-free language. The class of context-free languages is a proper subclass of the class of context-sensitive languages.

**Finite-state machines.** A finite-state automaton, or a finite-state machine, or a finite automaton, is a computational device having a fixed upper bound on the amount of memory it uses. It should be clear that the amount of memory for Turing machines, linear bounded automata, or push-down automata is unlimited. One approach to finite automata is through the concept of an acceptor. The finite automaton examines an input string (that is, a sequence of input symbols, located on the tape) in one pass from left to right. It has a finite number of states, among which one is specified as initial. The assumption is that the finite automaton starts scanning of input standing in its initial state. Some of the states are called accepting states. The finite automaton has a transition function (or next-state function) which maps each state and input symbol into the next state. In each step the finite automaton computes the next state and reads the next input symbol. If after reading the entire input string the last state is accepting, the string is accepted; otherwise it is rejected. The language of the finite automaton (called also a regular language or regular event) is the set of all strings over the set of input symbols that are accepted. The class of regular languages is a proper subclass of the class of context-free languages.

For example, consider the finite acceptor presented in **Fig. 2**. It has two input symbols, 0 and 1, and four states, $q_0$, $q_1$, $q_2$, and $q_3$, where $q_0$ is initial and $q_2$ is accepting (in the example there is just one accepting state). Actions are denoted by arrows. For example, if, in the initial state, the acceptor reads input symbol 0 on the tape, the next state is $q_3$. The regular language of this acceptor is the set consisting of the following strings: 11, 101, 1001, 10001, . . . .

Another approach to the definition of the finite automaton is presented below. A finite automaton is a quintuple $(S, \Sigma, \Omega, M, N)$, where $S$ is a finite nonempty set (state set), $\Sigma$ is a finite nonempty set (input set), $\Omega$ is a finite nonempty set (output set), $M$ is a function (next-state function, transition function) of $S \times \Sigma$ into $S$, and $N$ is a function (output function) into

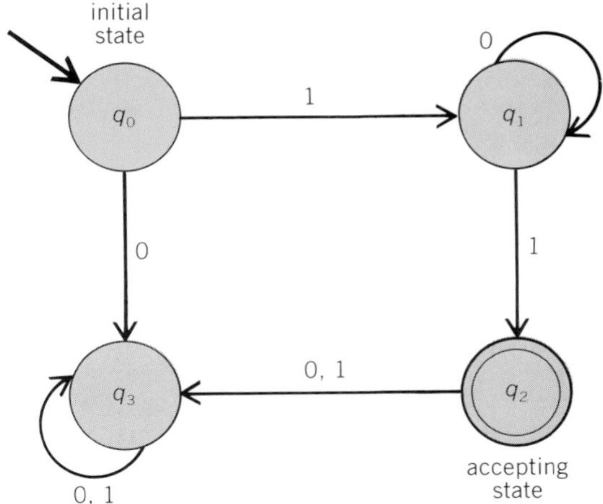


**Fig. 2. Finite acceptor with four states (*q*).**

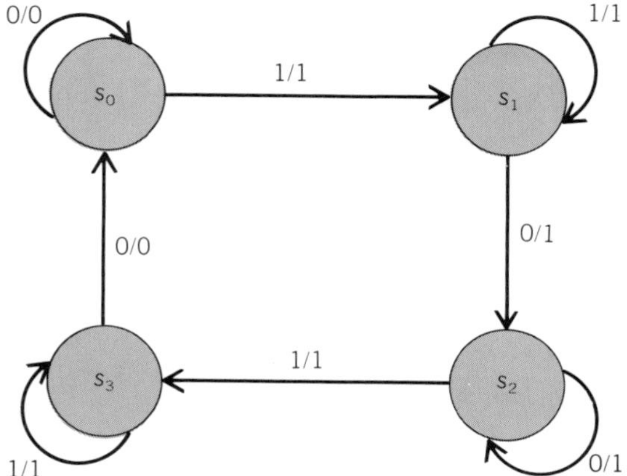


**Fig. 3. Finite automaton with four states (s).**

Ω in the case of Mealy automaton or $S$ into Ω in the case of Moore automaton.

A special case of the Moore automaton corresponds to the first approach to the definition of a finite automaton. Namely, it is necessary to select one state and call it initial, to set Ω equal to the set {0,1}, and to define $N$ by: $N(s) = 1$ if and only if $s$ is accepting. The difference between the two approaches is not fundamental.

Degenerated finite automata, defined as those with just one state, are called combinational automata or combinational networks.

An example consists of the ball-point pen with a button. Possible input symbols are: 0 (releasing the button of the pen) and 1 (pushing the button of the pen). Possible output symbols are also 0, which means that the pen cannot be used to write, and 1, which means that it can. As follows from the analysis of the pen, a finite automaton which models it has four states $s_0$, $s_1$, $s_2$, and $s_3$. Actions of a finite automaton, modeling a pen, are shown in **Fig. 3** as arrows labeled by fractions. A numerator of the fraction describes an input symbol, a denominator an output symbol. For example, an arc from $s_0$ to $s_0$, denoted by 0/0, should be interpreted as: if the state is $s_0$, and the input symbol is 0, then the next state is again $s_0$, and the output symbol is also 0.

*Jerzy W. Grzymala-Busse*

***Bibliography.*** Z. Bavel, *Introduction to the Theory of Automata*, 1983; J. L. Gersting, *Mathematical Structures for Computer Science*, 1982; J. Hartmanis and R. E. Stearns, *Algebraic Structure Theory of Sequential Machines*, 1966; J. E. Hopcroft and J. D. Ullman, *Introduction to Automata Theory, Languages, and Computation*, 1979; Z. Kohavi, *Switching and Finite Automata Theory*, 1970; R. McNaughton, *Elementary Computability, Formal Languages and Automata*, 1982.

## Automatic frequency control (AFC)

The automatic control of the intermediate frequency in a radio, television, or radar receiver, to correct for variations of the frequency of the transmitted carrier or the local oscillator. In high-fidelity broadcast receivers AFC keeps distortion due to detuning to a low figure. In the reception of long-haul telegraph signals, AFC reduces the error rate due to signal pulse distortion or interference from lower intensity signals in the same frequency band.

Single-sideband receivers receive signals which are transmitted with a carrier level that is reduced to as small a proportion as 5%, or less, of the sideband (intelligence) amplitude. Proper demodulation requires the generation locally of a carrier-frequency signal synchronized to the transmitted carrier by AFC. Since propagation at frequencies of 3–30 MHz is dependent upon reflections from the ionosphere, motion in this medium will speed up and retard the arrival of the wave, causing Doppler-effect frequency changes. Transmission to and from speeding aircraft will also suffer Doppler frequency drift. To reduce these effects, the carrier is transmitted for synchronization so that the frequency difference between the carrier and side frequency is maintained on reception.

AFC techniques are varied but are mainly of two types. One uses a discriminator to furnish a voltage whose magnitude and polarity are determined by the frequency change. This voltage is used to adjust the frequency of the local oscillator of the receiver, thereby keeping the intermediate frequency constant. The other uses two-polarity pulse accumulation which furnishes a dc potential proportional to frequency error.

To select only the carrier for AFC, very narrow bandwidths are utilized. As an example, a bandwidth of 30 Hz at 70% of maximum response is quite common. The response of the control circuits is usually designed to be slow and to be inactive below a determinable level of carrier input. These techniques reduce noise and interference as well as frequency-control capture by undesired adjacent carriers. *See Radar; Radio receiver; Television receiver.*

*Walter Lyons*

## Automatic gain control (AGC)

The automatic maintenance of a nearly constant output level of an amplifying circuit by adjusting the amplification in inverse proportion to the input field strength, also called automatic volume control (AVC). Almost all radio receivers in use employ AGC. In broadcast receivers AGC makes it possible to receive incoming signals of widely varying strength, yet have the sound remain at nearly the same volume. In communications receivers a type of AGC circuit called a squelch circuit is used to prevent noise during periods of no transmission, such as in the reception of on-off keying, frequency-shift keying, and phone. AGC is also useful in accelerating the switching action between receivers in diversity connection. *See Radio receiver.*

AGC action depends on the characteristic, possessed by most electronic tubes and transistors, of adjustment of gain by the variation of the applied bias

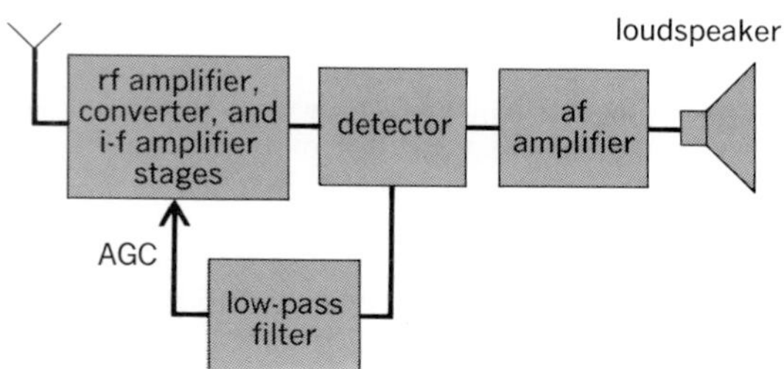


**Fig. 1. Block diagram of broadcast receiver using AGC.**

voltage. If the dc voltage applied to the control grid of a vacuum tube is made more negative, the amplification of that stage will be reduced.

In most broadcast receivers the AGC voltage is taken from the detector. This dc voltage, proportional to the average level of the carrier, adjusts the gain of the radio-frequency (rf) and intermediate-frequency amplifiers and the converter (**Fig. 1**). AGC tends to keep the input signal to the audio-frequency amplifier constant despite variations in rf signal strength. There are several modifications of this basic circuit.

Perfect AGC action would provide a constant output for all values of input signal strength. A slightly rising output characteristic with increased signal strength is generally desirable to facilitate proper tuning. The figure of merit applied to AGC action is given as the change in input required for a given output change. An example of a good figure of merit may be seen when an 80-dB change in input carrier signal results in an output change of no more than 3 dB. This applies to the unmodulated carrier strength only, since the modulation of the carrier must always vary as the modulation of the transmitter.

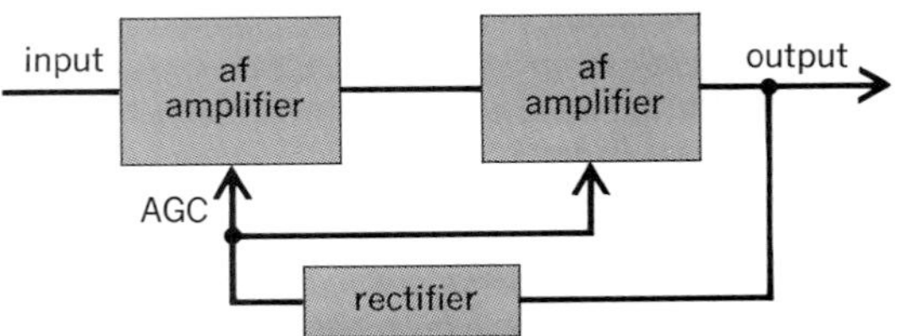


**Fig. 2. Block diagram of AGC of an audio amplifier.**

AGC circuits are also used in dictation recording equipment, public address systems, and similar equipment where a constant output level is desirable. **Figure 2** shows a typical block diagram for such equipment. *See Amplifier*.

*Walter Lyons*

## Backward-wave tube

A type of microwave traveling-wave tube in which energy on a slow-wave circuit flows opposite in direction to the travel of electrons in a beam. Chief characteristics of backward-wave tubes are regenerative feedback produced by interaction of circuit and beam, and a wide range of electrical tuning, easily produced by changing the beam voltage. Such tubes are useful as voltage-tuned oscillators for signal generators, as power sources for quick tuning transmitters, and as local oscillators in receivers for systems that have quick tuning transmitters. If backward-wave tubes are operated as regenerative amplifiers, they are useful as narrowband amplifers in wide-range rapidly tuned receivers.

**O-type backward-wave oscillator.** An O-type backward-wave oscillator (or O-carcinotron) may be similar in appearance to a forward-wave traveling-wave tube. An electron gun produces an electron beam; this beam is focused longitudinally throughout the length of the tube. A slow-wave circuit interacts with the beam, and at the end of the tube a collector terminates the beam (**Fig. 1**). *See Traveling-wave tube*.

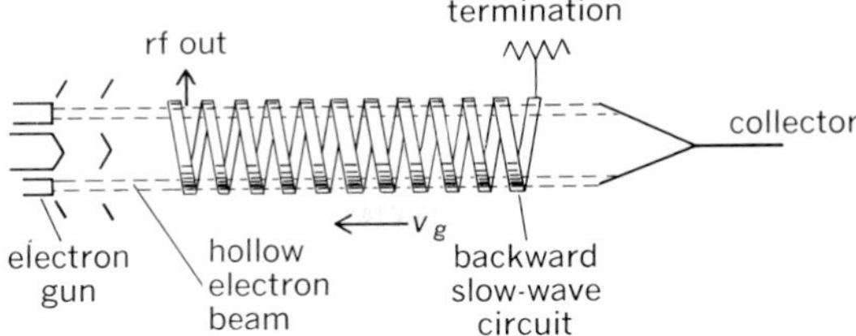


**Fig. 1. O-type backward-wave oscillator (or O-carcinotron), with a hollow cylindrical electron beam, which uses a helix as the slow-wave circuit.**

Energy in the slow-wave circuit travels from collector end toward the gun end of the tube. Hence, microwave energy is coupled out adjacent to the electron gun. At the collector end the slow-wave circuit is terminated with a matched load, usually internally, so that no microwave terminal is provided. For a tube in which the slow-wave circuit is a helix, the termination usually consists of lossy material sprayed on the collector end of the circuit.

The electron beam is usually hollow, the electrons thereby all being close to the helix. The electrons experience the strongest electric filed from the microwave signal when they pass a gap between two helix turns. Electron velocity is adjusted so that any one electron experiences approximately the same phase of the microwave signal as it passes successive gaps. Hence, axial forces due to the microwave field cause some electrons to speed up and others to slow down as they travel past successive gaps. These accelerations and decelerations cause the electrons to bunch in the axial direction. Average velocity of a bunch is such that it drifts into a retarding electric field as it travels down the tube; thus the bunched beam transfers energy to the slow-wave circuit. This action provides continuous feedback along the tube, the beam providing a forward flow of energy and the circuit a backward flow.

To examine the synchronism condition for backward-wave interaction, consider two successive gaps of a helix. The time required for an electron to travel from the first gap to the second equals $p/u_o$, where $p$ is helix pitch, and $u_o$ is electron velocity. During this transit time, a microwave signal of frequency $f$ on the helix will have changed its phase at any one gap by $2\pi fp/u_o$. In addition, at any instant the microwave fields at the two adjacent gaps differ in phase by $2\pi fp/v_g$, where $v_g$ is the velocity at which microwave energy travels along the helix toward the gun. Thus, an electron in moving from the first to the second gap experiences a total field phase change of $\phi$. This is defined in the equation below, where synchronism occurs when phase change $\phi$ is exactly one cycle or $2\pi$

$$2\pi fp/u_o + 2\pi fp/v_g = \phi$$

radians. Frequency of oscillation $f$ can be controlled by changing electron velocity $u_o$, which depends on the helix-to-cathode voltage.

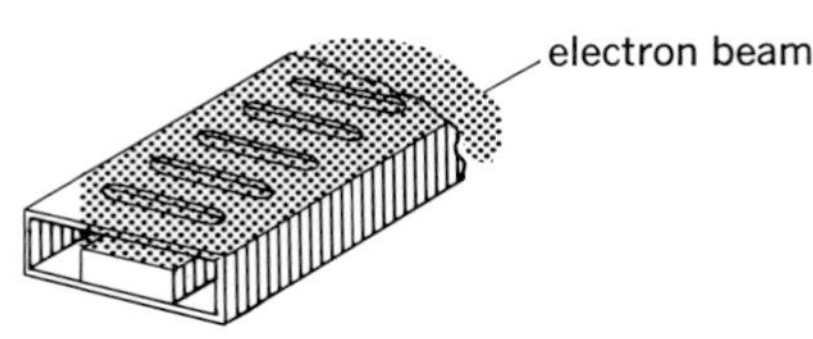


**Fig. 2. Karp circuit used at millimeter wavelengths.**

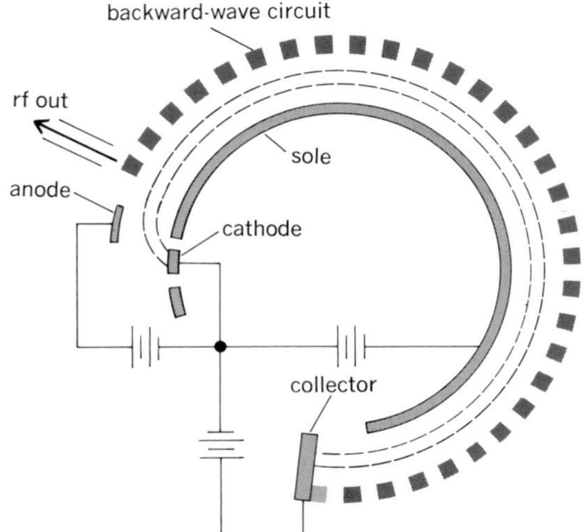


Fig. 3. M-type backward-wave oscillator with the beam focused by a static magnetic field directed into the plane of the page.

As in any feedback oscillator, gain must exceed internal losses. To obtain this minimum required gain, beam current is raised above a value called the start-oscillation current. Normally, operation is at a current in the order of twice the start-oscillation current. Too much beam current would permit higher-order electronic modes that interfere with the desired mode.

Backward-wave oscillators with a helix for the slow-wave circuit typically develop outputs of 10–200 milliwatts, with efficiencies of a few percent or less. Frequency can be voltage-tuned typically over a 2:1 range. Another slow-wave circuit, used at millimeter wavelengths, is the Karp circuit (**Fig. 2**).

**M-type backward-wave oscillator.** An M-type backward-wave oscillator (or M-carcinotron) is similar in principle to the O-type, except that focusing and interaction are through magnetic fields, as in magnetrons. In the M-type oscillator (**Fig. 3**), a transverse magnetic field and a static radial electric field between sole and backward-wave circuit structure confine the beam to the interaction space. Either the voltage connected to the sole or to the slow-wave circuit tunes the frequency. SEE MAGNETRON.

The commonest slow-wave circuit is an interdigital structure, consisting of an array of vertical bars alternating up and down. Efficiency of the M-type tube is considerably higher than that of the O-type tube, typical efficiencies being 20–30%. However, noise and spurious output power are also greater in the M-type tube. Continuous output powers of several hundred watts are typical.

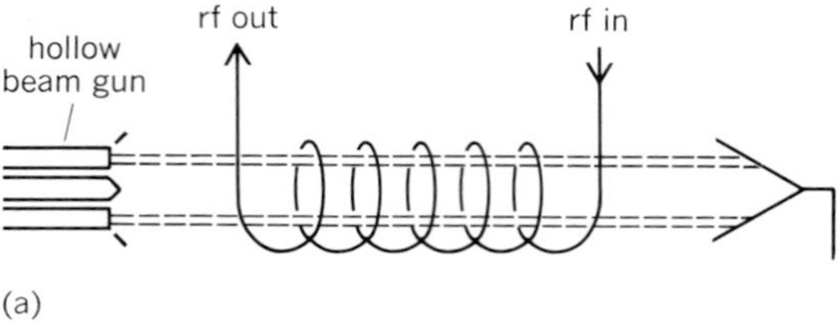


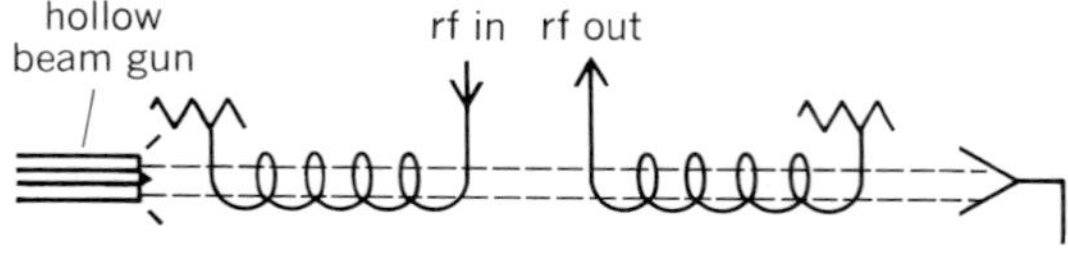


Fig. 4. Backward-wave amplifiers. *(a)* Single-circuit type. *(b)* Cascade type, used for increased stability.

**Backward-wave amplifier.** When either type tube is operated with currents below the start-oscillation value, narrow-band regenerative amplification is obtained. Amplifier frequency is electrically tunable over a wide range by change of beam voltage. Input to a backward-wave amplifier is at the collector end and output is at the gun end (**Fig. 4**). Separation of the slow-wave circuit into two or more parts enhances stability. A cascade backward-wave amplifier has a stable gain in excess of 20 dB, a bandwidth of a fraction of a percent, a tuning range easily of 2:1, and a noise figure as low as 3.5 dB. SEE MICROWAVE TUBE.

*J. W. Gewartowski*

**Bibliography.** J. W. Gewartowski and H. A. Watson, *Principles of Electron Tubes*, 1965; A. L. Lance, *Introduction to Microwave Theory and Measurements*, 1964; S. Ligo, *Microwave Devices and Circuits*, 1980.

## Band theory of solids

A quantum-mechanical theory of the motion of electrons in solids. Its name comes from the fact that it predicts certain restricted ranges, or bands, for the energies of electrons in solids.

Suppose that the atoms of a solid are separated from each other to such a distance that they do not interact. The energy levels of the electrons of this system will then be those characteristic of the individual free atoms, and thus many electrons will have the same energy. Now imagine the atoms being slowly brought closer together. As the distance between atoms is decreased, the electrons in the outer shells begin to interact with each other. This interaction alters their energy and, in fact, broadens the sharp energy level out into a range of possible energy levels called a band. One would expect the process of band formation to be well advanced for the outer, or valence, electrons at the observed interatomic distances in solids. Once the atomic levels have spread into bands, the valence electrons are not confined to individual atoms, but may jump from atom to atom with an ease that increases with the increasing width of the band.

Although energy bands exist in all solids, the term energy band is usually used in reference only to ordered substances, that is, those having well-defined crystal lattices. In such a case, an electron energy state can be classified according to its crystal momentum $\mathbf{p}$ or its electron wave vector $\mathbf{k} = \mathbf{p}/\hbar$ (where $\hbar$ is Planck's constant $h$ divided by $2\pi$). If the electrons were free, the energy of an electron whose wave vector is $\mathbf{k}$ would be as shown in Eq. (1), where $E_0$ is

$$E(\mathbf{k}) = E_0 + \hbar^2\mathbf{k}^2/2m_0 \qquad (1)$$

the energy of the lowest state of a valence electron and $m_0$ is the electron mass. In a crystal, however, the electrons are not free because of the effect of the crystal binding and the forces exerted on them by the atoms; consequently, the relation $E(\mathbf{k})$ between energy and wave vector is more complicated. The statement of this relationship constitutes the description of an energy band.

A knowledge of the energy levels of electrons is of fundamental importance in computing electrical, magnetic, optical, or thermal properties of solids.

**Allowed and forbidden bands.** The bands of possible electron energy levels in a solid are called al-

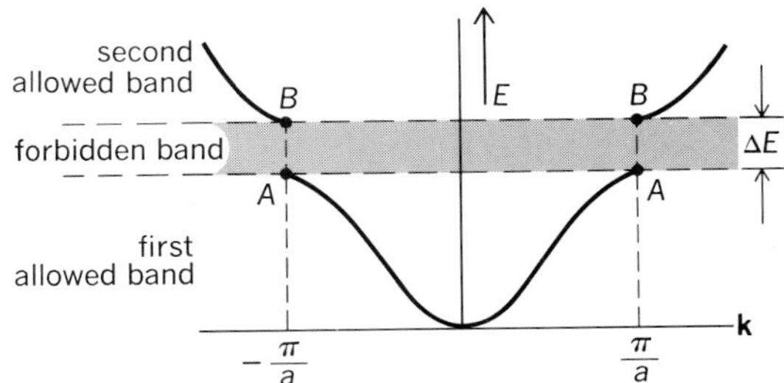


**Electron energy *E* versus wave vector k for a monatomic linear lattice of lattice constant *a*. (*After C. Kittel, Introduction to Solid State Physics, 2d ed., Wiley, 1956*)**

lowed energy bands. It often happens that there are also bands of energy levels which it is impossible for an electron to have in a given crystal. Such bands are called forbidden bands, or gaps. The allowed energy bands sometimes overlap and sometimes are separated by forbidden bands. The presence of a forbidden band, or energy gap, immediately above the occupied allowed states (such as the region *A* to *B* in the **illustration**) is the principal difference in the electronic structures of a semiconductor or insulator and a metal. In the first two substances there is a gap between the valence band or normally occupied states and the conduction band, which is normally unoccupied. In a metal there is no gap between occupied and unoccupied states.

The presence of a gap means that the electrons cannot easily be accelerated into higher energy states by an applied electric field. Thus, the substance cannot carry a current unless electrons are excited across the gap by thermal or optical means.

**Effective mass.** When an external electromagnetic field acts upon the electrons in a solid, the resultant motion is not what one would expect if the electrons were free. In fact, the electrons behave as though they were free but with a different mass, which is called the effective mass. This effective mass can be obtained from the dependence of electron energy on the wave vector, $E(\mathbf{k})$, in the following way.

Suppose there is a maximum or minimum of the function $E(\mathbf{k})$ at the point $\mathbf{k} = \mathbf{k}_0$. The function $E(\mathbf{k})$ can be expanded in a Taylor series about this point. For simplicity, assume that $E(\mathbf{k})$ is a function of the magnitude of $\mathbf{k}$ only, that is, is independent of the direction of $\mathbf{k}$. Then, by dropping terms higher than second order in the Taylor series, Eq. (2) results. By

$$E(\mathbf{k}) = E(\mathbf{k}_0) + {}^1\!/_2\,(\mathbf{k} - \mathbf{k}_0)^2 \left(\frac{d^2E}{dk^2}\right)_{\mathbf{k}_0} \qquad (2)$$

analogy with Eq. (1), a quantity $m^*$ with the dimensions of a mass can be defined by the relation in Eq. (3).

$$\hbar^2/m^* = \left(\frac{d^2E}{dk^2}\right)_{\mathbf{k}_0} \qquad (3)$$

The quantity $m^*$ is called the effective mass of electrons at $\mathbf{k}_0$. For many simple metals, the average effective mass is close to $m_0$, but smaller effective masses are not uncommon. In indium antimonide, a semiconductor, the effective mass of electrons in the conduction band is 0.013 $m_0$. In a semiclassical approximation, an electron in the solid responds to an external applied electric or magnetic field as though it were a particle of mass $m^*$. The equation of motion of an electron is shown in Eq. (4), where $\mathbf{v}$ is the

$$m^* \frac{d\mathbf{v}}{dt} = e(\mathbf{E} + \mathbf{v} \times \mathbf{B}) \qquad (4)$$

electron velocity, $\mathbf{E}$ the electric field, $\mathbf{B}$ the magnetic induction, and $e$ the charge of the electron.

It may happen that the energy $E(\mathbf{k})$ does depend upon the direction of $\mathbf{k}$. In such a case, the effective mass is a tensor whose components are defined by Eq. (5). Equation (4) remains valid with a tensor $m^*$.

$$\hbar^2/m_{ij}^* = \left(\frac{\partial^2E}{\partial k_i \partial k_j}\right)_{\mathbf{k}_0} \qquad (5)$$

Bismuth is an example of a metal in which the effective mass depends strongly on direction.

**Transitions between states.** Under external influences, such as irradiation, electrons can make transitions between states in the same band or in different bands. The interaction between the electrons and the vibrations of the crystal lattice can scatter the electrons in a given band with a substantial change in the electron momentum, but only a slight change in energy. This scattering is one of the principal causes of the electrical resistivity of metals. SEE ELECTRICAL RESISTIVITY.

An external electromagnetic field (for example, visible light) can cause transitions between different bands. In such a process, momentum must be conserved. Because the momentum of a photon $h\nu/c$ (where $\nu$ is the frequency of the light and $c$ its velocity) is quite small, the momentum of the electron before and after collision is nearly the same. Such a transition is called vertical in reference to an energy band diagram. Conservation of energy must also hold in the transition, so absorption of light is possible only if there is an unoccupied state of energy $h\nu$ available at the same $\mathbf{k}$ as the initial state. These transitions are responsible for much of the absorption of light by semiconductors in the visible and near-infrared region of the spectrum.

**Energy band calculation.** As is the case for any quantum mechanical system, the energy levels of electrons in solids are determined in principle by the solution of the Schrödinger wave equation for the system. However, the enormous number of particles involved makes exact solution of this equation impossible. Approximate methods must be employed. The atoms are regarded as fixed in their equilibrium positions. Each electron is regarded as having an individual wave function $\psi_n(\mathbf{k},\mathbf{r})$, in which $\mathbf{k}$ is the wave vector and the index $n$ designates a particular band. The wave function $\psi_n(\mathbf{k},\mathbf{r})$ is frequently called a Bloch function. The wave function of the many-electron system is written as a determinant of Bloch functions to satisfy the requirements of the Pauli exclusion principle. The general variational method of quantum mechanics may be employed to derive an equation for the individual Bloch functions. This equation, which is known as the Hartree-Fock equation, is similar to a one-electron Schrödinger equation in which each electron moves in the field of all the nuclei of the system and the average field of all the other electrons. An additional term, exchange, takes account of the reduction of the average electronic repulsion, because the probability of close encounters of electrons of parallel spin is reduced by the Pauli exclusion principle.

The Hartree-Fock equations are still quite complicated, and must be solved by the self-consistent field method. In this approach, some reasonable distribution of electrons is assumed to exist. An effective potential $V(\mathbf{r})$ can be calculated from this distribution, including the contribution from the nuclei. Usually it is an adequate approximation to include the exchange terms in this potential. Then the Bloch functions may be formed by solving Eq. (6), in which $V(\mathbf{r})$ is the

$$-\frac{\hbar^2}{2m_0}\Delta^2\psi_n(\mathbf{k,r}) + V(\mathbf{r})\psi_n(\mathbf{k,r}) = E_n(\mathbf{k})\psi_n(\mathbf{k,r}) \quad (6)$$

potential described above and $E_n(\mathbf{k})$ is the energy of an electron in band $n$ having wave vector $\mathbf{k}$. The potential $V(\mathbf{r})$ is periodic in space with the periodicity of the crystal. The wave function $\psi_n(\mathbf{k,r})$ obtained from Eq. (6) yields a new electron distribution from which the potential $V(\mathbf{r})$ may be calculated again. The process is repeated until the potential used in the solution of Eq. (6) agrees with that obtained from the solution $\psi_n(\mathbf{k,r})$ to sufficient accuracy.

The local density approximation is frequently used to obtain this potential. In the simplest formula of this type, the Kohn-Sham potential, $V(\mathbf{r})$ is given by Eq. (7). The first term represents the potential energy of

$$V(\mathbf{r}) = -e^2\sum_{\mu}\frac{Z_\mu}{|\mathbf{r}-\mathbf{R}_\mu|} + e^2\int\frac{p(\mathbf{r}')d^3r'}{|\mathbf{r}-\mathbf{r}'|} - 2e^2\left(\frac{3\rho(\mathbf{r})}{8\pi}\right)^{1/3} \quad (7)$$

an electron in the field of all the nuclei of the system. These nuclei are located at sites $\mathbf{R}_\mu$ and have charge $\mathbf{Z}_\mu$. The second term contains the average electronic repulsion of the electron distribution, and $\pi(\mathbf{r})$ is the electron density. The third term approximately describes the exchange interaction.

The self-consistent field procedure is evidently quite complicated. Since it may not be practical to repeat the calculations to obtain a self-consistent solution, it is desirable to choose an initial $V(\mathbf{r})$ which approximates the actual physical situation as closely as possible. Choice of an adequate crystal potential is the chief physical problem in the calculation of energy levels of electrons in solids.

Several techniques are available for solving wave equation (6) with a given $V(\mathbf{r})$. Those in common use include the Green's function method, the augmented plane wave method, the orthogonalized plane wave method, and the linear combination of atomic orbitals method. It is also possible to use experimentally determined energy levels and effective masses to obtain a suitable potential for use in Eq. (6). This procedure, which bypasses many of the difficulties of the self-consistent field approach, is known as the pseudopotential method and is now widely used. In simple metals (not transition metals) and wideband semiconductors, such as germanium and silicon, the pseudopotential is rather weak, and many properties can be calculated by using perturbation theory.

**Density of states.** Many properties of solids, including electron specific heat and optical and x-ray absorption and emission, are related rather simply to a basic function known as the density of states. This function, here denoted $G(E)$, is defined so that the number of electronic energy states in the range between $E$ and $E + dE$ is $G(E)dE$. It can be shown that $G(E)$ is given by Eq. (8), in which $E(\mathbf{k})$ is the energy

$$G(E) = \frac{\Omega}{4\pi^3}\int\delta(E - E(\mathbf{k}))\,d^3k = \frac{\Omega}{4\pi^3}\int\frac{dS_k(E)}{|\nabla_k E(\mathbf{k})|} \quad (8)$$

band function, $\delta$ is the Dirac delta function, $\Omega$ is the volume of a unit cell of the solid, and the constant multiplying the integral has been chosen so that the number of states is two (one for each spin direction) for each energy band. The first integral in Eq. (8) is taken over the Brillouin zone, the second over a surface of constant energy $E$ in the zone. The density of states will show structure in the neighborhood of energies corresponding to points where $|\nabla_k E(\mathbf{k})|$ vanishes. Such points, which are required to exist by reasons of crystal symmetry and periodicity, are known as Van Hove singularities. The energies of states at which Van Hove singularities occur can be determined from optical and (sometimes) x-ray measurements.

**Experimental information.** A considerable amount of experimental information has been obtained concerning the band structures of the common metals and semiconductors. In metals experiments usually determine properties of the Fermi surface (the surface in $\mathbf{k}$ space bounding the occupied states at zero temperature), since only electrons in states near the top of the Fermi distribution are able to respond to electric and magnetic fields. For example, the magnetic susceptibility of a metal exhibits a component which is an oscillatory function of the reciprocal of the magnetic field strength when the field is strong (de Haas–van Alphen effect). Measurement of the period of these oscillations determines the area of a cross section of the Fermi surface in a plane perpendicular to the direction of the magnetic field.

Other properties of the Fermi surface are obtained by studying the increase of the electrical resistance in a magnetic field, and from the magnetic field dependence of ultrasonic attenuation. The density of states (number of electron states per unit energy) at Fermi energy can be found from measurements of the electron contribution to the specific heat. Effective masses of electrons and holes can be determined by cyclotron resonance measurements in both semiconductors and metals.

Optical and x-ray measurements enable the determination of energy differences between states. The smallest width of the characteristic energy gap between valence and conduction bands in a semiconductor can be determined by measuring the wavelength at which the fundamental absorption begins. Application of a strong uniform magnetic field will produce an oscillatory energy dependence of this absorption, from which a precise determination of effective masses is possible.

In both semiconductors and metals, states removed in energy from the Fermi level can be studied optically. Measurements of the reflectivity will show structure at energies corresponding to transitions at symmetry points of the Brillouin zone where Van Hove singularities are likely to occur. To reveal such structure clearly against a background which frequently may be large, it is useful to subject the solid to a periodic perturbation, possibly an electric field, stress, or a change in temperature. This modifies the band structure slightly, particularly near Van Hove singularities, which tend to be sensitive to perturbations. As a result, the optical properties of the sample are slightly modulated, and this modulation is detected directly. It is possible to apply this technique in the soft x-ray wavelength region as well. Modulation of the soft x-ray emission by alternating stress (the piezo soft x-ray effect) enables the determination of the energies of transitions between band and deep core states.

Photoemission measurements can also yield information about energy bands below the Fermi energy. In these experiments, an electron is excited by a photon from a state of energy, $E_i$, below the Fermi energy to a state of high enough energy, $E_f$, such that the electron can escape from the crystal. The relation between the energies is $E_f = E_i + h\omega$, where $\omega$ is the angular frequency associated with the light. The number of emitted electrons is studied as a function of the angle between the direction of the outgoing electrons and that of the incident photon (often chosen to be perpendicular to the surface). The polarization of the light can also be controlled. If the surface of a single crystal sample is plane, the component of the electron momentum parallel to the solid ($\mathbf{k}_{\|}$) is conserved. The measurement is then sensitive to the distribution of electrons in energy along a line in the Brillouin zone parallel to the surface normal and with the specified value of $\mathbf{k}_{\|}$. The results can be interpreted to give the positions of the energy band in the initial state. *See Photoemission; Semiconductor.*

*Joseph Callaway*

**Bibliography.** P. W. Anderson, *Concepts in Solids*, 1964; N. W. Ashcroft and N. D. Mermin, *Solid State Physics*, 1976; R. H. Bube, *Electronic Properties of Crystalline Solids*, 1974; J. Callaway, *Quantum Theory of the Solid State*, 1974; M. Cardona, *Modulation Spectroscopy*, Suppl. 11 of *Solid State Phys.*, 1969; G. C. Fletcher, *The Electron Band Theory of Solids*, 1971; W. Jones and W. H. March, *Theoretical Solid State Physics*, 1973; C. Kittel, *Quantum Theory of Solids*, 1963; J. C. Slater, *Quantum Theory of Molecules and Solids*, vol. 2: *Symmetry and Energy Bands in Crystals*, 1965; J. M. Ziman, *Principles of the Theory of Solids*, 2d ed., 1972.

## Bandwidth requirements (communications)

The channel bandwidths needed to transmit various types of signals, using various processing schemes. Every signal observed in practice can be expressed as a sum (discrete or over a continuum) of sinusoids of various frequencies. The plot of amplitude versus frequency is the frequency spectrum of the signal. The difference between the highest and the lowest frequencies of components of significant amplitudes in the spectrum is called the bandwidth of the signal, expressed in the unit of frequency, hertz (Hz). Every communication medium (also called channel) is capable of transmitting a band or a spectrum of frequencies with reasonable fidelity. The difference between the highest and the lowest frequencies of components in the band over which the channel gain is constant (or within a specified variation) is called the channel bandwith. *See Waveform.*

**Signal processing.** Clearly, to transmit a signal with reasonable fidelity over a communication channel, the channel bandwidth must match and be at least equal to the signal bandwidth. Proper processing of a signal, such as modulation or coding, however, can increase or decrease the bandwidth of the processed signal. Thus, it is possible to transmit the information of a signal over a channel of bandwidth larger or smaller than that of the original signal.

Amplitude modulation (AM) with double sidebands (DSB), for example, doubles the signal bandwidth. If the audio signal to be transmitted has a bandwidth of 5 kHz, the resulting AM signal bandwidth using DSB is 10 kHz. Amplitude modulation with a single sideband (SSB), on the other hand, requires exactly the same bandwidth as that of the original signal. Amateur radio is an example of this scheme where the transmission bandwidth is 5 kHz. Vestigial sideband (VSB) modulation is a compromise between DSB and SSB. It requires a bandwidth slightly larger (typically 20–30%) than that of the message signal. Broadcast television is an example of this scheme. The television signal (video and audio) bandwidth is 4.5 MHz. It is transmitted by VSB modulation that requires a bandwidth of 6 MHz. *See Amplitude modulation; Amplitude-modulation radio; Single sideband; Television.*

DSB, SSB, and VSB modulation are examples of amplitude-modulation schemes. In broadcast frequency modulation (FM), on the other hand, audio signal bandwidth is 15 kHz (for high fidelity), but the corresponding frequency-modulated signal bandwidth is 200 kHz. In telephony, the audio signal bandwidth is 3 kHz and is transmitted over local lines of 3 kHz bandwidth, or over long distances (using SSB) requiring a transmission bandwidth of 4 kHz per telephone channel (3 kHz for the signal and a guard band of 1 kHz). On the other hand, a digitized telephone signal (processed by analog-to-digital conversion) requires a bandwidth of 32–64 kHz. Facsimile typically requires a bandwidth of 5 kHz for AM and 25 kHz for FM. In telegraphy, the bandwidth for transmission of 100 words per minute is 170–400 Hz. *See Analog-to-digital converter; Facsimile; Frequency modulation; Frequency-modulation radio.*

For digital communication, theoretically, a channel of bandwidth $B$ can transmit the information of $2B$ pulses per second accurately. But due to practical problems, the rate of most of the older digital schemes is $B$ pulses per second or less. The duobinary scheme (or partial response signaling) enables a transmission rate of $2B$ pulses per second and is increasingly used in digital communication. *See Modulation; Pulse modulation; Radio.*

**Shannon's equation.** C. E. Shannon demonstrated that over a channel of bandwith $B$ the rate of information transmission, $C$, in bits/s (binary digits/second) is given by the equation below, where

$$C = B \log_2 (1 + \text{SNR}) \quad \text{bits/s}$$

SNR is the signal-to-noise power ratio. This result assumes a white gaussian noise, which is the worst kind of noise from the point of view of interference. For any other noise the rate of information transmission will be at least as large as that indicated by Shannon's equation. *See Information theory; Signal-to-noise ratio.*

It follows from Shannon's equation that a given information transmission rate $C$ can be achieved by various combinations of $B$ and SNR. It is thus possible to trade $B$ for SNR, and vice versa. In a communication system, one of the two resources ($B$ or SNR) may be more precious than the other, and the communication scheme would be optimized accordingly. A typical voice-grade telephone circuit has a limited bandwidth (3 kHz) but a lot of power is available, whereas in communications satellites, large bandwidths are available but power is scarce. Hence the communication schemes required in the two cases are usually different.

**Broadbanding.** A corollary of Shannon's equation is that, if a signal is properly processed to increase its bandwidth, the processed signal becomes more immune to interference or noise over the channel. This means that an increase in transmission bandwidth (broadbanding) can suppress the noise in the received signal, resulting in a better-quality signal (increased SNR) at the receiver. Frequency modulation and pulse-code modulation (PCM) are two examples of broadband schemes where the transmission bandwidth can be increased as desired to suppress noise. The former transmits information in analog form (an analog scheme), while the latter digitizes the analog information and transmits the resulting digital data (a digital scheme). In general, digital schemes use increased bandwidth more efficiently than the analog schemes in suppressing noise. Amplitude modulation, on the other hand, is not a broadband scheme because its transmission bandwidth is fixed and cannot be increased.

Broadbanding is also used to make communication less vulnerable to jamming and illicit reception by using the so-called spread spectrum signal. The jamming signal can be considered as noise, and by using the proper technique of broadbanding (spread spectrum) the jamming signal can be rendered less effective (suppressed). Spread spectrum may use direct-sequence, frequency, time-hopping, and chirp systems. In spread spectrum systems, some signal function other than the information being sent is employed to determine the transmitted signal bandwidth. For this reason, conventional FM, where the signal bandwidth is determined only by the message signal, cannot be considered a spread spectrum system. *See* ELECTRICAL COMMUNICATIONS; SPREAD SPECTRUM COMMUNICATIONS.

*B. P. Lathi*

**Bibliography.** R. L. Freeman, *Telecommunication Transmission Handbook*, 2d ed., 1981; D. H. Hamsher, *Communication System Engineering Handbook*, 1967; Howard W. Sams Engineering Staff, *Reference Data for Radio Engineers*, 6th ed., 1975; B. P. Lathi, *Modern Digital and Analog Communication Systems*, 1983.

## Barium titanate

A dielectric crystalline material which exhibits the anomalous properties typical for ferroelectricity. Barium titanate, $BaTiO_3$, is a thoroughly studied important compound and is representative of the physically related materials crystallizing in the perovskite structure.

On lowering the temperature, cubic $BaTiO_3$ transforms to a tetragonal structure at about 266°F (130°C; Curie temperature), where the crystal spontaneously acquires an electric polarization (a permanent electric dipole moment). As the polarization can in general point in any one of the originally cubic crystal axes, the crystal consists, in the ferroelectric state, of regions (domains) which differ in the direction of the spontaneous polarization. An applied electric field can align the polarization in the whole crystal and can reverse the polarization direction whereby electric hysteresis occurs. At lower temperatures, 41 and −130°F (5 and −90°C), additional phase transitions take place. The spontaneous polarization successively changes its direction relative to the crystallographic axes and increases in absolute value. *See* FERROELECTRICS.

Many other compounds of the general formula $ABO_3$ have a perovskite-type structure and rather similar properties. As $BaTiO_3$ forms solid solutions with many of these compounds, its properties can be varied systematically over wide ranges. Such materials can be readily produced in a polycrystalline ceramic form which is fully adequate for many applications, some of which are discussed below.

Barium titanate has a high dielectric constant, typically 2000 for a ceramic sample at room temperature. Thus, capacitors of very small dimensions can be produced for electronics applications. As a further advantage, the temperature coefficient of capacitance can be varied over a range of positive and negative values by admixtures of other compounds, such as strontium titanate and lead titanate.

Barium titanate ceramics, when suitably doped with a trivalent oxide such as lanthanum oxide, for example, exhibit a variation of the electrical conductivity by a factor up to $10^6$ in the vicinity of the Curie temperature. This effect can be used for sensitive temperature-control devices.

Ceramics of barium titanate and, in particular, of a mixed lead titanate zirconate can be poled by an electric field and retain a substantial remanent polarization. These materials then have a strong piezoelectric effect. In addition, they are mechanically rugged and rather insensitive to temperature and humidity. Therefore, these ceramics find wide applications in devices such as microphones, ultrasonic and underwater transducers, and spark generators. *See* PIEZOELECTRICITY.

*H. Granicher*

**Bibliography.** M. Deri, *Ferroelectric Ceramics*, 1969; M. E. Lines and A. M. Glass, *Principles and Applications of Ferroelectrics and Related Materials*, 1977; T. Mitsui, *An Introduction to the Physics of Ferroelectrics*, 1976.

## Bias of transistors

The establishment of an operating point on the transistor volt-ampere characteristics by means of direct voltages and currents.

**Biasing biopolar transistors.** Since the transistor is a three-terminal device, any one of the three terminals may be used as a common terminal to both input and output. In most transistor circuits the emitter is used as the common terminal, and this common emitter, or grounded emitter, is indicated in **Fig. 1***a*. If the transistor is to be used as a linear device, such as an audio amplifier, it must be biased to operate in the active region. In this region the collector is biased in the reverse direction and the emitter in the forward direction. The area in the common-emitter transistor characteristics to the right of the ordinate $V_{CE} = 0$ and above $I_C = 0$ is the active region. Two more biasing regions are of special interest for those cases in which the transistor is intended to operate as a switch. These are the saturation and cutoff regions. The saturation region may be defined as the region where the collector current is independent of base current for given values of $V_{CC}$ and $R_L$. Thus, the onset of saturation can be considered to take place at the knee of the common-emitter transistor curves. *See* AMPLIFIER.

In saturation the transistor current $I_C$ is nominally $V_{CC}/R_L$. Since $R_L$ is small, it may be necessary to keep $V_{CC}$ correspondingly small in order to stay within the limitations imposed by the transistor on maximum-current and collector-power dissipation. In the cutoff region it is required that the emitter current $I_E$ be zero, and to accomplish this it is necessary to reverse-bias the emitter junction so that the collector current is approximately equal to the reverse saturation current $I_{CO}$. A reverse-biasing voltage of the order of 0.1 V across the emitter junction will ordinarily be adequate to cut off either a germanium or silicon transistor.

The particular method to be used in establishing an operating point on the transistor characteristics depends on whether the transistor is to operate in the active, saturation or cutoff regions; on the application under consideration; on the thermal stability of the circuit; and on other factors.

***Fixed-bias circuit.*** The operating point for the circuit of Fig. 1*a* can be established by noting that the required current $I_B$ is constant, independent of the quiescent collector current $I_C$, which is why this circuit is called the fixed-bias circuit. Transistor biasing circuits are frequently compared in terms of the value of the stability factor $S = \partial I_C/\partial I_{CO}$, which is the rate of change of collector current with respect to reverse saturation current. The smaller the value of $S$, the less likely the circuit will exhibit thermal runaway. $S$, as defined here, cannot be smaller than unity. Other stability factors are defined in terms of dc current gain $h_{FE}$ as $\partial I_C/\partial h_{FE}$, and in terms of base-to-emitter voltage as $\partial I_C/\partial V_{BE}$. However, bias circuits with small values of $S$ will also perform satisfactorily for transistors that have large variations of $h_{FE}$ and $V_{BE}$. For the fixed-bias circuit it can be shown that $S = h_{FE} + 1$, and if $h_{FE} = 50$, then $S = 51$. Such a large value of $S$ makes thermal runaway a definite possibility with this circuit.

***Collector-to-base bias.*** An improvement in stability is obtained if the resistor $R_B$ in Fig. 1*a* is returned to the collector junction rather than to the battery terminal. Such a connection is shown in Fig. 1*b*. In this bias circuit, if $I_C$ tends to increase (either because of a rise in temperature or because the transistor has been replaced by another), then $V_{CE}$ decreases. Hence $I_B$ also decreases and, as a consequence of this lowered bias current, the collector current is not allowed to increase as much as it would if fixed bias were used. The stability factor $S$ is shown in Eq. (1). This

$$S = \frac{h_{FE} + 1}{1 + h_{FE}R_L/(R_L + R_B)} \tag{1}$$

value is smaller than $h_{FE} + 1$, which is the value obtained for the fixed-bias case.

***Self-bias.*** If the load resistance $R_L$ is very small, as in a transformer-coupled circuit, then the previous expression for $S$ shows that there would be no improvement in the stabilization in the collector-to-base bias circuit over the fixed-bias circuit. A circuit that can be used even if there is zero dc resistance in series with the collector terminal is the self-biasing configuration of Fig. 1*c*. The current in the resistance $R_E$ in the emitter lead causes a voltage drop which is in the direction to reverse-bias the emitter junction. Since this junction must be forward-biased (for active region bias), the bleeder $R_1$-$R_2$ has been added to the circuit.

If $I_C$ tends to increase, the current in $R_E$ increases. As a consequence of the increase in voltage drop across $R_E$, the base current is decreased. Hence $I_C$ will increase less than it would have had there been

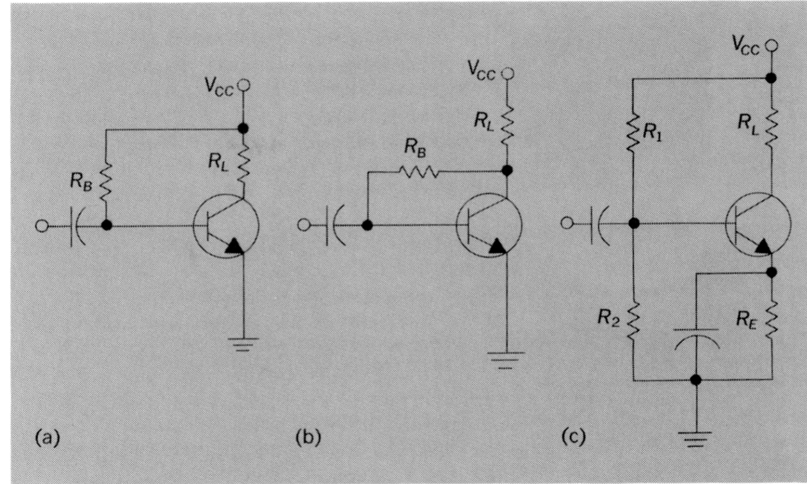


**Fig. 1. Transistor circuits. (*a*) Fixed-bias. (*b*) Collector-to-base bias. (*c*) Self-bias.**

no self-biasing resistor $R_E$. The stabilization factor for the self-bias circuit is shown by Eq. (2), where $R_B =$

$$S = (1 + h_{FE})\frac{1 + R_B/R_E}{1 + h_{FE} + R_B/R_E} \tag{2}$$

$R_1R_2/(R_1 + R_2)$. The smaller the value of $R_B$, the better the stabilization. Even if $R_B$ approaches zero, the value of $S$ cannot be reduced below unity.

In order to avoid the loss of signal gain because of the degeneration caused by $R_E$, this resistor is often bypassed by a very large capacitance, so that its reactance at the frequencies under consideration is very small.

**Biasing the FET and MOSFET.** The selection of an appropriate operating point ($I_D$, $V_{GS}$, $V_{DS}$) for a field-effect transistor (FET) amplifier stage is determined by considerations similar to those given to transistors, as discussed previously. These considerations are output-voltage swing, distortion, power dissipation, voltage gain, and drift of drain current. In most cases it is not possible to satisfy all desired specifications simultaneously.

***Source self-bias.*** The configuration shown in **Fig.** 2*a* can be used to bias junction FET devices or deple-

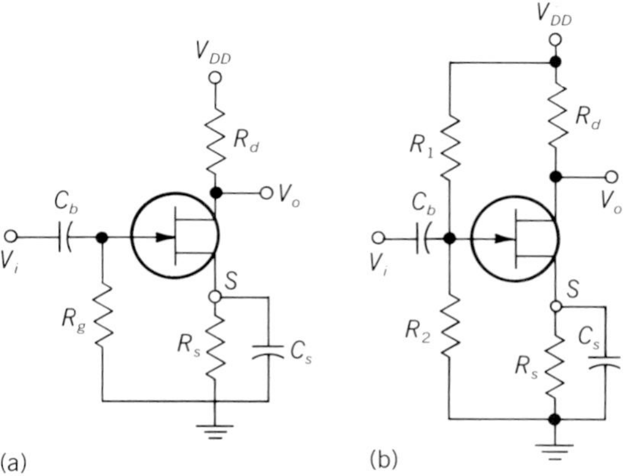


**Fig. 2. Biasing circuits for FETs and MOSFETs. (*a*) Source self-bias circuit for an FET and a depletion-type MOSFET. (*b*) Biasing circuit for an FET and an enhancement-type MOSFET. (*After J. Millman Microelectronics, McGraw-Hill, 1979*)**

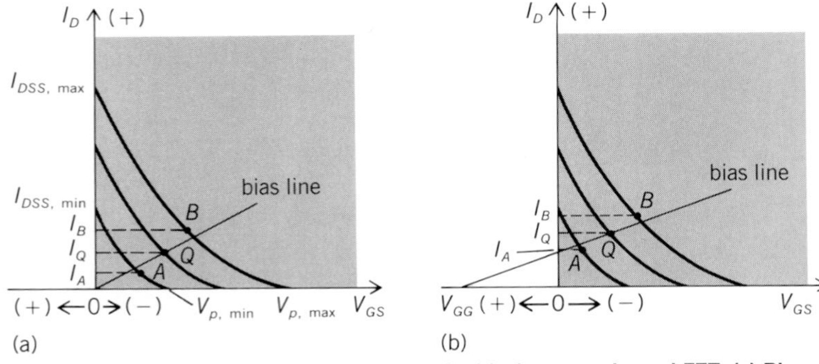


**Fig. 3. Maximum and minimum transfer curves for biasing an *n*-channel FET. (*a*) Bias line passes through origin. (*b*) Bias line does not pass through origin. (*After J. Millman, Microelectronics, McGraw-Hill, 1979*)**

tion-mode metal-oxide-semiconductor FETs (MOSFETs). For a specified drain current $I_D$, the corresponding gate-to-source voltage $V_{GS}$ can be obtained analytically or by using the plotted drain or transfer characteristics. Since the gate current (and, hence, the voltage drop across $R_g$) is negligible, the source resistance $R_s$ can be found as the ratio of $V_{GS}$ to the desired $I_D$.

***Biasing against device variation.*** FET manufacturers usually supply information on the maximum and minimum values of $I_{DSS}$ and $V_P$ at room temperature, where $I_{DSS}$ is the value of the drain current $I_{DS}$ with $V_{GS} = 0$, and $V_P$ is the pinch-off voltage. They also supply data to correct these quantities for temperature variations. The transfer characteristics for a given type of *n*-channel FET may appear as in **Fig. 3*a*** where the top and bottom curves are for extreme values of temperature and device variation. Assume that it is necessary to bias the device at a drain current which will not drift outside $I_D = I_A$ and $I_D = I_B$. Then the bias line $V_{GS} = -I_DR_s$ must intersect the transfer characteristics between the points *A* and *B*, as indicated in Fig. 3*a*. The slope of the bias line is determined by the source resistance $R_s$. For any transfer characteristic between the two extremes indicated, the current $I_Q$ is such that $I_A < I_Q < I_B$, as desired.

Consider the situation indicated in Fig. 3*b*, where a line drawn to pass between points *A* and *B* does not pass through the origin. This bias line satisfies Eq. (3). Such a bias relationship may be obtained by add-

$$V_{GS} = V_{GG} - I_DR_s \qquad (3)$$

ing a fixed bias to the gate in addition to the source self-bias, as indicated in Fig. 2*b*. This circuit requires only one power supply and satisfies Eqs. (4), where

$$V_{GG} = \frac{R_2V_{DD}}{R_1 + R_2} \qquad R_g = \frac{R_1R_2}{R_1 + R_2} \qquad (4)$$

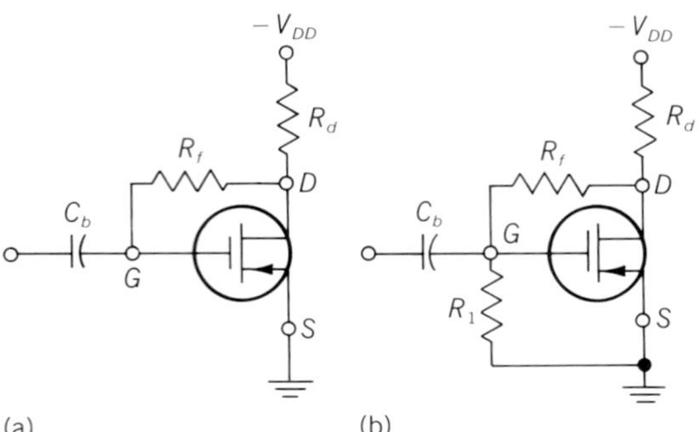


**Fig. 4. Drain-to-gate bias circuits for enhancement-type MOSFET. (*a*) Circuit with $V_{GS} = V_{DS}$. (*b*) Improved version, with $V_{GS} \neq V_{DS}$. (*After J. Millman, Microelectronics, McGraw-Hill, 1979*)**

it is assumed that the gate current is negligible. It is also possible for $V_{GG}$ to fall in the reverse-biased region, so that the line in Fig. 3*b* intersects the axis of abscissa to the right of the origin. Under these circumstances, two separate supply voltages must be used.

***Biasing the enhancement MOSFET.*** The self-bias technique of Fig. 2*a* cannot be used to establish an operating point for the enhancement-type MOSFET because the voltage drop across $R_s$ is in a direction to reverse-bias the gate, and a forward gate bias is required. The circuit of **Fig. 4*a*** can be used, and for this case $V_{GS} = V_{DS}$, since no current flows through $R_f$. If, for reasons of linearity in device operation or maximum output voltage, it is desired that $V_{GS} \neq V_{DS}$, then the circuit of Fig. 4*b* is suitable. In this case, $V_{GS} = [R_1/(R_1 + R_f)] \cdot V_{DS}$. Both circuits discussed here offer the advantages of dc stabilization through the feedback introduced with $R_f$.

The circuit of Fig. 2*b* is often used with the enhancement MOSFET. The dc stability introduced in Fig. 4 through the feedback resistor $R_f$ is then missing, and is replaced by the dc feedback through $R_s$. SEE TRANSISTOR.

*Christos C. Halkias*

***Bibliography.*** P. Horowitz and W. Hill, *The Art of Electronics*, 1980; J. Millman, *Microelectronics*, 1979.

## Bit

In the pure binary numeration system, either of the digits 0 or 1. The term may be thought of as a contraction of binary digit. SEE NUMBER SYSTEMS.

In a binary notation, bits are used as two different characters. For example, in the American National Standard Code for Information Interchange (ASCII), a seven-bit coded character set, the seven bits 1000111 represent the letter G.

Bit is widely used as a synonym for binary element, a constituent element of data that takes either of two values or states (on-off, yes-no, zero-one, and so forth). The brains of animals and registers, memories, and other storage devices of digital computers and electronic calculators store bits (binary elements) as the smallest unit of information.

During a meeting in the late winter of 1943/1944 in Princeton, New Jersey, convened by John von Neumann and Norbert Wiener, engineers, physiologists, and mathematicians found that it was convenient to measure information in terms of numbers of yeses and nos and to call this unit of information a bit. Strictly speaking, the bit of von Neumann, Wiener, and their associates is the binary element and not the binary digit.

A byte is a string of bits (binary elements) operated on or treated as a unit and usually shorter than a word. An eight-bit byte comprises eight bits. In precise usage, *n*-bit bytes are called quartet, quintet, . . ., octet, and so forth. Byte is derived from bite.

A word is a string of bits (binary elements) that consists of two or more bytes. The terms halfword, fullword, and doubleword are also used.

A computer word is a word stored in one computer location, usually 16, 32, 36, 48, or 64 bits in length, depending on the design of the computer.

In microcomputers or in particular applications, a nybble is a strong of bits (binary elements) operated on as a unit, larger than a bit, and smaller than a byte. Nybble is derived from nibble. *See Digital computer.*

In information theory, bit is a synonym for the new, preferred term shannon, a unit of measure of information equal to the decision content of a set of two mutually exclusive events. For example, the decision content of a character set of eight characters equals three shannons (the logarithm of 8 to base 2). A shannon also is called an information content binary unit. A hartley is the information content decimal unit. These unit names were adopted by the International Organization for Standardization (ISO) in 1975, honoring C. E. Shannon and R. C. L. Hartley. *See Information theory.*

*Helmut E. Thiess*

**Bibliography.** J. Aczel and Z. Daroczy, *Measures of Information and their Characteristics*, 1975; R. W. Hamming, *Coding and Information Theory*, 1980; M. H. Weik, *Standard Dictionary of Computers and Information Processing*, 2d ed., 1977; N. Wiener, *Cybernetics*, 2d ed., 1961.

## Blocking oscillator

A relaxation oscillator that generates a short-time-duration pulse using a single transistor or vacuum tube and associated circuitry. The input and output are coupled together by a transformer in a regenerative feedback arrangement, with the output current being periodically interrupted because of the regenerative action which drives the input far into the reverse-bias or cut-off region. The duration of the period between pulses, which coincides with the period during which the output current is blocked, is dependent upon the value of the *RC* (resistance–capacitance) time constant in the input circuit. The blocking oscillator may be made to operate in either a monostable or astable fashion. When operated as a monostable device, considerable control can be exercised over the shape and duration of the pulse, making the circuit useful as a pulse generator. *See Pulse generator; Relaxation oscillator.*

**Free-running astable type.** A simple astable blocking oscillator using an *npn* transistor is shown in **Fig. 1**. A field-effect transistor or vacuum tube may be used as an alternative. If one assumes initially that the transistor is forward-biased at cutoff level $V_{BEO}$ of the input waveform such that base current is just beginning to flow, the regenerative action will increase the current up to a maximum value corresponding to saturation level $V_{BES}$, as shown. At some such level the output will no longer drive the input to higher current levels because of transformer losses and decreased transistor input impedance. Then, the base current reverses and the voltage drops to the level $V_{BEO}$. This portion of the waveform corresponds to the negative going collector pulse, as shown. During this conducting period $T_1$, the capacitor voltage changes by an amount given by Eq. (1), with polarity as indicated.

$$V_{c1} = \int_0^{T_1} i_B dt \qquad (1)$$

At the end of the conducting interval, the voltage across the transformer winding in series with the base collapses, and the base voltage drops to the negative value $V_{B\min}$, as shown, which is approximately equal in magnitude to the change in capacitor voltage during the previous conducting interval. At this time the voltage at the base rises toward the supply voltage $V_{CC}$, according to Eq. (2). Time $T_2$ is the time taken

$$v_B = V_{B\ \min} + (V_{CC} - V_{B\ \min})\,(1 - e^{-t/(R_1C_1)}) \qquad (2)$$

to reach the point at which the transistor again conducts, and the entire process repeats itself.

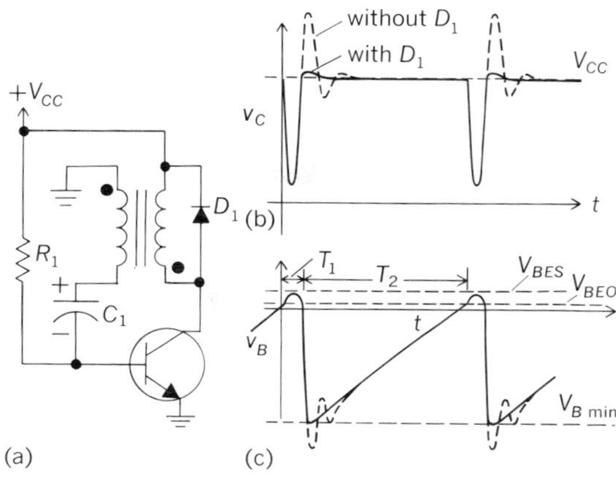


**Fig. 1. Typical free-running blocking oscillator. (*a*) Circuit. (*b*) Collector voltage. (*c*) Base voltage.**

**Synchronized type.** The blocking oscillator may be synchronized with external pulses occurring at a rate slightly faster than its own natural frequency in the same manner as multivibrators, as shown in **Fig. 2**. It may be used in the same manner as a frequency divider, as shown in **Fig. 3**. *See Multivibrator.*

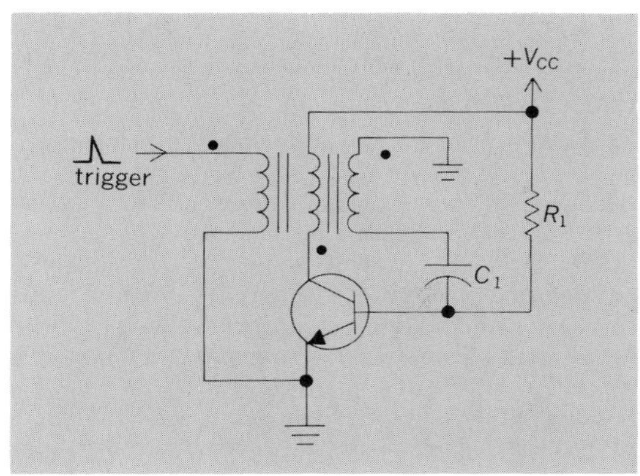


**Fig. 2. Synchronized blocking oscillator.**

The blocking oscillator becomes a monostable de-

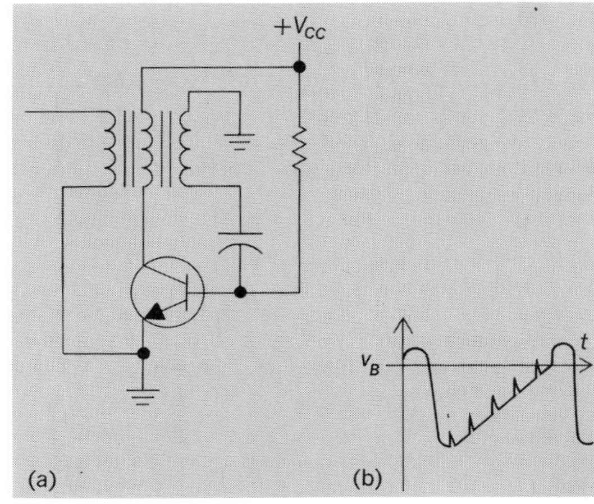


**Fig. 3. Blocking oscillator as a frequency divider. (*a*) Circuit. (*b*) Base voltage.**

vice if resistance $R_1$ is returned to a voltage sufficiently far in the reverse-bias direction so that an external trigger must be applied before an action can be initiated. There is more freedom of control of the circuit elements for control of pulse duration in the monostable circuit than in the astable circuit, if it is desired to use the blocking oscillator as a pulse generator.

*Glenn M. Glasford*

**Bibliography.** B. Chance et al. (eds.), *Waveforms*, 1949; D. G. Fink and D. Christiansen, *Electronics Engineers' Handbook*, 2d ed., 1982; G. M. Glasford, *Fundamentals of Television Engineering*, 1955; Howard W. Sams Engineering Staff, *Reference Data for Radio Engineers*, 6th ed., 1975; J. Millman and H. Taub, *Pulse, Digital, and Switching Waveforms*, 1965; L. Strauss, *Wave Generation and Shaping*, 1970.

## Boolean algebra

A branch of mathematics that was first developed systematically, because of its applications to logic, by the English mathematician George Boole, around 1850. Closely related are its applications to sets and probability.

Boolean algebra also underlies the theory of relations. A modern engineering application is to computer circuit design. *See* Digital computer; Switching theory.

**Set-theoretic interpretation.** Most basic is the use of boolean algebra to describe combinations of the subsets of a given set $I$ of elements; its basic operations are those of taking the intersection or common part $S \cap T$ of two such subsets $S$ and $T$, their union or sum $S \cup T$, and the complement $S'$ of any one such subset $S$. These operations satisfy many laws, including those shown in Eqs. (1), (2), and (3).

$$S \cap S = S \qquad S \cap T = T \cap S \qquad S \cap (T \cap U) = (S \cap T) \cap U \tag{1}$$

$$S \cup S = S \qquad S \cup T = T \cup S \qquad S \cup (T \cup U) = (S \cup T) \cup U \tag{2}$$

$$S \cap (T \cup U) = (S \cap T) \cup (S \cap U) \qquad S \cup (T \cap U) = (S \cup T) \cap (S \cup U) \tag{3}$$

If $O$ denotes the empty set, and $I$ is the set of all elements being considered, then the laws set forth in Eq. (4) are also fundamental. Since these laws are

$$O \cap S = O \qquad O \cup S = S \qquad I \cap S = S \qquad I \cup S = I \qquad S \cap S' = O \qquad S \cup S' = I \tag{4}$$

fundamental, all other algebraic laws of subset combination can be deduced from them.

In applying boolean algebra to logic, Boole observed that combinations of properties under the common logical connectives *and*, *or*, and *not* also satisfy the laws specified above. These laws also hold for propositions or assertions, when combined by the same logical connectives. *See* Logic circuits.

Boole stressed the analogies between boolean algebra and ordinary algebra. If $S \cap T$ is regarded as playing the role of $st$ in ordinary algebra, $S \cup T$ that of $s + t$, $O$ of 0, $I$ of 1, and $S'$ as corresponding to $1 - s$, the laws listed above illustrate many such analogies. However, as first clearly shown by Marshall Stone, the proper analogy is somewhat different. Specifically, the proper boolean analog of $s + t$ is $(S' \cap T) \cup (S \cap T')$, so that the ordinary analog of $S \cup T$ is $s + t - st$. Using Stone's analogy, boolean algebra refers to boolean rings in which $s^2 = s$, a condition implying $s + s = 0$.

Boolean algebra arises in other connections, as in the algebra of (binary) relations. Such relations $\rho$, $\sigma$, . . . refer to appropriate sets of elements $I$, $J$, . . . . Any such $\rho$ can be defined by describing the set of pairs $(x,t)$, with $x$ in $I$ and $y$ in $J$, that stand in the given relation—a fact symbolized $x \rho y$, just as its negation is written $x \rho' y$. Because of this set-theoretic interpretation, boolean algebra obviously applies, with $x(\rho \cap \sigma)y$ meaning $x \rho y$ and $x \sigma y$, and $x(\rho \cup \sigma)y$ meaning $x \rho y$ or $x \sigma y$.

**Abstract relationships.** Before 1930, work on boolean algebra dealt mainly with its postulate theory, and with the generalizations obtained by abandoning one or more postulates, such as $(p')' = p$ (brouwerian logic). Since $a \cup b = (a' \cap b')'$, clearly one need consider $a \cap b$ and $a'$ as undefined operations. In 1913 H. M. Sheffer showed one operation only $(a|b = a' \cap b')$ need be taken as undefined. In 1941 M. H. A. Newman developed a remarkable generalization which included boolean algebras and boolean rings. This generalization is based on the laws shown in Eqs. (5) and (6). From these assumptions, the

$$a(b + c) = ab + ac \qquad (a + b)c = ac + bc \tag{5}$$

$$a1 = 1 \qquad a + 0 = 0 + a = a \qquad aa' = 0 \qquad a + a' = 1 \tag{6}$$

idempotent, commutative, and associative laws (1) and (2) can be deduced.

Such studies lead naturally to the concept of an abstract boolean algebra, adefined as a collection of symbols combined by operations satisfying the identities listed in formulas (1) to (4). Ordinarily, the phrase boolean algebra refers to such an abstract boolean algebra, and this convention is adopted here.

The class of finite (abstract) boolean algebras is easily described. Each such algebra has, for some nonnegative integer $n$, exactly $2^n$ elements and is algebraically equivalent (isomorphic) to the algebra of all subsets of the set of numbers 1, . . . , $n$, under the operations of intersection, union, and complement. Furthermore, if $m$ symbols $a_1$, . . . , $a_m$ are combined symbolically through abstract operations $\cap$, $\cup$, and $'$ assumed to satisfy the identities of Eqs. (1) to (4), one gets a finite boolean algebra with $2^{2^m}$ elements—the free boolean algebra with $m$ generators.

**Infinite relationships.** The theory of infinite boolean algebras is much deeper; it indirectly involves the whole theory of sets. One important result is Stone's representation theorem. Let a field of sets be defined as any family of subsets of a given set $I$, which contains with any two sets $S$ and $T$ their intersection $S \cap T$, union $S \cup T$, and complements $S'$, $T'$. Considered abstractly, any such field of sets obviously defines a boolean algebra. Stone's theorem asserts that, conversely, any finite or infinite abstract boolean algebra is isomorphic to a suitable field of sets. His proof is based on the concepts of ideal and prime ideal, concepts which have been intensively studied for their own sake. Because ideal theory in boolean algebra may be subsumed under the ideal theory of rings (via the correspondence between boolean algebras and boolean rings mentioned earlier), it will not be discussed here. A special property of boolean rings (algebras) is the fact that, in this case, any prime ideal is maximal.

The study of infinite boolean algebras leads naturally to the consideration of such infinite distributive laws as those in Eqs. (7a) and (7b).

$$\begin{aligned} x \cap \left(\bigcup_B y_\beta\right) &= \bigcup_B (x \cap y_\beta) \\ x \cup \left(\bigcap_B y_\beta\right) &= \bigcap_B (x \cup y_\beta) \end{aligned} \qquad (7a)$$

$$\begin{aligned} \bigcap_C \left[\bigcup_{A\gamma} u_{\gamma,\alpha}\right] &= \bigcup_F \left[\bigcap_C u_{\gamma,\phi(\gamma)}\right] \\ \bigcup_C \left[\bigcap_{A\gamma} u_{\gamma,\alpha}\right] &= \bigcap_F \left[\bigcup_C u_{\gamma,\phi(\gamma)}\right] \end{aligned} \qquad (7b)$$

For finite sets $B$ of indices $\beta = 1, \ldots, n$, if

$$\bigcap_B y\beta$$

means $y_1 \cup \cdots \cup y_n$, and so on, the laws (7a) and (7b) follow by induction from (1) to (3). Also, if the symbols $x$, $y_\beta$, and so on, in (7a) and (7b) refer to subsets of a given space $I$, and if

$$\bigcup_B y_\beta \quad \text{and} \quad \bigcap_B y_\beta$$

refer to the union and intersection of all $y_\beta$ in $B$, respectively, then (7a) and (7b) are statements of general laws of formal logic. However, they fail in most infinite boolean algebras. This is shown by the following result of Alfred Tarski: If a boolean algebra $A$ satisfies the generalized distributive laws (7a) and (7b), then it is isomorphic with the algebra of all subsets of a suitable space $I$. A related result is the theorem of L. Loomis (1947) which states: Every $\sigma$-complete boolean algebra is isomorphic with a $\sigma$-field of sets under countable intersection, countable union, and complement.

In general, such completely distributive boolean algebras of subsets may be characterized by the properties of being complete and atomic. These properties may be defined roughly as the properties that (a) there exists a smallest element

$$\bigcup_B y\beta$$

containing any given set $B$ of elements $y_\beta$, and (b) any element $y > 0$ contains an atom (or point) $p > 0$, such that $p > x > 0$ has no solution (from Euclid, "A point is that which has no parts"). Condition (b) is also implied by the "descending chain condition" of ideal theory.

**Other forms.** Nonatomic and incomplete boolean algebras arise naturally in set theory. Thus, the algebra of measurable sets in the line or plane, ignoring sets of measure zero, is nonatomic but complete. The field of Borel sets of space is complete as regards countable families $B$ of subsets $S_\beta$, but not for uncountable $B$. Analogous results hold for wide classes of other measure spaces and topological spaces, respectively. In any zero-dimensional compact space, the sets which are both open and closed (which "disconnect" the space) form a boolean algebra; a fundamental result of Stone shows that the most general boolean algebra can be obtained in this way.

Many other interesting facts about boolean algebra are known. For instance, there is an obvious duality between the properties of $\cap$ and $\cup$ in the preceding discussion. However, so many such facts have natural generalizations to the wider context of lattice theory that the modern tendency is to consider boolean algebra as it relates to such generalizations. For instance, the algebras of $n$-valued logic, intuitionist (brouwerian) logic, and quantum logic are not boolean algebras, but lattices of other types. The same is true of the closed sets in most topological spaces.

*Garrett Birkhoff*

***Bibliography.*** G. Birkhoff, *Lattice Theory*, 3d ed., Amer. Math. Soc. Colloq. Publ., vol. 25, 1967; G. Birkhoff and S. MacLane, *Survey of Modern Algebra*, 4th ed., 1977; G. Boole, *An Investigation of the Laws of Thought*, 1854; H. Levitz and K. Levitz, *Logic and Boolean Algebra*, 1979; R. Sikorski, *Boolean Algebras*, 3d ed., 1969; G. F. South, *Boolean Algebra and its Uses*, 1974.

## Breadboarding

Assembling an electronic circuit in the most convenient manner on a board or other flat surface, without regard for final locations of components, to prove the feasibility of the circuit and to facilitate changes when necessary. Standard breadboards for experimental work are made with mounting holes and terminals closely spaced at regular intervals, so that parts can be mounted and connected without drilling additional holes.

Printed-circuit boards having similar patterns of punched holes, with various combinations of holes connected together by printed wiring on each side, are often used for breadboarding when the final version is to be a printed circuit. *See* Circuit (electronics); Printed circuit.

*John Markus*

## Breakdown potential

The potential difference at which an electrically stressed gas is tranformed from an insulator to a conductor. In an electrically stressed gas, as the voltage is increased, the free electrons present in the gas gain energy from the electric field. When the applied voltage is increased to such a level that an appreciable number of these electrons are energetically capable of ionizing the gas, the gas makes the transition from an insulator to a conductor; that is, it breaks down. The potential difference at which this transition occurs is known as the breakdown potential for the particular gaseous medium.

The breakdown potential depends on the nature, number density, and temperature of the gas; on the material, state, and geometry of the electrodes; on the type of voltage applied (steady, alternating, impulsive); and on the degree of preexisting ionization. Areas of surface roughness at the electrodes (especially the cathode) or the presence of conducting particles in the gas greatly reduces the breakdown potential because at such points the electric field is significantly enhanced, increasing the electron energies and thus gas ionization. The breakdown voltage varies considerably from one gaseous medium to another; it is very low for the rare gases, such as neon, for which a 0.394-in. (1-cm) uniform-field gap at 1 atm (101.3 kilopascals) breaks down at 0.53 kV; and very high for polyatomic, especially electronegative, gases such as sulfur hexafluoride ($SF_6$), for which a 0.394-in. (1-cm) uniform-field gap at 1 atm (101.3 kilopascals) breaks down at 88.9 kV.

The transition of a gas from an insulator to a conductor under an imposed electrical potential occurs in times ranging from milliseconds to nanoseconds, depending on the form of the applied field and the gas density. It depends on the behavior of electrons, ions, and photons in the gas, especially the processes which produce or deplete free electrons. Knowledge of these processes often allows predictionof the breakdown voltage of gases and the tailoring of gas mixtures which can withstand high electrical potentials for practical uses. *SEE ELECTRICAL CONDUCTION IN GASES*.

**Increasing the breakdown potential.** Fundamental research on the microscopic physical processes which take place in an electrically stressed gas—especially those involving the interaction of slow (less than about 20 eV) electrons with atoms and molecules—has led to a better understanding of the electrical "breakdown" of gases. It has also led to the realization that an effective way of increasing the breakdown potential is to prevent the free electrons in the gas from initiating the breakdown by attaching them to gas molecules forming negative ions, which—being much heavier than the electrons—do not ionize the gas. (In such cases the breakdown potential can be defined as that value of the applied potential for which the rate of electron production by ionization is equal to the rate of electron depletion by attachment.) The ability of molecules to capture free electrons is large in the extreme low-energy range (less than about 1 eV) and decreases as the electron energy increases. For this reason, the gas itself—or an additive to it, as in a gas mixture—must be capable of reducing the energies of the free electrons and effectively scattering them into the low-energy region, where they can be captured most efficiently. Knowledge of the electron-scattering properties of gases permits selection of suitable gases for the slowing down of free electrons in dielectric gas mixtures. Combinations of two or more electron-attaching and electron-slowing-down gases have been developed in this manner which effectively control the energies and number densities of free electrons in electrically stressed gases. This approach allows the systematic identification of unitary gases (for example, sulfur hexafluoride and perfluorocarbons) and the systematic development of multicomponent gaseous dielectrics (for example, sulfur hexafluoride–nitrogen; perfluorocarbon–nitrogen; and sulfur hexafluoride–perfluorocarbon–nitrogen) which are able to withstand very high potentials before breaking down and are suitable for many applications.

**Applications.** The systematic development of gaseous dielectrics with high dielectric strength (that is, high breakdown potential) is most significant for high-voltage technology, which has a multiplicity of gas insulation needs. Dielectric gases are widely used as insulating media in high-voltage transmission lines, circuit breakers, transformers, substations, high-voltage research apparatus, and other electrical equipment (such as Van de Graaff accelerators). In transmission lines the high-voltage conductor is held in place by solid insulators and is enclosed in a vacuum-tight pipe, the earthed electrode (often buried underground), which is filled with the insulating gas at pressures usually ranging from 1 to 10 atm (100 to 1000 kPa) depending on the voltage. The voltages in such systems can be higher than 1,000,000 V, resulting in considerable reduction of resistive losses and hence substantial energy savings. The use of compressed-gas–insulated transmission lines and other gas-insulated high-voltage electrical equipment is expected to continue increasing. *SEE TRANSMISSION LINES*.

*L. G. Christophorou*

**Bibliography.** L. G. Christophorou (ed.), *Gaseous Dielectrics III*, 1982; L. G. Christophorou, D. R. James, and R. Y. Pai, Gas breakdown and high voltage insulating gases, in *Applied Atomic Collisions*, vol. 5, pp. 87–167, 1982; E. E. Kunhardt and L. H. Luessen (eds.), *Electrical Breakdown and Discharges in Gases*, vols. 89a and 89b, NATO Advanced Science Institutes Series, 1983; J. M. Meek and J. D. Craggs (eds.), *Electrical Breakdown in Gases*, 1978.

## Bridge circuit

An electric network composed of four impedances forming a diamond-shaped network. These impedances, shown in the **illustration** as $Z_1$, $Z_2$, $Z_3$, and $Z_4$,

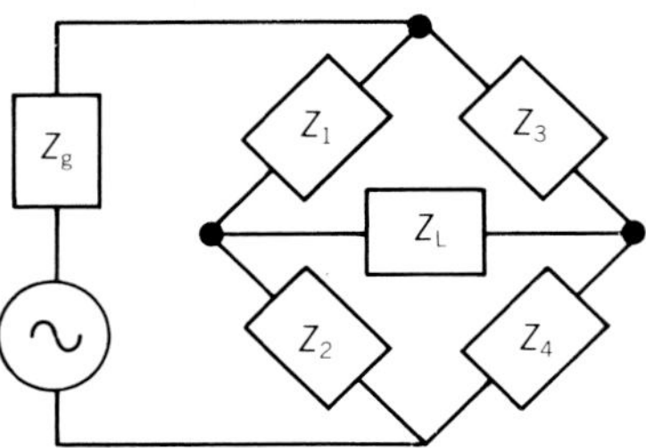


**Schematic diagram of bridge circuit. $Z_g$ is the impedance of the seat of the electromotive force.**

may be combinations of resistors, capacitors, and inductors. Bridge circuits perform numerous functions, depending upon the type of circuit elements used in the arms of the bridge. For example, the bridge circuit can be used to determine the value of an unknown resistance. This is done by making the arm impedances resistances with one of them the unknown. The load impedance $Z_L$ can be that of a measuring instrument, such as a galvanometer. The current through $Z_L$, and the voltage across it, will be zero when $Z_1Z_4 = Z_2Z_3$. With the proper combination of resistors and capacitors in the bridge arms, the voltage across $Z_L$ will be zero for some frequency. Thus, the bridge acts as a frequency-measuring device. *SEE FREQUENCY MEASUREMENT; WHEATSTONE BRIDGE*.

The property of the bridge circuit that the voltage across $Z_L$ will be zero for the proper arm impedances, and the proper frequency makes the circuit useful in an oscillator known as the Wien-bridge oscillator. It also has been used in the feedback path of some special amplifiers where its properties give the amplifier unusual characteristics. *SEE OSCILLATOR*.

*Harold F. Klock*

**Bibliography.** A. Budak, *Circuit Theory Fundamentals and Applications*, 1978; T. J. Maloney, *Electric Circuits: Principles and Applications*, 1984; R. E. Risdale, *Electric Circuits*, 1983; D. Tuttle, *Circuits*, 1977.

## Brush discharge

A particular form of corona discharge characterized by strongly ionized streamers. It generally occurs at a field slightly less than that required for complete breakdown. The conditions for a brush discharge are as follows: The pressure should be about atmospheric; one or both of the electrodes should have a radius of curvature small compared to the gap separation; and the gap itself should be large, at least of the order of a few centimeters. The ionized streamers take on a treelike form. The light originates from recombination and radiative transitions from excited states. *SEE BREAKDOWN POTENTIAL; CORONA DISCHARGE.*

*Glenn H. Miller*

## Calculators

Portable or desktop devices, primarily electronic, that are used to perform arithmetic and other numerical processing operations at the direction of an operator or a stored program.

**Mechanical calculators.** Early calculators were exclusively mechanical. An older mechanical calculator provides identical columns of numeral selection keys, one column for each digit of the operand range, with the units selection keys as the rightmost column. A numerical value is selected by depressing one or more keys, one in each column for which a nonzero value is desired. The selected operand is added to the accumulated sum or subtracted from the remaining difference either as the selection of value is made or as the operator takes some further action. The result is displayed in a mechanical accumulator register.

Mechanical calculators are best suited to addition and multiplication. Multiplication is accomplished by repeated addition of the multiplicand to form a series of partial sums. Additions for the units digit of the multiplier are made into the rightmost accumulator locations. A shift of one position to the left precedes the additions for each subsequent multiplier digit. Subtraction involves addition of the tens complement of the subtrahend. Division consists of repeated subtractions, beginning in the leftmost accumulator locations and shifting right by one location for each quotient digit to be determined. The operator must keep track of the location of any decimal point appearing in any calculation and must align decimal points for an addition or subtraction.

Improvement in mechanical calculators consisted of incorporating motors to effect additions upon key command and adding mechanisms to automatically control execution of the repeated additions needed in multiplication and division. Few mechanical units could perform any operations beyond the four basic arithmetic functions. Although some printing 10-key mechanical calculators are used in offices and small businesses, mechanical calculators have been almost completely replaced by quieter, more efficient, and more capable electronic units.

**Electronic calculators.** Calculators changed radically in the mid-1960s when transistorized models were developed to replace the mechanical units. The early electronic units were faster and quieter, but merely emulated their mechanical predecessors—only arithmetic operations were executed. As development continued, the capabilities of the electronic calculators increased and sizes decreased. By 1975, inexpensive hand-held calculators employing large-scale integrated circuits as processing elements were in wide use. *SEE ELECTRONICS.*

The rapid evolution of the electronic calculator has been made possible by technological improvements in integrated circuits. An integrated circuit with an area of less than 0.5 $in.^2$ (3 $cm^2$) can hold all the circuit elements needed to implement the algorithms and the control and timing functions of a calculator. Multiplication, for example, is still accomplished by multiple additions and shifts, but every step in the operation is under the direction of the integrated circuit. Forty or more algorithms may be held in memory, to be retrieved and used when requested by depression of a function key. A hand-held calculator may use a single integrated circuit to interpret key-switch closures, carry out the requested operation, and multiplex the individual digits of the result to the display. *SEE INTEGRATED CIRCUITS.*

Although most electronic calculators are similar with regard to basic operation, wide differences in functional capabilities exist between models. The user must evaluate the application and select a unit providing the needed features. Some of the differences in calculator capabilities are discussed in the following.

***Display.*** Several display formats are prevalent. The simple fixed-point display, in which the decimal point remains in a fixed position and answers are automatically aligned on the decimal point by the calculating unit, appeared in early electronic models but is seldom used in more recent designs. The floating-point format, in which the decimal point can appear in any display location, is more flexible. The processor carries information on decimal-point location along with each operand, aligns decimal points of operands involved in additions and subtractions, and calculates decimal-point locations for results of all other arithmetic processes, passing this information to the display.

More elaborate calculators employ either scientific notation or engineering notation or both. In scientific notation, any displayed result consists of a mantissa and a characteristic, the characteristic being the power of 10 associated with the number. The characteristic may be positive or negative. The mantissa always has one digit, which may be a zero, to the left of the decimal point. For example, the displayed value 4.86750 07 corresponds to the floating-point number $4.86750 \times 10^7$, or 48,675,000. A display of 2.13447-02 represents $2.13447 \times 10^{-2}$, or 0.0213447. Some units capable of scientific notation routinely display results in floating-point form and automatically shift to scientific notation when the results are too large or too small to be accurately represented in floating-point form. The calculator definition of floating-point format does not conform to the same expression in computer terminology, where scientific notation is considered floating-point.

Engineering notation is similar to scientific notation with the restrictions that the characteristic must be a multiple of three and from one to three nonzero digits must appear to the left of the decimal point. The examples provided earlier in scientific notation would appear as 48.6750 06 and 21.3447-03 in an engineering notation display. Since engineers and scientists often express units in powers of 3, engineering notation facilitates the use of common engineering prefixes such as mega ($10^{-6}$) and micro ($10^{-6}$).

The numbers of display digit locations vary with the calculator model and the mode of display. A floating-point display might have 8 digit positions and a sign location. Scientific and engineering formats usually occupy 12 or 14 display positions, with 8 or 10 digit locations for the mantissa, 2 for the characteristic, and 1 each for the sign of the mantissa and the sign of the characteristic. The operator can select the number of mantissa digits displayed and the display mode on some models.

Although the early electronic calculators used high-voltage gas discharge tubes for display, most hand-held units now utilize the more reliable and power-saving light-emitting diode (LED) displays, which are energized at a low voltage level and which can be readily multiplexed from the calculator integrated circuit. Since an LED display can account for most of the power consumed in a calculator, and therefore for battery drain, many units automatically remove power from the displays after a predetermined interval of inactivity, retaining the displayed value in semiconductor memory for recall. *SEE LIGHT-EMITTING DIODE.*

Some designs make use of liquid-crystal display (LCD) elements which avoid the current drain of LED displays. An LCD assembly provides a significant saving in power consumption over an LED display, but is less easily viewed by the operator, particularly in a bright light environment. *SEE LIQUID CRYSTALS.*

A display usually provides an overflow or underflow indication when answers exceed the range of the calculator, or an error indication, such as a blinking display, if an illegal operation is requested or unacceptable results are generated. Most displays also indicate impending battery discharge. *SEE ELECTRONIC DISPLAY.*

***Operand range.*** The range of operands that can be accepted, processed, and displayed by a calculator is a function of the display and the processing capabilities of the unit. An eight-digit floating-point display can exhibit numbers between .00000001 and 99,999,999, a 16-decade dynamic range. A 12-location scientific display can represent numbers from $1.0 \times 10^{-99}$ to $9.9999999 \times 10^{99}$, a range of about 200 decades. If the available range is exceeded, the operator must reformulate or rescale the problem.

***Entry notation.*** The user of a calculator must enter a sequence of operands and commands to direct the unit through the required processing. For entry, most calculators use either algebraic notation or reverse polish notation (RPN). With algebraic notation, the calculator accepts and processes data and commands in the order in which they would be written in an equation. If, for example, the operator wished to add 21 and 38 and divide the result by 14, the operator would enter, in sequence, the number 21, an add command (+), the number 38, a divide command (÷), the number 14, and a command to complete the calculation (=). Some calculators using algebraic notation must perform special operations or impose restrictions on the operator in order to handle the nesting of parentheses that occurs in more complex equations.

The RPN entry mode is more convenient for evaluation of complex expressions. This is also known as postfix notation because an operational command always follows the operand to which it applies. For the example provided previously, the operator would enter 21, an ENTER command, 38, an add command (+), 14 and a divide command (÷).

***Storage registers.*** Availability of registers in which operands and intermediate results can be stored is of importance in many applications. If storage is inadequate, the operator may be forced to record intermediate results by hand and reenter them as they are needed for the calculation. Most calculators supply at least one memory register, to be exercised by store and recall keys. Some units contain stacks of three or four registers each; selection of one register in a stack is made by shifting the contents of the registers through the visual display until the desired location reaches the display. Any of a number of scientific calculators provides 10 or more storage locations. Storage and retrieval (into the displayed register) are done by activation of the store or recall key and a location-designating key, in sequence.

***Speed.*** Calculators are designed to carry out computations previously performed by hand, the automation yielding speed and accuracy advantages. By computer standards, calculators are slow. A scientific calculator may require a second or more to execute one of its more complex operations. Execution time may also be dependent upon operand value since some operations involve iterative computations. The relatively slow speed of the calculator is seldom perceived as a handicap by the user.

**Programmable calculators.** Any calculator can be considered a computer in that it contains in nonvolatile memory a fixed set of algorithms for execution of the processing operations in its repertoire. These algorithms are available whenever power is applied to the unit. Programmable calculators (see **illus.**) are able to accept and act upon a higher level of programming that directs the units through sequences of processing steps without operator intervention other than operand entry. Programming may be done by the operator or, in advance, by the manufacturer, and storage of the program may be volatile or nonvolatile. Programming relieves the drudgery of repeated keystroke entry when a repetitive calculation must be made.

**Programmable calculator combined with printer. The calculator has an alphanumeric, liquid-crystal display. The thermal printer prints a variety of characters and is equipped with a plotting routine. (*Hewlett-Packard Co.*)**

Programming by the operator on the unit to be used for the calculation is known as keystroke programming. The desired sequence of operations is entered into calculator memory by depression of keys as though a calculation were being made, but with the unit in program mode. Each keystroke enters an instruction into the semiconductor memory of the unit. When the unit is returned to the normal run mode, the program sequence can be initiated by the operator through depression of a special function key on the keyboard. Three or more special function keys may be provided; a number of programs can simultaneously reside in memory.

The semiconductor storage in a calculator is usually volatile—program information is lost when power is removed. Some units can accept magnetic tape cartridges or miniaturized magnetic cards, from which the volatile memory can be loaded and to which the memory contents can be written. The magnetic medium provides a means of saving and reentering a program written by the keystroke method. Manufacturers also offer preprogrammed tapes and cards for specialized calculations in a wide range of fields, such as surveying, statistics, financial decisions, mathematics, and circuit analysis. A tape or card can customize a general-purpose calculator to a particular application. Since the miniaturized cards are easily carried with a calculator, the nonvolatile storage capacity greatly improves the computational capacity, and hence the value of a hand-held calculator, especially for use in the field.

Memory of the complementary metal-oxide semiconductor (CMOS) type, which exhibits very low power consumption when storage or retrieval is not under way, has been incorporated into several models. These units prevent program loss by continuously maintaining power on the memory section. The combination of a CMOS memory and an LCD readout can provide long battery life and protection against program loss in a self-sufficient calculator unit.

Several programmable calculators accept plug-in elements such as memory extender modules, read-only memory modules for specialized computations, magnetic card readers, and printers (see illus.). Programmer assistance in the form of prompting is provided in an alphanumeric display—a display capable of showing letters as well as numbers. A calculator with these capabilities could be likened to a numerical processing computer with peripheral devices. As the range of calculator expansion elements increases and calculation capabilities increase, the differences between calculators and computers will become even less distinct. *See Computer; Digital computer.*

**Special-purpose calculators.** Although any programmable calculator with sufficient capability can be specialized to a task by insertion of a program, some units are designed for particular applications. Calculators performing all the basic engineering, scientific, or statistical calculations are numerous. A financial calculator can carry out determinations of yields, compound interest, loan and mortgage amortization, depreciation, and many related items. Some calculators perform arithmetic in, and conversions between, the several number systems used in computer programming. A checkbook calculator maintains current balance in its memory. Several models serve as teaching aids by posing arithmetic problems to elementary students and evaluating answers. Calculatorlike units serve as teaching aids for spelling, in translation from one language to another, and in a variety of electronic games.

*W. W. Moyer*

## Calibration

The process of determining, by measurement or by comparison with a standard, the correct value of each scale reading on a meter or the correct value of each setting of a control knob. In a radio receiver, for example, calibration would mean adjusting the tuned circuits in the oscillator to make the readings of the tuning dial correspond exactly to the frequencies of the incoming signals.

With measuring instruments, calibration generally involves adjusting the values of internal components so that the indication is correct at a specified number of points on the indicating scale and approximately correct between these points. With highly accurate instruments, calibration involves the preparation of a graph or table that gives the exact value corresponding to each line on the indicating scale.

*John Markus*

## Capacitance

The ratio of the charge $q$ on one of the plates of a capacitor (there being an equal and opposite charge on the other plate) to the potential difference $v$ between the plates; that is, capacitance (formerly called capacity) is $C = q/v$.

In general, a capacitor, often called a condenser, consists of two metal plates insulated from each other by a dielectric. The capacitance of a capacitor depends on the geometry of the plates and the kind of dielectric used since these factors determine the charge which can be put on the plates by a unit potential difference existing between the plates.

For a capacitor of fixed geometry and with constant properties of the dielectric between its plates, $C$ is a constant independent of $q$ or $v$, since as $v$ changes, $q$ changes with it in the same proportion. This statement assumes that the dielectric strength is not exceeded and thus that dielectric breakdown does not occur. (If it does occur, the device is no longer a capacitor.) If either the geometry or dielectric properties, or both, of a capacitor change with time, $C$ will change with time.

In an ideal capacitor, no conduction current flows between the plates. A real capacitor of good quality is the circuit equivalent of an ideal capacitor with a very high resistance in parallel or, in alternating-current (ac) circuits, of an ideal capacitor with a low resistance in series.

**Properties of capacitors.** One classification system for capacitors follows from the physical state of their dielectrics. For a discussion based on this classification *see Capacitor.*

***Charging and discharging.*** These processes can occur for capacitors while the potential difference across the capacitor is changing if $C$ is fixed; that is, $q$ increases if $v$ increases and $q$ decreases if $v$ decreases. If $C$ and $v$ both change with time, the rate of change of $q$ with time is given by Eq. (1). Since the current $i$ flowing

$$\frac{dq}{dt} = C\frac{dv}{dt} + v\frac{dC}{dt} \tag{1}$$

in the wires leading to the capacitor plates is equal to $dq/dt$, Eq. (1) gives $i$ in the wires. In many cases, $C$ is constant so $i = C\,dv/dt$.

***Energy of charged capacitor.*** This energy $W_C$ is given by the formula $W_C = vq/2$, and is equal to the work the source must do in placing the charge on the capacitor. It is, in turn, the work the capacitor will do when it discharges.

***Geometrical types.*** The geometry of a capacitor may take any one of several forms. The most common type is the parallel-plate capacitor whose capacitance $C$ in farads is given in the ideal case by Eq. (2),

$$C = \frac{A\epsilon_r\epsilon_0}{d} \qquad (2)$$

where $A$ is the area in square meters of one of the plates, $d$ is the distance in meters between the plates, $\epsilon_0$ is the permittivity of empty space with the numerical value $8.85 \times 10^{-12}$ farad/m, and $\epsilon_r$ is the relative permittivity of the dielectric material between the plates. The value of $\epsilon_r$ is unity for empty space and almost unity for gases. For other dielectric materials, $\epsilon_r$ ranges in value from one to several hundred. In order for Eq. (2) to give a good value of $C$ for an actual capacitor, $d$ must be very small compared to the linear dimensions of either plate.

Each plate of a parallel-plate capacitor may be made up of many thin sheets of metal connected electrically with a corresponding number of thin sheets of metal making up the other plate. The sheets of metal and their intervening layers of dielectric are chosen and stacked in such a way that $A$ will be large and $d$ small without making the whole capacitor too bulky. The result is appreciable capacitance in a reasonable volume.

The spherical capacitor is made of two concentric metal spheres with a dielectric of relative dielectric constant $\epsilon_r$ filling the space between the spheres. The capacitance in farads of such a capacitor is given by Eq. (3), where $r_2$ is the radius in meters of the outer

$$C = 4\pi\epsilon_r\epsilon_0\frac{r_1 r_2}{r_2 - r_1} \qquad (3)$$

sphere and $r_1$ that of the inner sphere.

The cylindrical capacitor, as the name implies, is made of two concentric metal cylinders, each of length $l$ in meters, with a dielectric filling the space between the cylinders. If $r_2$ and $r_1$ are the radii in meters of the outer and inner cylinders, respectively, and $l$ is very large compared to $r_2 - r_1$, the capacitance $C$ in farads is given by Eq. (4), where $\epsilon_r$ is the

$$C = \frac{2\pi\epsilon_r\epsilon_0 l}{\ln (r_2/r_1)} \qquad (4)$$

relative dielectric constant of the dielectric and ln $(r_2/r_1)$ indicates the natural logarithm of the ratio $r_2/r_1$.

**Guard ring.** This is often used with a standard parallel-plate capacitor, as shown in the **illustration**, in order that Eq. (2) shall more accurately represent its capacitance. It is the fringing of the electric lines of force which makes Eq. (2) inaccurate for an actual capacitor and, as shown in illus. *c*, the fringing is nearly all at the outside edge of the guard ring, and thus is not associated with the charge $Q$ which is put onto plate $P_1$ while the capacitor is being charged. It is the charge $Q$ that determines the deflection of the ballistic galvanometer during the charging process. Then Eq. (2) gives the correct value of $C$ that is needed to relate $Q$ to the potential difference $\mathscr{E}$ across the plates by the equation $Q = C\mathscr{E}$. Thus, with $C$ known from Eq. (2) and $\mathscr{E}$ known from a potentiometer measurement, $Q$ may be computed and the ballistic galvanometer calibrated. This illustrates one use of a standard capacitor with a guard ring.

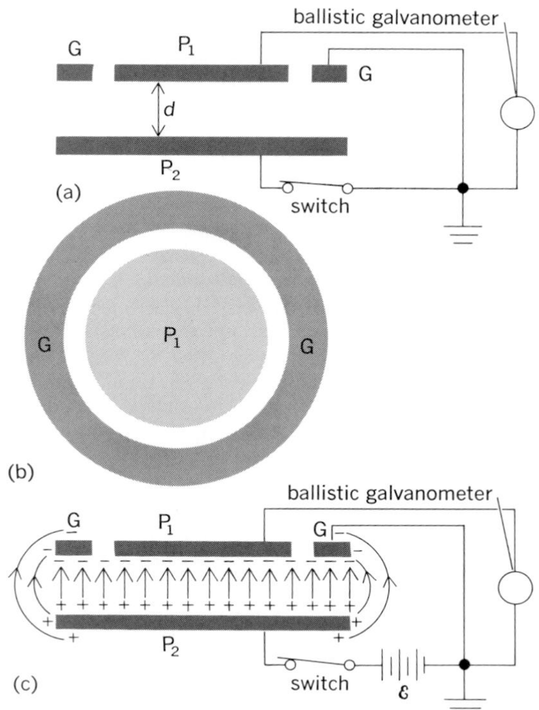


**Parallel-plate capacitor $P_1$, $P_2$ with guard ring GG. Spacing between guard ring and plate is exaggerated. (*a*) Cross section with all parts of capacitor at ground potential. (*b*) Top view showing plate $P_1$ surrounded by guard ring. (*c*) Cross section of capacitor charged from battery whose electromotive force is $\mathscr{E}$.**

**Body capacitance.** When a part of the human body, say the hand, is brought near a high-impedance network, the body serves as one plate of a capacitor and the adjacent part of the network as the other plate. This situation is the equivalent of a capacitor of very low capacitance, in parallel between that part of the network and ground, since the human body can usually be considered as being a grounded conductor. This capacitance is known as body capacitance and enters as a part of the distributed capacitance of the network. A high-impedance network must be well shielded in order to eliminate the variable and undesirable effects of body capacitance. *See* Capacitor.

*Ralph P. Winch*

***Bibliography.*** E. M. Purcell, *Electricity and Magnetism*, 2d ed., 1984; R. Resnick and D. Halliday, *Physics*, 3d ed., 1977; F. W. Sears et al., *University Physics*, 6th ed., 1981.

## Capacitance measurement

In a multiconductor system capacitances between each of the conductors may be defined. In general, these capacitances are functions of the total geometry, that is, the location of each and every conducting and dielectric body. When, as is usually true, one is inserted in the capacitance between two conductors only, the presence of other conductors is an undesirable complication. It is then customary to distinguish between two-terminal and three-terminal capacitors and capacitance measurements. In the case of a two-terminal capacitor, either one of the conductors of primary interest essentially surrounds the other, in which case the capacitance between them is independent of the lcoation of other bodies except in the vicinity of the terminals; or one accepts the somewhat indefinite contributions of the other conductors to the capacitance of interest.

A three-terminal capacitor consists of two active electrodes surrounded by a third, or shield, conductor. The direct capacitance between the two active electrodes is the capacitance of interest, and, when shielded leads are used, it is independent of the location of all other conductors except the shield. Only certain of the methods described are suitable for the measurement of three-terminal capacitors.

Every physically realizable capacitor has associated loss in the dielectric and in the metal electrodes. At a single frequency these are indistinguishable, and the capacitor may be represented by either a parallel or series combination of pure capacitance and pure resistance. The measurement of capacitance, then, in general involves the simultaneous measurement of or allowance for an associated resistive element.

Most capacitance measurements involve simply a comparison of the capacitor to be measured with a capacitor of known value. Methods which permit comparison of essentially equal capacitors by simple substitution of one for the other at the same point in a circuit are frequently possible and almost always preferable.

**Resonance method.** This method is suitable for two-terminal capacitance measurements when only moderate accuracy is required. The resonance method involves resonating an inductor with a calibrated variable capacitor which has a range of variation larger than the value of any capacitor to be measured. The parallel or series *LC* circuit is tuned to resonance by adjustment of the variable capacitor. The capacitor to be measured is then connected in parallel with the variable unit and the latter readjusted until resonance at the same frequency is again achieved. The value of the capacitor being measured is equal to the change in the variable capacitance standard.

A variety of techniques is available for determining when the resonance condition is achieved, some using series and some parallel resonance, but they differ significantly only in the way in which the source and detector are connected.

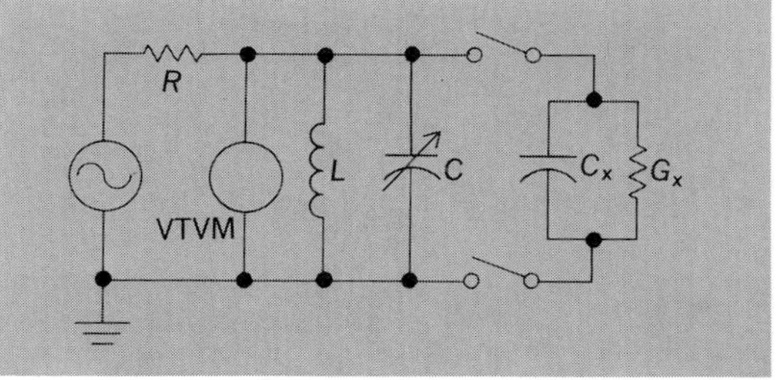


Fig. 1. Susceptance variation method.

**Susceptance variation.** This method is a resonance technique capable of yielding both the effective parallel capacitance and conductance components of a capacitor (**Fig. 1**). The calibrated variable capacitor $C$ is first adjusted to the value $C_1$ for which the vacuum-tube voltmeter (VTVM) indicates a maximum $V_m$. $C$ is then increased to a new value $C_2$ for which the VTVM reads $V_m/\sqrt{2}$. Simple network theory shows that the equivalent parallel conductance of the *LC* network is given by Eq. (1).

$$G_{\mathrm{eq}} = \omega\,(C_2 - C_1) \tag{1}$$

If now the capacitor to be measured, represented by the parallel combination $C_x$ and $G_x$, is connected across $C$ and the process repeated yielding values $C_1'$ and $G_{\mathrm{eq}}'$, the Eqs. (2) and (3) hold.

$$C_x = C_1' - C_1 \tag{2}$$

$$G_x = G_{\mathrm{eq}}' - G_{\mathrm{eq}} \tag{3}$$

Alternate resonance techniques include use of a parallel *LC* circuit as the frequency-determining element in an oscillator or as one arm of a Wheatstone bridge whose other three arms are resistors. In the latter case balance of the bridge defines the resonant condition and also provides a measure of the equivalent resistive component.

**Bridge methods.** When high accuracies are required, bridge methods must be adopted. *See* Bridge circuit; Wheatstone bridge.

***Resistance-ratio bridges.*** These are Wheatstone-bridge configurations in which two adjacent arms are resistors, as indicated in **Fig. 2**. Application of the generalized Wheatstone bridge equation, Eq. (4),

$$Z_1Z_x = Z_2Z_s \quad \text{or} \quad Y_1Y_x = Y_2Y_s \tag{4}$$

leads to Eqs. (5) and (6) for the parallel arrangement,

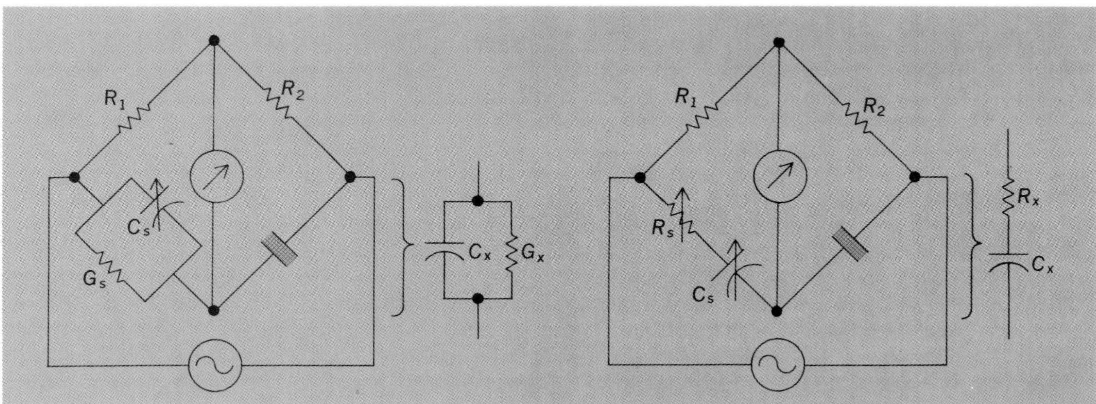


Fig. 2. Resistance-ratio bridges, in which two adjacent arms are resistors.

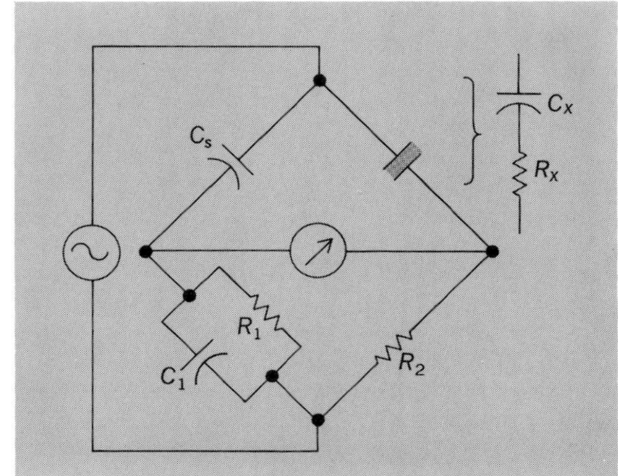


Fig. 3. Schering bridge for measurement of the equivalent series-circuit representation of a capacitor.

$$C_x = C_s \frac{R_1}{R_2} \quad (5)$$

$$G_x = G_s \frac{R_1}{R_2} \quad (6)$$

and to Eqs. (7) and (8) for the series arrangement.

$$C_x = C_s \frac{R_1}{R_2} \quad (7)$$

$$R_x = R_s \frac{R_2}{R_1} \quad (8)$$

These are the conditions for bridge balance as indicated by zero voltage across the detector terminals.

***Schering bridge.*** This bridge yields a measurement of the equivalent series-circuit representation of a capacitor (**Fig. 3**). The equations of balance are written as Eqs. (9) and (10).

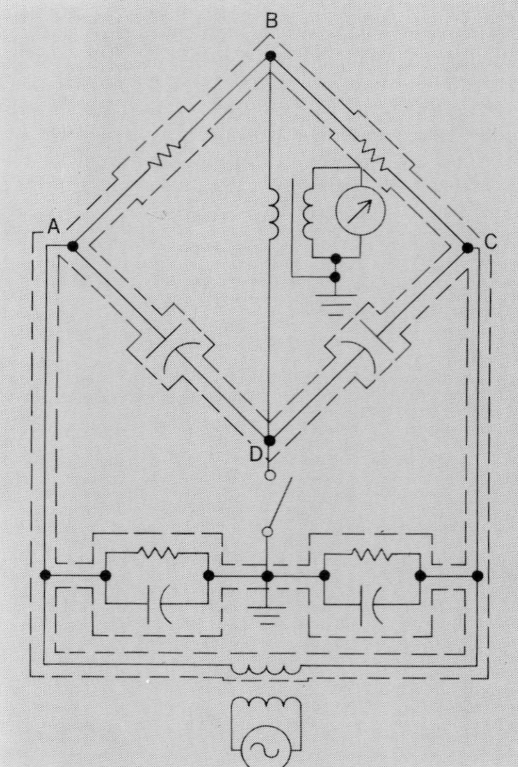


Fig. 4. Shielded resistance ratio-arm bridge with Wagner branch for three-terminal measurements.

$$C_x = C_s \frac{R_1}{R_2} \quad (9)$$

$$R_x = R_2 \frac{C_1}{C_s} \quad (10)$$

The arrangement shown is used when it is desirable for high voltages to be applied to the capacitor under test. The relative impedances are usually such that most of the applied voltage appears across the capacitors and, if balance is effected by varying $C_1$ and $R_1$ or $R_2$, the operator need not approach the high-voltage elements.

In general with a given applied voltage, higher sensitivity is obtained if the source and detector connections are interchanged; this so-called conjugate bridge is more frequently used for measurements of high precision. Because variable capacitors are less subject to errors from associated residuals than variable resistors, balance is then usually effected by varying $C_s$ and $C_1$; the standard capacitor $C_s$ is assumed to be free from loss.

***Wagner branch.*** The resistance-ratio and Schering bridges (**Fig. 4**) are useful for two-terminal capacitance measurements. Their use may be extended to three-terminal measurements and extended in accuracy and range by the introduction of shielding and the addition of the Wagner branch.

Balance is effected alternately by adjustment of the main bridge arms with the switch open, and by adjustment of the Wagner branch elements with the switch closed. The final balance may be considered to be that with the switch open. Capacitances to ground at both the A and C corners of the bridge then shunt the Wagner arms and do not affect the balance of the main bridge. Capacitances to ground at the B and D corners carry no current at balance and therefore cannot introduce error.

***Transformer ratio-arm bridges.*** These are particularly suitable for three-terminal capacitance measurements. Of the variety of inductive and transformer ratio-arm bridges that have been developed, the one shown in **Fig. 5** seems most suitable for capacitance measurements of high accuracy.

Capacitance to ground from b reduces sensitivity but does not affect the condition of balance. Capaci-

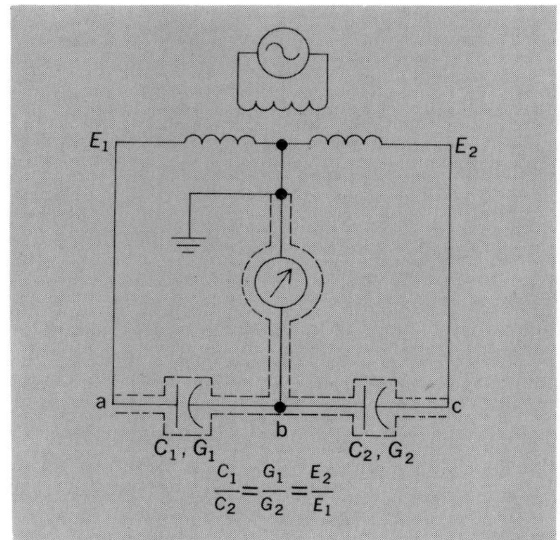


Fig. 5. Transformer ratio-arm bridge, used in capacitance measurements requiring high accuracy.

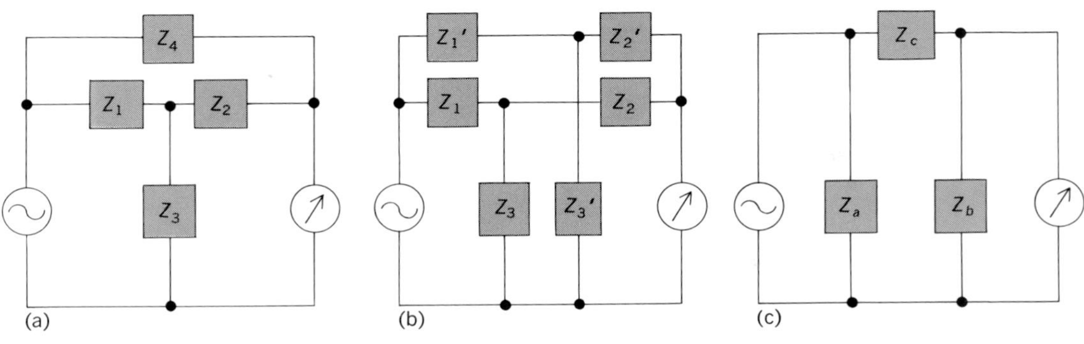


Fig. 6. T networks. (*a*) Bridged T. (*b*) Parallel T. (*c*) Equivalent circuit.

tances to ground from a and c introduce loads on the transformer secondaries, but with proper transformer design the errors introduced may be kept negligible.

Audio-frequency three-winding transformers with secondary open-circuit voltage ratios equal to the turns ratios within 10 parts in 1,000,000 are quite readily constructed. With care in design 1:1 and 10:1 transformers with ratio errors of the order of 1 part in $10^7$ are entirely feasible. The secondary-winding resistances and leakage inductances under conditions of use introduce departures from the open-circuit voltage ratio, and therefore this bridge circuit is most useful for the measurement of capacitors less than 1 microfarad at audio frequencies. Transformer design for radio-frequency use is more difficult. However, the bridge circuit is used with reduced accuracy at capacitance levels of the order of 100 picofarads and below, at frequencies up to 10 MHz.

***Bridged-T and parallel-T networks.*** These complex bridges possess a significant advantage over four-arm bridges for medium-accuracy radio-frequency measurements of capacitance; the source and detector have a common point of connection which may be grounded (**Fig. 6**).

Use of the Y-delta network transformation permits reduction of either the bridged-T or the parallel-T to the equivalent circuit shown. Balance, or null indication of the detector, is achieved by variation of the network components until the equivalent impedance $Z_c$ is infinite. In the application of the parallel-T network to capacitance measurements, as shown in **Fig. 7**, two balances are required, one with and the other without the unknown connected. The equivalent parallel components of the unknown admittance are obtained from the differences in the values of the two capacitors indicated.

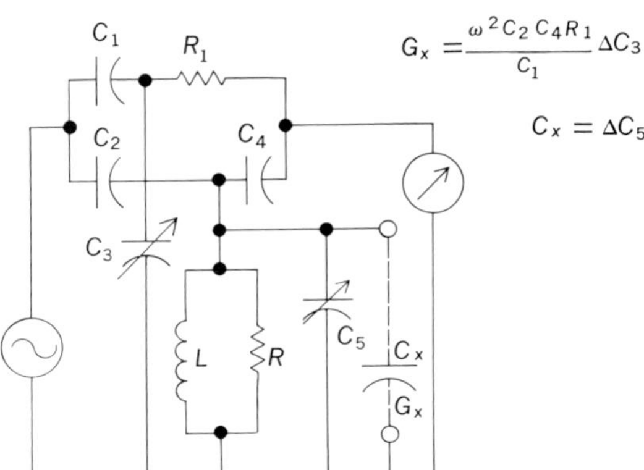


Fig. 7. Parallel-T network to measure capacitance.

**Time-constant methods.** If a direct voltage is suddenly applied to the series combination of a resistor and an initially discharged capacitor, the charge and the voltage on the capacitor increase exponentially toward their full magnitudes with a time constant equal in seconds to the product of the resistance in ohms and the capacitance in farads. Similarly, when a charged capacitor is discharged through a resistor, the charge and the voltage decay with the same time constant. Various methods are available for the measurement of capacitance by measurement of the time constant of charge or discharge through a known resistor. SEE TIME CONSTANT.

***Ballistic galvanometer method.*** This method (**Fig. 8**) compares the charge lost by the capacitor in a known time interval to the total charge. With the capacitor completely discharged the switch is closed, and the product of the galvanometer deflection and the multiplying factor of the shunt is proportional to the total

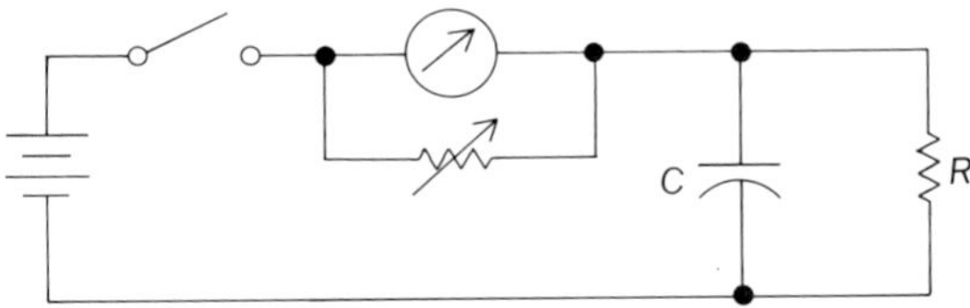


Fig. 8. Ballistic galvanometer method.

charge $Q_T$. The switch is opened for a measured time interval $\Delta t$ and again closed. The product of the galvanometer deflection and the shunt factor is then proportional to the charge $Q_a$ lost by the capacitor. Because Eq. (11) is valid, Eq. (12) holds.

$$Q_T - Q_a = Q_T e^{-\Delta t/RC} \quad (11)$$

$$C = \frac{-\Delta t}{R \ln [(Q_T - Q_a)/Q_T]} \quad (12)$$

***Integrating operational amplifier.*** In this method the time required for the output voltage of an amplifier to increase to a value equal to the step-function input voltage is determined by an electronic voltage-comparison circuit and timer (**Fig. 9**). Assuming ideal characteristics for the amplifier, such as infinite gain without feedback, infinite input impedance, and zero output impedance, the measured time interval is equal to the product of the values of the known resistance and the capacitance being measured.

**Distributed capacitance.** An inductor is a particularly impure circuit component. In addition to the series resistance of the winding, distributed capacitance is always present from turn to turn and layer to layer, making the effective inductance a function of frequency. It is customary to assume that the effect of the distributed capacitance in an inductance coil may

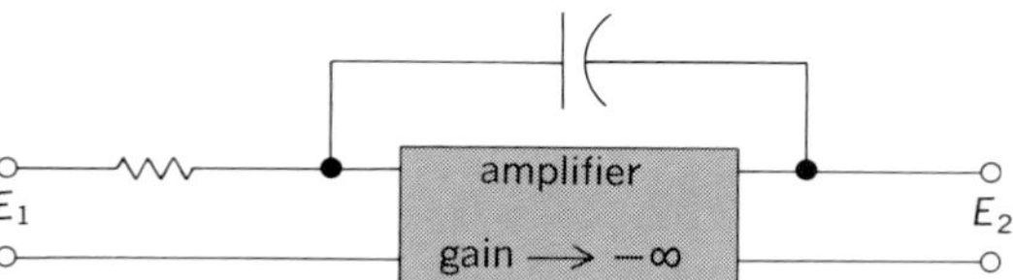


Fig. 9. Intergrating operational amplifier.

be represented by a single capacitor connected between the coil terminals. In some cases the value of this equivalent capacitor may be obtained by a determination of the self-resonant frequency of the coil; however, as a result of the distributed nature of both the inductance and the capacitance, the coil may exhibit several resonance modes, and a self-resonance determination is then ambiguous.

A procedure that usually surmounts this difficulty is that of determining the resonant frequency for several settings of a variable capacitor connected in parallel with the coil. A plot of the capacitance of the observed auxiliary capacitor against the reciprocal of the square of the corresponding resonant frequency and extrapolated to infinite frequency then gives a value for the lumped equivalent of the distributed capacitance.

*F. Ralph Kotter*

**Adjustment.** The effective value of a capacitor $C_e$ (the value that is measured at its terminals) may be affected by three factors. First, the series inductance $l$ increases the actual capacitance $C$, according to Eq. (13). Second, dielectric absorption in a capacitor with

$$C_e = \frac{C}{1 - \omega^2 lC} \qquad (13)$$

a solid dielectric normally causes a reduction in capacitance as the frequency is raised. Third, mechanical displacement of the electrodes due to the electric forces between them may alter the capacitance; this effect should be detectable only in air or gas dielectric capacitors, and it can be quite appreciable in high-voltage capacitors. SEE INDUCTANCE.

The series inductance can be obtained from a measurement of the self-resonant frequency $f$ of the capacitor with its terminals connected together by a link of low and calculable inductance. The total inductance is $1/(2\pi f)^2C$.

The effect of dielectric absorption is measured by ultimate reference to an air or gas dielectric capacitor which is free from this phenomenon.

The electric forces between the electrodes of standard capacitors produce capacitance changes that are usually too small to be significant, except when the highest accuracy is required at more than a single applied voltage.

**Thompson-Lampard capacitor.** The value of a capacitor of a fixed shape is proportional to its size; that is, a single dimension might be used to establish its value. A. M. Thompson and D. G. Lampard showed how this principle could be applied to a precise and practical capacitor. The value of such a capacitor requires only a single length to be measured accurately, and this is readily accomplished by interferometry. Thompson and Lampard's theorem relates to a capacitor which, in its simple form, comprises four equal electrodes of parallel round bars arranged with their axes at the corners of a square and with small gaps between adjacent bars. In vacuum, the cross-capacitance between diagonally opposite electrodes per unit length is given by Eq. (14). If the two cross-capaci-

$$C_0 = 1.95354902 \quad \text{pF/m} \qquad (14)$$

tances are not quite equal and differ by $\Delta C$, the mean capacitance is given approximately by Eq. (15).

$$C = C_0(1 + 0.0866(\Delta C/C)^2) \qquad (15)$$

The essential features of this capacitor are shown in **Fig. 10**. Grounded electric shields around the assembly and at the ends are omitted from the figure; these eliminate from a measurement all capacitances except the required internal ones. The capacitor is in an evacuated enclosure to avoid uncertainties arising from the relative permittivity and the refractive index.

If a grounded bar or tube is inserted into the central space between the electrodes, with a small gap between the bar and the electrodes, it forms an electric shield and the cross-capacitance is zero. A short, fixed tube is inserted at one end, and at the other there is a long tube that can be moved axially to alter the active length of the capacitor. The change of length is measured interferometrically; for this, interferometer plates are mounted at the inner ends of the fixed and movable tubes. There is a minimum separation of the tubes—about three times the space between opposing electrodes—below which the capacitance change with length becomes significantly nonlinear.

A practical cross-capacitor departs slightly from the ideal geometry in a number of ways, so that the accuracy is limited to about $1 \times 10^{-8}$ pF; if the working range of the capacitor is 0.5 pF (equivalent to a change of length of 10 in. or 25 cm), the overall accuracy on this account is 2 parts in $10^8$. The repeatability is appreciably better.

**Calibration of a fixed capacitor.** The first step in the measurement of capacitance is to calibrate a stable, fixed capacitor. A suitable one is the 10-pF fused quartz capacitor discussed below. For this purpose, the bridge shown in **Fig. 11** is convenient and flexible; it has a 10:1 low-impedance precision transformer, and a nine-dial inductive voltage divider is con-

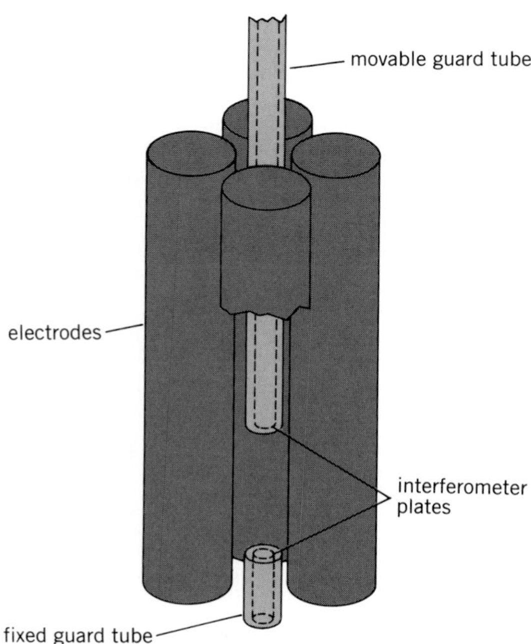


Fig. 10. Essential arrangement of a calculable capacitor with an interferometer for length measurement.

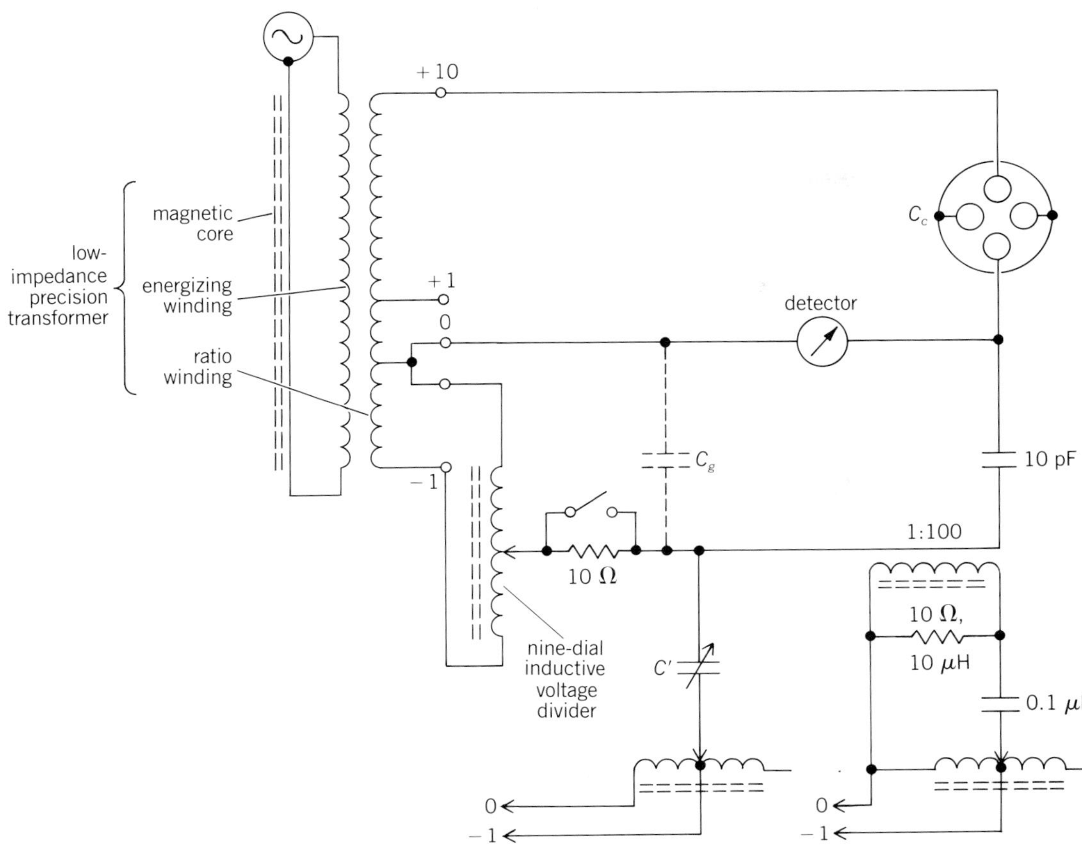


**Fig. 11. Transformer bridge for the calibration of a 10-pF capacitor against a calculable capacitor $C_c$.**

nected across the low-voltage winding to allow continuous variation of the potential applied to the 10-pF fixed capacitor. There is also a small adjustable voltage, accurately in quadrature, to effect a balance of the loss components of the capacitors. The ratio of the transformer has been measured with an accuracy of $10^{-9}$ at 1592 Hz—the normal working frequency—and the inductive voltage divider has also been measured with this accuracy of the input voltage. A low-noise preamplifier followed by a phase-sensitive detector with a 10-s time-constant gives a discrimination of $10^{-21}$ pF in the value of the calculable capacitor. The ground capacitance $C_g$, of the output termination of the nine-dial inductive voltage divider, is compensated by the capacitor $C'$ of value equal to the ground capacitance and supplied with a voltage twice that of the inductive voltage divider.

**Calibration of standard capacitors.** The 10-pF capacitor provides the starting point for the calibration of standard capacitors, which are compared in 1:10 steps by using an accurately calibrated transformer. When the highest accuracy of comparison is required, the capacitors must be four-terminal-pair components and used in an appropriate bridge, as in **Fig. 12**. A 4-terminal-pair impedance has two coaxial connections at the input and at the output terminations. The source is connected to one input connection, and the defining voltage appears at the other input connection; similarly, the current through the impedance passes through one output connector, while the potential difference at the other output connection is kept at zero. The defining conditions can be departed from, provided that the bridge balance is not thereby altered. For clarity in Fig. 12, all the screens and the outer conductors of the coaxial connections have been omitted; also, every mesh has a current equalizer which ensures that equal currents of opposite sign flow in the inner and the outer conductors of every coaxial connection. The transformer is of the two-stage type; thus there is an energizing winding on the first core followed by a winding which supplies the current to the impedances $Z_1$ and $Z_2$ to be compared, and finally, a second core and the overall winding, which provides a precise potential ratio for comparing the two four-terminal-pair impedances. The second core is energized with a small current which modifies the overall output potential without changing the potential ratio. The bridge is balanced by injecting a small known voltage (not shown in Fig. 12) into the potential circuit of one of the impedances and by the excitation of the second core. Adjustment of the combining network for the detector is also required. For this, the supply is transferred from the main transformer to the injection circuit and the combining network adjusted to obtain a balance. When the supply is removed from the injection circuit, it is replaced by a short circuit.

**Properties of standard capacitors.** The most stable capacitor is one with fused quartz dielectric having a value of 10 pF. The dielectric is a quartz disk about 2.8 in. (70 mm) in diameter and 0.4 in. (10 mm) thick. Electrodes are fired onto the two faces of the disk and a guard electrode fired onto the circumferential surface. Because fused quartz has a temperature coefficient of permittivity of about 5 parts per million per °F (10 parts per million per K) it is essential to measure the temperature accurately and a resistance thermometer is placed around the disk. The unit is in

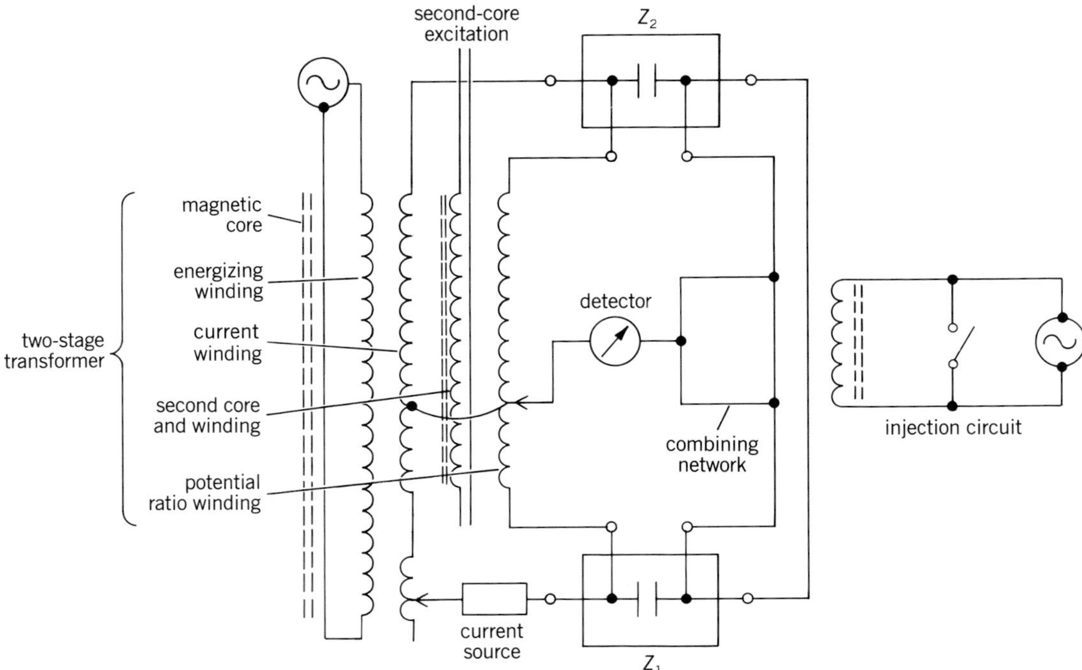


**Fig. 12. Two-stage transformer bridge for the precise comparison of two similar impedances $Z_1$ and $Z_2$.**

a hermetically sealed container and can be put in an oil-bath or other constant temperature enclosure.

Other good capacitors with values up to 1 nF have parallel plates or cylindrical electrodes; they are hermetically sealed and evacuated or filled with dry gas; capacitors of larger value have a solid dielectric, such as mica or polystyrene or other plastic film, and are less constant in value. When they are used as standards, a three-terminal arrangement is normal, and there is a screening case with a separate connection. A three-terminal capacitor can be measured satisfactorily if the screen can be maintained at the potential of one of the capacitor terminals, but at high frequencies—above about 100 kHz—it becomes increasingly difficult to satisfy this condition, and a two-terminal capacitor may be advantageous. The disadvantage of a two-terminal capacitor is the uncertainty arising from the fringing field of its terminals, which may be a few tenths of a picofarad; however, a change in capacitance will be precise if the fringing field is unaltered. For example, the difference in the value of two capacitors with identical terminal arrangements can be measured accurately even if their total capacitance cannot be determined with high accuracy. This applies even to capacitors with precision coaxial connectors for use up to a few GHz; with one type of such capacitor, when it is unmated, the inner conductor length can differ slightly from one connector to another, thereby giving a corresponding different capacitance for an unmated connector. Such capacitors have a series inductance of a few nanohenries, and they and transmission lines of accurately known dimensions provide the standards for high-frequency measurements.

At the other end of the frequency range, measurements are required on capacitors up to 1 F in value at frequencies around 100 Hz. The stability of these capacitors is such that the standards used in their measurement need have an accuracy of no better than 0.01% and are often considerably worse. For this

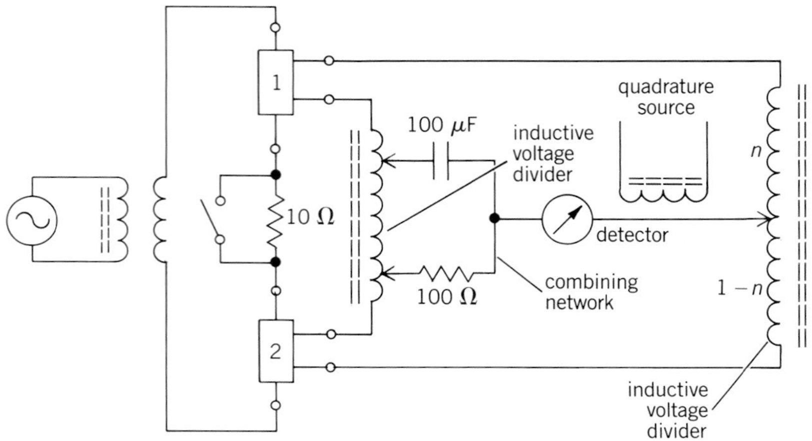


**Fig. 13. An ac double bridge suitable for the comparison of two similar, low-value impedances 1 and 2.**

range, the standards comprise a capacitor combined with transformers for the input and output connections. A single capacitor, which may be a 1-μF mica dielectric capacitor, and multitapped input and output transformers can be used to provide values between 1 μF and 1 F. However, a better performance is obtained if a transformer designed to give the optimum properties is used to provide each value of the capacitance, and plastic-film capacitors of value larger than 1 μF are used. A bridge circuit suitable for the comparison of such capacitors is shown in **Fig. 13**. It is basically an ac double bridge for the comparison of two similar impedances which are of the four-terminal type; for clarity, the outer conductors of the coaxial connections and current equalizers have been omitted. The ratio of the values of four-terminal impedances 1 and 2 is equal to the ratio $n/(1 - n)$ of the inductive voltage divider; the latter has a high input impedance and does not cause significant loading of the potential connections of the impedances 1 and 2. The bridge is made immune to the voltage appearing in the current circuit between 1 and 2 by adjusting the combining network so that a balance is maintained both with the 10-Ω resistor in circuit and with it shorted. Only one inductive voltage divider is shown for the resistor and the capacitor, but a separate inductive voltage divider may be used for each. *See Capacitance; Capacitor; Electrical measurements*.

*G. H. Rayner*

***Bibliography.*** W. K. Clothier, A calculable standard capacitance, *Metrologia*, 1:36–55, 1965; R. D. Cutkosky and L. H. Lee, Improved ten-picofarad fused silica dielectric capacitor, *J. Res. NBS*, 69C:173–179, 1965; S. Harkness, *Low Noise FET Amplifiers for Low-Loss Capacitative Sources*, Nat. Phys. Lab. Rep. DES 41, 1977; F. K. Harris, *Electrical Measurements*, 1952, reprint 1975; B. P. Kibble and G. H. Rayner, *Coaxial A. C. Bridges*, 1984; B. P. Kibble, G. H. Rayner, and M. J. Swan, *Comparing Capacitance Standards of Values Greater than a Microfarad*, Nat. Phys. Lab. DES Mem. 34, 1981.

## Capacitor

An electrical device capable of storing electrical energy. In general, a capacitor consists of two metal plates insulated from each other by a dielectric. The capacitance of a capacitor depends primarily upon its shape and size and upon the relative permittivity $\epsilon_r$ of the medium between the plates. In vacuum, in air, and in most gases, $\epsilon_r$ ranges from one to several hundred. *See Capacitance*.

**Classification.** One classification of capacitors comes from the physical state of their dielectrics, which may be gas (or vacuum), liquid, solid, or a combination of these. Each of these classifications may be subdivided according to the specific dielectric used. Capacitors may be further classified by their ability to be used in alternating-current or direct-current circuits with various current levels.

Capacitors are also classified as fixed, adjustable, or variable. The capacitance of fixed capacitors remains unchanged, except for small variations caused by temperature fluctuations. The capacitance of adjustable capacitors may be set at any one of several discrete values. The capacitance of variable capacitors may be adjusted continuously and set at any value between minimum and maximum limits fixed by construction. Trimmer capacitors are relatively small variable capacitors used in parallel with larger variable or fixed capacitors to permit exact adjustment of the capacitance of the parallel combination.

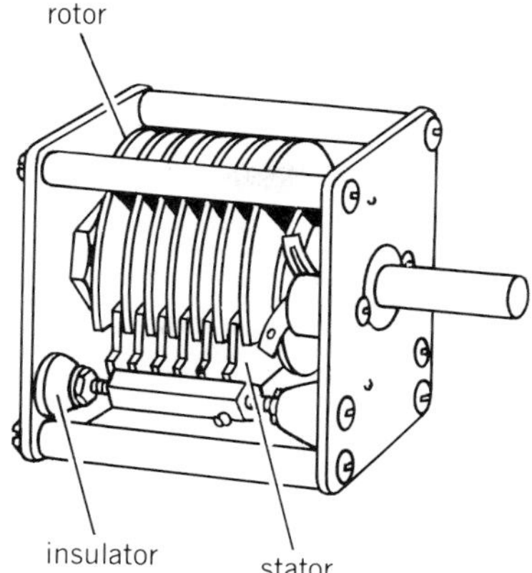

**Fig. 1. Variable air capacitor.**

**Air, gas, and vacuum types.** Made in both fixed and variable types, these capacitors are constructed with flat parallel metallic plates (or cylindrical concentric metallic plates) with air, gas, or vacuum as the dielectric between plates. Alternate plates are connected, with one or both sets supported by means of a solid insulating material such as glass, quartz, ceramic, or plastic. **Figure 1** shows a variable air capacitor. Gas capacitors are similarly built but are enclosed in a leakproof case. If the gas capacitor is variable, the shaft supporting the movable plates, or rotor, is brought out through a pressure-tight insulated seal. Vacuum capacitors are of concentric-cylindrical construction and are enclosed in highly evacuated glass envelopes.

The purpose of a high vacuum, or a gas under pressure, is to increase the voltage breakdown value for a given plate spacing. For high-voltage applications, when increasing the spacing between plates is undesirable, the breakdown voltage of air capacitors may be increased by rounding the edges of the plates. Air, gas, and vacuum capacitors are used in high-frequency circuits. Fixed and variable air capacitors incorporating special design are used as standards in electrical measurements. *See Capacitance measurement*.

**Solid-dielectric types.** These capacitors use one of several dielectrics such as a ceramic, mica, glass, or plastic film. Alternate plates of metal, or metallic foil, are stacked with the dielectric, or the dielectric may

**Dielectric materials used in capacitors**

| Dielectric material | Relative permittivity ($\epsilon_r$) | Power factor, % |
|---|---|---|
| Vacuum-air | 1 | 0 |
| Kraft paper | 4.0–6.5 | 3 |
| Polyester | 3.0 | 0.5 |
| Polypropylene | 2.2 | 0.01 |
| Glass | 6.7 | 0.06 |
| Mica | 6–8 | 0.02 |
| Aluminum oxide | 10.0 | 5–10 |
| Tantalum oxide | 11.0 | 5–10 |
| Barium titanate | 10.60 | 5–10 |

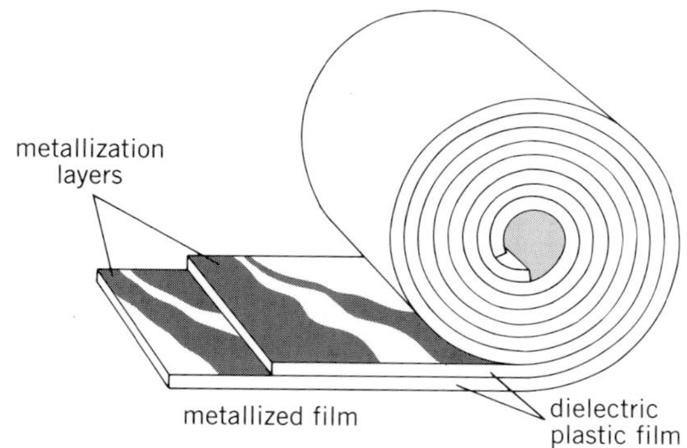


Fig. 2. Wound-roll construction of plastic film capacitor.

be metal-plated on both sides. Some of the more popular dielectric materials are listed in the **table**, along with their relative permittivities and power factors.

***Plastic-film types.*** These capacitors use dielectrics such as polypropylene, polyester, polycarbonate, or polysulfone with a relative permittivity ranging from 2.2 to 3.2. This plastic film may be used alone or in combination with Kraft paper. The dielectric thicknesses range from 0.06 mil (1.5 micrometers) to over 0.8 mil (20 micrometers). The most common electrodes are aluminum or zinc vacuum-deposited on the film, although aluminum foil is also used. These types generally utilize wound-roll construction (**Fig. 2**).

Plastic-film capacitors may be constructed in a dry roll for dc and low-voltage ac applications. For ac applications above about 250 volts ac, the capacitor winding is usually impregnated with a dielectric fluid to avoid degradation of the dielectric due to partial discharges.

***Mica types.*** These capacitors use thin rectangular sheets of mica as the dielectric. The relative permittivity of mica is in the range of 6–8. The electrodes are either thin sheets of metal foil stacked alternately with the mica sheets, or thin deposits of silver applied directly to the surface of the mica sheets. Mica capacitors are used chiefly in radio-frequency applications. They have a low dielectric loss at very high frequencies, good temperature, frequency, and aging characteristics, and low power factor, but have a low ratio of capacitance to volume or to mass. They are made with dc voltage ratings from a few hundred to many thousand volts and with radio-frequency current ratings up to about 50 A.

***Paper types.*** A dielectric of Kraft paper usually impregnated with mineral oil, or ester, is used in paper capacitors. Paper (**Fig. 3**) and plastic-film capacitors are constructed by stacking, or forming into a roll, alternate layers of foil and dielectric. Paper capacitors are gradually being replaced by metallized polypropylene and polyester films because of their lower cost, smaller size, and lower power factor.

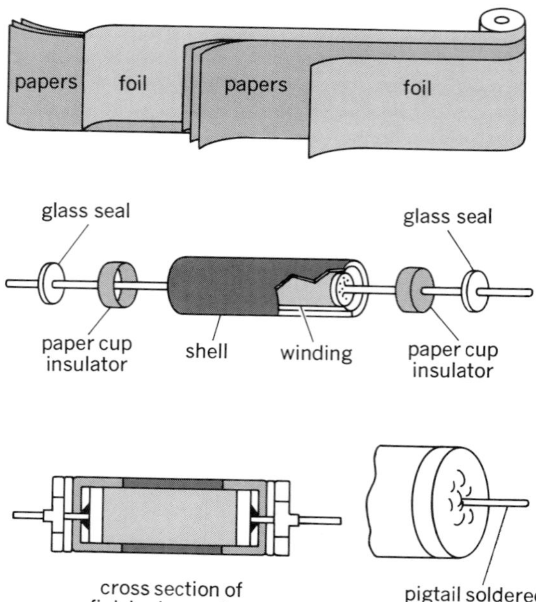


**Fig. 3. Components of extended-foil paper capacitor. (*After K. Henney and C. Walsh, eds., Electronic Components Handbook, McGraw-Hill, 1957*)**

***Ceramic types.*** The monolithic ceramic capacitor consists of dielectric layers interleaved with electrode layers; the assembly is then compressed and sintered to form a solid monolithic block (**Fig. 4**). The dielectric layer may be as thin as 0.8 mil (20 μm), and as many as 40–50 layers may be interleaved. The most common dielectric material is barium titanate. The electrodes are composed of materials such as a silver-palladium mixture. The end termination is usually composed of several layers of silver-palladium, nickel, and tin. These capacitors may be constructed in radial, axial, or chip form. The chip construction is especially popular for surface mounting on electronic circuits. These capacitors are known for their ability to withstand the 450°F (230°C) reflow solder and 540°F (280°C) wave solder mounting temperatures. SEE BARIUM TITANATE.

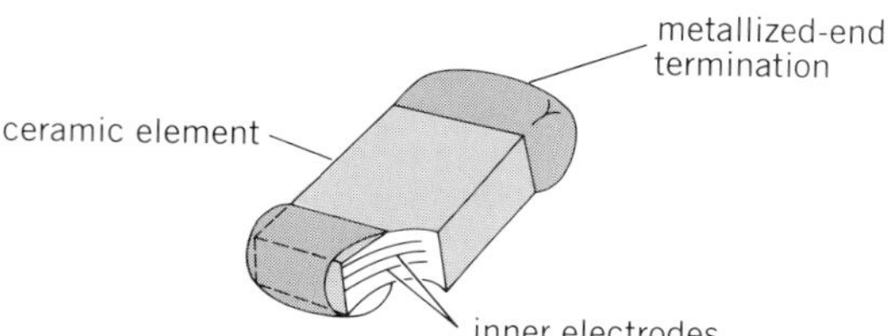


**Fig. 4. Ceramic capacitor constructed in chip form, showing cutaway of finished chip.**

***Electrolytic types.*** A large capacitance-to-volume ratio and a low cost per microfarad of capacitance are chief advantages of electrolytic capacitors. These use aluminum or tantalum plates (**Fig. 5**) on which an oxide film forms and acts as the dielectric. The characteristics of the oxide film depend on the polarity of the applied voltage. Such a device is said to be polarized. Polarized electrolytic capacitors must be connected to the circuit correctly. They can be used only in circuits in which the dc component of voltage across the capacitor exceeds the crest value of the ac ripple.

Another type of electrolytic capacitor utilizes compressed tantalum powder and the baking of manganese oxide ($MnO_2$) as an electrolyte. These capacitors may be constructed with either radial, axial, or chip configurations (**Fig. 6**).

Nonpolarized electrolytic capacitors can be constructed for use in ac circuits. In effect, they are two polarized capacitors placed in series with their polarities reversed.

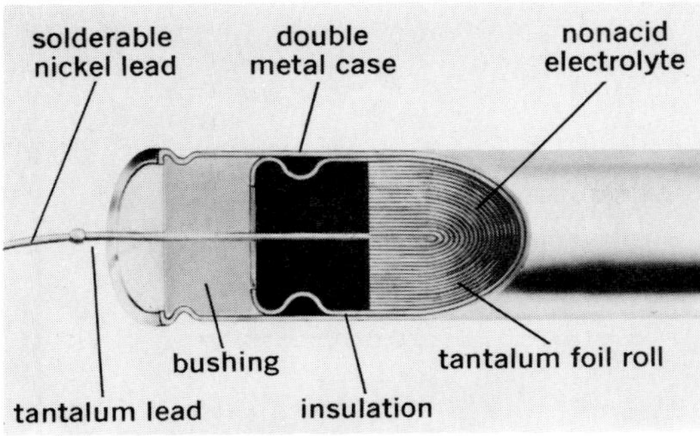


**Fig. 5. Tantalum electrolytic capacitor showing cross section. (*General Electric Co.*)**

**Thick-film types.** These capacitors are made by means of successive screen-printing and firing processes in the fabrication of certain types of microcircuits used in electronic computers and other electronic systems. They are formed, together with their connecting conductors and associated thick-film resistors, upon a ceramic substrate. Their characteristics and the materials are similar to those of ceramic capacitors. *SEE PRINTED CIRCUIT.*

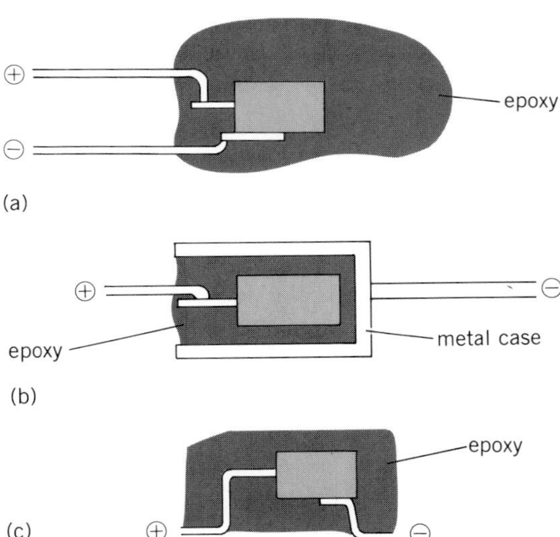


**Fig. 6. Typical structures of various types of tantalum capacitors. (*a*) Radial leads. (*b*) Axial leads. (c) Chip configuration.**

**Thin-film types.** Thin-film dielectrics are deposited on ceramic and integrated-circuit substrates and then metallized with aluminum to form capacitive components. These are usually single-layer capacitors. The most common dielectrics are silicon nitride and silicon dioxide. Thin-film dielectrics may be deposited by plasma deposition or sputtering. *SEE INTEGRATED CIRCUITS; SPUTTERING.*

*David G. Shaw*

***Bibliography.*** K. Henney and C. Walsh (eds.), *Electronic Components Handbook*, 1957; W. F. Mullin, *ABC's of Capacitors*, 1966; D. G. Shaw, S. W. Cichanowski, and A. Yializis, Changing Capacitor Technology—Failure Mechanisms and Design Innovations, *IEEE Transactions on Electrical Insulation*, EI-16:399–413, 1981.

## Carrier

Any wave to which modulation is subsequently applied. Common examples are a sinusoidal wave, a recurrent series of pulses, and a direct current or voltage. *SEE AMPLITUDE MODULATION; ANGLE MODULATION; FREQUENCY MODULATION; PHASE MODULATION.* For a definition of pulse carrier *SEE PULSE MODULATION;* for a definition of subcarrier *SEE MODULATION.*

It is not always necessary or even desirable to transmit the carrier wave; when not transmitted, it is termed a suppressed carrier. *SEE SINGLE SIDEBAND.*

*Harold S. Black*

## Cascode amplifier

A transistor amplifier consisting of a common-emitter stage in series with a common-base stage. The input resistance and current gain are nominally equal to the corresponding values for a single common-emitter stage (see **illus.**). The output resistance is approximately equal to the high output resistance of the common-base stage. The reverse open-circuit amplification parameter $h_r$ is very much smaller for the cascode connection than for a single common-emitter stage. The small value of $h_r$ makes this circuit particularly useful in tuned amplifier design where the collector load is replaced with a tuned circuit.

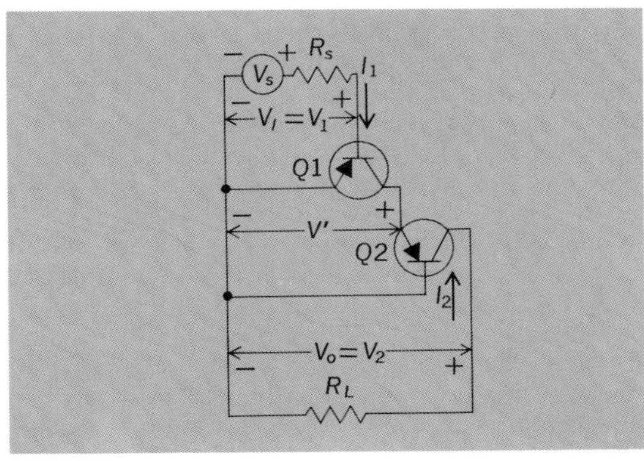


**Cascode configuration. Supply voltages are not shown.**

A vacuum tube version of the cascode amplifier is composed of a grounded cathode stage connected to a grounded grid stage. This circuit has the characteristics of a pentode, that is, a high amplification factor and a large plate resistance.

The cascode amplifier finds its principal application in the amplification of high-frequency signals of 25 MHz and higher. It is particularly useful in low-level input stages where the signal-to-noise ratio is a problem. One widespread use for the cascode circuit is in the tuner of a television receiver. In the fringe areas where the signal strength is small, an amplifier is needed which can amplify the signal the required amount without introducing an excessive amount of noise. *SEE TELEVISION RECEIVER.*

*Christos C. Halkias*

***Bibliography.*** B. Grob, *Electronic Circuits and Applications*, 1982; C. A. Holt, *Electronic Circuits: Digital and Analog*, 1978; J. Millman, *Microelectronics*, 1979.

## Cathode-ray tube

An electron tube in which a beam of electrons can be focused to a small cross section and varied in position and intensity on a display surface. In common usage, the term cathode-ray tube (CRT) is usually reserved for devices in which the display surface is cathodoluminescent under electron bombardment, and the output information is presented in the form of a pattern of light. The character of this pattern is related to, and controlled by, one or more electrical signals applied to the cathode-ray tube as input information. SEE CATHODOLUMINESCENCE; ELECTRON TUBE.

**Development.** The technology of the cathode-ray tube was both a product of certain late-nineteenth-century experiments which led to modern physics and an indispensable element in the conduct of such experiments. In particular, the discovery of x-rays in 1895 by William Roentgen and the discovery of the electron in 1897 by J. J. Thompson both resulted from experiments in which early cathode-ray devices were involved.

While experiments with cathode rays within partial vacuum devices had been conducted by various scientists for at least the previous 200 years, Ferdinand Braun is credited with inventing in 1897 a "cathode-ray indicator tube" from which all modern cathode-ray tubes are derived. Braun's interest in the cathode-ray tube was primarily as a device for the study of phenomena related to electricity. The cathode-ray tube was well suited to this use because of its ability to provide a visual indication of alternating electric currents at low frequencies. Oscillography was thus a natural first application for the new device. To this day, the cathode-ray oscilloscope continues to be an indispensable tool in nearly all fields of electronics.

Early experimenters in television who were attempting to develop electronic scanning realized the potential usefulness of the cathode-ray tube as a television display device. In the 1920s V. K. Zworykin developed a cathode-ray tube which was improved in ways which made it particularly suitable for the display of television images. This tube, the kinescope, first demonstrated in 1929, was the forerunner of the monochrome television picture tubes which were produced commercially in the late 1940s and the 1950s. Modifications to the kinescope, including the addition of a shadow mask, led to the commercial introduction of the color picture tube in 1953. SEE COLOR TELEVISION; PICTURE TUBE; TELEVISION.

During the 1930s, it had become apparent that the cathode-ray tube would make an excellent display device for use with the new radar technology. Many of the early television pioneers were recruited into the effort to complete the development of radar for use in World War II. SEE RADAR.

In the 1960s and 1970s the cathode-ray tube became established as a widely used device for the display of computer output information. Modifications have been made to television picture tubes, both monochrome and color, to improve characteristics which are of importance to observers of computer output information. Cathode-ray tubes specialized for this use are called data display tubes. Their use has grown rapidly, particularly because of the popularity of personal computers. SEE COMPUTER; MICROCOMPUTER.

**Basic elements.** In the following description of a typical cathode-ray tube, emphasis is given to those features which are common to most of the tubes now produced. Some of the variations in construction and function from this basic cathode-ray-tube configuration are described later in the article.

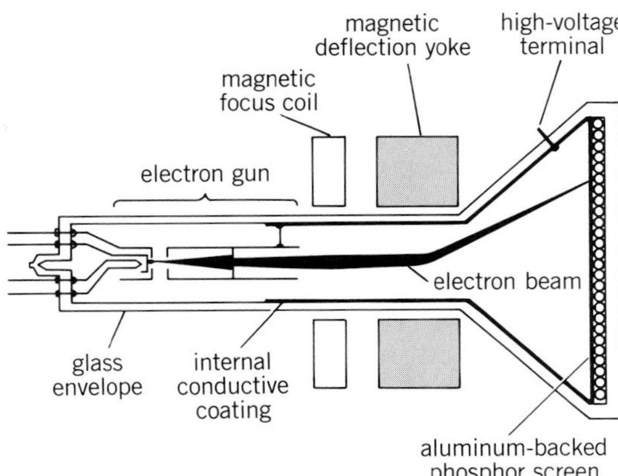


**Fig. 1. Elements of a cathode-ray tube.**

The three elements of the basic cathode-ray tube are the envelope, the electron gun, and the phosphor screen (**Fig. 1**).

***Envelope.*** The envelope is usually made of glass, although ceramic envelopes and metal envelopes have been used. The envelope is typically funnel-shaped. The small opening is terminated by the stem, a disk of glass through which pass metal leads that apply voltages to the several elements of the electron gun. A tubulation that passes through the stem is used to evacuate the air from the tube during manufacture, and is then sealed off. The electron gun is mounted within the neck portion of the envelope and is connected to the leads coming through the stem. The neck is often made sufficiently narrow to allow positioning of deflection and focusing components outside of it.

The large end of the funnel is closed by a faceplate, on the inside of which the phosphor screen is deposited. The faceplate is made of high-quality clear glass in order to provide an undistorted view of the display on the phosphor screen.

***Electron gun.*** The electron gun consists of an electrical element called a heater, a thermionic cathode, and an assemblage of cylinders, caps, and apertures which are all held in the proper orientation by devices such as glass beads, ceramic rods and spacers.

The cathode is a source of electrons when maintained at about 1750°F (1100 K) by thermal radiation from the heater. The heater requires from 0.5 to 5 W of input power, depending on its design. Electrons emitted by the cathode are formed into a beam, and controlled in intensity by other elements of the electron gun. Depending on the design and application of the cathode-ray tube, the current of the electron beam will have an instantaneous peak value from 0.5 to 5000 microamperes. Means are provided, either within the electron gun itself or externally, to focus the electron beam to a small cross section at its intersection with the phosphor screen and to deflect it to various locations on the screen. SEE ELECTRON EMISSION; ELECTRON OPTICS.

A monochrome cathode-ray tube is designed to display information in a single color, usually white, although green, orange, and other colors are used. A color cathode-ray tube, such as a color picture tube, is designed to display information in a full range of colors. In most cases, monochrome cathode-ray tubes employ a single electron gun. Nearly all color picture tubes employ the shadow-mask principle and use three electron guns.

The deflection path of the electron beam on the phosphor screen depends on the intended use of the cathode-ray tube. In oscillography, a horizontal trace is swept across the phosphor screen, with vertical excursions of the beam which coincide with variations in the strength of some electrical signal. In television, a raster of closely spaced horizontal lines is scanned on the phosphor screen by the electron beam, which is intensity-modulated to produce a visible picture. Radar makes use of a variety of specialized electron-beam scanning patterns to present information to an observer. It is also a common practice to apply scan-conversion techniques to the radar signals so that they may be displayed by using a television raster scan.

In the display of computer output information, two general approaches to beam deflection are used: The raster-scan technique may be identical in format to that used for television or may utilize a greater number of scanning lines for increased definition. The random-scan technique involves computer control to direct the electron beam to locations which may be anywhere on the tube face.

***Phosphor screen.*** The phosphor screen consists of a layer of luminescent material coated on the inner surface of the glass faceplate. Typically, the luminescent material is in the form of particles whose size is from 1 to 100 micrometers, depending upon the design and intended use of the cathode-ray tube. Monochrome cathode-ray tubes generally use a single layer of a homogeneous luminescent material. Color cathode-ray tubes typically utilize a composite screen made up of separate red-, green-, and blue-emitting luminous materials.

**Design considerations.** There are certain concerns which must be dealt with in the design of all types of cathode-ray tubes.

***Safety.*** Foremost is the matter of safety. While cathode-ray tubes now in use generally can be considered safe, when employed as intended by their manufacturer, there are potential health hazards which must be considered in the design both of the cathode-ray tubes and of the equipment incorporating them. For example, as discussed below, it is frequently desirable to operate cathode-ray tubes at high voltages and currents, for example, tens of kilovolts and hundreds to thousands of microamperes. Consequently, there are possible hazards of electrical shock, x-radiation, and high temperatures. Designers of cathode-ray tubes and equipment using the tubes are generally quite aware of these possible hazards and are able to effectively utilize designs without undue risk to health and safety.

***Vacuum maintenance.*** Another general concern is the absolute necessity of maintaining a high vacuum within the envelope of the cathode-ray tube so that the electron beam can travel unimpeded from the electron gun to the phosphor screen. Also, it is frequently not possible for the various electrodes within the cathode-ray tube to withstand electrical breakdown except under high vacuum. Cathode-ray tubes are exhausted by vacuum pumps for periods of up to several hours before being tipped off (permanently sealed at the exhaust tubulation). Cathode-ray tubes are typically raised to temperatures of a few hundred degrees Celsius during exhaust in order to outgas the internal parts. Internal pressure in a cathode-ray tube at tip-off is typically in the range of $10^{-4}$ to $10^{-8}$ torr ($10^{-2}$ to $10^{-6}$ pascal), the desired value being determined by the design and intended use of the cathode-ray tube.

With very few exceptions, commercial cathode-ray tubes are never again vacuum-pumped after tip-off, and are expected to maintain an acceptable high level of vacuum. Leaks through the vacuum envelope are extremely rare; those problems which do arise are generally from the outgassing of internal parts. In order to assist in maintaining a high internal vacuum throughout many years of storage and use, it is now a universal practice to include within the cathode-ray tube one or more small devices called getters. Getters, through chemical action, absorb residual gas molecules within an envelope, and will continue to do so usually for several years.

***Voltage control.*** Another general concern is the need to have several different voltages applied to structures within the cathode-ray-tube envelope. These voltages must be individually passed through the vacuum envelope, either through the stem leads or through metal buttons or pins sealed into the envelope. Frequently, an electrical cable carrying voltages as high as 50 kV will be encapsulated to a button terminal on the outside of the cathode-ray tube. Inside the cathode-ray tube, it is important that all envelope surfaces, as well as all electrode structures, be set at definite, known electric potentials. For this reason, conductive coatings which include materials such as graphite, iron oxide, stannous chloride, or evaporated aluminum are applied to nearly all interior envelope surfaces. This is one of the functions of the aluminum coating on the back of the phosphor screen. By these means, the path of the electron beam is fully established and controlled.

**Performance.** Two major considerations in cathode-ray-tube design are the choice of the overall operating voltage, that is, the potential difference between the cathode and the phosphor screen, and the electron-beam current to the phosphor screen. The product of the overall operating voltage (called the screen voltage) and the average value of the screen current gives the power input to the phosphor screen. For example, a cathode-ray tube operating at a screen voltage of 20 kV and screen current of 500 μA has 10 W of input power. A small fraction of this power, typically 10 to 20%, is converted into visible light by the phosphor. Less than 1% of the input power is converted into x-radiation, nearly all of which is absorbed within the glass walls of the envelope. The remainder of the input power is dissipated in the faceplate as heat. Most cathode-ray tubes operate at power levels such that this heat is allowed to radiate away or otherwise be removed by conduction and convection. Tubes which operate at very high voltages and currents, such as projection tubes, sometimes require special means, such as cooling fans, to remove heat from the faceplate.

The choice of operating screen voltage and current can have considerable effect on the design and construction of the cathode-ray-tube envelope, electron gun, and phosphor screen. It is important to consider the tradeoffs involved in making these choices. The higher the screen voltage, the greater the level of performance which can be obtained from the cathode-ray tube. The performance characteristics most directly

**Table 1. Characteristics of cathode-ray tubes**

| Type of cathode-ray tube | Screen voltage, kV | Screen current, μA | Brightness, footlamberts (candelas/m²) | Resolution expressed as spot size, in. (mm) | Typical application |
|---|---|---|---|---|---|
| Oscilloscope | 5 | 100 | 40 (137) | 0.050 (1.3) | Oscilloscope |
| Photorecording | 15 | 5 | 3 (10) | 0.001 (0.025) | Phototypesetter |
| Picture tube (monochrome) | 20 | 300 | 100 (340) | 0.015 (0.4) | Television or data display |
| Picture tube (color; 3 guns) | 30 | 400 | 100 (340) | 0.020 (0.5) | Television or data display |
| Projection | 45 | 2000 | 10,000 (34,000) | 0.004 (0.1) | Data display |

affected by choice of screen voltage and current are screen brightness and resolution. While higher values of screen voltage will improve both brightness and resolution, higher values of screen current will improve brightness but degrade resolution performance. For any particular cathode-ray-tube design, the upper level of screen current which can be utilized is set by the allowable level of resolution degradation. On the other hand, the upper limit of screen voltage that can be utilized is set by: (1) the capability of the internal tube elements, as well as the glass wall of the envelope, to withstand high potential gradients without electrical breakdown; (2) the practical problems involved in generating a very high voltage and delivering it to the cathode-ray-tube high-voltage terminal; (3) added power requirements for the deflection drive circuits; and (4) additional precautions necessary to ensure safe operation at high voltages as far as electrical and x-radiation safety are concerned.

A great deal of the design effort for any cathode-ray tube goes into obtaining the maximum attainable brightness and resolution at a selected screen voltage and current. The required brightness and resolution vary greatly, depending on the intended use of the cathode-ray tube (see **Table 1**).

**Envelopes.** Cathode-ray-tube envelopes have been made from metal, ceramic, and glass materials. Glass is now used more than any other material, because it has the most desirable combination of mechanical, electrical, and optical properties. A variety of specialized glasses have been developed for use in cathode-ray tubes.

***Electrical resistance.*** An important characteristic of glass for cathode-ray tubes is its electrical resistance. Early oscilloscope cathode-ray tubes, operating at voltages from 500 to 2000 V, were made by using a soda-lime-silica combination similar to that used in windows and bottles. This glass was found to be useless at higher voltages because of low electrical resistance. SEE ELECTRICAL RESISTANCE.

***X-ray absorption.*** A second important characteristic is produced any time that electrons traveling at high speed strike a stationary target. The amount of x-radiation produced is proportional to the square of the energy of the electron and to the first power of the atomic number of the constituents of the target material. The target material is that of the phosphor screen, the faceplate, and shadow mask, if one is present. The amount of x-radiation generated within the cathode-ray tube can be substantial at higher voltages. Manufacturers and users of cathode-ray tubes depend on the material of the envelope to absorb nearly all of this radiation. Absorption of x-radiation within the envelope depends on the thickness of the envelope and its composition, and is given by Eq. (1), where $I$ is the intensity of x-radiation at the out-

$$I = I_0 e^{-\mu t} \quad (1)$$

side surface of the cathode-ray tube; $I_0$ is the intensity of x-radiation at the inside surface of the cathode-ray tube; $\mu$ is the linear x-ray absorption coefficient of the particular type of glass used (usually expressed in units of 1/cm); and $t$ is the thickness of glass (usually expressed in cm).

***Optical properties.*** A third important characteristic for glass used in cathode-ray tubes is the optical properties of the faceplate glass. These properties vary widely, depending on the design and intended use of the cathode-ray tube. The best cathode-ray-tube faceplates have optical characteristics and quality equivalent to those of the finest photographic lenses. Cathode-ray-tube faceplates may be clear or may have intentionally reduced optical transmission in order to improve the contrast of the display. Special-purpose cathode-ray tubes have been built with fiber-optic faceplates which make possible direct-contact exposure of photosensitive film and paper.

***Shapes and sizes.*** **Figure 2** shows a variety of cathode-ray tubes having different shapes and sizes. Cathode-ray-tube envelopes are generally round or are rectangular with a 3 × 4 product aspect ratio, although numerous other shapes have been built. Extremes in sizes of cathode-ray tubes are exhibited by 1-in.-diameter (2.5-cm) and 36-in.-diameter (91-cm) round cathode-ray tubes.

Another parameter characterizing the shape of a cathode-ray tube envelope is its deflection angle. The deflection angle is related roughly to the angular dimension of the opening of the funnel. Cathode-ray tubes with deflection angles of from 15 to 110° have been built.

**Electron gun.** The electron gun and its associated neck components generate the electron beam and direct it toward the phosphor screen. This assembly may conveniently be broken down into three separate systems: the electron emission system, the focusing system, and the deflection system.

***Emission systems.*** An emission system may consist of the cathode with its associated heater, a control grid, also called grid #1, and an accelerating grid (**Fig. 3**).

The voltage applied to the accelerating grid sets up a field which penetrates the opening in the control grid and determines the magnitude of the space-charge–limited current drawn from the cathode. As the control grid is made more negative in potential, the penetration of the accelerating field and, consequently, the beam current are reduced.

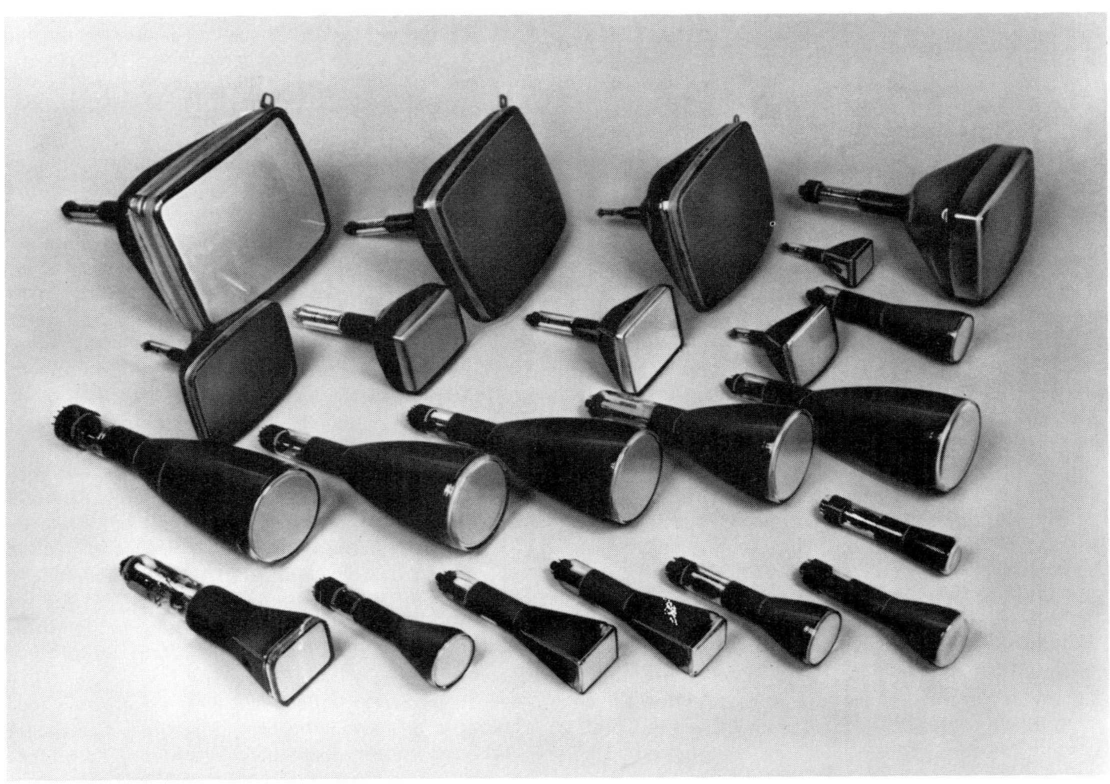

Fig. 2. Typical cathode-ray tubes.

The electrostatic field in the emission system of an electron gun is so shaped by the geometry of the several elements that electrons perpendicularly leaving the cathode enter trajectories which carry them across the axis of the system in the vicinity of the control-grid–accelerator-grid space. The location at which the electrons cross the axis is called the crossover point and represents the minimum beam cross section in the vicinity of the cathode surface. Beyond this point, beam electrons enter the field-free drift space within the cylindrical electrode attached to the accelerating grid and travel along straight diverging trajectories toward the focusing system. *SEE* ELECTRON MOTION IN VACUUM.

A key parameter for the emission system of an electron gun is the cutoff voltage, that voltage between the control grid and the cathode which is just necessary to extinguish the flow of electrons from the cathode. Depending on a particular design, this value may lie between −15 and −150 V, the grid being at a negative voltage with respect to the cathode.

The control grid can be modulated by a video signal, or otherwise varied in voltage between cutoff and zero volts, in order to produce a desired level of beam current. The total current from the cathode is given by Eq. (2), where $I$ is the actual cathode current in

$$I = KV_d^3 V_c^{-3/2} \tag{2}$$

microamperes, $K$ is a constant whose value typically is in the range of 3 to 5, $V_d$ is the grid drive which is equal to the difference between the actual voltage on the control grid and the cutoff voltage, and $V_c$ is the cutoff voltage. Absolute values are used for both $V_d$ and $V_c$.

Emission-system operation, as described above, in which the cathode is grounded and the control grid is modulated, is termed grid drive. Another mode of operation is cathode drive, in which grid #1 is grounded and the cathode is modulated. The formula for cathode current in the cathode-drive mode is more complicated than that given above for the grid-drive mode.

Often, a circular baffle termed a limiting aperture is introduced in the path of the electron beam. The limiting aperture intercepts the outer portions of the beam and prevents their reaching the phosphor screen, thus improving the resolution of the display. The portion of the beam intercepted may be from 0 to 98%, depending on the design and intended use of the cathode-ray tube. For this reason, the electron-beam current reaching the phosphor screen may be a small fraction of the current emitted by the cathode.

An emission system consisting of a cathode, a control grid, and an accelerating grid is termed a triode emission system. A tetrode emission system (**Fig. 4**) has an additional electrode, called grid #2, inserted between the control grid and the accelerating grid. A primary purpose of grid #2 is to electrically isolate the emission system from the focusing system and the high-voltage portion of the envelope, so that changes in focusing or anode voltage will not affect cutoff and

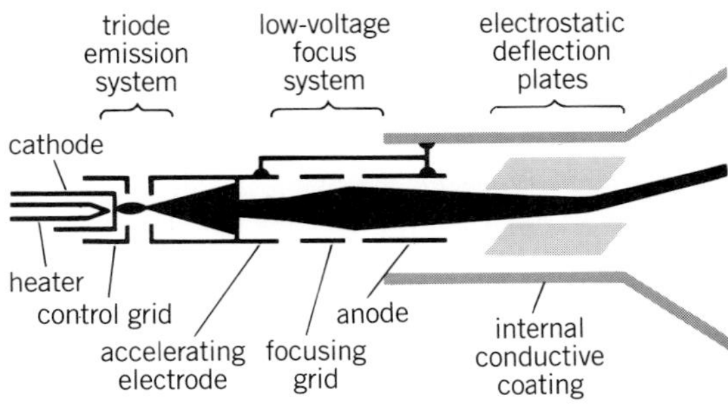


Fig. 3. Simplified electron gun with triode emission system, electrostatic focus, and electrostatic deflection.

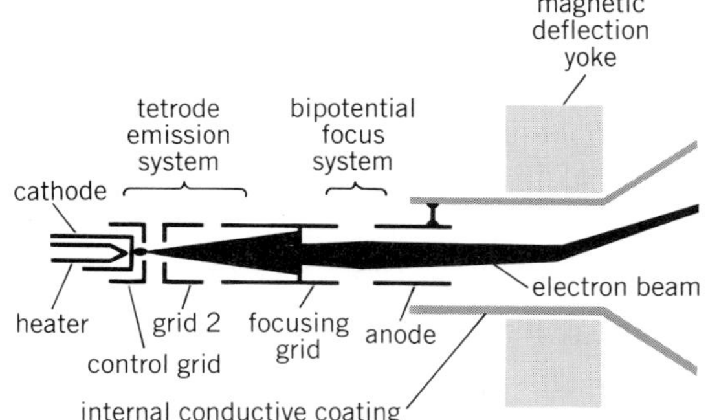


**Fig. 4. Simplified electron gun with tetrode emission system, electrostatic focus, and magnetic deflection.**

drive voltages. Grid #2 is typically operated within a range of 150 to 1500 V positive with respect to the cathode, depending on the design of the electron gun. Grid #2 may be adjusted in voltage to select a desired cutoff voltage. Increasing the grid #2 voltage will raise the magnitude of the cutoff voltage, and vice versa.

The element within the cathode-ray tube set at the highest voltage to which the electron beam is subjected prior to its deflection is termed the anode, or sometimes the ultor. Except in the special case of cathode-ray tubes which utilize postdeflection acceleration, the anode is the element at the highest positive direct-current voltage in the cathode-ray tube and is the element to which the aluminum backing of the phosphor screen is connected. In many cathode-ray tubes, the anode will function as the emission-system accelerating electrode.

***Focusing systems.*** Tht two basic types of focusing used in cathode-ray tubes, magnetic and electrostatic, have been extensively used in many different cathode-ray-tube designs with fully acceptable performance. Electrostatic focus has the advantage of being generally less costly and easier to implement for most applications. In certain applications where resolution at high beam current is required, there is usually a performance advantage in using magnetic focus.

1. Magnetic focusing. In magnetic focusing systems, a short focus coil is fitted externally to the neck of the envelope of the cathode-ray tube. The coil is arranged so that magnetic flux lines flow within the neck parallel to the direction of travel of the electron beam. The focus coil is positioned toward the phosphor screen from the anode portion of the electron gun, so that focusing will take place in a region free from electrostatic potential gradients. Current through the focus coil is adjusted to bring the electron beam to a sharp focus on the phosphor screen. Many designs will require dynamic changes in the focus current to maintain sharp focus as the electron beam is deflected to various positions on the tube face. *See* Magnetic lens.

2. Electrostatic focusing. In electrostatic focusing systems, an electrostatic lens is formed between two or more electrodes within the neck of the tube. Many different electrode arrangements which will give satisfactory focus are in use. Two frequently encountered arrangements are the bipotential lens (Fig. 4) and the low-voltage focus lens (Fig. 3). These lenses are often used with tetrode emission systems, where the presence of grid #2 serves to prevent variations in focus voltage from altering the emission-system cutoff voltage. The bipotential lens requires an additional electrode, the focus electrode, inserted between grid #2 and the anode. The focus electrode operates at an intermediate voltage between that of grid #2 and the anode. Typically, this voltage is in the range of 20 to 40% of the anode voltage, depending on lens design, and is adjusted in value for optimum focus. In the bipotential lens, the main focusing action takes place in the region between the focus electrode and the anode.

In the low-voltage lens, the anode is split into two separate cylinders and an additional electrode, the focus electrode, is inserted into the gap between them. This focus electrode operates at a potential which is only a few tens of volts above cathode voltage, compared to a few thousand volts for the bipotential focus electrode. The bipotential lens generally will provide superior focus quality.

Some newer designs for electrostatic focusing lens involve the introduction of several focusing electrodes stacked together, each operating at a slightly different voltage. *See* Electron lens; Electrostatic lens.

***Deflection systems.*** Two basic types of deflection are electrostatic deflection and magnetic deflection. In principle, either types of deflection can be used for any application, although each has advantages which have led to its being favored for certain classes of use.

1. Electrostatic deflection. With electrostatic deflection, it is possible to very quickly deflect the beam from one location to any other location on the screen. Electrostatic deflection is usually preferred over magnetic deflection for cathode-ray tubes intended for oscillography and other instrumentation applications, because operation is possible over a wider frequency range. The band pass of an electrostatic deflection system is limited in a practical sense by the amount of power the equipment designer can justifiably expend in achieving adequate display brightness and size. Laboratory oscilloscopes designed around conventional cathode-ray tubes and having useful band pass to the order of 50 MHz are readily obtained.

Deflection systems, particularly of the electrostatic type, invariably distort to some degree the circular cross section of an electron beam which undergoes deflection. This distortion increases with angle of deflection. Taking all factors into consideration, the designer of practical cathode-ray tubes with electrostatic deflection rarely attempts to design for angles of deflection much greater than 15° with respect to the gun axis.

In the electrostatic-deflection electron gun shown in Fig. 3, the deflecting system consists of a single pair of parallel electrodes mounted symmetrically about the axis of the gun. The electron beam entering and traversing the space between the electrodes does so at a constant axial velocity corresponding to the average potential of the electrodes. This potential is usually adjusted to be essentially that of the anode. Signals to be applied to the deflecting electrodes are first passed through a paraphrase amplifier in which two components equal in voltage but opposite in polarity are generated. These two components can be applied to the opposing deflecting electrodes without affecting the average potential in the space between them. Under the influence of the applied deflection signals, an electric field is set up between the electrodes. This field imparts an acceleration to the electron beam which is perpendicular to the direction of the constant beam velocity. In the space between the electrodes, therefore, the beam travels in a parabolic path. After leaving this transverse field, the beam continues to the phosphor screen on a straight path tangent to the parabola. The assumption is made that no postdeflection acceleration is present. If the signals applied to the electrodes vary linearly with time, a straight line is traced out upon the phosphor screen. In a practical tube, a second pair of deflecting electrodes is mounted farther along the gun axis at right angles to the first. These electrodes provide a second independent axis of deflection, orthogonal to the first.

The deflection produced by a pair of parallel electrodes is given by Eq. (3), where $y$ is the deflection

$$y = \frac{LbV_d}{2aV} \tag{3}$$

observed at the phosphor screen in any linear units, $L$ is the distance from the axial midpoint of the electrodes to the phosphor screen in the same linear units, $b$ is the deflecting-electrode length in the same linear units, $a$ is the deflecting-electrode spacing in the same linear units, $V_d$ is the potential difference between electrodes in volts, and $V$ is the beam acceleration potential in volts.

The effectiveness of a pair of deflecting electrodes is often described in terms of its deflection factor: the number of volts necessary to deflect the beam a unit distance (usually in inches) at the phosphor screen for a given accelerating potential (usually 1 kV).

Plane-parallel electrodes are rarely found in modern cathode-ray tubes. Overall improvements in performance are obtained by forming the electrodes so that the spacing between plates increases with distance in the direction of beam travel.

2. Magnetic deflection. Magnetic deflection systems generally require more time, perhaps tens of microseconds, to deflect the electron beam from one location on the screen to another. This is because a change in position requires a change in the value of the current through an inductive coil. Magnetic deflection systems do have an important advantage in that they can deflect the beam through a much wider deflection angle with less distortion in the shape of the cross section of the beam than is possible with electrostatic deflection. Also, with high anode voltages of 20–30 kV, the current required for magnetic deflection yokes can readily be provided; whereas the high dynamic voltages which would be required for electrostatic deflection plates, on the order of 3–4 kV peak to peak, cannot easily and economically be achieved. For these reasons, cathode-ray tubes employing magnetic deflection are widely used, particularly in television, radar, and data display.

An elementary magnetic deflection system takes the form of a pair of coils, each wound on a rectangular form, positioned externally to the cathode-ray tube with major planes parallel to beam direction on opposite sides of the neck. The magnetic field lines are thus perpendicular to the axis of the electron gun mounted therein. On entering this field, the beam electrons encounter forces which impart to them acceleration perpendicular to their velocity. If the flux density is uniform, the path followed by the electrons is circular and lies in a plane perpendicular to the lines of flux. On leaving the deflection field, the beam travels in a straight-line path tangent to the circle just described. The deflection given an electron beam which traverses a field of uniform flux density limited to the space between two planes perpendicular to the initial direction of the beam motion (that is, the tube axis) is given approximately by Eq. (4), where $y$ is

$$y \approx \frac{LbB}{3.37\sqrt{V}} \tag{4}$$

the deflection observed at the phosphor screen in centimeters (1 in. equals 2.54 cm), $L$ is the distance from the axial midpoint of the magnetic field to the phosphor screen in centimeters, $b$ is the axial extent of the magnetic field in centimeters, $B$ is the flux density in gauss (1 tesla equals $10^4$ gauss), and $V$ is the beam acceleration potential in volts. By an appropriate arrangement of the windings of a magnetic-deflection coil pair, more commonly called a deflecting yoke, it is possible to obtain useful total deflection angles up to 110°.

3. Postdeflection acceleration. As discussed above, brighter and sharper cathode-ray-tube displays can be obtained at higher anode voltages. It is apparent from Eqs. (3) and (4), however, that high anode voltages require either high levels of magnetic deflection flux or high peak-to-peak electrostatic deflection voltages. A variety of schemes have been employed in cathode-ray tubes to arrange for acceleration of the electron beam to a higher voltage after deflection, thus avoiding the need for very high deflection voltages or magnetic flux. While postdeflection acceleration, as it is called, can be used with either magnetic or electrostatic deflection, it is far more important in the case of electrostatic deflection. From Eq. (3) and (4) it follows that while electrostatic deflection varies inversely with anode voltage, magnetic deflection varies inversely only with the square root of the anode voltage.

The most successful scheme for providing postdeflection acceleration involves the addition of a shaped open-mesh electrode to the interior of the cathode-ray tube at some point between the electron gun and the phosphor screen, usually within the neck of the envelope. The mesh serves to separate the high- and low-voltage sections of the interior of the envelope. By suitable selection of voltages and appropriately shaping the mesh, scan magnification or enhancement can be attained in addition to postdeflection acceleration.

**Phosphor screen.** This element converts electrical energy to visible radiation. Materials known as phosphors are said to be luminescent; that is, they are able to emit light at temperatures substantially below those which produce incandescence. A phosphor which is excited to luminescence by electron bombardment is described as cathodoluminescent. In the case of phosphors for cathode-ray tubes, luminescence invariably persists after cessation of excitation. Luminescence which continues for more than $10^{-8}$ s after excitation is removed is called phosphorescence. Luminescence which is coincident in time with excitation is known as fluorescence.

A wide variety of materials display the property of cathodoluminescence. Phosphors used in commercially fabricated cathode-ray tubes are generally inorganic, nonmetallic, crystalline materials. Many phosphors now make use of materials which incorporate transition elements, such as yttrium, and the lanthanoid metals: lanthanum, cerium, europium, gadolinium, and terbium. Phosphors made from materials using these elements are known for their high luminous output, purity of color, and stability.

Some of these materials will emit radiation in the pure state. Most, however, display practical lumines-

**Table 2. Characteristics of some phosphor screens used in cathode-ray tubes**

| WTDS* designation | Previous EIA† designation | Base material (activator) | Color of luminous emission‡ | Persistence classification§ | Typical application |
|---|---|---|---|---|---|
| BE | P11 | Zinc sulfide (silver) | Blue | Medium short | Photorecording |
| BH | P47 | Yttrium silicate (cerium) | Purplish blue | Very short | Flying-spot scanner |
| BM | P55 | Zinc sulfide (silver) | Blue | Medium short | Projection, large screen |
| GH | P31 | Zinc sulfide (copper) | Green | Medium short | Data display, oscillography |
| GJ | P1 | Zinc orthosilicate (manganese) | Yellowish green | Medium | Projection, oscillography |
| GM | P7 | Zinc sulfide (silver) on top of zinc cadmium sulfide (copper) | Yellowish green | Long | Radar |
| GY | P43 | Gadolinium oxysulfide (terbium) | Yellowish green | Medium | Data display |
| KA | P20 | Zinc cadmium sulfide (silver) | Yellow green | Medium | Storage tubes |
| KG | P46 | Yttrium aluminate (cerium) | Yellow green | Very short | Flying-spot scanner |
| KH | P48 | Yttrium aluminate (cerium) and yttrium silicate (cerium) | Yellow green | Very short | Flying-spot scanner |
| KJ | P53 | Yttrium aluminum garnet (terbium) | Yellowish green | Medium | Data display |
| RF | P56 | Yttrium oxide (europium) | Red | Medium | Projection, large screen |
| WB | P45 | Yttrium oxysulfide (terbium) | White | Medium | Projection, large screen |
| WW | P4 | Zinc sulfide (silver) and zinc cadmium sulfide (silver) | White | Medium short | Monochrome television, data display |
| X | P22¶ | Zinc sulfide (silver) | Blue | Medium short | Color television, data display |
| | | Zinc cadmium sulfide (silver) | Green | Medium short | |
| | | Yttrium oxysulfide (europium) | Red | Medium short | |

*World Wide Type Designation System. Designation administered by the Electronic Industries Association.
†Electronic Industries Association.
‡Color shown is that of phosphorescence, that is, the color after cessation of phosphor excitation.
§Persistence categories are based upon time for radiant output to drop to 10% of initial level following interruption of excitation: very long, 1 s or more; long, 100 ms to 1 s; medium, 1 ms to 100 ms; medium short, 10 μs to 1 ms; short, 1 μs to 10 μs; very short, less than 1 μs.
¶Composite structured screen used in conjunction with shadow mask for full color display. The materials shown are one example of several sets of materials used for this screen.

cence only when activated by an impurity (see **Table 2**). These impurities, deliberately introduced in amounts ranging from 1 part in 100,000 to 1 part in 100, play a profound role in determining the efficiency, color, and persistence of the emission obtained from a given phosphor. **Figure 5** shows the spectral emission density curves which plot relative radiant energy versus wavelength for certain of these phosphor screens.

One of the criteria by which a phosphor material is judged is its ability to convert electrical energy to useful radiation. In many cases, cathode-ray-tube screens are intended to be viewed by human observers. It is appropriate, therefore, to speak in terms of visible flux output. The luminous efficiencies of practically all commercially significant phosphors are within the range 5–50 lumens per watt of exciting power. Light output increases with increasing bombarding-current density, eventually exhibiting evidence of saturation at current-density levels which are characteristic of particular phosphors. For some phosphors, saturation effects are quite evident at the 10 $\mu A/cm^2$ level. Others display relatively undiminished luminous efficiencies at levels of several hundred microamperes per square centimeter.

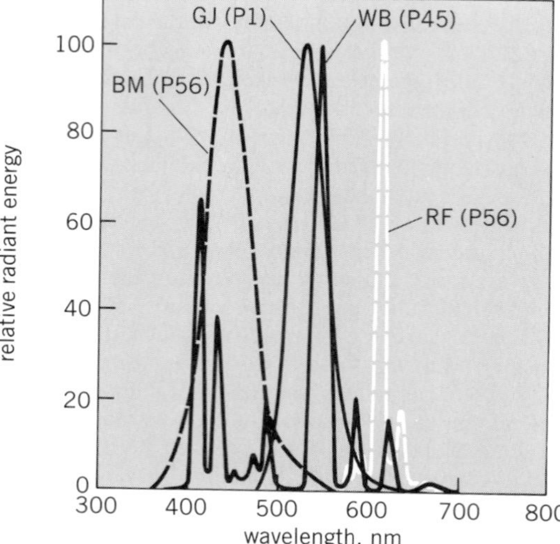


**Fig. 5.** Spectral emission density curves for phosphor screens.

The color of the emission from a phosphor is governed both by the base material and by the activator. The spectral-energy distributions of most phosphors are fairly broad, although colors of high saturation are readily obtained. Phosphors made from materials incorporating rare-earth and related elements are noted for having spectral-energy distributions in which the radiant energy is concentrated into very narrow emission bands at just a few wavelengths.

As is evident from Table 2, a wide range of colors is available; the tube designer is restricted in this matter only insofar as particular efficiencies and persistences must be achieved simultaneously with a given color.

A great majority of cathode-ray-tube screens now being produced are aluminized. The side of the phosphor screen facing the electron gun is coated with a thin electron-transparent film of aluminum by vacuum-deposition techniques. This process not only stabilizes the phosphor potential at the applied acceleration voltage, but also provides an increased light output because of the mirror effect of the highly reflective layer, which redirects radiation that could otherwise be lost in the interior of the envelope.

The fineness of detail in an image presented on a phosphor screen is limited to some extent by the granular nature of the screen. Both particle size and layer thickness affect performance. Phosphor screens intended for very high-resolution cathode-ray tubes employ thin layers of phosphor with particles as fine as 1 μm in size.

**Varieties of tubes.** A wide variety of available envelopes, electron guns, and phosphor screens are combined in different ways to fashion cathode-ray tubes which are specialized to meet the needs of a host of different applications. A few of these tubes are described here.

***Oscillography.*** Equipments to be used as oscilloscopes, spectrum analyzers, computer waveform analyzers, and related applications require cathode-ray tubes with fast deflection, high writing speed, and highly visible displays. Also important are small size, low weight, and ruggedness to fit a variety of working environments. Generally, less importance is given to resolution. Such tubes will usually employ electrostatic focus and deflection with small deflection angles of 10 to 15°, round or rectangular envelopes with a largest display dimension of 3 to 8 in. (7.5 to 20 cm), and a highly visible phosphor screen such as GH(P31) or GJ(P1) [see Table 2]. If there is a need for longer persistence due to a low refresh rate, a long-persistence phosphor such as GM(P7) may be used. These cathode-ray tubes generally use operating anode voltages of from 0.5 to 10 kV. Some envelopes for these tubes are made from ceramic materials. *See Oscilloscope*.

***Radar.*** The most widely used display mode for radar, the plan position indicator (PPI) mode, is readily adapted to electrostatic-focus, magnetic-deflection electron guns of moderate current capability and resolution, operating at 5 to 15 kV. Typically, round envelopes will be employed which are 1 to 36 in. (2.5 to 91 cm) in diameter, although the most common sizes are 5 to 10 in. (12.5 to 25 cm).

The most important requirement for cathode-ray tubes for use as radar-display indicators has been a long-persistent image. This is important because the refresh period of most radar antennas has been several seconds. The phosphor screen GM(P7), which has persistence at a low light level of several seconds, was developed during World War II to meet this need. After World War II, a special class of tubes called cathode-ray charge-storage tubes was developed to meet the need of providing a persistent radar display image. Such tubes have been in use in radar display indicators in both commercial and military aircraft for many years. *See Storage tube*.

In the 1970s, the availability of solid-state memory devices at acceptable cost levels obviated the need for special cathode-ray tubes with built-in capability of providing long-persistent images. Many radar displays since the early 1970s use cathode-ray tubes more closely related to those used for television and data display. The storage necessary for long-persistent radar images is provided by sold-state memory circuits external to the tube. The cathode-ray tube is fed an appropriate video signal at or near television scan rates.

***Pictorial.*** A large class of applications for cathode-ray tubes involves either the presentation on the cathode-ray-tube screen of an actual picture with a full black and white halftone range or with full color, such as is required for television, or the presentation of a computer-generated display which may consist of alphanumerics, graphics, or a variety of pictorial subjects. Tubes for the direct viewing of such presentations are required to have large display sizes, high brightness, high resolution, and in many cases a full halftone range and full color capability.

Cathode-ray tubes for these presentations have always employed magnetic deflection and generally electrostatic-focus electron guns operating at high voltages from 15 to 35 kV. Envelopes for television cathode-ray tubes have traditionally been rectangular, of 3 × 4 aspect ratio. Popular usable screen diagonals have been 10 to 27 in. (25 to 70 cm). Deflection angles have ranged from 10 to 110°.

Cathode-ray tubes for computer-generated data-display applications are very similar to television picture tubes but may use other rectangular or square display formats. The need for uniformity of resolution in the display, particularly from the center of the picture to the edge, is even more acute for tubes intended for data display than it is for tubes intended for television only. Particular attention is paid to this need in the design of cathode-ray tubes for data-display applications.

One special class of pictorial applications comprises displays for use in automobiles, airplanes, boats, and military vehicles of all types. While cathode-ray tubes for such applications are similar to those described above, they tend to be smaller and brighter, and they must be quite rugged.

Another special class is projection tubes, but these are not intended to be directly viewed. The display on the phosphor screen is projected by using an optical system, such as a lens, onto large screens. Screen sizes vary widely, the largest being those in theaters and sports arenas that are equipped for projection television.

Cathode-ray tubes for projection applications are usually of the general type described above but optimized for extremely high brightness and resolution capability. Projection cathode-ray tubes generally have a largest phosphor screen dimension of 3 to 8 in. (7.5 to 20 cm). This smaller size is compatible with available high-efficiency optical systems. Projection cathode-ray tubes generally operate at higher voltages than direct-view tubes. Tubes which can be operated at voltages as high as 80 kV have been built.

***Photorecording.*** Another class of cathode-ray tubes which are not intended for direct viewing by human observers comprises photorecording tubes. The applications for these tubes require that the phosphor screen display be projected by an optical system, such as a lens, onto a photosensitive medium, such as photographic film. Applications include electronic phototypesetting and the storage of computer output information on microfilm. Photorecording cathode-ray tubes are required to have extremely high resolution capability, to be extremely stable over long periods of time, and to have accurate and precise display geometry. A photorecording display may have 50 times the information content of a typical broadcast television picture.

Photorecording tubes usually employ magnetic deflection and may utilize either magnetic or electrostatic focus. They operate at anode voltages in the range 10 to 20 kV. Many photorecording cathode-ray tubes use envelopes with 3- or 5-in. (7.5- or 12.5-cm) round faceplates of optical quality. Displays on these faceplates are projected through a lens onto the photosensitive medium. Other photorecording tubes have faceplates made from fiber-optic plates which, in use, are in direct contact with the photosensitive medium.

A special cathode-ray tube which is closely related to the photorecording tube is the flying-spot scanner. The flying-spot-scanner display consists of a spot of light moving across the phosphor screen to scan a raster such as that used in television. This raster is blank and includes no video modulation other than retrace blanking. In a typical application, the raster will be projected through a lens onto a slide transparency. The light passing through the transparency is picked up by one or more photomultiplier tubes. The pictorial content of the transparency in this way is made available as a video signal, provided by the photomultiplier, which can then be displayed on a television monitor.

Phosphor screens having extremely short persistence, on the order of 150 nanoseconds, have been developed for use with flying-spot scanners. These are identified in Table 2. Short persistence is necessary to avoid severe distortion of the video signal.

***Competing technologies.*** Considering the length of time that the cathode-ray tube has been in use, and the number of uses to which it has been put, it must be considered one of the most successful electronic devices ever conceived. There are, nonetheless, certain drawbacks inherent in the use of the cathode-ray tube: (1) it must have a certain size and weight to provide a vacuum-tight enclosure and sufficient room internally for generation and deflection of the electron beam; (2) it has a long but finite lifetime, limited by degradation processes associated with the high temperatures at which the heater and cathode are operated; and (3) it is essentially an analog device which must be interfaced with other electronic devices, an increasing proportion of which are exclusively digital.

Display technologies not involving the use of cathode-ray tubes have been under development for many years. The more promising make use of plasma or gas discharge, electroluminescent, and liquid-crystal devices. Some of these devices have gained a degree of acceptance in data display applications which have also made use of cathode-ray tubes. *See Electronic display.*

In spite of certain drawbacks and the advent of other display technologies, there are advantages to the use of cathode-ray tubes which ensure their continuing presence: (1) the ease with which the electron beam can be deflected to address any desired display location; (2) the ease and efficiency with which electrical energy can be converted into radiant energy at visible wavelengths in the phosphor screen; and (3) the flexibility of cathode-ray-tube technology, which has allowed a high degree of customization to meet the special requirements of diverse applications. The cathode-ray tube is still the most widely used display device in those equipments which originally use the tube at the time of their introduction. These include the oscilloscope, the radar display, the television set, and the personal computer.

*Norman W. Patrick*

***Bibliography.*** A. M. Morrell et al., *Color Television Picture Tubes,* 1974; H. Moss, *Narrow Angle Electron Guns and Cathode Ray Tubes,* 1968; S. Sherr, *Electronic Displays,* 1979; Tube Engineering Panel Advisory Council, *Optical Characteristics of Cathode Ray Tube Screens,* TEP 116, Electronic Industries Association, 1980; V. K. Zworykin and G. A. Morton, *Television,* 2d ed., 1954.

## Cathode rays

The name given to the electrons originating at the cathodes of gaseous discharge devices. The term has now been extended to include low-pressure devices such as cathode-ray tubes. Furthermore, cathode rays are now used to designate electron beams originating from thermionic cathodes, whereas the term was formerly applied only to cold-cathode devices. *See Cathode-ray tube.*

The basis for the nomenclature is purely historical. The first outward evidence was fluorescence from the glass walls of cold-cathode discharge tubes. This fluorescence appeared as the pressure was reduced to the region where the mean free path became greater than the tube dimensions. At these pressures, the gas in the tube no longer emitted an appreciable amount of light. It was ascertained that the wall fluorescence had its origin in rays of particles coming from the cathode. Furthermore, it was demonstrated that these particles traveled in approximately straight lines. If an object was interposed between the cathode and the wall, the fluorescence disappeared in the optically shadowed region of the wall. In 1897 J. J. Thomson was able to show, using electric and magnetic fields, that the particles were negatively charged. In his experimental arrangement, he eliminated all but a very narrow beam of these rays. By producing an electrostatic deflection of the beam and then counteracting this with a magnetic deflection, he was able to determine the charge-mass ratio $e/m$. This was found to be the same as that of the electron, and resulted in the identification of these particles.

Thomson's measurements also form the basis for modern beta ray spectroscopy. In this case $e/m$ is known, so that either an electric or magnetic field may be used to determine the energy of the electrons which emanate from various radioactive materials, such as beta rays. *See Electrical conduction in gases; Electron emission.*

*Glenn H. Miller*

***Bibliography.*** D. Halliday and R. Resnick, *Physics,* 3d ed., 1978; F. K. Richtmyer et al., *Introduction to Modern Physics,* 6th ed., 1969; M. R. Wehr, J. A. Richards, and T. W. Adair, *Physics of the Atom,* 3d ed., 1978.

## Cathodoluminescence

A luminescence resulting from the bombardment of a substance with an electron beam. The major application of cathodoluminescence is in cathode-ray oscilloscopes and television picture tubes. In these devices a thin layer of luminescent powder is evenly deposited on the transparent glass face plate of a cathode-ray tube. The electron beam originating in the cathode, after undergoing acceleration, focusing, and deflection by various electrodes in the tube, impinges on the luminescent coating. The resulting emission is normally observed through the glass face plate of the tube, that is, from the unbombarded side of the coating. Depending on the type of signal information to be displayed on the tube, phosphors or phosphor blends of various emission colors and persistences are used. *See Cathode-ray tube.*

The brightness $B$ of a phosphor under cathode-ray bombardment depends linearly on the current density $j$ for sufficiently small values of $j$, but saturation effects set in at higher current densities. $B$ depends on the bombarding voltage according to the empirical relation $B = kf(j)(V - V_0)^q$, where $k$ is a constant of the face plate material, $f(j)$ represents the dependence of brightness on current density, $V$ is the accelerating voltage, $V_0$ is a so-called dead voltage, and $q$ is a constant for the particular phosphor, the values for different phosphors lying between 1 and 3. The efficiency of conversion of the electron-beam energy into light energy is at most about 20%, considerably less than the best efficiencies with photoluminescence. This relative inefficiency is due to the complex mechanism of excitation by the electron beam, which loses its energy by interaction with ions of the crystal lattice and consequently dissipates a large fraction of its energy before reaching a luminescent center.

An important requirement for a good cathodoluminescent phosphor is that it have good secondary electron emission properties; otherwise it will charge up negatively and decrease the effective potential of the bombarding beam. Phosphors in cathode-ray tubes are subject to deterioration by prolonged action of the electron beam and by bombardment by residual gas ions that remain in the tube or are generated at the electrodes or tube walls. SEE SECONDARY EMISSION.

*Clifford C. Klick; James H. Schulman*

## Cavity resonator

An enclosure capable of resounding or resonating and thereby intensifying sound tones or electromagnetic waves. Resonance is the phenomenon which results when the frequency of the impressed driving force is the same as the natural vibration of the cavity. Vibrating rods, the tuning fork, musical instrument strings, radio and television channel tuners, and so forth, constitute resonating systems as well. The cavity resonator enclosure has a volume which stores energy oscillating between one form and another. In the case of sound, the oscillation is between displacement and velocity of particles. In the case of electromagnetic waves, the energy oscillates between the magnetic and the electric fields.

**Sound-resonant pipes.** Cavity pipes are used as resonators in musical instruments such as pipe organs and flutes to increase their sonority. The frequency of resonance is determined (to a degree of approximation) by the length of the pipe, by the velocity of sound at the ambient temperature and pressure, by the intensity of the driving force, and by the condition at the ends of the pipe: closed or open. The resulting frequency is related to multiples of quarter-wavelengths or half-wavelengths (depending on the end conditions) contained in the length of pipe. The driving force, if sufficiently strong, can force oscillations to occur at overtone frequencies which are higher multiples of the lowest or fundamental frequency, as well as at the fundamental. **Figure 1** illustrates simple cavity resonators for sound for a pipe open at one end and closed at the other. Other resonators have both ends open or both ends closed, with a small hole through which the driving force is introduced. For the case of both ends open as well as for the case of both ends closed, the resonant frequencies are those frequencies for which the pipe length is a whole number of half-wavelengths.

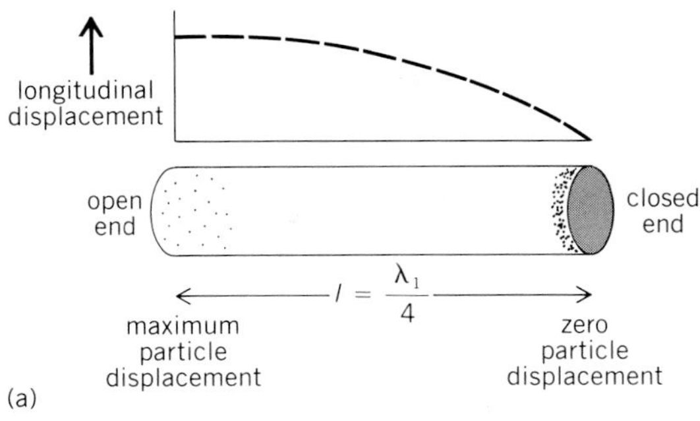


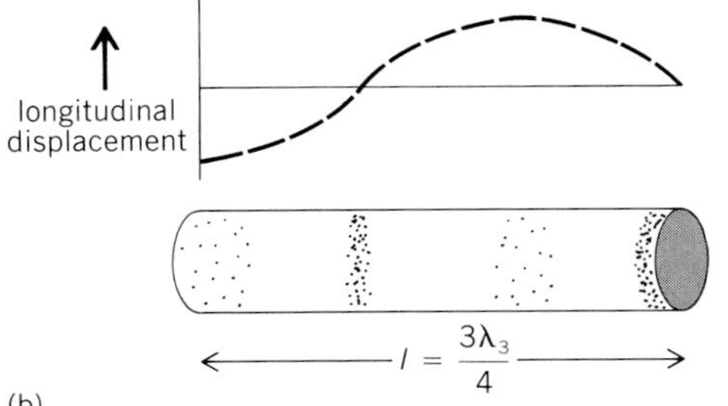


**Fig. 1. Closed-end sound pipe resonating (*a*) at the fundamental frequency $f_1$ (the first harmonic) with wavelength $\lambda_1$, and (*b*) at an overtone, $f_3 \approx 3f_1$ (the third harmonic), with wavelength $\lambda_3$.**

**Microwave-resonant cavities.** At very high radio frequencies, losses due to radiation can be eliminated and resistive losses can be minimized by using closed resonant cavities instead of lumped-circuit resonators. A cavity resonator stores both magnetic and electric fields, the energy oscillating between the two, losing energy only to the conducting walls if a perfect dielectric fills the space. The resonant frequency of the cavity is determined by the shape of the cavity and the mode, or allowable field distribution, of the electromagnetic energy that the cavity contains. The usual cavities consist of closed sections of cylindrical or rectangular waveguides, or of hollow spheres or other symmetrical shapes. The choice of the shape is determined by the ease of fabrication or by the cavity's application. In the case of the cylindrical cavity resonator, the resonant frequency $f_0$ is computed from Eq. (1)

$$f_0 = \frac{c}{2L}[1 + (2L/K_{nl}a)^2]^{1/2} \tag{1}$$

where $a$ = radius
$L$ = cavity length
$c$ = velocity of light
$K_{nl}$ = $l$th root of $J'_n(K) = 0$ for transverse electric (TE) modes
$K_{nl}$ = $l$th root of $J_n(K) = 0$ for transverse magnetic (TM) modes ($J_n$ is the $n$th-order Bessel function and $J'_n$ is its derivative)

If one of the end walls of the cavity is adjustable, the cavity can act as a wavemeter; that is, the resonance frequency can change as $L$ is adjusted. **Figure 2** illustrates how this can be done. SEE WAVELENGTH MEASUREMENT; WAVEMETER.

For the case of a rectangular cavity, the resonance frequency is determined by Eq. (2), where $a$, $b$, and

$$f_0 = \frac{c}{2}\left[\left(\frac{m}{a}\right)^2 + \left(\frac{n}{b}\right)^2 + \left(\frac{p}{d}\right)^2\right]^{1/2} \tag{2}$$

$d$ are dimensions of the cavity and $m$, $n$, and $p$ are integers (or zero in certain cases) as determined by the mode of the enclosed fields. SEE MICROWAVE; WAVEGUIDE.

**Coupling.** Coupling to cavities may be accomplished by: (1) introduction of a conducting probe or antenna oriented so it coincides with the direction of the electron field; (2) introduction of a conducting loop with plane normal to the magnetic field; (3) placement of a hole or iris between the cavity and a

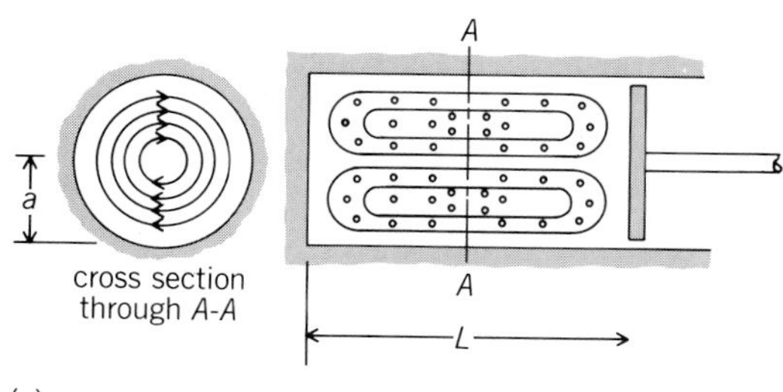


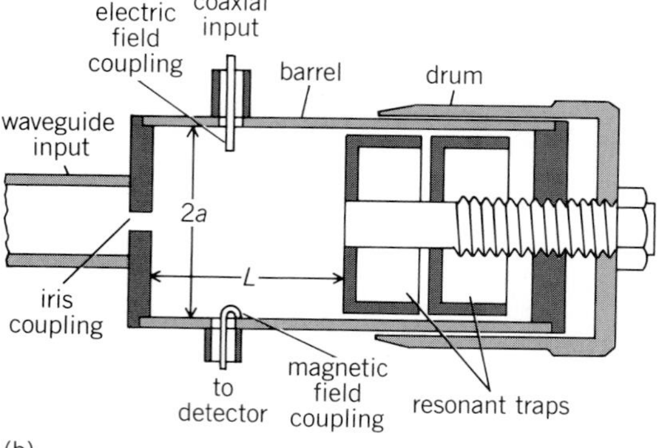


**Fig. 2. Wavemeters. (*a*) Wavemeter consisting of cylindrical cavity with an adjustable end-wall, resonating in the $TE_{011}$ mode. The free-space wavelength $\lambda_0$ corresponding to the resonant frequency $f_0$ is given by $\lambda_0 = 2L\,[1 + (2L/1.64a)^2]^{-1/2}$. (*b*) Practical wavemeter for the $TE_{111}$ mode.**

driving waveguide, the iris being placed so that a field component in the cavity mode has a common direction with one in the waveguide or other cavity; and (4) introduction of a pulsating electron beam passing through a small gap into the cavity and in the direction of the electric field of the cavity. The first three coupling methods are illustrated in Fig. 2*b*.

**Quality factor.** A good measure of the quality of a typical cavity resonator is expressed by the amount of stored energy as compared with the energy lost to the imperfectly conducting walls (and if present, to the imperfect dielectric of the cavity region).

More precisely defined, the quality factor is represented by Eq. (3). The formula for any particular cavity configuration operating in a particular mode is derived by calculating the energy stored (either in the magnetic field or in the electric field), determining the losses due to the currents flowing on the imperfect conducting walls, and substituting in Eq. (3) for $Q$. The formula then contains the dimensions of the cavity relevant to the mode of the field configuration and an expression for the surface resistance of the conducting walls.

$$Q = \frac{2\pi f_0 \times (\text{energy stored})}{\text{average power loss}} = \frac{\pi(\text{energy stored})}{\text{energy loss per half cycle}} \qquad (3)$$

If a resonant cavity which as a quality factor $Q$ is coupled to an external load which has a factor denoted by $Q_e$, the combination of the two leads to a loaded quality factor $Q_L$, which is related to the others by Eq. (4).

$$1/Q_L = 1/Q_e + 1/Q \qquad (4)$$

The Q can be measured by using two basic techniques. The first is to monitor the field intensity $E$ as the frequency of the driving force is increased and decreased off the resonance of the cavity. **Figure 3***a* shows the response of such a detuning. The two points representing a drop in field intensity to 0.707 or $1/\sqrt{2}$ of its peak value (half-power points) also represent the bandwidth, or $\Delta f$. Under this condition, it can be shown that $Q$ is given by Eq. (5).

$$Q = \frac{f_0}{\Delta f} \qquad (5)$$

Another approach is to make use of the damping properties which indicate the rate at which oscillations would decay if the driving source were removed. For this method the fields $E$ decay as given in Eq. (6),

$$E = E_0 e^{-(\pi f_0/Q)t} \qquad (6)$$

where $E_0$ is the initial field and $e$ = 2.718 . . . Consequently, if, as shown in Fig. 3*b*, a measure of the time taken for the field to drop to $(1/e)$th of its initial value is denoted as $\Delta t$, then $Q$ is given by Eq. (7),

$$Q = \pi f_0 \Delta t \qquad (7)$$

and, since $1/f_0$ *is* the period of the oscillation $T_0$, then Eq. (8) is valid.

$$Q = \pi \Delta t/T_0 = \pi \times [\text{number of cycles in } \Delta t] \qquad (8)$$

SEE Q (ELECTRICITY); RESONANCE (ALTERNATING-CURRENT CIRCUITS).

**Optical cavity resonators.** As the frequency of oscillation of the electromagnetic waves gets higher and well beyond the microwave range, the microwave cavity resonators described above become impractical. For lasers, with operation in the visible range,

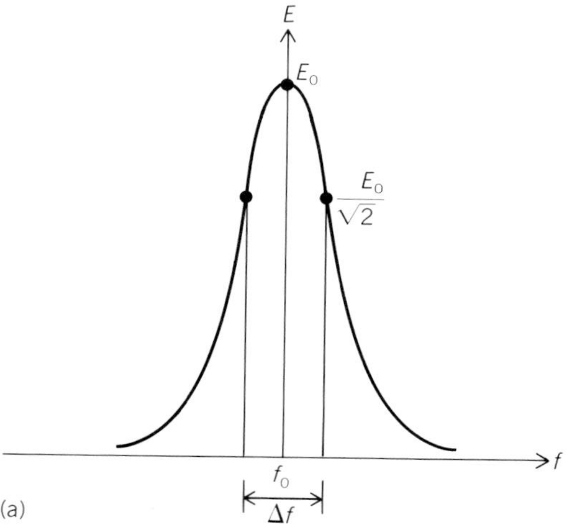


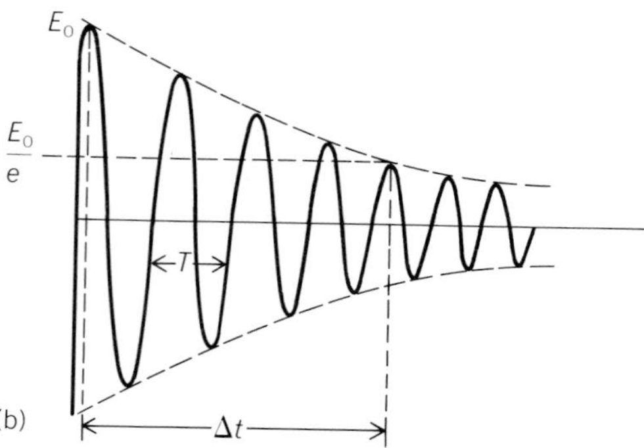


**Fig. 3. Determination of the Q of a cavity resonator by (*a*) measuring the bandwidth and (*b*) measuring the damping rate of the oscillations.**

the infrared, or ultraviolet, the corresponding wavelengths are of the order of micrometers. The resonant cavity would have to be extremely small. If one was constructed with dimensions of millimeters, then the resonances of the possible modes of operation would be extremely close together and it would be impractical to separate them. Removing the sides of a closed cavity eliminates a large number of modes which in the absence of walls would radiate and thus be damped out. It has been shown that proper shaping and placing of the ends does support low-loss modes. Parallel plane mirrors is one system. Another consists of curved mirrors facing each other. Combinations of curved-planar mirrors, confocal mirrors, concentric mirrors, and spherical mirror configurations also constitute optical resonators. The objective in each design is to stabilize (contain) low-loss modes. *See Laser.*

The system of parallel plane reflectors has been used in interferometry and is referred to as a Fabry-Perot resonator or etalon.

Optical resonators have also been made using loops of low-loss optical fibers, and in integrated optical circuits. *See Integrated optics.*

*Diogenes J. Angelakos*

**Bibliography.** R. E. Collin, *Foundations for Microwave Engineering*, 1966; J. D. Kraus and K. R. Carver; *Electromagnetics*, 2d ed., 1973; M. I. Skolnik, *Radar Handbook*, 1970; L. F. Stokes, M. Chodorow, and H. J. Shaw, Sensitive all-single-mode-fiber resonant ring interferometer, *J. Lightwave Technol.*, Lt-1:110–115, 1983.

## Character recognition

The technology of using machines to automatically identify human-readable symbols, most often alphanumeric characters, and then to express their identities in machine-readable codes. This operation of transforming numbers and letters into a form directly suitable for electronic data processing is an important method of introducing information into computing systems. *See Data-processing systems.*

Character recognition machines, sometimes called character readers, print readers, scanners, or reading machines, automatically convert printed alphanumeric characters or symbols into a machine-readable code at high speeds. The output of the character recognition machine may be temporarily stored on magnetic disks or magnetic tape. Alternatively, the recognition system may be operated on line with the data processor (**Fig. 1**). The first commercial application of character recognition was in the banking industry, which adopted magnetic ink character recognition (MICR). In most applications, the printed or typed characters are sensed optically; this process is called optical character recognition (OCR).

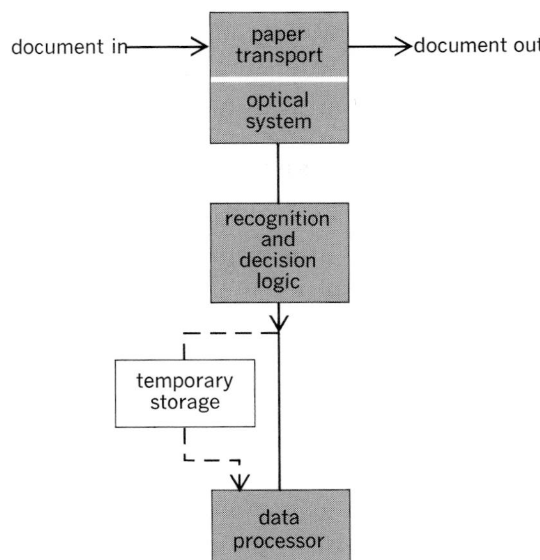


**Fig. 1. Diagram of optical character recognition system.**

Optical mark reading (OMR) refers to the simpler technology of optically sensing marks. The information being read is encoded as a series of marks such as lines or filled-in boxes on a test answer sheet, or as some special pattern such as the Universal Product Code (UPC). The UPC uses a predetermined and reproducible standard pattern which corresponds to each number in a 10-digit code. A relatively simple optical scanner detects the pattern and then decodes the number.

There are various manual alternatives to automatic character recognition equipment for data entry. These include keypunch, key tape, and key disk systems, in which the data are entered through a keyboard and are recorded on punched cards, magnetic tape, or rotating magnetic disks, respectively. Keyboard terminals are another approach to on-line data entry. Manual keystroking is a tedious and costly operation, and it is therefore advantageous to use automatic character recognition equipment whenever the form of the information to be entered is consistent with the capabilities of the character recognition system. Limited-vocabulary isolated-word voice recognition equipment is now available for data entry. However, voice input is also a slow process and would not be competitive with OCR in situations where the data already exist in printed or typed form.

### Pattern Recognition

The technology of automatically recognizing complex patterns is being developed in the context of numerous military and civilian applications such as: the analysis of aerial and satellite images obtained with visible, infrared, radar, and multispectral sensors, for the detection and classification of military objects, terrain types, weather patterns, and land use patterns; identification of individuals or medical conditions using fingerprint, palmprint, blood cell, tissue cell, chromosome, and x-ray images; processing of voice, sonar, electrocardiogram, electroencephalogram, seismic, and other waveforms to detect and classify "signatures" of different events or conditions: automatic detection of flaws in sheet glass, bottles, textiles, paper, printed circuit boards, and integrated circuit masks; recognition of alphanumeric characters or reading for the blind, and analysis, clustering, and classification of survey and experimental data obtained in diverse disciplines.

### Optical Character Recognition

Of all the above application areas, OCR is the single most important commercial application of pattern recognition technology.

**Functional systems.** The technologies used in OCR systems include optical, electronic, mechanical, and computer techniques. In general an OCR system has the following functional systems: input; transport;

scanner; preprocessor; feature extraction and classification logic; output.

***Transport.*** The problems of feeding, transporting, and handling paper, especially at high speeds, have caused much difficulty in some applications of OCR, for example, in postal address reading for mail sorting. Turnaround documents, such as credit card slips, have tight contraints on size and quality of paper and so are much easier to transport at high speeds than mail in which size, thickness, and paper quality have only recently become subject to some constraints. Page readers may have to handle only a couple of documents per second, but each page may contain up to 2000 characters. And in some applications, for example, the reading of sales tags with a hand-held ''wand,'' motion of the paper is completely avoided.

***Scanning.*** The scanner converts reflected or transmitted light into an electric signal which is then digitized by an analog-to-digital (A/D) converter. Although simpler to design, transmitted light scanning requires the additional step of making a (film) transparency of every image to be read, and hence is less suitable than reflected light scanning for high-volume applications unless the documents already exist in microfilm form or are routinely microfilmed for ease of storage. *See* ANALOG-TO-DIGITAL CONVERTER.

One categorization of optical scanners is whether they employ a flying-spot or a flying-aperture principle. In the first case a spot of light sequentially illuminates successive portions of the material to be read, and all the reflected or transmitted light is collected by a detector. An example is the cathode-ray-tube (CRT) flying-spot scanner, where the CRT beam may be moved to sequentially strike the phosphor on the tube face, and the glow of the spot on the phosphor screen illuminates the corresponding spot on the document. In flying-aperture devices the entire document is flooded with light, but light is collected sequentially spot by spot from the illuminated image. An example is Vidicon scanners in which a document is flooded with light from an ordinary light source, and the reflected or transmitted light impinges upon the photoconductive target of the Vidicon. The image on the surface causes a variation in the local charge concentration, which is converted into a video signal by sequentially scanning the photoconductive surface with an electron beam. *See* CATHODE-RAY TUBE; TELEVISION CAMERA TUBE.

Mechanical scanners, television cameras, CRT flying-spot scanners, solid-state linear and two-dimensional array scanners, and electrooptical scanners which use a laser as the source of illumination are the main scanning techniques which have been employed in commercial OCR systems.

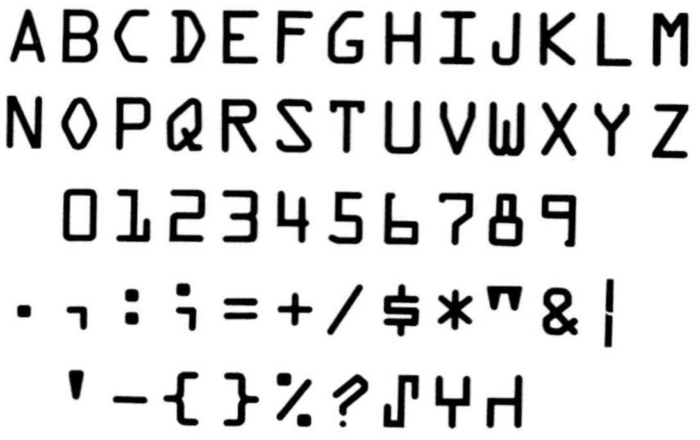

ABCDEFGHIJKLM
NOPQRSTUVWXYZ
0123456789
. ¬ : ; = + / $ * " & |
' - { } % ? ⑀ ⑂ ⑁

**Fig. 2. Character set (ISO-A) approved by the American Standards Association for use in optical character recognition applications.**

1234567890
ABCDEFGHIJKLM
NOPQRSTUVWXYZ
abcdefghijklm
nopqrstuvwxyz
* + - = / . , : ; " ' _
? ! ( ) < > [ ] % # & @ ^
¤ £ $ ¦ \ ¥ ■ ——

**Fig. 3. ISO-B character set for international usage.**

Mechanical motion of the document is usually used to scan successive lines of print. Earlier OCR systems also used a rotating or oscillating mirror or a prism to scan across each line of print, and to collect the signal from a single vertical column in a character or form an entire character using a photocell array.

In solid-state scanners, instead of mechanically or electronically scanning a single beam across the region of interest, the region is sampled in small, discrete, adjacent areas by electronically switching between elements in the array. Flying-spot devices use linear or two-dimensional light-emitting-diode (LED) arrays. Flying-aperture devices use arrays of photodiodes or phototransistors. *See* LIGHT-EMITTING DIODE; PHOTODIODE; PHOTOTRANSISTOR.

The most commonly used scan pattern is a raster scan in which the flying spot or flying aperture sequentially scans the character area by using a sawtooth pattern. A line-following pattern has been used in some hand-print readers. Because of microprocessors, completely programmable scanners are economically feasible, making it easier to rescan rejected characters, scan blank areas at low resolution for increased throughput, and perform various preprocessing functions.

***Preprocessing.*** Preprocessing refers to line finding, character location and isolation, normalization and centering, and related processing functions that may be needed prior to feature extraction and classification. The nature and degree of preprocessing needed depend on whether the material being read consists of stylized fonts, typescript, typeset text, or hand-printed characters.

Stylized font characters such as the ISO-A or OCR-A (**Fig. 2**) and ISO-B or OCR-B (**Fig. 3**) character sets have well-defined and closely controlled formats and line spacing. Documents using stylized font characters usually also have special symbols to guide the scanner to each field of data; special ink invisible to the optical scanner is used to print material not to be read by the OCR. Contrasted with these well-defined formats which are easy to handle automatically, are the format control problems created when reading general typeset material involving text interspersed with illustrations, tables, and so forth. In such situations, current commercial OCRs require human direction of the scanner to the appropriate data field.

Procedures available for line-finding include adaptive line-following algorithms which compensate for baseline drift in the lines of print. For situations where characters are not uniformly well spaced or in which easily detectable boundaries do not occur where expected, character segmentation may involve a scanning aperture smaller than that used for subsequent classification. Various heuristic procedures are used to separate touching characters, eliminate noise such as isolated dots, and smooth out gaps or breaks in line segments.

The extent of rotation and skew correction, character segmentation, size normalization, centering, and noise elimination achievable on individual characters prior to classification determines how sophisticated the feature extraction and algorithms must be for a given application. Many commercial OCRs use simple template matching classification logic, which gives adequate performance only if variations of the above type have been essentially eliminated.

***Feature extraction and classification.*** When simple template matching is inadequate, recognition is achieved by extracting distinctive features and using them in a decision logic to classify the characters. Decision logics are designed by using statistics of features obtained from sets of learning samples representative of the applications for which the OCR is intended.

Most high-speed commercial OCRs use special hardware for preprocessing, feature extraction, and classification, although there exists at least one high-performance, high-speed postal address reader which uses general multiprocessors and software recognition. Optical correlation, resistor summing networks, and parallel digital logic circuits represent some of the ways in which character and feature templates and weighted masks have been implemented in hardware. Centering of the character being scanned within a recognition "window," referred to as registration, may be done by shifting the digitized character through a discrete number of successive positions in a one- or two-dimensional shift register. Approaches to segmenting a line of print into individual characters include comparing successive vertical scans to give an explicit segmentation of the entire line or alternatively looking for peaks in the output of the classifier to implicitly segment each character.

**Element design.** The design of different elements of an OCR, that is, the transducer, the preprocessing, features, and classification logic, is determined by the type of characters and quality of material that is to be read. Some aspects which affect the design, such as line and character spacing, character-size and stroke-width variability, number of character classes, and differentiability of most similar characters, are a function of the character fonts that are used. Independent of the character fonts are other aspects, such as the reflectance of the paper, quality of the printing, and format of the document. Various standards by the American National Standards Institute (ANSI) contain specifications and recommendations for the paper, print quality, format rules, and measuring techniques for various classes of OCR applications.

0 1 2 3 4 5 6 7 8 9 A B C D E F G H I J

K L M N O P Q R S T U V W X Y Z + - . ,

ƀ ł " # $ % & ' ( ) * / : ; < = > ? @ \

^ _ [ ] ¿ A E I O U Á É Í Ó Ú À È Ì Ò Ù

Â Ê Î Ô Û Å Ø Ç Ñ ß £ ¥ 1 7

**Fig. 4. Proposed standard character set for hand-printed OCR applications.**

## OCR Applications

The classes of OCR applications range from highly controlled stylized fonts to unconstrained multifont typewritten, printed, and handwritten characters encountered by postal address readers. Important elements in rating the performance of an OCR are the error rate, the throughput, the number of fonts capable of being recognized, and the cost, size, and reliability of the machine. The error rate has two components: the undetected substitution rate and the reject rate, that is, the proportion of characters not classified into any character class.

**Stylized font characters.** Stylized characters are designed to make automatic recognition easier. Two widely used special fonts are the ISO-A (Fig. 2), which was the first character set standardized by the International Standards Organization, and ISO-B (Fig. 3), originally promoted in Europe as being more natural looking. ANSI has also proposed a standard for hand-printed characters (**Fig. 4**). Stylized fonts are used extensively on turnaround documents such as utility bills and gasoline credit card slips (**Fig. 5**). A common example of stylized font character recognition is the magnetic ink character recognition (MICR) system which is used on bank checks. This special font, adopted as a standard by the American Banking Association, is called E-13B (**Fig. 6**). Error rates for single-font stylized character readers can be about 1 substitution in 200,000 characters and 1 reject in 20,000.

Single-stylized-font OCR wands, that is, hand-held readers, are being used more and more in inventory and point-of-sale applications. User-programmable hand-held wands in which a microprocessor can be programmed through the wand by reading special codes in the stylized character set have been introduced.

**Postal address readers.** At the opposite end of the scale from stylized font characters is the variability of character fonts used in postal address readers. Postal

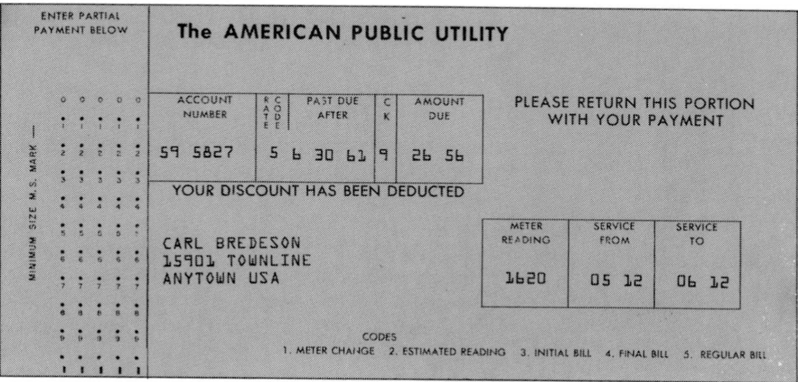
ENTER PARTIAL PAYMENT BELOW

The AMERICAN PUBLIC UTILITY

| ACCOUNT NUMBER | RATE CODE | PAST DUE AFTER | CK | AMOUNT DUE |
|---|---|---|---|---|
| 59 5827 | 5 | 6 30 61 | 9 | 26 56 |

YOUR DISCOUNT HAS BEEN DEDUCTED

PLEASE RETURN THIS PORTION WITH YOUR PAYMENT

CARL BREDESON
15901 TOWNLINE
ANYTOWN USA

| METER READING | SERVICE FROM | SERVICE TO |
|---|---|---|
| 1620 | 05 12 | 06 12 |

MINIMUM SIZE M.S. MARK —

CODES
1. METER CHANGE 2. ESTIMATED READING 3. INITIAL BILL 4. FINAL BILL 5. REGULAR BILL

**Fig. 5. Typical document for optical character recognition systems use.**

Fig. 6. E-13B font in magnetic ink on the bottom of a typical bank check to permit electronic processing.

address readers sort mail in a number of large cities in the United States, and additional OCR and bar code readers are to be installed. Together with the introduction of a nine-digit business zip code and special incentives for large-volume business mailers, this equipment improves service for large-volume mailers. High-volume business mailers already participate in a special "red tag" program in which batches of mail suitable for automatic reading and sorting are sorted and tagged before being sent to the post office for automatic mail sorting.

In the machine reading of outgoing mail one can make use of relationships between the city, state, and zip code on the last line of the address. Thus better recognition and missort rates can be expected on outgoing mail than on incoming mail. Performance figures on the postal address reader SARI show that the state of the art of postal address reading is well advanced. On a sample of 1,250,487 live mail pieces, a true throughput of 32,078 letters per hour was obtained with a recognition rate of 97% and a missort rate of 0.01% on outgoing mail, and a recognition rate of 93% and missort rate of 0.46% on incoming mail. On incoming mail the missort rate figure includes missorting of street numbers. The volume of mail is such that even when a substantial percentage is rejected by the OCR and diverted to subsequent manual sorting, automatic sorting of the rest can still be cost-effective.

The reading of hand-printed zip codes has been successfully accomplished in Japan by requiring that the numerals be carefully written in boxes preprinted on a standard location on the envelope. Such constraints avoid the problem of segmenting the characters and help humans adapt to the characteristics suitable for machine readability of hand-printed numerals. Preprinted boxes on envelopes are likely to be adopted by many postal services. To encourage experimentation and comparative evaluation of approaches to automatic reading of handwritten zip codes, the U.S. Postal Service has prepared two data bases. The first, CONSCRIPT, consists of multilevel digitized data tapes of the video scan from five-digit postal zip codes and six-digit numeric codes from constrained handwritten OCR forms. The second, ZIPSCRIPT, consists of multilevel digitized tapes of zip codes selected from samples or envelopes collected at dead-letter mail offices.

**Typewritten and typeset characters.** Many data-entry and word-processing applications are aided by the automatic reading of material typed in one of the various popular typewriter fonts. Performance figures similar to those quoted for stylized font characters may be obtained with certain typewriter fonts, that is, modified Courier, when typed on a specially aligned typewriter using carbon film ribbon, high-quality paper, and well-specified format conventions. In general, with standard typefaces, error rates are likely to be one or two orders of magnitude higher, depending on the typeface and print quality.

The large number of styles and the segmentation of variable-width characters make the automatic reading of typeset text much more difficult than typewritten material. There are a larger number of classes of characters in each font, many symbols, and combinations of characters called ligatures, for example, fi, ffi, and fl. OCR performance on variable-pitch typeset material is much lower than on typewritten and stylized OCR fonts; 1 in 100 characters may be incorrectly classified.

A major application for automatic reading of typeset text is computerized information retrieval. One application of mixed-font OCR is a commercially available reading machine for the blind. By coupling the reader to a speech synthesizer, the OCR's output is voiced at an adjustable rate between 100 and 300 words per minute. The human listener soon learns to make sense of the output even when a high fraction of the characters is incorrectly recognized.

**Hand-printed characters.** A number of manufacturers offer OCRs for constrained hand-printed numerics, and a few offer readers for constrained alphanumeric hand-printed characters. State payroll tax forms, driver's license applications, magazine subscription renewal forms, and other short forms with boxes and directions on how to print the characters give evidence of the business use of constrained hand-printed OCR. The recogniton performance depends, among other things, on the number of writers, the number of different character classes, and the training of the writers.

The problem of recognizing unconstrained hand-printed characters is a challenging one and is similar to the problem of classifying reasonably good-quality machine-printed characters from an unlimited number of fonts all mixed together. The variability of characters printed by the same individual is large, with an even larger variability encountered between different individuals. Performance figures of the order of 95–98% correct recognition for alphanumerics and 99.5% correct recognition for numerals only, have been found for an "untrained but motivated population." Providing feedback and display of rejected and misclassified characters to the writers can result in a much lower error rate. A commercially available OCR for reading unconstrained numerals handwritten on bank checks is in operation.

**Cursive writing.** On-line recognition of cursive writing by using features of the stylus motion appears to lead to the future possibility of devices for signature verification, and is being studied by a number of investigators. Non-real-time approaches to automatic recognition of cursive alphanumeric script have not gone beyond the laboratory investigation phase.

**Different alphabets.** In principle, OCR can be performed on characters of any alphabet belonging to any language. Work has been reported on OCR for Cyrillic, Devanagri (Hindi), Arabic, Chinese, and Katakana alphabets. One OCR recognizes Russian capital letters, digits, punctuation marks, and arithmetic and other symbols—53 characters in all. Chinese or Japanese character recognition is a very special problem in which the number of possible categories is very large—tens of thousands. But the variability in each character is very small, for the font as known in English does not exist. Thus a particular Chinese character in a newspaper or a book does not vary much from sample to sample. Moreover, the problems of character separation in Chinese or Japanese are easier to resolve than in English since a character usually has a definite size and constant pitch.

### Prospects

The increasing use of microprocessor technology is aimed at developing low-cost, decentralized OCR devices which can handle a wide variety of fonts and formats. Combinations of word-processing and OCR equipment, and OCR and facsimile store and forward communications are likely to lead to many new applications for OCR. *See* Computer; Digital computer; Microprocessor; Word processing.

*Laveen N. Kanal*

**Bibliography.** N. Ahuja and B. J. Schachter, *Pattern Models*, 1983; K. S. Fu, *Syntactic Pattern Recognition and Applications*, 1982; L. N. Kanal and A. Rosenfield (eds.), *Progress in Pattern Recognition*, vol. 1, 1982; G. Nagy, Engineering considerations in optical character recognition, *Proc. COMPCON*, San Francisco, IEEE Cat. 8OCH1491-OC, pp. 402–406, February 1980; C. Y. Suen, Automatic recognition of hand-printed characters: The state of the art, *Proc. IEEE*, 68:469–487, April 1980; S. Watanabe, *Pattern Recognition: Human and Mechanical*, 1984.

## Characteristic curve

A curve that shows the relationship between two changing values. A typical characteristic curve is that which shows how the changes in the control-grid voltage of an electron tube affect the anode current. When three variables are involved, a family of characteristic curves is frequently drawn, with each curve representing one value of the third variable. Other common examples of curves include speed-torque characteristics of motors, frequency-gain characteristics of amplifiers, and voltage-temperature characteristics of thermocouples. The curves are produced by making a series of measurements and plotting the results.

With appropriate electronic circuits the measurements can now be made automatically and fast enough so that the entire characteristic curve is visible on the screen of a cathode-ray oscilloscope. *See* Oscilloscope.

*John Markus*

## Charge-coupled devices

Semiconductor devices wherein minority charge is stored in a spatially defined depletion region (potential well) at the surface of a semiconductor, and is moved about the surface by transferring this charge to similar adjacent wells. The formation of the potential well is controlled by the manipulation of voltage applied to surface electrodes. Since a potential well represents a nonequilibrium state, it will fill with minority charge from normal thermal generation. Thus a charge-coupled device (CCD) must be continuously clocked or refreshed to maintain its usefulness. In general, the potential wells are strung together as shift registers. Charge is injected or generated at various input ports and then transferred to an output detector. By appropriate design to minimize the dispersive effects associated with the charge-transfer process, well-defined charge packets can be moved over relatively long distances through thousands of transfers.

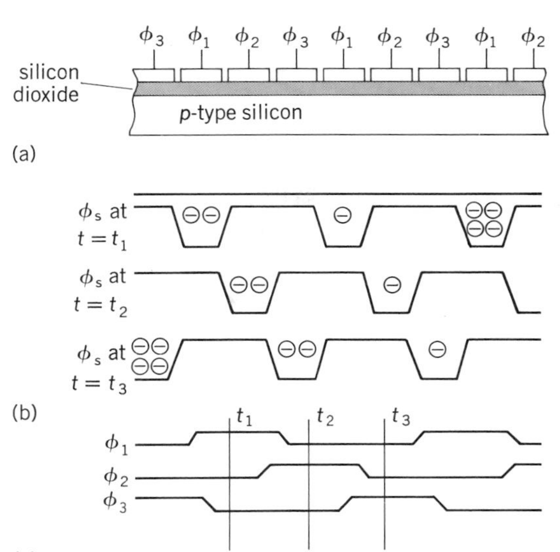


**Fig. 1. Operation of three-phase charge-coupled shift register. (*a*) Cross section of register through channel. (*b*) Profile of surface potential $\phi_s$ for three different clock time intervals $t_1$, $t_2$, and $t_3$. (*c*) Voltage waveforms $\phi_1$, $\phi_2$, and $\phi_3$ for the three-phase clocks.**

**Control of charge motion.** There are several methods of controlling the charge motion, all of which rely upon providing a lower potential for the charge in the desired direction. When an electrode is placed in close proximity to a semiconductor surface, the electrode's potential can control the near-surface potential within the semiconductor. The basis for this control is the same as for metal oxide semiconductor (MOS) transistor action. If closely spaced electrodes are at different voltages, they will form potential wells of different depths. Free charge will move from the region of higher potential to the one of lower potential. **Figure 1** shows a case where by alternating the voltage on three electrodes in proper phase, a charge packet can be moved to the right. **Figure 2** illustrates

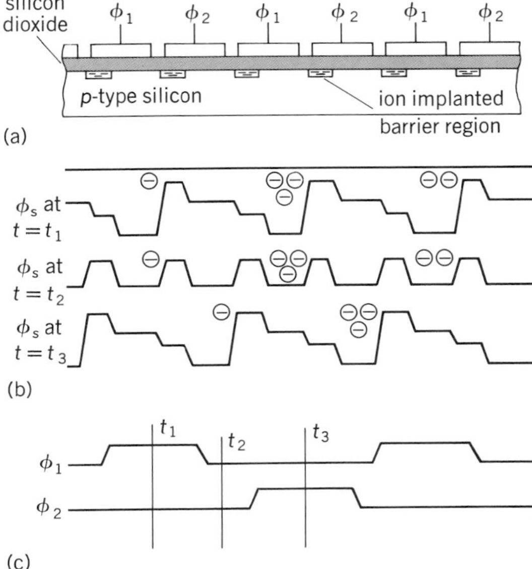


**Fig. 2. Operation of two-phase charge-coupled shift register. (*a*) Cross section of register through channel. (*b*) Profile of surface potential $\phi_s$ for three different clock time intervals $t_1$, $t_2$, and $t_3$. (*c*) Voltage waveforms $\phi_1$ and $\phi_2$ for the two-phase clocks.**

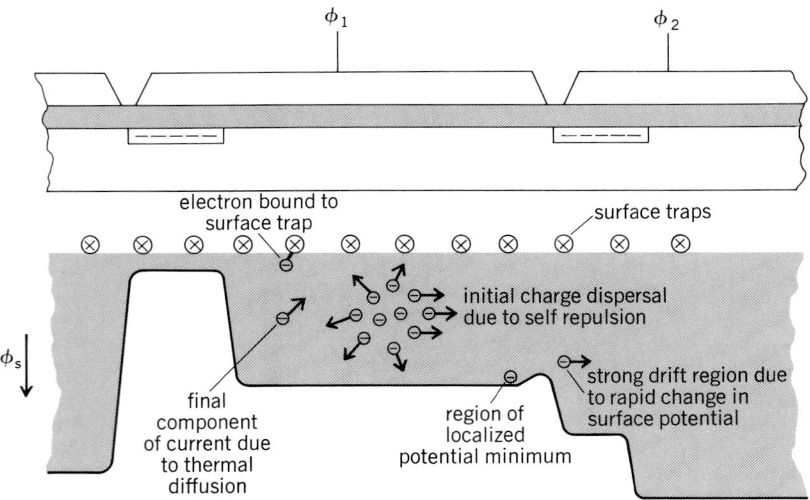


**Fig. 3. Mechanisms determining charge-transfer rate. The three terms contributing to charge transfer include self-induced drift, channel drift fields, and thermal diffusion. Charge is left behind due to electron traps and localized potential minima.**

another scheme whereby an asymmetry built into a well can direct the charge in a given direction. Asymmetries of this type are easily created by using implanted ion layers or varying dielectric thickness. The three-phase structure shown in Fig. 1 has the ability to reverse the charge direction by a change in electrical phase.

**Transfer efficiency.** An important property of a charge-coupled device is its ability to transfer almost all of the charge from one well to the next. Without this feature, charge packets would be quickly distorted and lose their identity. This ability to transfer charge is measured as transfer efficiency, which must be very good for the structure to be useful in long registers. Values greater than 99.9% per transfer are not uncommon. This means that only 10% of the original charge is lost after 100 transfers.

**Figure 3** shows a close-up of a stage of a charge-coupled device. Several mechanisms influence the transfer of charge from one well to the next. Initial self-induced drift acts to separate the charge. This repulsion of like charge is the dominant transfer mechanism for large signals, and is effective for the first 99% or so of the charge. Near the edge of the transfer electrode the potential gradient creates a field which sweeps the charge onward. Thermal diffusion accounts for the transfer of the remaining charge.

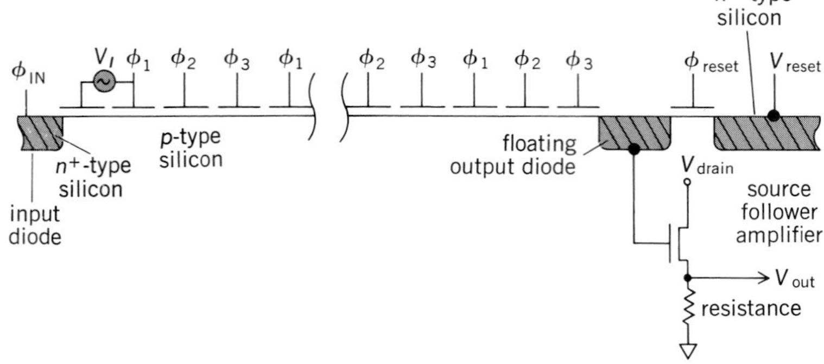


**Fig. 4. Charge-coupled register showing analog input and output ports.**

***Electron traps.*** It would appear that, given sufficient time, almost all of the charge could be transferred. Two other mechanisms are at work to counter this. Within the silicon and at its surface are sites that can act as electron traps. This is especially true at the surface, where numerous surface states exist. These traps collect charge when exposed to a large charge packet and then slowly release it during later cycles of small charge packets. By stringing a large number of empty charge packets together, the traps can be emptied completely. When the first packet containing charge arrives, it could be completely consumed, recharging the traps.

Other than process steps that minimize the trap density, there are two methods to alleviate the severity of this problem. The first is never to allow a series of completely empty charge packets to occur. Instead of an empty charge packet, a minimum charge quantity is always present. This charge, called a fat zero, can be 10–20% of the well capacity. Under some conditions, this can reduce the trapping effects to tolerable levels. The second approach is to use a channel for the charge whose potential minimum does not occur at the surface. This is called a buried channel device, as opposed to a surface channel device. Since the charge is located within the bulk silicon below the surface, it is not exposed to the surface-state traps. Bulk traps remain, but because of their low density they are almost insignificant.

The process to shift the channel potential minimum below the surface can be either an ion-implant layer or an epitaxy layer combined with an implant layer. Because the charge is further removed from the surface control electrode, the maximum charge density has been reduced by a factor of 2 to 3. For the same reason, the fringing fields are greater and charge transfer can be much faster. The charge also moves with bulk mobility rather than the lower surface mobility, further enhancing performance. Fractional charge losses of as low as $5 \times 10^{-5}$ at clock frequencies greater than 100 MHz have been reported for buried-channel charge-coupled device structures. This means that such a structure could transfer $10^6$ electrons from one well to another in less than 10 ns, leaving fewer than 50 electrons behind. SEE ION IMPLANTATION.

***Localized potential minima.*** In addition to electron-trapping sites, there is another reason that charge can be left behind. Where the two adjacent surface electrodes come together, there is necessarily a gap. This gap is usually quite small, and sometimes may even be covered by one of the electrodes. However, the gap represents a region of poorly controlled surface potential. It is possible, under some conditions, for the transition from one potential well to the next to have perturbations in it. These perturbations, or glitches, can trap charge. They represent a localized minipotential well within the larger one. Charge trapped by the glitch will be left behind after a transfer. If the glitch remained filled, continued clocking of the structure would not represent a problem. However, the size of the glitch may change, depending upon electrode clock amplitude. Also, charge is released over the glitch as thermionic emission over a barrier potential. Thus a glitch can be emptied by a series of empty charge packets to trap the next packet-containing charge. Many times, glitches occur at input or output ports without detriment to the structure's operation, since their effect may be small. However, if a glitch occurs within the repetitive register, the multiplication effect can have a serious impact on overall performance.

**Lifetime.** A second important property of a charge-coupled device register is its lifetime. When the surface electrode is clocked high, the potential within the semiconductor also increases. Majority charge is swept away, leaving behind a depletion layer. If the potential is taken sufficiently high, the surface goes into deep depletion until an inversion layer is formed and adequate minority charge collected to satisfy the field requirements. The time it takes for minority charge to fill the well is the measure of well lifetime. The major sources of unwanted charge are: thermal diffusion of substrate minority charge to the edge of the depletion region, where it is collected in the well; electron-hole pair generation within the depletion region; and the emission of minority charge by traps. Surface-channel charge-coupled devices usually have better lifetime, since surface-state trap emission is suppressed and the depletion regions are usually smaller.

**Input and output ports.** Once adequate transfer efficiency and sufficient lifetime have been achieved, input and output ports must be established. The port structure of a charge-coupled device depends upon its application. Analog registers require linear inputs and outputs with good dynamic range. Digital registers require precisely metered and detected ones and zeros. Imaging devices use photoemission at the register sites as input with analog-output amplifiers.

The most common input is shown in **Fig. 4**. This input structure relies upon a diode as a source of minority charge. Whenever the diode potential drops below the threshold potential of the adjacent gate, an inversion layer is formed beneath the gate. By pulsing the diode potential low or the adjacent gate potential high, charge can be injected into the register. To prevent the charge from returning to the diode, the next gate in the register immediately collects it. The amount of charge injected can be controlled by adjusting the channel potential difference between the first two gates.

Figure 4 also shows a common output circuit. The output diode is reset at the start of each cycle to the reset level. During the second part of the cycle, charge from the charge-coupled device register is dumped on the floating diode, causing its voltage to change. The diode is connected to a gate which can be used in an amplifier configuration. The example in Fig. 4 shows a source follower output. For digital applications, the output goes to a regenerative circuit with sufficient gain to produce full-level signals at the output.

*Mark R. Guidry*

**Applications.** Because of their unique properties, charge-coupled devices have found widespread use in a growing number of applications. Many solid-state imaging devices and analog-signal-processing devices have been successfully manufactured by using the principles of charge-coupling. Devices have been fabricated in both silicon and gallium arsenide, but silicon is the more prevalent.

***Imagers.*** The most common use of charge-coupled devices is in solid-state imagers. In a charge-coupled device imager, the photosites are used to convert an optical image into an electrical signal. Photons striking the surface of a semiconductor device will generate free electrons in an amount linearly proportional to their radiant energy. For a silicon device, electrons will be generated for incident photons with wavelengths of approximately 400–1100 nanometers, with the peak response occurring at 700–800 nanometers. This corresponds to the entire visible range of light, from blue to near-infrared. These photogenerated electrons can be collected in a regularly spaced array of photosites, each of which will then contain a charge packet of electrons. The amount of charge collected at each photosite will be directly proportional to the incident radiation of that photosite. If an image is focused on the surface of the device, the amounts of charge collected in the photosites will then be a faithful representation of the intensity of the image at each location. These charge packets correspond to picture elements, or pixels, each of which is a small part of the complete image. The number of photosites on the device determines the resolution of the final image. These charge packets are then transferred in parallel into a charge-coupled-device shift register, where they are then transferred serially to the output port. The output of the imager will be a series of electric signals whose amplitudes will represent the intensity of the image at each pixel.

Solid-state imagers offer many advantages over other imaging methods, including high reliability, high sensitivity, low power dissipation, and good spectral response over the entire visible spectrum. Charge-coupled-device imagers are produced in two formats, as linear arrays and as area arrays. Linear imaging devices (LIDs) consist of a single row of photosites, and scan images one line at a time. Area imaging devices (AIDs) consist of a matrix of photosites, and sense an entire field at one time. Linear imaging devices are used in applications where either the device or the image is moving at some constant speed, such as for inspection of objects on a conveyor belt. Other applications for linear imaging devices include use in facsimile equipment, photocopiers, mail sorters, and bar code readers, and for aerial mapping and reconnaissance.

Area imaging devices have been used in applications where neither the device nor the image is being moved in a regular manner, such as for closed-circuit television cameras, video cameras, and vision systems for robotics applications. Area imaging devices are also being used to replace conventional film for many kinds of astronomical observations. Charge-coupled-device imagers offer the astronomer many advantages over other detectors, such as good stability, linearity of output, and sensitivity of up to 50 times that of conventional film. When cooled to very low temperatures, on the order of −150°F (−100°C), charge-coupled-device imagers can allow exposure times of several hours. This allows astronomers to detect fainter objects than ever before possible. The output signals from these devices can be fed into a computer to enhance the images and to extract other important data. *See* Television camera; Television camera tube.

***Signal processing.*** Many applications for charge-coupled devices have been found in the processing of analog signal information. Since a charge-coupled device is an excellent analog shift register, it can be used as an analog delay line, where the delay is determined by the number of elements in the array and by the frequency at which it is clocked. The delay can be controlled externally by simply varying the clock frequency. It can also be used to scramble and de-scramble audio and video signals by varying the delay times of different sections of the signal. This could be used as a cable television descrambler, for example. By tapping a charge-coupled delay line, sampled analog filters can be produced that can be externally programmed to change their filter characteristics. Other uses for charge-coupled-device signal processors include applications as multiplexers and demultiplexers, correlators, and analog-to-digital converters. SEE COMPUTER STORAGE TECHNOLOGY; INTEGRATED CIRCUITS; SEMICONDUCTOR.

*David E. Weisner*

**Bibliography.** G. F. Amelio, Charge-coupled devices, *Sci. Amer.*, 230(2):22–31, February 1974; F. Bower, *CCD Fundamentals*, Fairchild Camera and Instrument Corp., February 1978; W. F. Kosonocky, Charge-coupled devices: An overview, *Western Electron Show and Convention Technical Papers*, vol. 18, pp. 2/1–2/20, September 1974; J. Kristian and M. Blouke, Charge-coupled devices in Astronomy, *Sci. Amer.*, 247(4):66–74, October 1982.

## Choke (electricity)

An inductor used in a low-pass filter in which the useful output is a direct current, as in the filter of a power rectifier. At usual power frequencies a filter choke has an iron core, with an air gap to minimize variation of inductance with direct current. In a choke-input filter (a filter in which the first element is an inductance) some economy is sometimes afforded by designing the choke so that its inductance is allowed to reduce because of saturation at high currents. Such a choke is called a swinging choke. SEE ELECTRONIC POWER SUPPLY.

*Wilbur R. LePage*

## Chopper

Usually an electromechanical component that synchronously switches a signal circuit. By extension, the term chopper is also applied to photoelectric, electronic, and transistor circuits adapted to perform the same function as a mechanical chopper. An older related device is an optical shutter arranged to sequentially pass and interrupt, or chop, a light beam.

Basically a chopper serves as a suppressed carrier square-wave modulator. Such a component is shown schematically in the **illustration**. An electromagnet

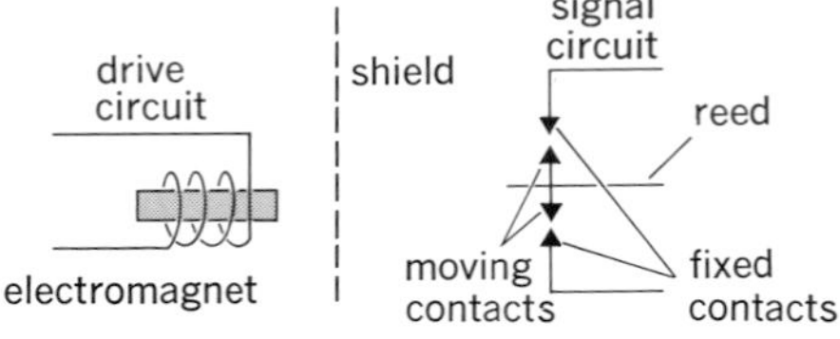


**Diagram of basic chopper structure.**

driven by a source of alternating current (typically 60 or 400 Hz, although higher frequencies may be used) sets a reed into vibration. The reed carries a moving contact that alternately contacts one and the other of two fixed contacts in a signal circuit. Thus the signal (typically in the order of 1 mW or less at 1 V) is periodically interrupted.

A usual chopper application is the inversion of a slowly varying signal into a rapidly varying one, the latter being the more readily amplified. An electrostatic shield and other design precautions minimize coupling between drive and signal circuits. A frame supports the parts, usually with some degree of vibration isolation.

*Frank H. Rockett*

## Chopping

The act of interrupting an electric current, beam of light, or beam of infrared radiation at regular intervals. This can be accomplished mechanically by rotating a vibrating mirror in the path of the beam to deflect it away from its intended source at regular intervals. A current can be chopped with an electromagnetic vibrator having contacts on its moving armature. A current can also be chopped electronically by passing it through a multivibrator or other switching circuit. Chopping is generally used to change a direct-current signal into an alternating-current signal that can more readily be amplified. Control systems for guided missiles make extensive use of chopping. SEE MULTIVIBRATOR.

*John Markus*

## Circuit (electricity)

A general term referring to a system or part of a system of conducting parts and their interconnections through which an electric current is intended to flow. A circuit is made up of active and passive elements or parts and their interconnecting conducting paths. The active elements are the sources of electric energy for the circuit; they may be batteries, direct-current generators, or alternating-current generators. The passive elements are resistors, inductors, and capacitors. The electric circuit is described by a circuit diagram or map showing the active and passive elements and their connecting conducting paths.

Devices with an individual physical identity such as amplifiers, transistors, loudspeakers, and generators, are often represented by equivalent circuits for purposes of analysis. These equivalent circuits are made up of the basic passive and active elements listed above.

Electric circuits are used to transmit power as in high-voltage power lines and transformers or in low-voltage distribution circuits in factories and homes; to convert energy from or to its electrical form as in motors, generators, microphones, loudspeakers, and lamps; to communicate information as in telephone, telegraph, radio, and television systems; to process

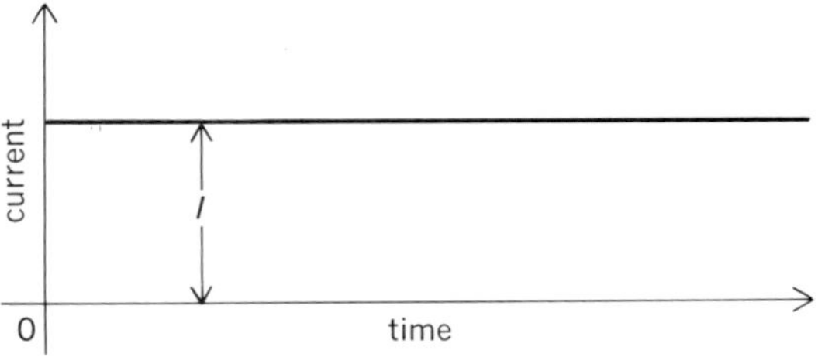


**Fig. 1. Direct current.**

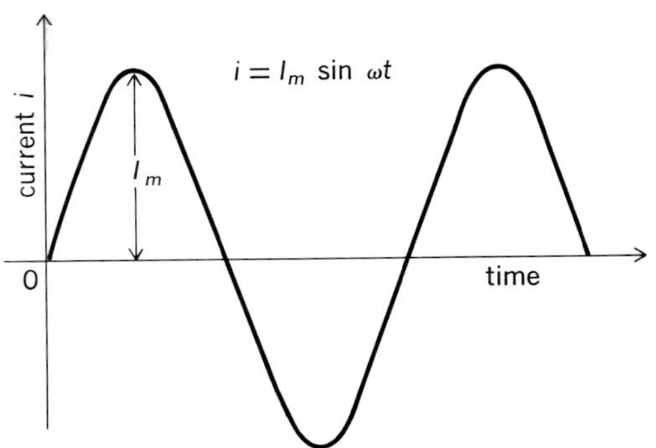


Fig. 2. Alternating current.

and store data and make logical decisions as in computers; and to form systems for automatic control of equipment.

**Electric circuit theory.** This includes the study of all aspects of electric circuits, including analysis, design, and application. In electric circuit theory the fundamental quantities are the potential differences (voltages) in volts between various points, the electric currents in amperes flowing in the several paths, and the parameters in ohms or mhos which describe the passive elements. Other important circuit quantities such as power, energy, and time constants may be calculated from the fundamental variables. For a discussion of these parameters SEE ADMITTANCE; CONDUCTANCE; ELECTRICAL IMPEDANCE; ELECTRICAL RESISTANCE; REACTANCE; SUSCEPTANCE; TIME CONSTANT.

Electric circuit theory is an extensive subject and is often divided into special topics. Division into topics may be made on the basis of how the voltages and currents in the circuit vary with time; examples are direct-current, alternating-current, nonsinusoidal, digital, and transient circuit thoery. Another method of classifying circuits is by the arrangement or configuration of the electric current paths; examples are series circuits, parallel circuits, series-parallel circuits, networks, coupled circuits, open circuits, and short circuits. Circuit theory can also be divided into special topics according to the physical devices forming the circuit, or the application and use of the circuit. Examples are power, communication, electronic, solid-state, integrated, computer, and control circuits. SEE CIRCUIT (ELECTRONICS); NEGATIVE-RESISTANCE CIRCUITS.

**Direct-current circuits.** In dc circuits the voltages and currents are constant in magnitude and do not vary with time (**Fig. 1**). Sources of direct current are batteries, dc generators, and rectifiers. Resistors are the principal passive element. For a discussion of direct-current circuits SEE DIRECT-CURRENT CIRCUIT THEORY.

**Magnetic circuits.** Magnetic circuits are similar to electric circuits in their analysis and are often included in the general topic of circuit theory. Magnetic circuits are used in electromagnets, relays, magnetic brakes and clutches, computer memory devices, and many other devices.

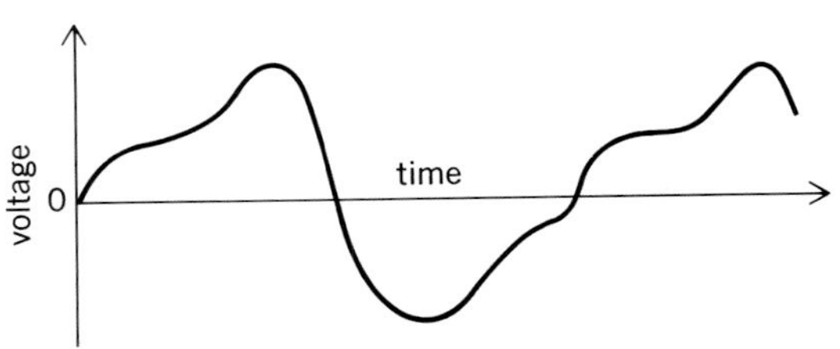


Fig. 3. Nonsinusoidal voltage wave.

**Alternating-current circuits.** In ac circuits the voltage and current periodically reverse direction with time. The time for one complete variation is known as the period. The number of periods in 1 s is the frequency in cycles per second. A cycle per second was named a hertz (in honor of Heinrich Rudolf Hertz's work on electromagnetic waves).

Most often the term ac circuit refers to sinusoidal variations. For example, the alternating current in **Fig. 2** may be expressed by $i = I_m \sin \omega t$. Sinusoidal sources are ac generators and various types of electronic and solid-state oscillators; passive circuit elements include inductors and capacitors as well as resistors. The analysis of ac circuits requires a study of the phase relations between voltages and currents as well as their magnitudes. Complex numbers are often used for this purpose. For a detailed discussion SEE ALTERNATING-CURRENT CIRCUIT THEORY.

**Nonsinoidal waveforms.** These voltage and current variations vary with time but not sinusoidally (**Fig. 3**). Such nonsinusoidal variations are usually caused by nonlinear devices, such as saturated magnetic circuits, electron tubes, and transistors. Circuits with nonsinusoidal waveforms are analyzed by breaking the wave form into a series of sinusoidal waves of different frequencies known as a Fourier series. Each frequency component is analyzed by ac circuit techniques. Results are combined by the principle of superposition to give the total response. SEE NONSINUSOIDAL WAVEFORM.

**Electric transients.** Transient voltage and current variations last for a short length of time and do not repeat continuously (**Fig. 4**). Transients occur when a change is made in the circuit, such as opening or closing a switch, or when a change is made in one of the sources or elements. For a discussion of dc and ac transients SEE ELECTRIC TRANSIENT.

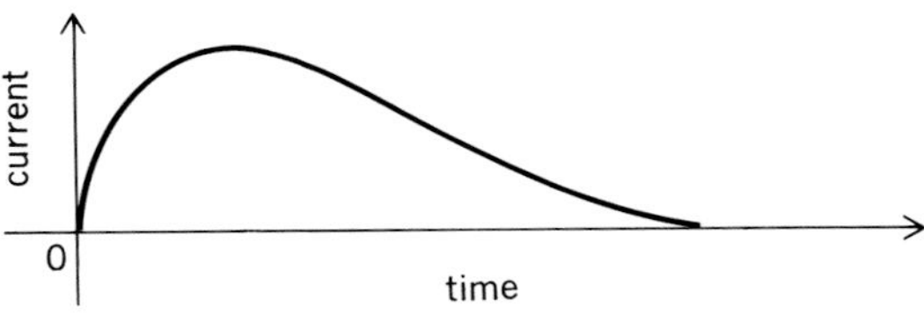


Fig. 4. Transient electric current.

**Series circuits.** In a series circuit all the components or elements are connected end to end and carry the same current, as shown in **Fig. 5**. SEE SERIES CIRCUIT.

**Parallel circuits.** Parallel circuits are connected so that each component of the circuit has the same potential difference (voltage) across its terminals, as shown in **Fig. 6**. SEE PARALLEL CIRCUIT.

**Series-parallel circuits.** In a series-parallel circuit some of the components or elements are connected in parallel, and one or more of these parallel combinations are in series with other components of the circuit, as shown in **Fig. 7**.

**Electric network.** This is another term for electric circuit, but it is often reserved for the electric circuit that is more complicated than a simple series or par-

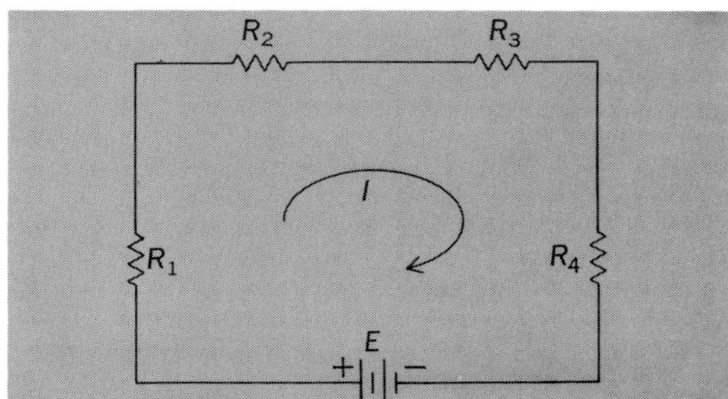


Fig. 5. Series circuit.

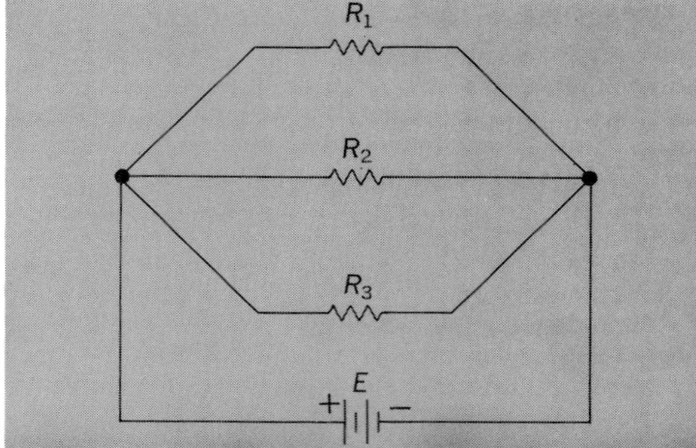


Fig. 6. Parallel circuit.

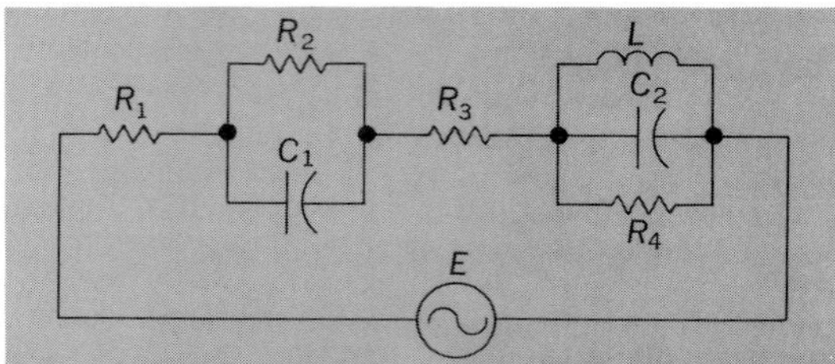


Fig. 7. Series-parallel circuit.

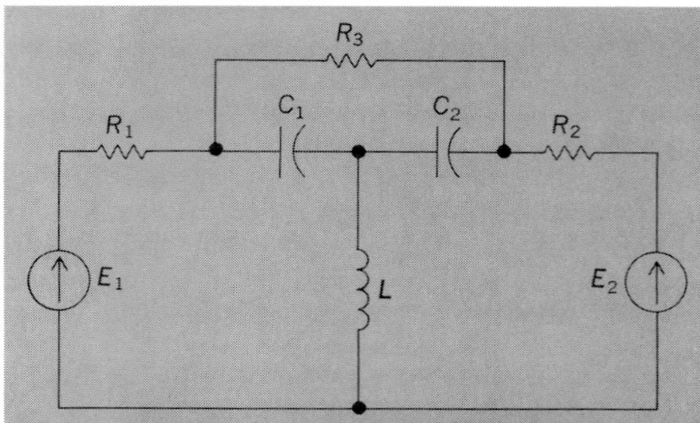


Fig. 8. A three-mesh electric network.

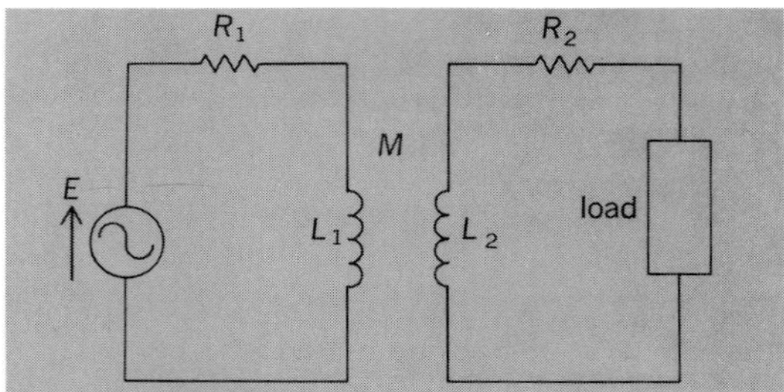


Fig. 9. Inductively coupled circuit.

allel combination. A three-mesh electric network is shown in **Fig. 8**. *See* N*etwork theory*.

**Coupled circuits.** A circuit is said to be coupled if two or more parts are related to each other through some common element. The coupling may be by means of a conducting path of resistors or capacitors or by a common magnetic linkage (inductive coupling), as shown in **Fig. 9**. *See* C*oupled circuits*.

**Open circuit.** An open circuit is a condition in an electric circuit in which there is no path for current flow between two points that are normally connected. *See* O*pen circuit*.

**Short circuit.** This term applies to the existence of a zero-impedance path between two points of an electric circuit.

**Integrated circuit.** In the integrated circuit the entire circuit is contained in a single piece of semiconductor material. Sometimes the term is also applied to circuits made up of deposited thin films on an insulating substrate. *See* I*ntegrated circuits;* S*emiconductor*.

Clarence F. Goodheart

***Bibliography.*** A. E. Fitzgerald et al., *Basic Electrical Engineering*, 5th ed., 1981; W. Hayt, Jr., and J. E. Kemmerly, *Engineering Circuit Analysis*, 3d ed., 1978; L. P. Huelsman, *Basic Circuit Theory*, 2d ed., 1984; D. E. Johnson et al., *Basic Electric Circuit Analysis*, 2d ed., 1984; T. J. Maloney, *Electric Circuits*, 1984; S. Oppenheimer, *Fundamentals of Electric Circuits*, 1984; R. E. Risdale, *Electric Circuits*, 2d ed., 1983; R. J. Smith, *Circuits, Devices, and Systems*, 3d ed., 1976.

## Circuit (electronics)

An electric circuit in which the equilibrium of electrons in some of the components is upset by a means other than an applied voltage. The means by which electron equilibrium is upset leads to further designation of electronic circuits. In circuits with thermionic tubes, electron equilibrium is upset by thermal emission. In solid-state circuits, electron equilibrium is upset by intentionally introduced imperfections of the crystals in use.

Electronic circuits are also classified by their functions. *See* A*mplifier;* D*etector;* D*igital counter;* E*lectronic power supply;* M*icroprocessor;* M*odulator;* O*scillator;* R*ectifier;* S*emiconductor memories;* S*weep generator;* S*witching circuit;* W*ave-shaping circuits*.

Electronic circuits can consist of discrete elements, coupled integrated circuits, or combinations of both kinds (**Fig. 1**). Integrated circuits can consist of groups of lumped components such as resistors, capacitors, and active devices, or of exotic combinations of passive and active components that are intended to have properties not normally available in lumped discrete-element networks. *See* I*ntegrated circuits*.

Electronic circuits find application in all branches of industry and in the home, both for entertainment equipment and increasingly for control. Because of their low power dissipation and fast response, they are excellent control circuits. Computers, communication systems, and navigation systems use many types of electronic circuits. *See* C*omputer;* E*lectrical communications*.

**Electronic components.** For an electric circuit to be classed as an electronic circuit, some of its components must be able to switch currents or voltages without mechanical switches, or to amplify or control voltages or currents without mechanical command or other nonelectrical command. Such devices as electron tubes, transistors, magnetic amplifiers, diodes, quartz crystals, resistors, capacitors, inductors, transformers, and ferrite devices are electronic components; tube sockets, interconnecting wires, and chassis for example, are not, although they form a part of the electronic circuit assembly. For a discussion of typical components *SEE CAPACITOR; ELECTRON TUBE; FERRITE DEVICES; INDUCTOR; INTEGRATED CIRCUITS; PIEZOELECTRIC CRYSTAL; RESISTOR; SEMICONDUCTOR; SEMICONDUCTOR DIODE; TRANSFORMER; TRANSISTOR.*

Typically, electronic components have the capability of dissipating, controlling, or storing electric energy, or some combination of these functions. In addition, the current and voltage applied to the component may bear a relatively linear relation to each other (as in a resistor), a nonlinear relation as a function of current and voltage (as in a diode, bipolar transistor, field-effect transistor, electron tube, or saturable reactor), a relation that is a function of frequency (as in an inductor, capacitor, or transformer), a time-controlled switching function (as in a thyratron, ignitron, unijunction transistor, or a silicon-controlled rectifier), or a combination of the relations. Current and voltage may be inversely related. *SEE CAPACITOR; GAS TUBE; INDUCTOR; SEMICONDUCTOR RECTIFIER.*

There are two kinds of negative-immittance devices, namely, negative-resistance and negative-conductance devices. These are significantly different in several respects. In the negative-immittance region, a negative-conductance device has a maximum (absolute) value of negative conductance, and for a range of currents there is more than one value of voltage at which that level of current can be generated. With a negative-resistance device, there will be more than one value of current for which a given value of voltage can be generated. Distinctions are drawn between these kinds of negative immittance in many countries, a negative-conductance device often being called a voltage-controlled negative resistance, and the converse, a current-controlled negative resistance. With the former device type, in the negative-conductance range the value of negative resistance goes from negative infinite to a minimum value; with the latter, it goes from zero to a negative maximum value. *SEE NEGATIVE-RESISTANCE CIRCUITS.*

Although a component may be intended to introduce only one or two of the voltage-current relations or characteristics into a given circuit, certain undesired or parasitic characteristics are also introduced. Because of the wide range of power levels at which electronic components must function, from less than $10^{-25}$ W to $10^7$ W and higher, and the wide range of frequencies, from direct current to over $10^{11}$ Hz, the parasitic characteristics are of great importance in circuit behavior. Noise generated in the components has importance in low-power circuits. *SEE ELECTRICAL NOISE.*

Some classes of electronic components, such as those for military, marine, or airborne service, are packaged to protect them from environmental conditions, whereas ordinary components are given little more than electrically insulating mechanical protection. Specially packaged components that are used in equipment required to give reliable operation must also be used conservatively, that is, derated in accordance with environmental conditions to fractions of their rated values of voltage, current, and power dissipation. Determination of deratings is a function of circuit design, and is discussed later in this article.

**Fig. 1.** Back of a television receiver, showing circuit technologies. Except for the picture tube, most of the components are on a few circuit boards. (*Zenith Electronics Corp.*).

Complex electronic systems often use assemblies of components interconnected as subassemblies. The most elaborate subassemblies, called integrated circuits, are collections of active and passive components formed by deposition, diffusion, or epitaxial growth on a common poorly conducting or insulating substrate (**Fig. 2**). They have many practical advantages compared with discrete-component circuits (including those of the welded cord-wood variety), and several disadvantages. Probably the most important advantage is the extremely small segment, or chip, required to support a relatively complex circuit. An operational amplifier having a gain in the tens of thousands or more may often be housed in a single transistor can whose size may be as small as 0.1 in. (2.5 mm)

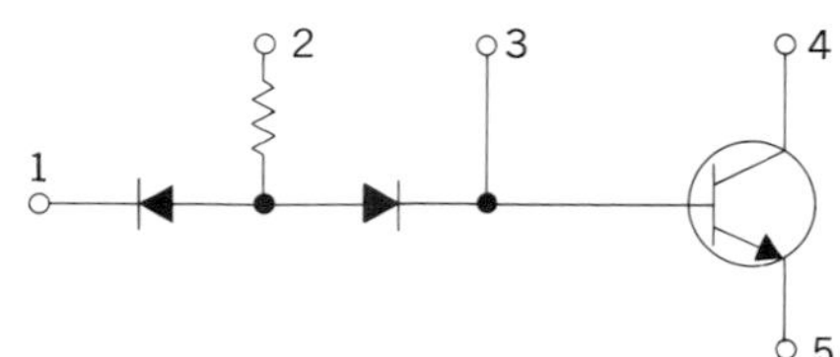


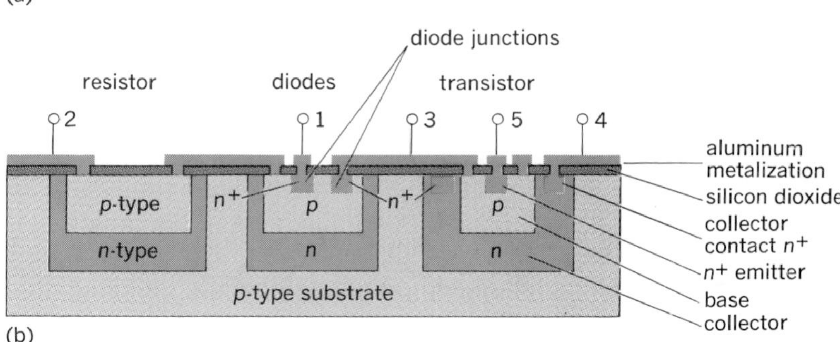


**Fig. 2.** An integrated circuit combines active and passive components on a single chip. (*a*) Schematic of discrete circuit. (*b*) Cross section of integrated equivilent circuit, with corresponding terminals numbered. (*After A. B. Phillips, Monolithic integrated circuits, IEEE Spectrum, 1(6):83–101, June 1964*)

**Fig. 3.** Development of digital computers. (*a*) ENIAC, first large-scale electronic digital computer, containing 18,000 vacuum tubes. Some of the computer racks are shown, with their patch panels for programming (*Ballistic Research Laboratory*). (*b*) TI-57-LCD hand-held programmable calculator, based on integrated circuits, which can carry out calculations that could not be done on ENIAC for lack of memory (*Texas Instruments*).

on a side. Previous equivalent tube-type designs typically required more than 10 in.$^3$ (160 cm$^3$) of space. (A complex integrated circuit like a microprocessor may have hundreds of thousands of active elements and can perform hundreds of different operations.)

Signal transmission times among integrated circuit components can be less by as much as two or more orders of magnitude compared with those of corresponding tube circuits because lead lengths can be reduced from many inches to as little as a few thousandths of an inch in a typical integrated circuit. These short lead lengths make possible circuit analysis based on lumped parameters both for operation at higher frequencies and for faster switching rates. As a consequence, a computer with the computation capability of the original electronic digital computer, the ENIAC, but based on integrated circuits, fits in a typical pocket calculator instead of approximately 50 racks for the ENIAC, and it could have at least 1000 times the speed of the ENIAC (**Fig. 3**). In addition, power requirements would be in fractions of a watt instead of hundreds of kilowatts.

**Electronic circuit design.** The design of electronic circuits is the process of establishing appropriate electrical and environmental conditions in a network to achieve a required reaction to a given stimulus. In the synthesis of design, both the form of the network as a whole and the kinds and sizes of the parts must be selected to assure proper operation on demand from the stimulus.

Design of an electronic circuit is also a process of compromise in that it is necessary to establish a steady-state electrical environment in which the required small-signal behavior can be achieved. Even reliable operation of a switching circuit depends, in the final analysis, on small-signal characteristics for its action in transferring between its rest states. In particular, switching between states occurs only if the instantaneous loop gain of the circuit as a whole exceeds unity. As a result, efficient circuit design depends on the engineering quality of specifications developed for the component characteristics, both nominal values and tolerances, and the ingenuity of the designer in evolving the circuit configuration.

In addition to electrical factors, such other environmental factors as mechanical and thermal must all be considered. Importance of these other factors is a function of (1) use of the circuit, (2) complexity of the system in which it operates, and (3) reliability of operation that is required.

Even simple circuits may use components having relatively wide electrical tolerances. For this reason it is important that the designer determine the relative importance of each design factor involved and that he or she know which factors can be specified most precisely and used most effectively in the design procedure. Some design procedures evolve through experience, but other procedures can be developed only after intensive study of both the physical fundamentals of specific devices and the practical requirements for their reliable operation.

**Component specifications.** It is a design tautology that an electronic circuit can be only as good as the information, electrical and otherwise, on which it is based. For example, a designer's understanding of the nonlinear characteristics of devices, particularly active nonlinear devices, is usually gained through extensive applicational experience. Because such experience can be applied only in a limited way to other devices, development of reliable electronic circuits has been restricted, in great degree, to linear operation. Even the best circuit engineers who have extremely able circuit technicians working with them usually use active devices with which they are well acquainted.

More fundamental description of active devices can aid circuit designers in carrying over experience from one device to another. The description can be based on more specific identification of a device in terms of precise physical properties or can be based on more inclusive classification of device production characteristics by statistical methods.

Careful analysis of properties of known active devices in the circuit configurations ordinarily encountered shows that there is a set of device specifications that can lead to efficient design and useful reliability. With these specifications, the most important parameters of devices can typically be specified accurately in terms of a prime device variable, such as a current that is directly controlled by the designer. For electron tubes, bipolar transistors, and field-effect transistors, the most important parameter is the Fermi constant $\Lambda$, which has the value of 39 siemens per ampere at room temperature. The reciprocal of 39 siemens per ampere is 26 millivolts or 26 ohm-milliamperes.

Traditional treatments of parameter relations and their applications to circuit design are based on the form of the specifications used by manufacturers to present data on resistors, capacitors, inductors, transistors, tubes, and similar devices. For entertainment applications, this convention, although not ideal, is adequate. With more stringent requirements placed on circuits for computers, controllers, and communication systems, designs based on these data have not always proved to be fully adequate. Two solutions have been found for this dilemma, one based on the choice of parameters that measure the primary properties of the device in question in terms of physical coefficients, and the other on use of statistical techniques for circuit design. The latter procedure helps to minimize the difficulties resulting from wide tolerances because the use of statistics is effective when the theoretically selected statistical distribution is reasonably similar to the distribution encountered with practical devices. The statistical procedure has become practical with the advent of large-scale high-speed computers.

Examination of parameter data on active devices in particular shows that the tolerances on some parameters must be wide, whereas other parameters can be more precisely controlled. Statistical procedures are required when design is based on such wide-tolerance derived parameters as transistor current gain, or $\beta$, which is a function of the ratio of one current to the small difference of two currents. Fundamental parameters, such as the Fermi constant, $\Lambda = q/kT$, where $q$ is electron charge, $k$ is Boltzmann's constant, and $T$ is absolute temperature, are truly independent of the methods by which they are measured. Use of fundamental parameters becomes increasingly important as integrated circuits encompass more elements.

The equations derived by Ebers and Moll, when changed into the commonmode format, can be used to facilitate design of many circuits involving not only bipolar transistors but also field-effect transistors and typical electron tubes. To accomplish this in simplest form, a transconductance-efficiency, or kappa, parameter is introduced, which measures the efficiency of control that the input signal on a device exercises over the output current flow. This parameter has a value of approximately unity for bipolar transistors, and there are regions of operation for both electron tubes and many field-effect transistor devices for which kappa has a value near unity. Typical values of kappa for these latter devices in their normal operating region are less than 0.01, however. This parameter can be used as a measure of the power-handling ability of a device, the power being inversely related to the value of the kappa factor.

The kappa for any typical device may be measured in terms of the voltage change required to generate a two-to-one change in output current. Dividing this voltage change into 0.018 V gives the approximate kappa, and the approximate usable output supply voltage may be found by dividing the measured voltage change by 0.009. Since these devices all have limitations on their maximum current-carrying capabilities, and voltage gains per stage must be limited for stability reasons, this parameter is one of the more important ones associated with circuit design.

From the above, it is evident that active devices should be used with the lowest possible output supply voltages. Using a higher voltage than is required for the allowed level of voltage gain leads to instability or, as a minimum, excessive power dissipation. This is because device transconductance is almost independent of output supply voltage, depending on output current alone. As a result, power dissipation can be sharply reduced, and reliability can be sharply increased.

Development and use of integrated circuit assemblies as fundamental building blocks simplify and at the same time complicate the design of electronic systems. Design is simplified insofar as a single mass-produced integrated circuit assembly can often replace a complex circuit constructed from discrete components. Design is complicated by the fact that this mass-produced integrated circuit consists of a complex of nonlinear elements which, although deposited in a specific configuration, differ from unit to unit. As a consequence, the transfer function, measuring the ratio of the circuit response to its input signal, differs for each unit from the required transfer function.

These differences limit the designers when they model or simulate a circuit during its development. Applicability of the model depends on two chief criteria: (1) conditions of operation in the model needed to duplicate those to which published specifications apply; and (2) there must be a unique and close correspondence between observable behavior in the model and published specifications. Implicit in these criteria is the need that published specifications for components intended to be used in circuits meaningfully describe characteristics and tolerances which are fundamental to circuit operation.

From the above, it follows that specifications placed on components, subassemblies such as integrated circuits, and circuit assemblies are important in the design of electronic circuits. Preparation and selection of specifications strongly influence use of a component or a subassembly; reliability and maintenance of the finished circuit, both of which contribute to its long-term costs, also depend on the adequacy of component specifications.

***Circuit specifications.*** Normally, characteristics of an existing or a required circuit are expressed as a performance specification. This specification states, often in considerable detail, performance limitations, leaving the choice of structural and circuit details that will meet these limits to the circuit designer. Such a specification typically includes, for an amplifier, bandwidth between half-power (3-dB) points (the lower and upper frequency limits at which power gain is half of the nominal value), overall power gain (typically given in decibels), power output (in watts), and permitted distortion or intermixing limit (expressed in a form such as harmonic distortion or intermodulation distortion). Other electrical characteristics important for the application at hand will be part of the specification. In addition, because electronic circuits are expected to perform satisfactorily over a wide range of environmental conditions, the specifications include the permissible change in characteristics of the circuit of the full range of temperatures.

Mechanical, chemical, atmospheric, and possibly other design requirements must also be met. Circuits may be required to withstand sinusoidal vibration and noise excitation, to undergo accelerations, and sometimes to sustain impulse loading without failing. Assemblies must withstand the chemical action of their own encapsulants and also the action of corrosive atmospheres at alternately elevated and depressed temperatures. A series of tests exposing the circuit to these environmental conditions is often specified to establish minimum requirements for acceptance. These tests reflect special environmental applications such as marine, military, aircraft, or space use. Such qualification tests are designed to measure compliance of production circuits to performance limits under electrical or environmental conditions that experience has shown may lead to difficulty or failure. Because new problems appear as rapidly as new techniques are developed, tests can only represent a starting point for evaluation of reliability.

***Reliability considerations.*** An electronic circuit may or may not function as intended during its expected life. The probability that it will function as intended is its reliability. Reliability of a circuit depends, in turn, on the reliability of each element or component as operated in the circuit in question. Consequently, reliable circuits are made from reliable components used under conditions that provide an additional margin of safety beyond the safe limits specified by the manufacturer.

Mechanical reliability of an electronic circuit depends largely on the number of interconnecting wires, the mechanical support provided to components, and the manner in which connections are made and connectors used. Mechanical design of parts, particularly connectors and relays, can also be important. Low reliability can be expected on interconnection wiring, particularly when soldering is involved. If such wiring is replaced with welded connections or, better still, with vacuum-deposited wiring, significantly improved operation generally can be achieved. With large-scale integration, external interconnections may be as few as 2% of those in a circuit wired between discrete components. The potential improvement in reliability is self-evident.

Disadvantages of integrated circuits are their low voltage and power ratings and their highly nonlinear parasitic leakage paths, which can exist in the semiconductor material. Typical integrated circuits should be operated at supply voltages less than 12–20 V. Their power dissipation capability depends on the amount of heat-conducting and -radiating material in the integrated circuit and the paths by which the heat developed on the chip can be conducted away or radiated. Unfortunately, a design which achieves low thermal resistance (high capability for conducting heat away from the chip) also tends to have high parasitic capacitances.

Whereas the circuits themselves should be operated at the lowest possible voltages, there can be problems in operating circuits containing electrical connections. Problems are most severe with low-voltage computer circuits and on the connections by which unit boards plug into motherboards, since the voltages are typically below 5 or 6 V. They can be particularly severe with sensor electrodes such as those used with electrocardiographs and similar instruments. One typical approach to correcting socketing problems, used where highest reliability is required, is to gold-plate the mating contact areas. Application of a non-oxidizing coating that will also have a lubricating effect can be helpful; some kind of petroleum jelly is an alternative. Most components are either soldered or welded onto circuit boards for this reason. When one is confronted by this kind of a problem in a practical system, it is good practice to rub all available contacts with a coarse eraser.

The nature of integrated circuits is such that parasitic diodes cannot be avoided in their structures, although their effects can be minimized, particularly on thin-film integrated circuits. Parasitic coupling effects often can be minimized by proper use of inverting barriers. *See Integrated circuits.*

***Component ratings.*** Circuit components are rated to indicate the conditions below which they can probably provide a specified kind of service without failure and above which they cannot function without excessive chance of failure. In reality, probability of failure is usually a continuous function of operating conditions. When a circuit must be designed to achieve a specified reliability and must simultaneously meet conflicting operating requirements, it is important to recall that the MTBF of electronic components is halved by temperature rises of 35–55°F (20–30°C). Since active devices in particular must be characterized in terms of their output currents, and the applied voltage is a secondary parameter, it is important to design for minimum supply voltage in the output circuit that will ensure proper operation. (This is another reason that the above-mentioned kappa is very important.) Applications where these considerations are critical are in aircraft and missile equipment and in much military equipment.

Ratings are normally a function of operating environment. For example, a pair of resistors may be able to dissipate 5 W of power each in a given environment; yet both might fail under the same environment if they were mounted in contact with one another. Common ratings are power dissipation, peak voltage or peak inverse voltage, peak pulse current or maximum average current, and insulation resistance or dielectric strength. Power dissipation is a sensitive function of such factors as heat radiation, convection, and conduction; it should be specified in terms of these factors.

The maximum voltage a component can withstand normally is a function of the temperature of the component, and may be a function of humidity, ambient air pressure, and similar factors. It may also be a function of the method of use. For example, a capacitor used in an electronic flash unit can be intermittently charged to a voltage significantly higher than the safe voltage at which it can be steadily operated as a filter component in a high-current power supply.

***Environmental factors.*** Environmental conditions under which any electronic circuit operates must be considered. Already mentioned is the importance of temperature; it may range between −50 and +150°F (−45 and +65°C) ambient. Equipment may encounter environmental conditions of up to 100% humidity with salt air conditions, air with high dust content, and atmospheric pressures from below sea level to interplanetary space.

Steps commonly taken to protect equipment against such adverse environments include selection of specially designed components or subassemblies, use of fungus-resistant insulating varnishes, drying and filtration of air, circulation of cooling air, and maintenance of a positive air pressure differential between the container housing the circuits and the external environment. Protection of circuits for field use requires specialized engineering experience.

***Stabilization of circuits.*** The stability of a circuit is a function of the ranges of environmental and operating conditions over which performance must remain within specified tolerances. Because characteristics of electronic circuits drift to a greater or lesser extent, they can change with both environment and with time. Control of these changes is simplified by designing circuits in terms of parameters having the least significant stability problems and in ways that minimize the effects of the remaining parameters.

Typical circuits using electron tubes or transistors are often stabilized by control of the steady-state current flowing in the output circuit because forward admittances can generally be specified with considerable precision in terms of instantaneous output current. When necessary, feedback or degeneration, achieved by introduction of output signal into the input of an amplifier, helps stabilize amplifier characteristics. Preaging, whereby a circuit operates in a prescribed environment for a predetermined time prior to testing or use, may cause it to complete most of its drifting so that, thereafter, operation remains adequately stable.

***Minimum phase considerations.*** Voltage gain in circuits is much more critical than current gain because the phase stability of a circuit can be severely degraded from feedback effects that are voltage-gain-sensitive. In particular, achieving minimum phase characteristics is very important in electronic instrumentation and in color television. The voltage-gain limitation of approximately 10 per stage was clearly documented during World War II, and it has been repeatedly confirmed since. Yet it is now very difficult to calculate the voltage gain as a function of operating conditions based on the data normally made available on active devices. The use of kappa largely circumvents this problem and helps both in the stabilization and in the improvement of MTBF for circuits and systems.

***Electronic circuit tests.*** Tests normally made on electronic circuits may be classified into (1) engineering design (worst case) tests, (2) production limit tests, (3) functional tests, and (4) failure (or repair) tests. Engineering design tests are performed to verify that the engineering design results in the required performance with production-tolerance components and that it will meet specifications under all conditions likely to be encountered in use. Production limit tests verify that tolerance limits established in design are met by production equipment. Limits may not be met because of changes in components resulting from procurement difficulties. Functional tests serve to assure that the unit continues to function within tolerances in the field-use environment. Failure tests are used to locate failure and diagnose its cause. The number, kind, and severity of the tests applied depend on the nature and intended function of the equipment.

Electronic equipment intended for home use (radios, televisions, hi-fi equipment, stereo equipment, computers, video recorders and players, tape recorders, intercoms, special telephone equipment, and so on) being sold in a highly competitive market may only be tested to ensure initial operation in such an environment. Equipment intended for a radio or a television station or for use as part of a computer or an industrial control system will be tested much more thoroughly, both for the relatively moderate environmental conditions it normally must survive and for stability during expected service life. Field equipment, particularly for military use, and other equipment on whose continued operation many lives may depend, are given extremely rigorous performance and environmental tests.

***Engineering design tests.*** After a trial design has been established, a laboratory model is constructed and tested to measure characteristics of the circuit. During these tests, values of components are varied, supply voltages are varied, and a variety of active devices or integrated circuits representing the full expected range of acceptable units is substituted within the model in a way to stress its capability of operating correctly in as severe a manner as appears to be meaningful. The extent of these tests depends on the application and the number of units to be made and on the innovations in earlier equipment of similar nature.

Tests on the engineering model are not necessarily conclusive, however. For example, a circuit may function as intended in the presence of parasitic conductances and capacitances existing in the model; yet it may not function in the prototype because these parasitic conductances and capacitances are significantly different from those in the engineering design. As a consequence, a series of engineering design tests is made on the final prototype model to determine whether production problems are likely to occur. Any significant change in test limits between engineering and prototype models, unless explainable in terms of known changes in the design or structure, may be cause for a further study. The prototype will be given the full spectrum of tests; for military equipment this includes temperature, cycling, humidity, salt spray, fungus, vibration, and mechanical shock, as required. Life tests to determine the mean-time-before-failure (MTBF) can also be applied, either normally or under overstress conditions as indicated in the performance specifications.

***Production line tests.*** Whereas the microprocessor has made possible greatly improved means for testing circuits, it has also resulted in vastly increased complexity in what can be done transparently (automatically) in military and space-probe instrumentation. The computers that run the automatic test equipment can control signal generators, waveform generators, synthesizers, and testing and measuring equipment of almost any sort. The main problem is the cost of the specialized equipment and operating software, and of the skilled operators. These requirements limit the applicability of sophisticated technology to either very large-volume-production items or to extremely costly and critical items. For complex circuits, simply verifying the correctness of wiring may require such automatic test procedures (**Fig. 4**).

In general, it is necessary that testing of assemblies be done as they are completed and before they are introduced into a higher level of assembly. This kind of testing will correct internal errors, and if the sources and sensors used are sufficiently similar to the actual operating environment, the test can ensure that the boards that pass are in fact compatible with the balance of the system. For such equipment as computers or guidance systems, a hierarchy of such in-line tests aid in ensuring that each subassembly has been properly manufactured before it is built into the next higher assembly.

Choice of circuit boundaries may be influenced as strongly by production test requirements as by circuit functions. That is, if packaging of a multiplicity of circuits into manufacturable subassemblies divides circuits into units that can be tested independently of each other, both production testing and field failure testing can give results directly related to the units under test. As a consequence, manufacturing can be more economically controlled, and field troubleshooting and maintenance can be more quickly completed.

Production tests may also call for a small percentage of production assemblies to be put through full engineering design final tests. This procedure gives further assurance that significant unexpected changes have not occurred to cause production tests to become meaningless.

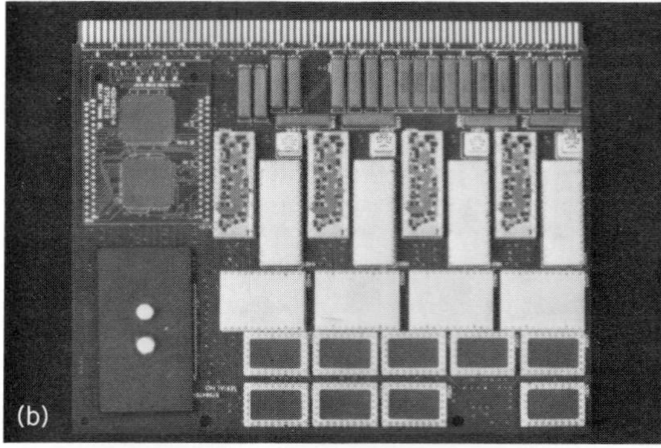


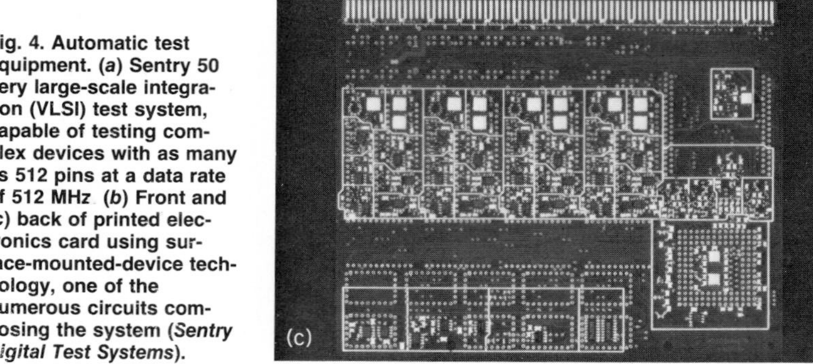


**Fig. 4. Automatic test equipment. (*a*) Sentry 50 very large-scale integration (VLSI) test system, capable of testing complex devices with as many as 512 pins at a data rate of 512 MHz (*b*) Front and (c) back of printed electronics card using surface-mounted-device technology, one of the numerous circuits composing the system (*Sentry Digital Test Systems*).**

***Automatic test equipment.*** The development of computers has led to interest and activity in the development of automatic test instrumentation. The military and NASA in particular have participated in the development of these systems, since in space flight or in battle the time lost in attempting to resolve failures can mean the difference between life and death. The development of an inexpensive microprocessor has proven to be the key to this problem, as it is possible to put a microprocessor in a system that is dedicated to the function of verifying the readiness of the system for operation, and to identify any problem areas that exist so that replacements can be substituted for apparently failed subsystems. These systems will actually print out information that for practical purposes defines the specific malfunction. They read sensors with the help of analog-to-digital converters, compare the results against data stored in a reference memory called a read-only memory (ROM), and print out the results. Tens of thousands of readings may be made every second, and a whole system can be evaluated in seconds. The result is that much more complex systems can be used effectively than was possible in the past. *See* Analog-to-digital converter.

***Statistical test methods.*** Because of the importance of failure-free operation during such activities as aircraft or space flights, accurately predictive test methods are essential. In the Department of Defense, a special set of production-limit tests has been developed for use in evaluating electronic circuits that must meet stringent requirements. These are based on statistical methods, because 100% testing is neither wise nor economical even if the tests can be nondestructive.

For statistical methods to be applicable, all circuits of a given type (the test population) must share common characteristics. Consequently, the first step in preparing for statistical tests is to sort out those factors that cannot be handled statistically and to test them separately. Tests may show that dissipation or voltage breakdown failures are occurring with one or two elements of a circuit. Such failure modes must then be analyzed independently. Any predominant cause of failure must be treated separately; only those causes of failure not occurring abnormally often can be treated statistically.

The Department of Defense, in particular, maintains a list of components meeting specific tests which it has found important in military applications. Such a list, called a qualified parts list (QPL), provides a basis for parts selection for an electronic circuit to which statistical methods could be applied. The fact that a component has a QPL designation does not necessarily assure that it will be satisfactory for a given application. The circuit designer should make certain that his method of application is compatible with all conditions for which the part was tested. In a circuit so designed, all parts can be expected to withstand the test conditions equally.

Another condition needed before statistical theory can be applied in electronics is the basis for defining acceptance. Too high an acceptance level raises the producer's risk, which in effect measures the probability that many circuits in a production lot will be satisfactory but that the test samples will fail. Too low a level increases the user's risk, which measures the probability that the user will accept some defective merchandise. These risks contribute to the determination of the acceptable quality level (AQL). Sufficient samples are then tested from a production lot to measure this level to the required confidence.

***Reliability.*** Many specifications now contain reliability clauses, requiring the contractor to estimate the expected MTBF to demonstrate compliance with the estimate. A test for circuit characteristics can be useful if data are properly used. The question is, what constitues a failure? In field equipment designed to be operated by an untrained, or relatively untrained, individual, any adjustment required by the equipment could represent a failure, whereas if the field equipment is meant to be operated by a trained technician thoroughly versed in its operation, only an unexpected interruption of operation might represent a failure.

***Functional tests.*** In such equipment as computers, radars, military electronic systems, and television networks, it is considered good practice to provide functional tests which measure the conformance of the equipment to the overall system specifications just prior to its use. This kind of test is particularly important in satellite and missile tracking systems and in electronics associated with expensive experiments. Typically, monitors serve this function for television stations, although much more elaborate backup measuring systems are used in the latest systems. These are made necessary by the phase stability requirements vital in color television. In addition, a variety of general-purpose test equipment is usable for function and repair tests.

***Failure tests.*** No electronic equipment or system can be made to be failure-free. As a consequence, it is necessary to have test equipment capable of diagnosing the causes of failure so that repairs may be made quickly and easily. Self-contained and easily accessible equipments such as radio and television receivers can often be tested adequately with such simple test equipments as a signal generator, an oscilloscope, and a volt-ohmmeter. This kind of testing is simplified through the use of schematics having supplementary tables of test-point voltages and resistances.

Failures of plug-in components or circuit assemblies are usually found relatively easily by substitution of a unit known to operate properly for the one suspected to be the cause of the failure.

With complex industrial and military equipment, construction is usually based on replaceable subassemblies, each such subassembly having test points for diagnostic systems. These test points serve, first, for location of the defective subassembly within the equipment and, second, for localization of the failure to a component or integrated circuit of the subassembly. *See* CIRCUIT (ELECTRICITY).

*Keats A. Pullen*

***Bibliography.*** Army Material Command, *Reliable electronic circuits*, AMCP 706–124, (NTIS 008-020-00602-5); P. M. Chirlian, *Electronic Circuits: Physical Principles, Analysis, and Design*, 1971; C. F. Coombs, Jr., *Printed Circuits Handbook*, 2d ed., 1979; C. A. Holt, *Electronic Circuits: Digital and Analog*, 1978; K. A. Pullen, On FET devices, *Electr. Device Lett.*, no. 69, p. 11, March 1984; K. A. Pullen, On some reliability implications of electronic circuit design, *IEEE Trans. Reliability*, R-32(1):106–110, April 1983; D. L. Schilling and C. Belove, *Electronic Circuits: Discrete and Integrated*, 2d ed., 1979.

## Clamping circuit

An electronic circuit that effectively functions as a switch to connect a signal point to a fixed-reference voltage or current level, either at a specific time interval or at some prescribed amplitude level of the signal itself. The circuit is also called, simply, a clamp. Clamps are frequently used to reset the starting level of periodic waveforms, such as sweep generators, and to establish a direct-current (dc) level in a signal which may have lost its dc component because of capacitance coupling. They are also used in many frequency and voltage comparison circuits and in control circuits.

The basic elements of a clamping circuit are shown in **Fig. 1**. The clamp between terminals *A* and *B* is shown as a switch *S* in series wtih reference voltage $V_R$, having a large resistance $r_R$ when the switch is open and a small resistance $r_F$ when it is closed.

**Voltage-amplitude-controlled clamp.** In **Fig. 2***a* the diode functions as a clamp whenever the potential at point *A* starts to rise above $V_R$; then the diode is in its forward-biased condition and acts as a very low resistance. Such a clamp is referred to as a voltage-amplitude-controlled, or continuous, clamp. The circuit of Fig. 2*b* is similar, except that the polarity is

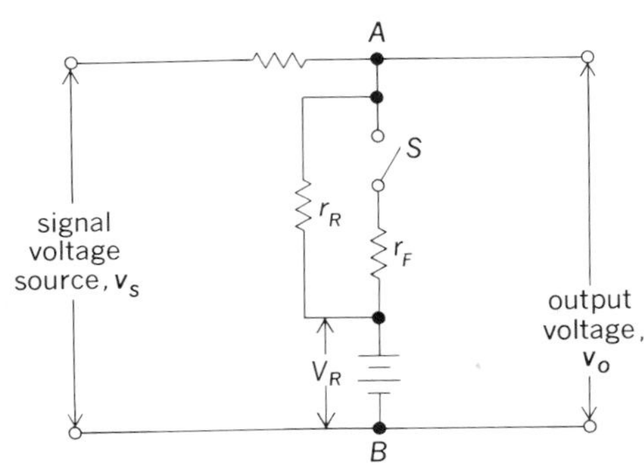


**Fig. 1. Clamp elements.**

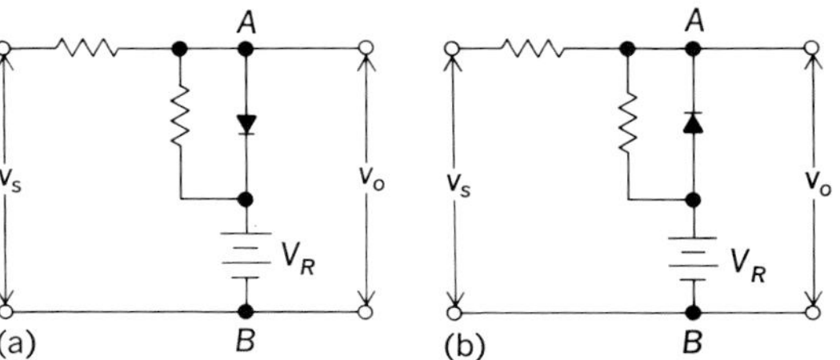


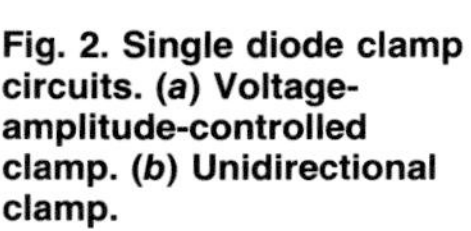
**Fig. 2. Single diode clamp circuits. (*a*) Voltage-amplitude-controlled clamp. (*b*) Unidirectional clamp.**

reversed. Point $A$ is connected to $V_R$ through a low resistance whenever the potential at point $A$ drops below $V_R$. These clamps function only when a fixed polarity of signal with respect to $V_R$ appears at point $A$, and are therefore referred to as unidirectional clamps.

**Keyed, or synchronous, clamp.** If a clamp functions at specific time intervals controllable from separate voltage or current sources rather than from the

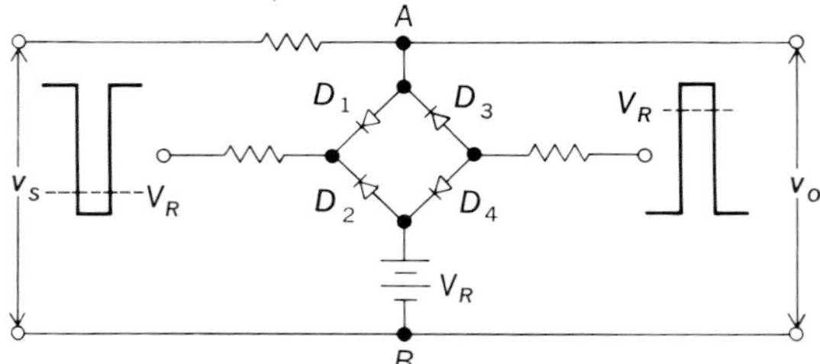


**Fig. 3. Four-diode bidirectional keyed clamp. *D* = diode.**

signal itself, it is a keyed, or synchronous, clamp, and the sources, usually pulses, used to actuate the clamping action are called keying, or clamping, pulses. Such a keyed clamp may be unidirectional but more often it is a bidirectional clamp, defined as a clamp that functions at the prescribed time irrespective of the polarity of the signal source at the time the keying pulses are applied.

A bidirectional clamp using four diodes with two opposite-polarity keying pulses is shown in **Fig. 3**. The peak of the negative pulse is established at a level negative with respect to $V_R$, casuing $D_2$ to conduct heavily when the pulse is applied, while that of the positive-going pulse is above $V_R$, causing $D_4$ to be forward-biased and to conduct heavily. If, at the same time, point $A$ is above $V_R$, $D_1$ conducts and point $A$ is clamped to $V_R$, while if it is below $V_r$, $D_3$ conducts and point $A$ is clamped to $V_R$. When point $A$ is exactly at $V_R$, all diodes are forward-biased and conducting. Between clamping pulse intervals, all diodes are reverse-biased, and the clamp is open. A unidirectional keyed clamp results if the left or right pair of diodes, together with their keying pulses, is eliminated.

In form, the bidirectional clamp is similar to the essential element of the diode transmission gate and the sample-and-hold circuit, and the voltage-controlled diode clamp is the main element of the limiter. *See* Gate circuit; Limiter circuit.

**DC restorer.** A dc restorer is a clamp circuit used to establish a dc reference level in a signal without modifying to any important degree the waveform of the signal itself. For this function to be performed, the signal must have a self-contained reference level which repeats at periodic intervals. A typical example of such a waveform is that comprising the video signal of the television system. *See* Television.

An example of a simple waveform, assumed to be periodic at intervals of $T$, applied to a single-diode voltage-controlled clamp is shown in **Fig. 4*a***. Restoration of the peak of the waveform to the level of $V_R$ depends upon current flowing through the capacitance when the input level is above $V_R$ and the diode is forward-biased. The capacitance charges in the direction shown during such successive peaks, and the peak level is finally established at $V_R$. The circuit does not operate if the peak of the waveform at point $A$ is not above the level of $V_R$ initially. The reverse time constant $[R_1 + R_2r_R/(R_2 + r_R)]C$ must be long compared to the period $T$, while the forward time

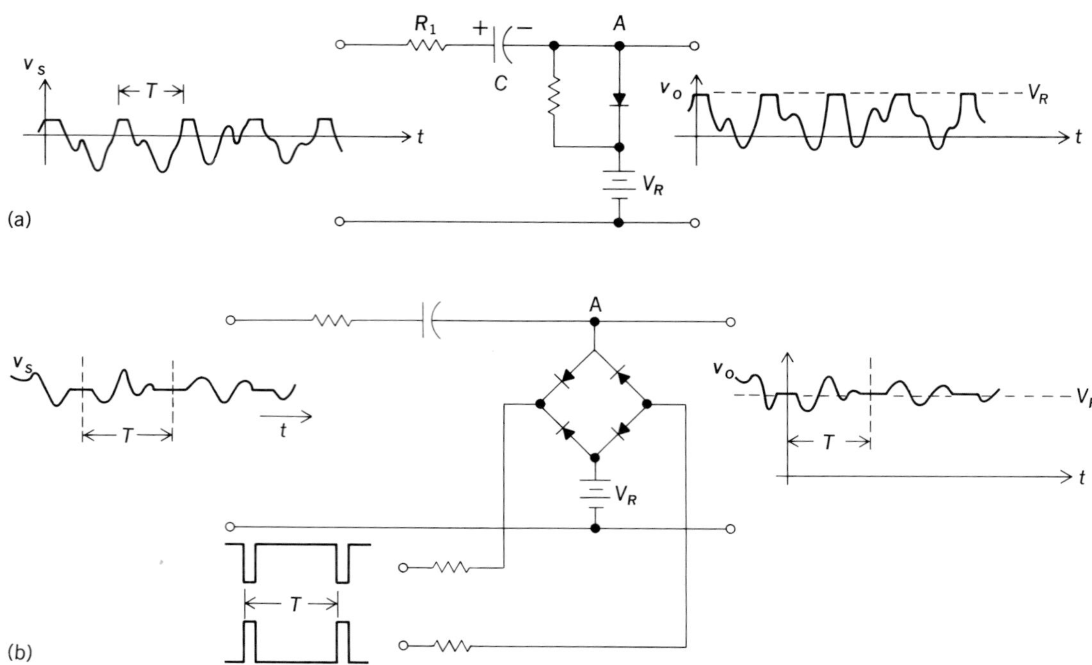


**Fig. 4. DC restorers. (*a*) Diode clamp. (*b*) Keyed clamp.**

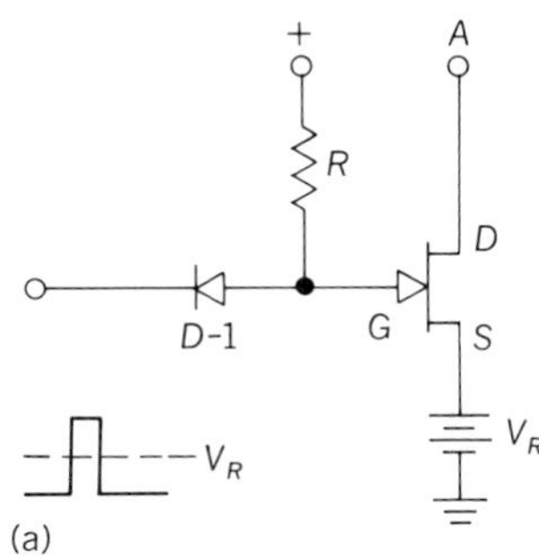


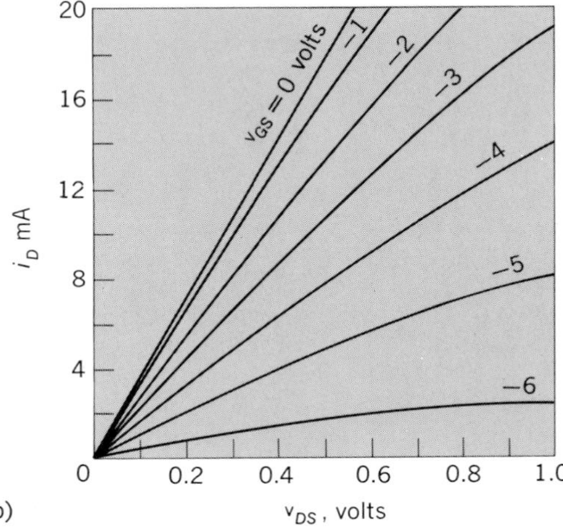


**Fig. 5. Example of bidirectional clamp which uses complementary field-effect transistors. (*a*) Circuit. (*b*) The low-voltage characteristics of a low-resistance field-effect transistor of the *n*-channel type.**

constant $(R_1 + r_F)C$ must be very short, with $(R_1 + r_F)$ as small as possible. A bidirectional keyed clamp is required to function as a dc restorer on the waveform shown in Fig. 4*b*. A bidirectional keyed clamp thus establishes the recurrent reference level regardless of the signal polarity between pulses.

**Triode clamp.** A three-terminal, high-impedance device such as a field effect transistor (FET) may be used as a keyed clamp to eliminate the need for balanced keying pulses. One common form of such a clamp is shown in **Fig. 5***a* using an *n*-channel junction FET having the low-voltage characteristics shown in Fig. 5*b*.

When no keying pulse is applied, diode *D*-1 conducts and the gate of the FET is held sufficiently negative with respect to the source that its drain current is cut off; hence, the drain-source terminals represent essentially an open circuit. When the keying pulse is applied, *D*-1 cuts off and sufficient gate current flows through *R* to cause the drainsource path through the FET to be a very low resistance, thus essentially short-circuiting point *A* to $V_R$. The junction FET is a symmetrical device with the source and drain interchangeable; therefore the clamp will function whether *A* is positive or negative with respect to $V_R$ before the clamp pulse is applied.

*Glenn M. Glasford*

***Bibliography.*** J. J. Brophy, *Basic Electronics for Scientists*, 4th ed., 1983; J. Millman, *Microelectronics*, 1979; J. Millman and H. Taub, *Pulse, Digital, and Switching Waveforms*, 1965; C. A. Schuler, *Electronics: Principles and Applications*, 1984.

## Clipping circuit

An electronic circuit that prevents transmission of any portion of an electrical signal exceeding a prescribed amplitude. The clipping circuit operates by effectively disconnecting the transmission path for the portion of the signal to be clipped.

**Diode.** A diode may be used as a switch to perform the clipping action. The direct-coupled circuit of **Fig. 1** represents a typical example. A time-varying signal voltage $v_s$ is applied to the input of the network containing a diode having terminals *p* and *n*. The diode functions as a very low resistance when *p* is positive and as a very high resistance when *p* is negative. Thus, if any portion of the waveform at *p* lies below the common reference or ground level, that portion will be removed, or clipped, and will not appear across output load resistance $R_L$, as illustrated by the three separate examples of output waveforms for load voltage $v_L$. If bias voltage $V_B$ is positive, the upper plot is typical; if it is zero, the upper half periods, as shown by the center waveform, will appear; and if it is negative, more than half of the peak-to-peak amplitude will be clipped, as shown by the lower waveform. The output waveforms are for a sinusoidal input as shown. In the plots of typical outputs, when $V_B \neq 0$, the dashed lines are the zero axis of this sinusoidal waveform from which the output is clipped. That is, the action of bias voltage $V_B$ is to displace the zero axis of the signal waveform from the zero axis of the output voltage. SEE DIODE.

In the circuit shown in Fig. 1, when the diode is nonconducting, assuming infinite diode resistance, the voltage $v_p$ at *p* is shown by Eq. (1), and when it is

$$v_p = \frac{R_2}{R_1 + R_2} v_s + \frac{R_1}{R_1 + R_2} V_B \qquad (1)$$

conducting, assuming zero diode resistance, it is shown by Eq. (2). The value of $v_p$ from both of these

$$v_p = \frac{R_2 v_s + R_1 V_B}{(R_1 + R_2)\left[1 + \dfrac{R_1 R_2}{R_L(R_1 + R_2)}\right]} \qquad (2)$$

equations must be the same at the time of transition from reverse to forward bias of the diode. Thus, the value of *v* that, when substituted into Eqs. (1) and (2), gives equal values of $v_p$ is the transition signal voltage $v_{s(\text{trans})}$. The value of this voltage is indicated by Eq. (3), which allows appropriate circuit constants

$$v_{s(\text{trans})} = -\frac{R_1}{R_2} V_B \qquad (3)$$

to be selected for a desired clipping level. The nonclipped waveform is attenuated by the divider network, which for a perfect diode is given by $v_L = v_p$ during signal transmission, in which case Eq. (2) applies for $v_L$. Clipping of the opposite polarity can be obtained by reversing the connections to the diode and the polarity of the bias voltage $V_B$.

Bidirectional clipping can be achieved by connecting two diodes as in **Fig. 2**. The circuit contains two bias voltages and a resistance network. Bias voltage $V_B$ is positive relative to point *b*, and bias voltage $V_A$ is negative relative to point *b*. In a region below a level determined by these voltages, network $R_1$, $R_2$, and $R_4$, and diode $D_1$, input voltage $v_s$ will produce no change in output voltage $v_L$; thus these parts of the

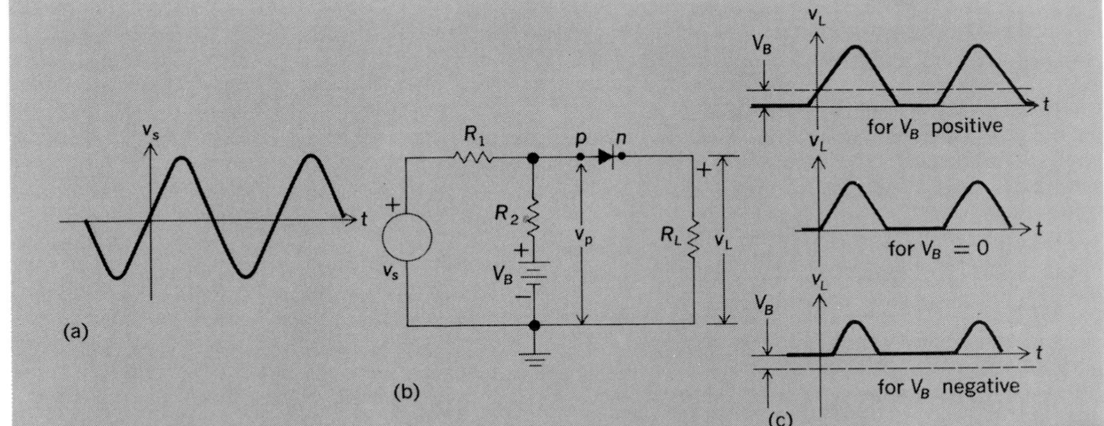


Fig. 1. An example of series diode clipping. (*a*) Waveform of time-varying input voltage. (*b*) Circuit diagram. (*c*) Waveform of output voltage $v_L$ when $V_B$ is positive, $V_B$ = 0, and $V_B$ is negative.

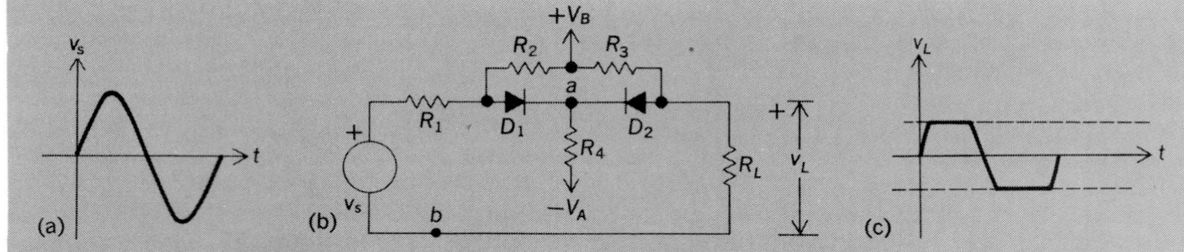


Fig. 2. Two-diode clipping. (*a*) Waveform of time-varying signal. (*b*) Circuit diagram. (*c*) Clipped waveform.

circuit set the lower clipping level. For signals $v_s$ above this level, both diodes can conduct up to a level at which the voltage at *a* rises above a value determined primarily by $V_B$, $V_A$, $R_3$, and $R_L$. When $v_s$ is above that value, $D_2$ becomes nonconductive. This action sets the upper clipping level. By proper choice of circuit values, clipping can be made approximately symmetrical about the axis, as shown by the output waveform $v_L$. Such a bidirectional clipper is sometimes referred to as a slicer, since it allows transmission of only a center section of a waveform.

**Triode clipper.** Clipping action may be achieved by using bipolar or field-effect transistors. To do so the bias at the input is set at such a level that output current cannot flow during a portion of the amplitude excursion of the input voltage or current waveform. A particular example, using a *p*-channel insulated-gate field-effect transistor, is shown in **Fig. 3**. Advantages of this particular device are that it operates normally with the gate forward-biased and that, with a single dc voltage supply in the source lead as shown, both the input and output voltages can be referenced to a common reference or ground potential. As indicated by load line $R_L$ on the set of characteristic curves, the gate is set at a dc voltage determined by $R_1$, $R_2$, and $V_{SS}$, so that at the output the axis of the

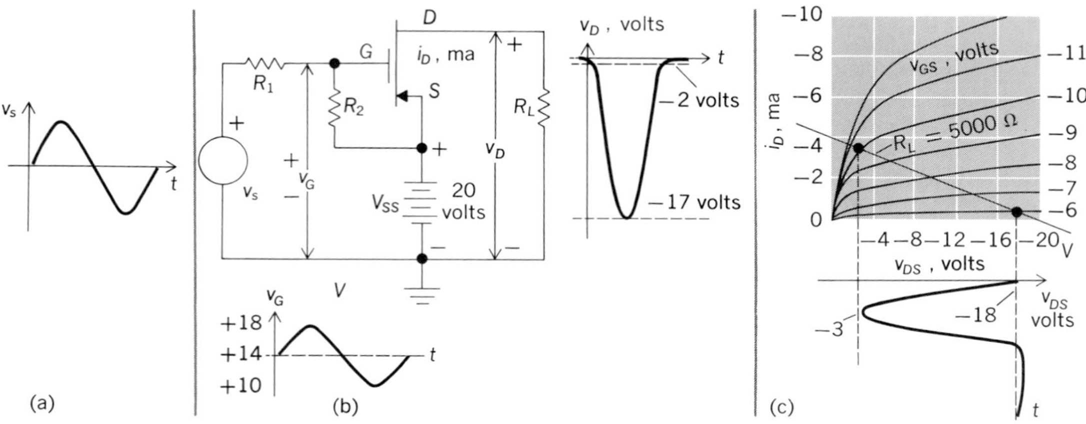


Fig. 3. Triode clipper using insulated gate transistor. (*a*) Input waveform $v_S$. (*b*) Circuit diagram with waveform of voltage $v_G$ from gate G to ground, and one of voltage $v_D$ across output load resistance $R_L$. (*c*) Relation of output waveform to transistor characteristic curves as determined by load line for an $R_L$ of 5000 ohms in circuit.

signal voltage waveform is near drain-current cutoff. Operation is along the load line determined by $R_L$. Excursions of the output waveform with respect to $V_{DS}$ as a reference, plotted directly below the set of characteristic curves, correspond to the actual output voltage waveform with respect to the common reference seen plotted to the right of the circuit.

This particular circuit can also function as a limiter if the input amplitude is increased, or if the input bias point is shifted such that the output-circuit saturation level is exceeded at very low values of $V_{DS}$. Likewise, clipping can be achieved using bipolar transistors by shifting their bias levels from the limiting conditions to values such that they have sufficient reverse bias to prevent output current from flowing for a portion of the amplitude excursion of the input voltage or current waveform. Slicing, as described above for the diodes, can be accomplished by a combination of limiting and clipping actions if the bias is adjusted properly and the input amplitude is sufficiently large. SEE LIMITER CIRCUIT; TRANSISTOR.

*Glenn M. Glasford*

**Bibliography.** J. J. Brophy, *Basic Electronics for Scientists*, 4th ed., 1983; A. P. Malvino, *Electronic Principles*, 3d ed., 1984; J. Millman and H. Taub, *Pulse, Digital, and Switching Waveforms*, 1965; J. Millman, *Microelectronics*, 1979; C. A. Schuler, *Electronics: Principles and Applications*, 2d ed., 1984.

## Closed-circuit television

A video communication system in which the signal is transmitted from the point of origin only to those specific receivers that have access to it by previous arrangement. Closed-circuit television enables visual information to be transmitted, often in parallel with audio information, to a selected audience or between selected groups of people. This private nature of closed-circuit television distinguishes it from broadcast television, in which all receivers in a given area have access to the broadcast signals.

**Applications.** The number of closed-circuit television installations is counted in the hundreds of thousands and far exceeds the number of television broadcast stations. These installations employ a wide variety of system arrangements tailored to the even wider variety of uses to which closed-circuit television is put. This article describes some of these applications.

***Monitoring.*** Closed-circuit television is used for a large number of different types of monitoring applications in which the remote viewing of an ongoing process or activity at a location provides economic, safety, or educational advantages. Examples include the monitoring of hazardous situations such as the input to a rock crusher, the interior of a furnace, or the operation of a process in a hostile environment. Closed-circuit television is used to monitor a number of remote locations from a centralized point, for example, to observe traffic flow in a city, for control; to observe critical locations in a bank or plant, for security reasons; or to read critical gages and instruments, for process control. It can be used to monitor microscopic or telescopic images, for greater ease of viewing; for example, closed-circuit television is used in hospital operating rooms so that new surgical techniques can be demonstrated to a large group of people. Often, a video tape recording is an integral part of the monitoring system, permitting later viewing or analysis.

***Educational applications.*** Educational institutions and corporations are also using closed-circuit television systems. A professor can lecture from a centralized classroom to students in a number of remote classrooms, or a corporate officer can make a presentation from company headquarters to employees in a number of remote office locations. Most of these applications consist of one-way television with two-way audio conference facilities to permit audience interaction. The development of economical video tape cassettes and associated recording, editing, and playback mechanisms has had a significant impact on the growth of closed-circuit television systems for educational purposes. The most rapid growth has been in connection with corporate training and employee information applications. Many businesses have found the use of video tape cassettes, coupled with internal closed-circuit television systems or a self-contained playback unit with a TV monitor, to be an economical, efficient way to communicate corporate policy, introduce a new product or sales program, and even conduct specialized training courses. In many of these applications, the video-taped program material is augmented by an individual who either broadcasts over the internal closed-circuit television system, as described earlier, or is actually present in the remote location. This person answers questions and makes possible audience interaction.

***Theater television.*** Because of nationwide and sometimes worldwide interest in certain sporting or entertainment events, one-way closed-circuit television systems are used to permit a number of geographically dispersed audiences to view the event simultaneously. In this application, the original television signal is transmitted and distributed to theaters which are equipped with large-screen television projection systems for displaying the received image to the paying audience.

***Video conferencing.*** Two-way closed-circuit television systems are used to permit groups of people in geographically separated locations to interact on both a visual and audio basis. With these systems, conference rooms or studios with specially equipped and controlled television cameras and monitors are used so that people can see and hear one another and exchange graphical information. Most conference rooms can comfortably accommodate four to nine active participants per location, with provision for additional people in the background. The systems are used by corporations, government organizations, and educational institutions as a substitute for, or supplement to, travel between the locations.

***Video telephone.*** Although usually intended to be used as a visual adjunct to telephony, video telephone equipment could serve many of the roles normally associated with closed-circuit television. SEE VIDEO TELEPHONE.

***Cable television.*** Community antenna television (CATV) or cable television systems are normally considered a type of closed-circuit television. As originally envisioned and implemented, these systems employ standard broadcast television signals which are received by a suitably located antenna and amplified and distributed through coaxial cables. This type of system can be used to provide reliable television reception in a community located beyond the useful range of broadcast television transmitters, or it can be used in an apartment building to avoid having each tenant install a separate antenna.

There are more than 3000 operating CATV systems franchised to provide service within defined geographic areas. Decisions by the Federal Communications Commission (FCC) have strongly influenced the development of these systems. As a result of FCC requirements, new systems must provide a capability of 20–40 television channels and two-way capability. Those cable television systems serving more than 3500 subscribers must be capable of television program origination and must devote some of this capacity to programming of community interest. Many of the largest cable television operators offer pay TV service, whereby subscribers have an adjunct to their home television set which permits them to receive special programs (first-run movies, sporting and cultural events) for an additional charge to their monthly service fee. Also, there is extensive ongoing experimentation to determine the feasibility of providing subscribers with customized services, including information retrieval, shop-at-home services, fire and burglar alarm monitoring, and other services which the large bandwidth and two-way nature of the new systems make possible.

**Technical considerations.** The range of signal formats and transmission means used in closed-circuit television is great. The signal formats are chosen to suit the particular use, and extend from high-resolution closed-circuit television applications, requiring bandwidths of 5–15 MHz, down to slow-scan television signals which require bandwidths as small as 2.5 kHz. The means of transmission range from broadband radio circuits to standard telephone message circuits.

The amount of visual information transmitted by a closed-circuit television system varies greatly, from color motion pictures for entertainment to monochrome still pictures for conveying information such as bank balances and signatures.

Pictures of moving objects require wide bandwidths and rapid scanning to provide adequate resolution and to avoid introducing a jerky characteristic into the motion. Common theater television systems, educational television systems, and video conferencing systems use the same scanning standards employed by broadcast television, with a bandwidth of about 4.2 MHz. A good-quality still picture can be transmitted over a narrowband circuit if the required transmission time can be accommodated.

The equation relating frame time $T$ in seconds, lines per picture height $N$, and bandwidth $B$ in hertz for a picture with a $4 \times 3$ aspect ratio (width to height) is $T/0.508\ N^2/B$. For a 525-line picture and a bandwidth of 4.2 MHz, $T = 1/30$ s, which is the frame period of standard broadcast television. For the same number of lines per picture and a bandwidth reduced to 2.5 kHz, $T = 56$ s.

Transmission facilities for systems located completely within a user's location and for distances up to 50 mi (80 km) normally use coaxial cable, shielded twisted-pair cable, or a short-haul microwave radio system. In certain cases, when conditions are favorable, laser-beam transmission systems are used. As a result of developments in the production of low-loss fiber optic cables, there has been extensive experimentation on the use of this medium for short-haul applications. Long-distance and intercity transmission are commonly provided as a service by a common carrier. Terrestrial microwave radio facilities are normally used in transmitting television signals for long distances. Increasingly, domestic and international satellite systems are used for transmission over greater distances or to reach otherwise isolated communities. Satellite systems are also being used to interconnect cable television systems for program sharing and for the distribution of signals for theater television applications. *See* Coaxial cable.

Technological advances in terminal equipment have broadened the potential applications for closed-circuit television systems. Among these developments are cameras that are capable of operating under very low ambient light conditions, and color cameras that are portable and simple to use. Developments in video tape cassette recording, editing, and playback mechanisms made the production of video program material easier and less expensive. Developments in video disk technology appear to have a great many potential applications, from mass entertainment to individual instruction in a variety of special fields.

The TV signal can be transmitted as a baseband video signal, with frequencies extending from only a few hertz to whatever bandwidth is required for the signal, or it can be modulated upon a carrier. For cable television, vestigial sideband modulation is normally used, and the signals are often placed at the same frequencies as those used for standard very-high-frequency (VHF) television broadcast channels. The latter approach permits the simultaneous transmission through a system of up to 12 different television signals, and a standard home television receiver can select the desired signal. The disadvantages of modulating the signal upon a carrier are the additional equipment required to perform the modulation, the wider bandwidth required in the transmission system, and the higher electrical attenuation, at higher frequencies, in coaxial cables. *See* Modulation; Television.

*Joseph J. Horzepa*

***Bibliography.*** R. Armstrong, *Closed-Circuit TV Installation, Maintenance, and Repair*, 1978; J. E. Cunningham, *Cable Television*, 2d ed., 1980; J. E. Cunningham, *Security Electronics*, 3d ed., 1983; N. J. Sambul, *The Handbook of Private Television*, 1982; L. A. Wortman, *Closed-Circuit Television Handbook*, 3d ed., 1974.

## Coaxial cable

An electrical transmission line comprising an inner, central conductor surrounded by a tubular outer conductor. The two conductors are separated by an electrically insulating medium which supports the inner conductor and keeps it concentric with the outer conductor. One version of coaxial cable is shown in **Fig. 1**, with periodically spaced polyethylene disks supporting the inner conductor. This coaxial is a building block of multicoaxial cables used in L-carrier systems. *See* Transmission lines.

The symmetry of the coaxial cable and the fact that the outer conductor surrounds the inner conductor make it a shielded structure. At high frequencies, signal currents concentrate near the inside surface of the outer conductor and the outer surface of the inner conductor. This is called skin effect. The depth to which currents penetrate decreases with increasing frequency. Decreased skin depth improves the cable's self-shielding and increases transmission loss. This loss (expressed in decibels per kilometer) increases approximately as the square root of frequency because of the skin effect. SEE ELECTRICAL SHIELDING.

Coaxial cables can carry high power without radiating significant electromagnetic energy. In other applications, coaxial cables carry very weak signals and are largely immune to interference from external electromagnetic fields.

A coaxial cable's self-shielding property is vital to successful use in broadband carrier systems, undersea cable systems, radio and TV antenna feeders, and community antenna television (CATV) applications.

Coaxial units are designed for different mechanical behavior depending upon the application. Widely used coaxials are classified as flexible or semirigid.

**Materials.** Conductors for coaxial cable are generally made of copper or aluminum. The low resistivity of these metals results in lower cable loss. A typical dielectric material is polyethylene; special grades are made with very low dielectric loss. Where mechanical factors allow, much of the space between inner and outer conductor is occupied by air. This may be done by using spaced insulating disks (Fig. 1) or expanded or spiraled insulation.

**Flexible coaxials.** These generally have a braided outer conductor and a stranded inner conductor. Insulation is made of solid or expanded plastic of a low-loss electrical grade. Since a single layer of braid has some air gaps between intersecting wires, a second layer of braid is placed over the first when shielding requirements are severe.

Flexible coaxials are used for high-frequency patch cords and intra- and interbay cabling. Very small-diameter coaxials are used to interconnect components on printed wiring boards. Since runs are short in these applications, loss is not generally important.

**Semirigid coaxials.** This class of coaxials finds the most extensive use in communications systems, such as cables used in long-distance terrestrial and undersea communications. Also, CATV and closed-circuit television often use semirigid coaxials. To minimize cable loss, the insulation may be of expanded plastic, effectively using air bubbles for up to 80% of the dielectric.

**Undersea coaxials.** To function reliably in a high-performance system in the ocean environment, undersea coaxials must meet severe requirements. Some of these are: (1) stable dimensions and predictable transmission characteristics under pressures of up to 11,000 psi (76 megapascals); (2) 25-year service lifetime; and (3) ability to withstand handling and scuffing. A solid polyethylene core withstands ocean pressure which would crush a cable with any air fill. The use of inert materials that resist attack by marine organisms assures the desired lifetime. The high-strength (300,000-psi or 2-gigapascals) steel strand and high-density jacket assure survival and continuity despite severe handling.

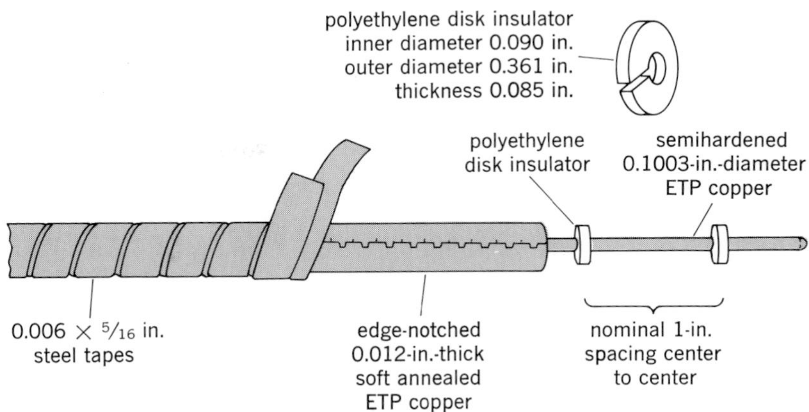


**Fig. 1. Air dielectric disk-insulated coaxial cable. 1 in. = 25 mm.**

The type of coaxial cable used in the most advanced analog undersea cable systems is shown in **Fig. 2**. The high-tensile steel strand provides longitudinal strength needed to lay or recover the cable in ocean depths of up to 4 nautical miles (7 km). The inner conductor is a high-conductivity copper tube, 0.48 in. (12 mm) in diameter, which is formed and swaged over the steel strand. Low-loss polyethylene is extruded over the inner conductor assembly to form the 1.7-in.-diameter (43.2-mm) cable core. To achieve an accurate (±0.001 in. or 0.025 mm) core diameter, the core is extruded slightly oversize and mechanically shaved.

In a further manufacturing operation, the 10-mil-thick (0.010-in. or 0.25-mm) copper outer conductor is formed over the cable core with an overlapped seam. A high-density polyethylene jacket, 2 in. (50 mm) in diameter, is extruded over the outer conductor to complete the cable.

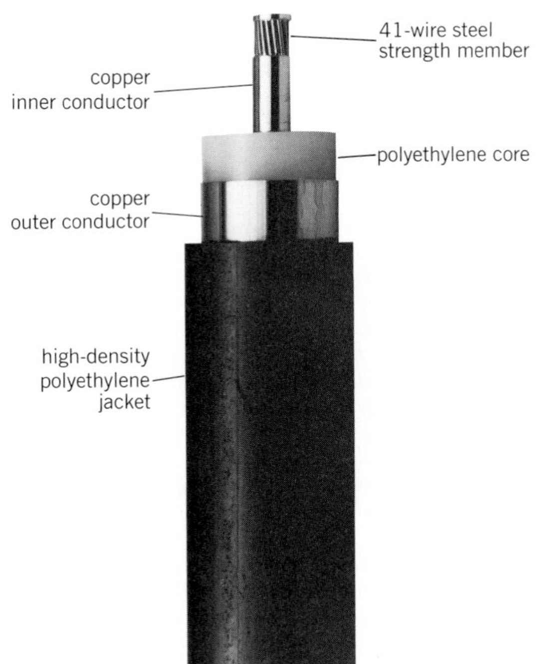


**Fig. 2. Deep-water armorless cable used in 4200-channel undersea systems.**

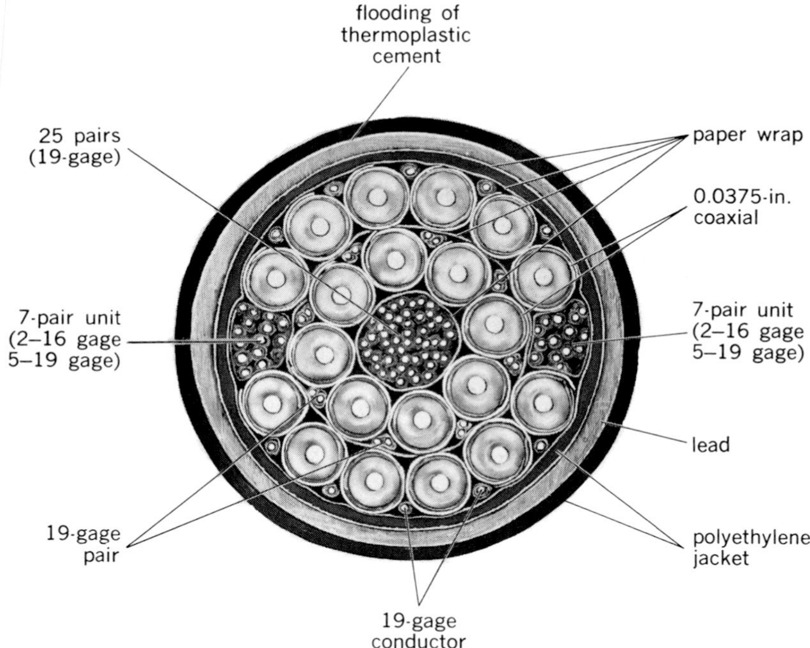


**Fig. 3. Construction of multicoaxial transmission line. 1 in. = 25 mm.**

**Terrestrial coaxials.** A single coaxial unit, which is used in the L3, L4, L5, and L5E carrier systems, is shown in Fig. 1. This unit uses polyethylene disks spaced 1 in. (2.5 cm) apart to keep the inner conductor centered. The outer conductor is then precision-formed around the disk-insulated inner conductor. Two layers of steel tape are overlapped to complete the unit. The tapes give the assembly mechanical stability and provide added shielding at low frequencies.

A coaxial unit such as that of Fig. 1 has low loss and excellent impedance characteristics. In the L5E system a pair of such coaxial units can carry 13,200 telephone calls. A cable carrying 20 of these coaxial units is shown in **Fig. 3**. A 22-unit coaxial version of this cable was used in later L5E installations. Fully equipped, this cable provides 132,000 telephone channel capacity over the 10 working coaxial pairs. The eleventh pair provides service protection for the 10 working pairs.

Very slight dimensional irregularities can result in small-impedance deviations in the cable. If such deviations are periodically spaced, they can produce reflections which cause large swings in the cable loss versus frequency. Hence, great care is taken in the design of the cable, and throughout manufacture. This care extends to raw materials, close dimensional control, careful machinery design and maintenance, precision qualification measurements, and quality control.

Two coaxial cables span the United States from east to west, with many intermediate and shorter installations. Such cables are widely used in North America, Japan, and Europe. Coaxial systems, along with microwave radio, provide most of the long-distance communication in the United States. *SEE COMMUNICATIONS CABLE*.

*S. Theodore Brewer*

## Coil

One or more turns of wire used to introduce inductance into an electric circuit. At power line and audio frequencies a coil has a large number of turns of insulated wire wound close together on a form made of insulating material, with a closed iron core passing through the center of the coil. This is commonly called a choke and is used to pass direct current while offering high opposition to alternating current.

At higher frequencies a coil may have a powdered iron core or no core at all. The electrical size of a coil is called inductance and is expressed in henries or millihenries. In addition to the resistance of the wire, a coil offers an opposition to alternating current, called reactance, expressed in ohms. The reactance of a coil increases with frequency. *SEE INDUCTOR*.

*John Markus*

## Coincidence amplifier

An electronic circuit that amplifies only that portion of a signal present when another enabling or controlling signal is simultaneously applied. The controlling signal may be such that the amplifier functions during a specified time interval, called time selection, or such that it functions between specified voltage or current levels, called amplitude selection. For example, the amplifier in a transmission gate operates on the basis of time selection where a control voltage of fixed amplitude is applied during a specific time interval. This voltage is the enabling waveform; it allows the amplifier to function normally only during the time it is applied. *SEE GATE CIRCUIT*.

A linear amplifier used to amplify a section of a waveform above or below specified voltage or current limits, as determined by a control signal, is an example of a coincidence amplifier that operates by amplitude selection. Limiting and clipping circuits that incorporate the function of amplification may be considered coincidence amplifiers. *SEE CLIPPING CIRCUIT; LIMITER CIRCUIT*.

A simple example of a coincidence amplifier that functions between two input voltage limits is shown in the **illustration**. This specific coincidence amplifier is sometimes referred to as a slicer of slicer amplifier. The transistor amplifier, in this case an emitter-coupled amplifier, is biased such that, until time $T_1$, input stage $Q_1$ functions as an emitter follower, but the voltage at the base of $Q_1$ is such that no current flows in its collector circuit until input level $V_1$ is reached. Between levels $V_1$ and $V_2$ both transistors are active, and an amplified output signal appears at the collector of $Q_2$. At time $T_2$, corresponding to level $V_2$, the input transistor becomes nonconducting and no further output is produced.

The same operation may be performed using *pnp* transistors with all bias and signal polarities reversed. The same function may also be performed using field-effect transistors or vacuum tubes as source-coupled or cathode-coupled amplifiers.

Such coincidence amplifiers, with their gains sometimes greatly magnified by positive feedback, are often used as elements in linear time-delay circuits. When such an amplifier is used and the interest is primarily in a pulse or other indication when a desired

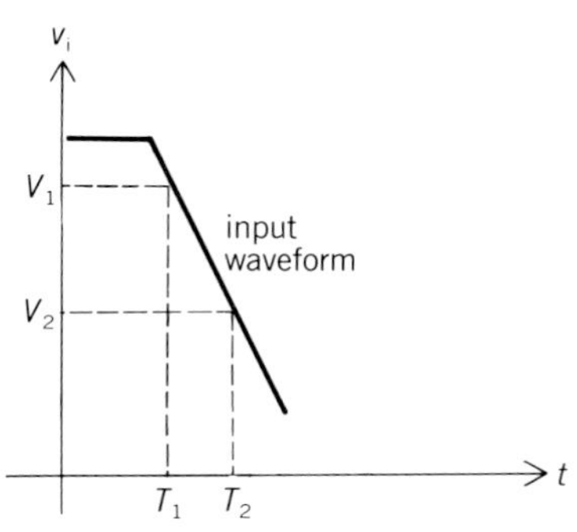


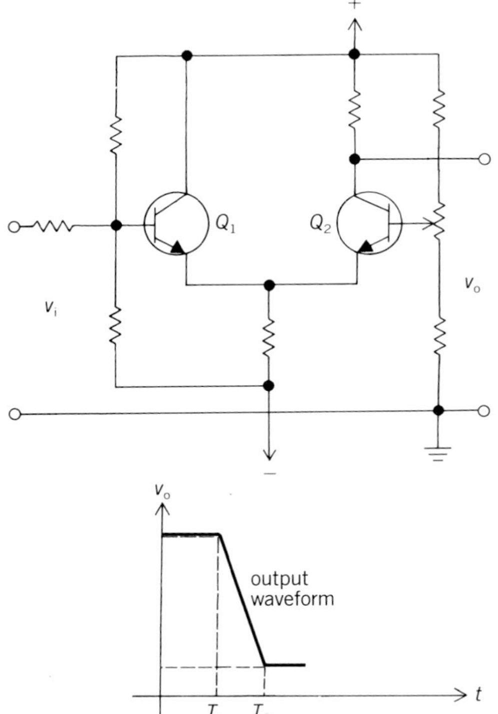


Simple coincidence amplifier.

level is reached rather than in preservation of the waveform itself, the term comparator is more often applied. However, the term coincidence circuit is sometimes used interchangeably when the concept of amplification is not specifically considered. In digital logic terminology the AND gate is an example of such a coincidence or comparator circuit. *See Comparator circuit*.

*Glenn M. Glasford*

## Color television

Transmission and reception of transient visual images in full color. The technique used for color television broadcasting in the United States is compatible with monochrome, or black-and-white, television. That is, color television signals are sufficiently similar to monochrome signals so that they produce acceptable monochrome pictures on black-and-white receivers while producing full-color pictures on color receivers. Conversely, a standard monochrome signal produces a satisfactory monochrome image on a color receiver. Compatible color television is based on a combination of the primary-color principle, conventional television technology, and special encoding techniques for combining primary-color television signals in such a way that they can be transmitted through a single broadcast channel.

**Use of primary colors.** Color television images are formed by combining three primary-color images. Although many sets of primary colors are theoretically possible (provided only that no combination of any two primaries in a set be capable of matching the third), the standard set which has proved to be most practical for color television consists of highly saturated red, green, and blue colors. The color kinescope, or picture tube, used to display the picture in a color television receiver can produce independent red, green, and blue images, usually in the form of tiny dots so closely intermingled that they cannot be resolved individually at the normal viewing distance. The three images are thus effectively fused by the visual system of the observer so that only the combined, full-color image is seen. *See Picture tube*.

**Color television cameras.** In the simplest type of color television system the three primary-color images

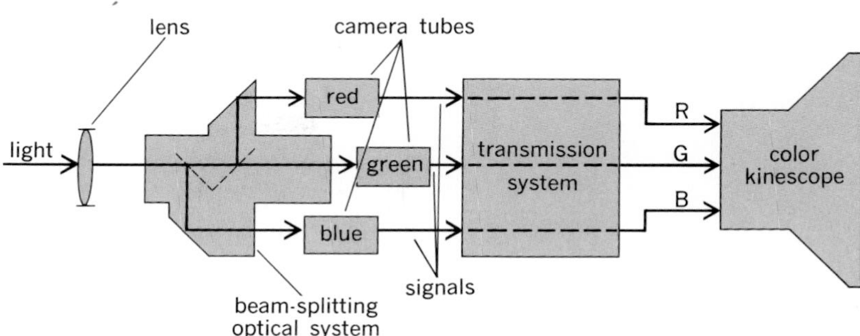


**Fig. 1. Simplified block diagram of a color television system.**

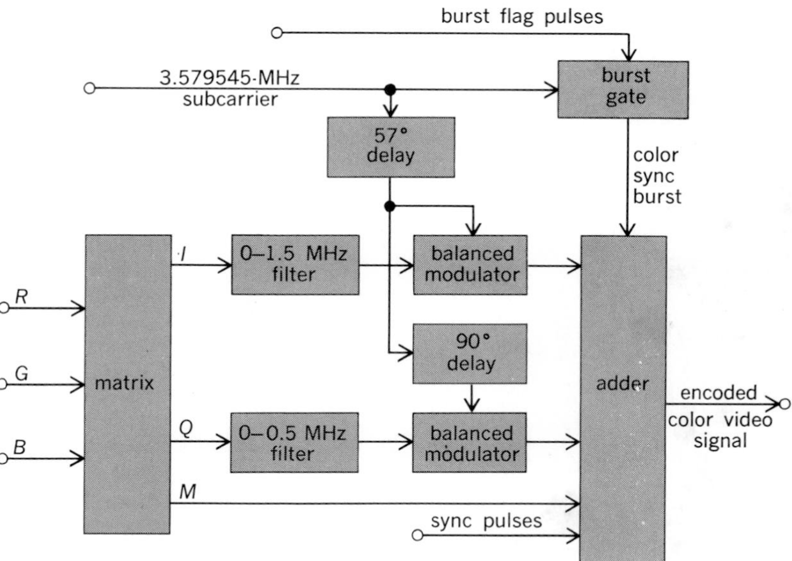


**Fig. 2. Block diagram of a compatible color encoder.**

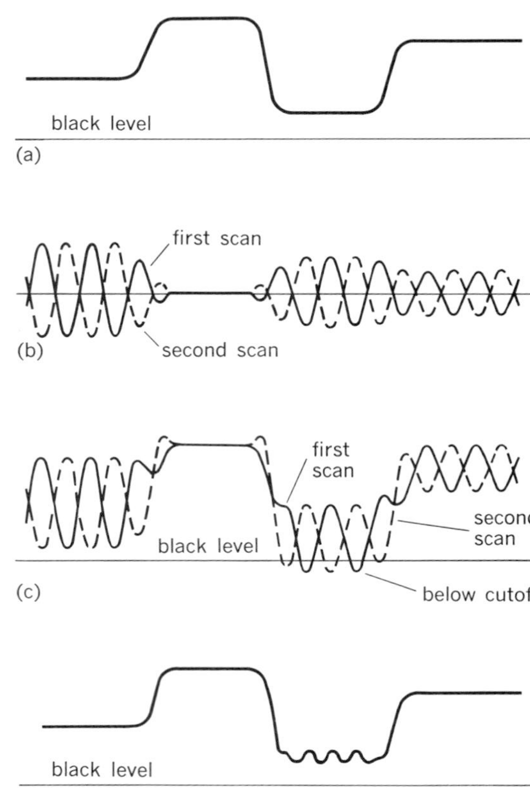


**Fig. 3. Several typical waveforms illustrating the frequency interlace technique. (*a*) Luminance signal. (*b*) Modulated subcarrier signal. (*c*) Sum of luminance and modulated subcarrier signals. (*d*) Average light output from two successive scans.**

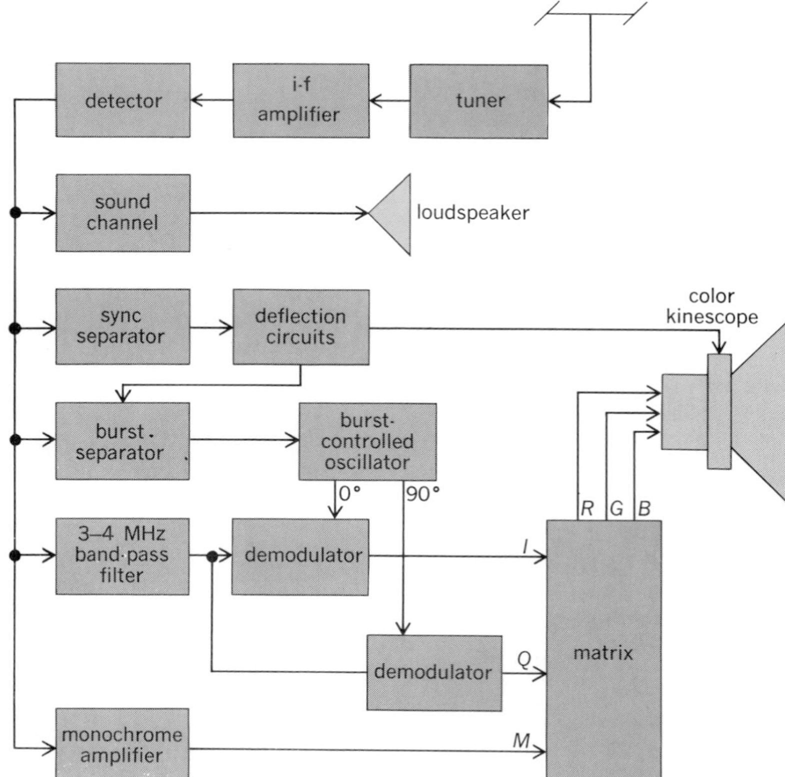


**Fig. 4. Simplified block diagram of a color television receiver.**

in the tricolor picture tube are controlled directly by video signals developed by three separate pickup tubes, adjusted to respond to red, green, and blue light **(Fig. 1)**. Close registration must be maintained among the three images so that the scanning beams in the three pickup tubes are always at the same relative points in their respective image areas. In most practical cameras beam splitters are used to form three separate optical images, and a common set of scanning circuits is used to drive three deflection yokes in parallel. The scanning pattern, horizontal and vertical deflection frequencies, and deflection-synchronizing techniques for compatible color television are the same as for monochrome television. *See Television camera; Television scanning*.

**Encoding and decoding.** Because of the great demand for television broadcast channels in the United States, it is not practical to utilize three separate channels for transmitting the red, green, and blue signals required to control a color kinescope. It is necessary, therefore, to encode the primary-color signals at the transmitter in such a way that they can be transmitted through a single television channel. The encoded color video signal contains three independent components, and is enough like a conventional monochrome signal to produce good images on monochrome receivers. Each color receiver contains decoder circuits (between the second detector and the kinescope) to retrieve from the color signal its red, green, and blue components.

***Color encoder.*** In a compatible color encoder **(Fig. 2)** the red ($R$), green ($G$), and blue ($B$) signals are first applied to a matrix, where they are cross-mixed in accordance with Eqs. (1)–(3). The signal desig-

$$M = 0.30\,R + 0.59\,G + 0.11\,B \quad (1)$$
$$I = 0.60\,R - 0.28\,G - 0.32\,B \quad (2)$$
$$Q = 0.21\,R - 0.52\,G + 0.31\,B \quad (3)$$

nated $M$ conveys luminance information; it is nominally equivalent to the signal that would be generated by a monochrome camera viewing the same scene as the color camera. That is, the $M$ or luminance signal controls the sensation of brightness. The $I$ and $Q$ signals convey chrominance information, which controls hue and saturation in the final image. The $I$ and $Q$ signals are reduced in bandwidth to about 1.5 and 0.5 MHz, respectively, in recognition of the fact that the human eye has limited resolving power for chrominance differences between small picture areas.

The $I$ and $Q$ signals are converted to modulated waves by means of a pair of balanced modulators. These modulated waves (including the necessary sidebands) are designed to fall within the 0–4.2 MHz video passband of a conventional television channel. The subcarrier inputs for the two modulators are both at the same frequency (3.579545 MHz), but are 90° apart in phase. When the modulated $I$ and $Q$ signals are added together, they form a two-phase-modulated wave (variable in both amplitude and phase) known as the chrominance subcarrier.

The complete color video signal is formed as the sum of (1) the chrominance subcarrier, (2) the monochrome or $M$ signal, (3) conventional synchronizing pulses, and (4) a special color synchronizing signal consisting of a brief sample (or burst) of the subcarrier frequency timed (by means of burst flag pulses) to occur shortly after each horizontal sync pulse. The purpose of the burst is to establish a frequency and phase reference for the receiver circuits that demodulate the chrominance subcarrier.

***Frequency interlace.*** The addition of a two-phase-modulated chrominance subcarrier does not prevent the monochrome component of a color signal from producing a satisfactory picture on black-and-white receivers because the subcarrier itself is frequency-interlaced. The subcarrier frequency is chosen as an odd multiple of one-half the horizontal scanning frequency, and is held in this relationship by counting circuits in the color sync generator. The waveform sketches of **Fig. 3** show how the frequency-interlace technique works. The top wave (Fig. 3*a*) is a small section of a typical luminance signal for one scanning line. Next is the modulated subcarrier signal (Fig. 3*b*) to be transmitted during the same interval. Because of its harmonic relationship to the scanning frequencies, the subcarrier reverses in polarity between successive scans (1/30 s), as indicated by the dotted line. There is usually no great change in the picture information from one frame to the next, so the luminance waveform and the modulation on the subcarrier remain essentially the same for the second scan. In Fig. 3 the complete color video signal (*c*) differs slightly from the luminance signal (*a*), but the subjective effect produced when two successive signals (*c*) are applied to a monochrome kinescope is approximately that represented by the average waveform (*d*). Persistence of vision tends to average the light output from several scans of each picture area, automatically cancelling most of the effect of the added subcarrier. The residual dot pattern, which results from imperfect cancellation, is not particularly objectionable.

***Color decoder.*** Basic functions performed in a color receiver are shown in **Fig. 4**. The tuner, intermediate frequency amplifier, detector, sound channel, sync separator, and deflection circuits are based on conventional designs. *SEE TELEVISION RECEIVER*.

The color decoder consists of the following circuits: (1) a burst separator, consisting of a gate circuit turned on by horizontal retrace pulses; the separated bursts are used to control a local subcarrier oscillator, which provides two carriers, 90° apart in phase, for demodulation of the chrominance subcarrier; (2) the monochrome channel, which passes the luminance signal component and rejects or attenuates the subcarrier frequency; (3) the chrominance channel, which consists of a band-pass filter centered at 3.579545 MHz, plus a pair of synchronous detectors to recover two independent components from the modulated subcarrier (these components need not necessarily be the same as the original *I* and *Q* signals; (4) a matrix that cross-mixes the monochrome signal and the demodulated chrominance signals to produce red, green, and blue signals suitable for driving the corresponding guns of a color kinescope.

*John W. Wentworth*

**Picture tube.** The color picture tube is an evacuated electronic device that transforms the electrical video signal into a full-color display. Its basic operation is similar to that of a black and white picture tube (or kinescope) in which a beam of high-velocity electrons, generated in an electron gun, is magnetically deflected so as to scan line by line the inside of the faceplate of the evacuated bulb. Light is produced by electron bombardment of the luminescent layer of phosphors. The intensity of the light is controlled by the video signal applied to the electron gun, which controls the number of electrons emitted at any given instant. *SEE CATHODE-RAY TUBE*.

To produce color, the color picture tube has a means to selectively excite one or more phosphors, each of which emits light of one of the three additive primary colors: red, green, and blue. Essentially, all present-day color picture tubes used in commercial television receivers employ the shadow-mask principle for selection of the primary colors.

In the shadow-mask tube, three electron guns provide three closely spaced, individually controllable electron beams which are deflected by a common magnetic deflection yoke. A shadow mask formed to the approximate spherical contour of the face of the picture tube is located about 0.6 in. (15 mm) behind the phosphor screen, which is deposited on the inner surface of the faceplate. The shadow mask is made of sheet steel and contains several hundred thousand small apertures. These apertures are associated with groups of screen elements of red, green, and blue light-emitting phosphors.

The relative position of the gun, shadow-mask apertures, and phosphor elements is such that the electron beam from one gun passes through the mask aperture and strikes only elements of one color-emitting phosphor. The mask shadows the other two phosphors. Thus, each gun can produce a picture in one of the three primary colors. The small size and large number of the phosphor elements make them blend together and appear indiscernible to the viewer's eye. By varying the relative brightness of each of the primary colors, a full-color picture or a black and white picture can be produced.

For many years the arrangement of phosphor elements was in the form of interlaced phosphor dots as shown in **Fig. 5**. For each trio of red, green, and blue light-emitting phosphor dots, there was a round aperture in the shadow mask. The diameters of the mask apertures were about 0.01 in. (0.25 mm), and each of the phosphor dots was about 0.013 in. (0.33 mm).

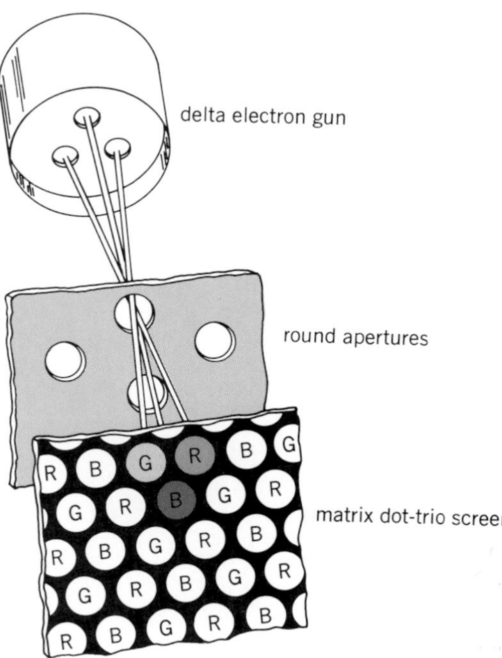


**Fig. 5. Diagram of dot-trio system, with red (R), green (G), and blue (B) phosphor dots. (*RCA Corp.*)**

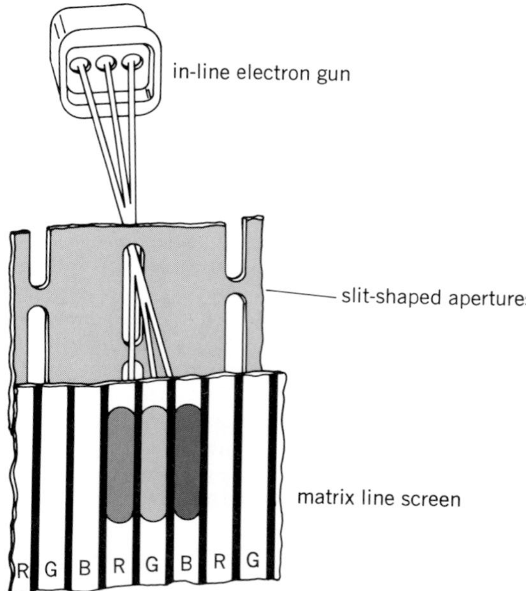


**Fig. 6. Diagram of in-line system with red (R), green (G), and blue (B) phosphor lines. (*RCA Corp.*)**

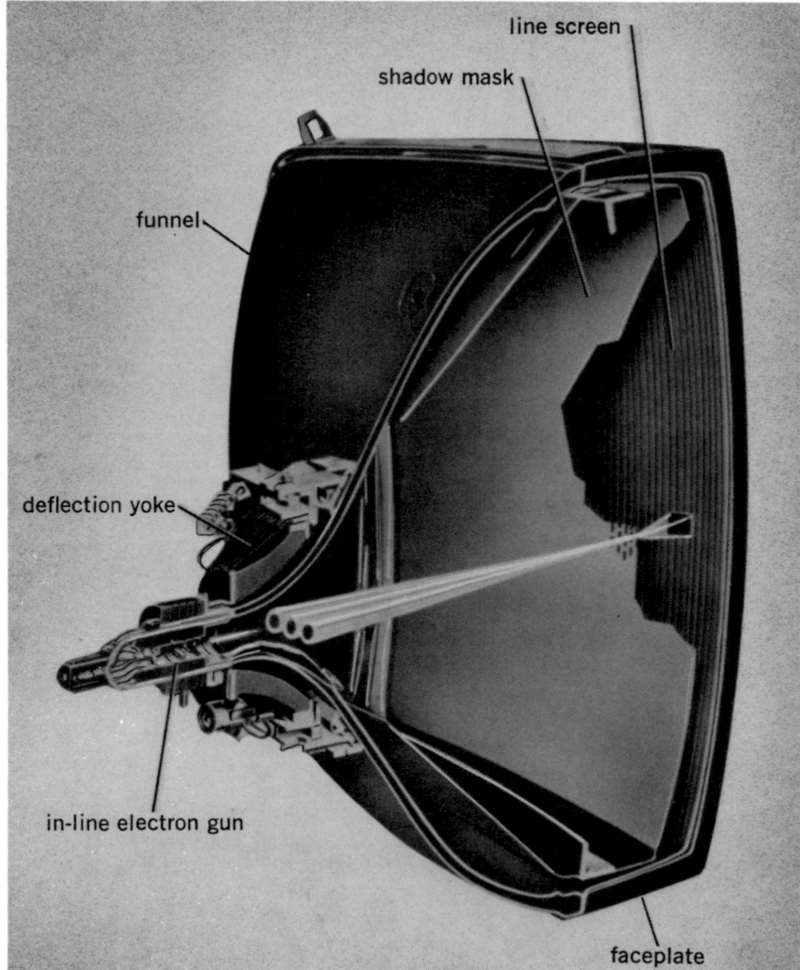


**Fig. 7. Cutaway view of a typical color picture tube. (*RCA Corp.*)**

The dot screen has been replaced by a line screen. In this system, vertical rows of alternate red, green, and blue phosphor lines form the screen. The shadow mask is composed of elongated apertures arranged in vertical rows, one for each trio of red, green, and blue phosphor lines on the screen. Small webs or crossties provide structural strength between the mask openings (**Fig. 6**). The width of the openings in the mask is about 0.006 in. (0.15 mm), and the width of each phosphor line is about 0.010 in. (0.25 mm).

The line screen is used with an in-line arrangement of the electron guns. This in-line arrangement permits ease in obtaining convergence or coincidence of the three beams at all points on the screen. Convergence is required to prevent color fringing that would result from noncoincidence of the three beams. The deflection yoke which scans the beams over the screen produces the convergence of the beam by its special field configuration. The position of the yoke must be precisely matched with the beam to obtain this condition.

To enhance contrast and light output, a black-matrix-type screen is used on most color tubes. In this type a black, light-absorbing material surrounds each phosphor element (Figs. 5 and 6). This black material, which covers about 30% of the screen area, reduces the reflection of ambient light and hence increases the contrast. The black matrix provides a "guard band" for any misalignment of the electron beam with respect to the desired phosphor element. A further improvement has been the use of a filtered or pigmented phosphor in which a red pigment is combined with the red light-emitting phosphor. These pigments reduce the reflection of ambient light and also enhance the contrast.

The bulb structure is made in two pieces (funnel and faceplate) for ease in fabrication of the tube. The mask is welded to a steel frame which is supported on leaf springs that engage tapered studs sealed in the sidewall of the faceplate. The two bulb parts are sealed together by a glass frit after the phosphor screen is deposited and the shadow mask inserted. A diagram of this type of picture tube is shown in **Fig. 7**. Tube manufacturing requires great accuracy: relative placement of phosphor lines and the shadow mask must be controlled to tolerances of a few micrometers. *See Television*.

*A. M. Morrell*

***Bibliography.*** D. G. Fink and D. Christiansen (eds.), *Electronic Engineers' Handbook*, 2d ed., 1982; C. N. Herrick, *Color Television: Theory and Servicing*, 2d ed., 1977; Howard W. Sams Editorial Staff, *Color-TV Field Service Guide*, 2 vols., 1971–1974; Howard W. Sams Editorial Staff, *Color-TV Training Manual*, 4th ed., 1977; R. G. Middletown, *Color TV Servicing Guide*, 3d ed., 1977; A. M. Morrell et al., *Color Television Picture Tubes*, 1974; A. M. Morrell, Design principles of RCA large screen 110° precision in-line color picture tube, *IEEE Trans. Consumer Electr.*, 22(1):1–7, 1976; T. Rzeszwski, *Color Television*, 1983; W. N. Sproson, *Color Science in Television and Engineering*, 1983.

## Communications cable

A cable that transmits information signals between geographically separated points. The heart of a communications cable is the transmission medium, which

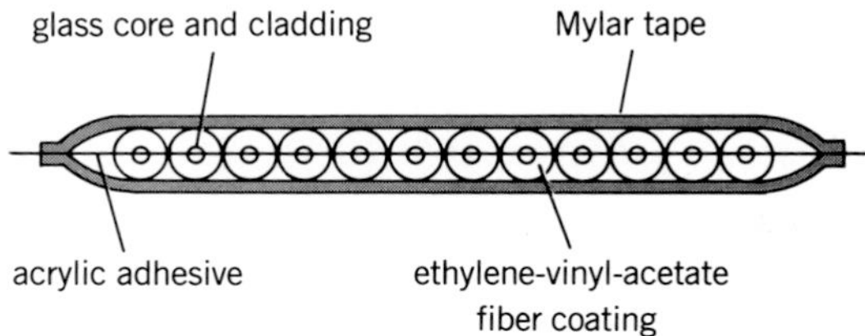


**Fig. 1. Cross section of optical fiber ribbon (12 fibers).**

may be optical fibers, coaxial conductors, or twisted wire pairs. A mechanical structure protects the heart of the cable against handling forces and the external environment. The structure of a cable depends on the application.

**Optical communications cables.** **Figures 1** and **2** show an optical communications cable for terrestrial use, where they may be installed aerially, or by direct burial, or in protective ducts. The cable used in the SL Undersea System is illustrated in **Fig. 3**. These cables were designed by Bell Laboratories for use in local and long-distance communications.

The terrestrial and undersea cables differ in several respects. First, the terrestrial cable requires only enough longitudinal strength to allow installers to pull the cable into ducts, or lay it in a trench. For the undersea cable, the high-strength steel strand allows it to be laid and recovered in ocean depths up to 4.5 mi (7315 m). A second difference is that the undersea cable must deliver as much as 1.6 amperes of direct current to the spaced, series-connected repeaters. Repeaters for the terrestrial system are generally located in buildings, and are powered from locally available sources. A third difference is due to the environment. Terrestrial cables are often installed in ducts. Hence, only limited protection is required against local hazards. The undersea cable, on the other hand, must withstand moderately severe handling in laying, and it sustains the full pressure of ocean depths. At 4.5 mi (7315 m) depth, this pressure is 10,700 psi (73.8 megapascals). To withstand this pressure, the cable is a filled design (no voids). The thick polyethylene outer layer provides electrical insulation for the power-carrying copper conductor, and is tough enough to resist severe handling. In addition to providing longitudinal strength, the steel strand overlaid with copper acts as a pressure cage to protect the core and fibers.

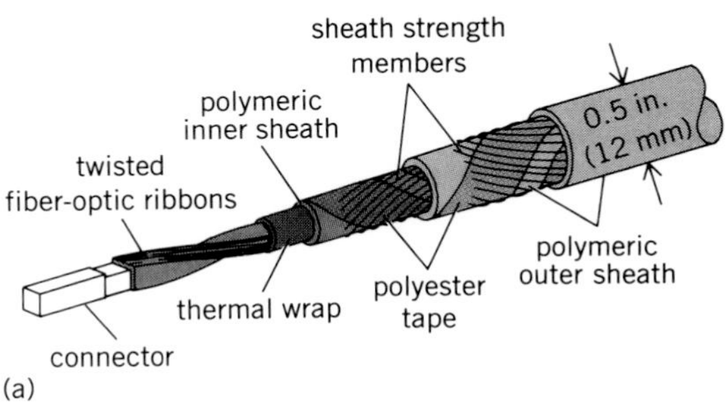


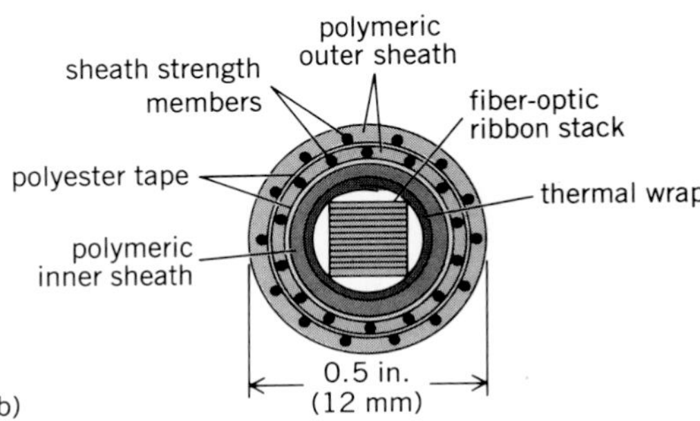


**Fig. 2. Multifiber cable for terrestrial use (144 fibers maximum). (*a*) Cutaway view. (*b*) Cross section.**

***Optical fibers.*** Signals in these cables are carried by light pulses which are guided down the optical fiber. In most applications, two fibers make up a complete two-way signal channel. The guiding effect of the fiber confines light to the core of the glass fiber and prevents interference between signals being carried on different fibers. The guiding effect also delivers the strongest possible signal to the far end of the cable.

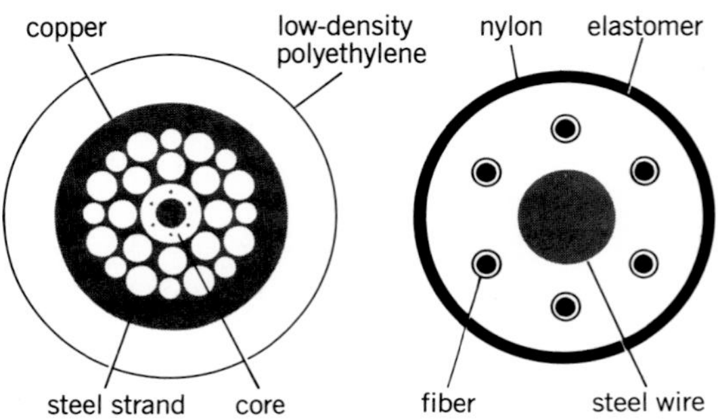


**Fig. 3. Optical-fiber cable for undersea systems. (*a*) Cross section. (*b*) Detail of cross section of core.**

Exceptionally pure silica glass in the fiber minimizes light loss for signals passing longitudinally through the glass fiber. Developers have realized fiber losses of 0.40 dB or less per statute mile (0.25 dB per kilometer), at a wavelength of 1550 nanometers. For such a fiber, the signal can travel 7.5 mi (12 km) before losing half its power, and can travel 50 mi (80 km) or more before requiring electronic regeneration. Coaxial cable systems require regeneration at much closer intervals. In the L5 and T4M Coaxial Cable systems, for example, signals are amplified or regenerated every mile (every 1.6 km).

***Signal regeneration.*** Optical cable systems are usually digital. Thus, information is coded into a train of off-or-on light pulses. These are detected by a photodetector at the far end of a cable span and converted into electronic pulses which are amplified, retimed, recognized in a decision circuit, and finally used to drive an optical transmitter. In the transmitter, a laser or light-emitting diode converts the electric signals back into a train of light pulses which are strong enough to traverse another cable span. By placing many spans in tandem, optical cable systems can carry signals faithfully for thousands of miles. *See* *Light-emitting diode*.

**Figure 4** shows an electronic regenerator for the SL Undersea Cable System. This regenerator will function in TAT-8 (the eighth United States–Europe transatlantic cable), scheduled for service in 1988. Six regenerators are mounted in a repeater housing. Thus, the repeater regenerates signals in three pairs of fibers. **Table 1** presents a summary of the characteristics of the TAT-8 cable system.

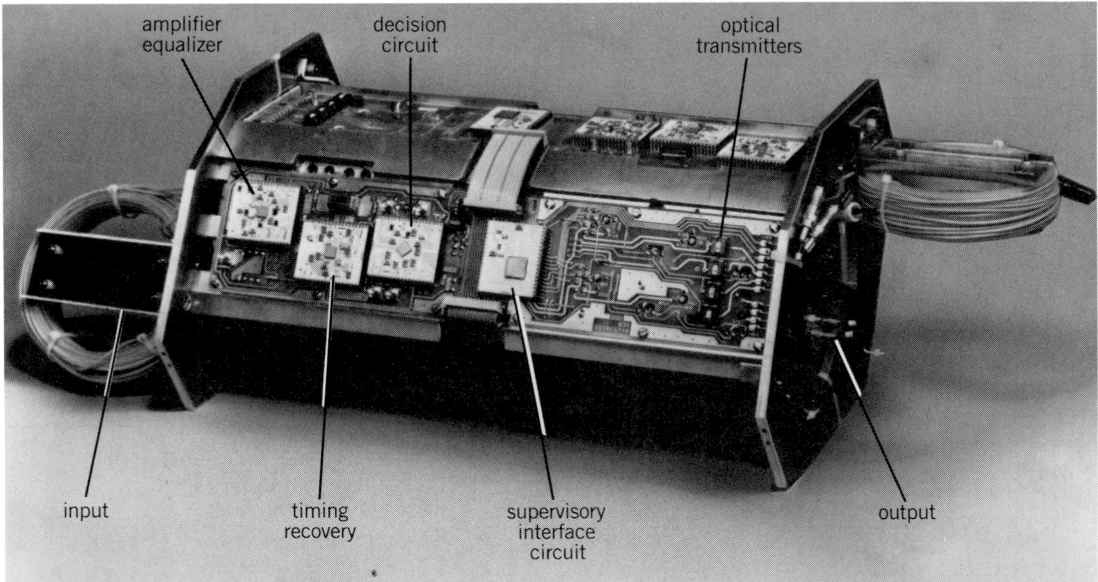


**Fig. 4. Regenerator for SL optical undersea cable communications system.**

**Table 1. Principal characteristics of eighth United States-to-Europe undersea cable system**

| Characteristic | Value |
|---|---|
| Line rate | 295.6 megabits/s |
| Number of service fibers | 4 |
| Number of protection fibers | 2 |
| Regenerators per repeater | 6 |
| Number of voice channels | 8000 |
| Number of conversations (with digital circuit multiplication equipment) | 40,000 |
| Optical wavelength | 1310 nm |

Optical communications cables are often used to carry input and output data to computers, or to carry such data from one computer to another. Then they are generally referred to as optical data links. The links are often short enough that intermediate regeneration of the signals is not needed.

***Repeaterless undersea cables.*** The trend toward lower fiber loss will allow the linking of mainland to offshore islands without undersea electronics and optics. Cable systems of up to 93 mi (150 km) are feasible, with future capability trending toward 125–150 mi (200–250 km). Parameters for a 93-mi (150-km) repeaterless cable system are shown in **Table 2**.

***Advantages.*** Optical communications cables have four key advantages over earlier metallic cables: much greater repeater spacings; enormous information capacity (many individual voice, data, or television channels); immunity from outside interference (other signals or noise); and smaller size and lower weight.

Because of these advantages and because optical cable technology is in its infancy, many additional applications can be expected to develop, and the cost of such communications cables can be expected to continue to decrease. Such communications cables require the conversion of the signal from optical to electronic mode and from electronic to optical at each regenerator. As the cost of lasers and optical detectors decreases, this complication will present less of a cost penalty. It also may become possible to achieve regenerators which process the signals optically. Such regenerators would eliminate the need for optoelectronic conversion, except at the ends of the entire link. *See* OPTICAL COMMUNICATIONS.

**Coaxial cable communications systems.** Coaxial communication systems evolved before optical systems. Most of these systems are analog in nature. Signals are represented by the amplitude of a wave representing the signal to be transmitted. In a multichannel system, each voice, data, or picture signal occupies its unique portion of a broadband signal which is carried on a shared coaxial conductor or "pipe." In the transmitting terminal, various signals are combined in the frequency-division transmitting multiplex equipment. At the receiving end of a link, signals are separated in the receiving demultiplex equipment. This combining and separation operates much as broadcast radio and television do, and the principles are identical. *See* AMPLITUDE MODULATION; ELECTRICAL COMMUNICATIONS; FREQUENCY MODULATION.

In order to carry as many channels as possible, the multiplexing and demultiplexing use single-sideband

**Table 2. Repeaterless cable system**

| Characteristic | Value |
|---|---|
| System length | 93 mi (150 km) maximum |
| Fiber type | SL, single-mode |
| Fiber proof stress | 200,000 psi (1.38 GPa) |
| Cable design | SL, embedded core |
| Optical wavelength | 1.55 μm |
| Optical source | Buried heterostructure laser |
| Optical detector | *pin* diode |
| Line data rate | 3.088 megabits/s |
| Line coding | Dipulse |

**Table 3. L-system characteristics**

| Characteristic | L1 | L3 | L4 | L5 | L5E |
|---|---|---|---|---|---|
| Service date | 1946 | 1953 | 1967 | 1974 | 1976 |
| Repeater spacing, mi (km) | 8 (12.9) | 4 (6.4) | 2 (3.2) | 1 (1.6) | 1 (1.6) |
| Voice-band channel capacity per ⅜-in. (9.5-mm) coaxial pair | 600 | 1860 | 3600 | 10,800 | 13,200 |
| Coaxial pairs | 4 | 6 | 10 | 11 | 11 |
| Working pairs | 3 | 5 | 9 | 10 | 10 |
| Channel capacity | 1800 | 9300 | 32,400 | 108,000 | 132,000 |

(SSB) transmission. The fixed carrier signals, which do not convey useful information, are suppressed in the transmitting multiplex and reintroduced in the receiving multiplex. This avoids unnecessary load on the system. *See* SINGLE SIDEBAND.

***Terrestrial cables.*** The channel capacity of terrestrial coaxial systems has increased dramatically over the years to meet increased long-distance calling. This has resulted in decreased cost per channel, which has stimulated still further demand. While demand was the driving force, it is improving technology which has allowed such tremendous increases in capacity. This historical evolution is summarized in **Table 3**.

The L1 and L3 systems used electron tubes as the amplifying device, while all later systems used transistors. The L5 system benefited by the use of thin-film integrated circuits. These advances were responsible for the 22-fold increase in the number of channels per coaxial pair, as shown in Table 3. Because the number of coaxial pairs per cable was also increased, the total route capacity was increased by a factor of 73 over the 30-year period covered in Table 3. **Figure 5** shows the 11-coaxial-pair cable used in the L5 and L5E systems. The overall diameter of this cable is 3 in. (76 mm). *See* ELECTRON TUBE; INTEGRATED CIRCUITS; TRANSISTOR.

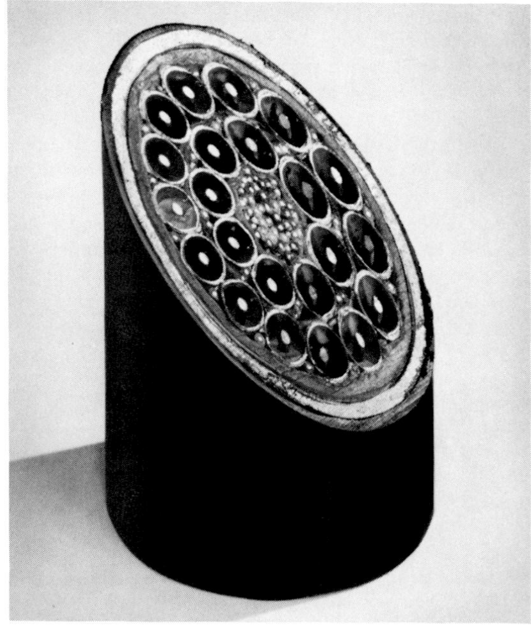

**Fig. 5. Multicoaxial cable used in the L5E communications system.**

Table 3 shows how repeater spacing decreases as the capacity rises. Multiplying channel capacity by 22 has meant going to higher frequencies, since each addition channel requires another 4 kHz of spectrum. At higher frequencies the cable has higher loss, and therefore such signals must be amplified at closer intervals.

In all of the above L-carrier systems, one of the coaxial pairs is reserved for protection of the working pairs. Since transfer to the protection pair is automatic upon failure of a working pair, this arrangement provides exceptionally high system reliability.

Since the various generations of L-carrier systems use the same basic coaxial unit, replacement of earlier electronics with the latest design can yield dramatic increases in channel capacity. As an example, if a cable with three working pairs of coaxials is upgraded from L-3 to L-5E, the capacity increases from 5580 to 39,600 channels. Since the cable and right of way are already established, this is a very economical method of enhancing the capacity of a route.

***Undersea cables.*** The history of undersea communications goes back to 1858, when the first transatlantic telegraph cable was completed by C. W. Field. This cable had no repeaters and thus was capable of carrying only a single slow-speed telegraph signal. Nevertheless, it allowed news to be communicated between North America and Europe without the long delay of surface mail. While telegraph cables were improved over the years, the next major breakthrough occurred in 1956, when the first transatlantic telephone cable was completed from Nova Scotia to Newfoundland, and then across the Atlantic to Scotland.

With the completion of TAT-1 (Transatlantic Telephone-1), callers could for the first time talk across the Atlantic Ocean as easily as they could within the continents. The response was a dramatic increase in use of overseas calling. Since 1956, cables have been installed throughout the world. England, France, Japan, and the United States have been active in designing and installing undersea communications cables.

Low delay is one respect in which undersea cables have a significant edge over satellites in a geosynchronous orbit. Delay is usually evaluated in terms of round-trip message time. For a telephone conversa-

**Table 4. Undersea cable systems from the United States to Europe**

| System designation | First service | Number of channels | Top frequency | Active devices |
|---|---|---|---|---|
| TAT-1 | 1956 | 36 | 0.164 MHz | Electron tubes |
| TAT-3 | 1963 | 138 | 1.1 MHz | Electron tubes |
| TAT-5 | 1970 | 840 | 6.0 MHz | Germanium transistors |
| TAT-6 | 1976 | 4200 | 30.0 MHz | Silicon transistors |
| TAT-8* | 1988 | 8000* | 295.6 megabits/s | Lasers, *pin* diodes, silicon integrated circuits |

*With digital circuit multiplication equipment, capability is 40,000 conversations. This is the first digital transatlantic light-wave system using optical-fiber communications cable.

tion, it is the extra time added between question and answer because of the transmission time. For the satellite connection, this delay is about 0.5 s. For a 4000-statute-mile (6400-km) undersea cable link, delay is only 0.06 s. Longer delay has two effects: it makes echo more bothersome to voice communications, and it requires more complex and less efficient protocols for data communications.

Traffic growth on the Atlantic route has exceeded 20% per year from the time of the first cable. In response to this rapid growth, AT&T Bell Laboratories designed five generations of communications cables. A summary of this technological evolution is presented in **Table 4**. SEE COAXIAL CABLE.

**Multipair communications cables.** These cables may contain from 6 to 4200 insulated twisted wire pairs in a protective sheath. Earlier cable designs used extruded lead sheaths. In new installations, sheaths using composites of metal and extruded plastic dominate the market. The wire pairs, which were insulated with paper pulp in early practice, are now more commonly insulated with extruded plastic. The conductors are most frequently copper, although aluminum is sometimes used for cost reasons.

***Development.*** Following the invention of the telephone in 1876, the first telephone systems used open wire lines. These lines differed from the earlier telegraph systems, which used a single wire with an earth return to complete the circuit. Such an arrangement would have produced intolerable noise and crosstalk at the higher frequencies (3500 Hz) used for telephony. Hence, open wire lines with a pair of spaced conductors for each circuit were employed. The two conductors were transposed periodically to further reduce noise and crosstalk. As the telephone grew in popularity, telephone poles became taller and carried more crossarms to hold the large number of open wire pairs. SEE CROSSTALK; ELECTRICAL NOISE.

At this point, the multipair cable was introduced, providing a flexible means of carrying large numbers of circuits. Within the cables, wires are grouped in bundles of 25 pairs. Each pair and bundle is individually color-coded.

***Types and uses.*** Paired cables are often classified according to application into three classes: exchange area cable, toll cable, and building or switchboard cable.

Exchange area cable connects the telephone subscriber to the central office, or one central office to another in the same area. Pulp paper insulation used in older cables has given way to plastic or expanded plastic insulation. Most new cables are buried rather than pole-mounted. Within the exchange area, subscriber loop carrier (SLC) csystems are being used to expand the capacity of existing cables and to avoid the need for installing new cables and ducts.

Toll cable connects central offices in different areas. As indicated above, optical communications and such means as L-carrier and microwave radio now carry a higher fraction of intercity traffic. In addition, T-carrier systems have been applied to existing multipair cables. Application of T-1, for example, provides 24 circuits over two pairs of conductors. Where carrier systems are applied, requirements of crosstalk, balance, and circuit impedance are more severe than for voice-frequency service.

Building or switchboard cable is for inside use, where fire resistance is of great importance. Because of this, polyvinyl chloride (PVC) is used for pair insulation and sheath. From a transmission point of view, PVC is inferior to paper or polyethylene, because its higher dielectric constant results in a cable with greater loss per unit length. This higher loss is generally not important because cable runs are relatively short.

***Pressure maintenance and waterproof cable.*** Lead-sheathed and other nonwaterproof cables are usually maintained by placing the entire inside of the cable under 6–10 psi (40–70 kilopascals) dry gas pressure. Each section may have a flow meter or pressure sensor whose information appears in the central office. This system quickly identifies a leak in the pressure-filled section before any electrical failure has occurred. Maintenance personnel can then pinpoint the sheath failure and make repair before moisture can damage the pairs.

To further ease maintenance, waterproof cables evolved (**Fig. 6**). The cable interstices are flooded with ''petroleum-based grease'' which prevents water penetration, even in the face of a damaged sheath. These waterproof cables do not require gas pressure and have greatly reduced problems due to moisture.

As cables have gone underground, they have been

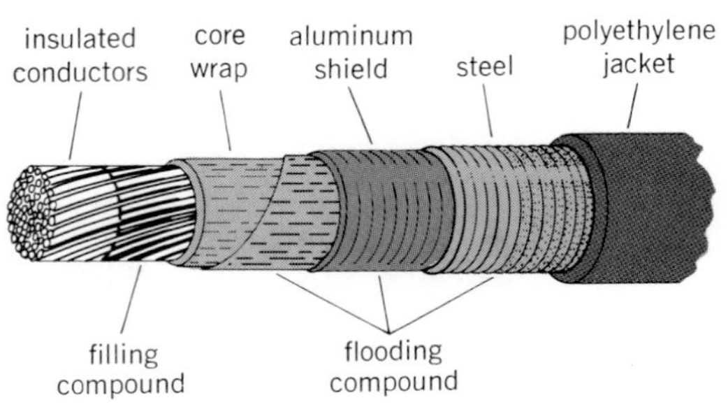


**Fig. 6. Waterproof cable design.**

better protected against storm damage but more continuously exposed to moisture. Hence, there is a strong preference for filled waterproof cable.

***Wire pair insulation.*** Early cables used paper pulp for insulation. To be effective, this insulation had to be kept dry. If the lead sheath or end seals were damaged, moisture could penetrate, causing noise and ultimately failure of the cable.

In the 1950s, high-speed plastic extrusion was first used to apply wire insulation. Thus, pulp gave way to polyethylene as an insulating material. Polyethylene has the advantage of excellent dielectric properties (high insulation strength and low dielectric constant).

The "grease" with which interstices of waterproof cables are filled has a dielectric constant of about 2.3. This grease replaces the air, which has a dielectric constant of 1.0. The result is an increase in the total capacitance of each pair, and hence an undersirable increase of cable loss. To overcome this effect, composite wire insulations were developed (**Fig. 7**). This design uses expanded plastic (about 50% air bubbles) to replace most of the insulation. A second, 50-μm-thick (0.002-in.) solid plastic layer gives moisutre protection and provides a carrier which can be color-coded for easy pair identification. The two layers are applied by tandem extrusion in a single insulation line. The dual-layer insulation allows the waterproof cable to have the same low-loss characteristics as the earlier air-filled cable, with no increase in outside cable diameter and minimal change in the amount of raw materials required.

***Sheaths.*** Lead is the sheath material of all early cables. It provides an excellent moisture barrier and good corrosion resistance. Since it can be extruded at low temperatures, it can be placed over the paper-wrapped core of pairs without damaging them. However, the ends of a lead-sheathed cable must be sealed.

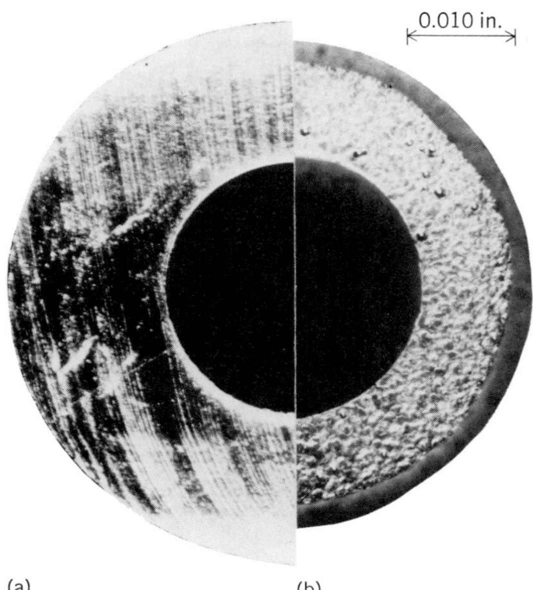


**Fig. 7. Comparison of (*a*) solid plastic insulation with (*b*) dual-layer expanded insulation (0.002-in. or 50-μm solid skin over 45% expanded core) showing both the structure and the smaller diameter of the dual-layer insulation compared with the solid insulation. Transmission properties are equivalent. (*Bell Telephone Laboratories*)**

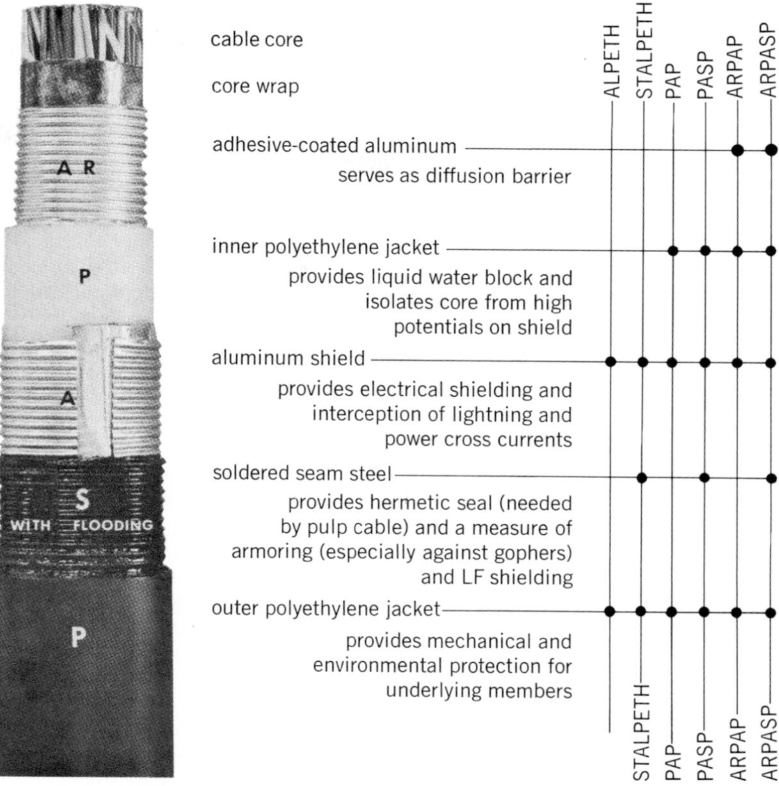


**Fig. 8. Representative sheath designs. The choice of layers incorporated in a particular design depends upon the type of cable core and environmental requirements.**

The development of newer materials, plus lead shortages, ultimately led to the evolution of composite sheaths, in which two or more layers provide the cable protection. One such design is shown in Fig. 6; the aluminum shield, the corrugated steel layer, and the polyethylene jacket replace the lead jacket.

The use of composite layers, which can be applied in a single in-line operation, gives great flexibility. Cables can be fabricated to meet widely differing environments. **Figure 8** represents some of the designs which have been manufactured. The particular designs are indicated by the column headings—acronyms which indicate the layers included in the particular design. Where there is a dot at a horizontal intersection, it indicates that this particular layer is included in that design. For example, the design shown as waterproof cable in Fig. 6 is a STALPETH design: It includes layers of steel, aluminum, and polyethylene.

***Installation methods.*** Earlier cables were usually installed aerially on poles, except in cities, where they were pulled into ducts. The vast majority of new cables are placed underground. In cities and larger towns, duct installation dominates. In smaller communities, cable may be installed in ducts or buried directly.

*S. T. Brewer*

***Bibliography.*** M. K. Barnoski (ed.), *Fundamentals of Optical Fiber Communications*, 1976; Bell Telephone Laboratories, *Transmission Systems for Communications*, 5th ed., 1982; R. D. Ehrbar, Undersea cables for telephony, *Commun. Mag.*, 21(5):18–27, August 1983; S. E. Miller and A. G. Chynoweth (eds.), *Optical Fiber Telecommunications*, 1979; *1980 World's Submarine Telephone Cable Systems*, U.S. Department of Commerce, NTIA-CR-80-6.

## Comparator circuit

An electronic circuit that produces an output voltage or current whenever two input levels simultaneously satisfy predetermined amplitude requirements. A comparator circuit may be designed to respond to continuously varying (analog) or discrete (digital) signals, and its output may be in the form of signaling pulses which occur at the comparison point or in the form of discrete direct-current (dc) levels.

**Linear comparator.** A linear comparator operates on continuous, or nondiscrete, waveforms. Most often one voltage, referred to as the reference voltage, is a variable dc or level-setting voltage and the other is a time-varying waveform. One common application of the comparator is in a linear time-delay circuit. Inputs consist of a sawtooth waveform of linearly increasing magnitude (ramp function) and a variable dc reference voltage. The reference voltage can be calibrated in units of time, as measured from the beginning of the sawtooth.

A clipper and a coincidence amplifier, together with a resistance-capacitance (*RC*) differentiating circuit, can perform the function of comparator. In **Fig. 1** the series clipper, usually called a pick-off diode for this application, does not conduct until the input reaches level $V_R$. The diode input is a sawtooth as shown. Consequently, only the portion of the sawtooth above $V_R$ appears at the output of the clipper. This output is applied to the *RC* differentiating network, which passes only the initial part of the rise. This short pulse is then amplified to produce the resultant output waveform. SEE CLIPPING CIRCUIT; COINCIDENCE AMPLIFIER.

The particular amplifier illustrated is a two-transistor high-gain amplifier with a relatively high input impedance and a low output impedance. A sharper pulse can be obtained if the amplifier is made regenerative. It may even take the form of a multivibrator or blocking oscillator to increase the gain at the point of coincidence. SEE BLOCKING OSCILLATOR; MULTIVIBRATOR.

**Regenerative comparator.** Multivibrators can be used in several ways directly as comparators without need for the pick-off diodes; such comparators sense the required coincidence accurately and introduce little additional delay. A simple type is the direct-coupled bistable circuit, sometimes known as the Schmitt circuit, one form being shown in **Fig. 2**. This example employs enhancement mode *p*-channel field-effect transistors and can be made to function from either negative or positive-going input waveforms. The example compares a negative-going input waveform with reference voltage $V_R$.

Under a variety of choice of supply voltage and resistances, the circuit will be bistable, that is, either of the two transistors can be conducting for a particular voltage at input gate $G_1$. Until a predetermined value of reference voltage is reached, $Q_1$ is nonconducting, and at time *T* it switches from nonconducting to conducting while $Q_2$ simultaneously switches from conducting to nonconducting. With dc coupling as shown in Fig. 2, three outputs of differing dc levels and polarities are produced. If *RC* differentiating circuits are added as indicated, sharp pulses can then be obtained. When the input waveform ends, all points in the circuit return to their initial states.

Direct-coupled regenerative comparators such as the Schmitt circuit are usually bidirectional, responding to inputs approaching the reference level $V_R$ from either the positive or the negative side. If the input starts at a value lower than $V_R$, the output voltage, $V_1$ will be at its high value until $V_R$ is reached and then shift to its low value. Polarities of the other output signals will be correspondingly reversed. Thus at the voltage coincidence of $V_i$ and $V_R$ there will be generated one of two possible output states definable as logic level (1) or logic level (0) in digital terminology. Because of design limitations in practical circuits, the input voltage at which the bistable circuit changes state is slightly less or greater than $V_R$ depending upon whether the input signal is positive-going or negative-going. This slight difference in level is referred to as the hysteresis of the circuit.

**Integrated circuit comparators.** High-gain dc operational amplifiers operated in the nonfeedback mode are often used to perform the comparator function, and many such amplifiers are classified as comparators because they are specifically designed to meet the needs for accurate voltage comparison applications. Such "op-amps" have two inputs, the output being inverting with respect to one and noninverting with respect to the other as shown in **Fig. 3**. The voltage gain (amplification) of the amplifier is so high that its output will swing through its entire dynamic range, $V_{min}$ to $V_{max}$, for very small changes in input voltage. Thus, for $V_i < V_R$ the amplifier will be cut off and the output voltage will be at $V_{max}$, and for $V_i > V_R$ the amplifier will saturate and the output will be at

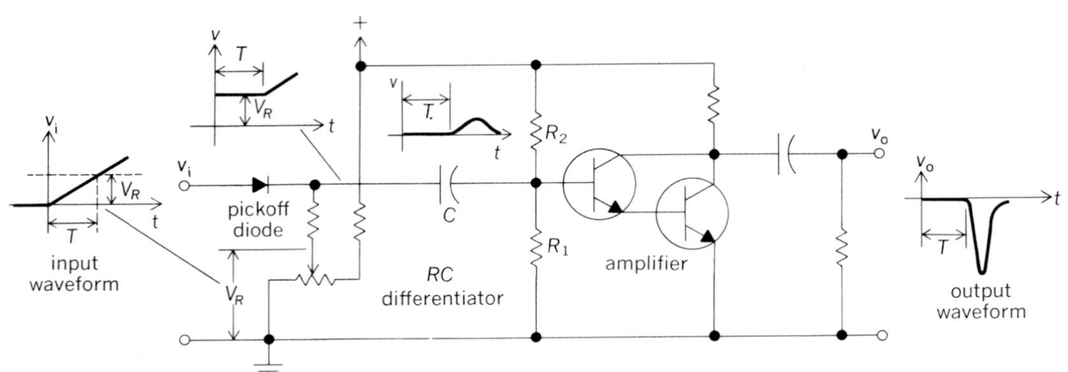


**Fig. 1. Simple comparator circuit using pick-off diode.**

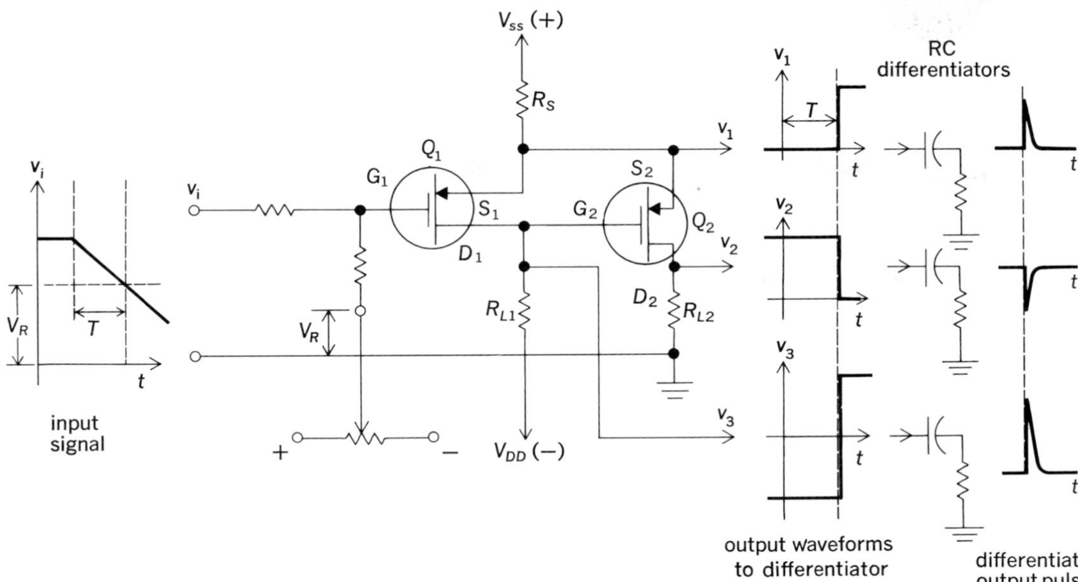


Fig. 2. Comparator using field-effect transistors in source-coupled bistable circuit.

$V_{min}$. For digital system applications, the output levels may be designed to coincide with logic level (0) and logic level (1) of the specific digital system and thus be suitable for converting a specific level in a continuously varying signal to a specific logic number assigned to the level. Arrays of such comparators connected to a common input, each designed to respond at a distinct reference voltage, and with the outputs connected to appropriate logic gates may be used to convert a range of signal levels to a specific digital code and as such form the basic building block of analog-to-digital converters. *SEE AMPLIFIER; ANALOG-TO-DIGITAL CONVERTER.*

The voltage gain and hence the timing precision of the operational amplifier comparator can be increased by converting it to a regenerative comparator as shown in **Fig. 4**. It then becomes an integrated circuit form of the Schmitt circuit shown in Fig. 2.

**Digital comparator.** The term "digital comparator" has historically been used when the comparator circuit is specifically designed to respond to a combination of discrete level (digital) signals, for example, when one or more such input signals simultaneously reach the reference level which causes the change of state of the output. Among other applications, such comparators perform the function of the logic gate such as the AND, OR, NOR, and NAND functions. More often, however, the term "digital comparator" is used to describe an array of logic gates designed specifically to determine whether one binary number is less than or greater than another binary number. Such digital comparators are sometimes called magnitude comparators or binary comparators. *SEE LOGIC CIRCUITS.*

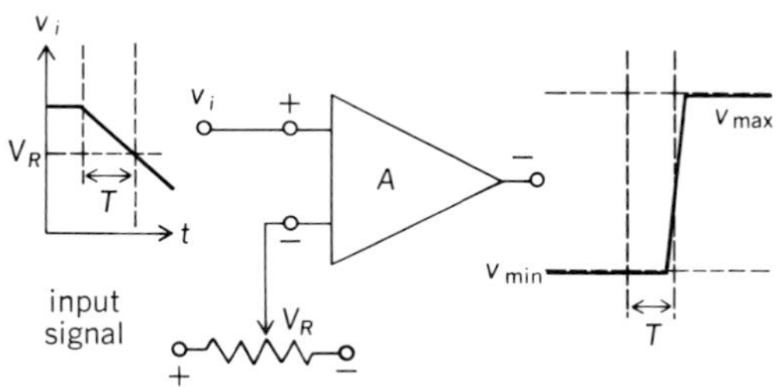


Fig. 3. Comparator circuit using integrated operational amplifier.

**Applications.** Comparators may take many forms and can find many uses, in addition to those which have been discussed. For example, the electronically regulated dc voltage supply uses a circuit which com-

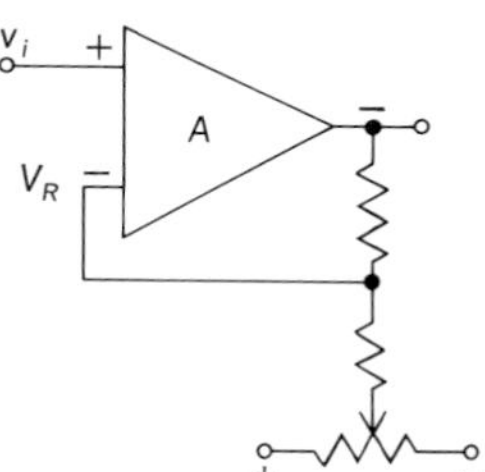


Fig. 4. Regenerative integrated circuit comparator.

pares the dc output voltage with a fixed reference level. The resulting difference signal controls an amplifier which in turn changes the output to the desired level. In a radio receiver the automatic gain control circuit may be thought of broadly as a comparator; it measures the short-term average of the signal at the output of the detector, compares this output with a desired bias level on the radio-frequency amplifier stages, and changes that bias to maintain a constant average level output from the detector. *SEE AUTOMATIC GAIN CONTROL (AGC).*

*Glenn M. Glasford*

**Bibliography.** J. J. Brophy, *Basic Electronics for Scientists*, 4th ed., 1983; J. A. Connelly (ed.), *Analog Integrated Circuits*, 1975; M. Kaufman and D. F. Stout, *Handbook of Operational Amplifier Circuit Design*, 1976; J. Millman, *Microelectronics*, 1979; J. Millman and H. Taub, *Pulse, Digital and Switching Waveforms*, 1965; S. Prensky, *Manual of Linear Integrated Circuits*, 1974; C. A. Schuler, *Electronics: Principles and Applications*, 2d ed., 1984.

## Computer

A device that receives, processes, and presents information. The two basic types of computers are analog and digital. Although generally not regarded as such, the most prevalent computer is the simple mechanical analog computer, in which gears, levers, ratchets, and pawls perform mathematical operations—for example, the speedometer and the watt-hour meter (used to measure accumulated electrical usage). The general public has become much more aware of the digital computer with the rapid proliferation of the hand-held calculator and a large variety of intelligent devices, ranging from typewriters to washing machines.

**Analog computer.** An analog computer uses inputs that are proportional to the instantaneous value of variable quantities, combines these inputs in a predetermined way, and produces outputs that are a continuously varying function of the inputs and the processing. These outputs are then displayed or connected to another device to cause action, as in the case of a speed governor or other control device.

The electronic analog computer is often used for the solution of complex dynamic problems. Electrical circuits, usually transistorized, perform the processing. Electronic amplifiers allow signals to be impressed upon cascaded circuits without significant electrical loss of attenuation through loading of prior stages, a feature absent in purely mechanical computers. Friction in a mechanical analog computer builds up and limits the complexity of the device.

Small electronic analog computers are frequently used as components in control systems. Inputs come from measuring devices which output an electrical signal (transducers). These electrical signals are presented to the analog computer, which processes them and provides a series of electronic outputs that are then displayed on a meter for observation by a human operator or connected to an electrical action device to ring a bell, flash a light, or adjust a remotely controlled valve to change the flow in a pipeline system. If the analog computer is built solely for one purpose, it is termed a special-purpose electronic analog computer.

General-purpose electronic analog computers are used by scientists and engineers for analyzing dynamic problems. A general-purpose analog computer receives its degree of flexibility through the use of removable control panels, each of which carries a series of mating plugs. Outputs from one component are routed to the input of another component by connecting an electrical conductor from one mating plug on the removable board (output) to another plug on the removable board (input). This process is called patching, and the removable panel is frequently called a patch board.

Thus, in any analog computer the key concepts involve special versus general-purpose computer designs, and the technology utilized to construct the computer itself: mechanical or electronic. In any case, an analog computer receives inputs that are instantaneous representations of variable quantities and produces output results dynamically to a graphical display device, a visual display device, or in the case of a control system a device which causes mechanical motion. *See* ANALOG COMPUTER.

**Digital computer.** In contrast, a digital computer uses symbolic representations of its variables. The arithmetic unit is constructed to follow the rules of one (or more) number systems. Further, the digital computer uses individual discrete states to represent the digits of the number system chosen.

***Electronic versus mechanical computers.*** The most prevalent special-purpose mechanical digital computers have been the supermarket cash register, the office adding machine, and the desk calculator. Each of these is being widely replaced by electronic devices allowing much greater logical decision making and greatly increased speed. For example, many products now carry a bar code, the Universal Product Code (UPC); in suitably equipped supermarkets, the code is scanned by a light-sensitive device, bringing information about each product into the point-of-scale (POS) terminal that has replaced the mechanical cash register. The POS terminal then computes total charges and provides a receipt for the customer. It may also communicate with a centralized computer system that controls inventory, accounts payable, salaries and commissions, and so on. While a mechanical cash register could carry out only a small number of operations each minute, and some electromechanical devices might handle several hundred operations per second, even a small general-purpose electronic computer can carry out its computations at speeds up to a million operations per second. *See* CALCULATORS.

***Stored program operation.*** A digital computer works with a symbolic representation of variables; consequently, it can easily store and manipulate numbers, letters, or graphical information represented by a symbolic code. Typically, a general-purpose electronic digital computer operates on numbers by using both decimal and binary number systems, and on symbolic data expressed in an alphabet. It contains both an arithmetic unit and a storage unit. As the digital computer processes its input, it proceeds through a series of discrete steps called a program. The storage unit serves to retain both the values of the variables and the program to process those variables. The arithmetic unit may operate on either variables or coded program instructions interchangeably, since both are usually retained in the storage unit in the same form. Thus, the digital computer has the capability to be adaptive because processing can be determined by the previously prepared program, by the data values supplied as input to the computation, and by the values generated during the course of the computation. Through the use of the stored program, the digital computer achieves a degree of flexibility unequaled by any other computing or data-processing devices. *See* DIGITAL COMPUTER PROGRAMMING.

***Applications.*** Most digital computers are occupied with performing applications related to bookkeeping, accounting, engineering design, or test data reduction. On the other hand, applications that were once considered esoteric have led to industrial applications, such as the use of robots on manufacturing assembly lines. Many of the heuristic techniques employed by these robots are based on algorithms developed in such artificial-intelligence applications as chess playing and remotely controlled sensing devices. Modern chess programs are capable of defeating even excellent human players, and computer chess tournaments are held routinely at national and international computer conferences. Of lesser difficulty, perhaps, but illustrative of the kind of information that can be manipulated is the solution of algebraic equations in symbolic form, to provide general algebraic solutions instead of numeric instances of solutions. SEE ARTIFICIAL INTELLIGENCE; ROBOTICS.

Another area of major societal impact is the application of digital computers to word processing, including the entire concept of office automation. The ability of even modest computer systems to store, organize, and retrieve very large amounts of information has brought about radical change in the very nature of many business offices. SEE DATA-PROCESSING SYSTEMS; DIGITAL COMPUTER; WORD PROCESSING.

Bernard A. Galler

**Bibliography.** R. C. Dorf, *Computers and Man*, 3d ed., 1982; R. W. Hamming, *Computers and Society*, 1972; D. H. Sanders, *Computers in Society*, 3d ed., 1980; G. A. Silver, *The Social Impact of Computers*, 1979.

## Computer-aided design and manufacturing

The use of computers in engineering design and manufacturing. Specifically, computer-aided design (CAD) refers to the use of computers to aid the designer from product conception to execution of engineering drawings. Computers can develop three-dimensional representations of engineering structures, analyze those structures, and make engineering drawings. Computer-aided manufacturing (CAM) refers to the use of computers to develop the optimum processing strategies for a given component. These strategies are converted to code for numerically controlled (N/C) machines which make the component. As more numerically controlled machines are installed, reorganization of the whole manufacturing process will occur, accompanied by increased plant productivity. In the early 1980s, the industrial robot became very important. Robotics and other high technologies are keys to a vastly more flexible and responsive manufacturing facility. SEE ROBOTICS.

The CAD/CAM technology provides a means of effectively using the computer-stored information for both CAD and CAM work in a common data base (data list). Thus the engineers need to input their ideas to the computer only once. SEE DATA-BASE MANAGEMENT SYSTEMS; DATA COMMUNICATIONS.

**CAD.** CAD/CAM was in its infancy in the early 1970s. The main developments were from industry, driven by the need to increase productivity of the engineering drawing process. Early CAD systems involved only basic automatic drafting; that is, the systems displayed the component in a line-type representation called a wire-frame model, on a televisionlike screen (cathode-ray tube). This provided a visual outline of the structure, but no detail of the interior of the component. Essentially, the representation was a natural selection because it had been used for many years for drafting. However, about the same time computer solids modeling was developed. With this capability, the design component is represented on the screen by the addition and subtraction of several primitive elements such as cylinders and cones. Even with the advantages of solids modeling, the wire-frame approach was selected, since this better met the industry goals of providing a basic drafting system.

***Finite element analysis.*** After the introduction of CAD systems, a demand grew for engineering analysis capability. At this point finite element analysis (FEA) was introduced. This analysis technique takes a complex solid structure and breaks it into a large number of simpler elements so that the engineering characteristics of the simpler elements are known. The computer assembles the elements and solves for the internal displacements and later the stress distribution. The engineer compares these stresses to the strength of the material. Redesign is carried out until all stress levels are acceptable. However, since the wire-frame model, with its lack of internal detail, was not a suitable data source for finite element analysis, other types of modeling capabilities were needed. Thus, CAD was expanded to include solids modeling, surface modeling (essentially the wire-frame model with surfaces hanging on the wire frame), and wire-frame capability.

***CAE.*** All engineering design decisions are not made on the basis of stress levels alone. The large number of engineering constraints on any particular design has resulted in a large number of specialized engineering analysis programs. Moreover, in complex design problems there are a large number of design variables; the best values for them are derived by optimization, a method which attempts through numerical procedures to adjust the variables so that the design meets some objective, for example, a minimum-weight design. The collection of analysis and optimization capabilities along with CAD and finite element analysis is sometimes called computer-aided engineering (CAE). SEE COMPUTER-AIDED ENGINEERING; OPTIMIZATION.

***CAT.*** In the late 1970s and early 1980s, computer-aided testing (CAT) was developed to satisfy the needs of testing and evaluation. In one application, automotive transmission life tests were automatically controlled by computers. Moreover, computer models of a newly designed automobile could be computationally crashed on the computer to predict the damage without actually crashing the prototype automobile. However, various automotive components still have to be statically tested to get enough data to complete the analysis.

***Experimental modal analysis.*** Experimental modal analysis combines both computational testing and CAD. This involves measuring, nondestructively, the dynamic properties of a prototype structure with subsequent computer analysis to provide a wire-frame model on the cathode-ray tube. The model is animated in a way that corresponds to its motion at some troublesome vibration or noise frequency. The motion provides the engineer with ideas on how to modify the prototype to correct the problem. Next, the computer extracts a mathematical model from the experimental data. Using this model, the designed can ask "what if" questions; the computer makes the proposed modification in its mathematical model and displays the characteristics of the modified structure. The major advantage is that no modifications need be made to the very expensive prototype. This area of CAD is important in the design of structures so complex that they are beyond economical evaluation even on modern computers.

**CAM.** The first breakthrough occurred in the mid-1950s, when the first N/C machines were introduced: workers no longer were required to control the machine tools completely, since most control was done by a coded paper tape; in most cases, the workers still had to load and unload the workpieces from the machines. However, N/C machines still represent only about 4% of machine tool sales in the United States.

A hindrance to the growth of N/C machines has been their programming complexity, although under CAM the programming is simplified. The computer has a N/C module that produces, from the geometry and the user-supplied tool sizes, speeds, feed rates, and tolerances, a programmed tool path needed to generate the part. This path is simulated on a color-graphics terminal screen in a different color from that of the component. **Figure 1** shows such a component. The cutter path is shown dotted at stations 1 and 2, with circles denoting the cutter positions. Once the path is verified by the user, the computer produces a N/C readable tape or disk file to be used in direct numerical control. **Figure 2** shows the N/C machine producing the component shown in Fig. 1. *See Computer graphics*.

**Robotics.** A significant entry in the CAM field is the robot. The first industrial robot was installed by a large United States automobile firm in 1961. A robot is a programmable piece of flexible machinery that can do many varied tasks even in hostile environments. During one type of robot training, the robot records movements in its memory and then replays the action on command. The tasks that robots can do are limited; for example, a robot alone could not inspect a product for visible defects. Machine vision can be added to provide the robot with the capability of performing inspection and quality control checks. Moreover, machine vision can enable some trained robots to modify their actions through adaptive control. For example, the machine vision may determine that a bolt to be installed in a certain spot is coming to the robot upside down. Through the adaptive control function, the robot turns the bolt around and inserts it properly. As robots are given more and more senses they will become the flexible element in the production system that will allow rapid manufacturing reconfiguration to reduce manufacturing lead time. *See Robotics*.

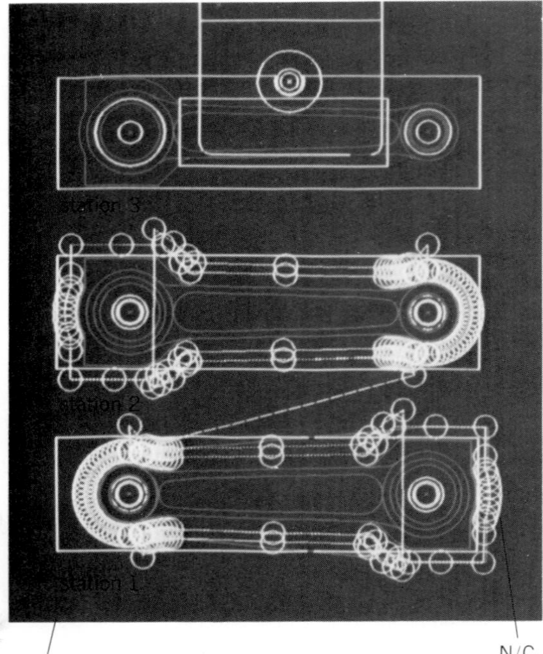


**Fig. 1. Computer-aided design and manufacturing display on a system that allows the engineer to create a cutter location file and interactively preview the cutter path before machining. (*Control Data Corp.*)**

**Fig. 2. Numerically controlled machine in profiling operation using data generated by an integrated computer-aided engineering and manufacturing (ICEM) system. (*Control Data Corp.*)**

**Integrated CAD/CAM.** The optimum results from CAD and CAM come from the combination of both technologies within the same facility. The CAD data base can be used for analysis, optimization, drafting, finite element analysis, interference checking, tool path definition, N/C tape generation, direct numerical control, inventory control, parts and service manual production, parts list, and many other things. In addition to the obvious efficiencies of the common data base, a data base that conforms to the International Graphics Engineering Standard (IGES) format provides data that can be assessed and used on entirely different CAD/CAM systems. The data may be supplied via computer to the potential job shops or suppliers that will bid on the production job, thus increasing response time and productivity. *See Computer; Computer-aided engineering; Digital computer; Digital computer programming; Nonlinear programming*.

*Larry D. Mitchell*

***Bibliography.*** P. F. Chenea, The engineer and the computer-A production partnership, *Comput. Mech. Eng.*, 1(3):35–37, January 1983; E. E. David, Jr., By 1990 all industries must be high tech, *High Tech.*, pp. 65–68, April 1983; J. K. Krouse, Industry gets serious about solids modeling, *Comput. Aided Eng.*, 1(2):22–26, November-December 1982; J. K. Krouse, Off-the-shelf software for mechanical design, *Mach. Des.*, pp. 47–52, April 21, 1983; J. R. Miller, Geometric modeling moves CAD one step closer to maturity, *Ind. Res. Develop.*, pp. 80–83, January 1983; A. P. Taylor, Getting a handle on factory automation, *Comput. Aided Eng.*, 2(3):74–80, May-June 1983; E. Teicholz, *CAD/CAM Handbook*, 1984.

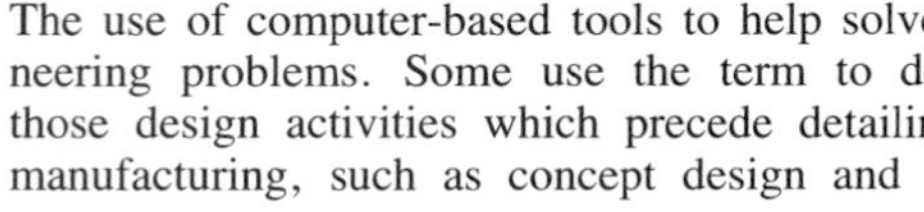

## Computer-aided engineering

The use of computer-based tools to help solve engineering problems. Some use the term to describe those design activities which precede detailing and manufacturing, such as concept design and performance analysis. Others use computer-aided engineering as an all-encompassing term for computer-assisted engineering activities, including mechanical, electrical, civil, process, and manufacturing. Most, however, agree that the potential applications of computer tools to engineering will prove as revolutionary as the application of electrical power to manufacturing.

Computer-aided engineering can be considered as a set of four interrelated problem-solving aids: computer data bases and communications; computer graphics and modeling; computer simulations and analyses; and data acquisition and control of physical prototypes and production processes. The applications of computer-aided engineering range up to final production, at which time similar computer applications are usually described as computer-aided manufacturing (CAM) or computer-integrated manufacturing (CIM). *SEE COMPUTER-AIDED DESIGN AND MANUFACTURING.*

Although successful applications of computers to engineering problems were evident in the 1960s and before, it was not until the 1970s that computer aids emerged as a common factor in engineering. The computer-using engineer who once might have relied upon a large mainframe computer in a batch (noninteractive) environment often migrated to interactive minicomputer systems and then to microcomputers. While dramatic decreases in computer costs have made computer-aided engineering cost-effective, the real key is applications software, because computer-aided engineering is, in effect, an evolving kit of software tools which are used by engineers to help create and evaluate alternative designs. *SEE MICROCOMPUTER.*

Engineers routinely use at least four kinds of "languages" to attack engineering problems. This approach is known as WRAP, an acronym for four modeling schemes: words, renderings, analyses, and prototypes. Various engineering disciplines bring special expertise to these four basic approaches: design engineers are particularly adept at graphical constructions, structural engineers at mathematical analyses, test engineers at acquiring data from physical prototypes, and so on.

Computers and computer software have revolutionized all four modes of problem solving, helping engineers to handle complex product development problems. There are, for example, specialized computers such as word processors and data-base machines to store and manipulate words. Similarly, there are graphics processors and computer-aided drafting systems; array processors and supercomputers dedicated to analytical simulations; and process computers dedicated to data acquisition and control of physical processes and prototypes.

**Data-base and data communications technology.** The complexity of many products outstrips the capacity of any single engineer to remember all the relevant information at any point in design. Access to the collective experience of the engineering team, as well as the experience embodied in references and standards, requires efficient organization of a project team, which may include hundreds of engineers.

Computers have emerged as a powerful aid to the management and communication of engineering information. For example, automobile manufacturers routinely make or purchase hundreds of different threaded fasteners. When a new component is being developed, it is usually much less expensive to order an additional quantity of an existing fastener than it is to design and procure a new one. Even so, manually sorting through the specifications for a thousand existing fasteners to find one that meets the new requirements (size, strength, corrosion resistance, and so forth) is so time-consuming that engineers rarely make the effort. However, a computer data base can be searched rapidly for appropriate existing fasteners and other items based on design requirements.

Other kinds of engineering information that companies have organized into computer data bases include test results, warranty reports, drawings, analysis results, cost and materials data, codes, design standards, component specifications, and documentation. Creating such a data base is a complex task. Furthermore, this information must often be organized in a way that takes into account all the future questions which engineers might want to ask. Thus, there is a possibility that a data base will become obsolete unless it is easy to update and retrieve information. There are several ways of organizing information in a computer. These include a simple file and increasingly flexible hierarchical, network, and relational data bases. The trade-off is generally future flexibility versus initial cost. However, as computer and memory costs have declined, more engineering information will be organized in relational data bases. This avoids the problem of having to predefine all possible questions. In addition, data management and control systems, essentially data-base programs to keep track of other data bases, have been developed. *SEE DATA-BASE MANAGEMENT SYSTEMS.*

Many of the greatest productivity improvements can come from taking people out of the loop when obvious decisions are involved. Thus a data base should be structured not only so that it is easy for people to use, but so that the information is in an unambiguous form which can be used directly by other computer programs. **Figure 1** shows the structure of an engineering data base. It would be ideal if the data base created on any drafting system could be used directly by any computer-controlled machine

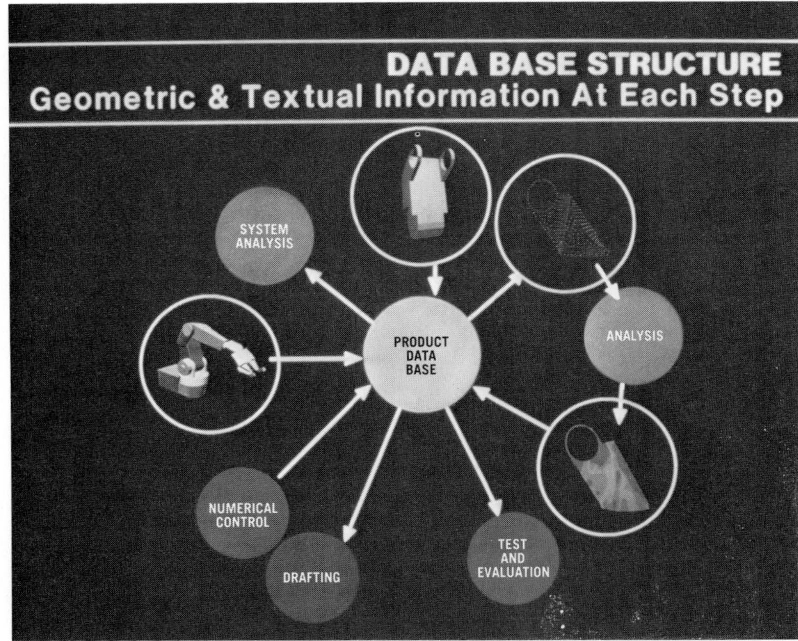


**Fig. 1. Diagram of the structure of an engineering data base. (*Structural Dynamics Research Corp.*)**

tool to manufacture that part. However, relatively few universally accepted standards in CAE exist today.

All the information in a data base is of limited value unless if is readily available to the user when needed. Advanced data communications technologies have become an important consideration in reducing overall project lead times, particularly for companies with engineers dispersed in many locations. Engineering applications often require both high bandwidths to handle the volume of information as well as multiple nodes to reach all those with a need for data-base access. SEE DATA COMMUNICATIONS; DATA-PROCESSING SYSTEMS.

**Computer graphics and modeling.** The language of design engineers is in the form of graphical renderings, that is, sketches, drawings, plots, histograms, maps, vectors, schematics, graphs, and projections. Computer graphic systems, which have made it possible for engineers to create and manipulate graphic representations much faster, are almost invariably tied to an alphanumeric data-base program, which names drawings and parts for retrieval. A computer-aided drawing system might be considered to be a power tool to replace manual drafting (**Fig. 2**).

The use of computer graphics goes beyond automating manual drawing tasks. One class of application is the visualization of abstract or mathematical results. For example, the numerical output from mathematical simulations such as finite element analysis may be a dense printout several inches thick. However, most of this information can be better portrayed with graphic displays. There are many programs available to convert test data and analysis results into plots, histograms, surface displays, animations, color contour maps, and schematics. This potential of computer graphics may be compared to the power of a microscope or telescope. All of these instruments reveal information which was previously obscured by perceptual limitations, including, in the case of computer graphics, the limited ability of people to deal with vast quantities of alphanumeric data.

Perhaps the most important graphic technology for engineering is solid modeling. With a traditional drawing or blueprint, the actual three-dimensional object to be manufactured is as much in the mind's eye as it is on paper. This is also the case with the first generations of computer-aided drafting systems, which automated the process of producing drawings. It was still necessary to interpret the results before giving instructions to computer-controlled manufacturing machines. A complete solids modeling program, however, allows the engineer to build an unambiguous data base which can be used directly by other programs to calculate masses and mass properties, to prepare a model for mathematical analysis, to check for interferences, to manufacture the part, and so on. Thus a solids modeling program allows the engineer to work with a much more complete representation of the product early in the design process.

Fig. 2. Typical turn-key CAD/CAM system. The use of two screens improves operator access to both geometric and textual information. (*General Electric Co.*)

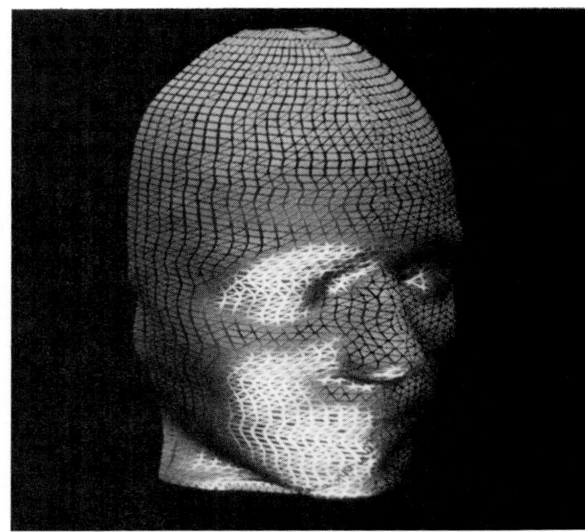

Fig. 3. Computer-generated solid model of a human face.

A logical assumption may be that solid modelers would simply set up a three-dimensional matrix of points and turn each one on or off to represent objects. However, with tolerances of 0.0001 in. (0.00025 cm) or so and geometrics which extend for many feet, or even miles in the case of mapping problems, this approach consumes far too much memory. Instead, the mathematical representation of a solid object typically follows one of two basic approaches. One approach is to build the object up out of a set of "primitives," much as with building blocks. The other approach is to represent the surfaces mathematically, and keep track of what is inside (solid) and what is outside. In order to make it easier for the engineer to create new geometries, hybrid methods have been developed. One program, for example, allows the user a great deal of flexibility in creating the geometry and keeps account of the results in a canonical form called rational B-splines.

The ability of some solid modeling programs to create free-form surfaces is very important, especially for cast, molded, and sculpted materials. **Figure 3** shows a model of a human face that was used in the design of face masks. The program also maintains a precise geometric data base which can be used for analysis and manufacturing functions. SEE COMPUTER GRAPHICS.

**Computer simulations and analyses.** Engineers are trained to model real-world systems with more or less analogous equations. This use of simulations can be thought of as building a mathematical prototype, which is often faster and cheaper to create than build-

Fig. 4. Computer-based testing system.

ing and testing the real thing. An added advantage of mathematical simulation is that it forces a better understanding of the system under investigation. Furthermore, it is relatively easy to try many variations in search of an optimal solution. However, not all problems are understood well enough to be modeled mathematically. Also, even with very powerful computers, some solvable problems, such as simulating aerodynamic flow around complex objects, require vast computing resources.

Finite element analysis techniques are an excellent example of the analytical applications of computer-aided engineering. The technique can be applied to any field problem, such as heat transfer, electrodynamics, and the behavior of structures. The response of a simple structure to loads, such as a single-degree-of-freedom spring, is easy to characterize mathematically. The response of a complex structure is far more difficult to characterize in a precise form. However, a reasonable approximation is possible by considering the structure as a network of interconnected finite elements, much as if it were a matrix of springs. Mathematically this results in a large number of linear equations, the solution of which is quite straightforward but much too time-consuming for manual methods. Finite element analysis software is well developed to solve these problems. SEE NUMERICAL ANALYSIS; SIMULATION.

**Data acquisitions and control.** Modeling with words, renderings, and analyses, even on the most powerful computers, rarely offers a complete understanding of product performance. Modern computer tools do allow far greater information to be understood in these forms, but there is still a role for building and testing prototypes prior to production. For example, computer finite element models require accurate input loads. Testing similar systems is a good way to determine these loads. The ideal, of course, is to have the best possible engineering design prior to building the first prototype of the product.

Computer tools have emerged to build prototypes faster through numerical control and computer-aided manufacturing techniques and to gain more insight into product performance through computer-aided testing techniques. In addition to general-purpose data acquisition and control programs, specialized testing techniques are well developed in the electronics industry and in the area of structural and vibrations testing (**Fig. 4**).

**Computer hardware trends.** Computer-assisted engineering applications use hardware similar to that in data processing, with input devices, central processors, main and auxiliary memory, and output devices. Some notable developments for engineering applications include very high-resolution graphic displays, a variety of easy-to-use graphic input devices, and specialized output devices such as plotters and machine controls. Robots might also be considered as specialized computer peripherals.

Another significant advancement has been the development of superminicomputers, which approach the performance of mainframe computers but at a much lower cost. Similarly, individual 32-bit microcomputers have been designed that approach the power of superminicomputers, but in desk-top work stations which can be networked to share resources and information (**Fig. 5**). The result is often a trend away from highly centralized computing to decentralized computing. SEE COMPUTER SYSTEMS ARCHITECTURE.

**Computer software trends.** Engineers orginally wrote many of their own programs to manipulate verbal, graphic, mathematical, and test data, often in the programming language FORTRAN. Today, many programs that are used to solve engineering problems are purchased, since they are generally more comprehensive, better validated, and better supported than the programs an individual engineer might develop. These programs are often written in structured programming languages such as Ada and C, making them easier to maintain and upgrade. Greater atten-

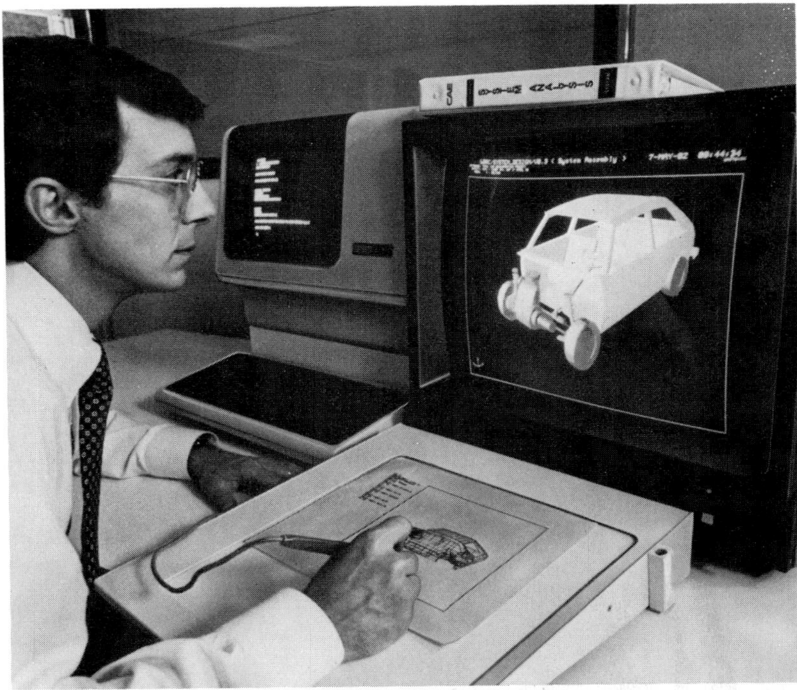

Fig. 5. Engineering work station with interactive access to data bases, solid models, analytical programs, and test results. (*Structural Dynamics Research Corp.*)

tion is also being given to simplifying and easing user interactions with user-friendly help messages, step-by-step command menus, and so on. To the extent that artificial-intelligence programming methods become feasible, engineers can expect that working with a computer system will become increasingly like a dialog with a colleague. *See* ARTIFICIAL INTELLIGENCE; NONLINEAR PROGRAMMING; PROGRAMMING LANGUAGES; SOFTWARE ENGINEERING.

**Implementation.** Most users of computer-aided engineering techniques go through several stages of implementation. The first stage is often to automate some isolated task, such as drafting. Here the basic work tasks are unchanged, but there are some isolated productivity improvements. Once users are comfortable with the use of computers in a familiar task, a second step is often to replace a traditional modeling strategy such as prototype testing with a newer and more cost-effective strategy such as analytical simulation. This involves changes to the current process of engineering with new functions and responsibilities. The organizational issues surrounding change are often a stumbling block. A third step may be the integration of various automation and simulation activities in an overall engineering system, moving engineering toward a continuous process rather than a department-to-department batch process.

*Peter A. Marks*

***Bibliography.*** P. Marks, *Managing Computer-Aided Engineering Technology*, 1983; Penton/IPC Publishing, *Computer-Aided Engineering* (magazine and annual reference issue), 1984.

## Computer graphics

The process of pictorial communication between humans and computers. The traditional (and still most widely used) means of inputting problems to computers and receiving answers has been the alphanumeric form—the letters, numbers, punctuation marks, and other symbols which can be handled by such input/output devices as punched-card and tape or disk peripherals, teletypewriters, and line printers. While any problem and its solution can be reduced to the alphanumeric form by suitable coding conventions, it is often an unnatural and time-consuming way for the human to think and work. An analogous situation would be the publication of a technical textbook without illustrations, with diagrams replaced by word descriptions, graphs by tables of numbers, and so forth. Anyone who has tried to visualize an odd-shaped plot of land from the usual word form of deed description "starting at bound mark, 321.26 feet northerly, thence 195.81 feet southeasterly, 82.64 feet easterly, . . ." can appreciate the difficulty of quickly comprehending a computer result presented in this way.

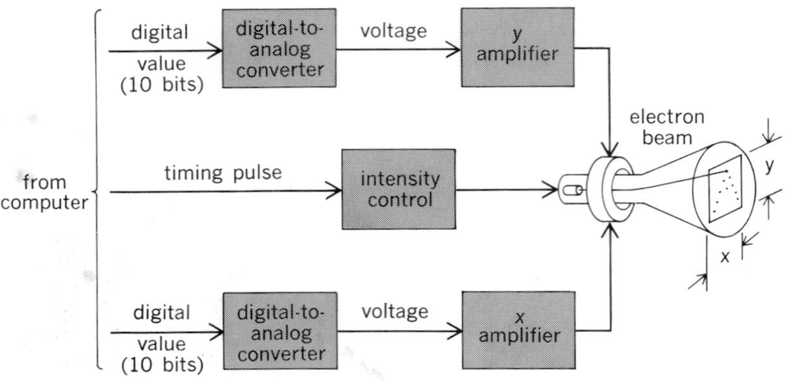


**Fig. 1. Point-plotting CRT output display.**

Output devices such as televisionlike cathode-ray-tube (CRT) displays and automatic mechanical plotting boards which operate under computer control permit the computer to draw almost any conceivable form of pictorial output. When a computer is equipped with such devices and suitable controlling programs, the user (the person desiring computations to be performed) can request in preparing a program and input data that the results of the calculations be output graphically, that is, as charts, drawings, or appropriate pictorial representation. Use of graphical output devices is showing a rapid increase, particularly in engineering applications. However, graphical output alone is only half the story—graphical input is also used in many situations. These will be discussed in turn. *See* CATHODE-RAY TUBE.

**Graphical output.** Graphical output devices are of two types: cursive writing and raster scan. In cursive writing, the CRT electron beam or the plotting pen is moved so as to trace out the lines and points making up the displayed output in sequential fashion, much as one draws with pencil and paper. Primarily line-type copy is produced. In a raster-scan output device, the beam or pen sweeps the entire display surface in a regular, repetitive pattern (as in television), and passes every location at a specific time. Drawing is therefore accomplished by energizing the beam or pen at appropriate times in the pattern cycle, and every point in the display area can be written in a single scan. Cursive writing formerly predominated in both graphic displays and hard-copy plotters, largely because of the much higher data requirements of raster scanning, where output data are required for every point, indicating whether it is to be visible or not. Beginning in the 1980s, however, advances in low-cost, solid-state circuits and memories have provided ready and inexpensive means of driving raster-scan displays. *See* INTEGRATED CIRCUITS; SEMICONDUCTOR MEMORIES.

***Cursive output.*** The simplest forms of cursive computer-controlled plotting boards or CRT displays are the point-plotting types. In these devices the computer specifies numerically the $x$ and $y$ coordinates of a point on the drawing surface or viewing screen, which causes an ink dot or spot of light to be made at the appropriate location. In the case of a CRT, it is usual to covert the numerical values to analog voltages by means of digital-to-analog converters, and then to use these voltages to drive the deflection system of the CRT (**Fig. 1**). It is common to divide each deflection axis into 1024 (10 binary digits) distinct addresses, which provides over a million possible dot locations. The speed of plotting depends upon the distance that the electron beam must move between dots, and varies from 1 microsecond for adjacent addresses to perhaps 30 microseconds for full-screen deflection between dots. Screen sizes are usually about 10 to 15 in. (25 to 38 cm) square, limited primarily by CRT cost and technology. *See* DIGITAL-TO-ANALOG CONVERTER.

Mechanical plotting boards, which must physically move the pen and the writing surface relative to each other, bear considerable resemblance to numerically controlled machine tools. Mechanical plotting is of course much slower than moving an electron beam in the CRT. Slowness of plotting, coupled with the fact that a picture element once drawn cannot be erased, makes plotting boards unattractive for interactive graphics. However, the resolution of plotting can be increased by simply making the writing surface bigger (up to 6 × 8 ft or 1.8 to 2.4 m in some models), permitting much more detailed drawings than can be displayed on a CRT. Also, plotters with multiple styli to write in color are available.

The point-plotting mode of operation described above, while seemingly rudimentary, provides a complete drawing capability. Closely spaced dots plotted in a row merge into continuous appearing lines, letters and numbers can be formed from arrays of dots similar to those used in football scoreboards, and so forth. The main disadvantage of point-plotting devices is that large amounts of data are required to produce a picture (20 or more binary digits for each point) which places a burden on the computer, and the plotting speed is limited. This latter factor is most important in CRT displays, where the entire picture must be "refreshed" (continuously rewritten) 30 or more times per second in order to provide a flicker-free presentation. For example, if the CRT is refreshed 30 times per second and the plotting time is 5–30 μs per point, pictures containing only up to a few thousand points can be displayed.

Most cursive display systems now include additional hardware to provide high-speed symbol and line (vector) drawing capabilities (**Fig. 2**). The point mode operates as described previously, but the other two modes produce an entire picture element with a single command from the computer, and at a much higher plotting rate than if it were drawn with individual points. Line generators operate with specification either of both end points or of the length of line to be plotted relative to current beam position. In either case all of the intermediate points on the line are automatically filled in by the line generator of the display system, by rapid point plotting (incremental digital technique) or by continuously sweeping the beam (analog technique).

Of the two techniques the analog technique is considerably faster, permitting a line to be drawn clear across the screen in as little as 30 μs. Symbol generators take many forms, the more common being based on arrays of dots, stroke techniques, or incremental tracing of the symbol shapes. The key feature of any of these is a local fixed memory which contains the detailed information about the shape of each symbol. Thus, the only input the symbol generator needs is the symbol code (6 to 8 binary digits) to tell it which symbol to plot. Current symbol generators permit as many as 4000 symbols to be displayed at a refresh rate of 30 frames per second. The capacity of a point-plotting display at the same refresh rate would be only 50–100 symbols, since 10–20 points are needed per symbol.

Some display systems have been designed with additional display functions to improve performance in special situations. Examples are generators for drawing circles or other common geometric curves with one command, hardware for scaling or rotating three-dimensional representations without requiring recomputation of the display data, and automatic insertion of perspective into three-dimensional representations.

***Raster-scan output.*** Raster-scan output has long been used in alphanumeric CRT displays, in which it is

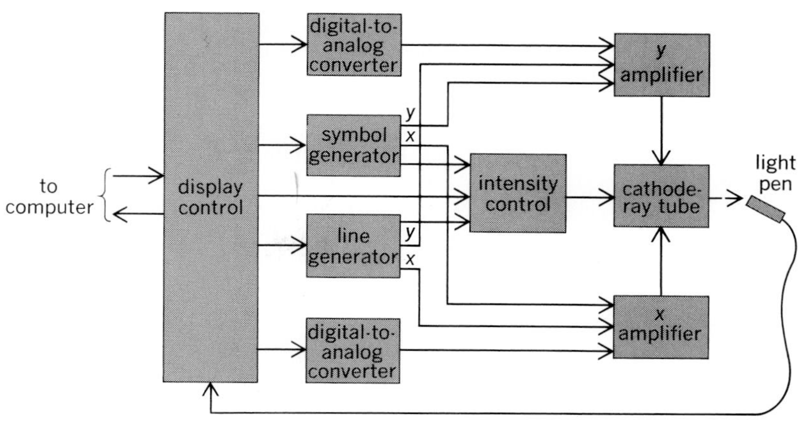


**Fig. 2. General display system organization.**

relatively easy to arrange a character generator to synthesize small symbols in synchronism with the scan. Simple, low-resolution graphics based on combinations of special symbols has also become feasible; this technique is used in teletext and videotext. High-resolution, synchronous graphics generation in scan format is, however, so much more difficult that new techniques had to be developed. A frame memory, or bit map, is one such technique (**Fig. 3**). The CRT intensity is controlled by reading out and decoding a sequence of words that the computer has stored in the memory, one word per $x,y$ location. The number of bits per word in the memory depends on the number of intensity levels (colors) desired. *See* VIDEOTEXT AND TELETEXT.

The memory is of two-port design, in which the scan-synchronous addressing for display readout has priority. Access time is sufficient, however, for the computer to write new display information into the memory. Display resolutions of up to 2000 by 2000 points are possible at frame rates of up to 60 per second (completely flicker-free), exceeding cursive display capabilities. No symbol or line generation elements are shown. These tasks are now accomplished in computer software, since they no longer have to be done in real time to drive the display, and can include area fill-in, shading, and hidden-line elimination for realistic display of solid objects. With the proper soft-

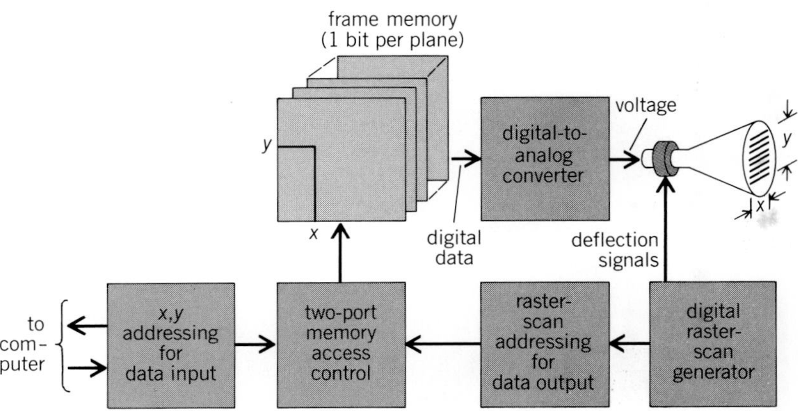


**Fig. 3. Frame-memory raster-scan display.**

ware, the more advanced raster-scan display systems can produce pictorial output approaching photographic quality (monochrome or color), but not necessarily at a fast enough new-frame rate to simulate real-time motion. There, cursive displays still have an advantage. Raster-scan displays, however, can be used to produce movie films, one frame at a time, and such computer animation is widely used.

In a different fashion, plotting technology has also advanced from a single, cursive writing stylus to linear arrays of individual styli (some spaced as finely as 200 to the inch or 8 to the millimeter) which draw complete pictures or text pages in one straight-line sweep across the display area. As in raster-scan CRTs, writing data must be supplied for every point in the display area, but no styli movement data are required.

**Graphical input.** Before discussing graphical input, it is necessary to distinguish between the two major ways of using a computer: batch operation and on-line operation. In batch operation the user has no direct access to the computer and is usually not present during the time when the job is running in the computer. A computing job must be completely prepared ahead of time, with detailed specification of input data and program, desired output, and alternate courses of action in case of certain error conditions. If an error occurs, the user must then review what results are received, make corrections in the input, and resubmit the job. This process may have to be repeated several times before all errors are corrected and a satisfactory run is achieved. Although graphical output as described in the preceding section is quite feasible, the forms of graphical input which require close human-computer interaction are not usually feasible.

In on-line operation, on the other hand, the user has direct input/output access to the computer through a console or terminal of some sort during the time a job is running in the computer. In this situation a result or partial result may be immediately presented to the user for decision as to correctness or the need for further input to correct errors or extend the solution, and the computer waits to receive further information before proceeding with the job. Turnaround time is reduced from the hours or days typical of batch operation to a few seconds, providing the intimate human-computer relationship needed for two-way (interactive) graphical communication. It is obvious, however, that having a large computer which can perform millions of operations per second wait idly while the user makes a decision and takes action is an inefficient use of valuable computer resources. Thus, on-line operation was at first restricted to experimental research facilities and special situations, such as air-traffic control and military systems, where rapid, joint human-computer decision making is essential. However, two developments in computer technology have acted to greatly increase adoption of on-line interaction: small, inexpensive computers, which can be used economically in a dedicated (one-user) mode of operation; and time-sharing techniques for large computers, which permit a computer to economically service a number (perhaps 10–100) of on-line users by switching instantly to work for another user when a particular job reaches a point where human decision is required. Both of these developments have sparked the growing interest in interactive computer graphics. SEE MICROCOMPUTER; MULTIACCESS COMPUTER.

Fig. 4. On-line interactive graphics console.

In noninteractive graphical input, specialized off-line equipment such as curve tracers and coordinate digitizers (human-guided or automatic) permit a sketch or drawing to be converted to the alphanumeric form on punched cards, punched tape, or magnetic tapes and disks. Such data can be used as input in batch computing but will be subject to the slow error-correction process.

The second, or interactive, form of graphical input requires on-line access to the computer. In this case, hand-held input devices, such as writing styli used with electronic tablets and light pens used with on-line CRT displays, permit the human to sketch a problem description, say, a bridge truss to be analyzed, in an on-line interactive mode in which the computer acts as a drafting assistant with unusual powers. For example, since the computer can analyze each element of a sketch as it is entered and apply precoded rules and constraints such as "all lines shall be either exactly vertical or exactly horizontal," it can instantly convert a rough freehand motion of the light pen into an accurate picture element. The computer can also establish connectivity between various picture elements so that the shape of the displayed object, say, a rectangle, can be altered by simply indicating with the light pen that one of the sides should be moved. As the computer knows which lines are connected together, it can automatically adjust lengths of the adjoining sides as any one side is moved.

There are two key concepts in this process. One is that the computer be continuously informed of the position of the hand-held input device as it is moved over the display screen or writing surface, and the other is that a displayed picture element may be identified to the computer for action such as moving it or erasing it by simply pointing to it with the input device. The action to be taken at any particular time is made known to the computer by additional manual input actions such as pushing one of a number of button switches on a panel, or pointing with the input device to one of a number of alternate commands (called light buttons or a pick list) displayed on the viewing screen along with the picture (usually along the bottom or one edge of the screen).

**Interactive input/output arrangements.** Devices used in interactive computer graphics include light pens, electronic tablets, the mouse, the touch screen, CRT recorders, and direct-view storage tube (DVST) displays.

***Light pens.*** The light pen, used for graphical input in conjunction with on-line CRT displays, consists of a photodetector mounted in a pen-shaped holder. When the pen is held over a displayed picture element, the pen senses the light created while the electron beam is writing that particular element and sends a signal to the computer (**Fig. 4**). Since the computer knows which element it is writing at any given time, the time of receipt of the signal from the pen immediately identifies to the computer which element in the picture the pen is pointing at, providing a convenient and natural method for the human user to "discuss" a picture with the computer. Because the light pen is a passive device which can only respond to displayed information, it provides no information to the computer when held over a blank part of the screen. Thus, in order to draw with a light pen, it is necessary to perform a process known as pen tracking. One way to do this is to continuously display a tracking cross, a cross-shaped pattern made up of dots, which is slightly larger than the field of view of the pen. As each dot is plotted, the pen reports whether or not it "saw" it, and by comparing the number of dots seen on each arm of the cross, the computer can keep the cross continuously aligned with the pen as the pen is moved over the viewing screen. The pen-tracking process is fairly effective for input drawing, but suffers from lack of precision and the use of a substantial amount of computing time to perform.

***Electronic tablets.*** The effort to find a better input means than the light pen produced a number of new devices, one of which is the electronic tablet. A number of different electronic detection principles are used in making tablets, but the end result is the same: The circuitry produces a pair of digital $x$ and $y$ coordinate values corresponding continuously to the position of a writing stylus upon the surface of the tablet. The advantage of the tablet is that no computer time is required for operation as in pen tracking (except to sample the input from the tablet). Also, the tablet can be placed on the table in front of the display screen, producing a more natural writing position for the user. Another advantage of tablets is that in most of them the stylus is capacitively coupled to the tablet surface, permitting the curves or drawings which already exist in paper form to be placed on the tablet surface and traced as input.

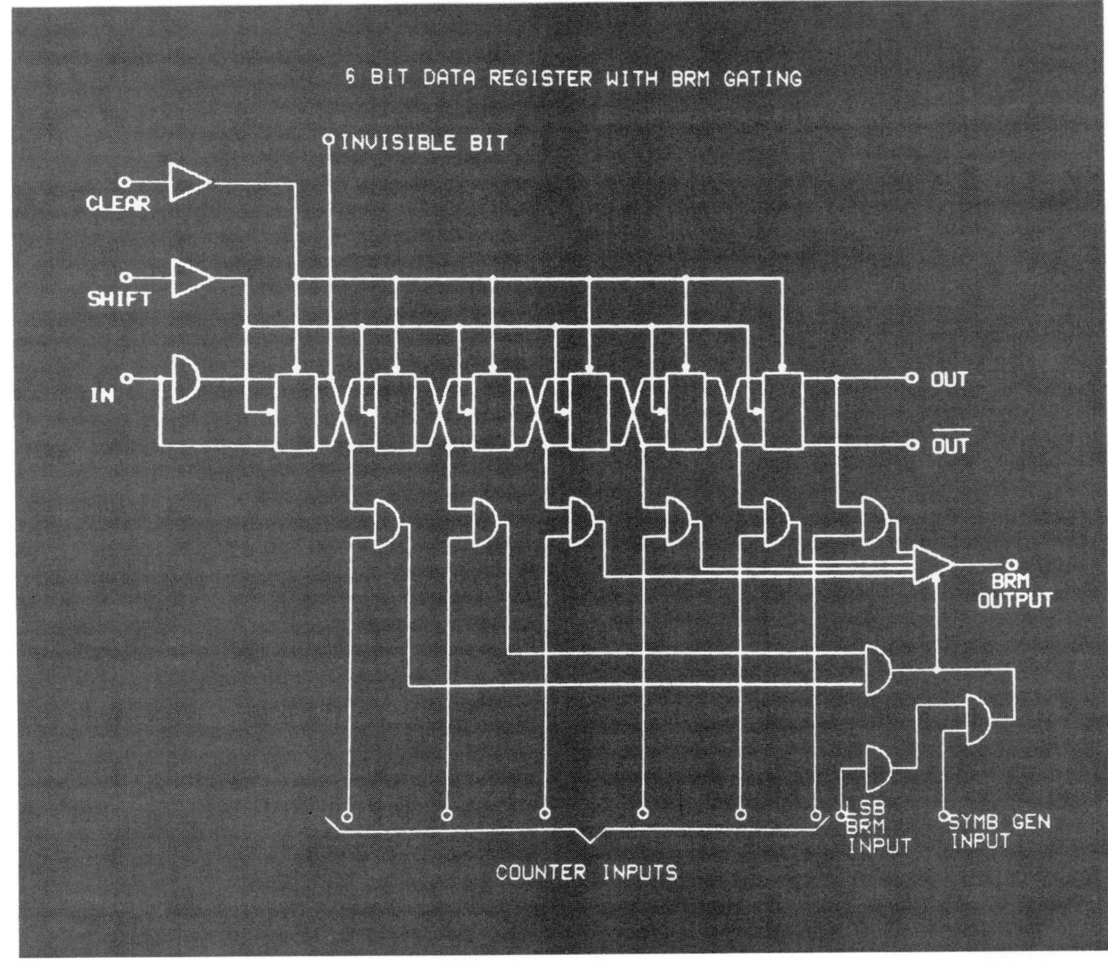


**Fig. 5. Display of electronic circuit.**

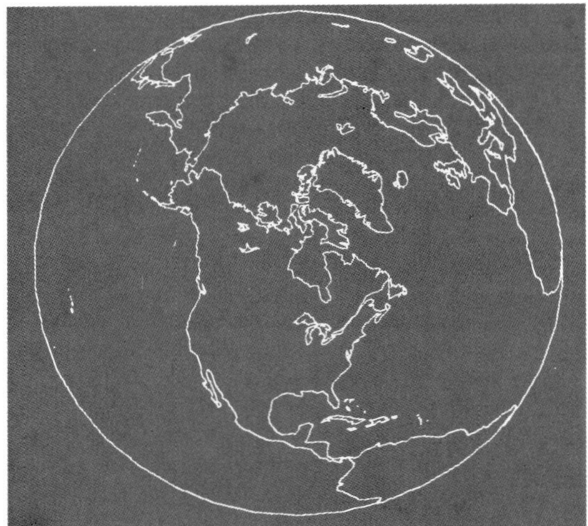

**Fig. 6. Example of computer-produced map.**

To provide interaction between the tablet and the display, it is usual to display a cursor (a dot or tracking symbol) corresponding to the current position of the stylus on the writing surface. The user then uses the stylus to steer this cursor around the screen to point to displayed objects, draw additional picture elements, and so forth. Other devices such as joy sticks, track balls, and slewing buttons are also used to steer cursors on the screen in many displays. These are all of relatively low cost and provide satisfactory pointing capability; however, the two-axis form of control that is characteristic of these devices is too awkward to permit drawing.

***Mouse.*** The mouse was developed in the 1960s, but only in the 1980s did it become popular in connection with graphical input for small personal computers. It is a small box about the size of a pack of cigarettes, with wheels mounted at right angles. As the mouse is held in the hand and moved over the surface of a table or drawing in a fixed orientation, it generates $x$ and $y$ signals similar to those from a tablet, and controls a cursor.

***Touch screen.*** Another interaction device from the 1960s that gained new popularity in the 1980s is the touch screen, which permits pointing at displayed objects with the finger. This has advantages for information screens in public places because there is no external device or wiring. Various implementations include arrays of sonic- or light-beam sensors interruptible by the finger, and crossed-wire matrices or transparent resistive sheets that sense and measure the point of finger contact. The precision of pointing is generally not as high as in the devices above, but is satisfactory for many purposes.

***CRT recorders.*** CRT recorders operate like CRT displays, but are desgined to record graphic images on film rather than display them for human viewing. This permits use of small, high-resolution CRTs with pu to 4000 dot addresses in each axis. Essentially, CRT recorders act like high-speed plotting boards capable of producing 2–10 pictures per second. One interesting use of CRT recorders is to produce animated movies.

***DVST displays.*** Direct-view storage tube (DVST) displays have come to the fore as a means of avoiding the refresh requirements fo standard CRT displays, particularly in low-cost remote display terminals driven over low bandwidth telephone-line connections. The DVST is analogous to the ''Etch-a-Sketch'' toy, maintaining any picture element once written until the entire screen is electronically erased. SEE STORAGE TUBE.

**Applications.** Graphic output from computers operated in batch mode has received wide acceptance in a variety of scientific and business applications (**Figs. 5** and **6**). Computer-produced graphs and charts are sufficiently readable to permit direct use in reports, eliminating laborious and costly manual plotting and drafting. In applications such as highway layout and piping layouts in ships and refineries, direct pictorial output is of great value. Interactive graphics is not yet used as widely because of its dependence on the availability of on-line computing facilities, but has already been applied in such diverse fields as integrated circuit design, dress-pattern layout (with automatic scaling of patterns for different sizes), aircraft design, and study of molecular structures. A whole field, called computer-adied design, depends on interactive computer graphics for the intimate, pictorial person-computer communications required. SEE COMPUTER; COMPUTER-AIDED DESIGN AND MANUFACTURING; DIGITAL COMPUTER.

*John E. Ward*

***Bibliography.*** J. Bertin, *Semiology of Graphics*, 1983; J. Deken, *Computer Images: State of the Art*, 1983; J. D. Foley and A. van Dam, *Fundamentals of Interactive Computer Graphics*, 1982; D. P. Greenberg and A. Marcus, *The Computer Image: Applications of Computer Graphics*, 1982; S. Harrington, *Computer Graphics: A Programming Approach*, 1983; J. E. Scott, *Introduction to Interactive Computer Graphics*, 1982; A. van Dam, Computer software for graphics, *Sci. Amer.*, 251(3):146–159, 1984; M. Waite and C. L. Morgan, *Graphics Primer for the IBM PC*, 1983.

## Computer hardware description languages

Notations and computer languages that facilitate the documentation, design, and manufacturing of digital systems. Extending beyond early applications in logic synthesis and simulation, these languages are now used to drive very large-scale integrated circuits, and combine program verification techniques with expert system design methodologies.

**Hierarchies of levels of detail.** Digital system descriptions use a hierarchy of levels of detail. A system is depicted as a network of components of a lower level, each of which is in turn a ''system'' composed of yet simpler components at an even lower level (see **table**). At some point, components are taken as primitive and their properties are not described in terms of lower-level elements.

**Evolution of CHDLs.** Computer hardware description languages (CHDLs) have been used since the 1950s, and their evolution has been tied to the maturity of the computer design process. Simpler notations were used to describe early systems at the gate and register transfer levels, and the primitive components were gates, registers, and so forth (transistors and capacitors being in some sense at a lower level but of more concern to electrical engineers and physicists than to most computer designers).

Starting in the late 1960s, instruction set processor description languages were introduced to aid the de-

**Hierarchy of levels of design**

| Component | Connection | Behavior |
|---|---|---|
| Gate<br>Flip-flop | Layout<br>Wire list | Timing diagrams<br>Boolean equation<br>Truth tables |
| Register<br>Arithmetic-logic unit (ALU) | Block diagram | State diagram<br>Register transfer |
| Processor | ? | Instruction set |
| Network | Processor-memory-switch (PMS) diagram | ? |

sign activities at a higher level. This was in response to the needs of computer architects who were more concerned with the behavior of the instruction set of the computer than with the implementation or realization of the data paths and control units. To a large extent, this evolution was triggered by the introduction of computer families, sharing the same instruction set but implemented with widely diverse technologies and cost-performance trade-offs. The notations borrow heavily from regular Algol-like programming languages, although the languages are tuned to the description of purely behavioral aspects of the system, ignoring implementation details. An instruction set processor description of an early minicomputer, the DEC PDP-8, is shown in the **illustration.** SEE COMPUTER SYSTEMS ARCHITECTURE.

Recently, processors, memories, and switches have appeared as primitive elements used to build multiprocessors and array processors of different kinds, leading to geographically distributed computer networks. There are few computer hardware description languages in use at this level because formal design methods are still evolving. SEE DISTRIBUTED SYSTEMS; MULTIPROCESSING.

Concurrently with the appearance of languages appropriate for the different levels of design, the domain of applications for the languages within each design level has also grown. This evolution is brought about by advances in computer programming technology. While the notations for early systems tended to be designed mostly for documentation and simulation, more formal applications of computer hardware description languages have become increasingly common.

As the complexity of hardware designs increases, hardware and software activities tend to blur. Current problems being addressed by designers of computer hardware description languages include correctness and verification, separate compilation facilities, access to program libraries, version control, and configuration management. Many good ideas have been developed to enhance the productivity of programmers and the correctness of the program development process, and a similar array of tools may soon be developed to aid the hardware design process. The commonality of activities has led some researchers to propose the use of regular programming languages, such as Ada, as computer hardware description languages. The migration of computer science results into hardware design is further illustrated by current approaches to very large-scale integration (VLSI) synthesis. SEE PROGRAMMING LANGUAGES.

**VLSI synthesis.** The use of very large-scale integration has made complete processors and memories available in a single silicon chip. Two aspects of this technological revolution are, first, that primitive components continue to increase in complexity and, second, that the rate of introduction of new components continues to increase.

While the increased power of the primitive components simplifies the design task, the rapid introduction of new, more complex components requires an acceleration in the design process if a new technology is to realize its potentiality—some estimates indicate an exponential growth in worker-hours per month required to design and lay out complex integrated circuits. This can be achieved only through automatic means.

Early design automation systems were constrained by a fixed, built-in set of components and by a direct or canonical implementation philosophy. That is, the designers specification would be translated into hardware in a manner very similar to a macroexpansion in an assembly programming language. A better approach is to eliminate the first constraint by taking as inputs both the designer's specification and the description of the components or building blocks from some design data base, thus speeding up the incorporation of new technologies into the design process. This works well when designing with standard packages, which are subject to common interconnection rules.

For a variety of reasons, a direct translation of the initial specification might not lead to an acceptable implementation. For example, the specification might have been written in a style that made it easy to read and perhaps extend by other designers. Thus, a more intelligent handling of the designer's specification is required. This is particularly true in the design of integrated circuits, where geometric constraints must be taken into account.

The design activity can be characterized as a constrained optimization problem along multiple dimensions, such as cost, speed, power dissipation, shape, size (or area), and component count, and the number of possible solutions (that is, implementations of a given behavioral specification) can be very large. Unfortunately, there are no algorithms that could lead a design automation program through the entire space of designs, evaluating them and retaining only those that meet some criteria of optimality. Emerging design automation systems rely instead on heuristic techniques to explore the design space and often borrow sophisticated methods developed in the field of artificial intelligence. At present, however, chip design remains an expensive, time-consuming labor-intensive activity. It will be a few years before the performance of artificial-intelligence-based tools becomes adequate for mass-produced designs in a truly automated silicon foundry. SEE ARTIFICIAL INTELLIGENCE; INTEGRATED CIRCUITS; OPTIMIZATION.

*Mario R. Barbacci*

**Bibliography.** Computer hardware description languages, *Computer*, special issue, vol. 18, no. 2, February 1985; G. Moore, VLSI; Some fundamental challenges, *IEEE Spectrum*, 16(4):30–37, April 1979; New VLSI tools, *Computer,* special issue, vol. 16, no. 12, December 1983; *Proceedings of the IFIP 6th International Symposium on Hardware Description Languages and Their Applications*, Pittsburgh, May 23–25, 1983; *Proceedings of the IFIP 7th Interna-*

*tional Symposium on Computer Hardware Description Languages and Their Applications*, Tokyo, August 29–31, 1985.

## Computer-integrated manufacturing

A system in which individual engineering, production, and marketing and support functions of a manufacturing enterprise are organized into a computer-integrated system. Functional areas such as design, analysis, planning, purchasing, cost accounting, inventory control, and distribution are linked through the computer with factory floor functions such as materials handling and management, providing direct control and monitoring of all process operations.

Computer-integrated manufacturing (CIM) may be viewed as the successor technology which links computer-aided design (CAD), computer-aided manufacturing (CAM), robotics, numerically controlled machine tools (NCMT), automatic storage and retrieval systems (AS/RS), flexible manufacturing systems (FMS), and other computer-based manufacturing technology. Computer-integrated manufacturing is also known as integrated computer-aided manufacturing (ICAM). Autofacturing includes computer-integrated manufacturing, but also includes conventional machinery, human operators, and their relationships within a total system. *SEE* COMPUTER-AIDED DESIGN AND MANUFACTURING; ROBOTICS.

**Factory of the future.** The term computer-integrated manufacturing was first popularized by Joseph Harrington in 1975. He predicted that future manufacturing success would be based more on effective management of data and information flow rather than on how efficiently either piece parts or finished products were manufactured. He postulated that in the CIM factory of the future there would be areas of "departmentalized" decision making. "Departments" would be defined as being process ("hard technology") based, that is, involving processes such as milling, drilling, routing, and grinding. "Nondepartments" are defined as being information ("soft technology") based, such as design engineering, process planning, and inventory management, the basic premise being that they are generic throughout an organization. For example, process planning considered as the function "planning" applies equally to all processes in the factory, whether they be machining of metal or lay-up of composite material. Investment made to computerize the function of process planning based on the assumption that it is generic will result in reuse of this investment many times throughout the organization. The computer-based process planning function will not change at all; but the data on which it operates will be specific to the process of the moment. Computer-aided design systems are the best example of the concept.

The CIM factory of the future will integrate the traditional hard or process-based technology factory (departments) with emerging softward of systems-based technology (nondepartments). **Figure 1** shows such a factory concept. The goal of this factory is to be efficiently integrated and continuously flexible and economical in the face of change.

***Effectiveness, efficiency, and economy.*** Efficiency is most often associated with transfer-line or assembly-line technology. The best-known developer of this technology was Henry Ford. His Model T factory could produce cars at an unprecedented rate, but the consumer had no choice at all about the specifications of the product. Flexibility is most often associated with robotics and other reprogrammable automation. Effectiveness is usually associated with the soft technology and organizational support structure of the enterprise.

Optimization of the CIM factory is based on specific criteria. By considering efficiency and flexibility and effectiveness, the CIM factory enables economy of scope. In economy of scope, flexibility is at least as important as efficiency, because the factory is seen to be an ever-changing dynamic environment which must always respond quickly to the needs of the marketplace, if not actually lead the need. The traditional factory with both rigid transfer-line technology and a rigid organizational structure cannot satisfy this objective; it strives for maximum volume of each product. In the ideal case, the CIM factory provides for profit with an order quantity of one, that is, when no two products are identical.

***Organization.*** The CIM factory concept is illustrated in Fig. 1: hard technology is shown in the upper half and soft technology in the lower half. Soft technology can be thought of as the intellect or brains of the factory, and hard technology as the muscles of the factory. The type of hard technology employed depends upon the products or family of products made by the factory. For metalworking, typical processes would include milling, turning, forming, casting, grinding, forging, drilling, routing, inspecting, coating, moving, positioning, assembling, and packaging. More important than the list of processes is their organization.

The CIM factory is made up of a part fabrication center, a component assembly center, and a product assembly center (Fig. 1). Centers are subdivided into work cells, cells into stations, and stations into processes. Processes comprise the basic transformations of raw materials into parts which will be assembled into products. In order for the factory to achieve maximum efficiency, raw material must come into the factory at the left end and move smoothly and continuously through the factory to emerge as a product at the right end. No part must ever be standing; each part is either being worked on or is on its way to the next work station. In conventional factories, a typical part is worked on about 5% of the time.

In the part fabrication center, raw material is transformed into piece parts. Some piece parts move by robot carrier or automatic guided vehicle (AGV) to the component fabrication center. Other piece parts (excess capacity) move out of the factory to sister factories for assembly. There is no storage of work in process and no warehousing in the CIM factory of the future. To accomplish this objective, part movement is handled by robots of various types. These robots serve as the focus or controlling element of work cells (**Fig. 2**) and work stations (**Fig. 3**). Each work cell contains a number of work stations. The station is where the piece part transformation occurs—from a raw material to a part, after being worked on by a particular process.

Components, also known as subassemblies, are created in the component assembly center. Here robots of various types, and other reprogrammable automation, put piece parts together. Components may then be transferred to the product assembly center, or out of the factory (excess capacity) to sister factories

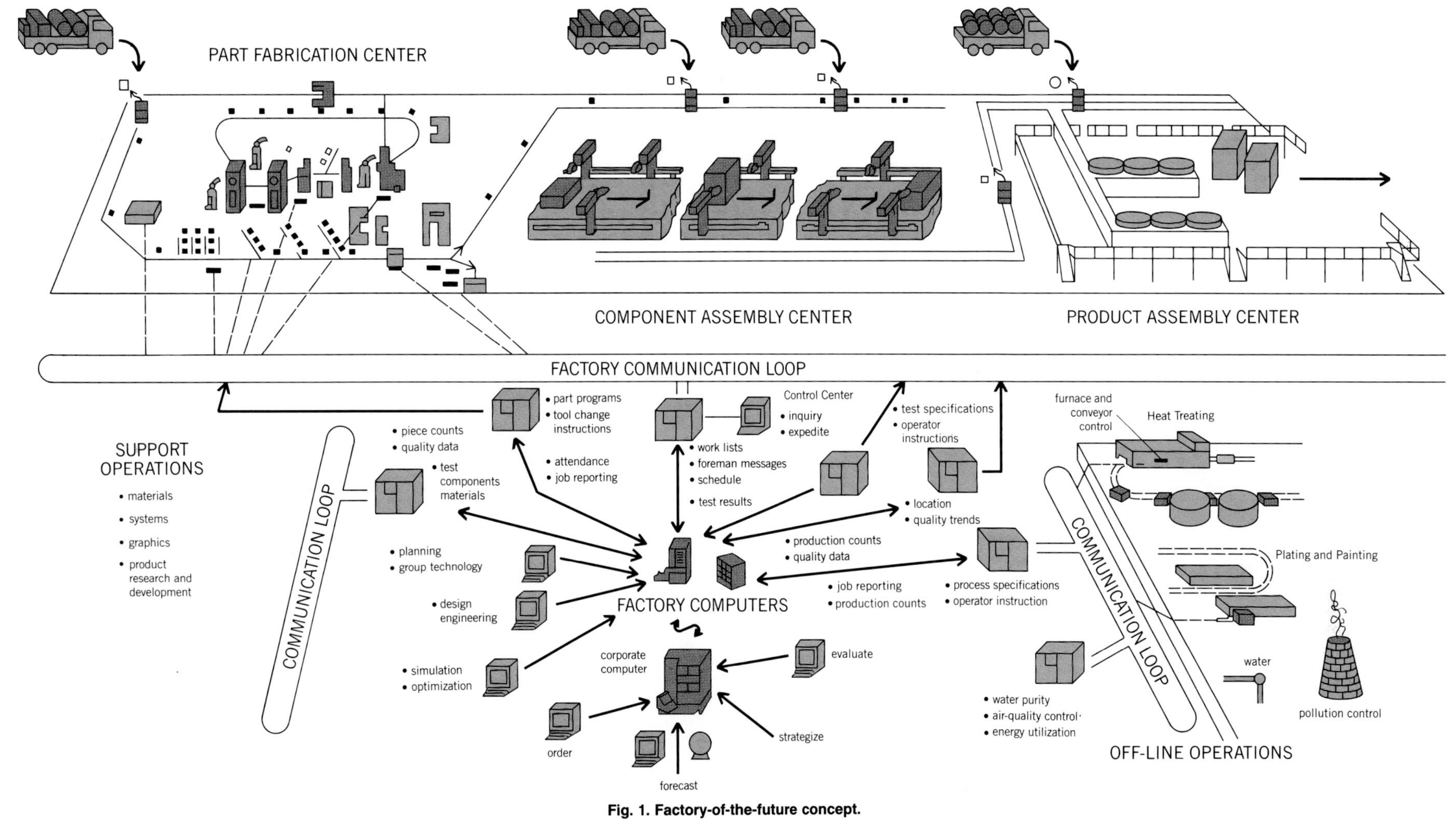


**Fig. 1. Factory-of-the-future concept.**

Fig. 2. Typical CIM work cell.

for final assembly operations there. Parts from other factories may come into the component assembly center of this factory, and components from other factories may come into the product assembly center of this factory. The final product moves out of the product assembly center to the end user.

**Integration.** The premise of CIM is that a network is created in which every part of the enterprise works for the maximum benefit of the whole enterprise. Independent of the degree of automation employed, whether it is robotic or not, the organization of computer hardware and software is essential (lower half of Fig. 1). The particular processes (upper half of Fig. 1) employed by the factory are specific to the product being made, but the functions performed (lower half of Fig. 1) can be virtually unchanged in the CIM factory of the future no matter what the product. These typical functions include forecasting, designing, predicting, controlling, inventorying, grouping, monitoring, releasing, planning, scheduling, ordering, changing, communicating, and analyzing.

It must be recognized that independent, optimum performance of the individual functions is not as important as their integration with one another, or their integration with the factory floor itself. This integration is brought about in two ways. The first is through an architecture of manufacturing which specifies precisely how and when each function is integrated with the other (**Fig. 4**). The second is through a cell controller and cell network.

The cell controller ensures integration of data between each machine, robot, automatic guided vehicle, and so forth, of the cell. The cell network (**Fig. 5**) actually performs this communication within the cell, and connects cells together into centers. In the cell network, communication is possible between each machine of the network and between different networks. The cell controller itself serves to perform such tasks as: downloading part programs from the CAD system to each machine in the cell, monitoring actual performance of each machine and comparing this performance to the plan, selecting alternate routing for a part if a machine is not operable, notifying operators of pending out-of-tolerance conditions, archiving historical performance of the cell, and trans

Fig. 3. Typical CIM work station.

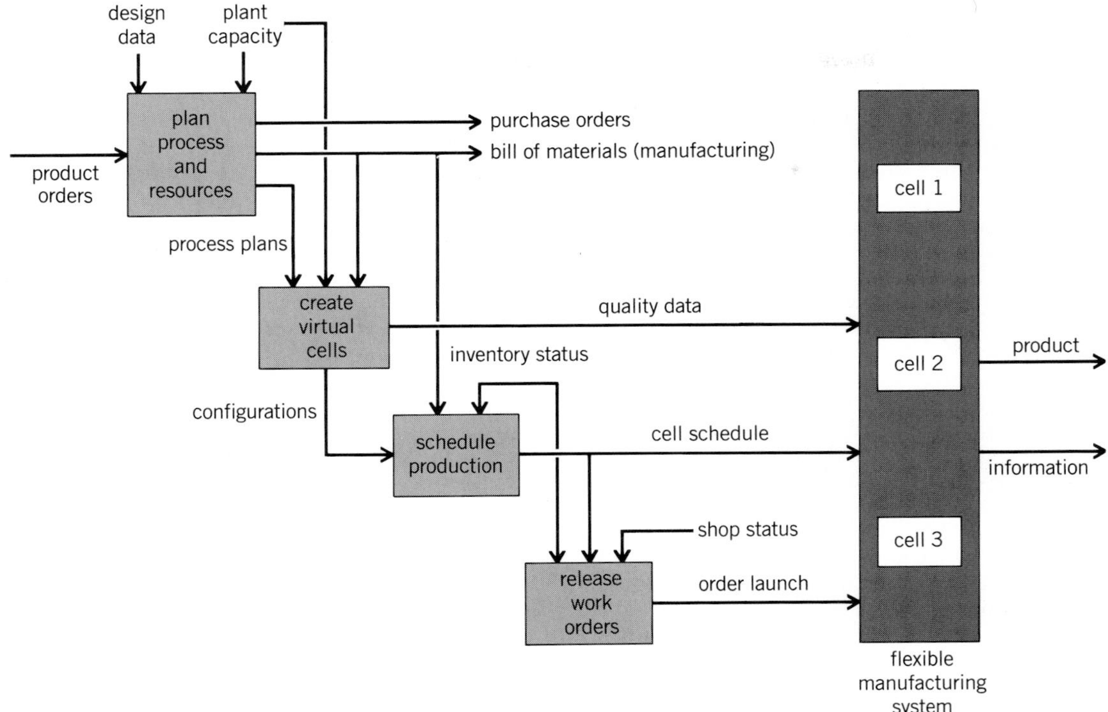


**Fig. 4. Diagram of the architecture of manufacturing. (*Designed by D. Shunk, GCA Corp.*)**

mitting to the center level on an exception basis the cell performance compared to plan. The center level of the CIM factory of the future is all of the policies and procedures that run the factory. These are embodied in computer software, which is in turn based upon an overintegration plan or architecture of manufacturing.

The purpose for the architecture of manufacturing is to provide a blueprint for employing CIM. While there are as many variations of the details of the ar-

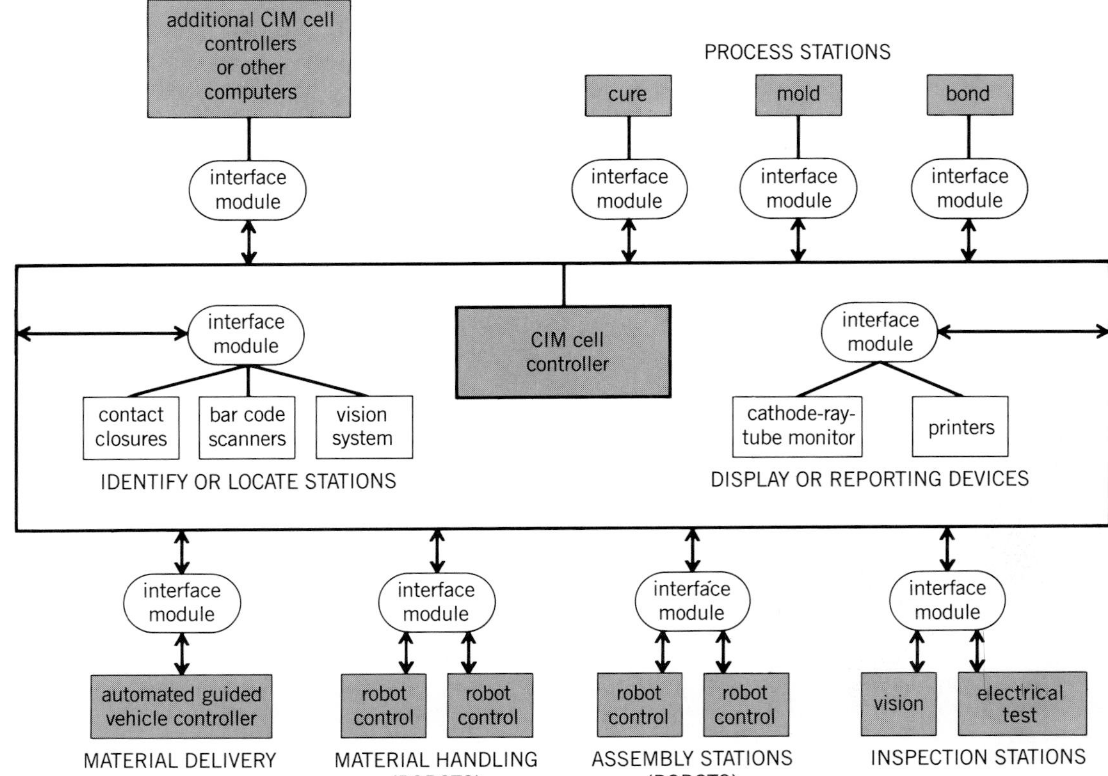


**Fig. 5. CIM production cell network.**

chitecture of the CIM factory of the future as there are factories, the structure of the architecture is generic. The focus is the flexible manufacturing system (FMS), which is made up of cells, stations, and processes. The information to be fed back to functions where decisions are made is more important than the product itself. In this example, the functions are defined very broadly and are used only to illustrate the absolute necessity for interaction between functions if the CIM factory is to be made to work efficiently, flexibly, and effectively.

Analysis of the first block of Fig. 4 illustrates the idea. Here input to the model is product forecast. The input is changed into output depending upon the status of the controls coming into the top of the function box. In this case, one control is design data. It should not be possible for an order to be accepted when design does not exist. A second control is plant capacity; an order cannot be accepted if it cannot be filled by the plant within cost and schedule.

In the ideal CIM factory of the future, before any real decision is made, it is tested on a computerized model of the architecture to determine its feasibility. Thereby, any mistakes are made in theory, not in practice. Several simulation software packages are routinely used for this purpose. For the true CIM factory of the future to be realized, it will be necessary to build a complete simulation model.

*Dennis Wisnosky*

**Bibliography.** J. Harrington, Jr., *Computer Integrated Manufacturing,* 1975, reprint 1979; R. M. Metcalf and D. R. Boggs (Xerox PARC), Ethernet: Distributed switching for local computer networks, *Commun. ACM,* 19:395–404, July 1976; A. B. Pritsker and C. D. Pegden, *Introduction to Simulation and SLAM,* 1979; C. M. Savage, Preparing for the factory of the future, *Mod. Mach. Shop,* October 1983.

## Computer networking

The connection of computers by systems that allow information to be directly transferred between them. A person with a computer can now send a letter across the United States by using a computer network for less cost than through the mail system. With a new computer network technology called packet switching, a letter sent coast to coast costs as little as one-half cent per 200 words. More significantly, a computer letter will arrive within seconds. SEE PACKET SWITCHING.

Even these costs will continue to decrease. The cost of electronic circuitry, the critical ingredient of computer and computer networking equipment, is falling at a rate of over 20% per year, so that circuits that cost $1000 today may cost only $328 in 5 years. Computers and computer networking facilities are also becoming easier for the layperson to use, and standards for exchanging information among diverse computers are being defined.

The future is likely to bring worldwide interconnected computer networks resembling the telephone system of today. Like the telephone system, these networks will have local components called local area networks (LANs), akin to a building or campus telephone system called the Private Branch Exchange (PBX), and components in the public domain called wide area networks (WANs). Access to computer networks will become as common as access to the telephone system, as prices reflect the circuit cost decreases and networking facilities become easier to use. Using computer networks, people will not only send letters but have access to a variety of information available from a new breed of electronics entrepreneur, the information provider.

**Development.** In a sense, the functions of the telegraph system developed during the nineteenth century more closely resembled a computer network than today's telephone network. The telegraph system, like the computer network, does not encourage direct interaction between the sender and receiver. A telegraph message, like a computer letter sent over a packet network, is stored at a number of intermediate stops along its path to the recipient.

In the 1950s it became useful to transfer computer information over the telephone system. At that time, computer information was actually first punched into computer cards or placed on magnetic tape before being sent long distances between two communicating card reader-punch machines or between two communicating magnetic tape machines. In the early 1960s, computers were redesigned to communicate directly without placing information on cards or magnetic tape. However, costs for circuits were high then, and the use of the telephone system for computer data was restricted by law. Not until the Supreme Court's "Carterfone decision" in 1969 was it deemed legal to attach equipment not owned by the telephone company to the telephone system.

The first wide area networks were government networks and a few private ones like airline reservation systems. One of these was to become the research vehicle for many other future wide area networks: the U.S. Department of Defense Advanced Research Projects Agency's (ARPA) network called the ARPANET. It was envisioned in a 1964 report as a packet network for computer sharing between government workers, and its initial version was completed in 1969. It became very useful as a test bed for computer networking principles. Instead of being used primarily for computer sharing, ARPANET rapidly became much more widely used as a vehicle for electronic mail between researchers in various computer science fields, including computer networking.

During the 1970s, wide area computer networks of two types, private and public, became available. Private networks, designed by computer manufacturers and owned by corporations and government organizations, provided information workers with data needed for daily operations. Digital Network Architecture (DNA) from Digital Equipment Corporation, and Systems Network Architecture (SNA) from International Business Machines Corporation were two prominent examples of these designs.

Public wide area networks, designed and owned by

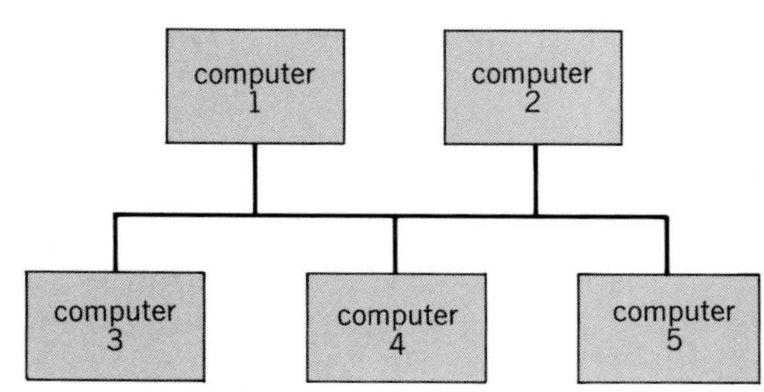


**Fig. 1. Bus configuration.**

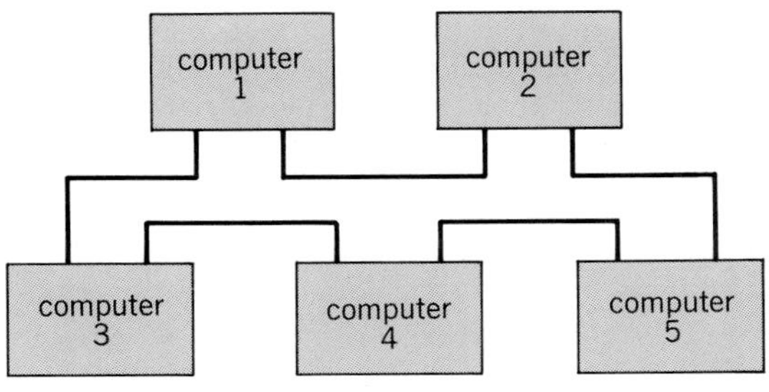


**Fig. 2. Ring configuration.**

telephone companies, gave people access to information and services from companies such as Dow Jones, which provided electronic financial information, and Mead Data, which provided electronic news. Datapac in Canada, Transpac in France, and Telenet and Tymnet in the United States were public networks through which these kinds of services were available.

During the 1970s local area networks became the subject of significant research, primarily as a result of the growing interest in moving the processing power of the computer to the user rather than asking the user to come to the computer room or share a large computer with other users. A number of different concepts, based on two physical network configurations, were proposed. Work was undertaken on a bus configuration (**Fig. 1**), using a mathematically based scheme called Carrier Sense Multiple Access (CSMA) to determine which computer has access to the bus at any given time.

A second configuration called the ring configuration (**Fig. 2**) was found to have the advantage of natural ordering. That is, each computer can determine which computer is before it and which follows it. For example, if the electrical signal flows clockwise in Fig. 2, computer 1 follows computer 5 and precedes computer 2; computer 2 follows computer 1 and precedes computer 3; and so on. This property allows a ''token'' or a permit to circulate to control access to ring at any given time. Until the ring is needed for message transmission, the token continues to circulate. Any station may remove it, send a message, and return it to the ring at any time. Thus, only one station will send a message at a given time. Both the ring and the bus were discovered to have the practical disadvantage that they would not be wired into a building in the traditional way. Traditionally, building wire extends outwardly radially from wiring centers

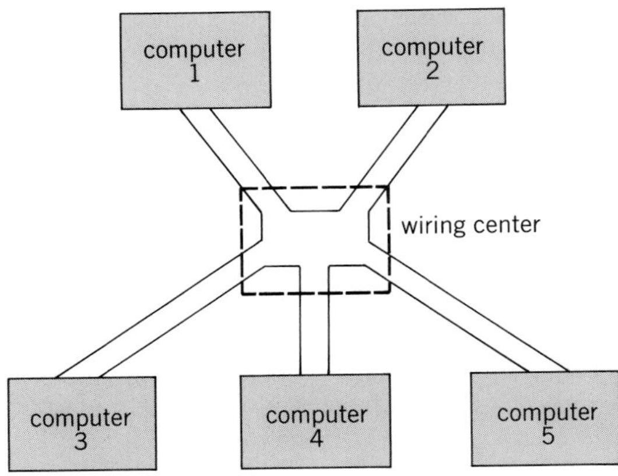


**Fig. 3. Star-ring configuration.**

in a ''star'' configuration. Researches then discovered that the ring could be made more reliable by wiring it as a star (**Fig. 3**). This configuration has replaced the pure ring in practical LANs. Other combinations have been developed from these two.

In the early 1980s the number of both public and private networks grew substantially. Almost every major noncommunist country had one or more public networks, and over 10,000 private networks were operational. The number and variety of information services available through computer networks also grew dramatically. By 1984 over 600 different data sources in the United States provided information almost instantly through computer networks. The technological differences between public networks and private networks were fading, and interconnection of both kinds of networks permitted information exchange between organizations. However, even with these advances, relatively little information in the form of images, graphics, or voice was transferred through computer networks.

**Principles.** The principles of computer networking are, in many ways, similar to the principles of vehicular traffic flow through the network of highways, bridges, and tunnels.

Three of the important problems of computer networking are addressing, routing, and flow control. Addressing is analogous to assigning names and numbers to the populated areas (city and town names) and routes between them (U.S. 70, I80, and so forth). The advantages of assigning designations that give information about the characteristics of the route (Interstate 80 is a better route than U.S. 70 which is better than Vt. 4) or the populated area (a city has more services than a town which has more services than a village) are obvious. Frequently, computer networks use a similar concept. A given node (analogous to a populated area) in a computer network may be designated, implicitly or explicitly, as a host, switching node, or terminal node. Similarly, a link (analogous to a piece of route connecting two adjacent populated areas) may be designated as a high- or low-capacity link.

Routing of messages in a computer network is similar to routing of cars and trucks from one location to another. Frequently, travelers unfamiliar with an area obtain the best route from one city to another through a travel service. A centralized routing service of this sort is used in many computer networks. The public network, Tymnet, has used the approach in the past, and private networks using SNA employ it in some small networks.

Another approach to traveling is simply to determine the best route from a map or from knowledge of geography. This normally works well, but can make traveling difficult if information about the terrain or road conditions is outdated. This technique is called source routing because the source (sender) determines the route the message will follow. Finally, a traveler may have no specific route in mind but make route decisions at each intersection. The network analogy to this semirandom approach is called fully distributed routing. This technique has been used in the ARPANET.

Flow control, used in computer networks, minimizes the ill effects of congestion. It has no universal analogy in the highway system. Data that enter a computer network at a high speed, say 8000 characters (a basic element of computer information, capable of representing a single letter or number) per second, may need to share the same telephone link with data entering from an unrelated terminal at a rate of 2000 characters per second. If the link which must accommodate the two data flows is able to carry only 6000 characters per second, there must be some technique that limits the two flows in a way which is fair to both. This is much like the problem of two highways coming together at a tunnel that is not able to accommodate the traffic from both highways. When this happens in a data network, flow control reduces the two data flows and may even limit the amount of data entering the network from the terminals. In the highway example, reducing the number of cars that enter the system would be akin to asking certain people to stay home since the tunnels are crowded.

**Prospects.** The future holds promise for tremendous growth and improvement in computer networks, both local area networks and wide area networks. It is likely that these networks will become as important economically and militarily as the highways and airways of today.

Computer networks will become more flexible, easier to use, and will perform better. Most importantly, computer networks will be easier to access from personal computers and terminals. As computer networks become as easy to use as the dictionary, the telephone book, and the automated bank teller, they will become important to a more diverse population of users.

The computer network will continue to improve its performance. This will be partly due to the improving underlying technologies, computers, and transmission systems, but will also be influenced by a demand for more rapid network response consistent with the human brain's reaction time.

The computer network will become more flexible so that it is easily able to accommodate a wide variety of information, either separately or mixed. For example, voice messages and pictures will be sent over the network in the same way that text messages or text documents can be sent today. These messages or documents may also have voice, text, graphics, and photographs all integrated into one information package. Computer networks will gradually change to accommodate, at lower costs and more rapidly, all of the information that can be sent through the mail today. *See Data communications; Electronic mail; Local-area networks; Video telephone; Wide-area networks.*

*Robert F. Steen*

**Bibliography.** P. Baran, F. Boehm, and P. Smith, *On Distributed Communications*, vols. 1–11, Rand Corp., August 1964; A. S. Tanenbaum, *Computer Networks*, 1981.

## Computer security

The preservation of computing resources against abuse or unauthorized use, especially the protection of data from accidental or deliberate damage, disclosure, or modification. Safeguards are both technical and administrative. Threats are both external (physical) and internal (logical) to the computer system.

Computing systems provide powerful tools for the storage and use of information. They are equally powerful tools for the misuse of the same information. Because of the pervasiveness of computers in modern society, the potential for abuse has triggered public awareness of the need for computer security. Computer abuse, financial fraud, invasion of individual privacy, industrial espionage, and problems with national security, are primary concerns. The right of privacy is the right of individuals or organizations to determine the degree to which information about them is collected, stored, and shared with others. Protection of privacy is an ethical and legal issue rather than a technical one, and is not unique to computing systems; however, computer security mechanisms can be used to protect information for privacy as well. Protection of data integrity is assurance that stored data will be accurate and consistent.

Computer security policies are rules of access to computing resources. Security mechanisms are the means by which policies are implemented. Discretionary access-control policies support the concept of data ownership by individual users and their right to share the data with other users. Nondiscretionary policies, used primarily by the military, rely on a built-in hierarchy of security classifications used to make access decisions. Security based on classification hierarchies is also called multilevel security. Authorization is the process of granting access rights to, and revoking the access rights of, various users of a discretionary system. Enforcement is the process of ensuring that all accesses which occur are in accordance with the current state of authorization.

Maintaining computer security is a management responsibility involving both technical and administrative problems. Management tasks include policy formulation, arrangements for physical security, cost modeling, and auditing procedures to validate the security controls and keep a record of system transactions. The primary function of management is to evaluate security threats, risks, policies, and mechanisms.

**Physical and logical security.** Physical and logical security are two important parts of computer security. Physical security measures, external to the hardware and software, are intended to prevent, or to facilitate recovery from, physical disasters such as fire, floods, riots, sabotage, and theft of physical resources. Logical security mechanisms, internal to the computing system, are used to protect against internal misuse of computing resources, such as the theft of computing time and unauthorized access to data.

Physical security includes the control of physical access to computing resources. In order to make decisions about who can have access to each terminal and each user account, as well as to the computer room itself, the installation must have one or more mechanisms for authenticating personal identification. Some physical access-control mechanisms are based on something a person has, such as a key for a lock or a magnetically striped card; or something a person knows, such as a password or the correct answers to an authentication dialog. Keys and cards can be lost or stolen, and passwords copied or forgotten—or sometimes even guessed. Thus, some personal identification mechanisms are based on something a person is, such as dermatoglyphics (for example, fingerprints or lip prints) or anthropometrics (for example, individual hand or head geometry). Analysis of the dynamics of pen movement and pressure during the signing of a person's signature is a promising research direction. Cryptographic digital signatures provide unforgeable and verifiable user authentication. Most of the physical security mechanisms, of course, are not limited to computer security.

The problems of logical security, on the other

hand, are more specific to computing. Logical computer security has several facets, including access controls, information flow controls, inference controls, and communication controls.

**Logical access controls.** All modern multiuser operating systems have some access controls for the sharing of resources, especially data. The objects protected by many systems are files. A coarse granularity of protection allows access to all of a file or none of it, and governs only a few access types, or operations on the objects, such as READ, WRITE, EXECUTE, or DELETE.

The access matrix (**Fig. 1**) is the basis for many methods of representing discretionary authorization information. The rows of the access matrix represent subjects, or users, of the system. The columns correspond to objects, or resources, of the system (mainly files). The authorization information contained in cell ($x$, $y$) of the table is a list of access types (allowable operations) that subject $x$ may apply to object $y$. Access matrix entries are created, propagated, modified, and revoked as part of the authorization process. The enforcement process uses the matrix to determine whether to allow a request by a given subject to perform a specified operation on a certain object. A row of an access matrix is a capability list, which contains the access rights of a given subject to various objects. A column of a matrix is an access control list, which contains the access rights of various subjects to a given object.

| Subjects \ Objects | File-1 | File-2 | ••• | SORT ROUTINE | ••• | File-*n* |
|---|---|---|---|---|---|---|
| SYSADMIN | -- | -- | | OWN READ EXECUTE | | -- |
| USER 1 | OWN READ | OWN READ WRITE | | EXECUTE | | -- |
| SORT ROUTINE | READ | WRITE | | -- | | -- |
| ••• | | | | | | |
| USER 17 | -- | READ | | -- | | OWN READ WRITE |

**Fig. 1. Access matrix for representing discretionary authorization information.**

The configuration of its access matrix at any point in time defines a system's protection state. The protection state is changed as a result of an authorization operation granting or revoking access rights, creating or deleting subjects or objects. These authorization operations are of course also subject to rights in the matrix. Theoretical results show that there is no general way to prove whether a given state of protection is safe, in the sense of whether it can leak an access right to an unauthorized cell in the access matrix. In practice, however, the safety question is trivially decidable for most real protection systems.

Access controls are also used in data-base management systems, but there are additional requirements. Data-base security needs a finer granularity (separate access decisions for small units of data). Access decisions must be based on a broader range of dependencies. For example, access might be conditional on data content, as in a policy which states that users in group X may not read any record from the personnel file for which the salary value is greater than $20,000. This policy cannot be implemented by the access matrix described above. Instead, the access condition (salary must be less than or equal to $20,000) is stored in the matrix and is evaluated at access time for each record that is about to be retrieved. This approach is called predicate-based protection. Procedural monitors, called formularies, have been used to evaluate access conditions. In another approach, called query modification, the access conditions are automatically combined with data-base queries before the data is retrieved. Queries thus modified cannot request unauthorized data. *See Data-base management systems*.

**Information flow controls.** While access controls protect access to data, they do not solve the problem of how to regulate what happens to the data after it is accessed. For example, someone authorized to read a top-secret file can make a copy of it. If access to the copy is not controlled as strictly as access to the original, the security of the information in the original can be compromised through the copy. Flow controls are concerned with labeling outputs of processes with authorization information consistent with the protection given the inputs. A multilevel protection policy called the star property expresses a flow restriction by not allowing information to flow from a given security classification to one that is lower (so that no one can later read the same information under a less strict access requirement). This property is extended in a lattice model of information flow, based on a hierarchy of security classes, which include both levels (for example, unclassified, confidential, secret, top secret) and sets of compartments (for example, NATO, nuclear, medical, financial) representing a need-to-know policy. Output from a program is not allowed to be sent to objects with security levels lower in the lattice than the highest level which has flowed from the inputs so far during the execution of the program. Alternatively, the security level of the file to which output is to be written can be raised, allowing the writing to proceed.

**Security kernels.** The difficulty of verifying a piece of software as large as an operating system had led to the concept of security kernels into which all security-related functions have been concentrated. An operating system kernel is a small, certifiably secure nucleus which is separate from the rest of the operating system. Nonkernel operating system software can then be allowed to run in a less protected environment. This new structure for operating systems, though achieved at the cost of a slight reduction in performance, has increased the trustworthiness of operating systems greatly over that of earlier systems with their defect-ridden, overly complicated patchworks of software. Most kernels implement multilevel, nondiscretionary security policies for access and flow controls. The simple security condition controls access by preventing a user operating at a given security level from reading data classified at a higher level. The star property controls flow by preventing the user from writing to a higher level. *See Operating system*.

**Inference controls.** Statistical data bases are intended to provide statistical information (for example, demographic data) about groups of people without allowing access to data about specific individuals.

However, it is often possible to infer data about an individual, given the statistical results for a group and some amount of prior knowledge about the individual. As an example, consider this query and its result:

COUNT (COLOR_EYES = GREEN AND
TOWN = LYONSDALE, NY) = 1

If it is known that a given individual fits this description, other details about that individual can illegally be deduced, for example, by:

COUNT (COLOR_EYES = GREEN AND
TOWN = LYONSDALE, NY
AND OCCUPATION = BOOKMAKER)

If this count is 1 also, that individual is a bookmaker. If small counts are not allowed in the responses, inference can still be made if information about the target individual is revealed in the difference between two large sets of people.

A mathematical device called a tracker provides a more general approach to inferring individual values. This approach is based on submitting statistical queries whose responses overlap. The overlapping process partitions the data base to form sets of records which act by inclusion and exclusion to isolate an individual record. Theoretical results indicate that very few statistical data bases can be made safe from all inference without becoming too restrictive for intended uses. For very large statistical data bases (for example, census data), it is effective to allow access only to randomly selected sample subsets of data which summarize the statistical characteristics of the full data base. Sometimes inference can be forestalled by introducing noise, in the form of slight random variations, into the data values.

**Cryptographic controls.** Cryptographic controls provide the means to encode data for storage or transmission so that even if an unauthorized person sees the data it will still be unreadable. Cryptographic controls thus protect transmitted data against electronic eavesdropping (for example, wiretapping). They also protect against the reading of data from tapes or disk packs that have been removed from their intended computers and therefore from access controls. Cryptographic controls protect the secrecy of the data and can provide proof of authenticity, so that a receiver of the data can be certain who sent it and that it is unmodified. Encryption is an encoding of the data, to be stored or transmitted, into a secret message by means of a key, which is the map to the encryption method. Decryption, also by a key, is necessary to return the data to its plainly readable form, called plaintext **(Fig. 2).** Transposition is a method of encryption that rearranges the symbols of the message. Substitution methods replace each message symbol with another symbol. Polyalphabetic substitution alternates between two or more sets of substitution alphabets for each plaintext symbol. If substitution is made from a table of symbols, the table is the key. Typically, the key is a parameter to an algorithm which computes the substitutions. For example, in a Caesar Cipher, for each letter in the alphabet the substitute is the letter which appears $x$ letters later in the alphabet. Here, $x$ is the key. If $x$ is 1, substitute B for A. If $x$ is 2, substitute C for A, and so on. The success of the system depends not on hiding the method of encryption, but on keeping the value of the key hidden. Thus, although the messages can be transmitted over open channels (channels susceptible to eavesdropping), the keys must be sent securely (perhaps hand-carried). Computer-generated pseudorandom sequences (sequences of nearly random numbers whose generation can be repeated) provide large, variable keys that are combined arithmetically (by multiplication, and so forth) with the numeric codes for the plaintext symbols to make encryptions which are very difficult to break.

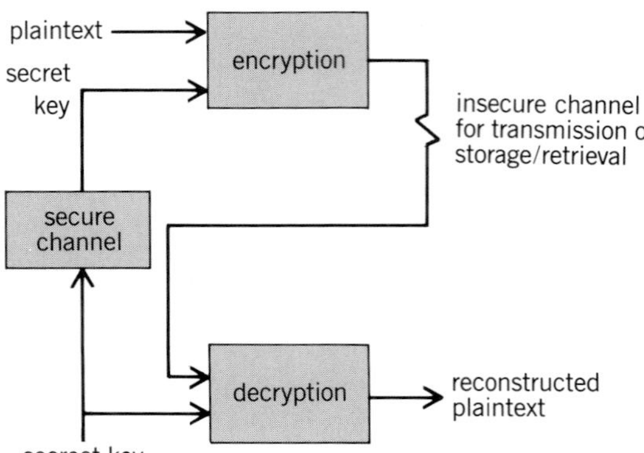


Fig. 2. Conventional encryption.

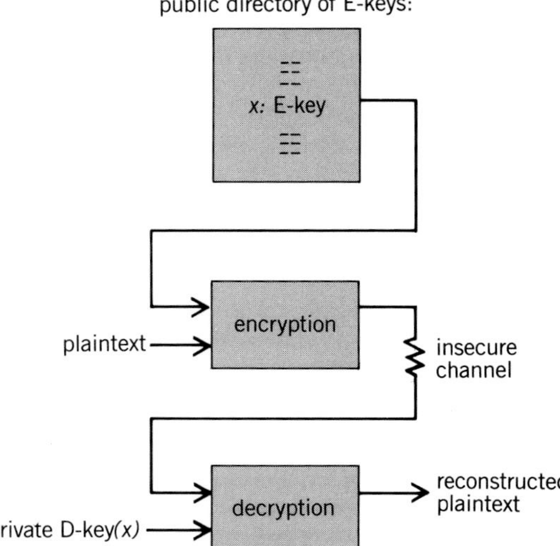


**Fig. 3. Public key encryption.**

In the interest of common hardware and communication interfaces, the National Bureau of Standards has produced a standard encryption algorithm, the Data Encryption Standard (DES), which has been mass-produced in integrated circuit microchips. The DES algorithm uses a combination of substitution and transposition and has been criticized for being too easy to break.

A recently developed method, called public-key encryption, uses two keys, one for encryption and a different one for decryption **(Fig. 3)**. The advantage is that the encryption key does not have to be transmitted in a secret way (for example, hand-carried). Anyone sending a message to party X uses X's encryption key, which is known publicly. The decryption key, however, is private to X. The two keys are related mathematically, but it is intended to be computationally too difficult to derive the decryption key from the public encryption key. *See Cryptography.*

*H. Rex Hartson*

***Bibliography.*** D. E. Denning, *Cryptography and Data Security*, 1982; E. B. Fernandez, R. C. Summers, and C. Wood, *Database Security and Integrity*, 1981; H. R. Hartson, Database security: Systems architecture, *Inform. Sys.*, 6:1–22, 1981; L. J. Hoffman, *Modern Methods for Computer Security and Privacy*, 1977.

## Computer storage technology

The techniques, equipment, and organization for providing the memory capability required by computers in order to store instructions and data for processing at high electronic speeds. In early computer systems, memory technology was very limited in speed and high in cost. Since the mid-1970s, the advent of high-density, high-speed random-access memory (RAM) chips has reduced the cost of computer main memory by more than two orders of magnitude. Chips are no larger than ¼ in. (6 mm) square and contain all the essential electronics to store tens to hundreds of thousands of bits of data or instructions. An analogous increase in magnetic recording density has increased the capacity and reduced the cost per bit of secondary memory. Traditionally, computer storage has consisted of a hierarchy of three or more types of memory storage devices (for example, RAM chips, disks, and magnetic tape units). *SEE BIT*.

### MEMORY HIERARCHY

Memory hierarchy refers to the different types of memory devices and equipment configured into an operational computer system to provide the necessary attributes of storage capacity, speed, access time, and cost to make a cost-effective practical system. The fastest-access memory in any hierarchy is the main memory in the computer. In most computers manufactured after the late 1970s, RAM chips are used because of their high speed and low cost. Magnetic core memories were the predominant main-memory technology in the 1960s and early 1970s prior to the RAM chip. The secondary storage in the hierarchy usually consists of disks. Significant density improvements have been achieved in disk technology, so that disk capacity has doubled every 3–4 years. Between main-memory and secondary-memory hierarchy levels, however, there has always been the ''memory gap.''

The memory gap noted by J. P. Eckert (a developer of the ENIAC computer in the 1940s) still presents a problem for the data-processing system designer. The memory gap for access time is bounded on one side by a 1-microsecond typical computer main memory cycle time and on the other by the 30-millisecond typical disk-drive access time. Capacity is bounded on the one side by a maximum mainframe memory capacity of 64 megabytes and on the other by multiple disks, each with a capacity of 100 to 2500 megabytes.

The last, or bottom, level (sometimes called the tertiary level) of storage hierarchy is made up of magnetic tape transports and mass-storage tape systems (**Fig. 1**). Performance (**Fig. 2**) is usually measured by two parameters: capacity and access time. (Speed or data rate is a third parameter, but it is not so much a function of the device itself as of the overall memory design.) Capacity refers to the maximum on-line user capacity of a single connectable memory unit. Access time is the time required to obtain the first byte of a randomly located set of data.

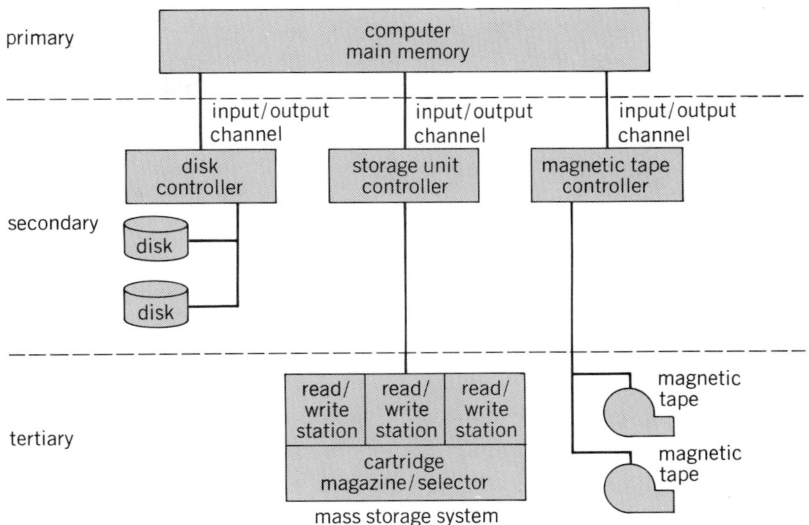


**Fig. 1. Memory hierarchy levels and equipment types.**

### MEMORY ORGANIZATION

The efficient combination of memory devices from the various hierarchy levels must be integrated with the central processor and input/output equipment, making this the real challenge to successful computer design. The resulting system should operate at the speed of the fastest element, provide the bulk of its capacity at the cost of its least expensive element, and provide sufficiently short access time to retain these attributes in its application environment. Another key ingredient of a successful computer system is an operating system (that is, software) that allows the user to execute jobs on the hardware efficiently. Operating systems are available which achieve this objective reasonably well. *SEE COMPUTER SYSTEMS ARCHITECTURE*.

The computer system hardware and the operating system software must work integrally as one resource. In many computer systems, the manufacturer provides a virtual memory system. It gives each programmer automatic access to the total capacity of the memory hierarchy without specifically moving data up and down the hierarchy and to and from the central processing unit (CPU). During the early years of computing, each programmer had to incorporate storage allocation procedures by determining at each moment of time how information would be distributed among the different hierarchic levels of memory, whenever the totality of information was expected to exceed the size of main memory. These procedures involved dividing the program into segments which would overlay one another in main memory. The programmer was intimately familiar with both the details of the machine and the application algorithms of the program. This all changed in the 1970s and was much improved in the 1980s, when sophisticated higher-level program languages and data-base management software became well established, to provide significantly greater problem-solving capability. Thus manufacturer-supported operating systems evolved, with complete built-in virtual memory support capabilities, which made it possible for the user to ignore the details of memory hierarchy internal software and hardware operations. *SEE DATA-BASE MANAGEMENT SYSTEMS; DIGITAL COMPUTER PROGRAMMING; OPERATING SYSTEM; PROGRAMMING LANGUAGES*.

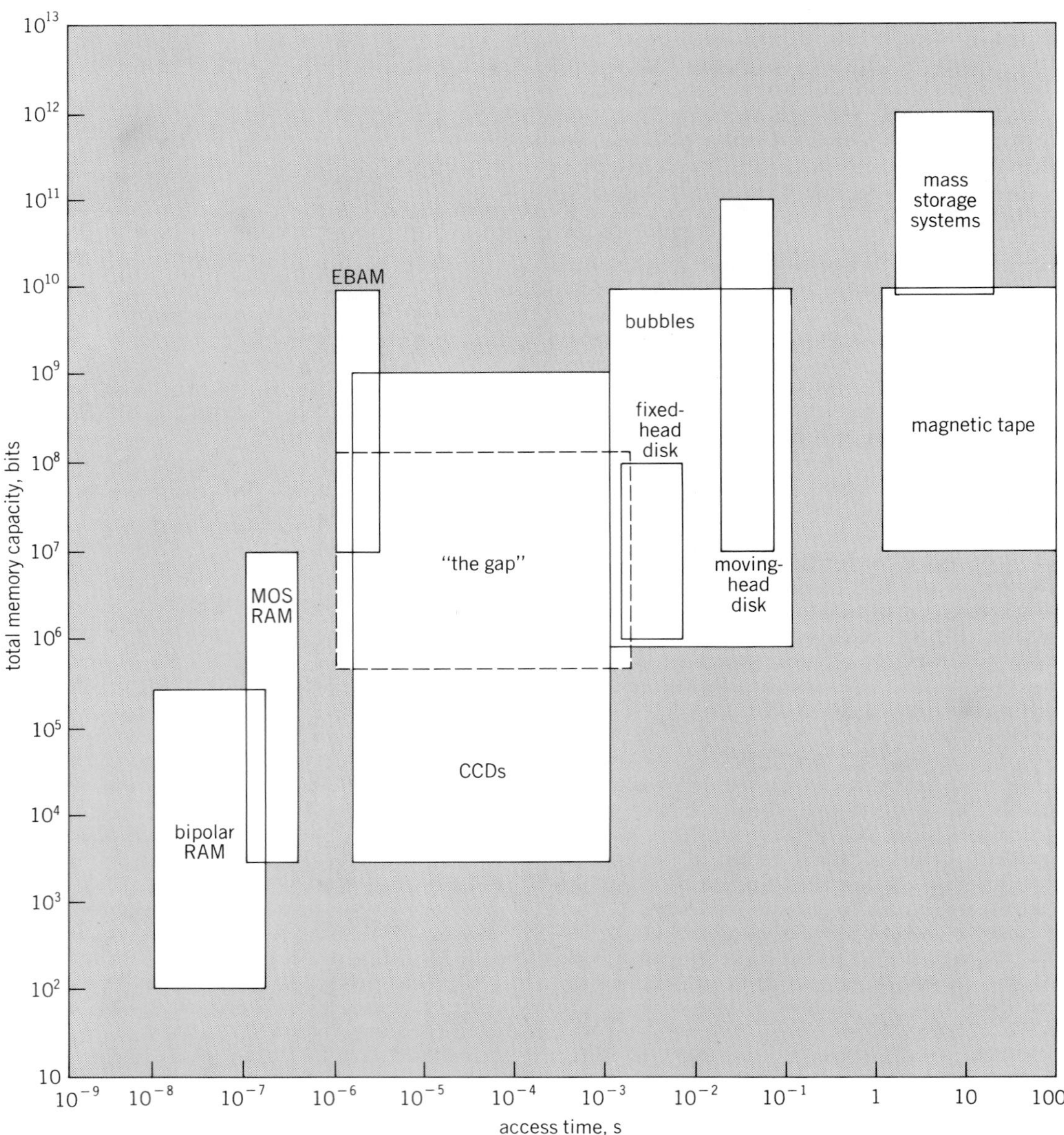


**Fig. 2. Memory capacity versus access time for various storage technologies.**

In the area of memory organization, two types of memory augmentation have been employed in the more widely used computers to enhance the overall computer performance capabilities. These two memory organization techniques are the cache memory, which speeds up the flow of instructions and data into the central processing unit from main memory, and an intelligent disk controller memory that is used as a staging buffer memory to queue up instructions and data for more rapid access into main memory.

**Cache memory.** A cache memory is a small, fast buffer located between the processor and the main system memory. Data and instructions in current use are moved into cache, producing two benefits. First, the average access time for the processor's memory requests is reduced, increasing the processor's throughput. Second, the processor's utilization of the available memory bandwidth, is thereby reduced, allowing other devices on the system bus to use the memory without interfering with the processor. Cache memory is thus used to speed up the flow of instructions and data into the central processing unit from main memory. This cache function is important because the main memory cycle time is typically slower than the central processing unit clocking rates. To achieve this rapid data transfer, cache memories are usually built from the faster bipolar RAM devices rather than the slower metal oxide semiconductor (MOS) RAM devices.

Performance of mainframe systems is very dependent upon achieving a high percentage of accesses from the cache rather than main memory. In typical systems 80–95% of accesses are to cache memory, with a typical cache size of 8K bytes. (1K bytes is equal to 1024 bytes.) Since the cache contents are a duplicate copy of information in main memory, writes (instructions to enter data) to the cache must eventually be made to the same data in main memory. This is done in two ways: write-through cache, in which write is made to the corresponding data in both cache and main memory; and write-back cache, in which main memory is not updated until the cache page is returned to main memory, at which time main memory is overwritten.

**Intelligent disk controller memory.** This is used as a cache memory between disk and main memories. Typically it consists of MOS RAM chips which overlap the disk operations, with their longer access time, to mask out the disk access delays so that main memory can execute subsequent tasks more rapidly and efficiently. Intelligent disk controllers provide the latest techniques to fill the memory gap with the best practical memory organization techniques for high performance. Microprocessors are also an integral part of intelligent disk controllers, and carry out many central processing unit operating system functions necessary for disk operations. This off-loads the mainframe computer from doing this kind of overhead processing to a large extent. *SEE MICROPROCESSOR*.

### Main Semiconductor Memory

The rapid growth in high-density large-scale integrated (LSI) circuits has advanced to a point where only a few applications require the tens to hundreds of thousands of transistors that can now be placed on a chip. One obvious exception is computer main memory, in which there is a continual demand for higher and higher capacity at lower cost. *SEE INTEGRATED CIRCUITS*.

In the 1960s and early 1970s, magnetic core memories dominated computer main-memory technology, but these have been completely replaced by semiconductor RAM chip devices of ever-increasing density. This transition started with the introduction of the first MOS 1K-bit RAM memory in 1971. This was followed with the 4K-bit RAM chip in 1973, the 16K-bit RAM chip in 1976, the 64K-bit RAM chip in 1979, and 256K-bit chip in 1982. **Figure 3** shows the progression of RAM chips, which follows the "rule of four," according to which the cost of development of a new RAM device generation can be justified only by a factor-of-four increase in capacity. *SEE SEMICONDUCTOR MEMORIES*.

**256K-bit RAM chips.** The 256K-bit MOS RAM has continued to push photolithographic fabrication techniques with feature sizes of 1 to 3 micrometers. For RAM chip densities of 256K bits or more per device, the integrated circuit industry has had to make a twofold improvement to maintain volume production and device reliability: better means, such as x-ray step-and-repeat equipment, to achieve features under 2 μm; and plasma-etching or reactive-ion-etching machines to achieve vertical profiles needed as horizontal dimensions decrease. Considerable progress has been made in the use of both x-ray and electron-beam techniques to achieve the submicrometer-size features needed to make even higher-density RAM chips. All 256K-bit RAMs are dynamic RAMs. The production techniques for dynamic and static RAM chips are identical. Therefore, the cost per unit quickly becomes the cost for mass-producing one chip. Since building costs per chip are about the same whether they store 4K bits or 256K bits, higher densities lead to lower costs per bit.

**RAM chip types and technologies.** RAM chips come in a wide variety of organizations and types. Computer main memories are organized into random addressable words in which the word length is fixed to some power-of-2 bits (for example, 4, 8, 16, 32, or 64 bits). But there are exceptions, such as 12-, 18-, 24-, 48-, and 60-bit word-length machines. Usually

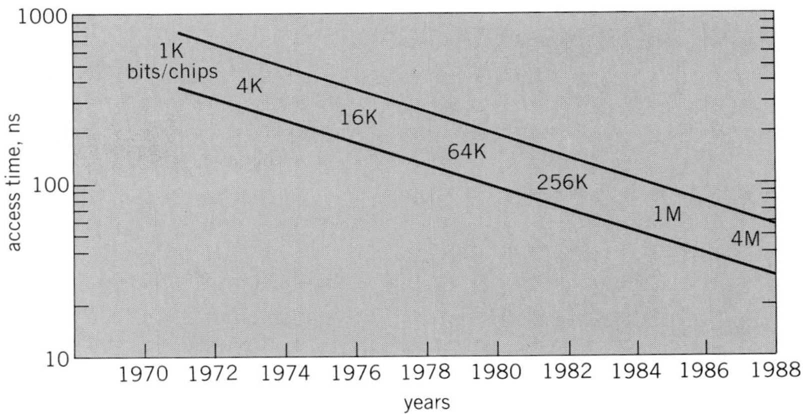


**Fig. 3. Trends in performance and density (in bits per chip) of dynamic RAM chips. 1K = 1024 bits; 1M = 1024 × 1024 bits = 1,048,576 bits.**

RAMs contain NK · 1 (for example, 64K · 1) bits, so the main memory design consists of a stack of chips in parallel with the number of chips corresponding to that machine's word length. There are two basic types of RAMs, static and dynamic. The differences are significant. Dynamic RAMs are those which require their contents to be refreshed periodically. They require supplementary circuits on-chip to do the refreshing and to assure that conflicts do not occur between refreshing and normal read-write operations. Even with those extra circuits, dynamic RAMs still require fewer on-chip components per bit than do static RAMs (which do not require refreshing).

Static RAMs are easier to design, and compete well in applications in which less memory is to be provided, since their higher cost then becomes less important. They are often chosen for minicomputer memory, or especially for microcomputers. Because they require more components per chip, making higher bit densities more difficult to achieve, the introduction of static RAMs of any given density occurs behind that of dynamic versions.

There is another trade-off to be made with semiconductor RAMs in addition to the choice between static and dynamic types, namely that between MOS and bipolar chips. Biopolar devices are faster, but have not yet achieved the higher densities (and hence the lower costs) of MOS. Within each basic technology, MOS and bipolar, there are several methods of constructing devices, and these variations achieve a variety of memory speeds and access times, as well as power consumption and price differences. Within the basic MOS technologies there are several types, such as the *n*-channel MOS referred to as NMOS and the complementary MOS solid-state structure referred to as CMOS. For bipolar there are several types such as transistor-to-transistor logic (TTL) and the emitter-coupled logic (ECL). **Table 1** provides a sampling of the many different memory chip types, where both the basic silicon technologies, MOS and bipolar semiconductor, are represented, and their varying characteristics. *SEE LOGIC CIRCUITS*.

***Memory cycle and access times.*** The RAM memory cycle time in a computer is defined as that time interval required to read or write one word of data. Access time is defined as the time interval in which the data are available after the initiation of the read cycle. From the user's point of view, cycle time is also an important characteristic because it has more impact on

**Table 1. Summary of characteristics of various memory chip types**

| Characteristics | Dynamic RAMs | Static RAMs | Static RAMs | ROMs | PROMs | PROMs | EPROMs | EEPROMs (EAROMs) |
|---|---|---|---|---|---|---|---|---|
| Chip technology | NMOS | NMOS CMOS | Bipolar (ECL) | CMOS | Bipolar | CMOS | MOS (UVPROMs) | MOS |
| Speed (access time) | 100 ns | 50–100 ns | 20 ns | 350 ns | 100 ns | 200 ns | 300 ns | 300 ns |
| Volatility | Volatile | Volatile | Volatile | Nonvolatile | Nonvolatile | Nonvolatile | Nonvolatile | Nonvolatile |
| Programmability | Easy | Easy | Easy | During manufacture | Once only | Once only | Many times, long procedure | Many times, easier and faster than EPROMs |
| Power dissipation | Low | Low | High | Low | High | Low | Medium | Medium |
| Chip density of currently available devices | 64K, 256K | 64K | 4K | 128K, 256K | 16K | 16K | 128K, 256K | 16K, 32K, 64K |

overall computational speed of the system. A new data read-write cycle does not begin until the previous read cycle is completed. The specified timing, signal overlap, and tolerances allowed vary with each RAM main memory system.

***Error checking and correction.*** Most computer main memories have a memory fault control consisting of a memory controller and a fault control subsystem which automatically corrects all single-bit errors and detects and reports all double-bit or three-bit errors. Each bit in a word is read from a separate RAM device. The fault control permits computer operation to continue even if a memory module is malfunctioning, and thus the computer will operate even if a memory chip is removed from the board. Failures are pinpointed to the specific chip by fault-indicating light-emitting diodes built into each array board. *See Light-emitting diode.*

***FIFO and LIFO chips.*** As memory chips increased in storage density and designers attempted to minimize interconnection circuitry, specialty memory function organizations such as first-in first-out (FIFO) buffers and last-in first-out (LIFO) buffers became available as chips. These kinds of chips are readily used in memory buffering applications to accommodate varying data rates between one element and another. The other complementary feature of FIFO and LIFO chips is the dual data paths (called ports) to allow simultaneous transfer of data into and out of these memory buffer chips. These chip types are commonly used on microcomputer boards and in the computer's peripheral interface and controller electronics.

***Gallium arsenide memory chips.*** All the memory chips discussed above are based on the predominant silicon technology. Reliable gallium arsenide (GaAs) intergrated circuits have been produced: 1K-bit and 4K-bit static RAM (SRAM) devices with 1-nanosecond access times. Development of 16K-bit SRAMs has been undertaken for military applications. Considering the need for and emphasis on increasingly-rapid computers, there is definite potential for high-speed gallium arsenide logic and memory devices.

**ROMs, PROMs, and EPROMs.** Microcomputers have evolved their own special set of semiconductor memory chips (see Table 1) to suit their application needs. Whereas large, medium-size, and minicomputers primarily use only RAMs that have read-write capability, microcomputers have found significant use for read-only memory (ROM) chips and programmable read-only memory (PROM) chips. Data and program storage in most microcomputer applications is separately allocated between RAMs and ROMs. ROMs provide protection, since the contents are fixed or hardwired and the chips are completely nonvolatile. During microcomputer program development, PROMs are typically used. A PROM can be written only once and involves the irreversible process of blowing polysilicon fuse links. These PROMs are neither erasable nor reprogrammable. Other kinds of devices, called an erasable PROM (EPROM), is cleared or rewritten by putting the EPROM chip under an ultraviolet light to zero out its contents and then using a PROM programmer to write in the new bit pattern for the modified program. After the microcomputer application program has completed final tests and acceptance, the final bit pattern in the EPROM can be put into ROMs or PROMs (using a chip mask) to facilitate quantity production. *See Microcomputer; Microcomputer development system.*

**EEPROMs.** There are also memory chip devices called electrically erasable programmable read-only memories (EEPROMs). They have an internal switch on the chip to permit a user to electrically rewrite new contents into them. This means EEPROMs do not have to be removed from the circuit in order to clear their contents to put in the new or modified bit pattern representing another program of instructions. Thus EEPROMs have met the need in microcomputer systems for a nonvolatile in-circuit reprogrammable random word access memory device.

EEPROMs use two distinctively different technologies. The more mature technology is metal nitride oxide semiconductor (MNOS), which is a very different gate insulator process technology from that used for MOS. The MNOS technology previously used the generic acronym EAROM (electrically alterable read-only memories) until EEPROMs became common in usage for both technologies. The other technology is floating-gate MOS (also called FAMOS). FAMOS technology was used for ultraviolet erasable EPROMs (UVPROMs) and was subsequently refined to provide an electrically erasable technology. Both technologies rely on Fowler-Nordheim tunneling to move the charge to be stored from the substrate to the gate. FAMOS stores the charge on the gate itself, whereas MNOS devices trap the charge in the nitride layer under the gate.

### Secondary Memory

High-capacity, slower-speed memory consists of two major functional types: random-access, which has been provided primarily by disk drives, and sequential-access, which has been provided primarily by tape drives. Since tape drives provide removability of the medium from the computer, tape is used for the majority of off-line, archival storage, although some disks are removable also. The on-line random-access disk devices are classed as secondary, and tape-based systems are classed as tertiary.

Over the history of electronic computers, while the technology for processors and main memory has been evolving from vacuum tubes to transistors to very large-scale integration (VLSI) chips, the predominant technology for secondary memory has continued to be magnetic recording on tape and disk. This has not been due so much to the absence of competing alternatives as to the continuous and rapid progression in magnetic recording capability. The increase in recording density on disks is shown in **Fig. 4**. The scale of the figure is logarithmic, so the rate of improvement has been exponential.

The current magnetic-disk technology will be discussed, and also the potential of new magnetic recording techniques such as thin-film, vertical recording, and bubble-memory devices; and a nonmagnetic technology, optical recording.

**Magnetic disk storage.** Conventional magnetic-disk memories consist of units which vary in capacity from the small 250-kilobyte floppy disks (used with microcomputers) to 2500-megabyte disk drives used with large-scale computers. Hard-disk memories are characterized by access times in the 20–80-millisecond region (versus access times of hundreds of nanoseconds to 1 microsecond for RAMs). **Figure 5** shows the historical progression in several performance factors: capacity, transfer rate, and access time.

***Capacity.*** The major area of development in disks has been the progressive and even spectacular increases in capacity per drive, particularly in terms of price per byte. There is a substantial economy of scale in storage capacity, in that the cost per byte goes down as the drive capacity goes up. Between small disks and top-end drives, the differences in access time and transfer rate may be only a factor of two to five, while the capacity difference is a factor of as much as 500, that is, from 5 megabytes to 2500 megabytes.

***Transfer rate.*** The rotation rate of the disk platter, like the action of the head actuators, is limited by considerations of physical dynamics, and major increases over the 3600-rpm rate of present large drives are not currently achievable. Increases in transfer rate will come from greater linear bit density around the track. In an absolute sense, transfer rates are not as often a system performance bottle neck as is access time.

***Average access time.*** Since the arm supporting the read-write head is one of the few moving mechanical parts in a computer system, it has not shown the multiple-orders-of-magnitude performance improvement over time that the electronic technologies have. Also, average access times for the highest-priced and lowest-prices disks do not vary by an enormous factor, being in the range of 40 to 80 milliseconds for a typical microcomputer hard (as opposed to floppy) disk, and 24 to 30 milliseconds for large disks on mainframe computers. There is nothing which indicates a breakthrough in the technology governing access time, even though greater capacities and transfer rates are still coming. Therefore, for random-access bottlenecks, the solution in the future will be the same as it is now: multiple smaller drives to allow overlapped seeks instead of a single large-capacity drive.

***Basic disk technology.*** Many significant advances in the capabilities of commercially available disk memory technology were made during the late 1970s. One of the major trends was toward larger-capacity disks, progressing from 100 megabytes to 2500 megabytes per disk drive. The majority of technology improvements to provide higher capacities, lower costs, and better reliabilities resulted from the Winchester technology. Prior to this technology, removable disk packs established themselves as the most advanced technology for large-capacity disks. The Winchester technology is characterized by nonremovable, sealed disk packs, which inherently provide more reliability due to less handling and make more stringent alignment tolerances practical.

The head, or read-write transducer, has undergone substantial refinement. Central to the advance in increasing disk-packing density was the reduction in the flying height of the read-write head. Because flux spreads with distance, reduced separation between the read-write head and the magnetic surface will decrease the area occupied by an information bit. This

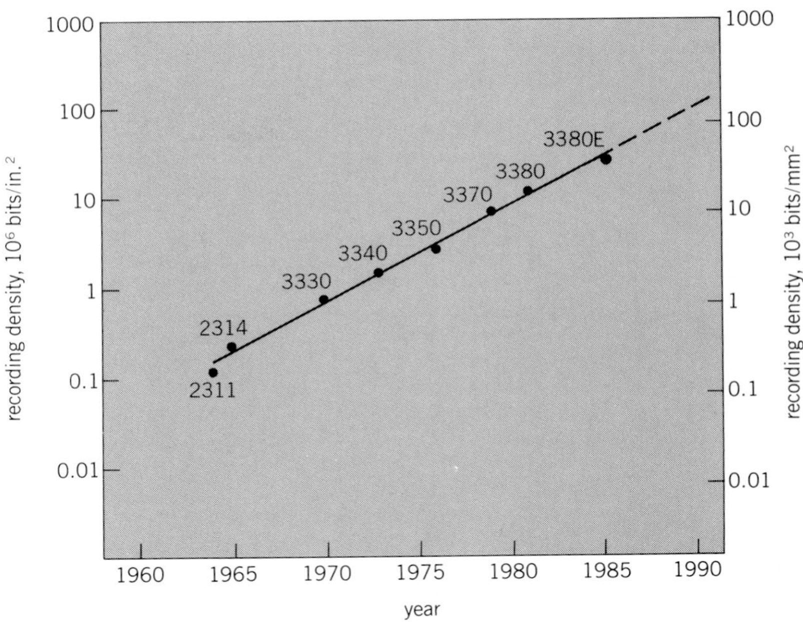


**Fig. 4. Increase in recording density on magnetic disk storage. Data points represent IBM models, and model numbers are indicated.**

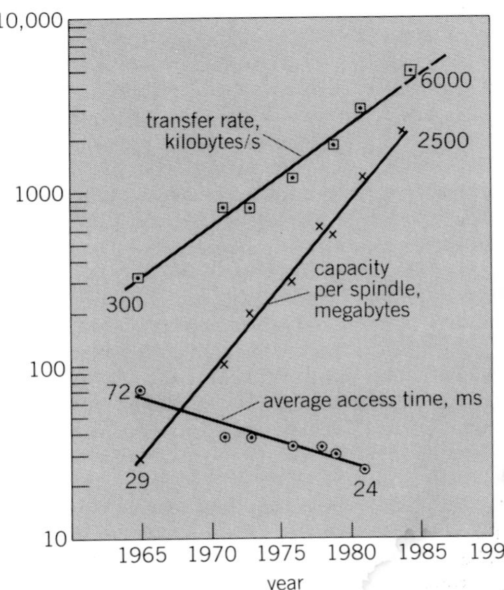


**Fig. 5. Development of magnetic disk performance factors.**

obviously limits the number of bits that can be defined along an inch of track and increases the minimum spacing between tracks. The ideal would be a direct contact between head and surface, which is the case with magnetic tape. But this is not possible with a rigid aluminum disk whose surface is traveling at rates that can exceed 100 mi/h (45 m/s). By applying a load on the head assembly, proper spacing is maintained. All movable media memories utilize an air-bearing mechanism known as the slider or flying head to space the transducer in proximity to the relatively moving media. The slider, when forced toward the moving surface of the medium, rests on a wedge of air formed between it and the medium by virtue of their relative motion. The thickness of the wedge can be controlled by the applied force, and the wedge in effect is an extremely stiff pneumatic spring. Head-to-medium spacings were well under 10 μin. (0.25 μm) in 1982. SEE TRANSDUCER.

Some standards have been developed for interfaces between the drive and the controller, to permit compatibility among drives of various capacities and manufacturers. One is the Storage Module Device (SMD) interface. Also in use is an American National Standards Institute (ANSI) standard.

In addition to fixed Winchester-type disk units of various capacities, disk storage is used in several removable forms.

***Cartridge disks.*** Removable storage cartridges containing single-disk packs are used extensively with minicomputer systems. The cartridge disk-drive unit has capacities ranging from 1 to 10 megabytes, depending on the recording density. Average access times range from 35 ro 75 milliseconds, and data transfer rates from 200 to 300 kilobytes per second. Physically, these plastic-encased cartridges are either top-loaded or front-loaded units. These units, besides having a removable disk, also have a fixed disk. The performance features of cartridge disks compete favorably with the larger-capacity disk pack storage equipment. A disadvantage of removable disk cartridges or disk packs is reduced reliability compared to fixed units.

***Floppy disks.*** Floppy disks have become the widely used random-access secondary memory for microcomputer systems. The floppy disk was originally developed by IBM in 1965 for internal use on its large 370 computers. The disk was designed to be a permanent nonvolatile memory storage device, written at the factory. However, large numbers of new and varied applications evolved for these relatively small, compact disk systems. Floppy disks derive their name from the recording medium, an oxide-coated flexible disk (similar to, but more flexible than, plastic 45-rpm music records) enclosed within a protective plastic envelope. The Mylar flexible disk is 7.875 in. (200 mm) in diameter, 0.003 in. (0.076 mm) thick, and records 3200 bits per inch (125 bits per millimeter) and 48 tracks per inch (1.9 tracks per millimeter). The disk is permanently enclosed in a protective envelope, and this package is 8 in. (203 mm) square, hence the common reference to the size as 8-inch. The protective envelope contains alignment holes for spindle loading, head contact, sector-index detection, and write-protect detection. The capacity of this easily transportable medium is 8 megabits, commonly laid out on 77 tracks, each divided into 26 sectors.

The flexible-disk drive subassembly consists of the metal base frame, the disk-drive motor that rotates the spindle (360 rpm for 8-in. or 203-mm, 300 rpm for 5¼-in. or 133-mm) through a belt drive, and a stepping motor with an integral lead screw to form the head-positioning actuator. The read-write head is mounted on a carriage that the lead screw moves. Head load is achieved by moving a load pad against the disk and restraining the disk between the head and the load pad to accomplish the head-to-disk compliance.

The removable floppy disk, called a diskette, was originally 8 in. (203 mm), in both single and double densities, and single- and double-sided. A variety of incompatible formats exist, particularly in double density, as the majority of suppliers use a common (IBM) format in single density. The most conspicuous format difference is in sector boundaries, hard-sector referring to boundaries of physical holes in the diskette, and soft-sector to boundaries that are software-formatted. As recording density increased and packaging considerations for microcomputers became important, a smaller, 5¼-in. (133-mm) diskette was introduced in 1976 and has become dominant, with a similar proliferation of formats as in 8-in. (203-mm). Newer systems are using yet smaller sizes such as 3, 3¼, and 3½ in. (76, 83, and 90 mm).

***Thin-film and vertical recording.*** Several technologies are in development for disk storage.

The recording technology for conventional magnetic disk recording has been based upon ferrite heads and a recording surface consisting of a coating embedded with ferrous oxide particles. One of the limiting factors is the thickness of the recording layer, which is 20 to 50 μin. (0.5 to 1.25 μm). With current products pushing the limits of recording density achievable with that approach, a successor technology has been developed, called thin-film.

The thin-film technique uses a continuous magnetic film of cobalt or nickel, applied by electroplating to a controlled thickness of as little as 1 μin. (25 nanometers). Either the head or the recording surface or both can use thin-film technology. Most of the major conventional large disks use thin-film heads and an oxide recording surface. Advanced models are designed to use a thin-film recording surface. Thin-film technology is the source for current progress in disk capacity and transfer rate. It was first introduced in small disks, partly due to greater ability to withstand the more portable environment of the small computer. The hardness of the medium which provides this resiliency also reduces both the likelihood and consequences of head crashes.

Another magnetic recording technique is vertical, or perpendicular, recording. In this approach the miniature magnets which are formed in the recording media are oriented downward into the surface rather than longitudinally along the surface. This allows closer packing of the magnetized spots, not just because of spatial compression, but also because of improved magnetic interaction between adjacent spots. The adjacent spots repel each other in the longitudinal case but attract in the vertical case. This technique offers the potential for significantly extending recording density and the accompanying performance parameters.

Recording density is the product of the bit density along the recording track, in bits per inch (or bits per millimeter), and the number of tracks per inch (or tracks per millimeter) across the recording surface. For a given rotation rate of the disk, the bit density along the track determines the transfer rate. A comparison of these characteristics for various recording techniques is given in **Table 2**.

The point at which vertical recording becomes attractive to develop into commercial products depends in part upon the level of capability which can ultimately be achieved with thin-film technology. The density level achieved by vertical recording technology may represent a limit for magnetic recording. If so, one possible answer to the question of how further levels of performance can be obtained is optical recording.

**Optical recording.** Optical recording is a nonmagnetic disk technology that uses a laser beam to burn pits in the recording medium to represent the bits of information, and a lower-power laser to sense the presence or absence of pits for reading. This technology has the potential for higher ultimate recording density than magnetic recording. The medium is removable and relatively inexpensive. The removability is significant in light of the nonremovability of most current and projected high-capacity magnetic disks. The recording density increase is apparent when it is noted that 4-gigabyte capacity is achieved on a single disk, whereas current-model large-capacity (2.5-gigabyte) magnetic drives typically consist of a cabinet containing two disk assemblies, each assembly having 16 platters.

One of the first optical disk mass-storage devices has 4 gigabytes on a removable, nonerasable, 14-in. (356-mm) disk. The transfer rate of 1.5 megabytes per second buffered or 3.0 megabytes streaming is similar to that of conventional magnetic disks (3.0 for the IBM 3380). The average access time is slower than that of high-performance magnetic disks at 84.7 milliseconds, versus the 3380's 24 milliseconds, but track-to track access is a comparatively fast 1.0 millisecond. The corrected bit error rate is 1 in $10^{13}$, which is compatible with magnetic disk standards.

In addition to the 14-in. (356-mm) disk for large-capacity systems, 12-in. (305-mm) optical disk systems in the 1-gigabyte capacity range have been produced for use with 16- or 32-bit microcomputer and minicomputer systems.

Optical technology has several disadvantages. First, the medium is not inherently erasable, although systems which can erase and rewrite are also in development. The primary problem in producing a commercial optical disk system has been getting the bit error rate down to an acceptable level, with sufficient recording density to be competitive with magnetic recording. To be competitive with magnetic tape, a bit error rate, after error detect and correct, of 1 in $10^{10}$ to $10^{11}$ is needed, and to compete with magnetic disk, 1 in $10^{13}$ to $10^{14}$. Through error detect and correct techniques, the 1 in $10^{13}$ level has been attained.

The bit error rate problem is far less critical for storage of documents and images, since bit dropout is seldom noticeable, in contrast with financial information, where it could be disastrous. This is the reason that optical disk recording was first used successfully in consumer and industrial systems for video-type image information, and for document storage and retrieval systems. *See Video disk recording.*

The nonerasability of the technology can be an advantage for some applications. Examples are data which must be kept for historical or audit-trail purposes, and applications where large amounts of data must be shipped among different locations.

When this technology matures, it will be an event of major significance, being a removable, large-capacity, random-access device using a recording technology with large potential for further growth. The potential for development of yet higher recording densities is perhaps the most significant factor, but in addition, having large capacity on a removable platter would allow some other kinds of system development. One possible system, referred to as a jukebox, would store on the order of 100 disks in an automatic retrieval and mounting device, so that a given disk could be fetched and accessed in around 5 seconds giving an on-line storage in the range of 500 gigabytes. Previous systems for very large on-line storage which have been delivered in significant quantity are the cartridge tape systems from IBM and CDC and automated tape libraries discussed below. The cartridge tape systems have capacities to 50 megabytes (IBM) and 8 megabytes (CDC) per cartridge; hence the optical system would provide a great improvement in the capacity available on the basic storage unit, and the automated tape libraries of course have the limitation of sequential data access.

**Bubble memory devices.** Bubble memories are chips rather than disks, but are different from semiconductor memories in that they are magnetic devices, in which the absence or presence of a magnetic domain is the basis for a binary 1 to 0. The performance characteristics of these devices makes them competitive as small-capacity secondary storage. A magnetic bubble is in reality a cylindrical magnetic domain with a polarization opposite to that of the magnetic film in which it is contained. These cylinders appear under a microscope as small circles (which give them their name) with diameters from 80 to 800 μin. (2 to 20 μm). The size of a bubble is determined by the material characteristics and thickness of the magnetic film.

Bubbles are moved or circulated by establishing a

**Table 2. Storage densities for various recording technologies**

| Technology | Bit density along track | | Track density | | Recording density | |
|---|---|---|---|---|---|---|
| | Bits/in. | Bits/mm | Tracks/in. | Tracks/mm | $10^6$ bits/in.$^2$ | $10^3$ bits/mm$^2$ |
| Magnetic recording | | | | | | |
| Conventional (IBM 3380) | 15,000 | 600 | 800 | 32 | 12 | 19 |
| Thin-film* | 25,000 | 1000 | 1,200 | 47 | 30 | 47 |
| Vertical* | 100,000 | 4000 | 1,200 | 47 | 120 | 190 |
| Optical recording | 15,000 | 600 | 15,000 | 600 | 225 | 350 |

*Figures are projections.

magnetic field through a separate conductor mounted adjacent to the bubble chip. A large portion of the bubble chip must be given over to circuitry for generating, detecting, and annihilating the bubbles. Magnetic-domain bubble devices typically operate in an endless serial loop fashion or in an organization with serial minor loops feeding major loop registers. Bubble memories are particularly well suited to applications such as portable recorders because of their physical advantages (low power requirements and light weight) and speed advantage over electromechanical devices such as cassettes and floppy disks. Like their electromechanical counterparts, bubble devices are nonvolatile; that is, they retain their contents when the power goes off.

The controller is central to any bubble memory system, which it serves as the interface between the bubble chip and the system bus. It generates all of the system timing and control functions and supervises the handshaking operations required to access and transfer data between the system bus and the bubble memory module. Usually a controller can operate more than one bubble chip module, in most cases up to eight modules. The function-driver integrated circuit produces the control currents required to generate and input or ouput tracks on the chip. The sense-amplifier integrated circuit converts the analog output signals produced by the bubble detector into a transmittable data stream that passes to the controller. The coil-driver integrated circuits excite the $x$ and $y$ coils of the bubble chip package with out-of-phase signals to produce the rotating field that moves the bubbles.

United States companies are producing 1-megabit and 4-megabit bubble memory chips. Under a cross-license and alternate source agreement, these companies have agreed to jointly adopt a low-height leaded package for complete component level interchangeability. Each company developed its peripheral chip set for the 4-megabit magnetic bubble module that will be compatible with the 1-megabit units.

For portable and other special applications, bubbles have definite advantages such as nonvolatility, low power, and high compactness. Performance capabilities relative to floppy disks are 100 kilobits per second for bubbles versus 200–250 kilobits per second for floppies, and 40 milliseconds average access time for bubbles versus 200–250 milliseconds for floppies. *See Magnetic bubble memory.*

**General trends.** The technologies which will provide the growth in performance in disk systems will also allow improved price-performance, so that the cost per byte on-line can be expected to continue to drop. Although this disscussion has concentrated on high-end disks in terms of performance parameters, small- and medium-range disks, including floppies, will benefit from the same technological and price-performance progression. Some of these technological developments in fact can appear first in the lower-end products, one such possibility being vertical recording in floppy diskettes.

In both hard disks and floppies, the higher recording densities permit progressively more compact packaging for microcomputers, but the constant change has aggravated the existing difficulties with lack of standardization, which is unfortunate for the potentially convenient interchange medium which the floppy diskette could provide. Although such possibilities as a 5-megabyte floppy diskette are impressive, the prospect for standards which would permit interchangeability are becoming less, with the proliferation of sizes and incompatible formats discussed above.

### Magnetic Tape Units

In magnetic tape units, the tape maintains physical contact with the fixed head while in motion, allowing high-density recording. The long access times to find user data on the tape are strictly due to the fact that all intervening data have to be searched until the desired data are found. This is not true of rotating disk memories or RAM word-addressable main memories. The primary use of tape storage is for seldom-used data files and as back-up storage for disk data files.

**Half-inch tapes.** Half-inch (12.7-mm) tape has been the industry standard since it was first used commercially in 1953. Half-inch magnetic tape drive transports are reel-to-reel recorders with extremely high tape speeds (up to 200 in. or 5 m per second), and fast start, stop (on the order of 1 millisecond), reverse, and rewind times.

Performance and data capacity of magnetic tape have improved by orders of magnitude, as shown in **Table 3**. Just prior to the 1970s came the single-capstan tape drive, which improved access times to a few milliseconds. These vacuum-column tape drives have such features as automatic hub engagement and disengagement, cartridge loading, and automatic thread operation. There are two primary recording techniques, namely, nonreturn-zero-inverted (NRZI) and phase-encoded (PE), used with packing densities of 800 and 1600 bytes per inch (31.5 and 63 bytes per millimeter). These typically use a 0.6-in. (15-mm) interrecord gap. In phase encoding, a logical ''one'' is defined as the transition from one magnetic polarity to another positioned at the center of the bit cell. ''Zero'' is defined as the transition in the opposite direction also at the center of the bit cell, whereas NRZI would involve only one polarity. The advantage of the phase-encoding scheme over NRZI is that there is always one or more transitions per bit cell,

**Table 3. Standard recording densities for magnetic tape**

| Year | Number of tracks | Bit density along track | | Area density | |
|---|---|---|---|---|---|
| | | bits/in. | bits/mm | bits/in.$^2$ | bits/mm$^2$ |
| 1953 | 7 | 100 | 4 | 1,400 | 2 |
| 1955 | 7 | 200 | 8 | 2,800 | 4 |
| 1959 | 7 | 556 | 22 | 7,784 | 12 |
| 1962 | 7 | 800 | 32 | 11,200 | 17 |
| 1963 | 9 | 800 | 32 | 14,400 | 22 |
| 1965 | 9 | 1600 | 63 | 28,800 | 45 |
| 1973 | 9 | 6250 | 246 | 112,500 | 174 |

which gives phase encoding a self-clocking capability, alleviating the need for an external clock. The disadvantage of phase encoding over NRZI is that at certain bit patterns the system must be able to record at twice the transition density of NRZI.

Computer-compatible magnetic tape units are available with tape drives of 6250 bytes per inch (246 bytes per millimeter). They have nine tracks, where eight bits are data and one bit is parity. Each track is recorded by a technique called group-coded record (GCR), which uses a 0.3-in. (7.6-mm) record gap. Every eighth byte in conjunction with the parity track is used for detection and correction of all single-bit errors. Thus, GCR offers inherently greater reliability because of its coding scheme and error-correction capability. It does, however, involve much more complex circuitry.

The on-line capacity is strictly a function of the number of tape drives that one controller can handle (eight is typical). A 2400-ft (730-m) nine-track magnetic tape at 6250 bytes per inch (246 bytes per millimeter) provides a capacity of approximately $10^9$ bits, depending on record and block sizes.

**Cassettes and cartridges.** The most frequently used magnetic tape memory devices for microcomputer systems are cassette and cartridge tape units. Both provide very low-cast storage, although their access times are long and their overall throughput performance is not as great as that of floppy disks. Cassette and cartridge units both use ¼-in. (6.35-mm) magnetic tape.

The digital cassette transport was orginally an outgrowth of an audio cassette unit. Unfortunately, the very low-cost audio-designed transport did not meet the endurance needs of true digital computer applications. There are two basic design approaches to digital cassette transports: capstan drive and reel-to-reel drive. Capstan tape drives are better for maintaining long-term and short-term tape-speed accuracy, while reel-to-reel transports have better mechanical reliability.

During the 1960s the first true digital tape cartridge was developed. With the cassette, a capstan must penetrate the plastic case containing the tape in order to make contact. There is no such penetration system with the cartridge because the transport capstan simply drives an elastomer belt by pressing against the rim of the belt's drive wheel. This simplicity eliminates a major source of tape damage and oxide flaking.

Cassettes have undergone evolution as a digital medium, and capacity has increased to 10 megabytes, at a density of 5120 bits per inch (202 bits per millimeter). Transfer rates are 24 kilobits per second at 30 in. (0.76 m) per second, or 72 kilobits per second at 90 in. (2.29 m) per second. The ¼-in. (6.35-mm) streaming tape cartridge has a typical capacity range of 10 to 30 megabytes, with some available with over 50 megabytes. Transfer rates are 30 to 90 kilobits per second, at densities of from 6400 to 10,000 bits per inch (252 to 394 bits per millimeter).

Half-inch (12.7-mm) tape is also used for back-up for microcomputer hard disk systems. Configured to standard microcomputer packaging sizes, these give 50-megabyte capacity in 5¼-in. (133-mm) form, and 300 megabytes in 8-in. (203-mm) form.

### Mass Storage Tape Systems

With the gradual acceptance of virtual memory and sophisticated operating systems, a significant operational problem arose with computer systems, particularly the large-scale installations. The expense and attendant delays and errors of humans storing, mounting, and demounting tape reels at the command of the operating system began to become a problem. Cartridge storage facilities are designed to alleviate this problem.

Their common attributes are: capacity large enough to accommodate a very large data base on-line; access times between those of movable-head disks and tapes; and operability, without human intervention, under the strict control of the operating system. The cartridge storage facility is included within the virtual address range. All such configurations mechanically extract from a bin, mount on some sort of tape transport, and replace in a bin, following reading or writing, a reel or cartridge of magnetic tape.

Cartridge storage systems are hardware devices that need operating system and data-base software in order to produce a truly integrated, practical hardware-software system. Users require fast access to their files, and thus there is a definite need to queue up (stage) files from the cartridge storage device onto the disks. The data-base software must function efficiently to make this happen. In general, users base their storage device selection on the file sizes involved and the number of accesses per month. Magnetic tape units are used for very large files accessed seldom or infrequently. Mass-storage devices are for intermediate file sizes and access frequencies. Disk units are used for small files or those which are accessed often.

In practice, most users have been satisfied with tapes and disks, and have not chosen to install mass storage systems. During the 1970s, two basic kinds were delivered, although some others were built and installed in the earlier years. In different ways, these units combine the low cost of tape as a storage medium with the operating advantages of on-line access. One is a mechanical selection and mounting unit to load and unload tape reels onto and off standard magnetic tape units; another is a mechanical selection and accessing unit to operate with special honeycomb short-tape units. The first type (sometimes called automated tape libraries) eliminated manual tape-mounting operations. The main objective of the short-tape honeycomb cartridge system is to improve access time. The shorter tape (770 in. or 19.6 m, versus 2400 ft or 730 m) results in better access time. Operationally, the honeycomb cartridge tape system and the mechanical standard tape-mounting units are capable of handling 100 to 300 cartridge or tape loads per hour.

The first type of fully automated tape library uses standard magnetic tape (½ in. or 12.7 mm wide). Under computer control, this equipment automatically brings the tapes from storage, mounts them on tape drives, dismounts the tapes when the job is completed, and returns them to storage. Accessing up to 150 reels per hour, this unit can store up to 7000 standard tapes or 8000 thin-line reels in a lockable self-contained library that can service up to 32 tape drives and that can interface with up to four computers.

The honeycomb cartridge storage system uses a storage component called a data cartridge. Housed in honeycomb storage compartments, these 2 × 4 in. (24 × 50 mm) plastic cartridges can each hold up to 50,000,000 bytes of information on 770 in.(19.6 m) of magnetic tape approximately 3 in. (76 mm) wide. Whenever information from a cartridge is needed by the computer, a mechanism selects the desired cartridge and transports it to one of up to eight reading stations. There the data are read out and transferred to the staging disk drives. *See Computer; Data-processing systems; Digital computer.*

*Michael Plesset; Douglas Theis*

***Bibliography.*** R. Brechtlein, Comparing disc technologies, *Datamation*, 24(1):130–150, January 1978; S. Chi, Advances in computer mass storage technology, *IEEE Comput.*, 19(5):60–74, May 1982; M. Elphick, Disk and tape memory systems, *Comput. Des.*, 22(1):85–126, January 1983; A. H. Eschenfelder, *Magnetic Bubble Technology,* 1980; E. R. Hnatek, *1982 Semiconductor Memories: An Update*, 1982; T. Moran, New developments in floppy disks, *Byte Mag.*, 8(3):68–82, March 1983; M. Plesset, Future developments in disc storage, *Data Process.*, 25(8):28–30, October 1983; R. M. White, Disk-storage technology, *Sci. Amer.*, 2432:(1)138–148, August 1980.

## Computer systems architecture

The discipline that defines the conceptual structure and functional behavior of a computer system. It is analogous to the architecture of a building, determining the overall organization, the attributes of the component parts, and how these parts are combined. It is related to, but different from, computer implementation. Architecture consists of those characteristics which affect the design and development of software programs, whereas implementation focuses on those characteristics which determine the relative cost and performance of the system. This division is necessary because of the existence of computer families. A family is a series of several computers (usually from the same manufacturer) that offers a variety of cost and performance options (different implementations) but can run the same software programs (that is, all have the same architecture).

The architect's main goal has long been to produce a computer that is as fast as possible, within a given set of cost constraints. This requires a strong background in electrical engineering. Over the years, other goals have been added, such as making it easier to run multiple programs concurrently or improving the performance of programs written in higher-level languages. Thus, the architect also needs a strong background in the software (programming) aspect of computing. *See Digital computer programming; Programming languages; Software engineering.*

A computer system consists of four major components (**Fig. 1**): storage, processor, peripherals, and input/output (communication). The storage system is used to keep data and programs; the processor is the unit that controls the operation of the system and carries out various computations; the peripheral devices are used to communicate with the outside world; and the input/output system allows the previous components to communicate with one another.

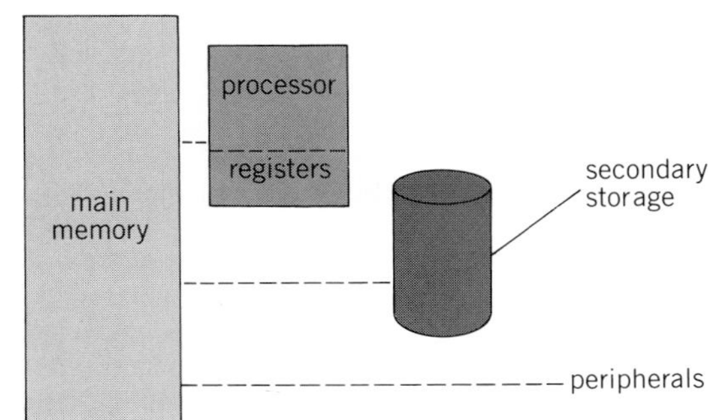


**Fig. 1. Overview of a computer system. Storage is made up of registers, main memory, and secondary storage. Broken lines indicate input/output.**

**Storage.** The storage or memory of a computer system holds the data that the computer will process and the instructions that indicate what processing is to be done. In a digital computer, these are stored in a form known as binary, which means that each datum or instruction is represented by a series of bits. Bits are conceptually combined into larger units called bytes (usually 8 bits each) and words (usually 8 to 64 bits each). *See Bit.*

A computer will generally have several different kinds of storage devices, each organized to hold one or more words of data. These types include registers, main memory, and secondary or auxiliary storage (**Table 1**).

***Registers.*** These are the fastest and most costly storage units in a computer (**Table 2**). Normally contained within the processing unit, registers hold data that are involved with the computation currently being performed. Registers are also used to hold information describing the current state of the computing process. Implementation of registers may vary with different members of the same architecture family.

***Main memory.*** This device holds the data to be processed and the instructions that specify what processing is to be done. Main memory consists of a sequence of words or bytes, each individually addressable and each capable of being read or written to. Two good measures of a computer system are how much main memory it can have and how fast that memory can be accessed. A major goal of the computer architect is to increase the effective speed and size of a memory system without incurring a large cost penalty. Two prevalent techniques for increasing effective speed are interleaving and cacheing, while virtual memory is a popular way to increase the effective size.

**Table 1. Storage characteristics of typical computers**

| Storage type | Capacity (words) | Access time, s | Typical uses |
|---|---|---|---|
| Registers | 1–128 | $10^{-8}$ to $10^{-6}$ | Computation |
| Main | 4,096–16,000,000 | $10^{-7}$ to $10^{-6}$ | Storage of programs and data |
| Secondary | 300,000–1,000,000,000 | $10^{-2}$ to $10^{-1}$ | Archival or long-term data and program storage |

**Table 2. Registers commonly found in computers**

| Register | Other names | Function |
|---|---|---|
| Instruction register | I register | To hold the instruction currently being executed by the processor |
| Accumulator | Arithmetic register | To hold the results of computation |
| Status register | State register | To indicate the results of tests, occurrence of unusual conditions, and status of certain activities |
| Program counter | Instruction pointer | To hold the address in main memory of the next instruction to be executed |
| Index register | Counter, B register | For counting (for example, number of times through a repeated computation) |
| Base register | Pointer register, address register | For pointing to (holding the address of) something in main memory |

Interleaving involves the use of two or more independent memory systems, combined in a way that makes them appear to be a single, faster system. In one approach, all words with even addresses come from one memory system and all words with odd addresses come from the other. When an even-numbered word is fetched, the next-higher odd-numbered word is fetched at the same time. If that odd-numbered word is requested next (a situation that occurs often), it has already been fetched and thus has an access time of zero. This nearly doubles the average access speed.

With cacheing, a small, fast memory system contains the most frequently used words from a slower, larger main memory. With careful design, cacheing can yield considerably improved average memory speeds.

Virtual memory is a technique whereby the programmer is given the illusion of a very large main memory, when in fact it has only a modest size. This is achieved by placing the contents of the large, "virtual" memory on a large but slow auxiliary storage device, and bringing portions of it into main memory, as required by the programs, in a way that is transparent to the programmer.

***Auxiliary memory.*** This portion of memory (sometimes called secondary storage) is the slowest, lowest-cost, and highest-capacity computer storage area. Programs and data are kept in auxiliary memory when not in immediate use, so that auxiliary memory is essentially a long-term storage medium.

There are two basic types of secondary storage: sequential and direct-access. Sequential-access secondary storage devices, of which magnetic tape is the most common, permit data to be accessed in a linear sequence. Thus, in order to access the 100th datum on such a device, the first 99 must be "passed over." For processes where sequential access is suitable, such as printing a list of names or merging two files of insurance records, sequential-access devices are very cost-effective.

A direct-access device is one whose data may be accessed in any order. Disks and drums are the most commonly encountered devices of this type, although certain low-speed semiconductor devices, such as bubble memory, are also used. Direct-access devices permit high-speed access to any block of data, regardless of its location on the device, and thus are well suited to situations where sequential access is not convenient, such as obtaining individual insurance records, at random, from a large file. *SEE MAGNETIC BUBBLE MEMORY; SEMICONDUCTOR MEMORIES.*

***Memory mapping.*** This is one of the most important aspects of modern computer memory designs. In order to understand its function, the concept of an address space must be considered. When a program resides in a computer's main memory, there is a set of memory cells assigned to the program and its data. This is known as the program's logical address space. If several programs reside in memory at the same time, each has its own logical address space.

The computer's physical address space is the set of memory cells actually contained in the main memory. In the simplest case, where only one program resides in main memory, the logical and physical address spaces may be identical. A more common situation (**Fig. 2**) is where several programs, and thus several logical address spaces, reside within the same physical address space. In such a case, it is desirable to design the system so that the program does not need to know in which part of the physical address space it resides; this anonymity permits the program to be placed anywhere. It is also desirable for the computer to prevent one program from accidentally accessing data in another program's memory. These goals are achieved by means of memory mapping.

Memory mapping is simply the method by which the computer translates between the computer's logical and physical address spaces. The most straightforward mapping scheme involves use of a bias register (**Fig. 3**). Suppose the physical address space begins at location 0, but the program is placed in memory at location 10,000. With the bias scheme, the program is written as though it began at location 0, and the number 10,000 is placed in the bias register. Each time memory is referenced by the program, the contents of the bias register are added to the memory address, thus offsetting the program addresses by the bias amount. Assignment of a different bias value to each program in memory enables the programs to coexist without interference.

Another strategy for mapping is known as paging. This technique involves dividing both logical and physical address spaces into equal-sized blocks called pages. Mapping is achieved by means of a page map,

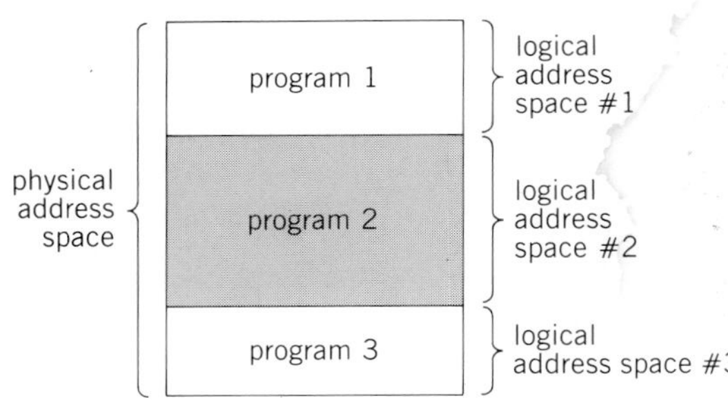


**Fig. 2. Several logical address spaces within a physical address space.**

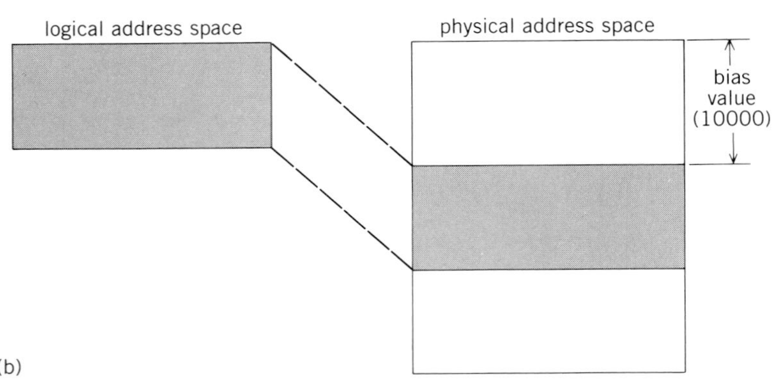


**Fig. 3. Memory mapping by means of a bias register. (*a*) Translation formula. (*b*) Memory structure.**

which can be thought of as a series of bias registers (**Fig. 4**). Each logical address is divided into a page number and an offset; the offset is combined with the page map value to yield a physical address.

A simple extension of paging, known as demand paging, allows implementation of virtual memory. In this scheme, the page map includes a "presence" bit for each page, indicating whether that page actually resides in main memory. For a page that is located in main memory, the operation is identical to that of simple paging. If, however, the presence bit indicates that the page is not in main memory, a page fault occurs, causing the computer to obtain the desired page from secondary storage and copy it into main memory. The above procedure is carried out by the operating system and is essentially unseen by the application program. SEE COMPUTER STORAGE TECHNOLOGY.

**Processing.** A computer's processor (processing unit) consists of a control unit, which directs the operation of the system, and an arithmetic and logic unit (ALU), which performs computational operations. The design of a processing unit involves selection of a register set, communication paths between these registers, and a means of directing and controlling how these operate. Normally, a processor is directed by a program, which consists of a series of instructions that are kept in main memory. Each instruction is a group of bits, usually one or more words in length, specifying an operation to be carried out by the processing unit. The basic cycle of a processing unit consists of the following steps: (1) fetch an instruction from main memory into an instruction register; (2) decode the instruction (determine what it indicates should be done); (3) carry out the operation specified by the instruction; and (4) determine where the next instruction is. Normally, the next instruction is the one immediately following the current one.

Each instruction must indicate an operation to be performed and the data to which the operation should be applied. The assembly language reference manual for any computer system will contain a good illustration of its repertoire of instructions, including both their formats and their functions. There is considerable variation between instruction sets from different computers, and selection of a set of instructions is a major job of the computer architect.

***Microprogramming.*** In the above discussion, it has been assumed that the process of decoding and executing instructions is carried out by logic circuitry. Although such is often the case, the complexity of instruction sets can lead to very large and cumbersome circuits for this purpose. To alleviate this problem, a technique known as microprogramming was developed. With microprogramming, each instruction is actually a macrocommand that is carried out by a microprogram, written in a microinstruction language. The microinstructions are very simple, directing data to flow between registers, memories, and arithmetic units. The microprograming cycle is similar to that described above for macroinstructions, except that the microinstructions are stored in a special microstore memory that cannot be used for storing regular programs and data.

The advantage of microprogramming is that the architect can create very complicated macroinstructions by simply increasing the complexity of the microprograms. The logic circuitry need not be made more complex, and the only cost is in providing a larger microstore to hold the increasingly complex microprograms.

It should be noted that microprogramming has nothing to do with microprocessors. A microprocessor is a processor implemented through a single, highly integrated circuit. SEE MICROPROCESSOR.

***Parallelism.*** There are limits to the speed of circuitry, determined by the state of technology and ultimately by the laws of physics. Efforts to design a

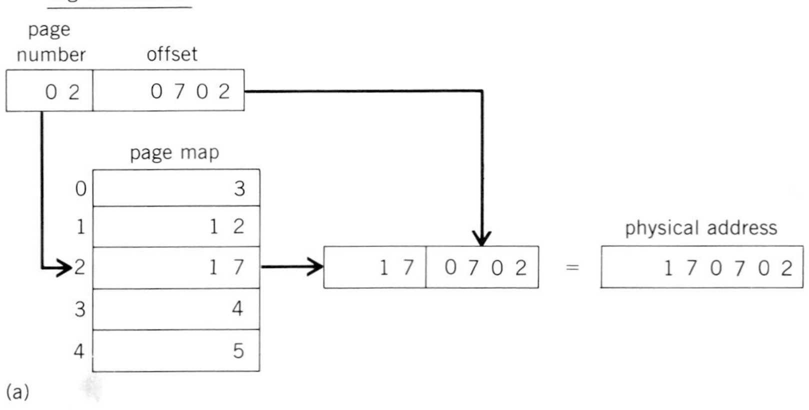


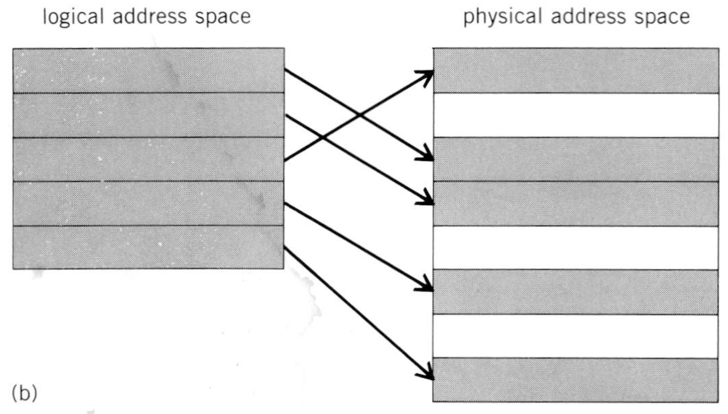


**Fig. 4. Memory mapping by means of a page table. (*a*) Translation formula. (*b*) Memory structure.**

faster computer often depend on parallelism. Because most techniques used to exploit parallelism belong to the area of implementation, they will be discussed only briefly.

Parallelism can occur in many ways. Parallel computer architectures have been categorized into four groups, depending on whether the instructions or the data are being handled in parallel. An example of the former is a system that fetches one instruction before it finishes with the previous one. An example of the latter is a system whose instructions specify groups of data to be processed at the same time (as in "add this vector to that one"). Perhaps the most widespread technique for parallelism, called pipelining, is similar to an assembly line in which the execution of an instruction is divided into stages, and there is a different instruction at each stage. *See* Concurrent processing; Data flow systems.

**Peripherals and communication.** A typical computer system includes a variety of peripheral devices such as printers, keyboards, and displays. These devices translate electronic signals into mechanical motion or light (or vice versa) so as to communicate with people. For example, as a person strikes a key (say, the letter K), a particular sequence of signals is transmitted to the computer. This sequence is interpreted as a string of bits, which the computer sees as the letter K. The details of how a peripheral device works are in the realm of mechanical and electrical engineering. The computer architect is more concerned with how the electrical signals are communicated to the computer. *See* Data-processing systems; Electronic display.

There are two common approaches for connecting peripherals and secondary storage devices to the rest of the computer: the channel and the bus. A channel is essentially a wire or group of wires between a peripheral device and a memory device (either main memory or a register). An input operation occurs when the memory receives data from the peripheral device, and an output operation occurs when the contents of the memory are transmitted to the device. A multiplexed channel allows several devices to be connected to the same wire.

A bus is a form of multiplexed channel that can be shared by large number of devices. The overhead of sharing many devices means that the bus has lower peak performance than a channel; but for a system with many peripherals, the bus is more economical than a large number of channels.

A computer controls the flow of data across buses or channels by means of special instructions and other mechanisms. In addition to the wires used to move data, a channel or bus has one or more wires that control what happens when. The simplest scheme is known as program-controlled input/output (I/O). In this approach, the computer has an instruction such as "read from channel n" which causes the processor to send a control signal across a particular channel. That control signal is interpreted by the device as a sign to transmit a word or byte of data across the channel. The data will be deposited in some register, and subsequent instructions will process that data or store the data into main memory for later use.

Direct memory access (DMA) I/O is a technique by which the computer signals the device to transmit a block of data, and the data are transmitted directly to memory, without the processor needing to wait. This is also a form of parallelism, for the processor may carry out other functions while the data transfer is taking place. Memory mapped I/O is a similar technique, except that the computer places commands to the device in a designated portion of memory rather than executing a special instruction.

Interrupts are a form of signal by which a peripheral device notifies a processor that it has completed transmitting data. This is very helpful in a direct memory access scheme, for the processor cannot always predict in advance how long it will take to transmit a block of data. Architects often design elaborate interrupt schemes to simplify the situation where several peripherals are active simultaneously. For example, there might be a separate interrupt signal for each peripheral, or a priority scheme so that, if two peripherals send interrupts at the same time, the more important one is transmitted to the processor first. *See* Computer; Data processing systems; Digital computer.

*Dennis J. Frailey*

**Bibliography.** P. J. Denning, Third generation computer systems, *ACM Computing Surveys,* 3(4):175–216, December 1971; M. J. Flynn, Very high-speed computing systems, *Proc. IEEE,* 54:1901–1909, December 1966; G. J. Myers, *Advances in Computer Architecture,* 2d ed., 1982; Special issue on computer architecture, *Communications of the ACM,* vol. 21, no. 1, January 1978.

## Computer vision

The use of digital computer techniques for extracting, characterizing, and interpreting information in visual images of a three-dimensional world; it is also known as machine vision. Visual sensing technology is receiving increased attention as a means to endow machines with the capability of exhibiting in a greater degree of "intelligence" in dealing with their environment. Thus, a robot or other machine that can "see" and "feel" should be easier to train in the performance of complex tasks while requiring less stringent control mechanisms than preprogrammed machines. A sensory, trainable system is also adaptable to a much larger variety of tasks, thus achieving a degree of universality that ultimately translates into lower production and maintenance costs.

The computer vision process may be divided into five principal areas: sensing, segmentation, description, recognition, and interpretation. These categories are suggested to a large extent by the way in which computer vision systems are generally implemented. It is not implied that human vision and reasoning can be neatly subdivided, nor that these processes are carried out independently of each other. For instance, it is logical to assume that recognition and interpretation are highly interrelated functions in a human. These relationships, however, are not yet understood to the point where they can be modeled analytically. Thus, the subdivision of functions discussed below may be viewed as a practical (albeit limited) approach for implementing computer vision systems, given the level of understanding and the analytical tools presently available.

**Visual sensing.** Visual information is converted to electrical signals by the use of visual sensors. The most commonly used visual sensors are vidicon cameras and solid-state diode arrays. Vidicons are the usual vacuum-tube cameras used as television imaging devices. An input video signal is digitized and transferred to a computer an an image of a size ranging typically from 64 × 64 to 512 × 512 discrete image elements, depending on the resolution requirements of a given application. SEE TELEVISION CAMERA.

Solid-state devices are available as linear and area arrays. If the scene to be imaged is in continuous, uniform motion (as in belt conveyors), a linear array can be used to scan a line across the conveyor, and the motion of an object in the direction perpendicular to scan produces the desired two-dimensional image. In a one-dimensional array each element is read every $N$ time intervals, where $N$ is the number of image elements in the line, whereas in a two-dimensional array each element is read every $N^2$ time intervals; therefore, the two-dimensional array maintains a higher output data rate while allowing a long integration time for noise reduction. Linear arrays with resolution exceeding 2048 elements are available.

In order for a vision system to be able to interact with its environment, a geometric relationship between the real world and the images in the picture seen by the system must be established. This relationship is a transformation of measurements from a three-dimensional coordinate system to the image coordinate system, or vice versa. Essential to the derivation of the object-image relationship is a precise mathematical description for the camera (that is, a camera model). The use of two or more cameras and their mathematical models allows extraction of three-dimensional information, such as depth.

Illumination of a scene is an important factor affecting the complexity of vision algorithms. Arbitrary lighting of the environment often results in low-contrast images, specular reflections, shadows, and extraneous details. When control of the illumination is possible, the lighting system should illuminate the scene so that the complexity of the resulting image is minimized, while the information required for analysis is enhanced. For instance, the so-called structured lighting approach used in some industrial vision systems projects points, stripes, or grids onto the scene. The way in which these features are distorted by the presence of an object simplifies the computer interpretation of the scene. Two examples of this approach are shown in **Fig. 1**.

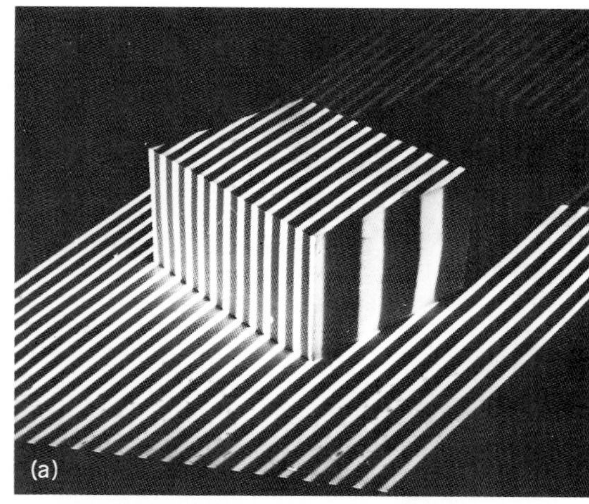


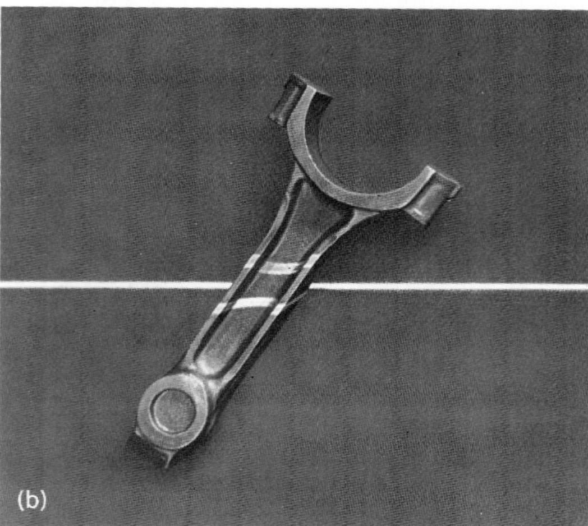


**Fig. 1. Two examples of scene illumination by structured lighting. (*a*) Illumination of a block by a series of parallel strips of light (*from W. Myers, Industry begins to use visual pattern recognition, Computer, 13(5):21–31, 1980.*) (*b*) Illumination of a workpiece by two strips of light which coincide at a background surface (*from F. Rocher and E. Keissling, Methods for analyzing three-dimensional scenes, Proceedings of the 1975 International Conference on Artificial Intelligence, American Association for Artificial Intelligence, pp. 669–673*).**

**Segmentation.** Segmentation is the process that breaks up a sensed scene into its constituent parts or objects. Hundreds of segmentation algorithms have been proposed since about 1970. This is still an active area of research because of its importance as the first processing step in any practical computer vision application. Although image segmentation has proved to be a difficult task in unconstrained situations such as automatic target detection, the problems encountered in industrial applications can be considerably simplified by special lighting techniques such as those discussed above.

Segmentation algorithms are generally based on one of two basic principles: discontinuity and similarity. The principal approach in the first category is edge detection. The principal approaches in the second category are thresholding and region growing. Most edge-detection techniques for industrial applications are based on the use of spatial convolution masks in order to reduce processing time. The idea is to move a mask over the entire image area, one image element location at a time and, at each location, to compute a measure proportional to discontinuity (for example, the gradient) in the image area directly under the mask. Thresholding is by far the most widely used approach for segmentation in industrial applications of computer vision. There are two reasons. First, thresholding techniques (in their simpler forms) are fast, and in addition, they are quite straightforward to implement in hardware. Second, the lighting environment is usually a controllable factor in industrial application; this results in images that often readily lend themselves to a thresholding approach for object extraction. Region-growing techniques are applicable in situations where objects cannot be differentiated from each other or the background by thresholding or edge detection. Although region growing has been used extensively in scene analysis, it has not found wide applicability in industrial applications because this method is usually impractical from a computational or hardware implementation point of view, and many of the problems which would require region growing for segmentation can usually be handled by special lighting or other enhancement techniques. A considerable amount of work has dealt with techniques that attempt to incorporate contextual information in the segmentation process. This includes the use of relaxation, plan-guided analysis and the use of semantic information.

**Description.** The description problem in computer vision is one of extracting features from an object for the purpose of recognition. Ideally, these features should be independent of object location and orientation and should contain enough discriminatory information to uniquely identify between objects. Descriptors for computer vision are based primarily on shape and amplitude (for example, intensity) information. Shape descriptors attempt to capture invariant geometrical properties of an object. Approaches for shape analysis and description are generally either global-oriented (region-oriented) or boundary-oriented. Global techniques include principal-axes analysis, texture, two- and three-dimensional moment invariants, geometrical descriptors such as $p^2/A$ (where $P$ is the length of the perimeter and $A$ is the area) and the extrema of a region, topological properties, and decomposition into primary convex subsets. Boundary-oriented techniques include Fourier descriptors, chain codes, graph representations, of which strings and trees are special cases, and shape numbers. Boundary feature extraction is often preceded by linking procedures which fit straight-line segments or polynomials to the edge points resulting from segmentation. An example of object description by extraction of its boundary and principal directional axes is shown in **Fig. 2**.

**Recognition.** Recognition is basically a labeling process; that is, the function of recognition algorithms is to identify each segmented object in a scene and to assign a label (for example, wrench, seal, or bolt) to that object. Recognition approaches presently in use may be subdivided into two principal categories: decision-theoretic and structural. Decision-theoretic techniques are based on the use of decision (discriminant) functions. Given $M$ object classes, $\omega_1$, $\omega_2$, . . . , $\omega_M$, the basic problem in decision-theoretic pattern recognition is to identify $M$ decision functions, $d_1(x)$, $d_2(x)$, . . . , $d_M(x)$, with the property that, for any pattern $x^*$ from class $\omega_i$, $d_i(x^*) > d_j(x^*)$, for $j = 1, 2, \ldots, M$, $j \neq i$. The objective is to find $M$ decision functions such that this condition holds for all classes with minimum error in classification. SEE DECISION THEORY.

Decision-theoretic methods deal with patterns on a quantitative basis and largely ignore structural interrelationships among pattern primitives. Structural methods of pattern recognition attempt to describe fundamental relationships among pattern primitives via discrete mathematical modes. Here, the most widely used method is syntactic pattern recognition in which concepts and results from formal language theory provide the basic mechanisms for handling structural descriptions. The existence of a recognizable and finitely describable structure is essential in the success of the syntactic approach. Basically, a formal grammar is developed to generate elements of a language that defines a pattern class, and an automaton (or equivalently, a parsing algorithm) is developed to recognize precisely that same language. Such a language may consist of strings of primitives and relational operators (for example, directed line segments along the boundary of a polygonal representation of a workpiece) or of higher-order data structures, such as trees, graphs, and webs.

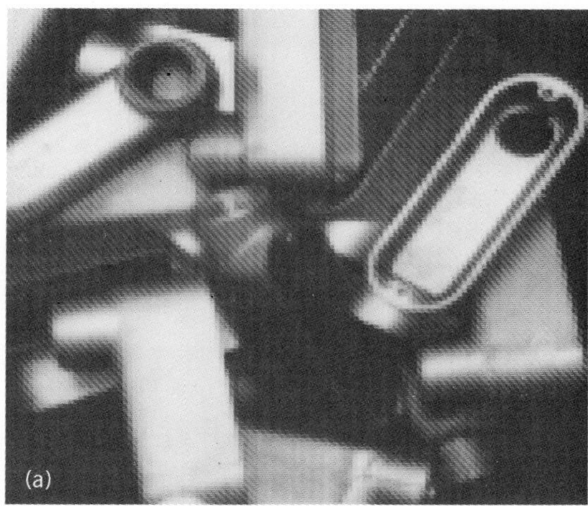


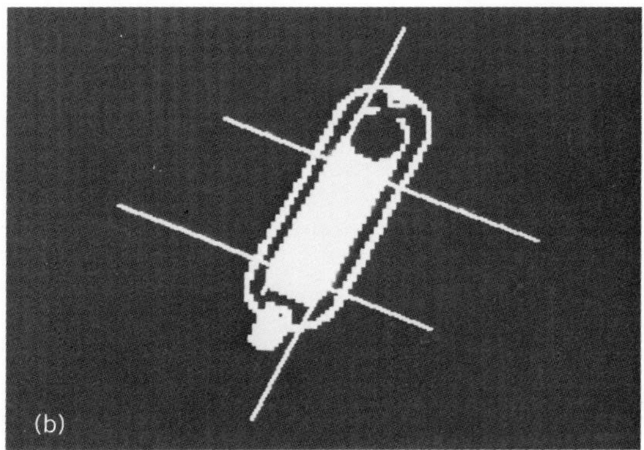


**Fig. 2. Description of an object by extraction of its boundary and principal directional axes. (*a*) Bin of workpieces. (*b*) Description of one of the segmented objects. (*From J. Birk, R. Kelley, and H. Martins, An orienting robot for feeding workpieces stored in bins, IEEE Trans. SMC, SMC-11:151–160, 1981*)**

One of the most significant recent extensions of syntactic techniques has been the inclusion of semantic evaluations simultaneously with syntactic analysis by means of attributed grammars. In this approach, a pattern primitive is defined by two components: a token or symbol from a finite alphabet, and an associated list of attributes consisting of logical, numerical, or vector values. The syntactic rules provide the basic structural description, while the semantic rules assign meaning to that description.

**Interpretation and models.** In this discussion, interpretation is viewed as the process which endows a vision system with a higher level of conception about its environment. Sensed information, tasks to be performed, and types of parts to be handled are all essential items in establishing the level of competence and adaptability of a vision system. Given the limited state of development in "truly intelligent" vision systems, careful definition of a constrained set of operating conditions is essential. This is usually accomplished via models.

The structure and complexity of a model depends on the stage of visual processing in which it is used. Computer vision techniques may be divided into three basic levels of processing: low-, medium-, and high-level vision. Although this division is somewhat arbitrary, it does provide a convenient method for categorizing the various processes that are inherent components of a computer vision system.

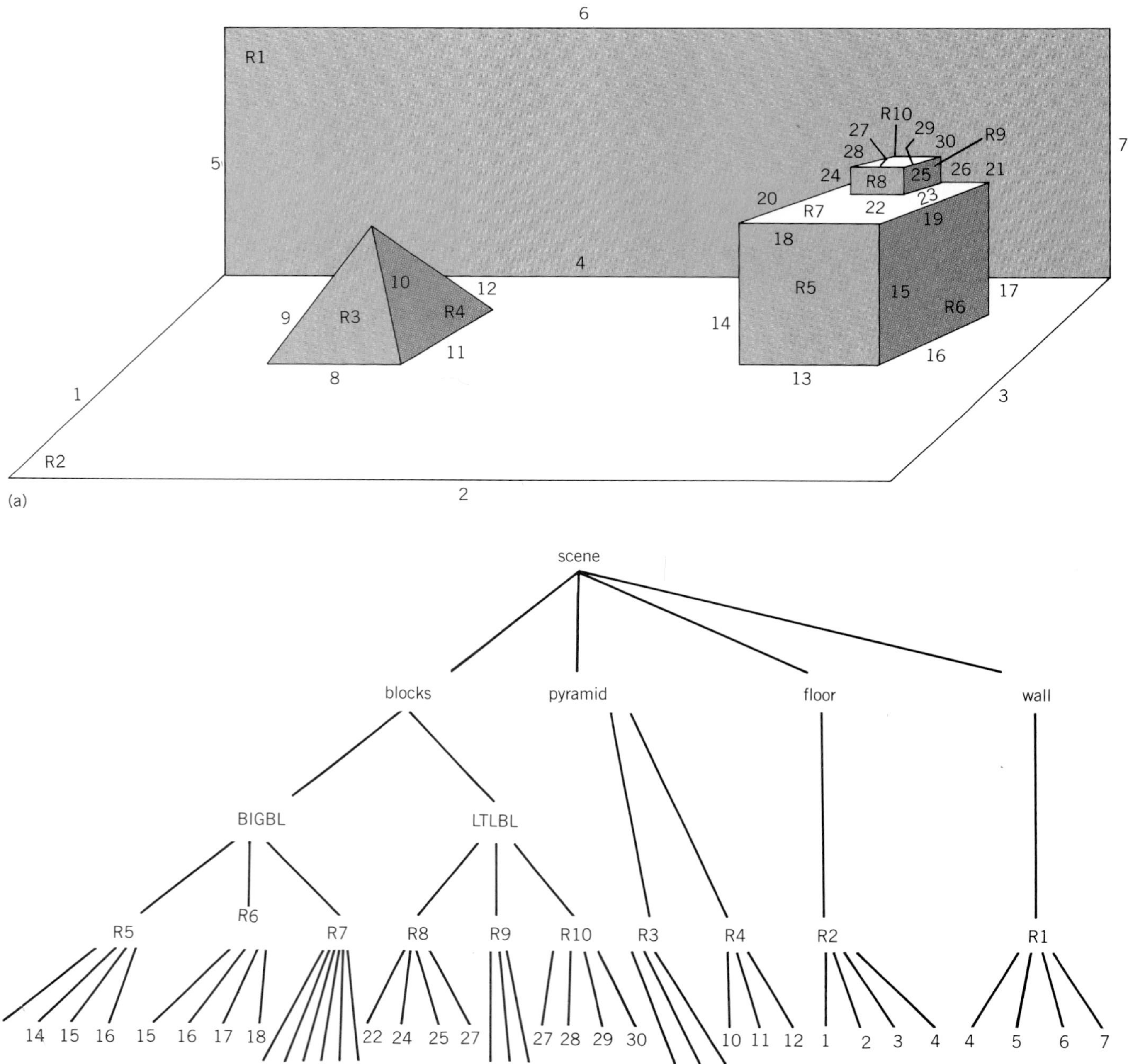


**Fig. 3. Hierarchical representation of a scene. (*a*) Scene with blocks, pyramid, floor, and wall. (*b*) Hierarchical representation. (*After M. G. Thomason and R. C. Gonzalez, Database Representation in Hierarchical Scene Analysis, in L. Kanal and A. Rosenfeld, eds., Progress in Pattern Recognition, Elsevier-North Holland, 1982*)**

Low-level vision techniques attempt to extract "primitive" information from a scene. Examples of the use of models in low-level vision procedures range from modeling the characteristics of incident and reflected light properties of a body, to the detection of edge segments in a scene by modeling an edge as an abrupt change in intensity amenable to detection by gradient operators. Medium-level vision refers to procedures which use the results from low-level vision to produce structures that somehow carry more meaning than the elements extracted by the low-level vision process. Medium-level vision processes include edge linking, segmentation, description, and recognition of individual objects. High-level computer vision may be viewed as the process that attempts to emulate cognition. At this level of processing, the present knowledge and understanding of a suitable model is considerably more vague and speculative. While models for low- and medium-level vision tend to be rather specific in nature, a model for high-level vision encompasses a considerably broader spectrum of processing functions, ranging from the actual formation of a digital scene through interpretation of interrelationships between objects in a scene.

**Figure 3** illustrates modeling of a scene by decomposing it into successively simpler elements. The simplest element considered in this case is an edge. Thus, regions are composed of edges, objects are composed of regions, and the scene is composed of objects. SEE ARTIFICIAL INTELLIGENCE; CHARACTER RECOGNITION; COMPUTER GRAPHICS; ROBOTICS.

R. C. Gonzalez

**Bibliography.** H. G. Barrow and J. M. Tenebaum, Computational vision, *Proc. IEEE*, 69:572–595, 1981; G. G. Dodd and L. Rossol (eds.), *Computer Vision and Sensor-Based Robots*, 1979; K. S. Fu, R. C. Gonzalez, and C. S. G. Lee, *Introduction to Robotics*, 1984; R. C. Gonzalez and R. Safabakhsh, Computer vision techniques for industrial applications and robot control, *Computer*, 15(12):17–32, 1982.

## Concurrent processing

The conceptually simultaneous execution of more than one sequential program on a computer or network of computers. The individual sequential programs are called processes. Two processes are considered concurrent only if they interact in some way. This interaction may range from cooperation (the exchange of information) to competition for scarce resources (such as the processor, the memory, or a printer). Concurrent processing is achieved on a single computer, that is, on a single processor, by interleaving the execution of the individual processes.

In comparison, distributed processing requires multiple processors for its implementation. According to this definition, all distributed programs are also concurrent programs, but the converse is not true. SEE DISTRIBUTED SYSTEMS.

**Advantages and disadvantages.** A common example of concurrent processing is a multiuser operating system, which allows more than one user process to be executed concurrently on the same processor. Many such systems do not allow the processes to communicate directly; they only coordinate the use of shared resources by the processes (for example, the static allocation of memory to the active processes or the dynamic allocation of processors to processes). This form of concurrency allows multiple users to share one processor, which is a necessity for time-sharing systems, without having the user programs complicated by codes dealing with the sharing of resources, scheduling, and so forth. This modularity is an advantage of most concurrent systems over sequential systems: different parts of a problem can be relegated to semi-independent processes that will communicate with one another only when necessary. SEE MULTIACCESS COMPUTER.

This form of concurrency has disadvantages as well. The operating system causes an overhead in the use of the processor; an operating system that executes user processes sequentially would spend very little time in allocating the processor's resources or in switching between tasks.

Distributed systems present additional advantages and disadvantages in comparison with centralized concurrent systems. Distributed systems eliminate some of the contention for the processor, because there are more processors available in the system. Furthermore, a centralized system does not lend itself to graceful degradation as does a distributed system. The failure of one processor in a distributed system need not cause the entire system to fail, if the remaining processors can take up where the failed processor left off.

Though distributed systems reduce contention for processors, they create contention for the communication network. In a centralized system, interaction can take place through shared memory protected by some synchronization mechanism; in a distributed system all interaction and communication must pass through the network. There also is a cost for the higher availability of distributed systems, especially where the processes are cooperating closely. Each processor (or its operating system) must keep track of the progress of the other processors in order to recover in the event of a failure.

**Specifying concurrency.** Many programming languages provide the user with the ability to write concurrent programs. Different languages allow parallelism with different degrees of concurrency.

Languages such as Ada, CSP, Concurrent Pascal, Mesa, and Module provide for statement-level (or procedure-level) concurrency. These languages have either a construct that causes a new process to be initiated, executing some statement or procedure in parallel with the current process, or a construct that causes a set of statements or procedures to be executed in parallel. In either case, the user tells the system what portions of the code will be executed concurrently.

In contrast, some data flow languages provide for operator-level concurrency. In such languages, the program is specified without reference to concurrency; the compiler breaks the program down into its component operations, often as small as add or multiply. When the program executes, all operators can be executed in parallel; an operator can execute as soon as it has received values for all of its input operands. Upon termination it forwards its result to those operators requiring that result as input. SEE DATA FLOW SYSTEMS; PROGRAMMING LANGUAGES.

**Communication and synchronization.** Interprocess communication invokes two classes of concurrent systems: synchronous and asynchronous. In a synchronous system, all processors work in lockstep; that is, they all execute the same instruction at the same time (on different data). In asynchronous systems each process (and processor) works independently of the others. Asynchronous processes need only synchronize temporarily to exchange information or to request a service. Such synchronization and communication takes place in one of two ways: by reading and writing shared memory or by exchanging messages.

In shared memory systems, processes communicate by modifying shared variables. Such variables contain values, such as the number of free tape drives or the identity of the next process to control the processor. Though shared, these variables must be protected from simultaneous access by multiple processes. The processor hardware usually prevents simultaneous writing of the same memory location (thereby preventing meaningless data from being stored), but that is not enough. Higher-level synchronization is required to prevent interference between processes. Problems arise when one process reads a shared variable, intending to change it, but a second process changes the variable before the first process performs its change. When the first process finally makes its change, the second process's update is lost. It is necessary for a process to be able to gain exclusive access to a variable for more than a read or write. The portion of a program in which a process has exclusive control over shared data is called a critical section. There are many mechanisms for obtaining such protection; one example is the monitor. Monitors protect shared variables by allowing processes to access these variables only through special procedures; only one process may execute a monitor's procedure at a time, thus preventing the destructive interference.

Message-passing systems communicate by send- and receiving messages. Sending a message is more expensive (in terms of computer time and resources) than modifying a shared variable. A message must be built out of the data provided by the sending process, and then copied to the address space of the receiving process. This may entail multiple copies if the data must be passed through intermediate processes and networks. On the other hand, message systems have no shared variables to protect from concurrent interference. There are different types of message-passing systems that depend on whether the sending process must wait until the receiving process actually receives the message, and if so, whether it must wait for a reply.

*Brent T. Hailpern*

**Bibliography.** G. R. Andrews, Synchronizing resources, *ACM Transactions on Programming Languages and Systems,* 3(4):405–430, October 1981; R. H. Kuhn and D. A. Padua (eds.), *Tutorial on Parallel Processing,* IEEE Computer Society, 1981; B. Liskov, Primitives for distributed computing, *ACM Proceedings of the 7th Symposium on Operating Systems,* pp. 33–42, 1979; P. D. Stotts, Jr., A comparative survey of concurrent programming languages, *ACM SIGPLAN Not.,* 17(9):76–87, September 1982.

## Conductance

The real part of the admittance of an alternating-current circuit. The admittance $Y$ of an alternating-current circuit is a complex number given by Eq. (1).

$$Y = G + jB \tag{1}$$

The real part $G$ is the conductance. The units of conductance, like those of admittance, are called siemens or mhos. Conductance is a positive quantity. The conductance of a resistor $R$ is given by Eq. (2).

$$G = 1/R \tag{2}$$

In general the conductance of a circuit may depend on the capacitors and inductors in the circuit as well as on the resistors. For example, the circuit in the **illustration** has impedance at frequency $\omega$ given by Eq. (3) and admittance given by Eq. (4), so that the

$$Z = R + jL\omega \tag{3}$$

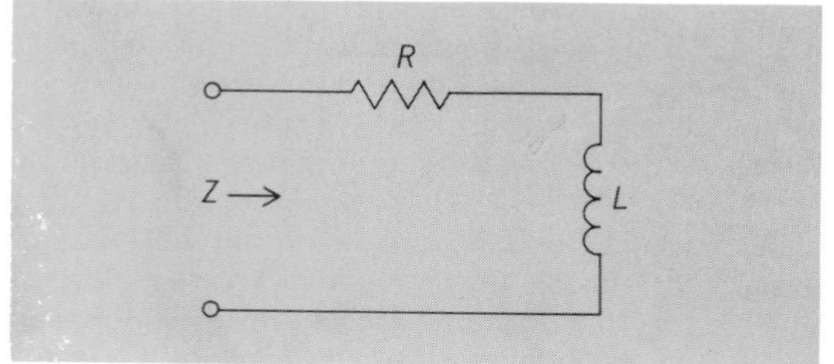


Circuit with a resistor and inductor in series.

$$Y = \frac{1}{R + jL\omega} \tag{4}$$

conductance, given by Eq. (5), depends on the induc-

$$G = \frac{R}{R^2 + L^2\omega^2} \tag{5}$$

tance $L$ as well as the resistance $R$. SEE ADMITTANCE; ALTERNATING-CURRENT CIRCUIT THEORY; ELECTRICAL IMPEDANCE.

*J. O. Scanlan*

## Conduction (electricity)

The passage of electric charges due to a force exerted on them by an electric field. Conductivity is the measure of the ability of a conductor to carry electric current; it is defined as the ratio of the amount of charge passing through unit area of the conductor (perpendicular to the current direction) per second divided by the electric field intensity (the force on a unit charge). Conductivity is the reciprocal of resistivity and is therefore commonly expressed in units of mhos (reciprocal ohms) per meter.

The magnitude of the conductivity of a material or system is determined by two properties: the number $n$ of its charges in unit volume that are free to move in the field, and how effectively the field can move them. Acted on by the field, which accelerates them, and by the resistance of the material to their motion, the free charges achieve a drift velocity that is proportional to the electric field intensity. The mobility $\mu$ of the charges is defined as the ratio of this drift velocity to the field. From the above definition of the conductivity $\sigma$, it follows directly that $\sigma = ne\mu$, where $e$ is the charge of a free carrier and $n$ is the number of free carriers per unit volume. In metals and semiconductors (such as germanium and silicon) the charges that are responsible for current are free electrons and holes (which, as missing electrons, act like positive charges). These are electrons or holes not bound to any particular atom and therefore able to move freely in the field. Conductivity due to electrons is known as $n$-type conductivity; that due to holes is known as $p$-type. SEE HOLES IN SOLIDS; SEMICONDUCTOR.

The conductivity of metals is much higher than that of semiconductors because they have many more free electrons or holes. In semiconductors the number of free electrons or holes is limited by the necessity for them to be excited across an energy gap; this requires energy that is usually provided by raising the temperature of the semiconductor. Thus the number of free electrons or holes, that is, free carriers, and the resulting conductivity usually increase rapidly with temperature. In metals the number of free carriers does not vary with temperature. Increasing temperature, however, causes the lattice atoms to vibrate more strongly, impeding the motion of the free carriers in the field and causing the conductivity to decrease. This effect also occurs in semiconductors, but the increase in number of free carriers with temperature is usually a stronger effect. At low temperatures the thermal vibrations are weak, and the impediment to the motion of free carriers in the field comes from imperfections and impurities, which in metals usually does not vary with temperature. At the lowest temperatures, close to absolute zero, certain metals become superconductors, possessing infinite conductivity. SEE SUPERCONDUCTIVITY.

Electrolytes conduct electricity by means of the positive and negative ions in solution. In ionic crystals, conduction may also take place by the motion of ions. This motion is much affected by the presence of lattice defects such as interstitial ions, vacancies, and foreign ions.

Ionic conduction can also take place in a gas by using a strong electric field to ionize the gas molecules. If sufficient ions are formed, there may be a spark. SEE ELECTRIC SPARK; ELECTRICAL CONDUCTION IN GASES.

Electric current can flow through an evacuated region if electrons or ions are supplied. In a vacuum tube the current carriers are electrons emitted by a heated filament. The conductivity is low because only a small number of electrons can be ''boiled off'' at the normal temperatures of electron-emitting filaments. SEE ELECTRON EMISSION; ELECTRON MOTION IN VACUUM.

*Esther M. Conwell*

**Bibliography.** C. Kittel, *Introduction to Solid State Physics*, 5th ed., 1976; L. B. Loeb, *Fundamental Processes of Electrical Discharge in Gases*, 1939; W. Shockley, *Electrons and Holes in Semiconductors*, 1950; P. Vashishta, J. N. Mundy, and G. K. Shenoy (eds.), Fast ion transport in solids, *Proceedings of the International Conference at Lake Geneva, Wisconsin*, May 21–25, 1979.

## Conduction band

The electronic energy band of a crystalline solid which is partially occupied by electrons. The electrons in this energy band can increase their energies by going to higher energy levels within the band when an electric field is applied to accelerate them or when the temperature of the crystal is raised. These electrons are called conduction electrons, as distinct from the electrons in filled energy bands which, as a whole, do not contribute to electrical and thermal conduction. In metallic conductors the conduction electrons correspond to the valence electrons (or a portion of the valence electrons) of the constituent atoms. In semiconductors and insulators at sufficiently low temperatures, the conduction band is empty of electrons. Conduction electrons come from thermal excitation of electrons from a lower energy band or from impurity atoms in the crystal. SEE BAND THEORY OF SOLIDS; SEMICONDUCTOR; VALENCE BAND.

*H. Y. Fan*

## Contact potential difference

The potential difference that exists across the space between two electrically connected metals; also, the potential difference between the bulk regions of a junction of two semiconductors. In **Fig. 1***a* consider two metals $M_1$ and $M_2$ with work functions $\phi_1$ and $\phi_2$, respectively. When the metals are brought in contact, the Fermi levels, that is, the levels corresponding to the most energetic electrons, must coincide, as in Fig. 1*b*. Consequently, if $\phi_1 > \phi_2$, metal $M_1$ will acquire a negative and metal $M_2$ a positive surface charge at the contact area. In the circuit indicated in **Fig. 2** there will thus exist a potential difference be-

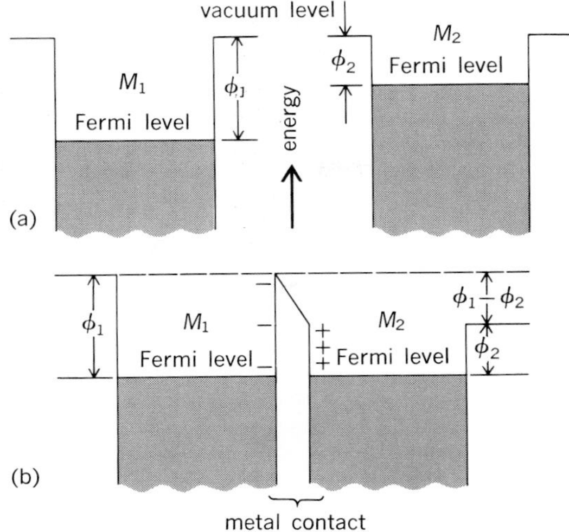


**Fig. 1. Energy-level diagram for conduction electrons of two metals. (*a*) Before contact. (*b*) After contact.**

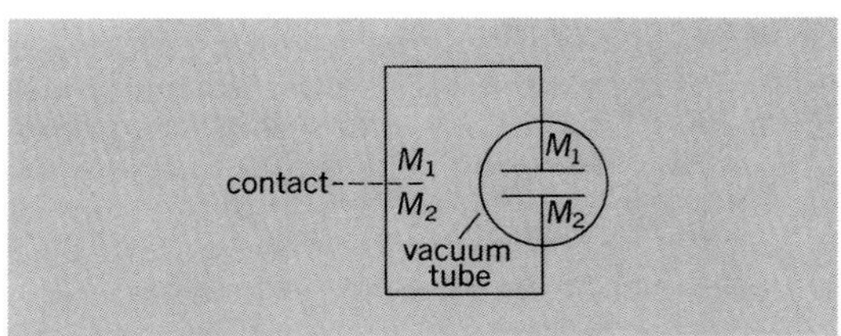


**Fig. 2. Two metallic plates in vacuum between which a contact potential difference may be measured.**

tween the plates such that $M_1$ is negative with respect to $M_2$; the magnitude of the contact potential is equal to $(\phi_1 - \phi_2)/e$ (of the order of a few volts or less) where $e = 1.6 \times 10^{-19}$ coulomb. Note that the contact potential is independent of the number of different materials used in the circuit external to the plates in vacuum. The contact potential difference may be measured by placing a variable electromotive force in the external circuit, which can be balanced to make the potential difference between the plates equal to zero. Contact potentials must be taken into account in analyzing physical electronics experiments. SEE WORK FUNCTION (ELECTRONICS).

*A. J. Dekker*

## Continuous-wave radar

A radar in which the transmitter output is uninterrupted, in contrast to pulse radar, where the output consists of short pulses. Among the advantages of continuous-wave (CW) radar is its ability to measure velocity with extreme accuracy by means of the Doppler shift in the frequency of the echo. The detected, reflected wave is shifted in frequency by an amount which is a function of the relative velocity between the target and the transmitter-receiver. Range data are extracted from the change in Doppler frequency with time. SEE DOPPLER RADAR.

In order to measure the range of targets, some form of frequency modulation (FM) of the continuous-wave output must be used. In one very effective form of modulation, the carrier frequency of the transmitted signal is varied at a uniform rate. Range is determined by comparing the frequency of the echo with that of the transmitter, the difference being proportional to the range of the target that produced the echo. Systems in which this is done are known as FM-CW radars. SEE FREQUENCY MODULATION.

A modified form of FM-CW radar employs long, but not continuous, transmission. This might be regarded as the same as transmitting extremely long pulses on an FM carrier. Systems of this type are referred to as pulse compression radars.

**Design objectives.** Design objectives for continuous-wave radar include: protecting the receiver from the transmitter output and close-by return echoes when a single antenna is used; resolving side-lobe ambiguity; resolving range ambiguity; eliminating noise and clutter; simultaneously measuring both target range and velocity; determining the shapes of targets; handling multiple targets; communicating with targets; and increasing the received signal-to-noise ratio.

***Receiver protection.*** One disadvantage of continuous-wave radar is that when a single antenna is used for both reception and transmission it is difficult to protect the receiver against the transmitter because, in contrast to pulse radar, both are on all the time. Use of isolation circuitry gives the receiver protection from a transmitter output up to 200 W. Use of magnetically biased yttrium-iron-garnet (YIG) provides three tuned, tandem-connected power-limiter stages in one X-band FM-CW radar. SEE FERRITE DEVICES.

In continuous-wave surveillance radars where wide bandwidth is required to meet range and range-rate measurement requirements despite clutter and other interfering environments, the transmitter output can be coded by pseudorandom binary signals that vary with range. This is an ideal waveform for permitting range measurements, retaining a capability for range-rate measurements, and rejecting the transmitter output and other nearby echoes.

***Side-lobe ambiguity.*** The problem of distinguishing between echoes from the main lobe and those from the side lobes has been addressed by providing a demodulated range response that has one polarity for the main-lobe echoes and the opposite polarity for side-lobe echoes.

***Range ambiguity.*** This ambiguity results from reception of echoes from targets beyond the range of interest and of second-time-around echoes. It can be resolved by range gates that make the radar insensitive to targets beyond the range of interest or by filters that put limits on range. Resolution of range ambiguity is very important in radars for personnel surveillance.

***Noise and clutter.*** Suppression of noise, clutter, chaff, and jamming has received a great deal of attention. In one approach, a fixed pair of amplitude-modulation (AM) sidebands is added and used to null out the noise.

Echo signal analyzers can be selectively adjusted for a certain moving-target size so that small targets are not detected. A series of digital range cells can be defined such that each cell represents the minimum allowable distance between two reflective points on a target. The radar also can be adaptively adjusted to attend to a desired average signal level.

Use of digitally controlled voltage-tunable radio-frequency generators permit frequency jumping to avoid jamming or spoofing. SEE ELECTRICAL NOISE.

***Range and velocity sensing.*** Several techniques are used to obtain simultaneous measurements of range and velocity. One involves transmitting sidebands of linearly increasing and decreasing frequency or using triangular modulation, and comparing the difference between transmitted and received frequencies with the difference between the received frequency and the transmitted frequency delayed by a period of time proportional to the range of the target. Phase-shift keying by a pseudorandom code also permits simultaneous measurement of range and velocity. SEE MODULATION.

***Target shape.*** Millimeter-wave FM-CW radar can be used to determine the shape of a target. These radars operate at frequencies in excess of 90 GHz. They often use Gunn oscillators as the source. SEE MICROWAVE SOLID-STATE DEVICES.

French and Soviet research suggests that in some applications it may be necessary to use space diversity in which two beams illuminate the target in order to compensate for nonlinearities in frequency scanning.

***Multiple targets.*** Discrete Fourier analysis of the video heterodyne (beat) signals using a digital computer permits multiple-target handling and achieves good resolution between approaching and receding targets. SEE SPECTRUM ANALYZER.

***Communicating with the target.*** In radar missile guidance, homing beacons, and identification–friend-or-foe, it is necessary to communicate with the target. This can be done by interrupting the range beat frequency at short intervals near its peak excursion and transmitting AM signals to the illuminated target.

***Signal-to-noise ratio.*** The signal-to-noise ratio can be improved by digitizing the beat frequency signals. Moreover, compressing the received signals to a sine-squared shape can increase the signal level more than 20 decibels. SEE SIGNAL-TO-NOISE RATIO.

**Applications.** Applications of continuous-wave radar include: missile guidance; detection of hostile targets; terrain clearance indication and ground surveillance; laser radar systems; atmospheric studies; automobile safety; surveillance of personnel; ice studies; remote sensing; and reproduction of the shape of a patient's pulse.

***Missile guidance.*** The principal use of continuous-wave radar is in short-range missile guidance. Typically the missile's course is tracked from the ground while the missile is simultaneously illuminated. Continuous-wave radar, in some cases the same radar, can be used for both tracking and illumination, although it is more common for pulse Doppler radar to be used for tracking.

Advances in the design of phased-array antennas have led to pulse Doppler radar becoming more attractive than continuous-wave radar even for illumination. However, at least one system allows the operator to select either continuous-wave or pulse Doppler radar for illumination.

Illumination radar is for target acquisition. Two signals are of interest. One, the directly received illumination of the missile, is called the rear signal. The other, the signal reflected from the target, is called the front signal. The front signal is shifted in frequency as the missile closes with the target. This shift occurs because of the Doppler effect. The shift, and therefore the range to the target, is obtained by coherently detecting the front signal against the rear signal. In an active guidance system, detection is performed on board the missile. Semiactive missile guidance is more frequently used, and in this system the signals are relayed over a data link for processing at the ground station.

A late version of the MPQ-34 tracking and acquisition radar for the Hawk ground-to-air missile incorporates the choice of either continuous-wave or pulse Doppler radar illumination. The ability of continuous-wave radar to discriminate against clutter made it attractive in this system, which was intended to be used againt low-flying aircraft.

Pulsed tracking radar with continuous-wave acquisition radar is used with the Sparrow air-to-air missile system and with the Tartar shipborne missile system.

A miss-distance indicator (MDI) is a special application of continuous-wave radar. It uses radio-frequency signals to determine the relative velocity between two objects, the time of intercept when the distance will be a minimum, and the actual value of that minimum distance. With the availability of real-time intercept information, a prior determination of guidance parameters that will produce a direct hit can be made.

***Detection of hostile targets.*** Modulated continuous-wave radar has been used to detect hostile military vehicles and personnel.

The Navy MK-92 fire-control system uses a linear FM-CW radar with multiple resonant filters.

An FM-CW naval radar operating at 95.6 GHz uses pseudorandom-coded phase-shift keying, digital signal processing, and microprocessor-controlled azimuth and elevation scanning. It can display the shape, range, velocity, and direction of vessels.

In the United States, Canada, and the United Kingdom, there has been interest in continuous-wave radar for detecting nonmetallic mines. One radar operates between 2 and 4 GHz and can detect plastic objects buried in 10 in. (25 cm) of wet sand.

***Terrain surveillance.*** One of the first uses of FM continuous-wave radar was in terrain clearance indicators or radar altimeters. Today intruder aircraft and air-breathing missiles obtain continuous guidance from that kind of equipment.

The ability of side-looking radar on reconnaissance aircraft and Earth-observation satellites to resolve targets has been enhanced by the use of synthetic-aperture radar. Although this technique usually requires a huge data rate and great processing complexity, special-purpose processors have been used to extract useful data economically. Such a processor on the *Seasat 1* was able to determine the direction of ocean wave movement from 800 mi (1300 km) up.

Earth surveillance has been hampered by some radar reflection phenomena, notably foreshadowing, which distorts distance; layover, which tends to fill in depressions; and shadow, which obscures features. These problems place limiting requirements on the size and contrast of images needed for successful interpretation. These limitations can be partially overcome by training radargrammetrists with simulators.

***Laser radar systems.*** An experimental modulated continuous-wave laser radar was built to track low-flying airborne targets from the ground. The system can determine both range and the rate at which the range is changing. An advantage of this system is its extreme precision. The divergence of the beam is less than 1 milliradian. The transmitter is a carbon dioxide laser operating at a wavelength of 10.6 micrometers. The infrared carrier is frequency-modulated with 10-MHz excursions occurring at a frequency of 1 kHz. SEE LASER.

***Atmospheric studies.*** The ability of FM-CW radar to measure distance and velocity despite smoke, dust, and thermal gradients makes it attractive for many industrial automatic control applications. The Naval Ocean Systems Center uses S-band continuous-wave radar to update refractive index profiles of the troposphere. This work forms the basis for radio interception and over-the-horizon targeting. In France, continuous-wave radar has been used to measure the electron temperatures in the ionosphere. The National Oceanic and Atmospheric Administration (NOAA) has used continuous-wave radar to measure wind in clear air.

***Automobile safety.*** An experimental continuous-wave radar which exploits the Doppler principle has been developed for use in automobiles. The radar can anticipate a crash when an obstacle is 30 ft (10 m) away in order to deploy air-cushion-type passive restraints. It can sense obstacles 500 ft (150 m) away to govern automatic braking and headway control. The source of carrier power is an X-band Gunn-type solid-state oscillator.

***Surveillance of personnel.*** A variant of continuous-wave radar is used to illuminate persons under surveillance by techniques employing semiconductor tracer diodes. These devices are secreted on or implanted in the subject's body without his or her knowledge, or else concealed in objects that are to be protected against theft. Despite the fact that pulsed X-band sources could provide the needed power levels more conveniently, the requirement to reduce clutter makes it desirable to use continuous-wave power.

These techniques are also used to sweep premises to discover clandestine listening devices and to guard protected locations against the introduction of concealed tape recorders.

Implementation of tracer-diode surveillance utilizes a single carrier frequency and looks for reflections of the third harmonic as evidence that the person sought has been acquired by the beam. The surveillance operations have been carried out from fixed posts, vans, and low-flying aircraft.

An improved version makes use of two carrier frequencies for illumination and depends upon coherent detection of the third and fourth harmonics of the sum and difference frequencies to signify acquisition of the target. SEE ELECTRONIC LISTENING DEVICES.

***Other applications.*** In Finland, a continuous-wave radar operating between 1 and 1.8 GHz has been used to measure ice and frost thickness in lakes and bogs. Continuous-wave radars operating at 1.5 and from 8 to 18 GHz have been used to discriminate among different types of Arctic Sea ice.

Continuous-wave radar has been used in the Netherlands to discriminate among different types of vegetation, crops, and bare soils.

With its antenna placed over a patient's wrist artery, continuous-wave radar has been shown to be able to reproduce the shape of the arterial pulse. SEE RADAR.

*John M. Carroll*

***Bibliography.*** D. F. Albanese, Pseudo-random code waveform design trade-offs for CW radar applications, *International Conference of the IEEE Aerospace and Electronic Systems Society,* October 1977; P. J. Martin, Direct determination of the two-dimensional image spectrum from raw synthetic aperture radar data, *IEEE Transactions on Geoscience and Remote Sensing,* GE-19; 194–203, 1981; H. E. Penrose and R. S. H. Boulding, *Principles and Practice of Radar,* 6th ed., 1959; *Proceedings of the European Microwave Conference,* 1980; *Proceedings of the IEEE International Microwave Symposium,* 1979;

*Proceedings of the IEEE International Radar Conference,* 1975; *Proceedings of the National Aerospace and Electronics Conference (NAECON),* 1983; A. B. Przedpelski, CW finds new uses in the '80s, *Microwaves,* 21(4):89–94, 1982; J. A. Stiles et al., The recognition of extended targets: SAR images for level and hilly terrain, *IEEE Transactions on Geoscience and Remote Sensing,* GE-20: 205–211, 1982.

## Controlled rectifier

A three-terminal semiconductor junction device with four regions of alternating conductivity type (*pnpn*), also called a thyristor. This switching device has a characteristic such that, once it conducts, the voltage in the circuit in which it conducts must drop below a threshold before the controlled rectifier regains control. Such devices are useful as high-current switches and may be used to drive electromagnets and relays.

The principle of operation can be understood by referring to the **illustration**. The central junction is reverse-biased (positive collector, grounded emitter). The wide *n* region between collector and base regions prevents holes injected at the collector junction from reaching the collector-to-base barrier by diffusion. The junction between emitter and base is the emitter. When operated as a normal transistor, this device shows a rapid increase of current gain of α (equal to $I_c/I_e$) with collector current. This effect may be due to a field-induced increase of transport efficiency across the floating *n* region, or to increased avalanching in the high-field barrier region, or to increased injection efficiency at the two forward-biased junctions, or to a combination of these phenomena.

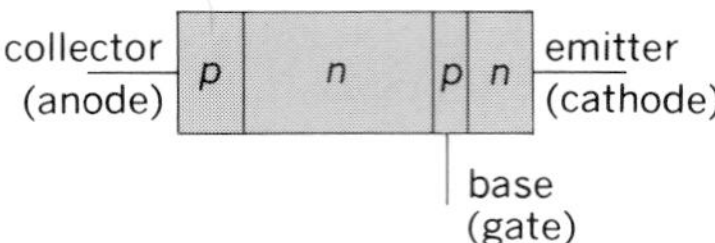


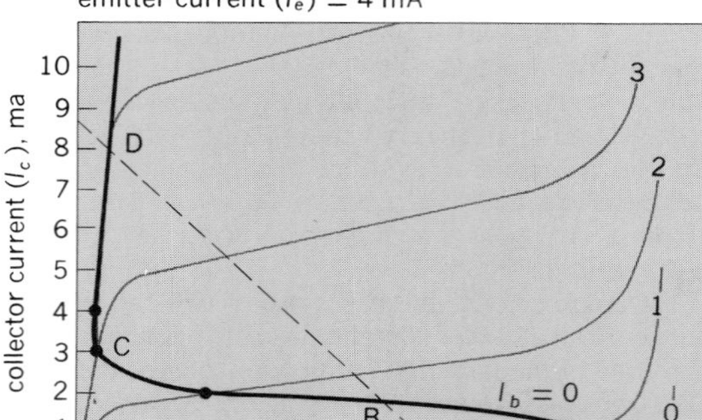


**Controlled rectifier diagram and characteristics.**

With a floating-base region ($I_b = 0$), the device is a two-terminal device and collector current $I_c$ must equal emitter current $I_e$.

By selecting the points on the illustrated characteristics where $I_c = I_e$, the characteristic for the base current $I_b = 0$ is shown as the heavy curve with the negative-resistance characteristic. This characteristic will be found in any transistor which shows an integrated α increasing from below unity at low collector currents to above unity at high collector currents.

If this device is operated as a three-terminal device, the switching between the nonconducting and conducting states can be controlled by the base. If in the grounded-emitter case the collector is biased to $+E_c$ as shown, the device will remain at point *A* until the base is pulsed positive by at least enough current to carry the emitter current to point *B*. At this point α exceeds unity and the device will spontaneously switch to point *D* in the conducting state. To reset the unit, either the emitter must be cut off or the collector voltage must be reduced so that the load line falls below the valley point *C*. The current of point *C* is called the holding current. Either of these results can be achieved by appropriate pulses on the base. Modern terminology usually refers to the rectifier terminals as anode and cathode and to the control terminal as the gate. *SEE SEMICONDUCTOR RECTIFIER*.

Overall current gain α may be maintained below unity for low anode-cathode currents by designing the junction between the anode and the floating *n* region and the junction between the gate and the cathode so each has a low-current injection efficiency below 0.5. For further discussion of four-layer devices *SEE TRANSISTOR*.

*Lloyd P. Hunter*

***Bibliography.*** S. M. Sze, *Physics of Semiconductor Devices*, 2d ed., 1981; E. S. Yang, *Fundamentals of Semiconductor Devices*, 1978.

## Corner reflector antenna

A directional antenna consisting of the combination of a reflector comprising two conducting planes forming a dihedral angle and a driven radiator or dipole which usually is in the bisecting plane. It is widely used both singly and in arrays, gives good gain in comparison with cost, and covers a relatively wide band of frequency.

The **illustration** shows the general configuration for a 90° corner reflector. The distance S from the driven radiator D to edge E need not be critically chosen with respect to wavelength; for a 90° reflector D may lie between 0.25 and 0.7 wavelength. The overall dimensions of the reflector need not exceed 2 wavelengths in order to approximate the performance obtained with very large reflectors. Gain, as compared with an isotropic radiator, is about 12 dB.

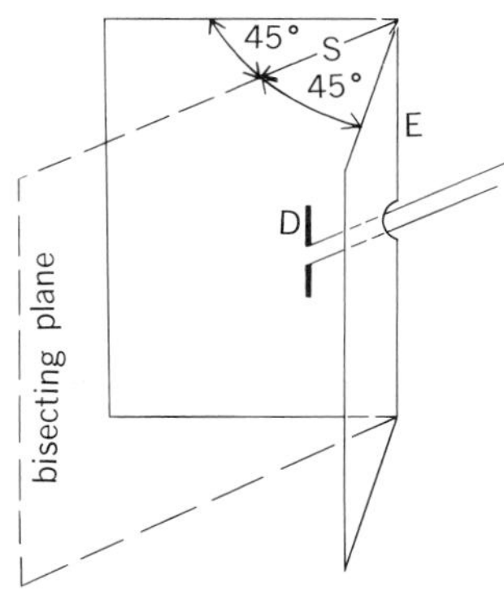


**Corner reflector antenna.**

The reflecting planes may be metal sheets or parallel wires separated by a small fraction of a wavelength and extending in the direction of current flow. SEE ANTENNA.

*J. C. Schelleng*

## Corona discharge

A type of electrical conduction that generally occurs at or near atmospheric pressure in gases. A relatively strong electric field is needed. External manifestations are the emission of light and a hissing sound. The particular characteristics of the discharge are determined by the shape of the electrodes, the polarity, the size of the gap, and the gas or gas mixture.

In some cases corona discharge may be desirable and useful, whereas in others it is harmful and attempts are made to minimize it. The effect is used for voltage division and control in direct-current nuclear particle accelerators. On the other hand, the corona discharge that surrounds a high-potential power transmission line represents a power loss and limits the maximum potential which can be used. Because the power loss due to $i^2r$ heating decreases as the potential difference is increased, it is desirable to use maximum possible voltage.

The shape of the electrodes has a very profound effect on the potential current characteristic. If the radius of curvature of the positive electrode is small compared to the gap between electrodes, the transition from the dark current region to the field-sustained discharge will be quite smooth. The effect here is to enable the free electrons to ionize by collision in the high field surrounding this electrode. One electron can produce an avalanche in such a field, because each ionization event releases an additional electron, which can then make further ionization. To sustain the discharge, it is necessary to collect the positive ions and to produce the primary electrons far enough from the positive electrode to permit the avalanche to develop. The positive ions are collected at the negative electrode, and it is their low mobility that limits the current in the discharge. The primary electrons are thought to be produced by photoionization (see **illus.**). For a discussion of ionic mobility SEE ELECTRICAL CONDUCTION IN GASES. SEE ALSO DARK CURRENT.

The situation at the negative electrode is quite important. The efficiency for ionization by positive ions is much less than for electrons of the same energy. Most of the ionization occurs as the result of secondary electrons released at the negative electrode by positive-ion bombardment. These electrons produce ionization as they move from the strong field at the electrode out into the weak field. This, however, leaves a positive-ion space charge, which slows down the incoming ions. This has the effect of diminishing the secondary electron yield. Because the positive ion mobility is low, there is a time lag before the high field conditions can be restored. For that reason the discharge is somewhat unstable.

From the preceding it may be seen that the electrode shape is important. The dependence on the gas mixture is difficult to evaluate. Electronegative components will tend to reduce the current at a given voltage, because heavy negative ions have a low mobility and are inefficient ionization agents. The excess electron will not be tightly bound, however, and may be released in a collision. The overall effect is to reduce the number of electrons that can start avalanches near the positive electrode. Further, if a gas with low-lying energy states is present, the free electrons can lose energy in inelastic collisions. Thus it is more difficult for the electrons to acquire enough energy to ionize. In electrostatic high-voltage generators in pressurized tanks, it is quite common to use Freon and nitrogen to take advantage of this effect to reduce corona. In a pure monatomic gas such as argon, corona occurs at relatively low values of voltage.

**Breakdown streamers in positive-point corona crossing from positive point to cathode below. (*From L. B. Loeb, Fundamental Processes of Electrical Discharge in Gases, Wiley, 1939*)**

In the potential current characteristic, the corona region is found above the dark current region and is field-sustained. Near the upper end it goes into either a glow discharge or a brush discharge, depending on the pressure. Higher pressure favors the brush discharge. SEE BRUSH DISCHARGE; GLOW DISCHARGE.

For still higher potential difference, breakdown takes place and a continuously ionized path is formed. SEE ELECTRIC SPARK.

*Glenn H. Miller*

***Bibliography.*** American Society for Testing and Materials, *Engineering Dielectrics*, vol. 1: *Corona Measurement and Interpretation*, 1979; L. B. Loeb, *Electrical Coronas*, 1965.

## Coupled circuits

Two or more electric circuits are said to be coupled if energy can transfer electrically or magnetically from one to another. If electric charge, or current, or rate of change of current in one circuit produces electromotive force or affects the voltage between nodes in another circuit, the two circuits are coupled.

Between coupled circuits there is mutual inductance, resistance, or capacitance, or some combination of these. The concept of a mutual parameter is based on the loop method of analysis. A mutual pa-

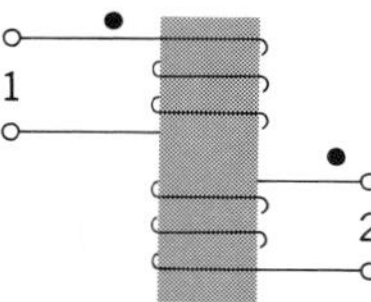


Fig. 1. Two coils wound on a single core, illustrating polarity.

rameter can be one that carries two or more loop currents; such a network has conductive coupling because electricity can flow from one circuit to the other. SEE NETWORK THEORY.

Also, there can be purely inductive coupling, which appears if the magnetic field produced by current in one circuit links the other circuit. A two-winding transformer is an application of inductive coupling, with energy transferred through the magnetic field only.

It is also possible to have mutual capacitance, with energy transferred through the electric field only. Examples are the mutual capacitance between grid and plate circuits of a vacuum tube, or the capacitive interference between two transmission lines, as a power line and a telephone line, that run for a considerable distance side by side.

**Polarity.** With inductive coupling, polarity may need to be known, particularly if two circuits are coupled in more than one way. Do two kinds of coupling produce voltages that add or subtract?

There are several ways to show the relative polarities of inductive coupling. **Figure 1** shows, somewhat pictorially, two coils wound on the same core. Current flowing into the upper end of coil 1 would produce magnetic flux upward in the core, and so also would current flowing into the upper end of coil 2. For this reason the upper ends of the two coils are said to be corresponding ends.

If a wiring diagram is drawn with some such semipictorial sketch of the coils, it is not difficult to determine which are corresponding ends. However it is easier, both in representation and in interpretation, to indicate the corresponding ends symbolically. For this purpose dots are placed on a diagram at the corresponding ends of coupled coils. Such dots are shown in Fig. 1, though these not needed there. Dots are also shown in **Fig. 2**, where they give the only means of identifying corresponding ends of the coils.

Note that the bottom ends of the coils shown in Fig. 1 are also corresponding ends, and that the two lower ends might have been dotted instead of the two upper ends; it makes no difference. But if the sense of winding of either coil 1 or coil 2 in Fig. 1 were reversed, then one dot (either one) would have to be shifted correspondingly.

**Voltage equations.** In addition to showing corresponding ends of two coils, Fig. 2 indicates that the two coils couple to each other. This coupling is identified as $L_{12}$. There is voltage from $a$ to $b$ in Fig. 2 if current $i_1$ is changing through the self-inductance $L_{11}$ of the coil in circuit 1. There is additional voltage from $a$ to $b$ if current $i_2$ is changing in circuit 2 because of the mutual inductance $L_{12}$ between the circuits. Thus, with circuit 1 coupled to circuit 2 and to any number of other circuits, Eqs. (1) and (2) hold.

$$v_{ab} = \left(L_{11}\frac{di_1}{dt} \pm L_{12}\frac{di_2}{dt} \pm \cdots\right) \tag{1}$$

$$v_{cd} = \left(\pm L_{21}\frac{di_1}{dt} + L_{22}\frac{di_2}{dt} \pm \cdots\right) \tag{2}$$

Here $L_{11}$ and $L_{22}$, the self-inductances of the circuits, are positive numbers (inductances measured in henrys). With regard to the mutual terms, two questions of polarity must be asked. Are the mutual inductances such as $L_{12}$ and $L_{21}$ always positive numbers? And are the signs before the mutual terms, shown as $\pm$ in Eq. (1), actually $+$ or are they $-$? Answers to these questions are not always the same, and may be different as given by different authors, but the most usual simple procedure to answer them is as follows:

1. Draw a circuit diagram, such as Fig. 2, with nominal positive directions of currents shown by arrows and with dots at corresponding ends of coupled coils.

2. Let each mutual inductance such as $L_{12}$ be a positive number.

3. Write equations such as Eqs. (1) and (2) with the following signs: First, if both arrows enter dotted end of a pair of coupled coils, or if both arrows enter undotted ends, use $+$ before the corresponding mutual-impedance term. Second, if one arrow enters a dotted end and the other an undotted end, use $-$ before the corresponding mutual-impedance term.

However, this simple procedure sometimes fails, for it may be impossible to dot corresponding ends of all pairs of coupled coils in a network if there are three or more coils. A more general method follows:

1. Draw a circuit diagram with nominal positive directions of currents shown by arrows; place dots at coil ends arbitrarily, as may be convenient.

2. Determine corresponding ends of pairs of coupled coils, considering the coils two at a time. For the mutual inductance between a pair of coils with corresponding ends dotted, use a positive number, such as $L_{12} = 5$. For mutual inductance between a pair of coils with noncorresponding ends dotted, use a negative number, such as $L_{12} = -5$.

3. Write equations according to rule 3, above.

**Steady-state equations.** The differential Eqs. (1) and (2) are quite general. For steady-state operation at a single frequency, it is often simpler to have phasor or transform equations. Such equations can be in terms of reactances instead of inductances ($X = \omega L = 2\pi fL$ where $f$ is frequency in cycles per second, or hertz). With the usual interpretation of phasor or transform equations, the steady-state relations corresponding to Eqs. (1) and (2) are shown in Eqs. (3) and (4). The rules in the foregoing paragraphs deter-

$$\begin{aligned} V_{ab} &= j\omega(L_{11}I_i \pm L_{12}I_2 \pm \cdots) \\ &= j(X_{11}I_1 \pm X_{12}I_2 \pm \cdots) \end{aligned} \tag{3}$$

$$\begin{aligned} V_{cd} &= j\omega(\pm L_{21}I_1 + L_{22}I_2 \pm \cdots) \\ &= j(\pm X_{21}I_1 + X_{22}I_2 \pm \cdots) \end{aligned} \tag{4}$$

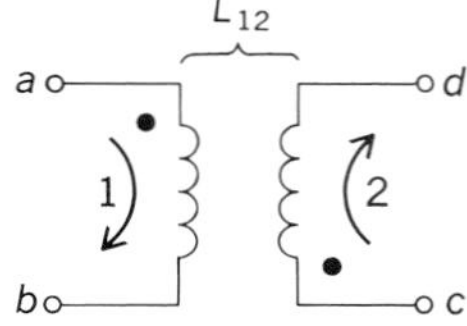


Fig. 2. Mutual inductance. Dots identify corresponding ends of coils.

mine the choice of + or − in these equations; also, a mutual reactance such as $X_{12}$ is a positive number (of ohms) if the corresponding mutual inductance such as $L_{12}$ is a positive number (of henrys), as determined by the above rules. *SEE ALTERNATING-CURRENT CIRCUIT THEORY.*

**Equality of mutual inductance.** Because of this equality it is not uncommon, if there are only two coupled coils in a network, to use the letter $M$ in place of both $L_{12}$ and $L_{21}$. This use of $M$ will be adopted in the following paragraphs.

**Coefficient of coupling.** The coefficient of coupling between two circuits is, by definition, Eq. (5). If the

$$k = M/\sqrt{L_{11}L_{22}} \qquad (5)$$

circuits are far apart or, because of orientation, have little mutual magnetic flux, they are loosely coupled and $k$ is a small number. Values of $k$ for circuits with loose coupling may be in the range between 0.01 and 0.10. For closely (or tightly) coupled circuits with air-core coils, $k$ may be around 0.5. In a transformer with a ferromagnetic core, $k$ is very nearly 1.00.

**Ideal transformers.** An ideal transformer is defined as one in which primary and secondary currents are related inversely as the number of turns in the windings; this is shown in Eq. (6). Voltages across the

$$I_1/I_2 = N_2/N_1 \qquad (6)$$

primary and secondary windings are in direct proportion to the numbers of turns, as shown in Eq. (7).

$$V_1/V_2 = N_1/N_2 \qquad (7)$$

An actual transformer may be almost ideal or not at all ideal, depending on how it is made, and construction in turn depends on the purpose for which it is to be used. In an ideal transformer $k = 1$; in any actual transformer $k$ is less than 1. In an actual transformer there is magnetizing current, so Eq. (6) is not exact. Also, an actual transformer has resistance and leakage reactance, so Eq. (7) is not exact. Nevertheless, the relations of ideal transformers are closely approximated by 60-Hz power transformers, and these relations are more or less close for other transformers that have ferromagnetic cores. *SEE TRANSFORMER.*

Whereas coupling $k$ is desirably as close as possible to unity in a transformer that couples power from one circuit to another, $k$ may purposefully be considerably less than unity in a transformer used for another purpose. In an oscillator, coupling need only be sufficient to sustain oscillation. In a band-pass amplifier, coupling is determined by bandwidth requirements. *SEE OSCILLATOR; RESONANCE (ALTERNATING-CURRENT CIRCUITS).*

**Equivalent circuits.** It is often convenient to substitute into a network, in place of a pair of inductively coupled circuits, an equivalent pair of conductively coupled circuits. Circuits so substituted are equivalent if the network exterior to the coupled circuits is unaffected by the change; in many cases this requirement implies that input current and voltage and output current and voltage are unaffected by the change.

Voltages and currents at the terminals of the coupled circuits of **Fig. 3** are related by Eqs. (8) and (9).

$$(R_1 + j\omega L_{11})I_1 - j\omega MI_2 = V_{ab} \qquad (8)$$

$$(R_2 + j\varphi L_{22})I_2 - j\omega MI_1 = V_{cd} \qquad (9)$$

Voltages and currents at the terminals of the network

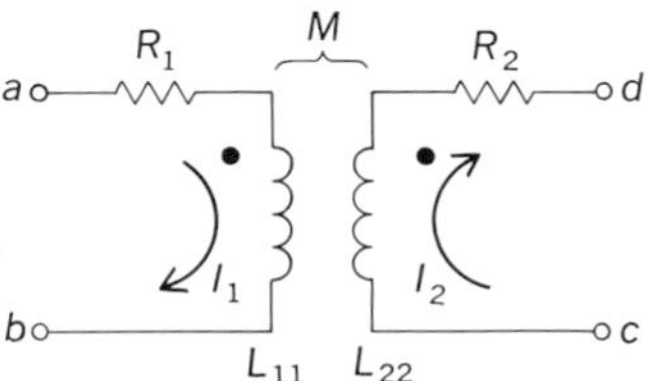


**Fig. 3. A pair of coupled circuits.**

of **Fig. 4** are also related by Eqs. (8) and (9), so the network of Fig. 4 is equivalent to the coupled circuits of Fig. 3. This is not immediately obvious, but it appears when loop equations for the network are simplified to a form that shows the requirement that $L_{11} = L_1 + aM$ and $L_{22} = L_2 + M/a$ and that $V_{c'd'} = aV_{cd}$, where $a$ is the turn ratio of the ideal transformer shown, equal to $N_1/N_2$ in Eqs. (6) and (7).

It seems at first that this substitution, resulting in the network of Fig. 4, has produced something more complicated than the circuit of Fig. 3, but the value of substituting will now be shown.

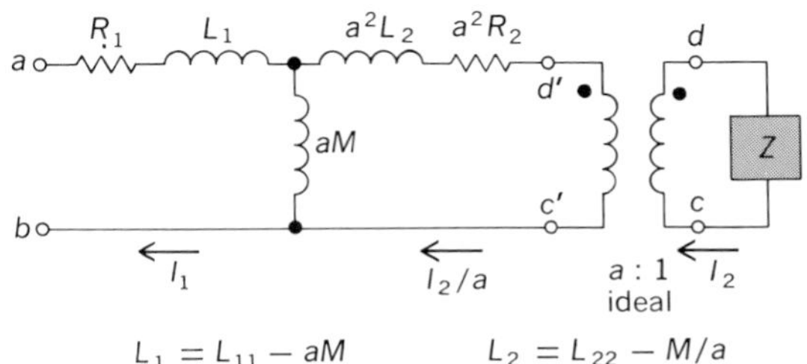


**Fig. 4. A network equivalent to coupled circuits, feeding a load of impedance Z.**

Mathematically, $a$ could be any number, but practically there are two particularly advantageous values for $a$. When the coupling between coils is loose so that $k$, the coefficient of coupling, is small, and if the coils have somewhere near the same number of turns, it is advantageous to let $a = 1$. With $a = 1$ the network of Fig. 4 is simplified to **Fig. 5**, leaving only the conductively coupled circuits with parameters $R_1$ and $L_1$, $M$, and $L_2$ and $R_2$, where $L_1 = L_{11} - M$, and $L_2 = L_{22} - M$. Many loosely coupled circuits particularly in radio circuits, are conveniently represented by this equivalent network with $a = 1$.

On the other hand, if coupling is close and especially when the two coupled coils have widely different numbers of turns (a situation that is typical of transformers), it is more convenient to let $a$ equal the actual turn ratio of the coils. If, for example, there are 10 times as many turns in the primary winding of

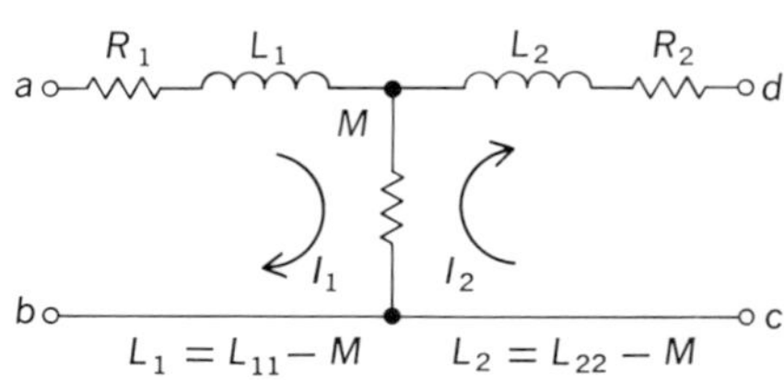


**Fig. 5. A conductive network equivalent to the coupled circuits of Fig. 3 (a = 1).**

a transformer as there are in the secondary winding, it is well to let $a = 10$. (Letting $a = 1$ in such a transformer would result in a negative value for $L_2$ which, though correct for analysis, is difficult to visualize.)

With $a$ equal to the actual transformer turn ratio, the following interpretation of Fig. 4 is usual and convenient. All causes of power loss and voltage drop have been put into the equivalent $T$ network. Only the turn ratio, the actual transforming function, remains in the ideal transformer. It now becomes possible to consider, to study, and even to design the separate functions independently.

**Transformers.** The equivalent circuit of Fig. 4 is so commonly used in transformer work that a number of the quantities have been given special names. With the concept that power is supplied to one winding of the transformer, this is called the primary winding; the other, the secondary winding, provides power to a load. There may be a third, or tertiary, winding, perhaps providing power to another load at a different voltage or with a different connection, and even other windings, on the same transformer core.

However, it is only when a transformer has become part of a system that there is any meaning in designating the windings as primary and secondary, for a two-winding transformer can be used to carry power in either direction. The terms "high-voltage side" and "low-voltage side" are preferable for a transformer that is not part of a system. In the following discussion the words primary and secondary really mean nothing more than the windings of the transformer that are designated by the subscripts 1 and 2.

Speaking of a transformer with $N_1$ primary turns and $N_2$ secondary turns, let $a$ be the turn ratio $N_1/N_2$. Then, referring to Fig. 4, $R_1$ is primary resistance; $L_1$ is primary leakage inductance; $aM$ is primary exciting inductance; $a^2L_2$ is secondary leakage inductance referred to the primary side; and $a^2R_2$ is secondary resistance referred to the primary side. Usually, operation of power transformers is described in terms of these leakage inductances (or leakage reactances), and in terms of resistances, inductances, or reactances all of which are referred to one side of the transformer or the other.

**Transformation of impedance. Figure 6** is the same as Fig. 4 except that the ideal transformer with turn ratio of $a$:1 has been eliminated and the impedance of the load has been changed from $Z$ to $a^2Z$. This conversion makes the network of Fig. 6 equivalent to that of Fig. 4 at the input terminals, and it suggests a concept that is quite useful in communications.

If a load with impedance $Z$ is preceded by an ideal transformer with turn ratio $a$, the input impedance to the transformer is $a^2Z$. Thus a load of impedance $Z$ can be made to act like a load with impedance $a^2Z$ by using an ideal transformer with turn ratio $a$. A useful application is to connect a load of one impedance to an incoming line that has a different terminal impedance through an impedance-matching transformer. By this means a transformer with turn ratio $a$ will match a load with resistance $R$ to a source with resistance $a^2R$, thereby providing for maximum power transfer to the load.

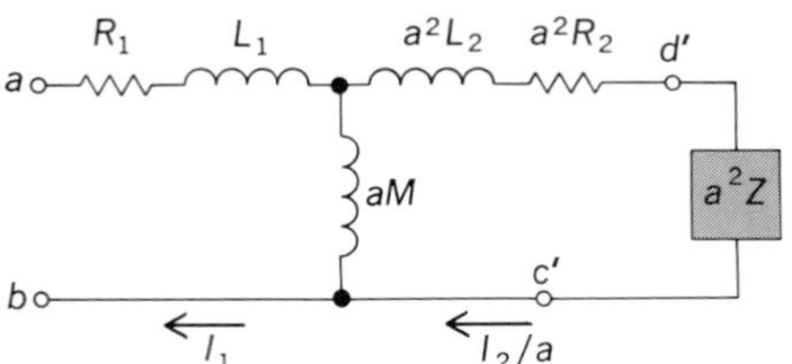

Fig. 6. Transformation of impedance from Fig. 4.

The preceding paragraph assumes an ideal transformer to provide a perfect impedance match. Figure 6 shows the $T$ network of resistances and inductances that an actual transformer introduces into the network. In practice, the transformer used must be good enough so that these resistances and inductances are acceptable.

**Core loss.** Neither the equations nor the circuits of this article have taken into account the power loss in a ferromagnetic core. Both eddy-current loss and hysteresis loss may be appreciable; these iron losses are commonly great enough to affect the economics of power transformers, and even to prohibit the use of metal cores with ratio-frequency current.

The relations of core loss are not linear and cannot accurately be included in linear equations, but a satisfactory approximation is used with power transformers for which frequency and applied voltage change little if at all. With these restrictions, core loss can be represented by the loss in a resistance shunted around mutual inductance $aM$ of Fig. 4. This approximation of loss is much better than neglecting core loss entirely, and is usual in work with power transformers. *SEE CIRCUIT (ELECTRICITY)*.

*Hugh H. Skilling*

***Bibliography.*** L. P. Huelsman, *Basic Circuit Theory*, 2d ed., 1984; D. E. Johnson, *Basic Electric Circuit Analysis*, 2d ed., 1984; R. E. Risdale, *Electric Circuits*, 2d ed., 1983.

## Critical path method (CPM)

A diagrammatic network-based technique, similar to the program evaluation and review technique (PERT), that is used as an aid in the systematic management of complex projects. The technique is useful in: organizing and planning; analyzing and comprehending; problem detecting and defining; alternative action simulating; improving (replanning); time and cost estimating; budgeting and scheduling; and coordinating and controlling. It has its greatest value in complex projects which involve many interrelated events, activities, and resources (time, money, equipment, and personnel) which can be allocated or assigned in a variety of ways to achieve a desired objective. It can be used to complete a multifaceted program faster or with better utilization of resources by reassignments, trade-offs, and judiciously using more or less assets for certain of the individual activities composing the overall project. *SEE PERT*.

CPM was introduced in 1957–1958 by E. I. du Pont de Nemours & Company. Present applications include: research and development programs; new product introductions; facilities planning and designs; plant layouts and relocations; construction projects; equipment installations and start-up: major maintenance programs; medical and scientific researches; weapons systems developments; and other programs in which cost reduction, progress control, and time management are important. It is best suited to large, complex, one-time or first-time projects rather than to repetitive, routine jobs.

A simplified example will show the features of the

**Table 1. CPM events table**

| Prior event | Event | Following event |
|---|---|---|
| — | A = Authorization to start received | B and C |
| A | B = Computing circuits designed | D and E |
| A | C = Video circuits designed | D |
| B and C | D = Keyboard and cabinets designed | G |
| B | E = Programming completed | F and H |
| E | F = Operating systems completed | G |
| D and F | G = Testing and debugging finished | H |
| E and G | H = Design specifications and programs finalized | — |

critical path method and the steps involved in constructing and using the network-based system:

Project: Design personal home-use computer.

Objective: Complete project as soon as possible.

Procedure: The CPM procedure for this project involves eight steps:

Step 1: List required events; arrange as to best guess of their sequence; assign a code letter or number to each. (See center column of **Table 1**.) [Events are accomplished portions or phases of the project. Activities are the resources applied to progress from one event to the next. This example has been greatly simplified for illustrative purposes. A real case could have several hundred events and activities and would be a candidate for computer analysis, for which programs are available.]

Step 2: Determine which event(s) must precede each event before it can be done and which event(s) must await completion of that event before it can be done. Construct a table to show these relationships. (See left and right columns of Table 1.)

Step 3: Draw the network, which is a diagram of the relationship of the events and their required activities that satisfies the dictates of Table 1 (see **Fig. 1**).

Step 4: List the required activities and enter the best estimate available of the time required to complete each activity. In PERT, three time estimates are entered: the most optimistic, the most likely, and the most pessimistic. This is the basic way in which PERT differs from CPM. Some users of CPM enter a second time estimate for each activity, the first being the normal time and the second being the crash (or fast at any price) time. **Table 2** shows the list of activities (AB designates the activity required in going from event A to event B), the expected normal time, the maximum number of weeks that each activity can be shortened under a crash program, and the cost per week to shorten, if it can be shortened.

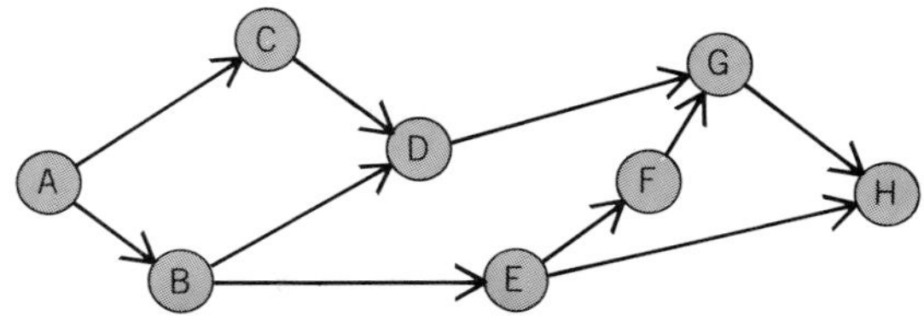


**Fig. 1. Network of relationship between events (circles) and their activities (arrows).**

Step 5: Write the normal expected time to complete each activity on the diagram (**Fig. 2**). Note that the relative lengths of the arrows (activities) have no relationship to their time magnitudes.

Step 6: Find the critical path, that is, the longest route from event A to event H. The longest path is the total time that the project can be expected to take unless additional resources are added or resources from some of the other paths in which there may be slack can be reallocated to activities which lie in the critical path. In the example shown in Fig. 2, the initial critical path is A–B–D–G–H, or 5 + 12 + 18 + 5 = 40 weeks. If the critical path time works out to be less or more than the target time to complete the project, there is then a positive or negative float.

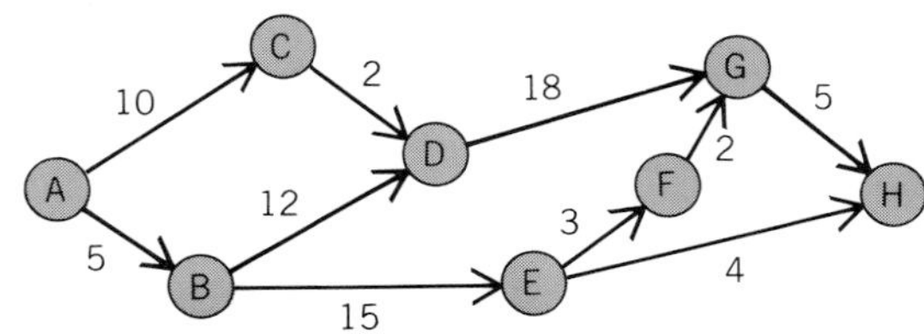


**Fig. 2. Network diagram modified to show time to complete activities. The critical path is indicated by the black arrows.**

**Table 2. Time and cost factors for activities**

| Activity | Expected time to complete, weeks | Maximum possible time reduction, weeks | Cost (per week) to reduce time |
|---|---|---|---|
| AB | 5 | 1 | $1000 |
| AC | 10 | 3 | 500 |
| BD | 12 | 3 | 1000 |
| BE | 15 | 2 | 500 |
| CD | 2 | 0 | — |
| DG | 18 | 4 | 500 |
| EF | 3 | 0 | — |
| EH | 4 | 1 | 2000 |
| FG | 2 | 0 | — |
| GH | 5 | 2 | 500 |

**Table 3. Costs of shortening activities**

| Reduce | | | Cost | | | |
|---|---|---|---|---|---|---|
| AB from | 5 weeks to | 4 weeks | 1 week | × $1000 | = | $1000 |
| BD | 12 | 9 | 3 | × 1000 | = | 3000 |
| DG | 18 | 14 | 4 | × 500 | = | 2000 |
| GH | 5 | 3 | 2 | × 500 | = | 1000 |
| Total | 40 | 30 | 10 | | | $7000 |

Step 7: Shorten the critical path. The stated objective for this example was to complete the project as soon as possible. Other projects might have different objectives. An examination of Table 2 and Fig. 2 suggests that the activities lying along the critical can be shortened for the costs shown in **Table 3**. The total expected time to complete the project can be shortened from 40 weeks to 30 weeks—a 25% improvement. A judgment can be made by those responsible for the project as to whether the 10-week time savings is worth the additional cost of $7000. In some cases, the critical path is so shortened that it is no longer the longest path, and another path becomes the critical one. Only reductions in the critical path time reduce the total project time, and activities in noncritical paths may run over or late to the limits of their floats without causing the project to be delayed. The floats are the differences between the total expected time required for each possible path in the network and the total time for the critical path, and are measures of spare time available.

Step 8: Construct a schedule of the project showing the earliest and latest permissible start and completion dates for each activity. To do this, the individual floats are calculated. With the slack in the critical path set at zero at the onset of the project's implementation, any slippage in the completion of any event along that path will result in a delay in the completion of the whole project, unless made up later.

The use of CPM adds another step to a project, and it requires continual updating and reanalysis as conditions change, but experience has shown that the effort can be a good investment in completing a project in less time, with less resources, with more control, and with a greater chance of ontime, within-budget completion.

*Vincent M. Altamuro*

## Crosstalk

Interference in a channel caused by signals present in other channels of a multichannel communications system. The channels of a multichannel system are used for simultaneous transmission of different signals from and to many users, and mutual interference is avoided by segregating the channels in space, frequency, or time. Economic and other constraints on actual systems preclude a complete segregation of channels, and this results in crosstalk, which depends on the segregation (that is, multiplexing) method used. Most common manifestations of crosstalk in the telephone network are bits and pieces of overheard conversation and call-progress tones (dial, address, and ringing signals, intended for other users).

**Multiplexing methods.** Three methods of multiplexing, and combinations of some or all of them in one system, are in common use.

***Space division.*** In this method, each signal is carried on a separate transmission medium (for example, a pair of wires in a multipair cable). Crosstalk is caused by the physical proximity of the different media and the resulting electromagnetic coupling. This coupling can be reduced by proper design, such as different twists for different pairs in the cable, shielding, and physical separation. Crosstalk in space-division systems is a linear phenomenon, independent of the signal levels, and is classified as either near-end cross talk (NEXT), when the disturbed receiver is located at the same end of the system as the disturbing transmitter, or far-end crosstalk (FEXT), when the disturbed receiver and disturbing transmitter are located at opposite ends of the system (see **illus.**). *SEE ELECTRICAL SHIELDING; ELECTROMAGNETIC COMPATIBILITY.*

***Frequency division.*** In this method, each signal is assigned a different frequency band and is shifted there by modulation; all the resulting signals are carried simultaneously by the common transmission medium (for example, broadcast radio). Nonlinearities in the medium (introduced, for instance, by the amplifiers used to extend the range of the system) create intermodulation distortion, which is the main cause of crosstalk in frequency-division systems. Intermodulation distortion in amplitude-modulation (AM) systems results in a replica of signals in two or more channels appearing in the frequency band of another channel. Angle modulated systems [frequency-modulated (FM) or phase-modulated (PM) ones] are immune to this interference, but are sensitive to phase nonlinearities, particularly those causing AM-to-PM conversion. These convert vestigial amplitude modulation in one channel into angle modulation in other channels. *SEE AMPLITUDE MODULATION; DISTORTION (ELECTRONIC CIRCUITS); FREQUENCY MODULATION; MODULATION; PHASE MODULATION.*

***Time division.*** In this method, each signal is assigned a series of discrete time intervals, called time slots, during which its discrete slices are transmitted by the common transmission medium. The time slots

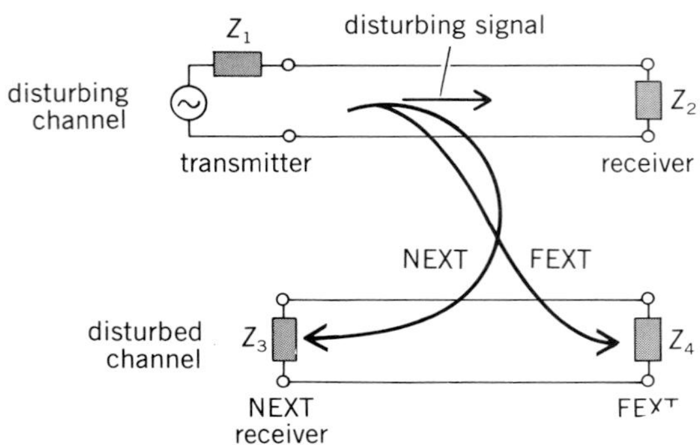


**Crosstalk types in a space-division system. $Z_1$, $Z_2$, $Z_3$, and $Z_4$ are impedances.**

of all the channels are interleaved in a periodic pattern, and the transmission medium is used by one channel at a time, once in every time frame which consists of all the time slots. This scheme is used most commonly in digital systems. Crosstalk in time-division systems occurs between adjacent and near-adjacent time slots and takes the form of intersymbol interference, a linear phenomenon caused by the limited bandwidth of the channel. *See Pulse modulation*.

**Crosstalk harm.** Received crosstalk signals can be either intelligible (that is, understood by an unintended recipient), or unintelligible. The reception of intelligible crosstalk is a violation of privacy, and as such it is especially annoying to the users of the communications network. The presence of the intended signal on the disturbed channel masks some of the intelligible crosstalk, but the problem may become acute during silent intervals in the desired signal. Unintelligible crosstalk is another source of noise, and therefore interferes with the reception of the desired signal. *See Electrical noise*.

**Mitigation.** Some of the factors that affect the impairment caused by crosstalk are beyond the control of the system designer. For instance, crosstalk is a problem only when both the disturbing and disturbed channels are active simultaneously; receiver acuity depends, among other characteristics, on the performance of the customer's equipment, be it a telephone set or a data terminal, and on ambient noise coming from other sources both inside and outside the transmission system. The main effort in the design of multichannel systems is expended on reducing interchannel coupling by the use of coaxial or optical fiber cables in space-division systems; the use of tight controls on the linearity of repeater characteristics and use of FM in frequency-division systems; and the use of wide-band transmission media, such as optical fibers, for transmitting the signals of time-division systems. Spectrum management is an important tool for controlling crosstalk interference since frequency bands, time slots, and maximum-signal-power levels can be assigned to different systems in a way that will allow efficient use of the transmission medium without unacceptable intersystem interference.

In addition to controlling the interchannel coupling by design, both the signal-to-interference ratio (which takes into account the masking of the interference by the desired signal) and the absolute level of the interference (to limit the disturbing effect during silent intervals in the desired signal) must be kept low at the receiver. Syllabic compandors are used in analog transmission systems to reduce the idle channel noise in voice communications (that is, the effects of crosstalk when the talker is silent). Pulse shaping in digital transmission systems is used to reduce crosstalk by reducing intersymbol interference. The need to maintain a proper signal-to-interference ratio constrains the number of repeaters and interrepeater span length. Thus, crosstalk can limit the total range of any transmission system. *See Electrical communications*.

*Reed Even*

***Bibliography.*** Bell Telephone Laboratories, *Transmission Systems for Communications*, 5th ed., 1982.

## Cryotron

A current-controlled switching device based on superconductivity for use primarily in computer circuits. The early version has been superseded by the tunneling cryotron, which consists basically of a Josephson junction. In its simplest form (see **illus.**) the device has two electrodes of a superconducting material (for example, lead) which are separated by an insulating film only about 10 atomic layers thick. For the electrodes to become superconducting, the device has to be cooled to a few degrees above absolute zero. The tunneling cryotron has two states, characterized by the presence or absence of an electrical resistance. They can be considered as the "on" and "off" states of the switch, respectively. Switching from on to off is accomplished by a magnetic field generated by sending a current through the control line on top of the junction. The device can switch in a few picoseconds and has a power consumption of only some microwatts. These properties make it an attractive switching device for computers, promising performance levels probably unattainable with other devices. *See Josephson effect; Superconducting devices; Superconductivity*.

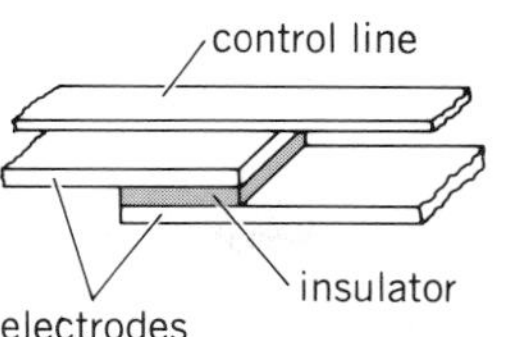


**The tunneling cryotron.**

*P. Wolf*

***Bibliography.*** W. Anacker, Computing at 4 degrees Kelvin, *IEEE Spectrum*, 16:26–37, May 1979.

## Cryptography

The various methods for writing in secret code or cipher. As society becomes increasingly dependent upon computers, the vast amounts of data communicated, processed, and stored within computer systems and networks often have to be protected, and cryptography is a means of achieving this protection. It is the only practical method for protecting information transmitted through accessible communication networks such as telephone lines, satellites, or microwave systems. Furthermore, in certain cases, it may be the most economical way to protect stored data. Cryptographic procedures can also be used for message authentication, personal identification, and digital signature verification for electronic funds transfer and credit card transactions. *See Computer security; Data-base management systems; Data communications; Digital computer; Electrical communications*.

**Cryptographic algorithms.** Cryptography must resist decoding or deciphering by unauthorized personnel; that is, messages (plaintext) transformed into cryptograms (codetext or ciphertext) have to be able to withstand intense cryptanalysis. Transformations can be done by using either code or cipher systems. Code systems rely on code books to transform the plaintext words, phrases, and sentences into codetext or code groups. To prevent cryptanalysis, there must be a great number of plaintext passages in the code book and the code group equivalents must be kept secret. To isolate users from each other, different codes must be used, making it difficult to utilize code books in electronic data-processing systems.

Cipher systems are more versatile. Messages are transformed through the use of two basic elements: a set of unchanging rules or steps called a cryptographic algorithm, and a set of variable cryptographic keys. The algorithm is composed of enciphering (**E**) and deciphering (**D**) procedures which usually are identical or simply consist of the same steps performed in reverse order, but which can be dissimilar. The keys, selected by the user, consist of a sequence of numbers or characters. An enciphering key (Ke) is used to encipher plaintext (X) into ciphertext (Y) as in Eq. (1),

$$\mathbf{E}_{Ke}(X) = Y \qquad (1)$$

and a deciphering key (Kd) is used to decipher ciphertext (Y) into plaintext (X) as in Eq. (2).

$$\mathbf{D}_{Kd}[\mathbf{E}_{Ke}(X)] = \mathbf{D}_{Kd}(Y) = X \qquad (2)$$

Algorithms are of two types—conventional and public-key (also referred to as symmetric and asymmetric). The enciphering and deciphering keys in a conventional algorithm either may be easily computed from each other or may be identical (Ke = Kd = K, denoting $\mathbf{E}_K$ (X) = Y for encipherment and $\mathbf{D}_K$ (Y) = X for decipherment). In a public-key algorithm, one key (usually the enciphering key) is made public, and a different key (usually the deciphering key) is kept private. In such an approach it must not be possible to deduce the private key from the public key.

When an algorithm is made public, for example, as a published encryption standard, cryptographic security completely depends on protecting those cryptographic keys specified as secret. *See Algorithm*.

**Unbreakable ciphers.** Unbreakable ciphers are possible. But the key must be randomly selected and used only once, and its length must be equal to or greater than that of the plaintext to be enciphered. Therefore such long keys, called one-time tapes, are not practical in data-processing applications.

To work well, a key must be of fixed length, relatively short, and capable of being repeatedly used without compromising security. In theory, any algorithm that uses such a finite key can be analyzed; in practice, the effort and resources necessary to break the algorithm would be unjustified.

**Strong algorithms.** Fortunately, to achieve effective data security, construction of an unbreakable algorithm is not necessary. However, the work factor (a measure, under a given set of assumptions, of the requirements necessary for a specific analysis or attack against a cryptographic algorithm) required to break the algorithm must be sufficiently great. Included in the set of assumptions is the type of information expected to be available for cryptanalysis. For example, this could be ciphertext only; plaintext (not chosen) and corresponding ciphertext; chosen plaintext and corresponding ciphertext; or chosen ciphertext and corresponding recovered plaintext.

A strong cryptographic algorithm must satisfy the following conditions: (1) The algorithm's mathematical complexity prevents, for all practical purposes, solution through analytical methods. (2) The cost or time necessary to unravel the message or key is too great when mathematically less complicated methods are used, because either too many computational steps are involved (for example, in trying one key after another) or because too much storage space is required (for example, in an analysis requiring data accumulations such as dictionaries and statistical tables).

To be strong, the algorithm must satisfy the above conditions even when the analyst has the following advantages: (1) Relatively large amounts of plaintext (specified by the analyst, if so desired) and corresponding ciphertext are available. (2) Relatively large amounts of ciphertext (specified by the analyst, if so desired) and corresponding recovered plaintext are available. (3) All details of the algorithm are available to the analyst; that is, cryptographic strength cannot depend on the algorithm remaining secret. (4) Large high-speed computers are available for cryptanalysis.

In summary, even with an unlimited amount of computational power, data storage, and calendar time, the message or key in an unbreakable algorithm cannot be obtained through cryptanalysis. On the other hand, although a strong algorithm may be breakable in theory, in practice it is not.

**Computational complexity.** The strength of a cryptographic scheme can be measured by the computational complexity of the task of cryptanalysis. The term complexity, when referring to a program or algorithm to accomplish a given task, means the number of elementary operations used by this program. The complexity of a task is the least possible number of elementary operations used by any program to accomplish this task. This is directly related to sequential time, or the time used by a conventional sequential computer. Of course, the time used by a faster computer will be less than that used by a slower computer. Other measures of importance are storage and parallel time, or the time used on a highly parallelized computer.

Given a particular algorithm (computer program) for solving a problem, analysis of the algorithm can involve probability theory, detailed knowledge of the problem at hand, and other disciplines, but meaningful estimates of the resource consumption of the algorithm can usually be provided. This gives an upper bound to the complexity of the given problem.

However, nontrivial lower bounds are very hard to obtain. This is a fundamental problem in the design of cryptographic systems: it is very difficult to ensure that a system is sufficiently hard to crack. Without a good lower bound, the possibility that someone will find a fast algorithm for cryptanalyzing a given scheme must always be anticipated.

***Problem classes P and NP.*** An important direction of theoretical work concerns the consideration (from computer science) of P versus NP. The class P consists of those problems which can be solved in polynomial time. That is, there are constants $c$ and $k$ such that, if the input to the problem can be specified in $N$ bits, the problem can be solved on a sequential machine in time $c \times N^k$. Roughly speaking, these are the tractable problems. They include multiplication of two large numbers, exponentiation modulo a large prime, running the Data Encryption Standard (discussed below), and roughly any straightforward problem which does not involve searching.

The class NP (nondeterministic polynomial time) consists of problems which can be solved by searching. Roughly speaking, a possible solution to a problem in NP is to guess in turn each of $2^N$ possible values of some $N$-bit quantity, do some polynomial-time work related to each guess, and if some guess turns out to be correct, report the answer.

An example of a problem in NP is the knapsack problem: Given a set of integers $\{A_1, A_2, \ldots, A_n\}$ and a target integer $B$, can a subset of the $A_i$ be selected without repetition (say $\{A_1, A_3, A_8\}$) such that their sum $(A_1 + A_3 + A_8)$ is the target $B$? One algorithm for solution is to try all possible subsets and just see whether any has the desired property. This algorithm requires exponential time, so called because the size of the input ($n$) occurs in the exponent of the formula expressing the running time (in this case, roughly $2^n$). In fact, all known algorithms for this problem require exponential time. But there may be an unknown algorithm which runs in polynomial time; no proof prohibiting this is currently known.

Certainly, any problem in P is also in NP. A major outstanding question in computer science is whether P equals NP or whether NP is strictly larger.

There is a particular collection of problems in NP, including the knapsack problem, which are termed NP-complete. These can be thought of as the hardest problems in NP. More precisely, either P = NP or P ≠ NP. If P = NP, then any problem in NP is also in P. If P ≠ NP, then there are problems that cannot be done in polynomial time on a conventional sequential computer but can be done in polynomial time on a nondeterministic computer. An important mathematical result states: if there are any such problems in NP but not in P, then each NP-complete problem is also in NP but not in P. This class has particular significance for cryptography.

In a good cryptographic system, certain operations (like decryption) are easy for those in possession of the key and difficult for those without the key. (In some public-key applications, encryption should be easy and decryption should be difficult.) The legitimate user, in possession of the key, should be able to easily decrypt messages, and this task should be polynomial-time on a conventional sequential machine. The cryptanalyst who could first guess and verify the correct key would be able to decrypt easily (in polynomial time). This could be done by searching over the space of possible keys and attempting to verify each one in polynomial time. Since the problem can be solved by searching, decryption is in NP.

If P = NP, then decryption would also be in P, and a good cryptographic system would most likely be difficult to design. Even if no way was seen to easily decrypt without the key, P = NP would guarantee the existence of an algorithm whereby the cryptanalyst could "easily" decrypt any message. Of course, this is not a proof, merely an intuitive argument. In particular, "easy" and "polynomial-time" are not exactly the same thing.

If P ≠ NP, then the NP-complete problems might form a good starting point for cryptographic system design. They are in NP, so that a machine endowed with fortunate guesses or inside information (that is, the key) can easily solve the problem (decrypt). But they are not in P, so that machines without such inside information would require time larger than any fixed polynomial (that is, the cryptanalyst's job would be "hard").

Unfortunately, mathematicians and cryptographers have not yet learned how to transform an NP-complete problem into a secure cryptographic system. In one attempt to do so, R. Merkle and M. Hellman devised a public-key scheme for encryption based on the knapsack problem. They showed how to choose a secret key K and generate from that key a set $\{A_i\}$ so that the legitimate user, knowing K, could easily solve a knapsack problem based on $\{A_i\}$, while the opponent, without K, would presumably have a difficult time. However, it turned out that the particular choice of $\{A_i\}$ prescribed in this scheme, chosen for ease of decoding by the legitimate user in possession of the key, rendered the scheme liable to attack by integer programming. Although some instances of knapsack problems are difficult, the special instances used by Merkle and Hellman were shown to be easy.

Even if an NP-complete problem is eventually transformed successfully into a cryptographic system, a proof of the difficulty of cryptanalysis of that system (or any other) can be expected to be taxing. Such a proof would probably also prove that P ≠ NP, and this conjecture has eluded computer scientists for several years. Thus, for now, the designers of cryptographic systems must rely on experience rather than rigorous proof of the difficulty of cryptanalysis.

***Examples.*** Examples of the most efficient known attacks on several popular cryptographic systems are discussed below. The Data Encryption Standard (DES) apparently requires key exhaustion in order to break it. That is, no known method is faster than trying in turn each of the $2^{56} \simeq 10^{17}$ keys, a task which would strain the largest computing facilities for years to come. An attack has been devised that allows this to be done in $2^{56}$ computations once and for all, storing a table of $2^{40} \simeq 10^{12}$ words, and using this table with a relatively modest amount of computation ($2^{40}$ steps) to break a given key, under the assumption of chosen plaintext or chosen ciphertext. This attack fails when chaining techniques are employed [such as cipher block chaining (CBC) and cipher feedback (CFB) modes of encryption], so that DES is still safe. The attack also fails against repeated encipherment with three independent keys. There is no guarantee against a more efficient, analytic attack, although none is known at present.

The RSA algorithm, also discussed below, is based on the difficulty of factoring large numbers. However, a family of algorithms has been developed for factoring such numbers. Fifty-digit numbers are routinely factored in a matter of hours, and sixty- or seventy-digit numbers will be handled in a matter of days or months, respectively, before long. If the modulus involved has, say, 200 digits, then RSA should be secure in the foreseeable future.

Another proposed number-theoretic cryptographic scheme is based on the difficulty of solving the discrete logarithm problem. This problem involves modular arithmetic. Two integers $a$ and $b$ are congruent for the modulus $m$ if their difference $(a - b)$ is divisible by the integer $m$. This is expressed by the symbolic statement $a \equiv b \pmod{m}$, where mod is short for modulus. If $P$ is a prime and $E$ is an integer, $E$ is a primitive element when $E^0 \bmod P$, $E^1 \bmod P$, $E^2 \bmod P$, . . ., $E^{P-2} \bmod P$ are all different, and take on each nonzero value mod $P$ exactly once. Equivalently, if $m$ is the least positive integer such that $E^m = 1 \bmod P$, $E$ is primitive when $m = P - 1$. SEE NUMBER THEORY.

If $P$ is a prime and $E$ a primitive element mod $P$, then given $X$ it is straightforward to compute $Y$ such that Eq. (3) is satisfied, while it is more difficult to

$$E^X \equiv Y \bmod P \tag{3}$$

recover $X$ given $Y$, $E$, and $P$. But a modification of the factoring algorithm discussed above handles this discrete logarithm problem as well. This algorithm recovers $X$ in a time given by expression (4) for some

$$e^{c\sqrt{(\log P \ \log \log P)}} \tag{4}$$

small constant $c$; this is eventually smaller than any fixed fractional power of $P$ such as $P^{1/6}$. Thus, this scheme also requires a large modulus $P$ for security.

In summary, an outstanding problem in the field of computational complexity is to devise a provably secure cryptographic system. A second, perhaps easier, problem is to devise a cryptographic system which is provably at least NP-hard.

**Privacy and authentication.** Anyone can encipher data in a public-key cryptographic system (**Fig. 1**) by using the public enciphering key, but only the authorized user can decipher the data through possession of the secret deciphering key. Since anyone can encipher data, message authentication is necessary in order to identify a message's sender.

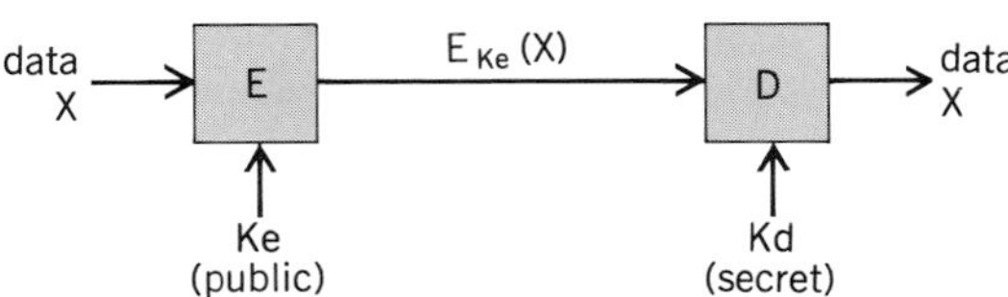


**Fig. 1. Public-key cryptographic system used for privacy only.**

A message authentication procedure can be devised (**Fig. 2**) by keeping the enciphering key secret and making the deciphering key public, provided that the enciphering key cannot be obtained from the deciphering key. This makes it impossible for nondesignated personnel to encipher messages, that is, to produce $\mathbf{E}_{Ke}(X)$. By inserting prearranged information in all messages, such as originator identification, recipient identification, and message sequence number, the messages can be checked to determine if they are genuine. However, because the contents of the messages are available to anyone having the public deciphering key, privacy cannot be attained.

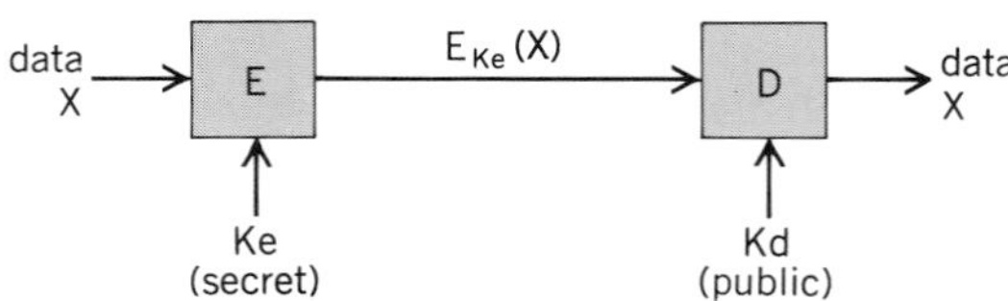


**Fig. 2. Public-key cryptographic system used for message authentication only.**

A public-key algorithm provides privacy as well as authentication (**Fig. 3**) if encipherment followed by decipherment, and decipherment followed by encipherment, produce the original plaintext, as in Eq. (5). A message to be authenticated is first deciphered

$$\mathbf{D}_{Kd}[\mathbf{E}_{Ke}(X)] = \mathbf{E}_{Ke}[\mathbf{D}_{Kd}(X)] = X \qquad (5)$$

by the sender (A) with a secret deciphering key (KAd). Privacy is ensured by enciphering the result with the receiver's (B's) public enciphering key (KBe).

Effective data security with public-key algorithms demands that the correct public key be used, since otherwise the system is exposed to attack. For example, if A can be tricked into using C's instead of B's public key, C can decipher the secret communications sent from A to B and can transmit messages to A pretending to be B. Thus key secrecy and key integrity are two distinct and very important attributes of

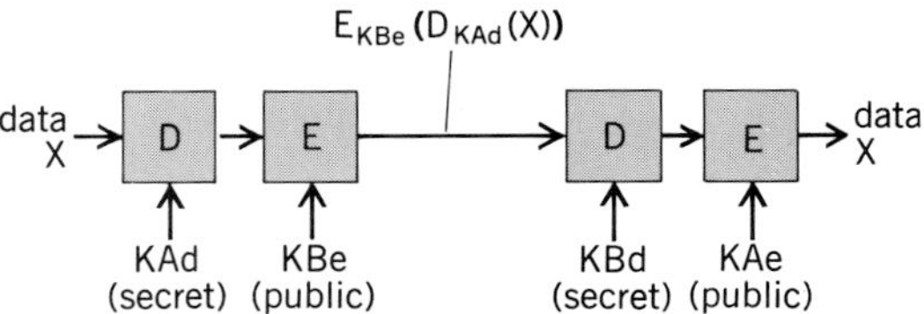


**Fig. 3. Public-key cryptographic system used for both message authentication and privacy. KAe and KAd are enciphering and deciphering keys of the sender (A). KBe and KBd are enciphering and deciphering keys of the receiver (B).**

cryptographic keys. While the requirement for key secrecy is relaxed for one of the keys in a public-key algorithm, the requirement for key integrity is not.

In a conventional cryptographic system, data are effectively protected because only the sender and receiver of the message share a common secret key. Such a system automatically provides both privacy and authentication (**Fig. 4**).

**Digital signatures.** Digital signatures authenticate messages by ensuring that: the sender cannot later disavow messages; the receiver cannot forge messages or signatures; and the receiver can prove to others that the contents of a message are genuine and that the message originated with that particular sender. The digital signature is a function of the message, a secret key or keys possessed by the sender and sometimes data that are nonsecret or that may become nonsecret as part of the procedure (such as a secret key that is later made public).

Digital signatures are more easily obtained with public-key then with conventional algorithms. When a message is enciphered with a private key (known only to the originator), anyone deciphering the message with the public key can identify the originator. The originator cannot later deny having sent the message. Receivers cannot forge messages and signatures, since they do not possess the originator's private key.

Since enciphering and deciphering keys are identical in a conventional algorithm, digital signatures must be obtained in some other manner. One method is to use a set of keys to produce the signature. Some of the keys are made known to the receiver to permit signature verification, and the rest of the keys are retained by the originator in order to prevent forgery.

**Data Encryption Standard.** Regardless of the application, a cryptographic system must be based on a cryptographic algorithm of validated strength if it is to be acceptable. The DES is such a validated conventional algorithm already in the public domain. (Since public-key algorithms are relatively recent, their strength has yet to be validated.)

During 1968–1975, IBM developed a crypto-

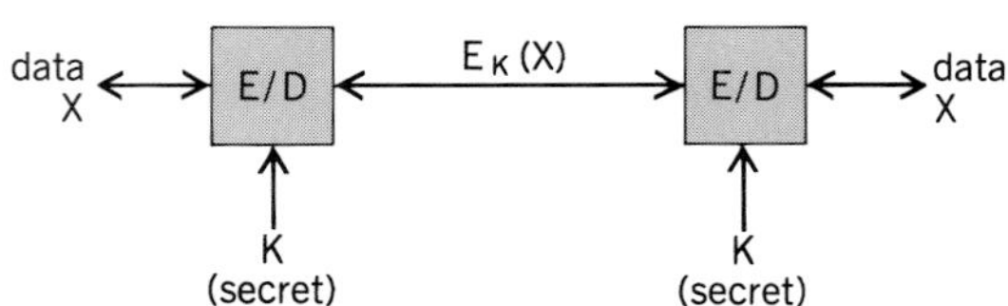


**Fig. 4. Conventional cryptographic system in which message authentication and message privacy are provided simultaneously. K represents a common secret key.**

graphic procedure that enciphers a 64-bit block of plaintext into a 64-bit block of ciphertext under the control of a 56-bit key. The National Bureau of Standards accepted this algorithm as a standard, and it became effective on July 15, 1977.

Conceptually, the DES can be thought of as a huge key-controlled substitution box (S-box) with a 64-bit input and output. With such an S-box, $2^{64}!$ different transformations or functions from plaintext to ciphertext are possible. The 56-bit key used with DES thus limits the number of usable functions to $2^{56}$.

A single huge S-box is impossible to construct. Therefore DES is implemented by using several smaller S-boxes (with a 6-bit input and a 4-bit output) and permuting their concatenated outputs. By repeating the substitution and permutation process several times, cryptographic strength "builds up." The DES encryption process consists of 16 iterations, called rounds. At each round a cipher function (f) is used with a 48-bit key. The function comprises the substitution and permutation. The 48-bit key, which is different for each round, is a subset of the bits in the externally supplied key.

The interaction of data, cryptographic key (K), and f is shown in **Fig. 5**. The externally supplied key consists of 64 bits (56 bits are used by the algorithm, and up to 8 bits may be used for parity checking). By shifting the original 56-bit key, a different subset of 48 key bits is selected for use in each round. These key bits are labeled $K_1$, $K_2$, . . ., $K_{16}$. To decipher, the keys are used in reverse order ($K_{16}$ is used in round one, $K_{15}$ in round two, and so on).

At each round (either encipherment or decipherment), the input is split into a left half (designated L), and a right half (designated R), (Fig. 5). R is transformed with f, and the result is combined, using modulo 2 addition (also called the EXCLUSIVE OR operation; see **Table 1**), with L. This approach, as discussed below, ensures that encipher and decipher operations can be designed regardless of how f is defined.

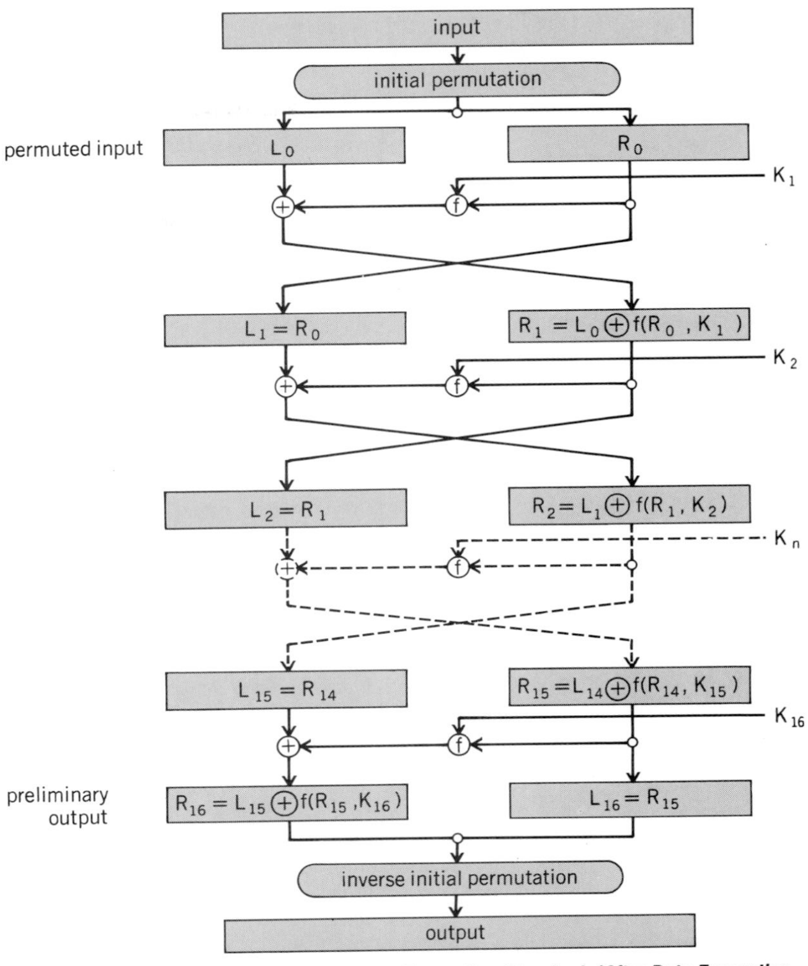


**Fig. 5. Enciphering computation in the Data Encryption Standard. (*After Data Encryption Standard, FIPS Publ.46, National Bureau of Standards, 1977*)**

**Table 1. Modulo 2 addition**

| A | B | A ⊕ B |
|---|---|---|
| 0 | 0 | 0 |
| 0 | 1 | 1 |
| 1 | 0 | 1 |
| 1 | 1 | 0 |

Consider the steps that occur during one round of encipherment (**Fig. 6**). Let the input block (X) be denoted $X = (L_0, R_0)$, where $L_0$ and $R_0$ are the left and right halves of X, respectively. Function f transforms $R_0$ into $f_{K_1}(R_0)$ under control of cipher key $K_1$. $L_0$ is then added (modulo 2) to $f_{K_1}(R_0)$ to obtain $R_1$, as in Eq. (6). The round is then completed by setting $L_1$ equal to $R_0$.

$$L_0 \oplus f_{K_1}(R_0) = R_1 \quad (6)$$

The above steps are reversible without introducing any new parameters or requiring that f be a one-to-one function. The ciphertext contains $L_1$, which equals $R_0$, and therefore half of the original plaintext is immediately recovered (**Fig. 7**). The remaining half, $L_0$, is recovered by recreating $f_{K_1}(R_0)$ from $R_0 = L_1$ and adding it (modulo 2) to $R_1$, as in Eq. (7).

$$R_1 \oplus f_{K_1}(R_0) = [L_0 \oplus f_{K_1}(R_0)] \oplus f_{K_1}(R_0) = L_0 \quad (7)$$

However, to use the procedure in Fig. 6 for encipherment as well as decipherment, the left and right

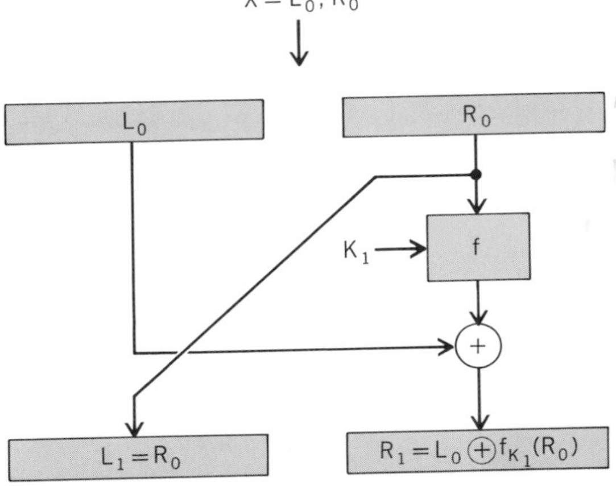


**Fig. 6. Transformation of input block ($L_0$, $R_0$). (*After C. H. Meyer and S. M. Matyas. Cryptography: A New Dimension in Computer Data Security, John Wiley and Sons, 1980*)**

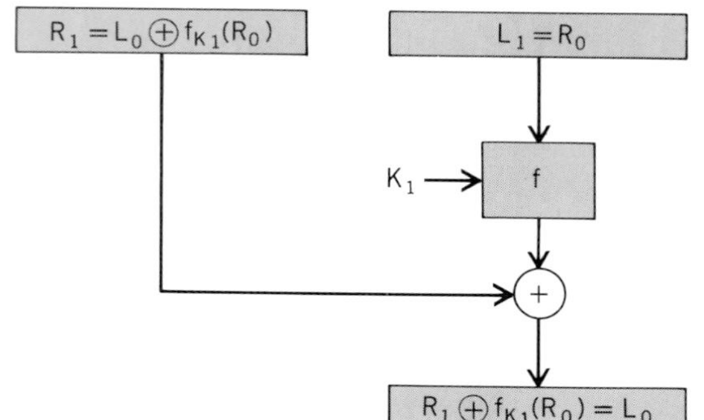


**Fig. 7. Recovery of $L_0$.** *(After C. H. Meyer and S. M. Matyas. Cryptography: A New Dimension in Computer Data Security, John Wiley and Sons, 1980)*

halves of the output must be interchanged; that is, the ciphertext (Y) is defined by Eq. (8). This modified

$$Y = [L_0 \oplus f_{K_1}(R_0)],\ R_0 \tag{8}$$

procedure easily extends to $n$ rounds, where the keys used for deciphering are $K_n, K_{n-1}, \ldots, K_1$.

**RSA public-key algorithm.** The RSA algorithm (named for the algorithm's inventors, R. L. Rivest, A. Shamir, and L. Adleman) is based on the fact that factoring large composite numbers into their prime factors involves an overwhelming amount of computation. (A prime number is an integer that is divisible only by 1 and itself. Otherwise, the number is said to be composite. Every composite number can be factored uniquely into prime factors. For example, the composite number 999,999 is factored by the primes 3, 7, 11, 13, and 37, that is $999{,}999 = 3^3 \cdot 7 \cdot 11 \cdot 13 \cdot 37$).

To describe the RSA algorithm, the following quantities are defined:

| | |
|---|---|
| $p$ and $q$ are primes | (secret) |
| $r = p \cdot q$ | (nonsecret) |
| $\phi(r) = (p-1)(q-1)$ | (secret) |
| Kd is the private key | (secret) |
| Ke is the public key | (nonsecret) |
| X is the plaintext | (secret) |
| Y is the ciphertext | (nonsecret) |

Based on an extension of Euler's theorem, Eq. (9),

$$X^{m\phi(r)+1} \equiv X \pmod{r} \tag{9}$$

the algorithm's public and private keys (Ke and Kd) are chosen so that Eq. (10) or, equivalently, Eq. (11)

$$\text{Kd} \cdot \text{Ke} = m\phi(r) + 1 \tag{10}$$

$$\text{Kd} \cdot \text{Ke} \equiv 1[\bmod \phi(r)] \tag{11}$$

is satisfied. By selecting two secret prime numbers $p$ and $q$, the user can calculate $r = p \cdot q$, which is made public, and $\phi(r) = (p-1)(q-1)$, which remains secret and is used to solve Eq. (11). (Tests are available to determine with a high level of confidence if a number is prime or not.) To obtain a unique solution for the public key (Ke), a random number, or secret key (Kd), is selected that is relatively prime to $\phi(r)$. (Integers $a$ and $b$ are relatively prime if their greatest common divisor is 1.) Ke is the multiplicative inverse of Kd, modulo $\phi(r)$, and Ke can be calculated from Kd and $\phi(r)$ by using Euclid's algorithm. Equation (9) can therefore be rewritten as Eq. (12), which holds true for any plaintext (X).

$$X^{\text{Kd}\cdot\text{Ke}} \equiv X \pmod{r} \tag{12}$$

Encipherment and decipherment can now be interpreted as in Eqs. (13) and (14). Moreover, because

$$\mathbf{E}_{\text{Ke}}(X) = Y \equiv X^{\text{Ke}} \pmod{r} \tag{13}$$

$$\begin{aligned}\mathbf{D}_{\text{Kd}}(Y) &\equiv Y^{\text{Kd}} \pmod{r} \\ &\equiv X^{\text{Ke}\cdot\text{Kd}} \pmod{r} \equiv X \pmod{r}\end{aligned} \tag{14}$$

multiplication is a commutative operation (Ke · Kd = Kd · Ke), encipherment followed by decipherment is the same as decipherment followed by encipherment [Eq. (5)]. Thus the RSA algorithm can be used for both privacy and digital signatures.

Finally, since $X^{\text{Ke}} \pmod{r} = (X + mr)^{\text{Ke}} \pmod{r}$ for any integer $m$, $\mathbf{E}_{\text{Ke}}(X) = \mathbf{E}_{\text{Ke}}(X + mr)$. Thus the transformation from plaintext to ciphertext, which is many-to-one, is made one-to-one by restricting X to the set $\{0, 1, \ldots, r-1\}$.

**Block ciphers.** A block cipher (**Fig. 8**) transforms a string of input bits of fixed length (termed an input block) into a string of output bits of fixed length (termed an output block). In a strong block cipher, the enciphering and deciphering functions are such that every bit in the output block jointly depends on every bit in the input block and on every bit in the key. This property is termed intersymbol dependence.

The following example (using DES) illustrates the marked change produced in a recovered plaintext when only one bit is changed in the ciphertext or key. Hexadecimal notation (**Table 2**) is used. If the plaintext 1000000000000001 is enciphered with a (56-bit) key 30000000000000, then the ciphertext 958E6E627A05557B is produced. The original plain-

**Table 2. Hexadecimal and binary notation**

| Hexadecimal digit | Binary digits |
|---|---|
| 0 | 0000 |
| 1 | 0001 |
| 2 | 0010 |
| 3 | 0011 |
| 4 | 0100 |
| 5 | 0101 |
| 6 | 0110 |
| 7 | 0111 |
| 8 | 1000 |
| 9 | 1001 |
| A | 1010 |
| B | 1011 |
| C | 1100 |
| D | 1101 |
| E | 1110 |
| F | 1111 |

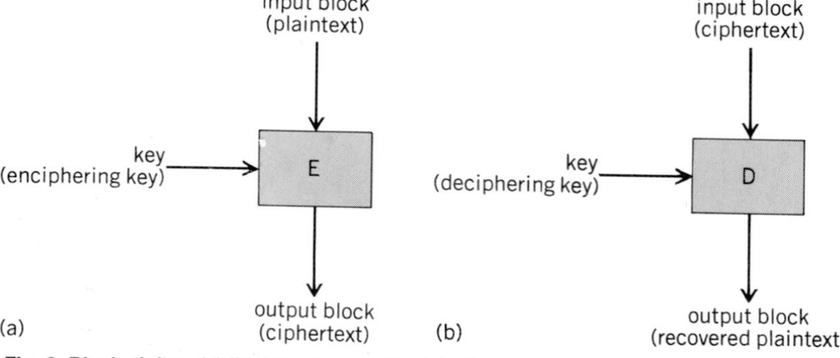


**Fig. 8. Block cipher. (*a*) Enciphering. (*b*) Deciphering.**

text is recovered if 958E6E627A05557B is now deciphered with 30000000000000. However, if the leading 9 in the ciphertext is changed to 8 (a one-bit change) and the ciphertext 858E6E627A05557B is now deciphered with key 30000000000000, the recovered plaintext is 8D4893C2966CC211, not 1000000000000001. On the other hand, if the leading 3 in the key is changed to 1 (another one-bit change) and the ciphertext 958E6E627A05557B is now deciphered with key 10000000000000, the recovered plaintext is 6D4B945376725395. (The same effect is also observed during encipherment.)

In the most basic implementation of DES, called block encryption or electronic codebook mode (ECB), each 64-bit block of data is enciphered and deciphered separately. Every bit in a given output block depends on every bit in its respective input block and on every bit in the key, but on no other bits.

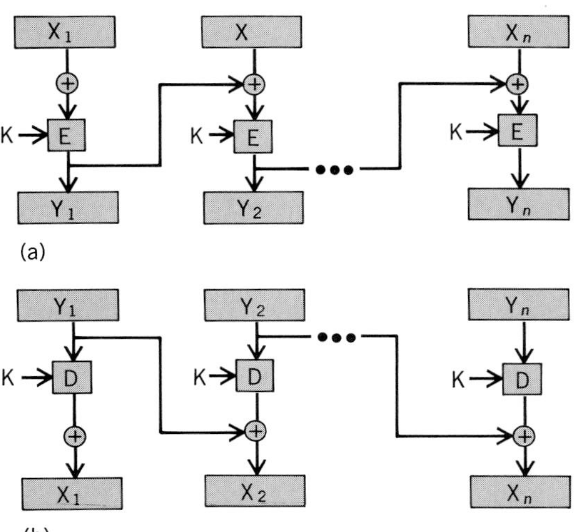


**Fig. 9. Block chaining with ciphertext feedback. (*a*) Enciphering. (*b*) Deciphering. (*After C. H. Meyer and S. M. Matyas. Cryptography: A New Dimension in Computer Data Security, John Wiley and Sons, 1980*)**

As a rule, block encryption is used to protect keys. A different method, called chained block encryption, is used to protect data. In chaining, the process of enciphering and deciphering is made dependent on other (prior) data, plaintext, ciphertext, and the like, also available at the time enciphering and deciphering takes place. Thus every bit in a given output block depends not only on every bit in its respective input block and every bit in the key, but also on any or all prior data bits, either inputted to, or produced during, the enciphering or deciphering process.

Sometimes data to be enciphered contain patterns that extend beyond the cipher's block size. These patterns in the plaintext can then result in similar patterns in the ciphertext, which would indicate to a cryptanalyst something about the nature of the plaintext. Thus, chaining is useful because it significantly reduces the presence of repetitive patterns in the ciphertext. This is because two equal input blocks encipher into unequal output blocks.

A recommended technique for block chaining, referred to as cipher block chaining (CBC), uses a ciphertext feedback (**Fig. 9**). Let $X_1, X_2, \ldots, X_n$ denote blocks of plaintext to be chained using key K; let $Y_0$ be a nonsecret quantity defined as the initializing vector; and let $Y_1, Y_2, \ldots, Y_n$ denote the blocks of ciphertext produced. The *i*th block of ciphertext ($Y_i$) is produced by EXCLUSIVE ORing $Y_{i-1}$ with $X_i$ and enciphering the result with K, as in Eq. (15),

$$\mathbf{E}_K(X_i \oplus Y_{i-1}) = Y_i \quad i \geq 1 \qquad (15)$$

where $\oplus$ denotes the EXCLUSIVE OR operation, or modulo 2 addition. Since every bit in $Y_i$ depends on every bit in $X_1$ through $X_i$, patterns in the plaintext are not reflected in the ciphertext.

The *i*th block of plaintext ($X_i$) is recovered by deciphering $Y_i$ with K and EXCLUSIVE ORing the result with $Y_{i-1}$, as in Eq. (16). Since the recovered plain-

$$\mathbf{D}_K(Y_i) \oplus Y_{i-1} = X_1 \quad i \geq 1 \qquad (16)$$

text $X_i$ depends only on $Y_i$ and $Y_{i-1}$, an error occurring in ciphertext $Y_j$ affects only two blocks of recovered plaintext ($X_j$ and $X_{j+1}$).

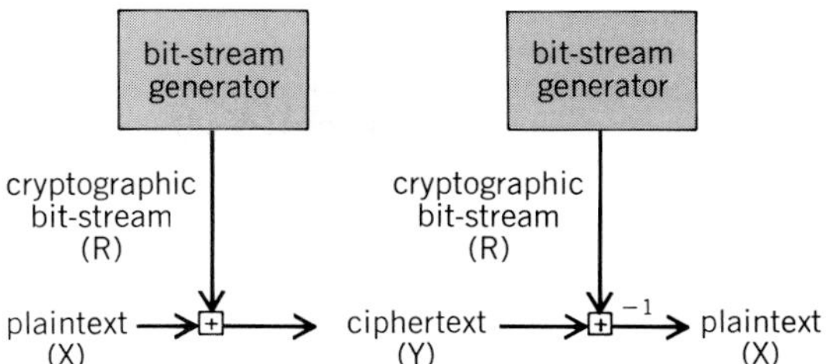


**Fig. 10. Stream cipher concept. (*After C. H. Meyer and S. M. Matyas. Cryptography: A New Dimension in Computer Data Security, John Wiley and Sons, 1980*)**

**Stream ciphers.** A stream cipher (**Fig. 10**) employs a bit-stream generator to produce a stream of binary digits (0's and 1's) called a cryptographic bit stream, which is then combined either with plaintext (via the ⊞ operator) to produce ciphertext or with ciphertext (via the $⊞^{-1}$ operator) to recover plaintext. (Traditionally, the term key stream has been used to denote the bit stream produced by the bit-stream generator. The term cryptographic bit stream is used here to avoid possible confusion with a fixed-length cryptographic key in cases where a cryptographic algorithm is used as the bit-stream generator.)

Historically, G. S. Vernam was the first to recognize the merit of a cipher in which ciphertext (Y) was

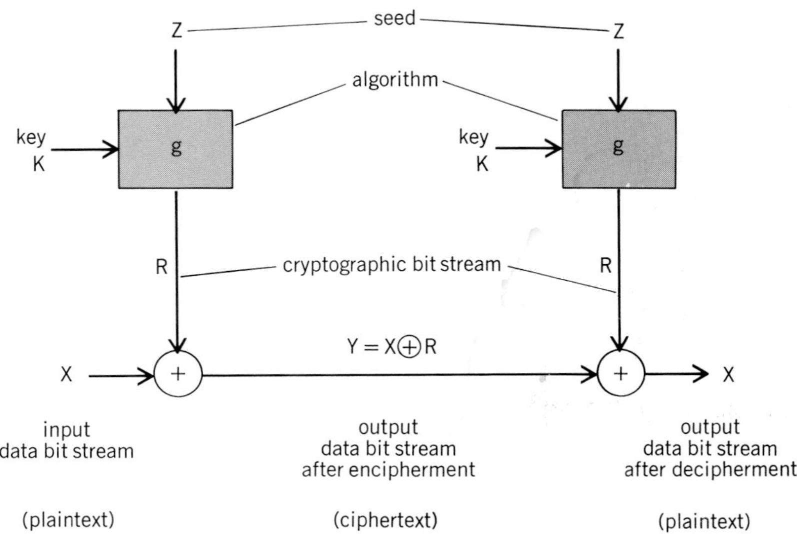


**Fig. 11. Stream cipher using an algorithmic bit stream generator, modulo 2 addition, and seed. (*After C. H. Meyer and S. M. Matyas. Cryptography: A New Dimension in Computer Data Security, John Wiley and Sons, 1980*)**

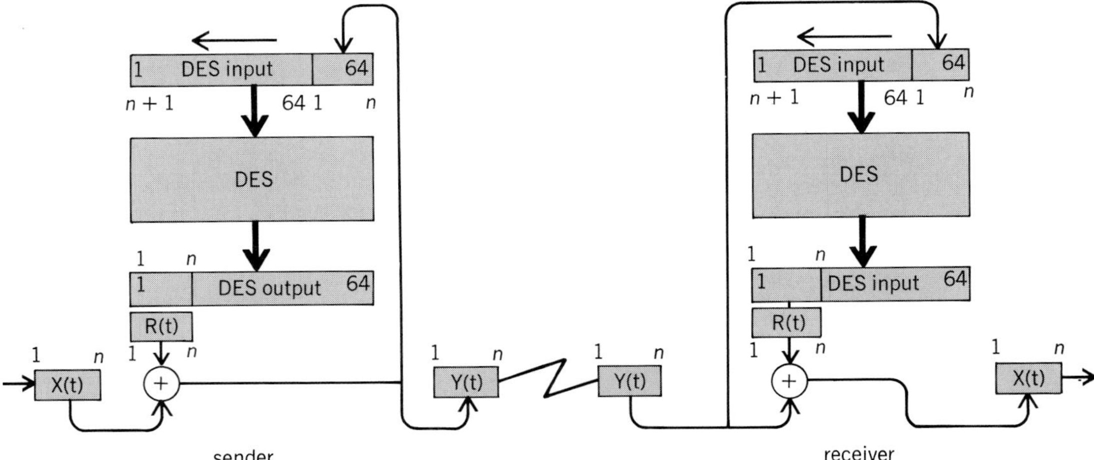


**Fig. 12. Cipher feedback.** *(After C. H. Meyer and S. M. Matyas. Cryptography: A New Dimension in Computer Data Security, John Wiley and Sons, 1980)*

produced from plaintext (X) by combining it with a secret bit stream (R) via a simple and efficient operation. In his cipher, Vernam used an EXCLUSIVE OR operation, or modulo 2 addition (Table 1), to combine the respective bit streams. Thus encipherment and decipherment are defined by $X \oplus R = Y$ and $Y \oplus R = X$, respectively. Therefore $\boxplus = \boxplus^{-1} = \oplus$. Modulo 2 addition is the combining operation used in most stream ciphers, and for this reason it is used in the following discussion.

If the bit-stream generator were truly random, an unbreakable cipher could be obtained by EXCLUSIVE ORing the plaintext and cryptographic bit stream. The cryptographic bit stream would be used directly as the key, and would be equal in length to the message. But in that case the cryptographic bit stream must be provided in advance to the communicants via some independent and secure channel. This introduces insurmountable logistic problems for heavy data traffic. Hence, for practical reasons, the bit-stream generator must be implemented as an algorithmic procedure. Then both communicants can generate the same cryptographic bit stream—provided that their algorithms are identically initialized. **Figure 11** illustrates a cryptographic bit stream produced with a key-controlled algorithm.

When modulo 2 addition is used as the combining operation, each bit in the output ciphertext (recovered plaintext) is dependent only upon its corresponding bit in the input plaintext (ciphertext). This is in marked contrast to the block cipher which exhibits a much more complex relationship between bits in the plaintext (ciphertext) and bits in the ciphertext (recovered plaintext). Both approaches, however, have comparable strength.

In a stream cipher the algorithm may generate its bit stream on a bit-by-bit basis, or in blocks of bits. This is of no real consequence. All such systems are stream ciphers, or variations thereof. Moreover, since bit streams can be generated in blocks, it is always possible for a block cipher to be used to obtain a stream cipher. However, because both the sender and receiver must produce cryptographic bit streams that are equal and secret, their keys must also be equal and secret. Therefore public keys in confirmation with a public-key algorithm cannot be used in a stream-cipher mode of operation.

For security purposes, a stream cipher must never predictably start from the same initial condition, thereby producing the same cryptographic bit stream. This can be avoided by making the cryptographic bit stream dependent on a nonsecret quantity Z (known as seed, initializing vector, or fill), which is used as an input parameter to the ciphering algorithm (Fig. 11).

In a stream cipher, Z provides cryptographic strength and establishes synchronization between communicating cryptographic devices—it assures that the same cryptographic bit streams are generated for the sender and the receiver. Initialization may be accomplished by generating Z at the sending device and transmitting it in clear (plaintext) form to the receiver.

**Cipher feedback.** A general approach to producing cryptographic bit streams is the automatic modification of the algorithm's input using feedback methods. In a key auto-key cipher, the cryptographic bit stream generated at time $t = \tau$ is determined by the cryptographic bit stream generated at time $t < \tau$. In a ciphertext auto-key cipher the cryptographic bit stream generated at time $t = \tau$ is determined by the ciphertext generated at time $t < \tau$. A particular implementation of a ciphertext auto-key cipher, recommended by the National Bureau of Standards, is called cipher feedback (**Fig. 12**).

In cipher feedback, the leftmost $n$ bits of the DES output are EXCLUSIVE ORed with $n$ bits of plaintext to

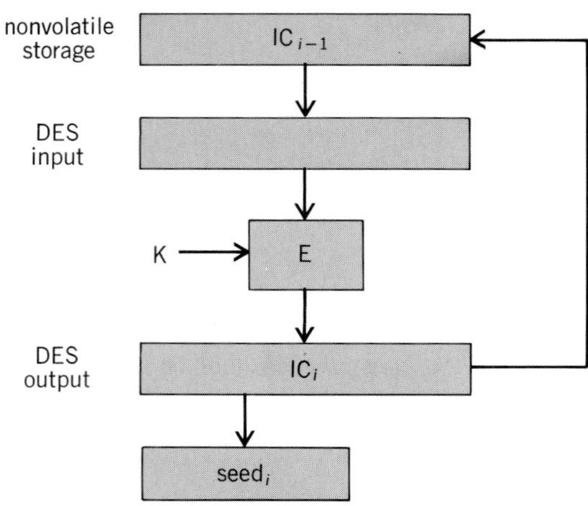


**Fig. 13. Seed generation using the DES algorithm.** *(After C. H. Meyer and S. M. Matyas. Cryptography: A New Dimension in Computer Data Security, John Wiley and Sons, 1980)*

| iteration | DES input at sender | | | | | | | | DES input at receiver | | | | | | | |
|---|---|---|---|---|---|---|---|---|---|---|---|---|---|---|---|---|
| 0 | 0 | 0 | 0 | S1 | S2 | S3 | S4 | S5 | 0 | 0 | 0 | S1 | S2 | S3 | S4 | S5 |
| 1 | 0 | 0 | S1 | S2 | S3 | S4 | S5 | $Y(t_1)$ | 0 | 0 | S1 | S2 | S3 | S4 | S5 | $Y(t_1)$ |
| 2 | 0 | S1 | S2 | S3 | S4 | S5 | $Y(t_1)$ | $Y(t_2)$ | 0 | S1 | S2 | S3 | S4 | S5 | $Y(t_1)$ | $Y(t_2)$ |
| 3 | S1 | S2 | S3 | S4 | S5 | $Y(t_1)$ | $Y(t_2)$ | $Y(t_3)$ | S1 | S2 | S3 | S4 | S5 | $Y(t_1)$ | $Y(t_2)$ | $Y(t_3)$ |
| 4 | S2 | S3 | S4 | S5 | $Y(t_1)$ | $Y(t_2)$ | $Y(t_3)$ | $Y(t_4)$ | S2 | S3 | S4 | S5 | $Y(t_1)$ | $Y(t_2)$ | $Y(t_3)$ | $Y(t_4)$ |
| 5 | S3 | S4 | S5 | $Y(t_1)$ | $Y(t_2)$ | $Y(t_3)$ | $Y(t_4)$ | $Y(t_5)$ | S3 | S4 | S5 | $Y(t_1)$ | $Y(t_2)$ | $Y(t_3)$ | $Y(t_4)$ | $Y(t_5)$ |
| 6 | S4 | S5 | $Y(t_1)$ | $Y(t_2)$ | $Y(t_3)$ | $Y(t_4)$ | $Y(t_5)$ | $Y(t_6)$ | S4 | S5 | $Y(t_1)$ | $Y(t_2)$ | $Y(t_3)$ | $Y(t_4)$ | $Y(t_5)$ | $Y(t_6)$ |
| 7 | S5 | $Y(t_1)$ | $Y(t_2)$ | $Y(t_3)$ | $Y(t_4)$ | $Y(t_5)$ | $Y(t_6)$ | $Y(t_7)$ | S5 | $Y(t_1)$ | $Y(t_2)$ | $Y(t_3)$ | $Y(t_4)$ | $Y(t_5)$ | $Y(t_6)$ | $Y(t_7)$ |
| 8 | $Y(t_1)$ | $Y(t_2)$ | $Y(t_3)$ | $Y(t_4)$ | $Y(t_5)$ | $Y(t_6)$ | $Y(t_7)$ | $Y(t_8)$ | $Y(t_1)$ | $Y(t_2)$ | $Y(t_3)$ | $Y(t_4)$ | $Y(t_5)$ | $Y(t_6)$ | $Y(t_7)$ | $Y(t_8)$ |
| 9 | $Y(t_2)$ | $Y(t_3)$ | $Y(t_4)$ | $Y(t_5)$ | $Y(t_6)$ | $Y(t_7)$ | $Y(t_8)$ | $Y(t_9)$ | $Y(t_2)$ | $Y(t_3)$ | $Y(t_4)$ | $Y(t_5)$ | $Y(t_6)$ | $Y(t_7)$ | $Y(t_8)$ | $Y(t_9)$ |

**Fig. 14. Self-synchronizing feature in cipher feedback. *(After C. H. Meyer and S. M. Matyas. Cryptography: A New Dimension in Computer Data Security, John Wiley and Sons, 1980)***

produce $n$ bits of ciphertext, where $n$ is the number of bits enciphered at one time ($1 \leq n \leq 64$). These $n$ bits of ciphertext are fed back into the algorithm by first shifting the current DES input $n$ bits to the left, and then appending the $n$ bits of ciphertext to the right-hand side of the shifted input to thus produce a new DES input used to the next iteration of the algorithm.

A seed value, which must be the same for both sender and receiver, is used as an initial input to the DES in order to generate the cryptographic bit stream. Federal Standard 1026 defines a 48-bit seed for all cipher feedback implementations, thus ensuring compatibility among users. The communicating nodes are synchronized by right-justifying the seed in the input to the DES and setting the remaining bits equal to 0.

One method to generate seed values with the DES is illustrated in **Fig. 13**. $IC_0$ (for initial condition) is a starting value supplied by the user and is placed in nonvolatile storage (where data remain permanent). $IC_1$ is produced by enciphering $IC_0$ with the (stored) cryptographic key, $IC_2$ is produced by enciphering $IC_1$, and so forth. At each iteration, $IC_i$ replaces $IC_{i-1}$, and seed$_i$ is the left-most $m$ bits ($m \leqslant 64$) of $IC_i$.

The cipher feedback approach is self-synchronizing, since any bit changes occurring in the ciphertext during transmission get shifted out of the DES input after 64 additional ciphertext bits are sent and received. If, for example, 8 bits are enciphered at one time, as shown in Fig. 12, and a bit is altered in $Y(t_1)$ changing it to $Y^*(t_1)$, then the sender's and receiver's inputs are as shown in **Fig. 14**, where the 40-bit seed is defined as S1, S2, . . . , S5. In this case, the blocks of ciphertext, given by $Y^*(t_1)$, $Y(t_2)$, . . . , $Y(t_8)$, can be correctly deciphered only at the receiver by chance since the DES input is incorrect in each case. After eight blocks of uncorrupted ciphertext have been received, given by $Y(t_2)$, $Y(t_3)$, . . . , $Y(t_9)$, both the sender's and receiver's cryptographic devices will have equal DES inputs again.

In general, any bit changes in an $n$-bit block of ciphertext can cause a change in any of the corresponding $n$ bits of recovered plaintext and in any of the 64 bits of recovered plaintext immediately following. However, a permanent "out-of-sync" condition will result if a ciphertext bit is added or dropped, since the integrity of the block boundary is lost. To recover from such an error, the sender and receiver would have to establish the beginning and ending of blocks of bits that are enciphered at one time ($n = 8$ bits in the given example).

On the other hand, if enciphering takes place on a bit-by-bit basis ($n = 1$), then the property of self-synchronization is maintained even when bits are lost or added. This is because blocks are bits, and therefore the block boundary cannot be disturbed. *SEE INFORMATION THEORY*.

*Carl H. Meyer; Stephen M. Matyas; Don Coppersmith*

**Bibliography.** *Data Encryption Standard*, FIPS Publ. 46, National Bureau of Standards, January 1977; W. Diffie and M. Hellman, New directions in cryptography, *IEEE Trans. Inform. Theory*, IT-22:644–654, November 1976; H. Feistel, Cryptography and computer privacy, *Sci. Amer.*, 228(5):15–23, May 1973; M. R. Garey and D. S. Johnson, *Computers and Intractability: A Guide to the Theory of NP-Completeness*, 1979; M. Hellman, The mathematics of public-key cryptography, *Sci. Amer.*, 241(2):146–157, August 1979; C. H. Meyer and S. M. Matyas, *Cryptography: A New Dimension in Computer Data Security*, 1982; R. L. Rivest, A. Shamir, and L. Adleman, Method for obtaining digital signatures and public-key cryptosystems, *Comm. ACM*, 21(2):120–126, February 1978; C. E. Shannon, Communication theory of secrecy systems, *Bell Syst. Tech. J.*, 28:656–715, 1949.

## Current measurement

The measurement of the flow of electric current. The unit of measurement, the ampere (A), is defined in the International System of Units (SI) through its electromagnetic reaction. One ampere of unvarying unidirectional current (direct current) flowing through a wire and returning through an adjacent parrallel wire will produce, when the two parallel wires are 1 m apart on centers, a force between the wires of 2 newtons for each length so positioned. This electromagnetic reaction was first studied by André Marie Ampère in 1820. The reaction or force is proportional to the current in each wire, or to the square of the current where it returns on itself, as in the definition. The force is also inversely proportional to the square of the distance between the wires.

In the practical determination of current value the

current-carrying wires are formed into circular coils. The moving coil may move up and down as in the Rayleigh balance, where the reaction is balanced by the force of gravity on known weights, or it may rotate as in the Pellat balance, being supported on a knife edge; here the force is balanced by an appropriate mass acting a known distance from the support.

**Direct and low-frequency currents.** The current balance is tedious to operate, and is ordinarily used only by the national laboratories of the various countries for the determination of the absolute ampere, whereby simpler (but less accurate) current-measuring devices may be calibrated.

The moving coil may rotate in jeweled bearings against the countertorque of a spiral spring. If a pointer is attached to the moving system rotating over an appropriately marked scale, calibrated in terms of the absolute current determinations of an ampere balance, the result is an indicating electrodynamometer ammeter. Such instruments are widely used as laboratory standards for both direct and alternating-current measurements and for the calibration of secondary instruments.

Direct current (dc) may also be measured by placing the movable coil in the magnetic field of a permanent magnet. This is the construction of the conventional type of dc ammeter. *SEE AMMETER.*

Structures incorporating a permanent magnet give a reversed deflection with reversed direction of current, and therefore are usable only on direct current. For the measurement of alternating current (ac) the instrument must take no account of current direction and, further, must give a reading of that function of the current oscillation which is to be measured. For example, only the peak value of current may be desired. An example is in the measurement of the maximum value of a lightning discharge to a transmission tower where a small magnetic link is magnetized by the peak value of the current; a test of the degree of its magnetization can be correlated to the peak current value.

In most cases it is desired to measure that value of the alternating current which is a measure of the power in a motor or of heat in a stove or lamp filament, namely, its root-mean-square (rms) value. The electrodynamometer ammeter indicates in these terms. If calibrated on direct current, it becomes a transfer instrument and may be used to calibrate other types of ac instruments in terms of true rms current value.

For ordinary switchboard or test indications of alternating current the fixed-coil, moving-iron type of instrument, with its high torque and quite adequate accuracy, is widely used. A fixed iron vane and a similar vane on a staff are magnetized by the current in the coil, the force between the vanes acting to rotate against a spring as a function of the rms value of the current.

The hot-wire ammeter, indicating the mechanically amplified stretch of a fine wire heated by the current, has been wholly replaced by the thermoammeter. In this instrument a short metal strip or wire is heated by the current in question; its temperature rise is measured by a contacting thermocouple connected, in turn, to a sensitive dc meter which deflects in proportion to the temperature rise. The scale is marked in terms of the heating current. This type of instrument is insensitive to variations in frequency and ambient temperature.

When direct currents of over a fraction of 1 A are to be measured, the bulk of the current is diverted around the instrument through a shunt or bypass circuit or, simply, a shunt. Large alternating currents, on the other hand, are connected to meters rated at 5 A through current stepdown transformers, or current transformers. Both are available in wide range variety and are of good accuracy.

Extremely heavy direct currents, above $10^4$ A, can be measured with a transductor, essentially an ac transformer with the iron core surrounding the dc bus. By properly proportioning the windings, the ac input, as indicated on an ammeter, is a measure of the direct current, and the scale can be so calibrated. *SEE TRANSFORMER.*

*John H. Miller/Jesse Beams*

**Very small currents.** The obvious method for measuring a very small current is to determine the voltage drop across a large resistor. A sensitive voltage detector having very low offset current is required, for example, an electrometer. Electrometers based on MOSFET (metal-oxide-semiconductor field-effect transistor) devices have overtaken other designs where they very highest resolution is required, as they can have offset current drifts less than $10^{-16}$ A. In order to provide a low impedance to the measured current, it is preferable to use the electrometer device in an operational amplifier configuration (see **illus.**).

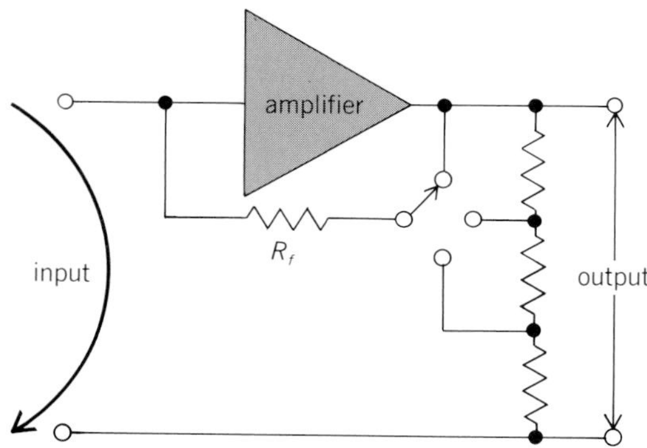


**Measurement of very small currents by using an operational amplifier.**

The input becomes a virtual ground, and so stray capacitance across the input connection does not degrade the rate of response of the circuit as seriously as in the simple connection. *SEE TRANSISTOR.*

The operational amplifier configuration can be extended to provide a variety of ranges from each high-value resistor. Driving the resistor from the amplifier output through a voltage divider of ratio $N$ gives a similar result to the use of a resistor $N$ times higher in value. This also has the advantage that extremely high-value resistors can be avoided.

Operational amplifiers suitable for this application are readily available, based not only on field-effect transistors but also on varactors. The latter are semiconductor equivalents to the mechanical vibrating capacitor electrometers. *SEE AMPLIFIER.*

*R. B. D. Knight*

**Current at high frequencies.** High-frequency current is usually measured by its heating effect. Thermocouple meters are most common, and available single-range commercial instruments are accurate to

1% up to 10 MHz. Special-purpose designs have been used to about 100 MHz. Bridges incorporating thermistor elements, in which resistance varies greatly with the heating, are also widely used. One of the best methods is to measure the voltage drop across a shunt with a diode-rectifier-type vacuum-tube voltmeter. At frequencies over a few hundred megahertz, current is seldom measured directly but is usually computed from impedance and power measurements. SEE ELECTRICAL MEASUREMENTS; MICROWAVE MEASUREMENTS; VACUUM-TUBE VOLTMETER; VOLTAGE MEASUREMENT.

*W. Norris Tuttle*

**Bibliography.** M. Braccio, *Basic Electrical and Electronic Tests and Measurement*, 1979; W. D. Cooper, *Electronic Instrumentation and Measurement Techniques*, 1978; B. A. Gregory, *An Introduction to Electrical Instrumentation and Measurement Systems*, 2d ed., 1981; F. K. Harris, *Electrical Measurements*, 1975; B. P. Kibble et al., The NPL moving coil ampere determination, *IEEE Trans. Instru. Meas.*, IM–32(1):141–143, March 1983; U.S. Department of Commerce, National Bureau of Standards, *Precision Measurement and Calibration, Electricity—Low Frequency*, Spec. Publ. 300, vol. 3., 1968.

## Cyclotron resonance experiments

The measurement of charge-to-mass ratios of electrically charged particles from the frequency of their helical motion in a magnetic field. Such experiments are particularly useful in the case of conducting crystals, such as semiconductors and metals, in which the motions of electrons and holes are strongly influenced by the periodic potential of the lattice through which they move. Under such circumstances the electrical carriers often have "effective masses" which differ greatly from the mass in free space; the effective mass is often different for motion in different directions in the crystal. Cyclotron resonance is also observed in gaseous plasma discharges and is the basis for a class of particle accelerators. SEE BAND THEORY OF SOLIDS.

The experiment is typically performed by placing the conducting medium in a uniform magnetic field $H$ and irradiating it with electromagnetic waves of frequency $\nu$. Selective absorption of the radiation is observed when the resonance condition $\nu = qH/2\pi m^*c$ is fulfilled, that is, when the radiation frequency equals the orbital frequency of motion of the particles of charge $q$ and effective mass $m^*$ ($c$ is the velocity of light). The absorption results from the acceleration of the orbital motion by means of the electric field of the radiation. If circularly polarized radiation is used, the sign of the electric charge may be determined, a point of interest in crystals in which conduction may occur by means of either negatively charged electrons or positively charged holes. SEE HOLES IN SOLIDS.

For the resonance to be well defined, it is necessary that the mobile carriers complete at least $1/2\pi$ cycle of their cyclotron motion before being scattered from impurities or thermal vibrations of the crystal lattice. In practice, the experiment is usually performed in magnetic fields of 1000 to 100,000 oersteds (1 oersted = 79.6 amperes per meter) in order to make the cyclotron motion quite rapid ($\nu \sim 10 - 100$ gigahertz, that is, microwave and millimeter-wave ranges). Nevertheless, crystals with impurity concentrations of a few parts per million or less are required and must be observed at temperatures as low as 1 K in order to detect sharp and intense cyclotron resonances.

The resonance process manifests itself rather differently in semiconductors than in metals. Pure, very cold semiconductors have very few charge carriers; thus the microwave radiation penetrates the sample uniformly. The mobile charges are thus exposed to radiation over their entire orbits, and the resonance is a simple symmetrical absorption peak.

In metals, however, the very high density of conduction electrons present at all temperatures prevents penetration of the electromagnetic energy except for a thin surface region, the skin depth, where intense sheilding currents flow. Cyclotron resonance is then observed most readily when the magnetic field is accurately parallel to the flat surface of the metal. Those conduction electrons (or holes) whose orbits pass through the skin depth without colliding with the surface receive a succession of pulsed excitations, like those produced in a particle accelerator. Under these curcumstances cyclotron resonance consists of a series of resonances $n\nu = qH/2\pi m^*c$ ($n = 1, 2, 3, \ldots$) whose actual shapes may be quite complicated. The resonance can, however, also be observed with the magnetic field normal to the metal surface; it is in this geometry that circularly polarized exciting radiation can be applied to charge carriers even in a metal.

Cyclotron resonance is most easily understood as the response of an individual charged particle; but, in practice, the phenomenon involves excitation of large numbers of such particles. Their net response to the electromagnetic radiation may significantly affect the overall dielectric behavior of the material in which they move. Thus, a variety of new wave propagation mechanisms may be observed which are associated with the cyclotron motion, in which electromagnetic energy is carried through the solid by the spiraling carriers. These collective excitations are generally referred to as plasma waves. In general, for a fixed input frequency, the plasma waves are observed to travel through the conducting solid at magnetic fields higher than those required for cyclotron resonance. The most easily observed of these excitations is a circularly polarized wave, known as a helicon, which travels along the magnetic field lines. It has an analog in the ionospheric plasma, known as the whistler mode and frequently detected as radio interference. There is, in fact, a fairly complete correspondence between the resonances and waves observed in conducting solids and in gaseous plasmas. Cyclotron resonance is more easily observed in such low-density systems since collisions are much less frequent there than in solids. In such systems the resonance process offers a means of transferring large amounts of energy to the mobile ions, which is a necessary condition if nuclear fusion reactions are to occur.

*Walter M. Walsh*

**Bibliography.** C. Kittel, *Introduction to Solid State Physics*, 5th ed., 1976; P. M. Platzman and P. A. Wolff, *Waves and Interactions in Solid State Plasmas*, 1973.

## Dark current

An ambiguous term used in connection with both gaseous-discharge devices and photoelectric cells or tubes. In gaseous-conduction tubes it refers to the region of operation known as the Townsend discharge. The name is derived from the fact that photons produced in the gas do not play an important part in the production of ionization. The initial ionization arises from independent effects such as cosmic rays, radioactivity, or thermionic emission. When applied to photoelectric devices, the term applies to background current. This is current which may be present as the result of thermionic emission or other effects when there is no light incident on the photosensitive cathode. *See Electrical conduction in gases; Townsend discharge.*

*Glenn H. Miller*

## Data-base management systems

Special data-processing systems or parts of data-processing systems which are developed to aid in the storage, manipulation, reporting, and managing of data. They may be considered as building blocks constructing a data-processing system which also acts as a mechanism for the effective control of the data.

**Cost of information systems.** An information (or data-processing) system consists of such hardware or physical devices as computers, storage units and input/output media controllers; also software and the people who build, maintain, and use the system. In the early days of computing, the cost of the system was mainly in the hardware, but during the 1970s the cost of hardware dropped radically. The ratio of software-to-hardware cost now falls between 1 and 10 for most industrial and commercial operations. The cost of people has not dropped; thus the concept of "hardware is expensive and should be used sparingly" has become obsolete. Emphasis must be placed on reducing the cost of software, both in building the system and in maintaining it, that is, all parts of the so-called software life cycle. *See Software engineering.*

Maintenance or modification occurs because of hardware changes, new ways of doing business, or different user orientation.

Software cost can be reduced in three ways:

1. While building the system, by using general system software. This spreads effort and cost over several applications. Early examples of this were such special packages or routines that took a square root, evaluated a trigonometric function, or even sorted (ordered) a set of data according to some numeric or alphabetic key.

2. When making modifications. This is achieved by making the system modular, such that only parts of it are affected by changes in the hardware configuration or by user-induced alterations. This modularity isolates system parts from one another, for example, the square-root routine need not be changed when its calling routine is modified.

3. By using a rapid-prototyping (RP) technique. This method involves the building of a model or "breadboard" of the system to be implemented. This is achieved relatively cheaply by use of a set of special interfaces provided in some commercial offerings. Such rapid-prototyping systems allow the users to "try out" their ideas before too much effort and resources have been expended, thereby allowing the prototype to be testing in much the same way as an engineering prototype is built before its design is finalized and the production line is started.

The success of early packages gradually led to the adoption of more complex ones, or system software to perform management functions. The most complex set of such packages is an operating system.

Some common functions have been identified to help with management, manipulation, and control of the data itself. Such a set of packages is generally called a data-base management system (DBMS) by its manufacturers although their specific design and implementation may differ.

**Management control of data.** Without data, the process of controlling any system is impossible. Data are the physical representation interpreted through work orders, experimental results or analyses, costs of operation, or tax schedules. Data can provide information to a worker on what job to perform next and what special problems to expect; data help the engineer to see how to improve a design; for the manager data can highlight operational inefficiencies; data help the bureaucrat to decide how to govern and what new laws are needed.

The computer provides business, industry, and government with the means to improve the speed and efficiency of the collection, manipulation, storage, reporting, and dissemination of data, and this has been advantageous. However, the advent of the data-base concept constitutes both an advantage and a potential threat. The threat has several aspects which show why control or management of data is very important.

***Organization of data.*** It has been estimated that a medium-sized corporation may need to retain $10^{10}$ characters of current important data in high-speed automated storage. By comparison, a book of 300 pages, 40 lines per page, and 12 words (each of about 6 characters) per line, contains about $10^6$ characters (including spaces between words) and thus the $10^{10}$-character "data base" could be stored in $10^4$ books, which is indeed a good-sized library. However, the organization of a library makes it relatively easy to find any book, but imagine a library that had no catalog, no librarians and no one putting the books back on the shelves. The cost of a library staff is similar to that of organizing data in a corporate data base: it is necessary if data must be found and used effectively. The old systems, without well-organized data, suffered from the problem that people knew data existed, but could not find the data easily and became frustrated. One reason for the development of data-base management systems was to solve this need.

Data become truly available when a large cross section of potential users know of their existence, when their location and format are known, and when there is a mechanism for retrieving the data. If the mechanism to locate its format is used by humans, the location is normally termed a directory, while the format is stored in a dictionary. If the locating device is embedded in the data-base system, the mechanism is termed a schema.

A schema is therefore a machine-readable version of the location and format of the stored data. The difference between the schema and its instances or occurrences is shown in **Fig. 1**. This simple schema contains information about a person: name, date of birth, and salary. The representation is: name 10 characters in length, left justified with blanks appended for shorter names; date of birth as year, month, and day, with two decimal digits representing each; and salary of up to $9999.99 per month. The model is defined in the schema, while the data are recorded in each instance.

In order for the data-base management system to retrieve or store data about a person, it must consult the schema to determine its form as well as its location in machine storage. This means that a data-base management system with a query language interface can respond to a request like FOR PERSON, FIND MONTHLY-SALARY, WHERE PERSON-NAME = "SINGER," or FOR PERSON, FIND PERSON-NAME AND DATE-OF-BIRTH, WHERE SALARY GREATER THAN 700.00

***Data security.*** This powerful capability of the data-base management system enables a wide variety of potential users to obtain information that would otherwise be unavailable. However, this also creates some social problems, because access to the data may become too easy. *SEE MULTIACCESS COMPUTER*.

The concept of privacy has been defined as the right to be left alone. If anyone can obtain someone else's date of birth, that person's privacy has been violated. There must be some restriction on who can obtain what data under which conditions (and maybe when). A certain clerk may be allowed to look at salary data and read and update it during the working day (but not at night or during the weekend). This authority to access data must be vested in and controlled through the data-base management system; it is usually termed a security technique.

Typically, security may be enforced by insisting that users of the data-base management system identify themselves both by name or employee number and by some password. Other mechanisms may involve the insistence on use of particular terminal devices at predefined locations, allowance of only certain types of command or programs to be initiated, and hiding of sensitive parts of the data base except to certain highly privileged users. Thus the data may be screened from the general user through various levels of security, even to the extend of encoding them (requiring automated decoding routines to make them meaningful for the authorized user).

***Integrity of data.*** Because the data are often stored in a device with moving parts they can be destroyed through mechanical or other failures. Data may also be lost through user carelessness or program malfunction. To protect the integrity of the data, several defensive steps may be taken. One major precaution is to take dumps, that is, copies of the data. This action is taken at regular intervals if the data are frequently changed; for example, the data may represent the quantity of various goods in a warehouse which changes every time an item is received or dispatched. In order to be able to restore a data base after it has been destroyed, it is merely necessary to get a copy of the last dump and update it. The updating makes use of an audit trail or log tape, which contains a history of the transactions affecting the data and generally also snapshots of data-base segments before and after a change. Thus by remaking all changes that were on the audit trail since the dump, the data base will be correctly restored to its most current image. The audit trail also allows the user to back-out an error (that is, to undo changes made in error) by going backward through the audit trail undoing all mistaken updates by using before-images of the data.

***Improved performance.*** The introduction of a data-base management system changes also the system's orientation. The emphasis on programs (that is, programs using data), shifts to data (that is, data used by programs). A new measurement of efficiency determines how effectively the data are used and stored, and how readily available the data are. The data-base management system becomes the focal point from which such measurement may be taken. They allow the data administrator to determine how well the schema fits user needs, and how well the storage structuring of the instances reflects the needs. Thus the data-base management system measurements help improve performance.

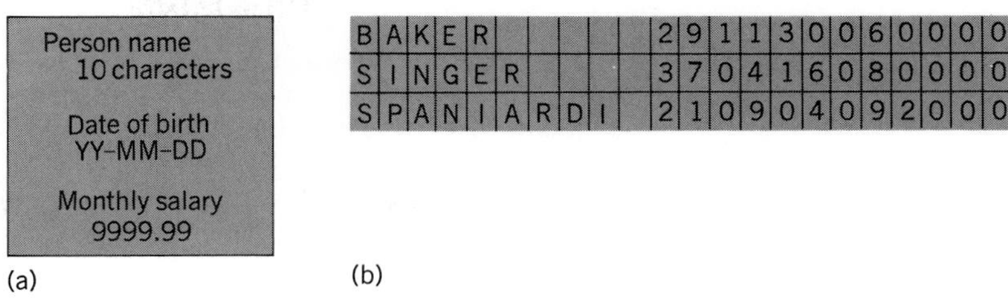


**Fig. 1. Simple schema representing (*a*) a very simple record structure and (*b*) its stored data base of three instances.**

In summary, the data-base management system provides a means for management of data by making available data to a large range of authorized users, while preserving the integrity of the data and improving the overall system performance.

**Architecture.** The somewhat simplified architecture of a data-base management system and its environment is shown in **Fig. 2**. It illustrates how a data request is satisfied. For example, consider the previous request for name and date of birth in the PERSON data base. An ad hoc user (that is, one who can query the system without having recourse to a previously coded program) goes to an input/output device with a keyboard or cathode-ray-tube (or both) combination. The person types in SIGNON JONES PASSWORD 51Z5QP, and

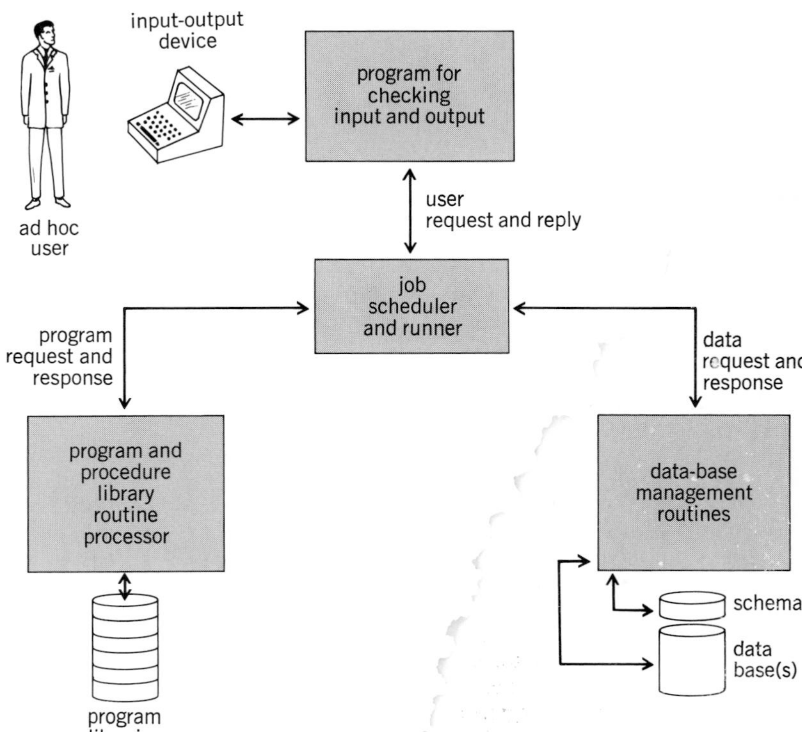


**Fig. 2. Architecture of a data-base management system.**

then (after some response) AD HOC DBMS FOR PERSON, FIND NAME AND DATE-OF-BIRTH WHERE SALARY GREATER THAN 700.00

The following operations will be performed: (1) The word SIGNON is transmitted by the checking program to the scheduler program which rquests the SIGNON program from its library. (2) The SIGNON program is run by the scheduler program to check that Jones has given the correct password. (3) The AD HOC program is called from the library and starts to look for more inputs. (4) The word PERSON is taken by this program as the name of the schema. (5) The scheduler program requests the data-base routine to load the PERSON schema from storage. (6) The next sentence is now checked to see whether NAME, DATE-OF-BIRTH, and SALARY are all valid words in the PERSON schema. (7) A search of the instances is made to determine which have a value of more than 700.00 in the SALARY item. In the above example, two people qualify. (8) The names and dates of birth of these two people are displayed for the user.

In this example, the authority of the user (Jones) to view any element (for example, date of birth) could be checked at step 6, if necessary.

This example demonstrates that the data-base management system consists of many routines that process data according to the schema. Many other special programs are associated with the data-base management system (such as the ad hoc query processor, the utilities to dump and restore the data base, and so forth). The data-base routines, in turn, use other operating system software such as access methods, input and output routines, and so forth. *SEE COMPUTER SYSTEMS ARCHITECTURE*.

**Modeling data.** Data can be used to represent important facts; a particular set of facts, with their relationships, are usage-dependent. For hiring a person, the attributes of importance (that is, the model needed) may be: date of birth, phone, address, sex, skills, and salary; however, for treating a person as a patient, the important model attributes are probably: date of birth, phone, address, sex, diseases, and so forth. Thus the important attributes represent the model of the entity under investigation.

Different data-base management systems model the data in different ways. The so-called relational system represents data as tables. The example in **Fig. 3** shows a unique identifier, or key, for a person (the Emp No, or employee number), and the person's date of birth, name, and salary. There must be only one line for each Emp No since this must be unique to a person. Moreover, the Education table, or Education relation, is linked to the person by the foreign key (Emp No) that has been added to the relation to identify which education relates to which person. The unique identifier for the Education relation is the concatenation of Emp No with School and Degree, since the three are needed to distinguish a line for a person who has two same degrees from different schools or two different degrees from the same school. No entry in the table contains more than one elementary value (for example, it would be impossible to have two salaries for BAKER).

Person

| Emp No | Date of birth | Name | Salary ($) |
|---|---|---|---|
| 204 | 29/11/30 | BAKER | 600. |
| 193 | 37/04/16 | SINGER | 900. |
| 067 | 21/09/04 | SPANIARDI | 920. |
| | | | |

Education

| Emp No | School | Degree | . . . |
|---|---|---|---|
| 067 | U OF MICH | BA | |
| 193 | HARVARD | BS | |
| 204 | OLD DOM | MS | |
| 204 | HARVARD | MS | |
| 193 | HARVARD | MS | |

**Fig. 3. Relational data base.**

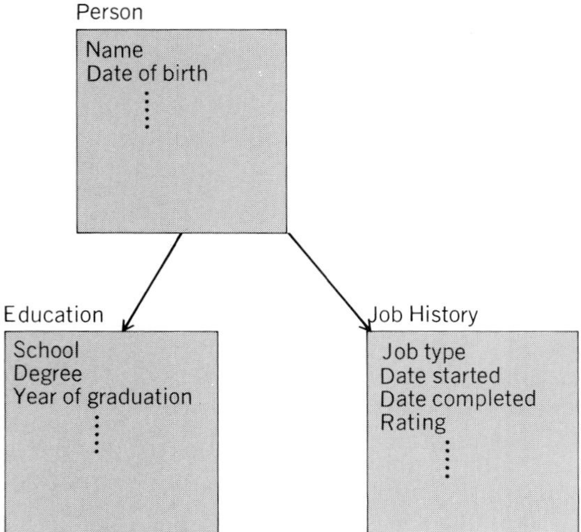


**Fig. 4. Hierarchical schema.**

The hierarchical system allows more structure. In this type of system, groupings of elements are connected by parent-child relationships (**Fig. 4**). Here, a particular person may have one or several different educational categories (high school, bachelor's degree, and so forth), as well as several job histories (office assistant, clerk, manager, president).

The network system has more structure and complexity, because it uses named relationships and more complexity. In the example given in **Fig. 5**, there are four groups (or record types) with four relations (or sets). Because these three types of systems are structurally different, most current commercial data-base management systems service only one type; future systems are expected to be able to allow the users to choose the best system to suit their special needs.

**Data-base administrator.** In order to utilize a data-base management system effectively, there must be one person or group within the organization that looks after the system and makes decisions about its control. Typical questions are: What is a good schema (that is, one that is effective for a mix of users with different needs)? How often should the data be dumped? How well is the system operating (that is, monitoring the time and volume of the data accesses, and so forth)? Such control parameters suggest the need for special skills, other than programming and management skills that were prevalent in the "old" data-processing environment. The role of data-base

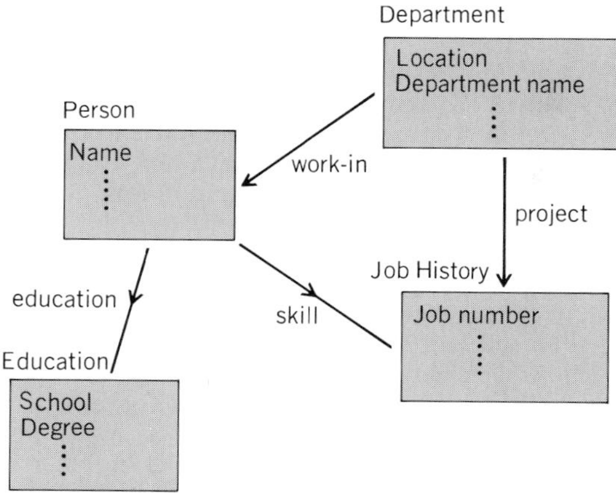


**Fig. 5. Network schema.**

administrator (DBA) has evolved to fill this need. The data-base administrator is a person or group that deals with corporate data, making decisions on the use, quality, access control, integrity needs, and so forth of all the data users of the organization.

**Data administration.** The management of the data in an organization involves both technical and administrative aspects, and implies more than a data-base administrator function, since the data-base administrator deals only with the technical part (for example, designing a data structure that is good for the set of organizational users). The more managerial role is assigned to a higher-level function, termed a data administrator (DA). This person is usually the manager of the data-base administrator.

The data administrator's position normally involves setting data policy, allocating resources in the data administrator group, and ensuring that the policies are carried out through control procedures enforced through the data administrator group. Naturally, because the data policy must mesh with the overall organizational policy, the data administrator acts as liaison officer with upper-level management in concerns affecting the data policy. The data administrator also acts as a liaison with user groups in all conflicts over data (such as ownership or sharing).

**Data dictionary.** Another essential function in a data-base management system is the recording of proper definitions of data entities. This implies some uniform way of storing and retrieving the information, and the software mechanism to achieve this is termed a data dictionary. The data dictionary requires a person or function termed the data dictionary administrator, reporting to the data administrator.

The data dictionary is like a schema; it records the names of data items and their structural relations, but it also carries definitions (in the form of a humanly understandable sentence or paragraph that describes the meaning or usage). This explanation aids in reducing misunderstanding due to homonyms and synonyms. A homonym occurs when two systems or users mean different things when they reference the same name (for example, a "full-time student" in an undergraduate school may differ from a "full-time student" in a medical school). A synonym occurs when two people give different names to the same entity (because neither knew that the other needed to use the same material). This may be an expensive problem because data may be unnecessarily collected and stored (when it already exists elsewhere), or it may be misused (when one user calls for it with the "wrong" name).

In addition, a data dictionary allows entitites other than data to be stored and manipulated, and relations may be defined between all entities. The implementor may ask: "What programs use the personnel file?" or "Which programmer wrote the accounts-receivable program?" This implies that there are entities like program, user, programmer, and so forth in the dictionary.

**Rapid prototyping.** As discussed above, the rapid-prototyping system is a means for easily defining a test system, so that users and implementers can try out their ideas and find if the requirements are being correctly stated or interpreted. The user of the rapid-prototyping system gives some input and output formats (generally through an interactive screen generator) and then relates the holes, or input positions, in the screen so generated to the data as defined in the schema and as recorded in the data dictionary. The user then provides the computational algorithms (usually in the form of a higher-level query language statement with parameters) and relates the algorithm/query to each screen, thereby showing which input screen triggers which algorithm and which screen is output from the data base using the algorithm. More complex control structures are normally allowed.

There are two somewhat different philosophies of rapid-prototyping systems:

1. Use the rapid-prototyping system as a proof of correctness of the original requirements specification; that is, ensure that the user will be satisfied if the ultimate system is designed and final-coded to the now approved specifications. The assumption here is that the inefficiencies of the rapid-prototyping–implemented system would be too great for a viable system, or that the prototype is a skeleton of the ultimate system. (Data validation and some batch transaction processing may be missing from the prototype.)

2. Iterate the rapid-prototyping system until it fully satisfies the customers and then freeze this as the production system. In this type of system, the user may be "paying" extra during running of the process, but have a good and sufficiently effective system to offset the added cost of a more efficient recoded system. Some systems are built with internal optimizers that allow the data administrator to improve the running by storage-device or schema adjustments and through a semicompilation step at the end of the rapid-prototyping system specification.

In the earliest use of this technique, in the late 1960s, users of the query-language interfaces of SYSTEM 2000 started to develop systems using the higher-level interface, and then (sometimes) made the implementation more efficient by coding the resulting system utilizing the COBOL or report generator interface. SYSTEM 2000 is a basically hierarchically modeled DBMS with any of the three possible means of data-base access (higher-level query language, report generator, and programming language, with the efficiency of the interface increasing in that order). Later, users of the NOMAD system (a combined hierarchical/relational DBMS) found also that it allowed them a fine rapid-prototyping capability. Some network models have sophisticated facilities for producing rapid-prototyping systems that are very efficient.

**Design and implementation.** The earliest commercially successful DBMS concentrated on the transaction processing market (which was the prime computing usage in the late 1960s). Possibly because of the preponderance of COBOL as a business programming language, estimated as the object language for 70% of all software systems, these systems often used a hierarchic approach. MARK IV and IMS (both having gone through many versions) are the major survivors from that era. The IMS system is essentially hierarchically structured, though it is possible to generate some internal structures that are networks, while retaining an essentially hierarchic programmer interface. The IMS system allows the data administrator to draw from four quite different accessing methods which have the indexed sequential access method (ISAM) and the direct (hashed) access method (DAM) as a general basis, but also allow the program to follow internal pointers that link repeating groups of the hierarchy.

The IDS (since upgraded as IDS II) was the earliest full data-base management system implementation on a commercial scale, and it introduced the network model. However, it was very effective as a transaction-processing system because the data administrator could choose the structures to have different accessing methods. For example, the Person record of Fig. 5 could be accessed by hashing (direct) accessing on the Emp No, while the Education record might be accessible only from the Person record by following pointers; meanwhile, the Department record might also be accessed by its name directly.

Both the early hierarchic and network styles of data-base management systems where primarily used as transaction-processing systems to implement systems that were mainly sequential in nature. However, by being able to follow pointers (logical or physical) around the data base, the programmer could plan a good implementation. This way of implementing a system has been termed a navigational system.

***Use of higher-level languages.*** The advent of systems that allowed the use of a higher-level language (such as SYSTEM 2000 and, later, the relational model) led to another type of system which had one major advantage: the user could formulate quite complex queries and present the answers in tabular or report form in a way well understood by most business and scientific personnel.

However, there was a potential disadvantage: there were possible inefficiencies in performing relatively complex operations, especially in handling large volumes of data in the interim (temporary) storage.

In practice, there are some difficulties in using a high-level language, because the user can be seduced into asking complex questions incorrectly (and getting the wrong answer but not knowing so). In fact, both SYSTEM 2000 and relational system users find it very easy for simple queries and some updates, but often experience difficulties in forming correct complex queries that involve quantifiers. On the other hand, the query languages are now driven by relatively sophisticated optimizers. These will generate a request for data that tries to minimize the volume of the data transferred while reducing the need for intermediate working storage.

***Optimization.*** Relational data-base management systems, as introduced theoretically in 1970, have been particularly studied with respect to optimization needs, and some effective heuristic algorithms have been developed. As an example, suppose a request, as formulated in some higher-level language, is: FOR PERSON, FIND NAME WHERE SALARY GREATER THAN 700.00 AND SCHOOL IS "HARVARD" (AND WHERE EMP NO IN PERSON = EMP NO IN EDUCATION). The parenthesized clause may not be needed if the system can infer the joining of the Person and Education relations based on the common named key (Emp No); this clause would also not be needed in a hierarchic structured system, such as SYSTEM 2000, where the relationship is explicit in the structure.

One possible way to implement the solution to this query is to take each clause and extract the necessary data for its solution, as follows:

1. Search the Person table to produce a temporary table (A) with those lines where salary is greater than 700.00.

2. Search the Education table to give a temporary table (b) where "school = 'Harvard.' "

3. Join A and B by using the common column "Emp No"—the combined table (C).

4. Eliminate all columns except name, but remove any duplicates to give the answer.

Assuming the tables of Fig. 3, the process is illustrated in **Fig. 6**.

Other methods are possible, such as:

1. Search the Person table to produce a temporary table (A) with those lines where salary is greater than 700.00.

2. Search the Education table for the same Emp No as in temporary table A to give temporary table D.

3. Eliminate from D those schools not Harvard.

4. Join D and A.

5. Eliminate all columns except name, but remove any duplicates to give the answer.

This is obviously similar to but not the same as:

1. Search the Education table to give a temporary table (B) where "school = 'Harvard.' "

Table A

| Emp No | Date of birth | Name | Salary ($) |
|---|---|---|---|
| 204 | 37/04/16 | SINGER | 900. |
| 193 | 21/09/04 | SPANIARDI | 920. |

Table B

| Emp No | School | Degree | |
|---|---|---|---|
| 193 | HARVARD | BS | |
| 204 | HARVARD | MS | |
| 193 | HARVARD | MS | |

Table C

| Emp No | Date of birth | Name | Salary ($) | School | Degree |
|---|---|---|---|---|---|
| 204 | 37/04/16 | SINGER | 900. | HARVARD | MS |
| 193 | 21/09/04 | SPANIARDI | 920. | HARVARD | BS |
| 193 | 21/09/04 | SPANIARDI | 920. | HARVARD | MS |

Answer table

| Name |
|---|
| SINGER |
| SPANIARDI |

**Fig. 6. Solution method for a relational query.**

2. Search the Person table to obtain only those lines with the same Emp No.

3. Eliminate all columns except name, but remove any duplicates to give the answer.

In discussing these solutions, the size of the intemediate tables and the number of operations will be seen to depend on the statistics of the data base, as well as the type and complexity of the question. If the question is changed slightly, the best solution for the original question may not be the best for the new one. For example, suppose there are 2000 people in the data base who went to Harvard, but only 5 with a salary greater than $700.00. It is then best to start by finding the Emp No that have a high salary and then see whether these went to Harvard. In contradistinction, if only 5 went to Harvard, but 2000 earn more than $700.00, the best method is to find the Harvardians, and see if they have the salary qualification.

The dilemma of writing generalized software is therefore being replaced by heuristic optimizers in the query language. These mechanisms work on a set of algorithms and sometimes use the probabilities of occurrence of an element as the way of constructing the best-path solution. Many artificial intelligence and operations research techniques are being incorporated, and sampling and branch and bound methods are very popular. Storage structure techniques, such as the availability of inverted keys (hashed values) and internal links (because even relational systems may benefit from internally maintained nontable structure), can also be included in the algorithm, and the resulting process may be quite different because of this. *See Artificial intelligence; Operational research.*

As a further example, the need for a search on school is greater if it is highly restrictive, yet some simple systems will always use an algorithm that selects on available inverted keys, thereby often giving large sets of possible intermediate values that are difficult to manipulate. For one large data base, the selection may be based on a person's nationality and date of birth. Now both of these columns have been inverted (their keys are in an inverted file structure), and a given nationality will produce several million possible answers while the date of birth gives only a hundred or so people. Unfortunately, the simple algorithm requires the two sets of selected records to be sorted and then merged: the consequent slow performance is not to user satisfaction.

In addition, a data dictionary allows entities other than data to be stored and manipulated, and relations may be defined between all entities. The implementor may ask: "What programs use the personnel file?" or "Which programmer wrote the accounts-receivable program?" This implies that there are entities like program, user, and programmer in dictionary.

***Success factors.*** Although commercial offerings of data-base mangement systems have existed since the early 1960s, they have not always been successful. The degree of success depends on the expectations and resources, and often the expectations have been too high and the resources too low.

Many early failures were due to poor planning, lack of corporate commitment to the concept, or misapplication. The truly integrated data base requires a good management structure, as described for the data administrator and good technical support through the data-base administrator and systems programmers. If integration needs are not carefully assessed, unnecessarily large, monolithic data bases are formed, the result being poor performance and extra expense. Equally, the data-base management system should not be considered a new toy or merely a sophisticated access method. Thus good planning is needed to decide what is right for each organization. The degree of commitment of upper-level management is also critical to the success of a data-base management system. Data policy must not be changed rapidly or radically; otherwise the data-base structure and procedures will be forced to change just as quickly and problems will result. Thus, the major success factor in the implementation of the information system is a good, stable organizational plan for the management of data, with proper resource allocation, and structural change to allow for the new data administrator and data-base administrator roles in the organization.

The second success factor results from everyone understanding the meaning and use of the data. This strongly implies the use of a data dictionary. The third success factor is a good data structure. There are several design aids that have been developed for specific data-base management systems. They allow the data-base administrator to try various data structures for an anticipated usage, and thus they provide a means of tuning the structure for good performance. Such design aids have become the most important tools for the data-base administrator. The fourth success factor is programming good systems to access the data. This implies the use of a professional application systems group who know and understand the use of data-base management systems in general, and the selected system in particular.

The final success factor is providing user facilities, which might involve query language interfaces. These are available in many modern commercial data-base management systems, and they can be added on. Report generators (RPG) are also effective tools for the end user. The usefulness of these facilities depends on the education and support functions provided by the data administrator office so that noncomputer professionals can formulate simple queries and request reports without contacting the data-processing professionals. *See Data-processing systems; Digital computer.*

**Three-schema data-base methodology.** The need to provide data to organizations in a controlled environment has led to the rapid adoption of the data-base technology, with still some distress on the part of users who need to have better access sooner. One of the problems that was addressed by a committee of the American National Standards Institute (ANSI), formed in 1972 to consider the need for standardization, was data independence. This is a somewhat misunderstood or ill-defined term; generally it is used to imply a minimum interaction between the way the user understands or "sees" the data and the way it is physically stored. However, as the above examples show, there is often a strange interaction between the logical and physical storage structure, and data independence is an attempt to reduce this. In particular, the relationships represented by the data and those relationships either explicitly stated or implied in the data are often very complex in an organization.

These considerations led to the idea that there were at least three kinds of schema needed by an organization:

1. External schema. This represented the data in the way that the users needed the data where users were considered as either programmers, transaction

processing initiators (for example, airline ticket agents or bank tellers), computer-aided design/computer-aided manufacturing (CAD/CAM) system users, or ad hoc query system users. Needs of these classes of user will span the entire range of possibilities of data models, from tables for some clerks and managers to complex hierarchies or networks for the representation of parts and components in a CAM system. Though some commercial systems now have multiple interfaces (for example, IDMS has both network and relational interfaces to the same data base), some problems still arise in general. The idea of a multiplicity of different model views is, however, now being realized.

2. Internal schema. The use of a single schema to represent the way the system stores and relates the data is central to the data-base concept. Thus the idea of an internal schema allows the data-base administrator to decide what internal efficiencies and storage methods are appropriate for the organization and possibly also how they are mapped to the external schema.

3. Conceptual schema. Having realized that the real problems in data independence occurred because the relationship between the internal and external schema was neither simple nor stable, the committee decided that there was a need to isolate them, if possible, by making them both map to something that was more stable, the enterprise view of the data. Presumably this was not changing very fast, and thus if it could be captured in a new schema, it could form a more stable basis for design and modification of the system. The idea was therefore to relate the two other schemas through the conceptual schema (**Fig. 7**), mapping each to it so that the resulting mappings (I-to-C and E-to-C) could be changed independently of one another.

Since the three-schema architecture was proposed, there have been many research and development efforts aimed at exploiting the idea. In some of these, the conceptual schema is considered to be merely the agglomeration of all other schema presented in some slightly more consistent and palatable form. However, this somewhat subverts the intent of the original proposal: to provide a stable platform in a time of change. However, all systems that have tried to implement the concept are in a reserach (noncommercial) state, and thus the feasibility of the concept has not been tested.

*Edgar H. Sibley*

**Bibliography.** S. Atre, *Data Base: Structured Techniques for Design, Performance, and Management*, 1980; *Database Engineering*, IEEE Computer Society Technical Committee, quarterly; H. C. Lefkovits, E. H. Sibley, and S. L. Lefkovits, *Information Resource/Data Dictionary Systems*, 1983; *Transactions on Database Systems*, Association for Computing Machinery, bimonthly; E. A. Unger, P. S. Fisher, and J. Slonim (eds.), *Advances in Data Base Management*, vol. 2, 1984.

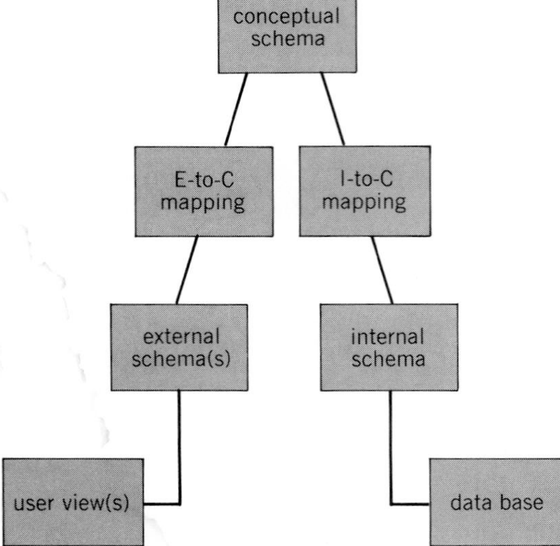


**Fig. 7.** Three-schema architecture. There will be as many user views as there are major classes of user. If there is a distributed data base, there may be several internal schema with consistency checks between them in the I-to-C mapping.

## Data communications

The function of electronically conveying digitally encoded information from a source to a destination where the source and destination may be displaced in space (distance) and time. Encoded information can represent alphabetic, numeric, and graphic forms. Such information may originate as keystrokes at a terminal, as images on a page, as motion of a hand-held stylus, as a signal from some electrical or mechanical measurement device, or as output from a computer. The data communications function includes management and control of connections as well as the actual transfer of information.

Digitally encoded information typically takes the form of a series of 1's and 0's called bits (contraction for binary digit). Groups of eight bits are often referred to as bytes. Standard codes (such as ASCII and EBCDIC) have been adopted to establish a correspondence between bytes (patterns of eight bits) and alphabetic, numeric, and commonly used graphic and control characters. These codes are used for the interchange of information among equipments made by different manufacturers. *See Bit.*

Data communications usually do not refer to the conveyance of voice and video, although these too may be digitally encoded and then conveyed in digital form just as data are conveyed. The increased use of computers in the design and implementation of communications systems and the efficiencies realized from the handling of digitally encoded information have markedly broadened the range of data communications, and tend to mask old distinctions between data communications and other forms of information transfer.

Data communications has evolved from a function serving simple terminal-to-terminal communications (telegraphy) to one dominated by communications with and among computers. Terminal-to-computer communications remains a sizable component of traffic, but the migration of intelligence into terminal systems (an aspect of distributed processing) is causing terminals to take on more of the communications characteristics of computers. Networks of terminals and computers are serving the needs of business, education, government, industry, medicine, recreation, and other forms of human endeavor. These systems, both publicly and privately owned and operated, manage and direct the movement of data between stations (terminals, computers, and other sources of digitally encoded information) and across networks. Where two stations are geographically separated, data communications manages the transfer of information as a displacement in space. Where there is value in delaying the transfer of information, data communications manages the transfer also as a displacement in time (**Fig. 1**). Access to and the movement of information have become activities of great social and commercial importance. *See Computer; Multiaccess computer.*

**Types of applications.** Data communications applications fall into three principal categories: transaction-oriented, message-oriented, and batch-oriented (**Fig. 2**). Transaction-oriented applications (Fig. 2*a*) involve the transfer of small amounts of data in the range of tens to hundreds of bytes and frequently require minimal delay in the transfer process. Transaction-oriented applications are typically bidirectional or conversational. Information is exchanged between source and destination stations. Examples are inquiry-response, information retrieval, and time-sharing, where people at terminals are communicating with large computers. For these applications, data communications serves stations displaced in space. Travel agents inquiring about seat availability, insurance agents inquiring about policy status, researchers accessing data banks, assembly-line process control, 24-hour bank tellers, merchants performing credit checks, computers monitoring life support systems, and retailers updating inventory status are examples of transaction-oriented applications.

Message-oriented applications (Fig. 2*b*) involve data transfers in the range of hundreds to a few thousand bytes or characters and are usually unidirectional, information flows from source to destination. Message applications frequently take advantage of time displacement (store and forward) as well as space displacement, and they exhibit data transfer options which go beyond the simple movement of information between two points. Examples of message-oriented applications are the transmittal of administrative messages within a corporate entity, the distribution of press releases, and price list updates being sent to field offices. Data entry uses, such as sales order processing, where information is collected from many sources for delivery to one or several destinations at some later time represent a large component of activity. Single messages carrying multiple addresses, addresses in the form of mnemonics (easily remembered names), requirements to journal (store) messages and to confirm the delivery of messages are examples of functions being served by data communications systems. Messages may be originated at terminals or in computers.

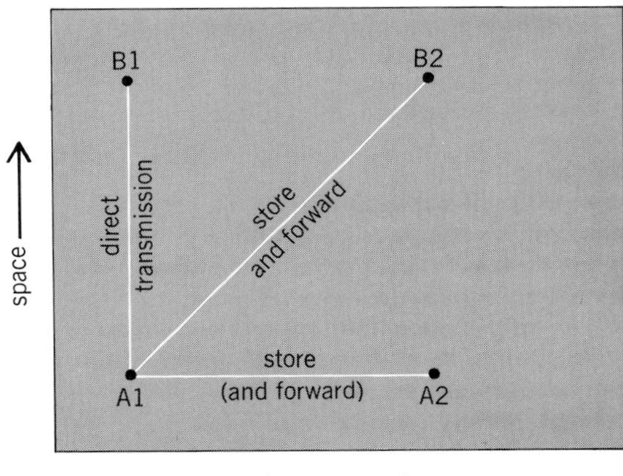


Fig. 1. Data communciations involving displacements in both space (distance) and time. Points A1 and B1 are separated by distance; the movement of data from A1 to B1 involves a displacement in space. Points A1 and B2 are separated by both distance and time; transfers between A1 and B2 require data to be stored by the data communications system before delivery. Points A1 and A2 are displaced in time but not in distance; for this case, data are transmitted, stored, and then returned to the originating station.

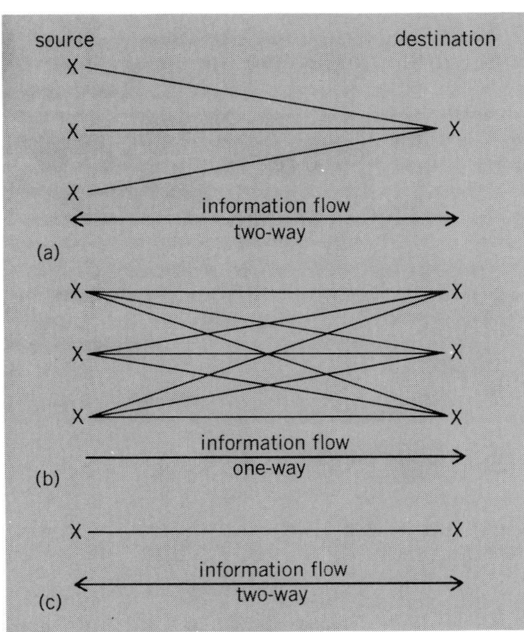


Fig. 2. Three principal categories of data communications. (*a*) Transaction-oriented. (*b*) Message-oriented. (*c*) Batch-oriented.

Batch-oriented applications (Fig. 2*c*) involve the transfer of thousands or even millions of bytes of data and are usually point-to-point (place-to-place) and computer-to-computer. Moving work from one computer to another (remote job entry), distributing the results of some centralized data-processing function, facsimile transmission, and updating distributed copies of data bases from some central site are examples of batch-oriented applications.

Transaction, message, and batch-oriented applications exhibit different needs in terms of total bytes transferred, delay, and special features. Consequently, they impose different demands upon the functional components of data communications: media conversion, communications processing, and transmission (**Fig. 3**).

**Media conversion.** Media conversion achieves the conversion of some input, such as a keyboard keystroke, graphic material, a signal representing some measurement, and information recorded on magnetic media such as tape or disk, into a digitally encoded signal which may be transmitted. Likewise, it achieves the conversion of a digitally encoded signal into similar forms of useful output. Typical media conversion devices such as card reader/punches, paper tape reader/punches, magnetic tape systems, and printers remain in use. However, the proliferation of data communications applications where people at terminals converse with computers has caused media conversion to be most often associated with the interactive terminal. Input is typically supported by a keyboard device, while output takes the form of a hard-copy printer or screen display. The latter may be a cathode-ray-tube device (television monitor), a plasma panel, or a light-emitting diode (LED) or liq-

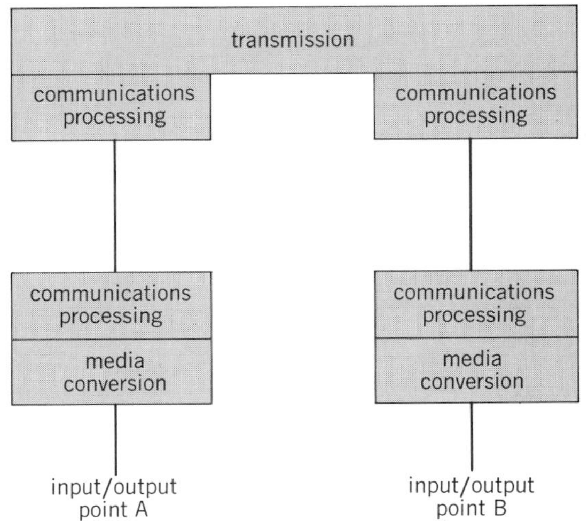


Fig. 3. Relationship of three functional components of data communications: media conversion, communications processing, and transmission.

uid-crystal array. Point-of-sale stations are interactive terminals which include both keyboard entry and laser- or magnetic-actuated pattern recognition devices for inputs.

The migration of intelligence into terminals in the form of storage and processing has enabled the use of all kinds of sensory devices as inputs and outputs. Optical character recognition, spoken-word recognition, tactile panels, light pens, facsimile devices, and x-y encoders all serve as input devices. Multicolor graphic displays, voice synthesizers, microfiche generators, and robots (mechanical servos) represent other important forms of output. Storage in the forms of floppy disks and magnetic bubble arrays are supplementing the more conventional cassette tape, and highly compact forms of storage such as video (optical memory) disks can be expected to be used as well. SEE CHARACTER RECOGNITION; COMPUTER GRAPHICS; COMPUTER STORAGE TECHNOLOGY; ELECTRONIC DISPLAY; SPEECH RECOGNITION; VOICE RESPONSE.

**Communications processing.** Communications processing provides the management and control in data communications systems. In the data terminal or media conversion system, it must at least manage the protocol (rules) used for intelligibly exchanging information with other stations including the administration of techniques designed to detect errors in transmission. Depending on the application, it may be necessary to perform code conversion and to multiplex or concentrate inputs from several terminals into a single output stream. It may also be desirable to augment variable data input via keyboard with fixed or automatically generated data such as date, time, operator identity, or location. The communications-processing function organizes encoded data into units suitable for transmission. Simple protocols demand that data be organized into single bytes. More complex and efficient protocols require the organization of bytes into blocks (hundreds of bytes) or bits into frames (**Fig. 4**). Blocks and frames typically begin with recognizable patterns of bytes and bits respectively. Still more sophisticated protocols include the organization and management of logical units of information ranging in size from 50 to about 1000 bytes called packets or messages.

For point-to-point transaction- or batch-oriented data communications applications involving only space displacement, little more is required of communications processing. For network applications, communications processing uses storage and processing to assure the proper addressing and formatting of packets and messages. To support time displacement, communications processing enables information to be stored for later retrieval, scheduled for later delivery, and delivered with return confirmation.

**Transmission.** Transmission accomplishes the physical transfer of data. It includes the provision of transmission channels, the signal conversions necessary to use such channels, and any required switching among channels.

Terminals and computers may be connected to transmission facilities via standardized interfaces. Where dedicated wire paths of up to a few miles can be established, so-called limited distance or baseband data sets (modems) enable the digital transmission of data at rates up to tens of thousands of bits per second (bps). At shorter distances, transmissions at more than 1,000,000 bits per second can be supported. Dedicated paths using optical fibers can support transmissions at rates of tens of millions of bits per second. Approaches such as infrared transmission enable open-air channels to be supported. Radio and satellite transmission are used as well. SEE OPTICAL COMMUNICATIONS.

***Use of telephone network.*** Since it is generally impractical to install privately owned cables beyond single buildings or campus environments and because transmission distances of more than a few miles are commonly of interest, the conventional approach is to use the telephone network for transmission facilities. Where such facilities are analog (such as channels which support voice signals), modems are required to convert the digitally encoded information produced at the terminal or computer into modulated analog form, and vice versa. Where digital facilities are available at a user's location, no analog-digital conversion is necessary, but a device to assure synchronization of timing signals and to perform other control functions must be used. SEE ANALOG-TO-DIGITAL CONVERTER; DIGITAL-TO-ANALOG CONVERTER; MODULATION.

Channels may be provided on a dedicated (private line) or switched (dial) basis. Dedicated channels may be used for multipoint connections which serve several terminals (**Fig. 5**). For such multipoint configurations, a polling scheme is used to assure that the channel is used by only one terminal at a time. Dedicated channels are commonly available to support rates up to 56,000 bits per second. Special arrangements can result in channels to support rates of

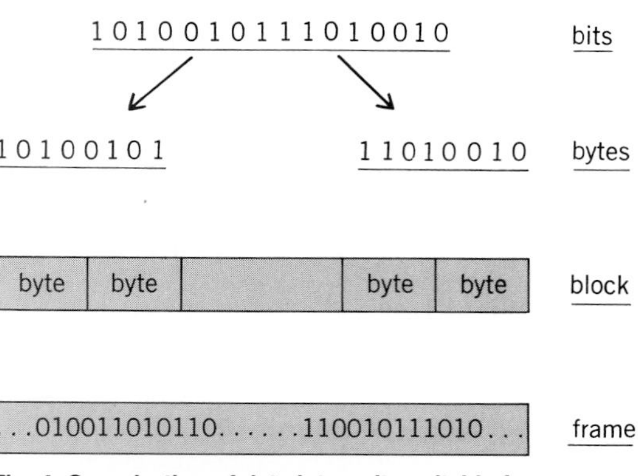


Fig. 4. Organization of data into units suitable for transmission.

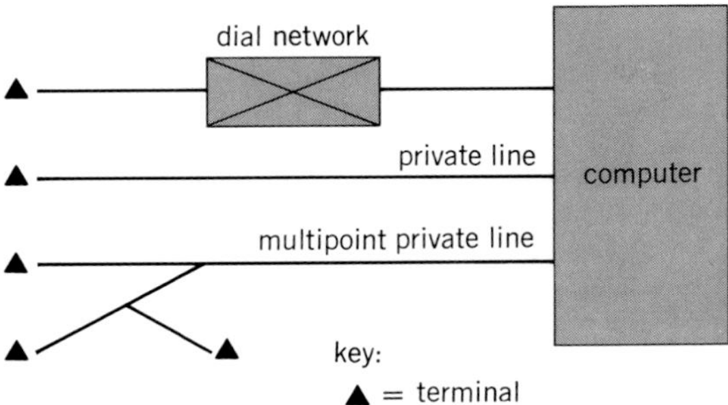


**Fig. 5. Connection arrangements for terminals and computers.**

230,400 and 1,544,000 bits per second. Dial channels typically support up to 4800 bits per second; higher rates may be supported under special circumstances.

***Asynchronous and synchronous transmission.*** Asynchronous and synchronous modes of transmission are used. In asynchronous transmission, bytes of data are transmitted independently of one another. Each byte begins with a start bit and ends with at least one stop bit. The time between bytes of data transmitted is variable. Asynchronous transmission is used at low speeds to support simple protocols used by low-cost terminals. Typical speeds are 75, 110, 134.5, 150, 300, 600, and 1200 bits per second full duplex (in both directions simultaneously). Synchronous transmission is more efficient than asynchronous transmission and is used to support more complex and efficient protocols. There are no start or stop bits. Data bits [for bit-synchronous protocols like X.25, derived by CLITT, an international standards body] or bytes [for byte-synchronous protocols like BSC (Binary Synchronous Communications) X3.28, defined by ANSI, an American standards body] follow one another in a precisely timed and correlated way.

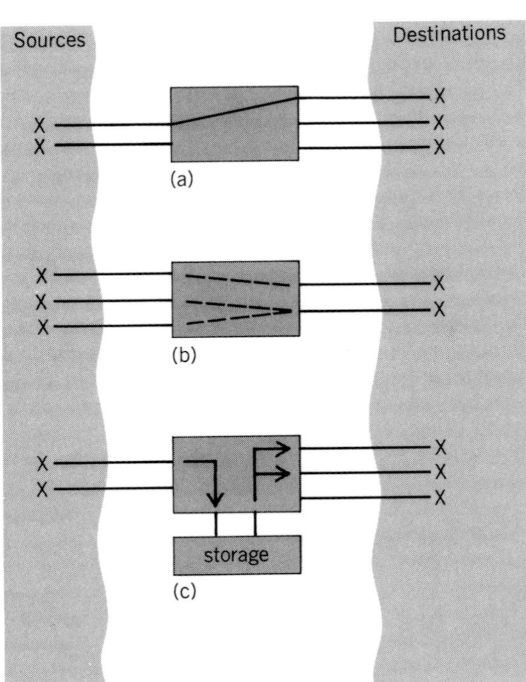


**Fig. 6. Switching in data communications system. (*a*) Circuit switch. (*b*) Packet switch. (c) Message switch.**

Typical speeds for dedicated channels are 2400, 4800, 9600, 19,200, and 56,000 bits per second full duplex. Typical dial speeds are 2400 and 4800 bits per second.

***Switching.*** To support applications where communications among multiple stations is required, data communications systems offer switching beyond that available in the dial switching capabilities of the telephone network. Circuit switching, packet switching, and message switching are the common forms (**Fig. 6**). Circuit (line) switching (Fig. 6*a*) results in the establishment of point-to-point channels, single-circuit paths where there is a direct connection between the incoming and outgoing lines to the switch, for the duration of a desired transmission. It is most suitable for batch-oriented applications.

Packet switching (Fig. 6*b*) permits a single access channel to be used for multiple concurrent transmissions. Data to be transmitted to different destinations are formed into packets to which addresses are assigned. These packets with variable addresses are output onto a transmission channel to be switched by a packet switch to their intended destinations. Likewise, packets received on a single transmission channel may have originated at different sources. In packet switching, packets are typically received, instantaneously stored, and then retransmitted over an appropriate outgoing line. There is no direct connection between the incoming and outgoing lines as in circuit switching. It is the role of a protocol handler to multiplex (mix or intersperse) packets into a single stream of data to be transmitted and to demultiplex (sort or separate) received packets into independent streams of data. Packet switching is most suitable for short transaction-oriented transmissions where multiple concurrent transmissions must be supported between a serving computer and remote terminals.

Message switching (Fig. 6*c*) is most suitable for message-oriented applications. A message switch performs communications processing as well as switching in managing the storage and distribution of messages. Whereas packets are most often created for the benefit of conveying information, including messages, messages are logical entities which represent the full informational content of a transaction and thus may be manipulated in more complex ways than packets. In message switching, a message is typically received, stored, and then retransmitted over an appropriate outgoing line at an appropriate time. As in packet switching, there is no direct connection between the incoming and outgoing lines. SEE ELECTRICAL COMMUNICATIONS; SWITCHING SYSTEMS (COMMUNICATIONS); VIDEOTEXT AND TELETEXT.

*Mark M. Rochkind*

***Bibliography.*** D. W. Davies et al., *Computer Networks and Their Protocols*, 1979; T. Housley, *Data Communications and Teleprocessing Systems*, 1979; M. E. Loomis, *Data Communications*, 1983; J. Martin, *Systems Analysis for Data Transmission*, 1972; R. Techo, *Data Communications: An Introduction to Concepts and Design*, 1980.

## Data compression

Reduction of the number of bits required to represent information. Information in a computer is represented as a sequence of bits. Usually, this representation is derived in a straightforward way, such as by using a

**Table 1. Huffman codes for "the cat saw the rat"**

| Character | Count | Probability, % | Information content | Huffman code |
|---|---|---|---|---|
| *space* | 4 | 21 | 2.25 | 000 |
| a | 3 | 16 | 2.66 | 001 |
| c | 1 | 5 | 4.25 | 0100 |
| e | 2 | 10 | 3.25 | 100 |
| h | 2 | 10 | 3.25 | 101 |
| r | 1 | 5 | 4.25 | 0101 |
| s | 1 | 5 | 4.25 | 0110 |
| t | 4 | 21 | 2.25 | 11 |
| w | 1 | 5 | 4.25 | 0111 |

7- or 8-bit code (for example, ASCII or EBCDIC) to represent each character in the alphabet. Data compression is the technique of finding a shorter bit representation for the same information. Compression is desirable in computer and communications systems for two principal reasons: first, current data bases contain vast amounts of data, and compression can reduce by two-thirds the amount of computer storage occupied. Second, large quantities of data are often transmitted rom one location to another, and reducing the number of bits for a given amount of information increases the effective rate of transmission.

All data compression schemes take advantage of the fact that some bit sequences are more common than others. The common sequences are given shorter representations at the expense of the uncommon ones which must be given longer representations. Overall, the average length of the data is less, although some sequences may be longer. Compression is of little use without expansion, the ability to reproduce the original information from its compressed form.

The field of mathematics known as information theory determines that the minimum number of bits required to represent a sequence (its entropy or information content) is given by expression (1), where $p$

$$-\log_2 p \tag{1}$$

is probability of the sequence in a given context. For example, in English, following the letter $q$ it may be predicted that the letter $u$ appears with 93.75% probability and that a period appears with 6.25% probability. In this context the information content of $u$ is 0.093 bits and the information content of a period is 4.0 bits. In an abstract sense, the problem of data compression is twofold: estimating the probability of each sequence, and determining a coding scheme whose length approximates the information content. In practical data compression methods, it is often difficult to separate the two.

**Huffman's method.** In a popular compression method due to D. Huffman, a sample of data is examined to count the number of times each character occurs. These counts are assumed to be proportional to the probability of each character, and a bit representation for each character is determined that is as close as possible to the predicted information content. Expansion is done in sequence; that is, the compressed bits are examined one at a time until the representation for a character is recognized. This process continues to recognize the next compressed character, and so on.

From the sample of data (2), the characters are counted and the Huffman codes in **Table 1** are determined. The compressed representation of (2) is there-

**"the cat saw the rat"** (2)

fore sequence (3). Huffman's method as described

**111011000000100001110000110001011100011101100000010100111** (3)

here can be expected to compress English text (including uppercase and lowercase, punctuation, and spacing) to between 4 and 5 bits per letter (as opposed to 7 or 8 bits for ASCII or EBCDIC).

The Huffman codes are calculated backward. The two least probable characters (in this example, **s** and **w**) will eventually be given codes that differ only in the last bit (the code for **s** ends in **0** and that for **w** ends in **1**). The code for the common prefix (**011**) is unknown at this stage, but its probability is equal to the sum of the two least probabilities (10.5%). In the remaining steps, this prefix is treated as an imaginary character (denoted **sw**) for which a Huffman code is to be found; the two individual characters are not considered further. With **sw** subsituted for **s** and **w**, the above process is repeated until only two characters remain. The complete sequence of steps is given in **Table 2**. (The *space* character is denoted by **β**.) After step 7, there are only two remaining prefixes: **βacrsw** and **eht**, which are given codes **0** and **1**, respectively. Next, **βa**, **crsw**, **eh**, and **t** are assigned **00**, **01**, **10**, and **11**. Once these codes are known, they can be constructed for **β**, **a**, **cr**, **sw**, **e**, and **h**: **000**, **001**, **010**, **011**, **100**, and **101**. Finally, the codes for **c**, **r**, **s**, and **w** are determined to be **0100**, **0101**, **0110**, and **0111**.

**Dictionary encoding.** In most text, such as English, longer sequences such as words can easily be recognized. Assuming these words are stored in a dictionary, each word in the data to be compressed may be replaced by a number which is the position of that word in the dictionary. Typically, these nubmers have a shorter representation than the words themselves.

**Table 2. Steps in calculation of Huffman code**

| Step | Least probable codes | | Common prefix |
|---|---|---|---|
| 1 | **s** (5.25%) | **w** (5.25%) | **sw** (10.5%) |
| 2 | **c** (5.25%) | **r** (5.25%) | **cr** (10.25%) |
| 3 | **e** (10.5%) | **h** (10.5%) | **eh** (21%) |
| 4 | **cr** (10.5%) | **sw** (10.5%) | **crsw** (21%) |
| 5 | **β** (21%) | **a** (16%) | **βa** (37%) |
| 6 | **eh** (21%) | **t** (21%) | **eht** (42%) |
| 7 | **βa** (37%) | **crsw** (21%) | **βacrsw** (58%) |

For example, with dictionary (4) and data (5), the

**cat, frog, garden, in, rat, saw, the** (4)

**"the cat saw the rat in the garden"** (5)

compressed representation would be sequence (6). In

**7 1 6 7 5 4 7 3** (6)

this example, **the** is replaced by **7** because it is the seventh word in the dictionary; **cat** is replaced by **1** because it is the first word in the dictionary; and so on. Since there are 7 words in the dictionary, each number can be represented as 3 bits, for a total size of 24 bits. In a large amount of text, such as a book, no more than a few thousand different words are expected; if there were 65,536 words, each word would be represented by 16 bits. For typical English text, the dictionary representation uses 3 to 4 bits per character. It is possible to apply Huffman's method to the codes produced by the dictionary method to achieve further compression.

A number of methods build a dictionary dynamically while compressing a sequence of data, rather than relying on an existing one. One approach is to keep a dictionary of only the most recent *n* words that have appeared in the data, where *n* is some constant, usually between 100 and 10,000. All commonly used words will remain in the dictonary, and exceptional words that are not in the dictionary are represented in some other manner (such as ASCII or EBCDIC). A very simple variant on this method is to store the entire sequence of data that has already been compressed. When a new sequence is to be compressed, the stored sequence is searched to see if it contains the new one. If it does, the new sequence is represented as its position in the stored one. For example, if the data process so far were given by (7), the next

**"the cat saw the rat in"** (7)

data **the** could be represented either as **1** or as **13**.

**Ziv-Lempel compression.** It is time-consuming to search the entire stored sequence, and a fast method has been developed by J. Ziv and A. Lempel that stores only some of the previous sequences but achieves results slightly better than the dictionary schemes. This method, unlike the dictionary methods, requires no prior knowledge about what constitutes a word in the data. For many practical applications, Ziv and Lempel's is the method of choice.

Ziv-Lempel compression begins with a dictonary containing every character in the alphabet. During compression, the dictionary is searched to find the longest string that is a prefix of the text yet to be compressed. The compressed representation of the string is its position in the dictionary. Then a new string, formed from the string just compressed and the upcoming character in the text, is added to the dictionary. Compression continues as described above, using the enlarged dictionary and the remainder of the text. For example, with the initial dictionary given by (8), the string (9) is encoded by the Ziv-Lempel method as sequence (10). The first letter **t** is encoded

**β a c e h r s t w** (8)

**"the cat saw the rat"** (9)

**8 5 4 1 3 2 8 1 7 2 9 1 10 12 6 15** (10)

as **8** and the string **th** is added to the dictionary. The second letter **h** is encoded as **5** and **he** is added to the dictionary, and so on. Eventually, the string **th** is encountered again (after compressing **"the cat saw"**) and is represented as **10** (its position in the dictionary). Then the string **the** is added to the dictionary. Following **th**, the string **eβ** is encoded as **12** and the new string **eβr** is added to the dictionary. Finally, **r** and **at** are encoded as **6** and **15**. At the end of the text the dictionary contains the entries given by (11).

**β a c e h r s t w th he eβ βc ca**
**at tβ βs sa as wβ βt the eβr ra** (11)

**Arithmetic coding.** Compression methods have been developed that separate the two aspects of data compression, that is, estimating the probability of each character and producing an optimal code based on the estimate. These methods hinge on arithmetic coding which, for any probability, can produce a representation that is arbitrarily close to the corresponding information content. Arithmetic coding involves representing a long string of characters as a single number.

Arithmetic coding is most simply illustrated by using a two-character alphabet (**a** and **b**) with fixed probabilites (80 and 20%, respectively). The text to be compressed is (12). Proceeding one character at a

**abaabaaabaaaab** . . . (12)

time, as many characters as possible are represented as an 8-bit number between 0 and 255. The range of possible values is partitioned in proportion to the probabilities of the characters: any number in the lower 80% of the range (0–204) represents **a** and any number in the upper 20% (205–255) represents **b**. Since the first character is **a**, the lower part of the range must be chosen, and the upper part is discarded. Again, this reduced range (0–204) is partitioned: the values 0–163 represent **a** and the values 164–204 represent **b**. The next character in the text is **b**, so the lower half of the range is discarded, and the encoded value must be in the range 164–204. This process of partitioning the range of values and encoding characters continues until the range contains only one number; that single number represents the string of characters. This example results in the sequence of ranges 0–255, 0–204, 164–204, 164–196, 164–189, 185–189, 185–188, 185–187, 187. The final value 187 represents string (13). From the char-

**abaabaaab** (13)

acter probabilities, the information content of this string is calculated to be 7.9 bits. Decoding takes place by reproducing the partitioning steps. At each step the number 187 is compared to see which partition it fits in: if it is in the lower range, the next decoded character is **a**, otherwise **b**. The range not containing the decoded character is discarded, and the process continues.

If each character is given a static probability, the amount of compression is nearly identical to that achieved by Huffman coding. However, it is not necessary to use unvarying estimates for the character probabilities; any knowledge whatsoever about the text may be used to predict upcoming characters. If a more accurate prediction is made, compression is improved. In example (12), it appears quite likely that the upcoming characters are given by (14). The prob-

**aaaaabaaaaaabaaaaaaab** . . . (14)

lem of making accurate probability estimates is a subject of current research. Current methods involve building a model to represent the data processed so far, and using that model to predict upcoming bits. Models that predict the next character based on the previous few characters can now compress English text to between 2 and 3 bits per character. C. Shannon conjectured that the actual information content of English is about 1.4 bits per character. Recent data compression techniques are challenging that bound.

**Special-purpose techniques.** In addition to the general techniques described above, a number of data compression methods developed with a particular purpose are in common use. These techniques generally rely on the data having a special form but still take advantage of the principles of information theory. Digram encoding relies on the fact that there are unused characters in the alphabet, and uses these characters to represent common pairs of characters. For example, English text could be reduced in size by replacing the digrams **th**, **an**, and **ie** by single characters. Run-length encoding encodes strings of the same character as a single number (a repetition factor). In English, run-length encoding is of little use, but in computer data, runs of special characters such as *space* or *underscore* might be expected. Difference encoding takes advantage of a sequence of data that differs little from one value to the next (for example, hourly temperature readings at a fixed location). Each value is encoded as the difference from the previous value. The advantage is that, because the differences are smaller than the actual values, they may be represented in fewer bits. Leading character elimination is used in dictionaries stored in alphabetical order. If the dictionary is large, adjacent entries tend to have several initial characters in common. The coding for each subsequent word has two parts: the number of characters in common with the previous word, and the unique suffix. These special-purpose techniques, while they do not outperform general methods, are used because they are simple and efficient to implement and because they aptly model some common forms of data. *SEE INFORMATION THEORY*.

*Gordon V. Cormack*

***Bibliography.*** D. Severance, A practitioner's guide to data base compression, *Inform. Syst.*, 8(1):51–62, 1983; T. A. Welch, A technique for high-performance data compression, *IEEE Comput.*, 17(6):8–19, June 1984; I. H. Witten and J. G. Cleary, Foretelling the future by adaptive modelling, *Abacus*, 3(3):16–73, 1986.

## Data flow systems

An alternative to conventional programming languages and architectures, in which values rather than value containers are dealt with, and all processing is achieved by applying functions to values to produce new values. These systems can realize large amounts of parallelism (present in many applications) and effectively utilize very large-scale-integration (VLSI) technology.

**Basic concepts.** Data flow systems use an underlying execution model which differs substantially from the conventional one. The model deals with values, not names of value containers. There is no notion of assigning different values to an object which is held in a global, updatable memory location. A statement such as $X := B + C$ in a data flow language is only syntactically similar to an assignment statement. The meaning of $X := B + C$ in data flow is to compute the value $B + C$ and bind this value to the name $X$. Other operators can use this value by referring to the name $X$, and the statement has a precise mathematical meaning defining $X$. This definition remains constant within the scope in which the statement occurs. Languages with this property are sometimes referred to as single assignment languages. The second property of the model is that all processing is achieved by applying functions to values to produce new values. The inputs and results are clearly defined, and there are not side effects. Languages with this property are called applicative. Value-oriented, applicative languages do not impose any sequencing constraints in addition to the basic data dependencies present in the algorithm. Functions must wait for all input values to be computed, but the order in which the functions are evaluated does not affect the final results. There is no notion of a central controller which initiates one statement at a time sequentially. The model described above can be applied to languages and architectures.

***Data dependence graphs.*** The computation specified by a program in a data flow language can be represented as a data dependence graph, in which each node is a function and each arc carries a value. Very efficient execution of a data flow program can be achieved on a stored program computer which has the properties of the data flow model. The machine language for such a computer is a dependence graph rather than the conventional sequence of instructions. There is no program counter in a data flow computer. Instead, a mechanism is provided to detect when an instruction is enabled, that is, when all required input values are present. Enabled instructions, together with input values and destination addresses (for the result), are sent to processing elements. Results are routed to destinations, which may enable other instructions. This mode of execution is called data-driven.

The **illustration** is an example of a machine language program for a data flow computer. Values are carried on tokens which flow on arcs of the graph. The graph in the illustration has four tokens initially. Tokens $x$ and $y$ carry input values; two control tokens have the value $F$. Iteration and conditional execution are achieved using the SELECT and DISTRIBUTE operators. SELECT routes a token to its output arc from either arc $T$ or arc $F$, depending on the value of the control token on the horizontal input arc. DISTRIBUTE routes a token on its input arc to either the $T$ or $F$ output, depending on the value of the control token. All operators remove the input tokens used and produce a number of identical result tokens, one for each destination. In the illustration the initial output of the upper SELECT is a token with value $x$, since the control token has a value $F$. The input tokens $x$ and $F$ are removed, and two output tokens are produced, one for the function $f$ and the other for the predicate $p$. It is a useful exercise to follow through the execution of the graph assuming that each arc is a first-in–first-out queue and can hold an unbounded number of tokens; and that $L$, $L^{-1}$, $D$, and $D^{-1}$ are the identity operations.

***Static and dynamic architectures.*** The execution model of a data flow computer as described above, though radically different from conventional processing, is the basis for most of the data flow machines

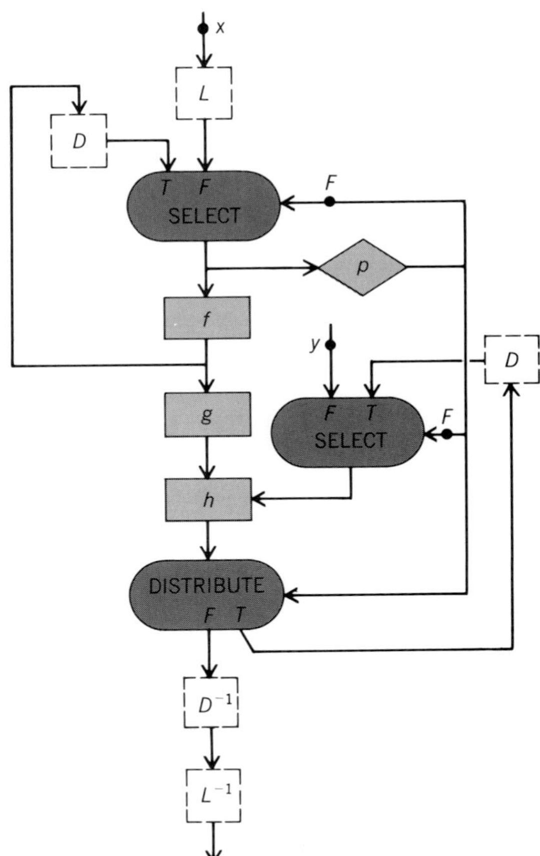


**Machine language program for a data flow computer, represented as a data dependence graph.**

now being investigated. Individual differences arise because of the amount of parallelism that can be realized, the mechanisms for detecting and scheduling enabled instructions, and the handling of data structures.

In static architectures, an instruction (like $h$ in the illustration) is represented in memory by a packet which has an operation code, and space to hold two input values and one or more destination addresses. Hardware is provided with the memory to detect the arrival of both input operands. One restriction in static data flow computers is that no arc in the graph can carry more than one token during execution. Control signals are sent from destination nodes to source nodes to indicate the consumption of previous values. Nevertheless, static machines can realize several different forms of parallelism. For example, $f$ and $p$ can be evaluated simultaneously. Also, $g$ and $h$ can be executed in parallel since they form two stages in a pipeline. However, one form of parallelism cannot be realized. Assume that $f$ and $h$ are simple functions which compute very fast and that $g$ is relatively slow. If the single-token-per-arc limitation is removed, then several tokens would accumulate at the input of $g$ and the possibility of invoking multiple, simultaneous instantiations of $g$ would arise. Dynamic data flow architectures can realize this form of parallelism.

Dynamic data flow architectures allow multiple tokens per arc. A token carries a value and a label. The label specifies a context, an iteration number, and a destination address. Each instruction knows its successors and sets the destination field of the result token appropriately. In addition, the $L$, $D$, $D^{-1}$, and $L^{-1}$ operators (ignored so far in the illustration) modify the context and iteration number. The $L$ operator creates a new context by stacking the previous context and iteration number, and also sets the new iteration number to 1. The $D$ operator increments the iteration number. The $D^{-1}$ operator resets the iteration number to 1, and the $L^{-1}$ operator restores the old context and iteration number (stacked by $L$). Dynamic data flow computers use an associative memory to hold tokens which are waiting for their partners to be produced. This mechanism is used to bring together tokens with identical labels. When this event occurs, the destination instruction is fetched and, together with the input values, is sent to a processing element. On completion, result tokens are produced with appropriate values. With this mechanism, simultaneous evaluations of $g$ are possible. Since $h$ may not be associative, successive evaluations of $h$ must proceed in the specified order. The token-labeling mechanism guarantees this, irrespective of the order in which the simultaneous evaluations of $g$ are completed. The token-labeling concept can be extended to handle recursion and generalized procedure calls.

***Data-driven and demand-driven execution.*** In data-driven execution, the sources of a node $N$ produce the input values and execution of $N$ is triggered when all input values are produced. With the second execution rule, called demand-driven, nothing happens until a result is demanded at a primary output of a graph. The corresponding node then demands its inputs. These demands flow opposite to the arcs in the graph until the primary inputs are reached. A node executes only if its result has been demanded and its own demands satisfied. An advantage of this approach is that the computations which occur are exactly those that are required. This rule is also called lazy evaluation.

**Comparison of conventional systems.** Conventional languages and architectures are characterized by the existence of a sequential controller and a global addressable memory which holds objects. Languages such as Fortran and PL/1 allow aliasing and side effects and impose sequencing constraints not present in the original algorithm. The compile step attempts to recover the parallelism obscured by the language and to generate a data dependence graph. Depending on the parallelism to be exposed, this can be a complex step. Code is then generated for a scalar processor, a vector processor, or a multiprocessor consisting of several uniprocessors sharing storage. Each alternative is examined below.

In uniprocessors, sequential decoding of instructions is necessary to place appropriate interlocks on storage and thereby guarantee the logical correctness of results. Techniques such as overlapping, pipelining, and out-of-sequence execution are used to design high-performance processors. However, because of the sequential decode, concurrency can be obtained only in a small window around the program counter. Furthermore, high-performance uniprocessors cannot effectively utilize VLSI technology.

The decoder limitation can be circumvented if a single instruction can initiate multiple operations on a data structure. This leads quite naturally to vector architectures. Portions of a program coded in instructions which have vector operands can be executed at very high speeds, limited only by hardware and memory bandwidth. However, not all applications with parallelism can be vectorized, and very sophisticated compiler analysis is needed to generate vector code automatically from sequential programs.

Conventional multiprocessing can utilize VLSI technology, but the key problem is the execution model with its global updatable memory. Since the processors execute asynchronously, the race conditions which can arise are prevented by embedding synchronization primitives in the code. Usually, the overhead for synchronization is large, and low-level parallelism cannot be realized. The code must be partitioned into relatively large blocks of computation with few synchronizing primitives. Moreover, if large amounts of parallelism are not obtained, the performance of the entire system can be critically dependent on processor-processor and processor-memory communications latency. The current state of development does not support compilation of sequential programs on a multiprocessor system. Also, multiprocessor code with embedded synchronization is extremely difficult to verify.

The complexity of the compile step for both vector and multiprocessor architectures can be reduced by extensions to sequential languages. However, this forces the programmer to consider parallelism explicitly, an added complexity.

**Advantages and limitations.** Data flow systems can overcome many of the disadvantages of conventional approaches. In principle, all the parallelism in the algorithm is exposed in the program and thus the programmer does not have to deal with parallelism explicitly. Since programs have mathematical properties, verification is simpler, and generation of the dependence graph from the program is a simple step. Systems of large numbers of flow-speed processors are possible, and the approach therefore exploits VLSI technology. If large amounts of parallelism are realized, then processor-memory and processor-processor communications latency is not as critical. Since there are constraints on the production and use of information, protection and security can be more naturally enforced.

Several important problems remain to be solved in data flow systems. The handling of complex data structures as values is inefficient, but there is no complete solution to this problem yet. Data flow computers tend to have long pipelines, and this causes degraded performance if the application does not have sufficient parallelism. Since the programmer does not have explicit control over memory, separate "garbage collection" mechanisms must be implemented. The space-time overheads of managing low levels of parallelism have not been quantified. Thus, though the parallelism is exposed to the hardware, it has not been demonstrated that it can be effectively realized. The machine state is large, and without the notion of a program counter, hardware debugging and maintenance can be complex. Data flow also shares problems with conventional multiprocessor approaches: program decomposition, scheduling of parallel activities, establishment of the potential of utilizing large numbers of slow processors over a variety of applications, and system issues such as storage hierarchy management and disk seek-time limitations. SEE DIGITAL COMPUTER PROGRAMMING; PROGRAMMING LANGUAGES.

*Tilak Agerwala*

**Bibliography.** T. Agerwala and Arvind (eds.), Data flow systems, *Computer*, special issue, 15(2):10–69, February 1982; P. C. Treleaven et al., Data-driven and demand-driven computer architecture, *Comput. Surv.*, 14(1):93–143, March 1982.

## Data-processing management

Managing the data-processing function, its people, and its equipment. This activity follows the well-recognized principles of planning, control, and operation. The basic prerequisites for data-processing management are therefore the same skills which are needed to manage any other enterprise.

Data processing is a continually evolving technology, and this fact differentiates data-processing management from many other managerial environments. Furthermore, data processing is most often a service function within an organization, and not an end product. Constant awareness of this aspect is essential to ensure successful discharge of data-processing managerial responsibilities.

**Organization of people.** Despite the apparently overwhelming and complex presence of computing equipment and its associated technology, the major and critical component in the data-processing function is people. To select, develop, and organize people for maximum effectiveness and efficiency should be the major concern. Many technical skills—if not experience—have been in short supply, making the organizational task more pressing. Providing an effective organizational environment which offers motivation through ongoing training and a competitive reward structure is one avenue to success. The other is to match the data-processing organization to the structure, the style, and the goals of the enterprise served. To achieve this, the products, the customers, the marketplace, even the politics and problems of the enterprise, must be understood by data-processing management. In turn, data-processing management must be a recognized, participating, and accepted part of the overall management structure of the enterprise.

**Products of data processing.** The products of the data-processing function are the developed application systems, which should be viewed as a portfolio of corporate assets, and the information output, processed efficiently through the computing equipment and often supported by telecommunications facilities.

***Application systems.*** Effective application systems development again depends on knowledge and understanding of the business activity, which implies full participation by and interaction with the users. Methodology and structure, that is, standards, are necessary to make systems developers—analysts and programmers—optimally productive. A formal plan, spanning 1–3 years, is needed to give direction and priority to the development tasks.

Application software for a particular need may also be available from vendors. The decision process to purchase rather than develop software should, of course, take the cost difference into consideration, but equally important is the fit of vendor software to the particular requirements. However, added to the acquisition price of the application software is the inevitable cost of conversion, education, modification, and installation.

***Information output.*** Converting input data into meaningful and relevant output is the real function of data-processing equipment. The technology employed, as well as the internal processes of the computer, are very complex. It is here that technical knowledge is paramount, making it very likely the most elusive area to manage. A high degree of reliance on a technically competent staff, either within or outside of the organization, is unavoidable. A fundamental knowledge of the technology on the part of data-processing management and frequent interaction with the technical staff are the best insurance that the technology stays within bounds and does not become the major driving force.

**Managerial control.** Continuous awareness of products offered by manufacturers and vendors, their capabilities, and their cost is a useful and effective means of maintaining the level of technical knowledge needed to exercise managerial control.

Inadequate control, manifested by failure to deliver output and projects within budget, is often cited as a problem of data-processing management. It is frequently unrecognized that the data-processing function contains an appreciable creativity factor, particularly in the development area. The inability to schedule creativity contributes to an on-time performance problem. The structuring of the work effort into manageable parts and clearly established responsibilities; keeping a constant watch on progress and work effort; immediately identifying problems; and determining resolutions can overcome this.

**Demands of computer technology.** Computer technology requires an unequivocal and exact representation of facts and figures. Its effective use makes particular demands on technicians and managers alike. Only what has been predetermined and planned will happen. Malfunctions aside, only that which has been programmed will be produced—no more, no less. Surprises can be minimized only by attention to detail and by exploration of ''what if'' consequences. Recognizing this is an essential ingredient of successful data-processing management. *See* COMPUTER; DATA-PROCESSING SYSTEMS; DIGITAL COMPUTER.

*Michael J. Samek*

## Data-processing systems

Electronic, electromechanical, or mechanical machines for transforming information into suitable forms in accordance with procedures planned in advance. The term data-processing system is also applied to the scheme, or procedure, that prescribes the sequence of operations to be performed in processing the information.

Typical business applications of data-processing systems include record keeping, financial accounting and planning, processing personnel information (including payroll processing), sales analysis, inventory control, production scheduling, operations research, and market research. Data-processing systems are also used to process correspondence and other information in business offices. These systems are called word processors. *See* WORD PROCESSING.

In science and engineering, data-processing systems are used in data reduction, statistical analysis of experimental data, planning and design of engineering projects, and the display in tabular and graphic form of the results of research and development. Special-purpose computer systems, which also fall within the definition of data-processing systems, are used to monitor and control such things as chemical processes, machine tools, typesetting equipment, and power generation plants. *See* DATA REDUCTION.

Data-processing systems can be broadly classified as manual, semiautomatic, or automatic, depending on the degree of human effort required to control and execute the procedures. The trend is to reduce human effort, and automatic methods are becoming the dominant mode of processing. In a manual system the operations are performed by one or more individuals without the aid of mechanical devices. Varying degrees of mechanization can be introduced into manual systems through the use of machines such as calculators and bookkeeping machines. Semiautomatic systems use machines to a greater extent. The principal semiautomatic systems employ punched cards, and are referred to as a tabulating system or electronic accounting machine (EAM) systems. Automatic systems are usually built around electronic digital computers and termed electronic data-processing (EDP) systems. *See* DIGITAL COMPUTER.

**Data-processing functions.** Virtually every data-processing system, regardless of the degree of automation, consists of six basic functions: recording, transmission, manipulation, reporting, storage, and retrieval—collectively termed the data-processing cycle.

***Recording.*** Before information can be processed, it must be recorded in some form that is meaningful to a person or a machine. The information may be written or typed on a paper document, or it may be coded as a pattern of punched holes on a card, pulses on magnetic disk, or varying-width vertical dark bars on the product label (Universal Product Code, UPC). Many business machines, such as typewriters and cash registers, can be equipped to record data in a machine-readable form as a by-product of their normal function. Patterns of holes on cards or pulses on disks can be created by using a keyboard entry device. Optical scanners are used to record the sequence of bars in the UPC.

At one time the principal medium used to enter information into computers was the punched card. The principal device used to record information for processing by computers was the keypunch. Subsequently keyboards linked to magnetic tapes (key to tape) or to magnetic disk (key to disk) systems became widely used. The information is usually recorded on a small reel of tape or a small disk first and then entered into the computer system later. These recording systems are being replaced in turn by key entry devices that are linked directly to the computer via communication lines. Intermediate recording, whether on punched cards, tape, or disk, is no longer required.

***Transmission.*** Once information has been recorded, it will usually need to be transmitted to another location for processing. The distance involved may range from a few feet to thousands of miles, and the information can be conveyed by personal delivery, mail, or wire. Where fast response is desirable and economically feasible, the data can be transmitted at high speeds by means of telephone or telegraph circuits, microwave links, or satellite channels. Numerous specialized business machines, such as airline reservation and credit authorization terminals, combine the recording and transmission functions by accepting data entered through a keyboard or read from credit cards or both and transmitting it directly to a distant computer system. *See* DATA COMMUNICATIONS.

***Manipulation.*** This is the stage in which most of the actual processing is performed. The operations involved can range from simple to highly complex. The most common types of operations are classifying, sorting, calculating, and summarizing. More specifically, the manipulation stage frequently involves (1) arrangement of the information into a sequence that will facilitate further processing; (2) determination of the exact procedure to be followed in processing each item of information; (3) references to files containing data that must be associated with the current information; (4) arithmetic operations upon the current information or file data or both; and (5) updating (changing) of the file data to reflect the current information.

***Report preparation.*** After information has been processed, it is usually necessary to report the results in a meaningful form. Reports are the people-oriented products of the data-processing activity. They should be timely, complete, understandable, and in a convenient format. Checks, letters that are ready to be mailed, and lists of purchases at supermarket checkouts, as well as more routine summaries of the results of data processing, are commonly prepared. The routine summaries are frequently presented in graphical as well as tabular form, and include substantial amounts of text in order to make the report more understandable. Most reports are printed-paper documents, but other media, such as cathode-ray-tube displays or microfilm, are used.

***Storage.*** Some or all of the processed information will need to be stored for future reference or retrieval. Information that is generated during one data-processing step frequently serves as a part of the input data for a later step, and must therefore be retained in a conveniently reusable form. The records of an organization may consist mainly of the contents of the storage generated by its data-processing system. Depending on the system, the information may be stored manually (as in ledgers or notebooks), electromechanically (as in punched cards or punched paper tape), or electronically (as in disk packs or magnetic tape).

***Retrieval.*** The importance of the contents of storage and the availability of transmission facilities have resulted in many automatic data-processing systems providing immediate retrieval of stored information at work stations. Questions regarding the contents of storage can be posed at remote locations, and responses can be prepared and transmitted to these locations in a few seconds. This is called an on-line query facility. Special capabilities that permit retrieval of stored information based on a more time-consuming, complex sequence of searches through the stored information are also available.

**Punched-card systems.** The first successful punched-card data-processing equipment was developed by Herman Hollerith for the U.S. Bureau of the Census in the 1880s. By 1930, a full line of machines was available for processing data recorded in cards, and punched-card accounting systems are in use around the world. Electronic data-processing systems, which offer greatly improved flexibility, speed, and economy, have been rapidly supplanting punched-card systems. The punched card itself, however, remains one of the principal means for recording data for entry into an EDP system.

The punched card is a piece of stiff paper in which data can be represented by punching holes in prescribed positions. The most commonly used type of card involves the Hollerith coding system and contains 80 vertical columns. Each column can represent a character (a digit, letter, or punctuation mark) by means of holes in 1, 2, or 3 of the 12 positions (**Fig. 1**). The card is 3.25 in. (82.55 mm) high, 7.375 in. (187.32 mm) wide, and 0.070 in. (1.78 mm) thick. Each card normally holds the data describing a single transaction, account, or record.

Punched-card accounting systems generally contain a separate machine to perform each processing function. Though many of the machines can process hundreds of cards per minute, a fairly high degree of manual effort is required to load and unload each machine to the next. The operation of most punched-card machines is controlled by plugboards. These are perforated boards whose holes (termed hubs) are manually interconnected by wires (termed patchcords) in a manner that will cause the machine to perform the desired functions. This method of control is far less flexible than the internally stored programs used by most digital computers.

There are many types of punched-card machines, but a fully mechanized system can contain as few as three machines: a key punch to record the information in punched cards, sorter to arrange the cards in the proper sequence, and a tabulator to prepare and print the reports.

**Electronic data-processing (EDP) systems.** EDP systems (**Fig. 2**) take advantage of the great speed and versatility of stored-program digital computers to process large volumes of data with little or no need

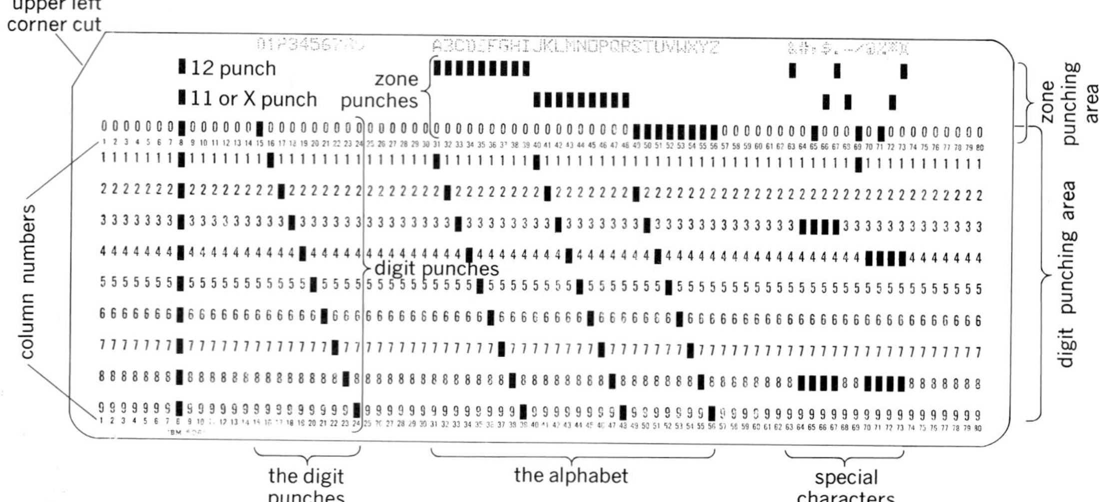


**Fig. 1.** An 80-column punched card showing the Hollerith coding for numeric and alphabetic information. *(After An Introduction to IBM Punched Card Data Processing, IBM Publ. F20-0074, November 1964)*

**Fig. 2. Large-scale electronic data-processing system. Disk drives are at the right, and tape drives at the left. Printers are in the foreground and to the right of the tape drives. The central processing unit and storage are in the center background. *(Sperry Univac Division, Sperry Rand Corp.)***

for human intervention. There is no fundamental difference between the computers currently used for business data processing and those used for scientific calculations; in fact, a single computer is often used for both types of applications. Scientific computers, however, tend to emphasize high computational speeds, while computers used for business data processing often place primary emphasis on fast, flexible input and output equipment.

Although large, high-performance computer systems cost hundreds of thousands or even millions of dollars, a wide variety of smaller systems is available at much lower prices for users with smaller volumes of data to be processed. These systems and others used in data communications take advantage of developments in microelectronics (**Fig. 3**) to deliver surprisingly high performance, along with compact dimensions and low prices (**Fig. 4**).

Every computer system has four basic functional parts: input equipment to permit data and instructions to be entered into the system; a storage unit to permit data and instructions to be stored until they are called for; a control unit, called the central processing unit (CPU), to interpret the stored instructions and direct their execution; and output equipment to permit the processed data to be removed from the system. *SEE COMPUTER STORAGE TECHNOLOGY; DIGITAL COMPUTER PROGRAMMING*.

The remainder of this article discusses the input and output equipment used in EDP systems. The common types of input and output devices, their recording media, and their typical speeds are summarized in the **table**. Magnetic tape and disk can also be viewed as storage media that supplement the storage available in the computer itself. They have been termed auxiliary storage.

***Disk pack units.*** Introduced in 1962, the disk pack has become the preeminent high-speed computer input/output medium. A disk pack typically consists of a stack of from 1 to 20 round stainless-steel plates mounted on a vertical spindle. Data are magnetically recorded on some or all of the surfaces of the disks. The disk pack can be conveniently mounted on a drive unit that spins it at 2400–3600 revolutions per minute. The drive unit also contains magnetic read/write heads mounted on a comblike access mechanism that moves horizontally between the disks in order to read and record information on them.

Disk packs have transfer rates from about 200,000 to nearly 2,000,000 characters per second and capacities of from about 10,000,000 to more than 600,000,000 characters per pack. The key advantage of disk packs that accounts for their preeminence is their rapid-access capability; any record stored in a disk pack can be located and read into the computer in a fraction of a second, whereas it may take as long as several minutes to locate a particular record stored in a reel of magnetic tape. Conversely, disk packs, on the basis of cost per character stored, currently cost several times as much as magnetic tape.

One development in magnetic disk technology deserves special mention. Flexible plastic disks, called diskettes or floppy disks, are widely used for applications in which low cost and ease of use are more important than high speeds and large data-storage capacities. Most diskettes are 8 in. (20.3 cm) or 5¼ in. (13.3 cm) in diameter, and may be housed in protective fiber-treated cardboard enclosures; the enclosure

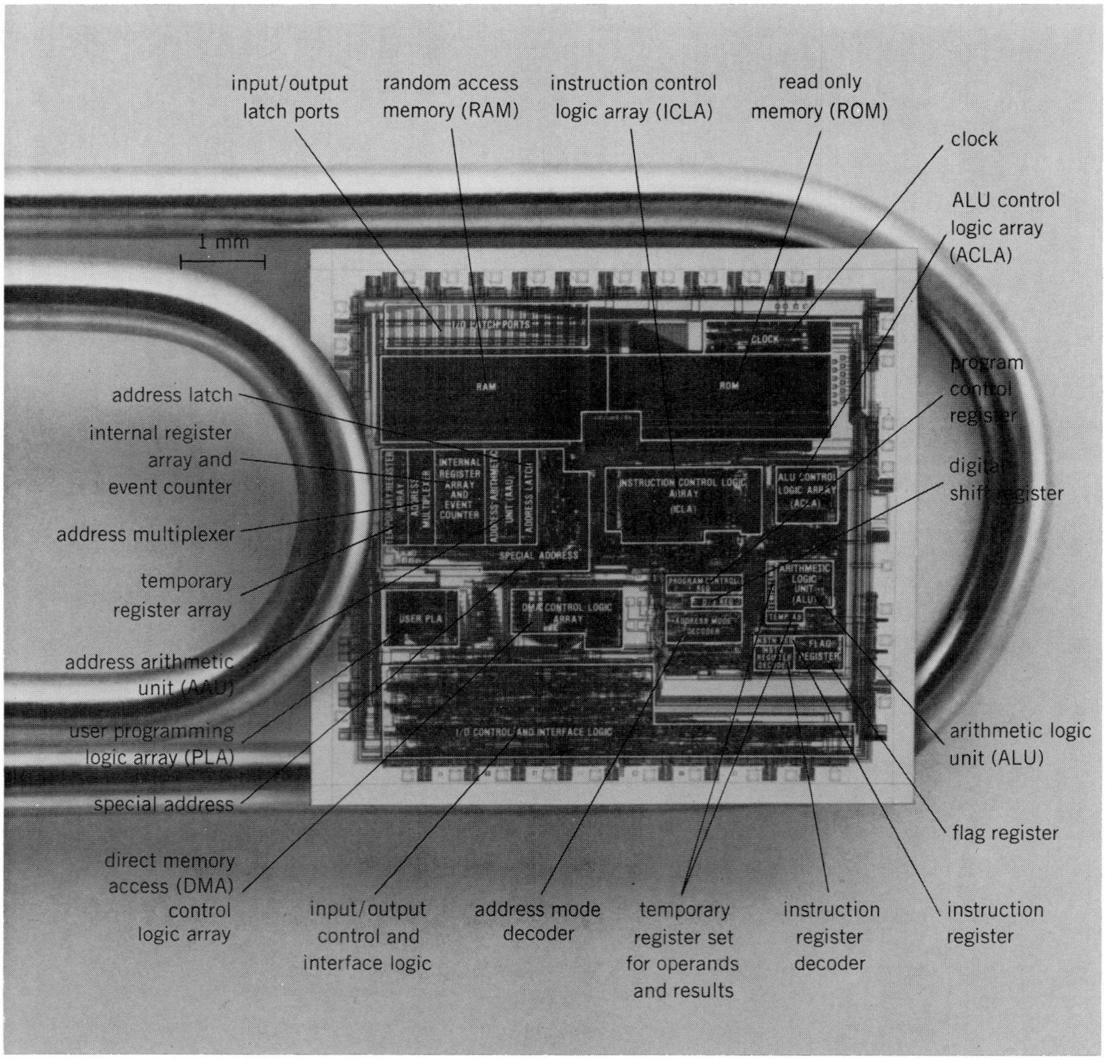

**Fig. 3. MAC-4 one-chip computer, developed for a variety of telecommunications applications, compared to a standard-sized paper clip. (*Bell Laboratories*)**

remains stationary while the drive unit spins the disk. Each diskette holds approximately 300,000 characters, and the data-transfer rate is about 30,000 characters per second.

***Magnetic tape units.*** Magnetic tape is an important input/output medium for EDP systems because it permits large quantities of information to be stored in a highly compact, economical, and easily erasable form. The tape is usually made of plastic with a magnetizable oxide coating on which data can be recorded in the form of magnetic spots. The tape transports must be capable of moving the tape past the read/write heads at high speeds (up to 250 in./s or 6.35 m/s) and of starting and stopping the tape movement within a few milliseconds.

The magnetic tape currently in widest use with EDP systems is ½ in. (12.7 mm) wide, is supplied in 2400-ft (732-m) reels with a diameter of 10.5 in. (26.67 mm), and is recorded with 9 parallel tracks across the tape at a density of 800, 1600, or 6250 frames per inch (31.5, 63.0, or 246.1 frames per millimeter). Each frame holds 9 bits (binary digits) and can represent one character of information. *See Bit.*

Transfer rates of magnetic tape units range from a few thousand to 1,250,000 characters per second. Though impressive, the transfer rates of both tape and disk fall far short of the internal processing speeds of the computer. As a result, the overall productivity of some data-processing systems are limited by the speed at which information can be entered into and removed from the system.

As an alternative to high-performance magnetic tape units, many EDP systems include smaller, less

**Fig. 4. Relatively low-cost EDP system. The system includes a keyboard, a cathode-ray-tube display, and a pair of diskette units. (*Digital Equipment Corp.*)**

**Input/output devices**

| Unit | Medium | Input or output | Typical approximate transfer rate in characters per second |
|---|---|---|---|
| Disk pack unit | Magnetic disks housed in interchangeable cartridges | Both | 200,000–2,000,000 |
| Diskette unit | Flexible magnetic disks | Both | Tens of thousands |
| Magnetic tape unit | Plastic tape with magnetizable coating, housed on reels | Both | Thousands–1,250,000 |
| Magnetic tape cartridge unit | Plastic tape with magnetizable coating, housed in cartridges | Both | Tens of thousands |
| Card reader | Punched cards | Input | 20–2000 |
| Card punch | Punched cards | Output | 20–700 |
| Paper tape reader | Perforated paper or plastic tape | Input | 10–1000 |
| Paper tape punch | Perforated paper or plastic tape | Output | 10–200 |
| Printer | Continuous paper forms | Output | 10–20,000 |
| Optical character reader | Paper or card documents | Input | 10–3000 |
| Magnetic ink character reader | Paper or card documents | Input | 200–3000 |
| Display unit | Cathode-ray tube or other display medium | Output* | 10–100,000 |
| Computer output microfilmer | Microfilm | Output | 2000–60,000 |

*Input capabilities are usually provided by an associated keyboard or light pen.

costly tape transports in which the data are recorded on shorter lengths of narrow magnetic tape, typically 0.15 or 0.25 in. (3.81 or 6.35 mm) wide, housed in conveniently interchangeable cartridges. The most commonly used type of cartridge is an adaptation of the Philips-type cassettes that are widely used in audio recording. The cartridge tape units have comparatively slow read/write speeds and small data-storage capacities; their offseting advantages are economy and convenience of use.

Magnetic tape is widely used to provide back-up for disk units and to permit the exchange of large volumes of information by sending reels of tape from one place to another. For example, computer programs that are purchased are often delivered on one or more reels of magnetic tape.

***Card reader and punch.*** The fact that most early computers replaced or augmented punched-card systems gave the punched card a strong head start as a computer input/output medium, and it is still used. The punched card is a highly flexible medium that has many advantages for use as a source document and as a storage medium for permanent records. In EDP systems its principal drawbacks are the difficulty of correcting errors in the punched data, the fixed upper limit on the amount of data a card can hold (usually 80 or 96 characters), and the comparatively low speeds of even the fastest card readers and punches (see table).

***Paper tape readers and punches.*** Paper tape can be punched and read by relatively simple, inexpensive equipment, making it practical to produce tape records as a direct by-product of the normal operations of many business machines, such as teletypewriters and cash registers.

Though generally called paper tape, the tape may be made of paper, plastic, metal, or laminated combinations of these materials. Data are recorded by punching round holes into the tape and read by sensing the holes either mechanically or photoelectrically. Nearly all paper tape in use at present is either 11/16, 7/8, or 1 in. (17.46, 22.22, or 25.4 mm) in width, and is recorded with 5, 7, or 8 data tracks at a density of 10 frames per inch (3.94 frames per centimeter). Each frame normally represents a single character using a code of 5–8 bits.

As with punched cards, the principal disadvantage of paper tape is the low speeds of the tape readers and punches available for use with computers. As a result, paper tape has been largely replaced by magnetic tape cassette units.

***Printers.*** Electromechanical printing devices are the primary means for making information processed by computers available to people. However, display units are overtaking printers in this regard. Computer printers can be broadly classified as either serial or line printers and as either impact or nonimpact printers. A serial unit prints one character at a time in the manner of a conventional typewriter, whereas a line printer prints a full line, usually consisting of 80 to 132 characters, at the same time. An impact printer uses direct mechanical force to produce character images on the paper, whereas nonimpact printers utilize various electrical or chemical processes to form the characters.

Most high-speed computer printing is currently done by line printers using on-the-fly impact printing techniques. In these devices, multiple rapid-action print hammers press continuous paper forms against an inked ribbon and a moving type element at the precise instants when the selected characters are in the appropriate positions. The type element may be a rotating drum, a horizontally moving chain of type slugs (**Fig. 5**), or a horizontally oscillating typebar. Speeds of 300 to 2000 lines per minute are typical for line printers.

Matrix printers may be impact or nonimpact. The most successful are nonimpact and use thermal-chemical or electrostatic processes to create an image. Typically a 5-by-7 matrix of dots is used to print each character. The set of dots that is printed provides an image of the character (**Fig. 6**). A matrix printer that is widely used, especially in offices using word processing, is the ink jet printer.

A thermal matrix printer uses either heat-sensitive paper or wax-coated dark paper as the medium for printing. The head-sensitive paper undergoes a chemical change when subjected to heat, producing a visible image. Speeds of about 10 to 100 characters per second are common for thermal printers, and they are relatively inexpensive—costing from a few hundred to a few thousand dollars. However, the quality of the

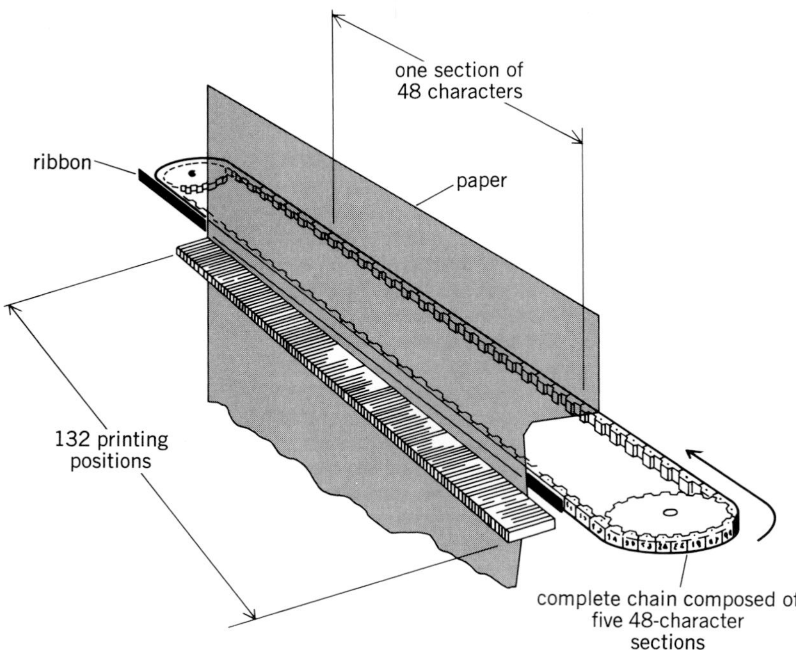


**Fig. 5. Schematic representation of a chain printer. (*After H. Maisel, Computers: Programming and Applications, Science Research Associates, 1976*)**

result is poor, and they may give off an offensive odor or accumulate wax debris.

Electrostatic printers are among the fastest and most versatile printers available. Speeds of several thousand characters per second can be achieved. The matrix printing approach accounts for their versatility. A 10-by-14 or even finger matrix can be used to obtain better printed images and a greater variety of characters.

A laser can be used to write the printed output on the light-sensitive surface of a drum. The image on this surface is then transferred to paper. Speeds of tens of thousands of characters per second can be realized by this type of printer. SEE LASER.

***Character reader.*** Optical character recognition (OCR) has been heralded as the solution to the great computer input bottleneck because it promises to reduce, and in some cases eliminate, the manual keystroke operations which are normally required in preparing the input data for machine processing. Machines capable of reading characters printed on paper documents by typewriters, cash registers, computer printers, and many other business machines are in use in applications such as utility billing and credit card processing. Moreover, machines that can read hand-printed characters are on the market, and extensive development work has been undertaken on machines to recognize ordinary handwriting. The principal barriers to wider use of optical character readers have been reliability problems and comparatively high costs.

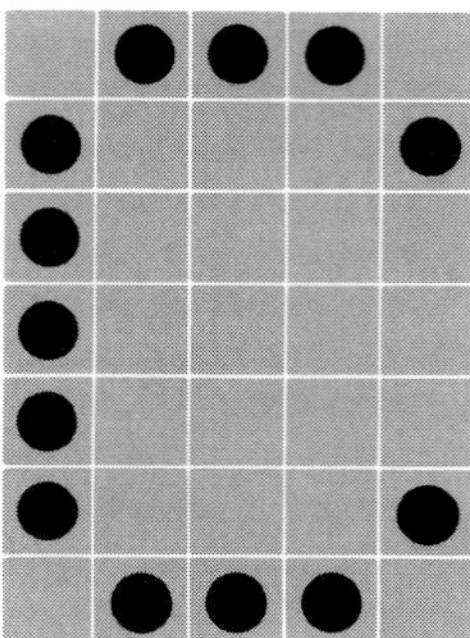

**Fig. 6. Matrix of dots used to represent the letter C.**

Optical recognition techniques can also be used effectively to read hand-made pencil marks or printed bar codes. Optical mark readers and bar-code readers are considerably less costly than character readers and are widely used in applications such as test scoring, survey analysis, credit-card processing, and supermarket checkout.

Magnetic-ink character recognition (MICR), unlike OCR, requires that the characters be printed with a special magnetic ink. This requirement limits the flexibility and applicability of the MICR technique, though it permits reliable readers to be built at a lower cost. The banking field, which adopted magnetic-ink encoding as the common language for checks in 1959, remains virtually alone in preferring MICR to the more flexible optical techniques. SEE CHARACTER RECOGNITION.

***Displays.*** Display units are widely used as ''electronic blackboards'' that provide rapid access to data stored in computer systems and facilitate human-machine communication. The great majority of current display units use cathode-ray tubes, but other technologies such as light-emitting diodes, liquid-crystal displays, and plasma (gaseous) displays are also used. The display units may be either connected directly to the computer or located remotely and connected by way of a data communications link. The displayed information may consist of characters or lines or both on the face of a cathode-ray tube. Most display units can also be used for input to the computer by means of either a keyboard or handheld light pen which the operator focuses upon particular points on the screen. SEE ELECTRONIC DISPLAY.

Two broad types of applications for which display units are particularly valuable are obtaining quick responses to inquiries (for example, about bank balances or airline reservations) through access to large, continually updated files of information; and providing convenient human-machine ''conversations'' which make it practical to construct programs and designs in step-by-step, trial-and-error fashion. Display units represent one of the most flexible and economical means for achieving communications between machines and people. Their most noteworthy weakness is their inability to produce permanent copies of the displayed information for future reference, and this can be overcome by equipping the display unit with an auxiliary printer.

***Computer output microfilmers.*** Microfilm has two noteworthy advantages over the printed paper reports that serve as the principal output from most EDP systems: printing on microfilm can be performed at considerably higher speeds, and the microfilmed reports require far less storage space. Conversely, the acceptance of microfilm as a computer output medium has suffered because the information cannot be read by humans without the use of special microfilm readers. The advantages of microfilm clearly outweigh the drawbacks for many computer users, and equipment available that can record computer-generated reports on microfilm at speeds ranging from 1200 to 30,000 lines per minute.

*Herbert Maisel*

**Bibliography.** E. M. Awad, *Business Data Processing*, 5th ed., 1980; G. B. Davis, *Computers and Information Processing*, 1978; W. Fuori and D. Tedesco, *Introduction to Information Processing*, 1983; M. R. Gore and J. W. Stubbe, *Computers and Information Systems*, 2d ed., 1984; H. Maisel, *Computers: Programming and Applications*, 1976; L. S. Orilia, *Introduction to Business Data Processing*, 2d ed., 1982; B. Robichaud, E. Muscat, and A. M. Hall, *Introduction to Data Processing*, 3d ed., 1983; D. Sanders, *Computers Today*, 2d ed., 1985.

## Data reduction

The transformation of information, usually empirically or experimentally derived, into corrected, ordered, and simplified form.

The term data reduction generally refers to operations on either numerical or alphabetical information digitally represented, or to operations which yield digital information from empirical observations or instrument readings. In the latter case data reduction also implies conversion from analog to digital form by human reading and digital symbolization or by mechanical means. SEE ANALOG-TO-DIGITAL CONVERTER; DIGITAL COMPUTER.

Data reduction is used to prepare data in a form suitable for scientific computation, statistical analysis, and control of industrial processes and operations, and for data processing in business applications. Examples are the preparation of data obtained from test runs in missile development, wind tunnel experiments, industrial product sampling, or from readings of sensing instruments in process control.

In applications where the raw data are already digital, data reduction may consist simply of such operations as editing, scaling, coding, sorting, collating, and tabular summarization.

More typically, the data reduction process is applied to readings or measurements involving random errors. These are the indeterminate errors inherent in the process of assigning values to observational quantities. In such cases, before data may be coded and summarized as outlined above, the most probable value of a quantity must be determined. Provided the errors are normally distributed, the most probable (or central) value of a set of measurements is given by the arithmetic mean or, in the more general case, by the weighted mean.

Data reduction may also involve operations of smoothing and interpolation, because the results of observations and measurements are always given as a discrete set of numbers, while the phenomenon being studied may be continuous in nature.

In a smoothing problem a function is empirically given (for example, positions of a body as a function of time) as a collection of points $(t_1,x_1)$, $(t_2,x_2)$, . . ., $(t_n,x_n)$ where the values of the variables, perhaps both independent and dependent, are inaccurate. A common procedure is to fit an $n$th-order (commonly second-order) parabola by least squares to the data points, thus obtaining a representation that will satisfy as nearly as possible all of the given pairs, but perhaps none exactly.

In interpolation a function is known in tabular form. The problem is to determine values between the tabulated points.

Any of the above-mentioned procedures may be carried out on a digital computer or built into a process control system or procedure.

*Raymond J. Nelson*

## Decision theory

A broad spectrum of concepts and techniques which have been developed to both describe and rationalize the process of decision making, that is, making a choice among several possible alternatives. In the broadest sense, one can differentiate between prescriptive decision theory, which formulates how decisions should be made, and descriptive decision theory, which deals with how people actually make decisions. Behavioral and social scientists and psychologists are trying to discover more elaborate descriptive models of the decision process in order to provide mathematicians, economists, strategists, business managers, and others with more sophisticated prescriptive decision-making procedures.

**Concepts and terminology.** The need for decisions in choosing one of several possible actions or series of actions is continuously present in everyday life. It starts with the decision on whether to get up in the morning when the alarm rings or to sleep an extra 15 min before deciding what to have for breakfast, or whether to skip breakfast altogether. Depending on the importance of an individual's position, decisions on various alternatives throughout the day may govern not only his personal future and well-being but also the fate and well-being of any number of other individuals. Thus decisions, having various degrees of importance, represent a critical part of an individual's life.

However, it is not the decisions themselves which are important but rather the consequences of the decisions. These consequences or outcomes are determined by two types of independent factors: (1) the controlled factors, represented by the courses of action or alternate strategies (in decision theory terminology) available to the decision maker; and (2) uncontrolled factors, or states of nature, which interact with the strategies.

The consequences of the chosen strategies are dependent quantities commonly termed outcomes ($O$). These can be measured in a variety of quantitative parameters such as dollars or number of items produced, and by subjective measures of outcome or, in decision theory terminology, by expected relative values or expected utilities.

Conceptually the decision problem is straightforward: From a set of (1) alternate strategies ($S_n$), choose the one which when combined with the relevant (2) states of nature ($N_j$) will produce the (3) outcomes ($O_{nm}$) which best satisfy the (4) goals or objectives of the decision maker. Some type of penalty or benefit criterion is used to evaluate the value or utility of the outcome. Decision theory implies that all four factors should be known to make a completely rational and meaningful decision. At the same time decision theory tries to explain why one often makes seemingly irrational decisions because one is either unable to adequately define the four ingredients or chooses to ignore the procedure.

By taking just the relatively simple decisions which have to be made before getting to work, one can demonstrate the possible difficulties and more of the relevant terminology. In **Fig. 1**, assume that the decision

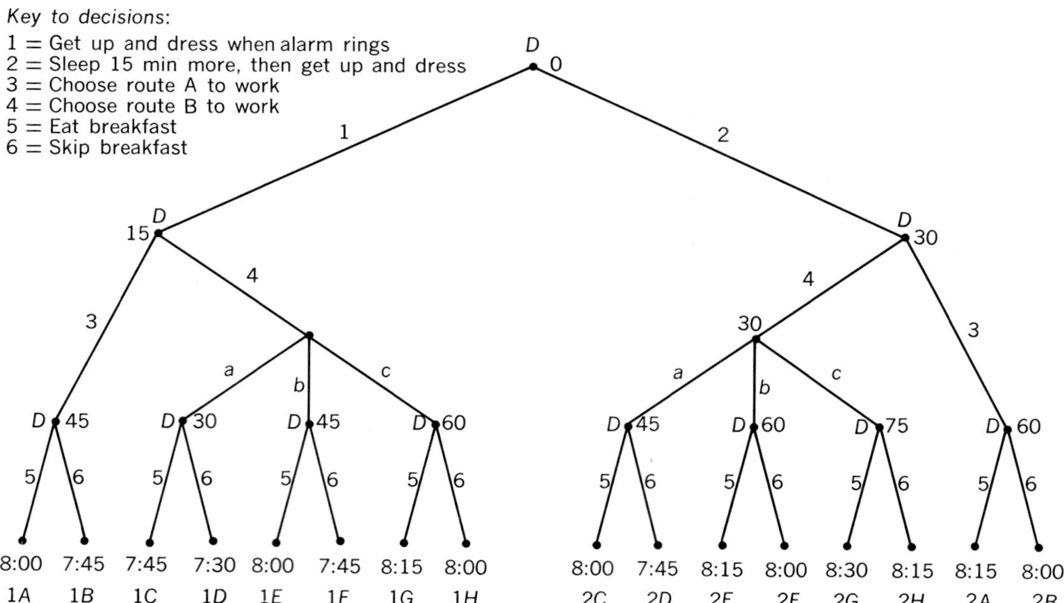


**Fig. 1. Decision tree for the decision problem given in text. Alarm rings at 7:00 A.M. Numbers at nodes represent times past 7:00 A.M. Numbers at branches refer to decision made or state of nature.**

maker has three basic decisions to make on his way to work: (1) He can get up at 7:00 A.M. (choice 1) or 7:15 A.M. (choice 2), with the associated consequence that after dressing he would depart at 7:15 or 7:30 A.M., respectively. (2) He can choose routes A or B (choices 3 and 4) with the expected outcomes that route A always takes 30 min while route B can take 15, 30, or 45 min ($a$, $b$, or $c$), depending on traffic conditions. (3) He can stop for breakfast, which takes 15 min or skip breakfast (choices 5 and 6).

The decision sequence is illustrated in Fig. 1 in the form of a decision tree. It shows all the possible intermediate and final outcomes which would result from all possible choices of alternatives posed by this example. The decision nodes at which decisions have to be made are marked *D*.

Several interesting observations can be made about the decision tree. (1) Although there are 16 possible outcomes, there are only 8 possible initial strategies since the choice $a$, $b$, $c$ is independent and is determined by a state of nature. (2) The decision problem has been bounded by enumerating all admissible strategies, states of nature, and outcomes. This has already involved some judgment in excluding other strategies, states of nature, and outcomes on the basis that they are unlikely to occur, or because the decision maker is specifically interested only in the alternatives presented. (3) Although the alternate strategies and outcomes are readily apparent from this particular decision tree, the fourth ingredient of a decision problem, the objectives of the decision maker, has not yet been defined. The objectives which generate the criteria for evaluating the decision problem represent the critical link in reaching the best decision for that particular decision maker at this particular time. In Fig. 1 it is clear that the decision on the best strategy to be followed is a function of the following objectives.

1. If the objective is to positively arrive at work at 7:45 A.M. sharp, no sooner, no later, then one can immediately eliminate all strategies which do not have 7:45 A.M. as their final outcome as inadmissible strategies. In this case the only admissible strategy would then be (1–3–6) since any other strategy might result in coming to work late.

2. If, on the other hand, the decision maker decides that breakfast is a vital function and will always insist on breakfast, he will eliminate all strategies which have a branch 6 in the decision tree. If his objective is still to get to work as early as possible, he will now be faced with the decision between strategy (1–3–5) and strategy (1–4–5), which may under certain circumstances get him to work faster than (1–3–5), that is, outcome *IC*. These two strategies dominate all other admissible strategies because under all circumstances they will get him to work faster than any of the other strategies. Thus when one strategy shows dominance over some other strategies, one can eliminate all but the dominant strategies from consideration. Strategies (1–3–5) and (1–4–5) do not dominate each other since under certain circumstances one or the other will have the more desirable outcome.

If strategy (1–3–5) is chosen, this is called decision making under certainty (DMUC) since the outcome is uniquely predictable and all states of nature are known. The outcome of strategy (1–4–5) depends on the traffic conditions ($a$, $b$, or $c$) or states of nature which are not under the decision maker's control. If he has no idea what the likelihood or probability of occurrence ($p_m$) of states $a$, $b$, or $c$ is, he will be faced with decision making under uncertainty (DMUU) and will employ one of the techniques described in the next section. If he can predict the probability of the states of nature $a$, $b$, or $c$ from past experience or from observations, then he can associate a probability with each of the possible outcomes. This represents decision making under risk (DMUR) with expected outcomes. The techniques used in these three types of decision making will be discussed further.

3. Except in very well-defined decision problems in which the outcomes are clearly represented by an objective parameter (such as dollars or time) there are conflicting objectives which require value judgments to determine the value or utility of each objective with respect to the others. This unescapable aspect of decision theory has led to the development of value the-

ory normally associated with decision theory. Value theory strives to evaluate relative utilities of simple and mixed parameters which can be used to describe outcomes. For example, the utility or value of $100,000 to a multimillionaire in a gambling decision is obviously quite different from its value to a person whose total possessions amount to $100,000. Similarly, the question of the relative values of 15 min extra sleep versus no breakfast versus coming to work late requires some resolution before the objectives and evaluation criteria for the decision problem can be established.

The general concepts of decision theory in trying to formalize and rationalize the decision-making process were indicated by the above discussion. Some techniques of actually using these concepts are described below. It should be emphasized that the major contributions of decision theory are to structure the decision problem and to define the scope and importance of various components so that each part of the decision can be evaluated and discussed before synthesizing the available information into a rational decision.

**Application and techniques.** Decision theory in various disguises has been applied with varying degrees of success to so many diverse areas of interest that it would be impossible to provide an inclusive list of the methods and techniques used. The bibliography at the end of the article represents a broad spectrum of application techniques and current research work. The formal procedures of decision theory are described below with an indication of the relative use and value of the techniques in various areas of modern society.

The information necessary for a rational decision is usually summarized in a decision matrix, as shown in **Fig. 2**. The alternate pure (independent from each other) or mixed (combinations of pure strategies) strategies are listed in the first column. These strategies ($S_1$ to $S_n$) can be generated by the decision maker, by his advisers, in group sessions, and so on, and should contain all possible and admissible courses of action which the decision maker can control. In business management these strategies could be money-borrowing strategies, sales and promotion strategies, and production and product mix strategies. In government it could be foreign policy strategies, military strategies, crime-fighting strategies, or government appointments.

Across the top all possible states of nature ($N_1$ to $N_m$) which might affect the outcome of the various strategies are enumerated. A business manager trying to raise capital may be interested in possible states of nature such as different interest rates and inflationary and deflationary trends. A military planner may be concerned with the possibilities of war in the Middle East or Europe or both. One can easily see that the decision matrix can become quite large and the trade-off between time and money expended on a decision compared with the value of a more or less reliable decision can become a decision problem in itself.

The probabilities of occurrence of various states of nature ($p_1$ to $p_m$) must be estimated and listed with the states of nature. Since these values will critically influence the decision, they should be as reliable as possible. In value theory one distinguishes between the subjective probability of occurrence which reflects the decision maker's opinion on what the probability is and the objective probability which is derivable mathematically or as a result of observations. Thus an optimist may consider the probability that he will get detained in traffic very unlikely and make his decision based on this assumption, while observation of traffic conditions over a period of time may indicate that 90% of the time he will be detained by traffic. Statistical theory plays an important role in defining these numbers.

Corresponding to each interaction of a strategy ($S_i$) and a state of nature ($N_j$), one determines a consequence or outcome ($O_{ij}$) in terms of some value or utility parameters. The outcome may sometimes be easily computed, for example, the interest cost on a business loan, but quite often must be based on insufficient data, past experience, or questionably valid assumptions, such as would be the case in trying to assess the outcome of a limited war. The generation of reliable outcome data can be expensive and time-consuming, and a probability of accuracy is often asso-

| States of nature | | $N_1$ | $N_2$ | — — | $N_j$ | — — — — — — | $N_m$ | Expected value |
|---|---|---|---|---|---|---|---|---|
| Probabilities of occurrence | | $p_1$ | $p_2$ | — — | $p_j$ | — — — — — — | $p_m$ | |
| Alternate strategies | $S_1$ | $O_{11}$ | $O_{12}$ | — — | $O_{1j}$ | — — — — — — | $O_{1m}$ | $EV_1$ |
| | $S_2$ | $O_{21}$ | $O_{22}$ | — — | $O_{2j}$ | — — — — — — | $O_{2m}$ | $EV_2$ |
| | \| | \| | \| | | \| | | \| | \| |
| | \| | \| | \| | | \| | | \| | \| |
| | $S_i$ | $O_{i1}$ | $O_{i2}$ | — — | $O_{ij}$ | — — — — — — | $O_{im}$ | $EV_i$ |
| | \| | \| | \| | | \| | | \| | \| |
| | \| | \| | \| | | \| | | \| | \| |
| | \| | \| | \| | | \| | | \| | \| |
| | $S_n$ | $O_{n1}$ | $O_{n2}$ | — — | $O_{nj}$ | — — — — — — | $O_{nm}$ | $EV_n$ |

**Fig. 2. Form of decision matrix. $O_{ij}$ = outcome of $j$th state of nature ($N_j$) intersecting with $i$th strategy ($S_i$).**

ciated with each outcome. The question of how to assess the relative value or utility of mixed parameters to present a single parameter for the outcome is still a paramount question in decision and utility or value theory, that is, establishing the utility of two apples versus one apple and one orange versus two oranges and so forth. The unit used to describe such a value parameter is a utile; its meaning must be adapted to each situation.

The information in the decision matrix is used to generate the last column which describes the overall expected outcome, or expected value (EV), or expected utility (EU), or expected profit for each strategy. Depending upon the confidence one places in the prediction of the probabilities of the states of nature, the decision process is classified as one of three types.

***Decision making under certainty (DMUC).*** In this case the state of nature which will interact with the strategies can be defined with sufficient certainty so that its probability is close to 1. This case reduces the decision matrix to one column showing the outcomes (profit, cost, and utility) of each strategy with the state of nature. Decision theory indicates that, assuming the alternate strategies are equal in all other respects, the one which will maximize the utility (maximize profit or minimize cost) should be selected. Since in many cases the dependent variable (outcome) is continuously related to the independent variable (strategy), one can obtain relationships which can be used to analytically find the strategy which will correspond to maximum utility. This process is normally termed optimization, which in its broadest interpretation refers to decision making under certainty.

***Decision making under risk (DMUR).*** This implies that, although a number of possible states of nature may interact with each strategy, the probability of occurrence of each of these is known with some degree of certainty. In the previous example, observation may show that 80% of the time it takes 15 min if decision 4 (Fig. 1) is chosen, 10% of the time 30 min, and 10% of the time 45 min. The objective (observed) probabilities for outcomes $a$, $b$, and $c$ would then be .8, .1, .1, respectively. The probabilities of occurrence of all states of nature must always add up to 1 (since one postulates that one of these states of nature will definitely interact with each strategy).

The expected value or utility for each strategy is obtained as a weighted average sum of the individual possible outcomes or, in mathematical terms,

$$(EV_i) = \sum_{j=1}^{m} p_j O_{ij}$$

Thus in the example the expected value for the branch 4 strategy would be $EV = (.8)15 + (.1)30 + (.1)45 = 19.5$ min.

When making decisions under risk, the intent is to choose the strategy which will minimize the expected value or utility. It should be emphasized again that the outcomes and expected values must be expressed by a parameter which adequately presents the objectives of the decision maker. If it does not, then a utility or value transformation is performed on the decision matrix to transform the outcomes into meaningful quantities. If minimum time to get to work is the major objective in the above example, then strategy 4 would be used since its expected value of 19.5 is lower than the expected value of 30 min for strategy 3 (in this particular case, strategy 3 involves no risk so that one is mixing DMUC with DMUR).

The condition of dominance is usually used to eliminate all strategies which are dominated. A dominant strategy has more desirable outcomes under any of the possible states of nature than the dominated strategy.

An additional insight into the reliability of a given decision can be obtained by a sensitivity analysis on the decision matrix. This involves incremental change of one or several probabilities of the states of nature to determine what effect this would have on a decision. This is particularly appropriate for probabilities which are of questionable accuracy.

***Decision making under uncertainty (DMUU).*** If the probabilities of the states of nature cannot be predicted, then the decision has to be made under conditions of uncertainty. For example, the probabilities of political incidents, riots, legal suits, wars, or accidental deaths cannot be accurately predicted.

Decision theory provides a number of techniques to deal with these. They are briefly outlined below without elaborating on their merits or shortcomings. Which of these will work best in a given situation is questionable, and their application depends primarily on the philosophical outlook of the decision maker.

1. Equal probability criterion: This is also known as the Laplace criterion and assumes that all states of nature considered are equally likely (that is, $p_j = 1/m$). The decision matrix is then used just as in DMUR.

2. Maxim criterion: This represents a pessimistic outlook in that it prescribes the strategy which will maximize the minimum profit; that is, in each row of the decision matrix one finds the worst possible outcome and then chooses the strategy which will give the best of the worst outcomes. Conceptually analogous is the minimax criterion which minimizes the maximum possible cost of the decision.

3. Maximax criterion: The optimist will like this one since it chooses the strategy which will maximize the maximum possible profit (the best of the best outcomes in each row).

4. Hurwicz criterion: A coefficient of optimism is defined as $\alpha = 1$ corresponding to a complete optimist, and $\alpha = 0$ corresponding to a complete pessimist ($\alpha$ can vary between 0 and 1 depending on the decision maker's state of optimism). The maximum possible profit for each strategy is then multiplied by $\alpha$ and the minimum profit by $(1 - \alpha)$ to find the best expected value.

5. Regret criterion: Also known as the Savage principle, this criterion is used to construct a regret matrix in which each outcome entry represents a regret defined as the difference between the best possible outcome and the given outcome. The matrix is then used as in DMUR with expected regret as the decision-determining quantity.

The techniques mentioned above only give an outline of the basic concepts of decision theory. The details of defining and quantifying the entries which constitute the decision matrix are determined by the area of application of the decision theory.

**Historical note.** Since humans have existed, they have been faced with decisions. The earliest decision theorists were concerned with gambling decisions as advisers to gamblers in the French court. The theory of games developed from these beginnings. Until fairly recently the bulk of decision theory was concerned with prescriptive decision making and was developed by economists and mathematicians for specific applications in economics, business, applied statistics, law, medicine, politics, and so on. The earliest notions of utility are attributed to Bernoulli, and these notions have developed into the modern utility and value theory concepts. Behavioral scientists are increasingly concerned with descriptive decision theory and, in particular, with the problems of measuring and describing the concepts of utility. Ordinal ranking, metric ranking, bounded interval measures, and other techniques are being developed for this purpose. Operations research has strong roots in decision theory both conceptually and in its wide use of optimization, statistical decision theory, and other decision-making techniques. *SEE GAME THEORY*.

Although decision theory has found extensive use in the past in various government agencies, for war games, operations research in the Defense Department, and so on, there is now more interest in providing a more rational basis for government decisions at all levels. Since resource allocation is a primary function of government agencies, cost-benefit analysis as a prescriptive technique of decision making has found increasingly sophisticated application in government decisions. It too has its concepts and techniques rooted in decision theory. Modern developments in information-processing techniques, data storage and retrieval, and high-speed computers have made it possible to automate the decision process for certain applications with vast amounts of operational and research data continuously updating the decision matrix and modifying strategies in response to new information. *SEE DIGITAL COMPUTER; OPTIMIZATION*.

*Igor Paul*

**Bibliography.** J. Byrd and L. T. Moore, *Decision Models for Management*, 1982; H. Chernoff and L. E. Moses, *Elementary Decision Theory*, 1959; G. Fandel and T. Gal (eds.), *Multiple Criteria Decision Making: Theory and Application*, 1980; P. C. Fishburn, *Mathematics of Decision Theory*, 1972.

## Delay line

A transmission line (as nearly dissipationless as possible) or an electric network approximation of it which, if terminated in its characteristic impedance, will reproduce at its output a waveform applied to its input terminals with little distortion but at a time delayed by an amount dependent upon the electrical length of the line.

If a transmission line is dissipationless, which will be the case if its series resistance is zero and its shunt conductance is also zero, it will have a characteristic impedance $Z_0$, as shown in Eq. (1), where $L$ is the

$$Z_0 = \sqrt{L/C} \tag{1}$$

series inductance and $C$ the shunt capacitance per unit length of the line.

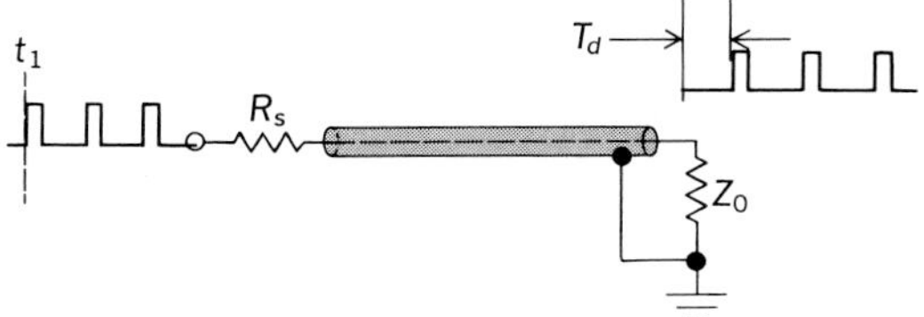


**Fig. 1. Transmission line as delay line.**

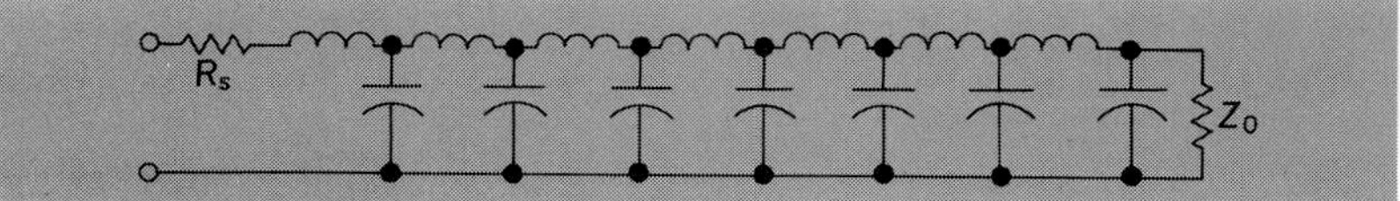


**Fig. 2. Lumped-circuit delay line.**

The velocity $v$ of propagation of a signal along the line is shown by Eq. (2).

$$v = \frac{1}{\sqrt{LC}} \tag{2}$$

Therefore the time required for the pulse to propagate a distance $x$ along the line is shown by Eq. (3).

$$T_d = x\sqrt{LC} \tag{3}$$

Such a line, terminated in its characteristic impedance, is shown in **Fig. 1**; and output pulses reproduce input at a delayed time $T_d$.

The lumped-circuit approximation of the transmission line is shown in **Fig. 2**. If the inductance and capacitance per section are $L_1$ and $C_1$, then the total time delay is shown by Eq. (4), where $n$ is the number of sections.

$$T_d = n\sqrt{L_1C_1} \tag{4}$$

If the delay line is not terminated in its characteristic impedance, there is multiple reflection back and forth along the line. For example, if the receiving end of the line is unterminated, as in **Fig. 3**, but the sending end is terminated in its characteristic impedance, the receiving-end reflection coefficient is positive, and a delayed pulse appears at the output, as given by Eqs. (3) and (4). In addition, a pulse of the same polarity appears at the input terminals, delayed by twice this amount (the time required for a pulse to travel to the end and back).

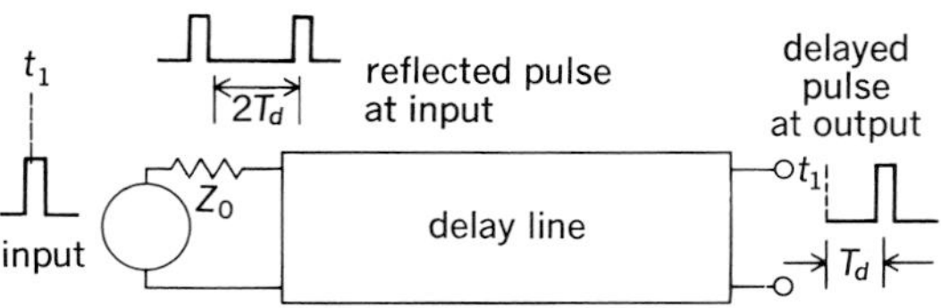


**Fig. 3. Reflection due to unterminated receiving end.**

If the receiving end is terminated in a short circuit as shown in **Fig. 4**, the receiving-end reflection coefficient is negative, and no pulse appears at the output, although an inverted pulse will appear at the input terminals with the same time delay as before.

Various applications make use of the short circuit and open circuit of delay lines, including line-controlled pulse generators. *SEE PULSE GENERATOR*.

Delay lines are also used for establishing a time sequence for the occurrence of events. A delay line with a total length equal to the greatest time delay required in a system may be used as a basic element. Pulses occurring at intermediate times may be obtained from taps at various points along the line. A specific application is found in the synchronizing signal generator of the television system. Also, the lumped-circuit delay line is an essential element of the wide-band distributed amplifier.

When a signal is digital in nature, or consists of a series of pulses, the series of pulses may be delayed

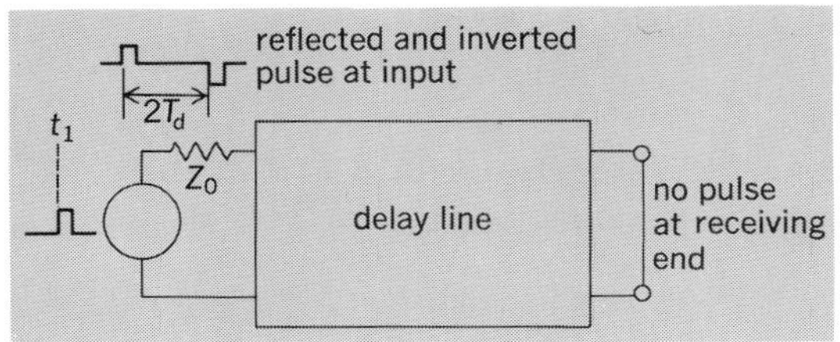


**Fig. 4. Reflection due to short-circuited receiving end.**

by using a shift register, which might, for example, consist of a chain of cascaded type D flip-flops. If the register has $n$ stages, the pulse series will appear at the output delayed by a time $(n - 1)T$, where $T$ is the periodicity of the pulses. The same function can be realized by using an array of charge-coupled devices. *See* CHARGE-COUPLED DEVICES; TRANSMISSION LINES.

*Glenn M. Glasford*

**Bibliography.** G. M. Glasford, *Linear Analysis of Electronic Circuits*, 1965; J. Millman, *Microelectronics*, 1979; J. Millman and H. Taub, *Pulse Digital and Switching Waveforms*, 1965.

## Demodulator

A device used to recover the original modulating signal from a modulated wave. A demodulator is also known as a detector.

In communications systems and in some automatic control systems, the information to be transmitted is first impressed upon a periodic wave called a carrier. The carrier is then said to be modulated. After reception of the modulated carrier, the original modulating signal is recovered by the process of demodulation or detection.

The amplitude, frequency, or phase of a carrier may be changed in the modulation process. Therefore, the process of demodulation and the practical circuits for accomplishing it differ in each case. However, all demodulators require the use of a nonlinear device in order to recover the original modulating frequencies, because these frequencies are not present in the modulated carrier and new frequencies cannot be produced by a linear device. *See* AMPLITUDE MODULATION; FREQUENCY MODULATION; PHASE MODULATION.

**AM types.** A semiconductor diode is frequently used to demodulate an amplitude-modulated (AM) carrier. A simple filter consisting of capacitance and resistance is used to eliminate the carrier and other undesired frequencies from the output of the demodulator. *See* ELECTRIC FILTER; RECTIFIER; SEMICONDUCTOR DIODE.

Another common AM detector uses a multiplier circuit, available as a semiconductor chip. The AM carrier is applied to one of the multiplier inputs, and an unmodulated carrier having the same frequency and phase as the modulated carrier is applied to the other multiplier input. A simple trigonometric identity shows that the multiplication produces the original modulating frequencies at the multiplier output. The unwanted frequencies are removed by a simple filter. The unmodulated carrier frequency of proper phase may be obtained in the receiver by the use of a phase-locked loop. This synchronous-type demodulator has less distortion and lower noise than the simpler diode detector. *See* PHASE-LOCKED LOOPS.

A square-law detector is often used to demodulate single-sideband (SSB) signals. A multiplier chip with both inputs tied together serves nicely as a squaring circuit and may be used as a low-distortion demodulator for SSB signals. *See* AMPLITUDE-MODULATION DETECTOR; SINGLE SIDEBAND.

**FM types.** Frequency-modulated (FM) signals and phase-modulated (PM) signals may generally be demodulated by the same type of circuits, the only difference being the filter circuits in their respective outputs.

There are two basic classes of FM or PM demodulators. The first type, known as discriminators, use tuned circuits to change frequency or phase variations into amplitude variations and then use amplitude-demodulating devices such as diodes or a multiplier to recover the modulating frequencies. The second class or type of FM demodulator is the phase-locked loop, which includes a phase detector that may be a multiplier, a low-pass filter, and a voltage-controlled oscillator that produces a frequency proportional to its control voltage. The output of the phase detector is proportional to the phase difference between the incoming FM or PM signal and the voltage-controlled oscillator output. This phase detector output, after filtering, is the desired original modulating signal and also provides the control voltage needed to keep the voltage-controlled oscillator locked to the incoming signal frequency. These phase-locked loops are available as integrated semiconductor circuits, or chips. *See* FREQUENCY-MODULATION DETECTOR; PHASE-MODULATION DETECTOR.

A special type of FM that is frequently used to transmit coded pulse signals is known as frequency-shift keying (FSK). In this type of modulation, only two different frequencies need to be transmitted to represent binary-coded signals: one to represent zeros and the other to represent ones. For example, the original carrier might represent a zero, and another nearby or shifted frequency would represent a one. A phase-locked loop is usually used as a demodulator in a communications system that uses FSK.

The phase-modulation equivalent of FSK is phase-shift keying (PSK). In this type of modulation the phase of the carrier is abruptly changed or shifted by approximately 180° when the modulating signal changes from a zero to a one, or vice versa. A phase-locked loop that has a long time-constant filter in the voltage-controlled oscillator circuit will demodulate the PSK signal. More complicated PSK modulations are used in special communications systems which shift the carrier phase less than 180°. A commonly used one is 4-0 PSK, where the carrier phase is shifted in increments of 90°.

**Modems.** Amplitude modulation and demodulation may be accomplished with the same device. For example, a multiplier performs both of these functions. In addition, phase-locked loops incorporate all the basic circuits needed for the modulation and demodulation of FM, PM, and AM signals. Therefore, circuits have been devised that will either modulate or demodulate FM, PM, and AM signals. These circuits are known as modems and are commonly used in modern communications systems.

**Optical demodulators.** The development of optical demodulators came with the advent of optical-frequency communications systems. *See* MODULATION; MODULATOR; OPTICAL COMMUNICATIONS; OPTICAL DETECTORS.

*Charles L. Alley*

**Bibliography.** J. J. DeFrance, *Communications, Electronics and Circuits,* 2d ed. 1972; S. Haykin, *Communications Systems,* 1983; R. Kellejian, *Electronic Communications, Circuits, Systems, Transmissions,* 1980.

## Desorption

A process in which atomic and molecular species residing on the surface of a solid leave the surface and enter the surrounding gas or vacuum. In stimulated desorption studies, species residing on a surface are made to desorb by incident electrons or photons. Measurements of these species provide insight into the ways that radiation affects matter, and are useful analytical probes of surface physics and chemistry. In thermal desorption studies, adsorbed surface species are caused to desorb as the sample is heated under controlled conditions. These measurements can provide information on surface-bond energies, the species present on the surface and their coverage, the order of the desorption process, and the number of bonding states or sites.

**Stimulated desorption.** Stimulated desorption from surfaces is initiated by electronic excitation of the surface bond by incident electrons or photons. The classical model of desorption is an adaptation of the theory of gas-phase dissociation, in which desorption results from excitation from a bonding state to an antibonding state. In this model the excitations for gas-phase dissociation and desorption from surfaces are identical, but the surface, which can absorb energy from the excited adsorbate before it can desorb, dramatically reduces the overall dissociation yield from surfaces. Thus, processes which are strong in the gas phase can be quenched on the surface, leading to a marked difference in the relative importance of competing mechanisms in the two environments. This model applies predominantly to neutral desorption of adsorbed molecular species.

Another model, proposed by M. L. Knotek and P. J. Feibelman, which is more applicable to the phenomenon of ion desorption, was first observed in studies of the desorption of positively ionized oxygen ($O^+$) from the surface of titanium(IV) oxide ($TiO_2$). Here it is found that $O^+$ is desorbed not by valence level excitation, but by ionization of the titanium and oxygen core levels. These levels, of course, have little to do with bonding. Furthermore, the fact that the oxygen is desorbed as an $O^+$ ion (whereas it is nominally at $O^{2-}$ on the surface) implies a large (three-electron) charge-transfer preceding desorption.

Titanium(IV) oxide is an ionic solid, and more importantly it is a maximal valency ionic compound. Maximal valency means that in the solid the titanium

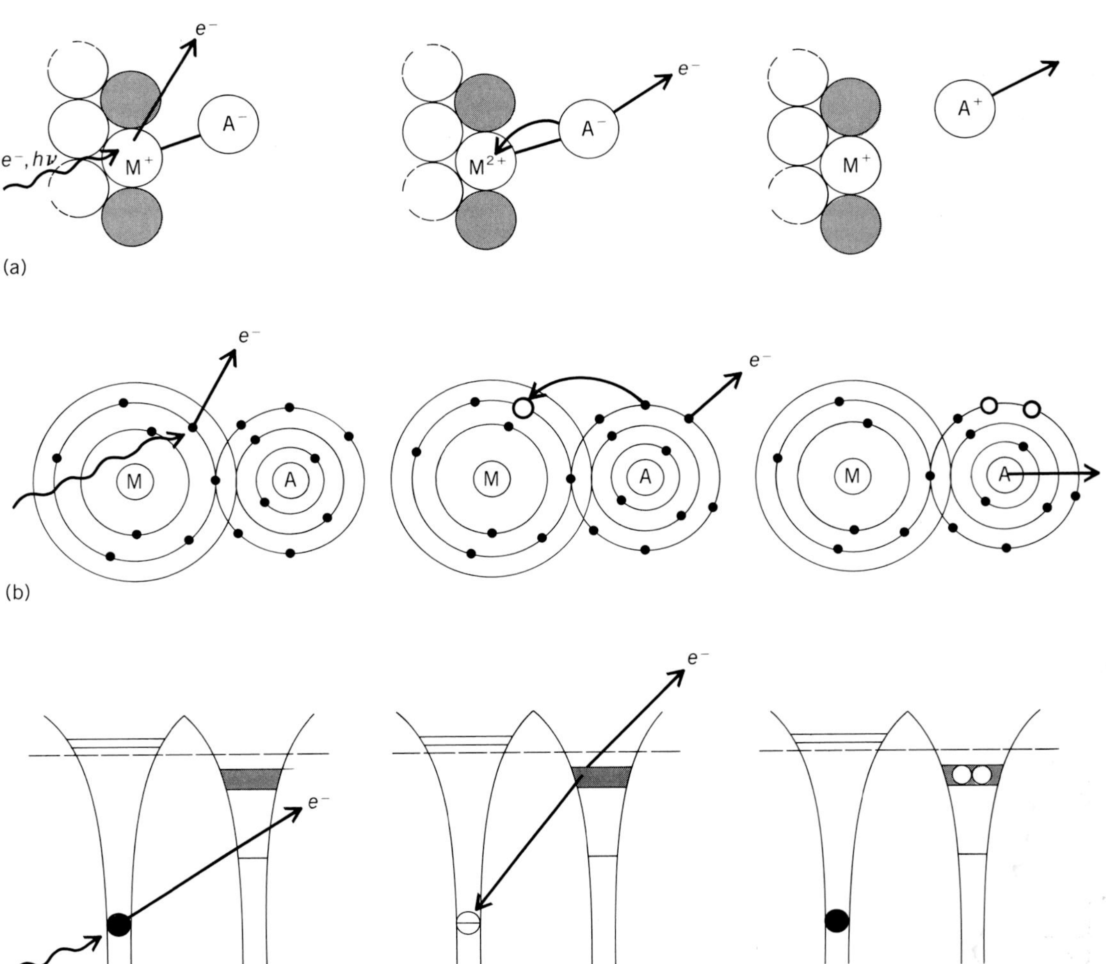


**Fig. 1.** Sequence of events leading to stimulated desorption by an electron ($e^-$) or photon ($h\nu$): (a) in the structural model, (b) in terms of orbitals, and (c) in terms of energy levels.

(Ti) is ionized to the noble-gas configuration $Ti^{4+}$, so that there are effectively no valence electrons on the Ti ion in the solid; its highest occupied orbital is 3*p* at about 30 eV below the Fermi level. The important thing about maximal valency ionic materials is that if a core level is ionized in either the cation or the anion, higher-lying valence electrons will decay into the deep hole left in the core level and give up the energy gained by emitting multiple-valence electrons from the solid (multiple Auger emission). Since valence electrons are only on the anion, the anion is selectively stripped in the process. In $TiO_2$ one electron is lost from $O^{2-}$ by decay into the core hole; in about 10% of the events two Auger electrons are emitted, transforming the $O^{2-}$ to an $O^+$ ion. An $O^+$ ion in a highly repulsive potential for positive ions results, which leads to $O^+$ desorption. In the general case of an ionic bond $M^+A^-$ (**Fig. 1**), the incident radiation ionizes the core level of the $M^+A^-$ pair. Auger decay of the core hole selectively removes charge from the $A^-$ ion and results in its being transformed into an $A^+$, and the resulting repulsion causes the $A^+$ to desorb. This model applies to a wide range of ionic materials, and explains why maximal valency materials like $TiO_2$, vanadium (V) oxide ($V_2O_5$), tungsten(VI) oxide ($WO_3$), molybdenum(VI) oxide ($MoO_3$), sodium fluoride (NaF), lithium fluoride (LiF), sodium chloride (NaCl), and so forth, are decomposed by irradiation.

This mechanism for desorption can also be effective for covalently bonded surface species. Covalently bonded structures differ from ionically bonded structures in that the electronic charge which bonds the atoms together is distributed more evenly through the structure. The electronic interaction between atoms is strong so that an electronic excitation produced on one atom can quickly move to a neighbor. Thus, a simple electronic excitation can quickly move off the site where it was created before dissociation can occur. It typically takes $10^{-12}$ s for bond dissociation to occur, whereas the motion of simple electronic excitations can occur in $10^{-16}$ s. However, an important attribute of states where two or more electrons are removed from the atom is that such multiply excited states are much more difficult to move to a neighbor and hence are localized for times long enough for desorption to occur. Several features of a covalent bond can enhance this tendency to localize on the atom—for example, reducing the number of neighbors (and hence bonds), or reducing the bond's ability to transport charge to the desorbing species to neutralize the excited state.

***Applications.*** Stimulated desorption studies are finding wide use. First, they can show the ways in which radiation affects the structure of solids. This will have important applications in the areas of radiation-induced damage and chemistry. Second, as an analytical tool, they offer a unique new way to study the physics and chemistry of atoms on surfaces which, when combined with the many other surface techniques based largely on electron spectroscopy, can provide new insight. Finally, models of the surface bond are put to a much sterner test in attempting to explain desorption phenomena.

***Analysis of surface structure.*** The techniques of electron- and photon-stimulated desorption can be very useful in the study of how atoms and molecules bond to surfaces. Since ions are desorbed only from the topmost layers of the solid, these techniques study only that outermost layer. By mass-analyzing the desorbed atomic and molecular species, the nature of the chemical species on the surface can be deduced. More importantly, an adsorbed species will be desorbed when the core level of its bonding-site atom is ionized. Since the energy of the electron or photon necessary to ionize a given atom's core level is well known and characteristic of that atom, the bonding sites of each of the desorbing species can be determined. Thus surface-, site-, and adsorbate-specific information can be obtained. Elaborate methods for deducing how the bonding site and adsorbate atoms are electronically and structurally configured can be utilized with this technique. The method is almost the only spectroscopy capable of detecting hydrogen, a classic problem in this field.

***Ion angular distributions.*** An additional important discovery is that ion angular distributions from stimulated desorption are not isotropic, but show that ions are emitted in relatively narrow cones which project along the nominal ground-state bond directions. An angular display shows an azimuthal pattern which reflects the symmetry of the bonding site, and a polar angular distribution which reflects the bonding angle relative to the surface normal. Thus this technique provides a direct display of the surface-bonding geometry.

There are a number of ways to measure the angular distributions of desorbed ions. One of the simplest employs an image intensifier. Individual ion events result in light pulses at a phosphor screen, and time-averaged photographs of the screen provide visual images of the distributions and thus allow a direct view of the arrangement of atoms and molecules on the surface (**Fig. 2**). The directness and simplicity of the technique make it particularly attractive to measure complicated surface adsorbate structures or chemical configurations which do not contain the long-range order necessary in many other techniques for measuring structure. *See* Light amplifier.

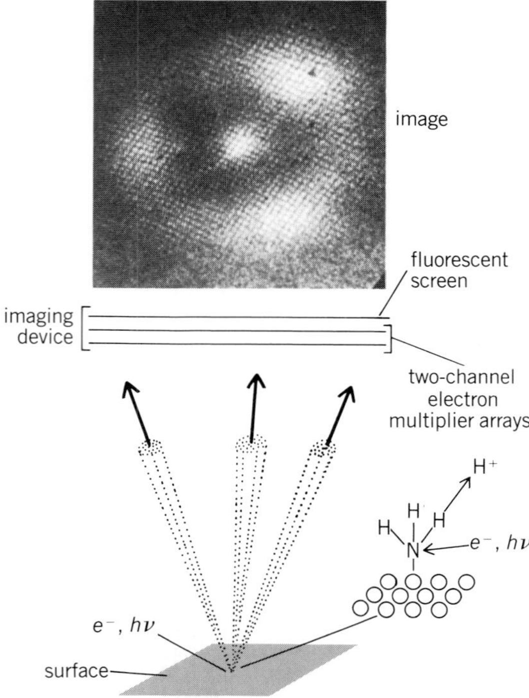


**Fig. 2. Measurement of the angular distribution of ions leaving a surface in stimulated desorption.**

**Thermal desorption.** Thermal desorption mass spectroscopy is possibly the oldest technique for the study of adsorbates on surfaces. Three primary forms of the thermal desorption experiment involve measurement of (1) the rate of desorption from a surface during controlled heating (temperature-programmed thermal desorption), (2) the rate of desorption at constant temperature (isothermal desorption), and (3) surface lifetimes and diffusion under exposure to a pulsed beam of adsorbates (molecular-beam experiments). Of the three, temperature-programmed thermal desorption is by far the most widely applied, and the discussion below is confined to it.

In thermal desorption measurements, a surface is first dosed with an adsorbate gas, and then the sample is heated at a controlled rate β while the rate of desorption of the adsorbed gas is measured with a mass-filter gas analyzer. The most straightforward information provided is the nature of the desorbed species from mass analysis, and a determination of the absolute coverage by the adsorbate, which is very difficult to obtain with other techniques. Coverage is determined by measuring the total amount of gas desorbed. The technique can also provide several important kinetic parameters of the desorption process as follows.

1. Since adsorption reactions are usually nonactivated, the desorption activation energy $E$, which thermal desorption can provide, is a good approximation to the differential heat of adsorption. Thus these studies provide information on surface-bond energies.

2. Desorption kinetics can be quite complex, especially when there are strong interactions between adsorbates. The general form of the $m$th-order desorption rate equation is given by Eq. (1), where $R(t)$ is

$$R(t) = \nu_0^{(m)} n^m \exp(-E/kT_s) \tag{1}$$

the rate of desorption as a function of time, $T_s$ is the substrate temperature, $\nu_0^{(m)}$ is the preexponential factor of the desorption-rate coefficient for order $m$, and $n$ is the two-dimensional adsorbate concentration. Desorption has been observed to obey zero-, first-, and second-order kinetics. Zero-order kinetics is observed for multilayers where removal of an adsorbed species does not lower the effective coverage feeding the desorption process. First-order kinetics is observed for simple desorption of an atomic or molecular species from a submonolayer of adsorbate. Second-order kinetics is often observed in systems where dissociative adsorption has occurred and recombination reactions occur before the desorption.

3. Desorption spectra can determine the number of binding states of an adsorbate on a surface, from the number of desorption peaks observed, and, coupled with structural models of the surface, can help determine both the nature of the bonding sites and the bonding geometries.

4. The preexponential factor of the desorption-rate coefficient, equivalent to an attempt frequency, the rate at which the desorbing particle attempts to leave the surface, not only is necessary to understand desorption kinetics, but helps in understanding the general problem of surface chemical dynamics.

5. The existence of indirect and direct interactions between coadsorbed species can be determined from

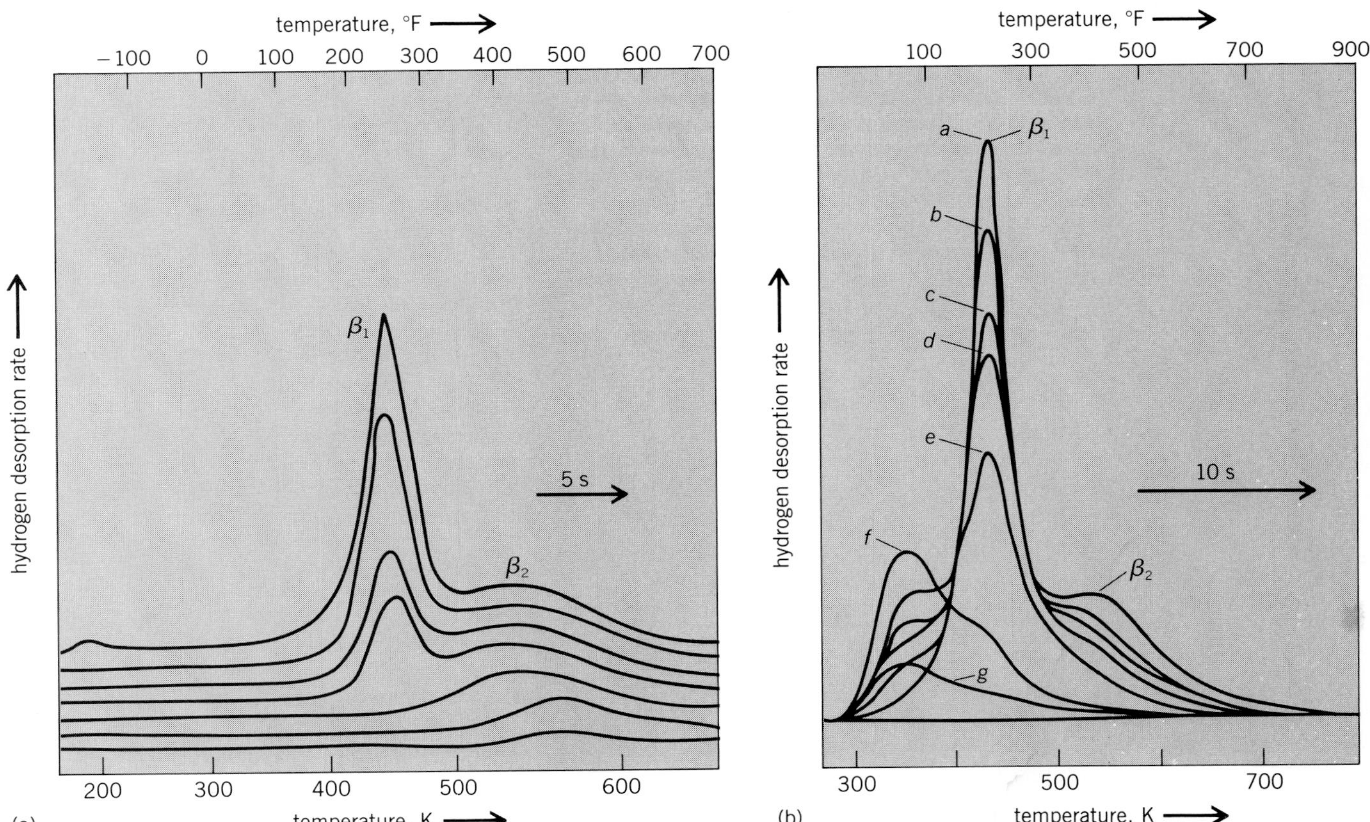


**Fig. 3. Hydrogen desorption rate as a function of sample temperature for a heating rate of approximately 10°C/s. (*a*) Successive curves from bottom to top represent increasing hydrogen coverage. (*b*) Desorption when carbon monoxide (CO) is added to the hydrogen-preadsorbed surface. Successive curves from *a* to *g* represent increasing carbon monoxide coverage. (*After T. E. Madey and J. T. Yates, Surf. Sci., 63:203–231, 1977*)**

thermal desorption. Knowledge of such interactions is directly applicable to such important problems as catalysis and corrosion.

There are several methods to derive the kinetic parameters of Eq. (1) experimentally. If a value is assumed for the preexponential factor $\nu_0$ (usually of the order of $10^{13}$), the desorption activation energy is given by Eq. (2) for first-order kinetics, and by Eq. (3) for second-order kinetics. Here β is the heating

$$E/kT_p = (\nu_0^{(1)}/\beta)\exp(-E/kT_p) \qquad (2)$$

$$E_k T_p^2 = (\nu_0^{(2)}\, n_0/\beta)\exp(-E/kT_p) \qquad (3)$$

rate, $n_0$ is the initial adsorbate concentration, and $T_p$ is the temperature of peak desorption rate. Alternatively, β can be varied and $E$ can be derived from Eq. (4) for first order; for second order, $E/k$ is deter-

$$E/kT_p = d(\ln\beta)/d(\ln T_p) \qquad (4)$$

mined from the slope of a plot of ln $(n_0T_p^2)$ versus $1/T_p$. It is also possible to derive the desorption energy from the width of the desorption peak.

One of the simplest of surface systems, hydrogen adsorbed on the (100) surface of tungsten (W), provides graphic examples how the above types of information manifest themselves and are analyzed. **Figure 3** shows molecular desorption of hydrogen as a function of sample temperature for heating rates β as shown in the figure. At low hydrogen coverages a single $\beta_2$ state is desorbed with second-order kinetics. At coverages above 0.2 monolayer of hydrogen, the $\beta_1$ state desorbs with first-order kinetics. When carbon monoxide (CO) is added to the preadsorbed hydrogen layer, it causes the depopulation of both the $\beta_1$ and $\beta_2$ states and introduces a weak state of lower binding energy. The $\beta_2$ state is now known to be hydrogen bound at reconstructed sites on the W(100) surface, while the $\beta_1$ state is hydrogen at unreconstructed sites.

While the thermal desorption techniques are among the simplest of surface probes, they remain indispensable because of their directness and the variety of information they convey. Thus while surface science moves to detailed methods involving extremely sophisticated apparatus, the simple thermal desorption methods remain an important part of the overall picture. *See Surface physics*.

*M. L. Knotek*

**Bibliography.** C. M. Chan, R. Aris, and W. H. Weinberg, An analysis of thermal desorption mass spectra, *Appl. Surf. Sci.*, 1:360–376, 1978; D. A. King, Thermal desorption from metal surfaces: A review, *Surf. Sci.*, 74:384–402, 1975; M. L. Knotek, Surface chemical information from electron- and photon-stimulated desorption, *Phys. Scripta*, T6:94–103, 1983; T. E. Madey and J. T. Yates, Desorption methods A: Probes of kinetics and bonding at surfaces, *Surf. Sci.*, 63:203–231, 1977; N. H. Tolk et al. (eds.), *Proceedings of the 1st International Workshop: Desorption-Induced Electronic Transitions*, DIETL, 1983.

## Detector

An electronic circuit in a radio receiver used to recover the original modulating signal, or intelligence, from the received signal. This type of circuit is more commonly called a demodulator in current electronic technology. *See Demodulator*.

Some measuring instruments such as impedance bridges and slotted lines for radio-frequency measurements use a meter or other device to indicate the signal strength at the point of interest. These indicating devices are also known as detectors but cannot be properly called demodulators. *See Microwave impedance measurements; Radio-frequency impedance measurements*.

*Charles L. Alley*

## Digital computer

Any device for performing mathematical calculations on numbers represented digitally; by extension, any device for manipulating symbols according to a detailed procedure or recipe. The class of digital computers includes microcomputers, conventional adding machines and calculators, digital controllers used for industrial processing and manufacturing operations, store-and-forward data communication equipment, and electronic data-processing systems. *See Calculators; Computer; Digital control*.

In this article emphasis is on electronic stored-program digital computers. These machines store internally many thousands of numbers or other items of information, and control and execute complicated sequences of numerical calculations and other manipulations on this information in accordance with instructions also stored in the machine. The first section of this article discusses digital system fundamentals, reviewing the components and building blocks from which digital systems are constructed. The following section introduces the stored-program general-purpose computer in more detail and indicates the characteristics by which system performance is measured. The final section traces the history of stored-program digital computer systems and shows how the requirements of new applications and the development of new technologies have influenced system design.

### Digital System Fundamentals

A digital system can be considered from many points of view. At the lowest level it is a network of wires and mechanical parts whose voltages and positions convey coded information. At another level it is a collection of logical elements, each of which embodies certain rules, but which in combination can carry out very complex functions. At a still higher level, a digital system is an arrangement of functional units or building blocks which read (input), write (output), store, and manipulate information.

**Codes.** Numbers are represented within a digital computer by means of circuits that distinguish various discrete electrical signals on wires inside the machine. Theoretically, a signal on a wire could be made to represent any one of several different digits by means of the magnitude of the signal. (For example, a signal from 0 to 1 V could represent the digit zero, a signal between 1 and 2 V could represent the digit one, and so on up to a signal between 9 and 10 V, the digit nine.) In practice, the most reliable and economical circuit elements distinguish between only two signal levels, so that a signal between 0 and 5 V may represent the digit zero and a signal between 5 and 10 V, the digit one. These two-valued signals make it necessary to represent numbers and symbols using a corresponding base-two or binary system. **Table 1** lists the first 20 binary numbers and their decimal

**Table 1. Counting from 0 to 19 by decimal and binary numbers**

| Decimal number | Binary number |
|---|---|
| 00 | 00000 |
| 01 | 00001 |
| 02 | 00010 |
| 03 | 00011 |
| 04 | 00100 |
| 05 | 00101 |
| 06 | 00110 |
| 07 | 00111 |
| 08 | 01000 |
| 09 | 01001 |
| 10 | 01010 |
| 11 | 01011 |
| 12 | 01100 |
| 13 | 01101 |
| 14 | 01110 |
| 15 | 01111 |
| 16 | 10000 |
| 17 | 10001 |
| 18 | 10010 |
| 19 | 10011 |

equivalents. For a detailed discussion of binary numbers *SEE NUMBER SYSTEMS*.

Data are stored and manipulated within a digital computer in units called words. The binary digits (called bits), which make up a word, may represent either a binary number or a collection of binary-coded alphanumeric characters. For example, the two-letter word "it" may be stored in a 16-bit computer word as follows, making use of the code shown in **Table 2**:

0100100101010100

The computer word merely contains a binary pattern of alternating 1's and 0's, and it is up to the computer user to determine whether that word should be interpreted as the English word "it" or as the decimal number 18,772. *SEE BIT*.

**Logical circuit elements.** Two kinds of logical circuits are used in the design and construction of digital computers: decision elements and memory elements. A typical decision element provides a binary output as a function of two or more binary inputs. The AND circuit, for example, has two inputs and an output which is 1 only when both inputs are 1. A memory element stores a single bit of information and is set to the 1 state or reset to the 0 state, depending on the signals on its input lines. And because such a circuit can be caused alternately to store 0's and 1's from time to time, a memory element is commonly called a flip-flop. *SEE SWITCHING THEORY*.

These two basic logical elements are all that are required to construct the most elaborate and complex digital arithmetic and control circuits. A simple example of such a circuit is shown in **Fig. 1**. Here the object is to perform a simple binary count, as shown in the table at the bottom of Fig. 1. As long as control signal $C$ is equal to 1, the counting continues. When the control input is 0, the counter is to remain in whatever state it had last counted to. Two flip-flops are used, labeled $Q1$ and $Q2$, and will be made to count through the sequence 0,1,2,3,0,1, . . . . To understand the design, it is necessary to introduce one more concept, the complementary output of a flip-flop. Each flip-flop generally has two output wires, which are always of opposite polarity. Whe flip-flop $Q1$ is storing a 1, output $Q1$ is 1 and the complementary output (which is labeled $\overline{Q1}$ and pronounced Q1 bar) is 0. When the flip-flop contains a 0, the $\overline{Q1}$ output is 1 and the $Q1$ output is 0.

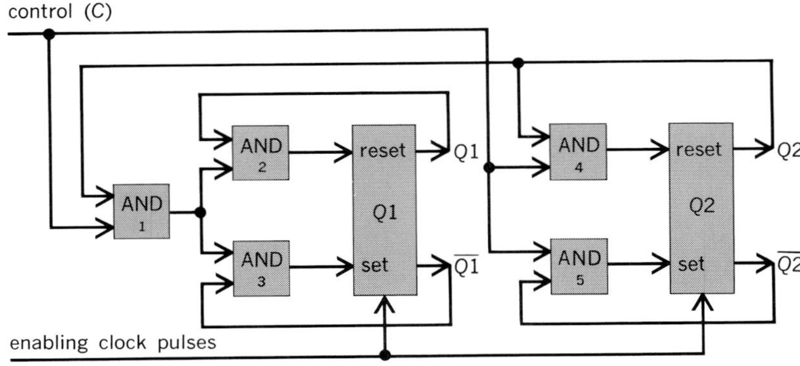


| Binary count: | | Logic equations: |
|---|---|---|
| Q1 | Q2 | $SQ1 = C \cdot Q2 \cdot \overline{Q1}$ |
| 0 | 0 | |
| 0 | 1 | $RQ1 = C \cdot Q2 \cdot Q1$ |
| 1 | 0 | |
| 1 | 1 | $SQ2 = C \cdot \overline{Q2}$ |
| 0 | 0 | |
| 0 | 1 | $RQ2 = C \cdot Q2$ |
| ... | ... | Note: $C \cdot Q2$ means C AND Q2 |

**Fig. 1. Simple digital counting circuit.**

To analyze the circuit, note first that, when control input $C$ is 0, the outputs of all AND gates are 0 and, because the reset and set inputs to both flip-flops are 0, the flip-flops will remain in whatever state they last reached. Now suppose that $Q1$ and $Q2$ both contain 0 and that the control input becomes 1. While flip-flop $Q2$ contains a 0, its $Q2$ output is also 0 and AND gate number 1 (labeled AND 1) is effectively turned off so that the reset and set inputs to $Q1$ are both 0. Thus flip-flop $Q1$ will remain in the 0 state. For the same reason AND gate 4 will also be turned off, and the reset input to flip-flop $Q2$ will be 0. However, from flip-flop $Q2$ complementary output $\overline{Q2}$ will be in the 1 state, and (while the control input is 1) AND gate 5 will be turned on and the set input to $Q2$ will be 1. Flip-flop $Q2$ will thus be turned on by the first clock

**Table 2. American standard alphabetic code for binary representation of letters**

| | | | |
|---|---|---|---|
| 11000001 | A | 11001110 | N |
| 11000010 | B | 01001111 | O |
| 01000011 | C | 11010000 | P |
| 11000100 | D | 01010001 | Q |
| 01000101 | E | 01010010 | R |
| 01000110 | F | 11010011 | S |
| 11000111 | G | 01010100 | T |
| 11001000 | H | 11010101 | U |
| 01001001 | I | 11010110 | V |
| 01001010 | J | 01010111 | W |
| 11001011 | K | 01011000 | X |
| 01001100 | L | 11011001 | Y |
| 11001101 | M | 11011010 | Z |

pulse to occur after $C$ is turned on; and from one clock pulse time to the next the two flip-flops will change from the (0,0) state to the (0,1) state. A careful review of the indicated circuits will show that the counter will indeed go through the count sequence as shown, as long as the control input is 1. The logic equations in Fig. 1 represent another way of describing the circuit and may be used in place of the more cumbersome diagram. *See* DIGITAL COUNTER; LOGIC CIRCUITS.

**Physical components.** The logical elements described in the paragraphs above are the fundamental conceptual components used in virtually all digital systems. The actual physical components which were used to realize conceptual gates and flip-flops in some specific piece of equipment are dependent on the status of electronic technology at the time the equipment was designed. In the 1950s the earliest commercial computers used vacuum tubes, resistors, and capacitors as components. A flip-flop typically required a dozen or more such components in these first-generation computers. Between the late 1950s and middle 1960s, solid-state transistors and diodes replaced the vacuum tubes, and the resulting second-generation systems were considerably more reliable than their first-generation predecessors; they were also smaller and consumed less power. But the number of electronic components per conceptual logical component remained about the same—a dozen or more for a flip-flop. *See* DIODE; TRANSISTOR; VACUUM TUBE.

Since the mid-1960s the integrated circuit (IC) has been the principal logical building block for digital systems. Early digital integrated circuits contained a single flip-flop or gate, and the use of these components permitted designers of the early third-generation systems to provide much more capability per component than was possible with the first- or second-generation technology. Since the mid-1960s integrated circuit technology has consistently improved, and typical large-scale-integration (LSI) circuits contain thousands of flip-flops and gates. *See* INTEGRATED CIRCUITS.

**System building blocks.** On a completely different conceptual level, a digital computer can be regarded as being composed of functional, system building blocks, containing (among other things) subassemblies of the fundamental logical components. A computer viewed at this level may be described in an oversimplified fashion by the diagram of **Fig. 2**. The computation and control block (often called the central processing unit, or CPU) is constructed entirely of logical elements of the kind described above. The main memory, which may store from a few thousand to several million binary digits, and the input/output and auxiliary memory devices (the so-called peripheral equipment) are specialized devices available over a range of speeds and operating characteristics. *See* COMPUTER SYSTEMS ARCHITECTURE.

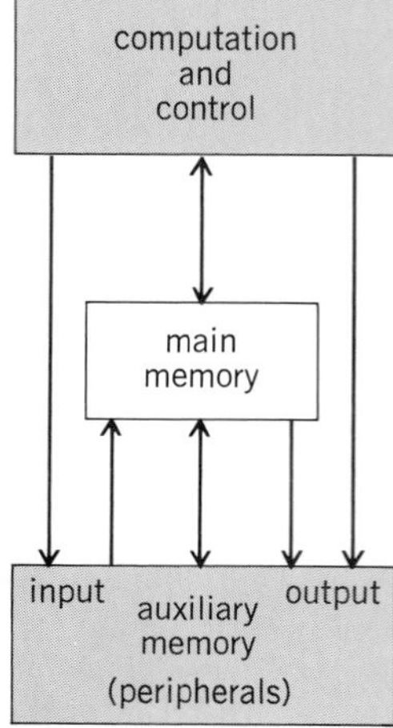


**Fig. 2. Block diagram of a digital computer.**

Main memory is a building block capable of storing data or instructions in bulk for use by the computation and control portion of the computer. The important characteristics of a memory are capacity, access time, and cost. Capacity is the amount of data that the computer can store. Access time is the maximum interval between a request to the memory for data and the moment when the memory can provide that data. Cost is measured by dividing total memory cost by the number of bits stored. For first-generation systems, designers used a variety of technologies in realizing main memory: mercury delay lines, electrostatic storage tubes, and magnetic drums all appeared in various products. But second- and third-generation systems were almost exclusively built using magnetic core main memories. Starting in the early 1970s, the integrated circuit memory was introduced, and is now the most widely used technology. *See* COMPUTER STORAGE TECHNOLOGY.

Input/output and auxiliary memory peripherals represent the other major computer building blocks. Equipment is now and has from the beginning been available for feeding information to the computer from paper tape and punched cards, and for receiving data from the computer and printing it, or punching it on tape cards. But in the intervening years, designers have provided additional output devices which record computer data on microfilm, or plot data on graphs, or use data to control physical devices such as valves or rheostats. They have also designed input equipment which feeds the computer data from laboratory instruments, and from devices which scan documents and ''read'' printed characters. Data can be transmitted to and from the computer over ordinary telephone lines, and a wide variety of devices generally called terminals, make it possible for people to send data to, or receive requested data from, a computer system located hundreds or thousands of miles away. *See* CHARACTER RECOGNITION; COMPUTER GRAPHICS; DATA COMMUNICATIONS; MULTIACCESS COMPUTER.

The earliest auxiliary memory equipment recorded data on reels of magnetic tape. Magnetic tape units are still very widely used, for although they are slow in comparison to the operating speeds of modern computers—it typically takes 2–30 min to read all the data on a 2400-ft (732-m) reel of tape, depending on the speed of the tape unit—they make it possible to store large volumes of data at low cost by virtue of the low cost of the tape itself. The other widely used auxiliary memory devices are the magnetic disk and drum, both of which provide faster access to data than do the tape units, but at higher cost per bit of data stored. *See* DATA-PROCESSING SYTEMS.

## Stored Program Computer

Components and building blocks described in the preceding paragraphs could be organized in a multitude of different ways. The first practical electronic computers, constructed during the latter part of World War II, were designed with the specific purpose of computing special mathematical functions. They did their jobs very well, but even while they were under construction, engineers and scientists had come to realize that it was possible to organize a digital computer in such a way that it was not oriented toward some particular computation, and could in fact carry out any calculation desired and defined by the user. The basic machine organization invented and constructed at that time was the stored-program computer, and it continues to be the fundamental basis for each of the hundreds of thousands of computing systems in use today. It has also become a system component, since the microcomputer is simply a stored program computer on a single integrated-circuit chip.

The concept of the stored-program computer is simple and can be described with reference to Fig. 2. Main memory contains, in addition to data and the results of intermediate computations, a set of instructions (or orders, or commands, as they are sometimes called); these specify how the computer is to operate in solving some particular problem. The computation and control section reads these instructions from the memory one by one and performs the indicated operations on the specified data. The instructions can control the reading of data from input or auxiliary memory peripherals, and (when the prescribed computations are completed) can send the result to auxiliary memory, or to output devices where it may be printed, punched, displayed, plotted, and so forth. The feature that gives this form of computer organization its great power is the ease with which instructions can be changed; the particular calculations carried out by the computer are determined entirely by a sequence of instructions stored in the computer's memory; that sequence can be altered completely by simply reading a new set of instructions into the memory through the computer input equipment.

**Instructions.** To understand better the nature of the stored-program computer, consider in more detail the kinds of of instructions it can carry out and the logic of the computation and control unit which interprets and implements the instructions. Because the instructions, like the data, are stored in computer words, one begins by examining how an instruction is stored in a word. As an example, assume one is looking at a small computer with words 16 bits long, and assume further that an instruction is organized as shown in **Fig. 3**. In this simple computer an instruction has two parts: the first 5 bits of the word specify which of the computer's repertoire of commands is to be carried out, and the last 11 bits generally specify the address of the word referred to by the command. A 5-bit command permits up to 32 different kinds of instructions in the computer, and an 11-bit address permits one to address up to 2048 different memory locations directly.

Typical instruction types for a computer of this kind are listed below.

***Load.*** Load the number from the prescribed memory location into the arithmetic unit.

***Store.*** Store the number from the arithmetic unit in the memory at the prescribed memory location.

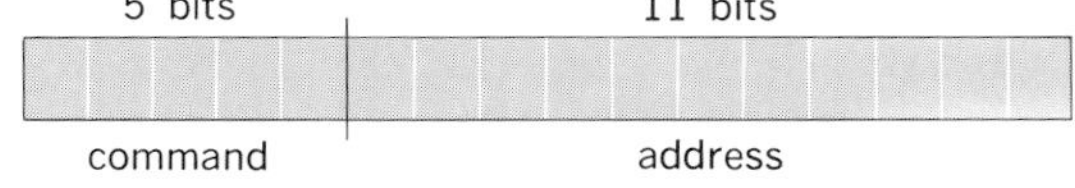

**Fig. 3. Sixteen-bit instruction.**

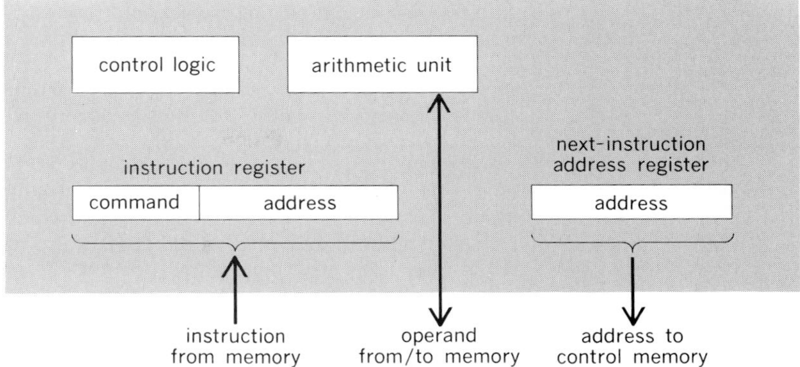

**Fig. 4. Computation and control unit.**

***Add.*** Add the contents of the addressed memory location to the number in the arithmetic unit, leaving the result in the arithmetic unit.

***Subtract.*** Subtract the contents of the addressed memory location from the number in the arithmetic unit, leaving the result in the arithmetic unit.

***Branch.*** If the number in the arithmetic unit is zero or positive, read the next instruction from the address in the next-instruction register as usual. If the number in the arithmetic unit is negative, store the address from the branch instruction itself in the next-instruction register, so that the next instruction carried out will be retrieved from the address given in the branch instruction.

***Halt.*** Stop; carry out no further instructions until the operator presses the RUN switch on the console.

***Input.*** Read the next character from the paper tape reader into the addressed memory location and then move the tape so a new character is ready to be read.

***Output.*** Type out the character whose code is stored in the right-hand half of the addressed memory location.

With the exception of the branch command, the preceding instructions are easy to interpret and to understand. The load and store commands move data to and from the arithmetic unit, respectively. The add and subtract commands perform arithmetic operations, each using the number previously left in the arithmetic unit as one operand, and a number read from a designated memory location as the other. The halt command simply tells the computer to stop and requires intervention by the operator to make the computer initiate computation again. The input and output commands make possible the reading of information into the computer memory from a paper tape input device, and the printing out of the results from previous computations on an output typewriter.

To understand the branch command, consider how the computation and control unit of **Fig. 4** uses the instructions in the memory. To begin with, the instructions which are to be carried out must be stored in consecutive storage locations in memory. Assume that the first of a sequence of commands is in memory location 100. Then the "next-instruction address register" in the computation and control unit (Fig. 4) contains the number 100, and the following sequence of four events takes place: (1) read, (2) readdress, (3) execute, and (4) resume.

***Read.*** The control logic reads the next instruction to be carried out from the memory location whose address is given by the next-instruction address register. The instruction coming from memory is stored in another register called the instruction register. (In this example the next-instruction address register started out containing the number 100, and so the instruction in memory location 100 is transferred to the instruction register.)

***Readdress.*** The control logic now adds unity to the number in the next instruction address register. (In the present example this changes the number in the next instruction address register from 100 to 101. The result is that, when the computer has interpreted and carried out the instruction from location 100, following the rules given in the third and fourth steps below, it will return to the read step above and next interpret and carry out the instruction from location 101.)

***Execute.*** The instruction from location 100 is now in the instruction register and must be carried out. The control logic first looks at the command portion of the instruction in the left-hand 5 bits of the register and interprets or decodes it to determine what to do next. If the instruction is add, subtract, load, or output, the control logic first uses the address in the instruction register—the address associated with the command—and reads the word from that addressed location in memory; it then proceeds to load the word into the arithmetic unit, add it to or subtract it from the number in the arithmetic unit, or transfer it to the output typewriter, depending on the command. If the command is store or input, the control logic collects a number from the arithmetic unit or the paper tape reader and then transfers that number to a location in the memory whose address is given in the instruction register. If the command is halt, the control logic simply prevents all further operations, pending a signal from the operator console.

If the command is branch, the control logic begins by looking at the number in the arithmetic unit. If that number is zero or positive, the control logic goes on to the fourth step below. If the number is negative, however, the control logic causes the address in the instruction register to be transferred to the next-instruction address register before going on to the fourth step. The computer will then continue with one sequence of commands if the previous arithmetic result was positive, and with another if the result was negative. This seemingly simple operation is one of the most important features a computer possesses. It gives the computer a decision-making capability that permits it to examine some data, compute a result, and continue with one of two sequences of calculations or operations, depending only on the computed result.

***Resume.*** As the fourth and final step in the sequence, when the command has been interpreted and carried out properly, the control logic returns to the read step and repeats the entire series of steps.

A sequence of instructions intended to carry out some desired function is called a program; collections of such programs are called software (as distinguished from the equipment, or hardware), and the act of preparing such programs is called programming. Because a computer can perform no useful function until someone has written a program embodying that function, the programming activity is an exceedingly important one and provides a basic limitation to the facility with which the computer can be applied to new areas. *SEE DIGITAL COMPUTER PROGRAMMING.*

**Computer characteristics.** A computer installation is complex. Consequently it is difficult to describe a system or to compare the characteristics of two systems without listing their instruction types and describing their modes of operation at some length. Nevertheless, certain important descriptors are commonly used for comparison purposes and are shown in **Table 3**, where salient characteristics of two typical systems are shown. Definitions of these characteristics can be stated as follows.

**Table 3. Typical computer characteristics**

| | Typical systems | |
|---|---|---|
| Characteristics | Large | Small |
| Memory cycle time | 0.03 μs | 0.90 μs |
| Add time | 0.07 μs | 2.84 μs |
| Main memory storage capacity | 4,000,000 words | 128,000 words |
| Word length | 64 bits | 16 bits |

Memory cycle time is the time required to read a word from main memory. Most modern computers have integrated-circuit memories with cycle times in the ranges shown in Table 3. Add time is the time required to perform an addition, including the time necessary to extract the addition instruction itself and the operand from memory. Main memory storage capacity is the number of words of storage available to the computation and control unit. Typically, a computer manufacturer gives the buyer some choice; the buyer can purchase enough memory to meet the needs of the expected application. This internal capacity refers to the high-speed internal storage only, and does not include disks, drums, or magnetic tape.

Word length is the number of bits in a computer word.

System cost may vary over a range of 5 or even 10 to 1 for a particular computer because of the great variety of options offered the buyer by the manufacturer—options such as memory size, special instructions for efficiency in certain calculations, and number and type of peripheral devices.

There are obviously a number of other measures which may be used to describe a computer. They include such characteristics as multiplication time, transfer rates between input/output equipment and memory, physical size, power consumption, and the availability of a variety of computing options and special features.

### EVOLUTION OF CAPABILITIES

The process by which new circuit and peripheral equipment technologies led to the development of a series of generations of computers was discussed above. But simultaneous with the changes in technology, there came changes in the structure or architecture of computers. These changes were introduced to improve the capability and efficiency of systems, as designers came to understand how computers were actually used.

**Computer efficiency.** One way of looking at system efficiency is indicated in **Fig. 5**, where the operation of a computer is shown broken down into the following four parts. (1) Operator time includes such activities as inserting cards into a card reader, loading magnetic tapes onto a tape unit, setting up controls on a computer operator's panel, and reviewing printed results. (2) Input comes to the computer from periph-

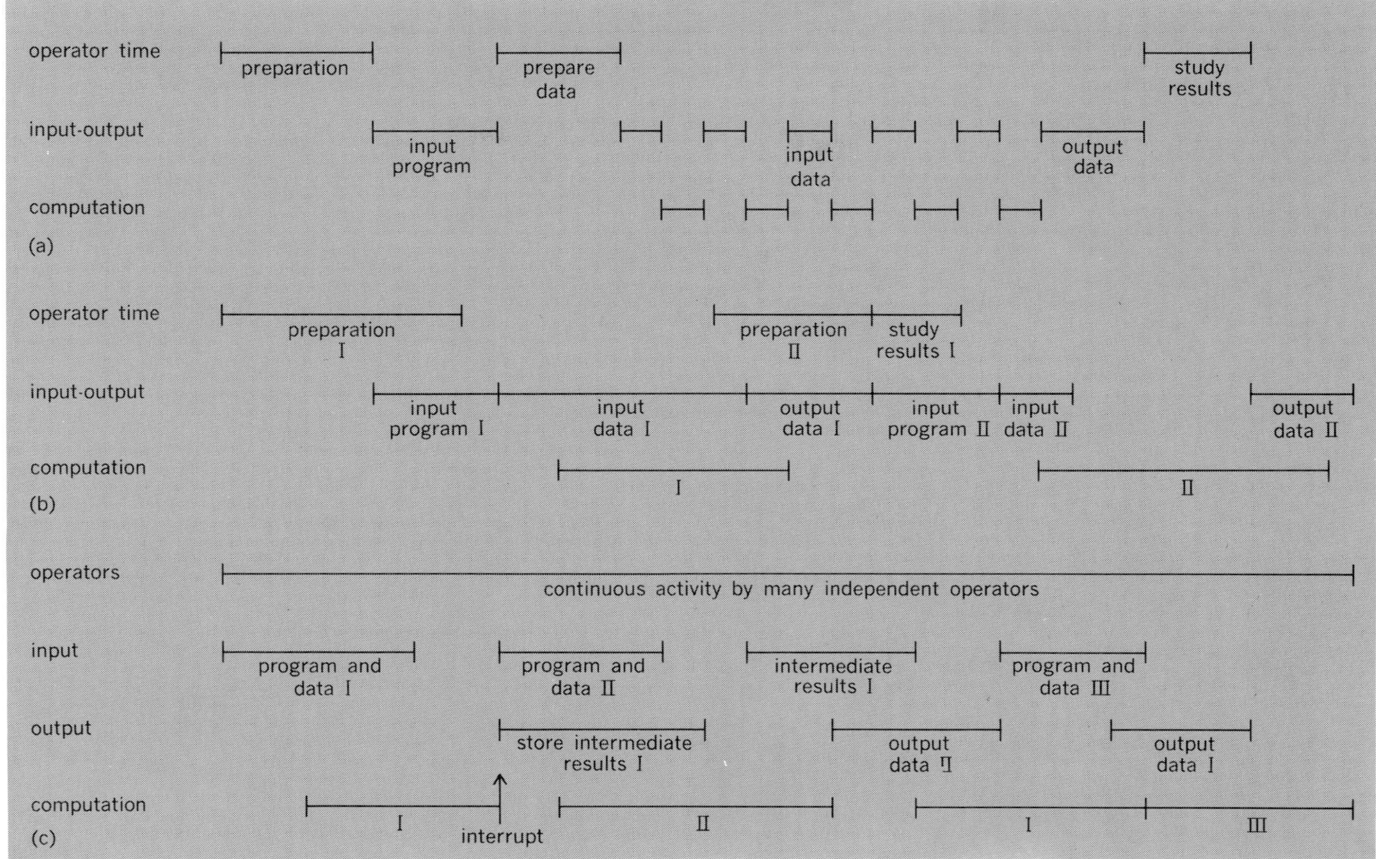


**Fig. 5. Comparison of efficiency for three generations of computers: (*a*) first, (*b*) second, and (c) third.**

eral devices or from auxiliary memory. The inputs include instructions from the operator, inputs of programs to be run, and inputs of data. (3) Computation, being the principal activity, should occupy relatively much of the total time. (4) Output includes storage of intermediate and final results in auxiliary memory, and printing of results along with instructions or warnings to the computer operator.

**First-generation computer.** In the first generation of computer equipment only one of these activities could be carried out at a time. Between jobs the computer was idle while an operator made ready for the next task. When the operator was ready, the program was read into the computer from some input device and the input data were then loaded. The program operated upon the data and performed necessary calculations. When the calculations were complete, the computer printed out answers, and the operator took steps to set up the next problem.

**Second-generation computer.** This series of operations was inefficient, and the designers of second-generation equipment removed some of the inefficiency by arranging input and output operations to be performed directly between the input/output peripherals and the computer memory without interfering with computations. As a result, second-generation computers were able to perform computations while reading in data and printing out replies, and efficiency was greatly enhanced. **Figure 6** indicates schematically the organizational change between generations of computers.

First-generation equipment was most efficient while performing tedious and lengthy computations. The input/output capabilities of the second generation made them useful in applications where large volumes of data had to be handled with relatively little computation—applications such as billing, payroll, and inventory control. At the same time, the great capability and increased reliability of second-generation systems encouraged engineers to apply them to situations where the computer acts as a control element. In military aircraft, in oil refineries and chemical plants, in research laboratories, and in factories, the computer received data directly from measuring instruments, performed appropriate calculations, and as a result made adjustments in the aircraft engine thrust, the flow of raw materials in the plant or factory, or the experimental setup in the laboratory. These new application areas led to two important developments in computer design. The first was a new set of input/output equipments that could be connected to process instruments, converting instrument signals into digital quantities and back again. *See* Analog-to-digital converter; Digital-to-analog converter.

The second development, which evolved from the use of the computer in second-generation control applications, was the interrupt. The processes or activities under control provided data to, and required action from, the computer at random times. These random requests to the computer required rapid response, either because the process required quick control action on the part of the computer or because the process data supplied by instruments were rapidly changing and had to be stored before the data were

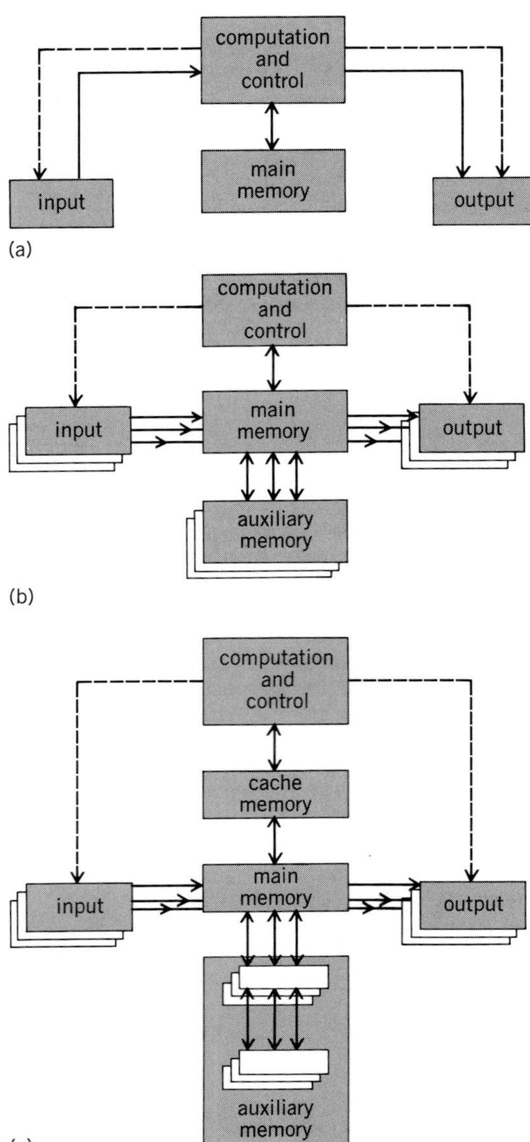


**Fig. 6. Evolution of organization for four generations of computers: (*a*) first; (*b*) second and third; (*c*) fourth.**

lost. The interrupt feature, built into the computation and control unit, solved these problems by providing circuits that could stop the computer after any given instruction, enable it to carry out some special program in response to the external interrupt, and finally permit it to return to precisely the position in the program where it had originally been interrupted.

The logic to achieve these ends is quite simple. When an interrupt signal is received from an external device, the logic circuitry waits until the computer has completed the current instruction and then stores the next instruction address in a specially reserved storage location. The logic substitutes a standard predetermined address in the next instruction address register and continues. The computer of course next executes the instruction at the standard address, and the rest is up to the programmer. The programmer must have inserted a special program at this standard address, and the program must respond to the conditions that caused the interrupt (by inputting data from instrumentation or by taking previously specified control action, for example) and then must return control to the original program at exactly the same place where the program was interrupted. Though the interrupt was originally used largely in control applications, it is now employed in virtually all systems to notify the computer when transfers to and from peripheral equipment are completed.

**Third-generation computer.** In the mid-1960s a new set of trends in computer applications was becoming apparent, and a third generation of computer systems became available to cope with those trends. The usefulness and flexibility of the stored-program computer, together with its improved cost-performance ratio, made it apparent that the computer had the basic power to perform a great variety of small and large tasks simultaneously. For example, the speed and capability of a computer were such that it could simultaneously collect data from a test run or experiment; maintain a file of inventory records on a disk memory; answer inquiries on status of specific items in inventory, such as inquiries entered at random from a dozen different cathode-ray-tube display devices; and assemble or compile programs for users at numerous terminals, all remote from the computer and all working independently on different problems.

A computer system which serves a number of users in this way is called a time-sharing system. To perform in such complex applications, third-generation computers required elaborations of the features found in second-generation computers (Fig. 6). Main and auxiliary memories became bigger and cheaper, more input/output equipments became available, input/output channels improved so that a larger number of simultaneous operations were possible, and interrupt structures grew more flexible. In addition, many new features appeared. Three of them, memory protection circuitry, rapid context switching, and the operating system, are worth discussing briefly.

To understand the implications of third-generation computers and the usefulness of these new features, consider the last portion of Fig. 5. Here the computer is engaged in a variety of different tasks, and it switches back and forth between them as it finishes one portion of a job or as it is interrupted to perform some high-priority job. This rapid switching from job to job led to the development of context-switching equipment. At the time of a changeover from one program to another, the programmer is able with a single instruction to interchange the instruction address register, together with the contents of various arithmetic and control registers, between the job he or she had previously been working on and the new job to be performed. Second-generation computers, without this context-switching feature, require a long sequence of commands every time a change is made from one task to another.

The memory protect feature is important for other reasons. Some programs executed in a time-sharing system such as that depicted by the third-genration portion of Fig. 6 would be new programs being run for the first time. Errors are common in such new programs, and it is the nature of the computer that such errors could have serious effects on system operation. For example, a user's program might accidentally store data in memory space reserved for supervisory or monitor programs—the programs that determine job priorities and reconcile conflicting input/output requirements. To keep such critical memory areas from being destroyed or modified by unchecked programs, designers have made it possible for the user to designate certain areas of memory as protected, and have ensured that only the monitor or supervisory programs can access these particular areas.

The operating system is the set of supervisory programs which manages the system, keeps it operating efficiently, and takes over many of the scheduling and monitoring functions which had previously been the function of the computer operator. It is typically supplied by the computer hardware manufacturer, and was first used with some second-generation systems, where it included little more than interrupt processing and error-handling routines, together with programs to control input/output operations for the user. Its size and importance have both grown with time, and it currently includes those early functions, as well as facilities for accessing compilers and utilities, scheduling jobs to maximize system throughput, managing data-communication facilities, controlling user access to protected data, maintaining records on system usage, and so forth.

**Fourth-generation systems.** Computer memory has become increasingly important with the passing generations, as users have found it useful to store more and more business, government, engineering, and scientific data in machine-readable form. Starting with the third generation, but increasingly with computers introduced in the early 1970s, computer system architects have provided a hierarchy of memory devices to improve system performance and give the user access to very large memory capacities. Figure 6*c* shows how a very large system may make use of such a hierarchy. A so-called cache memory has been interposed between the central processing unit and the main memory, and auxiliary memory has been split into two parts.

The cache is a relatively small but very high-speed memory which stores the data and programs currently being used by the central processing unit. When the central processing unit needs an instruction or data, it sends a main memory address to the cache memory. If the requested information is stored in the cache, it is immediately delivered to the central processing unit; if it is not in the cache, special cache memory hardware requests a block of information from main memory, and that block, which includes the data requested by the central processing unit, is delivered to the cache and displaces another block stored there. Because programs contain many branches, a typical program may repeatedly access a relatively small portion of the main memory, and so a small fast cache can be very effective in increasing the central processing unit's instruction-processing rate. (The cache's great speed makes it correspondingly expensive, and therefore not economical for use as main memory.)

A typical large fourth-generation system may make use of a similar hierarchical arrangement between main and auxiliary memory. Main memory in a large system may contain 750,000 words. But a system equipped with a virtual storage translator can give the user-programmer the illusion of working with 16,000,000 words. This is done by supplying the 750,000 words of real memory with temporary virtual addresses, and transferring data automatically from auxiliary to main storage as it is needed. For example, suppose the central processing unit needs a program which starts at address 2,500,000. The virtual storage translator may assign the virtual memory address 2,500,000 to the real address 700,000, and then transfer a block of (say) 1000 words from auxiliary memory to the main memory locations starting with 700,000. Now when the central processing unit next requests, for example, information from location 2,500,001, the translator locates it in real memory location 700,001, and sends it off to the cache.

Finally, in some very large systems there may also be an auxiliary memory hierarchy, in which a very large, cheap, but relatively slow auxiliary memory delivers data or programs as required to the primary auxiliary memory.

In all these hierarchical arrangements, the guiding principle is that the larger, slower, cheaper memory supplies data as needed to the smaller, faster, more expensive memory. The various levels of memory are invisible to the user; the hardware and, where necessary, the operating system make the various hierarchical levels deliver data and programs to the user without the necessity for any special action on his or her part.

**Fifth-generation systems.** In 1981 the Japanese government announced a 10-year program intended to encourage the development of "intelligent" computers. Japanese industry is participating in the program, whose object is to offer, in the 1990s, machines which can learn and reason, can "talk" to humans in everyday language, and can understand speech and pictures. The Japanese have called these machines fifth-generation computer systems. The American and European responses to Japan's ambitious project have been fragmented and disjointed, although the United

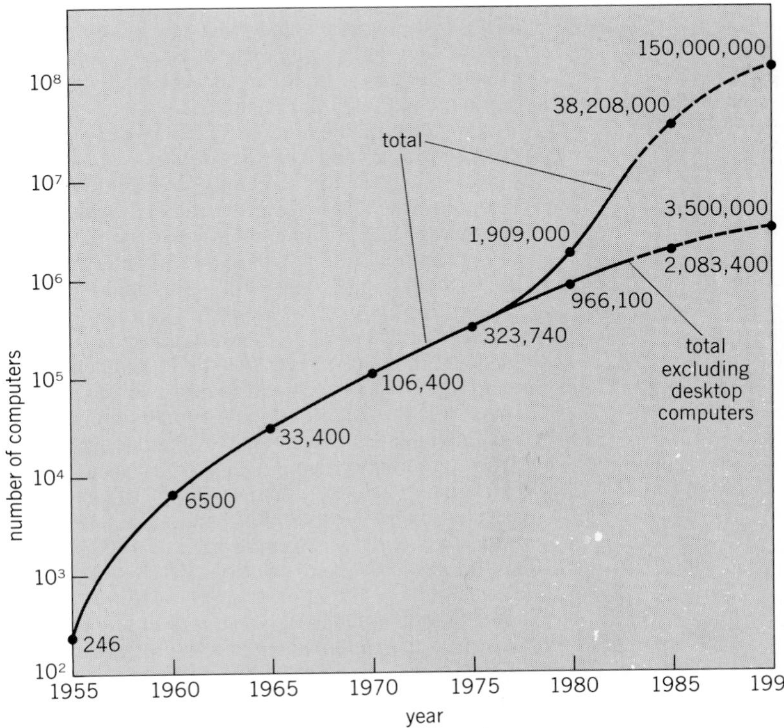


**Fig. 7. Worldwide growth in the number of computers (measured on a logarithmic scale) made by United States companies.**

States and many European countries continue to conduct research on all of the topics included in the Japanese study. SEE ARTIFICIAL INTELLIGENCE; SPEECH RECOGNITION; VOICE RESPONSE.

**Industry growth.** The versatility of the digital computer has led to its application in a wide variety of industries and activities. The evolution of the integrated circuit has made it possible for designers to provide ever-cheaper systems, and as a result, since the mid-1970s the desktop computer has become economical for use in small organizations, at the office worker's desk, and even in the home, where it can supply entertainment, educational, record-keeping, and computing capabilities. The net result of these developments is indicated in **Fig. 7**, which shows the growth in the number of computers in use each year, and forecasts how that growth will continue.

The influence of the digital computer is extending far beyond the realm of computing. The microcomputer has become a component in a variety of apparently noncomputing applications, being used in games, toys, robots, automobiles, appliances, tools, and many other artifacts. SEE MICROCOMPUTER; MICROPROCESSOR; ROBOTICS.

*Montgomery Phister, Jr.*

***Bibliography.*** C. G. Bell and A. Newell, *Computer Structures: Readings and Examples,* 1971; E. A. Feigenbaum and P. McCorduck, *The Fifth Generation,* 1983; M. Phister, Jr., *Data Processing Technology and Economics,* 1979; Special issue on computer architecture, *Commun. ACM,* vol. 21, no. 1, January 1978; Special issue on tomorrow's computers, *IEEE Spectrum,* vol. 20, no. 11, November 1983.

## Digital computer programming

The art of writing instructions to control the operation of a stored-program digital computer. More generally, programming refers to the analysis and planning of a problem solution, in which the phase of instruction writing is referred to as coding.

**Binary operation.** The programming process will be described in terms of the most common form of digital computer. This machine operates internally entirely in binary (base 2) arithmetic and logic, and is arranged so that information is stored and accessed in units termed words. A typical word size is 32 binary digits, or bits, although word sizes range in current practice from 8 to 60 bits. SEE INFORMATION THEORY.

**Notation.** The binary, word-oriented machines (now the dominant type) call for a notation that is either pure binary, or octal (base 8) or hexadecimal (base 16), the latter two being simply conveniences for programmers while they work. The discussion here is in terms of decimal, to simplify understanding of computer principles and to avoid lengthy digression to number systems other than decimal, such as binary, but it must be kept in mind that the basic nature of the machines is binary. SEE NUMBER SYSTEMS; COMPUTER.

**Number operations.** The purpose of a computer is to manipulate information that is stored within the machine in the form of binary numbers. These numbers can be treated as symbols and can represent alphabetic information or anything else the programmer wishes to manipulate. In the simplest case they are numbers and are to be treated arithmetically. Each word contains one number and its associated algebraic sign. The instructions which dictate the operations to be performed on such numbers (data) are also numbers and are also stored one per word in the same physical medium as the data. The stored programming concept presumes that there is no physical difference between these two types of numbers and that the instruction numbers may also be manipulated, in the proper context, as data.

**Addresses.** Each word in storage is assigned an address in order to refer to it, in a manner analogous to postal addresses. The addressing scheme is part of the hardware of the machine, and is wired in permanently. Word addresses range from zero to the storage size of the machine, typically from 00000 through 32,767. Any word may be loaded with any desired information. Some of this information is the data of the problem being processed; the rest is the instructions to be executed. The machine is designed basically to execute instructions in the order in which they are stored, advancing sequentially through the instruction words as addresses that increase by one.

**Instruction format.** Each instruction contains two basic parts: (1) a coded number that dictates what operation is to be performed, for example, ADD, MULTIPLY, and STORE; and (2) the address of the word (data) on which to perform that operation. Thus, suppose the data stored in words 12345, 12346, and 12347 are to be added together. The work is performed in a storage device called the accumulator, which is the same size as one storage word. Three operation codes are involved; namely, LOAD ACCUMULATOR, ADD, and STORE ACCUMULATOR, for which the corresponding operation codes might be 100, 123, and 234. The instructions must also reside in storage, say at addresses (called locations for instructions) 01017, 01018, 01019, and 01020. Then, the program shown in **Fig. 1** applies.

All the data and instruction numbers are in storage before execution begins. The logical sequence is controlled by a counting device called the instruction counter, which is set, for this program, to 01017. Line 1, when executed, causes the contents of the first data word to be moved to the accumulator, destroying the information previously stored there. During this operation the instruction counter advances by one, thus completing one cycle of operation, and the process repeats. Line 2 calls for the information in word 12346 to be added to the contents of the accumulator, and line 3 does the same for the information stored at 12347. Each of these operations involves moving stored information; all such moves follow the pattern that read-in (for example, to the accumulator) is destructive, but read-out (for example, from a referenced storage word) is nondestructive. Thus, after the additions, the data words are still in storage in their original form. Line 4 is the logical inverse of line 1; the information now in the accumulator is moved to word 12348 (and still remains in the accumulator).

Each computer type has a wired-in set of operation

| Location | Operation | Address | Line no. |
|---|---|---|---|
| 01017 | 100 | 12345 | 1 |
| 01018 | 123 | 12346 | 2 |
| 01019 | 123 | 12347 | 3 |
| 01020 | 234 | 12348 | 4 |

**Fig. 1. A straight-line program. Line numbers are for reference with comments made in the text.**

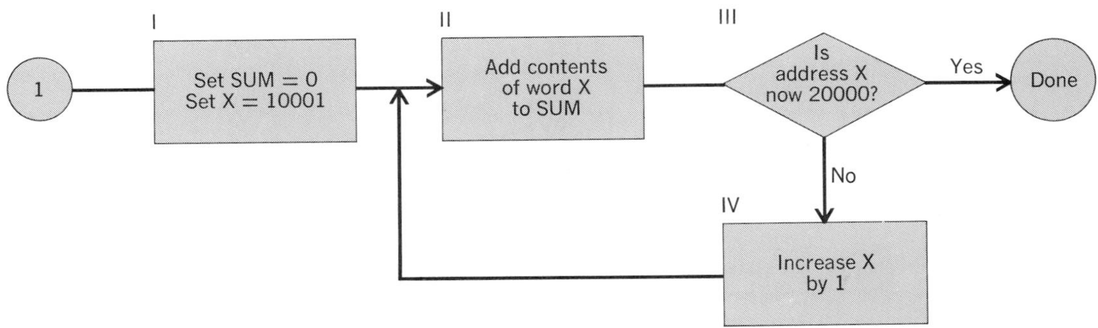


**Fig. 2. Flow chart for the program of Fig. 3.**

codes. Inexpensive machines may offer as few as 16; large machines have several hundred.

**Programming.** The program of Fig. 1 is a straight-line program; that is, its instructions are executed strictly in sequence as stored. The stored-program computer gains its power from two additional concepts. The first concept is derived naturally in that the words of information referenced by an instruction can be other instruction words; thus, a computer can manipulate its own instructions and alter them dynamically, particularly in their address portions, during the execution of a program. The second concept concerns the ability to branch, based on the condition of the accumulator at any given moment. Basically, the machine can interrogate the accumulator and, on the basis of its contents being negative, zero, or positive, call for operating on the instruction counter so that the next executed instruction is not at the location that is one more than the last excuted location, but is any other desired location. This branch of control may also be called for arbitrarily, that is, not based on the condition of the accumulator. For the available branch instructions the address portion is then the location of the next instruction rather than that of a data word. The operation codes are of the form BRANCH, BRANCH ON MINUS, BRANCH ON ZERO, BRANCH ON NONZERO, and so forth.

The program of Fig. 1 would serve to form the sum of three words of information, but would form a poor pattern if there were 10,000 words to be added. In the latter situation there would be 10,001 instruction words, all but two of which would be monotonously similar, differing only in the regular progression of 10,000 addresses. The capabilities of the computer allow for the larger task to be looped; that is, a few instructions can be used over and over.

**Flow-charting.** The logic of any problem situation can be expressed graphically in a flow chart. For the problem of summing the contents of 10,000 words, the flow chart of **Fig. 2** applies. Instructions are written to add the contents of one word (call its address X) to the word SUM. Prior to executing these instructions, it is arranged to set the contents of SUM to zero, and the value of address X to that of the first of the 10,000 words of data. After the contents of any word of data are added to SUM, a check is made to determine whether the word just added was the last word of data. If so, the repetitive task has been completed. If not, the address X is incremented by one, and the process continues. Programmed loops thus follow the pattern of initialization, performance of one case, a test for the last case, modification from case to case, and branch back to the performance block.

The program of **Fig. 3** implements, in the same hypothetical machine code, the loop shown. Following is a list of the operation codes used:

| | |
|---|---|
| 100 | Load accumulator |
| 234 | Store accumulator |
| 235 | Store the address portion of the accumulator |
| 123 | Add to the accumulator |
| 122 | Subtract from the accumulator |
| 002 | Branch if accumulator is zero |
| 001 | Branch unconditionally |

The distinct stages of the loop are marked off. The performance block is at locations 01004–01006. Line 5 calls for the word designated for the SUM to be loaded into the accumulator. The contents of one word, X, is added to it. The address of X is shown as zero, but will never be executed as such. The result of the addition is stored back at SUM (word 20001).

The contents of word 20001 must be set to zero; this is done by lines 1 and 2. Lines 3 and 4 ensure that X is preset to 10001. Lines 8–10 examine the instruction containing X (that is, all of the word at 01005) and effect an exit from the loop when the value of X is 20000. If the exit conditions are not met (as they will not be for 9999 traverses of the loop),

*Data and constants:*

| Address | Value |
|---|---|
| 10001–20000 | data words |
| 20001 | SUM |
| 20002 | 000 00000 |
| 20003 | 000 10001 |
| 20004 | 123 20000 |
| 20005 | 000 00001 |

*Instructions:*

| Location | Operation | Address | Line no. |
|---|---|---|---|
| 01000 | 100 | 20002 | 1 |
| 01001 | 234 | 20001 | 2 |
| 01002 | 100 | 20003 | 3 |
| 01003 | 235 | 01005 | 4 |
| 01004 | 100 | 20001 | 5 |
| 01005 | 123 | (00000) | 6 |
| 01006 | 234 | 20001 | 7 |
| 01007 | 100 | 01005 | 8 |
| 01008 | 122 | 20004 | 9 |
| 01009 | 002 | 01014 | 10 |
| 01010 | 100 | 01005 | 11 |
| 01011 | 123 | 20005 | 12 |
| 01012 | 234 | 01005 | 13 |
| 01013 | 001 | 01004 | 14 |
| 01014 | Continue with the problem | | |

**Fig. 3. A programmed loop. Line numbers are for reference with comments made in the text.**

**Frequently used high-level programming languages**

| Language | Description | How implemented | Features |
|---|---|---|---|
| FORTRAN | Language for scientific and engineering work | Compiled | The oldest high-level language; very widely used |
| COBOL | Language for business data processing | Compiled | Widely used in business |
| BASIC | Simplified language aimed at beginners; universally available on microcomputers | Interpreted | Easily learned, but limited in its scope |
| Pascal | Language for scientific and engineering work | Compiled | Encourages the constructs of structured programming; very popular in the academic community |
| LISP | Specialized language for list processing | Compiled | Leading language for work in artificial intelligence |

the branch to 01014 indicated on line 10 is not taken and the modification steps of lines 11–13 are executed, whose function is to increase the value of x by one. The four sections ruled off in Fig. 2 correspond directly to the boxes of the flow chart for Fig. 3; line 14 performs the unconditional branch back to block II.

**Programming languages.** Programming for a digital computer could be done as illustrated in Fig. 3, but is far more awkward in binary and, moreover, becomes increasingly difficult as programs get longer. For these and other reasons, programmers prefer to work in languages that are at a higher level than the machine language shown. The use of mnemonic operation codes (BZE for BRANCH ON ZERO, in place of the number 002) and the replacement of all absolute machine addresses by symbols greatly speed up the work of the programmer at the modest cost of an extra computer run whose sole function is the translation back to the language used in Fig. 3. The translating program is called an assembler, and the language used is assembly language. Generally, assembly language follows the format of the machine language and is one-for-one with it; that is, for every instruction written in assembly language, one machine language instruction will be produced.

Most programming is done in the language of compilers, for example, FORTRAN or COBOL. Compiler language permits a format that fits the problems rather than the machine, and is many-to-one. For example, a statement (instruction) in FORTRAN can be written Y=B**2−4.0*A*C to correspond to the algebraic expression $b^2-4ac$ (an asterisk being used for multiplication, and two adjacent asterisks denoting the raising to powers). As with assemblers, a separate machine run is needed to translate from the compiler language to the language of the machine; the translating program is called a compiler. The better compilers achieve a measure of machine independence in that programs in compiler language can be compiled into different machine languages without alteration.

The looping technique illustrated in Fig. 3 is one of the two basic building blocks of the programmer. The other is the closed subroutine. Both techniques have the purpose of allowing a small number of instructions to be executed many times. The typical example of the closed subroutine is the short program for the calculation of square root. Such a program might consist of 30 instructions and be needed at eight different places within a large program. The set of 30 instructions could be inserted eight times into the main program, but this would waste the programmer's time and storage space in the machine. The 30 instructions can be stored once, and simple arrangements can be made in the main program to cause their linkage and return at each of the eight points at which the square-root operation is needed.

The concept of the subroutine leads to systematic libraries of tested subroutines that build up for each machine type. Further extensions of this idea lead to whole packaged programs furnished by the manufacturers, to proprietary programs that are offered for sale, and to higher languages designed for specific problem areas.

The **table** describes the most frequently used high-level programming languages.

While the cost of nearly everything else in computing (central processors, storage devices, and input/output devices) continues to fall over the years, the cost of software (that is, computer programs) has risen. This is due in part to the greater complexity of the problems being attacked, and in part to the complexity of a computer system, which is the entity made up of the computer itself plus large control programs called operating systems. Attention has recently turned to methods and techniques, such as structured programming, for improving this situation. *SEE DIGITAL COMPUTER; PROGRAMMING LANGUAGES; SOFTWARE ENGINEERING.*

*Fred J. Gruenberger*

**Bibliography.** D. Cooper and M. Clancy, *Oh! Pascal*, 1982; G. B. Davis, *Computers and Information Processing*, 1978; B. Kernighan and P. J. Plauger, *The Elements of Programming Style*, 1978; D. E. Knuth, *The Art of Computer Programming*, 1975; D. D. McCracken, *Computing for Engineers and Scientists with Fortran 77*, 1984.

## Digital control

The use of digital or discrete technology to maintain conditions in operating systems as close as possible to desired values despite changes in the operating environment. Traditionally, control systems have utilized analog components, that is, controllers which generate time-continuous outputs (volts, pressure, and so forth) to manipulate process inputs and which operate on continuous signals from instrumentation measuring process variables (position, temperature, and so forth). In the 1970s, the use of discrete or logical control elements, such as fluidic components, and the use of programmable logic controllers to automate machining, manufacturing, and production facilities became widespread. In parallel with these developments was the accelerating use of digital computers in industrial and commercial applications areas, both for logic-level control and for replacing analog control systems. The development of inexpensive mini- and microcomputers with arithmetic and logical capability orders of magnitude beyond that obtainable with analog and discrete digital control elements resulted in the rapid substitution of conventional control systems by digital computer–based ones. With the introduction of microcomputer-based control systems into major consumer products areas (such as automobiles and video and audio electronics), it became clear that the digital computer would be widely used to control objects ranging from small, personal appliances and games up to large, commercial manufacturing and production facilities. Hence the focus of this discussion will be on computer-based control systems. *See* Analog computer; Microcomputer; Microprocessor.

**Computer/process interface.** The object that is controlled is usually called a device or, more inclusively, process. A characteristic of any digital control system is the need for a process interface to mate the digital computer and process, to permit them to pass information back and forth (**Fig. 1**).

***Digital control information.*** Measurements of the state of the process often are obtained naturally as one of two switch states; for example, a part to be machined is in position (or not), or a temperature is above (or below) the desired temperature. Control signals sent to the process often are expressed as one of two states as well; for example, a motor is turned on (or off), or a valve is opened (or closed). Such binary information can be communicated naturally to and from the computer, where it is manipulated in binary form. For this reason the binary or digital computer/process interface usually is quite simple: a set of signal-conditioning circuits for each measured or controlled signal and a set of registers to transfer the bits of digital information in each direction. Each register usually would contain the same number of bits as would be manipulated and stored within the digital computer.

***Analog control information.*** Process information also must be dealt with in analog form; for example, a variable such as temperature can take on any value within its measured range or, looked at conceptually, it can be measured to any number of significant figures by a suitable instrument. Furthermore, analog variables generally change continuously in time. Digital computers are not suited to handle arbitrarily precise or continuously changing information; hence, analog process signals must be reduced to a digital representation (discretized), both in terms of magnitude and in time, to put them into a useful digital form.

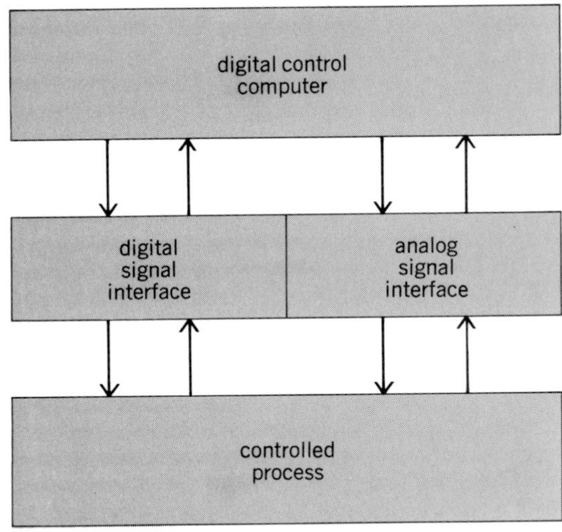

Fig. 1. Generalized digital computer control system.

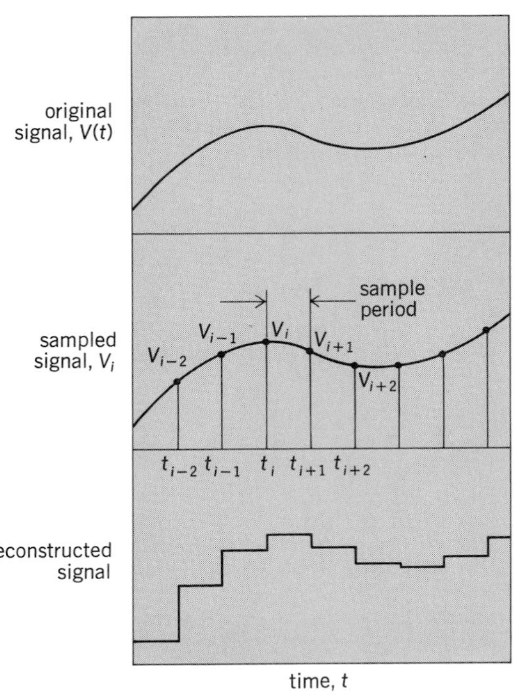

Fig. 2. Discretization in time of an analog signal.

The magnitude discretization problem most often is handled by transducing and scaling each measured variable to a common range, then using a single conversion device—the analog-to-digital converter—to put the measured value into digital form. An analog-to-digital converter suitable for measurement and control purposes typically will convert signals in the range −10 to +10 V direct current, yielding an output with 12 bits of accuracy in 10 to 50 microseconds. A multiplexer often is used to allow a number of analog inputs to be switched into a single analog-to-digital converter for conversion. High-level signals (on the order of volts) can be switched by a solid-state multiplexer; low-level signals (on the order of millivolts, from strain gages or thermocouples) would require mechanical relays followed by an amplifier to boost the signal to an acceptable input level for the analog-to-digital converter. Microcomputers contain integral analog conversion circuitry for several channels on the processor chip. *See* Analog-to-digital converter.

Discretization in time requires the computer to sample the signal periodically, storing the results in memory. This sequence of discrete values yields a ''staircase'' approximation to the original signal (**Fig. 2**), on which control of the process must be based. Obviously, the accuracy of the representation can be improved by sampling more often, and many digital systems simply have incorporated traditional analog control algorithms along with rapid sampling. However, newer control techniques make fundamental use of the discrete nature of computer input and output signals. Analog outputs from a computer most often are obtained from a digital-to-analog converter, a device which accepts a digital output from the computer, converts it to a voltage in several microseconds, and latches (holds) the value until the next output is converted. Usually a single digital-to-analog converter is used for each output signal. *SEE DIGITAL-TO-ANALOG CONVERTER.*

**Real-time computing.** In order to be used as the heart of a control system, a digital computer must be capable of operating in real time. Except for very simple microcomputer applications, this feature implies that the machine must be capable of handling interrupts, that is, inputs to the computer's internal control unit which, on change of state, cause the computer to stop executing some section of program code and begin executing some other section. Using its extraordinary computational abilities (on the order of a million instructions per second), the computer, which basically is a sequential or serial processor, can be made to appear to perform operations in parallel by proper design of its hardware and executive software. By attaching a very accurate oscillator (a so-called real-time clock) to the interrupt line, the computer can be programmed to keep track of the passage of real time and, consequently, to schedule process sampling and control calculations on a periodic basis.

The requirements of real-time computing also imply that the computer must respond to interrupts from the process. Thus a key process variable may be used to trigger an interrupt when it exceeds preset limits. The computer might be programmed to service such an interrupt immediately, taking whatever control action is necessary to bring the variable back within limits. The ability to initiate operations on schedule and to respond to process interrupts in a timely fashion is the very basis of real-time computing; this feature must be available in any digital control system.

**Programming considerations.** Much of the programming of computer control systems is done in a high-level language such as BASIC or FORTRAN; however, many microcomputer applications are carried out in machine (assembly) language. In either case the programmer must utilize program routines which access the devices in the process interface, for example, fetch the contents of a particular digital input register so as to check the status of some process digital element, or write out a digital result to a particular digital-to-analog converter channel. Additionally, the programmer will have the capability to schedule operations periodically or at particular times. *SEE PROGRAMMING LANGUAGES.*

Computer control systems for large or complex processes may involve complicated programs with many thousands of computer instructions. Several routes have been taken to mitigate the difficulty of programming control computers. One approach is to develop a single program which utilizes data supplied by the user to specify both the actions to be performed on the individual process elements and the schedule to be followed. Such an executive program, supplied by a control system vendor, might be utilized by a variety of users; and this approach often is taken for relatively standardized operations such as machining and sequential processing (manufacturing).

Another approach is to develop a rather sophisticated operating system to supervise the execution of user programs, scheduling individual program elements for execution as specified by the user or needed by the process. The multiple program elements, called tasks when used with a multitasking operating system, or called programs with a multiprogramming

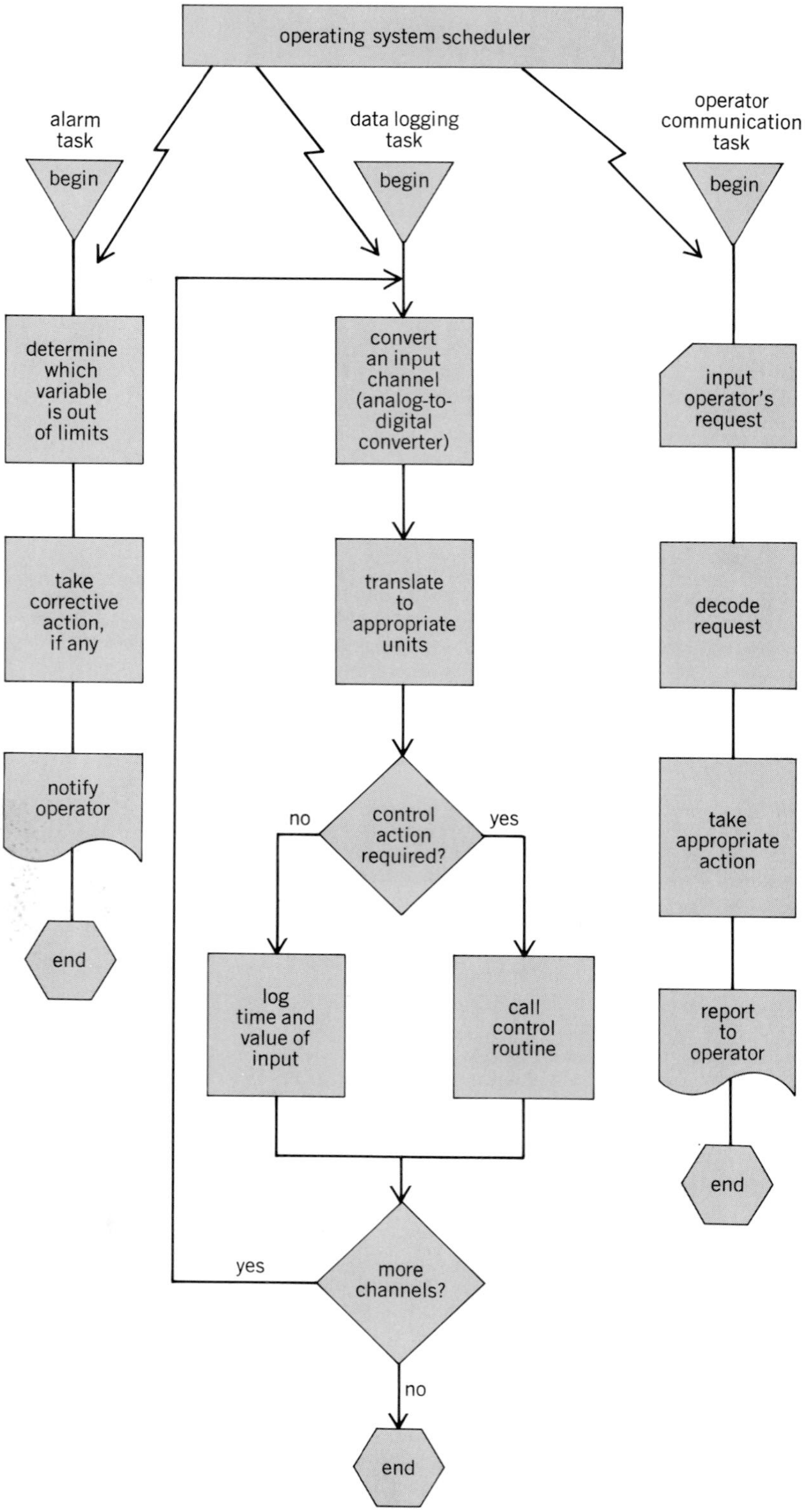

**Fig. 3. Example of a multitasked control program.**

system, will be scheduled individually for execution by the operating system as specified by the user (programmer) or needed by the process. A simple example is given in **Fig. 3** for three tasks—a data logging task which might be scheduled every 30 s, a process alarm task which would be executed whenever a process variable exceeds limits and causes an interrupt, and an operator communication task which would be executed whenever the operator strikes a key on the console. The operating system scheduler would resolve conflicts, caused by two or three tasks needing to execute simultaneously, on the basis of user-supplied priorities; presumably the alarm task would have the highest priority here. *SEE DIGITAL COMPUTER PROGRAMMING; SOFTWARE ENGINEERING.*

**Control algorithms.** Many applications, particularly machining, manufacturing, and batch processing, involve large or complex operating schedules. Invariably, these can be broken down into simple logical sequences, for example, in a high-speed bottling operation the bottle must be in position before the filling line is opened. Hence the control program reduces to a set of interlocked sequential operations. Some applications—in the chemical process industries, in power generation, and in aerospace areas—require the use of traditional automatic control algorithms.

Automatic control algorithms fall into two major categories: feedforward techniques, where process disturbances which would affect the controlled variable are measured and their effect canceled out or compensated by appropriate manipulation of a process input variable; and feedback techniques. In feedback control, which makes up the vast majority of applications, the controlled variable itself is measured and subtracted from a reference (set-point) variable equal to its desired value. The resulting deviation is the input to the controller, which then manipulates a process input variable through the final control element. If the controller is designed correctly, it should maintain the deviation quite small despite operator changes to the set point or despite environmental changes which cause disturbances to enter the control loop (**Fig. 4***a*).

***Digital implementation of traditional analog algorithms.*** Traditional algorithms for analog control of processes have been developed over many years. One very important example is the three-mode controller, so called because the algorithm for the controller output $U$ operates proportionally on the deviation $\epsilon$, the time integral of $\epsilon$, and the time derivative of $\epsilon$ as indicated in Eq. (1), where $U_0$ is the constant value

$$U = U_0 + K_c \left[ \epsilon + \frac{1}{\tau_I} \int_0^t \epsilon dt + \tau_D \frac{d\epsilon}{dt} \right] \quad (1)$$

that the controller output assumes when the controller first is turned on, and $K_c$, $\tau_I$, and $\tau_D$ are the controller proportional gain, and integral and derivative time constants, respectively. These controller parameters are chosen by the system designer appropriately for each control application.

In the digital implementation of a single-loop feedback control system (Fig. 4*b*), the digital computer implements the controller algorithm by using process information sampled through the analog-to-digital converter and a set point supplied by the operator. The symbolic switches and the subscript on the controller input $\epsilon_k$ (obtained from $R_k$ and $M_k$) in Fig. 4*b* are intended to indicate that the information is obtained by the computer only at discrete sampling times, $T$ time units apart. Similarly, the controller generates an output $U_k$ at each sampling time which it transmits through the digital-to-analog converter to the process's final control element. Implementation of

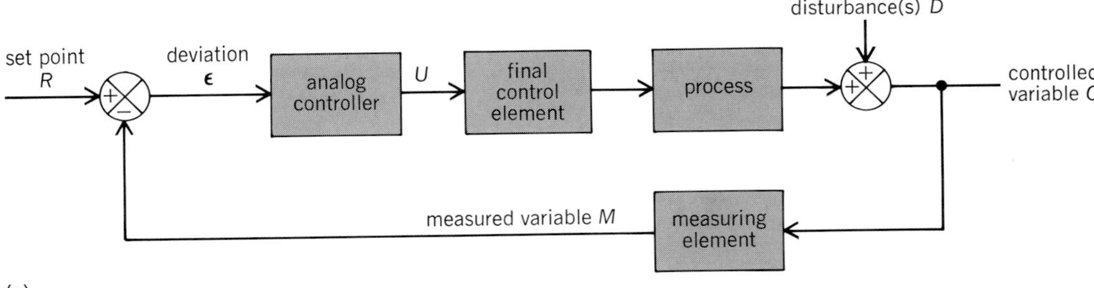


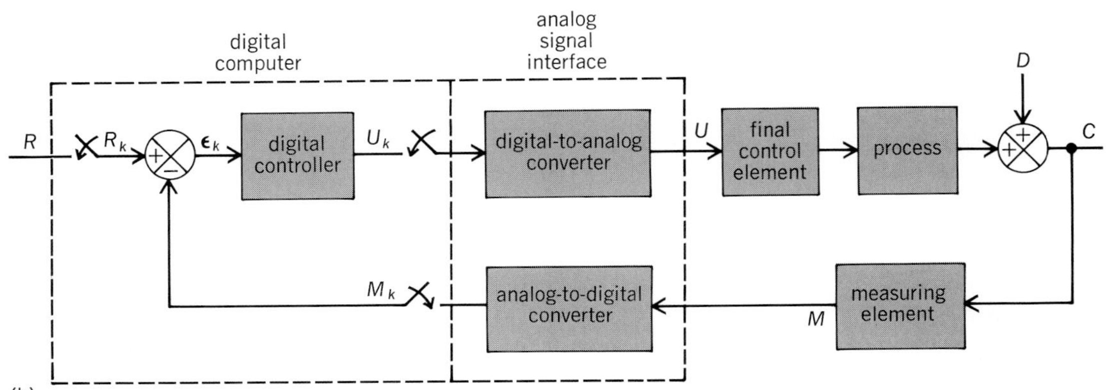


**Fig. 4. Single-loop feedback control system. (*a*) Traditional analog implementation. (*b*) Digital implementation.**

the three-mode algorithm in the digital (discrete) environment is straightforward. In the "velocity form" of the proportional-integral-derivative algorithm, so called because the change in $U$ from its previous value is calculated directly [Eq. (2)], the computer

$$U_k = U_{k-1} + K_c \left[ (\epsilon_k - \epsilon_{k-1}) + \frac{T}{\tau_I} \epsilon_k + \frac{\tau_D}{T} (\epsilon_k - 2\epsilon_{k-1} + \epsilon_{k-2}) \right] \quad (2)$$

need only store the controller output and two previous values of $\epsilon$ in order to calculate $U$ at the next sampling time. In actual application, digital versions of continuous control algorithms often utilize rapid sampling ($T$ is small) so that they respond in much the same way as analog systems do; hence the operational advantages and disadvantages of the two methods are equivalent.

***Purely digital algorithms.*** One disadvantage of the classical feedback algorithm of Eq. (1) or (2) is that it does not function well when the dynamics of the process contain significant time delay, that is, when a change in the process input has no effect on the controlled variable for a significant period of time (known as the dead time). So-called dead-time compensation algorithms have been available in analog form; however, only with the digital computer as controller has the implementation become so inexpensive that such applications can be widely justified. Hence the use of the three-mode algorithm in conjunction with a dead-time compensator is a common digital control approach, particularly for control of processes (where dead time is an important component of many, if not most, systems).

Attempts to expand the digital control medium through development of strictly digital control algorithms is an important and continuing trend. Such algorithms typically attempt to exploit the sampled nature of process inputs and outputs, significantly decreasing the sampling requirements of the algorithm (that is, making $T$ as large as possible). For example, in the "deadbeat" algorithm. Eq. (3), the controller

$$U_k = U_{k-1} + \frac{1}{K(N+1)(1 - e^{-T/\tau})}(\epsilon_k - e^{-T/\tau}\epsilon_{k-1}) \quad (3)$$

attempts to follow set-point changes in minimum time. The use of this algorithm presupposes that the process can be modeled approximately as a first-order-plus-dead-time system, where $K$ and $\tau$ are the process gain and time constant and $NT$ is the dead time. Hence a stepwise change in set point will cause the controlled variable to obtain its new, desired value in $N + 1$ sampling instants, the absolute minimum.

The deadbeat algorithm has a number of disadvantages, including its sensitivity to errors in the assumed process model. These often result in undesirable oscillations (ringing). Dahlin's algorithm, Eq. (4), is

$$U_k = U_{k-1} + \frac{1}{K[N(1 - e^{\lambda T}) + 1]}(\epsilon_k - e^{-T/\tau}\epsilon_{k-1}) \quad (4)$$

one of a number of attempts to eliminate the undesirable features of optimal, deadbeat control. In this instance, the use of an empirical tuning parameter, $\lambda$, relaxes the requirement of minimal response time, resulting in less ringing in the system response, particularly when the process dynamics change slightly from those assumed in the first-order model.

Dahlin's and the deadbeat algorithms, and other similar algorithms which are designed on the basis of set-point response, often respond more poorly to disturbances than the three-mode algorithm. Hence there is a continuing search for the "best" algorithm—one which is simple, responds well to both set-point changes and disturbances, requires little knowledge of process dynamics and is insensitive to changes in process dynamics, tolerates process constraints and nonlinearities, can be intended to multi-input/multi-output situations, is easy to implement and program, and so forth. Such a universal digit control algorithm likely will not be found, but the search has led in a number of interesting directions, including the development of self-tuning algorithms and the application of time convolution techniques for predictive control strategies. These approaches would not be possible without the digital computer and the ability to design and implement computer control systems. Additional demands are made as well in the analysis of digital control systems: discrete algebraic (difference) equations substitute for differential equations used traditionally to describe processes and analog controllers; and discrete transform techniques (the $Z$ transform) often replace the Laplace transform approach used in analyzing continuous systems. *SEE ALGORITHM; DIGITAL COMPUTER.*

*Duncan A. Mellichamp*

***Bibliography.*** D. M. Auslander et al., Direct digital process control: Practice and algorithms for microprocessor application, *Proc. IEEE*, 66:199–208, 1978; T. J. Harrison (ed.), *Minicomputers in Industrial Control*, Instrument Society of America, 1973; D. A. Mellichamp (ed.), *CACHE Monograph Series in Real-Time Computing*, vols. 1–8, 1977–1979; D. A. Mellichamp (ed.), *Real Time Computing: With Applications to Data Analysis and Control*, 1983; H. Meyer (ed.), *Real-Time Data Handling and Process Control*, 1980.

## Digital counter

An instrument which, in its simplest form, provides an output that corresponds to the number of pulses applied to its input.

**Types.** Counters may be categorized into two types: the Moore machine or the Mealy machine. The simpler counter type, the Moore machine, has a single count input (also called the clock input or pulse input), while the Mealy machine has additional inputs that alter the count sequence. Digital counters take many forms: geared mechanisms (tape counters and odometers are examples), relays (old pinball machines and old telephone switching systems), vacuum tubes (old test equipment), and solid-state semiconductor circuits (most modern electronic counters). This article will stress solid-state electronic counters.

Most digital counters operate in the binary number system, since binary is easily implemented with electronic circuitry. Binary allows any integer (whole number) to be represented as a series of binary digits, or bits, where each bit is either a 0 or 1 (off or on, low or high, and so forth). *SEE NUMBER SYSTEMS.*

**Figure 1** shows a four-bit binary counter that can

count from 0 to 15; the sixteenth count input causes the counter to return to the 0 output state and generate a carry pulse. This action of the counter to return to the 0 state with a carry output on every sixteenth pulse makes the four-bit binary counter a modulo 16 counter. The four binary-digit outputs $Q_D$, $Q_C$, $Q_B$, and $Q_A$ are said to have an 8-4-2-1 "weighting" because, if $Q_D$ through $Q_A$ are all ones, then the binary counter output is $1111_2 = 1 \times 2^3 + 1 \times 2^2 + 1 \times 2^1 + 1 \times 2^0 = 8 + 4 + 2 + 1 = 15_{10}$, where the subscripts indicate the base of the number system. In Fig. 1*a*, the counter state-flow diagram is shown. The word "state" refers to the number, the datum, in the counter; this datum is stored in four flip-flop devices, each of which is a memory bit that stores the current value of one binary digit. Each possible state is represented by the numerical output of that state inside a circle. Upon receiving a count pulse, the counter must change state by following an arrow from the present state to the next state. In Fig. 1*b*, a table is given showing the counter output after a given number of input pulses, assuming that the counter always starts from the 0 state. The counter output is listed in binary, octal, decimal, and hexadecimal. Figure 1*c* shows a block diagram of the counter built with *T* flip-flops, and Fig. 1*d* shows the counter waveforms through time, with a periodic count input. The *T* flip-flop is a device that has either a 0 or a 1 on its *Q* output at all times. When the count input *T* moves from the 1 state to the 0 state, the flip-flop output must change state, from a 0 to a 1 or a 1 to a 0. The carry output produces a 1-to-0 transition on every sixteenth count input, producing a divide-by-16 function. SEE MULTIVIBRATOR.

The four bits of the counter of Fig. 1 can be grouped together and used to represent a single hexadecimal digit; in Fig. 1*b*, each counter output state represents one hexadecimal digit. A two-digit hexadecimal counter requires two sets of four-bit binary counters, the carry output from the first set of counters driving the count input of the second set of counters.

A decimal counter built from four binary counters is shown in **Fig. 2**. Let four bits of data from the binary counter represent one decimal digit. The counter will work in the same way as the counter of Fig. 1, except that all the flip-flops are reset to the 0 state when the counter moves from the $1001_2 = 9$ state, instead of advancing to the $1010_2 = 10$ state. Besides the AND gate that is now used to detect the 1001 state of the counter and enable the resets, the circuit block diagram shows a new type of flip-flop. The "*SR*" flip-flop acts like a *T* flip-flop with an additional input that forces the *Q* output to a 1 state when the *S* (set) input is high and the *T* input has had a 1-to-0 transition applied. An *R* (reset) input acts as the *S* input does, except that the *Q* output goes to 0. This example decimal counter has an 8-4-2-1 weighted output that is known as binary coded decimal (B.C.D.). A seven-segment display is easily interfaced to the binary-coded-decimal counter by using a binary-coded-decimal-to-seven-segment decoder/driver circuit that is widely available.

**Applications.** Digital counters are found in much modern electronic equipment, especially equipment that is digitally controlled or has digital numeric displays. A frequency counter, as a test instrument or a channel frequency display on a radio tuner, consists simply of a string of decade counters that count the pulses of an input signal for a known period of time, and display that count on a seven-segment display. A digital voltmeter operates by using nearly the same idea, except that the counter counts a known frequency for a period of time proportional to the input voltage. SEE ANALOG-TO-DIGITAL CONVERTER; DIGITAL VOLTMETER.

A digital watch contains numerous counter/dividers in its large-scale integration (LSI) chip, usually implemented with complementary metal oxide semiconductor (CMOS) technology. A typical watch generates a 32,768-Hz crystal oscillator signal that is divided by $2^{15}$ (15 *T* flip-flop binary counters) to produce a 1-Hz signal that is counted as seconds by using two decimal counters that reset and produce a carry at every sixtieth count. That carry output is counted as a minutes display, generating another modulo 60 carry pulse for the hours display. The hours counters produce a carry at every twenty-fourth

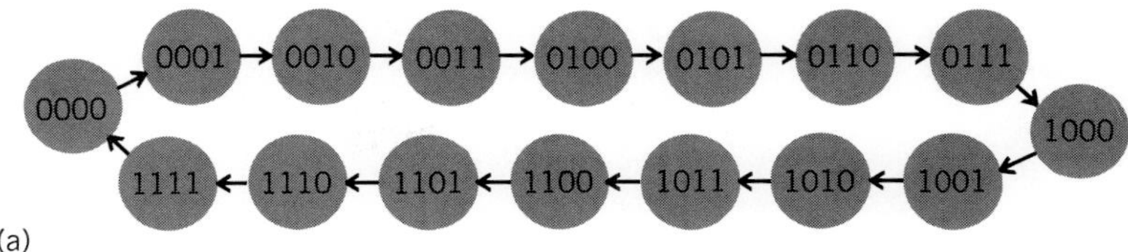


(a)

| number of count pulses | binary output | octal (base 8) | decimal (base 10) | hexadecimal (base 16) |
|---|---|---|---|---|
| 0 | 0000 | 0 | 0 | 0 |
| 1 | 0001 | 1 | 1 | 1 |
| 2 | 0010 | 2 | 2 | 2 |
| 3 | 0011 | 3 | 3 | 3 |
| 4 | 0100 | 4 | 4 | 4 |
| 5 | 0101 | 5 | 5 | 5 |
| 6 | 0110 | 6 | 6 | 6 |
| 7 | 0111 | 7 | 7 | 7 |
| 8 | 1000 | 10 | 8 | 8 |
| 9 | 1001 | 11 | 9 | 9 |
| 10 | 1010 | 12 | 10 | A |
| 11 | 1011 | 13 | 11 | B |
| 12 | 1100 | 14 | 12 | C |
| 13 | 1101 | 15 | 13 | D |
| 14 | 1110 | 16 | 14 | E |
| 15 | 1111 | 17 | 15 | F |
| 16 | 0000 | 0 | 0 | 0 |

(b)

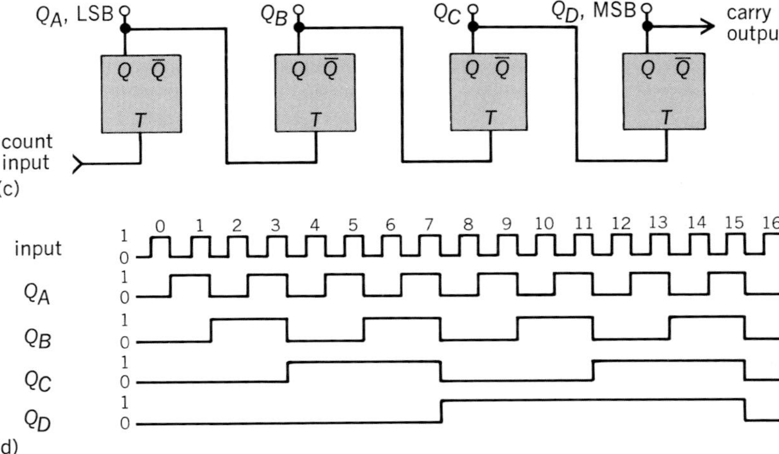


**Fig. 1. Four-bit binary counter using trigger flip-flops; this is a Moore machine. (*a*) State-flow diagram. (*b*) Table of the counter output in various number systems. (c) Circuit block diagram. LSB = least significant bit; MSB = most significant bit. (*d*) Output waveforms.**

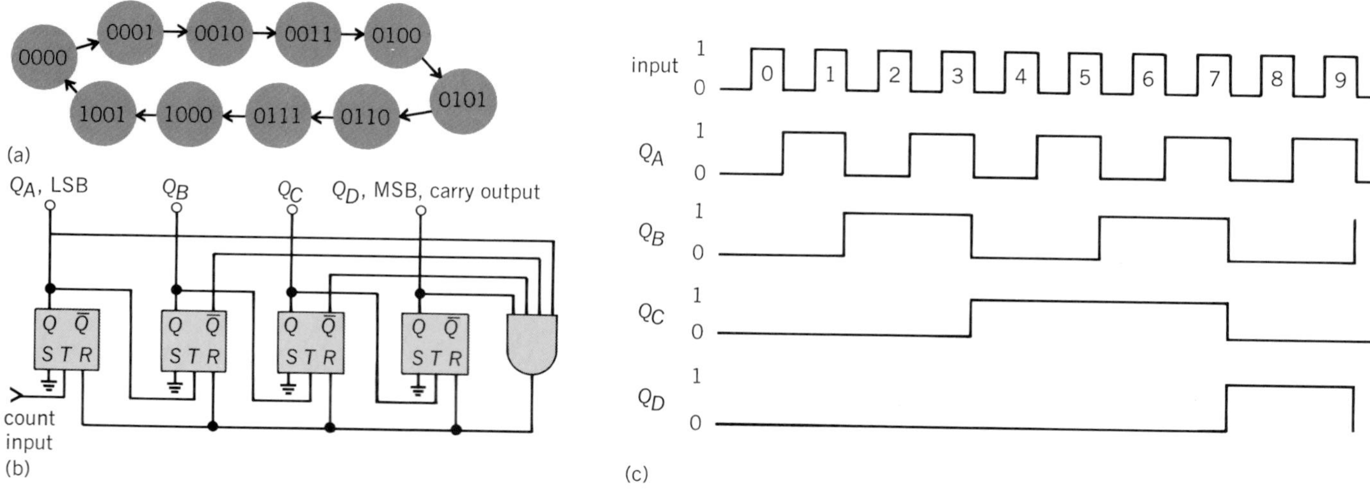


**Fig. 2. Four-bit binary counter modified to be a decimal counter. (*a*) State-flow diagram. (*b*) Circuit block diagram. LSB = least significant bit; MSB = most significant bit. (c) Output waveforms.**

count to run the days counter and display; that counter generates a carry pulse every 28 to 31 days, depending on the month. *SEE INTEGRATED CIRCUITS; WATCH.*

Digital computers may contain counters in the form of programmable interval timers that count an integral number of clock pulses of known period, and then generate an output at the end of the count to signal that the time period has expired. Most of the counters in a microprocessor consist of arithmetic logic units (ALU) that add one many-bit number to another, storing the results in a memory location. The program and data counters are examples of this kind of counter. *SEE DIGITAL COMPUTER; MICROPROCESSOR.*

**Counter specifications.** Counters have progressed from relays to light-wavelength-geometry very large-scale-integrated circuits. There are several technologies for building individual digital counters. Single counters are available as integrated circuit chips in emitter-coupled logic (ECL), transistor-transistor logic (TTL), and CMOS. The three technologies are listed in the order of decreasing speed and decreasing power dissipation. ECL will operate to 600 MHz, TTL to 100 MHz (Schottky-clamped), and CMOS to 5 MHz. Standard, high-volume production *n*-channel metal oxide semiconductor (NMOS) LSI can implement a 1-bit binary counter in a $100 \times 100\ \mu m^2$ ($39 \times 3.9\ mil^2$) area that will operate to 10 MHz. A gallium arsenide metal-semiconductor field-effect transistor (MESFET) master-slave *JK* flip-flop has been produced that operates at 610 MHz in a $390 \times 390\ \mu m^2$ ($15 \times 15\ mil^2$) surface area while consuming the power of an NMOS. *SEE SEMICONDUCTOR.*

*Michael E. Wright*

***Bibliography.*** C. H. Roth, *Fundamentals of Logic Design*, 1975; K. Suyama et al., Design and performance of GaAs normally-off MESFET integrated circuits, *IEEE Trans. Electr. Devices*, ED-27 (6):1092–1097, 1980.

## Digital-to-analog converter

A device for converting information in the form of combinations of discrete states or a signal, often representing binary number values, to information in the form of the value or magnitude of some characteristics of a signal, in relation to a standard or reference. Most often, it is a device which has electrical inputs representing a parallel binary number, and an output in the form of voltage or current.

**Figure 1** shows the structure of a typical digital-to-analog converter. The essential elements, found even in the simplest devices, are enclosed within the dashed rectangle. The digital inputs, labeled $u_i$, $i = 1, 2, \ldots, n$, are equal to 1 or 0. The output voltage $E_o$ is given by Eq. (1), where $V_{REF}$ is an analog reference voltage and $K$ is a constant. Thus, for a 5-bit binary converter with latched input code 10110, the output is given by Eq. (2).

$$E_o = KV_{REF}\,(u_1 2^{-1} + u_2 2^{-2} + u_3 2^{-3} + \cdots + u_n 2^{-n}) \qquad (1)$$

$$E_o = \left(\frac{16}{32} + \frac{0}{32} + \frac{4}{32} + \frac{2}{32} + \frac{0}{32}\right) KV_{REF} = \frac{11}{16} KV_{REF} \qquad (2)$$

Bit 1 is the "most significant bit" (MSB), with a weight of 1/2; bit $n$ is the "least significant bit" (LSB), with a weight of $2^{-n}$. The number of bits $n$ characterizes the resolution. *SEE ANALOG-TO-DIGITAL CONVERTER; NUMBER SYSTEMS.*

**Uses.** Digital-to-analog (D/A) converters (sometimes called DACs) are used to present the results of digital computation, storage, or transmission, typically for graphical display or for the control of devices that operate with continuously varying quantities. D/A converter circuits are also used in the design of analog-to-digital converters that employ feedback techniques, such as successive-approximation and counter-comparator types. In such applications, the D/A converter may not necessarily appear as a separately identifiable entity.

**Circuitry.** The fundamental circuit of most D/A converters involves a voltage or current reference; a resistive "ladder network" that derives weighted currents or voltages, usually as discrete fractions of the reference; and a set of switches, operated by the digital input, that determines which currents or voltages will be summed to constitute the output.

An elementary three-bit D/A converter is shown in

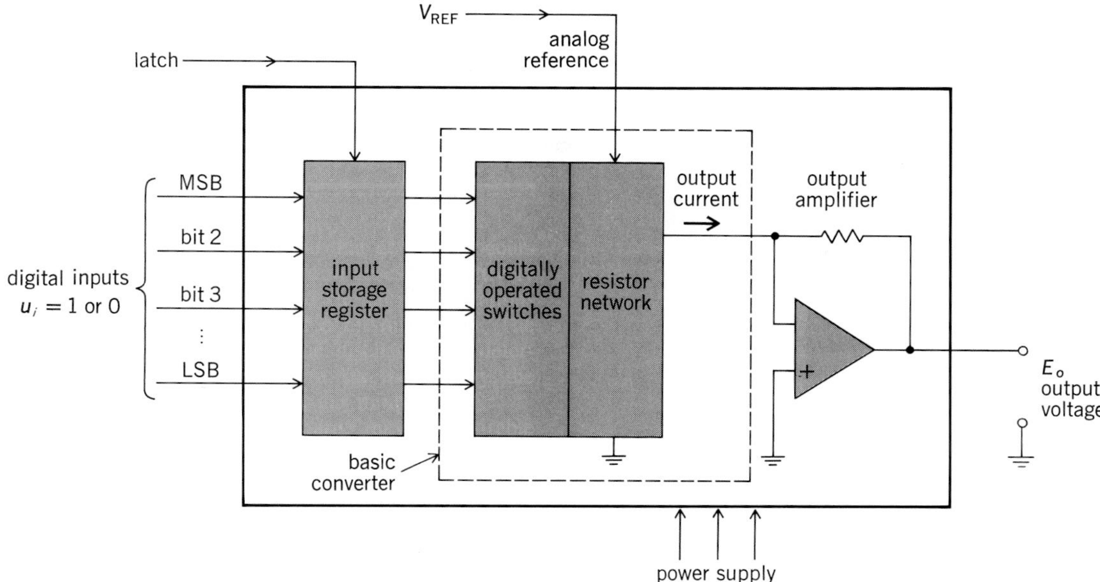


**Fig. 1.** Structure of a typical digital-to-analog converter.

**Fig. 2**. Binary-weighted currents developed in $R_1$, $R_2$, $R_3$ by $V_{REF}$ are switched either directly to ground or to the output summing bus (which is held at zero volts by the operational-amplifier circuit). The sum of the currents develops an output voltage of polarity opposite to that of the reference across the feedback resistor $R_f$. The **table** shows the binary relationship between the input code and the output, both as a voltage and as a fraction of the reference.

The output of the D/A converter is proportional to the product of the digital input value and the reference. In many applications, the reference is fixed, and the output bears a fixed proportion to the digital input. In other applications, the reference, as well as the digital input, can vary; a D/A converter that is used in these applications is thus called a multiplying DAC. It is principally used for imparting a digitally controlled scale factor, or "gain," to an analog input signal applied at the reference terminal. *See* Amplifier; Analog computer.

**Construction.** Except for the highest resolutions (beyond 16 bits), commercially available D/A converters are generally manufactured in the form of dual in-line-packaged integrated circuits, using bipolar, MOS, and hybrid technologies. A single chip may include just the resistor network and switches, or may also include a reference circuit, output amplifier, and one or more sets of registers (with control logic suit-

**Input and output of converter in Fig. 2**

| Digital input code | | | Analog output | |
|---|---|---|---|---|
| $u_1$ | $u_2$ | $u_3$ | $-E_o$, volts | $\frac{E_o}{V_{REF}}$ |
| 0 | 0 | 0 | 0 | 0 |
| 0 | 0 | 1 | 1.25 | 1/8 |
| 0 | 1 | 0 | 2.5 | 2/8 |
| 0 | 1 | 1 | 3.75 | 3/8 |
| 1 | 0 | 0 | 5.0 | 4/8 |
| 1 | 0 | 1 | 6.25 | 5/8 |
| 1 | 1 | 0 | 7.5 | 6/8 |
| 1 | 1 | 1 | 8.75 | 7/8 |

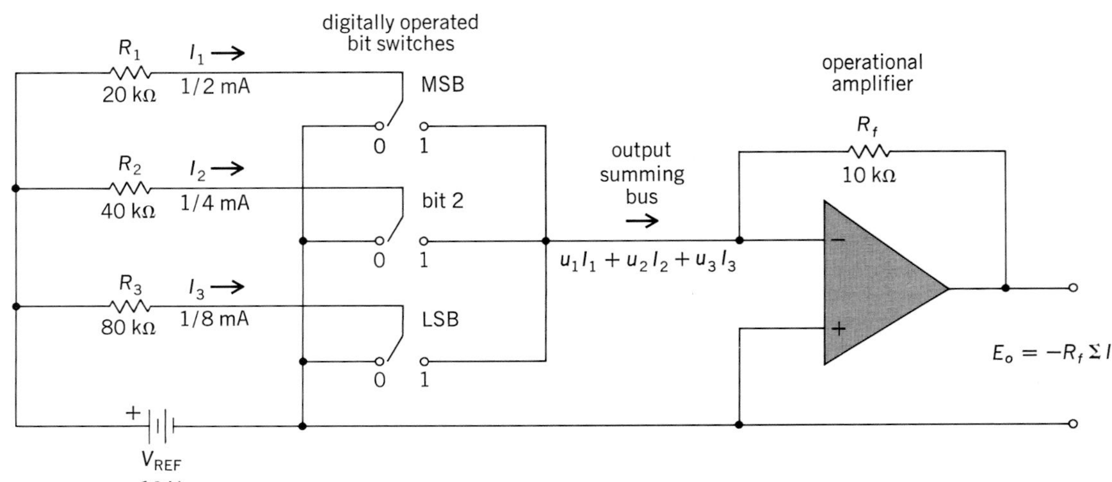


**Fig. 2.** Circuit of elementary 3-bit digital-to-analog converter.

able for direct microprocessor interfacing). *See Integrated circuits.*

*Daniel H. Sheingold*

**Bibliography.** D. J. Dooley (ed.), *Data Conversion Integrated Circuits*, 1980; *IEEE Transactions on Circuits and Systems*, special issue on analog/digital conversion, CAS-25, July 1978; D. Sheingold (ed.), *Analog-Digital Conversion Notes*, 1977; E.. Zuch (ed.), *Data Acquisition and Conversion Handbook*, 1979.

## Digital voltmeter

An electronic instrument which, in basic form, measures dc voltage and displays the result as a number (digits) instead of using a pointer against a graduated scale. It may also measure ac voltage, alternating and direct current, and resistance; hence it is often called a digital multimeter. The digital readout, coupled with features like automatic ranging, makes a digital voltmeter easier to use than a pointer instrument so that operator errors are less likely. *See Electronic display; Multimeter.*

Sizes vary, from battery-operated instruments which can be held in one hand to versions that are 17 in. (430 mm) wide and operate from power supply lines, for use on a bench or in automatic measurement systems.

Sensitivity (smallest change of reading) may be as low as 10 nanovolts, but 1 microvolt is usual; maximum input usually exceeds 1 kilovolt. Small, inexpensive instruments display three digits with accuracy (error) of 0.1%. More sophisticated products display up to nine digits with accuracy of a few parts per million.

Except in the smallest voltmeters, the digital reading can be passed to other equipment, such as a printer or computer, as a coded electrical signal. Additionally, the voltmeter functions can be controlled by coded commands sent to it. Communication is in ASCII or binary code, using the RS232C or IEEE488 standard. Many voltmeters can also be calibrated by external control, physical circuit adjustment being unnecessary. *See Computer; Data-processing systems; Teletypewriter.*

**Analog-to-digital conversion.** Digital voltmeters convert the analog input to a digital representation of the input. Speed of reading depends on the conversion technique. The fastest instruments, using successive approximation, may provide 10,000 readings per second. Each result is then a snapshot at one instant in time, there being no ability to integrate (or average), in order to reject interference which is often superimposed on low-level signals. *See Sampling voltmeter.*

Voltmeters for precision work integrate for a defined time which must be at least 16.67 ms to reject 60-Hz alternating current (20 ms for 50-Hz). Maximum speed is then 60 readings per second (50 at 20 ms). The dual-slope technique achieves this, but has the disadvantage that the input signal is disconnected and replaced by a reference voltage for up to half the measurement cycle. There is thus no ability to make a continuous average.

The pulse-width technique measures the input continuously, presenting a result on request. A voltmeter which uses pulse width can employ various integration times and scale lengths as determined by the user. *See Analog-to-digital converter.*

**Data processing.** Many digital voltmeters can process the measurements to provide results which are more useful. One example is to display temperature from a thermocouple measurement. Linear and polynomial equations may be used; statistics such as root-mean-square, variance, and standard deviation can be calculated; and high and low limits may be applied to sort results into different categories. Often a history file is included to store the most recent results (as many as 1000), which can then be reviewed or output electrically. *See Voltage measurement; Voltmeter.*

*J. Ralph Pearce*

## Diode

A two-terminal electron device exhibiting a nonlinear current-voltage characteristic. Although diodes are usually classified with respect to the physical phenomena that give rise to their useful properties, in this article they are more conveniently classified according to the functions of the circuits in which they are used. This classification includes rectifier diodes, negative-resistance diodes, constant-voltage diodes, light-sensitive diodes, light-emitting diodes, and capacitor diodes.

**Rectifier diodes.** A circuit element is said to rectify if voltage increments of equal magnitude but opposite sign applied to the element produce unequal current increments. An ideal rectifier diode is one that conducts fully in one direction (forward) and not at all in the opposite direction (reverse). This property is approximated in junction and thermionic diodes. Processes that make use of rectifier diodes including power rectification, detection, modulation, and switching.

In power rectification, a rectifier diode is connected in series with an alternating-voltage supply and a load. The current through the load consists of unidirectional pulses, which can be converted into essentially constant direct current by means of a filter network that removes the varying component of current. In the detection of amplitude-modulated voltage, a similar process transforms an alternating voltage of varying amplitude into a direct voltage, the magnitude of which is proportional to the amplitude of the alternating input voltage. In amplitude modulation, diode rectification is used to vary the amplitude of a carrier voltage in response to a signal voltage. *See Amplitude-modulation detector; Amplitude modulator; Electric filter; Electronic power supply; Rectifier; Semiconductor rectifier.*

Diode switching circuits include circuits in which output is obtained only in the presence or absence of one or more impressed control voltages. This is accomplished by the use of diodes that are normally maintained in the nonconducting (or conducting) state and are made conducting (or nonconducting) by the control voltages. Thus the diodes either provide a connection between the input and the output terminals or short-circuit the output terminals. Diodes can also be used to connect or disconnect two or more resistances in series or parallel between two terminals at selected values of input voltage and thus to synthesize a circuit that has a desired nonlinear current-voltage characteristic. *See Switching circuit.*

**Negative-resistance diodes.** Negative-resistance diodes, which include tunnel and Gunn diodes, are used as the basis of pulse generators, bistable counting and storage circuits, and oscillators. *See Negative-resistance circuits; Oscillator; Tunnel diode.*

**Constant-voltage diodes.** Breakdown-diode current increases very rapidly with voltage above the breakdown voltage; that is, the voltage is nearly independent of the current. In series with resistance to limit the current to a nondestructive value, breakdown diodes can therefore be used as a means of obtaining a nearly constant reference voltage or of maintaining a constant potential difference between two circuit points, such as the emitter and the base of a transistor. Breakdown diodes (or reverse-biased ordinary junction diodes) can be used between two circuit points in order to limit alternating-voltage amplitude or to clip voltage peaks. Severe clipping of a sinusoidal voltage wave produces an approximately rectangular voltage wave. *See Limiter circuit.*

**Light-sensitive and light-emitting diodes.** Light-sensitive diodes, which include phototubes, photovoltaic cells, photodiodes, and photoconductive cells, are used in the measurement of illumination, in the control of lights or other electrical devices by incident light, and in the conversion of radiant energy into electrical energy. Light-emitting diodes (LEDs) are used in the display of letters, numbers, and other symbols in calculators, watches, clocks, and other electronic units. *See Light-emitting diode; Photoelectric devices; Phototube; Photovoltaic cell.*

**Capacitor diodes.** Semiconductor diodes that are designed to have strongly voltage-dependent shunt capacitance between the terminals are called varactors. The applications of varactors include the tuning and the frequency stabilization of radio-frequency oscillators. *See Junction diode; Microwave solid-state devices; Point-contact diode; Semiconductor diode; Varactor.*

*Herbert J. Reich*

**Bibliography.** J. J. Brophy, *Basic Electronics for Scientists*, 4th ed., 1983; C. A. Holt, *Electronic Circuits*, 1978; H. L. Krauss, H. J. Reich, and J. G. Skalnik, *Theory and Applications of Active Devices*, 1966; J. Millman, *Microelectronics*, 1979; H. J. Reich, *Functional Circuits and Oscillators*, 1961; D. Schilling and C. Belove, *Electronic Circuits*, 2d ed., 1979.

## Direct-coupled amplifier

A device for amplifying signals with direct-current (dc) components. There are many different situations where it is necessary to amplify signals having a frequency spectrum which extends to zero frequency. Some typical examples are amplifiers in electronic differential analyzers (analog computers), certain types of feedback control systems, and some medical instruments such as the electrocardiograph. Amplifiers which have capacitor coupling between stages are not usable in these cases, because the gain at zero frequency is zero. Therefore, a special form of amplifier, called a dc (for direct-current) or direct-coupled amplifier, is necessary. These amplifiers will also amplify alternating-current (ac) signals. *See Amplifier.*

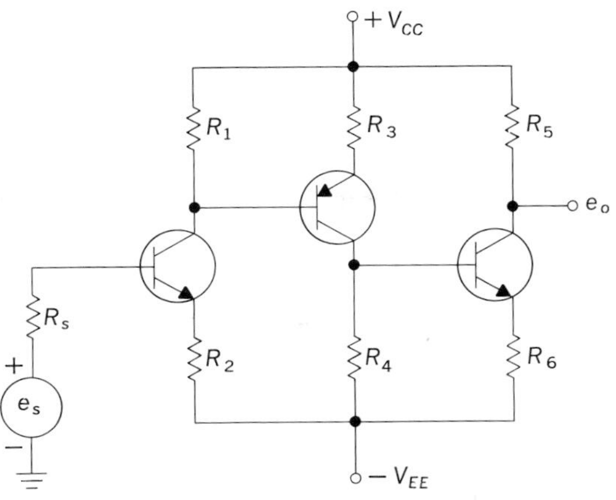


Fig. 1. Direct-coupled amplifier of the type which uses *npn* and *pnp* transistors.

Some type of coupling circuit must be used between successive amplifier stages to prevent the relatively large supply voltage of one stage from appearing at the input of the following stage. These circuits must pass dc signals with the least possible amount of attenuation.

Transistor direct-coupled amplifiers have a number of advantages and disadvantages relative to vacuum-tube amplifiers. Interstage direct coupling is much easier with transistors because of the availability of both *pnp* and *npn* transistors and Zener diodes. The circuit of **Fig. 1** is a direct-coupled amplifier. The main disadvantage of this amplifier is the temperature dependence of the transistor parameters, specifically the current gain $h_{FE}$, the base-to-emitter voltage $V_{BE}$, and the leakage current $I_{CBO}$. Very often a Zener diode is used to couple between stages, and in that case it is not necessary to use both *pnp* and *npn* transistors. The Zener diode has a range of values of current through the diode for which the voltage across it is nearly constant. In effect, the Zener diode acts like a battery.

**Differential dc amplifier.** It is generally recognized that the differential amplifier is the most stable dc amplifier circuit available. This is true because in this circuit the performance depends on the difference of the device parameters, and transistors can be manufactured using the planar epitaxial technique with very close matching of their parameters. **Figure 2** shows a differential amplifier with a constant current source in the emitter circuit.

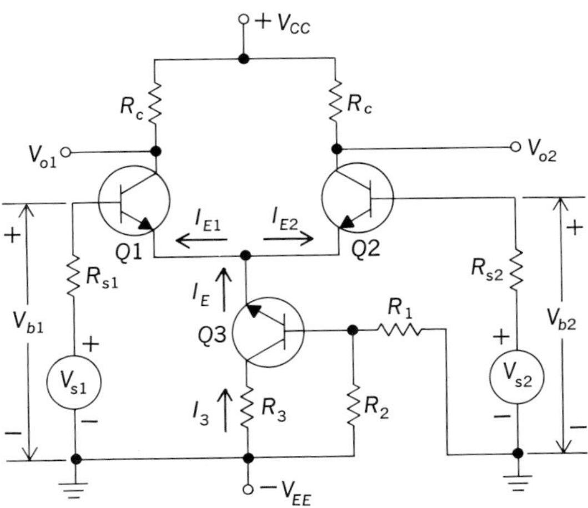


Fig. 2. Differential dc amplifier with constant-current stage in the emitter circuit.

**Carrier amplifier.** A method of amplifying dc (or slowly varying) signals by means of ac amplifiers is to modulate a carrier signal by the signal to be amplified, amplifying the modulated signal, and demodulating at the output. (In some applications, such as instrument servomechanisms, output in the form of a modulated carrier is required and no demodulation is necessary.) One arrangement is illustrated in block-diagram form in **Fig. 3**.

An analysis of an actual circuit would show that in order to have an output $e_o$ free from harmonics introduced by the modulation, the output low-pass filter cutoff frequency must be small compared to the modulation frequency. This limits the bandwidth of the input signal $e_s$ to a small fraction of the bandwidth of signals which can be amplified by the types previously discussed. This is a disadvantage in most cases, but there are cases, such as the output voltage from a thermocouple, where the required bandwidth is small.

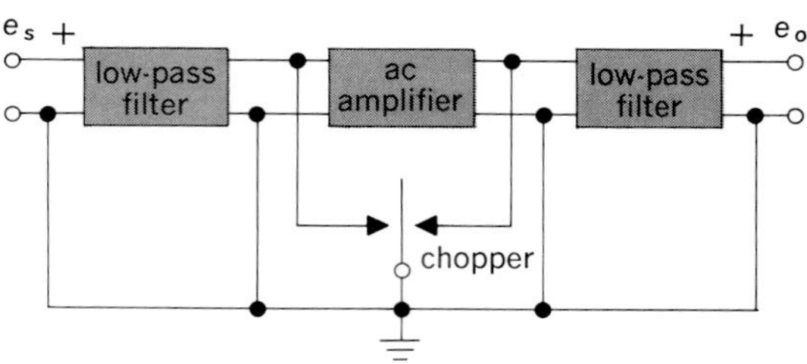


Fig. 3. Chopper amplifier.

Various types of choppers (bipolar transistors, field effect ransistors, and electromechanical devices) are used as modulators. An additional disadvantage is that the chopper must be carefully designed to reduce to a minimum the hum and noise which can be introduced by an electromechanical element and the offset voltage and leakage current of a transistor. However, this amplifier provides stable amplification of the input signal, and it is used in many industrial recording instruments. SEE MODULATION; VIBRATOR; VOLTAGE AMPLIFIER.

**Chopper-stabilized amplifiers.** A chopper-stabilized amplifier is composed of two amplifiers: One amplifier is a carrier amplifier employing a chopper to modulate and demodulate a portion of the signal to be amplified; the second amplifier is a straight dc amplifier. The success of this circuit in reducing to a very low value the amount of drift appearing at the output depends upon the fact that the drift is a very low-frequency phenomenon. A block diagram of a chopper-stabilized amplifier is illustrated in **Fig. 4**.

A component of the output signal $e_o$ is due to drift in the dc amplifier, and if it is fed back through the feedback resistor to the input of the chopper-modulated amplifier (it cannot be fed back to the dc amplifier because of the high-pass filter), the drift component will be amplified and returned to the dc amplifier. An analysis of the circuit shows that the input voltage $e_s$ to the dc amplifier is altered by a factor equal and opposite to the equivalent drift voltage appearing at the input. The net result is that the drift can be reduced to a negligible value.

A signal appearing at the input terminals is amplified partly in the dc amplifier and partly in the chopper-modulated amplifier, because the high-pass and low-pass filters direct the frequency components of the input signal into the separate amplifiers. Thus, for

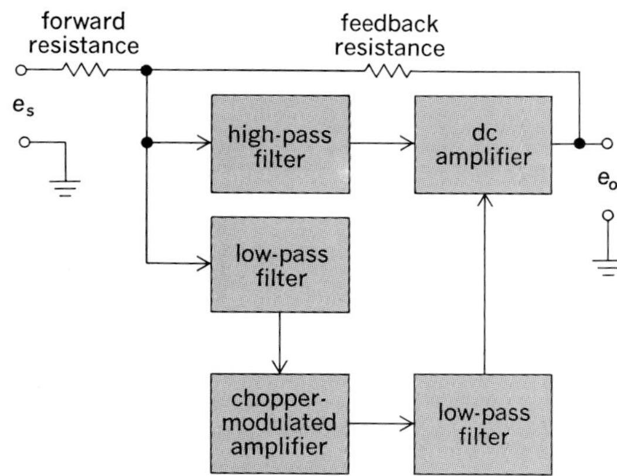


Fig. 4. Chopper-stabilized amplifier.

dc and very low frequency signals the open-loop gain is equal to the gain of the chopper amplifier times the gain of the dc amplifier, while for higher-frequency signals the gain is that of the dc amplifier alone. However, if the gains are large, then when the feedback network is connected, the gain is equal, to a good approximation, to the feedback impedance divided by the impedance in the forward path. The gain is, therefore, essentially independent of the open-loop gain, and the dc amplifier drift has been significantly reduced.

Chopper-stabilized amplifiers find wide application in analog computers, where they are used in integrating and summing amplifiers. In many problems solved on analog computers the time scale is reduced. This imposes strict requirements on the freedom from drift of the dc amplifiers. These requirements are met with amplifiers where a typical value for the dc amplifier gain is 100,000 and a typical value for the gain of the chopper-modulated amplifier is 1000.

*Christos C. Halkias*

***Bibliography.*** J. J. Brophy, *Basic Electronics for Scientists,* 4th ed., 1983; C. H. Evans, *Electronic Amplifiers: Theory, Design and Use*, 1979; D. G. Fink, *Electronics Engineer's Handbook,* 2d ed., 1982; C. A. Holt, *Electronic Circuits: Digital and Analog,* 1978; D. L. Schilling and C. Belove, *Electronic Circuits: Discrete and Integrated,* 1979.

## Direct current

Electric current which flows in one direction only through a circuit or equipment. The associated direct voltages, in contrast to alternating voltages, are of unchanging polarity. Direct current corresponds to a drift or displacement of electric charge in one unvarying direction around the closed loop or loops of an electric circuit. Direct currents and voltages may be of constant magnitude or may vary with time.

Batteries and rotating generators produce direct voltages of nominally constant magnitude (**illus.** *a*). Direct voltages of time-varying magnitude are produced by rectifiers, which convert alternating voltage to pulsating direct voltage (illus. *b* and *c*). SEE RECTIFIER.

Direct current is used extensively to power adjustable-speed motor drives in industry and in transportation (illus. *d*). Very large amounts of power are used in electrochemical processes for the refining and

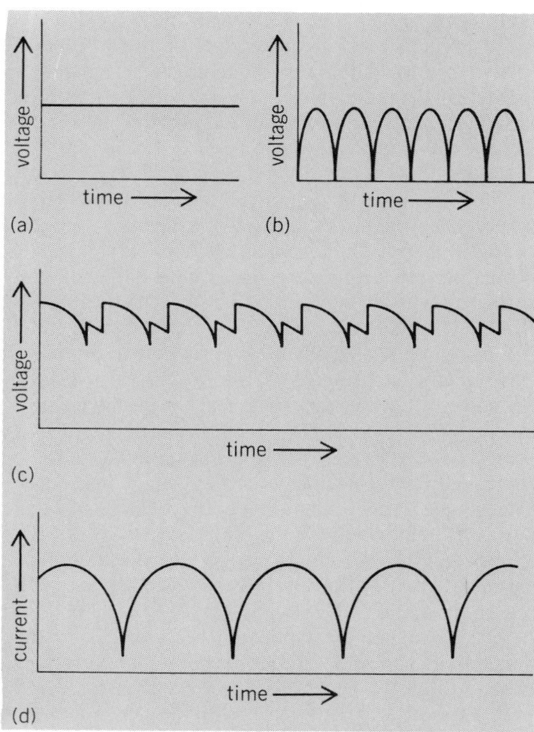


**Typical direct currents and voltages. (*a*) Output from a battery; (*b*) full-wave rectified voltage; (*c*) output of the rectifier station of a high-voltage dc transmission link (*after E. W. Kimbark, Direct Current Transmission, vol. 1, Wiley–Interscience, 1971*). (*d*) Current in a rectifier-supplied dc motor (*after A. E. Fitzgerald, C. Kingsley, and A. Kusko, Electric Machinery, 3d ed., McGraw-Hill, 1971*).**

plating of metals and for the production of numerous basic chemicals.

Direct current ordinarily is not widely distributed for general use by electric utility customers. Instead, direct-current (dc) power is obtained at the site whereit is needed by the rectification of commercially available alternating current (ac) power to dc power. Solid-state rectifiers ordinarily are employed to supplydc equipment from ac supply lines. Rectifier dc supplies range from tiny devices in household electronic equipment to high-voltage dc transmission links of at least hundreds of megawatts capacity. *See* Semiconductor rectifier.

Many high-voltage dc transmission systems have been constructed throughout the world. Very large amounts of power, generated as ac and ultimately used as ac, are transmitted as dc power. Rectifiers supply the sending end of the dc link; inverters then supply the receiving-end ac power system from the link. High-voltage dc transmission often is more economical than ac transmission when extremely long distances are involved. *See* Alternating current; Electric current; Transmission lines.

*D. D. Robb*

## Direct-current circuit theory

An analysis of relationships within a dc circuit. Any combination of direct-current (dc) voltage or current sources, such as generators and batteries, in conjunction with transmission lines, resistors, inductors, capacitors, and power converters such as motors is termed a dc circuit. Historically the dc circuit was the first to be studied and analyzed mathematically. *See* Circuit (electricity).

**Classification.** Circuits may be identified and classified into simple series and parallel circuits. More complicated circuits may be developed as combinations of these basic circuits.

***Series circuit.*** A series circuit is illustrated in **Fig. 1**. It consists of a battery of $E$ volts and three resistors of resistances $R_1$, $R_2$, and $R_3$, respectively. The conventional current flows from the positive battery terminal through the external circuit and back to the negative battery terminal. It passes through each resistor in turn; therefore the resistors are in series with the battery.

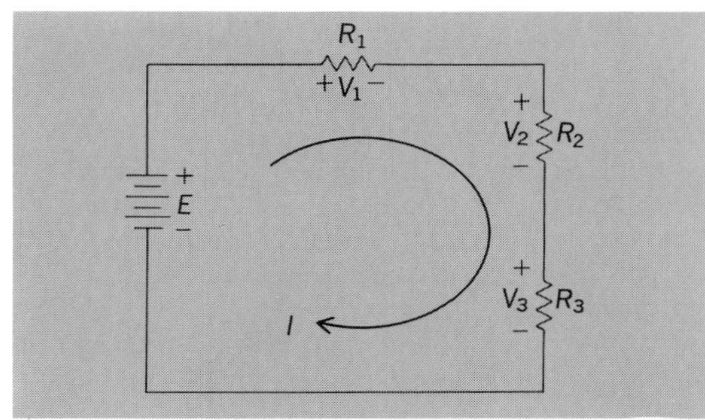


**Fig. 1. Simple series circuit.**

***Parallel circuit.*** The parallel circuit, shown in **Fig. 2**, consists of a battery paralleled by three resistors. In this chase the current leaving the positive terminal of the battery splits into three components, one component flowing through each resistor, then recombining into the original current and returning to the negative terminal of the battery.

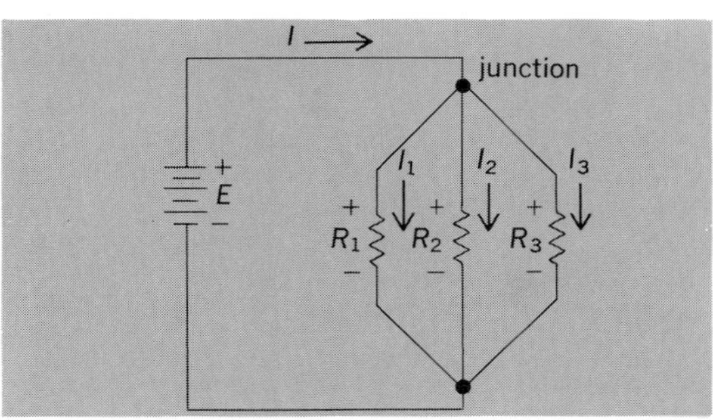


**Fig. 2. Simple parallel circuit.**

**Physical laws of circuit analysis.** The operation of the basic series and parallel circuits must obey certain fundamental laws of physics. These laws are referred to as Ohm's law and Kirchhoff's laws in honor of their originators.

***Voltage drops.*** When an electric current flows through a resistor, a voltage drop appears across the resistor, the polarity being such that the voltage is positive at the end where the conventional current enters the resistor. This voltage drop is directly proportional to the product of the current in amperes and the resistance in ohms. This is Ohm's law, expressed mathematically in Eq. (1). Thus in Fig. 1 the drop

$$V = IR \quad (1)$$

across $R_1$ is $V_1$ and has the polarity shown. SEE OHM'S LAW.

***Summation of voltages.*** The algebraic sum of all voltage sources (rises) and voltage drops must add up to zero around any closed path in any circuit. This is Kirchhoff's first law. In Fig. 1, the sum of the voltages about this closed circuit is as given by Eqs. (2),

$$E - V_1 - V_2 - V_3 = 0 \quad (2a)$$

$$E = V_1 + V_2 + V_3 \quad (2b)$$

where the minus signs indicate a voltage drop. Written in terms of current and resistance, this becomes Eq. (3). From this results the important conclusion

$$E = I(R_1 + R_2 + R_3) = IR_{\text{total}} \quad (3)$$

that resistors in series may be added to obtain the equivalent total resistance, as shown in Eq. (4).

$$R_{\text{total}} = R_1 + R_2 + R_3 + \cdots \quad (4)$$

SEE KIRCHHOFF'S LAWS OF ELECTRIC CIRCUITS.

***Summation of currents.*** The algebraic sum of all currents flowing into a circuit junction must equal the algebraic sum of all currents flowing out of the junction. In the circuit shown in Fig. 2, the current flowing into the junction is $I$ amperes while that flowing out is the sum of $I_1$ plus $I_2$ plus $I_3$. Therefore the currents are related by Eq. (5). This is Kirchhoff's

$$I = I_1 + I_2 + I_3 \quad (5)$$

second law. In this case the same voltage appears across each resistor. If the currents are expressed in terms of this voltage and values of the individual resistors by means of Ohm's law, Eq. (5) becomes Eq. (6). The equivalent resistance $R_{\text{eq}}$ that can replace the

$$I = \frac{E}{R_1} + \frac{E}{R_2} + \frac{E}{R_3} = \frac{E}{R_{\text{eq}}} \quad (6)$$

resistances in parallel can be obtained by solving Eq. (6) in the form of Eq. (7). Therefore, resistances in

$$R_{\text{eq}} = \left[\frac{1}{R_1} + \frac{1}{R_2} + \frac{1}{R_3} + \cdots\right]^{-1} \quad (7)$$

parallel are added by computing the corresponding conductances (reciprocal of resistance) and adding to obtain the equivalent conductance. The reciprocal of the equivalent conductance is the equivalent resistance of the parallel combination. SEE CONDUCTANCE.

**Sources.** Sources such as batteries and generators may be connected in series or parallel. Series connections serve to increase the voltage; the net voltage is the algebraic sum of the individual source voltages.

Sources in parallel provide the practical function of increasing the net current rating over the rating of the individual sources; the net current rating is the sum of the individual current ratings.

**Series-parallel circuits.** More complicated circuits are nothing more than combinations of simple series and parallel circuits as illustrated in **Fig. 3**.

***Single source.*** Circuits that contain only a single source are readily reduced to a simple series circuit. In the circuit of Fig. 3*a* the parallel combination of $R_1$ and $R_2$ is computed and used to replace the parallel combination. The resultant circuit is now a simple series circuit consisting of $R_3$ and $R_{\text{eq}}$ and can readily be solved for the series current if the voltage is known.

***Multiple sources.*** Circuits that contain two or more sources located in various branches cannot be reduced to a simple series circuit (Fig. 3*b*). The three basic laws of circuit theory still hold and may be directly applied to provide a simultaneous solution to the loop currents $I_A$ and $I_B$ flowing in each basic series circuit present in the overall network.

In this example the summations of voltages around the individual series circuits or loops are given by Eqs. (8) and (9), which may be solved for the math-

$$E_1 = (R_1 + R_3)I_A - R_1 I_B \quad (8)$$

$$-E_2 = -R_1 I_A + (R_1 + R_2)I_B \quad (9)$$

ematical loop currents $I_A$ and $I_B$. These loop currents can in turn be identified by reference to the circuit where $I_A$ is identical to $I$, and $I_B$ therefore, as stated by Eq. (10).

$$(I_A - I_B) = I_1 \quad (10)$$

This method may be used to solve any complicated combination of simple circuits. Other methods are also available to the circuit analyst. SEE NETWORK THEORY.

**Power.** The electric power converted to heat in any resistance is equal to the product of the voltage drop across the resistance times the current through the resistance, as stated by Eq. (11*a*). By means of Ohm's

$$P = VI \quad (11a)$$

$$P = VI = V^2/R = I^2R \quad (11b)$$

law, Eq. (11*a*) may also be written as Eq. (11*b*). The total power dissipated in a circuit is the arithmetic sum of the power dissipated in each resistance.

**Circuit response.** In the circuits mentioned thus far, the circuit responds in an identical manner from the moment the circuit is excited (switches closed) through any extended period of time. This is not true of circuits typified by those of **Figs. 4** and **5**.

For instance, when the switch of Fig. 4 is first closed, a momentary current limited only by resistance $R$ flows. As time passes, the capacitor, with capacitance $C$, charges and the voltage across it increases, eventually reaching a value equal to the applied voltage, at which time all flow of current ceases. The circuit current, given by Eq. (12), is in

$$i = (E/R)\epsilon^{-t/RC} \quad (12)$$

amperes. The product $RC$ is known as the time constant of the circuit. The energy $W$ in joules stored in a capacitance at any time is given by Eq. (13).

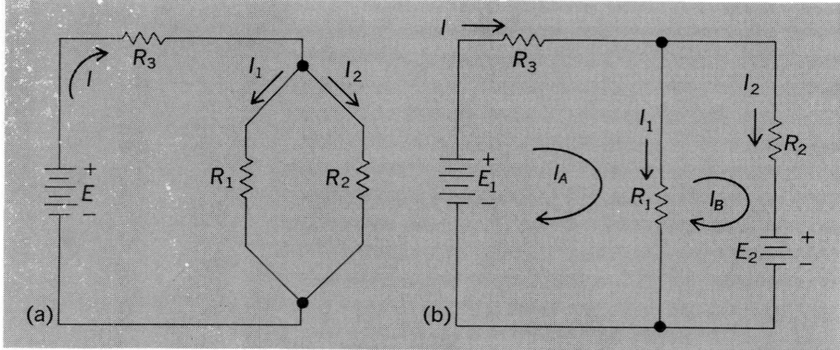


**Fig. 3. Series-parallel circuits. (*a*) Single source. (*b*) Multiple sources.**

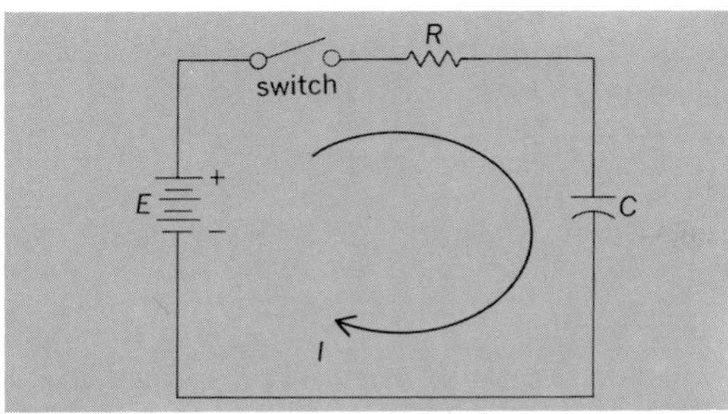


**Fig. 4. A series *RC* circuit.**

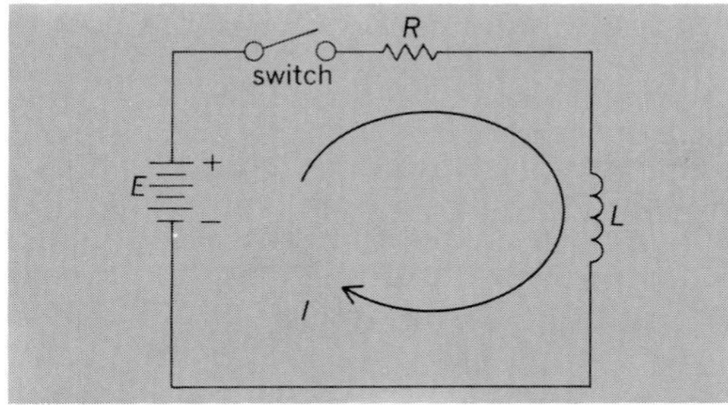


**Fig. 5. A series *RL* circuit.**

$$W = CE^2/2 \qquad (13)$$

SEE TIME CONSTANT.

For the circuit of Fig. 5, the initial current upon closing the switch is zero, since any attempt to cause a rate of change of current through the coil whose inductance is $L$ induces a counter emf across the coil or inductor. Eventually this counter emf disappears and a steady-state current $E/R$ flows indefinitely in the circuit.

The current at any time after closing the switch is given by Eq. (14) in amperes. The factor $R/L$ is the

$$i = (E/R)(1 - \epsilon^{-Rt/L}) \qquad (14)$$

time constant of the circuit. The energy $W$ stored in an inductance at any time is given by Eq. (15).

$$W = LI^2/2 \qquad (15)$$

For a complete discussion of transient phenomena SEE ELECTRIC TRANSIENT.

*Robert L. Ramey*

***Bibliography.*** L. P. Heulsman, *Basic Circuit Theory*, 2d ed., 1984; D. E. Johnson, *Basic Electric Circuit Analysis*, 2d ed., 1984; S. Oppenheimer, *Fundamentals of Electric Circuits*, 1984; R. E. Ridsale, *Electric Circuits*, 2d ed., 1982.

## Directional coupler

A four-port waveguide device (**Fig. 1**) in which an incoming wave at any one port (for example, A) appears at two others (C and D) but not at the fourth (B). This device finds numerous applications in waveguide networks such as microwave waveguides, integrated optics, and optical fibers. It is the equivalent of the hybrid induction coil used in conventional wire circuit telephony to provide side-tone balance. SEE TELEPHONE.

In Fig. 1, $P_A$ is the input power, and $P_B$, $P_C$, and $P_D$ are the powers of the output waves at ports B, C, and D respectively. Ideally, $P_B = 0$, and there is no spurious reflection from the input port: $P_{\text{back}} = 0$. As a system component, the performance of a directional coupler is quoted in terms of : (1) its coupling factor, 10 $\log_{10}$ $(P_D/P_A)$, in decibels (dB); (2) directivity, 10 $\log_{10}$ $(P_D/P_B)$, in dB; (3) insertion loss, 10 $\log_{10}$ $[(P_C + P_D)/P_A]$; (4) frequency band of operation; and (5) its matching impedance as measured by any spurious backward power flow from input port A. SEE ATTENUATION (ELECTRICITY); ELECTRICAL IMPEDANCE; IMPEDANCE MATCHING.

**Two-hole coupler.** Directional couplers are usually made by introducing some form of lumped or continuous coupling among several guides so that the coupled waves interfere constructively in some directions while canceling one another in other directions. Consider two identical microwave waveguides running adjacent to each other with two small holes of the same size and shape coupling between them (**Fig. 2**). These two holes will divert a small portion of the incoming wave at port A from the left-hand waveguide into the right-hand waveguide, thereby establishing four propagating components. The two forward-propagating components $1_F$ and $2_F$ have traveled different paths but equal distances from port A to port D. They are, therefore, always in phase and will combine constructively to produce the output wave at port D. As for the backward-propagating components, $1_B$ leads $2_B$ by a phase of $4\pi L/\lambda$ radians, where $L$ is the distance between the two holes and $\lambda$ is the wavelength of the propagating radiation. Evidently, if $L = \lambda/4$, $1_B$ and $2_B$ are 180° out of phase, and since they have the same amplitudes (due to the small-hole assumption), they will cancel each other and send no power to port B.

**Multipath and slot couplers.** The relation $L = \lambda/4$ and the smallness of the holes impose two limitations on the performance of the simple two-hole directional coupler: a narrow-frequency band over which the directivity is high, and a small coupling factor which is on the order of 10–30 dB; that is, $(P_D/P_A) = 10^{-1}$ to $10^{-3}$. To alleviate these problems, multipath couplers are used, where the backward cancellation is obtained through destructive interference among waves excited by three or more coupling elements (such as holes), usually spaced a quarter-wavelength apart. The coupling holes are not necessarily equal. Their coupling

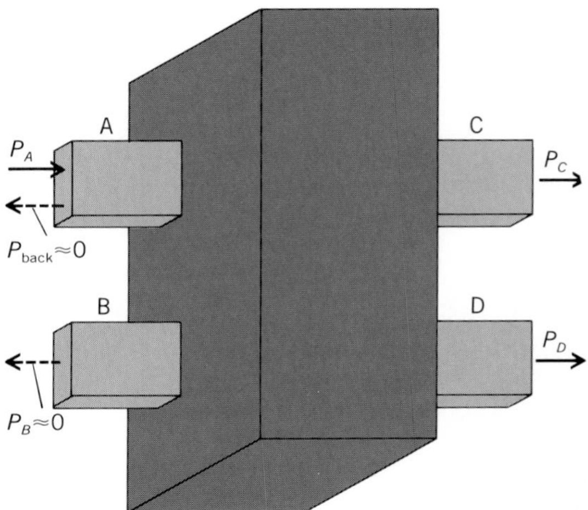


**Fig. 1. Four-port directional waveguide coupler.**

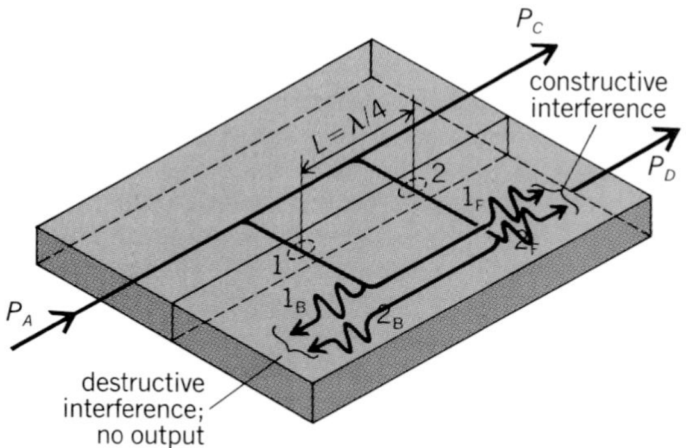


**Fig. 2. Two-hole directional coupler.**

is frequently arranged to be in a binomial series (for example, five holes with couplings proportional to 1:4:6:4:1) or according to some other tapering law. A natural extension to the multipath coupler is the slot coupler, where the coupling element is a continuous slot that is several wavelengths long and often tapered, and the coupling is continuously distributed along the length of the interaction.

**Couplers for open waveguides.** Holes and slots are appropriate coupling elements for closed metallic waveguides, where the propagating field is completely enclosed within the walls of the guide. Other design alternatives exist for open waveguides such as microwave striplines, diffused dielectric optical guides used in integrated optics, and optical fibers. In these guides, the propagating field extends beyond the physical dimensions of the guiding structure (for example, the metallic plates of the stripline or the core of the fiber), and proximity coupling becomes possible.

**Figure 3** shows a possible arrangement for a single-mode fiber-optic directional coupler. In a single-mode cylindrical fiber, optical power is carried in a very thin (5–10-micrometer diameter) core whose index of refraction is slightly higher than that of the surrounding cladding material. Similar to other dielectric waveguides, the electromagnetic field is not entirely confined within the core, and an exponentially decreasing, evanescent, nonradiating tail exists in the first few micrometers of the cladding. Fusion, etching, and mechanical polishing techniques may be used to bring two fiber cores close enough to each other to make possible the transfer of power from one core to the other through the interaction of the corresponding evanescent fields. The long interaction length (with respect to an optical wavelength) ensures an extremely high directivity (greater than 60 dB), and the gradual approach of the cores to each other virtually eliminates back reflections. As the separation between the cores decreases, a larger and larger percentage of the input power is coupled to port D, and a complete power transfer ($P_D = P_A$ and $P_C = 0$) is easily achieved. For even stronger coupling (smaller separation or longer interaction length), the power which was coupled to the lower fiber may couple back to the upper fiber, a condition known as overcoupling.

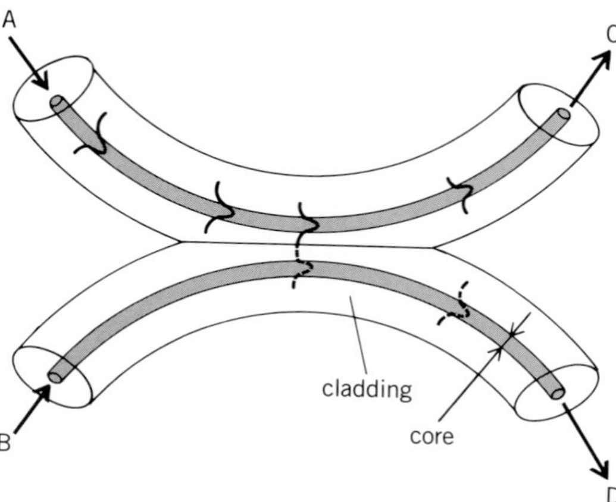


**Fig. 3. Single-mode fiber-optic directional coupler.**

**Relation of output to input.** Assume now that input waves are present at both port A and port B. Since directional couplers are linear devices, the output fields are linear combinations of the input fields. For simplicity, only the scalar case is considered where the input as well as the output waves have the same state of polarization. Thus, if $E_A$, $E_B$ and $E_C$, $E_D$ are, respectively, the amplitudes of the input and output fields, they are related to each other through Eq. (1), or, in a matrix form, through Eq. (2). (The $\{M_i\}$ are,

$$\begin{aligned} E_C &= M_1 \cdot E_A + M_2 \cdot E_B \\ E_D &= M_3 \cdot E_A + M_4 \cdot E_B \end{aligned} \tag{1}$$

$$\begin{bmatrix} E_C \\ E_D \end{bmatrix} = \begin{bmatrix} M_1 & M_2 \\ M_3 & M_4 \end{bmatrix} \cdot \begin{bmatrix} E_A \\ E_B \end{bmatrix} \tag{2}$$

in general, complex numbers.)

For a lossless coupler, the matrix $M$ is unitary; that is, the inverse of $M$ is also the complex conjugate of $M$. When the coupler is also symmetric, as in Figs. 2 and 3, $M$ has a much simpler form, given by Eq. (3),

$$\begin{bmatrix} E_C \\ E_D \end{bmatrix} = \begin{bmatrix} \sqrt{1-K} & j\sqrt{K} \\ j\sqrt{K} & \sqrt{1-K} \end{bmatrix} \cdot \begin{bmatrix} E_A \\ E_B \end{bmatrix} \tag{3}$$

where $K$ is the linear coupling factor and $j = \sqrt{-1}$. There is a phase difference of 90° between the coupled portion of the input wave ($M_3\,E_A$) and the uncoupled component ($M_1\,E_A$). This property which is also shared by bulk optic beam splitters, the waveguide magic tee, and the hybrid induction coil, is crucial for the understanding of the energy balance in various interferometers.

**Applications.** Directional couplers, whether fixed or variable, are extensively used in microwave and optical circuits. Weak couplers can selectively monitor either the forward or backward power flow in waveguides, and medium-to-strong couplers serve as amplitude combiners and splitters in various resonators and sensors. All of these applications require high directivity, low insertion loss, and negligible back reflections. Many other useful junctions are also based on the same physical principles. *See* INTEGRATED OPTICS; MICROWAVE MEASUREMENTS; MICROWAVE POWER MEASUREMENT; MICROWAVE TRANSMISSION LINES; OPTICAL COMMUNICATIONS; WAVEGUIDE.

*Moshe Tur*

**Bibliography.** M. J. F. Digonnet and H. J. Shaw, Analysis of a tunable single mode optical fiber coupler, *IEEE J. Quantum Electr.*, 18:746–754, 1982; S. Liao, *Microwave Devices and Circuits*, 1980; G. L. Matthaei, L. Young, and E. M. T. Jones, *Microwave Filters, Impedance-Matching Networks, and Coupling Structures*, 1964; A. Yariv, *Introduction to Optical Electronics*, 1976.

## Discriminator

A circuit that transforms a frequency-modulated or phase-modulated carrier into a wave that is amplitude-modulated as well as frequency-modulated. The amplitude modulation is then detected by a linear diode detector. Commonly used discriminators are the Foster-Seely discriminator and the ratio detector, which are popularly used in frequency modulated and television receivers. For these and other circuits SEE FREQUENCY-MODULATION DETECTOR.

*Charles L. Alley*

## Disk recording

The process of inscribing suitably transformed acoustical or electrical signals on a flat circular plate that may be played back at a subsequent time. Virtually all modern disk recorders and reproducers are used to record or reproduce sound signals, mainly music and voice.

This article discusses monophonic, stereophonic, and quadraphonic recording and reproducing systems and their compatibility, commercial phonographs, the manufacture and specifications of disk records, distortion and noise in record reproduction, and digital recording. For related information SEE AMPLIFIER; LOUDSPEAKER; MAGNETIC RECORDING; MICROPHONE; OPTICAL RECORDING.

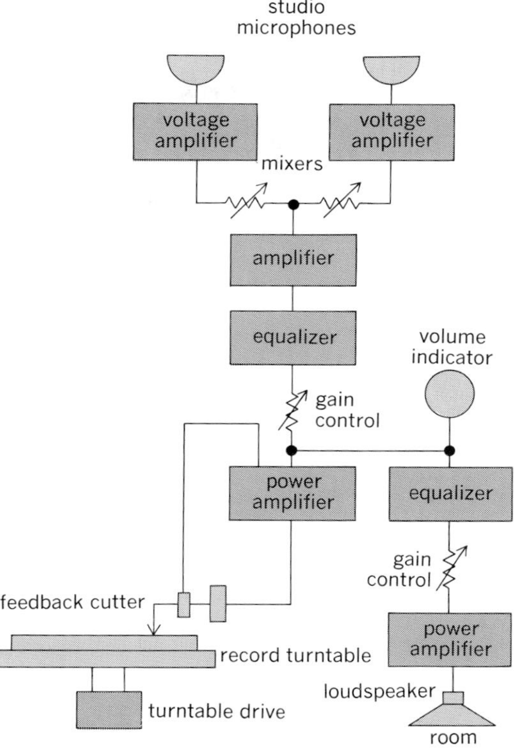


**Fig. 1. Schematic arrangement of apparatus in a complete monophonic disk recording system.**

### Monophonic System

A monophonic disk recording system consists of a disk record rotated by a turntable mechanism and a cutter for producing undulations in a groove in the disk corresponding to the sound signals. A monophonic disk reproducing system consists of a pickup and mechanism for rotating the disk record by means of which the recorded undulations in the disk record are converted into electrical signals of approximately like form.

**Recording system.** The elements in a complete monophonic disk recording system are shown in **Fig. 1**. The first element is the acoustics of the studio. The output of each microphone is amplified and fed to a mixer, a device having two or more inputs and a common output. If more than one microphone is used (for example, when an orchestra accompanies a soloist, there is one microphone for the orchestra and one for the singer), the outputs of the two microphones may be adjusted for the proper balance by means of the mixers. An electronic compressor is used to reduce a large amplitude range to that suitable for reproduction in the home. A corrective electrical network called an equalizer provides the recording characteristics, which are described later. The attenuator, or gain control, provides a given control on the overall level fed to the powerful amplifier. The cutter, actuated by the amplifier, cuts a wavy path in the groove of the revolving record corresponding to the undulations in the original sound wave striking the microphone. A monitoring system consisting of a volume indicator, complementary equalizer, attenuator or gain control, power amplifier, and loudspeaker is used to control the recording operation. The volume indicator employs a logarithmic or decibel scale calibrated in volume units (VU). The volume unit is defined as 10 times the common logarithm of the power ratio $p_2/p_1$, where the reference power level $p_1$ is selected as 1 and $p_2$ is the signal power level.

***Recorder.*** A phonograph recorder is an instrument for transforming acoustical or electrical signals into motion of approximately like form and inscribing such motion in an appropriate medium by cutting or embossing. For the recording of disk phonograph records, the electrical phonograph recorder (**Fig. 2**) replaced the mechanical recorder in the late 1920s. The lacquer disk used in recording the master record is placed on the recording turntable. The turntable is heavy, to ensure against spurious rotational motions. A suitable mechanical filter is placed between the driving motor and the turntable so that uniform rotational motion of the turntable will be obtained. The drive system is arranged so that records of all standard speeds can be cut. In general, the recording turntable is driven with a synchronous motor to ensure constant speed of rotation. The lead screw drives the cutter in a radial direction so that a spiral groove is cut in the record. Lead screws of different pitches

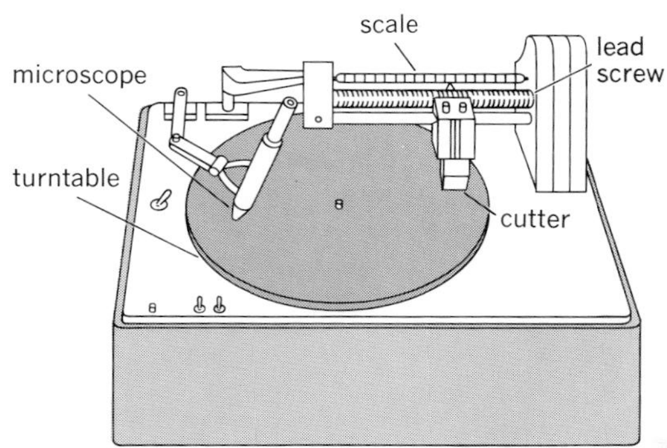


**Fig. 2. Disk phonograph recorder. Microscope is used for periodic inspection of groove. (*After H. F. Olson, Acoustical Engineering, Van Nostrand, 1957*)**

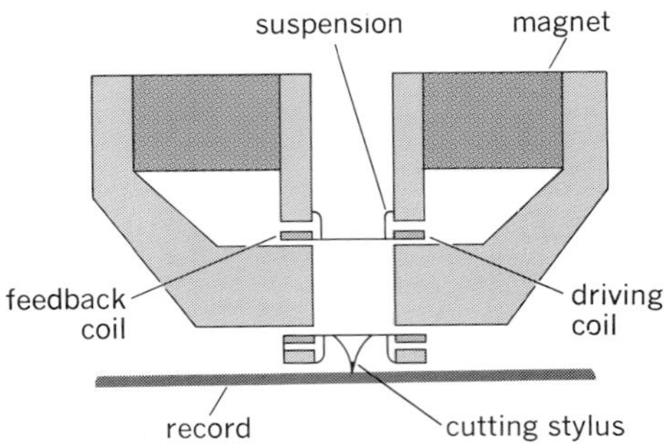


Fig. 3. Lateral feedback phonograph cutter.

are used, ranging from 100 to 500 grooves per inch (4 to 20 grooves per millimeter). In some recordings a variable pitch is used. In this procedure the spacing between the grooves is made to correspond to the amplitude—small spacing for small amplitudes and large spacing for large amplitudes. Under these conditions the maximum amount of information can be recorded on a record. The material removed in the cutting process, in the form of a fine thread, is pulled into the open end of a pipe, which is located near the cutting stylus and is connected to a vacuum system.

***Cutters.*** The electromechanical transducers used as cutters can be of either the lateral or the vertical type. In the lateral type of disk recording, the undulations are cut in a direction parallel to the surface of the record and perpendicular to the groove. A sectional view of a lateral feedback phonograph cutter is shown in **Fig. 3**. The vibrating system is of the dynamic type with two coils, one the driving coil and the other the sensing (feedback) coil, wound on a common cylinder. The cutting stylus is attached to the coil cylinder. The vibrating system is designed so that it exhibits a single degree of freedom (single type of movement) over the frequency range from 30 to 16,000 Hz with a fundamental resonant frequency at 700 Hz. The output of the sensing coil is fed to the input of the amplifier, as shown in Fig. 1. The output of the amplifier is fed to the driving coil in an out-of-phase relationship. With the feedback in operation, the velocity of the driving system is practically independent of frequency over the range from 30 to 16,000 Hz. The input to the amplifier is compensated to provide the desired recording characteristic.

The cutting stylus consists of a sapphire, synthetic ruby, or other hard material fashioned in the form of a pointed chisel (**Fig. 4**). The stylus is heated in recording and thereby imparts a smooth sidewall to the groove. This expedient results in considerable reduction in noise in reproduction. The stylus may be heated by a few turns of fine wire wound around it and operated from a low-voltage dc supply.

The original recording of disk records is made on a lacquer disk. The lacquer disk consists of a coating of

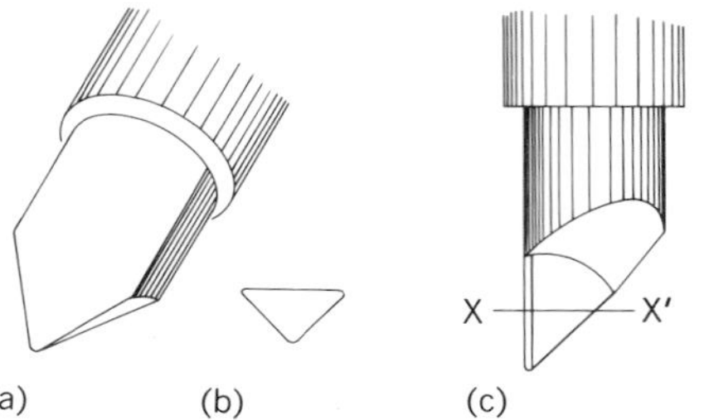


Fig. 4. Cutting stylus. (*a*) Perspective, (*b*) section, and (*c*) side views.

an acetate plastic on two sides of an aluminum disk. The grooves are cut in the plastic.

In the vertical (hill-and-dale) type of disk recording, the undulations of the groove are cut in a direction perpendicular to the surface of the record and perpendicular to the groove. The vertical cutter is similar to the lateral cutter except that the stylus is located on the end of the cylinder of Fig. 3, and the entire system is turned 90°.

The vertical disk phonograph system is used to a limited extent in broadcasting stations, but it is not used in home disk phonograph systems.

***Recording characteristics.*** The velocity-frequency-response characteristic of the groove in the phonograph disk record provides the velocity at the top of the stylus of the phonograph pickup as a function of the frequency.

Electrical transcriptions (a term applied to professional disk recordings) are cut with an orthacoustic recording characteristic on records 16 in. (406 mm) in diameter turning at 33⅓ rpm. The orthacoustic velocity-frequency characteristic for constant voltage input to the microphone voltage amplifier is shown in **Fig. 5**. This is essentially a constant amplitude frequency characteristic. In reproduction of the disk record, an inverse frequency-response characteristic is used to obtain a uniform overall frequency-response characteristic.

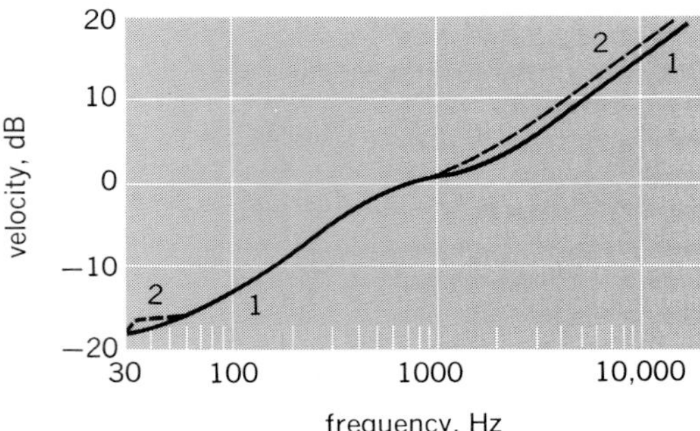


**Fig. 5. Velocity-frequency recording characteristics used in commercial records. Curve 1, Record Industry Association of America standard. Curve 2, Orthacoustic standard. (*After L. C. Smeby, Recording and reproducing standards, Proc. IRE, 30(8):355–356, 1942*)**

In the recording of commercial phonograph records, some form of high-frequency compensation has always been employed. The compensation that has been used since the advent of the disk phonograph has varied over wide limits. Fortunately, in 1954 the Record Industry Association of America standardized the velocity–frequency-response characteristic of the groove in the commercial lateral disk record. The RIAA standard velocity–frequency-response characteristic is shown in Fig. 5. In the reproduction of commercial disk phonograph records, an inverse frequency-response characteristic is employed in order to obtain a uniform overall frequency-response characteristic. Commercial standard frequency records exhibiting the RIAA frequency-response characteristic are used in the development, design, and service of disk phonograph instruments. *See Frequency-response equalization.*

***Record manufacture.*** The processes for the mass production of disk phonograph records are depicted in

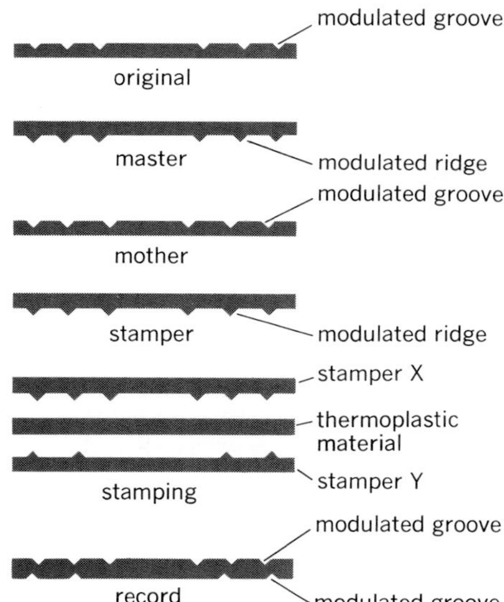


**Fig. 6. Steps in mass production of disk phonograph records from lacquer originals.**

**Fig. 6**. The original lacquer disk, termed the original, is metalized and then electroplated. The plating is separated from the lacquer and reinforced by backing with a solid metal plate. The assembly, called the master, is electroplated. This plating is separated from the master and reinforced by backing with a solid plate. The resulting assembly, the mother, is electroplated and reinforced by a solid metal plate, forming an assembly termed the stamper. Several stampers are made from each mother. One stamper containing a sound selection to be placed on one side of the final record is mounted in the upper jaw, and another stamper containing a sound selection to the placed on the other side of the record is placed in the lower jaw of a hydraulic press equipped with means for heating and cooling the stampers. A preform, or biscuit, of thermoplastic material such as a shellac compound or vinyl compound is placed between the two stampers.

The stampers are heated, and the jaws of the press are closed to bring the two stampers against the thermoplastic material. When an impression of the stampers has been obtained in the thermoplastic material, the stampers are cooled, thus cooling and setting the plastic record. The jaws of the hydraulic press are opened, and the record is removed from the press. The modulated grooves in the record correspond to those in the original lacquer disk. The stamping procedure is repeated again and again until the desired number of records is obtained. This process constitutes the mass-production technique for the production of phonograph records.

**Reproducing system.** The elements of a complete monophonic disk sound-reproducing system are shown in **Fig. 7**. The first element is the motor-driven turntable which turns the record at a constant rotational speed. The stylus or needle of the pickup follows the wavy groove in the record and the pickup transducer generates a voltage corresponding to the undulations in the record. The output of the pickup is amplified by a voltage amplifier. The amplifier is followed by an equalizer which complements the recording characteristic of the record. Filters and tone controls are provided for further equalization of the response according to the taste of the listener. The tone controls provide means for increasing or decreasing the low- and high-frequency response. In general, the increase or decrease in response starts at 1000 Hz with a gradual increase or decrease in both high and low directions. The maximum increase or decrease in response at the extreme ends of the frequency range covered is about $\pm 15$ dB. A volume control provides means for obtaining the desired level of sound in reproduction. The volume control is followed by an amplifier which drives the loudspeaker.

***Turntable and record changer.*** In an electrical record player and changer, the record is rotated by the turntable at the same angular speed as that used in recording. The turntable is rotated by means of an electric motor. The stylus or needle of the pickup follows the wavy spiral groove and generates a voltage corresponding to the undulations in the groove. (Pickups used in disk-record reproduction are described later.) A record player will play recordings at one or more of four rotational speeds: 16⅔, 33⅓, 45, and 78 rpm. A record changer may accommodate as many as eight records. A manual record player is the simplest type of disk-record reproducer, and involves placing the pickup arm on the record by hand and removing the arm at the conclusion of the record side. Such manual players include elaborate transcription types with very uniform rotational velocity and high-quality pickups.

***Pickups or cartridges.*** A phonograph pickup is an electromechanical transducer actuated by a phonograph record and delivering energy to an electrical system, the electric current having frequency components corresponding to those of the wave in the record. The following systems are used for converting the mechanical vibrations into the corresponding electrical variations: magnetic, condenser, electronic, dynamic, ceramic, and crystal.

Modern lateral pickups are of the crystal, ceramic, magnetic, or dynamic type. A crystal phonograph pickup depends for its operation on the piezoelectric effect. The crystal used is Rochelle salt. Top and sectional views of a typical crystal pickup used for commercial phonographs are shown in **Fig. 8***a* and *b*. The stylus driven by the record is coupled through an arm to the crystal and thereby produces a twist in the crystal. The open-circuit output of the crystal is proportional to the twist or displacement. The open-circuit voltage of a crystal pickup for an amplitude of 0.001 in. is about 0.5 V. The open-circuit voltage displacement characteristic makes the frequency equalization exceedingly simple because the recording character-

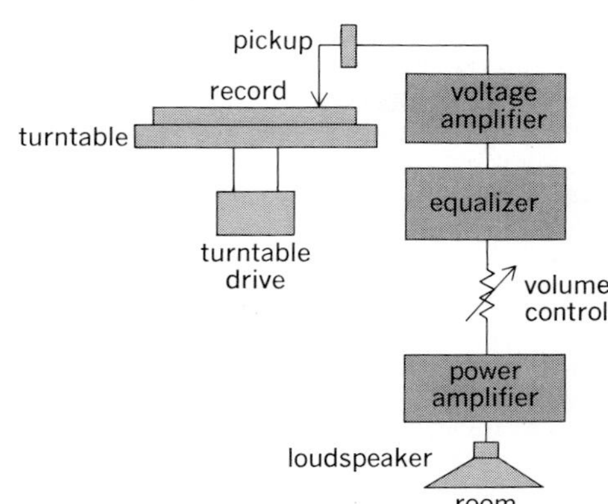


**Fig. 7. Schematic arrangement of apparatus in a complete monophonic disk sound-reproducing system.**

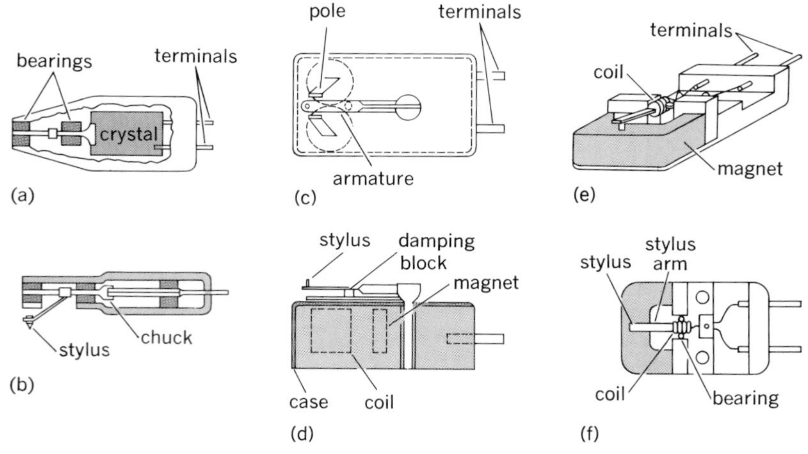


**Fig. 8. Phonograph pickups. (*a*) Crystal type in cutaway top view and (*b*) sectional view. (*c*) Magnetic type in bottom view and (*d*) sectional view. (*e*) Dynamic type in perspective view and (*f*) bottom view.**

istic shown in Fig. 5 exhibits a practically constant displacement frequency characteristic. The electrical capacitance of the crystal is of the order of 1000-2000 picofarads. The equivalent electrical circuit is the open-circuit voltage in series with the electrical capacitance. The electrical impedance presented to the crystal pickup must be larger than the electrical impedance of the crystal in order to prevent reduction of low-frequency response. Since the electrical impedance of the crystal is large in the low-frequency range, the electrical impedance presented to the crystal must be relatively large to prevent frequency discrimination against the low-frequency range. *See* Piezoelectricity.

A ceramic phonograph pickup depends for its operation on the electrostrictive effect. The ceramic used is barium titanate. The ceramic pickup may be made in designs similar to that of the crystal pickup. The characteristics are similar in all essential respects save that the sensitivity is somewhat lower than that of the Rochelle salt crystal. *See* Electrostriction.

A phonograph pickup which depends for its operation on the variation in magnetic flux through a stationary coil is called a magnetic pickup. A modern type is shown in Fig. 8*c* and *d*. The horizontal stylus also serves as the armature. This design makes it possible to obtain a relatively low mechanical impedance. The steady flux is supplied by a small permanent magnet. As the armature is deflected from the central position, the flux through one coil is increased and the flux through the other coil is decreased. The coils are connected in series so that the resultant voltages generated in the two coils are added. The open-circuit voltage generated in a coil is proportional to the time rate of change of magnetic flux through the coil, which in turn is proportional to the velocity of the armature. Thus, the open-circuit voltage generated in the coil will be independent of the frequency if the velocity of the armature is independent of the frequency. In a properly designed magnetic pickup, the open-circuit voltage frequency-response characteristic will correspond to the groove velocity frequency-response characteristic. For the recording characteristic of Fig. 5, frequency-compensating networks must be employed in order to obtain a uniform output frequency-response characteristic. The output of a typical magnetic pickup for an amplitude of 0.001 in. (25 μm) at 1000 Hz is of the order of 0.010 V. The electrical impedance is highly inductive and therefore the electrical impedance is nearly proportional to the frequency. The electrical impedance of a typical magnetic pickup for a 0.010-V output is 2500 ohms at 1000 Hz. The equivalent electrical circuit is the open-circuit voltage in series with the electrical impedance of the coils.

A dynamic phonograph pickup depends for its operation on the motion of a conductor in a magnetic field. A typical dynamic pickup is shown in Fig. 8*e* and *f*. The stylus arm is coupled to a coil located in a magnetic field. The open-circuit voltage developed in the coil is proportional to the rate of change of magnetic flux through the coil, and will be independent of frequency if the velocity is independent of frequency. In a properly designed dynamic pickup, the open-circuit voltage frequency-response characteristic will correspond to the groove velocity frequency-response characteristic. For the recording characteristic of Fig. 5, frequency-compensating networks must be employed in order to obtain a uniform output frequency-response characteristic. Since the vibrating system may be very small and light, it is possible to obtain a uniform velocity–frequency-response characteristic over a wide frequency range. The electrical impedance is practically an electrical resistance of about 25 ohms. The output at 1000 Hz for an amplitude of 0.001 in. (25 μm) is about 0.001 V. In general, a transformer is used to step up the output voltage and electrical impedance.

In the vertical type of disk recording, the undulations of the groove are perpendicular both to the plane of the disk and to the groove. Therefore, the vibration of the stylus of the pickup is in the vertical direction. Any of the lateral pickups just described may be used by turning the transducer 90°.

***Groove and stylus dimensions.*** A sectional view of the groove of a lateral disk record and the stylus is

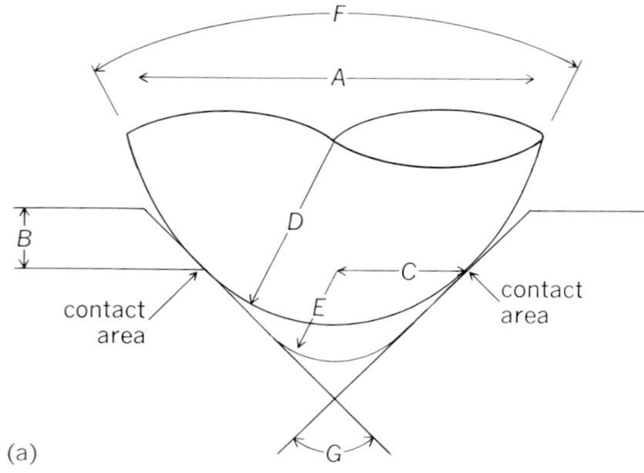


(b)

| Value | Coarse groove | Fine groove | Ultrafine groove |
|---|---|---|---|
| A, in. | 0.006 | 0.0027 | 0.001 |
| B, in. | 0.0008 | 0.0004 | 0.0004 |
| C, in. | 0.0019 | 0.0007 | 0.00017 |
| D, in. | 0.0027 | 0.001 | 0.00025 |
| E, in. | 0.0023 | 0.00027 | 0.00015 |
| F | 45° | 45° | 45° |
| G | 90° | 90° | 90° |

**Fig. 9. Stylus in groove. (*a*) Sectional view. (*b*) Values of dimensions and angles. (*After H. F. Olson, Acoustical Engineering, Van Nostrand, 1957*)**

shown in **Fig. 9***a*. The width of the groove at the surface of the record A, the angle of the walls of the groove G, the radius C of the stylus, the distance B below the surface of the record to the contact point of the stylus with the groove, and the width of the contact points are shown. The dimensions and angles for a coarse groove, fine groove, and ultrafine groove are given in Fig. 9*b*. The coarse groove is used in 78-rpm records, the fine groove in 45- and 33⅓-rpm records, and the ultrafine groove in 16⅔-rpm records.

The maximum nominal grooves per inch for the different-sized grooves are as follows: coarse groove, 125; fine groove, 275; and ultrafine groove, 550.

The maximum amplitudes, in inches, in the frequency range 200–2000 Hz for the different-sized grooves are as follows: coarse groove, 0.004–0.005 in. (102–127 μm); fine groove, 0.0015–0.002 in. (38–51 μm); and ultrafine groove, 0.0007–0.001 in. (18–25 μm).

### Commercial Disk Records

Commercial phonograph records are made in four speeds, namely, 78 (approximately), 45, 33⅓, and 16⅔ rpm. The 78-rpm records are made in three diameters, 12, 10, and 7 in. (305, 254, and 178 mm). The normal maximum playing times for full-width records are 5, 3½, and 2½ min, respectively. The 33⅓-rpm records are made in three diameters, 12, 10, and 7 in. The normal maximum playing times are 25, 17, and 8 min, respectively. The 45-rpm records are made in a diameter of 7 in. and have a normal maximum playing time of 8 min. The 16⅔-rpm records are made in a diameter of 7 in. The normal maximum playing time of the records with the large center hole is 30 min, while that for the small-hole records is 45 min for music and 60 min for speech. The overall diameter, the diameters of the first and last program groove, the label diameters, and the diameter of the center hole of the different records are shown in **Fig. 10**. It should be mentioned that the specifications of Fig. 10 and of the preceding discussion are representative and do not include all the variations.

### Distortion and Noise

Distortion is any undesired change in the waveform of a signal in a sound-reproducing system. Noise is any foreign, erratic, intermittent, or statistically random signal produced within a sound-reproducing system. Distortion and noise are the two major problems that must be solved to achieve high-fidelity performance in disk sound-reproducing systems.

**Distortion in reproduction.** The recording and reproducing of a phonograph record constitute a complicated process, with many sources of nonlinear distortion. The record does not present an infinite mechanical impedance to the stylus. As a consequence, the vibrating system of the pickup is shunted by the effective mechanical impedance of the record at the stylus. Nonlinear distortion will be introduced if this impedance of the record is variable. Other sources of distortion are tracking error and tracing distortion.

***Tracking distortion.*** A nonlinear distortion due to a deviation in tracking is commonly termed tracking error. The angle between the vertical plane containing the vibration axis of the pickup and the vertical plane containing the tangent to the record is a measure of the tracking error. If the vibration axis of the pickup passes through the tone arm pivot, the tracking error can be zero for only one point on the record. Tracking error can be reduced if the vibration axis of the

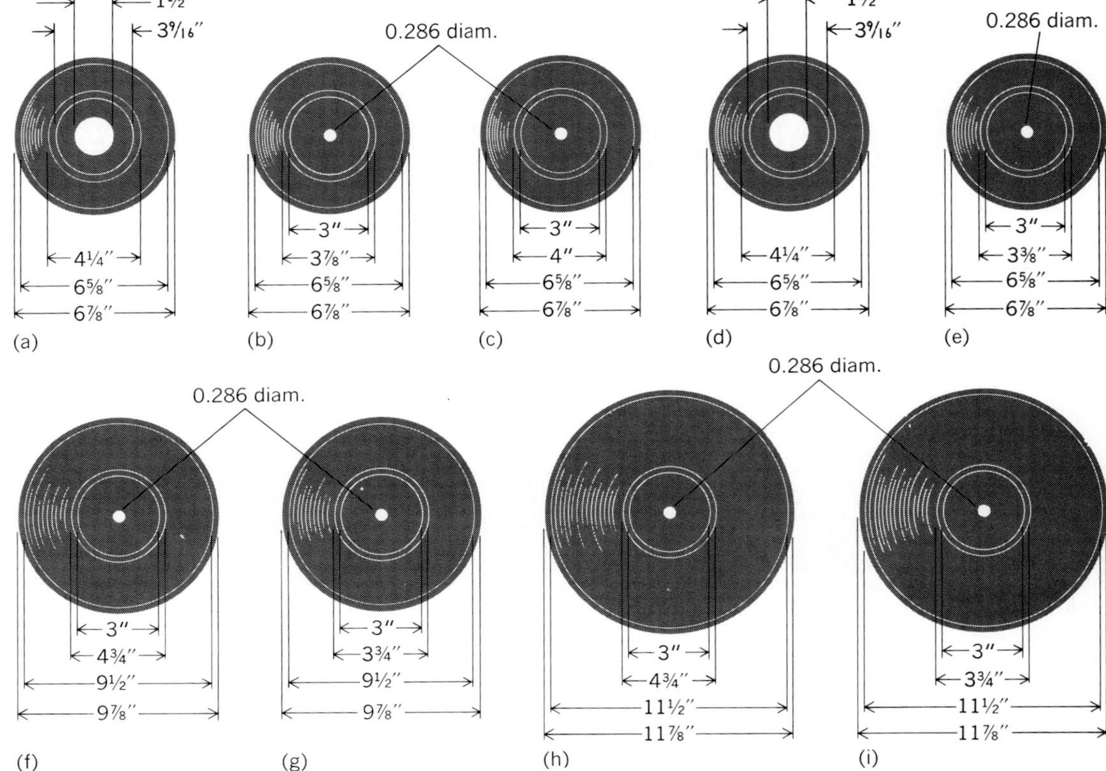


**Fig. 10. Typical dimensions of the commercial disk phonograph records. (*a*) 7 in. (178 mm), 16⅔ rpm, large hole. (*b*) 7 in., 16⅔ rpm, small hole. (c) 7 in., 33⅓ rpm. (*d*) 7 in., 45 rpm. (e) 7 in., 78 rpm. (*f*) 10 in. (254 mm), 33⅓ rpm. (*g*) 10 in., 78 rpm. (*h*) 12 in. (305 mm), 33⅓ rpm. (*i*) 12 in., 78 rpm. (*After H. F. Olson, Acoustical Engineering, Van Nostrand, 1957*)**

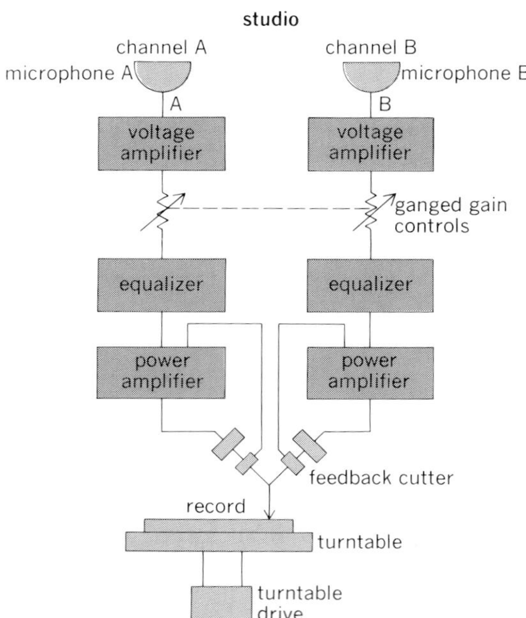


**Fig. 11. Schematic diagram of complete stereophonic disk recording system.**

pickup is set at an appropriate angle with respect to the line connecting the stylus point and the tone arm pivot, together with provisions for a suitable overhang distance between the stylus and the record axis.

***Tracing distortion.*** A form of distortion in lateral disk-record reproduction known as tracing distortion is a function of the diameter of the stylus, the lateral velocity, and the linear groove velocity. This distortion is due to the fact that there is not a one-to-one correspondence between the shapes of the cutting and reproducing styli (Figs. 4 and 9). The cutting stylus presents a triangular shape as it cuts the groove. Thus, it is seen that the groove narrows as the cutting stylus approaches the center position because the cutting stylus is moving at an angle with respect to the motion of the record. The reproducing stylus presents a spherical surface to the groove; therefore, as the reproducing stylus moves in the groove, it will rise as the groove narrows. The frequency of the rise is twice the frequency of the modulation. The narrowing of the groove is termed the pinch effect. The two sides of the groove are symmetrical; therefore, the stylus must execute symmetrical motion about the center line, which means that there should be no even harmonics. However, odd harmonics are produced.

***Other distortions.*** If the force which the stylus presents to the record is of such magnitude that it exceeds the yield point of the record material, the mechanical impedance of the record will not be a constant. The result is production of nonlinear distortion. Furthermore, if the force exceeds the yield point by a considerable amount, the record may be permanently damaged.

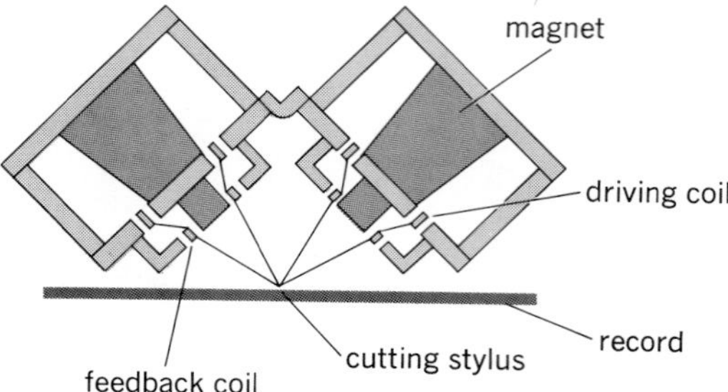


**Fig. 12. Sectional view of a feedback stereophonic disk phonograph cutter.**

As the needle or stylus is worn by the groove, the shape of the point changes from a spherical surface to a wedge shape. The wedge-shaped stylus introduces nonlinear distortion and a loss in the high-frequency response.

A consideration of the load and needle forces at the stylus tip shows that there is a force which is proportional to the tracking angle. This force, known as side thrust, is usually directed toward the center of the record and is applied to the inner boundary of the record groove; it is responsible for the unequal wear on the two sides of the stylus.

Another source of distortion results from the lack of correspondence between the linear groove speed in the recording and the ultimate reproduction. This type of distortion, which leads to a frequency modulation of the reproduced signal, is termed wow. Wow may be due to a nonuniform speed of the record turntable during recording or reproduction, misplacement of the center hole, or configuration distortion during the processing. In general, the major source of wow is the nonuniform speed of the reproducing turntable.

**Surface noise.** The record surface noise, in the absence of any signal, is one of the factors which limits the volume range and the frequency range of shellac phonograph records. The amount of surface noise for a given record is proportional to the frequency bandwidth. In order to reduce the surface noise to a tolerable value in shellac records, it is usually necessary to limit the high-frequency range in reproduction. A method of decreasing the effective surface noise is to increase the amplitude of the high-frequency response in recording and to introduce complementary equalization, as in the recording characteristic of Fig. 5.

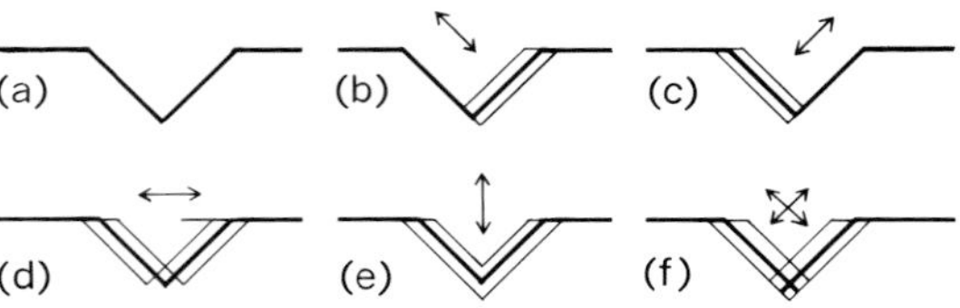


**Fig. 13. Schematic views of groove undulations in stereophonic disk phonograph system. Heavy line indicates zero amplitude or unmodulated groove. Light lines indicate maximum limit of groove modulation. Arrows indicate direction of motion of recording cutter and reproducing stylus. (*a*) Unmodulated groove. (*b*) Modulation in right channel. (c) Modulation in left channel. (*d*) Lateral modulation, combination of *b* and c in phase. (e) Vertical modulation, combination of *b* and c out of phase. (*f*) Combination of equal vertical and lateral amplitudes, combination of *b* and c with 90° phase shift.**

The noise of Vinylite records is extremely low and, in general, is not a problem. Adequate volume ranges can be obtained with Vinylite and similar plastics.

## Stereophonic System

Two-channel disk phonograph sound reproduction was commercialized in 1958. The stereophonic disk phonograph provides the reproduction of the original sound sources in auditory perspective; that is, the spa-

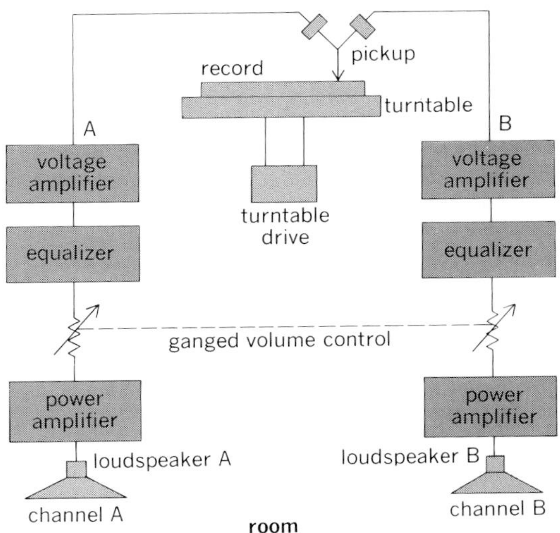


**Fig. 14. Schematic arrangement of complete stereophonic disk phonograph reproducing system.**

tial relations of the original sound are substantially retained in the reproduction of the recorded sound.

**Recording system.** The elements of a complete stereophonic disk recording system are shown in **Fig. 11**. There are two channels identical to the type shown in Fig. 1 except for the cutter. A two-channel disk phonograph dynamic-type feedback cutter is shown in **Fig. 12**. The two vibrating systems are arranged at right angles; therefore, the two channels in the groove are recorded at right angles. The modes of vibration in a plane normal to the surface of the record and normal to the groove axis are shown in **Fig. 13**. The motion of the cutting stylus is also shown in Fig. 13.

The same type of recorder described in the beginning of this article may be used in the recording of stereophonic records.

The recording characteristics that are employed in stereophonic disk recording are essentially the same as those that are used in monophonic disk recording.

**Reproducing system.** The elements of a complete stereophonic disk reproducing system are shown in **Fig. 14**. There are two identical channels following the pickup of the type shown in Fig. 7. A two-channel disk phonograph dynamic pickup is shown in **Fig. 15**. Each element of the stereophonic pickup consists of a transducer of the type employed in the single-channel lateral dynamic pickup shown in Fig. 8*e* and *f*. Reference to Figs. 13 and 15 shows that a vibration

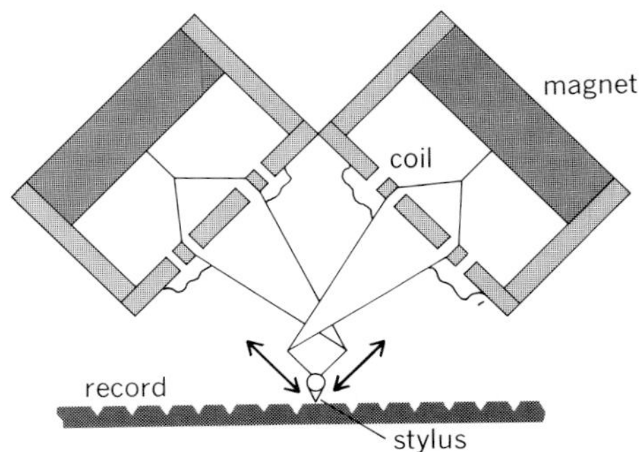


**Fig. 15. Sectional view of a dynamic stereophonic disk phonograph pickup.**

which excites one element will not excite the other. Other types of pickups have also been developed, for example, ceramic and magnetic pickups. A perspective view in schematic form depicting the elements of a ceramic pickup is shown in **Fig. 16**. The two ceramic elements are arranged with the vibrating planes at right angles and coupled to the stylus in such a manner that a vibration which excites one element

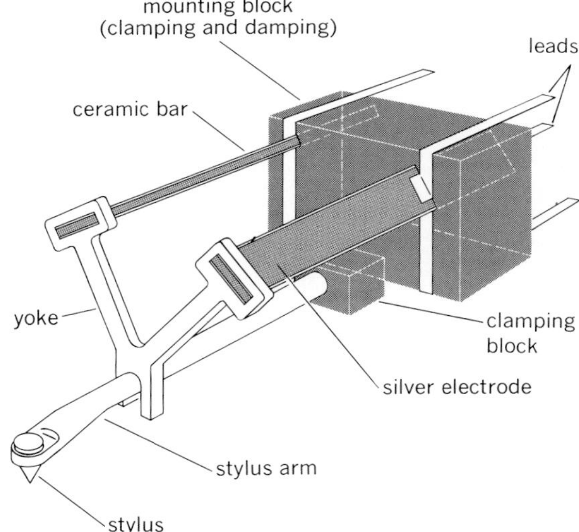


**Fig. 16. Ceramic stereophonic pickup. (*After H. F. Olson, Music, Physics and Engineering, Dover, 1967*)**

will not excite the other. A perspective view in schematic form depicting the elements of a magnetic pickup is shown in **Fig. 17**. The stylus is connected to a magnet. There are two magnetic circuits with coils arranged at right angles. The vibration of the

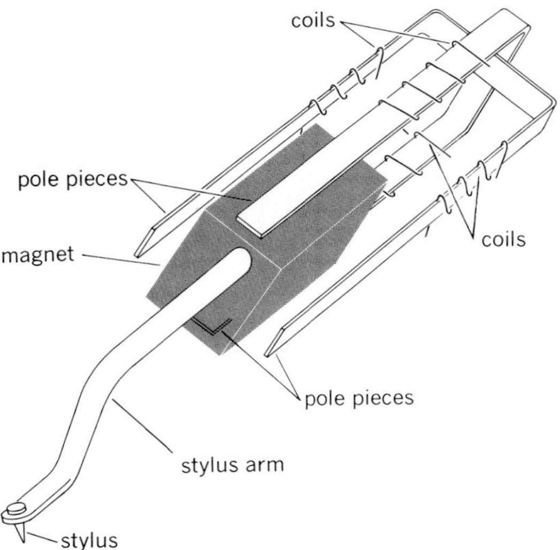


**Fig. 17. Magnetic stereophonic pickup. (*After H. F. Olson, Music, Physics and Engineering, Dover, 1967*)**

magnet leads to a variation in flux in the coils which in turn generates a voltage. A vibration which generates a voltage in one set of coils will not generate a voltage in the other set. The three types of stereophonic pickups shown in Figs. 15, 16, and 17 are the most common in use.

The groove used for the stereophonic disk record is shown in Fig. 9. A stylus with a tip radius of 0.00075 in. is a standard for use in the reproduction of stereophonic disk records. A stylus with an elliptical tip

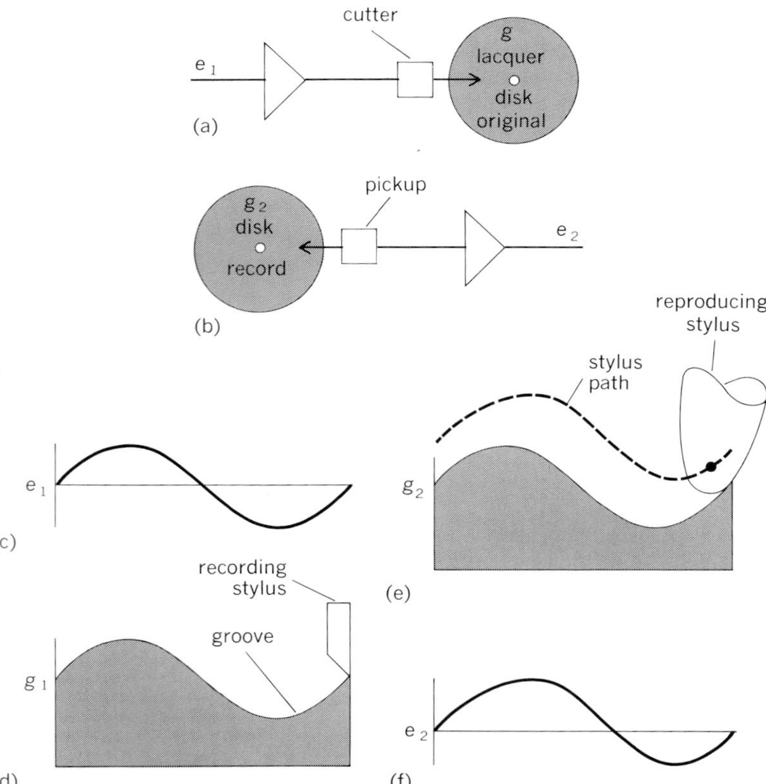


**Fig. 18.** The recording and reproducing process in a stereophonic disk system. (*a*) Recording system. (*b*) Reproducing system. (c) Input to recording system. (*d*) Groove cut in original lacquer disk record. (e) Path of reproducing stylus in the groove of the disk record. (*f*) Output of reproducing system.

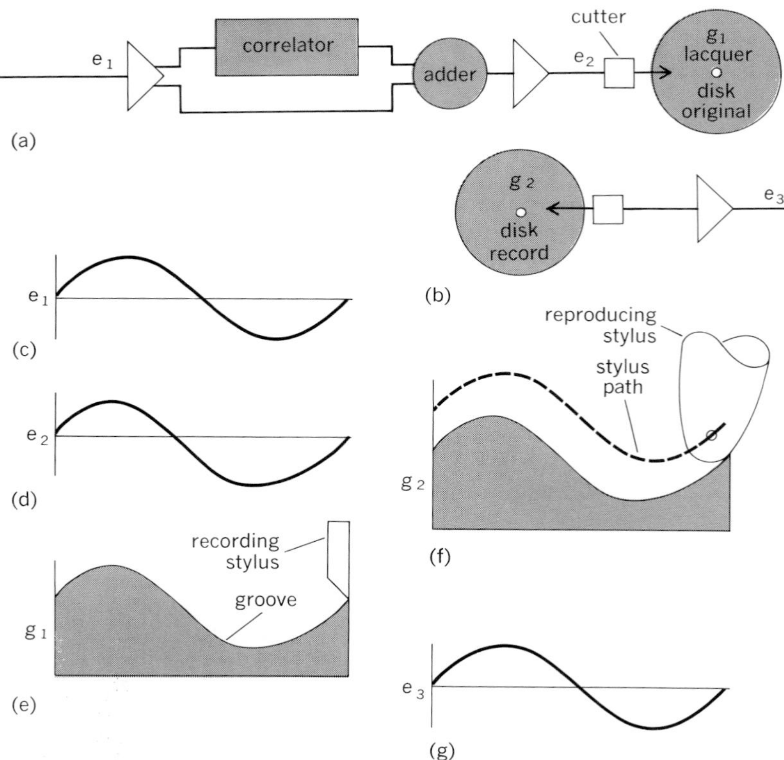


**Fig. 19.** The recording and reproducing process in a stereophonic disk system in which complementary distortion is introduced to reduce tracing distortion in reproduction. (*a*) Recording system. (*b*) Reproducing system. (c) Input to recording system. (*d*) Input to cutter. (e) Groove cut in original lacquer disk record. (*f*) Path of reproducing stylus in the groove of the disk record. (*g*) Output of reproducing system.

with a large ''radius'' of 0.00075 in. (19 μm) and a small ''radius'' of 0.00025 in. (6 μm) in contact with the record groove has also been used. The latter, smaller radius leads to a reduction in tracing distortion.

**Tracing distortion.** The master stereophonic disk record is cut with a chisel-type stylus and the replica is reproduced by a ball-tipped stylus. Therefore, there is a discrepancy between the motion of the cutting stylus which becomes more pronounced at the shorter wavelengths. This type of distortion is termed tracing distortion. The recording and reproducing process in one channel of a stereophonic disk system is depicted in **Fig. 18**. The input signal to the recording system $e_1$ is a sine wave. The groove $g_1$ cut in the original disk record is also a sine wave. The disk record $g_2$ is a replica of the original disk record $g_1$ and is also a sine wave. However, the path of the ball-tipped reproducing stylus is not a sine wave, but distorted in a manner characteristic of a vertical recording system. The wave of the electrical output of the reproducing system $e_2$ is unsymmetrical, which means that the major distortion component is a second harmonic.

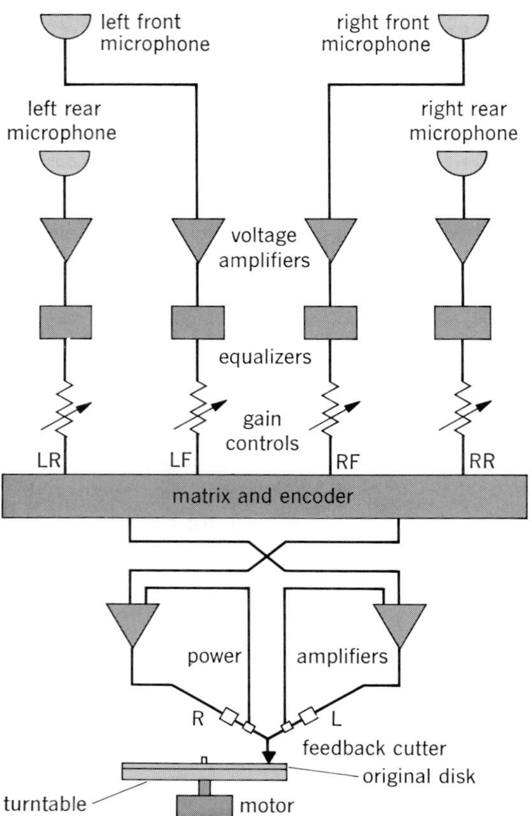


**Fig. 20.** Complete quadraphonic disk recording system employing matrixing and encoding for converting from four channels to two channels.

The distortion can be reduced by the introduction of complementary distortion, as depicted in **Fig. 19**. The input signal to the recording system is again a sine wave $e_1$. However, the correlator introduces nonlinear distortion which is added to $e_1$. The output of the adder and the input to the cutter $e_2$ is not a sine wave. The groove cut in the original disk record $g_1$ corresponds to $e_2$. The disk record $g_2$ is a replica of the original record $g_1$. The groove in the record is

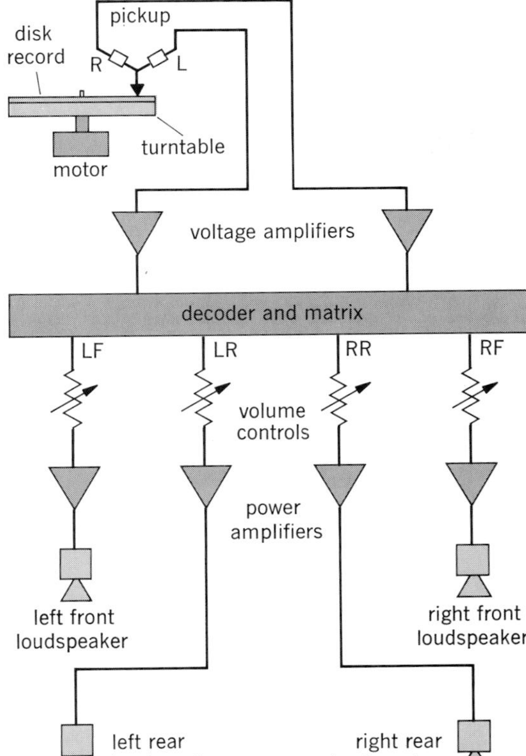


**Fig. 21. Complete quadraphonic disk reproducing system employing decoding and matrixing for converting two channels to four channels.**

distorted by the correlator so that the path of the reproducing stylus is a sine wave. The output of the reproducing system is a sine wave $e_3$. The mechanism of Fig. 19 indicates that the introduction of complementary distortion in the recording process will reduce distortion in the reproducing process. An electronic system which provides this type of distortion is termed a dynamic styli correlator. The distortion is reduced by a factor of more than 4 in actual practice.

**Vertical tracking angle.** A disparity between the effective vertical angle in the recording cutter cutting the modulated groove in the record and the vertical tracking angle of the pickup introduces harmonic and intermodulation in the output of the pickup. The standard vertical angle in stereophonic disk records is 15°. For this reason the angle between the axis of rotation of the vibrating system of the pickup and the plane of the record should be 15°.

**Side thrust.** A consideration of steady forces acting upon the stylus shows there is a force which is proportional to the horizontal tracking angle and is directed toward the center of the record. This places a permanent mechanical bias upon the pickup and may lead to distortion in stereophonic reproduction. This force can be corrected by the application of an equal and counter steady force applied to the pickup arm.

**Surface noise.** The signal-to-noise ratio in commercial stereophonic disk records is very large, of the order of 60 to 70 dB. Therefore, the noise in stereophonic disk records is not a problem for reproduction of sound in the home by means of disk records.

**Compatibility.** Monophonic and stereophonic records and phonographs are compatible as follows.

When a single-channel monophonic record is reproduced by a single-channel monophonic phonograph system, the single-channel output is reproduced by the two loudspeakers.

When a two-channel stereophonic record is reproduced by a single-channel monophonic phonograph reproducing system, the sound reproduced by the single loudspeaker is the sum of the two sound programs originally recorded on the two channels of the stereophonic recording system.

When the two-channel stereophonic record is reproduced by a two-channel stereophonic reproducing system, the stereophonic sound program is reproduced on the separate channels corresponding to the recording channels, and the sound from the two loudspeakers corresponds to the sound picked up by the respective microphones.

### Quadraphonic System

There are two approaches to quadraphonic sound reproduction by means of the disk record: first, the matrixing and encoding from four channels, to recording on a two-channel disk, and reproducing from a two-channel disk and decoding and matrixing to four channels; and, second, the recording and reproducing of four discrete channels by means of the disk record.

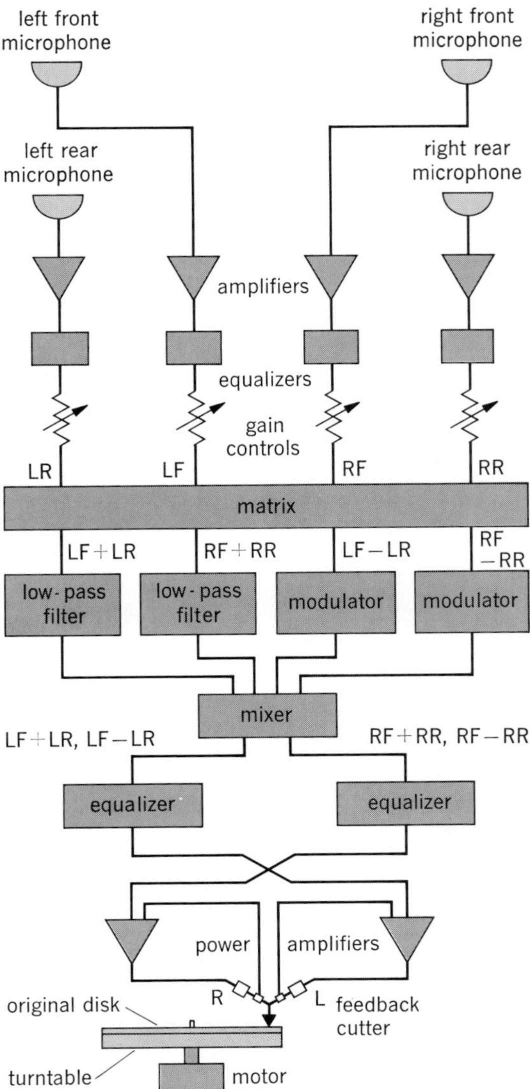


**Fig. 22. Complete discrete four-channel quadraphonic disk matrixing and recording system in which two channels are recorded in the conventional two-channel manner and the other two channels are recorded by modulation means.**

**Coding and matrixing system.** There are many different ways of matrixing and encoding from four channels to two channels and decoding and matrixing from two channels to four channels. The generic recording and reproducing systems employing coding and matrixing in these processes are depicted in **Figs. 20** and **21**. The four inputs LF, LR, RF, and RR, representing left front, left rear, right front, and right rear channels, are matrixed and encoded to the left, L, and the right, R, channels of the conventional two-channel stereophonic disk recording system, as shown in Fig. 20. Each of the two channels R and L contains a mixture of the four channels in such a manner that the four channels can be reconstituted in reproduction by means of the decoder and matrix which are illustrated in Fig. 21. In all of the coding and matrixing systems, the crosstalk separation that is achieved between LF, LR, RR, and RF signals is on the average 6 dB.

**Discrete system.** A discrete quadraphonic disk system, in which two channels are recorded in the conventional manner and the other two channels are recorded by modulation means in the region above 15,000 Hz, is depicted in **Figs. 22–24**. The left front, LF, plus the left rear, LR, signals are recorded in the left groove wall, and the right front, RF, plus the right rear, RR, signals are recorded in the right groove wall. These sets of signals are recorded in the conventional two-channel stereophonic mode and frequency range. The LF-minus-LR signals are recorded on a modulated carrier in the right groove wall, as shown in Fig. 22. The frequency-response characteristics are shown in Fig. 23. *See Modulation*.

In reproduction, the RF-plus-RR signals are separated by means of a low-pass filter. RF-minus-RR signals are separated and detected by means of a high-pass filter and detector, as shown in Fig. 24. The two signals are fed to a matrix. The output is the discrete RF and RR signals. The discrete LF and LR signals are obtained from the left groove in the same way. The cross-talk separation between the four discrete signals is of the same order as that between the LF and RF signals in the conventional two-channel stereophonic system. *See Detector; Electric filter*.

In general, the performance of the system with four discrete channels, as exemplified by auditory perspective and other spatial effects, is superior to that of the four-channel system derived from two channels by matrixing, encoding, and decoding processes.

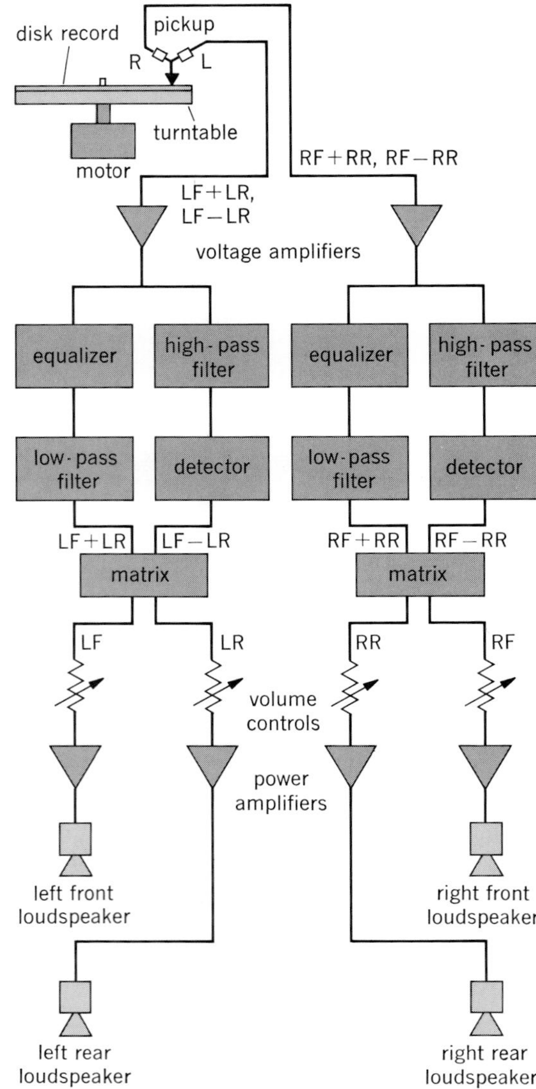


**Fig. 24. Complete discrete four-channel quadraphonic disk reproducing system in which two channels are reproduced in the conventional two-channel manner and the other two channels are reproduced by demodulation means employing a detector. Matrixing provides the four discrete channels.**

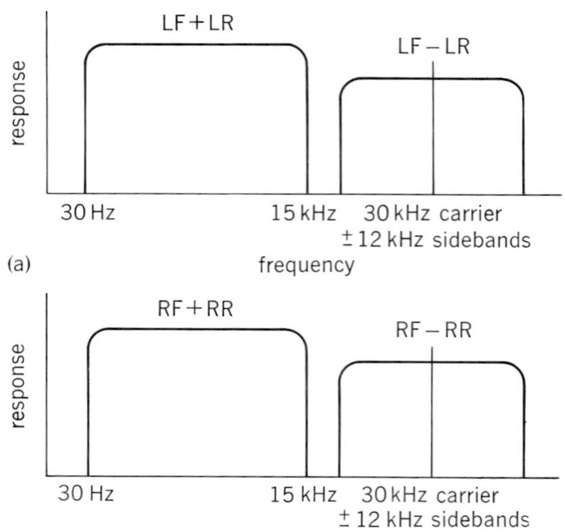


**Fig. 23. The spectrum allocation depicts the frequency ranges of the four channels. (*a*) Left side of groove. (*b*) Right side of groove.**

**Compatibility.** The quadraphonic system is compatible with monophonic and stereophonic systems. For example, if a quadraphonic record is reproduced on a one-channel monophonic system, the output will be the sum of the four signals LF, LR, RF, and RR. If a quadraphonic record is reproduced on a two-channel stereophonic system, the output on the L channel will be the sum of the LF and LR signals, and the output in the R channel will be the sum of RF and RR signals. If a monophonic record is reproduced on a quadraphonic system, all four channels LF, LR, RF, and RR will reproduce the same monophonic signal. If a stereophonic record is reproduced on a quadraphonic system, the L signal will be reproduced on LF and LR channels, and the R signal will be reproduced on RF and RR channels.

*Harry F. Olson / Constantine Trahiotis*

### Digital Recording

Advances in solid-state devices and in recording systems make it practical to extend the benefits of digital techniques to the recording and reproduction of music on disk records. During recording, the output of the microphone amplifier is converted to a stream of digital bits. Typically the sampling rate lies between 44,000 and 55,000 samples per second with 16 bits per sample. The digitized program is recorded on magnetic tape. Special encoding schemes involving the insertion of additional bits permit correction in playback of errors due to loss or misinterpretation of bits. Thus the digital signal may be rerecorded through many generations without deterioration of quality. Editing and mixing are done with the signals in digital form. *See Analog-to-digital converter.*

After editing and mixing, the digital signals are transferred from the tape to a disk rotating on the disk-recorder turntable. The recorded signal is carried in the form of microscopic indentations in a spiral track on the surface of the disk. Typically the indentations are less than 1 micrometer across and 0.15 micrometer deep (**Fig. 25**). The disk format and the recording techniques are those developed for video-disk recording of television signals. The master disk is used to form stampers for pressing vinyl records following the same processes used in the production of conventional phonograph records.

Players for the digital records resemble, and in some cases may be identical to, video-disk players. Depending on the record format offered by the manufacturers, the pickup in the player may be a capacitive, mechanical, or optical type. The digital output of the pickup and player circuits is error-corrected and stored temporarily in a memory. It is removed from the memory at a bit rate controlled by a precise quartz crystal, and is converted to analog audio signals to drive loudspeakers. Because the output bit rate is precisely controlled, any effects due to small fluctuations in speed of the tape recorders or of the disk turntables are removed from the analog output. *See Digital-to-analog converter; Video disk recording.*

The analog-to-digital and digital-to-analog converters are highly accurate devices, so that negligible distortion of the audio program results from digital processing. An effective dynamic range of about 90 dB is achieved in the magnetic recording stages. The bit rate is usually reduced to 14 bits per sample in the tape-to-disk transfer to yield an effective dynamic range of about 80 dB in disk playback, this being adequate for music reproduction in living rooms.

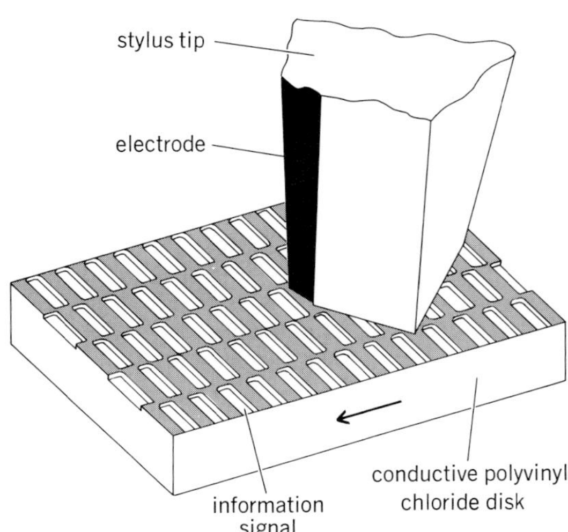


**Fig. 25. Schematic representation of high-density recorded surface of disk with capacitive-type pickup. (*Japan Victor Co.*)**

In the various prototype systems, disk diameters range from 4.5 to 12 in. (114 to 305 mm), and turntable rotation rates range from 200 to 900 rotations per minute. It is technically possible to digitally record more than 10 h of high-quality music on one side of a 12-in. (305-mm) disk, but this is considered impractical. Most offerings provide about 1 h of stereo per side. The Compact Disk Digital Audio System, the first commercially marketed system (1983), uses a laser readout. The disk diameter in this system is 4.7 in. (12 cm), the playing time is 74 min, and the rotation rate varies from 500 to 200 rotations per minute as the disk travels under the pickup at constant linear velocity. Digital records cannot be used on conventional phonographs and require their own players. Some record companies employ digital recording in making the master tapes, converting back to analog audio when recording the master disk. This procedure eliminates the loss of quality due to multiple generations of tape recordings, but does not remove the residual distortions and restrictions on dynamic range inherent in conventional phonograph reproduction.

*J. G. Woodward*

***Bibliography.*** B. B. Bauer, D. W. Gravereaux, and A. J. Gust, A compatible stereoquadraphonic (SQ) record system, *J. Audio Eng. Soc.*, 19:638, 1971; J. Borwick, *Sound Recording Practice*, 2d ed., 1980; J. Eargle, *Sound Recording*, 2d ed., 1980; J. B. Halter and J. G. Woodward, Vertical tracking errors in stereodisk systems, *J. Audio Eng. Soc.*, 12(1):8-14, 1964; T. Inove et al., A discrete four-channel disk and its reproducing system, *J. Audio Eng. Soc.*, 18(1):696, 1970; *NAB Disk Recording and Reproducing Standard*, 1963; H. F. Olson, *Modern Sound Reproduction*, 1972, reprint, 1978; H. E. Roys, *Disk Recording and Reproduction*, 1978; G. Stock, Digital recording: State of the market, *Audio*, 63(12):70–76, 1979; J. G. Woodward and E. C. Fox, Tracing distortion: Its cause and correction in stereodisk systems, *J. Audio Eng. Soc.*, 11(4):294–301, 1963.

## Distortion (electronic circuits)

Any undesired change in the waveform of an electric signal passing through a circuit, including the transmission medium. In the design of any electronic circuit one important problem is to modify the input signal in the required way without producing distortion beyond an acceptable degree. Amplifier and loudspeaker systems are examples where maximum effort has been expended to produce a design for faithful amplification of speech and music input signals. There are four general types of distortion: amplitude, frequency, phase, and cross modulation.

**Amplitude distortion.** This is generally considered to mean distortion produced by a nonlinear relationship between the input and output amplitudes of a device. Amplitude distortion is usually introduced by a transistor or vacuum tube. The change in collector current of a transistor is nearly proportional to the change in signal voltage only over a small range of signal voltage amplitude. For further increase, the collector current change begins to depart from proportionality. SEE TRANSISTOR.

To predict the amount of amplitude distortion that may be produced in a given case, a power series representation for the characteristic of the active device is often used. The relationship between output signal current $y$ and input signal $x$ is expressed as $y = G_1x + G_2x^2 + G_3x^3 + \cdots$. The coefficients must be evaluated for each active device and the operating point used.

The harmonic distortion is expressed in terms of percentages of the fundamental component of the collector current when the input signal is a sinusoid. If $A \sin \omega t$ is substituted for $x$ in the terms of the power series and the powers of $\sin \omega t$ are reduced by trigonometric identities to a fundamental and harmonic components, then the relative amplitudes of each of the harmonic components can be calculated for known values of the coefficients in the power series.

In addition to distortion introduced by nonlinear transistor or tube characteristics, distortion can be introduced in several other ways, all of which occur for large amplitude signals.

***Grid current.*** Distortion is produced when the signal which is applied to the input of a vacuum tube is so large that the grid becomes positive with respect to the cathode. The grid and cathode then form a diode, and current flows through the grid circuit. When this condition occurs, the dynamic input impedance can change appreciably and the stage amplification is adversely affected.

An additional form of distortion, called blocking, occurs in a resistance-capacitance coupled vacuum tube amplifier stage when grid current flows in the following tube. Under these conditions the coupling capacitor charges to nearly the plate voltage. When the plate voltage drops and grid conduction stops, the grid-to-cathode voltage of the following stage can become more negative than cutoff. This condition persists until the capacitor discharges (through a large resistance and therefore at a much slower rate than it charged) sufficiently to unblock the following stage. During the time that the stage is cut off, there will be no amplification. SEE VOLTAGE AMPLIFIER.

***Saturation.*** When the input signal to a transistor or tube is large enough to drive the device to saturation, a further increase in the signal voltage produces little change in the collector or plate voltage.

***Bottoming.*** This form of distortion is produced by a large input signal from a low-impedance source. No matter how large the input signal, the output current cannot exceed that value given by the ratio of the supply voltage divided by the load resistance. This type of distortion is called bottoming because the output voltage has fallen as low as possible.

***Cutoff.*** This form of distortion is produced by large input signals which drive the transistor or tube to cutoff. The collector or plate voltage is then at its maximum value. If the input signal goes more negative, the collector or plate voltage cannot increase and distortion results.

***Crossover distortion.*** An additional type of distortion is of importance in class B transistor power amplifiers. The input impedance varies inversely with emitter current and, for low values of current, may become appreciable compared with driver impedance. Under this circumstance a sinusoidal input voltage would not result in a sinusoidal output current. This is called crossover distortion.

**Frequency distortion.** This form of distortion is an inherent feature of all amplifiers but can be minimized by proper design. It occurs because the reactive elements and inherent reactances in the amplifier circuit do not allow the same amplification for all frequencies, and therefore some components of a signal are amplified more than others. Furthermore, in the case of audio amplifiers, the loudspeaker and enclosure characteristics affect the load presented to the amplifier in a manner which depends upon frequency. For a discussion of frequency response SEE AMPLIFIER.

The effects of frequency distortion may be considered in terms of an input signal composed of a fundamental and harmonic components, such as a square wave. If the amplifier gain is not a constant value for each frequency component, the output will not be an amplified replica of the input.

**Phase distortion.** Like frequency distortion, phase distortion is caused by the reactive elements in the circuit producing a phase shift that is not the same for each frequency component of the input signal. It is possible for an input signal to have frequency components with approximately constant magnitude amplification but not with a phase shift for each component which is proportional to the frequency. As a result, the output is not an amplified replica of the input. Fortunately, the ear is more tolerant of phase distortion than frequency distortion. This fact simplifies the design of a high-fidelity amplifier system.

If the gain magnitude is constant with frequency while the phase shift is proportional to the frequency, the output will be a replica of the input but delayed in time.

**Cross modulation.** Also called intermodulation, this effect is caused by nonlinear device characteristics. If two signals of different frequencies are applied to the input of a nonlinear transistor or vacuum tube stage, the output will contain the fundamental and harmonic components of each signal, frequency components equal to the sum and difference of the input signal frequencies, and sums and differences of the harmonics of the two input signals. Therefore, if the input is a signal composed of several frequencies, the nonlinearity will produce new frequencies not integrally related to those of the input signal. The distortion, if bad enough, is generally more noticeable than harmonic distortion.

**Reduction by feedback.** Distortion caused by nonlinear transistor or vacuum tube characteristics and by the frequency response of the amplifier can usually be reduced by the use of negative feedback. Amplitude distortion introduced in the last or next to last stages of a multistage amplifier can be reduced; distortion produced by the input stage cannot be reduced. Fortunately, in audio amplifiers distortion is generally produced in the last stage (the power output stage).

The use of negative feedback in a properly designed amplifier will make the amplitude more nearly constant and the phase shift more nearly proportional to frequency over a wider frequency range than in an amplifier without feedback. This extended frequency range can be made to include for all practical purposes the frequency range of music and speech signals. SEE FEEDBACK CIRCUIT.

*C. C. Halkias*

***Bibliography.*** J. D. Lenk, *Handbook of Modern Solid State Amplifiers*, 1974; J. Millman, *Microelectronics: Digital and Analog Circuits and Systems*, 1979; J. D. Ryder, *Electronic Fundamentals and Applications*, 5th ed., 1975.

## Distributed systems

Systems that implement related information-processing functions in two or more programmable devices, connected so that data can be exchanged, or they may also store segments of a data base on two or more computer systems. The subject of distributed systems thus encompasses both distributed processing and distributed data bases. Distributed processing is sometimes referred to as distributed data processing (DDP).

**Characteristics of distributed processing.** Distributed processing systems are distinguished from other types of computer-based systems by three characteristics. First, information-processing (application) functions are distributed. This excludes systems which consist of one information-processing computer surrounded by a network with programmable concentrators, network switches, or similar network-control devices. While such systems certainly include distributed functionality, they do not include distributed processing.

The second important characteristic is programmability in the distributed devices. Hard-wired terminals or terminal controllers, which provide management of only the terminal devices, do not fit within this definition. A central computer surrounded by terminals is not a distributed processing system. As unintelligent terminals are replaced by personal computers, many systems are evolving into distributed processing systems.

The final important characteristic is connection for data exchange. Two independent computer systems operated by the same organization, but without any linking network, are an example of decentralized, not distributed, processing. Admittedly there is some degree of ambiguity in this definition. If the two example computer systems exchange data via reels of magnetic tape or diskettes, which are created on one system and manually moved to the other for use as input, does this form a connection and transform these computers into a distributed system? The consensus is that in spite of the data transfer this is a decentralized system. Only a communications, cable, or bus connection between the computers would change this configuration into a distributed processing system.

There are situations in which components are linked together at some times and decoupled at others. For example, an organization might use personal computers or word-processing equipment mainly for local operations, in a free-standing, decentralized mode. At certain times, however, the local systems might be linked via dial-up connection to a central computer system, either to access data or services there or to send in data for processing. Whether this is considered a distributed or a decentralized system depends upon its major focus. If the local systems are selected and implemented as part of an overall system effort, but linked to the central site only occasionally to lower cost (or because only occasional connection is needed), this is best described as a distributed system. If the local systems are independently acquired, and operate mainly on local projects, but sometimes access the central system because it is convenient to do so, they are best described as decentralized systems.

**Evolution of distributed processing.** Centralized and decentralized processing were the typical modes of computer use prior to the introduction of minicomputers. Until then, the high cost of computer equipment made it most logical to concentrate processing to achieve economy of scale in both equipment and staff. In addition, data communications was a sufficiently unfamiliar technique, both to computer professionals and to the suppliers of voice-telephone-network facilities, that linking multiple computers into networks was seldom attempted.

At about the same time that minicomputers became generally available (in the late 1960s and early 1970s), the growing experience with data networks made these practical for use in more organizations. These two conditions came together to make possible the early attempts at distributed processing. Not long thereafter, the introduction of the microprocessor-based personal computer made it still more attractive to distribute functions rather than retaining and controlling them all centrally. *See* Computer networking; Data commmunications; Local-area networks; Microcomputer; Wide-area networks.

**Forms of distributed processing.** Although distributed systems are, in practice, extremely diverse, there are only two distributed processing structures, or ways in which to organize the functions within a distributed system. These can be used independently or can be combined.

***Hierarchical systems.*** Hierarchical systems represent the earliest form of distribution processing. In these systems, processing functions are distributed outward from a central computer, called the host system, to departmental systems or personal computers (**Fig. 1**). A system of this type is sometimes called a host-centered structure.

The terms host and departmental system are often equated to large system and minicomputer; however, those are not the true meanings. A host processor is typically located at some central site, where it serves as a focal point for the collection of data and often for the provision of services which cannot economically be distributed (for example, the management of large data bases, or simulations). Departmental systems are often installed to serve local work groups and provide a limited set of functions to support a specific department—for example, office automation, sales support, and engineering support. In other cases, departmental systems resemble local host systems and provide a wide range of capabilities—usually including transaction processing and data-base management—to support a variety of applications. Depending on the size of the department or work group, a departmental system may be based on a min-

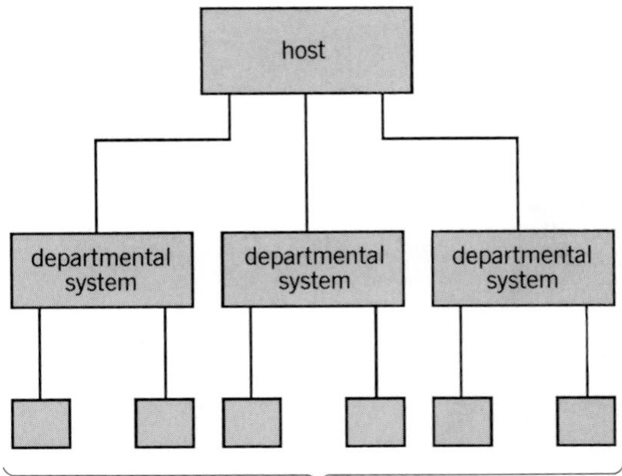


**Fig. 1. Hierarchical system. Processing functions are distributed outward from the host system to departmental systems or personal computers.**

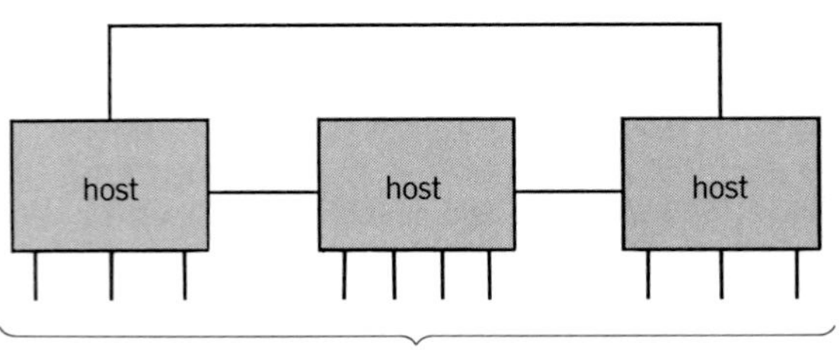


**Fig. 2. Horizontal system. Logically equivalent computers are connected.**

icomputer, a smaller model of the host, or a multiuser personal computer.

The first hierarchical systems consisted of a (usually) large host computer surrounded by minicomputers (initially called satellite processors), or in some cases by data-entry devices which might be either mini- or micro-based. Sometimes those structures resulted from conscious planning to install a distributed system; at other times they resulted from linking independently acquired local processors to an existing central system. In the latter case, it was often discovered that the local applications needed access to data or services available on an existing, larger central system.

Today hierarchical systems can be categorized as two-tier or three-tier configurations. Two-tier systems include a host system as the first tier of processing capability, and usually personal computers as the second tier. Occasionally a two-tier system consists of a host plus departmental systems and unintelligent workstations, but this configuration is becoming less common as personal computers proliferate.

Three-tier systems include a host as the first tier, departmental systems as the second tier, and personal computers as the third tier. Users at personal computers may be able to access both departmental systems and the host system. Depending on the network-connection scheme and the software used, access to the host may be either direct or via a departmental system.

***Horizontal systems.*** Horizontal systems form the other major structure for distributed processing. In this structure, two or more computers which are logically equivalent are connected **(Fig. 2).** The term logically equivalent means that there is no connotation of hierarchy or master/slave relationship, even though the systems may not be physically equal in their functional capability or processing capacity. This form is also called a peer structure or a host/host connection.

Sometimes the goal in a horizontal system is to-provide load leveling, to share the total workload among the available systems by transferring jobs and transactions (with their supporting data, if necessary) as needed. More often, the intersystem linkage allows resources to be shared among the systems; for example, remote access may be provided to unique data bases, programs, or peripheral devices. In many of these systems, the linkage supports data transfer, so that data collected or generated at dispersed locations can be consolidated at one computer system.

***Hybrid systems.*** Hybrid systems include both horizontal and hierarchical distribution **(Fig. 3).** Although this complex structure was originally very rare, it is becoming more common, especially as the merger of data processing and office automation becomes a goal for many organizations.

**Distributed data bases.** Distributed processing is often accompanied by a distributed data base. A distributed data base is a collection of logically related data, segments of which are stored on two or more computer systems. In addition, the distributed systems must allow users to access multiple segments of the distributed data base. Access may be provided by giving the user a direct connection to data stored on one or more remote systems or by allowing the user to copy remote data onto a local system (usually a personal computer) for use there. Unless this second criterion—access to multiple data-based segments—is met, the multiple sets of data are simply multiple data bases.

A typical example of a distributed data base **(Fig. 4)** is a bank that maintains its records of customer accounts in two geographically separate locations, attached to two seperate host systems. One system services customers in the western part of the state; the other services customers in the eastern part. Because customers travel, it must be possible to check an account in the western host when the customer wants to cash a check at a branch served by the eastern host. This kind of remote access is typically provided by sending a transaction from the eastern host, asking the western host to access its data base and check the customer's account.

This type of distributed data base is called a partitioned distributed data base, and ideally each partition contains only unique data. In practice, some data elements that are accessed frequently, but changed infrequently, are maintained in parallel in all partitions. An example is a partitioned airline reservation system in which each computer maintains a data base for specific flights; however, copies of flight schedules are most likely maintained at each location.

Such parallel data storage is characteristic of the other type of distributed data base, a replicated distributed data base. A typical example of such a data base is a manufacturing management system **(Fig. 5),** in which the production schedule for the entire factory is maintained by the host, while the schedule for each department is copied (replicated) on the departmental system for that part of the factory. In other applications, a replicated data base is maintained on a host and personal computers or on a departmental system and personal computers.

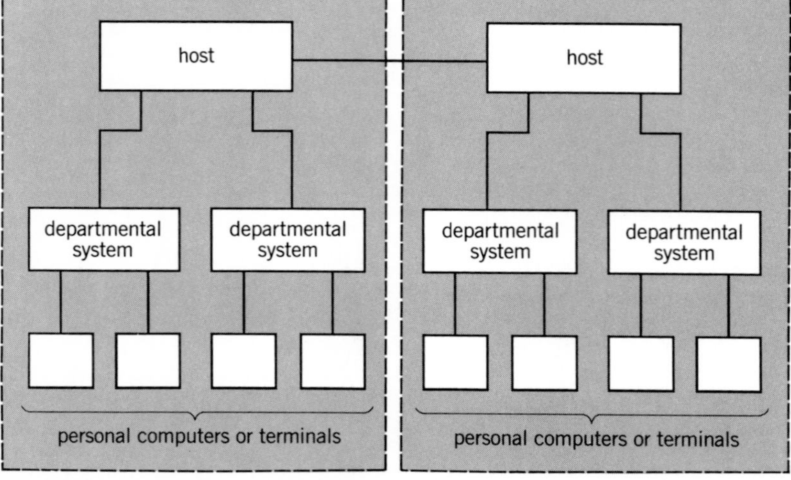


**Fig. 3. Hybrid system, including both horizontal and hierarchical distribution.**

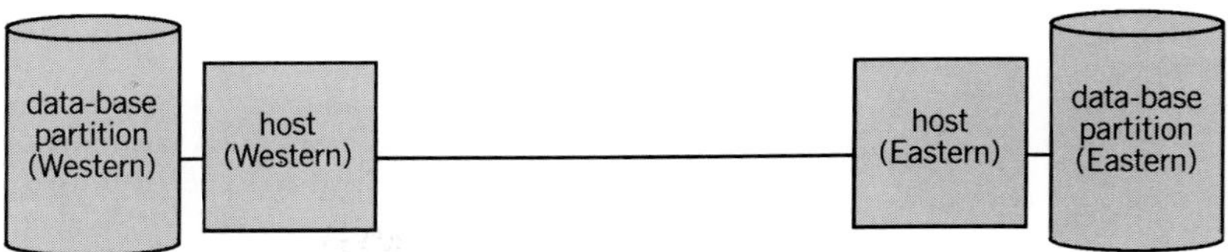

**Fig. 4. Partitioned data base. Customer accounts are partitioned according to most likely location of access.**

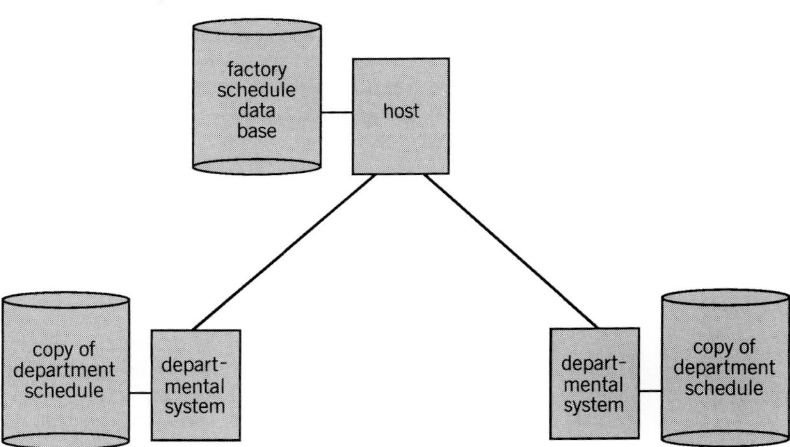

**Fig. 5. Replicated data base. The host maintains the master schedule for the factory; each departmental system maintains a copy of the schedule for its department.**

Deciding which type of distributed data base to use requires a thorough understanding of (1) how data elements are most likely to be accessed and (2) what kind of software capabilities are available to handle distributed data. In practice, the second factor is generally the limiting one, because very few systems have general-purpose distributed-data-base software. However, available software can handle the kinds of situations described in the preceding examples.

Knowing how data elements will be accessed is the key to the success of a distributed-data-base design. Access patterns that are clear and dependable can be used to partition a data base. For example, geographical patterns of access can often be used to partition a data base, as in the banking system mentioned above. Data bases in insurance and government have also been partitioned according to geographical access patterns, placing each partition in the appropriate part of the country or state. In almost all such cases, exceptions—involving access from outside the expected geographic area—are handled by exchanging transactions and responses between computers.

Time patterns of access and update can be used to replicate data, rather than partition data-based segments. For example, after a monthly, quarterly, or yearly closing, copies of financial data can be distribued to as many locations as need access to the data for applications such as trend analysis. Presumably there will be few, if any, changes in the data after closing, and so there is no problem with synchronizing the multiple copies at multiple locations. In other cases of replication, such as airline schedules, the copies can be tightly synchronized, and so provisions must be made to propagate changes when they occur, although presumably this will be on a relatively infrequent basis.

**Advantages.** Distributed processing can provide a number of advantages as compared to centralized or decentralized processing. These must, however, be considered potential advantages, as not all apply to every information system. The potential advantages are as follows: flexibility to change, because of the modularity of the distributed functions (modularity typically improves flexibility); the possibility of rapidexpansion of capacity, if this can be accomplished by adding more departmental systems or personal computers to the system; increased speed of response to users (especially to large numbers of users), because the processors are close to the users, and many processors can work in parallel; improved availability, because a distributed system is relatively invulnerable to single-point failures, and it may be possible to provide selective (rather than total) backup of only vital parts of the system; the potential for customization of functions, interfaces, reports, and so forth, to meet varying user needs; the possibility of less expensive data communications, especially if the departmental systems or personal computers are close enough to the users to be connected via local-area networks; and the fact that distributed processing mirrors the management control of most organizations, which is distributed (local managers have considerable responsibility and authority) rather than centralized.

**Prospects.** The earlier debate over whether organizations will implement distributed processing has been resolved by the realization that every organization—possibly excluding the very smallest—will move in this direction. In fact, a great many have already done so. This evolution reflects three basic trends: (1) the expanding use of personal computers, accompanied by the fact that many personal computer users need access to data maintained on host or departmental systems; (2) the slowly increasing availability of software to manage networks and provide a beginning at managing distributed data bases; and (3) the increasing integration of information-processing technology into the mainstream operations of many organizations.

On the other hand, factors that impede this evolution, in at least some organizations, include (1) lack of expertise in integrating personal computers, departmental systems, hosts, and networks, and (2) lack of well-defined methods to assess the payoff to be achieved with distributed processing. The second factor is especially evident when systems are used to support decision making, rather than to support more efficient operation. Improvements in efficiency, achieved through the use of distributed processing technology, are generally easy to quantify. Improvements in organizational effectiveness are less easily measured, making it more difficult to justify the investment necessary.

In spite of these barriers, indications are that integrated, distributed information systems will be the predominant form for essentially all users of computing and data processing equipment. *See* Digital computer.

*Grayce M. Booth*

***Bibliography.*** G. M. Booth, *The Design of Complex Information Systems*, 1983; M. Durr and D. Walker, *Micro to Mainframe: Creating an Integrated Environment*, 1985; F. A. Schreiber and W. Litwin (eds.), *Distributed Data Sharing Systems*, 1985; R. H. Sprague and B. C. McNurlin (eds.), *Information Systems Management in Practice*, 1986.

## Donor atom

An impurity atom in a semiconductor which can contribute or donate one or more conduction electrons to the crystal by becoming ionized and positively charged. For example, an atom of column V of the periodic table substituting for a regular atom of a germanium or silicon crystal is a donor because it has one or more valence electrons which can be detached and added to the conduction band of the crystal. Donor atoms thus tend to increase the number of conduction electrons in the semiconductor. The ionization energy of a donor atom is the energy required to dissociate the electron from the atom and put it in the conduction band of the crystal. *See Acceptor atom; Semiconductor.*

*H. Y. Fan*

## Doppler radar

A radar system used to measure the relative velocity of the system and the radar target. The operation of these systems is based on the fact that the Doppler frequency shift in the target echo is proportional to the radial component of target velocity.

**Airborne vehicular systems.** Airborne systems are used to determine the velocity of the vehicle relative to the Earth for such purposes as navigation, bombing, and aerial mapping, or relative to another vehicle for fire control or other purposes. Ground or ship equipment is used to determine the velocity of vehicular targets for fire control, remote guidance, intercept control, traffic control, and other uses.

The Doppler frequency shift $\Delta f$ is an extremely small fraction of the transmitter frequency $f$. It is given by the equation shown below, where $V$ is the

$$\Delta f = \frac{2Vf}{C} \cos \gamma$$

relative speed, $C$ is the speed of signal propagation, and $\gamma$ is the angle between the velocity and the direction of propagation (**Fig. 1**). The only practical way to measure the frequency shift is by adding the echo signal to a reference signal derived from the transmitter and observing the difference, or beat frequency. Some means of obtaining coherent detection is required.

Practical techniques have been devised for obtaining the requisite coherence in continuous-wave (CW), pulsed, and frequency-modulated transmission systems. *See Continuous-wave radar.* For a discussion of techniques similar to those in Doppler radar *see Moving-target indication.*

Doppler navigation radar is a type of airborne Doppler radar system for determining aircraft velocity relative to the Earth's surface. Such a Doppler velocity sensor (**Fig. 2**) consists of at least the following elements: transmitter, antenna, receiver, Doppler frequency measuring device, and output signal generators or displays. It is generally used with a navigation computer.

The signal from a single beam can provide only the velocity component in the direction of that beam. Complete velocity determination requires, therefore, the use of at least three beams. Most systems use four beams for symmetry (**Fig. 3**).

To relate the beam directions, and hence the measured velocity to an Earth-oriented coordinate system, a vertical reference must be provided. In newer systems the antennas are fixed to the aircraft. The Doppler frequencies and the vertical data, such as roll and pitch, are fed to a computer. Its outputs are electrical signals or displays representing the components of velocity. The components commonly displayed are those along-heading, across-heading, and vertical.

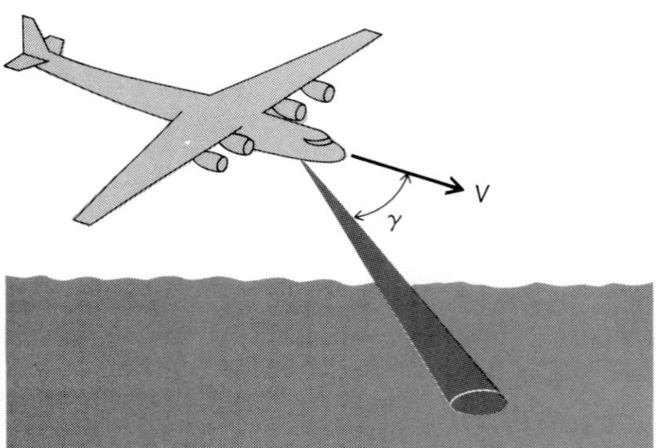


**Fig. 1. Doppler frequency measurement geometry.**

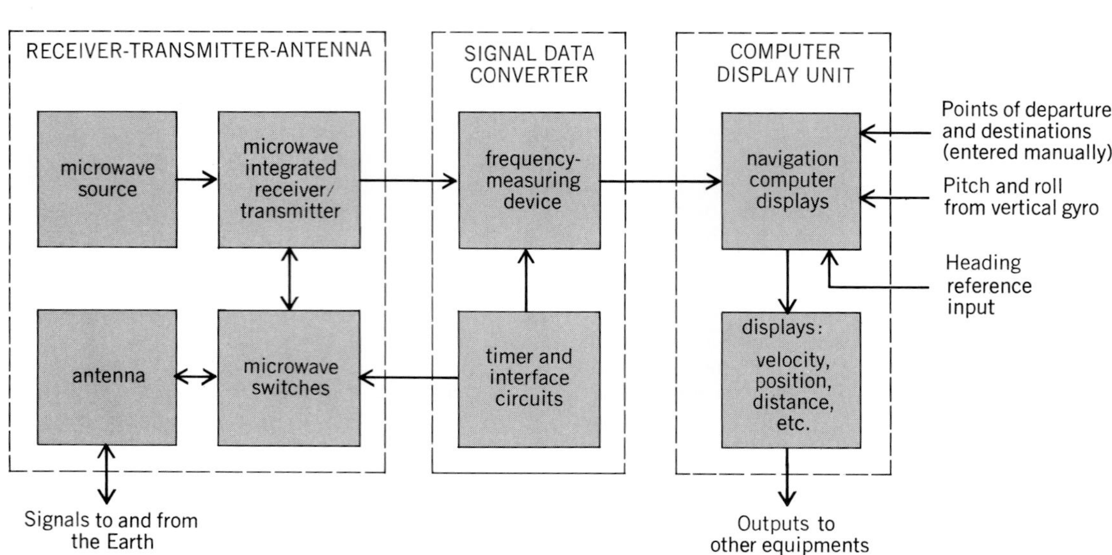


**Fig. 2. Block diagram of aircraft Doppler navigation system, the AN/ASN-128.**

Various types of antennas have found use in Doppler navigation radar. These include paraboloids, microwave lenses, and linear and planar arrays. Since both volume and radome cutout area should be small, various techniques are employed to enable each antenna to form (simultaneously or sequentially) more than one beam. Pencil beams of 3–5° width are used. The beams are directed 15–25° from the vertical. Larger values result in insufficient echo power over water. SEE ANTENNA.

Continuous-wave systems are coherent and are theoretically the most efficient. The chief difficulty is control of leakage of spurious signals from transmitter to receiver.

Pulsing enables the receiver to be rendered insensitive during transmission, thereby avoiding leakage signals. Coherence is achieved either by driving a transmitting power amplifier from a CW oscillator or by mixing at the detector a pair of pulse echoes received over different propagation paths.

A preferred technique is to employ sinusoidal frequency modulation. A sideband of the detected beat between echo and transmitter signal is used. Modulation index and rate and the sideband order are chosen such that echoes from nearby objects are rejected, while those from distant objects are accepted. Leakage noise is reduced at the expense of lowered efficiency.

An example of a system (**Fig. 4**) is the U.S. Army's standard airborne Doppler navigator which bears the nomenclature AN/ASN-128. It weighs 28 lb (12.7 kg), requires 89 W of power, and operates at 13.325-GHz frequency. In addition to velocities, outputs include present position, distance to go, desired track and bearing to destination, and steering signals. For helicopter use a steering hover indicator can also be provided. The system uses all-solid-state electronics and a printed grid planar array antenna. The velocity accuracy specifications are around a quarter of a percent of ground speed (and 0.2 knot or 0.1 m/s when hovering). The navigation accuracy specification is 1.3% of distance traveled when using a 1° accuracy heading reference.

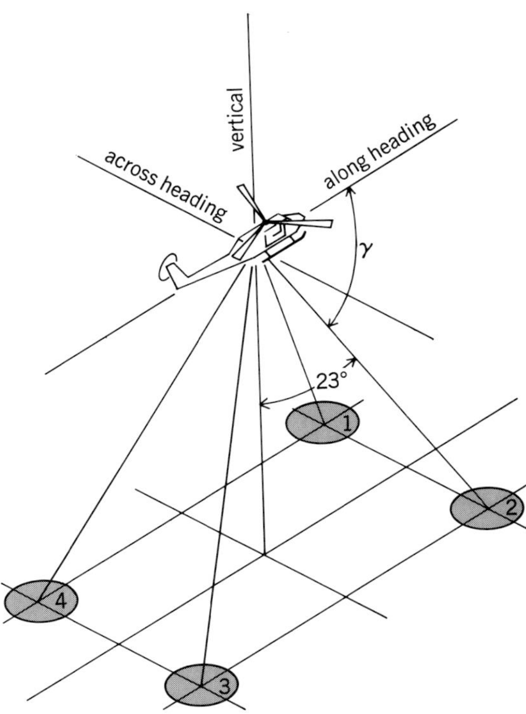


**Fig. 3. Typical antenna beam arrangement.**

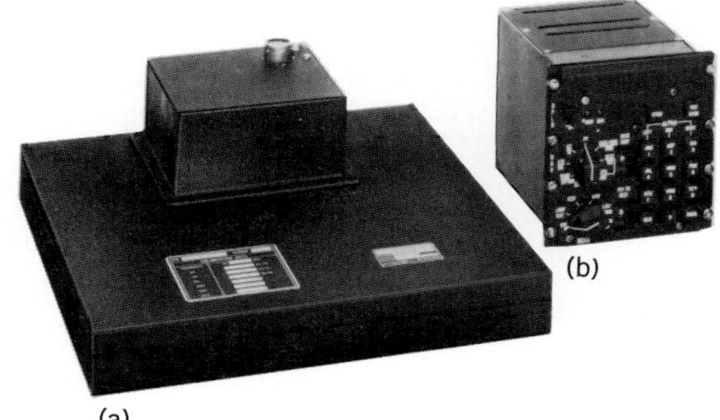


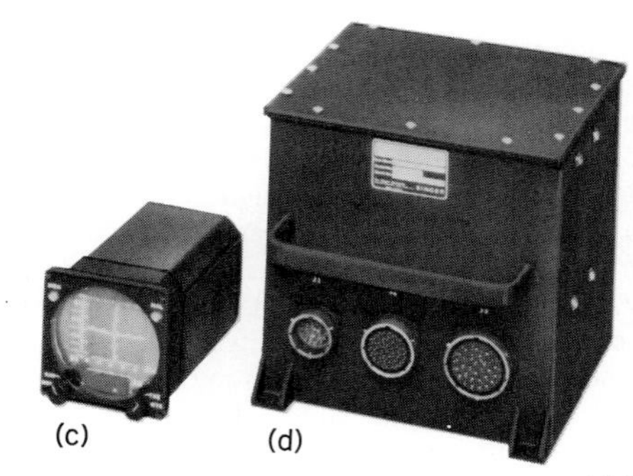


**Fig. 4. AN/ASN-128 Doppler navigation system. (*a*) Receiver-transmitter antenna. (*b*) Computer display unit. (*c*) Steering hover indicator. (*d*) Signal data converter. (*Singer Co., Kearfott Division*)**

*France B. Berger*

**Meteorological systems.** Pulse Doppler radars are useful tools for the observation of the movements of precipitation particles. The Doppler frequency shift associated with the velocity of atmospheric targets, such as precipitation particles or artificial chaff, is always a very small fraction ($10^{-6}$ to $10^{-8}$) of the radar operating frequency. The observation and measurement of such small frequency shifts require excellent radar system frequency-stability characteristics that are not usually found in conventional radars but can be added without a drastic increase in equipment cost. Pulse Doppler radar effectively samples the backscattered signal at the radar pulse repetition rate and can therefore provide unambiguous Doppler frequency observations only in the frequency range allowed by the sampling rate. The Doppler frequency shift for the radial velocity of a given target increases with the transmitted frequency. Decreasing the radar operating frequency thus increases the effective velocity coverage for the same sampling rate. Since the need for increasing velocity coverage would otherwise require an increase of the pulse repetition rate (which reduces the radar maximum range), it is advantageous to use the longest possible wavelength. The choice of wavelengths is limited, however, to centimetric waves if production of narrow radar beams with antennas of reasonable size is desired.

***Doppler spectrum.*** Since Doppler radars can observe and measure the radial velocity of targets, they are well suited for the observation of the motion of raindrops (precipitation). However, precipitation has the form of a "distributed" target; that is, there are numerous independent scatterers distributed in space. The backscattered signal that is selected at any given time after the transmitted pulse by a sampling circuit called a range gate is therefore due to the contribution of a finite scattering region that is determined by the radar beam cross-section area and half the radar pulse length in space (pulse volume). The backscattered signal sampled by the range gate is thus composed of a large number of separate scattering amplitudes, each having a Doppler frequency shift associated with the radial velocity of a particular scatterer. Therefore, a spectrum of frequency shifts (Doppler spectrum) is observed. This Doppler spectrum constitutes the basic velocity information acquired by the Doppler radar when it is used for the observation of precipitation systems.

At each range gate, a Doppler spectrum can be evaluated by processing the signal sampled at that range. The basic processing operation is a Fourier transform of the sampled signal. In order to take advantage of the radar resolution, the processing must be done at a large number of range gates, with the only limitation being that the gates must be spaced by more than one radar pulse width. The signals obtained at successive range gates can be digitized by analog-to-digital converters operating at high speed, with the digitized signals stored in a memory and then processed by a fast arithmetic system. Fast Fourier transform techniques are used for greatest computing efficiency. Although these systems are capable of processing several thousand spectra per second, they require large input memories and produce a volume of information that is difficult to handle.

***Mean Doppler.*** The amount of information can be reduced by considering only the first moment of the Doppler spectrum (mean radial velocity, or mean Doppler) and the spectrum width. Although the mean Doppler can be evaluated directly from the Doppler spectra, it can be more easily obtained by use of mean-frequency estimators that do not involve the computation of the whole spectrum through the Fourier transform operation.

With this technique, the mean Doppler can be easily processed simultaneously at a large number of range gates with relatively simple digital circuits. The spectrum variance can be measured by a slightly different approach.

***Probing motion in convective storms.*** It can be assumed that precipitation particles move with the air in their environment and are therefore good tracers for air motion. Observing the motion of precipitation particles inside convective storms therefore offers a unique technique for the study of kinematic processes in storms. However, the use of a single radar beam to scan the three-dimensional structure of a storm is of limited value, since only the radial velocity of precipitation particles can be observed. A more complete study of three-dimensional storm structure can be made by the simultaneous use of several scanning radars. For example, two Doppler radars installed at different locations, and operating independently with intersecting beams, will provide two different radial velocity components at the region where the beamsintersect. These two components can be used to evaluate the two-dimensional velocity in the tilted plane that is common to the two radar beams and the baseline between the radars. *See Radar.*

*Roger Lhermitte*

***Bibliography.*** D. J. Barlow, Doppler-radar, *Proc. IRE*, 37(4):340–355, 1949; F. B. Berger, The design of airborne Doppler velocity measuring systems, *IRE Trans.*, ANE-4(4):157–175, 1957; F. B. Berger, The nature of Doppler velocity measurement, *IRE Trans.*, ANE-4(3):103–112, 1957; H. Buell, Doppler radar systems for helicopter navigation, 36th Annual Meeting, Institute of Navigation, June 23–26, 1980; W. R. Fried, Principles and performance analysis of Doppler navigation systems, *IRE Trans.*, ANE-4(4):176–196, 1957; M. Kayton and W. R. Fried (eds.), *Avionics Navigation Systems*, 1969; R. Lhermitte, Meteorological Doppler radar, *Science*, 182(4109):258–262, 1973.

## Earphones

A class of energy tranducers capable of receiving alternating current and generating acoustic waves resembling very closely the characteristics of that current. The movement of an element (diaphragm) is accomplished by magnetic attraction, electrostatic attraction, or the piezoelectric effect (the expansion or contraction of certain crystalline substances in response to electric charges). Earphone systems include the driver element with its diaphragm and arrangements for magnetic flux, or electrostatic or direct electric charge, plus a casing, one or more acoustic cavities and ports, acoustic damping and insulation, and some arrangement for coupling the driver to the human ear. The wiring connecting the precedent amplifier to the driver, which may in modern systems be a complicated curcuit which feeds, for each of two stereophonic channels, some part of the current to each ear. The time delays and energy ratios at the two earphones (each of which may contain two drivers) can be appropriately adjusted so that the listener is given the illusion that the sound sources are not "within the head" but are externalized appropriately in all three planes of space. The various types of earphones are described below. *See Transducer.*

**Magnetic.** In this type, a permanently magnetized diaphragm is moved in and out by an electromagnet energized by alternating current. Early models had two poles attracting and repelling a relatively heavy metal diaphragm with complex vibrational modes, the frequency response being limited to about 300–2500 Hz. In one development, the heavy metal diaphragm was replaced by a thin sheet of aluminum held by a ring of magnetic metal. The coil through which the signal current traveled had to move only the relatively

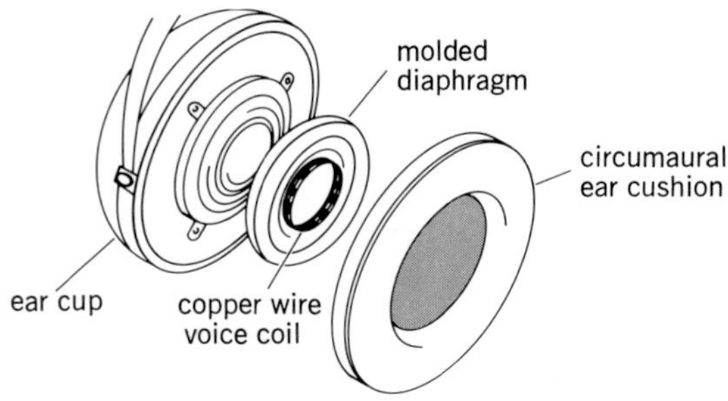


**Fig. 1. Exploded view of conventional dynamic earphone. (*After P. Milton, Headphones: History and Measurement, Audio, 26(5):90–94, May 1978*)**

low-weight ring, a greatly increased efficiency and with improved frequency response.

**Dynamic.** These earphones are actually small dynamic loudspeakers. In some, a small coil fed by the sound source is bonded to the membranous diaphragm (**Fig. 1**). Alternating current in the coil thus drives the diaphragm toward and away from a permanent magnet in the rear of the casing. In another configuration, the coil is relatively large and is attached to the diaphragm only at its edge; the diaphragm is a molded dome with a rolled edge and moves freely in the magnetic field. Such earphones are standard for high-fidelity communications.

**Miniature magnetic.** A common earphone is a small unit of which the output port fits snugly into a plastic olive in the ear canal (**Fig. 2**). These are widely used with small radios, with the more powerful hearing aids, by television commentators, in business transcription devices, and in many other communications situations. A coil fed by the signal current is wrapped around a pole and imparts in-and-out motion to the diaphragm proportional to the alternating current flow.

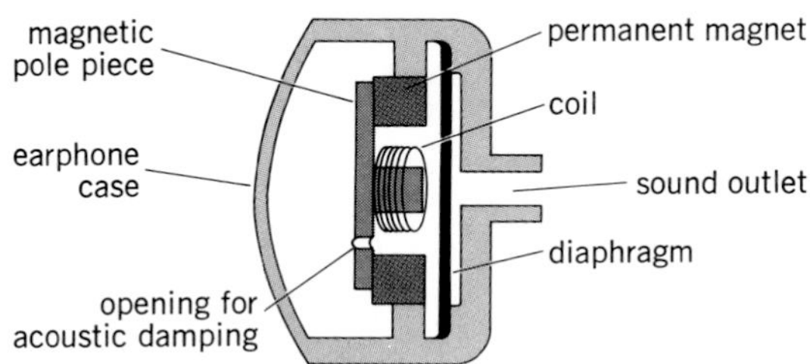


**Fig. 2. Cross section of external-type hearing aid earphone. (*After W. R. Hodgson and P. H. Skinner, eds., Hearing Aid Assessment and Use in Audiologic Habilitation, Williams and Wilkins, 1977*)**

Another configuration (**Fig. 3**) is incorporated inside the case of most ear-level and all-in-the-ear hearing aids. A metal armature has a free end between the two poles of a magnet. When alternating current is flowing in one direction, the armature at the free end is turned into a south pole and the armature moves toward the north pole of the permanent magnet. As the current changes direction, the free end is turned into a north pole and the armature moves in the other direction. The armature moves a diaphragm, creating sound which is ported into the ear canal.

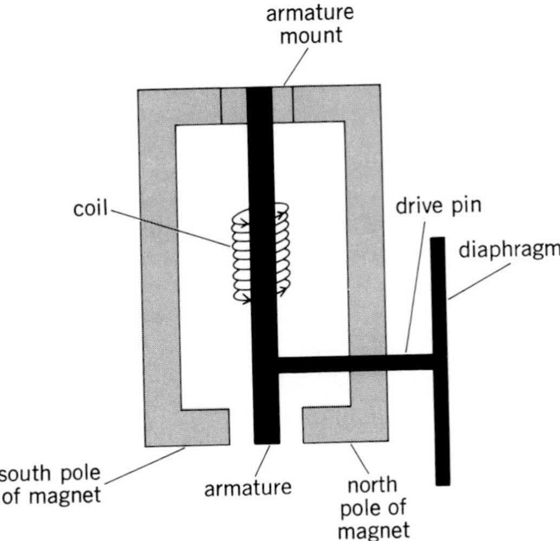


**Fig. 3. Cross section of internal-type hearing aid earphone. (*After W. R. Hodgson and P. H. Skinner, eds., Hearing Aid Assessment and Use in Audiologic Assessment, Williams and Wilkins, 1977*)**

The diaphragm can be of any light material, not necessarily magnetic, and can be formed into an efficient shape for producing and directing an acoustic wave. Such miniature earphones are now made so efficient as to compete favorably with much larger types with respect to acceptably flat frequency response in the octave above 10 kHz and with respect to sound power levels in the ear canal with acceptably low total harmonic distortion.

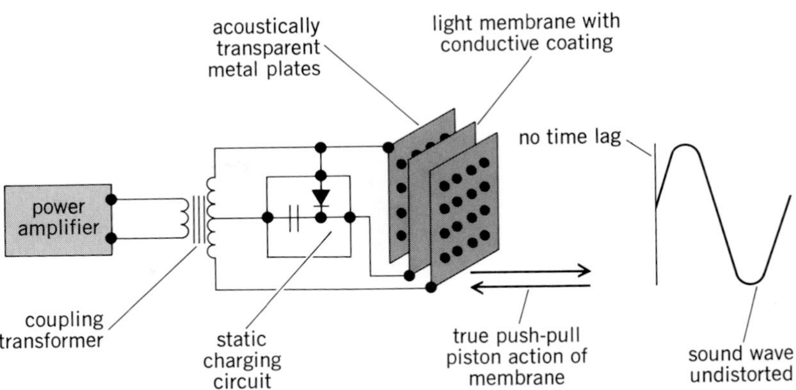


**Fig. 4. Block diagram of electrostatic earphone. (*After H. Souther, An Adventure in Headphone Design: The Model ESP-6 Electrostatic Headphone, Koss Electronics Inc., Cat. 111, 1969*)**

**Electrostatic.** Efficiency is increased if the mass of the diaphragm is reduced to a minimum. A thin (2.5–12 micrometers) metallized plastic film can be used, on which a large constant electrostatic charge is placed by an auxiliary unit, and the motion of the diaphragm is controlled by the audio signal impressed on perforated wire mesh plates on either side (the push-pull arrangement reduces second-harmonic distortion). The assembly is mounted in a relatively large cavity and coupled to the head by a circumaural cushion (that is, one which completely surrounds the auricle). Such earphones (**Fig. 4**) are light and comfortable and have excellent frequency-response and transient-distortion characteristics.

**Dynamic-electrostatic.** The diaphragm of a dynamic-electrostatic (or orthodynamic) earphone (**Fig. 5**) is a permanently polarized electret of fluorocarbon. Consequently the need for an added source of polarization voltage (a drawback inherent to electrostatic earphones) is eliminated. In one development, certain problems of such a system are avoided by separating the functions of the diaphragm and of the electret. The diaphragm can be of the thinnest (2.5 micrometers) metallized polyester, stretched between two electrets in push-pull. The diaphragm is matched in acoustic impedance very closely to the surrounding air, and the audio signal can be led directly to the electrets. *See* Electret transducer.

**Piezoelectric.** Certain crystalline substances expand and contract when alternating voltage is applied. In some piezoelectric earphones, a crystal element is coupled mechanically to the center of a small (about 2.5 cm diameter) cone. Such earphones can be lightweight, cheap, and useful in speech communication.

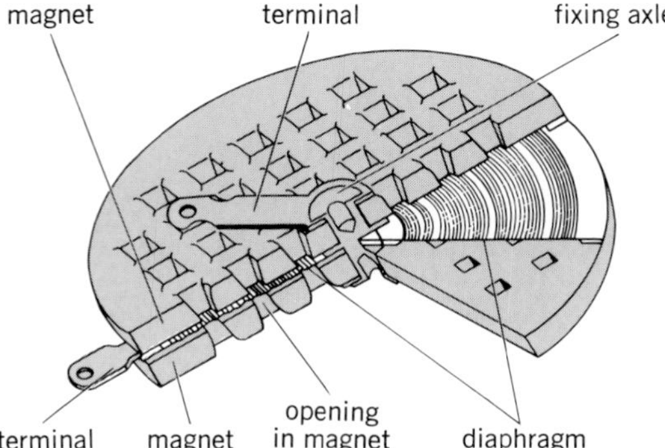


**Fig. 5. Construction of orthodynamic earphone driver. (*After P. Milton, Headphones: History and Measurement, Audio, 26(5):90–94, May 1978*)**

Substances other than quartz crystals, notably high-polymer films such as vinylidene fluoride, will expand and contract when an alternating current is applied. A thin sheet of such material can be stretched by a factor of 4, and aluminum vapor deposited over it. If a high dc voltage is now applied, and removed, the sheet will become and remain piezoelectric. Two sheets are bonded together back to back, and when alternating current is applied between the metallized faces the sheet will expand and contract. If a rectangular sheet is slightly curved and mounted rigidly top and bottom, much as a playing card might be grasped between the fingers, the movement in response to alternating current will be in and out in proportion and an acoustic wave will be created (**Fig. 6**). Earphones on this principle have desirable characteristics of stability, acoustic response, and cost, but require more amplification than an electret or other earphone to operate as efficiently. *SEE PIEZOELECTRIC CRYSTAL; PIEZOELECTRICITY.*

**Real-ear response.** An earphone system contains components which are in some respects as important as the driver. The configuration of the acoustic ports, for example, or the acoustic or other damping built into the system will help determine the eveness of the frequency response, while the cushions, whether circumaural or supraaural (fitting against the auricle), help determine the low-frequency real-ear response.

The effects of changes in these elements as reflected in acoustic differences at the eardrums of actual persons are not easy to determine. It is not difficult to couple an earphone system to a microphone by means of a standard cavity, perhaps incorporating a flat plate for the larger circumaural systems, but such a practice is useful primarily for manufacturer's quality control, and has limited relevance to the performance of the system on even the average human head. The reference equivalent threshold sound-pressure level of a certain earphone system, expressed in voltage applied as frequency changes, has to be determined by having a panel of normal-hearing listeners loudness-balance that system at each frequency against another (arbitrarily chosen) reference system.

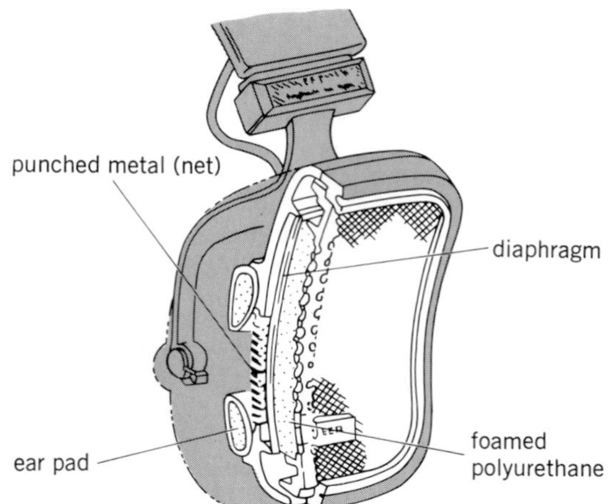


**Fig. 6. Cutaway view of rear of high-polymer piezoelectric earphone. (*After P. Milton, Headphones: History and Measurement, Audio. 26(5):90–94. May 1978*)**

The acoustic impedance of the several elements of the external ear, head, and torso have been measured, and artificial heads incorporating the results of such measurements are available. These devices allow fairly successful predictions as to how an earphone system will perform on an anthropometrically average person.

**Realistic simulation.** Any single-channel recording of a real acoustic event will, when played back to an earphone in one ear, sound ''in the head.'' Even stereo recordings from two channels played back to earphones on two ears, while furnishing the illusion of movement, still are not externally localized by the listener. Externalization is improved if some of the signal from the left channel is time-delayed and applied also to the right earphone (the same, of course, for the right channel to the left earphone), and it is also improved if a realistic ratio is achieved between the acoustic energy density ratio from the ''direct'' versus the ''indirect'' sound sources (as from reflective walls). Stereophonic earphone systems have been built which incorporate these time delays and ratios, and which furthermore feed the signal from the right channel of an artificial-head stereophonic recording to the left earphone (and the left channel to the right earphone) through frequency filters which simulate the differential acoustic effects at various frequencies of the head and external ears in the original recording situation. Thus the eardrums under earphones are presented with the exact acoustic conditions generated by a loudspeaker or other sound source in an actual room, and such earphone systems very materially advance the important psychoacoustic feature of externalization of sound and of acoustic

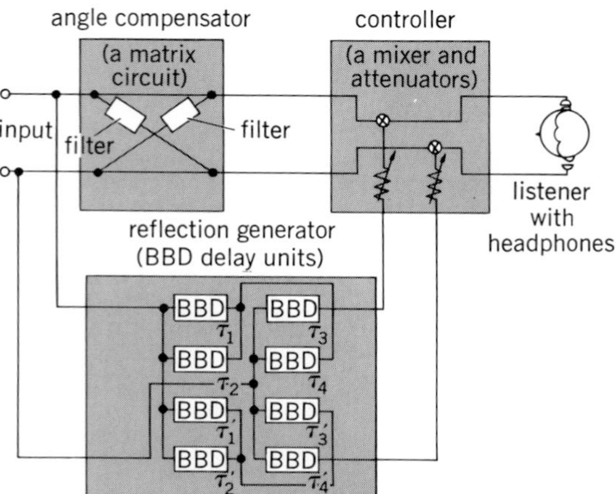


**Fig. 7. Block diagram of projected sound localization earphone system for stereophonic sources. BBD-bucket brigade device. (*After N. Sakamoto, T. Gotoh, and Y. Kimura, On "out-of-head" localization in headphone listening, J. Audio Eng. Soc., 24:710–716, 1976*)**

realism generally (see **Fig. 7**). *See* Loudspeaker; Microphone.

*J. Donald Harris*

## Echo box

A device used to check the output power and spectrum of a radar transmitter. It consists of a low-loss, tunable, resonant cavity connected to the antenna feed line through a fixed coupling circuit so that the fraction of output power supplied to the cavity is always constant. The signal level within the cavity depends on the strength of the portion of the transmitter output spectrum lying within the cavity's narrow passband, which can be tuned to traverse the entire frequency range of interest. A microammeter connected through a crystal rectifier to a loop within the cavity permits reading the signal level. The spectrum can be measured as the cavity is tuned to different frequencies.

A single test of the performance of the entire radar system, excluding only the antenna and antenna feed, can be made with the cavity tuned to the carrier frequency. Each transmitter output pulse causes a slowly damped oscillation in the cavity which feeds a signal back through the coupling circuit to the receiver. This signal appears as an echo at the receiver output (hence the name echo box). The time required for the echo to decay to the level of the receiver noise is proportional to the logarithmic difference, or difference in decibels, between the transmitter power level and the receiver noise level. This is an excellent overall figure of merit for the transmitter and receiver performance. If a dummy load is substituted in place of the antenna to absorb the output power, the radar can be tested without actually radiating, which may be useful in some military situations. *See* Radar.

*Robert I. Bernstein*

## Eddy current

An electric current induced within the body of a conductor when that conductor either moves through a nonuniform magnetic field or is in a region where there is a change in magnetic flux. It is sometimes called Foucault current. Although eddy currents can be induced in any electrical conductor, the effect is most pronounced in solid metallic conductors. Eddy currents are utilized in induction heating and to damp out oscillations in various devices.

**Causes.** If a solid conductor is moving through a nonuniform magnetic field, electromotive forces (emfs) are set up that are greater in that part of the conductor that is moving through the strong part of the field than in the part moving through the weaker part of the field. Therefore, at any one time in the motion, there are many closed paths within the body of the conductor in which the net emf is not zero. There are thus induced circulatory currents that are called eddy currents (**Fig. 1**). In accordance with Lenz's law, these eddy currents circulate in such a manner as to oppose the motion of the conductor through the magnetic field. The motion is damped by the opposing force. For example, if a sheet of aluminum is dropped between the poles of an electromagnet, it does not fall freely, but is retarded by the force due to the eddy currents set up in the sheet. If an aluminum plate oscillates between the poles, it will be stopped quickly when the switch is closed and the field set up. The energy of motion of the aluminum plate is converted into heat energy in the plate.

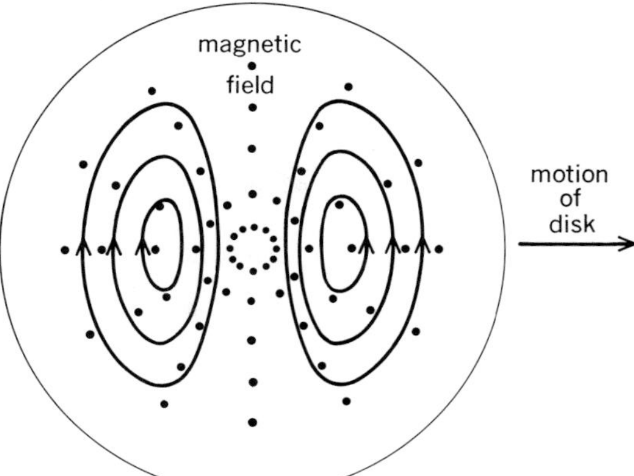


**Fig. 1. Eddy currents which are induced in a disk moving through a nonuniform magnetic field.**

Eddy currents are also set up within the body of material when it is in a region in which the magnetic flux is changing rapidly, as in the core of a transformer. As the alternating current changes rapidly, there is also an alternating flux that induces an emf in the secondary coil and at the same time induces emfs in the iron core. The emfs in the core cause eddy currents that are undesirable because of the heat developed in the core (which results in high energy losses) and because of an undesirable rise in temperature of the core. Another undesirable effect is the magnetic flux set up by the eddy currents. This flux is always in such a direction as to oppose the change that caused it, and thus it produces a demagnetizing effect in the core. The flux never reaches as high a value in the core as it would if there were no eddy currents present.

**Laminations.** Induced emfs are always present in conductors that move in magnetic fields or are present in fields that are changing. However, it is possible to reduce the eddy currents caused by these emfs by laminating the conductor, that is, by building the conductor of many thin sheets that are insulated from each other rather than making it of a single solid piece. In an iron core the thin iron sheets are insulated by oxides on the surface or by thin coats of varnish. The laminations do not reduce the induced emfs, but if they are properly oriented to cut across the paths of the eddy currents, they confine the currents largely to single laminae, where the paths are long, making higher resistance; the resulting net emf in the possible closed path is small. Bundles of iron wires or powdered iron formed into a core by high pressure are also used to break up the current paths and reduce the eddy currents.

*Kenneth V. Manning*

**Testing.** The testing of metallic materials through the detecting of eddy currents induced within them is widely used. A high-frequency alternating current in a coil placed close to a metallic material induces eddy currents within the material through electromagnetic induction. The flow of the eddy current is impeded by the material's electric resistance, which reflects characteristics such as hardness and chemical composition. Therefore, eddy current measurements reveal various properties of materials.

Flaws such as open cracks within materials cause eddy currents to detour around them and effectively

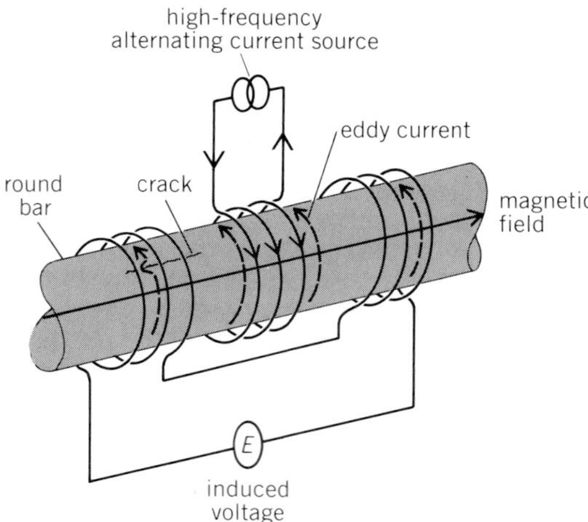


**Fig. 2. The alignment of coils used to inspect a long bar.**

enhance electric resistance; accordingly, eddy current testing can be used to detect flaws. Differences in thickness of foils and plating cause differences in the electric resistance; hence, eddy current testing is also convenient for estimating thickness. Stronger magnetic fields are induced within ferromagnetic materials undergoing testing, so that the magnetic permeability also affects the eddy current. The evaluation of the hardness of ferritic steel through eddy current testing is based upon this effect of permeability, which is very susceptible to hardness.

**Figure 2** shows the general alignment of coils to detect flaws within long bars. Annular coils encircle the round bar. The alternating current applied in the central coil generates a magnetic field inside of the coil and within the bar in the direction of their axis, and thereby induces eddy currents along concentric circular paths within the bar. Simultaneously this eddy current produces a counter magnetic field which is superimposed on the primary one. The combined magnetic field gives rise to electromotive forces, that is, voltages between terminals of each coil. Two coils on either side of the central coil are wound in opposite directions, connected in series. The voltage between terminals is monitored continuously. When a flaw within a moving bar enters one of the two coils, the voltage reading corresponds to the difference between the voltages of the coils. This alignment permits the detection of flaws with high sensitivity, because it eliminates noises that originate from irregularities in diameter or physical properties of materials, whose variation is negligibly small between the closely spaced coils.

Since eddy current testing is of the noncontacting type, it can detect flaws within materials moving at high speed and even those raised to red heat in hot-rolling mills. Inspection of the latter is advantageous to exclude the influence of variation in permeability, because ferromagnetism vanishes at temperatures above the Curie point (1416°F or 769°C for iron).

*Kazuo Watanabe*

**Braking and damping.** The principle outlined above, whereby a conductor which is moving through a nonuniform magnetic field experiences a retarding force, is used to brake or damp the oscillations of moving objects. In these applications, the field is that produced by a permanent magnet or an electromagnet supplied with direct current. The retarding force is proportional to the product of the flux produced by the magnet $\phi$ and the effective eddy current $I$ produced by it. The effective eddy current however, results from the rate of flux cutting, that is, the flux $\phi$ multiplied by the velocity of movement $v$. The retarding force is thus proportional to $\phi^2 v$. For a constant flux, which applies with a permanent magnet or electromagnet with constant current, the retarding force is proportional to the velocity of the moving object. With an electromagnet, the current can be varied, to adjust the ratio of retarding force to velocity. This ratio is also affected by the physical dimensions and materials used, for example, the resistivity of the moving object. Brakes are often fitted to rotating objects, and in these applications the retarding torque is proportional to the angular velocity $\omega$.

Eddy-current brakes are probably most widely used in the electromechanical energy meters which are installed in consumers' premises by electricity supply companies. In this application, the meters (**Fig. 3**) contain electromagnets which produce fluxes proportional to the system voltage and current. These fluxes induce emf's and eddy currents in a conducting disk, which is mounted in jewel bearings so that it may rotate freely. The eddy currents react with the fluxes to produce a torque proportional to the power being supplied. Eddy-current braking, produced by a flux from a permanent magnet cutting the disk, provides a retarding torque proportional to the disk speed. Because the frictional torques are negligible, the disk runs at a speed at which the driving and retarding torques are almost equal, and as a result the speed is proportional to the power being supplied to the consumer. A geared drive to indicating dials meshes with gear teeth on the disk's spindle.

The same form of braking is also employed widely in the induction-type relays to provide time-graded protection. Eddy-current brakes incorporating electromagnets are used to provide controllable load torques on test equipment for small machines.

Eddy-current damping is used to suppress undesirable mechanical oscillations. It is used widely in deflection-type indicating instruments. These instruments have very light movements which are mounted in jewel bearings. Such an instrument would oscillate over a wide range for a considerable period if the quantity being measured changed suddenly, and to

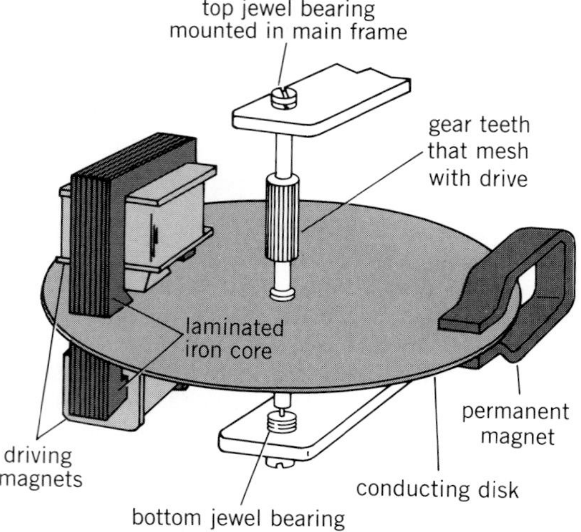


**Fig. 3. Basic construction of electromechanical energy meter.**

overcome this some form of damping is necessary. It is often obtained by attaching a thin aluminum disk or vane to the instrument spindle. The vane or disk fits between the poles of a permanent magnet. A retarding torque results to oppose motion in either direction of rotation, and oscillations are rapidly damped, the kinetic energy being converted to heat in the vane or disk.

*Arthur Wright*

**Bibliography.** B. Bleaney and B. I. Bleaney, *Electricity and Magnetism*, 3d ed.,1976; R. Hochshild, *Electromagnetic method of testing metals, Progress in Nondestructive Testing*, vol. 1, 1958; H. L. Libby, *Introduction to Electromagnetic Nondestructive Test Methods*, 1971; E. M. Purcell, *Electricity and Magnetism*, 2d ed., 1984; M. G. Say and E. O. Taylor, *Direct Current Machines*, 1980; A. Symonds, *Electrical Power Equipment and Measurements*, 2d ed., 1971.

## Electret

A solid dielectric with a quasipermanent electric moment. Electrets may be classified as real-charge electrets and dipolar-charge electrets. Real-charge electrets are dielectrics with charges of one polarity at or near one side of the dielectric and charges of opposite polarity at or near the other side, while dipolar-charge electrets are dielectrics with aligned dipolar charges. Some dielectrics are capable of storing both real and dipolar charges. An example of a charge arrangement of an electret metalized on one surface is shown in the **illustration**.

Modern electrets used in research and in applications are often films of 5–50 micrometers thickness (foil electrets) consisting of a suitable material. They are frequently metallized on one or both sides, depending on the intended use.

**Real-charge electrets.** In these electrets, the intrinsic conductivity and carrier mobility must be small enough so that excess charges can persist for long periods of time. Suitable materials are the organic polymers polytetrafluoroethylene (PTFE), its copolymer fluoroethylenepropylene (FEP), polycarbonate (PC), polyimide (PI), and polyethylene terephthalate (PETP), which can also assume a considerable dipole polarization, and inorganic materials such as silicon dioxide and aluminum oxide.

Charging of real-charge electrets, metalized on one side, can be achieved by treatment with a corona discharge; by application of an electric field at elevated temperatures through an electrode opposing the nonmetalized side of the dielectric; or by contacting with a biased, wet electrode. Another charging technique, allowing greater control than other methods, is electron injection with a nonpenetrating electron beam. In all cases, carriers of one polarity are deposited onto, or injected into, the insulator and trapped, and a compensation charge of equal magnitude but opposite sign flows into the sample electrode. Thus, the charge arrangement exhibits an electric moment. Another method, applied to photoconductors metalized on both sides with transparent electrodes, consists in the application of an electric field during irradiation with ultraviolet or visible light. Carrier generation by the light and charge separation by the field yield the desired electric moment, resulting in a photoelectret. SEE CORONA DISCHARGE; PHOTOCONDUCTIVITY.

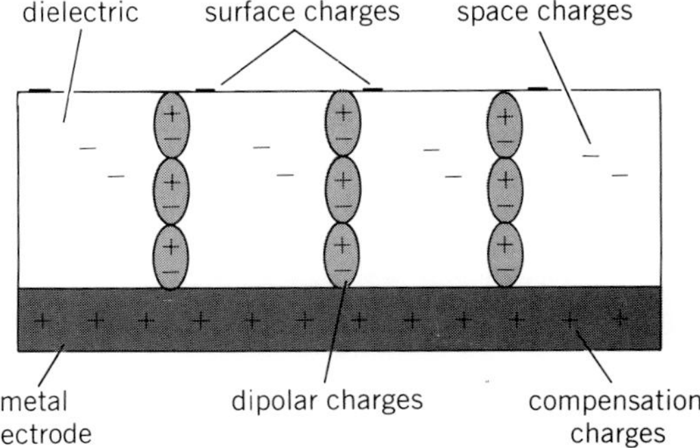


**Schematic cross section of an electret disk metallized on one side.**

PTFE and FEP are electronegative and therefore hold negative charges better than positive ones. Real-charge densities of up to 5 millicoulombs/m$^2$ (3.2 microcoulombs/in.$^2$) can be stored in these polymers. Electrets are stable over long periods of time. At the customarily used charge densities of about 0.2 millicoulomb/m$^2$ (130 nanocoulombs/in.$^2$), corresponding to surface potentials of approximately 250 V in a 25-μm-thick sample, the time constant of the decay of the surface potential of PTFE and FEP is about 200 years if storage is at room temperature and low relative humidity under shielded conditions. This time constant drops to about 10 years at 50°C (122°F) and 90% relative humidity. Silicon dioxide electrets show similar or better stability.

**Dipolar-charge electrets.** In these electrets, the relaxation time of the molecular reorientation has to be large enough that the dipole alignment persists for long periods of time. Most prominent among such materials are poly(vinylidenefluoride) [PVDF] and vinylidenefluoride–trifluoroethylene copolymers [VDF-TrFE] which exhibit piezoelectric and pyroelectric properties linked to the dipole polarization. Inorganic piezoelectric crystals and ceramics also belong to this category but are not discussed here. SEE PIEZOELECTRIC CRYSTAL; PIEZOELECTRICITY.

The preferred technique for the polarization of dipolar electrets is the above corona method applied to one-sided metalized samples. The injected charges set up a large field within the dielectric which aligns the dipoles. Another method consists in the direct application of a high field to a two-sided metalized sample at an elevated temperature.

In the case of PVDF, polarization densities of up to 0.1 coulomb/m$^2$ (65 microcoulombs/in.$^2$) can be achieved by corona charging at room temperature with fields of up to 400 MV/m (10 MV/in.) on samples prestretched to three to five times their original length. The stretching makes the material, which is semicrystalline, recrystallize in a polar form and also reorients the lamellar crystals so that the dipoles are more precisely aligned by the applied field.

PVDF has a relatively stable polarization at room temperature. At 100°C (212°F), the polarization decays initially (within minutes) to half its original value and stabilizes thereafter.

**Applications.** Important commercial applications of real-charge electrets are in electroacoustic and electromechanical transducers, in air filters, and in electret dosimeters. Also of interest are biological applications based on the blood compatibility of charged polymers or on their favorable influence on wound or fracture healing. Commercial applications of dipolar electrets are in piezoelectric transducers and in pyroelectric detectors. SEE ELECTRET TRANSDUCER.

*Gerhard M. Sessler*

**Bibliography.** D. A. Seanor (ed.) *Electronic Properties of Polymers*, 1982; G. M. Sessler (ed.), *Electrets*, vol. 33 of *Topics in Applied Physics*, 1980.

## Electret transducer

A device for the conversion of acoustical or mechanical energy into electrical energy, and vice versa, which utilizes a quasi-permanently charged dielectric material (electret). Examples are certain microphones, earphones, and phonograph cartridges. In the simplest implementation, such a transducer consists of a metal backplate (first electrode) covered by a mechanically tensioned diaphragm. The diaphragm is a foil electret carrying a metal coating (second electrode) on the side facing away from the backplate. Provisions are made to maintain a shallow air gap between electret and backplate. The air gap is occupied by an electrostatic field originating from the electret charges. Upon acoustical or mechanical deflection of the diaphragm, such a device generates an electrical output signal between its two electrodes; similarly, application of an electrical signal results in diaphragm deflections. Electret devices are therefore self-biased electrostatic or condenser transducers. They thus exhibit all the advantages of this transducer class, such as wide dynamic range and flat response over a frequency range of several decades, without requiring the external bias necessary in conventional transducers of this kind. SEE ELECTRET; TRANSDUCER.

**Foil electret.** The basic component of all modern electret transducers is a "foil electret" consisting of a thin film of insulating material that has been electrically charged to produce an external electric field. Strongly insulating materials capable of trapping charge carriers, such as the halocarbon polymers, in particular polyfluoroethylenepropylene (Teflon), are best suited for this purpose. Before charging, the material is either metallized on one side or backed up with a metal electrode.

In the presence of electrodes, the electret exhibits an external electric field extending from the electret to the electrodes. Such a foil electret is thus, as far as its external field is concerned, an electrostatic analog of a permanent magnet.

Charge storage on halocarbon polymers is relatively permanent. However, Teflon has less favorable mechanical properties because of stress relaxation, which causes a decrease in the mechanical tension of stretched films. As discussed below, this effect can be minimized in transducer applications.

**Electret microphones.** A simple implementation of the most widely used electret transducer is the foil-electret microphone (**Fig. 1**). The diaphragm, typically 0.5- or 1-mil (12- or 25-micrometer) Teflon metallized on one surface, is charged to 100–200 microcoulombs/m$^2$ (65–130 nanocoulombs/in.$^2$) corresponding to an external bias of about 200 V. The nonmetallized surface of this foil electret is placed next to a backplate, leaving a shallow air layer, the thickness of which (about 0.8 mil or 20 μm) is controled by ridges or raised points on the backplate surface. The stiffness of the air layer can be decreased (and thus the sensitivity of the microphone can be improved) by connecting the air layer to a larger cavity by means of small holes through the backplate. The backplate is either a metal disk or a metal-coated dielectric with a thermal expansion coefficient about equal to that of the diaphragm. The electrical output of the microphone is taken between the backplate, which is insulated from the outer case, and the metal side of the foil. The output is fed into a high-impedance preamplifier.

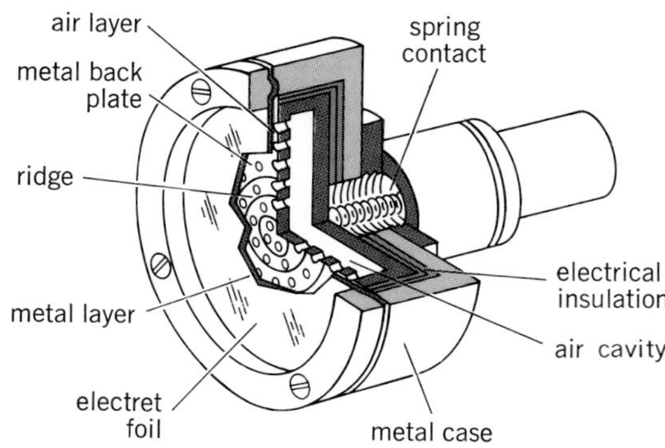


**Fig. 1. Cutaway drawing of a foil-electret microphone showing the basic elements. (*After G. M. Sessler and J. E. West, Electret transducers: A review, J. Acoust. Soc. Amer., 53:1589, 1973*)**

At frequencies below the resonance frequency the acoustical properties of electret microphones are largely governed by the restoring force on the diaphragm. Since the mechanical tension of the foil is generally kept at a relatively low value (about 0.7 lbf/ft or 10 newtons/m), the restoring force is determined by the compressibility of the air layer. Controlling the restoring force by the air layer is advantageous because changes in tension due to stress relaxation thus have only a minor effect on the sensitivity, which is largely independent of transducer area.

The problem of stress relaxation can be virtually eliminated by using a modified microphone design consisting of a metallic backplate coated with a layer of permanently charged Teflon (**Fig. 2**). A metal (or metallized polyester) diaphragm is stretched over this backplate. In this approach, the excellent electrical properties of the Teflon layer and the good mechanical behavior of the metal or polyester diaphragm are used to advantage.

Under open-circuit conditions, a displacement $d$ of

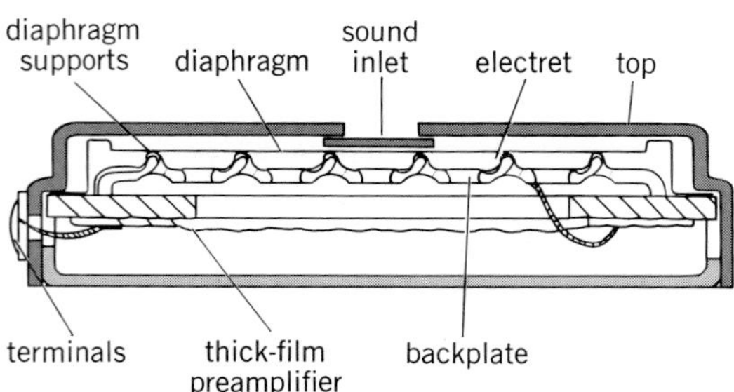


**Fig. 2. Schematic cross section of an electret microphone for use in hearing aids. The microphone has a Teflon electret bonded to a properly shaped backplate. (*After M. C. Killion, Vibration sensitivity measurements on subminiature condenser microphones, J. Audio Eng. Soc., 23:123–127, 1975*)**

the diaphragm of an electret microphone causes a frequency-independent output voltage given by Eq. (1),

$$v = Ed = \frac{\sigma D_1 d}{\epsilon_0(D_1 + \epsilon D_2)} \quad (1)$$

where $E$ is the (constant) electric field in the air layer of the transducer; $\sigma$ is the surface-charge density of the electret projected onto the surface; $D_1$ and $D_2$ are the thicknesses of electret film and air layer, respectively; $\epsilon_0$ is the permittivity of free space; and $\epsilon$ is the relative dielectric constant of the electret material. As in conventional electrostatic transducers, the displacement is proportional to the applied pressure in a wide frequency band extending from a lower cutoff given by a pressure-equalization leak in the back cavity to an upper cutoff determined by the resonance frequency. The voltage response for constant sound pressure is frequency-independent in this range.

Typical electret microphones designed for the audio-frequency range have constant sensitivities of 1–5 mV/microbar (70–350 V/psi or 10–50 mV/pascal) in the frequency range from 20 to 15,000 Hz. Nonlinear distortion is less than 1% for sound-pressure levels below 140 dB, and the impulse response is excellent, owing to the flat amplitude and phase characteristics. Other properties of electret microphones are their low sensitivity to vibration, owing to the small diaphragm mass, and their insensitivity to magnetic fields. Compared with conventional electrostatic transducers, electret microphones have the following advantages: they do not require a dc bias; they have three times higher capacitance per unit area, resulting in a better signal-to-noise ratio; and they are not subject to destructive arcing between foil and backplate in humid atmospheres and under conditions of water condensation.

Various electret microphones for operation at infrasonic and ultrasonic frequencies, covering the range from 0.001 Hz to 200 MHz, have been designed by properly positioning the upper and lower cutoff frequencies discussed above. Furthermore, transducers with directional characteristics such as cardioid, bidirectional, toroidal, and second-order unidirectional have been developed. *See Microphone*.

**Electret headphones.** Another group of electret transducers of interest are electret headphones. The above microphone designs can also be utilized in this case. They produce a certain amount of nonlinear distortion due to the partially quadratic dependence of the force $F$ per unit area, exerted on the diaphragm, on the applied ac voltage $v$, as can be seen from Eq. (2). This drawback can, however, be minimized in a

$$F = \frac{-\frac{1}{2}(D_1\sigma + \epsilon\epsilon_0 v)^2}{\epsilon_0(D_1 + \epsilon D_2)^2} \quad (2)$$

well-designed system, and high-voltage sensitivities have been achieved by making the air-gap thickness small. The distortion can be eliminated by the use of push-pull transducers and monocharge electrets.

The principle of a push-pull transducer is shown in **Fig. 3***a*. A diaphragm consisting of two electrets, each metallized on one side and with these metal layers in contact, is sandwiched between two perforated metal electrodes, forming a symmetrical system. Application of a signal voltage $\bar{v}$ in antiphase to the two electrodes causes the electrodes to exert forces $F_1$ and $F_2$ on the diaphragm. These forces are given by Eq.

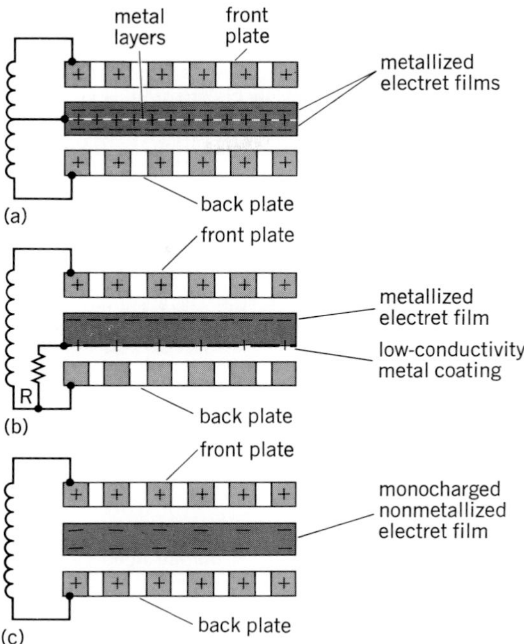


**Fig. 3. Schematic cross sections of push-pull electret headphones, showing static charge distributions. (*a*) Conventional double-electret transducer. (*b*) Single-electret transducer with metallized conventionally charged electret. (c) Single-electret transducer with nonmetallized monocharged electret.**

(2) if $\pm\bar{v}$ is substituted for $v$. The net force $F = F_1 - F_2$ on the diaphragm is determined by Eq. (3),

$$F = \frac{-2\bar{v}\sigma\,\epsilon D_1}{(D_1 + \epsilon D_2)^2} \quad (3)$$

which is linear in $\bar{v}$, indicating the absence of nonlinear distortion. The linearity, however, is maintained only if both air-layer thicknesses remain at the same value $D_2$. This is only possible if $D_2$ is relatively large, which makes such systems less sensitive than the above-described single-ended transducers.

This transducer can be simplified and improved by using the scheme shown in Fig. 3*b*. In this asymmetric system, a single electret coated on one side with a low-conductivity layer is used. The diaphragm holds an excess charge because of the presence of an induction charge on the front electrode. Thus, application of an ac signal causes a net force between diaphragm and plates which is linear if the resistivity of the coating (or the resistor $R$) prevents charge equalization during a period of lowest-frequency signal applied.

An interesting modification of the above push-pull transducers can be achieved by using nonmetallized monocharge electrets, which differ from customary electrets in that they carry only a single-polarity charge and no compensation charge. It is possible to form these electrets by electron injection or by the use of wet-contact charging methods. Since a compensating charge is absent, monocharge electrets have a strong external field that is independent of electrode distance. Thus, if such electrets are used in transducer configurations (Fig. 3*c*), large air gaps of the order of 0.04 in. (1 mm) can be used without loss in field strength. This in turn results in highly efficient transducers that can operate at large displacement amplitudes. *See Earphones*.

**Electromechanical transducers.** Apart from its use in electroacoustic transducers, such as microphones and earphones, the electret principle has been applied to electromechanical transducers. Examples are touch or key transducers, Korotkov sound pickups, impact-sensitive line transducers, phonograph cartridges, relay switches, and optical display panels.

Relatively close to the electroacoustic transducers described above are the first four of these groups. The touch or key transducers depend on the manual deflection of an electret relative to an electrode in a microphonelike structure. Large-voltage signals can be generated with such devices. Similarly, the Korotkov sound pickups are modified electret microphones which detect arterial pressure fluctuations. They may be used, for example, in blood-pressure-monitoring systems. Line transducers consist essentially of a coaxial cable with polarized dielectric in which the center conductor and the shield serve as electrodes. Mechanical excitation resulting in a deformation of the shield at any point along the length of such a cable produces an electrical output signal. Finally, the several types of electret phonograph pickups consist of a stylus which actuates in one way or another an electret transducer. SEE COAXIAL CABLE; DISK RECORDING.

Very different design principles are used in the relay switches and the optical display panels. The relay switches utilize the external fields of electrets mounted in bistable arrangements to open or close contacts. Such devices have power requirements 1000 times smaller than equivalent electromagnetic systems; thus considerable power conservation over present magnetic components is possible. A similar design is used in the optical display panels where illuminated channels are opened and closed by hinged and opaque electrets moved by electrostatic forces. Although relatively high voltages are required, the necessary currents are small and flow only during the switching operation. SEE ELECTRONIC DISPLAY.

**Applications.** Because of their favorable properties, simplicity, and low cost, electret transducers have been used in many applications, both as research tools and in the commercial market.

Among the research applications are microphones for use in acousto-optic spectroscopy, applied to the detection of air pollution and to the study of reaction kinetics of gases and optical absorption of solids. Because of the favorable noise performance of electret microphones, the detection threshold for air pollutants has been lowered by more than an order of magnitude. Other applications of electret microphones have been in aeronautics and shock-tube studies, in which the low vibration sensitivity of these transducers is crucial. The wide frequency range of electret transducers, discussed above, made possible their application in infrasonic atmospheric studies and in ultrasonic investigations of liquids and solids. In addition, ultrasonic arrays of electret microphones have been used in acoustic holography. Research uses of electromechanical electret transducers have been in such diverse areas as vibration analysis and leak detection in space stations. In these applications, the simplicity and reliability of electret transducers are of importance.

Of all commercial applications of electret devices, the high-fidelity electret microphone for amateur, professional, studio, and cassette recorder use is most prominent. Although the electret microphone was introduced only about 1970, about 100,000,000 of the instruments are produced annually, accounting for more than one-half of the entire output of high fidelity microphones. Other uses of electret microphones are in sound-level meters, noise dosimeters, movie cameras, and speaker phones. Miniature microphones are used in hearing aids, in telephone operators headsets, and in communication headsets, often as noise-canceling (first-order gradient) transducers. Ultrasonic electret microphones are used in burglar alarm systems and in remote TV control units. The success of the electret microphone in these applications is primarily due to its acoustic quality and low cost. It is noteworthy that, owing to their low vibration sensitivity, foil-electret microphones were the first transducers to be built directly into widely used tape recorders. In addition to electret microphones, there are single-backplate and push-pull electret earphones, also with monocharge electrets. The latter are believed to be among the highest-quality headsets available. Under study for commercial application are electret phonograph cartridges, optical display systems with mechanical electret gates, electret key transducers, and underwater transducers. SEE MAGNETIC RECORDING.

*Gerhard M. Sessler*

***Bibliography.*** G. M. Sessler (ed.), *Electrets*, 1980.

## Electric charge

A basic property of elementary particles of matter. One does not define charge but takes it as a basic experimental quantity and defines other quantities in terms of it. The early Greek philosophers were aware that rubbing amber with fur produced properties in each that were not possessed before the rubbing. For example, the amber attracted the fur after rubbing, but not before. These new properties were later said to be due to "charge." The amber was assigned a negative charge and the fur was assigned a positive charge.

According to modern atomic theory, the nucleus of an atom has a positive charge because of its protons, and in the normal atom there are enough extranuclear electrons to balance the nuclear charge so that the normal atom as a whole is neutral. Generally, when the word charge is used in electricity, it means the unbalanced charge (excess or deficiency of electrons), so that physically there are enough "nonnormal" atoms to account for the positive charge on a "positively charged body" or enough unneutralized electrons to account for the negative charge on a "negatively charged body."

The rubbing process mentioned "rubs" electrons off the fur onto the amber, thus giving the amber a surplus of electrons, and it leaves the fur with a deficiency of electrons.

In line with the previously mentioned usage, the total charge $q$ on a body is the total unbalanced charge possessed by the body. For example, if a sphere has a negative charge of $1 \times 10^{-10}$ coulomb, it has $6.24 \times 10^{8}$ electrons more than are needed to neutralize its atoms. The coulomb is the unit of charge in the SI system of units.

The surface charge density $\sigma$ on a body is the charge per unit surface area of the charged body. Generally, the charge on the surface is not uniformly distributed, so a small area $\Delta A$ which has a magnitude of charge $\Delta q$ on it must be considered. Then $\sigma$ at a point on the surface is defined by the equation below.

$$\sigma = \lim_{\Delta A \to 0} \frac{\Delta q}{\Delta A}$$

The subject of electrostatics concerns itself with properties of charges at rest, while circuit analysis, electromagnetism, and most of electronics concern themselves with the properties of charges in motion. SEE CAPACITANCE.

*Ralph P. Winch*

## Electric current

The net transfer of electric charge per unit time. It is usually measured in amperes. The passage of electric current involves a transfer of energy. Except in the case of superconductivity, a current always heats the medium through which it passes. For a discussion of the heating effect of a current SEE JOULE'S LAW.

On the other hand, a stream of electrons or ions in a vacuum, which also may be regarded as an electric current, produces no local heating. Measurable currents range in magnitude from the nearly instantaneous $10^5$ or so amperes in lightning strokes to values of the order of $10^{-16}$ A, which occur in research applications.

All matter may be classified as conducting, semiconducting, or insulating, depending upon the ease with which electric current is transmitted through it. Most metals, electrolytic solutions, and highly ionized gases are conductors. Transition elements, such as silicon and germanium, are semiconductors, while most other substances are insulators.

Electric current may be direct or alternating. Direct current (dc) is necessarily unidirectional but may be either steady or varying in magnitude. By convention it is assumed to flow in the direction of motion of positive charges, opposite to the actual flow of electrons. Alternating current (ac) periodically reverses in direction.

**Conduction current.** This is defined as the transfer of charge by the actual motion of charged particles in a medium. In metals the current is carried by free electrons which migrate through the spaces between the atoms under the influence of an applied electric field. Although the propagation of energy is a very rapid process, the drift rate of the individual electrons in metals is only of the order of a few centimeters per second. In a superconducting metal or alloy the free electrons continue to flow in the absence of an electric field after once having been started. In electrolytic solutions and ionized gases the current is carried by both positive and negative ions. In semiconductors the carriers are the limited number of electrons which are free to move, and the "holes" which act as positive charges.

**Displacement current.** When alternating current traverses a condenser, there is no physical flow of charge through the dielectric (insulating material), but the effect on the rest of the circuit is as if there were a continuous flow. Energy can pass through the condenser by means of the so-called displacement current. James Clerk Maxwell introduced the concept of displacement current in order to make complete his theory of electromagnetic waves. SEE ALTERNATING CURRENT; CONDUCTION (ELECTRICITY); DIRECT CURRENT; ELECTRICAL RESISTANCE; SEMICONDUCTOR; SUPERCONDUCTIVITY.

*John W. Stewart*

## Electric filter

A transmission network used in electrical systems for the selective enhancement (or reduction) of specified components of an input signal. The filtering is accomplished by selectively attenuating those frequency components of the input signal which are undesired, relative to those which it is desired to enhance.

The performance of any transmission network is measured by its transfer function $F$, which is the ratio of output to input signal (when these are described appropriately). The general form of such a transfer function is given by Eq. (1), where $s$ is the complex

$$F(s) = \frac{Hs(s^2 + \omega_0{}^2)\cdots}{(s^2 + a_1 s + a_0)(s^2 + b_1 s + b_0)\cdots} \quad (1)$$

frequency variable. (For the sinusoidal steady state, $s = j\omega$, where $j = \sqrt{-1}$ and $\omega$ is the angular frequency). Each quadratic factor in the denominator determines a pair of poles; the factors in the numerator determine the zeros.

A typical filter network having two ports is shown in **Fig. 1**. Since the output is generally smaller than the input, it is customary to specify the amplitude information as the amount of reduction of the input signal; the loss or attenuation is defined by Eq. (2), and

$$\alpha = -20 \log |F| \quad (2)$$

is measured in decibels. Whenever the output signal has an amplitude smaller than that of the input signal, $|F|$ will be less than 1, and its logarithm will be negative; thus the attenuation will have a positive value.

**Filter types.** An optical filter transmits, or passes, certain colors in the light spectrum and rejects, or stops, others. Electrical filters perform in a similar way. A band of frequencies which is rejected or greatly attenuated is called a stopband; a band which is transmitted with little attenuation is called a passband. Ideally, there should be zero attenuation in the passband and infinite attenuation in the stopband. More practically, a small amount of attenuation, say $\alpha_p$, can be tolerated in the passband, and a noninfinite attenuation, say $\alpha_s$, in the stopband. Two cases are illustrated in **Fig. 2**. The tolerable levels are shown by the horizontal dashed lines. The solid lines represent possible attenuation characteristics approximating the tolerable levels.

The first, in Fig. 2*a*, is the attenuation characteristic of a low-pass filter—one that transmits low frequencies with little attenuation, but stops high frequencies. The second (Fig. 2*b*) represents a band-pass filter—one that transmits an intermediate band of frequencies with little attenuation, but which greatly attenuates both low and high frequencies. A filter having the inverse performance of that of a low-pass filter—that is, one that stops low frequencies but passes high ones—is called a high-pass filter. The in-

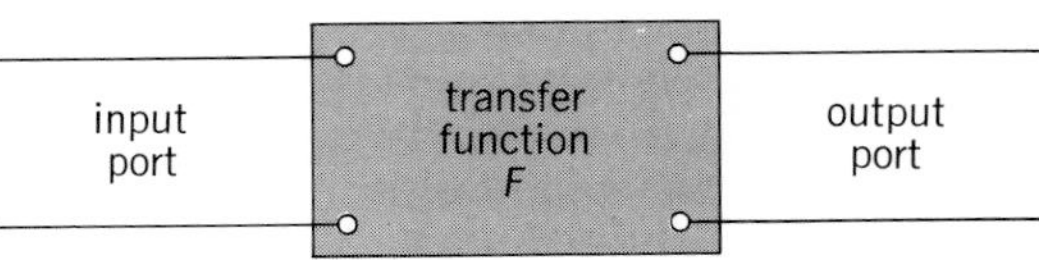


**Fig. 1. Two-port filter network.**

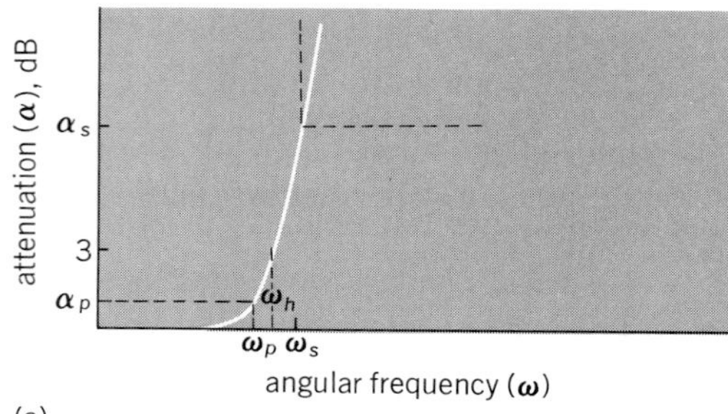


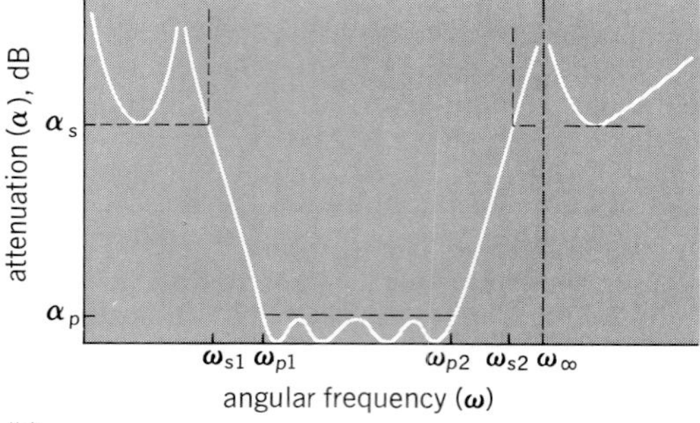


**Fig. 2. Attenuation characteristics. (*a*) Low-pass filter; (*b*) band-pass filter.**

verse of a band-pass filter is a band-stop filter, which stops an intermediate band but passes both low and high frequencies. Finally, there are filter-type networks which pass all frequencies equally well but modify the phase of input signals; they are called all-pass networks, or phase-correcting networks.

The region between the edge of the passband and that of the stopband—with angular frequencies labeled $\omega_p$ and $\omega_s$, respectively, in Fig. 2*a*—is a transition region. Similarly, the transition regions in Fig. 2*b* lie between $\omega_{p1}$ and $\omega_{s1}$, and between $\omega_{p2}$ and $\omega_{s2}$. The sharpness of the filter cutoff depends on the width of this transition region; the narrower the region, the sharper the cutoff is said to be. A particularly significant frequency is the half-power frequency. This is the frequency at which the power transmitted through the filter is half the power input. This occurs when the attenuation has risen to 3 dB from its nominal value (zero) in the passband. In Fig. 2*a* it is indicated by angular frequency $\omega_h = 2\pi f_h$, where *h* is half power (and $f_h$ is the corresponding frequency).

The maximum attenuation in the passband can be approximated in a maximally flat manner, as in the low-pass filter in Fig. 2*a*, or in an oscillatory equal-ripple (Chebyshev) manner, as in Fig. 2*b*. Similar approximations (monotonic or oscillatory) can be made to the stopband behavior.

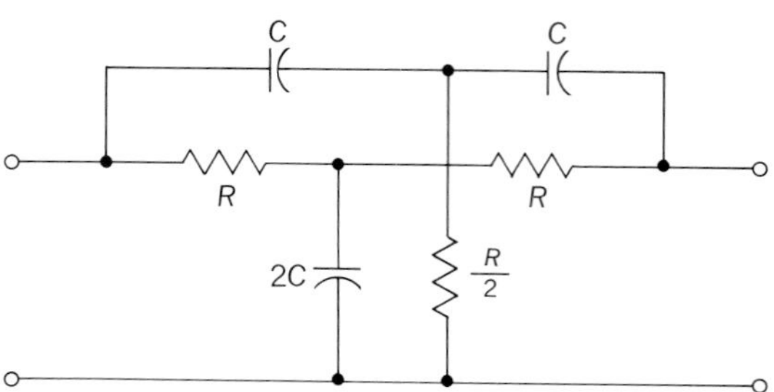


**Fig. 3. *RC* twin-tee null filter.**

**Applications.** Electrical filters are incorporated in almost all systems of electrical communications and control. Radio and television receivers contain filters in order to pass the particular channel selected and to stop others. The telephone network incorporates millions of filters in order to pass each conversation, which is carried by a different band of frequencies, to the appropriate telephone receiver and to stop all others. Bandwidths vary from a fraction of a hertz in control systems, to 3 kHz in telephone systems, to 20 kHz in AM radio systems, to 6 MHz in television systems. SEE AMPLITUDE-MODULATION DETECTOR; FREQUENCY-MODULATION DETECTOR; RADIO RECEIVER; TELEVISION RECEIVER.

Narrow-band band-rejection filters are often used to reduce interference from extraneous electrical noise, which may come from power lines or from industrial equipment. One example of such a null network is the twin-tee filter shown in **Fig. 3**. Ideally, this filter has infinite attenuation at an angular frequency $\omega = 1/RC$.

A common use of a filter is to smooth the output from a rectifier to make it more closely constant by attenuating the alternating-current component. The power supply in every radio and television receiver has such a low-pass filter. The transfer function of this power-supply filter is given in Eq. (3), under the

$$F(s) = \frac{V_2}{V_1} = \frac{1}{1 + s^2LC} \qquad (3)$$

assumption that there is negligible loading at the output port.

For direct current (dc), $s = j\omega = 0$; thus the transfer function is 1, and, according to Eq. (2), there is no attentuation. The components of ac voltage present at the input are 60 Hz or its harmonics, or both. (For a full-wave rectifier, the lowest frequency present is the second harmonic.) The *L* and *C* values are chosen so as to give an attenuation of at least 40 dB at the lowest ac frequency present. The ripple,which is the ac component of the output, will then be no more than 1% of the dc value.) If the transfer function of Eq. (3) is used in Eq. (2), with $s = j\omega$, this condition leads to the result shown in inequality (4). For a full-

$$20 \log |1 - \omega^2 LC| > 40 \qquad (4)$$

$$LC > \frac{10^2}{\omega^2}$$

wave rectifier, $\omega = 2\pi \times 120$. SEE ELECTRONIC POWER SUPPLY; RECTIFIER.

Another common use of a low-pass filter is as a decoupling network when several amplifier stages share the same power supply. A low-pass decoupling filter is placed between the power supply and each amplifier stage, thereby reducing interaction between the stages (**Fig. 4*b***). For this filter the transfer function is given by Eq. (5), again under the assumption

$$F(s) = \frac{V_2}{V_1} = \frac{1}{1 + sCR} \qquad (5)$$

that there is negligible loading at the output, which is usually the case. With direct current, $s = j\omega = 0$, and the transfer function equals 1. Hence, according to Eq. (2), direct current passes with zero attentuation. The half-power frequency is found by substituting the magnitude of *F* from Eq. (5), when $s = j\omega$, into the attenuation relation, Eq. (2), and setting the attenuation equal to 3 dB. The result is $\omega_h = 1/RC$.

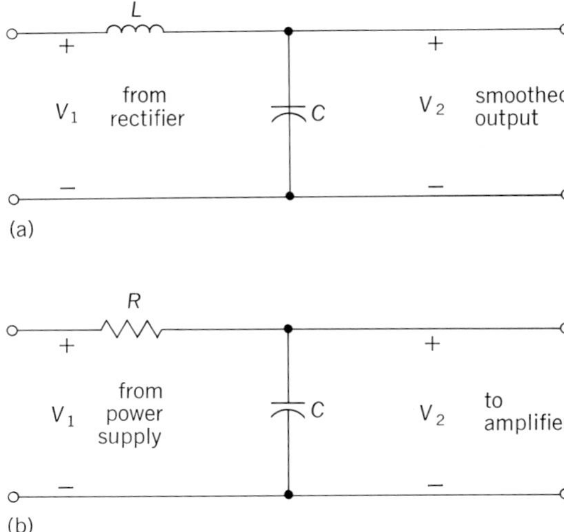


**Fig. 4. Simple low-pass filters. (*a*) Power-supply filter; (*b*) decoupling filter.**

**Design.** The filters mentioned in the preceding section are all relatively simple, with few components. Their design does not require deep knowledge and advanced techniques; the performance requirements imposed on such filters are not very stringent. However, in many applications in which sharp cutoffs and high stopband attenuation is required, simple procedures are inadequate, and more complicated design procedures are necessary.

From prescribed values of passband and stopband attenuation, half-power frequency, sharpness of cutoff, and so on, a transfer function is determined such that the filter constructed so as to have this transfer function meets the specifications to the required degree of approximation. Different design approaches can lead to different locations of poles and zeros of the transfer function; therefore these locations are not uniquely determined from a given set of specifications. The higher the order of the transfer function, the more extensive the filter. Thus the order of the transfer function should be as low as possible, consistent with the requirements of the specifications.

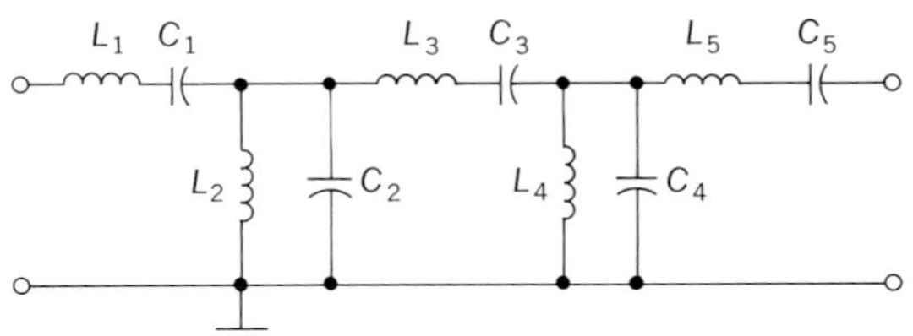


**Fig. 5. *LC* band-pass ladder filter.**

A very common filter design utilizes reactive components (inductors and capacitors), usually in a structure called a ladder. An example of a band-pass ladder is shown in **Fig. 5**. Low-pass and high-pass filters would have a similar structure except the values of the components would be different (and possibly some of the components would be absent). An efficient design procedure for such filters is the insertion-loss design. Extensive tables based on the insertion-loss design are available which give values of inductance $L$ and capacitance $C$ for ladder filters of this type for denominator orders from 3 to 10.

Once a filter has been designed and constructed, it is possible that the values of the components will change. This may occur because of aging, temperature variations, and so on. An important concern for a filter designer is the sensitivity of the attenuation to changes in the component values, that is, the percentage change in the attenuation as a result of a given percentage change in component values. In the most useful design, the sensitivity is as small as possible, other factors being equal. The low sensitivity of the ladder structure makes it a desirable design.

However, the trend in all electronic equipment is toward miniaturization. In fact, the trend is toward constructing as much as possible in the form of integrated circuits (tiny semiconductor chips which can be designed to perform rather complicated functions). Both because of their relatively bulky and heavy nature, and because they cannot be constructed in the form of integrated circuits, inductors are no longer popular. Designs that utilize resistors, capacitors, and active devices called active *RC* filters are increasingly being used. *See Integrated circuits*.

***Inductor simulation.*** One appealing type of design consists of the conventional *LC* filter in which the inductors have been replaced by appropriate combinations of active devices and resistors or capacitors. One such combination is called a gyrator. The physical construction of a gyrator can take many forms, some of which are more complicated than others. A particularly simple gyrator design, requiring just two operational amplifiers and four resistors, is shown in **Fig. 6*a***. Whatever the design might be, a simple schematic symbol, shown in Fig. 6*b*, is used to represent the gyrator in circuit diagrams. In some ways, a gyrator is like a transformer, and the gyration ratio $r$ is like the turns ratio $n$ of a transformer. A transformer transforms impedance; the equivalent impedance at one of the ports is directly proportional to the impedance connected to the other port, and the proportionality constant is the square of the turns ratio. The gyrator, on the other hand, has the property of impedance inversion; the equivalent impedance at one of the ports is inversely proportional to the impedance connected to the other port, the proportionality constant being the square of the gyration ratio $r$.

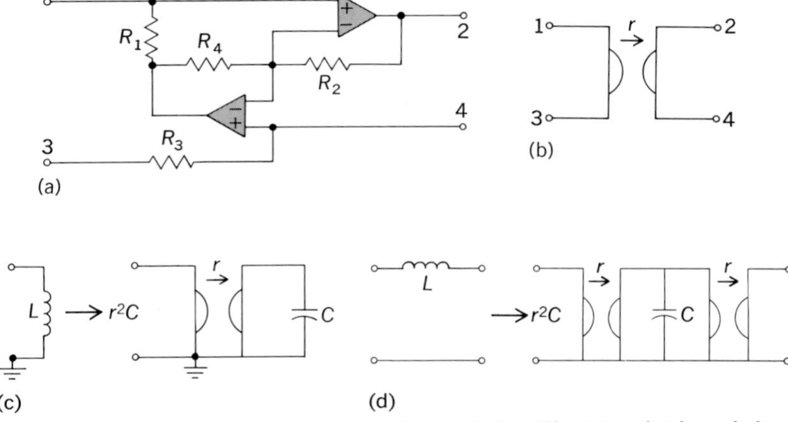


**Fig. 6. Gyrators and inductor simulation. (*a*) Gyrator design; (*b*) gyrator circuit symbol; (*c*) simulation of grounded inductor; (*d*) simulation of floating inductor.**

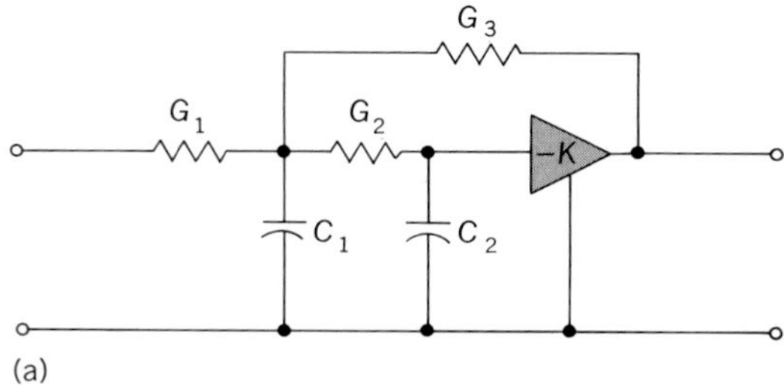


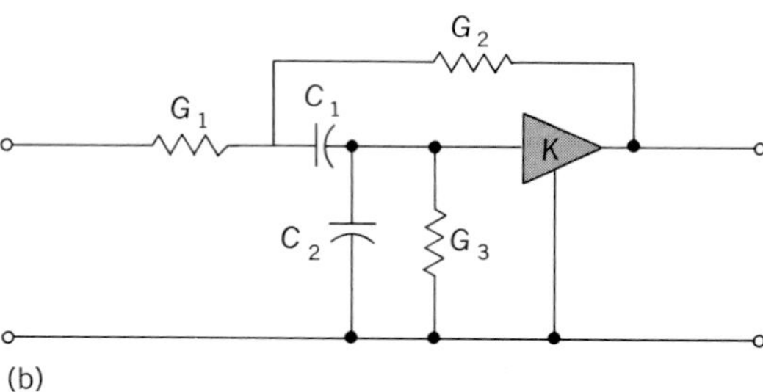


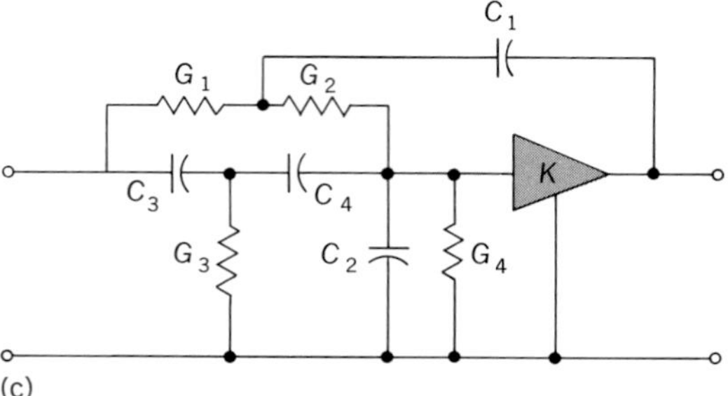


**Fig. 7. Feedback amplifier design. (*a*) Low-pass section; (*b*) band-pass section; (*c*) attenuation-peak-producing section.**

The connections of a capacitor and one or more gyrators which simulate an inductor are also shown in Fig. 6. Whenever an inductor is needed in a filter design, one of these combinations can be used instead.

Thus, in the filter of Fig. 5, each inductor with one terminal connected to ground can be replaced by the gyrator-capacitor combination in Fig. 6*c*. The "floating" inductors, like $L_1$, $L_3$, and $L_5$, which do not have one terminal connected to ground, require the more extensive arrangement with two gyrators shown in Fig. 6*d*. Although replacing the inductors in this manner seems to be a matter of converting a simple network to something more complex, this is not the case. Gyrators can be easily fabricated in the form of integrated circuits, which can be used to replace inductors in a classical design. *See* Gyrator; Transformer.

In fact, the gyrator-capacitor combinations can be fabricated in a single integrated-circuit unit. Whenever the classical design calls for an inductor, such a simulated inductor can be used in its place.

Other active devices can also be used to eliminate the inductors in a classical *LC* design. Among these are the general converter and the frequency-dependent negative-resistance converter. Each of these devices in itself is a rather extensive network. Nevertheless, each can be constructed in the form of an integrated circuit, either as a single unit or as a partial unit to which a few capacitors are connected externally. The design procedures utilizing these devices first require the *LC* filter to be designed. Then, appropriate combinations of these devices with resistors and capacitors eliminate the inductors.

Another virtue of inductor-elimination procedures, besides providing the ability to use the integrated circuit form, and consequently reducing costs, is that the low sensitivity of the ladder structure to changes in component values is retained.

***Feedback amplifier design.*** A variety of design procedures exist for obtaining an active *RC* filter directly, and the active device can take on one of several forms. For a given set of specifications, leading to a transfer function in the form of Eq. (1), two alternatives are possible. The entire transfer function can be realized as a filter all at once, or the transfer function can be written as a product of second-order functions (second-order denominator factors with appropriate factors of the numerator up to second order). Each second-order function is designed separately, and these partial designs are connected in cascade. (Other types of interconnection are also possible, requiring different ways of breaking up the original transfer functions.) Most direct active *RC* filter design procedures use the second alternative in order to reduce the sensitivity of the filter to component-value variations.

One method of design uses an ordinary amplifier in a feedback configuration. Three such second-order filters are shown in **Fig. 7**. Each triangle represents an amplifier; the amplifier gain is negative in the first one and positive in the other two. The third one provides a peak of attenuation, as in the attenuation curve in Fig. 2*b*, at the frequency labeled $\omega_\infty$. (The element values have been labeled in terms of their conductances *G* instead of resistances *R* because the design equations are thereby simplified.) Many other variations of these structures are possible. *See* Feedback circuit.

***Biquad.*** One of the most important active *RC* filter designs is shown in **Fig. 8**. It has been called the biquad because it can realize a general second-order (biquadratic) transfer function of the form shown in Eq. (6). The active devices in this design are operational amplifiers. *See* Amplifier.

$$F = \frac{a_2 s^2 + a_1 s + a_0}{s^2 + b_1 s + b_0} \tag{6}$$

For the simple low-pass characteristic—such as that obtained by the filter section in Fig. 7*a*—the summing amplifier at the bottom in Fig. 8 can be omitted and the output taken between the point labeled 5 and ground. Similarly, for a simple band-pass character-

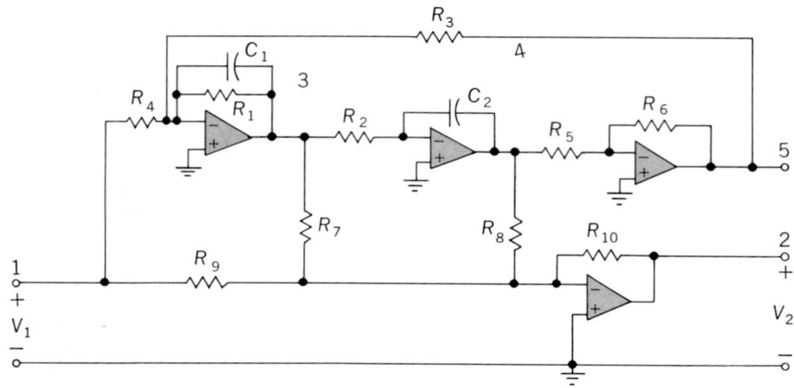


**Fig. 8. The biquad, an active *RC* filter.**

istic—such as that obtained by the section in Fig. 7*b*—the summing amplifier can again be omitted and the output taken between the point labeled 3 and ground.

The virtues of this design are that it can be easily constructed in the form of integrated circuits and that the sensitivity to variations in component values is quite small. Furthermore, the biquads can be interconnected so that higher-order filters can be obtained without interference between the sections occurring.

**Special filters.** Special categories of filters can be classified in accordance with either their application or the components used in their construction.

***Crystal and ceramic filters.*** Piezoelectric crystalline materials such as quartz have the property of electrical resonance when mechanically stressed along certain axes. This property can be used to replace electrical components in a filter. The resulting crystal filters are almost always used in band-pass applications. The incoming (and outgoing) electrical signals must be coupled to the mechanical vibrations of the crystal through transducers, which are themselves electrical elements.

The frequency range of crystal filters is from 2 MHz to 15 MHz, but it can reach as high as 200 MHz. Crystal filters can be made with extremely narrow bandwidths, as low as 0.01%. They have very low loss (with *Q*'s ranging from 10,000 up to 300,000; the higher the *Q*, the lower the loss). For these reasons they find application also in frequency standards. Although they are not smaller and lighter than active *RC* filters, they have the advantage of being passive and so do not generate internal noise.

Ceramic materials can also be used in place of crystals; the result is a ceramic filter. The losses are not quite as low as those of crystal filters (*Q*'s are of the order of 2000 or 3000), but this range is still superior to that of *LC* filters. Both crystal and ceramic filters compete favorably in cost both with conventional *LC* filters and with active *RC* filters. *SEE PIEZOELECTRIC CRYSTAL; Q (ELECTRICITY); RESONANCE (ALTERNATING-CURRENT CIRCUITS).*

***Mechanical filters.*** These filters have some characteristics in common with crystal filters, in that the resonant elements are mechanical. But they differ from crystal filters in that the coupling mechanisms between mechanical vibrations and electrical signals (the transducers) are also mechanical. Ferrites and iron-nickel alloys whose elastic modulus is constant over a temperature range are common materials from which mechanical filters are constructed. These filters also have narrow bandwidths (as low as 0.1%) and low loss (with *Q*'s ranging from 10,000 to 20,000), and their operating frequency range extends down to 3 kHz and up to 600 kHz. *SEE FERRITE DEVICES.*

***Microwave filters.*** These filters operate at microwave frequencies, generally considered to lie above 1 GHz. However, they can also be used in the much lower high-frequency (hf) range of 3–30 MHz. The components are no longer lumped elements, but consist of sections of transmission lines (called stubs), strip lines, coupled lines, and waveguide structures such as irises and posts. *SEE MICROWAVE TRANSMISSION LINES; WAVEGUIDE.*

***Distributed RC filters.*** These filters are made of thin-film integrated circuits or various large-area semiconductor devices. Since active devices, as well as resistors and capacitors, can be fabricated from integrated circuits, distributed *RC* filters (designated $\overline{RC}$) can be active or passive. All the components are fabricated by depositions of various thicknesses on the same substrate.

***Matched filters.*** A filter that is matched to the characteristics of an input signal of known time dependence is called a matched filter. The term is also applied to describe an impedence match between a filter and its termination. A matched filter has the property that, when the input consists of noise in addition to the desired signal, the output signal-to-noise ratio is the maximum that can be obtained by any linear filter. Accordingly, such filters are used (in radar and similar systems) to optimize the detection of weak signals. The impulse response of a matched filter is simply related to the input signal when the spectrum of interference is uniform.

***Switched filters.*** These filters are similar to other electrical filters except that a switch is incorporated into one of the branches. The switch is operated (turned on or off) in a periodic manner so that the switched filter is a time-varying linear network. Switched filters find particular application in modulators used in communications systems, both in frequency-division multiplexing (FDM) and in time-division multiplexing (TDM).

***Optimum filters.*** In some applications the desired output from a filter may be specified either as a function of frequency or as a function of time, more precisely than the attenuation maximum in the passband and minimum in the stopband in Fig. 2. Then the appropriately defined error between the actual output and the desired output is a measure of the performance of the filter. The most common measure is the mean square of the error. A filter designated so as to give the least mean-square error is called an optimum filter. This mean-square error minimization can be achieved under specific conditions, for example,in the presence of noise interference having a specified power spectrum. Optimum filters are used in predicting the future values of the input on the basis of its past values and the mean-square error.

**Digital filters.** An increasing amount of signal processing is being performed in digital form. A digital signal is one which takes on only a limited number of discrete values and only at discrete and equally spaced intervals of time. Signals may already be in digital form (for example, sent between digital computers and most business machines), or a continuous signal may be converted to digital form by sampling it at uniform intervals and digitally coding its values, for ease of transmission or some other reason. This digital signal is processed according to a set of instructions in order to regain the original information. The processing is performed by a digital filter.

Since the function performed by a digital filter is the processing of digital signals,the building blocks from which a digital filter is constructed are the same

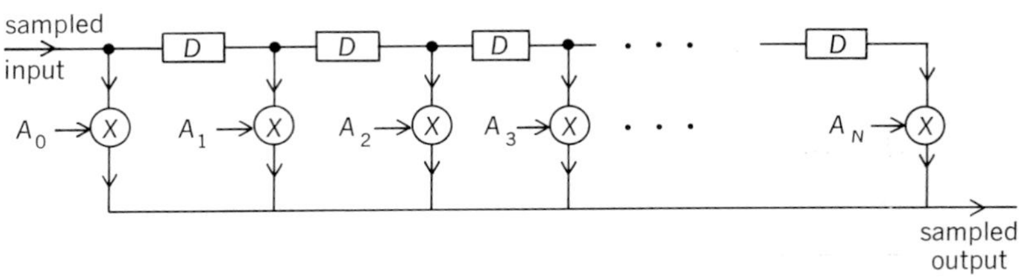


**Fig. 9. Tapped delay-line digital filter.**

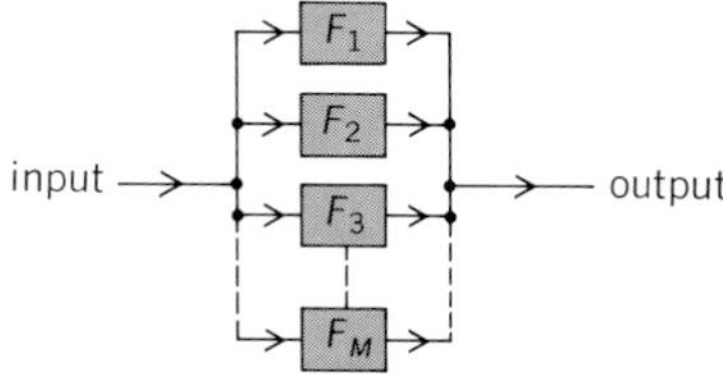


Fig. 10. Digital filter in parallel form.

as those in a digital computer—adders, multipliers, shift registers, memory units, and so on. A digital computer is a machine which processes data in accordance with a set of instructions, called the program. Therefore, not only is a digital filter a piece of equipment specially designed to perform a function but also from a conceptual standpoint, it can be viewed as the software (the program) which instructs a general-purpose digital computer. Thus a digital filter is inherently different from the other filters discussed in this article. SEE DIGITAL COMPUTER.

Digital filters can be designed by dealing with the representation of input and output signals either in the time domain or in the frequency domain. In the time domain, the filter is represented by its response in time to an impulse, called its impulse response. One form is which this representation can be implemented is shown in **Fig. 9**. The top row represents a delay line, with taps at uniform intervals in which each $D$ represents a fixed delay related to the sampling interval. (Mathematically, $D = e^{-sT}$, where $T$ is the sampling interval.) Each circle with an $x$ is a multiplier, and the $A$'s are the coefficients by which the delayed signal coming from the corresponding tap is multiplied.

The sampled input signal is a sequence of numbers. (In mathematical terms, it is said to be a sequence of impulses whose weights are the values of the input at the corresponding times.) The output is again a sequence of numbers obtained by adding the delayed outputs from the taps.

In the frequency domain, it is possible to express the digital transfer function as a sum of first-order and second-order terms. Each term is designed separately; the terms are then connected in parallel, as shown in **Fig. 10**. Designs of first-order and second-order digital filters are shown in **Fig. 11**. The circles with enclosed plus signs represent adders. Many other designs are also possible.

*Norman Balabanian*

**Bibliography.** P. Bowron and F. W. Stephenson, *Filters for Communication and Instrumentation*, 1979; C. Childers and A. Durling, *Digital Filtering and Signal Processing*, 1975; L. P. Huelsman and P. Allen, *Introduction to the Theory and Design of Active Filters*, 1980; D. E. Johnson, *Introduction to Filter Theory*, 1976; G. S. Moschytz, *Linear Integrated Networks: Design*, 1975; G. C. Temes and S. K. Mitra (eds.), *Modern Filter Theory and Design*, 1973.

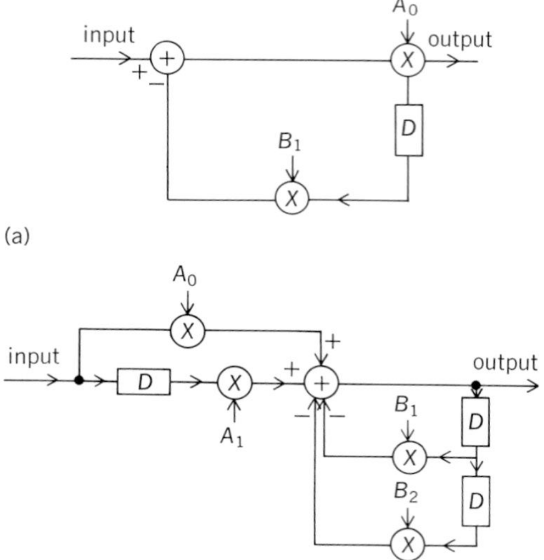


Fig. 11. Block diagrams of digital filter sections. (*a*) First order; (*b*) second order.

## Electric spark

A transient form of gaseous conduction. This type of discharge is difficult to define, and no universally accepted definition exists. It can perhaps best be thought of as the transition between two more or less stable forms of gaseous conduction. For example, the transitional breakdown which occurs in the transition from a glow to an arc discharge may be thought of as a spark.

Electric sparks play an important part in many physical effects. Usually these are harmful and undesirable effects, ranging from the gradual destruction of contacts in a conventional electrical switch to the large-scale havoc resulting from lightning discharges. Sometimes, however, the spark may be very useful. Examples are its function in the ignition system of an automobile, its use as an intense short-duration illumination source in high-speed photography, and its use as a source of excitation in spectroscopy. In the second case the spark may actually perform the function of the camera shutter, because its extinction renders the camera insensitive.

**Mechanisms.** The spark is probably the most complicated of all forms of gaseous conduction. It is exceedingly difficult to study, because it is a transient and because there are so many variables in the system. Some of these variables are the components of the gaseous medium, the gas pressure, the chemical form of the electrodes, the physical shape of the electrodes, the microscopic physical surface structure, the surface temperature, the electrode separation, the functional dependence of potential drop on time, and the presence or absence of external ionizing agents. One or more of these conditions may change from one spark to the next. Because of the great complexity, it will be impossible to do more than touch on some of the main features in this article.

The dependence of breakdown, or sparking, potential on pressure $p$ and electrode separation $d$ is considered first. It was shown experimentally by F. Paschen and theoretically by J. S. Townsend that the sparking potential is a function of the product $pd$ and not of $p$ or $d$ separately (**Fig. 1**). Further, there is a value of $pd$ for which the sparking potential is a minimum. Thus, if it is desired to prevent sparking between two electrodes, the region may be evacuated or raised to a high pressure. The latter method is used in accelerators of the electrostatic generator variety. Here the entire apparatus is placed in a pressurized tank.

Qualitatively, one of the aspects of a spark is that the entire path between electrodes is ionized. It is the photon emission from recombination and decay of excited states which gives rise to the light from the spark. Further, if the spark leads to a stable conduction state, the cathode must be capable of supplying the needed secondary electrons, and the conduction state produced must permit the discharge of the interelectrode capacitance at the very minimum. *See* Arc discharge; Electrical conduction in gases; Glow discharge.

In a consideration of the mechanism involved in the spark, the time required for the breakdown of the gas in a gap is an important element. L. B. Loeb pointed out that this time is often less than that required for an electron to traverse the gap completely. This implies that there must be some means of ionization present other than electron impact and that the velocity of propagation of this ionizing agent or mechanism must be much greater than the electron velocity. It seems definitely established that this additional method must be photoionization. In the intense electric field which is necessary for the spark, the initial electron will produce a heavy avalanche of cumulative ionization. Light resulting from the decay processes will produce ionization throughout the gas and electrons at the surfaces by the photoelectric effect (**Fig. 2**). The electrons resulting from this will in turn produce further avalanches through the entire region, so that in a time of the order of $10^{-8}$ the entire path becomes conducting. If the pressure is approximately atmospheric, the spark will be confined to a relatively narrow region, so that the conducting path, while not straight, will be a well-defined line. If the external circuit can supply the necessary current, the spark will result in an arc discharge. At lower pressure the path becomes more diffuse, and the discharge takes on either a glow or arc characteristic.

Figure 2 shows A, the electron multiplication of electrons by the cumulative ionization of a single electron liberated from the cathode by a photon; B, a secondary electron emitted from the cathode by a positively charged ion; C, the development and structure of an avalanche, with positively charged ions behind electrons at the tip; D, the avalanche crossing the gap and spreading by diffusion; and F, an older avalanche when electrons have disappeared into the anode. A positive space-charge boss appears on the cathode at F. Ion pairs out from the trail indicate the appearance of photoelectric ion pairs in the gas produced by photons from the avalanche. E shows a photoelectron from the surface of the cathode produced by the avalanche.

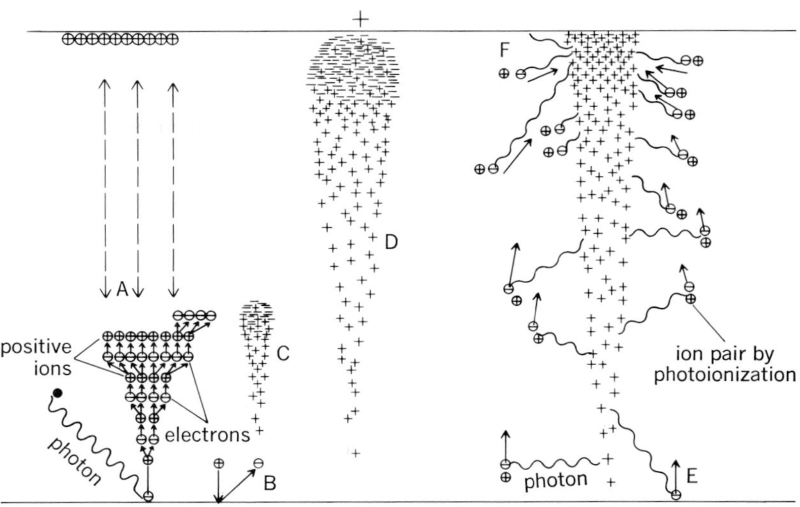


**Fig. 2. Electron multiplication and avalanching during an electric spark discharge. (*After L. B. Loeb and J. M. Meek, The Mechanism of the Electric Spark, Stanford University Press, 1941*)**

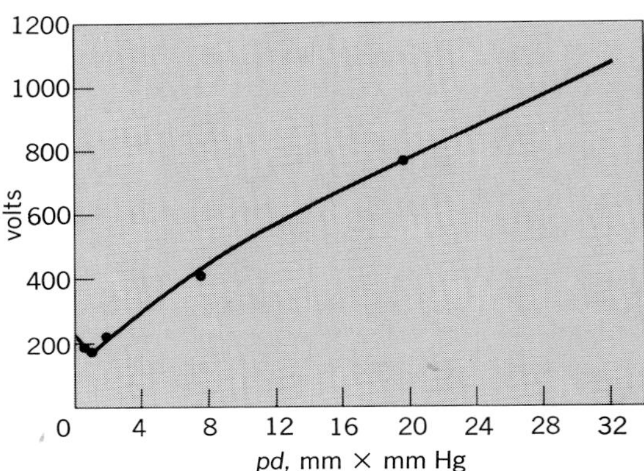


**Fig. 1. Dependence of sparking potential on *pd* for a sodium cathode in hydrogen gas. (*After L. B. Loeb and J. M. Meek, The Mechanism of the Electric Spark, Standford University Press, 1941*)**

**Theory.** Mathematically, the theory of Townsend predicts that the current in a self-sustained discharge of the glow variety will follow Eq. (1), where $I$ is the

$$I = I_0 \frac{e^{\alpha x}}{1 - \gamma e^{\alpha x}} \qquad (1)$$

current with a given plate separation $x$, $I_0$ is the current when $x$ approaches zero, and $\alpha$ and $\gamma$ are constants associated with the Townsend coefficients. This equation represents the case where the electrode separation is varied while the ratio of electric field to pressure is held constant. The condition for a spark is that the denominator approach zero, which may be stated as in Eq. (2). Loeb indicated that this criterion

$$\gamma = e^{-\alpha x} \qquad (2)$$

must be handled carefully. Townsend's equation really represents a steady-state situation, and it is here being used to explain a transient effect. If the processes which are involved are examined more carefully, it appears that there should be a dependence on $I_0$ as well.

*Glenn H. Miller*

***Bibliography.*** J. Beyon, *Conduction of Electricity through Gases*, 1972; J. D. Cobine, *Gaseous Conductors*, 1941; L. B. Loeb, Statistical factors in spark discharge mechanisms, *Rev. Mod. Phys.*, 20:151–160, 1948; D. Roller and D. H. C. Roller, *The Development of the Concept of Electric Charge*, 1954.

## Electric transient

A temporary component of current and voltage in an electric circuit which has been disturbed. In ordinary circuit problems, a stabilized condition of the circuit is assumed and steady-state values of current and voltage are sufficient. However, it often becomes important to known what occurs during the transition period following a circuit disturbance until the steady-state condition is reached. Transients occur only in circuits containing inductance or capacitance. In general, transients accompany any change in the amount or form of energy stored in the circuit. Both direct-current (dc) transients and alternating-current (ac) transients are treated following the introduction. SEE ALTERNATING-CURRENT CIRCUIT THEORY; DIRECT-CURRENT CIRCUIT THEORY.

**Introduction.** The study of transient phenomena is very broad. The mathematical requirements become severe and go far beyond the borders of all known mathematics. Transient analysis often requires the use of calculating machines, models, and tests. Fourier and Laplace transforms have proven indispensable in the modern treatment of transients and these disciplines need be mastered by anyone going far in the study of transients. The analysis of lumped-parameter circuits is comparatively easy and is all that will be described here, but transients of a much more complex nature occur on distributed-parameter circuits, such as transmission lines.

An electric circuit or system under steady-state conditions of constant, or cyclic, applied voltages or currents is in a state of equilibrium. However, the circuit conditions of voltage, current, or frequency may change or be disturbed. Also, circuit elements may be switched in or out of the circuit. Any change of circuit condition or circuit elements causes a transient readjustment of voltages and currents from the initial state of equilibrium to the final state of equilibrium to the final state of equilibrium. In a sense the transient may be regarded as superimposed on the final steady state, so that Eq. (1) applies.

$$\begin{pmatrix}\text{Instantaneous}\\ \text{condition}\end{pmatrix} = \begin{pmatrix}\text{final}\\ \text{condition}\end{pmatrix} + \begin{pmatrix}\text{transient}\\ \text{terms}\end{pmatrix} \qquad (1)$$

Furthermore, since the instantaneous condition at the first instant of disturbance (time zero) must be the initial condition, it may be described by Eq. (2).

$$\begin{pmatrix}\text{Initial}\\ \text{condition}\end{pmatrix} = \begin{pmatrix}\text{final}\\ \text{condition}\end{pmatrix} + \begin{pmatrix}\text{transient terms}\\ \text{at time zero}\end{pmatrix} \qquad (2)$$

A great deal of information may be obtained from these two "word equations" without recourse to mathematics. For example, if the weight on the end of a vertical spring is suddenly increased, its final displacement can be determined. Since the spring-weight combination is known to be an oscillating system, the amplitude of the transient oscillation follows from Eq. (2) as the difference between the initial and final displacements.

The nature of an electric transient is determined by three things: (1) the circuit or network itself—the interconnections of its elements and the circuit parameters (resistances $R$, inductances $L$, capacitances $C$, mutual inductances $M$); (2) the initial conditions of voltages, currents, charges, and flux linkages at the start of the transient; and (3) the nature of the disturbance which initiated the transient.

The circuit, or network, is usually defined by a diagram of connections showing all of the interconnections, junctions, meshes, circuit parameters, voltage and current sources and their polarities, and switches. Corresponding to the network a differential (or integral-differential) equation, or a set of such equations, may be written. These equations may also be written in terms of operational calculus, or as Laplace transforms, or in any other suitable mathematical equivalents. They are established in accordance with Kirchhoff's laws:

I. The sum of the currents $i$ at a junction is equal to zero: $\Sigma i = 0$.

II. The sum of the voltages $e$ around a mesh is equal to zero: $\Sigma e = 0$. SEE KIRCHHOFF'S LAW OF ELECTRIC CIRCUITS.

The voltage drops associated with a resistance, inductance, mutual inductance, and capacitance, respectively, are given by Eqs. (3). In applying Kirchhoff's law to a closed mesh, it is merely necessary (with due regard for signs and polarities) to equate the sum of all the voltage sources (such as generators and batteries) to the sum of all the voltage drops in the mesh, as in Eq. (4), where $m$ refers to any branch of

$$\begin{aligned} e_R &= Ri & e_L &= L\frac{di}{dt} \\ e_i &= M_{12}\frac{di_2}{dt} & e_C &= \frac{1}{C}\int i\,dt \end{aligned} \qquad (3)$$

$$\sum_m e_m = \sum_m \sum_n \left( R_{mn} i_n + L_{mn}\frac{di_n}{dt} + \frac{1}{C_{mn}}\int i_n\,dt \right) \qquad (4)$$

the mesh in question, and $n$ to any current causing a voltage drop in that branch (a branch may carry currents from meshes other than the mesh in question, or be mutually coupled with other branches). Equation (4) formulates the differential equation of the circuit in terms of the voltages and currents. It is sometimes convenient to make use of charges $q$ and fluxes $\phi$ by the substitutions of Eqs. (5).

$$i = \frac{dq}{dt} \quad \text{or} \quad q = \int i\,dt \quad \text{and} \quad N\phi = Li \qquad (5)$$

Since Eq. (4) contains an integral, it is convenient to eliminate it either by differentiating once or by substituting Eq. (5). Then Eqs. (6) follow.

$$\begin{aligned} \sum_m \frac{de_m}{dt} &= \sum_m \sum_n \left( R_{mn}\frac{di_n}{dt} + L_{mn}\frac{d^2 i_n}{dt^2} + \frac{i_n}{C_{mn}} \right) \\ \sum_m e_m &= \sum_m \sum_n \left( R_{mn}\frac{dq_n}{dt} + L_{mn}\frac{d^2 q_n}{dt^2} + \frac{q_n}{C_{mn}} \right) \end{aligned} \qquad (6)$$

SEE COUPLED CIRCUITS.

It is customary to factor out the current from Eq. (4) and write the equation in terms of a generalized impedance, operator $Z_{mn}$ defined by Eq. (7). Since an

$$\begin{aligned} \sum_m e_m &= \sum_m \sum_n \left( R_{mn} + L_{mn}\frac{d}{dt} + \frac{1}{C_{mn}}\int dt \right) i_n \\ &= \sum_m \sum_n Z_{mn} i_n \end{aligned} \qquad (7)$$

equation of this type can be written for each of the $N$-meshes of the network, the totality of the differential equations for the entire network constitutes a system of simultaneous differential equations in the form of Eqs. (8).

$$\begin{aligned} e_1 &= Z_{11}i_1 + Z_{12}i_2 + \cdots + Z_{1N}i_N \\ e_2 &= Z_{21}i_1 + Z_{22}i_2 + \cdots + Z_{2N}i_N \\ &\cdots\cdots\cdots\cdots \\ e_N &= Z_{N1}i_1 + Z_{N2}i_2 + \cdots + Z_{NN}i_N \end{aligned} \qquad (8)$$

In general, the process of solution of such a set of equations for any current leads to a differential equation of order $2N$; there will be $2N$ integration constants associated with it, and these integration constants must be determined from the initial conditions at the first instant of the disturbance.

Equation (9) is the solution of an ordinary differential equation with constant coefficients and is in two parts.

$$\begin{pmatrix}\text{Complete}\\ \text{solution}\end{pmatrix} = \begin{pmatrix}\text{particular}\\ \text{integral}\end{pmatrix} + \begin{pmatrix}\text{complementary}\\ \text{solution}\end{pmatrix} \tag{9}$$

The particular integral depends on the form of the applied voltage, and represents the final steady-state solution.

The complementary solution is independent of the form of the applied voltages, but depends on the initial conditions in the circuit, and represents the transient terms. Thus Eq. (9) is the mathematical equivalent of Eq. (1).

The opening of a switch may be simulated by superimposing an equal and opposite current and thereby canceling the current through the switch. Likewise, the closing of a switch may be simulated by canceling the voltage across its terminals by an equal and opposite voltage. The effect of a cancellation current (or voltage) may be superimposed on the currents and voltages already existing in the system, as in Eq. (10).

$$\begin{pmatrix}\text{Resultant}\\ \text{voltages}\\ \text{and}\\ \text{currents}\end{pmatrix} = \begin{pmatrix}\text{those which}\\ \text{would exist if}\\ \text{switches were}\\ \text{not operated}\end{pmatrix} + \begin{pmatrix}\text{those due to}\\ \text{``cancellation''}\\ \text{voltages or}\\ \text{currents}\end{pmatrix} \tag{10}$$

In many practical cases transients are one of three types:

1. Single-energy transients, in which only one form of energy storage (electromagnetic or electrostatic) is present; the transient exhibits simple exponential decay from the initial to the final conditions.
2. Double-energy transients, in which both forms of energy storage are present; the transient is either aperiodic or a damped sinusoid.
3. Combination of 1 and 2.

## DC Transients

Transients are initiated in dc circuits either when a switch is closed on a dc voltage, or when a switch is opened and the detached circuit is permitted to discharge its energy sources. The assumption is made that the suddenly applied dc voltage is sustained at a constant value for an indefinite period after the switching operation, and time is counted from the instant, $t = 0$, at which the switch is operated. It is further usually assumed, where possible, that all circuit parameters (resistances $R$, inductances $L$, and capacitances $C$) are constant, so that the resulting differential equations are linear.

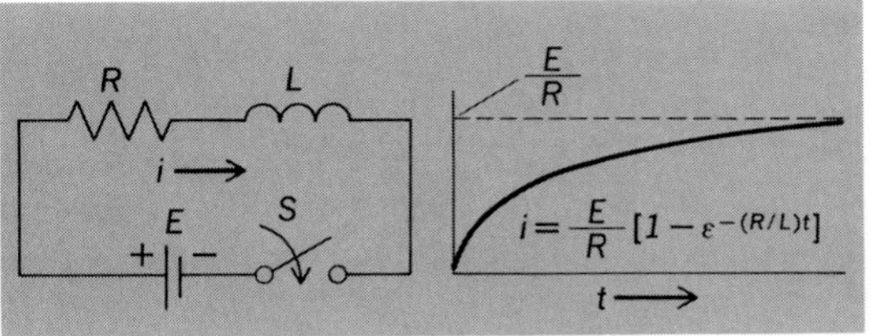


**Fig. 1. Resistance and inductance in series.**

The energy sources in dc systems comprise dynamoelectric machines, mercury-arc rectifiers, vacuum tubes, and electric batteries. Energy $W$ is stored in a circuit in inductances ($W = 1/2Li^2$) and capacitances ($W = 1/2Ce^2$). Energy is dissipated in circuit resistances ($W = Ri^2$).

**Resistance and inductance in series.** A lumped parameter circuit comprising a dc voltage source $E$, a resistance $R$, and an inductance $L$ is shown in **Fig. 1**. When the switch S is closed, the voltage $E$ is suddenly impressed on the series circuit. By Kirchhoff's second law the differential equation is given by Eq. (11).

$$E = Ri + L\frac{di}{dt} \tag{11}$$

Equating the right-hand side of Eq. (11) to zero, the complementary solution is found by assuming that Eq. (12), in which $I$ and $a$ are constants to be determined, applies. Upon substitution in Eq. (11), Eq. (13) results, from which follows $a = -R/L$.

$$i = I\epsilon^{at} \tag{12}$$

$$0 = RI\epsilon^{at} + aLI\epsilon^{at} = (R + aL)i \tag{13}$$

The particular integral is the final steady-state solution or $i(\infty) = E/R$. The complete solution, Eq. (14), is the sum of the complementary solution and the particular integral. But this expression contains the unknown integration constant $I$ which must be found from the initial conditions. At $t = 0$, the instant at which the switch is closed, there can be no current in the circuit, since it is impossible to store energy in an inductance instantaneously. Therefore $i(0) = 0$ and when this is put in Eq. (14), Eq. (15) is obtained.

$$i = E/R + I\epsilon^{-(R/L)t} \tag{14}$$

$$i(0) = 0 = E/R + I \quad \text{or} \quad I = -E/R \tag{15}$$

The complete solution by Eq. (14) therefore is given by Eq. (16), which is in the form of Eq. (1).

$$i = \frac{E}{R} - \frac{E}{R}\epsilon^{-(R/L)t} \tag{16}$$

Here $E/R$ is the final (steady-state) condition and $-(E/R)\epsilon^{-(R/L)t}$ is the transient term. Note also that at $t = 0$ this equation gives $i(0) = 0$, agreeing with Eq. (2). The graph of the transient is shown in Fig. 1, where the current starts at zero, rises exponentially, and approaches its steady-state value of $E/R$ as $t$ approaches infinity. See Electrical resistance; Inductance.

**Resistance and capacitance in series.** A resistance-capacitance series circuit is shown in **Fig. 2**. A residual charge $q_0$ is on the capacitor just prior to closing the switch S.

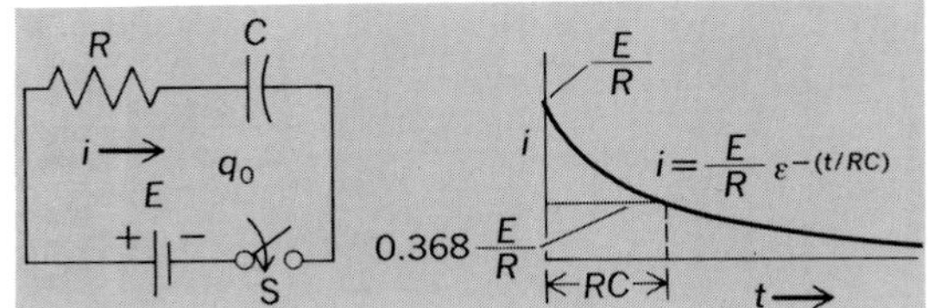


Fig. 2. Resistance and capacitance in series.

Equation (17) is the differential equation of the cir-

$$E = Ri + \frac{1}{C}\int i\,dt \tag{17}$$

cuit. This equation may be solved as it is, or converted to a linear differential equation, Eq. (18), by

$$0 = R\frac{di}{dt} + \frac{i}{C} \tag{18}$$

differentiation or restated in terms of the instantaneous charge on the capacitor by substituting $i = dq/dt$, giving Eq. (19).

$$E = R\frac{dq}{dt} + \frac{q}{C} \tag{19}$$

The solution to this equation, following precisely the steps of the previous paragraph, is given by Eq. (20), in which $Q$ is the integration constant. But ini-

$$q = Q\epsilon^{-(t/RC)} + CE \tag{20}$$

tially, at $t = 0$, there was a residual charge $q_0$ on the capacitance; therefore the relationship given by Eq. (21) pertains, and upon the substitution of Eq. (21) in

$$q(0) = q_0 = Q + CE \text{ or } Q = q_0 - CE \tag{21}$$

Eq. (20), Eq. (22) is obtained. This equation is in the

$$q = CE - (CE - q_0)\,\epsilon^{-(t/RC)} \tag{22}$$

form of Eq. (1), in which $CE$ is the final (steady-state) condition and the other term is the transient. Initially, at $t = 0$, $q = q_0$ in agreement with Eq. (2). The current is given by Eq. (23).

$$\begin{aligned} i &= \frac{dq}{dt} = \frac{CE - q_0}{RC}\,\epsilon^{-(t/RC)} \\ &= \left(\frac{E}{R} - \frac{q_0}{RC}\right)\epsilon^{-(t/RC)} \end{aligned} \tag{23}$$

Equations (22) and (23) have been plotted in Fig. 2 for the case $q_0 = 0$. *See* Capacitance.

**Resistance, inductance, and capacitance in series.** This circuit is shown in **Fig. 3**. The capacitor is assumed to have an initial charge $q_0$, or an initial voltage $V = q_0/C$. The differential equation of the circuit is given by Eq. (24).

$$E = Ri + L\frac{di}{dt} + \frac{1}{C}\int i\,dt \tag{24}$$

Differentiating once to clear the integral, Eq. (25)

$$0 = R\frac{di}{dt} + L\frac{d^2i}{dt^2} + \frac{i}{C} \tag{25}$$

is obtained. Equation (25) is a second-order linear differential equation with constant coefficients; since it is equal to zero, it will possess only a complementary solution. Equation (26) is assumed, which, upon

$$i = A\epsilon^{at} \tag{26}$$

substitution in Eq. (25), yields Eq. (27).

$$0 = aRA\epsilon^{at} + a^2LA\epsilon^{at} + (A/C)\epsilon^{at} \tag{27}$$

Canceling the constant $A$ and the exponential, there results a quadratic in $a$ whose solution gives the two possible values shown in Eqs. (28).

$$\begin{aligned} a_1 &= \frac{-RC + \sqrt{R^2C^2 - 4LC}}{2LC} \\ a_2 &= \frac{-RC - \sqrt{R^2C^2 - 4LC}}{2LC} \end{aligned} \tag{28}$$

Associating the integration constant $A_1$ with $a_1$ and $A_2$ with $a_2$, the solution takes the form of Eq. (29).

$$i = A_1\epsilon^{a_1t} + A_2\epsilon^{a_2t} \tag{29}$$

The voltage across the capacitor, Eq. (30), is ob-

$$\begin{aligned} e_C &= \frac{1}{C}\int i\,dt = E - Ri - L\frac{di}{dt} \\ &= E - (R + a_1L)A_1\epsilon^{a_1t} - (R + a_2L)A_2\epsilon^{a_2t} \end{aligned} \tag{30}$$

tained from Eq. (24).

Initially, at $t = 0$, the current must be zero because of the inductance, and the capacitor voltage is $e_C = V$. By the first of these conditions, $i(0) = 0$, in Eq. (29) it is seen that $A_2 = -A_1$. And by the second condition, $e_C(0) = V$, in Eq. (30), Eq. (31) is obtained.

$$\begin{aligned} V &= E - (R + a_1L)A_1 - (R + a_2L)A_2 \\ &= E - (a_1 - a_2)LA_1 \\ A_1 &= \frac{E - V}{(a_1 - a_2)L} = \frac{C(E - V)}{\sqrt{R^2C^2 - 4LC}} \end{aligned} \tag{31}$$

Then Eq. (32) is the complete solution.

$$i = \frac{C(E - V)}{\sqrt{R^2C^2 - 4LC}}(\epsilon^{a_1t} - \epsilon^{a_2t}) \tag{32}$$

There are three special cases of this solution, depending on the nature of the radical in Eq. (32).

***Nonoscillatory case***: $R^2C > 4L$. In this case the radical is positive, and the exponents $a_1$ and $a_2$ are real and negative, $a_1 = -\alpha + \beta$, $a_2 = -\alpha - \beta$, where $\alpha = R/2L$ and $\beta = \sqrt{R^2C^2 - 4LC}/2LC$. Then $i$ is given by Eq. (33), which is shown in Fig. 3,

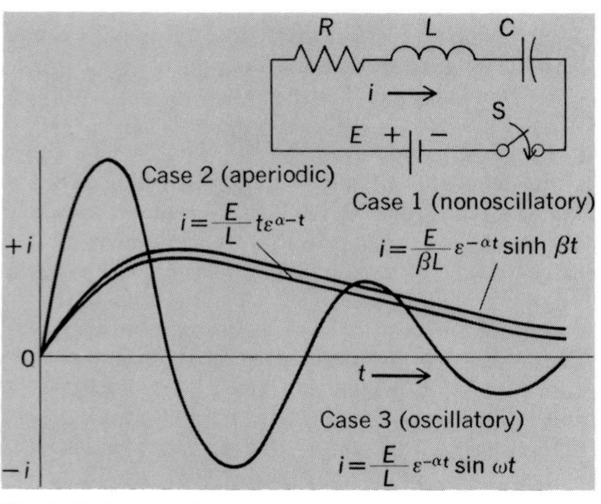


Fig. 3. Resistance, inductance, and capacitance in series for three cases.

$$i = \frac{C(E - V)}{\sqrt{R^2C^2 - 4LC}} \epsilon^{-\alpha t}(\epsilon^{+\beta t} - \epsilon^{-\beta t})$$
$$= \frac{2C(E - V)}{\sqrt{R^2C^2 - 4LC}} \epsilon^{-\alpha t} \sinh \beta t \qquad (33)$$

where $q_0$ is assumed to be 0 and $V = 0$.

***Aperiodic case***: $R^2C = 4L$. In this case $a_1 = a_2 = -R/2L$, and the radical in the denominator of Eq. (32) is zero, as is the numerator. The indeterminant is easily evaluated from Eq. (33) upon letting $\beta \to 0$, thus giving Eq. (34). This is the aperiodic or critical

$$i = \frac{2C(E - V)}{2LC\beta} e^{-\alpha t} \sinh \beta t \mid_{\beta \to 0}$$
$$= \frac{E - V}{L} e^{-\alpha t} t \qquad (34)$$

case, and is illustrated in Fig. 3.

***Oscillatory case***: $R^2C < 4L$. In this case the radical in Eq. (28) becomes imaginary and the exponents take the form of Eqs. (35), and Eq. (32) becomes Eq.

$$a_1 = \frac{-R}{2L} + j\frac{\sqrt{4LC - R^2C^2}}{2LC} = -\alpha + j\omega$$
$$a_2 = \frac{-R}{2L} - j\frac{\sqrt{4LC - R^2C^2}}{2LC} = -\alpha - j\omega \qquad (35)$$

(36). This is a damped oscillation and is illustrated in Fig. 3.

$$i = \frac{C(E - V)}{2j\omega LC} e^{-\alpha t}(\epsilon^{j\omega t} - \epsilon^{-j\omega t})$$
$$= \frac{E - V}{\omega L} \epsilon^{-\alpha t} \sin \omega t \qquad (36)$$

## AC Transients

Alternating-current transients differ from direct-current transients in two important respects: (1) The final condition, or steady state, is an alternating or cyclic one, and (2) the amplitudes of the transient terms depend on the point on the ac applied voltage wave at which the transient is initiated, and can therefore have many different values, or even change sign.

In the section on dc transients, solutions were carried out for *RL*, *RC*, and *RLC* circuits switched onto a voltage source. In the present section, the solution will be carried out in detail for the *RLC* circuit only; the others will be regarded as special cases of this general solution by putting $C = \infty$ and $L = 0$, respectively.

**Resistance, inductance, and capacitance in series.** Consider the circuit of **Fig. 4** in which an *RLC* circuit is suddenly switched onto an ac voltage $e = E \sin(\omega t + \gamma)$ at an electrical angle $\gamma$ displaced from $\omega t = 0$. Assume that a current $I$ is flowing in the circuit and a voltage $V$ is across the capacitance at the instant the switch is closed on the alternator. The voltage equation and the initial conditions then are given by Eqs. (37) and (38).

$$E \sin(\omega t + \gamma) = Ri + L\frac{di}{dt} + \frac{1}{C}\int i\,dt \qquad (37)$$

$$i = I \quad \text{and} \quad e_C = V \quad \text{at} \quad t = 0 \qquad (38)$$

Differentiating Eq. (37) once to clear it of the integral gives Eq. (39). The complementary solution of

$$\omega E \cos(\omega t + \gamma) = L\frac{d^2i}{dt^2} + R\frac{di}{dt} + \frac{i}{C} \qquad (39)$$

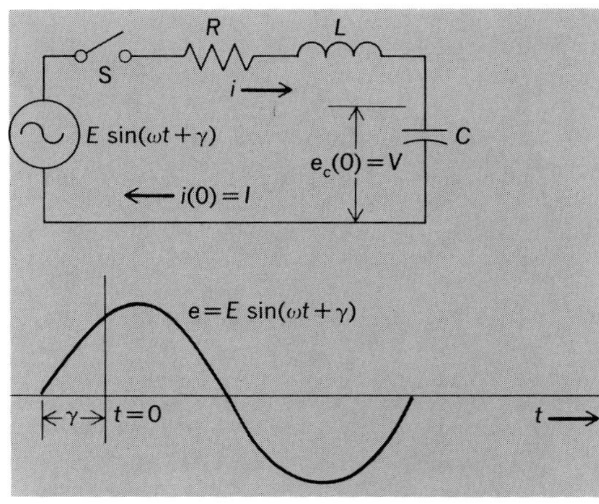


**Fig. 4.** ***RLC*** **circuit with alternating current source.**

this equation is the same as in the dc case of Eq. (25), that is, Eq. (29), where $a_1$ and $a_2$ are given in Eq. (28).

The particular integral of Eq. (39) is its final steady-state current. This is most easily obtained as Eq. (40), the ordinary ac solution for the current, to

$$i_{ac} = \frac{E}{Z} \sin(\omega t + \gamma - \theta) \qquad (40)$$

which Eqs. (41) and (42) apply.

$$Z = \sqrt{R^2 + (\omega L - 1/\omega C)^2} \qquad (41)$$

$$\tan \theta = \frac{\omega L - 1/\omega C}{R} = \frac{\omega^2 LC - 1}{\omega CR} \qquad (42)$$

The complete solution than is given by Eq. (43), in

$$i = \frac{E}{Z} \sin(\omega t + \gamma - \theta) + A_1\epsilon^{a_1 t} + A_2\epsilon^{a_2 t} \qquad (43)$$

which $A_1$ and $A_2$ are integration constants and $a_1$ and $a_2$ are given in Eq. (28).

The capacitor voltage is given by Eq. (44).

$$e_C = \frac{1}{C}\int i\,dt = -\frac{E}{\omega CZ}\cos(\omega t + \gamma - \theta)$$
$$+ \frac{A_1}{Ca_1}\epsilon^{a_1 t} + \frac{A_2}{Ca_2}\epsilon^{a_2 t} \qquad (44)$$

Now applying the initial conditions of Eq. (38) at $t = 0$, there results from Eqs. (43) and (44), respectively, Eqs. (45) and (46).

$$i(0) = I = \frac{E}{Z}\sin(\gamma - \theta) + A_1 + A_2 \qquad (45)$$

$$e_C(0) = V = \frac{-E}{\omega CZ}\cos(\gamma - \theta)$$
$$+ \frac{A_1}{Ca_1} + \frac{A_2}{Ca_2} \qquad (46)$$

Solving Eqs. (45) and (46) simultaneously for $A_1$ and $A_2$ and using Eq. (28), Eqs. (47)–(49) result.

$$A_1 = \frac{1}{\sqrt{R^2C^2 - 4LC}}\left\{\frac{I}{a_2} - CV\right.$$
$$\left. - \frac{E}{Z}\left[\frac{1}{\omega}\cos(\gamma - \theta) + \frac{1}{a_2}\sin(\gamma - \theta)\right]\right\} \qquad (47)$$

$$A_2 = \frac{-1}{\sqrt{R^2C^2 - 4LC}} \left\{ \frac{I}{a_1} - CV - \frac{E}{Z}\left[\frac{1}{\omega}\cos(\gamma - \theta) + \frac{1}{a_1}\sin(\gamma - \theta)\right]\right\} \quad (48)$$

$$a_1 = \frac{-R}{2L} + \sqrt{\left(\frac{R}{2L}\right)^2 - \frac{1}{LC}}$$
$$a_2 = \frac{-R}{2L} - \sqrt{\left(\frac{R}{2L}\right)^2 - \frac{1}{LC}} \quad (49)$$

These values, together with Eqs. (41) and (42), inserted in Eqs. (43) and (44) give the solution in a form suitable for the critically damped case. However, if $R^2C < 4L$, then the radicals in Eqs. (47)–(49) become imaginary and these expressions become the complex numbers given in Eqs. (50), whereupon Eq.

$$A_1 = \tfrac{1}{2}(M + jN) \qquad A_2 = \tfrac{1}{2}(M - jN)$$
$$a_1 = -\alpha + j\omega \qquad a_2 = -\alpha - j\omega \quad (50)$$

(43) takes the damped oscillatory form given in Eq. (51).

$$i = \frac{E}{Z}\sin(\omega t + \gamma - \theta) + \epsilon^{-\alpha t}(M\cos\omega t - N\sin\omega t) \quad (51)$$

It is evident from Eq. (43) or Eq. (51) that the final steady-state value, after the transient has died out, is the alternating current of Eq. (40). It is also clear from Eqs. (47) and (48) that the amplitudes of the transient terms depend upon the angle $\gamma$ on the ac applied voltage wave at $t = 0$.

**Resistance and inductance in series.** This may be regarded as a special case of Eq. (43), in which $C = \infty$ (the capacitance short-circuited) and $V = 0$. Consequently, the solution is given by Eq. (52). Thus the

$$i = \frac{E}{Z}\sin(\omega t + \gamma - \theta) + \left[I - \frac{E}{Z}\sin(\gamma - \theta)\right]\epsilon^{-(R/L)t} \quad (52)$$

transient starting from an initial value $I$ decays exponentially to its final ac steady-state value.

There will be no transient if the switch is closed at the angle $\gamma$ on the voltage wave such that Eq. (53) applies.

$$I = \frac{E}{Z}\sin(\gamma - \theta) \quad (53)$$

**Resistance and capacitance in series.** This may be regarded as a special case of Eq. (43), in which $L = 0$ and $I = 0$. Under these conditions the solution is given by Eq. (54) and the capacitor voltage is, by

$$i = \frac{E}{Z}\sin(\omega t + \gamma - \theta) - \left[\frac{V}{R} + \frac{E}{\omega CRZ}\cos(\gamma - \theta)\right]\epsilon^{-t/RC} \quad (54)$$

Eq. (44), defined by Eq. (55). Thus the transient,

$$e_C = \frac{-E}{\omega CZ}\cos(\omega t + \gamma - \theta) + \left[V + \frac{E}{\omega CZ}\cos(\gamma - \theta)\right]\epsilon^{-t/RC} \quad (55)$$

starting with a voltage $V$, decays exponentially to its final ac steady-state value. If the switch is closed at an angle $\gamma$ on the voltage wave such that Eq. (56)

$$V = -\frac{E}{\omega CZ}\cos(\gamma - \theta) \quad (56)$$

applies, there will be no transient.

*Loyal V. Bewley*

***Bibliography.*** J. B. Aidala and L. Katz, *Transients in Electric Circuits*, 1980.

## Electric uninterruptible power system

A system that provides protection against commercial power failure and variations in voltage and frequency. Uninterruptible power systems (UPS) have a wide variety of applications where unpredictable changes in commercial power will adversely affect equipment. This equipment may include computer installations, telephone exchanges, communications networks, motor and sequencing controls, electronic cash registers, hospital intensive care units, and a host of others. The uninterruptible power system may be used on-line between the commercial power and the sensitive load to provide transient free well-regulated power, or off-line and switched in only when commercial power fails.

**Types of systems.** There are three basic types of uninterruptible power system. These are, in order of complexity, the rotary power source, the standby power source, and the solid-state uninterruptible power system.

***Rotary power source.*** The rotary power source consists of a battery-driven dc motor that is mechanically connected to an ac generator. The battery is kept in a charged state by a battery charger that is connected to the commercial power line. In the event of a commercial power failure, the battery powers the dc motor which mechanically drives the ac generator. The sensitive load draws its power from the ac generator and operates through the outage.

***Standby power source.*** The standby power source (**Fig. 1**) consists of a battery connected to a dc-to-ac static inverter. The inverter provides ac power for the sensitive load through a switch. A battery charger, once again, keeps the battery on full charge. Normally, the load operates directly from the commercial

**Fig. 1. Standby power source. (*Topaz Electronics*)**

Fig. 2. A 250-kW on-line automatic reverse-transfer uninterruptible power system.

power line. In the event of commercial power failure, the switch transfers the sensitive load to the output of the inverter.

***Solid-state system.*** The solid-state uninterruptible power system has a general configuration much like that of the standby power system with one important exception. The sensitive load operates continually from the output of the static inverter. This means that all variations on the commercial power lines are cleaned and regulated through the output of the uninterruptible power system. A commercial power line, known as a bypass, is provided around the uninterruptible power system through a switch. Should the uninterruptible power system fail at some point, the commercial power is automatically transferred to the sensitive load through the switch. This scheme is known as an on-line automatic reverse-transfer uninterruptible power system (**Fig. 2**).

**Subsystems.** An uninterruptible power system consists of four major subsystems (**Fig. 3**): a method to put energy into a storage system, a battery charger; an energy storage system, the battery; a system to convert the stored energy into a usable form, the static inverter; and a circuit that electrically connects the sensitive load to either the output of the uninterruptible power system or to the commercial power line, the transfer switch.

***Battery charger.*** The purpose of the battery charger, also called the rectifier charger, is to deliver the power required to drive the static inverter and to charge the battery. When the commercial power line is present, the charger circuit supplies all the power used by the inverter and maintains the battery at full charge. Additionally the charger is sized to allow a safety margin for overload conditions at the output of the static inverter. Uninterruptible power systems that have a very long battery charge time require a charger that is only slightly larger than that of the inverter. In an uninterruptible power system where a short recharge time is required, the charger becomes much larger.

The battery charger is generally of the float type and exhibits very-well-regulated output voltage over a wide output current demand. This tight regulation is performed through the use of silicon controlled rectifiers for voltage regulation and silicon rectifiers to convert ac to dc. Current limiting is built into the circuit to protect the charger. The rating of the charger is determined by the requirements of the static inverter and the current necessary to recharge the battery after an uninterruptible power system has gone through a commercial power outage. *See Semiconductor rectifier.*

***Batteries.*** The battery used on an uninterruptible power system is sized to provide power to the inverter any time that the commercial power is removed. Power may be provided for anywhere from a few seconds to an hour or more. The battery necessary for power is dependent upon the sensitive load to be powered and the desired backup time.

The batteries are arranged in a series of racks called a battery bank. Each battery is made up of individual cells containing lead alloy plates and an electrolyte. Conductor size between batteries and current to be

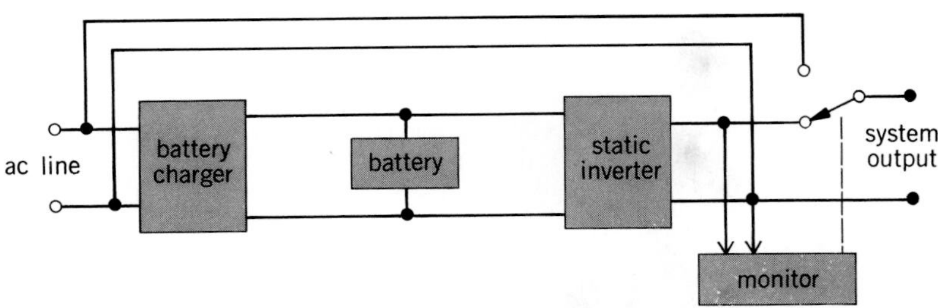


Fig. 3. Block diagram of an on-line automatic reverse transfer uninterruptible power system, showing subsystems. (*Topaz Electronics*)

handled by the static inverter determine the battery bank voltage. Small uninterruptible power systems use low voltages, while large uninterruptible power systems use battery banks of several hundred volts. In the smaller uninterruptible power systems the battery bank may be mounted adjacent to or inside the system.

Batteries may be any one of four different types. They are, in order of their frequency of use: lead antimony, nickel cadmium, gel electrolyte, and lead calcium. The cells within the lead antimony battery contain grids constructed of an alloy of lead and antimony and are surrounded by an electrolyte of sulfuric acid. This type of battery requires specialized charging techniques and a high level of maintenance. The nickel cadmium battery offers a high storage level at high cost. It is best used where the battery bank is subject to extremes of cold and physical space constraints. Once again, specialized charging techniques are required for this type of battery. The gel electrolyte type of battery is usually used in smaller uninterruptible power system installations where voltage and current demands will be at a relatively low level. Although generally more expensive than a liquid electrolyte lead acid battery, it is sealed and maintenance-free. In the lead calcium battery each cell uses calcium alloyed with lead and is filled with an electrolyte of sulfuric acid. This battery type has wider recharge tolerances, longer life, and substantially lower maintenance.

***Static inverter.*** The purpose of the static inverter is to change the dc voltage derived from the battery charger or battery bank to an ac voltage in order to power the sensitive load. The static inverter determines the quality of power used to drive the sensitive load. The ac output voltage must be stable and free from all interruptions. It is the most important subsystem of the uninterruptible power system. If the inverter should fail, the system is out of operation.

The most common static inverter types are, in order of complexity, the ferroresonant type, the quasi-square-wave type, the pulse-width-modulated type, and the step-wave type. The ferroresonant approach starts with a square-wave inverter system and a tuned output transformer. The output transformer performs all filtering, voltage regulation, and current limiting with magnetic regulation, allowing for the design of a very simple inverter. This technique is generally found in smaller, lower-power uninterruptible power systems. The quasi-square-wave approach uses a true electronic regulation technique. It consists of two square waves superimposed on each other to approximate the form of an ac sine wave. Regulation is achieved with a silicon controlled rectifier bridge and control circuit that change the relationship between the two square waves. This changes the pulse width and amplitude of the square wave, achieving regulation. An output LC filter is employed to filter and wave-shape the output sine wave. The pulse-width-modulated approach is essentially a square-wave inverter operating at high frequency. The pulse width, and not the amplitude, of the square wave is adjusted to approximate the sine wave. Once again, output filtering is employed to shape the output waveform. The stepped-wave approach is an extension of the pulse-width-modulated approach. Several pulses are provided per half cycle of the sine wave and are combined to develop an output voltage resembling a sine wave that needs very little filtering. This approach is complex and is found only in high-powered uninterruptible power system units. *See Electric filter; Function generator; Pulse modulation; Transformer.*

***Transfer switch.*** The switch that connects the sensitive load to either the inverter or the commercial power line is called the transfer switch. The major function of the switch is to provide an alternate source of ac power to the critical load should any of the components in the uninterruptible power system fail. The position of the switch is controlled by a monitor circuit as shown in Fig. 3. Generally the switch in an uninterruptible power system is a high-speed solid-state device that can transfer the load from one ac source to another with little or no break in power. The switch may be designed for uninterrupted make-before-break or interrupted break-before-make transfers.

*John Sullivan*

***Bibliography.*** *AC Power Handbook of Problems and Solutions*, 1979; K. G. Brill, *Mini-Micro Syst.*, 10(7):38–45, July 1977; N. L. Conger, *Instrum. Technol.*, 20(9):57–63, September 1973; J. J. Waterman, *Specifying Eng.*, 43(2):60–64, February 1980.

## Electrical breakdown

A large, ususally abrupt rise in electric current in the presence of a small increase in electric voltage. Breakdown may be intentional and controlled or it may be accidental. Lightning is the most familiar example of breakdown.

**Breakdown in gases and solids.** In a gas, such as the atmosphere, the potential gradient may become high enough to accelerate the naturally present ions to velocities that cause further ionization upon collision with atoms. If the region of ionization does not extend between oppositely charged electrodes, the process is corona discharge. If the region of ionization bridges the gap between electrodes, thereby breaking down the insulation provided by the gas, the process is ionization discharge. When controlled by the ballast of a fluorescent lamp, for example, the process converts electric power to light. In a gas tube the process provides controlled rectification. *See Arc discharge; Breakdown potential; Corona discharge; Electric spark; Electrical conduction in gases; Glow discharge; Ionization.*

In a solid, such as an insulator, when the electric field gradient exceeds $10^6$ V/cm, valence bonds between atoms are ruptured and current flows. Such a disruptive current heats the solid abruptly; the rate of local temperature rise may fracture the insulator, the high temperature may carbonize or otherwise decompose the insulation, or as occasionally happens when lightning strikes a tree, the heat may ignite the insulator.

In a semiconductor if the applied backward or reverse potential across a junction reaches a critical level, current increases rapidly with further rise in voltage. This avalanche characteristic is used for voltage regulation in the Zener diode. In a transistor the breakdown sets limits to the maximum instantaneous voltage that can safely be applied between collector and emitter. When the internal space charge extends from collector junction through the base to the emitter junction, even a voltage below the avalanche level can produce a short circuit, in which case the phenomenon is termed punch-through. *SEE SEMICONDUCTOR; TRANSISTOR; ZENER DIODE.*

*Frank H. Rockett*

**Laser-induced breakdown in gases.** For sufficiently high intensities, laser radiation can ionize (or breakdown) the gas atoms or molecules through which it is propagating. The laser radiation intensity required to produce ionization is dependent on the wavelength of the light and on the duration of the laser pulses as well as the gas species and pressure. In general, the breakdown by laser radiation can occur by two different mechanisms, a cascade- or collision-induced ionization, or a multiple-photon absorption process. The most often encountered mechanism is the cascade process, but multiple-photon ionization can be important under certain conditions.

***Multiple-photon ionization.*** Multiple-photon ionization occurs when an atom absorbs directly from the laser radiation field a sufficient number of photons to ionize the atom. The number of photons required is simply the ionization potential of the atom divided by the energy of a photon. For example, the photon energy of the ruby laser at 0.69-micrometer wavelength is 1.78 eV. Therefore, the multiple-photon ionization of argon having an ionization potential of 15.8 eV requires the simultaneous absorption of nine photons. Because of the nature of this process, the ionization is strongly dependent on the laser intensity and wavelength. Experimental measurements of multiple-photon ionization have shown that the threshold for air at pressures below 100 torr (2 psi or 13 kilopascals) is $10^{18}$ W/m$^2$ ($10^{17}$ W/ft$^2$) for a 50-picosecond-duration-pulse, 0.69-$\mu$m-wavelength laser. Multiple-photon ionization can be important for laser-induced breakdown at short wavelengths, short pulse durations, and low gas pressures. *SEE IONIZATION POTENTIAL.*

***Cascade breakdown.*** For the cascade breakdown process, a free electron is accelerated in the radiation field of the laser, but only gains an increment of energy upon collision with atoms. This energy absorption continues until the electron has sufficient energy to ionize an atom by an inelastic collision, producing a second electron. The two electrons then gain additional energy from the field, producing four electrons and so forth. Under breakdown conditions this process continues until the gas is fully ionized. An electron gaining energy from the laser radiation field can also lose energy by processes such as electronic excitation of atoms, or electrons can be lost from the breakdown process by diffusion out of the laser beam or by recombination or by attachment to form negative ions. The rate of ionization necessary to overcome these loss processes then defines the breakdown threshold intensity.

***Breakdown threshold.*** Since high-intensity lasers are usually pulsed devices, an important parameter affecting the breakdown threshold is the duration of the laser pulse. If the laser pulse is long compared to the characteristic electron-loss time, breakdown occurs when the rate of electron production just exceeds the losses; breakdown is determined by the laser intensity and is independent of the laser pulse duration. If the laser pulse is short relative to the characteristic loss times, breakdown occurs when there is sufficient fluence (energy per unit area) in the pulse to generate full ionization of the gas. For air at atmospheric pressure and large-diameter beams (such that electron diffusion is not important), the threshold is fluence-dependent for pulses less than approximately $10^{-7}$ s and is intensity-dependent for pulses having a longer duration. As an example, for air at atmospheric pressure and laser beams larger in diameter than $4 \times 10^{-3}$ in. ($10^{-2}$ cm), the threshold fluence for the 10.6-$\mu$m carbon dioxide ($CO_2$) laser wavelength is $10^5$ joules/m$^2$ ($10^4$ joules/ft$^2$) for pulse durations less than $10^{-7}$ s, and for longer pulses the intensity threshold is $3 \times 10^{13}$ W/m$^2$ ($3 \times 10^{12}$ W/ft$^2$). These theoretically predicted values have been experimentally verified.

***Conditions for occurrence.*** Two important factors affecting the occurrence of breakdown are the source of the initiating electron and the presence of aerosol particles. The electron required for initiating the cascade process must be provided by some mechanism other than the cascade, such as photoionization from natural causes or a spark or discharge. For visible-wavelength laser-induced breakdown, the initial electron can be the result of multiple-photon absorption ionization of impurities, but for long-wavelength radiation, certainly 10.6 $\mu$m, an external source must provide it. Particulate matter, such as naturally occurring aerosols in the atmosphere, can have a dramatic effect on the breakdown threshold of gases. For particles of 0.1 $\mu$m and larger, the interaction of the laser radiation with the particle vaporizes the particle, ionizes the vapor, and subsequently ionizes the surrounding gas. The threshold for this process can be several orders of magnitude lower than the threshold for gas breakdown in the absence of aerosols.

***Pressure dependence.*** The laser-induced gas breakdown has an interesting pressure dependence. The rate of laser energy absorption by free electrons increases with pressure because of the increase in the electron-atom collision frequency. This energy absorption increase continues as gas pressure increases until the collision frequency equals the oscillatory frequency of the laser radiation field. For pressures above this level, the rate of energy absorption decreases with increasing pressure, and the breakdown approaches that induced by a constant electric field in the high pressure limit. Therefore, there is a minimum in a plot of the threshold as a function of pressure that occurs when the collision frequency equals the oscillatory frequency. As an example, for atmospheric air and 10.6-$\mu$m-wavelength radiation this minimum occurs at approximately 44 atm (650 psi or 4.5 megapascals).

For gas pressures lower than the minimum, the gas breakdown threshold varies as the inverse square of the wavelength; that is, the shorter the wavelength, the more difficult it is to break down the gas. This behavior has been verified for wavelengths from 0.69 to 10.6 $\mu$m. The threshold for gas breakdown at pressures above the minimum is independent of the laser wavelength.

***Applications.*** Laser-induced gas breakdown is important as a limitation for propagating high-intensity laser radiation, and as a source for the production of a high-density, high-temperature plasma for a number of applications. Gas breakdown represents the first step in research leading to the study of laser-generated controlled fusion. The plasma produced by laser-induced breakdown can be used as a convenient source for soft x-rays and an intense source of ultraviolet or visible radiation for a fast-rise-time light source. *SEE LASER.*

*David C. Smith*

## Electrical communications

The science and technology by which information is collected from an originating source, transformed into electric currents or fields, transmitted over electrical networks or through space to another point, and reconverted into a form suitable for interpretation by a receiving entity.

**Sources.** Information to be transmitted comes from many sources. Some sources produce essentially continuously varying signals. Examples are speech, music, the output of TV cameras, and sensors of temperature, pressure, and the like. Others produce signals whose distinguishing characteristic is that they are on or off. Examples are the hand telegraph key, many operations of computers, above-or-below sensors of temperature, pressure, and so on.

**Transducers.** For transmission over an electrical communication channel, the original physical manifestation must be transformed into an analogous electrical signal—a speech sound in air by a telephone transmitter, variations in light intensity in a scanned picture by a television camera, temperature observations by the opening and closing of the switch of a thermostat. SEE TRANSDUCER.

**Information theory.** Many workers, especially the pioneers R. V. L. Hartley, N. Wiener and C. E. Shannon, have striven for a mathematical definition of information applicable to all the various sources, in a form that could be directly related to the fundamental characteristics of an electrical communication channel. The information unit chosen is the bit—an abbreviation of binary digit—which is the specification of a choice between only two alternatives, such as "yes" or "no". Finer gradations needed to describe the output from a continuously varying signal source can be determined by a sufficient but definite number of such choices or bits. Hartley and Shannon showed that the maximum practicable capacity $C$ which a communication channel can deliver is $C = B \log_2 (1 + S/N)$ bits/s, where $B$ is the bandwidth in hertz, and $S/N$ is the power ratio of the signal to the noise at the receiving end. Bandwidth and received signal-to-noise ratio are thus the fundamental characteristics of the electrical communication channel, however implemented. SEE BANDWIDTH REQUIREMENTS; ELECTRICAL NOISE; INFORMATION THEORY; SIGNAL-TO-NOISE RATIO.

**Transmission media.** Media commonly used for electrical communication can be divided into two classes: (1) Those carrying electrical currents, such as a pair of wires or coaxial cable. (2) Those in which a transducer must be used to change electrical currents into a form suited to the medium. Examples are electromagnetic fields in space, such as radio, for which the antennas are the transducers; electromagnetic fields in guiding structures, such as a waveguide; pressure waves in water (sonar); light waves in space or optical fibers. The various media have characteristics that are very different; relating these characteristics to the underlying physics is a very important field of study. But with appropriate transducers, the different media are simply alternative choices for carrying electrical communication channels. SEE ANTENNA; COAXIAL CABLE; COMMUNICATIONS CABLE; ELECTROMAGNETIC WAVE TRANSMISSION; MICROWAVE TRANSMISSION LINES; OPTICAL COMMUNICATIONS; SONAR; TRANSMISSION LINES; WAVEGUIDE.

**Network configurations.** Networks may be configured in several ways. Perhaps the most common is a channel between point A and point B. These may be direct connections for relatively long periods of time. They may, as in the telephone network, be switched on a call or message basis among the very large number of points available. Most point-to-point channels carry information in both directions. SEE SWITCHING SYSTEMS (COMMUNICATIONS).

Another configuration is a treelike structure in which the channel from one source is divided and subdivided to connect to many receivers. A cable television (CATV) system is an example of this type of configuration. Generally, though not always, the tree structures are one-way. SEE CLOSED-CIRCUIT TELEVISION.

The third configuration is typified by radio and TV broadcasting: a single source sends out radio waves, and any number of receivers in the area can pick them up on a one-way basis.

**Multilink channels.** The simplest channels are those having amplification, if any, only at the ends. One example is a telephone call to a neighbor involving only a few miles of wire between telephone instruments. Another is the radio channel from an astronaut on the Moon back to Earth. But whatever the transmission medium, the signal becomes weaker with distance, dropping nearer to the inevitable noise in the medium, thus reducing the $S/N$ ratio, and so limiting the information-carrying capacity of the channel. It becomes desirable to place one or more amplifiers at periodic intervals along the channel to raise the signal power and hence maintain the desired $S/N$ at the receiving end. For cable channels thousands of miles long, it would be completely impractical to pour in enough signal power at one end to have a useful $S/N$ at the other, whereas amplifiers with quite small power output at appropriate intervals can be satisfactory. Of course, the problems of designing amplifiers such that hundreds or thousands can be operated in tandem are themselves formidable. SEE AMPLIFIER.

**Frequency division multiplex.** Radio broadcasting is the best-known example of many channels sharing a common medium. Each transmitter is assigned a position in the frequency spectrum and is permitted to occupy a specified bandwidth. The receivers include selective networks or filters, which, when tuned to a selected channel, accept that channel and reject the others. This is an example of sharing the common medium by dividing the available frequency spectrum among the sharing channels, a technique known as frequency division multiplex. The process of shifting the input signal to the assigned frequency slot is called modulation, and the inverse process at the receiving end is called demodulation. The same processes are applied to the sharing of a common wire or coaxial cable medium. SEE ELECTRIC FILTER.

In amplitude modulation (AM), the amplitude of a steadily applied, continuous wave (carrier) is varied in accordance with the amplitude of the input signal. Mathematical analysis of the resulting wave shows that it includes three components: a large component of the carrier frequency, an upper sideband with a frequency width equal to that of the input signal, and an identical lower sideband. Obviously, all of the desired information is included in either sideband, so it is not necessary to transmit either of the other two components.

On cable systems, where the available useful bandwidth is limited, only one sideband is sent. This requires extra complexity of equipment, which is well justified by the more efficient utilization of the cable and its amplifiers. However, in radio broadcasting, the overriding consideration is to simplify the millions of home receivers, so double sideband is sent. *See* Amplitude modulation; Single sideband.

E. L. Armstrong pioneered the use of frequency modulation (FM). In this process, the steadily applied carrier wave is varied in frequency (rather than amplitude) according to the amplitude of the input signal. The resulting output wave occupies more bandwidth than with amplitude modulation, but it can be received successfully with a poorer *S/N* ratio. The system is used in radio broadcasting in the FM band (88–108 MHz) and has found wide application in many radio communication systems. *See* Frequency modulation.

In both AM and FM frequency division multiplex, the amplitude of the input signal controls the output. Hence they are well adapted to carry the continuously varying inputs like speech. However, the on-off sources require some special treatment to adapt them to the essentially analog nature of AM or FM. *See* Modulation.

**Time division multiplex.** There is another way for a multiplicity of channels to share a common medium, called time division multiplex. Each channel is assigned a short time slot during which it occupies the whole available bandwidth, with the channels occupying time slots in turn. When all channels have had their turn, a frame has been completed, and the roll call is repeated. Obviously, there has to be an identifying symbol at the beginning of each frame, so that the channel time slots can be identified.

It is not immediately evident that a continuously varying input signal can be transmitted through these repetitive, short time slots. However, H. Nyquist showed mathematically that if the amplitude of a wave is sampled for short intervals at a rate at least twice that of the highest frequency in the input, the wave can be reproduced without distortion from the samples. For speech, this "Nyquist rate" is commonly accepted to be 8 kHz, thus setting the length of the frame at 125 microseconds. The short samples of the varying amplitude of the input wave could be sent directly in the allotted time slots, a technique known as pulse amplitude modulation (PAM). But consideration of the tradeoffs that exist between bandwidth and *S/N* in the shared medium usually leads to more complicated methods. One example is pulse code modulation (PCM). The amplitude of the sample is not sent directly. Instead, a code of an appropriate number of pulses is sent, with one code word defining one amplitude. This involves a quantization of the signal, so that it is necessary to use enough pulses in the code word to keep distortion at an acceptable level. *See* Pulse modulation.

Clearly, the processing of continuously varying input sources is much more complicated than in frequency-division AM or FM systems. It involves sampling, quantizing, coding, and organizing into words and frames, with framing symbols and precise timing. When only vacuum tubes were available, the economics of the resulting tradeoffs were completely unfavorable. With the advent of the transistor, and the subsequent flowering of the solid-state art into integrated circuits, the whole economic picture changed dramatically. Complicated processing could be accomplished by tiny, inexpensive chips. The extra complexity in many cases was well justified by savings in the cable system and its amplifiers.

At the same time, there was a rapidly growing demand for communication of essentially on-off signals, as between computers and machines. The time division multiplex is very well suited to these signals, with little processing. For these reasons, there is a very rapidly expanding use of time division systems. However, the choice of method to be used is very complex, depending on the signals to be transmitted, the medium to be used, and the economics of the state of the art. In the case of radio, considerations of national policy affect the choices, since the radio spectrum is a limited and valuable national resource. *See* Electronics; Integrated circuits; Transistor.

For a discussion of major forms of electrical communication systems *see* Radar; Radio; Television.

*A. C. Dickieson*

**Bibliography.** Communications, special edition of *Sci. Amer.*, September 1972; S. Haykin, *Communication Systems*, 2d ed., 1983; G. Kennedy, *Electronic Communication Systems*, 2d ed., 1977; A. Marcus and W. Marcus, *Elements of Radio*, 6th ed., 1973; P. Z. Peebles, *Communication System Principles*, 1976; J. R. Pierce and E. C. Posner, *Introduction to Communication Science and Systems*, 1980; R. L. Shrader, *Electronic Communication*, 4th ed., 1980; H. Taub and D. L. Schilling, *Principles of Communication Systems*, 1971.

## Electrical conduction in gases

The process by means of which a net charge is transported through a gaseous medium. It encompasses a variety of effects and modes of conduction, ranging from the Townsend discharge at one extreme to the arc discharge at the other. The current in these two cases ranges from a fraction of 1 microampere in the first to thousands of amperes in the second. It covers a pressure range from less than $10^{-4}$ atm (10 pascals) to greater than 1 atm ($10^5$ pascals). *See* Arc discharge; Townsend discharge.

In general, the feature which distinguishes gaseous conduction from conduction in a solid or liquid is the active part which the medium plays in the process. Not only does the gas permit the drift of free charges from one electrode to the other, but the gas itself may be ionized to produce other charges which can interact with the electrodes to liberate additional charges. Quite apparently, the current voltage characteristic may be nonlinear and multivalued. *See* Semiconductor.

The applications of the effects encountered in this area are of significant commercial and scientific value. A few commercial applications are thyratrons, gaseous rectifiers, ignitrons, glow tubes, and gas-filled phototubes. These tubes are used in power supplies, control circuits, pulse production, voltage regulators, and heavy-duty applications such as welders. In addition, there are gaseous conduction devices widely used in research problems. Some of these are ion sources for mass spectrometers and nuclear accelerators, ionization vacuum gages, radiation detection and measurement instruments, and thermonuclear devices for the production of power.

The discussion of this complicated process will be divided into two parts. The first will deal with the basic effects involved, including production and loss of charges within the region and the motion of charges in the gas. The second part will deal with the mechanism of conduction.

**Basic effects.** To produce gaseous conduction, two conditions must obtain. First, there must be a source of free charges. Second, there must be an electric field to produce a directed motion of these charges. Considering the first of these, one finds that the free charge concentration is a result of a number of processes which produce and remove charges.

***Sources of free charges.*** In many gaseous devices, a thermionic-emission cathode is included. The process of electron emission from a heated electrode is well known. Closely related to this as a source of electrons is field emission. Here, a strong positive field at a metallic surface lowers the barrier for electron emission. Thus, the electron current from a surface at a given temperature may be significantly increased. *SEE THERMIONIC EMISSION.*

Both of these effects result in electron production. Another effect, photon absorption, may result only in electrons if the absorber is a solid. However, if the photon interacts with a gas molecule or atom, ionization may result and both an electron and a positive ion be obtained. The photon may come from some external source or it may be a secondary effect of the gaseous conduction. It may have a wavelength in the visible, ultraviolet, or x-ray region. *SEE PHOTOELECTRICITY.*

Conduction in flames is largely a result of the thermal production of ionization. This is a specialized field which has long been of interest in chemistry and combustion studies. To produce appreciable thermal ionization, the temperature must be high, as in a flame. If the effective temperature is known, the ionization concentration may be determined from statistical mechanics. Thermal ionization is also of tremendous importance in devices for production of power by thermonuclear processes, and in ion-propulsion equipment. A special form of this is surface ionization, in which a hot surface may cause ionization of a gas atom that comes in contact with it.

Another source of ionization is particle radiation due to cosmic rays, radioactive material in the walls or in the gas, or particles produced from an external source. These particles may then produce an ionized track in the gas. An example is the ionization produced by an α-particle from a polonium source in an ionization chamber.

In most of these methods of charge production, the sources are primary. That is, the presence of other free charges is not important in the production of ionization or electrons. Other processes are secondary in origin, although they may be of prime importance. It was pointed out that photons could originate either externally or as a secondary effect. Field emission could be a secondary effect, also. Other methods of ionization, however, are generally thought of as being secondary in origin. Ionization of the gas by electron impact is such a case. Here free electrons may gain enough energy in an electric field to interact with an atomic or molecular electron to produce an ion pair.

Cumulative ionization is an extension of ionization by impact. If the original electron and its offspring gain enough energy so each may produce another electron, and if this process is repeated over and over, the result is called an avalanche, and the ionization thus produced is referred to as cumulative ionization. This is the basis for particle detection in some ionization devices.

Another secondary source is electron emission from either electron or positive ion bombardment of a surface. This should not be confused with thermionic emission resulting from heating under bombardment. *SEE SECONDARY EMISSION.*

Other sources which may be important are atomic collisions, sputtering, and collisions of the second kind. In the first case, an atom or heavy ion may collide with an atom to produce ionization. This is quite unlikely until an energy of many times the ionization energy is obtained. The second is somewhat analogous to secondary electron emission. Here the positive ions strike a surface and knock out atoms or groups of atoms. Some of these come off as ions. In the third case, an excited atom may interact with an atom or molecule which is chemically different and has an ionization potential lower than the excitation potential of the excited atom. The result may be the decay of the excited state with ionization of the struck molecule or atom. Symbolically, this is shown by reaction (1), where A* is the excited atom, B the struck

$$A^* + B \longrightarrow A + B^+ + e^- \qquad (1)$$

atom or molecule, and $e^-$ an electron. *SEE EXCITATION POTENTIAL; IONIZATION POTENTIAL; SPUTTERING.*

***Free-charge removal.*** The net free-charge concentration is a balance between charge-production and charge-removal processes. Recombination is one such process. Here, an electron or heavy negative ion and a positive ion may recombine. The energy transition may appear as electromagnetic radiation or may be carried off by a third body, if one is present. There are a wide variety of conditions which may lead to recombination. Where the temperature and electric field are high, the recombination will occur predominantly at the walls.

The method of charge removal is important from the aspect of conduction, however. If the charges move to the appropriate electrodes under the influence of the field and there recombine, then they contribute to the current. If they simply diffuse to the walls and recombine there with ions of the opposite sign, or if they recombine in the gas volume, they may not appear as part of the external current.

***Motion of the charges.*** The motion of the charges within the gas will be largely influenced by the potential function. For the usual regular geometries, this could be calculated in principle if there were no charges present. However, in a gas with free charges distributed throughout, the problem is quite different. The charges modify the charge-free potential, but the potential itself determines how the charge will move. The motion of the charges further modifies the potential and so on. Although the situation can be described physically by Poisson's equation, it is generally impractical to carry out an analysis. As a practical result, the potential function must be determined by measurements which are made with probes. This requires careful procedures to obtain significant results.

***Diffusion of ions.*** Ion diffusion is a type of random motion which is always present and is the result of thermal or agitation energy. The randomness of the motion is brought about by the many collisions with molecules and other ions. A great difference exists in the motions of electrons and heavy ions. Because of low mass, electrons are easily deflected, so they move erratically. They diffuse badly, and follow field lines only generally. Again because the mass is small, an electron can give up appreciable energy only in an inelastic collision, in which excitation or ionization takes place. Hence, electron agitation and diffusion will be much greater in a pure inert gas than in a gas having many low-energy molecular states. Conversely, heavy ions exchange energy effectively at every collision. Diffusion is much less, so that they follow the electric field lines more closely than do electrons.

**Mechanism of conduction.** The ionic mobility $\mu$ relates drift velocity $v$ to electric field $X$ by Eq. (2).

$$v = \mu X \tag{2}$$

For electrons, the mobility is high, and a drift velocity of $10^6$ cm/s or greater may be obtained. The electronic mobility is not a true constant, but varies with field, pressure, temperature, and gas composition. For heavy ions, the mobility is much more nearly constant, but is still dependent on these quantities to some extent. Drift velocities are usually of the order of $10^3$–$10^4$ cm/s. Thus, in a typical conduction device, an electron may move from one electrode to the other before a heavy ion is displaced appreciably.

It would appear from the foregoing that if accurate information about the important processes existed, one could predict the characteristics of the conduction process under given conditions. Unfortunately this is not the case. Generally, the situation is so complicated that the theory can yield only qualitative predictions. Accordingly, most of the information concerning the various forms of gaseous conduction is empirical. In the present description, it will be possible to mention the main features of a few of these modes.

The **illustration** shows a sample voltage-current characteristic for a two-electrode device with constant pressure. It is assumed that there is a constant source of ionization which could be any of the primary sources previously discussed. In region $A$, the current first rises and then over a limited range is relatively constant as the voltage across the electrodes is increased. The initial rise is the result of the collection of charges which were either recombining or diffusing to the walls. The nearly constant current region is the result of the collection of almost all of the charges.

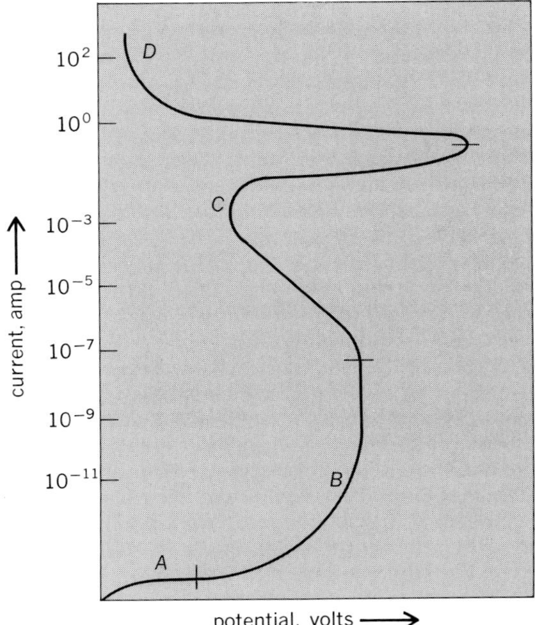


**Current-potential characteristics for a two-electrode device with constant pressure.**

In region $B$, further increase in voltage produces an increase in current. Here, ionization by electron impact is occurring. The situation is described by specifying that each free electron makes $\alpha$ additional ion pairs in traveling 1 cm in the direction of the field. The number of ion pairs produced per second in 1 cm at a distance $x$ from the cathode (assuming parallel plate electrodes) is given by Eq. (3), where $n_0$ is a

$$n = n_0 e^{\alpha x} \tag{3}$$

constant depending on the initial number of electrons. This is a form of the Townsend equation, and $\alpha$ is the first Townsend cofficient. In the region $B$ in the figure, the increase in current represents an increase in $\alpha$. Near the end of this region, the current increases more rapidly with applied field. Here, additional effects are taking place, such as the photoelectric process and secondary emission. This situation is described by Eq. (4), where $\beta$ is the second Townsend

$$i = i_0 \frac{(\alpha - \beta)\, e^{(\alpha - \beta)x}}{\alpha - \beta\, e^{(\alpha - \beta)x}} \tag{4}$$

coefficient, $i_0$ is the initial electron current at the cathode, and $i$ is the anode current as a function of plate separation $x$; $\beta$ is also a function of electric field.

At the end of the region, the slope becomes infinite, and if the external resistance is not too large, the current will jump in a discontinuous fashion. The transition is referred to as a spark, and the potential at which it occurs is the breakdown or sparking potential. The region $B$ is called a Townsend discharge and is not self-sustained. Thus, if the source of primary ionization were removed, the discharge would cease. *SEE BREAKDOWN POTENTIAL; ELECTRIC SPARK.*

As the potential reaches the sparking potential, a transition occurs to the region $C$. This is the self-sustained glow discharge region. Over an extensive current range, the voltage drop remains substantially constant. During the current increase, a glow occurs at the cathode, and at the upper end of the range, the cathode is completely covered. At this point, a further current increase can be achieved only if the potential drop across the discharge is increased. This portion of the characteristic is known as the abnormal glow. Throughout this portion of the discharge characteristic curve, secondary effects are quite important. Particularly vital are the effects of cumulative ionization and secondary emission at the cathode. *SEE GLOW DISCHARGE.*

Further increase in current leads to another mode of discharge, the arc. This is shown as region $D$ in the illustration. Characteristic of this mode is the low cathode potential fall and the very high current density. It is generally felt that the predominant effect in the production of the large number of electrons at the cathode necessary for the arc is thermionic emission. This is consistent with the very high temperatures known to exist either generally or locally on the cathode. Although the arc type of discharge has very great commercial value, the mechanism of its operation is not very well understood.

In addition to these general types of conduction,

there are very special cases of considerable interest. Some of these are the corona discharge, radio-frequency or electrodeless discharge, hot-cathode discharge, and discharges in the presence of a magnetic field.

*Glenn H. Miller*

**Bibliography.** J. Beynon, *Conduction of Electricity through Gases*, 1972; J. D. Cobine, *Gaseous Conductors*, 1941.

## Electrical impedance

The measure of the opposition that an electrical circuit presents to the passage of a current when a voltage is applied. In quantitative terms, it is the complex ratio of the voltage to the current in an alternating-current (ac) circuit.

The **illustration** shows a generalized ac circuit,

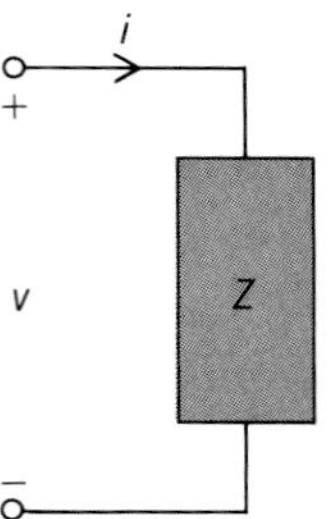


**Generalized alternating-current circuit.**

which may be composed of the interconnection of various types of circuit elements. If the voltage is $v = V_0 \sin(\omega t + \theta)$ and the current is $i = I_0 \sin(\omega t + \beta)$, then the circuit can be analyzed by considering a complex voltage $V = V_0 e^{j\theta}$ and a complex current $I = I_0 e^{j\beta}$. The impedance of the circuit is then given by Eq. (1), and $Z$ is a complex number given by Eq. (2). $R$, the real part of the impedance, is the resis-

$$Z = \frac{V}{I} \qquad (1)$$

$$Z = R + jX \qquad (2)$$

tance of the circuit, and $X$, the imaginary part of the impedance, is the reactance of the circuit. The units of impedance are ohms. SEE ELECTRICAL RESISTANCE; REACTANCE.

The modulus of the impedance is given by Eq. (3),

$$|Z| = \sqrt{R^2 + X^2} \qquad (3)$$

and this is the ratio of the maximum voltage to the maximum current. The phase angle of the impedance is given by Eq. (4), and this is the angle by which the

$$\psi = \tan^{-1} \frac{X}{R} \qquad (4)$$

current waveform lags the voltage waveform. The power factor of the circuit is $\cos \psi$ and is given by Eq. (5). The power dissipated in the circuit is given by Eq. (6).

$$\cos \psi = \frac{R}{\sqrt{R^2 + X^2}} \qquad (5)$$

$$P = \tfrac{1}{2}|V|\,|I| \cos \psi \qquad (6)$$

For a circuit composed of resistors, inductors, and capacitors, $R$ is always positive, but $X$ may be positive or negative. For example, in a circuit consisting of a resistor $R$ and inductor $L$ in series, the impedance at frequency $\omega$ is given by Eq. (7), so $R$ is greater

$$Z = R + jL\omega \qquad (7)$$

than 0 and $X$ is greater than 0. For a circuit consisting of a resistor $R$ and capacitor $C$ in series, the impedance at frequency $\omega$ is given by Eq. (8) so $R$ is greater

$$\begin{aligned} Z &= R + \frac{1}{jC\omega} \\ &= R - j\frac{1}{C\omega} \end{aligned} \qquad (8)$$

than 0 and $X$ is less than 0. SEE ALTERNATING-CURRENT CIRCUIT THEORY.

*J. O. Scanlan*

## Electrical instability

A persistent condition of unwanted self-oscillation in an amplifier or other electrical circuit. Instability is usually caused by excessive positive feedback from the output to the input of an active network. If, in an audio-frequency amplifier, instability is at a low audible frequency, the output will contain a putt-putt sound, from which such instability is termed motorboating. The instability may also be at a high audible frequency, or it may be at frequencies outside the audible range. Although such oscillations may not be heard directly, they produce distortion by driving the amplifier beyond its linear range of operation. SEE AMPLIFIER; MOTORBOATING.

Instability can arise if the load on an amplifier has a critical phase or magnitude. Similarly, instability arises in a closed-loop control system if the damping is too light relative to the response time. Such instability may result in the system hunting about a control condition instead of remaining steadily at the condition. SEE NEGATIVE-RESISTANCE CIRCUITS.

In a power distribution system, if the mechanical load on synchronous motors exceeds the steady-state stability limit or if an abruptly changed mechanical load causes the synchronous machines to exceed the transient stabiilty limit, the power system becomes unstable. It can also lose stability from a three-phase short circuit between generators and motors. High-speed circuit breakers and other protective devices guard against such instability. SEE CIRCUIT BREAKER.

*Frank H. Rockett*

## Electrical loading

The addition of inductance to a transmission line in order to improve its transmission characteristics over the required frequency band. Loading coils are often inserted in telephone lines, at spacings as close as 1 mi (1.6 km), to counteract the capacitance of the line and thus make the line impedance more closely equivalent to a pure resistance. Similar coils are used between sections of lines used for carrier transmission. SEE TRANSMISSION LINES.

With coaxial cables and waveguides, loading is placed at the end of the line to absorb all power reaching the end, thereby achieving a nonreflecting termination. The lossy sections used for this purpose may be tapered metal vanes, wedges of lossy dielectric material, or tapered sections of iron-dust core material that partly or completely fill the end of the line. *SEE COAXIAL CABLE; WAVEGUIDE.*

When an antenna is too short to give resonance at the desired frequency, a coil can be inserted in series with the antenna to give the required amount of loading needed for resonance. As an example, practically all auto radios have a loading coil in the antenna circuit, because the usual whip antenna is much too short for broadcast-band frequencies. *SEE ANTENNA.*

*John Markus*

## Electrical measurements

Measurements of the many quantities by which the behavior of electricity is characterized. The International System of Units (SI) is in universal use for all electrical measurements (although not yet for magnetic measurements). Electrical measurements are ultimately based on comparisons with realizations, that is, reference standards, of the various SI units. These reference standards are maintained by the National Bureau of Standards in the United States, and by the national standards laboratories of many other countries.

### DIRECT-CURRENT MEASUREMENTS

Direct-current (dc) measurements include measurements of resistance, voltage, and current in circuits in which a steady current is maintained.

**Resistance measurement.** Resistance is defined as the ratio of voltage to current, and for many conductors this ratio is nearly constant, but depends to a varying extent on temperature, voltage, and other environmental conditions. The best standard resistors are made from wires of special alloys chosen for low dependence on temperature and for stability. Exact equality of resistance can be established by an equal-arm Wheatstone bridge, using parallel resistors to provide for variations, and these parallel resistors can be of much lower accuracy than the resistors being compared. Higher values of resistance can thus be built up from the 1-ohm standard level. The use of switched series–parallel networks also provides a very accurate check, usually at resistance ratios of 100:1. The use of dc-comparator instruments, where the ratio measured depends on the ratio of the number of turns on the flux comparators, also provides accurate measurement over the range of resistance from fractions of an ohm to about 100 kΩ. The establishment of a resistance scale over a total range from microhms ($10^{-6}$ Ω) to terohms ($10^{12}$ Ω) is thus established from the 1-Ω standard essentially by a process of counting. *SEE RESISTOR; WHEATSTONE BRIDGE.*

For resistance values below about 1 kΩ, the greatest accuracy is achieved by the use of four-terminal measurements, although this introduces considerable complication into resistive bridges.

Resistors in series produce a value equal to their sum, but resistors in parallel produce a resistance whose reciprocal, called its conductance, is equal to the sum of the conductances of the components. For this reason it is sometimes more convenient to use conductance in siemens, rather than the resistance (in ohms); for example, a resistance of 0.1 Ω is equally well expressed as a conductance of 10 S. *SEE CONDUCTANCE.*

The principal instruments for accurate resistance measurement are bridges derived from the basic Wheatstone bridge, and resistance boxes. The achievement of constant resistance ratios is much easier than that of constant resistance, so that if a bridge is used only to measure the ratio between a standard resistor and an unknown, it need not be constructed of resistors of the high and expensive quality of the standard. When used in this way, many commercial bridges can provide considerably better accuracy than is available by using their built-in reference resistors.

Many digital multirange instruments measure resistance potentiometrically, that is, by measuring the voltage drop across the terminals to which the resistor is connected when a known current is passed through them. The current is then defined by the voltage drop across an internal reference resistor. For high values of resistance, above a megohm, an alternative technique is to measure the integrated current into a capacitor (over a suitably defined time interval) by measuring the final capacitor voltage. Both methods are capable of considerable refinement and extension. *SEE OHMMETER; RESISTANCE MEASUREMENT.*

**Voltage measurement.** The most stable room-temperature voltage standard is still the saturated Weston mercury-cadmium standard cell. There is enormous variation in the stabilities of such standard cells, but the best of them, selected by reference to a Josephson junction system, can provide a voltage of roughly 1.0186 V, which varies by less than 0.1 microvolt per year. They are very sensitive to environmental temperature and to the passage of current; to achieve this performance requires temperature control and measurement to within 1 millikelvin and extremely careful measurements. All national laboratories use these cells as their day-to-day working standards, and generally offer calibration services for standard cells with uncertainties of less than 1 μV. Standard cells are usually measured either by a potentiometer, that is, a resistive divider supplied with a constant current, or by a standard cell comparator in which two cells are connected back to back, and the resulting difference voltage is measured on a potentiometer of very limited range. Since the difference voltage will be very much smaller than the cell voltage, the measurement calls for much less accuracy and is thus easier. *SEE POTENTIOMETER (VOLTAGE METER).*

At the highest levels of accuracy, higher voltages are measured potentiometrically, that is, by using a null detector to compare the measured voltage against the voltage drop across a tapping of a resistive divider, which is standardized (in principle) against a standard cell. Dividers intended for this use up to 2 kV are usually called volt ratio boxes, and sometimes contain built-in self-calibration facilities. Resistive dividers for the accurate measurement of still higher voltages, up to about 500 kV, need increasing care to minimize the effects of the high electric fields, which may give errors due to current leakage through corona discharges. These can be avoided by the use of guarding techniques. *SEE CORONA DISCHARGE.*

Many commercial voltage-measuring instruments use built-in voltage references consisting of semiconductor junctions or Zener diodes. These are much more robust than standard cells, and can vary by as little as only a few parts per million per year. They are also available as laboratory voltage standards and as transfer standards, where their insensitivity to environment gives them considerable advantage over standard cells. *See* Semiconductor diode; Zener diode.

Most dc digital voltmeters, which are the instruments in widest use for voltage measurement, are essentially analog-to-digital converters which are standardized by reference to their built-in reference diodes. Some of these instruments may be microprocessor-controlled, in which case they may be remotely or automatically operated, and may include built-in error correction for linearity over the indicated range. The basic range in most digital voltmeters is between 1 and 10 V near the reference voltage. Other ranges are provided by ranging resistive dividers, or amplifiers where gain is stabilized by feedback resistance ratios. In this way these instruments provide measurements over the approximate range from 10 nanovolts to 10 kV. *See* Digital-to-analog converter; Microprocessor; Voltage measurement; Voltmeter.

**Current measurement.** Direct current measurement at maximum accuracy of currents less than about 1 A is made by measuring the voltage across the potential terminals of a resistor when the current is passed through it. It is important that the resistor has been calibrated under the conditions of use, or that allowances are made for the differences. Higher currents, up to about 50 kA, are best measured by means of a dc current comparator, which accurately provides the ratio of the high current to a much lower one which is measured as above. At lower accuracies, resistive shunts may be used up to about 5000 A, but the effective calibration of such shunts is a difficult process.

At the lowest levels of accuracy, for example, in instrument boards, moving-coil instruments are still widely used for dc measurements. These instruments usually give a full-scale deflection for a current of several milliamperes, and are converted to act as voltmeters by the addition of series resistance, or as ammeters by the addition of shunt conductance. *See* Current measurement.

## Power Frequency Measurements

The principal needs for accurate measurement at power frequencies (usually 60 or 50 Hz) arise from the sale of electrical energy. There are also widespread needs for less accurate measurement for the monitoring and control of generators, distribution systems, and plants.

**Alternating-current voltage and current measurements.** Alternating voltages are established with reference to the dc voltage standards by the use of thermal converters. These are small devices, usually in an evacuated glass envelope, in which the temperature rise of a small heater is compared by means of a thermocouple when heated sequentially by alternating-current (ac) and dc voltages. Suitable series resistors, which can be independently established to be free from variation with frequency, permit direct measurement of power frequency voltages up to about 1 kV. Greater accuracy is provided by multijunction thermal converters, although these are much more difficult and expensive to make. Thermal converters essentially measure the root-mean-square voltage. However, since alternating voltages and currents are fluctuating, the relation between the mean and peak values will depend on the waveform, which may be described in terms of a form factor or harmonic content. For a sinusoidal wave, the root-mean-square value is $0.5^{1/2}$ of the peak value. *See* Thermal converters.

Voltages above a few hundred volts are usually measured by means of a voltage transformer, which is an accurately wound transformer operating under lightly loaded conditions. These transformers are usually calibrated by comparison with a high-voltage capacitative divider, which can be independently evaluated. This permits the precise measurement of the voltage ratio and phase error of the transformer under its specified conditions of use.

The principal instrument for the comparison and generation of variable alternating voltages below about 1 kV is the inductive voltage divider. In principle, this resembles a series of tapped autotransformers connected to give a multidecade arrangement. Inductive voltage dividers are very accurate and stable devices, and at best provide an uncertainty of division of less than 1 in $10^8$. A principal source of error can arise from the accidental magnetization of the high-permeability magnetic cores, and simple demagnetization procedures can guard against this. Such dividers are widely used as the variable elements in bridges or measurement systems.

Alternating currents of less than a few amperes are measured by the voltage drop across a resistor, whose phase angle has been established as adequately small by bridge methods. Higher currents are usually measured through the use of current transformers, which are carefully constructed (often toroidal) transformers operating under near-short-circuited conditions. The performance of a current transformer is established by calibration against an ac current comparator, which establishes precise current ratios by the injection of compensating currents to give an exact flux balance.

Commercial instruments for measurement of ac quantities are usually dc measuring instruments, giving a reading of the voltage obtained from some form of ac–dc transducer. This may be a thermal converter, or a series of diodes arranged to have a square-law response, in which case the indication is substantially the root-mean-square value. Some lower-grade instruments measure the value of the rectified signal, which is usually more nearly related to the peak value.

**Power and energy measurements.** The principal complication in power measurement is that the power is the vector product of the voltage $V$ and current $I$, so a wattmeter is essentially a vector multiplier of these quantities. The wattmeters in widest use are dynamometers, in which the magnetic field is generated by coils energized by the current, and the moving coil carries a current proportional to the voltage. The total deflection is then proportional to the vector product $VI \cos \theta$, where $\theta$ is the phase angle. Such meters, whose accuracy can be confirmed by dc measurements, are used for the calibration of the energy meters which are universally used for the measurement of electricity to consumers as the basis of payment. These energy meters consist of revolving conducting disks driven by the interaction between induced currents due to voltage and current coils. They are remarkable for their accuracy (particularly at low energy levels), stability, and low cost. They are normally very well inside the limits of accuracy prescribed by legal requirements, where these exist.

The great majority of wattmeters work at levels of voltage and current less than about 10 A and 250 V, single phase. High-power levels such as the output from power stations at several hundred megawatts per phase are measured through the use of current and voltage transformers.

Several wattmeters have appeared in which the

multiplication is carried out electronically. In one method a pulse height is determined by the instantaneous value of one variable and the pulse width by the instantaneous value of the other. The integrated energy of the pulse string then gives the power. A second approach is direct sampling of the voltage and current, which are then reduced to digital values. The results of each sample pair are multiplied and stored, and their accumulated total gives the power. Another approach to power measurement is the use of the quarter-squares principle, using the identity below.

$$(V + I\cos\theta)^2 + (V - I\cos\theta)^2 = 4\,VI\cos\theta$$

This enables the use of two square-law devices whose outputs are summed to give a direct power reading. All these approaches have been shown to be capable of producing accuracy comparable to that of the best wattmeters of more conventional design.

#### Audio- and Radio-Frequency Measurements

At the highest level of accuracy, audio-frequency (af) voltages are measured in the same way as at power frequencies through the use of thermal converters, employing inductive voltage dividers to provide variable ratios. Such methods provide uncertainties of about 1 in $10^5$ at 1 kHz, increasing to about 0.1% at 100 kHz.

Both pointer and digital instruments for voltage measurement are similar to those in use at power frequencies. Current measurement is needed less often at these frequencies, and generally only small currents (less than about 1 A) are involved. These can readily be measured through a resistive transducer.

A large number of bridges are available for the measurement of impedance at these frequencies, and most of these are particularly suited to the measurement of particular parameters or ranges of values. The most accurate bridges are those based on transformers and inductive dividers, generally at frequencies below 100 kHz, and using coaxial systems throughout. *See* Capacitance measurement; Inductance measurement; Radio-frequency impedance measurements.

For power measurement, the range of dynamometer wattmeters is usually restricted to frequencies below 10 kHz. Electronic wattmeters, that is, those performing electronic vector multiplication, may often extend to 100 kHz or even up to 1 MHz, but in this frequency range the measurement of power by vector multiplication of voltage and current is superseded by the use of resistive bolometers or calorimeters, which receive a known fraction of the power to be measured, and this approach then extends to and beyond microwave frequencies.

#### Microwave Frequencies

At frequencies above about 300 MHz, where the circuit dimensions become an appreciable fraction of the wavelength, it becomes necessary to use totally enclosed circuits (waveguides), and the measurements of voltage, current, and lumped impedance are replaced by those of wave impedance, reflection and transmission coefficients, voltage standing-wave ratio, attenuation, and power. The measurement techniques, other than for power measurement, are drastically changed. *See* Attenuation (electricity); Microwave impedance measurement; Microwave measurements; Microwave noise standards; Microwave power measurement.

*Cyril H. Dix*

***Bibliography.*** C. H. Dix and A. E. Bailey, Electrical standards of measurement, *Proceedings of the IEE,* vol. 122, no. 10R, October 1975; S. Geczy, *Basic Electrical Measurements,* 1984; B. A. Gregory, *An Introduction to Electrical Instrumentation and Measurement Systems,* 2d ed., 1981; B. Hague, *Alternating Current Bridge Methods,* 5th ed., rev. 1957; F. K. Harris, *Electrical Measurements,* 1983; L. Heiserman, *Electrical and Electron Measuring Instruments*, 1983.

## Electrical noise

Interfering and unwanted currents or voltages in an electrical device or system. Electrical noise, or simply noise, has a significant effect on the design and operation of almost all electrical and optical systems which are used to communicate or process information. Noise is responsible for the familiar static observed on home radio receivers, the clicking sounds on frequency-modulation (FM) radios operating in fringe (near-threshold) areas, and the "snow"-type granularity on the viewing screen of a television receiver displaying a weak signal. In general, noise provides the fundamental limitation to the range over which radio or optical signals can be transmitted and received with integrity. Noise is, therefore, of great importance to the engineers who design and operate such systems.

It is convenient to differentiate between noise which results from human activity and that which is naturally occurring. Noise which results from human activity, such as that generated by an electrical appliance or an automotive ignition, can usually be eliminated or minimized by good design practice (shielding, filtering, equipment location, and so forth). Naturally occurring noise can be further subdivided into that which is irregular or erratic in nature and that which is more or less continuous. An example of noise which is irregular or erratic is that associated with an electrical storm. This type of noise is sometimes dealt with in the system design, but since it is only occasionally present, it does not ordinarily constitute a design limitation. On the other hand, naturally occurring noise which is essentially continuous in time is responsible for the fundamental limitation cited above. The remainder of the article therefore concentrates on this type of noise. *See* Crosstalk; Electric filter; Electrical shielding; Electromagnetic compatibility; Electronic equipment grounding.

**Sources.** Most noise generation is a consequence of the spontaneous fluctuations which occur within matter at the microscopic level. In electrical circuits these fluctuations give rise to what are commonly referred to as thermal noise and shot noise. Thermal noise is generated by the random motion of free electrons in a resistor or any conductor with resistance. The random motion, and thus the noise generated, is proportional to the temperature of the medium. At absolute zero temperature on the Kelvin scale (− 459.67°F), all motion ceases and no noise is generated. Shot noise is most commonly identified with the fluctuations in the current of a vacuum tube caused by the random emission of electrons from its heated cathode. Shot noise is also observed in semiconductor devices as random fluctuations in carrier density when an electric field is applied. There are other types of noise associated with electrical circuits, but shot noise and thermal noise are by far the most important. *See* SEMICONDUCTOR; VACUUM TUBE.

In a system in which signals are transmitted through the atmosphere [for example, amplitude-modulation (AM) or FM radio broadcast, or satellite communications], the receiving system will always receive noise as well as the desired signals. This noise is a result of thermal radiation from the Earth, planets, Sun, Moon, the galaxy (galactic noise), radio-emitting stars, and atmospheric gases. In addition, there is a small background level of thermal radiation, uniformly distributed, which is believed associated with the big bang origin of the universe. All of these noise sources, weighted by the directional characteristics of the receiving antenna, will contribute to the overall system noise.

In an optical communications system, a signal level is represented by a number of energy packets called photons. The mean arrival rate of the photons at the detector is proportional to the optical intensity or signal strength. At the detector (a photodiode), the photons are absorbed, each creating a hole-electron pair and thus a current in which the electrons are randomly positioned in time and in which the mean number of electrons is proportional to the optical intensity. The statistical nature of this process gives rise to fluctuations in the number of photons representative of a given level and, subsequently, the number of electrons generated to represent that level. If the detector has internal gain as in an avalanche photodiode, each hole-electron pair can create additional hole-electron pairs. This process, however, is statistical in nature, resulting in a mean value of gain but giving rise to additional fluctuations in the generated current. *See* MICROWAVE SOLID-STATE DEVICES; OPTICAL COMMUNICATIONS; OPTICAL DETECTORS; PHOTODIODE.

**Mathematical analysis.** Because of the statistical or random nature of noise, noise voltages and currents must be dealt with by using the branch of mathematics that deals with random variables, that is, probability theory. A random variable can be characterized by a probability density function $p(x)$. The definition of $p(x)$ is such that the probability that the random variable $x$ lies between $x_1$ and $x_2$ is given by Eq. (1).

$$\text{Prob}\,(x_1 < x < x_2) = \int_{x_1}^{x_2} p(x)\,dx \qquad (1)$$

Obviously, $p(x)$ can be normalized as shown in Eq. (2). Investigations have shown that fluctuation noise,

$$\int_{-\infty}^{\infty} p(x)\,dx = 1 \qquad (2)$$

in general, has a probability density function which is gaussian or normal, provided that the noise can be represented as a large number of independent overlapping samples. The gaussian distribution has the form given in Eq. (3), where $\sigma$ is the standard deviation, $x$

$$p(x) = \frac{1}{\sqrt{2\pi\sigma^2}}\, e^{-x^2/2\sigma^2} \qquad (3)$$

is the random variable (noise voltage or current), and the average value is zero.

If the average value is nonzero, the distribution will have the form illustrated by Eq. (4), where $V$ is the

$$p(x) = \frac{1}{\sqrt{2\pi\sigma^2}}\, e^{-(x-V)/2\sigma^2} \qquad (4)$$

average value. $V$ might be a signal voltage, for example, with the total instantaneous voltage fluctuating about that level.

In the foregoing, it has been assumed that the statistical properties of the random variable are invariant with time. The statistical process associated with such a system is said to be a stationary process. In experimentally collecting data to determine the probability distribution of a random variable (for example, a noise voltage), two methods are available. First, a large number of samples can be collected from a system at a sequence of times. Second, and alternately, the outputs of a large number of identical systems can be sampled simultaneously. The latter method is called the ensemble method. If the statistics collected by either of these methods are invariant with time, the process is stationary. Furthermore, if both methods yield identical statistics, the process is ergodic. Most noise processes are both stationary and ergodic. For such processes the mean value [$V$ in Eq. (4)] is just the time average of the noise, and the variance $\sigma^2$ is the average of the square of the fluctuations about the mean value.

Two additional functions that are useful in characterizing random noise are the autocorrelation function $R(\tau)$ and the power spectral density $G(w)$. $R(\tau)$ provides a measure of the dependence between any two values of the noise variable $x(t)$ and $x(t+\tau)$, as specified in Eq. (5). $G(w)$ gives the distribution of average

$$R(\tau) = \lim_{T\to\infty} \frac{1}{2T}\int_{-T}^{T} x(t)\,x(t+\tau)\,dt \qquad (5)$$

power in noise as a function of frequency $w$. $G(w)$and $R(\tau)$ are Fourier transform pairs; that is, they satisfy Eq. (6), where $j = \sqrt{-1}$. This is a useful relation-

$$\begin{aligned} G(w) &= \int_{-\infty}^{\infty} e^{-jw\tau} R(\tau)\,d\tau \\ R(\tau) &= \int_{-\infty}^{\infty} e^{-jw\tau} G(w)\,dw \end{aligned} \qquad (6)$$

ship because it relates the autocorrelation function of a noise voltage at the output of a linear system to a function $G(w)$ which can be expressed in terms of the transfer function of the system. For example, if white noise (uniform power spectrum) is passed through a system with transfer function $H(w)$, the autocorrelation function at the output of the system is simply the Fourier transform of $H(w)^2$.

Many network calculations involving shot noise and thermal noise can be handled simply by considering the noise sources as ordinary signal sources but with the distinction that mean-squared values are employed. Total voltages (or currents) can be determined by adding mean-squared values.

**Noise figure and noise temperature.** A quantity of considerable interest in describing the characteristics of an electrical or optical signal is the ratio of signal power to noise power ($S/N$) measured at various points in the system. In particular, the signal power–to–noise power ratio at the output of a network, $(S/N)_{\text{out}}$, can be related to the signal power–to–noise power ratio at the input of the network, $(S/N)_{\text{in}}$, by a term called the noise figure $F$, as expressed by Eq. (7). $F$ is a quality factor of the network because it

$$F = \frac{(S/N)_{\text{in}}}{(S/N)_{\text{out}}} \qquad (7)$$

provides a measure of the degradation introduced by the network to the signal-to-noise ratio. An ideal, lossless, noise-free network is one for which $F = 1$.

Frequently $F$ is expressed in decibels as shown by Eq. (8).

$$F_{dB} = 10 \log F \qquad (8)$$

*SEE SIGNAL-TO-NOISE RATIO.*

In radio astronomy and space communications and, in general, systems which employ very low-noise first-stage amplifiers in the receiving system (for example, masers and parametric amplifiers), it has become common practice to characterize the amplifier and, indeed, the system in terms of an equivalent noise temperature. The noise figure defined previously can be expressed in terms of this equivalent noise temperature, as shown in Eq. (9), where $T_e$ is

$$F = \frac{T_e}{T_o} + 1 \qquad (9)$$

the equivalent noise temperature and $T_o$ is the ambient temperature (usually taken as 290 K or 62°F). Then equivalent noise temperature is expressed in terms of noise figure by Eq. (10). Temperatures are always ex-

$$T_e = (F - 1)\, T_o \quad \text{K} \qquad (10)$$

pressed in kelvins. *SEE AMPLIFIER; MASER; PARAMETRIC AMPLIFIER.*

If the system consists of a series of cascaded networks, each with an equivalent noise temperature $T_i$ and gain $G_i$, it can be shown that the overall equivalent noise temperature referred to the input terminals of the first stage is given by Eq. (11). For this system

$$T_e = T_1 + \frac{T_2}{G_1} + \frac{T_3}{G_1G_2} + \cdots + \frac{T_n}{G_1G_2 \ldots G_{n-1}} \qquad (11)$$

or any system in which the overall equivalent noise temperature is known, the noise power spectral density is simply given by $kTe$ watts/hertz, where $k$ is Boltzmann's constant ($1.38 \times 10^{-23}$ joule/K) and $T_e$ is in kelvins.

**Thermal noise.** Spontaneous fluctuations in a resistor at temperature $T$ will give rise to a noise voltage at its terminals with mean-squared value given by Eq. (12), where $k$ is Boltzmann's constant, $R$ is the resis-

$$\overline{V_N^2} = 4kTRB \qquad (12)$$

tance in ohms, and $B$ is the bandwidth in hertz. Equation (12) is often referred to as the Nyquist formula and the thermal noise as Nyquist noise or Johnson noise in recognition of the original investigators.

Equation (12) is actually an approximate formula, but it is valid with useful accuracy over all radio and microwave frequencies of general interest. It is not, however, valid at optical frequencies. The Nyquist formula shows that the spectral density $4kTR$ is constant. Noise with a constant or uniform distribution with frequency is referred to as white noise.

In a communications system, thermal noise is evidenced throughout the receiving system: the antenna, the transmission lines, amplifiers, and so forth. In systems where very low noise is vital to operation (such as those used in space communications), cryogenic cooling of the first stage of amplification is frequently employed. Liquid helium and liquid nitrogen have commonly been used for this purpose. Receiver noise temperatures approaching 4 K (−452°F) have been demonstrated. In these systems, antenna noise temperature becomes very important.

Antenna noise temperature is defined formally in Eq. (13), where $A_e$ is the effective receiving area of

$$T_A = \frac{A_e}{\lambda^2} \int\int T(\theta,\phi)\, P_N(\theta,\phi)\, d\Omega \qquad (13)$$

the antenna in m$^2$, $\lambda$ is the wavelength in m, $P_N(\theta,\phi)$ is the normalized power pattern of the antenna, and $T(\theta,\phi)$ is the temperature distribution over all space in kelvins. $T(\theta,\phi)$ includes contributions from the atmosphere, the galaxy, radio-emitting stars, and so forth, as well as thermal radiation from the Earth itself. In Eq. (13), $\Omega$ is a solid angle and the integration is carried out over $4\pi$ steradians. $P_N(\theta,\phi)$ will depend on the pointing direction of the antenna; consequently, the antenna temperature will depend on the pointing direction of the antenna. At microwave frequencies, the antenna temperature is usually a minimum when the antenna is pointed to zenith. *SEE ANTENNA.*

**Shot noise.** Shot noise, like thermal noise, is thermal in origin. However, it differs from thermal noise in two significant ways: (1) for shot noise to be present in a circuit, a voltage (for example, cathode to anode) or electric field must be impressed; (2) shot noise is not characterized by a uniform, wide-band (white) spectral density, but rather has a high-frequency cutoff given approximately by the inverse transit time of an electron from cathode to anode.

The probability that $N$ electrons will be emitted from a heated cathode in a time interval $\tau$ is given by the Poisson distribution, Eq. (14), where $\bar{n}$ is the av-

$$P(N) = \frac{(\bar{n}\tau)^N e^{-\bar{n}\tau}}{N!} \qquad (14)$$

erage number of electrons emitted per second. If the electric field is sufficiently strong, all the emitted electrons are attracted to the anode, and the fluctuations in current are given by the fluctuations in emission. This is called the temperature-limited case, and the mean-squared noise current is given by the shot-effect formula of Eq. (15), where $e$ is the charge on

$$\overline{i_s^2} = 2e\bar{I}B \qquad (15)$$

an electron, $\bar{I}$ is the average current, and $B$ is the bandwidth in hertz.

If the applied electric field is not sufficiently strong to pull all the electrons to the anode, a negative space charge develops in the vicinity of the cathode which tends to inhibit shot-effect fluctuations. This is the space-charge-limited case, and the shot noise is then approximated by Eq. (16), where $\Gamma^2$ is a space-charge

$$\overline{i_s^2} = 2e\bar{I}\Gamma^2 B \qquad (16)$$

reduction factor varying commonly between 0.01 and 1. The value of $\Gamma^2$ depends on physical geometry, cathode temperature, and applied voltage. *SEE SPACE CHARGE.*

**Noise in optical detectors.** The reception of an optical signal involves the use of a photodetector in which the optical signal is converted to an electric current. Thus, both optical noise and electronic noise can be expected to influence the signal-to-noise ratio at the receiver output.

Optical noise relates to the random arrival of photons at the detector and subsequent generation of hole-electron pairs. The number of hole-electron pairs generated during the period $t$ to $t + \tau$ is a random variable having the Poisson distribution given by Eq.

(17), where $\Lambda$ is given by Eq. (18), where $\eta$ is the

$$P(n) = \frac{\Lambda^n e^{-\Lambda}}{n!} \tag{17}$$

$$\Lambda = \int_t^{t+\tau} \frac{\eta}{hf} p(t)\, dt \tag{18}$$

quantum efficiency (fraction of light absorbed), $h$ is Planck's constant, $f$ is the optical frequency, and $p(t)$ is the optical power.

For the case where $p(t)$ has a constant value $p_0$, an expression for the signal-to-noise ratio is given as Eq. (19), where $e$ is charge on the electron, $P_N$ is the

$$S/N = \frac{\left(\dfrac{\eta e p_0}{hf}\right)^2}{\dfrac{2\eta e^2 p_0}{hf} B + P_N} \tag{19}$$

mean-square thermal (electronic) noise power associated with amplification of the generated current, and $B$ is the bandwidth in hertz.

Many modern optical communications systems employ avalanche photodiodes. In the avalanche photodiode, a received photon creates a hole-electron pair, which in turn, by means of ionization collisions, creates additional hole-electron pairs. Thus the detector has internal gain. However, the process which gives rise to the gain is itself a random process, and therefore, additonal fluctuation noise is generated. The signal-to-noise ratio for the optical receiver employing an avalanche photodetector is given by Eq. (20),

$$S/N = \frac{\left(\dfrac{ne\, Gp_0}{hf}\right)^2}{\dfrac{2ne^2 G^2 F p_0 B}{hf} + P_N} \tag{20}$$

where $G$ represents the interval gain and $F$ is the excess noise factor.

If, in Eq. (19) or (20), the thermal noise term is sufficiently small compared to the optically generated noise so as to be neglected, the resulting $S/N$ is referred to as the quantum limit. In most present-day systems, however, thermal noise is found to be the dominant term.

**Noise measurement.** The most common apparatus used to measure noise is a total power receiver consisting of a wide-band amplifier, a square-law detector, an integrator, and an indicator. The sensitivity of the receiver (the minimum detectable noise fluctuation) is generally improved as the front-end bandwidth and the integration time is increased. Sensitive receivers of this type are called total power radiometers and are frequently employed in radio astronomy.

The noise temperature (or noise figure) of an amplifier can be determined by what is commonly called the $Y$-factor method. The measurement utilizes two calibrated noise sources and a power receiver of the type just described. One of the noise sources is connected to the input of the amplifier, and the output power is measured with the receiver. This is repeated with the second noise source. The ratio of power received in the two cases is recorded and denoted $Y$. The amplifier noise temperature is then given by Eq. (21), where $T_1$ and $T_2$ (where $T_2$ is greater than $T_1$)

$$T_{\text{amp}} = \frac{T_2 - YT_1}{Y - 1} \quad \text{K} \tag{21}$$

are the noise temperatures of the calibrated terminations. It is assumed that the amplifier has sufficiently high gain that the noise contribution from the receiver can be neglected.

The total system noise temperature can be measured by using the noise-adding method. In this method an increment of noise is injected into the system and the total received noise power is compared to the noise power without the added increment. Then the total system noise power is given by Eq. (22),

$$T_{\text{syst}} = \frac{\Delta T}{Y - 1} \quad \text{K} \tag{22}$$

where $Y$ is given by Eq. (23), and $\Delta T$ is the noise

$$Y = \frac{\text{system noise power} + \text{injected noise power}}{\text{system noise power}} \tag{23}$$

temperature of injected noise.

Modern test equipment is available which greatly simplifies the measurement of the noise performance of circuits. Automated instrumentation which provides output directly in terms of noise figures is, for example, readily available. SEE ELECTRICAL NOISE GENERATOR.

*Randall W. Kreutel*

**Bibliography.** M. K. Barnoski (ed.), *Fundamentals of Optical Fiber Communications,* 2d ed., 1981; W. B. Davenport, Jr. and W. I. Root, *Introduction to Random Signals and Noise,* 1958; J. D. Kraus, *Radio Astronomy,* 1966; J. E. Midwinter, *Optical Fibers for Transmission,* 1979; M. Schwartz, *Information, Transmission, Modulation and Noise,* 3d ed., 1980; A. Van Der Ziel, *Noise: Sources, Characterization and Measurement,* 1970.

## Electrical noise generator

A device which produces electrical noise for use in electrical measurements. Electrical noise generators are commonly employed to measure noise figure or noise temperature of radio receivers. They are also used in various other tests in radar and communications systems. Celestial noise sources are used to calibrate large antennas.

Some standard types of noise generators are hot-wire, diode, gas-discharge tube, hot and cold loads (terminations), and radio-star. A hot-wire noise source consists of the filament of a lamp heated by direct current. Thermal noise having spectral density $4kTR$, where $k$ is Boltzmann's constant and $T$ and $R$ are the temperature and resistance of the filament respectively, is generated across the terminals of the filament. A diode noise generator utilizes the temperature-limited shot effect to generate noise. At frequencies less than the reciprocal transit time of the diode, the noise spectral density is $2e\bar{I}$, where $e$ is the charge on the electron and $\bar{I}$ is the average anode current. A gas-discharge noise generator, commonly referred to as a noise tube, consists of a fluorescent light tube enclosed in a waveguide. Noise generation is essentially thermal. The noise tube is commonly employed at microwave frequencies. Hot and cold loads consist of well-matched terminations, either transmission line or waveguide, which are held at a given temperature by using an oven or by applying cryogenic refrigeration. Noise generation is thermal. Common temperatures for noise-generating terminations are nominally 80 and 300 K (−316 and +80°F).

Celestial radio sources (radio stars) are commonly employed as reference noise sources for evaluating the characteristics of very low-noise, high-gain space communications receiving terminals. There are a number of accurately calibrated sources available—the choice depending on system parameters (frequency, antenna gain, system noise temperature, elevation angle, and so forth) and physical location. The most common radio sources employed are Cassiopeia A, Taurus A, Cygnus A, and Orion A. The first three are classified as nonthermal sources in which radiation results from relativistic electrons interacting with an interstellar magnetic field. The electrons are rotated in a plane perpendicular to the magnetic field direction, and radiation is characterized by a component polarized parallel to that plane. The polarized component is small, however, and the major portion of the radiation is unpolarized. The nonthermal sources have flux densities which decrease with increasing frequency and, consequently, tend to have a cutoff frequency above which they are not usable. Orion A is a thermal source in which radiation occurs from a hot, ionized cloud. Orion A has a constant flux density at frequencies above 2 GHz. Other possible sources include the Sun, Moon, and the planets. It is important that variations in brightness over the source be corrected, that polarized components of flux be accounted for, and that attenuation characteristics of the intervening medium, the atmosphere, be included. SEE ELECTRICAL NOISE.

*Randall W. Kreutel*

**Bibliography.** J. D. Kraus, *Radio Astronomy,* chap. 8, 1966; R. W. Kreutel and A. O. Pacholder, The measurement of gain and noise temperature of a satellite communications earth station, *Microwave J.,* 12(10):61–66, October 1969; M. S. Gupta (ed.), *Electrical Noise: Fundamentals and Sources,* 1977; A. Van Der Ziel, *Noise: Sources, Characterization and Measurement,* 1970.

## Electrical resistance

That property of an electrically conductive material that causes a portion of the energy of an electric current flowing in a circuit to be converted into heat. In 1774 A. Henley showed that current flowing in a wire produced heat, but it was not until 1840 that J. P. Joule determined that the rate of conversion of electrical energy into heat in a conductor, that is, power dissipation, could be expressed by the relation given in notation (1).

$$H/t \propto I^2R \qquad (1)$$

The day-to-day determination of resistance by measuring the rate of heat dissipation is not practical. However, this rate of energy conversion is also $VI$, where $V$ is the voltage drop across the element in question and $I$ the current through the element, as in Eq. (2), from which the more conventional relationship implied by Ohm's law, Eq. (3), is apparent.

$$H/t \propto I^2R = VI \qquad (2)$$

$$R = V/I \qquad (3)$$

SEE OHM'S LAW; RESISTANCE MEASUREMENT; RESISTOR.

*Charles E. Applegate*

## Electrical shielding

The imposition of a metal or composite barrier between one or more sources of electrical noise and their victims with the objective of reducing or eliminating electrical interference. Examples of the barrier are the case or housing of equipment; shields covering interconnecting cables between equipment; large cabinets, racks, or consoles; shielded (screen) rooms; and entire shielded buildings or vehicles.

**Shielding effectiveness.** The principal measure of a shield's performance is the shielding effectiveness. It is defined by the equation below, where $SE_{dB}$ is the

$$SE_{dB} = 20 \log_{10} (F_b/F_a)$$

shielding effectiveness in decibels, $F_b$ is the electric (or magnetic) field strength before imposition of the barrier, and $F_a$ is the electric (or magnetic) field strength after imposition of the barrier.

Shielding is obtained by the combination of reflection loss and absorption loss. The former is due to the impedance mismatch between the wave impedance of an oncoming wave and the surface impedance of the interposed barrier. Absorption loss corresponds to the attenuation due to skin effect at higher frequencies, and is dependent upon the frequency, conductivity, permeability, and thickness of the barrier. Shielding effectiveness is the sum of both losses. SEE ATTENUATION (ELECTRICITY); RADAR-ABSORBING MATERIALS.

**Metal shields.** Most intentional shields are made of metal to ensure high reflection losses. Even thin metals, such as household aluminum foils (with a thickness of about 1.5 mil or 0.038 mm), offer shielding effectiveness in excess of 100 dB. At low frequencies, however, these foils become electromagnetically transparent (that is, they do not attenuate magnetic fields). Thus, if there is a shielding problem due to the selection and makeup of the metal barrier, it is likely to occur only for low-frequency magnetic fields.

To obtain significant shielding to magnetic fields at low frequencies, the metal barrier must be very thick or composed of a highly permeable material such as Mumetal, Supermalloy, or Hypernom. Often such shields are fabricated in two or more layers, frequently laminated, to obtain good shielding properties per unit size or weight.

**Leaky apertures.** The major problem encountered in achieving adequate shielding at other than low frequencies is leaky apertures, not the metal choice. To provide the integrity required of the basic shield metal, all apertures must be protected or secured, or special electrical components and gaskets should be used (see **illus.**).

**Shielded rooms.** Shielded enclosures, ranging in size from small rooms to entire buildings, are commercially available for performing as radiated emission and susceptibility test chambers, secure facility radiation containment, and protection for sensitive equipment from outside electromagnetic radiation. These enclosures typically provide in excess of 120

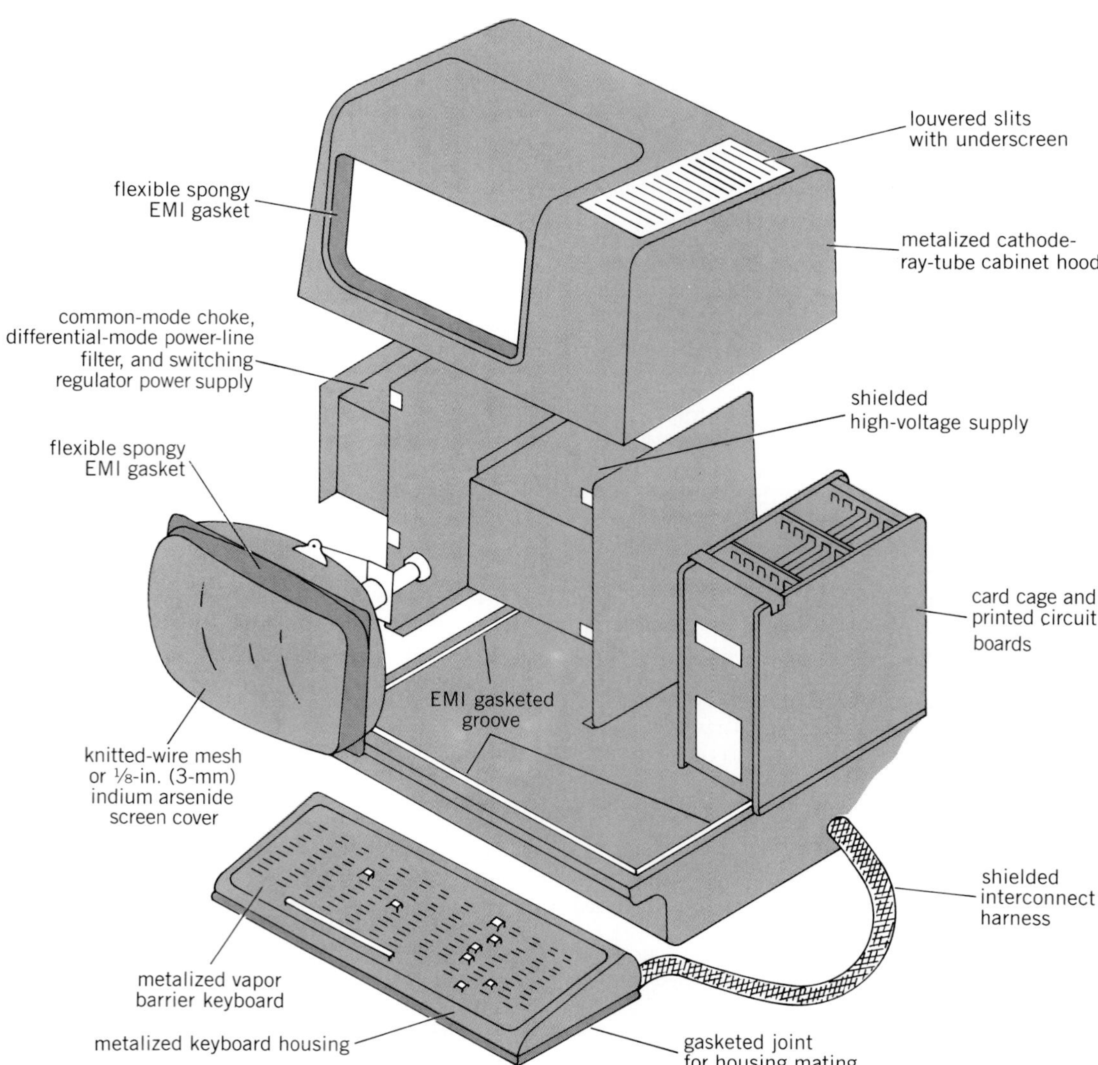


**Some measures for controlling electromagnetic interference in video display terminals.**

dB attenuation from 10 kHz to 1 GHz, and undergo reduced performance at lower and higher frequencies. Where extended performance is required, shielded rooms are usually made of solid seam-welded panels of galvanized steel. Special attention is given to leaky areas such as doors, and entrances where cables or wires such as power-line and telephone are brought in through filters. *See* ELECTRIC FILTER; ELECTROMAGNETIC PULSE (EMP).

**Cable shields.** Interconnecting cables between equipments often act as an "antenna farm" in which they behave as undesired pickup antennas and provide radiation escape from internal signals conducted along their length. Shielding such cables and harnesses is the dominant protection mechanism; other options include absorbers and filters. Cable shields may vary in complexity from one cover braid, through multibraids and composite braids or foils, to extruded tubes or conduits. *See* COMMUNICATIONS CABLE; ELECTRICAL NOISE; ELECTROMAGNETIC COMPATIBILITY.

*Donald R. J. White*

**Bibliography.** A. A. Smith, Jr., *Coupling of External Electromagnetic Fields to Transmission Lines*, 1977; Special issue on cables and connectors, *EMC Technol. Interfer. Control News*, 1(3):16–58, July 1982; D. R. J. White, *Handbook on Electromagnetic Shielding Materials and Performance*, 2d ed., 1980.

## Electrochromic displays

Devices that employ a reversible electrochemical reaction to cause a change in color of segments patterned to form alphanumeric characters.

Electrochromic displays (ECDs) are passive devices that only modulate ambient light, in contrast to a light-emitting diode (LED). Hence, they operate at low voltages, and have a low enough energy requirement that a watch-size display can be operated for about 1 year from a small commercial battery. In the off state, the segments are typically colorless; in the on state, they are brightly colored, for example, blue or purple. *See* LIGHT-EMITTING DIODE.

The structure of an electrochromic display package is shown in the **illustration**. It consists of a top glass piece with the transparent electrodes, typically vacuum-deposited indium and tin oxides, on the inside surface. The lead from each segment continues to the edge of the glass. An insulating layer of silicon diox-

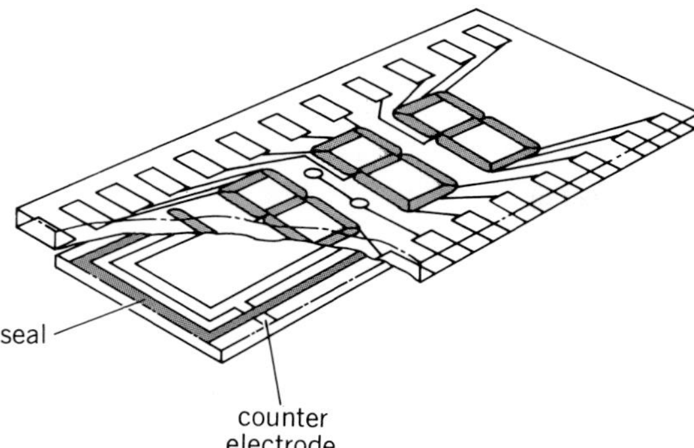


**Structure of an electrochromic display.**

ide ($SiO_2$) is deposited onto the leads to prevent their coloration. A counter electrode is deposited on the bottom piece. The two pieces are held together with a solder-glass, or epoxy, seal. To operate the device, a dc potential of 1–1.5 V is applied between the segments on the top plate and the counter electrode. Coloration and bleaching times are in the 200–500-millisecond range. Electrochromic displays can be categorized by the type of reaction that occurs when the potential is applied. Viologen electrochromic displays operate in an electroplating mode; with tungsten trioxide ($WO_3$) displays, the electrode material itself undergoes a color change. Electrochromic displays would be most efficiently utilized in applications requiring the display of large-format and slowly changing information, such as in clocks or message boards.

**Viologen displays.** The electrolyte is an aqueous solution of a dipositively charged organic salt, for example, a dialkyl derivative of 4.4′-bipyridinium bromide. When the appropriate negative potential is applied to the transparent electrode, the colorless cation in the electrolyte undergoes a one-electron reduction process to produce a purple radical cation. This species is insoluble in the aqueous electrolyte, hence it remains deposited on the electrode where it is formed. Since this precipitate is stable, the system possesses an open-circuit memory. To erase the segments, an appropriate positive potential is applied to the transparent electrodes. This oxidizes the purple film back to the soluble, colorless, doubly positive cation.

**$WO_3$ displays.** In these devices, a thin, colorless film of $WO_3$ is vacuum-deposited onto the transparent, patterned electrodes. Electrolytes are typically solutions of acids or lithium salts, such as $H_2SO_4$/glycerin or $LiClO_4$/propylene carbonate. When a negative potential is applied to this electrode, the reaction below occurs. Here a cation from the solu-

$$WO_3 + xM^+ + xe^- \longrightarrow M_xWO_3 \qquad M^+ = H^+, Li^+$$

tion and an electron from the electrode are simultaneously introduced into the $WO_3$ lattice. This changes the transparent $WO_3$ into a blue $M_xWO_3$, generally called a tungsten bronze. Since both states of this oxide are stable, the system has an open-circuit memory. To erase a segment, a positive potential is applied to the top electrode. This reverses the above reaction and renders the film colorless.

There are several other versions of these two concepts under development. However, fundamental to all these devices is the requirement that some chemical reaction take place reversibly, for millions of cycles. Due to various technical problems, for example, stability of the electrodes, side reactions, and the recrystallization of deposited films, the reliability necessary for commercial production of electrochromic displays has not yet been achieved. SEE ELECTRONIC DISPLAY.

*Gabriel G. Barna*

**Bibliography.** A. R. Kmetz and F. K. von Willisen (eds.), *Nonemissive Electrooptic Displays*, 1976.

## Electroluminescence

A luminescence resulting from the application of an electric field to a material, usually solid. Several different types of electroluminescence can be distinguished.

**Destriau effect.** In 1936, G. Destriau in France observed that when suitably prepared zinc sulfide phosphor powders, activated with small additions of copper, are suspended in an insulator and an intense alternating electric field is applied with capacitorlike electrodes, light emission results. The effect is the basis for modern electroluminescent lamps. The insulator may be either liquid (oil) or solid (glass or plastic). Thin films of tin oxide or metal are used as transparent electrodes.

Electroluminescent phosphors (or electroluminors) differ from phosphors that are excitable by cathode rays or ultraviolet radiation in that small regions of excess copper(I) sulfide ($Cu_2S$) cause the electrical properties to vary with location in the phosphor. This characteristic results in local intensification of the electric field, causing emission of light from a few small spots in each powder particle. A similar type of emission may be obtained from thin films of zinc sulfide (ZnS) prepared by vaporization in a vacuum; such films also emit if a direct voltage is applied.

Electroluminescence makes possible very thin large-area light sources. The active layer in a lamp for operation at 120 V may be about 1 mil (25 micrometer) thick, whereas evaporated films 1 μm thick may be operated at 20 V. The light output $L$ increases rapidly with increasing voltage $V$ according to the equation below, where $A$ and $B$ are constants.

$$L = A \exp\,(-B/V^{1/2})$$

Also the output increases slightly less than linearly as the frequency of the alternating voltage is increased until a saturation output is reached at frequencies of the order of 100,000 Hz. Maximum efficiency is not obtained for the same operating conditions as maximum brightness, and the efficiency is normally low compared to that of other light sources; for example, electroluminescence, 3–5 lumens/watt; incandescent lamp, 16 lm/W; fluorescent lamp, 75 lm/W. Some phosphors exhibit a change in emission color as the operating frequency is varied. In addition to their use in lamps, electroluminescent materials may be employed in display devices and, when used in conjunction with photoconductors, in light amplifiers and in logic circuits for computers, which are, however, slow compared to semiconductor logic circuits. SEE LIGHT AMPLIFIER; LIGHT PANEL.

**Injection electroluminescence.** Injection electroluminescence results when a semiconductor *pn* junction or a point contact is biased in the forward direction. This type of emission was first observed from silicon carbide (SiC) in England by H. J. Round in 1907. It is the result of radiative recombination of injected minority carriers with majority carriers across the energy band gap of the material. Such emission has been observed in a large number of semiconductors, including silicon (Si), germanium (Ge), diamond, cadmium sulfide (CdS), zinc sulfide (ZnS), zinc selenide (ZnSe), zinc telluride (ZnTe), zinc oxide (ZnO), and many of the so-called III–V compounds, such as gallium phosphide (GaP), gallium arsenide (GaAs), indium phosphide (InP), indium arsenide (InAs), indium antimonide (InSb), boron phosphide (BP), boron nitride (BN), and aluminum nitride (AlN). The wavelength of the emission corresponds to an energy equal, at most, to the forbidden band gap of the material, and hence in most of these materials the wavelength is in the infrared region of the spectrum. In some cases the efficiency is high, approaching one emitted photon for each carrier passing through the junction. In suitable structures the excitation intensity can become so high that stimulated rather than spontaneous emission predominates, and laser action results, with spectral narrowing and coherent emission. Direct electrical excitation is more convenient than optical excitation, but the beam divergence of injection lasers is normally much greater than that of gas lasers or the optically pumped solid type. *See* Junction diode; Laser; Semiconductor; Semiconductor diode.

**Other effects.** If a *pn* junction is biased in the reverse direction, so as to produce high internal electric fields, other types of emission can occur, but with very low efficiency. The presence of very energetic ("hot") carriers can result in emission at energies greater than the band gap of the material (avalanche emission). The emission in this case may be correlated with small active regions called microplasmas. Light emission may also occur when electrodes of certain metals, such as Al or Ta, are immersed in suitable electrolytes and current is passed between them. In many cases this galvanoluminescence is electroluminescence generated in a thin oxide layer formed on the electrode by electrolytic action. In addition to electroluminescence proper, other interesting effects (usually termed electrophotoluminescence) occur when electric fields are applied to a phosphor which is concurrently, or has been previously, excited by other means. These effects include a decrease or increase in steady-state photoluminescence brightness when the field is applied, or a burst of afterglow emission if the field is applied after the primary photoexcitation is removed.

*Clifford C. Klick; James H. Schulman*

**Bibliography.** P. Goldberg (ed.), *Luminescence of Inorganic Solids*, 1966; H. K. Henisch, *Electroluminescence*, 1962; H. F. Ivey, *Electroluminescence and Related Effects*, 1963; S. Larach (ed.), *Photoelectronic Materials and Devices*, 1965; J. I. Pankove (ed.), *Electroluminescence*, 1977; D. Theis, Application of thin film electroluminescent devices, *J. Lumin.*, 23:191–207, 1981; R. K. Willardson and A. C. Beer (eds.), *Semiconductors and Semimetals*, vol. 2, 1966.

## Electromagnetic compatibility

The situation in which electrical and electronic devices and systems work as intended, both within themselves and in their electromagnetic environment.

Electromagnetic interference (EMI) is said to exist when unwanted voltages or currents are present so that they adversely affect the performance of a device or system. Such voltages or currents may reach the victim circuit or device by conduction or by nonionizing radiation. In all cases, electromagnetic interference arises because of a combination of three factors: a source, a transmission path, and a response, at least one of which is unplanned. Electromagnetic interference control refers to the process of making design changes or adjustments of signal or noise levels in order to achieve electromagnetic compatibility (EMC). Examples of electromagnetic interference often experienced by the public are herringbone patterns on the television screen and buzzing and clicking sounds in the radio.

**Sources of interference.** Designers usually do not intend that their devices be sources of interference. However, what is a desired signal in one path may be an undesired signal, that is, noise, in a path into which it is inadvertently coupled. Interference may be unintentional, or nonfunctional, such as an arc discharge, radiation from a lightning stroke, a corona discharge from high-tension power lines, or a noise caused by a sudden change in current flow in a conductor. Functional intereference, while not usually produced for interference purposes, often includes sine waves, computer clock pulses, speech or video waves, or pulses forming data trains. An example of functional interference is signal leakage from cable television systems. Fluorescent lamps, commutators, automotive ignition systems, and industrial, scientific, and medical equipment such as diathermy machines all constitute sources of interference, as does the electromagnetic pulse (EMP) which accompanies a nuclear detonation. Short-wave radio listeners often experience interference from high-frequency radar from the Soviet Union. Interference also exists across national borders because of incomplete international agreement on the use of the radio-frequency spectrum. *See* Electromagnetic pulse (EMP).

**Interference coupling.** Electromagnetic interference always starts with a flow of current through a conductor (which may include a conducting gas), and always appears at the victim in the form of a current or a voltage. The coupling path, however, may be a conduction or a radiation path. Thus the actual paths include common wiring, capacitance between devices, mutual inductance between adjacent wiring, nonionizing radiation, or wires in an electromagnetic field. Such coupling is aided by the fact that all conductors, whether wires, printed circuit board traces, or the conductors within an integrated circuit, exhibit both resistance and inductance. Likewise, between wires, mutual inductance and capacitance exist, resulting in a variety of possible coupling paths. *See* Capacitance; Coupled circuits; Inductance.

**Grounds and bonds.** Grounding is the establishment of an electrically conductive path between an electrical or electronic element of a system and a reference point or plane known as the ground. Grounding thus is a circuit concept, whereas bonding refers to the physical implementation of that concept. Grounding may also refer to an electrical connection made to the earth.

Grounds for currents whose wavelength is long compared with circuit dimensions are best made directly to a single point in a system. For currents whose wavelength is comparable to, or shorter than, circuit dimensions, however, the multipoint ground must be used to avoid the situation in which the ground lead might be a significant fraction of a quarter-wavelength, and thus not serve as a low-impedance conductor. SEE ELECTRONIC EQUIPMENT GROUNDING.

**Shields.** The purpose of shielding is to confine radiated energy to a specific region, or to prevent radiated energy from entering a specific region. The most effective shield is a solid metallic enclosure, made of a permeable metal (for example, iron or steel) if frequencies below 100 kHz are to be shielded, or of any metal if higher frequencies are to be shielded. However, the solid shield does not permit light, air, water, or other substances to be passed through it, so shields with holes, including screens, braids, and honeycomb arrangements, as well as conductive glass may be needed. The widespread use of plastic enclosures has made thin film shields vital in achieving the needed shielding effectiveness in the use of such enclosures. SEE ELECTRICAL SHIELDING.

**Filters.** An electrical filter offers relatively little opposition to the passage of certain frequencies or direct current (dc) while blocking the passage of other frequencies. Accordingly, filters play a significant role in reducing conducted interference to the extent that such interference has a spectral content different from that of the desired signals.

A filter may be either reflective or lossy. Reflective filters present an impedance mismatch to unwanted frequencies, thereby returning them to the input, whereas lossy filters absorb unwanted frequencies. A filter may be designed on a time-domain basis as well as on a frequency-domain basis. SEE ELECTRIC FILTER; IMPEDANCE MATCHING.

**Mathematical models.** The complexity of electronic circuitry no longer allows the use of simple trial-and-error methods in achieving an electromagnetically compatible system design. System behavior can be expressed in terms of equations that describe source outputs, transmission or coupling characteristics, and susceptor responses. Such models have been incorporated into system analysis programs which not only predict system compatibility but also can be used to evaluate the effect of parameter changes on overall system performance, as may be needed in analyzing a proposed subsystem specification waiver, or in generating interface specifications for use within an overall system design. SEE SIMULATION.

**Standards.** Numerous standards have been developed for military as well as for industrial and consumer products. For military equipment, MIL-STD-461B, *EMI Characteristics Requirements for Equipment*, defines the emission and susceptibility limits applicable to units under various test conditions; MIL-STD-462, *Measurement of EMI Characteristics*, describes how the measurements are to be made.

Such organizations as the Institute of Electrical and Electronics Engineers (IEEE), the Society of Automotive engineers (SAE), the Electronic Industries Association (EIA), and the American National Standards Institute (ANSI) are active in promulgating standards for electronic equiment, including electromagnetic compatability aspects.

The Federal Communications Commission's (FCC) *Rules and Regulations*, Part 15, as amended by FCC Docket 20780, establishes emission limits on "computing devices," defined as any electronic devices or systems that use digital techniques. A class A computing device is destined for commercial, industrial, or business use. It must meet certain radiation limits (for frequencies of 30 to 100 MHz) at a 96-ft (30-m) distance, and conduction limits (for frequencies of 0.45 to 30 MHz) with respect to its power leads. A class B computing device is destined for residential use. It must meet certain radiation limits at a 10-ft (3-m) distance. Both its radiation limits and its conduction limits are more stringent than those of a class A device. SEE DIGITAL COMPUTER; MICROCOMPUTER.

**Mutual effects.** Digital systems, such as computers, tend to interfere with analog systems, such as voice and video communications, more readily than analog systems interfere with digital systems. Data streams to be transmitted over analog voice circuits thus are converted to a quasianalog tone form first. Computer clocks also may have to be shielded and their output circuits filtered to prevent interference to communication equipment. In addition, personal computers must be connected to television receivers so that the video output of the personal computer does not reach the television receiving antenna, which then would radiate such signals. SEE ELECTRICAL NOISE.

*Bernhard E. Keiser*

***Bibliography.*** Computer and Business Equipment Manufacturers Association, *Limits and Methods of Measurement of Electromagnetic Emanations from Electronic Data Processing Equipment and Office Equipment,* May 1977; Federal Communications Commission, Part 15: Radio Frequency Devices, Subpart J: Computing Device, *Rules and Regulations,* July 1981; Institute of Electrical and Electronics Engineers, *1983 International Symposium on Electromagnetic Compatibility,* pub. no. 83CH-1838-2, 1983; B. E. Keiser, *Principles of Electromagnetic Compatibility,* 1979.

## Electromagnetic pulse (EMP)

A transient electromagnetic signal produced by a nuclear explosion in or above the Earth's atmosphere. Though not considered dangerous to people, the EMP is a potential threat to many electronic systems.

**Discovery.** Though predicted by some scientists involved with the early development of nuclear weapons, EMP was not then considered to be a serious threat to people or equipment. However, in the early 1960s some of the high-altitude nuclear tests conducted in the Pacific led to some strange occurrences many miles from ground zero. In Hawaii, some 800 mi (1300 km) from the Johnston Island test, EMP was credited with setting off burglar alarms and turning off street lights. In tests conducted in Nevada, significant EMP-induced signals were coupled to cables.

**Initial nuclear radiation.** In a typical nuclear detonation, parts of the shell casing and other materials are rapidly reduced to a very hot, compressed gas, which upon expansion gives rise to enormous amounts of mechanical and thermal energy. At the same time the nuclear reactions release tremendous amounts of energy as initial nuclear radiation (INR). This INR is in the form of neutrons and high-energy electromagnetic radiation, called gamma rays. About a minute after the detonation, the radioactive decay of the fission products gives rise to additional gamma rays and electrons (or beta particles), known as residual nuclear radiation (RNR). The distribution of the total explosive energy of a hypothetical fission detonation in the atmosphere below an altitude of 6 mi

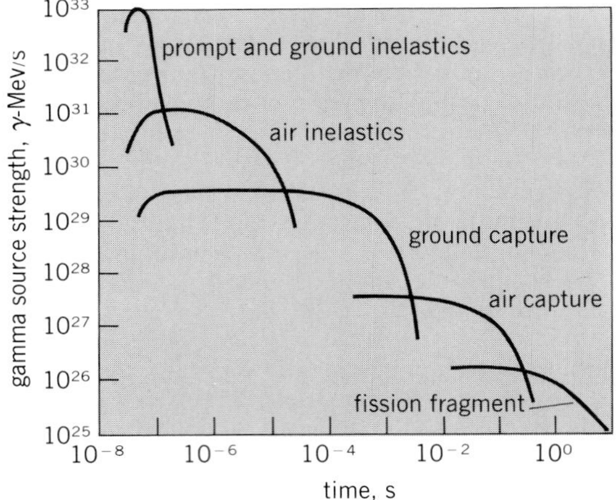


**Fig. 1. Total gamma source strength versus time for nominal 1-megaton surface burst. Both horizontal and vertical scales are logarithmic. (*After C. L. Longmire, On the electromagnetic pulse produced by nuclear explosions, IEEE Trans. Antennas Propag., AP-26(1):3–13, 1978*)**

(10 km) is 50% blast, 35% thermal, 10% RNR, and 5% INR. At higher altitudes where the air is less dense, the thermal energy increases and the blast energy decreases proportionately.

EMP is associated with the INR output, which is a small percentage of the total explosive energy. Nevertheless, EMP is still capable of transferring something of the order of 0.1–1 joule per square meter (0.1–0.01 ft-lbf/ft$^2$) onto a collector, more than enough to cause upset or damage to normal semiconductor devices.

Early research developed the physics of high-altitude EMP. In 1978 a consistent explanation was set forth of how EMP is generated, regardless of the detonation height above ground. **Figure 1** identifies six contributions to the gamma source for a hypothetical 1-megaton surface burst. As the detonation height is elevated, contributions from the ground and air sources decrease; for the high-altitude detonation (higher than 37 mi or 60 km; the EMP gamma source becomes essentially the prompt gammas from the nuclear burst. The gamma-source wave shape then approaches a smooth curve, approximating a double exponential, and since EMP is generated from the gamma source, it too approaches a double exponential wave shape.

**EMP generation in a high-altitude burst.** As the prompt gammas move away from a high-altitude nuclear detonation (**Fig. 2**), those gamma rays moving toward the Earth penetrate a more dense region of the atmosphere called the source or deposition region. In this region the highly energetic gamma rays interact with the air molecules to form 1-MeV Compton electrons and less energetic gamma rays, which then proceed in the same general direction as the original gamma rays. The fast Compton electrons slow down by stripping electrons from air molecules to form secondary electron-ion pairs. (Though these secondary electrons and ions do not contribute to the generation of the EMP, they do cause the region to become highly conductive, and therefore play an important role in determining the EMP wave shape and amplitude.) The very intense, short-duration pulse of Compton electrons is also deflected by the Earth's geomagnetic field, according to Eq. (1), where the

$$\vec{F} = q(\vec{v} \times \vec{B}) \qquad (1)$$

deflection force $\vec{F}$ is perpendicular to the geomagnetic field $\vec{B}$ and the velocity $\vec{v}$ of a Compton electron $q$. The Compton electrons then spiral about the geomagnetic lines as they slow down.

**Characteristics for a high-altitude burst.** For a high-altitude nuclear detonation the radiated EMP observed at large distances from the source region can be represented in time $t$ as an electric field $E(t)$, and a magnetic field $H(t)$, given by Eqs. (2) and (3), with

$$E(t) = E_0(e^{-\alpha t} - e^{-\beta t}) \qquad t \geqslant 0 \qquad (2)$$

$$H(t) = H_0(e^{-\alpha t} - e^{-\beta t}) \qquad t \geqslant 0 \qquad (3)$$

$E_0 = 5.2 \times 10^4$ V/m ($1.6 \times 10^4$ V/ft), $H_0 = 1.4 \times 10^2$ A/m ($4.2 \times 10$ A/ft), $\alpha = 4.0 \times 10^6$ s$^{-1}$, and $\beta = 5.0 \times 10^8$ s$^{-1}$. (In air, $E$ and $H$ are related by the impedance of free space, 377 ohms.) If the observer is directly below the detonation (ground zero), the polarization of both fields is predominantly horizontal; if the observer is at the horizon, the fields can have both horizontal and vertical components. The magnitude of these field components varies according to the latitude and longitude of the observer and the direction of the burst.

**EMP in a surface burst.** Should the nuclear detonation occur closer to the Earth, the EMP generation process becomes far more complex and the electric and magnetic fields become very complicated. The most dramatic change occurs with a surface burst (**Fig. 3**).

When the observer is somewhere within the source region of a near-surface burst, where the air conductivity varies between $10^{-4}$ and $10^{-2}$ siemens/m ($3 \times 10^{-5}$ and $3 \times 10^{-3}$ siemens/ft), the resultant electric field is predominantly vertical, and the resultant magnetic field is polarized perpendicular to the plane of the figure. The electric field polarization is due to the Compton-electron and ion-charge-separation fields which tend to become perpendicular to the conducting earth, leaving a resultant vertical electric field near the ground. As these Compton electrons move radially away from the detonation, they curve earthward and return to the detonation point through the conducting earth. This Compton current loop then gives rise to a resultant magnetic field. When the observer is far from the detonation (outside the source region), the electric and magnetic fields begin to approximate fields from a vertical dipole, decaying with distance ($r$) as $1/r$.

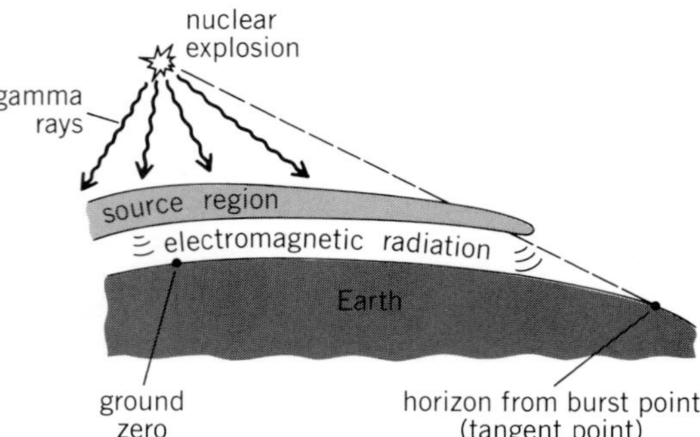


**Fig. 2. Schematic representation of the EMP in a high-altitude burst. The extent of the source region varies with the altitude and the yield of the explosion. (*After S. Glasstone and P. J. Dolan, eds., The Effects of Nuclear Weapons, U.S. Department of Defense and the Energy Research and Development Administration, 3d ed., 1977*)**

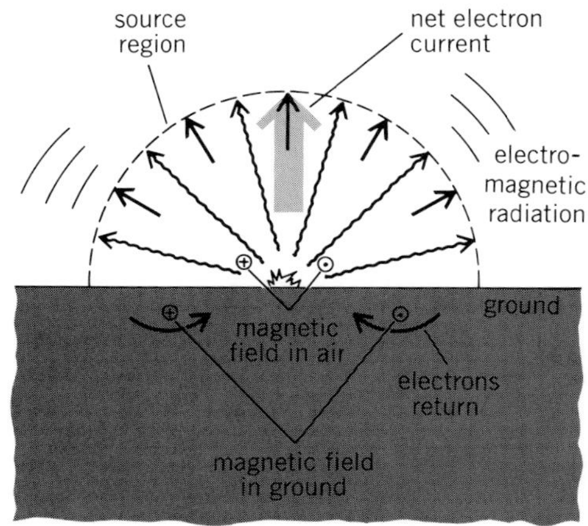


**Fig. 3. Schematic representation of the EMP in a surface burst. (*After S. Glasstone and P. J. Dolan, eds., The Effect of Nuclear Weapons, U.S. Department of Defense and the Energy Research and Development Administration, 3d ed., 1977*)**

**Internal EMP.** It is possible for INR to directly interact with systems, causing EMP signals internal to structures. This phenomenon has been called internal or system-generated EMP and is potentially a serious problem for satellites and electronics in metallic enclosures. These forms of EMP are generated by gamma rays impinging on the enclosures, producing currents of Compton electrons internally that then produce internal electromagnetic waves. They are very dependent upon the nuclear detonation, the system topology, and the relative position of one to the other.

**Coupling.** The coupling of these rather wide-band ($10^4$ to $10^8$ Hz) signals to systems of different topologies can be significant. For example, it is not unusual to predict voltage and current levels of hundreds of thousands of volts and a few thousand amperes coupled by high-altitude EMP onto extended systems. The exact level of coupling depends upon the size of the system and its orientation with respect to the incident field, and upon whether or not it is near an earth ground. For ground-based systems the incident field components can actually be enhanced or degraded, depending upon the polarization. Solving Maxwell's equations at the interface between an ideal conductor and a dielectric shows that the net horizontal electric field is zero at the interface and the net vertical electric field doubles. (For the magnetic field components the opposite is true.) Since the earth is not a perfect conductor, the field components do not completely cancel or quite double in amplitude.

An estimate of about 1 joule (0.7 ft-lbf) of EMP coupled energy is considered reasonable for many systems. Even if the coupling onto circuits is inefficient, as little as $10^{-13}$ J can upset some semiconductor devices and $10^{-6}$ J can cause damage. The potential for such upset and damage in critical electronic systems has led to the development of semiconductor devices which are "hardened" or protected against EMP. This development is particularly advanced in communications systems whose disruption by EMP is considered an important civil and military vulnerability.

*Robert A. Pfeffer*

***Bibliography.*** V. Gilinsky and G. Peebles, *J. Geophys. Res. Space Phys.*, 73(1):405–414, 1968; S. Glasstone and P. J. Dolan (eds.), *The Effects of Nuclear Weapons*, U.S. Department of Defense and the Energy Research and Development Administration, 3d ed., 1977; W. J. Karzas and R. Latter, *Phys. Rev.*, 157(5B):1369–1378, 1965; A. S. Kompaneets, *Sov. Phys.—JETP*, 35:1076–1080, 1959; C. Longmire, *IEEE Trans. Antennas Propag.*, AP-26(1):3–13, 1978.

## Electromagnetic wave transmission

The transmission of electrical energy by wires, the broadcasting of radio signals, and the phenomenon of visible light are all examples of the propagation of electromagnetic energy. Electromagnetic energy travels in the form of a wave. Its speed of travel is approximately 186,000 mi/s ($3 \times 10^8$ m/s) in a vacuum and is somewhat slower than this in liquid and solid insulators. An electromagnetic wave does not penetrate far into an electrical conductor, and a wave that is incident on the surface of a good conductor is largely reflected.

Electromagnetic waves originate from accelerated electric charges. For example, a radio wave originates from the oscillatory acceleration of electrons in the transmitting antenna. The light that is produced within a laser originates when electrons fall from a higher energy level to a lower one. SEE LASER.

The waves emitted from a source are oscillatory in character and are described in terms of their frequency of oscillation. Local telephone lines (not using carrier systems) carry electromagnetic waves with frequencies of about 200–4000 Hz. Medium-wave radio uses frequencies of the order of $10^6$ Hz, radar uses frequencies of the order of $10^{10}$ Hz, and a ruby laser emits light with a frequency of $4.32 \times 10^{14}$ Hz. The method of generating an electromagnetic wave depends on the frequency used, as do the techniques of transmitting the energy to another location and of utilizing it when it has been received. SEE RADAR.

The communication of information to a distant point is generally accomplished through the use of electromagnetic energy as a carrier. A familiar example is the telephone, in which sound waves in the range of frequencies from a few hundred to a few thousand hertz are converted into corresponding electromagnetic waves, which are then guided to their destination by a pair of wires. Another familiar example is radio, in which the signals are caused to modify an identifiable characteristic, such as the amplitude or frequency, of an electromagnetic carrier wave. The electromagnetic wave, thus modified, or modulated, is radiated from an antenna and can be received over a considerable region. SEE MODULATION.

**Features of electromagnetic waves. Figure 1** illustrates schematically some of the essential features of an electromagnetic wave. Shown in Fig. 1 are vectors that represent the electric field intensity $E$ and the magnetic field intensity $H$ at various points along a

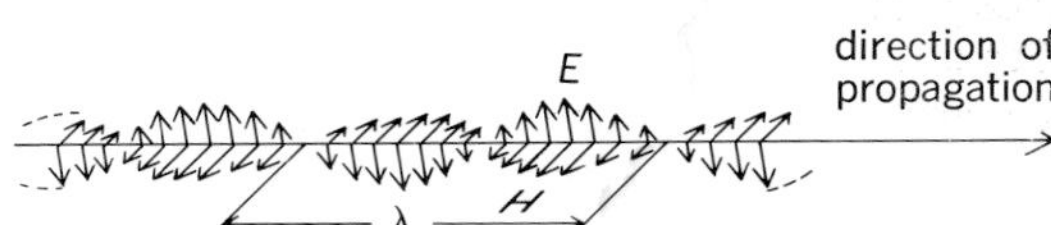


**Fig. 1. Representation of an electromagnetic wave at a particular instant of time.**

straight line taken in the direction of propagation of the wave. The electric field is in a vertical plane and the wave is said to be vertically polarized. The magnitude of the field, at a given instant, varies as a sinusoidal function of distance along the direction of propagation. The magnetic field intensity $H$ lies in a plane normal to that of $E$ and, at each point, is proportional in magnitude to $E$, as shown in Eq. (1),

$$\frac{E}{H} = \sqrt{\frac{\mu}{\epsilon}} \quad (1)$$

where $H$ is the magnetic field intensity in amperes/m, $E$ is the electric field intensity in volts/m, $\epsilon$ is the permittivity, or absolute dielectric constant, of the medium, and $\mu$ is the absolute permeability of the medium. For a vacuum, $\epsilon = 8.854 \times 10^{-12}$ farad/m and $\mu = 4\pi \times 10^{-7}$ henry/m; therefore for a vacuum the ratio $E/H$ is approximately 377 ohms. This ratio is termed the wave impedance of the medium.

The $E$ and $H$ waves travel along a straight line, as suggested in Fig. 1. Of the two possible directions along this line, the actual direction of travel can be determined by imagining a screw with a right-hand thread placed along the axis and turned from $E$ toward $H$; then the longitudinal direction of travel of the screw is the direction of propagation of the energy.

The velocity of travel of the wave is shown in Eq. (2). In a vacuum this is approximately $3 \times 10^8$ m/s.

$$v = 1\sqrt{\mu\epsilon} \quad (2)$$

The velocity in air is only slightly smaller.

The wavelength is the distance between two successive similar points on the wave, measured along the direction of propagation. The wavelength is denoted by $\lambda$ in Fig. 1.

As the wave travels past a stationary point, the values of $E$ and $H$ at the point vary sinusoidally with time. The time required for one cycle of this variation is termed the period, $T$ seconds. The number of hertz is the frequency $f$; and $f = 1/T$. In one cycle the wave, traveling at the velocity $v$, moves one wavelength along the axis of propagation. Therefore, $\lambda = vT$, or may be calculated by Eq. (3). Assuming a velocity of

$$\lambda = v/f \quad (3)$$

$3 \times 10^8$ m/s, an electromagnetic wave having a frequency of 60 Hz has a wavelength of $5 \times 10^6$ m, or approximately 3100 mi. At a frequency of 3 MHz ($3 \times 10^6$ Hz), $\lambda$ is 100 m, and at 3000 MHz, $\lambda$ is 10 cm. Visible light has a frequency of the order of $5 \times 10^{14}$ Hz and a wavelength of approximately $6 \times 10^{-5}$ cm.

The density of energy in an electric field is $\epsilon E^2/2$ joules/m$^3$, and that in a magnetic field is $\mu H^2/2$ joules/m$^3$. With the aid of Eq. (1), the relationships become those shown in Eq. (4). Therefore the electric

$$\mu H^2/2 = \mu(\sqrt{\epsilon/\mu}E)^2/2 = \epsilon E^2/2 \quad (4)$$

and magnetic fields carry equal energies in the electromagnetic wave. The total energy density at any point is equal to $\epsilon E^2$ joules/m$^3$. Since this is transported with a velocity equal to $1/\sqrt{\mu\epsilon}$, the rate of flow of energy per square meter normal to the direction of propagation is $\epsilon E^2 v$ or $E^2\sqrt{\epsilon/\mu}$ watts/m$^2$. In radio broadcasting a field of 50 millivolts/m is considered to be strong. An electromagnetic wave with this intensity has an average energy density of $2.2 \times 10^{-14}$ joule/m$^3$, and the average rate of energy flow per square meter is $6.6 \times 10^{-6}$ watt/m$^2$.

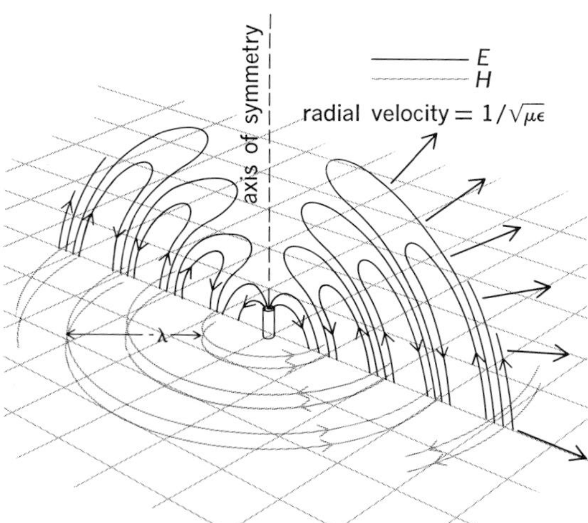


**Fig. 2. Configuration of electric and magnetic fields about a short vertical antenna.**

**Radiation from an antenna.** **Figure 2** illustrates the configuration of the electric and magnetic fields about a short vertical antenna in which flows a sinusoidal current of the form $i = I_{max} \sin 2\pi ft$ amperes. The picture applies either to an antenna in free space (in which case the illustration shows only the upper half of the fields), or to an antenna projecting above the surface of a highly conducting plane surface. In the latter case the conducting plane represents to a first approximation the surface of the Earth. The fields have symmetry about the axis through the antenna. For pictorial simplicity only selected portions of the fields are shown in Fig. 2. The magnetic field is circular about the antenna, is perpendicular at every point to the direction of the electric field, and is proportional in intensity to the magnitude of the electric field, as indicated by Eq. (1). All parts of the wave travel radially outward from the antenna with the velocity given by Eq. (2); the wave is described as spherical, with the antenna located at the center of the wave. The wavelength of the radiation is given by Eq. (3).

If a short antenna projecting above a highly conducting plane surface carries a current of $i = I_{max} \sin 2\pi ft$ that is uniform throughout the length of the antenna, the intensity of the electric field in the radiated wave is that shown in Eq. (5). where $l$ is the

$$E_{max} = \sqrt{\frac{\mu}{\epsilon}} \frac{I_{max}}{r} \frac{l}{\lambda} \cos\theta \quad \text{V/m} \quad (5)$$

length of the antenna, $r$ is the radial distance from the antenna, and $\theta$ is 0, and varies inversely with the distance from the antenna.

If the rate of flow of energy per unit area $E^2\sqrt{\epsilon/\mu}$ is integrated over an imaginary spherical surface about the antenna, the average power radiated is that shown by Eq. (6). The factor $(l/\lambda)^2$ is of partic-

$$P_{av} = \frac{2\pi}{3}\sqrt{\frac{\mu}{\epsilon}} I^2_{max}\left(\frac{l}{\lambda}\right)^2 \text{watts} \quad (6)$$

ular importance, for it indicates that a longer antenna is required at the longer wavelengths (lower frequencies). The radiation of appreciable energy at a very low frequency requires an impracticably long antenna.

The foregoing relations assume a uniform current throughout the length of the antenna. An approximation to this can be achieved in practice by connecting a long horizontal conductor to the top of the antenna. Where some such construction is not utilized, the current will not be uniform in the antenna and will, in fact, be zero at the tip. The results given by Eqs. (4) and (5) must be modified, but the qualitative features of the radiation remain as shown in Fig. 2. For further discussion SEE ANTENNA.

Often it is desired to concentrate the radiated energy into a narrow beam. This can be done either by the addition of more antenna elements or by placing a large reflector, generally parabolic in shape, behind the antenna. The production of a narrow beam requires an antenna array, or alternatively a reflector, that is large in width and height compared with a wavelength. The very narrow and concentrated beam that can be achieved by a laser is made possible by the extremely short wavelength of the radiation as compared with the cross-sectional dimensions of the radiating system.

**Propagation over the Earth.** The foregoing discussion shows some of the important features of the radiation of electromagnetic energy from an antenna, but is oversimplified insofar as communication to and from positions on or near the Earth is concerned. The ground is a reasonably good, but not perfect, conductor; hence, the actual propagation over the surface of the Earth will show a more rapid decrease of field strength than that indicated by the factor of $1/r$ in Eq. (5). Irregularities and obstructions may interfere. In long-range transmission the spherical shape of the Earth is important. Inhomogeneities in the atmosphere refract the wave somewhat. For long-range transmission, the ionized region high in the atmosphere known as the Kennelly-Heaviside layer, or ionosphere, can act as a reflector. The electric field of the wave produces oscillation of the charged particles of the region, and this causes the refractive index of the layer to be smaller than that of the atmosphere below. The result is that, if the angle of incidence is not too near the normal and if the frequency of the wave is not too high, the wave may be refracted back toward the Earth. Successive reflections between ionosphere and Earth can provide communication for long distances around the periphery of the Earth.

**Hollow waveguides.** When an electromagnetic wave is introduced into the interior of a hollow metallic pipe of suitably large cross-sectional dimensions, the energy is guided along the interior of the pipe with comparatively little loss. The most common cross-sectional shapes are the rectangle and the circle. The cross-sectional dimensions of the tube must be greater than a certain fraction of the wavelength; otherwise the wave will not propagate in the tube. For this reason hollow waveguides are commonly used only at wavelengths of 10 cm or less (frequencies of 3000 MHz or higher).

A single wave of the type in Fig. 1 cannot propagate longitudinally inside a tubular conductor since, at some portions of the inner surface of the conducting tube, the $E$ vector of the wave necessarily would have a component tangential to the surface. This is impossible because an electric field cannot be established along a good conductor, such as the wall of the tube. An electromagnetic wave can propagate along the interior of the tube only by reflecting back and forth between the walls of the tube. This reflection is a comparatively simple one between the plane surfaces of a rectangular tube, but is a complex reflection in tubes of other cross-sectional shapes.

A dielectric rod can also be used as a waveguide. Such a rod, if of insufficient cross-sectional dimensions, can contain the electromagnetic wave by the phenomenon of total reflection at the surface.

A hollow metallic waveguide of rectangular cross section is shown in **Fig. 3*a***. The simplest mode of propagation is indicated in Fig. 3*b*. The entire space is filled with a plane electromagnetic wave which moves obliquely to the left in the direction shown by the solid arrows. This wave has its $E$ vector normal to the paper and its $H$ vector in the plane of the paper. Any plane normal to the direction of propagation is a plane of uniform phase (thus the name plane wave), and one such plane is indicated in the illustration by a broken line. The wave strikes the wall at an angle $\theta$ from the normal and is reflected at an equal angle. As the wave is reflected, the direction of its $E$ vector reverses so as to make the tangential component of the electric field equal to zero at the conducting wall. The wave incident on the left wall thus is reflected to the right, where it is again reflected and moves to the left. By successive reflections the energy propagates longitudinally along the interior of the guide. As the wave incident upon the wall reflects and reverses the direction of its $E$ vector, electric currents are caused to flow in the conducting wall. Since the wall is not a perfect conductor, some of the energy of the wave is transformed into heat. Consequently the amplitude of the wave diminishes exponentially as it passed down the guide; this phenomenon is termed attenuation. For an electromagnetic wave with a frequency of 3000 MHz (wavelength of 10 cm) propagating down the interior of a rectangular copper waveguide with cross-sectional dimensions of 1.4 by 3.2 in (or 4 by 8 cm) half the power is lost in a distance of approximately 450 ft (150 m). Hollow waveguides are used chiefly for short-distance transmission, as from a transmitter to an antenna. SEE MICROWAVE TRANSMISSION LINES; WAVEGUIDE.

The requirements on the reflection of the wave, as outlined above, restrict the wavelength that can be propagated in a hollow guide. Consider the ray $ABC$ in Fig. 3. The wave propagates from $A$ to $B$, where it

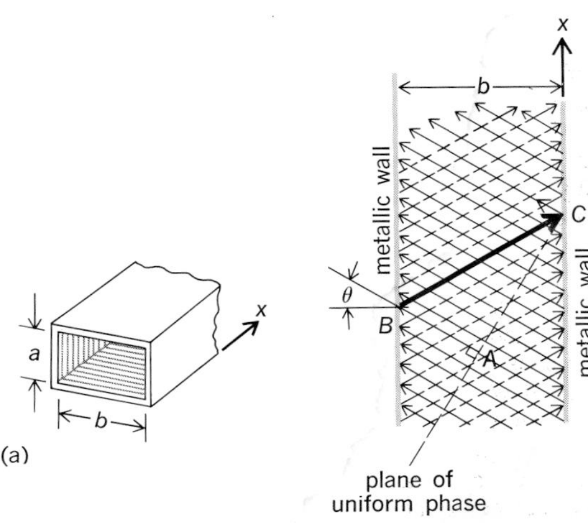


**Fig. 3. Hollow metallic waveguide of rectangular cross section. (*a*) Guide. (*b*) Paths of electromagnetic energy in the simplest mode of propagation.**

is reflected with reversal of the $E$ vector; thereupon it propagates from $B$ to $C$, where it is again reflected with another reversal of the $E$ vector. But $AC$ is a line of equal phase, and so the wave emerging from $C$ must have the same phase as that at $A$. Thus the distance $ABC$ must be an integral multiple of a wavelength, or $n\lambda$, where $n$ is a positive integer. The distance $ABC$ is $2b \cos \theta$ where $b$ is the breadth of the guide; hence, $n\lambda = 2b \cos \theta$. The condition for propagation down the axis of the guide is that $\theta > 0$; hence $\cos \theta < 1$, and the restriction on wavelength is $\lambda < 2b/n$. The greatest ratio of wavelength to breadth of guide is obtained when $n = 1$, whence $\lambda/b < 2$. Therefore, the breadth of the waveguide must be somewhat greater than $\lambda/2$.

In the simple mode of propagation described above, the fields are independent of distance in the direction of the dimension $a$, and this dimension has no influence on the propagation. The net electric vector caused by the sum of the two waves is everywhere transverse to the longitudinal axis of the guide, and so the mode is described as transverse electric (TE).

If the wavelength of the radiation is small enough in comparison with the cross-sectional dimensions of the guide, more complex modes of propagation are possible, in which the wave reflects obliquely against a side wall, proceeds to the top of the guide, and reflects from there to the other side wall, then to the bottom wall, and so on. With this type of reflection it is possible to have both transverse-electric and transverse-magnetic (TM) modes. In the latter the net $H$ vector is everywhere transverse to the axis of the guide.

When the dimensions of the guide are such that complex modes are possible, so also are the simple ones. The transmission of energy by a combination of modes introduces complications in abstracting the energy from the guide at the receiving end. Propagation in only the simplest mode is ensured by selecting the dimension $b$ to be greater than $\lambda/2$ but not as large as $\lambda$, and also by restricting the dimension $a$ so as to render complex modes impossible.

Waveguides of circular cross section are sometimes used. Analysis of these shows that the first TE mode is propagated if the diameter of the guide is greater than $0.586\lambda$, and that the first TM mode is propagated if the radius is greater than $0.766\lambda$.

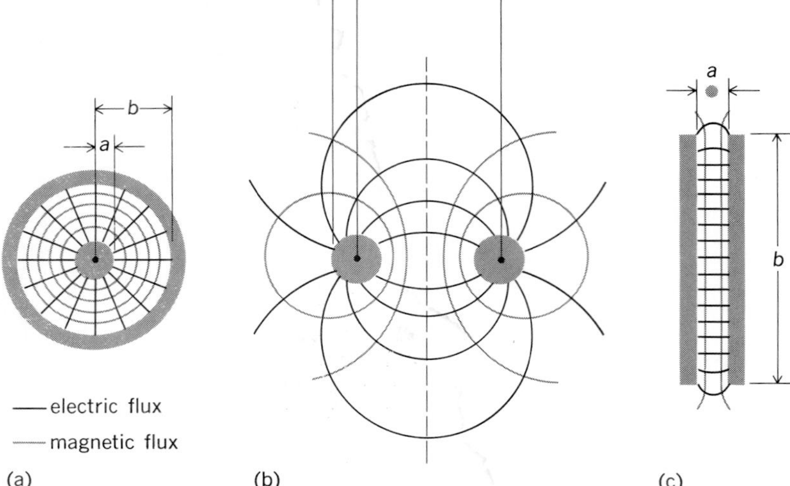


**Fig. 4. Cross sections of common two-conductor transmission lines. (*a*) Coaxial cable. (*b*) Two-wire line. (c) Parallel-strip line.**

**Two-conductor transmission lines.** Electromagnetic energy can be propagated in a simple mode along two parallel conductors. Such a waveguiding system is termed a transmission line. Three common forms are shown in **Fig. 4**. If the spacing between conductors is a small fraction of the wavelength of the transmitted energy, only one mode of propagation is possible. This corresponds to the wave of Fig. 1, with the direction of propagation taken longitudinally along the line. The $E$ and $H$ vectors are in the plane of the cross section, and the mode is termed transverse electromagnetic (TEM). The $E$ vector must be at right angles to a highly conducting surface, and the oscillating $H$ vector must be parallel with such a surface. With two separated conductors, there is for each geometrical arrangement of conductors one and only one cross-sectional field configuration which will satisfy the boundary conditions at the metal surface. The field configurations for coaxial and two-wire lines are shown in Fig. 4. At each point the ratio of $E$ to $H$ is as given by Eq. (1), and the velocity of propagation of the wave is as given by Eq. (2). Half of the propagated energy is contained in the electric field and half in the magnetic field. This mode of propagation is in contrast with the more complex modes required in a hollow metal pipe, where the conditions required at the boundaries can be satisfied only by means of reflections at the metal walls. As a result, the two-conductor transmission line does not have the upper limit on wavelength that was imposed on the hollow waveguide by the requirement of reflections; in fact, the two-conductor line operates completely normally at zero frequency (direct current).

At wavelengths that are small enough to be comparable with the cross-sectional dimensions of the line, more complex modes, involving reflections from the surfaces of the conductors, become possible. High-frequency energy can thus be propagated in several modes simultaneously. In a coaxial cable a rough criterion for the elimination of higher modes is that the wavelength should be greater than the average of the circumferences of the inner and outer conductors.

As the wave propagates along the line, it is accompanied by currents which flow longitudinally in the conductors. These currents can be regarded as satisfying the boundary condition for the tangential $H$ field at the surface of the conductor. The conductors have a finite conductivity, and so these currents cause a transformation of electrical energy into heat. The energy lost comes from the stored energy of the wave, and so the wave, as it progresses, diminishes in amplitude. The conductors are necessarily supported by insulators which are imperfect and cause additional attenuation of the wave. In a typical open-wire telephone line operating at voice frequencies, half the energy is lost in a distance of perhaps 60 mi (95 km). The losses increase with frequency, and for a typical air-insulated coaxial line operating at 5 MHz, half the energy is lost in a distance of less than 1 mi (1.6 km). At a frequency of 3000 MHz ($\lambda = 10$ cm), typical distances in which half the energy is lost are, for air-insulated coaxial cable, 82 ft (25 m); for flexible coaxial cable insulated with polyethylene, 33 ft (10 m).

***Noise.*** In a transmission line intended for the transmission of large amounts of power, such as the cross-country lines joining electrical generating stations to centers of population, the loss of an appreciable proportion of the power enroute is a serious matter. In a communication system, however, the average rate of flow of energy is rather small, and the intrinsic value of the energy itself is not of prime importance. The important characteristic of such a system is the accurate transmission of information, and the limiting factor is noise. Noise is always present in a transmission channel. Two common causes are thermal agitation and nearby electrical discharges. In a transmission system conveying information by an electromagnetic wave, the loss of energy in transmission becomes a serious matter if the wave is attenuated to the point where it is not large enough to override the noise. Amplifiers must be inserted in the transmission system at sufficiently close intervals, so that the signal never falls into the noise level, from which it could not be recovered and interpreted accurately.

***Circuit analysis of transmission lines.*** Because the conductors of a transmission line are almost always spaced much closer together than a quarter wavelength of the electromagnetic energy that they are guiding, it is possible to analyze their performance quantitatively by circuit theory. It is then possible to deal with the voltages between the conductors and the currents flowing along the conductors, instead of with the electric and magnetic fields that exist in the insulating medium.

The waveguiding properties of the transmission line can be examined most conveniently if losses of energy are ignored. If $L$ is defined as the inductance of the pair of conductors per unit length and $C$ the capacitance between the conductors per unit length, field theory shows that $L$ is $\mu F_g$ and $C$ is $\epsilon/F_g$, where $F_g$ is a geometrical factor that depends on the cross-sectional configuration of the conductors. For a coaxial line (Fig. 4*a*), $F_g = (1/2\pi) \log_\epsilon (b/a)$. For a two-wire line (Fig. 4*b*), $F_g = (1/\pi) \log_\epsilon (D/a)$. For a parallel-strip line (Fig. 4*c*), neglecting edge effects, $F_g = a/b$.

In the circuit analysis of a transmission line, the line can be visualized as being composed of a cascaded set of sections, each of short length $\Delta x$, as shown in **Fig. 5***b*. The partial differential equations which describe the voltage $e$ and the current $i$ are shown by Eqs. (7) and (8).

$$\frac{\partial e}{\partial x} = -L\frac{\partial i}{\partial t} \tag{7}$$

$$\frac{\partial i}{\partial x} = -C\frac{\partial e}{\partial t} \tag{8}$$

The solution of these equations is shown by Eqs. (9) and (10), where $f_1$ and $f_2$ are any finite, single-

$$e = f_1\,(x - t/\sqrt{LC}) + f_2\,(x + t/\sqrt{LC}) \tag{9}$$

$$i = \frac{1}{\sqrt{L/C}}\,[f_1\,(x - t/\sqrt{LC}) - f_2\,(x + t/\sqrt{LC})] \tag{10}$$

valued functions of the arguments $x - t/\sqrt{LC}$ and $x + t/\sqrt{LC}$, respectively. These are interpreted physically as traveling waves, the first traveling in the positive $x$ direction with the speed $1/\sqrt{LC}$ and the second traveling in the negative $x$ direction at the same speed. Substitution of the values for $L$ and $C$ for any configuration of conductors yields the velocity $1/\sqrt{LC}$, which equals $1/\sqrt{\mu\epsilon}$.

The quantity $\sqrt{L/C}$ has the dimensions of ohms, termed the characteristic impedance $Z_0$ of the line, as shown by Eq. (11). Thus, $Z_0$ is a real quantity (a re-

$$Z_0 = \sqrt{L/C} = \sqrt{\mu/\epsilon}F_g \tag{11}$$

sistance) and is equal to the wave impedance of the insulating medium, $\sqrt{\mu/\epsilon}$, multiplied by the geometrical factor, $F_g$, characteristic of the particular configuration of conductors. For the traveling waves of voltage and current, Eqs. (9) and (10), the ratio of voltage to current of the forward-traveling wave is $Z_0$; that of the backward-traveling wave is $-Z_0$.

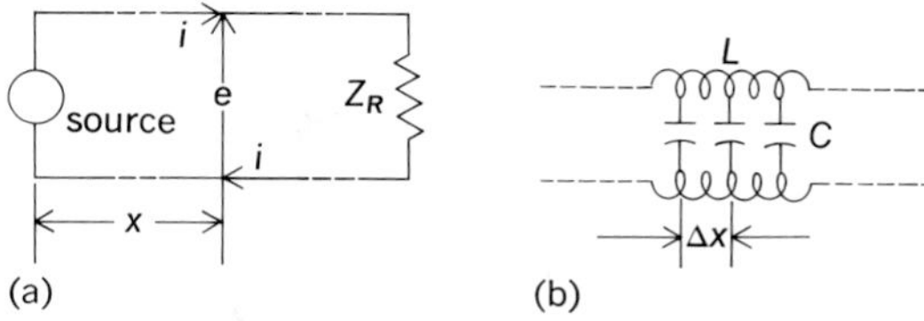


**Fig. 5. Schematic representation of a transmission line. (*a*) Circuit diagram. (*b*) Visualization of *L* and *C*.**

In Fig. 5*a*, a source of electrical energy is connected at one end of a transmission line and an electrical load is connected to the other. Electromagnetic energy is propagated from the sending end to the receiving end, and a portion of the energy is reflected back toward the sending end if the load impedance $Z_R$ is different from the characteristic impedance $Z_0$ of the line. If $Z_R$ equals $Z_0$, there is no reflection of energy at the load, and in Eqs. (9) and (10), the function $f_2$, representing leftward-traveling energy, is absent. This is the condition desired when the purpose of the line is to deliver energy from the source of the load. The sending-end impedance of the line is then equal to $Z_0$.

In addition to impedance matching to reduce reflections (echoes) along a transmission line, it is also necessary to minimize signal distortion, which consists of amplitude and phase (delay) distortion. If the line attenuation is frequency-dependent, then a signal consisting of a group of different-frequency components will undergo amplitude distortion due to the unequal attenuation of each component of the signal. Similarly, if the velocity of propagation along the line is frequency-dependent, then a delay in phase of each component will result in associated phase distortion of the signal.

Signal distortion can be minimized by the use of line loading, which is the addition of series impedances along the line and which is used to adjust the line parameters to obtain the so-called distortionless condition. Under distortionless operation the attenuation and velocity of propagation are independent of frequency. For a discussion of the distortionless line SEE TRANSMISSION LINES.

Instead of loading a line, one may employ equalizing circuits to compensate for the phase distortion along the line.

Short sections of transmission line are sometimes used to provide low-loss reactive impedances and resonant circuits at high frequencies. This is done by open-circuiting or short-circuiting the receiving end of the line to provide complete reflection of the incident energy. A short-circuited low-loss line provides the sending-end impedance shown by Eq. (12), measured

$$Z_s = jZ_0 \tan\,(2\pi fl/v) \tag{12}$$

in ohms. When $l$ equals $v/4f$, the line is a quarter

wavelength long, the argument $(2\pi fl/v)$ of the tangent function in Eq. (12) is $\pi/2$, and $Z_s$ approaches an infinite value. In actual practice, losses keep $Z_s$ to a finite value. However, at high frequencies the quarter wavelength is short and the losses are small, and such a short-circuited quarter-wave section can be used successfully as a low-loss insulator. Such a section is a resonant one and can be used as a substitute for a parallel-resonant *LC* circuit, for example, a tank circuit for a high-frequency oscillator. At low frequencies the required quarter wavelength is so large that losses impair the performance; also, the length becomes inconveniently great. At a frequency lower than $v/4l$, the sending-end impedance of the short-circuited line is inductive, and at frequencies between $v/4l$ and $v/2l$ the impedance is capacitive. This provides the possibility of using sections of short-circuited line as reactive elements in circuits.

*Walter C. Johnson*

**Bibliography.** A. G. Boardman, *Electromagnetic Surface Modes*, 1982; C. W. Davidson, *Transmission Lines for Communication and Digital Systems*, 1978; D. S. Jones, *Methods in Electromagnetic Wave Propagation*, 1979; E. C. Jordan and K. G. Balmain, *Electromagnetic Waves and Radiating Systems*, 2d ed., 1968; J. D. Kraus, *Electromagnetics*, 3d ed., 1984; S. Ramo, J. R. Whinnery, and T. Van Duzer, *Fields and Waves in Communication Electronics*, 1965; S. R. Seshadri, *Fundamentals of Transmission Lines and Electromagnetic Fields*, 1971; H. H. Skilling, *Electric Transmission Lines*, 1951, reprint 1979.

## Electromotive force (emf)

A measure of the strength of a source of electrical energy. The term is often shortened to emf. It is not, of course, a force in the usual mechanical sense (and for this reason has sometimes been called electromotance), but it is a conveniently descriptive term for the agency which drives current through an electric circuit. In the simple case of a direct current $I$ (measured in amperes) flowing through a resistor $R$ (in ohms), Ohm's law states that there will be a voltage drop (or potential difference) of $V = IR$ (in volts) across the resistor. To cause this current to flow requires a source with emf (also measured in volts) $E = V$. More generally, Kirchhoff's voltage law states that the sum of the source emf's taken around any closed path in an electric circuit is equal to the sum of the voltage drops. This is equivalent to the statement that the total emf in a closed circuit is equal to the line integral of the electric field strength around the circuit. *See Electric current; Electrical resistance; Ohm's law.*

A source of emf $E$ delivering a current $I$ supplies electrical energy at a rate of $EI$ (in watts). Hence the emf in a circuit is numerically equal to the work done in carrying a charge of 1 coulomb around the circuit.

**Open-circuit emf.** A source such as a battery has an internal resistance which causes an internal voltage drop when a current is drawn from it. Consequently the emf at the external terminals varies with the current. By extrapolating to zero current, the open-circuit emf may be derived. It is the open-circuit emf which is usually said to be the emf of a source; together with the value of the internal resistance, it enables the performance of the source in any circuit to be calculated.

**Types of emf.** An emf may be steady (direct), as for a battery, or time-varying, as for a charged capacitor discharging through a resistor. A class of time-varying sources of very great practical importance is that of generators of alternating (sinusoidal) emf. Emf's may be generated by a variety of physical, chemical, and biological processes. Some of the more important are:

1. Electrochemical reactions, as used in direct-current (dc) batteries, in which the emf results from the reactions between electrolyte and electrodes.

2. Electromagnetic induction, in which the emf results from a change in the magnetic flux linking the circuit. This finds application in alternating-current rotary generators and transformers, providing the basis for the electricity supply industry. *See Faraday's law of induction; Transformer.*

3. Thermoelectric effects, in which a temperature difference between different parts of a circuit produces an emf. The main use is for the measurement of temperature by means of thermocouples; there are some applications to electric power generation.

4. The photovoltaic effect, in which the absorption of light (or, more generally, electromagnetic radiation) in a semiconductor produces an emf. This is widely used for scientific purposes in radiation detectors and also, increasingly, for the generation of electric power from the Sun's radiation. *See Photovoltaic effect; Solar cell.*

5. The piezoelectric effect, in which the application of mechanical stress to certain types of crystal generates an emf. There are applications in sound recording, in ultrasonics, and in various types of measurement transducer. *See Disk recording; Microphone; Piezoelectricity; Transducer.*

For a more general discussion of the treatment of electric circuit quantities, including electromotive force, *see Alternating-current circuit theory; Direct-current circuit theory; Kirchhoff's laws of electric circuits.*

*A. Earle Bailey*

## Electron emission

The liberation of electrons from a substance into vacuum. Since all substances are built up of atoms and since all atoms contain electrons, any substance may emit electrons; usually, however, the term refers to emission of electrons from the surface of a solid.

The process of electron emission is analogous to that of ionization of a free atom, in which the latter parts with one or more electrons. The energy of the electrons in an atom is lower than that of an electron at rest in vacuum; consequently, in order to ionize an atom, energy must be supplied to the electrons in some way or other. By the same token, a substance does not emit electrons spontaneously, but only if some of the electrons have energies equal to, or larger than, that of an electron at rest in vacuum. This may be achieved by various means. If a substance is heated, the atoms begin to vibrate with larger amplitudes, and electrons may absorb sufficient energy from these vibrations to be emitted in the process known as thermionic emission. Electrons may also be liberated upon irradiation of the substance with light (photoemission). Electron emission from a substance may be induced by bombardment with charged particles such as electrons or ions in the phenomenon called secondary emission. Field emission, or cold emission, refers to the emission of electrons under influence of a strong electric field. Electrons may also be emitted from one solid into another, but this process is usually referred to as electron injection. For example, a metal may inject electrons into an insulator under certain circumstances. *SEE FIELD EMISSION; PHOTOEMISSION; SECONDARY EMISSION; THERMIONIC EMISSION.*

*Adrianus J. Dekker*

**Bibliography.** M. Cardona and L. Ley (eds.), *Photoemission in Solids*, 2 vols., 1978, 1979; P. H. Cutler and T. T. Tsong, *Field Emission and Related Topics*, 1978; L. N. Dobretsov and M. V. Gomoyunova, *Emission Electronics*, 1972; G. N. Hatsopoulos and E. P. Gyftopoulos, *Thermionic Energy Conversion*, 2 vols., 1979.

## Electron-hole recombination

The process in which an electron, which has been excited from the valence band to the conduction band of a semiconductor, falls back into an empty state in the valence band, which is known as a hole. *SEE HOLES IN SOLIDS.*

When atoms come together to form a crystal, the discrete atomic energy levels broaden into a level continuum. The periodic potential of the crystal produces gaps in the continuum, separating it into a number of energy bands. In a pure semiconductor crystal, bonding electrons fill the valence band, and above the valence band in energy is an empty conduction band. The two bands are separated by the band gap, which has no levels, and the extent of this band gap is a characteristic of each semiconductor. The band gap is of order 1 eV for common semiconductor materials such as silicon (Si) or gallium arsenide (GaAs). *SEE BAND THEORY OF SOLIDS.*

Light with photon energies greater than the band gap can be absorbed by the crystal, exciting electrons from the filled valence band to the empty conduction band (**Fig. 1***a*). The state in which an electron is removed from the filled valence band is known as a hole. It is analogous to a bubble in a liquid. The hole can be thought of as being mobile and having positive charge. The excited electrons and holes rapidly lose energy (in about $10^{-12}$ s) by the excitation of lattice phonons (vibrational quanta). The excited electrons fall to near the bottom of the conduction band, and the holes rise to near the top of the valence band, and then on a much longer time scale (of $10^{-9}$ to $10^{-6}$ s) the electron drops across the energy gap into the empty state represented by the hole. This is known as electron-hole recombination. An energy approximately equal to the band gap is released in the process. Electron-hole recombination is radiative if the released energy is light and nonradiative if it is heat.

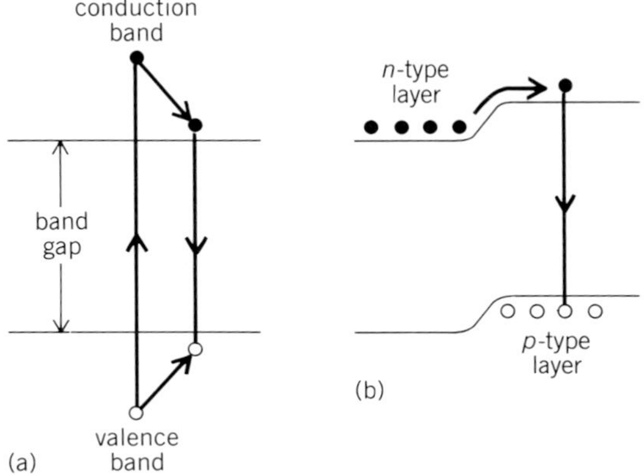


**Fig. 1.** Recombination of electrons and holes generated by (*a*) optical absorption and (*b*) a forward-biased *pn* junction.

**Recombination at pn junctions.** Electron-hole recombination requires an excited semiconductor in which both electrons and holes occupy the same volume of the crystal. This state can be produced by purely electrical means by forward-biasing a *pn* junction. The *pn* junction is formed by adjacent *p*-type and *n*-type layers containing excess holes and excess electrons, respectively. In the *n*-type layer, donor impurities replace some of the host atoms. Each donor impurity has one more electron in its outer shell than the host atom, and these extra electrons go into the conduction band. Likewise, in the *p*-type layer, acceptor impurities replace some of the host atoms. The acceptor atoms contain one less electron in their outer shell than the host atoms. They complete their valence bonds by taking a valence electron from elsewhere in the crystal, thereby creating holes in the valence band.

The *pn* junctions forms a barrier that keeps the electrons and holes separated. By contacting these layers and applying a forward-bias voltage to the *pn* junction, the barrier height can be reduced, enabling electrons to flow into the *p*-region or holes into the *n*-region, thus allowing electron-hole recombination to take place. The current passing through a *pn* diode in electrons per second equals the rate of electron-hole recombination (Fig. 1*b*). A major application of this phenomenon is the light-emitting diode (LED), which generates light by means of radiative electron-hole recombination resulting from forward-biasing the *pn* junction. *SEE LIGHT-EMITTING DIODE; SEMICONDUCTOR DIODE.*

**Radiative recombination.** Semiconductor materials may be divided into two types: direct-band-gap semiconductors and indirect-band-gap semiconductors. Efficient radiative recombination between free electrons and holes takes place only in direct-band-gap semiconductors. The continuous energy levels of electrons in the conductor and valence bands are characterized by a definite value of momentum (or more precisely, wave vector). During an optical transition, momentum is conserved, and since the photon carries away negligible momentum, transitions take place only between conduction-band and valence-band states having the same momentum. This is easily satisfied in direct-band-gap semiconductors, because electrons and holes collect at the conduction-band at minimum and the valence band at maximum, and both extrema have the same momentum (**Fig. 2***a*). However, for indirect-band-gap semiconductors (Fig. 2*b*), the conduction-band minimum and valence-band maximum have very different momenta, and consequently optical transitions between free electrons and holes are forbidden.

Radiative electron-hole recombination is possible in indirect-band-gap semiconductors when the transition

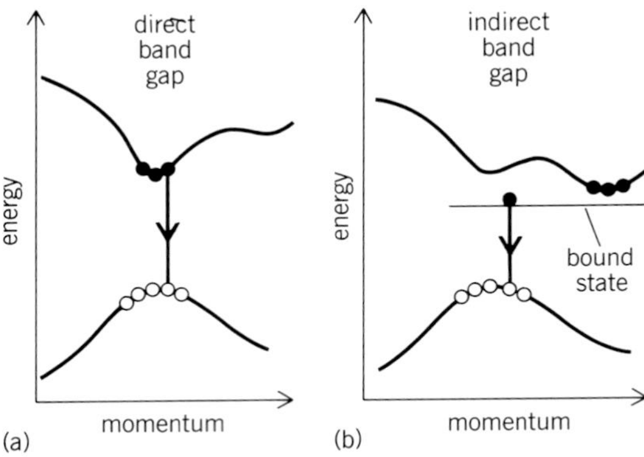


**Fig. 2. Energy versus momentum for the conduction-band and valence-band states of (*a*) a direct-band-gap semiconductor and (*b*) an indirect-band-gap semiconductor. Optical transitions in indirect-band-gap semiconductors take place through bound states that have a momentum distribution as indicated.**

is assisted by lattice phonons and impurities. Weak optical transitions can take place in which a momentum-conserving phonon is emitted along with the photon. Electrons can be trapped at impurities having energy levels within the energy gap. Unlike the free electron, the bound electron has a spread of momentum as a consequence of its localization (the uncertainty principle), with some components of momentum at the valence-band maxima (Fig. 2*b*). The isoelectronic impurity nitrogen substituted for phosphorus in gallium phosphide (GaP) and gallium arsenide phosphide (GaAsP) is used for this purpose. When heavily doped with nitrogen, these indirect semiconductors have moderate luminescence efficiency and are used as light-emitting diodes to generate green light. Bismuth impurities can be used in the same way to produce yellow light. It would be more desirable to use direct-band-gap semiconductors for this purpose, but currently there are no direct-band-gap semiconductors capable of forming *pn* junctions which emit these colors at room temperature.

Apart from its application in light-emitting diodes and laser operation, radiative recombination, especially at low temperatures (approximately 2 K or −456°F), has been a very important tool for studying the interaction of electrons and holes in semiconductor crystals. At low temperatures, many weakly bound states such as excitons are able to form stably. These states interact only weakly with lattice vibrations and consequently emit much of their recombination radiation in the form of sharp (zero phonon) spectral lines. For example, at low temperatures, electrons become trapped at donor sites and holes at acceptor sites. The spectrum of donor-acceptor recombination contains hundreds of resolvable lines, one for each crystallographically inequivalent donor-acceptor pair.

**Nonradiative recombination.** Competing with radiative recombination are the nonradiative recombination processes of multiphonon emission and Auger recombination. Nonradiative recombination of electrons and holes by multiphonon emission occurs in two steps. First, an electron is captured into a deep level near the middle of the energy gap, and subsequently the trapped electron state captures a hole from the valence band (**Fig. 3**). Multiphonon emission requires atoms very different from the host, or defects such as vacancy-impurity complexes, dislocations, or semiconductor-oxide interface states. Electron capture substantially alters the positions of the surrounding lattice, a process, known as lattice relaxation, that lowers the electronic energy of the bound electron (Fig. 3). The vibration of the lattice causes the electronic level to move within the energy gap and even cross into the bands. Capture takes place during the crossing.

In multiphonon emission, the energy lost during capture highly excites the vibrations of one or several atoms related to the defect site. This can greatly enhance the probability for an atom to jump to a different site, which also requires a highly excited atomic vibration. Such recombination-enhanced motion has been observed in detail for defects formed by ionizing radiation in GaAs and in Si. It is suspected that nonradiative recombination by multiphonon emission drives the movement of atoms at room temperature that are responsible for device degradation phenomena such as the climb of dislocations found in GaAs light-emitting diodes and lasers.

Another source of nonradiative recombination is the Auger effect, in which an electron or hole takes up the energy released in the recombination of a pair of other charge carriers. Auger recombination has been observed for excitons bound to neutral donors in Si and GaP, a complex of two electrons and a hole. In these cases, the Auger recombination rate is sev-

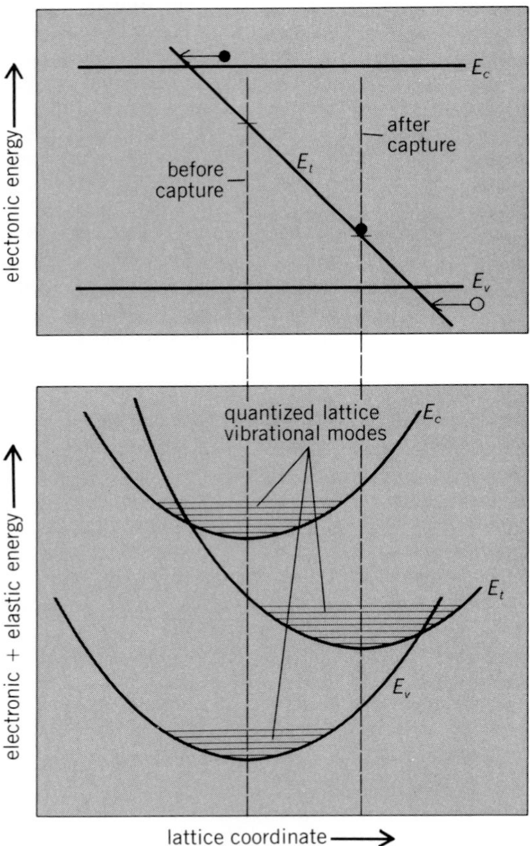


**Fig. 3. Electron and hole capture into a deep level by multiphonon emission. After capture the lattice relaxes, lowering the electronic energy of the bound state $E_t$. $E_c$ and $E_v$ are the minima of the conduction band and maxima of the valence band, respectively.**

eral orders of magnitude greater than the radiative rate. Auger recombination has been shown to limit the performance of long-wavelength (1.3–1.6 micrometer) lasers and light-emitting diodes used in optical communication systems. The Auger effect reduces light-emitting diode efficiency and greatly enhances the increase of laser threshold current with temperature. SEE LASER; OPTICAL COMMUNICATIONS; SEMICONDUCTOR.

*Charles H. Henry*

**Bibliography.** A. A. Bergh and P. J. Dean, *Light Emitting Diodes*, 1976; C. H. Henry, Deep level spectroscopy, low temperature defect motion and nonradiative recombination in GaAs and GaP, *J. Electr. Mater.*, 4:1037–1052, 1975; W. Schockley, *Electrons and Holes in Semiconductors*, 1950; A. Sugimura, Band to band Auger effect in long wavelength multilayer III-V alloy semiconductor lasers, *IEEE J. Quant. Electron.*, QE–18:352–363, 1982; S. M. Sze, *Physics of Semiconductor Devices*, 1981.

## Electron lens

An electric or magnetic field, or a combination thereof, which acts upon an electron beam in a manner analogous to that in which an optical lens acts upon a light beam. Electron lenses find application for the formation of sharply focused electron beams, as in cathode-ray tubes, and for the formation of electron images, as in infrared converter tubes, various types of television camera tubes, and electron microscopes.

Any electric or magnetic field which is symmetrical about an axis is capable of forming either a real or a virtual electron image of an object on the axis which either emits electrons or transmits electrons from another electron source. Hence, an axially symmetric electric or magnetic field is analogous to a spherical optical lens.

The lens action of an electric and magnetic field of appropriate symmetry can be derived from the fact that it is possible to define an index of refraction $n$ for electron paths in such fields. This index depends on the field distribution and the velocity and direction of the electrons. It is given by the equivalencies shown below. Here $e$ is the charge of the electron, $m$

$$n = \sqrt{\phi + \frac{2e\phi^2}{mc^2}} - \sqrt{\frac{e}{2m}}\,A\cos\chi$$

$$= \sqrt{\phi + 0.978 \times 10^{-6}\phi^2} - 0.297A\cos\chi$$

its rest mass, $\phi$ the potential of the point in space under consideration (so normalized that the kinetic energy of the electron vanishes for $\phi = 0$), $c$ the velocity of light, $A$ the magnetic vector potential, and $\chi$ the angle formed by the path of the electron with the direction of the magnetic vector potential. For an axially symmetric field the magnetic vector potential is perpendicular to the plane passing through the axis of symmetry and the reference point. Its magnitude is equal to the magnetic flux through the circle about the axis through the reference point divided by the circumference of that circle. The numerical coefficients in the final expression for $n$ apply if $\phi$ is measured in volts and $A$ in gauss-centimeters.

Electron lenses differ from optical lenses both in the fact that the index of refraction is continuously variable within them and that it covers an enormous range. Furthermore, in the presence of a magnetic field, $n$ depends both on the position of the electron in space and on its direction of motion. It is not possible to shape electron lenses arbitrarily. SEE ELECTROSTATIC LENS; MAGNETIC LENS.

*Edward G. Ramberg*

**Bibliography.** P. W. Hawkes, *Properties of Magnetic Electron Lenses*, 1982; S. Wischnitzer, *Introduction to Electron Microscopy*, 3d ed., 1981.

## Electron motion in vacuum

Motion of electrons in a space freed sufficiently from matter so that collisions with other particles play a negligible role. The motion of electrons in vacuum is controlled by electric and magnetic fields whose force on the electrons is proportional to their magnitude. Electric and magnetic fields may arise from the presence of electrodes, currents, and magnets surrounding the evacuated space in which a particular electron moves, as well as from the presence of other charged particles within this space. This article deals with the nonrelativistic motion of electrons in static electric and magnetic fields, the effect of space charge on the electron paths, and motion in the time-varying fields that are encountered, for example, in the cathode-ray oscilloscope.

**Static electric fields.** An electron moving in a plane of symmetry of an electric field will remain indefinitely in that plane because the electrical forces acting on the electron lie within the plane. A plane of symmetry is here defined as one for which the mirror image of the potential distribution in front of the plane coincides with the potential distribution in back of the plane. Newton's second law of motion for the electron moving in the plane with rectangular coordinates $x$, $y$ takes the form of Eqs. (1) and (2). Here

$$m\frac{d^2x}{dt^2} = -eE_x = e\frac{\partial\phi}{\partial x} \qquad (1)$$

$$m\frac{d^2y}{dt^2} = -eE_y = e\frac{\partial\phi}{\partial y} \qquad (2)$$

$-e$ and $m$ are the charge and mass of the electron, $t$ is time, $E_x$ and $E_y$ are the $x$ and $y$ components of the electric field, and $\phi$ is the electric potential, normalized as stated by Eq. (3). Newton's law as stated in

$$\frac{m}{2}\left[\left(\frac{dx}{dt}\right)^2 + \left(\frac{dy}{dt}\right)^2\right] = e\phi \qquad (3)$$

Eqs. (1) and (2) implies that the speed of the electron is small enough so that its mass can be regarded as constant. For an electron having an energy of 10 kilovolts, the increase in mass is about 1%.

***Path equation.*** Elimination of time from Eqs. (1) and (2) leads to the path equation, Eq. (4). If poten-

$$\frac{d^2y}{dx^2} = \frac{1}{2\phi}\left[1 + \left(\frac{dy}{dx}\right)^2\right]\left[\frac{\partial\phi}{\partial y} - \frac{dy}{dx}\frac{\partial\phi}{\partial x}\right] \qquad (4)$$

tial distribution $\phi(x,y)$ is known, and if position and velocity of the electron at one point within the field are also known, the electron's path can be determined by integrating Eq. (4). For simple electrode structures, the potential distribution can be determined analytically by solving Laplace's equation in the form of Eq. (5). More generally, it can be found by con-

$$\nabla^2\phi = \frac{\partial^2\phi}{\partial x^2} + \frac{\partial^2\phi}{\partial y^2} + \frac{\partial^2\phi}{\partial z^2} = 0 \qquad (5)$$

structing a large-scale model of the electrode structure and immersing it in an electrolytic tank so that the surface of the liquid (usually slightly acidified tap water) coincides with the plane of symmetry of interest. With potentials proportional to the actual potentials applied to the model electrodes, an equipotential line on the surface can be found by determining the points at which a probe at the potential in question draws no current.

The path equation, Eq. (4), leads to Eq. (6) for the

$$R = \frac{2\phi}{(\partial\phi/\partial n)} \qquad (6)$$

radius of curvature $R$ of the paths. Here $-\partial\phi/\partial n$ is the component of the electric field normal to the electron path. If an equipotential plot has been prepared, this relation permits graphical plotting of an electron path (**Fig. 1**). The path is approximated by a series of circular arcs, the radius of curvature between successive equipotential lines being computed from the preceding relation for $R$.

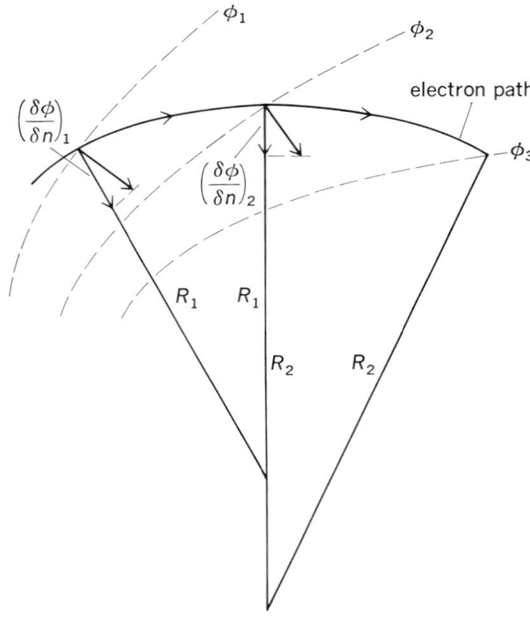


**Fig. 1. Path plotting in an electrostatic field. Broken lines $\phi_1$, $\phi_2$, and $\phi_3$ are equipotential lines. $R_1$ and $R_2$ are radii of curvature of the electron path.**

***Paraxial-ray equation.*** Electrostatic fields having not only a plane of symmetry but an axis of symmetry, which represents the intersection of an infinite family of planes of symmetry, have particular practical importance. Equation (4) still applies here, provided that $y$ is identified with $r$, the distance from the axis, and $x$ with $z$, the distance measured along the axis. The Laplace equation in the new coordinates $z$, $r$ takes the form of Eq. (7). Equation (7) is solved quite generally

$$\frac{\partial^2\phi}{\partial r^2} + \frac{1}{r}\frac{\partial\phi}{\partial r} + \frac{\partial^2\phi}{\partial z^2} = 0 \qquad (7)$$

by the series shown as Eq. (8), where $\Phi(z)$ is the

$$\phi(z,r) = \Phi(z) - \frac{r^2}{4}\frac{d^2\Phi}{dz^2} + \frac{r^4}{64}\frac{d^4\Phi}{dz^4} \cdots \qquad (8)$$

potential on the axis of symmetry. Thus, the potential everywhere within the axially symmetric electrode structure is fully determined by the potential variation along the axis. Substitution of $\phi$ from Eq. (8) into Eq. (4) with retention of terms of the first order only in $r$ and $dr/dt$ leads to the paraxial ray equation, Eq. (9). Equation (9) applies to electrons whose paths de-

$$\frac{d^2r}{dz^2} + \frac{1}{2}\frac{d\Phi}{dz}\frac{dr}{dz} + \frac{1}{4}\frac{d^2\Phi}{dz^2} r = 0 \qquad (9)$$

part relatively little, both in slope and in distance, from the axis of the field.

Equation (9) is linear in $r$. Thus, if one electron path intersects the axis in two points, all electron paths passing through one of the points also pass through the other. In brief, the electric field images the one point into the other. It can be shown further that this imaging property is not limited to the axis but applies to extended areas about the axis, so that the axially symmetric electric field acts on the paths of electrons in the same manner as glass lenses act on light rays. Departures of the exact path from the paraxial equation result in image defects or aberrations similar in character to those observed for glass lenses. *SEE ELECTROSTATIC LENS.*

**Magnetic fields.** A magnetic field exerts on an electron of velocity **v** a force **F** perpendicular to both the direction of motion and the direction of the field. In vector notation this Lorentz force is given by Eq. (10). Here, **b** is the magnetic induction. The compo-

$$\mathbf{F} = -e(\mathbf{v} \times \mathbf{b}) \qquad (10)$$

nents of the Lorentz force are given by Eqs. (11) – (13). Because this force is perpendicular to the direc-

$$F_x = e\left[b_y\frac{dz}{dt} - b_z\frac{dy}{dt}\right] \qquad (11)$$

$$F_y = e\left[b_z\frac{dx}{dt} - b_x\frac{dz}{dt}\right] \qquad (12)$$

$$F_z = e\left[b_x\frac{dy}{dt} - b_y\frac{dx}{dt}\right] \qquad (13)$$

tion of motion, it does no work on the electron, whose velocity consequently remains unchanged in magnitude. A uniform magnetic field parallel to the $z$ axis is described by Eqs. (14). Newton's second law

$$b_z = B \qquad b_x = b_y = 0 \qquad (14)$$

leads to a constant $z$ component of the velocity. The magnitude of the velocity component $v_{xy}$ in the $xy$ plane is similarly constant, the square of the total velocity being equal to the sum of the squares of the components, For the motion projected on the $xy$ plane, Newton's second law thus takes the form of Eq. (15). Here $R$ is the radius of curvature of the

$$mv_{xy}^2/R = ev_{xy}B \qquad (15)$$

projected path. $R$ is seen to be a constant, so that the projected path is a circle with radius given by Eq. (16). Here $\alpha$ is the angle which the electron path

$$R = \frac{mv_{xy}}{eB} = \frac{\sin\alpha}{B}\left(\frac{2m\phi}{e}\right)^{1/2} = \frac{3.37\phi^{1/2}}{B}\sin\alpha \qquad (16)$$

makes with the field direction, and $\phi$ is the accelerating potential of the electrons. If $B$ is measured in gauss, and $\phi$ in volts, $R$ is in centimeters. The fre-

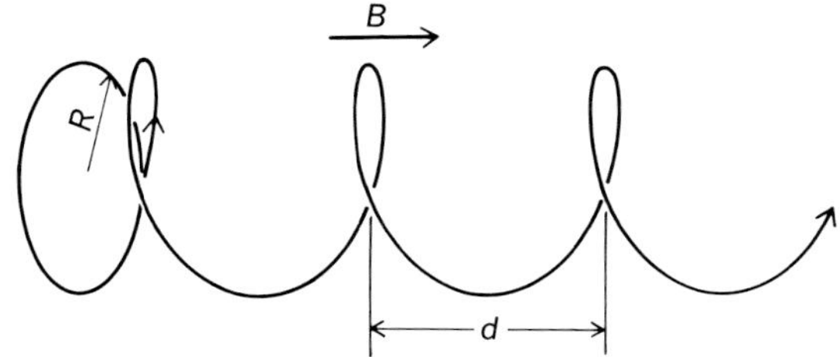


**Fig. 2. Motion of an electron in a uniform magnetic field. Its path is in general a helix with pitch *d*, radius *R*, and axis parallel to the field.**

quency with which the circle is traversed by the electron is given by Eq. (17). This frequency, in $s^{-1}$, the

$$f = v_{xy}/(2\pi R) = eB/(2\pi m) = 2.8 \times 10^6 B \quad (17)$$

cyclotron frequency, thus depends only on the magnetic field strength.

The complete motion of the electron (**Fig. 2**) is thus a helix about a magnetic line of force, with a pitch $d$ in centimeters given by Eq. (18). All electrons

$$d = v_z/f = \frac{2\pi \cos\alpha}{B}\left(\frac{2m\phi}{e}\right)^{1/2} = 21.08\,\frac{\phi^{1/2}}{B}\cos\alpha \quad (18)$$

passing through a point with equal axial velocity components pass through a series of points separated by $d$ on the same magnetic field line. An initially divergent electron beam is held together by a uniform magnetic field, because an electron path which intersects a particular field line can never depart from it by more than twice the radius $R$ of the helix. Uniform magnetic fields are widely used for keeping electron beams from spreading, for example, in traveling-wave tubes and klystrons. Electron beams will also follow magnetic field lines, if these are gently curved. This property is utilized in the magnetic deflection of beams in certain television camera tubes, such as the image orthicon and the vidicon. In these tubes, a weak transverse magnetic deflection field is superposed on a strong longitudinal magnetic focusing field. *SEE TELEVISION CAMERA TUBE.*

Motion in nonuniform magnetic fields with axial symmetry is conveniently treated as a special case of motion in combined electric and magnetic fields.

**Combined fields with axial symmetry.** Motion is now expressed by Eqs. (19)–(21). Coordinates $z$, $r$,

$$m\frac{d^2z}{dt^2} = e\left[\frac{\partial\phi}{\partial z} + b_r r\frac{d\theta}{dt}\right] \quad (19)$$

$$m\left[\frac{d^2r}{dt^2} - r\left(\frac{d\theta}{dt}\right)^2\right] = e\left[\frac{\partial\phi}{\partial r} - b_z r\frac{d\theta}{dt}\right] \quad (20)$$

$$m\frac{1}{r}\frac{d}{dt}\left(r^2\frac{d\theta}{dt}\right) = e\left[b_z\frac{dr}{dt} - b_r\frac{dz}{dt}\right] \quad (21)$$

and $\theta$ represent distance along the axis, perpendicular distance from the axis, and azimuthal angle about the axis. Terms $b_z$ and $b_r$ are the axial and radial components of the magnetic induction. From Eqs. (19)–(21), Eq. (22*a*), a path equation expressing the variation of the radial distance $r$ with the axial distance $z$, is derived, with $\phi^*$ defined by Eq. (22*b*). Here $\phi\, D^2$ is a shorthand symbol for the last term in Eq. (22*b*) and $C$ is, except for a universal multiplying constant, the angular momentum of the electron about the axis at a point where the magnetic field vanishes, given by Eq. (22*c*). Here $A$ is the magnetic vector potential,

$$\frac{d^2r}{dz^2} = \frac{1}{2\phi^*}\left[1 + \left(\frac{dr}{dz}\right)^2\right]\left[\frac{\partial\phi^*}{\partial r} - \frac{dr}{dz}\frac{\partial\phi^*}{\partial z}\right] \quad (22a)$$

$$\phi^* = \phi(1 - D^2) = \phi - \left[\frac{C}{r} + \left(\frac{e}{2m}\right)^{1/2} A\right]^2 \quad (22b)$$

$$C = r^2\frac{d\theta}{dz}\phi^{1/2}\left[\left(\frac{dr}{dz}\right)^2 + r^2\left(\frac{d\theta}{dz}\right)^2 + 1\right]^{-1/2} - \left(\frac{e}{2m}\right)^{1/2} rA \quad (22c)$$

which is numerically equal to the magnetic flux through a circle about the axis through the reference point divided by the circumference of that circle.

At the same time, the aximuth $\theta$ of the electron changes according to Eq. (23). Equations (22) can be

$$\theta = \phi_0 + \int_{z_0}^{z}\frac{D}{r(1 - D^2)^{1/2}} \cdot \left[1 + \left(\frac{dr}{dz}\right)^2\right]^{1/2} dz \quad (23)$$

solved by graphical and numerical methods useful for determining electron paths in electrostatic fields. The general paraxial equation is obtained by substituting the expansion of Eq. (24) into Eq. (22*b*). Here $B(z)$

$$A = \frac{r}{2}B(z) - \frac{r^3}{16}\frac{d^2B(z)}{dz^2}\cdots \quad (24)$$

is the magnetic induction along the axis. Substitution of Eq. (24) and that for the electrostatic potential and retention of terms of the first order in $r$ and $drPdz$ only lead to Eqs. (25). With $B$ in gauss, $\phi$ in volts, and $z$

$$\frac{d^2r}{dz^2} + \frac{1}{2\Phi}\frac{d\Phi}{dz}\frac{dr}{dz} + \left(\frac{1}{4\Phi}\frac{d^2\Phi}{dz^2} + \frac{eB^2}{8m\Phi} - \frac{C^2}{\Phi r^4}\right)r = 0 \quad (25a)$$

$$\theta = \theta_0 + \int_{z_0}^{z}\left[\frac{C}{r^2\Phi^{1/2}} + \left(\frac{e}{8m\Phi}\right)^{1/2} B\right] dz \quad (25b)$$

$$\frac{C}{r_0{}^2\Phi_0{}^{1/2}} = \left(\frac{d\theta}{dz}\right)_0 - \left(\frac{e}{8m\Phi_0}\right)^{1/2} B(z_0) \quad (25c)$$

in centimeters, $e/8m$ equals 0.022 volt/(gauss-cm)$^2$.

**Quadrupole fields.** The principal use of axially symmetric electrostatic and magnetic fields is to converge electron pencils; thus, in the cathode-ray tube, electrons diverging from a point in front of the emitter, called the crossover, are converged to a small spot on the viewing screen. Similarly, in an electron-imaging device such as the electron microscope, electrons diverging from a point on an object are brought to focus at a corresponding point of the image. However, this converging effect is only secondary; the primary effect of an axially symmetric electrostatic field is to accelerate or decelerate the electrons parallel to the axis, and the primary effect of an axially symmetric magnetic field is to give electrons diverging from a point on the axis a rotation about the axis. Correspondingly, the converging action or refractive power of a conventional electrostatic lens is proportional not to the first power but to the square of the

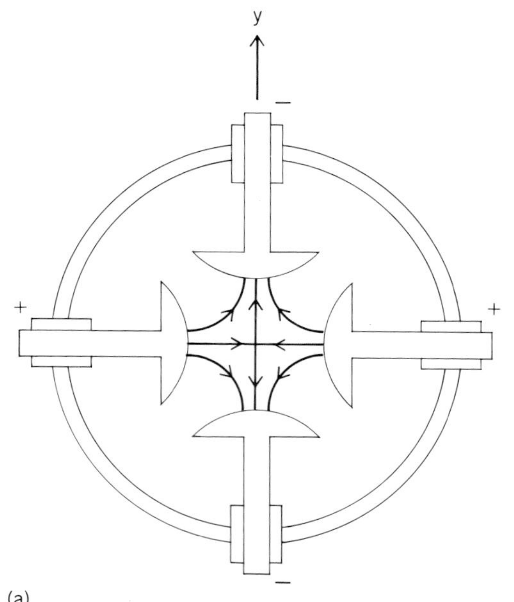


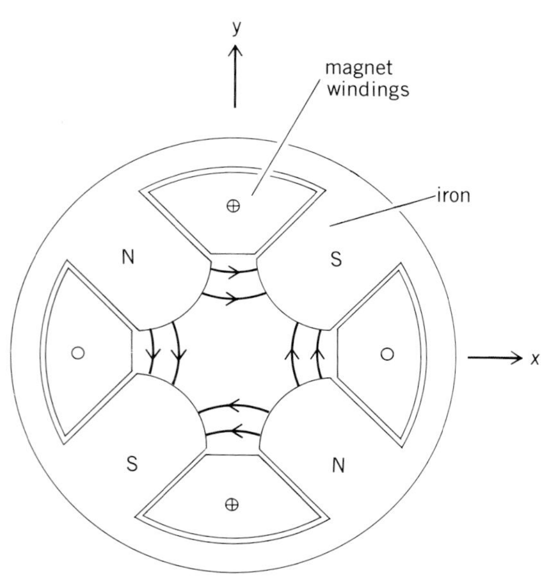


**Fig. 3. Two types of quadrupole lens. (*a*) Electrostatic quadrupole. (*b*) Magnetic quadrupole.**

ratio of the electrostatic field to the accelerating voltage, whereas the converging action of a conventional magnetic lens is proportional to the ratio of the square of the magnetic field to the accelerating potential at low electron energies (≪0.5 MeV) and to the square of the ratio of the field to the accelerating potential at high electron energies (≫0.5 MeV). Because breakdown phenomena place practical limits on the magnitude of electrostatic fields, and because pole-piece saturation limits (static) magnetic fields, conventional electron lenses are relatively ineffective in converging high-energy particles; they can be properly characterized as weak-focusing lenses.

Quadrupole fields, on the other hand, constitute strong-focusing lenses, insofar as their converging action is directly proportional to the electrostatic or magnetic field respectively. Consequently they (particularly magnetic quadrupole fields) have assumed great importance in the development of high-energy particle accelerators. In this application they permit the narrow confinement of the particle beam and consequently greatly reduce the cost of construction. Apart from the concentration and focusing of high-energy particle beams, strong-focusing lenses have found application as projector lenses (but not as objectives) of electron microscopes. Weak quadrupole fields (stigmators) also are used to compensate residual asymmetries in conventional electron lenses.

**Figure 3** shows sections normal to the lens axis of an electrostatic and a magnetic quadrupole lens. In the first instance the electrostatic potential is symmetric with respect to the two principal ($xz$ and $yz$) planes and antisymmetric with respect to the planes through the axis forming an angle of 45° with respect to the principal planes. In the second instance the magnetostatic potential is antisymmetric with respect to the principal planes. In the second instance the magnetostatic potential is antisymmetric with respect to the principal planes and symmetric with respect to the two 45° planes. Fulfillment of Laplace's equation. Eq. (5), now demands the form of Eq. (26) for the

$$\phi(x,y,z) = \frac{a}{2}(x^2 - y^2) - \frac{d^2a}{dz^2}\,2\,(x^4 - y^4)\cdots \qquad (26)$$

electrostatic potential. Magnetic field $B$, on the other hand, may be written as Eqs. (27)–(29). In Eqs. (26)–(29), $a$ and $A$ are functions of $z$. Neglecting the

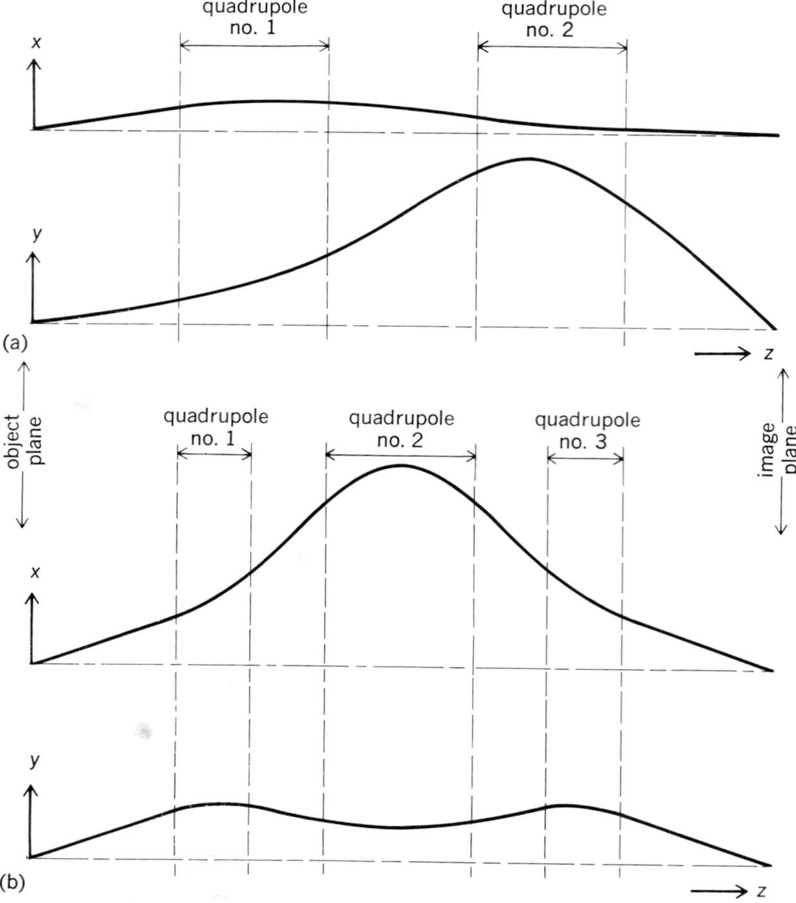


**Fig. 4. Diagrammatic representation of electron paths in principal planes of image-forming symmetrical (*a*) doublet and (*b*) triplet.**

$$B_x = Ay - \frac{1}{6}\frac{d^2A}{dz^2}\,y(3x^2 + y^2)\cdots \quad (27)$$

$$B_y = Ax - \frac{1}{6}\frac{d^2A}{dz^2}\,x(x^2 + 3y^2)\cdots \quad (28)$$

$$B_z = 0 - \frac{1}{6}\frac{d^3A}{dz^3}\,xy(x^2 + y^2)\cdots \quad (29)$$

higher-order terms, which become negligible for a long lens, one finds that the force exerted by the field on the electron is given by Eqs. (30)–(32).

| *Electrostatic lens* | | *Magnetic lens* | |
|---|---|---|---|
| $F_x = -ea\,x$ | (30*a*) | $F_x = -eAv_2x$ | (30*b*) |
| $F_y = ea\,y$ | (31*a*) | $F_y = eAv_zy$ | (31*b*) |
| $F_z = 0$ | (32*a*) | $F_z = 0$ | (32*b*) |

The force is thus, to a first approximation, entirely in a plane normal to the axis. In one principal plane it is such as to produce convergence (direction of force opposite to that of the displacement from the axis), and in the other, such as to produce divergence (direction of force equal to that of the displacement). Two successive quadrupole fields of opposite polarity (a doublet) are required to form a sharp, real image of an object on the axis. This image will have different magnifications in the two principal directions. If the image is to be undistorted, a triplet of three successive quadrupole fields is required. These electron paths are illustrated in **Fig. 4**.

The shaping of the poles influences only terms of the fifth and higher orders in the $x$ and $y$ coordinates in the field expressions. For long lenses all terms except the linear terms vanish if the poles are rectangular hyperbolic cylinders. In practice, circular-cylinder pole caps are more easily realized and give practically the same results. Like axially symmetric lenses, quadrupole lens systems exhibit aberrrations, although these are more complex in character. Octupole fields (**Fig. 5**), which produce transverse forces proportional to the third power of the displacement from the axis, opposite in polarity in the principal planes and in the 45° planes, are commonly employed to correct aberrations of quadrupole lens systems.

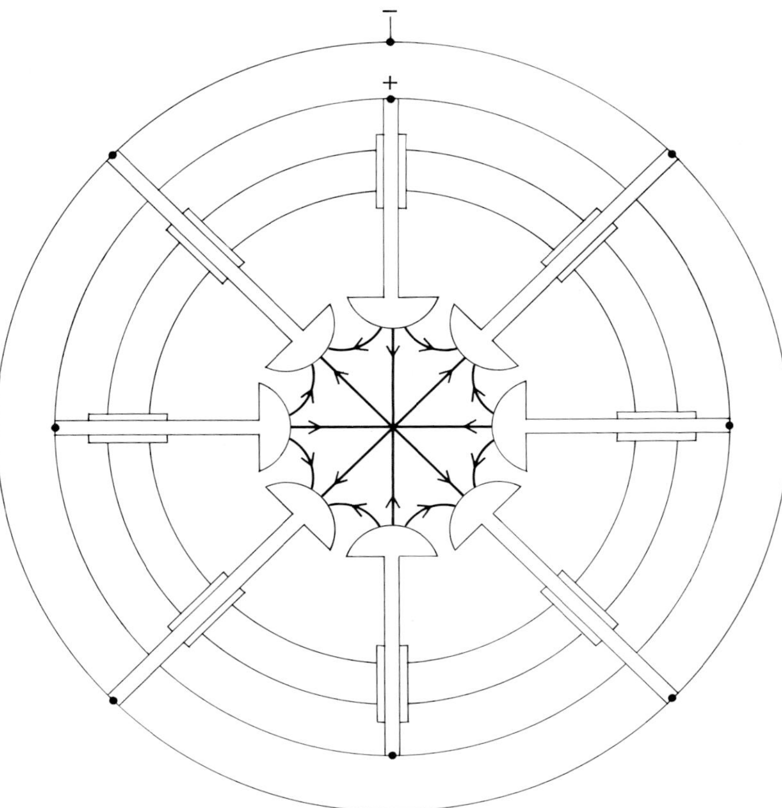


**Fig. 5. Electrostatic octupole.**

**Effect of space charge.** Space charge of either positive or negative sign can influence the paths of electrons. Space charge of positive sign is formed by electron beams passing through an imperfectly evacuated space. The beam electrons collide with gas atoms and ionize them. The heavy ions remain in the path of the electron beam for some time and prevent it from spreading. The luminous nodular or thread beams which are produced in this way are favorite objects for demonstration.

Electron beams in high vacuum, on the other hand, are subject only to the mutually repulsive forces between the electrons themselves. The repulsion is reduced, but never canceled, by the action of the magnetic fields that surround charges in motion; for two electrons moving with the same velocity $v$ parallel to each other, the ratio of the magnetic attractive force to the electrostatic repulsive force is $v^2/c^2$, where $c$ is the velocity of light. Hence, the magnetic force is significant only for electrons of very high energy.

The action of the remainder of the electrons in the beam upon any one electron can be approximated adequately by that of a continuous charge distribution equal to the average space-charge distribution. The behavior of the edge ray of a uniform circular beam of current $I$ aimed at a point of convergence a distance $L$ from the initial cross section of radius $r_B$ may serve as an example (**Fig. 6**). If the variation of the potential along the axis of the beam is neglected (that is, if $\phi$ is assumed to be constant), and the charge density $\rho$ is regarded as uniform within any beam cross section, $\rho$ is given by Eq. (33) and the path

$$\rho = \frac{I}{\pi r^2}\left(\frac{m}{2e\phi}\right)^{1/2} \quad (33)$$

equation becomes Eq. (34). Here $\epsilon$ is the dielectric

$$\frac{d^2r}{dz^2} = \frac{\pi\rho}{\epsilon\phi}\,r = \left(\frac{m}{2e}\right)^{1/2}\frac{I}{\phi^{3/2}}\,\frac{1}{\epsilon r} \quad (34)$$

constant of vacuum. As the result of the repulsive force of space charge, the ray under consideration

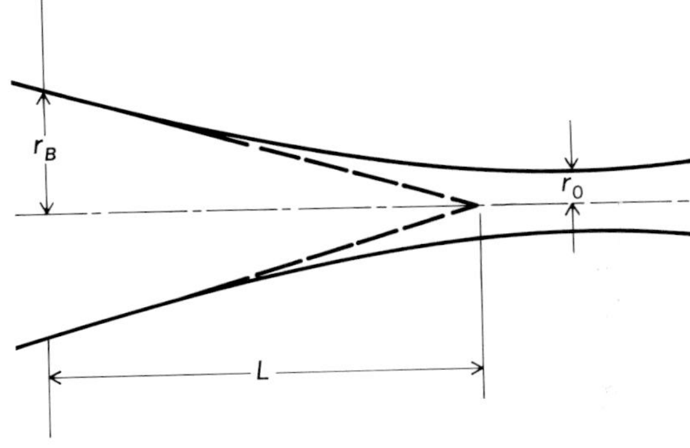


**Fig. 6. Widening of electron beam by space-charge repulsion as it traverses from left to right.**

does not cross the axis, but reaches a minimum separation $r_0$ from the axis and diverges from this point on. Integration of the differential equation, Eq. (34), gives the radius as Eq. (35). For example,

$$r_0 = r_B \exp\left[-\epsilon\left(\frac{e}{2m}\right)^{1/2}\frac{r_B{}^2\phi^{3/2}}{L^2I}\right] = r_B \exp\left[-3.3\times10^{-5}\frac{r_B{}^2\phi^{3/2}}{L^2I}\right] \quad (35)$$

if $r_B = 1$ mm, $\phi = 10{,}000$ volts, $L = 10$ cm, and $I = 0.001$ ampere, then $r_0 = 0.037$ mm.

**Time-varying fields.** In the preceding discussion, it was assumed that the electric and magnetic fields traversed by the electrons were constant in time. The total energy of the electron, or the sum of the kinetic energy and the potential energy, is then a constant. Because the potential energy is a function of position only, so is the kinetic energy. This is no longer true if the fields change appreciably in a period corresponding to the transit time of the electrons. For discussion of electron motion in time-varying fields, such as are encountered in microwave tubes, SEE KLYSTRON; MAGNETRON; TRAVELING-WAVE TUBE.

Beam deflection in the cathode-ray oscilloscope ceases to be proportional to the potential difference $V$ applied to the deflection plates if $V$ changes appreciably during the passage of the electron beam through the deflection field. If $V = V_0 \cos 2\pi ft$, an integration of the transverse impulse impressed on the electron passing between two parallel plates of length $l$ and separation $d$ expresses the deflection angle $\alpha$ in the form of Eq. (36). Here $\phi$ is the accelerating potential of the beam, and $t$ is the time the electron passes through the center of the deflection field. If $f$ (the frequency of the applied voltage) is measured in $s^{-1}$, $l$ in centimeters, and $\phi$ in volts, then Eq. (37) is

$$\tan\alpha = \frac{V_0 l}{2\phi d}\frac{\sin u}{u}\cos(2\pi ft) \quad (36)$$

$$u = \pi fl/(2e\phi/m)^{1/2} = 5.3\times10^{-8}\, fl/\phi^{1/2} \quad (37)$$

applicable. The quantity $(\sin u)/u$ represents the ratio of the deflection sensitivity at frequency $f$ to that at low frequencies ($f \rightarrow 0$) (**Fig. 7**). Thus, for a 10-kV beam and deflection plates 1 cm in length, the response is 95.4% at 1000 MHz ($10^9\ s^{-1}$), 82.3% at 2000 MHz, 40.2% at 4000 MHz, and it drops to zero at about 5930 MHz. In this discussion, the deflection field is assumed to be a sharply cutoff uniform field, with the effects of fringe fields neglected.

*Edward G. Ramberg*

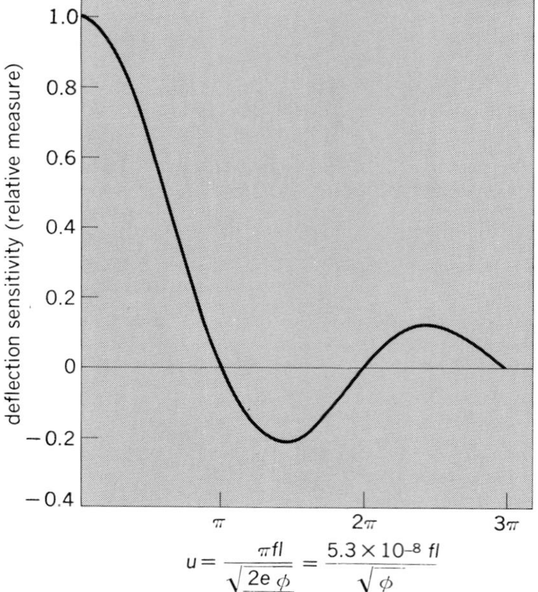


**Fig. 7.** Deflection sensitivity of cathode-ray oscilloscope as a function of frequency $f$.

**Bibliography.** P. Dahl, *Introduction to Electron and Ion Optics*, 1973; A. B. El-Kareh and J. C. El-Kareh, *Electron Beams, Lenses and Optics*, 1970; P. Grivet, *Electron Optics*, 1965; E. Hartung and F. H. Read, *Electrostatic Lenses*, 1976; O. E. Klemperer and M. E. Barnett, *Electron Optics*, 3d ed., 1970; A. Septier, Strong-focusing lenses, *Advan. Electron. Electron Phys.*, 14:85–170, 1961.

## Electron optics

The branch of physics concerned with the motion of free electrons under the influence of electric and magnetic fields. The term electron optics is derived from the fact that the laws governing electron paths in such fields are formally identical with those governing light rays in media of varying refractive index. Both may be derived from Fermat's law. This law states that the actual light ray or electron path passing through two prescribed points $A$ and $B$ is that which makes the integral (1) carried out over it a minimum. The refractive index $n$ is, for electrons, shown by Eq. (2).

$$\int_A^B n\, ds \quad (1)$$

$$n = \sqrt{\phi + \frac{2e\phi^2}{mc^2}} - \sqrt{\frac{e}{2m}}\, A\cos\chi \quad (2)$$

Here $-e/m$ is the charge-to-mass ratio of the electron, $c$ the velocity of light, $\phi$ the accelerating potential of the electron, $A$ the magnetic vector potential, and $\chi$ the angle formed by the electron path with the direction of the magnetic vector potential. Since for electrons of given kinetic energy $\phi$ and $A$ are unique functions of position, the refractive index $n$ is also a function of position and, in the presence of a magnetic field, of the direction of the electron path. A similar dependence of the refractive index on the direction of a light ray is encountered in crystal optics.

The study of electron paths, analogous to the study of light rays, is more properly called geometrical electron optics. The electron paths may be regarded as normals to electron waves, whose amplitude determines the statistical density of electrons, just as the amplitude of a light wave determines the density of light quanta, or photons. The study of the wave motion associated with electrons is called electron wave optics. It describes diffraction and interference effects between electron beams which are in every way similar to the diffraction and interference effects observed with light and x-rays.

Electron optics finds application in the formation of electron beams, as in cathode-ray tubes and television camera tubes; in the deflection of such beams by electric and magnetic fields; and in the formation of electron images, as in electron microscopes and image tubes. SEE CATHODE-RAY TUBE; ELECTRON LENS; ELECTRON MOTION IN VACUUM; ELECTROSTATIC LENS; MAGNETIC LENS.

*Edward G. Ramberg*

**Bibliography.** P. Dahl, *Introduction to Electron and Ion Optics*, 1973; P. Grivet, *Electron Optics*, 2d ed., 1972.

## Electron tube

A device in which conduction takes place by the movement of electrons or ions between electrodes through a vacuum or ionized gas within a gas-tight envelope. Electron tubes include all partially evacuated tubes whose electrical characteristics are derived from the flow of electrons through the tube. Two subclasses of electron tubes are vacuum tubes and gas-filled tubes. Vacuum tubes are evacuated to such a degree that their electrical characteristics are essentially unaffected by the presence of any residual gas or vapor. Gas-filled tubes have electrical characteristics that are substantially dependent upon the ionization of deliberately introduced gas or vapor. SEE VACUUM TUBE.

**Application.** The importance of electron tubes grew rapidly during the first half of the twentieth century. Although semiconductor devices have largely replaced vacuum tubes in many areas of application, tubes are still essential in a number of areas. Thus, cathode-ray tubes, which are a specialized form of vacuum tube, are at present indispensable to television receivers, oscilloscopes, and radar display units; camera tubes are used in television cameras; high-power tubes are used in broadcasting transmitters; and microwave tubes find many applications in radar, telephony, space communication and control, scientific research, and high-frequency ovens. Vacuum tubes are primarily used in applications where low noise and high frequency are involved. In contrast, gas tubes are used for high-current, low-frequency applications. They may be either simple diodes, which are used primarily as rectifiers, or control-type tubes having three or more electrodes for a variety of purposes. Gas tubes are used mainly in industrial applications where high power-handling ability and efficiency overshadow their frequency limitations. SEE CATHODE-RAY TUBE; SEMICONDUCTOR.

**Characteristics.** Electrical characteristics of electron tubes vary greatly among the many types, depending upon the number and configuration of the electrodes, the degree of evacuation, and the type and capability of the electron source. Power capability ranges from milliwatts to peak values of hundreds of megawatts, and the frequency of operation ranges from zero to the order of $10^{11}$ Hz. The evacuated envelope may be made of glass, quartz, ceramic, or metal.

**History.** Some of the phenomena associated with electron tubes were first noticed in the latter part of the century. In 1883 T. A. Edison observed some peculiar effects in light bulbs which were later recognized as due to electrons. H. Hertz observed photoelectric emission in 1887. W. C. Roentgen observed x-rays in 1895. The electron itself was probably first identified by J. J. Thomson, who in 1897 also measured its ratio of charge to mass. Probably the first electron tube was a cathode-ray tube built by K. F. Braun in 1897. A. Wehnelt discovered oxide emission in 1903, and this led to the development of the vacuum diode by J. A. Fleming in 1904. With the invention of the vacuum triode by L. DeForest in 1906, the age of electronics was ushered in. The tetrode was devloped in 1919 by W. Schottky and the pentode by G. Jobst and B. D. H. Tellegen in 1926. A. W. Hull developed the thyratron in 1929 and the magnetron in 1921. R. Varian and S. Varian invented the klystron in 1938, and R. Kompfner introduced the traveling-wave tube in 1946. SEE AUDION; GAS TUBE; MICROWAVE TUBE; NUMERICAL INDICATOR TUBE; PHOTOTUBE.

*Herbert J. Reich*

**Bibliography.** D. G. Fink and D. Christiansen, *Electronic Engineer's Handbook,* 2d ed., 1982; D. J. Harris and P. D. Robson, *The Physical Basis of Electronics,* 2d ed., 1974; Y. Koike, *Electron Tubes,* 1972; H. J. Reich, J. C. Skalnik, and H. L. Krauss, *Theory and Applications of Active Devices,* 1966.

## Electronic display

An electronic component used to convert electrical signals into visual imagery in real time suitable for direct interpretation by a human operator. It serves as the visual interface between human and machine. The visual imagery is processed, composed, and optimized for easy interpretation and minimum reading error. The electronic display is dynamic in that it presents information within a fraction of a second from the time received and continuously holds that information, using refresh or memory techniques, until new information is received. The image is created by electronically making a pattern from a visual contrast in brightness on the display surface without the aid of mechanical or moving parts.

The use of electronic displays for presentation of graphs, symbols, alphanumerics, and video pictures has doubled every several years. The biggest growth rate has been for utilitarian and industrial users. Electronic displays have largely replaced traditional mechanical and hardcopy (paper) means for presenting information. This change is due to the increased use of computers, microprocessors, low-cost large-scale

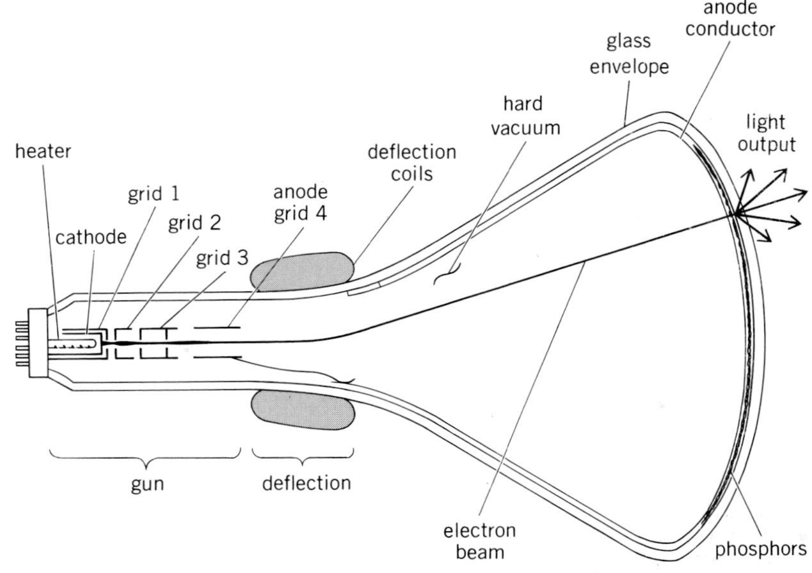


**Fig. 1. Cathode-ray tube using electrostatic and magnetic deflection.**

integration (LSI) electronics, and digital mass memories. The success of the hand-held calculator was directly attributable to the availability of low-cost LSI electronics and low-cost electronic numeric displays. *See Calculators; Computer; Computer graphics; Computer storage technology; Integrated circuits; Microprocessor.*

Electronic transducers and four-digit (or more) flat-panel displays have been used to replace the galvanometer movement, thermometer scale, barometer movement, and other forms of scientific instrumentation. Large signs, arrival and departure announcements, and scoreboards also use electronic means to portray changing messages and data. One of the major electronic displays applications is in home color television.

The computer terminal using a cathode-ray tube (CRT) is one of the most important industrial applications of electronic displays. The standard computer terminal displays 25 lines of 80 characters, for a total of 2000 characters, which correspond to one-half of a typed page. The computer terminal with a microprocessor, minicomputer, and mass memory serve to replace the office paper, typewriter, and file cabinet. *See Word processing.*

**Cathode-ray tube.** The primary applications of the cathode-ray tube are in home entertainment television, scientific and electrical engineering oscilloscopes, radar display, and alphanumeric and graphic electronic displays. *See Oscilloscope; Radar; Television.*

The basic elements of the cathode-ray tube are shown in **Fig. 1**. The viewing screen is coated with a phosphor which emits light when struck with a beam of high-energy electrons. The electrons are emitted from the cathode at the rear of the tube in a beam that is focused electrostatically (or magnetically) to a dot or spot on the phosphor screen and positioned in horizontal and vertical coordinates by magnetic (or electrostatic) forces. The cathode grids and electron-focusing lenses are incorporated into a subassembly called the gun. The beam is accelerated toward the phosphor by a high voltage (20 kV or more) at the anode grid conductor.

The cathode-ray-tube raster is shown in **Fig. 2**. Imagery is created on the screen as the raster is traced out. The video signal is applied, after amplification, directly to grid 2 of the gun, and controls the amplitude of the electron beam and thus the luminous output at the display surface. The deflection coils steer the beam to trace out the raster. The horizontal-scan deflection signal causes the beam to trace out the horizontal lines and then fly back for the next line. The vertical-scan deflection signal causes the beam to be stepped down the raster and then retraced to the top left corner at the beginning of each frame. Two fields are interlaced, with the raster lines of one traced between those of the other. The purpose of the interlace is to minimize flicker in the picture. *See Cathode-ray tube; Picture tube; Television receiver.*

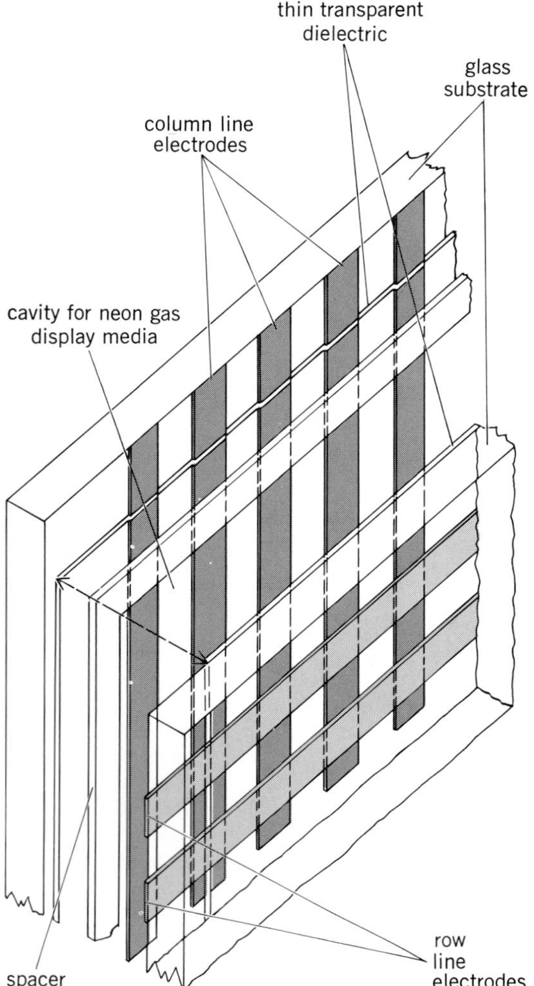


**Fig. 3. Diagram of an exploded section of a plasma flat-panel display.**

**Flat-panel displays.** Because of the depth dimension of the cathode-ray tube, there has been a concentrated effort to develop flat-panel displays. A primary motivating factor has been to achieve a flat television receiver which could be hung on a wall. The electrical phenomena most extensively developed for flat-panel displays are gas discharge (plasma), electroluminescence, light-emitting diode, cathodoluminescence, and liquid crystallinity. The cost of flat-panel displays is higher than cathode-ray tubes on a per-character basis for higher information content displays such as the 200-character computer terminal. The flat-panel technologies are utilized extensively in portable displays and numeric displays using several hundred characters and less. *See Cathodoluminescence; Electroluminescence; Light-emitting diode; Liquid crystals.*

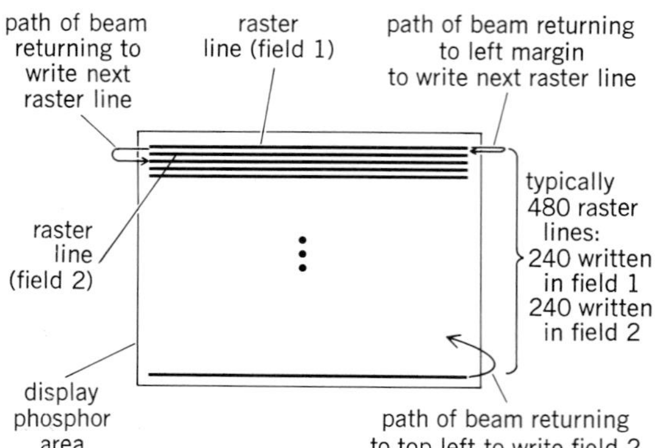


**Fig. 2. Cathode-ray-tube raster for television, using interlace.**

**Table 1. Flat-panel technologies**

| Technology | Phenomena |
|---|---|
| Emissive displays | |
| Gas discharge | Cathode glow from conducting gaseous discharge |
| Plasma panel | Alternating-current capacitively coupled gas discharge |
| Light-emitting diode | Electron injection in a forward-biased *pn* semiconductor junction |
| Vacuum fluorescence | Electron bombardment of phosphor in hard vacuum under control of a grid |
| Electroluminescence | Electron conduction in polycrystalline phosphors due to high electric field |
| Flat cathode-ray tube | Electron bombardment of phosphor in hard vacuum under control of a grid or cathode |
| Nonemissive displays | |
| Liquid crystallinity | Electrostatic rotation of organic compounds which exhibit liquid crystallinity |
| Electrochromism | Charging and discharging chemical systems (battery) which exhibit a color change in accordance with Faraday's law |
| Colloidal suspensions | Electrostatic transport or rotation of light-absorbing particles in a colloidal suspension |
| Electroactive solids | Ferroelectric and ferromagnetic materials with a significant electrooptic effect |
| Electromechanical | Mechanical motion of elements causing a contrast change |

Flat-panel displays are typically matrix-addressed. A row is enabled to accept display information in parallel via the column lines. The electronics commutate through the rows, serving the same purpose as the vertical deflection amplifier of the cathode-ray tube. The column data are shifted into the column drivers, and at the proper time applied to the column lines.

The flat-panel matrix addressing electrodes are shown in **Fig. 3**. The thickness is approximately 0.5 in. (1.3 cm). The row and column lines are spaced at 60 lines per inch (24 lines per centimeter). The intersection of each row line with each column line defines a pixel. A pixel or pel is a picture element, and denotes the smallest addressible element in an electronic display.

The flat-panel technologies are summarized in **Table 1**; each approach has unique advantages. The more important considerations include luminous efficiency, addressability, duty factor, gray scale, color, and cost. The capabilities in each area have evolved to the point of cost-effective applications to commercial and military products. For the vectorgraph and video display categories, liquid-crystal, electroluminescent, and gas-discharge or plasma displays have emerged as the most cost-effective approaches.

**Display categories.** Electronic displays can be categorized into four classifications, as shown in **Table 2**. Each classification is defined by natural technical boundaries and cost considerations. The categorization is useful in visualizing the extent to which electronic displays are used.

**Special-purpose displays.** The categorization of Table 2 emphasizes direct-view-type electronic displays which are of primary interest to industry. There are other special-purpose displays used in very sophisticated applications.

***Projection display.*** In the projection display an image is generated on a high-brightness cathode-ray tube or similar electronic image generator, and then optically projected onto a larger screen. To illuminate screens larger than approximately 3 × 4 ft (1 × 1.3 m) and in color, multiple cathode-ray tubes or light valves are used. The light valve is any direct view display optimized for reflecting or transmitting the image, with an independent collimated light source for projection purposes. Light valves create images to control the reflection of light to be projected onto the screen. This permits powerful light sources such as xenon lamps to be used independent of the image-generating technique. Oil-film light valves and liquid-crystal light valves are examples of devices used in large command and control and theater-size electronic display presentations.

***Three-dimensional imagery.*** True three-dimensional imagery can be created electronically by several techniques. One technique requires goggles using PLZT (lead zirconate titanate modified with lanthanum) electrooptical ceramic eyepieces over each eye. The eyepieces are electronically controllable shutters, with the ability to be reversibly switched from open to closed in microseconds. Two images from two television cameras placed to obtain the desired stereoscopic effects are electronically interlaced and displayed on one cathode-ray tube monitor. Each image is sequentially displayed from each camera at tv video rates. The goggles are synchronized to be opened and closed so that only the right eye sees the image from the right camera and the left eye sees the image from the left camera. The viewer sees true three-dimensional perspective while looking at the cathode-ray tube monitor through the goggles.

***Helmet-mounted and heads-up displays.*** Helmet-mounted displays (sometimes called visually coupled displays) and heads-up displays are used in aircraft. In both of these displays the image is projected, usually from a cathode-ray tube onto a combining glass, and collimated to be in focus at infinity. The combining glass screen is designed to reflect the display imagery to the viewer, usually at selected wavelengths of light, while being sufficiently transmissive for the viewer to see the scene beyond. The primary application for the heads-up display is to present critical aircraft performance, such as speed and altitude, on a combining glass at the windscreen for pilot monitoring while permitting the pilot to look out the window for other aircraft or the runway. The primary application for the helmet-mounted display is to present, on a combining glass within the visor of the helmet of a helicopter gunner, primary information for directing firepower. The angular direction of the helmet is sensed and used to control weapons to point in the same direction in which the gunner is looking.

**Color.** Color can be created on a cathode-ray tube equipped with a shadow mask duplicating quite closely all colors that occur in nature. This is done in the cathode-ray tube by using three different electron guns and three phosphors in a triad of red, green, and blue on the screen at each pixel. The shadow mask is a metal screen with a hole for each pixel. It is located in the path of the beam between the deflection area

**Table 2. Electronic display spectrum of applications**

| Classification | Characteristics | Applications | Electronic technologies |
|---|---|---|---|
| Pseudoanalog | Dedicated arrangement of discrete pixels used to present analog or qualitative information | Meterlike presentations, go/no-go messages, legends and alerts, analoglike (watch) dial | Gas discharge, light-emitting diodes, liquid crystal, incandescent lamps |
| Alphanumeric | Dedicated alphanumeric pixel font of normally less than 480 characters; most common is 4- and 8-character numeric displays | Digital watches, calculators, digital multimeters, message terminals, games | Liquid crystal, light-emitting diodes, vacuum fluorescent, gas discharge, incandescent lamps |
| Vectorgraphic | Large orthogonal uniform array of pixels which are addressable at medium to high speeds; normally, monochromatic with no gray scale; may have memory; normally, over 480 characters and simple graphics | Computer terminals, TWX terminals, arrivals and departures, scheduling terminals, weather radar, air-traffic control, games | Cathode-ray tube, plasma panels, gas discharge, vacuum fluorescent, electroluminescence, other technologies in advanced development |
| Video | Large orthogonal array of pixels which are addressed at video rates (30 frames per second); monochromatic with gray scale or full color; standardized raster scan addressing interface, arrays of pixels approximately 512 rows by 512 columns | Entertainment television, graphic arts, earth resources, video repeater, medical electronics, aircraft flight instruments, computer terminals, command and control, games | Cathode-ray tube, other technologies in advanced development |

and phosphor screen. Electron beams from each of three guns are constrained by each shadow mask hole to hit each respective phosphor dot. The gun, shadow-mask holes, and phosphor dots are aligned during manufacturing so that the three beams converge to pass through the single hole (or slit) in the shadow mask and then diverge as the beams emerge with sufficient separation to impact the three different phosphor dots. If all three guns are on simultaneously, the eye, upon close inspection, sees a red, a green, and a blue dot of light at each pixel. However, at a normal viewing distance, the three dots merge together in the retina of the eye, and from the laws of additive color, the pixel appears white. *SEE COLOR TELEVISION*.

Penetration phosphors are also used to create color on cathode-ray tube displays to eliminate the need for the shadow mask and extra guns. However, the color is limited and the brightness is low. Normally, two phosphors are placed on the screen in two layers or in microspheres of two layers. The gun and cathode-ray-tube anode are operated in two energy states to produce either a high-energy or a low-energy electron beam switchable in time. The high-energy beam penetrates the first phosphor layer and is stopped at the second layer. It then excites the second layer to produce its characteristic color. The low-energy beam is stopped by the first phosphor layer and excites it to produce its characteristic color. The two phosphor colors most often used are red and green. Intermediate-energy beams make it possible to fractionally excite both layers to get color combinations of red and green such as yellow and orange. Practical considerations limit this color approach to these four. Full color would require at least three primary colors such as red, green, and blue. Three layers of phosphors are limited in brightness due to practical considerations and have not been commercially available.

Monochromatic color is readily produced by flat-panel display technologies. Gas discharge is normally orange, owing to the neon gas. Other monochromatic colors are feasible. Light-emitting diode (LED) luminance is normally red, yellow, or green. A red or green state has been achieved which is switchable in a single diode by current control. Blue light-emitting diodes have been made in research devices. Electroluminescence is normally yellow or green, owing to the manganese or copper activator, respectively. Other monochromatic colors have been demonstrated in research devices. A wide range of color effects has been demonstrated in research devices with passive flat-panel displays such as liquid-crystal, electrophoretic, and electrochromic technologies. In flat-panel as in CRT displays, full color is produced by using a triad of red, green, and blue for each pixel.

Full color is very important for entertainment television displays. Most industrial electronic displays do not need or use full color. The most efficient monochrome from each display technology is normally used; for example, red for light-emitting diode, orange for gas discharge, and orange-yellow for electroluminescence. Limited color displays are sometimes used in industrial applications such as aircraft weather radar and artificial horizons, computer-aided multilayer circuit design, earth resources studies, air-route traffic control, and medical electronic displays. In all of these applications, the display instrument is usually a cathode-ray tube using the shadow-mask color technique.

**Display technique.** The essence of electronic displays is based upon the ability to turn on and off individual picture elements (pixels: **Fig. 4**). The pixel is the smallest controllable element of the display. A typical high-information-content display will have a quarter million pixels in an orthogonal array, each under individual control by the electronics. The pixel resolution is normally just at or below the resolving power of the eye. Thus, a good-quality picture can be created from a pattern of activated pixels.

The pixel concept for electronic displays has evolved from the modern flat-panel display technologies and digital electronics. It has been extended to the analog-raster-scan cathode-ray tube in the following way: The electron beam from the gun is deflected magnetically (or electrostatically), so as to sweep across the phosphor and thereby cause a line to lu-

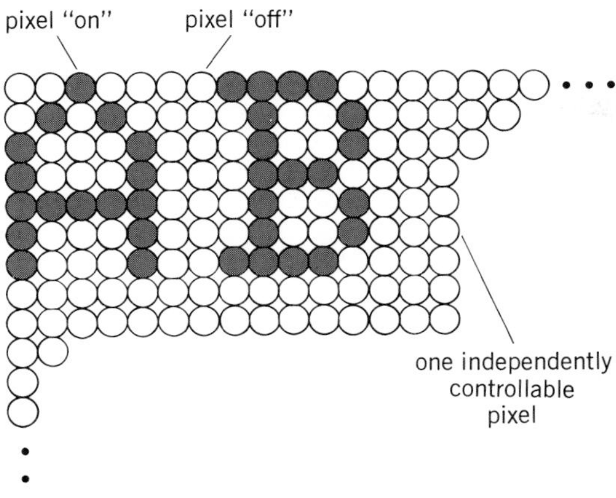


Fig. 4. Pixel array used for creating electronic display images.

minesce on the face of the cathode-ray tube. In digitally modulated cathode-ray tubes, the cathode is modulated by a sine wave as the beam is swept across the face of the cathode-ray tube. Here, instead of a continuous line, a string of dots results. Each dot corresponds to a pixel. Each pixel is on when the beam density is high, and off when the beam is off. The beam is turned off between pixels. The pixels are refreshed from 30 to 60 times per second on a cathode-ray tube.

Pixels are created in all the rows of the entire cathode-ray-tube raster in what is called a CRT-digital raster. This approach is commonly used in industrial applications and computer terminals, since it is easily interfaced with digital electronics. Home entertainment television uses an analog-raster-scan approach, as do nearly all video systems.

There are some applications in which a nonraster approach is used to create alphanumeric characters and vectors on cathode-ray tubes. The electron beam is deflected under control of the deflection amplifiers to stroke out each line of the image. When characters and vectors are generated this way, they are like Lissajous figures, as opposed to (digital or analog) raster characters and vectors. The Lissajous characters and vectors are best suited to large (25-in. or 63.5-cm diagonal) cathode-ray tubes and where there are numerous vectors, straight lines, and curves. Vectors and curves drawn with the raster technique have stair steps. Lissajous vectors and curves are always smooth and continuous. Lissajous techniques are yielding to the digital raster in newer designs as the cost of digital electronics improves.

**Font.** With flat-panel displays and cathode-ray-tube digital-raster displays, alphanumeric character fonts are created by turning on the appropriate pixels in an array. One standard size is a $5 \times 7$ array with two pixels between characters and two pixels between rows, (Fig. 4). All the letters and numbers can be created on this common array format. Several other combinations of pixels may be used to create the letter A. The viewer soon becomes accustomed to the minor variation. Readers do not read pixels but read letters and words, and therefore the exact detail of the character pixel pattern is of a secondary consideration. In general, the more pixels available in the basic array, the more esthetically pleasing is the character, at the cost of additional electronics to control the extra pixels. The viewing distance is normally far enough so that the pixels blur together.

Fig. 5. Seven-bar numeric font.

A very efficient and elegant array has evolved for portraying numeric characters only, called the seven-bar font (**Fig. 5**). Each bar is a pixel by definition. This font was initially considered crude when compared to the Leroy font and other more esthetic printer fonts. It is now universally accepted. A similar 14 bar font is sometimes used for alphanumeric characters.

**Display electronic addressing.** The numeric or alphanumeric display electronic drive may be performed in a single LSI metal oxide semiconductor (MOS) chip mounted in a single dual in-line package (DIP) suitable for direct assembly on a printed circuit board. All the timing, logic, memory, resistors, and drivers are contained in a single chip. A four- or seven-bit character code is serially fed into the chip for display (**Fig. 6**).

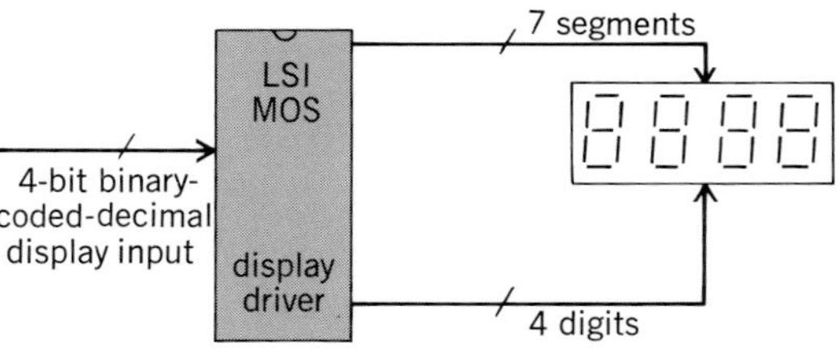


Fig. 6. Block diagram of LSI MOS electronic drive for numeric display.

A computer terminal (**Fig. 7**) will incorporate a microprocessor unit and a cathode-ray-tube controller to perform master control and cathode-ray-tube housekeeping tasks. A line of video data is loaded into the shift register for serial drive of the video amplifier at the time a raster line starts. The shift register is loaded during flyback time from the character generator. The character generator is a decoder transforming the alphanumeric information in coded form such as ASCII (American National Standard Code for Information Interchange) into pixel signals for each raster line. The ASCII code is stored in the display refresh memory. The entire cathode-ray-tube frame is stored in this memory, and is continuously displayed until changed under control of the microprocessor unit. New information can come from the mass memory, the keyboard, or other subsystems on the data bus and address bus, all under control of the microprocessor unit.

The cathode-ray-tube controller performs all the housekeeping tasks for proper cathode-ray-tube operation. These include the vertical- and horizontal-raster synchronization signals, the cursor control, blinking, blanking, interlace, paging, and scrolling. The cathode-ray-tube controller is a single LSI MOS chip, as are most of the other blocks shown in Fig. 7.

**Developing applications.** The market needs for electronic displays have accelerated the advancement

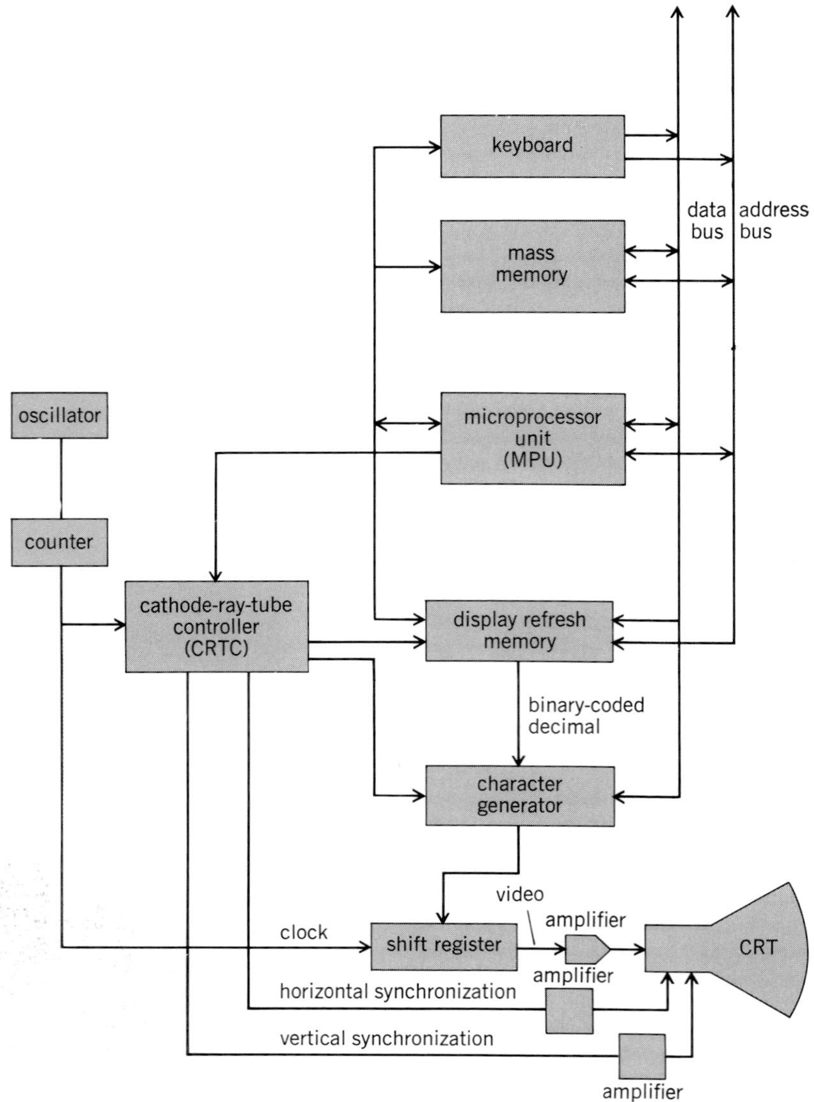


**Fig. 7. Block diagram of LSI electronics for a smart computer terminal cathode-ray-tube display.**

of the technology in three areas: personal computers, automotive panels, and portable television.

***Personal computers.*** These devices have evolved extremely rapidly with the development of better processors, larger memories, and more powerful software. There has been significant marketing pressure to make them more portable and smaller so as to use less desk space. There are four categories of personal computers dictated by size and power requirements which in turn are dictated mostly by the available display technologies. These four categories are: lap computers, portable computers, transportable computers, and desktop computers.

The lap computer, as the name implies, is small in size with limited functionality, operates with its own internal power, and uses a liquid-crystal display of approximately 320 alphanumeric characters.

The portable computer is, in its most simple definition, a fully functional computer with a handle and an internal power source. This segment of the family of personal computers is limited because of the display performance or cost. Liquid-crystal technology is used because it meets the cost, power, and 2000-character size requirement. However, the liquid-crystal technology performance is compromised when expanded upward to the larger character sets. The lack of adequate performance in conventional liquid-crystal techniques accelerated the development of active matrix addressing techniques such as cadmium selenide (CdSe) semiconductor polycrystalline thin-film transistors and amorphous silicon. These techniques improve the performance of the liquid-crystal display but at a cost penalty. Electroluminescent and electrophoretic displays are strong contenders for this application. The cathode-ray-tube and gas-discharge displays are too heavy and consume too much power to be used in portable computers.

The transportable computer differs from the portable computer primarily with regard to the power source. The power source for a portable computer consists of internally packaged batteries. The transportable computer relies on an external power source; it either uses a battery pack or is plugged into the house power. The biggest user of power is the display. The initial display technology was a scaled-down cathade-ray tube with compromises in performance. The flat-panel displays are most appropriate, since they are truly portable in briefcase size, without compromised performance. The most promising technology is the electroluminescent display with its excellent ergonomics and low power, and the gas discharge and plasma panels are next in contention. The gas discharge technologies are most limited by their weight and power efficiency.

The desktop computers use cathode-ray-tube displays almost exclusively. The use of flat-panel technologies could greatly improve the size and performance of the displays, however, cost is a major consideration. Flat-panel approaches using electroluminescent and gas-discharge displays are two to three times more expensive than cathode-ray tubes. This cost difference results from the extra supporting electronics for row and column drivers needed for matrix-addressed flat-panel displays. Finally, the element of a color display is a desired feature in desktop computers. The cost of a cathode-ray-tube color display is not much more than a black-and-white flat-panel display. *See Microcomputer.*

***Automotive panels.*** Automobiles require several displays: the integrated performance cluster including speed, engine status, and so forth; digital indicators including time, temperature, and so forth; and a high-resolution navigation display including map, position indication, and so forth. The sheer number of assemblies has presented serious difficulties for the display industry.

***Portable television.*** As with the portable transistor radio, cost and performance are the dominant factors determining the utilization of portable television. The most significant component which affects cost and performance is the display, and the most difficult performance goals to be achieved within cost limitations are low power, weight, and volume, and sunlight readability. Two approaches are a black-and-white flat cathode-ray tube and a color liquid-crystal display, both approaching a 4-in.-diagonal (10-cm) size. The cathode-ray tube is viewed from the back side of the faceplate, which greatly enhances its power efficiency and sunlight readability. The liquid-crystal display uses the twisted nematic mode of operation and amorphous silicon electronics for addressing the matrix of color triads for each pixel, and complementary-metal-oxide-semiconductor (CMOS) drivers for the row and column lines. The colors are created by strips of red, green, and blue filters for each row of pixels which are illuminated by a uniform rear area light source covering the entire display.

*Lawrence E. Tannas, Jr.*

**Bibliography.** L. E. Tannas, Jr., *Flat-Panel Displays and CRTs*, 1984.

## Electronic equipment grounding

The connecting of electronic equipment to an electromagnetic reference common to itself, its power source, its environment, and the environment of its users. Electronic equipment is grounded to protect users from shock, to protect the equipment from spurious currents or voltages, and especially to isolate it from noise that contaminates its environment.

**Need for thorough grounding.** Usually electronic equipment is powered from the electric service that supplies the building where the equipment is used. To provide security against hazards of electric shock or fire ignition, equipment frames and power-conductor enclosures are connected and grounded.

In addition, grounding (together with the shielding, isolation, compensation, and equalization) is applied to minimize the entrance of extraneous signals (noise) into the equipment. Basically, electronic equipment can be treated as a sensor or signal source, a signal circuit, and central equipment (**Fig. 1**). The sensor may be any of a wide variety of input devices, such as a tape reader, card reader, memory readout, medical sensor, industrial transducer, or microphone. Information from the sensor travels along the signal circuit in digital or analog form at low level. At the central equipment the signal is processed to be used for such purposes as recording or control. Reliability of the output use depends directly on the integrity of the signal received at the central equipment.

The sophistication of electronic equipment has advanced tremendously. The necessary intensity of electrical signals has been diminished generally to below 1 V. The amount of time allocated for the transmission of one bit of information has been progressively diminished to less than 1 μs. These advances aggravate the likelihood that spurious error signals will be of sufficient magnitude to create an error response. The effect of an error response, if not identified and corrected for, can produce tragic results in critical areas such as manned space flight. The controlling parameter can be expressed as the signal-to-noise ratio. The problem is ultimately one of ensuring acceptably high levels of signal-to-noise ratio. SEE ELECTRICAL NOISE.

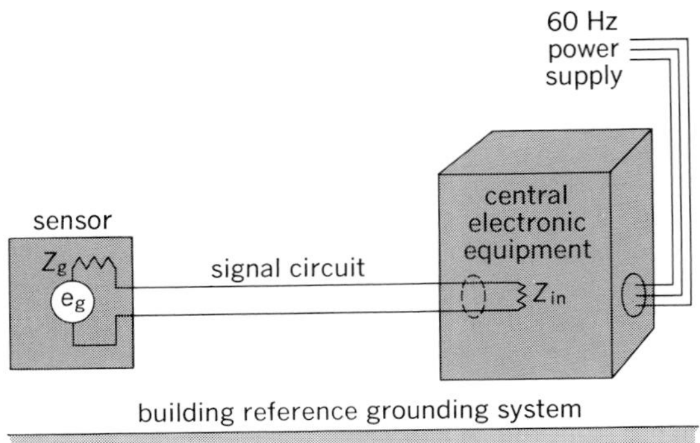


**Fig. 1. The three essential components for communicating information electrically.**

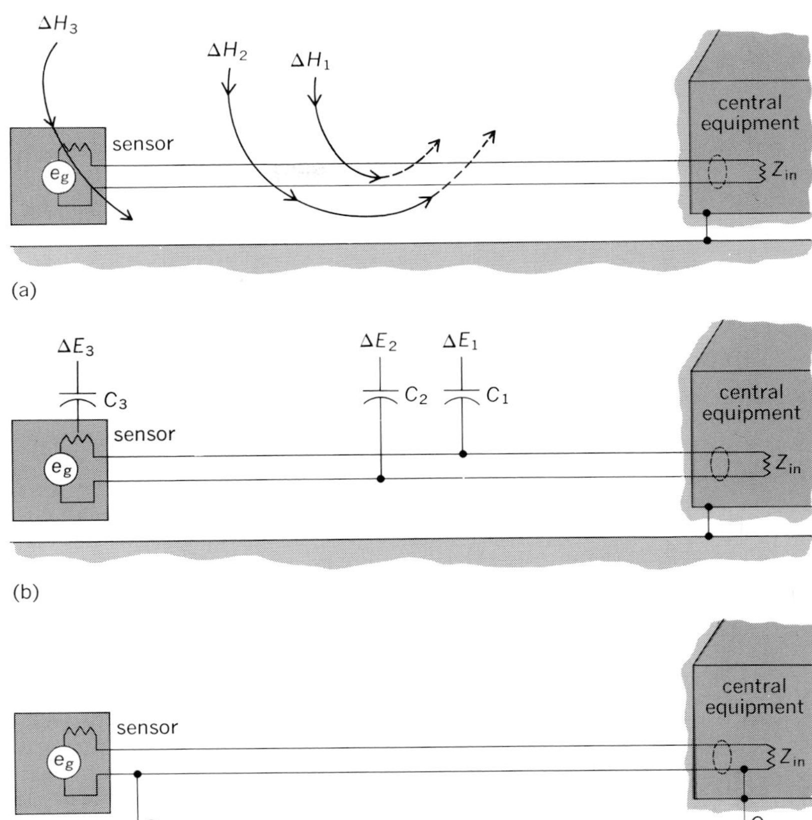


**Fig. 2. Common sources of error signals. (a) Electromagnetic coupling. (b) Electrostatic coupling. (c) Conductive coupling.**

The most vulnerable circuits are typically those associated with the information-gathering function, because they generally operate at low signal level and are followed by high-gain amplifiers within the data-processing system. Such an input circuit is shown in Fig. 1. The signal-sensing element may be in the next room, on a different floor of the same building, in a different building, or even in a different city. Techniques that are effective in establishing a high signal-to-noise ratio in this critical circuit, and techniques needed to handle the less critical circuits, are reviewed here.

**Noise coupling into signal circuit.** Spurious unwanted electric impulses (noise) may be mixed with true information signals in numerous ways, the most common and important being electromagnetic induction, electrostatic induction, and conductive coupling (**Fig. 2**).

***Magnetic induction.*** A changing magnetic field intensity in the space through which the signal circuits run (Fig. 2*a*) creates noise in the equipment. Such fields are present in the space surrounding any open conductor carrying substantial magnitudes of changing current. Intense fields exist around the anode leads of arc furnaces and the throat conductors of flash and spot welders. A helpful approach is to recognize that the inductive reactance of a current-carrying conductor, shown on the electrical engineer's one-line diagram as a property of the conductor, is in fact a property of the space-distributed magnetic field which surrounds the current-carrying conductor. Any electrical circuit which links a portion of such a space field will display a fractional part of the reactance voltage drop of the power conductor.

In Fig. 2*a* the fractional part of the changing space-distributed magnetic field $\Delta H_1$ which threads between the two signal-circuit conductors will induce a normal-mode error signal in that circuit. The terminal sensor is often an electromagnetic device which, in the presence of a changing space-distributed magnetic field $\Delta H_3$ in a particular direction, will display a normal-mode induced error voltage. A similar space field $\Delta H_2$ threading between the signal circuit conductors and the nearby conducting structure which connects the central processing framework with the remote terminal structure will induce a common-mode potential which can appear on the signal circuit.

***Electrostatic induction.*** A changing electrostatic space field (Fig. 2*b*) can induce a similar error voltage in the signal circuit by capacitive coupling. Electrostatic space-distributed fields will be created by unshielded, energized electrical conductors. Insulation over the conductor is not an attenuator. Intense fields can be expected in areas where ac high-potential testing is being done. Unshielded gaseous discharge lamps develop annoying space fields rich in harmonics and sharp step changes.

A changing-magnitude electrostatic field $\Delta E_1$, if coupled to one of the signal-circuit conductors through a capacitance $C_1$, will impart to that conductor an error voltage. To the other signal conductor will be communicated a similar error voltage produced by space field $\Delta E_2$ through coupling capacitance $C_2$. Even though $\Delta E_1$ equals $\Delta E_2$ and $C_1$ equals $C_2$, a normal-mode error signal voltage will be created if the signal circuit is not symmetrically balanced in its coupling to the central-equipment reference ground plane. Also, the terminal sensor may contain such parts as terminals, coils, and winding surfaces that are capacitively coupled to the ambient space field $\Delta E_3$. Unless coupling capacitance $C_3$ displays a symmetrical balance to the two signal conductors, a portion of the induced error voltage will be of the normal-mode type. Even an intentional grounding connection on the signal circuit at the central equipment, if not precisely balanced, will cause a fractional part of the common-mode, electrostatically induced voltage to appear as a normal-mode type.

The presence of large-magnitude, common-mode voltages on signal circuits may directly damage or even destroy electronic components and may create troublesome normal-mode error signals if only slight deviations from perfect symmetry occur on signal circuits.

***Conduction between units.*** Normal-mode error voltages are also created by conductive coupling (Fig. 2*c*). For the most part this origin of noise is identical with that commonly referred to as ground loop problems. The error voltage owes its origin to the fact that the reference grounding conductor system is not at a common potential throughout. Consider that one signal-circuit conductor is grounded at the central equipment in location $G_1$. This would be conventional practice when using coaxial signal circuits and is sometimes used on two-conductor wire circuits. The presence of a second ground connection on the same signal conductor at a different location $G_2$ will likely result in severe noise in low-level signal circuits. After making the first ground connection at $G_1$, it will be unlikely that another spot can be found along that conductor with a zero-voltage difference to the adjacent reference ground. When a second ground connection is made along a signal conductor, it forces the voltage difference, which had previously existed here, to vanish and appear as an impedance voltage drop (*IZ* drop) around the loop circuit formed by the second ground connection. SEE ELECTRICAL IMPEDANCE.

By reviewing the character of the impedance elements forming this loop, it becomes quite evident that the signal-circuit conductor between grounding points $G_1$ and $G_2$ will principally account for the ground loop impedance. The remainder of the loop will be made up of such low-resistance conductors as heavy building structural members and large pipes. Thus most of the voltage difference which, prior to the second ground connection, had existed between the signal conductor and the adjacent reference ground $G_2$ has, after the second ground connection, become an impedance voltage drop along only one signal conductor between locations $G_1$ and $G_2$. This voltage represents a normal-mode error voltage in the signal circuit.

***Conduction within one unit.*** At times the separation of only inches in the two ground connections can result in intolerable noise, as the following example illustrates. In a vacuum-tube amplifier (**Fig. 3**) the cathode and one heater lead are bonded to the chassis at point 1. One side of the filament transformer is bonded to the chassis at point 3; therefore, heater current flows through the chassis, as shown by the current flow lines. Normal to the current flow lines are equipotential lines, as shown. The grid resistor is bonded to the chassis at point 2. A noise signal $e_{12}$ is thereby inserted into the grid circuit, resulting from the potential drop along the chassis between cathode

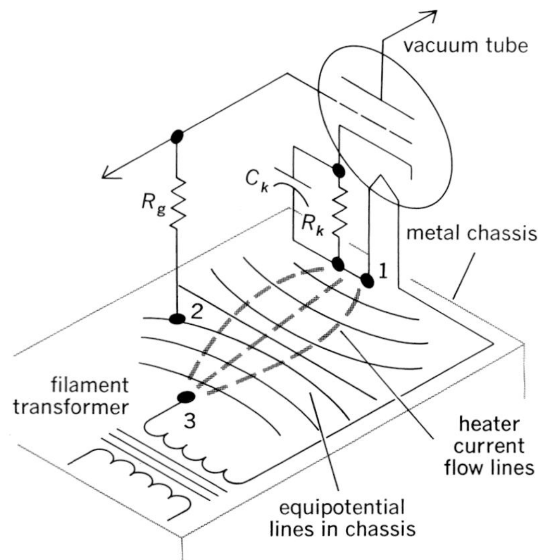


**Fig. 3. Improper grounding of an individual amplifier stage to a metal chassis, so that the noise voltage is coupled into the signal circuit.**

and grid bonding points. This drop may amount to only a few microvolts, but if it enters an early stage of a high-gain amplifier, excessive noise may be noticed in the output.

To avoid such problems, all bonding connections for a given stage should be made to only one point on the chassis. Also, the flow of large currents through the chassis of any high-gain amplifier, whether vacuum-tube or solid-state, must be avoided. Where high-gain amplifiers are controlling high-power ac or dc circuits having grounded terminals, it is best to insulate the amplifier chassis from the frames of the rest of the machinery and to provide a single ground strap from chassis to frame. This will prevent large currents from passing through the amplifier chassis. *See Circuit (electronics).*

In general, each stage of a high-gain amplifier should have its own chassis ground. Each individual amplifier should have its own ground lead to a common amplifier ground point. All machinery and other power devices should be bonded together, with a single lead to the amplifier ground point. Finally, if additional shielding is provided, such as a metal cabinet, it should have a single ground lead to the common ground point for the amplifier and the power equipment. This common ground point would then be grounded to earth by bonding to a cold-water pipe or by other methods in conformance with the local electrical codes.

**Ground gradients.** The medium- to high-voltage substation may display large voltage differences between the potential on the local station grounding conductors and remote earth. Information-gathering (or sensing) circuits associated with electronic equipment extending into or close to such a substation area will generally require extreme design care to avoid dangerous common-mode potentials. It is not unreasonable to expect steady-state voltage levels of as much as 50 volts. During a line-to-ground fault on an out-going overhead line, the potential of the substation ground mat might be elevated to several thousand volts, relative to remote mean earth potential by voltage gradients. Common-mode voltages from such causes can be compensated by insulating transformers or equalizing transformers or by other means of bridging large-magnitude, common-mode voltages.

The ordinary commercial building may present unexpected problems relative to common-mode voltage components due to voltage gradients in the building grounding conductor system. It is widely believed that the grounding requirements as spelled out in section NEC 250–23(a) of the National Electrical Code ensure that all electrical load current within the building will be returned to the service equipment (the point of electric service entrance) on power conductors, independent of the building structure.

An innocent-appearing exception can violate this concept. Section NEC 250–60 defines a grounding exception (rather generally used) for the frames of electric ranges, wall-mounted ovens, and counter-mounted cooking units. The code exception allows these appliance frames to be grounded by connection to the power system grounded conductor (white wire) if the electric service is a 240/120-V, single-phase, three-wire system or is taken from a 208Y/120-V, three-phase, four-wire system. It is unrealistic to assume that the appliance frames in question will not also be in contact with the building structure. The result is that the white load-current-carrying conductor becomes connected to the building frame through the heating appliance.

Thus a building devoted essentially to commercial activities, served with 208Y/120-V electric power, may have a snack bar installed on the sixth floor. Contained therein may be appliances grounded to the white wire as allowed by NEC 250–60. Instead of an electrically dry building frame, it may be found that between the sixth floor and the ground floor there is distributed the same electrical voltage drop as exists on the grounded power-system conductor between the snack bar connection and the service entrance.

When the service is three-phase and four-wire, all third-harmonic currents (and their multiples) in the entire array of line-to-neutral connected loads combine in an additive fashion in the neutral conductor (white wire) to aggravate the harmonic voltage drop along the white wire. In both the three-phase and single-phase power-supply cases, the increasing use of time-modulated (SCR-controlled) current in line-to-neutral connected devices (such as fans and lighting units) makes for the presence of much step-front hash in the voltage drop along the neutral conductor, which becomes voltage gradient in the building structure if the NEC 250–60 exception is employed. *See Semiconductor rectifier.*

Efforts have been made to restrict the use of the NEC 250–60 exception to appliance circuits which originate as branch circuits at the service equipment. It must be recognized, however, that the ground reference potential on one floor of an office building may differ from that of another floor by as much as several volts (third harmonic) and contain substantial fast-front hash.

Section NEC 250-23 of the National Electrical Code clearly prescribes that there shall be no grounding connection to the grounded power conductor of the electrical system downstream of the service equipment for that establishment. When this rule is respected, all of the load-system power current is returned to the grounded conductor at the service via insulated conductors. There is no opportunity for electrical noise, as it exists on the grounded power conductor (the white wire) to be conductively transferred to the system grounding conductors. There are three exceptions in the NEC text which may permit that rule to be bypassed. The first one applies to an in-plant separately derived electrical system located remote from the service equipment of the establishment. It is common to apply a permanent grounding connection at the supply-machine neutral. This will create a cross bond between the grounded conductor (white wire) and the grounding conductor downstream of the main service equipment. The second one applies to the case of an electric-supply circuit run to a second independent building. The NEC requires a cross bond between the grounded and the grounding conductor at the point of entry to the second building, unless an independent grounding conductor has been included with the power conductors from the supply point in the main building. The third exception, pertaining to ranges, countermounted cooking units, wall-mounted ovens, and clothes dryers, can be troublesome. While the National Electrical Code says merely that the power-circuit grounded conductor (white wire) may be used as the grounding conductor, it is commonly found that the appliance frames so grounded by connection to the white wire are also in contact with building metal frame or metal piping systems. It is this "back door" connection which allows communication of the electrical noise to the establishment grounding conductor system.

Progress is being made in restricting the use of the white wire as a grounding conductor.

A few instances of a cross-bond between the grounded power conductor and the equipment grounding conductor downstream of the service equipment have been observed as a result of an in-plant emergency or standby generator. These have been associated with 208Y/120-V and 480Y/277-V solidly grounded power systems serving hospitals, telephone exchanges, police centers, and other such important establishments. When operating on an emergency or standby basis, it is proper that a grounding connection exist at the local generator as prescribed for a separately derived electric power system in section NEC 250-26 of the National Electrical Code. It is common to find an intentional permanent grounding connection at the local-generator neutral junction. Unless the neutral line of the supplied load is switched, along with the phase conductors, the result is a permanent grounding connection on the "white wire" at the generator location, contrary to the planned design pattern. Location of the in-plant generator adjacent to the service equipment would eliminate the problem, as would also inclusion of the neutral conductor in the transfer switching operation.

There will occasionally occur brief intervals of much greater than normal voltage gradients along the building grounding conductor system. An insulation failure on a power conductor may permit a large-magnitude, ground-short-circuit current to flow through the building structure toward the service equipment location for the brief interval permitted by the overcurrent protector.

**Importance of low-noise environment.** The noise problems presented to the electronic equipment designer increase directly with increased ambient noise levels in the area. The quality level employed in grounding and shielding of power-system conductors has a marked effect on the ambient noise levels.

In an occupied building much can be learned of the general ambient noise levels by a study of the electric facility practices employed and by a general inspection of the building. Additional specific information may be obtained by test. It is important to look for unusual sources of high-energy radiation which may penetrate the building interior space. A nearby radio station antenna may create strong fields at one fixed frequency. High-power radar-scanning installations may be a source of annoying ambient fields of pulsed high frequency.

After an appraisal of the severity of the ambient electrical noise level, the problem of designing the grounding and shielding practices for the electronic equipment becomes a straightforward procedure.

**Grounding and shielding practices.** To establish an acceptably high signal-to-noise ratio demands that normal-mode noise be maintained at levels below a specified tolerable value.

***Choice of conductor.*** The construction geometry of the signal conductor (**Fig. 4**) plays a prominent part. Of the many possible varieties, the four most commonly used are random-selected wires in a multiconductor cable, parallel-wire twin-lead, twisted-pair, and coaxial lines. Because of the superiority of the twisted-pair relative to random wires or twin-lead at modest cost increase, its use is universal when noise reduction is a factor. A half twist every inch is both typical and effective.

An encircling metal raceway accomplishes substantial additional attenuation, particularly if it consists of steel conduit. In securing high-quality rejection of capacitively coupled noise voltages, it is common practice to avoid any grounding connection on the signal conductor (coaxial lines excepted) and to incorporate a balanced impedance connection to the central-equipment reference ground terminal in the input circuits of a differential amplifier.

The coaxial line (Fig. 4*d*) is a theoretically superior construction but may be faced with operating conditions which deteriorate these qualities. As it is inherently an unbalanced line, the exterior shell is commonly connected to the reference ground terminal at the central equipment. The existence of any connection to adjacent ground along the coaxial line (not easy to avoid) creates the ground loop situation described in Fig. 2*c* with a likely inevitable insertion of normal-mode error signal (noise). Even in the absence of a second ground connection, large-magnitude varying electric fields (Fig. 2*b*) can create measurable values of charging current flowing along the outer shell to the grounding connection at the central equipment, and in so doing can create an *IR* voltage drop along that conductor which will appear as a normal-mode noise voltage. An enclosing metal raceway grounded to the central-equipment ground reference terminal can be used to effectively suppress this noise source. SEE *IR* DROP.

***Conductor shielding.*** A multiplicity of signal circuits may be run within a common metal raceway, providing that the signal magnitude on these conductors is not great enough to create cross-coupled interference (cross talk). Of the various conductor geometries considered in Fig. 4, the random wire case in *a* would be most susceptible and would offer little hope for correction. With the conductor patterns in *b* and *c* the application of wrapped-on shielding tape (or equivalent concentric conducting shell) to each signal circuit, grounded at the central-equipment grounding terminal, would only accomplish high-quality cross-talk suppression. The coaxial line is inherently free of cross-talk interference if the outer conductor is grounded only at the central equipment.

It is possible (and not unlikely) that the outer terminal sensor may itself respond to ambient magnetic field noise (Fig. 2*a*) or electrostatic field noise (Fig. 2*b*) or both, and create normal-mode, signal-circuit noise. The magnetic field problem can be resolved by the application of appropriate magnetic shielding at the sensor, the enclosure of the complete sensor within a closed shell of conductive metal, or a combination of the two. The electrostatic problem can be

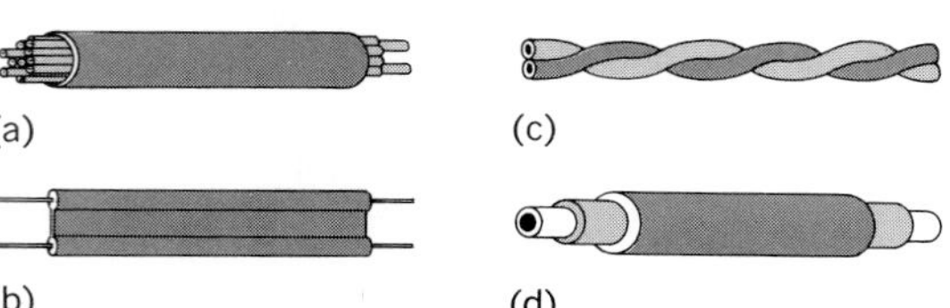


**Fig. 4. Common signal-circuit geometries. (*a*) Two random wires. (*b*) Straight twin-lead. (c) Twisted pair. (*d*) Coaxial line.**

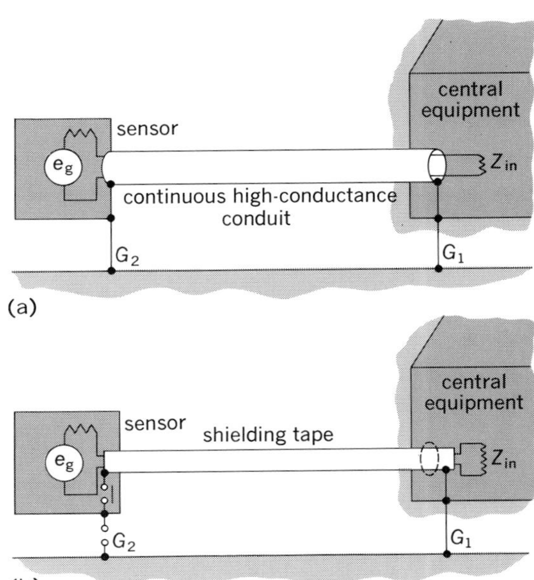


**Fig. 5. Practical grounding techniques. (*a*) High-conductance raceway. (*b*) Electrostatic shielding.**

resolved by enclosing the sensor winding and its circuit leads within a thin-wall shielding shell maintained at zero reference ground potential. The enclosing shell can be the same one used for magnetic induction suppression. The required connection to a zero potential reference point may require a unique grounding circuit extending from the central equipment (**Fig. 5**).

***Control of grounds.*** The remaining perplexing noise abatement problem relates to the creation of reference grounding terminals at peripheral equipment locations which appear to be at the same potential as the central-equipment grounding terminal; an example is the electrostatic suppression problem discussed in the previous paragraph. An earlier discussion (Fig. 2*c*) develops the fact that between a building ground-reference point $G_2$ and a widely separated central-equipment grounding terminal $G_1$ there will, more often than not, appear a difference in electrical potential. The difference voltage can create normal-mode, error-signal voltages in the several ways described.

If the remote terminal $G_2$ is not in the same building as is terminal $G_1$, or if it is located in an area where large common-mode noise voltages are expected, the use of insulating or equalizing transformers in the signal lines or the adoption of other common-mode suppression techniques should be considered.

If the remote equipment is in the same metal-frame building or in a location where common-mode voltage difference between reference ground terminals is known not to exceed perhaps 10 V, acceptable attenuation should be possible without the introduction of isolation techniques on the signal wires themselves.

The installation of a grounding conductor, run with the signal circuits, which interconnects grounding terminal $G_2$ with $G_1$ will be helpful but not as effective as might be expected. A substantial fraction of the original noise voltage will remain in the form of an *IZ* drop along the grounding conductor.

***High-conductance raceway.*** By modifying the form of this grounding conductor, a tremendous gain in attenuation can be achieved. By forming the conductive metal of the grounding conductor into a hollow tube through which the signal conductors are passed, its effectiveness is increased enormously. The resulting tubular grounding conductor, called a high-conductance raceway (Fig. 5*a*), interconnects grounding terminals $G_1$ and $G_2$ as did the cable grounding conductor. Voltage difference $e_{G1} - e_{G2}$ appears as an *IZ* drop along the raceway. The conductance (tube diameter, wall thickness, and type of metal) is selected so that only a small portion of the total *IZ* drop appears as a resistance drop along the metal tube. Almost the entire voltage difference between grounding terminals $G_1$ and $G_2$ is accounted for by a reactive-voltage drop *IX* created by an induced magnetic field encircling the tubular raceway. This magnetic field also links each signal conductor contained within the raceway and thus induces in each one identically the same *IX* voltage drop as in the raceway. With the *IX* voltage component equalized, or canceled out, only the *IR* drop along the high-conductance raceway appears as a voltage difference between signal conductors and adjacent ground at $G_2$.

It is important to note that this cancellation of the *IX* drop occurs only on those signal conductors run within the high-conductance raceway. If some critical signal circuits must take a different route, an independent high-conductance raceway to contain them will be needed to accomplish the desired high-magnitude attenuation.

The high-conductance raceway technique is applied extensively to interconnect the several independent housings marking up the central electronics equipment to establish a nearly quiet ground reference potential throughout the central equipment. One prominent item of the central equipment is designated as the reference unit and is bonded to the building reference ground, preferably at only one point. All other equipment frames in the group would, by design intent, permit conductive connection only to the central reference structure in the form of high-conductance raceways. Power conductors and other high-noise-level conductors should be run in raceways independent of the sensitive signal circuits.

In extremely severe situations where the *IR* drop in the high-conductance raceway creates intolerable noise levels, a dual concentric system may be substituted. The exterior high-conductance raceway is identical in design and function with the one just described. Within this is a second metallic tubular raceway, insulated from the former except for an intentional cross bond at the central equipment grounding terminal $G_1$. At the remote equipment locations, the construction consists of an outer enclosure bonded to the building ground terminal $G_2$. The electronic equipment chassis containing the active electronics components is insulated from the outer housing and bonded only to the internal concentric raceway. By this modification even the resistance voltage drop along the outer tubular raceway is prevented from appearing as a voltage difference between signal conductors and their enclosing raceway.

Should the remote sensor terminal be small and of simple character, with possible noise being essentially of electrostatic coupling origin, the simple circuit pattern illustrated in Fig. 5*b* may prove adequate. A lightweight shielding tape enclosing the signal conductors preserves a zero-potential reference plane surrounding the signal conductors. The sensor frame (or enclosing electrostatic shield) is connected to the signal-circuit shielding tape and kept insulated from the local grounding terminal $G_2$. The presence of high-intensity electric field noise at the outer terminal may demand a higher-conductance signal-circuit shield to avoid objectionable noise voltages of *IR* drop origin.

Grounding, electromagnetic shielding (and cancellation), electrostatic shielding, and insulation are intimately intertwined in effecting an acceptable solution.

**Data transmission.** To an ever-increasing extent the high-density channels of information handling (data transmission) are being accommodated by means other than metallic conductors. The prominent transmission avenues are microwave links and optic fibers. The problems of circuit grounding along these links are simply nonexistent. The interconnecting wire circuits between the distributed sensors and the central processing center, and between the various functional systems at the center, and the transmission to the output terminal at that location will face the same signal-to-noise ratio problem as in the past. *See* MICROWAVE; OPTICAL COMMUNICATIONS.

**Optical isolator.** In dealing with the aggravated problems associated with the large magnitudes of common-mode noise voltage encountered with circuits run to an outdoor electric substation, the optical isolator is a valuable tool. This device introduces a short optical transmission path into the electric signal circuit with a capability of withstanding several thousand volts of common-mode voltage without ill effects. *See* OPTICAL ISOLATOR.

*R. H. Kaufmann*

***Bibliography.*** W. W. Brown et al., System and circuit considerations for integrated industrial fiber optic data links, *IEEE Trans. Commun.*, 26(7):976–982, 1978; Communications and microwave technology, *IEEE Spectrum,* p. 38, January 1979; *Guide for Safety in Alternating Current Substation Grounding,* IEEE Stand, no. 80, 1976; R. L. Heider, Wiring practices for computer power and grounding, *Adv. Instrum.*, 34(1):257–264, 1979; Institute of Electrical and Electronics Engineers, The isolation concept for protection of wire line facilities entering electric power stations, *IEEE Trans. Power Apparatus Syst.*, PAS-95(4):1216, 1976; Institute of Electrical and Electronics Engineers, The neutralizing transformer concept for protection of wire line facilities entering electric power stations, *IEEE Trans. Power Apparatus Syst.*, PAS-96(4):1256, 1977.

## Electronic listening devices

Devices which are used to capture the sound waves of conversation originating in an ostensibly private setting in a form, usually as a magnetic tape recording, which can be used against the target by adverse interests.

There are two kinds of electronic listening devices. One takes advantage of equipment already present on the target's premises, such as a telephone, radio, phonograph, television set, public-address loudspeaker, or tape recorder, to act as a microphone, transmitter, or power supply. The other does not. In the former case, the target's equipment is said to have been compromised.

These practices are unlawful in the United States and Canada except when carried out by law enforcement officers acting under authority of a warrant. In the United Kingdom, electronic eavesdropping by private parties may contravene the laws against trespass and unauthorized use of telephone equipment or radio frequencies, but it is not unlawful in and of itself. The same situation is generally true in western European countries.

**Compromise.** Compromise of the target's own equipment takes advantage of the fact that any loudspeaker is capable of functioning just as well as a microphone, that convenient sources of dc power are available within the equipment, or that the equipment is connected to power or signal lines that can transmit the intercepted conversation to some place where recording can conveniently be accomplished.

The equipment most frequently compromised is the telephone handset. The act of compromise may be as simple as bypassing the switch hook with a Zener diode so that the instrument can transmit conversations to a wiretap, or high-impedance parallel connection off the premises, while not signaling a busy tone to someone attempting to dial in. *See* TELEPHONE; ZENER DIODE.

It can be as complex as the infinity transmitter, which is activated by the eavesdropper's dialing in and transmitting, before the telephone rings, an audio tone to a tuned relay concealed in the instrument.

**Bugs.** Eavesdropping devices that can stand alone are known commonly as "bugs." They take advantage of many developments of modern technology, such as microcircuits, miniature ceramic microphones, and miniature batteries. *See* INTEGRATED CIRCUITS; MICROPHONE.

The art of designing bugs has achieved its most advanced state of development in the national intelligence services of the Great Powers. One bug was discovered to have been inserted in the heel of a diplomat's shoe.

The smallest bug available to the private citizen is probably the Hong Kong "spider." It is no larger than a common postage stamp and less than a quarter-inch thick.

Electronically a bug is often just a two-stage frequency-modulated transmitter: an audio amplifier and a variable-frequency radio-frequency (rf) oscillator. *See* AMPLIFIER; OSCILLATOR; RADIO TRANSMITTER.

Bugs may operate on any frequency from 20 to 1000 MHz, but usually they snuggle up beside a powerful local frequency modulation (FM) or very high-frequency (VHF) television station.

A popular hybrid between a compromise device and a bug is the telephone drop-in. In this design, an FM transmitter is made in the form of a telephone microphone. The eavesdropper can casually unscrew the mouthpiece of the target's telephone handset and substitute the drop-in for the original microphone. The range of this device is about 250 ft (75 m). It has the added advantage of drawing its dc power from the telephone company central battery.

**Defenses.** The telephone line analyzer is used to defeat compromise devices. Under the control of a microcomputer, the line analyzer examines in turn each of the 50 or more telephone lines used by a typical commercial firm. It can detect the tiny amount of current flow into a Zener or other compromise device. A monotonically rising audio signal is then applied to trigger any infinity transmitter. If a compromise device is discovered, a pulse of 800 V is impressed upon the line to burn it out.

Technical surveillance sweeps, as they are known to the trade, are performed alternately with external signal lines connected and disconnected and with telephones on-hook and off-hook.

Often a sniffer is used to sense the presence of a bug. A sniffer may be a simple VHF diode detector with an output meter that reveals the presence of a local carrier. More sophisticated instruments sweep the frequency bands of interest and compare the audio output with locally generated signals, usually a tape recording of simulated business activity. Another type of sniffer affords discrimination between a genuine clandestine device and a strong local broadcasting station. *See Detector.*

If the presence of a clandestine device is indicated, the sweep team may employ a panoramic intercept receiver. This instrument displays the amplitude of received signals on a cathode-ray-tube trace calibrated in units of frequency. The frequency of the bug can be determined by observing which of the pips on the CRT trace appears to diminish and grow in direct response to the locally generated audio signal. Once its frequency is determined, the bug's physical location can be found by use of a tuned rf field-strength meter having a loop antenna. *See Antenna; Cathode-ray tube.*

The objective of a sweep such as the one described is to locate the device and discover its technical characteristics with a view toward feeding the device false information that may discredit or compromise the individuals responsible for planting it.

National security forces encounter clandestine devices which are switched on and off by an agent using a control transmitter. Such a device cannot be detected by the methods described above because they presuppose that the bug is continually on the air or can be activated by locally generated audio.

To detect silent bugs, advantage is taken of the fact that all subminiature transmitters contain one or more semiconductor junctions connected to an electromagnetic radiator. Inasmuch as these junctions are nonlinear impedances, a locally generated low-power ultra-high-frequency carrier will be reradiated by the bug, and the reradiated signal will contain strong harmonic components.

Natural devices such as rusty bedsprings will reradiate second-harmonic components, but only a real semiconductor junction will reradiate third (and higher) harmonics.

An ultra-high frequency (UHF) sweeper is equipped with a meter that produces a negative deflection in the presence of reradiated second-harmonic energy and a positive deflection in the presence of reradiated third-harmonic energy. Such a deflection discloses the presence of a bug, albeit a silent one not detectable by sniffers or panoramic receivers. The UHF sweeper is portable; it bears a resemblance to a household appliance for vacuuming drapes. Increasing positive deflection indicates to the sweep team member that he is approaching the bug. *See Harmonic analyzer.*

**Advanced devices.** Human capacity for designing electronic instruments to spy on one's neighbors appears to be boundless. Some of the more exotic include laser radar which responds to infinitesimal motion of windowpanes caused by conversation in a room, bugs which include miniature television cameras, and minicomputers which are programmed to intercept messages to a resource-sharing computer and to return answers which are spurious.

*John M. Carroll*

***Bibliography.*** D. A. Pollack, *Methods of Electronic Audio Surveillance*, 2d ed., 1979.

## Electronic mail

Any of various systems that transmit some form of electronic (usually digital) representation of a page or message from one location to another. The two locations may be as close as two adjacent terminals or as far as halfway around the world. Some forms of transmission capability have existed for a long time, but the term electronic mail appeared with the computer and integrated-circuit technology explosion. The emergence of inexpensive, high-speed scanners (which convert hard copy to an electronic representation) and error-free compression (a method of reducing the transmission time required) may be the primary catalysts that created the term electronic mail. The widespread usage of this term, however, probably results from the ability of large numbers of users to create electronic messages at readily available computer terminals. *See Integrated circuits.*

Because the term electronic mail is so commonly used in the field of communications, it has acquired a variety of meanings and interpretations, with regard to both the role of the originator and that of the recipient. The term has even been used to describe a communication that is received as a synthesized vocal output (voice), although this rare usage will probably not persist because, in general, electronic mail is applied to a communication that can be viewed by the recipient. The most used and meaningful definitions are discussed below.

**Small computers.** As late as 1970, home and small-business computers were experimental novelties; they were used mostly as stand-alones without being interconnected. Communication between such computers was either nonexistent or nearly impossible. As more people and companies became users, due primarily to decreasing costs and increasing capability, they began to see the advantages and economics of exchanging information through the electronic format in which the data existed. Software developers and common carriers were quick to make available what was needed to accomplish this interconnect capability. Most small computers are now able to communicate with one another and thus become electronic mail terminals. *See Computer; Microcomputer.*

The small-business-computer industry uses the term electronic mail to describe the ability to receive on one terminal a textual message that originated on another terminal. The output is normally a pictorial display on a computer monitor, which can be printed if the receiving terminal is so equipped.

**Facsimile.** Although the facsimile was invented in 1843 by Alexander Bain, the major practical use of a facsimile-type machine was by the wire news services to transmit pictures. These were called by various names, including wirephoto. These machines were slow compared to current technology, but were engineering marvels in the 1930s. It was not until the mid-1960s that a more general commercial facsimile machine became available.

The major problem in utilizing these machines then was that they were relatively expensive and could only be used to communicate with identical machines, which greatly reduced their value. Also, they were slow, usually taking 6 min to transmit a single page, which led to high operational line costs. In 1980 the Consulting Committee for International Telephone and Telegraph (CCITT), an international telecommunications organization, agreed to a standard for facsimile machines which could transmit a page in less than 1 min. These were called Group 3 machines. The popularity of this form of electronic mail is due to the high quality of the output copy. SEE FACSIMILE.

The term electronic mail is used in conjunction with compatible facsimile equipment for sending and receiving of memoranda, documents, sketches, tables, and so forth. This use of the term is primarily by the equipment manufacturers, in reference to the capability of the facsimile equipment to perform that function. The output of the high-resolution machines is a close reproduction of the original.

**Telegraphy.** Some services which have been available for a long time, such as telegrams, Telex, and TWX, have been referred to as the first electronic mail services. They have been undergoing a major modernization and image "facelifting," with computer-controlled switching and advanced designed terminal equipment, which may justify using a modern name such as electronic mail. The output is a text-only message.

The best known of this type of electronic mail, the telegram, has been available for over 100 years. A spinoff service which can fall within this definition is the Mailgram (of Western Union), which combines a textual input with high-speed electronic transmission to over 140 locations, where a hard copy is generated, enveloped, and placed into the regular daily delivery system of the U.S. Postal Service.

**Office automation systems.** The modern office automation systems industry uses the term electronic mail in conjunction with the ability of their equipment to transfer correspondence. The correspondence is generated on one terminal, stored in a central file, and retrieved by another compatible terminal with access to that central file. The output of these systems is, once again, text-only, but differs from that described above in that the format usually resembles a standard typewritten correspondence page.

Such systems are growing in acceptance. They usually have a communications capability that permits all or selected terminals and printers in the system to have access to messages stored in the central processor. However, their use will remain restricted to an individual company, and not interconnected with other companies, for security reasons. SEE WORD PROCESSING.

**Specially designed services.** Finally, the term electronic mail is applied to specially designed services that transfer a message page from one geographic location to another by electronic communication methods. This use of the term is usually without restriction as to the type of originating equipment, but the output is normally hard copy and most often hand-delivered to the addressee in an envelope, which makes it more like traditional mail. The major drawback in any such mail service is, of course, the ability of the originator to be able to complete the delivery of the message to the recipient. An example of this problem is that if the originator uses a computer to generate the message the recipient must have a compatible computer to accept the message. To overcome this problem and still make use of today's available high-speed transmission capability and maintain lower prices, the originator often makes use of the U.S. Postal Service's daily delivery of hard-copy mail. SEE ELECTRICAL COMMUNICATIONS.

*Victor P. Boyd*

**Bibliography.** S. Connell and L. A. Galbraith, *Electronic Mail: A Revolution in Business Communications*, 1980; Eastern Management Group, *Report on Electronic Mail*, January 1984; P. L. Probst, The subminute digital facsimile explosion, *Telecommunications*, pp. 53–54, September 1982; A. Simpson (ed.), *The Office of the Future*, no. 2: *Planning for Electronic Mail*, Gower Publishing, Great Britain, 1982.

## Electronic packaging

The physical support, protection, cooling, and electrical connections of semiconductor integrated circuit chips that constitute electronic circuits. Ceramic- and glass-metal packages were originally used for the interconnections and environmental protection of silicon and germanium devices, such as diodes and transistors. They are now used for intraconnections, substrates, power distribution, cooling, and inputs and outputs as well. As the number of circuits per chip increases, each of these functions takes on greater importance. SEE INTEGRATED CIRCUITS.

**Current technology.** There are three basic methods for joining silicon chips to their substrates: back bonding with gold connector wires, flip-chip bonding with solder pads, and decal bonding.

Back bonding, the original process which is still in use, bonds the silicon chips to the substrates with either a gold-silicon eutectic braze or a silver-loaded epoxy cement. The connections from the chip pads to those on the substrate are made with 0.001- to 0.003-in.-diameter (0.025- to 0.075-mm) gold wires which are ultrasonically or thermally bonded to both sets of pads.

In flip-chip bonding, up to 121 0.005-in.-diameter (0.125-mm) 95% lead–5% tin solder pads are deposited on each silicon chip. The pads on these chips are then placed on the vias in the ceramic substrate, held in place with a solder flux by surface tension, and then passed through a belt furnace at about 750°F (400°C). (Vias are holes in the ceramic layers, filled with metallic paste, which electrically connect the conductive pattern from layer to layer.) This method is used in manufacturing the thermal conduction module (see **illus.**).

Decal bonding uses a thin gold-plated copper foil which has been etched to mate with the pads on the chips and substrate. These patterns are the decals, and they are ultrasonically or thermally bonded to the chips and substrate. The chips are either backbonded to a substrate or encapsulated in an epoxy resin.

***Environmental protection.*** Silicon integrated circuit chips are usually coated with thick silica layers which provide adequate protection from the environment. In order to protect the aluminum conductors from humidity, the chips must be hermetically sealed. There are several approaches to achieve this. A thick plastic coating can be used which will delay the penetration of moisture, or glass-metal or ceramic-metal seals can be used. In the latter case a flange is brazed to the metallization on the ceramic and then a cover is welded or brazed to this flange. Another method, used with the newest version of the thermal conduction module (discussed below), is to directly seal the cover to the bare ceramic with the use of a C ring.

***Intraconnections.*** The intraconnection wiring determines the transmission speed of the signals within the substrate. **Table 1** lists several of the ceramics being used and those which are being considered for future use. It is important to reduce the permittivity of the ceramic because it determines the speed of the signal. As the dielectric constant of the ceramic is reduced, the characteristic impedance of the line $Z$ has to be maintained between 50 and 100 ohms, as determined by Eq. (1), where $L$ is the inductance of the line, and

$$Z = \sqrt{L/C} \qquad (1)$$

$C$ is the capacitance of the line to ground. Therefore, the thickness of the ceramic layers must be reduced to provide these values. As the layers become thinner, there is less space for the metallic components. Thus, the entire structure is subject to constraints which depend on the conductivity of the metal.

**Table 2** lists the properties of the metals in use now and those being considered for the future. Molybdenum and tungsten are the best compromises for adhesion, electrical conductivity, and thermal expansion for alumina substrates. As silicon chips increase in size, however, the thermal expansion of the ceramic should be reduced in order to minimize the stresses in the joints between the silicon and the ceramic. The Coffin-Manson equation (2) gives the

$$N_f = c/\epsilon^2 \qquad (2)$$

number of cycles to failure by fatigue, $N_f$, where $c$ is a constant for the system and $\epsilon$ is the strain. $N_f$ can be over 20,000 cycles with current ceramic materials and silicon. As the silicon chips get larger, however, fatigue failures will become a more serious problem due to the larger stresses.

***Power distribution.*** Higher-conductivity metals will be needed in multilayer ceramic structures for power distribution. Moybdenum and tungsten may be replaced with copper or gold when low-firing ceramic materials are used. Other alternatives could be the use of decoupling capacitors or bus-bars on the substrates.

***Cooling.*** There are two methods for removing the heat from chips on a module. Chips which are back-bonded to the substrate can have their heat removed through the substrate from the back of the chip. In the flip-chip technology, chips are cooled by aluminum pistons or ceramic or metal covers in contact with the back of the chips. Each of these configurations provides a direct path for heat to leave the module through a water or air exchange arrangement.

***Inputs and outputs.*** The leads on the substrates are used to provide a means of communication to the rest of the system. The lead reduction ratio parameter is a measure of the efficiency of the package. It is calculated from the total number of pads on all the chips divided by the total number of leads on the substrate. Early device packages had a lead reduction ratio of 1. As levels of integration grew, this value increased to 9 for the thermal conduction module.

**Advanced packages.** The thermal conduction module (see illus.) represents the most advanced ceramic package in the electronics industry. A new version of this module will be used in the next IBM series of large-scale computers. As in earlier versions, this substrate supports 133 chips, has 1800 pins, and is 3.5 in. (90 mm) square, but each chip now dissipates up to 6 W. The other major change is the elimination of the flange on the substrate, which has been replaced with a C-ring direct seal to the bare ceramic. This substrate also uses a 92% alumina ceramic with molybdenum.

Another type of substrate can have up to 41 ceramic layers, which are made from 55% alumina and 45% lead borosilicate glass. Each substrate can accommodate up to 76 chips, which are decal-bonded to the substrate by an ultrasonic thermal compression bonder. The metal is gold or 85% silver–15% palladium. These substrates are sintered at 1650°F (900°C) in order to prevent melting of the gold.

Another manufacturer uses a 96%-alumina ceramic with tungsten, which sinters about 2800°F (1550°C). Molybdenum-manganese pastes are used on the sur-

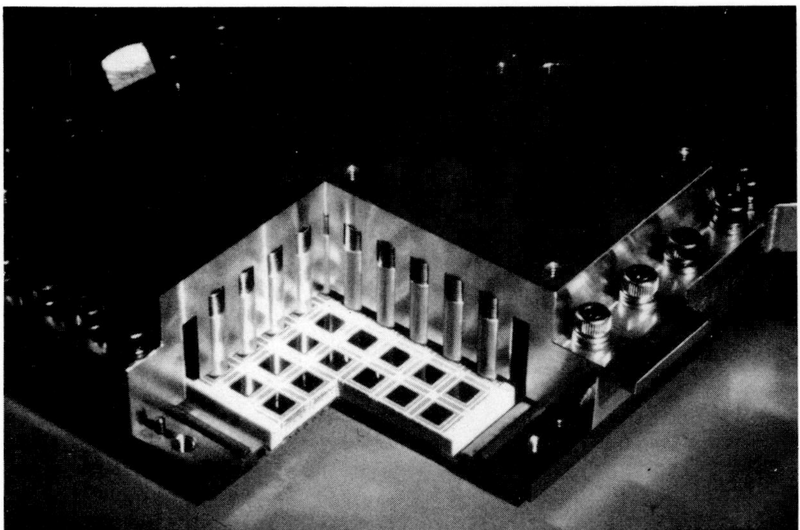
(a)

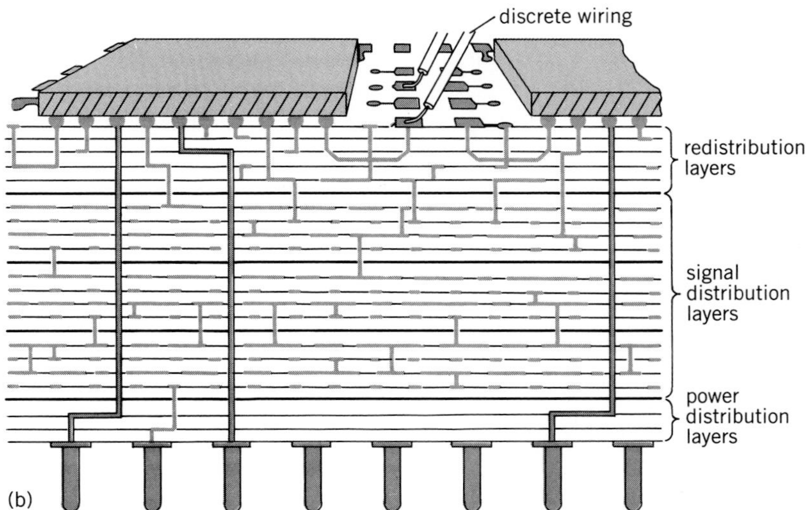


**Thermal conduction module. (*a*) Cutaway view. (*b*) Schematic cross section of multilayer ceramic substrate with chips and pins attached. The discrete wires are used to make engineering changes.**

**Table 1. Properties of ceramic materials**

| Material | Strength, kpsi (MPa) | Thermal conductivity, W/[m·°C] | Thermal expansion, $10^{-6}$/°C ($10^{-6}$/°F) | Relative permittivity [K] |
|---|---|---|---|---|
| Alumina ($Al_2O_3$) compositions | | | | |
| 92% | 46 (317) | 16.7 | 7.7 (4.3) | 9.5 |
| 96% | 40 (276) | 25.1 | 7.8 (4.3) | 10.2 |
| 55% + 45% glass | 43 (296) | 5.0 | 4.2 (2.3) | 7.5 |
| Future materials | | | | |
| Aluminum nitride (AlN) | 40 (276) | 210 | 4.5 (2.5) | 8.8 |
| Silicon nitride ($Si_3N_4$) | 85 (586) | 33.5 | 3.1 (1.7) | 6.0 |
| Silicon carbide (SiC) | 20 (138) | 340 | 3.1 (1.7) | 40 |
| Mullite | 24 (165) | 10 | 3.8 (2.1) | 5 |
| Cordierite | 15 (103) | 10 | 1.6 (0.9) | 6 |
| Glass-ceramic mixtures | 28 (193) | 3.5 | 6.5–7.5 (3.6–4.2) | 6.5–7 |

**Table 2. Properties of metals**

| Element | Melting point, °C (°F) | Resistivity, $10^{-8}$ ohm-m | Thermal expansion, $10^{-6}$/°C ($10^{-6}$/°F) |
|---|---|---|---|
| Tungsten (W) | 3415 (6179) | 5.5 | 4.5 (2.5) |
| Molybdenum (Mo) | 2625 (4757) | 5.2 | 3.5 (1.9) |
| Palladium (Pd) | 1552 (2826) | 10.8 | 11.0 (6.1) |
| Copper (Cu) | 1083 (1981) | 1.7 | 17.0 (9.4) |
| Gold (Au) | 1063 (1945) | 2.2 | 14.2 (7.9) |
| Silver (Ag) | 960 (1760) | 1.6 | 19.7 (10.9) |
| Aluminum (Al) | 660 (1220) | 3.7 | 23.9 (13.3) |

face of the modules, which are subsequently coated with up to five layers of polyimide and copper. The lines are 0.01 in. (0.25 mm) wide, with 0.02-in. (0.50-mm) spacings, and vias in the ceramic substrates have 0.008-in. (0.20-mm) diameters. The thin-film metal structures have 0.002-in. (0.05-mm) line widths with 0.005-in. (0.13-mm) spacings and vias with 0.0032-in. (0.08-mm) diameters in the polyimide.

**Future materials.** Ceramic materials being considered for future use include aluminum nitride (AlN), silicon nitride ($Si_3N_4$), silicon carbide (SiC), mullite-cordierite mixtures, and glass-ceramic mixtures.

Pure aluminum nitride has an extremely high thermal conductivity, a thermal expansion close to that of silicon, and a strength of 40,000 psi (276 megapascals). The problem with aluminum nitride is that it has to be sintered at very high temperatures. For example, with a 3% yttria addition as a sintering aid, this material has to be sintered at 3300°F (1800°C). Furthermore, this addition reduces its thermal conductivity.

Silicon nitride has a low thermal conductivity; however, it has a strength of 85,000 psi (586 MPa), a thermal expansion closer to that of silicon, and a dielectric constant of about 6. However, it also must be sintered at high temperatures and pressures to produce a dense material. Thin films can be produced by chemical vapor techniques.

Silicon carbide has the highest thermal conductivity of all the ceramic materials being considered, as well as a thermal expansion very close to that of silicon. Its dielectric constant, however, is about 40, and it has to be hot-pressed or hot-isostatically-pressed to obtain a high density.

Mixtures of mullite ($3Al_2O_3 \cdot 2SiO_2$) and cordierite ($2MgO \cdot 2Al_2O_3 \cdot 5SiO_2$) are also being studied in oxidizing or reducing atmospheres in the temperature ranges of 1800 to 2650°F (1000 to 1450°C). Their thermal expansions can be adjusted to match that of silicon, and dielectric constants are in an acceptable range of 5 to 6.

Various glass-ceramic mixtures are being developed in order to obtain low-firing materials which can be used with copper or noble metal pastes, such as gold or silver-palladium. A mixture of 35% alumina, 40% borosilicate glass, and 25% forsterite ($2MgO \cdot SiO_2$) ceramic has been developed and is being used with silver-palladium conductors for multilayer ceramic substrates. A low-temperature ceramic in the $ZnO$-$Al_2O_3$-$MgO$-$SiO_2$ system, cofired with gold, is also being developed for multilayer substrates. Finally, a 50% alumina—50% borosilicate glass multilayer substrate using copper metallurgy is being studied.

**New processes.** Doctor blading, the process now used to manufacture ceramic layers, can be extended to produce plasticized ceramic sheets as thin as 0.001 in. (0.025 mm). At this point other technologies, such as sputtering, evaporation, chemical vapor deposition, and sol-gel chemical synthesis, could be implemented in order to manufacture the next generation of ceramic or polymer substrates. Aluminum conductors could then be used with these processes because of their low operating temperatures. Also, these technologies are very suitable for making thin flims, which will permit the use of a much broader range of materials. SEE CIRCUIT (ELECTRONICS).

*Bernard Schwartz*

**Bibliography.** B. Schwartz, Microelectronics packaging, in *Electronic Ceramics*, Amer. Ceram. Soc. Spec. Publ. 3, pp. 12–15, May 3, 1969; B.

Schwartz, Review of multilayer ceramics for microelectronics packaging, *J. Phys. Chem. Solids*, 45:1051–1068, 1984.

## Electronic power supply

A source of electric energy employed to furnish the tubes and semiconductor devices of an electronic circuit with the proper electric voltages and currents for their operation. The more common sources of energy are chemical batteries and alternating-current mains or lines. Batteries are useful as portable sources but are expensive and have small capacities. Alternating-current mains are not portable but are relatively inexpensive and have a large capacity. *See Alternating current.*

One common method of classifying power supplies is by their use in electronic circuits. Most vacuum and gas tubes require a source of energy to energize their filaments or heaters; this type is known as a filament or heater power supply. Tubes require plate or anode voltages, and transistors need voltages for their collectors and emitters. These voltages are from a direct-current power supply which may provide about 4 to 40 V for circuits involving transistors and about 50 to 400 V for circuits using tubes. *See Gas tube; Semiconductor; Transistor; Vacuum tube.*

If the source is one of alternating voltage, a transformer is usually used to raise or lower the voltage to the required level. The alternating current (ac) usually must be changed to a direct current (dc); this is accomplished by a rectifier. A rectifier allows current to flow mostly in one direction, and a pulsating current results. This pulsating direct current is not suitable for most purposes and must be smoothed by a power-supply filter or voltage regulator. *See Rectifier.*

A power-supply filter stores energy when the current is high and give it up when the current is lower. The net result is to smooth out the variations in the current. The voltage regulator performs a similar function, but its operation is quite different. The Zener diode type of voltage regulator has a voltage which is nearly constant as the current is varied over a considerable range of values. The gas-tube type of voltage regulator has a characteristic constant voltage over a large range of current values. Vacuum-tube and transistor regulators usually operate as variable resistances; the resistance decreases when the load is heavy and increases when it is lighter. Voltage regulators deliver an almost constant output voltage in spite of variation in load or in input ac supply voltage. *See Voltage regulator; Zener diode.*

**Filament or heater power supply.** The filament or heater power supply is used to heat the filaments of vacuum or gas tubes so that electrons may be emitted from the filaments. If an indirectly heated cathode is used, a heater element inside the cathode must heat the cathode to a temperature at which electrons will be emitted.

Most of the present-day tubes heated by alternating current use 6.3 or 12.6-V heaters. A stepdown transformer is employed to change the 114 V of the ac lines to these voltages. As an example, the heaters of four tubes may be connected in parallel across the secondary of a heater transformer whose primary is connected to the 115-V ac lines. The center tap or one side of the secondary is often grounded. The tubes might take 0.5, 0.5, 1.0, and 2.0 A, respectively, for a total of 4.0 A. The heater transformer must have a rated capacity of at least 4.0 A to supply these tubes. The voltage that the insulation must withstand is also often stipulated. Some tubes require other heater voltages, such as 2.5, 5, and 25 V. Therefore, heater transformers with more than one secondary are useful.

Heater transformers are both heavy and expensive. To eliminate transformers, heaters may be connected in series across the ac line. Here each heater must take the same current, and the sum of the heater voltage ratings must be nearly equal to the ac line voltage. Other tubes use heaters made for direct connection across the ac lines.

For portable operation, batteries are usually used to heat the filaments. The tubes usually require 1–3 V, so that one or two cells of a dry battery or one cell of a wet battery will supply sufficient voltage. Tubes having 6.3- or 12.6-V heaters may be operated from a wet storage battery, such as an automobile battery, but the weight of the battery decreases its portability. The filaments of the tubes are connected in parallel and one side of the battery is connected to the plate supply, so a complete circuit exists for the electrons flowing in the tube.

**Direct-current power supply.** The dc power supply usually supplies direct current of about 5 to 30 or 40 V to transistor circuits, depending on the transistor type and its application. Similarly for tube circuits, the supply may deliver voltages of about 50 to 300 or 400 V. **Figure 1** shows the schematic diagram of a typical supply. The ac line energizes the primary of the transformer; the secondary is connected to the anodes of the rectifier diodes $D_1$ and $D_2$. The common diode connection is connected to the double-section $L$ filter. This is the positive side of the filter. The negative side, usually grounded, is connected to the center tap of the transformer secondary. The load resistance is shown at the other end of the filter. A bleeder resistor is sometimes connected across the load to prevent the output voltage from increasing to dangerous values when the load is light.

The power transformer should be selected to have a sufficiently high secondary voltage to supply the desired output voltage. Allowance must be made for the voltage drop or rise caused by the type of rectifier circuit employed, and for the voltage drop in the rectifier diodes and the filter elements caused by the combined load and bleeder currents. Also, the transformer secondary current rating must be sufficient to supply the combined currents. The rectifier diodes must have voltage ratings sufficiently large for the transformer secondary voltages, and current ratings sufficiently large for the combined load and bleeder

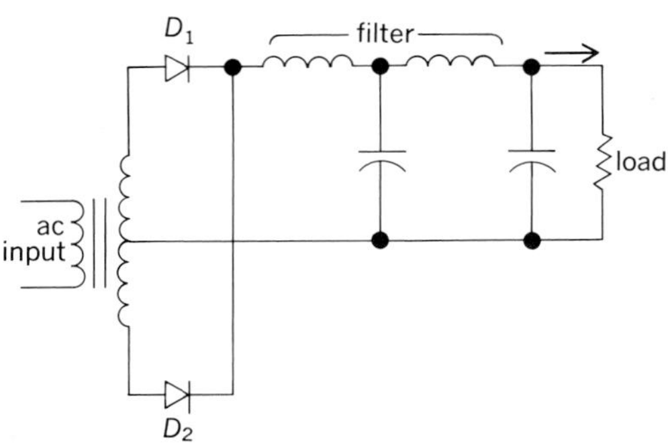


**Fig. 1. Typical direct-current power supply.**

currents and for the peak currents encountered in the particular rectifier circuit used. The filter capacitors should have sufficient capacitance for smoothing the ripple of the output voltage and sufficient voltage rating. The filter inductors should have sufficient inductance for smoothing, low resistance to the current carried, and high insulation voltage.

As the line-voltage fluctuates, the output dc voltage will also fluctuate. One method of reducing this fluctuation is to regulate the voltage of the ac lines by static ac voltage regulators.

**High-voltage power supply.** High-voltage power supplies are employed to supply dc voltages of 1–20 kV or more, usually at currents of a few milliamperes or less. Voltage-doubling and voltage-multiplying rectifier circuits are useful in such applications, which include the cathode-ray tube power supplies of television and radar. Another method of obtaining high voltages is to use a flyback power supply circuit with a half-wave rectifier and filter or with a voltage-multiplier circuit. For heavy-current high-voltage supplies, circuits such as that of Fig. 1 are almost always used. All components of the circuit must then be selected for the requirements of the high voltage and high currents. *SEE VOLTAGE-MULTIPLIER CIRCUIT.*

**Battery power supplies.** Batteries are useful for portable applications where lower voltages and lower currents are used, and this is particularly true for transistor circuits. Probably the voltages most used are 6 V produced by four dry cells in series and 9 V produced by six dry cells in series. The ordinary dry cells have a voltage that gradually decreases with use until the voltage is too low for satisfactory operation of the circuit. The more expensive mercury cells last several times longer than the ordinary cells, and the voltage remains more constant with use until the end of its life when the voltage falls abruptly. Dry battery units may also be used for some tube supply requirements, although wet storage batteries would be more common. The high dc voltages required for tube circuits may be obtained by the use of vibrator or dynamotor power supplies.

**Power-supply filters.** Power-supply filters are usually of the low-pass *LC* (inductance-capacitance) variety, with the cutoff frequency of the filter made as much below the fundamental frequency of the ripple voltage as is economically feasible. Occasionally, low-pass *RC* (resistance-capacitance) filters will be used if the load current requirements are small. Lower cutoff frequencies generally require larger inductances and capacitances.

There are two subdivisions of these filters. The first, called an inductive-input filter, has a series inductor immediately after the rectifier. The second is the capacitive-input filter, which has a shunt capacitor immediately after the rectifier. One or more sections may be used, as shown in **Fig. 2**. Figure 2*a* shows a single shunt capacitor as the smoothing element. Figure 2*b* shows a two-section inductive-input filter. Figure 2*c* gives a two-section capacitive-input filter. The inductive-input filter has the disadvantage of giving a lower output voltage but the advantage of a better voltage regulation. The capacitive-input filter has the important disadvantage of producing a much higher peak current in the rectifiers. The inductors, sometimes called choke coils, almost always have iron cores, and the resistance of the windings are kept low for high efficiency and good voltage regulation. Iron-cored inductors can be made to have an inductance that increases considerably as the load current approaches zero. These inductors, called swinging choke coils, help prevent the large rise in voltage at low load currents in capacitive-input filters. Capacitors for voltages below 500 V are almost always electrolytic capacitors, but above that voltage they have paper or plastic insulation. *SEE CAPACITOR; INDUCTOR.* For other types and general treatment of electronic circuits *SEE CIRCUIT (ELECTRONICS).*

*Donald L. Waidelich*

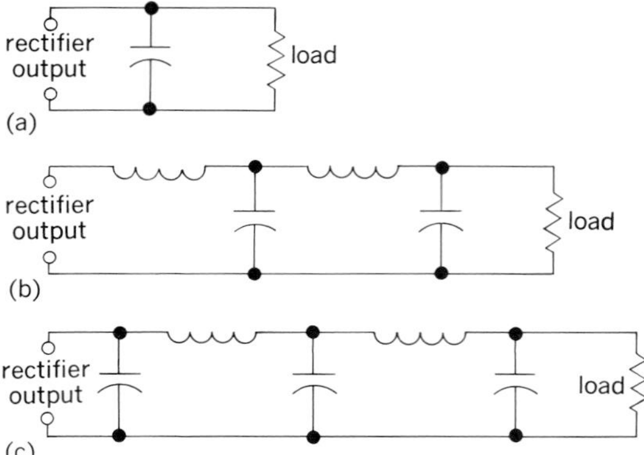


**Fig. 2. Smoothing filters. (*a*) Shunt capacitor. (*b*) Inductive-input filter. (*c*) Capacitive-input filter.**

***Bibliography.*** C. A. Holt, *Electronic Circuits: Digital and Analog,* 1978; A. P. Malvino, *Electronic Principles*, 3d ed., 1983; J. Millman, *Microelectronics*, 1979; D. L. Schilling and C. Belove, *Electronic Circuits: Discrete and Integrated*, 2d ed., 1979; C. A. Schuler, *Electronics: Principles and Applications*, 2d ed., 1983.

## Electronic switch

An electronic device to which two input waveforms can be applied and which delivers at a pair of output terminals a signal that is alternately a replica of each of the input signals. The transmission gate performs the basic switching function of the electronic switch, and sometimes such a gate circuit is itself defined as an electronic switch. However, the electronic switch is usually considered to be a separate instrument to which periodically recurrent input signals, of arbitrary waveform but with synchronously related periods, are connected. The output is switched between the two waveforms at a rate that is synchronous with the period of the input waveforms. One of the input signals often provides synchronizing information to supply periodic trigger pulses, which are then applied to the gate signal generators within the switch. *SEE GATE CIRCUIT.*

A frequent use of the electronic switch is to provide means for displaying two time-related signals on the screen of a cathode-ray oscilloscope without requiring two independent deflection systems within the cathode-ray tube. For this application, the time-based circuit of the display device is synchronized with the repetition rate of one of the two input signals, and the internal transmission gate of the switch alternately switches the signals to the output. At the same time a dc component, or pedestal, is added to each of the two signals so that they will appear at distinct levels on the screen of the display device.

A block diagram of an electronic switch is shown in the **illustration**. The two input waveforms are ap-

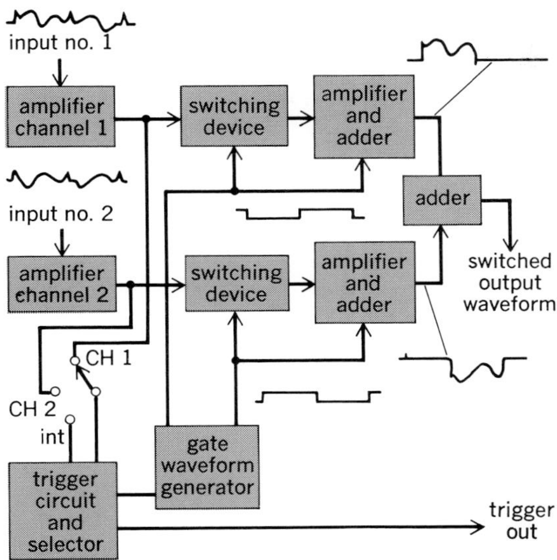


**Elements of an electronic switch.**

plied to amplifier channels. The amplified waveforms are then applied to switching devices and also to a trigger circuit, which generates trigger pulses that can be synchronized either internally or with one of the input signals. A gate waveform generator, usually a bistable multivibrator, is used to actuate a gating waveform to operate the switching devices alternately.

A controllable portion of the gating pulse may be combined with each switched channel to provide an amplitude separation of the two switched signals where separation is necessary for such applications as the cathode-ray tube display.

The trigger circuit might supply a trigger to the time-base generator of an oscilloscope, or when internal triggers are generated, it might be used to control the repetition period of the phenomena to be displayed. *See* SWITCHING THEORY; WAVE-SHAPING CIRCUITS.

*Glenn M. Glasford*

## Electronics

The branch of science and technology relating to the conduction and control of electricity flowing through semiconductor materials or through vacuum or gases. Electronics is concerned with the study and applications of the motions of charge carriers (electrons, holes, and ions) under the influence of externally applied voltage or current, or in relation to the incidence or production of radiant energy. While electronics is now a well-recognized part of electrical engineering, the latter term has in the past sometimes been reserved for applications involving power generation, distribution, and applications at low frequencies, for example, the 50- and 60-Hz power provided by utility systems. Since the 1960s, the dominant segment of electronics has been solid-state electronics, which involves semiconductor devices such as the transistor, the integrated circuit, and sources and detectors of radiant energy.

The electronics industry is concerned with the design, manufacture, and application of transistors, diodes, integrated circuits, and other semiconductor devices and, to a much lesser extent, vacuum tubes. The major uses of vacuum tubes, not yet taken over by solid-state devices, are the generation of large amounts of radio-frequency power, the perception and display of images (as in television camera tubes and picture tubes, and computer displays) and the production of x-rays. *See* CATHODE-RAY TUBE; ELECTRONIC DISPLAY; MICROWAVE TUBE; PICTURE TUBE; TELEVISION CAMERA TUBE.

Solid-state devices are used in a range of applications in the field of digital electronics, basic to the electronic calculator and computer. Since 1965, the reduction in size and cost of integrated circuits has been accompanied by a great increase in the density of devices contained in them. For example, a single integrated circuit no larger than a fingernail contains 450,000 transistors and performs all the computer functions of a 32-bit mainframe processing unit. Reducing the cost of a microprocessor chip, which performs all the functions of a computer except main data storage, made possible the personal computers, used as stand-alone units in homes, the professions and small businesses. They are priced in the hundreds or thousands of dollars and have capabilities equal to mainframe computers available no more than a decade earlier. The microprocessor also serves many specialized uses in industry: improving the fuel economy of automobiles and reducing pollution from them, controlling household appliances, satellite communications, financial transactions, industrial instrumentation and automation, medical devices and implants, and various functions in the aerospace and defense industries. To a degree not envisaged as late as 1980, solid-state electronics pervades nearly every area of human endeavor. *See* CALCULATOR; COMPUTER; MICROCOMPUTER; MICROPROCESSOR.

**History.** The history of electronics divides into two periods. The first began with the invention of the vacuum tube; the second, occupying the latter half of the twentieth century, is based on the invention of the transistor.

***Vacuum tubes.*** In the first period, the initial discovery, made by Thomas Edison in 1883, was that electric charges (electrons) are emitted by a hot filament and are attracted to a nearby positively charged metal plate, when filament and plate are enclosed in a vacuum. When a battery is connected so that the plate is charged negatively, however, the charges are repelled and no current flows. Thus, the current can flow between filament and plate on one direction only. The Edison effect was the first demonstration of the presence of freely moving negative-charge carriers, which were later named electrons. In 1887 J. A. Fleming made the first use of the unidirectional nature of the current flow in a detector for radio signals known as the Fleming valve. This device was the prototype of the vacuum-tube diode and of the solid-state diode that has replaced it in nearly all applications.

The second major step in electronics technology was taken by Lee De Forest in 1906. He introduced a third electrode, known as the grid, between the filament and the plate of the Fleming valve. Since the grid was composed of spaced wires, the electrons could pass through it to the plate. Moreover, the voltage between the filament and the grid would control the number of electrons passing through it. The polarity of the grid voltage was made negative with respect to the filament, so that electrons were not collected by the grid itself. But as the grid voltage was made successively more and less negative, the current to the plate was weakened and stengthened. The varying current reaching the plate was passed through a resistance, and the varying voltage appearing across the resistor was an enlarged replica of the varying voltage applied to the grid. This was the first example of electronic amplification, on which the subsequent growth of the industry was to depend. De Forest named his three-electrode tube the Audion, but the preferred term became triode, signifying its three active electrodes. As described here, the triode serves as a voltage amplifier. When appropriately connected to a current or power source, the triode may also serve as a current or power amplifier. Several modifications of the triode were developed by adding more grids, giving rise to the tetrode, pentode, and hexode versions. These have now been replaced by solid-state devices, the bipolar and field-effect transistors, and their embodiments in integrated circuits. SEE AUDION.

Over the first half of the twentieth century, during which time vacuum tubes dominated the field, three disadvantages had to be accepted: they required a source of power to heat their filaments; they required hundreds of volts of dc power to make their plates sufficiently positive; and their filaments (in later versions, the oxide surfaces of indirectly heated cathodes) eventually lost their ability to emit electrons. Thus electron tubes had to be replaced many times during the life of the equipment, and the times of replacement were difficult to predict. SEE ELECTRON TUBE; VACUUM TUBE.

***Transistors.*** These limitations were overcome in the transistor, invented in 1947 by John Bardeen, Walter Brattain, and William Shockley. The invention is based on the fact that semiconductors, notably germanium, when in the form of highly purified crystals of nearly perfect structure, can carry simultaneously two electric currents of opposite polarity when specified impurities are incorporated in the crystal in very minute amounts. Certain impurities, for example, phosphorus or antimony, produce *n*-type germanium, which has an excess of electrons, so that the major current is carried by the negative electrons. But a lesser positive current is also carried by holes, that is, electron vacancies in the crystal lattice. Other impurities, for example, boron or indium, produce *p*-type germanium, which has a deficiency of free electrons, so they become the carriers of the minority current, while the holes carry the majority current. When *n*-type and *p*-type germanium are arranged in intimate contact in the crystal lattice, for example, by changing the impurity during crystallization, a *pn* junction is formed. This junction has the property, like the Fleming valve, of preventing the reverse flow of majority carriers while permitting the minority carriers to pass. SEE JUNCTION DIODE; HOLES IN SOLIDS; SEMICONDUCTOR; SEMICONDUCTOR DIODE.

The transistor (the bipolar type that is widely used) consists of a single crystal of semiconductor in which two such junctions are present, forming two closely spaced parallel planes, so that the semiconductor is present in layered *n*, *p*, and *n* form (*npn* transistor) or in *p*, *n*, and *p* form (*pnp* transistor). The respective segments of the semiconductor are known as the emitter, base, and collector, which have functions roughly analagous to the filament, grid, and plate of a triode vacuum tube. When a varying voltage is applied, for example, between the emitter and base, it controls the flow of minority carriers across the second *pn* junction, where they are given additional energy before reaching the collector. A resistance receives the varying collector current, producing a voltage which is an amplified replica of the varying voltage applied between the emitter and base. No filament-heating power is needed, and the applied voltages are much smaller than those required by vacuum tubes. Most important, the motion and control of the holes and electrons are not destructive processes, so the transistor has an operating life as long or longer than that of other elements of electronic circuits. SEE TRANSISTOR.

Silicon, a much more abundant semiconductor than germanium, has been found to serve the same purposes in solid-state devices, with advantages in the production process, so it has become the preferred material for the manufacture of transistors and integrated circuits. For devices operating at extremely high frequencies, the compound semiconductor gallium arsenide is used. SEE MICROWAVE SOLID-STATE DEVICES.

Solid-state devices also serve as sources and sensors of visible and infrared radiation. The light-emitting diode (LED) emits radiation from junctions, typically composed of gallium phosphide, gallium arsenide-phosphide or gallium-aluminum arsenide. The semiconductor emits radiation (primarily in the infrared) from active layers containing compounds of such elements as gallium, arsenic, phosphorus, aluminum, indium, tin, tellurium, or lead. SEE LASER; LIGHT-EMITTING DIODE.

***Integrated circuits.*** Following the invention of the transistor as a discrete device, it was found in the 1950s that an assembly of solid-state diodes, transistors, capacitors, and resistors, with metallic connectors, could be produced on a flat substrate of silicon. This is known as an integrated circuit (IC), now the most widely used electronic device. Steady improvements in the methods of photodeposition, gaseous diffusion, and ion implantation to produce *p* and *n* layers have led to great increases in the number and density of devices that can be incorporated in chips of silicon ¼ in. (6 mm) on a side. Integrated circuits of this size having several hundred thousand individual circuit elements are routinely manufactured. SEE INTEGRATED CIRCUITS.

The most significant development in integrated circuits occurred in the early 1970s, when M. E. Hoff led a team to develop the microprocessor, an integrated-circuit chip incorporating all the elements of a computer's central processing unit. As noted above, this device has resulted in a variety of computer applications. The other major type of integrated circuit is the random-access memory chip, which is used in computers for storing data and instructions that can be retrieved selectively. SEE COMPUTER STORAGE TECHNOLOGY; SEMICONDUCTOR MEMORIES.

**Growth of electronics industry.** The extent to which high-density, large-scale, solid-state integrated circuits have permeated industry, commerce, financial institutions, and the home is now so great that electronics is one of the largest industries as measured by the value of its products. The rapid growth continues, particularly as the electronic computer has established the base of the information revolution, the impact of which may well exceed that of the Industrial Revolution.

**Applications.** The manifold applications of electronic devices depend on the fact that the force exerted on an electron or hole by the voltage applied to the device is very great in relation to the mass of the charge carrier. Consequently, the carrier is subject to very great acceleration and typically reaches its maximum velocity in $10^{-9}$ or less. This rapid reaction permits the device to amplify, or to generate, currents alternating at frequencies up to $10^{10}$ Hz or to respond to electric stimuli in less than $10^{-10}$ s. The same devices will, of course, generate or respond to signal frequencies lower than these limits.

While these numbers apply to low-power applications, other solid-state devices are designed for high-power use. The most important high-power device is the silicon controled rectifier (SCR), arrays of which can control as much as 1000 MW at commercial power frequencies. These devices also find use in the transformation and control of power in electric locomotives and other high-power applications. These heavy-current systems of generation and control are the subject of the field of power electronics. *SEE SEMICONDUCTOR RECTIFIER.*

***Communications.*** The major portion of all transoceanic traffic is now carried by geostationary satellites, which rotate synchronously with the Earth and hence occupy a fixed position over the Equator. The satellite transponders that relay telephone, data, and television traffic have steadily increased in power over the years, so that satellite television service direct to the home became feasible. Satellite communication does not have unlimited resources, since there is a limit to the number of orbital positions and to the frequency assignments that can serve during bad weather at the Earth's surface.

The limits of the traffic capacity of conventional cable and microwave circuits are being expanded manyfold by the use of optical fiber circuits. Infrared radiation, such as that produced by a semiconductor laser, is injected at one end of a very small glass fiber several miles long. Many segments of such fiber may be connected end-to-end. At the far end of each segment, another solid-state device, a photodiode, converts the infrared signal back into its electrical form. At this point the signal may, after amplification, be fed into the conventional telephone system, or passed on to the next segment of fiber cable through another laser. Typical optical cables contain 12 such fibers, capable of carrying 80,000 telephone conversations simultaneously, far more than can be accommodated by copper cable or microwave circuits. Extensive systems of fiber communications in corridors of heavy traffic were installed by the early 1980s. Their large capacity and freedom from electrical interference are important advantages that should lead them ultimately to replace copper circuits. *SEE OPTICAL COMMUNICATIONS.*

Another form of communication is known as videotex. This permits information to be requested from computer data banks and presented in the home on the screen of a television receiver. Such interactive, two-way circuits between home computers and distant data sources can be used for banking service, ordering from televised catalog displays, and a wide range of educational services. *SEE DATA COMMUNICATIONS; ELECTRICAL COMMUNICATIONS; VIDEOTEXT AND TELETEXT.*

***Consumer electronics.*** Aside from the communications services of telephone, radio, and television, the consumer has available a wide variety of electronic devices and equipment which employ the digital technology of the computer industry. The hand-held electronic calculator was joined by the portable programmable computer and the stand-alone personal microcomputer. Perhaps the most widely used digital device is the quartz-crystal–controlled timepiece, which in various forms has largely replaced spring-wound and escapement clocks and watches. In the late 1970s and early 1980s, video game-playing devices appeared in homes and arcades. These were followed by the keyboarded home computer, which adds computation, data storage, and word-processing functions. Similar equipment was also introduced to primary and secondary schools. To the home video tape recorder, several versions of video disk recorders were added, which have the capacity to store vast amounts of information that can be retrieved quickly and accurately. *SEE SPEECH RECOGNITION; VIDEO DISK RECORDING; VOICE RESPONSE; WORD PROCESSING.*

***Industry and commerce.*** Impressive as these applications of digital electronics are in the home, it seems certain that the major thrust of digital methods will continue to occur in commerce and industry. The basic commodity is information in all its forms. The collection, storage, retrieval, manipulation, display, and communication of information by computer systems now dominate information handling in nearly all forms of business and commerce, as well as the major fields of weapon systems and industrial manufacture. Information-controlled processes and automation have also been introduced into extractive industry, as well as in materials processing and power generation. *SEE COMPUTER-INTEGRATED MANUFACTURING; ROBOTICS.*

*Donald G. Fink*

***Bibliography.*** E. Braun and S. MacDonald, *Revolution in Miniature,* 1978; C. Evans, *The Micro Millennium,* 1979; D. Hanson, *The New Alchemists,* 1982; J. D. Ryder, *Engineering Electronics, with Industrial Applications and Control*, 2d ed., 1967; J. D. Ryder and D. G. Fink, *Engineers and Electrons,* 1984; S. Wang, *Solid State Electronics,* 1966.

## Electrostatic lens

An electrostatic field with axial or plane symmetry which acts upon beams of charged particles of uniform velocity as glass lenses act on light beams. The action of electrostatic fields with axial symmetry is analogous to that of spherical glass lenses, whereas the action of electrostatic fields with plane symmetry is analogous to that of cylindrical glass lenses. Plane symmetry as used here signifies that the electrostatic potential is constant along any normal to a family of parallel planes.

The action of an electrostatic lens on the paths of charged particles passing through it is most readily visualized with the aid of an equipotential plot of the fields in a plane of symmetry of the lens. The equipotential lines in the plot indicate the intersection with the plane of the drawing of surfaces on which the electrostatic potential is a constant. The paths of charged particles in the electrostatic field are bent toward the normals of the equipotentials as the particles are accelerated, and away from the normals as the particles are decelerated. *SEE ELECTRON MOTION IN VACUUM.*

**Axially symmetric lenses.** These lenses are generally formed at or between circular apertures and cylinders maintained at suitable potentials. A number of such lenses are shown with characteristic path plots in **Fig. 1**. For any of these it is possible to define

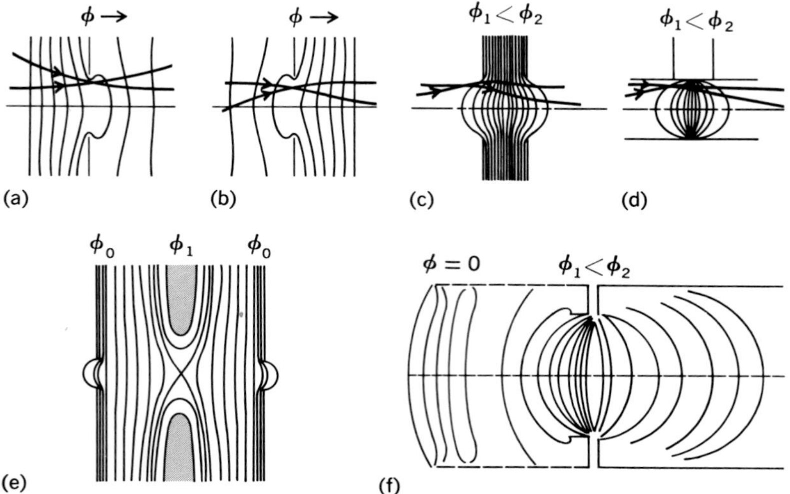


**Fig. 1.** **Axially symmetric electrostatic lenses. (*a*) Single-aperture lens (decreasing field). (*b*) Single-aperture lens (increasing field). (*c*) Two-aperature lens. (*d*) Two-cylinder lens. (*e*) Unipotential lens. (*f*) Cathode lens (image tube). (*After E. G. Ramberg and G. A. Morton, J. Appl. Phys., vol. 10, 1939, and V. K. Zworykin et al., Electron Optics and the Electron Microscope, Wiley, 1945*)**

focal points, principal planes, and focal lengths in the same manner as for light lenses and to determine with their aid image magnification for any object position (**Fig. 2**). For a thin electrostatic lens in particular, that is, a lens for which the extent of the variation in potential is small compared to its focal length, the object side focal length $f_0$ and the image side focal length $f$ are given by Eq. (1). Here $\phi(z)$ is the potential along

$$\frac{\phi_o^{1/2}}{f_o} = \frac{\phi_i^{1/2}}{f_i} = \frac{3}{16}(\phi_o\phi_i)^{1/4}\int\left(\frac{\phi'}{\phi}\right)^2 dz \tag{1}$$

the axis of the lens, $\phi$ its derivative with respect to $z$ (that is, the electric field along the axis), and $\phi_o$ and $\phi_i$ are the potential in object and image space, respectively. The integration is extended over the lens field. The quantity $\phi$ is here normalized so that it is equal to the accelerating potential of the particle in question.

Axially symmetric lenses are commonly divided into the four classes that follow.

***Simple aperture lenses.*** These are the lens fields formed about circular apertures in a plane metallic electrode at potential $\phi$ with different electrostatic fields $-\phi_o'$ and $-\phi_i'$ on the two sides. In most cases the focal length $f$ of such a lens is given to a sufficient degree of accuracy by the Davisson-Calbick formula for an aperture, Eq. (2). Simple aperture lenses are

$$\frac{1}{f} = \frac{\phi_i' - \phi_o'}{4\phi} \tag{2}$$

encountered as parts of more complex electrostatic lens systems, as well as at the mesh openings of metal screens employed as electrostatic shields in vacuum tubes.

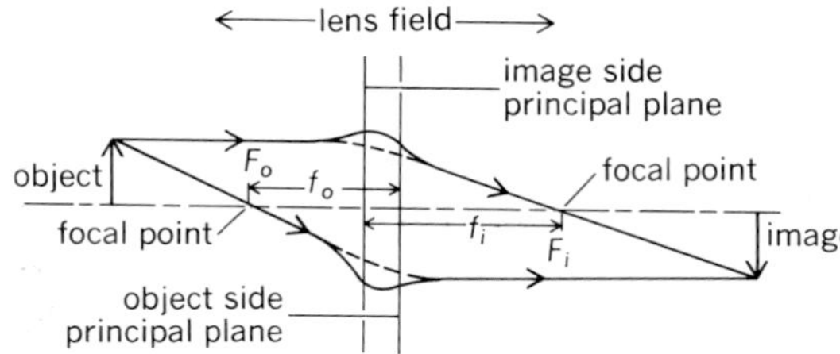


**Fig. 2. Definition of principal planes, focal points, and focal lengths for axially symmetric electrostatic lens.**

***Bipotential, or immersion, lenses.*** In these lenses image space and object space are field-free, but at different potentials. Typical examples are the lenses formed between apertures or cylinders at different potentials (Fig. 1*c* and *d*). If the separation $d$ of the two apertures is large compared to their diameters and if each component aperature lens satisfies the conditions for a validity of the Davisson-Calbick formula, the focal lengths of the bipotential aperture lens are given by Eq. (3). The distances of the principal planes from

$$\frac{1}{f_o} = \left(\frac{\phi_i}{\phi_o}\right)^{1/2}\frac{1}{f_i} = \frac{3}{8d}\left[1 - \left(\frac{\phi_o}{\phi_i}\right)^{1/2}\right]\left(\frac{\phi_i}{\phi_o} - 1\right) \tag{3}$$

the plane of symmetry are given by Eqs. (4) and (5).

$$h_o = \frac{-d}{2} - \frac{4d\phi_o}{[3(\phi_i - \phi_o)]} \tag{4}$$

$$h_i = \frac{d}{2} - \frac{4d\phi_i}{[3(\phi_i - \phi_o)]} \tag{5}$$

Generally, the principal planes are displaced from the plane of symmetry toward the low-potential side, with the image-side principal plane closer to object space than the object-side principal plane.

For two cylinders of equal diameter $D$, whose difference in potential is small compared to their mean potential, Eq. (6) gives the focal lengths.

$$\frac{1}{f_o} = \left(\frac{\phi_i}{\phi_o}\right)^{1/2}\frac{1}{f_i} = \left(\frac{\phi_i}{\phi_o}\right)^{1/4} 0.66\left(\frac{\phi_i - \phi_o}{\phi_i + \phi_o}\right)^2\frac{1}{D} \tag{6}$$

Bipotential lenses, in particular lenses formed between two cylinders at different potentials, find wide application in beam-focusing devices such as electron guns. Like unipotential lenses, they invariably act as converging lenses.

***Unipotential lenses.*** For this type the potentials are equal in object and image space. In their simplest form these lenses consist of three apertures of which the outer two are at a common potential $\phi_o$ and the central aperture is at a different, generally lower, potential $\phi_1$. For such lenses with a central aperture of diameter $D$ and the two outer apertures, of smaller diameter, separated a distance $D$ from the plane of symmetry, the weak-lens focal length is given by Eq. (7). As $\phi_1$ approaches zero, the quantity $1/f$ increases

$$\frac{1}{f} = \frac{0.2}{D}\left(\frac{\phi_o - \phi_1}{\phi_o}\right)^2 \tag{7}$$

more rapidly than indicated by this formula; it attains a value of $0.7/D$ for $\phi_1 = 0$. Unipotential lenses operated at high potentials (for example, $\phi_o = 50$ kilovolts, $\phi_1 = 0$) are employed as objectives and projection lenses in electrostatic electron microscopes. The electrodes are commonly made out of stainless steel and given a high polish.

***Cathode lenses or immersion objectives.*** Here the lens field extends from the emitter surface up to field-free image space. Examples are the cathode region of an electron gun, the electron-optical system of an electrostatic image tube or image converter, and the objective of an emission electron microscope. In the electron gun the cathode lens converges the electrons emitted by the cathode to a small spot, the crossover, which is imaged by a second electron lens as the scanning spot on the cathode-ray tube screen. SEE CATHODE-RAY TUBE.

In the image tube the cathode itself—a transparent photoemissive surface on which a light picture is projected—is imaged on a fluorescent screen beyond the cathode lens. Frequently a cathode lens consists essentially of a uniform accelerating field followed by a short lens. The image magnification $m$ is then given by Eq. (8). Here $u$ is the distance between cathode

$$m = \frac{v}{2u} \quad (8)$$

and short lens and $v$ is the distance between short lens and image. The quantity $v$ is given by Eq. (9), where

$$1v = \frac{1}{f} - \frac{1}{(2u)} \quad (9)$$

$f$ is the focal length of the short lens.

**Lenses of plane symmetry.** These lenses, analogous to cylindrical glass lenses, are formed between parallel planes and at slits, replacing the circular cylinders and apertures of lenses with axial symmetry. For the simple slit in an electrode at potential $\phi$ separating two regions of field $-\phi_o'$ and $-\phi_i'$, the focal length is given by the Davisson-Calbick formula for a slit as shown by Eq. (10).

$$\frac{1}{f} = \frac{\phi_i' - \phi_o'}{2\phi} \quad (10)$$

*Edward G. Ramberg*

## Electrostriction

A form of elastic deformation of a dielectic induced by an electric field; specifically, the term applies to those components of strain which are independent of reversal of the field direction. Electrostriction is a property of all dielectrics and is thus distinguished from the converse piezoelectric effect, a field-induced strain which changes sign upon field reversal and which occurs only in piezoelectric materials. SEE PIEZOELECTRICITY.

Electrostrictive strain is approximately proportional to the electric susceptibility, elastic compliance, and the square of the field strength, and is extremely small for most materials.

The electrostrictive effect in certain ceramics is employed for commercial purposes in electromechanical transducers for sonic and ultrasonic applications. SEE MICROPHONE.

*Robert D. Waldron*

## Embedded systems

Computer systems that cannot be programmed by the user because they are preprogrammed for a specific task and are buried within the equipment they serve. The term derives from the military, where computer systems are generally activated by the flip of a toggle switch or the push of a button. For example, an airplane pilot may wish to turn on the countermeasures equipment with the flip of a switch. There is no need for the pilot to be involved with the computer. The same holds true for a soldier who may direct a ground-to-ground missile against a target tank by the simple push of a button. In both cases, an embedded computer quickly goes to work.

The emergence of extremely small microcomputers on silicon chips about ¼ in. (6 mm) square made the concept of embedded systems for the military all the more desirable. As recently as 1960, it was difficult or impossible to embed a computer the size of a room into equipment which had to fit into, say, an airplane cockpit. The microcomputer changed all that.

The military establishment thus depends on microelectronics technology for the development of ever more sophisticated embedded systems. With very inexpensive microcomputer chips, not one but dozens of computers can be squeezed into a small piece of equipment the size of a lunch box, each preprogrammed to do a specific job. By doing only its own task, each microcomputer can devote its entire computational and analytical powers to that task, making possible extremely powerful military systems. SEE INTEGRATED CIRCUITS; MICROCOMPUTER; MICROPROCESSOR.

**VHSIC program.** A manifestation of the military's interest in microelectronics technology to further progress in embedded systems is the Department of Defense's Very High Speed Integrated Circuit (VHSIC) program. The VHSIC program provides the military with integrated circuit chips sufficiently advanced to enable the United States to maintain a qualitative superiority in weapons and armaments over its adversaries.

The VHSIC program is spread over four phases, 0 through III. The first three phases were run concurrently. Phase 0 was a 1-year effort to analyze approaches to be employed in phases I and II for the development of very high-speed digital signal–processing integrated circuits, with speeds on the order of $10^{10}$ Hz and line definitions on the order of 1 micrometer or less. Line definition refers to the smallest dimensions of the various structures that make up the integrated circuit chip.

Phase I, started in 1980, and planned to run for 6 years, has been aimed at the development of a brassboard version of the VHSIC devices that could later be reduced to even smaller sizes on integrated circuit chips.

Phase II will provide a system demonstration of the subsystems constructed in phase I, as well as the capability for improved system performance with higher-performance design concepts. Phase III supplements phases I and II and provides new or alternate technology directions not covered in phases I and II.

Phase I employs integrated circuits with on-the-chip structural geometries of 1.25 μm. Devices made under this phase operate at a minimum clock frequency of 30 MHz and a minimum gate-frequency product of $10^{11}$ gate-Hz/cm$^2$. (The gate-frequency product is the number of logic gates—the most basic elements of a chip—times the clock frequency at which the integrated circuit on the chip operates. The cm$^2$ denotes the area of silicon on the chip required to implement this performance.)

The gate-Hz/cm$^2$ quantity, also known as throughput capacity, is a measure of the capability expected from a VHSIC device. By comparison, conventional, commercially available microprocessor chips have throughput capacities of $10^{10}$ gate-Hz/cm$^2$, or an order of magnitude slower than that expected from VHSIC integrated circuits in phase I. The military, on the

**Major defense areas and weapons systems served by the VHSIC program***

| System area | Air Force | Army | Navy |
|---|---|---|---|
| Radar | Advanced medium-range air-to-air missile; advanced on-board signal processor; airborne warning and control system (AWACS); autonomous cruise-missile guidance; multifunction radar signal processor | Multimode fire-and-forget missile | Tactical air-to-air ground radar; surveillance radar |
| Imaging | Autonomous cruise-missile guidance | Target-acquisition/fire-control system; multimode fire-and-forget missile | Digital image processor |
| Antisubmarine warfare | | | Acoustic signal processor |
| Electronic warfare | Advanced defensive avionic system | High-mobility electronic-warfare weapons-targeting systems | Electronic systems module signal sorter |
| Command, Control and Communications ($C^3$) | Signal processor chip set for Joint Tactical Information and Distribution System | Battlefield information distribution system | Antijam modern; NATO identification system |

*From IBM Federal Systems Division, Manassas, Virginia.

other hand, is planning weapons systems with throughput capacities of $10^{13}$ gate-Hz/cm$^2$ or more. Such throughput rates mean that the smallest definable geometries of a VHSIC integrated circuit must be on the order of 1 μm or less, or total-system weights and power dissipation levels become too prohibitive.

All three branches of the armed services have major weapons programs designed with VHSIC chips, as can be seen from the **table**.

**Ada programming language.** In addition to the hardware digital-signal processors the military acquires from the VHSIC program, the Department of Defense needs software. The agency adopted Ada as the single high-level software programming language for all three branches of the service to simplify procurements, the interchange of software programs among the services' branches, and training. *SEE PROGRAMMING LANGUAGES.*

*Roger Allan*

***Bibliography.*** R. Allan, Special issue on military electronics, *Electr. Des. Mag.*, 29(16):87–119, August 1981; W. H. Lee, VHSIC functions for signal processing, *1982 Southcon Professional Program*; L. W. Sumney, Special issue on war and peace, *IEEE Spectrum Mag.*, 19(10):93–94, October 1982.

## Emitter follower

A circuit that utilizes a common-collector transistor which provides less than unity voltage gain but high input resistance and low output resistance. This circuit is used extensively to provide isolation or impedance matching between two electronic circuits.

A circuit diagram of a common-collector transistor amplifier is shown in the **illustration**. This amplifier is similar to the cathode follower in its operations, although there are four important differences. (1) This amplifier has a voltage gain which is very close to unity (much closer to unity for typical loads than the cathode follower). (2) The voltage drop across the emitter resistance (from emitter to ground) may be either positive or negative, depending on whether an *npn* or *pnp* transistor is used. In the case of the cathode follower the drop across the cathode resistor is always positive. (3) The input resistance of the emitter follower, although high (tens or hundreds of kilohms), is low compared with that of the cathode follower. (4) The output resistance of the emitter follower is much lower (perhaps by a factor of 10) than that of the cathode follower.

In cascading transistor amplifier stages, the emitter follower is not used as an intermediate stage because its input-to-input voltage gain is in general less than that of the common-emitter amplifier. This is due to the relatively high input resistance of the emitter follower.

The most common use for the emitter follower is as a device which performs the function of impedance transformation over a wide range of frequencies with voltage gain close to unity. In addition, the emitter follower increases the power level of the signal.

A typical emitter follower circuit is shown in the illustration. The input signal is applied across the parallel combination of $R_1$ and $R_2$, which constitute the biasing arrangement for this circuit. *SEE BIAS OF TRANSISTORS.*

The collector in the figure is connected directly to

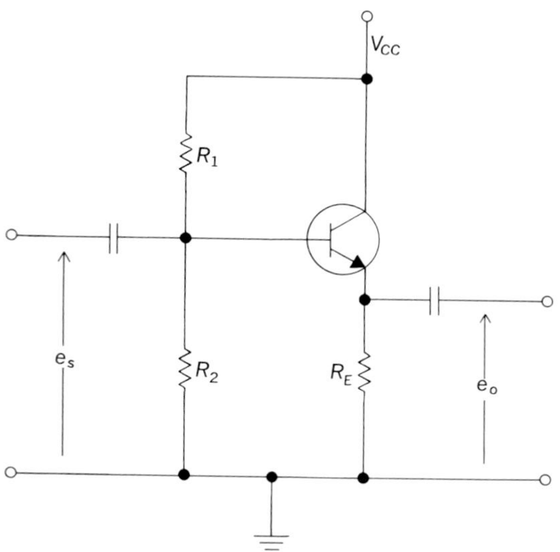


**Typical emitter follower.**

the power supply and hence is at ground potential for ac signals. In many practical applications a protective resistance $R_C$ is connected in series between the collector and the power supply to guard against transistor damage in the case of an accidental short circuit across $R_E$.

The emitter follower possesses negative feedback and results in reduced distortion. Its output is always in phase with the input, and typical values of voltage gain are about 0.95–0.99.

*Christos C. Halkias*

## Equivalent circuit

A representation of an actual electric circuit or device by a simplified circuit whose behavior is identical to that of the actual circuit or device over a stated range of operating conditions. These conditions depend on the elements contained in the actual circuit and may include such variables as frequency, temperature, and pressure, in addition to voltage and current. Equivalent circuits are often used by engineers to simplify circuit analysis since they show the relation between the variables more clearly than the actual circuit. SEE NETWORK THEORY.

Two types of equivalent circuits are used. One type is a simplification of an actual linear device, such as a transformer. In general, there are no restrictions on the magnitudes of applied voltages and currents in this type of equivalent circuit; therefore the equivalence holds over a wide range of operating conditions. SEE TRANSFORMER.

The second type of equivalent circuit is used to represent nonlinear devices, most commonly vacuum tubes and transistors. The actual circuit of the nonlinear device can be replaced by a fictitious generator and a simple network representing the operation of the actual device. Both the generator and network quantities depend on the parameters of the device. These parameters vary; therefore calculations made are necessarily limited to a portion of the characteristics over which the values of the parameters are reasonably constant. This type of circuit can, therefore, be used only for analysis of small signals. For large-signal analysis of nonlinear devices, it is necessary to use graphical methods on the characteristic curve of the device. SEE CIRCUIT (ELECTRICITY); CIRCUIT (ELECTRONICS); LOUDSPEAKER.

*Robert L. Ramey*

## Excitation

Application of energy to one portion of a system or apparatus in a manner that enables another portion to carry out a specialized function. Excitation establishes a condition essential to that function. In atomic physics, excitation means the addition of energy to an atom at ground state to produce an excited state. SEE EXCITATION POTENTIAL.

Excitation of a system or apparatus serves either to permit a transfer of energy or to control a flow of energy elsewhere in the system. Excitation energy may differ from the output energy in source, form, level, or location. Excitation produces a primary effect that is linked through an intermediate physical phenomenon to a dependent secondary effect (see **illus.**).

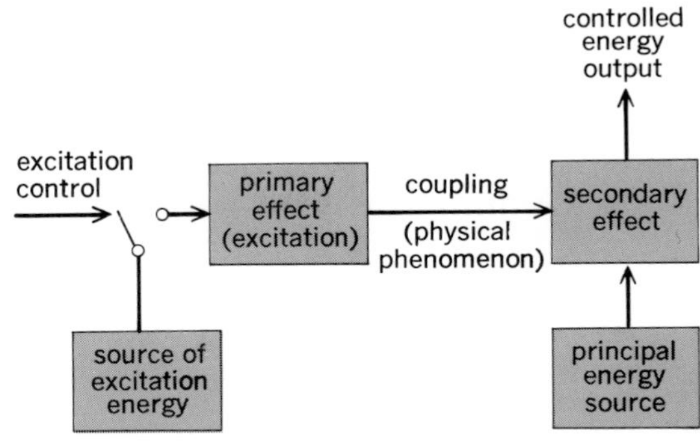


**System diagram showing function of excitation.**

Some examples will make this dependency apparent. A dynamic loudspeaker uses an excitatory current in a field coil to generate a magnetic field; when the voice coil receives an audio signal, it generates a second magnetic field, which interacts with the first to cause motion of the voice coil and the voice cone of the speaker. A sound motion-picture projector uses an excitatory lamp to provide a source of illumination; when the photosensitive pickup receives variations in illumination resulting from changes in the opaque area of the sound track through which the illumination must pass, it generates an audio signal output. A fluorescent lamp uses an excitatory current passing through an enclosed gas to generate ultraviolet radiation; when the phosphor coating inside the tube absorbs ultraviolet energy, it emits visible light. The human heart, to cite an example from biology, uses for excitation the decreasing electrical transmembrane potential of the pacemaker to generate an electrical impulse; when the surrounding striated muscle tissue receives this impulse, it transmits the electrical stimulus to other adjacent tissue and utilizes metabolic energy to contract, a response which produces the heartbeat. SEE OPTICAL RECORDING.

*William W. Snow*

## Excitation potential

The difference in potential between an excited atomic or molecular state and the ground state. The term is most generally used in connection with electron excitation, but it can be applied to excited molecular vibrational and rotational states.

A closely related term is excitation energy. If the unit of potential is taken as the volt and the unit of energy as the electronvolt, then the two are numerically equal. According to the Bohr theory, there is a relationship between the wavelength of the photon associated with the transition and the excitation energies of the two states. Thus the basic equation for the emission or absorption of energy is as shown below,

$$\frac{hc}{\lambda} = E_i - E_f$$

where $h$ is Planck's constant, $c$ the velocity of light, $\lambda$ the wavelength of the photon, and $E_f$ and $E_i$ the energies of the final and initial states, respectively. If the final state is the ground state, then the difference in energies is just the excitation energy of the initial state. If neither of the two states is the ground state, then the difference is numerically equal to the difference in excitation energies of the two states. This suggests that the excitation energy for many states may be determined spectroscopically. In fact, the careful measurement of the wavelengths associated with the transitions, along with the identification of the levels involved, permits the assignment of an excitation potential to each available energy state. This may be done by either emission or absorption spectra.

Measurements have also been made by using electron impact means. Here electrons from a hot filament are accelerated by a grid and collected on an outer electrode after passing through an intervening space where they can interact with a gas of molecular or atomic species. The potentials are so adjusted that the electrons can reach the collector only if they lose no energy after passing the grid. As the accelerating grid potential is increased, a series of sharp drops is noted in the collector current. Each of these is interpreted as representing a case where the electrons have obtained just enough energy to produce excitation, and hence no longer have the energy needed to climb the potential barrier to the collector. The evidence thus obtained is very direct, but the accuracy is not as good as that for spectroscopic data. SEE IONIZATION POTENTIAL.

*Glenn H. Miller*

**Bibliography.** S. Gasiorowicz, *Structure of Matter: A Survey of Modern Physics*, 1979; F. K. Richtmyer et al., *Introduction to Modern Physics*, 6th ed., 1969; I. Sobelman et al., *Excitation of Atoms and Broadening of Spectral Lines*, 1980; M. R. Wehr et al., *Physics of the Atom*, 3d ed., 1978.

## Expert systems

Methods and techniques for constructing human-machine systems with specialized problem-solving expertise. The pursuit of this area of artificial intelligence research has emphasized the knowledge that underlies human expertise and has simultaneously decreased the apparent significance of domain-independent problem-solving theory. In fact, a new set of principles, tools, and techniques have emerged that form the basis of knowledge engineering.

Expertise consists of knowledge about a particular domain, understanding of domain problems, and skill at solving some of these problems. Knowledge in any specialty is of two types, public and private. Public knowledge includes the published definitions, facts, and theories which are contained in textbooks and references in the domain of study. But expertise usually requires more than just public knowledge. Human experts generally possess private knowledge which has not found its way into the published literature. This private knowledge consists largely of rules of thumb or heuristics. Heuristics enable the human expert to make educated guesses when necessary, to recognize promising approaches to problems, and to deal effectively with erroneous or incomplete data. The elucidation and reproduction of such knowledge are the central problems of expert systems.

**Importance of expert knowledge.** Researchers in this field suggest several reasons for their emphasis on knowledge-based methods rather than formal representations and associated analytic methods. First, most of the difficult and interesting problems do not have tractable algorithmic solutions. This is reflected in the fact that many important tasks, such as planning, legal reasoning, medical diagnosis, geological exploration, and military situation analysis, originate in complex social or physical contexts, and generally resist precise description and rigorous analysis. Also, contemporary methods of symbolic and mathematical reasoning have limited applicability to the expert system area; that is, they do not provide the means for representing knowledge, describing problems at multiple levels of abstraction, allocating problem-solving resources, controlling cooperative processes, and integrating diverse sources of knowledge in inference. These functions depend primarily on the capacity to manipulate problem descriptions and apply relevant pieces of knowledge selectively. Current mathematics offers little help in these tasks.

The second reason for emphasizing knowledge is pragmatic: human experts achieve outstanding performance because they are knowledgeable. If computer programs embody and use this knowledge, they too attain high levels of performance. This has been proved repeatedly in the short history of expert systems. Systems have attained expert levels in several tasks: mineral prospecting, computer configuration, chemical structure elucidation, symbolic mathematics, chess, medical diagnosis and therapy, and electronics analysis.

The third motivation for focusing on knowledge is the recognition of its intrinsic value. Knowledge is a scarce resource whose refinement and reproduction creates wealth. Traditionally, the transmission of knowledge from human expert to trainee has required education and internship periods ranging from 3 to 20 years. By extracting knowledge from humans and transferring it to computable forms, the costs of knowledge reproduction and exploitation can be greatly reduced. At the same time, the process of knowledge refinement can be accelerated by making the previously private knowledge available for public test and evaluation.

In short, expert performance depends critically on expert knowledge. Because knowledge provides the key ingredient for solving important tasks, it reflects many features characteristic of a rare element: it justifies possibly expensive mining operations; it requires efficient and effective technologies for fashioning it into products; and a means of reproducing it synthetically would be "a dream come true."

**Distinguishing characteristics.** Expert systems differ in important ways from both conventional data processing systems and systems developed by workers in other branches of artificial intelligence. In contrast to traditional data-processing systems, artificial intelligence applications exhibit several distinguishing features, including symbolic representations, symbolic inference, and heuristic search. In fact, each of these characteristics corresponds to a well-studied core topic within artificial intelligence. Often a simple artificial intelligence task may yield to one of the formal approaches developed for these core problems. Expert systems differ from the broad class of artificial intelligence tasks in several regards. First, they perform difficult tasks at expert levels of performance. Second, they emphasize domain-specific problem-solving strategies over the more general, "weak" methods of artificial intelligence. Third, they employ self-knowledge to reason about their own inference processes and provide explanations of justifications for the conclusions they reach. As a result of these distinctions, expert systems represent an area of artificial intelligence research with specialized paradigms, tools, and system-development strategies.

**Accomplishments.** There have been a number of notable accomplishments by expert systems: PROSPECTOR discovered a molybdenum deposit whose ultimate value will probably exceed $100 million: R1 configures customer requests for computer systems; DENDRAL supports hundreds of international users daily in chemical structure elucidation; CADUCEUS embodies more knowledge of internal medicine than any human (approximately 80% more) and can correctly diagnose complex test cases that baffle experts; PUFF integrated knowledge of pulmonary function disease with a previously developed domain-independent expert system for diagnostic consultations and now provides expert analyses at a California medical center.

**Types of systems.** Most of the knowledge-engineering applications fall into a few distinct types, summarized in the **table**.

Interpretation systems infer situation descriptions from observables. This category includes surveillance, speech understanding, image analysis, chemical structure elucidation, signal interpretation, and many kinds of intelligence analysis. An interpretation system explains observed data by assigning symbolic meanings to them which describe the situation or system state accounting for the data. *See Character recognition; Speech recognition.*

Prediction systems present the likely consequences of a given situation. This category includes weather forecasting, demographic predictions, traffic predictions, crop estimations, and military forecasting. A prediction system typically employs a parameterized dynamic model with parameter values fitted to the given situation. Consequences which can be inferred from the model form the basis of the predictions.

Diagnosis systems predict system malfunctions from observables. This category includes medical, electronic, mechanical, and software diagnosis. Diagnosis systems typically related observed behavioral irregularities with underlying causes by using one of two techniques. One method essentially uses a table of associations between behaviors and diagnoses, and the other method combines knowledge of system design with knowledge of potential flaws in design, implementation, or components to generate candidate malfunctions consistent with observations.

Design systems develop configurations of objects that satisfy the constraints of the design problem. Such problems include circuit layout, building design, and budgeting. Design systems construct descriptions of objects in various relationships with one another and verify that these configurations conform to stated constraints. In addition, many design systems attempt to minimize an objective function that measures costs and other undesirable properties of potential designs. This view of the design problem can subsume goal-seeking behavior as well, with the objective function incorporating measures of goal attainment. *See Computer-aided design and manufacturing.*

Planning systems design actions. These systems specialize in problems with the design of objects that perform functions. They include automatic programming, robot, project, route, communication, experiment, and military planning problems. Planning systems employ models of agent behavior to infer the effects of the planned agent activities. *See Robotics.*

Monitoring systems compare observations of system behavior to features that seem crucial to successful plan outcomes. These crucial features, or vulnerabilities, correspond to potential flaws in the plan. Generally, monitoring systems identify vulnerabilities in two ways. One type of vulnerability corresponds to an assumed condition whose violation would nullify the plan's rationale. Another kind of vulnerability arises when some potential effect of the plan violates a planning constraint. These correspond to malfunctions in predicted states. Many computer-aided monitoring systems exist for nuclear power plant, air traffic, disease, regulatory, and fiscal management tasks, although no fielded expert systems yet address these problems.

Debugging systems prescribe remedies for malfunctions. These systems rely on planning, design, and prediction capabilities to create specifications or recommendations for correcting a diagnosed problem. Computer-aided debugging systems exist for computer programming in the form of intelligent knowledge base and text editors, but none of them qualify as expert systems.

Repair systems develop and execute plans to administer a remedy for some diagnosed problem. Such systems incorporate debugging, planning, and execution capabilities. Computer-aided systems occur in the domains of automotive, network, avionic, and computer maintenance, as well as others, but expert systems are just entering this field.

Instruction systems incorporate diagnosis and debugging subsystems which specifically address student behavior. These systems typically begin by constructing a hypothetical description of the student's knowledge. Then they diagnose weaknesses in the student's knowledge and identify an appropriate remedy. Finally, they plan a tutorial interaction intended to convey the remedial knowledge to the student.

An expert control system adaptively governs the overall behavior of a system. To do this, the control system must repeatedly interpret the current situation, predict the future, diagnose the causes of anticipated problems, formulate a remedial plan, and monitor its execution to ensure success. Problems addressed by control systems include air traffic control, business management, battle management, mission control, and others.

**Systems components.** The **illustration** shows an idealized representation of an expert system. No existing expert system contains all the components shown, but one or more components occur in every

**Generic categories of knowledge engineering applications**

| Category | Problem addressed |
|---|---|
| Interpretation | Inferring situation descriptions from sensor data |
| Prediction | Inferring likely consequences of given situations |
| Diagnosis | Inferring system malfunctions from observables |
| Design | Configuring objects under constraints |
| Planning | Designing actions |
| Monitoring | Comparing observations to plan vulnerabilities |
| Debugging | Prescribing remedies for malfunctions |
| Repair | Executing a plan to administer a prescribed remedy |
| Instruction | Diagnosing, debugging, and repairing students' knowledge weaknesses |
| Control | Interpreting, predicting, repairing, and monitoring system behaviors |

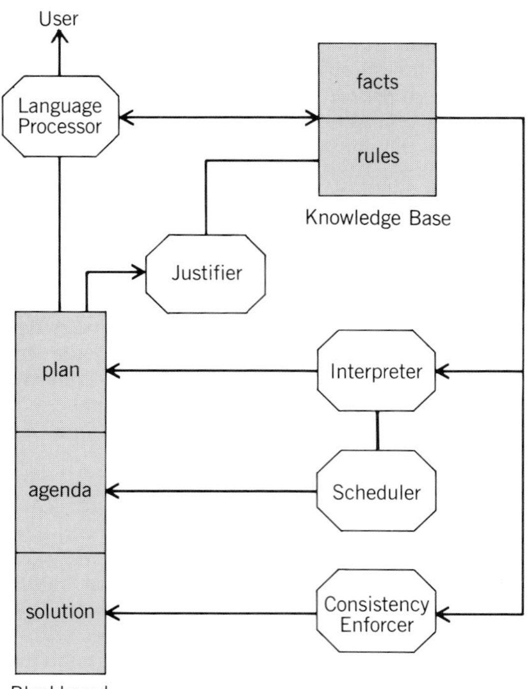


**Anatomy of an ideal expert system.**

system. The ideal expert system contains: a language processor for problem-oriented communications between the user and the expert system; a blackboard for recording intermediate results; a knowledge base comprising facts plus heuristic planning and problem-solving rules; an interpreter that applies these rules; a scheduler to control the order of rule processing; a consistency enforcer that adjusts previous conclusions when new data or knowledge alter their bases of support; and a justifier that rationalizes and explains the system's behavior.

The user interacts with the expert system in problem-oriented languages, usually some restricted variant of English, and in some cases through means of a graphics or structure editor. The language processor mediates information exchanges between the expert system and the human user. Typically, the language processor dissects, or parses, and interprets user questions, commands, and volunteered information. Conversely, the language processor formats information generated by the system, including answers to questions, explanations and justifications for its behavior, and requests for data. Existing expert systems generally employ natural language parsers written in INTERLISP to interpret user inputs, and use less sophisticated techniques exploiting ''canned text'' to generate messages to the user. *SEE PROGRAMMING LANGUAGES*.

The blackboard is a global data base that records intermediate hypotheses and decisions which the expert system manipulates. Every expert system uses some type of intermediate decision representation, but only a few explicitly employ a blackboard for the various types of ideal expert system decisions. The illustration shows three types of decisions recorded on the blackboard: plan, agenda, and solution elements. Plan elements describe the overall or general attack the system will use to solve the current problem, including current plans, goals, problem states, and contexts. For example, a plan may recommend processing all low-level sensor data first; formulating a small number of most promising hypotheses; refining and elaborating each of these hypotheses until the best one emerges; and, finally, focusing exclusively on that candidate until the complete solution is found. This kind of plan has been incorporated in several expert systems. The agenda elements record the potential actions awaiting execution. These generally correspond to knowledge-base rules which seem relevant to some decision placed on the blackboard previously. The solution elements represent the candidate hypotheses and decisions that the system has generated thus far, along with the dependencies, called links, that relate decisions to one another.

The scheduler maintains control of the agenda and determines which pending action should be executed next. Schedulers may utilize considerable abstract knowledge, such as ''do the most profitable thing next'' and ''avoid redundant effort.'' To apply such knowledge, the scheduler needs to prioritize each agenda item according to its relationship to the plan and to other solution elements. To do this, the scheduler generally needs to estimate the effects of applying the potential rule.

The interpreter executes the chosen agenda item by applying the corresponding knowledge-base rule. Generally, the interpreter validates the relevance conditions of the rule, binds variables in these conditions to particular solution blackboard elements, and then makes rule-prescribed changes to the blackboard. Interpreters of this sort are generally written in LISP because of its facilities for manipulating and evaluating programs. However, other languages are also suitable.

The consistency enforcer attempts to maintain a consistent representation of the emerging solution. This may take the form of likelihood revisions when the solution elements represent changing hypothetical diagnoses and when some new data are introduced. Alternatively, the enforcer might implement truth maintenance procedures when the solution elements represent changing logical deductions and their truth-value relationships. Most expert systems use some kind of numerical adjustment scheme to determine the degree of belief in each potential decision. This scheme attempts to ensure that plausible conclusions are reached and inconsistent ones avoided.

The justifier explains the actions of the system to the user. In general, it answers questions about why some conclusion was reached or why some alternative was rejected. To do this, the justifier uses a few general types of question-answering plans. These typically require the justifier to trace backward along blackboard solution elements from the questioned conclusion to the intermediate hypotheses or data that support it. Each step backward corresponds to the inference of one knowledge-base rule. The justifier collects these intermediate inferences and translates them to English for presentation to the user. To answer ''why not'' questions, the system uses a heuristic variant of this technique. Supposedly, it can identify a possible chain of rules that would reach the questioned conclusion but which did not apply because the relevance condition of some rule failed. The justifier explains the system's decision to reject a possible conclusion by claiming that such failed conditions impede all reasoning chains that can support the conclusion.

Finally, the knowledge base records rules, facts, and information about the current problem that may be useful in formulating a solution. While the rules of the knowledge base have procedural interpretations, the facts play only a passive role. *See Artificial intelligence; Data-processing systems.*

Frederick Hayes-Roth

**Bibliography.** D. Michie (ed.), *Expert Systems in the Microelectronic Age*, pp. 3–25, 1979; E. Shortliffe, *Computer Based Medical Consultations: MYCIN*, 1976; W. J. Van Melle, *System Aids in Constructing Consultation Programs*, 1981; R. Webster and L. Miner, Expert systems: Programming problem-solving, *Technology*, 2(1):62–73, 1982.

## Facsimile

Transmission of a fixed image as an electric signal over a communications channel. A scanner converts the original image into electrical impulses. A facsimile of the original image, similar to an office-copier reproduction, is made by a thermal or electrostatic recorder at the receiving unit. Telephone lines provide the communications channel.

Newspapers and magazines are published directly from full-page facsimile copies received from a central composing point. Almost all newspaper photographs of events other than local are sent by facsimile, with up to 2000 newspapers receiving the image at the same time. Weather networks cover the United States, constantly making copies of weather charts. Cloud-cover photographs and multispectral band images are recorded by facsimile from signals sent by orbiting satellites and by geostationary satellites.

Facsimile is the oldest office automation technology, predating the telephone and even the telegraph. The first facsimile transceiver, built in 1842, used a pendulum for synchronization and step-feed of the recording paper. Facsimile then became the sleeping giant of business-document communications for more than 100 years, while the telegram, teleprinter, teletypewriter exchange (TWX), and Telex also flourished. Analog facsimile gained a portion of this market in the early 1970s, but business facsimile became much more competitive with the development of digital facsimile in the late 1970s. The quality of the received copy is better than that made by many office copiers.

**Scanning.** This is the process by which the page to be transmitted by facsimile is represented by electric signals. An image of the original page is formed by a lens in a way similar to that of an ordinary camera (**Fig. 1**). A linear array of small photodiodes is substituted in facsimile in the place where film would be held in a camera. The portion of the image falling on the linear-diode array is a thin line, 0.005 in. (0.13 mm) high, across the top of the page being transmitted. Typically, 1728 diodes are used to view this line for a page 8½ in. (216 mm) wide. The photodiode corresponding to the upper left position on the page is first checked to determine whether the very small portion of the image it detects is white (the paper background) or black (a mark). The spot detected by a single photodiode is called a picture element (a pel for short if it is recorded as either black or white, or a pixel if a gray scale is used). Each of the 1728 diodes is checked in sequence, to read across the page. Then the original page is stepped the height of this thin line, and the next line is read. The step-and-read process repeats until the whole page has been scanned. This type of scanner, called flatbed, is used in most facsimile systems. Another type of flatbed scanner uses a single photomultiplier tube or a solid-state photosensor. The image is swept across this photosensor by either a galvanometer or a rotating multiface mirror. *See Optical detectors; Photodiode; Photomultiplier.*

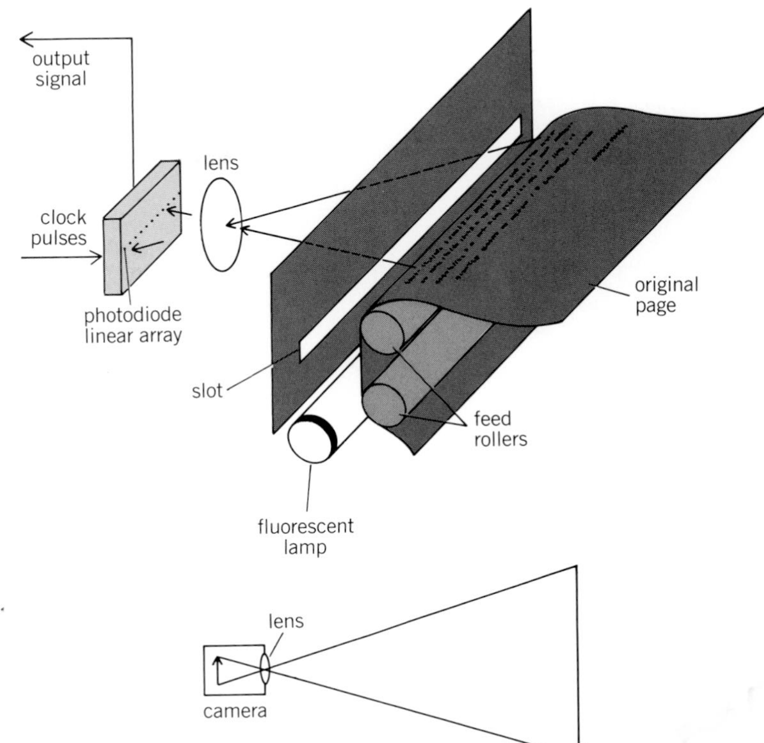


**Fig. 1. Photodiode facsimile scanner.**

With a drum-type scanner, the original sheet of paper is mounted on a drum that rotates while the scan head with a photosensor moves sideways the width of one scanning line for each turn of the drum. Very few modern designs use this type of scanner.

**Recording.** This is the process by which facsimile signals are converted into a copy of the original. One of the most commonly used systems is the thermal recorder. It has 1728 very fine wires positioned in a row across the recording paper. These wires touch the paper and produce very small hot spots as current passes through them. These hot-spot sections of the wires form a straight line across the page at a resolution of 200 dots per inch (8 dots per millimeter). Each wire takes only a few milliseconds to go from a cool, nonmarking condition to a hot, marking condition. Each recording wire corresponds to a photodiode in the linear array of the transmitting scanner.

Electrostatic recording is another multistylus system. A charge is applied on the recording paper under each stylus where a black mark is needed. This charge image is then made visible by a black-powder toner which sticks on the charged spots. Heat fuses the dots onto the paper, or they are squeezed into the paper by pressure rollers (**Fig. 2**). The main advantage of electrostatic recording over thermal recording is its much higher writing speed.

**Transmission.** Most analog facsimile units use the Public Switched Telephone Network (PSTN), also known as Direct Distance Dialing (DDD), to connect

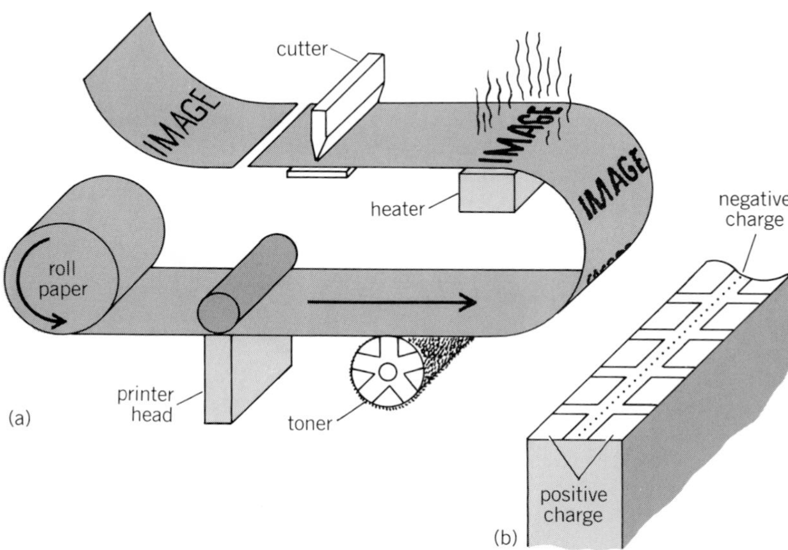


**Fig. 2. Electrostatic facsimile recording. (*a*) Recording system. (*b*) Printer head.**

the sending and receiving units. Calls are made to a distant facsimile unit in the same manner as for voice transmission, but the called unit often answers the call and records the message without help from a receiving operator. Analog facsimile equipment of older design takes 6 min to send a letter-size page. A simple built-in analog modem has an audio-frequency modulation system, whereby a 1500-Hz tone is sent for white areas of the original page and a 2400-Hz tone is sent for black marks, according to North American specifications. Shades of gray may be sent with intermediate tone frequencies. The international standard CCITT (Consultative Committee in International Telegraphy and Telephony) Group I specification of 1300 Hz for white and 2100 Hz for black is used by most countries outside North America. These incompatible standards prevent sending from one type of equipment to the other.

Later analog designs send the same letter-size page in 3 min with CCITT Group 2 standards. The Group 2 equipment achieves this doubling of speed with a combination of amplitude and phase modulation. A vestigial sideband (VSB) low-pass filter removes most of the upper sideband to reduce the bandwidth required. This method is similar to duo-binary modulation, sometimes used for data transmission. All countries use this Group 2 standard. *SEE AMPLITUDE MODULATION; PHASE MODULATION; SINGLE SIDEBAND.*

Digital facsimile designs which provide higher resolution and faster transmission speeds (CCITT Group 3) are employed in almost all modern office facsimile equipment. These digital facsimile units also transmit over Public Switched Telephone Network voice-type channels, but employ a built-in digital modem of the same type that data systems use. In the United States and other countries which have good telephone networks, transmission is usually at 9600 bits per second. If the telephone-line quality is not good enough for transmission at this rate, the receiver notifies the transmitter after initial handshake signals, and it automatically steps down to 7200 bits per second and tests the line again. This process continues if necessary at speeds of 4800 and 2400 bits per second for even poorer lines. *SEE PULSE MODULATION.*

A small percentage of facsimile systems are connected by dedicated (private) voice telephone lines instead of the Public Switched Telephone Network. Voice telephone lines used for office facsimile are seldom conditioned to correct for envelope delay distortion or amplitude-frequency distortion. For digital facsimile systems, the receiving modem automatically corrects for these distortions each time a new telephone call is made. *SEE DISTORTION (ELECTRONIC CIRCUITS).*

CCITT Group 4 facsimile standards have now been defined for a new type of office facsimile system which will send error-free copies over public data networks, but not over the Public Switched Telephone Network. Resolution should be 200 and 300 lines per in. (7.9 and 11.8 lines per millimeter), with 240 and 400 (9.4 and 15.7) optional. Direct interworking with Group 3 and mixed mode Teletex terminals is not possible.

Much higher-speed digital office facsimile systems have been built, but very few are in service. These may offer higher resolution of 300 or 400 lines per inch (11.8 or 15.7 lines per millimeter), sending a page in about 5 s for 56-kilobit systems or in about 1 s in even higher-speed systems.

**Facsimile systems.** The following facsimile systems have their own types of facsimile equipment and special features.

***Office facsimile.*** Unattended-reception capability allows transmission with automatic recording outside of regular business hours. An automatic document feeder transmits up to 50 unattended pages. Because this system has automatic dialing, unattended transmissions can be made at night, when telephone rates are lower; no operator is required at either the sending or receiving locations. Computer storage allows the same set of pages to be sent to many locations, or different pages to each location in the network. Polling allows one facsimile unit to call many stations automatically and collect documents from each. A polling code may be used to prevent unauthorized collection by another facsimile unit. The equipment prints out a daily use record, called an activity report, showing the facsimile unit identification and the following information: date, time, send or receive call, duration of the call, other party's identification code, number of pages sent, number of pages on each call, the total number of pages sent and received that day, and diagnostic codes. The following items are added automatically to the facsimile signal and print-out on each page recorded: sending-station identification, date, time, and page number. Some office facsimile systems incorporate encryption of the signal, so that only random black dots appear if the signals are intercepted and recorded. *SEE PRIVACY SYSTEMS (SCRAMBLING).*

***Newsphoto facsimile.*** Most pictures which newspapers print have been sent by facsimile. The Associated Press and United Press International have nationwide analog telephone networks which have been conditioned to reduce distortion of the received signals. Thousands of newspapers receive the latest news pictures at the same time by a broadcast operation. These circuits are also extended to transmit pictures of news events from almost anywhere in the world. Besides black and white, these systems reproduce the gray scale very well, providing 64 intermediate shades.

Associated Press uses a facsimile recorder which contains a helium-neon laser beam for a light source. This beam is swept across the recording paper by a galvanometer to expose the dry silver photographic material. The image is developed by heating the paper. United Press International uses an electrostatic type of facsimile recorder. Each pixel recorded has a black portion which varies form zero width for white to full width for black. The shape of the pixels has been selected to minimize moiré interference patterns with the screen dots used in the printing process. SEE LASER.

***Remote publishing.*** Newspapers and magazines are printed in plants which may be thousands of miles away from the place where the pages are composed. High-resolution facsimile equipment sends a full-size proof copy of each page to the printing location, with a few minutes per page. The facsimile recording may be directly onto a full-size plate which is then put on the press. One newspaper transmits simultaneously through a wide-band satellite channel to 21 printing plants located throughout the United States. For printing in color, three or four transmissions of each page may be made by using a color-separation process; in this process, each color sent is recorded separately on black-and-white film. The original page has already been screened in the areas where halftone reproduction of photographs and artwork is required. The resolution is usually 600 to 1500 dots per inch (24 to 59 dots per millimeter), for a total of 20–140 million dots per page. Plates made by this facsimile process deliver copies that cannot be distinguished from copies printed by ordinary methods. Laser recording may be used to write on photographic or xerographic materials. Both drum-type and flatbed scanners and recorders are used. Flatbed types can scan entire paste-ups, simplifying the preparation of the original page.

Pagination facsimile systems use a computer and a high-resolution cathode-ray tube to assemble and edit the newspaper page before it is transmitted to the printing plant. Text, photographs, and advertisements may be combined electronically rather than by conventional manual page makeup. SEE CATHODE-RAY TUBE; COMPUTER GRAPHICS.

***Meterorological facsimile.*** Many facsimile weather-map transmission networks operate at all hours providing a large variety of charts of weather conditions throughout the world. Some systems record on paper from a roll 18 in. (46 cm) wide, with map lengths up to 24 in. (61 cm) or more. The originals may be hand-drawn and sent by a facsimile transmitter or generated by a computer and sent directly from it without a hard-copy original. Most of the transmissions are charts, but cloud-cover photographs and infrared-scanned images are also sent. A resolution of 96 dots per inch (4 dots per millimeter) is commonly used. Many of the facsimile receivers still use the electrolytic recording process, which requires a wetted recording paper. Newer designs use electrostatic or thermal recording systems.

Cloud-cover photographs and multispectral infrared scans of the Earth are taken from orbiting or geostationary satellites 22,300 mi (35,900 km) above the Equator. One type of high-resolution cloud-cover photograph is produced by rotating the whole satellite, causing a telescopic optical scanner to sweep across the Earth. At each revolution the telescope points lower, until the entire globe is scanned in about 2000 revolutions, to produce a 2000-line facsimile recording.

***Police facsimile.*** A special type of facsimile equipment is used by police departments for transmission of fingerprint cards between police stations and the center for fingerprint records. The recorded image is built up using 200 dots per inch (8 dots per millimeter). The gray shadings of the original must be accurately reproduced to prevent loss of information in light areas and smudged areas with dark gray between the ridge marks. Facsimile networks exist among city police departments, county and state agencies, and the Federal Bureau of Investigation.

***Military facsimile systems.*** Tactical military facsimile equipment provides accurate copies of charts, drawings, photographs, and text under rugged operating conditions. Digital facsimile is used, with an algorithm which allows good copy to be received over very poor communications channels, where the error rate may be as high as 1 in 100 bits received.

*Kenneth R. McConnell*

***Bibliography.*** A. G. Cooley, Facsimile, in K. Henney (ed.), *Radio Engineering Handbook*, pp. 23-1 through 23-38, 1959; D. M. Costigan, *Electronic Delivery of Documents and Graphics*, 1978; N. Gilbert, The role of facsimile in telematics, *Telecommunications*, 17(10):71–76, October 1983; K. R. McConnell, Digital facsimile in the office automation environment, *IEEE Globecom '83*, Pap. 36.2.1, 1983; H. Ochi, K. Tateishi, and Tetsutani, Super high-speed facsimile equipment, *IEEE Globecom '83*, Pap. 36.3.2, 1983.

## Faraday's law of induction

A statement relating an induced electromotive force (emf) to the change in magnetic flux that produces it. For any flux change that takes place in a circuit, Faraday's law states that the magnitude of the emf $\epsilon$ induced in the circuit is proportional to the rate of change of flux as in expression (1).

$$\epsilon \propto -\frac{d\Phi}{dt} \qquad (1)$$

The time rate of change of flux in this expression may refer to any kind of flux change that takes place. If the change is motion of a conductor through a field, $d\Phi/dt$ refers to the rate of cutting flux. If the change is an increase or decrease in flux linking a coil, $d\Phi/dt$ refers to the rate of such change. It may refer to a motion or to a change that involves no motion.

Faraday's law of induction may be expressed in terms of the flux density over the area of a coil. The flux $\Phi$ linking the coil is given by Eq. (2), where $\alpha$

$$\Phi = \int B \cos \alpha \, dA \qquad (2)$$

is the angle between the normal to the plane of the coil and the magnetic induction $B$. The integral is taken over the area $A$ enclosed by the coil. Then, for a coil of $N$ turns, Eq. (3) holds.

$$\epsilon = -N\frac{d\Phi}{dt} = -N \int \frac{d(B \cos \alpha)}{dt} A \qquad (3)$$

SEE ELECTROMOTIVE FORCE (EMF).

*Kenneth V. Manning*

## Fault-tolerant systems

Systems, predominantly computing and computer-based systems, which tolerate undesired changes in their internal structure or external environment. Such changes, generally referred to as faults, may occur at various times during the evolution of a system, beginning with its specification and proceeding through its utilization. Faults that occur during specification, design, implementation, or modification are called design faults; those occurring during utilization are referred to as operational faults. Design faults are due to mistakes made by humans or by automated design tools in the process of specifying, designing, implementing, or modifying a system. The source of an operational fault may be either internal or external to the system. Internal operational faults are due to physical component failures or human mistakes (when humans are integral parts of the system). External operational faults are due to physical phenomena (temperature, radiation, and so forth) or improper actions on the part of external systems and humans interacting with the system.

**Fault prevention and fault tolerance.** Both design faults and operational faults affect a system's ability to perform during use, typically resulting in reduced performance or failure. Faults are thus the primary concern in efforts to enhance system reliability (the probability of no system failures during a specified period of time) or, more generally, system performability (the probability distribution of system performance during a specified period of time). In order to satisfy a given reliability or performability requirement, faults can be attacked by two basic approaches: fault prevention and fault tolerance. Fault prevention is the more traditional approach; it comprises techniques which attempt to eliminate faults by avoiding their occurrence (for example, design methodologies, quality control methods, radiation shielding) or by finding and removing them prior to system utilization (for example, testing or verification methods). The use of fault tolerance techniques is based on the premise that a complex system, no matter how carefully designed and validated, is likely to contain residual design faults and to encounter unpreventable operational faults.

**Faults and errors.** To describe how systems tolerate faults, it is important to distinguish the concepts of fault and error. Relative to a description of desired system behavior at some specified level of abstraction, an error is a deviation from desired behavior caused by a fault. Since desired behavior may be described at different levels of abstraction (for example, the behavior of computer hardware may be described at the circuit level, the logic level, or the register-transfer level), a variety of errors can be associated with a given fault. Moreover, a fault can cause an error at one level without causing an error at another level. A fault is latent until it does cause an error, and it is possible for a fault to remain latent throughout the lifetime of a system without ever causing an error.

The distinction between fault and error is particularly important in the case of design faults. For example, a software design fault (commonly referred to as a bug) may remain latent for years before the software is finally executed in a manner that permits the bug to cause an execution error. The sense in which a system tolerates a fault is typically defined as some form of restriction on the errors caused by that fault. This term is usually used to refer to the prevention of errors at a level that represents the user's view of desired system behavior. Errors at this level are known as system failures and therefore a fault is tolerated if it does not cause a system failure. A system is fault-tolerant if all faults in a specified class of faults are tolerated.

**Fault tolerance techniques.** A variety of fault tolerance techniques are employed in the design of fault-tolerant systems, particularly fault-tolerant computing systems. Generally, fault tolerance techniques attempt to prevent lower-level errors (caused by faults) from propagating into system failures. By using various types of structural and informational redundancy, such techniques either mask a fault (no errors are propagated to the faulty subsystem's output) or detect a fault (via an error) and then effect a recovery process which, if successful, prevents system failure. In the case of a permanent internal fault, the recovery process usually includes some form of structural reconfiguration (for example, replacement of a faulty subsystem with a spare or use of an alternate program) which prevents the fault from causing further errors.

Typically, a fault-tolerant system design will incorporate a mix of fault tolerance techniques which complement the techniques used for fault prevention. The choice of these techniques and, more generally, the specific nature of the system's hardware and software architecture is highly dependent on both the types of faults anticipated and the reliability or performability requirements imposed by the system's application environment. SEE SOFTWARE ENGINEERING.

*John F. Meyer*

**Bibliography.** T. Anderson and P. A. Lee, *Fault Tolerance: Principles and Practice*, 1981; T. Anderson and B. Randell (eds.), *Computing Systems Reliability*, 1979; A. Avizienis, Fault-tolerant systems, *IEEE Transac. Comput.*, C-25(12):1304–1312, Dec. 1976; D. P. Siewiorek and R. S. Swarz, *The Theory and Practice of Reliable System Design*, 1982.

## Feedback circuit

A circuit that returns a portion of the output signal of an electronic circuit or control system to the input of the circuit or system. When the signal returned (the feedback signal) is at the same phase as the input signal, the feedback is called positive or regenerative. When the feedback signal is of opposite phase to that of the input signal, the feedback is negative or degenerative.

The use of negative feedback in electronic circuits and automatic control systems produces changes in the characteristics of the system which improve the performance of the system. In electronic circuits, feedback is employed either to alter the shape of the frequency-response characteristics of an amplifier circuit and thereby produce more uniform amplification over a range of frequencies, or to produce conditions for oscillation in an oscillator circuit. It is also used because it stabilizes the gain of the system against changes in temperature, component replacement, and so on. Negative feedback also reduces nonlinear distortion. In automatic control systems, feedback is used to compare the actual output of a system with a desired output, the difference being used as the input signal to a controller. These two points of view will be considered separately in the following discussion. However, the analysis of both feedback amplifiers and electromechanical control systems can be made on a frequency-response basis; from the point of view of analysis the two have much in common.

**Amplifier feedback.** Feedback can be introduced into an amplifier by connecting to the input a fraction of the output signal. An amplifier will, in general, have better frequency-response characteristics when the system has feedback than when there is no feedback. The system can be designed to have a wider bandwidth and more nearly ideal frequency-response characteristics. Further, harmonic distortion due to nonlinear transistor or tube characteristics can be reduced by using feedback. *SEE DISTORTION (ELECTRONIC CIRCUITS)*.

The use of feedback in an improperly designed system, however, can produce a system with worse characteristics. Amplifiers can become oscillators when feedback is used in an improperly designed system. For a discussion of amplifier frequency response and bandwidth *SEE AMPLIFIER*.

A system with feedback can be analyzed by using the block diagram representation shown in the **illustration**. The sinusoidal input signal is $\mathbf{E}_s$ and the am-

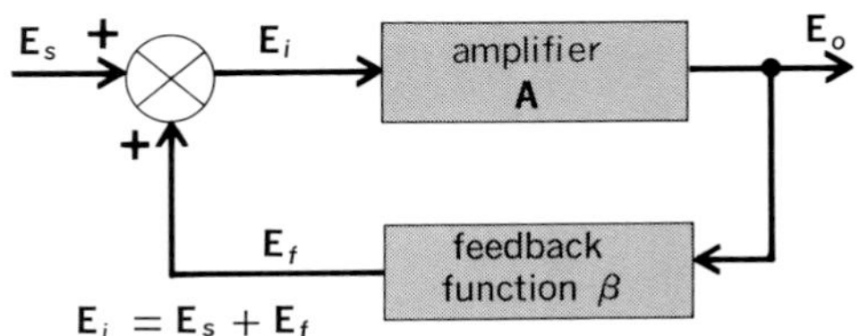


**Block diagram of feedback circuit.**

plifier gain is $\mathbf{A}$, which is a function of frequency. When there is no feedback, $\mathbf{E}_o = \mathbf{AE}_s$ because $\mathbf{E}_i = \mathbf{E}_s$. When there is feedback, $\mathbf{E}_i = \mathbf{E}_s + \mathbf{E}_f$.

Since $\mathbf{E}_o = \mathbf{AE}_i$, and $\mathbf{E}_f = \boldsymbol{\beta}\mathbf{E}_o$, the overall gain of the system with feedback is then shown by the equation below.

$$\frac{\mathbf{E}_o}{\mathbf{E}_s} = \frac{\mathbf{A}}{1 - \mathbf{A}\boldsymbol{\beta}}$$

This formula for the gain of an amplifier with feedback indicates the effect of feedback upon the frequency response of the amplifier without feedback. The $(1 - \mathbf{A}\boldsymbol{\beta})$ term in the denominator is a complex number. Therefore, the magnitude and phase angle of the gain of the amplifier with feedback will differ from the gain of the amplifier without feedback. The amount of the difference depends upon the value of the $\mathbf{A}$ and the $\boldsymbol{\beta}$ terms, and no general statements can be made.

If there is a frequency for which $\mathbf{A}\boldsymbol{\beta} = 1$, the denominator of the expression for the gain will be zero while the numerator will not be zero. When this occurs, the amplifier will oscillate at approximately the frequency for which $\mathbf{A}\boldsymbol{\beta} = 1$. Furthermore, if there is a frequency for which the magnitude of $\mathbf{A}\boldsymbol{\beta}$ is greater than unity and the phase angle of $\mathbf{A}\boldsymbol{\beta}$ is 0°, 360°, or any integral multiple of 360°, the amplifier will oscillate.

**Positive and negative feedback.** The terms positive feedback and negative feedback are used to denote the type of feedback found in certain electronic circuits. *SEE NEGATIVE-RESISTANCE CIRCUITS*.

When the magnitude of the denominator of the feedback equation is greater than unity, the overall gain with this (negative) feedback will be less than the gain with no feedback, and stable operation will result.

If the magnitude of the denominator in the displayed equation is less than unity, then the overall gain with this positive feedback will be greater than the gain without feedback. Under these circumstances the circuit may be unstable and oscillate.

It follows that both the magnitude and the phase angle $\theta$ of the product $\mathbf{A}\boldsymbol{\beta}$ are important in determining whether the feedback is positive.

The effect of feedback upon the frequency response of an amplifier can be determined from the expression $\mathbf{A}/(1 - \mathbf{A}\boldsymbol{\beta})$. The performance in a particular case depends upon the behavior of $\mathbf{A}$ and $\boldsymbol{\beta}$ as functions of frequency.

The usual method for analyzing the feedback amplifier to determine the possibilities of oscillation is the examination of the amplitude and phase of $\mathbf{A}\boldsymbol{\beta}$ over the frequency range from zero to a sufficiently high frequency (on the order of 100,000 Hz). The examination is often made by plotting the magnitude of $\mathbf{A}\boldsymbol{\beta}$ against the phase angle in polar coordinates.

An alternate method of analysis is to plot the logarithm of the magnitude of $\mathbf{A}\boldsymbol{\beta}$ against the logarithm of frequency and the phase angle $\mathbf{A}\boldsymbol{\beta}$ against the logarithm of frequency. The value of frequency at which the phase angle equals 180° is determined from the phase-angle-versus-log-frequency curve. If for this value of frequency the logarithm of $|\mathbf{A}\boldsymbol{\beta}|$ is greater than zero (the magnitude of $\mathbf{A}\boldsymbol{\beta}$ is greater than one), the amplifier will oscillate.

Several practical problems are found in the analysis of feedback amplifiers. One is that the values of the various circuit components, such as resistors, capacitors, and transformers, are only approximately known. For example, resistors may have a 20% tolerance and the values for transistor parameters may vary widely around a nominal value. Another problem is that all of the parameters which affect the performance, in particular stray capacitance introduced by the physical layout of components and writing, are not included in the expression for $\mathbf{A}\boldsymbol{\beta}$. This means that, in practice, mathematical analysis is only a guide; final design is refined by experiment.

**Input and output impedances.** The discussion has considered voltage feedback where the output voltage, or some function of it, is fed back to the input. Current feedback, where a voltage proportional to the output current or some function of the output current is fed back, may also be used. Furthermore, an amplifier may have both voltage and current feedback.

The input and output impedances of a feedback amplifier depend upon whether the output current or voltage is sampled and upon whether this signal is fed back in series or in parallel with the input excitation. It is possible for the impedance with feedback to be greater than or less than what it was before the feedback was added. An emitter-follower is an example of a feedback amplifier where the output impedance has been reduced to a very low value and the input impedance has been increased drastically.

**Oscillator feedback.** An oscillator can be viewed as a feedback amplifier with an input voltage supplied from its output. Referring to the illustration, this would mean that $\mathbf{E}_s$ equals zero and $\mathbf{E}_i$ equals $\mathbf{E}_f$.

From this viewpoint the condition for oscillation at a frequency $f_o$ is (to a first and usually very good approximation) that $\mathbf{A}\boldsymbol{\beta} = 1$ at $f = f_o$. This means that the feedback must be positive.

**Servomechanism feedback.** The purpose of feedback in a servomechanism is to obtain better control of the system. As an example, consider a position control system which is used to position an object at a point determined by a reference signal.

The command to move the object is derived by comparing the reference signal with a signal indicating the instantaneous location of the object. The command signal is an error signal derived from the comparison of the actual and desired signals; any error signal drives the system in such a direction as to reduce the error, that is, to make the actual position of the object agree with the desired reference position.

If feedback were not used in the position control system, a precisely calibrated control device would be needed to position the object in each position dictated by the reference. In general the required control could not be built with sufficient accuracy.

*Harold F. Klock*

**Bibliography.** J. D'Azzo and C. Houpis, *Linear Control System Analysis and Design*, 2d ed., 1981; J. Millman, *Microelectronics*, 1979; D. Schilling and C. Belove, *Electronic Circuits: Discrete and Integrated*, 1979.

## Ferrite devices

Electrical devices whose principle of operation is based upon the use of ferrites, which are magnetic oxides. By common usage, ferrite devices are referred to as those using magnetically soft ferrites, with the spinel or garnet crystal structure. Since the electrical resistivity of ferrites is typically $10^6$–$10^{11}$ times that of metals, ferrite components have much lower eddy current losses and are hence used at frequencies generally above about 10 kHz.

**Chemistry and crystal structure.** Modern ferrite devices stemmed from the contributions on spinel ferrites made by the Japanese and Dutch scientists during World War II. The general formula for the spinel is $MFe_2O_4$, in which M is a divalent metal ion. In special cases, the divalent ion M can be replaced by an equal molar mixture of an univalent and trivalent ion. Thus lithium ferrite can be thought of as having the formula $Li_{0.5}Fe_{0.5}Fe_2O_4$. However, the commercially practical ferrites are those in which the divalent ion represents one or more Mg, Mn, Fe, Co, Ni, Cu, Zn, and Cd ions. The trivalent Fe ion may also be substituted by other trivalent ions such as Al. The compositions are carefully adjusted to optimize the device requirements, such as permeability, loss, ferromagnetic-resonance line width, and so forth.

The ferrimagnetic garnets were discovered in France and the United States in 1956. The general formula is $M_3Fe_5O_{12}$, in which M is a rare-earth or yttrium ion. Single-crystal garnet films form the basis of bubble domain device technology. Bulk garnets have applications in microwave devices. *SEE MAGNETIC BUBBLE MEMORY.*

With the exception of some single crystals used in

**Summary of ferrite applications***

| Ferrite chemistry | Device | Device function | Frequencies | Desired ferrite properties |
|---|---|---|---|---|
| | | *Linear B/H, low flux density* | | |
| MnZn, NiZn | Inductor | Frequency selection network<br>Filtering and resonant circuits | <1MHz (MnZn)<br>~1–100 MHz (NiZn) | High μ, high μQ, high stability of μ with temperature and time |
| MnZn, NiZn | Transformer (pulse and wideband) | Voltage and current transformation<br>Impedance matching | Up to 500 MHz | High μ, low hysteresis losses |
| NiZn | Antenna rod | Electromagnetic wave receival | Up to 15 MHz | High μQ, high resistivity |
| MnZn | Loading coil | Impedance loading | Audio | High μ, high $B_s$, high stability of μ with temperature, time, and dc bias |
| | | *Nonlinear B/H, medium to high flux density* | | |
| MnZn, NiZn | Flyback transformer | Power converter | <100 kHz | High μ, high $B_s$, low hysteresis losses |
| MnZn | Deflection yoke | Electron-beam deflection | <100 kHz | High μ, high $B_s$ |
| MnZn, NiZn | Suppression bead | Block unwanted ac signals | Up to 250 MHz | Moderately high μ, high $B_s$, high hysteresis losses |
| MnZn, NiZn | Choke coil | Separate ac from dc signals | Up to 250 MHz | Moderately high μ, high $B_s$, high hysteresis losses |
| MnZn, NiZn | Recording head | Information recording | Up to 10 MHz | High μ, high density, high μQ, high wear resistance |
| MnZn | Power transformer | Power converter | <60 kHz | High $B_s$, low hysteresis losses |
| | | *Nonlinear B/H, rectangular loop* | | |
| MnMg, MnMgZn, MnCu, MnLi, etc. | Memory cores | Information storage | Pulse | High squareness, low switching coefficient, and controlled coercive force |
| MnMgZn, MnMgCd | Switch cores | Memory access transformer | Pulse | High squareness, controlled coercive force |
| MnZn | Magnetic amplifiers | | | |
| | | *Microwave properties* | | |
| YIG†, MgMn‡, Li§, NiZn | Isolators, attenuators, circulators, switches, modulators | Impedance matching, power level control, power splitting | 1–5 GHz (YIG), 2–30 GHz (YIG, MgMn, Li), 30–100 GHz (NiZn) | Controlled $B_s$, high resistivity, high Curie temperature, narrow resonance line width |

*After P. I. Slick, Ferrites for nonmicrowave applications, in I. P. Wohlfarth (ed.), *Ferromagnetic Materials*, vol. 2, North-Holland, 1980.
†May contain Al, Gd. ‡May contain Al, Zn. §May contain Ti, Zn.

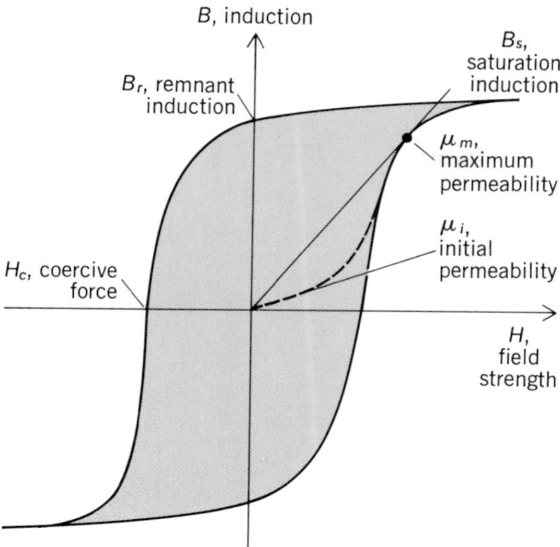


**Plot of magnetic induction *B* as a function of magnetic field strength *H*.**

recording heads and special microwave applications, all ferrites are prepared in polycrystalline form by ceramic techniques.

**Applications.** A summary of the applications of ferrites is given in the **table**. These may be divided into nonmicrowave and microwave applications. Further, the nonmicrowave applications may be divided into categories determined by the magnetic properties based on the $B/H$ behavior, that is, the variation of the magnetic induction or flux density $B$ with magnetic field strength $H$, as shown in the **illustration**. The plot in the illustration is termed a hysteresis loop, with the area encompassed by the loop being proportional to the power loss within the ferrite. The categories are: linear $B/H$, with low flux density; nonlinear $B/H$, with medium to high flux density; and highly nonlinear $B/H$, with a square or rectangular hysteresis loop.

***Linear B/H devices.*** In the linear region, the most important devices are high-quality inductors, particularly those used in filters in frequency-division multiplex telecommunications systems and low-power wide-band and pulse transformers. Virtually all such devices are made of either manganese zinc (MnZn) ferrite or nickel zinc (NiZn) ferrite, though perdominantly the former.

In the design of inductors, the so-called $\mu Q$ product of a material has been found to be a useful index of the quality of the material. In this product, $\mu$ is the initial permeability and $Q$ is equal to $\omega L/R$, where $\omega$ is the angular frequency, $L$ the inductance, and $R$ the effective series resistance arising from core loss. The higher the value of $\mu Q$, the better is the material, and ferrites have the highest $\mu Q$ product of any commercially available magnetic material. Typical $\mu Q$ values measured at 20 kHz for various materials are iron dust, 2000; Permalloy powder, 10,000; 12.5-micrometer-thick molybdenum Permalloy tape, 100,000; and MnZn ferrite, 250,000. Values of $\mu Q$ greater than $10^6$ at 20 kHz have been achieved commercially in specially prepared MnZn ferrites.

As compared with NiZn ferrites, MnZn ferrites have lower residual and hysteresis losses, higher permeabilities, and lower resistivities. A high permeability lowers the frequency of ferromagnetic resonance, which is accompanied by a large rise in losses. This factor, along with increased eddy current losses coming from lower resistivities, restricts the useful upper frequency range for MnZn ferrites in high-$Q$ inductors to about 1 MHz. Above that, NiZn ferrites are preferred. SEE ELECTRIC FILTER; INDUCTOR; Q (ELECTRICITY); TRANSFORMER.

For transformer applications the highest value of $\mu$ over the operating frequency range is desired. Values of $\mu$ in the 18,000 range (10 kHz) for MnZn ferrite are commercially available.

***Nonlinear B/H devices.*** The largest usage of ferrite measured in terms of material weight is in the nonlinear $B/H$ range, and is found in the form of deflecting yokes and flyback transformers for television receivers. The cores for these devices must have high saturation induction $B_s$ along with high maximum permeability $\mu_m$ at the knee of the $B/H$ curve to frequencies as high as 100 kHz, the effective flyback frequency used in scanning a television tube. Again, MnZn and NiZn ferrites dominate the use in these devices. SEE TELEVISION RECEIVER.

***Highly nonlinear B/H devices.*** The largest usage of ferrite measured in terms of number of parts is in the highly nonlinear $B/H$ range, and is used as square-loop toroidal cores for digital computer memories. The two stable states of magnetization represent the binary one and zero codes. The properties which are important here are a square hysteresis loop (with a high ratio of remanent induction to saturation induction, $B_r/B_s$), controlled coercivity, and fast switching time. For high packing density and fast access time, toroids with outside diameters as small as 0.02 in. (0.5 mm) have been achieved. The ferrites are primarily Mn, such as MnMg, MnCu, MnMgZn, MnCuNi, and MnLi. The last is exclusively used in small-size cores because of high Curie temperature for improved temperature stability, greater mechanical strength, and higher $B_s$ for greater output. The future for memory ferrites, however, was dimmed by the large-scale emergence in 1977 of semiconductor memories, which have progressively taken over the computer market. SEE COMPUTER STORAGE TECHNOLOGY.

***Microwave devices.*** Microwave devices make use of the nonreciprocal propagation characteristics of ferrites close to or at a gyromagnetic resonance frequency in the range of 1–100 GHz. The most important of such devices are isolators and circulators. Materials having a range of $B_s$ are needed for operation at various frequencies since for resonance, $B_s$ is less than $\omega/\gamma$ where $\gamma$ is the gyromagnetic ratio. In the 1–5-GHz range, yttrium iron garnet of $B_s$ = 0.02–0.18 tesla is used. In the 2–30-GHz range, MgMn, MgMnZn, MgMnAl, and Li ferrites of $B_s$ = 0.06–0.25 T are used along with the garnets. At 30–100 GHz, NiZn ferrites with $B_s$ up to 0.50 T are used. The garnets have highly desirable, small, ferromagnetic-resonance line widths, particularly in single-crystal form. In device development there is a strong trend toward realizing the conventional waveguide components in microstrip form whereby both the transmission and the gyromagnetic function are provided by a ferrimagnetic substrate, or the gyromagnetic function is provided by a ferrimagnetic insert on a nonmagnetic ferrite substrate. SEE GYRATOR; MICROWAVE; MICROWAVE TRANSMISSION LINES.

*Gilbert Y. Chin*

***Bibliography.*** C. Heck, *Magnetic Materials and Their Applications*, 1974; J. Smit and H. P. J. Wijn.

*Ferrites*, 1959; E. C. Snelling, *Soft Ferrites*, 1969; E. P. Wohlfarth (ed.), *Ferromagnetic Materials*, vol. 2, 1980.

## Ferroelectrics

Crystalline substances which have a permanent spontaneous electric polarization (electric dipole moment per cubic centimeter) that can be reversed by an electric field. In a sense, ferroelectrics are the electrical analog of the ferromagnets, hence the name. The spontaneous polarization is the so-called order parameter of the ferroelectric state, just as the spontaneous magnetization is the order parameter of the ferromagnetic state. The names Seignette-electrics or Rochelle-electrics, which are also widely used, are derived from the name of the first substance found to have this property, Seignette salt or Rochelle salt. SEE ROCHELLE SALT.

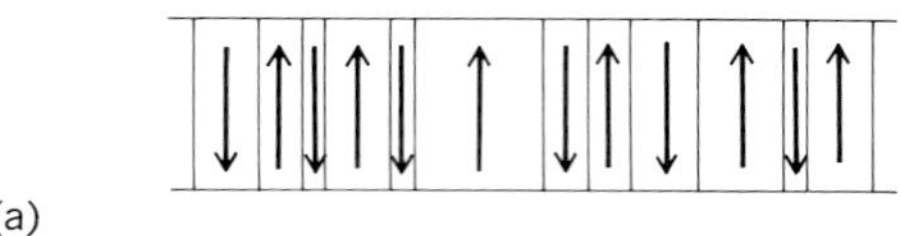
(a)

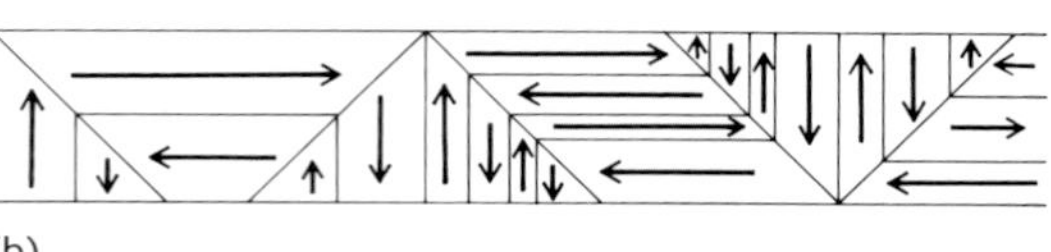
(b)

Fig. 1. Domain configurations (simplified) encountered in ferroelectric crystals. (*a*) First class. (*b*) Second class.

The reversibility of the spontaneous polarization is due to the fact that the structure of a ferroelectric crystal can be derived from a nonpolarized structure by small displacements of ions. In most ferroelectric crystals, this nonpolarized structure becomes stable if the crystal is heated above a critical temperature, the ferroelectric Curie temperature; that is, the crystal undergoes a phase transition from the polarized phase (ferroelectric phase) into an unpolarized phase (paraelectric phase). The change of the spontaneous polarization at the Curie temperature can be continuous or discontinuous. The Curie temperature of different types of ferroelectric crystals range from a few degrees absolute to a few hundred degrees absolute. As a rule, the ferroelectric phase is the low-temperature phase; however, there are crystals which are ferroelectric in a relatively narrow temperature range only, and others stay polarized up to the temperature of decomposition or melting.

Fig. 2. Ferroelectric domains in $BaTio_3$ photographed through a polarizing microscope. Ferroelectric domains range from macroscopic to submicroscopic size.

**Classification.** From a practical standpoint ferroelectrics can be divided into two classes. In ferroelectrics of the first class, spontaneous polarization can occur only along one crystal axis; that is, the ferroelectric axis is already a unique axis when the material is in the paraelectric phase. Typical representatives of this class are Rochelle salt, $KH_2PO_4$, $(NH_4)_2SO_4$, guanidine aluminum sulfate hexahydrate, glycine sulfate, colemanite, and thiourea.

In ferroelectrics of the second class, spontaneous polarization can occur along several axes that are equivalent in the paraelectric phase. The following substances, which are all cubic above the Curie point, belong to this class: $BaTiO_3$-type (or perovskite-type) ferroelectrics; $Cd_2Nb_2O_7$; $PbNb_2O_6$; certain alums, such as methyl ammonium alum; and $(NH_4)_2$-$Cd_3(SO_4)_3$. Some of the $BaTiO_3$-type ferroelectrics have, below the Curie temperature, additional transition temperatures at which the spontaneous polarization switches from one crystal axis to another crystal axis. For example, $BaTiO_3$ and $KNbO_3$ polarize with decreasing temperature first along a [100] axis, then the polarization switches into a [110] axis, and finally into a [111] axis.

From a scientific standpoint, one can distinguish proper ferroelectrics and improper ferroelectrics. In proper ferroelectrics, for example, $BaTiO_3$, $KH_3PO_4$, and Rochelle salt, the spontaneous polarization is the order parameter. The structure change at the Curie temperature can be considered a consequence of the spontaneous polarization. The unit cell of the crystal in the ferroelectric phase contains the same number of chemical formula units as the unit cell in the paraelectric phase. In improper ferroelectrics, the spontaneous polarization can be considered a by-product of another structural phase transition. The unit cell in the ferroelectric phase is an integer multiple of the unit cell in the paraelectric phase. Examples of such systems are $Gd(MoO_4)$ and boracites. The dielectric elastic and electromechanical behavior of the two types of ferroelectrics differ significantly.

**Ferroelectric domains.** The spontaneous polarization can occur in at least two equivalent crystal direction; thus, a ferroelectric crystal consists in general of regions of homogeneous polarization that differ only in the direction of polarization. These regions are called ferroelectric domains. Ferroelectrics of the first class consist of domains with parallel and antiparallel polarization (**Fig. 1***a*), whereas ferroelectrics of the second class can assume much more complicated domain configurations (Fig. 1*b*). The region between two adjacent domains is called a domain wall. Within this wall, the spontaneous polarization changes its direction. The wall between antiparallel domains is probably only a few lattice spacings thick, whereas the wall between domains that are polarized at a right angle to each other is probably thicker. Ferroelectric domains can be observed in a number of substances by means of the polarizing microscope (**Fig. 2**) because of their birefringence, or double refraction. The ferroelectric domains range in size from macroscopic (millimeters) to submicroscopic..

***Ferroelectric hysteresis.*** When an electric field is applied to ferroelectric crystal, the domains that are favorably oriented with respect to this field grow at the expense of the others, for example, by sidewise motion of domain walls. In addition, favorably oriented domains can nucleate and grow until the whole crystal becomes one single domain. When the field is reversed, the polarization reverses through the same processes. The relation between the resulting polarization $P$ of the whole crystal and the externally applied electric field $E$ is given by a hysteresis loop (**Fig. 3**). The shape of the hysteresis loop depends strongly upon the perfection of the crystal as well as upon the rate of change of the externally applied field $E$. A simple circuit that permits the observation of ferroelectric hysteresis loops by means of an oscilloscope is shown in **Fig. 4**. In some ferroelectrics, the polarization can be reversed within a fraction of 1 microsecond.

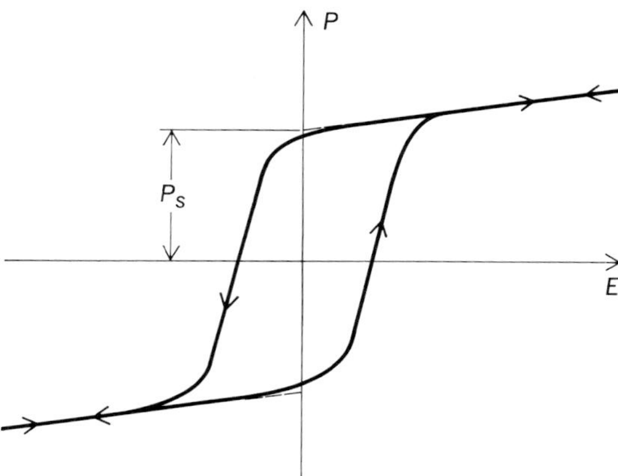


**Fig. 3. Net polarization *P* of a ferroelectric crystal versus externally applied electric field *E*.**

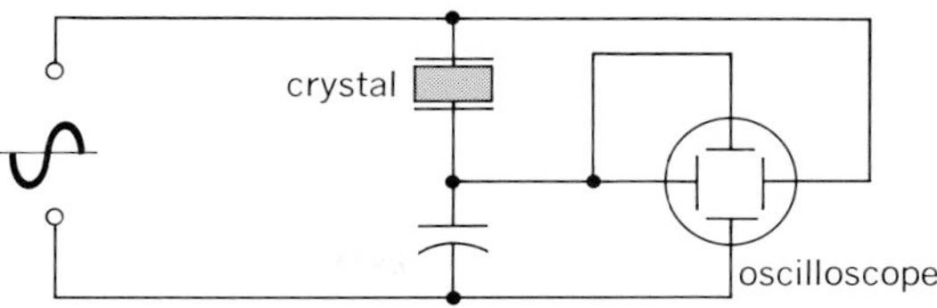


**Fig. 4. Circuit for the display of ferroelectric hysteresis loops on an oscilloscope.**

***Spontaneous polarization.*** The magnitude of the permanent or spontaneous polarization $P_s$ of a domain can be obtained from the hysteresis loop by extrapolating the saturation branch to zero external field (Fig. 3). For most ferroelectrics, the values of $P_s$ are between $10^{-7}$ and $10^{-4}$ coulomb/cm$^2$ (**Fig. 5**). In nonferroelectric dielectrics, electric fields between $10^5$ and $10^8$ V/cm would be necessary in order to achieve such large polarizations.

**Dielectric properties.** As a rule, the dielectric constant $\epsilon$ measured along a ferroelectric axis increases in the paraelectric phase when the Curie temperature is approached. In many ferroelectrics, this increase can be approximated by the Curie-Weiss law, shown in the equation below. Here $T$ designates the temperature of the crystal, and $T_0$ is equal to or somewhat smaller than the transition temperature. $C$ is the so-called Curie constant. For $BaTiO_3$, this law holds unaltered up to frequencies of $2.4 \times 10^{10}$ Hz. Dispersion sets in the far-infrared. The dielectric constant drops when the crystal becomes spontaneously polarized (**Fig. 6**). In the ferroelectric phase, the dielectric constant has two components. The first component is the dielectric constant of the individual domains. It is independent of the frequency and of the electric field generally up to far-infrared frequencies. The second component is due to domain wall motions, that is, to partial reversal of the spontaneous polarization. This process can give rise to large dielectric losses, and it depends strongly upon the frequency, the electric field strength, the domain structure, and the temperature. In uniaxial ferroelectrics, the dielectric constant measured perpendicular to the ferroelectric axis generally does not show a very pronounced anomaly near the Curie temperature, and in some cases it has even the same order of magnitude and temperature dependence as for any normally behaving dielectric crystal.

$$\epsilon = \frac{C}{T - T_0}$$

**Piezoelectric properties.** Ferroelectrics can be divided into two groups according to their piezoelectric behavior.

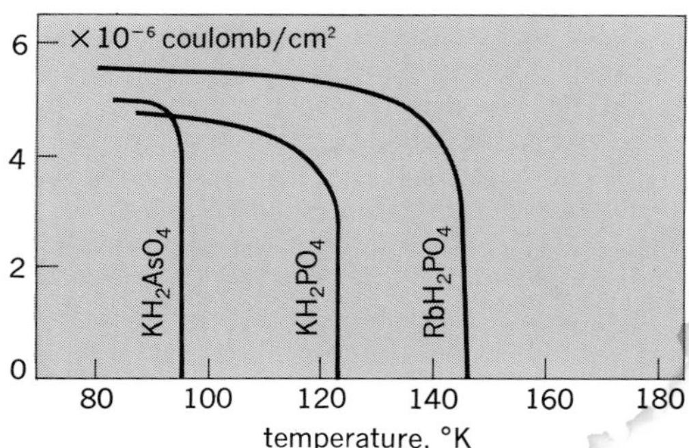


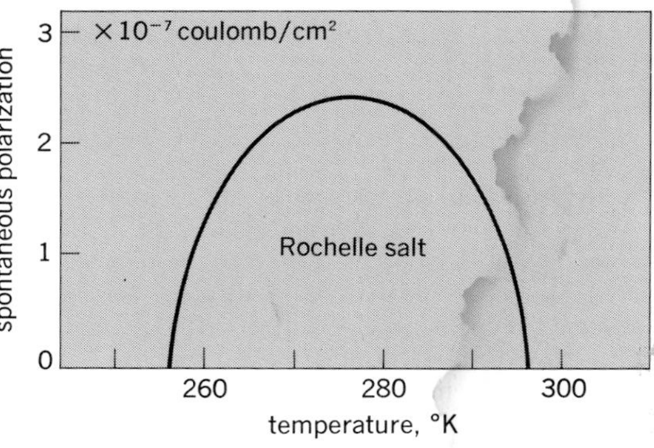


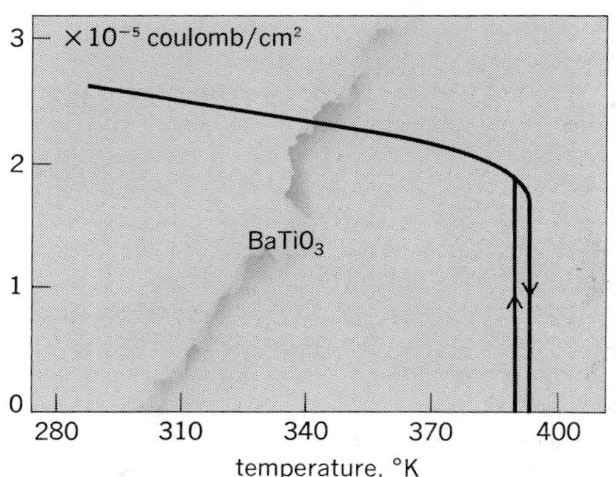


**Fig. 5. Dependence upon temperature of the spontaneous polarization of some ferroelectrics. °F = (K × 1.8) − 459.67. °C = K − 273.15.**

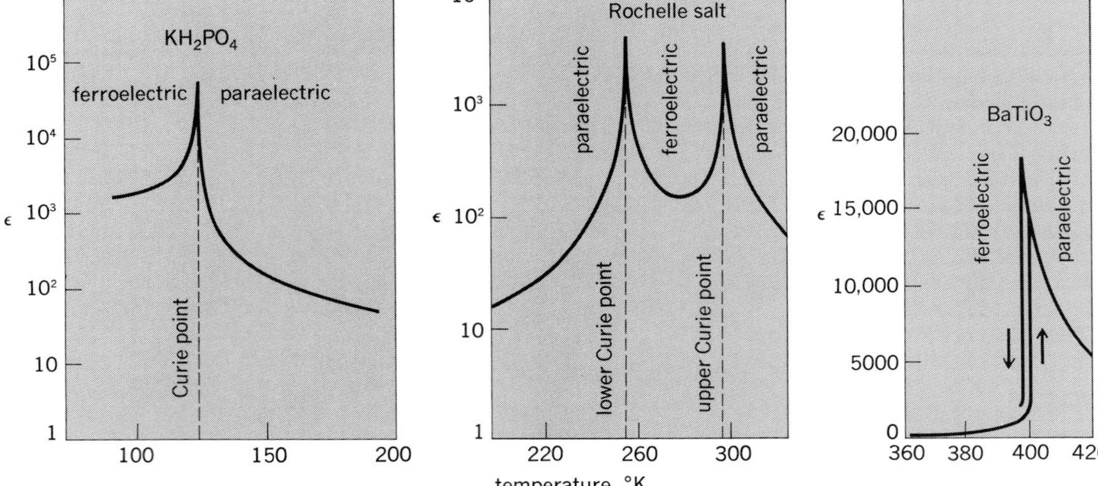


**Fig. 6. Anomalous temperature dependence of relative dielectric constant of ferroelectrics at transition temperature. °F = (K × 1.8) − 459.67. °C = K − 273.15.**

The ferroelectrics in the first group are already piezoelectric in the unpolarized phase. Those piezoelectric moduli which relate stresses to polarization along the ferroelectric axis have essentially the same temperature dependence as the dielectric constant along this axis, and hence become very large near the Curie point. The spontaneous polarization gives rise to a large spontaneous piezoelectric strain which is proportional to the spontaneous polarization. In $KH_2PO_4$-type ferroelectrics and in Rochelle salt, for example, this strain is a shear in the plane perpendicular to the axis of polarization. It reaches 27 min of arc in $KH_2PO_4$ and about 1.8 min of arc in Rochelle salt. The piezoelectric modulus decreases as the spontaneous polarization increases. But with sufficiently large stresses, it is possible to align the domains and reverse the spontaneous polarization (**Fig. 7**). The relation between the resulting polarization of the whole crystal and the mechanical stress is given by a hysteresis loop analogous to the loop of Fig. 3 (piezoelectric hysteresis). This effect can simulate a very large piezoelectric modulus.

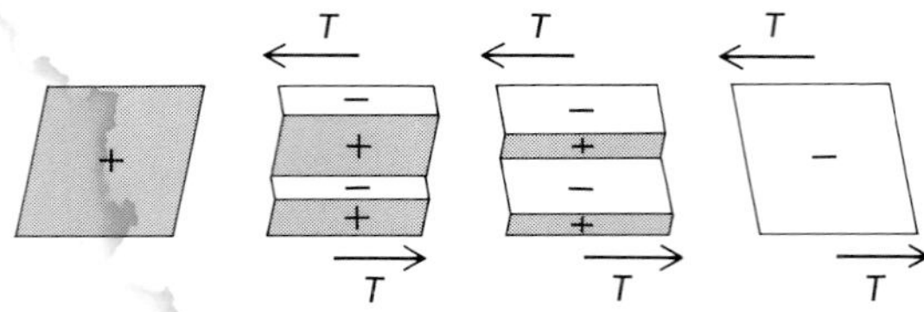

**Fig. 7. Schematic representation of the reversal of the spontaneous polarization by a mechanical shear stress *T* in $KH_2PO_4$ and Rochelle salt.**

The ferroelectrics in the second group are not piezoelectric when they are in the paraelectric phase. However, the spontaneous polarization lowers the symmetry so that they become piezoelectric in the polarized phase. This piezoelectric activity is often hidden because the piezoelectric effects of the various domains can cancel. However, strong piezoelectric activity of a macroscopic crystal or even of a polycrystalline sample occurs when the domains have been aligned by an electric field. The spontaneous strain is proportional to the square of the spontaneous polarization. In $BaTiO_3$, for example, the crystal (which has cubic symmetry in the unpolarized phase) expands along the axis of polarization and contracts at right angles to it. The strain is of the order of magnitude of 1%. The spontaneous polarization cannot be reversed by a mechanical stress in ferroelectrics of this group. SEE PIEZOELECTRIC CRYSTAL; PIEZOELECTRICITY.

**Crystal structure.** The structures of different types of ferroelectrics are entirely different, and it is not possible to establish a general rule for the occurrence of ferroelectricity. The structures of a number of ferroelectrics and the minute changes that they undergo when spontaneous polarization occurs are known in great detail from x-ray diffraction and neutron diffraction studies. In a qualitative way, the process of polarization is best understood for ferroelectrics of the $BaTiO_3$ type. **Figure 8** shows schematically the structure of the unit cell of a $BaTiO_3$ crystal in the unpolarized state, and the arrows indicate the direction in which the ions are slightly displaced when the lattice becomes spontaneously polarized along the axis *z*. The order of magnitude of the displacement is 1% of the unit cell dimension. However, these displacements do not account quantitatively for the observed

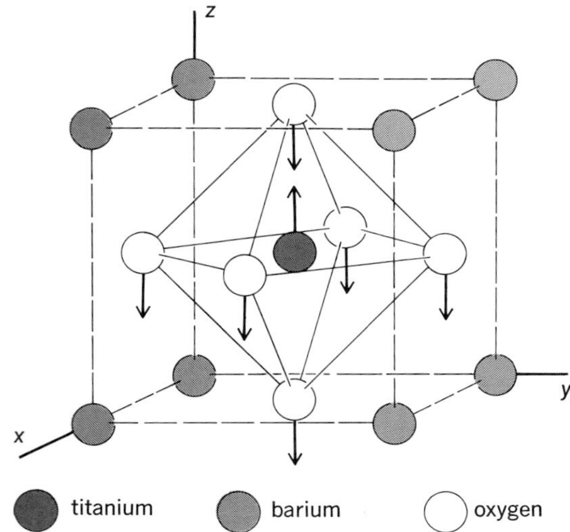


**Fig. 8. Crystal lattice of $BaTiO_3$. Arrows indicate displacements of the ions when crystal becomes polarized.**

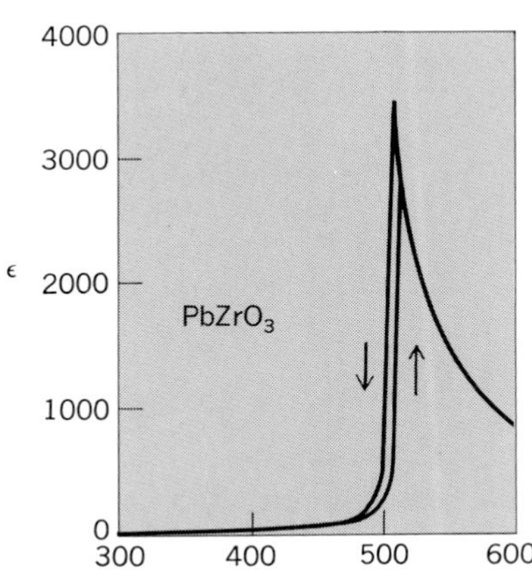

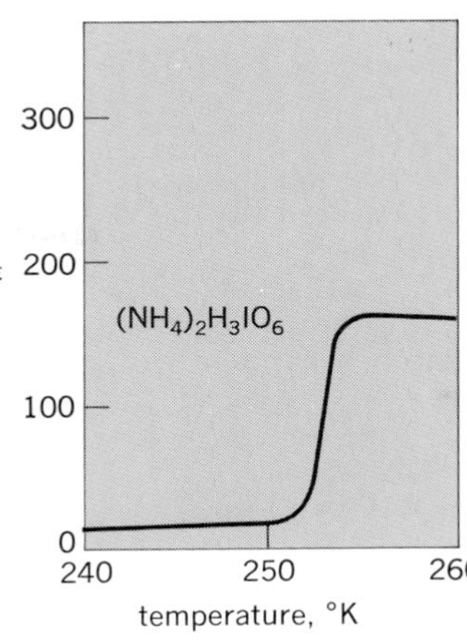

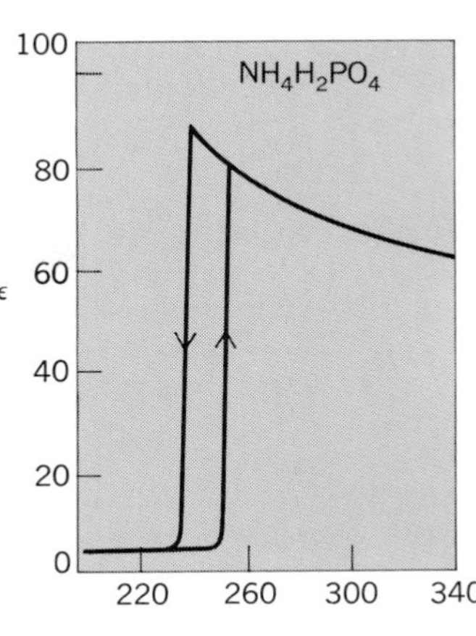


**Fig. 9. Anomalous temperature dependence of relative dielectric constant of antiferroelectric crystals. Note increase as transition temperature is approached and drop when antipolarization occurs. °F = (K × 1.8) − 459.67. °C = K − 273.15.**

polarization, because other changes of the electronic structure occur as well.

In $KH_2PO_4$-type ferroelectrics, hydrogen bonds O—H · · · O play an important part in the ferroelectric effect. Above the Curie temperature, the hydrogen ions are statistically distributed over the two possibilities O—H · · · O and O · · · H—O, whereas below the Curie point, one or the other of these two possibilities is strongly favored, depending upon the sign of the spontaneous polarization.

**Antiferroelectric crystals.** These materials are characterized by a phase transition from a state of lower symmetry (generally low-temperature phase) to a state of higher symmetry (generally high-temperature phase). The low-symmetry state can be regarded as a slightly distorted high-symmetry state. It has no permanent electric polarization, in contrast to ferroelectric crystals. The crystal lattice can be regarded as consisting of two interpenetrating sublattices with equal but opposite electric polarization. This state is referred to as the antipolarized state.

In a certain sense, an antiferroelectric crystal is the electrical analog of an antiferromagnetic crystal. In the high-symmetry phase, the sublattices are unpolarized and indistinguishable. In general, antiferroelectric crystals have more than one axis along which the sublattices can polarize. Therefore, the low-symmetry phase consists of regions of homogeneous antipolarization which differ only in the orientation of the axis along which antipolarization has occurred. These regions are called antiferroelectric domains and can be observed by the polarizing microscope. Because these domains have no permanent electric dipole moment, an electric field generally has little influence on domain structure.

The dielectric constant of antiferroelectric crystals is generally larger than it is for nonferroelectric crystals and has an anomalous temperature dependence. It increases as the transition temperature is approached and drops when antipolarization occurs (**Fig. 9**). In some antiferroelectrics the phase transition is discontinuous; in others it is continuous.

The structure of antiferroelectric crystals is generally closely related to the structure of ferroelectric crystals. Some antiferroelectrics even undergo phase transitions from an antipolarized state into a spontaneously polarized, ferroelectric state; in others a sufficiently strong electric field applied along an antiferroelectric axis reverses the polarity of one of the sublattices so that a ferroelectric state results. The crystal reverts, however, to the antiferroelectric state when the electric field is removed. **Figure 10** shows net polarization versus externally applied field for such a case.

Compounds with antiferroelectric properties are $PbZrO_3$, $PbHfO_3$, $NaNbO_3$ (isomorphous with ferroelectric $BaTiO_3$), $WO_3$ (structure related to $BaTiO_3$), $NH_4H_2PO_4$ and isomorphous $NH_4$ salts (isomorphous with ferroelectric $KH_2PO_4$), $(NH_4)_2H_3IO_6$, $Ag_2H_3IO_6$, and certain alums.

**Origin of phase transition.** The ferroelectric phase transition results from an instability of one of the normal lattice vibration modes. On approaching the transition temperature, the frequency of the relevant normal mode decreases (soft mode). The restoring force of the mode displacements tends to zero. When the stability limit is reached, the displacements corresponding to the soft mode freeze in, and the ferroelectric phase results. The ferroelectric soft mode is polar (infrared-active) and of infinite wavelength. The antiferroelectric phase transition, on the other hand, emerges from a soft lattice mode with a finite wavelength equal to an integer multiple of a lattice period.

**Applications.** The piezoelectric effect of ferroelectrics (and certain antiferroelectrics) finds numerous

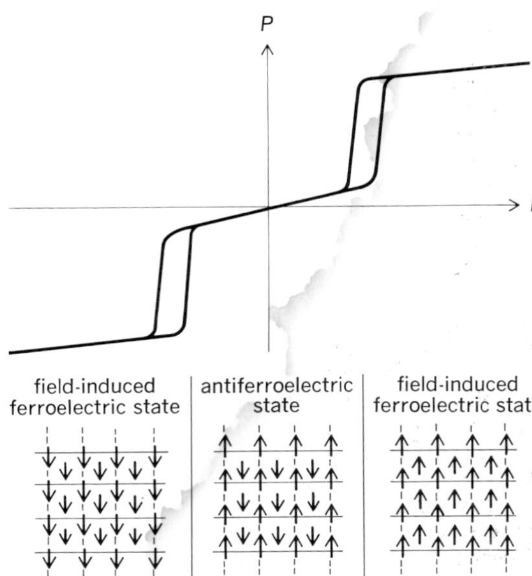


**Fig. 10. Polarization *P* of antiferroelectric $PbZrO_3$ versus externally applied electric field *E*. Strong fields "switch" the antiferroelectric crystal into a ferroelectric state, as shown here schematically.**

applications in electromechanical transducers. The large electrooptical effect (birefringence induced by an electric field) is used in light modulators. In certain ferroelectrics (for example, $BaTiO_3$, $LiNbO_3$, $KTaNbO_3$, and $LiTaO_3$), light can induce changes of the refractive indices. These substances can be used for optical information storage and in real-time optical processors. The temperature dependence of the spontaneous polarization corresponds to a strong pyroelectric effect which can be exploited in thermal and infrared sensors.

*Werner Kanzig*

**Bibliography.** R. Blinc and B. Žekš, *Soft Modes in Ferroelectrics and Antiferroelectrics*, 1974; V. M. Fridkin, *Ferroelectric Semiconductors*, 1980; V. M. Fridkin, *Photoferroelectrics*, 1979; M. E. Lines and A. M. Glass, *Principles and Applications of Ferroelectrics and Related Materials*, 1977; T. Mitsui, *An Introduction to the Physics of Ferroelectrics*, 1976; T. Mitsui et al., *Ferro- and Antiferroelectric Substances*, in K. M. Hellwege and A. M. Hellwege (eds.), Landolt-Bornstein Series, group 3, vol. 9, 1975.

## Fidelity

The degree to which the output of a system accurately reproduces the essential characteristics of its input signal. Thus, high fidelity in a sound system means that the reproduced sound is virtually indistinguishable from that picked up by the microphones in the recording or broadcasting studio. Similarly, a television system has high fidelity when the picture seen on the screen of a receiver corresponds in essential respects to that picked up by the television camera. Fidelity is achieved by designing each part of a system to have minimum distortion, so that the waveform of the signal is unchanged as it travels through the system. SEE DISTORTION (ELECTRONIC CIRCUITS).

*John Markus*

## Field emission

The emission of electrons from a metal or semiconductor into vacuum (or a dielectric) under the influence of a strong electric field. In field emission, electrons tunnel through a potential barrier, rather than escaping over it as in thermionic or photoemission. The effect is purely quantum-mechanical, with no classical analog. It occurs because the wave function of an electron does not vanish at the classical turning point, but decays exponentially into the barrier (where the electron's total energy is less than the potential energy). Thus there is a finite probability that the electron will be found on the outside of the barrier. This probability varies as $e^{-cA^{1/2}}$, where $c$ is a constant and $A$ the area under the barrier. SEE PHOTOEMISSION; THERMIONIC EMISSION.

For a metal at low temperature, the process can be understood in terms of the **illustration**. The metal can be considered a potential box, filled with electrons to the Fermi level, which lies below the vacuum level by several electronvolts. The distance from Fermi to vacuum level is called the work function, $\phi$. The vacuum level represents the potential energy of an electron at rest outside the metal, in the absence of an external field. In the presence of a strong field $F$, the potential outside the metal will be deformed along the line $AB$, so that a triangular barrier is formed, through which electrons can tunnel. Most of the emission will occur from the vicinity of the Fermi level where the barrier is thinnest. Since the electron distribution in the metal is not strongly temperature-dependent, field emission is only weakly temperature-dependent and would occur even at the absolute zero of temperature. The current density $J$ is given by the Fowler-Nordheim equation below, where $B$ is a field-independent

$$J = BF^2e^{-6.8\times10^7\phi^{3/2}/F}$$

constant of dimensions $A/V^2$ (A = amperes or state), $\phi$ is work function in electronvolts, and $F$ is applied field in V/cm. The factor $\phi^{3/2}/F$ is proportional to the square root of the area under the barrier at the Fermi level. Appreciable emission requires fields of $4–7 \times 10^7$ V/cm, depending on $\phi$. SEE WORK FUNCTION (ELECTRONICS).

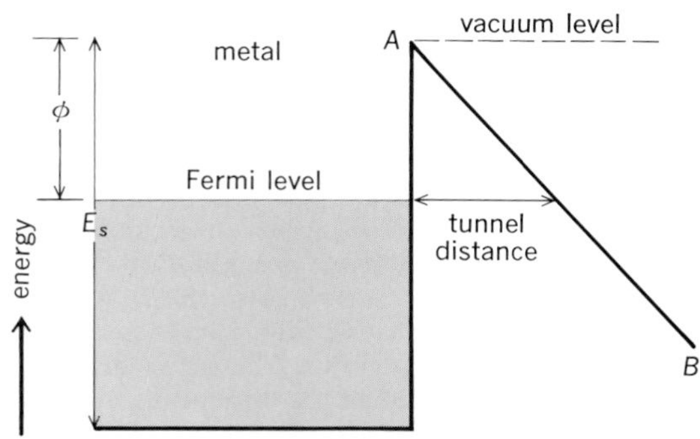


**Energy-level scheme for field emission from a metal at absolute zero temperature.**

Field emission is most easily obtained from sharply pointed metal needles whose ends have been smoothed into nearly hemispherical shape by heating. Tip radii $r_t$ equal to or less than 100 nanometers can be obtained in this way; because of its small size, the emitter is generally a single crystal. If an emitter is surrounded by a hemispherical anode raised to a voltage $V$, then the field $F$ is approximately $V/5r_t$ at the emitter. Thus, modest voltages suffice for emission. The electric lines of force diverge radially from the tip; since the electron trajectories initially follow the lines of force, they also diverge, and a highly magnified emission map of the emitter surface can be obtained, for instance, by making the anode a fluorescent screen. This constitutes a field emission microscope, invented by E. W. Müller in 1936. Since work function and hence emission are affected by adsorbed layers, the field emission microscope is very useful for studying adsorption, particularly surface diffusion. Field emitters are widely used in "ordinary" and scanning electron microscopes as high-brightness quasi-point sources of electrons, since emission occurs as if it originated from the center of the emitter cap.

Field emission can also occur from electrode asperities into insulating liquids, and thus isolated atoms or molecules in high fields, and is then called field ion ization. Field ionization forms the basis of the field ion microscope, and is a useful method of generating ions in analytical mass spectrometry. Internal field emission can occur from the valence to the conduction band of a semiconductor in a high field, and is then known as Zener breakdown. *See Electron emission*.

*Robert Gomer*

## Fourth-generation languages

A higher-level programming language that automates many of the basic functions which had to be spelled out in third-generation languages such as COBOL or PL/1. Such a language can obtain results with an order-of-magnitude less coding than the traditional languages because of its richer content of commands. Fourth-generation languages provide the programmer (who frequently is an end user) with the ability to execute complex functions with only a few commands. They provide speed, flexibility, and ease of use and they also move the systems development process back toward the user.

**Motivation.** Fourth-generation languages were created so that nonprogrammers could obtain results from computers, and the programming process could be greatly speeded up. There was a need to allow applications to be created, modified, and enhanced much more rapidly with fewer hours of professional expertise. Fourth-generation languages are easier to use; they place a powerful tool in the hands of end users, who require little training to master them. They substantially reduce the complexity of developing online and data-base inquiry systems. The required level of programming expertise is reduced, making all software developers more productive, whether system professionals or end users. In many cases, users have reported a 10-fold increase in productivity over conventional programming using COBOL or PL/1.

Fourth-generation languages were also created to permit skilled professionals to create more complex systems, enabling them to conceptualize the required actions and control structures.

**Using the languages.** Some fourth-generation languages, such as those that function as compiler languages or interpreters, require that the "programs" or language parameters be entered, validated, and then executed. Other fourth-generation languages, for example, data-base inquiry systems, are interactive; that is, commands are entered into the system individually and executed instantly. Most query languages provide the ability to store commands and command strings for future use.

***Procedural and nonprocedural languages.*** Fourth-generation languages can be categorized as procedural or nonprocedural. Some fourth-generation languages combine procedural and nonprocedural facilities. A procedural language specifies how something is accomplished. A nonprocedural language specifies what is accomplished but not in detail how it is accomplished. The traditional languages such as COBOL, FORTRAN, and PL/1 are procedural. Programmers must give precise detailed instructions for how each action is to be accomplished. Many fourth-generation languages, such as an application generator, where users fill in forms to tell the machine what to do, are nonprocedural. The user merely specifies what is to be done, and is not concerned with the detailed procedure for how it is done.

The fourth-generation languages that contain both procedural and nonprocedural statements differ widely in their syntax and capability. (No standards have yet been accepted.) Most fourth-generation languages are linked to a data-base system and allow users to create their own personal data bases. Some people create and employ relational data bases because these provide more powerful and flexible user commands than do the traditional data bases. Fourth-generation languages are user friendly, so that people can become competent at obtaining useful results after only a short training course.

***Intelligent capabilities.*** The fourth-generation language compiler or interpreter makes intelligent assumptions about the user's perceived needs. A relatively large amount of computer power is used for compiling or interpreting so that the user does not have to specify details of procedures. For example, the interpreter may automatically select a useful format for a report, put page numbers on it, select chart types for graphics displays, put labels on axes or on columnar headings, and query the user in an understandable manner when the interpreter needs more information. The user need not describe in code the format of a report or display screen. The interpreter selects a reasonable format, which the user can adjust if desired. Results can be obtained with brief nonprocedural statements such as:

LIST BY CUSTOMER AVERAGE (INVOICE TOTAL).

This is a complete program. It leaves the software to decide how the list should be formatted, when to skip pages, when to number pages, how to sort items into CUSTOMER sequence, and how to compute an average. If these so-called intelligent default assumptions are not correct, the user can adjust the results easily and quickly.

**Program generators.** These advances in programming languages have made possible the information center concept, whereby the user can develop applications quickly and easily. The application development tools that support automatic program generation are sometimes known as program generators. They are typically designed to provide logical view support through a central dictionary so that programmers need not know how to navigate through a data base in order to access information contained within it; the programmer simply needs to know the data required for a particular application. These packages are online and interactive, a characteristic that, together with logical view support, is vitally necessary for the application development tools to be fully effective. While these tools may yield somewhat inefficient code and require considerable resources, they generally provide impressive savings in personnel costs and are much less expensive than procedural languages. *See Data-base management systems*.

Generators may be used for most commercial data-processing applications, sometimes with the help of specially programmed subroutines. Data-base application generators may provide software for data entry, the creation of output, accuracy and validity checks, and restart and recovery after failures, as well as a simple means of creating the application logic. The best generators allow maintenance changes to be made quickly and easily. The result is that the applications may be adjusted constantly to meet the user's needs.

The increase in productivity, or in application development speed, with application generators is spectacular. They clearly play a vitally important role in the future of data processing and will greatly influence the systems analysis process.

**Prototyping.** Fourth-generation languages improve the productivity of systems professionals with much of the development of the problem solution going to the end user. Frequently, fourth-generation languages are referred to as prototyping tools, and the term prototyping is interchanged with software development using fourth-generation languages. Prototyping presents a different way of approaching systems development, and it addresses some of the problems associated with traditional approaches.

Prototyping allows users to become actively involved in the system design process; this involvement encourages them to make changes and helps ensure that the system is designed correctly. The low initial cost of developing prototypes invites experimentation with new applications of information systems. The user and the analyst typically work together to create a prototype of what the user has asked for, and together they refine it in a step-by-step fashion.

Prototypes were not used prior to the 1980s in any great number because it took almost as long to program the prototype as it did to program the live system. With the advent of fourth-generation languages, the use of prototypes became cost-justifiable and rapid. Using a good fourth-generation language, the analyst can create a prototype faster than by writing the specifications for it. An analyst working with an end user can create and demonstrate dialogues for data-base queries, report generation, and manipulation of screen information.

**Characteristics.** In summary, a fourth-generation language should have the following characteristics: (1) It is user-friendly. (2) A nonprofessional programmer can obtain results with it. (3) It employs a data-base management system directly. (4) Its procedural code requires an order-of-magnitude fewer instructions than COBOL or PL/1. (5) Nonprocedural code is used where possible. (6) The language makes intelligent default decisions about what the user wants. (7) It enforces or encourages structured code. (8) A user can easily understand and maintain another person's code. (9) The language is designed for interactive and online operation. (10) Users who are not data-processing professionals can master it in a very short period of training, 2 days or less. (11) It is designed for easy debugging of application software.

**DMS.** These properties of fourth-generation languages will be illustrated by discussing a particular language: IBM's DMS (Development Management System). It is a tool for generating interactive applications using DL/1 data bases. Often, complete applications are generated with it; sometimes it is used in conjunction with routines programmed in COBOL, PL/1, Assembler Language, or RPGII (Report Program Generator II). It forms a valuable tool for the systems analysis process when it is employed efficiently. Often, the systems analyst creates a prototype which needs to be tuned by a DMS expert or to have programmed routines written to supplement it. In either case, the systems analyst works with the end users and refines the results repeatedly until the users are satisfied with them and can use them efficiently.

DMS uses a so-called fill-in-the-blanks technique that makes it possible for online applications to be developed with little or no programming. Preprogrammed facilities are selected for functions such as data entry, inquiry, update, dialogue processing, and message switching.

The user describes data files, display screens called panels, and the application processing, either interactively through a terminal or offline through the use of a series of forms. With the interactive facility, DMS prompts the user through each step of the application definition. Specifications are validated to reduce errors. A HELP facility is provided which gives additional information and explains how data are to be entered.

Functions provided in DMS, in addition to the ability to perform calculations and editing, include those for data-base operation (search/browse, inquiry, update, amend/insert, deletion), data routing, program-to-program control, user processing, data validation, calculation (arithmetic and simple logic), application generation through forms, restart/recovery operations, audit control, and security and integrity functions. Data fields may be edited for validity by using such techniques as table lookup and comparison of one value with another. The user can select editing where it is needed or alter the sequence of processing as a result of any errors that are encountered.

The system can build an end user dialogue employing multiple screen panels which are logically linked. The user can capture data from a set of logically linked panels and construct from this logical file records of a data-base path involving up to four different files or data bases. The updating or creation of the data records occurs after the last panel of the set is processed.

Users in distributed locations may generate and test applications at a central point. Restart and recovery functions are provided to allow the user to save data and instructions previously entered if a system failure occurs. Audit procedures are available in which a log is kept, in some detail, of all terminal errors, allowing the auditors to check for inconsistencies.

Security is provided at various levels, including password protection at the terminal level. Integrity controls are provided to allow the user to identify and verify the contents of records. Search requests can produce listings of keys or records.

In general, systems produced with DMS are easier to design, avoid most of the need for programming, are easier to test, are self-documenting, and are much easier to maintain than conventionally produced systems. The analyst can specify the screens that will be used in an interactive dialogue, how the user may respond in the dialogue, and how the responses are processed. SEE PROGRAMMING LANGUAGES.

*Bartow Hodge*

**Bibliography.** B. Hodge, Implementing 4GL yields healthy DP environment, *Data Management*, 24(3):22–23, 1986; IBM, *Development Management System/Customer Information Control System/Virtual Storage: General Information Manual*, IBM Man. GH20-2195-2, 1980.

## Frequency (wave motion)

The number of times which sound pressure, electrical intensity, or other quantities specifying a wave vary from their equilibrium value through a complete cycle in unit time. The most common unit of frequency is the hertz; 1 Hz is equal to 1 cycle per second. In one cycle there is a positive variation from equilibrium, a return to equilibrium, then a negative variation, and return to equilibrium. This relationship is often described in terms of the sine wave, and the frequency referred to is that of an equivalent sine-wave variation in the parameter under discussion.

Frequency is a convenient means for describing the various ranges of interest in wave motion. For example, audible sound is between approximately 20 and 20,000 Hz. Infrasonic frequencies are below approximately 20 Hz; sound having frequencies above the audible is termed ultrasonic. Sound frequencies as high as $2.5 \times 10^{12}$ Hz have been obtained. Electromagnetic waves vary in frequency from less than 1 Hz for commutated direct current up to $10^{23}$ Hz for the most energetic $\gamma$-rays that have been observed. Within this range, typical approximate frequency ranges are: AM radio in the United States, 550 to 1700 kHz; FM radio, 88 to 108 MHz; visible light, $4 \times 10^{14}$ to $7.5 \times 10^{14}$ Hz. *SEE FREQUENCY MEASUREMENT*.

*William J. Galloway*

## Frequency counter

An electronic device capable of counting the number of cycles in an electrical signal during a preselected time interval. The modern high-speed electronic counter is a useful tool in the measurement of frequency when an accurate time base is available. It provides a digital counting or scaling device for registering the total number of events occurring during a given time interval.

Such electronic counting circuits operate reliably at rates of $10^7$ counts/s in many commercially available units and at rates up to approximately $5 \times 10^8$ counts/s by use of direct input with prescaling or aperiodic frequency-dividing input stages. For measurement of a frequency within the counting range of the digital circuits, the counter may be used directly with a standard frequency oscillator as a time-base control.

**Figure 1** shows a block diagram of an electronic digital counter. When $f_1$ is a standard frequency and $1/R$ is chosen to provide a standard time interval, the counter counts a number of cycles, or pulses, proportional to the frequency of $f_2$ in hertz (or other time intervals). When $f_1$ is not a standard frequency, the counter counts a number proportional to the ratio of $f_2$ to $f_1$. When $f_1$ is a standard frequency and $1/R$ is chosen to provide a time interval which is a fraction or a multiple ($1/N$ or $N$) of the nominal standard time interval, the counter indicator may be made direct reading for a harmonic ($N$) or submultiple ($1/N$) of $f_2$. When $f_1$ is a relatively low frequency, that is, its period corresponds to the time interval between two pulses, and $f_2$ is a standard frequency, the counter may be used to read the period or time interval by setting $R = 1$ and arranging the gate to open on the first pulse and close on the second.

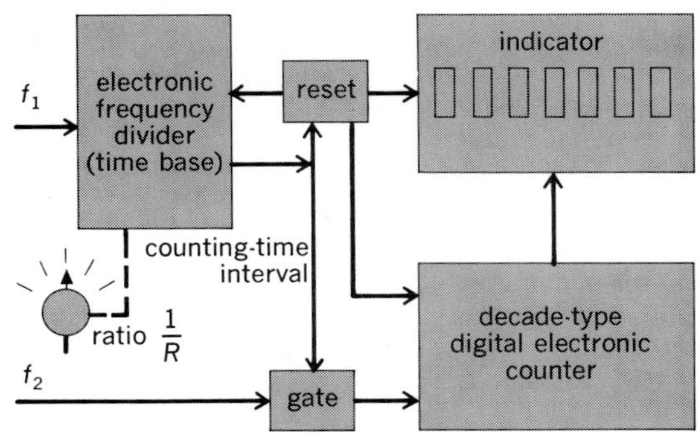


**Fig. 1. Block diagram of electronic digital counter.**

If the frequency to be measured is too high for direct counting, it is necessary to extend the range. A means commonly used is the heterodyning of the unknown signal by a standard frequency within 10 MHz of the unknown and the subsequent measuring of the beat frequency (**Fig. 2**). If the digital counter can count frequencies up to 10 MHz and the standard-frequency multiples are spaced by 10 MHz, continuous coverage is possible as far up in frequency as the standard frequencies are available. Typical electronic digital counters are shown in **Figs. 3** and **4**, with plug-in converter units for range extension. A multipurpose frequency, period, and time-interval electronic digital counter is shown in **Fig. 5**. *SEE HETERODYNE PRINCIPLE*.

The principal requirements are for signals of adequate level, free from interference and noise. With

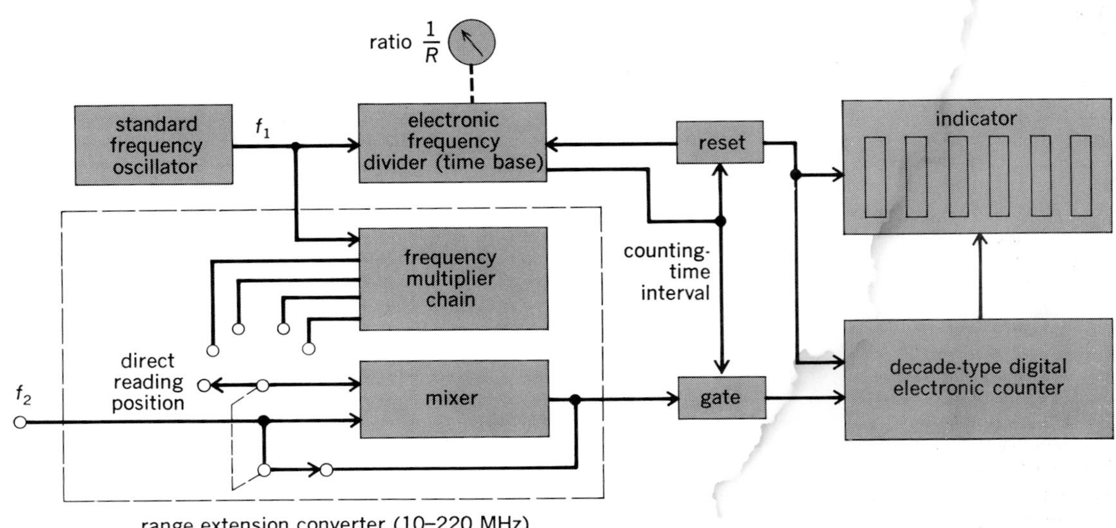


**Fig. 2. Electronic digital frequency counter with heterodyne extension of useful frequency range.**

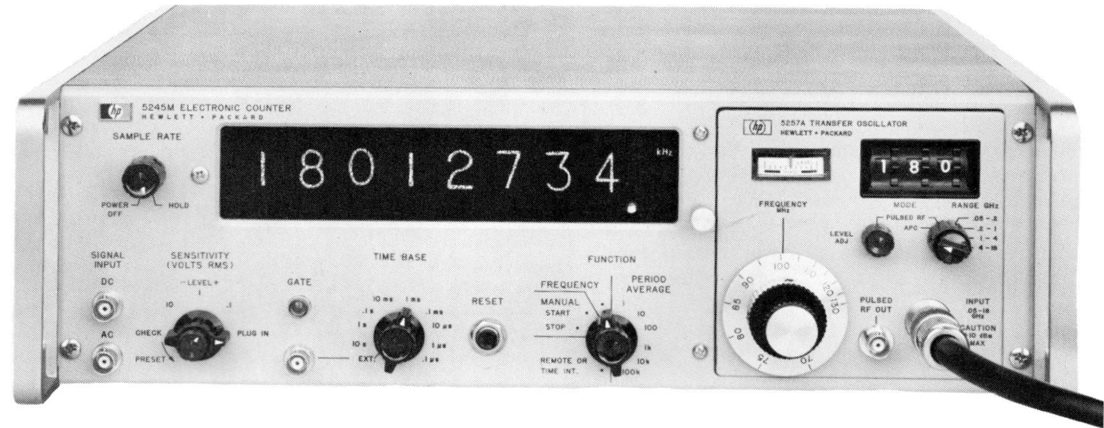


Fig. 3. Electronic digital counter which has been designed to accept plug-in units for function selection and for range extension. Phase-locking transfer oscillator shown installed, at right. (*Hewlett-Packard Co.*)

Fig. 4. Electronic counter with plug-in and add-on auxiliary units for range extension. (*Hewlett-Packard Co.*)

these conditions satisfied it is usually possible to obtain a precision of reading well beyond the stability of the overall system if a sufficiently long counting time is used. An extension of the frequency-measurement range is made possible by extending the range of the converter or heterodyning system. It is also feasible to add a transfer oscillator (**Fig. 6**) with harmonics available up into the microwave region.

The microwave frequencies are then measured as described above (transfer-oscillator method), using

Fig. 5. Electronic digital counter incorporating multiple functions which are selectable from panel, and using integrated circuits. (*General Radio Co.*)

the counter to measure the fundamental frequency of the transfer oscillator and with a beat detector and indicator to determine the beat note between the unknown and a harmonic of the transfer oscillator. A variation of this transfer-oscillator system provides for setting the time-base and zeroset conditions of the counter to give direct reading numbers valid for the particular harmonic of the transfer oscillator which is in use.

The electronic digital counter has been developed in commercial form to operate at counting rates up to 100 MHz or more, the cost increasing rapidly above 20–50 MHz. Extension of the frequency range covered by a given counter is possible by (1) prescaling, (2) using heterodyne systems which beat the signal against standard reference frequencies, (3) or using manual or automatic transfer oscillator systems. Transfer-oscillator and heterodyne range-extension systems operate satisfactorily into the microwave region (18 GHz or above). The limiting measurement accuracy depends on the excellence of the standard

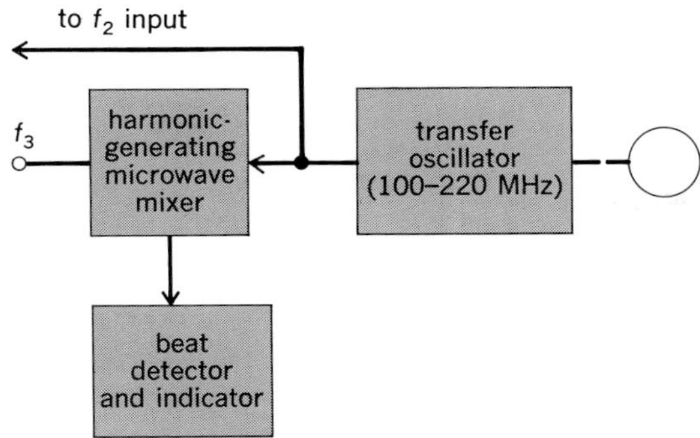


**Fig. 6. Microwave transfer oscillator.**

frequency source used for the time base and heterodyne converter reference. SEE ELECTRICAL MEASUREMENTS; FREQUENCY MEASUREMENT.

*Frank D. Lewis*

**Bibliography.** W. D. Cooper, *Electronic Instrumentation and Measurement Techniques*, 2d ed., 1978; P. Kantrowitz et al., *Electronic Measurements*, 1979.

## Frequency divider

An electronic circuit that produces an output signal at a frequency that is an integral submultiple of the frequency of the input signal.

Several information-processing and transmitting techniques require frequency division. In television, for example, it is essential to maintain a precise relationship between the horizontal-scanning frequency and the vertical-scanning frequency. Frequency division can be conveniently accomplished in two ways, digital division and division by triggering a subharmonic.

**Digital division.** Many circuits are available to count pulses. A bistable or flip-flop circuit produces one output pulse for every two input pulses. By cascading successive flip-flops, any desired degree of division can be obtained. Division by powers of 2 can be achieved simply by monitoring the output of the proper stage in the cascade. Division by other numbers can be achieved by gating to obtain the proper set of flip-flop conditions. Division by 10, or powers of 10, is readily obtained by using decade rings. SEE DIGITAL COUNTER; GATE CIRCUIT.

Reduction of the input to pulses can be accomplished when needed by amplifying, clipping, and differentiating the original signal. To provide an output that is a desired shape, the signal from the frequency divider can be used to synchronize a multivibrator to obtain a square wave and additional power. The square wave can be fed into a tuned circuit or filtered to obtain a sine wave, if that is needed. In many applications the input and output signals need no alteration. SEE MULTIVIBRATOR; WAVE-SHAPING CIRCUITS.

**Subharmonic triggering.** Any circuit which has a characteristic resonance responds to certain types of input energy by ringing, that is, by going through one or more cycles of electrical activity caused by the nature of the circuit rather than by the nature of the input. This characteristic can be used to accomplish frequency division, provided the input frequency does not vary over any extensive frequency range.

A triggered multivibrator can be used in this manner. Either an astable or a free-running type is selected such that the period for one cycle of the multivibrator will allow triggering only by a pulse that is an exact integral number of pulses from the last effective trigger. Thus one cycle of the multivibrator is initated every $n$ input pulses.

Similarly, other resonant or tuned circuits can be induced to supply submultiple outputs. Because the input may go through a large number of cycles for each output cycle, greater division per stage can be realized by this method than by digital division.

*William W. Snow*

## Frequency measurement

Measurement of the frequency of a periodic quantity, defined as the number of times a cyclic phenomenon occurs per unit of time. The second is the universally used unit of time. Conversely, time may be measured by observing the number of cycles occurring at constant frequency. The ordinary pendulum and household electric clocks are examples of such time-measuring devices. In the pendulum clock the pendulum completes one cycle of mechanical motion when it returns to its original position from the opposite direction. The electric clock completes one cycle in the electrical sense when the rotor of its motor has turned 360 electrical degrees. The alternating-voltage driving force starts a cycle from zero, passes through a maximum in one direction, returns to zero, passes through a maximum in the opposite direction, and again returns to zero, thereby completing one cycle of 360 electrical degrees. A two-pole synchronous motor consisting of one pair of north and south poles will turn 360 mechanical degrees for each cycle of 360 electrical degrees.

The measurements of frequency and time interval are probably the most precise measurements which can be made at present. Consequently, frequency and time measurement techniques find application in many areas where other measurement systems are either more difficult or not practical. Development of reasonably priced high-speed digital semiconductor integrated circuits has encouraged widespread use of electronic instrumentation, and has resulted in the development of digital counters which operate up into the 1-GHz range. Examples of the application of these techniques are the tracking of space vehicles, navigation systems such as loran C and Omega, and the precise measurement of distances and dimensions using modulated light beams or frequency-stabilizer lasers. Other examples are found in the circuits of analog-to-digital converters and digital voltmeters. These electronic systems have supplemented and even supplanted classical navigation systems based on astronomical observations and accurate time keeping. SEE ANALOG-TO-DIGITAL CONVERTER; DIGITAL COUNTER; DIGITAL VOLTMETER; INTEGRATED CIRCUITS.

**Standards of time and frequency.** The standard second is defined as the length of time required for 9,192,631,770 oscillations at the transition frequency of the cesium atom at zero magnetic field. This definition is thought to provide a constant time interval based on atomic constants. Ephemeris time is a uniform time scale based on the astronomical measurement of the time required for the Earth to orbit the Sun. The ephemeris second is 1/31,556,925.975 of the tropical year 1900 and is substantially equal to the atomic second. The time scale most widely used for navigation and daily living is based on the rotation of the Earth with respect to the Sun and is known as universal time (UT), and also as "mean solar time" or Greenwich mean time. Sidereal time is Earth rotation time measured with respect to a distant star. Universal time coordinated (UTC) is a standardized uniform time scale having an agreed offset value with respect to atomic time and being maintained in approximate agreement with observed universal time by step corrections. The agreed offset value and the step corrections are administered by the Bureau International de l'Heure (BIH), the UTC time scale being used by a majority of those countries providing radio dissemination of standard time. Time intervals on the atomic time scale may be derived from the frequencies of any of several atomic standard frequency broadcasting stations or from UTC broadcasts with a knowledge of the offset between UTC and atomic frequencies.

For calibration purposes, or for observations requiring accurate timing, a knowledge of the particular time scale being used is required. In any case calibration of a local time standard may be carried out by (1) reception of radio time signals, (2) use of a portable precision clock such as an atomic clock, or (3) astronomical measurement and computation. In most cases calibration to a given accuracy with respect to a specific time scale requires reference to a national observatory either through radio signals or a portable precision clock. In the United States the National Bureau of Standards maintains a standard frequency broadcasting service and also broadcasts standard time signals which are maintained within ±1 millisecond of UTC. The UTC scale is kept within approximately ±500 ms of corrected UT by the step corrections mentioned above. The time signals broadcast by the U.S. Naval Radio Service are also maintained to this accuracy. Accurate clock calibration may be obtained by carrying atomic clocks between the observatory and the clock to be calibrated or by such systems as satellite-borne radio relays using special terminal equipment.

Information on the accuracy of transmitted time and frequency broadcasts is available from the operating agencies. United States agencies are the National Bureau of Standards and the Naval Observatory. In Canada the service is provided by the National Research Council of Canada.

**Primary frequency standard.** The only primary frequency standards acceptable for use in national standards laboratories for frequency reference are atomic standards of the cesium-beam type. These devices provide intrinsic calibrations, independent of other reference standards. Atomic hydrogen masers are expected eventually to be developed as primary reference frequency standards. Cesium-beam atomic clocks have superseded other types of primary frequency standards as a consequence of the adoption of the atomic second as the unit of time.

**Secondary standard.** The frequency of a secondary standard is determined by comparison with a primary standard or by comparison with another secondary standard originally compared with a primary standard. Secondary standards include (1) quartz-crystal frequency standards, with or without clock indicators, and (2) gas-cell atomic standards such as rubidium-cell standards. Rubidium-cell standards are relatively rugged and can be made to exhibit low drift rates,

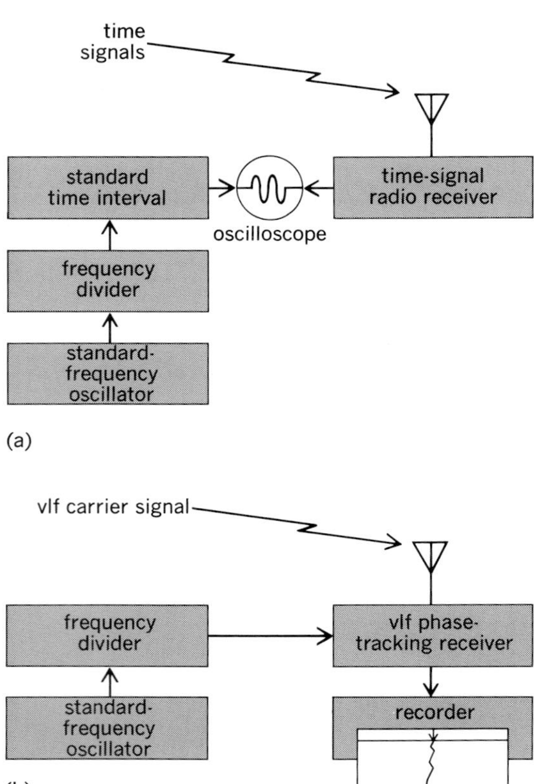


**Fig. 1. Secondary frequency standard calibration methods. Block diagram of (*a*) time signal method and (*b*) phase-recording method.**

thus enabling relatively long intervals between calibrations. Quartz-crystal frequency standards are the least expensive initially and may provide the most satisfactory working standards if calibration means are available. *See Quartz clock.*

Checking and calibrating a secondary standard may be accomplished by (1) use of a very-low-frequency (vlf) phase recording receiver with a vlf standard frequency signal, (2) comparison with loran-C signals on 100 kHz, or (3) use of an accurate clock indicator for comparison with radio time signals (**Fig. 1**). Somewhat less accuracy may be achieved using the high-frequency signals broadcast by station WWV and setting the standard to be calibrated to zero beat with the carrier frequency as received. The reduced accuracy arises from the propagation variations of the high-frequency signal.

*Frank D. Lewis*

**Audio-frequency meters.** A fairly wide variety of frequency meters has been developed and is commercially available. Broadly speaking they can be grouped into two classes, the resonant and ratiometer types. The resonant type may be further subdivided into instruments employing resonant reeds and those having electrically resonant circuits. The latter, as well as the ratiometer type, are classified as deflection-type instruments embodying moving systems with pointers and scales.

The moving systems of the conventional deflection type meters develop two opposing deflecting forces which cause the movement to come to rest when the two opposing torques are balanced. The net torque is directly dependent on the frequency being measured.

Deflection-type frequency meters, commonly used in power frequency applications around 25, 50, and 60 Hz, are also available in other ranges up to about 900. Their accuracies may be in the order of 0.14 Hz in the low frequency ranges and about 4 Hz in the higher frequency ranges.

Resonant-reed-type frequency meters are available in various ranges between 10 and 1000 Hz, with special designs ranging as low as about 7 Hz and as high as about 1500 Hz. Their accuracies, which are independent of their frequency ranges, can be in the order of ±0.1% of specified frequency.

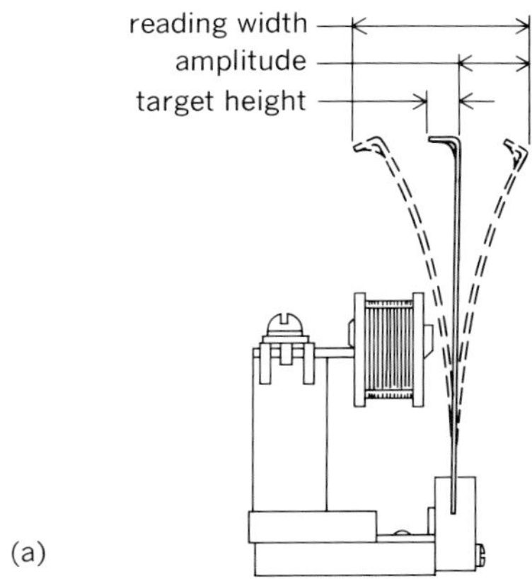


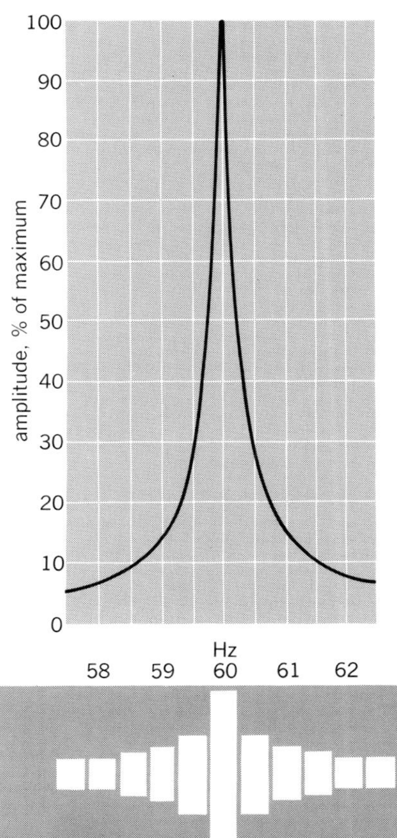


**Fig. 2. Reed-type frequency meter. (*a*) Actuating system of a Frahm frequency meter. (*b*) Resonance curve for 60-Hz reed showing the amplitude of vibration for the various applied frequencies.**

**Fig. 3. Cutaway view of an indirect-drive, switchboard-type frequency meter. (*James G. Biddle Co.*)**

***Reed-type frequency meters.*** This type of meter uses the principle of vibrating reeds. The reeds for such instruments, assembled into a so-called reed comb, are made of specially selected and properly tempered steel. They have bent tips which are enameled white for visibility. When the supply voltage is applied to the instrument, all of the reeds receive vibrational impulses; the effect is visible only in the reed or reeds which are in resonance. The reed in resonance behaves somewhat like a whip, the tip swinging through a readily visible arc, the natural period of vibration depending upon length and thickness. Resonance vibration extends over a limited visible range from about 2% below to 2% above the actual frequency (**Fig. 2**). Individual reeds can be tuned to a range of about ±0.1% of their rated frequencies.

The reeds in the comb are vibrated by an electromagnet energized from the source of which the frequency is to be measured. Depending upon design considerations, a permanent magnet may be used in conjunction with soft iron in the magnetic circuit. The magnetic-drive system usually takes one of two forms.

The direct-drive method drives the reeds magnetically by including them in the magnetic circuit (Fig. 2*a*). In the indirect-drive method the magnetic circuit includes a soft-iron pole piece or armature attached to the base of the reed comb, the armature indirectly transmitting its mechanical vibrations to the reeds. If no permanent magnet is used in the magnetic circuit, the reeds are vibrated at a frequency twice that of the source of voltage and consequent magnetic field. Biasing the magnetic field by use of a permanent magnet causes the reeds to vibrate at the same frequency as the source voltage. **Figure 3** is a cutaway view of a commercial switchboard-type frequency meter using an indirect drive.

***Moving-coil meters.*** **Figure 4** shows one design of a moving-coil resonant-type instrument. Two coils, A and B, are placed at right angles to form a moving element and are supplied through a resonant circuit. The coils are tuned to different frequencies, coil A to a frequency slightly below the lowest scale point and coil B an equal amount above the upper scale point. A fixed coil C divided into two parts carries the sum of the currents of the two circuits of coils A and B. When the frequency of the applied voltage equals the midscale frequency the currents in the two resonant

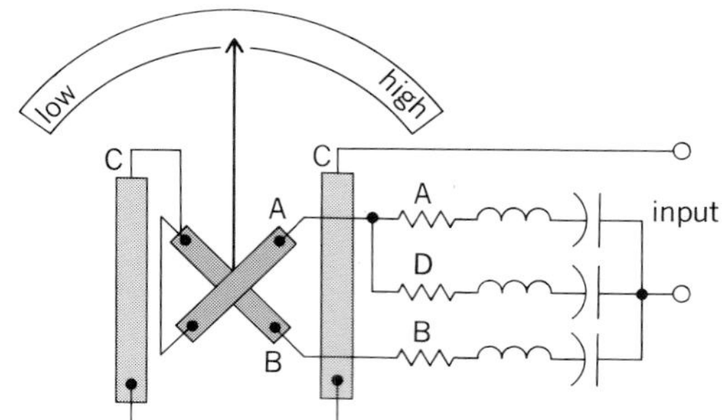


Fig. 4. Resonant-type moving-coil frequency meter.

circuits are practically equal and the phase lead of one coil equals the phase lag of the other with respect to the fixed-coil current. At frequencies near the low end of the scale, the moving element comes to rest with coil A approaching a position parallel to the fixed coil. As the circuit of coil A approaches resonance, the current in coil A is relatively high and in phase with the fixed-coil current and the current in coil B leads with respect to the fixed-coil current. At frequencies in the higher range, coil B approaches resonance and takes an equilibrium position parallel to the plane of the fixed coil. If the supply frequency is very low, the impedance of the circuit A and B being equal, the pointer will indicate a fictitious midscale reading. To rectify this misleading measurement, a third coil D is introduced in parallel with coil A and resonates at frequencies much less than the lowest scale point.

**Figure 5** shows a pictorial diagram of another moving-coil resonant-type frequency meter based on the electrodynamometer principle and usually called a mutual-induction-type instrument. The field structure comprises a laminated magnetic core which is shaped to provide space for a field winding. This construction provides a scale length of approximately 250° and covers a range of 56–65 Hz. An alternating flux produced by the field coil induces an electromotive force in the moving coil which varies with the deflection. This emf is opposed by the voltage drop across the tuned circuit. The resultant voltage causes a current to pass through the moving coil. A torque is developed by the interaction between the moving-coil current and the field flux and deflects the coil until it reaches a position where the in-phase component of its current becomes zero, which causes the torque also to become zero. The equilibrium position changes with frequency because the drop across the tuned circuit and the induced emf both vary with frequency.

***Moving-iron meters.*** A resonant-type frequency meter operating on the moving-iron principle is shown in **Fig. 6**. Two field coils are mounted opposite to each other and are connected so that their fluxes oppose. If $i_1$ and $i_2$ are moving-coil currents, the resultant field current will be $i_1 - i_2$. The moving system which lies between the field coils is comprised of an iron vane of magnetic material centered within the armature coils and rigidly attached to the shaft. Both the field coils are connected to series-resonance circuits in which resonance is produced below the operating range for one circuit and above the operating range for the other. Thus for a frequency range of 55–65 Hz the resonance may occur around 50 Hz for one circuit and 70 Hz for the other.

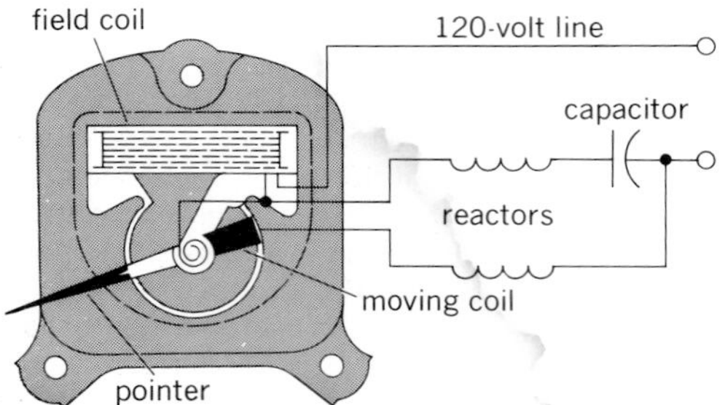


Fig. 5. Mutual-inductance-type frequency meter. (*General Electric Co.*)

Deflecting torque is produced by the reaction of the armature, or moving coil, field with the in-phase component of the field coils. This torque is proportional to the product of the resultant field flux, armature flux, and the cosine of the phase angle of the two fluxes.

In addition to this deflecting torque there is a countertorque produced by the action of the field flux in the magnetic vane of the moving element. When the deflecting torque causes the iron vane on the moving system to be out of alignment with the field flux, the iron vane exerts a torque opposite in direction (to the deflecting torque) because of its tendency to realign itself with the physical direction of the field flux. This countertorque is required to establish a position of equilibrium. This occurs when the magnitude of the countertorque is equal to the deflecting torque, which causes the pointer to take a position indicating the frequency.

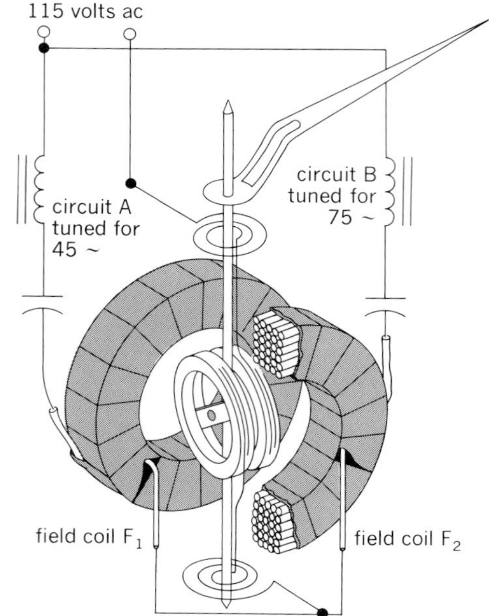


Fig. 6. Resonant-type frequency meter employing the moving iron principle. (*General Electric Co.*)

Another design of a moving-iron frequency meter, but of the ratiometer type, is shown in **Fig. 7**. Two coils A and B are arranged at right angles to each other. Coil A is in series with a resistance $R_A$, and this combination is in parallel with an inductance $L_A$. Similarly, coil B is in series with $L_B$ and the combination is in parallel with $R_B$. The complete circuit thus acts as a bridge network. When the bridge is balanced by suitable values of parameters, the cur-

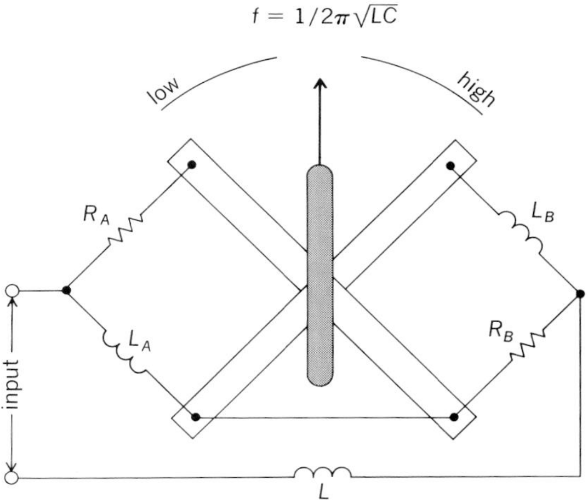


Fig. 7. Ratiometer-type Weston frequency meter which uses the moving-iron principle.

rents in the two coils are equal and the moving element, a pivoted soft-iron needle, will indicate the mean-frequency position as shown in the diagram. When the frequency increases the current increases in coil A and decreases in coil B. The interaction of the fields of the two coils will cause the needle to take up a new position. Hence for each change in frequency the needle tends to align itself along the resultant magnetic fields of the two coils. In this kind of meter the effects of distorted waveforms due to higher harmonics are almost nonexistent.

***Audio-frequency bridge methods.*** An ac bridge is generally made up of a four-arm network, where an ac source is applied to a pair of opposite terminals and a current-detecting device is connected to the remaining two terminals. With the bridge network energized, the current in the detecting device can be made zero by adjusting suitable values of resistance, capacitance, or inductance in the four bridge arms, a process known as balancing.

Bridge networks in which the balancing action depends upon the supply frequency may be used for frequency measurement. The choice of frequency bridge is dependent on the frequency range, the available apparatus, and the ease with which the bridge can be set up and balanced. *See Bridge circuit*.

A simple form of resonant-frequency bridge is shown in **Fig. 8**. Balance is obtained by adjustment

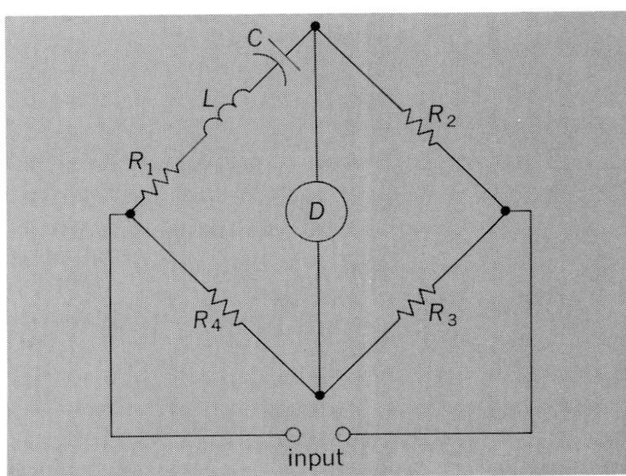


Fig. 8. Resonance-frequency bridge.

of $R_4$ and $C$, the detector D showing zero current. This will occur when $R_1/R_2 = R_4/R_3$ and $\omega L = 1/\omega C$ or $\omega^2 = 1/LC$. From this the frequency is found to be as in Eq. (1).

$$f = 1/2\pi\sqrt{LC} \quad (1)$$

The most commonly employed bridge is the Wien bridge, because it has many advantages of other bridge methods. **Figure 9** is the schematic diagram. $R_3$ and $R_4$ can be varied together. Condition of balance will be obtained when $R_3 = R_4$, $C_3 = C_4$, and $R_1 = 2R_2$.

The frequency of the source is written as Eq. (2).

$$f = 1/2\pi R_3C_4 \quad (2)$$

If the frequency to be measured is in the audio range, a pair of headphones may be used as a detector; for frequencies beyond the audio range an electronic voltmeter can be used.

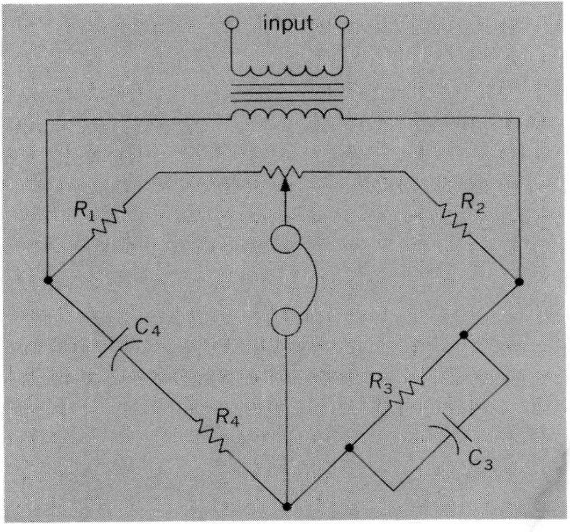


Fig. 9. Wien frequency bridge.

Campbell's bridge is shown in **Fig. 10**. This bridge is used because of its simplicity and fairly large range of frequency. Balance is obtained by adjusting the value of $M$ so that the detector current is zero. Under this condition the voltage induced in the secondary of the mutual inductor $M$ is equal in magnitude and 180° out of phase with the voltage drop across the capacitance $C$.

Hence at balance $\omega Mi = i/\omega C$ or $\omega^2 = 1/MC$, from which the frequency an be written as Eq. (3).

$$f = 1/2\pi\sqrt{MC} \quad (3)$$

***Direct-comparison methods.*** The most widely used of the simpler methods is aural comparison. An unknown frequency can be determined by direct comparison with a known adjustable standard frequency by using the ear. **Figure 11** shows a typical scheme where headphones are connected directly to the two audio sources. The unknown frequency is fed into one earpiece while the standard frequency supplied by a resistance-tuned or a beat-frequency oscillator is fed into another earpiece. A beat note between the two frequencies can be detected by the ear when the frequencies are not exactly equal.

A meter or an electric-eye indicator can take the place of the ear as a detector. An indicating ac voltmeter with a fast d'Arsonval movement may be used.

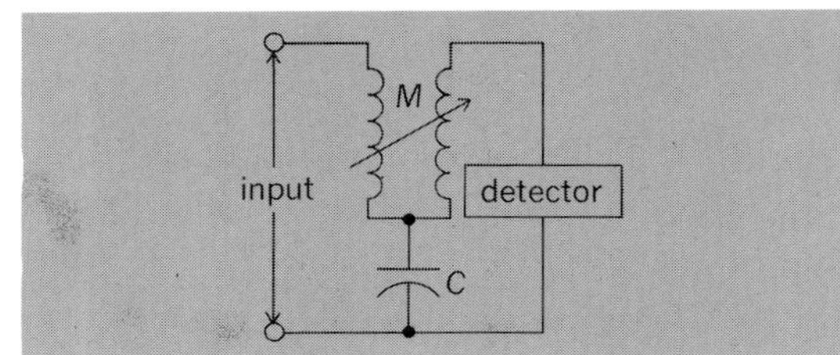

Fig. 10. Campbell's frequency bridge.

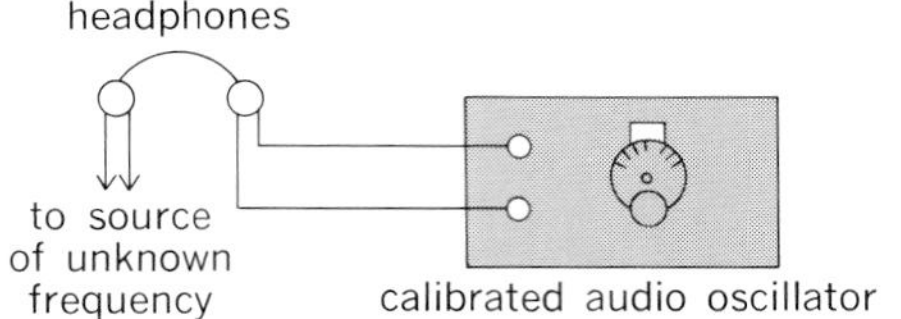

Fig. 11. Aural method of frequency measurement.

Under the influence of the beat note the pointer of the voltmeter vibrates about a mean value of the output voltage. For low values of frequency difference it swings back and forth; for high values it vibrates rapidly. Such a meter or an electric-eye indicator can detect frequency differences of very low values accurately, whereas in the ear method of detection the accuracy of adjustment is limited by the skill of the operator. *See Voltmeter*.

Cathode-ray oscilloscopes provide a most convenient means of comparing two frequencies. The usual method consists of applying a voltage of unknown frequency to one pair of deflecting plates and a voltage of known frequency to the other. The resulting patterns, known as Lissajous figures, are shown in **Fig. 12**. These patterns are a function of the difference in amplitude, frequency, phase, and the waveforms of the two applied voltages and their frequency ratio. Knowing one of the frequencies and determining the difference or the ratio of the frequencies, it is possible to calculate the second frequency. For example, the pattern with five vertical loops is produced by signals whose frequency ratio is 5:3 with the lower frequency on the horizontal plates. Any value of frequency in the audio range can be determined by this method, providing the ratio of the two frequencies does not exceed an approximate value of 10:1. *See Oscilloscope*.

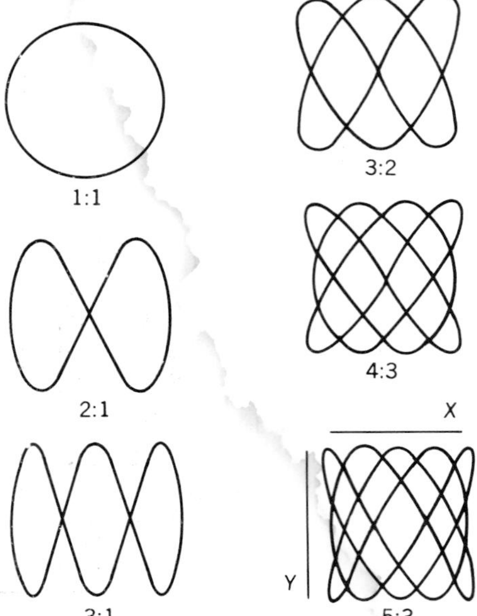

Fig. 12. Lissajous figures for various frequency ratios and phase angles.

***Frequency counters.*** For the basic measurement of audio frequencies one of the simplest methods is provided by frequency counters. In the simplest form, a mechanical counter is actuated by a polarized relay through an escapement or a linkage mechanism. The relay operates on each cycle of low-frequency voltage. The frequency values within the operating range can be determined by counting the number of cycles during a known period of time. Such counters are suitable only for very low frequencies; they are not satisfactory for frequencies even as high as 60 Hz.

For higher frequencies, electronic counters are useful. A block diagram of a commercial design is shown in **Fig. 13**. It shows a block diagram of an electronic counter, where the four stages consist essentially of so-called flip-flop circuits. Stages A, B, C, and D represent 1, 2, 4, and 8 counts, respectively. All the stages can be in two possible states, 1 or 2, signifying OFF and ON position of their neon lamps.

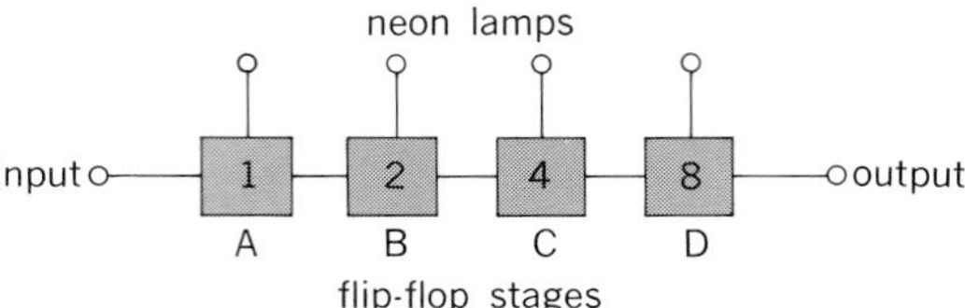

Fig. 13. Block diagram of electric counter.

Starting with all the stages in state 1, when a pulse is sent to the first stage A, it triggers into state 2 and its neon lamp starts glowing. A second pulse sent to stage A will put it back into state 1; however, the pulse will be directed to stage B and its lamp will glow. Stage B is now in state 2, signifying a count of 2. A third pulse will put stage A again into state 2, and now both the lamps of stages A and B will glow, indicating a count of three (1 + 2). A fourth pulse triggers both the stages A and B into state 1. A pulse is sent to stage C which triggers into state 2. The lamp of stage C starts glowing, representing a count of four. The next pulse will put stage A into state 2. The lamp for stage A and C will glow, indicating a count of five (1 + 4). The total count in all cases is equal to the sum of the counts represented by the stages which glow. Thus, if three stages A, B, and C glow, seven pulses will be received, indicating seven counts. Usually four-stage counters of this type are designed so that after nine pulses are received a pulse will be sent to the next counter.

In this type of counter the usual frequency range is 10 Hz to 100 kHz; however, in some cases counting rates of $10^6$ Hz (1 MHz) are possible. *See Frequency counter*.

*Edward B. Curdts*

**Radio-frequency measurements.** Precise measurement of frequencies above the audible range may be performed by various techniques. Basic measuring systems may consist of (1) a calibrated oscillator with some means of comparison with the unknown frequency, such as an oscilloscope or a heterodyne detector unit, (2) a digital counting or scaling device which registers the total number of events occurring during a given time interval, or (3) an electronic circuit for producing a direct current proportional to the frequency of its input signal which then may be indicated by a dc meter. In practice, each of these basic systems has an upper frequency limit for practical operation.

In order to extend the range of frequency measurement above the practical limits mentioned above, it is customary to generate a fixed standard frequency and to select a harmonic of it near the unknown frequency, after which the unknown frequency may be reduced to a lower value by subtraction of the standard-frequency harmonic in a mixer or heterodyne detector. This lower beat frequency may then be measured by application of the basic methods outlined above, which thus serve to interpolate between the known standard frequencies.

The complexity of the equipment required for a given frequency measurement is usually related to the nature of the unknown signal, the amount of manual operation of the controls required, and the precision required. If the unknown frequency is a pure sine wave of local origin or locally controllable, of adequate amplitude, and free from interfering signals, it is possible to measure its frequency by using (1) a digital counter with appropriate range-extending converter and frequency standard, (2) a heterodyne detection and interpolation system with a suitable frequency standard, (3) a calibrated oscillator and detector unit, called a heterodyne frequency meter, or (4) a calibrated absorption circuit such as a wavemeter or grid-dip meter if slightly lower precision is adequate. *See Wavemeter*.

If the unknown frequency is subject to interference, is intermittent in nature, is too low in amplitude to override noise, or otherwise requires selective filtering and identification, the simple systems outlined above require additional equipment and manipulation to produce acceptable measurements. Additional knowledge and skill are required of the operator. Measurements to high orders of precision require longer time intervals than less precise measurements.

***Microwave frequency measurements.*** The measurement of most electrical quantities becomes more difficult as the frequency becomes higher. Fortunately, the measurement of frequency, even in the microwave region, is not of unusual difficulty.

In the microwave range of frequencies the wavelengths involved are so short that it is easy to measure the wavelength and thus obtain the frequency by a simple calculation. Many absorption-type wavemeters are calibrated directly in frequency. The principal difference in technique at microwave frequencies is concerned with the generation of usable harmonics of fixed standard frequency oscillators or of tunable transfer oscillators in the range where measurements are required. Otherwise the use of either the digital counter or heterodyne system interpolation between standard-frequency harmonics is carried out as at lower radio frequencies.

If a microwave signal is locally controllable and of a reasonably steady, strong, and stable nature, it is possible to measure it directly by heterodyning it against a known standard frequency and measuring the resulting beat frequency. It is necessary to have a frequency standard, harmonic-generating multiplier chain, mixer, and either a heterodyne system or digital counter system for measuring the beat frequency. Added complexities requiring tunable receivers for selecting the beat frequency and tunable local oscillators for measuring the beat note are sometimes necessary if the beat frequency is not strong. A block diagram of a decade frequency standard and measuring system is shown in **Fig. 14**.

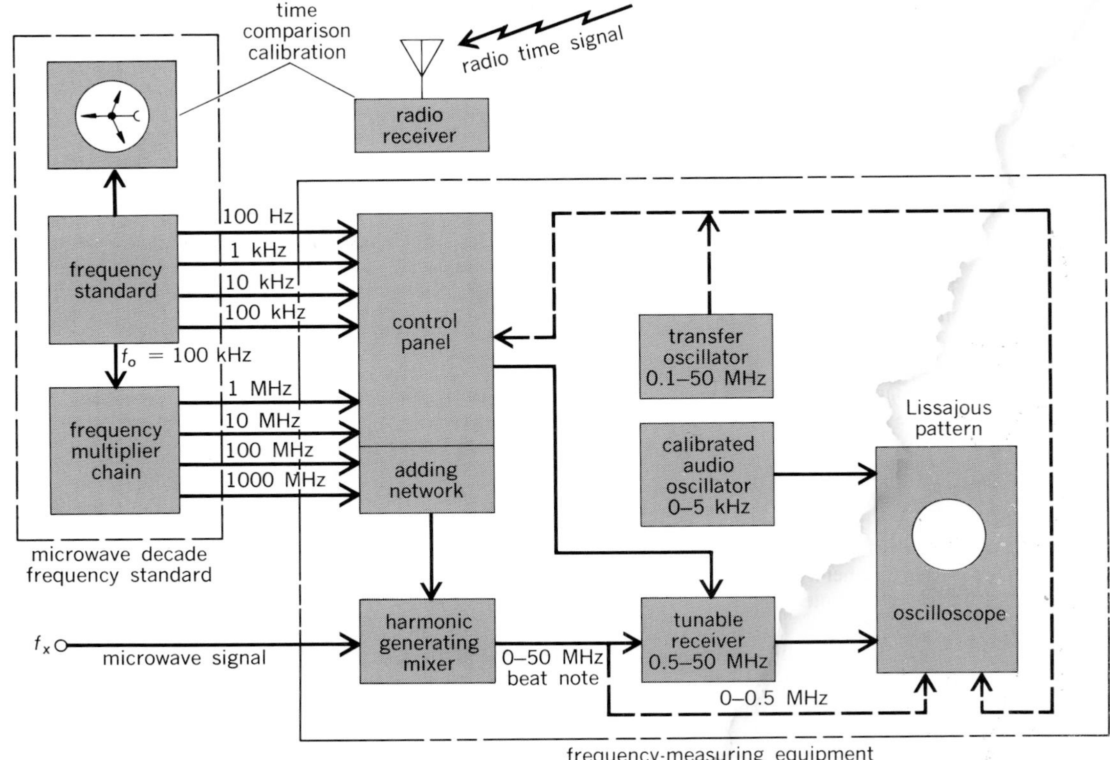


**Fig. 14. Block diagram of microwave frequency standard and frequency-measuring equipment.**

***Transfer oscillator methods.*** Calibrated oscillators may be used for interpolation between standard-frequency harmonics by using their dial calibrations and conventional interpolation methods. Microwave frequencies are usually measured by setting the frequency of the transfer oscillator so that a harmonic of it is at zero beat with the unknown frequency. In this way, it is possible to use the tunable oscillator to transfer the signal to a lower frequency range where it is easy to measure against a frequency standard by direct means. It is usual to provide a tuning range slightly greater than 2:1 for such a transfer oscillator in order to give continuous harmonic coverage at high frequencies.

Transfer oscillators require both high stability and high harmonic output, conditions which are not mutually compatible in one circuit. The stability is generally obtained by using a low-power oscillator with high-$Q$ tuned circuit, the harmonics by separate harmonic generators.

The development of controlled-frequency or synthesizer-type generators enables generation of accurately known stabilized frequencies and hence makes possible directly calibrated transfer oscillators or self-calibrated heterodyne frequency meters. The precision and accuracy of a frequency synthesizer depend on several factors, the limiting item ultimately being the frequency standard.

***Heterodyne frequency meters.*** The calibrated tunable oscillators mentioned above for use as transfer oscillators may be used directly for frequency measurement by their dial calibrations alone. A beat detector and indicator are necessary, as well as a harmonic generator covering the required frequency range; a diode mixer and suitable amplifier with headphones or meter indicator may be used. Unless a synthesizer-type stabilized controlled oscillator is used, the accuracy will not be as good as that obtainable by either the direct measurement or the transfer-oscillator method. Accuracies of 0.1% can be obtained with a well-designed portable heterodyne frequency meter. If an internal calibrating crystal oscillator is used, better accuracy may be obtained. Accuracy of the synthesizer-type approaches that of its reference frequency standard.

*Frank D. Lewis*

**Measurements of laser frequencies.** The frequency of an electromagnetic wave is the number of oscillations of its electric field occurring in 1 s. Electronic counters are available which directly count up to about $5 \times 10^8$ Hz. At higher frequencies, harmonic generation and mixing techniques must be used.

Harmonics of a known frequency $\nu_0$ are generated by radiating a nonlinear device which creates higher frequencies which are whole-number multiples $n$ of the fundamental frequency $\nu_0$. The resulting radiation at a frequency $n\nu_0$ is then subtracted from an unknown, higher frequency $\nu$ near $n\nu_0$ in a mixer to produce a difference or beat frequency $\nu_B$, which is usually at a lower and directly countable frequency. Thus, $\nu = n\nu_0 + \nu_B$, where $\nu_0$ is the known frequency, $\nu_B$ is the directly-counted beat frequency, and $\nu$ is the unknown frequency. At infrared frequencies a tungsten-nickel point-contact diode serves to perform both harmonic generation and mixing in a single device, and in the visible range crystal doublers are used. To measure laser frequencies, a whole series of measurements must be made because the harmonic number $n$ is typically less than 12. The result is an entire chain of frequency measurements linking the fundamental frequency standard (the cesium standard, at $9.3 \times 10^9$ Hz) with frequencies of the various lasers used in the chain. The highest frequency measured is in the visible at $5.2 \times 10^{14}$ Hz, some 56,000 times higher in frequency. SEE POINT-CONTACT DIODE.

The accuracy of frequency measurement is limited only by the stabilities of the oscillators themselves, and in the visible is about a thousand times greater than that of the wavelength measurements. Thus, the extension of frequency measurements to the visible in 1979 represented a major breakthrough in the measurements of electromagnetic radiation.

*Kenneth M. Evenson*

***Bibliography.*** K. M. Baird, Frequency measurements of optical radiation, *Phys. Today*, 36(1):52–57, January 1983; W. D. Cooper, *Electronic Instrumentation and Measurement Techniques*, 2d ed., 1978; E. Frank, *Electrical Measurement Analysis*, 1959, reprint 1977; F. K. Harris, *Electrical Measurements*, 1952, reprint 1975; H. Hellwig, K. M. Evenson, and D. J. Wineland, Time, frequency and physical measurement, *Phys. Today*, 31(12):23–30, December 1978; P. Kantrowitz et al., *Electronic Measurements*, 199; T. Laverghetta, *Microwave Measurements and Techniques*, 1976; *Proceedings of Annual Symposium on Frequency Control*, sponsored by U.S. Army Electronics Research and Development Command, Fort Monmouth, New Jersey; Special issue on time and frequency, *Proc. IEEE*, 60(5):473–648, May 1972.

## Frequency modulation

A special kind of angle modulation in which the instantaneous frequency of a sine-wave carrier is varied by an amount proportional to the magnitude of the modulating wave. In many so-called frequency-modulation (FM) applications, the angle modulation is neither FM nor phase modulation (PM), but one in which the angle changes in some other way in accordance with the modulating wave. SEE ANGLE MODULATION; PHASE MODULATION.

Either amplitude modulation (AM) or FM offers a solution to the important problem of how to impress the message wave to be communicated upon a high-frequency oscillation. Also, either AM or FM permits detection and faithful reproduction of the original message. However, unlike AM, FM does more than just enable communication. FM offers additional important advantages in exchange for extra bandwidth occupancy. Also, FM with negative feedback minimizes noise problems and receiver distortion. SEE MODULATION.

**Instantaneous frequency.** Frequency modulation is defined in terms of a generalized concept known as instantaneous frequency which is directly proportional to the time rate of change of the angle of a sine function, the argument of which is a function of time. When the argument is expressed in radians and the time in seconds, the instantaneous frequency in hertz is the time rate of change of the angle divided by $2\pi$.

In frequency modulation the instantaneous frequency is linearly proportional to the magnitude of the modulating wave.

**Principles.** The **illustration** depicts typical waveforms of AM and FM for increasing magnitudes of a sine-wave modulating signal. Louder tones with AM mean greater changes in amplitude. Louder tones with FM mean greater changes in frequency.

In AM, as the audio volume increases, the peak power of the modulated wave increases, the average power of each sideband increases, the carrier power is unchanged, and the zero crossings (zeros) of the modulated wave are unchanged and correspond to those of the unmodulated carrier, provided the modulation is short of being complete. SEE AMPLITUDE MODULATION.

In FM, as in any kind of angle modulation, the variable zero crossings of the modulated wave carry the information of the message to be communicated. Neither peak nor average power of the modulated wave changes. Even though the total average power remains constant, its distribution with frequency in the transmitted band changes continuously and in a nonlinear manner as a function of the modulating wave.

J. R. Carson in 1922 was the first to present a mathematical analysis demonstrating the wide band of frequencies involved in FM. However, E. H. Armstrong, in his patent in 1933, was the first to have a real appreciation of the noise-reducing properties of FM. At first, there was considerable skepticism about the practical utility of FM. Today, its vast multitude of uses and widespread acceptance are ample proof that for some purposes FM is better than either AM or single-sideband modulation (SSB). Single-sideband modulation conserves bandwidth, whereas FM uses extra bandwidth to reduce noise still lower.

**Advantages.** In radio broadcasting, provided the frequency deviation (peak difference between instantaneous and carrier frequencies) is large and provided multipath transmission effects are small, FM is capable of high-fidelity reception combined with the advantages of reduced noise, less interference between stations, and less transmitter power to cover a given area. Constant average power and constant peak power that is only twice the average power are two factors that permit a ready realization of a simple high-efficiency transmitter, simplify problems of automatic volume control, and allow amplifiers and other devices to operate closer to their maximum power capability without the penalties normally associated with nonlinearities.

**Spectrum.** The spectrum of any angle-modulated wave extends above and below the carrier frequency by amounts which theoretically extend indefinitely. For example, suppose the modulating signal is a single-frequency tone, 1000 Hz, and the carrier frequency is 1,000,000 Hz. The lower side-frequencies in Hz will be 999,000, 998,000, 997,000, and so on, corresponding to the difference between the frequency of the carrier and the frequency of the modulating signal and its harmonics. If $C$ and $V$ are the carrier and modulating-signal frequencies, the lower side frequencies are $C–V$, $C–2V$, $C–3V$, and so on. The upper side frequencies in hertz are 1,001,000, 1,002,000, 1,003,000, and so on, corresponding to $C + V$, $C + 2V$, $C + 3V$, and so on. In addition, the carrier amplitude is reduced when the modulating tone is applied and may even become zero.

This example might suggest that the side-frequency components of an FM wave would always be symmetrical about the carrier, independent of the waveform of the modulating wave. Such is not the case. Unlike the symmetrical spectra of the upper and lower

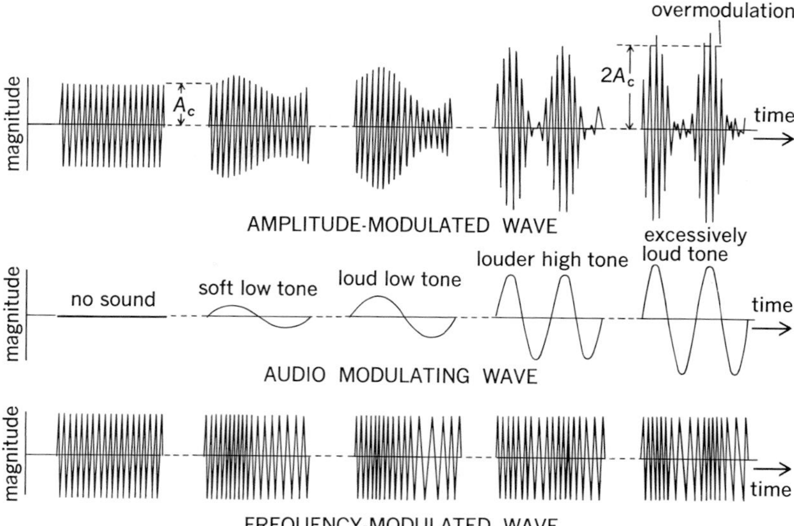


**Waveforms of AM carriers and FM carriers with varying degrees of modulation. (*After H. S. Black, Modulation Theory, Van Nostrand, 1953*)**

sidebands in AM, in FM unsymmetrical side-frequency spectra are a necessary consequence of an asymmetrical modulating wave.

Practically, when estimating approximate bandwidth occupancy, a rule of thumb states that angle modulation requires the band traversed by the instantaneous frequency plus the bandwidth of the modulating wave added at both top and bottom. For some purposes an even wider band may be required.

Moreover, unambiguous representation and recovery of the wanted message by angle-modulation techniques also require that the unmodulated carrier frequency comfortably exceed the sum of the frequency deviation in the down direction plus the bandwidth of the modulating wave. In other words, in FM the carrier frequency must be high compared to the maximum frequency deviation.

**Noise advantage.** For certain types of noise disturbance characterized by a noise spectrum that is uncorrelated and independent of frequency, the ratio of average signal power to average noise power in the output of the FM receiver will be proportional to the square of the peak-frequency deviation. Therefore under certain important conditions, the signal-to-noise ratio of an angle-modulation system improves 6 decibels for each 2:1 increase in bandwidth occupancy.

However, the noise advantage of FM cannot be increased indefinitely. As the bandwidth occupancy is continually increased to accommodate an increased frequency deviation, more noise reaches the FM detector. Presently, the assumption that the noise is less than the so-called improvement threshold is violated, whereupon the noise advantage of FM is quickly lost.

FM with negative feedback acts differently in that the improvement threshold is minimized and held constant, independent of the bandwidth occupied by the incoming FM signal.

***Improvement threshold.*** Any system that reduces noise in exchange for extra bandwidth occupancy is characterized by a threshold effect which becomes pronounced when the reduction is large. For a wideband FM system this threshold is a critical function of the signal-to-noise ratio at the receiver, after selection and before any nonlinear process such as amplitude limiting. When noise perturbations appreciably exceed this critical value, which is termed improvement threshold, the signal-to-noise ratio at the output of the FM receiver rapidly deteriorates. As the noise is still further increased, noise abruptly grabs control and the desired signal tends to be suppressed from the output.

***FM with negative feedback.*** This is accompanied by a decrease in distortion originating within the FM receiver and by an increased tolerance to noise falling within the frequency band occupied by the incoming FM signal. These two important advantages are not possessed by nonfeedback receivers. Substantial benefits are realized only when the amount of negative feedback is large. In common with nonfeedback FM systems, any large reduction in noise must be paid for by a corresponding increase in the bandwidth occupied by the transmitted FM signal.

FM with negative feedback provides an efficient method for the detection and tracking of narrow-band signals in the presence of wide-band noise, especially when the receiver must operate in the presence of large and continuously varying Doppler-frequency effects. In numerous other situations where the saving of power is vital and where extra bandwidth is available, FM with negative feedback may prove attractive, for example, in communications by means of satellites.

When the FM signal is carrying a number of communication channels as in a high-grade multiplex system, nonlinear distortion must be extremely small. This extraordinary degree of linearity is readily obtained with negative feedback. An FM receiver with negative feedback is also characterized by improved stability. With enough feedback, the output becomes virtually independent of such factors as fading of the input signal, power supply voltages, or changes in receiver amplification or detector efficiency.

In a typical nonfeedback receiver, the incoming FM signal is shifted to an intermediate frequency (i-f) by a product modulator fed by a beating oscillator. The instantaneous frequency variations of the i-f signal are then detected, thereby reproducing the original audio (modulating) signal.

With feedback, a portion of the receiver output is fed back and caused to modulate the frequency of the beating oscillator. The receiver output is increased or decreased according to whether the feedback is positive or negative. The amount of feedback is measured by the decibel change in output due to feedback. Negative feedback reduces the instantaneous frequency difference between the incoming FM signal and beating oscillator, thereby reducing the frequency swing (degree of modulation) of the i-f signal.

With sufficient negative feedback, the degree of modulation of the i-f signal is reduced to near zero, thereby reducing the i-f bandwidth to little more than twice the top audio frequency. By this means, the i-f signal is separated from most of the noise existing in the wider bandwidth occupied by the incoming FM signal. Under these conditions, regardless of the bandwidth occupied by the incoming FM signal, the transmitter power need only be enough to override noise in the narrow i-f band.

**Production and detection.** Many schemes are possible and nearly all use spectrum translation. For the production of FM most schemes resort to spectrum multiplication.

***Spectrum translation.*** Spectrum translation of an angle-modulated wave is accomplished by single-sideband modulation. The translated spectrum, with or without inversion, is centered about a new carrier. Otherwise its significant properties are unchanged.

***Spectrum multiplication.*** This implies angle multiplication. By generating the $x$th harmonic of an angle-modulated wave, the angle is multiplied by $x$. If the required multiplication is too great, then after a convenient number of multiplications the resulting spectrum may be translated downward and the multiplication resumed.

Angle multiplication by $x$ multiplies spectrum parameters by $x$. Typical parameters are significant band-width occupancy, carrier frequency, initial carrier phase, instantaneous frequency, instantaneous-frequency deviation, instantaneous-phase deviation, peak-frequency deviation, and peak-phase deviation.

***Preemphasis and deemphasis.*** Widespread use is made of the fundamental principle that by linearly distorting (equalizing) the modulating wave in a predetermined manner (thereby in effect creating a new modulating wave) any given angle modulator may be converted to another angle modulator having an arbitrary response. Similarly, appropriate equalization of the filtered output of a particular angle detector permits realization of an arbitrary detector response. In radio broadcasting, these procedures are termed preemphasis and deemphasis and are used to improve signal-to-noise ratio.

***FM modulators.*** For the most part FM modulators fall into two classes. In class I, a phase modulator is converted to a frequency modulator by first passing the audio signal through a circuit whose output is inversely proportional to frequency. The FM wave thus created normally goes to a spectrum multiplier to increase its frequency deviation. In Armstrong's experiments, this phase modulator consisted of a suppressed-carrier amplitude modulator. Carrier was not only supplied to this balanced modulator in the usual way but in addition was shifted in phase by 90° and then added to the modulator output. When this added carrier is sufficiently large, the resultant output approximates the output of a phase modulator. Armstrong intentionally limited the peak phase modulation resulting from this first step to a maximum range of only 30° in order to ensure reasonable linearity. Consequently, the phase had to be multiplied by several thousand by a succession of spectrum multipliers in order to produce a frequency swing of ± 75,000 Hz with peak audio input. Amplitude limiting in the first multiplier attenuated any residual amplitude modulation associated with the phase-modulation process.

In class II, a capacitance, inductance, potential of a control electrode, or other parameter is varied directly to change an oscillator frequency. Class II modulators usually require spectrum multiplication. *See* FREQUENCY MODULATOR.

***FM detectors.*** Ideally, these would produce output proportional to changes in instantaneous frequency, would not respond to amplitude modulation, and would limit output band to that allocated to the wanted message. In a practical receiver, frequency selection (filtering) is usually followed by spectrum translation and i-f amplification.

Finally, frequency detection is usually accomplished by an amplitude limiter followed by a balanced discriminator, followed by a low-pass filter.

The discriminator converts frequency variation to amplitude variation. *See Frequency-modulation detector.*

Harold S. Black

**Bibliography.** J. Betts, *Signal Processing, Modulation and Noise*, 1971; M. Schwartz, *Information, Transmission Modulation and Noise*, 3d ed., 1980.

## Frequency-modulation detector

Detection or demodulation of a frequency-modulated (FM) wave. FM detectors operate in several ways. In one class of detector, known as a discriminator, the frequency modulation is first converted to amplitude modulation, which is then detected by an amplitude-modulation detector. Another type of FM detector employs a phased-locked oscillator to recover the modulation. A still different type converts the frequency modulation to pulse-rate modulation, which can be converted to the desired signal by use of an integrating circuit. Examples of these types will be discussed here. *See Amplitude-modulation detector.*

**Discriminator.** An amplitude-modulation (AM) detector will demodulate an FM wave, providing the detector is detuned so the carrier frequency is on one side of the passband instead of in the center of the passband. Frequency variations are then converted into amplitude variations or modulation, as shown in **Fig. 1**, and an AM detector produces the desired output signal. This detection technique has serious limitations, however. Low distortion will be realized if the amplitude variation is linearly related to the frequency variation or deviation of the FM wave. This requirement confines the frequency deviation to a linear or straight-line portion of the tuned-circuit response curve. This restriction seriously limits the permissible deviation, and thus nullifies the advantages of FM that result from high deviation ratios. However, amateur radio operators sometimes use this detuning technique to receive narrow-band FM on an AM receiver. *See Frequency modulation.*

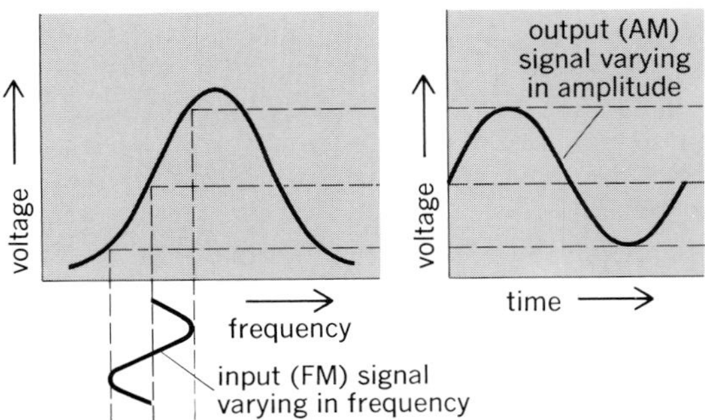


**Fig. 1. Resonant circuit used to convert frequency modulation to amplitude modulation.**

An improved demodulator, known as a phase-shift or Foster-Seely discriminator, is shown in **Fig. 2**. The transistor amplifier is not part of the discriminator, but is shown for completeness. In the circuit, voltage is induced in secondary coil $L_s$, and primary voltage $V_P$ is coupled to the center tap of secondary $L_s$ through capacitor $C$. The relative phase of the secondary current, and hence secondary voltage, changes rapidly with changes in input frequency because the secondary is tuned to the carrier or center frequency. A phasor diagram of primary voltage $V_p$, primary current $I_p$, and voltage $V_s$ induced in the secondary is given in **Fig. 3***a*. Primary current $I_p$ lags primary voltage $V_p$ by 90° because of the inductive reactance of the primary. Secondary voltage $V_s$ is either in phase or 180° out of phase with the primary, depending on the winding direction, because the induced voltage is proportional to the rate of change of the primary current. *See Alternating-current circuit theory.*

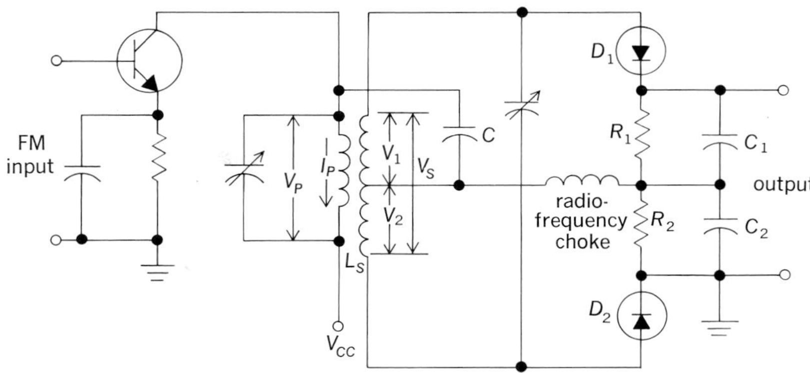


**Fig. 2. Phase-shift, or Foster-Seely, discriminator circuit.**

This situation is shown in Fig. 3*b*. The phasor sum of primary voltage $V_p$ and voltage $V_1$ across coil $L_1$ is applied to upper diode $D_1$ and its load resistor $R_1$. Similarly, voltage $V_{D2}$ is applied to lower diode $D_2$ and its load resistor $R_2$. Capacitors $C_1$ and $C_2$ bypass the radio frequency (rf) around the load resistors. The output voltage is the algebraic sum of the two load voltages, but because the current flows in opposite directions through these diode loads, the output voltage is actually the difference between the load voltages. Thus, if load resistance are equal, the output voltage is zero when the secondary is tuned to the input frequency.

When the input frequency rises above the resonant or center frequency, the secondary circuit is inductive, so the secondary current and the voltage across the secondary coils lag behind their resonant position, as shown in the phasor diagram of Fig. 3*c*. Voltage $V_{D1}$ applied to upper diode $D_1$ and its load resistor becomes larger than voltage $V_{D2}$ applied to lower diode $D_2$ and its load resistor. The difference between these two voltages produces an output voltage of positive polarity. Conversely, if the input frequency decreases from the resonance, the secondary becomes

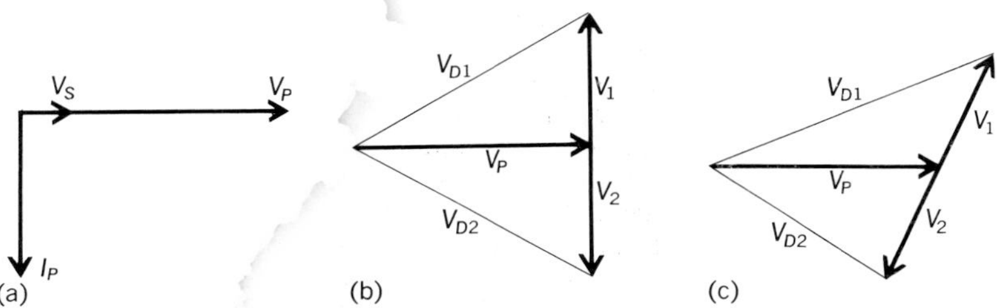


**Fig. 3. Phasor diagrams in a Foster-Seely discriminator. (*a*) Input conditions at resonance. (*b*) Output voltages at resonance. (*c*) Output voltages for input above resonance.**

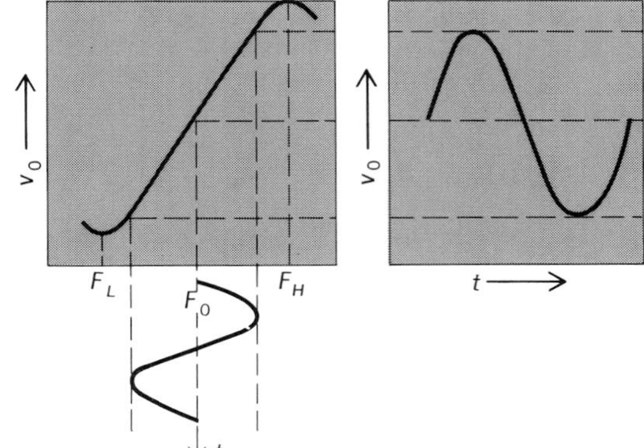


Fig. 4. Linearity and tuning characteristics of phase-shift, or Foster-Seely, discriminator.

capacitive and the secondary current shifts phase in a leading direction. Therefore, a net output voltage having negative polarity is produced.

The output voltage is essentially proportional to the frequency deviation as long as the frequency remains in the linear portion of the response curve of the coupled circuit. As the frequency approaches the edge of the passband, the change in output voltage for a given change in input frequency becomes less than near resonance because of the reduced amplitude of primary voltage $V_P$. Thus, for excursions beyond those for which the tuned circuits are designed, frequency discrimination in the coupling circuit produces waveform distortion in the output.

Linearity and tuning characteristics of the Foster-Seely discriminator are shown in **Fig. 4**. The carrier should be tuned to center frequency $F_0$. Edges of the useful passband are shown at $F_L$ and $F_H$. As illustrated, the output voltage is linearly related to the frequency deviation, providing the total deviation does not exceed about 70% of the passband. This degree of linearity is achieved with a double-tuned coupling circuit, as in Fig. 2, and a coefficient of inductive coupling adjusted to the critical value so that maximum linearity is obtained in the response curve. *See Resonance (alternating-current circuits).*

The Foster-Seely discriminator is sensitive to amplitude variations, or modulation, as well as to frequency modulation, as can be seen from the foregoing discussion. Therefore, a limiter should always precede the discriminator. The limiter removes amplitude variations from the FM signal. *See Limiter circuit.*

A ratio detector (**Fig. 5**) is a discriminator operating on the same principle as the Foster-Seely discriminator but less sensitive to amplitude modulation. The coupling circuit and the addition of the primary voltage to the center tap of the secondary may be identical to the corresponding portion of a Foster-Seely discriminator. However, in the ratio detector, the two diodes are connected so that their load voltages are additive rather than subtractive. In addition, a large capacitor (perhaps 20–100 microfarads) is connected across the series combination of the load resistors. Consequently, the total load voltage cannot follow short-term amplitude variations of the input signal, and the circuit is insensitive to amplitude modulation. However, the individual diode load voltages must vary in the manner described for the Foster-Seely discriminator. Thus, the ratio of the two load voltages changes with the input frequency, even though their sum is forced to remain essentially constant, and hence the name ratio detector.

The output voltage, which is obtained across either of the load resistors, is essentially a linear function of input frequency, providing the requirements placed on the Foster-Seely discriminator are met. In contrast to the Foster-Seely discriminator, the ratio detector has a dc component in the output even when the carrier is unmodulated and the circuit is properly tuned. This dc voltage is usually used for automatic gain control (AGC) when a limiter circuit is not used.

A third winding on the coupling coil, known as a tertiary winding, is often used to produce the voltage which is added to the secondary center tap in a discriminator instead of coupling the primary voltage through a capacitor. In fact, there are many variations of the typical discriminators shown, but they all operate on the same basic principles.

**Integrating detector.** A frequency-modulated wave can be converted to a pulse-rate modulated wave from which the original modulating signal can be recovered by the use of an integrator. The FM input signal is first converted to a low intermediate frequency (i-f) by mixing the input signal with a local oscillator signal in a nonlinear amplifier. *See Amplitude modulation.*

The local oscillator frequency is nearly equal to the carrier frequency, so the difference, or intermediate frequency, is low compared with the carrier frequency. Then the frequency deviation is a high percentage of the i-f. For example, the maximum frequency deviation of a standard broadcast FM signal at 100 MHz may be 150 kHz, or 1.5 parts per thou-

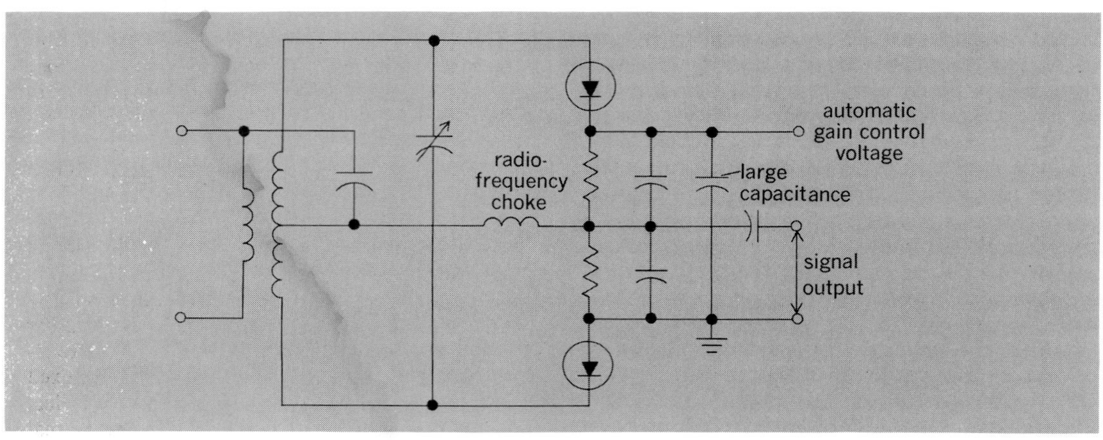


Fig. 5. Typical ratio-detector circuit.

sand. Then, if the i-f is only 200 kHz, the frequency deviation of the i-f is 750 parts per thousand. Thus, the i-f amplifier is normally an untuned low-pass amplifier. The i-f amplifier is followed by a limiter which clips the signal peaks and converts the sinusoidal i-f to a nearly square wave. This square wave is differentiated to obtain pulses which trigger the bistable multivibrator. The multivibrator then produces a rectangular pulse of constant amplitude and width for each input pulse. Therefore, the pulse rate is equal to the input frequency. If the frequency deviation is such that the input frequency is minimum, the pulses are widely spaced for a low-frequency input; on the other hand, the pulses are closely spaced when the deviation produces maximum input frequency. The integrator is basically a low-pass *RC* filter, which produces an output voltage proportional to the average value of the input voltage and filters out the high-frequency components of the pulses. Therefore, the output voltage is proportional to the pulse rate. The simple *RC* integrator can be replaced by an operational-amplifier-type integrator for improved filtering, linearity, and output voltage.

**Locked-oscillator detector.** A third type of FM detector is the locked-oscillator. In this type, a local oscillator follows, or is locked to, the input frequency. The phase difference between local oscillator and input signal is proportional to the frequency deviation, and an output voltage is generated proportional to this phase difference. The phase-locked loop is one of the most dependable and most linear of this type detector. *SEE PHASE-LOCKED LOOPS.*

*Charles L. Alley*

***Bibliography.*** C. Alley and K. Atwood, *Electronic Engineering*, 3d ed., 1973; R. G. Best, *Phase-Locked Loops: Theory, Design and Applications*, 1984; C. A. Schuler, *Electronics: Principles and Applications*, 2d ed., 1984.

## Frequency-modulation radio

Radio transmission accomplished by symmetrical variation of the carrier frequency by an analog input signal. The amount of swing from center frequency is dependent upon the peak value of the modulating voltage, as well as upon its frequency. The frequency of the modulation signal governs the rate at which the changes in carrier frequency occur. Frequency-modulation (FM) sidebands are formed during the modulation process and are separated from one another by an amount equal to the audio frequency. The amplitude of the sidebands diminishes progressively as the sidebands occur farther and farther from the center frequency, and the number of significant sidebands depends on the amplitude of the modulating signal. The deviation ratio of the carrier-frequency variation to the highest signal frequency transmitted may be any selected value, from fractional to large values. The greater the deviation ratio, the larger the bandwidth required for the transmission. Deviation ratios are standardized for various classes of service for optimum use of the radio-frequency spectrum by a large number of stations.

Because there is no amplitude change in the output of an FM transmitter, whatever the deviation ratio, this mode is an almost perfect cure for amplitude-related interference problems that plague radio-frequency reception. The FM receiver should respond only to frequency modulation; therefore, the signal is not amplified in a linear manner. In fact, the signal is amplified, clipped in a limiter, and amplified and clipped in several stages so as to remove completely any amplitude variation. The FM signal is converted to an amplitude-modulated (AM) signal in a frequency-discriminator detector circuit. The threshold for full quieting, noise-free reception occurs when the carrier-plus-noise-to-noise power ratio is about 12 dB. Another property of FM receivers is the relative freedom from interference between distant and local stations using the same channel; only the strongest signal is received, even if the wanted signal is only 3–6 dB stronger than the interfering one. This characteristic is known as the capture effect. In contrast, AM radio signals differing in strength by 35 dB result in noticeable interference. *SEE AMPLITUDE MODULATION; FREQUENCY-MODULATION DETECTOR.*

Since most FM receivers are equipped with a muting circuit (squelch) that silences the audio channel when no signal is present, an irritating hiss noise is not emitted from the loudspeaker when the frequency (or channel) being monitored is not in use. Frequency modulation is used mainly for transmissions above 25 megahertz (MHz). Typical uses are in broadcasting, television sound, mobile radio telephony, radio paging systems, space telemetry, intercity microwave relaying of all classes of public traffic including voice channels, teleprinting, facsimile, broadcast network programs, and television and computer data, and intercontinental telecommunications via satellite. Frequency modulation is used for both analog and digital communications, and phase modulation as well as frequency modulation is employed. The end result, with regard to output waveform, detection, and signal-to-noise improvement, is essentially the same whether phase-modulation (PM) or FM techniques are employed. *SEE PHASE MODULATION; SIGNAL-TO-NOISE RATIO.*

**FM broadcasting.** The frequency band 88–108 MHz is allocated to FM broadcasting in a large part of the world by international agreement. For a channel spacing of 200 kHz, there are 100 allocable channels for transmission of an audio range of 50–15,000 Hz, with a frequency-deviation ratio of 5. This means that there are five significant sidebands above and below the carrier, the carrier is deviated a maximum of ±75 kHz, and the emitted spectrum is twice this value. Because of the relatively small signal power in the modulating frequencies above 4 kHz, the received signal-to-noise ratio is improved substantially by preemphasis of the audio signal in transmission, necessitating complementary deemphasis in the receiver to restore natural program balance. In fact, preemphasis produces a sort of hybrid form of modulation, being pure frequency modulation at the lowest audio frequencies, and gradually changing to phase modulation at the highest. *SEE FREQUENCY MODULATION.*

***Subscription service.*** The large emission bandwidth of FM broadcast stations permits simultaneous transmission of other services by modulating at frequencies above the highest program frequencies. This is accomplished by frequency-division multiplexing. In one such use, one to three separate transmissions use FM subcarriers located between 25 and 75 kHz for subscription or other special services. Normal broadcast receivers will not respond to these multiplexed signals, but special receivers are employed to select at least one of them, to the exclusion of the normal broadcast program. These multiplexed special emissions are called special communication authorizations (SCA).

***Stereophonic broadcasting.*** Most FM stations broadcast stereophonic sound, that is, auditory perspective, because two microphones are used to pick up the program. The output of each microphone is separately routed through the transmitter (by multiplexing), transmitted on the same carrier, separated in the receiver, amplified, and reproduced by two loudspeakers.

Stereophonic transmission must also provide normal reception for nonstereophonic FM receivers. To accomplish this, the main channel modulation consists of combining, by additive polarities, the sum of the outputs from the left $L$ and right $R$ microphones. The multiplexed complementary stereophonic channel transmits the outputs for both $L$ and $R$ microphones, but with their polarities reversed. The main channel $L+R$ provides a complete natural signal from ordinary FM receivers. For stereophonic reception, the multiplexed channel contains the $L$-$R$ signal. Because the $L+R$ and $L$-$R$ signals are antiphased, high-volume peaks occur in one channel when the other is at its lowest. Each channel has access to almost half the total frequency deviation when its signal peaks to its highest volume. The available power is shared between the two, and the nonstereophonic receiver is unaffected by the multiplexed channel.

In this system, the $L$-$R$ channel is amplitude-modulated on a suppressed 38-kHz subcarrier, so that only symmetrical sidebands are transmitted. But transmission of a low-level pilot carrier at 19 kHz, from which the 38-kHz suppressed carrier frequency (2 times the 19-kHz pilot) was initially derived, also takes place.

Both the pilot frequency and the AM sidebands in turn frequency-modulate the main carrier. To be detected in the receiver, the 38-kHz subcarrier must be derived as a second harmonic of the 19-kHz pilot frequency, combined with the AM sidebands in proper phase and amplitude. An FM stereophonic system requires strict technological control throughout, especially in transmission.

A stereophonic FM station may also transmit an SCA service, which must be shifted to frequencies above those employed by the stereomultiplexed channel; a 67-kHz SCA subcarrier is commonly employed.

**Quadraphonic sound.** There was widespread interest in four-channel sound in the mid-1970s. The technology involved the employment of four microphones, left front, right front, left rear, and right rear, and the use of four similarly placed loudspeakers in playback was popularly nicknamed surround sound.

The primary difference between the various discrete and discrete–matrix systems proposed is the number and allocation of subcarrier signals used to scramble and unscramble the signal. Any system must work with existing monophonic and stereophonic equipment. However, there is a question as to whether such a system is worth the technical complexity. If a listener only wants surround sound, a version of it can be obtained by using the halfer connection, which feeds a rear pair of loudspeakers with a difference information available across the outputs of a conventional FM stereo receiver. This simple method provides signals from the rear from almost any program material, and the results can be highly acceptable.

**FM mobile transmission.** Millions of land, maritime, and aeronautical mobile FM transceivers are employed by police, fire fighters, public safety agencies, industrial and commercial enterprises, private citizens, and radio amateurs who desire the benefits of en-route telephony. The intensity of such usage has grown exponentially, mainly because of the availability of reliable, small, low-power-consumption solid-state equipments that are economical, and also because of the public realization of the benefits of having such communications. In fact, the increase in such usage became a major concern to managers of the radio-frequency spectrum when it became apparent that all available channels would be assigned in major city areas.

The channel width assigned for mobile radio telephony has been reduced in some bands to 15 kHz (12.5 kHz in the United Kingdom), from the wide-band frequency modulation initially employed, and state-of-the-art receivers provide intermediate-frequency (i-f) selectivities of $-100$ dB for $\pm 15$-kHz channel spacings. Additional bands have been allocated for mobile radio (800 MHz), and new techniques are being investigated as an alternative to FM, such as single-sideband (SSB), spread-spectrum, stored speech, and the virtual elimination of speech by the use of data transmission in those applications where standard forms of message predominate. SSB transmission, employing linear compression and expansion to combat the adverse effects of fading on SSB systems, has demonstrated that a minimum channel separation of about 6 kHz is possible compared with 15 kHz for FM transmission. SEE SINGLE SIDEBAND.

Typically, mobile telephony is intermittent, each station transmitting only to send. Receivers are open to receive incoming calls on their channel, or the receiver is activated only when certain signaling (touch) tones are received. Simplex transmission is the rule; that is, by means of a press-to-talk button on the handset or microphone, the transmitter is switched on to talk. Many stations can share a channel, each being informed of when the channel is clear.

Mobile transmitters have output powers of 10–30 W. Hand-held units employing powers of 1–6 W are also used. Base stations employ powers up to 250 W. Vertical polarization is used for FM radio telephony, since a mobile whip, which uses the vehicle as a ground plane, is the most practical antenna configuration. The geographical range of such stations is as much as 25 mi (40 km) with the most favorable terrain, but less in hilly or mountainous regions and heavily treed areas (for example, tropical forests). The use of repeaters favorably located on the top of high-rise buildings, or on the top of hills or mountains, increases the useful range for mobile-to-repeater communications to distances of 60 mi (100 km). In the ideal situation, therefore, mobile-to-mobile communication to twice this distance is possible. The repeater, as its name suggests, receives the input signal on one frequency and rebroadcasts it on another frequency, with higher transmitter power or high antenna gain, or both. Amateur radio 2M repeaters employ a frequency spacing of 600 kHz between input and output frequencies, necessitating high-$Q$ cavity duplexers so that the receiver and transmitter can employ a common high-gain antenna. The transmission signal must be attenuated by more than 100 dB, even with adequate receiver i-f selectivity, since the receiver must respond to signals as small as 0.2 microvolt or so in the presence of a transmission signal of tens of volts.

With increasing occupancy of the mobile radio bands by many nearby users operating on equally spaced channels, problems of intermodulation are a major limitation to further expansion in some congested areas. Intermodulation occurs when two or more frequencies combine external to, but usually in, the receiver front end to produce a difference frequency that is the same as the desired frequency. Typically, communication receivers experience intermodulation problems when the combination frequencies are about 80 dB above the receiver threshold, although improved performance is possible with state-of-the-art design.

Amateur radio repeaters have become very sophisticated, with tone burst, subaudible tones which can be used for remote control of the repeater functions, linking, and so on, and push-button autopatch (automatic connection and push-button dialing into the public switched telephone system). The numbers of amateur radio repeaters (simple or complex) have grown at a rate that exceeds development of commercial repeaters, and there are one or more repeaters serving most cities and surrounding areas in the United States and Canada. *SEE MOBILE RADIO*.

***Cellular systems.*** Cellular systems employ equipments operating in the 800-MHz band. The mobile user can move from cell to cell in an urban environment, and these movements are kept track of, whether the user is monitoring, initiating, or receiving a radio-to-telephone interconnect call. Such systems are necessarily oriented toward microprocessor control; in fact they must be if all the functions proposed are to be implemented. Cellular systems and trunking have a great deal in common.

***Radio paging service.*** These paging transmitters, which employ high power, a 600-W centrally located transmitter, or several 60-W transmitters frequency-synchronized to within a few hertz throughout the service area, so that reception is possible employing shirt-pocket-sized receivers and inefficient antennas inside buildings and automobiles, have increased difficulties due to intermodulation. "Beeper" and voice pagers are used. In the voice pager system, the voice of the calling telephone party is broadcast, so that the portable receiver, selectively called by a digital or dual-tone-multifrequency (DTMF) code sequence, receives the message. It is possible with light-emitting diodes (LED) to digitally display the telephone number the paged party is being asked to call. *SEE LIGHT-EMITTING DIODE; RADIO PAGING SYSTEMS*.

**Radio relaying.** Frequency modulation is used for microwave radio relaying over land, over water, and to great distances using satellites, sometimes carrying thousands of simultaneous telephone conversations or several television channels.

The advent of requirements for short-haul services, local distribution networks within cities, television relay, and a wide variety of optical communication services including high-speed computer communications, electronic mail, data transmission, and other services, where it may be cost-effective to avoid the local telephone loop, presents another application for FM radio relaying. While 11 GHz has been used to provide these office communications, an unused band centered on 18 GHz has been proposed as being well suited for such applications.

Frequency modulation is of special importance in this application because the signal amplitude remains constant throughout a substantial range of inevitable propagation path fading due to varying weather conditions. Instead, the background noise varies as the transmissions fade, but the signal level at the output of the limiter remains steady, a highly essential characteristic in a communication system.

In microwave communications, frequencies above 1 GHz and to about 18 GHz are used for terrestrial and satellite relaying. By these means, hundreds of telephone, teleprinter, television, and computer data channels of communications can be transmittted on a single microwave carrier. In large systems, as many as six or eight carriers operating in parallel over the same route, to achieve high capacity, are used.

High communications capacities are obtained by multiplexing, using large bandwidths. Two types of frequently employed carrier modulation are analog frequency-division multiplexing–frequency modulation (FDM/FM), which is more common, and digital phase-shift keying (PSK), which is growing in use. In digital communications the analog signal is sampled at some predetermined sampling rate, and the amplitude is quantized at this sample interval by an analog-to-digital converter. The main advantage of digital transmission consists in the possibility of "overcoming" noise and interference that are caused by human activities by means of special "coded signals" and by reception techniques which are optimum for the given conditions. In uncoded systems the signal-to-noise ratio increases linearly with increased signal bandwidth, whereas in coded systems the signal-to-noise ratio rises exponentially with increased signal bandwidth. This phenomenon can be explained as follows: Doubling of the spectrum width means doubling the number of pulses (or switch transitions) in the code combination, which, according to the rules that govern combinations, squares the number of signals which can be transmitted. *SEE ANALOG-TO-DIGITAL CONVERTER*.

When PSK or FSK (frequency-shift keying) are used with coherent reception, high frequency and phase synchronization are essential. This is a complicating requirement for this form of modulation, particularly since the PSK signal does not normally contain a component at the carrier frequency, and thus some method of synchronization is necessary.

Radio and television broadcasting using digital communications channels is possible. Although such systems are based on the principles of speech transmission, the system parameters are different, owing to the wider band of continuous signals and the necessary increase in the number of quantizing levels. Sophisticated high-speed digital communications equipments employ not just two-level PSK (0 to 180°) but quadraphase-shift keying (QPSK) modulation (0 or 180° as well as 90 or 270°), and thus provide double the transmission capacity.

Most systems employ analog FDM/FM. For example, a normal telephone signal occupying a range of 300–3400 Hz is used to modulate a suppressed carrier, commonly between 60–108 kHz. By means of electronic filters, only a single sideband (SSB) is selected, this being the original signal translated to a higher frequency. These subcarriers are spaced at 4 kHz, so that 12 conversations can fill the 60–108-kHz range. In turn, the 12 channels are multiplexed with other groups of 12, to form a supergroup of 60 channels, similarly transposed. Master groups of 600, 980, 1200, 1800, or 2700 channels are further extensions of the principle.

Finally, the carrier is frequency-modulated by this aggregate of individual channels to occupy a frequency band that may reach 8 MHz. The carrier peak-deviation ratio is fractional for overland relaying. Typical deviation per telephone channel is 2 kHz. Larger per-channel deviations are used for troposcatter systems and in satellite communications. The Canadian Anik satellite system has a maximum capacity of 4800 two-way voice circuits or 10 television channels. The American *Intelsat IVA* satellite was designed to have a capacity of about 10,000 two-way voice circuits or 20 television channels.

**Telegraphy.** Telegraphy, including teleprinting and binary digital data transmission, is based on shifting the carrier frequency or its phase between two limiting values, one of which represents a mark signal and the other a space signal. This frequency shift (or phase shift) is a form of FM signaling used over a wire, cable, or radio. A common approach is to use multiplexed audio tones, each deviated a few tens of cycles (or shifted in phase between two discrete levels), to carry individual messages. A normal voice channel can carry 16–24 such telegraph channels operating at standard teleprinter speeds. High-speed data transmission requires larger bandwidths and more elaborate equipment, but is based on the same principle of frequency or phase shift.

**Facsimile.** Black-and-white images (line drawings and typed copy) can be transmitted by employing the principles used in FM telegraphy; one limit frequency corresponds to black, and the other to white, on the image to be transmitted. It is necessary only that the original document be scanned (for example, by a photosensitive cell), that the scan at the recorder be synchronized with that at the transmitter, and that some means be employed, for example, using an electrosensitive or electrostatic (dry) process, to make the recording paper black when a black signal is received and leave it white for a white signal. A continuous gray scale can be transmitted and recorded if, instead of just two frequencies, a continuous frequency shift is employed between some low frequency (say, 1500 Hz) and some higher frequency (say, 2700 Hz), the exact frequency at any instant being proportional to the gray level of the image. The recorder employs a frequency-amplitude transducer, the response of which is the inverse of that at the transmitter. The audio-frequency tones can be sent over telephone lines; they can modulate an FM radio transmitter, or they can modulate an SSB transmitter. SEE FACSIMILE.

**Telemetry.** Frequency modulation is the preferred method for transmission of information or data from a remote or inaccessible location such as a rocket vehicle in flight. Each condition to be remotely observed actuates one subchannel, which, when multiplexed with other channels reporting other status conditions, modulates the radio carrier by frequency modulation. Telemetry is not much different in principle from FM and PM telegraphy, except that it is a one-way transmission system, with each channel containing a transducer which converts sensed phenomena into electrical signals. The signals may be either digitized coded pulses or continuous (analog) changes. At the receiver, each channel is suitably instrumented to record directly in real time the information reported by the transducer on that channel; or the FM signal can be frequency-translated and recorded directly on magnetic tape for subsequent analysis. Frequency or phase modulation is very useful for digital data recording, since, for example, phase modulation is effective against varying oxide thicknesses on the magnetic tape and varying signal strength. Telemetry systems exist in all degrees of sophistication, up to hundreds of data channels.

*John S. Belrose*

**Bibliography.** N. H. Crowhurst, *FM Stereo Multiplexing*, 1961; *FM and Repeaters for the Radio Amateur, ARRL*, 1974; *Reference Data for Radio Engineers*, 6th ed., 1975; M. Schwartz, *Information Transmission, Modulation and Noise*, 3d ed., 1980; R. L. Shrader, *Electronic Communication*, 4th ed., 1980; S. S. Sviridenko, *Fundamentals of Synchronization in Reception of Digital Signals*, 1974; C. E. Tibbs and G. G. Johnstone, *Frequency Modulation Engineering*, 1956; T. W. Washburn et al., *Development of HF Skywave Radar for Remote Sensing*, AGARD Conf. Proc. 263, 1979; W. R. Young et al., Advanced mobile phone service, *Bell Sys. Tech. J.*, 58(1):1–14, 1979.

## Frequency modulator

An electronic circuit or device producing frequency modulation. The frequency modulator changes the frequency of an oscillator in accordance with the amplitude of a modulating signal. If the modulation is linear, the frequency change is proportional to the modulating voltage.

High-frequency oscillators usually employ *LC* (inductance-capacitance) tuned circuits to establish the frequency of oscillation, and this frequency can be controlled by changing the effective capacitance or inductance in accordance with the modulating signal. A simple example of this type of modulator is a capacitor microphone used as the capacitive tuning element in an oscillator. The acoustic waves that strike the diaphragm of the microphone change the capacitance, which in turn changes the oscillator frequency. The acoustic pressures are usually so small that the capacitance change and the frequency change, or frequency deviation, are linearly related to the acoustic pressures. However, this modulation method is physically cumbersome and seldom used. Practical circuits usually employ either a reactance tube or a varactor diode to change the oscillator frequency in accordance with a modulating voltage.

**Varactor modulator.** The varactor diode is used commonly as a frequency modulator in modern equipment. A typical varactor modulator is shown in the **illustration**. In this circuit the collector voltage of the modulating amplifier controls the reverse bias across the diode. But since the junction capacitance of an abrupt junction diode is inversely proportional to the square root of the junction voltage, the oscillator tuning capacitance, which consists of capacitor $C$ and the diode in series, is therefore controlled by the modulation signal. The resistance of $R$ must be small in comparison with the reactance of either capacitor $C$ or the diode at all modulating frequencies. Otherwise, the high modulating frequencies will be attenuated. Also, the resistance of $R$ must be large in comparison with either the reactance of $C$ or the re-

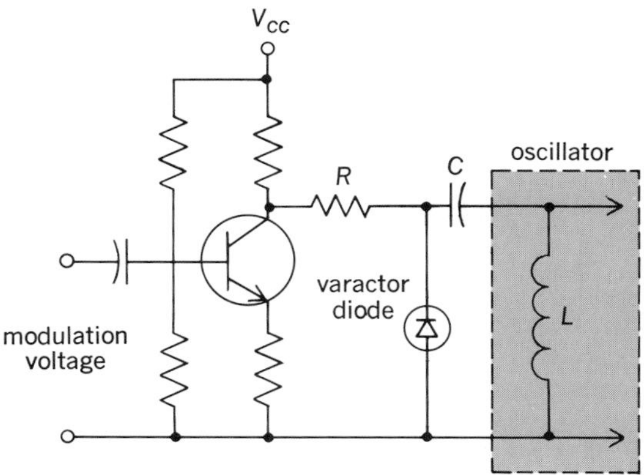


Elementary varactor-diode modulator.

actance of the diode at the oscillator frequency. Otherwise the $Q$ of the tuned circuit will be degraded.

**Linearity and bandwidth.** Because the frequency of oscillation is not linearly related to the tuning capacitance, modulation distortion will occur in either the reactance tube or the varactor modulators. This distortion can be limited to any desired value, however, by limiting the amplitude of the modulating signal. For example, the modulation distortion of the varactor-diode modulator will be less than 4% if the peak amplitude of the modulating signal is limited to one-tenth of the average bias voltage.

Frequency-modulation systems can be easily devised for low-frequency systems by controlling the base or gate bias supply voltages to relaxation oscillators such as multivibrators or unijunction oscillators. The frequency deviation of these oscillators is a fairly linear function of the modulating voltage. Sinusoidal voltages may be obtained, if desired, from these circuits by passing the output signal through a tuned amplifier. Frequency modulation can also be obtained by phase modulation.

**Voltage-controlled oscillators.** Oscillators having a linear relationship between their output frequency and a controlling voltage have been developed for use in phase-locked loops. Known as voltage-controlled oscillators, they are available in integrated-circuit form either as a separate chip or as a separately usable section of an integrated phase-locked loop. Voltage-controlled oscillators have excellent linearity over very wide frequency deviations and are available for frequencies up to 60 mHz. They may have many applications as frequency modulators. *See Phase-locked loops.*

There is no frequency-modulation index $m_f$ corresponding to the 100% amplitude modulation. The index $m_f$ is the ratio of the frequency deviation to the modulation frequency, and the optimum frequency deviation depends upon the bandwidth of the receiving system. This bandwidth must be approximately two times the sum of the frequency deviation and the modulation frequency. *See Frequency modulation; Phase modulation.*

*Charles L. Alley*

**Bibliography.** C. L. Alley and K. W. Atwood, *Electronic Engineering*, 3d ed., 1973; A. P. Malvino, *Electronic Principles*, 3d ed., 1984; C. A Schuler, *Electronics: Principles and Applications*, 2d ed., 1984.

## Frequency multiplier

An electronic circuit that produces an output frequency which is an integral multiple of the input frequency. There are two basic types of frequency multipliers. The first type is a nonlinear amplifier which generates harmonics in its output current and a tuned load that resonates at one of these harmonics. The second type uses the nonlinear capacitance of a junction (semiconductor) diode to couple energy from the input circuit, which is tuned to the fundamental, to the output circuit, which is tuned to the desired harmonic.

**Nonliner amplifier.** Harmonic-generating amplifiers are usually operated class C, biased so that the output current flows for only a small part of the input cycle, perhaps 90°. The output is then richer in harmonics, and higher efficiency is attained than with normal class C bias. The output circuit may be tuned to any harmonic, but the higher harmonics are weaker and the power output may be less than the power input if the selected harmonic is higher than the third or fourth. *See Amplifier.*

A highly efficient doubler can be devised by using two amplifiers, such as transistors, with their inputs driven with opposite polarity, obtained from opposite ends of a center-tapped coil, and their outputs connected in parallel.

These amplifier-type frequency multipliers are often used in crystal-controlled high-frequency transmitters. The crystal oscillator is desirable because of its excellent frequency stability, but crystals are available for only a limited frequency range. Therefore, a moderate crystal-oscillator frequency is multiplied to a high output frequency.

**Nonlinear coupler.** Diode-type multipliers are usually used in very high-frequency or ultrahigh-frequency solid-state transmitters. The frequency limit at which a transistor has useful power gain is highly dependent upon the power output capability of the transistor. Varactor-diode multipliers are often used to provide an output frequency for the transmitter that is several times as high as the frequency limit of the power transistor or transistors in the transmitter.

Efficiency is of prime importance in this type of multiplier because the transmitter power output is the power output of the final transistor amplifier minus the power loss in the multiplier. Fortunately, the efficiency of varactor-diode multipliers may be as high as 80–90% if the circuit and diode $Q$s are high and the multiplication in each stage is no greater than two or three. The multipliers can be advantageously connected in cascade if higher multiplication ratios are desired. A typical varactor-diode multiplier circuit is shown in the **illustration**. Coil $L_1$ and capacitor $C_1$

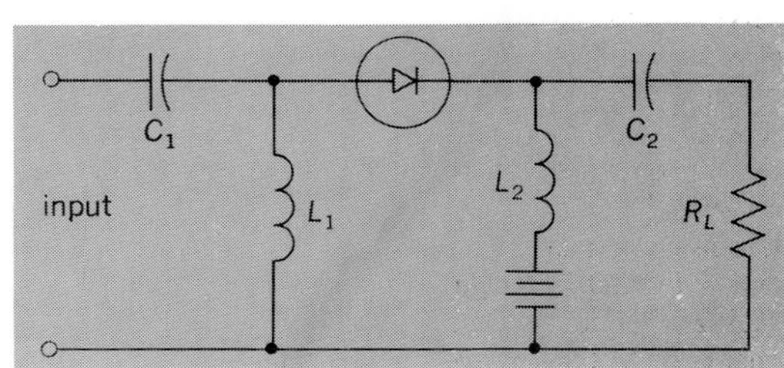


A varactor-diode multiplier.

resonate near the input frequency, while coil $L_2$ and capacitor $C_2$ resonate near the output frequency. *SEE SEMICONDUCTOR; VARACTOR.*

*Charles L. Alley*

## Frequency-response equalization

The process of obtaining a desired overall frequency-response characteristic in an audio-frequency circuit by introducing corrective electrical networks of various types, termed equalizers, into the circuit.

Equalizers are used both in communications networks and in systems for the recording and reproducing of photographic film, magnetic tape, and disk phonograph records. These equalizers are in the form of electrical networks of resistance, inductance, and capacitance. The position of the frequency-response characteristics with respect to frequency can be varied by a choice of values of $R$, $L$, and $C$. The maximum variation is 6 dB/octave. Larger variations can be obtained by cascading equalizers. Equalizers employing resistance and capacitance are shown in **illus.** *a*. Equalizers employing resistance and inductance are shown in illus. *b*. Equalizers employing resonant circuits consisting of resistance, inductance, and capacitance are shown in illus. *c*.

Referring to the figure, it will be seen that practically any type of equalization can be obtained from the systems and combinations of the systems shown. All major record companies in the United States use the RIAA (Record Industry Association of America) standard in their recordings; thus the provision of a large number of equalizing or playback settings on hi-fi amplifiers has become unnecessary. *SEE AMPLIFIER; DISK RECORDING.*

*Harry F. Olson*

## Function generator

An electronic instrument which generates periodic voltage or current waveforms that duplicate various types of well-defined mathematical functions. The simplest function generator usually generates a combination of square waves, triangular waves, and sine waves (**Fig. 1**).

One electronic circuit approach to the design of a simple function generator is to begin with a bistable multivibrator of "flip-flop" controlled in time by a succession of clock pulses which generates the square wave (**Fig. 2**). The triangular waveform is obtained by integrating the square wave through the use of the operational amplifier integrator. The sine wave is obtained by applying the triangular wave to a shaping circuit consisting of a combination of resistors and diodes. *SEE AMPLIFIER; MULTIVIBRATOR; WAVE-SHAPING CIRCUITS.*

Alternatively the sine wave may be generated by a sinusoidal oscillator (**Fig. 3**). From this output, the square wave may be obtained by amplication, limiting, and clipping of the sine wave. Then the triangu-

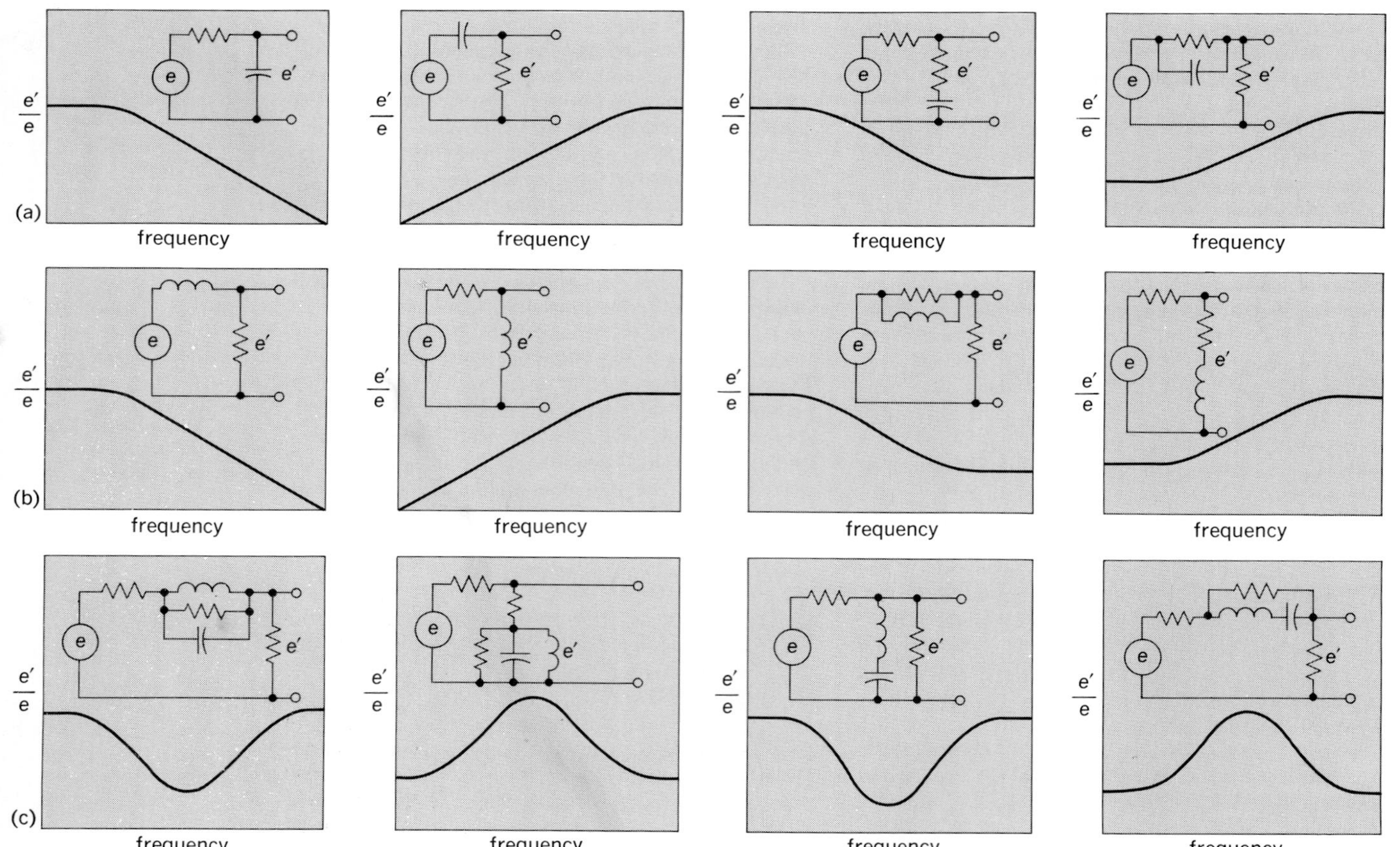


**Circuit diagrams and frequency-response characteristics of equalizers employing combinations of (*a*) resistance and capacitance. (*b*) resistance and inductance, and (c) resistance, inductance, and capacitance.**

Fig. 1. Waveforms generated by a simple function generator.

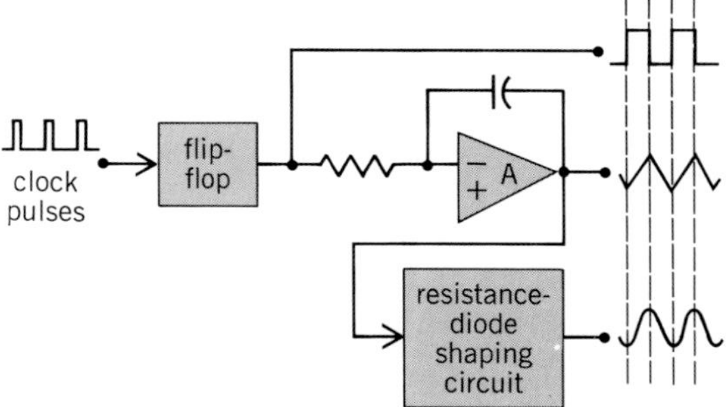


Fig. 2. Elementary function generator.

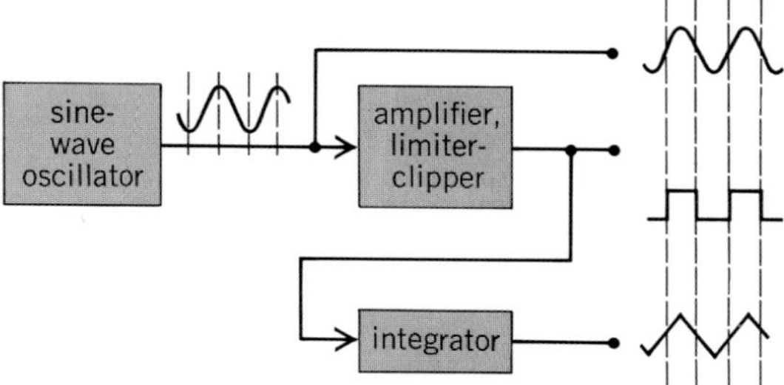


Fig. 3. Alternate form of a function generator.

lar wave may be obtained using an integrator as before. *See Clipping circuit; Limiter circuit.*

A still different configuration of a function generator consists of a circuit, which simultaneously generates triangular waves and square waves, whose rate is controllable by a direct-current level (**Fig. 4**). Such a circuit is identified as a voltage-controlled oscillator (VCO). One of the outputs can be applied to a resistor-diode shaping circuit to obtain the sine wave output. *See Frequency modulator; Phase-locked loops.*

More sophisticated function generators have circuits built in which will allow many other waveforms to be generated, such as parabolic waveforms and logarithmic functions, using combinations of resistor-diode combinations.

A combination of counters, programmed read-only memories (PROMS), and a digital-to-analog converter can be used as a function generator, generating almost any function desired to almost any degree of accuracy. *See Computer storage technology; Digital-to-analog converter.*

*Glenn M. Glasford*

**Bibliography.** J. A. Connelly, *Analog Integrated Circuits*, 1975; J. Millman and H. Taub, *Pulse, Digital, and Switching Waveforms*, 1965.

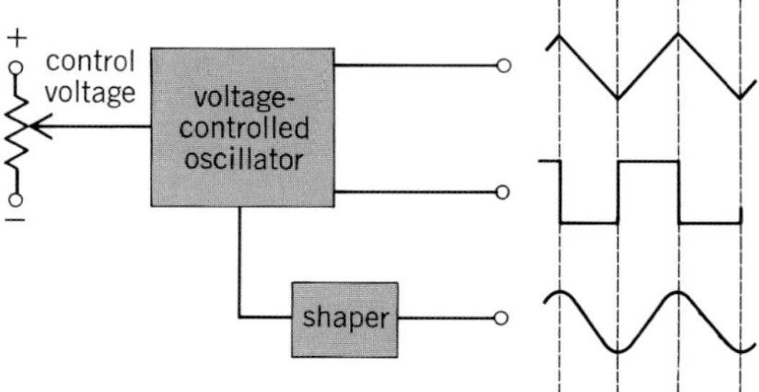


Fig. 4. Voltage-controlled oscillator as a function generator.

## Gain

A general term used to denote an increase in signal power or voltage produced by an amplifier in transmitting a signal from one point to another. The amount of gain is usually expressed in decibels above a reference level. *See Amplifier.*

Antenna gain is a measure of the effectiveness of a directional antenna as compared to a nondirectional antenna. It is usually expressed as the ratio in decibels of standard antenna input power to the power input to a directional antenna that will produce the same field strength in the desired direction. The more directional an antenna is, the higher is its gain. *See Antenna.*

*John Markus*

## Gas discharge

A system made up of a gas, electrodes, and an enclosing wall in which an electric current is carried by charged particles in response to an electric field, the gradient of the eletric potential, or the voltage between two surfaces. The gas discharge is manifested in a variety of modes (including Townsend, glow, arc, and corona discharges) depending on parameters such as the gas composition and density, the external circuit or source of the voltage, electrode geometry, and electrode material. A gas discharge can also be inductively coupled to an alternating-current (ac) circuit, eliminating the need for electrodes. Gas discharges are useful both as tools to study the physics existing under various conditions and in technological applications such as in the lighting industry and in electrically excited gas lasers. *See Laser.*

The study of gas discharges encompasses a broad range of topics in physics and engineering, only a few of which are mentioned here. New applications in gas insulation, in high-power electrical switching, and in materials reclamation and processing will assure a continuing effort to better understand all aspects of gas discharges. *See Gas tube.*

**Sources of electrons.** Electrons, rather than ions, are the main current carriers in gas discharges because their mass is smaller and their mobility is correspondingly much higher than that of ions. Electrons are produced by ionization of the gas itself, or they originate at the electrodes present in the system. Gas ionization can be accomplished in several ways, including electron impact ionization, photoionization, and associative ionization. Bombardment by photons, energetic ions or electrons, and excited neutral particles can cause secondary emission from the electrodes. A high-energy-per-unit electrode surface area can induce thermionic or field emission of electrons. Each of these means of producing electrons leads to a different response of the gas discharge as a circuit element. *See Electron emission; Field emission; Ionization; Photoemission; Secondary emission; Thermionic emission.*

**Townsend discharge.** A nonself-sustained discharge is one in which an agent external to the circuit is necessary to replenish the electrons lost from the system in order to maintain a flow of current; an example is a Townsend discharge. A Townsend discharge, considered here in a parallel plate electrode geometry, is a low-current (less than $10^{-5}$ A) discharge in which the primary source of current carriers is, for example, photoemission resulting from illumination of the cathode. The electrons gain energy from the electric field between the electrodes and lose energy to the gas through elastic and inelastic collisions with the neutral gas particles. Except in regions very near the electrodes, the energy gained by the electrons from the field balances that lost in collisions, and the discharge characteristics can be parametrized simply by the neutral gas composition and by the ratio of the field strength $E$ to the neutral gas density $n$. Townsend discharges have been widely used to study the physics of the interaction of electrons with neutral gas particles because external control of $E/n$ provides a convenient means for adjusting the electron energy. *See Townsend discharge*.

**Gas breakdown.** For $E/n$ greater than about $10^{-19}$ $V{\cdot}m^2$ (100 townsends) some of the electrons have sufficient energy to produce additional ionization in collisions with the neutral gas particles. The succeeding generation of electrons may also produce further ionization, and if the volume rate of ionization exceeds the volume losses due to diffusion and attachment, an exponential increase in the electron density results. This cascade is termed an electron avalanche. If the avalanche grows to the point where the gas loses its insulating properties and becomes highly conducting, gas breakdown is said to have occurred. The luminosity accompanying gas breakdown is due to electron impact excitation of the gas particles which then subsequently radiate. Lightning is a familiar example of the effect.

In determining the minimum voltage required for a self-sustained discharge, electron emission from the electrodes must be considered as well as the cascade ionization; that is, electrons originating from secondary emission at the electrodes must be considered in determining the minimum applied voltage for which the electron sources in the discharge balance the losses. The Paschen curve shows that this minimum voltage, or sparking potential, is a function of the product of the gas pressure $p$ and the electrode separation $d$. The sparking potential at a given value of $pd$ depends on gas composition, electrode material and geometry, and applied field frequency, but a minimum in the sparking potential always occurs at a finite value of $pd$. *See Breakdown potential; Electric spark*.

**Glow discharge.** At pressures lower than about 100 torr (13 kilopascals), but depending on the gas composition, a succession of overlapping avalanches between two electrodes leads to the very stable glow discharge, where space-charge fields adjust themselves so that the volume production of ionization, and the resulting secondary emission from the electrodes, balances the loss of the current carriers. The glow discharge is characterized by moderate current ($10^{-5}$ to $10^{-2}$ A) and voltage (on the order of 100 V), a particular field distribution due to the space-charge distortion of the applied field, and a well-defined luminosity pattern between the electrodes. In addition, the average electron energy is considerably higher than the average kinetic or internal energies of the neutral particles. In the normal glow discharge, the discharge voltage and the current density are nearly constant. An increase in current is achieved by reducing the external circuit impedance or by increasing the source voltage, which causes an increase in the electron-emitting area on the cathode surface. Once the glow covers the cathode surface, an additional increase in current is associated with an increase in the discharge voltage and in the current density. This regime is termed the abnormal glow. *See Glow discharge*.

**Arc.** By lowering the circuit resistance, or increasing the source voltage, a further increase in current can be realized. Past a certain current level, however, this increase is accompanied by an abrupt change in the discharge characteristics, and this high-current discharge mode is termed an arc. An arc is distinguished operationally from a glow by the large currents and the small voltage drop. A more fundamental distinction can be made by considering the sources of the ionization. A low-pressure arc is sustained by thermionic or field emission of electrons from the electrode surfaces; secondary electron emission and electron impact ionization are still present but are not very important as electron sources. At higher pressures, volume sources of electrons dominate, but the sources involve multistep, cumulative ionization through excited states, rather than the electron impact ionization predominantly from ground-state neutral particles, which is characteristic of most glow discharges. The range of applications of arcs is enormous. *See Arc discharge*.

**Glow-to-arc transition.** At pressures higher than about 100 torr (13 kPa), depending on the gas composition, the glow discharge is not stable and has a tendency to constrict to form an arc. The details of the mechanisms for the glow-to-arc transition are not clearly established, but involve changes in the kinetic and internal energy of the gas due to the large amounts of energy deposited in the gas. In a high-pressure arc, the gas is hot and highly excited, and collisions between electrons or neutral particles and excited gas particles produce most of the ionization; that is, the system approaches local thermodynamic equilibrium described by temperatures on the order of $10^3$ to $10^4$ K ($2 \times 10^3$ to $2 \times 10^4$ °F). Diffusion at the lower pressures tends to dissipate the energy in the gas and to stabilize the discharge in the glow mode, but the lower diffusion at higher pressures leads to nonuniform gas heating and excitation in the center of the discharge and the associated highly conducting arc. Any other nonuniformities in the system, either in the gas or on the electrodes, can also provide a seed for arc formation at high pressures. Arcs are undesirable in applications that depend on uniform volume excitation of the gas such as electrically excited gas lasers.

**Corona discharge.** This discussion has implicitly focused on parallel plate electrode geometries. Discharges in irregular geometries where the applied field confines the current density to localized regions are called corona discharges. These relatively low-current, high-voltage discharges occur in Townsend or glow discharges with point-plane electrode configurations or around conductors with a small radius of curvature, and are often intermittent. Corona discharges can represent significant power losses in high-voltage transmission lines. *SEE CORONA DISCHARGE; ELECTRICAL CONDUCTION IN GASES.*

*Leanne C. Pitchford*

**Bibliography.** J. D. Cobine, *Gaseous Conductors*, 1941; M. N. Hirsh and H. J. Oskam (eds.), *Gaseous Electronics*, vol. 1: *Electrical Discharges*, 1978; L. B. Loeb, *Fundamental Processes of Electrical Discharges In Gases*, 1939; J. M. Meek and J. D. Craggs (eds.), *Electrical Breakdown in Gases*, 1978.

## Gas tube

An electron tube, usually a diode (see **illus.**) or triode, containing a gas. The gas contributes two significant advantages: (1) The plasma, or gas of electrons and ions, that is formed in the gas during conduction allows space-charge effects to be overcome; and (2) the gas acts to reduce power dissipation at electrodes. These factors result in tubes that can conduct high currents and remain in use for long periods. Gas tubes are particularly important for high-power applications. Two important types are the thyratron and the gas-filled rectifier.

**Voltage and current characteristics.** The voltage and current characteristics of a gas tube differ from those of a vacuum tube. In a vacuum tube, quasifree charge, or space charge, is present. The power dissipated in a vacuum tube (which is the product of the voltage drop times the current) is usually larger because of the electric fields produced by space charge. This is described by the Child-Langmuir law, which states that the current in a vacuum diode is proportional to the voltage to the $3/2$ power. In addition, the charges between electrodes acquire significant energy from the applied voltage and release this energy when they strike the electrode. These two means of energy loss are reduced in a gas tube for the following reasons. As electrical breakdown occurs in a gas tube, a plasma is formed. A plasma is a mixture of electrons and ions that may be electrically neutral overall, because the electrons are provided by the ions, and thus the net charge is balanced. When a potential is applied, the positive charges move in a direction opposite to that of the electrons. Thus, it is possible to overcome the obstacle of the large electric fields due to space charge, and provide more charges besides, by producing a plasma. Most current is carried by the electrons, because their mass is much less than even the lightest of positive ions, and they move much faster than a heavy ion in the same potential field. The gas also acts to slow down electrons because of collisions between electrons and un-ionized atoms or molecules within the plasma. This reduces energy loss at the electrodes. *SEE ELECTRICAL CONDUCTION IN GASES; LANGMUIR-CHILD LAW; SPACE CHARGE; VACUUM TUBE.*

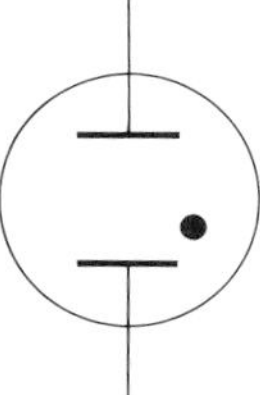

Symbol for a gas-filled diode.

Most of the potential fall in a tube occurs at the interface between the plasma and cathode. This region includes the cathode fall, which is a thin sheath that has a potential drop that corresponds to the energy required to ionize the gas in the tube. Thus, electrons are emitted from the cathode (requiring energy), and accelerated through a potential until they have sufficient energy to begin ionizing the gas that is present. This energy varies, depending on the ionization potential of the gas. *SEE IONIZATION POTENTIAL.*

**Choice of gas.** The gas is chosen with regard given to hold-off voltage and current-handling capabilities, as well as other factors related to specific applications, such as rate of rise of current (turn-on time), which is important for some pulsed applications. For example, mercury and xenon are used for high-current applications, and hydrogen is used for high-voltage applications.

**Thermionic cathode.** Many gas tubes use a thermionic or hot cathode, that is, a cathode that is heated and produces current through emission from a low-work-function material such as barium oxide. The development of improved cathodes remains an important technological problem. A good thermionic cathode allows a tube to operate for long periods with excellent repeatability and good current-handling capability. *SEE THERMIONIC EMISSION.*

**Applications.** Solid-state devices have replaced vaccum and gas tubes for many applications. Among the important remaining applications for gas tubes are high-power switching and pulsed-power applications requiring high power and rapid closing, or turn-on. For example, the hydrogen thyratron is still used as a radar modulator switch, and is also applied to the switching of high-power lasers. *SEE LASER; RADAR.*

**Types of tubes.** The hydrogen thyrattron is a triode that operates at hydrogen pressures between 300 and 900 millitorr (40 and 120 pascals). A plasma is formed, and a glow discharge may be seen in a glass-enclosed tube during the closed or on phase. Hydrogen thyratrons are rated for stand-off voltages up to about 50 kV, and peak currents up to about 5000 A (off the shelf). They also close, or turn on, rapidly. They use a thermionic cathode and have a reservoir of hydrogen within the tube. They achieve a high stand-off voltage through an interesting "trick." The grid is positioned very near the anode—about 0.1 in. (2 or 3 mm)—rather than away from it. The high stand-off voltage occurs because the average distance that an accelerated electron travels is comparable to the grid-anode separation, thus reducing the ionization of the gas, and therefore preventing breakdown. The stand-off voltage in one hydrogen thyratron may be 20 kV, but that tube can be switched on with only 100 to 200 V, applied between the grid and cathode. *SEE BREAKDOWN POTENTIAL; ELECTRICAL BREAKDOWN; GLOW DISCHARGE.*

Other gas-phase switches include the ignitron, where a pool of mercury serves as a cathode and mercury vapor is the conducting gas; the liquid-metal plasma tube, where a small amount of mercury is distributed over a metal cathode; the crossed-field tube, using a magnetic field to bend the paths of electrons; spark gaps; mercury rectifying tubes; and gas voltage regulators, which take advantage of a constant voltage across a glow discharge to clamp the voltage of an erratic source.

The spark gap has applications for very high voltages and currents. It operates in an arc mode, rather than a glow-discharge mode. The gas may be at atmospheric pressure, and gases such as nitrogen and helium are used. The spark gap tends to suffer from electrode degradation caused by arcing, but is able to stand off higher voltages and conduct higher currents than other gas-phase switches. *See* Arc discharge; Spark gap.

**Outlook.** Gas tubes are expected to retain their importance for higher-power applications, for example, voltages exceeding roughly 5 or 10 kV, along with high currents and fast turn-on. They are resilient to most perturbations. However, the continuing development of solid-state devices is expected to have increasing effect in this area as well: the thyristor (a *pnpn* semiconductor) has already made significant inroads. *See* Semiconductor rectifier.

*Martin Gundersen*

**Bibliography.** S. Flügge (ed.), Gas discharges, *Handbuch der Physik*, vols. 21 and 22, 1956; J. A. Kunc and M. Gundersen, A fundamental theory for high-power thyratrons, I and II, *Lasers and Particle Beams*, vol. 1, pt. 4, pp. 395–425, 1983; L. Marton (ed.), *Advances in Electronics and Electron Physics*, vol. 14, 1961; P. Parker, *Electronics*, 1950.

## Gate circuit

An electronic circuit having one output and one or more inputs, in which the output is a function of the inputs in a prescribed manner and in a controllable time sequence. Gate circuits may be classified as transmission gates or as switching gates, of which the logic gate is the most notable example.

**Transmission gate.** The transmission gate, sometimes called a sampling gate, delivers an output waveform that is a replica of a selected input during a specific time interval. The control signal, which determines the time interval, is called the gating signal or waveform; the gating generator is often a multivibrator. A simple transmission gate having one transmission signal input, *G*, is shown in **Fig. 1**. The gating signal from an external source, not shown, exists for period T. This gating signal is applied to the field-effect transistor, the gating signal allowing the transistor to amplify the signal which is applied to G only during interval T. *See* Transistor.

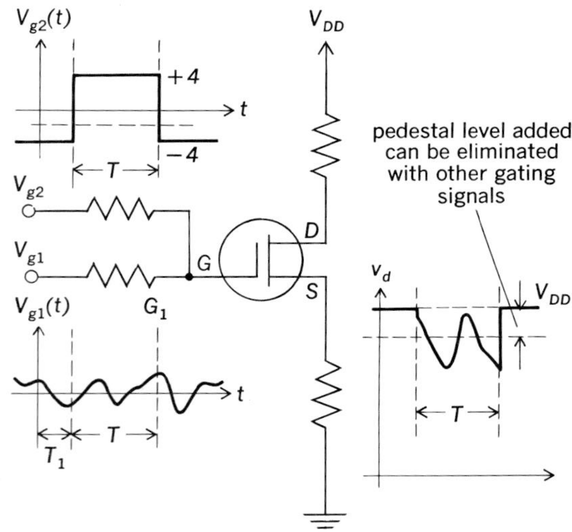


**Fig. 1. Transmission gate using field-effect transistor, showing typical operating levels.**

As a result of turning the device on from a completely off state, an additional level, or pedestal, appears at the output above the dashed line, as shown. Other signals could be mixed or gated in at other times by connecting the outputs of additional transistors in parallel and then applying such signals to the respective inputs of these transistors with gating waveforms applied to their G inputs. Also, gating signals applied to the parallel devices can be used to balance out the pedestal described above, if its existence is undesirable.

The function can also be performed by using the bases of emitter-coupled amplifiers for the signal and gate sources. Source-coupled field-effect transistors can function similarly.

Use of diodes in transmission gates is illustrated in **Fig. 2**. Here, gating waveforms of both positive and negative polarity are required from the gate generator. During the transmission interval, the diodes $D_5$ and $D_6$ are back-biased, or nonconducting. Meanwhile, dc voltages $+V$ and $-V$ ensure that $D_1$, $D_2$, $D_3$, and $D_4$ are forward-biased, or conducting. Thus, the signal waveform will be connected to the output through the low resistance of $D_1$, $D_2$, $D_3$, and $D_4$. During the nontransmission interval, the outputs of the gate generator are connected through $D_5$ and $D_6$, and the signal-path diodes are reverse-biased, or nonconducting. The balanced nature of the circuit is such that no pedestal is generated. *See* Diode.

The circuit of Fig. 1 illustrates the use of a clipping circuit as a transmission gate, while Fig. 2 uses a clamping circuit as a gate. *See* Clamping circuit; Clipping circuit.

An operational amplifier with a separate strobe input which internally disconnects the input from the

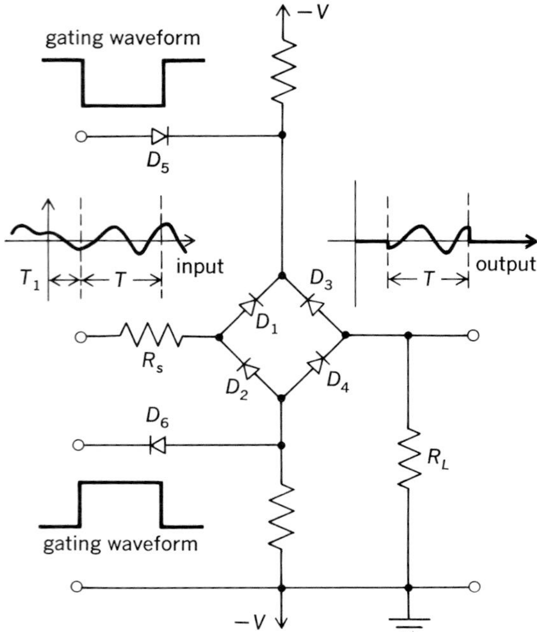


**Fig. 2. Diodes used in transmission gate.**

output sometimes functions as a transmission gate. The term analog switch is sometimes used synonymously with transmission gate. *See Amplifier*.

**Switching gate.** In the switching, or logical, gate an output having a constant amplitude is registered during a time interval if a particular combination of input signals exists. The output indicates only the existence of a particular combination of similar input signals. Examples are the OR, AND, NOR, and NAND circuits, which are basic building blocks of digital computers. Such circuits use combinations of transistors and diodes in much the same manner as transmission gates, and combinations of such functions are usually referred to as switching circuits.

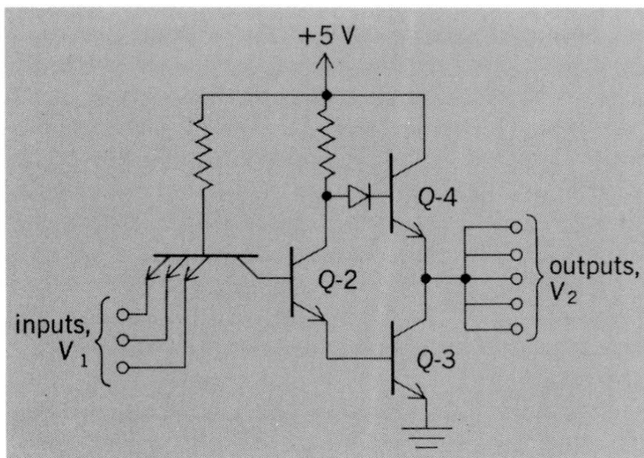


**Fig. 3.** Transistor-transistor logic ($T^2L$) circuit forming a NAND gate.

The transistor-transistor logic ($T^2L$) gate (**Fig. 3**) is an example. When all inputs are low, $V_1(0) = 0$, the output transistor, $Q$-3 is held nonconducting and the output is high, $V_2(0) = 3.5$ V. When all inputs are high, that is, $V_1(1) = 3.5$ V, the output transistor is at $V_2(1) = 0$. Such a circuit is referred to as a NAND gate. *See Logic circuits*.

*Glenn M. Glasford*

***Bibliography.*** J. Millman, *Microelectronics*, 1979; J. Millman and H. Taub, *Pulse, Digital, and Switching Waveforms*, 1965; C. Schuler, *Electronics: Principles and Applications*, 2d ed., 1984.

## GERT

A procedure for the formulation and evaluation of systems using a network approach. Problem solving with the GERT (graphical evaluation and review technique) procedure utilizes the following steps:

1. Convert a qualitative description of a system or problem to a generalized network similar to the critical path method–PERT type of network.
2. Collect the data necessary to describe the functions ascribed to the branches of a network.
3. Combine the branch functions (the network components) into an equivalent function or functions which describe the network.
4. Convert the equivalent function or functions into performance measures for studying the system or solving the problem for which the network was created. These might include either the average or variance of the time or cost to complete the network.

| network type | graphical representation | paths | loops | equivalent function |
|---|---|---|---|---|
| series | $w_a$, $w_b$ | $w_a\, w_b$ | — | $w_a\, w_b$ |
| parallel | $w_a$, $w_b$ | $w_a$, $w_b$ | — | $w_a + w_b$ |
| self-loop | $w_b$, $w_a$ | $w_a$ | $w_b$ | $\dfrac{w_a}{1 - w_b}$ |

**Fig. 1.** Calculation of the equivalent *w* function.

5. Make inferences based on the performance measures developed in step 4.

Both analytic and simulation approaches have been used to perform step 4 of the procedure. GERTE was developed to analytically evaluate network models of linear systems through an adaptation of signal flow-graph theory. For nonlinear systems, involving complex logic and queuing situations, Q-GERT was developed. In Q-GERT, a simulation of the network is performed in order to obtain statistical estimates of the performance measures of interest.

**GERTE.** The components of GERTE networks are directed branches and exclusive-or nodes. Two parameters are generally associated with each branch. These are the probability $p$ that the branch is taken, given that the node from which it emanated is realized; and the time $t$ (or cost, profit, and so on) required, if the branch is taken, to accomplish the activity which the branch represents. The time parameter can be a random variable.

For this type of network, the probability and time parameters can be combined into a single parameter, as in the equation below, where $M_t(S)$ is the moment-

$$w(s) = pM_t(s)$$

generating function of the time parameter. The calculation of the equivalent $w$ function is shown in **Fig. 1** for three basic types of networks. For general GERTE networks, an equivalent $w$ function can be calculated by using the topology equation or Mason's rule of signal flow–graph theory.

**Q-GERT.** For nonlinear systems, different node and branch types are required in order to obtain realistic network models. Q-GERT is used for such systems where branches represent activities and nodes are used to model milestones, decision points, and queues. Flowing through the Q-GERT network are items referred to as transactions. Transactions can represent physical objects, information, or a combination of the two. Different types of nodes are included in Q-GERT to allow for the modeling of complex queuing situations and project management systems. For example, activities can be used to rep-

(P or C) (D, PS)
A N

P = probability
C = condition
D = distribution type
PS = parameter set number
A = activity number
N = number of parallel servers

**Fig. 2.** Symbol and syntax for a Q-GERT activity.

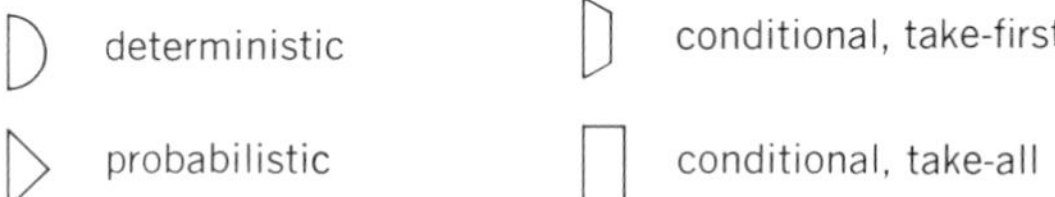

**Fig. 3. Routing types and symbols.**

resent servers of a queuing system, and Q-GERT networks can be developed to model sequential and parallel service systems.

The symbol to represent an activity is a branch with a syntax, as shown in **Fig. 2**. The distribution type and parameter set number characterize the time delay involved in the activity. The activity number is a label, and the number of parallel servers specifies a limit on the number of transactions that can proceed through the branch concurrently. The probability or condition specifies when the activity is to be taken and is used in conjunction with a routing type specified for a node. Routing characteristics are the means for directing transactions across activities and hence through the network. The routing types which may be specified for any node are shown in **Fig. 3**.

There are seven node types included in Q-GERT. These node types are shown in **Fig. 4**. The BASIC node type is used to create transactions, to terminate the existence of transactions, to accumulate transactions, and to collect statistics. The release requirement associated with the node specifies the number of incoming transactions required before an output is generated from the node. The choice criterion specifies the characteristics to be associated with any transaction leaving the node after it is released. Branching from the BASIC node is done in accordance with one of the routing types in Fig. 3. The Q-node provides a means for storing transactions waiting for service. The SELECT node is a means for selecting from among

BASIC — $R_f$ C / $R_s$ S #
$R_f$ = first release requirement
$R_s$ = subsequent release requirement
S = statistics or marking
C = choice criterion

Q-NODE — IQ / QC R #
IQ = initial queue length
QC = queue capacity
R = queue ranking rule

SELECT — QSR / SSR #
QSR = queue selection rule
SSR = server selection rule

MATCH — A > #
A = attribute number

ALLOCATE — QSR / RES / U #
QSR = queue selection rule
RES = resource number
U = number of units

FREE — RES / U # / ALLOC #S
RES = resource number
U = number of units
ALLOC #S = allocate node numbers

ALTER — RES / CC # / ALLOC #S
RES = resource number
CC = capacity change
ALLOC #S = allocate node numbers

**Fig. 4. Symbols and syntax of Q-GERT nodes.**

parallel queues and parallel servers. The MATCH node provides a mechanism for matching transactions prior to their continuation through the network.

The last three node types relate to the allocation of resources to transactions. Transactions requiring resources wait in Q-nodes which precede thd ALLOCATE node. If resources are available or when they become available, they are allocated to transactions at the ALLOCATE nodes. The number of units and the type of resource required are characteristics of the ALLOCATE node. Since many Q-nodes may precede an ALLOCATE node, a queue selection rule is specified for the ALLOCATE node. After a transaction has completed the activities for which the resources are required, the resources can be made available by routing the transaction through a FREE node. At the FREE node, the number of units of the particular resource to be freed is specified. Also indicated is the order in which ALLOCATE nodes should be polled in the attempt to reassign the freed resources. The last node type is the ALTER node, which allows the capacity of resources to be changed. When the capacity of a resource type is increased, a list of ALLOCATE nodes is appended to the ALTER node to specify where the newly created units are to be considered for allocation.

**Applications.** Many applications of GERT have been made. GERT networks have been designed, developed, and used to analyze the following situations: claims processing in an insurance company, production lines, quality control in manufacturing systems, assessment of job performance aids, burglary resistance of buildings, capacity of air terminal cargo facilities, judicial court system operation, equipment allocation in construction planning, refueling of military airlift forces, planning and control of marketing research, planning for contract negotiations, risk analysis in pipeline construction, effects of funding and administrative strategies on nuclear fusion power plant development, research and development planning, and system reliability. *SEE CRITICAL PATH METHOD (CPM); DECISION THEORY; PERT; SIMULATION.*

*A. Alan B. Pritsker*

***Bibliography.*** S. E. Elmaghraby, *Activity Networks*, 1978; L. J. Moore and E. R. Clayton, *Introduction to Systems Analysis with GERT Modeling and Simulation*, 1976; A. A. B. Pritsker, *GERT: Graphical Evaluation and Review Technique*, RM-4973-NASA, 1966; A. A. B. Pritsker, *Modeling and Analysis Using Q-GERT Networks*, 2d ed., 1980: G. E. Whitehouse, *Systems Analysis and Design Using Network Techniques*, 1973.

## Glass switch

A glassy, solid-state device used to control the flow of electric current. Useful solid-state devices can be made from glassy as well as crystalline semiconductors. Crystals possess long-range order; that is, given the position of any particular atoms and the orientation of the neighboring atoms, the location of any other atom is known, no matter how far away from the atom under consideration. A glass is a special case of a noncrystalline class of materials, namely, amorphous solids. These do not exhibit long-range order, althought they tend to have the same local structure (that is, short-range order) as the corresponding crystal. A glass is an amorphous solid that is formed by cooling rapidly from the liquid phase.

The first applications of glassy semiconductors were switches made from chalcogenide (that is, alloys containing tellurium, selenium, or sulfur) glasses. The two basic structures are known as the Ovonic Threshold Switch (OTS) and the Ovonic Memory Switch (OMS). They are active devices consisting simply of a thin film (about 1 micrometer or 0.000025 in. thick) of glass between two metallic contacts. The device characteristics depend on the bulk properties of the semiconductor material rather than on the contacts. Consequently, the switches are symmetrical in that they respond identically to voltages and currents of both polarities.

Amorphous semiconductors, as opposed to crystalline semiconductors, can be doped or made insensitive to the effects of impurities, depending on the desired application. For switching devices, it is ordinarily preferable to use an impurity-independent structure to take advantage of lower costs and stable operation. Ovonic switches are also highly resistant to the effects of radiation.

**Device characteristics.** Both the OTS and OMS show a rapid and reversible transition between a highly resistive and a conductive state effected by applied electric fields. The main difference between the two devices is that, after being brought from the highly resistive state to the conducting state, the OTS returns to its highly resistive state when the current falls below a holding current value. On the other hand, the OMS remains in the conducting state until a current pulse returns it to its highly resistive state. The OMS thereby remembers the last applied switching command, and it is from this property that the device receives its name.

Intermediate reistance states are also possible for OMS devices, which can be used in applications requiring a "gray scale." In all of these devices, the transitions between states are completely reversible.

The composition of the active material determines whether the device functions as an OTS or OMS, and also affects the values of certain device parameters. The device geometry, such as thickness and cross-sectional area of the active film, also affects the numerical values of the device parameters.

The current-voltage characteristics of the OTS are shown in **Fig. 1**. Conduction in the highly resistive state follows Ohm's law at fields below about $10^4$ V/cm. At higher fields the dynamic resistance $R_{\mathrm{dyn}}$ decreases monotonically with increasing voltage. Typical values are $R_{\mathrm{dyn}} = 2$–10 megohms at 1 V and $R_{\mathrm{dyn}} = 0.1$–0.5 megohm just prior to breakdown.

When the applied voltage exceeds a threshold voltage $V_T$, the OTS switches along the load line to the conducting state. The transition time $\tau_t$ of this switching process has been shown to be less than 150 picoseconds. $V_T$ is a function of both film thickness and active material composition and can be obtained in the range 2–300 V.

Current in the conducting state can be increased or decreased without significantly affecting the voltage drop across the device; the dynamic resistance is of the order of 1–10 ohms. Most of the voltage falls near the two contacts, due to barriers induced prior to switching; this accounts for about a 0.4-V drop. The field across the bulk is only about 1 kV/cm.

If the current is decreased below a critical value $I_H$, the OTS switches back to the original highly resistive state. $I_H$ depends on circuit parameters and also can be varied; typical values are 0.1–1 mA.

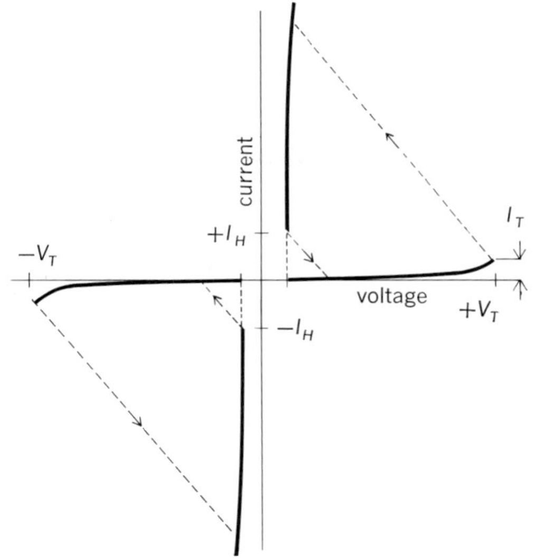


**Fig. 1. OTS current-voltage characteristics.**

The foregoing description of the static characteristics of the OTS holds for a slowly varying applied voltage. Upon application of a fast-rising pulse somewhat in excess of threshold voltage, the OTS ordinarily does not immediately switch to the conducting state but remains in the high-resistance state for a period of time $\tau_d$, called the delay time. The magnitude of this delay is strongly dependent on the extent to which the threshold voltage is exceeded. For an applied voltage pulse slightly greater than $V_T$, $\tau_d$ can be several microseconds. However, it rapidly decreases with increasing voltage in excess of threshold, and essentially vanishes above a critical voltage that is proportional to film thickness. Above this point, the speed of switching is only circuit-limited, and total switching times less than 150 picoseconds have been observed.

Switching is an electronic effect, induced by the appearance of a critical electric field across a part or all of the film. The field induces a sharp transition which increases the free-carrier concentration by a factor of about $10^8$. This results in a constant current density of approximately 10 kA/cm$^2$. At such current densities Joule heating effects are negligible. The high conduction occurs primarily through a central filament whose area varies proportionally with the current.

In the OMS the properties of the highly resistive state are essentially the same as for the OTS. As indicated in the current-voltage characteristics of **Fig. 2**, the OMS is switched to the conductive state when the threshold voltage is exceeded. It is switched back by a current pulse. The device remains in either state without power, a memory quality known as nonvolatility. Memory switching is a reversible amorphous-crystalline transition. It is preceded by a threshold switching, which provides a high density of free carriers. Under such conditions, crystallization proceeds at a greatly enhanced rate, a phenomenon known as electrocrystallization. Only the central part of the conducting filament crystallizes, but this converts to a semimetallic phase. Erasing is accomplished by providing a high-current pulse that preferentially appears through the conducting filament, thus exciting the crystalline phase. The surrounding amorphous material remains essentially unchanged during the entire

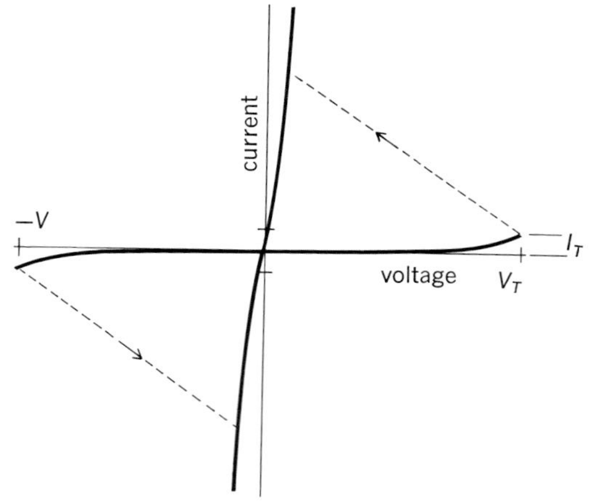


Fig. 2. OMS current-voltage characteristics.

process, and consequently acts as a heat sink which provides the rapid cooling necessary to reform the glass after the termination of the current pulse.

**Amorphous switch materials.** Materials used in an OTS are specifically chosen to meet several important requirements. First, the film should have high electrical resistivity to avoid Joule heating effects. Second, the amorphous phase should be sufficiently stable to prevent crystallization or other structural changes. Third, the material should be chosen so that irreversible breakdown does not occur. All of these conditions can be fulfilled by the use of chalcogenide glasses. Chalcogenides are alloys one of whose major components comes from one of the elements in group VI of the periodic table, ordinarily selenium or tellurium. These atoms ordinarily form polymeric-type chains in the solid state. Their electronic structure is such that they necessarily contain large but equal densities of positively and negatively charged traps in the amorphous phase. These traps keep the film resistivity high and retard irreversible breakdown. Structural stability is maintained by using alloys with relatively large densities or cross-linking atoms, ordinarily from groups IV and V of the periodic table.

Memory material is chosen to contain relatively weaker bonds and a smaller density of cross-linking atoms, so that structural changes are more easily attained. Crystallization involves only a small spatial diffusion of atoms. Under certain conditions, materials can be tailored such that other states intermediate between amorphous and crystalline can be attained. The lengths of the polymeric chains or the size of the crystalline grains can be varied depending on the amount and form of the energy of excitation.

**Applications.** Although Ovonic switches can be fabricated from bulk amorphous material, they are most conveniently produced as thin-film structures in which the active material and electrodes are vacuum-deposited or sputtered films, photolithographically defined. This economical process is compatible with transistor technology and with the methods used to produce passive components. It also lends itself to the fabrication of densely packed arrays.

***Read-only memories.*** Integrated arrays of OMSs can be used as electronically alterable read-only memories. They fill the gap in the computer memory spectrum between permanent read-only memories and volatile random-access memories. The array is nonvolatile, so the data are as permanent as in a hard-wired memory. Readout is extremely rapid (15 nanoseconds, limited only by the circuit) and nondestructive. The memory has many advantages over conventional technology, including a higher packing density, lower programming currents (5 mA), lower programming power (5 mW), and no fatigue problems. High-temperature operation (350°C or 660°F) and long lifetime (over $10^9$ write/erase cycles) have been achieved. SEE COMPUTER STORAGE TECHNOLOGY.

***Photographic films.*** Films have been developed in which the quality and amount of structural changes can be controlled by the amount of energy incident upon the film. Since these films do not contain silver, their cost does not vary with that of any precious metal. The MicrOvonic File is a completely updatable system for transferring original material onto a microfiche card. In addition, the MicrOvonic File Terminal, which accomplishes the same for electronic information, has also been developed.

***Transistors.*** A transistor, using an OTS as the emitter, has been developed. This can be used as a threshold amplifier, as a threshold latching amplifier, or as the basis for a computer using ternary logic. In the conducting state, OTSs can be used to provide a constant current density and to inject hot electrons into crystalline-semiconductor devices. Their threshold characteristics provide the opportunity for another important control function in these applications.

Other promising application areas include ac control where use is made of the inherent symmetry of these components, and microwave generation made possible by the inherently fast switching transition. It is anticipated that the exploration of new applications for amorphous switches will accelerate as knowledge of them becomes more widespread. SEE AMORPHOUS SOLID; SEMICONDUCTOR.

*Stanford R. Ovshinsky; David Adler*

***Bibliography.*** D. Adler, *Sci. Amer.*, 236(5):36–48, May 1977; D. Adler et al., Threshold switching in chalcogenide-glass thin films, *J. Appl. Phys.*, 51:3289–3309, 1980; S. R. Ovshinsky, Reversible electrical switching phenomena in disordered structures, *Phys. Rev. Lett.*, 21:1450–1453, 1968.

## Glow discharge

A mode of electrical conduction in gases. Glow discharge commonly occurs under conditions of relatively low pressure and generally in the pressure range of 1–10 mm of mercury (100–1000 pascals). The discharge typically gives off light, so that the region of the discharge appears to glow with considerable intensity. This glow is quite diffuse as contrasted to a higher-pressure discharge, such as a high-pressure arc. Typical currents may be of the order of tens or hundreds of milliamperes, whereas the potential drop may be of the order of 100 V.

The most important application of the glow discharge is in the so-called voltage regulator or voltage reference tube. This device maintains a relatively constant difference of potential across itself as the current is varied over an appreciable range, and consequently is very useful in cases where a constant reference potential is required.

In terms of the potential-current characteristic, the glow discharge occurs after the potential has been increased so that the Townsend region has been passed. Thus the discharge is field-sustained. On the other hand, a continued increase in current leads first to the region referred to as the abnormal glow and beyond this to the arc discharge. The transition from the abnormal glow to the arc generally is almost discontinuous and is accompanied by a spark. For a discussion of this relationship SEE ARC DISCHARGE; ELECTRIC SPARK; ELECTRICAL CONDUCTION IN GASES; TOWNSEND DISCHARGE.

**Regions of discharge.** There are three main regions of interest in the glow discharge, similar to those in the arc. These are the cathode fall, the positive column, and the anode region. These will be discussed separately, but it is appropriate first to examine some of the general features of the mode (see **illus.**). The appearance is that of successive more or less well-defined luminous and dark regions. Starting from the cathode, there is a dark space which generally extends for a few millimeters, the Aston dark space. This is followed by a luminous region, also of limited extent, known as the cathode glow. This is succeeded by a somewhat longer dark space, designated the Crookes or Hittorf dark space. After this comes the negative glow region, the boundaries of which are rather poorly defined. Following this is the Faraday dark space, which is also more extensive and poorly defined. This changes gradually into the positive column which is luminous and of length determined by the pressure and distance between electrodes. This region may or may not contain striations, and if present they may be either stationary or moving. At the end of the positive column is a thin layer of greater luminosity, designated the anode glow. Between this and the anode is the anode dark space.

***Cathode fall.*** The events occurring at the cathode are vital to the discharge. The current in the cathode circuit is primarily due to positive ions. However, it is necessary to produce enough electrons at the cathode to maintain the discharge. These electrons gain energy as they move in the electric field toward the anode, and produce excitation and ionization. It appears that these electrons are secondary electrons resulting from positive ion bombardment of the cathode surface. The drop in potential which occurs at the cathode depends on the kind of gas and the cathode material. Generally, this potential drop is a large fraction of the total potential drop across the discharge. The production of secondary electrons by this means is rather inefficient, which explains why the drop must be large.

Electrons starting at rest from the cathode must gain energy before they can produce excitation. This can be accomplished only by motion in the electric field, and hence there is a minimum distance which the electrons must move before they can produce excitation and consequent light emission. This explains the existence of the Aston dark space. It might be thought that the cathode glow could be explained by this also, but it is not likely that much of the light from this region is brought about by the secondary electrons. It appears that most of this light results from the positive ions that have struck the cathode and are returning to the ground state as neutral atoms. There are two facts of importance in this connection. First, the electron density is still rather low at such a short distance from the cathode. Second, the wavelengths present in the radiation indicate transitions involving states of a rather high degree of excitation. These high energy states probably could not be produced by the electrons from the cathode at this point.

The Crookes dark space is actually a region of nearly uniform electric field. Most of the cathode drop occurs in this region, and here the positive ions gain most of their energy before striking the cathode. The electrons from the cathode gain enough energy here to produce cumulative ionization near the end of the space. In the negative glow, which follows, the potential is relatively constant. Here electrons, both from the cathode and from cumulative ionization, lose energy by inelastic collisions and produce a large amount of excitation. The boundary at the anode end of this space is poorly defined because of the broad distribution in electron energy. The slowing down of the electrons at the end of this region results in a negative space charge. Thus the electrons that move into the Faraday dark space gain energy.

***Positive column.*** The beginning of the positive column is the result of excitation by these electrons. The situation in the positive column is the result of a balance between several processes. There is a nearly uniform potential drop which results in ionization throughout this entire region. On the other hand, there must be a loss of ions to make up for this production. This takes place primarily by diffusion to the walls, although there is also recombination. The electrons with their greater mobility diffuse to the walls, producing a slight negative potential relative to the center of the discharge. This negative potential both limits further electron diffusion and produces positive ion diffusion outward. This process is known as ambipolar diffusion. The positive column is not essential in maintaining the discharge. If the distance between electrodes is changed, with the pressure and current held constant, the extent of the positive column and the potential across the discharge change accordingly. The features of the anode and cathode regions remain unaltered under such a change up to the point where the positive column no longer exists.

A feature of this region is a succession of alter-

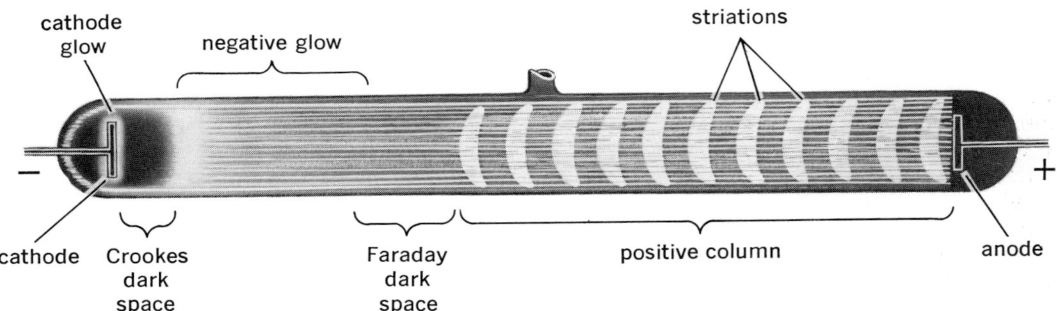


**Glow discharge at approximately 0.1 mm (13 Pa) pressure, showing successive more or less well-defined luminous and dark regions. (*After J. B. Hoag and S. A. Korff, Electron and Nuclear Physics, 3d ed., Van Nostrand, 1948*)**

nately luminous and dark regions, called striations, which usually occur when the discharge is operated at relatively high pressure; they may be stationary or moving. Their presence is related to the fact that in general the atomic species in the discharge are deexcited in times short compare to those required for them to diffuse through the positive column. Pure, inert gases do not show the effect, probably because they are excited into metastable, long-lived states.

***Anode region.*** At the anode end of the positive column, the positive ions are repelled. This produces an increase in electric field, which causes the electrons to gain energy and excite more effectively. Thus the positive column ends in a region of increased luminosity, the anode glow.

**Other aspects.** There are many other aspects of the glow discharge that are interesting and important. One such phenomenon is cathode sputtering. Here the positive ions that are accelerated into the cathode knock out atoms or groups of atoms from the surface. Another aspect is that of abnormal glow. The voltage across the discharge remains nearly constant while the current is increased in the normal glow mode. This current increase is accompanied by an increase in the area of the cathode glow. When the glow has completely covered the cathode, a further current increase results in an increase in the cathode potential drop, and hence the potential drop across the discharge. This is the abnormal glow. It is characterized by more intense light emission and increased sputtering. *SEE SPUTTERING.*

It should be stated that many of the details of the discharge are uncertain. The processes are generally quite complicated. Reliable and accurate measurements are difficult at best, and most of the information is of a qualitative nature.

*Glenn H. Miller*

***Bibliography.*** J. Beynon, *Conduction of Electricity Through Gases*, 1972; M. N. Hirsh and H. J. Oskam (eds.), *Gaseous Electronics*, vol. 1: *Electrical Discharges*, 1978; P. Llewellyn-Jones, *The Glow Discharge and an Introduction to Plasma Physics*, 1966; L. B. Loeb, *Basic Processes of Gaseous Electronics*, 1955.

## Grain boundaries

The surfaces separating individual crystals, or grains, in a crystalline solid. Many solids, especially metallic and ceramic materials, are characterized by a periodic internal structure. This structure is defined by arrangement of atoms (or ions) in a precise three-dimensional array to form a crystal. The extent of the arrangement is large with respect to the size of the atom or ion. Although solids may be a single crystal, it is much more common for solids to be composed of many crystals, which retain their characteristic structure but are misoriented with respect to neighboring crystals by a relative rotation of their principal axes. The boundary separating these individual grains is known as a grain boundary and is characterized by a two-dimensional structure which may be related to the structure of neighboring grains. Therefore, grain boundaries represent planar defects in an otherwise perfect crystalline material. Grains and grain boundaries are ubiquitous in nature; for example, a polycrystalline cube, measuring 0.4 in. (1 cm) on an edge, could easily contain over 1,000,000,000 grains and 10 $ft^2$ (1 $m^2$) of grain boundary area.

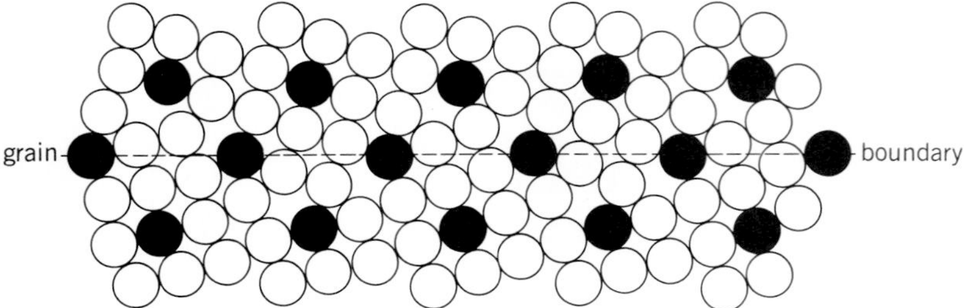


**Fig. 1. A grain boundary in a cubic structure, produced by rotation of one grain with respect to the other by 36.9° about a cube axis. In this particular case, a sublattice (solid circles) extends across the boundary without interruption.**

**Microscopic structure.** It was first believed that grain boundaries were composed of an amorphous (structureless) layer measuring many atomic diameters in thickness. However, mounting experimental and theoretical evidence indicates that grain boundaries not only are nearer to a single atomic diameter in thickness, but also are characterized by a periodic structure, regardless of the degree of misorientation between adjacent grains. One special type of structure is illustrated in **Fig. 1**, for two grains, characterized by cubic crystal structures and rotated with respect to one another by an angle of 36.9° about a common cube axis. This particular grain boundary merely provides an example of one possible boundary structure; the structure of other boundaries may vary considerably, depending on degree of misorientation between adjacent grains and inclination of the boundary plane with respect to these grains.

The structure of grain boundaries may conveniently be divided into three categories: low-angle boundaries, random high-angle boundaries, and special high-angle boundaries. Low-angle grain boundaries separate two adjacent grains which have been rotated (tilted or twisted) by a small angle (generally less than 15°) with respect to one another. For low-angle grain boundaries, the transition from one grain to another is only slightly perturbed, usually by a series of line defects aligned in the plane of the boundary (**Fig. 2**). These line defects are known as dislocations and consist of an elastic stress field and a (noncrystalline) core region. As the angle of misorientation between adjacent grains increases, the spacing between dislocations decreases until the dislocation cores overlap, thus defining a high-angle grain boundary. These boundaries may be composed of a disordered (random) atomic array due to close proximity of adjacent dislocation cores, or may be composed of an ordered (special) atomic array, wherein the boundary assumes a certain two-dimensional periodic structure. Such special high-angle boundaries often are assigned special names, such as twin boundaries, stacking faults, and coincidence boundaries. One example of a (special) coincidence boundary is illustrated in Fig. 1. It is evident that this misorientation (36.9° about a cube axis) represents a special case, resulting in a periodic grain boundary structure and an extension of a sublattice of the original lattice (solid circles) across the boundary.

**Effects on macroscopic properties.** The microscopic structure of grain boundaries is intimately related to many macroscopic properties, such as electrical resistivity, corrosion resistance, tensile strength, and fracture toughness. Moreover, in a macroscopic

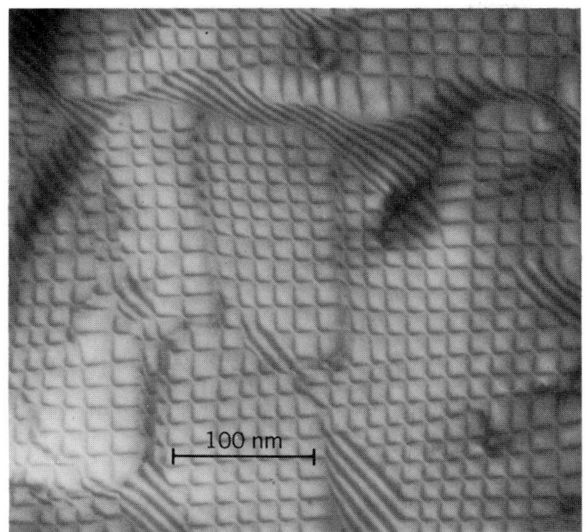


**Fig. 2. High-resolution transmission electron micrograph of a low-angle grain boundary in gold, wherein a cross-grid of dislocations, characterized by spacing of about 15 nm, is resolved. (*Courtesy of F. Cosandey*)**

sense, grain boundaries may be characterized by a surface tension, which requires a certain balance of forces at intersections of grain boundaries with other boundaries, with external (free) surfaces, or even with boundaries separating dissimilar crystallographic materials (phases). The behavior of grain boundaries closely resembles that of a soap froth, since both are governed by capillarity. Unlike soap films, however, surface tension of grain boundaries is not only a function of the degree of misorientation between adjacent grains, but also a function of inclination of the boundary plane with respect to these grains. Therefore, many properties associated with grain boundaries are antisotropic.

***Segregation of impurities.*** The fact that grain boundaries are characterized by a more open structure than their neighboring grains encourages segregation of impurities, especially if the diameter of the impurity atom differs significantly from that of the parent material. Accordingly, a material containing a small fraction of an impurity, on the average, could actually contain a large fraction of this impurity localized at grain boundaries. Localization of impurities at grain boundaries are often imparts undesirable properties to the overall material, such as susceptibility to corrosion and fracture. Moreover, the degree of segregation at grain boundaries depends on structure of the boundary, which, in turn, depends on degree of misorientation between adjacent grains and inclination of the boundary plane with respect to these grains. Therefore, effects of segregation of impurities at grain boundaries in polycrystalline materials depend on both amount and character of existing boundaries, as well as characteristics of the impurity itself.

***Mass transport.*** In contrast to segregation of impurities at grain boundaries, which is a dynamic equilibrium effect, impurities can also diffuse much more rapidly along grain boundaries, which is a kinetic effect. Accordingly, mass transport may occur either through grain interiors or along grain boundaries in a given (polycrystalline) material. Mass transport is especially severe in thin films, since not only is the film thickness small, but also the grain size is small, thus providing many short-circuit (grain boundary) paths for diffusion. Grain boundaries also play an important role in promoting solid-state phase transformations by providing internal surfaces for (heterogeneous) nucleation of a new phase.

***Mobility of boundaries.*** At sufficiently high temperatures, grain boundary movement can occur by removal of atoms from one grain and reattachment to the adjacent grain. Since the case of disattachment and reattachment of atoms depends on local grain boundary structure, grain boundaries are characterized by a spectrum of mobilities; that is, velocity per unit pressure. Accordingly, special and low-angle grain boundaries are relatively immobile, whereas random high-angle boundaries are relatively mobile. These particular factors are important during recrystallization, grain growth, and texture formation. In these processes, numerous grains are nucleated in a deformed matrix and grow in such a manner as to convert the entire matrix to its original state. The resultant polycrystalline material is often characterized by preferential orientation or texture of existing grains. Conversely, proper choice of deformation and annealing conditions may be used to control (refine) grain size. At elevated temperatures, grains may continue to grow due to imbalances of surface tension.

***Mechanical properties.*** Perhaps the effect of grain boundaries on mechanical properties is more important than on any other class of properties. In general, strength and ductility are controlled by the motion of dislocations under the influence of applied forces, which is responsible for plastic deformation. Grain boundaries provide an effective barrier to this motion so that strength increases and ductility decreases with decreasing grain size. Curiously, the role of grain boundaries is reversed at elevated temperatures, at which small grain size, that is, a large amount of grain boundary area, facilitates plastic deformation by mass transport of constituent atoms along these boundaries. This phenomenon, known as creep, often limits usefulness of materials at elevated temperatures. Fine-grained polycrystalline materials sometimes exhibit extraordinarily large degrees of plasticity, termed superplasticity, actually is an accelerated form of creep involving rapid diffusion of constituent atoms along grain boundaries in order to relieve the applied stress.

Even when motion of dislocations is sufficiently suppressed to severely limit plastic deformation, for example, at low temperatures, failure may occur by fracture. This phenomenon may occur either by nucleation of cracks and subsequent propagation along grain boundaries (intergranular) or by subsequent propagation through the interior of grains (transgranular). A very important technical problem that is associated with the presence of grain boundaries is stress-corrosion cracking. This phenomenon involves selective corrosion at grain boundaries under a mechanical stress until eventual failure occurs.

*Charles L. Bauer*

**Electronic properties of semiconductors.** From the above discussion of microscopic structure, it is clear that rather severely perturbed electronic energy levels might be expected in the vicinity of grain boundaries. For instance, when edge dislocations are present, a significant number of grain boundary atoms find themselves in environments with less than the normal number of nearest neighbors. This leads to severe disruption of the normal crystal bonding, or sharing of valence electrons, and usually gives rise to states for electrons in the forbidden energy gap of a semiconductor. The consequences of this are shown in **Fig. 3***a*, which illustrates a thin, electrically neutral, grain boundary region as it would exist if it could be placed between two semi-infinite, nearly adjacent crystals without any electrons being allowed to transfer from one to any other of the parts, so that the grain boundary region remains in a neutral state. The adjacent crystals are shown as being separated physically from the grain boundary region in Fig. 3*a* to emphasize that no charge flow to the boundary has yet occurred. Here $E_V$ and $E_C$ are the energies of the top of the valence band and the bottom of the conduction band, $\zeta$ is the energy separation between the highest filled (Fermi) level and the bottom of the conduction band. $E_{FG}$ is the energy of the highest filled electron state in the grains, and $E_{FB}$ is the corresponding quantity for the boundary region. Because of the defective structure of the grain boundary region, it contains numerous empty electron states (drawn as open circles) lying below the filled level of the crystalline regions. An *n*-type semiconductor which has electrons as the majority carriers is shown here, but similar phenomena occur in *p*-type materials.

If the hypothesis is continued, and the electrons in all three parts are allowed to find a common energy level (by joining), the structure of Fig. 3*b* results. Electrons (shown as minus signs) flow from the crystals to fill some of the empty states of lower energy in the grain boundary. This flow results in a negative charging of the center of the grain boundary and the formation of an electrostatic repulsive barrier which stops further electron flow by raising the energy levels of all the electron states at the center of the boundary until the energy of the highest filled state is the same everywhere. Here $\phi_B$ is the amount of electrostatic bending of the energy bands. If some of the defect states at the center of the boundary remain unfilled, they will play an important role in the electronic behavior of the boundary.

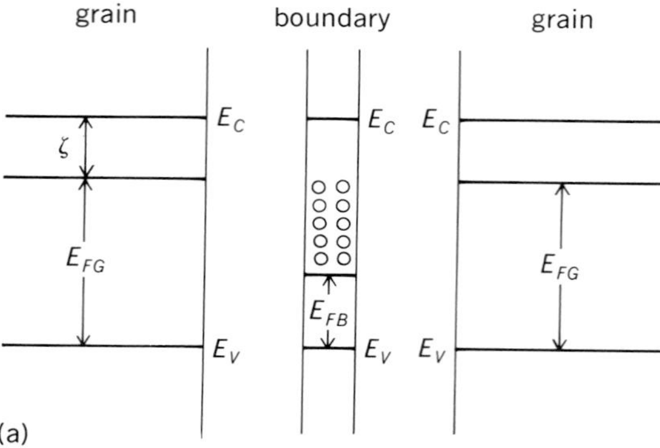


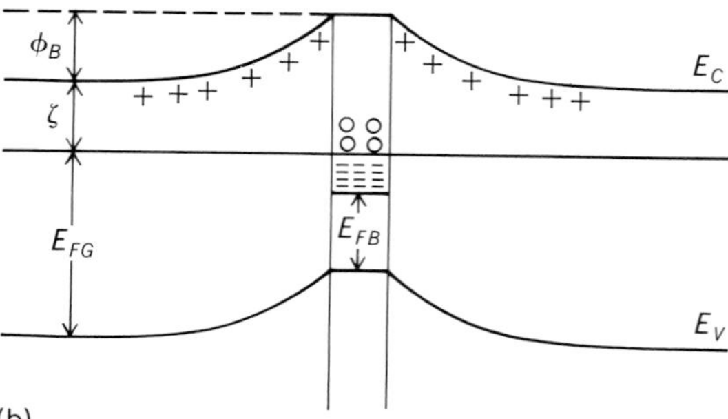


**Fig. 3. Process of grain boundary charging in semiconductors. (*a*) Electronic energy levels of two adjacent crystallites and their intervening grain boundary region, as they would exist if electron transfer between the three regions could not take place. (*b*) Electronic energy levels as they actually exist, after the three regions are joined.**

**Transport of charge.** The accumulation of majority carriers at semiconductor grain boundaries has been verified in a variety of materials, including silicon (Si), germanium (Ge), gallium arsenide (GaAs), cadmium sulfide (CdS), lead sulfide (PbS), and zinc oxide (ZnO). This charging effect has a profound influence on the electrical properties of polycrystalline semiconductors. In order for current to flow across such charged boundaries, the carriers must have an energy considerably in excess of their normal thermal energy (0.025 eV at room temperature). The number of electrons having this extra energy at any time is small, and hence the conductance such a potential barrier has when current flows across it is low and strongly temperature-dependent. The temperature dependence frequently seen is an exponential function of inverse absolute temperature—much like the leakage current across a *pn* junction device. Because of the small magnitude of this grain boundary conductance, polycrystalline aggregates frequently offer conductance to current flow which is many decades lower than that of single crystals of similar purity.

The exponential temperature dependence of the electrical conductance $G$ measured across a single silicon grain boundary is shown in **Fig. 4**. The grains in this case are doped *n*-type to a level of $1.3 \times 10^{16}$ $cm^{-3}$. The data points fit a formula of the type given below (indicated by the straight line in Fig. 4), where

$$G = G_0 \exp\left[-(\phi_B + \zeta)/kT\right]$$

$k$ is Boltzmann's constant, $G_0$ is a constant, $T$ is the absolute temperature, and $(\phi_B + \zeta)$ is 0.62 eV in this case. This result shows that electrons crossing the grain boundary are thermally emitted over a potential energy barrier of total height $(\phi_B + \zeta)$. This is the energy difference between the highest filled energy state and the top of the barrier (Fig. 3*b*).

**Applications.** Because of the narrow width of the grain boundary space charge regions, the capacitance of such a structure can also be large. This effect is put to use in boundary-layer capacitors, which are polycrystalline devices made of materials like barium titanate. These are useful for high-capacitance-value applications where circuit element size is an important consideration. *See* Capacitor.

Another useful property of grain boundaries—employed in devices called varistors—is their voltage-dependent resistance. As voltage is applied across a grain boundary, the presence of unfilled trapping states causes the potential barrier for current flow to remain large. However, continued application of larger and larger voltages eventually fills these states, and further bias causes a rapid reduction in this barrier. Drastic increases in current occur above this filled trap threshold, and the grain boundary turns on. Varistors made of materials such as polycrystalline zinc oxide exhibit this effect. They are used as voltage regulators and surge protectors in a variety of applications. *See* Varistor.

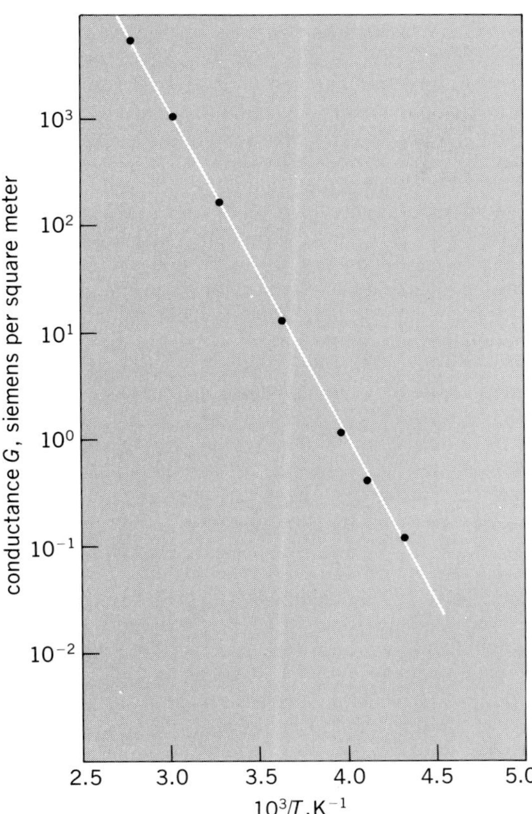


**Fig. 4. Temperature dependence of the electrical conductance measured across a single silicon grain boundary.**

Minority carriers are also strongly influenced by the presence of grain boundaries. An example is the photovoltaic cell, in which light-generated minority carriers must diffuse substantial distances to a collecting junction for current to be generated; here the presence of grain boundaries is quite harmful. The same grain boundary potential barrier which repels majority carriers attracts minority carriers and traps them until they recombine. This results in a short minority carrier lifetime, a property which has traditionally made polycrystalline semiconductors less than ideal for a variety of semiconductor devices such as transistors and photovoltaic cells. SEE PHOTOVOLTAIC CELL; PHOTOVOLTAIC EFFECT; SOLAR CELL.

Research has shown that hydrogen diffused into silicon removes grain boundary defect states, thereby considerably improving the electrical properties of polycrystalline silicon; chemical methods to alter grain boundary properties in other semiconductors have also been investigated. It is believed that improved polycrystalline devices will result from these efforts.

*C. H. Seager*

***Bibliography.*** G. A. Chadwick and D. A. Smith (eds.), *Grain Boundary Structure and Properties*, 1976; P. Chaudhari and J. W. Matthews (eds.), *Grain Boundaries and Interfaces*, Surf. Sci. Spec. Vol. no. 31 (1972); H. J. Leamy, G. E. Pike, and C. H. Seager (eds.), *Grain Boundaries and Semiconductors*, 1982; D. McLean, *Grain Boundaries in Metals*, 1957; L. E. Murr, *Interfacial Phenomena in Metals and Alloys*, 1975.

## Graph theory

A branch of mathematics that belongs partly to combinatorial analysis and partly to topology. Its applications occur (sometimes under other names) in electrical network theory, operations research, organic chemistry, theoretical physics, and statistical mechanics, and in sociological and behavioral research. Both in pure mathematical inquiry and in applications, a graph is customarily depicted as a topological configuration of points and lines, but usually is studied with combinatorial methods.

**Origin of graph theory.** Graph theory and topology are said to have started simultaneously in 1736 when L. Euler settled the celebrated Königsberg bridge problem. In Königsberg, there were two islands linked to each other and to the banks of the Pregel River by seven bridges. **Figure 1** illustrates both this

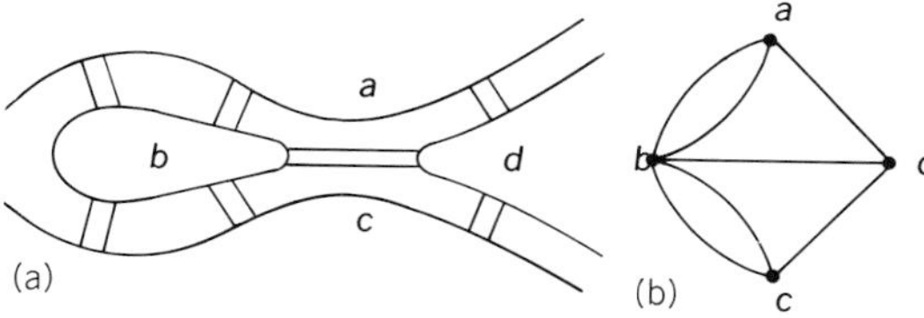


**Fig. 1. Königsberg bridge problem. (*a*) The seven bridges of Königsberg. (*b*) Corresponding graph.**

setting and its topological abstraction as a graph. The points $a$, $b$, $c$, $d$ correspond to land areas, and the connecting lines to bridges. The problem is to start at one of the land areas and to cross all seven bridges without ever recrossing a bridge. Euler proved that there is no solution, and he established a rule that applies to any connected graph: such a traversal is possible if and only if at most two points are odd, that is, each is the terminus for an odd number of lines. Euler also proved that the number of odd points in a graph is always an even number. Thus, a complete traversal without recrossing any lines is possible if the number of odd points is zero or two. If zero, the complete traversal ends at the starting point.

In geometry a graph might arise as the set of vertices and edges of a convex, three-dimensional polyhedron, such as a pyramid or a prism. Euler derived an important property of all such polyhedra. Let $V$, $E$, and $F$ be the numbers of vertices, edges, and faces of such a polyhedron. Euler proved that $V - E + F = 2$, which is now called the Euler equation. For instance, a cube has $V = 8$, $E = 12$, and $F = 6$, so that $8 - 12 + 6 = 2$. Euler's observations have been extended to a theorem about imbeddings of graphs in surfaces and to the Euler-Poincaré characteristic for cell complexes in combinatorial topology.

**Definitions.** A graph consists of a set of points, a set of lines, and in incidence relation that designates the end points of each line. In many applications no line starts and ends at the same point. (Such a line

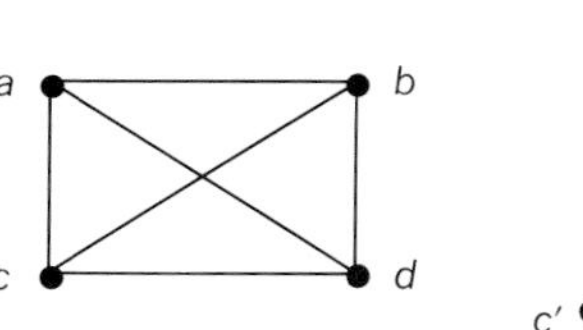


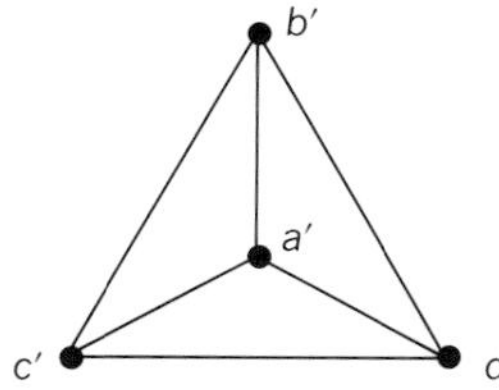


**Fig. 2. Two isomorphic graphs.**

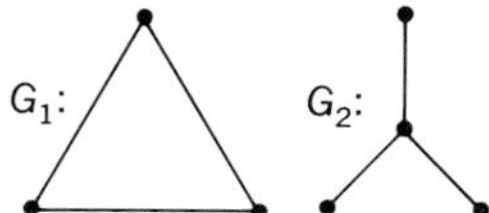


Fig. 3. Two graphs for which either a 120° rotation or a vertical reflection is an automorphism.

would be called a loop.) Also, no two lines have the same pair of end points. A graph whose lines satisfy these conditions is called simplicial. The valence of a point is the number of lines incident on it, calculated so that a loop is twice incident on its only end point. Two graphs are isomorphic if there is one-to-one correspondence from the point set and line set of one onto the point set and line set, respectively, of the other that preserves the incidence relation. The point correspondence $a \rightarrow a'$, $b \rightarrow b'$, $c \rightarrow c'$, $d \rightarrow d'$ indicates an ismorphism between the two graphs of **Fig. 2**.

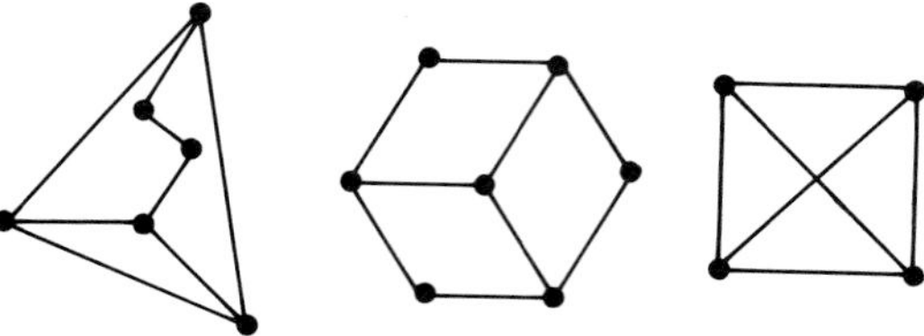

Fig. 4. Homeomorphic but nonisomorphic graphs.

An automorphism of a graph is an isomorphism of a graph with itself. For instance, a plane rotation of 120° would yield an automorphism of either of the two graphs in **Fig. 3**. A plane reflection through a vertical axis would also yield an automorphism of either of them. The set of all automorphisms of a graph $G$ forms the automorphism group of $G$. R. Frucht proved in 1938 that every finite group is the automorphism group of some graph. Two graphs are homeomorphic (**Fig. 4**) if, after smoothing over all points of valence 2, the resulting graphs are isomorphic.

**Map coloring problems.** Drawing a graph on a surface decomposes the surface into regions. One colors the regions so that no two adjacent regions have the same color, rather like a political map of the world. It is a remarkable fact that for a given surface, there is a single number of colors that will always be enough no matter how many regions occur in a decomposition of the surface. The smallest such number is called the chromatic number of that surface. It is easy to draw a plane map, as in **Fig. 5**, that requires four colors. In 1976 K. Appel and W. Haken settled a problem dating back to about 1850, by showing that four colors are always enough for plane maps.

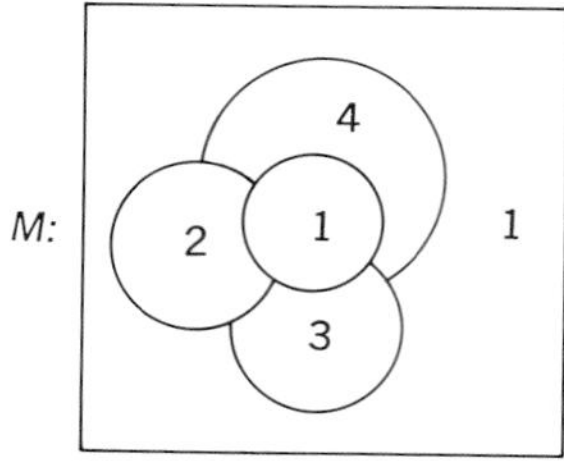


Fig. 5. Plane map requiring four colors.

Some maps on more complicated surfaces require more than four colors. For instance, **Fig. 6** illustrates a map on a torus (the surface of a doughnut) that needs seven. To obtain the toroidal map from the rectangular drawing, first match the top to the bottom to get a cylindrical tube. Then match the left end of the cylinder to the right end to complete the torus. Whereas, before this matching, region 7 meets only regions 1 and 6, after the matching it also meets region 2 along $FG$, region 3 along $GH$, region 4 along $AB$, and region 5 along $BC$. In fact, after the matching, each of the seven regions borders every other region. It follows that seven colors are necessary. No map on the torus needs more than seven colors, as P. J. Heawood proved in 1890. G. Ringel and J. W. T. Youngs completed a calculation in 1968 of the chromatic numbers of all the surfaces except the plane or sphere.

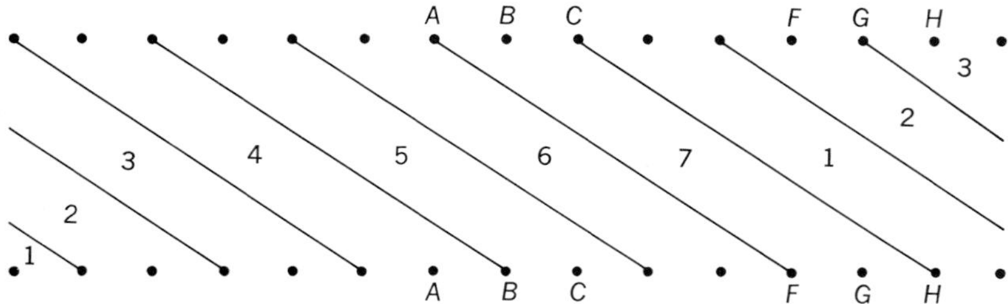


Fig. 6. Map on a torus (doughnut) that requires seven colors. To form the torus, paste opposite sides of the rectangle together.

**Planarity.** A graph is planar if it can be drawn in the plane so that none of its lines cross each other. Neither of the two graphs in **Fig. 7** can be drawn in the plane. K. Kuratowski proved in 1930 that a graph is planar if and only if it contains no subgraph homeomorphic to either of two two graphs. Testing all the subgraphs might be a very tedious process,.even on a fast computer. In 1974 J. Hopcroft and R. Tarjan obtained an extremely fast alternative planarity test. The time it takes a computer to perform the Hopcroft-Tarjan test is linearly proportional to the time it takes to read its point set into the computer.

There are methods to decide for any graph and any surface whether the graph can be drawn on the surface without edge crossings. The time to execute such methods is unfeasibly large for most graphs and most surfaces except the plane or the sphere. Ringel has constructed many important special drawings on higher-genus surfaces.

**Variations.** In a directed graph, or digraph, each line $ab$ is directed from one end point $a$ to the other end point $b$. There is at most one line from $a$ to $b$. The adjacency matrix $M = (m_{ij})$ of a digraph $D$ with points $b_1, b_2, \ldots, b_n$ has the entry $m_{ij} = 1$ if the line $b_ib_j$ occurs in $D$; otherwise $m_{ij} = 0$ (**Fig. 8**).

An oriented graph is obtained from an ordinary graph by assigning a unique direction to every line. If there is one line between ever pair of points and no loops, an ordinary graph is called complete. An oriented complete graph is called a tournament (**Fig. 9**).

**Applications.** A. Cayley reformulated the problem of counting the number of isomers of saturated hydrocarbons ($C_nH_{2n+2}$) in graphical language (**Fig. 10**). Each isomer is a tree all of whose vertices have valence 1 for hydrogen, or 4 for carbon. G. Polya devised a general theorem in 1937 for enumeration to provide a solution to such problems. F. Harary and others have solved many related problems by applying and extending Polya's theorem. Extremely effective use of Polya's theorem occurs in theoretical physics, where G. Ford and G. Uhlenbeck solved

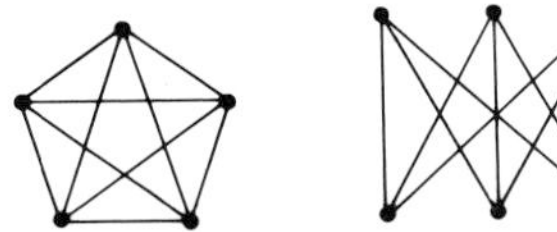

Fig. 7. Prototypes of all nonplanar graphs.

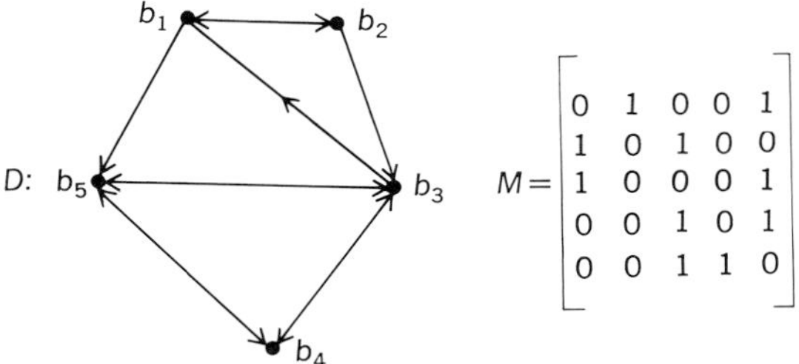


Fig. 8. A digraph and its adjacency matrix.

several graphical enumeration problems arising in statistical mechanics.

Suppose that some of the points of a graph correspond to workers $x_1, \ldots, x_m$, that the rest of the points correspond to jobs $y_1, \ldots, y_m$, and the presence of a line between $x_i$ and $y_j$ means that worker $x_i$ is capable of performing job $y_j$. The personnel assignment problem is to find $m$ lines so that each worker $x_i$ is matched to exactly one possible job. In the optimal assignment problem, labels on the lines tell how well a worker can do a particular job. An algorithm due to H. Kuhn and J. Munkres solves the optimal assignment problem.

If the points of a graph represent cities and the lines between them are labeled with distances, one might want to find the shortest path from one point to another. An efficient method to determine a shortest path was developed by E. Dijkstrain in 1959. K. Menger proved in 1927 that if $A$ and $B$ are disjoint sets of a connected graph $G$, then the minimum number of points whose deletion separates $A$ from $B$ equals the maximum number of disjoint paths between $A$ and $B$. L. Ford and D. Fulkerson generalized Menger's theorem into a method for solving network flow problems. SEE LINEAR PROGRAMMING.

According to the physical laws of G. Kirchhoff and G. Ohm, any set of voltages applied to the input

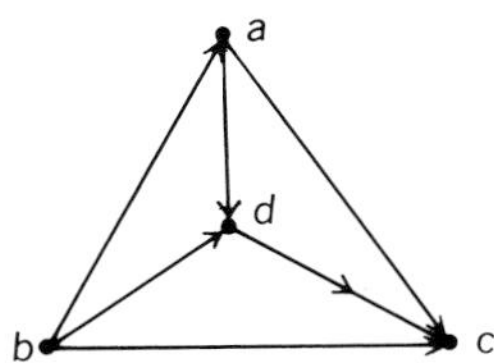


Fig. 9. A tournament.

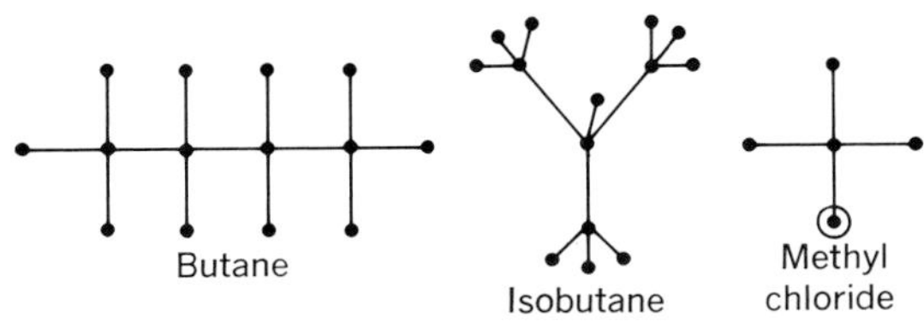


Fig. 10. The two isomers of a saturated hydrocarbon.

nodes of an electrical network determines the voltages at all other nodes and the currents on every branch. Kirchhoff also proved the result known as the matrix-tree theorem: Let $G$ be a connected graph with points $b_1, \ldots, b_n$, and let $A = (a_{ij})$ be the matrix such that $a_{ij}$ is the valence of $b_i$ and, for $i \neq j$, $a_{ij} = -1$ if $b_i$ is adjacent to $b_j$ or 0 otherwise. Then the cofactor of each entry $a_{ij}$ equals the number of spanning trees of $G$, that is, the number of trees in $G$ that includes every point of $G$ (**Fig. 11**). SEE NETWORK THEORY.

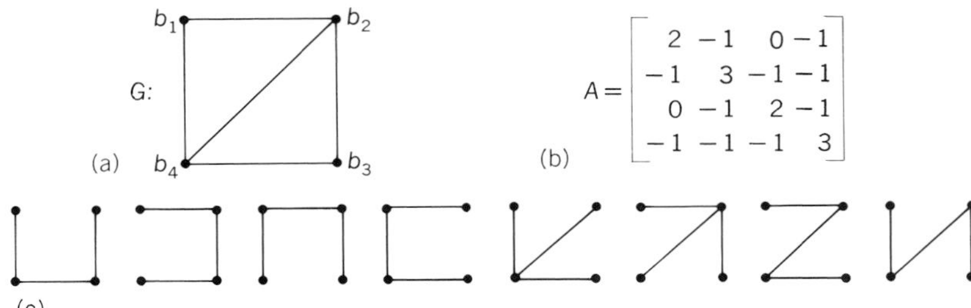


Fig. 11. Matrix-tree theorem, (*a*) Graph G. (*b*) Corresponding matrix *A*. (c) Spanning trees of G.

Numerous applications of graph theory to social and behavioral science have been developed, many by Harary and his coauthors. If points represent persons and lines represent such interrelationships as communication, linking, or power, then a graph may depict various aspects of social organization. For instance, anthropologists use graphs to describe kinship, and management scientists use them to display corporate hierarchy.

Graph theory is presently in a phase of rapid growth. Two of the major branches not described here are external graph theory, founded by P. Turan and developed by P. Erdös, and hypergraph theory, developed by C. Berge. Material theory, originated by H. Whitney and expanded by W. Tutte, is closely related to graph theory. Tutte is also responsible for important results in many other areas of graph theory and combinatorial research, including connectivity, decomposition, and chromatic numbers.

*Jonathan L. Gross*

***Bibliography.*** L. Beineke and R. Wilson (eds.), *Selected Topics in Graph Theory*, 1978; C. Berge, *Graphs and Hypergraphs*, 2d ed., 1976; N. Biggs, E. Lloyd, and R. Wilson, *Graph Theory 1736–1936*, 1976; B. Bollobas, *External Graph Theory*, 1978; B. Bollobas, *Graph Theory and Combinatorics*, 1984; A. Bondy and R. Murty, *Graph Theory with Applications*, 1976, reprint 1979; F. Harary, *Graph Theory*, 1969; F. Harary and E. Palmer, *Graphical Enumeration*, 1973; G. Ringel, *Map Color Theorem*, 1974; A. V. Temperly, *Graph Theory and Applications*, 1982; W. Tutte, *Introduction to the Theory of Matroids*, 1971.

## Gyrator

A linear, passive, two-port electric circuit element whose transmission properties are such that it is effectively a half wavelength longer for one direction of transmission than for the other direction of transmission. Thus a gyrator is a device that causes a reversal of signal polarity for one direction of propagation but not for the other. (A two-port element has a pair of

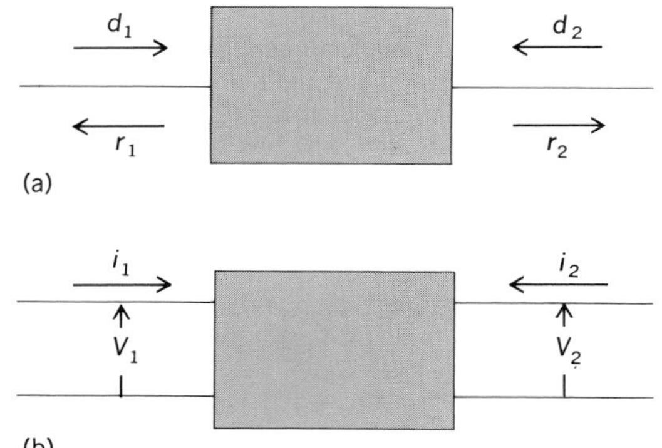


**Fig. 1.** Two-port microwave network. (*a*) Scattering matrix representation. (*b*) Currents and voltages.

input terminals and a pair of output terminals.) This device is novel, since it violates the theorem of reciprocity. *SEE RECIPROCITY PRINCIPLE.*

Until the early 1950s, all known linear passive electrical networks obeyed the theorem of reciprocity. However, several different types of nonreciprocal networks are now widely applied, principally at microwave frequencies. These devices are used to control the direction of signal flow and to protect or isolate components from undesired signals. One common application of a three-port nonreciprocal network, called a circulator, is to permit connection of a transmitter and a receiver to the same antenna. This is accomplished with minimum interference and virtually no power loss of either transmitted or received signal. *SEE CONTINUOUS-WAVE RADAR; NETWORK THEORY.*

**Reciprocity.** The theorem of reciprocity can be stated in many equivalent forms, and perhaps the simplest to consider and understand is the particular form it takes when it is expressed especially for a two-port microwave network, as shown in **Fig. 1***a*. Here $d_1$ represents the wave propagating away from the network on the same side, and $d_2$ and $r_2$ represent the same quantities on the other side. In a linear network the relationship between the waves can be expressed as shown in Eqs. (1). Thus $r_1$ consists of a part which arises from the partial reflection of $d_1$ at the input port and a part contributed by the fraction of $d_2$ which is transmitted through the network. The reflection and transmission properties of the network are described by the coefficients $S_{ij}$, which are termed the scattering parameters of the network.

$$\begin{aligned} r_1 &= S_{11}d_1 + S_{12}d_2 \\ r_2 &= S_{21}d_1 + S_{22}d_2 \end{aligned} \tag{1}$$

The network can be characterized by selectively setting one of the input waves to zero and measuring the resulting response. Thus when $d_2$ is zero, Eq. (2)

$$S_{21} = \frac{r_2}{d_1} \tag{2}$$

holds. The quantity $S_{21}$ gives the amplitude and phase of the wave emerging from the right-hand side of the network when a unit wave, with zero phase angle, is incident on the left-hand side. The significance of the other scattering parameters can be deduced by similar arguments. If there is no reflection of the incident waves, then $S_{11}$ and $S_{22}$ are zero, and the network is said to be matched.

The theorem of reciprocity is stated by Eq. (3).

$$S_{12} = S_{21} \tag{3}$$

That is, the network has the same transfer characteristics for one direction of propagation as it has for the other. Thus, if a matched network causes a particular insertion loss and phase shift for signals transmitted from left to right, signals transmitted from right to left must suffer the same loss and phase shift. An ideal gyrator is one which has the scattering matrix given in Eq. (4).

$$[S] = \begin{bmatrix} S_{11} & S_{12} \\ S_{21} & S_{22} \end{bmatrix} = \begin{bmatrix} 0 & -S_{21} \\ S_{21} & 0 \end{bmatrix} \tag{4}$$

The terminal currents $i_1$, and $i_2$ and voltages of $V_1$, and $V_2$ of the network (Fig. 1*b*) are related by impedances $Z_{ij}$ as shown in Eqs. (5). The theorem of reciprocity now requires the condition of Eq. (6).

$$\begin{aligned} V_1 &= Z_{11}i_1 + Z_{12}i_2 \\ V_2 &= Z_{21}i_1 + Z_{22}i_2 \end{aligned} \tag{5}$$

$$Z_{12} = Z_{21} \tag{6}$$

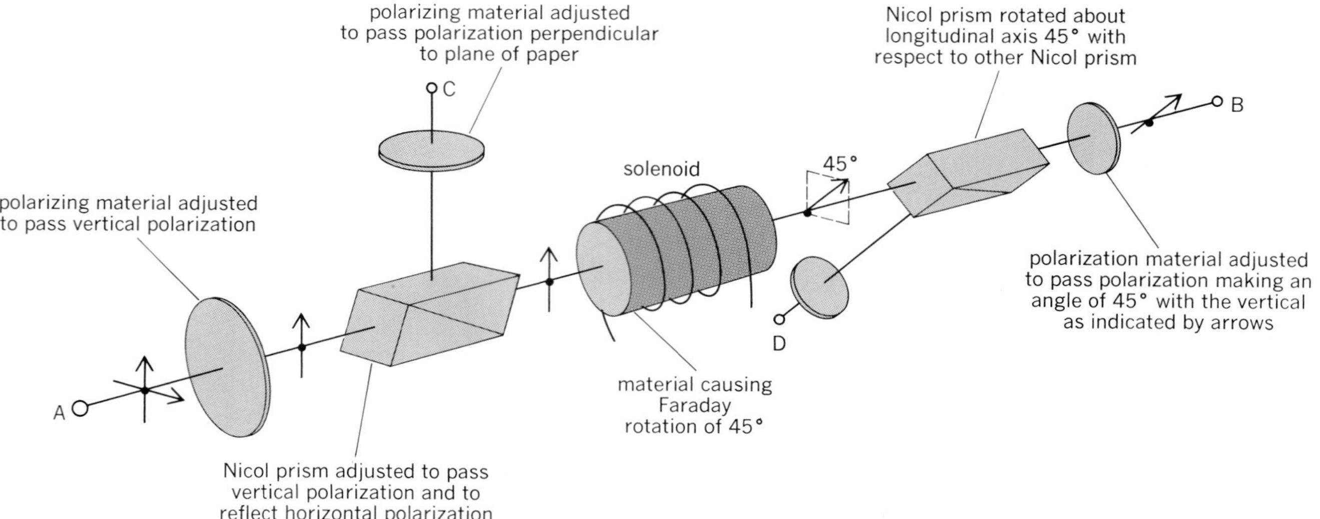


**Fig. 2.** Nonreciprocal optical device.

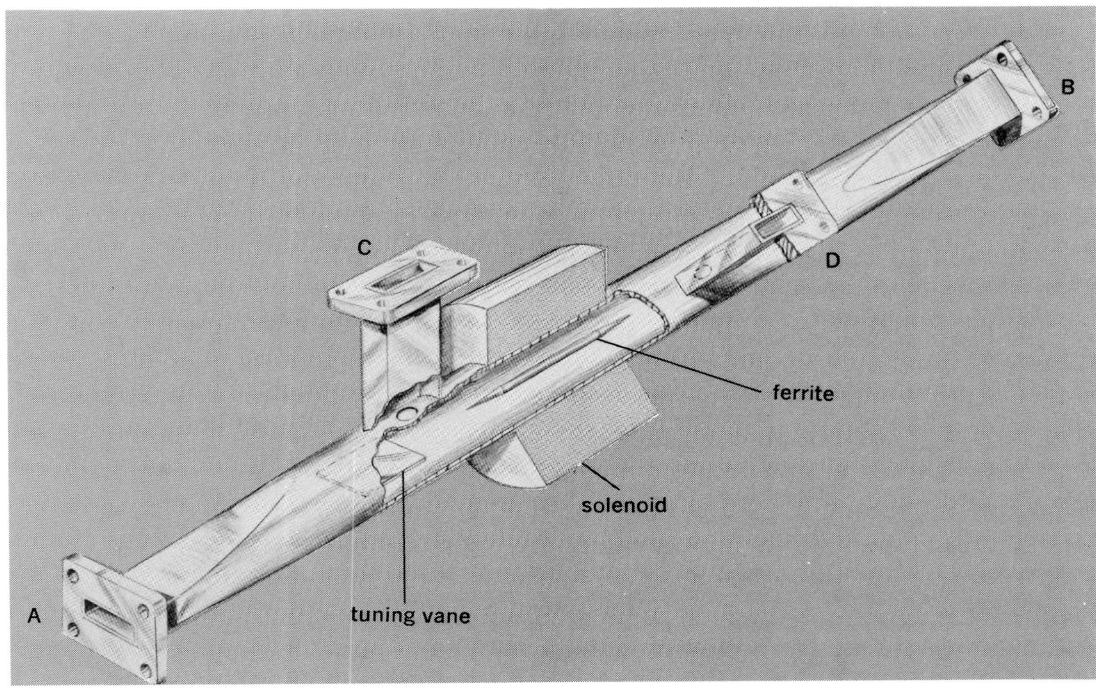


Fig. 3. Microwave analog of nonreciprocal optical device.

**Theoretical gyrators.** The first comprehensive treatment of nonreciprocal two-port networks was given in 1948 by B. D. H. Tellegen, who applied the word gyrator to describe such networks. Tellegen restricted his analysis to an ideal gyrator whose impedance matrix has the form given in Eq. (7). It may be

$$\begin{bmatrix} Z_{11} & Z_{12} \\ Z_{21} & Z_{22} \end{bmatrix} = \begin{bmatrix} 0 & -R \\ R & 0 \end{bmatrix} \tag{7}$$

easily shown that for such a gyrator to be nondissipative, the $Z_{ij}$ must be real. However, it is not necessary that the diagonal terms, $Z_{11}$ and $Z_{22}$, be zero. Furthermore, this restriction on the diagonal terms is not needed in order to realize two of the most important properties of the gyrator, namely, the construction of one-way transmission systems and the phase inversion of signal polarity for one direction of transmission.

Tellegen's ideal gyrator has the additional property of impedance inversion. If the gyrator is terminated by an impedance $Z_L$, Eq. (8), the input impedance $Z_{in}$ of the gyrator for Eq. (5) is given by Eq. (9). This

$$Z_{zL} = \frac{V_2}{i_2} \tag{8}$$

$$Z_{in} = \frac{V_1}{i_1} = \frac{R^2}{Z_L} \tag{9}$$

property of impedance inversion is not, however, unique to nonreciprocal networks. Indeed, if one makes the same requirement on a nondissipative reciprocal two-port, that $Z_{11} = Z_{22} = 0$, the input impedance $Z_{in}$ of the terminated networks is that given by Eq. (10), where $X_{12}$ is the transfer reactance

$$Z_{in} = \frac{V_1}{i_1} = \frac{X_{12}^2}{Z_L} \tag{10}$$

of a nondissipative network, $Z_{12} = jX_{12}$. Such a reciprocal impedance-inverting network can be easily realized.

**Practical gyrators.** The theorem of reciprocity has in the past been considered so universally valid that present-day textbooks still make the statement that if the condition stated in Eq. (6) is valid, the two-port is passive, and that if the condition does not hold for a particular network, it cannot be a passive one.

Although reciprocity is as universally valid in mechanical, acoustical, or optical systems as it is in electrical ones, there are passive systems that can be constructed in each of these areas which are nonreciprocal. For example, it has been long known that a mechanical system which contains a gyroscopic coupler does not obey the theorem of reciprocity.

Perhaps the first passive nonreciprocal system was an optical one proposed by Lord Rayleigh, making use of the rotation of the plane of polarization of light when it passed through a transparent material in the presence of a magnetic field. This phenomenon is called Faraday rotation. If polarized light is propagated through a transparent medium along the direction of the magnetic field, the plane of polarization of the light is rotated through some angle θ per unit length, which is determined by the properties of the

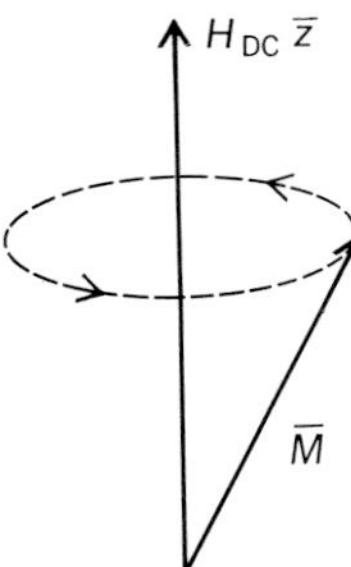


Fig. 4. Precessional motion of the ferrite internal magnetization vector, $\bar{M}$, with a static magnetic field $H_{DC}$ applied in the $\bar{z}$ direction.

medium and the strength of the magnetic field. Faraday rotation is unusual in that it is nonreciprocal. Thus the sense (clockwise or counterclockwise) of the rotation is the same whether the light travels parallel to the applied magnetic field direction or contraparallel to it. Hence, if the plane of polarization is rotated through an angle $\theta$ in traversing the Faraday cell and the ray is reflected back through the cell toward its source, it will again be rotated through an angle $\theta$, so that when it arrives back at the source, the plane of polarization will have been rotated through a total angle $2\theta$.

Lord Rayleigh's one-way system, shown in **Fig. 2**, consisted of two polarizing Nicol prisms oriented so that their planes of acceptance made an angle of 45° with each other. The material causing the Faraday rotation was placed between them. If the Faraday rotator is adjusted to cause a 45° rotation, light which is passed by the first crystal is passed by the second also. In the reverse direction, however, the 45° rotation added by the Faraday cell produces light rays polarized horizontally which are reflected by the Canada balsam cement in the first Nicol prism and directed toward point C in the figure. Thus light admitted to the device at point A is transmitted to point B; light admitted at point B is transmitted to point C; light admitted at point C is transmitted to point D; and light admitted at point D is transmitted to point A.

The microwave analogy of Lord Rayleigh's device was proposed by C. L. Hogan and is shown in **Fig. 3**. Since it circulates microwave power from waveguide A to B, from B to C, from C to D, and from D to A, it has been called a (four-port) circulator. The nonreciprocal medium used here is a ferrimagnetic material called ferrite. In such a material, infinitesimal magnetic dipole moments which arise from the electronic structure of the material act gyroscopically when a steady magnetic field is applied, as shown in **Fig. 4**. They precess about the applied field direction in a counterclockwise sense, thus permitting strong coupling to the component of a microwave-frequency magnetic field which is circularly polarized in the same sense. The component with the opposite sense of polarization is weakly coupled. Thus energy exchange between the magnetic dipoles and the microwave field is polarization-sensitive. *SEE FERRITE DEVICES.*

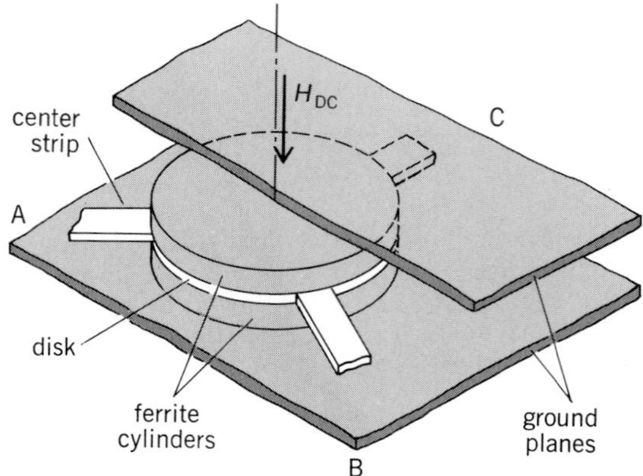


**Fig. 5. Stripline Y-junction circulator. (*After C. E. Fay and R. L. Comstock, Operation of ferrite junction circulator, IEEE Trans. Microwave Theory Tech., MTT-13:1–13, January 1965*)**

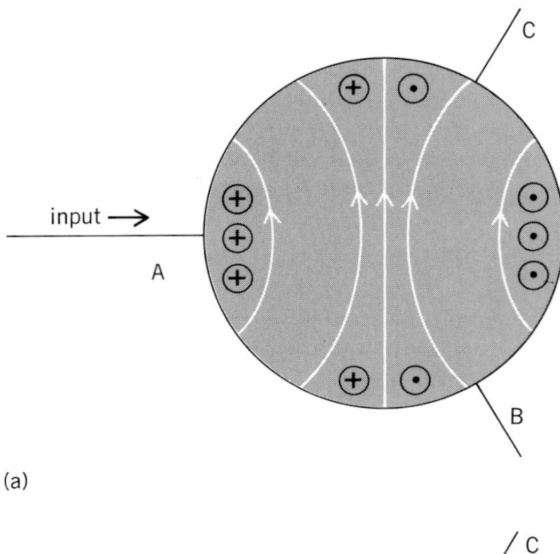


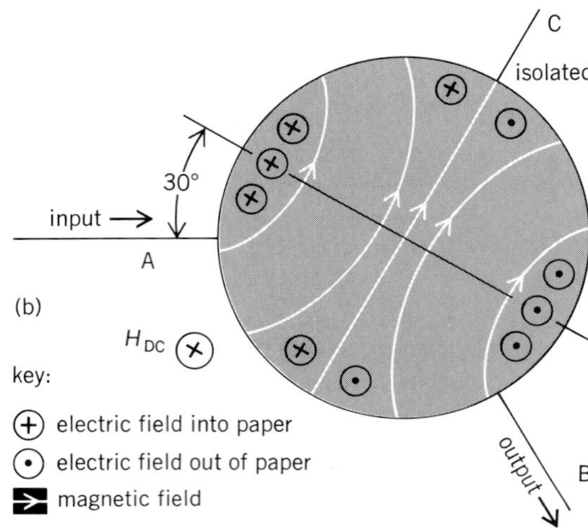


**Fig. 6. Stationary electromagnetic field pattern in disk resonator of stripline circulator. (*a*) Junction is not magnetized, resulting in symmetric coupling to ports B and C. (*b*) Junction is magnetized to rotate pattern 30°, for circulation. Port C is isolated. (*After C. E. Fay and R. L. Comstock, Operation of ferrite junction circulator, IEEE Trans. Microwave Theory Tech., MTT-13:1–13, January 1965*)**

Present-day circulators utilize the properties of electromagnetic fields in ferrite loaded microwave circuits. Consider the three-port circulator shown in **Fig. 5**, which comprises a circular disk resonator filled with ferrite connected to three transmission lines. When microwave energy is transmitted to the resonator along one of the transmission lines, an electromagnetic field is established in the resonator which is stationary in space, as shown in **Fig. 6**. The application of a dc magnetic field perpendicular to the plane of the disk resonator will rotate this stationary pattern through an angle dependent on the strength of the applied field. The field pattern is dipolar in nature, and hence has a region where the microwave magnetic field intensity is low. If the pattern is oriented to position this low-intensity region at one of the output transmission line ports, very little microwave power will leave the resonator via this port: it is isolated from the input. From the symmetry of the junction, this stationary pattern will advance 30° if the ports are excited sequentially. Thus energy at port A will be transmitted to port B, energy incident on port B will be transmitted to port C, and energy incident on port

C will be transmitted to port A. The ideal three-port scattering matrix of this junction circulator is given in Eq. (11).

$$[S] = \begin{bmatrix} 0 & 0 & S_{13} \\ S_{21} & 0 & 0 \\ 0 & S_{32} & 0 \end{bmatrix} \qquad (11)$$

Devices based on this pattern rotation principle have been realized in a variety of transmission line geometries, including rectangular waveguide, stripline, and microstrip. High performance can be obtained over wide microwave-frequency bandwidths (with ratio of upper to lower frequency limit less than or equal to 2:1) with isolation in the order of 0.01 of the incident power and with about 95% of the power transmitted to the desired port. These devices are found in most microwave systems, where they are employed to control the flow of microwave signals. For example, their use permits a radar transmitter and a radar receiver to share the same antenna. In another use, if a microwave absorber is connected to one of the ports of a three-port circulator, a one-way transmission device results, known as an isolator.

*Fred J. Rosenbaum*

**Bibliography.** H. Bosma, Junction circulators, *Advan. Microwaves*, vol. 6, 1971; J. Helszajn, *Passive and Active Microwave Circuits*, 1978; C. L. Hogan, The microwave gyrator, *Bell Syst. Tech. J.*, 31(1):1–32, 1952; B. Lax and K. J. Button, *Microwave Ferrites and Ferrimagnetics*, 1962; S. Liao, *Microwave Devices and Circuits*, 1980; B. D. H. Tellegen, The gyrator: A new electric network element, *Phillips Res. Rep.*, 3(2):81–101, 1948.

## Gyrotron

One of a family of microwave generators, also called cyclotron resonance masers, in which cyclotron resonance coupling between microwave fields and an electron beam in vacuum is the basis of operation. This type of coupling has the advantage that both the electron beam and the associated microwave structures can have dimensions which are large compared with a wavelength. Thus, cyclotron resonance masers are potentially greatly superior to conventional microwave tubes with respect to power capability at short wavelengths.

The development of these power sources is particularly significant for magnetically confined plasma fusion experiments. Microwave heating is considered an attractive method of supplying the energy needed to bring a reactor to ignition temperature, and gyrotrons provide a potential means of producing sufficient microwave power at the very short wavelength required. Gyrotrons also have potential application in millimeter-wave radar and communications systems.

**Basic characteristics.** The basic cyclotron resonance condition is given by Eq. (1), where $\omega$ is the

$$\omega = n\omega_c \qquad (1)$$

operating frequency, $n$ is an integer, and $\omega_c$ is the cyclotron frequency or angular velocity of the electron given by Eq. (2). Here, $B$ is the dc magnetic

$$\omega_c = \frac{eB}{\gamma m_o} \qquad (2)$$

field, $e$ is the electron charge, $m_o$ is the rest mass, and $\gamma$ is the relativistic mass factor. The fundamental

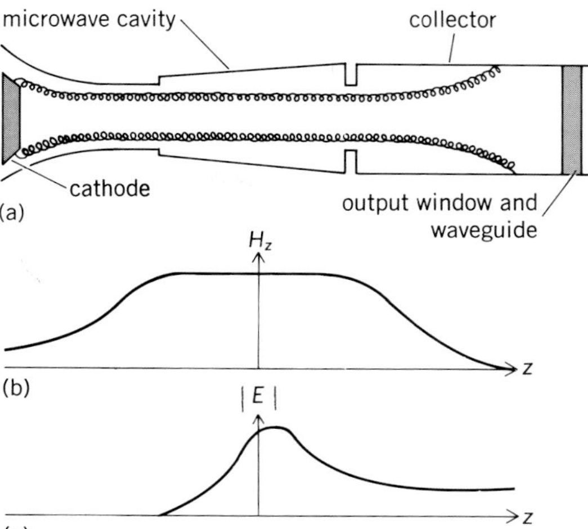


**Fig. 1. Gyrotron. (*a*) Schematic diagram, showing elements. (*b*) Plot of typical dc magnetic field $H_z$ as function of distance *z* along axis. (*c*) Plot of representative microwave electric field intensity |*E*|.**

cyclotron resonance occurs when $n = 1$. This is the strongest and most useful interaction. The resonance condition requires that very high magnetic fields be used for high-frequency devices. For example, a frequency of 120 GHz requires a magnetic field of about 45 teslas. Generally, the very-high-frequency gyrotrons have used superconducting magnets.

Larger values of $n$ allow corresponding reductions in the required dc magnetic field. Practical devices have generally been limited to values of $n$ no larger than 2 (second-harmonic operation).

The most important microwave field component in the gyrotron is the electric field tangential to the orbit of the electron. With the fundamental cyclotron resonance interaction, any spatial variation of the microwave fields is of little importance. It is this property that allows the gyrotron to use cross-section areas which are large compared with a wavelength.

Electron bunching in the gyrotron occurs by virtue of the relativistic mass effect included in Eq. (2). The transverse microwave electric field introduces a sinusoidal modulation of $\gamma$ depending on the angular po-

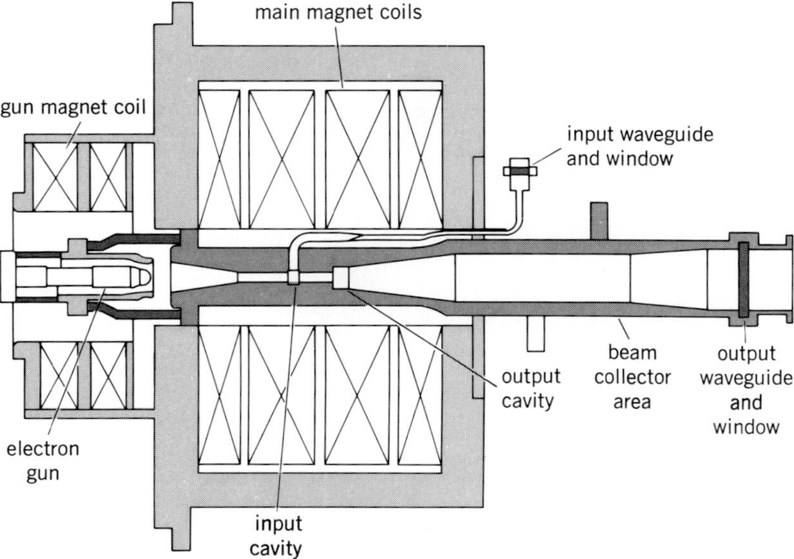


**Fig. 2. Simplified cross section of pulsed gyroklystron amplifier.**

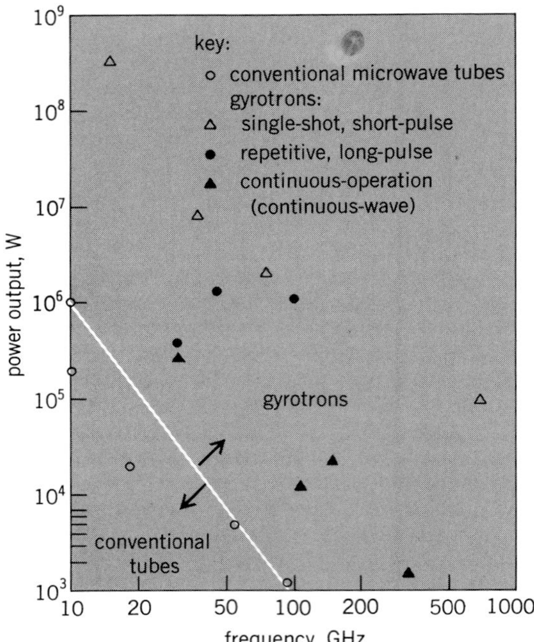


**Fig. 3. Power output versus frequency typical of gyrotrons compared with that of conventional microwave tubes.**

sition of the electron in its orbit relative to the direction of the electric field. The modulation of $\gamma$ results in a modulation of angular velocity as given by Eq. (2). As the beam drifts, this converts to angular bunching in the coordinate system centered on each electron orbit. By proper adjustment of phase conditions, the bunched beam can give up most of its energy to microwave energy.

A number of tube configurations are possible using the cyclotron resonance interaction. The simplest form, and that used for most practical gyrotrons to date, is an oscillator using a single resonant cavity. A gyroklystron amplifier employing two or more cavities is another alternative; and in a third variation a traveling-wave circuit, in analogy to a traveling-wave tube, is used.

A schematic representation of a gyrotron (single-cavity oscillator) is shown in **Fig. 1**, along with a typical dc magnetic field profile $H_z$ and a representative microwave electric field distribution $|E|$. The electron beam is a hollow beam with all electrons having helical motion. For efficient operation, all electrons must have a large fraction of their total energy contained in motion transverse to the device axis. A simplified cross section of a pulsed gyroklystron amplifier is shown in **Fig. 2**.

**Capabilities.** A summary of gyrotron demonstrated power output versus frequency is shown in **Fig. 3**, along with power capabilities of conventional klystrons and traveling-wave tubes. In the case of the pulsed devices, it is the peak power output that is shown on the graph. The single-shot, short-pulse results refer to devices using intense relativistic beams which are not suitable for repetitive pulsing. The gyrotron results indicate a clear capability for producing higher power at high frequency. SEE KLYSTRON; MICROWAVE TUBE; TRAVELING-WAVE TUBE.

*Howard R. Jory*

***Bibliography.*** A. A. Andronov et al., *Infrared Phys.*, 18:385–394, December 1978; V. A. Flyagin et al., *IEEE Trans.*, MTT-25:514-521, June 1977; J. L. Hirshfield and V. L. Granatstein, *IEEE Trans.*, MTT-25:522–527, June 1977; H. R. Jory, *Digest of the 1977 International Electron Devices Meeting*, IEEE, December 1977.

## Hall effect

An effect whereby a conductor carrying an electric current perpendicular to an applied magnetic field develops a voltage gradient which is transverse to both the current and the magnetic field. It was discovered by E. H. Hall in 1879. Important information about the nature of the conduction process in semiconductors and metals may be obtained through analysis of this effect.

**Theory.** A simple model which accounts for the phenomenon is the following. For a magnetic field of strength $B$ in the $z$ direction (**Fig. 1**), particles flowing with speed $v$ in the $x$ direction suffer a Lorentz force $F_L$ in the $y$ direction given by Eq. (1), where $q$ is the

$$F_L = -qvB \qquad (1)$$

charge of the particles. This force deflects the particles so that a charge imbalance develops between opposite sides of the conductor. Deflection continues until the electric field $E_y$ resulting from this charge imbalance produces a force $F_y = qE_y$ which cancels the Lorentz force. In practice, the equilibrium condition $F_L + F_y = 0$ is achieved almost instantaneously, giving a steady-state Hall field as in Eq. (2). The cur-

$$E_y = vB_2 \qquad (2)$$

rent density is $J_x = nqv$, where $n$ is the carrier density. The Hall resistivity, defined by Eq (3), is thus given by Eq. (4). For a sample of thickness $t$ and

$$\rho_{yx} = \frac{E_y}{J_x} \qquad (3)$$

$$\rho_{yx} = \frac{B}{nq} \qquad (4)$$

width $w$, the Hall voltage is $V_H = -E_y w$ and the total current is $I = J_x tw$ so that the Hall resistance, defined by Eq. (5) (which is the experimentally measured quantity), obeys Eq. (6) and is independent of the

$$R_H = \frac{V_H}{I} \qquad (5)$$

$$R_H = \frac{-B}{nqt} \qquad (6)$$

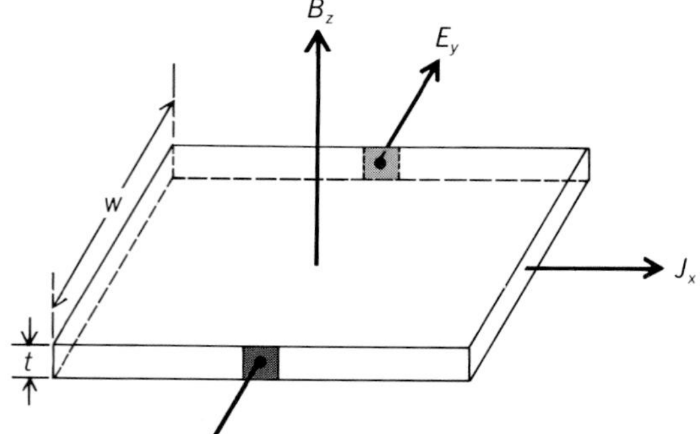


**Fig. 1. Configuration of fields and currents in the Hall effect experiment.**

**Hall coefficients of elemental metals**

| Element | Nominal valence | $R_{EXP}(10^{-10}$ m³/C) | $R_{EXP}/R_0$ |
|---|---|---|---|
| Lithium | 1 | −1.70* | +1.27 |
| Sodium | 1 | −2.34† | +0.99 |
| Potassium | 1 | −4.45† | +1.00 |
| Rubidium | 1 | −5.0* | +0.93 |
| Silver | 1 | −0.90* | +0.84 |
| Gold | 1 | −0.72* | +0.68 |
| Beryllium | 2 | +2.4* | −9.5 |
| Aluminum | 3 | +1.02† | −3.0 |
| Indium | 3 | +1.60† | −2.99 |

*At room temperature.
†At 4 K (−452°F).

width but inversely proportional to the sample thickness. The Hall coefficient, defined by Eq. (7), satisfies Eq. (8) and thus $R_0$ provides a measure of the

$$R_0 = \frac{\rho_{yx}}{B} \tag{7}$$

$$R_0 = \frac{1}{nq} \tag{8}$$

sign and magnitude of the mobile charge density in a conductor. Within the free-electron theory of simple metals, $q$ is expected to be the electron charge $-e$, and $n$ is taken to be $n = Zn_A$, where $Z$ is the valence of the metal and $n_A$ is the density of the atoms. This yields Eq. (9).

$$R_0 = \frac{1}{n_A Ze} \tag{9}$$

The **table** lists Hall coefficients at moderately high fields for various elemental metals. $R_{EXP}$ is the measured Hall coefficient and $R_0$ is the theoretical value calculated by using Eq. (9). If Eq. (9) were exact, all the entries in the last column of the table would be + 1.0. As can be seen from the table, Eq. (9) is approximately valid in simple monovalent metals but fails drastically for other materials, often even giving the wrong sign. The reason for this is that Eqs. (8) and (9) are based on a simple theory that does not take into account collisions between the electrons and the atoms and among the electrons themselves. These effects can be properly described only within a quantum-mechanical theory. Indeed, the explanation of the failures of Eq. (9) was one of the great early triumphs of the quantum theory of solids. The theory of band structure shows how collisions with the periodic array of atoms in a crystal can cause the current carriers to be holes which have an effective positive charge which changes the sign of the Hall coefficient. Band structure theory also accounts for the observed dependence of $R_0$ on the orientation of the current and the magnetic field relative to the crystal axes, an effect which is very useful for studying the topology of the Fermi surface. *See Band theory of solids; Holes in solids.*

**Effect in semiconductors.** Because of band structure effects, semiconductors generally contain two types of carriers and their number density is highly temperature-dependent. The presence of two types of carriers causes the Hall coefficient to vary with the strength of the magnetic field. This effect can be used to deduce the relaxation times of each carrier species. *See Semiconductor.*

**Effect in magnetic materials.** In a magnetic material the Hall resistivity has the form $\rho_{yx} = R_0B + R_SM$, where $M$ is the magnetization and $R_S$ is the anomalous (or extraordinary) Hall coefficient. The contribution of the anomalous term due to the magnetization may be as large as 100 to 1000 times that of the ordinary term due to the Lorentz force. The origin of this intrinsically quantum-mechanical effect is the asymmetry of the scattering of the electrons from the atoms when there is a net magnetization. The electrons scatter more frequently to the right (say) than the left, producing an extra transverse force distinct from the Lorentz force. An example is illustrated in **Fig. 2**, which gives the Hall resistivity and the magnetization of amorphous ferromagnetic cobalt as a function of applied field. The initial sharp rise in the resistivity is due to the increase in the normal component of magnetization of the sample and the resulting anomalous Hall effect. The magnetization reaches its saturation value $M_S$ at an applied field of about 1.8 teslas. The subsequent linear decrease in the Hall resistivity is due to the ordinary Hall effect, which happens to have the opposite sign.

**Quantization of Hall resistance.** In certain special field-effect transistors, it is possible to create an electron gas which is effectively two-dimensional. The Hall resistance for an idealized system in two dimensions is given by Eq. (10), where $n_S$ is the density of

$$R_H = \frac{B}{n_S e} \tag{10}$$

electrons per unit area (rather than volume). The measured value of $R_H$ (actually, of $V_H = IR_H$ at constant current $I$) for a high-quality (low-disorder) device is plotted in **Fig. 3** as a function of $B$. The linear behavior predicted by Eq. (10) is observed only at low fields. At high fields the Hall resistance exhibits plateau regions in which it is a constant independent of $B$. Furthermore, the values of $R_H$ on these plateaus are given quite accurately by the universal relation of Eq. (11), where $h$ is Planck's constant and $i$ is an

$$R_H = \frac{h}{e^2 i} \tag{11}$$

integer (Fig. 3). The precision and reproducibility of measurements of the quantized values of $R_H$ have reached a few parts in $10^8$. The absolute accuracy with which Eq. (11) has been verified is better than 1 part in $10^6$.

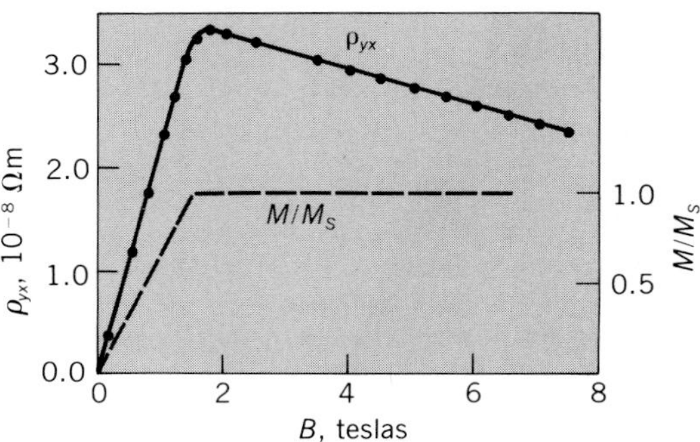


**Fig. 2.** Hall resistivity $\rho_{xy}$ of amorphous ferromagnetic cobalt as a function of applied field $B$, and ratio of magnetization $M$ to its saturation value $M_S$. (*After G. Bergmann, The normal Hall-effect of random close packed cobalt, Phys. Lett., 60A:245–246, 1977*)

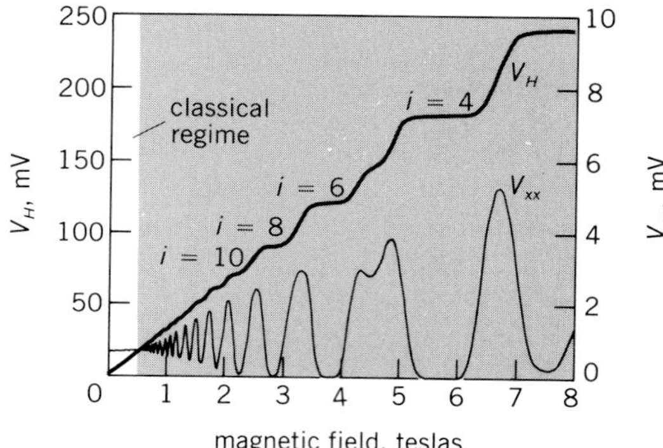


**Fig. 3. Hall voltage $V_H$ for a current of 25.5 microamperes in a GaAs–AlGaAs heterostructure at a temperature of 1.11 K (−457.67°F) as a function of magnetic field. $V_{xx}$ is the longitudinal voltage drop along the device. (*After M. E. Cage, R. F. Dziuba, and B. F. Field, U.S. National Bureau of Standards, unpublished*)**

This extremely accurate quantization of $R_H$ may allow the realization of a new standard of resistance based solely on fundamental constants of nature. In addition, the quantum unit of Hall resistance, $h/e^2 \cong$ 25,812.80 ohms, determines the fine-structure constant.

The explanation of this remarkable phenomenon involves several subtle quantum-mechanical effects. Figure 3 shows that in the quantum regime (small $i$), $V_{xx}$, which is the dissipative (longitudinal) voltage drop, approaches zero on the Hall plateaus. The quantization of the Hall resistance is intimately connected with this fact. It is speculated that at zero temperature the dissipation is zero and that Eq. (11) is then obeyed exactly.

**Anomalous quantum Hall effect.** A further striking phenomenon is observed at magnetic fields even higher than those shown in Fig. 3. Additional plateaus occur corresponding to quantum numbers which are simple rational fractions such as $i = 1/3$ or $i = 2/5$. This is known as the anomalous quantum Hall effect and is believed to arise from the mutual Coulomb repulsion among the particles.

*S. M. Girvin*

***Bibliography.*** N. W. Ashcroft and N. D. Mermin, *Solid State Physics*, 1976; G. Bergmann, The anomalous Hall effect, *Phys. Today*, 32(8):25–30, 1979; M. E. Cage and S. M. Girvin, The quantum Hall effect I, *Comments Solid State Phys.*, 11:1–16, 1983; C. L. Chien and C. R. Westgate (eds.), *The Hall Effect and Its Applications*, 1979; S. M. Girvin and M. E. Cage, The quantum Hall effect II, *Comments Solid State Phys.*, 11: 47–58, 1983; C. Kittel, *Introduction to Solid State Physics*, 5th ed., 1976.

## Harmonic analyzer

An instrument to measure the amplitudes, frequencies, and sometimes the phases of the components of a nonsinusoidal waveform. It is usually associated with audio and low frequencies, typically up to 100 kHz. A spectrum analyzer is a type of harmonic analyzer. *SEE SPECTRUM ANALYZER.*

A nonsinusoidal waveform (**Fig. 1***a*) can be viewed in the time domain by using an oscilloscope, but this only shows the wave shape and indicates that there may be distortion or unwanted signals. A harmonic analyzer separates out each signal component to isolate the Fourier series components of the waveform (Fig. 1*b*). *SEE OSCILLOSCOPE; NONSINUSOIDAL WAVEFORM; WAVEFORM.*

There are many types of analyzer; each is used for different applications.

**Tunable filter analyzer.** This type, also known as a sweeping filter analyzer, is the simplest. A band-pass filter which is either manually or automatically tuned isolates each component of the input signal in turn. The display for this, and for all types of analyzers, can be a moving-coil meter, digital display, chart recorder, $x$-$y$ plotter, or cathode-ray tube. The device is calibrated so that the levels and frequencies of the harmonic components can be accurately determined. *SEE CATHODE-RAY TUBE; ELECTRIC FILTER.*

**Stepped filter analyzer.** The signal to be analyzed is applied simultaneously to an array of band-pass filters, each with a different center frequency. The detector is switched to each filter output in turn, so that the display gives the level of signal corresponding to each filter frequency.

This method is cumbersome and expensive; a refinement, which achieves a similar effect, is to use just two filters whose tuned frequency can be changed by changing the values of the filter components. The two filters step up alternately in frequency so that one filter is being changed while the other is used to take a measurement.

**Heterodyne analyzer.** A heterodyne analyzer, usually known as a wave analyzer, uses the principle of a superheterodyne radio receiver to convert the signals to be analyzed to a chosen fixed frequency at which filtering takes place. The tunable oscillator is

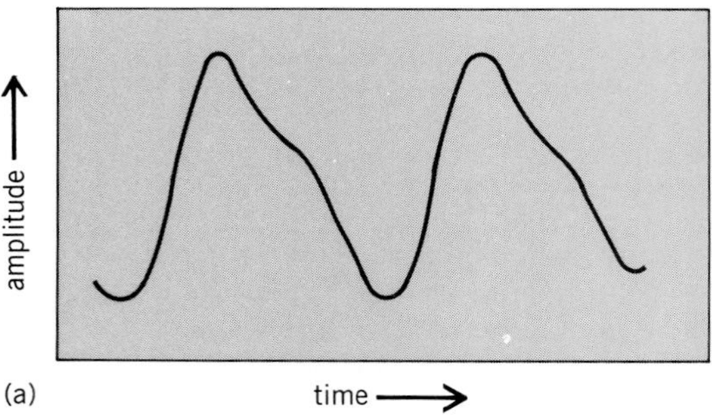


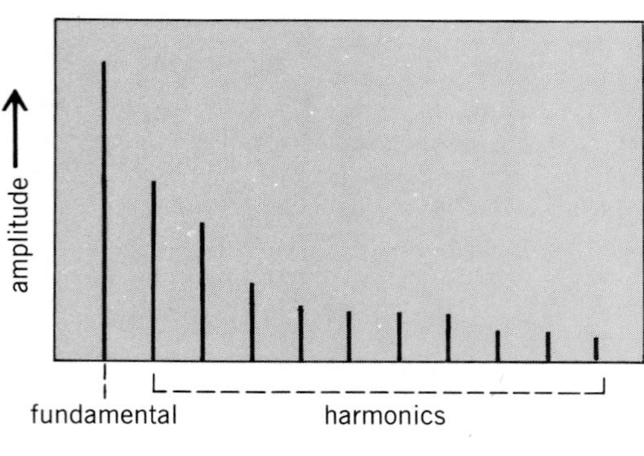


**Fig. 1. Nonsinusoidal waveform displays. (*a*) Oscilloscope display, giving time domain representation. (*b*) Harmonic analysis display, giving frequency domain representation.**

thus changed rather than the filter. The advantage of this method is that measurements are made with a filter whose characteristics, such as bandwidth and shape, are fixed. Since only one filter is required, this type of analyzer is generally more selective than the variable or switched filters. A spectrum analyzer is essentially an automatically swept heterodyne analyzer. *SEE HETERODYNE PRINCIPLE; RADIO RECEIVER.*

**Parallel filter analyzer.** The analyzers described above, which are known as serial or sequential analyzers, have a serious limitation for some applications: they need an input signal which remains constant while the measurement is made. To analyze varying waveforms such as speech, a real-time analyzer is required which can display all frequency components of a waveform simultaneously. A parallel filter analyzer is such a real-time analyzer. It uses a bank of filters, each tuned to a different frequency. It is of mainly historical interest since other methods have largely superseded it. The main limitation of this method is that high selectivity is not economically achievable, and that only a limited number of filters, typically 30, are practical so fine resolution is not possible.

**Time compression analyzer.** The time compression analyzer (**Fig. 2**) measures all frequency components almost simultaneously and is thus termed a real-time analyzer. It is a variant of the heterodyne analyzer, but it has a digital processing section preceding the mixer. This digital section stores the input signal, compresses it in time, and then repeatedly plays back the replica of the input signal while the tunable oscillator tunes the instrument over the required frequency range. *SEE ANALOG-TO-DIGITAL CONVERTER; DIGITAL-TO-ANALOG CONVERTER.*

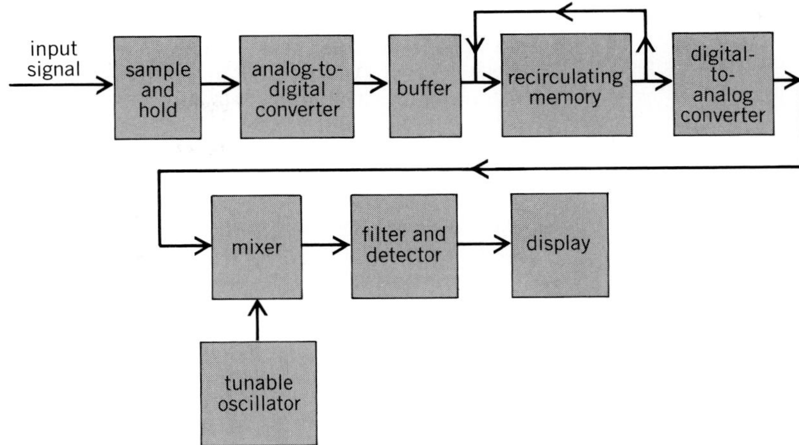


**Fig. 2. Block diagram of a time compression analyzer.**

**Fast Fourier transform analyzer.** While the time compression analyzer uses digital techniques to enhance an analog analyzer, a fast Fourier transform (FFT) analyzer uses digital techniques exclusively. The FFT analyzer computes the harmonic content of a waveform by using an algorithm to calculate the Fourier transform.

One of the main advantages of an FFT analyzer is that the phases of the harmonic components may also be measured. Another advantage is that further digital processing is possible, including zoom and autocorrelation. Further processing may also be carried out to determine other parameters such as the power cepstrum, which is the logarithm of the power spectrum.

**Distortion factor meter.** A distortion factor meter does not give absolute frequencies and amplitudes; instead it expresses the unwanted or distortion components as a proportion of the wanted or fundamental signal. Such an instrument is used to measure the distortion of audio equipment where the lack of detailed discrete information is not a problem since only a "figure of merit," the distortion factor, is required.

**Figure 3** shows the concept of such an instrument. The tunable rejection filter is switched in after a reference level has been established so that the level of unwanted signals can be evaluated against the level of the rejected fundamental.

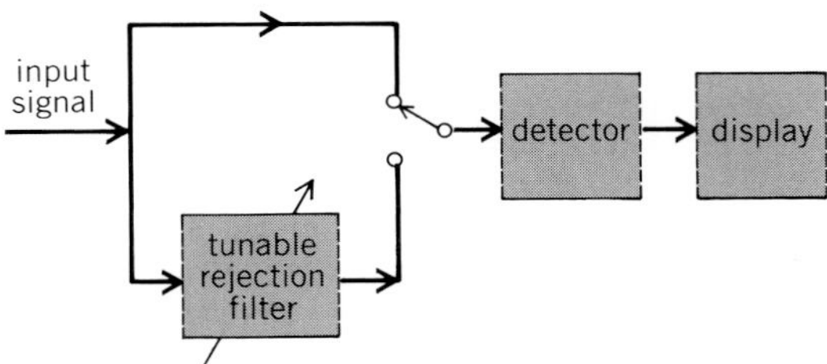


**Fig. 3. Block diagram of a distortion factor meter.**

**Applications.** Harmonic analyzers of the types described are used in a variety of applications. The most obvious use is the measurement of distortion and unwanted signals in all types of audio equipment from recording and broadcast studios to amplifiers used in the home. *SEE SOUND RECORDING; SOUND-REPRODUCING SYSTEMS.*

Further uses include the analysis of speech waveforms, measurement of vibration and resonances in mechanical equipment and structures, and determination of echo delays in seismic signals. Other applications include the investigation of noise such as from aircraft engines, analysis of sonar signals used to detect objects underwater, and study of ultrasonic waves to determine the internal structure of objects such as human tissue and metal castings. *SEE SPEECH RECOGNITION.*

*S. J. Gledhill*

**Bibliography.** J. S. Bendat and A. G. Piersol, *Engineering Applications of Correlation and Spectral Analysis*, 1980; J. W. Cooley and J. W. Tukey, An algorithm for the machine calculation of complex Fourier series, *Math. Computat.*, 19(90):297–301, April 1965; M. Engelson and F. Telewski, *Spectrum Analyzer Theory and Applications*, 1974; G. M. Jenkins and D. G. Watts, *Spectral Analysis and Its Applications*, 1968; R. B. Randall, *Application of B&K Equipment to Frequency Analysis*, 1977; Rockland Systems Corp., *Spectrum Analysis: Theory Implementation and Applications*, 1979.

## Heterodyne principle

The basic principle underlying the operation of a superheterodyne radio, television, or other receiver, wherein two alternating currents that differ in frequency are mixed in a nonlinear device to produce two new frequencies, corresponding to the sum and the difference of the input frequencies. Only the difference frequency is commonly used in a superheterodyne receiver, where it serves as the input to the intermediate-frequency amplifier. The heterodyne principle permits conversion of a wide range of different input frequencies to a predetermined, lower intermediate-frequency value that can be amplified more efficiently. Some frequency meters also use the heterodyne principle when comparing an unknown input frequency with a calibrated frequency standard. *See* Radio receiver; Superheterodyne receiver; Television receiver.

*John Markus*

## High-electron-mobility transistor

A high-speed field-effect transistor (FET) whose rapid response is based on the high mobilities of two-dimensional electrons. The need for fast electron devices is constantly increasing. These devices are used to improve the performance of microwave amplifiers in communication equipment as well as to enhance switching speed in large-scale computers. The high-electron-mobility transistor (HEMT) has been developed to meet such requirements. It switches on or off in about 10 picoseconds with the maximum oscillation frequency exceeding 100 GHz. Since 1980 considerable research has been done on the fabrication and characteristics of the device as well as on its microwave and digital applications. The device is also called by various other names: two-dimensional electron gas FET (TEGFET), selectively doped heterojunction transistor (SDHT), and modulation-doped FET (MODFET), all descriptive of various aspects of the operation or structure of the device.

**Structure and operating principles.** The device is made of gallium arsenide (GaAs) and gallium aluminum arsenide (GaAlAs) with a Schottky metal contact on the gallium aluminum arsenide layer and two ohmic contacts penetrating into the gallium arsenide layer, serving as the gate, the source, and the drain, respectively (**Fig. 1**). Schottky and ohmic contacts exhibit rectifying and nonrectifying characteristics, respectively. The device's fast response to the signal is attibuted to the fact that two-dimensional electrons

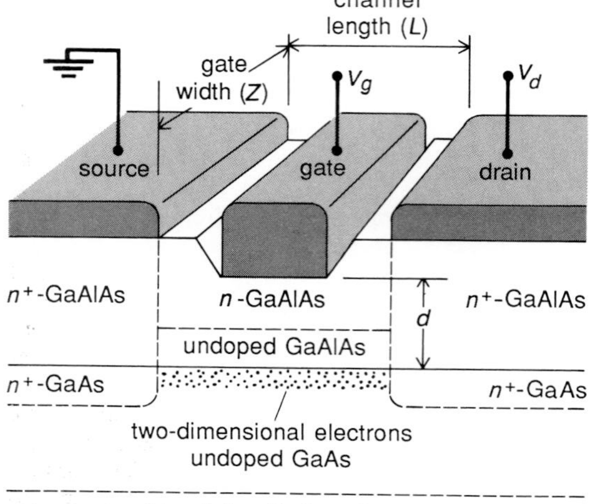


**Fig. 1. Cross section of a high-electron-mobility transistor (HEMT). The source, gate, and drain are metal electrodes; the source and gate are usually gold-germanium alloys and the drain is typically aluminum.**

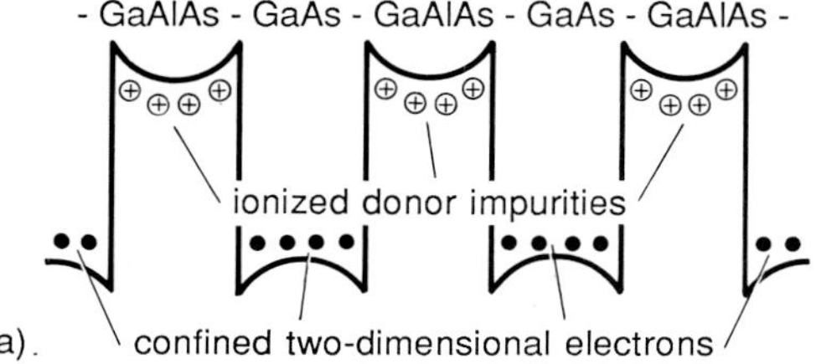


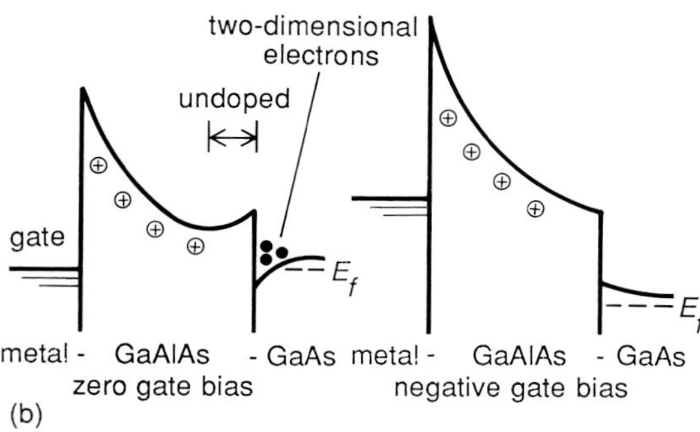


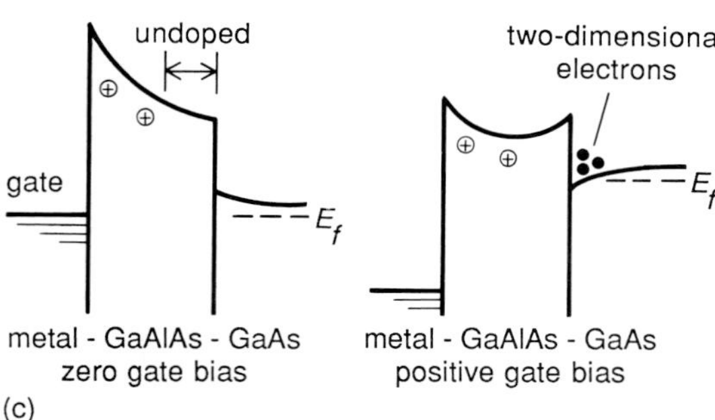


**Fig. 2. Energy diagrams of modulation doping. (*a*) Superlattice. (*b*) Depletion-mode HEMT (D-HEMT), without and with negative gate bias voltage. $E_f$ = Fermi level. (c) Enhancement-mode HEMT (E-HEMT), without and with positive gate bias voltage.**

(discussed below) at the interface between gallium arsenide and gallium aluminum arsenide have high mobilities and move very rapidly from source to drain.

The high-electron-mobility transistor evolved from work on gallium arsenide–gallium aluminum arsenide superlattices, periodic structures prepared by deposition of alternating ultrathin layers of gallium arsenide and gallium aluminum arsenide (**Fig. 2*a***). Usually free carriers—electrons and holes created in a semiconductor by impurity doping—suffer from impurity scattering. In superlattices, however, it is possible to spatially separate free carriers and their parent impurity atoms by doping impurities in the potential barriers of gallium aluminum arsenide. Electrons from donor impurities transfer to the potential well of gallium arsenide, forming a layer of so-called two-dimensional free electrons (Fig. 2*a*) that are free to move in the two dimensions parallel to the layers but are confined to bound quantum states in the well with respect to motion perpendicular to the layers. Such two-dimensional electrons suffer less from impurity scattering because of their spatial separation from the impurities, and thus have high mobilities. This concept of modulation doping was proposed together with the superlattice concept in 1969, and was first successfully implemented in 1978, resulting in the observation of high electron mobilities in gallium arsenide. Modulation doping also can be used to achieve high mobility for two-dimensional electrons confined in the potential well formed at the interface between gallium arsenide and gallium aluminum arsenide where, again, electrons transfer from donor impurities in gallium aluminum arsenide to the potential well of gallium arsenide. *SEE* ARTIFICIALLY LAYERED STRUCTURES; SEMICONDUCTOR HETEROSTRUCTURES.

The high-electron-mobility transistor employs this modulation-doping technique to obtain high electron mobilities: impurities are doped only in the gallium aluminum arsenide. Figure 2 shows the energy diagrams for two types of high-electron-mobility transistors: depletion-mode (D-HEMT; Fig. 2*b*) and enhancement-mode (E-HEMT; Fig. 2*c*) without and with negative and positive bias voltages for the gate Schottky barrier, respectively. A narrow portion of gallium aluminum arsenide close to the gallium arsenide is kept undoped. This further separates impurities and electrons, resulting in more enhancement on electron mobilities.

The high-electron-mobility transistor structure (Fig. 1) is fabricated on semi-insulating gallium arsenide substrates by the advanced thin-film growth techniques of molecular beam epitaxy or metal organic (or organometallic) chemical vapor deposition. Such techniques enable growth of high-quality heterostructures having designed potential profiles and impurity distributions with dimensional control close to interatomic spacing (approximately 0.2 nanometer), and with virtually defect-free interfaces in a lattice-matched pair such as gallium arsenide–gallium aluminum arsenide. This great precision in epitaxy is required in order to fabricate both D-HEMTs and E-HEMTs on the same wafer and achieve precise control of their threshold voltages.

The principle of operation of the high-electron-mobility transistor is similar to that of the silicon metal-oxide-semiconductor FET (MOSFET). In D-HEMTs, the thickness of the doped gallium aluminum arsenide under the gate is great enough for two-dimensional electrons to be present when there is no bias voltage (the device is normally on), and a negative gate bias depletes them (Fig. 2*b*); in E-HEMTs, that thickness is small enough for two-dimensional electrons to be absent when there is no bias voltage (the device is normally off), and a positive gate bias induces them (Fig. 2*c*). In practice, a small amount of recessing of the gate electrode (Fig. 1) is done by etching; the amount of the recess determines the type of device, either depletion-mode or enhancement-mode.

**Performance characteristics.** In the linear region, at low drain voltages, the transconductance $g_m$ is given by Eq. (1), where $Z$ and $L$ are the gate width

$$g_m = \frac{Z}{L}\mu C V_d \qquad (1)$$

and the channel length, respectively (Fig. 1); $\mu$ is the electron mobility; the capacitance $C$ is given by $\epsilon/d$ (where $\epsilon$ is the permittivity and $d$ is the thickness of gallium aluminum arsenide under the gate); and $V_d$ is the drain voltage. The high-electron-mobility transistor exhibits a high transconductance because of high electron mobilities as well as a large value of the relative permittivity, 1.3 for gallium arsenide as compared with 3.9 for silicon dioxide ($SiO_2$). At high bias voltages where the electron velocity saturates, the transconductance is given by Eq. (2), where $v_s$ is the

$$g_m = ZCv_s \qquad (2)$$

saturation electron velocity that is characteristic of gallium arsenide, which is considerably faster than that of silicon. Typical values for $L$ and $d$ are 1.2 micrometers and 35–40 nm, respectively.

For high-speed operations, there are two factors that limit the frequency response of a field-effect transistor, the $RC$ time constant and the transit time. The $RC$ time constant is a measure of how rapidly the charge associated with the capacitance $C$ of the device can be acquired and lost. The high electron mobility helps to reduce the resistance $R$ and thus reduces the $RC$ time constant. The transit time $\tau$ is the time required for electrons to travel from source to drain. In the linear region it is given by Eq. (3), and when the

$$\tau = \frac{L^2}{\mu} V_d \qquad (3)$$

velocity is saturated it is given by Eq. (4). The high

$$\tau = L/v_s \qquad (4)$$

mobility, high saturation velocity, and short channel length all contribute to improvements in the frequency response. The electron mobilities in the high-electron-mobility transistor increase considerably at low temperatures. Thus, the device performance at −321°F (77 K; liquid-nitrogen temperature) is substantially better than that at 80°F (300 K; room temperature).

**Applications.** D-HEMTS for microwave low-noise amplifiers have been developed and are commercially available, for instance, in satellite communication systems. A noise figure of 1.8 dB and associated gain of 8 dB at a frequency of 20 GHz have been reported.

E-HEMTs have been used for switching, because of their low power dissipation, in high-speed integrated digital circuits, where D-HEMTs with gate shorted to source serve as two-terminal loads. Three basic circuits, a NOR gate, a NAND gate, and a cross-coupled flip-flop memory cell, are illustrated in **Fig. 3**, where so-called direct-coupled FET logic circuit configurations are implemented. By using the flip-flop cell, a 4000-bit static random access memory (SRAM) has been reported with minimum address access time of 2.0 nanoseconds at −321°F (77 K) and 4.4 ns at 80°F (300 K). By using the NOR gate, a 1500-gate array has been reported with multiplication time of 3.1 ns at −321°F (77 K) and 4.9 ns at 80°F (300 K) in an 8 × 8 parallel multiplier. These figures, particularly those at −321°F (77 K), probably represent the highest speed recorded. *SEE* LOGIC CIRCUITS; SEMICONDUCTOR MEMORIES.

Recently, high hole mobilities with gallium arsenide and gallium aluminum arsenide heterostructures have been achieved by a modulation-doping technique similar to that described above, except that doping is carried out with acceptors such as beryllium (Be) ins70ad of donors such as silicon (Si). An attempt was then made to fabricate a high-hole-mobility transistor, which would complement the high-electron-mobility transistor.

Obviously, the production of high electron or hole mobilities by the modulation-doping technique is not limited to gallium arsenide and gallium aluminum arsenide heterostructures and, indeed, has been obtained with heterostructures such as gallium indium

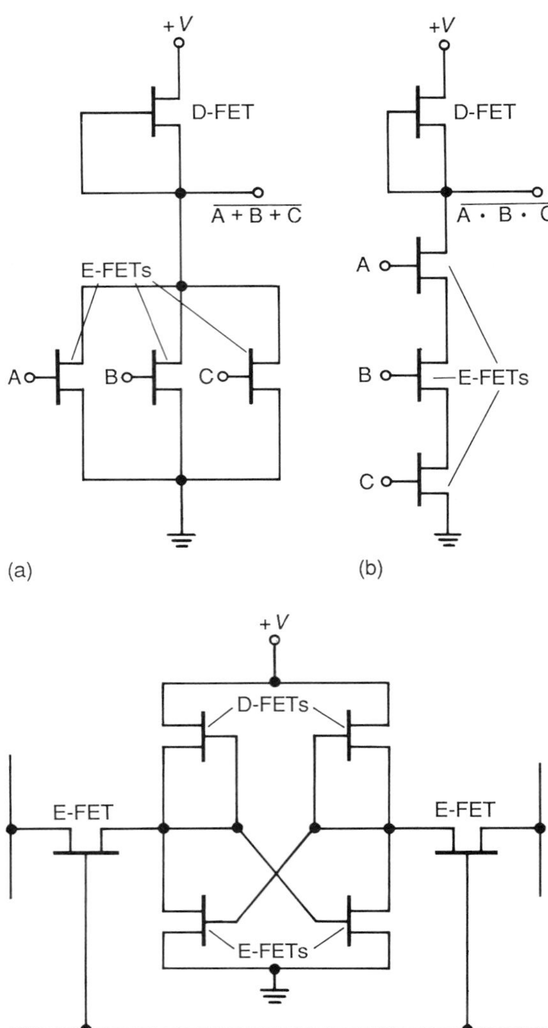


**Fig. 3.** Basic circuits employing high-electron-mobility transistors. (*a*) NOR gate with inputs A, B, and C, and output $\overline{A + B + C}$. (*b*) NAND gate, with inputs A, B, and C and output $\overline{A \cdot B \cdot C}$. (c) Cross-coupled flip-flop memory cell.

arsenide–indium phosphide (GaInAs-InP) and gallium indium phosphide—gallium arsenide (GaInP-GaAs). It is certainly possible to fabricate high-electron-mobility transistors with those heterostructures, some of which may outperform the conventional high-electron-mobility transistor for some purposes.

In summary, the high-electron-mobility transistor possesses many of the attributes required for high-speed operation. With more advanced material and fabrication technologies, better performance and larger integration for supercomputers can be expected in the near future. *See Integrated circuits; Microwave solid-state devices; Transistor.*

*Leo Esaki*

**Bibliography.** R. Dingle et al., Electron mobilities in modulation-doped semiconductor heterojunction superlattices, *Appl. Phys. Lett.*, 31:665–667, 1978; L. Easki and R. Tsu, Superlattice and negative conductivity in semiconductors, *IBM J. Res. Dev.*, 14:61–65, 1970; H. Morkoc and P. M. Solomon, The HEMT: A superfast transistor, *IEEE Spectrum*, 21(2):28–35, 1984; P. M. Solomon and H. Morkoc, Modulation-doped GaAs/AlGaAs heterojunction field-effect transistors (MODFETs), ultra high-speed device for supercomputers, *IEEE Trans. Electr. Devices*, ED-31:1015–1027, 1984.

## High-polymer transducer

A transducer that uses a piezoelectric high-polymer film, consisting of polyvinylidene fluoride. Of particular interest are high-polymer loudspeakers and high-polymer stereophonic headphones. As the film is very thin and flexible, an omnidirectional high-polymer loudspeaker has been developed by making the film into a cylindrical shape. The loudspeaker has perfect omnidirectional patterns in the horizontal plane. The high-polymer headphones have wide frequency range, flat frequency response, low distortion, light weight, thin shape, and high stability in the presence of moisture and dust.

**Piezoelectric high polymers.** Studies on the piezoelectric properties of the high polymers have been conducted since the discovery of the piezoelectricity of wood in the 1940s. In the 1950s the piezoelectricity of biological substances, such as collagen, bone, and silk, was investigated. In the 1960s the piezoelectricity of synthetic high-polymer polypeptides was found by E. Fukada.

The piezoelectricity of polyvinylidene fluoride film ($PVF_2$ film) was discovered by H. Kawai in 1969. Studies to improve the piezoelectricity of polyvinylidene fluoride have been conducted mainly in Japan. The first commercial product, a high-polymer stereophonic headphone, was disclosed in 1974.

At present, the largest piezoelectric constant is found in uniaxially stretched and polarized $PVF_2$ films. Polyvinylidene fluoride is a fluorocarbon resin, in which every other pair of hydrogen atoms in polyethylene is replaced by a pair of fluorine atoms. Because of its high weather resistance, one of the main applications of polyvinylidene fluoride is as a coating material.

The process which gives piezoelectricity to polyvinylidene fluoride consists of the following steps: (1) Extruded films are uniaxially stretched up to four times the original length at 60 to 100°C (140 to 212°F). (2) Aluminum is evaporated on both surfaces of the film as electrodes. (3) The films are polarized with a high direct-current electric field of 600 kV/cm (600 V for a film 10 μm thick) at 80 to 100°C (176 to 212°F) for 1 h. This procedure is very similar to that used for piezoelectric ceramics. This indicates that the piezoelectricity in polyvinylidene fluoride is due to remanent polarization after the polarization process, as in the ceramics. If a high alternating-current field is applied to the film, a hysteresis loop between the applied field and the polarization is observed similar to that of ferroelectric crystals. *See Ferroelectrics.*

The properties of $PVF_2$ film and of common piezoelectric materials are compared in the **table**. Piezoelectric properties are compared in the case of the transverse piezoelectric effect, in which the direction of the applied electric field is perpendicular to the direction of the resultant stress. The Young's modulus of the $PVF_2$ film is more than one order smaller than those of the usual piezoelectric materials. This property of the film is very important for the applications to high-quality audio transducers. The *d* constant of the film, which is a coefficient of an induced strain by an applied field, is rather small in comparison with that of the ceramics. But this order of magnitude of the *d* constant is sufficient to use the material in a loudspeaker because the applied electric field between the surfaces of the thin film is about one order higher

**Comparison of piezoelectric materials in the case of the transverse effect***

| Material | Density (ρ), g/cm³ or (kg/m³) × $10^{-3}$ | Young's modulus (*E*), (dyne/cm²) × $10^{10}$ or (N/m²) × $10^9$ | Relative dielectric constant ($\epsilon/\epsilon_0$) | Piezoelectric constants: *d*, (C/N) × $10^{-12}$ | Piezoelectric constants: *g*, (m²/C) × $10^{-3}$ | Electromechanical coupling coefficient (*k*), % |
|---|---|---|---|---|---|---|
| Usual piezoelectric materials | | | | | | |
| Quartz | 2.66 | 77.3 | 4.5 | 2.0 | 50.1 | 10 |
| Rochelle salt | 1.77 | 17.7 | 350 | 272.3 | 90 | 73 |
| PZT† (lead zirconate titanate) ceramics | 7.5 | 75 | 1700 | 126.7 | 11.1 | 34.4 |
| Piezoelectric high polymers ($PVF_2$ film) | 1.79 | 3.6 | 12 | 26.4 | 251.1 | 15.5 |

*After M. Tamura et al., Electroacoustic transducers with piezoelectric high polymer films. *J. Audio Eng. Soc.*, 23:21–26, 1975; courtesy of Journal of the Audio Engineering Society.

†PZT is the trademark for piezoelectric ceramics produced by the Clevite Corporation in the United States.

than in the case of ceramics. The *g* constant is a coefficient of an induced voltage by an applied force, and is important for the microphone application. The relative dielectric constant and the dimensions of a transducer determine the transducer's electrical impedance. The electromechanical coupling coefficient is defined, by analogy with an alternating-current transformer, as the ratio of the mutual elastodielectric energy density in the piezoelectric material to the square root of the product of the stored elastic and dielectric energy densities. Hence, the efficiency of the piezoelectric transducer depends on this coefficient directly. SEE PIEZOELECTRIC CRYSTAL; PIEZOELECTRICITY.

The piezoelectricity of the $PVF_2$ film is quite stable, even at a high temperature of 100°C (212°F) for many months. Since piezoelectricity is a bulk effect, the $PVF_2$ film is not affected by moisture and dust. This property is one of the good features of the $PVF_2$ film compared with electrets, whose use in transducers depends on surface charges of dielectrics. SEE ELECTRET TRANSDUCER.

**Direct radiator loudspeakers.** In order to use the $PVF_2$ film effectively in transducers, a very simple structure has been devised by utilizing the advantage of the thin-film form. In **Fig. 1***a*, when a sinusoidal electric field is applied to the $PVF_2$ film along the *z* axis, the $PVF_2$ film vibrates in a transverse direction (along the *x* axis), that is, in the stretching direction. Next, if the $PVF_2$ film is curved as shown in Fig. 1*b*, the transverse vibration is converted into a pulsating movement and generates sound waves. This is the common structure for the direct radiator loudspeakers, stereophonic headphones, and microphones using the $PVF_2$ films.

One of the most interesting applications of the above-mentioned structure is a perfect omnidirectional high-frequency loudspeaker as indicated in **Fig. 2**. To make a cylindrical shape, a perforated cylinder is placed between top and base plates. Next, a polyurethane foam backing is put on the perforated cylinder. Finally, a polarized $PVF_2$ film, whose thickness is typically 27 μm, is stretched over the polyurethane foam backing.

In order to cover the frequency range from 2 to 20 kHz, two coaxial cylinders are used, with one mounted above the other. The diameter of the larger unit is 120 mm (4.8 in.); the frequency range is 2 to 5 kHz. The diameter of the smaller one is 60 mm (2.4 in.); the frequency range is 5 to 20 kHz. To utilize these high-polymer loudspeakers in combination with a conventional low-frequency loudspeaker with impedance of 4 to 8 Ω, a step-up transfer is required because the impedances of the $PVF_2$ films are essentially capacitive and the loudspeaker impedances are relatively high in the operating frequency ranges. The step-up ratio of the transformer is about 1:10.

Because of the polyurethane foam backing, a sufficient mechanical damping is provided; therefore a smooth frequency response is easily obtained between 2 and 20 kHz. Perfect omnidirectional patterns have been realized up to 20 kHz. Another favorable feature of the high-polymer loudspeaker is its linearity over a wide range of input power up to 100 W. SEE LOUDSPEAKER.

**Stereophonic headphones.** The first practical application of the $PVF_2$ film to audio transducers was a stereophonic headphone. The structure of high-polymer headphone is quite simple, as shown in **Fig. 3**. The $PVF_2$ film, typically 7 μm in thickness, is stretched loosely over a rectangular framework aligning the stretching axis (*x* axis) to the shorter axis of the rectangle. The $PVF_2$ film is then placed in the base, and a bias force is applied through a polyurethane foam backing by a perforated plate.

In this headphone, the whole surface of the $PVF_2$ film is driven by the applied voltage, and the headphone has as good sound quality as the electrostatic type. A small input voltage, such as 3 V, is sufficient to produce a sound pressure level of 100 dB; thus, the headphones can be driven directly from the headphone terminals of a conventional amplifier in the same manner as in the moving coil type without using

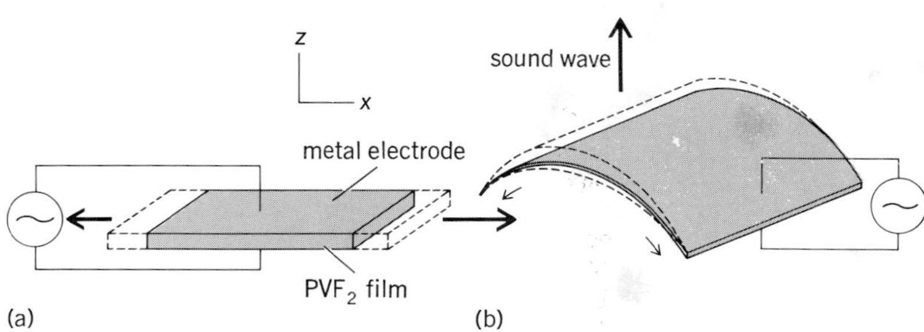


**Fig. 1. Generation of pulsating motion in a $PVF_2$ film. (*a*) Conversion of sinusoidal voltage along z axis into transverse motion along x axis. (*b*) Conversion of transverse vibration into pulsating motion. (*After M. Tamura et al., Electroacoustic transducers with piezoelectric high polymer films, J. Audio Eng. Soc., 23:21–26, 1975; courtesy of Journal of the Audio Engineering Society*)**

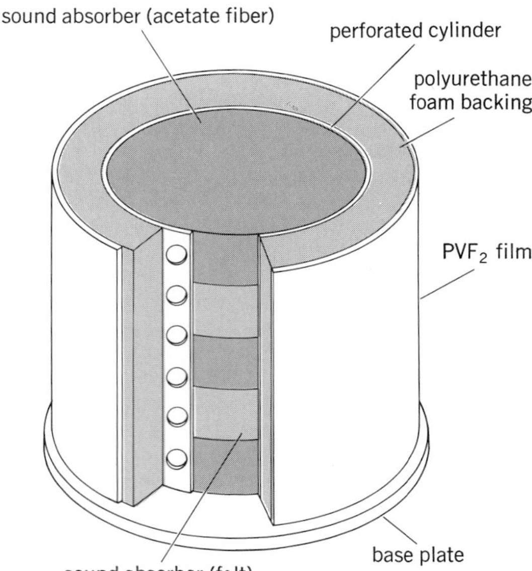


**Fig. 2. Structure of the omnidirectional high-polymer direct radiator loudspeaker. (*After M. Tamura et al., Electroacoustic transducers with piezoelectric high polymer films, J. Audio Eng. Soc., 23:21–26, 1975; courtesy of Journal of the Audio Engineering Society*)**

a step-up transformer, which must be employed in the electrostatic type.

In addition, the high-polymer headphones have the following advantages: no bias source is needed, and no irritating noises are produced even at a high input power. Also, the harmonic distortions are not greater than 1% even at an output sound pressure level of 110 dB. SEE EARPHONES.

**Microphones.** Another application of the $PVF_2$ film to electroacoustic transducers is in microphones. In recent years various types of electret microphones have been used because of their wide and flat frequency response, simple structure, and low cost.

An experimental high-polymer microphone has been developed which has a structure similar to that of the high-polymer headphone. The output signal can be taken from the terminals connected to both surfaces of the film. The diameter is 15 mm; the thickness of the $PVF_2$ film is 27 $\mu$m. The microphone can be simply built with only a thin $PVF_2$ film and a polyurethane foam backing. Furthermore, the accuracy of each part may be less exact that that required in the case of electrostatic microphones.

The response is similar to that of the electrostatic type. The sensitivity is $-74$ dB (0 db $=$ 1 V/$\mu$bar); the capacitance is about 700 pF. This capacitance value is about two orders greater than those of conventional electrostatic microphones. This means that the signal-to-noise ratio of the high-polymer microphone is fairly good in comparison with electrostatic microphones.

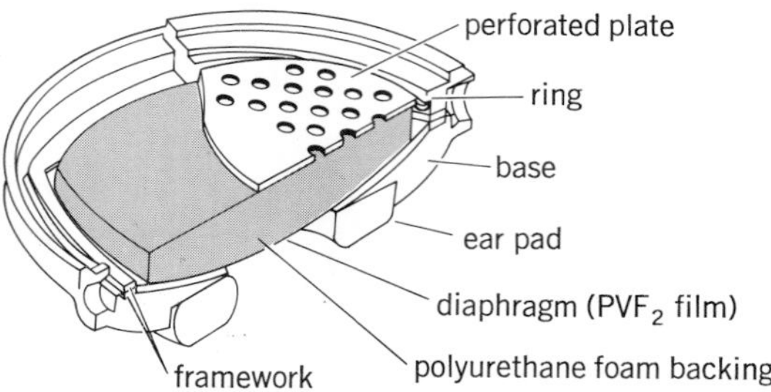


**Fig. 3. Cross-sectional view of high-polymer headphone. (*After M. Tamura et al., Electroacoustic transducers with piezoelectric high polymer films, J. Audio Eng. Soc., 23:21–26, 1975; courtesy of Journal of the Audio Engineering Society*)**

A noise-canceling microphone using a $PVF_2$ bimorph diaphragm has been proposed. The diameter is 5 mm; the thickness of the film is 32 $\mu$m. The fundamental resonance frequency is about 4 kHz.

Even with many good features, the high-polymer microphone has not yet been commercialized, because the cost of the $PVF_2$ film is not competitive with the electret film.

An experimental hydrophone has also been tested. The result indicates that the high-polymer hydrophone is a fairly promising one. SEE MICROPHONE.

**Electromechanical transducers.** Apart from its use in electroacoustic transducers such as described so far, piezoelectric high polymer has been tested for electromechanical transducers. Examples are phonograph cartridges and accelerometers.

***Phonograph cartridges.*** Because of the low stiffness of $PVF_2$ film, a very-high-compliance vibrating system can be easily designed. A high resonance frequency is realized due to the light weight of the small, thin element. The $PVF_2$ film is cut into small strips 1 mm wide and 2 mm long. Two small $PVF_2$ film elements have been used in an experimental high-polymer phonograph cartridge with a structure similar to that of the ceramic cartridge. SEE DISK RECORDING.

***Accelerometers.*** An experimental accelerometer has been developed. The $PVF_2$ film is cut out into a strip 2 mm wide and 15 mm long. The longitudinal axis of the strip is perpendicular to the stretching axis ($x$ axis). The ends of the strip are cemented together to form a ring. A small mass is attached to the top of the ring to produce a force. The output voltage can be taken from the terminals connected to the conductive layers on both surfaces of the film. The sensitivity and the frequency range are almost the same as those of conventional accelerometers.

**Range of applications.** Of all commercial applications of $PVF_2$ films, high-frequency loudspeakers and stereophonic headphones are most prominent. These devices were introduced only a few years ago. The range of applications of the $PVF_2$ film is not very wide yet because of the cost of this polarized product. But many applications to various transducers can be expected in the near future because the film has many good features, such as flexibility, light weight, thin shape, flat frequency response, low distortion, good sound quality, and stability against moisture and dust. SEE TRANSDUCER.

*Takeo Yamamoto; Mashiko Tamura*

***Bibliography.*** J. F. Sear and R. Carpenter, *Electron. Lett.*, 11:532–533, 1975; M. Tamura et al., *J. Appl. Phys.*, 48:513–521, 1977; M. Tamura et al., *J. Audio Eng. Soc.*, 23:21–26, 1975; Y. Wada and R. Hayakawa, *Japan. J. Appl. Phys.*, 15:2041–2057, 1976.

## High-temperature electronics

The technology of electronic components capable of operating at high temperatures (above 300°C or 570°F). The need for electronic devices for geothermal well probes, planetary space probes, jet-engine controls, and nuclear power plant instruments is supplying the impetus for advancements in this area, since conventional silicon diodes, transistors, and integrated circuits will not function in this temperature range. The research has been carried out in three primary areas: new silicon devices, compound semiconductor devices, and integrated thermionic circuits. Some of these devices have the potential of extending the operational range of electronic circuits up to 800°C (1470°F).

**Silicon devices.** Semiconductor devices can be divided into two categories: minority carrier devices, such as diodes and bipolar transistors, and majority carrier devices, such as the field-effect transistor (FET). Minority carrier devices made from silicon do not work well above 250°C (480°F). This is because the energy bandgap in silicon is only 1.1 eV, and at temperatures above 250°C (480°F) a large number of minority carriers are generated by thermal excitation.

The density of these thermally generated carriers in silicon is approximately $10^{10}/cm^3$ at room temperature and increases by about 6 orders of magnitude at 400°C or 750°F (to approximately $10^{16}/cm^3$). The large density increase in thermally generated carriers causes a large increase in reverse leakage current of *pn* junctions and makes the performance of minority carrier silicon devices, such as bipolar transistors and diodes, marginal above 250°C (480°F).

Majority carrier devices in silicon (such as field-effect transistors) do not depend on minority carriers for their operation and therefore can be made to operate at higher temperatures. Enhancement-mode metal-oxide semiconductor FET (MOSFET) devices have been made to operate at 350°C (660°F). To achieve this operating temperature it is necessary to remove the input-gate-protection bypass diodes and use dielectrically isolated (rather than junction-isolated) devices because of diode leakage. The upper limit of operating temperature for the silicon MOSFET is not known definitely. Problems that occur at high temperatures are oxide degradation in the gate and leakage at the source-drain *pn* junctions. It is generally felt that small-area devices may be eventually made to operate at 400°C (750°F). *See Junction diode; Transistor*.

**Compound semiconductor devices.** The basic need for a simple high-temperature rectifier diode and moderate power devices with gain have led to high-temperature research on compound semiconductors. Many of the group III–V compound semiconductors have energy bandgaps larger than silicon. For example, the semiconductor bandgap in gallium phosphide (GaP) is 2.2 eV. The thermally generated minority carrier density in gallium phosphide at 400°C (750°F) is approximately $10^{12}/cm^3$ (4 orders of magnitude less than silicon). This level is small enough that it is possible to build minority carrier devices at high temperatures by using this and other wide-bandgap semiconductor materials. Diodes and transistors have been demonstrated at 450°C (840°F) in GaP material. **Figure 1** shows a scanning electron photograph of a gallium phosphide bipolar transistor. The device in the photograph is a grown-junction *pnp* transistor made by liquid-phase epitaxy. The center contact is the emitter, the two outside pads are base contacts, and the collector contact is the bottom of the chip. Compound semiconductor devices of this type are estimated to be operational up to approximately 525°C (980°F), with moderate power-handling ability. Allowable current densities in these devices can be up to 100 $A/cm^2$, even at 400°C (750°F). While this current-carrying capacity is about 1 order of magnitude lower than that used in room-temperature silicon devices, it is still adequate for most high-temperature applications.

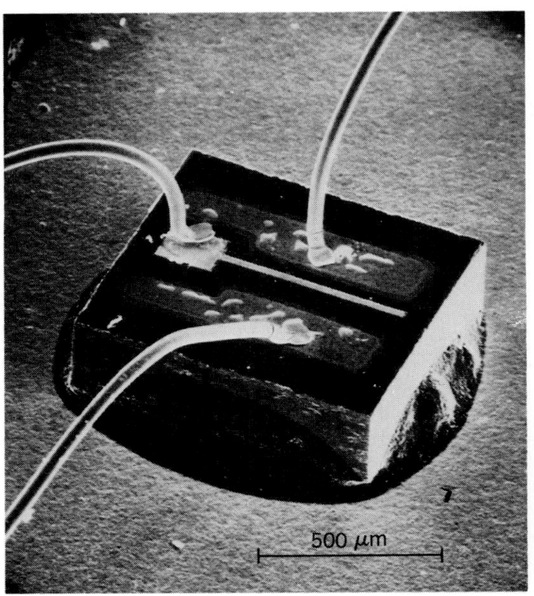


**Fig. 1. Gallium phosphide bipolar transistor for use at temperatures up to 450°C (840°F). Center contact is the emitter, base contacts are two outside pads, and collector contact is the bottom of the chip. Chip size is 500 × 750 μm.**

Research is also being carried out on compound semiconductor heterojunction devices. These are *pn* junctions made from dissimilar semiconductor materials such as gallium arsenide and gallium aluminum arsenide (GaAs and GaAlAs). The physics of junctions of dissimilar semiconductors can be exploited to reduce leakage currents which plague high-temperature devices, making successful high-temperature minority carrier devices possible. *See Semiconductor heterostructures*.

**Integrated thermionic circuits.** A dramatic departure from semiconductor technology is the integrated thermionic circuit. This technology combines photolithographically defined subminiature thin-film metal patterns with planar vacuum-tube technology. The result is a technology that allows fabrication of active circuits with a density approaching that of present room-temperature silicon integrated circuits. **Figure 2** shows a cutaway view of a single integrated-thermionic-circuit active device. In this structure the grids

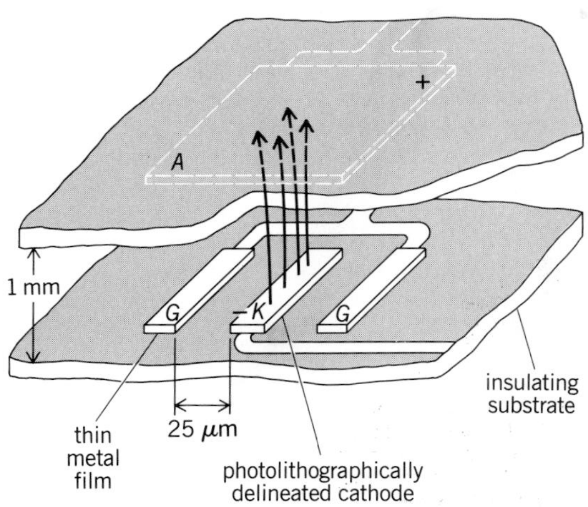


**Fig. 2. Integrated thermionic circuit. (*After Proceedings of the High Temperature Electronics and Instrumentation Conference, December 1981, Sandia National Laboratories Rep. SAND82-0425*)**

(*G*) are coplanar with the cathode (*K*) on the lower plane; the anode (*A*) is on the upper plane, and the space between the cathode and anode is evacuated. The grid metal and oxide-coated cathode are photolithographically defined on a sapphire substrate. During normal operation a resistance heater is used to heat this substrate to approximately 800°C (1470°F) to produce electron emission from the cathode. A positive voltage is applied to the anode to collect these electrons, and a voltage is applied to the grid lines to set up an electric field which controls this current flow in a manner similar to that of a conventional triode vacuum tube. The resulting devices produce current densities of approximately 0.1 A/cm$^2$. Because of this limitation these devices are low-power devices, operating at power densities about 3 orders of magnitude less than room-temperature silicon devices. Thus, they are not suitable for use in power-conditioning or line-driving applications. The small size of these small-signal devices does allow the integration of analog and digital circuits with device densities of several thousand per square centimeter. Integrated thermionic circuits have been life-tested at 500°C (930°F) for several thousand hours with no detectable degradation. An upper temperature limit is not known, but it is presumed that, with suitable packaging techniques to reduce outgassing problems, device temperatures should be able to approach the cathode temperature of 800°C (1470°F). These devices are also capable of surviving severe radiation environments and may be applicable to nuclear power reactor instrumentation. *See* Integrated circuits; Vacuum tube.

**Use of amorphous metal films.** One of the weak links in semiconductor technology at high temperatures is the metallization used. All semiconductor metallizations are presently made from polycrystalline metals. Failures that occur with room-temperature semiconductor devices are usually attributed to metal failures due to diffusion, corrosion, or electromigration of the thin metal films used to contact and interconnect the semiconductor devices. Since these failures are due to thermally activated processes, they occur even more rapidly at elevated temperatures. In order to make reliable high-temperature semiconductor devices with reasonable lives this problem must be solved. It is known that most of these metal failures occur along grain boundaries in the polycrystalline metals. A potential solution to this problem is the use of amorphous metal films (which have no grain boundaries) in place of the polycrystalline metals. Recent experimental results have demonstrated that amorphous metal films on semiconductors are several orders of magnitude less susceptible to these failures at high temperatures, and these films can be produced by processes compatible with the semiconductor industry. *See* Grain boundaries.

*Roger J. Chaffin*

**Bibliography.** *Proceedings of the Conference on High Temperature Electronics*, Tucson, March 1981, IEEE Rep. 81CH1658-4; *Proceedings of the High Temperature Electronics and Instrumentation Conference*, Houston, December 1981, Sandia National Laboratories Rep. SAND82-0425.

## Holes in solids

Vacant electron energy states near the top of an energy band in a solid are called holes. A full band cannot carry electric current; a band nearly full with only a few unoccupied states near its maximum energy can carry current, but the current behaves as though the charge carriers are positively charged. The situation can be understood in terms of the definition of the effective mass: if the energy band is specified by a function $E(k)$, where $k$ is the magnitude of the wave vector $\mathbf{k}$, the effective mass for a spherical band is given by the equation here, where $\hbar$ is Planck's

$$m^* = \hbar^2 \left(\frac{\partial^2 E}{\partial k^2}\right)^{-1}$$

constant divided by $2\pi$. Near a maximum of the band, the second derivative of the energy is negative, so the effective mass is negative. States for which the effective mass is negative are defined as hole states. Carriers in such states behave under the influence of an external electromagnetic field as though they carry positive charge. *See* Band theory of solids.

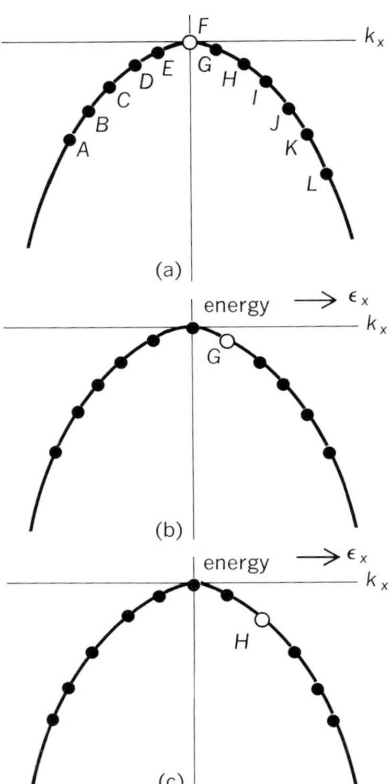


**Process of hole conduction. (*a*) At time $t$ = 0, energy states *A* through *L* are filled except *F*. (*b*) An electric field $\epsilon_x$ is applied in the +*x* direction. The force on the electrons is in the $-k_x$ direction, and all electrons make transitions in the $-k_x$ direction, moving the hole to *G*. (*c*) After a further interval, the electrons move farther along, and the hole is now at *H*. (After C. Kittel, *Introduction to Solid State Physics*, 3d ed., John Wiley and Sons, 1956)**

The process of conduction in such a system may be visualized in the following way. An electron moves against an applied electric field by jumping into a vacant state. This transfers the position of the vacant state, or propagates the hole, in the direction of the field, as shown in the **illustration**. Whether conduction occurs by electrons or holes is determined experimentally from the sign of the Hall emf. If a current is carried in the presence of a magnetic field perpendicular to the current, an emf is developed perpendicular to the current and to the field. The sign of this emf depends on the charge on the carriers. *See Hall effect.*

Hole conduction is important in many semiconductors, notably germanium and silicon. The occurrence of hole conduction in semiconductors can be favored by alloying with a material of lower valence than the "host." Semiconductors in which the conduction is primarily due to holes are called *p* type. Hole conduction is also observed in some metals, including iron and chromium. In other metals, including aluminum and bismuth, both holes and electrons may be present in equilibrium. *See Semiconductor.*

*Joseph Callaway*

**Bibliography.** N. W. Ashcroft and N. D. Mermin, *Solid State Physics*, 1976; C. Kittel, *Introduction to Solid State Physics*, 5th ed., 1976; W. Shockley, *Electrons and Holes in Semiconductors*, 1950, reprint 1976.

## Image processing

Manipulating data in the form of an image through several possible techniques. An image is usually interpreted as a two-dimensional array of brightness values, and is most familiarly represented by such patterns as those of a photographic print, slide, television screen, or movie screen. There are fundamentally two ways to process an image: optically, or digitally with a computer. This article focuses on digital processing of an image to perform one of three separate tasks: enhancement, restoration, or compression.

**Digitization.** To digitally process an image, it is first necessary to reduce the image to a series of numbers that can be manipulated by the computer. If the image is in the form of a photographic transparency, this digitization can be done by a scanning device that moves a spot of light over the transparency in a rasterlike fashion similar to a television scan. When the light falls on a particular area of the transparency, the amount of light transmitted at that point can be recorded by a photodetector, the signal digitized to, say, eight bits (yielding a possible $2^8$, or 256, gray levels), and stored. The spot is then moved a distance equal to its width, and the process is repeated, recording the entire transparency in this way as a long string of numbers. The smaller the spot and the finer the scan (up to the limit of the film grain), the more accurate the description of the transparency will be. Each number representing the brightness value of the image at a particular location is called a picture element, or pixel. A typical digitized image may have $512 \times 512$ or roughly 250,000 pixels.

Once the image has been digitized, there are three basic operations that can be performed on it in the computer. For a point operation, a pixel value in the output image depends on a single pixel value in the input image. For local operations, several neighboring pixels in the input image determine the value of an output image pixel. In a global operation, all of the input image pixels contribute to an output image pixel value. These operations, taken singly or in combination, are the means by which the image is enhanced, restored, or compressed.

**Enhancement.** An image is enhanced when it is modified so that the information it contains is more clearly evident, but enhancement can also include making the image more visually appealing. An example is noise smoothing. Given the image of **Fig. 1***a*, by replacing the value of randomly chosen pixels

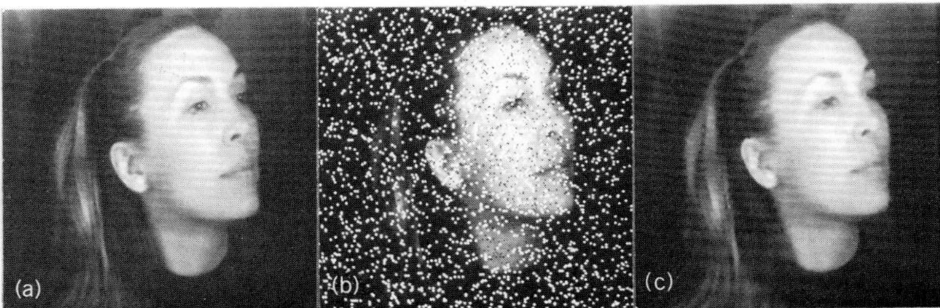

**Fig. 1.** Noise smoothing. (*a*) Original $256 \times 256$ pixel image. (*b*) Original image corrupted by spike noise. (*c*) Corrupted image filtered by a $3 \times 3$ pixel median filter.

by 150 (bright gray) or 0 (black), the noisy image of Fig. 1*b* results. This kind of noise might be produced, for example, by a defective solid-state TV camera. To smooth the noisy image, median filtering can be applied with a $3 \times 3$ pixel window. This means that the value of every pixel in the noisy image is recorded, along with the values of its nearest eight neighbors. These nine numbers are then ordered according to size, and the number with as many numbers above it as below it (the median) is selected as the value for the pixel in the new image. The location of this pixel in the new image is the same as the location of the center of the $3 \times 3$ window in the old image. Eventually, as the window is moved one pixel at a time across the noisy image, the filtered image is formed, as in Fig. 1*c*. This is an example of a local operation, since the value of a pixel in the new image depends on the values of nine pixels in the old image.

Another example of enhancement is contrast manipulation, where each pixel's value in the new image depends solely on that pixel's value in the old image; in other words, this is a point operation. Contrast manipulation is commonly performed by adjusting the brightness and contrast controls on a television set, or by controlling the exposure and development time in printmaking. Another point operation is that of pseudocoloring a black-and-white image, by assigning arbitrary colors to the gray levels. This technique is popular in thermography (the imaging of heat), where hot objects (high pixel value) are assigned the color red, and cool objects (low pixel value) are assigned blue, with other colors assigned to intermediate values.

**Restoration.** The aim of restoration is also to improve the image, but unlike enhancement, knowledge of how the image was formed is used in an attempt to retrieve the ideal (uncorrupted) image. Any image-forming system is not perfect, and will introduce artifacts (for example, blurring, aberrations) into the final image that would not be present in an ideal image. To illustrate, the image of **Fig. 2***a* is "imaged" on a computer that simulates an out-of-focus lens, producing Fig. 2*b*. The image of a point object through this system would look like Fig. 2*c*; this is called the point spread function of the system. Such blurring can be referred to as a local operation, in that the value of a pixel in the blurred image is an average of the values of the pixels around (and including) that pixel location in the original image. The averaging function is the blurring point spread function (Fig. 2*c*). The blurring process is mathematically referred to as a convolution of the original object with the point spread function.

Another point spread function, called a filter, can be constructed that "undoes" the blurring caused by

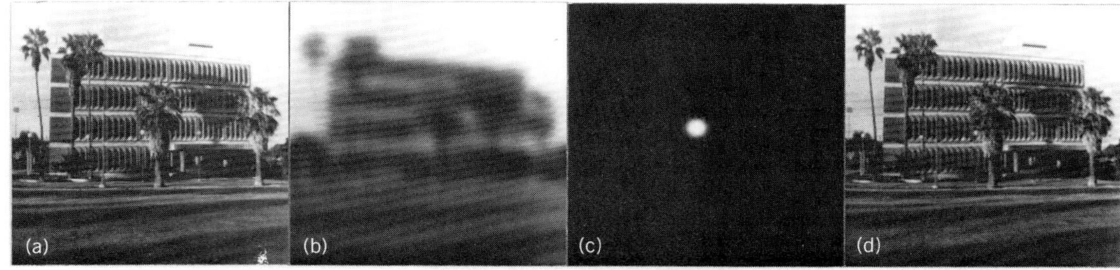

Fig. 2. Example of restoration. (*a*) Original 256 × 256 pixel image (*courtesy of Richard Murphy*). (*b*) Blurred version of the original image. (c) The image of a point subject to the same blurring that produced the blurred version of the original image. (*d*) The results of the inverse filter applied to the blurred version of the original image.

the point spread function of Fig. 2*c*. Such a point spread function (not shown) has both positive and negative values, even though the blurring point spread function has only positive values. A general rule is that blurring point spread functions are positive, and sharpening point spread functions have both positive and negative values. By imaging Fig. 2*b* with the filter point spread function, the restored image of Fig. 2*d* results. The filter point spread function is spread out more than the blurring point spread function, bringing more pixels into the averaging process. This is an example of a global operation, since perhaps all of the pixels of the blurred image can contribute to the value of a single pixel in the restored image. This type of deblurring (called inverse filtering) will not work well if noise is added to the blurred image before the deblurring operation. A more sophisticated approach, modifying the deblurring filter according to the properties of the noise, is then required.

There exist mathematical transformations that can be performed on images to facilitate deblurring, as well as other operations. An extremely useful one in image processing is the Fourier transform, which decomposes the image into two-dimensional sine waves of varying frequency, direction, and phase. In fact, convolution of an image with a point spread function (the imaging process) can be carried out in the Fourier domain by simply multiplying the Fourier transform of the image by the Fourier transform of the point spread function, and taking the inverse Fourier transform of this product to get the final image. This process was used in the example of Fig. 2.

**Compression.** Compression of an image is a way of representing the image by fewer numbers, at the same time minimizing the degradation of the information contained in the image. There are two ways to perform compression: in the image space or in transform space (for example, Fourier). Compression in image space is discussed in the following example.

**Figure** 3*a*, representing the image to be compressed, contains 256 × 256 pixels, with each pixel having a possible 256 gray levels, so that 8 bits are required on a computer to store each pixel. Thus a total of roughly 500,000 bits is required to store or transmit the image. If the number of bits per pixel is reduced to 3 (8 gray levels), Fig. 3*b* results. The total number of bits have been reduced by ⅜ or 0.375, but at the price of contouring the image. However, if a spatially variable contrast transformation is first applied to Fig. 3*a* with the resulting image then reduced to 3 bits, followed by a geometric distortion that shrinks areas of little variation (the wall and jacket) and leaves areas of large variation (the face) alone, Fig. 3*c* results. The geometric shrinking reduces the number of bits by a factor of 0.500, and the gray-level reduction to 3 bits further reduces the number by ⅜ to a total reduction of 0.188, or roughly ⅕ of the original number of bits required to represent the image. Applying the inverse geometric and contrast transformations to Fig. 3*c* results in Fig. 3*d*, an improvement over Fig. 3*b*, with a greater compression factor than Fig. 3*b* as well.

**Applications.** Due to its vast scope, image processing is an active area of research in such diverse fields as nuclear medicine, astronomy, electron microscopy, seismology, and many others. The concept of an image is expanding to include three-dimensional data sets (volume "images"), and even four-dimensional volume-time data sets. An example of the latter is a volume image of a beating heart, obtainable with computerized tomography. Advances in computer technology are making efficient processing of the huge data sets required in these problems possible, and such technology promises to bring sophisticated

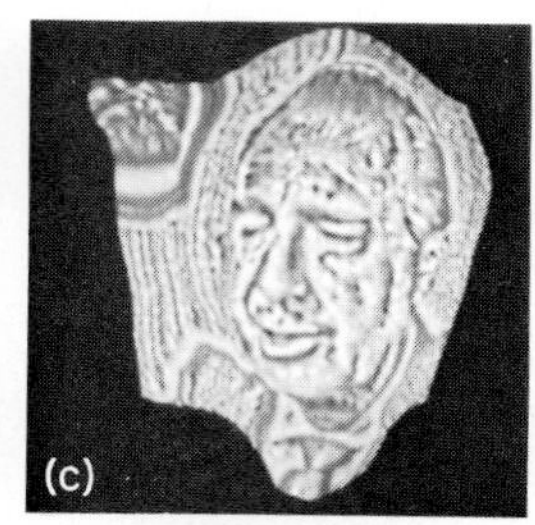

Fig. 3. Example of compression. (*a*) Original 256 × 256 pixel image, 8 bits per pixel (256 gray levels). (*b*) Original image, reduced to 3 bits per pixel (8 gray levels), for a bit reduction of 0.375. (c) Original image, with contrast and geometric transformations applied, followed by a reduction to 3 bits per pixel, for a total bit reduction of 0.188. (*d*) The inverse contrast and geometric transformation applied to c, to "decompress" the image. (*From R. N. Strickland and W. E. Smith, Stationary Transform Processing of Digital Images for Data Compression, Appl. Opt., 22:2161–2168, July 15, 1983*)

image processing into the home. *SEE* DIGITAL COMPUTER.

*Warren E. Smith*

**Bibliography.** H. C. Andrews and B. R. Hunt, *Digital Image Restoration*, 1977; H. H. Barrett and W. Swindell, *Radiological Imaging: The Theory of Image Formation, Detection, and Processing*, 1981; R. C. Gonzalez and P. Wintz, *Digital Image Processing*, 1982; W. K. Pratt, *Digital Image Processing*, 1978.

## Immittance

The impedance or admittance of an alternating-current circuit. It is sometimes convenient to use the term immittance when referring to a complex number which may be either the impedance (ratio of voltage to current) or the admittance (ratio of current to voltage) of an electrical circuit. The units of impedance and admittance are, of course, different and so units cannot be assigned to an immittance. However, in certain theoretical work it may be necessary to deal with general functions which afterward will be specialized to become either an impedance or an admittance by the assignment of suitable units; in such cases it is convenient to refer to the functions as immittances. *SEE* ADMITTANCE; ALTERNATING-CURRENT CIRCUIT THEORY; ELECTRICAL IMPEDANCE.

*J. O. Scanlan*

## Impedance matching

The use of electric circuits and devices to establish the condition in which the impedance of a load is equal to the internal impedance of the source. This condition of impedance match provides for the maximum transfer of power from the source to the load. In a radio transmitter, for example, it is desired to deliver maximum power from the power amplifier to the antenna. In an audio amplifier, the requirement is to deliver maximum power to the loudspeaker. *SEE* ELECTRICAL IMPEDANCE.

The maximum power transfer theorem of electric network theory states that at any given frequency the maximum power transfer theorem of electric network theory states that at any given frequency the maximum power is transferred from the source to the load when the load impedance is equal to the conjugate of the generator impedance. Thus, if the generator is a resistance, the load must be a resistance equal to the generator resistance for maximum power to be delivered from the generator to the load. When these conditions are satisfied, the power is delivered with 50% efficiency; that is, as much power is dissipated in the internal impedance of the generator as is delivered to the load.

**Impedance matching network.** In general, the load impedance will not be the proper value for maximum power transfer. A network composed of inductors and capacitors may be inserted between the load and the generator to present to the generator an impedance that is the conjugate of the generator impedance. Since the matching network is composed of elements which, in the ideal case of no resistance in the inductors and perfect capacitors, do not absorb power, all of the power delivered to the matching network is delivered to the load. An example of an L-section matching network is shown in the **illustration**. Matching networks of this type are used in radio-frequency circuits. The values of inductance and capacitance are chosen to satisfy the requirements of the maximum power transfer theorem. The power dissipated in the matching network is a small fraction of that delivered to the load, because the elements used are close approximations of ideal components.

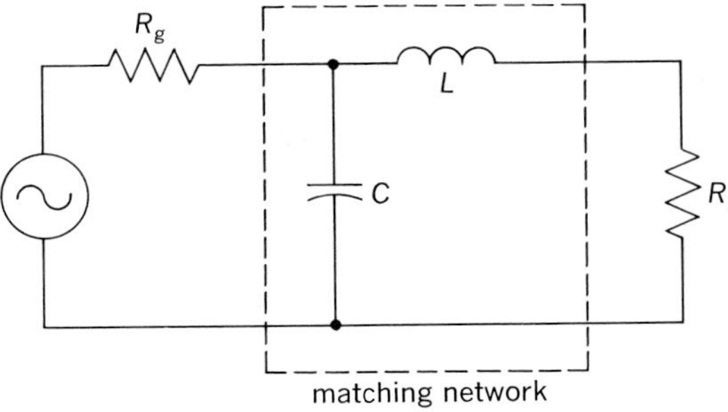


L-section impedance matching network.

**Transformers.** The impedance measured at the terminals of one winding of an iron-cored transformer is approximately the value of the impedance connected across the other terminals multiplied by the square of the turns ratio. Thus, if the load and generator impedances are resistances, the turns ratio can be chosen to match the load resistance to the generator resistance for maximum power transfer. If the generator and load impedances contain reactances, the transformer cannot be used for matching because it cannot change the load impedance to the conjugate of the generator impedance (the L-section matching network can). The turns ratio can be chosen, however, to deliver maximum power under the given conditions, this maximum being less than the theoretical one.

Iron-cored transformers are used for impedance matching in the audio and supersonic frequency range. The power dissipated in the core increases with frequency because of hysteresis. Above the frequency range at which iron-cored transformers can be used, the air-core transformer or transformers with powdered-iron slugs can be used effectively. However, in these cases the turns-ratio-squared impedance-transforming property is no longer true. Since the transformer is usually part of a tuned circuit, other factors influence the design of the transformer.

The impedance-transforming property of an iron-cored transformer is not always used to give maximum power transfer. For example, in the design of power-amplifier stages in audio amplifiers, the impedance presented to the transistor affects distortion. A study of a given circuit can often show that at a given output power level, usually the maximum expected, there is a value for the load resistance which will minimize a harmonic component in the harmonic distortion, such as the second or third harmonic. The transformer turns ratio is selected to present this resistance to the transistor. *SEE* TRANSFORMER.

**Emitter follower.** In electronic circuitry a signal source of large internal impedance must often be connected to a low-impedance load. If the source were connected directly to the load, attenuation of the signal would result. To reduce this attenuation, an emitter follower is connected between the source and the load. The input impedance of the emitter follower is high, more nearly matching the large source impedance, and the output impedance is low, more nearly matching the low load impedance. If the object were the delivery of maximum power to the load, it might be possible to design the emitter follower to have an output resistance equal to the load resistance, assuming that the load is a resistance. (Special audio amplifiers have been designed to use emitter followers, rather than a transformer, to connect the loudspeaker to the power amplifier.) In many cases, maximum power transfer is not the goal; the emitter follower is introduced primarily to reduce to a minimum the attenuation of the signal

There exist a number of applications where the emitter follower is not useful as an impedance matching circuit. For example, if a very low-impedance source must be matched to a high-impedance load, then a transistor is used in the common base configuration. SEE EMITTER FOLLOWER; VOLTAGE AMPLIFIER.

*Christos C. Halkias*

**Bibliography.** C. A. Schuler, *Electronics: Principles and Applications*, 2d ed., 1984; R. L. Thomas, *A Practical Introduction to Impedance Matching*, 1976; M. E. Van Valkenburg, *Network Analysis*, 3d ed., 1974.

## Inductance

That property of an electric circuit or of two neighboring circuits whereby an electromotive force is induced (by the process of electromagnetic induction) in one of the circuits by a change of current in either of them. The term inductance coil is sometimes used as a synonym for inductor, a device possessing the property of inductance. SEE ELECTROMOTIVE FORCE (EMF); INDUCTOR.

**Self-inductance.** For a given coil, the ratio of the electromotive force of induction to the rate of change of current in the coil is called the self-inductance $L$ of the coil, given in Eq. (1), where $e$ is the electromotive force at any instant and $dI/dt$ is the rate of change of the current at that instant. The negative sign indicates that the induced electromotive force is opposite in direction to the current when the current is increasing ($dI/dt$ positive) and in the same direction as the current when the current is decreasing ($dI/dt$ negative). The self-inductance is in henrys when the electromotive force is in volts, and the rate of change of current is in amperes per second.

$$L = -\frac{e}{dI/dt} \tag{1}$$

An alternative definition of self-inductance is the number of flux linkages per unit current. Flux linkage is the product of the flux $\Phi$ and the number of turns in the coil $N$. Then Eq. (2) holds. Both sides of Eq. (2) may be multiplied by $I$ to obtain Eq. (3), which may be differentiated with respect to $t$, as in Eqs. (4).

$$L = \frac{N\Phi}{I} \tag{2}$$

$$LI = N\Phi \tag{3}$$

$$L\frac{dI}{dt} = N\frac{d\Phi}{dt} = -e \quad \text{or} \quad L = -\frac{e}{dI/dt} \tag{4}$$

Hence the second definition is equivalent to the first.

Self-inductance does not affect a circuit in which the current is unchanging; however, it is of great importance when there is a changing current, since there is an induced emf during the time that the change takes place. For example, in an alternating-current circuit, the current is constantly changing and the inductance is an important factor. Also, in transient phenomena at the beginning or end of a steady unidirectional current, the self-inductance plays a part. SEE ELECTRIC TRANSIENT.

Consider a circuit of resistance $R$ and inductance $L$ connected in series to a constant source of potential difference $V$. The current in the circuit does not reach a final steady value instantly, but rises toward the final value $I = V/R$ in a manner that depends upon $R$ and $L$. At every instant after the switch is closed the applied potential difference is the sum of the $iR$ drop in potential and the back emf $L\, di/dt$, as in Eq. (5),

$$V = iR + L\frac{di}{dt} \tag{5}$$

where $i$ is the instantaneous value of the current. Separating the variables $i$ and $t$, one obtains Eq. (6). The solution of Eq. (6) is given in Eq. (7).

$$\frac{di}{(V/R) - i} = \frac{R}{L}\,dt \tag{6}$$

$$i = \frac{V}{R}(1 - e^{-(R/L)t}) \tag{7}$$

The current rises exponentially to a final steady value $V/R$. The rate of growth is rapid at first, then less and less rapid as the current approaches the final value.

The power $p$ supplied to the circuit at every instant during the rise of current is given by Eq. (8). The first term $i^2R$ is the power that goes into heating the circuit. The second term $Li\, di/dt$ is the power that goes into building up the magnetic field in the inductor. The total energy $W$ used in building up the magnetic field is given by Eq. (9). The energy used in building up the magnetic field remains as energy of the magnetic field. When the switch is opened, the magnetic field collapses and the energy of the field is returned to the circuit, resulting in an induced emf. The arc that is often seen when a switch is opened is a result of this emf, and the energy to maintain the arc is supplied by the decreasing magnetic field.

$$p = iV = i^2R + Li\, di/dt \tag{8}$$

$$W = \int_0^t p\, dt = \int_0^t Li\frac{di}{dt}\,dt = \int_0^I Li\, di = \tfrac{1}{2}LI^2 \tag{9}$$

**Mutual inductance.** The mutual inductance $M$ of two neighboring circuits $A$ and $B$ is defined as the ratio of the emf induced in one circuit $\mathscr{E}$ to the rate of change of current in the other circuit, as in Eq. (10).

$$M = -\frac{\mathscr{E}_B}{(dI/dt)_A} \tag{10}$$

The mks unit of mutual inductance is the henry, the same as the unit of self-inductance. The same value is obtained for a pair of coils, regardless of which coil is taken as the starting point.

The mutual inductance of two circuits may also be expressed as the ratio of the flux linkages that are produced in circuit $B$ by the current in circuit $A$ to the current in circuit $A$. If $\Phi_{BA}$ is the flux threading $B$ as a result of the current in circuit $A$, Eqs. (11) are ap-

$$\mathscr{E}_B = -N_B\frac{d\Phi_{BA}}{dt} = -M\frac{dI_A}{dt} \quad \text{or} \quad N_B\, d\Phi_{BA} = M\, dI_A \tag{11}$$

plicable. Integration leads to Eq. (12).

$$M = \frac{N_B \Phi_{BA}}{I_A} \quad (12)$$

SEE INDUCTANCE MEASUREMENT.

Kenneth V. Manning

## Inductance measurement

The measurement of self- or mutual inductance. As with any other electrical impedance, these quantities are the ratios of a current through the device to the voltage having the appropriate phase which appears across specified terminals. These ratios are often measured by commercial instruments in terms of the ratio associated with a noninductive resistor. SEE ELECTRICAL IMPEDANCE.

**Precautions.** Some practical precautions must be taken if meaningful, accurate results are to be obtained. If the magnetic circuit of a coil includes magnetic material whose permeability depends on the magnetic flux caused by a direct current flowing in the coil, or by its previous magnetic history, its inductance will also be current- or history-dependent and these conditions must be specified if the measurement is to be meaningful. Also, any magnetic field associated with the inductor must not interact significantly with magnetic or conducting material in the vicinity of the inductor, inasmuch as its field, and therefore the inductance, would be altered. The varying magnetic field of an inductor will induce eddy currents in any nearby conducting material, which will in turn produce a magnetic field which interacts with the inductor and measuring system. Errors in a measurement of inductance may also arise from the interaction of the magnetic field of an inductor with the rest of the measuring circuit. Capacitance to other parts or to the surroundings of an inductor arising from its associated electric field will affect the impedance or apparent inductance of an inductor by a frequency-dependent amount. Capacitive currents associated with the measuring circuit, however, can be routed in such a way as not to affect the measurement. SEE EDDY CURRENT; INDUCTOR.

The electrical property of self- or mutual inductance is only defined for complete circuits. Since a measuring device or network forms part of the complete circuit when it is connected to an inductor to perform a measurement, it is necessary to ensure that either the inductance associated with the measuring circuit is negligible or that the change in inductance occurring when the unknown is replaced by a short circuit is defined as the measured quantity. The former procedure is usual for mutual inductors, and the latter for self-inductors.

**Phase defect.** In a mutual inductor the changing magnetic flux resulting from a varying current $i$ in one coil induces a varying voltage $V$, 90° out of phase, in another coil. A perfect mutual inductor would have negligible energy losses associated with the interactions between the changing electric and magnetic fields of the device and nearby resistive conductors, including the conductors of the coils themselves. The energy loss per cycle in a practical air-cored mutual inductor amounts to only a few parts per million of the total stored magnetic energy of the device. The effect of this loss is that the phase of the voltage induced in the secondary will lead that of the current in the primary by slightly less than 90°. The departure

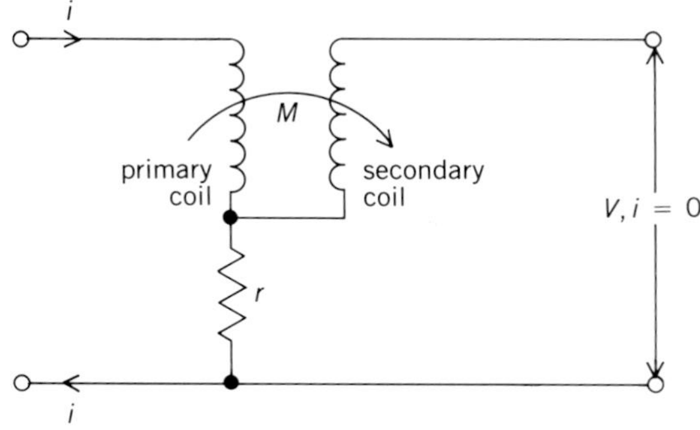


**Fig. 1.** Equivalent circuit representing loss in a mutual inductor.

from 90° is called the phase defect of the device. It is usual to define a configuration for a mutual inductor in which one specified end of the primary coil is connected to a specified end of the secondary coil; the effect of a phase defect can then be represented by the equivalent circuit shown in **Fig. 1**, in which the primary and secondary share a common fictitious path of small resistance $r$. This resistance has nothing to do with the actual resistance of the primary coil, which is irrelevant as far as the mutual inductance of the device is concerned.

In a self-inductor, however, primary and secondary coils are the same, and therefore the voltage induced in the secondary includes the potential drop of the current in the primary as it flows through the actual resistance of the coil. Self-inductors therefore have large, frequency-dependent phase defects, and this makes measuring them difficult. Their phase defect may be represented by an equivalent circuit in which a resistor whose value $R$ is closely equal to the actual resistance of the coil is in series with an inductor whose value $L$ is the inductance of the device in this representation.

Comparing mutual inductors and deriving their values in terms of other electrical standards requires different methods from those used for self inductors. The measurement of each will be discussed separately, taking account of the above considerations.

**Measuring self-inductance.** Capacitance and resistance standards have replaced inductance standards as the primary standards of impedance, and a scale of self-inductance may be established by finding the value of a self-inductor in terms of the reactance of a known variable capacitance $C$. If these components are connected in parallel so that the combination appears to be purely resistive when measured in a suitable bridge at a frequency $f$, then Eq. (1) is satisfied.

$$2\pi f L = \frac{1}{2\pi f C} \quad (1)$$

SEE CAPACITANCE MEASUREMENT; RESISTANCE MEASUREMENT.

This procedure measures the inductance parameter associated with a parallel equivalent circuit in which a resistance $R'$ is in parallel with the inductance of value $L'$. If the alternative representation of a series equivalent circuit is required, as is usually the case, the conversion between these representations is given by Eqs. (2), where $D = 2\pi f L'/R' = R/2\pi f L$ is the

$$L = \frac{L'}{(1 + D^2)} \qquad R = \frac{R'D^2}{(1 + D^2)} \quad (2)$$

reciprocal of the Q factor of the inductor.

The value of a standard of self-inductance is defined by specifying an alteration in the complete cir-

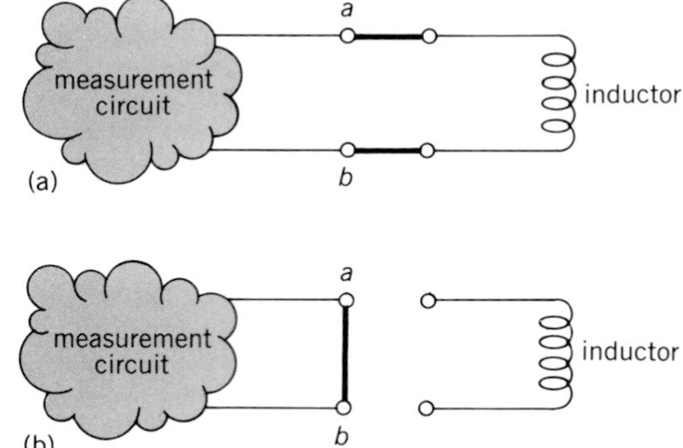


**Fig. 2. Definition of the value of a self-inductor. (*a*) Circuit with self-inductor. (*b*) Circuit with self-inductor replaced by shorting link between terminals *a* and *b*.**

cuit containing it, usually by breaking the circuit at terminals *a* and *b* (**Fig. 2***a*) and substituting a shorting link (Fig. 2*b*).

Self-inductors can be compared in a bridge in which the ratio of voltages $V_1/V_2$ across them is equated to the voltage ratio of a tapped autotransformer, otherwise called an inductive voltage divider. A noninductive variable resistance $R_v$ in series with the inductor having the higher value of the ratio $L/R$ enables the magnitude and phase of these voltage ratios to be equated when the detector is nulled (**Fig. 3**). Then Eqs. (3) are satisfied.

$$L_1 = \frac{V_1}{V_2} L_2 \qquad R_1 = \frac{V_1}{V_2} R_2 - R_v \tag{3}$$

If the inductors have any significant external magnetic field, interaction of the one with the other or with the measuring circuit can be avoided by placing the inductors far apart with their coil axes in perpendicular directions, and by constructing the measuring circuit, including the leads to the inductors, as twisted conductor pairs or as coaxial cables whose inner and outer conductors carry equal and opposite currents.

The effect on the measurement of an alternating magnetic field emanating from the bridge or leads to the inductor can be eliminated by reversing the connections to the inductor, repeating the measurement, and taking the mean of the two results. Additionally, if the bridge is of the type described above which compares an unknown inductor with a standard, the effect of any small remaining coupling between the inductors once they have been placed with their axes perpendicular can be eliminated by also reversing the connections to the standard. When the reversal of the unknown inductor is repeated, the mean of the resulting four measurements will eliminate all unwanted magnetic couplings between the inductors and the bridge.

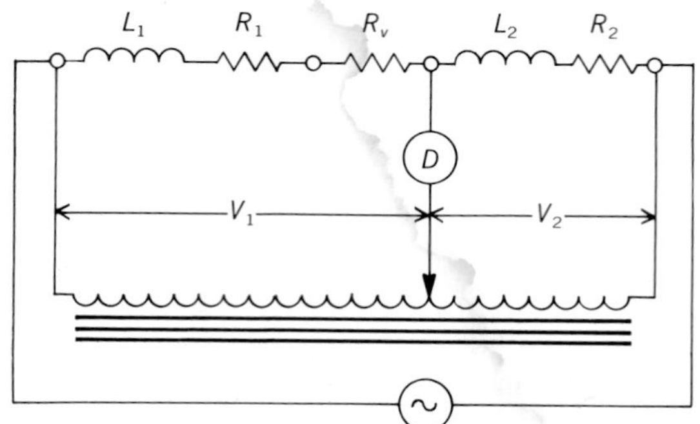


**Fig. 3. Comparison of self-inductor using an inductive voltage divider.**

The accuracy of any measuring instrument can be reduced to the fulfillment of two requirements: that the readings at two points on its scale, preferably near either end, are correct and that it is linear (that is, its readings are proportional to the value of the unknown presented to it) over its measurement range. In the case of an inductance-measuring instrument, the first condition is assured if the change in value of a known standard inductor on substituting its shorting link is recorded correctly. The second condition can be verified at one point on its scale by using the instrument to measure the values of two self-inductors separately and seeing if the measured values of the inductors connected in series are the sum of these separate values. In making the last measurement, it is especially important to minimize and take account of any magnetic field of one inductor interacting with the other by repeating the measurement with the connections to one inductor reversed.

Apparent lack of linearity might be due, among other possibilities, to insufficient rejection by the measuring instrument of the resistive component of the inductor's impedance. This can be tested by connecting a resistor of value comparable with that of the inductor and of negligible inductance in series or parallel with the inductor to be measured. Having paid due regard to the lumped circuit representation of the inductor assumed by the instrument and any necessary consequent conversion given be Eq. (2), the inductance value given by the measuring instrument ought to be unaffected by the presence of the resistor.

**Measuring mutual inductance.** If losses and capacitative effects between windings and to other parts of the circuit are neglected, mutual inductance is linearly additive. That is, the voltages induced in two or more secondary coils of a mutual inductor can be added simply by connecting the windings in series. Moreover, a mutual inductor is inherently a four-terminal device having separate current and potential terminals. Its impedance is defined as the ratio of the voltage across the potential terminals to the current flowing into and out of the current terminals. These two considerations make measuring and comparing mutual inductances easier and more exact than comparing self-inductances, but it is still important that no significant magnetic fields other than those of the devices being compared are produced by the measuring circuits, and that the field of one device does not interact with another.

Two mutual inductors $M_1$ and $M_2$ can be compared by using the circuit of **Fig. 4**, which again uses an inductive voltage divider as a device of known voltage ratio.

The same current can be made to flow in the primary windings of two mutual inductors by connecting them in series across the bridge source. The ratio of the two voltages induced in the secondary coils can then be compared with the voltage ratio of the inductive voltage divider. Should the input impedance of the inductive voltage divider be insufficiently large so that the secondary coils are loaded by it to an unacceptable extent, then it is necessary to supply the energizing current for the inductive voltage divider directly from the source in such a way that the defining condition of no current in the conductors at A and B is realized. Then the ratio of the inductors is given by

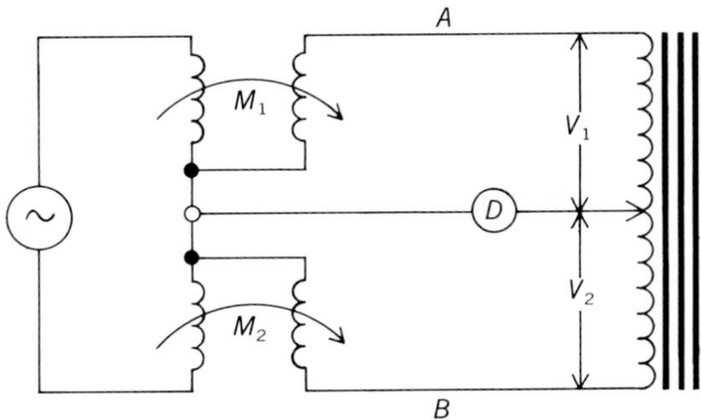


**Fig. 4. Comparison of mutual inductors using an inductive voltage divider.**

Eq. (4) to an accuracy of the order of $(r/2\pi fM)^2$,

$$\frac{M_1}{M_2} = \frac{V_1}{V_2} \quad (4)$$

where $r$ represents the loss of a mutual inductor $M$ as in the equivalent circuit of Fig. 1. This accuracy will usually be sufficient for all ordinary purposes.

The Heydweiller or Carey-Foster bridge (**Fig. 5**) is a convenient classical four-armed bridge for mutual inductance; $L$ and $R_m$ are respectively the inductance and resistance of the current-carrying windings of the mutual inductor. As can be seen, the source and detector share a common terminal, which simplifies the problem of using shields to prevent stray capacitive impedances from affecting the measurement.

If the parameter $r$ which represents the phase defect of a mutual inductor can be neglected, the bridge balance equations are Eqs. (5) and (6).

$$M = R_a\,(R_m + R)C \quad (5)$$

$$L = (R_c + R_a)\,(R_m + R)C \quad (6)$$

$R_m$ must be known, or separately measured, but $R$ can often be chosen to be much larger than $R_m$, so that no great accuracy for $R_m$ is required.

A mutual inductor can also be measured in terms of a known self-inductance, using for example the bridge in Fig. 4. The primary and secondary coils are connected in series in the same and opposing senses, and the respective total self-inductances $L_1$ and $L_2$ measured. The mutual inductance $M$ can then be calculated from Eq. (7).

$$M = \frac{(L_1 - L_2)}{4} \quad (7)$$

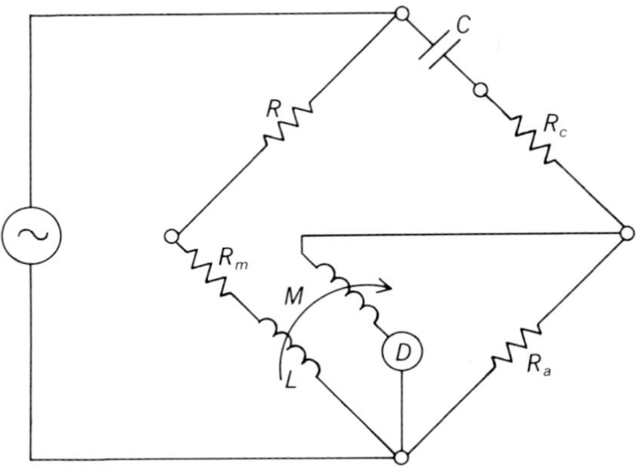


**Fig. 5. Heydweiller bridge.**

**Shielding of capacitive currents.** In all the circuits described above, it is to be understood that appropriate electrical screens maintained at the potential of the detector terminals (but not directly connected to them) surround the conductors and components of the measuring circuit. This may be accomplished by connecting these screens to the output of a suitably adjusted potential divider connected across the source. In this way, capacitive currents from all parts of the circuit are intercepted and diverted back to the source so that they do not flow through the detector and influence the bridge balance.

A further improvement in technique is to construct the measurement system with fully screened components interconnected with coaxial cables. There are methods to ensure that the currents in the coaxial inner conductors are balanced by equal and opposite currents in the coaxial outer conductors. In this way unwanted magnetic interactions between the various parts of the network can also be avoided. *See Coaxial cable; Electrical measurements; Electrical shielding; Inductance.*

*Bryan P. Kibble*

**Bibliography.** B. Hague and T. R. Foord, *Alternating Current Bridge Methods*, 6th ed., 1971; B. P. Kibble and G. H. Rayner, *Coaxial A.C. Bridges*, 1984.

## Inductor

A device for introducing inductance into a circuit. The term covers devices with a wide range of uses, sizes, and types, including components for electric-wave filters, tuned circuits, electrical measuring circuits, and energy storage devices.

Inductors are classified as fixed, adjustable, and variable. All are made either with or without magnetic cores. Inductors without magnetic cores are called air-core coils, although the actual core material may be a ceramic, a plastic, or some other nonmagnetic material. Inductors with magnetic cores are called iron-core coils. A wide variety of magnetic materials are used, and some of these contain very little iron. Magnetic cores for inductors for low-frequency, or high-energy storage, use are most commonly made from laminations of silicon steel. Some iron-core inductors with cores of compressed powdered iron, powdered permalloy, or ferrite are more suitable for higher-frequency applications.

**Fixed inductors.** In fixed inductors coils are wound so that the turns remain fixed in position with respect to each other. If an iron core is used, any air gap it has is also fixed and the position of the core remains unchanged within the coil.

A toroidal coil is a fixed inductor wound uniformly around a toroidal form (see **illus.**). Because of the closed magnetic circuit, such an inductor has practically no leakage flux and is little affected by the presence of stray magnetic fields. High-accuracy standard inductors are commonly made in this form. Powdered cores are used to increase the $Q$ of the coil and reduce the size required for a specified inductance. Ceramic-core toroidal coils supported in cork are used as standard inductors of high stability and accuracy.

**Adjustable inductors.** These either have taps for changing the number of turns desired, or consist of several fixed inductors which may be switched into various series or parallel combinations.

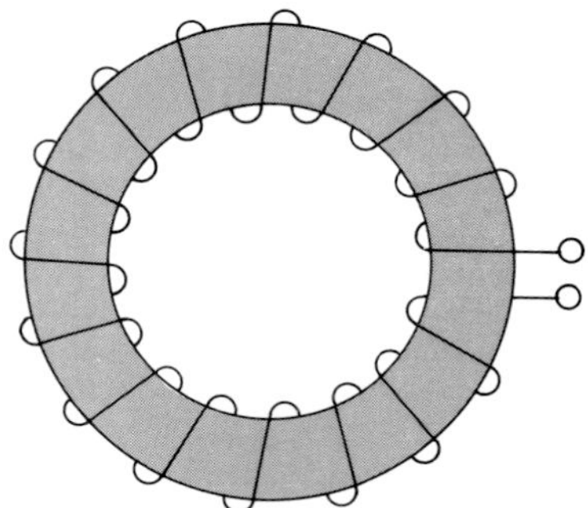

Toroidal coil, a type of fixed inductor.

**Variable inductors.** Such inductors are constructed so that the effective inductance can be changed. Means for doing this include (1) changing the permeability of a magnetic core; (2) moving the magnetic core, or part of it, with respect to the coil or the remainder of the core; and (3) moving one or more coils of the inductor with respect to one of more of the other coils, thereby changing mutual inductance. *See* Alternating-current circuit theory; Inductance.

*Burtis L. Robertson; Wilson S. Pritchett*

## Information theory

A branch of communication theory devoted to problems in coding. A unique feature of information theory is its use of a numerical measure of the amount of information gained when the contents of a message are learned. Information theory relies heavily on the mathematical science of probability. For this reason the term information theory is often applied loosely to other probabilistic studies in communication theory, such as signal detection, random noise, and prediction. *See* Electrical communications.

Information theory provides criteria for comparing different communication systems. The need for comparisons became evident during the 1940s. A large variety of systems had been invented to make better use of existing wires and radio spectrum allocations. In the 1920s the problem of comparing telegraph systems attracted H. Nyquist and R. V. L. Hartley, who provided some of the philosophy behind information theory. In 1948 C. E. Shannon published a precise general theory which formed the basis for subsequent work in information theory. *See* Modulation.

In information theory, communication systems are compared on the basis of signaling rate. Finding an appropriate definition of signaling rate was itself a problem, which Shannon solved by the use of his measure of information, to be explained later. Of special interest are optimal systems which, for a given set of communication facilities, attain a maximum signaling rate. Optimal systems provide communication-systems designers with useful absolute bounds on obtainable signaling rates. Although optimal systems often use complicated and expensive encoding equipment, they provide insight into the design of fast practical systems.

**Communication systems.** In designing a one-way communication system from the standpoint of information theory, three parts are considered beyond the control of the system designer: (1) the source, which generates messages at the transmitting end of the system, (2) the destination, which ultimately receives the messages, and (3) the channel, consisting of a transmission medium or device for conveying signals from the source to the destination. Constraints beyond the mere physical properties of the transmission medium influence the designed. For example, in designing a radio system only a given portion of the radio-frequency spectrum may be available. The transmitter power may also be limited. If the system is just one link in a larger system which plans to use regenerative repeaters, the designer may be restricted to pulse-transmission schemes. All such conditions are considered part of the description of the channel. The source does not usually produce messages in a form acceptable as input by the channel. The transmitting end of the system contains another device, called an encoder, which prepares the source's messages for input to the channel. Similarly the receiving end of the system will contain a decoder to convert the output of the channel into a form recognizable by the destination. The encoder and decoder are the parts to be designed. In radio systems this design is essentially the choice of a modulator and a detector.

***Discrete and continuous cases.*** A source is called discrete if its messages are sequences of elements (letters) taken from an enumerable set of possibilities (alphabet). Thus sources producing integer data or written English are discrete. Sources which are not discrete are called continuous, for example, speech and music sources. Likewise, channels are classified as discrete or continuous according to the kinds of signals they transmit. Most transmission media (such as transmission lines and radio paths) can provide continuous channels; however, constraints (such as a restriction to use pulse techniques) on the use of these media may convert them into discrete channels.

The treatment of continuous cases is sometimes simplified by noting that a signal of finite bandwidth can be encoded into a discrete sequence of numbers. If the power spectrum of a signal $s(t)$ is confined to the band $O$ to $W$ hertz (cycles per second) then Eq. (1) applies. Equation (1) reconstructs $s(t)$ exactly

$$s(t) = \sum_{n=-\infty}^{\infty} s\left(\frac{n}{2W}\right) \frac{\sin 2\pi W\left(t - \dfrac{n}{2W}\right)}{2\pi W\left(t - \dfrac{n}{2W}\right)} \tag{1}$$

from its sample values (Nyquist samples), at discrete instants $(2W)^{-1}$ s apart. Thus, a continuous channel which transmits such signals resembles a discrete channel which transmits Nyquist samples drawn from a large finite set of signal levels and at the rate of $2W$ samples per second.

***Noiseless and noisy cases.*** The output of a channel need not agree with its input. For example, a channel might, for secrecy purposes, contain a cryptographic device to scramble the message. Still, if the output of the channel can be computed knowing just the input message, then the channel is called noiseless. If, however, random agents make the output unpredictable even when the input is known, then the channel is called noisy. *See* Privacy systems (scrambling).

**Encoding and decoding.** Many encoders first break the message into a sequence of elementary blocks; next they substitute for each block a representative code, or signal, suitable for input to the channel. Such encoders are called block encoders. For example, telegraph and teletype systems both use block en-

**Three possible binary codes for four-letter alphabet**

| Letter | Code I | Code II | Code III |
|---|---|---|---|
| A | 0 0 | 0 0 0 | 0 0 0 0 0 |
| B | 0 1 | 0 1 1 | 0 0 1 1 1 |
| C | 1 0 | 1 0 1 | 1 1 0 0 1 |
| D | 1 1 | 1 1 0 | 1 1 1 1 0 |

coders in which the blocks are individual letters. Entire words form the blocks of some commercial cablegram systems. The operation of a block encoder may be described completely by a function or table showing, for each possible block, the code that represents it.

It is generally impossible for a decoder to reconstruct with certainty a message received via a noisy channel. Suitable encoding, however, may make the noise tolerable. For illustration, consider a channel that transmits pulses of two kinds. It is customary to let binary digits 0 and 1 denote the two kinds of pulse. Suppose the source has only the four letters A, B, C, D. One might simply encode each single-letter block into a pair of binary digits (code I of the **table**). In that case the decoder would make a mistake every time noise produced an error. If code II is used, the decoder can at least recognize that a received triple of digits must contain errors if it is one of the triples 001, 010, 100, or 111 not listed in the code II column. Because an error in any one of the three pulses of code II always produces a triple that is not listed, code II provides single-error detection. Similarly code III provides double-error detection, because errors in a single pulse or pair of pulses always produce a quintuple that is not listed.

As an alternative, code III may provide single-error correction. In this usage, the decoder picks a letter for which code III agrees with the received quintuple in as many places as possible. If only a single digit is in error, this rule chooses the correct letter.

Even when the channel is noiseless, a variety of encoding schemes exists and there is a problem of picking a good one. Of all encodings of English letters into dots and dashes, the Continental Morse encoding is nearly the fastest possible one. It achieves its speed by associating short codes with the most common letters. A noiseless binary channel (capable of transmitting two kinds of pulse 0, 1, of the same duration) provides the following example. Suppose one had to encode English text for this channel. A simple encoding might just use 27 different five-digit codes to represent word space (denoted by #), A, B, . . . , Z; say # 00000, A 00001, B 00010, C 00011, . . . , Z 11011. The word #CAB would then be encoded into 00000000110000100010. A similar encoding is used in teletype transmission; however, it places a third kind of pulse at the beginning of each code to help the decoder stay in synchronism with the encoder. The five-digit encoding can be improved by assigning four-digit codes 0000, 0001, 0010, 0011, 0100 to the five most common letters #, E, T, A, O. There are 22 quintuples of binary digits which do not begin with any of the five four-digit codes; these may be assigned as codes to the 22 remaining letters. About half the letters of English text are #, E, T, A, or O; therefore the new encoding uses an average of only 4.5 digits per letter of message. *SEE* TELETYPEWRITER.

More generally, if an alphabet is encoded in single-letter blocks, using $L(i)$ digits for the $i$th letter, the average number of digits used per letter is shown in Eq. (2), where $p(i)$ is the probability of the $i$th letter.

$$L = p(1)L(1) + p(2)L(2) + p(3)L(3) + \cdots \qquad (2)$$

An optimal encoding scheme will minimize $L$. However, the encoded messages must be decipherable, and this condition puts constraints on the $L(i)$. The code lengths of decipherable encodings must satisfy the relationships shown in inequality (3). The real

$$2^{-L(1)} + 2^{-L(2)} + 2^{-L(3)} + \cdots \leqq 1 \qquad (3)$$

numbers $L(1)$, $L(2)$, . . . , which minimize $L$ subject to inequality (3) are $L(i) = -\log_2 p(i)$ and the corresponding minimum $L$ is shown in Eq. (4), which pro-

$$H = -\sum_i p(i) \log_2 p(i) \qquad (4)$$

vides a value of $H$ equal to a number of digits per letter.

The $L(i)$ must be integers and $-\log_2 p(i)$ generally are not integers; for this reason there may be no encoding which provides $L = H$. However, Shannon showed that it is always possible to assign codes to letters in such a way that $L \leqq H + 1$. A procedure for constructing an encoding which actually minimizes $L$ has been given by D. A. Huffman. For (27-letter) English text $H = 4.08$ digits per letter, as compared with the actual minimum 4.12 digits per letter obtained by Huffman's procedure.

By encoding in blocks of more than one letter, the average number of digits used per letter may be reduced further. If messages are constructed by picking letters independently with the probabilities $p(1)$, $p(2)$, . . . , then $H$ is found to be the minimum of the average numbers of digits per letter used to encode these messages using longer blocks.

**Information content of message.** The information contained in a message unit is defined in terms of the average number of digits required to encode it. Accordingly the information associated with a single letter produced by a discrete source is defined to be the number $H$. Some other properties of $H$ help to justify using it to measure information. If one of the $p(i)$ equals unity, only one letter appears in the messages. Then nothing new is learned by seeing a letter and, indeed, $H = 0$. Second, of all possible ways of assigning probabilities $p(i)$ to an $N$-letter alphabet, the one which maximizes $H$ is $p(1) = p(2) = \cdots = 1/N$. This situation is the one in which the unknown letter seems most uncertain; therefore it does seem correct that learning such a letter provides the most information. The corresponding maximum value of $H$ is $\log_2 N$. This result seems reasonable by the following argument. When two independent letters are learned, the information obtained should be $2H = 2 \log_2 N$. However, such pairs of letters may be considered to be the letters of a larger alphabet of $N^2$ equally likely pairs. The information associated with one of these new letters is $\log_2 N^2 = 2 \log_2 N$. Although $H$ given by Eq. (4) is dimensionless, it is given units called bits (a contraction of binary digits). Occasionally the information is expressed in digits of other kinds (such as ternary or decimal). Then bases other than 2 are used for the logarithm in Eq. (4).

The majority of message sources do not merely pick successive letters independently. For example in

English, H is the most likely letter to follow T but is otherwise not common. The source is imagined to be a random process in which the letter probabilities change, depending on what the past of the message has been. Statistical correlations between different parts of the message may be exploited by encoding longer blocks. The average number of digits per letter may thereby be reduced below the single-letter information $H$ given by Eq. (4). For example, by encoding English words instead of single letters, 2.1 digits/letter suffice. Encoding longer and longer blocks, the number of digits needed per letter approaches a limiting minimum value. This limit is called the entropy of the source and is interpreted as the rate, in bits per letter, at which the source generates information. If the source produces letters at some fixed average rate, $n$ letters/s, the entropy may also be converted into a rate in bits per second by multiplying by $n$. The entropy may be computed from tables giving the probabilities of blocks of $N$ letters ($N$-grams). If in Eq. (4) the summation index $i$ is extended over all $N$-grams, then the number $H$ represents the information in $N$ consecutive letters. As $N \to \infty$, $H/N$ approaches the entropy of the source. The entropy of English has been estimated by Shannon to be about 1 bit/letter. However, an encoder might have to encode 100-grams in order to achieve a reduction to near 1 digit/letter. Comparing English with a source which produces 27 equally likely letters independently (and hence has entropy $\log_2 27 = 4.8$ bits/letter), this result is often restated: English is 80% redundant. Other common sources are also very redundant. Facsimile, for example, can be speeded by a factor of 10 by means of practical encoding techniques.

**Capacity.** The notion of entropy is more widely applicable than might appear from the discussion of the binary channel. Any discrete noiseless channel may be given a number $C$, which is called the capacity. $C$ is defined as the maximum rate (bits per second) of all sources that may be connected directly to the channel. Shannon proved that any given source (which perhaps cannot be connected directly to the channel) of entropy $H$ bits/letter, can be encoded for the channel and run at rates arbitrarily close to $C/H$ letters/s.

By using repetition, error-correcting codes, or similar techniques, the reliability of transmission over a noisy channel can be increased at the expense of slowing down the source. It might be expected that the source rate must be slowed to 0 bits/s as the transmission is required to be increasingly error-free. On the contrary, Shannon proved that even a noisy channel has a capacity $C$. Suppose that errors in at most a fraction $\epsilon$ of the letters of the message can be tolerated ($\epsilon > 0$). Suppose also that a given source, of entropy $H$ bits/letter, must be operated at the rate of at least $(C/H) - \delta$ letters/s ($\delta > 0$). No matter how small $\epsilon$ and $\delta$ are chosen, an encoder can be found which satisfies these requirements.

For example, the symmetric binary channel has binary input and output letters; noise changes a fraction $p$ of the 0s to 1 and a fraction $p$ of the 1s to 0 and treats successive digits independently. The capacity of this channel is shown by Eq. (5), where $m$ is the

$$C = m\{1 + p \log_2 p + (1 - p) \log_2 (1 - p)\} \quad (5)$$

number of digits per second which the channel transmits.

A famous formula is shown by Eq. (6), which

$$C = W \log_2 \left(1 + \frac{S}{N}\right) \quad (6)$$

gives the capacity $C$ of a band-limited continuous channel. The channel consists of a frequency band $W$ Hz wide, which contains a gaussian noise of power $N$. The noise has a flat spectrum over the band and is added to the signal by the channel. The channel also contains a restriction that the average signal power may not exceed $S$.

Equation (6) illustrates an exchange relationship between bandwidth $W$ and signal-to-noise ratio $S/N$. By suitable encoding a signaling system can use a smaller bandwidth, provided that the signal power is also raised enough to keep $C$ fixed. *SEE BANDWIDTH REQUIREMENTS*.

Typical capacity values are 20,000 bits/s for a telephone speech circuit and 50,000,000 bits/s for a broadcast television circuit. Speech and TV are very redundant and would use channels of much lower capacity if the necessary encodings were inexpensive. For example, the vocoder can send speech, only slightly distorted, over a 2000-bits/s channel. Successive lines or frames in television tend to look alike. This resemblance suggests a high redundancy; however, to exploit it the encoder may have to encode in very long blocks.

Not all of the waste in channel capacity can be attributed to source redundancies. Even with an irredundant source, such as a source producing random digits, some channel capacity will be wasted. The simplest encoding schemes provide reliable transmission only at a rate equal to the capacity of a channel with roughly 8 dB smaller signal power (the 8-dB figure is merely typical and really depends on the reliability requirements). Again, more efficient encoding to combat noise generally requires larger-sized blocks. This is to be expected. The signal is separated from the noise on the basis of differences between the signal's statistical properties and those of noise. The block size must be large enough to supply the decoder with enough data to draw statistically significant conclusions. *SEE ELECTRICAL NOISE*.

**Algebraic codes.** Practical codes must use simple encoding and decoding equipment. Error-correcting codes for binary channels have been designed to use small digital logic circuits. These are called algebraic codes, linear codes, or group codes because they are constructed by algebraic techniques involving linear vector spaces or groups.

For example, each of the binary codes I, II, and III in the table contains four code words which may be regarded as vectors $C = (c_1, c_2, \ldots, c_n)$ of binary digits $c_i$. Define the sum $C + C'$ of two vectors to be the vector $(c_1 + c_1', \ldots, c_n + c_n')$ in which coordinates of $C$ and $C'$ are added modulo 2. Codes I, II, and III each have the property that the vector sum of any two code words is also a code word. Because of that, these codes are linear vector spaces and groups under vector addition. Their code words also belong to the $n$-dimensional space consisting of all $2^n$ vectors of $n$ binary coordinates. Codes II and III, with $n = 3$ and 5, do not contain all $2^n$ vectors; they are only two-dimensional linear subspaces of the larger space. Consequently, in Codes II and III, the coordinates $c_i$ must satisfy certain linear homogeneous equations. Code II satisfies $c_1 + c_2 + c_2 = 0$. Code III satisfies $c_2 + c_4 = 0$, $c_2 + c_3 + c_5 = 0$, $c_1 + c_2 = 0$, and other equations linearly dependent on these three. The sums in such equations are performed modulo 2; for this reason the equations are called parity check equations. In general, any $r$ linearly independent parity check equations in $c_1, \ldots, c_n$ determine a linear subspace of dimension $k = n - r$. The $2^k$ vectors in this subspace are the code words of a linear code.

One may transform the $r$ parity checks into a form which simplifies the encoding. This transformation consists of solving the original parity check equations for some $r$ of the coordinates $c_i$ as expressions in which only the remaining $n - r$ coordinates appear as independent variables. For example, the three parity check equations given for Code III are already in solved form with $c_1$, $c_4$, $c_5$ expressed in terms of $c_2$ and $c_3$. The $k = n - r$ independent variables are called message digits because the $2^k$ values of these coordinates may be used to represent the letters of the message alphabet. The $r$ dependent coordinates, called check digits, are then easily computed by circuits which perform additions modulo 2.

At the receiver the decoder can also do additions modulo 2 to test if the received digits still satisfy the parity check equations. The set of parity check equations that fail is called the syndrome because it contains the data that the decoder needs to diagnose the errors. The syndrome depends only on the error locations, not on which code word was sent. In general, a code can be used to correct $e$ errors if each pair of distinct code words differ in at least $2e + 1$ of the $n$ coordinates. For a linear code that is equivalent to requiring the smallest number $d$ of "ones" among the coordinates of any code word (excepting the zero word $(0, 0, \ldots, 0)$) to be $2e + 1$ or more. Under these conditions each pattern of $0, 1, \ldots, e - 1$, or $e$ errors produces a distinct syndrome; then the decoder can compute the error locations from the syndrome. This computation may offer some difficulty. But at least it involves only $r$ binary variables, representing the syndrome, instead of all $n$ coordinates.

***Hamming codes.*** The $r$ parity check equations may be written concisely as binary matrix equation (7).

$$HC^T = 0 \qquad (7)$$

Here $C^T$ is a column vector, the transpose of $(c_1, \ldots, c_n)$. $H$ is the so-called parity check matrix, having $n$ columns and $r$ rows. A Hamming single-error correcting code is obtained when the columns of $H$ are all $n = 2^r - 1$ distinct columns of $r$ binary digits, excluding the column of all zeros. If a single error occurs, say in coordinate $c_i$, then the decoder uses the syndrome to identify $c_i$ as the unique coordinate that appears in just those parity check equations that fail.

***Shift register codes.*** A linear shift register sequence is a periodic infinite binary sequence $\ldots, c_0, c_1, c_2, \ldots$ satisfying a recurrence equation expressing $c_j$ as a modulo 2 sum of some of the $b$ earlier digits $c_{j-b}, \ldots, c_{j-1}$. A recurrence with two terms would be an equation $c_j = c_{j-a} + c_{j-b}$, with $a$ equal to some integer $1, 2, \ldots$, or $b - 1$. The digits of a shift register sequence can be computed, one at a time, by very simple equipment. It consists of a feedback loop, containing a shift register to store $c_{j-b}, \ldots, c_{j-1}$ and a logic circuit performing modulo 2 additions. This equipment may be used to implement a linear code. First, message digits $c_1, \ldots, c_b$ are stored in the register and transmitted. Thereafter the equipment computes and transmits successively the $n - b$ check digits $c_j$ obtained from the recurrence equation with $j = b + 1, \ldots, n$. By choosing a suitable recurrence equation, one can make the period of the shift register sequence as large as $2^b - 1$. Then, with $n$ equal to the period $2^b - 1$, the code consists of the zero code word $(0, 0, \ldots, 0)$ and $2^b - 1$ other code words which differ from each other only by cyclic permutations of their coordinates. These latter words all contain $d = 2^{b-1}$ "ones" and so the code can correct $e = 2^{b-2} - 1$ errors. SEE SWITCHING CIRCUIT.

***Intermediate codes.*** The Hamming codes and maximal period shift register codes are opposite extremes, correcting either one or many errors and having code words consisting either mostly of message digits or mostly of check digits. Many intermediate codes have been invented. One of them requires $n + 1$ to be a power of 2; say $n + 1 = 2^q$. It then uses at most $qe$ check digits to correct $e$ errors.

***Perfect codes.*** Although each pattern of $0, 1, \ldots, e$ errors produces a distinct syndrome, there may be extra syndromes which occur only after more than $e$ errors. In order to keep the number of check digits small, extra syndromes must be avoided. A code is called perfect if all $2^r$ syndromes can result from patterns of $0, 1, \ldots, e - 1$, or $e$ errors. Hamming codes are all perfect. M. J. E. Golay found another perfect binary code having $n = 23$, $r = 11$ check digits, and correcting $e = 13$ errors.

***Orthogonal parity codes.*** Orthogonal parity codes are codes with especially simple decoding circuits which take a kind of majority vote. Suppose the parity check equations can be used to derive $2e + 1$ linear equations in which one digit, say $c_1$, is expressed with each of the remaining digits $c_2, \ldots, c_n$ appearing in at most one equation. If at most $e$ errors occur, then the received digits satisfy a majority of the $2e + 1$ equations if and only if $c_1$ was received correctly. For example, the recurrence $c_j = c_{j-2} + c_{j-3}$ generates a maximal period shift register code with $n = 7$, $r = 4$, $e = 1$. Set $j = 1, 3$, and 4 in the recurrence equation. One obtains three of the parity check equations, $c_1 = c_5 + c_6$, $c_1 = c_3 + c_7$, and $c_1 = c_2 + c_4$, after using the fact that the shift register sequence has period 7. These three equations are already in the form required for decoding $c_1$ by majority vote. Similar equations, obtained by permuting $c_1, \ldots, c_7$ cyclically, apply for $c_2, \ldots, c_7$. Then the decoder can be organized so that most of the equipment used to decode $c_1$ can be used again in decoding $c_2, \ldots, c_7$.

*Edgar N. Gilbert*

***Bibliography.*** R. B. Ash, *Information Theory*, 1965; E. R. Berlekamp, *Algebraic Coding Theory*, 1968; C. Cherry, *On Human Communications: A Review, a Survey, and a Criticism*, 3d ed., 1980; S. Guiasu, *Information Theory With New Applications*, 1977; R. W. Hamming, *Coding and Information Theory*, 1980; S. Lin, *An Introduction to Error-Correcting Codes*, 1970; M. Schwartz, *Information Transmission, Modulation, and Noise*, 2d ed., 1970; C. E. Shannon and W. Weaver, *The Mathematical Theory of Communication*, 1949.

## Infrared imaging devices

Devices that convert an invisible infrared image into a visible image. Infrared radiation is usually considered to span the wavelengths from about 0.8 or 0.9 micrometer to several hundred micrometers; however, most infrared imaging devices are designed to operate within broad wavelength regions of atmospheric transparency, that is, the atmospheric windows. At sea level, for horizontal paths of a few kilometers' length, these are approximately at 8–14 μm, 3–5 μm, 2–2.5 μm, 1.5–1.9 μm, and wavelengths shorter than 1.4 μm. The radiation available for imaging may be emitted from objects in the scene of interest (usually at the longer wavelengths called thermal radiation) or reflected. Reflected radiation may be dominated by sunlight or may be from controlled sources such as lasers used specifically as illuminators for the imaging device. The latter systems are called active, while those relying largely on emitted radiation are called passive. Active optical imaging systems were developed to achieve a nighttime aerial photographic capability, and work during World War II pushed such systems into the near-infrared spectral region. Development of passive infrared imaging systems came after the war, but only the advent of lasers allowed creation of active infrared imagers at wavelengths much longer than those of the photographic region. Striking advances have been made in active infrared systems which utilize the coherence available from lasers, and hybrid active-passive systems have been studied intensively. *See Laser.*

Although developed largely for military purposes, infrared imaging devices have been valuable in industrial, commercial, and scientific applications. These range from nondestructive testing and quality control to earth resources surveys, pollution monitoring, and energy conservation. Infrared images from aerial platforms are used to accomplish "heat surveys," locating points of excessive heat loss. An example is shown in **Fig. 1***a*. As discussed below, calibration allows association of photographic tones in this figure with values of apparent (that is, equivalent blackbody) temperatures. Dark areas in the figure are "colder" than light ones.

**Scanning systems.** Infrared imaging devices may be realized by electrooptical or optomechanical scanning systems. All have an optical head for receiving the infrared radiation and a display for the visible image. These are connected by electronics for the passage of electrical signals from the detector element(s) to the display input. Signal processing may be incorporated in the electronics to selectively enhance or reduce features in the produced visible image. For example, in Fig. 1*b* a "level-slice" technique presents in white all areas (mainly rooftops) with apparent temperatures between −7.9 and −8.9°C or 17.4 and 15.6°F. (The ambient air temperature was −5°C or 23°F) Black regions in the figure correspond to apparent temperatures below or above the narrow "sliced" temperature range of the white regions.

**Fig. 1.** Thermal imagery in the wavelength range 10.4–12.5 μm obtained during flights over Ypsilanti, Michigan, at 2400 hours, November 23, 1975, by the Airborne Multispectral Scanner operated by the Environmental Research Institute of Michigan. (*a*) Calibrated thermal imagery. (*b*) Signal-processed thermal imagery of same scene. (*From F. Tannis, R. Sampson, and T. Wagner, Thermal imagery for evaluation of construction and insulation conditions of small buildings, Environmental Research Institute of Michigan, ERIM Rep. 116600-12-F, July 1976*)

Optomechanical methods such as rotating prisms or oscillating mirrors may be used to sample or scan the spatial distribution of infrared radiation in either the object or image plane. Electrooptical imaging devices may use an electron beam (for example, vidicons) or charge transport in solids (for example, charge-coupled devices, or CCDs) to scan the infrared image formed by the optics of the device. This image-plane scanning places more stringent requirements upon the optics for image quality off-axis than does use of mechanically moved optical elements placed before the entrance aperture of the system. Intensive development of pyroelectric vidicons, detector arrays, and infrared charge-coupled devices (IRCCDs) has taken place, reflecting the critical role played by the detector element in all infrared systems. The spectral, spatial, and temporal responses of detectors are the major factors in determining the wavelength regions, the spatial resolution, and the frequency response (that is, the time constant) of imaging devices. *See Charge-coupled devices.*

**Detector arrays.** Optomechanical scanning methods often stress the response time of the detector-electronics package. As a result, multiple detectors or detector arrays are sometimes incorporated in the focal planes, resulting in partially electronically scanned optomechanical systems. The technology for use of a linear array of detector elements (often lead selenide and indium antimonide detectors for the 3–5-μm region, and mercury-doped germanium and mercury cadmium telluride for the 8–14-μm window) is well developed, and the use of a two-dimensional array or matrix of detectors has been studied. Optomechanical imagers incorporating such arrays allow the use of time delay and integration (TDI) of the signals to improve the resulting signal-to-noise ratios.

Solid-state components such as charge-coupled devices afford the opportunity for implementation of signal processing directly at the focal plane. Two approaches have been undertaken to attain the focal-plane array technology of infrared charge-coupled devices. In one, the development of a hybrid device, an infrared detector matrix of any suitable photodetector material, for example, indium antimonide, mercury cadmium telluride, and lead tin telluride, is mated with a conventional silicon charge-coupled device. Thus two solid-state wafers or "chips" are integrated to obtain an infrared charge-coupled device. In the other, the goal is a monolithic chip, one incorporating the photo-detection, charge generation, and charge transfer in a structure made of essentially one material. Candidate materials include impurity-doped silicon, indium antimonide, and mercury cadmium telluride. The hybrid device technology can be implemented more readily than that needed for monolithic infrared charge-coupled devices. The development of infrared charge-coupled devices with the number of detecting elements in a sufficiently closely packed array required for high-performance infrared imaging devices involves additional difficulties.

***Scanning motion.*** Some optomechanical imagers produce a two-dimensional scan entirely by movement of components of the device itself; others utilize the motion of a platform such as an aircraft or satellite. The first kind of system includes the forward looking infrared (FLIR) or framing imagers which usually scan in television-like raster patterns and display, synchronously if done in real time, a visible image corresponding to the spatial distribution of infrared radiation. These visible image outputs have been named thermographs and thermograms. Commercially available imaging devices of this type have used horizontally and vertically rotating germanium prisms, mirrors oscillated in orthogonal directions, two mirrors and a six-sided rotating prism, and other schemes to produce images at relatively slow rates from 16 per second to less than a quarter of a frame per second. Higher-performance systems have been produced for military purposes. The second class of imaging systems includes those often called line scanners or thermal mappers. One such system, the 12-channel Airborne Multispectral Scanner operated by the Environmental Research Institute of Michigan (ERIM; **Fig. 2**), includes two thermal radiation channels, at 8.2–9.3 μm and 10.4–12.5 μm, whose magnetic-tape recorder output was processed to produce the thermal imagery in Fig. 1.

**Characterization of output.** The instantaneous field of view (IFOV) or resolution element of imaging systems is always geometrically filled by the radiating source, so that the output of the device is a response to changes in amount of radiation from field of view to field of view. These changes are best characterized in terms of radiance $L$, the radiant flux per unit area per unit solid angle, usually in a selected spectral band of wavelengths, $\Delta\lambda$. Even in the infrared regions, the radiance variation may be ascribed to changes in reflectance, incident radiation, emissivity, or temperature. By restriction to wavelengths dominated by emission, the so-called thermal wavelengths longer than 3.5 μm, the radiance change can be described by the equation below, where $T$ is the absolute temperature and $\epsilon$ is the emissivity. Contributions due to $\Delta\epsilon$ are usually treated as changes in an equivalent blackbody temperature by setting $\epsilon = 1$ and $\Delta\epsilon = 0$. Then $T$ represents an equivalent blackbody temperature, and the radiance variation can be ascribed entirely to a value of $\Delta T$. That value of $\Delta T$ corresponding to a radiance difference which will just produce a signal-to-noise ratio of 1 is called the noise equivalent temperature difference (NETD). One can also characterize the performance of an imaging system by a noise equivalent emissivity difference or even a noise equivalent reflectivity difference. The use of noise equivalent temperature difference as a figure of merit for thermal imagers is obviously more appropriate. For the higher-performance forward-looking infrared systems, a useful figure of merit is the minimum resolvable temperature difference (MRTD), a figure of merit which includes the characteristics of the display and of the observer as well.

$$\Delta L = \frac{\partial L}{\partial T}\Delta T + \frac{\partial L}{\partial \epsilon}\Delta\epsilon$$

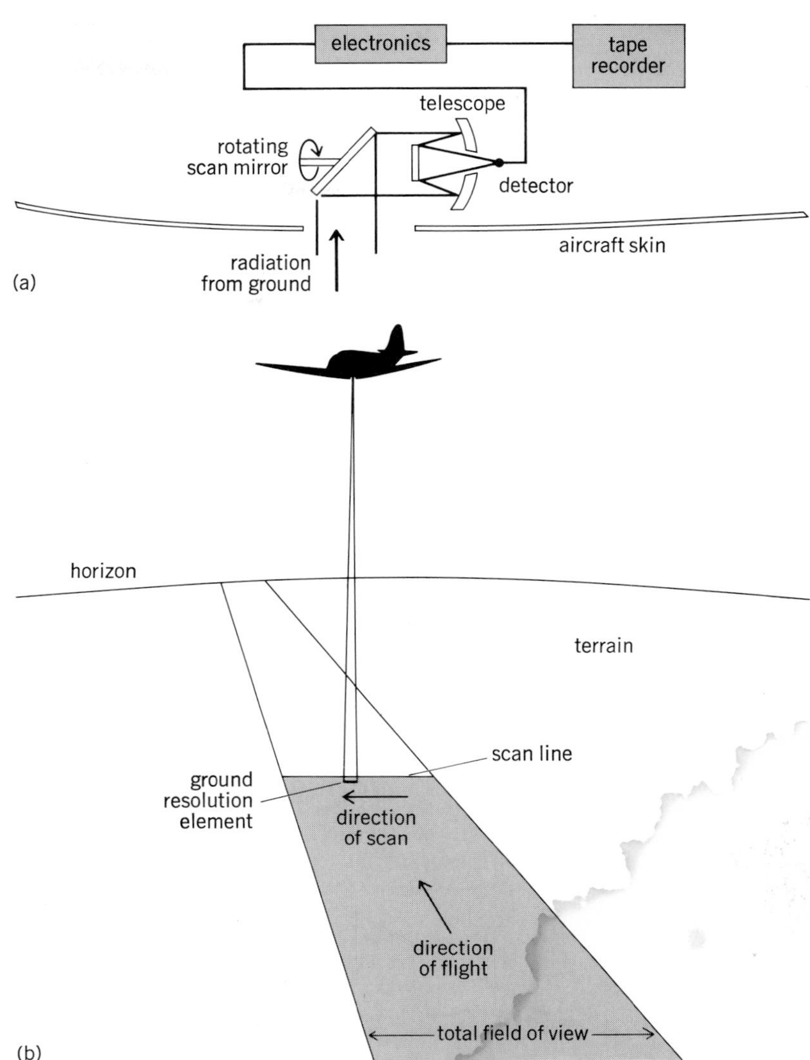


**Fig. 2.** **Airborne Multispectral Scanner. (*a*) Schematic diagram of equipment. (*b*) Scanning operation, utilizing motion of aircraft. (*After F. Tannis, R. Sampson, and T. Wagner, Thermal imagery for evaluation of construction and insulation conditions of small buildings, Environmental Research Institute of Michigan, ERIM Rep. 116600-12-F, July 1976*)**

**Display.** The visible image which is the output of infrared imaging devices may be displayed in the same manner as a conventional television picture by means of a cathode-ray tube (CRT). Cathode-ray-tube technology has been developed to a level that is suitable, and research has been undertaken toward creation of satisfactory flat panel displays using liquid crystal elements, light-emitting diodes, or plasma panels. Systems not requiring a real-time image display may utilize analog or digital data storage or transmission systems, which then are used to produce permanent visual records such as photographs. High-resolution "hard copy" images can be produced by sophisticated systems using electron-beam or laser recording on film. Complex signal-processing techniques are easily introduced before the final image recording is made. *See* Cathode-ray tube; Light-emitting diode; Liquid crystals.

George J. Zissis

***Bibliography.*** J. M. Lloyd, *Thermal Imaging Systems*, 1975; *Proceedings of the IEEE: Special Issue* *on IR Technology for Remote Sensing*, vol. 63, pp. 1–208, January 1975; F. Tanis, R. Sampson, and T. Wagner, *Thermal Imagery for Evaluation of Construction and Insulation Conditions of Small Buildings*, Environmental Research Institute of Michigan, ERIM Rep. 116600-12-F, July 1976; W. Wolfe and G. Zissis (eds.), *The Infrared Handbook*, Infrared Information and Analysis Center, Environmental Research Institute of Michigan, 1978.

## Integrated circuits

Miniature electronic circuits produced within and upon a single semiconductor crystal, usually silicon. Integrated circuits range in complexity from simple logic circuits and amplifiers, about 1⁄20 in. (1.3 mm) square, to large-scale integrated circuits up to about 1⁄3 in. (8 mm) square. They contain hundreds of thousands of transistors and other components which provide computer memory circuits and complex logic subsystems such as microcomputer central processor units. SEE SEMICONDUCTOR.

Since the mid-1960s, integrated circuits have become the primary components of most electronic systems. Their low cost, high reliability, and speed have been essential in furthering the wide use of digital computers. Microcomputers have spread the use of computer technology to instruments, business machines, automobiles, and other equipment. Other common uses of large-scale integrated circuits are in pocket calculators and electronic watches. For analog signal processing, integrated subsystems such as FM stereo demodulators and switched-capacitor filters are made. SEE CALCULATORS: DIGITAL COMPUTER; ELECTRONICS; MICROCOMPUTER.

Integrated circuits consist of the combination of active electronic devices such as transistors and diodes with passive components such as resistors and capacitors, within and upon a single semiconductor crystal. The construction of these elements within the semiconductor is achieved through the introduction of electrically active impurities into well-defined regions of the semiconductor. The fabrication of integrated circuits thus involves such processes as vapor-phase deposition of semi-conductors and insulators, oxidation, solid-state diffusion, ion implantation, vacuum deposition, and sputtering.

Generally, integrated circuits are not straight-forward replacements of electronic circuits assembled from discrete components. They represent an extension of the technology by which silicon planar transistors are made. Because of this, transistors or modifications of transistor structures are the primary devices of integrated circuits. Methods of fabricating good-quality resistors and capacitors have been devised, but the third major type of passive component, inductors, must be simulated with complex circuitry or added to the integrated circuit as discrete components. SEE TRANSISTOR.

Simple logic circuits were the easiest to adapt to these design changes. The first of these, such as inverters and gates, were produced in the early 1960s primarily for miniaturization of missile guidance computers and other aerospace systems. Analog circuits, called linear integrated circuits, did not become commercially practical until several years later because of their heavy dependence on passive components such as resistors and capacitors. The first good-quality operational amplifiers for analog computers and instruments were produced in 1966. SEE AMPLIFIER; ANALOG COMPUTER; LOGIC CIRCUITS.

### Types of Circuits

Integrated circuits can be classified into two groups on the basis of the type of transistors which they employ: bipolar integrated circuits, in which the principal element is the bipolar junction transistor; and metal oxide semiconductor (MOS) integrated circuits, in which the principal element is the MOS transistor. Both depend upon the construction of a desired pattern of electrically active impurities within the semiconductor body, and upon the formation of an interconnection pattern of metal films on the surface of the semiconductor.

Bipolar circuits are generally used where highest logic speed is desired, and MOS for largest-scale integration or lowest power dissipation. Linear circuits are mostly bipolar, but MOS devices are used extensively in switched-capacitor filters.

**Bipolar integrated circuits.** A simple bipolar inverter circuit using a diffused resistor and an *npn* transistor is shown in **Fig. 1**. The input voltage $V_{in}$ is applied to the base of the transistor. When $V_{in}$ is zero or negative with respect to the emitter, no current flows. As a result, no voltage drop exists across the resistor, and the output voltage $V_{out}$ will be the same as the externally applied biasing voltage, + 5 V in this example. When a positive input voltage is applied, the transistor becomes conducting. Current now flows through the transistor, hence through the resistor: as a result, the output voltage decreases. Thus, the change in input voltage appears inverted at the output.

The circuit symbol and the changes in input and output voltages during the switching process just described are illustrated in **Fig. 2**. The change in the

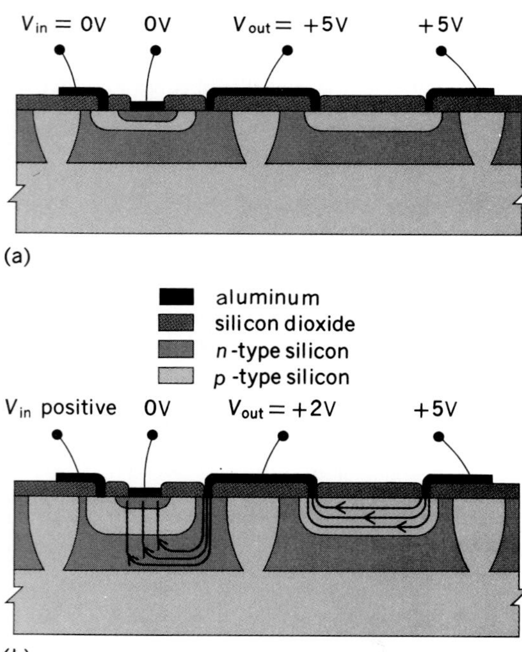


**Fig. 1. Operation of bipolar inverter circuit. (*a*) Input voltage $V_{in}$ is zero. (*b*) Positive input voltage applied; arrows indicate direction of current flow.**

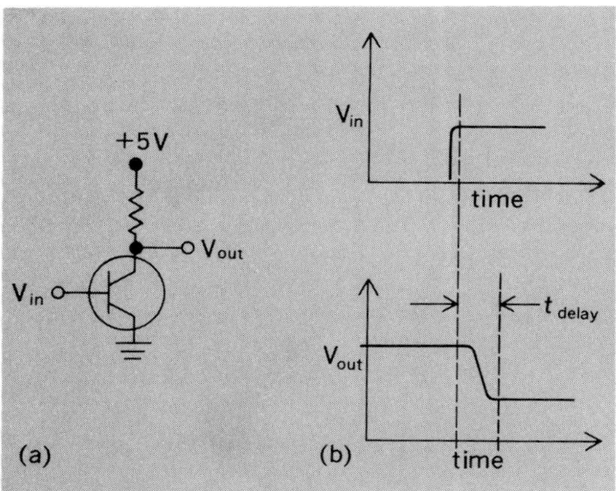


**Fig. 2. Characteristics of the inverter circuit of Fig. 1. (*a*) Circuit symbol. (*b*) Switching waveforms.**

output voltage occurs slightly later than the change in the input voltage. This time difference, called propagation delay, is an important characteristic of all integrated circuits. Much effort has been spent on reducing it, and values less than one-billionth of a second have been achieved.

Most simple digital circuits can be fabricated much as the inverter circuit described above. As an example, a photomicrograph of an early logic gate circuit is shown in **Fig. 3**. This circuit is one of the earliest digital integrated circuits, introduced commercially in 1961. For comparison, a 16-bit microcomputer digital integrated circuit introduced in 1983 is shown in **Fig. 4**. This circuit contains more than 3000 times as much circuitry, illustrating the tremendous increase in density that has occurred.

This tendency toward increased complexity is dictated by the economics of integrated circuit manufacturing. Because of the nature of this manufacturing process, all circuits on a slice are fabricated together. Consequently, the more circuitry accommodated on a slice, the cheaper the circuitry becomes. Because testing and packaging costs depend on the number of chips, it is desirable, in order to keep costs down, to crowd more circuitry onto a given chip rather than to increase the number of chips on a wafer.

***Linear circuits.*** Integrated circuits based on amplifiers are called linear because amplifiers usually exhibit a linearly proportional response to input signal variations. However, the category includes memory sense amplifiers, combinations of analog and digital processing functions, and other circuits with nonlinear characteristics. Some digital and analog combinations include analog-to-digital converters, timing controls, and modems (data communications modulator-demodulator units). *SEE ANALOG-TO-DIGITAL CONVERTER; DATA COMMUNICATIONS.*

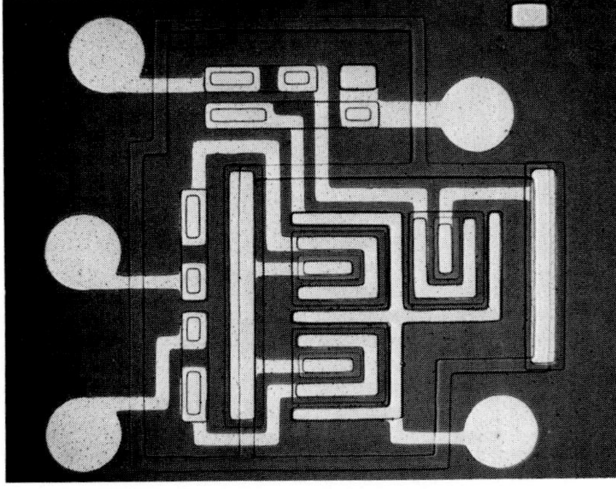

**Fig. 3. Photomicrograph of early bipolar logic gate circuit. (*Fairchild Semiconductor*)**

A long-standing drawback in these circuits was the lack of inductors for tuning and filtering. That was overcome by the use of resistor-capacitor networks and additional circuitry. For low-frequency circuits the resistor in these networks is being replaced by the switched capacitor. At the higher frequencies, an oscillator-based circuit called the phase-locked loop provides a general-purpose replacement for inductors in applications such as radio transmission demodulation. *SEE PHASE-LOCKED LOOPS; SWITCHED CAPACITOR.*

At first, the development of linear circuits was slow because of the difficulty of integrating passive components and also because of undesirable interactions between the semiconductor substrate and the operating components. Thus, much greater ingenuity was required to design and use the early linear circuits.

In addition, manufacturing economics favors digital circuits. A computer can be built by repetitious use of simple inverters and gates, while analog signal processing requires a variety of specialized linear circuits.

***Semiconductor devices.*** In the continuing effort to increase the complexity and speed of digital circuits, and the performance characteristics and versatility of linear circuits, a significant role has been played by the discovery and development of new types of active and passive semiconductor devices which are suitable for use in integrated circuits. Among these devices is the *pnp* transistor which, when used in conjunction with the standard *npn* transistors described above, lends added flexibility to the design of integrated circuits.

Two types of *pnp* transistor structures, both compatible with standard integrated circuit technology, are shown in **Fig. 5**. Figure 5*a* shows the so-called lateral *pnp*, which is a *pnp* transistor formed between two closely spaced *p*-type diffuse regions. Since these can be formed using the same diffusion step, described below, by which the base of the *npn* transistor and the resistor are formed, this structure can be fabricated simultaneously with the rest of the circuit. The same is true of the substrate *pnp* shown n Fig. 5*b*, except here the *p*-type substrate is employed as the collector.

Other possibilities involve means of producing integrated circuits with resistors of high resistance values. In the standard resistor process, described below, high resistances require long resistors, which in turn require large chips to accommodate them. An alternate approach is to use the *n* region between the diffused *p* region and the substrate as the resistor. This semiconductor region has a significantly higher resistance than that formed by the *p*-type diffusion. However, due to the reverse bias between the *n* region and the two *p* regions enclosing it from top and bottom, such resistors have highly nonlinear current-voltage characteristics. An alternate scheme involves the use of a very thin film of high-resistivity metal deposited by evaporation or sputtering on top of the insulating silicon dioxide layer. Such films can display resistiv-

**Fig. 4. Photomicrograph of 16-bit bipolar microprocessor. (*Fairchild Semiconductor*)**

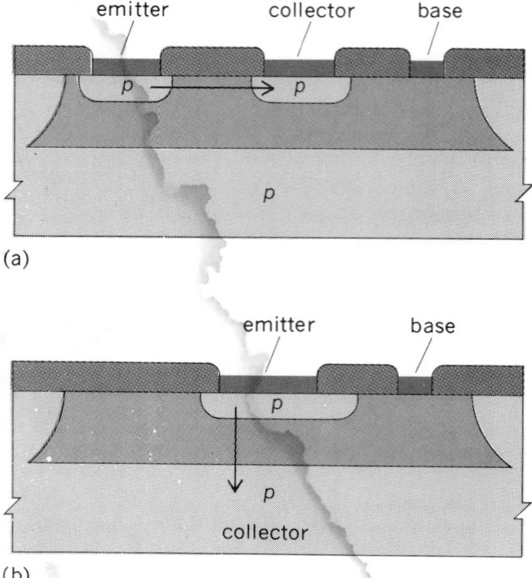


**Fig. 5. Types of *pnp* transistor structures. (*a*) Lateral *pnp* transistor. (*b*) Substrate *pnp* transistor. Arrows indicate direction of useful transistor action.**

ities as much as a hundred times higher than that of the diffused *p* region, and since their deposition is performed after the entire semiconductor structure is complete, they can be used in conjunction with any type of integrated circuit.

Several alternatives to *pn*-junction isolation are in use. These involve etching around the transistor regions, so that oxide or air isolates the components. Called dielectric isolation, the technique was initially used in military circuits to stop radiation-induced currents from flowing through and destroying the circuits. It is now used commercially to reduce circuit capacitance, thus speeding up operation, and to reduce the silicon area required for each transistor. It is not yet widely used, however, because it complicates the basic process.

**MOS integrated circuits.** The other major class of integrated circuits is called MOS because its principal device is a metal oxide semiconductor field-effect transistor (MOSFET). It is more suitable for very large-scale integration (VLSI) than bipolar circuits because MOS transistors are self-isolating and can have an average size of less than a millionth of a square inch ($5 \times 10^{-5}$ mm$^2$). This has made it practical to use over 1,000,000 transistors per circuit. Because of this high density capability, MOS transistors are used for high density random-access memories (RAMs; **Fig. 6**), read-only memories (ROMs), and microprocessors. *See* Computer storage technology; Microprocessor; Semiconductor memories.

Several major types of MOS device fabrication technologies have been developed since the mid-1960s. They are: (1) metal-gate *p*-channel MOS (PMOS), which uses aluminum for electrodes and interconnections; (2) silicon-gate *p*-channel MOS, employing polycrystalline silicon for gate electrodes and the first interconnection layer; (3) *n*-channel MOS (NMOS), which is usually silicon gate; and (4) complementary MOS (CMOS), which employs both *p*-channel and *n*-channel devices. In 1984 the silicon gate NMOS and CMOS were the dominant technologies, with CMOS using silicon gates becoming the most attractive for new designs.

Both conceptually and structurally the MOS transistor is a much simpler device than the bipolar transistor. In fact, its principle of operation has been known since the late 1930s, and the research effort that led to the discovery of the bipolar transistor was originally aimed at developing the MOS transistor. What kept this simple device from commercial utilization until 1964 is the fact that it depends on the properties of the semiconductor surface for its operation, while the bipolar transistor depends principally on the bulk properties of the semiconductor crystal. Hence MOS transistors became practical only when understanding and control of the properties of the oxidized silicon surface had been perfected to a very great degree.

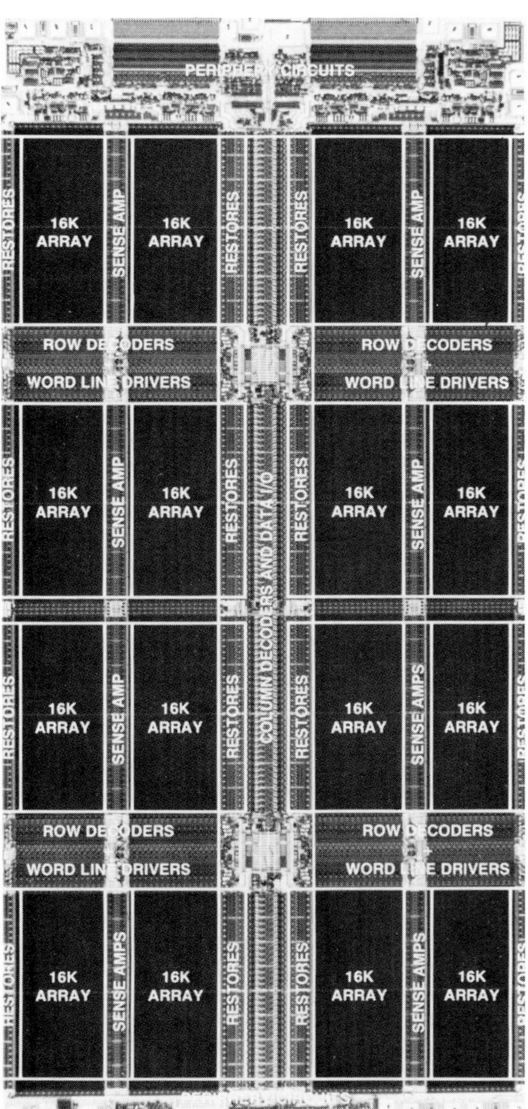


**Fig. 6.** **Photomicrograph of MOS LSI circuit used as 262,144-bit random-access memory (RAM).** (*Intel Corp.*)

***CMOS.*** A simple CMOS inverter circuit is shown in **Fig. 7** and a circuit schematic in **Fig. 8**. The gates of the *n*-channel and *p*-channel transistors are connected together as are the drains. The common gate connection is the input node while the common drain connection is the output node. A capacitor is added to the output node to model the loading expected from the subsequent stages on typical circuits.

When the input node is in the "low state", at 0 V, the *n*-channel gate to source voltage is 0 V while the *p*-channel gate to source voltage is −5 V. The *n*-channel transistor requires a positive gate-to-source voltage, which is greater than the transistor threshold voltage (typically 0.5–1 V), before it will start conducting current between the drain and source. Thus, with a 0-V gate-to-source voltage it will be off and no current will flow through the drain and source regions. The *p*-channel transistor, however, requires a negative voltage between the gate and source which is less than its threshold voltage (typically −0.5 to −1.5 V). The −5-V gate-to-source potential is clearly less than the threshold voltage, and the *p*-channel will be turned on, conducting current from the source to the drain, and thereby charging up the loading capacitor. Once the capacitor is charged to the "high state" at 5 V, the transistor will no longer conduct because there will no longer be a potential difference between the source and drain regions.

When the input is now put to the "high state" at 5 V, just the opposite occurs. The *n*-channel transistor will be turned on while the *p*-channel will be off. This will allow the load capacitor to discharge through the *n*-channel transistor resulting in the output voltage dropping from a "high state" at 5 V to a "low state" at 0 V. Again, once there is no potential difference between the drain and source (capacitor discharged to 0 V), the current flow will stop, and the circuit will be stable.

This simple circuit illustrates a very important feature of CMOS circuits. Once the loading capacitor has been either charged to 5 V or discharged back to 0 V, there is no current flow, and the standby power is very low. This is the reason for the high popularity of CMOS for battery-based systems. None of the other MOS technologies offers this feature without complex circuit techniques, and even then will typically not match the low standby power of CMOS. The bipolar circuits discussed above require even more power than these other MOS technologies. The price for CMOS's lower power are the additional fabrication steps required (10–20% more) when compared to NMOS.

***Sampled-data devices.*** In addition to the digital logic applications discussed above with the simple inverter circuit, MOS devices also offer unique features for some analog circuit applications. These include signal-processing applications that are based on sampled-data techniques. Two classes of devices, namely, charge-coupled devices (CCD) and switched-capacitor networks, play the major role in these applications.

In CCDs the stored charge at the semiconductor surface can also be made to propagate along the surface via potential wells created by a series of these MOS structures. The storage cell in the RAM circuit of Fig. 6 can be viewed as using a single CCD element for each bit. *See Charge-coupled devices*.

The capacitance $C$ from the MOS structure can be integrated with MOS transistors, which are used as switches, to form a switched-capacitor circuit (**Fig. 9**). One of the switches $\phi_1$ is closed when the other switch $\phi_2$ is open, and vice versa. The circuit is equivalent to a resistor with a value of $R = T/C$, where $T$ is the sampling interval. The advantage of the technique is the high quality and the high value of resistors that can be put on an integrated circuit.

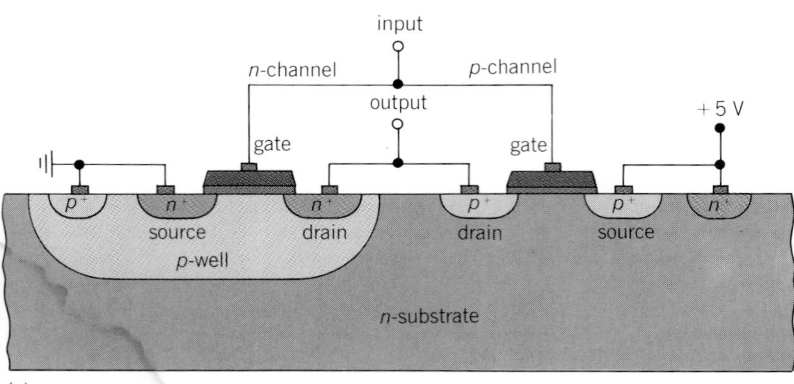


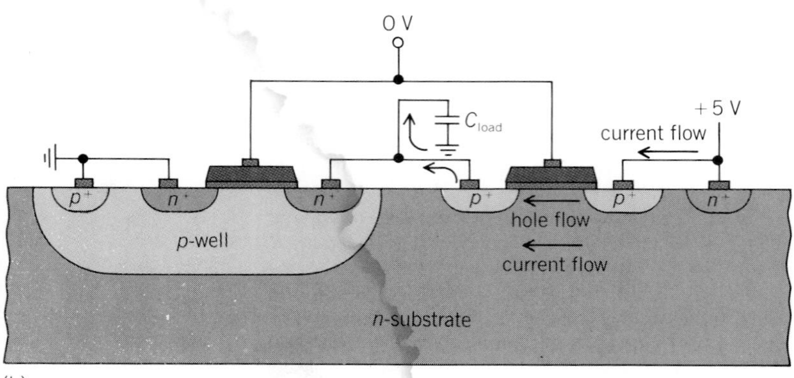


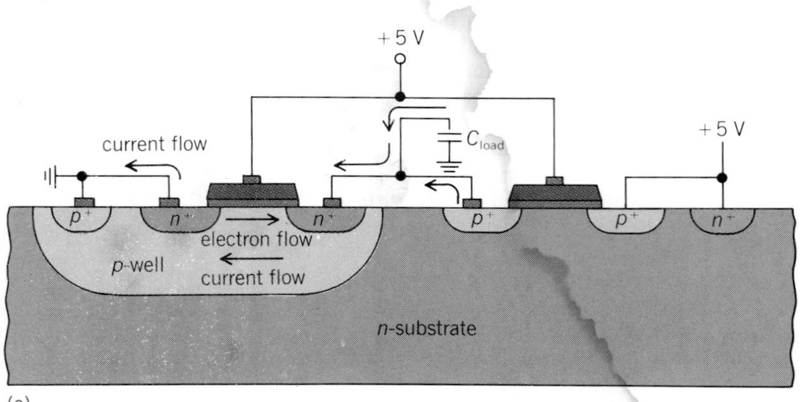


**Fig. 7. Simple CMOS inverter circuit. (*a*) Schematic cross section. (*b*) Current flow when input is "low" at 0 V. (c) Current flow when input is "high" at 5 V.**

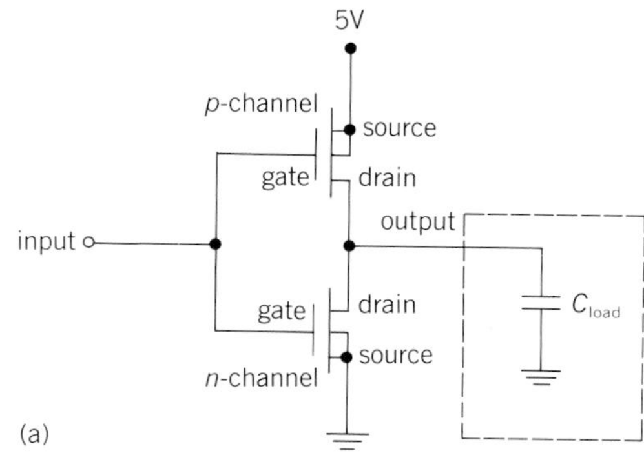


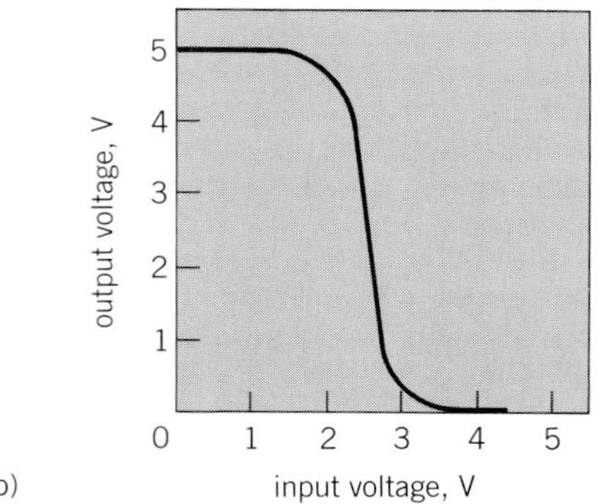


**Fig. 8. Characteristics of the CMOS inverter circuit shown in Fig. 7. (*a*) Circuit diagram. (*b*) Transfer characteristics.**

These resistors combined with capacitors and operational amplifers (all made with MOS technology) can be used to make active filters. Since many stages of these filters can be integrated into one chip, precise filters are now possible with integrated circuit technology. These filters are having a tremendous impact on low-frequency filters (frequencies less than 100 kHz) and will be used extensively in telecommunication equipment. *See Electric filter*.

## Integrated Optical Devices

Semiconductors have long been used as light sensors. Advances in large-scale integration (LSI) have enabled large arrays of sensors, such as solid-state television cameras, to be made commercially. MOS LSI is now preferred for sensor arrays because it permits large amounts of control logic to be fabricated in the same circuit as the sensors. *See Television camera; Television camera tube*.

In MOS optical arrays, the sensors are MOS devices or CCD elements. The sensor portion of the circuit views the scene through a transparent window. Light variations in the scene viewed cause variations in charge, producing signals transferable in shift-register fashion to processing stages such as amplifiers. These arrays have numerous applications, ranging from measuring and sorting objects on production lines to optical character readers, which automatically translate written information into digital computer input codes. *See* CHARACTER RECOGNITION; OPTICAL DETECTORS.

### Microcomputers

The LSI development having the most profound effect on electronic equipment economics and design in general is the microcomputer. The complexity and capability of these circuits, introduced in 1971, have expanded greatly. Initially these integrated circuits were applied to dedicated functions with the tailoring of that function being done with the ROM circuits on the chip. However, there are now many different types of microprocessor circuits ranging from the simple microcontroller types of functions to very complex computers on a chip such as the 16-bit microprocessor shown in **Fig. 10**.

This rapid development has been a result of both the technology which allows more circuits to be placed on a chip and circuit innovation. The technology has increased the number of transistors on a chip from a few thousand in 1971 to over 400,000 in 1984. The circuit innovations include both digital techniques and the combination of analog and digital processing functions on the same chip. Both analog-to-digital and digital-to-analog data conversion circuits have been combined with the digital processor into one integrated circuit.

As the technology enables the development of more complex circuits, the problem becomes not one of how to build these complex circuits but of what to build. The application of these circuits is rapidly becoming limited by the effort in programming them, rather than by their inherent capability. The emphasis in the future will be to apply circuit design features to reduce the rapidly increasing complexity of programming.

Although these LSI circuits are being used in calculators, automobiles, instruments, appliance controls and many other applications, realization of their potential is just beginning. As the power of the computer is captured in the relatively inexpensive integrated circuit, the role of integrated circuits will continue to expand rapidly.

*Ron Burghard; Youssef El-Mansy; Neil Berglund*

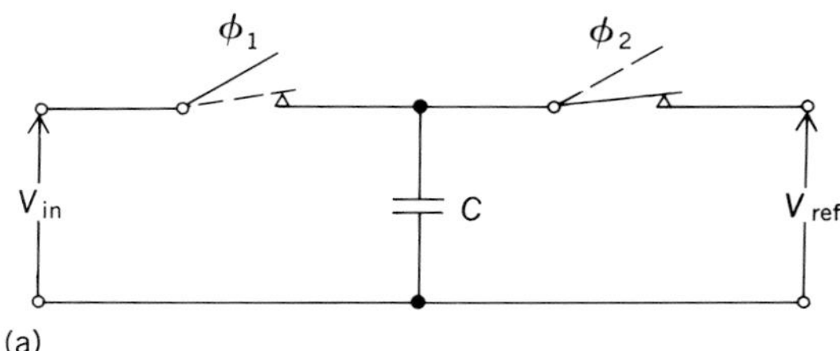


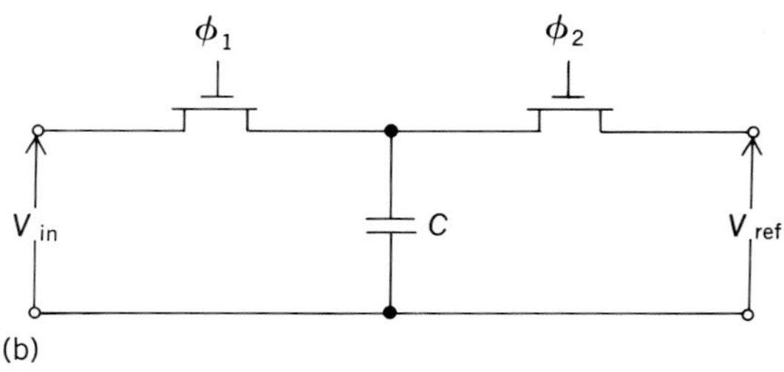


**Fig. 9. Switched-capacitor circuit. (*a*) Schematic of an *RC* section. (*b*) Implementation of the switches with MOS transistors with clocks applied to their gates.**

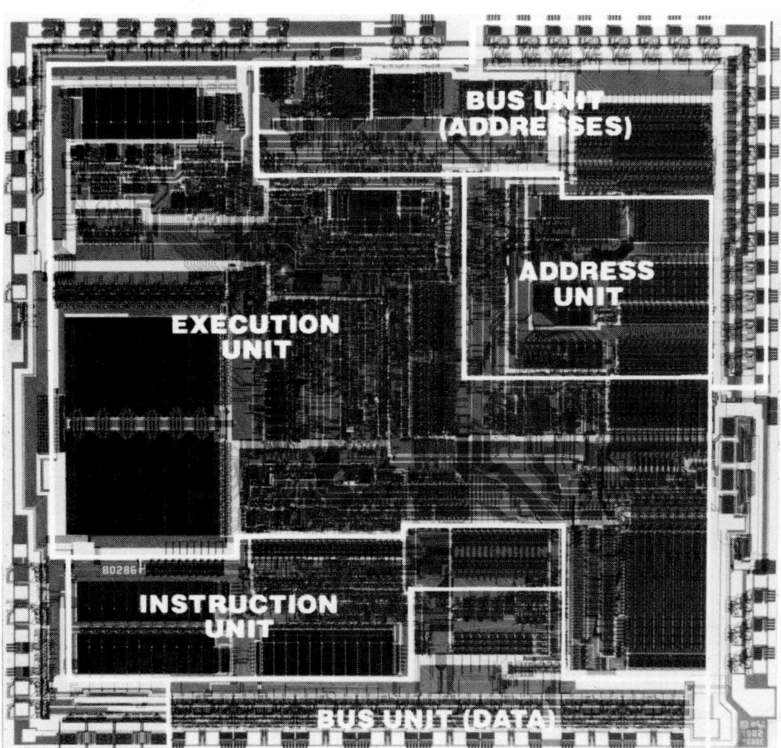


**Fig. 10. Photomicrograph of 16-bit MOS microprocessor. (*Intel Corp.*)**

### Fabrication

Integrated-circuit fabrication begins with a thin, polished slice of high-purity, single-crystal semiconductor (usually silicon) and employs a combination of physical and chemical processes to create the integrated-circuit structures described above. Junctions are formed in the silicon slice by the processes of thermal diffusion or high-energy ion implantation. Electrical isolation between devices on the integrated circuit is achieved with insulating layers grown by thermal oxidation or deposited by chemical deposition. Conductor layers to provide the necessary electrical connections on the integrated circuit are obtained by a variety of deposition techniques. Precision lithographic processes are used throughout the fabrication sequence to define the geometric features required.

**Requirements.** The integrated-circuit fabrication process is quite sensitive to both particulate and impurity contamination. Airborne particulates must be minimized during the fabrication sequence, since even small (1-micrometer) particles on the wafer surface can cause defects. A particulate-free fabrication ambient is normally achieved by the use of vertical laminar-flow clean rooms or benches (**Fig. 11**). Lint-free garments are worn to minimize operator-borne particulates. To minimize impurity contamination effects, the chemicals, solvents, and metals which are used must be of the highest possible purity (electronic

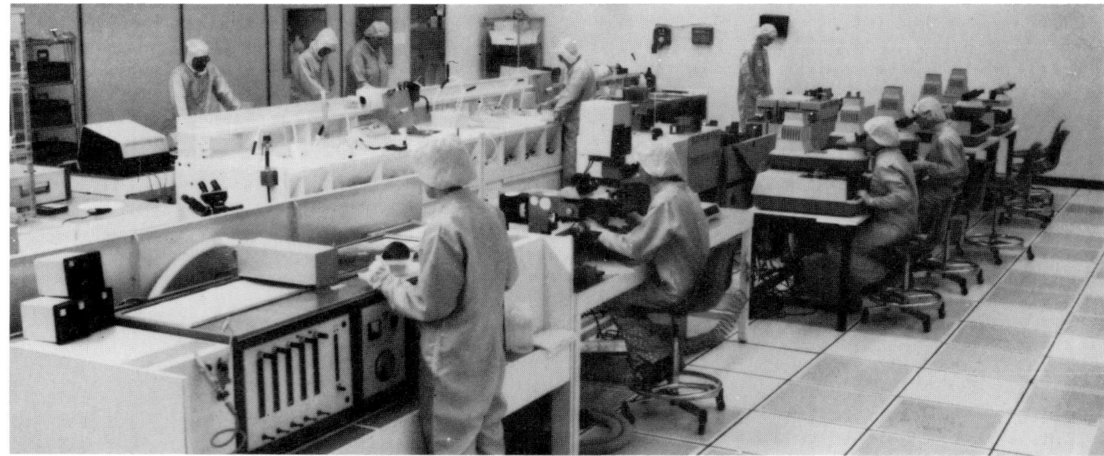

Fig. 11. Vertical laminar-flow clean room for integrated-circuit fabrication.

grade). Yellow light is necessary in the clean room because of the ultraviolet-sensitive photolithographic processes employed.

The precision and cleanliness requirements of integrated-circuit processing necessitate high discipline throughout the process sequence. This is achieved by extensive operator training, in-process tests and inspection with continual feedback, and a high degree of equipment calibration and control. The physical environment and operator attitude in an integrated-circuit fabrication facility are important factors for successful operation.

**Processes.** The basic relationship between the major processes in integrated-circuit fabrication is shown schematically in **Fig. 12**. Film formation is normally followed by impurity doping or lithography. Lithography is generally followed by etching, which in turn is followed by impurity doping or film formation. Impurity doping is normally followed by film formation or lithography. A complete integrated-circuit process sequence requires many cycles through the flow diagram in Fig. 12. For example, metal gate CMOS requires seven cycles through lithography. The complete flow time for a CMOS process is approximately 2 to 6 weeks, depending on process complexity.

***Film formation.*** Film formation employs thermal oxidation to produce silicon dioxide ($SiO_2$) films, chemical vapor deposition to produce silicon, silicon dioxide, or silicon nitride ($Si_3N_4$) films, or vacuum evaporation/sputtering to produce metal films.

The atoms on the surface of a silicon single crystal from which integrated circuits are manufactured are chemically bound only in the direction of the bulk of the crystal, and not in the other or free direction. The resultant so-called silicon dangling bonds are very reactive and may bond to oxygen or nitrogen or other impurities from the atmosphere, so that a large variety of reactions can occur. Each of these reactions will result in different electrical properties for the silicon surface, a serious problem in designing a manufacturing process in which extremely large numbers of identically operating and reliable devices are produced on silicon chips. The solution to this dilemma is to tie up the dangling bonds with a chemically stable and electrically insulating film that will not interfere with the electrical characteristics of the silicon surface. A material with these properties that can be easily prepared in thin-film form on silicon is silicon dioxide.

The silicon dioxide film is made by the reaction of a carefully cleaned and polished single-crystal silicon surface with an oxidant gas, usually oxygen or steam, at temperatures ranging from 1500 to 2200°F (800 to 1200°C) in a quartz-walled furnace tube (**Fig. 13*a***). The reaction occurs rapidly and exothermically on the silicon surface. As the oxide film grows, the rate of oxidation decreases, because the oxidant must transport to the silicon surface through the growing film. For large film thicknesses and at high oxidation temperatures, this transport controls the film growth kinetics, while for thin films the surface reaction is dominant.

Chemical vapor deposition (CVD) is a gas-phase process where a film deposit is obtained by combining the appropriate gases in a reactant chamber at elevated temperatures. A typical CVD reaction (silox process) is given below. Figure 13*b* shows a cold-

$$SiH_4 + O_2 \xrightarrow[\text{(750–930°F)}]{\text{(400–500°C)}} \underset{\text{(Deposits as film)}}{SiO_2\downarrow} + 2H_2\uparrow$$

walled, atmospheric-pressure CVD system where the silicon slice is heated by rf energy. Figure 13*c* shows a low-pressure CVD system where the slices and process gases are heated in a partially evacuated furnace tube. This low-pressure process produces very uniform film thicknesses.

Evaporation or sputtering of metal coatings is performed in a vacuum, with metal transport being produced either by heat (evaporation) or bombarding ions (sputtering). The vacuum evaporator in Fig. 13*d* uses fixturing with planetary motion during evaporation. This achieves uniform metal thickness over surface topology on the silicon slice. SEE SPUTTERING.

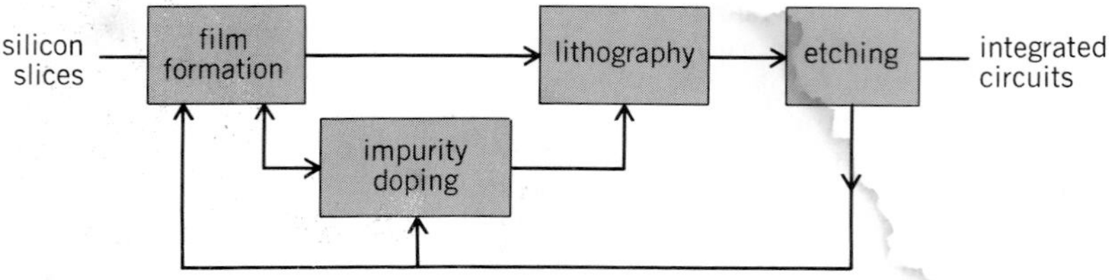


Fig. 12. Integrated-circuit fabrication sequence form. Fabrication normally proceeds in the direction of the arrows.

***Impurity doping.*** The unique electronic properties of semiconductors are produced by substituting selected impurities at silicon lattice positions in the silicon crystal, a process called doping. The distortions in the chemical bonding due to the presence of impurities at lattice positions cause some of the bonding electrons in the crystal to have a higher energy than in a perfect crystal lattice and therefore be available for electronic conduction. Similarly, holes, which are the absence of bonding electrons, are produced by other kinds of impurities. Both electrons and holes can carry electric current. In order to construct complex integrated circuits, the impurities must be placed in adjacent regions in the semiconductor surface. The two predominant methods of doping semiconductor surfaces are thermal diffusion in high-temperature furnaces (Fig. 13*a*) and ion implantation.

In the diffusional doping process, the regions of the silicon surface to be doped are exposed to a concentration of the dopant while maintaining a high temperature. Boron and phosphorus are dopants which can be introduced by thermal diffusion at temperatures from 1500 to 2200°F (800 to 1200°C). At these temperatures the silicon lattice contains a significant number of vacant lattice sites, that is, crystal lattice sites with missing silicon atoms. The impurity atoms can migrate from vacant site to vacant site. The driving force for this diffusion process is the concentration gradient of impurity atoms. Near the silicon surface there exists a large concentration of dopant, while in the silicon only a small number of impurities exist. There is a tendency for these concentrations to be equalized, thereby eliminating the gradient. When the impurity has diffused to the proper depth and is in the appropriate concentration in the silicon, the process is stopped. Other regions that are not to receive dopant are masked by using impenetrable films known as diffusion masks.

**Fig. 13. Modern integrated-circuit fabrication equipment. (*a*) Diffusion furnace. (*b*) Atmospheric-pressure chemical vapor deposition (CVD). (*c*) Low-pressure CVD. (*d*) Vacuum evaporator. (*e*) Ion implanter. (*f*) Contact mask aligner. (*g*) Direct step-on-water machine. (*h*) Plasma etcher.**

As device requirements become more stringent, very sharp diffusion profiles are needed so that the device size can be reduced. The solid-state diffusion process does not afford sufficient control for the most advanced device processes. For this purpose, the use of the direct implantation of impurity ions (electrically charged atoms) into the silicon lattice has been developed.

Ion implantation is also used when greater precision of dopant concentration is required or when a reduced temperature cycle is advantageous. Ion implantation makes use of intense, uniform beams of high-energy ions (typically 10–500 keV) of the desired dopant. These beams are formed in specialized accelerators such as Van de Graaff generators under high vacuum conditions (Fig. 13*e*). The beams can be focused, accelerated, and purified by using mass spectrometry techniques such as electrostatic plates and magnetic fields. The desired beam is them made to impinge on the silicon substrate which has appropriate masking so that the dopant beam impinges on the proper area of the silicon surface. The energy is sufficient for the ions in the beam to penetrate the silicon surface, leaving a distribution of dopant. The position of the peak of the distribution can be altered by altering the beam energy. The amount of dopant can be altered by the beam current and time of exposure. Damage is caused by the collisions of the ions in the beam with the atoms in the silicon lattice, but much of the damage can be removed by thermal annealing at temperatures of about 1500°F (800°C). Remarkably sharp dopant profiles of precise concentration can be achieved by using this technique. SEE ION IMPLANTATION.

***Lithography.*** Lithography is necessary to define the small geometries required in integrated circuits. In lithography the silicon slice is coated uniformly with a thin film of photosensitive material called resist. If the lithography is to be performed optically, the integrated-circuit pattern to be transferred to the resist is first created on a glass plate or "mask." This pattern can then be transferred to the resist by a number of optical techniques. These techniques range from direct contact printing using a collimated source of ultra-violet light (Fig. 13*f*), to optical projection of a single integrated-circuit pattern with associated reduction (for example, 10:1, 1:1) and a precise *x-y* motion of the silicon slice (direct step-on-wafer; Fig. 13*g*). Electron-beam direct patterning can be performed, without a mask, by using a controllable electron beam and an electron-sensitive resist. Lithography has also been achieved with x-rays, by their projection through a special mask in close proximity to the slice. Direct step-on-wafer photolithography, the most advanced of the optical lithographic techniques, is capable of defining 1 μm ($4 \times 10^{-5}$ in.) geometries. Electron-beam and x-ray lithography have demonstrated the capability to define features substantially smaller than 1 μm.

***Etching.*** Etching is necessary to transfer the resist pattern achieved through lithography to the underlying surface. Traditionally, integrated-circuit fabrication has employed wet chemical processes to etch lines and features. These techniques utilize the chemical reactivity with an etchant of the material to be etched. The difference between the etch rate of the masking material and that of the substrate is related to this chemistry. The chemical etching of crystalline materials can be either isotropic or anisotropic. In isotropic etching the etchant attacks the crystal equally in all directions without regard to the different densities of atoms and structural features in the different directions in a crystal. Amorphous materials etch isotropically. Anisotropic etching takes advantage of different reactivities of the different crystal planes due to bonding and density differences. Usually anisotropic etches are milder etches that take full advantage of chemical differences. Anisotropic etching enables the construction of intricate patterns in silicon surfaces and therefore permits the practice of constructing devices in etched regions or on unetched mesa areas.

As with diffusion, wet chemical etching is limited in terms of size of the lines or features to be formed (no less than 3–4 μm or $1.2–1.6 \times 10^{-4}$ in.) and, more important, the aspect ratio of the features, that is, their height-to-width ratios. Dense packing and small device size require high-aspect-ratio etching. Dry plasma etching, reactive ion etching, and ion milling are advanced techniques being developed to overcome the limits of chemical etching. In plasma etching (Fig. 13*h*), the most advanced of these techniques, the vertical etch rate can be adjusted to be much greater than the lateral etch rate. This enables the etching of fine lines and features without loss of definition, even in films approaching 1 μm in thickness.

For plasma etching, a plasma is formed above a masked surface to be etched by adding large amounts of energy to a gas at low pressures. This is commonly accomplished by electrical discharges in gases at about $10^{-3}$ atm ($10^{-2}$ Pa). A plasma contains ions, free radicals, and neutral species, all with high kinetic energies. By adjusting the electrical potential of the substrate to be etched, the charged species in the plasma can be directed to impinge on the substrate and thereby impact the nonmasked regions. The force of the high-energy impact can knock out substrate atoms. This plasma etching process can be made more effective with the use of gases in the plasma that are reactive with the material to be etched. In particular, the reactants should form volatile products that can be carried away by the vacuum system. Such gases usually contain halogens (fluorine, chlorine, and bromine). Reactive ion etching combines the energetic etching effects of the plasma with the reactivity of the gases and the formation of energetic reactive species in the plasma.

*Bob L. Gregory; Eugene A. Irene*

**Bipolar process flow.** The principal steps involved in the fabrication of the simple bipolar inverter circuit of Fig. 1 are shown schematically in **Fig. 14**. An inverter requires only a transistor and resistor, shown in cross section. Complete digital integrated circuits generally contain tens to hundreds of inverters and gates interconnected as counters, arithmetic units, and other building blocks. As indicated by Fig. 14*g*, hundreds of such circuits may be fabricated on a single slice of silicon crystal. This feature of planar technology—simultaneous production of many circuits—is responsible for the economic advantages and wide use of integrated circuits.

The starting material is a slice of single-crystal silicon, more or less circular, up to 6 in. (150 mm) in diameter, and a fraction of an inch (a few millimeters) thick. Typically, this material is doped with *p*-type impurities (Fig. 14*a*). A film of semiconductor, less than 0.001 in. (25 μm) thick, is then grown upon this substrate in a vapor-phase reaction of a silicon-con-

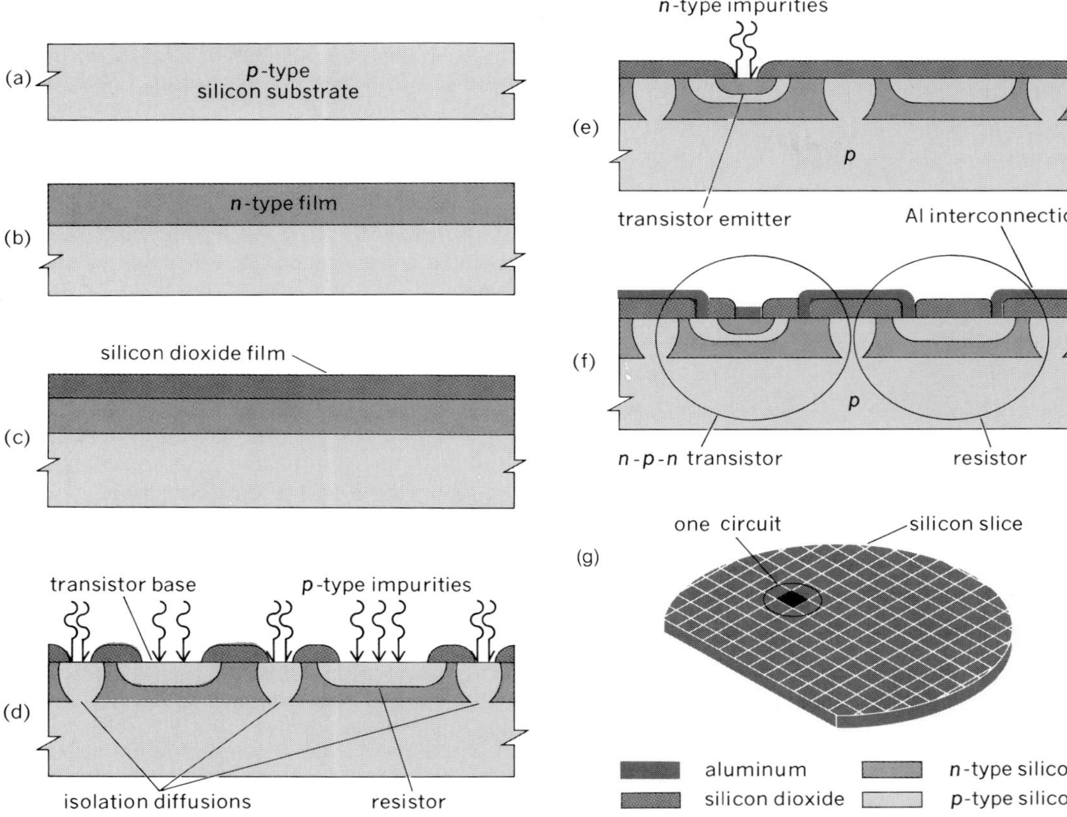


**Fig. 14. Steps in fabrication of bipolar inverter circuit. (*a*) Initial *p*-type substrate. (*b*) Growth of *n*-type film. (*c*) Growth of oxide film. (*d*) Opening of windows in oxide layer and formation of isolation regions, transistor base, and resistor. (*e*) Regrowth and formation of windows in oxide layer, and formation of transistor emitter. (*f*) Opening of contacts and deposit of metal. (*g*) Numerous circuits incorporated on a silicon slice.**

taining compound. The conditions of this reaction are such that the film maintains the single-crystal nature of the substrate. Such films are called epitaxial (Greek for ''arranged upon''). By incorporating *n*-type impurities into the gas from which the film is grown, the resulting epitaxial film is made *n*-type (Fig. 14*b*).

Next, the silicon slice is placed into an oxygen atmosphere at high temperatures ( 2200°F or 1200°C). The silicon and oxygen react, forming a cohesive silicon dioxide film upon the surface of the slice that is relatively impervious to the electrically active impurities. (Fig. 14*c*).

To form the particular semiconductor regions required in the fabrication of electronic devices, however, *p*- and *n*-type impurities must be introduced into certain regions of the semiconductor. In the planar technology, this is done by opening windows in the protective oxide layer by photoengraving techniques, and then exposing the slice to a gas containing the appropriate doping impurity. In the case of an integrated circuit, the isolation regions—*p*-type regions which, together with the *p*-type substrate, surround the separate pockets of the *n*-type film—are formed first by the diffusion of a *p*-type impurity. This is followed by a shorter exposure to *p*-type impurities during which the base region of the transistors and the resistors are formed (Fig. 14*d*). *See Junction transistor*.

Next, the slice is again covered with oxide, smaller windows are cut over the transistor base regions, and *n*-type impurities are permitted to diffuse in these regions to form the emitters of the transistors (Fig. 14*e*). As the lateral and vertical dimensions of these devices become smaller, control of the number and position of these impurities becomes more important. This has resulted in the increased use of ion implantation to introduce these impurities into the silicon.

Openings are cut in the oxide layer at all places where contact to the silicon is desired. Then a metal, aluminum for example, is deposited over the entire slice by vacuum evaporation or sputtering, and finally the undesired aluminum is removed by photoengraving, leaving behind aluminum stripes which interconnect the transistor and the resistor (Fig. 14*f*).

The preparation of the thousands of inverter circuits on the silicon slice is now complete. The slice is cut apart, much as a pane of glass is cut, and the individual circuits are tested and packaged.

Both the transistor and the resistor are formed within a separate pocket of *n*-type semiconductor surrounded on all sides by *p*-type regions. When the inverter circuit is operated, a reverse bias develops between the *n*-type pocket and its surroundings. The depletion region separating the *n*- and *p*-type regions has a very high resistance; consequently, the individual transistors and resistors are electrically isolated from each other, even though both of them have been formed within the same semiconductor crystal.

**CMOS process flow.** The principal steps in fabricating the simple CMOS inverter circuit of Fig. 7 are illustrated in **Fig. 15**. Again, as in the bipolar case, the process starts with the highly polished single slice of silicon crystal. For CMOS the first step is typically to put in the *p*-well regions for the *n*-channel devices, if the original silicon wafer is *n*-type (Fig. 15*a*). It is also possible to start with a *p*-type wafer in which *n*-well regions are introduced for the *p*-channel transistors. This discussion will be confined to the *p*-well case.

After the wells have been introduced, thick oxide

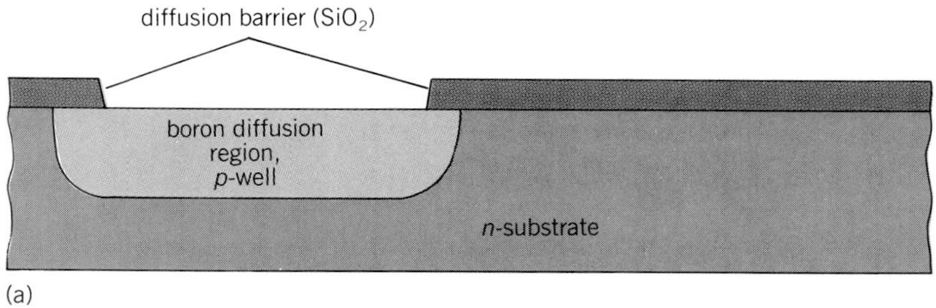


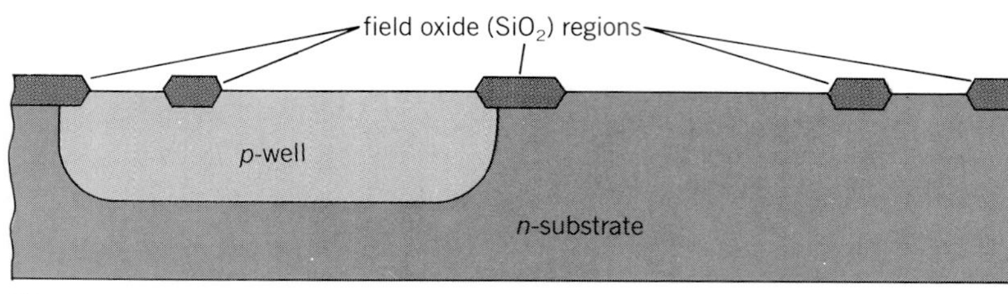


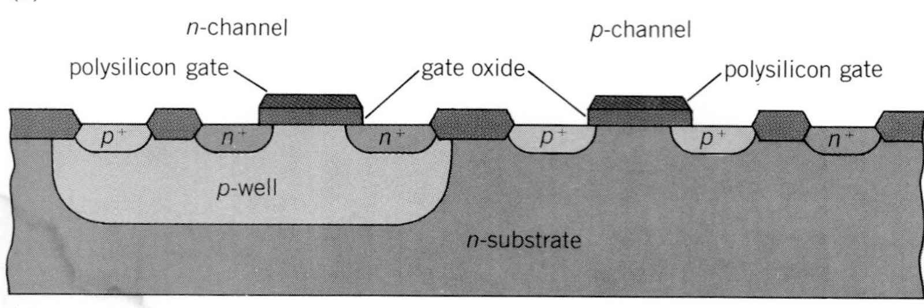


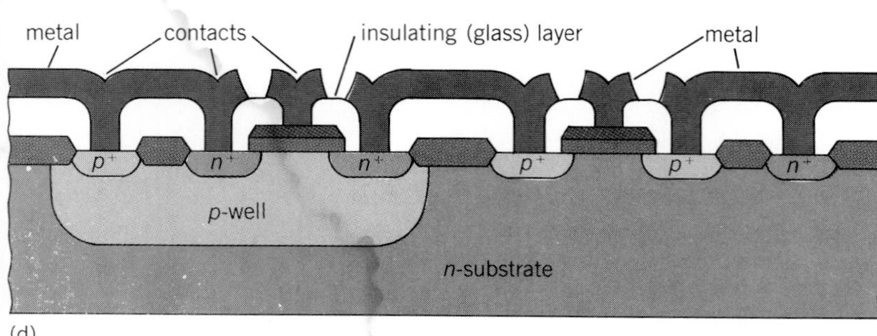


**Fig. 15.** Steps in fabrication of CMOS inverter circuit. (*a*) Introduction of *p* well. (*b*) Growth of field oxides. (*c*) Addition of gate oxides, polysilicon gates, and junctions. (*d*) Deposit of insulating layer, opening of contacts, and deposit of metal.

layers (0.5–1 μm or 2–4 × $10^{-5}$ in. thick) are grown in specific regions to isolate the transistor junctions from each other (Fig. 15*b*). Next the transistor gate oxides (typically 0.02–0.1 μm or 1–4 × $10^{-6}$ in. thick) are grown. Prior to the silicon gate deposition, implants may be used to control the threshold voltages of the transistors. Polysilicon is then deposited for the gate regions and doped with impurities to reduce the resistance. The gate regions are then defined by using photoresist and lithography, and the polysilicon and thin gate oxide is removed where it is not wanted. The transistors are now ready for the introduction of impurities for the source and drain junctions. With CMOS, separate masking steps are required to introduce the phosphorus or arsenic for the *n*-channel source and drain junctions and the boron for the *p*-channel source and drain junctions (Fig. 15*c*).

An insulating layer (typically a glass) to isolate the polysilicon gate conductor from the aluminum metallization is now deposited. Openings in the glass layer are made for the metal to make contact to the polysilicon lines and junctions. The metal is then deposited and the regions to be removed are etched away after using photoresist and lithography techniques (Fig. 15*d*). Finally a scratch protection passivation layer is deposited over the metal with openings made at the bond pad areas for the bond wire connections.

As in the bipolar case, the isolation of the transistors is accomplished by reverse-biased junctions. The substrate is always at the highest chip voltage while the *p*-well is always at the lowest chip voltage.

**Changes in technology.** Integrated-circuit fabrication technology changes rapidly due to the steadily decreasing feature size of the individual circuit elements, the improvements in yields allowing large chip sizes and the advances in equipment required for the

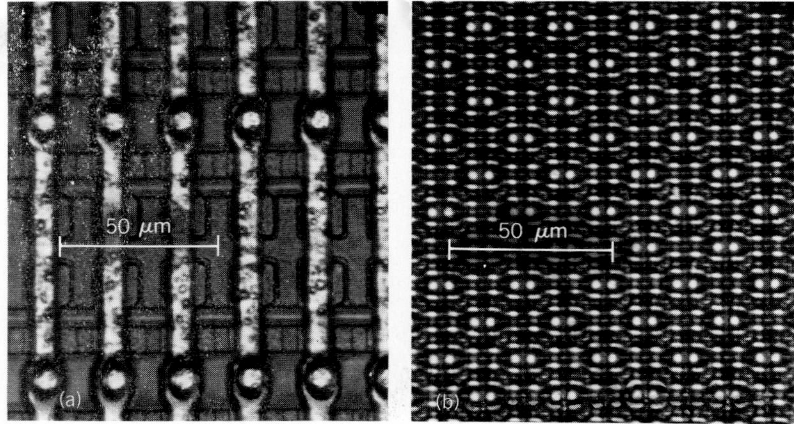


**Fig. 16.** Increased density from advanced technology as seen in cell areas of (*a*) 4096-bit random-access memory (1974) and (*b*) 262,144-bit random-access memory (1984). (*Intel Corp.*)

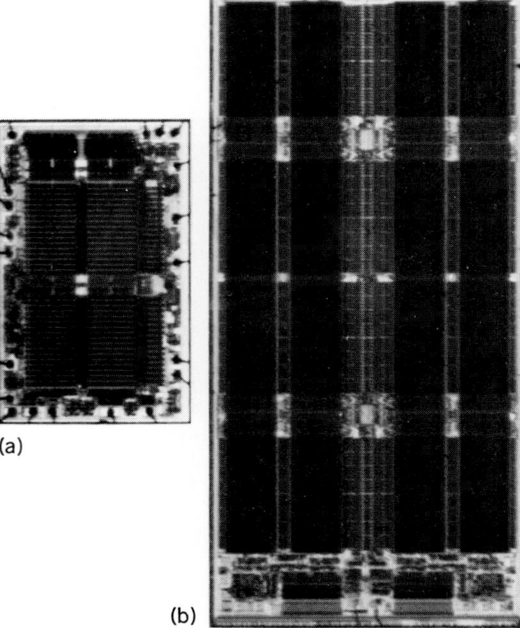


**Fig. 17.** Increase in die (chip) size from (*a*) 4096-bit random-access memory (1974) to (*b*) 262,144-bit random-access memory (1984). (*Intel Corp.*)

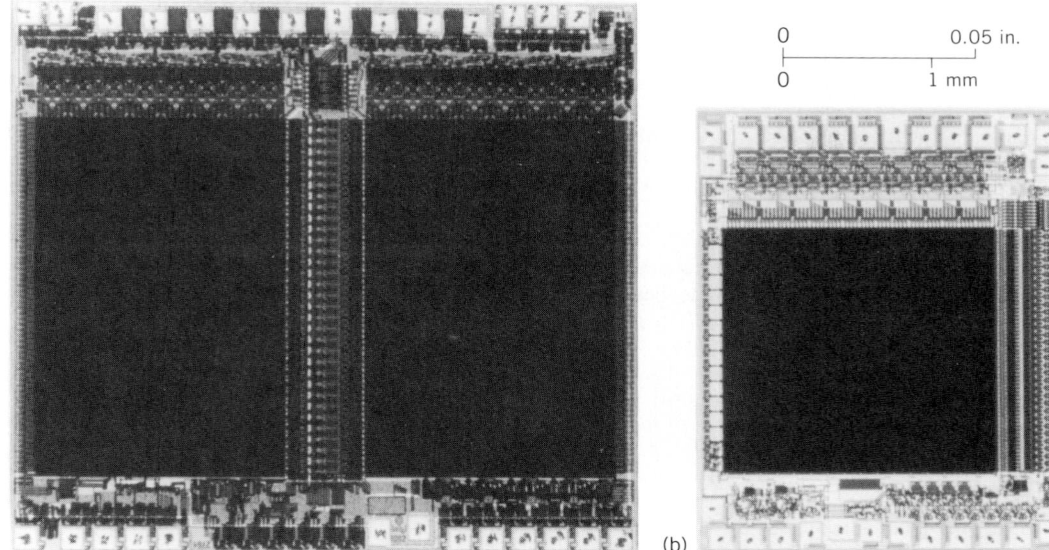


Fig. 18. Photographs of 65,536-bit electrically programmable read-only memory (EPROM) circuits. (*a*) 1981 manufacturing technology; chip area of 24,025 square mils (15.5 mm$^2$). (*b*) 1984 manufacturing technology; chip area of 11,500 square mils (7.4 mm$^2$). (*Intel Corp.*)

finer features and increasing wafer sizes. Because of these rapid changes a fabrication facility will remain state of the art in capability for no more than 3–5 years without making major equipment and process changes.

The sizes of the circuit elements continue to decrease as improvements in the lithography and etching techniques are incorporated (**Fig. 16**). This reduction in feature sizes has a direct impact on the chip sizes (**Fig. 18**). In addition to making smaller feature sizes which result in smaller chips for the same circuitry, the tendency has also been toward a rapid increase in circuit density. The outcome is that the chip sizes actually increase as more circuits are added than what would be gained by the smaller feature sizes (**Fig. 17**). This has allowed the density of memory circuits to quadruple every 3 years instead of 4–5 years.

One of the major reasons that it has been economical to increase the chip size is that the size of the silicon wafer used during processing continues to increase (**Fig. 19**). Where in 1970 2-in. (50-mm) wafers were common, by 1980 4-in. (100-mm) wafers were the choice for new manufacturing lines. During the mid-1980s, the 6-in. (150-mm) wafer was the direction of new manufacturing lines. The larger wafer plus the smaller feature sizes of the newer technolo-

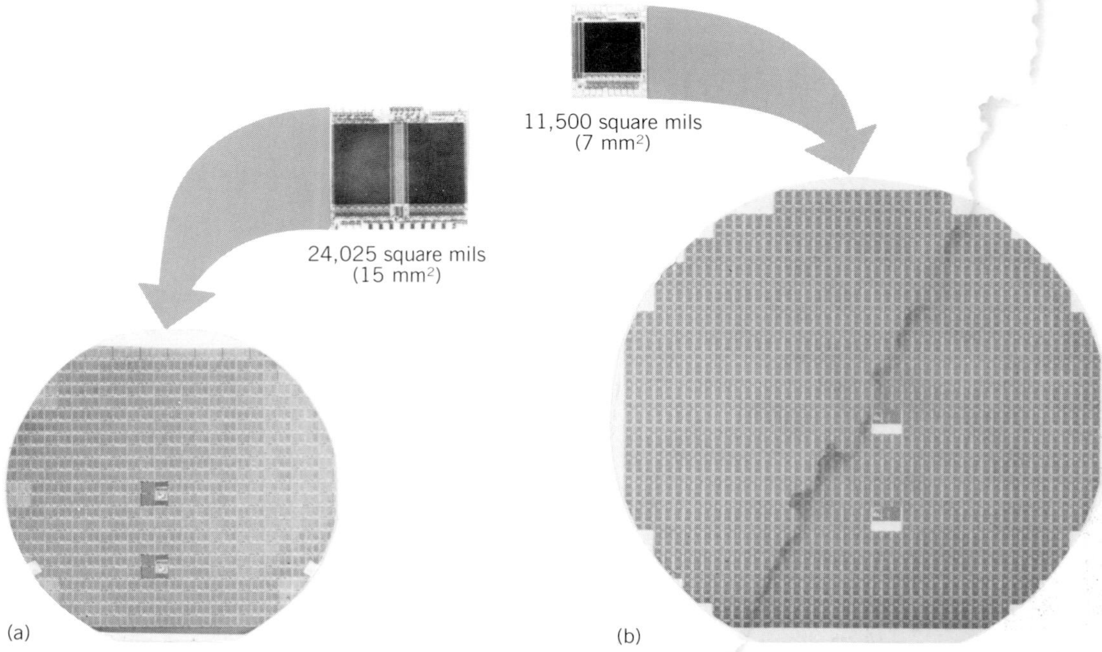


Fig. 19. Increased die per wafer available when decreasing the chip area plus increasing the wafer area. (*a*) 4-in. (100-mm) wafer. (*b*) 6-in. (150-mm) wafer. (*Intel Corp.*)

gies continue to decrease the cost of integrated circuits. This tendency is showing signs of slowing down, however, due to the fact that new manufacturing equipment results in a fixed cost per square inch of silicon. Two examples are the step-and-repeat photolithography and ion implanters which have slower throughput for the large wafers.

*Ron Burghard; Youssef El-Mansy; Neil Berglund*

## Gallium Arsenide Circuits

Integrated circuits based on gallium arsenide (GaAs) have come into increasing use since the late 1970s. The major advantage of these circuits is their fast switching speed.

**Galium arsenide FET.** The gallium arsenide field-effect transistor (GaAs FET) is a majority carrier device in which the cross-sectional area of the conducting path of the carriers is varied by the potential applied to the gate (**Fig. 20**). Unlike the MOSFET, the gate of the GaAs FET is a Schottky barrier composed of metal and gallium arsenide. Because of the difference in work functions of the two materials, a junction is formed. The depletion region associated with the junction is a function of the difference in voltage of the gate and the conducting channel, and the doping density of the channel. Be applying a negative voltage to the gate, the electrons under the gate in the channel are repelled, extending the depletion region across the conducting channel. The variation in the height of the conducting portion of the channel caused by the change in the extent of the depletion region alters the resistance between the drain and source. Thus the negative voltage on the gate modulates the current flowing between the drain and the source, as shown by the linear region of operation in Fig. 20*c*. As the height of the conducting channel is decreased by the gate voltage or as the drain voltage is increased, the velocity of charge carriers (electrons for *n*-type gallium arsenide) under the gate increases (similar to water in a hose when its path is constricted by passing through the nozzle). The velocity of the carriers continues to increase with increasing drain voltage, as does the current, until their saturated velocity is obtained (about $10^7$ cm/s or $3 \times 10^5$ ft/s for gallium arsenide). At that point the device is in the saturated region of operation; that is, the current is independent of the drain voltage.

The high-frequency operation of a device is limited by the transit time of the carriers under the gate. The time during which the velocity of electrons (output signal) is modulated by the voltage on the gate (input signal) must be short compared to any change of the input voltage. Because electrons in gallium arsenide have a high saturated velocity, GaAs FETs operate at very high frequencies. The high-frequency performance is also improved by decreasing the gate length (the length of the path of the electrons under the gate) by using special lithographic techniques to define the gate during processing. Gallium arsenide FETs with gate lengths as short as 0.1 μm ($4 \times 10^6$ in.) have been fabricated resulting in a potential frequency of operation of approximately 100 GHz.

**Fast switching speed.** As noted above, the major advantage of gallium arsenide integrated circuits over silicon integrated circuits is the faster switching speed of the logic gate. The reason for the improvement of the switching speed of GaAs FETs with short gate lengths (less than 1 μm or $4 \times 10^{-5}$ in.) over silicon FETs of comparable size has been the subject of controversy. In essence, the speed or gain-bandwidth product of a FET is determined by the velocity with which the electrons pass under the gate. The saturated drift velocity of electrons in gallium arsenide is twice that of electrons in silicon; therefore the switching speed of gallium arsenide might be expected to be only twice as fast.

However, this simplified model neglects several important aspects of the problem. One way to determine the switching speed of a logic circuit is to calculate the total capacitance that must be charged or discharged as the logic level is switched, and the current drive available. The larger the current drive and the smaller the capacitance, the faster the switching speed. Since gallium arsenide integrated circuits are fabricated on semi-insulating substrates, the parasitic capacitance to ground is much smaller than for silicon integrated circuits. The only comparable small-capacitance silicon technology is CMOS/SOS (silicon on sapphire). Also, because of the higher mobility, the transconductance of a GaAs FET is much higher than for a silicon FET, and the associated parasitic resistances are lower. Thus, there is more current change for a given amount of input voltage. Finally, the mobility of gallium arsenide is six to eight times that of silicon, and even though the saturated velocities of gallium arsenide and silicon are within a factor of two, the electrical field necessary for the carriers to reach velocity saturation in gallium arsenide (about 4 kV/cm) is much less than in silicon (about 40 kV/cm). Therefore, when operating at the low voltages typical of GaAs FETs, the speed ratio of similar gallium arsenide and silicon FETs is approximately proportional to their low-field mobilities. At higher voltages, the speed ratio decreases because the carrier velocity (current) continues to increase in silicon whereas the carriers are saturated in gallium arsenide; however, this increase in speed is at the expense of increased power dissipation. This effect explains the experimental results plotted in **Fig. 21**, where the

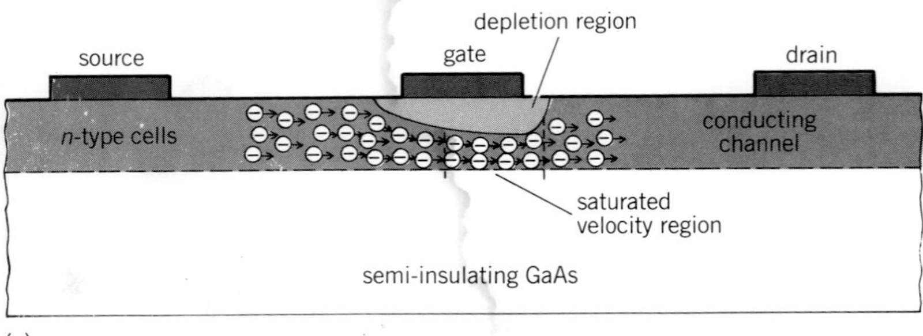


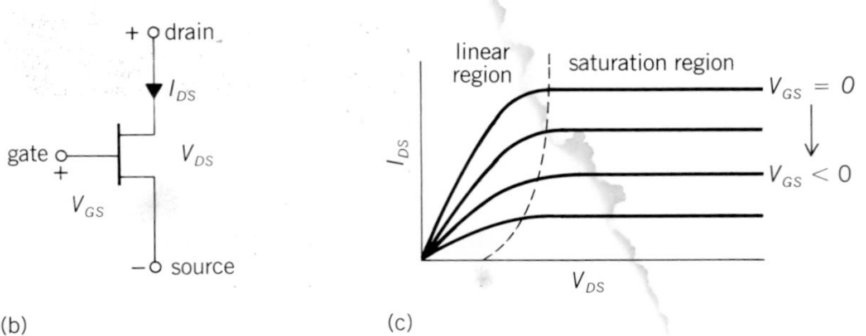


**Fig. 20. Gallium arsenide FET. (*a*) Cross section. (*b*) Circuit symbol. (*c*) Current-voltage characteristics. $I_{DS}$ = drain source current. $V_{DS}$ = drain source voltage. $V_{GS}$ = gate source voltage.**

power-delay products of silicon and gallium arsenide inverters with 1-μm-gate-length ($4 \times 10^{-5}$ in.) FETs are plotted as functions of power dissipation.

**Device technologies.** There are several device choices for high-speed gallium arsenide integrated circuits, each with certain advantages and disadvantages.

***Depletion-made FET (DFET).*** This is the most mature of the device technologies (**Fig. 22**). The DFET has the largest current drive capacity per unit device width for an all-GaAs FET device. This contributes to its high speed and high power dissipation. The pinchoff voltage of the DFET is determined by the channel doping and thickness under the Schottky barrier gate. This voltage can be made quite large (about −2.5 V) in order to improve the noise immunity of logic gates in which they are used.

***Enhancement-mode FET (ENFET).*** This low-current, low-power device is realized by increasing the pinchoff voltage to zero or above. The logic swing for the ENFET is limited to the difference between the pinchoff voltage (approximately 0 V) and the forward turn-on voltage of the Schottky barrier gate (approximately + 0.5 V), thus providing a significantly lower noise immunity for logic gates using ENFETs. The realization of medium-scale integration (MSI) and LSI chips in which the noise margins are small requires stringent process controls to fabricate devices across the wafer with very small variations in pinchoff voltage.

***Enhancement mode junction FET (E-JFET).*** In this device the Schottky barrier of the ENFET is replaced with an implanted *p* region that forms a *pn* junction for the gate (**Fig. 23**). The E-JFET has all the advantages of the ENFET with respect to low power plus the additional advantage of a slightly larger logic swing due to the larger turn-on voltage of the *pn* junction. The ultimate speed of the E-JFET will be less than an ENFET of similar dimesions because the added side wall gate capacitance of the *pn*-junction gate is a significant fraction of the total gate capacitance at submicrometer gate lengths.

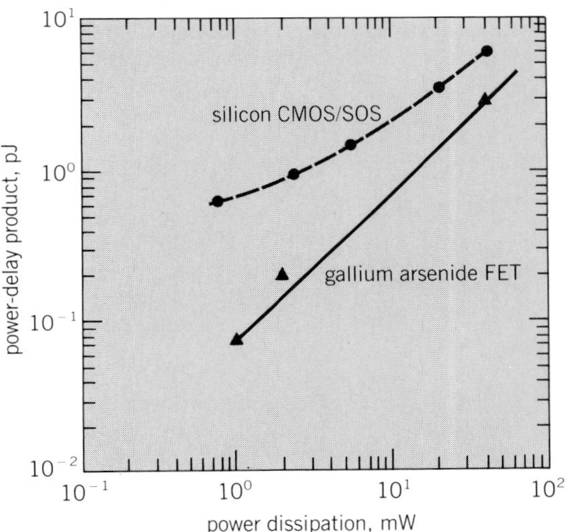


**Fig. 21. Comparison of gallium arsenide and silicon inverter performance.**

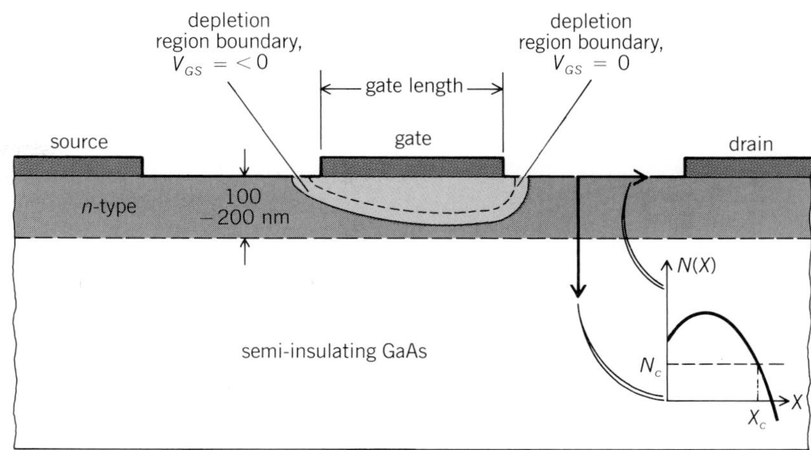


**Fig. 22. Depletion-mode FET (DFET). Graph shows doping density *N(X)* as function of depth *X*. $N_c$ = compensation density; $X_c$ = channel thickness.**

**Logic gate configurations.** Three different logic gate configurations (**Fig. 24**) are presently the most popular approaches to high-speed gallium arsenide logic circuits. The buffered-FET logic (BFL) gate is the fastest gate for reasonable fanouts but dissipates the most power (approximately 5–10 mW/per gate). The Schottky diode FET logic (SDFL) gate dissipates about one-fifth the power of the BFL; however, it is slower by about a factor of two. Finally, direct-coupled FET logic (DCFL) gates using enhancement-mode FETs have the lowest power consumption (about 50 μW/per gate) at gate delays two to four times those of BFL for complex logic circuits.

The BFL gate using DFETs requires level shifting to make the input and output logic levels compatible. This extra circuitry adds both delay to the switching time of the gate and extra power consumption; however, it provides buffering to the next stage and therefore has very good fanout (fanout is the number of identical logic gates it must drive) and on-off chip drive capabilities. Because of the high power dissipation and the large device count per gate, BFL will not be suitable for circuits with the complexity of large scale integration (greater than 1000 gates).

The SDFL gate incorporates very small Schottky

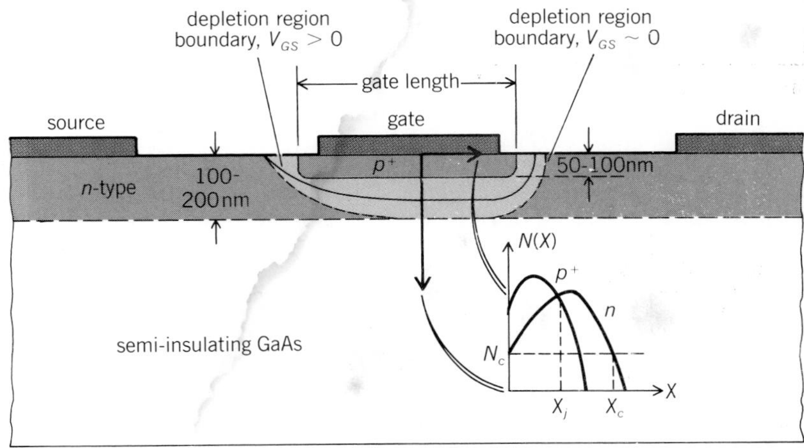


**Fig. 23. Enhancement-mode junction FET (E-JFET). Graph shows doping density *N(X)* as function of depth *X* in both *n* and $p^+$ regions. $N_c$ = compensation density; $X_c$ = channel thickness; $X_j$ = junction depth.**

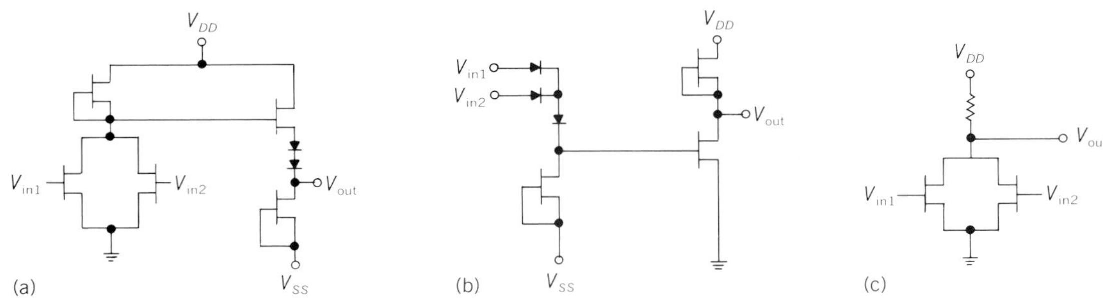


**Fig. 24. High-speed gallium arsenide logic gates. (*a*) Buffered FET logic (BFL) NOR gate. (*b*) Schottky diode FET logic (SDFL) NOR gate. (*c*) Direct-coupled FET logic (DCFL) NOR gate. $V_{in}$ = input voltage, $V_{out}$ = output voltage, $V_{DD}$ = drain supply voltage, $V_{SS}$ = source supply voltage.**

**Gallium arsenide logic gate applications and issues**

| Gallium arsenide technology | Target applications | Feasibility issues | Competing silicon technology |
|---|---|---|---|
| Buffered FET logic (BFL) | SSI (small-scale integration) - MSI (medium-scale integration) superfast logic-prescalers, multiplexers, demultiplexers, fast cache memory | Most producible, uses large logic swings with good noise margin; tolerant of FET threshold variations; least area efficient. | Emitter-coupled logic (ECL) and submicrometer MOS |
| Schottky diode FET logic (SDFL) | High-speed LSI (large scale integration), for example, 8 × 8 multiplier; arithmetic-logic unit (ALU), gate arrays | Replaces FETs with diodes for logic function; usually smaller noise margin than BFL, but still fairly tolerant of threshold variations; circuit design is complicated by fanout sensitivity | Bipolar LSI; 1-μm MOS LSI |
| Direct-coupled FET logic (DCFL) | Low power or VLSI (very large scale integration) applications, memory, gate arrays | Uses enhancement FETs; low-noise margin; requires excellent threshold control | 1-μm MOS VLSI |

barrier diodes ($1 \times 2$ μm or $4 \times 10^{-5}$ by $8 \times 10^{-5}$ in.) to perform the input logical-OR function and to provide level shifting. The invert function is performed by the DFETs in the second stage. Because of the lower power dissipation and small diodes, packing densities of more than 1000 gates/mm$^2$ (645,000 gates/in.$^2$) are achievable. Large fan-in does not require any significant chip area because of the small diodes; however, SDFL gates are very fanout-sensitive, and for fanouts of greater than 3 either buffers or much wider DFETs must be incorporated to maintain the speed. Because of the medium power dissipation and high packing density, SDFL is suitable for large-scale integration applications but not for circuits with the complexity of very large-scale integration (more than 10,000 gates).

DCFL incorporating ENFETs is inherently much simpler than BFL or SDFL since there is no need for level shifting. The very low power consumption and circuit simplicity lead to high packing density (more than 5000 gates/mm$^2$ or $3.2 \times 10^6$ gates/in.$^2$) at only slightly slower speeds.

The **table** lists the projected applications for each of the three logic gates, along with the competing silicon technology. *See* Circuit (electronics); Printed circuit.

*Paul T. Greiling*

**Bibliography.** D. J. Elliott, *Integrated Circuit Fabrication Technology*, 1982; P. R. Gray and R. G. Meyer, *Analysis and Design of Analog Integrated Circuits*, 1981; P. T. Greiling, The future impact of GaAs digital ICs, *IEEE Journal on Selected Areas in Communications*, 1985; A. S. Grove, *Physics and Technology of Semiconductor Devices*, 1976; E. H. Nicollian and J. R. Brews, *MOS (Metal Oxide Semiconductor) Physics and Technology*, 1982; S. M. Sze, *Physics of Semiconductor Devices*, 2d ed., 1981; R. M. Warner, Jr., and J. N. Fordemwalt (eds.), *Integrated Circuits: Device Principles and Fabrication*, 1965; W. Wisseman (ed.), *Gallium Arsenide, VLSI Electronics, Microstructures Science*, 1985.

## Integrated optics

The study of optical devices that are based on light transmission in planar waveguides, that is, dielectric structures that confine the propagating light to a region with one or two very small dimensions, on the order of the optical wavelength. The principal motivation for these studies is to combine miniaturized individual devices through waveguides or other means into a functional optical system incorporated into a small substrate. The resulting system is called an integrated optical circuit (IOC) by analogy with the semiconductor type of integrated circuit. An integrated optical circuit could include lasers, integrated lenses, switches, interferometers, polarizers, modulators, detectors, and so forth. Important uses envisioned for integrated optical circuits include signal processing (for example, spectrum analysis and analog-to-digital conversion) and optical communications through glass fibers, which are themselves circular (or elliptical) waveguides. Integrated optical circuits could be used in such systems as optical transmitters, switches, repeaters, and receivers. *See Integrated circuits; Optical communications.*

The advantages of having an optical system in the form of an integrated optical circuit rather than a conventional series of components include (apart from miniaturization) reduced sensitivity to air currents and to mechanical vibrations of the separately mounted parts, low driving voltages and high efficiency, robustness, and (potentially) reproducibility and economy. As in the case of semiconductor integrated circuits, an integrated optical circuit might be fabricated on or just within the surface of one material (the substrate) modified for the different components by shaping structures (using etching, for example) or incorporating suitable substitutes or dopants, or alternatively, by depositing or expitaxially growing additional layers. It is also possible to construct independent components which are then attached to form the integrated optical circuit. This option, called hybrid, has the advantage that each component could be optimized, for example, by using gallium aluminum arsenide lasers as sources for an integrated optical circuit and silicon detectors. In the former case, the integrated optical circuit is called monolithic, and is expected to have the advantage of ease of processing, similar to the situation for monolithic semiconductor integrated circuits. Perhaps the most promising materials for monolithic integrated optical circuits are direct band-gap semiconductors composed of III–V materials such as gallium aluminum arsenide [(GaAl)As] and indium gallium arsenide phosphide [(InGa)(AsP)] since with suitable processing they may perform almost all necessary operations as lasers, switches, modulators, detectors, and so forth.

**Guided waves.** The simplest optical waveguide is a three-layer or sandwich structure with the index of refraction largest in the middle or waveguiding layer (**Fig. 1**). The lower and top layers are usually the substrate and superstrate, respectively. Often, the top layer is air and the waveguide layer is referred to as a film. Sometimes, too, the outer regions are called cladding layers. A guided wave does not have light distributed uniformly across the waveguide, but is a pattern that depends on the indices of refraction of all three layers and the guide thickness. The waveguide is usually designed by selecting its refractive index and thickness, so that only one such characteristic pattern propagates with no change in shape. This pattern, referred to as the fundamental or lowest-order mode, travels down the guide with a characteristic velocity.

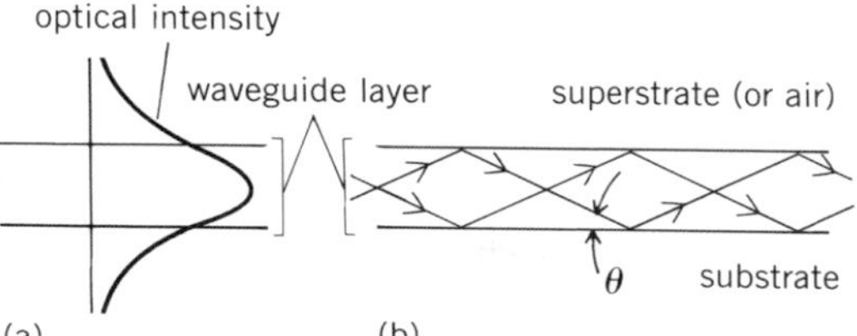


**Fig. 1. Optical waveguide. (*a*) Optical intensity of the fundamental guided mode. (*b*) Ray picture of the guided mode.**

A mode pattern such as that of Fig. 1*a* may be viewed as the superposition of two progressive waves moving at a particular slight angle θ to the propagation direction as shown in Fig. 1*b*. If the ray directions are sufficiently near grazing incidence, the large refractive index of the waveguide layer will cause total internal reflection at the interfaces and the mode will propagate along the waveguide without loss. *See Waveguide.*

**Materials and fabrication.** Waveguides have been made of many different materials, most of which may be categorized as ferroelectric, semiconductor, or amorphous. Examples of these classes are lithium niobate, gallium arsenide/gallium aluminum arsenide [GaAs/(GaAl)As], and glass, respectively. Methods for fabricating a waveguide layer at the surface of lithium niobate include heating the crystal in a vacuum to drive off lithium oxide or diffusing titanium metal into the crystal. Both processes create a region of high refractive index near the surface; air is the superstrate. Although the refractive index of the waveguide layer decreases with depth rather than being constant, the guided mode is similar to that shown in Fig. 1. A semiconductor waveguide is fabricated, for example, by growing successively crystalline layers of $(Ga_{0.7}Al_{0.3})As$, GaAs, and $(Ga_{0.7}Al_{0.3})As$. The thin GaAs waveguide layer of high refractive index is thus interposed between thicker cladding regions of the lower-index $(Ga_{0.7}Al_{0.3})As$. Glass waveguides may be formed, for example, by sputter deposition of a relatively high-refractive-index glass on a lower-index glass substrate. *See Ferroelectrics; Semiconductor heterostructures.*

Waveguides that confine light in two dimensions, rather than one as shown in Fig. 1, utilize refractive index differences in both transverse directions. Examples of these are the rib guide (**Fig. 2*a***) and the titanium-diffused channel guide (Fig. 2*b*). In fabricating a rib guide, photolithography is employed to delineate the stripe, followed by chemical or dry etching to remove the undesired material. The channel guide is produced by etching away all but a strip of metal prior to diffusion.

**Coupling of external light beams.** An external light beam may be coupled into a waveguide by introducing the light at the end of the guide at an edge of the substrate or through the surface of the waveguide. The former approach may employ a lens to focus the light beam onto the guide end. Alternatively, the laser or an optical fiber is placed against or in close proximity to the guide end, which is referred to as butt coupling. Light may also be injected through the guide surface with an auxiliary element. Simply illuminating that surface will not suffice since the refractive index difference needed for effective waveguiding prevents light from entering at the required angle. The necessary angle, which is exactly that of the propagating waves shown in Fig. 1*b*, may be obtained by passing the light through a high-refractive-index prism whose surface is so close to the guide layer that waveguiding is disturbed in that region. The prism

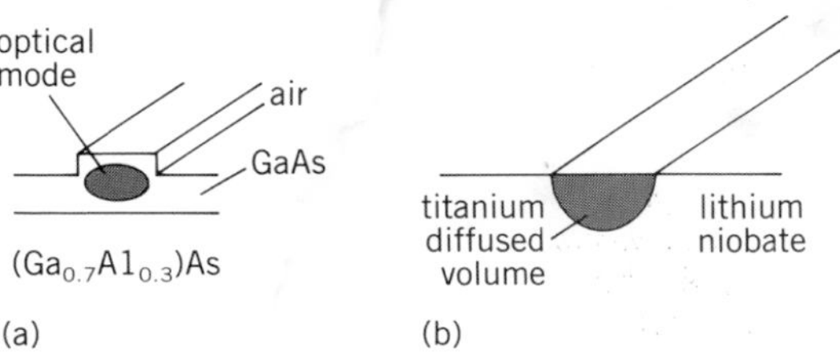


**Fig. 2. Two-dimensional transverse waveguiding. (*a*) Rib waveguide. (*b*) Diffused channel guide.**

not only permits the introduction of light, but also acts to couple light from the waveguide. For this reason, the light must illuminate the guide near the end of the prism (**Fig. 3**). The angle of light incident on the surface of the waveguide layer can also be modified so as to coincide with the internal angle of the propagating wave by a periodic structure or grating on the waveguide surface. Such a grating may be made by a multiple-step process which begins by depositing a light-sensitive material called photoresist and concludes with etching and cleaning. The grating also functions as an output coupler. By reversing the incident and output beam directions in Fig. 3, the roles of the prism and grating couplers are interchanged.

**Lasers and distributed feedback.** The diode laser is already an integrated optics device in a sense since the lasing medium is a waveguide laser interposed between two cladding layers. The waveguide layer may be GaAs, in which case the outer regions are composed of $(Ga_{0.7}Al_{0.3})As$, for example. When used as a separate source, the crystal facets act as end reflectors. The diode laser's high efficiency, low-voltage operation, small size, and physical integrity cause it to be the laser of choice in many hybrid integrated optics applications. Moreover, it lends itself to integration in an integrated optical circuit where reflectivity may be provided by introducing an appropriate periodic structure. This could be a thickness variation in the waveguide layer. Devices utilizing such structures are called distributed feedback or distributed Bragg reflector lasers. SEE LASER.

**Switches and modulators.** Both lithium niobate and gallium arsenide belong to the family of electro-optically active crystals. When an electric field is applied to these materials, their refractive indices are modified. This effect is employed in integrated optical circuit switching and modulation applications. To construct a switch, gold or other conducting electrodes are deposited on a lithium niobate integrated optical circuit surface parallel to two closely spaced waveguides. If the electrodes and waveguides are suitably designed, the applications of specific small voltages to the electrodes will cause the transfer of optical power from one waveguide to its neighbor with high efficiency and little residual power in the initial guide. Shown in **Fig. 4** is a "4 by 4" switching network in which each of four input optical signals, possibly from optical fibers butt-coupled to the waveguide inputs, may be switched to any one of the four output ports. Such an integrated optical circuit serves to interconnect four computers through optical fibers, for example.

A switch is in effect a modulator as well. Modulation is a process in which information is encoded onto an optical or other electromagnetic wave. Pulse modulation results simply by interrupting or connecting a light wave in a manner intelligible to the receiver. (Morse code is an unsophisticated example.) By transferring light into or out of a waveguide in response to an electric signal at a switching electrode, the output optical wave becomes modulated; that is, the switch operates as a modulator. SEE OPTICAL MODULATORS.

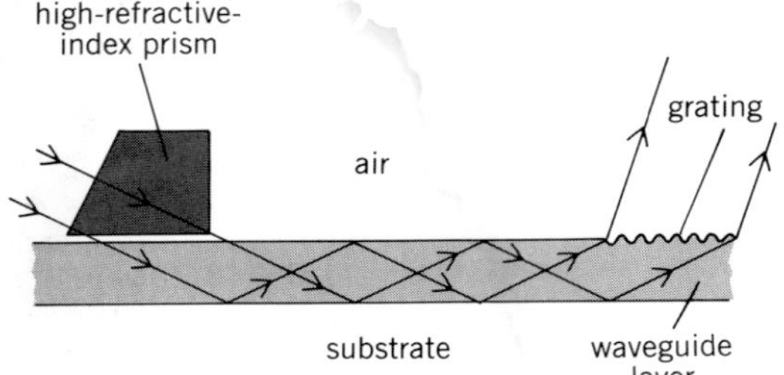


Fig. 3. Prism input coupling and grating output coupling. With the ray directions reversed, the grating acts as an input coupler and the prism as an output coupler.

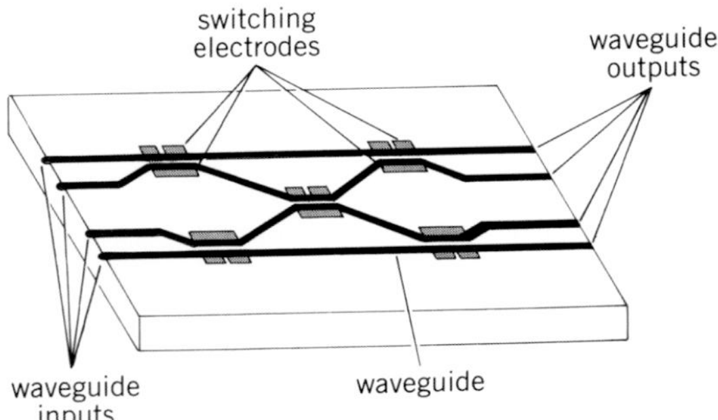


Fig. 4. A "4 by 4" directional coupler switch.

**Spectrum analyzer.** Light propagating in an integrated optical circuit within a one-dimensional waveguide may be deflected by interacting with an acoustic wave. The deflection angle is a function of the acoustic frequency. This interaction forms the basis of an integrated optics spectrum analyzer (**Fig. 5**). An acoustic wave is generated by an electric signal whose frequencies are being analyzed. The acoustic wave interacts with a guided optical wave and the deflected light is focused onto a detector array. The one or more detectors which respond determines the previously unknown frequencies. The integrated optical circuit incorporates lenses which focus the light and a transducer to generate the acoustic wave. The lenses may be fabricated by depositing additional high-refractive-index material in an area so as to decrease locally the propagation velocity of the guided wave. The transducer is made of a piezoelectric material (such as lithium niobate) which has the property of converting an electric field into a strain field. If lithium niobate is used for the integrated optical circuit, the transducer consists of a sophisticated interdigital electrode structure deposited on the waveguide surface. SEE SPECTRUM ANALYZER.

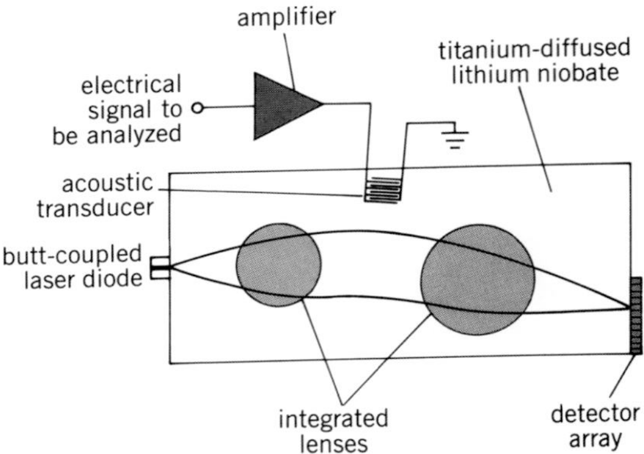


Fig. 5. Top view of an integrated optics spectrum analyzer.

*William Streifer*

**Bibliography.** F. J. Leonberger, Applications of guided wave interferometers, *Laser Focus Fiberopt. Tech.*, 18:125–129, 1982; Optical Society of America, Integrated and guided wave optics, *Tech. Dig.*, January 6–8, 1982; T. Tamir (ed.), *Integrated Optics*, 1975; P. K. Tien, Integrated optics and new wave phenomena in optical waveguides, *Rev. Mod. Phys.*, 49(2):361–420, 1977.

## Intelligent machine

Any machine that can accomplish its specific task in the presence of uncertainty and variability in its environment. The machine's ability to monitor its environment allowing it to adjust its actions based on what it has sensed, is a prerequisite for intelligence. The term intelligent machine is an anthropomorphism in that intelligence is defined by the criterion that the actions would appear intelligent if a person were to do it. A precise, unambiguous, and commonly held definition of intelligence does not exist.

Examples of intelligent machines include industrial robots equipped with sensors, computers equipped with speech recognition and voice synthesis, self-guided vehicles relying on vision rather than on marked roadways, and so-called smart weapons, which are capable of target identification. These varied systems include three major subsystems: sensors, actuators, and control. The class of computer programs known as expert systems is included with intelligent machines, even though the sensory input and output functions are simply character-oriented comcmunications. The complexity of control and the mimicking of human deductive and logic skills makes expert systems central in the realm of intelligent machines. SEE EXPERT SYSTEMS; ROBOTICS; SPEECH RECOGNITION; VOICE RESPONSE.

**Intelligent control.** Since the physical embodiment of the machine or the particular task performed by the machine does not mark it as intelligent, the appearance of intelligence must come from the nature of the control or decision-making process that the machine performs. Given the centrality of control to any form of intelligent machine, intelligent control is the essence of an intelligent machine. The control function accepts several kinds of data, including the specification for the task to be performed and the current state of the task from the sensors. The control function then computes the signals needed to accomplish the task. When the task is completed, this also must be recognized and the controller must signal the supervisor that it is ready for the next assignment (**Fig. 1**).

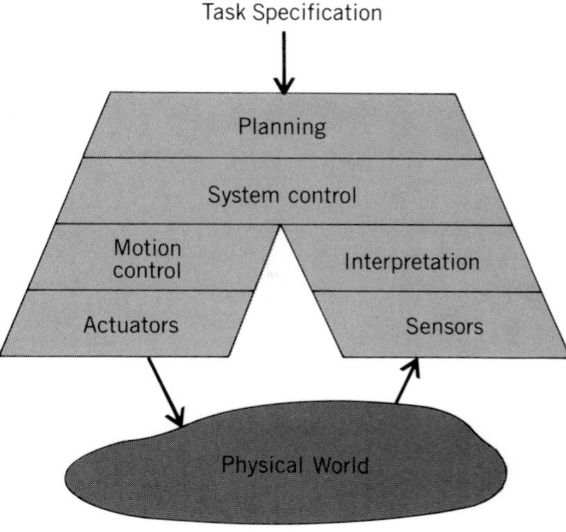


**Fig. 1. Flow of information and data in a typical intelligent machine.**

Automatic, feedback, or regulatory systems such as thermostats, automobile cruise controls, and photoelectric door openers are not considered intelligent machines. Several important concepts separate these simple feedback and control systems from intelligent control. While examples could be derived from any of the classes of intelligent machines, robots will be used here to illustrate five concepts that are typical of intelligent control. (1) An intelligent control system typically deals with many sources of information about its state and the state of its environment. A robot may contain a vision system and tactile sensors in addition to the internal position sensors that allow calculation of its spatial location. Given multiple sources of information, the intelligent control function evaluates them as needed based on the nature of the functions that must be performed at any instant. (2) An intelligent control system can accommodate incomplete or inconsistent information. For example, a robot expecting to pick up a single object from a conveyor belt may be confronted with two overlapping objects or no objects. (3) Intelligent control is characterized by the use of heuristic methods in addition to algorithmic control methods. A heuristic is a rule of thumb, a particular solution or strategy to be used for solving a problem that can be used for only very limited ranges of the input parameters. A possible heuristic for solving a particular robot-implemented insertion task would be to move the part incrementally along an outward spiral path, retrying the insertion, if the original attempt should fail. This heuristic could be repeated many times until an area large compared to positional uncertainties was covered. Clearly, such a heuristic is applicable only to a very small fraction of robot tasks. (4) An intelligent machine has a built-in knowledge base that it can use to deal with infrequent or unplanned events. An intelligent robot would have mechanisms, both sensors and heuristics, ensuring its own and its operator's safety. (5) An algorithmic control approach assumes that all relevant data for making decisions is available. The heuristic approach is predicted on the knowledge that all relevant data cannot be made available, even in principle, and that the control system will have to resolve ambiguous cases.

**Intelligent robots.** To clarify these very general concepts and to illustrate them with more detail, a sensor-equipped robot performing an electronics assembly task will be described. The task is to pick a part from an egg-carton-like pallet, inserting it into a test fixture, and, if it tests acceptably, to insert it into the appropriate place on the printed wiring board being assembled. A human worker, especially one with some experience in production line assembly, could be instructed in this task in a few minutes and would also know, without further instruction, what actions to take for the many exceptional conditions that can arise in this type of activity. Outlining the steps that must be taken to program a robot to accomplish the same task will illustrate the amount of prior knowledge possessed by a person and the general level of complexity of programming in an environment where all relevant data and actions must be stated completely and unambiguously. The robot program will be given in verbal outline form rather than coded in a particular robot programming language. The numbers are used both for specifying branches in the flow of control and for referencing in the discussions that follow. *SEE ROBOTICS.*

1. Wait for a printed wiring board to enter the assembly station.

2. Take an image of the parts presentation pallet: an egg-carton arrangement that separates and loosely orients the parts.

3. Locate a part in the image.

4. If the pallet is empty, move it to the stacking area and signal the conveyor to move a fresh pallet into position. Resume at step 2.

5. If a part is present, pick up the part and position it in the visual inspection station. Take an image of the bottom of the part. Determine the location and orientation of the pin field.

6. If an incorrect pin field is seen, deposit the part in the reject bin and resume at step 2.

7. If the pin field is correct, orient the robot hand based on the observed orientation of the part and insert the part into the electrical test station.

8. Signal the electrical test to begin.

9. If the test fails, remove the part from the test fixture and deposit it in the reject bin. Then resume at step 2.

10. If the electrical test was passed, regrasp the part to ensure it is accurately held by the robot. Remove it from the test fixture and move it to a point just above the insertion location on the printed wiring board.

11. Insert the part in the printed wiring board by moving it vertically downward while monitoring the force. When the vertical force reaches a specified value, stop the robot's vertical motion.

12. Check the vertical position of the robot hand when it stopped moving. If it is at a height indicating that the part was inserted, release the part, retract the robot hand, and resume at step 1.

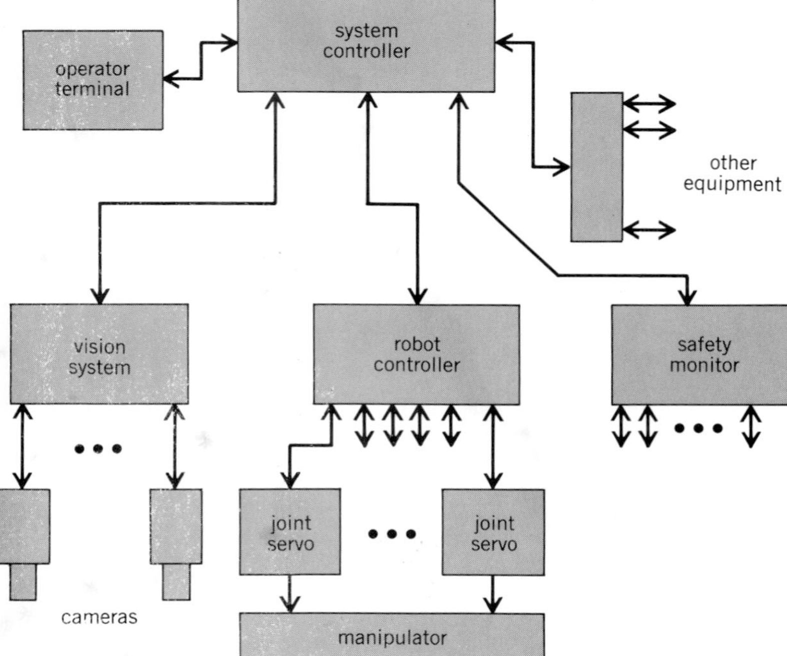


**Fig. 2. Interconnection of processors forming a sensor-based robot.**

13. If the part was not inserted correctly, move the robot hand in the plane of the printed wiring board by a small increment along a prescribed path and resume at step 11.

Several comments can be made about a robot that is following the above program and the program itself. Such a robot would appear to be intelligent given the definition in the beginning of the article. There is variability in the robot's environment, and it is using a variety of sensory data to guide its actions. However, the program is incomplete. There are many things that can go wrong that have not been accounted for: If a hole in the printed wiring board for the part is missing, the insertion cannot be successfully accomplished. In this case, program steps 11, 12, and 13 form an apparent infinite loop. Many other similar problems lurk in this program. The program also presupposes significant capabilities and data in the robot and related vision system. The vision system and robot must be calibrated; that is, a procedure must be periodically executed that calculates the transformations between the robot and vision system coordinates. The vision system must be programmed to recognize first what the part looks like in the context of the pallet (step 3) and second what a correct pin field looks like (step 5). The precise locations of all points of reference for the robot must be determined. The search strategy to be followed if the part is not inserted correctly (step 13) must be carefully defined. The calibration and teaching programs required to accomplish these steps may be as complex as the primary task.

Execution of the assembly program and all of the implied subsidiary functions defines the control capability of the robot. The threshold of intelligent control is reached when the system can deal with many of the infrequent and exceptional conditions without requiring outside intervention or assistance. A second part of intelligent control is the development of the detailed programs given a high-level statement of the task requirements. This is the planning function (Fig. 1). Systems of this level of complexity are primarily found in robotics research laboratories. The automatic planning of complex robot control programs given high-level task descriptions is an area of research.

**Control hierarchy.** The control function in an intelligent machine is generally implemented as a hierarchy of processes. The upper levels are responsible for global decision-making processes and for the planning phases of the task. The lower levels implement critical time-dependent subtasks. In **Fig. 2** the interconnection of a group of processors forming a vision-controlled robot is diagrammed. The manipulator arm is itself controlled by a two-level hierarchy. The lower level consists of a processor that performs the servo function for each joint of the arm. The robot controller converts world coordinates supplied by the system controller into the values for each joint required to place the robot hand in the desired location. The robot controller also divides complete movement specifications into a series of short steps that result in coordinated motion and controlled velocity of the robot.

The control program outlined in the robot example would be executed on the system-level control processor. In addition to the vision, manipulator, and safety subsystems, the system-level controller would also be the interface with the robot operator and the factory communications system. The partitioning of subtasks onto autonomous communicating processors is a natural and economic way to obtain increased system performance by using multiple microprocessors. *SEE MICROPROCESSOR.*

**Computer vision.** A computer vision system interprets the contents of a large array (256 × 256 is common) of intensity values that is the computer representation of a frame of a television image. Interpret in this context means to find, recognize, or inspect a prespecified object or group of objects. The first processing step is to isolate or segment the image of the object from the background image. The most common technique in use is to create a high-contrast image, typically by backlighting the object of interest, which allows a simple threshold to be used for the segmentation. Objects in the image are found at those locations where the intensity value is less than some prespecified constant. Lower-contrast images, such as a part in a pallet, require segmentation techniques that rely on rapid changes in brightness (edges) or differences in intensity between two images, or techniques that look for specific visual features by using any of a large number of matched filter techniques. The amount of computation required to segment a low-contrast image is significantly greater than that required by thresholding. Once an object image is segmented from the background, a set of parameters known as features is calculated. The set of features, which may include the object area, perimeter, number of holes and any other enumerable parameter, is compared to a model of the object either to ascertain its identitity or to compare it to some inspection criteria. The specific set of features needed for a specific visual recognition problem depends on the exact appearances of the objects in complex ways with the result that the feature set is normally determined empirically. Similarly, orientation and location quantities are also computed for the segmented image. Generally, an image represents a two-dimensional projection of a three-dimensional object. Correction to the perceived shape and location may have to be made based on the location of the object relative to the viewing camera. No matter what complexity of techniques are used in its construction, a computer vision system is invariably implemented with a dedicated processor.

**Expert systems.** The control schemes outlined above are algorithmic even if the resulting system behavior appears intelligent. The explicit programming methods described do not lend themselves to situations where several alternative actions could be rationally considered. In the explicit programming of a complex task, there is very little opportunity to use default actions for many infrequent conditions. The method of expert systems is expected to provide a paradigm for a better way of robot task planning and execution. Expert systems consist of a knowledge base and an inference procedure for obtaining a result consistent with the contents of the knowledge base, given an arbitrary set of input conditions. The knowledge base is represented by a collection of condition-action statements (rules). The primary difficulties are in obtaining an adequate collection of rules for the task and in defining an appropriate strategy for resolving inconsistencies or ambiguities when applying rules to a given problem. A specific robot task would be programmed by adding a set of rules, describing the particular operation to be formed, to an existing, and probably much larger, set of rules that defined the default and exception-handling behavior of the robot. *SEE EXPERT SYSTEMS.*

**Interconnection of machines.** Another trend expected in the area of intelligent machines is their interconnection into cooperating groups to address larger tasks. Standardization of information exchange protocols and languages describing various fields of work are prerequisites to any extensive development of interconnected, cooperating systems.

Slow, steady improvements may be expected in intelligent machine capabilities. Progress will follow in microprocessors with the availability of other functions implemented as very large-scale integrated (VLSI) circuits. *SEE INTEGRATED CIRCUITS.*

*John F. Jarvis*

***Bibliography.*** F. Hayes-Roth, D. A. Waterman, and D. B. Lenat, *Building Expert Systems*, 1983; C. S. G. Lee, R. C. Gonzalez, and K. S. Fu (eds.), *Tutorial on Robotics*, 1983. R. Nevatia, *Machine Perception*, 1982; R. P. Paul, *Robot Manipulators: Mathematics, Programming and Control*, 1981.

## Intermediate-frequency amplifier

A tuned amplifier employed in the amplification of the signals produced by the mixer in a radio receiver. Because the carrier frequency of the modulated signal from the mixer is essentially constant, the resonant frequency of the amplifier is fixed.

The proper design of the intermediate-frequency (i-f) amplifier is essential for good selectivity and reproduction of the original transmitted signal. If the amplifer is tuned too sharply, the high-frequency components of the modulating signal will be lost. To avoid this, stagger-tuning of the individual stages may be used. In a stagger-tuned amplifier the resonant frequency of each stage is slightly different from the carrier frequency, with the result that the gain is essentially constant over the bandwidth of the modulated signal. The gain decreases rapidly at frequencies outside this band.

The standard i-f frequency for broadcast radio receivers is 455 kHz; other frequencies used depend upon the application, such as television receivers or radar receivers. *SEE AMPLIFIER.*

*Harold F. Klock*

## Ion beam mixing

A process in which bombardment of a solid with a beam of energetic ions causes the intermixing of the atoms of two separate phases originally present in the near-surface region. In the well-established process of ion implantation, the ions are incident instead on a homogeneous solid, into which they are incorporated over a range of depths determined by their initial energy. In the simplest example of ion beam mixing, the solid is a composite consisting of a substrate and a thin film of a different material (**Fig. 1***a*). Ions with sufficient energy pass through the film into the substrate, and this causes mixing of the film and substrate atoms (Fig. 1*b*). If the ion dose is large enough, the original film will completely disappear (Fig. 1*c*). This process may result in the impurity doping of the substrate, in the formation of an alloy or two-phase mixture, or in the production of a stable or metastable solid phase that is different from either the film or the substrate. *SEE ION IMPLANTATION.*

Like ion implantation, ion beam mixing is a solid-state process that permits controlled change in the

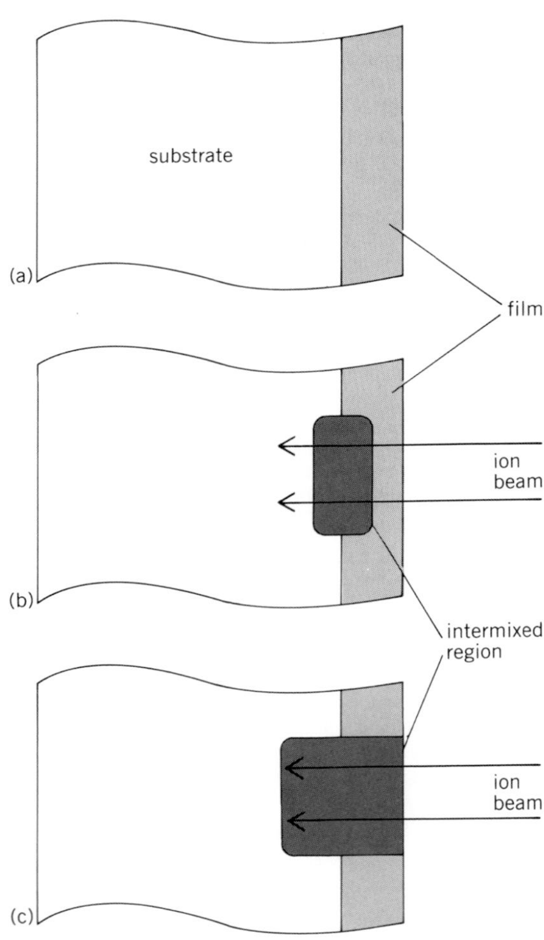


**Fig. 1. Ion beam mixing of film and substrate. (*a*) Before ion bombardment. (*b*) Partial intermixing. (*c*) Complete intermixing.**

composition and properties of the near-surface region of solids. Although not yet employed commercially, it is expected to be useful for such applications as the surface modification of metals and semiconductor device processing. In conjunction with thin-film deposition technology, ion beam mixing should make it possible to introduce many impurity elements at concentrations too high for ion implantation to be practical.

**Mixing mechanisms.** The ion beam mixing of a film and substrate takes place by the following mechanisms, in increasing order of complexity: recoil implantation, cascade mixing, and radiation-enhanced diffusion. In recoil implantation, an atom is driven from the film into the substrate as a result of a direct collision with an incident ion. Cascade mixing takes place when the recoil of an atom from such a collision initiates a series of secondary collisions among the film and substrate atoms. These collisions produce both forward and backward displacements and therefore lead to transfer of atoms from the substrate into the film as well as from the film into the substrate. Both recoil implantation and cascade mixing are kinematic mechanisms whose effectiveness generally increases with the mass and energy of the incident ions and with the masses of the film and substrate atoms but is relatively insensitive to temperature. These phenomena usually yield a ratio of intermixed atoms to incident ions no greater than about 10 to 1. Since they are coincident with the atomic collisions, they occur in only about $10^{-11}$ s, roughly the transit time of the incident ions through the film. Mixing of the film and substrate atoms by the mechanism of radiation-enhanced diffusion requires much longer times, and the rate is strongly temperature-dependent because diffusion is a thermally activated process. This mechanism is a consequence of the increase in interdiffusion coefficients that results because additional lattice defects (of which the simplest are vacancies and interstitial atoms) are formed by the atomic displacements produced by ion bombardment. Intermixing of several hundred atoms per incident ion can be achieved by heating a bombarded sample to temperatures where the defects become sufficiently mobile for rapid diffusion.

**Stable- and metastable-phase formation.** When a sample is subjected to ion beam mixing, the nature of the solid phase obtained depends upon the composition of the intermixed region. For samples initially consisting of a thin film on a substrate, the composition obtained by complete mixing is determined by the thickness of the film. An alternate sample configuration is prepared by depositing alternating thin films of different elements on a substrate (**Fig. 2**), and passage of the energetic ions homogenizes the films on an atomic scale. For this configuration the intermixed composition can be adjusted by varying the relative thickness of the different films.

If the composition produced by ion beam mixing corresponds to a solid phase that is thermodynamically stable, this is the phase that will be obtained. Such a phase could be a solid solution of one constituent in the other, or it could be a chemical compound of the two constituents. In addition, ion beam mixing can also produce metastable phases, because it is a highly nonequilibrium process in which the kinetic energy of the bombarding ions is transferred to the target atoms and then very rapidly dissipated by atomic collision and rearrangement. For example, this technique has been used to prepare a continuous series of silver-copper solid solutions, in which the lattice constant varies almost linearly with alloy composition, and the solid solubility of nickel in silver has been increased to more than 40 times the equilibrium value. Splat cooling, the extremely rapid solidification of a liquid phase, is another nonequilibrium technique for producing metastable materials such as supersaturated solid solutions or amorphous phases. However, single-phase solid compositions can be achieved only to the extent that the constituents are miscible in the liquid phase. Thus in the silver-nickel system the effectiveness of splat cooling in increasing the solid solubility is limited by the immiscibility in

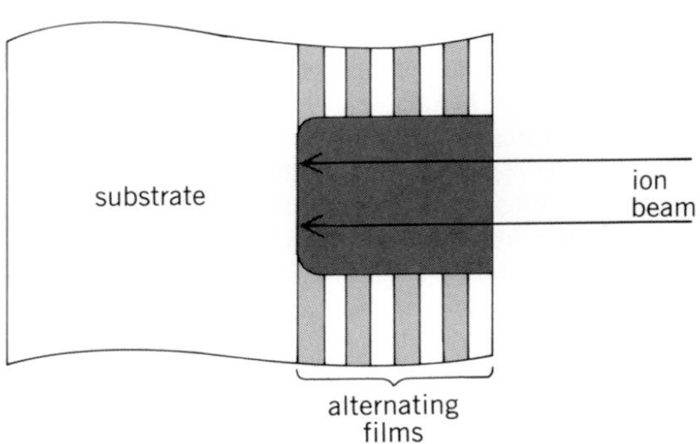


**Fig. 2. Ion beam mixing of alternating films.**

the liquid phase. As a solid-state process, ion beam mixing is not subject to this limitation.

**Applications.** While ion implantation is a well-established technique for modifying the near-surface physical and chemical properties of metals in order to improve such characteristics as wear and corrosion resistance, this technique has the disadvantage that relatively high ion doses may be necessary for effective surface modification. Thus doses of $10^{17}$–$10^{18}$ cm$^{-2}$ are usually required to achieve impurity concentrations of 1–10 at. % in the near-surface region. To obtain such doses in a reasonable length of time requires high beam intensities that may be difficult to achieve for metallic elements, which are generally the ones used for direct implantation. This disadvantage can be overcome by the use of ion beam mixing, not only because the ratio of intermixed ions to bombarding ions is much greater than one, but also because the bombarding species can be ions of gases such as nitrogen and argon, for which high beam intensities are easily produced in long-life sources that are commercially available. In an initial demonstration of surface modification by ion beam mixing, the wear resistance of titanium alloys has been substantially improved by the intermixing of a tin film bombarded with nitrogen ions.

In silicon integrated circuits, metal silicides such as titanium silicide ($TiSi_2$) and tungsten silicide ($WSi_2$) are widely used for low-resistance contacts and interconnects. These materials have conventionally been formed by deposition of a metal film on the silicon wafer and subsequent thermal reaction between the metal and silicon. Ion beam mixing offers the advantage of reducing the temperature required for silicide formation, since penetration of the bombarding ions through the metal-silicon interface disperses interfacial impurities (particularly native oxides of silicon), which generally form a diffusion barrier that impedes reaction. Silicides formed by ion beam mixing exhibit good surface morphology and electrical properties. *See* INTEGRATED CIRCUITS.

*Bor-Yeu Tsaur*

**Bibliography.** J. E. E. Baglin and J. M. Poate (eds.), *Thin Film-Interface and Interactions*, 1979; R. E. Benenson et al., *Ion Beam Modification of Materials*, 1981; G. K. Hubler et al., *Ion Implantation and Ion Beam Processing of Materials*, 1984; S. T. Picraux and W. J. Choyke, *Metastable Materials Formation by Ion Implantation*, 1982.

## Ion implantation

A process of introducing impurities into the near-surface region of solids by directing a beam of energetic ions at the solid (**Fig. 1**). When ions of sufficient energy are directed toward a crystal surface, they will penetrate the surface and slow to rest within the solid. Ion implantation differs from the normal thermal equilibrium means of introducing atoms into a solid, which is usually carried out either by adding the elements during growth of a solid from a liquid or vapor phase, or by diffusing the atoms into the solid at elevated temperatures. The advantages of the implantation process are: precise control of the type of impurity to be introduced, the amount of impurity introduced, and the impurity distribution in depth. In addition, since any atoms can be added to any solid, mixtures can be formed which would not normally be found in nature, that is, systems which are not in thermal equilibrium. Most of the work in developing and understanding the ion implantation processes has taken place since the middle 1960s. A major area of application of ion implantation has been to semiconductor device fabrication, where the process is a standard technique. Additional applications have been developed in metals, where unexpectedly beneficial effects on surface-sensitive properties have been found, and in insulators, and research in ion implantation has been undertaken for the purpose of developing scientific understanding and technological applications.

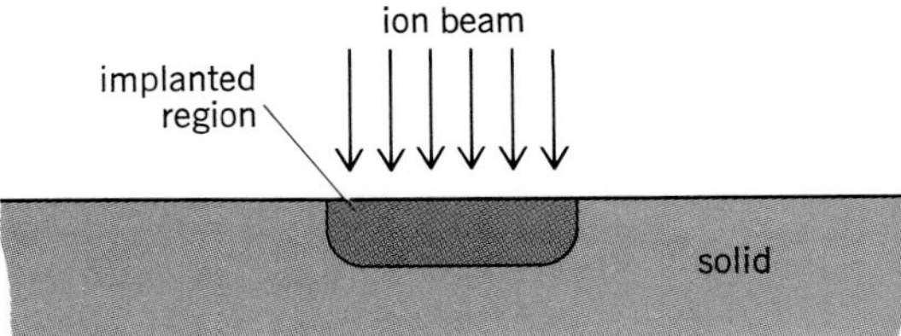


**Fig. 1. Ion implantation into a solid.**

### Implantation Process

Any atom can be implanted into a solid. An ion implantation system is shown schematically in **Fig. 2**. First the atom must be ionized, which is the process of changing the number of electrons associated with an atom and thus leaving it with a net positive or negative charge. This is done in an ion source, usually by a plasma discharge. As the ions are formed, they are continuously extracted from the plasma and accelerated through a voltage difference $V$. This gives each ion an energy $E = qV$, where $q$ is the charge of the ion. Typical acceleration voltages are 10,000 to 500,000 V. The ion beam is then passed through a transverse magnetic field so that the different mass ions of energy $E$ will be deflected by different angles, and in this way ions of particular energy and mass are selected. Varying electric fields are often used to sweep the selected ion beam laterally so that an area can be uniformly implanted with the ions. The region between the ion source and the solid target is kept under vacuum since the ions would travel only very short distances in air. The total number of ions incident on the target is determined by measuring the current to the sample during ion implantation. By integrating this current to obtain the total ion charge and using the known charge per ion, the number of ions implanted in the target can be precisely controlled.

As the energetic ions penetrate a solid, they encounter electrons and atoms with which they have collisions. In this manner they transfer their energy to

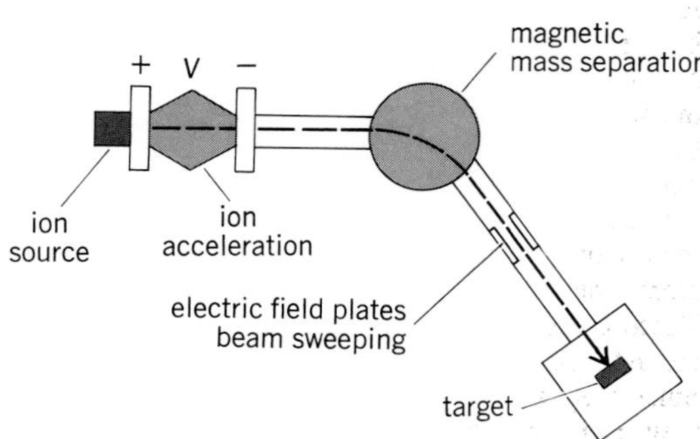


**Fig. 2. Ion implantation system.**

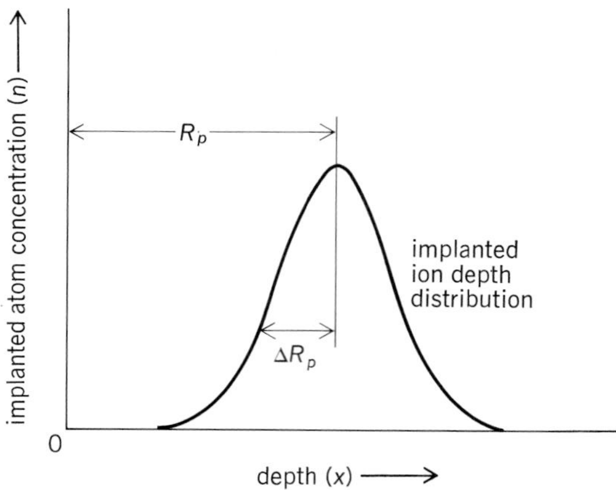


**Fig. 3. Implanted ion depth profile.**

the electrons and atoms in the solid until they finally come to rest. In the process of transferring energy to electrons and atoms, radiation damage is produced in the target. For example, in a single crystal target some atoms will be given enough energy to be knocked off normal lattice sites, and the ion thus leaves a track of damage as it comes to rest. Each of the collision events usually results in a loss of only a small fraction of the ion energy, and in many cases the collisions can be treated as statistically independent events. In this case, the final profile of the ions after they come to rest will be very close to a gaussian distribution in depth. The concentration of implanted atoms $n$ as a function of depth $x$ can then be described by the equation shown, where $N$ is the total number

$$n = \frac{N}{\sqrt{2\pi}\Delta R_p} \exp\left[-\left(\frac{x - R_p}{\sqrt{2}\Delta R_p}\right)^2\right]$$

of atoms implanted per unit surface area (**Fig. 3**). In this description there are two important parameters which describe the final distribution of the ions which have been implanted into the solid: $R_p$ is called the projected range of the ion, and $\Delta R_p$ is referred to as the spread in this projected range. For a given ion energy, ion mass and target material $R_p$ and $\Delta R_p$ have unique values, which can be predicted theoretically. For example, boron ions implanted into silicon with an energy of 100,000 eV would have a projected range of $R_p = 290$ nm and a range spread of $\Delta R_p = 71$ nm. This description of the composition in the implanted region is important in understanding the changes which result in an ion-implanted solid.

## Applications

The ion implantation process changes the chemical composition of the near-surface region of a solid and introduces radiation damage into this region. These changes provide the possibility of modifying an extremely wide range of near-surface physical and chemical properties of solids.

**Semiconductors.** Ion implantation is most widely used in the controlled doping of semiconductors for the microelectronics industry. Here ion implantation is used instead of diffusion to dope semiconductors chemically, for the fabrication of such things as resistors, diodes, and MOS transistors. The advantage of implantation over diffusion is its ability to control very precisely the number of impurities that are introduced, and to form depth distributions of the impurities which may not be easily obtainable by diffusion. A complication introduced by implantation is the introduction of radiation damage, but this has been overcome for most applications by heating the semiconductor material to sufficiently high temperatures. The compatibility with the planar technology used in forming integrated circuits has allowed rapid acceptance of ion implantation in semiconductor device manufacturing. Examples of use include the formation of more accurate and higher-value resistors within smaller areas, and more precise control of the gate voltages of MOS transistors. The selected use of ion implantation to form better devices in terms of operation, speed, reliability, and precision has been an important contribution to the steady advance of microelectronics technology. *See Integrated circuits; Semiconductor; Semiconductor diode; Transistor.*

**Insulators.** Changes in properties of insulators can also be accomplished by ion implantation. One potential application involves a class of materials known as magnetic garnets. Films of these materials are used for storing and moving reversed magnetic domains called magnetic bubbles and can be used for memories in much the same way that certain forms of large silicon integrated circuits are used. The implantation process allows better control of the nature and paths of motion of magnetic bubbles. Implantation in optical materials involving both insulators and semiconductors may find important applications as the technology of integrated optics is developed. Here the processing and handling of light signals is envisioned in much the same way that electrical signals are stored and processed in integrated circuits. *See Computer storage technology.*

**Metals.** Most applications to metals require the introduction of many more ions than for semiconductors, so that the final impurity-atom concentrations may be as high as 1 to 10% of the target, in contrast to semiconductor applications where impurity concentrations in the parts per million are usually desired.

*Samuel T. Picraux*

***Surface-sensitive mechanical properties.*** The friction, wear rates, fatigue life, and cavitation erosion of various metals have been found to be beneficially affected by an ion-implanted alloyed layer to an unexpectedly high degree. It would be anticipated that any improvement in properties would be short-lived because of the limited thickness of the alloyed layer. However, this is not found to be the case, as exemplified by the improvements observed in the wear resistance of steel implanted by various species, such as titanium. The depth of the wear track far exceeds the range of implantation and, in the case of implanted nitrogen in steel, nitrogen is detected at the base of tracks 100 times deeper than the initial ion range. This suggests that deformation-induced transport of the implanted species may be responsible for the persistence of the beneficial effects. However, such a mechanism is not likely to be available for all implanted species in all host materials and, therefore, the persistence of the effects may be very specific. For example, the implantation of boron has no effect on the wear resistance of steel, while the implantation of titanium imparts considerable improvement.

***Oxidation and corrosion resistance.*** Ion implantation is exploited both for potential practical applications to enhance resistance and as a research tool for increasing the understanding of oxidation and corrosion processes. High-temperature oxidation resistance in metallic alloys requires the formation of a stable, adherent oxide film which has a low ionic conductivity (and, preferably, a low electronic conductivity also) and, therefore, a very low growth rate. Such properties are generally obtained by either bulk alloying, for example, of aluminum into copper alloys or chromium into steels, by diffusing the appropriate species into the surface layer at high temperatures, or by coating the part. Ion implantation of a species which enhances the growth of such a film has the following advantages over these conventional techniques. (1) The properties of the alloy are not affected as they are by bulk alloying. (2) Very little of the alloying species is required, thus minimizing the use of expensive or strategic materials. (3) There are no solid solubility limitations to the choice of solute, thereby permitting implantation of species which enhance the oxidation resistance but are normally insoluble. (4) The process is a low temperature one and so is not limited by diffusion rates, segregation of solutes, or annealing of the part. (5) The resultant surface alloy is an integral part of the material and will not suffer from decohesion as do many coatings. (6) The process does not alter the dimension of the part and so may be applied to the finished product.

These advantages of ion implantation also hold for improving aqueous corrosion in which the corrosion rate is determined, not simply by the oxide film, but also by the potential at its surface. Species may be implanted into a base metal, therefore, either to alter the corrosion potential or to provide a passive film. Noble metals such as platinum have been investigated for the former process. For the latter process, tantalum, which is insoluble in iron, can be implanted into the surface, and has been found to be even more effective than chromium in passivating iron and reducing its corrosion rate.

**Other properties.** Other areas in which ion implantation is being used or is being considered for use include the simulation of neutron radiation damage, the formation of catalysts, the synthesis of high-critical-temperature ($T_c$) superconductors, and research on basic metallurgical parameters. In the first application, short exposures of a material to an ion beam can produce damage similar to that produced by many years' exposure to neutrons in a nuclear reactor and, thereby permitting accelerated testing of the response of materials to the nuclear environment. For catalytic action, the impetus for using ion implantation is the potential cost saving of precious metals such as platinum. The efficiency of many chemical reactions such as the electrolysis of water or the oxidation of carbon monoxide is enhanced by various metals, particularly those of the platinum group, platinum being the most effective. Because of its costs and limited availability, there is every incentive to use as little as possible. Laboratory tests indicate that implantation of platinum ions, which uses much smaller amounts of the metal than do coating techniques, provides a surface electrocatalytic activity approaching that of platinum itself. For superconductivity, ion implantation is being used to synthesize metallic compounds, for example, $Nb_3Si$, which do not exist in equilibrium but are theoretically predicted to have high superconducting transistion temperatures. As a research tool, ion implantation makes it possible to study such factors as lattice site location of impurities, defect structures, diffusion characteristics, and solute interactions in alloys which are otherwise impossible to prepare. *See* Superconductivity.

**Prospects** The number and type of engineering components treated by ion implantation are currently very limited. Components include: nitrogen-implanted press tools and mill rolls, to reduce their adhesive wear; nitrogen-implanted dies and molds used in the injection molding of plastic, to reduce their abrasive wear; chromium-implanted ball bearings, to reduce their corrosion, and boron-implanted beryllium bearings, to increase their hardness and reduce wear. Nevertheless, the rapid increase in the understanding of the ion implantation process and its advantages and limitations, coupled with a greater availability of implantation facilities, is being accompanied by its increased exploitation as a competitive industrial process.

*Carolyn M. Preece*

**Bibliography.** G. Dearnaley et al., *Ion Implantation*, 1973; J. K. Hirvonen, *Treatise on Materials Science and Technology*, vol. 18: *Ion Implantation*, 1980; J. W. Mayer, L. Eriksson, and J. A. Davies, *Ion Implantation in Semiconductors*, 1970; F. F. Morehead and B. L. Crowder, Ion implantation, *Sci. Amer.*, 228(4):64–71, 1973; S. T. Picraux, E. P. EerNisse, and F. L. Vook, *Applications of Ion Beams to Metals*, 1974; C. M. Preece and J. K. Hirvonen, *Ion Implantation Metallurgy*, 1980.

## Ionization

The process by which an electron is removed from an atom, molecule, or ion. This process is of basic importance to electrical conduction in gases, liquids, and solids. In the simplest case, ionization may be thought of as a transition between an initial state consisting of a neutral atom and a final state consisting of a positive ion and a free electron. In more complicated cases, a molecule may be converted to a heavy positive ion and a heavy negative ion which are separated.

Ionization may be accomplished by various means. For example, a free electron may collide with a bound atomic electron. If sufficient energy can be exchanged, the atomic electron may be liberated and both electrons separated from the residual positive ion. The incident particle could as well be a positive ion. In this case the reaction may be considerably more complicated, but may again result in a free electron. Another case of considerable importance is the photoelectric effect. Here a photon interacts with a bound electron. If the photon has sufficient energy, the electron may be removed from the atom. The photon is annihilated in the process. Other methods of ionization include thermal processes, chemical reactions, collisions of the second kind, and collisions with neutral molecules or atoms. *See* Electrical conduction in gases.

*Glenn H. Miller*

**Bibliography.** H. D. Beckey, *Field Ionization and Field Desorption Mass Spectrometry*, 1980; E. Nasser, *Fundamentals of Gaseous Ionization and Plasma Electronics*, 1971; H. Rusotti, *The Study of Ionic Equilibria: An Introduction*, 1978; A. H. Von Engel, *Ionized Gases*, 2d ed., 1965.

## Ionization potential

The potential difference through which a bound electron must be raised to free it from the atom or molecule to which it is attached. In particular, the ionization potential is the difference in potential between the initial state, in which the electron is bound, and the final state, in which it is at rest at infinity.

The concept of ionization potential is closely associated with the Bohr theory of the atom. Although the simple theory is applicable only to hydrogenlike atoms, the picture furnished by it conveys the idea quite well. In this theory, the allowed energy levels for the electron are given by the equation below, where $E_n$ is

$$E_n = -k/n^2 \quad n = 1, 2, 3, \ldots$$

the energy of the state described by $n$. The constant $k$ is about 13.6 eV for atomic hydrogen. The energy approaches zero as $n$ becomes infinite. Thus zero energy is associated with the free electron. On the other hand, the most tightly bound case is given by setting $n$ equal to unity. By the definition given above, the ionization potential for the most tightly bound, or ground, state is then 13.6 eV. The ionization potential for any excited state is obtained by evaluating $E_n$ for the particular value of $n$ associated with that state.

The ionization potential for the removal of an electron from a neutral atom other than hydrogen is more correctly designated as the first ionization potential. The potential associated with the removal of a second electron from a single ionized atom or molecule is then the second ionization potential, and so on.

Ionization potentials may be measured in a number of ways. The most accurate measurement is obtained from spectroscopic methods. The transitions between energy states are accompanied by the emission or absorption of radiation. The wavelength of this radiation is a measure of the energy difference. The particular transitions that have a common final energy state are called a series. The series limit represents the transition from the free electron state to the particular state common to the series. The energy associated with the series limit transition is the ionization energy.

Another method of measuring ionization potentials is by electron impact. Here the minimum energy needed for a free electron to ionize in a collision is determined. The accuracy of this type of measurement cannot approach that of the spectroscopic method.

*Glenn H. Miller*

**Bibliography.** A. Beiser, *Concepts of Modern Physics*, 3d ed., 1981; S. Gasiorowicz, *Structure of Matter: A Survey of Modern Physics*, 1979; M. R. Wehr et al., *Physics of the Atom*, 4th ed., 1984.

## IR drop

That component of the potential drop across a passive element (one which is not a seat of electromotive force) in an electric circuit caused by resistance of the element. This potential drop, by definition, is the product of the resistance $R$ of the element and the current $I$ flowing through it. The $IR$ drop across a resistor is the difference of potential between the two ends of the resistor.

In a simple direct-current circuit containing a battery and a number of resistors, the sum of all the $IR$ drops around the circuit (including that of the internal resistance of the battery itself) is equal to the electromotive force of the battery. This is an important circuit theorem useful in the analytic solution of electrical networks. SEE ELECTRICAL RESISTANCE; KIRCHHOFF'S LAWS OF ELECTRIC CIRCUITS; NETWORK THEORY.

*John W. Stewart*

## Josephson effect

The passage of paired electrons (Cooper pairs) through a weak connection (Josephson junction) between superconductors, as in the tunnel passage of paired electrons through a thin dielectric layer separating two superconductors.

**Nature of the effect.** Quantum-mechanical tunneling of Cooper pairs through a thin insulating barrier (on the order of a few nanometers thick) between two superconductors was theoretically predicted by Brian D. Josephson in 1962. Josephson calculated the currents that could be expected to flow during such superconductive tunneling, and found that a current of paired electrons (supercurrent) would flow in addition to the usual current that results from the tunneling of single electrons (single or unpaired electrons are present in a superconductor along with bound pairs). Josephson specifically predicted that if the current did not exceed a limiting value (the critical current), there would be no voltage drop across the tunnel barrier. This zero-voltage current flow resulting from the tunneling of Cooper pairs is known as the dc Josephson effect. Josephson also predicted that if a constant nonzero voltage $V$ were maintained across the tunnel barrier, an alternating supercurrent would flow through the barrier in addition to the dc current produced by the tunneling of unpaired electrons. The frequency $\nu$ of the ac supercurrent is given by Eq. (1),

$$\nu = 2eV/h \tag{1}$$

where $e$ is the magnitude of the charge of an electron and $h$ is Planck's constant. The oscillating current of Cooper pairs that flows when a steady voltage is maintained across a tunnel barrier is known as the ac Josephson effect. Josephson further predicted that if an alternating voltage at frequency $f$ were superimposed on the steady voltage applied across the barrier, the ac supercurrent would be frequency-modulated and could have a dc component whenever $\nu$ was an integral multiple of $f$. Depending upon the amplitude and frequency of the ac voltage, the dc current-voltage characteristic would display zero-resistance parts (constant-voltage steps) at voltages $V$ given by Eq. (2), where $n$ is any integer. Finally, Josephson pre-

$$V = nhf/2e \tag{2}$$

dicted that effects similar to the above would also occur for two superconducting metals separated by a thin layer of nonsuperconducting (normal) metal. In 1963 the existence of the dc Josephson effect was experimentally confirmed by P. W. Anderson and J. M. Rowell, and the existence of the ac Josephson effect was experimentally confirmed by S. Shapiro. SEE TUNNELING IN SOLIDS.

**Theory of the effect.** Superconducting state has been described as a manifestation of quantum mechanics on a macroscopic scale, and the Josephson effect is best explained in terms of phase, a basic concept in the mathematics of quantum mechanics and wave motion. For example, two sine waves of the same wavelength $\lambda$ are said to have the same phase if their maxima coincide, and to have a phase difference equal to $2\pi\delta/\lambda$ if their maxima are displaced by a distance $\delta$. An appreciation of the importance that phase can have in physical systems can be gained by considering the radiation from excited atoms in a ruby rod. For a given transition, the atoms emit radiation of the same wavelength; if the atoms also emit the radiation in phase, the result is the ruby laser.

According to the Bardeen-Cooper-Schrieffer (BCS) theory of superconductivity, an electron can be attracted by the deformation of the metal lattice produced by another electron, and thereby be indirectly attracted to the other electron. This indirect attraction tends to unit pairs of electrons having equal and opposite momentum and antiparallel spins into the bound pairs known as Cooper pairs. In the quantum-mechanical description of a superconductor, all Cooper pairs in the superconductor have the same wavelength and phase. It is this phase coherence that is responsible for the remarkable properties of the superconducting stage. The common phase of the Cooper pairs in a superconductor is referred to simply as the phase of the superconductor. SEE PHASE.

The phases of two isolated superconductors are totally unrelated, while two superconductors in perfect contact have the same phase. If the superconductors are weakly connected (as they are when separated by a sufficiently thin tunnel barrier), the phases can be different but not independent. If $\phi$ is the difference in phase between superconductors on opposite sides of a tunnel barrier, the results of Josephson's calculation of the total current $I$ through the junction can be written as Eq. (3), where $I_0$ is the current due to single

$$I = I_0 + I_1 \sin \phi \tag{3}$$

electron tunneling, and $I_1 \sin \phi$ is the current due to pair tunneling. The time dependence of the phase is given by Eq. (4). In general, the currents $I$, $I_0$, and $I_1$

$$\partial\phi/\partial t = 2\pi(2eV/h) \tag{4}$$

are all functions of the voltage across the junction. For $V = 0$, $I_0$ is zero and $\phi$ is constant. The value of $I_1$ depends on the properties of the tunnel barrier, and the zero-voltage supercurrent is a sinusoidal function of the phase difference between the two superconductors. However, it is not the phase difference that is under the control of the experimenter, but the current through the junction, and the phase difference adjusts to accommodate the current. The maximum value sin $\phi$ can assume is 1, and so the zero-voltage value of

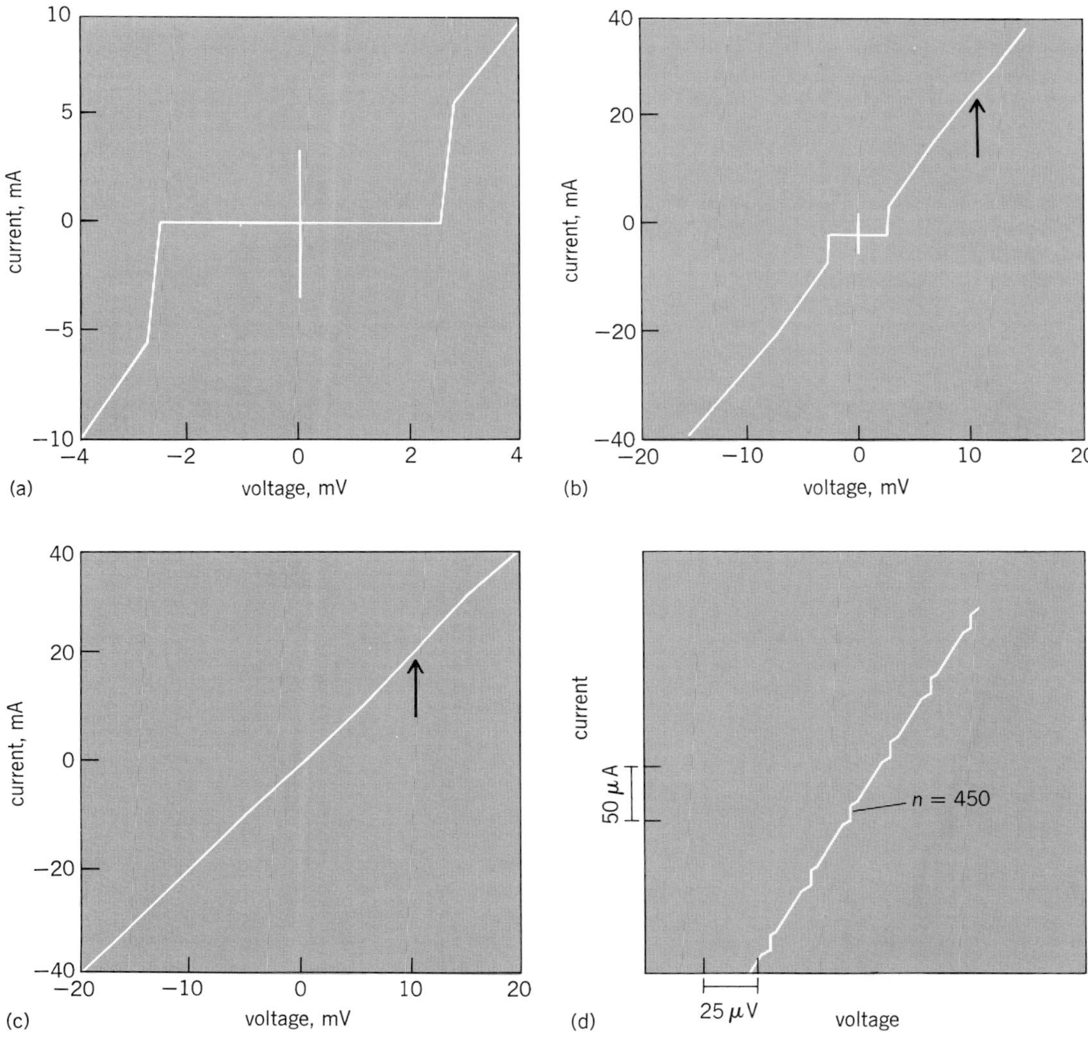


**Fig. 1. DC current-voltage characteristics of lead–lead oxide–lead Josephson tunnel junction at 1.2 K. (*a*) Without microwave power. (*b*) Same characteristic with reduced scale. (c) 11-GHz microwave power applied. (*d*) Expanded portion of c; arrow indicates a constant-voltage step near 10.2 mV corresponding to $n = 450$ in Eq. (2). This voltage is also indicated by arrows in b and c. (*After T. F. Finnegan, A. Denenstein, and D. N. Langenberg, AC-Josephson-effect determination of e/h: A standard of electrochemical potential based on macroscopic quantum phase coherence in superconductors, Phys. Rev. B, 4:1487–1522, 1971*)**

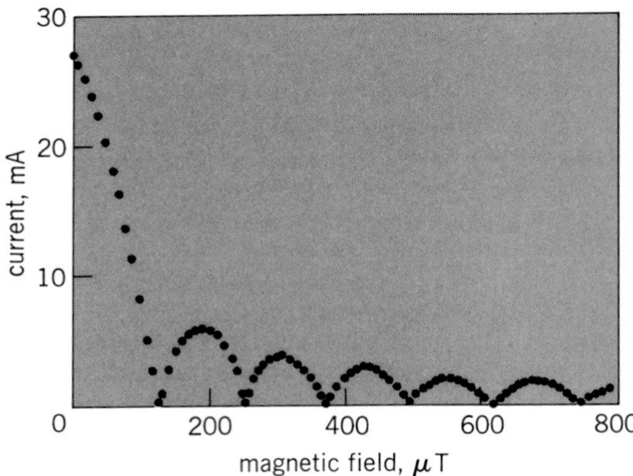


**Fig. 2. Magnetic field dependence of the critical current of a Josephson tunnel junction. Data are for a tin–tin oxide–tin junction at 1.2 K, with the magnetic field in the plane of the barrier. (*After D. N. Langenberg, D. J. Scalapino, B. N. Taylor, The Josephson effects, Sci. Amer., 214(5):30–39, May 1966*)**

$I_1$ is the critical current of the junction.

Integration of Eq. (4) shows the phase changes linearly in time for a constant voltage $V$ maintained across the barrier, and the current through the barrier is given by Eq. (5), where $\phi_0$ is a constant. The su-

$$I = I_0 + I_1 \sin [2\pi(2eV/h)t + \phi_0] \quad (5)$$

percurrent is seen to be an ac current with frequency $2eV/h$. The supercurrent time-averages to zero, so the dc current through the barrier is just the single-electron tunneling current $I_0$.

If the voltage across the junction is $V + v \cos 2\pi ft$, Eqs. (3) and (4) give Eq. (6) for the current. The

$$I = I + I_1 \sin [2\pi(2eV/h)t + \phi_0 + (2ev/hf) \sin 2\pi ft] \quad (6)$$

expression for the supercurrent is a conventional expression in frequency-modulation theory and can be rewritten as expression (7), where $J_n$ is an integer-

$$I_1 \sum_{n=-\infty}^{n=\infty} +(-1)^n J_n(2ev/hf) \times \sin [2\pi(2eV/h)t - 2\pi nft + \phi_0] \quad (7)$$

order Bessel function of the first kind. This expression time-averages to zero except when $V = nhf/2e$, in which case the supercurrent has a dc component given by $(-1)^n I_1 J_n(2ev/hf) \sin \delta_0$. As for the zero-voltage dc supercurrent, the phase difference $\phi_0$ adjusts to accommodate changes in current at this value of $V$, and the dc current-voltage characteristic of a Josephson tunnel junction with and without a microwave-frequency ac voltage is shown in **Fig. 1**. The straightening of the current-voltage characteristic in the presence of microwave power displayed in Fig. 1*c* is due to the phenomenon of photon-assisted tunneling, which is essentially identical to classical rectification for the junction and frequency in question.

Josephson pointed out that the magnitude of the maximum zero-voltage supercurrent would be reduced by a magnetic field. In fact, the magnetic field dependence of the magnitude of the critical current is one of the more striking features of the Josephson effect. Circulating supercurrents flow through the tunnel barrier to screen an applied magnetic field from the interior of the Josephson junction just as if the tunnel barrier itself were weakly superconducting. The screening effect produces a spatial variation of the transport current, and the critical current goes through a series of maxima and minima as the field is increased. **Figure 2** shows the variation of the critical current with magnetic field for a tunnel junction whose length and width are small in comparison with the characteristic screening length of the junction (the Josephson penetration depth, $\lambda_J$). The mathematical function which describes the magnetic field dependence of the critical current for this case is the same function as that which describes the diffraction pattern produced when light passes through a single narrow slit.

**Josephson junctions.** The weak connections between superconductors through which the Josephson effects are realized are known as Josephson junctions. Historically, superconductor-insulator-superconductor tunnel junctions have been used to study the Josephson effect, primarily because these are physical situations for which detailed calculations can be made. However, the Josephson effect is not necessarily a tunneling phenomenon, and the Josephson effect is indeed observed in other types of junctions, such as the superconductor-normal metal-superconductor junction. A particularly useful Josephson junction, the point contact, is formed by bringing a sharply pointed

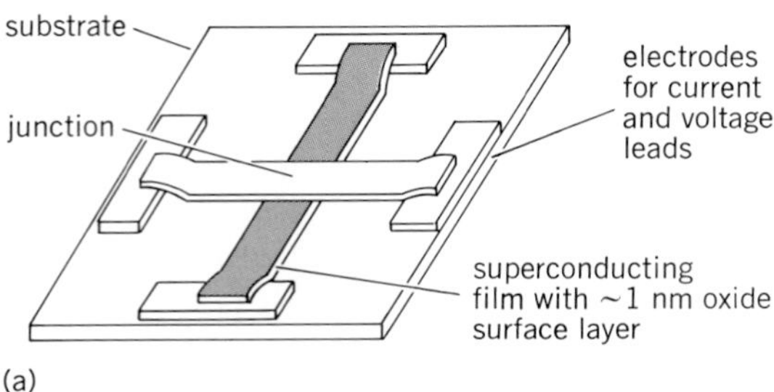


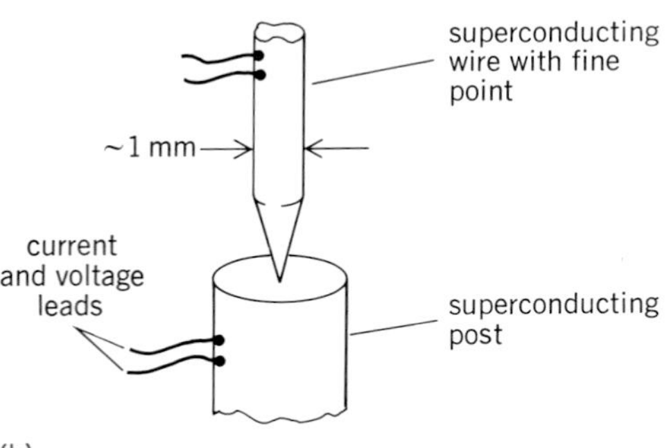


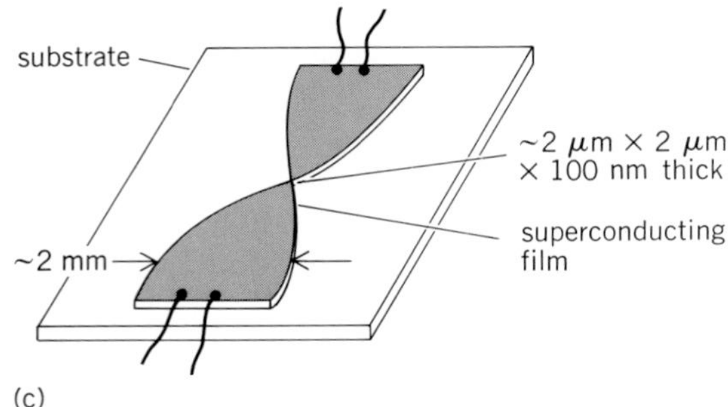


**Fig. 3. Some types of Josephson junctions. (*a*) Thin-film tunnel junction. (*b*) Point contact. (c) Thin-film weak link. (*After E. Burstein and S. Lundqvist, eds., Tunneling Phenomena in Solids, Plenum, 1969*)**

superconductor into contact with a blunt superconductor. The critical current of a point contact can be adjusted by changing the pressure of the contact. The low capacitance of the device makes it well suited for high-frequency applications. Thin-film microbridges form another group of Josephson junctions. The simplest microbridge is a short narrow constriction (length and width on the order of a few micrometers or smaller) in a superconducting film known as the Anderson-Dayem bridge. If the microbridge region is also thinner than the rest of the superconducting film, the resulting variable-thickness microbridge has better performance in most device applications. If a narrow strip of superconducting film is overcoated along a few micrometers of its length with a normal metal, superconductivity is weakened beneath the normal metal, and the resulting microbridge is known as a proximity-effect or Notary-Mercereau microbridge. Among the many other types of Josephson junctions are the superconductor-semiconductor-superconductor and other artificial-barrier tunnel junctions, superconductor-oxide-normal metal-superconductor junctions, and the so-called SLUG junction, which consists of a drop of lead-tin solder solidified around a niobium wire. Some different types of Josephson junctions are illustrated in **Fig. 3**.

The dc current-voltage characteristics of different types of Josephson junctions may differ, but all show a zero-voltage supercurrent, and constant-voltage steps can be induced in the dc characteristics at voltages given by Eq. (2) when an ac voltage is applied. The dc characteristics of a microbridge and a tunnel junction are compared in **Fig. 4**.

**Applications.** The United States legal volt, $V_{NBS}$, is now defined by Eq. (1) through the assigned value given by Eq. (8), and it is maintained at the National

$$2e/h = 483593420 \text{ MHz}/V_{NBS} \tag{8}$$

Bureau of Standards to an accuracy of within a few parts in $10^8$ using the ac Josephson effect; the standards of voltage of most other nations as well as the international volt are similarly defined and maintained. This developed as a natural consequence of extremely precise measurements of $2e/h$ via the Josephson effect, and the recognition that a Josephson junction is a precise frequency-to-voltage converter and that atomic frequency standards are inherently more stable than electrochemical voltage standards.

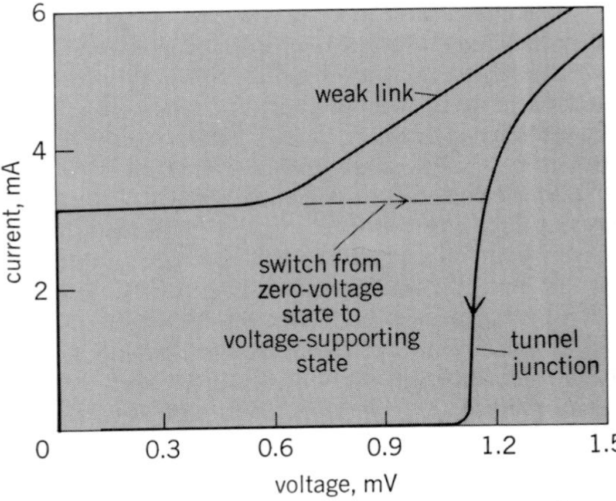


**Fig. 4. DC current-voltage characteristics for a weak link and a tunnel junction. (*After E. Burstein and S. Lundqvist, eds., Tunneling Phenomena in Solids, Plenum, 1969*)**

The Josephson effect permits measurement of absolute temperature: a voltage drop across a resistor in parallel with a Josephson junction causes the junction to emit radiation at the frequency given by Eq. (1), but voltage fluctuations resulting from thermal noise produce frequency fluctuations which depend on absolute temperature. The temperature scale below 1 K is maintained at the National Bureau of Standards via this noise thermometry in conjunction with nuclear-orientation thermometry.

Josephson junctions, and instruments incorporating Josephson junctions, are used in other applications for metrology at dc and microwave frequencies, frequency metrology, magnetometry, detection and amplification of electromagnetic signals, and other superconducting electronics such as high-speed analog-to-digital converters and computers. A Josephson junction, like a vacuum tube or a transistor, is capable of switching signals from one circuit to another; a Josephson tunnel junction is capable of switching states in as little as 6 ps and is the fastest switch known. Josephson junction circuits are capable of storing information. Finally, because a Josephson junction is a superconducting device, its power dissipation is extremely small, so that Josephson junction circuits can be packed together as tightly as fabrication techniques will permit. All the basic circuit elements required for a Josephson junction computer have been developed. It has been predicted that the first computer to be made will fill a cube 5 cm on a side and will have a cycle time of 2 nanoseconds, at least 10 times faster than an equivalent high-speed semiconductor-based computer. *SEE SUPERCONDUCTING DEVICES; SUPERCONDUCTIVITY.*

*Louis B. Holdeman*

***Bibliography.*** E. Burstein and S. Lundqvist, *Tunneling Phenomena in Solids*, 1969; D. N. Langenberg, D. J. Scalapino, and B. N. Taylor, The Josephson effects, *Sci. Amer.*, 214(5):30–39, May 1966; J. Matisoo, The superconducting computer, *Sci. Amer.*, 242(5):50–65, May 1980; L. Solymar, *Superconductive Tunnelling and Applications*, 1972.

## Joule's law

A quantitative relationship between the quantity of heat produced in a conductor and an electric current flowing through it. As experimentally determined and announced by J. P. Joule, the law states that when a current of voltaic electricity is propagated along a metallic conductor, the heat evolved in a given time is proportional to the resistance of the conductor multiplied by the square of the electric intensity. Today the law would be stated as $H = RI^2$, where $H$ is rate of evolution of heat in watts, the unit of heat being the joule; $R$ is resistance in ohms; and $I$ is current in amperes. This statement is more general than the one sometimes given that specifies that $R$ be independent of $I$. Also, it is now known that the application of the law is not limited to metallic conductors.

Although Joule's discovery of the law was based on experimental work, it can be deduced rather easily for the special case of steady conditions of current and temperature. As a current flows through a conductor, one would expect the observed heat output to be accompanied by a loss in potential energy of the moving charges that constitute the current. This loss would result in a descending potential gradient along the conductor in the direction of the current flow, as usually defined. If $E$ is the total potential drop, this loss, by definition, is equal to $E$ in joules for every coulomb of charge that traverses the conductor. The loss conceivably might appear as heat, as a change in the internal energy of the conductor, as work done on the environment, or as some combination of these. The second is ruled out, however, because the temperature is constant and no physical or chemical change in a conductor as a result of current flow has ever been detected. The third is ruled out by hypothesis, leaving only the generation of heat. Therefore, $H = EI$ in joules per second, or watts. By definition, $R = E/I$, a ratio which has positive varying values. Elimination of $E$ between these two equations gives the equation below, which is Joule's law as stated

$$H = RI^2$$

above. If $I$ changes to a new steady value $I'$, $R$ to $R'$, and $H$ and $H'$, then $H' = R'I'^2$ as before. The simplest case occurs where $R$ is independent of $I$. If the current is varying, the resulting variations in temperature and internal energy undoubtedly exist and, strictly speaking, should be allowed for in the theory. Yet, in all but the most exceptional cases, any correction would be negligible.

This phenomenon is irreversible in the sense that a reversal of the current will not reverse the outflow of heat, a feature of paramount importance in many problems in physics and engineering. Thus the heat evolved by an alternating current is found by taking the time average of both sides of the equation. Incidentally, the changes in internal energy, if they were included in the theory, would average out. Hence the equation continues to have a similar form, $\overline{H} = R\overline{I^2}$, for ac applications. SEE OHM'S LAW.

*Lewellyn G. Hoxton / John W. Stewart*

## Junction diode

A semiconductor rectifying device in which the barrier between two regions of opposite conductivity type produces the rectification (**Fig. 1**). Junction diodes are used in computers, radio and television, brushless generators, battery chargers, and electrochemical processes requiring high direct current and low voltage. Lower-power units are usually called semiconductor diodes, and the higher-power units are usually called semiconductor rectifiers. For a discussion of conductivity types, carriers, and impurities SEE SEMICONDUCTOR.

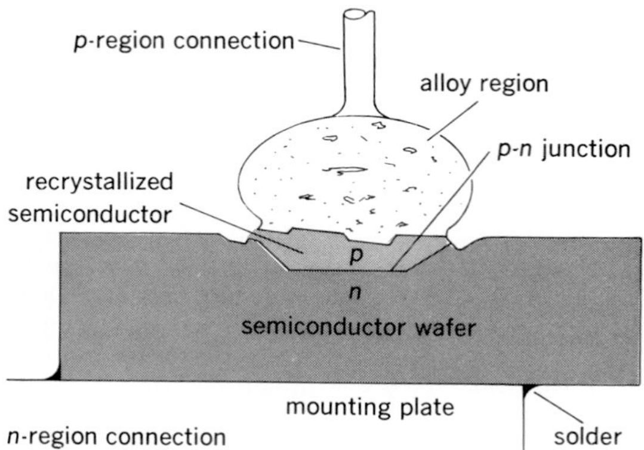


**Fig. 1.** Section of a bonded or fused junction diode.

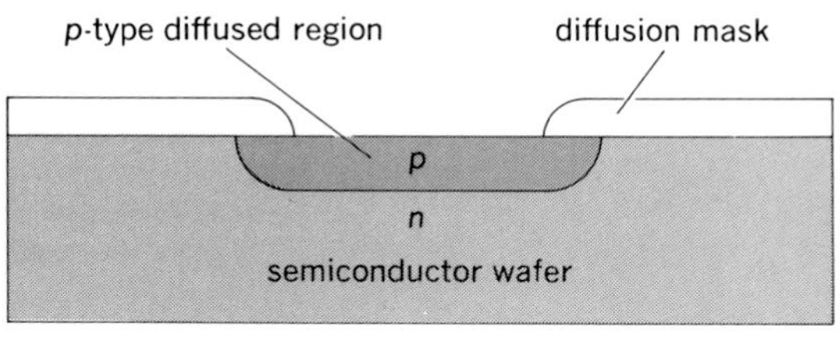


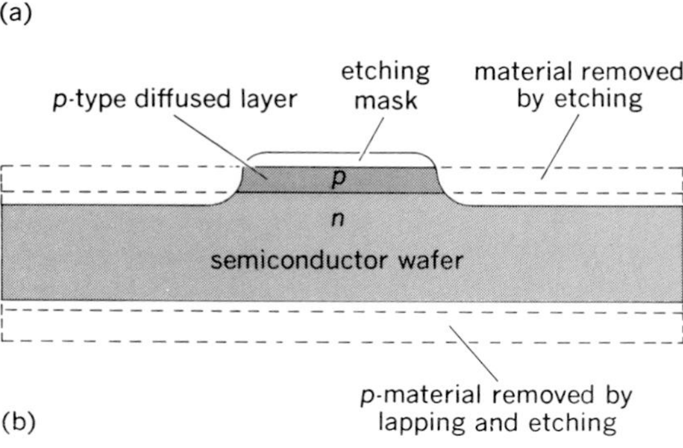


**Fig. 2.** High-speed diffused silicon diodes. (*a*) Mesaless structure. (*b*) Mesa structure.

Junction diodes are classified by the method of preparation of the junction, the semiconductor material, and the general category of use of the finished device. By far the great majority of modern junction diodes use silicon as the basic semiconductor material. Germanium material was used in the first decade of semiconductor diode technology, but has given way to the all-pervasive silicon technology, which allows wider temperature limits of operation and produces stable characteristics more easily. Other materials are the group III–V compounds, the most common being gallium arsenide, which is used where its relatively large band-gap energy is needed. A partial list of silicon types includes the diffused silicon switching diode, alloyed silicon voltage reference diode, epitaxial planar silicon photodiode, and diffused silicon rectifier. Other types include the ion-implanted varactor diode and the gallium arsenide light-emitting diode.

In silicon units nearly all categories of diodes are made by self-masked diffusion, as shown in **Fig. 2*a***. Exceptions are diodes where special control of the doping profile is necessary. In such cases, a variety of doping techniques may be used, including ion implantation, alloying with variable recrystallization rate, silicon transmutation by neutron absorption, and variable-impurity epitaxial growth. The mesa structure shown in Fig. 2*b* is used for some varactor and switching diodes if close control of capacitance and voltage breakdown is required. SEE DETECTOR; ELECTRONIC SWITCH; SEMICONDUCTOR DIODE; RECTIFIER.

**Fabrication methods.** The alloy and mesa techniques are largely historical, but were important in the development of junction diodes. The alloy junction section (Fig. 1) is produced by placing a pill of doped alloying material on the clean flat surface of a properly oriented semiconductor wafer and heating it until the molten alloy dissolves a portion of the semiconductor immediately beneath it. Upon cooling, the dissolved semiconductor, now containing the doping impurity, recrystallizes upon the surface of the undissolved semiconductor, reproducing its crystal structure and creating a *pn* junction at the position marking the limit of the solution of the original wafer.

If such a junction is held at the peak temperature of its alloying cycle for sufficient time to allow diffusion of the alloy impurity beyond the limit of the dissolved semiconductor into the solid semiconductor, the junction produced is called alloy-diffused.

The planar diffused junction section (Fig. 2*a*) is produced in silicon by first polishing the top surface of a large silicon wafer and then oxidizing the surface by heating the wafer at about 1000°C (1800°F) in the presence of wet oxygen. After about 0.5 micrometer of oxide has grown on the surface, the wafer is cooled, and an array of holes is opened in the oxide by high-precision etching geometrically controlled by a photoresist technique. A very heavily doped thin oxide layer is chemically deposited in the holes opened in the oxide. This predeposition step is followed by a drive-in diffusion at a higher temperature, causing the deposited impurity to penetrate the substrate, thereby forming diffused *pn* junctions beneath each hole. Subsequently the individual junctions are separated out of the large wafer by scribing and breaking and are encapsulated as individual diodes. Such planar diffused diodes have relatively high breakdown voltages and low leakage currents. The ends of the junction are automatically protected by the oxide mask so that such diodes show long-term stability. This protection by the oxide is often referred to as passivation.

Planar diodes and planar transistors are used in integrated circuits. The diodes in integrated circuits usually consist of the emitter junction or collector junction of a transistor structure rather than being fabricated as a separate diode. Most discrete diodes are power rectifiers, voltage regulators, varactors, or light-emitting diodes. SEE INTEGRATED CIRCUITS; VARACTOR; VOLTAGE REGULATOR.

The mesa structure (Fig. 2*b*) is produced by diffusing the entire surface of the large wafer and then delineating the individual diode areas by a photoresist-controlled etch that removes the entire diffused area except the island or mesa at each diode site.

Still another method of doping control used in modern diodes is through epitaxially deposited material. In this process the polished wafer is subjected at an elevated temperature to a vapor containing a compound of the semiconductor together with a compound containing the appropriate doping element. These compounds decompose upon contact with the surface of the wafer and cause the semiconductor to grow a layer of doped material on its surface. Under proper conditions of cleanliness and growth rate, the underlying crystal structure is propagated into the growing layer, which is then said to be epitaxial in character. In this way either localized areas or entire surfaces of either conductivity type may be produced. In diode fabrication it is typical to use the epitaxially grown material as a lightly doped layer over the original substrate material of the same conductivity type. The junction is then formed in the lightly doped layer by masked diffusion of the opposite-conductivity-type material. By this means the thickness of the web of lightly doped material immediately beneath the diffusion can be controlled to give both a desired reverse breakdown voltage and a relatively constant capacitance. Forward-bias recovery time can be controlled in a trade-off with reverse breakdown voltage in such a structure.

A method of doping control used when special doping concentration profiles are needed, or when localized doping must be accomplished without self-masking oxide, is ion implantation. At present the largest use of this technique in *pn* junction fabrication is to replace the chemical predeposition step in the planar diffusion process. Here ion implantation gives a much more precise control of the sheet resistivity of the diffusion, and it can be accomplished without opening holes in the protective oxide. Crystal damage is automatically healed during the subsequent drive-in diffusion. SEE ION IMPLANTATION.

**Junction rectification.** Rectification occurs in a semiconductor wherever there is a relatively abrupt change of conductivity type. In any semiconductor the product of the concentrations of the majority and minority current carriers is a temperature-dependent equilibrium constant. The conductivity is proportional to the majority carrier concentration and inversely proportional to the minority-carrier concentration. When a *pn* junction is reverse-biased (*p*-region negative with respect to the *n*-region), the majority carriers are blocked completely by the barrier, and only the minority carriers can flow under the barrier. This minority carrier current is the sum of the individual currents from the *m*- and *p*-regions, and each component is inversely proportional to the conductivity of its region. In addition, there is a thermal regeneration current of minority carriers generated in the depletion region of the reverse-biased junction. In silicon the regeneration current dominates and is about $10^{-3}$ A/m$^2$ at room temperature.

When a *pn* junction is forward-biased (*p*-region positive with respect to the *m*-region), the majority hole and electron distributions can flow into the opposite region because the bias has markedly lowered the barrier. Since electrons flowing into a *p*-region or holes flowing into an *n*-region represent a great increase in minority-carrier concentration, the thermodynamic equilibrium of the holes and electrons is disturbed, and the product of their concentrations increases as the junction is approached. The resistivity of both the *n*- and *p*-type regions is considerably lowered by these excess minority carriers, and the forward current is greater than the current through a geometrically equivalent bar of material containing no *pn* junction.

The electrons in an *n*-type semiconductor are given up to the conduction process by donor impurity atoms which remain as fixed, positively charged centers. Similarly, the holes of a *p*-region are created by the capture of electrons by acceptor impurity atoms which remain as fixed, negatively charged centers. In both cases the space charge of the ionized impurity centers is neutralized by the space charge of the majority carriers.

At a *pn* junction the barrier that keeps majority carriers away consists of a dipole layer of charged impurity centers, positive on the *n*-type side and negative on the *p*-type side. When a reverse bias is applied, the barrier height increases and requires more charge in the dipole layer to produce the required step in voltage. To add to the charge, the layer must widen, because ionized impurities are in fixed positions in the crystal. As the layer widens, the capacitance of the junction decreases since the plates of the capacitor are farther apart. Therefore, a *pn* junction acts as a variable capacitance as well as a variable resistance.

**Optical properties.** When light of sufficient energy is absorbed by a semiconductor, excess minority car-

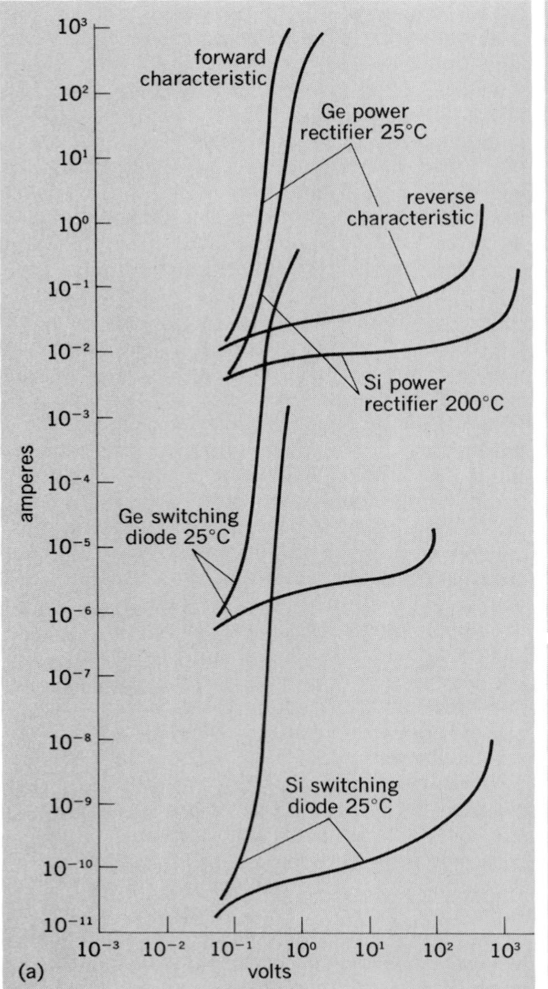


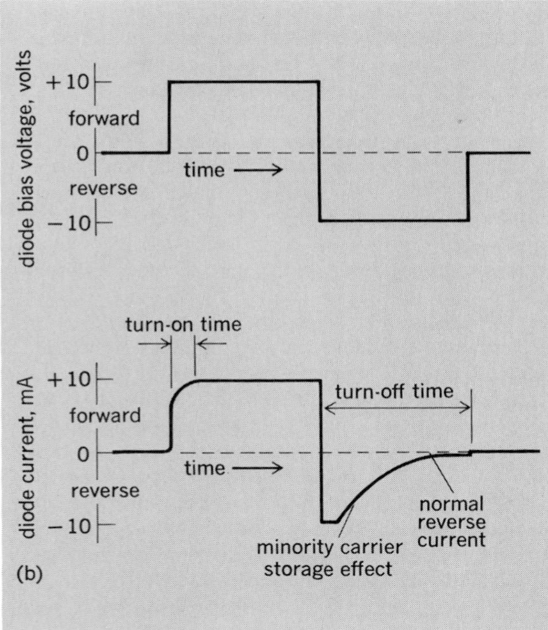


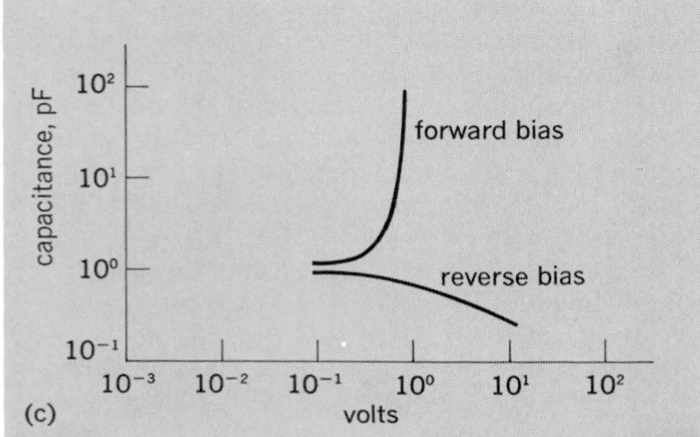


**Fig. 3. Junction diode characteristics. (*a*) Rectification. (*b*) Switching. (*c*) Silicon switching diode capacitance. °F = (°C × 1.8) + 32.**

riers are created. In a *pn* junction device these excess carriers will increase the reverse-bias leakage current by a large factor if they are within diffusion distance of the junction. If the junction is open-circuited, a forward voltage will develop to oppose the diffusion of the excess carriers generated by the light absorption. This photovoltaic response is the basis of the operation of solar cells and most photographic exposure meters. *SEE PHOTOVOLTAIC CELL; PHOTOVOLTAIC EFFECT; SOLAR CELL.*

The inverse of the above effect also exists. When a *pn* junction in a so-called direct-gap semiconductor is forward-biased, the electrically injected excess minority carriers recombine to generate light. This is the basis of light-emitting diodes and injection lasers. Typical direct-gap semiconductors (suitable for light-emitting diodes) are compounds between III and V group elements of the periodic table such as gallium arsenide. *SEE LASER.*

**Characteristics.** Typical rectification, switching, and capacitance characteristics of a junction diode are shown in **Fig. 3**. Rectification characteristics (Fig. 3*a*) show that silicon units provide much lower reverse leakage currents and higher voltage breakdowns and can operate up to 200°C (392°F).

For switching purposes, turn-on and turn-off times are most important (Fig. 3*b*). The turn-on time of a diode is governed by its junction capacitance and is usually short. The turn-off time, usually the critical characteristic, is governed by the time required to remove all of the excess minority carriers injected into the *n*- and *p*-regions while the diode was in the forward-bias state. This is called the minority carrier storage effect, and it is of the order of a few microseconds for good switching diodes. Silicon diodes are usually somewhat superior to germanium units in this respect. The limits of operation of present junction diodes are about 2500 V reverse-standoff voltage and 1500 A forward current in power rectifiers; about 1.0 nanosecond reverse recovery time and 100 picoseconds rise time for fast-switching diodes; a minimum reverse leakage current in a small signal diode is about 0.01 nA.

For further discussion of the properties of *pn* junctions *SEE JUNCTION TRANSISTOR; TRANSISTOR. SEE ALSO POINT-CONTACT DIODE.*

*Lloyd P. Hunter*

**Bibliography.** J. J. Brophy, *Basic Electronics for Scientists*, 1983; S. M. Sze, *Physics of Semiconductor Devices*, 2d ed., 1981; E. S. Yang, *Fundamentals of Semiconductor Devices*, 1978.

## Junction transistor

A transistor in which emitter and collector barriers are formed by *pn* junctions between semiconductor regions of opposite conductivity type. These junctions are separated by a distance considerably less than a minority-carrier diffusion length, so that minority carriers injected at the emitter junction will not recombine before reaching the collector barrier and therefore be effective in modulating the collector-barrier impedance. Junction transistors are widely used both as discrete devices and in integrated circuits. The discrete devices are found in the high-power and high-frequency applications. Junction transistors range in power rating from a few milliwatts to about 300 W, in characteristic frequency from 0.5 to 2000 MHz, and in gain from 10 to 50 dB. Silicon is the most widely used semiconductor material, although germanium is still used for some applications. Junction transistors are applicable to any electronic amplification, detection, or switching problem not requiring operation above 200°C (392°F), 700 V, or 2000 MHz. Not all these limits can be achieved in one device, however. Junction transistors are classified by the number and order of their regions of different conductivity type, by the method of fabricating and structure, and sometimes by the principle of operation. Most modern transistors are fabricated by the silicon self-masked planar double-diffusion technique. The alloy technique and the grown-junction technique are primarily of historical importance. For a general description and definition of terms used here and a description of the mechanism of operation SEE TRANSISTOR.

**Alloy-junction transistors.** Also called fused-junction transistors, these are made in the *pnp* and *npn* forms. The emitter and collector regions are formed by recrystallization of semiconductor material from a solution of semiconductor material dissolved in some suitably doped metal alloy. The major metal of the alloy serves as the solvent for the semiconductor, while the minor element serves as a source for doping impurity in order to render the recrystallized material opposite in conductivity type to the original wafer.

Alloy junctions are abrupt and allow for bidirectional operation. They usually show a low series resistance, and were therefore used in high-power transistors.

**Figure 1** compares several transistor profiles which show how the impurity content varies through the structure. In these profiles $C_p$ is the concentration of the *p*-type impurity; $C_n$ is the concentration of the *n*-type impurity. The net impurity content determines the conductivity type and magnitude. The profile of the alloy transistor shows that there are abrupt changes of impurity concentration at emitter and collector junctions and that the conductivities of emitter and collector regions are therefore high compared to those of the base region. Such a structure shows good emitter-injection efficiency but only moderate collector-voltage rating and relatively high collector capacitance. SEE SEMICONDUCTOR.

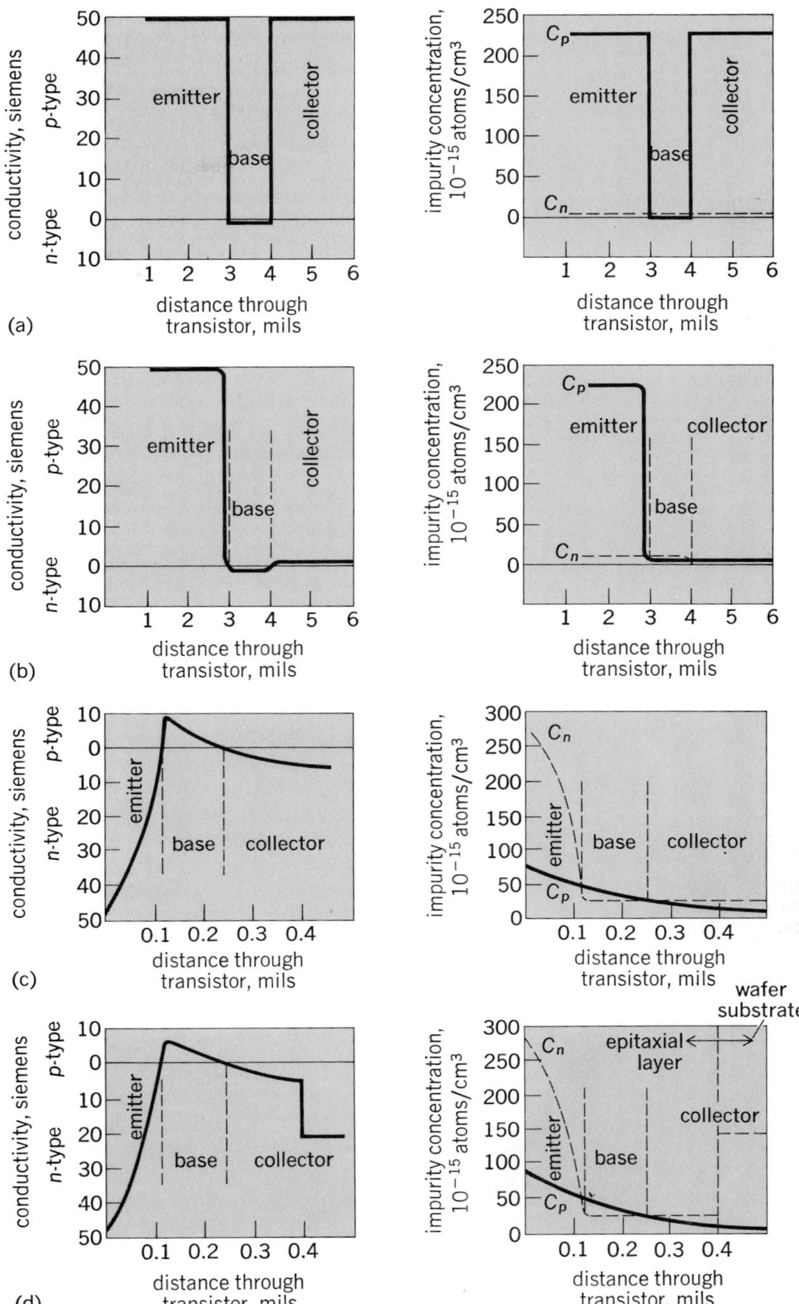


**Fig. 1.** Conductivity and impurity profiles of typical junction transistors. (*a*) *pnp* alloy-junction type. (*b*) *pnp* grown-junction type. (*c*) *npn* double-diffused-junction type. (*d*) *npn* epitaxial double-diffused-junction type. 1 mil = 25.4 μm.

**Grown-junction transistors.** These are made in the *pnp* and *npn* forms, as well as in more complicated forms. There are several variations of the grown-junction technique. The simplest consists of successively adding different types of impurities to the melt from which the semiconductor crystal is being grown.

A semiconductor crystal is usually grown by dipping the end of a seed crystal into molten semiconductor and by arranging the thermal gradients so that new semiconductor solidifies on the end of the seed as it is slowly withdrawn. The solid-liquid interface is roughly a plane perpendicular to the axis of withdrawal. A *pnp* structure can be grown by starting with a *p*-type melt; by adding, at one point in the crystal growth, enough *n*-type impurity to give a slight excess over the *p*-type impurity originally present; and, after growth has continued for a few micrometers, by adding an excess of *p*-type impurity to the melt. The last-grown region will be the emitter region, and the original *p*-type crystal will be the collector region. The impurity profile of such a structure is shown in Fig. 1*b*.

The high-conductivity emitter region gives a good injection efficiency, and the junction between the base and collector regions is gradual enough so that the unit will show a relatively low collector capacitance and a high breakdown voltage. The one disadvantage of this method is that both the collector and base regions show relatively high series resistances.

**Planar diffused epitaxial transistors.** The structure of this transistor is shown in section in **Fig. 2**, and the doping profile through the emitter, base, and collector is shown in Fig. 1*d*. In this structure both collector and emitter junctions are formed by diffusion of impurities from the top surface, as shown in Fig. 2. Using silicon, the structure is formed by growing a diffusion mask of native oxide (silicon dioxide) on the previously polished wafer. A hole is opened in the oxide by a photoresist etch technique (Fig. 2*a*) to define the area of the collector buried layer. For a *p*-type substrate a heavy concentration ($n^+$) of *n*-type impurity such as phosphorus is diffused into the substrate through the opening in the masking oxide. The oxide is etched away, and an epitaxial layer of lightly doped (*n*-) silicon is grown over the entire wafer by vapor decomposition at a temperature low enough to prevent significant diffusion of the $n^+$ material out of the buried layer (Fig. 2*b*). A new oxide layer is grown on the surface of the epitaxial layer, and an opening is etched in it to define the limits of the *p*-type base diffusion (Fig. 2*c*). (This automatically controls the collector junction geometry and capacitance.) The masking oxide is again stripped and regrown for the masking of the $n^+$ diffusion used to form the emitter and collector contact region (Fig. 2*d*). Next the emitter mask is removed, and an impervious layer of oxide is formed over the surface of the crystal. A layer of glass is bonded to the crystal by means of the oxide layer. The glass must match the expansion coefficient of silicon fairly well, and the oxide must be sufficiently impervious to the glass at the bonding temperature to prevent the diffusion of impurities from the glass into the silicon transistor structure. Finally, holes are etched in the glass-oxide structure so that electrical contact can be made to the various regions of the transistor (Fig. 2*e*).

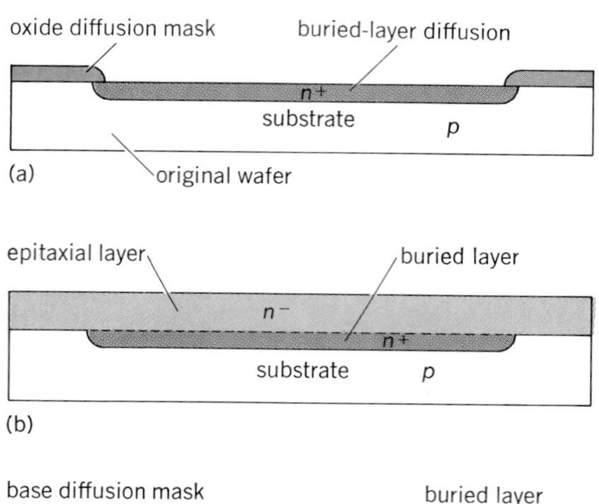


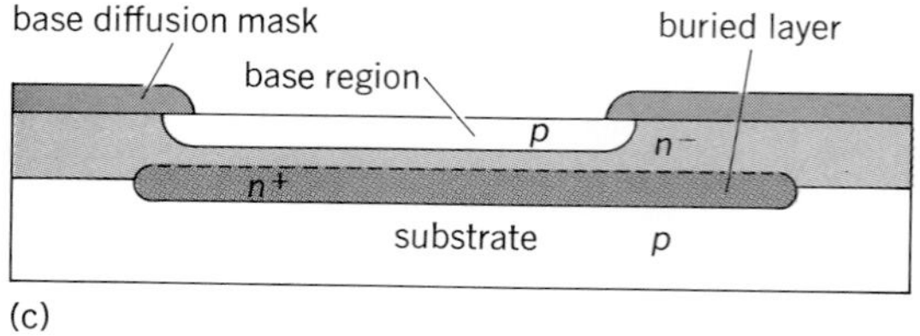


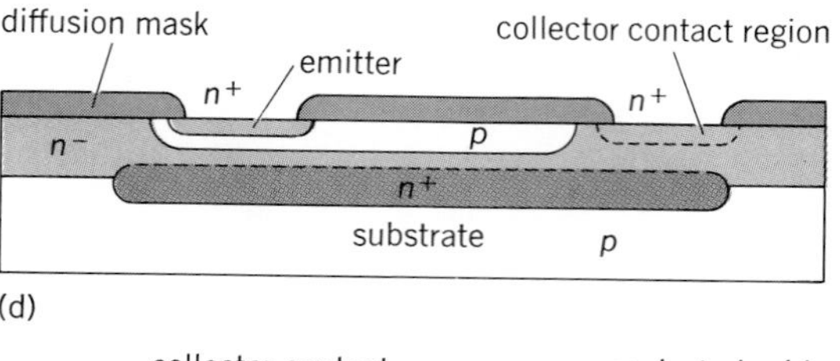


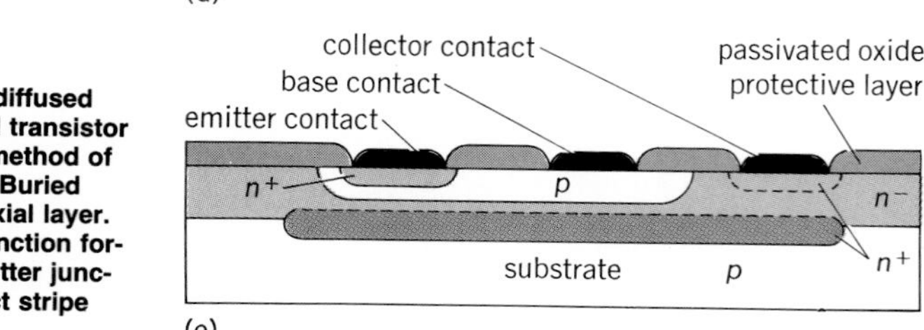


**Fig. 2. Double-diffused planar epitaxial transistor structure and method of fabrication. (*a*) Buried layer. (*b*) Epitaxial layer. (*c*) Collector junction formation. (*d*) Emitter junction. (*e*) Contact stripe placement.**

In modern technology the above-described base and emitter diffusions are carried out in two steps: a predeposition step, in which a very thin layer of heavily doped oxide is chemically deposited over the open surface of the silicon in the hole opened in the masking oxide; and a drive-in diffusion step, in which the deposited dopant is diffused into the silicon at a higher temperature than that used for the predeposition. This typically controls the sheet resistance of the final diffusions to about $\pm 10\%$ of the design value. The forward current-transfer ratio of the transistor is determined by the ratio of these sheet resistances through the medium of the injection efficiency of minority carriers.

The chemical predeposition step is being replaced by ion implantation directly through the oxide. The masking is accomplished by placing a layer of photoresist on top of the oxide. This eliminates the oxide etching step and allows an accurately metered deposition by controlling the time of bombardment and the current of the ion beam. This modification of the process promises to keep the emitter and base region sheet resistivities within about $\pm 1\%$ of the design value. *See* ION IMPLANTATION.

In this transistor, formation of the base region by diffusion from the emitter side produces a steep doping gradient and thereby a strong electric field in the base region. In the typical alloy-junction transistor (uniform base doping) the minority-carrier transport across the base is achieved by a relatively slow diffusion process. In this diffused base type (sometimes called a drift transistor) the base region shows a high conductivity gradient, decreasing from the emitter to the collector (Fig. 1*d*). This conductivity gradient means that the majority-carrier concentration is much greater near the emitter than near the collector. In order to cancel the natural diffusion of majority carriers from the high- to the low-concentration region, an electric field must exist of such a polarity as to tend to drive majority carriers back toward the emitter. This polarity of field then tends to drive minority carriers from the emitter to the collector; when normal bias is applied to the device, excess injected minority carriers will be accelerated across the base by this field.

The buried layer of $n^+$ doped material has very low resistance and acts as a shorting bar between the area immediately beneath the emitter and the area immediately beneath the collector contact stripe, thus maintaining a low collector series resistance even if the $n^-$ material of the epitaxial region is of quite high resistivity. The collector breakdown voltage may be maintained at a reasonably high value and the collector capacitance at a low value by controlling the thickness of the $n^-$ material between the base and the buried layer and by keeping the doping level of the $n^-$ material quite low.

**Mesa transistors.** These transistors minimize the collector capacitance by limiting the collector junction area. This area limitation is achieved by etching away the surrounding material so that the entire transistor structure stands up from the body of the wafer like a small mesa. This structure gave the highest frequency response for many years. It is now replaced by the planar type of structure.

**Power transistors.** These are used in the output stage of an electronic circuit both as switches and as amplifiers. Depending on the load, a high voltage rating, a high current rating, or a high power rating may be required. With any of these, heat dissipation within the device is a serious limitation. In order to obtain high current capability in a power transistor, a large emitter junction area is required. The base-region recombination current produces a lateral voltage drop between the center of the emitter area and the center of the base contact area in a planar device. This voltage tends to bias the center of the emitter area to off and concentrate the injection current at the periphery of the emitter. Modern silicon power transistors minimize this effect by using emitter junctions with a large perimeter-to-area ratio, usually in the form of a multipronged fork with base contacts interdigitated between the tines. This preserves high forward current-transfer ratio to large values of emitter current. SEE CONTROLLED RECTIFIER.

**Unijunction transistor.** This device is really a diode in which the resistance of a portion of the base region is modulated by minority carriers injected by forward-biasing its single junction. Its structure typically consists of a lightly doped base region with ohmic contacts at opposite ends. The single junction is formed over a narrow range near the center of the base region by a shallow diffusion of heavily doped material of the opposite conductivity type. If a bias current is set up from end to end in the base, the potential at the junction can be set at a desired reverse bias relative to ground. If a signal is applied to the junction electrode, the device will turn on when the signal exceeds the original reverse-bias potential of the base at that point. Once forward-biased, the junction injects sufficient minority carriers into the base to short the region beneath the junction to the ground end of the base, and the device remains conducting until reset, either by the base bias or by the emitter signal. These devices show a typical negative resistance characteristic and are used for timing, control, and sensing circuits.

**Summary.** Silicon planar passivated transistors show a wide range of performance with characteristic frequencies up to 2000 MHz, voltage ratings of 12–700 V and power dissipation ratings of 100 mW–300 W. The highest-frequency devices range up to 4000 MHz. Silicon planar technology is used in fabricating integrated circuit chips. The general form of the transistor structure displayed in Fig. 2 is used in integrated circuits. Such a structure is used for diodes as well as transistors since, for example, it is necessary only to connect the base and collector contacts to use the collector junction as a diode. SEE INTEGRATED CIRCUITS.

Lloyd P. Hunter

**Bibliography.** J. J. Brophy, *Basic Electronics for Scientists*, 4th ed., 1983; L. P. Hunter, *Handbook of Semiconductor Electronics*, 3d ed., 1970; S. M. Sze, *Physics of Semiconductor Devices*, 2d ed., 1981; E. S. Yang, *Fundamentals of Semiconductor Devices*, 1978.

## Kelvin bridge

A specialized version of the Wheatstone bridge network designed to eliminate, or greatly reduce, the effect of lead and contact resistance and thus permit accurate measurement of low resistance. The circuit shown in the figure accomplishes this by effectively placing relatively high-resistance-ratio arms in series with the potential leads and contacts of the low-resistance standards and the unknown resistance. In this circuit $R_A$ and $R_B$ are the main ratio resistors, $R_a$ and $R_b$ the auxiliary ratio, $R_x$ the unknown, $R_s$ the standard, and $R_y$ a heavy copper yoke of low resistance connected between the unknown and standard resistors.

By applying a delta-wye transformation to the network consisting of $R_a$, $R_b$, and $R_y$, the equivalent Wheatstone bridge network shown in the **illustration** is obtained, where Eqs. (1) hold. By an analysis similar to that for the Wheatstone bridge, it can be shown that for a balanced bridge Eq. (2) holds. If Eq. (3) is valid, the second term of Eq. (2) is zero, the measurement is independent of $R_y$, and Eq. (4) is obtained.

$$R'_s = \frac{R_y R_a}{R_y + R_a + R_b} \qquad R'_x = \frac{R_y R_b}{R_y + R_a + R_b} \qquad R'_G = \frac{R_a R_b}{R_y + R_a + R_b} \tag{1}$$

$$R_x = \frac{R_B}{R_A} R_s + R_y \left(\frac{R_b}{R_a + R_b + R_y}\right)\left(\frac{R_B}{R_A} - \frac{R_b}{R_a}\right) \tag{2}$$

$$\frac{R_B}{R_A} = \frac{R_b}{R_a} \tag{3}$$

$$R_x = \frac{R_B}{R_A} R_s \tag{4}$$

As with the Wheatstone bridge, the Kelvin bridge for routine engineering measurements is constructed using both adjustable ratio arms and adjustable standards. However, the ratio is usually continuously adjustable over a short span, and the standard is adjustable in appropriate steps to cover the required range. SEE WHEATSTONE BRIDGE.

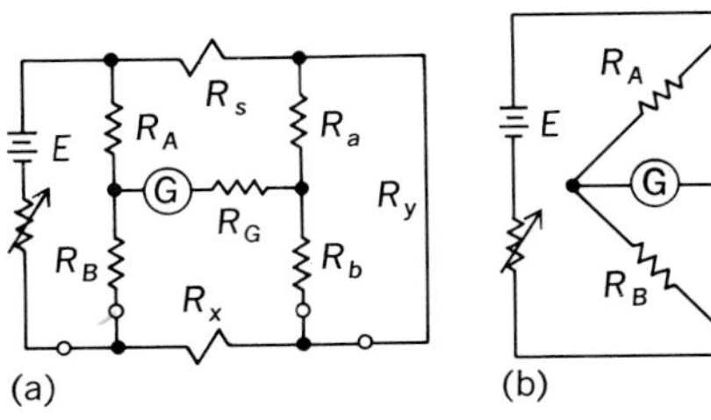


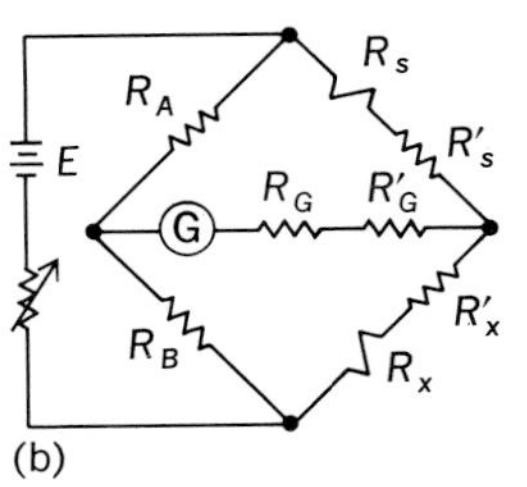


Kelvin bridge. (*a*) Actual circuit. (*b*) Equivalent Wheatstone bridge circuit.

**Sensitivity.** The Kelvin bridge sensitivity can be calculated similarly to the Wheatstone bridge. The open-circuit, unbalance voltage appearing at the detector terminals may be expressed, to a close degree of approximation, as in Eq. (5).

$$e = E \frac{r}{(r+1)^2} \frac{\Delta R_x}{R_x + R_y \left(\frac{r}{r+1}\right)} \quad (5)$$

The unbalance detector current for a closed detector circuit may be expressed as in Eq. (6).

$$I_G = \frac{E\left(\frac{\Delta R_x}{R_x}\right)}{\frac{R_G}{r/(r+1)^2} + R_A + R_B + R_a + R_b} \quad (6)$$

The Kelvin bridge requires a power supply capable of delivering relatively large currents during the time a measurement is being made. The total voltage applied to the bridge is usually limited by the power dissipation capabilities of the standard and unknown resistors.

**Errors.** Kelvin bridge resistance-measurement errors are caused by the same factors as for the Wheatstone bridge. However, additional sources of error, as implied by the second term of Eq. (2), must be evaluated since these factors will seldom be reduced to zero. For minimum error the yoke resistance should be made as low as possible by physically placing the commonly connected current terminals of the unknown and standard as close together as possible and connecting with a low-resistance lead.

The ratio resistors each include not only the resistance of the resistors but also that of the interconnecting wiring and external leads and the contact resistance of the potential circuit contacts. The external leads are most likely to cause errors, and they should therefore be of the same resistance so that Eq. (3) will be fulfilled as nearly as possible. In addition, they should be relatively short, since the addition of a large resistance (long leads) will introduce an error in the calibrated ratio $R_B/R_A$. For precise measurements, trimmer adjustments are required in the ratio-arm circuits and provision is made to connect the bridge resistors into two different Wheatstone bridge configurations. By successively balancing first the Kelvin network and then each of the Wheatstone networks, these additive errors are virtually eliminated. SEE BRIDGE CIRCUIT; RESISTANCE MEASUREMENT.

*Charles E. Applegate*

## Kirchhoff's laws of electric circuits

Fundamental natural laws dealing with the relation of currents at a junction and the voltages around a loop. These laws are commonly used in the analysis and solution of networks. They may be used directly to solve circuit problems, and they form the basis for network theorems used with more complex networks.

In the solution of circuit problems, it is necessary to identify the specific physical principles involved in the problem and, on the basis of them, to write equations expressing the relations among the unknowns. Physically, the analysis of networks is based on Ohm's law giving the branch equations, Kirchhoff's voltage law giving the loop voltage equations, and Kirchhoff's current law giving the node current equations. Mathematically, a network may be solved when it is possible to set up a number of independent equations equal to the number of unknowns. SEE CIRCUIT (ELECTRICITY); NETWORK THEORY.

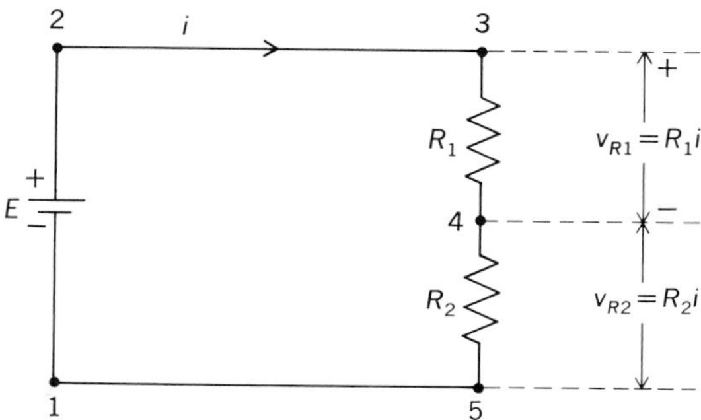

Fig. 1. Simple loop to show Kirchhoff's voltage law.

When writing the independent equations, current directions and voltage polarities may be chosen arbitrarily. If the equations are written with due regard for these arbitrary choices, the algebraic signs of current and voltage will take care of themselves.

**Kirchhoff's voltage law.** One way of stating Kirchhoff's voltage law is: "At each instant of time, the algebraic sum of the voltage rise is equal to the algebraic sum of the voltage drops, both being taken in the same direction around the closed loop."

The application of this law may be illustrated with the circuit in **Fig. 1**. First, it is desirable to consider the significance of a voltage rise and a voltage drop, in relation to the current arrow. The following definitions are illustrated by Fig. 1.

A voltage rise is encountered if, in going from 1 to 2 in the direction of the current arrow, the polarity is from plus to minus. Thus, $v_{R1} = R_1 i$ is a voltage drop from 3 to 4. The application of Kirchhoff's voltage law gives the loop voltage, Eq. (1).

$$E = v_{R1} + v_{R2} = R_1 i + R_2 i \quad (1)$$

In the network of **Fig. 2** the voltage sources have the same frequency. The positive senses for the branch currents $I_R$, $I_L$, and $I_C$ are chosen arbitrarily, as are the loop currents $I_1$ and $I_2$. The voltage equations for loops 1 and 2 can be written using instantaneous branch currents, instantaneous loop currents, phasor branch currents, or phasor loop currents.

The loop voltage equations are obtained by applying Kirchhoff's voltage law to each loop as follows.

By using instantaneous branch currents, Eqs. (2) and (3) may be obtained. By using instantaneous

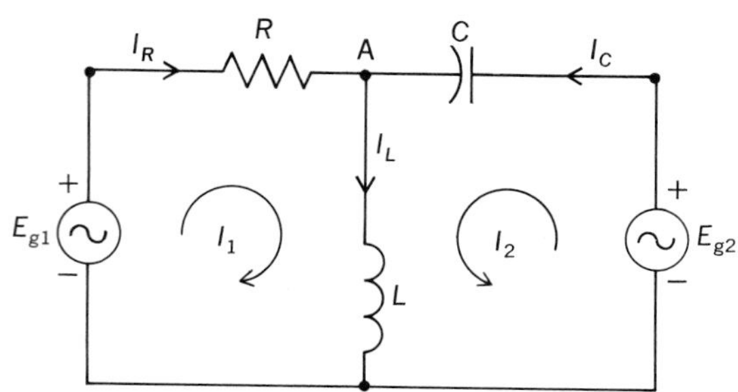

Fig. 2. Two-loop network demonstrating the application of Kirchhoff's voltage law.

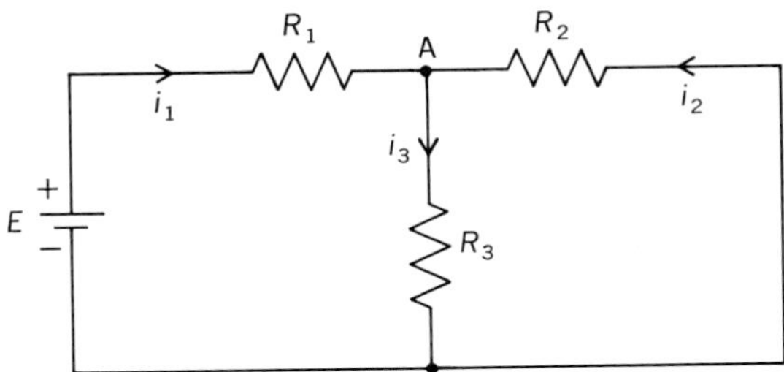

Fig. 3. Circuit demonstrating Kirchhoff's current law.

$$e_{g1} = Ri_R + L\frac{di_L}{dt} \tag{2}$$

$$e_{g2} = \frac{1}{C}\int i_C dt + L\frac{di_L}{dt} \tag{3}$$

loop currents, Eqs. (4) and (5) are obtained. Equations

$$e_{g1} = Ri_1 + L\frac{d(i_1 + i_2)}{dt} \tag{4}$$

$$e_{g2} = \frac{1}{C}\int i_2\, dt + L\frac{d(i_2 + i_1)}{dt} \tag{5}$$

(6) and (7) are obtained by using phasor branch cur-

$$\mathbf{E}_{g1} = R\mathbf{I}_R + j\omega L\mathbf{I}_L \tag{6}$$

$$\mathbf{E}_{g2} = -j\frac{1}{\omega C}\mathbf{I}_C + j\omega L\mathbf{I}_L \tag{7}$$

rents. By using phasor loop currents, Eqs. (8) and (9) may be obtained.

$$\mathbf{E}_{g1} = R\mathbf{I}_1 + j\omega L(\mathbf{I}_1 + \mathbf{I}_2) \tag{8}$$

$$\mathbf{E}_{g2} = -j\frac{1}{\omega C}\mathbf{I}_2 + j\omega L(\mathbf{I}_2 + \mathbf{I}_1) \tag{9}$$

**Kirchhoff's current law.** Kirchhoff's current law may be expressed as follows: "At any given instant, the sum of the instantaneous values of all the currents flowing toward a point is equal to the sum of the instantaneous values of all the currents flowing away from the point."

The application of this law may be illustrated with the circuit in **Fig. 3**. At node *A* in the circuit in Fig. 3, the current is given by Eq. (10).

$$i_1 + i_2 = i_3 \tag{10}$$

The current equations at node *A* in Fig. 2 can be written by using instantaneous branch currents or phasor branch currents.

By using instantaneous branch currents, Eq. (11) is obtained.

$$i_R + i_C = i_L \tag{11}$$

By using phasor branch currents, Eq. (12) is obtained.

$$\mathbf{I}_R + \mathbf{I}_C = \mathbf{I}_L \tag{12}$$

SEE DIRECT-CURRENT CIRCUIT THEORY.

K. Y. Tang / Robert T. Weil

## Klystron

An evacuated electron-beam tube in which an initial velocity modulation imparted to electrons in the beam results subsequently in density modulation of the beam. A klystron is used either as an amplifier in the microwave region or as an oscillator. For use as an amplifier, a klystron receives microwave energy at an input cavity through which the electron beam passes. The microwave energy modulates the velocities of electrons in the beam, which then enters a drift space. Here the faster electrons overtake the slower to form bunches. In this manner, the uniform current density of the initial beam is converted to an alternating current. The bunched beam with its significant component of alternating current then passes through an output cavity to which the beam transfers its ac energy. SEE MICROWAVE.

**Klystron amplifier.** In a typical klystron (**Fig. 1**), a stream of electrons from a concave thermionic cathode is focused into a smaller cylindrical beam by the converging electrostatic fields between the anode, cathode, and focusing electrode. The beam passes through a hole in the anode and enters a magnetic field parallel to the beam axis. The magnetic field holds the beam together, overcoming the electrostatic repulsion between electrons which would otherwise make the beam spread out rapidly. The electron beam goes through the cavities of the klystron in sequence, emerges from the magnetic field, spreads out, and is stopped in a hollow collector where the remaining ki-

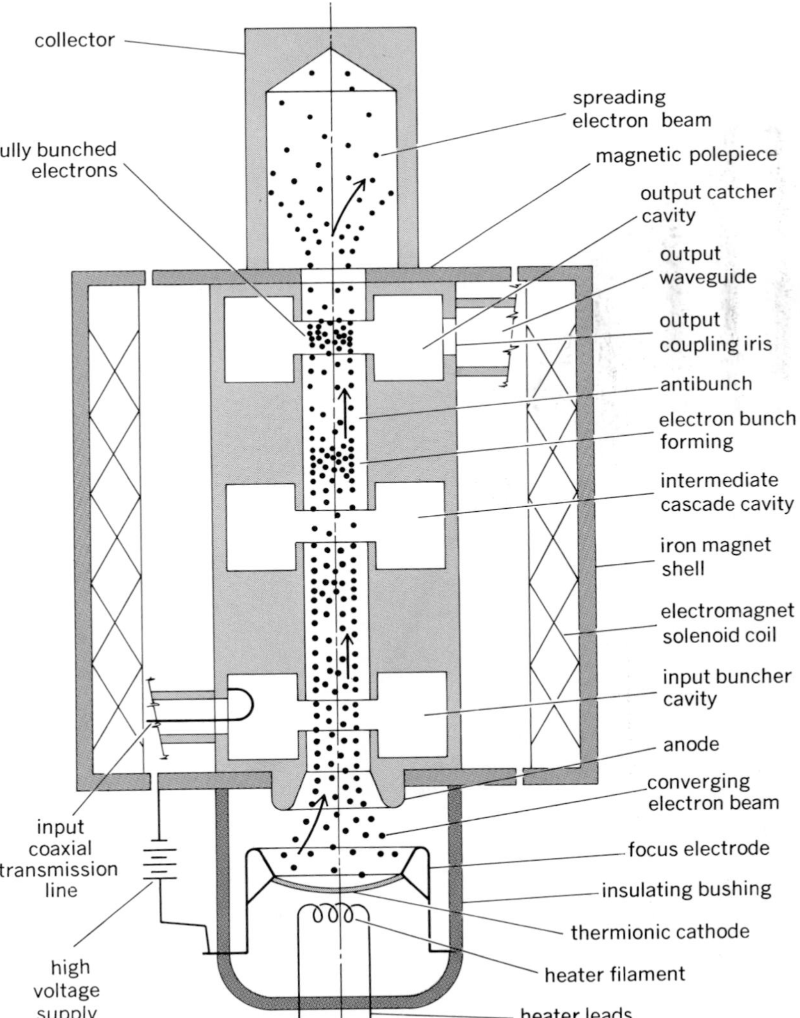

Fig. 1. Cross section of cascade klystron amplifier. (*Varian Associates*)

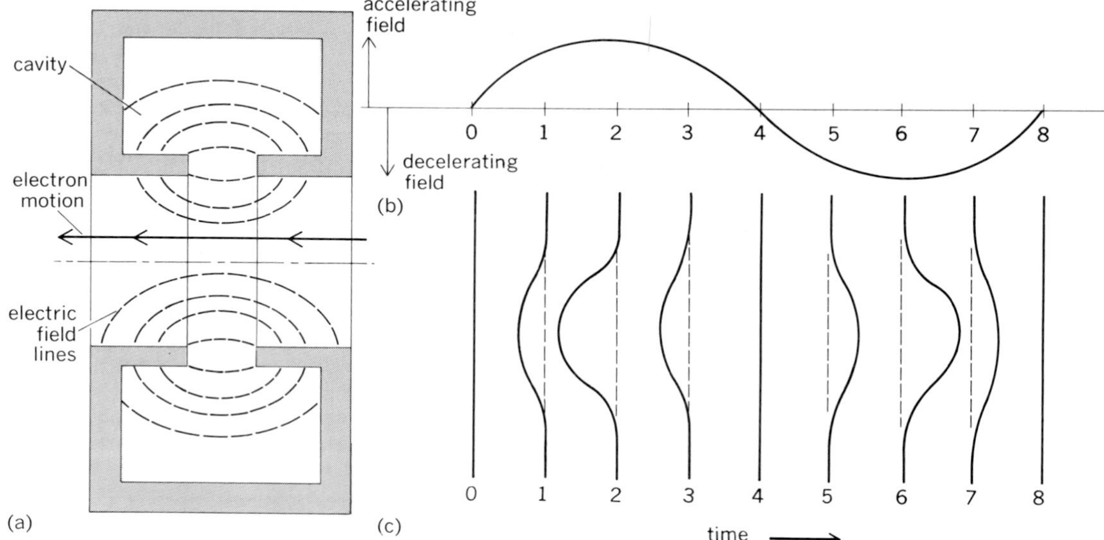


**Fig. 2. Cavity concentrates electric field between the reentrant noses. As field varies sinusoidally with time, an electron crossing in the gap between the noses experiences an electric field whose strength and direction depend on the instantaneous phase of the field. (*a*) Map of instantaneous field. (*b*) Cycle variation of field. (*c*) Profile of field on the axis at various times in the cycle. (*Varian Associates*)**

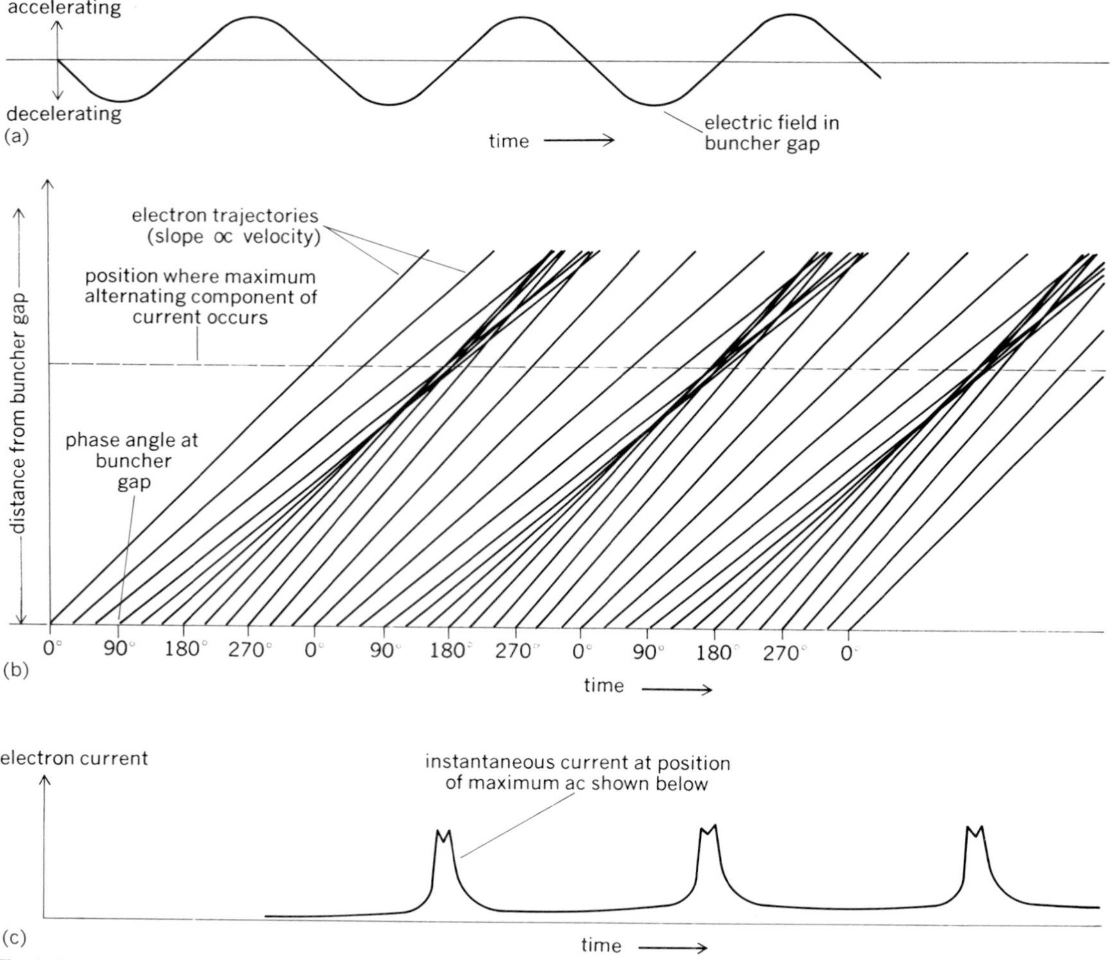


**Fig. 3. Bunching the electron stream. (*a*) As the electric field varies periodically, electrons traversing the cavity are speeded up or slowed down. (*b*) Distance-versus-time lines graph the gradual formation of bunches. (*c*) Current passing a fixed point becomes periodic, that is, it becomes alternating. (*Varian Associates*).**

netic energy of the electrons is dissipated as heat. *SEE ELECTRON MOTION IN VACUUM*.

The signal wave to be amplified is introduced into the first, or buncher, cavity through a coaxial transmission line. This hollow metal cavity is a resonant circuit, analogous to the familiar inductance-capacitance combination, with the electric field largely concentrated in the reentrant noses so that the highest voltage occurs between them. The inductance may be considered as a single-turn conductor formed by the outer metal walls. In Fig. 1 the current in the center conductor of the input transmission line flows through a loop inside the cavity and back to the outer conductor. The magnetic flux generated in the loop links through the cavity inductance, as in a transformer. At the resonant frequency of the cavity, the voltage across the reentrant section through which the electron beam passes is built up by the cavity configuration to 10–100 times the voltage in the input line. *SEE CAVITY RESONATOR*.

**Figure 2** shows the pattern of the electric field in the cavity and how it varies cyclically with time. As electrons pass through the gap in which the cavity field is concentrated (Fig. 2*a*), they are accelerated or decelerated (Fig. 2*b*), depending on the instantaneous direction of the field.

**Figure 3** illustrates graphically the effect of these velocity changes. Each slanted line represents the flight of an electron as a function of time measured in electrical degrees as the electron travels from the buncher gap. The slope of a line is thus the velocity of that electron. The velocities leaving the buncher vary sinusoidally with time, as determined by the instantaneous field. The horizontal broken line represents a fixed point beyond the buncher. The flow of electrons past this point is given by the time sequence in which the electron paths cross the broken line. Figure 3 shows how the electrons have gathered into bunches. The rate of current flow is now periodic with time so that the current has an alternating component.

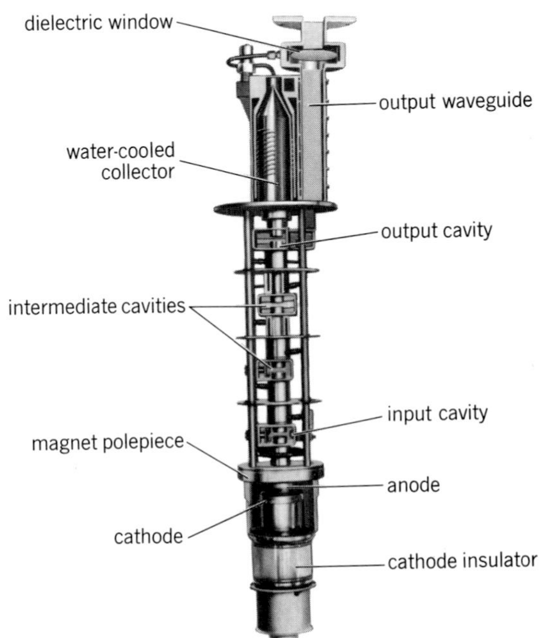


**Fig. 4. Cutaway view of four-cavity amplifier. (*Varian Associates*)**

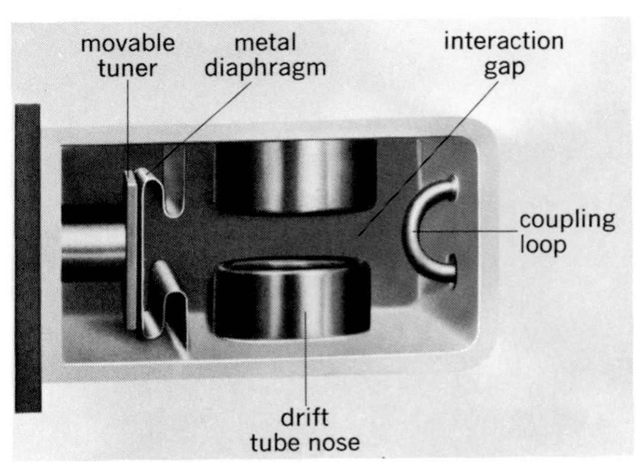


**Fig. 5. Detail of input cavity for four-cavity klystron amplifier of Fig. 4. (*Varian Associates*)**

When the bunched beam passes through a second cavity, its space charge induces in the walls of this cavity an alternating current of opposite sign to the electron current. The cavity is tuned to the input frequency so that it has a high resonant impedance; the induced current flowing through this impedance generates voltage in the cavity.

In Fig. 1 the second cavity is not coupled to any outside circuits. Voltage built up here by the beam current produces further velocity modulation in the beam. The resulting alternating current component is about 10 times greater than the initial current. More of these uncoupled cascade cavities can be added for increased amplification.

The final output cavity is coupled into a transmission line (a waveguide in Fig. 1) which carries off the generated power to its useful destination. Because the cavity is tuned to resonance, its reactance is canceled. The induced current flowing through its pure resistive impedance generates in-phase voltage in the direction opposing the current flow. Thus the field in the gap is at its maximum decelerating value at the time a bunch of electrons passes. Most of the electrons therefore are slowed down, and there is a net transfer of kinetic energy of the electrons into electromagnetic energy in the cavity. Klystron amplifiers are used in transmitters for radar and one-way radio communication, for driving particle accelerators, and for dielectric heating. The useful range of frequencies is from 400 MHz to 40 GHz. Power levels range from a few watts up to 400 kW of continuous power or 20 MW for short pulses. Amplification is about 10 dB for a two-cavity tube. With more cavities, gains up to 60 dB are practical.

**Figure 4** shows the construction of a four-cavity amplifier rated at 2 MW pulsed output at 2.8 GHz. It operates in a solenoid magnet, as in Fig. 1. The cavities are tuned to the operating frequency by moving one flexible inner wall of the box-shaped cavity, changing its volume and its effective inductance. In **Fig. 5** the details of the input cavity are enlarged.

**Reflex oscillator.** Klystrons may be operated as oscillators by feeding some of the output back into the input circuit. More widely used is the reflex oscillator in which the electron beam itself provides the feedback. **Figure 6** illustrates the operation. The beam is focused through a cavity, as in the amplifier. No magnetic field is needed to keep the beam focused because the total travel distance is short and the amount of natural spreading is tolerable. The cavity

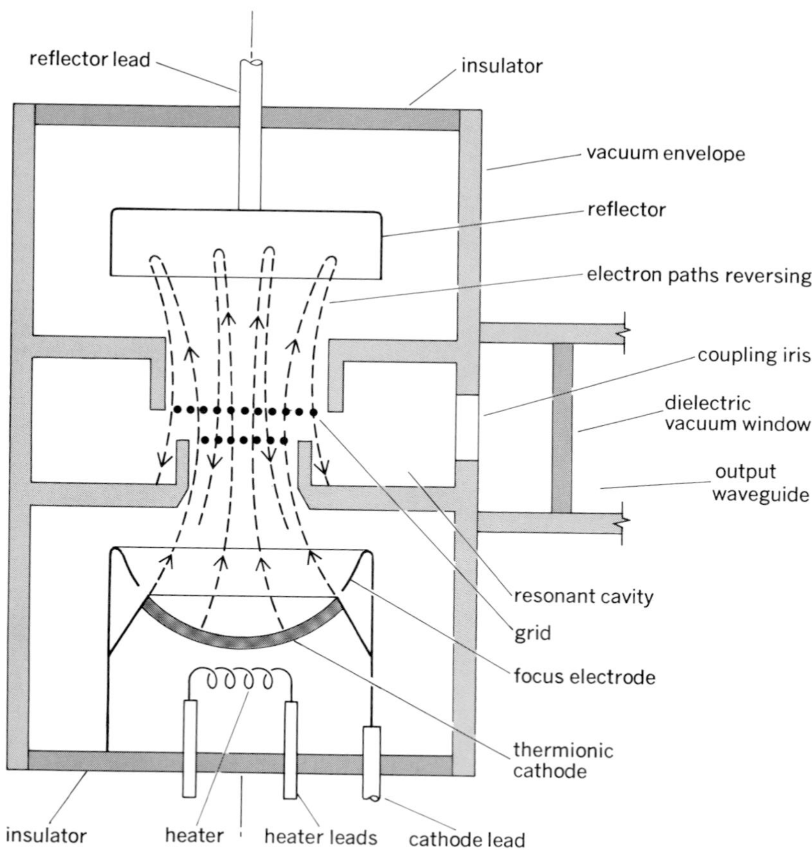


**Fig. 6. Schematic cross section of reflex oscillator. (*Varian Associates*)**

usually has grids with open mesh through which the electrons can penetrate. The purpose of the grids is to concentrate the electric field in a short space so that the field can interact with a slow, low-voltage electron beam.

In the cavity the beam is velocity-modulated as in the amplifier. Leaving the cavity, the beam enters a region of dc electric field opposing its motion, produced by a reflector electrode operating at a potential negative with respect to the cathode. The electrons do not have enough energy to reach the electrode, but are reflected in space and return to pass through the cavity again. The points of reflection are determined by electron velocities, the faster electrons going farther against the field and hence taking longer to get back than the slower ones.

A trajectory plot for the reflex oscillator is shown in **Fig. 7**. In a uniform retarding field the space-versus-time curves are parabolas. As in Fig. 3, velocity modulation produces bunches of electrons. If the voltages are adjusted so that the average time to return is $n + 3/4$ cycles ($n$ = integer), the bunches cross the cavity when the alternating field is maximum in the decelerating direction. This transfers beam energy to the cavity.

Because the reflex klystron has only one cavity, it is easy to tune its frequency with a single adjustment. Power output is from 10 mW to a few watts. Reflex oscillators are used as signal sources from 3 to 200 GHz, as the transmitter tubes in line-of-sight radio relay systems, and in low-power radars.

A cutaway of a typical reflex klystron is shown in **Fig. 8**. This tube is tuned by deforming the upper cavity wall, which varies the spacing between the

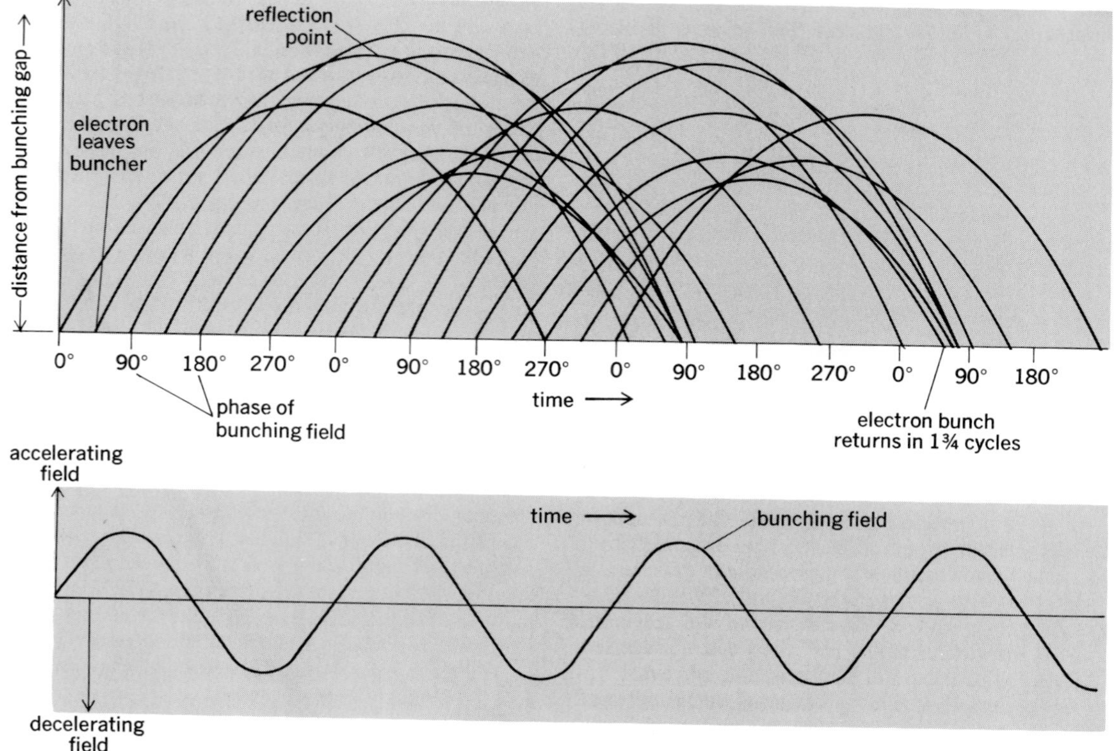


**Fig 7. Trajectories show bunching in a reflex oscillator. Electrons are turned back by a retarding field, faster ones going farther and taking longer. The bunched beam returns through the cavity. (*Varian Associates*)**

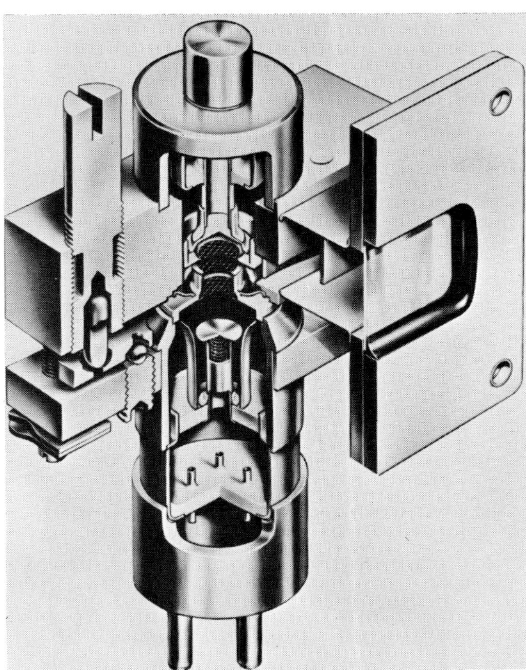

**Fig. 8. Cutaway of reflex oscillator shows (at left) the screw that deforms the flexible bottom wall of the cavity to change its resonant frequency. The beam passes through honeycomb grids in the cavity. The cathode leads come out at the bottom socket, and the reflector lead comes out at the top. The output waveguide has a mica vacuum window. (*Varian Associates*)**

grids and hence the effective capacitance of the cavity resonator.

*Richard B. Nelson*

**Bibliography.** J. Coleman, *Microwave Devices,* 1982; L. Ginzton, The klystron, *Sci. Amer.*, 190(3):84–88, March 1954; S. Liao, *Microwave Devices and Circuits*, 1980; J. R. Pierce and W. G. Shepherd, Reflex oscillators, *Bell Syst. Tech. J.*, 26:460–681, 1947; R. F. Soohoo, *Microwave Electronics,* 1971.

## Langmuir-Child law

A law governing space-charge-limited flow of electron current between two plane parallel electrodes in vacuum when the emission velocities of the electrons can be neglected. It is often called the three-halves power law, and is expressed by the formula below.

$$j(\text{A/cm}^2) = \frac{\epsilon}{9\pi}\left(\frac{2e}{m}\right)^{1/2}\frac{V^{3/2}}{d^2} = 2.33 \times 10^{-6}\,\frac{V(\text{volts})^{3/2}}{d(\text{cm})^2}$$

Here $\epsilon$ is the dielectric constant of vacuum, $-e$ the charge of the electron, $m$ its mass, $V$ the potential difference between the two electrodes, $d$ their separation, and $j$ the current density at the collector electrode, or anode. The potential difference $V$ is the applied voltage reduced by the difference in work function of the collector and emitter. The Langmuir-Child law applies, to a close approximation, to other electrode geometries as well. Thus for coaxial cylinders with the inner cylinder the cathode, it leads to a deviation from the true value of the current density of 13% at most.

*Edward G. Ramberg*

## Laser

A device that uses the principle of amplification of electromagnetic waves by stimulated emission of radiation and operates in the infrared, visible, or ultraviolet region. The term laser is an acronym for light amplification by stimulated emission of radiation, or a light amplifier. However, just as an electronic amplifier can be made into an oscillator by feeding appropriately phased output back into the input, so the laser light amplifier can be made into a laser oscillator, which is really a light source. Laser oscillators are so much more common than laser amplifiers that the unmodified word "laser" has come to mean the oscillator, while the modifier "amplifier" is generally used when the oscillator is not intended. *See Maser.*

The process of stimulated emission can be described as follows: When atoms, ions, or molecules absorb energy, they can emit light spontaneously (as in an incandescent lamp) or they can be stimulated to emit by a light wave. This stimulated emission is the opposite of (stimulated) absorption, where unexcited matter is stimulated into an excited state by a light wave. If a collection of atoms is prepared (pumped) so that more are initially excited than unexcited, then an incident light wave will stimulate more emission than absorption, and there is net amplification of the incident light beam. This is the way the laser amplifier works.

A laser amplifier can be made into a laser oscillator by arranging suitable mirrors on either end of the amplifier. These are called the resonator. Thus the essential parts of a laser oscillator are an amplifying medium, a source of pump power, and a resonator. Radiation that is directed straight along the axis bounces back and forth between the mirrors and can remain in the resonator long enough to build up a strong oscillation. (Waves oriented in other directions soon pass off the edge of the mirrors and are lost before they are much amplified.) Radiation may be coupled out as shown in **Fig. 1** by making one mirror partially transparent so that part of the amplified light can emerge through it. The output wave, like most of the waves being amplified between the mirrors, travels along the axis and is thus very nearly a plane wave.

**Comparison with other sources.** In contrast to lasers, all conventional light sources are basically hot bodies which radiate by spontaneous emission. The electrons in the tungsten filament of an incandescent

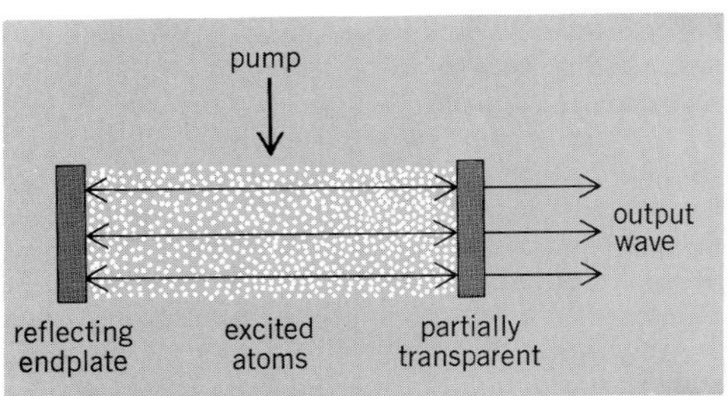


**Fig. 1. Structure of a parallel-plate laser.**

lamp are agitated by, and acquire excitation from, the high temperature of the filament. Once excited, they emit light in all directions and revert to a lower energy state. Similarly, in a gas lamp, the electron current excites the atoms to high-energy quantum states, and they soon give up this excitation energy by radiating it as light. In all the above, spontaneous emission from each excited electron or atom takes place independently of emission from the others. Thus the overall wave produced by a conventional light source is a jumble of waves from the numerous individual atoms. The phase of the wave emitted by one atom has no relation to the phase emitted by any other atom, so that the overall phase of the light fluctuates randomly from moment to moment and place to place. The lack of correlation is called incoherence.

Hot bodies emit more or less equally in all directions radiation whose wavelength distribution is dictated by the Planck blackbody radiation curve. For example, the surface of the Sun radiates like a blackbody at a temperature of about 6000 K, and emits a total of 7 $kW/cm^2$, spread out over all wavelengths and directions. Light from gas lamps can be more monochromatic (wavelengths radiated are restricted by the quantized energies allowed in atoms), but radiation still occurs in all directions. In contrast to this, an ideal plane wave would have the same phase all across any wavefront, and the time fluctuations would be highly predictable (coherent). The output of the parallel-plate laser described above is very nearly such a plane wave and is therefore highly directional. This arises because in the laser oscillator atoms are stimulated to emit in phase with the stimulating wave, rather than independently, and the wave that builds up between the mirrors matches very closely the mirrors' surfaces. The output is powerful because atoms can be stimulated to emit much faster than they would spontaneously. It is highly monochromatic largely because stimulated emission is a resonance process that occurs most rapidly at the center of the range of wavelengths that would be emitted spontaneously. Since atoms are stimulated to emit in phase with the existing wave, the phase is preserved over many cycles, resulting in the high degree of time coherence of laser radiation.

The various types of lasers are discussed below, classified according to their pumping (or excitation) scheme. The function of the pumping system is to maintain more atoms in the upper than in the lower state, thereby assuring that stimulated emission (gain transitions) will exceed (stimulated) absorption (loss transitions). This so-called population inversion ensures net gain (amplification greater than unity).

**Optically pumped lasers.** One way to achieve population inversion is by concentrating light (for example, from a flash lamp or the Sun) onto the amplifying medium. Alternatively, lasers may be used to optically pump other lasers. For example, powerful continuous-wave (cw) ion lasers can pump liquid dyes to lase, yielding watts of tunable visible and near-visible radiation. Molecular lasers, like carbon dioxide ($CO_2$), can pump gases, like deuterium cyanide (DCN), to lase powerfully in the far infrared, operating out to several hundred micrometers wavelength. Optical pumping can be employed to pump gases at very high pressures (for example, 42 atm or 4.3 megapascals) to obtain tunability where other excitation methods would be difficult if not impossible to implement.

Many lasers are three-level lasers; that is, ground-state atoms are excited by absorption of light to a broad upper-energy state, from which they quickly relax to the emitting state. Laser action occurs as they are stimulated to emit radiation and so return to the original ground state. Crystalline, glass, liquid, and gaseous systems have been found suitable, but many possible materials remain to be explored. Solid three-level lasers usually make use of ions of a rare-earth element, such as neodymium, or of a transition metal, such as chromium, dispersed in a transparent crystal or glass. For example, ruby, which is crystalline aluminum oxide containing a fraction of a percent of trivalent chromium ions in place of aluminum ions, has been used for lasers to produce red light with wavelengths of 693 to 705 nm. The chromium ions have broad absorption bands in which pumping radiations can be absorbed. Thus broad-band white light can be used to excite the atoms.

Many rare-earth ion lasers use a fourth level above the ground state. This level serves as a terminal level for the laser transition, and is kept empty by rapid nonradiative relaxation to the ground state. This means that, relative to three-level systems, a population inversion is easier to maintain, and therefore such materials require relatively low pumping light intensity for laser action. Neodymium ions can provide laser action in many host materials, producing outputs in the infrared, around 1 micrometer. In glass, which can be made in large sizes, neodymium ions can generate high-energy pulses or very high peak powers (**Fig. 2**). Lasers using neodymium ions in crystals such as yttrium aluminum garnet (YAG) can provide continuous output powers up to a kilowatt. The output of either type (in glass or in crystals) can be converted to visible light, near 500 nm, by a harmonic generator crystal, as discussed below. Optically pumped solid-state lasers provide relatively high peak output powers. Tens of kilowatts can easily be obtained in a pulse lasting 100 μs. Much higher peak powers can be obtained by special techniques described below.

The structure of an optically pumped solid-state laser can be as simple as a rod of the light-amplifying material with parallel ends polished and coated to reflect light. Pumping radiation can enter either through the transparent sides or the ends. Other structures can be used. The mirror ends can be spherical rather than plane, with the common focal point of the two mir-

**Fig. 2. High-power laser amplifier stage, with a 30-cm (1 ft) aperture, using liquid-cooled slabs of neodynium glass. (*Lawrence Livermore National Laboratory*)**

rors lying halfway between them. Still other structures make use of internal reflection of light rays that strike the surface of a crystal at a high angle.

Liquid lasers have structures generally like those of optically pumped solid-state lasers, except that the liquid is generally contained in a transparent cell. Some liquid lasers make use of rare-earth ions in suitable dissolved molecules, while others make use of organic dye solutions. The dyes can lase over a wide range of wavelengths, depending upon the composition and concentration of the dye or solvent. Thus tunability is obtained throughout the visible, and out to a wavelength of about 0.9 μm. Fine adjustment of the output wavelength can be provided by using a diffraction grating or other dispersive element in place of one of the laser mirrors. The grating acts as a good mirror for only one wavelength, which depends on the angle at which it is set. With further refinements, liquid-dye lasers can be made extremely monochromatic as well as broadly tunable. They may be pumped by various lasers to generate either short, intense pulses or continuous output. Dyes may also be incorporated into solid media such as plastics or gelatin to provide tunable laser action. Then the tuning may be controlled by a regular corrugation in the refractive index of the host medium, which acts as a distributed Bragg reflector. The reflection from any one layer is small, but when the successive alternations of refractive index provide reflections in phase, the effect is that of a strong, sharply tuned reflection.

Certain color centers in the alkali halides can be optically pumped to make efficient, tunable lasers for the region 0.8 to 3.3 μm, thus taking over just where the organic dyes fail. Both pulsed (10 kW) and continuous (watts) operation have been achieved.

In several infrared regions, tunable laser action can be obtained by using an infrared gas laser to pump a semiconductor crystal in a magnetic field, giving amplification by stimulating spin-flip Raman scattering from the electrons in the semiconductor. Tuning is achieved by varying the magnetic field.

**Gas-discharge lasers.** Another large class of lasers makes use of nonequilibrium processes in a gas discharge. At moderately low pressures (on the order of 1 torr or $10^2$ Pa) and fairly high currents, the population of energy levels is far from an equilibrium distribution. Some levels are populated especially rapidly by the fast electrons in the discharge. Other levels empty particularly slowly and so accumulate large numbers of excited atoms. Thus laser action can occur at many wavelengths in any of a large number of gases under suitable discharge conditions. For some gases, a continuous discharge, with the use of either direct or radio-frequency current, gives continuous laser action. Output powers of continuous gas lasers range from less than 1 μW up to about 100 W in the visible region. Wavelengths generated span the ultraviolet and visible regions and extend out beyond 700 μm in the infrared. They thus provide the first intense sources of radiation in much of the far-infrared region of the spectrum.

The earliest, and still most widely used, gas-discharge laser utilizes a mixture of helium and neon. Various infrared and visible wavelengths can be generated, but most commonly they produce red light at a 632.8-nm wavelength, with power outputs of a few milliwatts or less, although they can be as high as about a watt. Helium-neon lasers can be small and inexpensive. Argon and krypton ion gas–discharge lasers provide a number of visible and near-ultraviolet wavelengths with continuous powers typically about 1 to 10 W, but ranging up to more than 100 W. Unfortunately, efficiencies are low.

Many molecular gases, such as hydrogen cyanide, carbon monoxide, and carbon dioxide, can provide infrared laser action. Carbon dioxide lasers can be operated at a number of wavelengths near 10 μm on various vibration-rotation spectral lines of the molecule. They can be relatively efficient, up to about 30%, and have been made large enough to give continuous power outputs exceeding tens of thousands of watts.

Many gas-discharge lasers, for example, helium-neon, produce only very small optical gain; thus losses must be kept low. Consequently, mirrors with very high reflectivity (greater than 99%) must generally be used. Diffraction losses can be kept low by using curved mirrors. One common arrangement, which combines relatively low diffraction losses with good mode selection, uses a flat mirror at one end and a spherically concave mirror at the other. The spacing between mirrors is made equal to the radius of curvature of the spherical mirror. On the other hand, in some of the higher-power, higher-gain lasers even the plane-parallel mirror structure does not give sufficient discrimination against those undesired modes of oscillation which cause the beam to be excessively divergent. It is then helpful to use "unstable" resonators, with at least one of the mirrors convex toward the other.

A smooth, small-bore dielectric tube can guide a light wave in its interior with little loss. Thus a light wave can be amplified by a long, narrow medium without spreading or diffraction. A gas discharge in a hollow optical waveguide can be run at high pressure and benefits from cooling by the nearby walls, so that relatively high-power outputs (watts) can be obtained from a small volume. Wave-guide structures are also useful when a medium is pumped optically by another laser, whose narrow beam can be confined within the bore of the tube. For example, pumping of various molecules, such as methyl fluoride, by a carbon dioxide laser has been used to generate coherent light in the very far-infrared (submillimeter-wavelength) region.

**Pulsed gas lasers.** Pulsed gas discharges permit a further departure from equilibrium. Thus pulsed laser action can be obtained in some additional gases which could not be made to lase continuously. In some of them the length of the laser pulse is limited when the lower state is filled by stimulated transitions from the upper level, and so introduces absorption at the laser wavelength. An example of such a self-terminating laser is the nitrogen laser, which gives pulses of several nanoseconds duration with peak powers from tens of kilowatts up to a few megawatts at a wavelength of 337 nm in the ultraviolet. They are easy to construct and are much used for pumping tunable dye lasers throughout the wavelength range from about 350 to 1000 nm. Very powerful laser radiation in the vacuum ultraviolet region, between 100 and 200 nm, can be obtained from short-pulse discharges in hydrogen, and in rare gases such as xenon at high pressure. (High pressure leads to higher power.) When the gas pressure is too high to permit an electric discharge, excitation may be provided by an intense burst of fast electrons from a small accelerator, the so-called E beam.

Some gases, notably carbon dioxide, which can provide continuous laser action, also can be used to generate intense pulses of microsecond duration. For this purpose, gas pressures of about 1 atm ($10^5$ Pa) are used, and the electrical discharge takes place across the diameter of the laser column, hence the name transverse-electrical-atmospheric (TEA) laser.

**Chemical lasers.** It is also possible to obtain laser action from the energy released in some fast chemical reactions. Atoms or molecules produced during the reaction are often in excited states. Under special circumstances there may be enough atoms or molecules excited to some particular state for amplification to occur by stimulated emission. Usually the reacting gases are mixed and then ignited by ultraviolet light or fast electrons. Both continuous infrared output and pulses up to several thousand joules of energy have been obtained in reactions which produce excited hydrogen fluoride molecules.

Pulsed laser action in the ultraviolet (193 to 353 nm) has been obtained from excimer states of rare gas monohalides (for example, KrF, XeF, KrCl, XeCl, XeBr). Such molecules have ground states which are unstable, thereby making a population inversion easy to achieve. Although these lasers require an electrical source for initial gas reaction, laser pumping is dependent on chemical reactions.

**Photodissociation lasers.** Intense pulses of ultraviolet light can dissociate molecules in such a way as to leave one constituent in an excited state capable of sustaining laser action. The most notable examples are iodine compounds, which have given peak 1.3-μm pulse powers above $10^9$ W from the excited iodide atoms.

**Nuclear lasers.** Laser action in several gases has also been excited by the fast-moving ions produced in nuclear fusion. These fusion products excite and ionize the gas atoms, and make it possible to convert directly from nuclear to optical energy.

**Gas-dynamic lasers.** When a hot molecular gas is allowed to expand suddenly through a nozzle, it cools quickly, but different excited states lose energy at different rates. It can happen that, just after cooling, some particular upper state has more molecules than some lower one, so that amplification by stimulated emission can occur. Very high continuous power outputs have been generated from carbon dioxide in large gas-dynamic lasers.

**Semiconductor lasers.** Another method for providing excitation of lasers can be used with certain semiconducting materials. Laser action takes place when free electrons in the conduction band are stimulated to recombine with holes in the valence band. In recombining, the electrons give up energy corresponding nearly to the band gap. This energy is radiated as a light quantum. Suitable materials are the direct-gap semiconductors, such as gallium arsenide. In them, recombination occurs directly without the emission or absorption of a quantum of lattice vibrations. A flat junction between *p*-type and *n*-type material may be used. When a current is passed through this junction in the forward direction, a large number of holes and electrons are brought together. This is called recombination and is accompanied by emission of radiation. A light wave passing along the plane of the junction can be amplified by stimulating such recombination of electrons and holes. The ends of the semiconducting crystal provide the mirrors to complete the laser structure. In indirect-gap semiconductors, such as germanium and silicon, only a small amplification by stimulated emission is possible because of their requirement for interaction with the lattice vibrations.

Semiconductor lasers can be very small, less than 1 mm in any direction. They can have efficiencies higher than 50% (electricity to light). Power densities are high, but the thinness of the active layer tends to limit the total output power. Even so, maximum continuous powers are comparable with those of other moderate-size lasers. Since semiconductor lasers are so small, they can be assembled into compact arrays of many units, so as to generate higher peak powers. An alternative excitation method, bombardment of the semiconductor by a high-voltage beam of electrons, may provide laser action in larger crystal volumes, but it is likely to cause damage to the crystal.

Early semiconductor lasers required cooling and pulsed operation, emitting light only in the infrared. Great progress has been made, making possible room temperature, continuous operation. Monochromaticity has been improved to degrees almost comparable with gas lasers. SEE SEMICONDUCTOR.

**Free-electron lasers.** Free-electron lasers are of interest because of their potential for efficiently producing very high-power radiation, tunable from the millimeter to the x-ray region. The principle of operation, so far demonstrated only at 3.4 μm and at very low-power levels, involves passage of electrons through a spatially varying magnetic field which causes the electron beam to "wiggle" and hence to radiate. The large Doppler upshift due to relativistic electron velocities can be adjusted, resulting in tunable emission at optical frequencies.

**High-power, short-pulse lasers.** The output power of pulsed lasers can be greatly increased, with correspondingly shorter pulse durations, by the Q-switch technique. In this method, the optical path between one mirror and the amplification medium is blocked by a shutter. The medium is then excited beyond the degree ordinarily needed, but the shutter prevents laser action. At this time the shutter is abruptly opened and the stored energy is released in a giant pulse (1–100 MW peak power, lasting 1–30 ns for optically pumped solid-state lasers). Still higher peak powers can be obtained by passing this output through a traveling-wave laser amplifier (without mirrors). Peak powers in excess of 100 MW have been obtained in this way.

Still shorter, and higher-power, pulses can be generated by mode-locking techniques. A typical laser without mode locking usually oscillates simultaneously and independently at several closely spaced wavelengths. These modes of oscillation can be synchronized so that the peaks of their waves occur simultaneously at some instant. The result is a very short, intense pulse which quickly ends as the waves of different frequency get out of step. Mode-locked lasers have generated pulses shorter than 1 ps. Since such brief pulses tend to produce somewhat less damage to materials, they can be amplified to very high peak intensities. Power outputs of picosecond pulses as high as 10–100 MW have been obtained, limited as in the Q-switch case by material damage.

For the highest peak power, the output may be further intensified by additional stages of laser amplification. The beam diameter is increased by some optical arrangement, such as a telescope, so as to expand (dilute) the beam and thereby prevent damage to the laser material and optics. Sometimes the amplifying medium is divided into flat slabs separated by cooling liquid (Fig. 2). Here the open faces of the light-amplifying slabs present a large area to receive pumping light and liquid cooling.

Development of very large multistage lasers has been undertaken for research on thermonuclear fusion. In a particularly large one, at Lawrence Livermore Laboratory, a single neodymium-glass laser oscillator is designed to drive 20 amplifier chains of glass rods and disks, each delivering a pulse of more than $10^{12}$ W. Focusing all these pulses onto the surface of a small pellet of heavy hydrogen is designed to heat and compress the pellet by ablation, until it is so hot that the hydrogen nuclei fuse to produce helium and release large amounts of nuclear energy. Ultimately this type of controlled laser fusion may become an important source of thermal, electrical, and chemical energy.

The technology of scaling up lasers to higher and higher powers has been so successful that the limitations are often set by material damage thresholds of the laser medium or associated optics. At the high-power densities attainable by focusing laser beams, the electric fields of the light can be large. Thus when the light intensity is $10^{12}$ W/cm$^2$, the corresponding electric field is $10^7$ V/cm. To such large fields, many transparent materials have a nonlinear dielectric response. This nonlinearity can be large enough to permit the generation of optical harmonics. It is possible, with careful design and good nonlinear materials, to obtain substantially complete conversion of a laser's output to the second harmonic, at twice the frequency, even for continuous lasers near 1-W output power. Nonlinear dielectrics can be used as mixers to give the sum or difference of two laser frequencies. They also permit the construction of optical parametric oscillators which, when pumped by a laser, can generate coherent light tunable over a wide range of wavelengths.

**Applications.** The variety of technological uses for lasers has increased steadily since their appearance in 1960. Among the noticeable applications are those that utilize high-speed controllability of the tiny focal spot of a laser beam. For example, high-speed automatic scanners identify library cards, ski passes, and supermarket purchases and perform a variety of functions known as optical processing. Other uses for the laser beam's programmable control include information storage and retrieval (including three-dimensional holography and video disk reading), laser printing, micromachining, and automated cutting. Further applications involving high power include weaponry, laser welding, laser surgery (self-cauterizing), laser fusion, and materials processing. Optical communications utilize the laser's high frequency, which makes possible high information capacity (**Fig. 3**). Except for space applications, laser light communication is primarily done through glass fibers. Fiber-optic laser telephone systems are presently in operation in many cities around the world. Low-loss optical fibers are far more compact, light weight, and economical than copper wires. Bright laser beams are used by the construction industry to align straight excavations and for surveying. Some applications include rotation rate sensing (laser gyros), laser velocity sensing (laser radar or lidar), optical testing, metrology (including the distance to the Moon), laser spectroscopy (including pollution monitoring), pumping other lasers to produce beams of coherent light at other wavelengths, from millimeters to x-rays, and exploration of ultrafast phenomena (by using picosecond laser pulses). *SEE* CHARACTER RECOGNITION; CONTINUOUS-WAVE RADAR; INTEGRATED OPTICS; OPTICAL COMMUNICATIONS; PHOTOACOUSTIC SPECTROSCOPY; VIDEO DISK RECORDING.

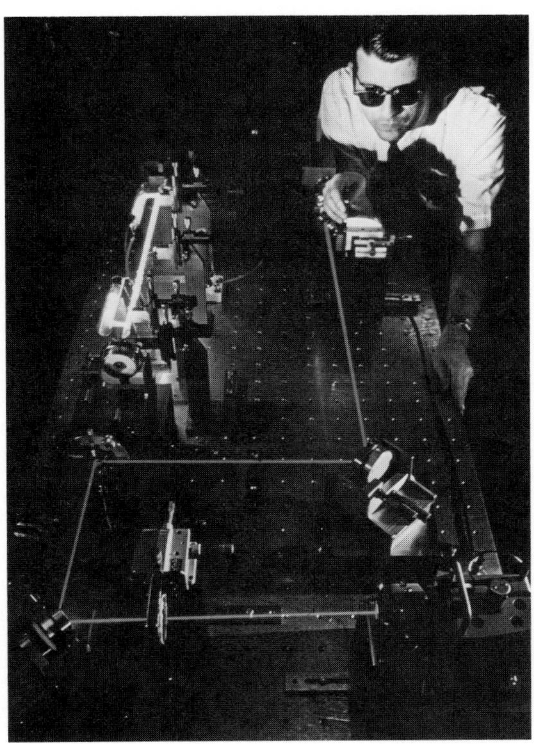

**Fig. 3. Experimental arrangement to impress pulse-code modulation on a laser beam for optical communication. (*Bell Laboratories*)**

*Stephen F. Jacobs; Arthur L. Schawlow*

**Bibliography.** S. F. Jacobs et al. (eds.), *Free Electron Generators of Coherent Radiation*, vols. 7–9, 1980–1982; S. F. Jacobs et al., *Laser Photochemistry, Tunable Lasers, and Other Topics*, 1976; L. Marton and C. Marton, *Methods of Experimental Physics*, vol. 15, 1979; D. C. O'Shea, W. R. Callen, and W. T. Rhodes, *An Introduction to Lasers and Their Applications*, 1977; A. E. Siegman, *Introduction to Lasers and Masers*, 1971; D. C. Sinclair and W. E. Bell, *Gas Laser Technology*, 1969; O. Svelto, *Principles of Lasers*, 2d ed., 1982; A. Yariv, *Introduction to Optical Electronics*, 1976.

## Laser-solid interactions

Interactions of laser light with solids. The term usually refers to the thermal effects of absorption of high-intensity laser beams.

One of the unique features of lasers is their ability to concentrate the energy of light so that a surface can be exposed to a photon flux of $10^6$ to $10^{12}$ W/cm$^2$. These extraordinarily high power densities are attainable even with lasers of moderate size and average output of only a few watts, since light can be emitted in pulses of a few nanoseconds or even less than 1 picosecond duration and a coherent beam can be focused into spots as small as 1 micrometer in diameter. The high power densities allow melting and even vaporization of any solid material that is sufficiently opaque at a given wavelength or photon energy. This

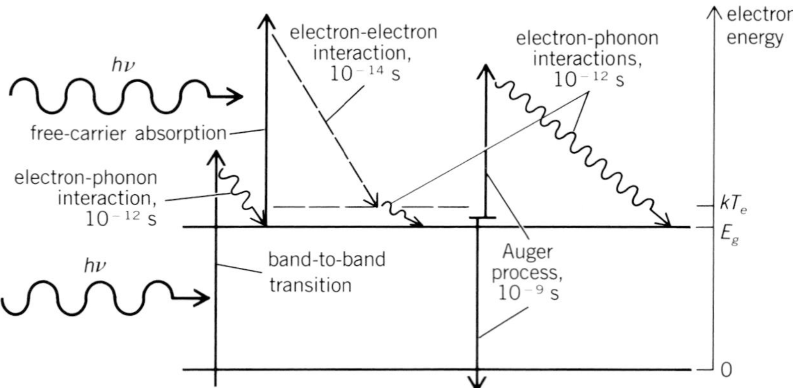


**Fig. 1. Absorption of light and energy transfer mechanism for a very intense flux ($10^7$ – $10^9$ W/cm$^2$) of photons with energy $h\nu$ exceeding the band-gap energy $E_g$. Approximate times for processes to take place are given. The quantity $kT_e$ is the average thermal energy per electron, the product of Boltzmann's constant $k$ and the electron temperature $T_e$.**

has led to a number of applications involving cutting and drilling of ceramics and other brittle materials, even diamonds. Welding of components from the smallest wires to huge steel plates is done commercially with high-power lasers. Metal alloying in surface regions is also a domain of lasers. Modification of semiconductors with intense laser irradiations has emerged as one of the most exciting fields of scientific discovery while at the same time promising substantial practical benefits for the semiconductor device industry. *See Semiconductor.*

**Photon-electron-phonon interactions.** Photons with energy exceeding the fundamental band-gap energy $E_g$ of the semiconductor are absorbed near the surface, exciting electrons from the valence to the conduction band and forming electron-hole pairs. For direct band-gap semiconductors, such as gallium arsenide (GaAs), indium phosphide (InP), and indium antimonide (InSb), light is absorbed within 100 nanometers of the surface. For indirect band-gap semiconductors, such as silicon and germanium, the transition from transparency to absorption is a more gradual function of the light wavelength, because for each transfer of energy from a photon to an electron a phonon has to be created or annihilated to assure conservation of momentum. *See Band theory of solids.*

For photon energies less than $E_g$, semiconductors are largely transparent, at least at moderate light intensities. Some photons are still absorbed by exciting electrons and holes within the conduction and valence bands to higher energies (free-carrier absorption), but unless the semiconductor is heavily doped with impurities that lead to a large concentration of free carriers, the light beam can penetrate to a depth of 0.04 in. (1 mm) or more before it is fully absorbed. Far-infrared light can interact directly with the lattice vibrations or phonons, that is, the energy of photons can be directly transformed into heat, but this absorption mechanism is quite weak. The low absorption channels are often very important at high photon fluxes, as they can initiate surface heating that tends to make solids more opaque. This feedback mechanism facilitates laser melting and vaporization of almost any solid substance. In semiconductors, free-carrier absorption by electrons and holes generated by optically and thermally stimulated band-to-band transitions contributes a large component to the total absorption at high power densities.

Excited electrons and holes share energy with one another very rapidly through electron-electron and electron-plasmon interactions. They release energy to other electric carriers and to phonons until they reach the lowest energy possible within their respective energy bands. Then they recombine by one of several mechanisms: radiatively by emitting a photon, nonradiatively by transferring the amount of energy $E_g$ into heat or by an Auger process that transfers the energy to a third particle (electron or hole), exciting it to an energy higher by $E_g$ (**Fig. 1**). Auger interactions are very important for a high density of photoexcited carriers. Although they do not reduce the energy of the electronic system, they convert the band-gap energy into kinetic energy of carriers that can be dissipated rapidly into heat by phonon emission. All the photon energy absorbed by the solid is transformed into heat in about 1 ps, that is, almost instantaneously.

**Annealing of ion-implanted layers.** Ion implantation has become a dominant method of introducing controlled quantities of impurities near the surface of silicon and other semiconductors for the purpose of adjusting their electrical conductivity and forming diodes, transistors, and entire integrated circuits. The implanted layers need a heat treatment to repair the displacement damage caused by bombardment with energetic ions and to move the implanted impurity ions into lattice locations where they replace host atoms and become electrically active. Laser heating is particularly suitable for annealing since only the im-

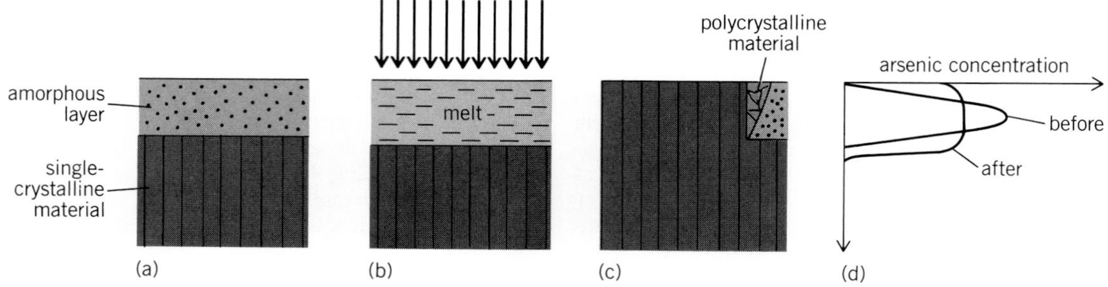


**Fig. 2. Pulsed laser annealing by liquid-phase epitaxy. (*a*) Cross section of a crystalline semiconductor with a thin (typically 100 nm thick) amorphous surface layer formed by ion implantation. (*b*) The entire thickness of the amorphous film and some of the underlying crystal melted by a laser pulse. (c) Molten layer recrystallized from the crystalline template to the surface. At the edge of the laser-irradiated spot, where the melt has not reached the crystalline substrate, the material is polycrystalline. (*d*) Typical depth profiles of arsenic implanted into silicon, before and after pulsed laser annealing.**

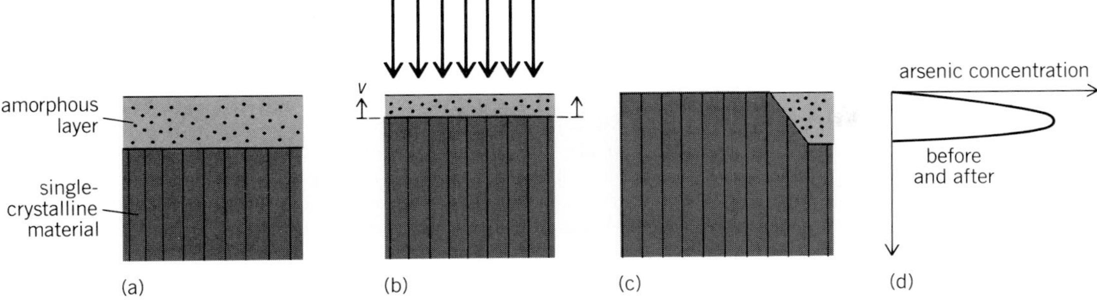


**Fig. 3. Continuous-wave laser annealing by solid-phase epitaxy. (*a*) Cross section of the starting structure. (*b*) Crystalline-amorphous interface propagating toward the surface with a velocity *v* that depends on temperature induced by the laser beam. (*c*) The irradiated region fully recrystallized, except at the edge of the laser-heated spot where the interface has a wedge shape. (*d*) Depth profiles of arsenic implanted into silicon, the same before and after continuous-wave laser annealing.**

planted regions are heated. This capability of delivering heat selectively to a very thin layer is the basis of "laser annealing" of semiconductors. SEE ION IMPLANTATION.

***Pulsed laser annealing.*** A short, high-intensity laser pulse melts the layer of silicon damaged by ion implantation. As soon as the pulse is over, the layer freezes, starting at the unmelted single crystal (**Fig. 2**). The single crystal forms a template on which the melt solidifies, preserving the perfection of the template. This process of liquid-phase epitaxy is the same as conventional crystal growth from the melt, except that the solid-liquid interface moves at a velocity of many feet per second, driven by the temperature gradients of about $10^7$ degrees/in. The quality of the crystalline structure is not diminished by the rate of growth, but some new phenomena appear. For example, most impurities that are present in the liquid are incorporated into the solid more completely than during slow crystal growth. Maximum concentrations of some impurities in the crystalline semiconductor can exceed by orders of magnitude the near-equilibrium solid solubilities.

Pulse irradiation allows investigation of the physical limits of crystal growth and the thermodynamic properties of different phases. For example, it was determined that amorphous silicon melts at a lower temperature than crystalline silicon, confirming theoretical predictions based on Gibbs free-energy considerations. When the solidification rate of molten semiconductors exceeds about 50 ft/s (15 m/s; this is accomplished with pulses shorter than 2 ns and short-wavelength irradiation), the liquid is supercooled so much that it transforms into an amorphous layer instead of a single crystalline layer. Therefore, depending on irradiation conditions, amorphous → crystalline and crystalline → amorphous phase transitions are achievable, even with the same laser.

***Continuous-wave.*** Laser beams can anneal implantation displacement damage without melting, by solid-phase epitaxy. At elevated temperature the atoms rearrange themselves into an orderly crystalline structure. The process starts at the boundary between crystalline and damaged regions, and this interface moves through the amorphous film (**Fig. 3**), at a velocity determined by the activation energy $E_a$ (for silicon $E_a = 2.7$ eV).Typically about 1 millisecond time is required to regrow ion-implanted surface layers. Pulses of such duration could be used, but better results are obtained with a continuous-wave laser beam scanned across the surface at a velocity that yields about 1 ms dwell time. This type of laser annealing is physically equivalent to furnace annealing, but there are some important differences. Heating is so brief that practically no diffusion of impurities take place. The impurity profiles after annealing are indistinguishable from as-implanted depth profiles. In contrast, furnace annealing at high temperatures that are necessary for complete defect removal causes significant diffusion of doping impurities. Laser heating is localized both in depth and in a lateral direction. Small areas can be selectively annealed with a tightly focused beam, and micrometer-size patterns can be written in implantation amorphized material. Since high surface temperatures are attained with a laser in less than 1 ms, measurements of solid-phase epitaxial regrowth rates up to the melting temperature became possible, broadening the understanding of solid-phase epitaxy.

**Silicon on insulator.** Thin films of single-crystalline silicon over an insulating substrate are very attractive for high-speed integrated circuits. An important approach to the formation of such films is the controlled melting of thin polycrystalline layers deposited over fused silica substrates or over oxidized silicon wafers. Through a careful control of temperature gradients around the molten spot, by shaping the laser beam or patterning the film, single-crystalline regions can be obtained. One particularly successful approach involves growing single-crystalline films from openings in the oxide where the melt is in contact with the single-crystalline template (**Fig. 4**). The formation of silicon-on-insulator structures will lead in the future to three-dimensional circuits, with sev-

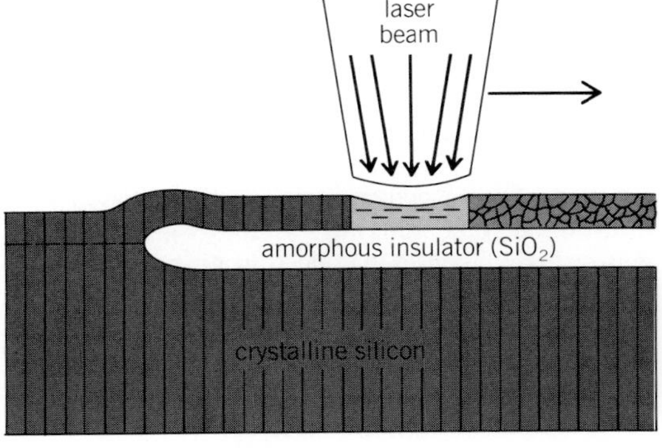


**Fig. 4. Melting with a scanning continuous-wave laser beam, allowing lateral epitaxial regrowth of crystalline silicon over a layer of silicon dioxide ($SiO_2$).**

eral levels of transistors on the same chip. *See Integrated circuits*.

**Laser-induced-damage gettering.** At high power densities, Q-switched laser pulses can vaporize material from the surface of a solid and form microscopic craters. Shock waves associated with vaporization stress the surface and lead to formation of dislocations. The laser-induced surface damage helps in removing undesirable impurities from the device regions of silicon to an inactive area such as the back side of a wafer. The fast-diffusing impurities become trapped or gettered at the damage sites, from where they do not affect device operation. *See Laser*.

*George K. Celler*

***Bibliography.*** G. K. Celler, *Modification of Silicon Properties with Lasers, Electron Beams, and Incoherent Light*, CRC Critical Reviews in Solid State and Material Science, vol. 12, pp. 193–265, 1984; S. S. Charschan, *Lasers in Industry*, 1972; *Materials Research Society Proceedings*, annual volumes since 1979; J. M. Poate and J. W. Mayer, *Laser Annealing of Semiconductors*, 1982.

## Light amplifier

In the broadest sense, a device which produces an enhanced light output when actuated by incident light. A simple photocell relay–light source combination would satisfy this definition. To make the term more meaningful, common usage has introduced two restrictions: (1) a light amplifier must be a device which, when actuated by a light image, reproduces a similar image of enhanced brightness; and (2) the device must be capable of operating at very low light levels without introducing spurious brightness variations (noise) into the reproduced image. The term is used synonymously with image intensifier. The light amplifier increases the brightness of an image which is below the visual threshold to a level where it can be readily seen with the unaided eye. It is, of course, impossible to see under conditions of complete darkness. Indeed, there is a fundamental lower limit of illumination under which an image of a given quality can be recognized. This limitation arises because of the corpuscular nature of light.

Photons arriving through a lens, or other optical system, onto an image area are random in time. If the number of photons per unit area arriving during the time allotted for image formation (for example, the period of the persistence of vision) is too low, the statistical fluctuation will be greater than the variation in number due to true differences in image brightness. Under these circumstances, image recognition is impossible.

**Image-intensifier tubes.** Intensifier tubes may consist of a semitransparent photocathode which emits electrons with a density distribution proportional to the distribution of light intensity incident on it. Thus, when a light image falls on one side of the cathode, an electron-current image is emitted from the other side. An electron optical system, which acts on electrons in much the same way as does a glass lens system on light, focuses the electron image onto an intensifier element. This electron optical system may be purely electrostatic or may utilize magnetic focusing. The intensified electron image from the other side of the intensifier element is again focused, by a second electron lens, onto a second intensifier element (if additional amplification is required) or onto a fluorescent viewing screen, where the electron energy is converted to visible light.

Proximity tubes are a class of intensifiers in which the photocathode and the fluorescent viewing screen are parallel and separated by only a short distance. No focusing is required for a proximity tube, since the electrons generated at the photocathode are accelerated along the tube axis by the high electric fields.

The spectral response of the image-intensifier tube depends on the type of photocathode employed, and the tube may serve as a wavelength converter as well as an intensifer. *See Electron optics*.

***Intensifier elements.*** Two types of intensifier elements are ordinarily employed. One consists of a transparent support (either a thin film or a fiber optics plate) with a phosphor screen on the side on which the electron image is incident, and a photocathode on the other. An electron striking the phosphor produces a flash of light which causes a release of 50 or more electrons from the photoemitter directly opposite the point of impact. Thus, the intensifier element increases the electron-image current density by a factor of 50. Two such intensifier elements in cascade give a gain of 2500. The **illustration** shows a three-stage electrostatic image-intensifier tube.

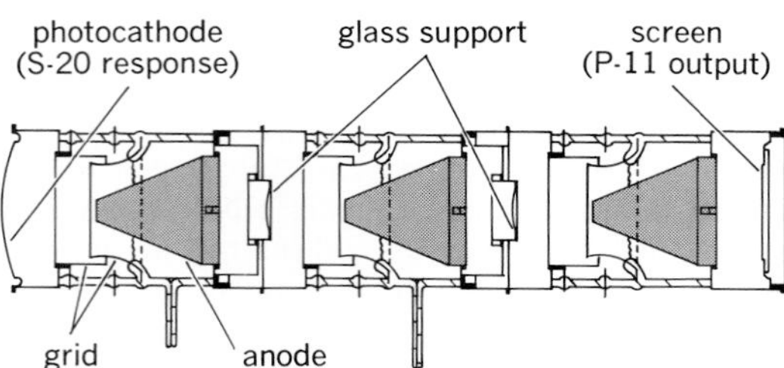


**Three-stage electrostatically focused image tube.**

A second type of high-gain intensifier element is a thin secondary-emission current amplifier called a microchannel plate, which is placed between the photocathode and screen. It consists of a parallel bundle of small, hollow glass cylinders, where the inside walls of the cylinders are coated with a secondary emitting material. Electrons emitted from the photocathode strike the inside walls of the cylinders, causing secondary electron generation. These secondary electrons in turn continue to cascade down the inside walls of the cylinders, resulting in a high total current gain.

***Television camera tube.*** The intensifier image device can be combined with television pickup tubes to make a television camera whose sensitivity is very close to the threshold determined by the photon "shot noise" from the scene being televised. A SIT (silicon intensifier target) camera tube has a wide dynamic range and operates at very low light levels. In the SIT tube, the photoelectrons accelerated from the photocathode are focused onto a thin silicon target consisting of an array of *pn* junctions. The high-energy photoelectrons generate multiple hole-electron pairs in the silicon target, resulting in gain. The signal is read out by scanning the reverse side of the silicon target with an electron beam, similar to the method used in vidicon camera tubes. In other types of EBS (electron-bombarded silicon) tubes, the silicon *pn* junction target is replaced with scanned photodiode arrays or with CCD (charge-coupled device) imagers. In these cases, the electronic readout of the silicon targets is accomplished without the use of a scanned electron beam, and this results in even lower light-level performance. SEE TELEVISION CAMERA TUBE.

**Solid-state image intensifiers.** A greal deal of exploratory work has been done on solid-state light amplifiers. The form which has been extensively investigated consists of a photoconductive film in contact with an electroluminescent screen. Current flows through the photoconductor at illuminated areas, causing light to be generated in the electroluminescent layer. This type of intensifier gives considerable image enhancement at intermediate light levels, but fails at very low light levels because of extreme time lag. SEE ELECTROLUMINESCENCE.

Another type of solid-state light amplifier which works at intermediate light levels is the liquid-crystal light valve. The light valve consists of an electrically biased multilayer sandwich which has a liquid-crystal layer on the front face and a photoconductive layer on the rear face. In this system, the incident light is focused on the photoconductive side, while a bright, polarized light is projected onto the liquid-crystal side. The incident light from the photoconductive side causes an increase in voltage drop across the liquid crystal. This increased voltage causes a rotation in the orientation of the liquid-crystal molecules, which in turn modulates the polarization of the reflected projection light. Only the modulated reflected light is allowed to be viewed.

**Applications.** In addition to their application for night vision, light amplifiers have been useful in many fields of science, such as astronomy, nuclear physics, and microbiology.

*Dean R. Collins*

***Bibliography***. D. R. Collins et al., Development of a CCD for ultraviolet imaging using a CCD photocathode combination. *Proceedings of the Symposium on Charge Coupled Device Technology for Scientific Imaging Applications,* Jet Propulsion Laboratory, pp. 163–174, 1975; A. D. Jacobson et al., A new color-TV projector, *SID77 Digest,* Society for Information Displays, pp. 106–107, 1977; *RCA Electro-Optics Handbook,* 1974.

## Light-emitting diode

A rectifying semiconductor device which converts electric energy into electromagnetic radiation. The wavelength of the emitted radiation ranges from the green to the near infrared, that is, from about 550 to over 1300 nanometers. Blue light-emitting diodes (LEDs) have also been reported, but they are not available commercially.

**Fabrication methods.** Most commercial light-emitting diodes, both visible and infrared, are fabricated from group III–V compounds. These compounds contain elements such as gallium, indium, and aluminum of group III and arsenic and phosphorus of group V of the periodic table. With the addition of the proper impurities, III–V compounds can be made *p*- or *n*-type, to form *p-n* junctions. They also possess the proper band gap to produce radiation of the required wavelength and are efficient in the conversion of electric energy into radiation. The fabrication of light-emitting diodes begins with the preparation of single-crystal substrates usually made of gallium arsenide (GaAs), 250–350 micrometers (0.010–0.014 in.) thick. Both *p*- and *n*-type layers are formed over this substrate by depositing layers of semiconductor material from a vapor or from a melt.

The most commonly used light-emitting diode is the red light-emitting diode, made of gallium arsenide-phosphide on gallium arsenide substrates (**Fig. 1***a*). An *n*-type layer is grown over the substrate by vapor-phase deposition followed by a diffusion step to form the *p-n* junction. Ohmic contacts are made by evaporating metallic layers to both *n*- and *p*-type materials. The arrows indicate the emitted light at the *p-n* junction. The light generated at any point is uniformly distributed in all directions. Only a small fraction of the light striking the top surface of the diode can escape, however, due to the large difference in the refractive indices between semiconductor and air. Most of the light is internally reflected and absorbed by the substrate. Hence a typical red light-emitting diode has only a few percent external quantum efficiency, that is, only a few percent of the electric energy results in useful light. More efficient and therefore brighter light-emitting diodes can be fabricated on a gallium phosphide substrate, which is transparent to the emitted radiation and permits the light to escape upon reflection from the back contact. Although more expensive than light-emitting diodes made of gallium arsenide, these high-efficiency light sources compete favorably in brightness with miniature incandescent lamps.

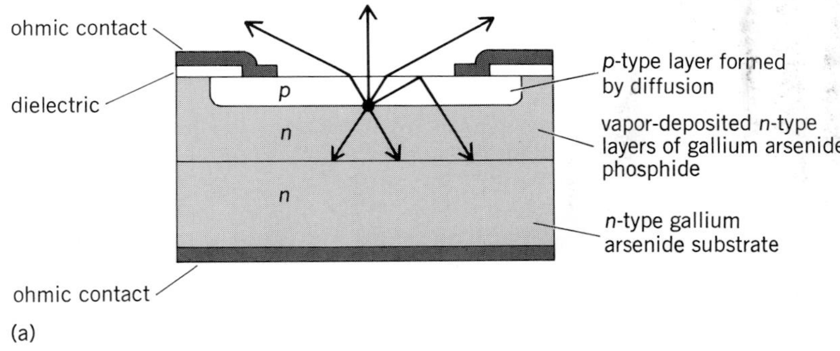


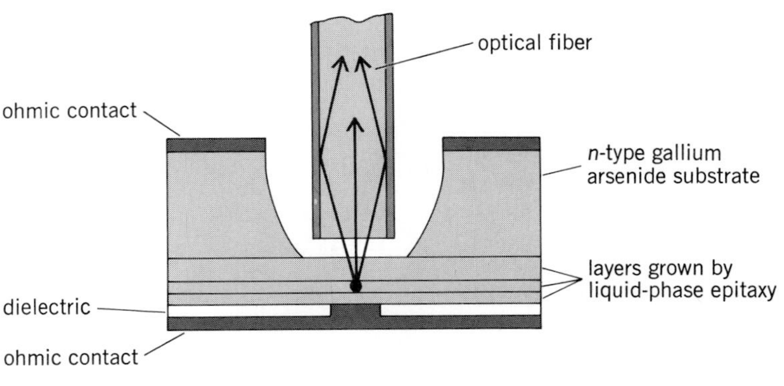


**Fig. 1. Diagrams of light-emitting diodes. (*a*) Red-emitting gallium arsenide-phosphide LED. (*b*) Infrared, etched-well LED designed for coupling radiation into an optical fiber.**

Extracting the infrared radiation into an optical fiber is even more challenging since the fiber has a narrow (10–15°) acceptance angle. It is also necessary to shorten the response time of the light-emitting diode for high data-rate transmission. This is accomplished by introducing several changes into the light-emitting diode design (Fig. 1*b*). First, the light-emitting diode structure is turned around compared with that of the red diode (Fig. 1*a*), and the radiation is extracted through an etched well on the side of the substrate. A dielectric layer separates most of the ohmic contact on the other side, limiting the active area of the junction to the size of the optical fiber. Finally, one or several additional layers are deposited (4 in Fig. 1*b*) to increase quantum efficiency and response time. The optical power from the light-emitting diode is limited by the heat dissipation of the semiconductor chip, which is usually mounted on a gold heat sink. Although some light-emitting diodes of this type are commercially available, development is being directed toward longer-wavelength devices (peak emission at 1.3 μm compared with 0.85 μm for the above light-emitting diodes) using layers containing four elements, gallium, indium, arsenic, and phosphorus, grown on indium phosphide substrates. These light-emitting diodes can send higher data rates over longer distances in the optical fibers.

**Applications.** Visible light-emitting diodes are used as solid-state indicator lights and as light sources for numeric and alphanumeric displays. Infrared light-emitting diodes are used in optoisolators and in optical fiber transmission in order to obtain the highest possible efficiency.

***Indicators and displays.*** The advantages of light-emitting diodes as light sources are their small size, ruggedness, low operating temperature, long life, and compatibility with silicon integrated circuits. They are widely used as status indicators in instruments, cameras, appliances, dashboards, computer terminals, and so forth, and as nighttime illuminators for instrument panels and telephone dials. Visible light-emitting diodes are commercially available in red, orange, yellow, and green. Blue-light emitters have been made in the laboratory on wide band-gap materials such as silicon carbide, gallium nitride, and zinc sulfide. These devices have different structures than the *p-n* junctions described above, their fabrication is more expensive, and their brightness is lower by approximately two orders of magnitude than that of other light-emitting diodes, and hence they are not employed commercially.

Some of the most commonly used light-emitting diode structures are shown in **Fig. 2**. The metal-flanged, single-lead design (Fig. 2*a*) is very rugged and easy to insert; the lead-frame package (Fig. 2*b*) can easily incorporate built-in voltage regulators so that the light-emitting diodes can be operated over a range of input voltages such as 3–15 V. Some packages have provisions to focus or redistribute the light, such as the lead frame with a built-in reflector (Fig. 2*c*). Light-emitting diodes can also be employed to light up a segment of a large numeric display, used for example on alarm clocks; or a small numeric display with seven light-emitting diodes can be formed on a single substrate, as commonly used on watches and hand-held calculators.

***Optoisolators.*** Infrared light-emitting diodes with solid-state photodetectors provide an optical interface in electric circuits. In the simplest optical interface, the optoisolator, a light-emitting diode and a photodetector are optically coupled, but electrically isolated, in a small package. This device can be used, for example, at the interface between two different circuits, such as the switching equipment in a telephone central office and the connecting loop circuit which carries the signals to the telephone sets. The electric signal from the central office is converted to radiation by the light-emitting diode, which in turn is converted back into an electric signal by the photodetector before it enters the loop circuit. This type of interface is traditionally provided by electromechanical relays or isolation transformers. The electrical isolation resulting from the optical path protects the central office from electromagnetic interferences such as lightning which hits telephone wires or surge currents from electromechanical relays. Light-emitting diodes are ideal for this application because they are small, rugged, efficient, reliable, and can be modulated to carry high-frequency signals.

In a typical optoisolator structure (**Fig. 3**), the light-emitting diode and the phototransistor are mounted on separate metal lead frames, and the two components are coupled optically through a transpar-

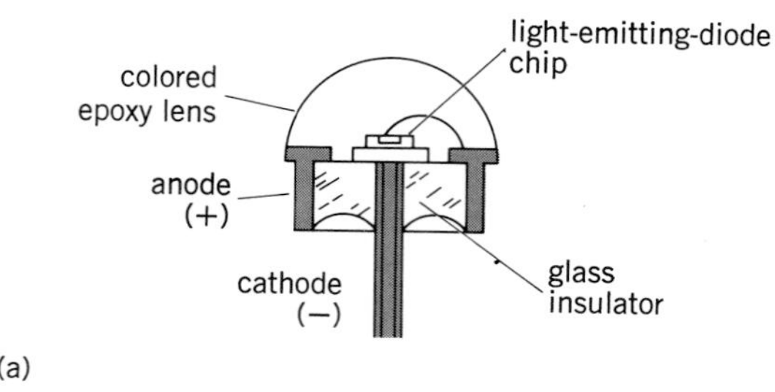


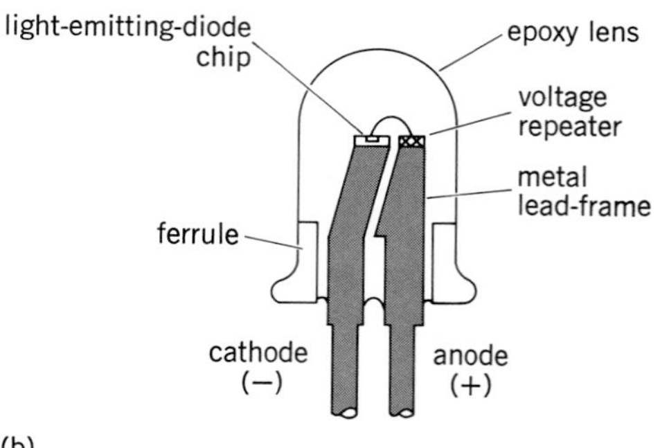


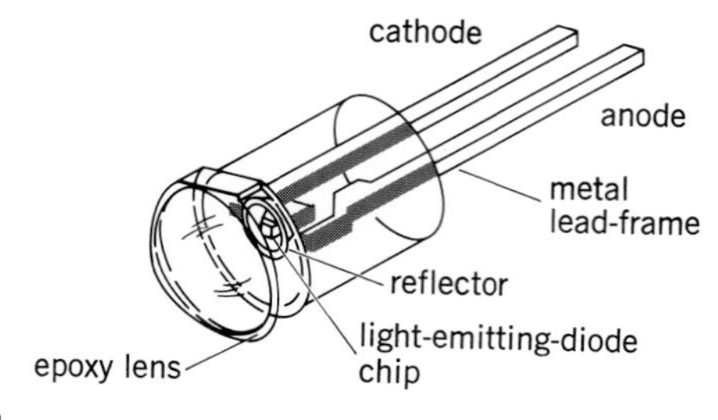


**Fig. 2. Light-emitting diode lamps. (*a*) Metal-flanged single-lead header. (*b*) Lead-frame package with built-in resistor. (c) Lead-frame package with built-in reflector.**

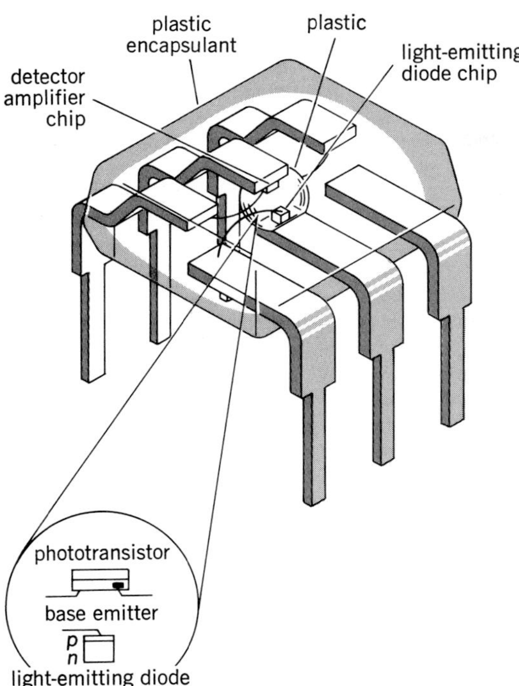


**Fig. 3. Typical optoisolator in plastic-encapsulated dual in-line package.**

ent plastic encapsulant. This plastic is also the source of electrical isolation, typically on the order of 2500 V. Final encapsulation is completed with a black, opaque overmold which also provides mechanical stability. Optoisolators are compatible with silicon integrated circuits in size, reliability, and performance parameters, giving them a prominent role in modern solid-state circuits. *See* Optical isolator.

***Optical fiber transmission.*** Another rapidly evolving application of infrared light-emitting diodes is in optical fiber transmission. The optical signal is fed into a thin (50–100 μm or 0.002–0.004 in. in diameter) optical fiber and transmitted over distances ranging from several hundred meters to over 10 km (6 mi). At the other end of the fiber, a photodetector converts the optical signals back to electric signals similar to those in optoisolators. This fiber, which replaces coaxial cables, is smaller in volume, less expensive, and immune to electromagnetic interference. It also transmits higher data rates and provides longer repeater spacings than metal conductors. Since doped silica fibers exhibit both low loss and minimum material dispersion near 1.3 μm, light-emitting diode sources at this wavelength can achieve a repeater spacing of 10 km (6 mi) at a data rate of 250 megabits per second. This will provide a major market for high-performance light-emitting diodes and support the development of long-wave-length light-emitting diodes. *See* Optical communications.

For further discussion of the properties of *p-n* junctions and light generation in solid-state devices *see* Electroluminescence; Junction diode; Junction transistor; Laser.

*A. A. Bergh*

***Bibliography.*** A. A. Bergh and P. J. Dean, *Light Emitting Diodes*, 1976; C. H. Gooch, *Injection Electroluminescent Devices*, 1973; S. E. Miller and A. G. Chynoweth, *Optical Fiber Telecommunications*, 1979; E. W. Williams and R. Hall, *Luminescence and the Light Emitting Diode*, 1978.

## Light panel

A surface-area light source that employs the principle of electroluminescence to produce light. Light panels are composed of two sheets of electrically conductive material, one a thin conducting backing and the other a transparent conductive film, placed on opposite sides of a plastic or ceramic sheet impregnated with a phosphor, such as zinc sulfide, and small amounts of compounds of copper or manganese. When an alternating voltage is applied to the conductive sheets, an electric field is applied to the phosphor. Each time the electric field changes, it dislodges electrons from the edges of the phosphor crystals. As these electrons fall back to their normal atomic state, they affect the atoms of the slight ''impurities'' of copper or manganese, and radiation of the wavelength of light is emitted. *See* Electroluminescence.

In contrast to incandescent, vapor-discharge, and fluorescent lamps, which are essentially point or line sources of light, the electroluminescent light panel is essentially a surface source of light. Complete freedom of size and shape is a fascinating aspect of luminescent cells (see **illus.**).

Brightness of the panel depends upon the voltage applied to the phosphor layer and upon the electrical frequency. In general, higher voltage and higher frequency both result in a brighter panel. Blue, green, red, or yellow light can be produced by the choice of phosphors, and the proper blend of these colors produces white light. Color can be varied for a particular phosphor by changing the frequency of the applied voltage. Increasing the frequency shifts the color toward the blue end of the spectrum.

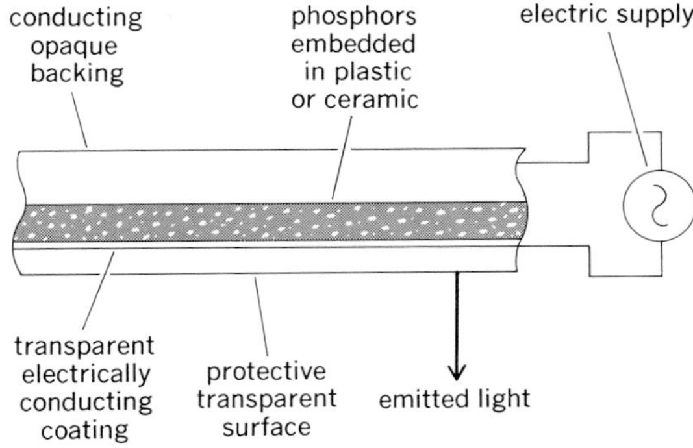


**Simplified diagram of an electroluminescent cell; the sketch is not drawn to scale.**

The efficiency of these light panels is only a fraction of that of the most efficient fluorescent lamps. Theoretical limits indicate, however, that the efficiency can be further improved, probably to exceed that for fluorescent lamps. Because panel lights employ no filaments and no evacuated or gas-filled bulbs, replacement of units is virtually eliminated. Glareless uniform distribution of light from large-area sources is possible without shades, louvers, or other control devices.

*Warren B. Boast*

## Limiter circuit

An electronic circuit used to prevent the amplitude of an electrical waveform from exceeding a specified level while preserving the shape of the waveform at amplitudes less than the specified level. The limiting action takes place by effectively shunting a normal load resistance with a much lower resistance at and above the specified limiting level.

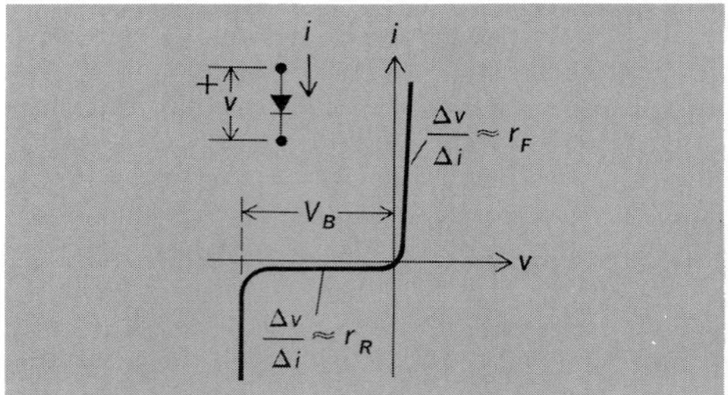

**Fig. 1. Voltage-current characteristic of junction diode shows instantaneous diode current *i* as a function of instantaneous voltage *v*.**

**Diode limiters.** Limiting action is usually accomplished by use of the highly nonlinear or "switching" voltage-current characteristic of an electronic device. A semiconductor diode used as a clamp is often the essential element in a limiter circuit. The action of such a diode may be understood with reference to the voltage-current characteristic of a typical semiconductor diode shown in **Fig. 1**. In the first quadrant, the diode is forward-biased, conduction depends on forward resistance $r_F$, and the characteristic can be approximated by a linear resistance of a very low value, ranging from a few ohms to several hundred ohms. In the third quadrant, the diode is reverse-biased. Until the breakdown point is reached, this portion of the characteristic can be approximated by a very large re-

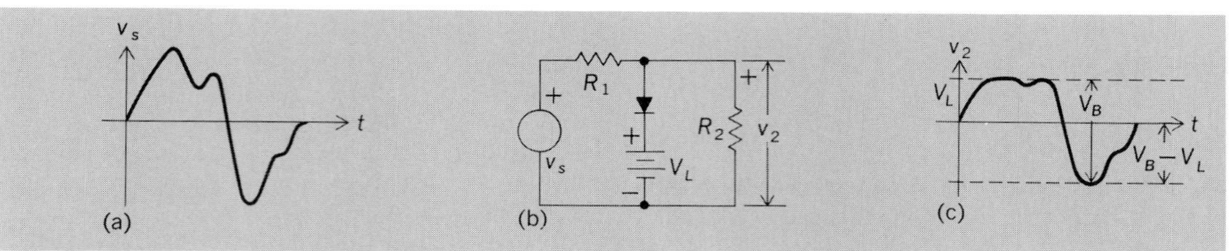

**Fig. 2. In combined forward-bias and reverse-breakdown limiting, (*a*) input voltage applied to (*b*) limiting circuit produces (*c*) output voltage.**

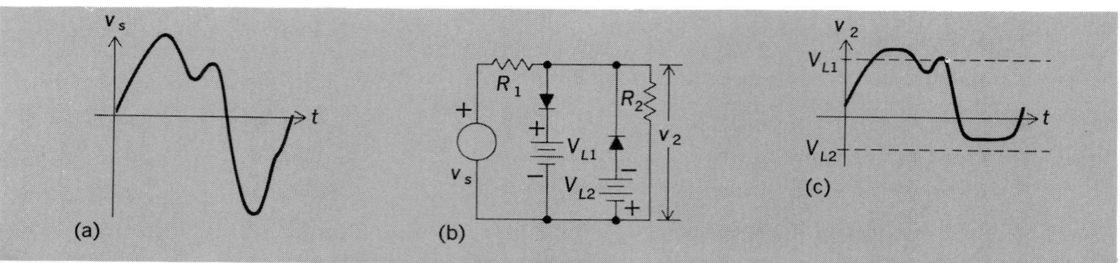

**Fig. 3. For bidirectional limiting (*a*) input voltage can be limited in both directions by (*b*) circuit. (*c*) Bias voltage $V_{L1}$ sets positive limit level and independent voltage $V_{L2}$ sets negative level to produce output voltage.**

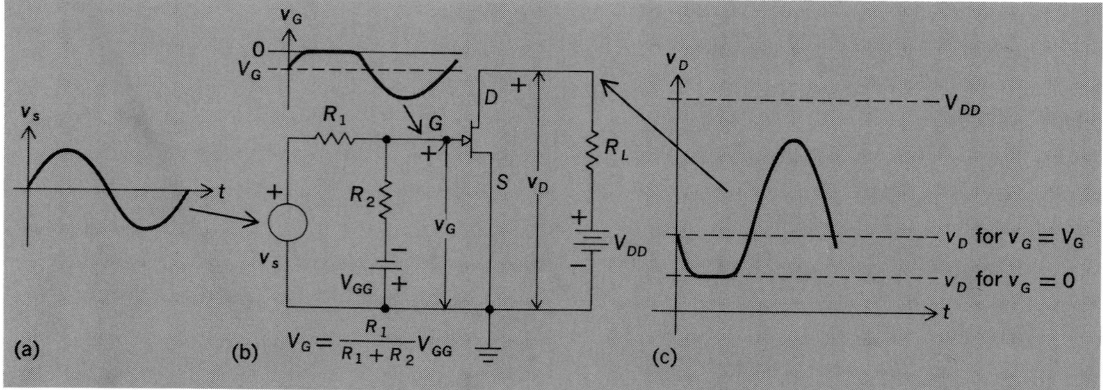

**Fig. 4. In a gate-current limiter using a junction FET, (*a*) input voltage $v_s$ is limited in (*b*) the gate circuit to produce gate voltage $v_G$. This voltage is then amplified and inverted in the drain circuit to produce (*c*) output voltage $v_D$. Gate bias voltage $V_{GG}$ and the divider composed of the resistances $R_1$ and $R_2$ determine the quiescent level $V_G$ which corresponds to $v_s$ = 0.**

sistance $r_R$, ranging up to several megohms. At the breakdown point a sharp change occurs. For the semiconductor diode, this point is known as the Zener or avalanche breakdown region and can range from a few volts upward. After the breakdown, current becomes essentially independent of voltage. Either the sharp transition between reverse- and forward-bias regions or the avalanche transition may be used as a limit. *SEE CLAMPING CIRCUIT; SEMICONDUCTOR DIODE.*

**Use of both limits.** Use of both limits simultaneously is illustrated in **Fig. 2**, where input voltage $v_s$ and output voltage $v_2$ are shown as functions of time $t$. The positive amplitude of the output waveform is limited at reference voltage $V_L$; negative amplitude is limited at a level $V_L - V_B$. Sharp limiting in the forward-bias direction is achieved when forward resistance $r_F$ is small compared to reverse-bias resistance $r_R$ and when $r_F$ is small compared to series limit resistance $R_1$. A vacuum diode may be used as the limiter at its transition between reverse- and forward-bias regions, but it has no well-defined breakdown level comparable to the avalanche region of a junction diode. Either positive or negative limiting at the reverse–forward-bias transition can be obtained with semiconductor or vacuum diodes by choice of polarities, voltage, and diode. If bidirectional limiting is desired, the circuit of **Fig. 3** can be used with two diodes and two separate bias voltages.

**Triode limiters.** Bipolar or field-effect transistors can also be used as limiters, in either the input or output circuits. For example, in the circuit of **Fig. 4**, if the input waveform becomes sufficiently positive, the gate-source circuit becomes a forward-based diode, and limiting takes place as it does in the diode circuit. The drain current is limited at a value corresponding to the positive gate drive if $R_L$ is sufficiently low that output limiting does not take place simultaneously. *SEE TRANSISTOR.*

**Limiting by saturation.** Saturation characteristics of the output circuit of a field-effect transistor or bipolar transistor can also produce limiting action. **Figure 5** illustrates this action for an *n*-channel junction field-effect transistor. The characteristics shown are those of drain current $i_D$ as a function of drain voltage $v_D$ for successive values of input, or gate voltage $V_G$ through the normal range. The input voltage bias level and the load resistance are so chosen that limiting takes place in the output circuit when drain current saturation level is reached. The corresponding output voltage waveform is plotted.

The bipolar transistor functions in a similar manner, with the output characteristics that are similar to those of Fig. 5 being collector current as a function of collector voltage, for a range of values of input or base current (rather than input voltage) because the bipolar transistor is a low-input-resistance device. Such a circuit is shown in **Fig. 6** for an *npn* transistor with the base-emitter circuit forward-biased.

All polarities can be reversed by using *p*-channel field-effect transistors or *pnp* transistors in place of the transistors of Figs. 5 and 6, respectively.

The term limiter is often defined in sufficiently broad terms to include the related operation of clipping, which also results in deletion of a portion of a waveform. Some authors even use the terms interchangeably. Limiters and clippers are often used together, rather than bidirectional limiters alone, where both negative and positive peaks of a waveform are to be removed. *SEE CLIPPING CIRCUIT.*

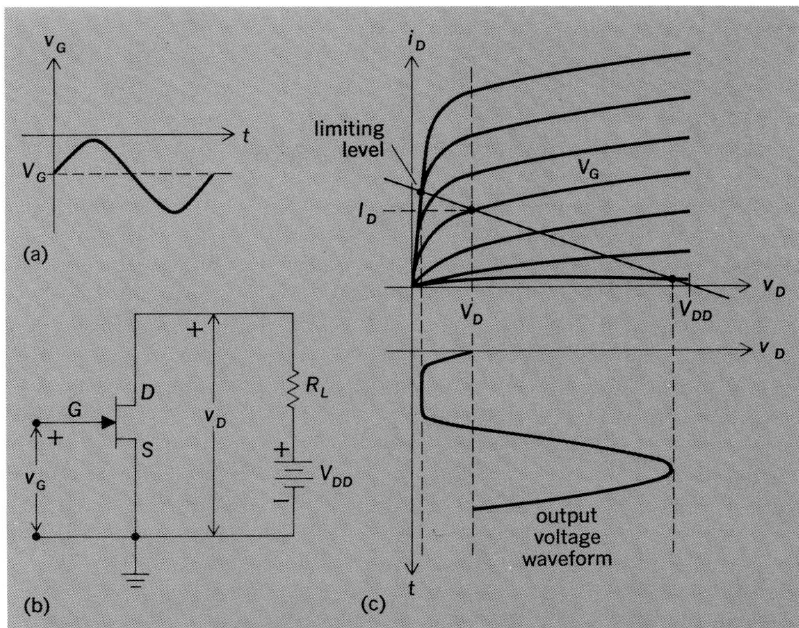


**Fig. 5.** Output saturation limiting using *n*-channel junction field-effect transistor limits (*a*) input voltage in (*b*) circuit because of saturation of drain current, as shown on (c) the $v_D - i_D$ characteristic curves, to produce output voltage.

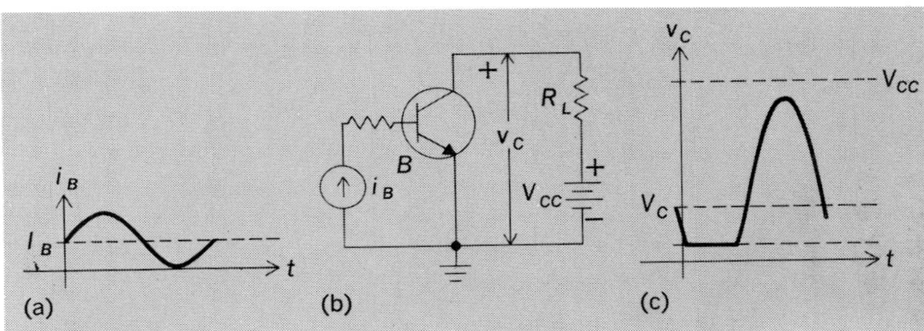


**Fig. 6.** When (*a*) the input voltage is applied to (*b*) the circuit with an *npn* transistor, the collector current limiting produces (c) the output voltage.

*Glenn M. Glasford*

**Bibliography.** J. Millman, *Microelectronics*, 1979; C. A. Schuler, *Electronics: Principles and Applications*, 2d ed., 1984; H. Taub and D. Schilling, *Digital Integrated Electronics*, 1976.

## Linear programming

A mathematical subject whose central theme is finding the point where a linear function defined on a convex polyhedron assumes its maximum or minimum value. Although contributions to this question existed earlier, the subject was essentially created in 1947, when G. B. Dantzig defined its scope and proposed the first, and still most widely used, method for the practical solution of linear programming problems. The largest class of applications of linear programming occurs in business planning and industrial engineering. Its basic concepts are so fundamental, however, that linear programming has been used in almost all parts of science and social science where mathematics has made any penetration. Furthermore, even in cases where the domain is not a polyhedron, or the function to be maximized or minimized is not linear, the methods used are frequently adaptions of linear programming. SEE NONLINEAR PROGRAMMING; OPERATIONS RESEARCH.

**General theory.** A typical linear programming problem is to maximize expression (1), where $x_1$,

$$c_1x_1 + \cdots + c_nx_n \qquad (1)$$

$\ldots, x_n$ satisfy the conditions shown by notation (2).

$$\begin{array}{c} x_j \geqq 0 \\ a_{11}x_1 + \cdots + a_{1n}x_n \leqq b_1 \\ \cdots\cdots\cdots\cdots \\ a_{m1}x_1 + \cdots + \alpha_{mn}x_n \leqq b_m \end{array} \qquad (2)$$

The $a_{ij}$, $c_j$, and $b_1$ are constants; $x_1, \ldots, x_n$ are variables.

Sometimes the problem may be to minimize rather than to maximize; sometimes some of the variables may not be required to be nonnegative; sometimes some of the inequalities $a_{i1}x_1 + \cdots + a_{in}x_n \leqq b_i$ may be reversed, or be equalities.

The linear inequalities, which the variables satisfy, correspond algebraically to the fact that the variable point $x = (x_1, \ldots, x_n)$ lies in a convex polyhedron. Hence, the principal mathematical bases for linear programming are the theory of linear equalities, a part of algebra, and the theory of convex polyhedra, a part of geometry. The most important theoretical foundations are as follows.

If the function $c_1x_1 + \cdots + c_nx_n$ does not get arbitrarily large for points $x = (x_1, \ldots, x_n)$ on the convex polyhedron, then a maximum is attained at a vertex of the polyhedron.

If there is a maximum in the stated problem, then there is a minimum in the dual problem of minimizing $b_1y_1 + \cdots + b_my_m$, where notation (3) applies.

$$\begin{array}{c} y_i \geqq 0 \\ a_{11}y_1 + \cdots + a_{m1}y_m \leqq c_1 \\ \cdots\cdots\cdots\cdots \\ a_{1n}y_1 + \cdots + a_{mn}y_m \leqq c_n \end{array} \qquad (3)$$

Further, the maximum and minimum are the same number. This duality theorem is essentially equivalent to the minimax theorem. Both the duality theorem and the minimax theorem are algebraic paraphrases of the geometric fact that if a point is not contained in a convex polyhedron then a hyperplane can be found which separates the point from the polyhedron. The duality theorem is also closely related to the concept of Lagrange multipliers.

In an important class of linear programming problems, there is imposed an additional requirement that some or all of the variables must be whole numbers. If the numbers $b_1, \ldots, b_n$ are whole numbers, and if every square submatrix of $(a_{ij})$ has determinant 0, 1, or $-1$, then the integrality requirement will be automatically satisfied. In any case, the faces of the convex hull of the integral points inside a polyhedron can be found by a finite process in which, at each stage, a new inequality is determined by taking a nonnegative linear combination of previous inequalities and replacing each coefficient by the largest integer not exceeding it.

**Methods of calculation.** The most popular method for solving linear programs, that is, the finding of the $x = (x_1, \ldots, x_n)$ which maximizes $c_1x_1 + \cdots + c_nx_n$, is the simplex method, developed by Dantzig in 1947. The method is geometrically a process of moving from vertex to neighboring vertex on the convex polyhedron, each move attaining a higher value of $c_1x_1 + \cdots + c_nx_n$, until the vertex yielding the greatest value is reached. Algebraically, the calculations are similar to elimination processes for solving systems of algebraic equations. The computer programs used try to take advantage of the fact that almost all the matrices $(a_{ij})$ arising in practice have very few nonzero entries.

The popularity of the simplex method rests on the empirical fact that the number of moves from vertex to vertex is a small multiple (about 2–4) of the number of inequalities in most of the thousands of problems handled, although it has never been proved mathematically that this behavior is characteristic of "average" problems.

There have also been developed methods of calculation specifically tailored for special classes of problems. One such class (network flows) is exemplified by the transportation problem described below. Another important class is where most of the columns of $(a_{ij})$ are not known explicitly in advance, but consist of all columns which satisfy some particular set of rules. The idea used here (known in different contexts as the column-generation principle or the decomposition principle) is that the new vertex prescribed by the simplex method can be found if a solution is achieved for the problem of maximizing a linear function defined on the set of columns satisfying the particular rules.

The technology of solving integer linear programming problems is not stabilized. Methods vary from testing integral points near the optimum fractional point to systematic methods for generating relevant faces of the convex hull of the integral points satisfying the given inequalities.

**Applications.** Let $a_{ij}$ denote the number of units of nutrient $j$ present in one unit of food $i$. Let $c_j$ be the minimum amount of nutrient $j$ needed for satisfactory health, $b_i$ be the unit price of food $i$. Let the variables $y_i$ denote respectively the number of units of food $i$ to be bought. Then the dual problem is the so-called diet problem, to maintain adequate nutrition at least cost. It has been used in planning feeding programs for several varieties of livestock and poultry. With a different interpretation of the symbols, the same format describes the problem of combining raw materials in a chemical process to produce required end products as cheaply as possible.

In another situation, let $c_{ij}$ be the cost of shipping one unit of a given product from warehouse $i$ to customer $j$ for all $m$ warehouses $i$ and all $n$ customers $j$ pertaining to a business. Let $a_i$ be the amount available at warehouse $i$, and $b_j$ the amount required by customer $j$. The transportation problem is to ship the required amounts to the customers at least cost. Thus, if $x_{ij}$ is the amount to be shipped from $i$ to $j$, then minimize notation (4), where $x_{i1} + \cdots + x_{in} \leqq a_i$

$$c_{11}x_{11} + \cdots + c_{mn}x_{mn} \qquad (4)$$

($i = 1, \ldots, m$) and $x_{1j} + \cdots x_{mj} = b_j$ ($j = 1, \ldots, n$).

The foregoing are representative of the business applications of linear programming, several hundred of which have now been reported. The best-known applications outside business have been to economic theory and to combinatorial analysis. In both instances, the duality theorem has been used to illuminate and generalize previous results.

*Alan J. Hoffman*

***Bibliography.*** V. Chavatal, *Linear Programming*, 1983; S. I. Gass, *Linear Programming*, 4th ed., 1975; J. P. Ignizio, *Linear Programming in Single and Multiple Objective Systems*, 1982; K. Murty, *Linear Programming*, 1983; N. Wu and R. Coppins, *Linear Programming and Extensions*, 1981.

## Linearity

The relationship that exists between two quantities when a change in one of them produces a directly proportional change in the other. Thus, an amplifier has good linearity when doubling of its input signal strength always doubles the output signal strength. A transistor displays good linearity when doubling of the instantaneous base voltage serves to double the instantaneous value of collector current.

In television, uniform linearity of scanning is essential for uniform spacing of picture elements in each horizontal line and uniform vertical spacings between scanning lines. Poor linearity causes the picture to be compressed or stretched in some area, so that circles of test patterns become eggshaped or even more greatly distorted. *SEE SAWTOOTH-WAVE GENERATOR.*

*John Markus*

## Liquid crystals

A state of matter that mixes the properties of both the liquid and solid states. Liquid crystals may be described as condensed fluid states with spontaneous anisotropy. They are categorized in two ways: thermotropic liquid crystals, prepared by heating the substance, and lyotropic liquid crystals, prepared by mixing two or more components, one of which is rather polar in character (for example, water). Thermotropic liquid crystals are divided, according to structural characteristics, into two classes, nematic and smectic. Nematics are further subdivided into ordinary and cholesterics.

When the solid which forms a liquid crystal is heated it undergoes transformation into a turbid system that is both fluid and birefringent. The consistency of the fluid varies with different compounds from a paste to a free-flowing liquid. When the turbid system is heated, it is converted into an isotropic liquid (optical properties are the same regardless of the direction of the measurement). These changes in phases can be represented schematically as follows:

$$\text{Solid} \underset{\text{cool}}{\overset{\text{heat}}{\rightleftharpoons}} \text{liquid crystal} \underset{\text{cool}}{\overset{\text{heat}}{\rightleftharpoons}} \text{liquid}$$

On cooling the system, the process reverses and goes from isotropic liquid to liquid crystal and finally to the solid.

Lyotropic liquid crystals often have an amphiphilic component, a compound with a polar head attached to a long hydrophobic tail. Sodium stearate and lecithin (a phospholipid) are typical examples of amphiphiles. Starting with a solid amphiphile and adding water, the lamellar structure (molecular packing in layers) is formed. By step-wise addition of water, the molecular packing may take on a cubic structure, then hexagonal, then micellar, followed by true solution. The process is reversed by withdrawing water. Thousands of compounds will form liquid crystals on heating, and still more will do so if two or more components are mixed. A few representative compounds are listed in the **table**.

**Classification and structure.** Conventionally, matter is considered to have only three states: solid, liquid, and gas. In the solid state, the molecules or atoms show small vibrations about rigidly fixed lattice positions, but they cannot rotate. A liquid will take the shape of its container and will bound itself at the top with its own free surface. The liquid state is characterized by relatively unhindered rotation and no long-range order. The space in a system constituting a gas is sparsely occupied. The molecules are free to occupy the entire volume of their container.

Liquid crystals are a state of matter that combines a kind of long-range order (in the sense of a solid) with the ability to form droplets and to pour (in the sense of waterlike liquids). They also exhibit properties of their own such as the ability to form monocrystals with the application of a normal magnetic or electric field; an optical activity of a magnitude without parallel in either solids or liquids; and a temperature sensitivity which results in a color change in certain liquid crystals. Thermotropic liquid crystals are either nematic or smectic.

***Nematic structure.*** Nematic liquid crystals are subdivided into the ordinary nematic and the cholesteric-nematic. The molecules in the ordinary nematic structure maintain a parallel or nearly parallel arrangement to each other along the long molecular axes (**Fig. 1***a*). They are mobile in three directions and can rotate about one axis. This structure is one-dimensional.

When the nematic structure is heated, it is generally transformed into the isotropic liquid (Fig. 1*b*). The nematic structure is the highest-temperature me-

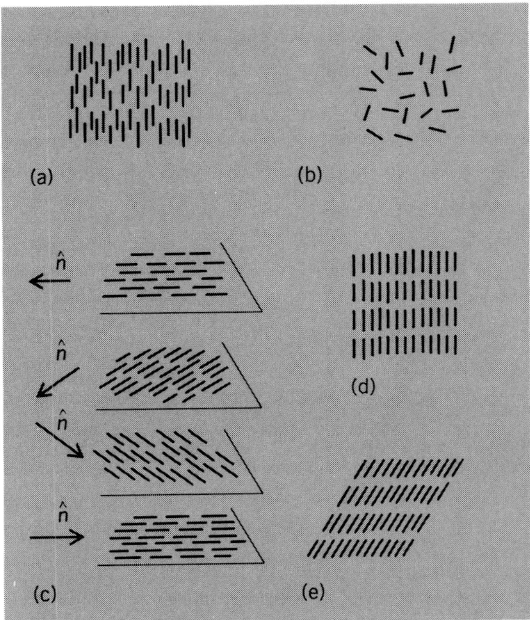


**Fig. 1. Schematic representation of the molecular arrangement in the (*a*) ordinary nematic liquid crystal; (*b*) isotropic liquid; (c) cholesteric-nematic liquid crystal; (*d*) smectic A liquid crystal; and (e) smectic C liquid crystal. (*After G. H. Brown and J. J. Wolken, Liquid Crystals and Biological Structures, Academic Press, 1979*)**

**Name, formula, and liquid crystalline range of selected compounds**

| THERMOTROPIC LIQUID CRYSTALS | |
|---|---|
| *1. Nematic liquid crystals* | |
| $H_3C-O-C_6H_4-CH=N-C_6H_4-C_4H_9-n$ <br> *p*-Methoxybenzylidene-*p*′-butylaniline (MBBA) | 70–117°F (21–47°C) |
| $H_{11}C_5-C_6H_4-C_6H_4-CN$ <br> 4-Cyano-4′-*n*-pentyl-biphenyl | 75–95°F (24–35°C) |
| $H_{11}C_5-C_6H_4-C_6H_4-C_6H_4-CN$ <br> 4-Cyano-4″-*n*-pentyl-*n*-terphenyl | 268–464°F (131–240°C) |
| $H_3C-O-C_6H_4-N=N(\rightarrow O)-C_6H_4-O-CH_3$ <br> *p*-Azoxyanisole (PAA) | 243–279°F (117–137°C) |
| *2. Cholesteric esters* | |
| $CH_3(CH_2)_7-C(=O)-O-$ (cholesteryl; side chain $-CH(CH_3)-(CH_2)_3-CH(CH_3)_2$) <br> Cholesteryl nonanoate | 293–354°F (145–179°C) |
| *3. Noncholesteryl, chiral-type compound* | |
| $H_3C-O-C_6H_4-CH=N-C_6H_4-CH=CH-C(=O)-O-CH_2-CH(CH_3)-C_2H_5$ <br> (−)-2-Methylbutyl-*p*-(*p*′-methoxy-benzylideneamino) cinnamate | 169–257°F (76–125°C) |

sophase in thermotropic liquid crystals. The energy required to deform a nematic liquid crystal is so small that even the slightest perturbation caused by a dust particle can distort the structure considerably.

In the cholesteric-nematic structure (Fig. 1*c*), the direction of the long axis of the molecule in a given layer is slightly displaced from the direction of the molecular axes of the molecules in an adjacent layer. If a twist is applied to this molecular packing, a helical structure is formed. The helix has a pitch which is temperature-sensitive. The helical structure serves as a diffraction grating for visible light. Chiral compounds show the cholesteric-nematic structure (twisted nematic), for example, the cholesteric esters.

***Smectic structure.*** The term smectic covers all thermotropic liquid crystals that are not nematics. At least seven smectic structures have been described. Indications are that two more can be added, making a total of nine from smectic A($S_A$) to smectic I ($S_I$). The alphabetic subscripts only indicate the order in which the smectic structures were first recognized and identified. In most smectic structure, molecules are arranged in strata. The molecules (except in smectic D) are arranged in layers with their long axes parallel to each other. They can move in two directions in the plane and can rotate about one axis. Those within layers can be in neat rows or randomly distributed.

Smectic liquid crystals may have structured or unstructured strata. Structured smectic liquid crystals have long-range order in the arrangement of molecules in layers to form a regular two-dimensional lattice. The most common of the structured liquid crystals is smectic B. Molecular layers are in well-defined order, and the arrangement of the molecules within the strata is also well ordered. The long axes of the molecules lie perpendicular to the plane of the layers. In the smectic A (Fig. 1*d*) structure, molecules are also packed in strata, but the molecules in a stratum are randomly arranged. The long axes of the molecules in the smectic A structure lie perpendicular to the plane of the layers. Molecular packing in a smectic C (Fig. 1*e*) is the same as that in smectic A, except the molecules in the stratum are tilted at an angle to the plane of the stratum.

There is also a unique kind of liquid crystal known

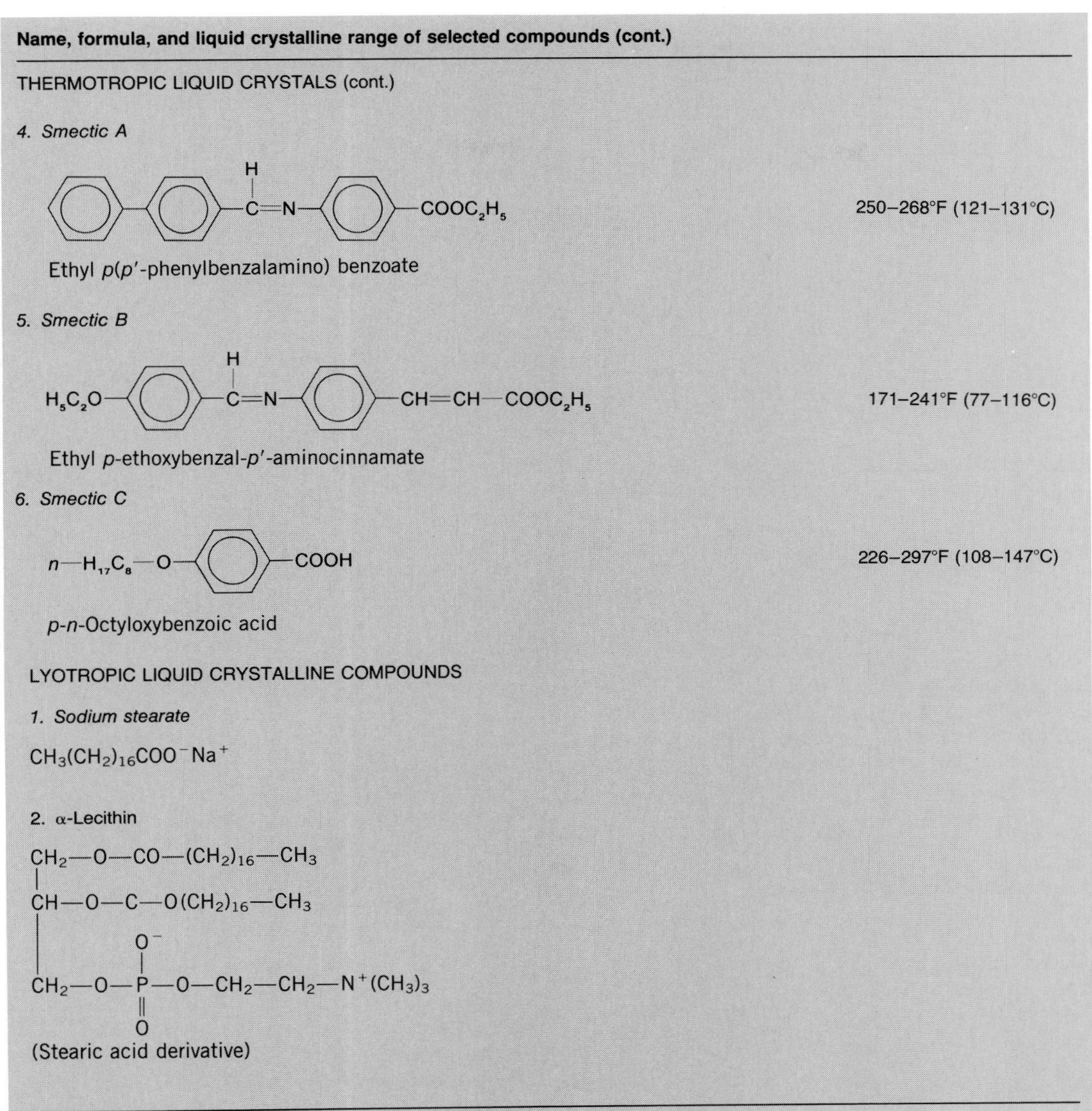

**Name, formula, and liquid crystalline range of selected compounds (cont.)**

THERMOTROPIC LIQUID CRYSTALS (cont.)

*4. Smectic A*



250–268°F (121–131°C)

Ethyl *p*(*p*′-phenylbenzalamino) benzoate

*5. Smectic B*



171–241°F (77–116°C)

Ethyl *p*-ethoxybenzal-*p*′-aminocinnamate

*6. Smectic C*



226–297°F (108–147°C)

*p*-*n*-Octyloxybenzoic acid

LYOTROPIC LIQUID CRYSTALLINE COMPOUNDS

*1. Sodium stearate*

$CH_3(CH_2)_{16}COO^-Na^+$

2. α-Lecithin

$CH_2$—O—CO—$(CH_2)_{16}$—$CH_3$
CH—O—C—O$(CH_2)_{16}$—$CH_3$
$O^-$
$CH_2$—O—P—O—$CH_2$—$CH_2$—$N^+(CH_3)_3$
O

(Stearic acid derivative)

as the smectic D which is isotropic, but nevertheless shows three-dimensional order in the molecular packing of the structure.

**Applications.** Liquid crystals have many applications. They are used as displays in digital wristwatches, calculators, panel meters, and industrial products. They can be used to record, store, and display images which can be projected onto a large screen. They also have potential use as television displays.

***Displays.*** The two features which make them more desirable for displays than other materials are lower power consumption and the clarity of display in the presence of bright light. The power requirements are often so low that a digital display on a wristwatch requires about the same power as does the mechanism which runs the watch. The two modes most widely used in liquid crystal displays are dynamic-scattering and field-effect.

In displays, the liquid crystal cell design usually begins with a thin film of a room-temperature liquid crystal sandwiched between two transparent electrodes (glass coated with a metal or metal oxide film). The thickness of the liquid crystal film is 6–25 micrometers and is controlled by a spacer which is chemically inert. The cell is hermetically sealed in order to eliminate oxygen and moisture, both of which may chemically attack the liquid crystalline material.

In dynamic scattering, if no electric field is applied, the cell is transparent. However, on addition of electric field to the liquid crystal, the cell becomes opaque. The field-effect display utilizes twisted nematic liquid crystals. The cell is prepared by rubbing the glass surface directionally or by chemically treating the surface and by adding a chiral compound to nematic liquid crystals. Digital displays are made by photoetching a seven-segment pattern onto one or both of the indium–tin oxide–coated glass plates. Reflection displays have one of the plates coated with a reflecting layer. Transmissive displays have etched surfaces on both plates.

The field-effect display is more widely used in watch and pocket-calculator displays. In a liquid crystal watch that displays hours and minutes (**Fig. 2**), the quartz crystal accurately controls the oscillating cir-

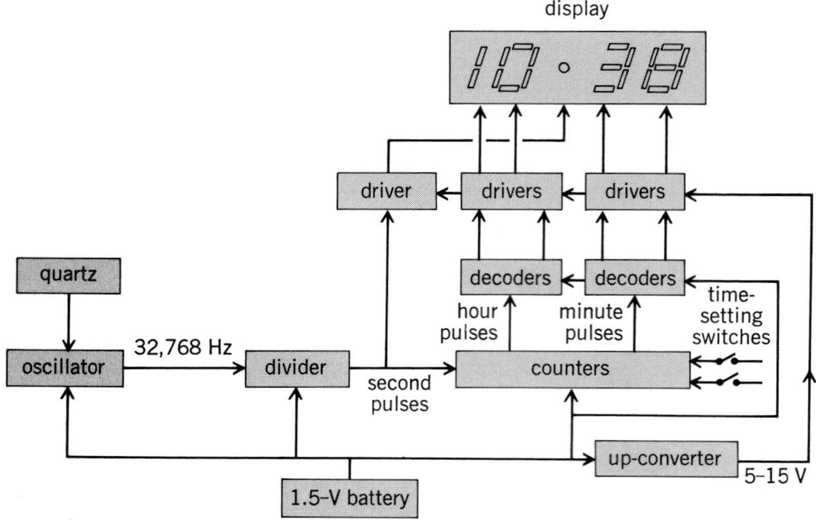


**Fig. 2. Block diagram of a liquid crystal watch.** ***(After F. D. Saeva, ed., Liquid Crystals: The Fourth State of Matter, Marcel Dekker, 1979)***

cuit. The oscillator frequency is typically 32,768 Hz. Each of the time pulses is decoded to give outputs that are needed for seven-segment displays. All electronic watches operate on the same principles, regardless of the display technique (for example liquid crystals and light-emitting diodes). Newer display techniques, such as multiplexing, will reduce the number of electrical leads to the segments in digital and bar-graph displays.

The electronics for the wristwatch display is complex, and the dividers, driver circuits, decoders, and counters contain about 1500 transistors. All of these transistors can be collected on a silicon area of approximately 0.10 by 0.16 in. (0.25 by 0.40 cm). The display for field-effect requires low voltages (1.5 to 5.0 V), and little power.

The optics of the liquid crystal display are shown in **Fig. 3**. The cell with the nematic liquid crystal is placed between two crossed polarizers. Polarized light entering the cell follows the twist of the nematic liquid crystal, is rotated 90°, and as such can allow passage of the light through the second polarizer (Fig. 3*a*). Application of an electric field changes the molecular alignment in the liquid crystal such that the polarization is not altered in the cell and no light is transmitted. If a mirror is used behind the second polarizer, the display will appear black (Fig. 3*b*) when voltage is applied. If, in addition, one of the electrodes is shaped in the pattern of segments of digits, then a numeric display will appear when the voltage is on. By changing the direction of the polarizers, the digit can be made to appear white on a black background. *SEE ELECTRONIC DISPLAY*.

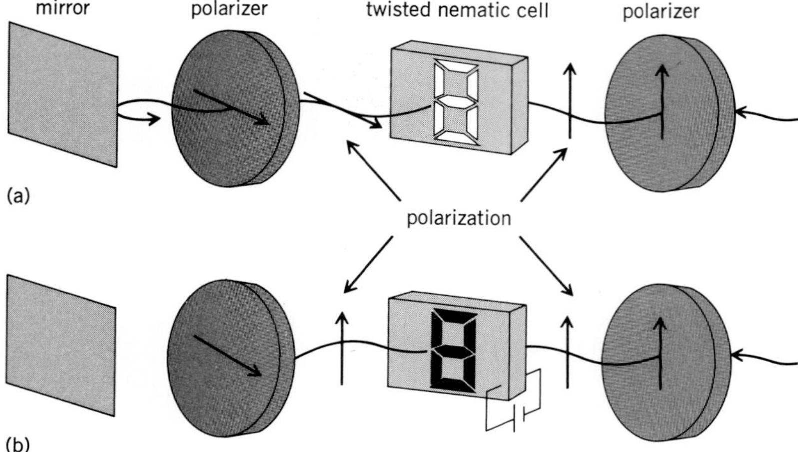


**Fig. 3. Optics of field-effect display device when a twisted nematic cell is utilized. (*a*) Optics without electric field applied to liquid crystal cell. (*b*) Optics with electric field applied.**

***Nondestructive testing.*** Cholesteric-nematic liquid crystals undergo a change in color with a small change in temperature, a property that can be used for nondestructive testing.

***Thermometers.*** Desk thermometers are available which use cholesteric-nematic liquid crystals. Observation of skin temperature changes following blockage of the sympathetic nervous system enables the physician to determine if neurological and vascular pathways are open. Monitoring skin temperature over extended areas provides a more detailed and readily interpreted indication of circulatory patterns than point measurements with thermocouples and thermistors.

*Glenn H. Brown*

***Bibliography.*** G. H. Brown and J. J. Wolken, *Liquid Crystals and Biological Structures,* 1979; J. D. Margerum and L. J. Miller, Electro-optical applications of liquid crystals, *J. Coll. Int. Sci.,* 58: 559–580, 1977; F. D. Saeva (ed.), *Liquid Crystals; The Fourth State of Matter,* 1979; A. Skoulios, Amphiphiles: Organization et diagrammes des phases, *Ann. Phys.,* 3:421–450, 1978.

## Load line

A line drawn on the output characteristic curves of a vacuum tube or transistor, used to determine the operating range and the quiescent point (the operating point for zero signal input voltage or current). In the case of vacuum tubes, this graphical construction is necessary because the mathematical function relating plate current to plate voltage and grid voltage is not known analytically. A set of plate current curves with a load line drawn is shown in the **illustration**. *SEE VACUUM TUBE*.

If the tube has fixed bias, as shown in the circuit diagram in the illustration, the procedure for drawing the load line is simple. The load line is drawn to intersect the plate-voltage axis at a value equal to $V_{PP}$, the plate supply voltage, and the vertical axis at a value of plate current which is equal to $V_{PP}/R_L$, where $R_L$ is the load resistance. The quiescent plate current $I_P$ and plate voltage $V_P$ are read at the point $Q$, where the curve for the value of grid bias intersects the load line.

If the tube is self-biased with a cathode resistor, $R_K$, then the load line is drawn to intersect the plate-voltage axis at $V_{PP}$ and the vertical axis at $V_P/(R_L + R_K)$. A bias line is constructed corresponding to the equation $v_C = -i_P R_K$ (assuming that $V_{GG} = 0$ and a grid-leak resistor is used). The point of intersection of the bias line and load line gives the quiescent point on the tube characteristics.

Load lines similarly constructed may also be used

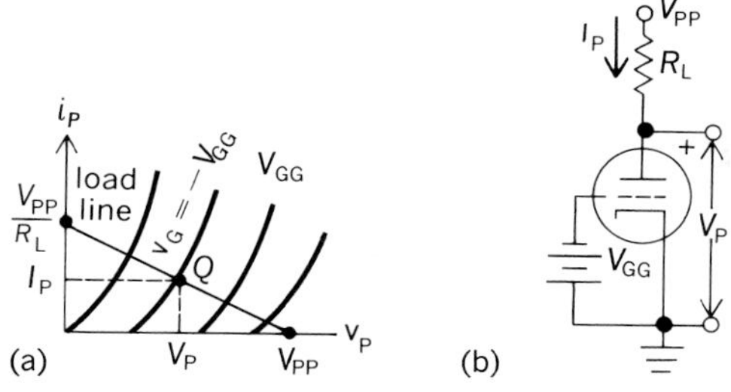

**Graphical construction for load line. (*a*) Load line drawn on plate current characteristics. (*b*) Tube with load resistor.**

with transistor circuits and other nonlinear devices to determine the quiescent point. SEE TRANSISTOR.

*Christos C. Halkias*

## Local-area networks

A system consisting of a set of nodes that are interconnected by a set of links. The nodes and links cover a relatively small geographic area, ranging from a few feet to a mile. The nodes may be terminals, microcomputers, minicomputers, mainframes, printers, hard disks, or work stations. The links may be coaxial cable, twisted-pair wires, or fiber-optic cable. SEE COAXIAL CABLE; COMMUNICATIONS CABLE; DATA-PROCESSING SYSTEMS; DIGITAL COMPUTER; MICROCOMPUTER; OPTICAL COMMUNICATIONS.

**Purposes.** There are many reasons for developing and using local-area networks (LANs), including message communication, resource sharing, improved productivity, file transfer, application performance improvement, and combinations of these functions.

***Message communication.*** With a local-area network it is possible to provide an electronic mail capability because the nodes are connected, thus allowing for the transfer of a message from one node to another. SEE ELECTRONIC MAIL.

***Resource sharing.*** As microcomputers proliferate, it becomes increasingly expensive for management to provide every worker with a fully equipped machine, including disks, printers, modems, and software. A more economical alternative is to provide only a minimal work station capability for hundreds of workers and to provide a few expensive devices which can be shared by many users. In some cases, certain users have repositories of software and files which many users wish to access. Accessibility is improved significantly if users can access these resources electronically by file transfer from a server node (for example, a relatively expensive microcomputer which contains a hard disk and printer) to their work station or by using the server as a remote computer.

***Improved productivity.*** Lagging productivity of office workers and professional people is of great concern to industry. One of the first steps taken to alleviate this problem was the widespread use of personal computers in the office. This movement represented only a limited attack on the problem. Although each worker had access to his or her own data, two important ingredients were missing: ability to communicate electronically with other workers and access to corporate data. Without going through an expensive mainframe, data accessibility was not available laterally from worker to worker or vertically from worker to management, and vice versa. If there is one aspect that characterizes the modern work force, it is multichannel communication. A local-area network facilitates this communication through its internodal message paths and, when equipped with the necessary hardware and software, provides communication with corporate mainframe computers.

***File transfer.*** A frequent need of computer users is to transfer a file that is stored on one local computer to another local computer. The file may consist of a program, data, or both. There can be many reasons for doing a file transfer, including the following:

1. The program or data is needed at a particular local computer in order to execute a program.
2. The file resides on a server node and the user wants to transfer it to his or her work station. Typically, the copy at the server node is read-only so important information cannot be altered by unauthorized users; the system manager controls access and updating action. However, a copy can be transferred to the user's work station where the data can be both read and written, and the copy treated as a private file.
3. The user receives a request to transfer a file to another user.

***Application performance improvement.*** Access to more and better software packages and hardware via a network should result in improvement of the functional performance of the user's applications. This is a principal motivation for networking. The advantage of greater accessibility to resources must be weighed against the following possible disadvantages: slower response time caused by the use of communication facilities; increased complexity of operations engendered by being a member of a local-area network; and temporary lock-out from file access to server nodes caused by concurrent multiple-user activity.

***Multiple applications.*** Seldom is a local-area network built for a single application (for example, electronic mail) or reason, but more likely for a number of the reasons given above. Since local-area networks are built from general-purpose computers, it is possible to provide for a variety of applications in a single local-area network. Thus a user can integrate the applications of, perhaps, data-base management, electronic mail, and word processing. SEE DATA-BASE MANAGEMENT SYSTEMS; WORD PROCESSING.

**Architectures.** The three characteristics that differentiate local-area network architectures are control, topology, and communication technology.

***Control.*** Control refers primarily to the techniques used for allowing access to the communications medium and resolving contention. There are three major control techniques: carrier sense, mutliple access with collision detection (CSMA/CD); token passing; and centralized switching.

In CSMA/CD systems, nodes are connected to a bus and have multiple, or concurrent, access to the communication medium (for example, coaxial cable). Nodes listen for existing transmissions to determine whether it is safe to transmit; hence, the terminology "carrier sense," or sensing the carrier. Unfortunately, this terminology is a misnomer in those local-area networks which do not use modulated transmission. If no transmission is detected, a node will transmit. Due to signal propagation delay, a node cannot be certain that no other node is transmitting. Therefore, overlapping transmissions, or collisions, can occur. Nodes are designed to detect a collision. When a nodes does so, it transmits a jam signal so that all transmitting nodes can recognize it and abort their transmission. Affected nodes probabilistically reschedule their next attempt to transmit. This technique is inexpensive and has good performance at low to medium loads; performance is significantly degraded at high loads. Due to repeated collisions, a node may be delayed in transmitting for an indefinite amount of time. (If collisions persist beyond a system-specified limit, an error is reported.) Thus there is no upper limit on response time, and performance must be described probabilisitically.

Token passing is a control technique that guarantees an upper limit on response time (that is, deterministic performance), but is more complex and expensive than CSMA/CD. This technique is used on rings and buses and uses a control message called the token for granting permission to a node to transmit. In a ring local-area network, for example, the token is rotated in the ring until a node that has data to transmit captures it. Since the node which acquires the token must release it after transmitting and the token returns to the transmitting node, every node is guaranteed to have access to the communication medium within a calculable time. Generally, this method has poorer performance than CSMA/CD at light loads (more overhead) and better performance at high loads (no collisions).

Centralized switching is used primarily in private automatic branch exchange (PABX) systems, which were first used for voice communication, and are challenging other types of local-area networks for market supremacy by emphasizing the integration of voice and data in one network. This technique is used in star configurations where all data are sent from the origin, through a switch, and out to the destination. Its performance is usually worse than the other two techniques but has the significant advantage that the telephones in every office and the switching equipment in many of them can be naturally extended for use in data communication.

***Topology.*** Topology refers to the way in which nodes are connected. There are three major arrangements: bus, ring, and star. The mutual interdependence of the control technique and the topology of a local-area network may be demonstrated as follows:

1. When nodes are connected to a bus, they can all access the bus simultaneously; therefore, there must be an arbitration technique like CSMA/CD to referee access. An alternative is to use token passing on a bus, but this requires a complex control mechanism.

2. When nodes are connected in a ring, there is the opportunity to regulate their access to the communication medium by circulating a token in the ring which must be captured by a node in order for it to acquire the right to transmit.

3. The star topology is natural for centralized switching because every node is connected to the hub of the network; this central node performs switching and routing.

***Communication technology.*** There are two major communication technologies: baseband and broadband. Baseband is unmodulated transmission; it transmits at the original frequency of the digital data. It is used with CSMA/CD, coaxial cable, or twisted-pair wire transmission, and a ring topology. A fiber-optic bus is also a possibility, but it is more natural to use it on a ring, as fiber-optic transmission is unidirectional. Since transmission on a bus spreads in both directions simultaneously from the source, it is difficult to control multiple reflections in a bus-type fiber-optic cable. Since baseband is unmodulated transmission and does not transmit in different frequency bands, it is usually limited to a single service (for example, data).

Broadband transmission is modulated and is based on community antenna television (CATV) technology. It is used with CSMA/CD, coaxial transmission, and bus topology. Systems can be single-cable or dual-cable. In the former, transmissions are directed to a frequency translator called the headend which converts all transmitted frequencies to higher received frequencies. The headend retransmits at the higher frequency to the receiving node. This method is necessary to distinguish transmission and reception on a single cable. It is unnecessary on a dual-cable system because one cable is used for transmitting and the other for receiving. The dual-cable system has twice the capacity of a single-cable system but it is more expensive. A feature of any broadband system is its multiservice capability. This is the result of its multichannel communication characteristic, wherein different frequency bands can be used for different services (for example, data, voice, and television).

The PABX uses a different communication technology. Pulse-code modulation is used to quantize the analog voice signal into a binary bit stream for efficient digital transmission. This method is also compatible with integrating voice with data, since the data are already in digital form and can be merged with the digitized voice information. *See* Data communication; Pulse modulation.

*Norman F. Schneidewind*

***Bibliography.*** R. Bernhard, The quandry of office automation, *IEEE Spectrum*, 19(9):34–39, September 1982; D. D. Clark et al., An introduction to local area networks, *Proc. IEEE*, 66:1497–1517, 1978; L. W. Davies, *Computer Networks and Their Protocols*, 1979; W. R. Franta and I. Chlamtac, *Local Networks*, 1981; J. M. McQuillan, Local network architectures, *Computer Design*, pp. 18–26, May 1979; A. S. Tanenbaum, *Computer Networks*, 1981.

## Lock-in amplifier

An instrument for the measurement of periodic signals which are contaminated by noise and interference. The operation of a lock-in amplifier depends on the provision of a reference voltage that is synchro-

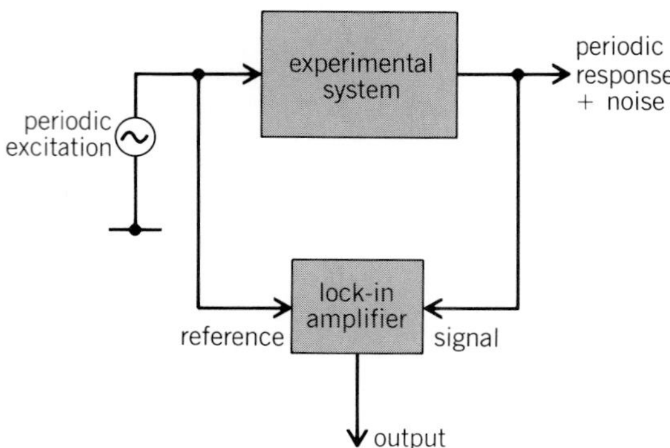


**Fig. 1. Measurement of a noisy signal using a lock-in amplifier. The reference voltage is derived directly from the experiment excitation source.**

nized to the signal to be measured. In a typical experimental application the reference is derived directly from the excitation source (**Fig. 1**). *SEE ELECTRICAL NOISE*.

**Operating principles.** The internal arrangement of a lock-in amplifier is shown in **Fig. 2**. The signal channel contains a variable-gain alternating-current (ac) amplifier. The reference channel generates a precision square-wave voltage triggered from the applied reference, and incorporates a variable phase shifter. The variable phase shifter is used to adjust the relative phase of the signal and square-wave reference voltages appearing at the phase-sensitive detector (PSD). *SEE AMPLIFIER; FUNCTION GENERATOR*.

The phase-sensitive detector consists of a switching multiplier followed by a low-pass filter and will only detect (or rectify) signal voltages that are synchronous with the reference voltage. **Figure 3** illustrates the waveforms appearing at the multiplier output for a sine-wave signal and synchronous reference. The direct-current (dc) component is transmitted to the final output by the low-pass filter and has a value that depends on the signal amplitude $V_s$ and the phase difference θ between signal and reference as given by the equation below. The user is able to maximize the re-

$$V_{DC} \propto V_s \cos \theta$$

sponse to a signal of interest by adjusting the reference phase from the front panel of the lock-in amplifier. *SEE ELECTRIC FILTER*.

The response of the multiplier to asynchronous noise inputs is a fluctuating ac voltage with zero average value. The response to a synchronous signal is therefore quite unambiguous because there is no error due to rectified noise components. In practice, residual noise at the final output can be smoothed by reducing the bandwidth of the low-pass filter. This represents the main mechanism for signal-to-noise ratio improvement in lock-in amplifiers.

**Dynamic range.** The dynamic range of a lock-in amplifier reflects its ability to measure with precision a synchronous voltage in the presence of large-scale interference. Modern systems can offer an overall measurement resolution of the order of 0.1% while withstanding the effects of interference voltages several thousand times greater than the signal.

**Heterodyne lock-in amplifiers.** The basic system shown in Fig. 2 is characterized by spurious responses at odd harmonics of the reference and hence the signal frequency. In a heterodyne lock-in amplifier, phase-sensitive detection is carried out at a relatively high, fixed frequency following a stage of frequency translation of the applied signal. Since the phase-sensitive detector now operates at a frequency that bears no harmonic relationship to the applied signal, the odd harmonic responses are effectively suppressed.

**Applications.** Lock-in amplifiers operate over many decades of frequency without tuning or adjustment and are therefore suited to swept-frequency measurements. Because the detection process is phase-sensitive, the same instrument can be used in a range of measurements on signals and systems. Lock-in amplifiers are widely employed as precision vector voltmeters, selective microvoltmeters, frequency-response analyzers, and spectrum analyzers covering a frequency range from less than 1 Hz to several

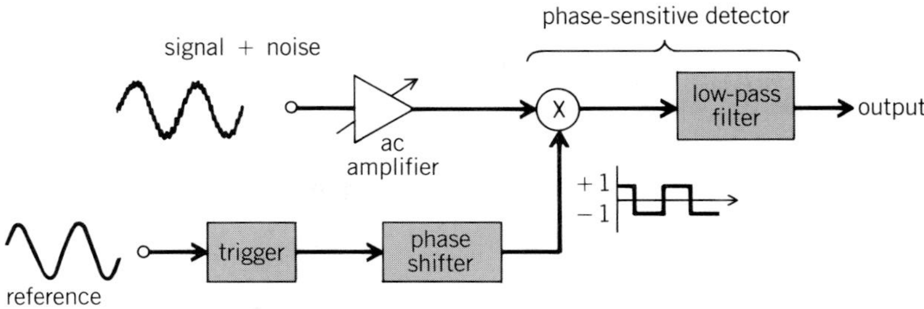


**Fig. 2. Basic lock-in amplifier.**

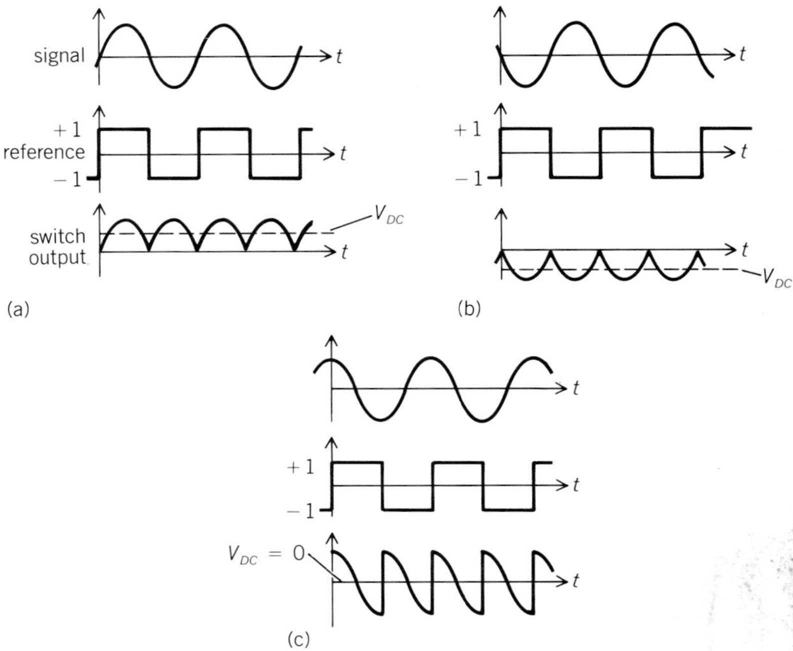


**Fig. 3. Waveforms at the multiplier output for a sine-wave signal at different values of reference phase shift θ. (*a*) θ = 0°. (*b*) θ = 180°. (c) θ = 90°.**

hundred kilohertz. *SEE SPECTRUM ANALYZER; VOLTMETER*.

*M. L. Meade*

**Bibliography.** M. L. Meade, *Lock-in Amplifiers: Principles and Applications*, 1983.

## Logic circuits

The basic building blocks used to realize consumer and industrial products that incorporate digital electronics. Such products include digital computers, video games, voice synthesizers, pocket calculators, and robot controls. *SEE CALCULATORS; DIGITAL COMPUTER; ROBOTICS; VOICE RESPONSE*.

The change that has enabled widespread economical use of digital logic once found only in very expensive, room-sized computers has been a dramatic evolution in device technology. Logic circuits which comprise several basic electronic devices (typically transistors, resistors, and diodes) were once designed with each device as a separate physical entity. Now, very large-scale integration of devices offers up to several hundred thousand equivalent basic devices on one small piece of silicon, typically rectangular with maximum dimensions of a few tenths of an inch

(1 in. = 25 mm) per side. *See Integrated circuits.*

This dramatic reduction in size has been accompanied by a number of effects. The cost and power consumption per logic device have been greatly reduced. The modestly priced digital watch that can run for over a year on a tiny battery exemplifies these effects.

**Logic circuit operation.** Logic circuits process information encoded as voltage or current levels. The adjective ''digital'' derives from the fact that symbols are encoded as one of a limited set of specific values. While it would be feasible to encode information using many distinct voltage levels (for example, each of 10 voltage levels might correspond to a distinct decimal digit value), there are several reasons for using binary or two-valued signals to represent information: the complexity of the sending and receiving circuit is reduced to a simple on-off switch type of operation corresponding to the two-valued signals; the speed of operation is far greater since it is not necessary to wait until a changing signal has had time to converge to a final value before interpreting its binary value; and the on-off operation makes the circuitry very tolerant of both changing characteristics of devices due to aging or temperature-humidity environment and electromagnetically induced noise added to the voltage levels.

Since signals are interpreted to be one of only two values (denoted as 0 and 1), a group of four such signals must be used to represent a decimal digit, as an example. A very commonly used convention in computers and terminals is to use a group of eight binary signals to represent alphabetic, numeric, and in general any keyboard-derived symbol. The eight signals enable encoding any of 256 character or symbol values.

More generally, the binary digits, or bits, are used in a number system with digit weights that change by multiples of 2 rather than multiples of 10 as in the decimal system. In this system, successive digits or bits have weights of 1, 2, 4, 8, . . . , in contrast to the decimal system where successive digits have weights of 1, 10, 100, . . . . *See Number systems.*

**Types of logic functions.** All logic circuits may be described in terms of three fundamental elements, shown graphically in **Fig. 1**. The NOT element has one input and one output; as the name suggests, the output generated is the opposite of the input in binary. In other words, a 0 input value causes a 1 to appear at the output; a 1 input results in a 0 output. Two NOT elements in series, one output driving the input to the other, simply reproduce a copy of the input signal.

The AND element has an arbitrary number of inputs and a single output. (Electrical characteristics of devices used or physical packaging of devices result in some practical limit to the number of inputs allowed.) As the name suggests, the output becomes 1 if, and only if, all of the inputs are 1; otherwise the output is 0. The AND together with the NOT circuit therefore enables searching for a particular combination of binary signals. If, for example, a signal is needed that goes to 1 only when signals $A$, $B$, and $C$ are 1, 0, and 1, respectively, then the circuit indicated in **Fig. 2** will generate the desired output.

The third element is the OR function. As with the AND, an arbitrary number of inputs may exist and one output is generated. The OR output is 1 if one or more inputs are 1.

The operations of AND and OR have some analogies

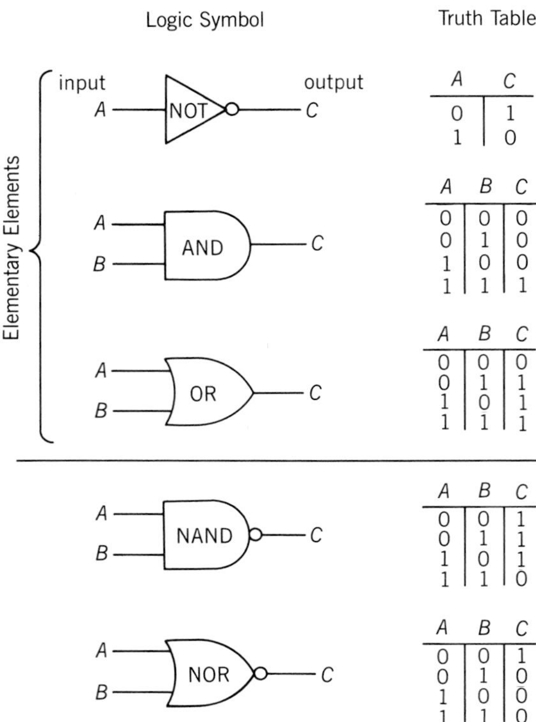


Fig. 1. Logic elements.

to the arithmetic operations of multiplication and addition, respectively. The collection of mathematical rules and properties of these operations is called Boolean algebra.

While the NOT, AND, and OR functions have been designed as individual circuits in many circuit families, by far the most common functions realized as individual circuits are the NAND and NOR circuits of Fig. 1. A NAND may be described as equivalent to an AND element driving a NOT element. Similarly, a NOR is equivalent to an OR element driving a NOT element. (The reason for this strong bias favoring inverting outputs is that the transistor, and the vacuum tube which preceded it, are by nature inverters or NOT-type circuit devices when used as signal amplifiers.) An interesting property of the NAND or NOR circuits is that all logic functions may be accessed using either type of circuit. A NOT element, for example, is realized as a one-input NAND. An AND element is realized as NAND followed by a NOT element. An OR element is realized by applying a NOT to each input individually and then applying the resulting outputs to the NAND as inputs.

**Combinational and sequential logic.** As the names of the logic elements described suggest, logic circuits respond to combinations of input signals. In an arithmetic adder, for example, a network of logic elements

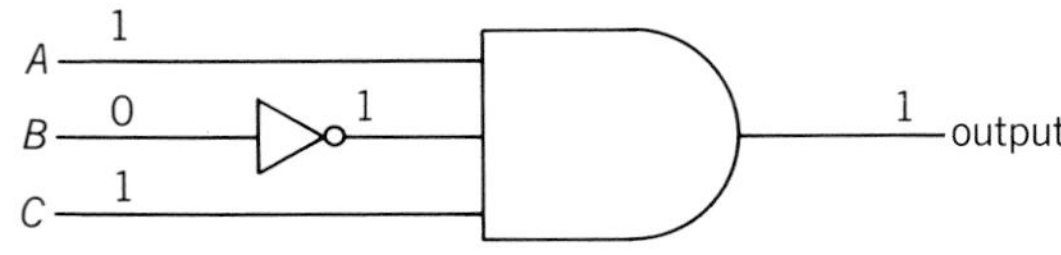


Fig. 2. Logic circuit whose output is 1 only when input signals *A*, *B*, and *C* are 1, 0, and 1, respectively.

is interconnected to generate the sum digit as an output by monitoring combinations of input digits; the network generates a 1 for each output only in response to those combinations in the addition table that call for it.

Logic networks which are interconnected so that the current set of output signals is responsive only to the current set of input signals are appropriately termed combinational logic.

An important further capability for processing information is memory, or the ability to store information. In digital systems, the memory function has been provided for by a variety of technologies, including magnetic cores, stored charge, magnetic bubbles, and magnetic tape. The logic circuits themselves must provide a memory function if information is to be manipulated at the speeds the logic is capable of. The logic elements defined above may be interconnected to provide this memory by the use of feedback. *SEE COMPUTER STORAGE TECHNOLOGY.*

The circuit indicated in **Fig. 3** illustrates a basic and perhaps the most commonly used form of memory circuit. Normally both inputs *A* and *B* to the cross-coupled NAND gates are at the voltage corresponding to logic 1; if a 0 is applied to signal *A*, outputs *C* and *D* assume the values 0 and 1, respectively, based on the definition of NAND operation; the outputs retain these values after input *A* is returned to the quiescent value of 1. Conversely, if *B* is set to 0 while *A* is 1, then the outputs *C* and *D* become 1 and 0, respectively, and again retain these values after *B* is returned to a value of 1. In the jargon of logic circuit design, this circuit is variously called a flip-flop, toggle, or trigger. Like the light switch on the wall, the circuit retains one of two stable states after the force initiating change to that state is removed. This circuit is therefore well matched to the storage of binary or two-valued signals. Logic circuit networks that include feedback paths to retain information are termed sequential logic networks, since outputs are in part dependent on the prior input signals applied and in particular on the sequence in which the signals were applied. *SEE SWITCHING CIRCUIT.*

**Logic circuit embodiment.** Several alternatives exist for the digital designer to create a digital system.

Ready-made catalog-order devices can be combined as building blocks. In this case, manufacturers have attempted to provide a repertoire of logic networks that will find common usage and generality. Some examples of the types of circuits found in digital circuit manuals or catalogs are: arrays of individual logic gates (typically four to six) with outputs and inputs available as external connections to the device; arrays of memory elements (flip-flops) used to hold a collection of binary signals or digits; arithmetic adders capable of adding four corresponding binary digits from each of two binary numbers and of being cascaded to produce an adder for any multiple of four digits; and multipliers capable of forming the product of two 16-bit numbers in a single step (that is, a combinational multiplier).

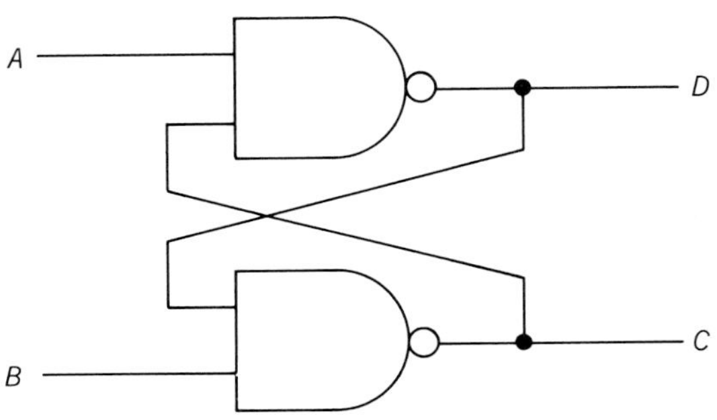


**Fig. 3. Memory element.**

The significance of these examples is that the number of gates or logic elements realized on individual devices ranges from a few to several thousand. Clearly a design that can use the devices with larger gate counts is likely to be more compact and more economical.

A second and increasingly common realization of logic gates is custom-designed devices. Two factors which make this practical are computer-aided-design (CAD) tools and libraries of subnetworks that can be used as building blocks. Custom design of a logic network implies the generation of highly complicated artwork patterns, called masks, for use in photographic-development-like steps used to produce the integrated circuit networks. The availability of a library of subnetworks for which this artwork has already been generated reduces the additional artwork required to interconnection patterns among these library elements to set up the desired logic network. *SEE COMPUTER-AIDED DESIGN AND MANUFACTURING.*

A third option is gate-array devices. In this case, the device vendor manufactures devices comprising a two-dimensional array of logic cells. Each cell is equivalent to one or a few logic gates. The final layers of metallization that determine the exact function of each cell and interconnect the cells to form a specific network are deferred until the customer orders such a device. This procedure uses the advantage of mass production for the majority of processing steps necessary to manufacture a device, including most of the necessary artwork. Since the interconnecting metallization layers are a relatively small and simple part of the total device fabrication, the customization cost and time can be reduced significantly by this method relative to a totally custom fabrication. The sacrifice in this approach is that the packing density of the two-dimensional array will tend to be less than a custom-designed layout, since routing channels must allow for reasonably general interconnection patterns.

A fourth option in realizing logic functions is programmable logic arrays, or PLAs. The manufactured part has the potential for realizing any of a large number of different sets of logic functions; the particular functions produced are determined by actually blowing microscopic fuses built into the device, in effect removing unwanted connections. In one device, each of 16 device-input signals is an input to each of 48 AND gates; the 48 AND outputs are input signals to 8 OR gates that generate the device outputs. Selective removal of inputs to the AND gates, and between the AND and OR gates, enables implementation of a wide variety of functions.

A fifth embodiment of logic network functions involves the use of table look-up. A logic network has several binary input signals and one or more binary outputs. The transformation of input signal combinations to output signal values need not be realized by AND-OR-type logic elements at all; instead, the collection of input signals can be grouped arbitrarily as ad-

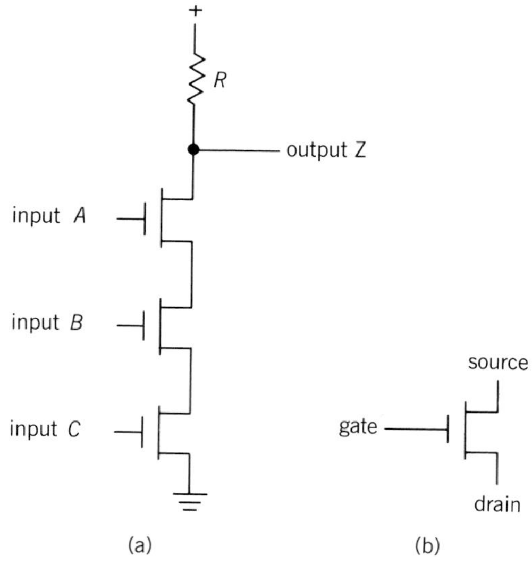


**Fig. 4. MOS NAND gate. (*a*) Circuit configuration. (*b*) MOS transistor (*n* or *p*), the basic circuit device.**

dress digits to a memory device. In response to any particular combination of inputs the memory device location that is addressed becomes the output. For example, a logic network function involving 10 binary inputs and 8 binary output signals could be realized with a single memory device that holds 1024 memory cells, with 8 bits stored in each cell. (Ten bits addresses $2^{10}$ = 1024 locations.)

The form of memory device used for table look-up is usually read-only, that is, memory contents are defined as part of the manufacturing process by means of the last layer of metallization, or one of a number of other means is used to fix the memory cell contents so that it is not necessary to reload the memory after each turn-off of power.

Typically, this approach may lead to slower operation than the use of logic circuits, but in some cases can lead to very significant economies.

The last form of logic network embodiment that will be discussed is the microcomputer. A microcomputer is a single device that includes a read-only memory to hold a program, a processor capable of reading and executing that program, and a small read-write memory for scratch working space. Just as a memory device provides an efficient realization of a combinational network, the equivalent of a highly complex sequential network can be had with a microcomputer, as evidenced by electronic games. Two important advantages of this approach are that little or no custom-device fabrication is required, and the programmability permits utilization of complicated and modifiable equivalent networks. *See* MICROCOMPUTER; MICROPROCESSOR.

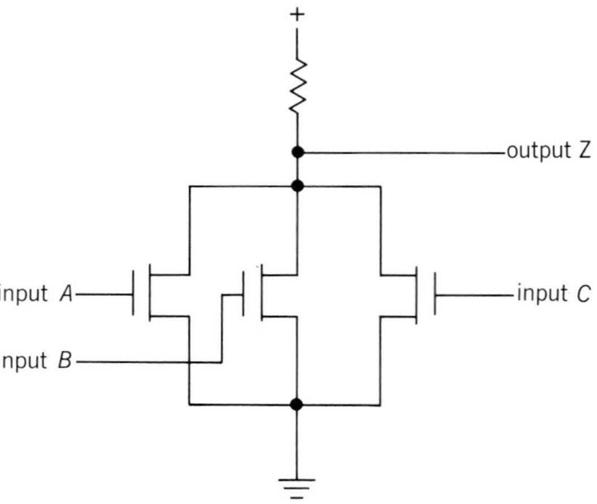


**Fig. 5. MOS NOR gate.**

As with table look-up, the principal disadvantage of this approach is that the speed of operation may be slower than if an actual network of high-speed logic circuits were used.

**Technology.** There are basically two logic circuit families in widespread use: bipolar and metal-oxide-semiconductor (MOS).

The basic MOS device is formed by using a silicon substrate which has been doped in such a way as to greatly increase the hole/electron relative density, forming a *p*-type substrate. In addition to the substrate, two diffused *n*-type regions are formed. A layer of metal, insulated from the substrate by a deposit of oxide, is situated between the two *n* regions. This metal connection is known as the gate, and the two *n* regions are called the source and drain; since the device is symmetrical in every respect, source and drain are functionally interchangeable. When a sufficient voltage exists between the metal gate and the substrate, electrons are conducted between the drain and source connections, essentially shorting the two together. Otherwise, a high resistance exists between the two. Thus, the gate input is analogous to the control lever of a switch. In like manner, an *n*-type doping of the substrate, along with a *p*-type source and drain, may be used to implement the switch. This will result in hole migration between source and drain when the gate is turned on. *See* TRANSISTOR.

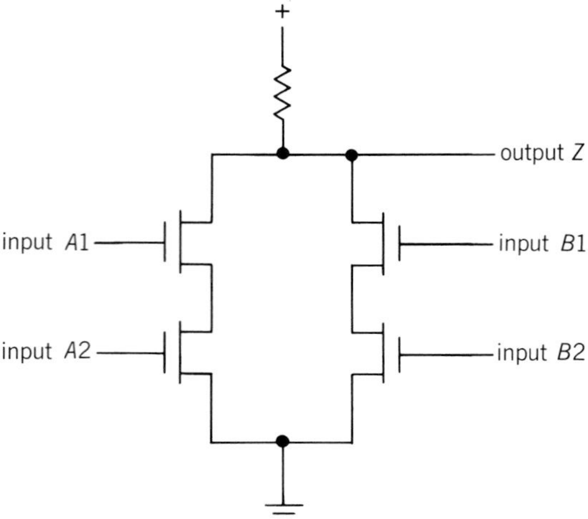


**Fig. 6. MOS A-O-I (AND-OR-INVERT) gate.**

The simplest MOS logic structure is the transmission gate (also known as pass transistor and steering logic); only one transistor is used to implement the function, where source and gate leads represent the two input variables, and the drain becomes the output value. The transistor is turned on when the gate voltage is above the threshold voltage that assures sufficient current flow through the channel; in other words, it acts as a short between source and drain. This is analogous to a mechanical switch in the ''on'' position. When the gate is below the threshold potential the switch is opened, thus performing an AND-like function on the inputs.

The NAND logic function is also easily derived with MOS circuits. **Figure 4** shows a sample NAND circuit in which the transistors *A*, *B*, and *C* are configured in series and must therefore all be in the "on" state for a conduction path from output *Z* to ground to be established. If *A*, *B* and *C* are all above threshold, output *Z* is shorted to ground or is forced to logical zero. On the other hand, if any of *A*, *B*, or *C* are off, an open circuit essentially exists between *Z* and ground. In this case, output node *Z* exhibits much less resistance to the power source ($R \ll R_a + R_b + R_c$) and therefore will be at the voltage potential of the power source.

This NAND circuit can be reconfigured into the NOR circuit of **Fig. 5**. Here, the transistors *A*, *B*, and *C* are in parallel instead of in series, and it is easily seen that when any of the inputs are turned on the output will be grounded. Otherwise, *Z* will be pulled up to the power supply voltage.

Another useful MOS logic structure is the AND-OR-INVERT, which performs the logic functions exactly as stated in the name. The A-O-I is shown in **Fig. 6** to be a combination of the NAND and NOR configurations. Output *Z* is low only if the function (*A*1 AND *A*2) OR (*B*1 AND *B*2) is high.

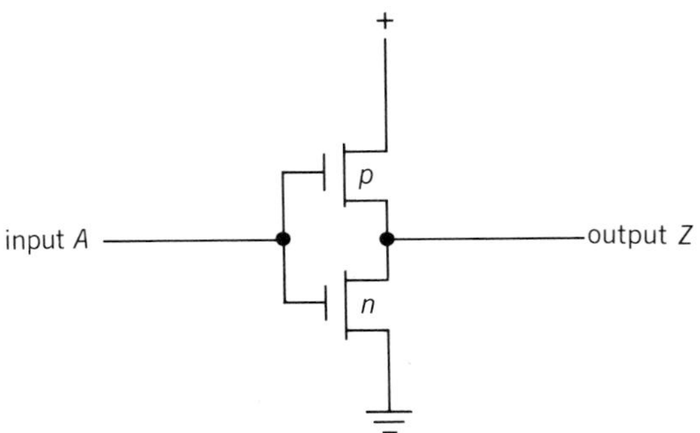


**Fig. 7. CMOS inverter.**

As described earlier, either an *n*-channel substrate (NMOS) or a *p*-channel substrate (PMOS) may be used to implement the logic structures. Additionally, both types may be used concurrently in the logic circuit to fabricate a more sophisticated device. **Figure 7** shows an inverter built with both NMOS and PMOS devices. When the input is low, the NMOS transistor is cut off and the PMOS transistor conducts, shorting the output to the power source. On the other hand, when the input is high, the PMOS gate is shut off and the NMOS gate shorts the output to ground, thus performing the inverter function. The advantage of such a complementary configuration, known as CMOS, is primarily one of power dissipation. Owing to the fact that only one complementary transistor conducts at any time (other than the short overlap during switching), there is always a very high resistance from the power source to ground, and therefore very little current flows through the pair. The primary disadvantage of CMOS over the common MOS circuit is the increased fabrication complexity due to the *n* and *p* substrates occupying the same chip, and the secondary disadvantage is the increased area needed to build the

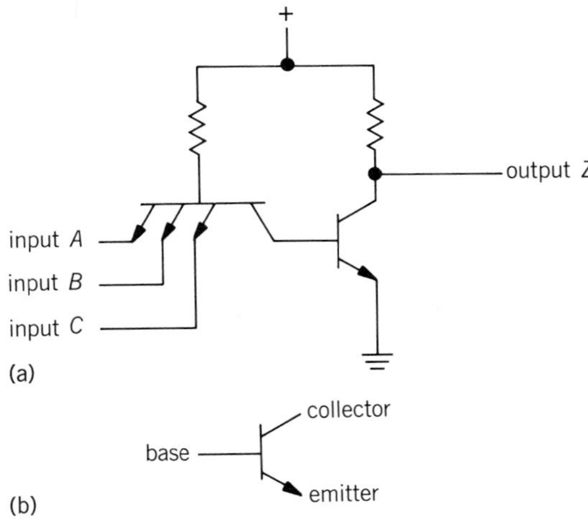


**Fig. 8. TTL (transistor-transistor-logic) NAND gate. (*a*) Circuit configuration. (*b*) Bipolar junction transistor (*npn*), the basic circuit device.**

CMOS structure because of the use of complementary pairs.

The charge carriers in an MOS transistor are either free electrons or holes. For this reason, MOS is known as a unipolar device. In contrast, devices which utilize both free electrons and hole migration are made. These are known as bipolar devices, such as the junction transistor. Although general comparisons are hard to make, these devices typically exhibit much less input resistance and demand a more sophisticated fabrication technique than do MOS devices, but offer the advantage of accentuated high-frequency response. In terms of logic realization, the bipolar family encompasses many common circuit types. Perhaps the best-known and most widely used implementation of logic switches is the bipolar transistor-transistor logic, or TTL. Shown schematically in **Fig. 8**, the basic TTL NAND gate is formed by a multiemitter transistor (turned on only if every input is high) followed by an output transistor that acts as a pullup/buffer. Thus, the first transistor performs an AND operation on the inputs and the second transistor completes the NAND by performing an inversion. *SEE JUNCTION TRANSISTOR*.

TTL transistors are operated in the saturation mode;

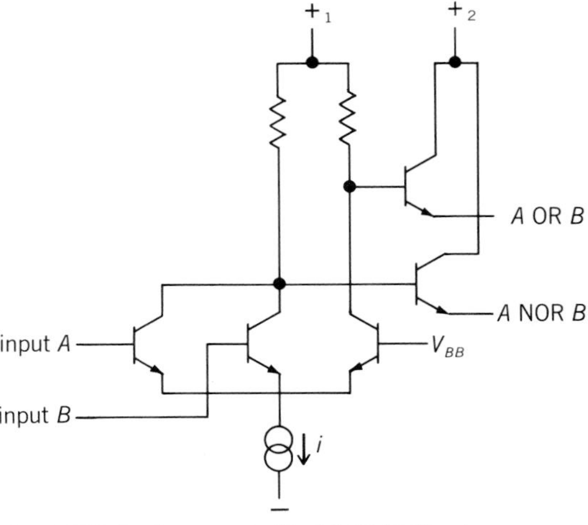


**Fig. 9. ECL (emitter-coupled-logic) OR/NOR gate.**

in other words, the transistors are driven hard to either the cutoff or the saturation limits. This overdriving introduces a time delay that does not exist if the transistors are operated in the nonsaturated mode. Such nonsaturating logic, while inherently faster, is more susceptible to noise since it is biased in the linear region.

Current-mode logic, or CML, is a popular form of nonsaturation logic and most often takes the configuration of emitter-coupled logic, or ECL. The basic ECL gate is shown in **Fig. 9** to be composed of current-steering transistors that perform an OR operation on the inputs. Typically, the gate output is amplified by an emitter-follower transistor, and both the true and complement signals can be made available with no added delay as outputs.

*R. R. Shively; W. V. Robinson*

***Bibliography.*** M. Mandl, *Introduction to Digital Logic Techniques and Systems*, 1983; J. Millman, *Microelectronics*, 1979; N. M. Morris, *Logic Circuits*, 3d ed., 1984; H. Taub, *Digital Circuits and Microprocessors*, 1982; H. Taub and D. L. Schilling, *Digital Integrated Electronics*, 1977; C. A. Wiatrowski and C. H. House, *Logic Circuits and Microcomputer Systems*, 1980.

## Loudspeaker

A device that converts an electrical signal from an amplifier into sound. Loudspeakers are designed for the reproduction of audio signals which have a frequency range of approximately 20 Hz to 20 kHz and a pressure range of approximately $10^{-5}$ to 50 pascals or $10^{-9}$ to $7 \times 10^{-3}$ lbf/in.$^2$ (1 atm is $1.013 \times 10^5$ pascals or 14.7 lbf/in.$^2$). Electroacoustic transducer is a more general term used to describe any device which converts an electrical signal into sound, including subsonic or ultrasonic sound, underwater sound, or sound in a solid material. The term driver (or unit) is used to indicate a transducer mechanism without a structural radiation aid such as a horn, baffle, or enclosure. A loudspeaker system normally consists of one or more drivers, an electrical network (which divides the electrical signal into the optimum frequency band for each driver), and an enclosure (or baffle). Loudspeakers (drivers or systems) are used in many different consumer products such as home and car stereos, television and radio receivers, electronic musical instruments, and toys. Professionally, they are used in broadcast stations, recording studios, and concert halls, stadiums and arenas, theaters, discotheques, and many other public places. A good understanding of how the loudspeaker works is essential for its appropriate use, since some of its characteristics are more important than others, depending on the purpose of the sound-reproducing system under consideration. SEE TRANSDUCER.

**Types.** Loudspeakers are classified in several ways. The classification criteria and the corresponding categories are as follows:

Radiation
1. Direct
2. Horn-loaded

Driving element
1. Magnetic
   a. Dynamic (moving-coil, ribbon, and so on)
   b. Moving-armature
   c. Magnetostrictive
2. Electrostatic (condenser)
3. Piezoelectric (crystal, ceramic, polymer)
4. Ionophone
5. Air-jet

Reproduction range
1. Low-frequency (woofer, subwoofer)
2. Mid-frequency (midrange, squawker)
3. High-frequency (tweeter, supertweeter)
4. Full-range

Diaphragm shape
1. Cone (straight, parabolic, flared)
2. Dome
3. Flat

The three most commonly used loudspeaker types are the dynamic (moving-coil) direct-radiator loudspeaker, the horn loudspeaker, and the electrostatic loudspeaker.

***Dynamic (moving-coil) direct-radiator loudspeaker.*** In this type of loudspeaker (**Fig. 1**), the permanent magnet produces a high flux density in the narrow air gap in which the voice coil (moving coil) is located. The interaction of the flux and the current produces a force given by Eq. (1) where $F^1$ is the force in newtons, $B$

$$F^1 = BlI \tag{1}$$

is the flux density in webers per square meter, $l$ is the effective length of the wire in meters, and $I$ is the current in amperes. This force activates the vibrating assembly (voice coil, diaphragm, outer suspension or surround, and inner suspension or spider), producing sound. The diaphragm is expected to move as a piston and to exactly follow the alternately changing force. The inner and outer suspension is necessary to maintain the diaphragm and the voice coil in their proper positions without preventing a free movement in the axial direction. This type of loudspeaker is often called a cone-type or a dome-type loudspeaker depending on the shape of the diaphragm. Nonflat diaphragm shapes are generally employed since they give a much larger mechanical strength to the diaphragm. The cone-type loudspeaker can be used in any frequency range either as a low-frequency

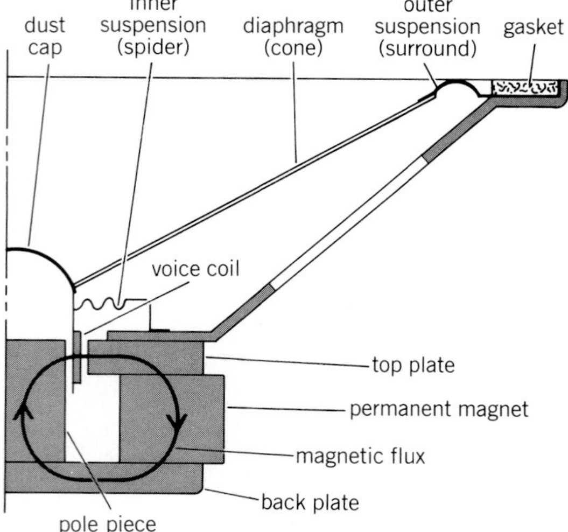


**Fig. 1. Half cross-sectional view of a moving-coil direct-radiator loudspeaker.**

driver (woofer) or as a high-frequency driver (tweeter), but the dome-type loudspeaker is mostly used in the mid- to high-frequency ranges.

The moving-coil direct-radiator loudspeaker is the most widely used type since it has a simple structure and is easily assembled. The motion of the vibrating system is basically linear, making it possible to reproduce a sound with high fidelity. One disadvantage of this type is that it has a low radiation efficiency (ratio of sound output power to electrical input power), typically 0.5–4%. This is because the air is too light compared to the vibrating assembly. The horn loudspeaker is used to overcome this problem.

***Horn loudspeaker.*** In a horn loudspeaker (**Fig. 2**), the horn is a curved tube usually made of metal, plastic, or wood, with a gradually increasing cross section. One end is adjacent to the diaphragm and is called the throat, and the other end, which radiates sound into the air, is called the mouth. Some horn loudspeakers have phase plugs in front of the diaphragm to effectively focus the wavefront of the sound radiated from different areas of the diaphragm. The horn is combined with different types of drivers such as dynamic (moving coil, ribbon), electrostatic, piezoelectric, and ionophone drivers. The function of the horn may be understood from the common experience that the voice of a person can travel much farther in an open space if two hands are placed by the mouth to simulate a horn. The horn increases the radiation efficiency (due to the increased acoustical load) and changes the directivity of the sound. The increase in efficiency normally ranges from 10 to 100 times (10 to 20 dB). Horn loudspeakers are almost always used for sound reinforcement in large rooms and in open spaces (outdoors) because of their high efficiency and directivity. For high-fidelity sound reproduction, they must be designed carefully to avoid coloration of the sound due to the horn loading, and the nonlinear distortion produced around the throat.

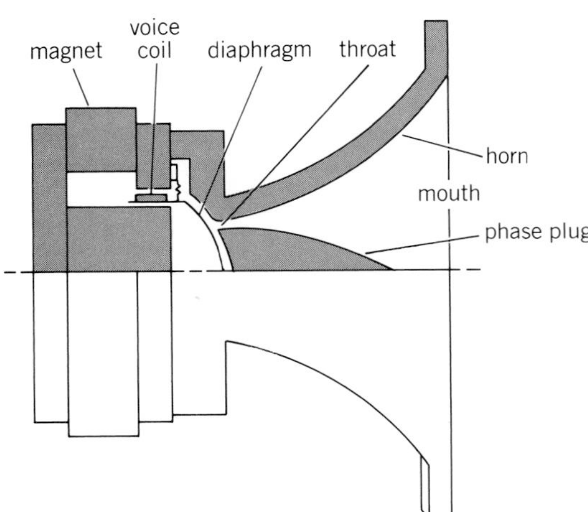


**Fig. 2. Cross-sectional view of a horn-type loudspeaker.**

***Electrostatic loudspeaker.*** The electrostatic loudspeaker is also called a condenser-type loudspeaker. It comprises two electrodes, a flexible conductive sheet (usually a metallic foil or evaporated film) and a solid conductive back plate, placed close to each other, and direct-current (dc) voltage source polarizing them. (Two fixed electrodes, one on each side of the movable electrode, are used in push-pull types.) The flexible sheet is pulled toward the plate by a static force due to the electrical charge. When an alternating-current (ac) voltage is applied from a power amplifier, the flexible sheet is alternately pulled and pushed, resulting in the radiation of sound waves. In order to increase the radiation efficiency, the area of the diaphragm and the dc bias voltage must be increased, and the distance between electrodes must be reduced. These requirements are difficult to fulfill for the reproduction of large sound output in the low-frequency range. The necessity of the dc voltage source and a step-up transformer for impedance matching is another disadvantage of this type of loudspeaker. Some listeners, however, prefer the natural sound quality of a well-designed electrostatic loudspeaker.

**Equivalent electrical circuit.** An equivalent electrical circuit models the mechanical and acoustical components of a loudspeaker by electrical components. In the impedance analogy, a force is represented by a voltage, a velocity by a current, a mass by an inductance, a compliance (inverse of spring constant) by a capacitance, and a mechanical resistance by an electrical resistance. (The other type of analogy is called the mobility analogy.)

The general equivalent electrical circuit of a moving-coil direct-radiator loudspeaker in an infinite baffle or in free air is shown in **Fig. 3*a*** (according to the impedance analogy; see also **Table 1**). The interaction between the electrical and mechanical parts is represented by an ideal gyrator, which can be replaced by a transformer when the mobility analogy is used. *See* Gyrator.

The circuit shown in Fig. 3*b* is obtained when the units of the mechanical elements including the air load are converted to electrical units by removing the gyrator. This circuit is convenient for an analysis of the electrical properties of the loudspeaker. A form

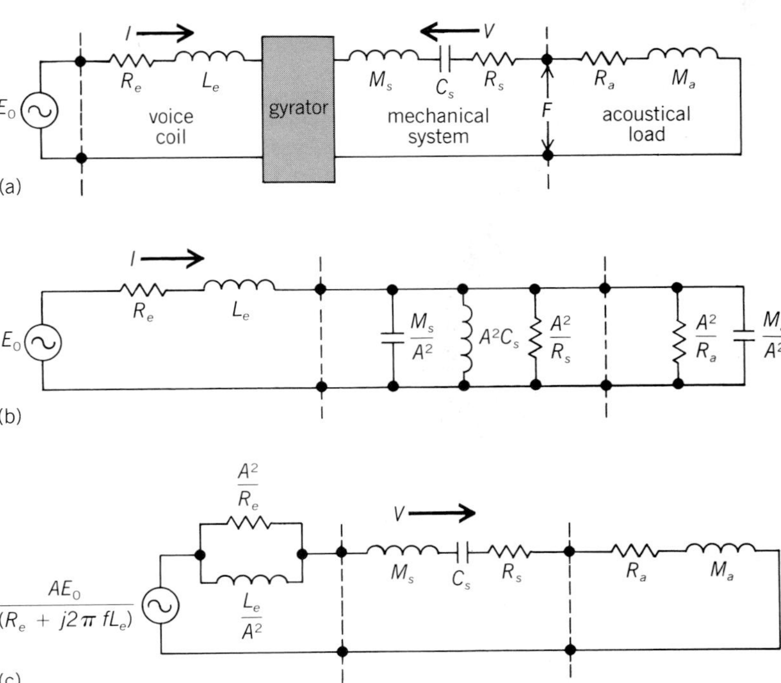


**Fig. 3. Equivalent electrical circuits of a loudspeaker (*a*) electrical and mechanical units, (*b*) electrical units only, and (c) mechanical units only. The symbols are explained in Table 1.**

**Table 1. Symbols used in representing equivalent circuits**

| Symbol | Quantity | SI unit |
|---|---|---|
| $f$ | Signal frequency | Hertz (Hz) |
| $E_0$ | Power amplifier output voltage | Volt (V) |
| $I$ | Power amplifier output current | Ampere (A) |
| $R_e$ | Voice coil resistance | Ohm (Ω) |
| $L_e$ | Voice coil inductance | Henry (H) |
| $A$ | Force factor: product of flux density $B$ and effective length of wire $l$ | Newton per ampere (N/A) |
| $V$ | Diaphragm velocity | Meter per second (m/s) |
| $M_s$ | Effective diaphragm mass | Kilogram (kg) |
| $C_s$ | Compliance of suspension | Meter per newton (m/N) |
| $R_s$ | Mechanical resistance | Newton-second per meter (N-s/m) |
| $F$ | Reaction force of air | Newton (N) |
| $R_a$ | Radiation resistance | Newton-second per meter (N-s/m) |
| $M_a$ | Radiation mass | Kilogram (kg) |
| $j$ | Imaginary unit ($\sqrt{-1}$) | |

used for the analysis of the mechanical properties of the loudspeaker is given by Fig. 3*c*, where the electrical units are converted to mechanical units. Figure 3*c* shows that the function of the loudspeaker is described by a simple equivalent electrical circuit, which is valid as long as the diaphragm vibrates as a piston and proper magnitudes are assigned to the radiation impedance. From Fig. 3*c*, the fundamental resonance frequency $f_s$, which generally determines the lowest limiting frequency of the reproduction range, and the quality factor $Q_t$, which is the indicator of the sharpness of the resonance, are given by (discarding the small term $L_e/A^2$) Eqs. (2) and (3). The

$$f_s = 1/2\pi[(M_s + M_a)C_s]^{1/2} \quad (2)$$

$$Q_t = 2\pi f_s(M_s + M_a)/(R_s + R_a + A^2/R_e) \quad (3)$$

electromagnetic damping $A^2/R_e$ is the major factor in determining $Q_t$ since $A^2/R_e$ is much greater than $R_s + R_a$. SEE Q (ELECTRICITY).

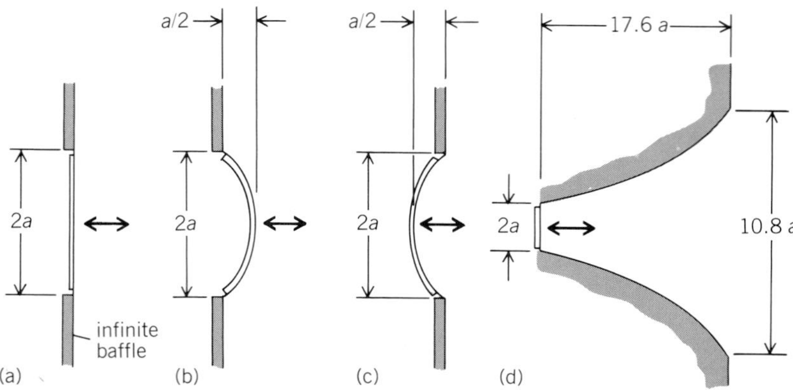


**Fig. 4. Geometries of ideally rigid diaphragms with radius *a* in an infinite baffle. (*a*) Flat. (*b*) Convex dome. (*c*) Concave dome. (*d*) Flat diaphragm with an additional rigid horn.**

**Radiation impedance.** The radiation impedance is defined as the complex ratio of the reacting force of the air on the diaphragm to the velocity of the diaphragm ($F/V$ in Fig. 3). The real part of the radiation impedance is the radiation resistance $R_a$, and the imaginary part is called the radiation reactance. The acoustic power is given by $W = R_aV^2$, in the same way as the electrical power. Therefore, a large radiation resistance is required for efficient sound radiation.

The radiation impedance of a diaphragm in an infinite baffle is dependent on the diaphragm geometry (**Fig. 4**). The radiation resistances of the diaphragms in Fig. 4 are shown by the curves in **Fig. 5** as a function of normalized frequency $ka$, where $k$ is the wave number given by $2\pi/\lambda$ and $\lambda$ is the wavelength. The resistances are normalized to $\rho_0 c\pi a^2$ and are given on a decibel scale as 10 log $(R_a/\rho c\pi a^2)$, where $\rho_0$ is the density of the air and $c$ is the speed of sound. For $ka$ less than 1.0, the radiation resistance increases at a rate of approximately 6 dB/octave for the diaphragms without the horn. This is the region in which a direct-radiator loudspeaker usually operates. As Fig. 3*c* indicates, the velocity of the diaphragm $V$ decreases by a rate of 6 dB/octave above the fundamental resonance frequency $f_s$ and, therefore the radiated acoustical power, $W = R_aV^2$, becomes theoretically constant in this reproduction range. The convex and concave domes have significant differences in their radiation resistances for $0.8 \leq ka \leq 2.2$. The larger radiation resistance of the concave dome in this region is due to its cavity resonance. The on-axis sound pressure of a convex dome is much lower than that of the concave dome for the same velocity of the diaphragm since the convex dome has a lower radiation resistance and a wider directivity pattern. The differences of the sound quality among loudspeakers with cone, dome, and flat diaphragms may be partly explained by the difference of their radiation characteristics. SEE CAVITY RESONATOR.

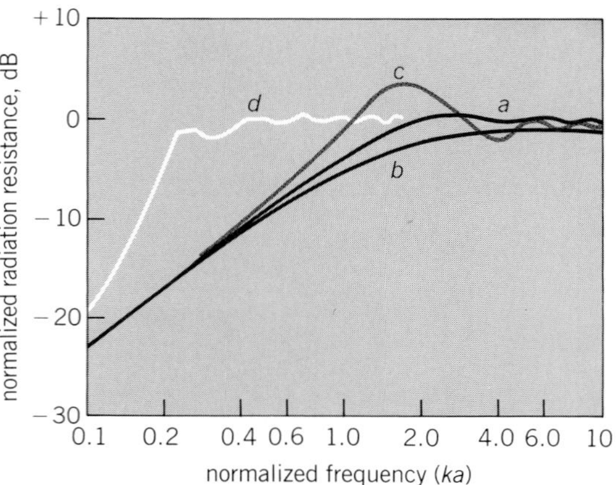


**Fig. 5. Normalized radiation resistances of the diaphragm shown in Fig. 4 as a function of normalized frequency.**

Curve *d* in Fig. 5, when compared with the other curves, clearly shows that the horn load increases the radiation resistance in the range $0.1 \leq ka \leq 1.0$. For the same output power, a horn loudspeaker with the geometry shown in Fig. 4*d* requires approximately one-tenth (−10 dB) of the input power required for a direct-radiator loudspeaker.

The radiation mass of a flat piston in an infinite baffle in the low-frequency range is given by Eq. (4).

$$M_a = 8\rho_0\pi a^3/3 \tag{4}$$

For a concave diaphragm, the mass of the air in the cavity must be added.

**Physical performance characteristics.** Several physical performance characteristics are important for the evaluation of a driver or a loudspeaker system. In the discussion below, the measured characteristics of a commercial three-way loudspeaker system (that is, one with three drivers—a woofer, a midrange, and a tweeter) with a closed-box type of enclosure are used as an example.

***Pressure response–frequency characteristic.*** This is the most important characteristic of the loudspeaker since it shows the reproduction range, sensitivity, and smoothness of the response. Normally, it is shown as a frequency dependence of the sound-pressure level (SPL) in decibels measured in an anechoic chamber at 3.3 ft (1 m) from the loudspeaker (on axis) when a sinusoidal electrical input of 1 W is applied. As a general criterion for a high-fidelity stereo system, a reproduction range from 50 Hz to 15 kHz or wider, an average sensitivity of 85–95 dB SPL/W at 3.3 ft (1 m), and a response deviation within ±5 dB is required. The curve giving the on-axis response in **Fig. 6** is the pressure response–frequency characteristic of the sample loudspeaker system. This curve shows that this loudspeaker has, approximately, a reproduction range from 50 Hz to 15 kHz, a sensitivity of 87 dB SPL/W, and a response deviation of ±3 dB.

***Input impedance.*** The electrical input impedance is defined as the ratio of the applied sinusoidal voltage across the terminals of the loudspeaker to the resulting current. It is important to make sure that the input impedance of a specific loudspeaker is not too low or too high before it is connected to an amplifier, since if it is too low, the amplifier will be damaged, and if it is too high, not enough sound output will be produced. The input impedance–frequency characteristic is also important since it reveals some of the hidden characteristics of the loudspeaker driver or system.

The input impedance of the equivalent electrical circuit of Fig. 3*b* is given by Eq. (5), where $\omega$ (equal

$$Z_e = (R_e + j\omega L_e) + A^2/[(R_s + R_a) + j\omega(M_s + M_a) + 1/j\omega C_s] \tag{5}$$

to $2\pi f$) is the angular frequency. The second term of the right-hand side of Eq. (5) is called the motional impedance, and it becomes zero when the diaphragm is blocked. Figure 6 shows the impedance curve of the sample loudspeaker system. The response gives several important constants of the system: the fundamental resonance frequency (with the enclosure) $f_c$, the mechanical quality factor $Q_m$, the total quality factor $Q_{tc}$, and the minimum impedance $Z_{\min}$, given by Eqs. (6)–(9). The fundamental resonance frequency

$$f_c = 40 \text{ Hz} \tag{6}$$

$$Q_m = f_c/(f_2 - f_1) = 5 \tag{7}$$

$$Q_{tc} = Q_m \cdot R_e/Z_{\max} = 1.1 \tag{8}$$

$$Z_{\min} = 6 \text{ ohms} \tag{9}$$

$f_c$ (with the enclosure) is normally considered as the lower limiting frequency of the reproduction range, and $f_1$ and $f_2$ are the frequencies near the resonance at which the impedance drops to 0.707 of the maximum impedance $Z_{\max}$. The dc resistance ($R_e$ = 5.2 ohms in this case) is measured directly by using an ohmmeter. Generally speaking, a wide and large peak around $f_c$ indicates that a large magnetic voice coil system (that is, one with a large force factor $A$) is used. The impedance curve also indicates that the system has crossover frequencies at approximately 400 Hz between the woofer and the midrange and at 4 kHz between the midrange and the tweeter.

***Directional characteristics.*** The loudspeaker has omnidirectional characteristics in the low-frequency region where the wavelength is much larger than the diameter of the loudspeaker. The sound radiation, however, becomes more directional as the frequency rises. For a normally designed woofer or midrange, $ka$ = 2.0 (720 Hz for $a$ equal to 0.15 m or 6 in.) may be considered as the upper limit on the reproduction range that results from the loudspeaker's directional characteristics. The pressure response–frequency characteristics of the sample loudspeaker system measured at 3.3 ft (1 m) from the speaker and

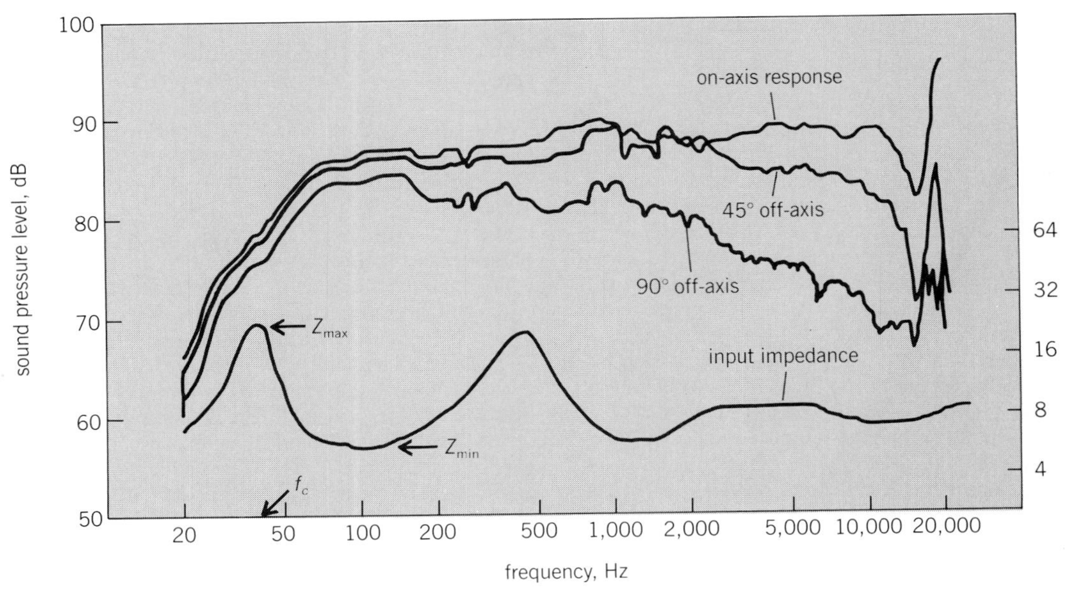


**Fig. 6. Sound pressure response of a sample loudspeaker system with a 1 W input, measured at points 3.3 ft (1 m) from the system, on axis, 45° off axis, and 90° off axis. The input impedance of the loudspeaker is also shown.**

45° and 90° off axis are shown in Fig. 6. In the low-frequency region, there is little difference among the curves, indicating the omnidirectional characteristics of the system. The radiation is directional around the crossover frequencies and in the high-frequency region. The relationship between the optimum directivity characteristics and the acoustic listening environment for high-fidelity reproduction is very important. Too wide or too narrow a directivity in the middle- to high-frequency region is not preferred. For a sound-reinforcement system in a large area, a specially designed loudspeaker array system is frequently used to increase directivity and hence to reduce unwanted reflections and reverberation.

***Distortion.*** If the loudspeaker output contains frequency components other than those contained in the input signal, the new components are called nonlinear distortion products. Harmonic distortion is of this type. When a sinusoidal input with frequency $f$ is applied, the output contains components which are integral multiples of this frequency, such as $2f$, $3f$, etc. If the levels are $e_1$, $e_2$, $e_3$, etc., the $n$th harmonic distortion is $e_n/e_1$ and the total harmonic distortion is $(e_2^2 + e_3^2 + \ldots)^{1/2}/e_1$. In the moving-coil direct-radiator loudspeaker, distortion components higher than the second and third harmonics are mostly insignificant. Harmonic distortion is caused by several processes such as the nonlinearities of the force factor $A$ and the suspension at the low frequencies, the current distortion due to the hysteresis characteristic of the magnetic circuit in the middle- to high-frequency region, and the bending motion of the diaphragm (commonly known as cone breakup) in the same region. In the horn loudspeaker, the nonlinearity of air contributes to the harmonic distortion, since the air is subject to high pressure around the throat. If the second and third harmonics are each 50 dB or more below the fundamental with an average output level of 90 dB SPL measured at 3.3 ft (1 m) on axis from the loudspeaker, the system may be considered to have a good harmonic distortion level for high-fidelity reproduction.

Another type of nonlinear distortion is the intermodulation distortion. If a high-frequency ($f_2$) component of the loudspeaker output is amplitude- or frequency-modulated by a low-frequency ($f_1$) component, the components with frequencies given by Eq. (10) are called intermodulation distortion

$$f_i = f_2 \pm nf_1 \qquad n = 1, 2, \ldots \tag{10}$$

products. The frequency modulation is caused by the Doppler effect. The amplitude modulation is partly caused by the change of the radiation efficiency of the high-frequency driver when the diaphragm position of the low-frequency driver is gradually changed by the low-frequency input signal. A difference-frequency distortion is the new component of the frequency $f_2 - f_1$ created when an input with components of two relatively close frequencies $f_1$ and $f_2$ is given to the loudspeaker.

The other kind of distortion is linear distortion, which is independent of the input level. This kind of distortion is produced by an imperfect pressure–frequency response or phase response–frequency characteristic. A loudspeaker with better pressure and phase responses has a better transient response. The loudspeaker system which is designed especially for a good phase response is called a linear–phase loudspeaker.

**Diaphragm material.** Since the loudspeaker is expected to reproduce any kind of audio sound without coloration, the loudspeaker diaphragm should have a wide frequency range of pistonlike motion or, in other words, should be free from resonances as much as possible. Any mechanical structure, however, shows resonances in the frequency range where the wavelength of the sound in the structure becomes comparable to the size of the structure. A stiffer, lighter, and smaller structure has resonances at higher frequencies. If a structure has large damping (mechanical loss), the resonances become less prominent. This is also true for loudspeaker diaphragms. The diaphragm resonances provide the factor that determines the upper frequency limit of a driver's reproduction range. Therefore, a large Young's modulus $E$, a small density $\rho$, and a large loss factor ($\tan \delta$) are the properties required for a loudspeaker diaphragm. Paper has been used almost exclusively as the diaphragm material of the moving-coil direct-radiator loudspeaker since it was invented. Paper has a relatively high sound velocity (equal to $\sqrt{E/\rho}$) and a reasonable loss factor, and it is inexpensive. Some other materials, however, have come into use to achieve higher fidelity and consistent quality.

**Table 2** shows several diaphragm materials with their Young's moduli, densities, longitudinal sound velocities, and loss factors. Metal diaphragms show large sound velocities and small loss factors. They are mostly used for midranges and tweeters. Composite materials have much higher sound velocities than paper, and yet maintain large loss factors. They are normally used for woofers and midranges. A honeycomb surfaced with a stiff light material or similar structure is most appropriate for a flat diaphragm since its large thickness effectively increases the resonance frequencies. Plastic diaphragms are low cost, give a smooth high-end response due to their large loss factor, and provide consistent quality. No ideal diaphragm material has yet been found or invented, and different diaphragm materials are chosen to meet different design requirements.

**Crossover network.** Most loudspeaker systems employing two or more drivers incorporate an electrical network. The electrical input signal is divided into frequency bands by the crossover network. Each driver is then fed with only those frequencies that it is designed to reproduce. This is necessary to provide a smooth pressure response–frequency characteristic and efficient energy conversion, to protect the drivers from overload, and for other reasons. The response of an $n$th-order dividing network changes proportional to the $\pm n$th power of frequency outside the pass band. This means that for $n$ equal to 1, 2, and 3, the response has a slope of $\pm$ 6, $\pm 12$, and $\pm 18$ dB/octave, respectively. **Figure 7** shows two typical crossover networks, a two-way first-order network with crossover frequency $f_1$, and a three-way second-order network with crossover frequencies $f_1$ and $f_2$, where the circuit elements satisfy Eqs. (11)–(14). The first-order network satisfies two conditions; it has a constant input impedance $Z_{\text{in}} = R$ over the entire frequency range, and the $-3$-dB (half-power) points of the low- and high-pass filter responses fall at the crossover frequency $f_1$. These two conditions are also approximately satisfied by the second-order network if the two crossover frequencies $f_1$ and $f_2$ are not too close to each other. However, the pressure, phase, and impedance of real loudspeakers vary in a complex

**Table 2. Acoustic properties of materials used for loudspeaker diaphragms***

| Material | Young's modulus (E), $10^{10}$ N/m$^2$ ($10^6$ lbf/in.$^2$) | Density (ρ), kg/m$^3$ (lbm/ft$^3$) | Sound velocity ($\sqrt{E/\rho}$), m/s (ft/s) | Loss factor (tan δ) |
|---|---|---|---|---|
| *Metals* | | | | |
| Boron | 42 (61) | 2300 (144) | 13,500 (44,300) | <0.01 |
| Beryllium | 28 (41) | 1840 (115) | 12,300 (40,400) | <0.01 |
| Aluminum | 7.4 (10.7) | 2690 (168) | 5200 (17,100) | <0.01 |
| Titanium | 10.5 (15.2) | 4510 (282) | 4830 (15,850) | <0.01 |
| *Composites* | | | | |
| Carbon fiber–reinforced plastic + aluminum honeycomb | 0.9 (1.3) | 100–300 (6–19) | 5000–9000 (16,000–30,000) | 0.01–0.05 |
| Graphite flake + polyvinyl chloride + polyvinylidene chloride | 4–7 (6–10) | 1600 (100) | 5000–7000 (16,000–23,000) | 0.01–0.05 |
| Graphite + fiberglass + polyimide | 2.0 (2.9) | 1800 (112) | 3300 (10,500) | 0.02–0.03 |
| *Plastics* | | | | |
| Polyolefin | 0.12 (0.17) | 890 (56) | 1160 (3800) | 0.09 |
| Rubber-modified high-impact polystyrene + polyvinyl acetate | 0.19 (0.28) | 1000–1300 (62–81) | 1200–1300 (4000–4300) | 0.05–0.10 |
| *Paper* | 0.2–0.4 (0.3–0.6) | 300–600 (19–37) | 2000–3000 (6500–10,000) | 0.03–0.05 |

*Values shown should be considered as representative.

manner, and therefore the constants given in Eqs. (11)–(14) should be considered only as a first approximation.

$$L_1 = R/2\pi f_1 \quad (11)$$

$$C_1 = 1/2\pi f_1 R \quad (12)$$

$$L_2 = R/2\pi f_2 \quad (13)$$

$$C_2 = 1/2\pi f_2 R \quad (14)$$

Modification of the network elements is generally required after measurement and listening tests. SEE NETWORK THEORY.

**Enclosure.** When a diaphragm vibrates in free space, positive and negative sound pressures are produced alternately in front of and behind the diaphragm. Cancellation between the positive and negative pressures occurs at low frequencies since the loudspeaker has an omnidirectional characteristic at these frequencies. In an enclosure, the pressure radiated behind the diaphragm is contained, so that it does not negatively interfere with the sound generated in front of the diaphragm. The three enclosure types most commonly used for loudspeaker systems are the closed-box type, the acoustic suspension (or bookshelf) type, and the bass-reflex (or vented-box) type.

***Closed-box type.*** The intereference problem is solved when a woofer is installed in a closed rigid box with a sufficient amount of absorbing material. However, another problem arises if the internal volume of the enclosure $V$ is not adequate. The effective mechanical compliance working on the loudspeaker diaphragm is given by Eq. (15), where $S_d$ is the effective area of the diaphragm.

$$C_c = V_c/\rho_0 c^2 S_d^2 \quad (15)$$

This compliance is connected in series to the radiation impedance in the equivalent circuit of Fig. 3c. Then, the fundamental resonance frequency of the loudspeaker with the enclosure and the system quality factor are given by Eqs. (16) and (17). As Eq. (16) indicates, the resonance frequency in the box is significantly raised if the enclosure compliance $C_c$ is small compared to the loudspeaker suspension compliance $C_s$. The closed-box type of enclosure is used when a relatively large internal volume is available.

$$f_c = [(C_s + C_c)/C_c]^{1/2} f_s \quad (16)$$

$$Q_{tc} = [(C_s + C_c)/C_c]^{1/2} Q_t \quad (17)$$

***Acoustic-suspension (bookshelf) type.*** There are two ways to keep the resonance frequency $f_c$ low even when the enclosure volume is relatively small. First, the resonance frequency of the loudspeaker (without enclosure) $f_s$ can be made low if a loudspeaker with a large mass $M_s$ and a large compliance $C_s$ is used, as can be seen from Eq. (2). Second, by the addition of a great amount of absorbing material inside the enclosure, the effective compliance $C_c$ can be made large. By employing these two techniques, a loudspeaker system with a small enclosure that still has a low resonance frequency $f_c$ is made possible. Since this type of loudspeaker system has a low efficiency, a power amplifier with a large output is required for a high sound-reproduction level.

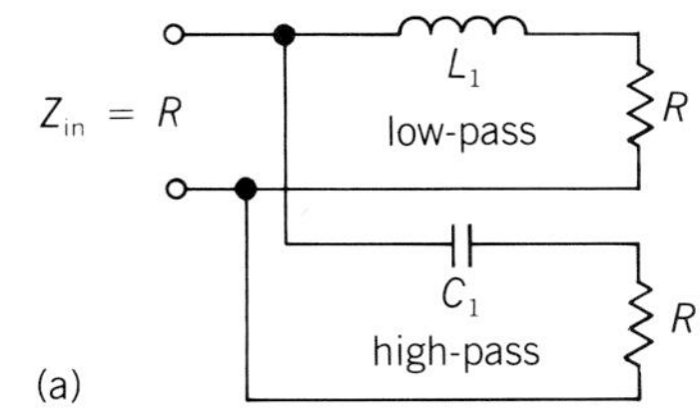


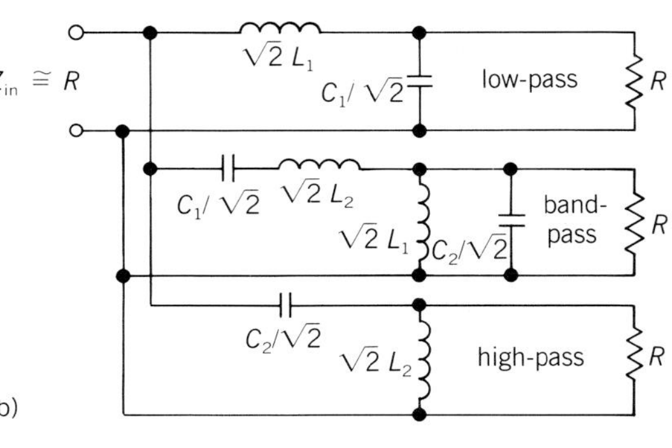


**Fig. 7. Typical crossover networks. (*a*) Two-way first-order network. (*b*) Three-way second-order network.**

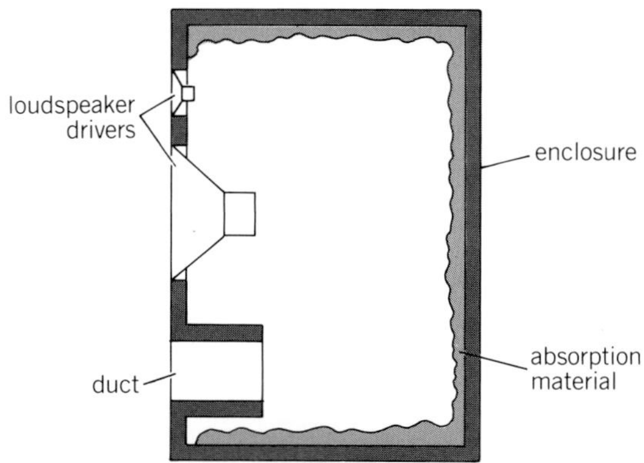


**Fig. 8. Cross-sectional view of a loudspeaker system with a bass-reflex type of enclosure.**

***Bass-reflex (vented-box) types.*** When a duct (or vent) is added to a closed box, the mass of air inside the duct and the springlike compliance of the air in the enclosure constitutes a resonance circuit (**Fig. 8**). If the resonance is properly tuned, the sound radiated through the duct opening from inside the enclosure effectively adds to the direct sound and can improve the response near the low cut-off frequency. Below the enclosure resonance, however, the pressure response decays very sharply as the frequency decreases due to the interference between the direct and indirect sounds. In the equivalent circuit, the mass in the duct is taken care of by adding the effective (mechanical) mass $(S_d/S_p)^2M_p$, in parallel with the enclosure compliance $C_c$ of the closed-box type of system, where $S_p$ is the duct opening area and $M_p$ is the mass of the air inside the duct including the radiation mass at the opening. The resonance of the enclosure is then given by Eq. (18). This is tuned near the resonance frequency of the loudspeaker in free air, $f_s$, depending on the parameters of the woofer and the enclosure, and the required response.

$$f_b = [\rho_0 c^2 S_p^2/(M_p \cdot V_c)]^{1/2}/2\pi \qquad (18)$$

*Hideo Suzuki*

***Bibliography.*** Audio Engineering Society Inc., *An Anthology of Articles of Loudspeakers from the Papers of the Journal of the Audio Engineering Society,* I, vols. 1–25, 1978, and II, vols. 26–31, 1984; L. L. Beranek, *Acoustics,* 1954; M. Colloms, *High Performance Loudspeakers,* 2d ed., 1979; L. E. Kinsler et al., *Fundamentals of Acoustics,* 3d ed., 1980; H. S. Knowles, Loudspeakers and room acoustics, *Radio Engineers Handbook,* pp. 760–761, 1950; H. F. Olson, *Music, Physics and Engineering,* 1967.

## Magnetic bubble memory

A memory storage technology which uses localized magnetized regions to store information. Magnetic bubble memory (MBM) is the integrated-circuit analogy to rotating magnetic memories such as disks and tapes.

**Principles of operation.** Magnetic bubble memories employ materials that are easily magnetized in one direction but are hard to magnetize in the orthogonal direction. The most commonly used materials are magnetic garnets which are deposited on a nonmagnetic substrate to form the basis of a bubble memory chip. A thin film of one of these materials, with the easy direction perpendicular to the surface, will allow only two natural directions of magnetization—up or down in the easy direction. When no external magnetic field is applied, the magnetic garnet film forms serpentine patterns of upward and downward magnetization. When a magnetic field is applied by sandwiching the film between two permanent magnets, cylindrical-shaped magnetic domains are formed in place of the serpentine structure. These cylinders are called magnetic bubbles and have a magnetization pointing in the opposite direction of the surrounding area. In effect, magnetic bubbles are magnetic islands in a magnetic sea of opposite magnetic polarity.

***Storage locations.*** To make a memory of these magnetic bubbles, several functions must be performed. A bit of storage is represented as the presence or absence of a bubble at a given storage location. There are several methods of defining the storage locations, but the most common way is to use the chevron patterns shown in **Fig. 2**. These chevrons are made of a soft ferromagnetic material such as permalloy and are deposited on the surface of the magnetic garnet. There can be one bubble for each chevron.

***Loop organization.*** The chevrons also serve as the path for bubble movement when the information is accessed. To organize the bubble memory bits, the chevron patterns are deposited to form loops along which the bubbles can travel. The simplest organization is one single, large loop. The drawback is that the bubbles must travel the entire length of the loop before the information can be retrieved, and this is time-consuming. Most bubble memory chips now use a more sophisticated architecture called the major/minor loop (**Fig. 1**). In these multiple storage loops, the length and the time taken to traverse a minor loop is much smaller than for one major, large loop. The information is retrieved by waiting until the desired bubbles are at the top of the minor loops. At that point one bubble from each minor loop is transferred to the major loop. This "bubble train" traverses the major loop, during which time the information can be read or new information can be substituted. When the bubble train has traveled once around the major loop, all the bubbles are transferred back into the minor loops. The commensurate lengths of the major loops and minor loops are such that the bubble train retains its original position in the minor loops.

***Information retrieval.*** To move the bubbles along the loops, a rotating magnetic field must be generated. For each rotation of the magnetic field each bubble moves synchronously from one chevron to the next. In other words, the magnetic bubbles move within the material, but no physical motion takes place. This is the opposite of what takes place in other magnetic memories such as disks and tapes. Disks and tapes also store information as small magnetized regions. However, to retrieve this information, disks and tapes must physically move the magnetized regions past a read/write head. The "motion" of bubble memories is accomplished by using two orthogonal coils which are wound around the bubble memory chip.

**Figure 3** shows the main components and operation of magnetic bubble memories, including the memory chip, the magnetic garnet material where bubbles are formed, the permalloy patterns which guide and control bubble movements, the two coils that power bubble movement, and the two permanent magnets that retain the information when power is removed giving the memory the property of nonvolatility. Various types of interfacing circuitry which are needed to make a complete bubble memory system are also shown.

**Technology status.** The fundamentals of bubble memories were discovered in the late 1960s. The bubble technology advanced very rapidly thereafter, and today 1,000,000 bits can be stored on a chip which is about 15 mm square. This chip, when enclosed inside two coils and two permanent magnets, is about a 1 in. square (25 mm square) package.

Bubble memory manufacturing is similar to semiconductor production. The materials are different, but the manufacturing steps are nearly identical. For this reason, major semiconductor manufacturers, as well as computer companies in the United States and other countries, have invested in the magnetic bubble memory technology.

The average time to retrieve the information depends on the length of the minor loops and speed of bubble memory shifting. The shift rate is typically 100 kHz and this is also the rate of information transfer, that is 100 kilobits per second. The 1,000,000-bit chips have minor loops lengths of about 2000 bits, and this gives an average information access time of approximately 10 milliseconds.

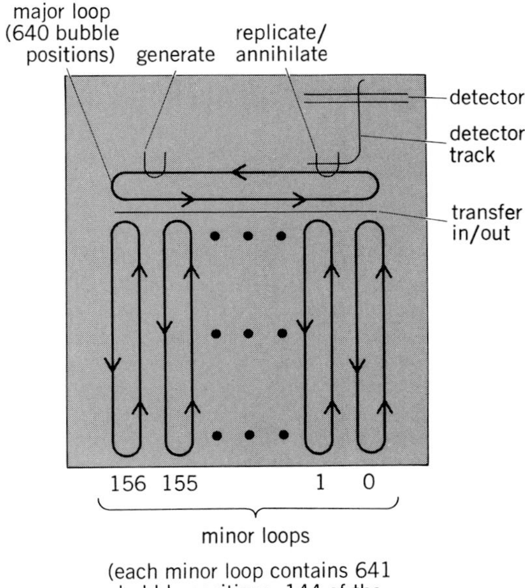


**Fig. 1. Diagram of the major/minor loop architecture of a 100,000-bit magnetic bubble memory chip. With multiple storage loops, the time to traverse a minor loop is much reduced as compared with one major, large loop.**

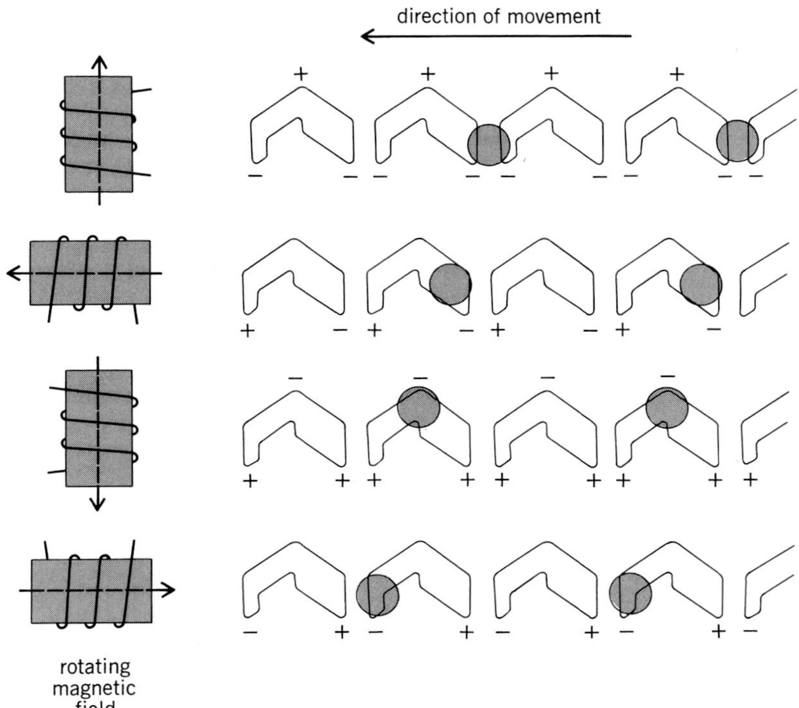


**Fig. 2. Movement of magnetic bubbles under pattern of conductive chevrons.**

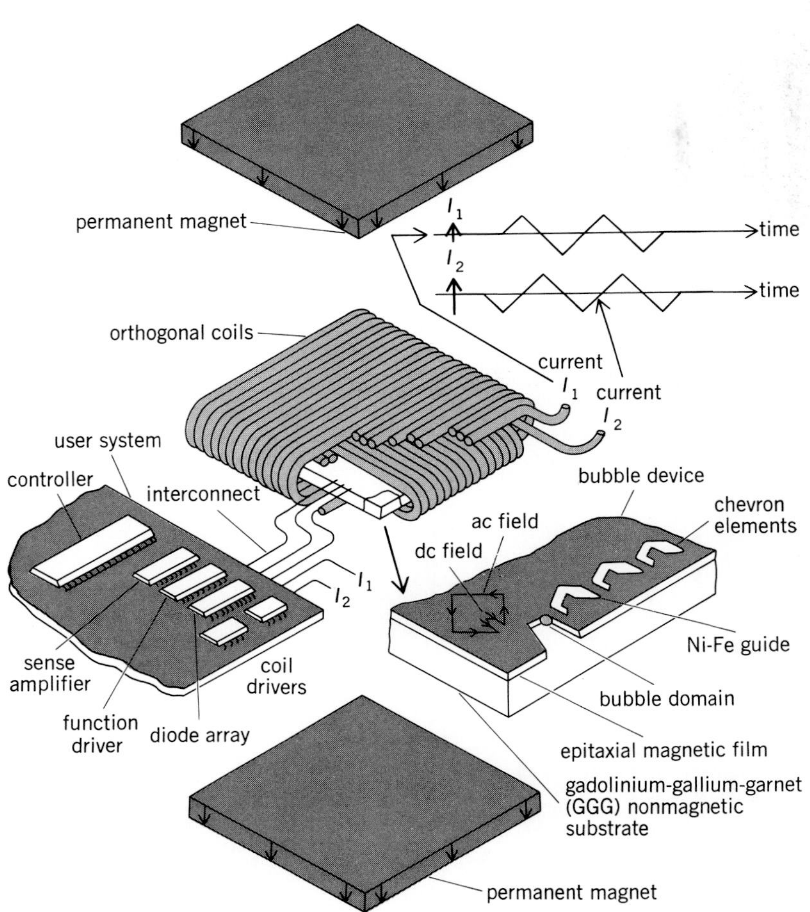


**Fig. 3. Principal components and operation that are utilized in magnetic bubble memory.**

Compared to competing technologies, magnetic bubble memories have many desirable features and few disadvantages. Compared with both disks and floppy disks, magnetic bubble memories have lower access time, lower entry price, smaller physical size, and simpler interfacing, but have the disadvantage of lacking media removability. However, removable bubble memory cartridges have been introduced. Magnetic bubble memories also have the disadvantages of higher bit price and lower transfer rate compared with disks (other than floppy disks). On the other hand, compared with semiconductor memories, magnetic bubble memories have nonvolatility, lower bit price and more bits per chip, but have the disadvantages of higher access time, complex interfacing, and lower transfer rate. The advantages for bubble memories are strongest when a relatively small amount of secondary storage is needed—a few million bits or less. Application examples are terminals, desk-top computers, computer-controlled machinery, test equipment, and similar microcomputer-based systems. SEE COMPUTER STORAGE TECHNOLOGY; INTEGRATED CIRCUITS.

*J. Egil Juliussen*

**Bibliography.** H. Chang, Major activity in MBM technology, *Comput. Des.*, 18(11):117–125, November 1979; G. Cox, Trio of dense bubble memories has large supporting cast, *Electronics*, 52(23):123–128, November 8, 1979; J. E. Juliussen, The competitive status of bubble memories, *Proceedings of Electro '79 Conference*, New York, April 26, 1979.

## Magnetic lens

A magnetic field with axial symmetry capable of converging beams of charged particles of uniform velocity and of forming images of objects placed in the path of such beams. Magnetic lenses are employed as condensers, objectives, and projection lenses in magnetic electron microscopes, as final focusing lenses in the electron guns of cathode-ray tubes, and for the selection of groups of charged particles of specific velocity in velocity spectrographs.

As shown in the **illustration**, magnetic lenses may be formed by solenoids or helical coils of wire traversed by electric current, by axially symmetric pole pieces excited by a coil encased in a high-permeability material such as soft iron, or by similar pole pieces excited by permanent magnets. In the last two instances the armatures and pole pieces serve to concentrate the magnetic field in a narrow region about the axis.

Magnetic lenses are always converging lenses. Their action differs from that of electrostatic lenses and glass lenses in that they produce a rotation of the image in addition to the focusing action. For the simple uniform magnetic field within a long solenoid the image rotation is exactly 180°. Thus a uniform magnetic field forms an erect real image of an object on its axis. This image has unity magnification and is at a distance from the object equal to $(8\pi^2 m\phi/eB^2)^{1/2} = 21.08\phi^{1/2}/B$, where $m$ is the mass of the particles, $e$ their charge, $\phi$ the accelerating potential of the particles, and $B$ the magnetic induction on an axis of symmetry of the field. The numerical coefficient 21.08 applies for electrons, with $\phi$ in volts and $B$ in gauss.

For short magnetic lenses, or lens fields which are short compared to the focal length, both the magnification and image position depend on the position of the object. The focal length $f$ is given by Eq. (1). The

$$\frac{1}{f} = \frac{e}{8m\phi} \int B^2\, dz = \frac{0.022}{\phi} \int B^2 \cdot dz \text{ cm}^{-1} \quad (1)$$

integration is carried out over the extent of the lens field along the axis of symmetry (the $z$ axis). The numerical coefficient 0.022 again applies for electrons. At the same time the field produces an image rotation through an angle $\phi$, as given in Eq. (2). Thus the

$$\theta = \left(\frac{e}{8m\phi}\right)^{1/2} \int B\, dz = \frac{0.147}{\phi^{1/2}} \int B\, dz \quad (2)$$

magnetic lens field formed by two identical coils in tandem, traversed by oppositely directed currents, is

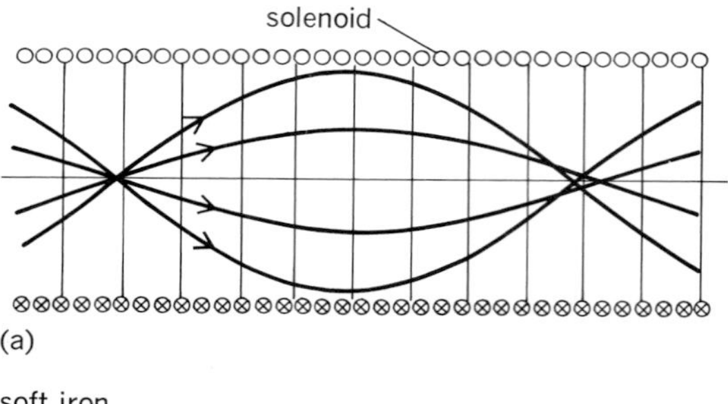


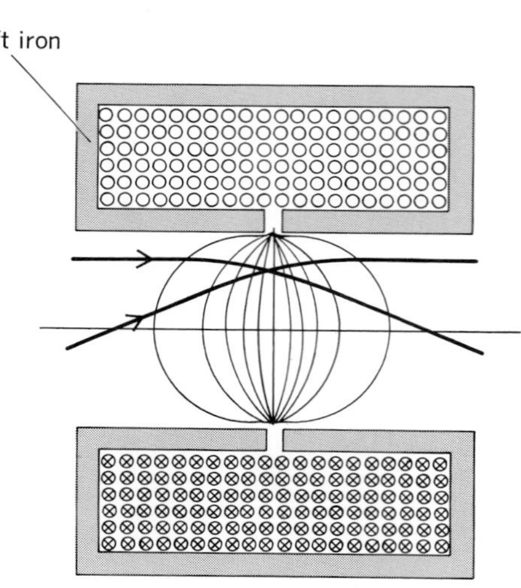


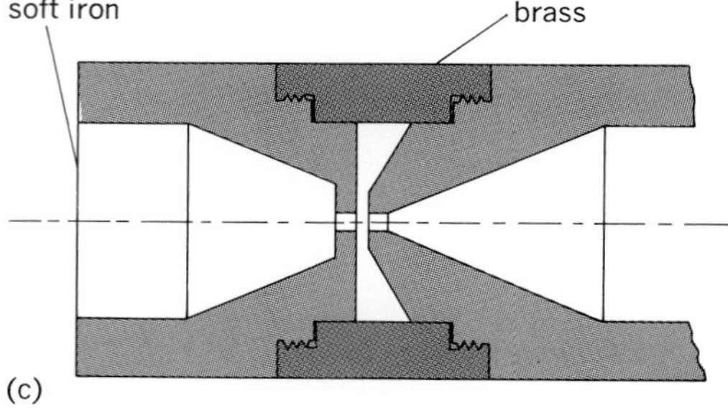


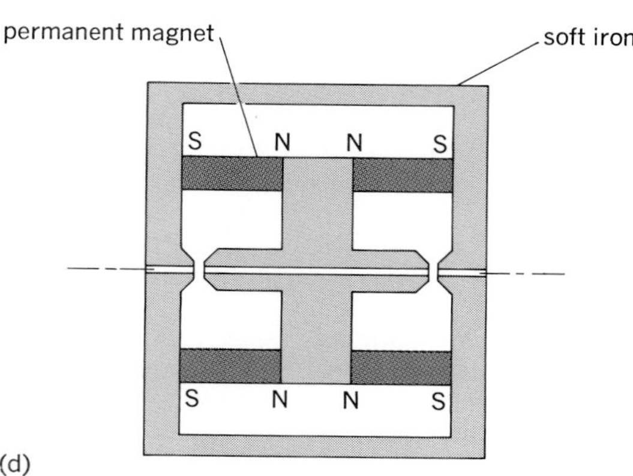


**Magnetic lenses. (*a*) Uniform magnetic field. (*b*) Short magnetic lens formed at gap in soft-iron casing about coil. (c) Pole pieces for magnetic electron microscope objective. (*d*) Double magnetic lens excited by permanent magnets. (*After E. G. Ramberg and G. A. Morton, J. Appl. Phys., vol. 10, 1939, and J. Hillier and E. G. Ramberg, J. Appl. Phys., vol. 18, 1947*)**

rotation free. As a specific example of a short lens, a single circular loop of wire of radius $r$ traversed by current $I$ produces a lens with focal length $f = 96.8r\phi/I^2$ cm. Here $\phi$ is in volts and $I$ in amperes. The image rotation for this lens is $\theta = 0.185I/\phi^{1/2}$ radian. *SEE ELECTRON MOTION IN VACUUM.*

*E. G. Ramberg*

***Bibliography.*** P. Dahl, *Introduction to Electron and Ion Optics*, 1973; A. B. El-Kareh and J. C. El-Kareh, *Electron Beams, Lenses and Optics*, 2 vols., 1970; P. Grivet, *Electron Optics*, 2d ed., 1972; P. W. Hawkes, *Properties of Magnetic Electron Lenses*, 1982; O. E. Klemperer and M. E. Barnett, *Electron Optics*, 3d ed., 1970.

## Magnetic recording

The technique of storing electric signals as a magnetic pattern on a moving magnetic surface. In magnetic recording a time-varying electric current produces a corresponding time-varying magnetic field in a recording head. This field then lays down a spatially varying pattern of magnetization in a sheet or strip of magnetic material moving past the head. When this recorded pattern moves past a playback head, a time-varying electric output is generated in the head corresponding to the original electric signal. A common form of magnetic recorder is diagrammed in **Fig. 1**. Magnetic tape from the supply reel moves past an erase head which removes any previously recorded pattern and leaves the tape in a demagnetized condition. An electric signal fed to the recording head lays down the desired new pattern on the tape. This recorded pattern induces an electric output as it moves over the playback head. Since the magnetization pattern remains in the tape until erased or otherwise altered, the tape may be rewound onto the supply reel and replayed as often as desired, with the erase and recording heads inactivated. The motor-driven capstan and pinch roller pull the tape over the heads at a uniform, controlled speed during recording and playback.

Audio and video magnetic recorders have become indispensable in innumerable areas of modern society. Audio recorders are sold by the millions as consumer products in reel-to-reel, cartridge, and cassette formats. Tape recorders are central in professional sound-recording studios and in radio and television broadcasting. They serve as mass-storage memories in computer systems and are used as instrumentation recorders for collecting data in research, industry, and military applications. They are employed in satellites and spacecraft for delayed transmission of data to earth stations.

### Principles of Operation

The principles of magnetic recording were first demonstrated in 1898 by V. Poulsen. Despite early attempts, however, there were almost no practical applications until the 1930s and 1940s. The earlier recorders of this era used steel ribbon or steel wire as the recording medium; wire recorders using 0.004-in.-diameter (100-micrometer) stainless steel wire were popular throughout the 1940s. Eventually they were supplanted by tape recorders using thin plastic tapes coated with magnetic iron oxide. Such tape was introduced in 1935 for the German Magnetophone.

Regardless of the nature of the application and of the mechanical configuration of the recorder, all magnetic recorders rely on the same basic magnetic behavior for their operation.

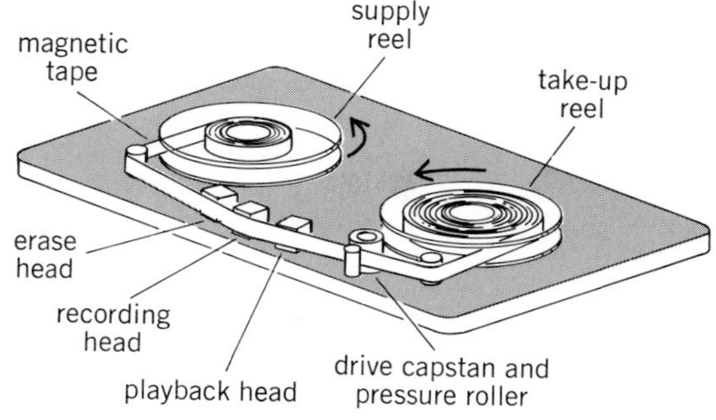


**Fig. 1. Common form of magnetic tape recorder.**

**Recording medium.** The plastic base for magnetic tapes is now almost universally a polyester film between 0.0005 and 0.0015 in. (12.5 and 37.5 μm) in thickness. The magnetic coating most frequently used is acicular gamma ferric oxide ($\gamma Fe_2O_3$) particles. Premium-grade tapes with higher energies may use particles of chromium dioxide ($CrO_2$), cobalt-modified ferric oxide, or ferric metal alloy particles. These particles (**Fig. 2**) are dispersed in a binder and coated uniformly on the base film. While the coating is still liquid, a magnetic field may be applied to orient the particles in the direction of recording. The freshly coated film, in a web 12 in. (30 cm) or more in width, is then dried and finally slit into tapes of the required widths. Depending on the application, the coating thickness is usually between 0.00005 and 0.0002 in. (1.2 and 5 μm).

Each of the particles in a tape coating is a tiny permanent magnet embedded in the resin so it cannot move. However, the direction of the particle's magnetization can be reversed by an external magnetic field of sufficient strength. The bulk magnetic char-

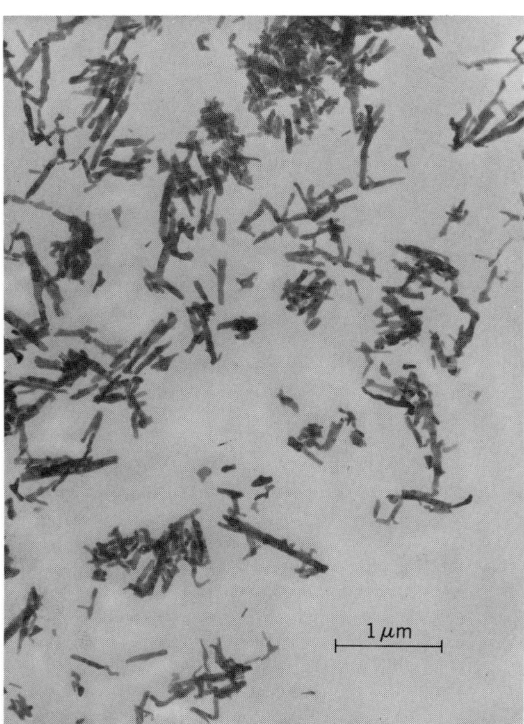


**Fig. 2. Photomicrograph of particles of the type used in magnetic recording media. In an actual coating the particles would be much more densely packed.**

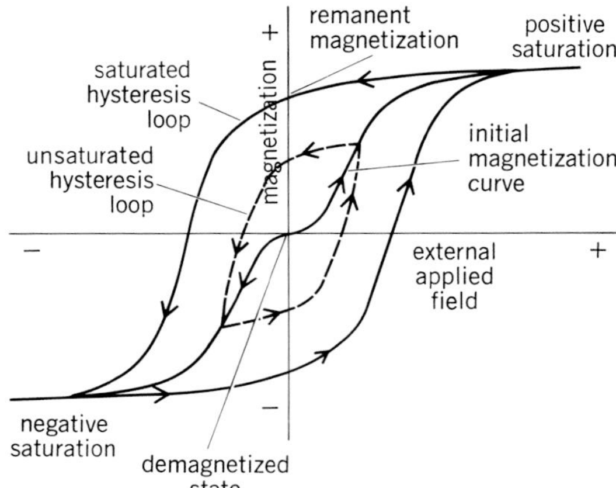


Fig. 3. Magnetization characteristics of recording tape.

acteristics measured for a tape coating are the sum of the states of all of the particles as an aggregate. Thus, when a tape is demagnetized it means that the contributions of some particles exactly cancel the contributions of other particles to yield zero field outside the coating. When an external magnetizing field is applied and gradually increased in strength, more and more particles will switch the direction of their magnetization to conform to the direction of the applied field. The tape is magnetically saturated when all of the particles have been switched. When the external field is removed, some of the particles will reverse their magnetization due to the influence of the fields of neighboring particles, and the tape will be left in a remanent state of magnetization that is somewhat weaker than the saturated state. If an external field in the opposite direction is applied, increased, and removed, saturation and remanence of the tape occur in the opposite polarity. The bulk result yields the familiar form of a magnetic saturated hysteresis loop shown in **Fig. 3**.

**Magnetic heads.** While magnetic heads may differ widely in geometrical details, they are basically of the form sketched in **Fig. 4**, whether they are recording or playback heads. Frequently, the same head is used for both functions. A coil of wire is wound on a core of material that very readily carries magnetic flux (that is, a high-permeability material). Iron and some of its alloys are such materials. Certain ceramiclike ferrites are others. A nonmagnetic gap is formed in the core at some point. When an electric current passes through the coil, magnetic field lines associated with the current follow paths around the high-permeability core. At the gap, some of the lines spread outside the core to form a fringing field. The

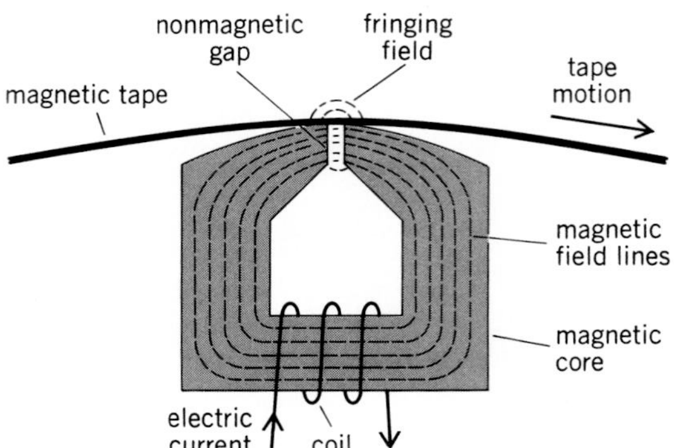


Fig. 4. Schematic representation of a magnetic recording head.

recording medium passes through the fringing field above the gap and is magnetized there during recordings.

The width of the track on the recording medium is determined by the thickness of the core at the gap. Several cores, each with its own coil, may be mounted side by side in a single structure to form a multitrack head.

**Recording process.** During recording, the fringing field is the external applied field mentioned in connection with Fig. 3. Starting with erased (demagnetized) tape, if the strength of the fringing field is gradually increased, the tape magnetization will increase while following the initial magnetization curve depicted in Fig. 3. As a segment of tape passes away from the recording gap, the strength of the fringing field falls to zero and the tape is left with a remanent magnetization. If a smaller value of current is fed to the coil, the remanent magnetization will have a lesser value, as indicated by the remanence for an unsaturated hysteresis loop in Fig. 3. The remanence always corresponds to the strongest magnetizing field experienced by an element of tape in passing through the fringing field, provided that the field does not reverse while the element is under its influence.

**Playback process.** The structure represented in Fig. 4 can function as a playback head. In this case no current is fed to the coil and no fringing field is produced at the gap. Rather, the ''magnets'' previously recorded on the tape are moved over the head. These generate their own external magnetic field lines, many of which enter the core of the head. Some of these pass directly across the gap in the core and reenter the tape to complete their loop. These lines have no role in the playback process. Other lines follow the longer route around the core and pass through the coil. This time-varying playback flux threading through the coil generates a voltage in the coil that is amplified to produce the output signal of the recorder. *SEE FARADAY'S LAW OF INDUCTION.*

**High-frequency bias.** The recording process described above produces in the tape a remanent magnetization corresponding generally to the current in the coil. However, the process is highly nonlinear because of the sharp curvature in the initial magnetization curve near the origin. This introduces distortion that is unacceptable for some applications, including audio recording. The process can be linearized and the distortion reduced to very low values by the use of a high-frequency bias during recording. The frequency of the bias must be several times higher than the highest frequency to be recorded. For example, if the highest signal frequency of interest in audio recording is 15 kHz, the bias frequency should be in the 75–100-kHz range. The signal and bias currents are simply added together in the recording head, with the bias current being the larger of the two and of constant amplitude approximating saturation of the tape. As an element of tape passes through the fringing field, the bias swings the element through several trips around the major hysteresis loop before the element moves beyond the gap and the fringing field falls to zero. This ''anhysteretic'' magnetization process leaves the tape magnetized in direct proportion to the strength of the signal current. The bias frequency is usually too high to be recorded by the system and does not appear in the playback. This magnetization process is quite complicated and, while several theoretical models offer insights and explanations, analysis complete in all details is still elusive. Nevertheless, high-frequency-bias recording has been routinely and successfully used in audio recorders for several decades.

**Digital recording.** Magnetic recording is naturally adapted to the use of digital signals consisting of binary states represented by ones and zeros. The two digital states are made to correspond to the two polarities of magnetic saturation of the recording medium. Since only saturation is involved, there is no concern with linearity of recording and high-frequency bias is not needed, nor is erasure of the recording medium. While nearly all digital recording systems depend on switching between the two saturation states, several data-encoding schemes have been devised to use the magnetic medium more efficiently by detecting the time at which each magnetism reversal occurs instead of, or in addition to, the direction of reversal for identifying ones and zeros.

While the most widespread use of digital recording is in computers, it is also used in instrumentation recorders, satellite and telecommunication recorders, machine-tool controllers, electronic games, and audio and video recorders. *See Analog-to-digital converter.*

**FM recording.** In frequency-modulation (FM) recording the information to be stored in the magnetic tape is carried as frequency modulation of a high-frequency carrier. The carrier is recorded on and played back from the tape, being demodulated after playback to retrieve the original information. Since only changes in the frequency of the carrier must be detected, linearity in recording is not important, and high-frequency bias is not essential. However, the tape should be erased prior to recording a new signal. FM recording is in widespread use in instrumentation recorders and in video recorders. *See Frequency modulation.*

**Noise and wavelength limitations.** The information-carrying capacity of every communications or recording system is limited by the background noise inherent in the system and by the range of frequencies it can handle. In magnetic recording, the basic noise limitation in a well-designed system arises from nonuniformities in the recording medium. Inevitable statistical variations in the size and dispersion of the particles are reflected in small fluctuations of the magnetic properties in the coating, as well as in imperfect smoothness of its surface. When manufacturing tapes to be used in high-quality systems, great pains are taken in dispersing the particles and in polishing the coating surface.

The range of signal frequencies that can be handled in a magnetic recorder is limited by the abrupt falling off of the record-playback response at high frequencies. The fundamental factors responsible for the falloff are geometrical in nature and are more correctly described as short-wave-length losses. When a signal consisting of only a single frequency is recorded, the distance occupied along the track by one cycle of the signal is its wavelength. The wavelength is equal to the speed of the tape moving past the head divided by the frequency. Therefore, shorter wavelengths correspond to higher frequencies at any head-to-tape speed. Some of these short-wavelength losses are intrinsic in the recording process, arising from self-demagnetization of the recorded signals and from a too gradual falling off of the fringing field at the trailing edge of the gap. Both effects cause a smearing out of the recorded pattern, with smearing being more severe at shorter wavelengths.

Two further losses occur in playback. One is a separation loss due to imperfect contact between the tape coating and the surface of the playback head. This loss amounts to 55 dB (about 1/600) for a separation of one wavelength. The other loss is called gap loss and is related to the length of the head gap in the direction of tape motion. Gap losses are increasingly serious as the recorded wavelengths are made short enough to be comparable to the gap length. The output falls to zero when the wavelength and gap length are equal, since the head now receives equal fluxes from the two opposite magnetization polarities of each recorded cycle on the tape.

The principal motivation for extending system response to ever-shorter wavelengths is to increase the density of information on the recording medium. Greater densities mean that less tape is needed for recording a given amount of information. All magnetic recording systems can benefit by extending the response to shorter wavelengths, since the short-wavelength response is usually the limiting factor in performance. The benefit may be used, as it becomes available through improved tapes and heads, to extend the response to higher frequencies, to increase the signal-to-noise ratio, to improve the system stability, to reduce the tape speed, or to achieve some optimal combination of these, depending on the requirements of the system. *See Electrical noise; Signal-to-noise ratio.*

### Types of Recording System

Some of the most common and most important recording systems are described below.

**Audio recorders.** The earliest significant use of magnetic recording was in the audio-frequency domain, and today audio tape recorders greatly outnumber other types. Machines for professional use in recording studios require the highest possible linearity, signal-to-noise ratio, and speed constancy. They operate at standard tape speeds of 15 in./s (38 cm/s) and 30 in./s (76 cm/s), since short-wavelength losses are reduced at these speeds. By contrast, the cassette recorders sold in the mass consumer market have a tape speed of only 1⅞ in./s (4.8 cm/s). Certain other recorders requiring only low-grade voice quality, such as dictation machines and recorders for long-term monitoring purposes, operate at even slower tape speeds. Stereo-8 cartridge players operate at 3¾ in./s (9.5 cm/s). Reel-to-reel consumer machines operate at selectable speeds of 3¾ and 7½ in./s (9.5 and 19 cm/s).

Of the numerous attempts to eliminate the inconvenience of threading tape through its path from the supply reel to the take-up reel in a recorder, only two have received widespread acceptance. They are the endless-loop cartridge and the coplanar-hub cassette.

***Cartridge.*** In the cartridge, the tape is wound on a single hub. Tape is drawn out of the wound stack at the hub, pulled past a playback head by a capstan, and returned to the outside of the stack, with the two ends of the length of tape being spliced together to form an endless loop (**Fig. 5**). Since adjacent layers of the tape in the stack are continuously sliding past one another, low-friction coating is applied to the side of the tape opposite the magnetic coating during manufacture of the tape to permit smooth motion of the tape without application of excessive pulling forces.

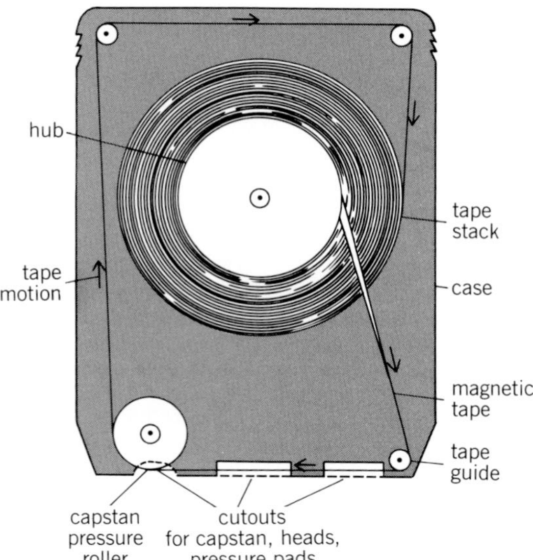


**Fig. 5. Diagram of a Stereo-8 audio tape cartridge.**

The hub, with its wound stack, is contained in a plastic case that also has posts and rollers to guide the tape past the head and capstan on the player. Cutouts in one edge of the case allow a short span of tape to engage the head and capstan when the cartridge is inserted in a slot in the player.

A common use of endless-loop cartridges is for commercial messages in radio stations. Endless-loop cartridges have received popular acceptance for music reproduction in the home and in automobiles. In this application eight tracks are recorded side by side along the ¼-in.-wide (0.63-cm) tape, and the package is designated Stereo-8. The tracks are used in pairs for stereophonic sound reproduction. Thus, four passes of the loop occur before a recorded program repeats itself. Usually a player carries a sensor to detect the splice in the loop, and the playback head is automatically advanced to the next pair of tracks at that point. Any desired pair of tracks may be selected manually at any time. Stereo-8 players usually do not have provision for recording and are used with prerecorded cartidges.

***Cassette.*** In an audio cassette the tape is wound in a stack on a hub, with one end of the tape being permanently attached to the hub. The other end of the tape is permanently attached to an identical hub in the same plane as the first and symmetrically located in the flat plastic case. The tape path between the hubs is determined by guide posts in the case, and the tape travels from one hub to the other. Cutouts in one edge of the case allow a span of tape to engage the capstan and heads in the player when the cassette is inserted (**Fig. 6**). The tape is 0.15 in. (0.38 cm) wide and carries four tracks. Depending on the player, the tracks may be used for monophonic reproduction or for stereophonic reproduction. One pair of tracks is used for one direction of tape motion and the other pair for the opposite direction, the direction reversal usually being achieved by removing the cassette and reinserting it with the other side up. Most cassette players have a provision for recording as well as playback.

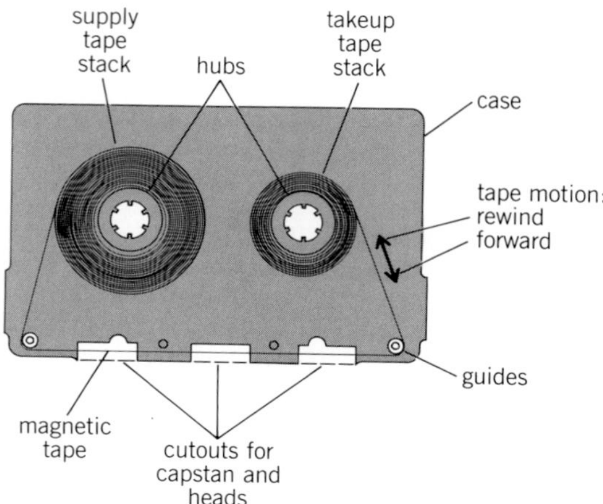


**Fig. 6. Diagram of a coplanar-hub audio tape cassette.**

***Reel-to-reel recorders.*** Reel-to-reel recorders were the earliest form of audio-tape machine, and they still are the form employed when the highest-possible quality of reproduced sound is desired. The high quality in reel-to-reel machines is due partly to the higher tape speeds available, partly to wider tracks on the tape, and partly to the more precise construction of the elements in the tape transport mechanism. The consumer products use tape that is ¼ in. (0.63 cm) wide. Monophonic machines generally have two tracks, one playing in the forward direction and the other in the reverse direction of tape travel. Much more common are stereophonic machines that have two tracks in each direction (four tracks total). Quadraphonic machines use all four tracks simultaneously in one direction.

There is much greater diversity in the equipment used professionally in recording studios. The simplest machine in this category records two tracks on tape having a width of ¼ in. (0.63). Next in the hierarchy are machines that record two, four, or eight tracks on ½-in. (1.25-cm) tape. Other machines record up to 16 tracks on 1-in. (2.5-cm) tape and, finally, the most complex machines can record 24 or 32 tracks on 2-in. (5-cm) tape. The large number of tracks are desired in studio recording sessions to permit an exclusive track assignment for an individual instrument or performer in a musical ensemble.

***Sound quality.*** Professional-grade equipment running at a tape speed of 30 in./s (76 cm/s) can yield a signal-to-noise ratio between 60 and 70 dB in the original recording. However, in each subsequent generation of rerecording, the tape copy suffers some reduction in signal-to-noise ratio, along with an increase in distortion. Since several generations are normally involved in the production of a working master tape, the sound quality of this tape may be marginal. An improvement of 10 dB or so in the signal-to-noise ratio is obtained by employing electronic noise-reduction systems. Various approaches are used in these systems but, in essence, relatively quiet signals are raised in level during recording and reduced in a complementary way in playback so that even low-level signals are kept above the background noise generated by the tape.

Consumer recorders operating at lower tape speeds cannot provide such low noise and distortion levels. In the case of prerecorded music on cassettes which are played at only 1⅞ in./s (4.7 cm/s) and are several generations removed from the original studio recording, signal-to-noise ratios between 45 and 50 dB are to be expected. However, improvements in tapes and the incorporation of electronic noise reduction in prerecorded cassette tapes and in some of the more expensive players can keep the ratio close to or somewhat above the upper value of this range.

***Digital recorders.*** The problems of distortion and noise have prompted the development of digital magnetic tape recorders for audio use. In digital recording, the output of the microphone amplifiers in the studio is immediately converted from its analog form to digital, and the signals are recorded in digital codes on the tracks on the tape. The signals remain in digital form throughout all subsequent mixing, editing, and rerecording procedures and are not converted to analog form until the final playback from digital tape or digital disk for reproduction from loudspeakers. The advantages of digital recording are that signal-to-noise ratios greater than 90 dB are readily attainable and that there is no degradation in quality during rerecording, regardless of the number of generations. SEE DISK RECORDING.

**Video recorders.** The purpose of video tape recorders is to record and play back television signals. The television signal frequency-modulates a carrier which is recorded on the magnetic tape, with frequencies in excess of 15 MHz being involved in high-band professional video recorders. High head-to-tape speeds are required for recording these high frequencies. High head-to-tape speeds are obtained by mounting the heads on a rapidly rotating wheel that sweeps the heads more or less transversely across the tape from edge to edge. Two types of recorders that function in this manner have come into use, namely, the Quadruplex and the helical scan (sometimes called slant-track).

***Quadruplex recorders.*** In Quadruplex recorders, four equally spaced heads are mounted on the rim of a headwheel having a diameter of 2 in. (5 cm). In the United States, Canada, Japan, and a few other countries that adopted the National Television System Committee (NTSC) standards, the headwheel rotates at 14,400 revolutions/min to give a peripheral head-to-tape speed of 1556 in./s (3952 cm/s). In countries following other television standards the headwheel speed is somewhat different. The tape is 2 in. (5 cm) wide. It is pulled by a capstan and moves from a supply reel to a take-up reel at a uniform speed of 15 in./s (38 cm/s) or 7½ in./s (19 cm/s). As it approaches the headwheel, the tape is formed into a circular, concave surface by a vacuum guide. This allows the heads to maintain contact with the tape throughout their scan across the tape. The combination of rapid scan across the tape and slow forward motion of the tape results in a series of parallel video tracks making a nearly 90° angle with the direction of tape motion (**Fig. 7**). Downstream from the headwheel a straight guide restores the tape to travel in a plane before reaching fixed heads that record audio signals in a conventional way on tracks along the edges of the tape. Quadruplex machines are used only in broadcasting and other television-related enterprises.

***Helical-scan recorders.*** While helical-scan recorders have been available for a number of years, only in the late 1970s did they become sufficiently advanced to meet the stringent requirements of broadcast television. Recorders are available in several formats, but all are designed around the same underlying principle, which will be discussed with reference to the type of helical-scan recorder preferred for professional use in broadcast studios. In the type C helical recorder the tape is 1 in (2.5 cm) wide and moves from a supply reel to a take-up reel at a speed of 9.6 in./s (24 cm/s), being pulled through its path by a capstan and pressure roller. In one portion of its path the tape makes a nearly 360° helical wrap around the outside of a hollow circular cylinder, with the magnetic coating against the surface of the cylinder. The recording heads are carried on a drum rotating inside, and concentric with, the cylinder. The heads protrude through a slot in the cylinder wall to contact the coating of the tape. The drum rotation is 3600 revolutions/min, and the peripheral head-to-tape speed is 1000 in./s (25 m/s). The head-to-tape speed and the helix combine to lay down a series of parallel video tracks across the tape, making an angle of 2°34′ with the edges of the tape (**Fig. 8**). After leaving the cylinder, the tape moves past a series of stationary heads that lay down audio and control tracks along the edges of the tape.

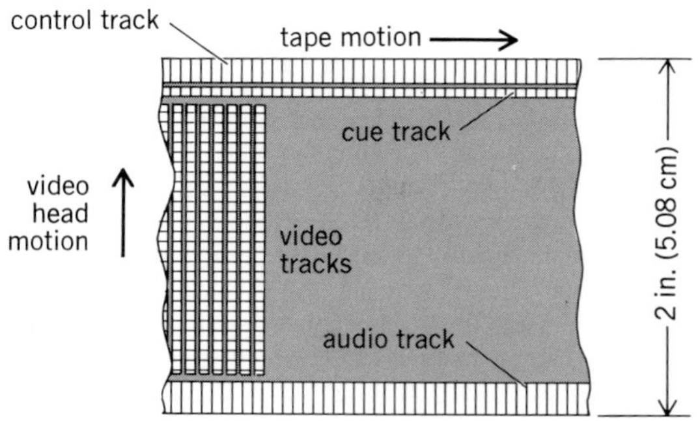


**Fig. 7. Track format of a Quadruplex video recorder.**

Other types of helical-scan recorders of lesser performance are Beta and VHS formats, in widespread use for educational and entertainment purposes. Most of these use ½-in.-wide (1.25-cm) tape. Nearly all require the tape to be stored in a cassette that is basically similar to, though larger than, the audio cassette described above. The video tape players incorporate ingenious mechanical devices to extract a length of tape from the cassette and wrap it in the helix on the cylinder before forward motion of the tape commences. SEE TELEVISION.

**Recorders for computers.** From the inception of electronic computers, magnetic tape recorders have been an indispensable element in the hierarchy of computer memories. During the 1960s and 1970s, magnetic disk files assumed an equally important function in the hierarchy. All recording associated with computers employs digital signals. Since the loss of even a single bit in a digital number can have near-catastrophic results, much effort goes into assuring precision and reliability in the manufacture and fabrication of tapes, disks, heads, and mechanical structures involved in the recorders.

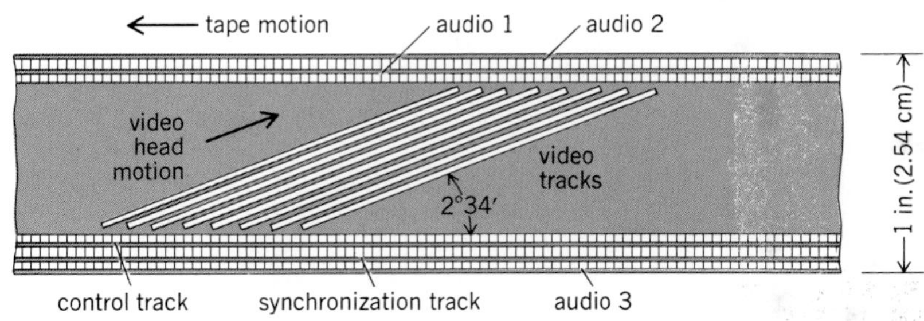


**Fig. 8. Track format for a television-broadcast helical-scan (slant-track) video recorder.**

***Computer tape recorders.*** Computer tape recorders usually are of the reel-to-reel type, although cassettes are employed in certain applications. The computer tape recorders differ from the reel-to-reel recorders described above in that tape motion in both directions is required, together with very short start-up intervals. Computer recorders have two counterrotating capstans, one on each side of the record/playback head. Solenoid-operated pressure rollers engage the tape with one or the other capstan to determine the direction of motion. Several feet (a few meters) of tape from the supply and take-up reels are stored loosely in bins between the capstans and the reels, so that when a ''start'' command is received the activated capstan must accelerate only the miniscule mass of a short length of tape. The high-inertia reel can be accelerated much more slowly by a separate motor to eventually make up the supply of tape removed from the bin by the capstan. With this arrangement, a reversal from full speed in one direction to stop, and to full speed in the opposite direction, can be accomplished in milliseconds.

The most common computer-tape width is ½ in. (1.25 cm). Multiple tracks, typically nine, are used with stacked heads to record the bits of a digital word in parallel in a line across the tape, with the tape moving at selected speeds up to 120 in./s (305 cm/s). To increase reliability, the packing density is kept lower than in noncomputer applications. Standard densities are 200, 556, 800, 1600, or 6250 bits/in. (79, 219, 315, 630, or 2461 bits/cm).

***Disk file.*** In a disk file the most common recording medium is a very smooth aluminum disk, 14 in. (35.6 cm) in diameter, having both of its surfaces coated with magnetic oxide. Data are recorded in concentric tracks on both surfaces with track densities of up to about 1000 tracks per inch (254 per centimeter) along the radius. The disk rotation rate is 3600 revolutions per minute. Up to 10 disks are contained in a module, called a disk pack, that may be mounted on the spindle of a disk drive unit. The disks in the pack are clamped one above the other, with space between disks to allow entry of two record/playback heads, one for an upper and one for a lower surface of adjacent disks. The tiny ferrite heads are carried in a highly polished ceramic plate called a slider, having a carefully contoured surface facing the surface of the disk. The high-speed motion of the disk surface carries air along with it, and the contour of the slider gives rise to an aerodynamic flotation providing a constant, controlled separation between disk and head. The separation is required to prevent rapid wear of disks and heads, since the disk files run continuously whenever their computer is in operation. Aerodynamic separations between 0.00001 and 0.0001 in. (0.25 and 2.5 μm) are used in various disk systems.

The head assemblies are mounted on an actuator that moves them in and out radially, so any track on any surface may be selected for use upon command from the computer. The average time to change from one track to any other is measured in milliseconds. Modern disk packs have a capacity of as much as $5 \times 10^9$ bits. Several drives are usually used in each computer installation to give even greater storage capacity.

One version of disk file has packs that are removable and interchangeable among drives. Another form of disk file is the Winchester type, in which the disks are nonremovable, being permanently sealed in a chamber with heads and actuators. The sealed protected environment allows higher densities, greater reliability, and longer life than with removable disks. Winchester files are also made with 8-in-diameter (20-cm) and 5¼-in.-diameter (13-cm) disks.

***Flexible disk.*** The flexible disk (floppy disk, diskette) was introduced as a computer storage medium in the 1970s. In these disks the substrate is a plastic 0.003 in. (76 μm) thick coated on one or both sides with magnetic oxide. The disk is permanently enclosed in a square jacket lined with a slippery fibrous cloth that allows the disk to turn while heads contact the disk through slots in the jacket. Disk diameters of 8 in. (20 cm) and 5¼ in. (13 cm) are standard, with smaller versions about 3½ in. (8.8 cm) also available. Storage capacity per disk is about 0.3 to 1.0 megabytes. Flexible disks have become an indispensible part of personal computers, where they store programs (software) and serve as medium scale memories. *See* COMPUTER STORAGE TECHNOLOGY; MICROCOMPUTER.

**Instrumentation recorders.** The purpose of an instrumentation recorder is the storing of electric signals so they may be reproduced at a later time for detailed analysis. Examples for which instrumentation recorders are used are geophysical exploration; medical diagnosis; radar surveillance; measurement of explosions and supersonic shock waves; measurement of mechanical stress and vibration of structures; testing of jet, rocket, and internal combustion engines; and flight testing of aircraft and missiles. Any environmental, physical, chemical, or physiological parameter that can be converted to an electric signal by a suitable transducer is a candidate for instrumentation recording.

The design of instrumentation recorders is as varied as the applications in which they are employed. All of the types of recorder discussed above, as well as several not mentioned, have been used in instrumentation work. Depending on the nature of the signal and the type of recorder, the signals enter the recording medium in any of the following forms: direct analog, digital, pulse-code modulation, frequency modulation, and multiplexed frequency modulation. *See* PULSE MODULATION.

**Tape duplication.** The ability to copy a recorded program from one tape onto another is an important feature of magnetic recording. In principle all that is required for the copying process is two recorders, one for playback and a second one for recording the output of the first. When multiple copies are desired, this simple procedure is inefficient and time-consuming. It is preferable to feed the playback output to several recorders and to record several copies simultaneously. The playback unit is the ''master'' and the recording units are ''slaves.'' Simple duplicators are available to churches, educational institutions, and other enterprises that may rather frequently wish to make only a few copies of material recorded on a cassette.

In commercial duplication large numbers of copies are required, and the duplicating procedures are modified in the interests of manufacturing efficiency. There may be as many as 20 slave units, and the tape is moved at faster-than-normal speed to reduce the copying time. The same arrangement is used for duplicating audio tapes for cassettes, Stereo-8, and reel-to-reel products.

In a large operation the program to be copied is

recorded on a working-master tape, ½ in. (1.25 cm) wide, at its normal speed. This tape is unwound from its reel and fed into a loose stack in a storage bin. The ends of the tape are spliced to form an endless loop that runs continuously through the master playback machine, generating the signals that are fed to the bank of slave recorders. The supply of tape in each slave is in a large reel carrying up to 7200 ft (2194 m) of tape, which is sufficient to make a number of copies before reloading. The master tape is run at 120 in./s (305 cm/s), which is 64 times the normal cassette speed, 32 times the Stereo-8 speed, and either 32 times or 16 times the reel-to-reel speeds. When the copying is finished, the tape is transferred from the slave to an editing machine where leaders are spliced on, and the tape is cut at the end of each program and wound onto hubs or reels for the final product.

In this high-speed duplication process all signal frequencies from the master tape are raised in the same ratio as the tape speeds. Thus, in the 64-times case a 15 kHz signal becomes 960 kHz. Also, the high-frequency bias in the slave recorder now ought to be in the neighborhood of 6.4 MHz. The duplicator must be provided with heads and electronics capable of operating at these high frequencies.

Video cassette tapes also are duplicated by the master/slave procedure. Some of the video-frequency components that must be copied lie in the 5–10-MHz range. Since no head materials are known that perform efficiently above 20 MHz, it is not possible to greatly reduce the copying time by high-speed duplication as in audio duplication. High-speed contact-printing techniques have been demonstrated as alternatives to the master/slave approach.

*J. G. Woodward; Marvin Camras*

**Bibliography.** S. W. Athey, *Magnetic Tape Recording*, National Aeronautics and Space Administration, NASA SP-5038, 1966; M. Camras, *Magnetic Recording Handbook*, 1985; M. Camras, *Magnetic Tape Recording*, 1985; G. L. Davies, *Magnetic Tape Instrumentation*, 1961; A. S. Hoagland, *Digital Magnetic Recording*, 1963, reprint 1983; F. Jorgenson, *The Complete Handbook of Magnetic Recording*, 1980; C. B. Mee, *The Physics of Magnetic Recording*, 1964; J. F. Robinson, *Videotape Recording*, 1975.

## Magnetic thin films

Sheets of magnetic material with thicknesses of a few micrometers or less, used in the electronics industry. Magnetic films can be single-crystalline, polycrystalline, or amorphous in the arrangement of their atoms. Applications include magnetic bubble technology, magnetoresist sensors, thin-film heads, and recording media. *See* Magnetic bubble memory; Magnetic recording.

**Fabrication.** Thin films are usually directly deposited on a substrate. The techniques of deposition vary from high-temperature liquid-phase epitaxy such as that used in the fabrication of garnet films, through electroplating, to vapor deposition and sputtering. Permalloy, for example, can be both electroplated and sputtered or vapor-deposited.

**Magnetic order.** Both ferro- and ferrimagnetic films are used. The ferromagnetic films are usually transition-metal-based alloys. For example, permalloy is a nickel-iron alloy. The ferrimagnetic films, such as garnets or the amorphous films, contain transition metals such as iron or cobalt and rare earths. The ferrimagnetic properties are advantageous in bubble applications where a low overall magnetic moment can be achieved without a significant change in the Curie temperature. They are also useful for magnetooptic applications.

**Magnetic anisotropy.** In an isotropic bulk magnetic sample the overall magnetization does not prefer a particular direction. However, the same material in the form of a thin film has a lower energy when the magnetization lies in the plane of the film. This shape-induced anisotropy is useful in applications such as permalloy drive or sensor patterns used in bubble technology. However, there are other situations where it is advantageous to have perpendicular rather than in-plane anisotrophy. For example, magnetic bubble and magnetooptic memory materials have perpendicular anisotropy. This is obtained by using anisotropic crystals, by growing films in a magnetic field or directional deposition, and by annealing in a magnetic field or applying an anisotropic stress.

**Domain structure.** Depending upon the nature of anisotropy (perpendicular to planar), a variety of domain patterns can be obtained. For example, when the perpendicular anisotropy is large relative to shape-induced anisotropy, stripe domains are observed. These form cylindrical domains if an external magnetic field is applied perpendicular to the plane of the films. Such cylindrical domains are called magnetic bubbles. The domain structure can be observed in an optical microscope with polarized light using either the Faraday or Kerr effect. It can also be observed using ferrofluids. Domains and domain wall structure are also observable by electron microscope techniques.

**Coercivity.** The coercivity of thin film varies with applications. For most applications a low coercive force is desired. Coercivity is generally associated with inhomogeneities such as stress fields, compositional fluctuations, defects, and surface roughness.

*Praveen Chaudhari*

**Bibliography.** P. Chaudhari and D. Turnbull, Structure and properties of metallic glasses, *Science*, 199:11–21, 1978; I. S. Jacobs, Magnetic materials and applications: Quarter century overview, *J. Appl. Phys.*, 50:7294–7306, 1979.

## Magnetron

The oldest of a family of crossed-field microwave electron tubes wherein electrons, generated from a heated cathode, move under the combined force of a radial electric field and an axial magnetic field. By its structure a magnetron causes moving electrons to interact synchronously with traveling-wave components of a microwave standing-wave pattern in such a manner that electron potential energy is converted to microwave energy with high efficiency. Magnetrons have been used since the 1940s as pulsed microwave radiation sources for radar tracking. Because of their compactness and the high efficiency with which they can emit short bursts of megawatt peak output power, they have proved excellent for installation in aircraft as well as in ground radar stations. In continuous operation, a magnetron can produce a kilowatt of microwave power which is appropriate for rapid microwave cooking.

The magnetron in an oscillator; it generates radio-frequency energy, usually over limited portions of the microwave frequency range of 1–40 gigahertz. It can produce microsecond pulses of peak power as high as 10 megawatts but with low duty-cycle ratios (ratio of pulse length of pulse repetition period). Mechanical tuning of the magnetron microwave circuit can change the center frequency of the output radiation by about ±5%.

**Configuration.** Raw materials of a magnetron are chiefly copper, iron, and ceramic welded and brazed together to form a vacuum tube. A slow-wave microwave circuit, made of copper to reduce ohmic losses, serves to provide a traveling wave that can interact with the electrons. Iron pole pieces guide the magnetic flux from externally attached horseshoe-shaped magnets (**Fig. 1**). Pole pieces shape the kilogauss magnetic field in the electron-microwave interaction region to be perpendicular to the electric field and to constrain the electrons to the interaction region. Ceramic (or sometimes glass) serves as a standoff insulator for the tens of kilovolts applied between cathode and anode. Ceramic is also used as the microwave window to couple the power generated inside the magnetron through the vacuum enclosure to externally attached waveguides. The breakdown limit of this window may be the chief factor in setting the peak power output obtainable from a magnetron.

The magnetron is a device of essentially cylindrical symmetry (**Fig. 2**). On the central axis is a hollow cylindrical cathode. The outer surface of the cathode carries electron-emitting materials, primarily barium and strontium oxides in a nickel matrix. Such a matrix is capable of emitting electrons when current flows through the heater inside the cathode cylinder. *See Vacuum tube.*

At a radius somewhat larger than the outer radius of the cathode is a concentric cylindrical anode. The anode serves two functions: (1) to collect electrons emitted by the cathode and (2) to store and guide microwave energy. The anode consists of a series of quarter-wavelength cavity resonators symmetrically arranged around the cathode. *See Cavity resonator.*

A radial dc electric field (perpendicular to the cathode) is applied between cathode and anode. This electric field and the axial magnetic field (parallel and

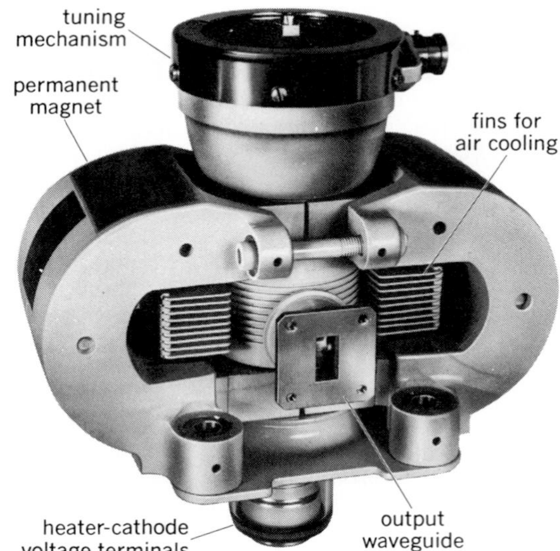


**Fig. 1. Coaxial cavity magnetron with horseshoe-shaped magnets. (*After J. W. Gewartowski and H. A. Watson, Principles of Electron Tubes, Van Nostrand, 1965*)**

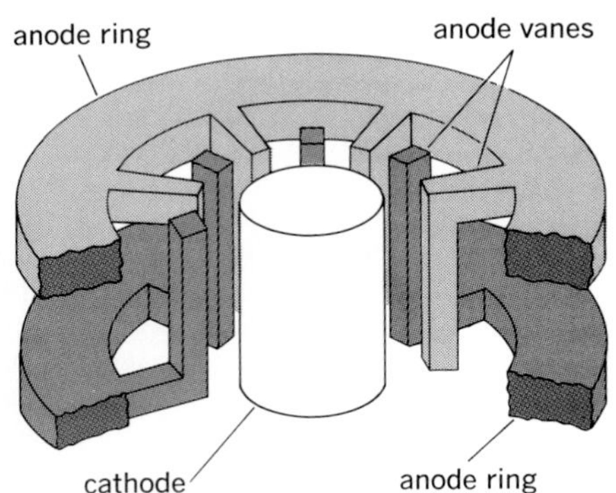


**Fig. 2. Interdigital-vane anode circuit and cathode, indicating the basic cylindrical geometry. (*After G. D. Sims and I. M. Stephenson, Microwave Tubes and Semiconductor Devices, Blackie and Son, London, 1963*)**

coaxial with the cathode) introduced by pole pieces at either end of the cathode, as described above, provide the required crossed-field configuration.

**Microwave generation.** Provided that the magnitudes of the electric field and the magnetic field are properly adjusted, an electron emerging from the heated cathode proceeds to orbit the cylindrical cathode, moving on the average in a direction perpendicular to both applied fields (**Fig. 3**). The totality of electrons emitted by the cathode form a swarm or hub of negative charge rotating about the cathode axis. The hub thickness extends from the cathode surface outward to a radius intermediate between cathode and anode radii. Motion of the rotating swarm of electrons past the surface of the concentric-anode microwave circuit induces a noise current in the copper circuit. This noise shock excites the resonators so that microwave fields build up at the resonant frequency. The velocity of the electrons, as determined by the applied voltage and magnetic field, is made to be close to or synchronous with the slow-wave phase velocity characteristic of the microwave circuit. Consequently, as the electron swarm rotates, it concentrates into bunches that deliver microwave energy to the resonators. Thus, as in most oscillators, the process begins with noise; then electromagnetic fields build up at the resonant frequency. These fields react, in turn, upon the electrons, remove some of their potential energy, and cause them to approach the circuit more closely, whereupon the process intensifies. Buildup of the microwave field is limited by internal ohmic losses in the circuit, external loading of the output coupling, and the electron energy available for conversion to microwave energy.

**Electron bunching.** Bunching of electrons plays a prominent role in the generation of microwave power in the magnetron, as it does in most microwave tubes. The applied radial electric field $E$ and the axial field $B$ constrain the average motion of the hub electrons to a direction perpendicular to both fields and hence circumferential about the cathode. (There is cycloidal motion superimposed on the average, as well.) The average circumferential electron velocity, called drift velocity, has a magnitude $u = E/B$. The microwave circuit is designed to support a traveling wave whose phase velocity $v$ is equal to $u$. If $u = v$, the electron hub rotation is said to be synchronous with the rotating traveling wave. Under these conditions, one can consider the interaction of electrons with microwave fields from the anode in a frame of reference which rotates at the synchronous velocity.

The quarter-wave cavity resonators, which support the rotating microwaves and surround the electron hub, present at the hub a rotating microwave field configuration consisting of electric fields having strong circumferential components. These components are 180° out of phase (oppositely directed) for neighboring cavities, as shown in Fig. 3. This set of alternating fields can be considered as composed of two sets of uniformly directed fields (each internally inphase), one set 180° out of phase with the other and the two interlaced. (Such a microwave field configuration is called a $\pi$ mode, the two sets of fields being phased $\pi$ radians from each other.) In the frame of reference rotating in synchronism with these two sets of microwave fields, the circumferential components of the microwave electric fields can be regarded as steady or static fields crossed with the applied axial magnetic field.

Those hub electrons rotating in phase and under the influence of one of the sets of microwave fields, because of the crossed-field situation, are constrained to move radially toward the anode (average electron motion is always perpendicular to both electric and magnetic crossed-field directions). In doing so they contribute to the strength of the microwave field, converting their potential energy in the applied electric field to microwave energy. The process continues until the electrons finally fall through the entire hub-to-anode potential and are collected on the anode. As a consequence, the distribution of electrons in the interaction region between cathode and anode looks like a hub with spokes, all rotating together at drift velocity $E/B$ (Fig. 3). In this sense the electrons are bunched. Throughout the interaction the electrons continue to rotate at close to synchronous velocity, remaining in phase with the wave and continuing to convert dc potential energy into microwave energy until striking the anode. This staying-in-synchronism results in high energy conversion efficiency (values may be as high as 65–75%) of the magnetron in contrast to those microwave tubes that depend on differential velocities of electrons for bunching. It also means that the anode must be rugged enough to absorb the full kinetic energy of the electrons ($mu^2/2$, where $m$ is the electron mass). *See Klystron*.

Those electrons in phase with the remaining set of microwave fields (the set 180° out of phase with the first) will be constrained to move radially back through the hub toward the cathode. This motion results in an increase of electron potential energy at the expense of the microwave field. However, the loss in microwave energy is small because such electrons move out of high microwave field regions toward weaker ones and so move to minimize their interaction. On striking the cathode these electrons heat up the cathode and reduce the required heater power. The phenomenon of electron bunching, wherein certain in-phase electrons give up their potential energy to the microwave field while other out-of-phase electrons are forced out of the microwave field region to prevent their extracting microwave energy, is further abetted by the shape of the microwave fields near the anode. The field shape is such as to cause electrons approaching the anode to become even more closely in phase so as to deliver maximum power to the circuit.

**Microwave circuit.** The only aspect of the magnetron that is not symmetric is the output coupler. Being an oscillator and generating its own signal starting from noise-induced fields, the magnetron must maintain enough energy in its resonant circuit to keep the generation process going. On the other hand, only the microwave energy coupled out of the magnetron is useful to the radar operator. Thus some compromise must determine the fraction of the generated power which is coupled out through the output coupling slot, the ceramic window, and output waveguide.

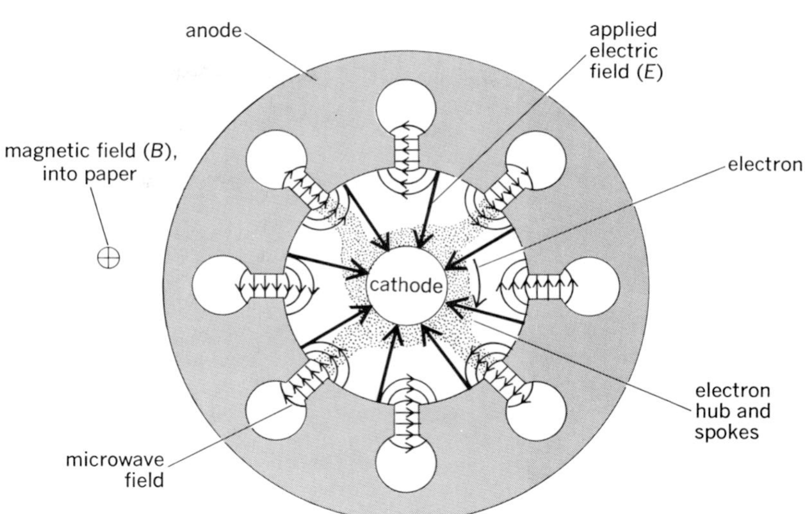


**Fig. 3. Electron motion in magnetron interaction region under action of applied electric and magnetic fields and generated microwave field. (*After C. H. Dix and W. H. Aldous, Microwave Valves, Illiffe Books, London, 1966*)**

The $\pi$-mode electromagnetic field configuration is desirable for interaction with the electrons as described above, and the output coupling is generally designed for such a resonant condition. However, the microwave circuit can sustain other resonant modes which can interact with the electrons and which are

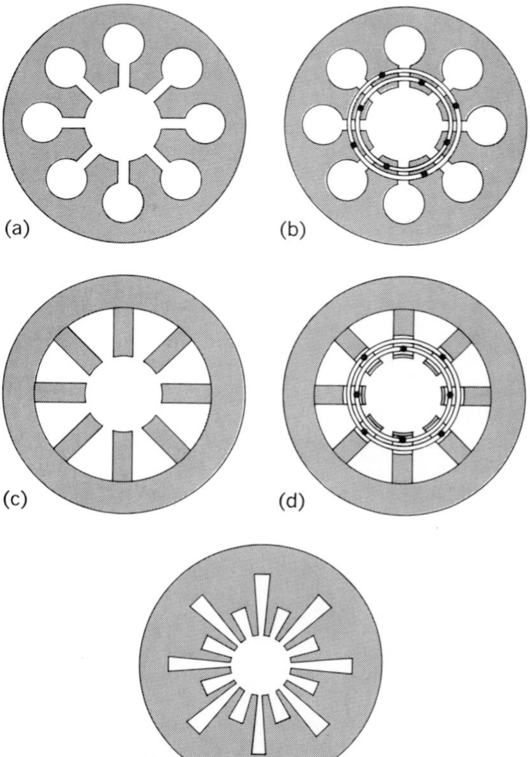


**Fig. 4. Magnetron slow-wave circuits. (*a*) Unstrapped cavity. (*b*) Strapped cavity. (*c*) Unstrapped vane block. (*d*) Strapped vane block. (*e*) Rising-sun block. (*After C. H. Dix and W. H. Aldous, Microwave Valves, Iliffe Books, London, 1966*)**

generally less efficient. Some of these undesirable modes can so orient themselves as to present a null in the microwave field pattern at the output. All the energy converted from interaction with electrons is then stored inside the magnetron in such modes, and none is usefully coupled out. The fields in the interaction region can become high enough to block operation in the $\pi$ mode. Such undesirable modes can be close in frequency to the $\pi$ mode, and unless special circuit design is incorporated, they are difficult to discriminate against. Much of the design of magnetron microwave structures has to do with maximizing efficiency of $\pi$-mode interaction while inhibiting electron interaction with other undesirable modes.

A variety of shapes have been used in the design of the quarter-wavelength cavities whose open-end, capacitative section provides the electric fields for interaction with the electrons. There are vane-type cavities and hole-and-slot versions (**Fig. 4**). These may be strapped (alternate cavities tied together with a copper strap to promote $\pi$-mode operation), or alternate cavities can be elongated (rising-sun configuration) to separate the undesirable modes from the $\pi$ mode. Such circuits are generally tuned in frequency by inserting copper pins into the induction sections of the quarter-wave cavities. Voltage tuning has been achieved in certain low-power magnetrons.

**Coaxial cavity magnetron.** A more recent magnetron design, the coaxial cavity magnetron (**Fig. 5**), achieves mode separation, high efficiency, stability, and ease of mechanical tuning by coupling a coaxial high Q cavity to a normal set of quarter-wavelength vane cavities. *See* Cavity resonator; Q (electricity).

The high Q cavity is resonant in the $TE_{011}$ mode, a mode in which current flow on the inner conductor is circumferential and phase is not a function of circumferential position. To couple microwave energy from the slow-wave circuit into the coaxial cavity, slots are cut into the backs of alternate quarter-wavelength cavities. If the rotation of the electron hub induces current flow on the vanes, so that a $\pi$-mode resonant buildup of microwave fields commences there, the slot coupling geometry is correct to also stimulate the buildup of the $TE_{011}$ mode in the outer coaxial cavity. Because alternate vane cavities are in phase in $\pi$-mode operation, the current coupled into the high Q cavity through slots cut only in alternate cavities will also be in phase. This is the condition required to induce the $TE_{011}$ mode in the coaxial cavity. The output frequency can be tuned merely by altering the axial length of the outer coaxial cavity (a tuning piston is employed). Most stored microwave energy is in the coaxial cavity, and its high Q ensures efficient storage. The coaxial cavity magnetron has replaced many earlier designs for airborne radar.

Some characteristics typical for the coaxial cavity magnetron are as follows.

| | |
|---|---|
| Frequency (tunable) | 15.5–17.5 GHz |
| Peak output power | 125 kW |
| Peak applied voltage | 17.5 kV |
| Peak anode current | 19 A |
| Pulse duration | 3 μs |
| Duty cycle | 0.001 |
| Magnetic field | 0.74 weber/in.$^2$ (1150 teslas) |
| Overall efficiency | 43% |

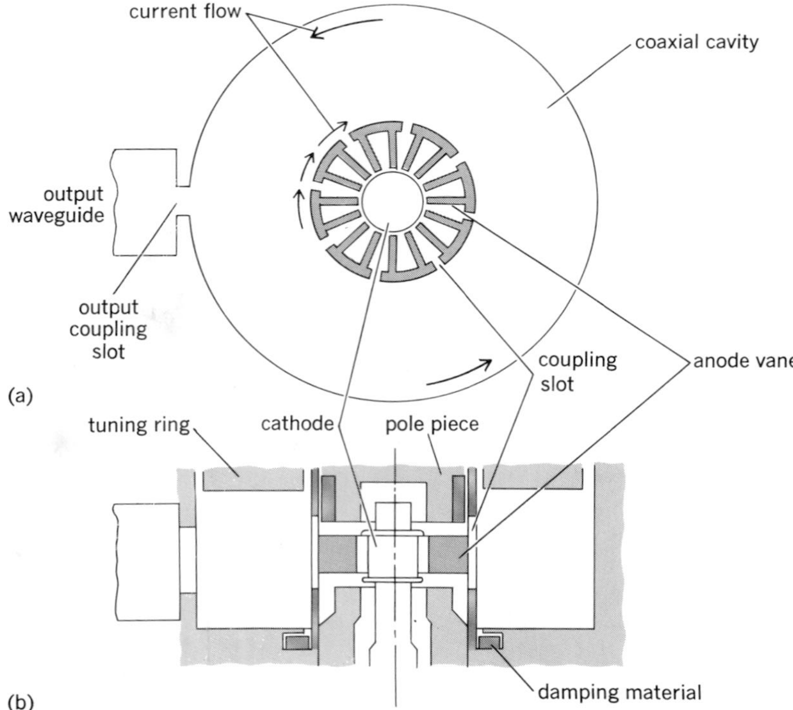


**Fig. 5.** Coaxial cavity magnetron. (*a*) End view. (*b*) Cross-sectional view. (*After J. W. Gewartowski and H. A. Watson, Principles of Electron Tubes, Van Nostrand, 1965*)

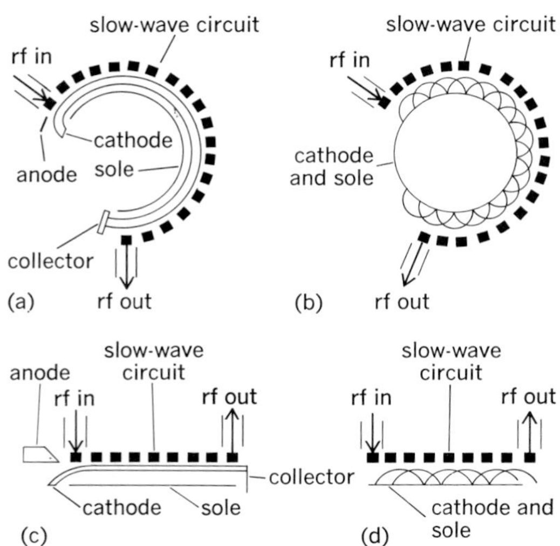


**Fig. 6.** Magnetron amplifiers. (*a*) Circular type with beam injection. (*b*) Circular type with continuously emitting sole. (*c*) Linear type with beam injection. (*d*) Linear type with continuously emitting sole.

**Other crossed-field tubes.** The magnetron is a member of the crossed-field family of devices. Other members are platinotrons, amplitrons, forward-wave crossed-field amplifiers, non-reentrant-beam crossed-field amplifiers, and carcinotrons. Some of these devices are oscillators and others amplifiers (**Fig. 6**). Some interact with backward slow waves, others with forward waves. Some employ an electron gun, others an emitting sole. The magnetron oscillator itself has both a reentrant electron beam and a reentrant microwave circuit. (The electron flow is continuous in the circumferential direction, orbiting the axial cathode, while the quarter-wavelength cavities are symmetrically disposed around the cathode with no beginning or end.) *See Backward-wave tube.*

Power generation in an oscillator begins with noise, and the resonant nature of the circuit produces the high electric fields required to further react with the electrons. Amplifiers, on the other hand, have nonreentrant circuits with a definite input and output. The input signal provides the initial microwave field to begin interaction between electrons and circuit. The electron beam may be reentrant or not, depending on the geometry of the circuit—whether the cavities are arranged with cylindrical or linear symmetry.

The magnetron and related crossed-field amplifiers and oscillators are rather noisy devices and operate best in the high-output-power region. As amplifiers, they have generally low gain, but their output power is high. Compactness and high efficiency are the most attractive features of crossed-field electron tubes. Conversion of electron potential energy to microwave energy in characteristic of all crossed-field devices (M-type carcinotrons) in contrast to conversion of kinetic energy in the case of traveling-wave tubes (O-type devices). *See Traveling-wave tube.*

*R. J. Collier*

**Bibliography.** J. Coleman, *Microwave Devices*, 1982; C. H. Dix and W. H. Aldous, *Microwave Valves*, 1966; J. W. Gewartowski and H. A. Watson, *Principles of Electron Tubes*, 1965; S. Liao, *Microwave Devices and Circuits*, 1980; E. Okress (ed.), *Crossed-Field Microwave Devices*, vols. 1 and 2, 1961; R. F. Soohoo, *Microwave Electronics*, 1971.

## Maser

A device for coherent amplification or generation of electromagnetic waves by use of excitation energy in resonant atomic or molecular systems. The word is an acronym for *m*icrowave *a*mplification by *s*timulated *e*mission of *r*adiation. The device uses an unstable ensemble of atomic or molecular particles which may be stimulated by an electromagnetic wave to radiate excess energy at the same frequency and phase as a stimulating wave, thus providing coherent amplication. Masers, however, are not limited to the microwave region; this type of amplification has been extended to include a frequency range from audio to infrared or optical frequencies. Maser-type amplifiers and oscillators are also sometimes referred to as molecular, or quantum-mechanical, since they involve processes on a molecular scale, and since some types cannot be adequately described by classical mechanics, but show characteristic quantum-mechanical phenomena.

Maser amplifiers can have exceptionally low noise, and come close to effectively amplifying a single quantum of radiation in the microwave region; that is, they approach the limits, set by the uncertainty principle, on the precision with which phase and energy of a wave may be amplified. Their inherently low noise makes maser oscillators that use very narrow atomic or molecular resonances extremely monochromatic, providing a basis for frequency standards. Since atoms or molecules may have resonances and effective amplification over a wide frequency range and to very short wavelengths, masers are useful as coherent amplifiers of millimeter, infrared, optical, and perhaps also ultraviolet wavelengths, where older types of circuit elements are not effective.

Because of their low noise and high sensitivity, maser amplifiers are particularly useful for reception and detection of very weak signals in radio astronomy, microwave radiometry, long-distance radar, and long-distance microwave communications. They also provide research tools for very sensitive amplification or detection of electromagnetic radiation.

Thermodynamic equilibrium of an ensemble of particles—such as atoms, molecules, electrons, or nuclei—which have discrete energy levels and which may radiate electromagnetic energy, requires that the number $n_1$ of particles in a lower level 1 be related to the number $n_2$ in an upper level 2 by the Boltzmann distribution condition $n_1/n_2 = e^{(E_1 - E_2)/kT}$, where $E_1$ and $E_2$ are the respective energies of the two levels; $k$ is Boltzmann's constant; and $T$ is the absolute temperature, a positive number. Thermodynamic equilibrium also requires that phases of oscillation of the particles, or relative phases of quantum-mechanical wave functions for the various states, be random. A violation of either condition can result in instabilities which may release electromagnetic radiation. The frequency $\nu$ of radiation released is given by $h\nu = E_2 - E_1$, where $h$ is Planck's constant.

The particles may be stimulated by an electromagnetic wave to make transitions from the lower to the upper level, absorbing energy from the wave, or from the upper to the lower level, imparting energy to the wave, and thereby increasing the wave amplitude coherently. Stimulated transitions from the upper to the lower state and those from the lower to the upper state are equally probable. For equilibrium at any positive temperature, the Boltzmann distribution requires that $n_1$ be greater than $n_2$. Therefore, there is a net absorption of energy from the wave, because particles which absorb are more numerous than those which emit. If the condition $n_2 > n_1$ occurs, the system may be said to have a negative absolute temperature, because the Boltzmann conditions is fitted only by a negative value of $T$. If there are not too many counterbalancing losses from other sources, this condition allows a net amplification, because particles which emit energy are more numerous than those which absorb.

**Gas masers.** An amplifier where $n_2 > n_1$ is the beam-type maser (**Fig. 1**). Operated in 1954, this was the first type of maser to be suggested. Ammonia gas issues from a small orifice into a vacuum system to form a molecular beam. Molecules in the lower of the two states are deflected away from the axis of the

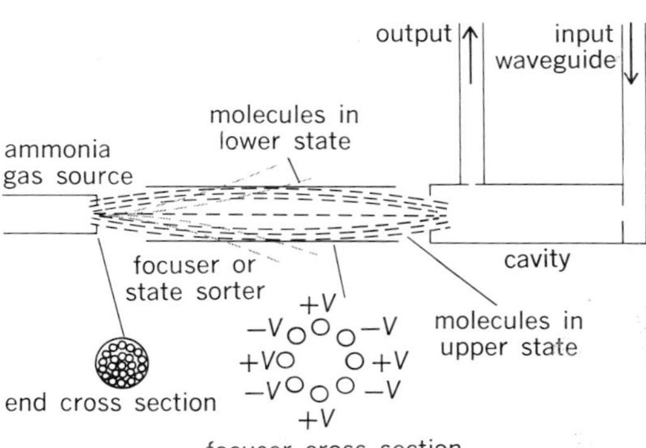


**Fig. 1.** Schematic of beam-type maser.

state sorter or focuser by inhomogeneous electric fields which act on their dipole moments. Those molecules in the upper state are deflected toward the axis and sent into the microwave-resonant cavity. If losses in the cavity walls and coupling holes are sufficiently small, or if the number of molecules is sufficiently large, amplification or oscillation will occur. This maser is particularly useful as a frequency or time standard because of the relative sharpness and invariance of resonances of the ammonia beam.

The condition for oscillations to occur is given by Eq. (1), where $h$ is Planck's constant, $V$ the cavity

$$n_2 - n_1 \geqq hV\Delta\nu/8\pi\mu^2 Q \quad (1)$$

volume, $\Delta\nu$ the width at half maximum of resonant response of the molecules, $\mu$ the molecular dipole moment (matrix element), and $Q$ the quality factor of the loaded cavity. The maximum power output is approximately $h\nu$ multiplied by the rate at which molecules enter the cavity, and is very small. A wave impinging on the cavity will be amplified on reflection if it occurs near the resonant response and if $n_2 - n_1 \geqq hV\Delta\nu/8\pi\mu^2 Q_0$, where $Q_0$ is the quality factor of the unloaded cavity.

Other masers using gaseous molecules have been proposed which involve production of a nonequilibrium distribution by excitation of the gas by means of externally applied radiation of shorter wavelength. Normally, such a system requires molecules with at least three energy levels, two used for amplifying a wave and a third higher level to which molecules are excited from the lowest level, as indicated in **Fig. 2**. In decaying from the higher level, molecules return, at least in part, to fill up the intermediate level and to satisfy the condition $n_2 > n_1$. If it is light radiation which excites molecules to higher levels, the system is said to use optical pumping.

**Solid-state masers.** Solid-state masers usually involve the electrons of paramagnetic atoms or molecules in a static or slowly varying magnetic filed. In the simplest case, the two-level solid-state maser, only one electron on each molecule is affected. The energy of the electron is quantized into two levels, according to whether the magnetic moment, associated with the electron spin, is parallel or antiparallel to the magnetic field. At thermal equilibrium there are more magnetic moments parallel than antiparallel to the field, corresponding to $n_1 > n_2$. This situation may be reversed, so that $n_2 > n_1$, by interchanging the two populations $n_1$ and $n_2$. The interchange is accomplished by rapid variation of the frequency of an intense electromagnetic field through resonance, by application of a pulse of resonant electromagnetic radiation, or in principle by sudden reversal of the magnetic field.

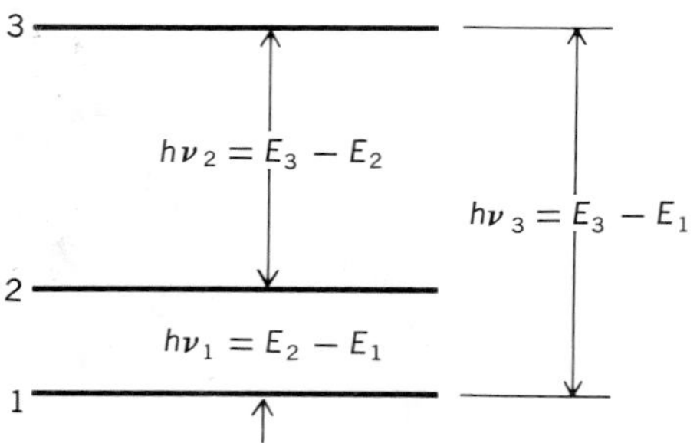


Fig. 2. Energy levels for a three-level maser.

Electron-spin moments are more weakly coupled to the eletromagnetic field than are molecular electric-dipole moments (by a factor of about $10^4$). A much larger preponderance in the upper state is required than for the maser of Fig. 1. If requirements for amplification are met, however, electron-spin moments give correspondingly greater power output. Furthermore, their resonant frequencies are easily tunable by variation of the magnetic field, because their energies involve interaction between electronic magnetic moments and the field. In the simplest cases, the resonant frequency in megacycles is approximately 2.8 times the magnetic field strength in oersteds. Electron-spin resonances in paramagnetic materials allow amplification over broader bandwidths (one to a few hundred megahertz) than do gas systems. Favorable conditions are usually obtainable only at very low temperatures, such as occur in a liquid-helium cryostat; hence, cryogenic problems are often involved and materials used are normally solids rather than liquids. The two-level solid-state maser is most easily operated in pulses, between which the populations of the two levels are readjusted.

The popular three-level solid-state maser also uses paramagnetic material containing electronic magnetic moments in a magnetic field. It has many of the characteristics of the two-level solid-state maser, but can be operated continuously with much more convenience. In Fig. 2, the spacing between the three levels is shown to correspond to microwave frequencies $\nu_1$, $\nu_2$, and $\nu_3$. Usually a few milliwatts of microwave power at frequency $\nu_3$, called the pumping frequency, are sufficient and amplification occurs at a lower frequency with a maximum power output of a few microwatts. Under the simplest assumptions, the number of systems in levels 1 and 3 is equal and the number in level 2 is greater if $\nu_1 < \nu_2$, giving amplification at frequency $\nu_1$. If $\nu_1 > \nu_2$, simple assumptions predict amplification for frequency $\nu_2$.

For three suitable levels to occur in a paramagnetic material, each paramagnetic center must involve the magnetic moment of more than one electron, and must interact with a surrounding array of atoms which are not cubically arranged. The energy levels and frequencies still respond to an externally applied magnetic field. They are, however, no longer simply related to it but may vary widely in accordance with fields internal to the crystalline material. This allows responses at high frequencies with relatively low applied fields.

Three-level solid-state maser amplifiers have been made which have a noise temperature less than about 5 K (noise figure $\leqq$ 1.02). Although a wide variety of paramagnetic materials may be used, synthetic ruby, containing paramagnetic chromic ($Cr^{3+}$) ions, is favored. It has provided amplification both in resonant cavities and in traveling-wave structures.

**Optical and infrared masers.** Optical and infrared masers utilize a variety of principles for excitation of the nonequilibrium distribution. All involve multimode cavities, usually consisting of two optically flat plates between which the radiation is reflected many times through the excited medium. Such masers are particularly valuable as oscillators, producing coherent light that is extremely monochromatic and can be focused either to a very intense small spot or radiated in a remarkably parallel beam. *See Laser.*

Maser oscillators in the megahertz and audio range have been proposed; they use nuclear moments in an applied magnetic field or, with pumping at a higher frequency, in internal crystalline fields. The magnetic moments of protons in liquid water have provided a successful maser of this type. Small impurities of a paramagnetic ion furnish the higher energy level needed and transfer their excitation to the protons. The proton resonances in a magnetic field must be extremely narrow. Such a maser may be used as a very monochromatic oscillator with frequency proportional to the magnetic field strength. Hence it serves as a very precise magnetometer.

Deviation from thermodynamic equilibrium of the second type, involving phase coherence, also allows master-type amplification and is present in many masers. In the beam-type maser oscillator, molecules decay toward the lower state. They continue to amplify after the probability of their being found in the lower state in greater than that of being found in the upper, because they oscillate coherently and in such a phase that they transfer energy to the electromagnetic field.

Raman-type masers rely on a type of phase coherence. Molecules with two levels, separated by energy $h\nu_1$, may be strongly driven by an electromagnetic field of frequency $\nu_2$. If the majority of systems is in the lower state, and if $\nu_2 > \nu_1$, the Raman effect can allow amplification at frequency $\nu_2 - \nu_1$. This requires an intense driving field or a very strong coupling of the systems to the field, such as occurs in ferromagnetic electron resonances. In ferromagnetic materials, large numbers of electrons act in unison, thus providing coupling to an oscillating field which is strong enough to make Roman effects prominent. This can also be discussed in terms of classical theory if nonlinearities are allowed for, and is closely related to ferromagnetic amplifiers and to other parametric amplifiers. SEE PARAMETRIC AMPLIFIER.

**Circuits.** Maser circuits characteristically involve atoms or molecules which provide resonant reactances, positive or negative resistances, and coupling between two or more frequencies or circuit components. They also use certain elements of spectroscopic systems and a wide variety of components found in other radio-frequency and microwave devices.

In the simplest cases the molecular resonances behave like a resonant $LC$ circuit with a positive or negative series resistor, or like a large number of such circuits in parallel and tuned over a distribution of frequencies.

The more classical circuit elements normally involved in masers supply the following functions:

1. Means of ensuring sufficiently strong interaction of an electromagnetic wave with material which amplifies the wave by stimulated emission.
2. Input and output coupling for the wave.
3. Auxiliary circuits which take appropriate advantage of maser characteristics in an overall system.
4. Where electromagnetic excitation is used, circuits which supply energy to the material and produce an unstable state which can radiate.
5. Magnetic field or other components for controlling frequencies of resonance of the material. The schematic of a three-level solid-state maser amplifier, shown in Fig. 3, illustrates each of these functional parts.

The resonant cavity, fulfilling function 1, must have sufficiently low internal losses and produce a sufficiently intense oscillating field (in this case a magnetic field) in the region of the amplifying material. If the cavity is uniformly filled with this material, the condition that amplification be obtainable is given by Eq. (2), where $Q_0$ is the unloaded quality

$$Q_0 \geqq -Q_M = \frac{h\Delta\nu V}{8\pi\mu^2 (n_1 - n_2)} \qquad (2)$$

factor of the cavity, $h$ is Planck's constant, $\Delta\nu$ is the width of the molecular or atomic resonance, $V$ is the cavity volume, $n_1$ is the number of particles in the upper state, $n_2$ is the number in the lower state, and $\mu$ is the effective dipole moment (matrix element) of the atoms or molecules.

A maser of this type is very similar to any other amplifier with positive feedback. There is an effective negative resistance with which may be associated the negative quality $Q_M$, giving a fractional gain per cycle in energy stored of $2\pi/|Q_M|$. As the losses, characterized by the loaded $Q$ of the cavity, are decreased, the amplifier gain increases until it becomes unstable and oscillates when $1/Q + 1/Q_M \leqq 0$. Here $1/Q = 1/Q_0 + 1/Q_E$, where $Q_E$ applies to the external coupling. The power gain is $G = [(2Q/Q_E) - 1]^2$. The bandwidth $B$ Decreases with gain in such a way that the bandwidth-voltage gain product is nearly constant under typical conditions, as in Eq. (3), where $\nu$ is the

$$(\sqrt{G} + 1)\,B = 2\nu/Q_E \qquad (3)$$

frequency for maximum gain. Thus, for given characteristics of the maser material specified by $Q_M$, the gain and bandwidth can be adjusted over certain limits by variation of the cavity losses, or $Q_O$, and the coupling, or $Q_E$.

The noise temperature $T$ for the amplifier alone (**Fig. 3**) is given by Eq. (4), where $k$ is Boltzmann's

$$T = \frac{h\nu}{k \ln\left[\dfrac{n_2}{n_1} + \dfrac{n_1 - n_2}{n_1}\dfrac{Q_M}{Q_0}\right]} \qquad (4)$$

constant. Minimum noise temperatures require a $Q_O$ appreciably larger than $Q_M$ and a small ratio $n_2/n_1$. A noise temperature of $h\nu/k$, or near 1 K for microwave frequencies, is the minimum needed, since this allows effective amplification of approximately one quantum, the limit set by quantum mechanics.

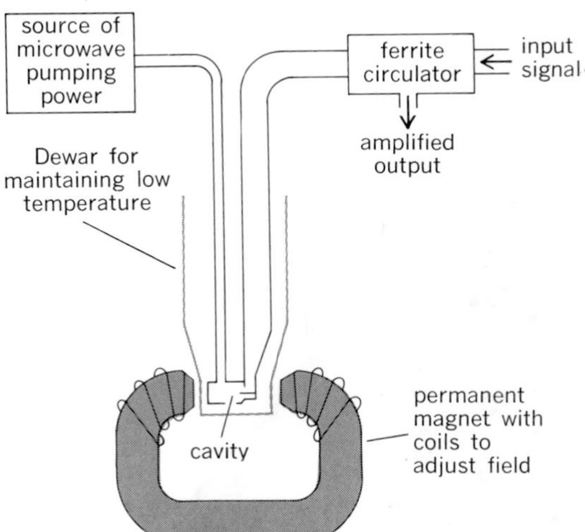


**Fig. 3. Maser amplifier system for 9000 MHz.**

The input and output use the same coupling hole in Fig. 3, and require a directional coupler, or preferably a circulator, for this separation. Separate input and output coupling holes may be used, but this tends to decrease the gain-bandwidth product and to increase noise.

To take full advantage of the low noise in the maser amplifier, the input and output circuits must be prevented from radiating excess noise into the amplifier. For example, attenuation in parts of the input wave guide and in the circulators, which are not at low temperature, results in noise radiation into the amplifier. If there is 0.1 dB loss in some part which is at room temperature, noise radiation into the amplifier corresponding to about 7 K (−480°F) will result. Since most solid-state maser amplifiers operate at low temperatures, some components of the input or output circuits may conveniently be cooled to minimize their noise radiation. If input and output coupling holes are used, the output wave may be passed through a cooled isolator to avoid noise radiation from warm components of the output circuit.

If energy is supplied to the amplifying material by an electromagnetic drive, the circuits used for this purpose must provide a sufficiently strong controllable drive (usually constant in amplitude and frequency). If the interaction between the driving or pumping radiation and the material is strong, a relatively small amount of power may be needed. In Fig. 3 the cavity must be resonant at both the pumping and the amplifying frequencies. In some cases the orientation of fields at both frequencies must also be carefully controlled. Usually excess pumping power is available so that careful design for coupling it to the amplifying material is not essential.

Masers using a resonant cavity may also be operated as superregenerative amplifiers, for which various components such as the driving field, the cavity losses, the couplings, or the "static" magnetic field may be modulated.

Traveling-wave masers normally use slow-wave structures, which need only be effective over the range of response of the maser material. Amplification of a reflected wave may be controlled in the usual ways by matching, by attenuators or isolators, or by arrangement of the maser material itself to absorb a reflected wave.

The overloading of a maser amplifier is qualitatively like that of any other amplifier, the overload occurring when the molecular energy becomes exhausted. Recovery times vary between microseconds and seconds, depending especially on the maser material used; *TR* (transmit-receive) devices are sometimes necessary. *SEE RADAR*.

Maser oscillators used as frequency standards require especially stable cavities, in which the field is strongly coupled to the excited molecules. The cavities should be decoupled from external circuits, as by an attenuator or isolator.

Amplification or generation of electromagnetic waves at infrared or optical frequencies by maser techniques requires circuits which superficially appear quite different from those at lower frequencies but which serve the same functions. The resonant circuit is usually provided by two surfaces between which the radiation is reflected. The short wavelengths in this region imply that all manufactured circuit elements are large compared with a wavelength. Partially transparent surfaces, multilayers of dielectrics, lenses, and other normal infrared and optical components fill the role of circuit elements.

*Charles H. Townes; J. P. Gordon*

**Bibliography.** M. Bertolotti, *Masers and Lasers: An Historical Approach*, 1983; T. K. Ishii, *Maser and Laser Engineering*, 1980; A. E. Siegman, *Introduction to Lasers and Masers*, 1971; H. G. Unger, *Introduction to Quantum Electronics*, 1970; A. Yariv, *Quantum Electronics*, 2d ed., 1975.

## Metallic-disk rectifier

A rectifier that consists of one or more disks of metal in contact with coatings or layers of a semiconductor material. Alternating current is changed into pulsating direct current by the rectifying action that occurs at the junction interface between a metal disk and its mating semiconductor layer. The most common examples are the selenium and copper-oxide rectifiers. In a selenium rectifier a thin layer of selenium is deposited on one side of an aluminum plate and a conductive metal coating is sprayed or otherwise deposited on the selenium; electrons flow much more readily in the direction from the metallic coating to the selenium. In a copper-oxide rectifier rectification occurs at the junction between a copper disk and a coating of cuprous oxide. For a more detailed discussion *SEE SEMICONDUCTOR RECTIFIER*.

*John Markus*

## Microcomputer

A digital computer whose central processing unit (CPU) resides on a single semiconductor integrated circuit chip. The development of the microcomputer is of such historical significance that the event may be compared to the invention of the Gutenberg printing press. Just as the printed word made knowledge available on an unprecedented scale, so has the microcomputer made unprecedented computational power widely available. Indeed, the potential for the microcomputer far exceeds that of the published word, since the machine offers a much more intimate mode of interaction with information.

The microcomputer has already had an extraordinary impact upon technology and society since its introduction in 1975. The "computer on a chip," a product of large-scale integration of digital circuits, has evolved from a special-purpose dedicated device to a general-purpose system. Microcomputers control machines of all kinds, from home appliances to Earth satellites. The general-purpose implementations, in the form of personal and professional computers, support a variety of applications, from video games to business reports to labortory analysis.

**Hardware.** The microcomputer is an electronic device consisting of a microprocessor central processing unit, memory input/output (I/O) capabilities, and a power supply. This self-contained unit provides all that is needed for digital data processing. The term microcomputer is often used as a synonym for the heart of the unit, the microprocessor. The microprocessor resides on a single chip of silicon and provides the computational and control capabilities of the system. The microcomputer itself usually consists of a printed circuit (PC) board upon which are mounted the microprocessor and other large-scale integrated (LSI) chips for memory and input/output. All of these devices are connected by metal circuits printed on the board. SEE INTEGRATED CIRCUITS; MICROPROCESSOR; PRINTED CIRCUIT.

***Architecture.*** The microprocessor central processing unit consists of the same components as most digital computers: a control unit (CU), an arithmetic and logic unit (ALU), special memory units called registers, high-frequency clocks, and input/output devices. The control unit is responsible for fetching and decoding programmed instructions and managing the system. The arithmetic and logic unit performs computations and data manipulations such as addition, subtraction, comparison, and logical (boolean) AND and OR operations. The registers are very fast memory units which store data for the central processing unit and the arithmetic and logic unit and for input/output. The clock is needed to provide a continuous pulse which triggers and synchronizes events for the computing device. Input/output devices, or drivers, are needed to communicate with the world outside the chip. SEE COMPUTER SYSTEMS ARCHITECTURE.

***Word size.*** The size of a microcomputer is usually measured in terms of the width of its registers in units of bits (binary digits capable of storing either a 1 or a 0). Some devices have 4-bit registers, while others have 32 or more. The first generation of personal computers was based upon 8-bit devices. Since it requires 8 bits to represent a single character, or byte, the register size (or word size) is an important measure of the speed and power of a central processing unit. SEE BIT.

***Clocks.*** Another important measure of the microcomputer's power is the clock rate. Just as the register size measures how much data the device can process at a time, so the clock frequency determines how fast the device can process the information. Commercial microprocessors operate in the range of 1 to 25 MHz. This high level of activity is maintained by a quartz crystal oscillator made to vibrate with great consistency by using the piezoelectric effect. Outside the central processing units, other clocks are used for timing [such as the programmable interval timer (PIT)] and for input/output. SEE OSCILLATOR; PIEZOELECTRIC CRYSTAL; QUARTZ CLOCK.

***Data bus.*** Input/output between the microprocessor and the rest of the microcomputer system is performed over a bus. This is simply a data path. A data bus connects all components of the system, while an address bus is used to determine where data are located, and a control bus is used to monitor and manage the system. The bus width is yet another measure of the power of a microcomputer. It is quite common for the bus to be half the width of the register (word) size; for example, 16-bit registers may be used with an 8-bit bus. The control bus may consist of 100 or more lines of communication to the components of the system. Multiplexing is often used to allow both data and status codes to be simultaneously passed along a bus.

***Data storage.*** The memory available to the microcomputer is also an important determination of its power. Memory is available in several forms, including random-access memory (RAM) chips and read-only memory (ROM) chips. The total amount of memory permitted for a particular machine is its address space. This is a function of the register size of the central processing unit and the overall design of the machine. A 16-bit device, for example, may be able to address more than 64 k (1 k = 1024) bytes (characters) of memory. Various programming schemes are available which allow a device to access memory beyond its hardware limit, up to millions of bytes. SEE SEMICONDUCTOR MEMORIES.

In addition to the general-purpose memory available to the central processing units, there are various kinds of special-purpose memories. The ROMs are preprogrammed with commonly used instructions such as the bootstrap program for initializing the system, the nucleus of the operating system, input/output routines, and even interpretive computer languages. The RAMs may be configured to provide for buffers and caches for quick access to data retrieved from or transmitted to slower devices. Both RAMs and magnetic bubble memories are used to provide high-speed bulk storage for data as electronic disks. SEE MAGNETIC BUBBLE MEMORY.

For larger stores of data, more economical (in cost per bit) secondary storage devices are used. These include floppy disks and hard disks. The floppies are useful for smaller quantities of related data, such as word-processing text files. The hard disks, which have a capacity of several megabytes, are suitable for larger data bases of information. A microcomputer can support several secondary storage units or drives. Often a cassette tape unit is used to archive data which is not currently needed from the active storage units. Work on such technologies as laser disks promises even more economical mass storage with extremely large storage capacities. SEE COMPUTER STORAGE TECHNOLOGY; DATA-BASE MANAGEMENT SYSTEMS; WORD PROCESSING.

***Input and output.*** The impression the microcomputer makes upon the user is closely related to the mechanisms used for input and output. Unlike its cumbersome predecessors, the microcomputer offers a very rich selection of input and output mediums. For general character and numeric data, the keyboard remains an important source of input, but it is accompanied by such devices as the optical mouse, the light pen, the joystick, and the graphics tablet. All of these pointing devices rely upon software to communicate with the system. For certain printed material, optical character recognition is available. Voice input can be very effective, although the vocabulary of the machine is usually limited to a relatively small set of words spoken and passed by the user. SEE CHARACTER RECOGNITION; SPEECH RECOGNITION.

The output produced by the microcomputer can be especially impressive. One or more color graphics displays can be used to preset text and graphics in virtually limitless variations. The use of bit-mapped graphics memories and special-character and figure generation devices has made this possible. The bits of data stored in the memories are related directly to the picture elements (pixels) on the screen, permitting complex graphical manipulations simply by turning bits on and off and copying data into the memory. Multiple planes of video memory can be used to overlay one image upon another. The effect is especially dramatic when used with simulations, such as a flight simulator, but is also useful in business presentations. Voice output is also achievable with microcomputers although, like the voice input, the intelligible vocabulary is somewhat limited. Of course, hard-copy output devices such as printers and plotters remain an important part of the microcomputer system. SEE COMPUTER GRAPHICS; DATA-PROCESSING SYSTEMS; VOICE RESPONSE.

***Additional devices.*** Modern microcomputers include several intellgént devices in addition to the primary central processing unit. For numerical computations, special floating–point microprocessors serve as a companion to the controlling processor. Memory access is managed by special devices which provide for direct memory access (DMA). Secondary storage is handled by satellite processors called device controllers. Each input/output device may have its own microprocessor, including viewing screens, keyboards, and printers. The microcomputer is developing into a network of microprocessors working together to perform one or more parallel or serial tasks.

***Microprocessors and computing power.*** Among the most popular microprocessors are the Intel 8086 family of processors and the Motorola 68000 family. These 16-bit devices evolved from their 8-bit predecessors, the original micocomputers. The two families of chips have resulted in two rather different families of microcomputers. Both processors have advantages and disadvantages and can serve equally well in most applications. The original 8-bit chips, the Intel 8080 and Motorola 6502, are also still used in personal computers and in control applications. These microprocessors, and many other popular devices, provide considerable computing power for many personal applications, while the 16-bit machines are more suitable for professional, business, and engineering use.

The generation of 32-bit microprocessors makes available as much computing power as was available in large mainframe computers at the time when the microcomputer was introduced. These desktop computers have the capacity to support several users performing concurrent programming, word processing, financial analysis, and data-base searches. Tied to computer networks, these systems make great resources available to the individual. The Motorola 68000–based systems and those using true 32-bit devices are fast enough to provide for multiprocessing and timesharing. These systems have provided a basis for implementations of the UNIX operating system. SEE LOCAL-AREA NETWORKS; MULTIACCESS COMPUTER; MULTIPROCESSING; OPERATING SYSTEM; WIDE-AREA NETWORKS.

At the other end of the spectrum are a variety of small briefcase- and notebook-size machines which make all of the power of the original microcomputers available in a conveniently transportable package. These devices serve for data collection, calculation, word processing, and on-the-spot computing. Their ability to communicate with larger machines permits them to be used as terminals for data input and retrieval in the field.

**Software.** Taken as is, the microcomputer may not appear to have much to offer. It can accept data in its own (machine language) form and manipulate it in rather basic ways at a very fast rate. It cannot, however, perform useful work without first being given a program. Ultimately this program must be a set of instructions in the form of binary code which directs the actions of the machine. Each device has its own instruction set of allowable operations. This concept of the stored-program computer is attributed to John Von Neumann, and is the basic form of most modern digital computers. With the appropriate program, and connections to the outside world, the computer exhibits a certain intelligence. It becomes an extension of the mind just as conventional machines become an extension of muscle power. The possibilities for programs are without limit. SEE DIGITAL COMPUTER PROGRAMMING.

Fortunately, microcomputers evolved at a time when a very substantial body of knowledge about programming was available. The techniques used to develop software for large mainframe computers and intermediate minicomputers have been applied to microcomputers. Not only has software been borrowed or converted, but much new code has been written as well. Microcomputers have provided an opportunity to greatly improve the software which is still used on most larger computers. This fresh start has resulted in a highly interactive and very productive kind of personal computing.

***Levels.*** Microcomputers provide several levels of software that, together, can meet the needs of almost anyone. Many video game cartridges are programmed directly into machine code (microcode). For programmers and some engineers there are low-level assemblers which translate mnemonic instructions into machine code. These professionals along with business analysts and students take advantage of high-level compilers and interpreters that translate Englishlike syntax into machine code. Popular compilers include Pascal, C, Cobol, and Fortran. The most popular interpreter is BASIC. Compilers usually require a significant amount of memory and so are available ony for the larger machines. Programs written in assembly language usually run faster, but are more difficult to develop and to debug (correct). SEE PROGRAMMING LANGUAGES.

***Application software.*** Many individuals and software vendors have used software tools such as compilers and assemblers to develop a vast range of application software to meet the needs of professional and personal users. General-purpose systems for word processing, spreadsheet calculations, graphics, communication, and other applications make the microcomputer a powerful tool for manipulating words, numbers, or symbols. General-purpose software for storing information in computer files on floppy or hard disks is available which rivals that available on mainframe computers. These file management and data-base management systems allow data to be stored in a convenient form and then sorted, searched, processed, and reported in a variety of ways. All of this general-purpose application software is complex and would require much time for an individual to develop. This software is a significant resource for the microcomputer user.

***Integration.*** Although each of these software tools is powerful in itself, a quantum leap in utility has been achieved through their integration. Software for microcomputers has evolved beyond a collection of generally unrelated components to a unified set of tools where each application can share the data produced by any other application. This integration is usually based upon a common set of data definition and directory information referred to as a data dictionary. This concept, which was derived from the mainframe software environment, provides for the commonality of the application software available to the microcomputer user.

**Applications.** The continuation of the trend toward applying faster and more powerful machines to a broad range of problems presents profound implications for the future.

***Education.*** In education, the microcomputer is available from grade school through graduate school. It serves as a replacement for the typewriter and calculator as essential tools for the college student, and it is likely to pervade education at all levels. In addition to their application to homework, the machines are providing the basis for interactive computer-assisted instruction (CAI). The language Logo was developed expressed to teach programming and to allow children to express themselves creatively.

***Libraries.*** Although the machines are far too small to store the contents of an institution's books, they are powerful enough to process specific information garnered from the stacks. Research papers, statistical analysis, charts, and graphs can all be produced by using these library resources.

***Home computers.*** Home computers have outgrown computer games and are being effectively applied to record keeping, financial management, word processing, and education. These machines can communicate with one another over telephone lines. As a result, hundreds of personal computer networks exist for exchanging information. Communication links also provide for access to a variety of information sources including financial data, government reports, airline schedules, current events, and abstracts of publications in many fields. With the advent of fiber-optic communications channels, Videotex systems are capable of providing a variety of two-way services as the home microcomputer communicates with a central system. Individual financial institutions established their own timesharing arrangements to permit their customers to conduct transactions from the convenience of their homes. SEE OPTICAL COMMUNICATIONS; VIDEOTEXT AND TELETEXT.

***Business.*** Business organizations, both large corporations and small firms, find the microcomputer to be essential to growth and profitability. Each machine can send information to the company's large computers for storage and processing and can also receive information from virtually any other machine. The electronic mail capability of microcomputer networks has been one important reason for their success, since it allows messages, reports, and graphics to be transmitted at high baud rates to a given destination or broadcast to many terminal points. The machines are essential tools for financial analysts, and managers are able to control information much more directly than with centralized computing. SEE ELECTRONIC MAIL.

***Engineering.*** For engineering organizations and engineers the microcomputer offers more power than many mainframe machines of the 1970s. Not only can analysis and design computations be perfomed, but interactive graphics as well. Computer-aided design (CAD) systems using microcomputers permit engineers to design and test a mathematical model of a new product in a fraction of the time required by traditional procedures. The machines can feed information directly into microprocessor controlled milling machines and robots for computer-aided manufacturing (CAM). SEE COMPUTER-AIDED DESIGN AND MANUFACTURING; COMPUTER-AIDED ENGINEERING.

***Smart systems.*** Microprocessors and microcomputers not only are employed in the design and manufacture of products, but embedded (built-in) in the products as well. This created a new generation of intelligent machines, and smart systems for managing the environment at home, controlling office machines at work, and monitoring the functioning of communications, transportation, and energy systems. Although these systems are often inconspicuous, their contribution to society is considerable. SEE ARTIFICAL INTELLIGENCE; EMBEDDED SYSTEMS.

***Military electronics.*** The microcomputer provides many advantages because of its small size, light weight, low power requirements, and capacity for adding intelligence to weapons systems and supporting equipment. Militarized microcomputers assist in the control of aircraft, surface vessels, and submarines. The microcomputer is responsible for the capabilities of military satellites as well. With the development of very high-speed integrated circuits (VHSIC) these systems will be able to perform even better in real-time environments. SEE DIGITAL COMPUTER.

*Larry D. Tindell*

***Bibliography.*** M. Dahmke, *Microcomputer Operating Systems*, 1982; H. D'Angelo, *Microcomputer Structures*, 1981; C. J. Date, *An Introduction to Database Systems*, 2 vols., 3d ed., 1982; Digital Equipment Corp., *A Guide to Personal Computing*, 1982; General-purpose microprocessors: Performance and features, *Electr. Des.*, 30(21):118–141, October 14, 1982; J. E. Haugo, *Introduction to Microcomputers*, 1982; Intel Corp., *An Introduction to ASM86*, 1981; P. Norton, *Inside the IBM PC: Access to Advanced Features and Programming*, 1983; A. Osborne, *An Introduction to Microcomputers*, 2 vols., 1976; Sybex, Inc., *International Microcomputer Dictionary*, 1981; R. Zaks, *From Chips to Systems: An Introduction to Microprocessors*, 1981.

## Microcomputer development system

A complete microcomputer system used to test and develop both the hardware and software of other microcomputer-based systems, from initial development through debugging of final prototypes.

A typical microcomputer development system includes assembler facilities, a text editor, debugging facilities, and hardware emulation capabilities. Often a microcomputer development system will also include a test board for peripheral interfaces and other hardware, a floppy disk storage system, a video display terminal, a keyboard or keypad input device, and a provision for using a printing peripheral. A few microcomputer development systems include provisions for programmable read-only memory (PROM) devices.

The assembler permits instructions for the microcomputer to be written as mnemonics, which are then translated by the assembler into hexadecimal or binary machine language. The machine language program, known as an object file, is loaded into the microcomputer for execution. The program written in mnemonics is known as the source code, and is generated by the text editor. SEE DIGITAL COMPUTER PROGRAMMING.

A key component is the emulator, a combination of hardware and software which permits the MDS to emulate programs written for other microcomputer systems. Many emulators can execute source code programs for different microprocessors. A few emulators can also execute high-level languages such as BASIC, FORTRAN, and PASCAL. *See Programming languages*.

An MDS normally includes several software development and debugging tools. One common debugging facility is the trace function. This allows program execution to be halted at desired points so that central processing unit (CPU) registers or memory contents may be examined.

If true emulator and debugging facilities are not included in an MDS, a cross assembler will usually be provided. This is an assembler which accepts source code for one microprocessor type and compiles it by using a system for another microprocessor. However, it is not possible to run or debug programs by using a cross assembler.

Typical MDS random-access memory (RAM) capacity is 64K bytes or greater. A floppy disk–based mass storage system is now part of almost all available microcomputer development systems. *See Computer storage technology; Semiconductor memories*.

Most microcomputer development systems support the development of just one microprocessor or family of microprocessors. However, microcomputer development systems have been introduced which can support several different microprocessors and high-level languages. *See Microcomputer; Microprocessor*.

*Harry L. Helms*

## Microphone

An electroacoustic device containing a transducer which is actuated by sound waves and delivers electric signals proportional to the sound pressure. Microphones are usually classified with respect to the transducer principle used. Their directional characteristics are also of interest, that is, the voltage output as a function of the direction of incidence for constant sound pressure. *See Directivity; Sound; Sound pressure; Transducer*.

In addition to directional characteristics, some other important characteristics of microphones include open-circuit sensitivity, equivalent noise level, dynamic range, and vibration sensitivity.

Open-circuit sensitivity is defined as the ratio of open-circuit output voltage and sound pressure. The pressure sensitivity refers to the actual pressure acting upon the diaphragm of the microphone, while the free-field sensitivity refers to the pressure that existed in the sound field before insertion of the microphone. Pressure sensitivity and free-field sensitivity are equal at low frequencies. Sensitivities are measured in volt/pascal (V/Pa).

Equivalent noise level is equal to the level of a sound pressure which generates an output voltage of the microphone corresponding to its inherent A-weighted noise voltage. It is measured in dB(A).

Dynamic range is defined as the range of sound pressure levels in decibels (dB) extending from the equivalent noise level to the level where the nonlinear distortion reaches 3%.

Vibration sensitivity is defined as the ratio of the output voltage of the microphone as a result of acceleration of its case to the magnitude of the acceleration. Vibration sensitivities are measured in volt/$g$, where $g$ is the acceleration of the Earth's gravity, or in volt/(m/s$^2$).

Some aspects of the acoustic performance of a few microphones are given in the **table**. Only microphones of current interest have been considered.

### Microphone Types

The various microphone types differ by the transducers used for converting the acoustic into electric signals. Most commonly used are electrostatic, piezoelectric, dynamic, magnetic, and carbon transducers. The first four transducer principles are reversible, that is, the microphones can also be used as sound generators, while the carbon transducer is nonreversible. *See Loudspeaker*.

**Electrostatic (condenser) microphones.** These consist of a fixed electrode (the backplate), a movable electrode (the diaphragm), and an air gap between the electrodes. To decrease the acoustic stiffness of the airgap, which is generally about 0.8 to 1.2 mils (20 to 30 micrometers) thick, the backplate is often perforated with holes connecting the air gap to a larger air cavity. The diaphragm is a thin [typically 0.16 to 0.24 mil (4 to 6 μm) thick] nickel, Duralumin, or

**Acoustic characteristics of microphones**

| Microphone type | Frequency range, Hz | Sensitivity, mV/Pa | Equivalent noise level, dB(A) | Directional characteristics |
|---|---|---|---|---|
| **Condenser** | | | | |
| Measuring microphone, dc-biased, 1-in. (25-mm) diameter | 3–8,000 | 50 | 10 | Omnidirectional |
| Measuring microphone, dc-biased, 0.12-in. (3-mm) diameter | 7–140,000 | 1.0 | 55 | Omnidirectional |
| Measuring microphone, electret, 0.5-in. (12-mm) diameter | 7–12,500 | 50 | 14 | Omnidirectional |
| Low-noise measuring microphone, dc-biased, 1-in. (25-mm) diameter | 7–12,500 | 100 | − 2.5 | Omnidirectional |
| Studio microphone, rf-biased | 20–20,000 | 20 | 24 | Omnidirectional |
| Lavalier microphone, electret | 50–20,000 | 10 | 30 | Omnidirectional |
| Studio "shotgun" microphone, rf-biased | 40–20,000 | 40 | 22 | Club-shaped |
| Miniature microphone, electret, 0.16 × 0.12 × 0.08 in. (4 × 3 × 2 mm) | 100–5,000 | 10 | 25 | Cardioid |
| **Piezoelectric** | | | | |
| Telephone transmitter, unimorph | 300–3,400 | 4 | | Omnidirectional |
| **Dynamic** | | | | |
| Studio microphone | 30–20,000 | 1.3 | 30 | Omnidirectional |
| Directional studio | 30–20,000 | 1.8 | 30 | Superdirectional |

metalized plastic (for example Mylar) foil under mechanical tension. The resonance frequency of the microphone is determined by the mass of the diaphragm and by the restoring forces, consisting of the tension of the diaphragm and the stiffness of the air gap. Below resonance, the system is controlled by the restoring forces and has a frequency-independent sensitivity. The two electrodes form a capacitor whose capacitance is very small, typically between 2 and 100 picofarads. The electrical impedance of the transducer is therefore relatively large. *SEE CAPACITANCE; CAPACITOR; ELECTRICAL IMPEDANCE.*

Impinging sound waves produce a motion of the diaphragm and a corresponding variation of the capacitance. This variation can be utilized in various ways to generate electrical output signals. Accordingly, three types of condenser microphones are customary, namely direct-current–biased systems, electret-biased systems, and radio-frequency–biased systems.

In the dc-biased system (**Fig. 1***a*), a polarizing voltage of about 200 V (or 20 V in portable systems) is applied between the microphone electrodes. Electrical output signals are thus generated by the diaphragm deflections. These are fed into a cathode follower with an input impedance $R$ of typically $10^8$ ohms or more. For frequencies $\omega$ larger than $1/RC$, where $C$ is the microphone capacitance, the voltage delivered to the cathode follower is proportional to

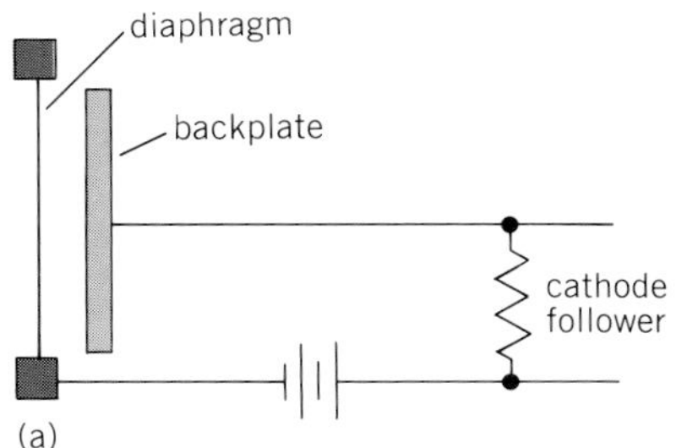


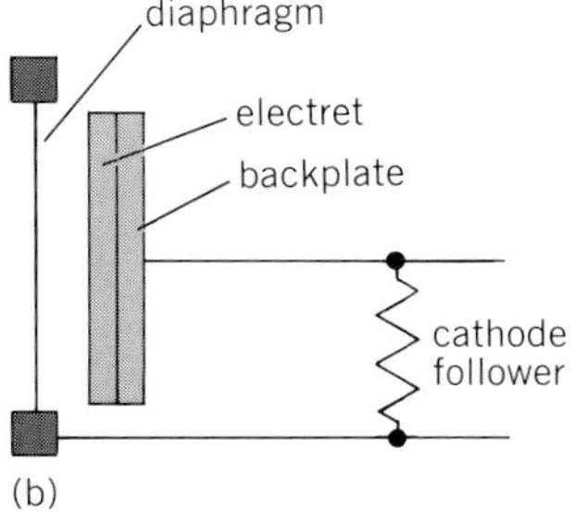


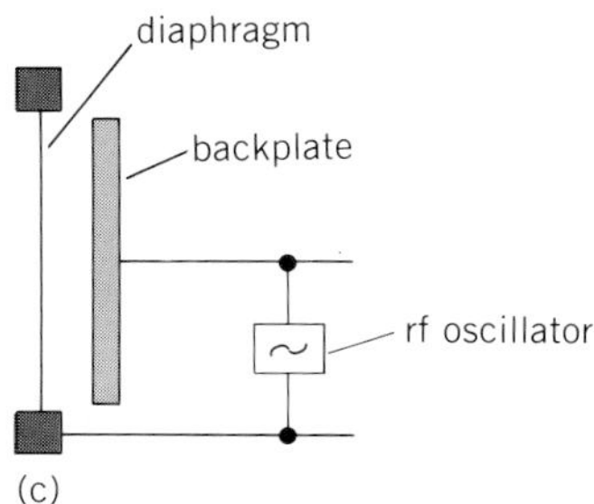


**Fig. 1. Electrostatic transducers: (*a*) dc-biased system, (*b*) electret-biased system, (c) rf-biased system.**

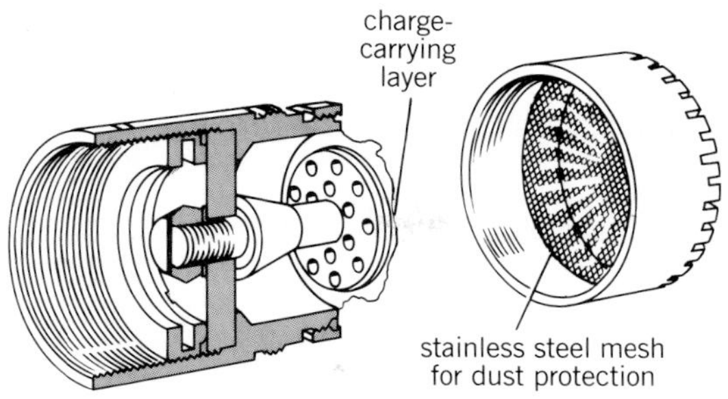


**Fig. 2. Measuring condenser microphone. (*Brüel and Kjaer*)**

the sound pressure. To avoid capacitive loading of the transducer by stray capacitances and to eliminate electric pickup, the cathode follower is directly built into the microphone case.

In the electret-biased system (Fig. 1*b*), a permanently charged dielectric (electret) is inserted between the two electrodes of the transducer. The electret, usually made of a 0.5 to 1.0 mil (12 to 25 μm) polymer film, such as Teflon, either is cemented onto the backplate or is metalized on one side and used as the diaphragm of the microphone. The amount of charge is chosen so that it corresponds to a bias voltage of about 200 V. As in dc-biased systems, the electric output signal of the transducer is fed into a cathode follower. *SEE ELECTRET TRANSDUCER.*

In the rf-biased system (Fig. 1*c*), the capacitance of the transducer determines the frequency of oscillation of an rf circuit, usually about 10 MHz. Motion of the diaphragm produces a frequency-modulated signal. Upon demodulation, a low-frequency signal corresponding to the sound pressure is obtained. As opposed to dc-biased systems, the rf-biased transducer has no low-frequency cutoff. *SEE FREQUENCY MODULATION.*

Condenser microphones are renowned for their excellent acoustic qualities such as high sensitivity, large dynamic range, and small vibration sensitivity. Also important is their suitability for miniaturization, with the smallest units having dimensions of only about 0.12 × 0.12 × 0.08 in. (3 × 3 × 2 mm). They can be designed as precision instruments (**Fig. 2**) and as such are widely used in measurement. Other applications are in high-fidelity sound reproduction, in cassette recorders, and in hearing aids. In some countries, electret microphones have been introduced in telephones as a replacement for the carbon transmitter. Condenser microphones, particularly of the electret-biased type, are now the most widely used microphones. *SEE MAGNETIC RECORDING; TELEPHONE.*

**Piezoelectric microphones.** These consist of a material having piezoelectric properties. A deformation of the material leads to the generation of a voltage which corresponds to the deformation. Piezoelectric materials can be crystals, polycrystalline ceramics, or semicrystalline polymers. The best-known piezoelectric crystals are quartz and ammonium dihydrogen phosphate (ADP). Representative of polycrystalline ceramics are lead zirconate titanate (PZT) and barium titanate, which are initially electrostrictive; they have to be poled, that is, exposed to a high electric field at elevated temperatures, to become piezoelectric. An example of a semicrystalline polymer is poly(vinylidenefluoride) [PVDF]. It is also made piezoelectric by poling. *SEE ELECTRET; ELECTROSTRICTION; PIEZOELECTRIC CRYSTAL; PIEZOELECTRICITY.*

Piezoelectric microphones for audio and near-ultrasonic frequencies are made from these materials in the form of flexure-mode transducers, such as bimorphs, unimorphs, or curved benders.

The bimorph consists of two piezoelectric disks, usually made of PZT, which are cemented together. Either the disks are poled in the same direction with the outputs connected in parallel (**Fig. 3***a*), or they are poled in opposite directions with the outputs connected in series (Fig. 3*b*). Since bending of the structures shortens one disk and lengthens the other, the voltage signals from the two disks add in both cases. The unimorph (Fig. 3*c*) consists of a single piezoelectric disk cemented to a thin metal plate. It has the advantage of being less fragile than the bimorph. Bimorphs and unimorphs are made in rectangular, square, or circular shapes.

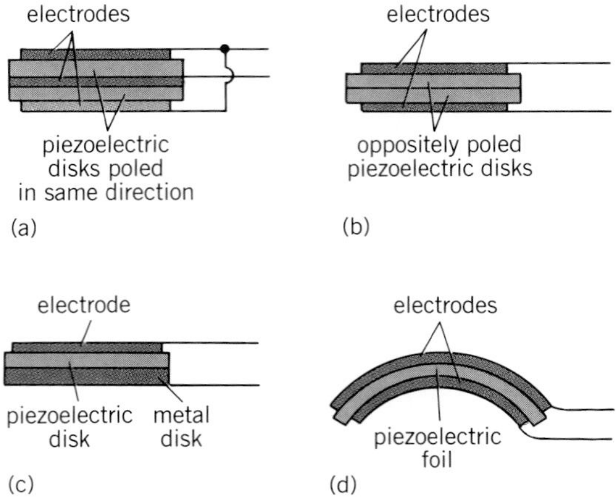


**Fig. 3. Piezoelectric transducers: (*a*) parallel bimorph, (*b*) series bimorph, (c) unimorph, (*d*) curved bender.**

To be operational, these elements have to be mounted in some way. Frequently applied is edge mounting along the entire edge or, for rectangular disks, cantilever mounting at one of the short sides of the rectangle. The transducers are then either directly actuated by the sound waves or actuated by means of a membrane connected by a stylus to some properly chosen point of the system.

The single-element bender (Fig. 3*d*) consists of a curved piezoelectric foil, usually PVDF, which is clamped around part of its edge. Preferred geometries are cylindrical sections or domes. If actuated by a sound wave, a voltage signal is generated due to the piezoelectric effect.

In piezoelectric microphones, the resonance frequency is placed at the upper end of the response range. At much lower frequencies, the system is stiffness-controlled. Since the output voltage is proportional to the displacement, a constant sensitivity results in this range. Because the resonance is very prominent, it has to be damped to ensure relatively constant sensitivity around this frequency.

Well-designed piezoelectric microphones have acceptable quality. A drawback is the relatively high vibration sensitivity. Directly actuated unimorph microphones have been introduced in telephones as a replacement for carbon transmitters in some countries.

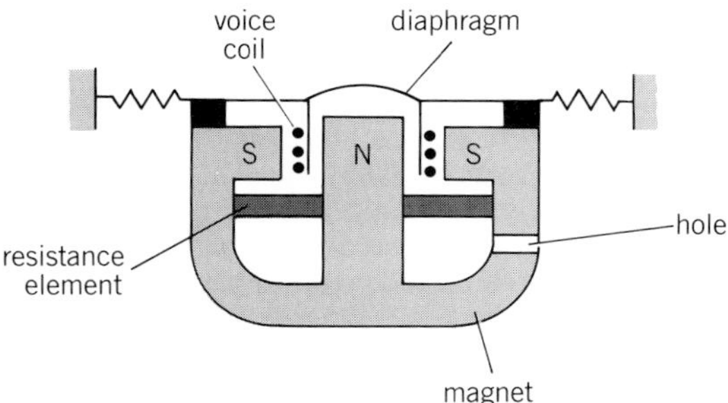


**Fig. 4. Dynamic microphone of the moving-coil type.**

**Dynamic microphones.** These consist of a conductor located in the gap of a permanent magnet. Motion of the conductor produces a voltage proportional to its velocity. Depending on the kind of conductor used, moving coil and ribbon microphones are distinguished.

In the moving-coil microphone (**Fig. 4**) the coil, often referred to as voice coil, is connected to a diaphragm actuated by the sound waves. Motion of the coil induces a voltage proportional to its velocity. To obtain a frequency-independent sensitivity, the coil must respond to the sound pressure with frequency-independent velocity. This is accomplished by resistance-controlling the system: the acoustical resistance is made larger in magnitude than the acoustical reactance due to the mass of the diaphragm and coil and due to the compliance of the suspension. A silk cloth or a piece of felt placed behind the voice coil is used for this purpose. The major resonance frequency of the system is usually placed in the range of 500 to 1000 Hz. To equalize the sensitivity in the lower and upper parts of the audio range, other resonances of the microphone are used. In modern moving-coil microphones, the diaphragm is made of a plastic film, for example, 0.6-mil (15-μm) Mylar. The impedance of the voice coil is typically 200 to 1000 ohms.

In the ribbon microphone, a metallic ribbon is placed in a magnetic field. As in the moving-coil microphone, the ribbon has to be terminated into an acoustical resistance that is large compared to the reactance of the system if a frequency-independent sensitivity is desired.

Dynamic microphones are relatively complicated systems. If well designed, they are of good quality. Drawbacks are the difficulties encountered in minia-

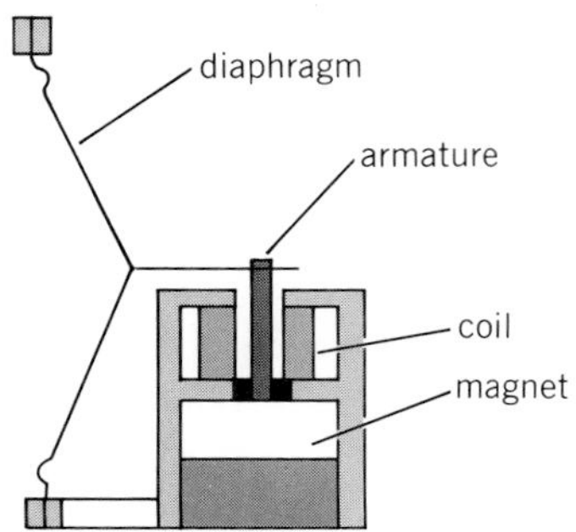


**Fig. 5. Sectional view of magnetic microphone of the balanced-armature type. (*After H. F. Olson, Acoustical Engineering, Van Nostrand, 1957*)**

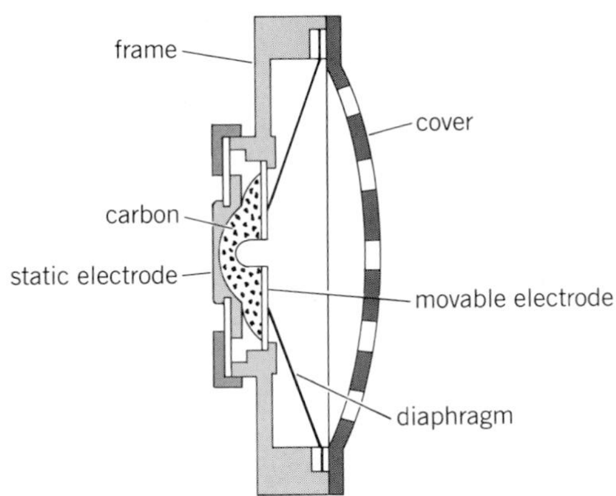


**Fig. 6. Sectional view of carbon microphone.**

turization and the relatively high vibration sensitivity. Moving-coil microphones are still widely used in high-fidelity and radio applications. In many other areas they have been replaced by electret microphones. Ribbon microphones were very popular in the past but are now rarely employed.

**Magnetic microphones.** These consist of a diaphragm connected to an armature which, when vibrating, varies the reluctance in a magnetic field (**Fig. 5**). The variation in reluctance leads to a variation in the magnetic flux through a surrounding coil and therefore to an induced voltage. This voltage is proportional to the velocity of the armature. To obtain a frequency-independent sensitivity, the velocity of the armature must be independent of frequency. As in dynamic microphones, this is accomplished by resistance-controlling the system, for example, by placing an acoustic resistance behind the diaphragm.

Magnetic microphones are relatively complicated and have poor frequency response and high vibration sensitivity. While never extensively used, they have now disappeared completely.

**Carbon microphones.** These consist of a diaphragm connected to a movable electrode which together with a stationary electrode forms a cup containing carbon granules (**Fig. 6**). A polarizing current is passed through the electrodes and the carbon granules. Motion of the diaphragm varies the resistance of the carbon element. To obtain constant sensitivity, the amplitude of the diaphragm must be independent of the frequency. Therefore, the system must be stiffness-controlled. This can be accomplished by placing the resonance frequency of the diaphragm and carbon-element assembly at or near the upper limit of the response range. The electrical impedance of the carbon element is a resistance of the order of 100 to 200 ohms.

Carbon microphones have a poor frequency response, large nonlinear distortion (up to 30%), and pronounced sensitivity fluctuations, and consume a relatively large current. Yet, because of their high sensitivity and low cost, they were almost universally employed in telephony until 1970. Since then they have been gradually replaced by electret and piezoelectric microphones.

### Directional Characteristics

The microphones described above are inherently nondirectional (omnidirectional) as long as they are small compared to the wavelength and if the microphone case shields the rear side of the diaphragm from the sound waves. This means that they pick up sound from all directions with equal sensitivity. They are therefore referred to as pressure microphones since pressure is a scaler and not a vector quantity.

In many applications, however, microphones with other-than-omnidirectional characteristics are desired. Such microphones reject signals from certain directions and thus yield an improvement of the signal-to-noise ratio. A great variety of directivity patterns can be achieved with microphones based on either the gradient or the dimensional scheme. Combinations of both principles are also useful.

**Gradient scheme.** The directivity of a first-order gradient microphone depends on the pressure difference between two microphone elements separated by a distance that is small compared to the wavelength. Second-order gradients are formed by subtracting the outputs of two displaced first-order gradients. Analysis shows that the directivity of such systems is always independent of frequency and transducer dimensions as long as the above condition about the separation of the elements holds. Three common directivity patterns achievable with first-order gradients are shown in **Fig. 7**.

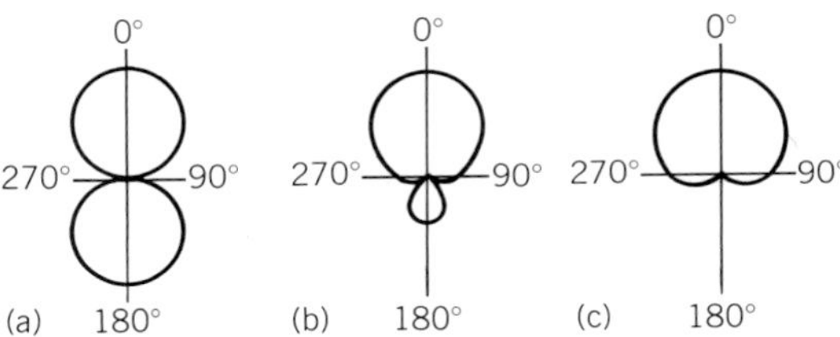


**Fig. 7. Polar directivity patterns: (*a*) bidirectional, (*b*) superdirectional, (c) unidirectional.**

A simple gradient microphone with the bidirectional sensitivity pattern shown in Fig. 7*a* is obtained by exposing the diaphragm of a transducer to the sound field from both sides. Such microphones, because of the large sensitivity in the backward direction, are infrequently used.

Of great practical use, however, is the undirectional microphone based on the gradient principle. A system employing a condenser transducer is schematically depicted in **Fig. 8**. An acoustical resistance is located behind the diaphragm to provide resistance control of the vibrating system. The back of the diaphragm is coupled to the acoustic inertance of the ports in the side of the case and an acoustic resistance and acoustic capacitance of the air volume in the case. The phase shift introduced by the acoustic net-

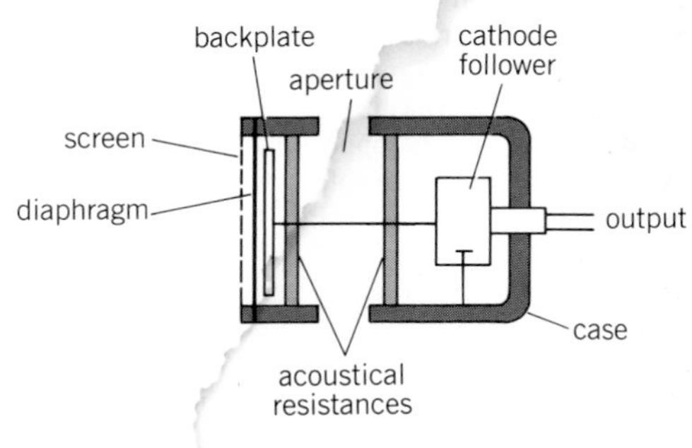


**Fig. 8. Sectional view of a unidirectional microphone employing condenser transducer.**

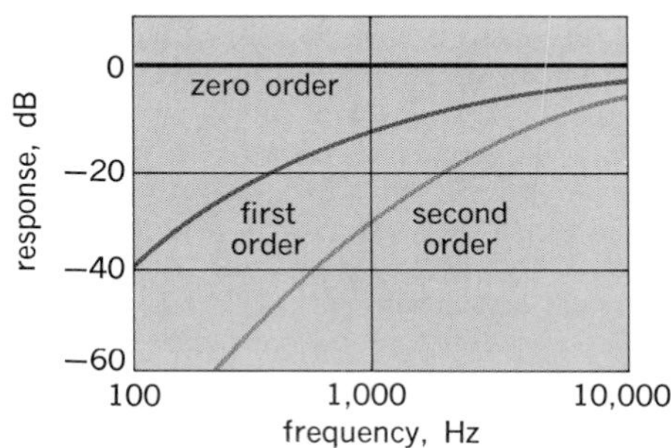


**Fig. 9. Frequency-response characteristics of zero-, first-, and second-order gradient microphones, assuming a frequency-independent characteristic of the zero-order system.**

work consisting of the inertance, resistance, and capacitance corresponds to the distance from the ports to the front of the diaphragm. As a result, for sound arriving from the back, the forces on the front and back of the diaphragm are almost equal in phase and amplitude, and the response is low. The phase shift is at a maximum for sound arriving in a forward direction, with resultant maximum sensitivity. Thus, a unidirectional directivity pattern is obtained.

As compared to the sensitivity of a pressure (zero-order gradient) microphone, the sensitivity of a first-order gradient microphone to plane waves from a far sound source decreases with decreasing frequency. This is shown in **Fig. 9** where a flat response for the zero-order gradient has been assumed. An even

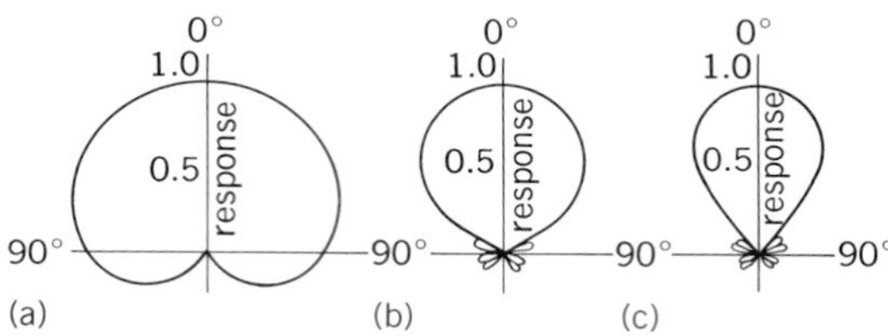


**Fig. 10. Directivity patterns for a line microphone at different frequencies. The response maximum is arbitrarily chosen as unity. (*a*) Length of line = λ/2, where λ = wavelength. (*b*) Length of line = 2λ. (*c*) Length of line = 8λ.**

greater sensitivity loss toward low frequencies is found in second-order gradients. However, all gradients will show equal sensitivity to the spherical waves of a close sound source. The first- and second-order gradients can thus be used as "close-talking" microphones, having the advantage of suppressing the low-frequency components from far-away noise sources.

**Dimensional scheme.** The dimensional-directivity scheme depends on interference of signals with phase differences which are exclusively due to the geometry of the system. For the microphone to be directive, the dimensions of the transducer have to be comparable to the wavelength. As opposed to gradient-type microphones, the directivity of such microphones is dependent on the ratio of linear dimensions to wavelength, as shown in **Fig. 10** for a line microphone, that is, a microphone picking up sound along a line. Other examples of dimensional microphones are transducer arrays and reflectors.

An implementation of the dimensional scheme in the form of a line microphone consists of a long tube which has a large number of sound inlets along its side. The transducer is placed at the end of the tube (**Fig. 11**). For incidence along the axis of the tube in the direction toward the microphone, the sound waves propagating alongside and inside the tube are in phase, the interference is constructive, and maximum sensitivity results. For incidence at other angles, phase differences between the sound waves impinging on the tube and those propagating in the tube appear, and the interference is fully or partially destructive. The directivity patterns are those of Fig. 10. Systems

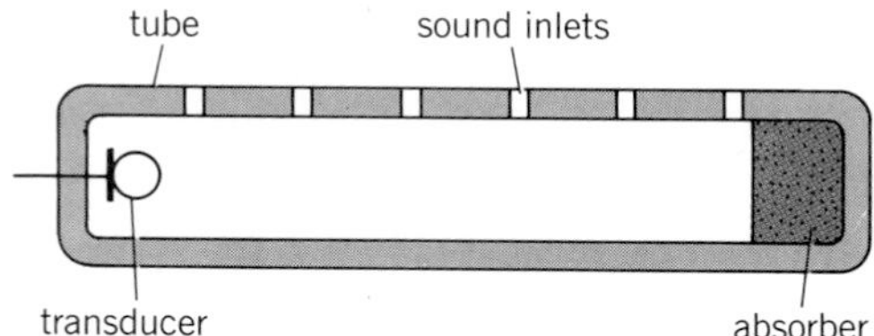


**Fig. 11. Schematic section of a line microphone.**

of this kind are referred to as "shotgun" microphones.

The dimensional scheme is often combined with the gradient principle to improve the directivity of cardioid or supercardioid microphones at higher frequencies.

### Sensitivity Calibration

A number of methods may be employed for determining the sensitivity of microphones. The pistonphone and the reciprocity calibration are widely used.

A pistonphone is used to calibrate pressure-type microphones (**Fig. 12**). The small piston is driven by a crank and thus produces a pressure that can be exactly calculated from the geometry of the system. The pistonphone method is useful for calibrating microphones in the low-frequency range. The upper limit is governed by the permissible speed of the mechanical system, which corresponds to approximately 300 Hz. Pressure and free-field sensitivities do not differ in this range. The accuracy of the pistonphone-calibration method is ±0.2 dB.

The reciprocity method allows sensitivity measurements in the entire audio-frequency range and beyond, and can be adapted to yield either the pressure or the free-field sensitivity of microphones. In both cases, an auxiliary reversible transducer $S_1$ and an auxiliary loudspeaker $S_2$ are required in addition to the microphone $M$ to be calibrated. A number of ex-

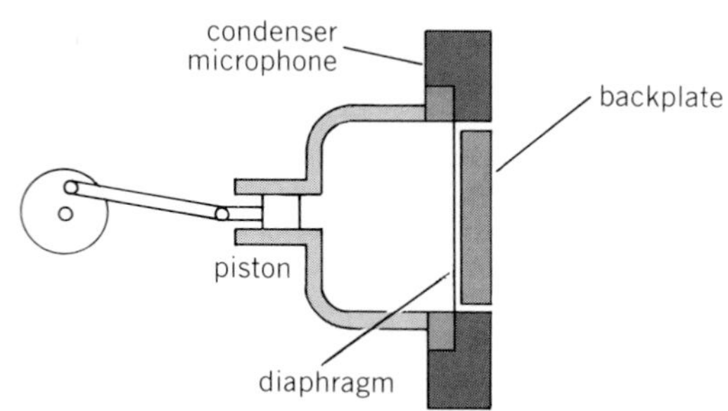


**Fig. 12. Sectional view of a pistonphone.**

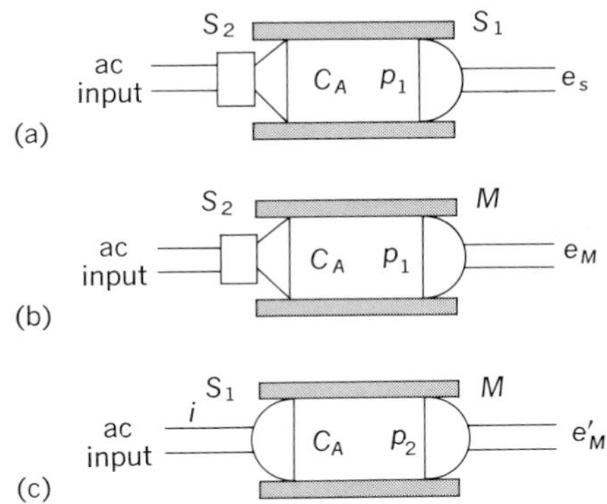


**Fig. 13.** The three experiments of the reciprocity calibration for obtaining the pressure sensitivity of a microphone. (a) The open-circuit voltage $e_S$ of the reversible microphone loudspeaker $S_1$ when used as a microphone and actuated by a sound pressure $p_1$. (b) The open-circuit voltage $e_M$ of the microphone $M$ to be calibrated, when actuated by a sound pressure $p_1$. (c) The open-circuit voltage $e'_M$ of the microphone $M$ to be calibrated, when actuated by a sound pressure $p_2$ produced by the reversible microphone loudspeaker $S_1$ used as a loudspeaker with a current input $i$ and a volume coupling $C_A$.

periments have to be performed to determine the sensitivity of $M$.

The procedure for the pressure-response calibration is schematically shown in **Fig. 13**. In Fig. 13*a*, an alternating current is fed to the loudspeaker $S_2$. A sound pressure $p_1$ is produced in the volume having an acoustical compliance $C_A$. It generates an open-circuit voltage $e_S$ of $S_1$. In the next experiment (Fig. 13*b*), the same current is fed to the loudspeaker $S_2$, resulting in an open-circuit voltage $e_M$ of the microphone $M$. In the third experiment, a current $i$ is fed to $S_1$ which is now used as a loudspeaker. This produces the output voltage $e'_M$ of $M$. The sensitivity $K_M$ of the microphone $M$ is then given by Eq. (1), where

$$K_M = \sqrt{\frac{j\omega C_A e_M e'_M}{e_S i}} \tag{1}$$

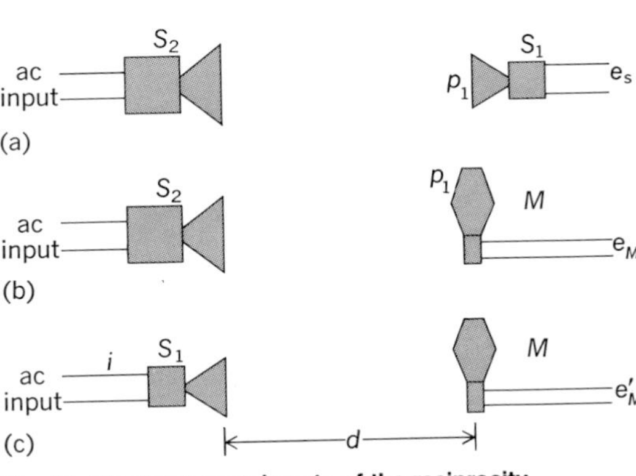


**Fig. 14.** The three experiments of the reciprocity calibration for obtaining the free-field sensitivity of a microphone. (a) The open-circuit voltage $e_S$ of the reversible microphone loudspeaker $S_1$ when used as a microphone and actuated by a sound pressure $p_1$. (b) The open-circuit voltage $e_M$ of the microphone $M$ to be calibrated, when actuated by a sound pressure $p_1$. (c) The open-circuit voltage $e'_M$ of the microphone $M$ to be calibrated, when actuated by a sound pressure produced by the reversible microphone loudspeaker $S_1$ used as a loudspeaker with a current input $i$ and a spatial separation $d$.

$\omega = 2\pi f$, $f$ being the frequency. The acoustical compliance $C_A$ is obtained from the dimensions of the cavity.

The free-field calibration by means of the reciprocity procedure is shown in Fig. 14. In this case, the sensitivity $K_M$ of the microphone $M$ is given by Eq. (2), where $e_S$, $e_M$, $e'_M$, and $i$ are obtained from the

$$K_m = \sqrt{\frac{2d\lambda e_M e'_M}{r_A i e_S}} \tag{2}$$

experiments in **Fig. 14**, $d$ is the distance as shown in the figure, $\lambda$ is the wavelength of the sound wave, and $r_A$ is the characteristic impedance of air.

The reciprocity calibration is a very accurate method since it depends solely on measurements of electrical quantities and length dimensions. Its accuracy is estimated to be $\pm 0.05$ dB.

*Gerhard M. Sessler*

***Bibliography.*** L. E. Kinsler et al., *Fundamentals of Acoustics*, 3d ed., 1982; H. F. Olson, *Modern Sound Reproduction*, 1971, reprint 1978.

## Microprocessor

A central processor unit (CPU) on a single integrated circuit (IC) chip. The physical size of a typical microprocessor wafer is around 0.2 in. × 0.2 in. (5 mm × 5 mm), but may vary from one microprocessor to another. **Figure 1** is a magnified view of a typical microprocessor. Based on its word size (bits), the commercially available microprocessors can be classified as 4-bit, 8-bit, 16-bit, 32-bit, or bit-sliced. The physical size and the number of pins of a microprocessor chip are proportional to its word size. The longer the word size, the bigger the chip, and the greater the number of pins required. The first and shortest word-size microprocessor was the Intel 4004, manufactured by Intel Corporation in 1970. Since then, the microprocessor has grown continually bigger and more powerful.

**Architecture and instruction set.** Each microprocessor has its own architecture, which encompasses the general layout of its major components, the principal features of these components, and the manner in which they are interconnected. However, the major components of all microprocessors are the same: (1) the clock; (2) control unit, comprising the program counter (PC), instruction register (IR), processor status word (PSW), and stack pointer (SP); (3) control memory; (4) bus control; (5) working register; (6) arithmetic/logic unit (ALU); (7) internal memory or stack. Their general layout is shown in **Fig. 2**. They are also called the hardware of a microprocessor. Besides the hardware, a microprocessor has its instruction set or software. According to the type of operations that the instructions perform, an instruction set can be subdivided into group operations for arithmetic, data transfer, branching, logic, and input/output (I/O). A set of logically related instructions stored in memory is referred to as a program. The microprocessor "reads" each instruction from memory in a logically determinate sequence, and uses it to initiate processing actions.

**Fundamentals of operations.** Even though the architectures and instruction sets of different microprocessors are different, their fundamentals of operation are the same. For example, the pin configuration and

**Fig. 1. Typical microprocessor (Intel 8085).** ***(Intel Corp.)***

the block diagram of the architecture of Intel 8085, one of the commonly used microprocessors, are shown in **Fig. 3**. The 8085 contains a register array with both dedicated and general-purpose registers: (1) a 16-bit program counter; (2) 16-bit stack pointer; (3) six 8-bit general-purpose registers arranged in pairs: BC, DE, HL; (4) temporary register pair: WZ; (5) serial I/O register pair; (6) interrupt control register.

The 16-bit program counter fetches instructions from any one of $2^{16}$ or 65,536 possible memory locations. When the RESET IN pin of 8085 is made logic 0, the program counter is reset to zero; when the RESET IN pin is returned to logic 1, the control unit transfers the contents of the PC to the address latch, providing the address of the first instruction to be executed. Thus, program execution in the 8085 begins with the instruction in memory location zero.

8085 instructions are 1 to 3 bytes in length. The first byte always contains the operation code (OP code). During the instruction fetch, the first byte is transferred from the memory by way of the external data bus through the data bus buffer latch into the instruction register. The PC is automatically incremented so that it contains the address of the next instruction if the instruction contains only 1 byte, or the address of the next byte of the present instruction if the instruction consists of 2 or 3 bytes.

In the case of a multibyte instruction, the timing and control section provides additional operations to read in the additional bytes. The timing and control section uses the instruction decoder output and external control signals to generate signals for the state and cycle timing and for the control of external devices. After all the bytes of an instruction have been fetched into the microprocessor, the instruction is executed. Execution may require transfer of data between the microprocessor and memory or an I/O device. For these transfers, the memory or I/O device address placed in the address latch comes from the instruction which was fetched or from one of the register pairs used as a data pointer: HL, BC, or DE.

The six general-purpose registers in the register array can be used as single 8-bit registers or as 16-bit register pairs. The temporary register pair, WZ, is not program-addressable and is only used by the control unit for the internal execution of instructions. For example, to address an external register for a data transfer, WZ is used to hold temporarily the address of an instruction read into the microprocessor until the address is transferred to the address and address/data latch.

The 16-bit stack pointer, SP, always points to the top of the stack allocated in external memory. The stack, as previously indicated, primarily supports interrupt and subroutine programming.

The 8085's arithmetic/logic unit performs arithmetic and logic operations on data. The operands for these operations are stored in two registers associated with the ALU: the 8-bit accumulator and the 8-bit temporary register. The accumulator is loaded from the internal bus and can transfer data to the internal bus. Thus, it serves as both a destination and source register for data. The temporary register stores one of the operands during a binary operation. For example, if the contents of register B are to be added to the contents of the accumulator and the result left in the accumulator, the temporary register holds a copy of the contents of register B while the arithmetic operation is taking place.

Associated with the ALU is the 5-bit flag register, F, which indicates conditions associated with the results of arithmetic or logic operations. The flags indicate zero, a carry-out of the high-order bit, the sign (most significant bit), parity, and auxiliary carry (carry-out of the fourth bit). *SEE DIGITAL COMPUTER PROGRAMMING.*

**Bit-sliced microprocessors.** Bit-sliced microprocessors achieve a high performance level which the

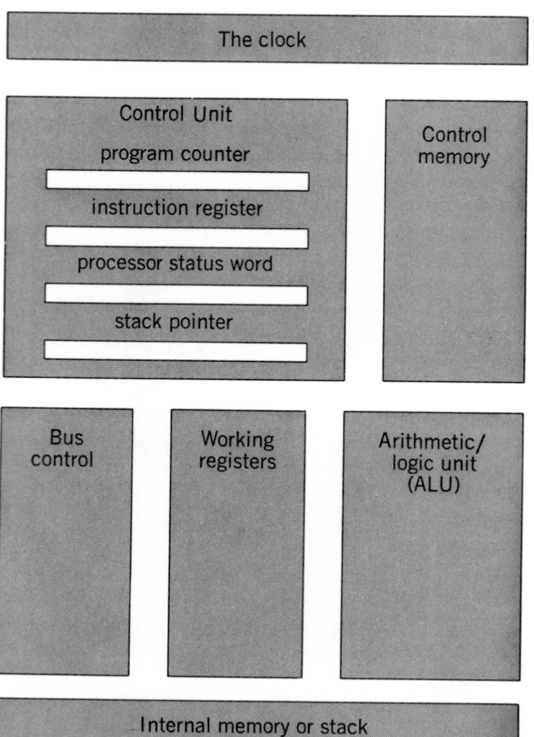


**Fig. 2. Components of a microprocessor.**

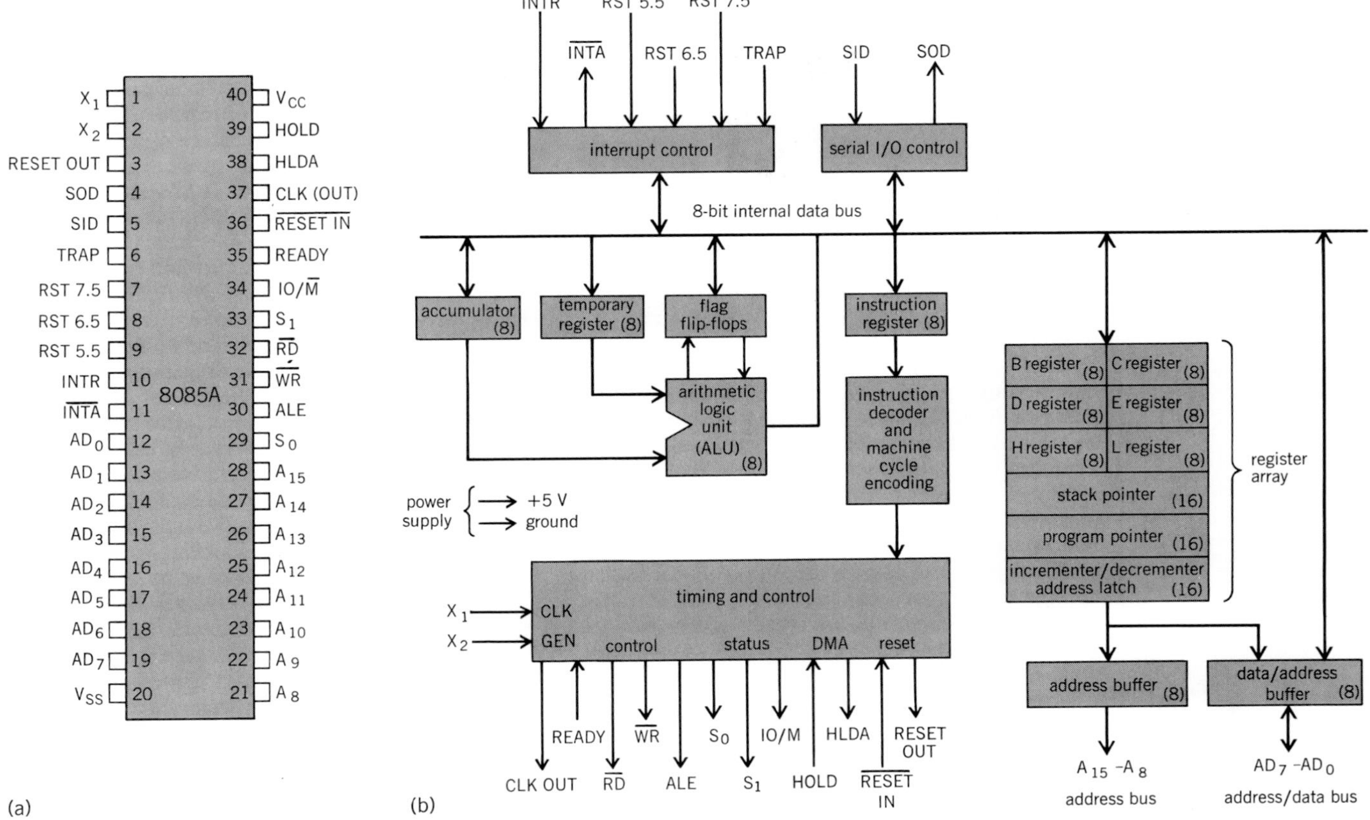


**Fig. 3. Intel 8085 microprocessor. (*a*) Pin configuration. (*b*) Block diagram. (*Intel Corp.*)**

single-chip microprocessors are unable to provide. The major logic of a central processor is partitioned into a set of large-scale-integration (LSI) devices as opposed to being placed on a single chip. The chip set is used as the basic building block to construct a microprogrammed central processor which can be configured in various ways. Unlike the single-chip microprocessor, several identical processor elements can be wired in parallel to achieve a desirable word length. The microprogrammed architecture allows the addition of new instructions without modifying the hardware wiring, and consequently provides a flexibility that is very desirable.

**Digital system design.** The main difference between the microprocessor digital system design and the hard-wired logic digital system design is that the former uses the microprocessor to replace hard-wired logic by storing program sequences in the read-only memory (ROM) rather than implementing these sequences with gates, flip-flops, counters, and so on. After the design is completed, any modifications or changes may be made by simply changing the program in the ROM. The microprocessor digital system design is now widely used because of the following advantages:

1. Manufacturing costs of industrial products can be significantly reduced.
2. Products can get to the market faster, providing a company with the opportunity to increase product sales and market share.
3. Product capability is enhanced, allowing manufacturers to provide customers with better products, which can frequently command a higher price in the marketplace.
4. Development costs and time are reduced.
5. Product reliability is increased, while both service and warranty costs are reduced. *See* SEMICONDUCTOR MEMORIES.

**Applications.** The list of possible application areas includes: industrial sequence controllers; machine tool controllers; point-of-sale terminals; intelligent terminals; instrument processors; traffic light controllers; weather data collection systems; and process controllers. *See* DIGITAL COMPUTER; INTEGRATED CIRCUITS; MICROCOMPUTER.

*Samuel C. Lee*

**Bibliography.** D. L. Cannon and G. Luecke, *Understanding Microprocessors*, 2d ed., 1984; S. Evanczuk, *Microprocessor Systems: Software, Hardware, and Architecture*, 1984; C. M. Gilmore, *Introduction to Microprocessors*, 1982; D. V. Hall, *Microprocessors and Digital Systems*, 2d ed., 1983; F. J. Hall, F. J. Hill and G. R. Peterson, *Digital Logic and Microprocessors*, 1984; B. S. Walkers, *Understanding Microprocessors*, 1981.

## Microwave

Electromagnetic energy with wavelengths ranging roughly from 0.3 to 30 cm (**Fig. 1**). In general, regions of the electromagnetic spectrum can be characterized by the types of low-loss transmission lines in common use to convey radiation from one point to another: Hollow rectangular or circular metal pipes, called waveguides, are used to transmit energy in the microwave region. At wavelengths longer than the microwave region, coaxial and twisted pairs of wires

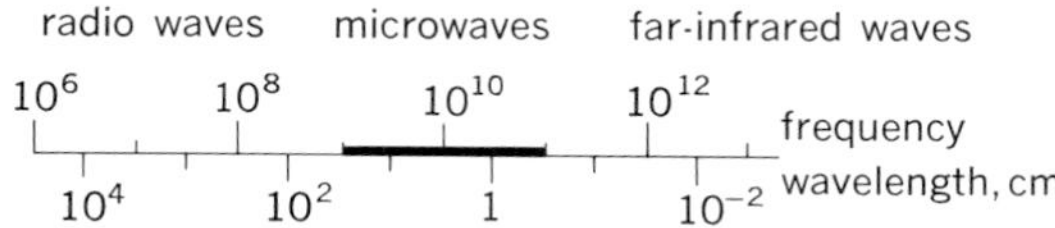


**Fig. 1. Portion of the electromagnetic spectrum, with microwave range indicated.**

are used, and at shorter wavelengths optical means are used. There are no sharp boundaries between the microwave region and these neighboring spectral regions. *SEE COAXIAL CABLE; ELECTROMAGNETIC WAVE TRANSMISSION; TRANSMISSION LINES.*

The frequencies and wavelengths corresponding to these spectral regions are shown in Fig. 1. Frequency, wavelength, and the velocity of electromagnetic propagation are related by Eq. (1), where $f$ is the fre-

$$f\lambda = v \qquad (1)$$

quency, $\lambda$ is the wavelength, and $v$ is the velocity of propagation. Both wavelength and velocity of propagation depend upon the physical properties of the transmission medium; only the frequency is invariant. Figure 1 is derived from this equation using the velocity of propagation in free space of $3 \times 10^{10}$ cm/s. In terms of frequency, the microwave region extends from about 1 to about 100 GHz. *SEE FREQUENCY (WAVE MOTION).*

**Development.** The early study of microwaves was only one phase of the developing knowledge of electromagretic waves in general. The existence of electromagnetic waves was predicted theoretically by James Clerk Maxwell in 1864 and proved experimentally by Heinrich Hertz in 1888. Maxwell formulated in mathematical terms—Maxwell's equations—the laws of physics which govern the behavior of electromagnetic phenomena. Practical development of microwave applications began in the 1930s, was accelerated by the substantial improvement in the performance of microwave generators in that decade, and took a great leap forward with the development of radar during World War II.

**Generation.** For most applications, microwaves are generated in electronic devices that produce tunable, single-frequency, continuous-wave (CW) oscillations, also called coherent oscillations: vacuum-tube generators include klystrons, magnetrons, and backward-wave oscillators; solid-state generators include tunnel diodes, Gunn diodes, IMPATT diodes, transistor oscillators, masers, and harmonic generators using varactor diodes. All of the solid-state generators and the backward-wave oscillator were developed after World War II. The vacuum-tube generators are used to produce higher powers, which can be as much as thousands of kilowatts. Solid-state generators were formerly limited in power to a few watts. By combining many transistors on a common substrate, powers of many tens of watts are obtained. *SEE BACKWARD-WAVE TUBE; GYROTRON; KLYSTRON; MAGNETRON; MICROWAVE SOLID-STATE DEVICES; MICROWAVE TUBE; TRAVELING-WAVE TUBE.*

For some applications, microwave noise is useful. This noise, generated in ordinary fluorescent light bulbs mounted in waveguides is uniform across a wide band of frequencies, and the power emitted is known accurately and is quite stable with respect to time. Generators of this type are used in measuring the noise performance of receivers and, after amplification to high power, as a jamming signal for radar and communication systems. Microwave noise is also generated by current passed through a solid-state diode. *SEE ELECTRICAL NOISE; MICROWAVE NOISE STANDARDS.*

**Circuit elements.** Physical elements which produce specific effects on microwaves are called circuit elements. Microwave circuit elements bear little resemblance to circuit elements at lower frequencies because the shorter wavelength leads to an entirely different method of transmitting microwaves from place to place within a system (**Fig. 2**).

***Waveguide.*** The most common method of microwave transmission within a system is through hollow circular or rectangular metal tubes of uniform cross section called waveguides. The microwave energy is confined within these tubes and guided along them.

In general, microwave energy is conveyed by an electromagnetic field whose components are the electric and magnetic intensities, denoted by $E$ and $H$ respectively. In a waveguide, only certain specific patterns of $E$ and $H$, known as modes, can exist. The exact nature of the modes is determined by Maxwell's equations and the boundary conditions; the latter consist of the cross-sectional dimensions and the electromagnetic properties of the waveguide. Two types of mode can exist in a hollow waveguide, the transverse electric (TE) and the transverse magnetic (TM) modes.

The cross-sectional dimensions of a waveguide determine a frequency and a corresponding free-space wavelength below which no transmission is possible for each mode; this is the cutoff frequency or wave-

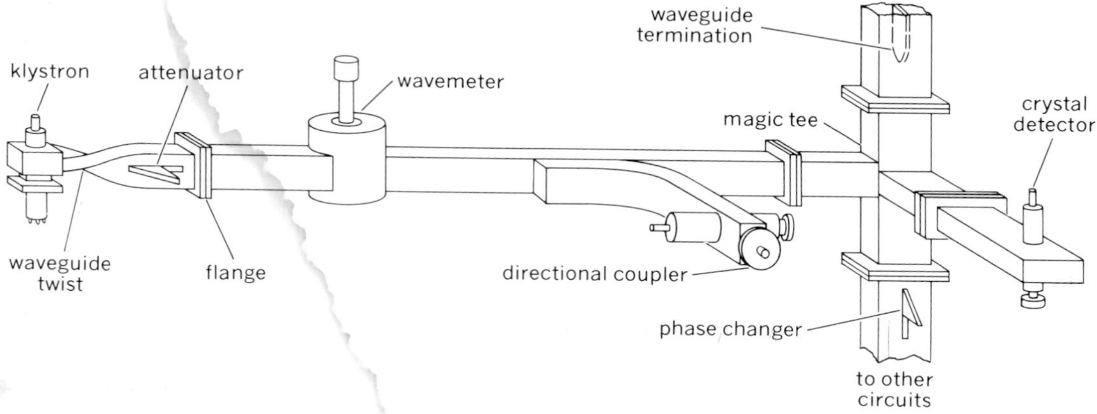


**Fig. 2. Sample microwave circuit illustrating some microwave components.**

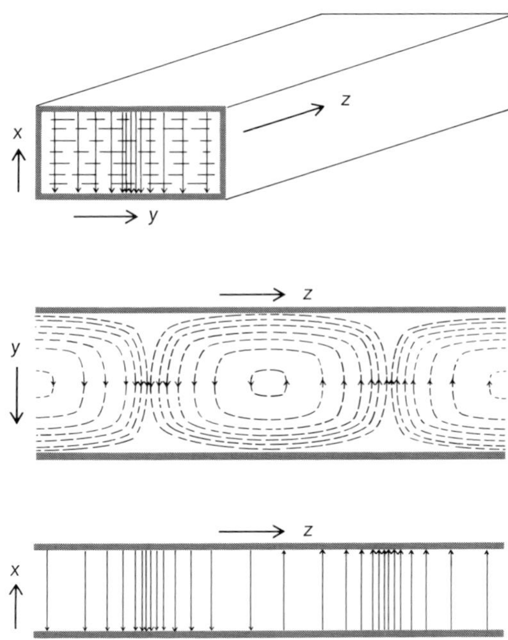


**Fig. 3. Instantaneous field pattern for the $TE_{01}$ wave in a rectangular waveguide. The wave propagates in the z direction. Solid lines indicate the electronic intensity *E*, and broken lines the magnetic intensity *H*.**

length. The mode which has the lowest cutoff frequency is called the dominant mode, and the other modes are called higher-order modes. In most applications, the waveguide dimensions are chosen so that transmission can occur only in the dominant mode, the other modes having cutoff frequencies well above the operating frequency. **Figure 3** illustrates the electric and magnetic intensities for the dominant TE mode in a rectangular waveguide.

Most waveguides are rectangular in cross section. They are used to carry microwaves between other circuit elements and as integral parts of other circuit elements such as attenuators and phase shifters. The points at which microwaves enter or leave a circuit element are called ports; a length of waveguide has two ports. *SEE MICROWAVE TRANSMISSION LINES; WAVEGUIDE.*

***Stripline.*** A stripline is a thin, narrow strip of metal placed a short distance above a metal ground plane, parallel to it, and separated by a thin strip of dielectric material. Microwaves are almost completely confined between the strip and the ground plane, and the transmission, like that in two-wire line, is via the transverse electromagnetic mode. A stripline is lossier than a waveguide, but it is smaller and cheaper, and several circuit elements can be constructed above a single ground plane. Any circuit element that can be built with a waveguide can also be built with a stripline.

***Microwave filter.*** Two vertical posts inside a waveguide and parallel to the electric field *E* form a resonant cavity when placed about one-half wavelength apart. Transmission through this cavity resembles transmission through a single-tuned circuit at lower frequencies; the output power is a maximum at the resonant frequency and falls off on either side. Cavities, arranged in sequence, form filters with frequency characteristics suitable for microwave systems. Cavities called wavemeters are also used to measure the frequency of a signal. *SEE CAVITY RESONATOR; ELECTRIC FILTER; WAVELENGTH MEASUREMENT; WAVEMETER.*

***Attenuator, phase shifter, and termination.*** A thin sheet of plastic can be used to alter the amplitude or phase of microwaves. If the sheet is coated with powdered carbon with appropriate electrical conductivity and placed in a waveguide with the lossy material parallel to the lines of electrical intensity, it will absorb microwave power. Variable attenuation can be achieved by mechanically inserting more or less of the lossy strip into the path of the wave. *SEE ATTENUATION (ELECTRICITY).*

A phase shifter changes the phase of a microwave without changing its amplitude. It can be constructed in the same manner as an attenuator without the lossy material.

An attenuator which has a very large loss and is closed at one end is called a termination; it absorbs all the power transmitted into it, reflecting none.

***Detector.*** The most common microwave detector is a silicon diode designed for high frequencies and mounted in a waveguide or a stripline. One terminal of the diode is connected to the waveguide, and the other is connected to a wire post, which is parallel to the direction of the electric field *E* and and brought out of the waveguide through a small hole. The diode rectifies the microwave signal, producing an average current which can be indicated by a direct-current meter connected between the diode terminals; a typical diode detector produces a current of approximately 1 mA for a microwave power input of 1 mW. If the microwave signal is modulated in amplitude, the modulation will appear in the output current. *SEE AMPLITUDE MODULATION; SEMICONDUCTOR DIODE.*

The bolometer is a detector which absorbs microwave power, causing a temperature increase and a corresponding change in resistance. The bolometer does not respond fast enough to detect modulation. It is often used as one arm of a resistance bridge circuit in microwave power meters. *SEE DETECTOR; MICROWAVE POWER MEASUREMENT.*

***Antenna.*** A transmitting antenna takes microwave power from a waveguide and converts it into a plane wave that propagates through space to a distant receiving antenna. Two important characteristies of antennas are efficiency and directivity, efficiency being the ratio of the power delivered into space to the power available in the waveguide. High directivity is accomplished by large antennas which focus the microwave energy in the same way a searchlight focuses a beam of light. In the parabolic antenna, a small waveguide feed horn (**Fig. 4**) illuminates a large paraboloidal dish which concentrates the energy in a narrow angular beam. In the horn-reflector antenna, a waveguide is expanded into a horn to illuminate a large paraboloidal surface (**Fig. 5**) which reflects the microwave energy in a narrow angular beam in the direction shown. Directivity is described by the beam width *W* of an antenna which is approximately given in radians by Eq. (2), where $\lambda$ is the wavelength and

$$W = \lambda/D \tag{2}$$

*D* is the dimension of the antenna aperture. For circular antennas, *D* is the diameter. For rectangular antennas, *D* is either dimension, the beamwidth applying in the plane of the dimension. Directivity is also related to the gain of the antenna, which is the ratio of the power received at a distant receiver to the power that would be received if the transmitted power

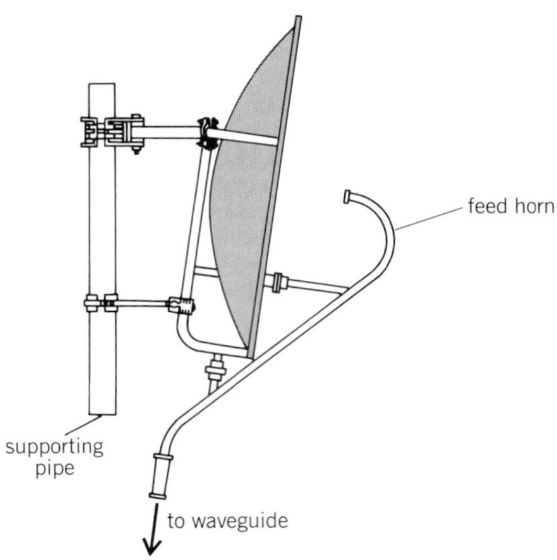


**Fig. 4. Parabolic microwave antenna. (*After K. L. Dumas and L. G. Sands, Microwave Systems Planning, Hayden Book Co., 1967*)**

were radiated from an antenna with a uniform spherical pattern. Most microwave applications require highly directive antennas; gains of several thousand are not unusual, corresponding to beamwidths ranging from a fraction of a degree to several degrees.

When receiving, an antenna intercepts power from the incident microwave proportional to the area of the antenna aperture. The gain and directivity of an antenna are the same whether it is used to transmit or receive. Efficiency of large antennas ranges from 50% to nearly 100%. SEE ANTENNA.

***Gyrator, circulator, and isolator.*** In 1948 B. D. H. Tellegen introduced the gyrator, a lossless, nonreciprocal, two-port circuit which has 180° more phase shift in one direction than in the other. This principle is used in the broadband microwave circulator. The three-port circulator has the property that all the power into port 1 exits at port 2, all the power into port 2 exits at port 3, and all the power into port 3 exits at port 1 (**Fig. 6**). The nonreciprocal phase shift is achieved in a magnetic ferrite placed in the waveguide junction and magnetized with an external permanent magnet. An isolator is a circulator with one port terminated, resulting in a circuit which transmits power in one direction and not the other. The input circuit is thus isolated from the output circuit. When the terminated port is internal, the isolator appears to be a two-port element. SEE GYRATOR.

**Varactor.** This is a solid-state diode whose capacitance changes with applied voltage. Varactors are used as harmonic generators to obtain microwave power efficiently from lower-frequency sources such as quartz crystal–controlled oscillators in the 10–100-MHz range. Varactors are also used in up-converters and down-converters performing the same functions as similar circuits using resistive diodes, but more efficiently and at the expense of narrower bandwith. SEE OSCILLATOR.

***Amplifier.*** A microwave amplifier converts a low-power input signal to a higher-power output signal while preserving one or more characteristics. A linear amplifier preserves the amplitude, frequency, and phase of the input signal. When a linear amplifier is overloaded, it becomes saturated: the output amplitude tends to remain constant, and only the phase and frequency of the input signal is preserved.

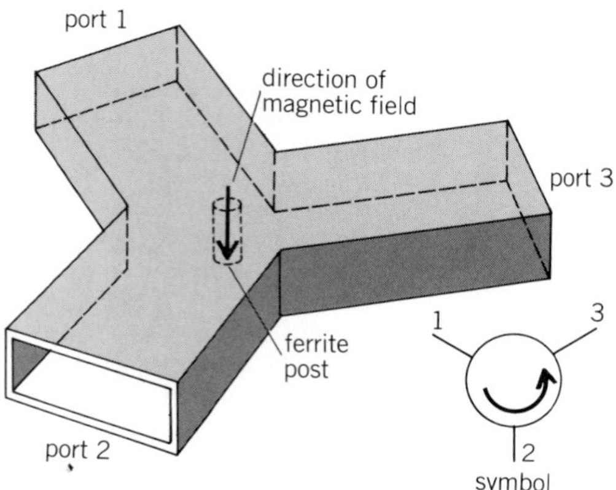


**Fig. 6. Microwave circulator. (*After G. J. Wheeler, Introduction to Microwaves, Prentice-Hall, 1963*)**

In an injection-locked–oscillator amplifier, a high-amplitude oscillator is locked in phase and frequency to a low-amplitude input signal coupled into the oscillator circuit. The output of the oscillator is unaffected by the input signal; therefore only the phase and frequency of this type of amplifier are preserved.

High power output is achieved with klystron and traveling-wave tube (TWT) amplifiers, both of which can be operated in the linear or saturated modes; the traveling-wave tube amplifier has the larger bandwidth, and the klystron has the higher power. Moderate power can be achieved with transistor amplifiers at frequencies up to about 20 GHz in the linear or saturated modes. At higher frequencies, solid-state oscillators such as the IMPATT diode can be operated as injection-locked oscillator amplifiers in the saturated mode. These are one-port amplifiers, the ouput power emerging from the input port, and a circulator is used to convert them into two-port amplifiers.

Very low noise levels are achieved in the maser and the parametric amplifier, both of which require power at a single frequency to pump the active element. In the maser, energy is pumped from one atomic level to another, and in the parametric amplifier a varactor is driven by the pumping signal to pro-

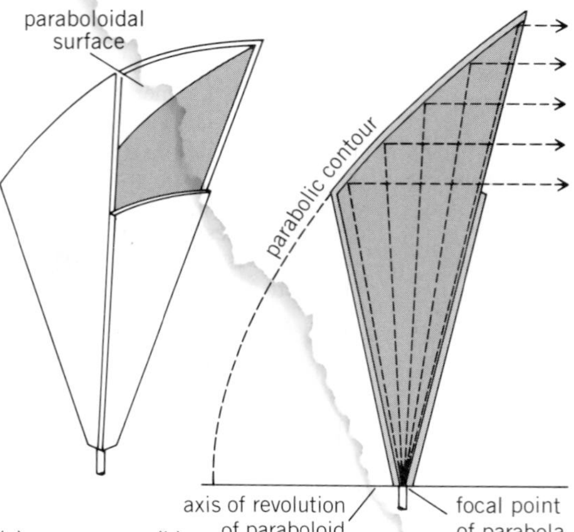


**Fig. 5. Horn-reflector antenna. (*a*) Oblique view. (*b*) Cross section. (*After S. A. Schelkunoff and H. T. Friis, Antenna Theory and Practice, John Wiley and Sons, 1952*)**

vide the nonlinear capacitance required for amplification. SEE MASER; PARAMETRIC AMPLIFIER.

***Monolithic microwave integrated circuits.*** Microwave circuit elements are beginning to be built on semiconductor chips similar in size to those used for computer circuits. An amplifier with a frequency response from 2 to 18 GHz has been built by using the semiconductor Gallium arsenide (GaAs). This amplifier has a gain of 25 dB, a power output of 50 mW, and automatic gain control. It occupies a space of 0.5 × 0.2 × 0.015 in. (13 × 5.1 × 0.38 mm). Another amplifier, which has a bandwidth of 12 GHz and a power output of 25 milliwatts, has an area of 0.02 × 0.04 in. (0.5 × 1.0 mm). SEE INTEGRATED CIRCUITS.

**Polarization.** An important property of a microwave is its polarization, the direction of its electric field $E$ with respect to a fixed plane. A microwave transmitted parallel to the Earth is said to be vertically polarized if $E$ is perpendicular to the Earth's surface. Two superimposed waves of the same frequency and magnitude, and in both time and phase quadrature, result in a circularly polarized wave in which the electric field direction rotates either clockwise or counterclockwise.

Circuit elements can be constructed whose effect is polarization-sensitive. For example, closely spaced, vertical wires in a plane normal to the direction of a wave will completely reflect a vertically polarized wave and pass, without modification, a horizontally polarized wave.

**Microwave receiver.** The most simple microwave receiver is a silicon diode detector followed by an amplifier; amplitude modulation on the input signal is detected directly and amplified to a suitable level. This receiver is insensitive and noisy and cannot be used with frequency or phase modulation. SEE FREQUENCY MODULATION; MODULATION; PHASE MODULATION.

The first active element in nearly all microwave receivers is a silicon diode operated as a down-converter. In this type of receiver, a strong, continuous-wave local oscillator signal is used to pump the diode over its nonlinear resistance range. In this manner, the local oscillator and the input signal are multiplied, shifting the input signal down to an intermediate frequency (i-f), which is the difference between the frequencies of the local oscillator signal and the received signal. Intermediate frequencies of a few tens of megahertz are common. Frequency, phase, or amplitude modulation on the received signal appears in the detector output at the intermediate frequency. A band-pass intermediate-frequency amplifier, providing most of the gain of the receiver, follows the detector, after which a demodulator converts the modulation on the intermediate-frequency signal to usable form, for example, an audio or a television signal. SEE RADIO RECEIVER.

If extremely low-noise performance is required, the first active component is a maser or a parametric amplifier. These are expensive and are not required in most applications.

**Microwave transmitter.** The main components of a microwave transmitter are a microwave power source, a modulator, and, if necessary, a power amplifier. Among the vacuum-tube power sources, the reflex klystron and the backward-wave oscillator are frequency-modulated, and the magnetron is pulse amplitude-modulated, by a signal on an electrode. In solid-state transmitters, by contrast, the modulator is usually separate from the continuous-wave power source. The modulation can be done directly at microwave frequencies or it can be performed at intermediate frequency and shifted to the microwave frequency in an up-converter, which is very much like a down-converter. A common frequency modulator consists of an intermediate-frequency oscillator tuned by the modulation signal applied to a varactor. SEE PULSE MODULATION.

The power amplifier can be a klystron or traveling-wave tube when higher powers are required. For solid-state transmitters, transistor or injection-locked-oscillator amplifiers are common.

**Microwave propagation.** In free space, microwaves travel in straight lines as do optical waves. Near the Earth, however, the atmosphere has an index of refraction which normally decreases with distance above the Earth and causes the wave to travel in a circular path which bends slightly toward the Earth. The radius of the circular path is larger than the radius of the Earth so normally a wave traveling above the surface of the Earth and parallel to it will not intercept the Earth even though it bends slightly toward it. Microwaves are reflected and refracted by objects just as are optical waves. SEE MICROWAVE OPTICS.

Occasionally during the summer, atmospheric conditions exist which cause microwaves transmitted from an antenna to travel to a receiver via two or more paths. These waves interfere at the receiver and may cause large decreases in the received signal amplitude with a resulting system failure. This phenomenon, called multipath fading, is a serious problem in microwave transmission parallel to the surface of the Earth. Other atmospheric conditions exist which cause the microwave to bend away from the Earth and miss the receiver entirely. This problem is solved by placing the transmitting and receiving antennas on tall towers; the wave initially heads toward the Earth, bends away before intercepting the Earth, and reaches the receiver if it is high enough. If the towers are not sufficiently high, the wave is intercepted by the Earth, resulting in what is known as earth-bulge fading. When microwaves are directed well above the horizon, neither of these two problems occurs. Thus satellite microwave systems do not suffer from either multipath or earth-bulge fading.

At frequencies above about 10 GHz, rain absorbs microwave energy, resulting in large signal losses. Both satellite and point-to-point microwave systems are seriously affected by rain attenuation.

For most frequencies the attenuation of microwaves by the Earth's atmosphere is very small. There are, however, bands of frequencies for which the loss is higher due to molecular absorption. Attenuation due to water vapor occurs in several bands, the first one appearing at about 30 GHz. A larger attenuation, due to oxygen absorption, occurs at 60 GHz.

**Applications of microwaves.** Areas in which microwave radiation is applied include radar, communications, radiometry, medicine, physics, chemistry, and cooking food.

***Radar.*** This is an acronym for radio detection and ranging. In one form a pulse of electromagnetic energy is transmitted in a narrow beam toward a target, and part of the energy is reflected to the receiver. The time difference between the transmitted and received pulses provides the distance to the target, and the direction of the antenna beam provides the target's direction. Radar is used in military applications, remote sensing of the atmosphere, and astronomy.

The high antenna directivity and the excellent propagation characteristics of microwaves in the atmosphere make this the preferred band for radar applications. Radars in the microwave band have the best combination of range and resolving power. *See* Radar.

***Communications.*** There is 100 times as much frequency space available for communications in the microwave band as in the entire spectrum below microwaves, which includes AM and FM broadcasting, television, low-frequency and high-frequency radio communication, mobile radio, amateur radio, and citizen's band radio. In addition, the high directivity obtainable at microwave frequencies allows reuse of these frequencies many times in the same area, practice not possible at lower frequencies. The high directivity also makes possible communication to satellites and deep-space probes.

Most Western countries are crisscrossed with microwave point-to-point communications systems carrying telephone and television signals. A single microwave channel with one modulated frequency typically carries thousands of telephone signals or one television signal, and a system will have from one to more than a dozen channels. The microwave signals are periodically picked up and rebroadcast by repeaters mounted on towers that are spaced from a few miles to a few tens of miles depending upon the frequency, the prevailing weather conditions, and the terrain. A repeater consists of a receiver followed by a transmitter for each microwave channel. Systems operate from the low microwave range up about 40 GHz.

Many countries have microwave communication satellites. These resemble point-to-point systems, but higher transmitter power, larger ground station antennas, and low-noise amplifiers are required to bridge the great distance between the Earth and the satellite. Most satellite systems operate at frequencies between 4 and 12 GHz.

Communication between the Earth and deep space probes is accomplished with microwaves because of the great antenna directivity and receiver sensitivity that can be achieved at microwave frequencies. Signals of very narrow bandwidth must be used to reach the great distances required.

***Radiometry.*** All objects, including liquids and gases, emit electromagnetic radiation in the form of noise, the amount of the noise being proportional to the absolute temperature of the object. A noise temperature $T$ can be assigned to the object corresponding to the amount of noise radiating from it. The determination of the noise temperatures of selected noise sources, including background radiation from outer space, rain, clouds, stars, and the Earth, is called radiometry.

A microwave radiometer is a sensitive receiver which measures the noise power received by an antenna; from this measurement, the noise temperature of the source object can be determined. The noise powers measured are so small that receivers with very high gain are required, and the accuracy of the measurements is severely limited by small time variations in the gain. R. H. Dicke solved this problem in 1946 by switching the receiver input between the antenna and a reference noise source at a rate faster than the gain changes in the amplifier. The detected output of the receiver is also switched synchronously at the same rate resulting in two output signals, one due to the noise received by the antenna and the other to the reference noise source. These two signals are subtracted to form an output signal proportional to the difference in the input noise temperatures. The reference noise power can then be adjusted until the output signal is zero, indicating the received noise power is equal to the known reference noise power.

Radiometers are used extensively for remote sensing. Atmospheric temperature, water vapor density over oceans, soil moisture content, and the liquid water content of clouds can be determined from radiometer measurements, some of which are made from satellites. Microwave radiometers are used to study astronomical sources of noise and to observe planets from deep space probes. *See* Passive radar.

***Physiological effects.*** Exposure to microwave power of 100 mW/cm$^2$ for several minutes can lead to pathophysiologic effects in laboratory animals. The microwaves penetrate beneath the skin and heat the tissue, and tissue destruction can result if the temperature rise is faster than the control mechanisms of the body can handle. It is assumed that human tissue reacts to microwave exposure in the same manner, and safety standards have been proposed. In the United States the maximum recommended exposure is 10 mW/cm$^2$ for durations greater than 6 min. In the Soviet Union the maximum recommended exposure is much less, illustrating the controversy in this subject.

Applications of mcrowaves in medicine include: (1) thermography, the measurement of tissue temperature (cancer causes a temperature rise of about 2°F or 1°C which can be detected with a microwave radiometer); (2) hyperthermia, microwave heating used in the treatment of cancer and in the treatment of hypothermic subjects; and (3) biomedical imaging, the use of microwaves to study the structure of tissue beneath the skin.

***Physics and chemistry.*** Microwave energy is used in large particle accelerators to accelerate charged particles such as electrons and protons to very high energies and cause them to collide. From experiments of this type, knowledge of the binding forces of the particles and of matter is obtained.

Knowledge of the structure of matter is also obtained from microwave spectroscopy, which is used to study the frequencies and amplitudes of the microwave resonances of molecules. Microwaves are also used in the study of the crystal structure.

***Microwave oven.*** Several hundred watts of microwave power at about 3 GHz are used in microwave ovens to cook food. The microwaves are absorbed throughout the food, heating it more or less uniformly throughout, instead of from the outside as occurs in more conventional ovens, with the result that the cooking is faster. Metal containers must not be used because they shield the microwaves from the food and prevent cooking.

**Beyond microwaves.** Applications of electromagnetic radiation in the millimeter-wave region, which extends from about 100 to about 300 GHz, are much like those in the microwave region. Beyond this range, and throughout the long infrared wavelengths, suitable power for many of these applications is not available.

At the shorter infrared wavelengths and in the visible optical range, the light-emitting diode (LED) and the laser provide the power, and solid-state detectors the necessary efficiency, for communication and other applications. Optical communication (including the infrared) is feasible through the atmosphere but is seriously affected by fog, haze, rain, and snow. The advent of the optical fiber has greatly accelerated the application of these wavelengths to communications. Fibers are made from glass, are as small as a human hair, and can be made very low loss, a few decibels per kilometer. Transmission through fibers is unaffected by atmospheric conditions. The communication capacity of an optical fiber system can be very large: as many as 1 billion pulses per second can be transmitted over a single fiber. Optical fiber systems have been built for use inside buildings, between cities, and across oceans. SEE JUNCTION DIODE; LASER; LIGHT-EMITTING DIODE; OPTICAL COMMUNICATIONS; OPTICAL DETECTORS.

*Clyde L. Ruthroff*

**Bibliography.** K. C. Gupta, *Microwaves*, 1980; J. Helszajn, *Passive and Active Microwave Circuits*, 1978; Joint special issue on monolithic microwave IC's, *IEEE Transactions on Electron Devices*, vol. ED-31, no. 12, and *IEEE Transactions on Microwave Theory and Techniques*, vol. MTT-31, no. 12, December 1984; S. Liao, *Microwave Devices and Circuits*, 1980; R. F. Soohoo, *Microwave Electroncs*, 1971; F. T. Ulaby, R. K. Moore, and A. K. Fung, *Microwave Remote Sensing: Active and Passive*, 1981.

## Microwave free-field standards

The means for setting up electromagnetic fields of precisely determined intensity at microwave frequencies in unbounded regions of space. Such standards are used to evaluate field probes and antennas for measuring field strength and power density. The standardization of these devices is necessary before they are used for determining the performance of radar and communications systems or for assessing such systems for health and safety risks or electromagnetic compatibility. SEE MICROWAVE.

**Near fields and far fields.** An electromagnetic field can be launched into an unbounded region by applying an oscillating voltage or current to a radiating structure or antenna. The energy radiating from an antenna passes through several distinct stages before the final pattern emerges. The true near field comprises induction and static fields which decrease in magnitude as the inverse-squared and inverse-cubed of distance $R$ respectively; they thus become negligibly small a few wavelengths from the antenna and are rarely significant in practice. The radiated field decreases in intensity as the inverse of distance and thus becomes predominant beyond a few wavelengths. SEE ANTENNA.

Radiating antennas carry alternating currents which can be thought of as an array of monochromatic sources spread over the structure according to the Huygens-Fresnel principle, and these sources will give rise to elemental wavefronts which arrive at a point distant from the antenna with phases which impose an interference-type pattern on the wavefront, those at the extremities of the structure having the greatest phase differences. The complex wavefront is obtained by the superposition of these elementary wavelets. The distance at which a 90° phase shift obtains on the elemental wavefronts is known as the Rayleigh distance, and is equal to $D^2/2\lambda$ where $D$ is the maximum aperture dimension and $\lambda$ the wavelength of the radiation. The region of the field within this distance is the radiated near field, and because of its complex nature it is commonplace free-field measurement practice to use $2D^2/\lambda$ as a minimum working distance for antenna measurements. However, even at this distance the path phase differences are 22.5° and the power density, being proportional to $1/R^2$, is accurate only to 5%. For 1% uncertainty the required separation is at least $10D^2/\lambda$.

**Standard antennas.** Antennas used in free-field standards are usually either half-wave dipoles or waveguide horns.

***Half-wave dipole.*** The half-wave dipole is a collinear device with a length of approximately one-half of the free-space wavelength of the radiated wave. The radiation pattern is doughnut-shaped and symmetrical about the axis of the dipole. The gain of a simple dipole can be shown to be 2.16 dB.

***Waveguide horns.*** An open-ended waveguide will radiate effectively and, as the aperture dimensions are comparable with the wavelength, its pattern is very broad; an open-ended waveguide has a power gain of about 6 dB. Flaring the aperture decreases the beamwidth and results in a pyramidal horn. Horns can be made with gains ranging from about 8 to about 30 dB, depending on frequency and acceptable size. The gain and pattern characteristics of a pyramidal horn can be calculated to accuracies of about ±0.2 dB; however, the reflections at the throat and aperture discontinuities significantly influence the gain-frequency characteristic and calibration is usually necessary. SEE WAVEGUIDE.

**Free-field measuring sites.** The ideal environment for making measurements on antennas is a large unobstructed volume which is free of reflecting objects and electromagnetically interfering signals—that is, a free-space condition.

***Anechoic chambers.*** A practical solution is to use an anechoic chamber to set up simulated free-space conditions in a bounded environment. Low reflection of electromagnetic signals from the walls of such a chamber is achieved by the use of an electromagnetic-wave absorbent layer covering all of the reflecting surfaces within the room or chamber, the outer shell of which is a metallic structure to give shielding against interfering signals encroaching on the test region.

Anechoic chambers can be of rectangular or tapered form. For rectangular chambers the width of the chamber is ideally chosen so that the angle of incidence for the reflected ray from the side wall is of the order of 70° or less. The receiving antenna is placed about half the width of the chamber from the back wall so that coupling to the back wall absorbers is minimal. These considerations suggest an optimum length-to-width (and height) ratio of about 3:1. The "tapered" anechoic chamber consists of a pyramidal tapered anechoic section joined to a cubical anechoic section and is an alternative construction suitable for some antenna measurements. The tapered section may be thought of as a large horn antenna terminating in a large waveguide in which a single mode in the form of a plane wave is to be generated.

The size of field strength monitor or antenna which can be measured in an anechoic chamber is determined by the size, and shape, of its quiet zone, which is the volume in which the reflections from the internal surfaces of the chamber are below a specified acceptable signal level compared to the direct radiated

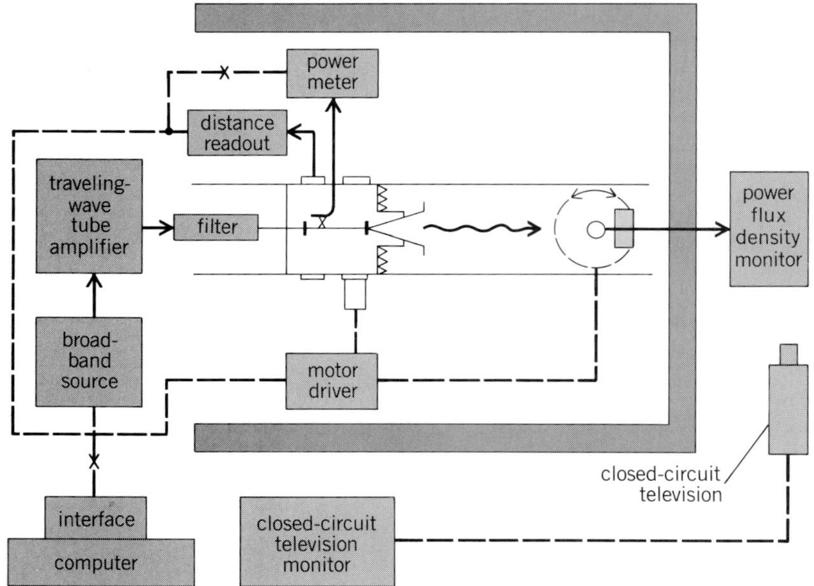


**Fig. 1. Microwave free-field calibration system.**

value of the field. The measure of the quiet-zone performance, the reflectivity, will vary with position in the zone as well with frequency. For antenna measurements using pseudo-far-field methods the quiet zone needs to be as long as possible with respect to the operating wavelength; this is in order for the separation between receiving and transmitting antennas to be at least equal to several Rayleigh distances at the lowest operating frequency. For normal pattern measurements a reflectivity level of −40 db in the quiet zone is acceptable; for high-precision gain measurements, with uncertainties of 0.1 dB, −50 dB reflectivity is necessary.

For near-field scanning applications, in which the sampling or detecting probe scans within a few wavelengths of the test antenna, interfering reflections and resonances from the environment which may contaminate the test region can be controlled with a fairly modest application of electromagnetic absorber materials.

***Open field sites.*** Clear open sites can be used at low frequencies, or for high-gain antennas where far-field measurements require such large distances that enclosed or anechoic environments are impractical. The horizontal plane can be readily made free of obstruction, as can the upward vertical plane. However, since electromagnetic waves are strongly reflected by a ground plane, this effect must be accommodated, and one of two courses can be adopted. One is to do measurements as far above the ground as possible. The alternative is to make use of the ground plane by working close to it—if necessary, enhancing its reflection with a metal ground plane or grid—and by making allowance for the reflection in the analysis of performance.

**Measurements on antennas.** Probably the single most important parameter of a standard antenna, when considered for metrological applications, is the boresight or maximum gain, and a number of methods of determining this parameter have been devised.

***Three-antenna method.*** The basis of this method is a measurement of the transmission between two polarization-matched antennas (1 and 2), which is expressible in terms of the antenna gains by the Friis formula, Eq. (1), where $P_t$ and $P_r$ are the transmitted and

$$P_r = P_t G_1 G_2 (\lambda/4\pi D)^2 \quad (1)$$

received powers, $\lambda$ the wavelength, and $D$ the separation. Only the product of the gains can be obtained; however, with three antennas the measured combinations will yield the gain of each antenna uniquely. Small corrections are required due to imperfect matching in the waveguide systems.

***Extrapolation method.*** The extrapolation technique is probably the most accurate method known for determining absolute gain and polarization. The method is one of determining the transmission characteristic between two antennas as the transmission path is increased through about 4 to 10 Rayleigh distances. With good metrology it is possible to get a sufficiently accurate characterization to allow extrapolation to the true far-field range.

***Near-field scanning.*** Antenna metrology has increasingly concentrated on near-field techniques with the objective of improving antenna characterization, particularly at very high (VHF) and ultrahigh (UHF) frequencies where the lack of low-reflectivity far-field ranges has been acute. In this method a probe antenna is used to sample the magnitude and phase, for orthogonal polarizations, of the radiated fields over a well-defined surface, which can be a plane, a cylinder, or a sphere, a few wavelengths from the antenna under test. The objective of the near-field to far-field technique is to mathematically transform the data determined in the near field into the required far-field properties. For a large antenna the number of samples required to define the near field adequately can be large enough to require substantial measurement and computational time. The features of the technique are that complete characteristics can be obtained for any distance, near-field or far-field, for the test antenna and that measurements may be made indoors as close as desired to the antenna in a simple anechoic environment.

**Calibration.** The essential requirement for the calibration of devices for measuring power flux density or field strength is the creation of a substantially plane wave of known power density which encompasses the effective aperture of the device to be tested. This is effected by launching a known power through an antenna or transverse-electromagnetic (TEM) cell of

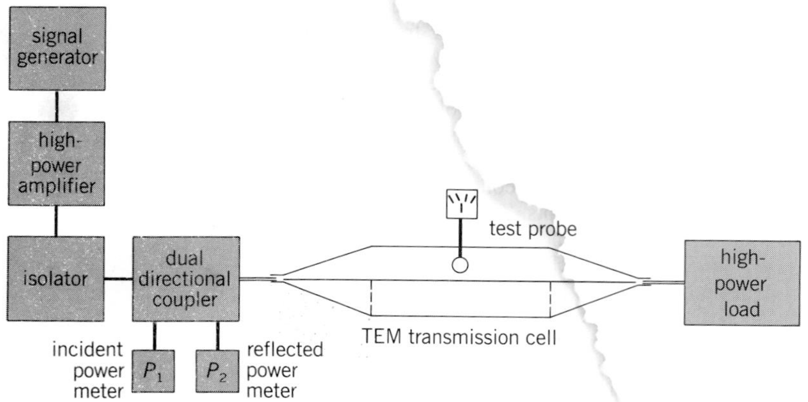


**Fig. 2. Guided-wave test facility based on Crawford transverse-electromagnetic (TEM) cell.**

known characteristics and calculating the field strength or power density from the appropriate equation. The techniques used fall into two groups which are conveniently divided by frequency.

***Frequencies above 500 MHz.*** At frequencies above a nominal 500 MHz the conventional technique for calibrating power density or field monitors is to set up a standard field in an anechoic space and position the probe at some prescribed position in front of the waveguide horn.

A practical system for setting up standard fields or power densities involves a small anechoic chamber (**Fig. 1**) about 15 ft (5 m) long, lined on five sides with electromagnetic absorber. One end is left open for access to the generating and measuring systems. The microwave signal is generated by a broadband signal generator operating into a traveling-wave-tube power amplifier. The output of the latter is filtered to remove spurious harmonics and linked to the monitoring coupler and power meter combination and output (horn) antenna by a low-loss coaxial cable. The instrument under test is mounted on a low-loss dielectric pedestal which is positioned about 3 ft (1 m) from the end wall of the chamber and on the axis of the radiating antenna, which places the test probe in the quiet zone. A computer can be used to control the measurement process and apply corrections. The uncertainties associated with this measurement are about 0.3 dB (equivalent to about 7%). *SEE SIGNAL GENERATOR; TRAVELING-WAVE TUBE.*

***Frequencies below 500 MHz.*** The Crawford transverse-electromagnetic transmission cell is commonly used for setting up radio-frequency fields. This consists of a transmission line with a rectangular outer conductor, 1.5–3 ft (0.5–1 m) in size, and an inner conductor in the form of a flat plate or septum (**Fig. 2**). The input and output ends are tapered so as to form a transition to a conventional coaxial cable. The wave within the cell is essentially plane and can be made to have free-space impedance by proper choice of width and height dimensions. The field distribution within the cell, and thus its uniformity, can be calculated. The electric field within the working area is given approximately by dividing the voltage between the plates by the separation of the plates. The voltage is determined by calculation from the power $P$ transmitted through the cell divided by the line impedance $Z$ (equal to 50 ohms). The power density is then expressed by Eq. (2), where $Z_0$ is the impedance of free

$$\text{Power density} = PZ_0/b^2Z \quad \text{W/m}^2 \qquad (2)$$

space (376.7 ohms) and $b$ is the separation of the plates. The uncertainties associated with transverse-electromagnetic cell measurements are of the order of 0.5 to dB. *SEE COAXIAL CABLE.*

The upper limit to the operating frequency range of transverse-electromagnetic cells is determined by resonances within the cell; also, it is not good practice to more than half fill the gap between the plates. As a consequence, the larger the test object, the larger must be the cell, and thus the lower its maximum frequency. This problem can be reduced to some extent by placing electromagnetic absorber material in the cell, but this expedient renders the cell suitable for comparison purposes only.

*Ralph W. Yell*

***Bibliography.*** M. L. Crawford, Generation of standard EM fields using TEM transmission cells, *IEEE Trans. EMC*, 16:189–195, 1974; Institute of Electrical and Electronics Engineers, *IEEE Standard Test Procedures for Antennas,* ANSI IEEE Std. 149–1979, 1979; W. H. Kummer and E. C. Gillespie, Antenna measurements, *Proc. IEEE*, 66:483–507, 1978; A. W. Rudge et al., *The Handbook of Antenna Design*.

## Microwave impedance measurement

The determination of parameters, associated with microwave propagation in transmission lines or waveguides, which are generalizations of the impedance concept at lower frequencies and are derived from ratios of complex electric or magnetic field amplitudes.

As an outgrowth of popular usage the term impedance measurement, at microwave frequencies, has acquired a more general interpretation than the one associated with it at lower frequencies. Throughout the lower portion of the radio frequency spectrum, impedance is generally defined as the (complex) ratio between voltage and current. Although the low-frequency concepts of voltage and current can be generalized in such a way as to be useful in the microwave region, the almost universal practice is to use the scattering description. Instead of voltage and current, the basic parameters are now the complex electric- or magnetic-field traveling-wave amplitudes in the (assumed) uniform transmission line or waveguide by which the components of interest are interconnected. The coaxial transmission line and rectangular waveguide (where the center conductor is absent) are common examples. *SEE ALTERNATING-CURRENT CIRCUIT THEORY; COAXIAL CABLE; ELECTRICAL IMPEDANCE; MICROWAVE TRANSMISSION LINES; TRANSMISSION LINES; WAVEGUIDE.*

For a given transmission line or waveguide, there is a preferred band of operating frequencies throughout which the solution of Maxwell's equations is given by a pair of complex numbers $a$ and $b$ which represent the electric or magnetic traveling-wave amplitudes to the left and right (**Fig. 1**). Let a voltage $v$ and current $i$ be defined by Eqs. (1) and (2), where

$$v = b + a \qquad (1)$$

$$i = (b - a)/Z_0 \qquad (2)$$

$Z_0$ is a property of the transmission line, called characteristic impedance. These definitions of voltage and current are consistent with the ones in common use at lower frequencies. Obviously, Eqs. (1) and (2) can be solved for $a$ and $b$ in terms of $v$ and $i$ so that the information content is the same in either description; the mode of expression, however, is different.

As a counterpart to the lower-frequency definition of impedance (the complex ratio of $v$ to $i$), a reflection coefficient (which is usually represented by the Greek letter Γ) can now be defined as the complex ratio

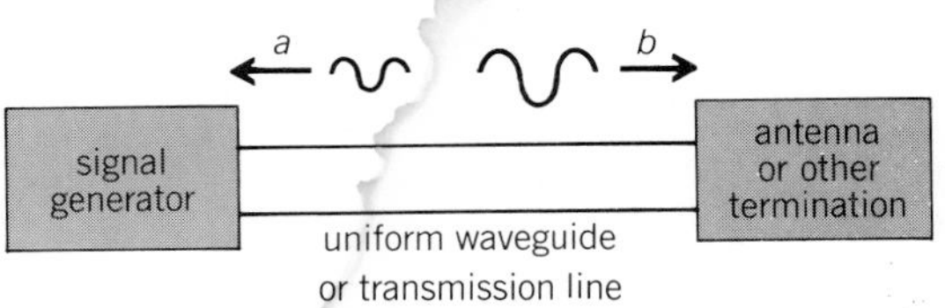


**Fig. 1. Microwave system, with complex traveling-wave amplitudes *a* and *b* that are generally used to describe the electric and magnetic fields.**

given by Eq. (3). The measurement of reflection coef-

$$\Gamma = \frac{a}{b} \quad (3)$$

ficient is usually included if not primarily implied by the term impedance measurement at microwave frequencies. In its more restricted definition, the impedance $Z$ is given by the ratio of Eqs. (1) and (2). From here it is easy to show that Eqs. (4) and (5) are valid.

$$\Gamma = \frac{Z - Z_0}{Z + Z_0} \quad (4)$$

$$Z = Z_0 \frac{1 + \Gamma}{1 - \Gamma} \quad (5)$$

**Scattering parameters.** Linear electrical circuits can be completely characterized by parameters measured at the input and output ports. Several different parameter sets can be used. At low frequencies, $h$, $y$, and $z$ parameters are frequently encountered; for example, the network shown in **Fig. 2***a* can be characterized by $y$ parameters by using Eqs. (6) and (7),

$$i_1 = y_{11}v_1 + y_{12}v_2 \quad (6)$$

$$i_2 = y_{21}v_1 + y_{22}v_2 \quad (7)$$

where $v_1$ and $v_2$ are the voltages across the input and output ports respectively and $i_1$ and $i_2$ denote the currents entering the network. SEE NETWORK THEORY.

To measure $h$, $y$, or $z$ parameters, it is necessary to excite the two ports in turn with an open-circuit or short-circuit connected to the other port. At microwavelengths (0.3–30 cm) this measurement is difficult to carry out for several reasons: (1) Lead inductance makes it difficult to get a good short circuit. (2) Stray capacitance makes it difficult to create a good open circuit. (3) Microwave amplifiers sometimes oscillate when their ports are open-circuited or short-circuited. (4) Voltages and currents are rarely measured at microwavelengths, but equipment that yields reflection and transmission coefficients is frequently employed.

For all of these reasons, scattering parameters, rather than $h$, $y$, and $z$ parameters, are widely used to characterize microwave networks. Let $a_1$ and $a_2$ in Fig. 2*b* represent the complex wave amplitudes entering ports 1 and 2 respectively, and let $b_1$ and $b_2$ denote the complex wave amplitudes emerging from ports 1 and 2 respectively. The relationships between these complex wave amplitudes are given by Eqs. (8) and (9).

$$b_1 = s_{11}\, a_1 + s_{12}\, a_2 \quad (8)$$

$$b_2 = s_{21}\, a_1 + s_{22}\, a_2 \quad (9)$$

***Interpretation.*** When a generator is connected to port 1 and a nonreflecting (that is, perfectly matched) termination is connected to port 2, $a_2 = 0$, and from Eq.(8) it follows that Eq. (10) is satisfied. Thus, $s_{11}$

$$s_{11} = \frac{b_1}{a_1} \quad (10)$$

is the voltage reflection coefficient looking into port 1 when port 2 is perfectly matched. Under the same conditions, it is seen from Eq. (9) that Eq. (11) is

$$s_{21} = \frac{b_2}{a_1} \quad (11)$$

valid. Thus, $s_{21}$ is the ratio of the complex-wave amplitude emerging from port 2 to the complex-wave amplitude incident on port 1 when port 2 is perfectly matched. After interchanging the generator and matched termination, expressions for $s_{22}$ and $s_{12}$ are found in a similar way.

***Matrix notation.*** The scattering coefficients are often written in matrix notation. For a two-port network, the scattering matrix has the general form shown in Eq. (12).

$$[S] = \begin{pmatrix} s_{11} & s_{12} \\ s_{21} & s_{22} \end{pmatrix} \quad (12)$$

For a device with $m$ ports, the scattering matrix has $m$ rows and $m$ columns. For the $n$th port, some workers let $|a_n|$ and $|b_n|$ represent the root-meansquare values of the incident and reflected voltages; but the expressions for reciprocity and losslessness with unequal port characteristic impedances become more simple if $|a_n|^2$ and $|b_n|^2$ represent the incident and reflected powers respectively. Using this latter convention, the following rules apply:

1. In a linear reciprocal two-port network, Eq. (13) is valid.

$$s_{12} = s_{21} \quad (13)$$

2. In a linear lossless two-port network, Eqs. (14–16) are satisfied, where $s_{11}{}^*$ denotes the complex con-

$$s_{11}\, s_{11}{}^* + s_{21}\, s_{21}{}^* = 1 \quad (14)$$

$$s_{12}\, s_{12}{}^* + s_{22}\, s_{22}{}^* = 1 \quad (15)$$

$$s_{11}\, s_{12}{}^* + s_{21}\, s_{22}{}^* = 0 \quad (16)$$

jugate of $s_{11}$, and so forth. In mathematical language, $S$ is a symmetric, unitary matrix when the two-port network is linear, reciprocal and lossless.

These rules remain valid when the two ports have different characteristic impedances. There are corresponding rules for multiport networks. The scattering matrices for many two-, three-, and four-port networks are given in standard works and are widely used when analyzing microwave systems.

The scattering matrix for a perfectly matched lossless line of length $x$ is given by Eq. (17), where $\beta =$

$$[S_x] = \begin{pmatrix} 0 & e^{-j\beta x} \\ e^{-j\beta x} & 0 \end{pmatrix} \quad (17)$$

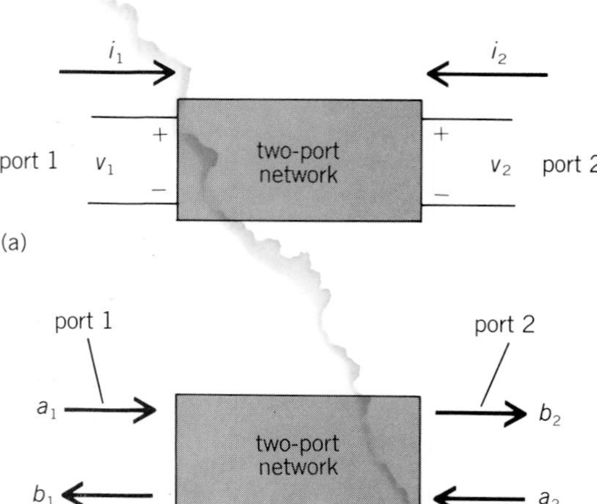


**Fig. 2. Two-port network showing (*a*) the voltages and currents used in *y*-parameter definitions, and (*b*) the incident and reflected complex-wave amplitudes used in scattering-parameter definitions.**

$2\pi/\lambda$ is the phase constant of the line and $\lambda$ denotes the wavelength in it. The rules stated above are all seen to be satisfied by this matrix.

*Frank L. Warner*

**Slotted line.** Among the most conceptually simple and oldest methods of measuring microwave impedance is the slotted line. In its basic form, a longitudinal slot is cut in the transmission line of interest, which permits the fields to be sampled by means of a movable probe at different positions along the axis of the line. A mechanical transport mechanism is provided so that the depth of penetration or coupling between the probe and internal fields remains fixed as the probe moves along the slot.

At any instant of time, the phase of $a$ or $b$ depends upon the phase of the generator and the propagation time delay between the generator and the probe position where $a$ or $b$ is measured. As the probe is moved along the line, this time delay will be increased for $a$ and decreased for $b$, or vice versa, depending upon the position of the generator and the direction of the motion. Thus the phase difference between $a$ and $b$ will depend upon the probe position.

In the existing practice, the designs of most probes are such that their response is proportional only to the total field amplitude which is given by $|a + b|$ or $|v|$ [according to Eq. (1)]. Since motion along the line is accompanied by changes in the phase difference between $a$ and $b$, the magnitude of the sum changes as required by the laws governing the addition of two complex numbers. In particular, if $a$ and $b$ are in phase, the maximum probe response is obtained, and this is proportional to $|a| + |b|$. At the minimum, the response is proportional to $\big||a| - |b|\big|$. By definition, the ratio between these two responses is the voltage-standing-wave-ratio (VSWR) and is given by Eq. (18). (The reciprocal of this definition is also in use.)

$$\text{VSWR} = \frac{|a| + |b|}{\big||a| - |b|\big|} \tag{18}$$

The measurement of VSWR also falls within the scope of "impedance measurement" at microwave frequencies. Ordinarily, the directions of wave propagation associated with $a$ and $b$ are chosen such that $|a| \leq 1$. Equations (3) and (18) may now be combined to obtain Eqs. (19) and (20).

$$\text{VSWR} = \frac{1 + |\Gamma|}{1 - |\Gamma|} \tag{19}$$

$$|\Gamma| = \frac{\text{VSWR} - 1}{\text{VSWR} + 1} \tag{20}$$

The foregoing procedure determines the magnitude of $\Gamma$ but not its phase. In many applications, however, the interest in the phase of $\Gamma$ is minimal. The reason is that the generation of energy is far more difficult at microwave than at the lower frequencies. As a consequence, the interface between different components is usually arranged so as to achieve maximum power transfer. As a general rule, this calls for wave propagation in one direction only. Loosely speaking, the magnitude of $\Gamma$ usually represents an indication of the extent of departure from the system design objectives.

On the other hand, it is possible to obtain the phase by a rather simple extension of the foregoing technique. While the phases of $a$ and $b$ change with respect to line position, their magnitudes and thus $|\Gamma|$ remain constant. At the position of the minimum probe output, the phase of $\Gamma$ is 180° since this corresponds to a minimum value of the sum $|a + b|$. To find the phase of $\Gamma$ at any other position in the line, it is only necessary to note that since the phases of $a$ and $b$ move in opposite directions, the phase of $\Gamma$ changes at twice the rate of either of them and undergoes a total of 360° between two successive minima. By observing the positions of two minima, the phase of $\Gamma$ at any other location can then be determined provided that its distance from the position of the minimum is known. SEE PHASE-ANGLE MEASUREMENT.

**Reflectometer.** In the case of the slotted line, the probe typically consists of a short length of circular rod which projects into the waveguide in a direction perpendicular to its axis. The reflectometer is based on a different type of coupling mechanism, a simple example of which is illustrated in **Fig. 3**. Here the secondary waveguide is coupled to the primary one by means of a pair of small holes spaced a quarter wavelength apart. On an individual basis, each of these holes is a source of waves in the secondary guide which tend to be of equal amplitude in both directions. When taken as a pair of holes, however, the geometry is such that the waves tend to combine in phase in the forward direction and out of phase (and thus cancel) in the reverse direction. (From a given point in the primary guide to the left of the coupling holes, the distance to a point in the secondary guide to the right of these two holes is the same via either of them. In the reverse direction, however, that is, to a point in the secondary guide to the left of the two holes, there is a half-wavelength difference in the path length associated with each of the holes. This leads to a reinforcement of the total wave amplitude in one direction and to a cancellation in the other.)

The foregoing waveguide circuit is aptly called a directional coupler, which is the basic element in a reflectometer. If the wave in the primary guide in Fig. 3 is propagating to the left instead of to the right, the coupled wave in the secondary arm will also be primarily to the left. Let each of the secondary arms be terminated by a suitable detector such as a diode or bolometer. These devices respond to the powers which they absorb and which are proportional to $|a|^2$ and $|b|^2$. The square root of the ratio of the detector responses thus gives $|\Gamma|$. SEE DIRECTIONAL COUPLER; MICROWAVE POWER MEASUREMENT.

As before, only the magnitude of $\Gamma$ is obtained, but this time there is no simple extension of the method

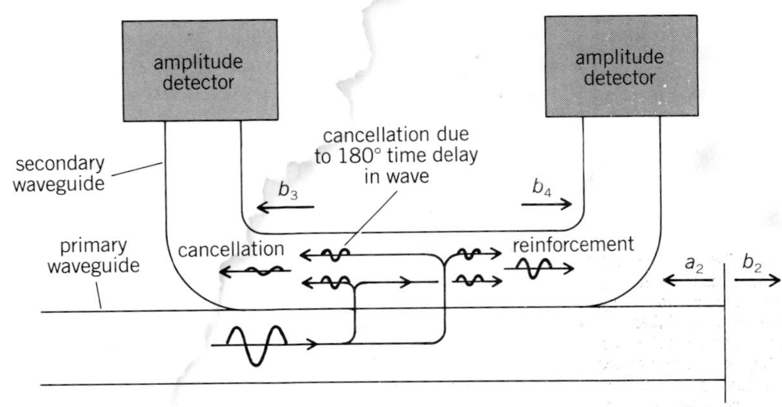


**Fig. 3. Directional coupler which forms the basic element of a microwave reflectometer.**

which yields the phase. If required, the phase can be obtained by one of the techniques described below.

The foregoing methods have the advantage of requiring only the most simple of microwave detectors, usually either a bolometer or diode, but yield only the amplitude (as contrasted with phase) of the detected signals. On the other hand, the accuracy of these methods is limited by the impossibility of constructing either slotted lines or directional couplers which completely satisfy the simple description outlined above. With regard to the reflectometer, techniques based on the use of tuning transformers have been devised which substantially improve its operation at a single frequency, but these methods become time-consuming in a practical application where measurements at multiple frequencies are required.

**Network analyzer.** The limitations on accuracy and multiple-frequency operation noted above are largely avoided by the network analyzer, which is a multipurpose instrument with applications in the measurement of attenuation, and possibly power, as well as of impedance.

Let $a_2$ and $b_2$ in Fig. 3 represent the wave amplitudes in the primary line, while $b_3$ and $b_4$ represent those in the secondary or coupled line. In general, $b_3$ can be expressed by Eq. (21), where $A$ and $B$ are two

$$b_3 = Aa_2 + Bb_2 \tag{21}$$

complex constants which are functions of the scattering parameters of the directional coupler and its associated detectors. The magnitudes $|A|$ and $|B|$ indicate how tightly the secondary line is coupled to the primary line, while their ratio is a measure of the directive properties of the coupling. In a similar way, $b_4$ can be expressed by Eq. (22), where $C$ and $D$ are

$$b_4 = Ca_2 + Db_2 \tag{22}$$

additional complex constants. For an ideal reflectometer, one has $B = C = 0$, and taking the ratio of Eqs. (21) and (22) yields Eq. (23), so that if the de-

$$\left|\frac{b_3}{b_4}\right| = \left|\frac{A}{D}\right| \cdot \left|\frac{a_2}{b_2}\right| = \left|\frac{A}{D}\right| \cdot |\Gamma| \tag{23}$$

tectors measure $|b_3|$ and $|b_4|$ their ratio is proportional to the reflection coefficient. The constant term $|A/D|$ can be easily determined by observing $|b_3/b_4|$ in conjunction with a known value of $|\Gamma|$, usually a short for which $|\Gamma| = 1$. Thus the system is a reflectometer as described above.

In the network analyzer mode of operation, Eqs. (21) and (22) are combined to yield Eq. (24).

$$\frac{a_2}{b_2} = \Gamma = \frac{\dfrac{b_3}{b_4} - \dfrac{B}{D}}{\dfrac{Cb_3}{Db_4} + \dfrac{A}{D}} \tag{24}$$

Equation (23) gives $\Gamma$ in terms of the complex ratio $b_3/b_4$, which means that the detection system must provide the phase difference between $b_3$ and $b_4$. In addition, the ratios $A/D$, $B/D$, and $C/D$ are also required. These are properties of the coupling network and must be determined at each operating frequency by a suitable calibration procedure. The network analyzer has the advantage that errors due to nonzero values of $B$ and $C$ are in principle eliminated. In addition to the calibration requirement, however, an alternative detection system is required which provides the phase difference between $b_3$ and $b_4$. Ordinarily, this calls for heterodyne conversion to a lower frequency which preserves the phase information and where phase detection techniques are well known. SEE HETERODYNE PRINCIPLE.

**Six-port network analyzer.** The six-port network analyzer derives its name from the use of a six-port, rather than four-port, coupling network and the use of four amplitude detectors rather than a complex-ratio ($b_3/b_4$) detector. Each detector satisfies Eq. (25), sim-

$$|b_3| = |Aa_2 + Bb_2| \tag{25}$$

ilar to Eq. (21), where the absence of phase response is reflected by the use of absolute values.

Equation (25) may be factored to yield Eq. (26), where $q_3 = -(B/A)$.

$$|b_3| = |b_2| \cdot |A| \cdot |\Gamma - q_3| \tag{26}$$

Because of the absolute value sign, it is not possible to solve Eq. (26) for $\Gamma$. In the complex plane, $|\Gamma - q_3|$ represents the distance between $q_3$ and $\Gamma$ but gives no indication of the direction. The values of $\Gamma$ which satisfy Eq. (26) lie on a circle whose center is at $q_3$ and whose radius is determined by $|b_3|$, $|A|$, and $|b_2|$. Here $|b_3|$ is measured by one of the detectors, while $|A|$ and $q_3$ are parameters of the six-port network.

The term $|b_2|$, however, is an unknown whose value (in common with $\Gamma$) depends upon the excitation conditions, and whose determination usually falls within the scope of power rather than impedance measurement. It can be eliminated from consideration in the present context by taking the ratio between two detectors. Here it will prove convenient to assume initially that this second detector is described by Eq. (22) but where $C = 0$. Then, Eq. (27) is satisfied.

$$\left|\frac{b_3}{b_4}\right| = \left|\frac{A}{D}\right| \cdot |\Gamma - q_3| \tag{27}$$

By use of the remaining two detectors, it is possible to form two more equations similar to Eq. (27), but where the six-port design is such that the values of $q_3$ are different. Each of these equations fixes the

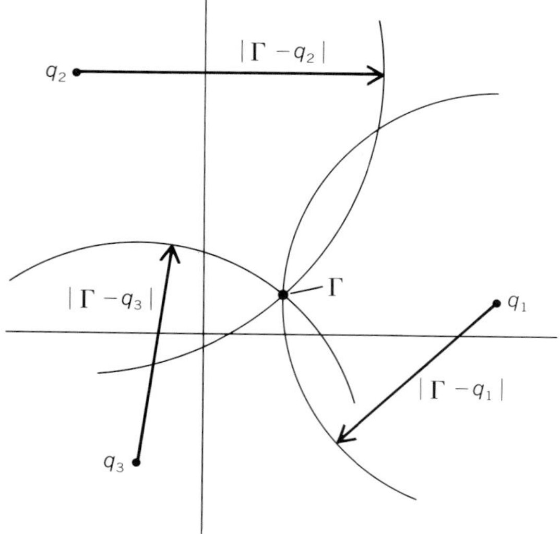


**Fig. 4. Geometric construction used with six-port reflectometer to determine the complex reflection coefficient from the intersection of three circles.**

distance between $\Gamma$ and three arbitrary points (circle centers). It is convenient to visualize the operation as providing the value of $\Gamma$ through the intersection of three circles (**Fig. 4**). Here the circle centers, $q_1$, $q_2$, and $q_3$, are parameters of the six-port, while their radii are given by the detector responses. In practice, where the value of $C$ is usually different from zero, the circle centers as well as their radii depend upon $\Gamma$, so that the foregoing description is only an approximate one.

The six-port network analyzer has the advantage of simplicity in the detection system, since the requirement for frequency conversion has been eliminated. On the other hand, since the detectors tend to be broadband, it is important for the signal source to be free of harmonics. In addition, if bolometric detectors are employed to achieve the best accuracy, a considerable increase in the signal power is required.

**Swept-frequency reflectometry.** In the above discussion, the problems associated with multiple-frequency operation have been largely ignored. As a practical matter, it is frequently important to know how the impedance (or reflection coefficient) varies with frequency. One of the more simple methods of achieving this is with the swept-frequency reflectometer. This is nothing more than the reflectometer described above in conjunction with a swept signal source whose frequency varies smoothly from an initial to a final value and then returns quickly to the starting value for a repeat of the sweep. If the reflectometer output is displayed on an oscilloscope, the reflection coefficient magnitude can be obtained as a function of frequency.

In response to increasing frequency range and accuracy requirements, however, this method has been largey replaced by automated versions of the network analyzers described above. The automatic network analyzer (ANA) typically includes a small digital computer for making the necessary computations and for controlling the signal source. It is thus possible to make a rapid succession of measurements at closely spaced frequencies. Moreover, the phase as well as magnitude of the reflection coefficient is usually obtained.

**Time-domain reflectometer.** In a typical application, the wave amplitude $b$ in Fig. 1 has its source in a generator (to the left) which is delivering energy, via the transmission line, to an antenna or other termination on the right. Provided that the antenna impedance is equal to $Z_0$, it is evident from Eqs. (3) and (4) that the amplitude of the wave, $a$, will equal zero. In a practical application, if $a$ is found to be nonzero, it may be desirable to determine whether the source of this reflected wave is the antenna or possibly some other discontinuity in the transmission line. Although it is possible to answer this question given the results of impedance measurements at a number of different frequencies, a more simple approach, at least conceptually, is to use a different form of test signal. In **Fig. 5** are shown the basic components of a time-domain reflectometer. In one mode of operation the generator output is a series of short pulses. These will travel down the line and be reflected at discontinuities within the line itself (if they exist) or at the antenna (or other termination) if its impedance is different from $Z_0$. Provided that the pulse width is short in comparison with the transit time from the generator to the discontinuity, or termination, the oscilloscope responses to the generator pulse and to the reflected pulse will be separated by twice the transit time to the reflection and thus will be displaced from one another along the horizontal time axis. Apart from having confined the transmitted energy to a waveguide rather than free space, the operation is basically the same as radar. Another useful waveform in time-domain reflectometry is the step function. By examining the waveform associated with the reflection, it is possible to learn a great deal about the nature of the discontinuity which produced it. *SEE FUNCTION GENERATOR; PULSE GENERATOR; RADAR.*

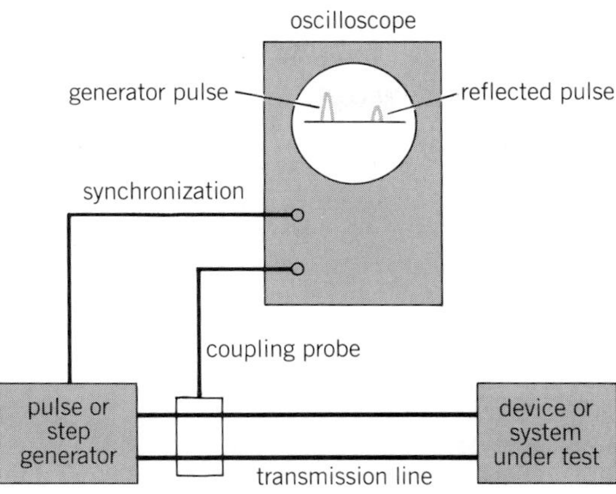


**Fig. 5. Basic elements of a time domain reflectometer.**

As an alternative to generating these specialized waveforms, it is also possible to synthesize the time-domain response from measurements at a collection of suitably chosen discrete frequencies. The basis for this is found in Fourier analysis. In particular, any arbitrary repetitive waveform (including, for example, a series of short pulses) can be synthesized by the superposition (or addition) of a (usually infinite) number of harmonically related frequencies of the proper amplitude and phase. (As a practical matter, the synthesis is limited to a finite number of frequencies, and the desired waveform is only approximated.) The system response to the synthesized waveform may be obtained by mathematically combining the system responses to this collection of discrete frequencies, usually with the help of a digital computer.

**Locating reflectometer.** Another method of determining the position of waveguide discontinuities is provided by the locating reflectometer, which uses a swept-, rather than stepped-, frequency source. This technique is also based upon Fourier analysis, but the Fourier transformation is obtained by analog rather than digital methods, and the need for a (digital) computer is eliminated. On the other hand, the associated waveguide circuit tends to be more complicated.

**Comparison reflectometer.** As noted above, much of the motivation for the network analyzer is to eliminate errors caused by nonzero values of $B$ and $C$, which in turn are due to imperfections in the directional coupler. An alternative technique for dealing with this problem is provided by the comparison reflectometer. The solution of Eq. (24) for $|b_3/b_4|$ yields Eq. (28). If $|\Gamma|$ is small, the term $C\Gamma$ may ordinarily

$$\left|\frac{b_3}{b_4}\right| = \frac{|A\Gamma + B|}{|C\Gamma + D|} \tag{28}$$

be neglected in comparison with $D$. On the other hand, $A\Gamma$ and $B$ may be comparable in magnitude so that the nonzero value of $B$ represents a major source of error. In the comparison reflectometer the directional coupler is separated from the item being measured by a long length of waveguide. This has the effect of causing the phase of Γ to vary rapidly with frequency. A small variation in source frequency will thus cause the terms $A\Gamma$ and $B$ to combine in and out of phase, while ordinarily $A$ and $B$ may be assumed to be constant if the frequency excursion is not too large. The separate contributions of $A\Gamma$ and $B$ to the reflectometer response may then be obtained by techniques similar to those described in conjunction with the slotted line. SEE MICROWAVE MEASUREMENTS; RADIO-FREQUENCY IMPEDANCE MEASUREMENTS.

Glenn F. Engen

**Bibliography**. S. F. Adam, *Microwave Theory and Applications*, 1969; J. L. Altman, *Microwave Circuits*, 1964; E. L. Ginzton, *Microwave Measurements*, 1957; K. C. Gupta, *Microwaves*, 1979; D. M. Kerns and R. W. Beatty, *Basic Theory of Waveguide Junctions and Introductory Microwave Network Analysis*, 1967; P. A. Matthews and I. M. Stephenson, *Microwave Components*, 1968; C. G. Montgomery, *Technique of Microwave Measurements*, 1947; M. Sucher and J. Fox, *Handbook of Microwave Measurements*, 1963; F. L. Warner, *Microwave Attenuation Measurement*, 1977.

## Microwave measurements

A collection of techniques particularly suited for development of devices and monitoring of systems where physical size of components varies from a significant fraction of an electromagnetic wavelength to many wavelengths. SEE MICROWAVE.

Virtually all microwave devices are coupled together with a transmission line having a uniform cross section. The concept of traveling electromagnetic waves on that transmission line is fundamental to the understanding of microwave measurements. SEE MICROWAVE TRANSMISSION LINES.

At any reference plane in a transmission line there are considered to exist two independent traveling electromagnetic waves moving in opposite directions. One is called the forward or incident wave, and the other the reverse or reflected wave. The electromagnetic wave is guided by the transmission line and is composed of electric and magnetic fields with associated electric currents and voltages. Any one of these parameters can be used in considering the traveling waves, but the measurements in the early development of microwave technology made principally on the voltage waves led to the custom of referring only to voltage. One parameter in very common use is the voltage reflection coefficient Γ, which is related to the incident, $V_i$, and reflected, $V_r$, voltage waves by Eq. (1).

$$\Gamma = \frac{V_r}{V_i} \tag{1}$$

**Impedance.** The voltage reflection coefficient Γ is related to the impedance terminating the transmission line and to the impedance of the line itself. If a wave is launched to travel in only one direction on a uniform reflectionless transmission line of infinite length, there will be no reflected wave. The input impedance of this infinitely long transmission line is defined as its characteristic impedance $Z_0$. An arbitrary length of transmission line terminated in an impedance $Z_0$ will also have an input impedance $Z_0$. SEE ELECTRICAL IMPEDANCE.

If the transmission line is terminated in the arbitrary complex impedance load $Z_L$, the complex voltage reflection coefficient $\Gamma_L$ at the termination is given by Eq. (2).

$$\Gamma_L = \frac{Z_L - Z_0}{Z_L + Z_0} \tag{2}$$

Even when there is no unique expression for $Z_L$ and $Z_0$ such as in the case of hollow uniconductor waveguides, the voltage reflection coefficient Γ has a value because it is simply a voltage ratio. In general, the measurement of microwave impedance is the measurement of Γ. Both amplitude and phase of Γ can be measured by direct probing of the voltage standing wave set up along a transmission line by the two opposed traveling waves, but this is a slow technique. Directional couplers have been used for many years to perform much faster swept frequency measurement of the magnitude of Γ, and more recently the use of automatic network analyzers under computer control has made possible rapid, accurate measurements of amplitude and phase of Γ over very broad frequency ranges. SEE DIRECTIONAL COUPLER; MICROWAVE IMPEDANCE MEASUREMENT.

**Power.** A required increase in microwave power is expensive whether it be the ouput from a laboratory signal generator, the power output from a power amplifier on a satellite, or the cooking energy from a microwave oven. To minimize this expense, absolute power must be measured. Most techniques involve conversion of the microwave energy to heat energy which, in turn, causes a temperature rise in a physical body. This temperature rise is measured and is approximately proportional to the power dissipated. The whole device can be calibrated by reference to low-frequency electrical standards and application of appropriate corrections. SEE MICROWAVE POWER MEASUREMENT.

The power sensors are simple and can be made to have a very broad frequency response. A power meter can be connected directly to the output of a generator to measure available power $P_A$, or a directional coupler may be used to permit measurement of a small fraction of the power actually delivered to the load.

Microwave power measurements provide a good illustration of some of the differences between low-frequency and microwave measurement problems. Consider the simple connection of a load to a generator at low frequency (**Fig. 1**). The equivalent circuit of the generator consists of a source of constant voltage $V$, connected in series with $Z_G$, the internal impedance of the generator. The load has impedance $Z_L$.

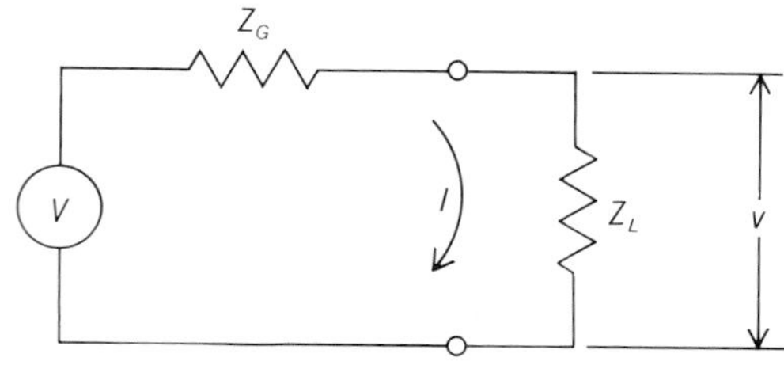


**Fig. 1. A load connected to a generator.**

If the circulating current in Fig. 1 is taken as $I$ and the voltage drop across $Z_L$ as $v$, Eqs. (3) and (4) follow from Ohm's law. These are all vector quantities having both a magnitude and a phase angle. SEE ALTERNATING-CURRENT CIRCUIT THEORY.

$$I = \frac{V}{Z_G + Z_L} \quad (3)$$

$$v = IZ_L \quad (4)$$

The power $P_L$ delivered to $Z_L$ is a scalar quantity and can be calculated from Eq. (5), where $I^*$ is the complex conjugate of the current $I$ and the symbol Re{ } stands for the real part of the complex number enclosed inside the brackets.

$$P_L = \text{Re}\{vI^*\} \quad (5)$$

Substituting Eqs. (3) and (4) in Eq. (5) yields Eq. (6) for $P_L$ in terms of the parameters of the circuit.

$$P_L = \text{Re}\left\{\frac{VZ_LV^*}{(Z_G + Z_L)(Z_G + Z_L)^*}\right\} \quad (6)$$

It can be shown that the maximum power which the generator can deliver is available only when the load has impedance $Z_G^*$, the complex conjugate of the generator impedance. This power is defined as the available power $P_A$, a fundamental parameter of the generator, and its value is obtained by substituting $Z_G^*$ for $Z_L$ in Eq. (6) and simplifying to obtain Eq. (7).

$$P_A = \frac{VV^*}{4\text{Re}\{Z_G\}} \quad (7)$$

The actual power delivered to $Z_L$ relative to the available power may be determined by taking the ratio of Eq. (6) divided by Eq. (7) to obtain Eq. (8).

$$\frac{P_L}{P_A} = \frac{4\text{Re}\{Z_G\}\text{Re}\{Z_L\}}{|Z_G + Z_L|^2} \quad (8)$$

The same simple circuit can also be considered at microwave frequencies. The same power ratio can be written as Eq. (9), where the voltage reflection coefficient $\Gamma_G$ of the generator is given by Eq. (10). The expression in Eq. (9) is called a mismatch factor because it would be equal to 1 if the impedances $Z_G$ and $Z_L$ were equal (matched) to $Z_0$. Since usually the magnitudes $|\Gamma_L|$ and $|\Gamma_G|$ are measured, the denominator of the mismatch factor can commonly be determined only to be within certain limits about 1.

$$\frac{P_L}{P_A} = \frac{\{1 - |\Gamma_L|^2\}\{1 - |\Gamma_G|^2\}}{|1 - \Gamma_L\Gamma_G|^2} \quad (9)$$

$$\Gamma_G = \frac{Z_G - Z_0}{Z_G + Z_0} \quad (10)$$

If a uniform transmission line is introduced between the generator and load, the voltage on the line can be considered constant at low frequency, but at microwave frequencies both the phase and the amplitude of the voltage will vary along the line. For example, if the forward-traveling voltage wave has value $V_f$ at a certain reference plane on the transmission line, it will have a value $V_fe^{-\gamma x}$ at a distance $x$ from that reference plane measured in the direction of travel. The parameter $\gamma$ is the propagation constant and has a real and imaginary part so that the factor $e^{-\gamma x}$ modifies both amplitude and phase of $V_f$ to account for the power loss in the transmission line and the finite time taken for the forward wave to travel the distance $x$.

**Scattering coefficients.** While the measurement of absolute power is important, there are many more occasions which require the measurement of relative power which is equivalent to the magnitude of voltage ratio and is related to attenuation. Also there arises frequently the need to measure the relative phase of two voltages. Measurement systems having this capability are referred to as vector network analyzers, and they are used to measure scattering coefficients of multiport devices. The concept of scattering coefficients is an extension of the voltage reflection coefficient applied to devices having more than one port. The most simple is a two-port. Its characteristics can be specified completely in terms of a 2 × 2 scattering matrix, the coefficients of which are indicated in **Fig. 2**. The incident voltage at the reference plane of each port is defined as $a$, and the reflected voltage is $b$. Voltages $a$ and $b$ are related by matrix equation (11), where $(S_{nm})$ is the scattering matrix of the junction. Writing Eq. (11) out for a two-port device gives Eqs. (12) and (13). Examination of Eq. (12) shows, for example, that $S_{11}$ is the voltage reflection coefficient looking into port 1 if port 2 is terminated with a $Z_0$ load ($a_2 = 0$).

$$(b_n) = (S_{nm})(a_m) \quad (11)$$

$$b_1 = S_{11}a_1 + S_{12}a_2 \quad (12)$$

$$b_2 = S_{21}a_1 + S_{22}a_2 \quad (13)$$

**Attenuation.** To define attenuation and illustrate the use of the scattering equations, it is useful to consider the case in which the two-port is a microwave attenuator. The insertion loss of the attenuator will first be defined, and the attenuation will follow. Consider a source connected to its load as shown in **Fig. 1**. The power which will be delivered to $Z_L$ is a function of $V$, $Z_G$, and $Z_L$, and is defined as $P_L$.

Now if an attenuator is inserted between the source and the load as shown in **Fig. 2**, the power $P_T$ which will be delivered to $Z_L$ is now a function of $V$, $Z_G$, $Z_L$ and the scattering matrix $(S_{nm})$ of the attenuator. The insertion loss $L_I$ of the attenuator is defined by Eq. (14). Although $L_I$ is a power ratio, independent of physical units, it is conveniently expressed as 10 times the logarithm to base 10 and assigned the unit name decibel (dB). SEE DECIBEL.

$$L_I = 10 \log_{10} \frac{P_L}{P_T} \quad (14)$$

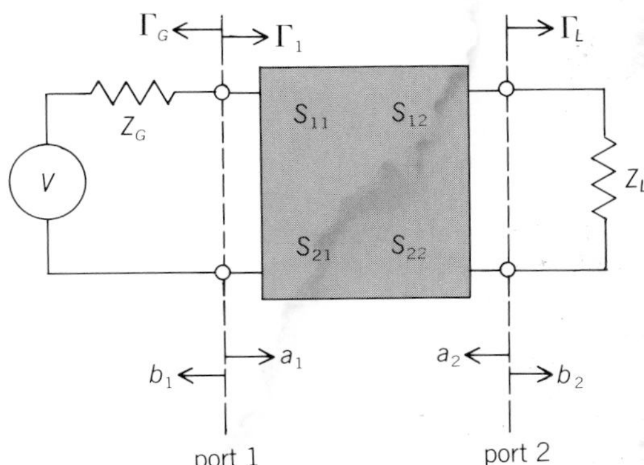


**Fig. 2. A two-port inserted between a load and a generator. $S_{nm}$ are the scattering coefficients of the two-port.**

It can be shown that the insertion loss is given by Eq. (15), where the reflection coefficient $\Gamma_1$ is the input reflection coefficient of the attenuator-load combination.

$$L_I = 10 \log_{10} \left| \frac{(1 - \Gamma_G\Gamma_1)(1 - S_{22}\Gamma_L)}{S_{21}(1 - \Gamma_G\Gamma_L)} \right|^2 \qquad (15)$$

The attenuation $A$ of the attenuator may now be defined, and it is the particular value of insertion loss which the attenuator causes when inserted between a generator and load both having zero reflection coefficients. Therefore the expression for $A$ is Eq. (16), and

$$A = L_I \Big|_{\Gamma_G, \Gamma_L = 0} = 10 \log_{10} \left| \frac{1}{S_{21}} \right|^2 \qquad (16)$$

the remaining part of the expression in Eq. (15) will be the mismatch factor whose limits may be estimated or whose value may be calculated and applied as a correction if attenuation measurement is being made by using a source and load whose impedances are not matched to the transmission line. SEE ATTENUATION (ELECTRICITY).

**Heterodyne.** The heterodyne principle is used for scalar attenuation measurements because of its large dynamic range and for vector network analysis because of its phase coherence. The microwave signal at frequency $f_s$ is mixed with a microwave local oscillator at frequency $f_{LO}$ in a nonlinear mixer. The mixer output signal at frequency $f_s - f_{LO}$ is a faithful amplitude and phase reproduction of the original microwave signal but is at a low, fixed frequency so that it can be measured simply with low-frequency techniques. One disadvantage of the heterodyne technique at the highest microwave frequencies is its cost. Consequently, significant effort has been expended in development of multiport network analyzers which use several simple power detectors and a computer analysis approach which allows measurement of both relative voltage amplitude and phase with reduced hardware cost. SEE HETERODYNE PRINCIPLE.

**Noise.** Microwave noise measurement is important for the communications field and radio astronomy. The noise figure of an amplifier is a measure of the amount of noise added to a signal in the process of amplification. If the amplifier adds a lot of noise, the signal must be correspondingly larger at the input to the amplifier to maintain the minimum signal-to-noise ratio required at the output of the amplifier, for example, to obtain appropriate television picture clarity or insignificant errors in digital communication. If measurement of noise figure shows that one amplifier has a lower noise figure than another, a smaller antenna or a lower transmitter power may be used in a telecommunications link which incorporates the less noisy amplifier.

The measurement of thermal noise at microwave frequencies is essentially the same as low-frequency noise measurement, except that there will be impedance mismatch factors which must be carefully evaluated. The availability of broadband semiconductor noise sources having a stable, high, noise power output has greatly reduced the problems of source impedance mismatch because an impedance-matching attenuator can be inserted between the noise source and the amplifier under test. SEE ELECTRICAL NOISE; ELECTRICAL NOISE GENERATOR; MICROWAVE NOISE STANDARDS.

**Sources, detection, and automation.** Microwave sources should be stable in both amplitude and frequency for accurate microwave measurements. The amplitude is stabilized by using an amplitude sensor and a negative-feedback loop. Frequency synthesis which permits automatic frequency adjustment with great precision and stability is now in fairly common use.

Microwave diodes are very often used as detectors. With their extremely low capacitance, their output can follow rapid changes in the amplitude of the microwave input, which is useful for rapid measurements. Although the diode output response varies from square law at low-level inputs to linear at high-level, careful calibration permits use of the diode over a wide dynamic range. A small penalty in accuracy is paid for the simplicity of the detection hardware. SEE DIODE; MICROWAVE SOLID-STATE DEVICES.

The need to apply calculated corrections to obtain the best accuracy in microwave measurement has stimulated the adoption of computers and computer-controlled instruments. An additional benefit of this development is that measurement techniques that are superior in accuracy but too tedious to perform manually can now be considered. An example is the multiport network analyzer using power detectors mentioned above.

*Richard F. Clark*

**Bibliography.** A. J. Estin (ed.), *Precision Measurement and Calibration: Selected NBS Papers on Electricity-Radio Frequency*, NBS Spec. Publ. 300, vol. 4, 1970; H. Fukui (ed.), *Low Noise Microwave Transistors and Amplifiers*, 1981; K. C. Gupta, *Microwaves*, 1980; D. M. Kerns and R. W. Beatty, *Basic Theory of Waveguide Junctions and Introductory Microwave Network Analysis*, 1967; A. Lance, *Introduction to Microwave Theory and Measurements*, 1964; T. S. Laverghetta, *Microwave Measurements and Techniques*, 1976; S. Saad, R. C. Hansen, and G. J. Wheeler (eds.), *Microwave Engineers Handbook*, 1971; F. L. Warner, *Microwave Attenuation Measurement*, 1977.

## Microwave noise standards

Electrical noise generators which produce calculable noise intensities at microwave frequencies, and which are used to calibrate other noise sources by using comparison methods. A factor limiting the performance of microwave communications and radar systems is receiver sensitivity (signal-to-noise ratio). To measure this, a reference noise source is needed. SEE RADAR; SIGNAL-TO-NOISE RATIO.

**Blackbody radiator.** Noise standards are based upon the blackbody or thermal radiator and generate noise power according to Eq. (1), which is derived

$$S = k \cdot T \cdot P(f) \qquad \text{W/Hz} \qquad (1)$$

from quantum mechanics. Here $k$ is the Boltzmann constant ($1.38 \times 10^{-23}$ joule/kelvin), $T$ the absolute temperature in kelvins, and $P(f)$ the Planck function given by Eq. (2), where $h$ is the Planck constant ($6.62$

$$P(f) = (hf/kT)\{\exp(hf/kT) - 1\}^{-1} \qquad (2)$$

$\times 10^{-34}$ J-s) and $f$ the frequency in Hz. The quantity $T \cdot P(f)$ is referred to as the noise temperature and is used as a convenient measure of available noise power from a source. In the microwave region and at room temperature $P(f)$ is nearly equal to 1, and thus $S = kT$ W/Hz.

The practical realization of a blackbody in the microwave region may best be understood by reference to Kirchhoff's law of radiation, which states that for any body the ratio of emissivity $E$ to absorptivity $A$ is equal to the emissivity $E_b$ of a blackbody; that is, Eq. (3) holds. To realize a blackbody the absorptivity $A$

$$E/A = E_b \qquad (3)$$

is set equal to 1. A microwave absorber with unity absorptivity can be achieved by using a transmission line terminated in its characteristic impedance, or in microwave terminology a matched termination. SEE MICROWAVE TRANSMISSION LINES; TRANSMISSION LINES.

**Temperature.** The range of sources which require calibration and the desire to obtain low uncertainties dictate that microwave thermal noise standards are required with temperatures both above and below the ambient temperature. Sources have been developed with temperatures in the range from 4 to 1300 K (−452° to 1900°F). The low temperatures are normally achieved by immersion of the matched termination in a cryogenic liquid of which liquid nitrogen (77 K or −321°F) is the most common. Standards for measurement of high-temperature sources have the termination in a heated oven. A transition section supports the temperature gradient from the thermal termination to the ambient temperature output which connects to the measurement system (**Fig. 1**). The structures are produced in transmission lines with well-established characteristics such as coaxial lines or waveguides. Complications in the design of microwave thermal noise standards arise principally in the transition and output sections. These are lossy elements with nonzero absorptivity and are thus themselves thermal noise generators. Because the absorptivity $A$ is less than 1 for these elements, the noise power which they contribute is proportional to $k \cdot A \cdot T$. If the transmission coefficient of the lossy element is represented by Eq. (4), then for a two-port com-

$$\tau = (1 - A) \qquad (4)$$

ponent at a temperature $T_A$ with an input noise temperature $T_{in}$, the output noise temperature is given by Eq. (5). The transition and output sections thus re-

$$T_{out} = T_{in}\,\tau + (1 - \tau)T_A \qquad (5)$$

duce the noise output from the blackbody termination and add some noise themselves. The combined effect is such that the output noise temperature relative to the termination temperature is lower for an above-ambient source and higher for a below-ambient source. SEE COAXIAL CABLE; WAVEGUIDE.

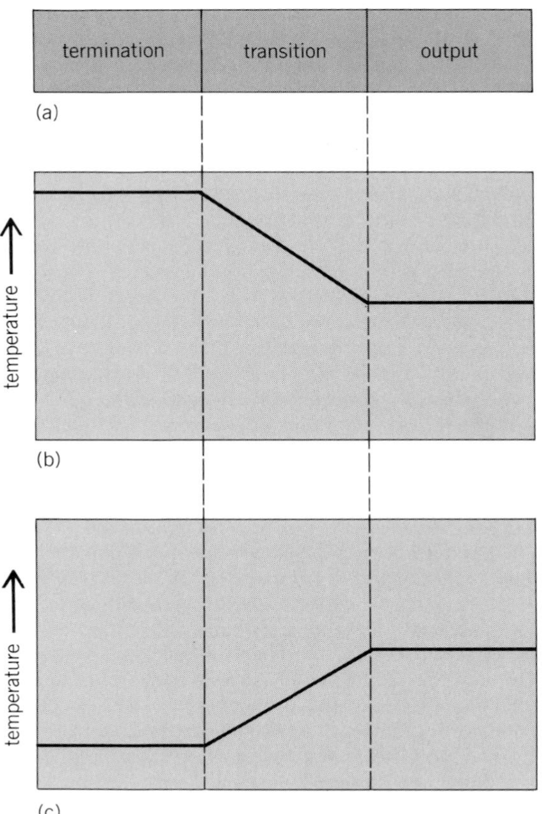


**Fig. 1. Microwave noise standard. (a) General form. (b) Temperature variation in a standard with termination at a temperature above ambient. (c) Temperature variation in a cryogenic standard.**

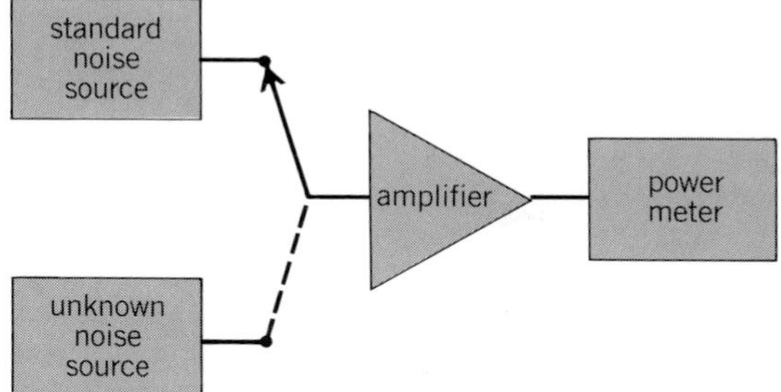


**Fig. 2. Total-power radiometer.**

**Radiometers.** Measurement of microwave noise involve comparison between an unknown source and a thermal noise source or a secondary standard which has been compared previously with a thermal source. The measurement systems are classified under the general heading of radiometers, which simply compare the noise powers of the standard and unknown noise sources. The most simple type of radiometer is the total power radiometer (**Fig. 2**).

The standard and unknown noise sources are connected to the input of the amplifier in turn and the output observed on the power meter. The unknown noise source may be calculated by using Eq. (6),

$$T_x = YT_s + T_R(Y - 1) \qquad (6)$$

where $T_x$ and $T_s$ are the noise temperatures of the unknown and standard sources, and $Y$ is the ratio of the power meter readings when $T_x$ and $T_s$ are connected respectively. $T_R$ is the input noise temperature of the amplifier system and is determined separately by using two known sources at the system input. The sensitivity of the system is given by Eq. (7), where $T_{in}$

$$\Delta T = T_{in}/(BC)^{1/2} \qquad (7)$$

is the sum of the receiver and source noise temperatures at the input, $B$ is the amplifier bandwidth, and $C$ is the time constant associated with the power meter. $\Delta T$ represents the minimum change at the system input which may be detected at the output. The total power radiometer may be used for measurement of above- and below-ambient sources. For the below-ambient (cryogenic) sources the value of $T_R$ must be as low as possible to retain good sensitivity. *SEE MICROWAVE; MICROWAVE MEASUREMENTS*.

*Malcolm W. Sinclair*

**Bibliography.** D. A. Bell, *Electrical Noise*, 1960; A. J. Estin et al., Absolute measurement of temperature of microwave noise sources, *IRE Trans. Instrum.*, I-9:209–213, 1960; W. W. Mumford and E. H. Scheibe, *Noise Performance Factors in Communication Systems*, 1968; M. W. Sinclair, *Noise Measurements*, Lecture no. 25, 25/1–25/31, IEE Microwave Measurements Vacation School, University of Kent, Canterbury, September 18–24, 1983; J. McA. Steele et al., Electrical standards of measurement, part 2: R. F. and microwave standards, *Proc. IEE*, 122:1037–1053, 1975; C. T. Stelzried, Microwave thermal noise standards, *IEE Trans. Microw. Theory Techniq.*, MTT-16:646–655, 1968; A Van Der Ziel, *Noise: Sources, Characterization, Measurement*, 1970.

## Microwave optics

The study of those properties of microwaves which are analogous to the properties of light waves in optics. The fact that microwaves and light waves are both electromagnetic waves, the major difference being that of frequency, already suggests that their properties should be alike in many respects. But the reason microwaves behave more like light waves than, for instance, very low-frequency waves for electrical power (50 or 60 Hz) is primarily that the microwave wavelengths are usually comparable to or smaller than the ordinary physical dimensions of objects interacting with the waves.

In his classical experiments to verify Maxwell's theory, H. Hertz first demonstrated the optical properties of damped decimeter waves, such as rectilinear propagation, reflection, refraction, and polarization. It is virtually taken for granted that microwaves inherently possess all these properties, and the language of geometrical or physical optics is freely used wherever allowed by the situation.

**Rectilinear propagation.** As is the case with light, a beam of microwaves propagates along a straight line in a perfectly homogeneous infinite medium. This phenomenon follows directly from a general solution of the wave equation in which the direction of a wave normal does not change in a homogeneous medium. In the use of radar, a microwave beam is justifiably presumed to travel in a straight line before and after reflection by an object. For microwave communication in cases when two distant stations are not along the line of sight, the waves would be blocked by the Earth's surface. The difficulty is remedied by the use of microwave relay links so that straight-line propagation is maintained in each section. *SEE MICROWAVE TRANSMISSION LINES*.

**Reflection and refraction.** Consider a plane boundary between two semi-infinite media having different physical properties (**Fig. 1**). If a plane-polarized microwave is incident from medium 1, the boundary conditions generally require the presence of a reflected wave back to medium 1 and a transmitted (refracted) wave into medium 2. In the case of two in-

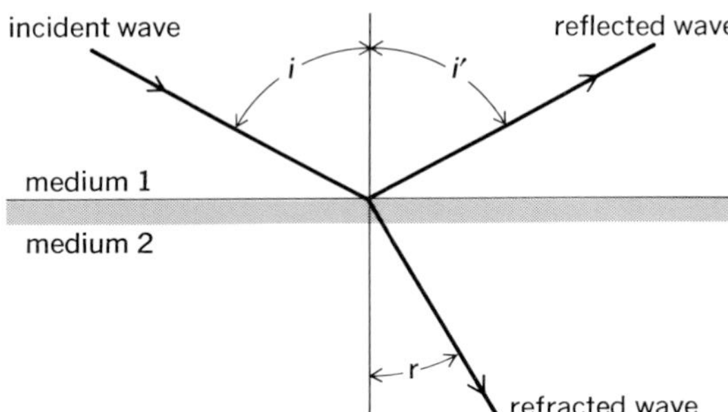


**Fig. 1. Reflection and refraction of microwaves at a plane boundary between two insulating media.**

sulating media, the familiar relations in optics shown in Eqs. (1) and (2) hold, where the angles $i$, $i'$, and $r$

$$i = i' \qquad \text{for reflection} \tag{1}$$

$$\frac{\sin i}{\sin r} = \sqrt{\frac{\epsilon_2}{\epsilon_1}} = N \qquad \text{for refraction} \tag{2}$$

are as indicated in Fig. 1, $\epsilon_1$ and $\epsilon_2$ are the dielectric constants of media 1 and 2, respectively, and $N$ is the index of refraction of medium 2 relative to medium 1. The reflected and refracted intensities depend upon whether the incident electric intensity is polarized in the plane of incidence or perpendicular to it. In any case, the well-known Fresnel equations of optics can all be applied to this case.

With some modification the laws of reflection and refraction can be applied to the propagation of microwaves inside a dielectric-filled metallic waveguide. The usual case is that of a vertical incidence to the plane boundary between two dielectric media perpendicular to the lengthwise direction of the waveguide. The reflection coefficient can be obtained by measuring the standing-wave ratio in the waveguide. Another interesting application is associated with the microwave analog of total internal reflection in optics. It may be seen from Eq. (2) that if $\epsilon_1 > \epsilon_2$ (that is, if the wave is incident from a denser medium), there is a total internal reflection for the wave when $i > \sin^{-1}\sqrt{\epsilon_2/\epsilon_1}$. This means that a properly designed dielectric rod (without metal walls) can serve as a waveguide by totally reflecting the elementary plane waves. Still another case of interest is that of a microwave lens. By using either a natural dielectric of a certain shape or an artificial dielectric consisting of an array of thin metal plates of a certain design, a microwave lens can be constructed which has the required index of refraction. Such lenses have been used as microwave antennas. *SEE ANTENNA; WAVEGUIDE*.

The reflection of a microwave by a conducting plane has all the characteristics of the reflection of a light wave by a metallic mirror. The amplitude of the reflected wave is practically identical to that of the incident wave, with the angle of reflection equal to the angle of incidence. The wave in the conducting medium does not go much beyond a "skin depth" and is of little practical consequence. Examples of reflection of microwaves by conductors are found in parabolic reflectors used as antennas and in targets for radar beams.

**Diffraction.** In an analogous manner to light, a microwave undergoes diffraction when it encounters an obstacle or an opening which is comparable to or

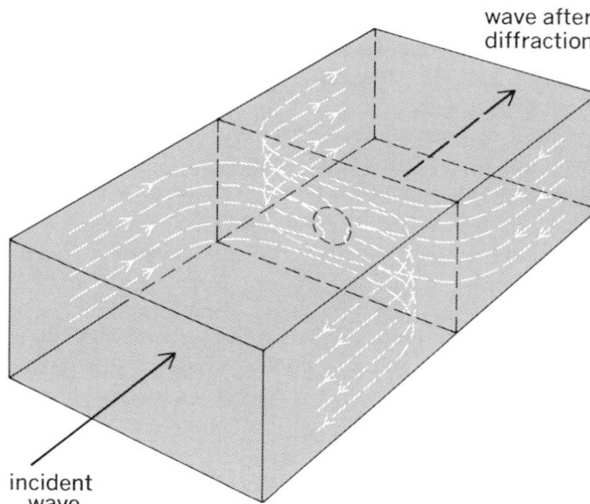


**Fig. 2.** Diffraction of microwaves through a small aperture between two waveguides. Only magnetic lines of force are shown for the field pattern.

somewhat smaller than its wavelength. Diffraction problems have been much studied but the results are generally too complicated for a simple description. One case of considerable importance, however, may be cited as an illustration. Let two waveguides be coupled through a small hole in a metallic partition as shown in **Fig. 2**. The radius of the hole is assumed to be much smaller than $\lambda/2\pi$, where $\lambda$ is the wavelength. A wave in one waveguide will leak through the hole by diffraction into the other waveguide. While an exact calculation is difficult, a satisfactory treatment can be worked out by regarding the diffraction effect as being equivalent to the presence of an electric and magnetic dipole placed at the position of the hole. The radiation fields of the dipoles supply the necessary wave coupling between the two waveguides.

**Polarization.** The polarization of an electromagnetic wave is specified by the direction of the electric and magnetic intensities. For simplicity, consider a plane wave propagating in the $z$ direction. The electric and magnetic intensities are always mutually perpendicular to each other in the $xy$ plane. It is, consequently, only necessary to consider the polarization of the electric intensity alone. If the electric intensity is polarized along one direction, say the $x$ axis, then the wave is said to be plane polarized. If there are components $E_x$ and $E_y$ equal in amplitude but differing in phase by 90°, the wave is circularly polarized (right-handed for $E_y$ lagging $E_x$ and left-handed for $E_y$ leading $E_x$). Lastly, if the wave is neither plane nor circularly polarized, it must be elliptically polarized.

The preceding essentially optical description holds true for microwaves in free space or wherever there is a transverse electric and magnetic (TEM) wave. Since a hollow waveguide does not support a TEM wave, the description of the polarization of the wave is much more complicated. However, the general notions expressed here are still valid and useful. For instance, the electric intensity of the dominant mode ($TE_{01}$) in a rectangular waveguide is plane polarized. This situation is also approximately true for the dominant mode ($TE_{11}$) in a circular waveguide. A circular waveguide is particularly useful in transforming plane-polarized electric intensity into circularly polarized electric intensity by a technique equivalent to the use of a quarter-wave plate in optics. For this purpose, it suffices to use a thin slab of dielectric material, such as mica, to introduce a 90° phase shift for one of the two equal components of the electric intensity. For information on TEM waves SEE MICROWAVE.

**Faraday effect for microwaves.** In optics, the Faraday effect is the rotation of the plane of polarization of a light beam which propagates in a dense transparent medium placed in a magnetic field along the direction of propagation. In microwaves, a similar phenomenon has been discovered and has led to many interesting applications.

Consider, for example, a circular waveguide which contains a slender rod of ferrite (a magnetic material of very low conductivity), as shown in **Fig. 3**. Place a steady magnetic field along the axial direction. If a wave with vertical electric polarization is incident from the left, then in passing through the ferrite zone its plane of polarization is rotated by an angle $\theta$ as indicated in the figure. This Faraday effect can be explained by the action of precessing elementary magnets in the magnetized ferrite upon the phase of the propagating wave. The initial plane-polarized electric intensity is equivalent to two oppositely rotating circularly polarized components. Only one of the components is affected (principally in the phase factor) by the precessing magnets because the latter can only precess in a unique direction corresponding to a given direction of the magnetic field. In the output, the combination of two circularly polarized waves with a relative phase shift is equal to a plane-polarized wave having its polarization rotated by an angle with respect to the initial plane.

If the output wave is sent back to pass by the ferrite from right to left, the plane of polarization of the backward wave rotates another $\theta$ degrees in the same direction as the initial rotation. In other words, the polarization of the new output wave on the left is rotated from the initial plane by $2\theta$, instead of zero degrees as might be expected by the principle of reciprocity. Thus this system constitutes a nonreciprocal circuit element and is sometimes called a gyrator to signify the gyrating motion of the elementary magnets. SEE GYRATOR; RECIPROCITY PRINCIPLE.

One of the most important applications of a gyrator is found in unidirectional transmission. Suppose a plane-polarized wave is introduced from a rectangular to a circular waveguide containing a gyrator and finally to another rectangular waveguide oriented to suit the polarization of the output wave. If the angle of rotation, which defines the output polarization, is adjusted to 45°, any wave from the output which is fed back to the input will be at right angles with the input intensity and hence will not be accepted by the rectangular waveguide. Another important application of gyrators is known as a circulator, a simple example

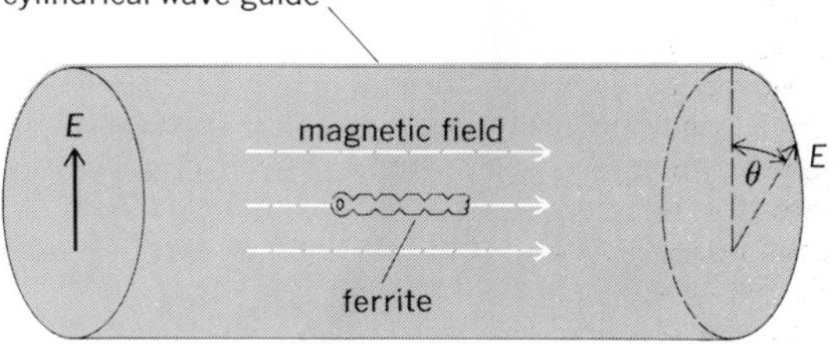


**Fig. 3.** Rotation of the plane of polarization of a microwave by a ferrite rod in a longitudinal magnetic field. *E* represents electric intensity.

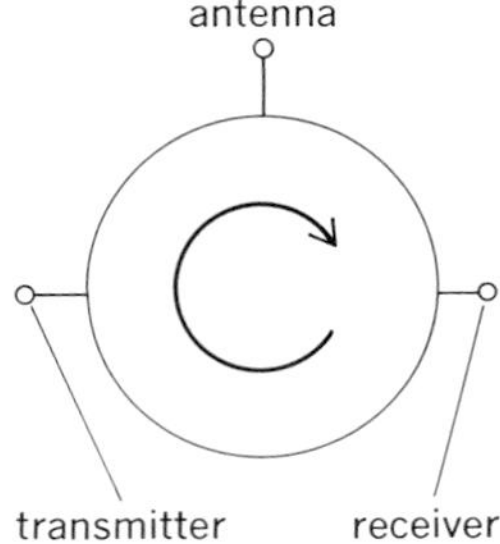


**Fig. 4. Circulator formed by one or more gyrator elements for nonreciprocal application.**

of which is given in **Fig. 4**. By means of one or more gyrators, a circulator such as the one depicted will allow a wave from the transmitter to go to the antenna but not to the receiver and will let a wave from the antenna go to the receiver but not to the transmitter. SEE MICROWAVE TRANSMISSION LINES.

*C. K. Jen*

***Bibliography.*** A. J. Baden-Fuller, *Microwaves: An Introduction to Microwave Theory and Techniques*, 1979; K. C. Gupta, *Microwaves*, 1980; L. Lewin, *Theory of Waveguides*, 1975.

## Microwave power measurement

Determination of the rate at which energy is transmitted by microwave propagation. Power is one of the fundamental parameters measured at microwave frequencies. Since the physical dimensions of the microwave system are comparable with the wavelength, the voltage along a conductor is no longer constant. Further, for energy transmitted inside a hollow, unicon-ductor waveguide, the voltage difference between two points is not uniquely defined and varies as a function of the path taken to pass from one point to the other. Thus voltage standards, basic to low-frequency electrical measurements, give way to power standards at microwaves. Power meters are connected either temporarily, to measure all the power, in place of the normal termination, or permanently to measure a fixed portion of the power. SEE MICROWAVE.

**Terminating power meters.** A terminating power meter absorbs a power $P_M$ at its one input port. The effective efficiency $\eta_e$ of the terminating power meter is defined by Eq. (1), where $P_I$ is the power indicated

$$\eta_e = \frac{P_I}{P_M} \qquad (1)$$

by the power meter. A parameter designated the calibration factor $K$ of a terminating power meter is defined by Eq. (2). In this case the power incident has

$$K = \frac{P_I}{\text{power incident}} \qquad (2)$$

a rather special meaning. It is the energy per second flowing in the electromagnetic wave incident on the power meter as measured an infinitesimal distance ahead of the power meter input.

In order to relate the two parameters, $\eta_e$ and $K$, consider the terminating power meter connected to a short section of transmission line having characteristic impedance $Z_0$ which has electromagnetic energy fed into its opposite end (**Fig. 1**). If the incident electromagnetic wave is assumed to have voltage $V$ at an infinitesimal distance $\delta$ in front of the power meter input, the reflected electromagnetic wave at the same plane will have voltage $\Gamma_M V$, where $\Gamma_M$ is the voltage reflection coefficient of the power meter. SEE ELECTRICAL IMPEDANCE; MICROWAVE IMPEDANCE MEASUREMENT; TRANSMISSION LINES.

Since the energy flow in the traveling waves is proportional to the square of the voltage, assuming an ideal section of transmission line connected to the power meter, it follows that Eq. (3) is valid, where

$$\frac{P_M}{\text{power incident}} = 1 - |\Gamma_M|^2 \qquad (3)$$

$|\Gamma_M|$ is the magnitude of the voltage reflection coefficient. Hence the relation between $K$ and $\eta_e$ is given by Eq. (4).

$$K = \eta_e(1 - |\Gamma_M|^2) \qquad (4)$$

While $\eta_e$ and $K$ are both useful parameters for a terminating power meter, $\eta_e$ should be considered the more fundamental since it is independent of the characteristic impedance of the connecting line and of the impedance of the power meter. Furthermore, the two parameters are very simply related, and either one may be determined through knowledge of the other one and an impedance measurement.

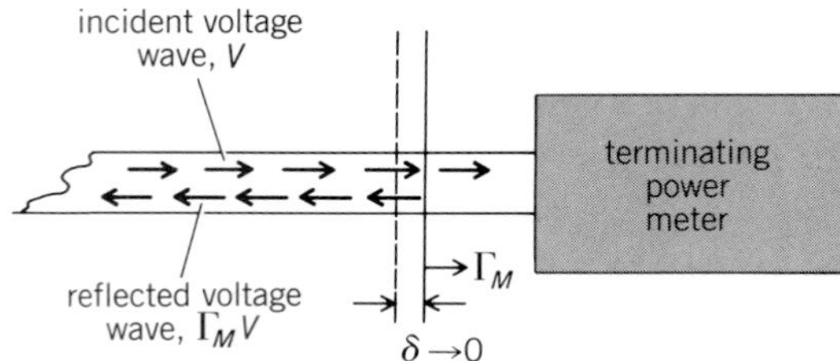


**Fig. 1. Microwave power incident on a terminating power meter.**

The power $P_0$ that a microwave source would deliver to a termination with characteristic impedance $Z_0$, as measured by the terminating power meter, is given by Eq. (5), where $\Gamma_G$ is the voltage reflection

$$P_0 = \frac{P_I}{K}|1 - \Gamma_G\Gamma_M|^2 \qquad (5)$$

coefficient of the source. Usually the impedance portion of the expression in Eq. (5) is not calculated, but is included in the error budget of the measurement.

**Two-port power monitor.** The use of a two-port power monitor was proposed as a technique for assembling a standard power source. The general form of this type of device consists of a stable three-port network converted to a two-port power monitor by permanent connection of a power meter to one of its ports. An excellent power monitor (**Fig. 2**) has a ter-

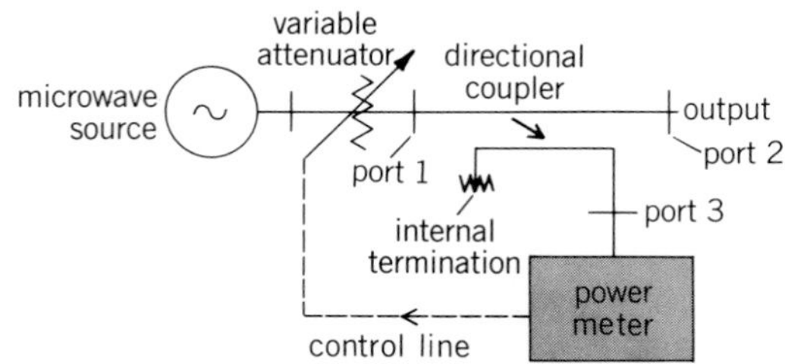


**Fig. 2. A standard source of microwave power stabilized by a power meter.**

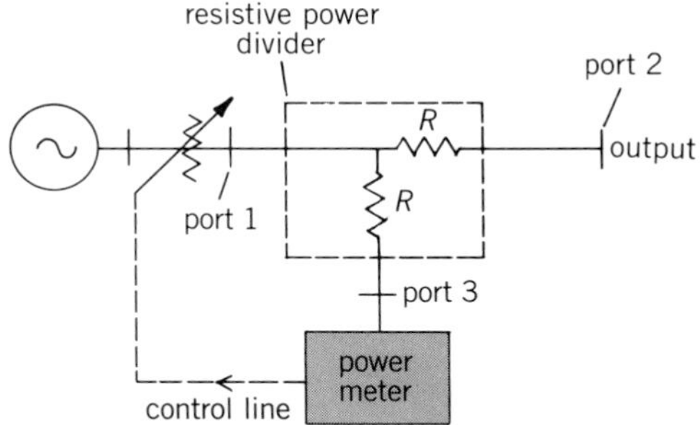


**Fig. 3.** A standard microwave source having very broad frequency range.

minating power meter connected to the side-arm, port 3, of a three-port directional coupler. The output from port 3 is proportional to the microwave energy traveling in the main line of the directional coupler in the direction from port 1 to port 2. The fourth port of the directional coupler is terminated internally. A source of radio-frequency energy with adjustable amplitude is connected to port 1. Port 2 becomes the output of a standard source with power available and output impedance given by the power meter reading and the characteristics of the three-port. The variable attenuator may be adjusted manually for a desired power meter reading, or, as suggested by the broken line, an electrical output from the power meter may be used to automatically control the attenuator to maintain a constant power available from port 2. SEE DIRECTIONAL COUPLER.

A calibration factor may be assigned to the directional coupler with side-arm power monitor. The calibration factor of interest is $K_2$ and is defined by Eq. (6), where $P_{I_3}$ is the power indicated by the power

$$K_2 = \frac{P_{I_3}}{P_{0_2}} \quad (6)$$

monitor at port 3 when the power delivered to a load with characteristic impedance $Z_0$ connected at port 2 is $P_{0_2}$. Calibration of the coupler-power monitor is thus performed by connection of a power meter having known characteristics to the output port 2 and determination of $P_{0_2}$ for a particular power monitor reading. Use is made of Eq. (5) for this measurement.

The directional coupler-power monitor must now be regarded as a single device and must remain connected together permanently as a calibrated feed-through power monitor. The advantage of this coupler-power monitor is that it can have a very low insertion loss and yet have a very low effective source reflection coefficient. However, its bandwidth is limited by the directional coupler.

For cases in which the low insertion loss is not necessary, it is possible to assemble an extremely broadband feed-through power meter (**Fig. 3**). The power splitter has no low-frequency cutoff, but three-fourths of the power available from the source is lost. In the particular case where $R$ is 50 ohms, the effective source reflection coefficient has magnitude zero in a 50-ohm transmission line system. This is due to the fact that a monitored T junction behaves as a zero impedance voltage source.

**Power sensors.** A number of techniques have been used to sense microwave power. These include (1) conversion of the microwave power to heat and sensing the thermal effect on a calorimetric body, (2) measurement of the force caused by microwave radiation pressure, (3) measurement of a microwave Hall effect, (4) measurement of electron acceleration caused by a microwave electric field, and (5) rectification of microwave voltage by using diodes. Rectification of microwave voltage is the most simple and most sensitive technique, but conversion of microwave power to heat is by far the most widely used because of its long term stability. Two versions of detector, based on conversion to heat are bolometers and thermocouples. SEE DIODE; HALL EFFECT; RECTIFIER.

***Bolometer mounts.*** A bolometer is a component whose resistance varies with temperature. Very small bolometers are inside a bolometer mount having a transmission line input. The bolometer is located so that it can simultaneously absorb microwave power and dc power. By using electronic instrumentation, the bolometer resistance is held constant by automatic adjustment of the dc bias power dissipated in the bolometer. When microwave power is fed into the mount, the dc power is automatically reduced to keep the bolometer resistance constant, and the change in dc power required is a measure of the microwave power. The most used type of bolometer is the thermistor with a negative temperature coefficient of resistance. Since this is a power substitution technique, any long-term drift or instability in the thermistor is compensated by an automatic change in dc bias power.

***Thermocouple detectors.*** A type of power detector in which the microwave power is dissipated directly on the warm junctions of a thermopile has largely replaced the coaxial thermistor mount for general usage. The electronic instrumentation is simply a low-noise dc amplifier-voltmeter combination to measure the thermopile output. Also, manufacturers have achieved a better impedance match over a broad frequency range with this detector than with a thermistor mount. One complication is the inclusion of a stable radio-frequency reference source into the electronic part of the measurement system to permit checking of the long-term stability of the detector.

**Standards.** The power sensors and their associated electronics are the standards for measurement of microwave power throughout industry and in the laboratory. The electronic portion can usually be calibrated by reference to dc standards. The efficiency and calibration factor of the microwave power sensors are compared through a hierarchy of laboratories to fundamental standards of microwave power. These fundamental standards are essentially the calorimetric type mentioned above, but are configured so that their efficiency is either calculable or measurable.

In one type of fundamental standard, referred to as a coaxial calorimeter, microwave power is dissipated in a resistor and the temperature rise of the resistor and its mounting is measured by a thermopile. Direct-current power for the same temperature rise is fed into the calorimeter through the same input port as was used for microwave power. The calorimeter is constructed so that the microwave and direct currents in the resistor are as nearly as possible the same. The difference between the microwave loss and the dc loss in the thermally insulating input to the resistor is measured and used to calculate the reduction in efficiency of the calorimeter at high measurement frequencies.

A second type of fundamental standard involves

again a calorimetric measurement, but in this case a thermistor mount is placed in thermal isolation inside an enclosure. The dc bias power causes the thermistor mount to heat up relative to its immediate surroundings, and a thermopile indicates this relative temperature rise. When microwave power is applied, the dc power automatically decreases to maintain constant power dissipation in the thermistor. However, any microwave power not dissipated in the thermistor itself causes an increase in thermopile output which is interpreted as a measure of the inefficiency of the thermistor mount. SEE MICROWAVE MEASUREMENTS.

*Richard F. Clark*

**Bibliography.** A. J. Estin (ed.), *Precision Measurement and Calibration; Selected NBS papers on Electricity–Radio Frequency*, NBS Spec. Publ. 300, no. 4, pp. 1–72, June 1970; *Fundamental of RF and microwave power measurements*, Hewlett-Packard Applicat. Note 64-1, 1977; T. S. Laverghetta, *Microwave Measurements and Techniques*, 1976; T. S. Laverghetta, *Handbook of Microwave Testing*, 1981; T. S. Laverghetta, *Practical Microwaves*, 1984.

## Microwave reflectometer

A form of directional coupler that is used for measuring the power flowing in both directions in a waveguide. A pair of single-detector couplers appropriately positioned on opposite sides of the waveguide can be used for this purpose, with one detector positioned to monitor transmitted power and the other detector positioned to measure power reflected back from a discontinuity in the line. Each coupler receives a constant small fraction of the energy flowing in one direction in the waveguide, the energy being extracted from the waveguide through two small holes drilled ¼ wavelength apart along the length of the guide. SEE DIRECTIONAL COUPLER; MICROWAVE IMPEDANCE MEASUREMENT.

*John Markus*

## Microwave solid-state devices

Semiconductor devices for the generation, amplification, detection, and control of electromagnetic energy in the frequency range of about 1–100 GHz. Devices that generate or amplify microwave energy are referred to as active microwave devices. The most important active solid-state microwave devices are microwave transistors, transferred electron (Gunn) devices, avalanche diodes, and tunnel diodes. Devices that detect or control microwave energy are referred to as passive microwave devices. The most important passive solid-state microwave devices include PIN diodes, varactor diodes, and point-contact and Schottky-barrier detector diodes. SEE MICROWAVE; MICROWAVE TUBE; SEMICONDUCTOR DIODE; TRANSISTOR.

### ACTIVE DEVICES

At the lower microwave frequencies, transistors are the most widely used active solid-state devices. Two types of microwave transistors are commercially available: silicon bipolar transistors and gallium arsenide (GaAs) field-effect transistors (FETs). Microwave transistors that have been under development include high-electron-mobility transistors (HEMTs) on modulation-doped FETs (MODFETs), and gallium indium arsenide (GaInAs) metal-insulator-semiconductor FETs (MISFETs).

At the higher microwave frequencies, the usefulness of transistors is severely limited by high-frequency effects, and two-terminal negative resistance devices such as transferred-electron devices, avalanche diodes, and tunnel diodes predominate. In a negative resistance, the current and voltage are 180° out of phase. A current $I$ flowing through a negative resistance $-R$ produces a voltage rise $V = -IR$, and a power $P = I^2R$ is generated by the power supply associated with the negative resistance. In microwave applications, the negative-resistance device is usually mounted in a circuit placed at the end of a transmission line, and a ferrite circulator is used to separate input power from the amplified output power. SEE FERRITE DEVICES; NEGATIVE-RESISTANCE CIRCUITS.

**Silicon bipolar transistors.** Most modern silicon bipolar microwave transistors are epitaxial diffused *npn* structures. **Figure 1***a* shows a cross-sectional view of a modern microwave transistor, a double-diffused epitaxial device. An epitaxial *n* layer is deposited on a heavily doped $n^+$ substrate. A *p* base is diffused into the epitaxial layer and many heavily doped *n* emitters are diffused into the base with $p^+$ plugs used to reduce the base spreading resistance. Silicon oxide layers are used as diffusion masks and for insulation. Contacts are made through openings in the oxide. Figure 1*b* shows three surface geometries that are widely used in microwave power transistors.

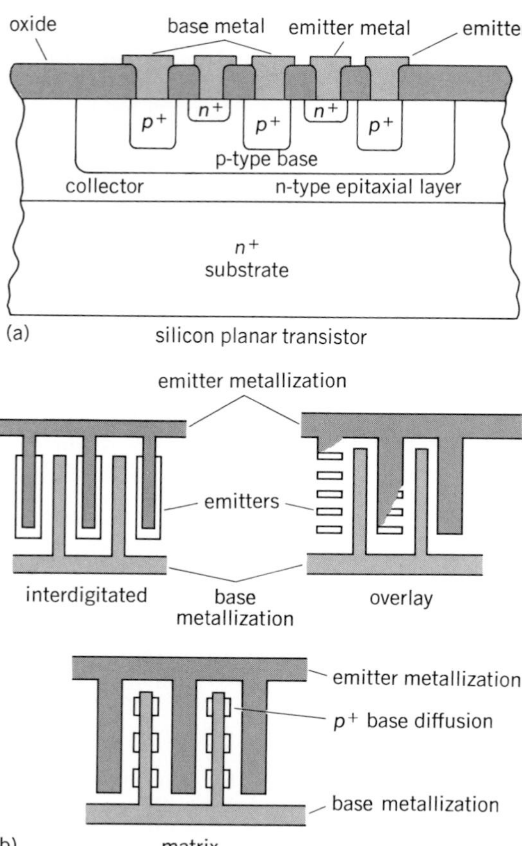


**Fig. 1. Planar silicon bipolar-power microwave transistor. (*a*) Cross section of transistor. (*b*) Surface geometries. (*After H. Sobol and F. Sterzer, Microwave power sources, IEEE Spectrum, 9(4)20–33, 1972*)**

The width of the emitter in Fig. 1*b* may be as small as 1 micrometer.

The basic principles of operation of bipolar microwave transistors are the same as those of low-frequency bipolar transistors. However, because of the higher frequencies involved, the requirements on dimensions, process control, packaging, heat sinking, and radio-frequency (rf) circuitry are much more severe for microwave transistors than for low-frequency transistors. The **table** lists the continuous-wave (CW) performance of typical silicon microwave power transistors. The pulsed power outputs that can be obtained are significantly higher than the CW power outputs. For example, peak power outputs of 600 W can be obtained from single transistors operating at 1 GHz. The noise figure of silicon bipolar transistors specifically designed for low-noise operation ranges from about 1.2 dB at 1 GHz to about 2.5 dB at 4 GHz.

**Typical CW performance of microwave silicon power transistors (28-V bias)**

| Frequency, GHz | Power, W | Gain, dB | Efficiency, % |
|---|---|---|---|
| 1 | 60 | 10 | 60 |
| 2 | 50 | 7 | 50 |
| 4 | 5 | 6 | 35 |

**GaAs field-effect transistors.** Microwave GaAs FETs are a type of microwave transistor that provides improved performance over silicon microwave transistors. Low-noise, low-power, and medium-power GaAs FETs are commercially available. **Figure 2** shows the cross section of a typical GaAs FET. An epitaxial *n* layer of GaAs is deposited on a semi-insulating GaAs substrate. Ohmic source and drain contacts and a Schottky-barrier gate contact are formed on the *n* layer. In a typical power microwave FET, the *n* layer is 0.3 μm thick, the source-drain spacing is about 2 μm, and the gate length ranges from about 0.5 to 1 μm.

In operation of the FET, the gate is biased negative with respect to the source, while the drain is biased-positive. The microwave input signal is applied between gate and source, and modulates the depth of the depletion layer that is formed underneath the gate. Since the electrons flowing from source to drain must move around the depletion layer, the source-drain current flow is modulated by the microwave input signal. The amplified signal is taken from a load resistor in the source-drain circuit. GaAs rather than silicon is used in the construction of FETs designed for operation at microwave frequencies, because the mobility of electrons in GaAs is several times as high as in silicon. This higher mobility is particularly important at microwave frequencies, since it leadsto lower series resistance and larger device dimensions for devices designed for operation at a given frequency.

The best noise figures obtained from GaAs FETs range from about 0.4 dB at 4 GHz to about 1.0 dB at 12 GHz and 6 dB at 30 GHz. CW power outputs range from 20 W at 4 GHz to 4 W at 12 GHz and 1.0 W at 20 GHz. Conversion efficiencies of over 40% at 10 GHz and 70% at 4 GHz have been obtained with devices operating class B (dc gate bias just sufficient to shut off direct current flow between source and drain).

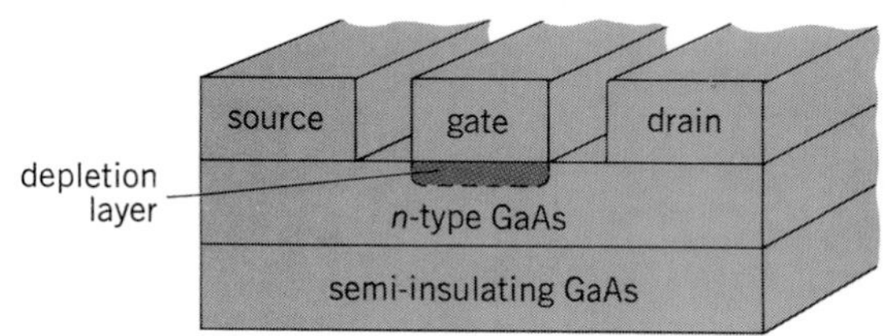


**Fig. 2. Cross-sectional view of a typical GaAs Schottky-barrier FET.**

**Transferred-electron (Gunn) devices.** In transferred-electron devices (TEDs), negative resistance is achieved by taking advantage of the negative differential mobility ($\mu = dv/dE$; $v$ = velocity of charge carriers, $E$ = electric field) of electrons in certain *n*-type III–V compounds, particularly GaAs. The basic theoretical concepts underlying the operation of TEDs were developed during the early 1960s, and the first experimental TED was described in 1963 by J. B. Gunn.

**Figure 3** shows graphs of electron drift velocity versus electric field for silicon and GaAs. The drift velocity for silicon exhibits a "normal" behavior, increasing monotonically with increasing electric field. In GaAs, on the other hand, the drift velocity decreases with increasing field above about 3 kV/cm. The negative differential mobility of GaAs is caused by the transfer of electrons from high- to low-mobility energy bands, hence the name transferred electron devices. *SEE SEMICONDUCTOR*.

Structurally, TEDs are particularly simple semiconductor devices. They consist merely of a bar of transferred electron material of length $L$ with ohmic cathode and anode contacts. The anode is biased positive with respect to the cathode at a magnitude larger than the threshold voltage $V_{TH} = E_{TH} \times L$ ($E_{TH}$ is the field at which maximum electron drift velocity occurs). Therefore, part of the device is biased into the negative mobility region. Excess electron space charge introduced at the cathode moves through the device under the influence of the applied field. The charge grows exponentially as it traverses the negative mobility region, since in a negative mobility region charges of like polarity attract one another and any accumulation of space charge grows with time at the rate exp $t/|\tau_r|$ ($\tau_r$ = dielectric relaxation time = $\epsilon/en\mu$; $\epsilon$ = dielectric constant, $e$ = electronic charge, $n$ = carrier concentration). If the space-charge growth in the device is not too large ($nL \gtrsim 7.6 \times 10^{11}/\text{cm}^2$ for GaAs), then the space-charge distribution in the device will be stable with time and the device will exhibit a stable negative resistance over a

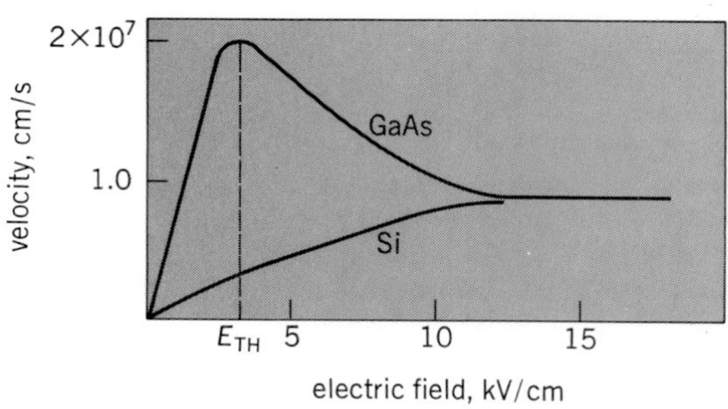


**Fig. 3. Curves of electron drift velocity versus electric field for silicon and gallium arsenide. (*After H. Sobol and F. Sterzer, Microwave power sources, IEEE Spectrum, 9(4):20–33, 1972*)**

wide range of frequencies, and can be used as the active element in a negative-resistance amplifier. For GaAs, the center frequency of the negative-resistance region is approximately given by Eq. (1).

$$f(\text{GHz}) \approx \frac{100}{L(\mu m)} \quad (1)$$

If the space-charge growth in a TED is sufficiently large ($nL$ greater than between 1 and a few times $10^{12}$ $\text{cm}^2$ for typical GaAs TEDs), the electric field distribution becomes a function of time. Several different time-varying field distributions (modes) useful for oscillator applications are then possible. For example, in the transit time mode, the domain of charges is nucleated at the cathode of the TED. The domain grows exponentially while moving toward the anode until the voltage across it is so large that the field in the parts of the TED outside the domain falls below threshold. The fully formed or "mature" domain disappears when it is collected at the anode. As it is being collected, the electric field throughout the TED rises above threshold, a new domain is nucleated at the cathode, and the cycle repeats itself. Short current pulses are generated while this process is going on. The spacing of the current pulses is approximately the transit time of the domains ($\sim L/v$). Another mode is the limited space-charge accumulation (LSA) mode. In the LSA mode, the formation of traveling domains is suppressed by an rf voltage whose amplitude is large enough to drive the TED below threshold during every rf cycle. The frequency of the rf voltage must also be high enough so that there is not enough time for a domain to form during the part of the rf cycle when the device voltage is above threshold. Frequency of oscillation in the LSA mode is independent of the transit time of the charge carriers and is determined solely by the circuit around the TED. At any given frequency, a TED operating in the LSA mode can be made much thicker than a TED operating in the domain mode.

The CW power outputs that can be obtained from TEDs range from 1 to 2 W at 10 GHz to about 60 mW at 90 GHz. The latter results were obtained with TEDs fabricated from indium phosphide (InP). Conversion efficiencies of commercially available devices are typically only a few percent, but in the laboratory, efficiencies in the 10–20% range have been obtained. The noise figure of transferred-electron amplifiers ranges typically from 10 to 20 dB. Several kilowatts of peak power can be obtained at the lower microwave frequencies from TEDs operating in the LSA mode. Unfortunately, high-power pulsed TEDs require thick $n$ layers that are difficult to heat-sink. The duty cycle of such thick devices is usually limited to a small fraction of 1%.

**Avalanche diodes.** Avalanche diodes are junction devices that produce a negative resistance by appropriately combining impact avalanche breakdown and charge-carrier transit time effects. Avalanche breakdown in semiconductors occurs if the electric field is high enough for the charge carriers to acquire sufficient energy from the field to create electron-hole pairs by impact ionization. For silicon and gallium arsenide, the semiconductors most commonly used to fabricate avalanche diodes, the threshold field for breakdown is on the order of a few hundred thousand volts per centimeter. Transit time effects occur if the time the charge carriers spend traversing the diode becomes an appreciable fraction of an rf period. If the current injected at the cathode of a thick diode is $I_0 \cos \omega t$, then the current flowing through the external circuit of the diode is given by Eq. (2), where $\omega$ is

$$I_T = I_0 \frac{\sin(\omega\tau/2)}{\omega\tau/2} \cos[\omega\tau - \omega\tau/2] \quad (2)$$

the angular frequency and $\tau$ is the time it takes the charge carriers to move from the cathode to the anode of the diode.

The two most important classes of avalanche diodes are IMPATT diodes (impact avalanche and transit time diodes) and TRAPATT diodes (trapped-plasma avalanche-triggered transit diodes). In IMPATT diodes, best operation is usually obtained when the transit angle of the carriers traversing the diode is of the order of 180°. In TRAPATT diodes, the transit angle is usually much smaller than 180°.

The basic operation of IMPATT diodes can be most easily understood by reference to the first proposed avalanche diode, the Read diode. The theory of this device was presented in 1958 by W. T. Read, and the first experimental diode was described in 1965. A model of the Read diode and the dc electric field distribution when a large reverse bias is applied across the diode are shown in **Fig. 4**. It is assumed for purposes of the illustration that the diode has been placed in an rf circuit or cavity and that the total field across the diode is the sum of the dc and ac fields. The diode bias is chosen so that the field in the avalanche region is high enough to cause breakdown during the positive half of the rf voltage cycle, but is below the critical field required for breakdown during the negative part of the voltage cycle. As a result, the hole current generation in the avalanche region grows during the positive half of the rf voltage cycle and dies down during the negative half. The hole current therefore reaches its maximum value one-quarter of a cycle after the voltage reaches its maximum; that is, the hole current lags the rf voltage by 90°. During the entire rf cycle, the electric field in the drift region is kept high enough to cause the injected holes to travel with the constant limiting drift velocity. The length of the drift region is chosen to make $\omega\tau = \pi$, so that from the transit time equation, Eq. (2), $I_T$ lags $I$ by 90°, and the phase difference between the applied voltage and $I_T$ is 180°; that is, the diode acts as a negative resistance.

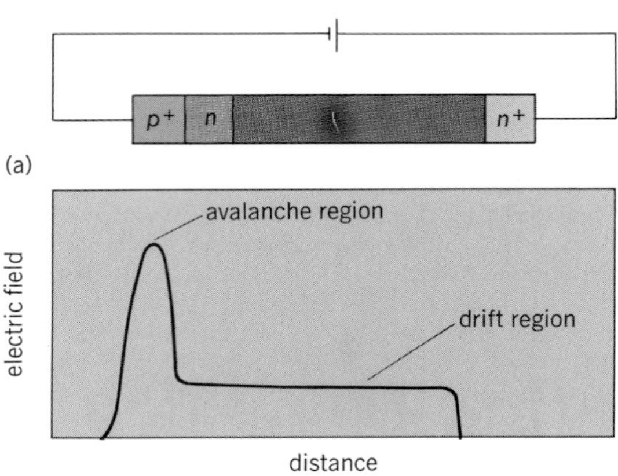


**Fig. 4. Two characteristics of a Read-type IMPATT diode. (*a*) Doping profile. (*b*) Electric field distribution. (*After H. Sobol and F. Sterzer, Microwave power sources. IEEE Spectrum, 9(4):20–33, 1972*)**

Most practical IMPATT diodes differ from the Read diode in that avalanching is not confined to a narrow, well-defined region, but occurs over a significant portion or over the entire depletion region. These types of diodes behave similarly to Read diodes and also exhibit negative resistance when the transit time of the charge carriers becomes a significant fraction of an rf period. The semiconductor materials favored for microwave IMPATT diodes are silicon and gallium arsenide.

TRAPATT diodes are typically $p^+nn^+$ or $n^+pp^+$ silicon diodes. In operation, a diode is placed in a circuit containing high-$Q$ resonators and is back-biased into avalanche. As the diode breaks down, a highly conducting electron-hole plasma quickly fills the entire $n$ region, and the voltage across the diode drops to a low value. The plasma is then extracted from the diode by the low residual electric field, thus causing a large current flow even though the voltage is low. Once extraction of the plasma is completed, the current becomes very small and the voltage rises to a high value. Eventually, the reactive energy stored in the resonant circuits raises the voltage above breakdown, and the cycle repeats.

The CW power outputs that can be obtained from IMPATT diodes range from several watts at 10 GHz to 2 W at 40 GHz and 50 mW at 250 GHz. Peak powers as high as 50 W can be obtained at 10 GHz. The best efficiencies obtained to date are on the order of 35%. TRAPATT diodes are particularly well suited for generating high peak powers. Peak power outputs of TRAPATT diodes range from several hundred watts at 1 GHz to tens of watts in the 10–15-GHz range. The best pulsed efficiencies range from about 60% at 1 GHz to about 30% at 10 GHz.

**Tunnel diodes.** Tunnel diodes were first described by L. Esaki in 1958. They are heavily doped *pn* junctions that exhibit a negative differential resistance over part of their current-voltage characteristics. The negative resistance is caused by processes (quantum-mechanical tunneling) that are so fast that there are no transit time effects even at the highest microwave frequencies. Tunnel diodes can be fabricated from a host of different semiconductor materials, but only diodes from germanium, gallium arsenide, and gallium antimonide are used at microwave frequencies.

Tunnel diodes are used in oscillators, low-noise amplifiers, and detectors at microwave frequencies. However, the power output of tunnel diode oscillators and amplifiers is limited to a few milliwatts at most, and for this reason tunnel diodes are being replaced by some of the newer solid-state microwave devices, particularly by GaAs field-effect transistors. *SEE TUNNEL DIODE.*

### PASSIVE DEVICES

The oldest passive microwave device is the point-contact diode, a diode that was widely used in World War II radars. More modern passive microwave solid-state devices include Schottky-barrier diodes, PIN diodes, and varactor diodes.

**Point-contact and Schottky-barrier diodes.** Point-contact and Schottky-barrier diodes are majority-carrier rectifiers that are used as the nonlinear element in passive microwave-frequency down-converters and in rectifiers. The rectification characteristics of these diodes are similar to those of *pn* junction diodes, but unlike *pn* junction diodes they do not exhibit any minority-carrier charge storage capacitance. This lack of charge-storage capacitance makes point-contact and Schottky-barrier diodes particularly attractive for down-converter applications, since variations in capacitance are in general undesirable in down-conversion. In point-contact diodes, a pointed tungsten wire is forced down on a semiconductor wafer (usually silicon). In Schottky-barrier diodes, the rectifying junction is formed at the interface of a deposited metal layer and a semiconductor crystal, usually silicon or gallium arsenide. The metal-semiconductor interface is planar, and as a result the contact potential and the current distribution are nearly uniform over the entire junction. This is in contrast to point-contact diodes, where the interface between the sharp tungsten point and the semiconductor wafer is nearly hemispherical, and both contact potential and current distribution are therefore in general nonuniform. Because of their greater uniformity, Schottky-barrier diodes have lower series resistance, lower noise figures, greater dynamic range, and greater resistance to pulse burnout than point-contact diodes. With GaAs Schottky-barrier diodes, conversion losses as low as 2.5 dB can be obtained when down-converting a 12 GHz signal to 70 MHz. *SEE POINT-CONTACT DIODE.*

**PIN diodes.** PIN diodes are junction diodes in which the $p$ and $n$ regions are separated by a relatively thick high-resistivity intrinsic layer. These diodes are widely used in microwave switches, electronically variable microwave attenuators, and microwave limiters. When a PIN diode is back-biased, the intrinsic region of the diode is swept free of holes and electrons, and the series resistance of the diode is very large. Under forward bias, on the other hand, the $p$ and $n$ regions inject holes and electrons into the intrinsic region, forming a highly conductive plasma, and the series resistance becomes very small. Because of the high resistivity and thickness of the intrinsic layer, the junction capacitance of a PIN diode is not a function of bias voltage at microwave frequencies, and the value of capacitance for a given junction area is much smaller in a PIN diode than in a conventional *pn* junction diode. The power-handling capability of PIN diode arrays can be as high as 1 MW peak and 1 kW average. *SEE JUNCTION DIODE.*

**Varactor diodes.** A varactor (variable-capacitance) diode is a *pn* junction diode that is specifically designed for applications that make use of the voltage dependence of the diode depletion-layer capacitance. The voltage-dependent junction capacitance $C_j$ of an ideal varactor diode is given by Eq. (3), where $K$ is a

$$C_j = K(\phi - V_j)^{-n} \tag{3}$$

constant, $\phi$ is the contact potential, $V_j$ is the voltage across the junction, and $n$ is a coefficient whose value depends on the doping profile of the junction ($n = 1/3$ for a graded junction, $n = 1/2$ for an abrupt junction, $n = 1$ for a hyperabrupt junction).

Microwave varactor diodes are usually fabricated from either silicon or gallium arsenide. They are widely used as tuning elements in voltage-controlled filters and oscillators, in harmonic generators, and in parametric amplifiers and frequency converters. An important figure of merit of varactor diodes is their cutoff frequency $f_c$, which is defined in Eq. (4),

$$f_c = \frac{1}{2\pi R_S C_j} \tag{4}$$

where $R_S$ is the series resistance of the diode. GaAs varactor diodes with cutoff frequencies (measured at breakdown) of many hundreds of gigahertz are commercially available. *See* Varactor.

#### Optically Controlled Devices

The characteristics of microwave solid-state devices can be modified or controlled by optically generating free carriers (electron-hole pairs) in the semiconductors of the devices. Optically generated free carriers change the device characteristics because they increase the conductivity of the semiconductors in which they are generated. Furthermore, free carriers produce photovoltaic voltages, particularly if the carriers are generated in or near semiconductor junctions. *See* Photoconductivity; Photovoltaic effect.

Most of the experimental work on optically controlled solid-state microwave devices has been carried out with GaAs FETs. It has been demonstrated that it is possible to optically control the gain of GaAs FET amplifiers, as well as the frequency of GaAs FET oscillators. It has also been shown that GaAs FET oscillators can be phase-locked with optical signals, and that GaAs FETs can be used as fast photodetectors. *See* Optical detectors.

*Fred Sterzer*

**Bibliography.** P. Bhartia and I. J. Bahl, *Millimeter Wave Engineering and Application*, 1984; B. G. Bosch and R. W. H. Engelman, *Gunn-Effect Electronics*, 1975; J. V. DiLorenzo and D. D. Khandelwal, *GaAs FET Principles and Technology*, 1982; C. P. Snapp, Bipolars quietly dominate, *Microwave Sys. News*, pp. 45–67, November 1979; R. Soares et al., *Applications of GaAs MESFETS*, 1983; H. Sobol and F. Sterzer, Microwave power sources, *IEEE Spectrum*, 9(4):20–23, 1972; S. M. Sze, *Physics of Semiconductor Devices*, 1982; H. A. Watson, *Microwave Semiconductor Devices and Their Circuit Applications*, 1969.

## Microwave transmission lines

Structures used for transmission of electromagnetic energy at microwave frequencies from one point to another.

Electromagnetic fields can be transmitted from one position to another in free space. Electromagnetic waves propagating in free space travel at the velocity of light $c$, equal to $3 \times 10^8$ m/s or $1.86 \times 10^5$ mi/s. When the electromagnetic waves travel in a lossless, dielectric, nonmagnetic medium, their velocity is reduced from that in free space by the square root of the relative permittivity. Microwaves are characterized by free-space wavelengths of less than 1 m, corresponding to frequencies higher than 300 MHz. *See* Electromagnetic wave; Permittivity.

Microwaves can also be guided within conducting or metallic boundaries. If the conducting boundaries are composed of two or more conducting surfaces of uniform cross sections in the direction of propagation, then the most simple mode of propagation is a transverse electromagnetic (TEM) mode, whose propagation velocity is the same as that of a wave propagating in the same medium without boundaries. Examples of such two-conductor lines are two-wire lines (such as used for power transmission at 60 Hz), coaxial lines, and strip lines. At microwave frequencies, coaxial lines find the widest application of these configurations, while strip lines are used particularly for microwave integrated circuits that employ planar geometries with such technologies as silicon-on-sapphire and gallium arsenide. *See* Integrated circuits; Microwave solid-state devices.

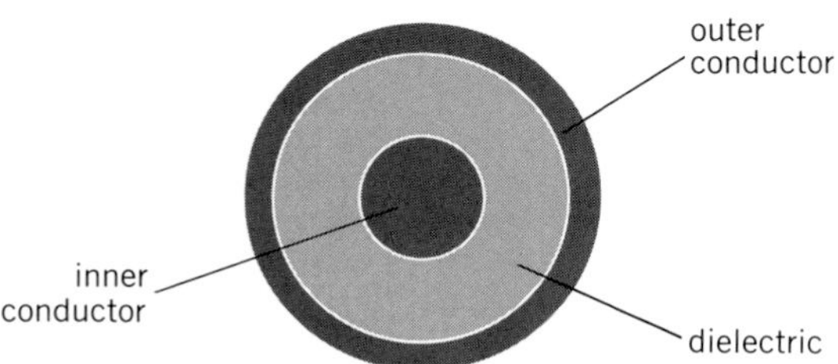

**Fig. 1.** Cross-sectional view of coaxial transmission line.

**Coaxial transmission lines.** Coaxial transmission lines consist of a dielectric material bounded by two coaxial, cylindrical conducting walls; the electromagnetic fields travel in the dielectric medium (**Fig. 1**). In theory, such lines can propagate in the transverse electromagnetic mode at frequencies from zero to infinity (including the microwave range). To limit propagation to transverse electromagnetic mode, the mean circumference of the line must be less than one wavelength. Since coaxial transmission lines cannot be made indefinitely small, there is an upper bound on the frequencies at which such lines may be used exclusively for only transverse electromagnetic propagation. Above this bounding frequency, where the mean circumference is greater than one wavelength, transverse electric (TE) and transverse magnetic (TM) modes also propagate on the line. These modes are of the same types that propagate in waveguides.

In general, coaxial lines exhibit skin effect loss in the conductors, and dielectric loss in the dielectric. Skin effect loss increases with increasing frequency, and thus limits the upper frequency of operation. The center conductor may be supported by the dielectric material in flexible coaxial cables, or by dielectric beads or shorted one-fourth–wavelength stubs in rigid coaxial lines. Neither beads nor one-fourth–wavelength stub supports affect the propagation characteristics of rigid coaxial lines significantly. *See* Coaxial cable.

**Strip transmission lines.** Microwave strip lines are constructed with a metal strip above a metal plane or with a metal strip between two metal planes (**Fig. 2**). In either case, a dielectric material is used to insulate the metal strip and the ground plane or planes. Microwave integrated circuits made from these elements can be built to include various passive circuit elements, and active circuit elements can then be connected to them. As the technology of microwave integrated circuits improves, it is expected that active microwave frequency devices will increasingly be

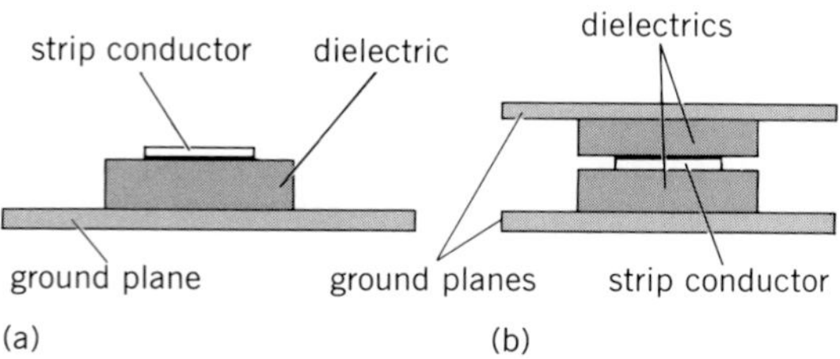

**Fig. 2.** Cross-sectional view of microwave strip lines (*a*) with a strip over a plane or (*b*) with a strip between two planes.

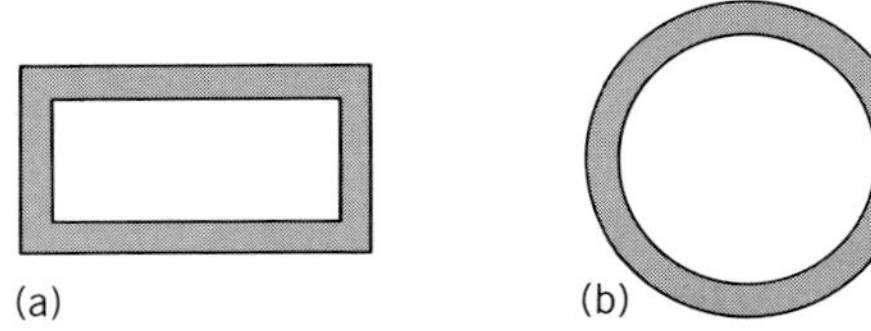


**Fig. 3.** Cross-sectional view of (*a*) rectangular and (*b*) circular waveguide configurations.

fabricated in the circuits by using strip transmission lines.

**Waveguides.** In general, waveguides are hollow pipes which do not exhibit propagation down to zero frequency because the transmission line does not have two conductors but is composed of only one conducting boundary (**Fig. 3**). Thus, all such waveguides have a low-frequency cutoff, and operation can be achieved only for frequencies above this cutoff. The dimensions of the hollow pipe determine the cutoff wavelength corresponding to the cutoff frequency, so that the pipe dimensions and cutoff wavelength are of the same order of magnitude. When the mean circumference of a coaxial transmission line is larger than a wavelength, then coaxial lines also exhibit propagation modes with lower-frequency cutoffs. Above the cutoff frequency, the waves propagated are transverse electric or transverse magnetic modes and the velocity of propagation is a function of frequency. Since all transverse electric and transverse magnetic modes have velocities which are frequency-sensitive, the dimensions or the design of the transmission line or waveguide are ordinarily chosen to propagate only the desired mode. Coaxial lines are generally operated in the transverse electromagnetic mode to avoid this difficulty, and waveguides are usually operated in the modes with the lowest cutoff frequency (dominant modes) to avoid moding problems. *SEE WAVEGUIDE.*

**Phase and group velocity.** Any plane wave is characterized by two velocity parameters, the phase velocity $v_p$ and the group velocity $v_g$, both of which depend in turn on the phase number $\beta$ and the radian frequency $\omega$. The phase number $\beta$ is the rate at which the phase of the wave changes with distance in the direction of propagation, and is equal to $2\pi/\lambda$, where $\lambda$ is the wavelength. The radian frequency $\omega$ is the rate at which the phase of the wave changes with time, and is equal to $2\pi/T$, where $T$ is the period of the wave.

The phase velocity is defined in terms of the phase difference observed at two different points in a plane wave. It is considered to be the velocity of a single frequency wave and is defined as the ratio of the radian frequency to the phase number, Eq. (1). If there

$$v_p = \frac{\omega}{\beta} \tag{1}$$

is a modulation impressed on a carrier, then the modulation (envelope) pattern travels at a velocity called the group velocity. Analysis of the velocity of the modulation envelope shows that the group velocity is equal to the rate of change of the radian frequency with respect to the phase number, Eq. (2). In a mod-

$$v_g = \frac{\partial\omega}{\partial\beta} \tag{2}$$

ulated wave, the carrier has a velocity $v_p$ and the envelope has a velocity $v_g$. *SEE MODULATION.*

In a medium where the phase velocity is independent of frequency, the group velocity equals the phase velocity, and any signal will propagate without phase distortion. In a medium where the phase velocity is a function of frequency, this is no longer the case and the medium is said to be dispersive. A vacuum is nondispersive, but all material media are dispersive. In general, the phase velocity is a function of frequency, density, and temperature, so the dispersion problem can be very complex. Generally, however, the dielectric materials used in transmission lines are isotropic.

A useful representation of the phase and group velocities is a graph of the radian frequency $\omega$ versus the phase number $\beta$. The slope of the chord from a point on the curve to the origin is the phase velocity $v_p$, and the slope of the tangent of the curve at the same point is the group velocity $v_g$ (**Fig. 4**). These slopes are identical in a nondispersive medium.

**Propagation impedance.** The characteristic impedance of free space is equal to 377 ohms, being given by $\sqrt{\mu_0/\epsilon_0}$, where $\mu_0$ and $\epsilon_0$ are the permeability and permittivity of free space, respectively. In a lossless, nonmagnetic medium, the impedance is reduced from that of free space by the square-root of the relative permittivity. Ferrites have values of permeability greater than the permeability of free space. For a transmission line, the characteristic impedance is also a function of the line's transverse cross section. This characteristic impedance is defined as the voltage impressed across the line divided by the current flowing in the line.

For lossless lines, the characteristic impedance is equal to $\sqrt{L/C}$, where $L$ and $C$ are the inductance and capacitance per unit length. For coaxial transmission lines, the characteristic impedance depends on the inner radius of the outer conductor, the outer radius of the inner conductor, and the relative permittivity of the dielectric medium. This impedance is adjusted to 50 or 75 ohms in many standard cables by the choice of these three parameters. For strip transmission lines, the characteristic impedance depends on the width of the line, the spacing between the strip and the ground plane, and the relative permittivity of the dielectric material. These parameters can be chosen to achieve a particular value of characteristic impedance. *SEE ALTERNATING-CURRENT CIRCUIT THEORY; ELECTRICAL IMPEDANCE.*

**Reflections and standing waves.** Traveling waves can propagate in either direction on transmission lines. Whenever there are changes in the cross-sectional dimensions of the line or transitions to other

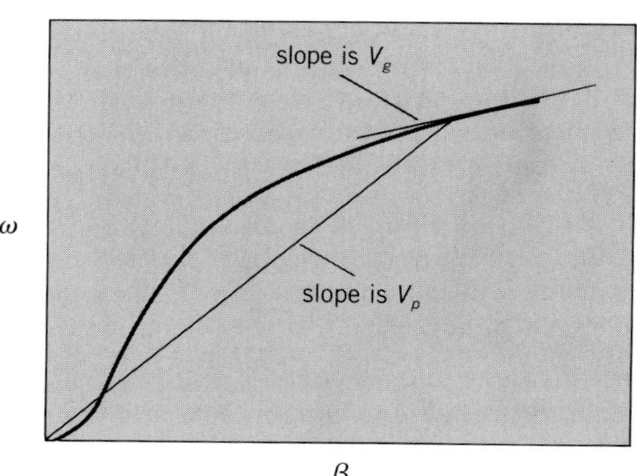


**Fig. 4.** Representation of the phase velocity $v_p$ and the group velocity $v_g$ on a plot of radian frequency $\omega$ versus phase number $\beta$.

lines or other passive elements, reflections can occur at the junction or transition points. At these points, a portion of the wave is reflected and a portion is transmitted past the junction. The reflection coefficient ρ may be defined in terms of the reflected and incident waves by Eq. (3), where $V_1'$ is the reflected voltage

$$\rho = \frac{V_1'}{V_1} \tag{3}$$

and $V_1$ is the incident voltage. This coefficient can also be defined in terms of the impedance of the line before the junction, $Z_1$, and the impedance beyond the junction, $Z_2$, by Eq. (4).

$$\rho = \frac{Z_2 - Z_1}{Z_2 + Z_1} \tag{4}$$

The presence of both the incident wave $V_1$ and the reflected wave $V_1'$ leads to standing waves between the source and the reflection points. These can be observed with a standing-wave detector. The absolute magnitude of the ratio of the maximum and minimum voltages resulting from the sum and differences of the incident wave $V_1$ and the reflected wave $V_1'$ is defined as the voltage standing-wave ratio (VSWR). The reflection coefficient ρ and the voltage standing wave ratio are related by Eq. (5). If the impedance $Z_2$ of

$$\text{VSWR} = \frac{1 + |\rho|}{1 - |\rho|} \tag{5}$$

the line beyond the junction is equal to the impedance $Z_1$ of the line before the junction, then the reflection coefficient equals 0 and the voltage standing-wave ratio equals 1, corresponding to a matched load condition at the junction. Alternately, a short circuit or an open circuit at the junction gives a $|\rho|$ of unity and a voltage standing-wave ratio of infinity. The voltage standing-wave ratio is particularly useful in determining the effectiveness of the match between the impedances at a junction. SEE MICROWAVE IMPEDANCE MEASUREMENT; STANDING-WAVE DETECTOR.

**Matching techniques.** It is often necessary to impedance-match a transmission line to a load. The optimum method is to make the load impedance equivalent to the transmission line impedance. Sometimes this is not possible, and special techniques are then necessary to eliminate the reflected wave. One technique is to introduce a second reflection of the same magnitude and to position it so the two reflections cancel in phase and amplitude. A slide screw tuner can be used to accomplish this matching. This technique can also be accomplished in a two-wire transmission line by connecting another line across the first and adjusting its length and position to cancel the reflection from the load. Combinations of two or more such stub tuners are frequently used for impedance matching. Another technique for matching to a load is to use an approximately quarter-wavelength long section of line between the transmission line and the load, with the inserted section having a characteristic impedance equal to the geometric mean of the load and transmission line impedances.

These are resonant techniques that depend on using sections of transmission line of the proper length to achieve a good match. However, because the wavelength λ is a function of frequency, matches of this kind cannot be made of indefinitely wide bandwidth. Since only a limited bandwidth can be achieved with resonant techniques, nonresonant tapering is often preferred for impedance matching. A tapered section of transmission line is used between the two impedances to be matched, with a length of at least one-half wavelength at the lowest frequency for which a good match is desired. Various charts are used to facilitate the matching process, the most widely used of which is the Smith chart. SEE ELECTROMAGNETIC WAVE TRANSMISSION; IMPEDANCE MATCHING; MICROWAVE; TRANSMISSION LINES.

*Richard W. Grow*

**Bibliography.** A. J. Baden-Fuller, *Microwaves: An Introduction to Microwave Theory and Techniques*, 1979; R. G. Brown et al., *Lines, Waves and Antennas: The Transmission of Electric Energy*, 2d ed., 1973; C. H. Durney and C. C. Johnson, *Introduction to Modern Electromagnetics*, 1969; O. P. Gandhi, *Microwave Engineering and Applications*, 1981; K. C. Gupta, *Microwaves*, 1980; L. Lewin, *Theory of Waveguides*, 1975; S. Liao, *Microwave Devices and Circuits*, 1980.

## Microwave tube

A high-vacuum tube designed for operation in the frequency region from approximately 3000 to 300,000 megahertz. Two considerations distinguish a microwave tube from vacuum tubes used at lower frequencies: the dimensions of the tube structure in relation to the wavelength of the signal that it generates or amplifies, and the time during which the electrons interact with the microwave field.

**Effect of tube geometry.** In a vacuum tube the active region is where the electrons travel through the evacuated space from the cathode, through the grid, to the plate (**Fig. 1**). The circuit in which the tube operates extends from this active region along the internal tube structure, through the enclosing vacuum-tight envelope, and onto the portions of the circuit external to the tube. In the microwave region wavelengths are in the order of centimeters; resonant circuits are in the forms of transmission lines that extend a quarter of a wavelength from the active region of the microwave tube. With such short circuit dimensions the internal tube structure constitutes an appreciable portion of the circuit.

For these reasons a microwave tube is made to

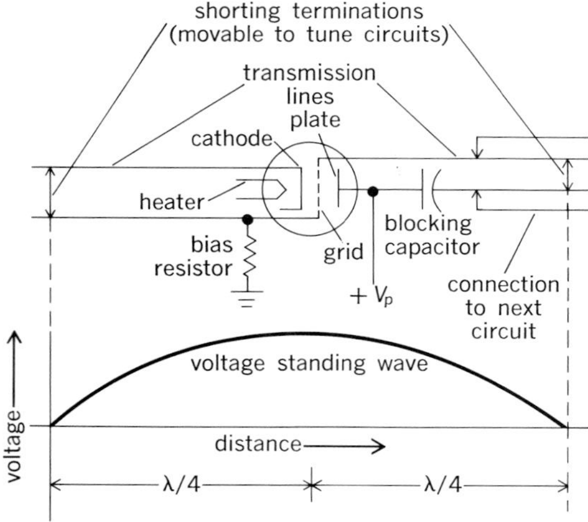


**Fig. 1. Schematic of microwave triode in a circuit of two transmission lines. Usually the tube has circular symmetry and fits directly into coaxial lines.**

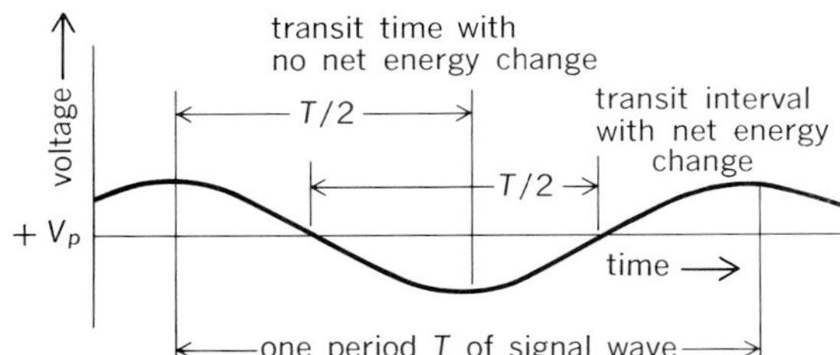


**Fig. 2. Diagram of transit time. For efficient tube operation, the transit time during which an electron passes through the signal field needs to be short compared to the period of the signal.**

form part of the resonant circuit. Leads from electrodes to external connections are short, and electrodes are parts of surfaces extending through the envelope directly to the external circuit that is often a coaxial transmission line or cavity. Design of the tube and of the circuit in which it is to operate thus become closely related. *See* CAVITY RESONATOR; TRANSMISSION LINES.

**Effect of transit time.** At frequencies well below the microwave region, the time during which any one electron travels through the active region within a tube is so short compared to the period of the signal as to be negligible. At microwaves the period of the signal is in the range of 0.001–1 nanosecond. If transit time is comparable to the period of the signal, an electron experiences an inappreciable net change in energy. Even if transit time is reduced to half the signal period, an electron that is in transit when the signal reverses polarity experiences little net change in energy (**Fig. 2**). Only if transit time is less than a quarter of the signal period do significant numbers of electrons exchange appreciable energy with the signal field.

Transit time is reduced in several ways in microwave tubes. Electrodes are closely spaced and made planar in configuration. Spacings of 0.025 mm (0.001 in.) are practical, but to be effective require that electrodes be closely parallel to each other. High interelectrode voltages also decrease transit time by their acceleration of electrons; however, the voltage stresses that glass vacuum seals can withstand place a practical limit on the voltage. *See* VACUUM TUBE.

**Alternative designs.** Tubes designed by the foregoing principles are effective for wavelengths from a few meters to a few centimeters. At longer wavelengths lumped-constant circuits are effective and tubes can be designed for optimum internal characteristics. At shorter wavelengths different principles are necessary. To obtain greater exchange of energy between the electron beam and the electromagnetic field several alternative designs have proved practical.

Instead of collecting the electron beam at a plate formed by the opposite side of the resonant circuit, the beam is allowed to pass into a field-free region before reacting further with an external circuit. The electron could can be deflected by a strong static magnetic field so as to revolve and thereby react several times with the signal field before reaching the plate. *See* KLYSTRON; MAGNETRON.

Instead of producing the field in one or several resonant circuits, the field can be supported by a distributed structure along which it moves at a velocity comparable to the velocity of electrons in the beam. The electron beam is then directed close to this structure so that beam and field interact over an extended interval of time. *See* BACKWARD-WAVE TUBE; TRAVELING-WAVE TUBE.

Such structures as these greatly extend the region over which useful gains, low signal-noise ratios, and significant powers can be produced, although the design of any one microwave tube can usually be optimized for only one of these characteristics at a time. Even so, dimensions and tolerances limit the wavelengths for which such tubes can be manufactured. For operation at shorter wavelengths entirely different techniques are necessary, such as those using quantum behavior within molecules or the intermodulation of signals within a nonlinear device. *See* MASER; MICROWAVE SOLID-STATE DEVICES; MICROWAVE TRANSMISSION LINES; PARAMETRIC AMPLIFIER.

*Frank H. Rockett*

**Bibliography.** D. Allen and K. Ryan, *Microwave Engineering*, 1982; J. Coleman, *Microwave Devices*, 1982; R. E. Collin, *Foundations for Microwave Engineering*, 1966; S. Liao, *Microwave Devices and Circuits*, 1980; R. F. Soohoo, *Microwave Electrontics*, 1971.

## Mixer

A device having two or more signal inputs, usually adjustable, and one common output. It is used in audio amplifiers to combine the outputs of individual microphones and other audio-signal sources linearly and in desired proportions to produce one audio output signal. In television, a mixer serves similarly to combine the outputs of two or more television cameras or other video signal sources. The mixer stage in a superheterodyne receiver combines the incoming modulated radio-frequency (rf) signal with the signal of a local rf oscillator to produce a modulated intermediate-frequency (i-f) signal. Crystal diodes are used as mixers in radar and other microwave equipment. *See* MICROPHONE; RADIO RECIEVER.

*John Markus*

## Mobile radio

Radio communication in which at least one end of the radio path terminates in equipment carried in a vehicle or on a person and can function with one or both terminals in motion. Mobile radio is the short form of the term "land mobile radio service" as defined in the United States by the Federal Communications Commission (FCC). Other categories of mobile communications not technically included in the term are amateur radio, ship-to-shore (high seas), citizens' band, and wireless telephone extensions. These will not be treated in this article. *See* AMATEUR RADIO.

**Uses.** Mobile radio has found extensive use in the United States: by 1978 there were over 8,000,000 two-way mobile units in service, and by 1984 the estimated number was 15,000,000. There is also substantial use worldwide, particularly in Europe and Japan.

The list of uses includes, but is not limited to, police, fire, health emergency, state-highway maintenance, electric utility and telephone company maintenance, gas and petroleum pipeline maintenance, outside construction, doctors, realtors, forestry, commercial agriculture, long-haul trucking, railroads, short-haul delivery, commercial urban services (plumber, cleaner, florist, appliance and furnace repair), taxis, news services, airplane-to-ground systems, commercial and pleasure boats, and buses.

**Types of system.** Many users are not organized into any structured system but simply own equipment that allows them to talk with others who have similar equipment. Examples are very high-frequency (VHF) Maritime Mobile units installed on boats, at Coast Guard stations, bridges, marinas, and harbor masters' locations.

***Dispatch systems.*** A much more prevalent configuration, however, is the dispatch system, which typically has a land-based transmitter and receiver used by a dispatcher or other home-office contact to communicate with a few to many mobile units within a useful service area. Each of these systems is privately owned and operated (that is, there is no common carrier) by the agency or company which uses it. The useful coverage area of such a system typically has a radius of 20 to 25 mi (32 to 40 km), though many systems cover more or less than this, with the land radio at the center. Transmission to the mobile units is generally better than in the reverse direction because the land transmitter may have as much as 250 W of power, whereas the mobile unit is limited to 30 W.

The use of tone-coded squelch allows many users to share a channel without having to listen to all conversations on the channel. This is a system in which 19 audio tones below 300 Hz are selected to identify various land transmitters operating on the same frequency in the same area so that each will enable the audio output of only its own mobile units. Sharing of a channel by more than one fleet (none of which needs the full capacity of a channel) is a necessity because of the large pressure to find enough spectrum space to meet the demands for service.

In addition to voice communication, adjuncts are available, such as pushbuttons, lights, printers, and keyboards, for more effective communication in some circumstances (for example, delivering a message to a vehicle when the occupants are away, or enabling the mobile unit to access directly a land computer for needed information). These digital adjuncts can also aid in conserving channel-usage time.

Large public-safety systems are designed to incorporate data processing (with its associated memory) to provide assistance to dispatchers by automatically keeping the log on assigned cars, assigned areas, and unassigned cars. Different systems have been advanced to enter automatically the cars' latest locations into a computer that can assist the dispatcher by, for example, diplaying this information on a map.

Whenever security is required, voice signals, as well as digital codes, can be scrambled quite readily with microelectronic devices. *See* Privacy systems (scrambling).

***SMR service.*** The FCC has allowed a configuration which it calls Specialized Mobile Radio (SMR) Service. Companies which are not common carriers are permitted to supply a communication service for rent to clients who are themselves entitled to licenses under the rules for private services. This permits the service needs of small companies or agencies to be combined for a more economical and spectrum-efficient service. SMRs operate on a group of radio channels set aside for this use. Each of their customers' mobile units can be served on any of these channels, thus obtaining the service advantage of not encountering call blocking unless all channels of the group are busy.

SMRs provide an arrangement called community repeater, in which the voice output of a land-based radio receiver which receives on channel $f_1$, is transmitted outward on channel $f_2$. The receiver-transmitter pair is usually located centrally in the desired coverage area, and the antennas are placed high above the street for good coverage. Transmission on $f_1$ from any user station, mobile or fixed, will be received and relayed over $f_2$ to another user station, mobile or fixed. These two users must not transmit simultaneously for they will not hear each other. One receiver-transmitter is required for each pair of channels, and arrangements for selecting a particular pair for a given conversation are provided.

***Public-correspondence systems.*** Another system configuration, which has been in existence since the 1940s, is used for public correspondence. The FCC calls this Domestic Public Mobile Radio Service. Common carriers provide the land-based radio equipment, and they may also lease the mobile radio equipment in the customers' vehicles, to afford radio connection into the wireline telephone network from points all over a service area. The many existing systems, taken together, provide coverage in all of the medium and large cities, and many other smaller areas as well. Public correspondence service is provided by the wireline common carriers (WLCC), both Bell System and independents, and by Radio Common Carriers (RCC) [who provide no other common carrier service]. The two categories of companies are in competition for subscribers in more than 1000 cities and towns in the United States.

In all of the systems, channels are assigned and used in pairs, one for the land transmitter and the other for the mobile transmitter. This permits full-duplex transmission, where signals pass in both directions simultaneously. This avoids the need for push-to-talk operation in the vehicle, which is considered strange and objectionable by telephone-type users. In most of these systems, the mobile units are equipped to operate on any of the channels assigned to the system of which they are a part. Where there are sufficient channels available in a given service area, the mobile unit can be served over any available channel and the trunk-group advantage is obtained. A trunk group can handle more traffic with smaller probability of a call being blocked for lack of an available channel.

In all of the early public-correspondence systems, the control of calls was by an operator, who responded to a service request by a mobile unit, or who called a particular mobile unit by dialing a number to its selective-calling circuit. Now many of these systems provide for automatic calling through the telephone network directly to a mobile unit. They also provide for dialing from the mobile unit into the telephone network. They further provide for automatic selection of the channel to use, for both inward and outward calling.

A valuable feature of the public-correspondence systems is the accommodation of roamers—users of vehicles who are normally based and served in one city, but who demand service in other cities or on intercity highways. This feature is not normally available in the private and dispatch systems.

The number of mobile units in public-correspondence systems is relatively small because of the very small allocation of channels. There are approximately 150,000 mobile units, using, altogether, 54 channels which are arranged in small groups scattered about the radio spectrum from 30 to 500 MHz. However, the number of units increased with the introduction of cellular mobile radio.

All of the systems discussed so far employ one or a pair of channels for each conversation that is taking place at a given moment in the whole of the area covered by the system. That channel or channel pair cannot be used for another conversation at the same time in the same service area, or within a radius of 60–100 mi (100–150 km) of it, without high likelihood of interference. This is wasteful of spectrum. Cellular Mobile Radio Service was devised to improve spectrum utilization.

***Radio paging.*** Radio paging is an important one-way service. When a land party wishes to address a particular page receiver, which is usually worn in a person's pocket or on a belt, the information supplied by the originator causes a coded selective signal to be radiated. The signal is received by all of the active page receivers on that channel, but only the one which expects that code responds. It produces some sort of signal to alert the wearer: a steady tone, a series of beeps, or a light. Systems vary in complexity. Some add more code words to cause one or more digits to be displayed. Some, called tone-and-voice, follow the tone alert with a brief voice message. In any case, the paged person knows by convention what the message means. In the most simple one, a tone means that the person paged should call the home office over regular telephone facilities, where someone has taken a message to be relayed.

In the most simple system, the selective code is the whole message and takes a fraction of a second to transmit. Because of this and because the frequency of calling any subscriber is low, it is possible to serve more than 30,000 pagers on a single channel (in a given coverage area) without causing an objectionable queuing delay. The number of possible different call-codes is typically 100,000. On the other hand, if voice messages are relayed to the pager, the number that can be served is no more than a few hundred.

The number of pagers served by common carriers is estimated to be over 2,500,000. The bulk of these are customers of the radio common carriers. About 20% are customers of the wireline common carriers. In addition, there are uncounted private paging systems.

For many years radio paging was limited to a very small number of channels near 150 and 450 MHz. However, 120 channels (including future reserves) have been made available near 930 MHz for this service. SEE RADIO PAGING SYSTEMS.

**Development.** The first practical use of radio transmission to a moving automobile for dispatch service is credited to the Detroit Police Department in 1922. The Detroit and other early police radio installations provided only one-way communication to the vehicles, and employed amplitude modulation, first in the broadcast band and later in the medium-frequency bands. The high-seas public correspondence service was started in 1929. By 1932 there was a two-way system for Coast Guard vessels and harbor craft. By the middle to late 1930s, the concept of using radio to direct the movement of people in cars had advanced to the point that the FCC set aside some frequencies in the VHF band (30–40 MHz), thereby eliminating much but not all of the interference from sky-wave propagation of interfering signals and reducing the level of ignition-noise interference that had previously hampered operations at lower frequencies. SEE AMPLITUDE-MODULATION RADIO.

Narrow-band frequency modulation (±15 kHz compared with ±75 kHz used in broadcasting) was proposed not only as a remedy against noise but also as a means for providing more precise limits on area coverage by virtue of the capture effect, in which a strong frequency-modulation (FM) signal in an FM receiver suppresses a weaker signal on the same frequency. The first statewide two-way FM system was installed by the Connecticut State Police just before World War II. At first the modulation deviation was ±15 kHz for the maximum capture effect and minimal noise impact, but in the mid-1950s, as the radio spectrum became increasingly crowded, ±5 kHz became the standard. SEE FREQUENCY-MODULATION RADIO.

At the conclusion of World War II, the Radio Technical Planning Board laid out a comprehensive spectrum-allocation plan that set aside a total of 43 MHz of spectrum in the United States for commercial use in the frequency bands of 25–50, 152–162, and 450–470; frequencies for nonmilitary federal government use were also designated at 162–174 and 406–420 MHz. The FCC allocated specific sets of channels for the private Land Mobile systems for various user categories, including industrial, business, public safety (police, fire, and so forth), and land transportation. Most of these operate as dispatch systems. Other sets of channels were allocated for maritime mobile use, for airplane-to-ground systems, and for radio paging.

Service was begun by the Bell System in 1946 on the first of the public-correspondence mobile telephone systems, designed to cover the urban and suburban areas in St. Louis. This operated on some of the channels in the 152–162-MHz band. The following year, a system of land stations was established along the highway between New York and Boston to serve vehicles traveling that route. It operated in the 35–44-MHz band.

Originally the FCC dedicated six pairs of channels for urban service, and in 1949 allocated a different six pairs for the use of radio common carriers. The original channel spacing of 60 kHz was halved to 30 kHz around 1955 in order to create five more pairs in each group. The year 1956 saw the addition of new assignments near 450 MHz: 12 pairs for the wire line common carriers and 12 for the radio common carriers.

Initially, all of the systems functioned on a manual basis, that is, operator-controlled. In 1964 the Bell System introduced an improved system for the 152–162-MHz band that provided dialing from a land customer directly to a vehicle, and dialing from the vehicle to a land customer (or another vehicle). Channel selection was automatic, and push-to-talk operation was no longer necessary. In 1969 these capabilities were extended to the systems at 450 MHz. Similar systems are available now around the world.

Recognizing the large potential for Domestic Public Land Mobile Radio Service, the Bell System in 1947 started a series of requests to the FCC for allocation of a sufficient number of channels to respond to that need. The systems proposed for such an allocation promised substantial improvements over existing technology in spectral efficiency and traffic capacity, based on improved system-layout possibilities and the use of the trunk-group mode for handling traffic. Early in this period the increase in spectral efficiency and traffic capacity achievable by the cellular-service-area concept was known but not included in these proposals because the required technology had not matured until the 1960s. This led in 1969 to the Bell System advancing a proposal for a cellular system.

**Cellular mobile radio.** This is a concept in which a system coverage area, such as a large city with its suburbs, is divided into many smaller cells, each of which is served by its own land transmitters and receivers. This requires mobile units to be tunable upon system command to appropriate new channels when the unit moves from one cell's coverage area to another's. The control and switching required to do this demands a highly sophisticated electronic switching system with its computer-type control. The great benefit of this system is a very substantial increase in traffic capacity and grade of service, combined with a large increase in spectral efficiency. These benefits follow from the possibility of reuse of the same channels at much shorter distances than in conventional systems. Efficiency here is thought of as getting more effective talk per unit area per unit of assigned spectrum. *See Switching systems (communications).*

***Channel assignment.*** In the cellular concept, a channel assigned to one cell is not used in any nearby cell because of the possibility of interference, but may be used in cells that are sufficiently far away that the probability of interference is small. The cells that make up the total service area are served by other channels, assigned in as efficient a pattern as possible while meeting the above constraints. In a typical application, this means dividing the total frequency allocation to this service into seven parts and assigning the parts to the cells in a repetitive geographical pattern.

***Expandability.*** An especially attractive feature of the cellular system is its ability to grow in geographical size and in the density of traffic that it can handle, without interruption of service. A system can be started with a few large cells (even only one cell), typically of 8-mi (13-km) radius, and only a few channels implemented with land radio and control equipment. When more area coverage is required, additional cells can be designated and equipped. When traffic begins to overload any part of the system, more channels can be put into use, up to the limit of channels available. Further increase in traffic can be accommodated by dividing the cells into smaller ones, say of radius 4 mi (6.5 km)—that is, adding base stations between the existing ones—and implementing them with additional radio and control equipment. Still finer division of cells results in still more traffic capacity.

***Implementation.*** The FCC made final its allocation of radio channels and its rules and regulations for the Domestic Public Cellular Radio Telecommunications Service in March 1982. It allocated a total of 40 MHz of spectrum, 825–845 and 870–890 MHz, divided into channels of 30-kHz width, and specified division of these bands between wireline common carriers and radio common carriers. This was the culmination of a process begun by an FCC request in 1968 for proposals for cellular systems. A tentative allocation was reached in 1974, whereupon the Bell System proceeded with a development system. This system, installed in 1978, operated in the Chicago area to serve selected customers, and amply proved the practicality of the cellular system. In 1981, service started on a compatible but somewhat different developmental cellular system in the Washington, D.C., area.

The first commercial version of the cellular system in the United States began service on October 13, 1983, serving Chicago and its suburbs. This system, with 17 cells serving a total of about 2400 mi$^2$ (6200 km$^2$) has a capacity to serve up to 100,000 subscribers.

By early 1985 cellular systems were in service in all the major cities in the United States.

Canada has joined the United States in standards for cellular radio.

A system for the United Kingdom began operation in 1985. It was based upon the system described above, adapted to United Kingdom standards of channel spacing and frequency band.

A cellular system which now covers Tokyo, Osaka, and Nagoya, Japan, was inaugurated in 1979. The system differs considerably from the United States system.

A cellular system started operating in 1981 in Denmark, Finland, Norway, and Sweden. While it operates at 450 MHz, there are plans to operate in the region of 900 MHz in the late 1980s. This system differs from the United States system and the Japanese system.

**Prospects.** The ever-increasing demands for mobile communications in the face of limited available spectrum exert pressure to find ways to increase the efficiency of spectrum utilization. This must be measured, as stated above, in terms of more effective talk per unit area per unit of assigned spectrum. The use of single-sideband (SSB) modulation, digitally coded modulation, and spread spectrum techniques instead of the current FM has received much attention, but there is so far no consensus that any of these techniques will achieve the desired improvement in spectral efficiency. *See Modulation; Single sideband; Spread spectrum communication.*

When the mobile unit is moving at normal vehicular speeds, the amplitude and phase of the received radio signal fluctuates rapidly (at frequencies up to more than 100 Hz) because of the standing waves along the transmission path. In a single-sideband system, it is particularly difficult to mitigate the effects of this fluctuation on the voice modulation.

In spread spectrum, the voice signal is digitized, and that signal is used to control the shifting of the radio carrier in discrete steps and in a pseudorandom manner over a large frequency band. This procedure may turn out not to be as wasteful as it might seem, since many radios, each carrying a different conversation, can transmit in the same wide band with acceptably low interference with each other.

Efforts have continued to find a way of serving mobile radio by digitally encoding voice and suitably modulating the carrier. There is hope that such a system might be more spectrally efficient and that security encoded speech (of any desired degree of security) would be more simply provided without any further loss of voice quality.

New technology is expected to result in more affordable equipment, particularly the mobile units. Also, smaller hand-carried two-way units and smaller paging receivers can be expected. The attraction of small lightweight units is strong; and if battery technology can provide more power in a smaller lighter cell, a portable pocket telephone can be expected. *See Radio*.

*W. Rae Young*

**Bibliography.** W. C. Jakes, *Microwave Mobile Communications*, 1974; W. C. Y. Lee, *Mobile Communications Engineering*, 1982; R. Northcott, Bright future for mobile telecommunications services, *Telephony*, 205(18):90–92, October 24, 1983; Special issue on cellular mobile radio, *Bell Sys. Tech. J.*, vol. 58, no. 1, January 1979.

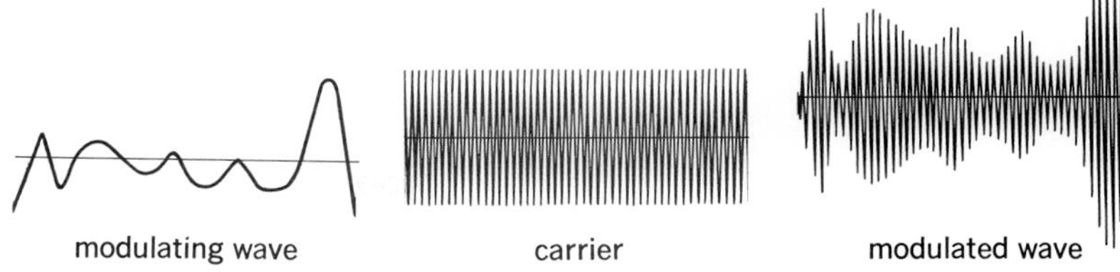


**Fig. 2. Typical waveforms in amplitude modulation of a sine-wave carrier by a voice-frequency–modulating wave. (*After H. S. Black, Modulation Theory, Van Nostrand, 1953*)**

## Modulation

The process or result of the process whereby a message is changed into information-bearing signals that not only unambiguously represent the message but also are suitable for propagation over the transmitting medium to the receiver.

The vehicle for the propagation of electric signals from one region in space to another is always an electromagnetic field, and when this field changes with time it takes the form of a wave.

At the distant end the receiver is waiting to be informed; this is accomplished by the arrival of the propagated wave, which, it is important to note, must change in a way the receiver cannot predict. Here, too, modulation is the process whereby in response to the received wave either the original message or information pertaining to the original message is made available in the form desired and is delivered when and where it is wanted. The terms demodulation and detection are often used to denote the recovery of the wanted message from a modulated signal.

Modulation is fundamental to communication. No matter how, when, or where communication takes place, modulation is encountered. Many kinds of modulation are possible, but a characteristic common to all is change. *See Electrical communications*.

Modulation implies bandwidth occupancy. For any signal to change in a way that cannot be predicted implies necessarily that the signal occupy a nonzero band of frequencies. For example, the spoken word occupies a band from a few hundred to several thousand hertz.

Ordinary telephony (**Fig. 1**) is a good example of these modulation concepts. Longitudinal sound waves generated by the spoken word constitute the information-bearing signals to be communicated. The telephone transmitter, acting as a modulator, changes this acoustic energy into electric energy suitable for high-speed propagation to a distant point. At the receiving end, demodulation in the telephone receiver changes the electric signals back to pressure waves in the air. *See Telephone*.

Defined broadly, modulation is the process or result of the process whereby some parameter of one wave is varied in accordance with another wave. As is customary in the treatment of modulation, the word wave is used as a generic term intended to include such concepts as signal, voltage, current, pressure, displacement, and the like, whether these are constant or changing.

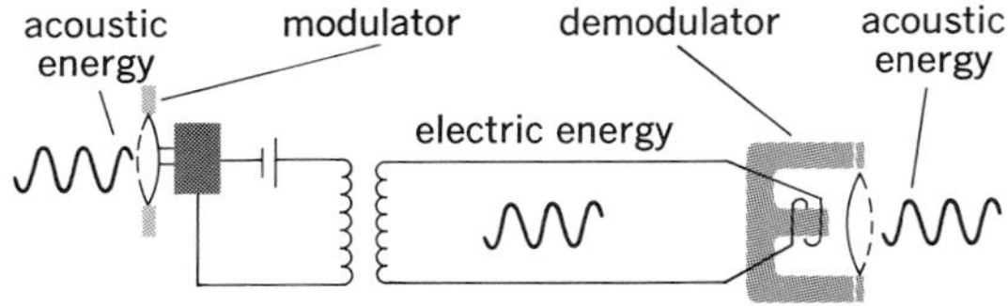


**Fig. 1. Diagram of ordinary telephony sequence. (*After H. S. Black, Modulation Theory, Van Nostrand, 1953*)**

This broad definition of modulation, which may be illustrated by a familiar example of amplitude modulation, implies three fundamental concepts: modulating wave, carrier, and modulated wave (**Fig. 2**). A modulating wave changes some parameter of the wave to be modulated; a carrier is a wave suitable for modulation by the modulating wave; a modulated wave has some parameter changed in accordance with the modulating wave.

**Amplitude modulation (AM).** In amplitude modulation the amplitude of a carrier is the parameter subject to change by the modulating wave.

In a more restrictive sense, AM is defined to mean modulation in which the amplitude factor of a sine-wave carrier is linearly proportional to the modulating wave. Analysis shows that the modulated wave depicted in Fig. 2 is composed of the transmitted carrier, which conveys no information (apart from its amplitude, frequency, and phase), plus the familiar upper and lower sidebands, which convey identical and therefore mutually redundant information. Thus, AM doubles bandwidth occupancy. *See Amplitude modulation; Sideband*.

Assuming adequate knowledge of the carrier, either sideband alone unambiguously defines the message. Accordingly, carrier-suppressed single-sideband transmission (SSB) conserves both power and frequency space and, when combined with frequency division multiplexing, is widely used for long-distance telephony. *See Single sideband*.

**Angle modulation.** Instead of conserving bandwidth, bandwidth occupancy may be intentionally increased in exchange for improved performance. Angle modulation is one of the simplest ways of sacrificing frequency space for reduced noise. In angle modulation the angle (entire argument) of a sine-wave carrier is the parameter changed by the modulating wave. Frequency and phase modulation are particular forms of angle modulation. Often the term frequency modulation is used to connote angle modulation. *See Angle modulation*.

A fundamental concept in angle modulation is that of instantaneous frequency. It is proportional to the time rate of change of the angle of a sine function, the argument of which is a function of time. When the argument is expressed in radians and time in seconds, Eq. (1) may be formulated.

$$\text{Instantaneous frequency} = \frac{1}{2\pi}\frac{d}{dt}(\text{angle}) \quad (1)$$

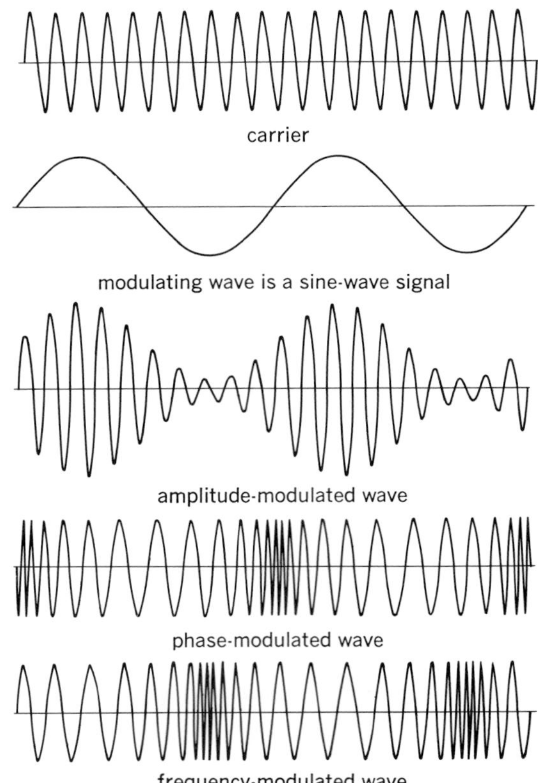


**Fig. 3. Amplitude, phase, and frequency modulation of a sine-wave carrier by a sine-wave signal. (*After H. S. Black, Modulation Theory, Van Nostrand, 1953*)**

***Frequency modulation (FM).*** FM is angle modulation in which the instantaneous frequency of a sine-wave carrier is caused to depart from the carrier frequency by an amount proportional to the instantaneous value of the modulating wave (**Fig. 3**). *SEE FREQUENCY MODULATION.*

***Phase modulation (PM).*** PM is angle modulation in which the angle of a sine-wave carrier is caused to depart from the carrier angle by an amount proportional to the instantaneous value of the modulating wave. The instantaneous frequency deviates from its unmodulated value by an amount proportional to the time derivative of the modulating wave (Fig. 3). *SEE PHASE MODULATION.*

FM and PM are similar in the sense that any attempt to shift frequency or phase is accomplished by a change in the other. The terms FM and PM simply indicate which parameters of the complete argument (angle) of the sine function are being modulated.

**Pulse modulation.** In pulse modulation the carrier may be a train of regularly recurrent pulses. Modulation may control the amplitude, duration, position, or mere presence of the pulses so as to represent the message to the communicated. These forms of pulse modulation are commonly called, respectively, pulse-amplitude modulation (PAM), pulse-duration modulation (PDM), pulse-position modulation (PPM), and pulse-code modulation (PCM). Ease of multiplexing channels by time division is one of the important economic advantages of all forms of pulse modulation. All but pulse-amplitude modulation can exchange extra bandwidth occupancy for noise reduction. Pulse-code modulation is a digital system transmitting ''on'' or ''off'' pulses and thereby offering major transmission advantages not possible with an analog system. *SEE PULSE MODULATION.*

*Harold S. Black*

**Digital modulation.** To make the transition from analog pulse modulation to digital modulation, the samples of the original waveform have to be quantized and then encoded (say, through PCM). Once a baseband data sequence of digital pulses is available, some digital modulation format is used to allow the transmission of the information to the receiver.

There are many types of digital modulation formats, and they can be either binary or $M$-ary ($M > 2$). The two most common binary techniques are phase-shift keying (PSK) and frequency-shift keying (FSK). In binary PSK, the phase of the transmitted carrier is changed by $\pi$ radians to distinguish one symbol from the other. That is, if the baseband symbol 0 is to be transmitted, the waveform given by Eq. (2) is sent over the channel for $T$ seconds, where $A$ is

$$s(t) = A \cos \omega_0 t \qquad (2)$$

a constant amplitude and $\omega_0$ is a constant frequency. If, on the other hand, the baseband symbol 1 is to be transmitted, the waveform given by Eq. (3) is sent

$$s(t) = A \cos (\omega_0 t + \pi) = -A \cos \omega_0 t \qquad (3)$$

over the channel for $T$ seconds.

An alternative to binary PSK is binary FSK. In this case, the frequency of the transmitted waveform is changed according to what baseband symbol is to be conveyed to the receiver. The performance of binary PSK is superior to that of binary FSK, but often the receiver for FSK is much simpler than that for PSK.

Digital modulation formats are especially suitable for communication with spread spectrum systems. Specifically, spread spectrum communications consist of transmitting the desired signal in a bandwidth much larger than the information bandwidth. This is sometimes accomplished by modulating the digital information sequence with a wide-bandwidth binary-coded waveform [typically a so-called pseudonoise (PN) sequence]. Such a system is referred to as a direct-sequence (DS) spread spectrum system. *SEE SPREAD SPECTRUM COMMUNICATION.*

There are many uses for spread spectrum systems, with the most important being in the area of rejection of interference (either intentional or unintentional). However, these same spreading sequences have properties that make them attractive for use in designing waveforms that can be used to combat multipath interference, that can be used for accurate ranging and navigation, and that can ''hide'' the transmitted signal in the background noise, thus making it difficult for an unauthorized listener to detect the presence of the signal.

*Laurence B. Milstein*

**Multiple modulation.** Practical applications of modulation often utilize what is commonly referred to as multiple modulation, a succession of modulating processes in which the modulated wave from one process becomes the modulating wave for the next. A typical example is a system in which position-modulated pulses are used to modulate the amplitude of a sine-wave carrier. Such a system is abbreviated PPM-AM (pulse-position modulation–amplitude modulation) inasmuch as it is customary to list the processes in the order in which the message to be conveyed encounters them. A subcarrier is any carrier used in an intermediate step of multiple modulation.

**Engineering applications.** The principal application and major fields of use of these various kinds of

**Typical kinds of modulation, with principal advantages, disadvantages, and uses (*cont.*)**

| Kind | Advantages | Disadvantages | Uses |
|---|---|---|---|
| **Digital modulation** | | | |
| Phase-shift keying (PSK) | Excellent performance for binary and quaternary systems; good bandwidth efficiency for $M$-ary systems | Poorer performance for $M$-ary systems when $M > 4$ | Voice, data, and video over satellite and terrestrial channels |
| Frequency-shift keying (FSK) | Simple receiver structure; excellent performance for $M$-ary systems when $M > 4$ | Poor performance of binary system; bandwidth occupancy grows as $M/\log_2 M$ in $M$-ary system | Voice, data, and video over satellite and terrestrial channels |
| **Multiple modulation** | Many, depending upon circumstances; often accomplishes what cannot be done in one step | Extra steps usually add extra complexity | A feature of all but the simplest transmitters and receivers |

modulation are indicated by the technical comparisons and typical examples in the **table**.

*Harold S. Black*

**Bibliography.** F. R. Connor, *Modulation*, 2d ed., 1982; J. K. Holmes, *Coherent Spread Spectrum Systems*, 1982; Howard W. Sams Engineering Staff, *Reference Data for Radio Engineers*, 6th ed., 1975; W. C. Lindsey and M. K. Simon, *Telecommunication Systems Engineering*, 1973; J. G. Proakis, *Digital Communications*, 1983; M. Schwartz, *Information, Transmission, Modulation and Noise*, 3d ed., 1980.

## Modulator

Any device or circuit by means of which a desired signal is impressed upon a higher-frequency periodic wave known as a carrier. The process is called modulation. The modulator may vary the amplitude frequency, or phase of the carrier. SEE MODULATION.

**Amplitude modulator.** An amplitude modulator varies the amplitude of the carrier in accordance with the modulating signal. The envelope of the carrier then has the same waveform as the modulating signal if the modulation is distortionless. There are many ways to accomplish amplitude modulation, but in all cases a nonlinear element or device must be employed. The modulating signal controls the characteristics of the nonlinear device and thereby controls the amplitude of the carrier. For example, the modulating signal may be used to control the bias currents and thus the transconductance of radio-frequency amplifier. Then the output of the amplifier is proportional to the amplitude of the modulating signal, provided the carrier amplitude is equal to or greater than that of the modulating signal. Thus the modulator is essentially a multiplying circuit. In fact, a multiplier integrated circuit is commonly used as a low-power, or low-level, modulator having low distortion. The distortion is zero if the transconductance is directly proportional to the modulating voltage. Class B or class C amplifiers are frequently used as the nonlinear element or multiplying device when high-power, or high-level, signals are to be modulated. Other devices, such as a diode or a nonlinear resistance, may be used as the modulating element. SEE AMPLIFIER; AMPLITUDE MODULATION; AMPLITUDE-MODULATION DETECTOR; AMPLITUDE MODULATOR; DIODE; INTEGRATED CIRCUITS.

Trigonometric identities can be used to show that the multiplication process produces new frequencies which are the sum of the carrier frequency $f_c$ and the modulating frequencies $f_m$, or $f_c + f_m$, and also the difference frequencies $f_c - f_m$. Therefore the passband of the modulator must extend from $f_c - f_m$ to $f_c + f_m$ and have a bandwidth of at least $2f_m$, where $f_m$ is the highest modulating frequency of interest.

**Frequency modulator.** The frequency modulator changes the frequency of the carrier in accordance with the modulating signal while the amplitude remains constant. The frequency modulator usually changes the effective capacitance or inductance in the frequency-determining $LC$ circuit of the oscillator. However, other techniques can be used. For example, a multivibrator can be used to generate carrier frequencies up to a few megahertz, and the multivibrator frequency can be modulated by controlling the base, gate, or grid bias supply voltage. An integrated circuit known as a voltage-controlled oscillator is commercially available and has an output frequency that is a linear function of its control voltage. The voltage-controlled oscillator may be used as an inexpensive, linear frequency modulator if the carrier-frequency stability requirements are not too high. SEE FREQUENCY MODULATION; FREQUENCY-MODULATION DETECTOR; FREQUENCY-MODULATION RADIO; FREQUENCY MODULATOR; MULTIVIBRATOR.

**Phase modulator.** The phase modulator varies the phase of the carrier in accordance with the modulating signal. Phase modulation is very closely related to frequency modulation. Phase modulation will produce the characteristics of frequency modulation if the frequency characteristics of the modulating signal are altered. SEE PHASE MODULATION; PHASE-MODULATION DETECTOR; PHASE MODULATOR; PULSE MODULATION; PULSE MODULATOR.

*Charles L. Alley*

**Bibliography.** J. J. DeFrance, *Communications, Electronics and Circuits*, 2d ed., 1972; S. Haykin, *Communications Systems*, 2d ed., 1983; R. Kellejian, *Applied Electronic Communications: Circuits, Systems, Transmission*, 1980.

## Molecular electronics

The systematic use of molecular materials to produce new or improved electronic devices. Conventional devices mostly rely on inorganic semiconductors, metals, and conductors, but molecular materials can fulfill many similar functions. Molecular materials also have specific advantages. These include controllability of molecular size, shape, and properties obtainable by chemical modification; reproducibility of material dimensions and properties implicit in the molecular structure; and selectivity of physical and chemical behavior governed by the molecular constitution and packing. A growing number of devices therefore employ molecular materials to produce novel or significantly enhanced performance.

**Polymers.** Many devices use polymers, which are generally strong and easily processed by low-energy methods. Conventional technology for very large-scale integration uses polymer resists to mask selected areas of a silicon wafer while other areas are processed. Progress toward smaller, faster, low-power devices depends on reducing feature sizes, which requires improved resists with controlled response to the light or ionizing radiation which delineates the mask. Resists are essential for the processing step but are absent from the final device. However, conventional devices often incorporate polyimide dielectrics (I). This was the first, and probably remains the most

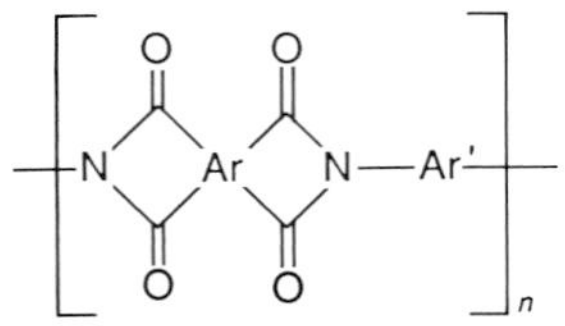

Ar, Ar′= aryl groups

(I)

widespread, use of a molecular material as a constituent element of a device; polymers also find extensive use as encapsulating layers around devices. *See* Electronic packaging; Integrated circuits.

Electroactive polymers are of considerable importance. Aromatic and heteroaromatic materials are often effective photoconductors, conducting electric current when exposed to light. They can be adapted for use in photocopiers if attached to a polymer backbone, allowing large-area thin films to be prepared; a commercial example is poly(*N*-vinylcarbazole) [PVK; II]. Piezoelectric and pyroelectric polymers are also

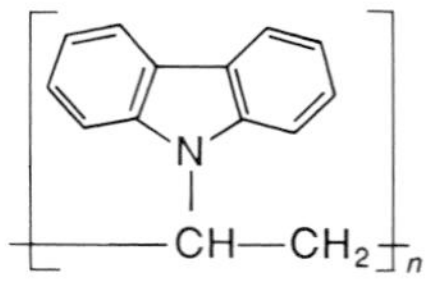

(II)

found, the main example being poly(vinylidene fluoride) [PVDF; III]. These two classes of polymers re-

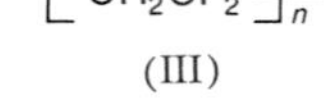

$$-[CH_2CF_2]_n-$$

(III)

spond electrically to pressure and temperature changes, and conversely they develop a mechanical distortion or a temperature charge when subjected to an electric field. They are therefore used as transducers in compact lightweight microphones, infrared detectors, and sensors.

Much attention is being devoted to conducting polymers. Polymer structures allowing electron delocalization along the backbone can often be doped (chemically oxidized or reduced) to achieve conductivities up to metallic levels of 1000 siemens/cm in the best cases, for example, poly(acetylene) [$(CH)_n$; IV]. Polymers of aromatic species such as

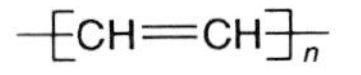

$$-[CH{=}CH]_n-$$

(IV)

poly(phenylene)[V], poly(phenylene sulfide) [VI], poly(pyrrole) [VII], and poly(thiophene) [VIII] have

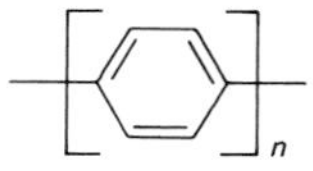

(V) 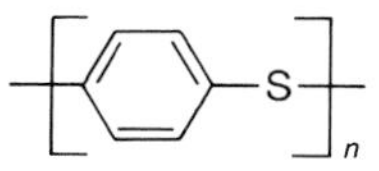 (VI)

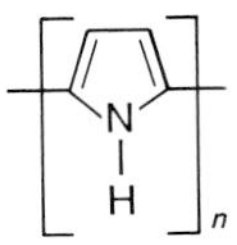

(VII) 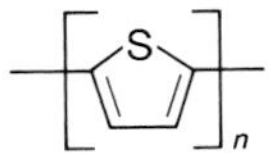 (VIII)

advantages in ease of preparation, tractability, or stability. Conducting polymers are expected to find applications in lightweight electromagnetic screening, novel battery systems, and the connection of active molecular elements to conventional inorganic elements in hybrid devices. In one demonstration device,

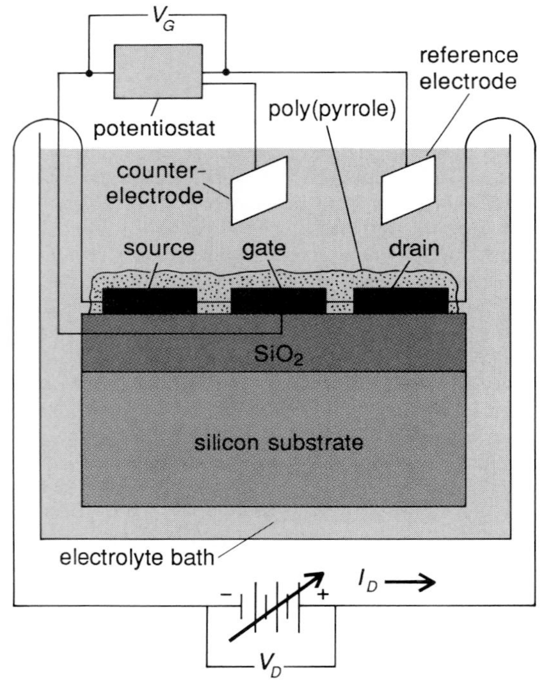


**Molecule-based transistor. The silicon dioxide ($SiO_2$) layer is about 0.45 micrometer thick on a 0.3-mm-thick substrate. The gold source, drain, and gate electrodes are about 3 μm wide, 140 μm long, and 0.12 μm thick, and are coated with about $10^{-7}$ mol/cm$^2$ poly(pyrrole). The whole assembly is immersed in electrolyte solution. $I_D$ = current between source and drain; $V_D$ = voltage between source and drain; $V_G$ = gate potential. (*After H. S. White, G. P. Kittelsen, and M. S. Kittelsen, and M. S. Wrighton, Chemical derivatization of an array of three gold microelectrodes with polypyrrole: Fabrication of a molecule-based transistor, J. Amer. Chem. Soc., 106:5375–5377, 1984*)**

poly(pyrrole) immersed in an electrolyte exhibits behavior analogous to that of a transistor: the current between source and drain microelectrodes increases greatly once the potential of a central gate electrode exceeds that required to oxidize the poly(pyrrole), so that the gate voltage is amplified (see **illus.**).

**Langmuir-Blodgett films.** Amphiphilic molecules containing both hydrophilic and hydrophobic groups may adsorb at a water-air interface. The surface layer can then be compressed into a floating monolayer and transferred to a substrate by dipping. The resulting film is called a Langmuir-Blodgett (LB) film. These films are highly ordered and free of voids or pinholes, but noncrystalline, with many features useful for electronics applications. The thickness of one layer is determined reproducibly by the molecular dimensions, and multilayers (possibly of different species) can be prepared by repeated dipping. Specific properties can be incorporated by using molecules with suitable electric, magnetic, optical, or chemical behavior.

Polymerizable Langmuir-Blodgett films have been developed. Uniform polymerization improves stability through covalent bonding in the film while retaining the film thickness precisely; for this purpose, diacetylene Langmuir-Blodgett films are attractive because they polymerize with minimal disruption. Selective polymerization defines microstructures for integrated circuits or integated optics. For instance, the terminally unsaturated long-chain molecule ω-tricosenoic acid (IX) makes a good negative resist under electron-

$$H_2C = CH(CH_2)_{20}CO_2H$$

(IX)

beam polymerization.

Langmuir-Blodgett films find uses in processing of enhanced-performance devices as insulating layers of precisely determined thickness; their fabrication requires much lower temperatures than does the oxidation of silicon, and they are available for semiconductors that lack oxides suitable for use in electronic devices. Examples are a solar cell based on cadmium telluride and an electroluminescent diode based on gallium phosphide, each markedly more efficient with two or three Langmuir-Blodgett monolayers between the metal and the semiconductor than with none. A metal-insulator-semiconductor-semiconductor (MISS) structure, such as metal–Langmuir-Blodgett film–*n*-type gallium arsenide (GaAs)–$P^+$-type gallium arsenide, acts as a switch, and will serve as a sensor if the Langmuir-Blodgett film contains an organic species sensitive to some external influence which affects the switching characteristics.

Other sensors are based on measurable changes that occur in a surface Langmuir-Blodgett film when it adsorbs a target species, even at the parts-per-million level. These changes are detected by surfaceplasmon resonances on a metal, surface acoustic waves on a quartz oscillator, or surface electronic states on an inorganic semiconductor. Such sensors have been demonstrated for the detection of several molecular species, including nitrogen oxides and acetic acid. *See Surface acoustic-wave devices*.

Pyroelectric Langmuir-Blodgett films serve as infrared detectors. Such devices require a noncentrosymmetric sample, achieveable as a single layer or as alternating layers of different species. As the figure of merit for such detectors depends inversely on the film thickness, excellent response is obtained as compared with thicker polymer or ceramic detectors. Noncentrosymmetric Langmuir-Blodgett films are also employed for their nonlinear optical properties such as second-harmonic generation or parametric oscillation, important in optical communications. The response of such films increases quadratically with the number of layers, and two different layers may enhance one another's response. *See Nonlinear optical devices*.

**Optical materials.** Molecular materials possess optical properties valuable in electronics applications such as information storage and display, optoelectronics, and communications. The nonlinear response already mentioned for Langmuir-Blodgett films can be achieved also in doped polymers and in molecular crystals. The molecules can be tailored to optimize the nonlinear response, optical absorption, and crystal packing. A classic example ocurs in the nitroanilines, where a single isolated molecule of the para compound (X) has high nonlinear response but the crystal

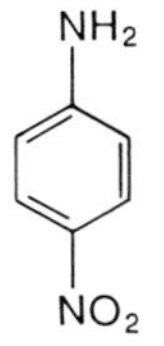

$NH_2$

$NO_2$

(X)

structure is inactive for second-harmonic generation, while the meta compound (XI) has a lower molecular

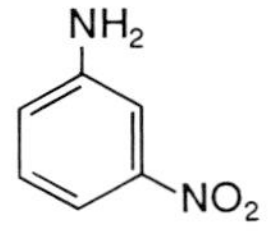

$NH_2$

$NO_2$

(XI)

response but an active crystal structure; adding a methyl group at the meta position in *para*-nitroaniline to form methylnitroanaline (XII) retains a high molec-

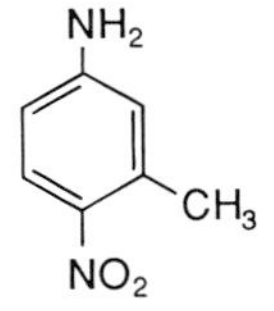

$NH_2$

$CH_3$

$NO_2$

(XII)

ular response and an active crystal structure. The resulting material has an excellent figure of merit with respect to both second-harmonic generation and the Pockels linear electrooptic effect; moreover, like most molecular materials, it is highly resistant to optical damage. *See Optical modulators*.

Liquid-crystal devices fall within the above definition of molecular electronics, although they are often excluded from this field and regarded as a separate topic. Their well-known use in low-power displays has required effective systematic molecular design to meet the technological objectives of these devices; and their development has continued. Recently, liquid-crystal side-chain polymers have been applied to information storage. An unaligned scattering state can be selectively aligned electrically above the polymer glass-transition temperature $T_g$ to give negative contrasting clear regions which persist on cooling toward

$T_g$. Alternatively, an electrically aligned material can have positive contrasting regions written in by a laser beam which provides temporary local heating; this gives good contrast and spatial resolution with simple erase and rewrite capabilities. *See Liquid crystals.*

Information can be stored also as colored spots produced by a laser beam in a photochromic material. Here individual molecules change color on illumination, so that grain size no longer limits resolution as in conventional storage media, and developing and fixing are unnecessary. Practical photochromic storage media must be thermally stable in both colorless and colored forms, while being optically readable and preferably optically erasable. Molecules tailored to meet these conditions include the fulgides (XIII), de-

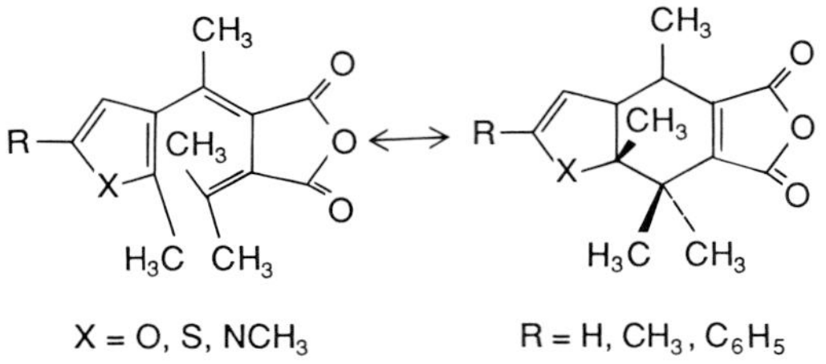

X = O, S, $NCH_3$ R = H, $CH_3$, $C_6H_5$

(XIII)

rivatives of bismethylene succinic anhydride, which function by exploiting the Woodward-Hoffman rules governing electrocyclic reactions: optical and thermal reactions proceed by different stereochemical pathways, and the thermal one is blocked by bulky side groups. Optical techniques are limited in resolution by the wavelength of the laser light, but this restriction can be circumvented by storing information at various wavelengths in the same physical region of a sample consisting of photoactive molecules that are dispersed in an amorphous medium and have a distribution of adsorption maxima. This technique, persistent spectral hole burning, has been demonstrated in systems, including the phthalocyanines (XIV).

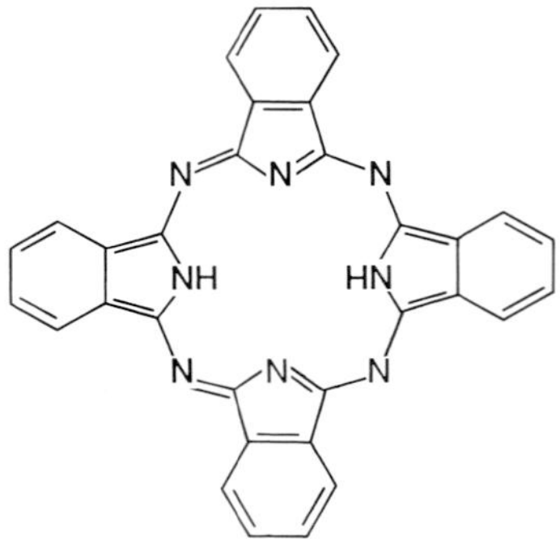

(XIV)

Molecular electrochromic media change color on oxidation or reduction at a suitable potential and can be used for displays. One type uses viologens (XV),

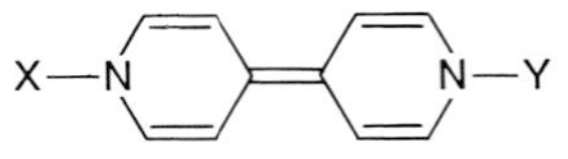

(XV)

whose color changes depend on the substituents X and Y (typically alkyl or aryl groups) and counterions, which also modify the display response times and durability. Another possibility is use of poly(pyrrole) (VII), which is dark in the conducting form prepared electrochemically but transparent green in the insulating form, while poly(isothianaphthene) (XVI) is transparent in its conducting form.

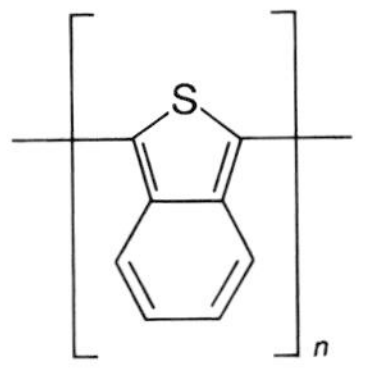

(XVI)

*See Electrochromic displays; Optical communications; Optical information systems.*

**Prospects.** Molecular electronics is already successful in the areas outlined above, in most of which devices are at the prototype stage or beyond, and active development continues. The components in microelectronic circuits are now so small that they will soon be reduced to molecular dimensions. Molecular electronics will then have to treat whole systems of molecules rather than individual molecular elements. Such systems will have to largely assemble themselves specifically and spontaneously under the influence of their intermolecular forces, as biological system do. After assembly, the constituent molecules will interact nonlinearly (and not necessarily electronically), leading ultimately to supermolecular arrays for information processing.

*R. W. Munn*

**Bibliography.** F. L. Carter (ed.), *Molecular Electronic Devices*, 1982; *J. Mol. Electr.*, 1985– ; G. G. Roberts, An applied science perspective of Langmuir-Blodgett films, *Ad. Phys.*, 34(4):475–512, 1985.

## Monopulse radar

A radar that obtains a complete measurement of the target's angular position from a single echo pulse. Together with the range measurement performed with the same pulse, the target position in three dimensions is determined completely. Usually a train of echo pulses is then employed to make a large number of repeated measurements and produce a refined estimate, but this is not intrinsically necessary.

The antenna receiving characteristics are especially pertinent to monopulse performance. It is usually convenient, but not necessary, to use the same antenna to illuminate the target. The monopulse operation is implemented by means of two pairs of feed points appropriately located at the antenna. The two feeds for determining azimuth information are located in the same horizontal plane on either side of the beam axis. The main lobe belonging to one is directed slightly to the left of the beam axis, and the main lobe belonging to the other is tilted slightly to the right. A target located exactly on the beam axis produces the same signal in both feeds, but a target located to one side of the beam axis produces a stronger signal in one feed than the other. The difference between the signals received by the two feeds indicates the azimuth separation between the beam axis and the line of sight to the target. The sum of the signals received by the two feeds indicates the gross signal strength and is used as a normalizing factor. *See Antenna*.

A similar arrangement is used to measure elevation angle, with the two feeds located in the same vertical plane above and below the beam axis. There is nothing to prevent simultaneous measurement of azimuth and elevation.

The same antenna can also be used for transmission by connecting the four feed points in parallel. The radiation pattern thereby produced is almost the same as the pattern produced by a single feed, except that the beam width is slightly smaller, the gain slightly higher, and the lobe pattern is symmetrically positioned with respect to the beam axis instead of being tilted.

The sum and difference signals can be formed either at the carrier frequency or after conversion to a lower frequency. It is of some advantage to obtain the sum and difference results immediately at the carrier frequency to minimize the possibility of subsequent circuits introducing errors. The operations can be performed conveniently at microwave frequencies by the use of waveguide hybrid mixers. Only the sum and difference signals, in both azimuth and elevation, would then be conveyed beyond this point in the receiver.

An important advantage of a monopulse tracking radar over one employing conical scan is that the instantaneous angular measurements are not subject to errors caused by target scintillation. In a conical-scan system the angular information is derived from the phase and amplitude of the modulation envelope on the echo pulse train. The conical mutation frequency usually lies in the range between 20 and 40 Hz, and the scintillation spectrum of most targets possesses nonnegligible components within this band. The scintillation produces random modulation at the nutation frequency which cannot subsequently be differentiated from the signal, leading to tracking errors. A monopulse tracking radar is not susceptible to this difficulty because each pulse provides an angular measurement without regard to the rest of the pulse train. There is no opportunity for radar cross-section fluctuations to affect the measurement.

An additional advantage of monopulse tracking as compared to conical scan is that no mechanical action is required in monopulse. In a precise and highly maneuverable tracking radar it is helpful not to have to accommodate a whirling scanner. For discussion of conical scan *see Radar*.

*Robert I. Bernstein*

**Bibliography.** D. K. Barton (ed.), *Radar: Monopulse Radars*, vol. 1, 1974; M. I. Skolnik, *Introduction to Radar Systems*, 2d ed., 1980.

## Motorboating

A form of oscillation that occurs at a very low audio frequency in a system, circuit, or component. It is caused by excessive amount of audio feedback at low frequencies. This oscillation is a succession of pulses; when these occur in a circuit that is feeding a loudspeaker, the pulses result in putt-putt sounds resembling those made by a motorboat.

Feedback through a common power supply is one cause of motorboating and can be suppressed by using resistance-capacitance decoupling filters between the power supply and the plate circuit of each tube. Another solution is to cause the amplification to fall off sharply immediately below the useful range of frequencies, so that the motorboating frequencies are inherently suppressed. *See Amplifier*.

*John Markus*

## Moving-target indication

A method of presenting pulse-radar echoes in a manner that discriminates in favor of moving targets and suppresses stationary objects. Moving-target indication (MTI) is almost a necessity when moving targets are being sought over a region from which the ground clutter echoes are very strong. The most common presentation of the output of a radar with MTI is a plan position indicator (PPI) display. The moving targets appear as bright echoes, while ground clutter is suppressed.

**Principles of operation.** MTI is based upon the use of the Doppler effect; that is, the carrier frequency of the echo from a target moving toward or away from the radar shifts by an amount proportional to the product of radial velocity and transmitted frequency (see **illus**.). A stable oscillator in the receiver is synchronized with the transmitter, providing a continuous reference of the transmitter frequency and phase. Echoes are heterodyned with the reference oscillator. Stationary objects supply echoes having a carrier phase shift which is constant from pulse to pulse, because the time for the signal to travel to a stationary object and back is always the same. Therefore the

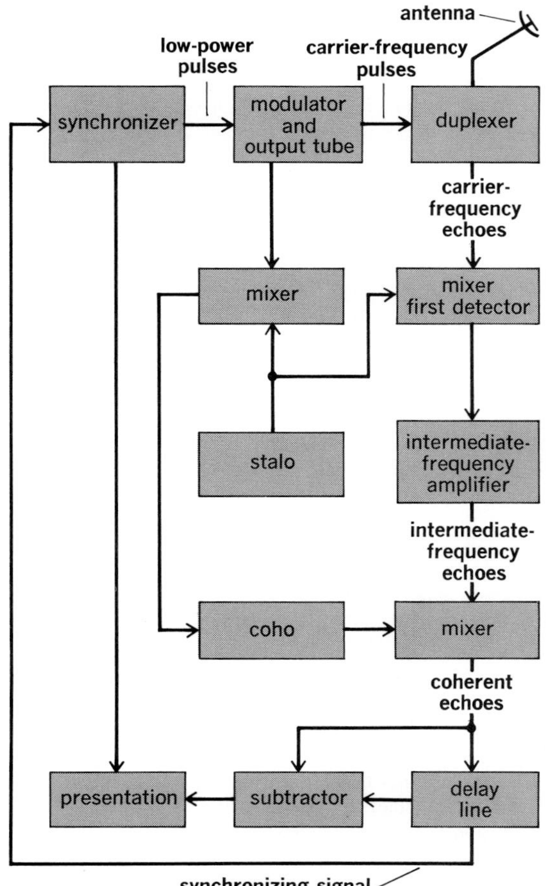


Diagram of radar system with moving-target indication.

heterodyner output for stationary echoes does not change in phase from pulse to pulse. However, phase shift in echoes from moving targets changes from pulse to pulse because of the change in signal propagation time. *See* DOPPLER RADAR.

To utilize the lack of pulse-to-pulse phase difference to discriminate against clutter echoes, the heterodyner output is fed to a delay line which stores the signal for a period of time exactly equal to the period between pulses. Then the output of the delay line is subtracted from the freshly produced output of the heterodyner. If the two outputs are identical, as will be the case for clutter, the difference is zero. But this difference is not zero for moving targets because of their pulse-to-pulse phase shift. The difference between consecutive echoes is presented as the MTI output. The delay line usually employed utilizes acoustic propagation within fused quartz.

A variety of internal arrangements are in use for assuring that the reference oscillator is synchronized with the transmitter output. The reference oscillator may be at the carrier frequency but usually operates at an intermediate frequency, because better stability can be obtained in a low-frequency oscillator. This arrangement requires that the local oscillator used for conversion from the carrier frequency to the intermediate frequency be extremely stable, and the term stalo (stable local oscillator) is used to denote circuits that satisfy this requirement. The reference oscillator is called the coho (coherent oscillator) to denote that it remains coherent (fixed phase relation) with the transmitter output.

**Measures of merit.** The figure of merit of an MTI system, clutter suppression factor, is defined as the ratio of root-mean-square (rms) clutter amplitude before MTI to rms clutter fluctuation after MTI. It is the amount by which the clutter is suppressed. It depends in turn upon several other factors, some of which are system parameters and thus controllable, and some of which are functions of terrain and weather.

Another measure of merit for MTI radar is the signal-to-clutter ratio (SCR). However, it has been found that increasing the SCR simultaneously reduces the signal-to-noise ratio (SNR), a measure of merit of the sensitivity of the radar. Targets in a clutter-free environment are less detectable with MTI than without it because of reduced SNR. A parallel bank of Doppler filters can provide a simultaneous improvement in both SCR and SNR. *See* SIGNAL-TO-NOISE RATIO.

**Use of charge-transfer devices.** Charge-transfer devices can be utilized to implement MTI with excellent capability for canceling clutter. A charge-transfer device is a capacitorlike semiconductor device of the bucket-brigade variety. As used in MTI, samples of the returned radar signal are stored and processed as discrete quantities of electrical charge. This implementation has become known as discrete-signal moving-target indication (DSMTI). Metal oxide semiconductor field-effect transistors are used as charge-transfer devices to provide the delay that permits subtracting a radar return delayed by one pulse-repetition interval (PRI) from the currently incoming radar return.

**Adaptive MTI.** Radar systems designers have long appreciated that the best target range and velocity resolution are obtained by using recurrent pulses whose duration is short compared with the PRI. However, this practice gives rise to ambiguities in determining the range and velocity of the target. In fact, it causes the radar to be blind to targets moving at certain velocities when MTI is in use. A way to avoid blind velocities is to implement a random staggering of the radar's pulse-repetition frequency (PRF). Fast changes in the PRF combined with filtering systems and integration methods that adapt automatically to these changes permit ambiguities in determining the range and velocity of the target to be resolved in a single look at the target. Clutter filters switched in synchronism with the PRF also reduce undesirable clutter sidebands even when the PRF is switched at a high rate, and the irregular pulse spacing alleviates the problem of blind velocities. The clutter filter can be a notch-type filter that has its rejection band centered about the carrier frequency. *See* ELECTRIC FILTER.

This adaptive MTI (AMTI) proved to be useful in achieving acceptable detection of targets in the presence of natural precipitation static and chaff dispersed by the enemy as a defensive measure against radar. *See* RADAR.

*John M. Carroll*

**Bibliography.** A. Andrews, *ABC's of Radar*, 1961; *Proceedings of the IEEE International Radar Conference*, 1975; M. I. Skolnik, *Introduction to Radar Systems*, 2d ed., 1979.

## Multiaccess computer

A computer system in which computational and data resources are made available simultaneously to a number of users. Users access the system through terminal devices, normally on an interactive or conversational basis. A multiaccess computer system may consist of only a single central processor connected directly to a number of terminals (that is, a star configuration), or it may consist of a number of processing systems which are distributed and interconnected with each other as well as with the user terminals.

The primary purpose of multiaccess computer systems is to share resources. The resources being shared may be simply the data-processing capabilities of the central processor, or they may be the programs and the data bases they utilize. The earliest examples of the first mode of sharing are the general-purpose, time-sharing, computational services. Examples of the latter mode are airlines reservation systems in which it is essential that all ticket agents have immediate access to current information. Both of these classes of systems are still popular, with the proportion and importance of distributed application systems continuing to increase in areas such as corporate management and operations. *See* DATA-BASE MANAGEMENT SYSTEMS.

There are a number of economic factors supporting the growth of multiaccess systems. Primary among these are improvements in hardware performance and economics, with the latter being the principal factor. Digital-computer hardware continues to exhibit rapidly decreasing costs while its operational capabilities increase. At the same time most of the other cost factors involved with corporate operations such as labor, travel, and communications are increasing, and the cost of time delays in operations such as inventory management and confirming orders, as well as the cost of investment funding, is becoming significant.

**System components.** The major hardware components of a multiaccess computer system are terminals or data entry/display devices, communication lines to interconnect the terminals to the central processors, a central processor, and on-line mass storage.

Terminals may be quite simple, providing only the capabilities for entering or displaying data. Also utilized in multiaccess systems are terminals having an appreciable amount of "local intelligence" to support simple operations like editing of the displayed text without requiring the involvement of the central processor. Some terminals provide even more extensive support, such as the local storage of small amounts of text. It is also possible to assemble clusters of terminals to share local logic and storage.

The interconnecting communication lines can be provided by utilizing the common-user telephone system or by obtaining leased, private lines from the telephone company or a specialized carrier. Another important source of data circuits is a value-added network specializing in providing data transmission services. *See* DATA COMMUNICATIONS.

The communications interface for the processor may be provided by an integral hardware component or by a separate device known as a communications controller or front-end (communications) processor. The detailed operations involved in the control of a single communications line are not very great; however, servicing a large number of such lines may present an appreciable load to the central processor; therefore, separate hardware for communications interfacing is almost essential in a multiaccess computer system.

A central processor suitable for use in a multiaccess system must include the capability to support a large central memory as well as the communications interface mentioned above and the on-line mass storage discussed below.

The desirable characteristics of a mass storage device are: the ability to quickly locate any desired data; the ability to transfer data at a very high speed; the provision of economical storage for a large quantity of data; and a high degree of reliability.

The most common form of mass storage is rotating magnetic disks. Originally, magnetic drums were utilized for this purpose; however, the price, performance, and capacity of disks have resulted in their replacing drums. *See* COMPUTER STORAGE TECHNOLOGY.

**System operating requirements.** A multiaccess system must include the following functional capabilities: (1) multiline communications capabilities that will support simultaneous conversations with a reasonably large number of remote terminals; (2) concurrent execution of a number of programs with the ability to quickly switch from executing the program of one user to executing that of another; (3) ability to quickly locate and make available data stored on the mass storage devices while at the same time protecting such data from unauthorized access.

The ability of a system to support a number of simultaneous sessions with remote users is an extension of the capability commonly known as multiprogramming. In order to provide such service, certain hardware and software features should be available in the central processor. Primary among these is the ability to quickly switch from executing one program to another while protecting all programs from interference with one another. These capabilities are normally provided by including a large central memory in the processor, by providing hardware features that support rapid program switching, and by providing high-speed transfers between the central memory and the mass storage unit on which the programs and the data they utilize are stored.

Memory sharing is essential to the efficient operation of a multiaccess system. It permits a number of programs to be simultaneously resident in the central memory so that switching execution between programs involves only changing the contents of the control registers. The programs that are resident in central memory are protected from interfering with one another by a number of techniques. In earlier multiprogramming systems, this was accomplished by assigning contiguous memory space to each program and then checking every access to memory to ensure that a program was accessing only locations in its assigned space. The drawback to this type of memory allocation is that the entire program had to be loaded into memory whenever any portion of it was to be executed. A popular memory management technique is the utilization of paging. The program is broken into a number of fixed-size increments called pages. Similarly, central memory is divided into segments of the same size called page frames. (Typical sizes for pages and page frames are 512 to 4096 bytes.) Under the concept known as demand paging, only those pages that are currently required by the program are loaded into central memory. Page frames may be assigned to a given program in a random checkerboard fashion. Hardware capabilities are provided to automatically manage the assignment of page frames as well as to make them appear to the program as one continuous address space. At the same time, the hardware provides memory access protection.

**Software capabilities.** The control software component of most interest to an interactive user is the command interpreter. It is only one portion of a larger control program known as the operating system; however, in multiaccess systems it differs greatly from the command interpreter in a system providing batch multiprogramming service on a noninteractive, nonterminal-oriented bases. This routine interacts directly with users, accepting requests for service and translating them into the internal form required by the remainder of the operating system, as well as controlling all interaction with the system.

The operating system must also have the capability for controlling multiprogramming; that is, the concurrent execution of a number of user programs quickly switching from one to another during their execution as well as controlling memory sharing. The capability to page the memory as outlined above can be utilized to provide users with the impression that each has available a memory space much larger than is actually assigned. Such a system is said to provide a virtual memory environment. Similarly, the ability of the operating system to quickly change context from one executing program to another will result in users' receiving the impression that each has an individual processor. This is especially true when considering the large difference between the response and thinking time of a human compared to the computer's processing time. For the interactive users, such a capability results in the impression of having a private virtual machine.

The mass storage device mentioned above as hardware required for a multiaccess system must be supported by an efficient file management system. The latter is responsible for maintaining current information as to the physical location of the data stored on the mass storage device as well as providing a capability for quickly locating those data and controlling their transfer to the central memory for utilization. In addition, the file management system must provide protection of data from unauthorized access. *See* Data-processing systems; Digital computer.

Philip H. Enslow, Jr.

**Bibliography.** D. Davies et al., *Computer Networks and Their Protocols*, 1979; D. Doll, *Data Communications*, 1978; J. Martin, *Introduction to Teleprocessing*, 1972; A. S. Tanenbaum, *Computer Networks: Toward Distributed Processing Systems*, 1981.

## Multimeter

A common term for a volt-ohm-milliammeter, also called an analyzer or circuit analyzer. A much less common usage applies to a self-contained test instrument containing two or more single- or multiscale indicating instruments for measuring simultaneously two or more electrical quantities. *See* Volt-ohm-milliammeter.

Isaac F. Kinnard/Edward C. Stevenson

## Multiplexing

Various techniques which are used to enable the transmission of multiple messages through a common channel. The term multiplexing is sometimes reserved for those systems which combine the various messages at a common point, say, at the input to a channelized bank of filters. In contrast, the term multiple access refers to systems wherein many users access a channel from, in general, different geographical points. An example of the latter would be the common amplitude-modulation (AM) radio channel whereby many different stations broadcast their programs simultaneously. In the discussion below, this distinction between the two terms is loosely applied.

**Frequency division.** The two classical techniques for either multiplexing or multiple accessing are frequency division and time division. In frequency-division multiple access (FDMA) or multiplexing, each user is given its own frequency band, and all users are allowed to transmit simultaneously. One obvious consideration in designing such a system is to ensure that there is no overlap (or at least a minimal degree of overlap) between the frequency spectra of the different users. This is accomplished by band-limiting the transmissions of the different users and also by allowing for guard bands between the spectra of adjacent signals. A second problem that often arises with systems of this type is intermodulation distortion. This refers to the generation of frequencies at the output of some nonlinearity when a sum of signals at different carrier frequencies is the input to the nonlinearity. *See* Distortion (electronic circuits).

**Time division.** A time-division multiplexed system [or a time-division multiple-access (TDMA) system] can be used to circumvent both of these problems. In this case, each user is the sole user of the channel during the portion of time it is transmitting, but can access the channel only a fraction of the total time. In other words, the different users now transmit sequentially in time, rather than simultaneously in time. The key virtue in this technique is that it eliminates the intermodulation problem. The difficulty in employing the technique is that accurate synchronization between the transmitters and receivers must be established and maintained. For multiplexed signals which originate at a common point this is not a serious problem, but for multiple-access systems this can be quite difficult to implement.

**Code division.** A third technique, used primarily in a multiple-access setting, is called code-division multiple access (CDMA), or sometimes spread-spectrum multiple access. In this scheme, all users occupy the total channel bandwidth and all transmit simultaneously in time. However, each user has superimposed upon its data sequence a wide-bandwidth code, or spreading sequence. Each spreading sequence is unique to a given user, and the joint properties of the set of such sequences enable each receiver, when properly synchronized to the spreading sequence of the user of interest, to receive the signal of that user and sufficiently attenuate the signals of the other users to keep the overall interference level to a tolerable value. *See* Spread spectrum communication.

**Choice of technique.** With respect to which modulation formats are most appropriate, frequency-division multiplexing is in a sense the most versatile of the three multiplex or multiple-access schemes in that it can, in principle, be used with either analog or digital modulation. In practice, however, it is most often used with analog modulation techniques. On the other hand, both time and code division are commonly employed with digital modulation formats, although time-division multiplexing could be used with analog pulse modulation (for example, pulse amplitude modulation). *See* Modulation; Pulse modulation.

Under ideal conditions, for a given number of users, each of the three techniques requires the same amount of bandwidth. Indeed, it is only when nonideal conditions such as nonlinear elements and imperfect synchronization are considered that the differences in performance of the schemes become evident. *See* Electrical communications.

Laurence B. Milstein

**Bibliography.** W. D. Gregg, *Analog and Digital Communications*, 1977; H. Taub and D. L. Schilling, *Principles of Communication Systems*, 1971; R. E. Ziemer and W. H. Tranter, *Principles of Communications*, 1976.

## Multiprocessing

An organizational technique in which a number of processor units are employed in a single computer system to increase the performance of the system in its application environment above the performance of a single processor. In order to cooperate on a single application or class of applications, the processors share a common resource. Usually this resource is primary memory, and the multiprocessor is called a primary memory multiprocessor. A system in which each processor has a private (local) main memory and shares secondary (global) memory with the others is a secondary memory multiprocessor, sometimes called a multicomputer system because of the looser coupling between processors. The more common multiprocessor systems incorporate only processors of the same type and performance and thus are called homogeneous multiprocessors; however, heterogeneous multiprocessors are also employed. A special case is the attached processor, in which a second processor module is attached to a first processor in a closely coupled fashion so thatthe first can perform input/output and operating system functions, enabling the attached processor to concentrate on the application workload. *SEE COMPUTER STORAGE TECHNOLOGY; OPERATING SYSTEM.*

**Classification.** Multiprocessor systems may be classified into four types: single instruction stream, single data stream (SISD); single instruction stream, multiple data stream (SIMD); multiple instruction stream, single data stream (MISD); and multiple instruction stream, multiple data stream (MIMD). Systems in the MISD category are rarely built. The other three architectures may be distinguished simply by the differences in their respective instruction cycles:

In an SISD architecture there is a single instruction cycle; operands are fetched serially into a single processing unit before execution. Sequential processors fall into this category.

An SIMD architecture also has a single instruction cycle, but multiple sets of operands may be fetched to multiple processing units and may be operated upon simultaneously within a single instruction cycle. Multiple-functional-unit, array, vector, and pipeline processors are in this category. *SEE SUPERCOMPUTER.*

In an MIMD architecture, several instruction cycles may be active at any given time, each independently fetching instructions and operands into multiple processing units and operating on them in a concurrent fashion. This category includes multiple processor systems in which each processor has its own program control, rather than sharing a single control unit.

MIMD systems can be further classified into throughput-oriented systems, high-availability systems, and response-oriented systems. The goal of throughput-oriented multiprocessing is to obtain high throughput at minimal computing cost (subject to fail-soft equipment redundancy requirements) in a general-purpose computing environment by maximizing the number of independent computing jobs done in parallel. The techniques employed by multiprocessor operating systems to achieve this goal take advantage of an inherent processing versus input/output balance in the workload to produce balanced, uniform loading of system resources with scheduled response.

High-availability multiprocessing systems are generally interactive, often with never-fail real-time online performance requirements. Such application environments are usually centered on a common data base and are almost always input/output-limited rather than computer-limited. Tasks are not independent but are often interdependent at the data-base level. The operating system goal is to maximize the number of cooperating tasks done in parallel. Such systems may also process multiple independent jobs in a background mode. The additional hardware redundancy in a fault-tolerant system over a general-purpose multiprocessor can be considered a trade-off against software complexity and the time required for software check-pointing in a sequential mainframe system. *SEE FAULT-TOLERANT SYSTEMS; REAL-TIME SYSTEMS.*

The goal of response-oriented multiprocessing (or parallel processing) is to minimize system response time for computational demands. Applications for such systems are naturally computer-intensive, and many such applications can be decomposed into multiple tasks or processes to run concurrently on multiple processors. In the past, successful SIMD and MIMD parallel processors were often special-purpose machines dedicated to a single class of scientific or real-time signal processing applications. The interest in high-performance, low-cost computers able to handle combined numeric, symbolic, and signal processing tasks concurrently, for so-called fifth-generation applications, together with the availability of low-cost very large-scale integrated-circuit (VLSI) microprocessors has rekindled interest in response-oriented multiprocessing. *SEE CONCURRENT PROCESSING; INTEGRATED CIRCUITS; MICROPROCESSOR.*

**Throughput-oriented multiprocessing.** The performance of a classical shared-memory multiprocessor is limited by the so-called bandwidth of its shared memory (the total data transfer capacity of the memory bus). Access conflicts further reduce effective bandwidth and thus overall system performance. Studies on early multiprocessors showed interesting results on throughput loss as a function of effective memory bandwidth. For example, if a single processor had one unit of throughput, its dual processor had only 10% less throughput than two single processor systems, and a triple processor had 20% less throughput than three individual systems in a multicomputer rather than multiprocessor configuration. This was not a high penalty to pay for fail-soft function in an airline reservation system with 3000 remote agent terminals. Multiprocessors now exhibit similar performance characteristics up to six processors, that is, up to their effective memory bandwidth performance limit which has been enhanced by a higher degree of memory interleaving over earlier multiprocessor systems. Operating system software provides the key fail-soft capability in a throughput-oriented multiprocessor. The performance cost of software checkpointing is higher in sequential processors than in a multiprocessor. Since system protective tasks are redundant, the more processors the better, up to the effective bandwidth limits of the system's shared resources.

**High-availability multiprocessing.** Fault-tolerant multiprocessor systems were a natural development from throughput-oriented multiprocessor systems. While the trade-off that achieves fault tolerance is a hardware one—that is, more hardware units are used in order to achieve greater system availability—the technology employed is primarily a software one. Lower-level hardware redundancy is used in many such systems, but its successful deployment in applications is still a software issue. The basic requisite for a highly available system in most applications is that each major hardware and software component must at least be duplicated. The system requires two or more processors, two paths connecting the processors, and two paths from the processors to the data base. The system's disk controllers and communication controllers must be multiported, so that they may be connected to multiple processors. A high-availability data-base-oriented system requires five essential software ingredients: a network-communication subsystem, a data-communication subsystem, a data-base manager, a transaction manager, and an operating system. The network communication subsystem supports interprocess communication within a cluster of locally distributed processors. If the highly available system is also a node on a geographically distributed system, the communication subsystem must also support internode communication. *SEE DATA-BASE MANAGEMENT SYSTEMS; DATA COMMUNICATIONS.*

**Response-oriented multiprocessing.** The ideal performance characteristic for an $N$-processor system, on which a given problem could be partitioned into $N$ or more similar tasks, would be a linear relationship between performance (the rate at which the system can solve a problem, in units of single-processor performance) versus the number of processors. M. Minsky was skeptical of this ideal, conjecturing that for large $N$ the best hope was for $\log_2 N$ performance. In 1967 G. Amdahl suggested Amdahl's (second) law, stating that if a computer has two speeds of operation the slower mode will dominate performance even if the faster mode is infinitely fast. This leads to a $N/\log N$ performance in a multiprocessor performing a single application in multitask mode.

Minsky's conjecture now seems much too pessimistic, and parallel processing performance gains even greater than those predicted by Amdahl's law have become the goal. A sophisticated technique has been developed for the extraction of parallelism from FORTRAN DO-loops that can routinely exceed Amdahl's law for SIMD machines. While 100% efficiency is probably not attainable, many highly tailored applications based on careful manual extraction of parallelism have achieved efficiency ratings in the 80–90% range. *See* Programming languages.

Most computer engineers and architects see a high degree of multiprocessing or parallel processing as essential for achieving performance requirements for future computer systems for scientific computation, for fifth-generation or artificial intelligence (AI) applications, and for dedicated and embedded multiprocessors in control or automation systems. It is also widely accepted that a new parallel application and programming technology must be developed to make effective use of multiprocessors having hundreds or thousands of processors. The promise of high-performance computer systems made up of low-cost high-volume components (for example, microprocessor chips) rather than high-cost low-volume components draws computer architects and applications specialists toward the development of parallel processing technology. *See* Artificial intelligence; Computer systems architecture; Digital computer; Embedded systems.

*Peter C. Patton*

**Bibliography.** G. M. Amdahl, Validity of single processor approach to achieving large scale computing capabilities, *AFIPS Conf. Proc.*, 30:483–485, 1967; P. H. Enslow, Jr. (ed.), *Multiprocessors and Parallel Processing*, 1974; M. J. Flynn, Some computer organizations and their effectiveness, *IEEE CT*, 21(9): 948–960, 1972; P. C. Patton, Multiprocessors: Architecture and applications, *IEEE Comput.*, June 1985.

## Multivibrator

A form of relaxation oscillator consisting normally of two or more active devices, such as transistors, interconnected by electric networks. In a multivibrator a portion of the output voltage or current of each active device is applied to the input of the other with such magnitude and polarity as to maintain the devices alternately conducting over controllable periods of time. The transition time of each device from one state to the other is extremely short. As a consequence the voltage waveform from the output of each of the devices is essentially rectangular in form.

Multivibrators are classified by the manner in which the reversal-of-state action of each device is initiated and by the method of control of the time interval in each state, whether from external sources or from the decay of voltage across a capacitor in circuits containing RC (resistance-capacitance) time constants within the multivibrator itself.

**Symmetrical bistable multivibrator.** In bistable multivibrators either of the two devices may remain conducting, with the other nonconducting, until the application of an external pulse. Such a multivibrator is said to have two stable states.

***JFET circuits.*** The original form of bistable multivibrator made use of vacuum tubes and was known as the Eccles-Jordan circuit, after its inventors. It was sometimes called a flip-flop or binary circuit because of the two alternating output voltage levels. The junction field-effect transistor (JFET) circuit (**Fig. 1**) is a modern version of the Eccles-Jordan circuit. Its resistance networks between positive and negative supply voltages are such that, with no current flowing to the drain of the first JFET, the voltage at the gate of the second is slightly negative, zero, or limited to, at most, a slightly positive value. The resultant current in the drain circuit of the second JFET causes a voltage drop across the drain load resistor; this drop in turn lowers the voltage at the gate of the first JFET to

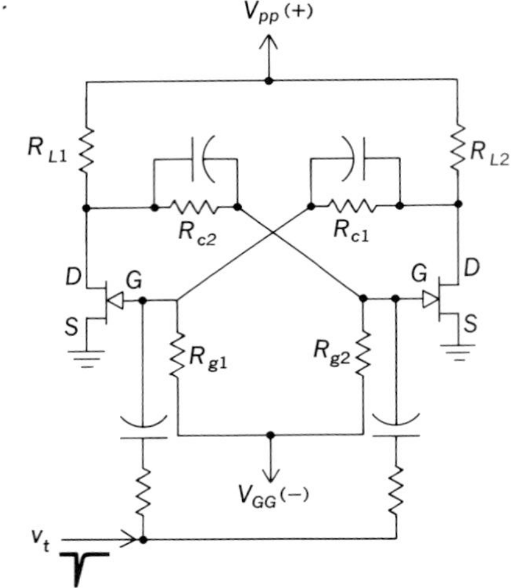


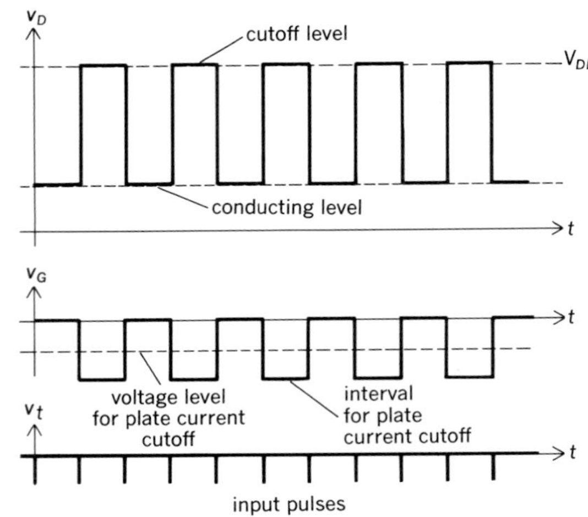


**Fig. 1. Bistable multivibrator with triggering, grid, and plate waveforms shown for one tube.**

a sufficiently negative value to continue to reduce the drain current to zero. This condition of the first device OFF and the second ON will be maintained as long as the circuit remains undisturbed.

If a fast negative pulse is then applied to the gate of the ON transistor, its drain current decreases and its drain voltage rises. A fraction of this rise is applied to the gate of the OFF transistor, causing some drain current to flow. The resultant drop in drain voltage, transferred to the gate of the ON transistor, causes a further rise at its drain. The action is thus one of positive feedback, with nearly instantaneous transfer of conduction from one device to the other. There is one such reversal each time a pulse is applied to the gate of the ON transistor. Normally pulses are applied to both transistors simultaneously so that whichever device is ON will be turned off by the action. The capacitances between the gate of one transistor and the drain of the other play no role other than to improve the high-frequency response of the voltage divider network by compensating for the input capacitances of the transistors and thereby improving the speed of transition.

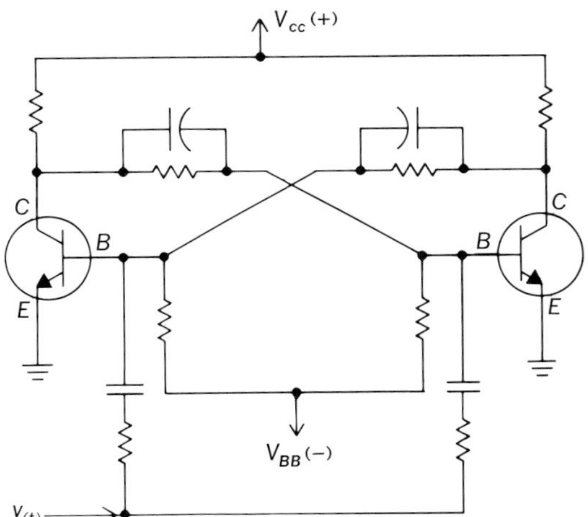


**Fig. 2. Bistable multivibrator using *npn* bipolar transistors. Action is similar to vacuum-tube circuit.**

***Bipolar transistor circuits.*** A bipolar transistor counterpart of the JFET bistable multivibrator with *npn* bipolar transistors is shown in **Fig. 2**. The base of the transistor corresponds to the gate, the emitter to the source, and the collector to the drain. Although waveforms are of the same polarity and the action is roughly similar to that of the JFET circuit, there are important differences. The effective resistance of the base-emitter circuit, when it is forward-biased and being used to control collector current, is much lower than the input gate resistance of the JFET when used to control drain current (a few thousand ohms compared to a few megohms). This fact must be taken into account when the divider networks are designed. If *pnp* transistors are used, all voltage polarities and current directions are reversed.

***IGFET circuits.*** Insulated-gate field-effect transistors (IGFETs) may be used effectively in multivibrators. Use of enhancement-mode insulated-gate field-effect transistors permits direct cross-coupling with considerable simplification (**Fig. 3**).

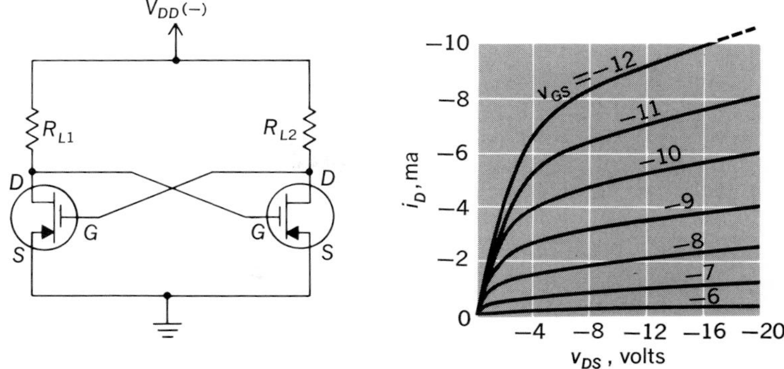


**Fig. 3. Direct-coupled, bistable multivibrator which uses *p*-channel enhancement-mode, field-effect transistors, resulting in considerable simplification.**

**Unsymmetrical bistable circuits.** Bistable action can be obtained in the emitter- or source-coupled circuit with one of the set of cross-coupling elements removed (**Fig. 4**). In this case, regenerative feedback necessary for bistable action is obtained by the one remaining common coupling element, leaving one emitter or gate free for triggering action. Biases can be adjusted such that device 1 is ON, forcing device 2 to be OFF. In this case, a pulse can be applied to the free input in such a direction as to reverse the states. Alternatively, device 1 may initially be OFF with device 2 ON. Then an opposite polarity pulse is required to reverse states. Such an unsymmetrical bistable circuit, historically referred to as the Schmitt trigger circuit, finds widespread use in many applications.

A Schmitt trigger circuit often employs a high-gain operational amplifier of the type normally used as a comparator in a positive-feedback or regenerative mode (**Fig. 5**). When $V_i > V_F$, the output is in its low state $V_{OL}$, with $V_F$ in turn determined by $V_{OL}$, $V_{REF}$, $R_1$, and $R_2$. When $V_i < V_F$, the output will be in its high state $V_{OH}$, and $V_F$ will be at a correspondingly higher level. Thus if the input $V_i$ switches between two levels, the output will switch between its low and high states. These switching levels are different depending upon whether $V_i$ is increasing or decreasing. The difference in $V_i = V_F$ for the two levels is known as the hysteresis of the circuit. When the input $V_i$ is between the low and high $V_F$ levels, the output can be in either its high or low state depending upon the previous turn-on history; hence the term bistable circuit.

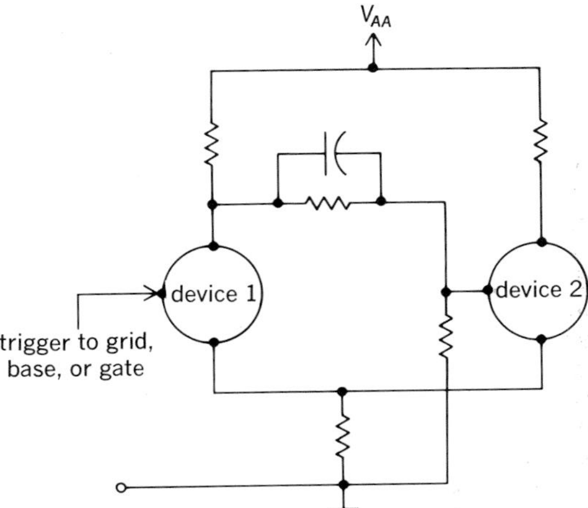


**Fig. 4. Unsymmetrical bistable multivibrator.**

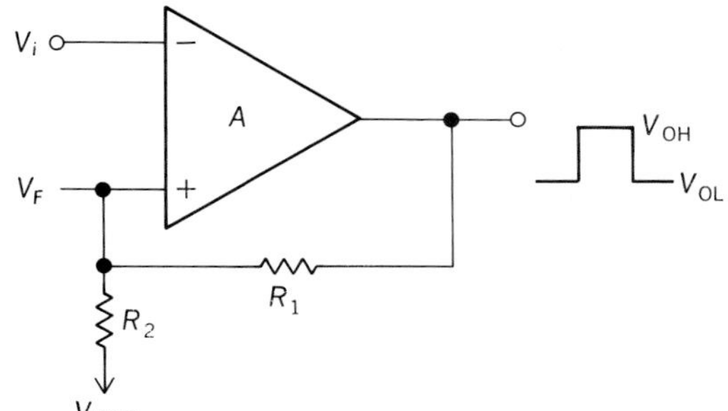


**Fig. 5. Operational amplifier comparator used as Schmitt trigger circuit.**

**Monostable multivibrator.** A monostable multivibrator has only one stable state. If one of the normally active devices is in the conducting state, it will remain so until an external pulse is applied to make it nonconducting. The second device is thus made conducting and remains so for a duration dependent upon *RC* time constants within the circuit itself.

A typical monostable multivibrator is shown in **Fig. 6**. The input of field-effect transistor (FET) 1 is capacitance-coupled to the output of FET 2. In the absence of external pulses, FET 1 is conducting, with its gate at zero potential, or limited to a slight positive value by saturation. The resultant drain current limits the drain voltage to a value that makes the gate of FET 2 sufficiently negative to keep FET 2 cut off. If a negative pulse is applied to the gate of FET 1, this FET is cut off and FET 2 conducts. The circuit action is similar to that of the bistable circuits except that the voltage drop at the drain of FET 2 is transferred to the gate of FET 1 through the capacitance $C_c$. This change, or transition, cannot be maintained indefinitely because the current flowing through $C_c$ and $R_{G1}$ causes a decrease in voltage with time across $C_c$ and rise in voltage at the gate of FET 1, as shown. The initial drop is of the same magnitude as that at the drain of FET 2 at the time the trigger is applied. The ensuing rise is exponential in form and (if $R_{G1}$ is much greater than $R_{L2}$) is given by Eq. (1). When the

$$V_{G1} = (V_{GG} - V_{DD}) \exp\left[-t/R_{G1}C_c\right] + V_{DD} \quad (1)$$

rising voltage reaches the level $V_{c1}$, drain current again flows in FET 1. Positive feedback quickly causes FET 1 to become fully conducting and limited by gate current saturation. The duration of the nonconducting interval for FET 1 time ($T_1$ in Fig. 6) is found by solving Eq. (1) for time $t = T_1$ and for $V_{G1} = V_{c1}$. The result is Eq. (2). The circuit will remain

$$T_1 = -R_{G1}C_c \ln \frac{V_{c1} - V_{DD}}{V_{GG} - V_{DD}} \quad (2)$$

in this state until another initiating trigger is applied.

**Astable multivibrator.** The astable multivibrator has capacitance coupling between both of the active devices and therefore has no permanently stable state. Each of the two devices functions in a manner similar to that of the capacitance-coupled half of the monostable multivibrator, as shown in **Fig. 7**. It will therefore generate a periodic rectangular waveform at the output with a period equal to the sum of the OFF periods of the two devices. The duration of each of the two periods is governed by an equation of the form of Eq. (2), with the appropriate values for each of the two parts of the circuit used. The transistor astable multivibrator similarly functions as the combination of two transistor monostable sections coupled together.

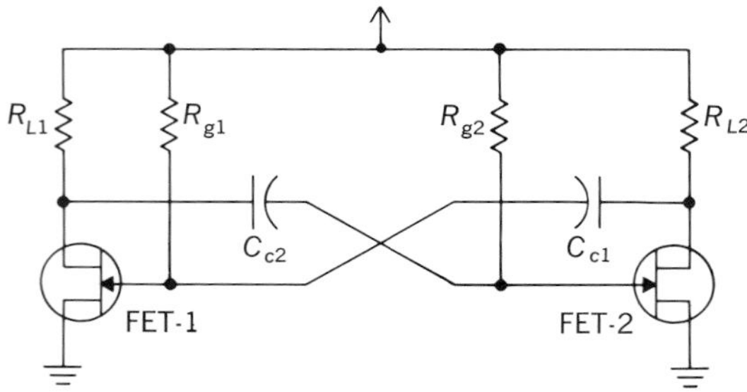


**Fig. 7. Astable or free-running multivibrator.**

Astable multivibrators, although normally free-running, can be synchronized with input pulses recurrent at a rate slightly faster than the natural recurrence rate of the device itself. This is illustrated in **Fig. 8**, which shows the relation between the internal waveform and the applied synchronizing pulses. If the synchronizing pulses are of sufficient amplitude, they will bring the internal waveform to the conduction level at an earlier than normal time and will thereby determine the recurrence rate.

**Triggering of multivibrators.** The period of the bistable, the monostable, and the synchronized astable multivibrator is controlled by pulses (triggers) from an external source. These triggers may be applied to the circuit in various fashions. The initiating trigger should be sufficiently wide for the circuit to respond (as limited by its high-frequency response) before the pulse is over, but not so wide as to interfere with normal action of the multivibrator once the transition has taken place. The trigger should be cou-

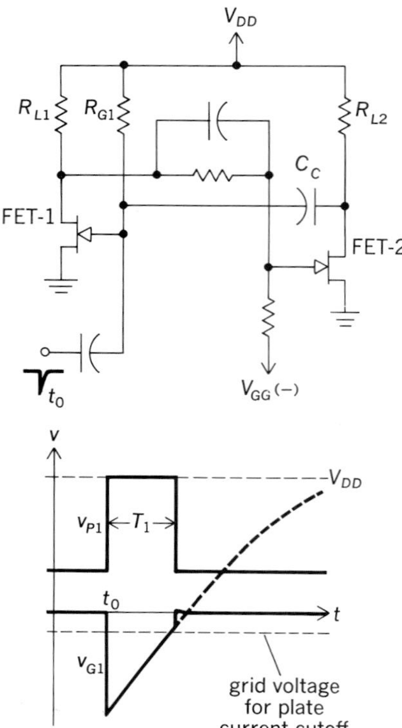


**Fig. 6. Basic monostable multivibrator using vacuum triodes. Almost identical characteristics are obtained with *n*-channel junction, field-effect transistors.**

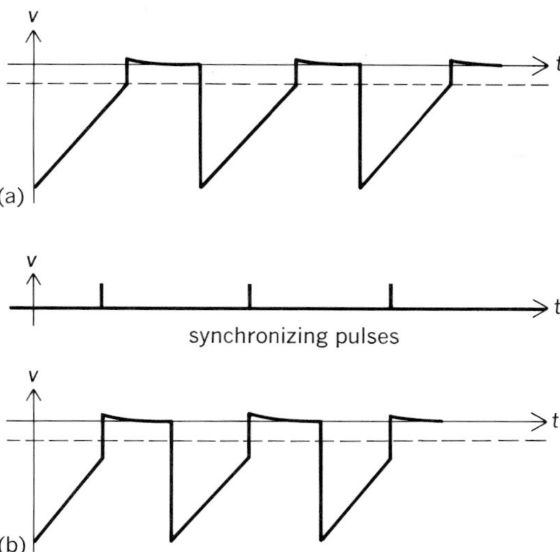


**Fig. 8. Comparison of the free-running and synchronized multivibrator waveforms. (*a*) Free-running waveform. (*b*) Synchronized waveform.**

pled to the multivibrator through a small capacitance so that loading by the trigger source is negligible. Usually a faster transition can be achieved if triggers turn off a normally ON device. Triggers are usually applied to the appropriate input, but they may also be applied to the outputs and reach the inputs through the coupling networks. In some cases any coupling between trigger source and multivibrator is objectionable, and an isolating amplifier is used with its plate and the plate of the multivibrator connected together. Auxiliary diodes are frequently used to provide trigger isolation and to improve triggering stability. *SEE TRIGGER CIRCUIT*.

Also, particularly where bistable circuits are used in computer logic systems, it is necessary to reset initial states so that the desired device is ON before a subsequent set of triggers are applied. Such a multivibrator provides extra available terminals for triggering purposes, as illustrated in **Fig. 9**. *SEE DIGITAL COMPUTER*.

**Logic gate multivibrators.** Multivibrators may be formed by using two cross-coupled logic gates, with the unused input terminals used for triggering purposes. Such circuits are usually referred to as flip-flops. For example, the circuit of **Fig. 10**, which is like that of Fig. 2, may be thought of as the cross connection of two, two-input RTL (resistor-transistor-logic) gates. The two extra inputs are available for set-reset triggering functions. The inputs and outputs are at standard logic levels. (0) and (1). The output levels after inputs at *R* and *S* are removed depend

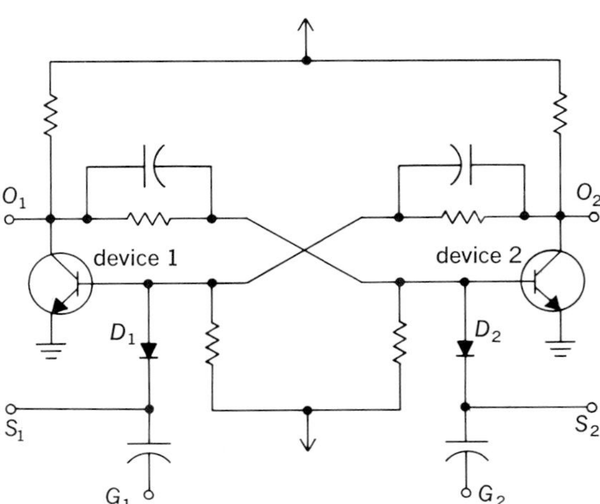


**Fig. 9. Multivibrator triggering techniques.**

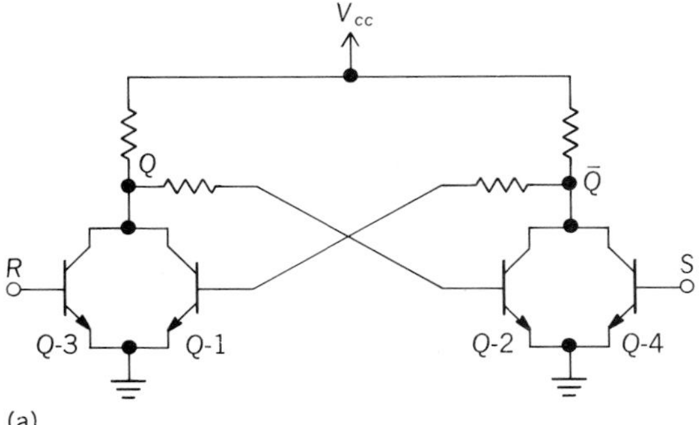


(a)

| $Q_n$ | $\bar{Q}_n$ | R | S | $Q_{n+1}$ | $\bar{Q}_{n+1}$ |
|---|---|---|---|---|---|
| 1 | 0 | 0 | 0 | 1 | 0 |
| 0 | 1 | 0 | 0 | 0 | 1 |
| 1 | 0 | 1 | 0 | 0 | 1 |
| 0 | 1 | 0 | 1 | 1 | 0 |
| 0 | 1 | 1 | 0 | 0 | 1 |
| 1 | 0 | 0 | 1 | 1 | 0 |
| 1 | 0 | 1 | 1 | ? | ? |
| 0 | 1 | 1 | 1 | ? | ? |

(b)

**Fig. 10. Cross-coupled RTL gates as R-S flip-flop. (*a*) Circuit. (*b*) Truth table.**

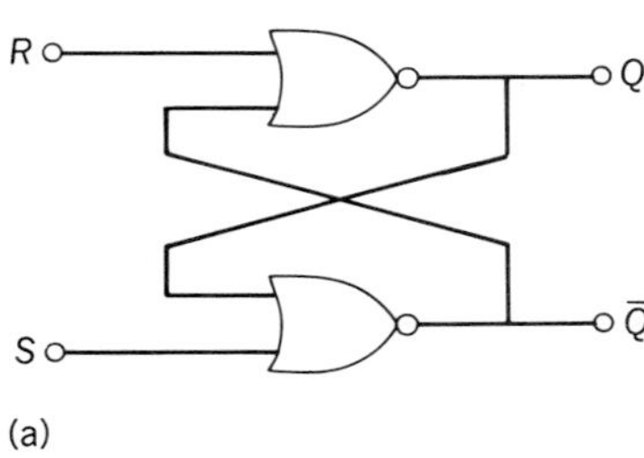


(a)

| R | S | $Q_{n+1}$ | $\bar{Q}_{n+1}$ |
|---|---|---|---|
| 0 | 0 | $Q_n$ | $\bar{Q}_n$ |
| 1 | 0 | 0 | 1 |
| 0 | 1 | 1 | 0 |
| 1 | 1 | not used | |

(b)

**Fig. 11. NOR gate R-S flip-flop. (*a*) Symbolic representation. (*b*) Abridged truth table.**

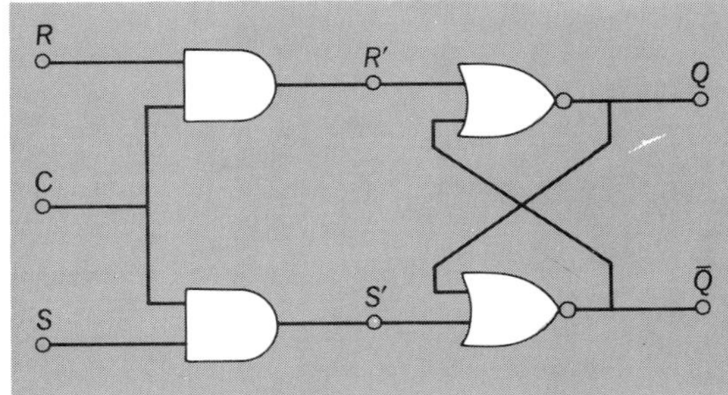


**Fig. 12. Clocked R-S flip-flop.**

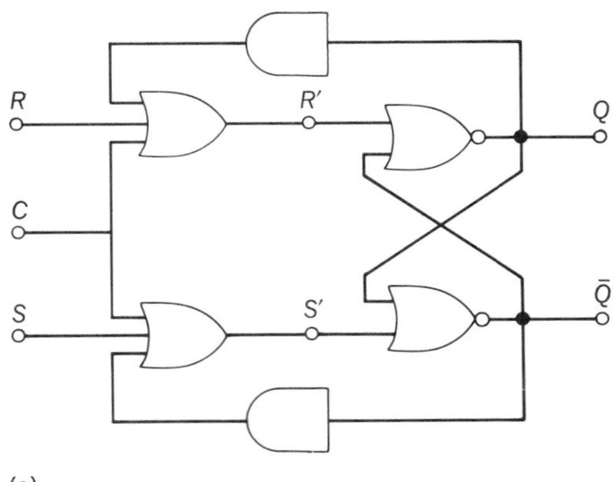


(a)

| R | S | $Q_{n+1}$ | $\bar{Q}_{n+1}$ |
|---|---|---|---|
| 0 | 0 | $Q_n$ | $\bar{Q}_n$ |
| 1 | 0 | 0 | 1 |
| 0 | 1 | 1 | 0 |
| 1 | 1 | $\bar{Q}_n$ | $Q_n$ |

(b)

**Fig. 13. Pulse-triggered R-S flip-flop. (*a*) Circuit. (*b*) Truth table.**

J C K J–K Q Q̄

(a)

| J | K | $Q_{n+1}$ | $\bar{Q}_{n+1}$ |
|---|---|---|---|
| 0 | 0 | $Q_n$ | $\bar{Q}_n$ |
| 0 | 1 | 0 | 1 |
| 1 | 0 | 1 | 0 |
| 1 | 1 | $\bar{Q}_n$ | $Q_n$ |

(b)

**Fig. 14. J-K flip-flop. (*a*) Symbolic representation. (*b*) Truth table with standard output designation.**

upon the input gate combinations. This is illustrated by the accompanying truth table, where $Q_n$ and $\overline{Q}_n$ are the output states before the input gate signals are applied, and $Q_{n+1}$ and $\overline{Q}_{n+1}$ are the outputs after signals at $R$ and $S$ are removed. The outputs are independent of the prior states unless $R$ and $S$ are both zero, in which case they remain unchanged. Also if both inputs are logic (1) the output is indeterminate, since if they both go to (0) at the same time the outputs may return to either bistable condition. This combination is generally indicated as ''not used.'' The RTL flip-flop is representative of two cross-coupled NOR gates shown symbolically in **Fig. 11** with an abridged truth table leaving out the unnecessary initial state columns. The circuit function illustrated by these two circuits is generally referred to as an *R-S* flip-flop. Such flip-flops identified by the same truth table can be constructed by using cross-coupled NAND gates with inverting stages added at the inputs.

If the *R-S* flip-flop inputs are preceded by AND gates [**Fig. 12**, where $R'$ or $S'$ can be (1) only if both inputs to the AND gate are (1)] with a precisely timed ''clock'' pulse applied during the existence of the $R$ and $S$ functions, the output state of the flip-flop is set at the time that the clock pulse is applied. This is called a clocked *R-S* flip-flop and has the same truth table as the unclocked version.

If a clocked *R-S* flip-flop uses a three-input NAND gate at the inputs with a feedback path consisting of a single-gate noninverting delay (**Fig. 13**), the inputs are ''steered'' in such a way that the not-used state is removed as indicated by the accompanying truth table. This works only if the clock pulse is very narrow so that it is removed before the feedback action is completed. Such as circuit is often referred to as a pulse-triggered *R-S* flip-flop.

Additional circuits which make the operation of the flip-flop independent of pulse width result in a circuit known as a *J-K* flip-flop, shown symbolically in **Fig. 14** with a truth table which identifies $J$ and $K$ inputs in a standard manner.

Sometimes problems exist with *J-K* flips-flops for slow rising pulses at inputs $J$ and $K$. Additional circuits are sometimes used whereby one flip-flop called a master drives another flip-flop called a slave with feedback connections such that relative independence of clock pulse width or rise and fall times is achieved. Such a circuit is called a master-slave *J-K* flip-flop. The truth table is that of the ordinary *J-K* flip-flop. *SEE LOGIC CIRCUITS; TRANSISTOR.*

*Glenn M. Glasford*

***Bibliography.*** J. J. Brophy, *Basic Electronics for Scientists*, 4th ed., 1983; J. Millman, *Microelectronics*, 1979; H. Taub and D. Schilling, *Digital Integrated Electronics*, 1977.

## Natural language processing

Computer analysis and generation of natural language text. The goal is to enable natural languages, such as English, French, or Japanese, to serve either as the medium through which users interact with computer systems such as data-base management systems and expert systems (natural language interaction), or as the object that a system processes into some more useful form such as in automatic text translation or text summarization (natural language text processing). *SEE DATA-BASE MANAGEMENT SYSTEMS.*

In the computer analysis of natural language, the initial task is to translate from a natural language utterance, usually in context, into a formal specification that the system can process further. Further processing depends on the particular application. In natural language interaction, it may involve reasoning, factual data retrieval, and generation of an appropriate tabular, graphic, or natural language response. In text processing, analysis may be followed by generation of an appropriate translation or a summary of the original text, or the formal specification may be stored as the basis for more accurate document retrieval later. Given its wide scope, natural language processing requires techniques for dealing with many aspects of language, in particular, syntax, semantics, discourse contest, and pragmatics. (Analysis and generation of spoken natural language, not discussed in this article, also involve techniques for dealing with acoustic phonetics, phonology, stress, and intonation.) *SEE SPEECH RECOGNITION; VOICE RESPONSE.*

**Parsing.** The aspect of natural language processing that has perhaps received the most attention is syntactic processing, or parsing. Most current techniques for parsing an input string of words involve (1) a description of the allowable sentences of the language (the grammar); (2) an inventory of the words of the language with their inflectional, syntactic, and possibly semantic properties (the lexicon); and (3) a processor which operates on the grammar, the lexicon, and the input string (the parser). This processor (1) simply accepts the input string, if grammatically well formed, or rejects it (a recognizer); (2) associates the string, if well formed, with its structure (or structures, if ambiguous) according to the grammar (an analyzer); or (3) associates the string with some other representation, for example, a semantic characterization (a transducer). Syntactic processing is important because certain aspects of meaning can be determined only from the underlying structure and not simply from the linear string of words.

One of the oldest parsing techniques, called augmented transition networks (ATNs), grew out of a system for parsing context-free (CF) languages, called recursive transition networks (RTNs). A recursive transition network parser consists of a set of named graphs or networks, each consisting of a set of nodes or states connected by a possibly ordered set of directed labeled arcs. The labels correspond to (1) words or classes of words that can be recognized or ''consumed'' on the arc; (2) the empty symbol, indicating an arc that can be taken without consuming any input; or (3) the name of a network, which indicates that the next segment of the input string must be recognizable by that network. Each network has a start state and one or more end states. If the parser can move through a network from start to end by consuming a segment of the input string, that segment is said to be recognizable by that network. *SEE GRAPH THEORY.*

An augmented transition network adds to the basic recursive transition network framework the ability to set and test variables or registers, thereby giving it the power to recognize a wider class of languages than a recursive transition network. An augmented transition network is appearing because its grammar is relatively easy to specify. Its weaknesses lie in the simple, uniform control structure provided by the basic augmented transition network (that is, unguided backtracking) and in its power, felt to be more than is needed for recognizing a natural language.

Current trends are to construct parsers and grammars which appear to follow more closely human parsing strategies and which have less power. In particular, researchers have begun to give almost context-free descriptions of natural languages, thereby allowing them to use slightly extended versions of efficient context-free parsing techniques. Such descriptions include generalized phrase structure grammar (GPSG), immediate dominance/linear precedence (ID/LP) grammar, and tree adjoining grammar (TAG).

**Semantic analysis.** A second phase of natural language processing, semantic analysis, involves extracting context-independent aspects of a sentence's meaning. These include the semantic roles played by the various entities mentioned in the sentence. For example, in the sentence ''John unlocked the toolbox,'' ''John'' serves as the agent of the unlocking and ''the toolbox,'' serves as the object; in ''This key will unlock the toolbox,'' ''this key'' serves as the instrument. Context-independent aspects of sentence meaning also include quantificational information such as cardinality, iteration, and dependency. For example, in the sentence ''In every car, the mechanic checked to see that the engine was working,'' the checking is iterated over each car; the identity of the engine depends on the identity of the car, while that of the mechanic does not; and the cardinality of engines per car is one. Thus there are as many engines as cars, but possibly only one mechanic. The representational formalism used by the system for semantic analysis (for example, first-order predicate calculus, case grammar, conceptual frames, procedures, and so forth) is usually chosen for its ability to convey those aspects of semantics that the system requires for later processing. For example, if temporal position (past/present/future) is not significant, it will not be captured in the formalism.

Most semantic analysis is done by applying pattern-action rules either during parsing or afterward. The pattern part of a rule consists of clauses, each of which specifies the presence of a particular lexical item, usually the head of some syntactic substructure (for example, the main verb of a clause or sentence or the head noun of a noun phrase); or a particular syntactic substructure (for example, a relative clause, to be interpreted as a restriction on the class described by the rest of the noun phrase). A pattern clause may also specify a test on another part of the current substructure. The action part of a rule usually calls for building a piece of semantic representation, often requiring the semantic analysis of some other part of the syntactic substructure. For example, there may be a pattern-action rule associated with ''unlock'' as the main verb of a clause. A test in the pattern may require that the subject of the clause be interpretable as an animate agent. The rule's action may call for the inclusion of a conceptual frame for the concept ''unlock'' as part of the semantic representation of the sentence. The rule's action may further specify that the agent role of the frame be filled by the semantic interpretation of the subject of the clause, and that the object role be filled by the semantic interpretation of the direct object. In some systems, a rule can have optional pattern clauses and actions: thus, the rule pattern for ''unlock'' might optionally specify a ''with'' prepositional phrase whose noun phrase object can be interpreted as a tool. If so, the rule action might additionally call for instantiating the instrument role in the frame with the semantic interpretation of the prepositional phrase object.

**Contextual analysis.** Given that most natural languages allow people to take advantage of discourse context, their mutual beliefs about the world, and their shared spatio-temporal context to leave things unsaid or say them with minimal effort, the purpose of a third phase of natural language processing, contextual analysis, is to elaborate the semantic representation of what has been made explicit in the utterance with what is implicit from context. Two major linguistic devices that contextual analysis must deal with are ellipsis and anaphora.

***Ellipsis.*** Ellipsis involves leaving something unsaid. To handle ellipses computationally, techniques are required for recognizing that something is indeed missing and for recovering the ellipsed material. When the utterance is a sentence fragment and not a complete sentence, it is fairly easy to recognize that something is missing. An example appears in the following sequence:

User: What is the length of the JFK?
System: ⟨some number of feet⟩
User: The draft?

On the other hand, since parsers are usually designed for well-formed input, either the system's grammar must be revised to accept sentence fragments or a special error-recovery routine must take over after the parser fails. When an utterance is syntactically well formed, it may still be elliptic in that some needed conceptual material is missing, as in the following example:

User: What maintenances were performed on plane 3 in May 1971?
System: ⟨list of maintenances⟩
User: What maintenances were performed on plane 48?

In the user's second question, the time period of interest is missing, and the question should not be answered until it is recovered. (It is clearly May 1971.)

The primary technique for recovering ellipsed material is a simple one, based on semantic features. For sentence fragment ellipses, the previous discourse is searched for the most recent utterance containing a constitutent with the same features as the fragment. The utterance minus that constituent is taken as the ellipsed material. For conceptual ellipses in a syntactically well-formed sentence, the previous discourse is searched for the most recent utterance with a constituent having the required semantic features. That constituent is taken to be the ellipsed material. In each case, a new well-formed sentence is then constructed and processed as if the ellipsis had never occurred. For instance, in the first example, both "length" and "draft" are properties of ships. Thus, given the fragmentary utterance "The draft?," What is ___ of the JFK?" is found as the ellipsed material. The question "What is the draft of the JFK?" is then interpreted and answered normally. This technique works often, but does not constitute a general solution. A more powerful solution has been developed based on recognizing a user's goals in producing an utterance, but has been found conputationally efficient only in very narrow task-oriented domains. This will be discussed below.

***Anaphora.*** Anaphoric expressions are very simple words or phrases which cospecify something previously evoked by the discourse or are strongly associated with something so evoked. Instances of anaphora include definite pronouns such as "he," "she," "it," "they," and definite noun phrases such as "the mechanic" and "the cars." The problem is that anaphora can be interpreted only in context, and the semantic interpretation of a sentence is not complete until all anaphoric expressions are resolved and the cospecified entities identified.

Early computational approaches to anaphora resembled those for dealing with ellipses: entities described in previous sentences were searched for the most recently mentioned one with appropriate semantic features. Now recency has been replaced by the notion of focus as a basis for anaphora resolution. Immediate focus reflects the particular thing the speaker is talking about; global focus involves things associated with it or in which it participates, and gives a sense of what may be talked about next. Techniques have been developed for tracking immediate focus, projecting ahead from the current utterance what may be focused on in the next one. This is useful for resolving anaphora, in that it predicts what entities are likely to be respecified anaphorically.

***Pragmatics.*** A fourth phase of natural language processing, pragmatics, takes into account the speaker's goal in uttering a particular thought in a particular way—what the utterance is being used to do. In an interaction, this will influence what constitutes an appropriate response. For example, an utterance which has the form of a yes/no question or an assertion may have the goal of eliciting information (for example: "Do you know how to delete a control-Z?," "I can't get the set file protection command to work."). Because it is inappropriate (and possibly at times dangerous) to take a user's utterances literally or to assume that the user will take those of the system literally, computational techniques must be devised for relating the syntactic shape and semantic content of an utterance to its pragmatic function.

***Plan recognition.*** One important approach to this problem has been to view language understanding as plan recognition. The actions (either communicative or physical) that constitute the plan may be motivated in one of two ways: goals in the world that the person wants to accomplish, for which he or she needs to elicit or offer aid or information; or aspects of an already ongoing interaction that need attention—for example, confusion over the speaker's foregoing utterance may lead the listener to seek clarification.

A user seeking particular information from the system illustrates clearly a plan-recognition approach to language understanding. The user's utterance—a well-formed sentence or an ellipsed fragment—is taken as a request for information that the user believes he or she needs in order to accomplish some goal, a goal which is not as yet presumed to be known to the system. Just as a medical diagnosis system uses rules which link findings back to those diseases which commonly manifest them, the plan-recognition system uses rules which link utterances back to those domain goals which need the intended information in order to be achieved. For example, consider the utterance "The train to Windsor?" made to a system serving as train information clerk. The system interprets this as a request: the user wants to know some property of that train in order to fulfill his or her goal. The system then tries to figure out what that goal is, in order to figure out what information the user might be requesting. There are only two possible goals considered: meeting a train and boarding one. The description "train to X" does not match that of incoming train, so the user's goal is taken to be boarding the Windsor train. To board a train, one needs to know its departure time and track. Since the system does not have evidence of the user's knowing either of these properties, it responds with both: "It leaves at 3:15, from track 7." Currently, it is only by limiting the domain, and hence the range of possible goals the system needs to consider, that such a plan-based approach to pragmatics and natural language processing becomes feasible.

***Cooperative principle.*** Because pragmatics acknowledges language use, it also acknowledges expectations that speakers and listeners have about the form and content of utterances, based on normal conventions of use. This has been well described by the philosopher Paul Grice, who noted that speakers acknowledge a "cooperative principle" of conversation (by either upholding it or purposely flouting it), which he further specified in terms of conversational maxims of quantity, quality, manner, and relation. For example, the quantity maxim states: "Make your contribution as informative as is required (for the current purposes of the exchange). Do not make it more informative than is required."

The cooperative principle and its maxims are important to natural language processing because, if a system does not behave in accord with normal conventions of use, the user is likely to be confused or misled by the system's behavior. Conversely, if the system does not interpret the user's behavior in terms of normal conventions of use, the system is unlikely to understand the user correctly, if at all. In particular, the cooperative principle and its maxims reveal a method of implicit communication which Grice termed implicature. An implicature is basically an aspect of an utterance's interpretation which makes no contribution to its truth value (that is, semantics) but constrains its appropriateness in discourse. For example, consider the following discourse:

Q: Is there a gas station on the next block?
R: Yes.

The simple "yes" answer implicates to Q that, as far as R knows, the gas station is able to provide its normal services and hence fulfill Q's probable goal. Q reasons that if R knew that the gas station was closed and hence could not fill Q's needs, R would have said so: that is, R would have said "Yes, but it's closed." Thus a system must be as aware of implicatures (both the user's and its own) as it is aware of what is communicated explicitly.

**Overall organization.** As for fitting the pieces together, there is no single way that natural language analysis is done. Some systems have a single processor for syntactic, semantic, contextual, and pragmatic analysis, with no distinction made as to the source of that knowledge. Some systems keep the knowledge sources separate but apply them simultaneously, extracting whatever can be derived at the moment and using whatever information is available. Other systems are very modular, separating the knowledge sources and specifying when they should be applied. Efficiency, extensibility, and transportability are some of the important issues to be considered when evaluating a system for natural language analysis.

**Natural language generation.** The bulk of early research in natural language processing was formerly directed at natural language analysis. Now researchers have taken up seriously the task of natural language generation. Generation is not just the reverse of analysis because the status of user and system are fundamentally different. Systems can be developed which tolerate users' mechanical errors (for example, spelling, typing, and grammatical mistakes), treating them as insignificant variations. Users, on the other hand, may not be able to figure out which aspects of the system's natural language behavior reflect simple nonfluencies (for example, those due to limited lexical or grammatical options) and which embody significant aspects of communication. Moreover, the system's sense of language must be more highly developed for generation, lest it confuse or mislead the user by what it communicates or how. Work on explanation is also a significant aspect of natural language generation. *See* ARTIFICIAL INTELLIGENCE.

Bonnie Webber

***Bibliography.*** *Proceedings of the Association for Computational Linguistics*; *Proceedings of the International Conference on Computational Linguistics*; H. Tennant, *Natural Language Processing*, 1981; T. Winograd, *Language as a Cognitive Process*, 1982.

## Negative-resistance circuits

Circuits or devices whose static (direct-current) current-voltage characteristic at one or more ports has a range in which the slope is negative. **Figure 1** shows two typical negative-resistance characteristics in which a positive increment of voltage is accompanied by a negative increment of current. Strictly, the term also includes circuits whose static current-voltage characteristics do not have negative-slope ranges, but in which the input impedance or admittance at one or more ports has a negative real component. The negative resistance may arise from inherent properties of a device or from the proper choice of electrical circuit configuration and operating conditions. Only circuits having static characteristics of the general form of Fig. 1 are treated in this article. Negative-resistance circuits and the circuits based upon them find many applications in counting or information storage, in the generation of pulses or alternating voltages, in instrumentation, in the control of current and power, and in physical realization of idealized (lossless) or hypothetical circuits.

**Basic circuits.** A port having a characteristic of the form of Fig. 1*a* is said to be voltage-stable (voltage-controllable) because at any value of voltage there is only one value of current, but over a range of current

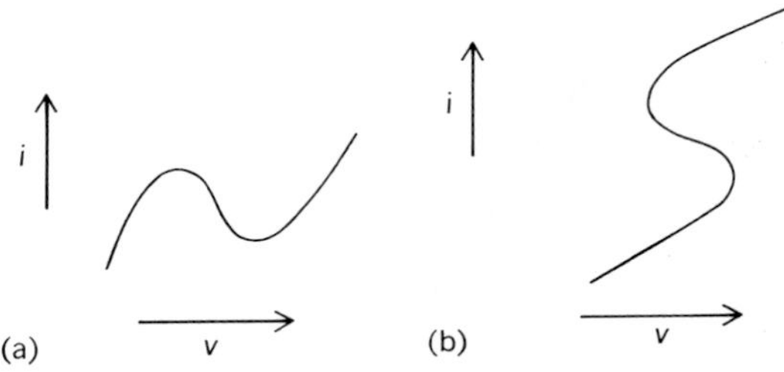


**Fig. 1. Examples of (*a*) voltage-stable and (*b*) current-stable current-voltage characteristic curves.**

there are three values of voltage, between which transition may take place spontaneously or under excitation. Similarly, a port having a characteristic of the form of Fig. 1*b* is said to be current-stable (current-controllable) because for each value of current there is only one value of voltage, but over a range of voltage there are three values of current, between which transition may take place. In general, negative-resistance circuits may have both voltage-stable and current-stable ports. Because the negative-slope portion of the current-voltage characteristic, or the entire characteristic, may be located anywhere with respect to the origin of coordinates, the origin is not shown in Fig. 1.

**Figure 2** shows one type of negative-resistance circuit. The indicated direction of input current $\Delta i$ resulting from a positive increment of input voltage $\Delta v$ is that which would obtain if the input resistance of the port were positive (dissipative). If the voltage amplification $A$ of the amplifier is positive and greater than unity, the output voltage $A\Delta V$ is of the same sign as the input voltage and greater in magnitude. The current $\Delta i_r$ through the resistance $R$ is then in the direction shown. If this current exceeds the current $\Delta i_i$ into the amplifier input, $\Delta i$ must be opposite in direction to that shown. In other words, the positive increment of impressed voltage produces a negative increment of current, and the slope of the characteristic relating current $i$ with voltage $v$ is negative. Because the range of input voltage over which the amplifier has an amplification greater than unity is limited, the negative-slope portion of the characteristic is also limited with respect to voltage, and the characteristic is the voltage-stable form shown in Fig. 1*a*. A similar analysis shows that a voltage-stable port can be formed across the output terminals of the amplifier and that current-stable ports can be formed in place of resistor $R$ or by opening the connection between the lower input and output terminals. Voltage-stable and current-stable ports can in general also be formed within the amplifier itself. *SEE AMPLIFIER*.

A more general form of the circuit of Fig. 2 is shown in **Fig. 3*a***. As in the circuit of Fig. 2, feedback must be positive (regenerative), and the open-loop amplification of the circuit must be positive and greater than unity. *SEE FEEDBACK CIRCUIT*.

Another generalized form of negative-resistance circuit is shown in Fig. 3*b*, in which positive feedback from output to input of the amplifier is produced by the coupling resistance $R_{12}$. In this circuit, voltage-stable ports can be formed in place of $R_{12}$ or across the input or output terminals of the amplifer, and current-stable ports can be formed in place of $R_1$ or $R_2$

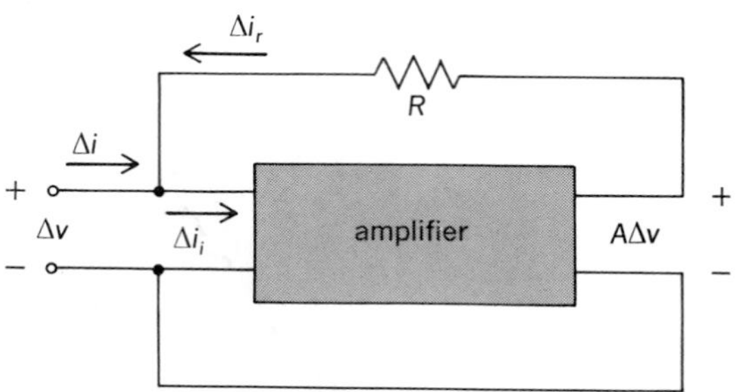


Fig. 2. Example of a circuit that has a voltage-stable current-voltage characteristic.

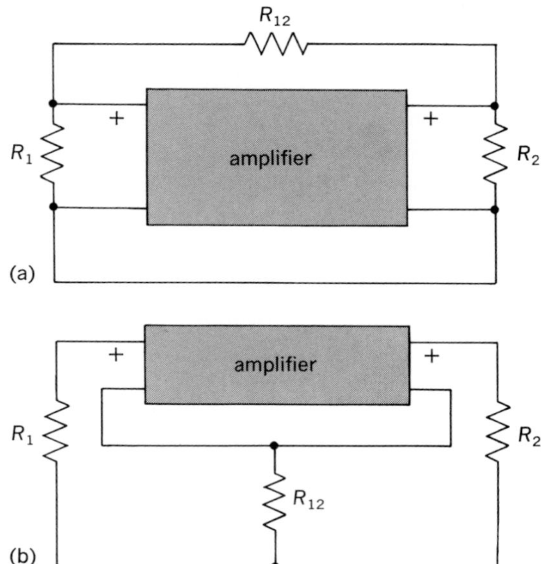


Fig. 3. Generalized negative-resistance circuits. (*a*) Generalization of circuit in Fig. 2. (*b*) Circuit in which positive feedback is produced by the coupling resistance $R_{12}$.

or in series with the lower input or output terminal of the amplifier.

The two essentials of a negative-resistance circuit are amplification and positive feedback; any circuit modification that tends to increase the open-loop amplification of the amplifier and feedback network is favorable to the production of negative resistance. In order that negative resistance can be obtained under static conditions, it is necessary that the amplifier be capable of amplifying increments of direct voltage.

**Typical circuits.** All negative-resistance circuits are of the general form of Fig. 3*a* or *b* or variants thereof. They differ with respect to details of the amplifier. Although only transistor circuits are discussed in the remainder of this article, any type of dc amplifier may be used. In the most commonly used circuit, the Eccles-Jordan circuit, the amplifier consists of two resistance-coupled common-emitter stages. The amplifier is used in the circuit of Fig. 3*a*, as shown in **Fig. 4*a***. The complete circuit is usually drawn in the symmetrical form of Fig. 4*b*. Because of the symmetry, ports formed across or in place of $R_1'$, $R_{12}'$, and $R_2'$ have the same forms of current-voltage characteristics as those formed across or in place of $R_1'$, $R_{12}'$, and $R_2$, respectively. This fact justifies for this circuit the statement that negative-resistance ports can in general be formed within the amplifiers of Fig. 3.

Typical current-voltage characteristics measured in the circuit of Fig. 4 are shown in **Fig. 5**. Characteristic *a* is that of a port formed in place of $R_2$ or $R_2'$. Characteristic *b* is obtained between the two collectors, and the current-stable characteristic *c* is observed at a port formed in place of either $R_{12}$ or $R_{12}'$. Symmetrical current-stable characteristic *d* is obtained between the two emitters when additional equal resistances are inserted between each emitter and the voltage supply.

**Figure 6** shows a form of the circuit of Fig. 3*a* in which the amplifier consists of a common-base stage directly coupled to a common-collector stage. Voltage-stable characteristic *b* is observed at a port

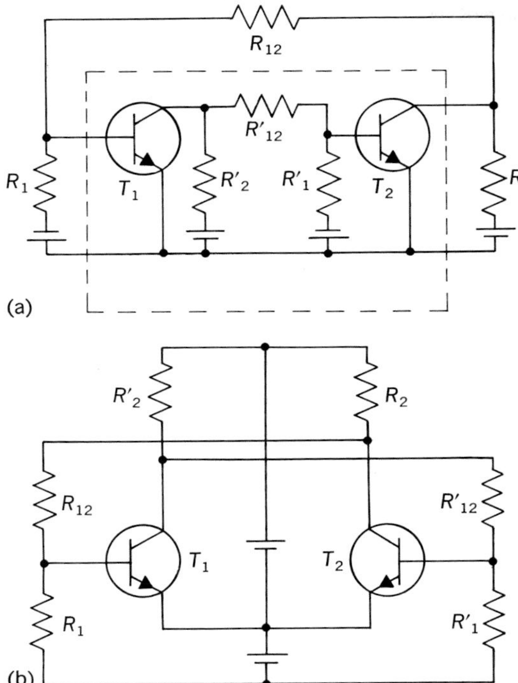


**Fig. 4. Eccles-Jordan negative-resistance circuit (*a*) drawn to show amplifier in Fig. 3*a*, and (*b*) drawn in symmetrical form.**

formed in place of $R_{12}$; current-stable characteristic *c* is observed at a port formed in place of $R_1$. A current-stable characteristic is also observed between the two emitters.

**Bistable circuits.** Any negative-resistance circuit or device can be converted into a bistable circuit simply by connecting a resistance $R$ of proper magnitude in series with a properly chosen voltage $V_s$ across any port, as in **Fig. 7***a*. That such a circuit can be multistable is shown by the diagrams of Fig. 7. In these diagrams the straight line of slope $-1/R$ is the locus of all corresponding values of current through resistance $R$ and of resulting voltage $v$ across the port, determined by the relation $v = V_s - iR$. In Fig. 7*b* the negative-resistance characteristic is that of a voltage-stable port of the internal negative-resistance circuit. It is the locus of all possible combinations of voltage across the port and current into the port. In the complete circuit, because the current through the resistance is also the current into the port, intersections of the resistance line with the negative-resistance characteristic give possible equilibrium values of current and voltage across the port.

If the slope of the resistance line in Fig. 7*b* is less than the maximum slope of the negative-slope portion of the characteristic, as it will be if resistance $R$ exceeds the magnitude of the negative resistance, there are three intersections. Analysis of the circuit with inherent capacitances taken into consideration shows that point 3 is always unstable. If the current $i$ and the voltage $v$ initially have values corresponding to point 3, any small circuit disturbance causes the voltage to decrease or increase until it reaches the value at point 1 or that at point 2, both of which correspond to stable conditions of equilibrium. Similarly, three intersections may be obtained with a current-stable characteristic if the resistance $R$ is less than the magnitude of the negative resistance, as in Fig. 7*c*. Transition from one stable state to the other can be initiated by changing (1) the magnitude of $R$ and therefore the slope of the resistance line, (2) the value of $V_s$ and thus the voltage intercept of the resistance line, or (3) one or more biasing voltages in the amplifier and hence the position or shape of the current-voltage characteristic. It follows that the basic negative-resistance circuits of Fig. 3 are in themselves bistable circuits if resistances and supply voltages are properly chosen. Reference to Fig. 5, or to similar characteristic curves for other two-transistor negative-resis-

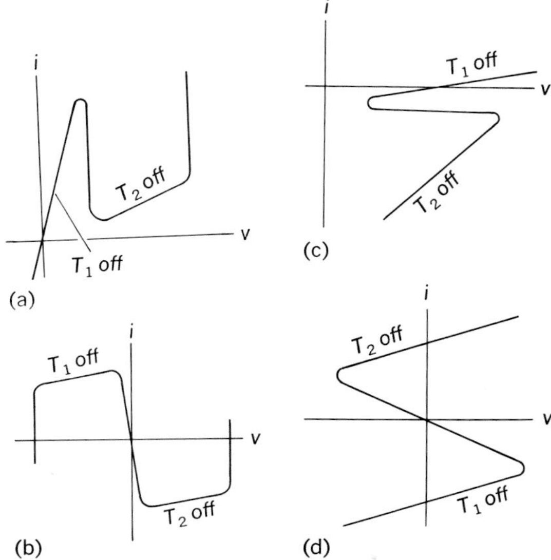


**Fig. 5. Current-voltage characteristics at various ports of the circuit of Fig. 4: (*a*) at port formed in place of $R_2$ or $R'_2$; (*b*) between the two collectors; (*c*) at port formed in place of either $R_{12}$ or $R'_{12}$; (*d*) between the two emitters when additional equal resistances are inserted between each emitter and the voltage supply.**

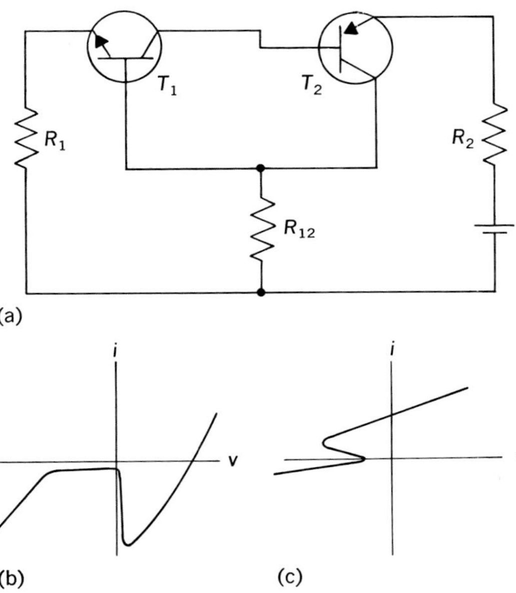


**Fig. 6. Negative-resistance circuit based on circuit of Fig. 3*b*. (*a*) Circuit diagram. (*b*) Characteristic at port formed in place of $R_{12}$. (*c*) Characteristic at port formed in place of $R_1$.**

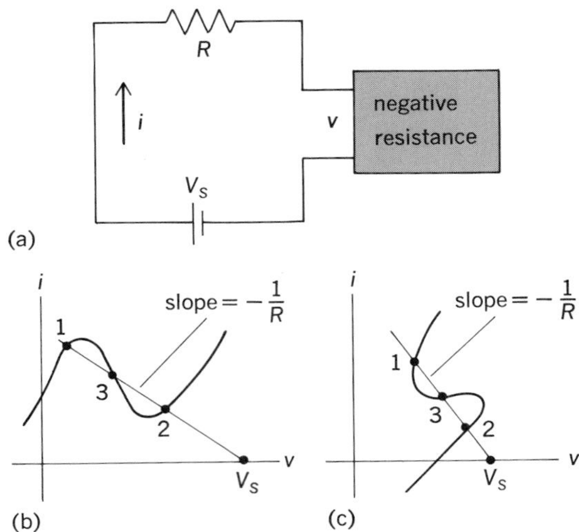


**Fig. 7. Bistable circuit. (*a*) Circuit diagram. (*b, c*) Current-voltage characteristics.**

tance circuits, shows that one transistor is off and the other conducts in each stable state.

The usual means of initiating transition from one stable state to the other in bistable circuits is the application of short triggering pulses of voltage to one or more electrodes of the amplifier transistors. The fact that a change from one stable state to the other is an indication that a triggering pulse has occurred makes possible the use of bistable circuits in pulse counting and in the storage of information in digital computers. Bistable circuits have also found numerous applications in electronic instrumentation.

**Astable circuits.** An astable circuit (relaxation oscillator for the generation of nonsinusoidal voltages and currents) can be formed by shunting any voltage-stable port of a negative-resistance circuit by inductance in series with resistance, provided that this resistance is smaller than the magnitude of the negative resistance. In general, such a circuit oscillates over a wide range of inductance and with values of resistance ranging from zero to thousands of ohms. In a similar manner an astable circuit can be formed by shunting any current-stable port by capacitance in parallel with resistance, provided that this resistance is larger than the negative resistance. Relaxation oscillation occurs over wide ranges of capacitance and resistance. The frequency of oscillation of these oscillators is varied by changing the time constant $L/R$ or $RC$, or one or more operating voltages. The output waveform in general consists of two or more exponential sections or of exponential and sinusoidal sections. A simple oscillator of this type is formed by shunting $R_1$ or $R_2$ in the circuit of Fig. 6*a* by a capacitor, or inserting an inductor in series with, or in place of, $R_{12}$.

Astable circuits may be looked upon as modifications of bistable circuits. Addition of one or more capacitors or inductors to a bistable circuit converts the two stable states of equilibrium into two quasi-stable states, in each of which the circuit remains for periods determined by the time constants. Transition from one state to the other is followed by charging or discharging of the capacitors or inductors, and thus by gradual changes of electrode voltages. When the voltage of a control electrode reaches a critical value, transition to the previous state of equilibrium occurs. This transition is again followed by discharging or charging of the capacitors or inductors until transition occurs once more, and the cycle repeats.

One of the most useful relaxation oscillators is the multivibrator, which is formed from the Eccles-Jordan circuit of Fig. 4 by replacing the resistors $R_{12}$ and $R_{12}'$ by capacitors. Thus capacitors shunt the current-stable ports between the collector of each transistor and the base of the other. If the circuit is made symmetrical with respect to resistances, capacitances, and voltages, symmetrical voltage waves are produced between the collectors and between the bases. The frequency of oscillation is adjusted by means of the resistors or capacitors or by means of the base supply voltage.

**Monostable circuits.** The operating voltages of the transistors of an astable circuit can be adjusted so that only one state of equilibrium is quasistable while the other is stable. Under standby conditions the circuit remains in the stable state. Application of a triggering pulse to the circuit causes transition to the quasi-stable state, followed by charging or discharging of one or more capacitors or inductors, and thus by a gradual change of electrode voltages. At a critical value of an electrode voltage the circuit rapidly returns to the stable state. The output of such a circuit is a pulse of length determined by the $RC$ or $L/R$ time constants and by one or more supply voltages. The output voltage can be made to approximate a rectangular pulse by proper choice of circuit resistances, capacitances, and supply voltages.

**Sine-wave oscillators.** A sine-wave oscillator can be formed from a negative-resistance circuit or device by shunting any voltage-stable port by a resonator consisting of inductance and capacitance in parallel, or any current-stable port by a resonator consisting on inductance and capacitance in series. Circuit parameters and voltages must be such that the resistance line corresponding to the dc resistance between the terminals of the resonator intersects the current-voltage characteristic only in the negative-resistance range. A particularly useful oscillator of this type is formed by connecting a parallel resonator between the collectors of the Eccles-Jordan negative-resistance circuit of Fig. 4, as shown in **Fig. 8**. SEE OSCILLATOR.

Advantages of negative-resistance sine-wave oscil-

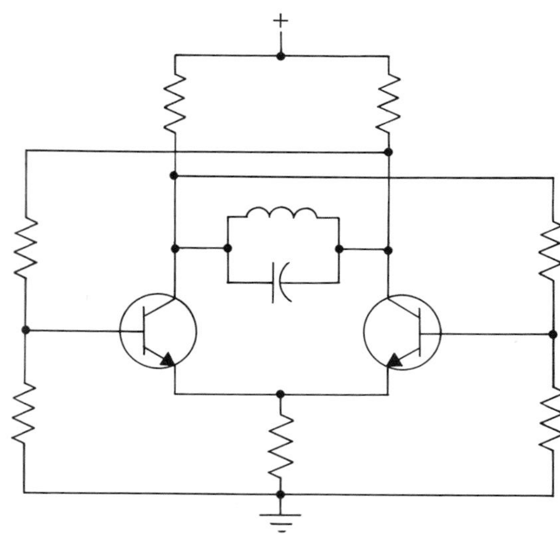


**Fig. 8. Sine-wave oscillator based on circuit of Fig. 4.**

lators include relatively small dependence of oscillation frequency upon supply voltages, and the simplicity of the circuits in comparison with feedback oscillators. The symmetry of the current-voltage characteristic used in the oscillator of Fig. 8 and the monotonically decreasing slope of the characteristic with increase of voltage magnitude (Fig. 5*b*) make possible low amplitude of oscillation and associated low harmonic content of the voltage across the resonator.

Improved amplitude limitation and stabilization can be achieved by any of a number of circuit modifications. One means of limiting the amplitude of oscillation is by rectifying the resonator voltage and using the rectified voltage to reduce the forward bias of the transistor bases, and hence the amplification of the transistors. This in turn reduces the slope of the negative-resistance portion of the current-voltage characteristic as the amplitude of oscillation increases.

Another method of amplitude limitation is using in series with the inductor a resistor that has a positive temperature coefficient of resistance, or in parallel with the resonator a resistor that has a negative temperature coefficient of resistance. Amplitude limitation occurs because heating of the resistor by the current through it causes the resonator losses to increase with amplitude of oscillation. A third method of amplitude limitation is the use of two oppositely connected diodes in parallel with the resonator. Decrease of the effective resistance of the diodes with increase of voltage across them causes the circuit losses to increase rapidly with increase of amplitude.

Simultaneous oscillation at two or more frequencies can be produced by a modification of the circuit of Fig. 8 in which parallel resonators of different frequencies are connected in series between the collectors. Each resonator must incorporate its own temperature-sensitive resistor or pair of diodes. SEE CIRCUIT (ELECTRONICS); NETWORK THEORY.

**Negative-resistance devices.** Two examples of current-stable negative-resistance devices are the *pnpn* transistor and the unijunction transistor; two examples of voltage-stable devices are the tunnel (Esaki) diode and the Gunn diode. An advantage of negative-resistance devices over circuits that incorporate two transistors to achieve negative resistance is the simplicity of bistable, monostable, and oscillator circuits in which they are used. Tunnel and Gunn diodes have the additional very important advantage that their rapid response makes them ideal for use in amplification and power generation at very high microwave frequencies (as high as 100 GHz) and in high-speed switching circuits.

The *pnpn* transistor, which consists of four alternate layers of *p*-type and *n*-type semiconductor, is equivalent to the two directly coupled transistors of Fig. 6*a*, the inner *n*-type layer serving both as the collector of $T_1$ and the base of $T_2$, and the inner *p*-type layer as the collector of $T_2$ and the base of $T_1$. As the *pnpn* transistor is usually used, $R_1$ is zero. The supply voltage $V_s$ and the load resistance $R_2$ are then directly between the two outer elements (layers), which correspond to the two emitters in the circuit of Fig. 6*a*. Typical current-voltage characteristics observed between these elements at two values of current $i_G$ into one of the inner elements, called the gate, are shown in **Fig. 9**, together with the resistance line corresponding to the load resistance $R_2$ and supply voltage $v_s$. Transition from a very low value of current at point 1 to a high value at point 2 can be initiated by a change of gate current from $i_{G1}$ to $i_{G2}$. Because the voltage across the device is small in the high-current state, this device affords an efficient means of controlling the current of motors and lights. Another important application is in the conversion from alternating to direct current (rectification) and from direct current to alternating current (inversion). Units designed for the control or rectification of large currents are called (silicon) controlled rectifiers. SEE CONTROLLED RECTIFIER; SEMICONDUCTOR RECTIFIER.

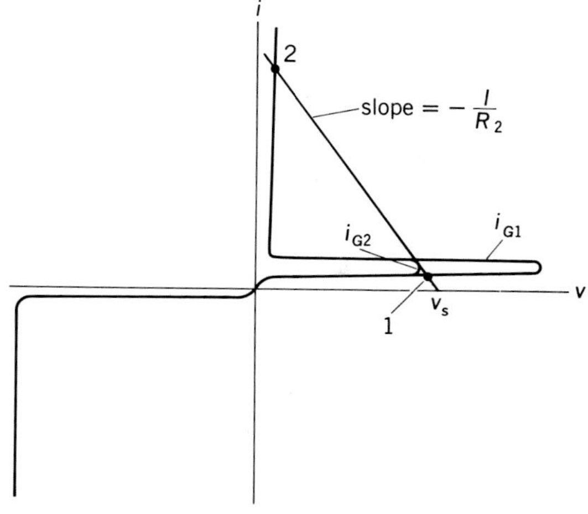


**Fig. 9.** Current-voltage characteristic of *pnpn* transistor at two values of gate current, $i_{G1}$ and $i_{G2}$.

The unijunction transistor owes its negative resistance to increase of conductivity of a semiconductor region as the result of increase in the number of injected minority carriers with increase of current. The negative resistance of the tunnel diode is produced by tunneling of electrons across a junction that has a high potential barrier. Small capacitance and the rapidity with which tunneling takes place account for the excellent high-frequency response of the tunnel diode. In microwave negative-resistance amplifiers, the negative resistance of a diode is used to compensate for the positive resistance of other circuit elements and thus increase the amplification. SEE MICROWAVE SOLID-STATE DEVICES; TRANSISTOR; TUNNEL DIODE.

*Herbert J. Reich*

**Bibliography.** J. J. Brophy, *Basic Electronics for Scientists*, 4th ed., 1982; H. J. Reich, *Functional Circuits and Oscillators*, 1961; H. J. Reich, H. L. Krauss, and J. G. Skalnik, *Theory and Applications of Active Devices*, 1966.

## Neper

A unit of attenuation used in transmission-line theory. On a uniform transmission line having waves traveling in only one direction, the magnitudes of voltage $E$ and of current $I$ decrease with distance $x$ traveled, as given by Eq (1), where $E_0$, $I_0$, and $\alpha$ are constants.

$$\frac{E}{E_0} = \frac{I}{I_0} = \epsilon^{-\alpha x} \tag{1}$$

The attenuation in nepers between the points where $E_0$ and $I_0$ are measured and where $E$ and $I$ are measured is given by Eq. (2), in which ln denotes the

$$\alpha x = \ln \frac{E_0}{E} = \ln \frac{I_0}{I} \tag{2}$$

natural (or napierian) logarithm.

The word neper originated from a misspelling of

the proper name Napier. One neper equals 8.686 dB, the decibel being the practical unit of attenuation. SEE TRANSMISSION LINES.

*Edward W. Kimbark*

## Network theory

The systematizing and generalizing of the relations among the elements of an electrical network. To be precise, certain terms will be defined. SEE ALTERNATING-CURRENT CIRCUIT THEORY.

**Elements.** The elements of a network model are resistance, inductance, and capacitance (the passive elements) and sources of energy (the active elements), which may be either independent sources or controlled, that is, dependent, sources. An independent-voltage source produces voltage between its terminals that is independent of all currents and voltages, although it may be a function of time, as an alternating source would be; an independent-current source carries current that is indpendent of all voltages or currents but may be a function of time. SEE CAPACITANCE; ELECTRICAL RESISTANCE; ELECTROMOTIVE FORCE (EMF); INDUCTANCE.

A number of definitions, together with theorems that relate them, are taken from the mathematical subject of topology, which deals with certain aspects of form. Two or more elements are joined at a node (**Fig. 1**). If three or more elements are connected together at a node, that node is called a junction. (The term major node may be used instead of junction; topological terminology varies among authors.) An element extends from one node to another. A branch of a network extends from one junction to another an may consist of one element or several elements in series. A loop, or circuit, is a single closed path for current. A mesh, or window, is a loop with no interior branch.

Figure 1 shows a network with 13 elements, 12 passive and 1 active. Nodes are indicated by dots; of the 9 nodes, 6 are junctions. There are 10 branches of which 5 come together in a single node or junction at the bottom of the figure.

Equation (1) is an extension of Ohm's law, where

$$V = IZ \qquad (1)$$

$I$ is the current in an element, $Z$ is the impedance of that element, and $V$ is the voltage or potential difference between the nodes that terminate that element; this applies to every passive element of an electrical network. [Equation (1) may be a phasor equation for steady alternating current, in which case impedance is a function of frequency and $V(j\omega) = I(j\omega)Z(j\omega)$, or it may more generally be the transform of the differential equation, $V(s) = I(s)Z(s)$.] The number of elements (active or passive) in a network may be designated $E$. SEE ELECTRICAL IMPEDANCE; OHM'S LAW.

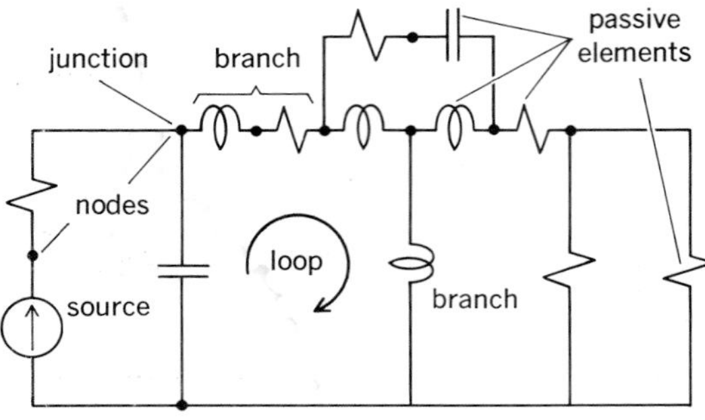


**Fig. 1.** Parts of a network. (After H. H. Skilling, Electrical Engineering Circuits, 2d ed., John Wiley and Sons, 1965)

At every node of an electrical network the sum of currents entering that node is zero. Equation (2) expressed Kirchhoff's current law. An equation of this

$$\Sigma I = 0 \qquad (2)$$

form can be written for each node, but in a fully connected network one of these equations can be derived from the others; hence the number of independent node equations is one less than the number of nodes. The number of independent node equations, called $N$, equals in a fully connected network the number of nodes minus one. SEE KIRCHHOFF'S LAWS OF ELECTRIC CIRCUITS.

Around every loop of an electrical network the sum of the voltages across the elements is zero. Equation (3) expresses Kirchhoff's voltage law. A network

$$\Sigma V = 0 \qquad (3)$$

such as that of Fig. 1 can have many possible loops and hence many equations of this form, but only a limited number are independent. If $L$ is the number of independent loops, topology gives Eq. (4), from

$$E = N + L \qquad (4)$$

which $L$ can be computed, $E$ and $N$ having been counted. Thus in Fig. 1 there are 13 elements and 9 nodes, hence 8 independent nodes, so that there are 13–8 or 5 independent loops; that is, $L = 5$.

If a network is planar (flat) and fully connected, the number of independent loops is equal to the number of meshes, or windows. Figure 1 shows such a network, and the number of meshes is obviously 5, so again $L = 5$.

**Branch equation.** There are $E$ elements in a network. Suppose that all impedances are known. Across each element there is a voltage, and through each element there is a current; hence there are $2E$ voltages and currents to be known. One equation is provided by each element; either the element is a source for which voltage or current is given, or it is an impedance for which there is a relation given by Ohm's law in the form of Eq. (1). Hence there are $E$ equations from the elements. From Eqs. (2) and (3) the nodes and loops provide $N + L = E$. Thus there are $2E$ equations relating voltages and currents.

In an actual solution for current and voltage in a network, it is probably desirable to reduce the number of equations by combining elements that are in series. This can reduce the number of elements to the number of branches and the number of nodes to the number of junctions; the network is then described by $2B$ branch equations.

These branch equations are easy to write but tedious to solve, unless an electronic computer is used. Two modifications have been devised, however, that eliminate a great deal of the labor and reduce the number of equations from $2B$ to either $L$, the number of independent loops, or $N$, the number of independent nodes, as will be described in following paragraphs.

***Linearity.*** Although branch equations can be written for networks of either linear or nonlinear elements, the solution is tremendously more difficult for nonlinear networks. A linear network is one that gives rise to linear systems of equations, which are subject to special methods of solution, and with which the prin-

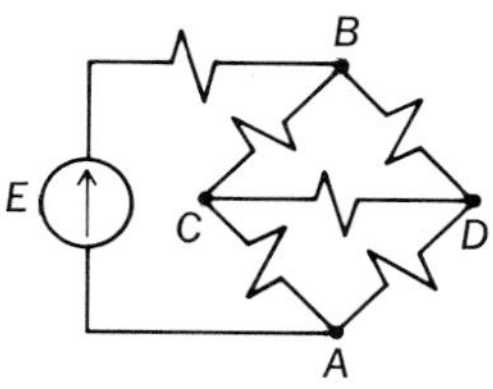


**Fig. 2. Network of six branches. (*After H. H. Skilling, Electrical Engineering Circuits, 2d ed., John Wiley and Sons, 1965*)**

ciple of superposition can be applied, permitting the use of loop or node equations. In a linear system the values of resistance, inductance, and capacitance are constant with respect to voltage and current, and a controlled source produces a voltage or a current that is proportional to another voltage or current. SEE SUPERPOSITION THEOREM (ELECTRIC NETWORKS).

Fortunately, many electrical networks are linear or are nearly enough linear to be so considered, at least in the useful range of operation or in a piece-wise linear fashion. Examples of branch, loop, and node equations are given below for linear systems.

***Examples.*** Using Ohm's law six times, the branch equations for the network of **Fig. 2** are shown in Eqs. (5).

$$\begin{aligned} V_{BC} &= Z_{BC}I_{BC} & V_{CD} &= Z_{CD}I_{CD} \\ V_{BD} &= Z_{BD}I_{BD} & V_{DA} &= Z_{DA}I_{DA} \\ V_{CA} &= Z_{CA}I_{CA} & V_{BA} &= Z_{BA}I_{BA} + E \end{aligned} \tag{5}$$

The source electromotive forces and branch impedances are assumed to be known, and all currents and branch voltages are to be found. There are, then, 6 equations with 12 unknowns, the unknowns being voltage and current of each branch. (Although a source is indicated in only one of these branches, the method can be applied in the same way if there are sources in any or all of the branches.) Clearly, 6 more equations are needed.

The 6 needed equations may be called connection equations, and they are found from Kirchhoff's laws. The current law gives Eqs. (6), called node equations

$$I_{BC} + I_{BD} + I_{BA} = 0 \tag{6a}$$
$$I_{BC} + I_{CD} + I_{CA} = 0 \tag{6b}$$
$$I_{AC} + I_{AD} + I_{AB} = 0 \tag{6c}$$

or junction equations. Equation (6*a*) shows the sum of the currents flowing out of junction *B* to be zero. Equations (6*b*) and 6*c*) make similar statements with regard to junctions *C* and *A*.

Three more equations may be obtained from Kirchhoff's voltage law. The sum of the voltages around loop *BCD* must be zero, Eq. (7*a*); the sum of the

$$V_{BC} + V_{CD} + V_{DB} = 0 \tag{7a}$$
$$V_{CA} + V_{AD} + V_{DC} = 0 \tag{7b}$$
$$V_{AB} + V_{BC} + V_{CA} = 0 \tag{7c}$$

voltages around loop *CAD* must be zero, Eq. (7*b*); and the sum of the voltages around loop *ABC* must be zero, Eq. (7*c*).

There are now 12 equations. Recognizing that $I_{BC} = -I_{CB}$, and so on with other currents and voltages, there are still 12 unknowns, for the 6 connection equations of Eqs. (6) and (7) have added no new unknowns. The 12 equations can be solved simultaneously for the 12 unknowns. The actual solution is not particularly interesting and will not be pursued.

It would seem to be possible to write a fourth junction equation at junction *D*: $I_{BD} + I_{CD} + I_{AD} = 0$. This proposed equation contains no new information, however, for it could have been derived from the other three equations. It results from adding Eqs. (6*a*), (6*b*), and (6*c*) and canceling equal and opposite quantities. Although it is a true equation, it is not an independent equation. The solution for 12 unknowns requires the use of 12 independent equations.

A somewhat similar observation can be made about the independence of loop equations. The three loops for which equations are written are not the only possible ones. For example, there is also loop *ACBD*, but this loop will not give another independent equation, nor will any of the other possible loops.

**Loop equations.** The ingenuity of the loop method lies in the selection of currents to be determined. It is necessary to find only as many different currents as there are independent loops, instead of finding as many different currents as there are branches.

Thus in the network of **Fig. 3** a current which can be called $I_1$ flows around loop 1. (This is the current in the source $E_1$ and in the impedance $Z_a$.) The convention generally adopted is to take the reference direction for all loop currents as clockwise, and this will be taken as the reference direction of $I_1$. The reference direction of the current called $I_2$ that flows around loop 2 is also clockwise. This is the current in the source $E_2$ and in impedance $Z_c$. Loop currents $I_1$ and $I_2$ both flow in $Z_b$. The reference direction of one is downward and that of the other is upward. Thus the total current downward in $Z_b$ is $I_1 - I_2$. When $I_1$ and $I_2$ are known, every current in the network is determined.

The first step in solving for these currents is to write network equations in terms of $I_1$ and $I_2$. Kirchhoff's voltage law is used to write Eq. (8),

$$E_1 - Z_aI_1 - Z_b(I_1 - I_2) = 0 \tag{8}$$

which says that the sum of all voltages about loop 1 is zero. Rearranged, Eq. (8) becomes Eq. (9). This

$$(Z_a + Z_b)I_1 - Z_aI_2 = E_1 \tag{9}$$

equation is valid when there is current in both loops of the network.

Similarly, Eq. (10) is written for loop 2 of the network. This is done from Fig. 3 without further explanation. The first term is the voltage in loop 2 when the only current is $I_2$, and the second term is the volt-

$$(Z_b + Z_c)I_2 - Z_bI_1 = E_2 \tag{10}$$

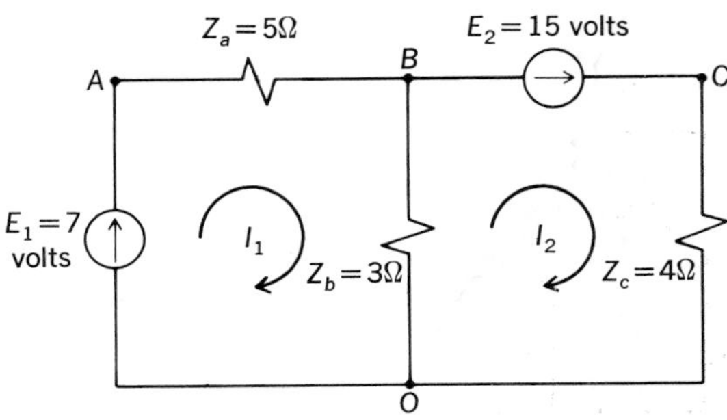


**Fig. 3. Network of two loops. (*After H. H. Skilling, Electrical Engineering Circuits, 2d ed., John Wiley and Sons, 1965*)**

age in loop 2 caused by $I_1$. Since $E_2$ has the same reference direction as $I_2$, it is positive.

Equations (9) and (10) are a pair of equations with only two unknowns, $I_1$ and $I_2$. They can be solved simultaneously by Eqs. (11*a*) and (11*b*). By way of

$$(Z_a + Z_b)I_1 - Z_bI_2 = E_1 \qquad (11a)$$

$$-Z_bI_1 + (Z_b + Z_c)I_2 = E_2 \qquad (11b)$$

illustration let the electromotive forces and impedances be given numerical values and solve for the currents as follows. It is assumed that the equations are linear (see above), which implies that the resistances are constant, and that the electromotive forces are independent of current and voltage.

***Examples.*** If the impedances shown in Fig. 3 are pure resistances and with the values shown, Eqs. (12) and (13) may be written. The electromotive forces

$$8I_1 - 3I_2 = 7 \qquad (12)$$

$$-3I_1 + 7I_2 = 15 \qquad (13)$$

may be either dc values or phasors of alternating voltages (the solution is the same). These are linear equations that can be solved by any convenient means. Using determinants and Cramer's rule, they are solved in Eqs. (14) and (15), where $D$, the denomi-

$$I_1 = \frac{\begin{vmatrix} 7 & -3 \\ 15 & 7 \end{vmatrix}}{\begin{vmatrix} 8 & -3 \\ -3 & 7 \end{vmatrix}} = \frac{49 + 45}{56 - 9} = \frac{94}{47} = 2 \qquad (14)$$

$$I_2 = \frac{\begin{vmatrix} 8 & 7 \\ -3 & 15 \end{vmatrix}}{D} = \frac{120 + 21}{D} = \frac{141}{47} = 3 \qquad (15)$$

nator of $I_2$, is the same as the denominator of $I_1$. The results are two loop currents in amperes. SEE LINEAR SYSTEMS OF EQUATIONS.

Now all unknown quanitites in the network may be easily found. Current in the central branch is $I_{BO} = I_1 - I_2 = -1$ ampere. The negative sign indicates that 1 amp is flowing upward. If the bottom node (node $O$) is taken to be the reference node at an assumed zero potential, then the potential at node $B$ is $-3$ volts. The potential at node $A$ is $-3 + 5 \cdot 2 = 7$ volts, which is also the electromotive force of the source $E_1$. The potential at node $C$ is $-3 + 15 = 12$ volts, which can also be found (across $Z_c$) as $4 \cdot 3 = 12$ volts. The most convenient way to specify all the voltages of a network is to give the potentials at the various nodes with reference to some one node that is arbitrarily assumed to be at zero potential.

***Standard notations.*** It is customary to use a standard system of symbols for writing loop equations. Equations (11) are specific examples of the general form shown in Eqs. (16). Equations (16) are a set of $L$

$$Z_{11}I_1 + Z_{12}I_2 + Z_{13}I_3 + \cdots + Z_{1L}I_L = V_1 \qquad (16a)$$

$$Z_{21}I_1 + Z_{22}I_2 + Z_{23}I_3 + \cdots + Z_{2L}I_L = V_2 \qquad (16b)$$

$$Z_{31}I_1 + Z_{32}I_2 + Z_{33}I_3 + \cdots + Z_{3L}I_L = V_3 \qquad (16c)$$

$$\cdots\cdots\cdots\cdots\cdots\cdots$$

$$Z_{L1}I_1 + Z_{L2}I_2 + Z_{L3}I_3 + \cdots + Z_{LL}I_L = V_L \qquad (16d)$$

simultaneous linear equations, applying to the $L$ loops of a network; the network may be any network and $L$ may be any number. In writing the equations, the following conventions are used. Each loop current is numbered, as $I_1$, $I_2$, and so on. $V_1$ is a voltage in loop 1 that is not taken into account by the terms of the left-hand side of the equation. It may be, as it was in Eq. (9), an independent electromotive force. It may be the sum of several voltages, and must include all voltages that appear in loop 1 when all the other loops are open. Note that its nominal positive direction is taken to be that of $I_1$.

The total impedance about loop 1 is $Z_{11}$. In Eq. (11), which applies to Fig. 3, $Z_{11}$ is $Z_a + Z_b$. It might include many more elements if the network were more complicated. $Z_{11}$ is called the self-impedance of loop 1. It could be measured by means of a bridge or other impedance-measuring instrument connected in place of the source in loop 1, all other loops of the network being opened during the measurement. Each loop has its self-impedance: $Z_{22}$, $Z_{33}$, and so on.

Certain branches are common to two loops. Thus $Z_b$ in Fig. 3 is in both loop 1 and loop 2. In such a case, current in one loop produces voltage in another loop, and there is said to be mutual impedance. By definition, the mutual impedance is the ratio of such a voltage in one loop to the current in another loop that produces it. That is, if current in loop 2 is $I_2$ and mutual impedance with loop 1 is $Z_{12}$, then the resulting voltage in loop 1 is $Z_{12}I_2$. For example, Eq. (11) shows that the voltage produced in loop 1 of Fig. 3 by the current in loop 2 is $-Z_bI_2$. By definition, then, $Z_{12} = -Z_b = -3$. The negative sign results from the fact that in the common element the reference direction of $I_2$ is opposite to the reference direction of $I_1$. If positive $I_1$ produces a positive voltage, positive $I_2$ in the same element produces a negative voltage. In network computations the reference directions are commonly assumed in such a way that the mutual impedances (such as $Z_{12}$, $Z_{23}$, and so on) are negative quantities. However, it is not wrong to direct the arrows that indicate the nominal positive direction of current in such a way that mutual impedances are positive.

In Eq. (16*b*) the first term contains $Z_{21}$. Comparison with Eq. (11) shows that, for the network of Fig. 3, $Z_{21} = -Z_b$. $Z_{21}$ is therefore equal to $Z_{12}$. When two loops contain resistors or coils or capacitors in a common branch, current in loop 1 will produce the same voltage in loop 2 that equal current in loop 2 would cause in loop 1; therefore $Z_{21} = Z_{12}$. The general form for this relation is given in Eq. (17). Al-

$$Z_{pq} = Z_{qp} \qquad (17)$$

though less evident, this relation is still true if two circuits are coupled by a magnetic field (as in a transformer); whatever the turn ratio, the mutual inductance $L_{21}$ equals the mutual inductance $L_{12}$. If the coupling between the loops is by means of an electric field through mutual capacitance with no conductive connection, Eq. (17) is again valid. Indeed, it fails only for circuit elements that are not bilaterally symmetrical. (For example, a transistor or a vacuum tube is not bilateral.)

The order of the subscripts attached to $Z$ has the following significance. The first subscript is the number of the equation in the array of Eqs. (16) and therefore agrees with the subscript attached to $V$ in that equation. The second subscript is the number of the term in the equation and therefore agrees with the subscript attached to $I$ in that term. Thus $Z_{pq}I_q$ is a voltage in circuit $p$ produced by a current in circuit $q$.

**Node equations.** Loop equations are written starting with the concept of loop currents. This makes it unnecessary to give any attention to Kirchhoff's cur-

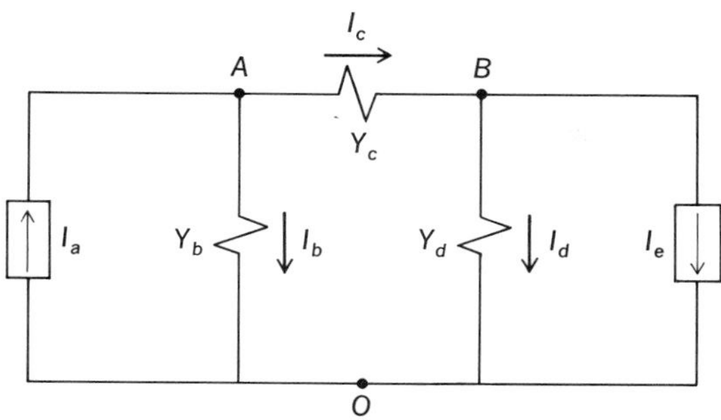


**Fig. 4. Network with two independent nodes; a third one is the reference node O. (*After H. H. Skilling, Electrical Engineering Circuits, 2d ed., John Wiley and Sons, 1965*)**

rent law, for loop currents necessarily add to zero at every node, and Kirchhoff's current law is automatically satisfied. The loop-current concept therefore reduces the number of equations that must be solved simultaneously from the $2B$ equations of the branch method to $L$, the number of independent loops, which is usually about one-fourth as many.

In the node-equation method, the simplifying concept is the idea of measuring voltage from all the nodes of the network to one particular node that is called the reference node, or the datum node. This makes it unnecessary to give any attention to Kirchhoff's voltage law. It is only necessary to satisfy Kirchhoff's current law at each node, for the voltage law is automatically satisfied. Thus the number of simultaneous equations is reduced to the number of independent nodes $N$, a number much smaller than $2B$ and comparable with $L$.

Whether the node method or the loop method is the more convenient depends on the network. Some networks have fewer loops than nodes, and some have fewer nodes than loops. Other factors also affect the relative convenience, as will be seen.

**Figure 4** shows a network with two independent nodes; that is, it has three nodes, one of which is the reference node $O$, and the others are marked $A$ and $B$. Kirchhoff's current law is used for node $A$, Eq. (18), and node $B$, Eq. (19). Assume that the potential

$$I_a = I_b + I_c \tag{18}$$

$$I_e = -I_d + I_c \tag{19}$$

at node $O$ is zero; if the potential at node $A$ is called $V_A$, then $I_b = Y_bV_A$. Also, $I_d = Y_dV_B$ and $I_c = Y_c(V_A - V_B)$. Equations (20) and (21) may now be-

$$\begin{aligned} I_a &= Y_bV_A + Y_c(V_A - V_B) \\ &= (Y_b + Y_c)V_A - Y_cV_B \end{aligned} \tag{20}$$

$$\begin{aligned} I_e &= -Y_dV_B + Y_c(V_A - V_B) \\ &= Y_cV_A - (Y_c + Y_d)V_B \end{aligned} \tag{21}$$

solved for $I_a$ and $I_e$.

It will be found with practice that it is easy to write the final form of Eqs. (20) and (21) directly. To write Eq. (20), note that the independent value $I_a$ of incoming current is set equal to the current that would flow from node $A$ if all other nodes were at zero potential, that is, $(Y_b + Y_c)V_A$, from which is subtracted the current that would flow to node $A$ if it were at zero potential while all other nodes were at their actual potentials, that is, $Y_cV_B$. To write the first term, assume that all nodes except $A$ are short-circuited to node $O$; to write the second term, assume that node $A$ alone is short-circuited to node $O$.

To write Eq. (21) at node $B$, the independent incoming current $-I_c$ is equated to current that would flow from node $B$ if node $A$ were at zero potential, that is, $(Y_c + Y_d)V_B$, less the current that would flow to node $B$ if it alone were at zero potential, in this case $Y_cV_A$; the result, with all signs changed, is Eq. (21).

***Standard notations.*** There is a standard form for writing node equations similar to the standard form for loop equations. For a network of $N$ independent nodes, Eqs. (22) may be written. $Y_{AA}$ is called the

$$\begin{aligned} Y_{AA}V_A + Y_{AB}V_B + Y_{AC}V_C + \cdots + Y_{AN}V_N &= I_A \\ Y_{BA}V_A + Y_{BB}V_B + Y_{BC}V_C + \cdots + Y_{BN}V_N &= I_B \\ Y_{CA}V_A + Y_{CB}V_B + Y_{CC}V_C + \cdots + Y_{CN}V_N &= I_C \\ \cdots\cdots\cdots\cdots\cdots\cdots\cdots\cdots\cdots \\ Y_{NA}V_A + Y_{NB}V_B + Y_{NC}V_C + \cdots + Y_{NN}V_N &= I_N \end{aligned} \tag{22}$$

self-admittance at node $A$, and in the example it is equal to $(Y_b + Y_c)$. Note that $Y_{AA}$ is the sum of all admittances attached to node $A$. $Y_{BB}$, $Y_{CC}$, . . . are self-admittances at the other nodes.

$Y_{AB}$ is the mutual admittance between nodes $A$ and $B$. In the example $Y_{AB} = -Y_c$; $Y_{BA}$ also equals $-Y_c$. Both $Y_{AB}$ and $Y_{BA}$ are the sum of all admittances connected directly between nodes $A$ and $B$ but written with a negative sign.

$I_A$ is another current flowing toward node $A$. In the example it is the source current designated $I_a$ in the diagram. Similarly, $I_B$ is current toward node $B$, and in the example given it is the source current $-I_c$.

It will be noted that every term in the node Eqs. (22) is a current, as every term in the loop Eqs. (16) is a voltage.

***Examples.*** As a numerical example, the following values are given to the impedances and the source currents of Fig. 4, and then voltage at the two independent nodes $A$ and $B$ and current in the three impedances are obtained. Note that the source currents are taken to be real numbers, implying either that they are direct current, or (if ac sources) that they are in phase with each other; the impedances are taken to be real, and this implies pure resistance. In a practical problem one voltage and all impedances might well be complex, and this would complicate the arithmetic but not change the method of solution. Given that $I_a = 2$ amperes, $I_e = 5$ amperes, $Y_b = 1/4$ mho, $Y_c = 1$ mho, and $Y_d = 1/2$ mho, node equations (22) are written as Eqs. (23) and (24).

$$(1/4 + 1)V_A - 1V_B = 2 \tag{23}$$

$$-1V_A + (1 + 1/2)V_B = -5 \tag{24}$$

These equations may be solved for $V_A$ and $V_B$ using Cramer's rule; they are shown as Eqs. (25) and (26).

$$V_A = \frac{\begin{vmatrix} 2 & -1 \\ -5 & 3/2 \end{vmatrix}}{\begin{vmatrix} 5/4 & -1 \\ -1 & 3/2 \end{vmatrix}} = \frac{-2}{7/8} = -\frac{16}{7} \text{ volts} \tag{25}$$

$$V_B = \frac{\begin{vmatrix} 5/4 & 2 \\ -1 & -5 \end{vmatrix}}{7/8} = \frac{-17/4}{7/8} = -34/7 \text{ volts} \tag{26}$$

Currents $I_b$, $I_c$, and $I_d$ are given in Eqs. (27)–(29).

$$I_b = V_A Y_b = -\ {}^{16}\!/_7\ {}^1\!/_4 = -\ {}^4\!/_7 \text{ amperes} \qquad (27)$$

$$I_c = (V_A - V_B)Y_c = \left(-\ {}^{16}\!/_7 + {}^{34}\!/_7\right) 1 = {}^{18}\!/_7 \text{ amperes} \qquad (28)$$

$$I_d = V_B Y_d = -\ {}^{34}\!/_7\ {}^1\!/_2 = -\ {}^{17}\!/_7 \text{ amperes} \qquad (29)$$

Equations (30) and (31) confirm these results. Note

$$I_a = I_b + I_c = -\ {}^4\!/_7 + {}^{18}\!/_7 = 2 \text{ amperes} \qquad (30)$$

$$I_e = I_c - I_d = {}^{18}\!/_7 + {}^{17}\!/_7 = 5 \text{ amperes} \qquad (31)$$

that currents $I_b$ and $I_d$ both turn out to be upward because of the large value of the source current $I_e$, and that therefore the two nodes $A$ and $B$ are both at negative potential compared with node $O$.

**Thévenin's theorem.** It is often convenient before applying network theory to simplify a problem by means of Thévenin's theorem. This theorem and its dual, Norton's theorem, may be expressed in many ways, but the following is among the more useful: Open-circuit voltage $V_\theta$ and short-circuit current $I_\theta$ are measured (or computed) at a pair of terminals of an active linear network. The active network is equivalent at these terminals to either an independent voltage source $V_\theta$ in series with an impedance $Z_\theta = V_\theta/I_\theta$, or alternatively to an independent-current source $I_\theta$ in parallel with the same $Z_\theta$ (**Fig. 5**). The former alternative is Thévenin's theorem, the latter is Norton's. A proof is not given; however, Eqs. (32–37) illustrate the application. *SEE THÉVENIN'S THEOREM (ELECTRIC NETWORKS).*

For the example of node equations Fig. 4 is used with the data given above to find currents and voltages in the network, using Thévenin's theorem.

Thévenin's theorem is applied twice to Fig. 4 to obtain the circuit of **Fig. 6**. Voltage $V_1$ and impedance $Z_1$ are equivalent to current $I_a$ and admittance $Y_b$; similarly $V_2$ and $Z_2$ are equivalent to $I_e$ and $Y_d$, as follows.

In Eqs. (32) the open-circuit voltage is computed

$$V_1 = \frac{I_a}{Y_b} = \frac{2}{{}^1\!/_4} = 8 \qquad (32a)$$

$$V_2 = \frac{I_e}{Y_d} = \frac{5}{{}^1\!/_2} = 10 \qquad (32b)$$

at each pair of terminals with $Z_c$ open.

Short-circuit current is computed with each of nodes $A$ and $B$ short-circuited to node $O$ in Eqs. (33).

$$I_1 = 2 \qquad (33a)$$

$$I_2 = 5 \qquad (33b)$$

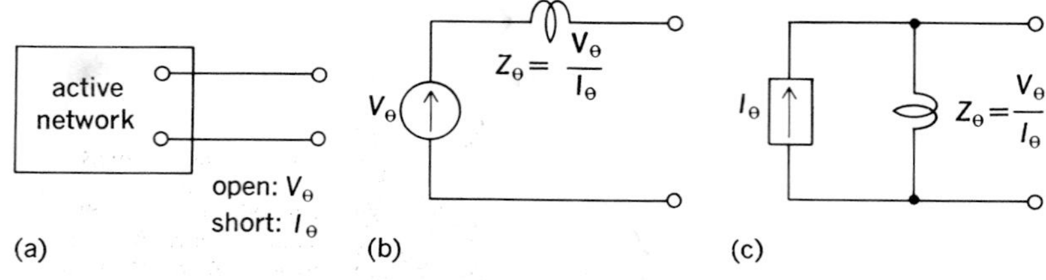


**Fig. 5.** Networks: (*a*) active, (*b*) Thévenin equivalent, and (*c*) its Norton equivalent. (*After H. H. Skilling, Electrical Engineering Circuits, 2d ed., John Wiley and Sons, 1965*)

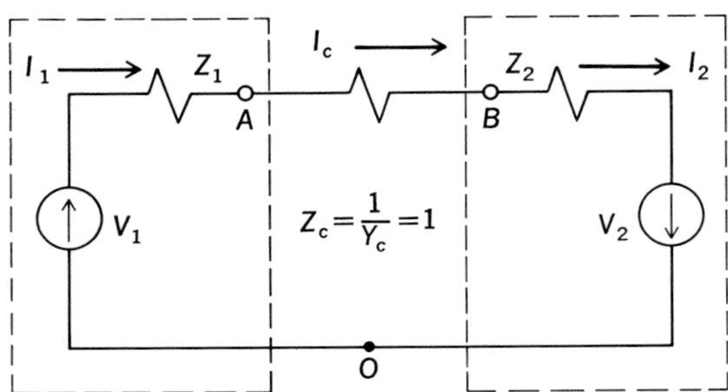


**Fig. 6.** Thévenin equivalent of Fig. 4.

The impedances, Eqs. (34), may be obtained from

$$Z_1 = \frac{V_1}{I_1} = {}^8\!/_2 = 4 \qquad (34a)$$

$$Z_2 = \frac{V_2}{I_2} = {}^{10}\!/_5 = 2 \qquad (34b)$$

Eqs. (32) and (33).

The current $I_c$ may be obtained from Fig. 6, Eq. (35).

$$I_c = \frac{V_1 + V_2}{Z_1 + Z_c + Z_2} = \frac{8 + 10}{4 + 1 + 2} = {}^{18}\!/_7 \text{ amperes} \qquad (35)$$

Voltages $V_A$ and $V_B$ at nodes $A$ and $B$ are given by Eqs. (36) and (37). These answers are, of course, the

$$V_A = V_1 - Z_1 I_c = 8 - 4({}^{18}\!/_7) = -\ {}^{16}\!/_7 \text{ volts} \qquad (36)$$

$$V_B = -(V_2 - Z_2 I_c) = -[10 - 2({}^{18}\!/_7)] = -\ {}^{34}\!/_7 \text{ volts} \qquad (37)$$

same as those obtained by node equations (25) and (26).

Many other network theorems are available, but perhaps none are as useful as Thévenin's and Norton's.

*Hugh Hildreth Skilling*

**Bibilography.** V. K. Aatre, *Network Theory and Filter Design,* 1980; H. H. Skilling, *Electric Networks*, 1974; G. Temes and J. Lapatra, *Introduction to Circuit Synthesis*, 1977; T. N. Trick, *Introduction to Circuit Analysis*, 1977; D. Tuttle, *Circuits*, 1977; M. E. Van Valkenburg, *Network Analysis*, 3d ed., 1974.

## Nonlinear optical devices

Devices based on a class of optical effects that result from the interaction of electromagnetic radiation from lasers with nonlinear materials. Nonlinear means that the effect depends on the intensity of the light. Nonlinear effects are due to the nonlinear contribution to the polarization of the medium, which can be expressed as a power series expansion in the incident electric field $E$ by Eq. (1), where $\chi^{(1)}$ is the linear,

$$P = \epsilon_0(\chi^{(1)} E + \chi^{(2)} E^2 + \chi^{(3)} E^3 + \cdots) \qquad (1)$$

and $\chi^{(2)}$ and $\chi^{(3)}$ are second- and third-order susceptibilities, respectively. $\chi^{(2)}$ has a nonzero value only in materials that do not possess inversion symmetry, but $\chi^{(3)}$ is usually nonzero in all materials. Second-order nonlinearities, which arise from $\chi^{(2)}$, can cause second-harmonic generation, optical parametric amplification, and oscillation. Four-wave mixing and phase conjugation are examples of third-order, $\chi^{(3)}$ nonlinear effects. Optical bistability, which can also be expressed as a $\chi^{(3)}$ mechanism, occurs when the nonlinearity is coupled with feedback.

Nonlinear optical devices can be classified roughly into two categories: $\chi^{(2)}$ devices that generate light at new frequencies and $\chi^{(3)}$ devices that process optical signals. The first category covers second-harmonic generators and optical parametric oscillators, while the second category contains four-wave-mixing beam deflectors, phase-conjugate mirrors, etalon switches and logic devices, and waveguide couplers. *SEE OPTICAL PHASE CONJUGATION.*

**Devices for frequency generation.** Generation of laser frequencies in the ultraviolet region of the spectrum is of considerable importance in many applications such as laser fusion and laser isotope separation. Second-harmonic generators and optical parametric oscillators have produced tunable coherent radiation for these and other applications. *SEE LASER.*

***Optical parametric oscillators.*** When an intense pump beam of frequency $\omega_3$ and a weak "signal" beam of frequency $\omega_1$ are simultaneously incident on a nonlinear crystal, an "idler" wave at frequency $\omega_2 = \omega_3 - \omega_1$ is generated. Also, the "signal" beam at $\omega_1$ is amplified at the expense of the pump photons. This process is called optical parametric amplification. If only the pump frequency $\omega_3$ is present and the crystal is placed inside an optical cavity, then under appropriate conditions, frequencies $\omega_1$ and $\omega_2$ will build up from noise and oscillate inside the resonator. This so-called optical parametric oscillation occurs when the conservation of momentum (phase-matching condition) is satisfied, namely, Eq. (2), where the **k**'s are

$$\mathbf{k}_1 + \mathbf{k}_2 = \mathbf{k}_3 \tag{2}$$

propagation constants. For a collinear geometry, each wave satisfies Eq. (3), where $n$ is the index of refraction of the crystal and $c$ is the speed of light. The

$$k = \frac{n\omega}{c} \tag{3}$$

phase-matching condition can then be expressed in terms of the indices of refraction of the crystal for the three waves as Eq. (4). The conservation of energy

$$\omega_3 n_3 = \omega_1 n_1 + \omega_2 n_2 \tag{4}$$

requires Eq. (5), and efficient parametric generation

$$\omega_3 = \omega_1 + \omega_2 \tag{5}$$

therefore requires that Eqs. (4) and (5) be satisfied simultaneously. A variation in the temperature of the crystal or a change in crystal orientation will change the three indices of refraction and will tune $\omega_1$ and $\omega_2$. The tuning of the "signal" and "idler" frequencies over a large range results from the nonresonant nature of the nonlinear mechanism in materials such as lithium niobate ($LiNbO_3$).

***Second-harmonic generators.*** Second-harmonic generation is a special case of parametric generation where $\omega_1 = \omega_2 = \omega$. The interaction of a beam of frequency $\omega$ with the nonlinear crystal causes the generation of a wave at twice the frequency, $2\omega$. Second-harmonic generators are widely used with neodymium:yttrium-aluminum-garnet (Nd:YAG) lasers and in correlation techniques for measurement of the time profile of fast (picosecond and subpicosecond) optical pulses. Quartz, potassium dihydrogen phosphate (KDP), and ammonium dihydrogen phosphate (ADP) are among the crystals used for second-harmonic generation. Rare gases are often used for second- and higher-harmonic generation of ultraviolet light because they are more transparent at shorter wavelengths than most materials.

**Devices for optical signal processing.** Nonlinear optical devices may be used in digital signal processing and optical computing. The parallel nature of light, which may make the simultaneous operation of many devices possible, together with the high speed of optical components, promises very large bandwidths for number crunching computation and information processing. Many counterparts of electronic circuit elements such as transistors and gates have already been demonstrated by using optical technology. Methods for optical interconnections within electronic computers have been considered.

***Etalon devices.*** When a nonlinear material is sandwiched between two partially reflecting mirrors, a nonlinear Fabry-Perot etalon is formed. Normally, a thin semiconductor slab is used to provide the nonlinearity. Such a semiconductor etalon is capable of performing logic operations, switching, and controlling one light beam with another. The principle of operation of such optical transistors can be described as follows. The incident laser frequency $\omega_L$ is initially detuned from the resonances (transmission peaks) of the Fabry-Perot etalon, resulting in low transmission; the device is in its "off" state (**Fig. 1***a*). To switch the device to its "on" state, a second laser beam is directed toward the same spot on the device. The primary function of the second laser is to change the index of refraction of the semiconductor by any of several physical mechanisms: heating the etalon, creating free carriers that screen an exciton feature or partially fill the conduction band, and so forth. The index change causes the nearest etalon resonance to shift toward $\nu_L$, resulting in an abrupt increase in the transmission and the consequent turn "on" of the switch (Fig. 1*b*). Optical switching can be accomplished with a single laser beam also. In this case, when the device

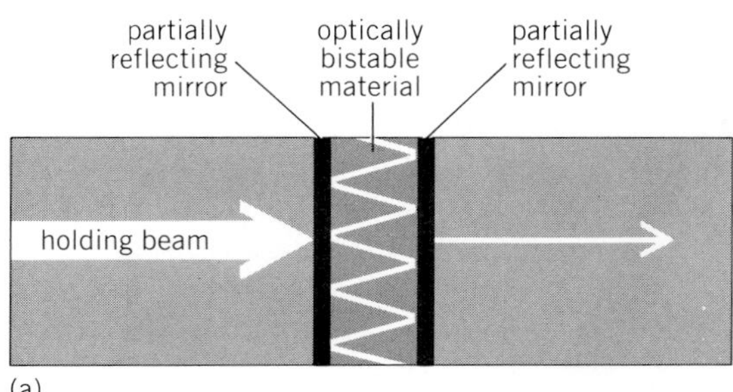

**Fig. 1. Operations of a nonlinear optical switch. (*a*) Switch in its "off" state. (*b*) Switch abruptly turns "on" by the application of a second switching beam.**

is initially "off," increasing the laser intensity beyond a critical value results in an abrupt turn "on" of the device while turning "off" can be performed by decreasing the intensity. Optical bistability refers to situations where the intensities for turning "on" and "off" are not the same. A typical optical bistability hysteresis curve is shown in **Fig. 2**. *See* Optical bistability; Semiconductor.

Operations of bistable devices have been realized in many semiconductors, including bulk gallium arsenide (GaAs), gallium arsenide–aluminum gallium arsenide (GaAs-AlGaAs) superlattices, copper chloride (CuCl), indium arsenide (InAs), indium antimonide (InSb), zinc sulfide (ZnS), zinc selenide (ZnSe), cadmium sulfide (CdS), and cadmium mercury telluride (CdHgTe). The ideal practical device should be small (with micrometer or submicrometer sizes) and fast (with picosecond switching times), require very little switching energy (of the order of $10^{-15}$ joule) and low holding power (submilliwatts), and operate at a convenient temperature and wavelength. Gallium arsenide is the most promising candidate: It can operate with a few milliwatts of power at room temperature; and switch-on times of a few picoseconds and switch-off times of a few nanoseconds have been demonstrated by using a few-micrometers-square spot on a gallium arsenide etalon. Operation at submilliwatt power levels at −307°F (85 K) has been accomplished. The response time of a gallium arsenide NOR gate was measured to be approximately 1 picosecond (**Fig. 3**). Even though the NOR gate responds in 1 picosecond, the next NOR gate operation cannot be performed for a few nanoseconds because it takes that long for the free carriers to recombine or diffuse out of the illuminated region and to allow the index of refraction to return to its initial value. For the NOR gate operation, the device is initially made totally transmitting by tuning one of the etalon resonances to the laser frequency. The application of one or two input beams shifts the etalon peak away from the laser frequency, resulting in a decrease in transmission. *See* Logic circuits; Semiconductor heterostructures.

Etalon devices are most suitable for parallel processing because many beams could be focused on a single etalon, thereby defining a two-dimensional array of pixels. Employing parallel processors in optical computing could considerably enhance the speed of computations. For example, simultaneous operation of $10^6$ pixels at a rate of 100 MHz per pixel results in an effective bandwidth of $10^{14}$ operations per second. Computer architecture approaches are based on parallel computations, and fifth-generation supercomputers will surely employ parallel architecture techniques. *See* Computer systems architecture; Concurrent processing; Optical information systems; Supercomputers.

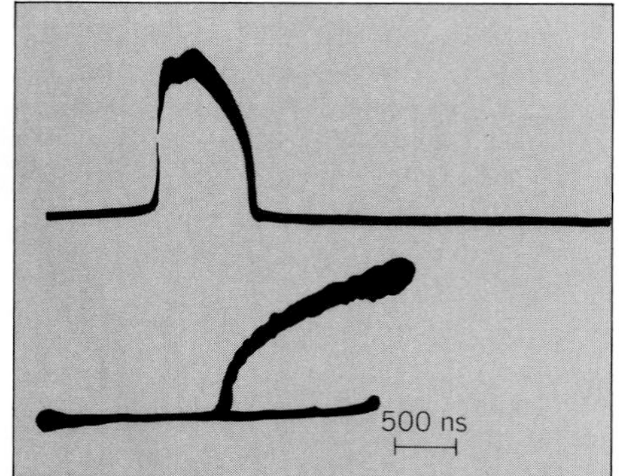


**Fig. 2. Room-temperature optical bistability in a gallium arsenide–aluminum gallium arsenide (GaAs–AlGaAs) nonlinear optical device. The top trace is the output transmission of the device versus time. The bottom trace is the output intensity versus input intensity, showing hysteresis. The input pulse versus time has a triangular shape and is not shown.**

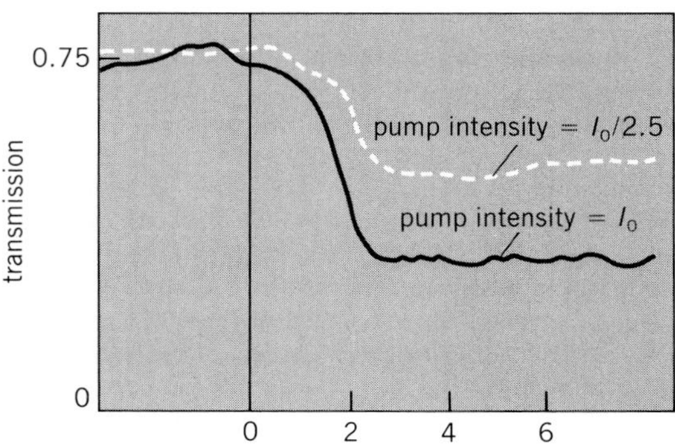


**Fig. 3. Transmission of a gallium arsenide–aluminum gallium arsenide (GaAs–AlGaAs) optical NOR gate versus time at two pump intensities, $I_0$ and $I_0/2.5$, showing a 1-picosecond response time for the device.**

***Waveguide devices.*** When light travels in a medium with an index of refraction larger than the surrounding material, light traveling at a shallow enough angle is trapped in the higher-index medium by total internal reflection. Such waveguiding can occur in one dimension only (as in many multimode diode lasers) or in both transverse dimensions (as in rib waveguides, single-transverse-mode diode lasers, or optical fibers). The guided-wave devices confine the light over a long interaction length (a fraction of an inch or few millimeters), thereby permitting high intensities in the guided region. (The intensity $I$ is related to power $P$ by $I = P/A$, where $A$ is the focused light area; therefore, for a small $A$, intensity can be high.) Also, the long interaction length permits the use of materials with weaker nonlinearities to obtain the phase shift (of the order of 180°) needed for logic devices. However, absorption in the guided material usually limits the extent of the interaction length.

***Four-wave-mixing beam deflectors.*** Optical techniques for intracomputer communications have become increasingly popular because of the limit imposed by the electronic interconnections on the scale-downs of computer circuits. One method that has been assessed for optical interconnection is the use of holographic elements to diffract the light to the desired locations. Holographic arrays may someday replace the huge number of wires or buses that are used inside the computer to transfer information. However, conventional holograms are not programmable and would have to be replaced every time a different set of pixels was to be accessed. Four-wave mixing is one of the avenues that has been investigated to perform real-time programmable holography. Dynamic gratings that are generated by four-wave mixing may be able to deflect light that has originated from a source on a very large-scale integrated circuit (VLSI) chip to a spot on the same chip or to another VLSI chip. If the light is desired to illuminate a different spot, the direction of the grating must be changed; this can be accomplished by changing the angle at which the two "write" beams intersect. SEE NONLINEAR OPTICS.

Nasser Peyghambarian; Hyatt M. Gibbs

**Bibliography.** H. M. Gibbs, *Optical Bistability: Controlling Light with Light*, 1985; A. Lattes et al., An ultrafast all-optical gate, *IEEE J. Quant. Electr.*, QE-19:1718–1723, 1983; A. Migus et al., One-picosecond optical NOR gate at room-temperature with a GaAs-AlGaAs multiple-quantum-well Fabry-Perot etalon, *Appl. Phys. Lett.*, 46:70, 1985; D. A. B. Miller and T. H. Wood, Quantum-well optical modulators and SEED all-optical switches, *Opt. News*, 10(6):19–20, 1984; N. Peyghambarian and H. M. Gibbs, Optical nonlinearity, bistability and signal processing in semiconductors, *J. Opt. Soc. Amer. B*, 2:1215, 1985; N. Peyghambarian and H. M. Gibbs, Optical bistability for optical signal processing and computing, *Opt. Eng.*, 24:68–73, 1975.

## Nonlinear programming

An area of applied mathematics concerned with finding the values of the variables which give the smallest or largest value of a specified function in the class of all variables satisfying prescribed conditions. The function which is to be optimized is called the objective function, and the functions defining the prescribed conditions are referred to as the constraint functions or constraints. This general problem is called the nonlinear programming problem. The study of the theoretical and computational aspects of the nonlinear programming problem is called nonlinear programming, mathematical programming, or optimization theory. When there are no constraints, the nonlinear programming problem is said to be unconstrained; otherwise the problem is said to be constrained. If the objective function and the constraint functions are linear, the nonlinear programming problem is said to be a linear programming problem. When the objective function is quadratic and the constraints are linear, the nonlinear programming program is said to be a quadratic programming problem. SEE LINEAR PROGRAMMING.

**General theory.** The general nonlinear programming problem can be stated as notation (1), where

$$\begin{aligned} &\text{minimize } f(x) \\ &\text{subject to } g_i(x) \geq 0, \quad i = 1, \ldots, m \\ &\qquad\qquad h_j(x) = 0, \quad j = 1, \ldots, p \end{aligned} \tag{1}$$

$x = (x_1, \ldots, x_n)$ are the variables of the problem, $f$ is the objective function, $g_i$ are the inequality constraints, and $h_j$ are the equality constraints. By changing $f$ to $-f$, a maximization problem is transformed to a minimization problem. Moreover, an inequality constraint in the form $g_i(x) \geq 0$ is equivalent to $-g_i(x) \leq 0$. Consequently the format of problem (1) can handle both types of inequality constraints and both minimization and maximization problems.

The basic theory deals with conditions which a solution of the nonlinear programming problem (1) must satisfy. In the case when the objective function and the constraint functions are differentiable, the most important necessary conditions are the Karush-Kuhn-Tucker conditions. Consider the lagrangian function (2) whose added variables $u = (u_1, \ldots, u_m)$ and

$$L(x,u,w) = f(x) - \sum_{i=1}^{m} u_i g_i(x) + \sum_{j=1}^{p} w_j h_j(x) \tag{2}$$

$w = (w_1, \ldots, w_p)$ are called Lagrange multipliers. The Karush-Kuhn-Tucker theory says that if $x$ solves problem (1), then there exists $u$ and $w$ so that the triple $(x,u,w)$ satisfies system (3) of equations and inequalities.

$$\begin{aligned} &\nabla f(x) - \sum_{i=1}^{m} u_i \nabla g_i(x) + \sum_{j=1}^{p} w_j \nabla h_j(x) = 0 \\ &g_i(x) \geq 0, \quad i = 1, \ldots, m \\ &h_j(x) = 0, \quad j = 1, \ldots, p \\ &u_i g_i(x) = 0, \quad i = 1, \ldots, m \\ &u_i \geq 0, \quad i = 1, \ldots, m \end{aligned} \tag{3}$$

The notation $\nabla f(x)$ is used to denote the gradient of $f$ at $x$ or the vector of partial derivatives at $x$ with respect to the $n$ independent variables. In order for this theory to be valid, an additional assumption called the constraint qualification must be made. Numerous constraint qualifications have been formulated; a useful but somewhat restrictive constraint qualification requires the gradients of the constraints which are actively involved in the solution to form a linearly independent set.

While the Karush-Kuhn-Tucker conditions (3) are only necessary conditions—meaning that, in general they are not sufficient to ensure that $x$ will solve problem (1)—in the case that $f$ and the $g_i$ are convex and the $h_j$ are affine, these necessary conditions are also sufficient conditions. The Lagrange multipliers are also called dual variables. In many problems in business, economics, and engineering, the dual variables have a useful interpretation in terms of sensitivity of the objective function to a particular constraint.

The branch of nonlinear programming which does not require the functions in problem (1) to be differentiable is called nondifferentiable programming or nondifferentiable optimization. Although this area has not received as much attention as the differentiable case, it has become the subject of considerable research activity and has increased in importance.

**Scope of application.** Many of the quantitative problems in business, economics, and engineering design can be expressed as nonlinear programming problems. General computational methods have been designed and implemented on large digital computers. Many problems which were considered large in 1970 are now considered small and can be solved efficiently. While considerable progress has been made in both the design and algorithms and computer technology, there are still many practical large nonlinear programs which cannot be solved. Research has been aimed at taking advantage of the structure of the particular problem in question. One important example of structure is sparseness. Sparseness would occur if the nonlinear programming problem had many variables, but the objective function and each constraint function involved only relatively few variables. SEE OPERATIONS RESEARCH.

**Computational methods.** Computational methods for the unconstrained optimization problem are well understood. For the unconstrained optimization problem, the Karush-Kuhn-Tucker conditions specialize to $\nabla f(x) = 0$. The preferred class of algorithms for this problem is the class of quasi-Newton methods which approximate the solution by the iterates given by Eq. (4), where $B_k$ is an $n \times n$ matrix and the superscript

$$x^{k+1} = x^k - \alpha^k B_k^{-1} \nabla f(x_k) \quad (4)$$

$-1$ denotes the process of matrix inversion. The scalar $\alpha_k$ in Eq. (4) is chosen to approximately solve the one-dimensional optimization problem in $\alpha$: minimize $f[x^k - \alpha B_k^{-1} \nabla f(x^k)]$. The special case of the quasi-Newton method, Eq. (4), which arises by choosing $B_k$ equal to the identity matrix is the gradient method, while the special case which arises by choosing $B_k = \nabla^2 f(x^k)$ (the hessian matrix of $f$ at $x^k$, that is, the matrix of second-order partial derivatives of $f$ at $x^k$) is Newton's method. The gradient method is so slow that it should generally not be used, and Newton's method requires so much work per iteration that it is of questionable value. The class of quasi-Newton methods called secant methods requires that $B_{k+1}^{-1} y = s$ in Eq. (4), where $s = x^{k+1} - x^k$ and $y = \nabla f(x^{k+1}) - \nabla f(x^k)$. This class of methods seems to be the best currently available, and the preferred formula for $B_{k+1}^{-1}$ is the Broyden-Fletcher-Goldfarb-Shanno (BFGS) secant update formula, Eq. (5), where the superscript $T$ denotes matrix transposition.

$$B_{k+1}^{-1} = \frac{B_k^{-1} - [sy^T B_k^{-1} + (B_k^{-1} y - s)s^T]}{\left( \dfrac{s^T y + ss^T (y^T B_k^{-1} y)}{(s^T y)^2} \right)} \quad (5)$$

The BFGS secant method is substantially faster than the gradient method, but not as fast as Newton's method. It requires more work than the gradient method, and less than Newton's method per iteration. Overall it is the preferred algorithm. The choice of $\alpha_k$ in Eq. (4) is important and the subject of current research.

There is lack of agreement of computational methods for attacking the constrained optimization problem. However, a reasonable approach to extending the successful secant methods from unconstrained optimization to constrained optimization appears to be the method of successive quadratic programming. Specifically the solution $x$ is approximated by the iterates $x^k$ which satisfy Eq. (6), where $\Delta x$ solves the

$$x^{k+1} = x^k + \alpha_k \Delta x \quad (6)$$

quadratic programming problem of notations (7).

$$\begin{aligned} &\text{minimize } q(\Delta x) = \nabla f(x^k)^T \Delta x + 1/2 \Delta x^T B_k \Delta x \\ &\text{subject to } \nabla g_i(x^k)\Delta x + g_i(x^k) \geq 0, \quad i = 1, \ldots, m \\ &\qquad \nabla h_j(x^k)\Delta x + h_j(x^k) = 0, \quad j = 1, \ldots, p \end{aligned} \quad (7)$$

The BFGS secant update for the matrix $B_k$ is given by Eq. (8), where $s = x^{k+1} - x^k$ and $y =$

$$B_{k+1} = \frac{B_k + yy^T}{s^T y} - \frac{B_k ss^T B_k}{s^T B_k s} \quad (8)$$

$\nabla_x L(x^{k+1}, u^{k+1}, w^{k+1}) - \nabla_x L(x^k, u^{k+1}, w^{k+1})$, with the multipliers $u^{k+1}$, and $w^{k+1}$ obtained from the solution of the quadratic programming problem (7). The notation $\nabla_x L$ denotes the vector of partial derivatives of $L$ taken with respect to the $x$ variables. The choice of the scalar $\alpha_k$ in Eq. (6) is the subject of current research. It is known that in the case of unconstrained optimization and constrained optimization of the choice $\alpha_k = 1$ for large $k$ is optimal.

There is considerable activity in the general area of algorithms for constrained optimization problems, and the development of effective and efficient algorithms for this general problem can be expected. However, there is still a considerable amount of work to be done in this area. SEE OPTIMIZATION.

*Richard A. Tapia*

**Bibliography.** M. Avriel, *Nonlinear Programming*, 1976; J. E. Dennis and J. J. Moré, Quasi-Newton methods, motivation and theory, *SIAM Rev.*, 19:46–89, 1977; O. Mangasarian (ed.), *Nonlinear Programming 4*, 1981.

## Nonsinusoidal waveform

The representation of a wave that does not vary in a sinusoidal manner. Electric circuits containing nonlinear elements, such as electron tubes, iron-core magnetic devices, and transistors, commonly produce nonsinusoidal currents and voltages. When these are repetitive functions of time, they are called nonsinusoidal electric waves. Oscillograms, tabulated data, and sometimes mathematical functions for segments of such waves are often used to describe the excursions throughout one cycle. A cycle corresponds to $2\pi$ electrical radians and covers the time interval $T$ seconds in which the wave repeats itself.

These electric waves can be represented by a constant term, the average or dc component, plus a series of harmonic terms in which the frequencies of the harmonics are integral multiples of the fundamental frequency. The fundamental frequency $f_1$, if it does exist, has the time span $T = 1/f_1$ s for its cycle. The second-harmonic frequency $f_2$ then will have two of its cycles within $T$ seconds, and so on.

**Fourier series representation.** The series of terms stated above is known as a Fourier series and can be expressed in the form of Eq. (1), where $y(t)$, plotted

$$\begin{aligned} y(t) &= B_0 + A_1 \sin \omega t + A_2 \sin 2\omega t + \cdots \\ &\quad + A_n \sin n\omega t + B_1 \cos \omega t + B_2 \cos 2\omega t \\ &\quad + \cdots + B_n \cos n\omega t \\ &= B_0 + C_1 \sin (\omega t + \phi_1) + \cdots \\ &\quad + C_n \sin (n\omega t + \phi_n) \\ &= \sum_{n=0}^{\infty} C_n \sin (n\omega t + \phi_n) \end{aligned} \quad (1)$$

over a cycle of the fundamental, gives the shape of the nonsinusoidal wave. The terms on the right-hand side show the Fourier series representation of the wave where Eqs. (2) and (3) apply. Here $A_0$ is iden-

$$C_n = \sqrt{A_n^2 + B_n^2} \quad (2)$$

$$\phi_n = \arctan \frac{B_n}{A_n} \quad (3)$$

tically zero, and $B_0 = C_0$ in Eq. (1). The radian frequency of the fundamental is $\omega = 2\pi f_1$, and $n$ is either zero or an integer. $C_1$ is the amplitude of the fundamental ($n = 1$), and succeeding $C_n$'s are the amplitudes of the respective harmonics having frequencies corresponding to $n = 2, 3, 4$, and so on, with respect to the fundamental. The phase angle of the fundamental with respect to a chosen time reference axis is $\phi_1$, and the succeeding $\phi_n$'s are the phase angles of the respective harmonics.

The equation for $y(t)$ shows all its separate components, which, in general, include an infinite number of terms. In order to represent a given nonsinusoidal wave by a Fourier series, it is necessary to evaluate each term, that is, $B_0$, and all $A_n$'s and all $B_n$'s. In practical problems the first several terms usually yield an approximate result sufficiently accurate for portrayal of the actual wave. The degree of accuracy desired in representing faithfully the actual wave determines the number of terms that must be used in any computation.

The constant term $B_0$ is found by computing the average amplitude of the actual wave over one cycle. Assuming any reference time $t = 0$ on the wave, $B_0$ is given by Eq. (4), where the angle $\omega t$ is replaced by

$$B_0 = \frac{1}{T}\int_0^T y(t)\,dt = \frac{1}{2\pi}\int_0^T y(\omega t)\,d\omega t = \frac{1}{2\pi}\int_0^T y(\theta)\,d\theta \qquad (4)$$

$\theta$. Since $B_0$ is a constant, or dc, term, it merely raises or lowers the entire wave and does not affect its shape.

The coefficients of the sine series are obtained by multiplying the wave $y(\theta)$ by $\sin n\theta$, integrating this product over a full cycle of the fundamental, and dividing the result by $\pi$. Thus, $A_n$ is given by Eq. (5).

$$A_n = \frac{1}{\pi}\int_0^{2\pi} y(\theta)\sin n\theta\,d\theta \qquad (5)$$

The coefficients of the cosine terms are obtained in like manner, except that $\cos n\theta$ replaces $\sin n\theta$. Thus, $B_n$ is given by Eq. (6).

$$B_n = \frac{1}{\pi}\int_0^{2\pi} y(\theta)\cos n\theta\,d\theta \qquad (6)$$

If mathematical expressions describe $y(\theta)$, Eqs. (4), (5), and (6) give the coefficients of the series directly through analytical methods. If oscillograms or tabulated data describe $y(\theta)$, then graphical or tabular forms of integration are used.

**Effect of even harmonics.** Figure 1 shows waves composed of a fundamental and a second harmonic only. In Fig. 1*a*, both $\phi_1$ and $\phi_2$ are zero. In Fig. 1*b*, $\phi_1$ is zero and $\phi_2$ is $+\pi/2$ radians with respect to one cycle of the second harmonic. In the example given in Fig. 1*b* the negative part of the overall wave is completely unlike the positive portion. Also, in general, these two sections will have different time intervals. Even harmonics give unsymmetrical waves.

**Effect of odd harmonics.** Figure 2 shows waves composed of a fundamental and a third harmonic. In Fig. 2*a*, both $\phi_1$ and $\phi_3$ are zero. In Fig. 2*b*, $\phi_1$ is zero and $\phi_3$ is $+\pi$ radians with respect to one cycle of the third harmonic. In Fig. 2*c*, $\theta_1$ is zero and $\theta_3$ is

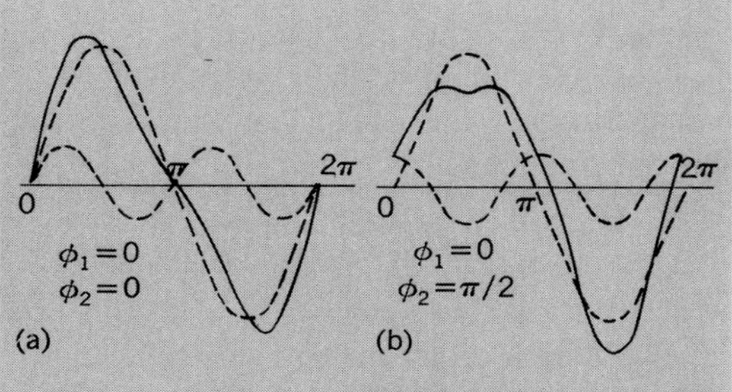


**Fig. 1.** **Addition of a fundamental and a second harmonic. (*a*) $\phi_1 = 0$, $\phi_2 = 0$. (*b*) $\phi_1 = 0$, $\phi_2 = +\pi/2$ radians.**

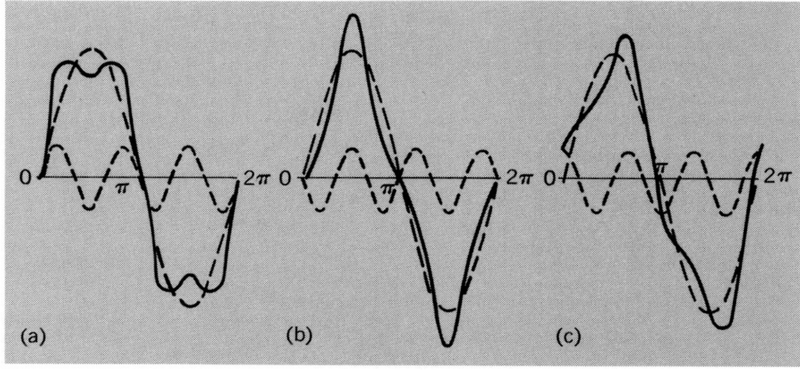


**Fig. 2.** **Addition of a fundamental and a third harmonic. (*a*) $\phi_1 = 0$, $\phi_3 = 0$. (*b*) $\phi_1 = 0$, $\phi_3 = +\pi$ radians. (*c*) $\phi_1 = 0$, $\phi_3 = +\pi/2$ radians.**

$+\pi/2$ radians on the third-harmonic time scale. In these diagrams the negative and positive parts of the overall waves are alike and both embrace $\pi$ radians of the fundamental. Odd harmonics lead to symmetrical waves.

**Symmetry.** To determine symmetry of nonsine waves, the constant term $b_0$ is first removed. This means moving the wave down or up by the value of $B_0$. After this, if the wave from $\pi$ to $2\pi$ is rotated about the horizontal axis and moved forward $\pi$ radians, and then coincides exactly with the section from 0 to $\pi$, the total wave is said to have half-wave symmetry. Often the wave is said merely to be symmetrical. This means that in such cases $y(\theta + \pi) = -y(\theta)$. If, in turn, each half of the wave is symmetrical about the vertical axes of $\pi/2$, or $3\pi/2$, the wave is said to have quarter-wave symmetry as well. Half-wave and quarter-wave symmetry do not necessarily accompany each other.

All three waves of Fig. 2 have half-wave symmetry. The first two have quarter-wave symmetry also, but that of Fig. 2*c* does not. Waves having only a fundamental and odd harmonics show half-wave symmetry. Conversely, half-wave symmetry indicates that only the fundamental, if it exists, and odd harmonics are present in the total wave. Half-wave symmetry permits Eqs. (5) and (6) to be integrated over the interval $\pi$, with the result multiplied by two. Quarter-wave symmetry permits integration over one-quarter cycle of the fundamental, with the result multiplied by four.

Half-wave symmetry means that the fundamental and all odd harmonics may pass through their zero values at times quite distinct from each other. With quarter-wave symmetry the fundamental and the odd harmonics all pass through their zero values at the same time; therefore all phase angles $\phi_n$ are either zero or 180°.

The wave of Fig. 1*a* has no symmetry of the kind discussed above. Waves containing only the fundamental and even harmonics, or even harmonics alone, are unsymmetrical. Although half-wave symmetry is absent, quarter-wave symmetry may exist. A wave which is the same from $\pi$ to $2\pi$ as it is from 0 to $\pi$, that is, $y(\theta) = y(\theta + \pi)$, is unsymmetrical. Only even harmonics are present, and the wave has no fundamental component. The output from a full-wave rectifier, for example, contains only the average term $B_0$ and even harmonics.

Waves that do not meet any of the special conditions noted above can be expected to contain both even and odd harmonics, and probably both sines and cosines also. Any doubt arising on the harmonic content of a wave is resolved by assuming all components of the Fourier series to be present. Analysis will show exactly those that actually exist.

**Even and odd functions.** The time origin of a wave can be chosen arbitrarily. If the reference axis $t = 0$ is such that the wave to the left is merely the wave to the right rotated about this axis, then $y(-\theta) = y(\theta)$, which is said to be an even function. Only cosine terms will be present in the Fourier series for the wave. On the other hand, if the wave to the left is the wave to the right rotated about the $t = 0$ axis, and then rotated about the horizontal axis, $y(-\theta) = -y(\theta)$, which is said to be an odd function. Only sine terms will appear in the Fourier series. Neither case precludes the possibility of the presence of both even and odd harmonics.

**The rms value of nonsinusoidal wave.** A nonsinusoidal wave has an rms value obtained through the following steps:

1. Combine all terms of the same frequency so as to have a single $A_1, A_2, \ldots, A_n; B_1, B_2, \ldots, B_n$; or a single $C_1, C_2, \ldots, C_n$. Terms such as $\sin(n\omega t \pm \alpha)$ and $\cos(n\omega t \pm \beta)$ each have sine and cosine components which can be separated out by trigonometric expansion.
2. Form the series $y(\theta)$ as in Eq. (1).
3. The rms value of the wave is then given by Eq. (7).

$$y_{\text{rms}} = \left(B_0^2 + \frac{A_1^2}{2} + \frac{A_2^2}{2} + \cdots + \frac{A_n^2}{2} + \frac{B_1^2}{2} + \frac{B_2^2}{2} + \cdots + \frac{B_n^2}{2}\right)^{1/2}$$
$$= \left(B_0^2 + \frac{C_1^2}{2} + \frac{C_2^2}{2} + \cdots + \frac{C_n^2}{2}\right)^{1/2} \qquad (7)$$

If $y_{\text{rms}}$ represents a voltage or a current, this value is shown by an electrodynamometer or iron-vane voltmeter or ammeter. The rms of the wave is merely the square root of the sum of the squares of the rms values of all of the frequency components.

**Power.** An indicating wattmeter with a nonsinusoidal voltage impressed on its potential circuit and a nonsinusoidal current in its current coils indicates the average power taken by the circuit. Designating peak values of the component voltages and currents by $E_n$'s and $I_n$'s in place of $C_n$'s results in Eq. (8). Each coef-

$$\text{Average power} = \frac{1}{2\pi}\int_0^{2\pi} ei\, d\theta$$
$$= E_0I_0 + \frac{E_1I_1}{2}\cos\theta_1 + \cdots + \frac{E_nI_n}{2}\cos\theta_n \qquad (8)$$

ficient is simply the product of arms voltage and current. No cross-product terms involving different frequencies result from the integration. That is, no power can be contributed by a voltage of one frequency and a current of another frequency.

**Power factor.** The apparent power taken by a circuit carrying nonsinusoidal voltage and current is the product of the rms values of these quantities. Power factor for such a case is defined only by the ratio of the average power to the apparent power. Thus, the power factor is given by Eq. (9). Power factor is

$$\text{Power factor (pf)} = \frac{\text{watts average power}}{\text{rms volts} \times \text{rms amperes}} \qquad (9)$$

hence the ratio of instrument readings as stated. All circuits have a power factor, but pf = $\cos\theta$ only for a sine wave voltage and current of the same frequency. There is no average or representative phase angle for a circuit carrying nonsinusoidal waves.

**Example of nonsinusoidal waves.** Assume a series circuit to have 8 ohms resistance and 15.91 millihenries inductance and that the impressed voltage is given by Eq. (10). The problem is to calculate the

$$e = 100 \sin 377t + 80 \sin 1131t \qquad (10)$$

rms voltage and current, the average power, and the power factor. The voltage has a fundamental component of 60 cycles ($f_1 = \omega_1/2\pi = 377/2\pi$) and a third harmonic of 180 cycles ($f_3 = \omega_3/2\pi = 1131/2\pi$).

At 60 cycles:

$$X_{L_1} = 377 \times 0.01591$$
$$= 6.0 \text{ ohms inductive reactance}$$
$$Z_1 = \sqrt{8^2 + 6^2} = 10 \text{ ohms impedance}$$
$$I_1 = 100/10 = 10 \text{ A max fundamental current}$$
$$\theta_1 = \arctan(6/8) = 36.87°$$

At 180 cycles:

$$X_{L_3} = 3 \times 6 = 18 \text{ ohms inductive reactance}$$
$$Z_3 = \sqrt{8^2 + 18^2} = 19.70 \text{ ohms impedance}$$
$$I_3 = 80/19.7$$
$$= 4.06 \text{ A max third-harmonic current}$$
$$\theta_3 = \arctan(18/8)$$
$$= 66.06° \ (= 22.02° \text{ on fundamental scale})$$

The equation for the current is

$$i = 10 \sin(377t - 36.87°) + 4.06 \sin(1131t - 22.02°)$$

$$E_{\text{rms}} = \sqrt{\frac{100^2}{2} + \frac{80^2}{2}} = 90.06 \text{ volts}$$

$$I_{\text{rms}} = \sqrt{\frac{10^2}{2} + \frac{4.06^2}{2}} = 7.63 \text{ amperes}$$

$$\text{Apparent power} = 90.06 \times 7.63$$
$$= 687 \text{ volt-amperes}$$
$$\text{Average power} = I^2R = 7.63^2 \times 8 = 466 \text{ watts}$$
$$\text{Power factor} = \frac{466}{682} = 0.678$$

SEE ALTERNATING-CURRENT CIRCUIT THEORY.

Burtis L. Robertson; W. S. Pritchett

**Bibliography.** R. E. Ridsdale, *Electric Circuits for Engineering Technology*, 2d ed., 1984; C. S. Siskind, *Electric Circuits, Direct and Alternating Current*, 2d ed., 1965; D. D. Weiner and J. F. Spina, *The Sinusoidal Analysis and Modeling of Weakly Nonlinear Circuits: With Application to Nonlinear Interference Effects*, 1980.

## Number systems

Integral numbers may be represented as linear combinations of powers of any convenient and arbitrarily chosen base. The choice of the base is not always made on a rational basis, the number systems have been based on 5, 6, 10, and 60. More recently, systems based on 2 and 8 have proved quite useful in computer applications. The duodecimal number system, in which numbers are represented as linear combinations of powers of 12, has certain advantages because 12 has the factors 1, 2, 3, 4, 6, and 12.

**Decimal system.** Every positive integer is uniquely a polynomial in 10 with coefficients, called digits, taken from 0, 1, . . . , 9. The fact that

$$205714 = 4 + 1 \cdot 10 + 7 \cdot 10^2 + 5 \cdot 10^3 + 0 \cdot 10^4 + 2 \cdot 10^5$$

is nearly always lost in present-day teaching, and in the hurried application of ordinary arithmetic. In fact, numbers are likely to be thought of as merely an orderly arrangement of decimal digits.

The decimal method of representing numbers comes from India and Arabia and is only a few centuries old in Europe. The base, 10, is due to the biological fact that humans have that many articulate fingers and thumbs. The positional significance, including the meaning and usefulness of zero, is of oriental origin.

The operations of addition and multiplication consist of the corresponding operations with polynomials, together with rules that serve to keep the results inside the system so that they can be used in future operations. In the case of addition of two numbers, use is made of either the familiar ''carry'' rule or the addition table, while for multiplication, use is made of the multiplication table to help represent the product of two digits as a two-digit number. These apparently nonalgebraic operations are so dominant that the basic polynomial structure of the numbers is obscured. Thus, the multiplication of polynomials is done by a more intelligent method than that used for numbers. For example, the multiplication of 2057 by 3416 can be carried out as follows:

```
      2 0 5 7
      3 4 1 6
  -------------
  6,1 7,3 3,4 2
    8,5 3,3 7
  -------------
  7 0 2 6 7 1 2
```

Commas separate those pairs of digits that arise from sums of products of pairs of digits taken one each from the original numbers, and having equal significance. Thus, 53, the fourth most significant contribution, is given by

$$53 = 2 \cdot 6 + 0 \cdot 1 + 4 \cdot 5 + 3 \cdot 7$$

This process can be carried out either from right to left or from left to right, and in the latter case, may be terminated when half done if the least significant half on the product is not needed.

In connection with the design and use of automatic computers, in which numbers of a limited size only may be added and multiplied at one time, precautions against overflow in addition, and approximation by rounding in multiplication further complicate the execution of ordinary arithmetic. This creates a system that, strictly speaking, fails to satisfy the axioms of arithmetic. This causes serious difficulties in some problems involving millions of additions and multiplications.

Subtraction introduces negative numbers that may be handled by introducing a special digit called a sign digit with its own rules of combination, or by introducing complementation in which the digits of a number are subtracted from 9, except for the last nonzero digit which is subtracted from 10. Thus to subtract 20570 from 34162, 20570 may be complemented, and 34162 added to it to obtain the desired difference, 13592:

```
. . . 99979430
. . . 00034162
--------------
. . . 00013592
```

Numbers that begin with a run of nines are considered negative in this system. Of course care must be taken to guard against overflow in which a very large positive number might be confused with a very small negative one.

Division is a process that can be carried out only rarely with absolute exactness in the decimal system, the process usually being nonterminating. This introduces the notion of infinite decimal expansions and the more or less theoretical operations with such numbers. In practice, truncation and rounding are used as in $2/3 = .66667$, with consequent errors and departure from the axioms of arithmetic. In this case a quantity like $ab/c$ is not unique but may depend upon the order in which the indicated operations are performed. For complicated and extensive problems involving only the four rational operations of arithmetic, an adequate analysis of the errors involved may be very costly indeed.

Automatic calculation in this simulated real number system may be facilitated by the use of a normalizing coding device called ''floating arithmetic.'' In this system a positive real number is expressed as a truncated decimal between .1 and 1 times the appropriate power of 10. Thus the number $\pi$ on a 10-digit decimal machine could be coded 3141592751. In interpreting this ''word,'' the machine separates the last two digits, 51, and subtracts 50 to get the exponent (possibly negative) of the power of 10 by which the mantissa .31415927 would have to be multiplied to obtain $\pi$ correct to eight decimals. Rules for multiplying and adding in this system are easily formulated. They involve inspection, comparison, and manipulation of the exponents, followed by appropriate shifting right or left of the mantissas, and finally a normalization and reassembly of the answer as a ''floating word.'' The system has the advantage of greater control over numbers of widely varying orders of magnitude. The disadvantages include slower operation, often by a factor of 5 or more, and occasional unpredictable loss of information.

Besides the operation of complementation, there are other nonarithmetic operations with decimal numbers, for example, comparison. Two numbers may be compared for size by a simple inspection of their corresponding digits, beginning from the left and stopping at the first case of inequality. This simple but important property is worth mentioning because comparison is almost impossible in certain other systems. An unusual use of decimal digits is the so-called middle-of-the-square method of generating random numbers. By this method the next 10-digit random number is obtained from the preceding one by squaring the latter and selecting from the square the central 10 digits.

There are many interesting properties of the digits of integer numbers. The simpler ones depend on the theory of congruences. The most familiar fact of this sort is the statement that a number is even if, and only if, its last digit is even. A similar statement is true with respect to divisibility by 5. If a number is diminished by the sum of its digits, the result is a multiple of 9. This fact is the basis for the scheme for checking arithmetic by ''casting out nines,'' at one time known to every school boy. Elevens may be cast out in like manner if the digits are added with alternating signs. Thus, $34162 - (2 - 6 + 1 - 4 + 3) = 34166$, is a multiple of 11. Similarly, grouping the digits by threes, $44535599 - (599 - 535 + 44) = 44535491$ is a multiple of $1001 = 7 \cdot 11 \cdot 13$. This fact is sometimes used to check desk calculator computations by casting out 100s. It is also used to decide quickly whether a given number is divisible by 7, 11, or 13. The number 44535599 is not divisible by 7, 11, or 13 since $599 - 535 + 44 = 108$ is not.

Squares of integers have digital properties. For example, the final digit of a square is either 0, 1, 4, 5, 6, or 9, never 2, 3, 7, or 8. There are only 22 combinations of two digits in which a square can end, and so on. Such facts are sometimes used in finding the factors of a given number by expressing is as a difference of two squares. The rapid recognition of nonsquares is also helpful in many other diophantine problems.

The representation of real numbers requires infinite, that is, unending, decimals. If the digits of such a decimal ultimately become periodic, the decimal is the ratio $P/Q$ of two integers, and conversely. The length of the period is a complicated function of $Q$, depending on the prime factors of numbers of the form $10^n - 1$. If, and only if, $Q$ is of the form $2^a5^b$, the decimal expansion of $P/Q$ terminates. In such cases $P/Q$ has in reality two expansions. Thus $7/5 = 1.4000 \ldots = 1.3999 \ldots$

The great majority of decimals do not become periodic, or in other words, almost all real numbers are irrational. The class of irrational algebraic numbers, such as the square root of 2, that are roots of polynomials with integer coefficients, is almost completely obscured by other real numbers in their decimal representation. There are only a few statements that can be made about the digits of such numbers other than the obvious one of nonperiodicity. For example, if $k$ consecutive zeros occur, then they cannot occur "too soon" for an infinity of $k$. On the other hand, almost all real numbers have perfectly normal decimal expansions in the sense that each digit occurs, on the average, one-tenth of the time, each ordered pair one-hundredth of the time, and so on. Whether $\pi$, $e$, or $\sqrt{2}$ are normal is not known. The totality of all known examples of normal numbers is countable.

Almost everything that has been said so far about the decimal system applies with equal force and very little modification to a general system based on an integer $b > 1$ instead of 10. The fact that people "know" all the powers of 10 but not the powers of 7 or 12 is purely psychological and based on tradition. Beyond the fact that 10 is even, there is little to recommend it as a base. The Babylonians used 60, a large but useful base that is still in vogue for measurement of time and angles. The mathematician J. d'Alembert and many others after him urged the adoption of $b = 12$ with its six divisors. The advent of electronic computers has made a good case for $b = 8$ or some other power of 2. Probably base 8 is used by humans more than any base except 10. For $b > 10$, new characters are needed to represent the extra digits. Although there is no agreement as to which characters to adopt, the modern tendency is to use roman letters because they are easily available on the typewriter. The adoption of a second system brings up the question of translating or converting numbers from one system to the other. Methods for doing this are explained in following sections on binary and octal systems.

**Binary system.** In the binary system every positive integer is the sum of distinct powers of 2 in just one way. Thus $434 = 2^8 + 2^7 + 2^5 + 2^4 + 2^1$, and this expressed by writing 110110010. The digits corresponding to $2^0$, $2^2$, $2^3$, and $2^6$ are zero, since these powers do not occur in 434. The first dozen integers are written as follows:

| | | | | | | | |
|---|---|---|---|---|---|---|---|
| 1 | 1 | 4 | 100 | 7 | 111 | 10 | 1010 |
| 2 | 10 | 5 | 101 | 8 | 1000 | 11 | 1011 |
| 3 | 11 | 6 | 110 | 9 | 1001 | 12 | 1100 |

The great advantage of the binary system lies in the fact that there are only two kinds of binary digits, or "bits," namely 0 and 1. This not only gives a simplified arithmetic but provides a language in which to treat two-valued functions or bistable systems. Among its disadvantages is the fact that the binary system requires nearly three times as many digits to represent a given number as does the familiar decimal system.

Digital computers invariably use the binary system. Computers code the decimal digits into binary form, while the purely binary machines use full binary arithmetic.

The physical representation of binary numbers, or information, is possible in many forms. A row of lights, some on and some off, may be interpreted as a binary number. A set of condensers, some charged and some not, a set of high and low voltages, or a set of magnets with fluxes in one direction or another are electronic examples of media for the processing and retention of data in the binary system. The fact that there are only two states to recognize accounts for the great reliability of such computing systems.

The conversion of decimal, or base 10, integers into the binary system can be done in two ways. First, one may substract from the given integer the highest power of 2 not exceeding this number and record a 1 in the binary position corresponding to this power of 2. The remainder of this subtraction, if not zero, now replaces the original number and the process is repeated until a zero remainder is obtained.

Alternatively, one may divide the given number by 2 and record the remainder, 0 or 1, as the final binary digit. The quotient in this division now replaces the given number and the process is repeated and continued until a quotient of zero is reached. The two methods are illustrated in the case of converting 434 to the binary system:

| | | | |
|---|---|---|---|
| 434 | | 434 | |
| −256 | | 217 | 0 |
| 178 | 1 | 108 | 10 |
| −128 | | 54 | 010 |
| 50 | 11 | 27 | 0010 |
| −32 | | 13 | 10010 |
| 18 | 1101 | 6 | 110010 |
| −16 | | 3 | 0110010 |
| 2 | 11011 | 1 | 10110010 |
| −2 | | 0 | 110110010 |
| 0 | 110110010 | | |

Both processes have obvious inverses for going from the binary system to the decimal system. In the first case, the indicated powers of 2 are simply added together, and in the second case, a sequence of doubling operations is used, followed by the addition of

0 or 1 as specified by the given binary number. For numbers between 0 and 1 similar procedures are available. Either the subtraction of powers of 2 (negative powers) can be continued or the given number can be doubled, followed by subtraction of whichever of the numbers 0 or 1 will make the remainder lie between 0 and 1, and the operation continued with the remainder as before. The reader may wish to test his understanding by verifying that 43.4294 has the binary representation

$$101011.01101101111011010\ldots$$

Arithmetic in the binary system is remarkably simple. For addition, only $1 + 1 = 10$ is needed, while the multiplication table reduces to $1 \cdot 1 = 1$. Examples of addition and multiplication are

$$\begin{array}{rl} 110101 & (53) \\ \underline{11001} & (25) \\ 1001110 & (78) \end{array} \qquad \begin{array}{rl} 1101 & (13) \\ \underline{1011} & (11) \\ 1101 & \\ 1101\phantom{0} & \\ \underline{1101\phantom{000}} & \\ 10001111 & (14) \end{array}$$

Such simple operations are readily performed electronically with extreme rapidity and reliability.

The binary system is useful not only to represent numbers but also to record and process information. In fact the unit of information is a binary digit. For example, given a set $S$ of objects and a property $P$, it is possible to record which obects have the property $P$, and which do not, by assigning a binary position to each object of $S$ and recording there a 1 or 0 according as the property $P$ is, or is not, possessed by the corresponding object. Thus if the objects are the first odd numbers and $P$ is the property of primality, the binary number

$$N = .01110110110100110010\ldots$$

is equivalent to the list of odd primes

$$3, 5, 7, 11, 13, 17, 19, 23, 29, 31, 37, \ldots$$

A binary computer, with its ability to extract and examine a given binary digit, can use this compact method of storing information. The operation $N + N$ replaces $N$, which shifts the digits one place to the left and produces overflow if, and only if, the corresponding number is a prime, can be used in general to select the successive members of $S$ having a property $P$. Other combinatorial processes involving several coded binary numbers can be used to advantage with a binary computer. For example, one can make a search for those objects of $S$ that have a set of specified properties $P_1, P_2, \ldots$.

The binary system is implicit in a number of different arithmetical operations and games. The so-called Russian peasant method of multiplying by doubling and halving is a case in point. To multiply 323 by 146, form two columns of figures (in the decimal system)

| | |
|---|---|
| 146 | 323 |
| 73 | 646 |
| 36 | 1292 |
| 18 | 2584 |
| 9 | 5168 |
| 4 | 10336 |
| 2 | 20672 |
| 1 | 41344 |
| | 47158 |

Each term of the first column is the integer part of half the preceding term. Each term of the second column opposite an even number in the first column is struck out. The sum of the remaining numbers give the desired product 47158. The method works because, in forming the first column, one is, in effect, converting 146 to the binary system.

Another operation in which binary representation is effective is that of raising a given base $B$ to a high integer power. Suppose that

$$n = b_k b_{k-1} \ldots b_2 b_1 b_0$$

is the binary representation of the integer $n$. To compute $B^n$ most efficiently, form recursively the numbers $w_i$, defined by

$$\begin{aligned} w_0 &= B^{b_k} = B \\ w_1 &= B^{b_{k-1}} (w_0)^2 \\ &\ldots\ldots\ldots\ldots \\ w_i &= B^{b_{k-i}} (w_{i-1})^2 \end{aligned}$$

Then $w_k = B^n$. In fact

$$w_k = B^{b_0} (w_{k-1})^2 = B^{b_0 + 2[b_1 + 2(b_2 + \cdots)]}$$

so that the exponent is

$$b_0 + 2b_1 + 2^2 b_2 + \cdots + 2^k b_k = n$$

**Octal system.** To write a number in the octal system, once it has been expressed in the binary system, one merely groups the binary digits by threes, beginning at the binary point and working to the left and right. Thus the decimal number 43.4294 gives

$$(101)(011).(011)(011)(011)(110)(110)(10.)$$

or simply 53.333664, where the last digit should perhaps be 5. On the other hand, decimal to octal conversion can be accomplished directly by either of the two methods that correspond in an obvious way to those given for decimal to binary conversion. Thus, by subtracting appropriate multiples of powers of 8, beginning with the largest possible power,

$$5280 = 1 \cdot 8^4 + 2 \cdot 8^3 + 2 \cdot 8^2 + 4 \cdot 8$$

so that in the octal system there are 12240 feet in a mile. Alternatively, one may divide 5280 by 8, getting 0 as remainder and 660 as quotient. Dividing 660 by 8, 4 and 82 are obtained. Dividing 82 by 8 gives 2 and 10. Dividing 10 by 8 gives 2 and 1. This gives the digits in reverse order.

Octal to decimal conversion may be effected by the use of a convenient table of powers of 8, a sample of which follows:

| $n$ | $8^n$ | $n$ | $8^n$ |
|---|---|---|---|
| 0 | 1 | −1 | .125000 |
| 1 | 8 | −2 | .015625 |
| 2 | 64 | −3 | .001953 |
| 3 | 512 | −4 | .000244 |
| 4 | 4096 | −5 | .000031 |
| 5 | 32768 | −6 | .000004 |

The octal system with its eight digits $0, 1, \ldots, 7$ affords a convenient way of condensing the lengthier display of the binary system. Arithmetic in the octal system resembles the familiar decimal arithmetic. The addition and multiplication tables are as shown:

Addition

| | 0 | 1 | 2 | 3 | 4 | 5 | 6 | 7 |
|---|---|---|---|---|---|---|---|---|
| 0 | 0 | 1 | 2 | 3 | 4 | 5 | 6 | 7 |
| 1 | 1 | 2 | 3 | 4 | 5 | 6 | 7 | 10 |
| 2 | 2 | 3 | 4 | 5 | 6 | 7 | 10 | 11 |
| 3 | 3 | 4 | 5 | 6 | 7 | 10 | 11 | 12 |
| 4 | 4 | 5 | 6 | 7 | 10 | 11 | 12 | 13 |
| 5 | 5 | 6 | 7 | 10 | 11 | 12 | 13 | 14 |
| 6 | 6 | 7 | 10 | 11 | 12 | 13 | 14 | 15 |
| 7 | 7 | 10 | 11 | 12 | 13 | 14 | 15 | 16 |

Multiplication

| | 0 | 1 | 2 | 3 | 4 | 5 | 6 | 7 |
|---|---|---|---|---|---|---|---|---|
| 0 | 0 | 0 | 0 | 0 | 0 | 0 | 0 | 0 |
| 1 | 0 | 1 | 2 | 3 | 4 | 5 | 6 | 7 |
| 2 | 0 | 2 | 4 | 6 | 10 | 12 | 14 | 16 |
| 3 | 0 | 3 | 6 | 11 | 14 | 17 | 22 | 25 |
| 4 | 0 | 4 | 10 | 14 | 20 | 24 | 30 | 34 |
| 5 | 0 | 5 | 12 | 17 | 24 | 31 | 36 | 43 |
| 6 | 0 | 6 | 14 | 22 | 30 | 36 | 44 | 52 |
| 7 | 0 | 7 | 16 | 25 | 34 | 43 | 52 | 61 |

Examples of addition and multiplication in the octal system are

$$\begin{array}{r} 4375 \\ \underline{3704} \\ 10301 \end{array} \qquad \begin{array}{r} 5734 \\ \underline{16} \\ 43450 \\ \underline{5734\phantom{0}} \\ 123010 \end{array}$$

Octal arithmetic can be checked by "casting out sevens" (instead of nines) by adding the digits. Thus for the addition problem above,

$$4375 \equiv 4 + 3 + 7 + 5 = 23$$
$$\equiv 2 + 3 = 5 \pmod 7$$
$$3704 \equiv 3 + 7 + 0 + 4 = 16$$
$$\equiv 1 + 6 \equiv 0 \pmod 7$$
$$10301 \equiv 1 + 3 + 1 = 5 \pmod 7$$

Checking by casting out nines involves taking the octal digits with alternating signs. Thus,

$$4375 \equiv 5 - 7 + 3 - 4 = -3 \equiv 6 \pmod 9$$
$$3704 \equiv 4 - 0 + 7 - 3 = 8 \pmod 9$$
$$10301 \equiv 1 + 3 + 1 = 5 \equiv 6 + 8 \pmod 9$$

The octal system requires only 10% more digits than the decimal system to represent the same amount of information. Some computing systems use base 16, in which case binary information is handled in sets of four bits. This system is more compact than the decimal system, 100 hexodecimals being equivalent to 120 decimals, but it requires a multiplication table with nearly three times as many entries.

Computing systems of binary type have subroutines for the conversion of any kind of decimal information into binary information during input, and vice versa during output, so that a facility in octal arithmetic is needed only rarely during checking and testing of a new problem. *See* Digital computer; Numerical analysis.

*Derrick H. Lehmer*

**Bibliography.** R. H. Bruck, *Survey of Binary Systems,* 3d ed., 1971; T. Danzig, *Number, the Language of Science,* 4th ed., 1967; C. Reid, *From Zero to Infinity,* 2d ed., 1960; H. Schmid, *Decimal Computation,* 1974, reprint 1983; E. Sondheimer and A. Rogerson, *Numbers and Infinity: An Historical Account of Mathematical Concepts,* 1981.

## Numerical analysis

The development and analysis of computational methods (and ultimately of program packages) for the minimization and the approximation of functions, and for the approximate solution of equations, such as linear or nonlinear (systems of) equations and differential or integral equations. Originally part of every mathematician's work, the subject is now often taught in computer science departments because of the tremendous impact which computers have had on its development. Research focuses mainly on the numerical solution of (nonlinear) partial differential equations and the minimization of functions. *See* Computer.

Numerical analysis is needed because answers provided by mathematical analysis are usually symbolic and not numeric; they are often given implicitly only, as the solution of some equation, or they are given by some limit process. A further complication is provided by the rounding error which usually contaminates every step in a calculation (because of the fixed finite number of digits carried).

Even in the absence of rounding error, few numerical answers can be obtained exactly. Among these are (1) the value of a piecewise rational function at a point and (2) the solution of a (solvable) linear system of equations, both of which can be produced in a finite number of arithmetic steps. Approximate answers to all other problems are obtained by solving the first few in a sequence of such finitely solvable problems. A typical example is provided by Newton's method: A solution $c$ to a nonlinear equation $f(c) = 0$ is found as the limit $c = \lim_{n\to\infty} x_n$, with $x_{n+1}$ a solution to the linear equation $f(x_n) + f'(x_n)(x_{n+1} - x_n) = 0$, that is, $x_{n+1} = x_n - f(x_n)/f'(x_n)$, $n = 0, 1, 2, \ldots$ . Of course, only the first few terms in this sequence $x_0, x_1, x_2, \ldots$ can ever be calculated, and thus one must face the question of when to break off such a solution process and how to gauge the accuracy of the current approximation. The difficulty in the mathematical treatment of these questions is examplified by the fact that the limit of a sequence is completely independent of its first few terms.

In the presence of rounding error, an otherwise satisfactory computational process may become useless, because of the amplification of rounding errors. A computational process is called stable to the extent that its results are not spoiled by rounding errors. The extended calculations involving millions of arithmetic steps now possible on computers have made the stability of a computational process a prime consideration.

**Interpolation and approximation.** Polynomial interpolation provides a polynomial $p$ of degree $n$ or less which uniquely matches given function values $f(x_0), \ldots, f(x_n)$ at corresponding distinct points $x_0, \ldots, x_n$. The interpolating polynomial $p$ is used in place of $f$, for example in evaluation, integration, differentiation, and zero finding. Accuracy of the interpolating polynomial depends strongly on the placement of the interpolation points, and usually degrades drastically as one moves away from the interval containing these points (that is, in case of extrapolation).

When many interpolation points (more than 5 or 10) are to be used, it is often much more efficient to use instead a piecewise polynomial interpolant or spline. Suppose the interpolation points above are ordered, $x_0 < x_1 < \ldots < x_n$. Then the cubic spline interpolant to the above data, for example, consists of cubic polynomial pieces, with the $i$th piece defining the interpolant on the interval $[x_{i-1}, x_i]$ and so matched with its neighboring piece or pieces that the resulting function not only matches the given function values (hence is continuous) but also has a continuous first and second derivative.

Interpolation is but one way to determine an approximant. In full generality, approximation involves several choices: (1) a set $P$ of possible approximants, (2) a criterion for selecting from $P$ a particular approximant, and (3) a way to measure the approximation error, that is, the difference between the function $f$ to be approximated and the approximant $p$, in order to judge the quality of approximation. Much studied examples for $P$ are the polynomials of degree $n$ or less, piecewise polynomials of a given degree with prescribed breakpoints, and rational functions of given numerator and denominator degrees. The distance between $f$ and $p$ is usually measured by a norm, such as the $L_2$ norm $(\int |f(x) - p(x)|^2 dx)^{1/2}$ or the uniform norm $\sup_x |f(x) - p(x)|$. Once choices 1 and 3 are made, one often settles 2 by asking for a best approximation to $f$ from $P$, that is, for an element of $P$ whose distance from $f$ is a small as possible. Questions of existence, uniqueness, characterization, and numerical construction of such best approximants have been studied extensively for various choices of $P$ and the distance measure. If $P$ is linear, that is, if $P$ consists of all linear combinations

$$\sum_{i=1}^{n} a_i p_i$$

of certain fixed functions $p_1, \ldots, p_n$, then determination of a best approximation in the $L_2$ norm is particularly easy, since it involves nothing more than the solution of $n$ simultaneous linear equations.

**Solution of linear systems.** Solving a linear system of equations is probably the most frequently confronted computational task. It is handled either by a direct method, that is, a method which obtains the exact answer in a finite number of steps, or by an iterative method, or by a judicious combination of both. Analysis of the effectiveness of possible methods has led to a workable basis for selecting the one which best fits a partcular situation.

***Direct methods.*** Cramer's rule is a well-known direct method for solving a system of $n$ linear equations in $n$ unknowns, but it is much less efficient than the method of choice, elimination. In this procedure the first unknown is eliminated from each equation but the first by subtracting from that equation an appropriate multiple of the first equation. The resulting system of $n - 1$ equations in the remaining $n - 1$ unknowns is similarly reduced, and the process is repeated until one equation in one unknown remains. The solution for the entire system is then found by back-substitution, that is, by solving for that one unknown in that last equation, then returning to the next-to-last equation which at the next-to-last step of the elimination involved the final unknown (now known) and one other, and solving for that second-to-last unknown, and so on.

This process may break down for two reasons: (1) when it comes time to eliminate the $k$th unknown, its coefficient in the $k$th equation may be zero, and hence the equation cannot be used to eliminate the $k$th unknown from equations $k + 1, \ldots, n$; and (2) the process may be very unstable. Both difficulties can be overcome by pivoting, in which one elects, at the beginning of the $k$th step, a suitable equation from among equations $k, \ldots, n$, interchanges it with the $k$th equation, and then proceeds as before. In this way the first difficulty may be avoided provided that the system has one and only one solution. Further, with an appropriate pivoting strategy, the second difficulty may be avoided provided that the linear system is stable. Explicitly, it can be shown that, with the appropriate pivoting strategy, the solution computed in the presence of rounding errors is the exact solution of a linear system whose coefficients usually differ by not much more than roundoff from the given ones. The computed solution is therefore close to the exact solution provided that such small changes in the given system do not change its solution by much. A rough but common measure of the stability of a linear system is the condition of its coefficient matrix. This number is computed as the product of the norm of the matrix and of its inverse. The reciprocal of the condition therefore provides an indication of how close the matrix is to being noninvertible or singular.

***Iterative methods.*** The direct methods described above require a number of operations which increases with the cube of the number of unknowns. Some types of problems arise wherein the matrix of coefficients is sparse, but the unknowns may number several thousand; for these, direct methods are prohibitive in computer time required. One frequent source of such problems is the finite difference treatment of partial differential equations (discussed below).. A significant literature of iterative methods exploiting the special properties of such equations is available. For certain restricted classes of difference equations, the error in an initial iterate can be guaranteed to be reduced by a fixed factor, using a number of computations that is proportional to $n \log n$, where $n$ is the number of unknowns. Since direct methods require work proportional to $n^3$, it is not surprising that as $n$ becomes large, iterative methods are studied rather closely as practical alternatives.

The most straightforward iterative procedure is the method of substitution, sometimes called the method of simultaneous displacements. If the equations for $i = 1, \ldots, n$ are shown in Eq. (1), then the $r$th

$$\sum_{j=1}^{n} a_{ij} x_j = b_i \tag{1}$$

iterate is computed from the $r - 1$st by solving the trivial equations for $x_i^{(r)}$ shown in Eq. (2) for $i =$

$$\sum_{j \neq i} a_{ij} x_j^{(r-1)} + a_{ii} x_i^{(r)} = b_i \tag{2}$$

$1, \ldots, n$, where the elements $x_i^{(0)}$ are chosen arbitrarily. If for $i = 1, \ldots, n$, the inequality

$$\sum_{j \neq i} |a_{ij}| \leq |a_{ii}|$$

holds for some $i$, and the matrix is irreducible, then $x_i^{(r)} \underset{r}{\rightarrow} x_i$ is the solution. For a matrix to be irreducible, the underlying simultaneous system must not have any subset of unknowns which can be solved for independently of the others. For practical problems for which convergence occurs, analysis shows the expected number of iterations required to guarantee a fixed error reduction to be proportional to the number of unknowns. Thus the total work is proportional to $n^2$.

The foregoing procedure may be improved several ways. The Gauss-Seidel method, sometimes called the method of successive displacements, represents the same idea but uses the latest available values. Equation (3) is solved for $i = 1, \ldots, n$. The

$$\sum_{j<i} a_{ij}x_j^{(r)} \; a_{ii}x_i^{(r)} + \sum_{j>i} a_{ij}x_j^{(r-1)} = b_i \qquad (3)$$

Gauss-Seidel method converges for the conditions given above for the substitution method and is readily shown to converge more rapidly.

Further improvements in this idea lead to the method of successive overrelaxation. This can be thought of as calculating the correction associated with the Gauss-Seidel method and overcorrecting by a factor $\omega$. Equation (4) is first solved for $y$. Then

$$\sum_{j<i} a_{ij}x_j^{(r)} + a_{ii}y + \sum_{j>i} a_{ij}x_j^{(r-1)} = b_i \qquad (4)$$

$x_i^{(r)} = x_i^{(r-1)} + \omega(y - x_i^{(r-1)})$. Clearly, choosing $\omega = 1$ yields the Gauss-Seidel method. For problems of interest arising from elliptic difference equations, there exists an optimum $\omega$ which guarantees a fixed error reduction in a number of iterations proportional to $n^{1/2}$, and thus in total work proportional to $n^{3/2}$.

A number of other iterative techniques for systems with sparse matrices have been studied. Primarily they depend upon approximating the given matrix with one such that the resulting equations can be solved directly with an amount of work proportional to $n$. For a quite large class of finite difference equations of interest, the computing work to guarantee a fixed error reduction is proportional to $n^{5/4}$. The work requirement proportional only to $n \log n$ quoted earlier applies to a moderately restricted subset.

***Overdetermined linear systems.*** Often an overdetermined linear system has to be solved. This happens, for example, if one wishes to fit the model

$$p(x) = \sum_{j=1}^{n} a_j p_j$$

to observations $(x_i, y_i)_{i=1}^{m}$ with $n < m$. Here one would like to determine the coefficient vector $\mathbf{a} = (a_1, \ldots, a_n)^T$ so that $p(x_i) = y_i$, $i = 1, \ldots, m$. In matrix notation, one wants $A\mathbf{a} = \mathbf{y}$, with $A$ the $m$-by-$n$ matrix $[p_j(x_i)]$. If $n < m$, one cannot expect a solution, and it is then quite common to determine $\mathbf{a}$ instead by least squares, that is, so as to minimize the "distance" $(\mathbf{y} - A\mathbf{a})^T(\mathbf{y} - A\mathbf{a})$ between the vectors $\mathbf{y}$ and $A\mathbf{a}$. This leads to the so-called normal equations $A^TA\mathbf{a} = A^T\mathbf{y}$ for the coefficient vector $\mathbf{a}$. But unless the "basis functions" $p_1, \ldots, p_n$ are chosen very carefully, the condition of the matrix $A^TA$ may be very bad, making the elimination process outlined above overly sensitive to rounding errors. It is much better to make use of a so-called orthogonal decomposition for $A$.

Assume first that $A$ has full rank (which is the same thing as assuming that the only linear combination $P$ of the functions $P_1, \ldots, p_n$ which vanishes at all the points $x_1, \ldots, x_m$ is the trivial one, the one with all coefficients zero). Then $A$ has a $QR$ decomposition, that is, $A = QR$, with $Q$ an orthogonal matrix (that is, $Q^T = Q^{-1}$), and $R$ an $m$-by-$n$ matrix whose first $n$ rows contain an invertible upper triangular matrix $R_1$, while its remaining $m$-$n$ rows are identically zero. Then $(\mathbf{y} - A\mathbf{a})^T \cdot (\mathbf{y} - A\mathbf{a}) = (Q^T\mathbf{y} - R\mathbf{a})^T(Q^T\mathbf{y} - R\mathbf{a})$ and, since the last $m$-$n$ entries of $2R\mathbf{a}$ are zero, this is minimized when the first $n$ entries of $R\mathbf{a}$ agree with those of $Q^T\mathbf{y}$, that is, $R_1\mathbf{a} = [(Q^T\mathbf{y})(i)]_1^n$. Since $R_1$ is upper triangular, this system is easily solved by back-substitution, as outlined above. The $QR$ decomposition for $A$ can be obtained stably with the aid of Householder transformations, that is, matrices of the simple form $H = I - (2/\mathbf{u}^T)\mathbf{u}\mathbf{u}^T$, which are easily seen to be orthogonal and even self-inverse, that is, $H^{-1} = H$. In the first step of the process, $A$ is premultiplied by a Householder matrix $H_1$ with $\mathbf{u}$ so chosen that the first column of $H_1A$ has zeros in rows $2, \ldots, m$. In the next step, one premultiplies $H_1A$ by $H_2$ with $\mathbf{u}$ so chosen that $H_2H_1A$ retains its zeros in column 1 and has also zeroes in column 2 in rows $3, \ldots, m$. After $n - 1$ such steps, the matrix $R := H_{n-1} \ldots H_1A$ is reached with zeros below its main diagonal, and so $A = QR$ with $Q := H_1 \ldots H_{n-1}$.

The situation is somewhat more complicated when $A$ fails to have full rank or when its rank cannot be easily determined. In that case, one may want to make use of a singular value decomposition for $A$, which means that one writes $A$ as the product $USV$, where both $U$ and $V$ are orthogonal matrices and $S = (s_{ij})$ is an $m$-by-$n$ matrix that may be loosely termed "diagonal," that is, $s_{ij} = 0$ for $i \neq j$. Calculation of such a decomposition is more expensive than that of a $QR$ decomposition, but the singular value decomposition provides much more information about $A$. For example, the diagonal elements of $S$, the so-called singular values of $A$, give precise information about how close $A$ is to a matrix of given rank, and hence make it possible to gauge the effect of errors in the entries of $A$ on the rank of $A$.

**Differential equations.** Classical methods yield practical results only for a moderately restricted class of ordinary differential equations, a somewhat more restricted class of systems of ordinary differential equations, and a very small number of partial differential equations. The power of numerical methods is enormous here, for in quite broad classes of practical problems relatively straightforward procedures are guaranteed to yield numerical results, whose quality is predictable.

***Ordinary differential equations.*** The simplest system is the initial value problem in a single unknown, $y' = f(x,y)$, and $y(a) = \eta$, where $y'$ means $dy/dx$, and $f$ is continuous in $x$ and satisfies a Lipschitz condition in $y$; that is, there exists a constant $K$ such that for all $x$ and $y$ of interest, $|f(x,y) - f(x,z)| \leq K|y - z|$. The problem is well posed and has a unique solution.

The Euler method is as follows: $y_0 = \eta$, Eq. (5)

$$y_{i+1} = y_i + hf(x_i, y_i) \qquad (5)$$

holds, and $i = 0, 1, 2, \ldots, (b - a)/h$. Here $h$ is a small positive constant, and $x_i = a + ih$. Analysis shows that as $h \to 0$, there exists a constant $C$ such that $|y_k - y(x_k)| \leq Ch$, where $y(x_k)$ is the value of the unique solution at $x_k$, and $a \leq x_k \leq b$. This almost trivial formulation of a numerical procedure thus guarantees an approximation to the exact solution to the problem that is arbitrarily good if $h$ is sufficiently small, and it is easy to implement. A trivial extension of this idea is given by the method of Heun, Eq. (6).

$$y_{i+1} = y_i + 1/2h[(f(x_i,y_i) + f(x_i + h, y_i + hf(x_i,y_i))] \quad (6)$$

The method of Heun similarly is guaranteed to approximate the desired solution arbitrarily well since there exists another constant $C_1$ such that the $\{y_i\}$ satisfy relation (7). This is clearly asymptotically better

$$|y_k - y(x_k)| \leq C_1h^2 \quad (7)$$

than the method of Euler. It is readily found to be practically superior for most problems. Further improvement of this type is offered by the classical Runge-Kutta method, Eq. (8), where $\phi(x,y,h) =$

$$y_{i+1} = y_i + h\phi(x_i,y_i,h) \quad (8)$$

$\frac{1}{6}[k_1 + 2k_2 + 2k_3 + k_4]$, and $k_1 = f(x,y)$, $k_2 = f(x + h/2, y + hk_1/2)$, $k_3 = f(x + h/2, y + hk_2/2)$, and $k_4 = f(x + h, y + hk_3)$. For this method there exists a constant $C_2$ such that $|y_k - y(x_k)| \leq C_2h^4$.

The foregoing methods are called single-step since only $y_i$ is involved in the computation of $y_{i+1}$. The single-step methods yielding the better results typically require several evaluations of the function $f$ per step. By contrast, multistep methods typically achieve high exponents on $h$ in the error bounds without more than one evaluation of $f$ per step. Multistep methods require use of $y_{i-\alpha}$ or $f(x_{i-\alpha},y_{i-\alpha})$ or both for $\alpha = 0, 1, \ldots, j$ to compute $y_{i+1}$. Typical is the Adams-Bashforth method for $j = 5$, Eq. (9).

$$y_{i+1} = y_i + \frac{h}{1440}[4277\,f(x_i,y_i) - 7923\,f(x_{i-1},y_{i-1}) + 9982\,f(x_{i-2},y_{i-2}) - 7298\,f(x_{i-3},y_{i-3}) + 2277\,f(x_{i-4},y_{i-4}) - 475\,f(x_{i-5},y_{i-5})] \quad (9)$$

Analysis shows the solution of this Adams-Bashforth procedure to satisfy relation (10) for some con-

$$|y_k - y(x_k)| \leq C_3h^6 \quad (10)$$

stant $C_3$. A large number of valuable multistep methods have been studied. If $f$ is nontrivial to evaluate, the multistep methods are less work to compute than the single-step methods for comparable accuracy. The chief difficulty of multistep methods is that they require $j$ starting values and, therefore, cannot be used from the outset in a computation.

***Partial differential equations.*** Methods used for partial differential equations differ significantly, depending on the type of equation. Typically, parabolic equations are considered for which the prototype is the heat flow equation, Eq. (11), with $u(x,0)$ given on

$$\frac{\partial^2 u}{\partial x^2} = \frac{\partial u}{\partial t} \quad (11)$$

$x\epsilon[0,1]$, say, and $u(0,t)$ and $u(1,t)$ given for $t > 0$. A typical finite difference scheme is shown in Eq. (12),

$$(w_{i,n})_{x\bar{x}} = \frac{w_{i,n+1} - w_{in}}{k} \quad (12)$$

where $i - 1, \ldots, 1/h - 1$, $w_{0,n} = u(0,t_n)$, and $w_{1/h,n} = u(1,t_n)$, with $(w_i)_x = (w_{i+1} - w_i)/h$, $(w_i)_{\bar{x}} = (w_{i-1})_x$, and $w_{i,n}$ is the function defined at $x_i = ih$, $t_n = nk$. Analysis shows that as $h,k\rightarrow 0$, the solution $w_{i,n}$ satisfies $|w_{i,n} - u(x_i,t_n)| < C(h^2 + k)$ for some constant $C$ if $k/h^2 \leq 1/2$, but for $k/h^2$ somewhat larger than $1/2$, $w_{i,n}$ bears no relation at all to $u(x_i,t_n)$.

The restriction $k/h^2 \leq 1/2$ can be removed by using the implicit difference equation, Eq. (13), but now

$$(w_{i,n+1})_{x\bar{x}} = \frac{w_{i,n+1} - w_{in}}{k} \quad (13)$$

simultaneous equations must be solved for $w_{i,n+1}$ each step. The inequality, $|w_{i,n} - u(x_i,t_n)| < C(h^2 + k)$, still holds for some constant $C$. An improved implicit formulation is the Crank-Nicolson equation, Eq. (14).

$$1/2(w_{i,n} + w_{i,n+1})_{x\bar{x}} = \frac{w_{i,n+1} - w_{i,n}}{k} \quad (14)$$

As $h,k \rightarrow 0$, solutions satisfy relation (15) for some constant $C$; again $h/k$ is unrestricted. Such techniques can readily extend to several space variables and to much more general equations. The work estimates given above for iterative solution of simultaneous equations, such as Eq. (14), apply for two-space variables.

$$|w_{i,n} - u(x_i,t_n)| < C(h^2 + k^2) \quad (15)$$

Work using variational techniques to approximate the solution of parabolic and elliptic equations has been most fruitful for broad classes of nonlinear problems. The technique reduces partial differential equations to systems of ordinary differential equations. Analysis shows that solutions obtained approximate the desired solution, as within a constant multiple of the best that can be achieved within the subspace of the basis functions used. Practical utilization suggests this to be the direction for most likely future developments in the treatment of partial differential systems.

*Carl de Boor*

***Bibliography.*** P. G. Ciarlet, *The Finite Element Method for Elliptic Problems*, 1978; S. Conte and C. de Boor, *Elementary Numerical Analysis*, 3d ed., 1980; L. W. Johnson and R. D. Riess, *Numerical Analysis*, 1982; M. J. Maron, *Applied Numerical Analysis*, 1982; J. L. Morris, *Computational Methods in Elementary Numerical Analysis*, 1983; J. M. Ortega and W. C. Rheinboldt, *Iterative Solution of Nonlinear Equations in Several Variables*, 1970; R. D. Richtmyer and K. W. Morton, *Difference Methods for Initial-Value Problems*, 2d ed., 1967; J. H. Wilkinson, *The Algebraic Eigenvalue Problem*, 1965.

## Numerical indicator tube

Any electron tube capable of visually displaying numerical figures. Some varieties also display alphabetical characters and commonly used symbols. In many electronic circuits and equipments it is desirable to indicate numbers or characters. Such a tube can be one of a set which displays, for instance, the magnitude and polarity of voltage in digital form. This is similar to electrical clocks which display the time in numerical form.

A simple and extensively used form is a cold-cathode gas tube in which there is a series of cathodes which light up because of the cathode glow surrounds any cathode in a gas discharge (see **illus.**). A common anode is used. The cathodes are shaped to correspond to the different numerical digits, zero through nine. These cathodes may also be shaped to form alphabetical characters of other symbols, such as (+) and (−). The desired cathode is selected by any suitable switching scheme. The cathodes are made by photoetching the desired shape from a suitable metal. They are insulated and stacked one above the other, so that any particular number can be read when the

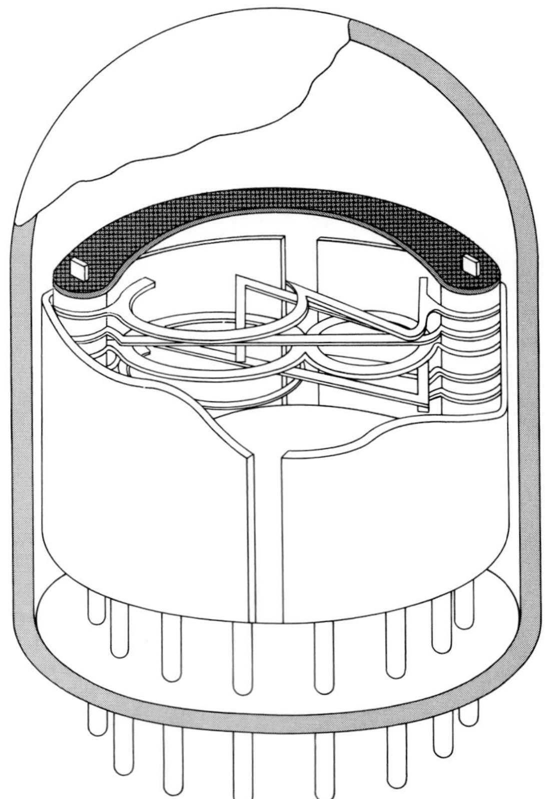

Cold-cathode gas-type numerical indicator tube.

corresponding cathode is energized. SEE ELECTRICAL CONDUCTION IN GASES; GAS TUBE.

A cold-cathode gas tube is shown in the illustration. The metal cup surrounding the cathodes is used as the common anode and also provides a dark background to minimize reflections from the tube base and to increase the viewing contrast. This type of indicator tube is bright enough to be used in daylight, although there are sometimes disturbing reflections on the glass envelope. These reflections can be overcome by placing a polaroid screen in front of the tubes.

These devices have declined in use with the growth of other display technologies such as liquid crystals and light-emitting diodes. SEE ELECTRONIC DISPLAY; LIGHT-EMITTING DIODE; LIQUID CRYSTALS.

*Roger W. Wolfe*

## Octal number system

A system in which numbers are represented as linear combinations of powers of 8. Below is shown the relationship between the octal system and the decimal system.

| *Decimal notation* | *Octal notation* |
|---|---|
| $12 = 8^1 + 4$ | $= 14$ |
| $31 = 3 \times 8^1 + 7$ | $= 37$ |
| $123 = 1 \times 8^2 + 7 \times 8^1 + 3$ | $= 173$ |

The octal system has come into importance because of its value in computer applications. SEE NUMBER SYSTEMS.

*Marvin Yelles*

## Ohmmeter

A small, portable instrument using a microammeter and associated circuitry to measure resistance by the voltmeter-ammeter method. Additional circuits are usually included to measure alternating and direct-current volts and amperes, and the instrument is called a volt-ohm-milliammeter, or multimeter (**Fig. 1**). SEE RESISTANCE MEASUREMENT.

A typical resistance-measuring circuit is shown in **Fig. 2***a*. Figure 2*b* shows a simplified schematic diagram of the $\times 100$ range of the circuit. In operation, the instrument is first adjusted for full-scale deflection of the meter with the measuring leads shorted. When the unknown resistance is added to the circuit, the current through the meter decreases according to the equation shown below. The various resistances are

$$R_x = \left[\frac{I_{RO}}{I_{RX}} - 1\right]\left[\frac{R_M R_s}{R_M + R_s} + R_p\right]$$

identified in Fig. 2*b*. $I_{RO}$ is the current required for full-scale deflection of the meter when $R_x$ is 0, and $I_{RX}$ is the meter current with the unknown resistor $R_x$ in the circuit. The meter deflects according to the value of $I_{RX}$.

Since $R_x$ is a function if $1/I_{RX}$, the scale, calibrated in resistance units, is a reciprocal function. Full-scale deflection of the meter always corresponds to zero ohms, and no deflection indicates an open circuit.

**Fig. 1. Volt-ohm-milliammeter. (*Simpson Electric Co.*)**

The scale relation between these two points is arbitrary and is governed by the choice of one other scale point, such as the resistance for half-scale current. The scale of the instrument in Fig. 1 is based on a half-scale resistance of about 12 ohms. In common with any measuring equipment having an error stated in terms of full-scale deflection, the absolute error

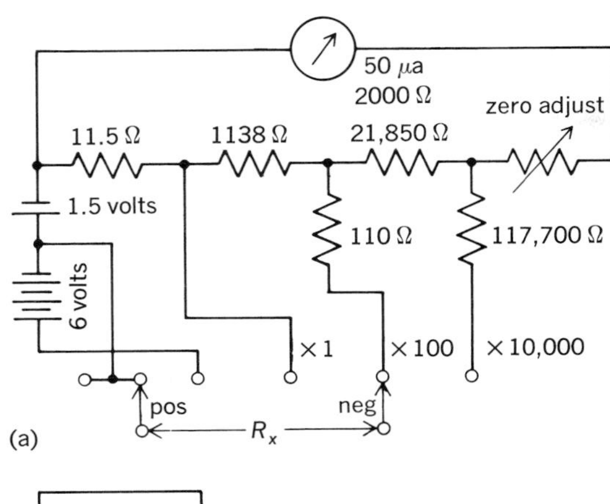


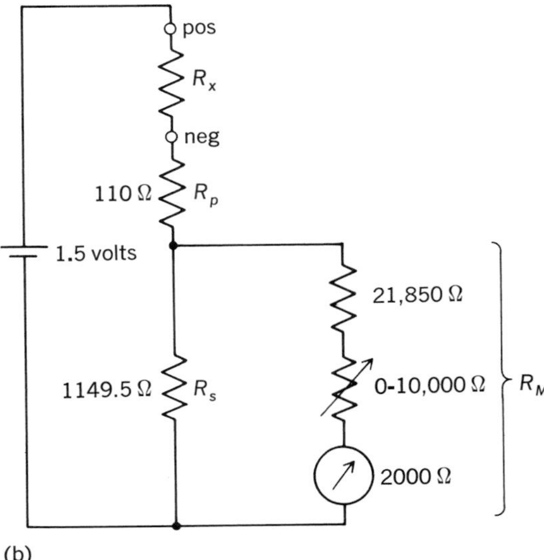


**Fig. 2. Ohmmeter circuits. (a) Typical basic circuit. (b) Simplified circuit of the ×100 range.**

(error of the reading) is large for small deflections.

Voltage and current ranges for this equipment are obtained in the usual fashion with resistance multipliers for extended voltage ranges, current shunts for multiple current ranges, and a copper-oxide rectifier for alternating-current operation. A vacuum-tube voltmeter (VTVM) usually incorporates a resistance-measuring circuit for convenience. SEE AMMETER; SAMPLING VOLTMETER; VACUUM-TUBE VOLTMETER; VOLTMETER.

*Charles E. Applegate*

## Ohm's law

The direct current flowing in an electrical circuit is directly proportional to the voltage applied to the circuit. The constant of proportionality $R$, called the electrical resistance, is given by $V = RI$, in which $V$ is the applied voltage and $I$ is the current. This relationship was first described by Georg Simon Ohm in 1827 and was based on his experiments with metallic conductors. Since that time numerous deviations from this simple, linear relationship have been discovered. SEE ELECTRICAL RESISTANCE; RESISTANCE MEASUREMENT; SEMICONDUCTOR.

*Charles E. Applegate*

## Open circuit

A condition in an electric circuit in which there is no path for current between two points; examples are a broken wire and a switch in the open, or off, position. SEE CIRCUIT (ELECTRICITY).

Open-circuit voltage is the potential difference between two points in a circuit when a branch (current path) between the points is open-circuited. Open-circuit voltage is measured by a voltmeter which has a very high resistance (theoretically infinite), such as a vacuum-tube voltmeter.

*Clarence F. Goodheart*

## Operating system

A set of programs to control and coordinate the operation of hardware and software in a computer system. Operating systems typically consist of two sets of programs. Control programs direct the execution of user application programs and support programs. They also supervise the location, storage, and retrieval of data (including input and output to various peripherals) and allocate the resources of the computer system to the different tasks entered into the system. Processing programs include applications programs; utility programs; system diagnostics; and language translators, such as compilers and interpreters.

There are five general types of operating systems:

1. Real-time. Processing functions are executed within narrow time limits, as in updating a data bank or reading and evaluating input from a sensor or transducer. SEE REAL-TIME SYSTEMS.

2. Serial or batch. Tasks or jobs are run one at a time according to a schedule determined by the operating system.

3. Multiprogramming. Two or more jobs may be run concurrently in the same system.

4. Time sharing. Multiple users have simultaneous access to the system. A user is not aware that others have access to the system; the impression is that of exclusive use of the system. SEE MULTIACCESS COMPUTER.

5. Multiprocessing. Two or more processing units are coupled together to execute a single job. SEE MULTIPROCESSING.

**Control programs.** The control program has an executive function and a system resource allocation and management function. The executive function arranges the computer system environment necessary to run a job. One task of the executive function is to schedule the jobs. Jobs may be scheduled sequentially, but many operating systems permit scheduling on the basis of assigned priorities. The executive function directs communications between the computer system and human operator, and communications between the processor and various input and output peripherals.

The system resource allocation and management function is sometimes referred to as the supervisor. A key task of the supervisor is to allocate, monitor, and control the computer system's main memory space. The supervisor controls and synchronizes the tasks necessary to execute the instructions in a program as well. The supervisor also manages data within the system. For example, it allocates space on disks for data storage. It is responsible for constructing and developing data structures, and it maintains directories of data files within the system.

Modern supervisors are increasingly sensitive to the problem of data security, particularly unauthorized access to data files. The most common security device is the password, a code which must be correctly entered into a computer system before a user can have access to a computer system's data files. The supervisor may also record all users of a system along with the data files accessed and the amount of time each user spent using the system. *See Computer security*.

**Processing programs.** Processing programs include applications developed for use with a computer system, and translators which convert high-level languages such as COBOL, FORTRAN, and BASIC into the assembly language used by the processor. *See Digital computer programming; Programming languages*.

Several software development and diagnostic support aids are also part of the processing programs. A common feature is the presence of several debugging aids to assist in the proper development and use of applications programs. Commonly, these aids will indicate why a program failed to execute properly. These aids give an output to the user, known as a diagnostic. Most systems also include several utilities, which permit the user to accomplish such tasks as transferring data from one storage medium to another or duplicating storage disks.

**Time-sharing applications.** Much effort in recent years has been directed toward the development of operating systems for time sharing and multiprogramming tasks. Many commercial companies have been organized which sell access time to a large computer system on a time-sharing basis. The customers have a terminal at their place of business and are linked to the computer by telephone lines. Customers are billed according to the amount of time they use the computer. Such systems require a supervisor which restricts access to customers and adequately protects against unauthorized or fraudulent use. Large commercial users of computers need multiprogramming capability, which allows jobs to be run according to priority. Some multiprogramming systems permit programs to be run during off-peak hours. This allows a computer system to be utilized around the clock, giving more efficient use of computing resources.

**Microcomputer systems.** The growth of microcomputers has resulted in the development of operating systems specifically designed for them. Perhaps the most widely used is CP/M (control program for microprocessors), an operating system developed by Digital Research Corporation. CP/M is used with 8-bit microprocessor microcomputers. Another system is Unix, developed by Bell Labs for use with the C programming language. Unix has been adopted for several 16-bit microprocessor microcomputers.

Work has been done on the development of multiprocessing operating systems for microcomputers. In these systems, for example, a 16-bit microprocessor could be used for such tasks as actual computation and an 8-bit microprocessor could be used for such tasks as input and output. The essential task of these operating systems is to coordinate the activities of the two microprocessors. This task is often complicated by the fact that various microprocessors operate at different speeds. However, interest in multiprocessing operating systems for microcomputers can be expected to spread since multiple microprocessors can perform certain tasks more effectively than single microprocessors. *See Digital computer; Microcomputer; Microprocessor*.

*Harry L. Helms*

**Bibliography.** G. M. Wiederhold, *Database Design*, 2d ed., 1982.

## Operations research

The application of scientific methods and techniques to decision-making problems. A decision-making problem occurs where there are two or more alternative courses of action, each of which leads to a different and sometimes unknown end result (**Fig. 1**). Operations research is also used to maximize the utility of limited resources. The objective is to select the best alternative, that is, the one leading to the best result. Often, however, is is not simply a matter of searching a table, as there may literally be an infinity of outcomes. More intelligent means are needed to seek out the prime result.

To put these definitions into perspective, the following analogy might be used. In mathematics, when solving a set of simultaneous linear equations, one states that if there are seven unknowns, there must be seven equations. If they are independent and consistent and if it exists, a unique solution to the problem is found. In operations research there may be figuratively "seven unknowns and four equations." There may exist a solution space with many feasible solutions which satisfy the equations. Operations research is concerned with establishing the best solution. To do so, some measure of merit, some objective function, must be prescribed.

There are several terms associated with the subject matter of this program: operations research, management science, systems analysis, operations analysis, and so forth. While there are subtle differences and distinctions, the terms can be considered nearly synonymous.

The field can be divided into two general areas with regard to methods. These are those that can be termed mathematical programming and those associated with stochastic processes. While computers are heavily used to solve problems, the term programming should not be considered in that sense, but rather in the general sense of organizing and planning. Also, the tools of probability and statistics are used to a considerable extent in working with stochastic processes. These

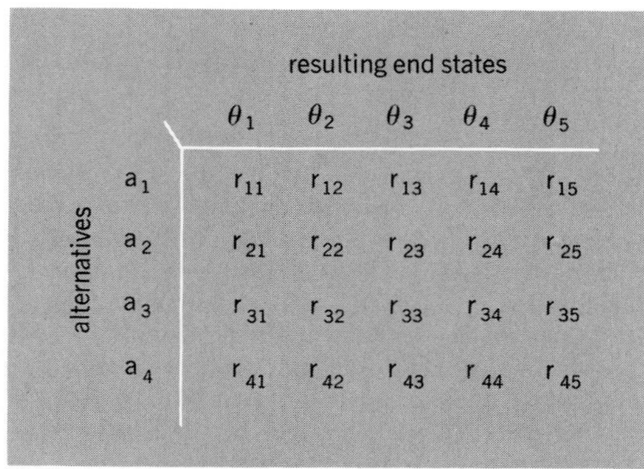


**Fig. 1. End states for alternatives in a decision-making process.**

areas will be explored in greater detail in a later section. With regard to areas of applications, there are very few fields where the methods of operations research have not been tried and proved successful. Following is a brief history of the field, and then the general approach to solving problems.

### History

While almost every art and every science can reach back into antiquity for its roots, operations research can reach back less than a century to find its beginnings. During World War I, F. W. Lancaster developed models of combat superiority and victory based on relative and effective firepower. Thomas Edison studied antisubmarine warfare, and in 1915 F. Harris derived the first economic order quantity (EOQ) equation for inventory. Starting in 1905 and continuing into the 1920s, A. Erlang studied the flow of calls into a switchboard and formed the basis of what is now known as queueing theory.

**Empiricists.** The formal beginning of operations research was in England during World War II, where the term was and still is operational research. Early work concerned air and coastal defense—the coordination of fighter aircraft, antiaircraft guns, barrage balloons, and radar. Typical of the research groups formed was "Blackett's Circus." This interdisciplinary group consisted of three physiologists, two math physicists, an astrophysicist, an army officer, one surveyor, one general physicist, and two mathematicians. The basic mode of operation was to observe the problem area, and then call on the expertise of the various disciplines to apply methods from other sciences to solve the particular problem. In retrospect, this was an era of "applied common sense," and yet it was novel and highly effective.

**Pragmatists.** Following World War II, operations research continued to exist mainly in the military area. The operations research groups formed during the war stayed together, and a number of civilian-staffed organizations were established—RAND (1946), ORO (1948), and WSEG (1948). The real impetus to this era and to the whole field was the work done by George Dantzig and colleagues at RAND on Project Scope, undertaken for the U.S. Air Force in 1948. In attacking the problem of assigning limited resources to almost limitless demands, they developed the techniques of linear programming. Perhaps no other method is more closely associated with the field. Its use quickly spread from the military to the industrial area, and a new dimension was added to operations research. No longer was it simply "observe, analyze, and try." For the first time the field became "scientific." It could now "optimize" the solutions to problems. *See Linear programming.*

It was during this time that formal courses in operations research were first offered. It was also during this time that operations research suffered its first lapse. Linear programming soon was looked to as the cure for too many of industry's ills. Unfortunately, industry's problems were not all linear, and "straightening them out" to fit resulted in many aborted projects and reports that were simply shelved instead of implemented. The early 1950s saw a growth in the number of industrial operations research groups; by the end of the decade, many had disappeared.

**Theorists.** Toward the end of the 1950s a number of highly skilled scientists emerged who made some substantial contributions to the field. Operations research came of age and matured. In fact, the movement was so far advanced toward developing a sound theoretical base that a new problem arose—the practicality gap.

### Methodology

Operations research today is a maturing science rather than an art—but it has outrun many of the decision makers it purports to assist. The success of operations research, where there has been success, has been the result of the following six simply stated rules:

1. Formulate the problem.
2. Construct a model of the system.
3. Select a solution technique.
4. Obtain a solution to the problem.
5. Establish controls over the system.
6. Implement the solution (**Fig. 2**).

The first statement of the problem is usually vague, inaccurate, and sometimes not a statement of the problem at all. Rather, it may be a cataloging of observable effects. It is necessary to identify the decision maker, the alternatives, goals, and constraints, and the parameters of the system. At times the goals may be many and conflicting; for example: Our goal is to market a high-quality product for the lowest cost yielding the maximum profit while maintaining or increasing our share of the market through diversifications and acquisitions; yielding a high dividend to our stockholders while maintaining high worker morale through extensive benefits, without the Justice Department suing us for constraint of trade, competition, price fixing, or just being too big.

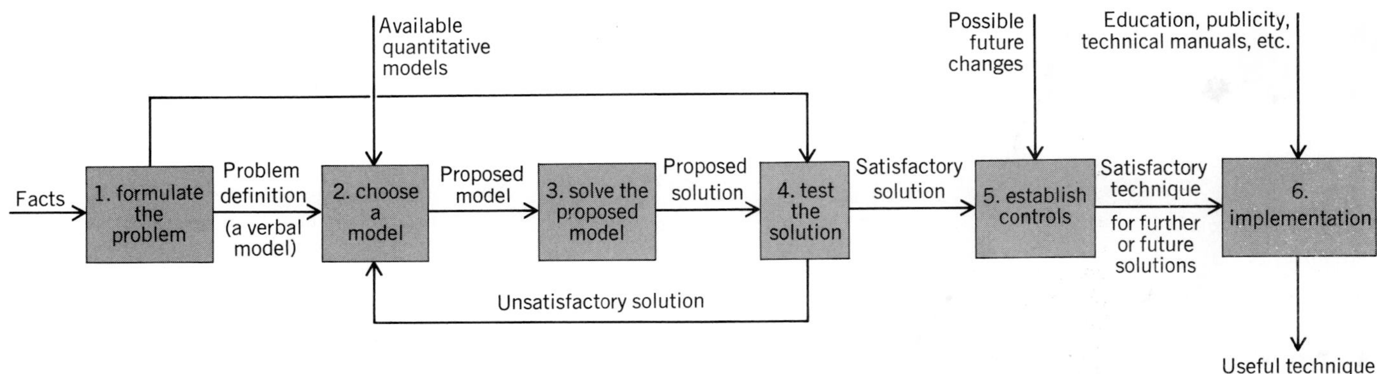


**Fig. 2. Operations research approach: the six basic rules of success.**

More properly, a statement of the problem contains four basic elements that, if correctly identified and articulated, greatly eases the model formulation. These elements can be combined in the following general form: "Given (the system description), the problem is to optimize (the objective function), by choice of the (decision variable), subject to a set of (constraints and restrictions)."

In modeling the system, one usually relies on mathematics, although graphical and analog models are also useful. It is important, however, that the model suggest the solution technique, and not the other way around. Forcing a model to fit a preferred technique led to some of the bad operations research of the past.

With the first solution obtained, it is often evident that the model and the problem statement must be modified, and the sequence of problem-model-technique-solution-problem may have to be repeated several times. The controls are established by performing sensitivity analysis on the parameters. This also indicates the areas in which the data-collecting effort should be made.

Implementation is perhaps of least interest to the theorists, but in reality it is the most important step. If direct action is not taken to implement the solution, the whole effort may end as a dust-collecting report on a shelf. Given the natural inclination to resist change, it is necessary to win the support of the people who will use the new system. To do this, several ploys may be used. Make a member of the using group also a member of the research team. (This provides liaison and access to needed data.) Educate the users about what the system does—not to the extent of making them experts, but to alleviate any fear of the unknown. Perhaps the major limitation to successful use of operations research lies in this phase.

## Mathematical Programming

Probably the one technique most associated with operations research is linear programming. The basic problem that can be modeled by linear programming is the use of limited resources to meet demands for the output of these resources. This type of problem is found mainly in production systems, but is not limited to this area. Since this method is so basic to the operations research approach, its use will be illustrated.

**Linear program model.** Consider a company that produces two main products—X and Y. For every unit of X it sells, it gets a $10 contribution to profit (selling price minus direct, variable costs), and for Y it gets a $15 contribution. How many should they sell of each? Obviously there must be some limitations—on demand and on productive capacity. Suppose they must, by contract, sell 50 of X and 10 of Y, while at the other end the maximum sales are 120 of X and 90 of Y. Unfortunately they have only 40 total hours of productive capacity per period, and it takes 0.25 h to make an X an 0.4 h to make a Y. What is their optimal strategy? First, the problem must be formally stated: "Given a production system making two products, the problem is to maximize the contribution to profit, by the choice of how many of each product to make, subject to limits on demand (upper and lower) and available production hours."

If X equals the number of first products made and Y the number of the second products made, the system can be modeled as follows:

| | | *Constraint line in Fig. 3* |
|---|---|---|
| Maximize | | |
| Profit contrib. | $= 10X + 15Y$ | |
| Subject to | $X \geq 50$ | 1 |
| | $X \leq 120$ | 2 |
| | $Y \geq 10$ | 3 |
| | $Y \leq 90$ | 4 |
| | $.25X + .40Y \leq 40$ | 5 |

The first two constraints are the lower and upper bounds of demand on X, the next two are for Y, and the last constraint refers to the productive capacity.

The problem is illustrated in **Fig. 3**. Any point in the feasible region of solution and the edges will satisfy all the demand and capacity constraints. To pick the best, the objective—"maximize contribution to profit"—is used. Several isoprofit lines, that is, lines where the profit is a constant value, have been added to Fig. 3. Note that the $600 line is below the feasible region, the $1800 line is above it, and the $1200 line runs through it. If other lines were formed between $1200 and $1800, one could graphically find the maximum-profit-level line that still had one point in the feasible region. This would occur at the interesection of the second and fifth constraints. At this point, the solution:

$$\text{Profit contrib.} = \$1575 \qquad X = 120 \qquad Y = 25$$

It is fairly easy to verify that this is the optimal solution, that all the constraints are satisfied, and that no larger profit can be found.

While this simple example did not pose much of a computational problem, actual cases do, in that there may be thousands of variables and thousands of constraints. Problems of scheduling the product mix from a refinery where a blend of different crudes can be used (each with different costs and properties) are in this category. Efficient algorithms and computer codes have been developed to solve these problems.

**Other models.** There are a number of other linear programming models that relate to specific types of problems. However, advantage is taken of the special structure of the model to develop special and more efficient methods of solution.

***Transportation problem.*** While the transportation problem can be modeled as a linear programming model, it is not efficient to solve it in that manner. Consider the tableau shown in **Fig. 4**. This shows the

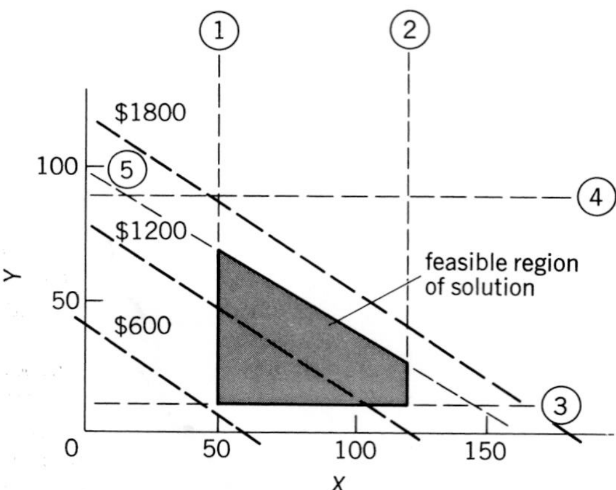


**Fig. 3. Graphical presentation of production problem; circled numbers refer to the constraints.**

unit profit of shipping a common item from four plants to six regional distribution points. Supply refers to the number of units that each source can provide. Demand refers to the number of units that each destination requires. The "dummy" column is added to the supply-demand matrix so as to make the supply equal the demand. In Fig. 4, a dummy demand of 300 units is added to make it equal the total 3600 units of supplies available from four sources. Most transportation problems simply minimize the cost of transportation. This example includes variable selling price, variable production cost, and transportation costs that depend on the distance between the plant and destination.

If the problem were to be modeled as a linear programming model, there would be a decision variable for each combination of shipment. For the example problem there are 4 sources and 6 possible destinations, resulting in 24 decision variables: the amount shipped from each source to each destination. There would be 10 constraints—4 indicating the capacity limits on the plants and 6 reflecting the demand constraints. In general, there will be $S \times D$ variables and $S + D$ constraints, where $S$ is the number of sources and $D$ is the number of constraints. For a more realistic problem, there might be a dozen sources and five dozen destinations. Then the linear programming model would have 720 variables and 72 constraints.

Another factor is that the linear programming model matrix will be composed entirely of 0s and 1s. Also these 1s will be regularly placed. Because of this regular structure, more efficient methods have been found to solve the problem. These algorithms typically have two phases, just as in linear programming.

In the first phase, the objective is to find a feasible solution. One such heuristic is called the North-West Corner rule. Simply stated, the solution process starts in the upper left-hand corner of the tableau, and either the minimum of supply or demand is assigned to the first cell. The next step is to move either horizontally or vertically, depending upon where the demand has been satisfied or the capacity has been all used. The result is a set of assignments that generally move down the main diagonal of the tableau.

A more efficient alogrithm is known as Vogel's approximation method (VAM). Again using the transportation tableau, the procedure is to examine each row and column to determine the difference between the highest unit profit and the next highest unit profit. Where only costs are considered, the procedure would be to determine the difference between the lowest cost and the next lowest cost.

These differences are examined to determine the largest difference, and a transportation assignment is made to the highest unit profit that caused this largest difference. The assignment is to ship either the remaining capacity of the plant or the remaining unsatisfied demand of the destination—whichever is smaller.

The basic philosophy of Vogel's approximation method is that these differences represent a measure of "regret"—that is, how much would be lost (or how much more would have to be paid) if the row or column representing highest unit profit was not used. That is, if it is not used, then it might be necessary to settle for "second best." Choosing the largest difference is an attempt to minimize regret.

Vogel's approximation method then proceeds to re-

| INCREMENTAL PROFIT MATRIX | | | | | | | | |
|---|---|---|---|---|---|---|---|---|
| | DESTINATIONS | | | | | | | |
| SOURCES | St. Louis | Kansas City | Little Rock | Dallas | Houston | Mont-gomery | dummy | source supply |
| Atlanta | 25.00 | 27.60 | 40.50 | 22.50 | 32.00 | 48.50 | 0.00 | 1200 |
| Austin | 12.00 | 18.50 | 30.00 | 18.00 | 28.50 | 32.00 | 0.00 | 500 |
| Memphis | 32.60 | 35.20 | 48.70 | 30.80 | 39.80 | 52.00 | 0.00 | 1200 |
| Tulsa | 21.40 | 28.00 | 37.70 | 22.50 | 30.50 | 38.00 | 0.00 | 700 |
| destination demand | 750 | 500 | 150 | 750 | 1000 | 150 | 300 | 3600 |

**Fig. 4. Transportation problem tableau, showing the incremental profit and the supply-demand matrices of sources and destinations.**

calculate these differences for the remaining row and columns (one row or column is eliminated at each iteration) and to repeat the procedure. When the method is completed, the result will not only be a feasible solution but an extremely good one—and possibly the optimal.

After either approach, the result is an initial basic feasible solution. The next steps are to determine if the solution is optimal. The specific algorithm is too lengthy to present here.

***Assignment problem.*** The assignment problem is also a linear programming model and a variation of the transportation problem. It can be stated as: Given a set of $N$ tasks to be performed by $N$ people and a table of values showing the cost or time it takes each person to perform each task, the problem is to minimize the total time or cost it takes to perform the $N$ tasks by choice of which task is assigned to each person, with the restrictions that each task must be done and each person is assigned to only one task.

This can be considered a special form of the transportation problem where there are $N$ sources (tasks) and $N$ destinations (people). Also, the capacities are each 1. The linear programming simplex method to solve the problem can be used. There would be $N \times N$ variables and $2N$ constraints. The matrix also would be all 0s and 1s. The transportation algorithm could also be used, but would run into many degenerate solution points.

The special structure of the model is used to form a special algorithm to efficiently solve this model. It is known as the Hungarian method and consists of the following steps:

1. The smallest element in each row of the cost-time matrix is subtracted from each element in that row. (This will create at least one element that is 0.)
2. The same procedure is repeated for each problem.
3. An attempt is made to make one assignment to each row and column using the elements that are 0 as candidates. (The recommended procedure is to start with those rows and columns with only one 0.)
4. If a complete set of assignments has been made, then the optimal solution has been found; if not, the next step in the procedure is followed.
5. Using a minimum number of lines either horizontal or vertical, the 0s in each row and column are crossed out. (This can always be done, as many lines are assignments in the current solution.)

6. The smallest element not crossed out is selected, and it is subtracted from each element not crossed out and added to each element at the intersection of a vertical and horizontal line. (This will result in the creation of at least one new 0 as a candidate for assignment and may result in the loss of one or more 0s if they happened to be at the intersection of two lines.

The entire process is repeated (steps 1–6) until the optimal solution is found.

The solution process is reasonably simple, and even modestly large problems can be solved by hand. Besides the generic assignment problem, this approach has been used for such diverse applications as the machine change-over problem (the sequence of jobs to be run on a machine to minimize setup time; assigning students to projects; allocating parking spaces to employees; and so forth).

**Network models.** There is another set of linear programming models that fall under the general category of network models:

The shortest-path problem determines the shortest path from one node to another. (The reverse of this is the critical path method used in project management.) *See Critical path method (CPM).*

The max flow problem determines the capacity of a network such as a pipeline or highway system.

The min cost problem is a variation of the transportation problem.

***Integer linear programming.*** There is a class of problems that have the linear programming form, but in which the variables are limited to being integer values. These represent the most difficult set to solve, especially where the variables take on values of 0 or 1. (This problem occurs, for instance, in project selection—the project is either funded, 1, or not funded, 0.) While a number of algorithms have been developed, there is no assurance that a given problem will be solved in a reasonable amount of computer time. These algorithms fall into two general categories—the cutting plane method, which adds constraints that cut off noninteger solution points, and the branch and bound method, which examines a tree network of solution points. *See Algorithm.*

***Nonlinear programming.*** Another category of problems arises where either the objective function or one or more of the constraints, or both, are nonlinear in form. A series of methods have been developed that have varying degrees of success, depending on the problem structure.

***Geometric programming.*** One of the techniques developed relates to a certain class of nonlinear models that use the arithmetic-geometric mean inequality relationship between sums and products of positive numbers. Such models result from modeling engineering design problems, and at times can be solved almost by inspection. Because of the ease of solution, a considerable effort has been made to identify the various problems that can be structured as a geometric programming model.

***Dynamic programming.*** This technique is not as structured as linear programming, and more properly should be referred to as a solution philosophy rather than a solution technique. Actually, predecessors of this philosophy have been known for some time under the general classification of calculus of variation methods. Dynamic programming is based on the principle of optimality as expressed by Richard Bellman: "An optimal policy has the property that whatever the initial state and initial decision are, the remaining decision must constitute an optimal policy with regard to the state resulting from the first decision." *See Optimization.*

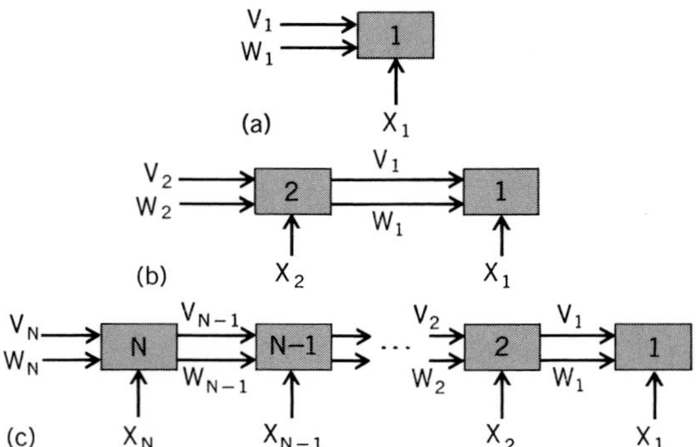


**Fig. 5. Dynamic programming problems. (*a*) Final decision stage. (*b*) Two-stage problem. (*c*) "N"-stage problem.**

The operative result of this principle is to start at the "end" of the problem—the last stage of the decision-making process—and "chain back" to the beginning of the problem, making decisions at each stage that are optimal from that point to the end. To illustrate this process, the fly-away-kit problem (also known as the knapsack problem) will be briefly described: Given a set of components, each with a unit weight and volume, the problem is to maximize the value of units carried to another location, by choice of the number of each to be taken, subject to limitations on volume and weight that can be carried.

In this problem each component will represent a stage at which a decision is to be made (the number to be included in the kit), and the amount of volume and weight left are defined as state variables. The end of the problem, then, is where there is only one more component to consider (**Fig. 5*a***).

Usually at this stage the solution is almost trivial. As many of the last components ($X_1$) are selected as can be within the limits of available volume ($V_1$) and weight ($W_1$). In practice, all possible values of these two state variables are solved for, since it is not known how much will be left when the last stage is reached. To this solution is now "chained" the problem of how to select the second-last component (Fig. 5*b*).

Here is considered the problem that, for each level of volume and weight, a choice must be made between taking one or more of component 2 or passing it on to the last stage. Combinations of components 1 and 2 must now be looked at to find the best mix, considering the available resources. In like manner, the solution is "chained back" to the beginning of the problem (Fig. 5*c*).

The measures of value can be in any terms. If the components are simple cargo, they could have a monetary value. If they are spare parts for some system, a reliability measure could be used.

### Stochastic Processes

A large class of operations research methods and applications deals with stochastic processes. These can be defined as processes in which where one or more of the variables take on values according to some, perhaps unknown, probability distribution. It takes only one of these random variables to make the process stochastic.

In contrast to the mathematical programming methods and applications, there are not many optimization techniques. The techniques used tend to be more diagnostic than prognostic; that is, they can be used to describe the "health" of a system, but not necessarily how to "cure" it. This capacity is still very valuable.

**Queueing theory.** Probably the most studied stochastic process is queueing. A queue or waiting line develops whenever some customer seeks some service that has limited capacity. This occurs in banks, post offices, doctors' offices, supermarkets, airline check-in counters, and so on. But queues can also exist in computer centers, repair garages, planes waiting to land at a busy airport, or at a traffic light.

Queueing theory is the prime example of what can be said about the state of the system but not how to improve it. Fortunately, the improvements can be made by increasing the resources available. For example, another teller opens up a window in a bank, or another check-out stand is opened in the supermarket. Other possible changes are more subtle. For example, the "eight items or less" express lane in a supermarket minimizes the frustration of a customer in line behind another with two full shopping carts. Some post offices and banks have gone to a single queue where the person at the head of the line goes to the next available window.

While it is not possible to generalize the results of queueing analysis, it is possible to provide some general measures. One is the load or traffic factor. This is the ratio of arrival rate to combined service rate, considering the number of service centers in operation. It is possible to plot queueing statistics against this factor as shown in **Fig. 6**.

When the load factor (ρ) is low, there is excess serving capacity. There may be occasional lines, but not often. As the load factor rises, a fairly linear rise is obtained in any queueing statistics until approximately the point where $\rho = 0.75$. After this there is a sharp and continuous rise in the lengths of line and waits. The system is becoming saturated. If $\rho = 1.00$, the best that can be said is, "the larger the line, the larger the wait."

The following problem is an example of the type of analysis that can be done on a simple queueing system. A check-out counter at a small market can handle customers at a rate of 20 per hour (3 min per customer). Since the number of customers will vary considerably throughout the day and throughout the days of the week, the arrival rate of customers at the check-out counter will also vary considerably. The manager wishes to know when to open up a second check-out counter.

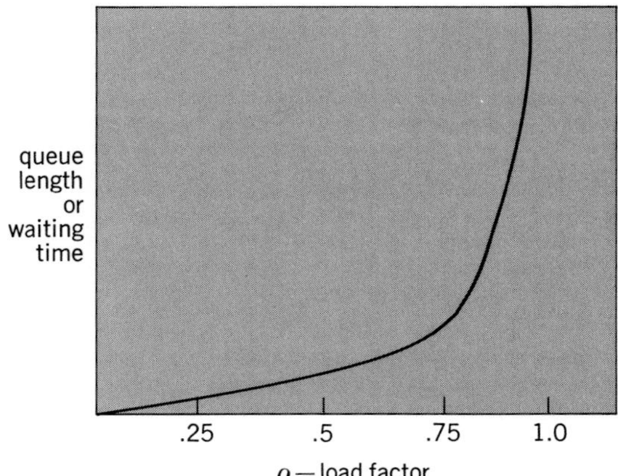


**Fig. 6. Plot for general queues relating load factor to serving capacity.**

The basic set of queueing formulas are given in Eqs. (1)–(5). If the arrival rate varies from a low

$$\rho = \lambda/\mu \tag{1}$$

$$L = \lambda/(\mu - \lambda) \tag{2}$$

$$L_q = \rho^2/(1 - \rho) \tag{3}$$

$$W_q = \lambda/\mu(\mu - \lambda) \tag{4}$$

$$W = W_q + 1/\mu \tag{5}$$

where $\lambda$ = the arrival rate
$\mu$ = the service rate
$\rho$ = the traffic factor
$L$ = the average number of customers in the system
$L_q$ = the average number of customers in the check-out queue
$W_q$ = the average waiting time for service
$W$ = the average time in the check-out system

value to one approaching the service rate, the effects on the system can be examined. These results are presented in the **table**. From this table, it is evident that the queue builds up very rapidly as the traffic factor increases beyond 0.75. The store manager would need to monitor the actual number of customers in the queue and open another check-out counter when this number exceeds 4 or 5.

**Analysis of a simple queueing system**

| Arrival rate (λ) | Traffic factor (ρ) | Average number of customers in the system ($L$) | Average number of customers in the check-out queue ($L_q$) | Average waiting time for service ($W_q$) | Average time in checkout system ($W$) |
|---|---|---|---|---|---|
| 1 | .05 | .053 | .0026 | .0026 | .0526 |
| 5 | .25 | .333 | .0833 | .0166 | .0666 |
| 10 | .50 | 1.000 | .5000 | .0500 | .1000 |
| 15 | .75 | 3.000 | 2.2500 | .1500 | .2000 |
| 16 | .80 | 4.000 | 3.2000 | .2000 | .2500 |
| 17 | .85 | 5.667 | 4.8161 | .2833 | .3333 |
| 18 | .90 | 9.000 | 8.1000 | .4500 | .5000 |
| 19 | .95 | 19.000 | 18.0500 | .9500 | 1.0000 |

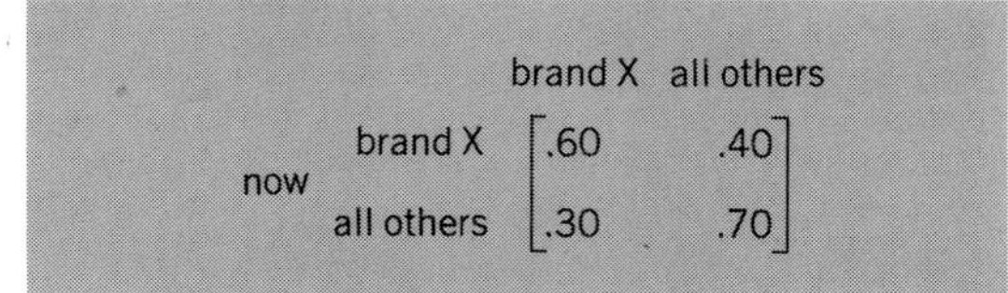


**Fig. 7. Probability matrix for brand-switching model.**

The mathematics of the probability distributions of arrival rates and service times often define closed-form solutions, that is, being able to directly solve for an answer. In these cases another technique has proved very useful.

**Simulation.** Simulation is defined as the essence of reality without reality itself. With stochastic processes, values are simulated for the random variables from their known or assumed probability distributions, a simpler model is solved, and the process is repeated a sufficient number of times to obtain statistical confidence in the results.

As a simple example of this, assume that someone makes the statement that the average female student at a university is of a certain height. To verify this assumption the actual heights of all female students could be measured, but this may be a long process. As an alternative, a hopefully random sample may be taken, the heights measured, the average determined, and an inference made as to the whole female population.

Many stochastic processes do not lend themselves to such a direct approach. Instead an assumption is made as to what the underlying probability distributions of the random variables are, and these are sampled. This sampling is done with random numbers. True random numbers are difficult to obtain, so pseudorandom numbers are generated by some mathematical relationship. This apparent paradox is justified by the fact that the numbers appear to be random and pass most tests for randomness. As an example, a queueing system could be modeled by having two wheels of fortune—one with numbers in random order from 1 to 15, and the other from 1 to 20. The first could represent the number of arrivals into the system per 10-min period, and the other the number served during the same period. In this manner a system with a load factor of 0.75 could be simulated. Many simulation computer languages have been developed to ease the work of analyzing queueing systems. SEE SIMULATION.

**Markov processes.** This class of stochastic processes is characterized by a matrix of transition probabilities. These measure the probability of moving from one state to another. Such methods have been used to determine the reliability of a system, movement of a stock in the stock market, aging of doubtful accounts in credit analysis, and brand switching. This last application will be illustrated.

A company is considering marketing a new product. A preliminary market survey indicates that if a customer uses the product, there is a 60% probability that he or she will continue to do so. Likewise, the advertising campaign is such that 70% of those using all other products will be tempted to switch. The question is, what market share will the product be expected to finally obtain? The probability matrix is shown in **Fig. 7**.

Initially the market share of brand X is 0%, but after one period this will rise to 30%; that is, the advertising campaign will induce 30% to try brand X. In the next period, only 60% of these 30% will continue to purchase brand X, but 30% of the other 70% will switch, for a total market share of 39%.

Period by period, there will be transitions from state to state, but soon the variations will dampen out and a steady state will be achieved. This can be found for this problem by matrix value, and the final market share for brand X is 42.8%.

**Decision trees.** While not originated by the field of operations research and not strictly in its domain, decision trees are an important tool in the analysis of some stochastic processes. More properly, they are a part of what may be considered statistical decision making. Their use can be illustrated with an example from the oil industry.

An oil company is developing an oil field and has the option to lease the mineral rights on an adjacent block of land for $100,000. An exploratory well can be drilled at a cost of $250,000. If the well is considered moderate or good, it will cost an additional $50,000 to complete before production can start.

For simplicity, it can be assumed that the well, if good, has either moderate or good production. Also, the present worth of the net returns on all the future production is $1,000,000 and $3,500,000 for these two states. The problem facing the oil company is what they should do.

To analyze this problem, some subjective probabilities must be estimated. It is assumed that the probability that the well is dry is 70%, that the flow is moderate is 20%, and that it is good is 10%. With these percentages, a decision tree can be constructed (**Fig. 8**).

By a process of "folding back" the values and probabilities, the expected value at each decision point is seen to be represented by a square in Fig. 8. Actually, while there are three sequential decisions—lease, drill, and complete the well—once the decision to lease is made, the sequence is fixed unless the well is discovered to be dry. The expected value of this decision can be calculated as follows:

$$
\begin{aligned}
E[\text{lease} - \text{drill}] \\
&= -100{,}000 - 250{,}000 + 0.70(0) \\
&\quad + 0.20(-50{,}000 + 1{,}000{,}000) \\
&\quad + 0.10(-50{,}000 + 3{,}500{,}000) \\
&= \$185{,}000
\end{aligned}
$$

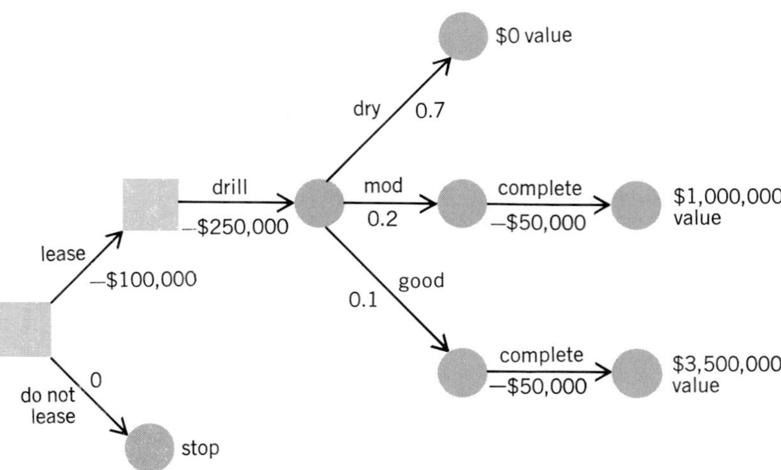


**Fig. 8. Decision tree for an oil well problem.**

This expected value is slightly positive. In reality one of three things will happen—the well is dry, and the loss is $350,000; the well is moderate, with a net gain of $600,000; or the well is good, with a net gain of $3,100,000. This expected value can be interpreted as follows: If a large number of wells are drilled, 70% will be dry at a loss of $350,000 each, 20% will be moderate, and 10% will be good. The average gain will be $185,000.

### Scope of Application

There are numerous areas where operations research has been applied. The following list is not intended to be all-inclusive, but is mainly to illustrate the scope of applications: optimal depreciation strategies; communication network design; computer network design; simulation of computer time-sharing systems; water resource project selection; demand forecasting; bidding models for offshore oil leases; production planning; assembly line balancing; job shop scheduling; optimal location of offshore drilling platforms; optimal allocation of crude oil using input-output models; classroom size mix to meet student demand; optimizing waste treatment plants; risk analysis in capital budgeting; electric utility fuel management; public utility rate determination; location of ambulances; optimal staffing of medical facilities; feedlot optimization; minimizing waste in the steel industry; optimal design of natural-gas pipelines; economic inventory levels; random jury selection; optimal marketing-price strategies; project management with CPM/PERT/GERT; air-traffic-control simulations; optimal strategies in sports; system availability/reliability/maintainability; optimal testing plans for reliability; optimal space trajectories.

It can be seen from this list that there are few facets of society that do not have an application for operations research. *See Decision theory; GERT; PERT.*

*William G. Lesso*

**Bibliography.** R. E. Bellman and S. E. Dreyfus, *Applied Dynamic Programming*, 1962; V. N. Bhat, *Elements of Applied Stochastic Processes*, 1972; F. S. Hillier and G. Lieberman, *Introduction to Operations Research*, 3d ed., 1980; H. A. Taha, *Operations Research*, 3d ed., 1982.

## Optical bistability

A phenomenon whereby an optical device can have either of two stable output states, labeled 0 and 1, for the same input (**Fig. 1***a*). Optical bistability is an expanding field of research because of its potential application to all-optical logic and because of the interesting physical phenomena it encompasses. A bistable optical device can function as a variety of logic devices or as an optical memory element. Under slightly modified operating conditions, the same device can exhibit the optical transistor characteristic of Fig. 1*b*. For input intensities close to $I_{gain}$, small variations in the input light are amplified in much the same way that a vacuum tube triode or transistor amplifies electrical signals. The characteristic of Fig. 1*b* can also be used as a discriminator; inputs above $I_{gain}$ are transmitted with far less attenuation than those below. Finally, there is limiting action above $I_{gain}$: large changes in the input hardly change the output. There is hope that bistable devices will revolutionize optical processing, switching, and computing. Since the first observation of optical bistability in a passive, unexcited medium in 1974, bistability has been observed in many different materials, including tiny semiconductor etalons. Research has focused on optimizing these devices and developing smaller devices of better materials which operate faster, at higher temperatures, and with less power. *See Amplifier; Computer storage technology; Limiter circuit; Logic circuits; Transistor; Vacuum tube.*

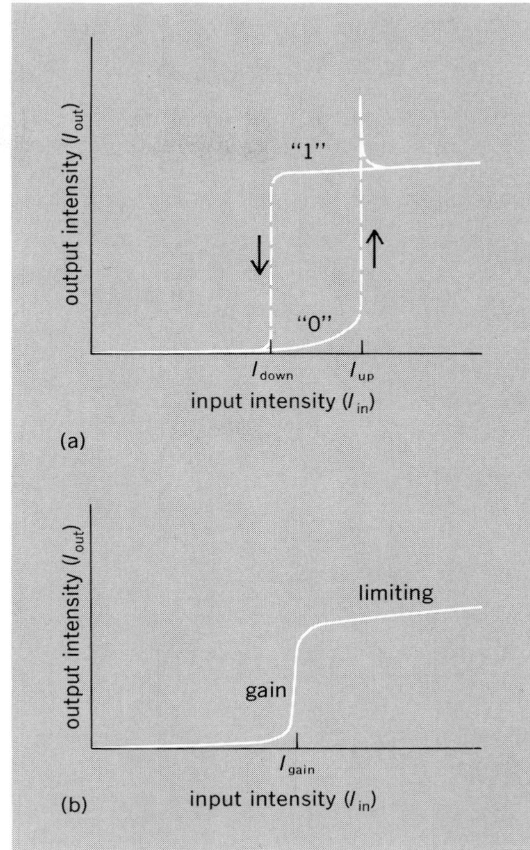


**Fig. 1. Transmission of a typical bistable optical device, under conditions of (*a*) bistability (memory) and (*b*) high ac gain (optical transistor, discriminator, or limiter).**

Optical bistability has also attracted the attention of physicists interested in fundamental phenomena. In fact, a bistable device often consists of a nonlinear medium within an optical resonator; it is thus similar to a laser except that the medium is unexcited (except by the coherent light incident on the resonator). Such a device constitutes a simple example of a strongly coupled system of matter and radiation. The counterparts of many of the phenomena studied in lasers such as fluctuations, regenerative pulsations, and optical turbulence can be observed under better-controlled conditions in passive bistable systems. *See Laser.*

**All-optical systems.** The transmission of information as signals impressed on light beams traveling through optical fibers is replacing electrical transmission over wires. The low cost and inertness of the basic materials of fibers and the small size and low loss of the finished fibers are important factors in this evolution. Furthermore, for very fast transmission systems, for example, for transmitting a multiplexed composite of many slow signals, optical pulses are best. This is because it is far easier to generate and transmit picosecond optical pulses than electrical pulses. With optical pulses and optical transmission, the missing component of an all-optical signal processing system is an optical logic element in which one light beam or pulse controls another. Because of the high frequencies of optical electromagnetic radiation, such all-optical systems have the potential for subpicosecond switching and room-temperature operation. Although any information processing and transmitting system is likely to have electrical parts, especially for powering the lasers and interfacing to humans, the capability of subpicosecond switching appears unique to the optical part of such a system. *SEE OPTICAL COMMUNICATIONS; OPTICAL INFORMATION SYSTEMS.*

**Bistable optical devices.** Bistable optical devices have been constructed which have many of the desirable properties of an all-optical logic element. A device is said to be bistable if it has two output states for the same value of the input over some range of input values. Thus a device having the transmission curve of Fig. 1*a* is said to be bistable between $I_{down}$ and $I_{up}$. This device is clearly nonlinear; that is, $I_{out}$ is not just a multiplicative constant times $I_{in}$. In fact, if $I_{in}$ is between $I_{down}$ and $I_{up}$, knowing $I_{in}$ does not reveal $I_{out}$. To accomplish this behavior, an all-optical bistable device requires feedback. Even though a nonlinear medium is essential, the nonlinearity alone only means that $I_{out}$ versus $I_{in}$ is not a straight line. The feedback is what permits the nonlinear transmission to be multivalued, that is, bistable. *SEE FEEDBACK CIRCUIT.*

***Fabry-Perot interferometer.*** The most nearly practical devices so far are tiny semiconductor etalons, that is, tiny Fabry-Perot interferometers consisting of a gallium arsenide (GaAs) or indium antimonide (InSb) crystal with flat parallel faces sometimes coated with dielectrics to increase the reflectivity to about 90% (**Fig. 2**). In these etalons the Fabry-Perot cavity provides the optical feedback, and the nonlinear index of refraction $n_2$ is the intensity-dependent parameter. The bistable operation of such a Fabry-Perot cavity containing a medium with a nonlinear refraction can be pictured as follows. In the off or low transmission state, the laser is detuned from one of the approximately equally spaced transmission peaks of the etalon and most of $I_{in}$ is reflected (**Fig. 3***a*). The refractive index is approximately $n_0$, its value for weak light intensity. In the on state the index is approximately $n_0 + n_2I_c$, where the intensity inside the cavity is $I_c$. This change in index shifts the etalon peak to near coincidence with the laser frequency, permitting a large transmission and a large $I_c$. Clearly there must be a consistency between the index and the laser frequency; each affects the other through the feedback. As the input is increased from low values, the frequency $\nu_{FP}$ of the Fabry-Perot peak begins to shift when $n_2I_c$ becomes significant. But this shift increases $I_c$, which further increases $n_2I_c$, and so on. This positive feedback continues until, at $I_{up}$, the effect runs away, the device turns on, and the transmission reaches a value on the negative feedback side of the etalon peak consistent with $n = n_0 + n_2I_c$ (Fig. 3*b*). Once the device is turned on, $I_c$ is larger than $I_{in}$ because of the storage property of the cavity. Therefore $I_{in}$ can now be lowered to a value below $I_{up}$, and the large $I_c$ will keep the device on. Thus the hysteresis of the bistability loop arises from the fact that, for the same input intensity, the intracavity intensity and index contribution are small in the off or detuned state and large in the on or in-tune state. *SEE SEMICONDUCTOR.*

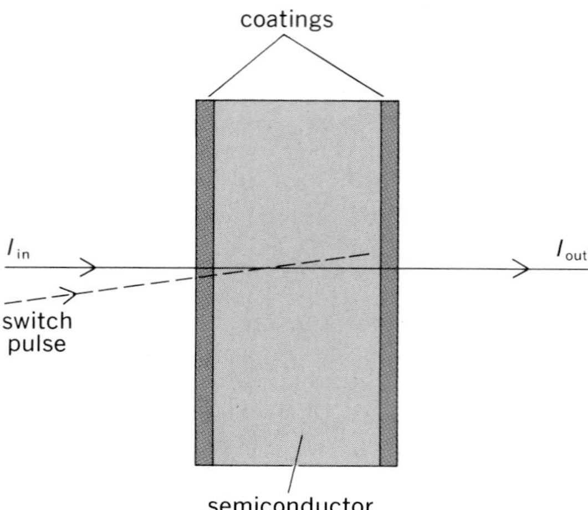


**Fig. 2. Bistable optical etalon.**

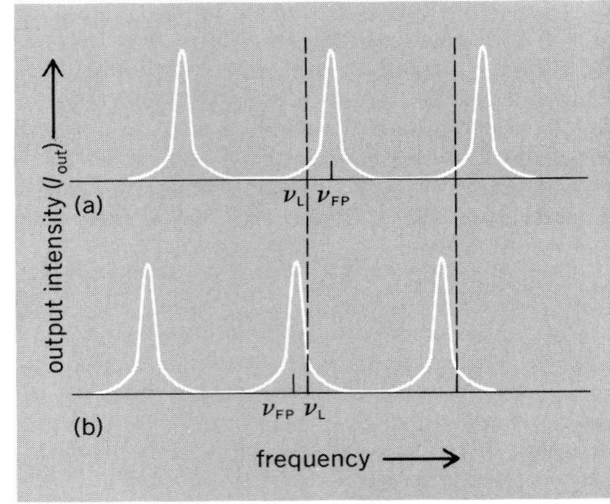


**Fig. 3. Transmission function of a nonlinear Fabry-Perot interferometer: (*a*) device off, index $n \cong n_0$, and (*b*) device on, $n \cong n_0 + n_2I_c$. The laser frequency $\nu_L$ is fixed, but the cavity peak frequency $\nu_{FP}$ changes with light intensity via $n_2$.**

Clearly, a device with the transmission characteristic of Fig. 1 can serve as an optical memory. If $I_{in}$ is maintained between $I_{down}$ and $I_{up}$, the value of $I_{out}$ reveals the state of the device. Light pulses can be used to switch the device on and off, just as for an electrical flip-flop. A simple analysis of a nonlinear Fabry-Perot cavity and experiments show that by changing the initial detuning this device can perform a whole host of optical operations. Bistable optical devices have been operated as an all-optical differential or ac amplifier (also called an optical transistor and a transphasor), limiter, discriminator, gate, oscillator, and pulse shaper. *SEE GATE CIRCUIT; OSCILLATOR; PULSE GENERATOR.*

***Properties.*** A GaAs device has been fabricated that was only 5 micrometers thick, and the laser beam diameter on the etalon was only 10 μm—about one-tenth the diameter of a human hair. The device was switched on by a 10-ps pulse in a time shorter than the 200-ps detector response time, and a time of a few picoseconds is believed possible. The GaAs device operates at a convenient wavelength (0.83 μm) and is constructed of a material used for electronics and diode lasers, facilitating interfacing and integration. But all the properties of the demonstrated device are not ideal. The switch-down time is about 40 nanoseconds, presumably arising from the lifetime of the free carriers and excitons created by the intense light in the on state. The minimum input power is about 100 mW, and the minimum switch-on energy about 1 nanojoule, far more than a practical device can have. And the highest operating temperature is −244°F (120 K), because the free exciton resonance used to produce $n_2$ decreases, and the undesirable band-tail absorption increases, with increased temperature. However, measurements of the intrinsic properties of pure GaAs reveal the switching times and energy should be greatly reduced in optimized etalons.

The InSb etalons are longer (a few hundred micrometers), operate at longer wavelengths (approximately 5 μm), and hence have larger transverse dimension limitations than GaAs, have demonstrated switching times of a few hundred nanoseconds, operate at least up to −321°F (77 K), and have functioned with as little as 8-mW input power. And, just as for GaAs, it is unlikely that the InSb devices are optimized.

The results of these first experiments seeking practical devices point to obvious areas currently under intense research. The physics of semiconductors is being challenged to identify giant nonlinearities at convenient wavelengths and at higher temperatures. In addition to the GaAs free exciton and InSb below-edge band-to-band saturation mechanisms already observed, electron-hole plasma and biexciton mechanisms have been proposed. Other bistable configurations are being sought to better utilize the nonlinearities and minimize the power required: thin etalons, nonlinear interfaces, self-focusing devices, and guided-wave structures.

**Fundamental studies.** In addition to work on the application of optical bistability to practical devices, a comparable effort is being directed toward the properties of these devices, whose operation depends on the nonlinear coupling between electronic material and light. Figure 1 shows a discontinuity in the transmission, reminiscent of a first-order phase transition. The input light maintains the system in equilibrium which is far from thermal. Fluctuations and transient behavior of such systems are of great interest. A sluggishness in response, called critical slowing down, has already been observed for $I_{in}$ close to $I_{up}$. Regenerative pulsations have also been seen in which competing mechanisms cause the device to switch on and off repeatedly, forming an all-optical oscillator.

***Hybrid devices.*** Many of these fundamental studies have been conducted with hybrid (mixed optical and electronic) bistable devices in which the intensity dependence of the intracavity index results from applying a voltage proportional to the transmitted intensity across an intracavity modulator. In fact, the cavity is not necessary, since electrical feedback is present. Placing the modulator between crossed polarizers provides the required nonlinearity. Integrated hybrids are being considered for practical devices, but the ultimate in shortening the detector-to-modulator wire length is to place the detector inside the cavity. The distinction between hybrid and intrinsic then fades. The best device may have a voltage across the semiconductor to increase its speed and sensitivity. Arrays of hybrid devices have been used to study image processing using bistable elements; eventually bistable arrays could be used for parallel computing, for example, for propagation problems with transverse effects. SEE IMAGE PROCESSING.

***Optical turbulence.*** Hybrid devices have been considered to be completely analogous to intrinsic devices. It has been predicted that an intrinsic ring-cavity device subjected to a steady input will exhibit periodic oscillations and turbulence or chaos if the medium response time is short compared with the cavity round-trip time. The hybrid analogy is to delay the feedback by a time longer than the detector-feedback-modulator response time. Optical chaos, observed in such a hybrid, has been used to study the evolution, from a stable output, through periodic oscillations, to chaos as the input is increased. The optical turbulence studies interface to phenomena in many other disciplines, such as mathematics, genetics, and hydrodynamics, emphasizing the basic similarity of these seemingly diverse phenomena, in agreement with some recent mathematical findings. SEE NONLINEAR OPTICAL DEVICES.

*Hyatt M. Gibbs*

***Bibliography.*** H. M. Gibbs, S. L. McCall, and T. N. C. Venkatesan, Optical bistable devices—The basic components of all-optical systems? *Opt. Eng.*, 19:463–468, 1980; H. M. Gibbs et al., Observation of chaos in optical bistability, *Phys. Rev. Lett.*, 46:474–477, 1981; S. D. Smith and D. A. B. Miller, Computing at the speed of light, *New Sci.*, 85:554–556, February 21, 1980; P. W. Smith and W. J. Tomlinson, Bistable optical devices promise subpicosecond switching, *IEEE Spectrum*, 18(6):26–33, 1981.

## Optical communications

The transmission of speech, data, video, and other information by means of the visible and the infrared portion of the electromagnetic spectrum. A communication system consists of a transmitter, a transmission medium, and a receiver (see **illus.**).

Optical communication is one of the newest and most advanced forms of communication by electromagnetic waves. In one sense, it differs from radio and microwave communication only in that the wavelengths employed are shorter (or equivalently, the frequencies employed are higher). However, in another very real sense it differs markedly from these older technologies because, for the first time, the wavelengths involved are much shorter than the dimensions of the devices which are used to transmit, receive, and otherwise handle the signals.

The advantages of optical communication are threefold. First, the high frequency of the optical carrier (typically of the order of 300,000 GHz) permits much more information to be transmitted over a single channel than is possible with a conventional radio or microwave system. Second, the very short wavelength of the optical carrier (typically of the order of 1 micrometer) permits the realization of very small, compact components. Third, the highest transparency for electromagnetic radiation yet achieved in any solid material is that of silica glass in the wavelength region 1–1.5 μm. This transparency is orders of magnitude higher than that of any other solid material in any other part of the spectrum.

Communication by means of light is not a new concept. A. G. Bell patented the "photophone" in

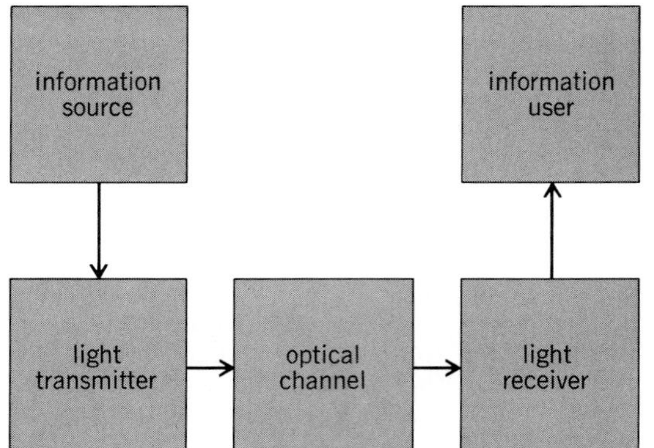


**Block diagram of a simplified optical communication system.**

1880. In this device, the sound waves from a speaker's voice caused a mirror to vibrate and this in turn caused a beam of sunlight to be modulated. At the receiver, a selenium detector converted the sunlight into electronic current to recreate the speech. Nevertheless, optical communication in the modern sense of the term dates from about 1960, when the advent of lasers and light-emitting diodes (LEDs) made the exploitation of the wide-bandwidth capabilities of the light wave practical. During the 1960s much effort was devoted to utilizing light waves which were propagating through the atmosphere. But in 1970 an optical fiber which was orders of magnitude more transparent than any of its predecessors was made. The advent of this low-loss fiber stimulated a worldwide effort in what is now known as fiber optics. The result has been a tremendous increase in the transparency of silica fibers. (In the best fibers available prior to 1970, light waves retained only about 1% of their energy after traveling a distance of 65 ft or 20 m. By 1984 light waves in the best fibers retained about 10% of their energy after traveling over 12 mi or 20 km.) SEE LASER; LIGHT-EMITTING DIODE.

Although the majority of the effort in optical communication is now in the area of optical fiber systems, they were not the only or the first systems considered or used. Other optical channels which have been considered include light beams in free space (between satellites), light beams through the atmosphere, and light beams through tubes which control the atmosphere.

In addition to categorizing optical communication systems by the type of transmission medium, it is possible to categorize them by wavelength, by the characteristics of the signal transmitted, and by type of source.

**Free-space optical communications.** A free-space optical channel exists, for example, between orbiting satellites. A free-space channel between satellites is, in some sense, ideal; it does not distort or attenuate the light beam. For this application the laser is the best source because its spatially coherent radiation can be confined to a much smaller angle of divergence than can the incoherent radiation from other sources. Lasers particularly well suited to this application are the carbon dioxide gas laser and the neodymium yttrium-aluminum-garnet (Nd:YAG) solid-state laser. The beam can be launched at the transmitter and picked up at the receiver by telescopes with apertures limited only by the weight and by the precision with which they can be pointed at each other. Pointing is a severe limitation since light beams less than 1 second of arc wide may be required, a beam width attainable with a 4-in. (10-cm) telescope at visible wavelengths. For this reason, lightwave systems have had difficulty competing with millimeter-wave systems for satellite-to-satellite communication.

**Atmospheric optical communications.** For satellite-to-Earth communications and terrestrial communications through the air, the Earth's atmosphere strongly influences the light transmission. In the visible wavelength band and in a few narrow windows in the near-infrared, transmission losses are low in clear weather. However, minute temperature gradients along the path of the light beam cause the beam to broaden and bend so that even in clear air the degradation can be severe over longer paths. Rain, fog, and snow cause even more severe transmission degradations. Attenuation of the light beam power to less than 1/1000 the clear weather value can occur in a 2-mi (3-km) path.

The primary source of excess attenuation in an Earth-to-satellite path is clouds. Fog and snow, rather than rain, are the most serious offenders on terrestrial paths. In neither case would the transmission reliability be considered satisfactory for most communication purposes. But for very short transmission paths the probability of outage may be low enough to be acceptable. For example, it is sometimes feasible to provide data links between nearby buildings over optical beams.

In a shielded atmosphere (such as in a room or in a pipe) the effects of precipitation can be avoided so that attenuation is quite low. Optical communication systems which guide light beams along a path inside a pipe with the help of lenses and mirrors have been studied. Even in a confined atmosphere, however, thermal effects must be very well controlled to prevent degradation of the light beams. The information-carrying capacity of a pipe carrying many such light beams could be very high, perhaps a few million telephone conversations. But the installation and maintenance costs would be very high, and the demand for such a system may never be sufficient to justify the expense of its development.

**Optical fiber communications.** Optical fiber bundles had been used to transmit light and even images for many years when the use of silica-based optical fibers to transmit data was proposed in 1966. With the development of extremely low-loss optical fibers during the 1970s, optical fiber communication became a very important form of telecommunication almost instantaneously. For fibers to become useful as light waveguides (or light guides) for communications applications, transparency and control of signal distortion had to be improved dramatically and a method had to be found to connect separate lengths of fiber together.

The transparency objective was achieved by making glass rods almost entirely of silica. These rods could be pulled into fibers at temperatures approaching 3600°F (2000°C).

Reducing distortion over long distances required modification of the method of guidance employed in early fibers. These early fibers (called step-index fibers) consisted of two coaxial cylinders (called core and cladding) which were made of two slightly different glasses so that the core glass had a slightly higher index of refraction than the cladding glass. Light rays that strike the core-cladding interface at a grazing angle are reflected into the core by means of a theoretically lossless process called total internal reflection, and thus are confined there. Depending on the angle of incidence, therefore, the rays follow different paths and hence require different lengths of time to travel down the fiber. This difference in propagation time results in distortion of the signal—a broadening and overlapping of the pulses in a digital signal, for example. Because the propagation time increases with path length, this effect places a limit on the transmission distance for a given pulse rate.

Two modifications of the step-index fiber have led to large improvements in the transmission of high data rates over large distances: (1) By causing the index of refraction to decrease continuously according to a particular formula, the effect of this delay distortion can be greatly reduced. This happens because in a properly designed fiber the light which travels the greatest distance spends more time farther from the axis in a region of lower index and therefore travels at a greater velocity. These graded-index fibers were widely used in first-generation optical fiber transmission systems, and they will continue to be used in certain applications in the future. However, an alternative approach is more attractive and is the method of choice in most long-distance systems. (2) By reducing the core size and the index difference in a step-index fiber, it is possible to reach a point at which only axial propagation is possible. In this condition, only one mode of propagation exists and determines the travel time. These single-mode fibers are capable of transmitting rates in excess of $10^9$ pulses per second over distances of 75 mi (120 km). In fact, it will become feasible in the near future to provide individual offices and even individual homes with the capability of receiving and sending data at rates in excess of $2 \times 10^9$ bits per second. SEE WAVEGUIDE.

The problem of joining fibers together was solved in two ways. For permanent connections, fibers can be spliced together by carefully aligning the individual fibers and then epoxying them together or fusing them together. In fact, permanent connection of fiber ribbons—linear arrays of several fibers—can be achieved by splicing the entire ribbon as a single unit. Fusion splices have been made with losses of less than 3% while epoxied splices typically have losses of about 12%.

For temporary connections, or for applications in which it is not desirable to make splices, fiber connectors have been developed. Connector losses for good connectors are typically less than 12%.

***Terrestrial systems.*** Almost every major metropolitan area in the United States has a light-wave transmission system in service connecting telephone central offices. These systems typically operate at either 45 or 90 megabits per second. The older systems use a wavelength of 0.825 μm and require repeaters every 7 mi (11 km). The newer ones use a wavelength of 1.3 μm and require a repeater every 26 mi (42 km). In 1983 construction began on an intercity transmission system from Boston through New York to Washington. This system uses multimode fibers and operates at a data rate of 90 Mb/s. A similar system has been installed between Los Angeles and Sacramento.

It is anticipated that light-wave systems will gradually be installed in the telephone loop plant—that is, the portion of the telephone plant which connects the individual subscriber to the telephone central office. It will then become feasible to provide high-speed digital services such as digital video, high-speed facsimile, and high-speed data transfer to business and eventually residential customers. SEE DATA COMMUNICATIONS; FACSIMILE.

***Undersea cable.*** The eighth transatlantic telephone cable, to be laid in 1988, will be an optical fiber cable running from Tuckerton, New Jersey, to a branch point near the European coast. From this branch point, two fiber cables will run, one to Widemouth in Great Britain and the other to Penmarch in France. Each cable will contain two active fiber pairs and one standby pair. The fibers will use pulse-code modulation and transmit at a rate of 295.6 Mb/s. By means of highly efficient coding, each fiber can carry up to 20,000 voice circuits.

The fibers will be single-mode fibers operating at a wavelength of 1.3 μm. The transmitters will be indium gallium arsenide–phosphide lasers and the receivers will be indium gallium arsenide detectors. Avalanche photodetectors will not be used because of the reasons cited below, as well as the fact that they are not yet proven sufficiently reliable. Reliability is the overriding consideration in an undersea system, where repair of a faulty component is extremely expensive. The reliability target for the system is three repairs over the 25-year lifetime of the system. All new components are protected by the third fiber pair which can be switched into service as required. In addition, there is a cold standby backup for every laser in the system. The distance between repeaters in the system varies from 24 mi (39 km) on the continental shelf to 39 mi (63 km) in the deep ocean.

A novel system continuously monitors selected critical voltages and currents in the repeaters and predicts failures before they become service-affecting. The system from the North American coast to the branch point will be built by the United States; the branches from that point to Great Britain and France will be built by those respective countries.

**Optical transmitters.** In principle any light source could be used as an optical transmitter. In modern optical communication systems, however, only lasers and light-emitting diodes are generally considered for use. The most simple device is the light-emitting diode which emits in all directions from a fluorescent area located in the diode junction. Since optical communication systems usually require well-collimated beams of light, light-emitting diodes are relatively inefficient. In particular, since optical fibers accept only light entering the core in a relatively narrow solid angle about the axis, only a small portion of the emitted light is captured and transmitted by the fiber. In fact, the acceptance angle for single-mode fibers is so small that light-emitting diodes are not well suited for use with them unless a high loss can be tolerated. On the other hand, light-emitting diodes are less expensive than lasers and, at least until recently, have exhibited longer lifetimes.

Another device, the semiconductor laser, provides comparatively well-collimated light. In this device, two ends of the junction plane are furnished with partially reflecting mirror surfaces which form an optical resonator. (In practical semiconductor lasers the partially reflecting mirrors are formed by simply cleaving the two sides of the junction.) The device enhances the light bouncing back and forth between these mirrors by means of stimulated emission. As a result of cavity resonances, the light emitted through the partially reflecting mirrors is well collimated within a narrow solid angle, and a large fraction of it can be captured and transmitted by an optical fiber.

Both light-emitting diodes and laser diodes can be modulated by varying the forward diode current. Typically, the message is a digital sequence of pulses which are used to turn the diode on and off. The light injected into the optical channel is a faithful representation of the information sequence.

It is also possible to fabricate a laser directly in an optical fiber by doping the core glass with ions of an element such as neodymium and pumping this active medium with light-emitting diodes of the proper wavelength. Lasers of this type require external modulators which make them less attractive than the diode lasers described above. Such lasers are still in the early experimental stage, but they show potential for use as amplifiers in long-haul systems.

**Optical receivers.** Semiconductor photodiodes are used for the receivers in virtually all optical communication systems. There are two basic types of photodiodes in use. The most simple comprises a reverse-biased junction in which the received light creates electron-hole pairs. These carriers are swept out by the electric field and induce a photocurrent in the external circuit. The minimum amount of light needed for correct reconstruction of the received signal is limited by noise superimposed on the signal by the following circuits. Such a photodiode must collect more than 100 nanowatts of signal in order to receive a signal of $10^8$ pulses per second with sufficient fidelity. SEE PHOTODIODE.

Avalanche photodiodes provide some increase in the level of the received signal before it reaches the external circuits. They achieve greater sensitivity by multiplying the photogenerated carriers in the diode junction. This is done by creating an internal electric field sufficiently strong to cause avalanche multiplication of the free carriers. Unfortunately, the avalanche gain process is a random phenomenon and introduces additional noise into the signal. This excess noise becomes the limiting factor in the amount of avalanche gain which can be beneficially obtained. Nevertheless, the improvement available from avalanche detectors is significant. A reduction in required signal power of between 10 and 100 times (depending on the type of devices used) is routinely realizable. Avalanche photodiodes are used only when the extra sensitivity which they provide is required because they are more expensive than simple photodiodes, they require much more expensive power supplies than simple photodiodes, and they require very careful temperature stabilization. SEE MICROWAVE SOLID-STATE DEVICES; OPTICAL DETECTORS.

*W. M. Hubbard*

***Bibliography.*** A. H. Cherin, *An Introduction to Optical Fibers*, 1983; C. K. Kao, *Optical Fiber Systems: Technology, Design, and Applications*, 1982; S. E. Miller and A. G. Chynoweth (eds.), *Optical Fiber Telecommunications*, 1979; S. D. Personick, *Fiber Optics: Technology and Applications*, 1985.

## Optical detectors

Devices that generate a signal when light is incident upon them. The signal may be observed visually in reflected or transmitted light, or it may be electrical. The eyes of animals and the leaves of plants, for example, perform this function. Light, as well as other forms of electromagnetic energy, can also be detected by observing the temperature change which is produced in a body absorbing it. Furthermore, it can be detected by the color changes its absorption produces in certain materials. However, the need for high sensitivity or fast response or both usually leads, in optical technology, to detectors based on other mechanisms.

One of the most widely used optical detectors is photographic film. This method of detection is based on a photochemical process in particles embedded in the film. This fairly sensitive technique is more effective than others in detecting or recording, or both, the large amount of information usually contained in an image or a complicated optical spectrum. Disadvantages are its insensitivity to wavelengths longer than those in the optical range and the need to develop film after exposure.

In many cases, fast detector response is needed to detect rapid changes in incident light; also, an electrical output signal may be desired. The optimum detector here would be based on external or internal photoemission.

In an externally photoemitting device, the light incident upon a surface causes an emission of electrons from that surface into a vacuum. These electrons can be amplified in number by using electric and magnetic fields to cause them to impinge on other surfaces, thereby producing secondary electrons. Detectors of this type can be fabricated in such a way as to detect images. These detectors are limited to wavelengths in the visible region or shorter, but are capable of a sensitivity and speed of response higher than any other type. SEE PHOTOMUTIPLIER; PHOTOTUBE.

In an internally photoemitting device, incident light produces free charge carriers within a body and is detected through the effect of these charge carriers on the electrical impedance of the body. In its simplest and most widely used form, the body is a photoconductor whose impedance is high in the absence of incident light. Such detectors are less sensitive and slower than external photoemitters, but they require no vacuum envelope and operate at low voltages. They also have the advantage that some of them are sensitive to all wavelengths shorter than about 40 micrometers, far into the infrared. In general, however, operation at the longer wavelengths requires that the device be cooled. Detectors of this type can also be built in such a way as to detect images. This, however, is generally done with an electron beam as part of the read-out circuit and does require a vacuum envelope. SEE PHOTOCONDUCTIVE CELL; PHOTOCONDUCTIVITY.

A development among internal photoemitting detectors is the reverse-biased semiconductor diode, which takes advantage of a large electric field at the reverse-biased semiconductor *pn* junction to give a response faster than that of the devices simply based on photoconductivity in bulk samples. The device, when made of germanium, is sensitive to all wavelengths shorter than 1.6 μm. Its advantages are further increased by operating it at voltages which cause avalanche processes to follow each absorption of a photon. This gives rise to internal gain, and thereby increases the figure of merit of the device if, as is often the case, other sources of noise are dominant. It is difficult to produce avalanche diodes so that the properties of successive diodes are identical. This problem has been solved for the nonavalanching devices, however. Thus it has been possible to fabricate arrays which have potential for use in vidicons as image detectors. SEE OPTICAL COMMUNICATIONS; OPTICAL MODULATORS; PHOTODIODE; SEMICONDUCTOR DIODE.

*J. K. Galt*

**Bibliography.** L. K. Anderson and B. J. McMurty, High speed photodetectors, *Appl. Opt.*, 5:1573–1587, October 1966; H. Melchior, M. B. Fisher, and F. R. Arams, Photodetectors for optical communication systems, *Proc. IEEE*, 58:1466–1486, 1970; T. P. Pearsall, Long wavelength photodetectors, *Fiber Integr. Opt.*, 4:107–128, 1982; G. H. S. Rokos, Optical detection using photodiodes, *Opto-Electronics*, 5:351–366, 1973; G. E. Stillman and C. M. Wolfe, Avalanche photodiodes, in R. W. Willardson and A. C. Beer (eds.), *Semiconductors and Semimetals*, vol. 12, 1977; L. R. Tomasetta et al., High sensitivity optical receivers for 1.0–1.4 μm fiber-optic systems, *IEEE J. Quantum Electron.*, QE-14:800–804, 1978.

## Optical information systems

Devices that use light to process information. Optical information systems or processors consist of one or several light sources; one- or two-dimensional planes of data such as film transparencies, various lenses, and other optical components; and detectors. These elements can be arranged in various configurations to achieve different data processing functions. As light passes through various data planes, the light distribution is spatially modulated proportional to the information present in each plane. This modulation occurs in parallel in one or two dimensions, and the processing is performed at the speed of light. The high-speed and parallel-processing features of optical information processors, together with their small size and low power dissipation, are their attractive features. The processing speed is limited in practice by the rate at which new planes of data can be introduced into the system and the rate at which processed data can be removed from the output detectors.

Practical systems employ real-time and reusable spatial light modulators rather than film. These devices include various liquid, ferroelectric, magnetooptic, electrooptic, and acoustooptic crystals to convert optical data (for example, an ambient scene) or electrical data into a form suitable for spatially modulating the light passing through the system. (Usually, coherent laser light is employed.) Lenses, mirrors, computer-generated holograms, holographic optical elements, and fiber optics are used to manipulate and control the light as it passes through the system and thus to provide a quite versatile collection of architectures for diverse applications. Optical information processors can be grouped into three major classes: optical image processors, optical signal processors, and optical computers. The architecture of the optical system and the type of processing functions performed in each case differ considerably. SEE LASER.

**Optical image processing.** The basic optical image processing functions are shown in **Fig. 1**. An image $g(x,y)$ is placed in plane $P_1$ and illuminated with laser light. The light distribution incident on $P_2$ is the two-dimensional Fourier transform $G(u,v)$ of the input image $g(x,y)$. This Fourier-transform distribution is a representation of the spatial frequencies $(u,v)$ present in the input image. Lower spatial frequencies (corresponding to larger input shapes) lie closer to the center of $P_2$, and higher spatial frequencies (corresponding to smaller input image regions) lie further from the center of $P_2$. The orientation of each input object is reflected in the angular location of its corresponding spatial frequency distribution in $P_2$. Detectors placed in $P_2$ can feed this Fourier-coefficient information to a digital postprocessor for subsequent analysis and classification of the type of input object and its size and orientation. This is one form of optical extraction for pattern recognition and precise measurement of object size and orientation.

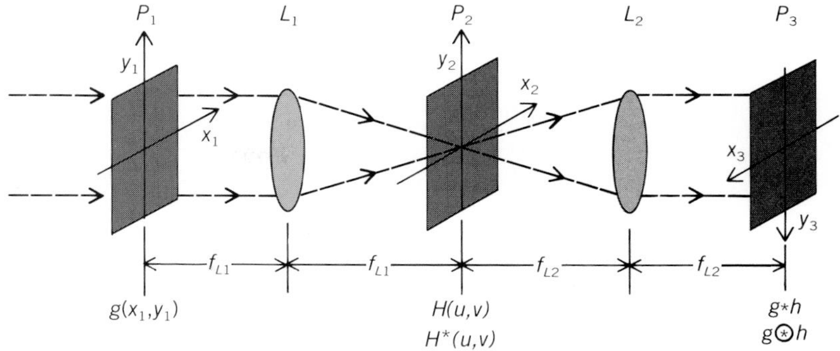


**Fig. 1. Optical Fourier transform and correlation image processor. Lenses $L_1$ and $L_2$ have focal lengths $f_{L1}$ and $f_{L2}$.**

Other architectures can optically compute other features of an input object such as its geometrical moments and its chord histogram distribution (the length and angle of all chords that define the object), which a digital postprocessor can analyze to determine the final class and orientation of the input object. Such feature extraction systems are the simplest form of optical pattern recognition image processors.

However, the full optical system of Fig. 1 can also perform the correlation operation. In this case, the transmittance of $P_2$ is made proportional to $H^*(u,v)$, the conjugate Fourier transform of a reference function $h(x,y)$. The $H^*(u,v)$ filter function at $P_2$ is formed by holographic techniques. Then, the $P_3$ pattern is the correlation of the two space functions $g$ and $h$, written $g\circledast h$. The correlation of two functions is equivalent to translating $h$ spatially over $g$ and, for each translation, forming the product and sum of $h$ and the associated region of $g$. The regions of an input scene $g$ that most closely match the reference function $h$ being searched for yield the largest output. This template matching operation can thus locate the presence and positions of reference objects in an input image. This object pattern recognition operation is achieved with no moving parts and is quite effective for extracting objects in clutter or high noise and for locating multiple occurrences of an object. Advanced filter synthesis techniques allow such systems to operate independent of scale, rotation, and other geometrical distortions between the input and reference object. Character recognition, robotics, missile guidance, and industrial inspection are the major applications that have been pursued for such architectures. If $H(u,v)$ rather than $H^*(u,v)$ is recorded at $P_2$, the $P_3$ output is an image, $g{*}h$, that is a filtered version of the input. The filter function of the system can be controlled by spatially varying the contents of $P_2$ to achieve image enhancement and restoration of blurred and degraded images.

*See* Character recognition; Computer vision; Image processing; Robotics.

**Optical signal processing.** Signal processing systems are used in radar, sonar, electronic warfare, and communications to determine the frequency and direction of arrival of input signals, and for correlation applications. These systems generally employ acoustooptic transducers to input electrical signals to the optical processor. The electronic input to an acoustooptic cell is converted to a sound wave which travels the length of the cell. If the cell is illuminated with light, the amplitude of the light leaving the cell will be proportional to the strength of the input signal, and the angle at which the light leaves will be proportional to the frequency of the input signal. Since the device and system are linear, if $N$ input signals are simultaneously present, $N$ light waves leave the cell at $N$ angles and strengths. A lens behind the cell focuses each light wave to a different spatial location in an output detector plane. Thus, an optical spectrum analyzer results (**Fig. 2**). Compact systems of this type exist, and bandwidths in excess of 2 GHz can be achieved and up to 1000 signals can be simultaneously processed. If a multichannel acoustooptic cell is used with input signals from different antennas or antenna elements, the two-dimensional Fourier transform of its output provides a two-dimensional display of the simultaneous frequency and direction of arrival of all received signals within the bandwidth of the cell. The angle at which light is deflected can be varied by varying the frequency of the input signal to the acoustooptic cell; a beam deflector or scanner based on this principle is used in most xerographic reproduction systems and laser printers. Other architectures using multiple cells can correlate two or more signals. These systems are used for simultaneous range and Doppler processing and for demodulation and synchronization of signals for communication applications. *See* Radar; Spectrum analyzer.

**Optical computing.** The optical processors described above are special-purpose architectures. The parallel and high-speed features of optical systems can also be used to fabricate rather general-purpose optical computers (which can be used to perform general functions). Much research has been done on the optical realization of parallel processors for multiplication and addition. A parallel two-dimensional multiplication occurs when a two-dimensional spatially modulated light beam is passed through a two-dimensional transparency. Certain two-dimensional spatial light modulators can also produce an output that is the difference between two successive two-dimensional inputs or contains only the moving objects within a two-dimensional input scene. The addition of two two-dimensional data planes occurs if two spatially modulated beams are incident on a detector array simultaneously or sequentially. Various number representations have been used (such as residue arithmetic) to design efficient parallel optical and numerical computers. *See* Computer systems architecture; Concurrent processing; Digital computer.

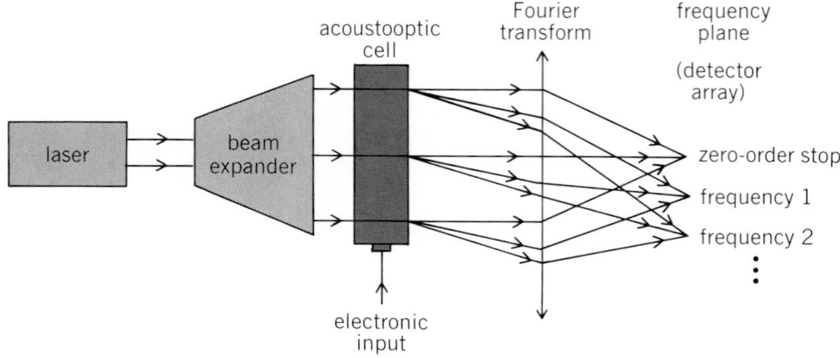

**Fig. 2. Acoustooptic signal spectrum analyzer.**

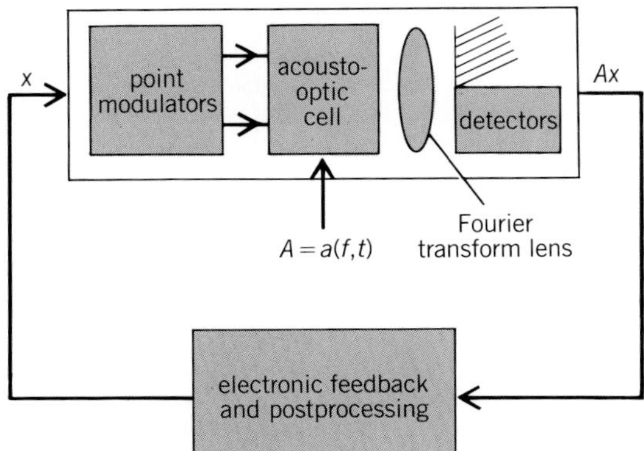

**Fig. 3. Optical linear algebra processor.**

The most attractive class of general-purpose optical computers is presently optical linear algebra processors. These systems perform matrix-vector operations and similar linear algebra algorithms, often in a systolic form. The architecture for one rather general form of such a processor (**Fig. 3**) exemplifies the basic concepts. This system consists of a linear array of input point modulators (for example, laser diodes), each of which is imaged through a different spatial region of an acoustooptic cell. The Fourier transform of the light distribution leaving the cell is formed on a linear output detector array. If the elements of $N$ input vectors are fed simultaneously at time $t$ to the acoustooptic cell, each vector on a different frequency $f$, then the transmittance of the cell will be $N$ vectors (that is, a matrix $A$). If the input point modulators are fed in parallel with the elements of another vector $x$, then the product of the input vector and the $N$ vectors in the cell is formed, and each vector inner product is produced (by the Fourier-transform lens) on a separate output detector. Thus, the system performs $N$ vector inner products or a matrix-vector multiplication in parallel. With various frequency, time, and space encoding techniques, different electrical postprocessing, and various feedback configurations, all of the major linear algebra operations required in modern signal processing can be achieved on this one system. Use of multichannel acoustooptic cells and related architectures can increase the processing capacity of the system and allow optical processing of data to the accuracy possible on digital computers.

*David Casasent*

**Bibliography.** N. J. Berg and J. N. Lee (eds.), *Acousto-Optic Signal Processing: Theory and Practice,* 1983; D. Casasent, Coherent optical pattern recognition, *Opt. Eng.,* 24:26–32, January 1985; Special issue on acousto-optic signal processing, *Proc. IEEE,* vol. 69, January 1981; Special issue on optical computing, *Proc. IEEE,* vol. 72, July 1984.

## Optical isolator

A very small four-terminal electronic circuit element that includes in an integral package a light emitter, a light detector, and, in some devices, solid-state electronic circuits. The emitting and detecting devices are so positioned that the majority of the emission from the emitter is optically coupled to the light-sensitive area of the detector. The device is also known as an optoisolator, optical-coupled isolator, and optocoupler. The device is housed in an integral opaque package so that the only optical emission impinging on the detector is that produced by the emitter. This configuration of components can perform as a solid-state electronic transformer or relay, since an electronic input signal causes an electronic output signal without any electrical connection between the input and the output terminals.

Optical isolators are particularly useful to electronic circuit and systems designers because two circuits often have a large voltage difference between them and yet it is necessary to transfer a small signal between them without changing the basic voltage level of either.

Before optical isolators were developed, this circuit function was performed by such devices as isolation transformers or signal relays. The optical isolator provides a number of advantages over such devices in that it is much smaller, much faster, has no contact bounce (unlike a relay), has no inductance (unlike a transformer), and provides a very high voltage isolation between the input and output circuits.

In order to discuss applications of the optical isolator, it is necessary to identify the different types of optical isolators that can be produced through the use of different light emitter-detector combinations.

**Optical emitters.** The optical emitter most commonly selected for use in optical isolators is the gallium arsenide light-emitting diode (LED), which emits in the infrared or near-infrared regions of the spectrum. The typical wavelength of the emission is 850 nanometers. The LED is extremely small (about the size of a transistor chip) and provides extremely fast infrared light pulses. Photodetectors fabricated from silicon are particularly sensitive to the wavelength of light emitted by the gallium arsenide LED, so that the transfer of a signal from the input to the output of the optical isolator is particularly efficient.

The other input devices commonly used are gas-discharge and incandescent lamps. These emitters tend to be somewhat larger and slower than LEDs, but are used when their particular electronic characteristics are desired, and in conjunction with detectors that have a spectral peak in the visible portion of the spectrum. *See* Light-emitting diode.

**Optical detectors.** The light detectors that are used in the construction of optical isolators include light-dependent resistors (such as photocells), light-sensitive devices that generate a voltage without any electrical input (such as photovoltaic devices), light-sensitive devices that switch from one state to another (such as photothyristors), and light-sensitive devices that modify a voltage or current (such as phototransistors, photodiodes, and photodetector-amplifier combinations).

Having such a wide variety of emitter and detector combinations available means that circuitry and system designers can use them over a wide range of applications. For example, the combination of a photocell and an incandescent lamp produces a device with entirely different characteristics from those of the combination of an LED and a phototransistor. Each combination is described below and its primary application identified.

***Incandescent lamp–photocell optical isolators.*** In these devices the resistance of the photocell varies from about 10 megohms to 1000 megohms, as the input light is varied from off to maximum brightness. If the input changes instantaneously, the output resistance change occurs in 20 ms (typical). If the input voltage changes gradually, the resistance of the photocell varies somewhat proportionally to the input voltage. As a result of this variable-resistance characteristic, the device whose schematic is shown in **Fig. 1** can be used as a remote-controlled rheostat where there is no electrical connection between the control wire and the circuit being controlled. In applications where signals are required for two separate circuits, without an electrical connection between any of the three circuits, devices are used with two photocells built into the case of the optical isolators.

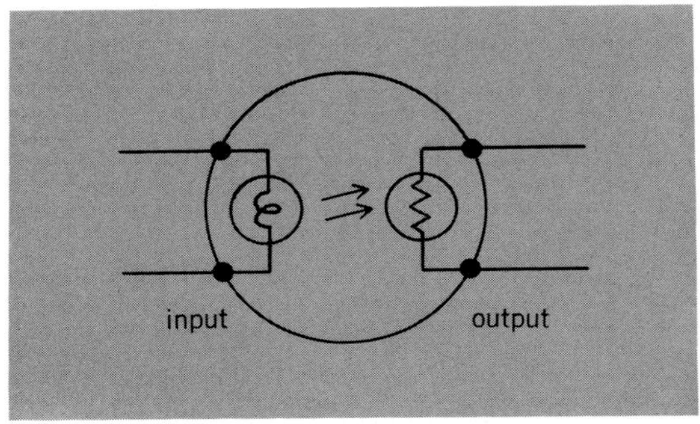


**Fig. 1. Schematic diagram of incandescent lamp–photocell optical isolator.**

***Neon lamp–photocell combinations.*** These devices have output characteristics similar to the incandescent lamp–photocell devices. However, the input characteristics vary dramatically, because the neon lamp does not emit light (ignite) until the input voltage reaches about 70 V. Also, the current after ignition is very small. These devices are employed where large input voltage swings are typical and where long life is required. A schematic diagram is shown in **Fig. 2**.

***LED-silicon detector combinations.*** All of the optical isolators that employ silicon photodetectors have LED emitters. The most common photodetector is the phototransistor. A schematic diagram of a type of LED-

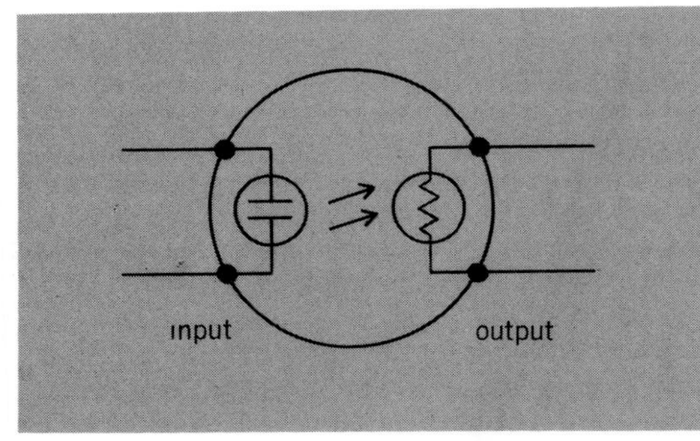


**Fig. 2. Schematic diagram of neon lamp–photocell optical isolator.**

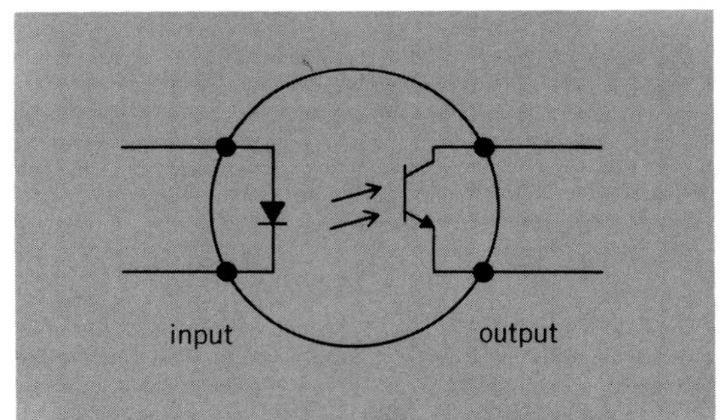


Fig. 3. Schematic diagram of LED-phototransistor optical isolator.

phototransistor optical isolator is shown in **Fig. 3**. In such devices the light from the LED causes the phototransistor current to vary as a function of the amount of light impinging on the photosensitive area of the phototransistor. The devices can isolate circuits that differ by as much as 5000 V. The devices are very fast, with the output current changing in some devices in as little as 10–20 ns after the occurrence of an input pulse. This fast response time means that these devices are particularly useful in computer circuit applications where such fast pulses are common. Not only do these devices provide high voltage isolation between circuits, but because the phototransistor has built-in gain, the detected signal is amplified. These devices are also immune to certain types of noise and are extremely small, the package being just larger than a typical transistor can. The devices can be used in most circuits that require an isolation transformer, and provide the additional advantages of higher speed and higher voltage ratings. Such devices also can perform as a solid-state relay (no mechanical wear, so no contact bounce), as a high-speed chopper, and as a pulse amplifier.

A similar type of optical isolator that produces a higher output amplitude for the same input employs a photo-Darlington sensor and output device. The photo-Darlington is in reality two phototransistors that are integrally connected. Although it does have increased amplification, it is a much lower speed device.

***LED-photodetector-amplifier.*** In some optical isolators, integrated circuits are also included in the package to provide specific output characteristics. For example, one optical isolator includes an integrated circuit amplifier so that the optical isolator can perform like a broadband pulse transformer that is compatible with diode-transistor-logic (DTL) computer circuitry as well as provide a frequency response to zero frequency. A schematic diagram of an LED–photodiode–integrated-circuit optical isolator is shown in **Fig. 4**. *SEE CIRCUIT (ELECTRONICS); OPTICAL DETECTORS; SEMICONDUCTOR DIODE.*

*Robert D. Compton*

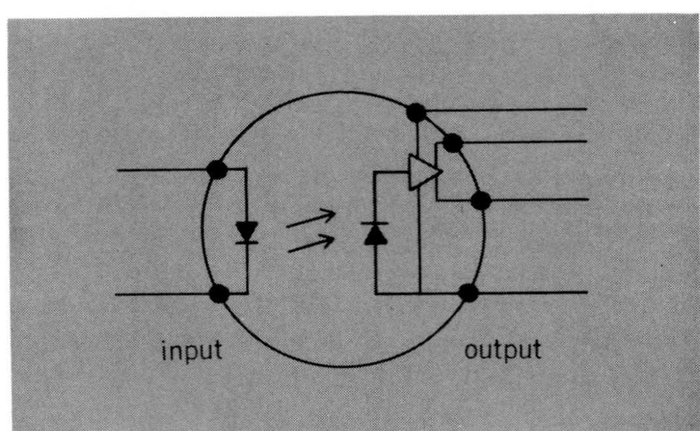


Fig. 4. Schematic diagram of LED–photodiode–integrated-circuit optical isolator.

## Optical modulators

Devices that serve to vary some property of a light beam. The direction of the beam may be scanned as in an optical deflector, or the phase or frequency of an optical wave may be modulated. Most often, however, the intensity of the light is modulated.

Rotating or oscillating mirrors and mechanical shutters can be used at relatively low frequencies (less than $10^5$ Hz). However, these devices have too much inertia to operate at much higher frequencies. At higher frequencies it is necessary to take advantage of the motions of the low-mass electrons and atoms in liquids or solids. These motions are controlled by modulating the applied electric fields, magnetic fields, or acoustic waves in phenomena known as the electrooptic, magnetooptic, or acoustooptic effect, respectively.

For the most part, it will be assumed that the light to be modulated is nearly monochromatic—either a beam from a laser or a narrow-band incoherent source.

**Electrooptic effect.** The quadratic or Kerr electrooptic effect is present in all substances and refers to a change in refractive index, $\Delta n$, proportional to the square of the applied electric field $E$. The liquids nitrobenzene and carbon disulfide and the solid strontium titanate exhibit a large Kerr effect. *SEE KERR EFFECT.*

Much larger index changes can be realized in single crystals that exhibit the linear or Pockels electrooptic effect. In this case, $\Delta n$ is directly proportional to $E$. The effect is present only in noncentrosymmetric single crystals, and the induced index change depends upon the orientations of $E$ and the polarization of the light beam. Well-known linear electrooptic materials include potassium dihydrogen phosphate (KDP) and its deuterated isomorph (DKDP or KD*P), lithium niobate ($LiNbO_3$) and lithium tantalate ($LiTaO_3$), and semiconductors such as gallium arsenide (GaAs) and cadmium telluride (CdTe). The last two are useful in the infrared (1–10 micrometers), while the others are used in the near-ultraviolet and visible regions (0.3–3 μm). *SEE FERROELECTRICS; SEMICONDUCTOR.*

The phase increment $\Phi$ of an optical wave of wavelength $\lambda$ that passes through a length $L$ of material with refractive index $n$ is given by Eq. (1). Thus

$$\Phi = \frac{2\pi}{\lambda} nL \qquad (1)$$

phase modulation can be achieved by varying $n$ electrooptically. Since the optical frequency of the wave is the time derivative of $\Phi$, the frequency is also shifted by a time-varying $\Phi$, yielding optical frequency modulation. *SEE MODULATION.*

The refractive index change is given in terms of an electrooptic coefficient $r$ by Eq. (2), where typical

$$n(E) = n(0)\,\frac{-n^3rE}{2} \qquad (2)$$

values for $n$ and $r$ are 2 and $3 \times 10^{-11}$ m/V, respectively.

**Electrooptic intensity modulation.** Intensity modulation can be achieved by interfering two phase-modulated waves as shown in **Fig. 1**. The electrooptically induced index change is different for light polarized parallel ($p$) and perpendicular ($s$) to the modulating field; that is, $r_p \neq r_s$. The phase difference for the two polarizations is the retardation $\Gamma$ given by Eq. (3), which is proportional to the applied voltage $V$. If

$$\Gamma(V) = \Phi_p - \Phi_s = \frac{2\pi}{\lambda}(n_p - n_s)L \qquad (3)$$

it is assumed that $n_p(0) = n_s(0)$ for $V = 0$, then $\Gamma(0) = 0$. Further assume that $\Gamma(V') = \pi$. Then incident light polarized at 45° to the field may be resolved into two equal, in-phase components parallel and perpendicular to the field. For $V = 0$, they will still be in phase at the output end of the electrooptic crystal and will recombine to give a polarization at +45° which will not pass through the output polarizer in Fig. 1.

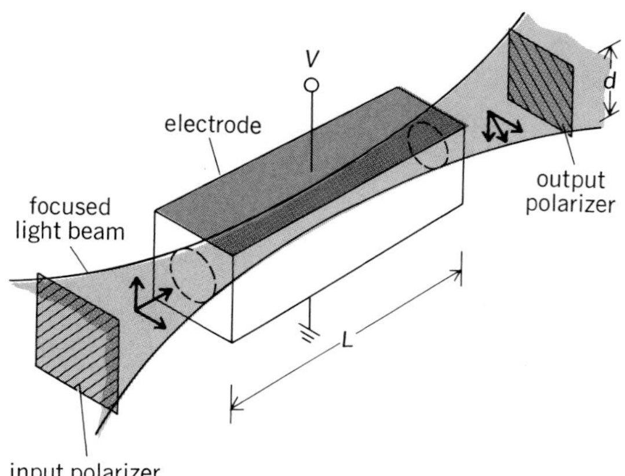


**Fig. 1. Electrooptic intensity modulator.**

For $V = V'$, however, the two components will be out of phase and will recombine to give a polarization angle of −45° which will pass through the output polarizer. The switching voltage $V'$ is called the half-wave voltage and is given by Eq. (4), with $d$ the

$$V' = \frac{\lambda d}{n^3 r_c L} \qquad (4)$$

thickness of the crystal and $r_c$ an effective electrooptic coefficient. A typical value for $n^3 r_c$ is $2 \times 10^{-10}$ m/V.

Electrooptic devices can operate at speeds up to several GHz.

**Acoustooptic modulation and deflection.** All transparent substances exhibit an acoustooptic effect—a change in $n$ proportional to strain. Typical materials with a substantial effect are water, glass, arsenic selenide ($As_2Se_3$), and crystalline tellurium dioxide ($TeO_2$).

An acoustic wave of frequency $F$ has a wavelength given by Eq. (5), where $C$ is the acoustic velocity,

$$\Lambda = \frac{C}{F} \qquad (5)$$

which is typically $3 \times 10^3$ m/s. Such a wave produces a spatially periodic strain and corresponding optical phase grating with period $\Lambda$ that diffracts an optical beam as shown in **Fig. 2**. A short grating

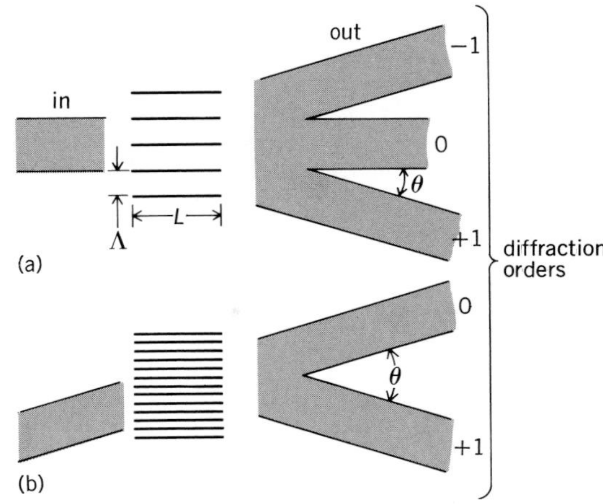


**Fig. 2. Acoustooptic modulator-deflector. (*a*) Raman-Nath regime. (*b*) Bragg regime.**

($Q < 1$) produces many diffraction orders (Raman-Nath regime), whereas a long grating ($Q > 10$) produces only one diffracted beam (Bragg regime). The quantity $Q$ is defined by Eq. (6). If one detects the

$$Q = \frac{2\pi L \lambda}{n\Lambda^2} \qquad (6)$$

Bragg-diffracted beam (diffraction order + 1), its intensity can be switched on and off by turning the acoustic power on and off.

The Bragg angle $\theta$ through which the incident beam is diffracted is given by Eq. (7). Thus the beam

$$\sin\frac{\theta}{2} = \frac{\lambda}{2\Lambda} \qquad (7)$$

angle can be scanned by varying $F$.

Acoustooptic devices operate satisfactorily at speeds up to several hundred megahertz.

**Optical waveguide devices.** The efficiency of the modulators described above can be put in terms of the electrical modulating power required per unit bandwidth to achieve, say, 70% intensity modulation or one radian of phase modulation. For very good bulk electrooptic or acoustooptic modulators, approximately 1 to 10 mW is required for a 1-MHz bandwidth; that is, a figure of merit of 1 to 10 mW/MHz. This figure of merit can be improved by employing a dielectric waveguide to confine the light to the same small volume occupied by the electric or acoustic field, without the diffraction that is characteristic of a

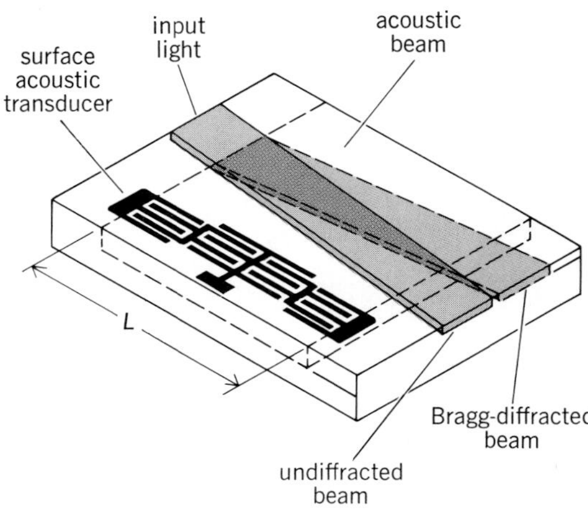


**Fig. 3. Waveguide acoustooptic modulator-deflector.**

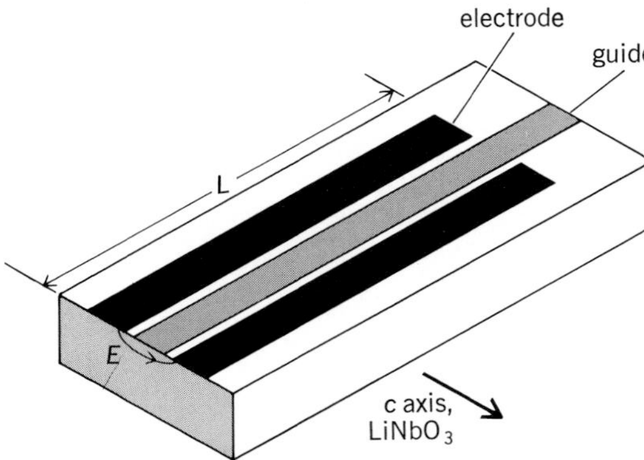


Fig. 4. Titanium-diffused $LiNbO_3$ strip waveguide with coplanar electrodes for electrooptic phase modulation.

focused optical beam. This optical waveguide geometry is also compatible with optical fibers and lends itself to integrated optical circuits. *See* INTEGRATED OPTICS; OPTICAL COMMUNICATIONS.

An optical wave can be guided by a region of high refractive index surrounded by regions of lower index. A planar guide confines light to a plane, but permits diffraction within the plane; a strip or channel guide confines light in both transverse dimensions without any diffraction.

Planar guides have been formed in semiconductor materials such as $Al_xGa_{1-x}As$ by growing epitaxial crystal layers with differing values of $x$. Since the refractive index decreases as $x$ increases, a thin GaAs layer surrounded by layers of $Al_{0.3}Ga_{0.7}As$ will guide light. If one of the outer layers is $p$-type and the other two layers are $n$-type, a reverse bias may be applied to the $pn$ junction to produce a large electric field in the GaAs layer. Very efficient electrooptic modulators requiring about 0.1 mW/MHz at $\lambda = 1$ μm have been realized in such junctions. Further improvement has been realized by loading the planar guide with a rib or ridge structure to provide lateral guiding within the plane. Ridge devices 1 mm long require about 5 V to switch light on or off, with a figure of merit of 10 μW/MHz.

Both planar and strip guides have been formed in $LiNbO_3$ by diffusing titanium metal into the surface in photolithographically defined patterns. Planar guides with surface acoustic wave transducers (**Fig. 3**) have been employed in waveguide acoustooptic devices. Strip guides (**Fig. 4**) have been used to make electrooptic phase modulators 3 cm long requiring 1 V to produce $\pi$ radians of phase shift at $\lambda = 0.63$ μm; the figure of merit is 2 μW/MHz. In order to make an intensity modulator or a $2 \times 2$ switch, a

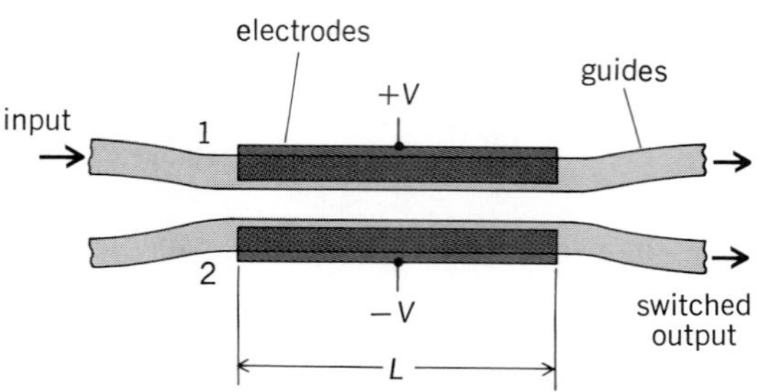


Fig. 5. Directional coupler waveguide modulator switch.

directional coupler waveguide pattern is formed, and electrodes are applied as shown in **Fig. 5**. With no voltage applied and $L$ the proper length, light entering guide 1 will be totally coupled to and exit from guide 2; with the proper applied voltage, the phase match between the two guides will be destroyed, and no light will be coupled to guide 2, but will all exit from guide 1. Switches and modulators operating at speeds up to 5 GHz have been realized in this way. *See* SURFACE ACOUSTIC-WAVE DEVICES.

*Ivan P. Kaminow*

**Bibliography.** R. C. Alferness, Guided wave devices for optical communication, *IEEE J. Quart. Elec.*, 17(6), June 1981; I. P. Kaminow, *An Introduction to Electrooptic Devices*, 1974; J. F. Nye, *Physical Properties of Crystals*, 1960; T. Tamir, *Integrated Optics*, 1975.

## Optical recording

The process of recording sound signals on a photosensitive medium so that they may be reproduced at a subsequent time. Photographic film has been widely used as the photosensitive medium, but in the late 1970s development of another kind of medium, the so-called optical disk, was undertaken. The introduction of the laser as a light source greatly improves the quality of reproduced sound signals. The pulse code modulation (PCM) techniques make it possible to obtain extremely high-fidelity reproduction of sound signals in optical disk recording systems. This ar-

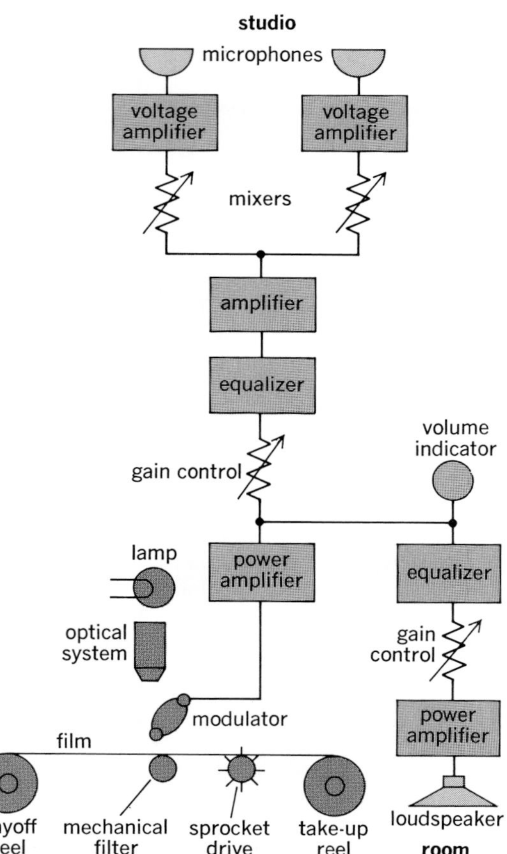


Fig. 1. Schematic arrangement of apparatus in a complete optical sound motion picture recording system.

ticle first describes optical film recording and then introduces some of more modern optical recording methods.

**Optical film recording system.** Optical film recording is also termed motion picture recording or photographic recording. A sound motion picture recording system consists basically of a modulator for producing a modulated light beam and a mechanism for moving a light-sensitive photographic film relative to the light beam and thereby recording signals on the film corresponding to the electrical signals. A sound motion picture reproducing system is basically a combination of a light source, optical system, photoelectric cell, and mechanism for moving a film carrying an optical record by means of which the recorded photographic variations are converted into electrical signals of approximately like form.

***Recording system.*** The elements in a complete monophonic sound motion picture recording system are shown in **Fig. 1**. The output of each microphone is amplified and fed to a mixer, a device having two or more inputs and a common output. If more than one microphone is used, as for example when there are two actors, one microphone for each, the outputs of the two microphones may be adjusted for the proper balance by means of the mixers. An electronic compressor is used to reduce the amplitude range to that suitable for reproduction in the home. An equalizer provides the standard motion picture recording characteristic. The gain control provides means for controlling the overall signal level fed to the power amplifer. The light modulator, actuated by the amplifer, records a photographic image upon the film corresponding to the electrical input. The narrow bands used for the sound record on motion picture film are called sound tracks. A monitoring system consisting of a volume indicator, complementary equalizer, gain control, power amplifier, and loudspeaker or headphone is used to control the recording operation. *SEE FREQUENCY-RESPONSE EQUALIZATION*.

***Modulator.*** In the variable-area recording system the transmitted light amplitude is a function of the amount of unexposed area in the positive print. This type of sound track is produced by means of a mirror galvanometer which varies the width of the light slit under which the film passes. The elements of a variable-area recording system are shown in **Fig. 2**. The triangular aperture is uniformly illuminated by means of a lamp and lens system. The image of this triangular aperture is reflected by the galvanometer mirror focused on the mechanical slit, which in turn is focused on the film. The galvanometer mirror swings about an axis parallel to the plane of the paper. The triangular light image on the mechanical slit moves up and down on the mechanical slit. The result is that the width of the exposed portion of the negative sound track corresponds to the rotational vibrations of the galvanometer. In the positive record, the width of the unexposed portion of the track corresponds to the signal.

A variable-density system has also been used, but it has been largely replaced by the variable-area system. The reproducer can play either one.

***Recording film transport.*** The film-transport mechanism used in recording sound on film consists of a positive drive of the perforated film and a constant-speed drive of the film where the modulated light beam strikes the film. A film-transport mechanism of this type is shown in **Fig. 3**. Positive drive of the film is obtained by the sprocket drive, which is interlocked with the camera drive so that synchronism of picture and sound will be obtained. When the film passes over the sprocket drive, variations in the motion of the film at the sprocket-hole frequency are produced. These variations in the film speed must be removed at the recording point to eliminate spurious frequency

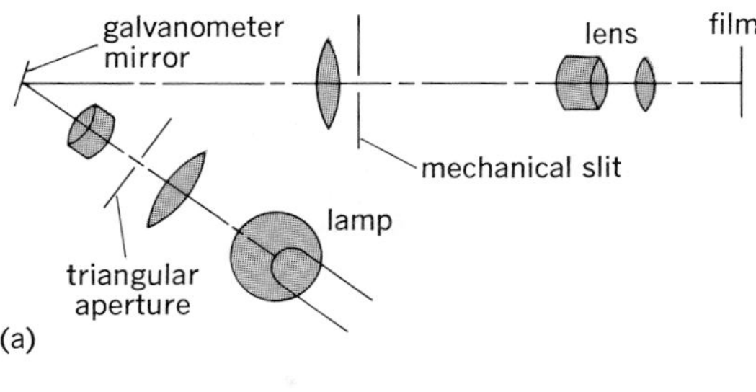


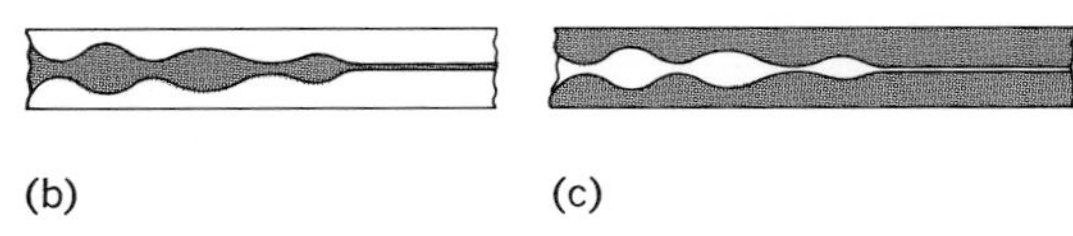


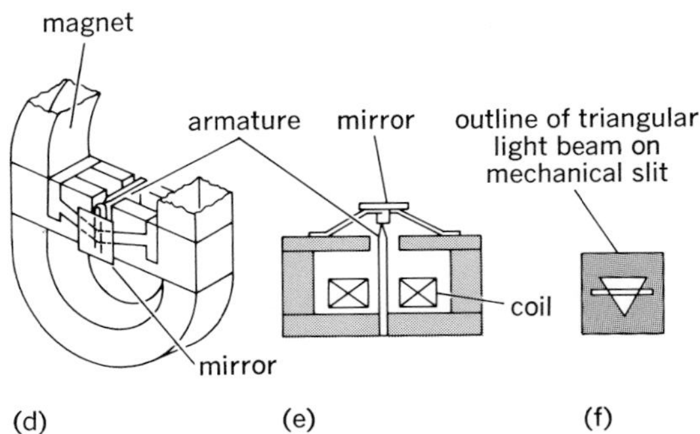


**Fig. 2. Elements of a variable-area sound motion picture film recording system. Transmitted light amplitude is a function of the amount of unexposed area in the positive print. (*a*) Schematic of a recording system. (*b, c*) Negative and positive sound tracks. (*d*) Perspective view. (*e*) Sectional view. (*f*) Mechanical slit.**

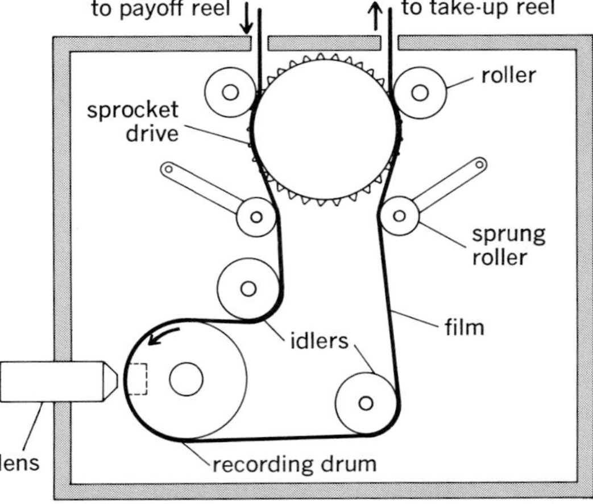


**Fig. 3. Photographic film-transport mechanism in a motion picture film sound recorder. (*After H. F. Olson, Modern Sound Reproduction, Van Nostrand, 1972*)**

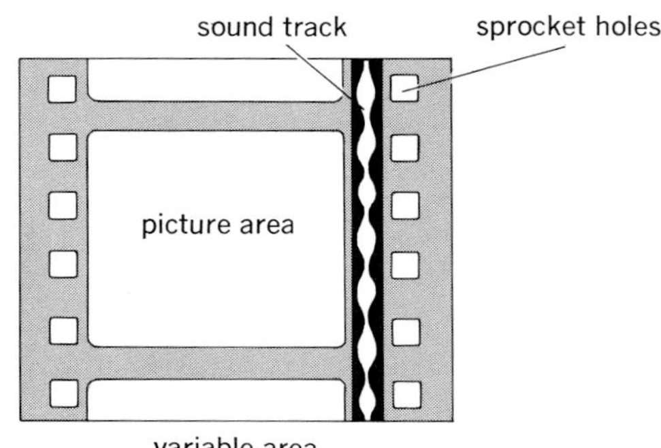


Fig. 4. Position of the picture and variable area sound track in a 35-mm sound motion picture film. (*After H. F. Olson, Modern Sound Reproduction, Van Nostrand, 1972*)

modulation of the image on the film. Uniform speed at the recording point is provided by a mechanical contrivance called a filter. It is located between the sprocket drive and recording point and consists of the inertia of the recording drum and the compliance of the film between the recording drum and the sprocket drive. The recording drum is driven by a magnetic system from the motor which drives the sprocket and thereby imparts a slight amount of drive to the film. The magnetic drive isolates the variations in the rotational speed of the motor drive from the rotating drum. The combination of the isolating filter and magnetic drive provides a system with very uniform motion of the surface of the drum. The image of the modulator is focused on the film while it is in contact with the drum.

***Film and sound track.*** In the recording of sound motion pictures, the picture and sound are recorded on separate photographic films. The camera and sound recorder must be synchronized. This is accomplished by the use of an interlock system between the camera and sound recorder and the use of perforated film in the form of sprocket holes along the two edges of the film for both the camera and sound recorder.

The sound track on 35-mm film occupies a space about 0.1 in. (2.5 mm) wide just inside the sprocket holes, as shown in **Fig. 4**.

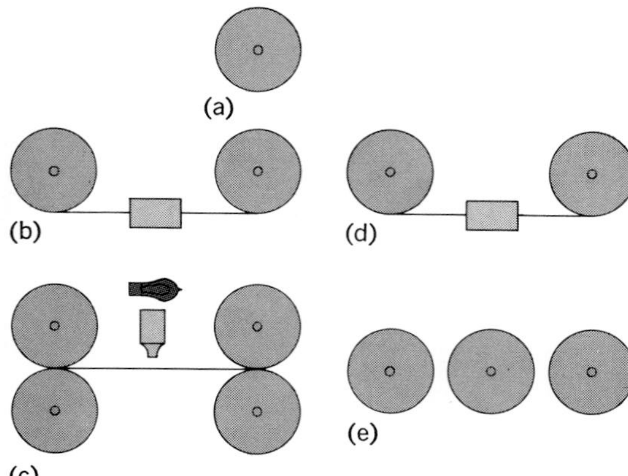


Fig. 5. Steps in the process for the production of motion picture positive film from negative film. (*a*) Undeveloped negative record on film. (*b*) Negative developer. (*c*) Developed negative record on film printer. Printed positive record on film. (*d*) Positive developer. (*e*) Positive film records on reels. (*After H. F. Olson, Modern Sound Reproduction, Van Nostrand, 1972*)

***Film developing and printing.*** The processes used in the film laboratory for the mass production of motion picture positive prints are shown in **Fig. 5**. The negative record of Fig. 5*a* is developed as shown in Fig. 5*b*. Then the required number of positive prints of both picture and sound is printed from the negative record as shown in Fig. 5*c*. These positive records are developed as shown in Fig. 5*d*. The positive records of Fig. 5*e* are used for sound reproduction and picture projection in the theater.

***Reproducing system.*** The elements in a complete sound motion picture reproducing system are shown in **Fig. 6**. The first element is the optical system, consisting of a lamp and a lens arrangement which produces an illuminated slit of light upon the film. The light beam passes through the film and falls upon the photoelectric cell. When the film is pulled past the slit, the variations in light, which are due to the variable-density or variable-area recording on the film, fall upon the photoelectric cell and are converted into the corresponding electrical variations. The output of the photoelectric cell is fed to an amplifier followed by a filter, which is used to cut the ground noise (residual noise in the absence of the signal) due to the film above the upper limit of reproduction, and by equalizers, which are used to adjust the frequency characteristic to that suitable for the best sound reproduction in the theater. The volume control (gain con-

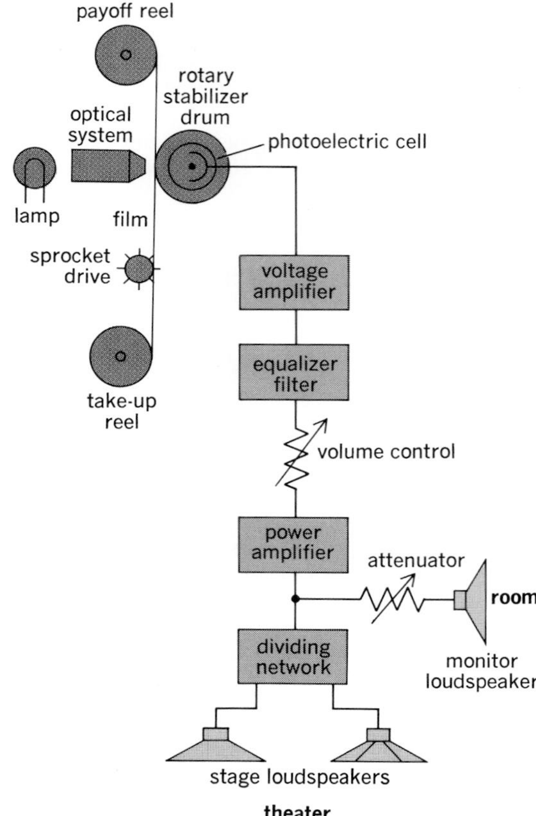


Fig. 6. Schematic arrangement of apparatus in a complete optical sound motion picture reproducing system.

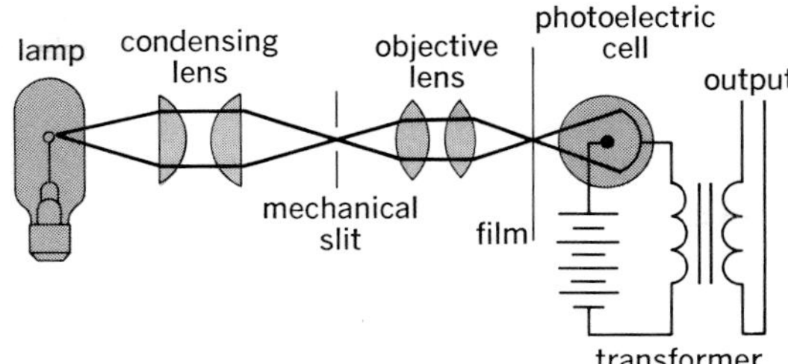


**Fig. 7. Diagrammatic arrangement of elements of a motion picture film sound-reproducing system.**

trol) is used for adjusting the level of sound output. The output of the power amplifier feeds the stage loudspeakers, located behind the screen, and the monitoring loudspeaker. Except for the stage loudspeakers, the entire equipment including the monitoring loudspeaker is located in the projection booth.

***Optical electronic reproducer.*** The elements of a motion picture film sound-reproducing system are shown in **Fig. 7**. The light source, in the form of an incandescent lamp, is focused upon a mechanical slit by means of a condensing lens. The mechanical slit in turn is focused on the negative film. The height of the image on the film is usually about 0.00075 in. (19 micrometers). Under these conditions the amount of light which impinges upon the photocell is proportional to the unexposed portion of the sound track in variable-area recording. When the film is in motion, the resultant light undulations which fall upon the photocell correspond to the voltage variations applied to the recording galvanometer. The voltage output of the photocell is proportional to the amount of light which falls upon the cathode.

***Reproducing film transport.*** The film transport used in reproducing sound on photographic film consists of a positive drive of the perforated film and a constant-speed drive where the light passes through the film to the photoelectric cell. A film transport mechanism of this type is shown in **Fig. 8**. Positive drive of the film is obtained by means of the two sprocket drives. The sprocket drives are geared with the positive picture drive so that a constant loop of film is maintained between the sound head and the picture head. The positive drive also ensures that the film speed in reproduction will be the same as that in recording. There is a loose loop of film between the picture head and the sound head, and for this reason variations in the picture drive will not be imparted to the sound head.

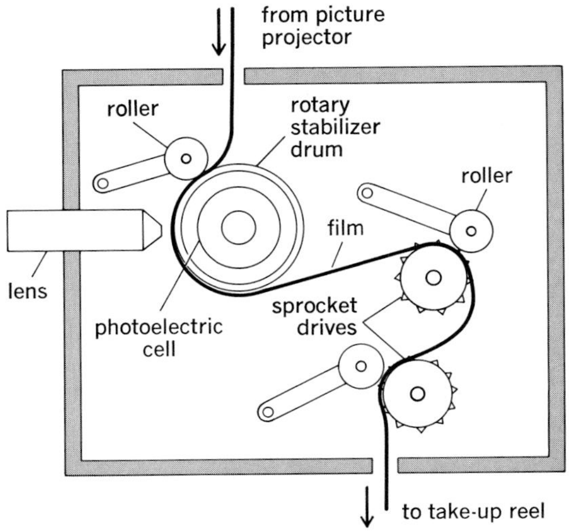

**Fig. 8. Photographic film transport mechanism of a motion picture film sound reproducer. (*After H. F. Olson, Modern Sound Reproduction, Van Nostrand, 1972*)**

After the film enters the sound head, it passes over a drum. The light beam of the reproducing system passes through the film to the photocell located inside the drum while the film is on the drum. The drum is driven by the first sprocket drive. The compliance of the film between the film and the sprocket provides a mechanical filter system and thereby reduces the sprocket-hole ripple at the drum. Under these conditions, the drum is rotated at a constant speed, and as a consequence the film will move past the light beam at a constant speed. The second sprocket isolates the takeup reel from the reproducing system.

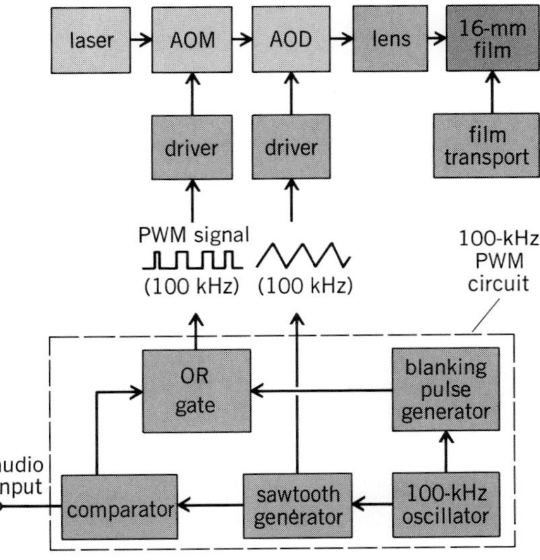


**Fig. 9. Block diagram of the laser sound recorder. (*After T. Taneda et al., A high quality optical sound recording system using a scanned laser beam, SMPTE J., 89:95–97, 1980*)**

***Distortion and noise in reproduction.*** Most commonly, distortion in an optical reproducing system is due to the inherent nonlinear characteristics of the photographic process. This type of distortion can be reduced to a low value by the use of proper illumination in the recording or duplicating process. The developing processes must also be accurately controlled in order to achieve a low value of nonlinear distortion.

Noise in clean film is due to the inherent grain structure of the photographic medium. Scratches and foreign particles on the film add additional noise.

Another source of distortion is a nonuniform motion of the film in the recording and reproducing process. This is manifested as a frequency modulation of the reproduced signal and is termed flutter and wow.

**Laser-beam film recording.** An optical film system which utilizes a laser as a light source and a combination of an acoustooptical modulator (AOM) and an acoustooptical deflector (AOD) instead of a galvanometer was developed in the late 1970s (**Fig. 9**). A

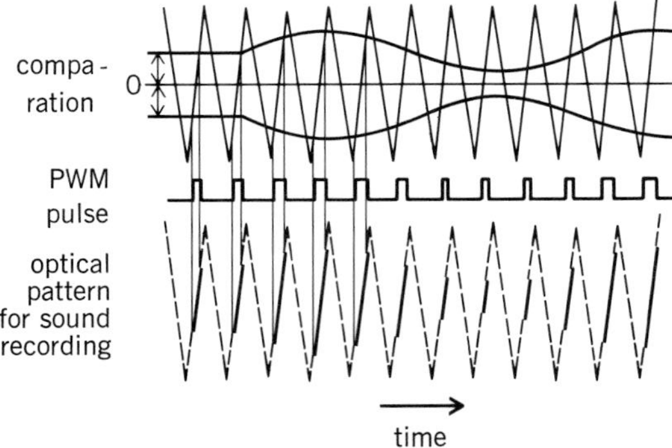


**Fig. 10. Schematics of the sound track waveform generation of the laser sound recorder. (*After T. Taneda et al., A high quality optical sound recording system using a scanned laser beam, SMPTE J., 89:95–97, 1980*)**

100-kHz pulse width modulation (PWM) circuit converts the audio input signal into a PWM signal. The laser beam is made to continuously scan the sound track area at right angles to the direction of the film transport. This is done by means of the AOD, which in turn is driven by a 100-kHz sawtooth signal. Simultaneously, the laser beam is pulse-width-modulated by means of the AOM, which is driven by a 100-kHz PWM signal. The AOD scanning signal and the AOM pulse-width-modulated signal combine and generate the variable-area sound track exposure on the film (**Fig. 10**). Because the actual distance between successive scans is much smaller than shown in Fig. 10, the traces of successive scans are fused into a pattern of variable-area recording.

The layout and operation of the laser beam are illustrated in **Fig. 11**. The light from laser is at first pulse-width-modulated in the AOM at 10 microsecond (0.01-kHz) intervals in response to the amplitude of the audio signal. As is normal for acoustooptical modulation, the modulated beam is separated into a zeroth-order (nondeflected) and a first-order (deflected) beam. Only the first-order beam is used, and the zeroth-order beam is blocked by an optical stop. Next, the diameter of the first-order beam is expanded to the size of the aperture. The beam is then deflected by the AOD and is again separated into a first-order and zeroth-order beam. Both beams are now converged to form spot images by means of a pair of cylindrical lenses. The first-order beam is focused on the film, while the zeroth-order beam is blocked by a fixed optical spot just in front of the film. Owing to the nature of the recording system, a wide-band frequency response can be obtained. A comparison of recorded sound tracks obtained by the laser-beam method and the conventional one (**Fig. 12**) indicates that sharper peaks and dips are obtained by the laser-beam method, clearly demonstrating that wider frequency response is achieved by the laser-beam method than by the conventional one. *See Laser; Pulse modulation.*

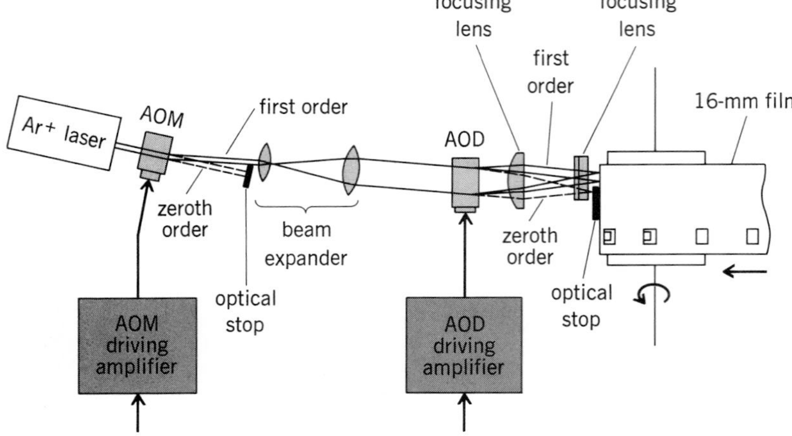


**Fig. 11. Basic layout of the main optical components of the laser-beam sound recorder. (*After T. Taneda et al., A high quality optical sound recording system using a scanned laser beam, SMPTE J., 89:95–97, 1980*)**

**PCM optical sound disk player.** The development of an optical disk was undertaken in the late 1970s. It allows a color television program of about 30 minutes' duration to be reproduced from a recording on a phonographlike disk 30 cm (12 in.) in diameter. Owing to its wide frequency range characteristics, up to several megahertz, it can also serve to record or reproduce digitized (plus code modulation or PCM) audio signals. The PCM optical sound disk player has the following superior characteristics which are not available from the conventional disk: (1) wide-frequency-range (up to 20 kHz) audio signals; (2) extremely large dynamic range; and (3) the complete absence of various distortions inherent in conventional records such as tracing distortion, pinch effect, and flutter and wow. These are direct results of PCM techniques applied to audio signal recording.

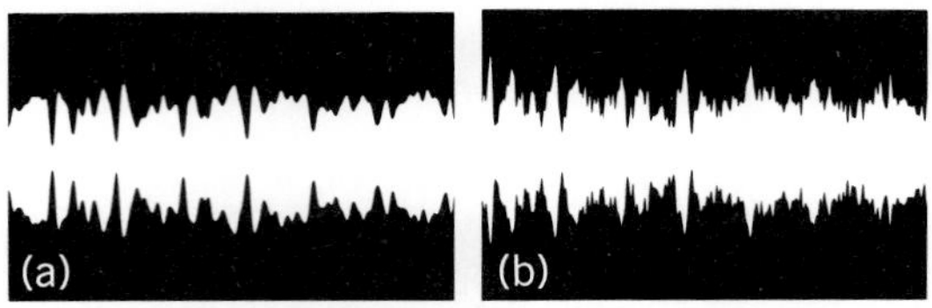


**Fig. 12. Comparison of two microscopic photographs of recorded waveform on sound track obtained by (*a*) conventional optical recorder and (*b*) laser-beam sound recorder.**

***Process of PCM disk recording.*** In the recording system (**Fig. 13**), an originating disk is obtained by coating a thin layer of evaporated metal on one side of a glass disk. The audio signal is passed through a PCM coding circuit for conversion into a digital signal which is then frequency-modulated. This frequency-modulated signal is then applied to the optical modulator which chops the continuous beam of light from the argon laser. The laser-beam intensity corresponding to the frequency modulation is then focused into a spot of about 0.8-micrometer (0.00003-in.) diameter by the optical condenser. The information is thus recorded as a series of pits in thin metal film on the disk (**Fig. 14**). In order to maintain the laser spot upon the disk at this constant value, an automatic optical focusing system is provided. The track pitch is 1.6 micrometers.

***Optical disk record manufacture.*** The optical PCM disk record is produced simply by the normal pressing techniques. The original disk is used to make the regular type of master, mother, and stamper. The stamper is then used to make a pressing of transparent polyvinylchloride. The surface on which PCM signals are recorded is plated with an aluminum or other metal film, and then this surface is protected with plastic coating. SEE DISK RECORDING.

***Disk reproducing process.*** The PCM laser sound disk player (**Fig. 15**) rotates the disk at the correct speed. Its optical system directs and focuses a low-power (1-mW) helium-neon laser beam to a small read spot on the surface of the disk and then collects the reflected optical energy and directs it to a single photodetector. The received energy at the photodetector changes according to the presence of recorded pits. Its electronic circuits process the received signal into digitized form, and the subsequent digital-to-analog converter converts the digital signals into the audio output signals with high fidelity. The player has several servo systems that make it possible to position the read spot on the disk surface correctly. SEE DIGITAL-TO-ANALOG CONVERTER.

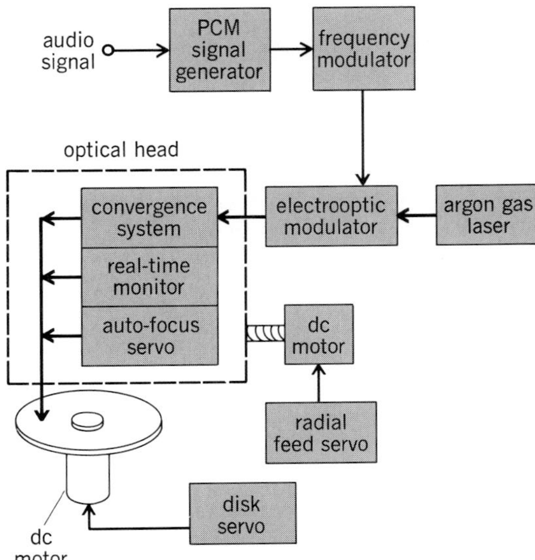


**Fig. 13. Block diagram of recording apparatus for the PCM laser-beam sound disk. (*After S. Itoya et al., Development of the PCM laser sound disc player, IEEE Trans. Consumer Electr., CE-24:443–452, 1978*)**

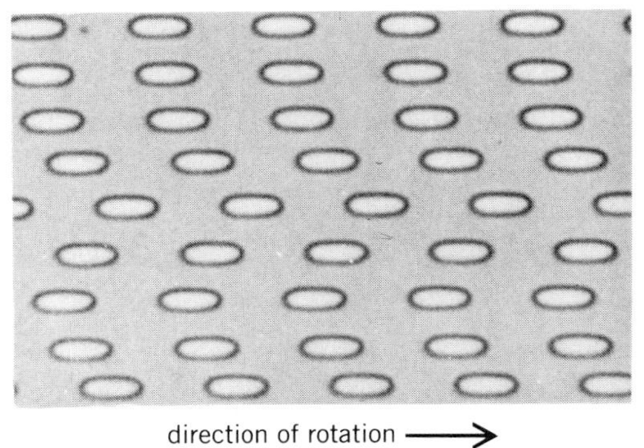


**Fig. 14. Microscopic photograph of the pattern of recorded pits on the PCM laser sound disk player.**

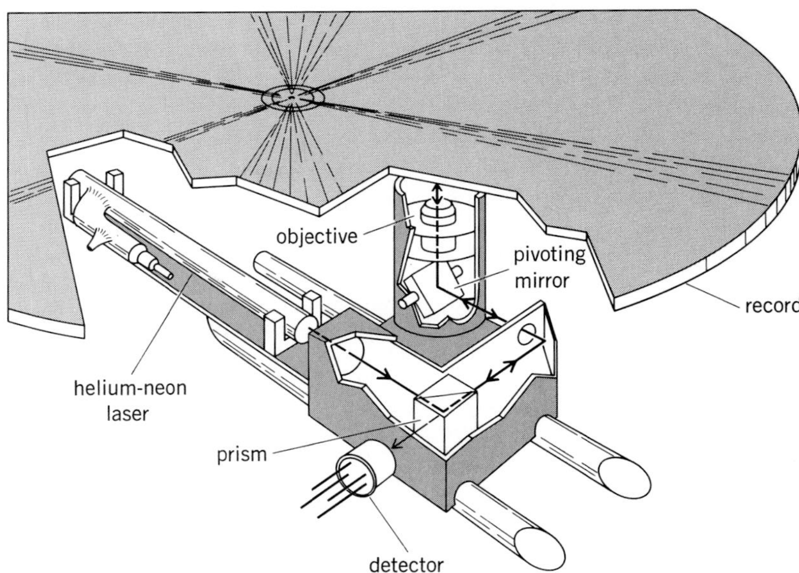


**Fig. 15. PCM laser sound disk player.**

*H. Date*

***Bibliography.*** S. Itoya et al., Development of the PCM laser sound disc player, *IEEE Trans. Consumer Electr.*, CE-24:443–452, 1978; H. F. Olson, *Modern Sound Reproduction*, 1972; T. Taneda et al., A high-quality optical sound recording system using a scanned laser beam, *SMPTE J.*, 89:95–97, 1980.

# Optimization

In its most general meaning, the efforts and processes of making a decision, a design, or a system as perfect, effective, or functional as possible. Formal optimization theory encompasses the specific methodology, techniques, and procedures used to decide on the one specific solution in a defined set of possible alternatives that will best satisfy a selected criterion. Because of this decision-making function the term optimization is often used in conjunction with procedures which more appropriately belong in the more general domain of decision theory. Strictly speaking, formal optimization techniques can be applied only to a certain class of decision problems known as decision making under certainty.

## Concepts and Terminology

Conceptually, the formulation and solution of an optimization problem involves the establishment of an evaluation criterion based on the objectives of the optimization problem, followed by determination of the optimum values of the controllable or independent parameters that will best satisfy the evaluation criterion. The latter is accomplished either objectively or by analytical manipulation of the so-called criterion function, which relates the effects of the independent parameters on the dependent evaluation criterion parameter. In most optimization problems there are a number of conflicting criteria and a compromise must be reached by a trade-off process which makes relative value judgements among the conflicting criteria. Additional practical considerations encountered in most optimization problems include so-called functional and regional constraints on the parameters. The former represents physical or functional interrelationships which exist among the independent parameters (that is, if one is changed it causes some changes in the others); the latter limits the range over which the independent parameters can be varied.

**Application.** Before proceeding with a detailed description of the steps involved in formulating and solving optimization problems in general, a simple problem is briefly discussed below to demonstrate the overall concepts and terminology.

A common optimization problem is solved in tuning a bad-reception TV channel. Because the tuning knob position for the best picture is usually different from the position giving the best sound quality, it is impossible to have both optimum sound and picture simultaneously. In this case the position of the knob becomes the independent parameter (it can be controlled by the person performing the optimization) whose value determines the resulting value of the criteria, which in this case are picture clarity and sound quality. The relative importance of the two conflicting criteria in regard to his objectives must be judged by the optimizer in order for him to arrive at an optimum setting of the tuning knob. If, for example, the viewer is interested in reading some printed information displayed on the screen he will optimize the picture resolution at the expense of sound quality, while sound quality may be the primary criterion in watching a concert on TV. For general viewing a setting which represents a trade-off between the two criteria might be chosen. This setting would be suboptimum with respect to picture resolution and sound quality, but would be optimum with respect to the combined criteria of sound and picture. In this example picture resolution and sound quality have been considered as the conflicting criteria. Both of these can have rather broad interpretation and for a more formalized optimization it is necessary to define some measurable, quantitative parameters which would serve to describe the criteria. In that case, it is possible experimentally to obtain two criterion functions which would show the behavior of the picture criterion and the sound criterion as a function of tuning knob setting, as shown schematically in **Fig. 1***a* and *b*. Regional constraints on the range of possible knob positions might be imposed by the fact that an unbearable noise develops at knob settings below a certain value or that the picture blacks out completely at knob settings above a certain value.

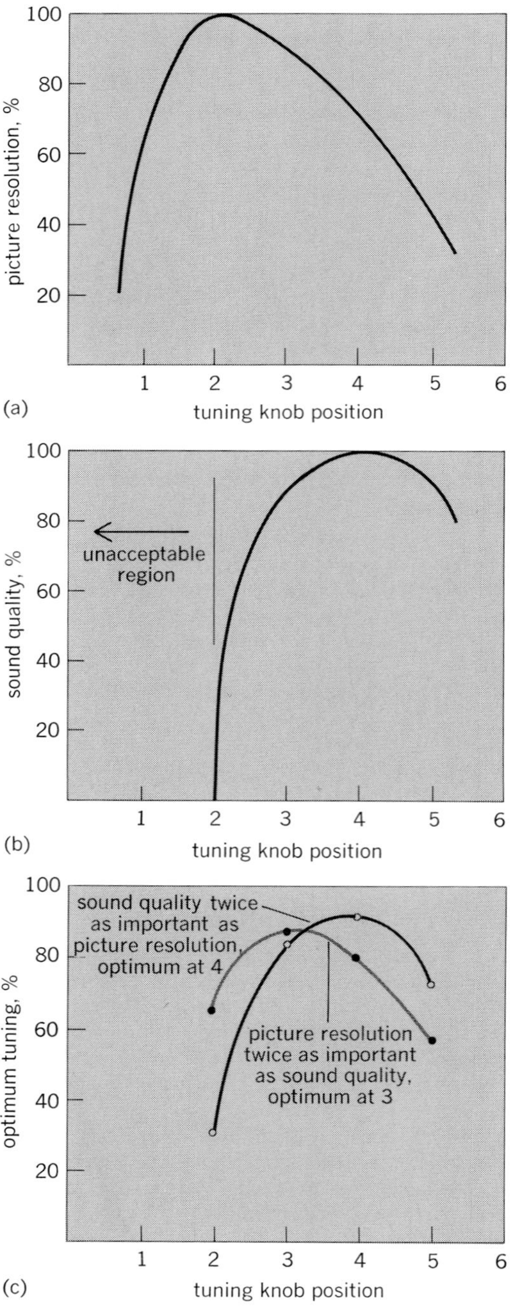


**Fig. 1. Effects of tuning knob positions on the quality of the television picture. (*a*) Picture quality. (*b*) Sound quality. (*c*) Two overall criterion functions.**

After a value judgment with respect to the relative importance of the two criteria has been made, an overall criterion function can be established. Figure 1*c* shows two overall criterion functions: one with units of picture resolution twice as important as units of sound quality, and the other with the relative importance of the criteria reversed. It is easily observed that the optimum setting of the knob (at which the value of the overall criterion is at a maximum) is different for the two cases.

**Other parameters.** It should be emphasized that optimization techniques only work for a specific system or configuration which has been described to a point where all criteria and parameters are defined within the system and are isolated and independent from other parameters outside the boundaries of the defined system. Formal optimization is not a substitute for creativity in that it depends on a clear definition of the system to be optimized, and even though an optimum solution for a given system configuration is obtained, this does not guarantee that a better solution is not available.

This can best be demonstrated by expanding the example given above. After the optimum tuning knob setting has been determined, someone may come along and change the direction of the TV antenna (a parameter which was not included in the original problem), thus producing perfect picture and sound, or someone may suggest that the viewer watch the program on a portable TV which has perfect reception of the particular channel in question. Both of these solutions are obviously more optimal than the original one but would not be identified by formal optimization techniques. This very vital deficiency of optimization theory is frequently overlooked. Realistically speaking, formal optimization theory should be used only to find optimum parameters in well-defined, preferably analytically describable systems with unique, quantitative-dependent and -independent parameters, criterion function, and functional and regional constraints. When several system configurations are possible, each should be optimized and then compared with the others.

### Optimization Problem Formulation

To further demonstrate formal optimization procedures and solution techniques, a step-by-step description of the procedures follows and is applied to an example.

**Definition.** This is a critical part of problem formulation and consists of:

(1) A description of the system configuration to be optimized, including definition of system boundaries to an extent that system parameters become isolated and independent of external parameters.

(2) Definition of a single, preferably quantitative, parameter which will serve as the overall evaluation criterion for the specific optimization problem. This is the dependent parameter (it depends upon the choice of the optimum solution) which measures how well the solution satisfies the desired objectives of the problem and this is the parameter which will be maximized or minimized to satisfy the objectives. As mentioned earlier, the process of finding a single evaluation parameter can become quite complex because normally specification of the optimum solution is complicated by conflicting criteria.

A compromise or trade-off between conflicting criteria must be reached by making value decisions based on value judgment of the relative importance of each criterion. The relative value of each criterion with respect to the others depends on the objectives of the optimization problem. Thus, in a complicated optimization problem all criteria relevant to the objectives must be enumerated, their relative importance established, and this information combined into a single parameter that will serve as the optimization criterion.

(3) Definition of controlled or independent parameters that will have an effect on the criterion. These are the parameter or parameters whose values determine the value of the criterion parameter and these should include all controllable parameters which influence the criterion and are within the boundaries of the defined problem.

**Criterion function.** The most critical aspect of formulating a formal optimization problem is the establishment of a satisfactory criterion function that describes the behavior of the evaluation criterion as a function of the independent parameters. The criterion function, often also referred to as the pay-off or objective function, usually takes the form of a penalty or cost function (which attempts are made to minimize) or a merit, benefit or profit function (which attempts are made to maximize by choosing the optimum values of the independent variables). In order to apply formal solution methods, the criterion function should be expressed graphically or analytically. In symbolic form the criterion function can be expressed as: criterion parameter = function of independent parameters $x_1, x_2, \ldots, x_n$. This may be represented by Eq. (1).

$$C = f(x_1, x_2, \ldots, x_n) \tag{1}$$

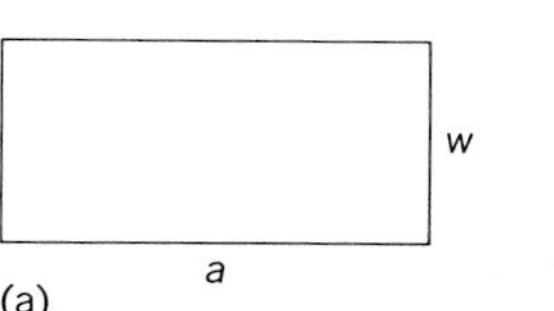

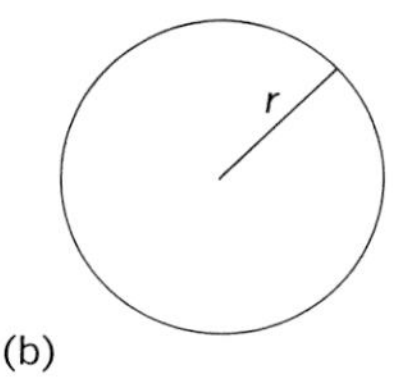


**Fig. 2.** Possible shapes for garden plots. (*a*) Rectangular. (*b*) Circular.

At this point it should be helpful to introduce another example to illustrate the steps described so far. The problem of optimizing the shape of a vegetable garden so as to maximize the available planting area which can be enclosed by a given length of fence will be considered.

To formalize the problem, a system configuration must be chosen. Several obvious possibilities come to mind, such as triangular, rectangular, elliptical, or even polyhedral shapes, or randomly shaped, closed curves. Consideration will be limited to the two shapes shown in **Fig. 2**, namely, a rectangular configuration and a circular configuration. It should be noted that, based on some objective judgments, some possible configurations which may give a better solution than the chosen shapes have been eliminated.

The implied criterion is the maximization of the area of the garden, which emerges as the principal criterion even though secondary considerations such as esthetics and compatibility with the surroundings may have already influenced the choice of the configurations actually being optimized.

The independent parameters in the two suboptimization problems which have developed become the length $a$ and width $w$ of the rectangular plot and the radius $r$ of the circular plot. The respective criterion functions for the three choices are given by Eqs. (2).

$$A = aw \tag{2a}$$

$$A = \pi r^2 \tag{2b}$$

To continue the example it is necessary to return to the optimization steps.

**Functional constraints.** Physical principles of operation which govern the relationship among the various independent parameters of the problem represent functional constraints. Symbolically, this becomes functional constraints = functions of independent parameters $x_1, x_2, \ldots, x_n$. This is represented by Eqs. (3). The number of independent functional constraints

$$fc_1 = f_1\,(x_1, x_2, \ldots, x_n) \tag{3a}$$

$$fc_2 = f_1\,(x_1, x_2, \ldots, x_n) \tag{3b}$$

$$fc_m = f_m\,(x_1, x_2, \ldots, x_n) \tag{3c}$$

must always be less than the number of independent parameters; otherwise all independent parameters can be eliminated from the criterion function, resulting in a single solution without a choice for optimization.

In the example the respective functional constraints relating the problem parameters become Eqs. (4).

$$2a + 2w = L \text{ (rectangle)} \tag{4a}$$

$$2\pi r = L \text{ (circle)} \tag{4b}$$

Since the circle only has one independent parameter, $r$, the single functional constraint eliminates that parameter when combined with the criterion function; for example, $A = \pi r^2$ and $r = L/2\pi$ (from the constraint) so that Eq. (5) is obtained. This result indi-

$$A = \frac{\pi L^2}{2\pi} = \frac{L^2}{4\pi} \quad (5)$$

cates that, regardless of the size of the radius chosen, the relationship between the area and the total length of the fence is unique and given by Eq. (6).

$$A = L^2/4\pi \quad (6)$$

In general, when an optimization problem includes functional constraints, these can be used to eliminate the number of independent parameters that can be varied (as will be indicated further in discussing solution methods).

**Regional constraints.** Most optimization problems involve practical limits on the range over which each parameter or function of the parameters can be varied. Symbolically these regional constraints are expressed as the inequalities in Eqs. (7).

$$l_1 \leq r_1 (x_1, x_2, \ldots, x_n) \leq l_2 \quad (7a)$$

$$l_3 \leq r_2 (x_1, x_2, \ldots, x_n) \leq l_4 \quad (7b)$$

$$l_{2p-1} \leq r_p (x_1, x_2, \ldots, x_n) \leq l_{2p} \quad (7c)$$

There can be any number of regional constraints to limit the analytical region of independent parameters over which one can search for the optimum. For the respective configurations in the above example, it is possible to stipulate the regional constraints given in Eqs. (8).

$$L \leq 100 \text{ ft} \quad (8a)$$

$$a \leq 50 \text{ ft} \qquad w \leq 50 \text{ ft} \quad (8b)$$

**Solution of optimization problems.** The reliability and the sophistication of the solutions of optimization problems increase as the problem becomes better defined. In the early stages of optimization of a complex problem, the considerations may be primarily objective judgments based on the optimizer's judgments of the relevant parameters. As alternative subsystem and system configurations evolve through a process of conceptualization, analysis and evaluation, and elimination of undesirable system configurations, a clearer configuration of parts of the problem can be defined, together with the relevant criteria, parameters, and constraints. Although these initial stages are often also referred to as optimization, the techniques of searching for alternate strategies and determining the single best choice are more generally referred to as decision theory. Procedures for defining competing systems or alternate strategies and formulating the problem in order to apply formal optimization techniques are also common to operations research, systems analysis, and systems design.

The most general formal optimization problem is formulated in terms of the three types of equations discussed above: the criterion function, the functional constraints, and the regional constraints [Eqs. (1), (3), and (7), respectively]. The techniques used for solving the optimization problem depend on the complexity of the optimization equations. Detailed treatment of the various techniques for solving Eqs. (1), (3), and (7) represent the major part of the literature on optimization. Only a very cursory description of the most popular techniques is presented here since the mathematics is beyond the scope of this discussion.

***Graphical analysis.*** Simple optimization problems with one or two independent variables can be solved by graphically representing the objective function as a function of the independent variables (over the constrained parameter range) and then picking the appropriate maximum or minimum. Figure 1*a* demonstrates

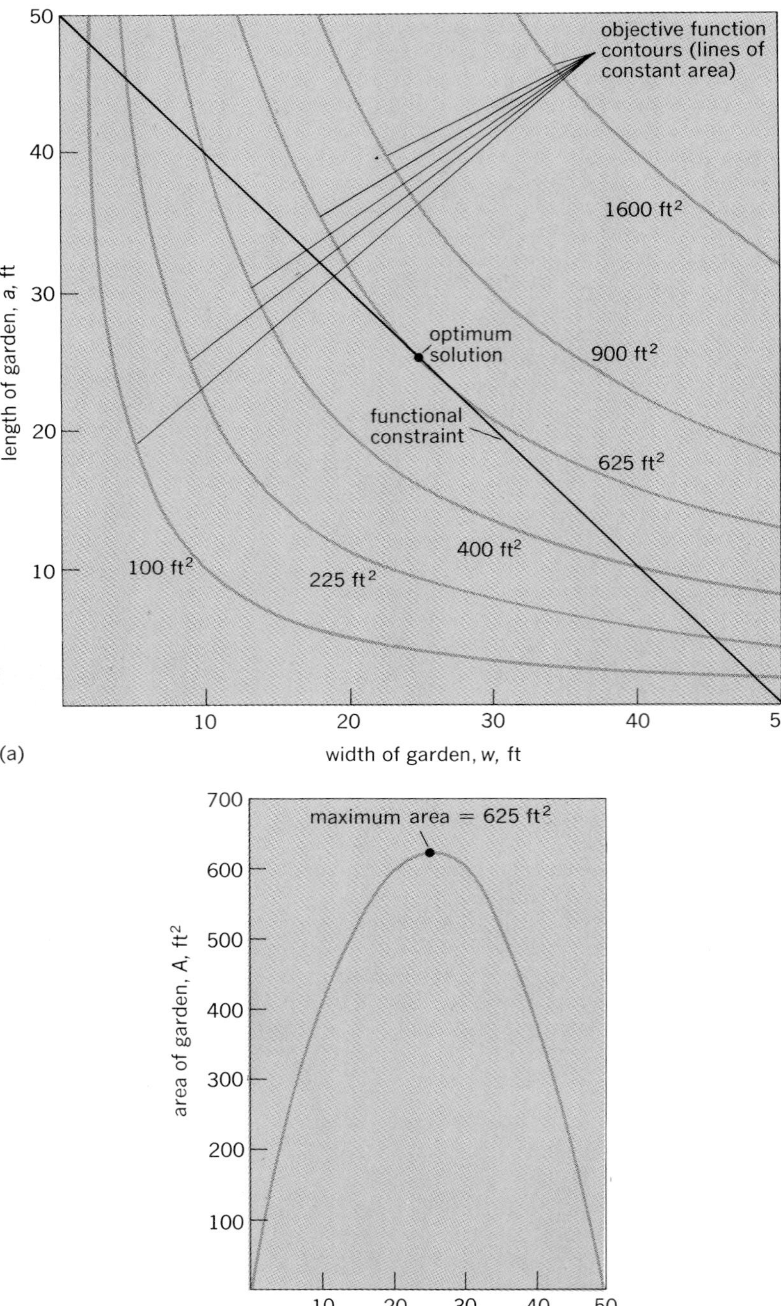


**Fig. 3. Graphical analysis. (*a*) Graphical solution of the criterion function and functional constraint for the rectangular garden plot of Fig. 2*a*. (*b*) Graphical solution with single independent variable. 1 ft = 0.3 m. 1 ft² = 0.09 m².**

this technique for one independent parameter where picture resolution represents the evaluation criterion to be maximized and tuning knob position represents the independent parameter. For two independent parameters the profit or penalty parameter can be graphically represented as contour lines with the two independent parameters as axes. This is shown in **Fig. 3*a*** for the example of the rectangular garden plot of Fig. 2*a*. Each contour line indicates the combination of length and width of the plot which will result in the value of the profit variable (area in this example) shown on the contour lines. These profit function contours can be shown over the full permissible range of the independent parameters. To find the solution, however, the functional constraint must also be considered. The functional constraint $2a + 2w = 100$ is shown as the straight line in Fig. 3*a*. Only combinations of length and width lying on this line are permissible. One can easily see that the maximum area is obtained when the functional constraint line intersects the highest profit function contour. In this case it occurs at $a = w = 25$ ft, for which the area is 625 $ft^2$ ($1\ ft^2 = 0.09\ m^2$). Thus the optimum solution for the rectangular plot is a square.

In many cases the functional constraints can be substituted directly into the criterion function to reduce the number of independent parameters. In the example (Fig. 2), Eq. (4*a*) can be solved for *a* and substituted into Eq. (2*a*) to obtain Eq. (9), which has

$$A = 50w - w^2 \tag{9}$$

only one independent parameter, *w*. Solutions to Eq. (9) plotted in Fig. 3*b* again give 625 $ft^2$ as the optimum solution.

Although in the solutions illustrated, the evaluation parameter has a simple maximum, in more general cases the criterion parameter may be complicated, as shown in **Fig. 4**, with relative maxima and minima, inflection points, and so on.

Graphical methods result in the most descriptive solutions. However, they are usually restricted to problems with at most two independent parameters, because one can only visualize in three dimensions (one for the evaluation criterion and two for the independent parameters). But graphical solutions serve

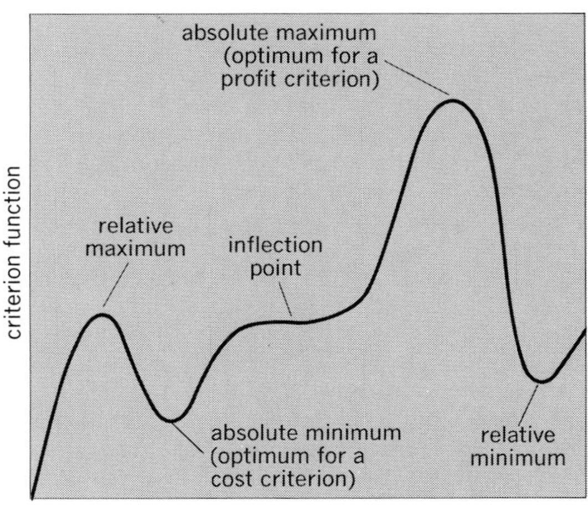


**Fig. 4. Maximum and minimum values of a criterion function. Concepts of local and absolute minima and maxima can be extended to *n*-dimensional criterion functions.**

as a good conceptual starting point for the more general optimization problem in which one is looking for a maximum or minimum of a function in *n*-dimensional space. Analytical and numerical techniques must be used for these purposes.

***Analytical approach.*** The classical analytical methods involve reduction of the number of independent parameters by substituting the functional constraints into the objective function, differentiating the resulting objective function with respect to each of the *n*-independent variables, and setting these first derivatives equal to zero. This results in a set of *n* simultaneous equations in *n* unknowns which are then solved by various mathematical techniques (for example, Jacobian or Newton-Raphson methods). The classical Lagrange multiplier technique is a variation of these differential methods of finding an extremum for a function in *n*-dimensional space.

For the simple example (Fig. 2), equating the first derivative of Eq. (9) to zero gives Eqs. (10) and (11).

$$\frac{dA}{dw} = 50 - 2w = 0 \tag{10a}$$

$$w = 25\ \text{ft} \tag{10b}$$

$$A = aw = 625\ \text{ft}^2 \tag{11}$$

It should be noted that although the optimum solution for a rectangular plot gives 625 $ft^2$, this is only a suboptimum in the example, since a circular plot would give an area of $A = L^2/4 = 796\ ft^2$, using 100 ft of fence.

Some optimization problems involve optimization of a whole function rather than a single operating point (for example, optimum lunar landing trajectories). The calculus of variations is used in that case to maximize or minimize the objective function.

***Recursive methods.*** Among the recursive, step-by-step techniques for finding an extremum, the best known are linear and dynamic programming and random search methods.

Linear programming can be applied only to problems having linear objective functions and linear functional constraints. For a number of practical problems, such as production scheduling, product mix decisions, capacity allocation, and dispatching strategies, which can be formulated in terms of linear equations, linear programming has become an important optimization technique.

The more sophisticated dynamic programming technique transforms sequential *n*-dimensional optimization problems into a sequence of single-stage problems having only one variable each. It can be used on both linear and nonlinear problems.

Both of these techniques are programmed on digital computers and are routinely used to solve problems with 30–40 independent variables and 50–70 constraints.

***Random search methods.*** A number of random search techniques have been developed to arbitrarily sample the *n*-dimensional space to find an extremum of the function. The Monte Carlo method is one of these. The more sophisticated random search techniques use secondary information, such as local gradients, to narrow the random search region.

With the development of computers the application of optimization techniques (particularly linear and dynamic programming and random search techniques) to multivariable optimization problems has prospered, and these techniques are routinely used in business management, resource allocation, military and economic planning, engineering design and manufacture, and other areas. *See Decision theory; Digital computer.*

*Igor Paul*

**Bibliography.** W. Conley, *Computer Optimization Techniques,* 1980; H. Eschenauer and N. Olhoff (eds.), *Optimization Methods in Structure Design,* 1983; J. H. Faupel and F. E. Fisher, *Engineering Design,* 2d ed., 1981; N. L. Svensson, *Introduction to Engineering Design,* 1977; J. P. Vidosic, *Elements of Design Engineering,* 1969.

## Oscillator

An electronic circuit that converts energy from a direct-current source into a periodically varying electrical output. If the output voltage is a sine-wave function of time, the generator is called a sinusoidal, or harmonic, oscillator. Only sinusoidal oscillators are discussed in this article. If the output waveform contains abrupt changes in voltage, such as occur in a pulse or square wave, the device is called a relaxation oscillator. *See Relaxation oscillator; Wave-shaping circuits.*

**Basic principles.** The fundamental laws governing sinusoidal oscillators are the same for all oscillator circuits. These basic concepts are illustrated in **Fig. 1**. The amplifier provides an output voltage $v_o$ as a consequence of an external input signal voltage $v_s$. The voltage $v_o$ is applied to a circuit called a feedback network whose output is $v_f$. If the feedback voltage $v_f$ were made identically equal to the input voltage $v_s$, and if the external input were disconnected and the feedback voltage connected to the amplifier input terminals 1 and 2, the amplifier would continue to provide the same output voltage $v_o$ as before. This requires that the instantaneous values of $v_f$ and $v_s$ be exactly equal at all times. Since no restriction was made on the waveform, it need not be sinusoidal.

If the entire circuit operates linearly and the amplifier or feedback network or both contain reactive elements, the only periodic wave that will preserve its form is the sinusoidal waveform, and such a circuit will be a sinusoidal oscillator. For sinusoidal oscillators the condition where $v_s$ equals $v_f$ requires that amplitude, phase, and frequency of $v_s$ and $v_f$ be identical. The phase shift introduced in a signal while being transmitted through a reactive network is invariably a function of the frequency, and there is usually only one frequency at which $v_f$ and $v_s$ are in phase. Therefore, a sinusoidal oscillator operates at the frequency for which the total phase shift of the amplifier and feedback network is precisely zero (or an integral multiple of $2\pi$). The frequency of a sinusoidal oscillator, provided the circuit oscillates at all, is therefore determined by the condition that the loop phase shift is zero.

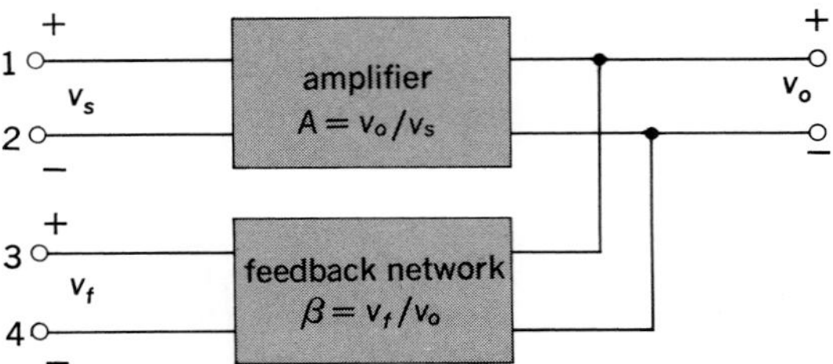


**Fig. 1. Amplifier and feedback network which is not yet connected to form a closed loop.**

Another condition, which must clearly be met if the oscillator is to function, is that the magnitude of $v_s$ and $v_f$ must be identical. If the amplifier has a voltage amplification, or gain, $A$, then $v_o$ applied to the input through the feedback network is called the feedback factor $\beta$. Therefore, Eqs. (1) are obtained. If $v_f$ is to

$$v_f = \beta v_o \qquad v_f = \beta A v_s \tag{1}$$

equal $v_s$, then $\beta A$ must equal 1. $\beta A$ is called the loop gain.

An oscillator will not function if, at the oscillator frequency, the magnitude of the product of the gain of the amplifier and the feedback factor of the feedback network is less than unity. The condition of unity loop gain is called the Barkhausen criterion.

Referring again to Fig. 1, if $\beta A$ at the oscillator frequency is precisely unity and the feedback voltage is connected to the input terminals, the circuit will operate with the external generator removed. If $\beta A$ is less than unity, the removal of the external generator will immediately result in a cessation of oscillations. If $\beta A$ is greater than unity, 1 volt appearing initially at the input terminals will, after a trip around the loop, appear at the input as a voltage larger than 1 volt. After another trip around the loop this larger voltage will be still larger, and so on. It seems, then, that if $\beta A$ is larger than unity, the amplitude can continue only as long as it is not limited by nonlinearity of operation in the active devices associated with the amplifier. Such a nonlinearity becomes more marked as the amplitude of oscillations increases. This onset of nonlinearity to limit the amplitude of oscillations in an essential feature of the operation of all practical oscillators because all oscillators operate with $\beta A$ greater than one. The condition that $\beta A$ equal 1 imposes a single and precise condition of operation which is not practical in electronic design. Even if the circuit were initially designed to satisfy this condition, it could not be maintained because circuit components (especially active devices) change characteristics (drift) with age, temperature, and voltage. Therefore, if the oscillator is left to itself, in a short time $\beta A$ will become either less than or larger than unity. An oscillator in which the loop gain is exactly unity is an abstraction that is completely unrealizable in practice. A practical oscillator always has a $\beta A$ somewhat larger than unity (say 5%) to ensure that, with incidental variations in transistor and circuit parameters, $\beta A$ does not fall below unity.

**Phase-shift oscillator.** The phase-shift oscillator, **Fig. 2**, exemplifies the principles set forth above. A field-effect-transistor (FET) amplifier of conventional design is followed by three cascaded arrangements of a capacitor $C$ and a resistor $R$, the output of the last $RC$ combination being returned to the gate. The phase of the signal is shifted 180° by the amplifier, and the network of resistors and capacitors shifts the phase by an additional amount. At some frequency the phase shift introduced by the $RC$ network is precisely 180°, and the total phase shift around the circuit is exactly zero. At this particular frequency the circuit will oscillate, provided that the magnitude of the amplification is sufficiently large.

The frequency at which the phase shift for the $RC$ network is 180° is given by Eq. (2). At this frequency

$$f = 1/(2\pi RC\sqrt{6}) \tag{2}$$

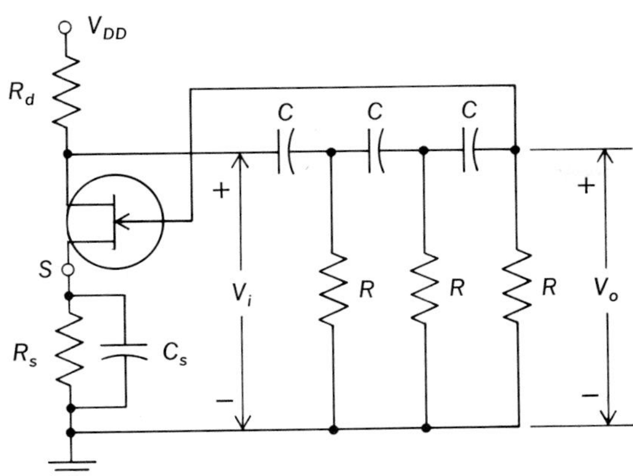


**Fig. 2. FET phase-shift oscillator.**

of oscillation β equals $-(1/29)$. For $\beta A$ to be greater than unity, $A$ must be at least 29. The oscillator then cannot be made to work with an FET for which $g_mR_d < 29$, where $g_m$ is the transductance of the FET.

The phase-shift oscillator is particulary suited to frequencies from several hertz to several hundred kiliohertz and so includes the range of audio frequencies. At frequencies in the range of megahertz it has no marked advantage over circuits employing a tuned $LC$ network. In fact, at the higher frequencies, the impedance of the phase-shifting network may become quite small, and the loading of the amplifier by the phase-shifting network may become serious. On the other hand, if $R$ and $C$ are made large but still well within the range of commercially available values, frequencies of 1–2 Hz are easily attained. Inductors suitable for use in $LC$ tuned oscillators for this frequency range are often impractical.

The frequency of the oscillator may be varied by changing the value of any of the impedance elements in the phase-shifting network. For variations of frequency over a large range the three capacitors should be varied simultaneously. Such a variation will keep the input impedance to the phase-shifting network constant and keep constant also the magnitude of β and $\beta A$. Hence the amplitude of oscillation will not be affected as the frequency is adjusted.

If a bipolar transistor were used as the active elements in Fig. 2, the output $R$ of the feedback network

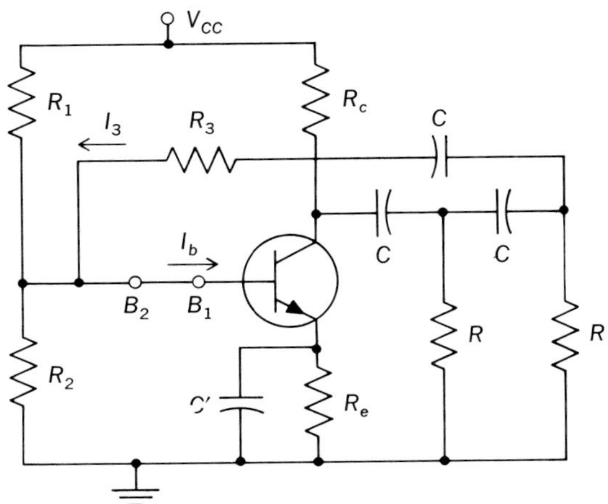


**Fig. 3. Transistor phase-shift oscillator.**

would be shunted by the relatively low input impedance of the transistor. Hence the circuit of **Fig. 3** is used, where the feedback signal is the current $I_3$ applied in shunt with the base current $I_b$. The resistor $R_3 = R - R_i$, where $R_i$ is the input resistance of the transistor. This choice makes the three $RC$ sections of the phase-shifting network alike and simplifies the calculations. It is assumed that the biasing resistors $R_1$, $R_2$, and $R_e$ have no effect on the signal operation, and these are neglected in the following analysis.

The Barkhausen condition that the phase of $I_3/I_b$ must equal zero leads to Eq. (3), the expression for

$$f = \frac{1}{2\pi RC}\frac{1}{\sqrt{6 + 4k}} \tag{3}$$

the frequency of oscillation, where $k \equiv R_c/R$. The requirement that the magnitude of $I_3/I_b$ must exceed unity in order for oscillations to start leads to the inequality in Eq. (4), where $h_{fe}$ is the small-signal com-

$$h_{fe} > 4k + 23 + \frac{29}{k} \tag{4}$$

mon-emitter short-circuit current gain. The value of $k$ which gives the minimum $h_{fe}$ turns out to be 2.7, and for this optimum value of $R_c/R$, it is found that $h_{fe} = 44.5$. A transistor with a small-signal common-emitter short-circuit current gain less than 44.5 cannot be used in this phase-shift oscillator.

**A general form of oscillator circuit.** Many radio-frequency oscillator circuits fall into the general form shown in **Fig. 4**. The active device may be a bipolar

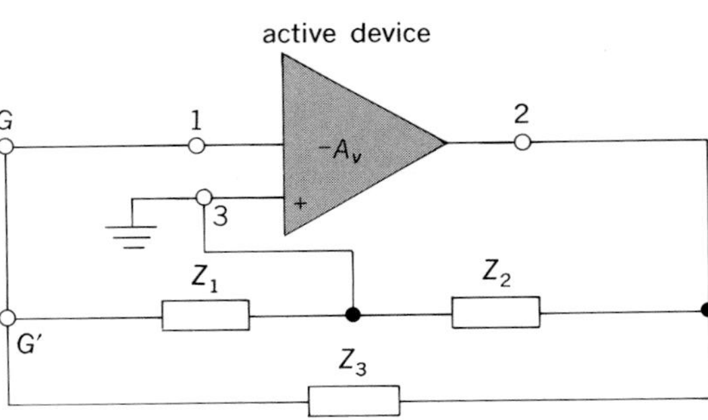


**Fig. 4. Basic configuration for many resonant-circuit oscillators.**

transistor, an FET, or an operational amplifier. In the analysis that follows it is assumed that the active device has very high input resistance which does not load down $Z_1$. If it is assumed that the impedances $Z$ are pure reactances $X$ (either inductive or capacitive), then, from the Barkhausen criterion, the circuit will oscillate at the resonant frequency of the series combination of $X_1$, $X_2$, and $X_3$. Also, the loop gain is given by Eq. (5).

$$A_v = \frac{+X_3}{X_2} \tag{5}$$

Since β must be positive and at least unity in magnitude, then $X_1$ and $X_2$ must have the same sign. In other words, they must be the same kind of reactance, either both inductive or both capacitive. Then $X_3 = -(X_1 + X_2)$ must be inductive if $X_1$ and $X_2$ are capacitive, or vice versa.

If $X_1$ and $X_2$ are capacitors and $X_3$ is an inductor, the circuit is called a Colpitts oscillator. If $X_1$ and $X_2$ are inductors and $X_3$ is a capacitor, the circuit is called a Hartley oscillator. In this latter case, there

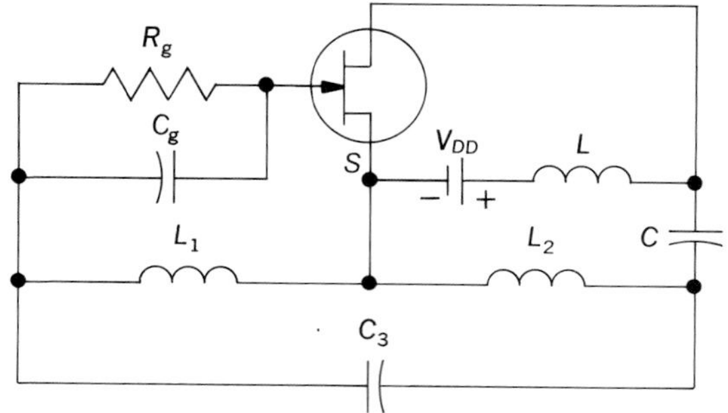


Fig. 5. FET Hartley oscillator.

may be mutual coupling between $X_1$ and $X_2$. If $X_1$ and $X_2$ are tuned circuits and $X_3$ represents the gate-to-drain interelectrode capacitance, the circuit is called a tuned-drain, tuned-gate oscillator. Both gate and drain circuits must be tuned to the inductive side of resonance.

A practical form of a Hartley oscillator is shown in **Fig. 5**. The drain voltage $V_{DD}$ is applied through the inductor $L$, whose reactance is high compared with $X_2$. The capacitor $C$ has a low reactance at the frequency of oscillation. However, at zero frequency it acts as an open circuit. Without this capacitor the supply voltage would be short-circuited by $L$ in series with $L_2$. The parallel combination of $C_g$ and $R_g$ acts to supply the bias. The circuit operates in class C, and the gate current charges up $C_g$ to provide the $X_2$ bias voltage.

The Hartley oscillator may be modified by substituting $L_1$ and $L_2$ with a transformer having separate primary and feedback windings. A bipolar version of such a circuit is shown in **Fig. 6**, which is known as the tuned-collector oscillator. In this design, the quiescent bias is determined by $R_1$, $R_2$, and $R_e$. If $R_1$ were omitted, then initially the transistor currents would be zero, $g_m$ would be zero, and the circuit would not oscillate. With $R_1$ in place, the transistor is biased in its active region, oscillations build up, and the dynamic self-bias is obtained from the $R_2C''$ combination due to the flow of base current. This action results in class C operation.

A transistor Colpitts oscillator is indicated in **Fig. 7**. Qualitatively, this circuit operates in the manner described above. However, the detailed analysis of a transistor oscillator circuit is much more difficult than that of an FET circuit, for two fundamental reasons. First, the low input impedance of the transistor shunts $Z_1$ in Fig. 4 and hence complicates the expressions for the loop gain given above. Second, if the oscillation frequency is beyond the audio range, the simple low-frequency $h$-parameter model is no longer valid and the more complicated high-frequency hybrid-$\pi$ model must be used.

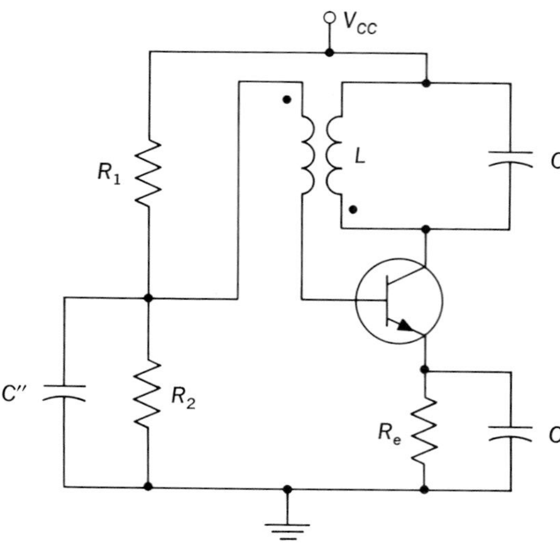


Fig. 6. Tuned-collector oscillator.

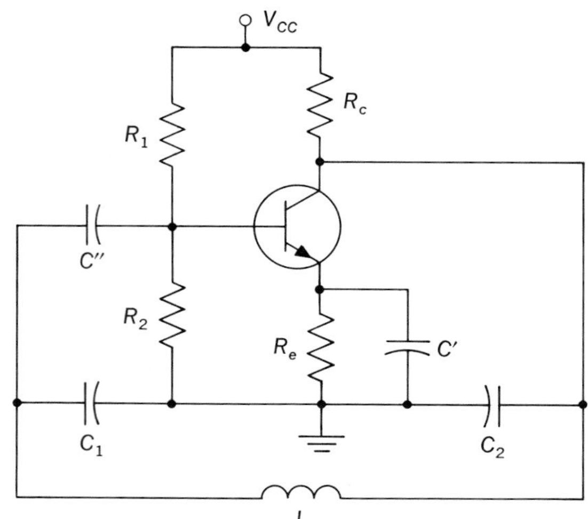


Fig. 7. Transistor Colpitts oscillator.

**Very high-frequency (vhf) oscillators.** These operate in the range of from a few to several hundred megahertz. The basic configuration of these oscillators is similar to that indicated in Fig. 4. However, usually the impedances in the circuit are not lumped elements but are rather distributed (a parallel-wire transmission line or a coaxial cable). These elements are adjusted so that they appear as pure reactances. Sometimes a tuning element called a butterfly is used with a vhf oscillator. This element is similar to a variable air capacitor except that the stator plates have holes cut in them in the shape of the wings of a butterfly. As the rotor is turned the inductance (the magnetic energy storage) as well as the capacitance (the electrostatic energy storage) is varied. Hence, tuning over a wide frequency range is possible.

High-frequency transistors, both bipolar and FET types, are available in the 100-MHz to 5-GHz range. In particular, the gallium arsenide (GaAs) and metal-semiconductor field-effect transistor (MESFET) is capable of oscillating beyond 15 GHz.

**Bridge oscillators.** In a bridge circuit the output is in phase with the input at the balance frequency $\omega_0$. Hence, this circuit may be used as the feedback network for an oscillator, provided that the phase shift through the amplifier is zero. This condition is satisfied in the Wien-bridge oscillator shown in **Fig. 8**. The frequency of oscillation is precisely the null frequency of the balanced bridge, namely, $f_0 = 1/(2\pi RC)$.

The output of a balanced bridge is zero when $\omega$ equals $\omega_0$; therefore $\beta$ and $\beta A$ are both 0 at this frequency. To satisfy the Barkhausen condition ($\beta A = 1$), the bridge must be unbalanced, but in such a way that the phase shift remains zero. This is accomplished by making the ratio $R_2/(R_1 + R_2)$ smaller than 1/3. In Fig. 8, the coupling capacitors are made large

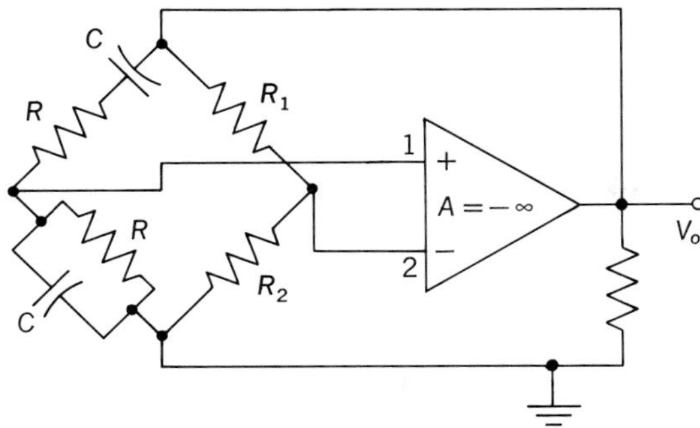


**Fig. 8. Wien-bridge oscillator.**

enough so that they introduce no appreciable phase shifts even at the lowest frequencies of operation. Maximum frequency of oscillation is limited by the slow rate of the amplifier.

Continuous variation of frequency is accomplished by varying simultaneously the two capacitors $C$ (ganged variable air capacitors). Changes in frequency range are accomplished by simultaneously switching in different values for the two identical resistors $R$.

If in Fig. 8 the resistor $R_2$ is replaced by a sensistor, the amplitude is stablized against variations due to the aging of transistors and circuit components. The regulation mechanism introduced by the sensistor automatically changes $\beta$ to keep $\beta A$ more nearly constant whenever the value of $A$ should change, as when amplifier loading changes. The resistance of a sensistor increases with temperature, and the temperature is in turn determined by the root-mean-square value of the current which passes through it. An alternate method makes use of the nonlinear characteristic of diodes so that the gain is reduced when the output amplitude exceeds a given value.

Other types of bridge networks, such as the twin-T and bridge-T, may be used as feedback elements to form an oscillator. The general principles enunciated above are applicable to these bridge-type oscillators, although the practical details are different.

**Crystal oscillators.** If a piezoelectric crystal, usually quartz, has electrodes plated on opposite faces and if a potential is applied between these electrodes, forces will be exerted on the bound charges within the crystal. When properly mounted, deformations take place within the crystal, and an electromechanical system is formed which will vibrate when properly excited. The resonant frequency and the $Q$ depend upon the crystal dimensions, how the surfaces are oriented with respect to its axes, and how the device is mounted. Frequencies ranging from a few kilohertz to a few megahertz and $Q$s in the range from several thousand to several hundred thousand are commercially available. These extraordinarily high values of $Q$ and the extremely stable characteristics of quartz with respect to time and temperature account for the exceptional frequency stability of oscillators using crystals. SEE PIEZOELECTRIC CRYSTAL.

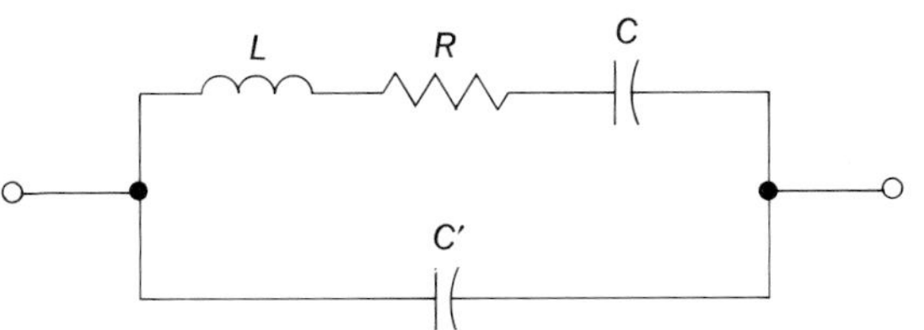


**Fig. 9. Electrical equivalent circuit of a piezoelectric crystal.**

The electrical equivalent circuit of a crystal is indicated in **Fig. 9**. The inductor $L$, capacitor $C$, and resistor $R$ are the analogs of the mass, the compliance (the reciprocal of the spring constant), and the viscous damping factor of the mechanical system. Typical values for a 90-kHz crystal are in $L$ of 137 henrys, a $C$ of 0.0235 picofarad, and an $R$ of 15 kilohms, corresponding to a $Q$ of 5500. The dimensions of such a crystal are 30 × 4 × 1.5 mm. Since $C'$ represents the electrostatic capacitance between electrodes with the crystal as a dielectric, its magnitude (≅3.5 pF) is much larger than $C$.

If one neglects the resistance $R$, the impedance of the crystal is a reactance $jX$ whose dependence upon frequency is given by Eq. (6), where $\omega_s^2 = 1/LC$ is

$$jX = -\frac{j}{\omega C'}\frac{(\omega^2 - \omega_s^2)}{(\omega^2 - \omega_p^2)} \tag{6}$$

the series resonant frequency (the zero-impedance frequency) and $\omega_p^2 = (1/L)(1/C + 1/C')$ is the parallel resonant frequency (the infinite-impedance frequency). Since $C'$ is much greater than $C$, then $\omega_p \cong \omega_s$. For the crystal whose parameters are specified above, the parallel frequency is only 0.3 of 1% higher than the series frequency. For $\omega_s < \omega < \omega_p$ the reactance of the crystal is inductive; outside this frequency range it is capacitive, as indicated in **Fig. 10**.

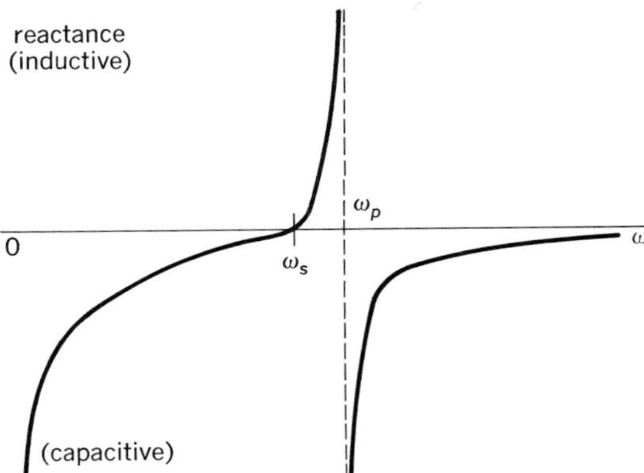


**Fig. 10. Reactance function of a crystal (whose resistance has been neglected).**

A variety of crystal oscillator circuits is possible. If in the basic configuration of Fig. 4, a crystal is used for $Z_1$, a tuned $LC$ combination for $Z_2$, and the capacitance $C_{dg}$ between drain and gate for $Z_3$, the resulting circuit is as indicated in **Fig. 11**. From the theory given above, the crystal reactance, as well as that of the $LC$ network, must be inductive. In order for the loop gain to be greater than unity, $X_1$ cannot be too small. Hence the circuit will oscillate at a frequency which lies between $\omega_s$ and $\omega_p$ but close to the parallel-resonance value. Since $\omega_p \approx \omega_s$, the oscillator frequency is essentially determined by the crystal and not by the rest of the circuit.

**Integrated oscillators.** The unavailability of an integratable inductance necessitates a fundamental change in the approach of oscillator design in inte-

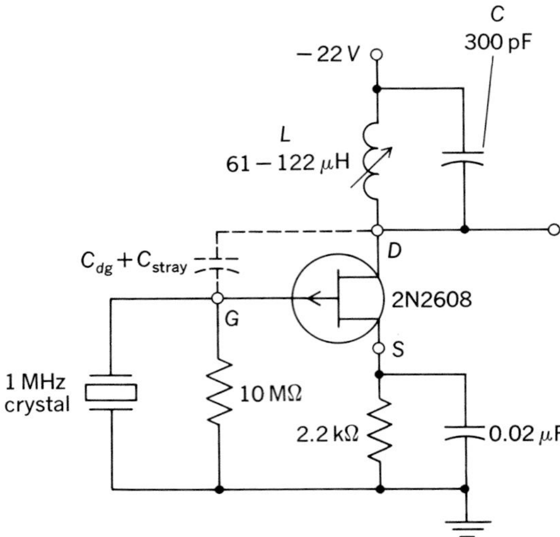


Fig. 11. A 1-MHz FET crystal oscillator. (*Siliconix Co.*)

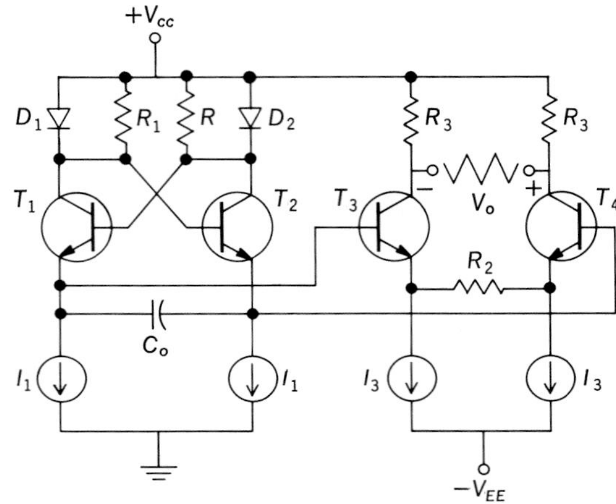


Fig. 12. Oscillator circuit for generating a symmetrical triangular waveform.

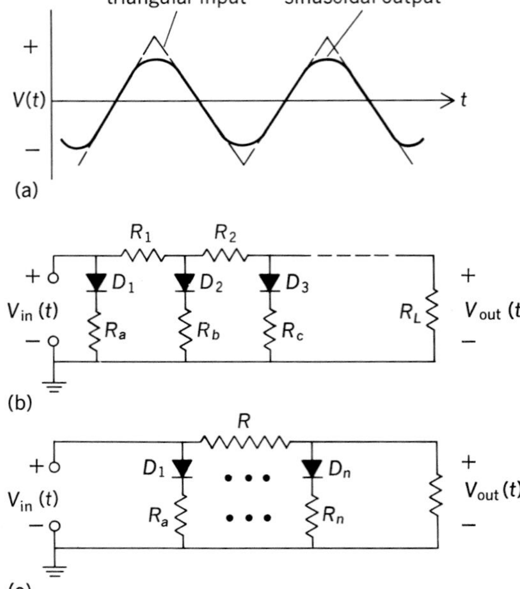


Fig. 13. Conversion of a symmetrical triangular waveform into a sinusoid by the use of a diode-resistor clipping network. (*a*) Input and output waveforms. (*b*) Lumped diode-resistor chain. (*c*) Distributed diode-resistor chain. Sections shown for positive half-cycle clipping. (*After A. S. Grebene, Monolithic waveform generation, IEEE Spectrum, 9(4):34–40, April 1972*)

grated circuits. In general, an integrated sinusoidal oscillator is obtained by using a relaxation oscillator to generate a periodic waveform which is then processed through a wave-shaping network. For example, a triangular waveform is readily available in the *RC*-coupled multivibrator shown in **Fig. 12**. The triangular waveform may be converted into a sine wave by rounding off its peaks with the aid of a diode-resistor network (**Fig. 13**). By using eight or more diodes, a symmetrical triangular wave input can be converted into a sinusoidal output with less than 0.5% harmonic distortion. Furthermore, one may use the distributed nature of the *pn* junction in an integrated diffused resistor structure to effect the conversion.

An alternative approach to realize a harmonic oscillator makes use of the digital signal synthesis technique. By combining a digital clock, a programmable read-only memory (ROM) and control circuitry, nearly ideal sinusoidal waveforms are obtainable.

**Heterodyne oscillator.** In the heterodyne, or beat-frequency, oscillator circuit the voltage from one radio-frequency oscillator is mixed with the output from a similar device tuned to a slightly different frequency. The difference frequency, or beat note, may be varied over the audio or video range by means of a tuning capacitor.

**Microwave oscillators.** Special tubes and semiconductor devices are used for generating waveforms whose frequency range lies between a few hundred and several tens of thousands of megahertz. *See* Microwave solid-state devices; Microwave tube.

*Edward S. Yang*

***Bibliography.*** J. J. Brophy, *Basic Electronics for Scientists*, 4th ed., 1983; A. B. Grebene, Monolithic waveform generation, *IEEE Spectrum*, 9(4):34–40, April 1972; J. Millman, *Microelectronics*, 1979; B. Parzen, *Design of Crystal and Other Harmonic Oscillators*, 1983.

## Oscilloscope

An electronic measuring instrument which produces a display showing the relationship of two or more variables. In most cases it is an orthogonal ($x,y$) plot with the horizontal axis being a linear function of time. The vertical axis is normally a linear function of voltage at the signal input terminal of the instrument. Because transducers of many types are available to convert almost any physical phenomenon into a corresponding voltage, the oscilloscope is a very versatile tool useful for many forms of physical investigation. *See* Transducer.

Oscilloscopes are one of the most widely used electronic instruments because they provide an easily understood waveform display and are capable of making measurements over an extremely wide range of voltage and time. The **table** summarizes the performance ranges of currently available types of general-purpose oscilloscopes. No one oscilloscope type covers the entire ranges shown.

Oscilloscope screens are typically divided into 8 vertical divisions and 10 horizontal divisions. Thus, an oscilloscope with a maximum sensitivity of 10 mV per division will have a minimum full-screen voltage of 80 mV. Similarly, an oscilloscope with a maximum sweep speed of 10 nanoseconds per division will have a minimum full-screen time of 100 nanoseconds.

**Approximate performance ranges of general-purpose oscilloscopes**

| Type | Voltage/division | | Time/division | | Bandwidth | Rise time |
|---|---|---|---|---|---|---|
| | Minimum | Maximum* | Minimum | Maximum | | |
| Nonstorage oscilloscopes | | | | | | |
| Real time | 10 μV | 100 V | 200 ps | 5 s | 0(dc)–1 GHz | 350 ps |
| Equivalent time | 2 mV | 0.5 V | 10 ps | 5 ms | 0(dc)–14 GHz | 25 ps |
| Storage oscilloscopes | | | | | | |
| Cathode-ray tube (CRT) | 10 μV | 100 V | 500 ps | 5 s | 0(dc)–400 MHz | 0.88 ns |
| Digital | 10 mV | 100 V | 200 ns | 60 min | 0(dc)–50 MHz | 7.0 ns |

*May be extended with suitable probes.

The four major types of oscilloscopes may be classified into two groups: Nonstorage oscilloscopes, either real-time or equivalent-time (sampling); and storage oscilloscopes, comprising cathode-ray tube (CRT) and digital. Each type has certain unique measurement capabilities with corresponding components and techniques used.

### Nonstorage Oscilloscopes

Real-time nonstorage oscilloscopes are the oldest and most widely used type of oscilloscope. They will be described in some detail since many of the techniques used are common to all other types. Equivalent-time nonstorage oscilloscopes are also called sampling oscilloscopes.

**Real-time nonstorage oscilloscope.** The front panel of a typical oscilloscope is shown in **Fig. 1**. This oscilloscope has a bandwidth of 150 MHz, two main vertical channels plus two auxiliary channels, two time bases (one usable for delay), and a 3.2 × 4 in. (8 × 10 cm) cathode-ray-tube display area. It includes on-screen readout of some control settings and measurement results. A typical oscilloscope is composed of five basic elements: (1) the cathode-ray tube and associated controls; (2) the vertical or signal amplifier system with input terminal and controls; (3) the time base, which includes sweep generator, triggering circuit, horizontal or $x$-amplifier, and unblanking circuit; (4) auxiliary facilities such as a calibrator and on-screen readout; (5) and power supplies.

The first four elements will be described in detail; power supplies are used in all electronic equipment and require no special description. SEE ELECTRONIC POWER SUPPLY.

***Cathode-ray tube.*** The central component in a cathode-ray oscilloscope is the cathode-ray tube, which, in its simplest form, consists of an evacuated glass container with a fluorescent screen at one end and a focused electron gun and deflection system at the other.

Either magnetic or electric fields may be used for focusing and deflection. Electrostatic deflection is almost universally used for oscilloscopes because it is capable of superior high-frequency response.

The cathode-ray-tube designer is faced with four primary technical objectives: (1) high deflection sensitivity up to the desired frequency; (2) a bright image for ease of observation and photography; (3) small spot size relative to the image area; and (4) accurate deflection geometry. All of these are interdependent so that each tube design is a compromise chosen to best meet the needs of the intended users. SEE CATHODE-RAY TUBE.

***Vertical amplifier.*** The signal to be observed is generally applied to the vertical or $y$ axis of the oscilloscope. The vertical amplifier is required to provide sufficient gain so that small signals may be displayed with suitable amplitude on the cathode-ray tube. All modern oscilloscope vertical amplifiers are dc-coupled so as to allow accurate observation of slowly changing signals. The vertical amplifier must amplify the signal so as to minimize distortion in its wave shape. It is thus required to be highly linear and have a suitable frequency, phase, and transient response. In addition, because it is desirable to view the signal that triggers the time base, a signal delay is incorporated in the vertical amplifier to allow the time base to start before the vertical signal reaches the cathode-ray-tube vertical deflection plates. A delay line, either with coaxial cables or of a specially wound type, is generally used for this purpose and is located in the vertical amplifier after the trigger pick-off point. SEE AMPLIFIER; DELAY LINE; DIRECT-COUPLED AMPLIFIER.

To obtain a suitable image size on the cathode-ray tube, a convenient means of varying the amplifier gain is needed. The method used must vary the gain without introducing frequency or amplitude distortion. Generally, a high-impedance frequency-compensated attenuator switched in an accurate 1-2-5 sequence is used before the amplifier input, and a continuously variable control covering a range of at least 2.5:1 is used within the amplifier to bridge between the steps of the input attenuator. SEE ATTENUATION (ELECTRICITY).

All oscilloscope vertical amplifiers provide for var-

**Fig. 1. Four-channel 150-MHz oscilloscope. (*Tektronix*)**

iable positioning on the cathode-ray-tube screen and a choice of ac or dc coupling for the input signal. The positioning control inserts a variable current controllable by the user at a suitable point in the vertical amplifier, and the input coupling control inserts a capacitor in series with the input terminal when ac coupling is chosen. AC coupling is typically used when a small ac signal is present together with a large dc signal which would otherwise deflect the display off-screen.

Most oscilloscope signal amplifiers have one terminal, usually called the ground terminal, connected to the chassis of the instrument. This is normally satisfactory because most waveforms being observed also have a common or ground reference. Sometimes, however, it is necessary to observe the waveforms between two points, neither of which is grounded. For this purpose a balanced or differential amplifier is needed. The output of this type of amplifier is proportional to the algebraic difference of the signals applied to its two input terminals. Thus, signals common to both terminals are canceled, but potential differences between the terminals are amplified. In high-sensitivity differential amplifiers the amplification of the desired signal may be as much as 100,000 times the common-mode signal. This property makes it possible to observe a small differential signal in the presence of a large common-mode interfering signal.

Most oscilloscopes incorporate a multitrace vertical system which provides for the simultaneous display of two or more different signals for comparison purposes. The most common method used to achieve a multitrace display is to incorporate a vertical input amplifier complete with all controls for each channel and then electronically switch between them at a rate faster than the human persistence of vision. In this case the display will appear flicker-free. To achieve this result, two alternative switching methods are employed with a choice available to the user. One method is to switch during the sweep return time (alternate mode) so that succeeding sweeps display first one channel, then another, and then repeat. This gives a flicker-free display provided the sweep repetition rate is high enough. If this is not the case, then the chopped mode must be used. Here the switching between channels is done continuously at a high rate with cathode-ray-tube beam blanking used to avoid displaying the switching waveform itself.

Some applications require that two simultaneous high-speed signals occurring only once (single shot) or at a very low repetition rate be observed or photographed. Neither of the switching systems above is suited for this measurement, and a dual-beam oscilloscope must be employed. A dual-beam oscilloscope comprises two completely independent vertical amplifiers feeding two separate sets of cathode-ray-tube vertical deflection plates. Either one or two time bases and cathode-ray-tube horizontal deflection systems may be employed. Since the vertical systems are independent, there are no compromises imposed by having to choose between alternate or chopped modes as in a time-shared multitrace oscilloscope. Dual-beam oscilloscopes are more expensive than single-beam types and in general have poorer matching between the transfer response of the vertical channels.

***Time bases.*** In the standard oscilloscope waveform presentation the horizontal axis on the cathode-ray tube represents a linear function of time. This is achieved by the use of a linear sweep generator feeding the cathode-ray-tube horizontal deflection plates via the horizontal amplifer. For a satisfactory display the sweep generator must be correctly triggered and the cathode-ray-tube beam blanked except when a sweep is present.

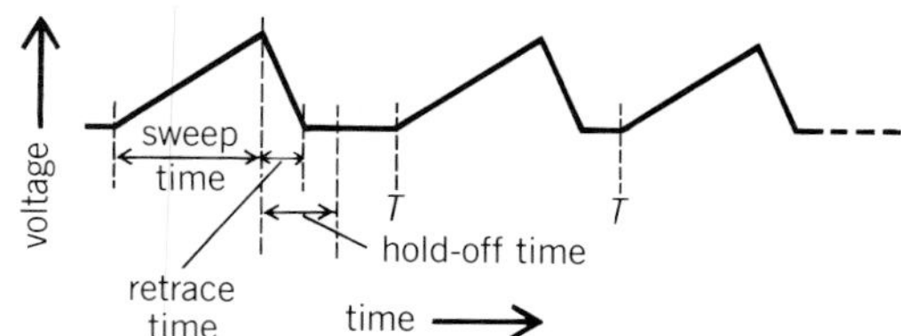


**Fig. 2. Sweep generator waveform. T = time at which sweep generator is triggered.**

A cathode-ray-tube presentation that is a linear function of time requires that a voltage changing linearly with time be applied to the cathode-ray-tube plates, generally in push-pull to avoid geometrical distortion in the cathode-ray tube itself. The waveform generated by the sweep generator is shown in **Fig. 2**.

The sweep generator is started (triggered) by a very fast signal derived from a signal that is time-related to the oscilloscope's vertical input signal. The sweep generator provides a linearly increasing voltage which is amplified by the horizontal amplifier and applied to the cathode-ray-tube horizontal deflection plates. When the cathode-ray-tube spot reaches the end of its desired excursion on the screen, the time-base generator rapidly returns to its original voltage during the retrace time. The sweep generator circuits require a finite time to recover and be ready for the receipt of a new trigger signal; there is thus a dead time, called the hold-off time, provided for this purpose. At the end of the hold-off period the sweep generator is ready to start on the receipt of a new triggering signal. This covers one complete cycle of operation of the time base generator. The cycle is repeated every time the sweep generator is prepared to receive a new triggering signal. The sweep time is controlled by the setting of the time/division control on the oscilloscope's front panel. *SEE SWEEP GENERATOR*.

The unblanking amplifier switches the cathode-ray tube on (at its grid-cathode) during the sweep time and switches it off at all other times, and thus ensures that the retrace is not seen and that a bright spot is not displayed when the sweep generator has returned to its quiescent state and is waiting for the next triggering signal.

In many cases, for example, with a long train of dissimilar pulses, the standard 4 in. (10 cm) of horizontal display is insufficient to allow examination of the waveform in the necessary detail. In this case a second, slower time base is used to delay the start of the higher-speed time base to the point where detailed examination is required. The display thus uses a high-speed time base to give sufficient resolution, but the segment of the wave form to be displayed may be changed by varying the time delay of the start of the high-speed time base relative to the triggering signal. This method increases the time resolution by a factor of at least 1000 and also improves the accuracy of time measurements. A delay time control covering a very wide range selects the delay time. The selected time may be either obtained from the control setting or displayed on the cathode-ray tube.

***Trigger generator.*** To ensure a stable display of the incoming signal, each sweep must start at a time corresponding to precisely the same point on the signal waveform. The information needed by the sweep generator to accomplish this may come either from the signal itself or from another signal which has a consistent time relationship to the signal to be observed. The input of the trigger generator is thus capable of being switched between several sources, the most commonly used being a portion of the signal at a suitable point before the delay line in the vertical amplifier. Whatever its source, the signal is applied to a circuit which generates a very fast output pulse every time the incoming signal reaches a certain voltage. This pulse is used to start the sweep generator, providing the hold-off time has ended. Front panel controls allow selection of the slope and voltage of the incoming signal that result in a trigger signal being generated. Most oscilloscopes have an automatic mode of triggering which arranges the trigger circuit to sense the input signal and provide a trigger pulse output at a point on the waveform which will generally result in a satisfactory display. When no signal is present the time base is made to run, resulting in a bright horizontal line (baseline) being displayed which assists the user in selecting the kind of display that is needed. *See Trigger circuit.*

***Calibrators.*** Most oscilloscopes incorporate an accurate square-wave calibrator which is used to check the vertical gain calibration and adjust the probe, if used, for optimal response. In addition, some calibrators may be sufficiently accurate in time to allow the oscilloscope time-base calibration to be checked.

**Equivalent-time nonstorage oscilloscope.** The limit of speed of vertical response of real-time nonstorage oscilloscopes is determined by the design of the vertical amplifier and by the cathode-ray-tube deflection plate bandwidth. The fastest general-purpose oscilloscope available has a bandwidth from O (direct current) to 1 GHz; wider bandwidths are possible, but cost and power consumption rapidly increase. Equivalent-time or sampling oscilloscopes provide much higher bandwidths at reasonable cost and power consumption, but the technique requires that the signal to be observed is repetitive at a suitable minimum rate. It makes use of extremely short pulses which are used to sample the incoming signal. Samples are taken at a slightly later time at each recurrence of the trigger pulse. The samples are amplified, lengthened in time, and displayed at a relatively slow sweep speed. Some important limitations of this type of oscilloscope are that single transients cannot be observed and that it may take a considerable time to build up a complete picture of the incoming signal if its repetition rate is low. A variation on the sampling technique described above is to take samples in a random fashion and then reconstitute the samples in the correct equivalent time and again display at a relatively slow sweep speed. Both sampling methods are used in commercially available oscilloscopes with bandwidths from 0 (dc) to over 10 GHz. *See Sampling voltmeter.*

### Storage Oscilloscopes

It is often desirable to store a waveform for further use after the originating signal has ceased to exist. This is essential for single transients, for later reproduction (hard copy), and for modifications to the stored waveform using computer techniques.

The simplest method of recording a waveform is to photograph it on the screen of a nonstorage oscilloscope. Photographic recording is, however, inconvenient, time-consuming, and liable to error; in addition, the signal is not digitized and is thus unsuitable as an input for computer processing. Two broad types of oscilloscopes have evolved with the capability of storing a waveform, or its representation, for an extended period of time.

**CRT storage oscilloscope.** This type of instrument is based on the real-time oscilloscope, but substitutes a storage cathode-ray tube for the standard type. There are several types of storage cathode-ray tube, but all have the property of being able to display a waveform for a limited length of time after the originating signal has disappeared. The storage time is at least sufficient for convenient photography and for relatively leisurely visual observation. Most storage oscilloscopes provide several modes of operation such as (1) nonstorage operation similar to a nonstorage oscilloscope; (2) medium-speed storage with long storage time; and (3) high-speed storage with relatively short storage time.

Storage cathode-ray tubes differ from nonstorage types in that they incorporate a target, in some cases the actual phosphor, which changes its electrical state after being scanned by the electron beam and results in a lingering charge storage pattern representing the original waveform. After the original signal has ended, the cathode-ray-tube operating voltages are changed so as to display a replica of the charge storage pattern; simultaneously, all further vertical input signals are stopped from affecting the cathode-ray tube until the user reactivates the oscilloscope. Cathode-ray-tube storage oscilloscopes are available which are capable of storing waveforms at up to 400 MHz. Except for the cathode-ray tube and its associated power and control circuits, circuits used in cathode-ray-tube storage oscilloscopes are similar to those used in nonstorage types.

**Digital storage oscilloscope.** This type differs greatly from all previous types in that the signal is converted from analog to digital form prior to display. In its simplest form a digital storage oscilloscope comprises six basic elements: (1) analog vertical input amplifier; (2) high-speed analog-to-digital converter and digital waveform memory; (3) time base, including triggering and clock drive for the analog-to-digital converter and waveform memory; (4) waveform reconstruction and display circuits; (5) display, generally, but not restricted to, a cathode-ray tube; (6) power supplies and ancillary functions.

***Analog vertical input amplifier.*** This device performs functions identical to those of a vertical amplifier in a real-time oscilloscope; however, its output feeds a high-speed analog-to-digital converter instead of the cathode-ray tube.

***High-speed analog-to-digital converter.*** This samples the incoming vertical signal at a rate dependent upon the time-base time/division setting selected by the user. Each sample encodes the instantaneous value of the incoming signal into one of $n$ levels; $n$ is commonly 256 levels (8 bits), but 10 or more bits of resolution are used where better precision is required. The digitally encoded level is fed to the digital waveform memory. The process is repeated until sufficient samples have been taken for the resolution required in the display or for further digital processing. For display purposes 256 or more samples are commonly acquired. Longer records may be taken when subsequent digital processing is required. Multitrace operation requires two or more analog input amplifiers, two or more analog-to-digital converters (or one converter, time-shared at a reduced maximum rate), and additional digital waveform memory. *SEE ANALOG-TO-DIGITAL CONVERTER.*

***Time base.*** The time base clocks the analog-to-digital converter at a rate selected by the user. A triggering circuit processes a signal derived from or time-related to the vertical signal in a way similar to the trigger generator of a real-time oscilloscope. The time base normally runs continuously, and hence the digitized waveform is updated at every sample. The output from the trigger generator is used to stop the time base and thus "freeze" the digitized waveform. In practice, provision is generally made for the oscilloscope to remember and subsequently display the signal before, at, or after the trigger event time as selected by the user. This feature dispenses with the need for a delay line in the vertical channel and enables a variable amount of equivalent vertical delay to be selected at will.

***Waveform reconstruction and display.*** The digitized input signal, now in memory, is used along with the knowledge of the original digitizing rate to reconstruct an oscilloscope-type display of amplitude versus time. The display device used is generally a cathode-ray tube, but since the reconstructed display rate can be chosen independently of the original signal speed, other types of display devices may be selected if their characteristics are more desirable. The reconstructed display may display one dot for each sample or may use straight or curved lines to join the dots to make the display easier to interpret.

***Advantages and limitations.*** Digital storage oscilloscopes have evolved rapidly. The highest-speed analog-to-digital converters do not now compete in time resolution or signal bandwidth with the highest-speed cathode-ray-tube storage oscilloscopes, but they do offer equal or better time and amplitude resolution and accuracy within their basic speed limits. Because the waveform is stored in "permanent" digital memory, it is possible to process and use it in ways inherently unavailable in any other type of oscilloscope. For example, new types of display may be created by using the mathematical manipulating capabilities of a computer, either built into or external to the oscilloscope. Hard copy is easy to produce by using a standard *x-y* plotter or printer. Because the input signal is sampled at discrete points in time, a digitized signal can contain no information at a frequency greater than half the digitizing frequency; thus a digital storage oscilloscope with a 100-MHz maximum sampling rate cannot provide any information above 50 MHz. Even at 50 MHz only two points per cycle are available, and the subsequent display may not be very useful. In addition, it is possible for a digital storage oscilloscope to give a misleading display if the incoming signal is sampled at too low a rate. This defect is sometimes called aliasing and a user must be alert to its possible occurrence. At the time of acquisition it is possible to check whether aliasing is occurring, but once the original signal has ceased it is impossible to know whether or not aliasing has occurred.

***Combined instruments.*** A combination of real-time nonstorage and digital storage oscilloscopes is a common way of achieving the advantages of both types and allows some savings in size, weight, and cost over two separate instruments. As the performance and cost of analog-to-digital converters improve, it can be expected that there will be less need for combined instruments and that digital storage oscilloscopes will gradually displace cathode-ray-tube storage oscilloscopes initially, and subsequently real-time nonstorage types. A combination of sampling techniques and digital storage gives all the advantages of both, except for high-speed single-shot storage.

### Photography of Waveforms

The cathode-ray tubes of nonstorage oscilloscopes are frequently photographed to preserve for future study and comparison an image of both repetitive and single transient waveforms. Photography of repetitive waveforms is relatively easy since a suitable record can be obtained by using normal films and exposure techniques. Similarly, stored traces on storage oscilloscopes can be easily recorded if a permanent record is required.

To photograph fast single transients on nonstorage oscilloscopes requires a high-speed camera lens, high-speed film, and suitable photographic techniques. There are thus two basic types of oscilloscope cameras. Slow-speed cameras for repetitive or stored signals typically have a lens aperture of *f* 8 to *f* 16 and only a few shutter speeds, and are relatively inexpensive and easy to use. For high-speed transient photography of nonstorage oscilloscopes, cameras with lens apertures of *f* 1.4 to *f* 2 are available which have a wide range of shutter speeds and make use of the highest-speed Polaroid film available, at present 20,000 ASA/ISO. Most oscilloscopes of 100-MHz bandwidth and over have sufficient cathode-ray-tube brightness to be able to record single transients at their highest sweep speed settings, provided the correct camera and film are chosen. The highest cathode-ray-tube spot speed which can be satisfactorily recorded with a given camera-film combination is called the writing speed, generally specified in centimeters per microsecond or per nanosecond.

### Plug-in Oscilloscopes

Often, one oscilloscope will not cover the whole range of measurement needs of a user, and because many users' needs change from time to time, plug-in oscilloscopes are available which provide for changing only the vertical and time base capabilities without the need to buy a complete new oscilloscope whenver unanticipated needs arise. Because of this versatility, some relatively uncommon performance capabilities such as sampling and wide-bandwidth differential measurements are available only in plug-in oscilloscope lines. Plug-in oscilloscopes are in general more expensive and larger than non-plug-in types of equivalent performance.

### Oscilloscope Selection

The wide variety of oscilloscope types available makes selection complex. The first essential step is to decide on the approximate characteristics of the signals that are to be measured. Estimates must be made of signal amplitude, frequency, or rise time, repetition rate, and number of signals to be viewed simultaneously. After an initial selection, further narrowing of the choice will depend upon which desirable, but not essential, features are most wanted.

**Signal amplitude.** The lowest expected signal amplitude should provide over two divisions of deflection at the oscilloscope's minimum deflection factor, and the highest amplitude no more than full screen, typically eight divisions. Probe attenuation must be taken into account.

**Rise time.** The fastest rise time of the signal and the degree of acceptable measurement error determine the needed rise time of the oscilloscope. If $n$ is the maximum percentage error acceptable when viewing a signal having a rise time of $t_s$, then the oscilloscope's rise time must be no more than that approximately given by expression (1). For instance, if $n$ =

$$[(1 + n/100)^2 - 1]^{1/2} \times t_s \quad (1)$$

10% and $t_s$ = 10 ns, then the oscilloscope's rise time must be no more than 4.6 ns.

Conversely, the true rise time of a signal may be approximately estimated from the measured rise time, $t_m$, and the oscilloscope's known rise time, $t_0$, using Eq. (2).

$$\text{True rise time} = (t_m^2 - t_0^2)^{1/2} \quad (2)$$

**Oscilloscope bandwidth.** The bandwidth of a nondigitizing oscilloscope is the frequency at which the vertical amplitude response is 3 dB (about 30%) below its low-frequency value. Rise time and bandwidth are related approximately by Eq. (3).

$$\text{Bandwidth (in MHz)} = \frac{350}{\text{rise time (in ns)}} \quad (3)$$

**Signal repetition rate.** If single-shot transient measurements are necessary, then either a camera must be used with a nonstorage oscilloscope or some kind of storage oscilloscope selected. The oscilloscope must be capable of recording the highest-speed signal expected. For photography of nonstored traces, the film and camera to be used must be known. Storage oscilloscope specifications generally include information on the maximum speed of signal that can be recorded. If two high-speed single-shot transients must be recorded simultaneously, then the choice narrows to either a dual-beam oscilloscope (plus camera) or a two-channel digital storage oscilloscope.

**Number of signals.** Most modern oscilloscopes have two vertical channels, and some have three or more. Very few oscilloscopes, except plug-in types, provide four identical general-purpose channels.

### Signal Acquisition

Oscilloscopes of up to 300-MHz bandwidth generally have an input impedance of their signal input equivalent to 1 megohm with 15–30 picofarads capacitance in parallel. Connection to the circuit under test is generally done by using probes. In order to increase the impedance connected to the test circuit, probes with 10 times attenuation are most commonly used. These have a typical input impedance at their tip equivalent to 10 megohms with 10 pF in parallel. The probes are carefully designed to introduce minimum distortion in the signal they transmit. Above 200–300 MHz, the 10-pF-probe input capacitance has an undesirably low reactance (10 pF has a reactance of 53 ohms at 300 MHz), and other methods are needed. Most common is the provision of an accurate 50-ohm input to the oscilloscope. The user can either terminate the signal at the oscilloscope input, or a low-impedance probe can be used which again divides by 10 times, but has an impedance represented by 500 ohms and about 2 pF; at 300 MHz this gives an impedance of 236 ohms and is thus higher than in the previous case. Active probes are also available; they contain a miniaturized input circuit in the probe itself and transmit the signal over a 50-ohm line to the oscilloscope's input. Active probes provide the highest input impedance in the range of 100–1000 MHz but are expensive and relatively fragile. SEE ALTERNATING-CURRENT CIRCUIT THEORY; ELECTRICAL IMPEDANCE.

*Oliver Dalton*

**Bibliography.** J. D. Lenk, *Handbook of Oscilloscopes,* 1982; B. M. Oliver and J. M. Cage, *Electronic Measurements and Instrumentation,* 1971; S. Prentiss, *The Complete Book of Oscilloscopes,* 1983; S. Prentiss, *Oscilloscopes,* 1980; R. Van Erk, *Oscilloscopes: Functional Operation and Measuring Examples,* 1978.

## Packet switching

A software-controlled means of directing digitally encoded information in a communication network from a source to a destination. Switching and transmission are the two basic functions that effect communication on demand from one point to another in a communication network, an interconnection of nodes by transmission facilities (see **illus.**). Each node functions as a switch in addition to having potentially other nodal functions such as storage or processing.

**Switching techniques.** Switched (or demand) communication can be classified under two main categories: circuit-switched communication and store-and-forward communication. Store-and-forward communication, in turn, has two principal categories: message-switched communication (message switching) and packet-switched communication (packet switching).

In circuit switching, an end-to-end path of a fixed bandwidth (or speed) is set up for the entire duration of a communication or call. The bandwidth in circuit switching may remain unused if no information is being transmitted during a call. In store-and-forward switching, the message, either as a whole or in parts, transits through the nodes of the network one node at a time. As the name implies, the entire message, or a part of it, is stored at each node and then forwarded to the next.

In message switching, the switched message retains its integrity as a whole message at each node during its passage through the network from the source node to the destination node. For very long messages, this

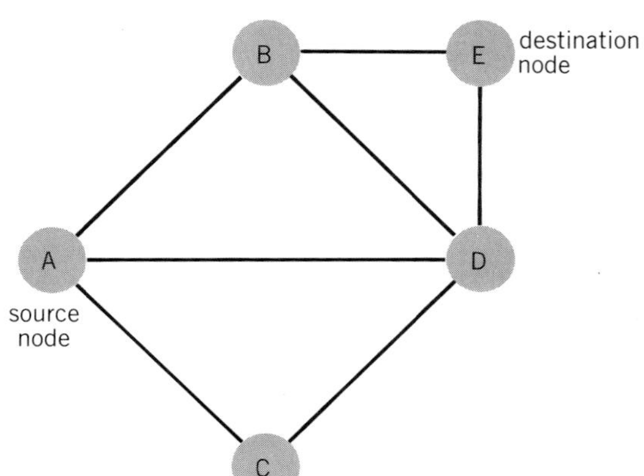


**Communication network with five switching nodes interconnected by transmission facilities. Information arriving at the originating or source node can be switched to the destination node through a variety of possible end-to-end paths, for example, ABE, ADE, ABDE, ACDE.**

requires large buffers (or storage capacity) at each node. Also, in situations where one or more intermediate nodes are involved, the constraint of receiving the very last bit of the entire message before forwarding its first bit to the next node may result in unacceptable delays. Packet switching can be viewed as a technique which breaks a large message into fixed-size, small packets and then switches these packets through the network as if they were individual messages. This approach reduces the need for large nodal buffers and "pipelines" the resources of the network so that a number of nodes can be active at the same time in switching a long message, reducing significantly the transit delay of the original message through the network. One important characteristic of packet switching is that network resources are consumed only when data are actually sent.

Being a class of store-and-forward switching, packet switching can readily accommodate source and destination end points that are operating at different speeds within the limits imposed by the network. The underlying link-layer protocol (discussed below) in packet switching can also incorporate error detection and correction capability based on error detection by cyclic redundancy coding (CRC) and correction by retransmission of the packet in error. SEE INFORMATION THEORY.

Packet switching requires the use of one technique to break a message successively into smaller packets—usually 128 octets long—and another technique to reassemble the packets at the destination node, in sequence, to recreate the original message. Different packets coming from a single message could take different paths between the source and the destination nodes, although this procedure is not currently used in commercial implementations.

**Packet format.** The International Organization for Standardization (ISO) has formulated a conceptual model, known as the open system interconnection (OSI) model, for exchange of information between dissimilar entities. The link-layer and the network-layer protocols represent the second and the third layers in this hierarchy. Briefly, the link-layer protocol is responsible for ensuring the integrity of data across a single link. The network-layer protocol is responsible for delivering statistically multiplexed data transparently across a network.

During their passage through the network, the user data are contained within a packet which is itself contained within (link-layer) frames which are transmitted from one node to the next. The link-layer and network-layer protocols ensure that packets in error are retransmitted with their original packet numbers so that the integrity of the message is maintained as well as the integrity of the packet reassembly process.

**Packet networks.** The practicality and efficiency of a geographically large network using packet switching was first demonstrated in the early 1970s by ARPANET, developed by the Advanced Research Project Agency of the U.S. Department of Defense. A number of subsequent public packet networks have been developed, including Telenet and Accunet in the United States, Datapac in Canada, Transpac in France, and DDX in Japan.

All public packet networks require that terminals and computers connecting to the network use a standard access protocol such as X.25, standardized by the CCITT (International Telegraph and Telephone Consultative Committee), which is an arm of the International Telecommunication Union, an agency of the United Nations. Interconnection of one public packet network to others is carried out by using X.75, another CCITT standardized protocol.

Packet networks can provide three services: switched virtual circuits, known as virtual calls; permanent virtual circuits; and datagrams. A virtual circuit is a bidirectional, transparent, flow-controlled path between a pair of logical or physical ports. (A transparent path or connection implies that all bit patterns, including all data and control characters, will be transferred across that path without any mutilation.) A switched virtual circuit is a temporary association, while a permanent virtual circuit is a permanent association between two communicating end points (also called data terminal equipments, or DTEs) of a packet network. A datagram is a self-contained user data unit containing sufficient information to be routed to the destination DTE (independently of all other data units) without the need for a call to be established. The datagram service is not presently available on any public packet network. The standard X.25 protocol does not support datagram service.

Charges for the use of public packet networks are usually based on the number of packets (or octets) switched and, in some cases, connect time or user requests for special capabilities. This is in contrast to circuit switching where users are charged for usage of the network by connect time only.

**Applications.** Data communication (or computer communication) is the primary application for packet networks. Computer communication traffic characteristics are fundamentally different from those of voice traffic. Data communication at speeds from several hundred bits to 56–64 kilobits per second is quite common. Data traffic is usually bursty, lasting from several milliseconds in an inquiry response application to several minutes or hours in an application involving the transmission of long files with millions of bits. The holding time for data traffic is also widely different from one application to another. These characteristics of data communication make packet switching an ideal choice for most applications. SEE DATA COMMUNICATIONS.

The possibility of voice communication using packet switching has been explored. Packet switching can allow better use of transmission resources because unused bandwidth can be allocated to other users while a speaker is listening, saving on overall transmission resources. However, several technical factors concerning speech communication by packet switching still await economic solutions. These obstacles, coupled with the large investment in the circuit-switched public network for voice (the telephone network), make it unlikely that packet switching will find wide application for voice communication in the near future. SEE SWITCHING SYSTEMS (COMMUNICATIONS).

*Pramode K. Verma*

**Bibliography.** P. Baran, Some perspectives on networks past, present, and future, *Inform. Process.*, 77:459–464, 1977; P. E. Green, Jr. (ed.), *Computer Network Architectures and Protocols*, 1983; L. Kleinrock, On communications and networks, *IEEE Transac. Comput.*, C-25:1326–1335, 1979; R. D. Rosner, *Packet Switching*, 1982; Special Issue on Packet Communication Networks, *Proc. IEEE*, vol. 66, no. 11, November 1978.

## Parallel circuit

An electric circuit in which the elements, branches (elements in series), or components are connected between two points with one of the two ends of each component connected to each point. The **illustration** shows a simple parallel circuit. In more complicated electric networks one or more branches of the network may be made up of combinations of series or series-parallel elements. *SEE CIRCUIT (ELECTRICITY).*

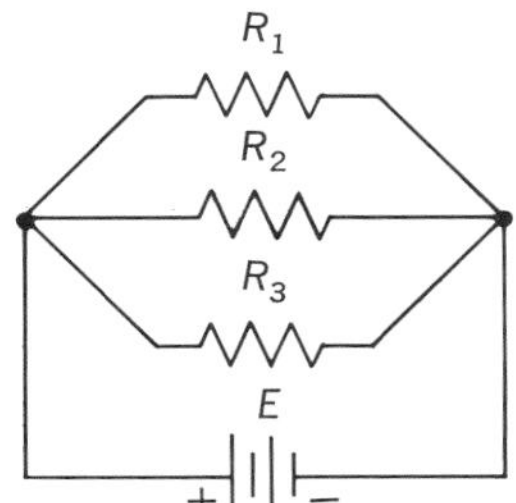


**Schematic of a parallel circuit.**

In a parallel circuit the potential difference (voltage) across each component is the same. However, the current through each branch of the parallel circuit may be different. For example, the lights and outlets in a house are connected in parallel so that each load will have the same voltage (120 V), but each load may draw a different current (0.50 A in a 60-W lamp and 10 A in a toaster).

For a discussion of parallel circuits *SEE ALTERNATING-CURRENT CIRCUIT THEORY; DIRECT-CURRENT CIRCUIT THEORY.*

*Clarence F. Goodheart*

## Parametric amplifier

A highly sensitive low-noise amplifier for ultrahigh-frequency and microwave radio signals, utilizing as the active element an inductor or capacitor whose reactance is varied periodically at another microwave or ultrahigh frequency. A varactor diode is most commonly used as the variable reactor. The varactor is a semiconductor *pn* junction diode, and its junction capacitance is varied by the application of a steady signal from a local microwave oscillator, called the pump. Amplification of weak signal waves occurs through a nonlinear modulation or signal-mixing process which produces additional signal waves at other frequencies. This process may provide negative-resistance amplification for the applied signal wave and increased power in one or more of the new frequencies which are generated. *SEE VARACTOR.*

The parametric amplifier operates through a periodic variation of a circuit parameter, in this case, the capacitance of the varactor. Similar amplification is possible by using a periodically variable inductor which may utilize a saturable magnetic material such as a ferrite. The inductive form of this device has not found application because it requires much larger amounts of pumping power to vary the inductance significantly at microwave frequencies.

**Effects.** Parametric effects are also found with variable resistive elements such as the varistor or rectifying diode. These elements do not commonly provide amplification of signals but are widely used as frequency converters in radio receivers to translate signals from high frequencies to lower or intermediate frequencies for more convenient signal amplification. *SEE VARISTOR.*

The varactor diode is a simple *pn* junction semiconductor device designed to maximize the available reactance variation, to minimize signal losses in electrical resistance, and to require low microwave power from the pump. The junction is biased with a low dc voltage in the nonconducting direction and the applied voltage of the microwave pump wave causes the total bias to vary periodically at the microwave pumping frequency. The capacitance of a reverse-biased semiconductor diode varies with voltage, decreasing as the bias voltage is increased. Common diodes with an abrupt junction between the *p* and *n* regions have a capacitance variation according to the equation shown below, where $C$ is the capacitance in farads, $k$ is a

$$C = \frac{k}{\sqrt{V_i + V_b}}$$

constant depending upon the area of the junction and the doping concentrations of impurities in the two semiconductor regions, $V_i$ is an internal or "built-in" voltage (a few tenths of a volt in most diodes), and $V_b$ is the applied bias voltage (in the nonconducting direction). When used in a parametric amplifier, $V_b$ includes a steady dc component plus a microwave ac value, varying periodically with time at a very high rate.

There are several possible circuit arrangements for obtaining useful parametric amplification. The two most common are the up-converter and the negative-resistance amplifier. In both types, the pump frequency is normally much higher than the input-signal frequency. In the up-converter, a new signal wave is generated at a higher power than the input wave. In the negative-resistance device, negative resistance is obtained for the input-signal frequency, causing an enhancement of signal power at the same frequency. *SEE NEGATIVE-RESISTANCE CIRCUITS.*

When a varactor is energized with two simultaneous voltage waves of different frequencies, such as a pump wave at a frequency $f_p$ and a signal wave at a frequency $f_s$, the current induced may have a complex waveform which contains other frequencies. Mathematical analysis shows that the first-order and most significant of these new frequencies are the sum ($f_p + f_s$) and the difference ($f_p - f_s$). Depending upon the varactor characteristics and the strength of the applied waves, still other frequencies can be produced which can have frequencies such as $nf_{p.} \pm mf_s$, where $m$ and $n$ are integers of any value, including zero. Normally only the sum or the difference frequency is utilized.

Analysis also shows that, if the varactor and its surrounding network are so tuned that significant power is generated by the varactor and dissipated at the new frequency $f_p - f_s$ and not at $f_{p.} + f_s$, the varactor will present a negative-resistive input impedance to an input wave at the frequency $f_s$. Instead of being absorbed by the amplifier network, the input wave will be reflected back down the input transmission line with an increased power. The wave at the frequency $f_p - f_s$ is not utilized outside the amplifier and is called, therefore, the idler frequency. This is

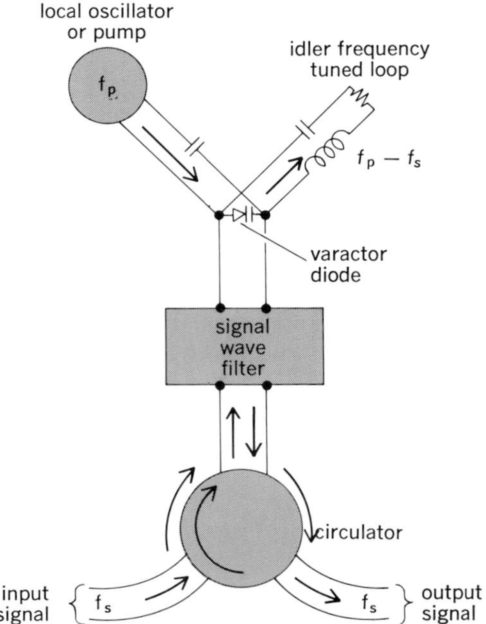


**Negative-resistance-type parametric amplifier.**

the mechanism of the negative-resistance form of the parametric amplifier, the most common type. A functional block diagram of this type of amplifier is shown in the **illustration**.

Alternatively, if the network is so designed that the sum frequency $f_p + f_s$ is generated and transmitted out by a second transmission line, and if significant energy is not generated or dissipated at the difference frequency $f_p - f_s$, the power output at $f_p + f_s$ can be greater than the power input at $f_s$ by a factor which may approach the ratio of these two frequencies $(f_p + f_s)/f_s$. This is the mechanism of the up-converter form of the parametric amplifier, so named because the signal wave is converted to a new higher frequency band.

**Advantages.** The most important advantage of the parametric amplifier is its low level of noise generation. In most other amplifiers, current flows through the active device by discretely charged electrons passing from one electrode to another. Random fluctuations in the rate of such flow normally occur, providing a finite background level of electrical noise (called shot noise) in the output which may override very weak signals, destroying their usefulness. Similar weak fluctuation noise is generated by resistive elements at normal temperatures in amplifier networks (called thermal noise). In the parametric amplifier, relatively very few electrons pass from one electrode to another in the varactor, reducing the shot-noise effects. Resistance and thermal noise generation effects are also minimized by proper diode and network design.

The parametric amplifier finds its greatest use as the first stage at the input of microwave receivers where the utmost sensitivity is required. Its noise performance has been exceeded only by the maser. Maser amplifiers are normally operated under extreme refrigeration using liquid helium at about 4° above absolute zero. The parametric amplifier does not require such refrigeration but in some cases cooling to very low temperatures has been used to give improved noise performance that is only slightly poorer than the maser. SEE MASER.

*M. E. Hines*

**Bibliography.** J. C. Decroly et al., *Parametric Amplifiers*, 1973.

## Parasitic oscillation

An undesired oscillation which may occur in any type of circuit, such as an audio-, video-, or radio-frequency amplifier, oscillator, modulator, or pulse waveform generating circuit. For example, it often happens that with no apparent input signal to an amplifier an output voltage of considerable magnitude is obtained. The amplifier may be oscillating because some part of the output is inadvertently being fed back into the input. This feedback may result from the output impedance of the power supply. If feedback does occur through the power supply impedance, the oscillations can usually be stopped by the use of appropriately placed decoupling networks. Such a filter is obtained by placing a resistor in series with the plate load and bypassing the resistor to ground with a large capacitor. SEE AMPLIFIER; FEEDBACK CIRCUIT; OSCILLATOR.

Feedback may also occur through the interelectrode capacitance from grid to plate of a tube, through lead inductances, stray wiring, and other paths, which are often difficult to determine exactly. Parasitic oscillations are particularly prevalent in circuits where physically large tubes are used, in circuits where tubes or transistors are operated in parallel or push-pull, and in power stages. The frequency of oscillation may be in the audio range but is usually much higher. Often it is so high (hundreds of megahertz) that its presence cannot be detected with an oscilloscope. A low-wattage neon bulb insulated from ground may be used as an indicator. When the lamp is brought near the portion of the circuit which is oscillating, the lamp will glow.

Parasitic oscillations represent a waste of power, a distortion of the desired waveform, or a complete malfunctioning of the circuit. Hence these oscillations must be eliminated. This can usually be accomplished by a change in circuit parameters, a rearrangement of wiring, some additional bypassing of shielding, a change of tube or transistor, the use of an rf inductor in the plate circuit, the use of rf chokes in series with filament lead, and other methods. A small resistance (50–1000 ohms) placed in series with a grid and as close to the grid terminal as possible is often effective in reducing high-frequency oscillations.

Even if the circuit is not oscillating, an output voltage may be present in a vacuum-tube amplifier in the form of hum from the use of ac heated filaments. Some hum may also appear from pickup resulting from stray magnetic fields of the power transformer or from the fields produced by the heater current in the connecting leads. It is also possible to pick up rf signals radiated through space. Spurious output voltages caused by vibrations of the electrodes because of mechanical or acoustical jarring of the tube are called microphonics. The undesired waveforms discussed here should not be confused with true parasitic oscillations. SEE ELECTRICAL NOISE; ELECTRICAL SHIELDING; ELECTRONIC EQUIPMENT GROUNDING.

*Jacob Millman*

## Passive radar

A receive-only radar used for search, tracking, surveillance, identification, guidance, and mapping. The techniques used are similar to those in radiometry; passive radar could be said to be a branch of radiometry. Military applications are quite different, however, from other uses of radiometry in that the source is usually not known to exist until detected by the radar, and the operator has no control over the position of the source but must determine it and sometimes track it. There are often other sources in the vicinity, so that discriminating between competing sources is important in military applications. The operation of passive radars depends upon the detection of microwave or infrared radiation from warm bodies. *SEE MICROWAVE.*

All bodies, solid, liquid, and gaseous, emit electromagnetic radiation in the form of noise, the amount of noise depending upon the absolute temperature of the body. Energy is radiated at all frequencies, including microwaves, with a maximum in the infrared range. In many applications, very high-gain receivers are required, and the accuracy of the measurements is severely limited by small time variations in the gain of the amplifiers. R. H. Dicke solved this problem in 1946 with a radiometer in which the receiver input is switched between the antenna and a known reference noise source at a rate faster than the gain variations of the amplifiers. The detected output of the receiver is switched synchronously at the same rate, resulting in two output signals, one due to the noise received by the antenna and the other to the reference noise source. These two signals are subtracted to form an output signal proportional to the difference in the input noise temperatures. The reference noise power can be adjusted until the output signal is zero, indicating that the received noise power is equal to the known reference noise power. Radiometers of this type can be used to measure the absolute power received from a source, and this is required in some applications. In military applications, however, it is usually only necessary to separate a noise source from its surroundings, so an adjustment of the known reference noise source is not necessary.

Many potential military targets radiate high noise power: ships at sea, exhaust from trucks, tanks, missiles, and airplanes, and factory chimneys, to name a few. Unlike an active radar, a passive radar cannot determine the range to a target. However, using the high antenna directivity obtainable at microwave and infrared wavelengths, a passive radar can locate a source of radiation accurately in direction and discriminate between nearby targets. The angular resolution is given approximately by the equation $A = 1.22\lambda/D$, where $A$ is the angular resolution in radians, $\lambda$ is the wavelength, and $D$ is the diameter of the antenna used. An antenna with a diameter of 39 in. (100 cm) has an angular resolution of about 0.0037 radian at a frequency of 100 GHz; an angular resolution of 1 milliradian can be achieved at infrared with a 12-in. (30-cm) antenna diameter.

A passive radar can track a target closely and be used to direct weapon fire toward it. A passive radar, mounted on a missile, can be used to home the missile in on a target by using just the pointing information provided by the radar. The power required to operate such a radar is quite small because there is no transmitter. Ground surveillance and mapping can be accomplished with an airborne ground scanner. This type of radar provides an infrared picture of the terrain and any targets which may be present. Radars of this type can often see through visual camouflage.

The absence of transmitted power makes the location, and even the existence, of a passive radar difficult to determine. Even if the position of a passive radar is known, its frequency cannot be determined; for this reason and because of the high angular resolution, it is difficult to jam. *SEE RADAR.*

*Clyde L. Ruthroff*

**Bibliography.** M. R. Holter et al., *Fundamentals of Infrared Technology*, 1962; F. T. Ulaby, R. K. Moore, and A. K. Fung, *Microwave Remote Sensing: Active and Passive*, 1981.

## PERT

An acronym for program evaluation and review technique; a planning, scheduling, and control procedure based upon the use of time-oriented networks which reflect the interrelationships and dependencies among the project tasks (activities). The major objectives of PERT are to give management improved ability to develop a project plan and to properly allocate resources within overall program time and cost limitations; and to control the time and cost performance of the project, and to replan when significant departures from budget occur.

**Background.** In 1958 the U.S. Navy Special Projects Office, concerned with performance trends on large military development programs, introduced PERT on the Polaris weapons system. Since that time the use of PERT has spread widely throughout the United States and the rest of the industrialized countries. At about the same time that the Navy was developing PERT, the DuPont Company, concerned with the increasing cost and time required to bring new products from research to production, and to overhaul existing plants, introduced a similar technique called the critical path method (CPM). *SEE CRITICAL PATH METHOD (CPM).*

**Requirements.** The basic requirements of PERT, in its time or schedule form of application, are the following:

1. All individual tasks required to complete a given program must be visualized in a clear enough manner to be put down in a network composed of events and activities. An event denotes a specified program accomplishment at a particular instant in time; in effect, it represents a state of the project system. An activity represents the time and resources that are necessary to progress from one event to the next. Emphasis is placed on defining events and activities with sufficient precision so that there is no difficulty in monitoring actual accomplishment as the program proceeds. **Figure 1** shows a typical operating-level PERT network from the electronics industry. Events are shown by squares, and activities are designated by arrows leading from predecessor to successor events.

2. Events and activities must be sequenced on the network under a logical set of ground rules. The activity sequencing is not arbitrary, but rather it is based on technological constraints; a foundation must be dug before the concrete can be poured. The network

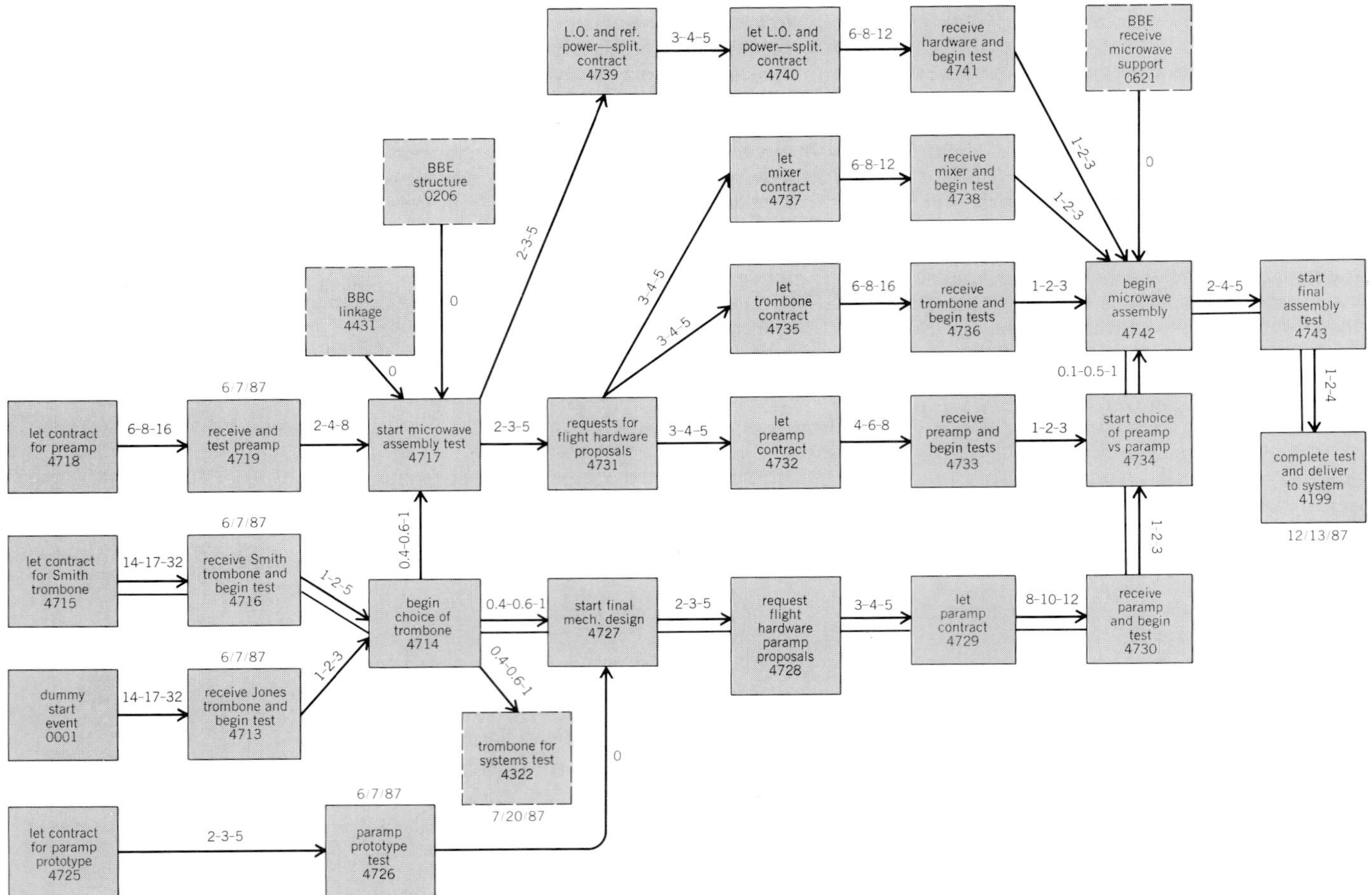


**Fig. 1. Typical PERT network of an electronic module development project. Arrows and lines denote the critical path. (*Applied Physics Laboratory, Johns Hopkins University*)**

logic is merely the requirement that an event is said to occur when all predecessor activities are completed, and only then can the successor activities begin. The initial event, without predecessors, is self-actuated when the project begins, and the occurrence of the final event (without successor activities) denotes completion of the project. This logic requires that all activities in a network must be completed before the project is complete, and no "looping" of activities in the network is allowed. Another technique, called GERT, relaxes these logic constraints. *See GERT*.

3. Time estimates can be made for each activity of the network on a three-way basis (the three numbers shown along the arrows in Fig. 1). Optimistic (minimum), most likely (modal), and pessimistic (maximum) performance time figures are estimated by the person or persons most familiar with the activity involved. The three-time estimates are used as a measure of uncertainty of the eventual activity duration; they represent the approach used in PERT to express the probabilistic nature of many of the tasks in development-oriented and nonrepetitive programs. It is important to note, however, that for the purposes of critical path computation and reporting, the three-time estimates are reduced to a single expected time $T_E$, and it is used in the same way that CPM employs a single (deterministic) time estimate of activity duration time.

4. Finally, critical path and slack times are computed. The critical path is that sequence of activities and events on the network that will require the greatest expected time to accomplish. Slack time is the difference between the earliest time that an activity may start (or finish) and its latest allowable start (or finish) time, as required to complete the project on schedule. Thus, for any event, it is a measure of the spare time that exists within the total network plan. If total expected activity time along the critical path is greater than the time available to complete the project, the program is said to have negative slack time. This figure is a measure of how much acceleration is required to meet the scheduled program completion date.

5. The difference between the pessimistic ($b$) and optimistic ($a$) activity performance times is used to compute the standard deviation ($\sigma$) of the hypothetical distribution of activity performance times [$\hat{\sigma} = (b - a)/6$]. The PERT procedure employs these expected times and standard deviations ($\sigma^2$ is called variance) to compute the probability that an event will be on schedule, that is, will occur on or before its scheduled occurrence time. The procedure merely adds the expected time ($T_E$) and variances ($\sigma^2$) of the activities on the critical path to get the mean and variance of the hypothetical distribution of project duration times. [See columns headed EXP TIME and EXP VAR in **Fig. 2**, and the total values of 28.6 and 1.9,

respectively, for the last activity (4004-743 to 4004-199) on the critical path.] The normal distribution is then used to approximate the probability of meeting the project schedule, as the area under the normal distribution curve to the left of (earlier than) the project scheduled completion date.

A computer-prepared analysis of the illustrative network contains data on the critical path (first group of activities in the table) and slack times for the other, shorter network paths. Note that the events (points in time) are labeled in the network, but the computer output is by activities (identified by event numbers) which also have descriptive labels. Under the column heading PROB(ability), note the figure 0.12 for the final activity on the critical path (4743-4199). This analysis indicates that the expected completion time of 12/25/87 results in a low probability of meeting the scheduled time of 12/13/87. This computer output (slack order report) is the most important of a number of outputs provided by most PERT computerized systems. Other reports may give greater or lesser details for different levels of management; they may deal with estimated and actual costs by activities (system called PERT COST); and so forth.

In the actual utilization of PERT, review and action by responsible managers is required, generally on a biweekly basis, concentrating on important critical path activities. Where necessary, effective means of shortening critical path time must be found by applying new resources or additional funds, often obtained from those activities that can afford them because of their slack condition. Alternatively, sequencing of activities along the critical path may be compromised to reduce overall duration. A final alternative may be a change in the scope of the work along the critical path to meet a given program schedule. Utilization of PERT requires constant updating and reanalysis, since the outlook for completion of activities in a complex program is constantly changing. Systematized methods of handling this aspect have been developed.

**Advantage.** A major advantage of PERT is the kind of planning required to create an initial network. Network development and critical path analysis reveal interdependencies and problem areas before the program begins that are often not obvious or well defined by conventional planning methods. Another advantage, especially where there is a significant amount of uncertainty, is the three-way estimate. If there is a minimum of uncertainty, the single-time approach may be used while retaining the advantages of network analysis.

In summary, it should be stated that while the developments of PERT and CPM were independent, they are both based on the same network logic to represent the project plan. PERT emphasizes the time performance of a project, including a probabilistic treatment of the uncertainty in the activity performance times and scheduled completion dates, while CPM treats time deterministically and addresses the problem of minimizing total (direct plus indirect) project cost as a function of scheduled project duration. The acronym PERT has become a generic term for network-based project management schemes that have evolved over the years. These schemes are hybrids of both PERT and CPM, but they are most often referred to as PERT. Finally, mention should be made of

RUN 1 ENDING EVENT
BY PATHS OF CRITICALITY DATE 06-07-87
CHART AJ LR SN 9 ELECTRONIC MODULE (ILLUSTRATIVE NETWORK) SYSTEM W 034

| EVENT PREDECESSOR | SUCCESSOR | NOMENCLATURE | DEP | DATE EXPECTED | DATE ALLOWED | DATE SCHD/ACT | PROB | SLACK | EXP TIME | EXP VAR |
|---|---|---|---|---|---|---|---|---|---|---|
| 4004-715 | 4004-716 | REV DATE (SMITH TROMBONE RECD-BEG TEST) | 98 | | 05-26-87 | A06-07-87 | | -1.6 | + | |
| 4004-716 | 4004-714 | SMITH TROMBONE TESTED | 0146 | 06-23-87 | 06-12-87 | | | -1.6 | + 2.3 | .4 |
| 4004-714 | 4004-727 | TROMBONE CHOSEN-BEGIN MECH DESIGN | 0146 | 06-28-87 | 06-16-87 | | | -1.6 | + 3.0 | .5 |
| 4004-727 | 4004-728 | RFP PARAMP FLIGHT HARDWARE | 0146 | 07-20-87 | 07-08-87 | | | -1.6 | + 6.1 | .7 |
| 4004-728 | 4004-729 | PARAMP CONTRACT LET | 0146 | 08-17-87 | 08-05-87 | | | -1.6 | +10.1 | .8 |
| 4004-729 | 4004-730 | PARAMP RECEIVED | | 10-26-87 | 10-14-87 | | | -1.6 | +20.1 | 1.3 |
| 4004-730 | 4004-734 | PARAMP TESTED | 0146 | 11-09-87 | 10-28-87 | | | -1.6 | +22.1 | 1.4 |
| 4004-734 | 4004-742 | CHOICE BETWEEN PREAMP-PARAMP | 0146 | 11-13-87 | 11-01-87 | | | -1.6 | +22.6 | 1.4 |
| 4004-742 | 4004-743 | COMPL MICROWAVE ASSY | 0146 | 12-09-87 | 11-28-87 | | | -1.6 | +26.5 | 1.6 |
| 4004-743 | 4004-199 | COMPL FINAL TEST MICWAVE ASSY-DELIVERED | 0146 | 12-25-87 | 12-13-87 | 12-13-87 | .12 | -1.6 | +28.6 | 1.9 |
| 4000-001 | 4004-713 | REV DATE (JONES TROMBONE RECD-BEG TEST) | 99 | | 05-29-87 | A06-07-87 | | -1.3 | + | |
| 4004-713 | 4004-714 | JONES TROMBONE TESTED | 0146 | 06-21-87 | 06-12-87 | | | -1.3 | + 2.0 | .1 |
| 4004-714 | 4004-717 | TROMBONE CHOSEN-BEGIN MICWAVE ASSY TEST | 0146 | 06-28-87 | 07-02-87 | | | + .5 | + 3.0 | .5 |
| 4004-717 | 4004-731 | RFP FOR FLIGHT HDW-MIXER-TROMB-PREAMP | 0146 | 07-20-87 | 07-24-87 | | | + .5 | + 6.1 | .7 |
| 4004-717 | 4004-739 | COMPL MICWAVE ASSY TEST-RFP LOC OSCIL | 0146 | 07-20-87 | 07-24-87 | | | + .5 | + 6.1 | .7 |
| 4004-731 | 4004-735 | TROMBONE CONTRACT LET | 0146 | 08-17-87 | 08-21-87 | | | + .5 | +10.1 | .8 |
| 4004-731 | 4004-737 | MIXER CONTRACT LET | 0146 | 08-17-87 | 08-21-87 | | | + .5 | +10.1 | .8 |
| 4004-739 | 4004-740 | CONTRACT LET FOR LOC OSCIL AND PWR SPLT | 0146 | 08-17-87 | 08-21-87 | | | + .5 | +10.1 | .8 |
| 4004-735 | 4004-736 | TROMBONE RECEIVED | | 10-14-87 | 10-18-87 | | | + .5 | +18.5 | 1.8 |
| 4004-737 | 4004-738 | MIXER RECEIVED | | 10-14-87 | 10-18-87 | | | + .5 | +18.5 | 1.8 |
| 4004-740 | 4004-741 | LOC OSC-PWR SPLITTER RECEIVED | | 10-14-87 | 10-18-87 | | | + .5 | +18.5 | 1.8 |
| 4004-736 | 4004-742 | TROMBONE TESTED | 0146 | 10-28-87 | 11-01-87 | | | + .5 | +20.5 | 1.9 |
| 4004-738 | 4004-742 | MIXER TESTED | 0146 | 10-28-87 | 11-01-87 | | | + .5 | +20.5 | 1.9 |
| 4004-741 | 4004-742 | LOC OSC-PWR SPLITTER TESTED | 0146 | 10-28-87 | 11-01-87 | | | + .5 | +20.5 | 1.9 |

**Fig. 2. Typical PERT computer output. First three paths of Fig. 1 are shown here. (*After J. J. Moder and C. R. Phillips, Project Management with CPM and PERT, 2d ed., Van Nostrand–Reinhold, 1970*)**

GERT, which denotes a generalization of the PERT/CPM network logic to complex situations where branching at events and closed loops of activities are required to adequately portray a complex project plan in the form of a network.

*Joseph J. Moder*

**Bibliography.** D. G. Malcolm et al., Applications of a technique for R and D program evaluation, *Operations Res.*, 7(5):646–669, 1959; J. J. Moder and S. E. Elmaghraby, *Handbook of Operations Research, Models and Applications*, vol. 2, 1978; J. J. Moder and C. R. Phillips, *Project Management with CPM and PERT*, 2d ed., 1970.

## Phase

The fractional part of a period through which the time variable of a periodic quantity (alternating electric current, vibration) has moved, as measured at any point in time from an arbitrary time origin. In the case of a sinusoidally varying quantity, the time origin is usually assumed to be the last point at which the quantity passed through a zero position from a negative to a positive direction. It is customary to choose the origin so that the fractional part of the period is less than unity.

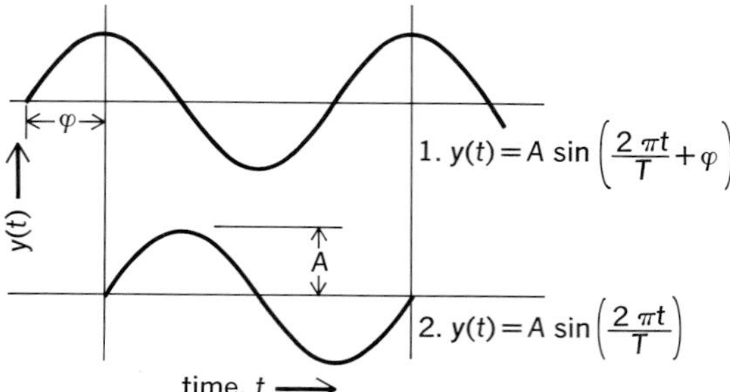


**Illustration of the meaning of phase for a sinusoidal wave. The difference in phase between waves 1 and 2 is *φ* and is called the phase angle. For each wave, *A* is the amplitude and *T* is the period.**

In comparing the phase relationships at a given instant between two time-varying quantities, the phase of one is usually assumed to be zero, and the phase of the other is described, with respect to the first, as the fractional part of a period through which the second quantity must vary to achieve a zero of its own (see **illus.**). In this case, the fractional part of the period is usually expressed in terms of angular measure, with one period being equal to 360° or $2\pi$ radians. Thus two sine waves of a given frequency are said to be 90°, or $\pi/2$, out of phase when the second must be displaced in time, with respect to the first, by one-fourth period in order for it to achieve a zero value. SEE PHASE-ANGLE MEASUREMENT.

*William J. Galloway*

## Phase-angle measurement

The determination of the relative times at which alternating currents and voltages in a circuit take on zero values. If two voltages $v_1$ and $v_2$ are zero at the same instant, they are in phase, with zero phase difference (or out of phase with 180° difference). If one voltage $v_1$ passes through zero 1/8 cycle before a second voltage $v_2$, it leads by 360°/8 or 45° (**Fig. 1**). The com-

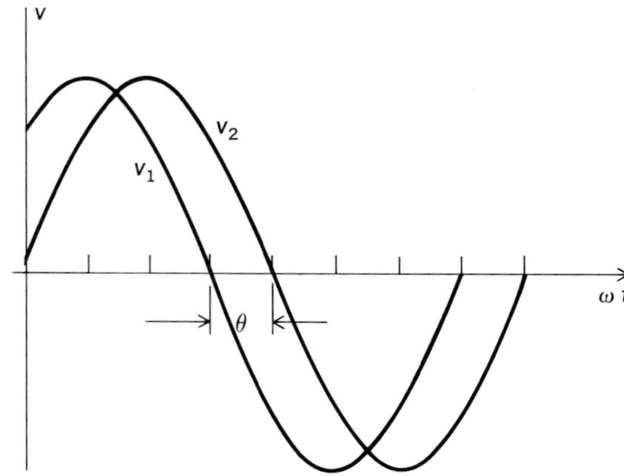


**Fig. 1. Phase angle between two voltages.**

mon phase meter, a commercial device for determining the angle between current and voltage, can be used when its presence will not disturb the circuits under measurement. When phase angles to be measured are in high-impedance or low-power circuits, this device is unsatisfactory and other measurement methods must be used.

**Three-voltmeter method.** This method can be used when the voltages involve a common point. **Figure 2*a*** shows three terminals *a*, *b*, and *c*. If the voltages $v_{ab}$, $v_{bc}$, and $v_{ca}$ are measured by a high-impedance voltmeter (one voltmeter is sufficient), the magnitudes can be plotted to give a triangle, Fig. 2*b*. The angle $\theta$ between $v_{ab}$ and $v_{bc}$ can be determined from the law of cosines in trigonometry, as shown by Eq. (1).

$$v_{ca}^2 = v_{ab}^2 + v_{bc}^2 + 2v_{ab}v_{bc}\cos\theta \tag{1}$$

**Electronic phase-angle meter.** This instrument gives the angle $(\pi - \theta)$ of Fig. 2 directly. One such instrument converts the two voltage waves to square waves by repeated amplification and limiting. The zero crossings of the square waves are identical to the zero crossings of the original voltage waves. The two square waves are applied to the input of a circuit that

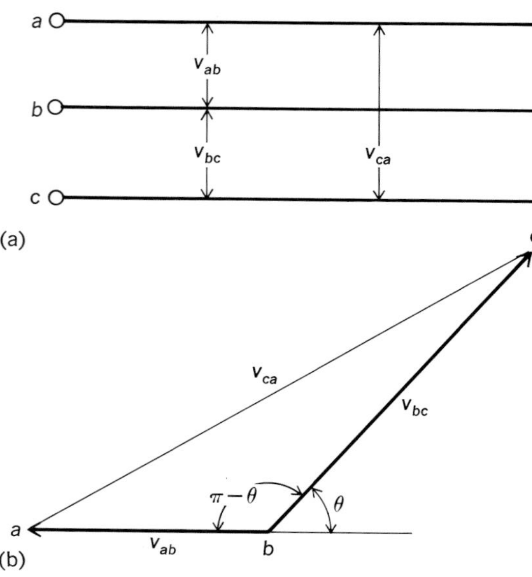


**Fig. 2. Voltages employed in three-voltmeter method. (*a*) Circuit diagram. (*b*) Vector diagram.**

will pass current only when both square waves are positive. In this case the greater the lag of one voltage, the smaller the overlap of the positive portions and the lower the average current. The current in this case is proportional to $\theta$ of Fig. 2.

This circuit has the theoretical limitation that each input voltage must be greater than a critical minimum value. In practice the critical value is determined by the noise on the amplifier input. If the voltage is too low, this noise causes a random zero-crossing shift and the results would be subject to this uncertainty.

A precision phase-angle meter for high-frequency voltages uses a variable delay line, and its operation is based on the fact that the difference of two voltages of constant amplitude is a minimum when the two are in phase. One of the two voltages to be compared is connected to both inputs of a variable-delay line, which is then adjusted to give a minimum output. The change in the delay-line setting gives the time delay of one voltage relative to the other. When the frequency is known, the time delay can be computed as angle of lag. If $\Delta t$ is the change in the delay-line setting and the frequency is $f$ hertz, the phase angle is given by $2\pi f\,\Delta t$ radians or $360f\,\Delta t$ degrees.

**Oscilloscope methods.** Phase-angle measurements by oscilloscopes are popular in the laboratory when quick approximate results are required. If one voltage is connected to the vertical amplifier and the other to the horizontal amplifier, a Lissajous figure is obtained.

If the two voltages are of the same frequency, as is the case when phase angles are measured, the basic figure is an ellipse. A straight line with a positive slope implies that the two waves are in phase. If one leads the other, the cathode-ray beam starts back in one direction before it reaches a maximum in the other and the ray traces an ellipse.

If the amplifiers are adjusted so that the horizontal amplitude is equal to the vertical amplitude, the slope of the straight line for in-phase signals is 45°. The ellipse widens to a circle when the phase angle is 90°. Intermediate values are indicated by Eq. (2), where $\phi$

$$\tan\frac{\phi}{2} = \frac{b}{a} \tag{2}$$

is phase angle sought, $b$ is width of the ellipse, and $a$ is its length. *SEE OSCILLOSCOPE*.

Another method of utilizing an oscilloscope, developed by H. Sohon, may be illustrated by the following considerations. If a signal is applied across the input of the bridge circuit shown in **Fig. 3***a*, the output voltages $v_1$ and $v_2$ will be 90° apart, and if $r$ equals $x$ (equals $1/2\pi fC$), they will be equal in amplitude. Now if $v_1$ and $v_2$ are applied to the vertical and horizontal amplifiers of an oscilloscope, the resulting trace will be a circle. If $r$ and $x$ are interchanged as in Fig. 3*b*, the trace will again be a circle, but the spot will trace the circle in the opposite direction.

If these two circuits are combined so that the sums of the outputs are applied, the spot cannot go around the circles in opposite directions at the same time, and it will trace a straight line instead. As the phase of one voltage is advanced, say by the angle $\Delta\theta$, the straight line will rotate on the screen through the angle $2\Delta\theta$. A scale can be marked on the screen and either end of the straight line used for reference. The presence of harmonics and slight errors in the $r = x$ relationship or in the equality of the input voltages will cause the line to open into a narrow ellipse. The slope of the major axis of the ellipse in this case is used for the slope of the straight line. **Figure 4** shows a working circuit. It is built so that $r = x$ at the operating frequency, and $R$ is several times $r$ so that the voltages are added without appreciable loading of the bridge circuits.

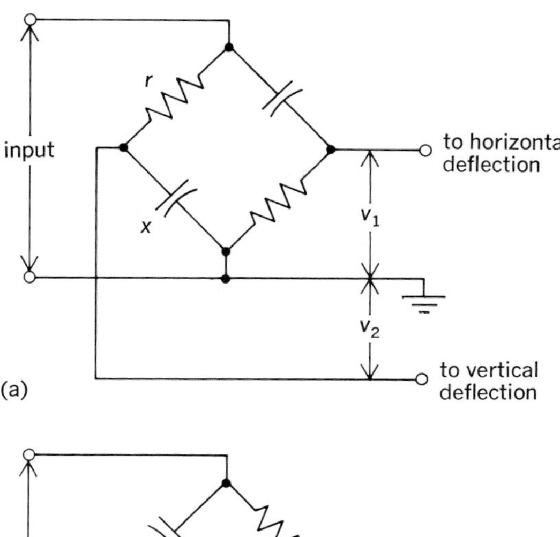


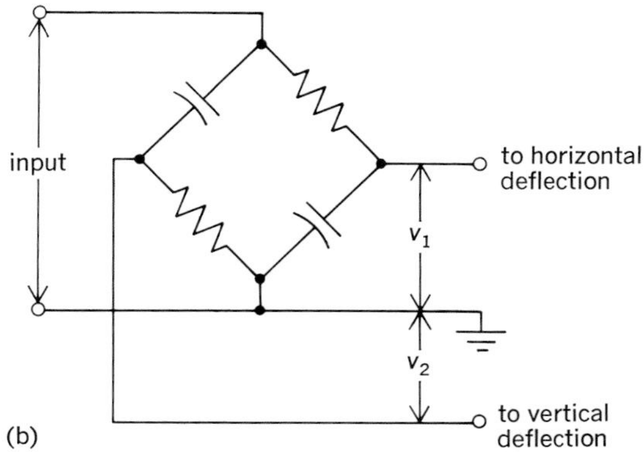


**Fig. 3.** Basic circuits for measuring the phase angle with an oscilloscope. (*a*) Clockwise circular sweep generated. (*b*) Counterclockwise circular sweep generated.

**Electronic switch.** An electronic switch can be used with an oscilloscope as a phase-angle meter. The switch permits the oscilloscope to display first one wave and then the other. If the linear sweep is at the same frequency as the waves being compared, the two waves will be superimposed on the screen. The phase difference and the period can be measured on the screen in inches, the ratio giving the phase angle as a fraction of 360°.

**Phase-order indicators.** These devices are used to indicate which phase voltage of a polyphase circuit leads or lags another. If the voltage vectors of a three-phase generator are as indicated in **Fig. 5***a*, the voltage from neutral to line 2 reaches a maximum 1/3 cycle (or period) after the voltage of line 1 and 1/3 cycle before the voltage of line 3. The voltage of phase 2 lags that of phase 1 and leads that of phase

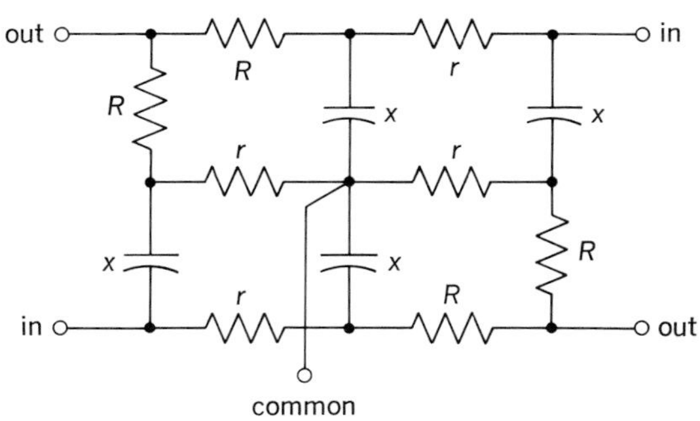


**Fig. 4.** An actual circuit for measuring phase angle with an oscilloscope.

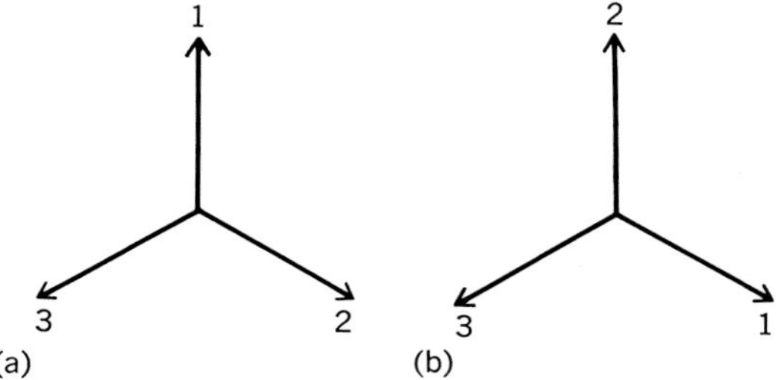


Fig. 5. Phase sequence. (*a*) Sequence 1–2–3. (*b*) Sequence 1–3–2.

3. The phase order or phase sequence is then said to be 1–2–3.

Relative motion between the armature conductors and the magnetic field induces the voltages in an alternator. Therefore, if the alternator were rotated in the opposite direction, the order in which the phase voltages reached maximum would be reversed. The phase sequence would be 1–3–2 as shown in Fig. 5*b*.

A miniature three-phase motor designed to rotate clockwise when connected to a three-phase system possessing a phase sequence 1–3–2 is used as a phase-sequence indicator. Counterclockwise rotation would indicate a 1–2–3 phase sequence.

A common type of phase-order indicator consists of an inductance and two lamps connected in Y to the three-phase lines as in **Fig. 6***a*. If it is assumed that the inductive reactance is very high, the common connection on the Y is at a voltage nearly equal to the midpoint of line 2–3 in Fig. 6*b* and *c*. The voltage across the reactor is $v_{n1}$, and the current lags by 90° and lies on *n*2 in Fig. 6*b* and on *n*3 in Fig. 6*c*. This current divides, part going through each lamp. The result is to increase the current in lamp 2 when the phase sequence is 1–2–3, and to increase the current in lamp 3 when the phase sequence is 1–3–2.

**Phase-relation indicators.** These devices are used to indicate the instant when two generators or sources of alternating voltage are in phase with one another. If two voltages reach maximum at the same time, they are in phase. When two sources are to be connected in parallel, they should have the same voltage, frequency, and phase. A voltmeter and a tachometer can be used to indicate when the voltages and frequencies are nearly equal. The phase relation between the two sources is shown by means of phasing lamps or by means of a synchroscope or synchronizer.

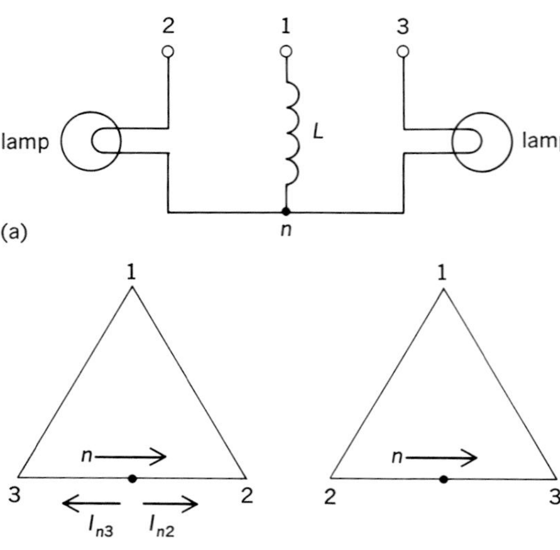


Fig. 6. Phase-sequence indicator. (*a*) Circuit diagram. (*b*) Vector diagram for sequence 1–2–3. (*c*) Vector diagram for sequence 1–3–2.

Phasing lamps placed across the open switch used to parallel two generators will often suffice to indicate an in-phase condition (**Fig. 7**). Depending upon the relative phase of the two machines, the lamp voltage varies from the sum to the difference of the machine voltages. As the two frequencies approach one another, the lamps flicker, changing from full bright to dim at a decreasing rate. If the two frequencies are equal, the lamp will maintain a fixed brilliance. Usually the oncoming machine is set with a slightly higher frequency so that it will take up some load rather than be an additional load on the system. As the lamps slowly go through the dim phase, the switch is closed, connecting the machine to the system.

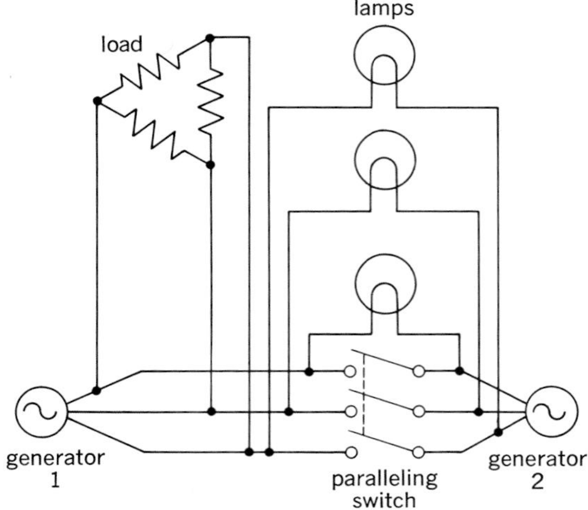


Fig. 7. Paralleling a second generator with a first generator which is already under load.

**Synchronizer or synchroscope.** This is a variation of the Tuma phase meter. The current in the fixed coil is supplied by one machine; the current in the movable crossed coils is supplied by the other machine. If the two machines are in synchronism, their frequencies are equal and the crossed coils will take a position depending upon the relative phase angle. If the frequency of one machine is slightly higher, the phase will continue to vary and the crossed coils will rotate in a direction determined by whether the speed is too low or too high. Generally the incoming machine is given a slightly higher speed and is connected to the line when the synchroscope pointer drifts past the zero mark. *See* Electrical measurements.

*Harry Sohon; Edward C. Stevenson*

***Bibliography.*** S. Geczy, *Basic Electrical Measurements*, 1984; B. A. Gregory, *An Introduction to Electrical Instrumentation and Measurement Systems*, 2d ed., 1981; R. L Heiserman, *Electrical and Electronic Measuring Instruments*, 1983.

## Phase inverter

A circuit having the primary function of changing the phase of a signal by 180°. The phase inverter is most commonly employed as the input stage for a push-pull amplifier. Therefore, the phase inverter must supply two voltages of equal magnitude and 180° phase difference. A variety of circuits are available for the phase inversion. The circuit used in any given case depends upon such factors as the overall gain of the phase inverter and push-pull amplifier, the possibility that the input to the push-pull amplifier may require power, space requirements, and cost. *See* PUSH-PULL AMPLIFIER.

Overall fidelity of a phase inverter and push-pull amplifier can be adversely affected by improper design of the phase inverter. The principal design requirement is that frequency response of one input channel to the push-pull amplifier be identical to the frequency response of the other channel. In this respect popular phase-inversion circuits are capable of providing precisely 180° phase difference only after careful selection of components. Some phase-inverter circuits can perform inversion at only one frequency; at other frequencies distortion is introduced because of unequal frequency response characteristics.

**Transformer inverter.** The simplest form of phase-inverter circuit is a transformer with a center-tapped secondary (**Fig. 1**). Careful design of the transformer assures that the secondary voltages are equal. The transformer forms a good inverter when the inverter must supply power to the input of the push-pull amplifier. The turns ratio can be adjusted for maximum power transfer. *See* TRANSFORMER.

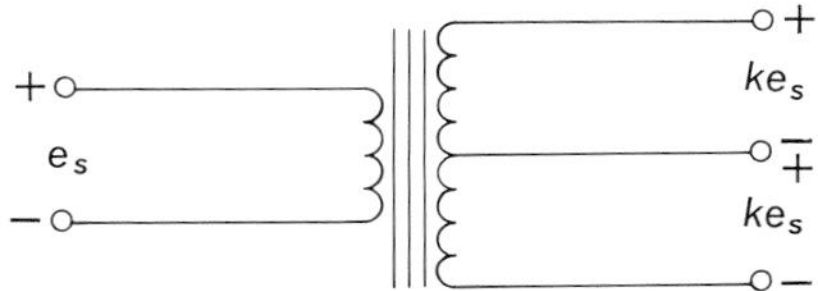


**Fig. 1. Transformer, simplest form of phase-inverter circuit. The turns ratio is represented by *k*.**

The transformer inverter has several disadvantages. It usually costs more, occupies more space, and weighs more than a transistor or vacuum-tube circuit. Furthermore, some means must be found to compensate for the frequency response of the transformer, which may not be as uniform as that which can be obtained from solid-state or vacuum-tube circuits.

**Paraphase amplifiers.** An amplifier that provides two equal output signals 180° out of phase is called a paraphase amplifier. If coupling capacitors can be omitted, the simplest paraphase amplifier is illustrated in **Fig. 2**. Approximately the same current flows through $R_L$ and $R_E$, and therefore if $R_L$ and $R_E$ are equal, the ac output voltages from the collector and from the emitter are equal in magnitude and 180° out of phase. The gain of the circuit is less than unity, which is one factor that limits its applicability. A second important factor is that the addition of coupling capacitors and biasing resistors, necessary when the circuit is coupled to the push-pull stage, causes the phase inversion to be other than 180° over the frequency range of expected operation. One of the most stable and important paraphase amplifiers is the emitter-coupled phase inverter (**Fig. 3**). If the emitter resistance $R_E$ is large compared to the impedance seen looking into the emitter of each transistor, current $i_1$ will equal $i_2$. Under this condition the voltage at one collector is exactly the negative of that at the other collector, and push-pull operation is achieved. The collector-to-collector gain is equal to the gain which would be provided by a single-transistor grounded-emitter amplifier with collector load $R_L$.

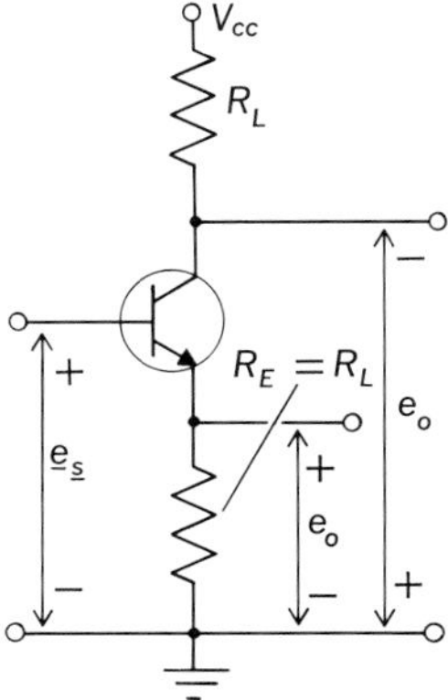


**Fig. 2. Single-transistor inverter.**

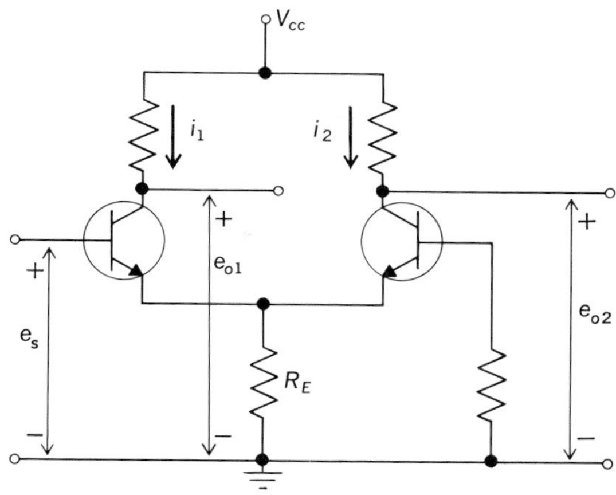


**Fig. 3. Emitter-coupled phase inverter.**

If the phase-inverter circuit is to produce two voltages 180° out of phase, the equivalent circuits governing the behavior of the two output voltages must be identical. The mid-frequency gain of each must be identical and the phase-shift functions must be identical. The phase-shift requirements are often compromised in the interests of simplicity of the final circuit and freedom from critical adjustments of key circuit parameters. *See* PHASE; PHASE-ANGLE MEASUREMENT; SEMI-CONDUCTOR.

*Harold F. Klock*

## Phase-locked loops

Electronic circuits for locking an oscillator in phase with an arbitrary input signal. A phase-locked loop (PLL) is used in two fundamentally different ways: (1) as a demodulator, where it is employed to follow (and demodulate) frequency or phase modulation, and (2) to track a carrier or synchronizing signal which may vary in frequency with time. When operating as a demodulator, the PLL may be thought of as a matched filter operating as a coherent detector. When used to track a carrier, it may be thought of as a narrow-band filter for removing noise from the signal and regenerating a clean replica of the signal. *See* DEMODULATOR; ELECTRIC FILTER.

**Basic operation.** The basic components of a phase-locked loop are shown in **Fig. 1**. The input signal is a sine or square wave of arbitrary frequency. The voltage-controlled oscillator (VCO) output signal is a sine or square wave of the same frequency as the input, but the phase angle between the two is arbitrary. The output of the phase detector consists of a direct-current (dc) term, and components of the input frequency and its harmonics. The low-pass filter removes all alternating-current (ac) components, leaving the dc component, the magnitude of which is a function of the phase angle between the VCO signal and the input signal. If the frequency of the input signal changes, a change in phase angle between these signals will produce a change in the dc control voltage in such a manner as to vary the frequency of the VCO to track the frequency of the input signal.

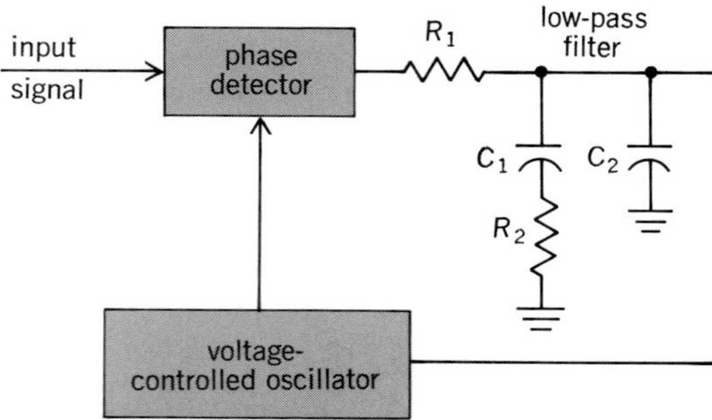


**Fig. 1. Phase-locked loop.**

Two qualities of the loop specify its performance. One is the hold-in range, while the other is the pull-in range. The hold-in range is the maximum change in input frequency for which the loop will remain locked. It is governed by the dc gain of the loop. As the input frequency is changed, the change in phase of the two signals to the phase detector will produce a dc control voltage that will change the frequency of the VCO. As the input frequency is further changed, the phase angle will continue to increase until it reaches 0 or 180°, when the loop will unlock. If an amplifier is added to the loop, a greater control voltage will be generated which will decrease the phase error in the phase detector, and hence further detuning can occur before unlocking takes place.

The pull-in range is that range of frequencies that the loop will lock to if it is initially unlocked. Suppose the loop is unlocked and the VCO is running at frequency $f_1$. If the input signal $f_2$ is applied, but out of the pull-in range, a beat note $f_1 - f_2$ will appear at the output of the phase detector. The filter components will govern the amplitude of this beat note at the input to the VCO. If the frequency difference is reduced, the frequency of the beat note will decrease and the amplitude at the VCO input will increase. At some point, the amplitude will drive the VCO far enough over in frequency to match the input frequency and locking will occur. The lower the roll-off frequency of the loop filter, above which its attenuation begins to increase, the less will be the pull-in range.

Phase-locked loops are generally designed to have narrower pull-in range than hold-in range. This is the advantage of a PLL over more conventional types of filters. The pull-in range is analogous to filter bandwidth and may be made as narrow as desired by suitable choice of the resistance-capacitance (*RC*) filter, while the center frequency may be any desired value.

**Voltage-controlled oscillators.** Voltage-controlled oscillators may take many forms, two common types being the reactance modulator and the varactor modulator. These circuits are commonly used in narrow-band PLLs where narrow hold-in and pull-in ranges are desired. *See Varactor.*

Another common form of voltage-controlled oscillator utilizes a multivibrator type of circuit where the timing capacitor charging current may be varied by a dc control voltage. This circuit relies on the fact that the time required to charge the timing capacitance is inversely proportioned to the frequency of oscillation, hence the control voltage will vary the frequency of the oscillator. *See Multivibrator.*

Reactance- and varactor-type modulators are used with crystal-controlled oscillators where tuning ranges of 0.25–0.5% are desired, or with *LC* oscillators where tuning ranges of 5% can be achieved. Multivibrator types of circuits are used where wide tuning ranges of up to 1000 to 1 have been achieved. Conversely, phase noise and stability are best with crystal-controlled oscillator and least with multivibrator-type circuits.

**Phase detectors.** Two commonly used phase detectors are the diode phase detector and the double-balanced phase detector. The diode phase detector has been used historically because of lower cost and better performance at high frequencies (above 50 MHz). With the advent of monolith integrated circuits, the double-balanced phase detector has become useful at lower frequencies.

In the diode detector (**Fig. 2**) the voltage applied to the two peak rectifiers are the sum and difference of the two input signals $e_r$ and $e_s$. Rectified output voltages are equal to the amplitudes of each of the sums $E_a$ and $E_b$. The phase detector output voltage $E_d$ is equal to the difference of the two rectified voltages, $E_a - E_b$. Considering that $e_r$ and $e_s$ are sinusoidal waves of the same frequency but varying phase angle, the dc output $E_d$ will be zero when the two input signals are in quadrature (90°), a maximum positive value when in phase, and a maximum negative value when 180° out of phase.

The double-balanced phase detector (**Fig. 3**) works well at low frequencies. The upper four transistors

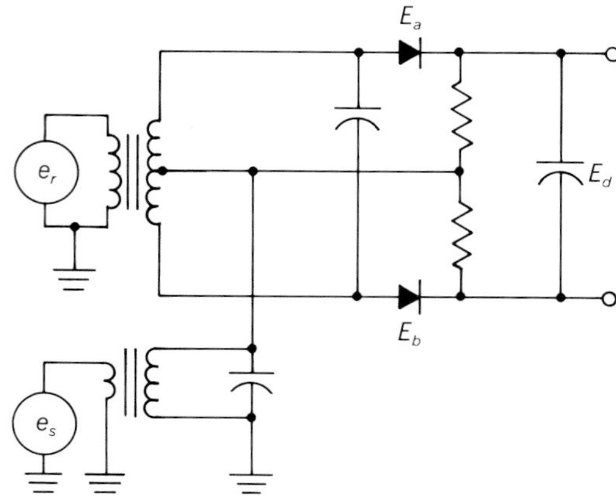


**Fig. 2. Diode phase detector.**

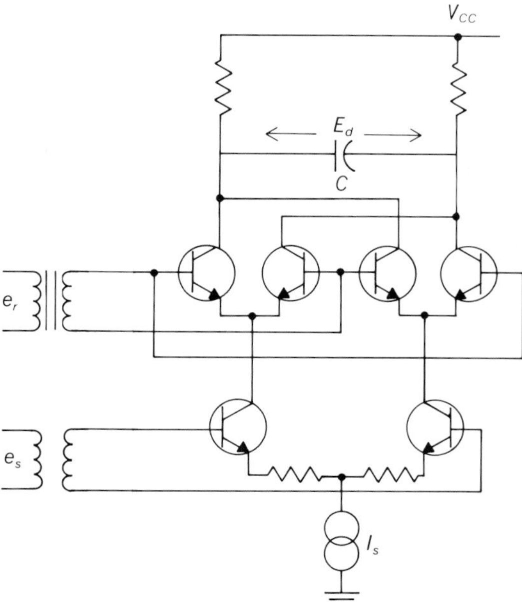


Fig. 3. Double-balanced phase detector.

operate as a double-pole double-throw switch driven by the reference signal $e_r$. The lower transistors operate as an amplifier, their collector currents being proportional to the input signal $e_s$. **Figure 4** shows the output waveform for different phase angles between the two input signals. The output signal shown is that which would be obtained if the filter capacitor $C$ were removed.

The loop filter determines the dynamic characteristics of the loop: its bandwidth and response time. This filter is generally composed of a lag-lead network (Fig. 1). The transfer function of the VCO has the characteristic of an integrator: a step change in the dc control voltage will produce a ramp change in output phase, increasing without bound. The low-pass filter characteristic begins attenuating frequencies above its break point determined by $R_1C_1$; at a higher frequency determined by $R_2C_1$, no further attenuation occurs. This is important because the phase shift associated with the VCO is 90°, and that associated with the roll off due to $R_1C_1$ is also approaching 90°. With a phase shift of 180° the loop will oscillate and become unstable. The leading phase shift associated with $R_2C_1$ reduces the phase shift around the loop and enhances stability.

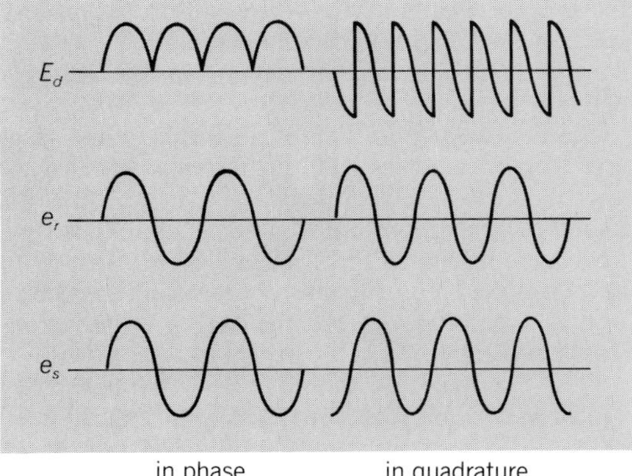


Fig. 4. Waveforms in double-balanced phase detector.

**Uses of phase-locked loops.** The most widespread use of phase-locked loops is undoubtedly in television receivers. Synchronization of the horizontal oscillator to the transmitted sync pulses is universally accomplished with a PLL; here it is desirable to have a stable, noise-free reference source to generate the scanning line since the eye is intolerant of any jitter (or phase noise). The color reference oscillator is often synchronized with a phase-locked loop; here it is necessary to maintain less than 5° of phase error between the transmitted color reference signal and the locally generated reference in the receiver. In both of these applications, the VCO signal is the useful output, and the design of the loop filter is such as to produce a narrow-band characteristic so that noise is reduced and the filter "remembers" the proper phase during short periods of noise and loss of signal.

Phase-locked loops are also used as frequency demodulators. Since the VCO is locked to the incoming carrier frequency, and the control voltage is proportional to the VCO frequency, as long as the loop remains locked, the control voltage will be a replica of the modulating signal. Phase-locked loops may also be used as frequency multipliers. The VCO is operated at $N$ times the input frequency $f_1$ and divided by $N$ in a digital divider (**Fig. 5**). If a wide-range VCO

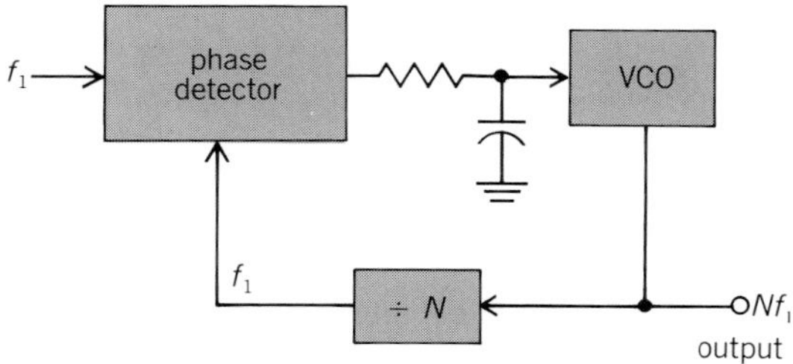


Fig. 5. Frequency multiplier.

is used, the circuit will operate over a wide range of input frequencies. The loop filter must remove the components of carrier appearing at the output of the phase detector or phase modulation of the VCO will occur.

Phase-locked loops have been applied to stereo decoders made on silicon monolithic integrated circuits. This design technique eliminates the coils used in previous decoder designs. The circuit consists of a 76-kHz VCO, which, after being divided by 4, is locked to the transmitted 19-kHz pilot carrier. The PLL therefore acts as a carrier regenerator (or narrow-band filter). The 76 kHz is also divided by 2 to obtain 38 kHz that is applied to a double-balanced demodulator, which decodes the stereo signal into left and right channels.

High-performance amplitude demodulators may be built using phase-lock techniques. If, instead of using a diode detector, a double-balanced demodulator is used, the lower port of which is driven with the signal to be demodulated, and the upper port is driven with a noise-free replica of the carrier, a very linear (low distortion) demodulator results. The phase-locked loop (**Fig. 6**) consisting of phase detector 1 and the VCO locks to the carrier frequency; the loop filter

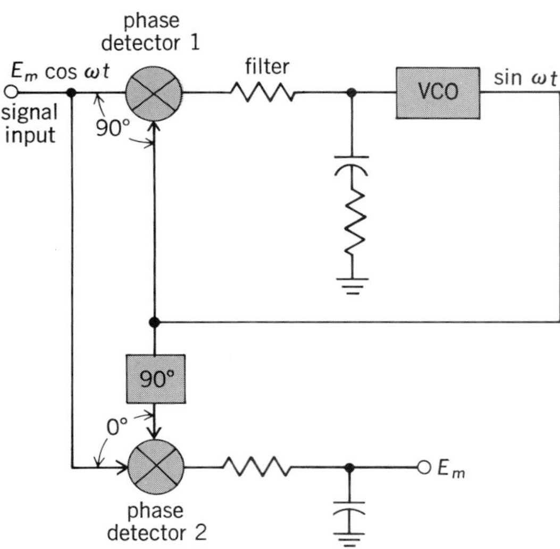


**Fig. 6. Amplitude-modulation demodulator.**

should be narrow enough that modulation is not present in the PLL. Since the first phase detector is driven in quadrature with the input signal, very little amplitude information is demodulated in the loop. The VCO signal is also phase-shifted 90° and applied to phase detector 2, which is also driven with the signal to be demodulated. Since the carrier and reference are in phase in this detector, the output will be proportional to the amplitude of the incoming carrier. Demodulators using this technique have been built with linearity better than 0.5% distortion for 90% modulated signals. SEE AMPLITUDE-MODULATION DETECTOR.

*Thomas B. Mills*

**Bibliography.** F. M. Gardner, *Phase-Lock Techniques*, 2d ed., 1979.

## Phase modulation

A special kind of angle modulation in which the linearly increasing angle of a sine-wave carrier has added to it a phase angle that is proportional to the instantaneous value of the modulating wave (message to be communicated). Phase modulation (PM) is a scheme for impressing the message to be communicated upon a high-frequency sine-wave carrier. There is a direct proportionality between the message to be communicated and the phase variations imparted to the modulated wave propagated to the receiver. For basic concepts, technical terms, and supplementary information SEE MODULATION. SEE ALSO ANGLE MODULATION.

**Advantages and applications.** Like other forms of angle modulation, PM reduces noise at the cost of extra bandwidth occupancy, transmits constant average signal power, transmits constant peak power equal to twice the average signal power, and has a channel-grabbing property whereby, if two signals reach the PM detector, the larger signal is accepted to the near exclusion of the smaller.

Important applications include certain types of telegraph, telemetering, and data-processing systems. PM is used in certain microwave radio relay systems; some carry telephone conversations and television programs simultaneously. PM techniques are used in many types of measuring and control systems.

The sharp limitation of range (channel grabbing) is especially important for some services. Typical examples using PM include mobile and fixed radio systems for police, airway, and military applications.

**Noise response.** Noise appearing in the output of an angle-modulation detector depends upon the kind of angle modulation, other factors being equal. When the noise disturbance has the characteristics of resistance noise, the average noise power in the output of a PM detector is uniformly distributed with respect to frequency. Under the same conditions, the distribution of root-mean-square noise currents in the output of a frequency-modulation (FM) detector is a distribution increasing linearly with frequency. Other kinds of angle modulation are characterized by other kinds of noise spectra. Normally, the angle modulation used would be that giving the best signal-to-noise ratio. SEE ELECTRICAL NOISE; FREQUENCY MODULATION.

**Fundamental properties.** Instantaneous phase variations imply and are necessarily accompanied by uniquely related instantaneous frequency variations, and conversely. Also, given one, it is possible to reproduce the other.

For example, in PM the instantaneous phase variations imparted to the modulated wave are directly proportional to the modulating wave. The resulting variations in instantaneous frequency are, however, directly proportional to the time derivative of the modulating wave.

Similarly, in FM the instantaneous frequency of the modulated wave is linearly proportional to the modulating wave. However, the resulting variations in instantaneous phase are directly proportional to the time integral of the modulating wave.

Actually, PM and FM are not essentially different. A circuit whose output is inversely proportional to frequency (zero frequency excepted) preceding a phase modulator converts PM to FM, and following an FM detector, converts frequency to phase detection. Similarly, a circuit whose output is directly proportional to frequency (zero frequency excepted) preceding a frequency modulator converts FM to PM, and following a PM detector, converts phase to frequency detection.

Angle modulation manifests itself by the zeros of the angle-modulated wave. These zeros are the exact instants of time that the angle-modulated wave passes through zero. Theoretically, given the zeros, it is possible to determine for all values of time the instantaneous frequency deviations from the fixed frequency of the unmodulated carrier, and also the instantaneous phase deviations corresponding to the instantaneous frequency deviations. In other words, the zeros, which are nothing more than a distribution of points along the time axis, unambiguously identify the original message.

When detecting an angle-modulated wave perturbed by noise, nonsignificant information must be ignored, because only by this means can the full noise advantage of angle modulation be realized. The limiter in a conventional PM detector ignores nonsignificant information by completely destroying the waveform of the received wave, leaving only the zeros. SEE PHASE-MODULATION DETECTOR; PHASE MODULATOR.

*Harold S. Black*

**Bibliography.** F. R. Connor, *Modulation*, 2d ed., 1982; M. Schwartz, *Information, Transmission, Modulation and Noise*, 3d ed., 1980.

## Phase-modulation detector

A device which recovers or detects the modulating signal from a phase-modulated carrier. Any frequency-modulation (FM) detector with minor modifications will detect phase-modulated waves. *See* FREQUENCY-MODULATION DETECTOR; PHASE MODULATION.

**Modification of FM detector.** In standard FM broadcast, the only difference between FM and phase modulation (PM) is the manner in which the modulation index varies with the modulating frequency. The modulation index is independent of the modulating frequency in PM but is inversely proportional to the modulating frequency in FM. Therefore an FM detector, when used to detect a phase-modulated wave, produces an output voltage which is proportional to the modulating frequency, assuming the original modulating signal to be of constant amplitude. Consequently, a low-pass filter with a single reactive element, such as an *RC* (resistance-capacitance) filter, is needed in the output of the FM detector which is used to detect a phase-modulated wave.

A simple *RC* filter which might be used to convert an FM detector into a PM detector is shown in **Fig. 1**. The *RC* time constant of the filter should equal the reciprocal of the lowest modulating frequency component in radians per second. However, the resistance $R$ involved in the time constant is the total resistance in parallel with the capacitance $C$, not just the resistance $R_F$. Commercial FM broadcasting ordinarily utilizes the characteristics of FM for modulating frequencies below about 2100 Hz and the characteristics of PM for frequencies above 2100 Hz for the purpose of maintaining improved signal-to-noise ratio at high modulating frequencies, as compared with pure FM. This technique is usually known as preemphasis. Then the FM detector must include a filter such as the *RC* filter shown in Fig. 1, but the crossover frequency must be approximately 2100 Hz instead of the lowest modulating frequency. This filter is usually known as a deemphasis filter and has a time constant of approximately 75 microseconds ($RC = 1/6.28 \times 2100$). This filter must be added to an FM detector to convert it into a PM detector. *See* ELECTRIC FILTER.

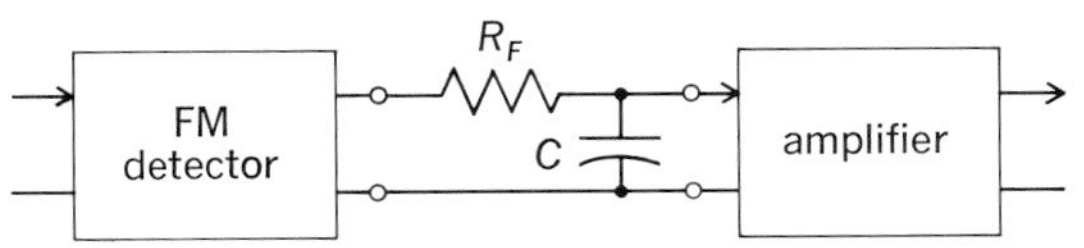


**Fig. 1.** An *RC* filter which is used to convert a frequency-modulation detector into a phase-modulation detector.

**Multiplier circuit.** A multiplier circuit or chip may be used as a phase detector, provided its frequency capability, or passband, includes the carrier frequency. **Figure 2** shows how the multiplier serves as a phase detector. The phase-modulated carrier is applied to one multiplier input while the unmodulated carrier frequency is applied to the other input. These signals are shown as square waves because PM and FM are usually severely clipped to remove amplitude modulation with its associated noise. Also Fig. 2 is easier to understand with square waves. The output is maximum positive when the inputs $V_1$ and $V_2$ are in phase (Fig. 2*a*), but the average value of the output decreases to zero as the relative phase of the two inputs shifts to 90° (Fig. 2*b*). Then as the relative input phase increases to 180°, the output becomes maximum negative (Fig. 2*c*). After the carrier and other high frequencies are filtered from the output, the output voltage is a linear function of the phase difference between the two inputs (Fig. 2*d*). The unmodulated carrier may be generated in the receiver by the use of a phase-locked loop (PLL). *See* AMPLITUDE MODULATOR; PHASE-LOCKED LOOPS.

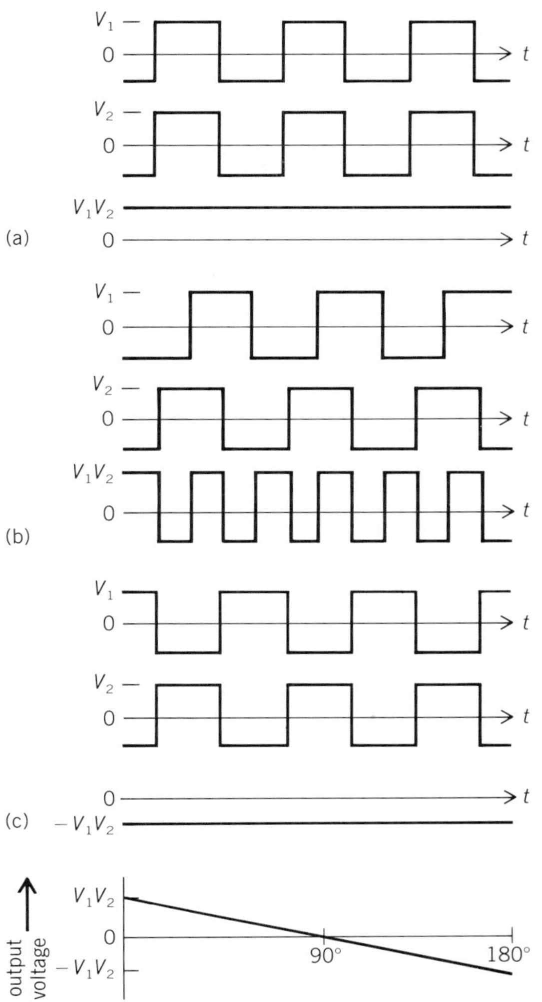


**Fig. 2.** Phase detection by multiplication. (*a*) Inputs $V_1$ and $V_2$ are in phase. (*b*) Relative phase of inputs is 90°. (*c*) Relative phase of inputs is 180°. (*d*) Output voltage as a function of phase difference between the inputs.

**Demodulation of PSK.** Phase-modulation detectors are often called upon to demodulate a type of pulse-code modulation known as phase-shift keying (PSK). In PSK modulation the carrier phase shifts abruptly by 180° whenever the pulse-code modulating signal changes from the zero level to the one level, or vice versa (**Fig. 3**). When the multiplier-type demodulator is used for PSK, the output filter must allow the output voltage to change from maximum positive to maximum negative during a time that is short compared with the time allotted to either a one or a zero in the pulse-code modulation. *See* PULSE MODULATION.

Since a PLL has both a phase detector and a voltage-controlled oscillator (VCO), the PLL may be used as a complete phase demodulator, including the

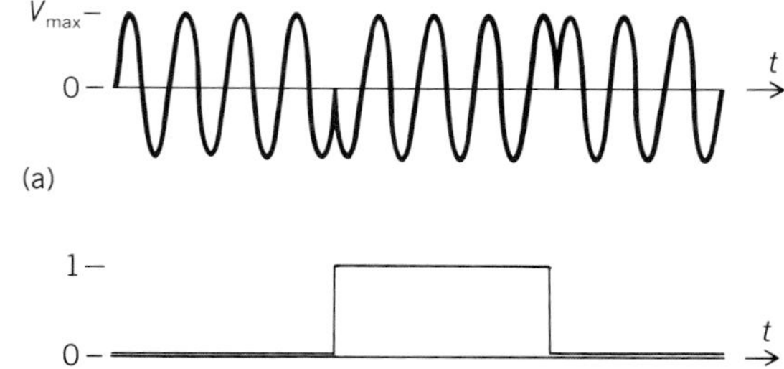


Fig. 3. Phase-shift keying modulation. (*a*) Modulated signal. (*b*) Pulse-code modulating signal.

carrier regeneration. Only a long-time-constant filter is needed between the phase detector output and the VCO to provide a quasi-dc voltage to the VCO in order to maintain its lock to the carrier frequency.

**Demodulation of FSK.** Another commonly used type of pulse-code modulation is frequency-shift keying (FSK), in which the carrier frequency changes abruptly by an amount $\Delta f$ as the modulating signal changes from the zero level to the one level, or vice versa. Therefore, FSK is basically a type of FM, and any type of FM demodulator may be used to recover the pulse-code modulating signal. However, phase-locked loops are commonly used. Thus a phase-locked loop may be used to detect either FSK or PSK, but an additional long-time-constant filter is required between the output and the VCO in the PSK detector in order to hold the VCO at the carrier frequency without abrupt changes in phase.

Although the fidelity of a PLL in demodulating an FM signal is as good as the linearity of the VCO frequency to its control voltage, this linearity is not important in the reception of FSK because the only requirement is to faithfully identify the two different voltage levels in the output of the PLL. The same is true for the reception of PSK, except that the linearity of the phase detector instead of the VCO would be involved in this case. SEE MODULATION; MODULATOR.

*Charles L. Alley*

**Bibliography.** J. J. DeFrance, *Communications, Electronics and Circuits*, 2d ed., 1972; S. Haykin, *Communication Systems*, 2d ed., 1983; R. Kellejian, *Applied Electronic Communications: Circuits, Systems, Transmission*, 2d ed., 1980.

## Phase modulator

An electronic circuit that causes the phase angle of the modulated wave to vary (with respect to the unmodulated carrier) in accordance with the modulating signal. Since frequency is the rate of change of phase, a phase modulator will produce the characteristics of frequency modulation (FM) if the frequency characteristics of the modulating signal are so altered that the modulating voltage is inversely proportional to frequency. Commercial FM transmitters normally employ a phase modulator because a crystal-controlled oscillator can then be used to meet the strict carrier-frequency control requirements of the Federal Communications Commission. The chief disadvantage of phase modulators is that they generally produce insufficient frequency-deviation ratios, or modulation index, for satisfactory noise suppression. Frequency multiplication can be used, however, to increase the modulation index to the desired value, since the frequency deviation is multiplied along with the carrier frequency. Many different types of phase modulators have been devised. A few of the typical and more commonly used modulators are described in this article. SEE FREQUENCY MODULATION; PHASE MODULATION; PHASE-MODULATION DETECTOR.

**Types.** A simple modulator is shown in **Fig. 1**. In this circuit the modulating voltage changes the capacitance of the varactor diode. The phase shift depends upon the relative magnitudes of the capacitive reactance of the varactor diode and the load resistance $R$. Therefore the phase shift varies with the modulating voltage and phase modulation (PM) is accomplished. However, the phase shift is not linearly related to the modulating voltage if the PM exceeds a few degrees, because the phase shift is not linearly related to the capacitance and the capacitance of the varactor diode is not linearly related to the modulating voltage. SEE VARACTOR.

**Figure 2** illustrates the principle of operation of a phase modulator which provides greater phase shift for a given distortion than the simple phase modulator of Fig. 1. The block diagram of Fig. 2*a* shows that the oscillator signal is passed through two channels, 1 and 2. In channel 1 the phase of the signal is shifted 90°, and in channel 2 the signal is amplitude-modulated. The outputs of channel 1 and channel 2 are then recombined and passed through a limiter to remove the residual amplitude modulation (AM). The phasor diagram shows how PM is produced when the amplitude-modulated carrier voltage $V_2$ is added to the 90° phase-shifted carrier voltage $V_1$. The phasor sum $V_0$ is the hypotenuse of the phasor triangle and varies in phase with respect to the channel 1 voltage as the channel 2 voltage varies in amplitude. The phasor sum $V_0$ also varies somewhat in amplitude, but a limiter can be used to remove this AM, as previously mentioned and shown in Fig. 2. This phase modulator is linear, or distortionless, providing first, that the AM is distortionless and second, that the change in phase is proportional to the change in amplitude of the amplitude-modulated signal from channel 2.

But elementary trigonometry and Fig. 2*b* show that the phase of $V_0$ is the angle whose tangent is $V_2/V_1$. Therefore linear modulation is attained only for small phase angles where the tangent of the angle is approximately equal to the angle itself. This requirement limits the total phase variation to about 20° if the distortion is limited to 54. This limit would permit only 10° phase deviation on each side of the unmodulated, or carrier, position.

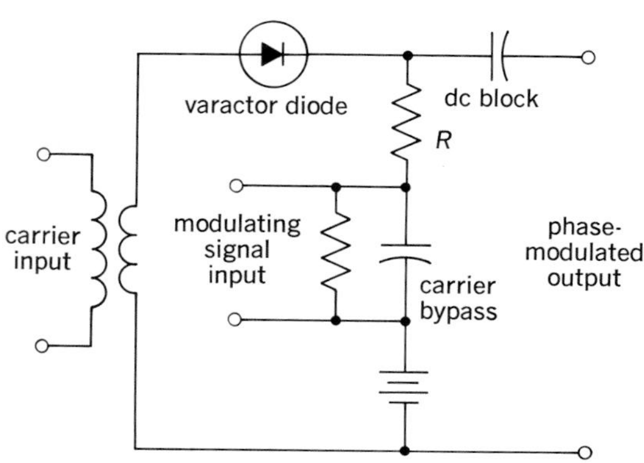


Fig. 1. A simple phase modulator.

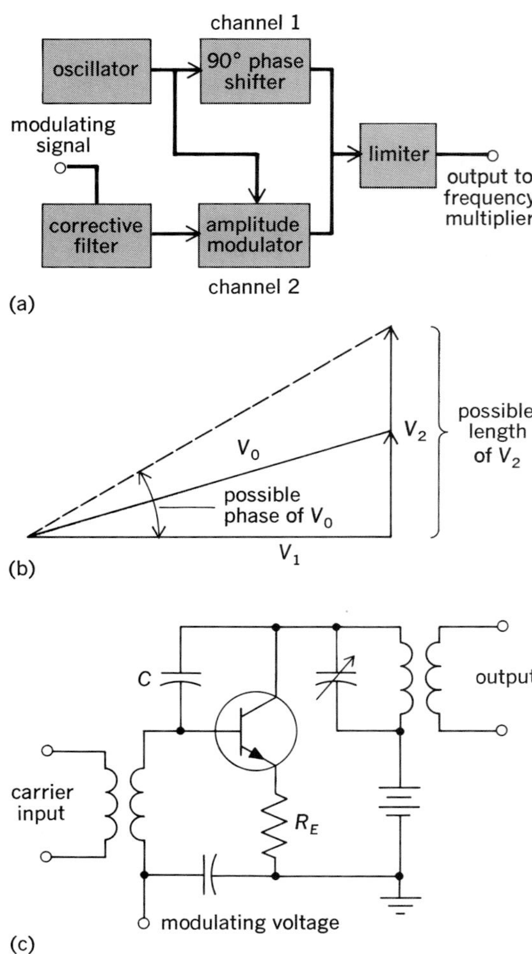


**Fig. 2. A method for the production of phase modulation. (*a*) Block diagram. (*b*) Phasor diagram showing the combination of voltages. (c) A circuit which performs the necessary functions, except corrective filtering and limiting, in a single transistor circuit.**

A simple circuit employing a single transistor can perform the basic functions of a phase modulator, as shown in Fig. 2*c*. The transistor is a base-modulated amplifier which has low gain because of the unbypassed resistor $R_E$ in the emitter circuit. The current through the small capacitance $C$ leads the input voltage by approximately 90° and adds to the amplitude-modulated collector current in the collector load. The small voltage gain, perhaps less than 1, is required in the transistor amplifier for two reasons. First, the current through capacitor $C$ is then essentially proportional to the carrier input, which is essentially constant, as assumed in the phasor diagram of Fig. 2*b*. Second, the capacitance $C$ can cause the amplifier to be unstable unless the voltage gain is low.

The phase deviation can be doubled for a given distortion level if the base-modulated amplifier of Fig. 2 is replaced by a balanced modulator. The reason for this improvement is that the carrier is suppressed in the balanced modulator output and only the sideband frequencies are present in channel 2 output to add to channel 1 output. Thus the carrier is not present to produce the unmodulated phase offset shown by the solid line labeled $V_0$ in Fig. 2*b*. The improvement gained by suppressing the AM carrier can be visualized if the modulating signal is a single frequency so there are only two side frequencies. Each of these side frequencies can be viewed as a rotating phasor which adds vectorially to the carrier phasor. The upper side frequency is higher than the carrier. Therefore when the carrier phasor is used as a reference, the upper side frequency appears to rotate counterclockwise. Similarly, the lower side-frequency phasor appears to rotate clockwise because its frequency is lower than the carrier frequency. The vector sum of these three phasors produces AM as shown in **Fig. 3***a*. However, PM is produced when the side frequencies are shifted 90° in phase with respect to the carrier (or vice versa) as shown in Fig. 3*b*. Then the phase is seen to deviate symmetrically on either side of the phase-shifted carrier and the peak-to-peak deviation can be at least twice as great for a given distortion as when the phase deviates only in one direction. The peak-phase deviation may be about 30° if 8% harmonic distortion is tolerable. A simple balanced modulator circuit is shown in Fig. 3*c*. *See* AMPLITUDE MODULATION.

When the balanced modulator is used in the block diagram of Fig. 2*a* and the frequency multiplier and a power amplifier follow the limiter, a complete FM transmitter results and is known as the Armstrong system of phase (or frequency) modulation.

**Phase-shift keying (PSK).** A comparatively simple circuit may be used to phase-modulate a pulse-coded signal. In this type of signal, only two different voltage levels are used to represent ones and zeros in binary coded signals. Therefore, a simple phase inverter and switching circuit may be used to obtain 180° phase-shift modulation as the signal changes from a zero to a one, or vice versa. Such a circuit is shown in **Fig. 4**, where the carrier is applied through a transformer to the single-pole double-throw transistor

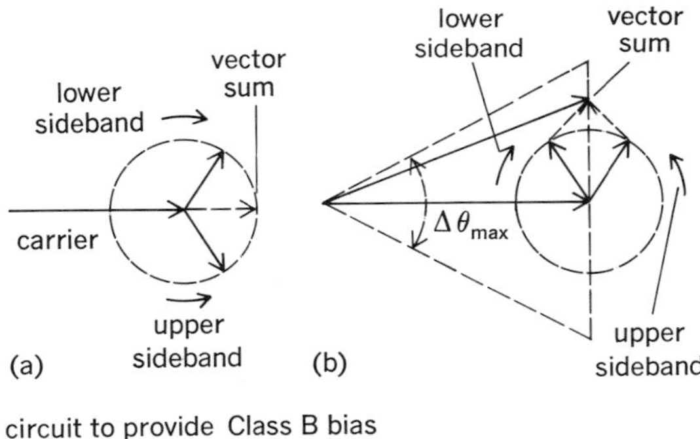


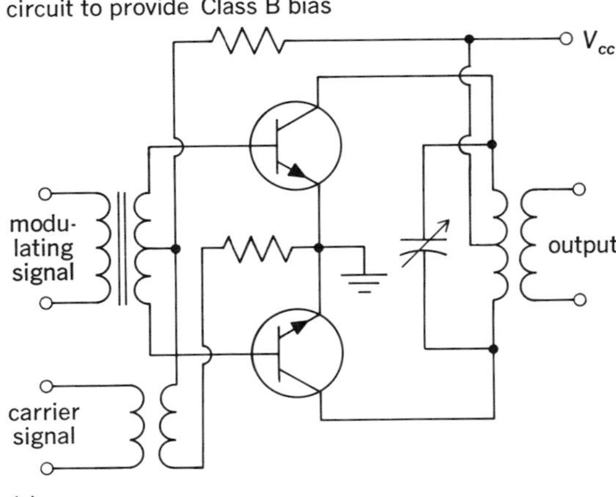


**Fig. 3. Illustration of the principle of phase modulation using a balanced modulator. (*a*) Amplitude modulation. (*b*) Phase modulation. (c) A balanced modulator.**

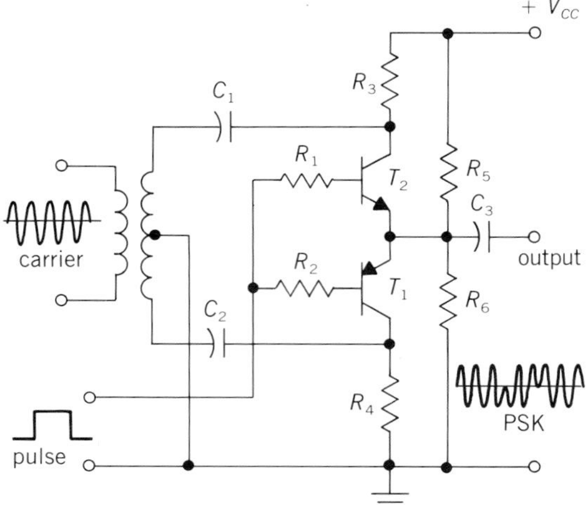


**Fig. 4. Phase modulators for phase-shift keying.**

switch. When the modulating signal is at "zero level", transistor $T_1$ is forward-biased to saturation so the lower end of the input transformer is connected through the low-saturation resistance of $T_1$ through the dc blocking capacitor $C_5$ to the output terminal. As the modulating signal changes to "one" level, transistor $T_1$ is cut off and transistor $T_2$ becomes saturated, thus connecting the top end of the input transformer through $T_2$ to the output. Since the signal at the upper end of the transformer is 180° out of phase with the signal at the lower end, the center tap being the reference, the output phase shifts 180° at each transition between zero and one, or vice versa. Capacitors $C_1$ and $C_2$, like $C_3$, block dc so proper bias levels may be maintained on the transistors. Thus their reactances need to be negligible at the carrier frequency. Resistors $R_1$, $R_2$, $R_3$, and $R_4$ control the transistor bias currents, and resistors $R_5$ and $R_6$ maintain the average voltage, or dc component, at the emitters of the two transistors at about $V_{CC}/2$ volts. The carrier frequency is limited by the switching characteristics of the transistors, but may be above 100 MHz with careful transistor selection. At high frequencies, the input transformer should either be tuned or be bifilar-wound. *See* MODULATION; PULSE MODULATION.

The examples given above are typical of the many different phase-modulating schemes that may be used.

*Charles L. Alley*

***Bibliography.*** S. Haykin, *Communications Systems*, 2d ed., 1983; R. Kellejian, *Applied Electronic Communications: Circuits, Systems, Transmission*, 2d ed., 1980; M. Schwartz, *Information Transmission Modulation and Noise*, 3d ed., 1980.

## Photoacoustic spectroscopy

A technique for measuring small absorption coefficients in gaseous and condensed media, involving the sensing of optical absorption by detection of sound. It is frequently called optoacoustic spectroscopy. Although the technique dates back to 1880 when A. G. Bell used chopped sunlight as the source of radiation, it remained dormant for many years, primarily because of the lack of suitable powerful sources of tunable radiation. However, the usefulness of optoacoustic detection for spectroscopic applications was recognized early in its development, and pollution monitoring instruments (called spectrophones) dedicated for detection of specific gaseous constituents have been used intermittently since Bell's work.

**Methods of measuring absorption.** During the transmission of optical radiation through a sample (gas, liquid, or solid), the absorption of radiation by the sample can be measured by at least three techniques. The first one is the straight-forward detection technique which requires a measurement of the optical radiation level with and without the sample in the optical path. The transmitted power $P_{\text{out}}$ and the incident power $P_{\text{in}}$ are related through Eq. (1), where $\alpha$

$$P_{\text{out}} = P_{\text{in}}e^{-\alpha l} \tag{1}$$

is the absorption coefficient and $l$ is the length of the absorber. With this technique, the minimum measurable $\alpha l$ is of the order of $10^{-4}$ unless special precautions have been taken to stabilize the source of radiation.

The second of the techniques is the derivative absorption technique where the frequency of the input radiation is modulated at a low radio frequency or audio frequency, $\omega_m$. The transmitted radiation then contains a time-varying component at $\omega_m$, if the optical path contains absorption which has a frequency-dependent structure. (For structureless absorption, modulated absorption spectroscopy does not provide a signal that can characterize the amount of absorption.) For situations where the absorption has well-defined structure, the modulation absorption spectroscopy can be used to measure $\alpha l$ as small as about $10^{-8}$ for sufficiently high input powers. The ability to measure the small absorption effects is independent of the input and output power levels for the straight-forward measurement technique as long as the noise contributed by the detector is not a factor in determining the signal-to-noise ratio. For the derivative absorption technique, the smallest $\alpha l$ that can be measured varies as $(P_{\text{in}})^{-1}$ until the shot noise of the detector begins to be appreciable.

The third technique, optoacoustic detection, is a calorimetric method where no direct detection of optical radiation is carried out but, instead, a measurement is made of the energy, with power $P_{\text{abs}}$, absorbed by the medium from the incident radiation, Eq. (2). Thus the optoacoustic signal, $V_{\text{oa}}$, is given

$$P_{\text{abs}} = P_{\text{in}}(1 - e^{-\alpha l}) \tag{2}$$

by Eq. (3), where $K$ is the constant describing the

$$\begin{aligned} V_{\text{oa}} &= K\{P_{\text{in}}(1 - e^{-\alpha l})\} \\ &\approx KP_{\text{in}}\alpha l \qquad (\text{for } \alpha l \ll 1) \end{aligned} \tag{3}$$

conversion factor for transforming the absorbed energy into an electrical signal using an appropriate transducer. It has been tacitly assumed that the absorbed energy is lost by nonradiative means rather than by reradiation. The optoacoustic detection scheme implies that the absorbed energy will be converted into acoustic energy for eventual detection.

From Eq. (3), the optoacoustic signal is proportional to the incident power and the absorption-length product $\alpha l$. Thus, for given sources of noise from the detection transducers, the signal-to-noise ratio improves as the incident energy is increased. Put differently, the smallest amount of absorption that can be measured using the optoacoustic technique varies as

$(P_{in})^{-1}$ with no limitation on the level to which $P_{in}$ can be increased for detecting small absorptions. Values of $\alpha l$ as small as $10^{-10}$ can be measured in the gas phase. The techniques generally used for gases and those used for condensed-phase optoacoustic spectroscopy differ in detail somewhat.

**Gases.** If optical radiation is amplitude-modulated at an audio frequency, the absorption of such radiation by a gaseous medium that has been confined in a cell with appropriate optical windows for the entrance and exit of the radiation and the subsequent nonradiative relaxation of the medium, will cause a periodic variation in the temperature of the column of the irradiated gas (**Fig. 1**). Such a periodic rise and fall in temperature gives rise to a corresponding periodic variation in the gas pressure at the audio frequency. The audio-frequency pressure fluctuations (that is, sound) are efficiently detected using a sensitive gas-phase microphone. The intrinsic noise limitation to the optoacoustic detection scheme arises from the Brownian motion of gas atoms/molecules, and Kreuzer showed that the minimum detectable absorbed power is $P_{min} \approx 3.6 \times 10^{-11}$ W for a 11.9-cm-long (4.7-in.) cell. Substituting $P_{min}$ for $P_{abs}$ in Eq. (2), and noting, as in Eq. (3), that $(1 - e^{-\alpha l}) \cong \alpha l$ for $\alpha l \ll 1$, it follows that $\alpha_{min}$ varies as $(P_{min}/P_{in})$ as indicated above. The usefulness of the optoacoustic detection for measurement of small absorption coefficients became evident with the development of a variety of tunable high-power laser sources which could take advantage of the $(P_{in})^{-1}$ dependence. Using a spin-flip Raman laser tunable in the 5.0- to 5.8-micrometer range, with a power output of approximately 0.1 W, C. K. N. Patel and R. J. Kerl were able to detect $\alpha_{min}$ of approximately $10^{-10}$ cm$^{-1}$ for a cell length of 10 cm (4 in.). These studies used a miniature optoacoustic cell (**Fig. 2**) with a total gas volume of approximately 3 cm$^3$ (0.18 in.$^3$). The absorber used was nitric oxide diluted in nitrogen. It is estimated that for a signal-to-noise ratio of approximately 1, and a time constant of 1 s, it is possible to detect a nitric oxide (NO) concentration of approximately $10^7$ molecules cm$^{-3}$, corresponding to a volumetric mixing ratio of approximately $1{:}10^{12}$ at atmospheric pressure. SEE LASER.

The capability of measuring extremely small absorption coefficients and correspondingly small concentrations of the absorption gases has many applications, including high-resolution spectroscopy of isotopically substituted gases, excited states of molecules and forbidden transitions, and pollution detection. In the last application, both continuously tunable lasers, such as the spin-flip Raman laser and dye lasers, and step tunable infrared lasers, such as the carbon dioxide ($CO_2$) and carbon monoxide (CO) lasers, have been used as sources of high power radiation. The pollution measurements have demonstrated that the optoacoustic spectroscopy technique in conjunction with tunable lasers can be routinely used for on-line real-time in-place detection of undesirable gaseous constituents at sub-parts-per-billion levels. Specific examples include the measurement of nitric oxide on the ground and in the stratosphere (where nitric oxide plays an important role as a catalytic agent in the stratospheric ozone balance) and measurements of hydrocyanic acid (HCN) in the catalytic reduction of $CO + N_2 + H_2 + \cdots$ over platinum catalysts. These studies point toward expanding use in the future of optoacoustic spectroscopy in pollution detection. SEE LASER.

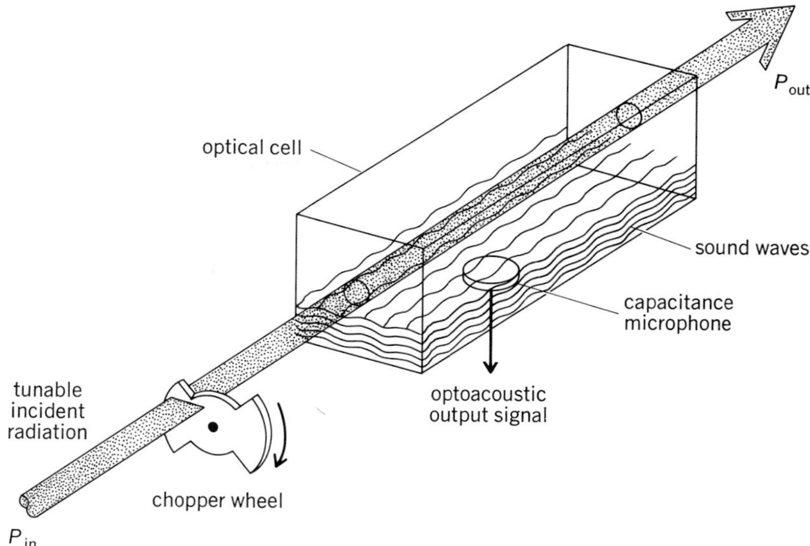


**Fig. 1. Optoacoustic cell for gaseous spectroscopy.**

**Condensed-phase spectroscopy.** A straightforward application of the gas-phase optoacoustic spectroscopy technique to the study of condensed phase (liquid or solid) spectra involves enclosing the condensed phase material within the gas-phase optoacoustic cell (**Fig. 3**). The "photoacoustic" signals generated in the sample due to the absorption of optical radiation are communicated to the gas-phase microphone via coupling through the gas filling the chamber. The inefficiency of such a system is high because of the very poor acoustical match (coupling efficiency approximately $10^{-5}$) between the condensed-phase sample and the gas. In reality, because of the large acoustical mismatch, the detection scheme is really "photothermal" rather than "photoacoustic," and this scheme provides a capability of measuring frac-

**Fig. 2. Sensitive optoacoustic gaseous spectroscopy cell.**

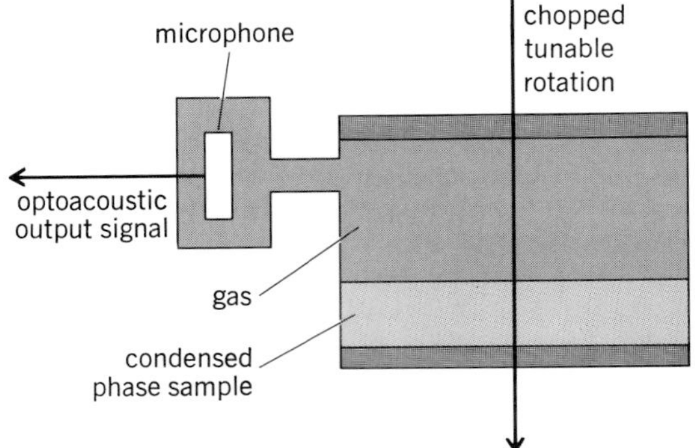


**Fig. 3. Arrangement for condensed-phase photoacoustic spectroscopy.**

tional absorption at a level of approximately $10^{-4}$ when a continuous-wave laser power of approximately 10 W is used. A more severe drawback of the scheme, however, lies in the difficulty of interpretation of the data because of the intimate dependence of the observed optoacoustic signal from the microphone on the chopping frequency, absorption depth, and heat diffusion depth. However, in spite of its shortcomings, the gas-phase microphone technique for condensed-phase optoacoustic spectroscopy has found applications.

A very sensitive calorimetric spectroscopic technique has been developed for the study of weak absorption in liquids and solids. This technique uses a pulsed tunable laser for excitation and a submerged piezoelectric transducer, in the case of a liquid, or a contacted piezoelectric transducer, in the case of a solid, for the detection of the ultrasonic signal generated due to the absorption of the radiation and its subsequent conversion into a transient ultrasonic signal (**Fig. 4**). The major distinction between the above condensed-phase "photoacoustic" spectroscopy technique and the pulsed-source, submerged or contacted piezoelectric transducer technique, is the high coupling efficiency of approximately 0.2 for the ultrasonic signal in the liquid to the submerged transducer, or an efficiency of approximately 0.9 for coupling the ultrasonic wave in a solid to a bonded transducer. Because of this high efficiency, the pulsed-laser, submerged or bonded optoacoustic spectroscopy technique has been shown to be useful for measuring fractional absorptions (that is, values of $\alpha l$) as small as $10^{-7}$ when using a laser source with pulse energy of approximately 1 millijoule, pulse duration of approximately 1 microsecond, and a pulse repetition frequency of 10 Hz. There is room for improvement by increasing the laser pulse energy. There is a possibility of the electrostriction effect giving rise to an unwanted background signal, but this signal is not dependent on the light wavelength, and can be minimized by proper choice of experimental parameters.

The pulsed-laser, submerged or bonded piezoelectric transducer technique has a further advantage that time-gating of the ultrasonic signal output can be utilized for the rejection of spurious signals since the sound velocity in condensed media is known and hence the exact arrival time of the real optoacoustic pulse can be calculated. This technique has been used for measurement of very weak overtone spectra of a variety of organic liquids, optical absorption coefficients of water and heavy water in the visible, two-photon absorption spectra of liquids, Raman gain spectra in liquids, absorption of thin liquid films, spectra of solids and powders, and weak overtone spectra of condensed gases at low temperatures. Because of the capability of measuring very small fractional absorptions, the technique is clearly applicable to the area of monitoring water pollution, impurity detection in thin semiconductor wafers, transmission studies of ultra-pure glasses (used in optical fibers for optical communications), and so forth. Further, even though in all of the present studies use is made of only the optical radiation, there is no reason to restrict "optoacoustic" spectroscopy to the optical region. By using pulsed x-ray sources, such as the synchrotron light source or pulsed electron beams, the principle described above for a pulsed-light-source, submerged or bonded piezoelectric transducer, gated-detection technique can be extended to x-ray acoustic

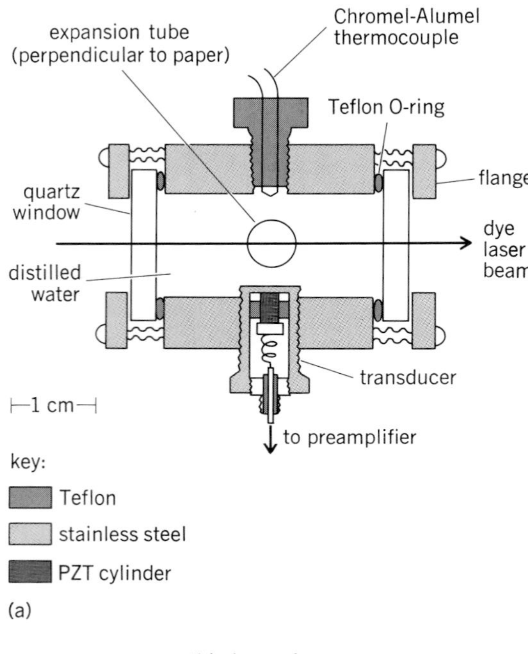


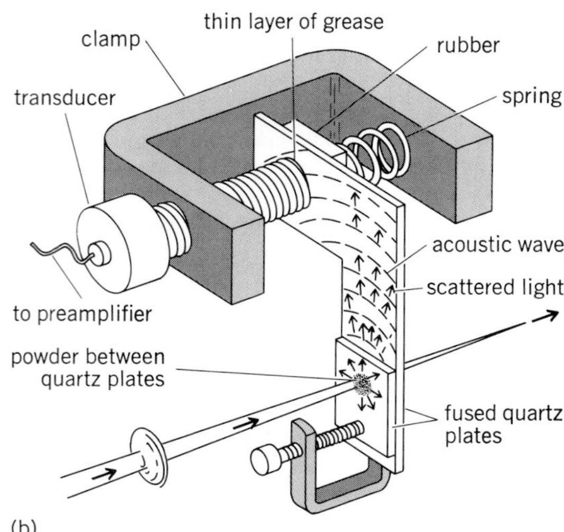


**Fig. 4. Arrangement for pulsed-laser (*a*) immersed and (*b*) contacted piezoelectric transducer optoacoustic spectroscopy.**

spectroscopy and electron-loss acoustic spectroscopy. These extensions are likely to have major impact on materials and semiconductor fabrication technology.

*C. K. N. Patel*

**Bibliography.** A. G. Bell, On the production and reproduction of sound by light, *Proc. Amer. Ass. Adv. Sci.*, 29:115–129, 1880; L. B. Kreuzer, The physics of signal generation and detection, in Y.-M. Pao (ed.), *Optoacoustic Spectroscopy and Detection*, 1977; C. K. N. Patel, Spectroscopic measurements of stratosphere using tunable infrared lasers, *Opt. Quantum Electr.*, 8:145–154, 1976; C. K. N. Patel and R. J. Kerl, A new optoacoustic cell with improved performance, *Appl. Phys. Lett.*, 30:578–579, 1977; C. K. N. Patel and E. D. Shaw, Tunable simulated Raman scattering from conduction electrons in InSb, *Phys. Rev. Lett.*, 24:451–454, 1970; C. K. N. Patel and A. C. Tam, Pulsed optoacoustic spectroscopy of condensed matter, *Rev. Mod. Phys.*, 53:517–550, 1981; M. B. Robin and W. R. Harshbarger, The opto-acoustic effect: Revival of an old technique for molecular spectroscopy, *Acc. Chem. Res.*, 6:329, 1973; M. Rosencwaig, Photoacoustic spectroscopy of solids, *Optics Commun.*, 1:305, 1973.

## Photoconductive cell

A device for detecting electromagnetic radiation (photons) by variation of the electrical conductivity of a substance (a photoconductor) upon absorption of the radiation by this substance. During operation the cell is connected in series with an electrical source and current-sensitive meter, or in series with an electrical source and resistor. Current in the cell, as indicated by the meter, is a measure of the photon intensity, as in the voltage drop across the series resistor.

Photoconductive cells are made from a variety of semiconducting materials in the single-crystal or polycrystalline form. There are elemental types such as germanium, silicon, and tellurium; binaries such as lead sulfide, cadmium sulfide, and indium arsenide; ternaries such as mercury cadmium telluride, lead tin telluride, indium arsenide antimonide, and other combinations of elements. The semiconductor detectors respond to photons that exceed a material-related threshold energy. The bolometer is another important detector and consists of a blackened material having a temperature-sensitive conductivity. This device detects photons over a broad spectrum, utilizing the heating effect of photons. The cells are prepared by growth of the semiconducting materials as nearly pure single crystals, or as polycrystalline films deposited chemically or by evaporation on suitable substrates.

Cadmium sulfide cells are used in the visible spectrum for street lighting control and camera exposure meters. Lead sulfide and mercury cadmium telluride, sensitive to infrared radiation, are used for night vision. Infrared photoconductive cells are used for detecting energy loss from buildings and for early detection of breast cancer.

The choice of cell type depends on the application requirements, which include operating temperature, wavelength to be detected, and response time. SEE PHOTOCONDUCTIVITY; PHOTOELECTRIC DEVICES.

*Sebastian R. Borrello*

**Bibliography.** S. Larach (ed.), *Photoelectronic Materials and Devices*, 1965; W. L. Wolfe and G. J. Zissis (eds.), *The Infrared Handbook*, Environmental Research Institute of Michigan, 1978.

## Photoconductivity

The increase in electrical conductivity caused by the excitation of additional free charge carriers by light of sufficiently high energy in semiconductors and insulators. Effectively a radiation-controlled electrical resistance, a photoconductor can be used for a variety of light- and particle-detection applications, as well as a light-controlled switch. Other major applications in which photoconductivity plays a central role are television cameras (vidicons), normal silver halide emulsion photography, and the very large field of electrophotographic reproduction. The phenomena related to photoconductivity have also played a large part in the understanding of electronic behavior and crystalline imperfections in a variety of different materials. SEE OPTICAL DETECTORS; OPTICAL MODULATORS; PHOTOCONDUCTIVE CELL; TELEVISION CAMERA TUBE.

Since the electrical conductivity $\sigma$ of a material is given by the product of the carrier density $n$, its charge $q$, and its mobility $\mu$ [Eq. (1)], an increase in

$$\sigma = nq\mu \tag{1}$$

the conductivity $\Delta\sigma$ can be formally due to either an increase in $n$, $\Delta n$, or an increase in $\mu$, $\Delta\mu$. Although cases are found in which both types of effects are observable, photoconductivity ($\Delta\sigma$) in single-crystal materials is due primarily to $\Delta n$, with only small effects at low temperatures due to $\Delta\mu$ if photoexcitation decreases the density of charged impurities that scatter charge carriers. In polycrystalline materials, on the other hand, where transport may be limited by potential barriers between the crystalline grains, an increase in mobility $\Delta\mu$ due to photoexcitation effects on these intergrain barriers may dominate the photoconductivity.

The increase in carrier density $\Delta n$ can be conveniently related to the photoexcitation density $f$ (excitations per unit volume per second) by the simple relation (2), where $\tau$ is the lifetime of the photoexcited carrier, that is, the length of time that this carrier stays free and able to contribute to the conductivity before it loses energy and returns to its initial state via recombination with another carrier of opposite type (that is, electrons with holes, or holes with electrons). In Eq. (2) the photoexcitation term $f$ includes

$$\Delta n = f\tau \tag{2}$$

all the processes of optical absorption (excitation across the bandgap of the material, excitation from or to imperfection states in the material, generation of excitons that are thermally dissociated to form the free carriers), and the lifetime $\tau$ includes all the processes of recombination (free electron with free hole, free electron with trapped hole, free hole with trapped electron). An understanding of the detailed processes of photoconductivity therefore requires a comprehensive understanding of the variation of optical absorption with photon energy, and of the dependence of recombination on imperfection density, capture cross section, photoexcitation intensity, and temperature. SEE BAND THEORY OF SOLIDS; ELECTRON-HOLE RECOMBINATION; HOLES IN SOLIDS.

**Photosensitivity.** Although all insulators and semiconductors may be said to be photoconductive, that is, they show some increase in electrical conductivity when illuminated by light of sufficiently high energy to create free carriers, only a few materials show a large enough change, that is, show a large enough photosensitivity, to be practically useful in applications of photoconductors. There are several ways that the magnitude of the photosensitivity can be defined, depending on the application in mind.

***Lifetime-mobility product.*** Comparison of Eqs. (1) and (2) shows that the basic measure of material photosensitivity is given by the $\tau\mu$ product in the common case where $\Delta\sigma$ results primarily from $\Delta n$. The mobility does vary from material to material, but in most practical photoconductors $\mu$ has values between $10^2$ and $10^4$ cm$^2$/V-s at room temperature, and of course the choice of a particular material is usually dominated by its desirable optical absorption characteristics. The free carrier lifetime $\tau$, on the other hand, can take on a wide range of values from $10^{-9}$ to $10^{-2}$ s, depending on the particular density and properties of imperfections that are present in the material.

***Detectivity.*** One of the major applications for photoconductors has been in the detection of small signals in the infrared portion of the spectrum, where the principal objective is to be able to detect the smallest signal possible with the detecting system. Since in this case the photoconductivity is usually much smaller than the dark conductivity, an ac technique is used in which the light signal is chopped and ac amplification stages are used. The limit to detectability is reached when the light-generated signal is comparable to the electrical noise in the photoconductor. Thus the photosensitivity in this particular case is often defined as a detectivity, which is a normalized radiation power required to give a signal equal to the noise. *See Electrical noise.*

***Gain.*** A third device-oriented definition of photosensitivity is that of photoconductivity gain. The gain is defined as the number of charge carriers that circulate through the circuit involving the photoconductor for each charge carrier generated by the light. The time required for a charge carrier to pass through the photoconductor from one electrode to the other, called the transit time, $t_r$, is given by Eq. (3), where

$$t_r = L^2/\mu V \tag{3}$$

$L$ is the distance between electrodes and $V$ is the applied voltage. The gain is given then by $\tau/t_r$ for each type of possible charge carrier, giving Eq. (4) for the

$$\text{Gain} = (\tau_e\mu_e + \tau_h\mu_h)V/L^2 \tag{4}$$

total gain if both electrons and holes contribute. Gains of hundreds or thousands can be readily achieved if the lifetimes are sufficiently long. Gains greater than unity require electrical contacts to the photoconductor that are able to replenish charge carriers that pass out of the opposite contact in order to maintain charge neutrality; such contacts are called ohmic contacts. If nonohmic contacts are used, so that charge carriers cannot be replenished, the maximum gain is simply unity, since only the initially created charge carrier contributes to the current flow. Historically, unity-gain currents of this latter type have been called primary photocurrents, whereas high-gain currents described by Eq. (4) have been called secondary photocurrents.

**Spectral response.** The variation of photoconductivity with photon energy is called the spectral response of the photoconductor. The curves in the **illustration** typically show a fairly well-defined maximum at a photon energy close to that of the band gap of the material, that is, the minimum energy required to excite an electron from a bond in the material into a higher-lying conduction band where it is free to contribute to the conductivity. This energy ranges from 3.7 eV, in the ultraviolet, for zinc sulfide (ZnS) to 0.2 eV, in the infrared, for cooled lead selenide (PbSe). Photoconductivity associated with excitation across the band gap of the material is called intrinsic photoconductivity. For photon energies smaller than the band gap, the light is not strongly absorbed by the material, and the photoconductivity decreases. For photon energies larger than the band gap, the optical absorption is large, and absorption takes place close to the surface of the material; since the surface has in general more imperfections than the bulk, the carrier lifetime at the surface is generally smaller, and hence the photoconductivity decreases. If the bulk of the material contains a sufficiently high density of imperfections contributing localized levels within the band gap of the material, it is often possible to detect photoconductivity corresponding to optical excitation from an occupied imperfection level to the conduction band or to an unoccupied imperfection level from the valence band of the material. This photoconductivity occurs for photon energies smaller than the band gap, and is called extrinsic photoconductivity.

**Speed of response.** A third major characteristic of a photoconductor of practical concern is the rate at which the conductivity changes with changes in photoexcitation intensity. If a steady photoexcitation is turned off at some time, for example, the length of time required for the current to decrease to $1/e$ of its initial value is called the decay time of photoconductivity, $t_d$. The magnitude of the decay time is determined by the lifetime $\tau$ and by the density of carriers

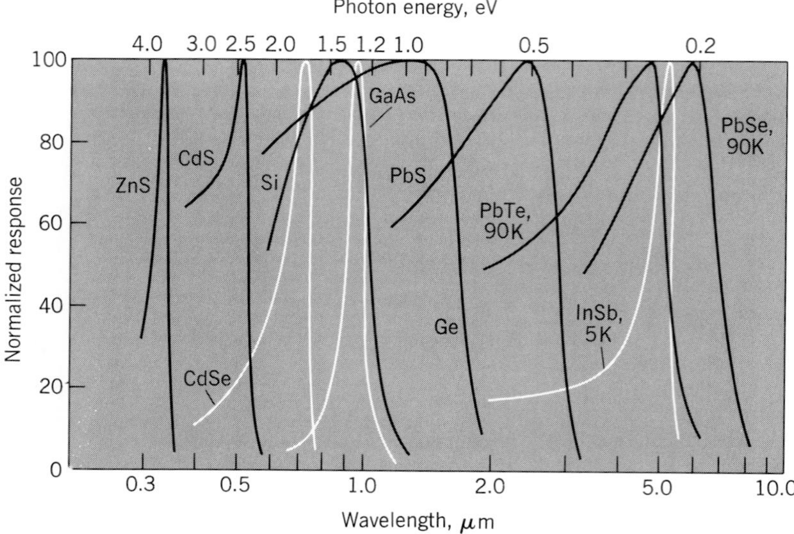


**Spectral response of photoconductivity for 10 common photoconducting materials (*After R. H. Bube, Photoconductivity of Solids, John Wiley and Sons, 1960; reprint, Krieger, 1978*)**

trapped in imperfections as a result of the previous photoexcitation, which must now also be released in order to return to the thermal equilibrium situation. If the photoexcitation intensity is high, or the density of imperfections is small, the decay time $t_d$ approaches the lifetime $\tau$ as a minimum limiting value. For low light intensities or high imperfection densities, where the density of trapped carriers is much larger than the density of free carriers, the decay of photoconductivity is controlled not by the free carrier recombination rate but by the rate of thermal freeing of trapped carriers, and can be many orders of magnitude larger than the lifetime.

**Device forms.** Photoconductivity detectors may be made in the form of single-crystal devices or as polycrystalline films, in which the bulk material is homogeneous, or in the form of semiconductor junction diodes. Such junction diodes may be prepared in the form of Schottky barriers, *np* homojunctions, *np* heterojunctions, or more complex *npn* or *pnp* double-junction devices with gain greater than unity. *See Junction diode; Microwave solid-state devices; Semiconductor heterostructures.*

Polycrystalline film photodetectors can be made from a variety of methods involving vacuum evaporation, powder sintering, and chemical solution deposition. The photoconductive behavior can be dominated by quite different effects in different materials systems. For example, the photoconductivity in cadmium sulfide (CdS) films deposited by spray pyrolysis is usually controlled by the modulation of intergrain barriers by photoexcitation, so that $\Delta\mu \gg \Delta n$. On the other hand, standard infrared detecting films of lead sulfide (PbS), deposited from chemical solution, exhibit a photoconductivity for which $\Delta n \gg \Delta\mu$, even though the effects of intergrain barriers are clearly measurable in the mobility.

The television camera vidicon and electrophotography are two applications of photoconductivity in which the device form is dictated by the specific nature of the information processing system involved. In both cases an electrical charge is deposited on one side of a high-resistivity photoconducting material; subsequent illumination of the material increases the conductivity locally and allows the charge to leak off through the material. The local absences of charge are then detected and used to produce or reproduce the original light pattern. The material involved must have special characteristics: it must have a high enough dark resistivity so that the deposited charge does not leak off by ordinary dark conduction, and a high enough photosensitivity so that the charge will leak off as quickly as desired. In the vidicon the charge is deposited by scanning by an electron beam; absence of charge is detected by current flow in a subsequent scanning by the beam. In electrophotography the charge is deposited by a corona discharge; absence or presence of charge is fixed by a subsequent printing process.

*Richard H. Bube*

**Bibliography.** R. H. Bube, Photoconductivity of semiconductors, in H. Eyring, D. Henderson, and W. Jost (eds.), *Physical Chemistry*, vol. 10: *Solid State*, pp. 515–578, 1970; R. H. Bube, *Photoconductivity of Solids*, 1960, reprint 1978; J. Mort and D. M. Pai (eds.), *Photoconductivity and Related Phenomena*, 1976; A. Rose, *Concepts in Photoconductivity and Allied Problems*, 1963, reprint 1978.

## Photodiode

A semiconductor two-terminal component with electrical characteristics that are light-sensitive. All semiconductor diodes are light-sensitive to some degree, unless enclosed in opaque packages, but only those designed specifically to enhance the light sensitivity are called photodiodes.

Most photodiodes consist of semiconductor *pn* junctions housed in a container designed to collect and focus the ambient light close to the junction. They are normally biased in the reverse, or blocking, direction; the current therefore is quite small in the dark. When they are illuminated, the current is proportional to the amount of light falling on the photodiode. For a discussion of the properties of *pn* junctions *see Junction diode.*

Photodiodes are used both to detect the presence of light and to measure light intensity. *See Photoelectric devices.*

*W. R. Sittner*

## Photoelectric devices

Devices which give an electrical signal in response to visible, infrared, or ultraviolet radiation. They are often used in systems which sense objects or encoded data by a change in transmitted or reflected light. Photoelectric devices which generate a voltage can be used as solar cells to produce useful electric power. The operation of photoelectric devices is based on any of the several photoelectric effects in which the absorption of light quanta liberates electrons in or from the absorbing material. *See Photovoltaic cell; Solar cell.*

Photoconductive devices are photoelectric devices which utilize the photoinduced change in electrical conductivity to provide an electrical signal. Thin-film devices made from cadmium sulfide, cadmium selenide, lead sulfide, or similar materials have been utilized in this application. Single-crystal semiconductors such as indium antimonide or doped germanium are used as photoelectric devices for the infrared spectrum. The operation of these devices requires the application of an external voltage or current bias of relatively low magnitude. *See Photoconductive cell.*

Photoemissive systems have also been used in photoelectric applications. These vacuum-tube devices utilize the photoemission of electrons from a photocathode and collection at an anode. Photoemissive devices require the use of a relatively large bias voltage. *See Photoemission.*

Many photoelectric systems now utilize silicon photodiodes or phototransistors. These devices utilize the photovoltaic effect, which generates a voltage due to the photoabsorption of light quanta near a *pn* junction. Modern solid-state integrated-circuit fabrication techniques can be used to create arrays of photodiodes which can be used to read printed information. *See Photodiode; Phototransistor.*

Photoelectric devices can be used in systems which read coded or printed information on data cards and packages. Similar systems are used to sense and control the movement of objects in perimeter guard systems which sense an intruder by the interruption of a light beam. *See Character recognition.*

Most visible and ultraviolet photoelectric devices

for use in the infrared must be cooled with the longer-wavelength response devices requiring the most cooling. SEE PHOTOELECTRICITY.

*Richard A. Chapman*

**Bibliography.** M. Buresch, *Photovoltaic Energy Systems: Design and Installation,* 1983; R. P. Turner, *Solar Cells and Photocells,* 1980.

## Photoelectricity

The process by which electromagnetic radiation incident on a solid, liquid, or gas liberates electrical charge, which is detectable in an electric field. The process is strictly quantum in nature.

Historically, this phenomenon was first explained in 1905 by Albert Einstein, who invoked the quantum character of electromagnetic radiation, namely the photon, with characteristic energy $h\nu$, where $h$ is Planck's constant and $\nu$ the frequency. The liberation of electrons from matter is governed by Einstein's photoelectric equation $E = h\nu - \phi$. where $E$ is the kinetic energy of the emitted electron and $\phi$ represents the binding energy of the electron.

Early photoelectric experiments involved the photoemission of electrons from the surface of metals into a vacuum, or the liberation of electrons and positively charged ions in a gas by the process of photoionization. Values of $\phi$ for these processes typically are a few electronvolts, and as such these experiments were limited primarily to the visible and ultraviolet regions of the spectrum. The common photomultiplier tube is an example of a photoemissive device.

The quantum nature of electromagnetic radiation also manifests itself in the liberation of electrons and postive holes within the interior of a solid, giving rise to photoconductive and photovoltaic effects. These phenomena are readily observable in the class of solids known as semiconductors. The binding energy $\phi$ of electrons and holes in semiconductors can be as little as a few millielectronvolts, and as such the region of the spectrum involved transcends both the visible and the infrared, out into the far infrared. Devices based upon these effects are in widespread use in the fields of thermal imaging, solar energy conversion, security monitoring, data readout, and product control. SEE PHOTOCONDUCTIVITY; PHOTOELECTRIC DEVICES; PHOTOEMISSION; PHOTOVOLTAIC EFFECT.

*Michael A. Kinch*

## Photoemission

The ejection of electrons from a solid (or less commonly, a liquid) by incident electromagnetic radiation. Photoemission is also called the external photoelectric effect. The visible and ultraviolet regions of the electromagnetic spectrum are most often involved, although the infrared and x-ray regions are also of interest. For important practical applications of photoemission SEE PHOTOTUBE; TELEVISION CAMERA TUBE.

The salient experimental features of photoemission are the following: (1) There is no detectable time lag between irradiation of an emitter and the ejection of photoelectrons. (2) At a given frequency the number of photoelectrons ejected per second is proportional to the intensity of the incident radiation. (3) The photoelectrons have kinetic energies ranging from zero up to a well-defined maximum, which is proportional to the frequency of the incident radiation and independent of the intensity.

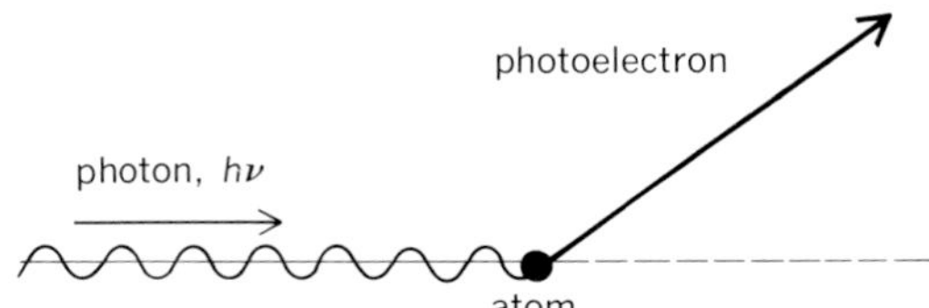


**Fig. 1. External photoelectric effect.**

**Einstein photoelectric law.** These characteristics cannot be explained by J. C. Maxwell's theory of electromagnetic waves. In 1905 Albert Einstein made the clarifying assumption that the radiation had characteristics like those of particles when it delivered energy to electrons in the emitter. In Einstein's approach the light beam behaves like a stream of photons, each of energy $h\nu$, where $h$ is Planck's constant, and $\nu$ is the frequency of the photon (**Fig. 1**). The energy required to eject an electron from the emitter has a well-defined minimum value $\varphi$ called the photoelectric threshold energy. When a photon interacts with an electron, the latter absorbs the entire photon energy.

For $h\nu$ values below the threshold, photoelectrons are not ejected. Even though the electrons absorb photon energy, they do not receive enough to surmount the potential barrier at the surface, which normally holds the electrons in the solid. The threshold energy $\varphi$ is associated with a threshold frequency $\varphi/h$ and a threshold wavelength $ch/\varphi$, where $c$ is the velocity of light. For photoelectrons range from zero up to a maximum value, $E = h\nu - \varphi$. This is the Einstein photoelectric law, and $E$ is commonly termed the Einstein maximum energy. Careful photoelectric experiments by R. A. Millikan in 1916 fixed $h$ in Einstein's law with considerable precision and furthered its identification with the constant which M. Planck had used in his theory of blackbody radiation. For a discussion of the surface potential barrier SEE SCHOTTKY EFFECT.

**Metals.** The Einstein law is based only on the photon hypothesis and on the conservation of energy. It does not take into account momentum, which must also be conserved. The incident photon has a momentum $h\nu/c$ which is negligible compared to the change in momentum of the electron when it gains the energy $h\nu$. Thus, it is not possible for a free electron to absorb the entire energy of a photon. In order for this to happen the electron must be bound to another body, which takes up the recoil momentum.

**Figure 2** shows an energy diagram of the electrons in the metal sodium. There is a potential barrier at the surface, which the electrons must surmount before they can escape. The most easily ejected electrons must acquire 2.3 eV of additional energy from photons in order to do this. This 2.3 eV is the electronic work function, which for a metal is equal to the photoelectric threshold energy. Inside the metal the electrons occupy a band of energies about 3 eV wide. These electrons are said to be quasi-free. This means that they behave in many ways like a gas of free, noninteracting electrons; nevertheless they move in the periodic potential due to the positive sodium ions, and in this sense they are bound. SEE WORK FUNCTION (ELECTRONICS).

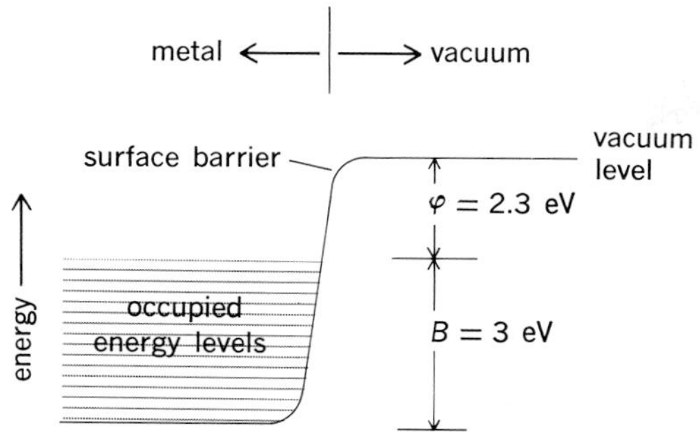


**Fig. 2. Energy diagram for electrons in sodium. The photoelectric threshold energy is $\varphi$; in a metal $\varphi$ is equal to the electronic work function. The band of energy levels occupied by almost free electrons has a width *B*.**

In this situation two types of photoemission are theoretically possible, the surface effect and the volume effect. In the surface effect, recoil momentum is communicated to the crystal because the electron is coupled to the barrier at the surface during photon absorption. In the volume effect the electron is coupled to the internal periodic potential.

Experimental determination of the relative importance of surface and volume photoeffects in metals is difficult. Experiments by H. Mayer and his collaborators indicate that for potassium the volume effect is predominant for photon energies from the threshold value at 2.1 eV to at least 4 eV. Thus the photoelectric emission increases as the thickness of a potassium film increases. (This would not be true for the surface effect.) Photoelectrons can escape from depths greater than $10^{-6}$ cm when excited by light in the threshold region.

Thus far the photoelectric threshold has been treated as a sharply defined quantity. This is precisely true for metals only at temperatures near absolute zero. At higher temperatures the upper edge of the band of occupied electron energy states in Fig. 2 is no longer sharp. It becomes diffuse because of thermal agitation. Electrons may be then emitted for photon energies less than the threshold value $\varphi$. At ordinary room temperatures, for example, measurable photoemission appears for photon energies as much as 0.2 eV below the threshold. R. Fowler has developed a convenient graphical technique, known as a Fowler plot, for determining the absolute-zero threshold from data taken at higher temperatures on the spectral dependence of the photoelectric yield, which is the number of photoelectrons ejected per incident photon. L. A. DuBridge has developed a similar technique using either the temperature dependence of the photoelectric yield or the distribution of photoelectrons in energy at fixed frequency. These treatments show that the photoelectric yield is approximately proportional to the quantity $(h\nu - \varphi)^2$ when the photon energy $h\nu$ is within about 1 eV of the threshold energy $\varphi$. **Figure 3** shows a graph of the spectral dependence of photoelectric yield for some typical emitters. **Figure 4** shows typical energy distributions. Photoelectric yields from metals are of the order of $10^{-3}$ electron per incident photon when $h\nu - \varphi$ is 1 eV. Photoelectric threshold energies range from 2 eV for cesium to values such as 5 eV for platinum. They vary for different types of crystal faces on the same crystal, and they are exceedingly sensitive to small traces of adsorbed gases.

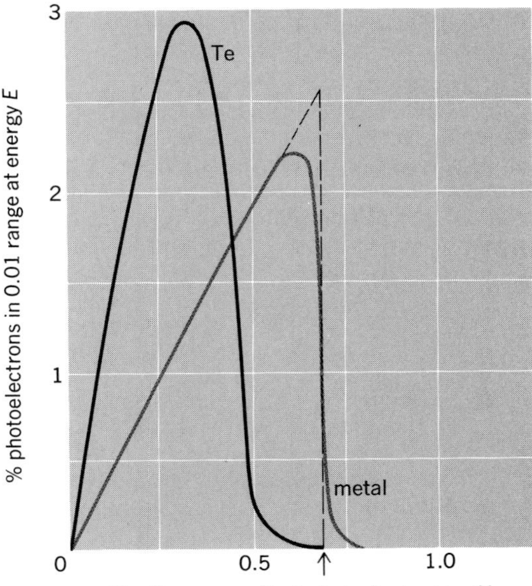


**Fig. 4. Energy distributions of photoelectrons from tellurium and a metal having the same work function. Solid line for the metal shows results for room temperature, and broken line for absolute zero. Arrow marks Einstein maximum energy; photon energy is 5.42 eV.**

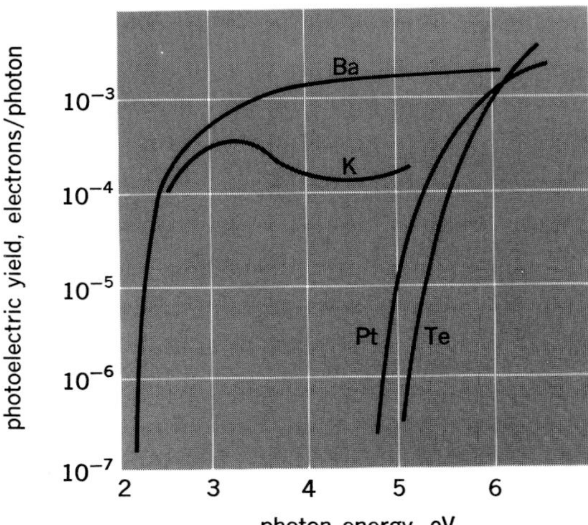


**Fig. 3. Spectral distribution of the photoelectric yield from typical samples of barium, Ba; potassium, K; platinum, Pt; and tellurium, Te. Platinum and tellurium have practically the same electronic work function. Note the higher threshold and more steeply rising curve for tellurium, which is a typical elemental semiconductor.**

**Semiconductors.** The photoelectric behavior of semiconductors, such as germanium or tellurium, differs from that of metals. As shown in **Fig. 5**, the electrons in a semiconducting emitter completely occupy a closed band of energies, which lies just below a so-called forbidden energy band. The electrons behave quite differently from those in metals. As a result, the photoelectric threshold energy $\varphi$ is larger than the electronic work function *W*. Thus, a semiconductor exhibits a higher photoelectric threshold energy than a metal having the same work function.

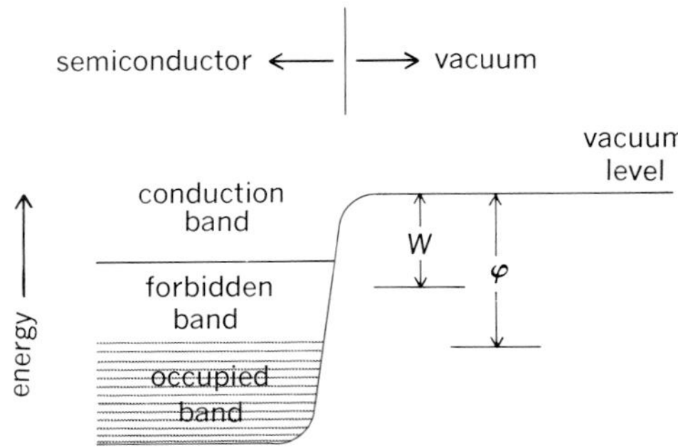


**Fig. 5. Energy diagram for electrons in a semiconductor. Occupied band is filled with bound electrons that behave differently from the electrons in metals. As a result, the electronic work function *W* is smaller than the photoelectric threshold energy $\varphi$.**

An example of this is shown for the metal platinum and the semiconductor tellurium in Fig. 3. Both this particular platinum sample (Pt) and the tellurium (Te) have the same electronic work function, about 4.8 eV. The photoelectric threshold of the platinum is equal to the work function, whereas that for the tellurium is clearly higher. Spectral and energy distributions are shown in Figs. 3 and 4. Clean surfaces of silicon, germanium, and certain semiconducting chemical compounds have been made by cleaving single crystals in ultrahigh vacuum. Both the surface photoelectric effect and the volume effect have been measured. From the measurements of the volume effect, valuable information on the detailed nature of the electron energy bands has been deduced from structure that occurs in photoelectron energy distributions. *SEE BAND THEORY OF SOLIDS*.

A particularly interesting and important kind of photoemitter is typified by cesium antimonide, $Cs_3Sb$. This material is a semiconductor having a forbidden energy band about 1.5 eV wide. The photoelectric threshold energy is only slightly higher than this. Electrons excited from the occupied energy band by incident photons cannot assume energies lying in the forbidden band. They must remain in the conduction band shown in Fig. 5. Thus even the slowest ones must retain energies only slightly less than that required for escape. The probability of photoemission is higher than for metals (or for semiconductors that have threshold energies greater than twice the width of the forbidden energy band). $Cs_3Sb$ is sensitive over much of the visible range and can give very high yields, in excess of 0.2 electron per incident photon. It is widely used in practical phototubes. Related compounds can be made with enhanced photoelectric response in the red or ultraviolet regions of the spectrum.

**Alkali halides.** Three basically different kinds of photoemission are possible for alkali halides: intrinsic, extrinsic, and exciton-induced photoemission.

***Intrinsic photoemission.*** This is characteristic of the ideally pure and perfect crystal. It is thus analogous to the emission already described for metals and semiconductors. It appears only for photon energies higher than the intrinsic threshold. For example, potassium iodide, KI, is an alkali halide having this intrinsic threshold in the far ultraviolet near 7 eV. Apparently the width of the forbidden electron energy band in KI is only about 1 eV less than this. For the same reason that was mentioned for the semiconductor $Cs_3Sb$, the photoelectric yields are high, in excess of 0.1 electron per incident photon, as shown by section C of the curve in **Fig. 6**.

***Extrinsic photoemission.*** A second kind of emission occurs when a KI crystal contains imperfections in the form of negative ion vacancies (lattice sites from which negative iodine ions are missing). These vacancies can be filled by electrons. Color centers, which absorb visible light, are formed. They may reach concentrations as high as $10^{20}$ per cm$^3$. External photoelectrons may be ejected directly from these centers by photons. It is termed an extrinsic process since the light is absorbed by a crystal defect; it is also called direct ionization. The threshold energy for this process is about 2.5 eV. The yields can reach values of the order of $10^{-4}$ electron per incident photon, as shown in section A of the curve in Fig. 6. The exact value of the yield depends on the concentration of color centers. Most of the incident radiation is lost because it is not intercepted by the centers, which present a limited cross-section to the incident photons.

***Exciton-induced photoemission.*** When color centers are present, another photoelectric process takes place in two stages. Potassium iodide has a sharp optical absorption band, peaking at a photon energy of 5.6 eV. This is the first fundamental or intrinsic optical absorption band. Energy absorbed in this peak does not release free electric charges in the crystal. Rather, it leads to a kind of nonconducting excited state called an exciton state. The exciton can transfer enough energy to color centers to eject photoelectrons from the crystal. This two-stage process is termed exciton-induced photoemission. It appears in the peak B on the curve in Fig. 6. It is more efficient than direct ejection of photoelectrons from color centers. The entire crystal is capable of the primary photon absorption, and the energy can be transferred rather efficiently to color centers. Thus the process avoids much of the

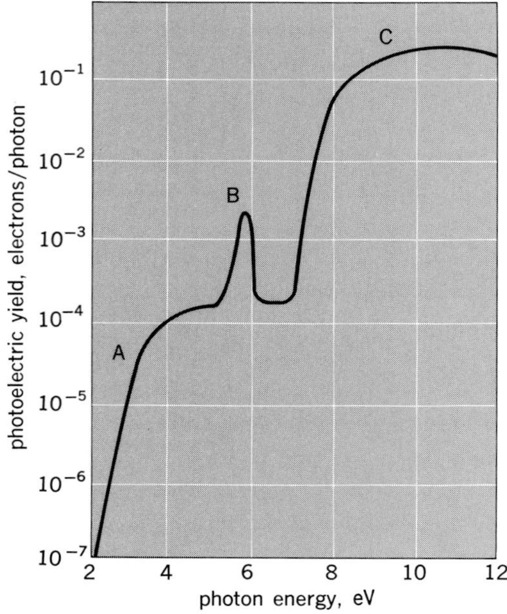


**Fig. 6. Spectral distribution of photoelectric yield from potassium iodide containing color centers. Region *A* of the curve is due to direct ejection of photoelectrons from color centers; the peak *B* is due to exciton-induced emission; *C* is due to intrinsic emission.**

loss in incident energy that arises from the limited cross section of color centers when they absorb photons directly.

**Other compounds.** Other ionic crystals, such as barium oxide, behave much like the alkali halides. Direct ejection of photoelectrons from chemical impurities and from energy levels or defects localized at the crystal surface can be important. In addition to these extrinsic processes, exciton-induced emission and intrinsic photoemission both occur.

Compounds such as zinc sulfide behave somewhat like germanium but have higher intrinsic threshold energies, of the order of 7 eV. The photoelectric yields are comparatively low, as for germanium. Extrinsic processes, such as direct ejection of electrons from chemical impurities (or defects), are sometimes detectable but are usually weak.

Certain complex photoemitters are made by letting cesium react with silver oxide to form cesium oxide and silver. They are valuable because they have threshold energies below 1 eV, and thus they are sensitive in the infrared. The photoelectrons appear to be directly ejected either from cesium adsorbed on the oxide surface or from discrete energy levels in the cesium oxide. The yields are about $10^{-3}$ electron per incident photon. Intrinsic emission from cesium oxide (with yields above 0.01) occurs for photon energies above the intrinsic threshold at about 4 eV.

*L. Apker*

***Bibliography.*** L. Azaroff and J. J. Brophy, *Electronic Processes in Materials,* 1963; M. Cardona and L. Ley (eds.), *Photoemission in Solids,* 2 vols., 1978, 1979; B. Feuerbacher, B. Fitton, and R. F. Willis, *Photoemission and the Electronic Properties of Solids,* 1978; A. Sommer, *Photoemissive Materials,* 1968, reprint 1980; A. Van der Ziel, *Solid State Physical Electronics,* 3d ed., 1976.

## Photoferroelectric imaging

The process of storing an image in a ferroelectric material by utilizing either the intrinsic or extrinsic photosensitivity in conjunction with the ferroelectric properties of the material. Specifically, photoferroelectric (PFE) imaging refers to storing photographic images or other optical information in transparent lead-lanthanum-zirconate-titanate (PLZT) ferroelectric ceramics.

**Imaging devices.** The photoferroelectric imaging device consists simply of a thin (0.1–0.3 mm), flat plate of optically polished PLZT ceramic with transparent electrodes deposited on the two major faces. The image to be stored is made to illuminate one of the electroded faces by using near-ultraviolet illumination in the intrinsic photosensitivity region (corresponding to a band-gap energy of approximately 3.35 eV) of the PLZT. Simultaneously, a voltage pulse is applied across the electrodes to switch the ferroelectric polarization from one stable remanent state to another. Images are stored both as spatial distributions of light-scattering centers in the bulk of the PLZT and as surface deformation strains which form a relief pattern of the image on the exposed surface. The light scattering and surface strains are related to spatial distributions of ferroelectric domain orientations introduced during the image-storage process. These spatial distributions replicate the brightness variations in the image to which the PLZT is exposed.

Stored images may be viewed directly or may be projected by using either transmitted or reflected light. For projection, the image contrast is usually improved by using collimated light and a schlieren optical system.

Either total or spatially selective erasure of stored images is accomplished by uniformly illuminating the area to be erased with near-ultraviolet light and simultaneously applying a voltage pulse to switch the ferroelectric polarization back to its initial remanent state, that is, to switch it to the polarization state prior to image storage.

The solid-solution PLZT ceramics can be fabricated with a wide range of compositions and sintering conditions to produce an associated wide range of ferroelectric, dielectric, and electrooptic properties. For example, an important factor in determining the maximum resolution of stored images is the ceramic grain size, which can be controlled to a large extent by the sintering temperature and pressure. Images with resolutions as high as 2500 line pairs per inch (100 line pairs per millimeter) can be stored in plates with 2-micrometer grain size, while the maximum image resolution achieved in 5-micrometer grain size plates is about 1000 line pairs per inch (40 line pairs per millimeter).

Important potential applications of photoferroelectric imaging devices include temporary image storage with periodic update, projection-type display, spatial-temporal light modulation, and high-density optical information storage. Various types of image processing, including image contrast enhancement, are also offered by the capability of switching from a positive to a negative stored image in discrete steps. Nonvolatile photographic images with gray scale ranges extending from an optical density of about 0.15 to more than 2.0 and with resolutions as high as 1000 line pairs per inch (40 line pairs per millimeter) are routinely stored in PLZT plates with 5-μm grain size (**Fig. 1**). SEE IMAGE PROCESSING; OPTICAL INFORMATION SYSTEMS; OPTICAL MODULATORS.

**Fig. 1. Photographic image with high resolution and gray scale stored in a photoferroelectric imaging device.**

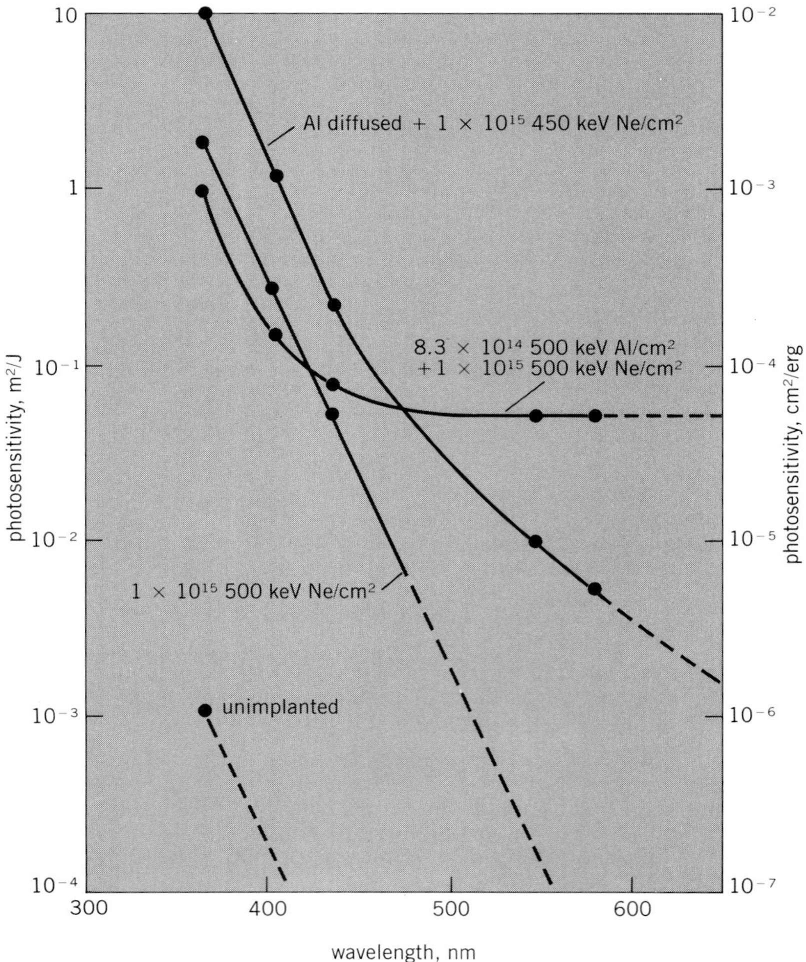


**Fig. 2. Wavelength dependence of the photoresponse for aluminum-diffused-plus-neon-implanted PLZT compared to neon-implanted and neon-plus-aluminum-implanted PLZT. The near-ultraviolet response for unimplanted PLZT is also shown.**

**Intrinsic PFE effect.** The intrinsic photoferroelectric effect is characterized by a photoinduced reduction of the coercive voltage $V_C$ (the externally applied voltage required to switch the ferroelectric polarization from a saturation remanent state to an average value of zero) produced by irradiating the PLZT surface with band-gap or higher energy light. The reduction in $V_C$ occurs because the absorbed near-ultraviolet light photoexcites charge carriers into the conduction state, and these carriers are transported, under the influence of the applied field, to the ceramic underlying the absorption region, where they contribute to ferroelectric domain nucleation and reorientation. Retrapped carriers establish space charge fields which, in combination with the photocurrent, provide the mechanisms for the photoinduced reduction of $V_C$. In any given localized area of the ceramic surface, $V_C$ is reduced by an amount proportional to the exposure energy $W_{ex}$ (product of near-ultraviolet light intensity and image exposure time) in that area. As a result, the stored images faithfully reproduce the gray scale of the input image. *See Band theory of solids.*

**Photosensitivity enhancement.** The exposure energy $W_{ex}$ required to store photographic images in unmodified PLZT is 1–5 × $10^3$ joules/m$^2$ (1–5 × $10^6$ ergs/cm$^2$). The relatively high value of $W_{ex}$ (compared to electrophotographic processes or photographic film) tends to limit the scope of practical applications of photoferroelectric imaging devices. Because of the many attractive features of photoferroelectric imaging devices, including erasable and reusable image storage, image contrast enhancement, high-resolution optical information processing, and other optical storage and processing capabilities, various techniques to improve the photosensitivity and to extend the photoresponse from the near ultraviolet throughout the visible spectral region have been explored. Dramatic improvement of the near-ultraviolet photosensitivity, involving reduction of threshold $W_{ex}$ from about $10^3$ to $10^{-1}$ J/m$^2$ ($10^6$ to $10^2$ ergs/cm$^2$), has been achieved by implantation of inert ions, such as argon, neon, and helium, and significant photoresponse throughout the visible spectral region has been achieved by co-implantation of chemically active (for example, aluminum or chromium) and inert ions. It has also been found that the combination of thermal diffusion of aluminum followed by neon implantation yields photosensitivity improvement in the near-ultraviolet and blue spectral regions comparable to or better than that obtained by the ion implantation alone. *See Ion implantation.*

The primary effect of the surface modifications described above is to decrease the dark conductivity of the near-surface region, relative to that of unmodified PLZT, due to implantation-induced defects. These defect states result from atomic displacements produced by energy deposited in nuclear collision processes. In the surface-modified PLZT, a significant fraction of the externally applied voltage can be dropped in the thin (~ 1 μm), low-conductivity, damaged layer to produce very high drift fields in this near-surface region. Photogenerated charge carriers in this region experience extremely high electric fields and have a high probability of being swept into the underlying ceramic to nucleate and reorient ferroelectric domains. The resulting high photocurrents provide the basis of the ion-implantation enhancement of the photosensitivity.

The photosensitivity $S$ (inverse of $W_{ex}$) versus wavelength is compared for aluminum-diffused plus neon-implanted and aluminum-plus-neon-implanted PLZT in **Fig. 2**. Also included in Fig. 2 are data for neon-implanted and unimplanted PLZT. Comparison of these data indicates that the major factor contributing to the visible photoresponse is the absorption states associated with aluminum rather than disorder-related defect states produced by the neon implantation. However, the neon implantation is the major contributor to the near-ultraviolet photosensitivity enhancement. This latter conclusion is supported by other published data for PLZT co-implanted with the inert ions argon, neon, and helium which shows that the near-ultraviolet photosensitivity approaches that of aluminum-diffused PLZT, but the visible photoresponse is similar to that of the neon-implanted PLZT.

The dramatic photosensitivity enhancements in both the near-ultraviolet and the visible spectral regions have greatly expanded the variety of possible applications of PLZT as an erasable and reusable photoferroelectric imaging device. *See Electronic display; Ferroelectrics; Photoconductivity.*

*Cecil E. Land*

**Bibliography.** C. E. Land, Optical information storage and spatial light modulation in PLZT ceramics, *Opt. Eng.*, 17:317–326, 1978; C. E. Land and P. S.

Peercy, Photoferroelectric effects in PLZT ceramics, *Ferroelectrics*, 22:677–679, 1978; C. E. Land and P. S. Peercy, A review of the effects of ion implantation on the photoferroelectric properties of PLZT ceramics, *Ferroelectrics*, 45:25–43, 1982; C. E. Land, P. D. Thacher, and G. H. Haertling, in R. Wolfe (ed.), *Applied Solid State Science*, vol. 4: *Electrooptic Ceramics,* 137–233, 1974; P. S. Peercy and C. E. Land, Photographic image storage in ion implanted ceramics, *Nucl. Instrum. Meth.*, 209/210:1167–1178, 1983.

## Photomultiplier

A very sensitive vacuum-tube detector of light or radiant flux containing a photocathode which converts the light to photoelectrons; one or more secondary-electron-emitting electrodes or dynodes which amplify the number of photoelectrons; and an output electrode or anode which collects the secondary electrons and provides the electrical output signal. It is less frequently known as a multiplier phototube or photomutiplier tube. Because of the very large amplification provided by the secondary-emission mechanism, and the very short time variation associated with the passage of the electrons within the device, the photomultiplier is applied to the detection and measurement of very low light levels, especially if very high speed of response is required.

The first photomultipliers were developed during the late 1930s; applications were generally in astronomy and spectrometry. Development of photomultipliers was stimulated beginning in the late 1940s by their application to scintillation counting. Variations in electron-optical design and the introduction of a variety of photocathode, dynode, and envelope materials led to the use of photomultipliers in a wide variety of applications. Active design programs continue despite the competition from various solid-state detectors. Photomultiplier tubes are available in sizes ranging fron ½ in. (13 mm) in diameter to 5 in. (127 mm), with photocathodes useful for detecting radiation having wavelengths from 110 nanometers, the deep ultraviolet (using a lithium fluoride window), to 1100 nanometers, the infrared (with special photocathodes), and with amplification factors ranging from $10^3$ to $10^9$.

**Operation and design.** The schematic of a typical photomultiplier in **Fig. 1** illustrates its operation. Light incident on a semitransparent photocathode located inside an evacuated envelope causes photoelectron emission from the opposite side of the photocathode. (Some photomultipliers are designed with the photocathode mounted inside the vacuum envelope to provide for photoemission from the same side of the photocathode on which the light is incident.) The efficiency of the photoemission process is called the quantum efficiency, and is the ratio of emitted photoelectrons to incident photons (light particles). Photoelectrons are directed by an accelerating electric field to the first dynode, where from 3 to 30 secondary electrons are emitted from each incident electron, depending upon the dynode material and the applied voltage. These secondaries are directed to the second dynode, where the process is repeated and so on until the multiplied electrons from the last dynode are collected by the anode.

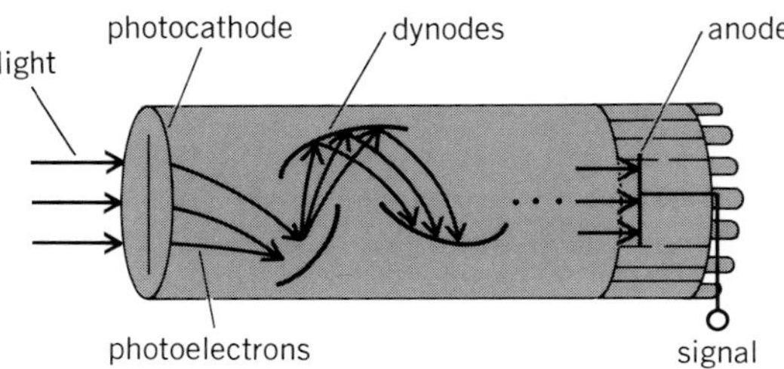

**Fig. 1.** Schematic of a photomultiplier. (*After R. W. Engstrom, Photomultipliers—then and now, RCA Eng., 24(1):18–26, June–July 1978*)

A typical photomultiplier may have 10 stages of secondary emission and may be operated with an overall applied voltage of 2000 V. In most photomultipliers the focusing of the electron streams is done by electrostatic fields shaped by the design of the electrodes. Some special photomultipliers designed for very high speed utilize crossed electrostatic and magnetic fields which direct the electrons in approximate cycloidal paths between electrodes. Because the transit times between stages are nearly the same, anode pulse rise times as short as 150 picoseconds are achieved.

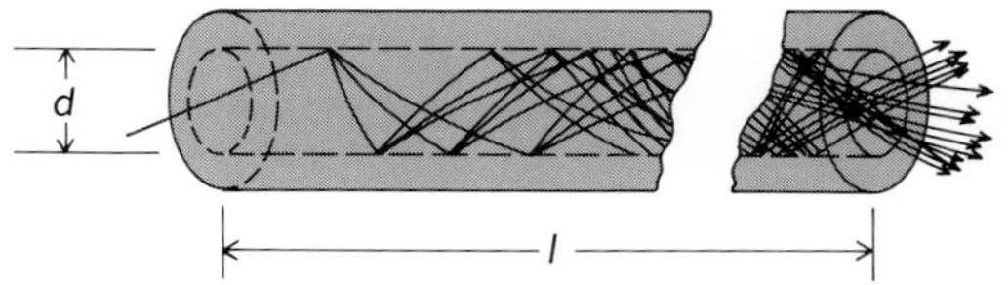

**Fig. 2.** Continuous-channel multiplier structure. (*After RCA Photomultiplier Manual, Tech. Ser. PT-61, 1970*)

Another special photomultiplier design is based on the use of microchannel plates. A single-channel multiplier is schematically shown in **Fig. 2**. The channel is coated on the inside with a resistive secondary-emitting layer. Gain is achieved by multiple electron impacts on the inner surface as the electrons are directed down the channel by an applied voltage over the length of the channel. The gain of the channel multiplier depends upon the ratio of its length $l$ to its diameter $d$; a typical ratio is 50:1. A microchannel plate is formed by combining a large number of the channels in parallel with spacings on the order of 40 micrometers. A very high-speed photomultiplier utilizes a microchannel plate mounted in a closely spaced parallel arrangement between a photocathode and an anode. Time resolutions of less than 100 ps are achieved.

**Dynode materials.** Common dynode materials used in photomultiplier tubes are cesium antimonide ($Cs_3Sb$), magnesium oxide, and beryllium oxide. The surface of the metal-oxide dynodes is modified by activation with an alkali metal such as cesium which lowers the surface potential barrier, permitting a more efficient escape of the secondary electrons into the vacuum.

Materials characterized as negative-electron affinity (NEA) have been developed and utilized in photomultipliers for both dynodes and photocathodes. A typical NEA secondary-emission material is gallium phosphide (GaP) whose surface has been treated with cesium (GaP:Cs). **Figure 3** shows the energy band model of an NEA material. The surface barrier is reduced by the electropositive cesium layer, and band-

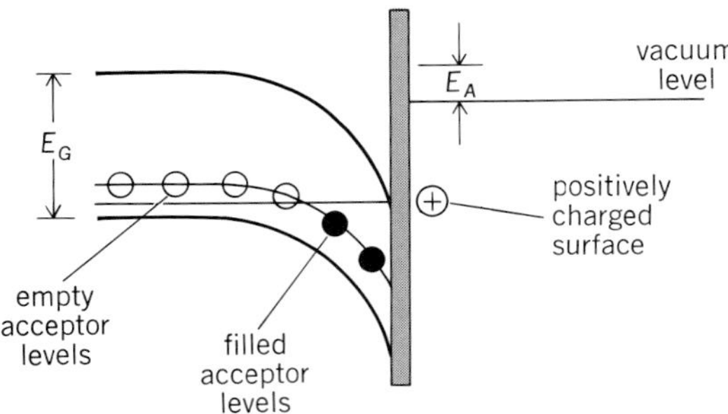


**Fig. 3. Semiconductor energy-band model showing negative electron affinity, $E_A$. Band-gap energy = $E_G$. *(After RCA Photomultiplier Manual, Tech. Ser. PT-61, 1970)***

bending occurs so that the conduction band may actually lie above the vacuum level as indicated.

When a primary electron impacts an NEA material, secondary electrons are created within the material, and even low-energy electrons escape to the vacuum. The result is a much higher secondary-emission ratio than that achieved in other secondary emitters, especially at higher primary energies when the primary electrons penetrate more deeply into the material. Secondary electrons within an emitter lose energy before reaching the surface, so that in ordinary materials the secondary emission actually decreases with increase in voltage above an energy of perhaps 500 eV. For example. $Cs_3Sb$ reaches a maximum secondary emission of about 8:1 at 500 V. At the same primary voltage GaP:Cs has a secondary emission of 25:1, and secondary emission increases linearly with voltage to a ratio of at least 130:1. *See Secondary emission; Semiconductor.*

**Photocathode materials.** The first photomultipliers developed utilized a photocathode of silver oxide activated with cesium (Ag-O-Cs). Although the quantum efficiency of this photocathode is quite low (less than 1% at the wavelength of its maximum response), it is still used because of its near-infrared response out to 1.1 μm.

Most photomultipliers today have photocathodes classed as alkali-antimonides: $Cs_3Sb$, $K_2CsSb$, $Na_2KSb$, $Na_2KSb$:Cs, Rb-Cs-Sb. These photocathodes have good quantum efficiency in the visible-wavelength range—in some cases exceeding 20%. The NEA type of photocathodes such as GaAs:Cs and InGaAs:Cs have even higher quantum efficiency and response through the visible and into the near infrared. However, they are difficult to fabricate and are more readily damaged by excessive photocurrents. *See Phototube.*

**Detection limits.** Because there is very little noise associated with the amplification process in a photomultiplier, detection limits are primarily determined by the quantum efficiency of the photocathode, by the thermionic or dark emission of electrons from the photocathode, and by the bandwidth of the observation. A typical photomultiplier limited by dark emission is capable of detecting $10^{-12}$ lumen—the equivalent of the flux on 1 $cm^2$ from a l-candlepower lamp at a distance of 6 mi (10 km). By selecting a photomultiplier having a photocathode with low dark emission, restricting the effective photocathode area magnetically, and cooling the tube to reduce dark emission further, a background count as low as one or two electrons emitted from the photocathode per second can be achieved. Against this background, with a photocathode having 20% quantum efficiency, the incidence of a flux of only 10 photons per second can be detected in an observation time of perhaps 10 s. In this technique, referred to as photon counting, each electron originating at the photocathode results in an output pulse which is counted. An evaluation must be made by statistically comparing the cases of source-on and source-off. Such techniques were applied successfully in 1969 in the laser-ranging experiments using a retroreflector placed on the Moon by the *Apollo 11* astronauts. *See Thermionic emission.*

**Applications.** Ever since their invention, photomultipliers have been found useful in low-level photometry and spectrometry. The many applications of photomuliplers include high-speed inspection of small objects such as fruits, seeds, toys, and other industrial products; pollution monitoring; laser ranging; and process control with transmitted or reflected light to detect flaws in various solid, liquid, or gaseous manufacturing operations. *See Laser.*

***Scintillation counting.*** The most important applications of photomultipliers are related to scintillation counting. In a scintillation counter, gamma rays produce light flashes in a material such as NaI:Tl. A photomultiplier is optically coupled to the scintillator and provides a count of the flashes and a measure of their magnitude. The magnitude of the scintillation flash is proportional to the energy of the gamma ray, thus enabling the identification of particular isotopes. A whole science of tracer chemistry has developed using this technique and is applied to agriculture, medicine, and industrial problems.

***Gamma-ray camera.*** The gamma-ray camera developed in the late 1950s has proved to be a very valuabel medical tool. In this application, a radioactive isotope combined in a suitable compound is injected into or fed to a patient. Certain compounds and elements concentrate preferentially in particular organs, glands, or tumors: for example $^{131}I$ concentrates in the thyroid gland. Gamma rays which are then emitted are detected by a large scintillator, and an array of photomulitiplier tubes provides spatial data on the gamma-ray source. The technique is widely applied in diagnostic medicine, especially in the locating of tumors.

***Computerized tomography.*** The CT or CAT (computerized axial tomographic) scanner is a similar medical instrument developed during the 1970s. This instrument uses a pencil or fan-beam of x-rays that rotates around the patient. Several hundred photomultiplier-scintillator combinations surround the patient and record density from many different positions. These data are analyzed by a computer, thus providing a cross-section density map of the patient. The CT scanner is particularly useful because of the two-dimensional data provided, although it does not supply the functional information of the gamma-ray camera. Since 1980, silicon photocells have been replacing photomultipliers as the detectors of the scintillations.

***Positron camera.*** A similar development is the positron camera. This device uses radioisotopes, such as $^{11}C$, $^{13}N$, and $^{15}O$, that have short half-lives and emit positrons. When a disintegration occurs, the positron is annihilated by an electron, and the result is a pair of oppositely directed gamma rays detected in coincidence with photomultiplier-scintillator detectors on opposite sides of the patient. Functional information is provided and analyzed in a manner similar to that of a CT scanner.

*Ralph W. Engstrom*

**Bibliography.** Detectors: Photo/optical, *IEEE Trans. Nucl. Sci.*, vol. NS-26, no. 1, pt. 1, pp. 338–421, 1979; *RCA Photomultiplier Handbook*, Tech. Ser. PMT-62, 1980; H. Rougeot and C. Baud, Negative electron affinity photoemitters, in L. Marton (ed.), *Advances in Electronics and Electron Physics*, vol. 48, pp. 1–36, 1979.

## Phototransistor

A semiconductor device with electrical characteristics that are light-sensitive. Phototransistors differ from photodiodes in that the primary photoelectric current is multiplied internally in the device, thus increasing the sensitivity to light. For a discussion of this property *SEE TRANSISTOR*.

Some types of phototransistors are supplied with a third, or base, lead. This lead enables the phototransistor to be used as a switching, or bistable, device. The application of a small amount of light causes the device to switch from a low current to a high current condition. *SEE PHOTOELECTRIC DEVICES*.

*W. R. Sittner*

## Phototube

An electron tube comprising a photocathode and an anode mounted within an evacuated glass envelope through which radiant energy is transmitted to the photocathode. A gas phototube contains, in addition, argon or other inert gas which provides amplification of the photoelectric current by partial ionization of the gas. The photocathode emits electrons when it is exposed to ultraviolet, visible, or near-infrared radiation. The anode is operated at a positive potential with respect to the photocathode. *SEE ELECTRICAL CONDUCTION IN GASES; ELECTRON TUBE*.

**Characteristics.** A phototube responds to radiation over a limited range of the spectrum that is determined by the photocathode material. Radiant sensitivity, shown in the **illustration** as a function of wavelength, is the photoelectric current emitted per unit of incident monochromatic radiant power. Sensitivity on the short-wavelength side of the curves is limited by the transmittance of the glass envelope. Electron affinity of the photocathode determines the long-wavelength threshold of sensitivity. *SEE PHOTOEMISSION*.

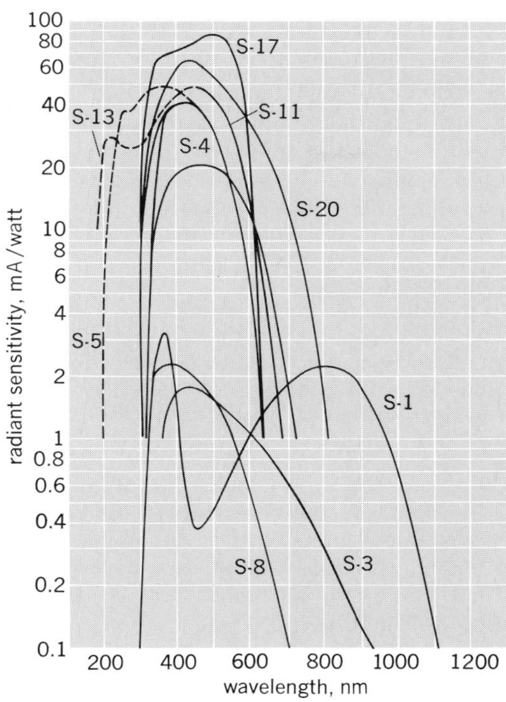


**Curves of the average spectral sensitivity characteristics of some typical phototubes.**

Typical phototube characteristics are summarized in the **table**. Quantum efficiency, or photoelectron yield, is the number of electrons emitted per incident photon. It is tabulated at the wavelength of maximum response. For photometric applications a useful parameter is luminous sensitivity: the photoelectric current per lumen incident from a specified source of light. A source commonly used is a tungsten-filament lamp operated at a color temperature of 4700°F (2870 K).

**Photocathodes.** Photocathodes are semiconductors which contain one or more of the alkali metals sodium, potassium, rubidium, or cesium chemically combined with bismuth, antimony, or silver oxide. The cathode surface contains a critical excess of the alkali metal which enhances photoelectric emission by

**Average cathode characteristics**

| Spectral sensitivity characteristic* | Cathode material | Wavelength of maximum response, nm | Peak radiant sensitivity, mA/W | Peak cathode quantum efficiency, % | Luminous sensitivity, μA/lumen† | Remarks |
|---|---|---|---|---|---|---|
| S-1 | $Cs_2O$, Ag | 800 | 2.2 | 0.3 | 25 | |
| S-3 | $Rb_2O$, Ag | 420 | 1.8 | 0.5 | 6.5 | |
| S-4 | $Cs_3Sb$ | 400 | 40 | 12.4 | 40 | |
| S-5 | $Cs_3Sb$ | 340 | 49 | 17.8 | 40 | Ultraviolet transmitting window |
| S-8 | $Cs_3Bi$ | 365 | 2.3 | 0.8 | 3 | |
| S-10 | Bi, Ag, O, Cs | 450 | 20.3 | 5.6 | 40 | Semitransparent |
| S-11 | $Cs_3Sb$ | 440 | 48 | 13.5 | 60 | Semitransparent |
| S-13 | $Cs_3Sb$ | 440 | 47 | 13.2 | 60 | Semitransparent; ultraviolet transmitting window |
| S-17 | $Cs_3Sb$ | 490 | 85 | 21.4 | 125 | Semitransparent, on reflecting substrate |
| S-20 | (NaKCs)Sb | 420 | 64 | 18.8 | 150 | Semitransparent |

*These characteristics, shown in the figure, refer to typical phototubes rather than to photocathodes.
†Light source is a tungsten-filament lamp operated at a color temperature of 4700°F (2870 K).

decreasing the affinity of the surface for electrons. Negative affinity for electrons is achieved with the gallium arsenide:cesium (GaAs:Cs) and indium gallium arsenide:cesium (InGaAs:Cs) photocathodes used in photomultipliers. Phototubes also emit electrons thermionically at ambient temperatures. This "dark current," observed in the absence of all irradiance, increases almost exponentially with temperature. Thermionic emission from the cesium antimonide (CsSb) photocathode is about $10^{-15}$ A/cm$^2$ at 68°F (20°C). SEE PHOTOMULTIPLIER; SEMICONDUCTOR.

**Applications.** Vacuum phototubes are used as detectors of radiant energy in the spectral range from 200 to 1100 nanometers. Since the photoelectric current is directly proportional to the intensity of the radiation, these tubes are used in radiometers, photometers, and colorimeters. By virtue of their narrow pulse response, vacuum phototubes are also used to measure the intensity of very short pulses of light generated by lasers and visible nuclear radiation. Gas phototubes can be used in light-operated relays and for the reproduction of sound from motion picture film, although their response to intensity-modulated light is limited to frequencies below 15 kHz. Vacuum as well as gas phototubes have been replaced in many applications by semiconductor photodiodes and photovoltaic cells. SEE LASER; PHOTODIODE; PHOTOVOLTAIC CELL.

*James L. Weaver*

**Bibliography.** M. Cardona and L. Ley (eds.), *Photoemission in Solids*, 1978 and 1979; A. Sommer, *Photoemissive Materials*, 1968.

## Photovoltaic cell

A device that detects or measures electromagnetic radiation by generating a current or a voltage, or both, upon absorption of radiant energy. Specially designed photovoltaic cells are used in solar batteries, photographic exposure meters, and sensitive detectors of infrared radiation. An important advantage of the photovoltaic cell in these particular applications is that no separate bias supply is needed—the device generates a signal (voltage or current) simply by the absorption of radiation.

Most photovoltaic cells consist of a semiconductor *p-n* junction or Schottky barrier in which electron-hole pairs produced by absorbed radiation are separated by the internal electric field in the junction to generate a current, a voltage, or both at the device terminals. The influence of the incident radiation on the current-voltage characteristics of a photovoltaic cell is to shift the current-voltage characteristic downward by the magnitude of the photogenerated current as shown in the **illustration**. Under open-circuit conditions (current $I = 0$) the terminal voltage increases with increasing light intensity (points A), and under short-circuit conditions (voltage $V = 0$) the magnitude of the current increases with increasing light intensity (points B). When the current is negative and the voltage is positive (point C, for example), the photovoltaic cell delivers power to the external circuit. In this case, if the source of radiation is the Sun, the photovoltaic cell is referred to as a solar battery. When a photovoltaic cell is used as a photographic exposure meter, it produces a current proportional to the light intensity (points B), which is indicated by a low-impedance galvanometer or microammeter. For use as sensitive detectors of infrared radiation, specially designed photovoltaic cells can be operated with either low-impedance (current) or high-impedance (voltage) amplifiers, although the lowest noise and highest sensitivity are achieved in the current or short-circuit mode. SEE JUNCTION DIODE; PHOTODIODE; PHOTOELECTRIC DEVICES; PHOTOVOLTAIC EFFECT; SEMICONDUCTOR; SOLAR CELL.

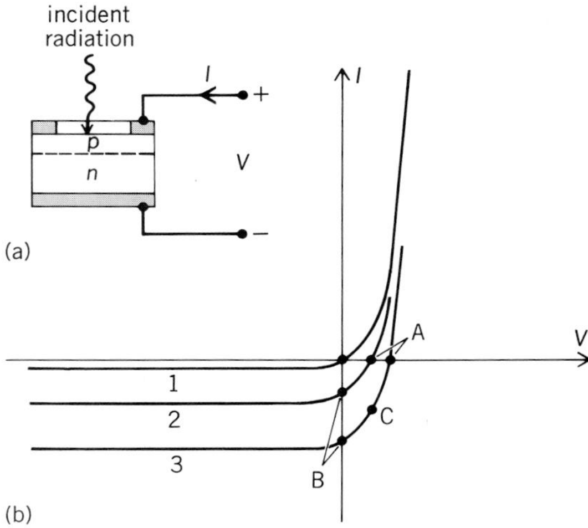


**The *p-n* junction photovoltaic cell. (*a*) Cross section. (*b*) Current-voltage characteristics. Curve 1 is for no incident radiation, and curves 2 and 3 for increasing incident radiation.**

*Gregory E. Stillman*

**Bibliography.** H. J. Hovel, *Solar Cells*, vol. 11 of R. K. Willardson and A. C. Beer (eds.), *Semiconductors and Semimetals*, 1975; D. Long, Photovoltaic and photoconductive infrared detectors, in R. J. Keyes (ed.), *Optical and Infrared Detectors*, pp. 101–145, 1977; W. F. Wolfe and G. J. Zissis (eds.), *The Infrared Handbook*, 1978.

## Photovoltaic effect

The conversion of electromagnetic radiation into electric power through absorption by a semiconducting material. Devices based on this effect are used as power sources in remote terrestrial locations and for satellites and other space applications. Photovoltaic powered calculators and other consumer electronic products have been manufactured, and solar photovoltaic automobiles and aircraft have been demonstrated.

**Principles.** The basic requirements for the photovoltaic effect are: (1) the absorption of photons through the creation of electron-hole pairs in a semiconductor; (2) the separation of the electron and hole so that the electric field within the semiconductor can be altered; and (3) the collection of the electrons and holes, separately, by each of two current-collecting electrodes so that current can be induced to flow in a circuit external to the semiconductor itself.

There are many approaches to achieving these three requirements simultaneously. A very common approach for separating the electrons from the holes is to use a single-crystal semiconductor, for example, silicon, into which a *pn* junction has been diffused. Silicon is often chosen because its optical band gap permits the absorption of a substantial portion of solar photons through the production of electron-hole pairs. The fabrication of such a device structure causes a local transfer of negative charges from the *n* layer into the *p* layer, bending the conduction and valence bands in the vicinity of the junction, and thereby creating a rectifying junction. Electrons generated in the *p* region can lower their energy by migrating into the *n* region, which they will do by a random walk process in the electric-field-free region far from the junction, or by drift induced by the electric field in the vicinity of the junction. Holes created in the *n* region, conversely, lose energy by migrating into the *p* region. Thus the presence of such a junction leads to the spontaneous separation of the photogenerated carriers, thereby inducing a voltage difference between current-carrying electrodes connected to the *p* and *n* regions. This process will continue until the difference in potential between the two electrodes is large enough to flatten the bands in the vicinity of the junction, canceling out the internal electric field existing there and so eliminating the source of carrier separation. The resulting voltage is termed the open-circuit voltage $V_{oc}$, and approximates the built-in voltage associated with the *pn* junction in the dark, a value which cannot exceed the band gap of the semiconductor. *See* HOLES IN SOLIDS; SEMICONDUCTOR; SEMICONDUCTOR DIODE.

In the limit when the device is short-circuited by the external circuit, no such buildup of potential is permitted. In this case, one electron flows in the external circuit for each electron or hole which crosses the junction, that is, for each optically generated electron-hole pair which is successfully separated by the junction. The resulting current is termed the short-circuit current $J_{sc}$ and, in most practical photovoltaic devices, approaches numerically the rate at which photons are being absorbed within the device. Losses can arise from the recombination of minority carriers (for example, electrons in the *p*-type region, holes in the *n*-type region) with majority carriers. *See* ELECTRON-HOLE RECOMBINATION.

**Power generation.** For a photovoltaic device to generate power it is necessary to provide a load in the external circuit which is sufficiently resistive to avoid short-circuiting the device. In this case, the voltage will be reduced compared to the open-circuit voltage because a continuing requirement exists for carrier separation at the junction; thus some band bending and its associated internal field must be retained. A maximum power conversion point in the available current-voltage (*I-V*) output plane exists for any photovoltaic device operating in a given photon flux. Device efficiency is then expressed as this maximum power output divided by the incident radiative power. The maximum power is usually expressed as the product of $V_{oc}$, $J_{sc}$, and F.F.; here F.F., the fill factor, is the ratio of the area in the *I-V* plane defined by the maximum power output divided by the area defined by the product of $V_{oc}$ and $J_{sc}$.

**Alternative materials.** While this explanation of the photovoltaic effect has been given in terms of the familiar crystalline silicon *pn* photovoltaic device, many alternative materials and device structures have been explored since the discovery of the photovoltaic effect in the nineteenth century. In fact, the first all-solid-state photovoltaic device appears to have used a semiconducting layer of glassy selenium illuminated through a semitransparent gold electrode in what would now be considered a metal-semiconductor Schottky barrier configuration.

Amorphous materials tend to have low carrier mobilities and, therefore, short diffusion lengths of minority carriers prior to recombination. Thus, devices utilizing amorphous materials tend to require internal electric field–induced carrier drift in order to achieve efficient carrier separation. Fortunately, the optical absorption of amorphous films can be matched so well to the incident solar radiation that devices as thin as 0.5 micrometer can be utilized, thus permitting the presence of electric fields throughout most of the absorbing layer thickness. *See* AMORPHOUS SOLID.

**Multiple-layered devices.** Various multiple-layered device configurations based on doped and undoped alloys of amorphous silicon have been developed for photovoltaic devices used in applications ranging from solar watches and calculators to remote power generators. The photovoltaic effect in these devices is particularly intriguing since it is possible to build up so-called tandem devices by stacking one device electrically and optically in series above another. In addition to the increased voltage and concomitant reduction in the required current-carrying capability of electrode grid structures, such devices permit, in principle, an increased efficiency of solar photovoltaic energy conversion. This is achieved by matching the band gap in the outer device with the higher–photon energy portion of the solar spectrum, thereby achieving a higher voltage, while matching the inner device with the lower–photon energy portion, thus utilizing a higher portion of these lower-energy photons than could be efficiently achieved in a single device. While band bending and internal fields are implicitly combined to create rectifying junctions in a single material (homojunctions), these two charge-separating mechanisms can be utilized independently, in principle, in heterojunctions, which are junctions created between two dissimilar semiconductor materials. Extension of the thin-film deposition techniques now used to create tandem amorphous devices appears to have the potential for creating structures in which the Fermi level and the conduction and valence band energies are independently controllable, through composition and structure, throughout the device thickness. Such control would permit the consideration of practical photovoltaic device structures which today exist only as theoretical possibilities. *See* SEMICONDUCTOR HETEROSTRUCTURES; SOLAR CELL.

*John P. de Neufville*

**Bibliography.** C. E. Backus (ed.), *Solar Cells*, 1976; L. P. Hunter (ed.), *Handbook of Semiconductor Electronics*, 3d ed., 1970; Special issue on photovoltaics, *IEEE Trans. Electr. Devices*, vol. ED-31, no. 5, May 1984; S. M. Sze, *Physics of Semiconducting Devices*, 2d ed., 1981.

## Picture tube

A cathode-ray tube used as a television picture tube, also called a kinescope. It might be referred to as a television picture reproducer. Modern television picture tubes use large glass envelopes (**Fig. 1**) that have a light-emitting layer of luminescent material deposited on the inner face. A modulated stream of high-velocity electrons scans this luminescent layer in a series of horizontal lines so that the picture elements (light and dark areas) are recreated.

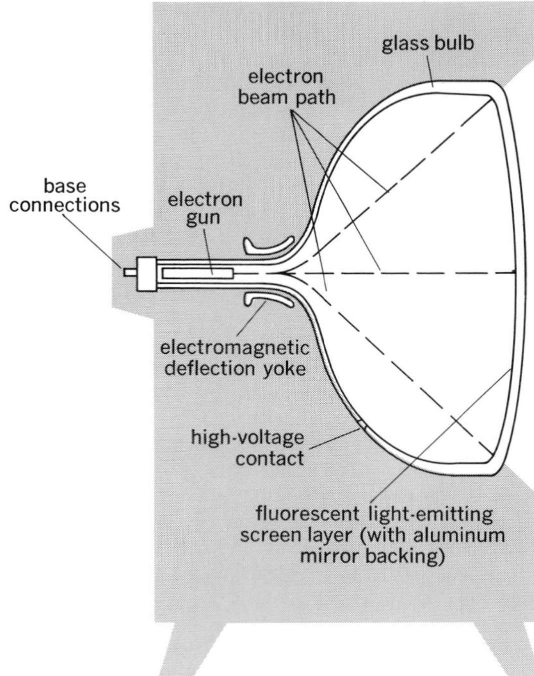


**Fig. 1. Black-and-white kinescope.**

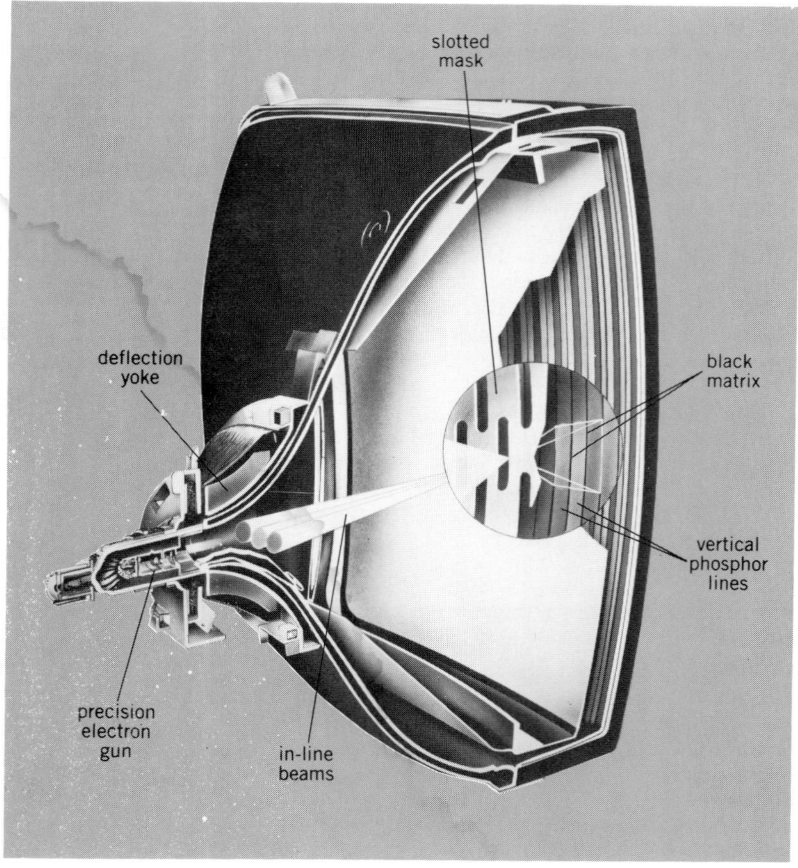


**Fig. 2. Color picture tube.**

The number of electrons in the system at any instant of time is varied by electrical pulses corresponding to the signal sent out by the television transmitter. These electrical pulses (picture information) were originally generated by a studio television camera. The home television receiver picks up the signal, and after suitable amplification and detection the picture information is supplied to the picture tube to recreate the original picture.

**Construction.** This article discusses construction of television picture tubes. For detailed discussion of cathode-ray tube construction *SEE* CATHODE-RAY TUBE.

***Glass envelope.*** A special-composition glass is used in making the envelope to minimize optical defects and to provide electrical insulation for high voltages. It also provides protection against x-radiation and has a light-absorption characteristic that improves picture contrast when it is viewed under bright illumination. In manufacturing the tube, air is evacuated from the glass bulb, and the tube is designed to withstand more than three times the force of atmospheric pressure to provide a safety margin. However, care must be taken in handling evacuated glass bulbs to avoid a dangerous implosion.

***Phosphor screen.*** The luminescent screen is made of a thin layer of phosphors (density of about 3 mg/cm$^2$). The phosphor materials for monochrome picture tubes are primarily zinc cadmium sulfide (which emits yellow light) and zinc sulfide (which emits blue light). By careful proportioning and mixing of these two phosphors the resultant emanation is a blue-white light.

The phosphor screen is aluminized by vacuum evaporation from a small molten aluminum pellet. The layer of aluminum, approximately 200 nanometers thick, is deposited on a smooth plastic film placed on top of the luminescent screen. The plastic film is subsequently volatilized and removed in the high-temperature processing of the tube. In the operation of the completed tube, the high-velocity electron beam penetrates the aluminum film, and its energy is transferred primarily to the phosphor screen. Only a small percentage of the electron-beam energy is converted into useful light energy, but this amount is sufficient to produce a brightness of several hundred footlamberts (1 footlambert = 3.4 candelas/m$^2$) in the picture highlights. The reflection of light by the aluminum mirror increases the picture brightness and improves picture contrast by preventing stray light from illuminating the back side of the phosphor screen.

***Wall coating.*** The inside walls of the bulb are coated with graphite to provide electrically conducting surfaces between the screen and the electron gun, and to provide a unipotential field through which the electron beam may travel without being disturbed by stray electrostatic fields. Graphite is a sufficiently poor conductor to minimize eddy-current power absorption from the electromagnetic fields generated by the external deflecting yoke. *SEE* EDDY CURRENT.

***Electron gun.*** The electron gun produces a stream of high-velocity electrons which are focused to a small spot at the phosphor screen. The electrons are generated by an indirectly heated nickel cathode coated with barium and strontium oxides. A cloud of electrons from the cathode is focused to a crossover point near the cathode by the electric fields between the cathode and the first two grids. This crossover of electrons is then focused electrostatically in a narrow beam by the main lens composed of the next two or more elements of the gun to produce a small spot on the phosphor screen. The voltage on the last element of the gun and on the screen is of the order of 15–25 kV. The intensity of the beam is controlled by the voltage between the cathode and the first grid. This voltage is modulated by the video signal to produce the range of brightness on the screen.

***Electromagnetic deflection.*** The electron beam is deflected electromagnetically to cause it to scan the picture area. This deflection is accomplished by a deflecting yoke, made up of two pairs of shaped coils which fit around the neck of the picture tube (Fig. 1). When pulsating electric currents of proper wave shape and phase are supplied to these coils, they generate magnetic fields which cause the electron beam to bend as it passes through them. By changing the magnitude and direction of the magnetic field, the electron beams are made to scan the screen in a systematic raster of horizontal lines which are sequentially stepped from top to bottom of the screen.

**Color picture tube.** A color television picture tube differs in several ways from the monochrome picture tube (**Fig. 2**): (1) The light-emitting screen is made up of small elemental (phosphor) areas laid in interlaced arrays, each capable of emitting light in one of the three additive primary colors (red, green, and blue). (2) The electron gun produces three beams, one for each of the primary-color phosphors. (3) A shadow mask assures that each of the three electron beams strikes only the color of phosphor elements intended. Red, green, and blue pictures are superimposed to produce a full range of perceived colors.

***Glass envelope.*** The glass bulb is made in two pieces, the face panel and the funnel-neck region. The separate face panel allows the fabrication of the segmented phosphor screen and the mounting of the shadow mask. The two glass pieces are sealed together by a special frit to provide a strong vacuum-tight seal.

***Face panel assembly.*** The light-emitting colored phosphors on the segmented screen can be either in dot arrays or, now more commonly, in line arrays. Typically, the trios of vertical phosphor lines are spaced 0.6–0.8 mm apart. Most modern tubes use a black matrix screen in which the phosphor lines are separated by opaque black lines. This black matrix reduces reflected light, thereby giving better contrast, and also provides a tolerance for the registration of the electron beam with the phosphor lines.

The shadow mask is made of a thin (0.10–0.17 mm) steel sheet in which elongated slits (one row of slits for each phosphor-line trio) have been photoetched. It is formed to a contour similar to that of the glass panel and is mounted at a precise distance from the glass. The width of the slits and their relative position to the phosphor lines are such that the electron beam from one of the three electron guns can strike only one of the sets of color phosphor lines. The shadow mask "shadows" the beam from the other two sets of phosphor lines.

***Electron gun.*** The electron gun for color is similar to that for monochrome except that there are three guns, usually arranged side by side, or in-line. This triple gun has common structural elements, but uses three independent cathodes with separate beam forming and focusing for each beam.

***Deflection yoke.*** The electromagnetic deflection yoke deflects or bends the beams, as in a monochrome tube, to scan the screen in a television raster. In addition, the yoke's magnetic field is shaped so that the three beams will be deflected in such a way that they land at the same phosphor trio on the screen at the same time. This convergence of the beams produces three images, one in red, one in green, and one in blue, that are superimposed to give a full-color picture. *See Television*.

*A. M. Morrell*

***Bibliography.*** E. G. Bylander, *Electronic Displays*, 1979; A. M. Dhake, *Television Engineering*, 1980; A. M. Morrell et al., *Color Television Picture Tubes*, 1974; S. Sherr, *Electronic Displays*, 1979.

## Piezoelectric crystal

A crystalline substance which exhibits the piezoelectric effect. This "pressure electricity" was first positively identified by the Curies in 1880, when they discovered that some crystals produced electric charges on parts of their surface when the crystals were compressed in particular directions, the charge disappearing when the pressure was removed. It was later discovered that these crystals become strained when subjected to electric fields; the piezoelectric deformation is directly proportional to the field and it reverses in sign as the sign of the field is reversed. These basic properties of piezoelectric crystals are used in electromechanical transducers, such as ultrasonic generators, microphones, phonograph pickups, and electromechanical resonators, such as frequency-controlling quartz crystals. *See Piezoelectricity*.

**Piezoelectric materials.** The principal piezoelectric materials used commercially are crystalline quartz and rochelle salt, although the latter is being superseded by other materials, such as barium titanate. Quartz has the important qualities of being a completely oxidized compound (silicon dioxide), and is almost insoluble in water. Therefore, it is chemically stable against changes occurring with time. It also has low internal losses when used as a vibrator. Rochelle salt has a large piezoelectric effect, and is thus useful in acoustical and vibrational devices where sensitivity is necessary, but it decomposes at high temperatures (131°F or 55°C) and requires protection against moisture. Barium titanate provides lower sensitivity, but greater immunity to temperature and humidity effects. Other crystals that have been used for piezoelectric devices include tourmaline, ammonium dihydrogen phosphate (ADP), and ethylenediamine tartrate (EDT). *See Barium titanate; Rochelle salt*.

The quartz crystal resonator is the most important class of piezoelectric device. Its principal application is in the fields of frequency control and electric-wave filters. It is also used in transducers, especially where heat or moisture are factors.

**Characteristics and manufacture.** The electrical properties of quartz crystals as circuit elements, including their temperature coefficient of frequency, motional inductance and capacitance, series resistance, and electrode or shunt capacitance, are largely determined by the dimensions and angles of rotation of the resonator surfaces with respect to the crystal axes. In commercial practice, raw quartz crystals are oriented by means of x-ray goniometers, the required angles of rotation are measured on the mounting jig, and the required blanks (unfinished slabs) cut from the mother crystal by diamond-faced saws. The blanks are then ground to the required frequency us-

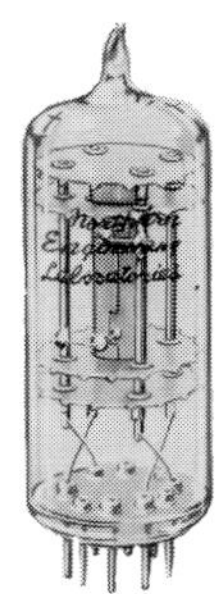
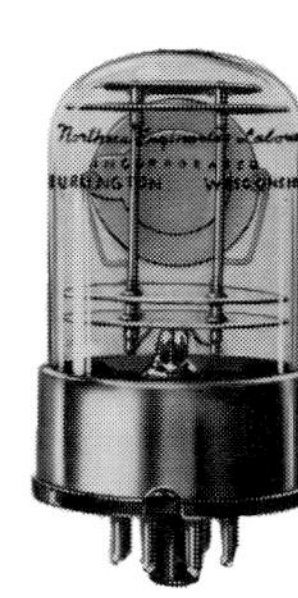

Fig. 1. Three typical vacuum-mounted quartz resonators. (*Northern Engineering Laboratories*)

ing lapping techniques with graduated sizes of abrasives to obtain a smooth finish. Some high-quality crystals are given optically polished surfaces. It is common practice to etch the surface of the crystal with fluorine compounds to remove microscopic surface irregularities.

Electrodes may be applied directly to the surface of the crystal, or they may be mounted externally in close proximity to the quartz element. Crystals with electrodes on their surfaces are frequently mounted by means of wires, which may also provide the connections to the electrodes. Containers for crystals may be hermetically sealed for protection from atmospheric effects, and some crystals are mounted in evacuated envelopes to improve $Q$ and reduce aging drift. Examples of vacuum-mounted quartz crystals are shown in **Fig. 1**. Vacuum-mounted crystals are not capable of handling much power (usually less than 1 or 2 mW maximum dissipation). Therefore, sealed crystals for power oscillators are usually mounted in an inert gas, such as nitrogen or helium.

The crystal-resonator cut chosen for a given application usually is dictated by the frequency at which the crystal must operate and the temperature range over which the crystal must work. A plot of typical frequency versus temperature curves for several different crystal cuts is shown in **Fig. 2**. A chart of frequency ranges covered by widely used crystal cuts is shown in **Fig. 3**.

**Applications.** Quartz crystal resonators are used for stabilizing the frequency of oscillators. The degree of stabilization depends on several factors, the principal ones being the $Q$ of the resonator, the type of crystal cut used and temperature range of operation, the type of circuit used, and the amount of power dissipated in the resonator. Thermostatic ovens are often used to enhance oscillator stability. The application of quartz crystals for oscillator stabilization has made possible the modern radio and television broadcasting industry and mobile radio communications with aircraft and ground vehicles. *See Oscillator*.

Quartz crystal resonators are also used in electric-wave, or frequency-separation, filters. Many thousands of such crystals are used in telephone systems for carrier-frequency separation, and in radio communication equipment for selecting a desired signal frequency band while rejecting undesired frequencies. *See Electric filter*.

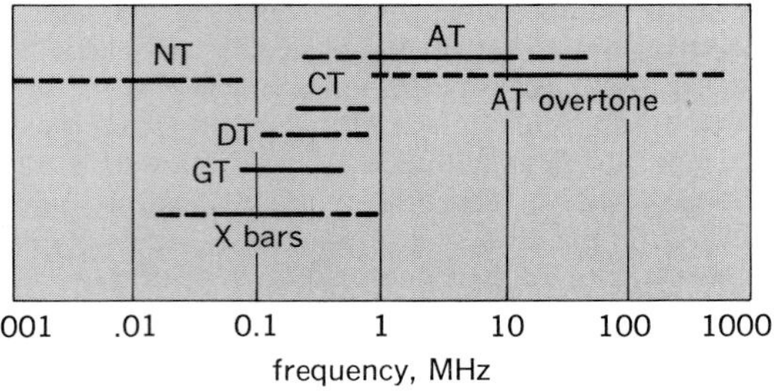


Fig. 3. Frequency range of various crystal cuts.

Transducers using piezoelectric elements are used for converting vibrations into electrical signals in such applications as crystal microphones, phonograph pickups, vibration pickups, and dynamic pressure-sensing elements. The inverse piezoelectric effect is used for converting electrical signals into mechanical vibrations. Thus, piezoelectric transducers are used in such applications as underwater sound ranging equipment (sonar, asdic), and in ultrasonic cleaning devices, which use a liquid medium for washing small to medium-sized objects.

*Frank D. Lewis*

**Bibliography.** W. G. Cady, *Piezoelectricity*, 1964; R. J. Mathys, *Crystal Oscillator Circuits*, 1983; J. Van Randeraat and R. E. Setterington, *Piezoelectric Ceramics*, 2d ed., 1974.

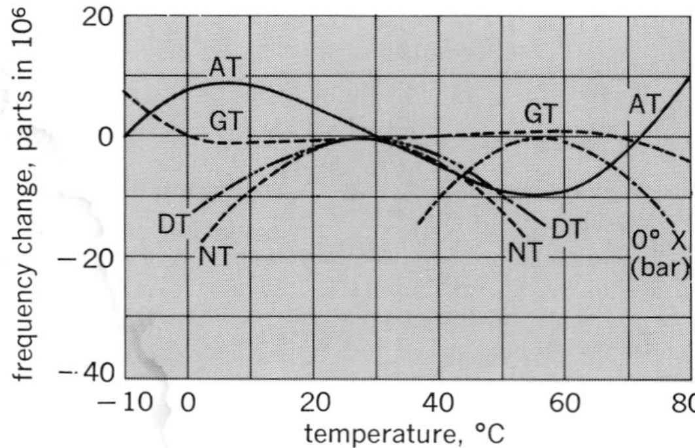


Fig. 2. Crystal frequency as a function of temperature for several different crystal cuts. The X bar is a rectangular bar with edges parallel to the crystal axes, and elongated parallel to the X or reference axis. The other cuts (AT, DT, GT, and so forth) are at orientations oblique to the crystal axis that have been found to have a small or vanishing temperature coefficient of the crystal frequency near the desired operating temperature. °F = (°C × 1.8) + 32.

## Piezoelectricity

Electricity, or electric polarity, resulting from the application of mechanical pressure on a dielectric crystal. The application of a mechanical stress produces in certain dielectric (electrically nonconducting) crystals an electric polarization (electric dipole moment per cubic meter) which is proportional to this stress. If the crystal is isolated, this polarization manifests itself as a voltage across the crystal, and if the crystal is short-circuited, a flow of charge can be observed during loading. Conversely, application of a voltage between certain faces of the crystal produces a mechanical distortion of the material. This reciprocal relationship is referred to as the piezoelectric effect. The phenomenon of generation of a voltage under mechanical stress is referred to as the direct piezoelectric effect, and the mechanical strain produced in the crystal under electric stress is called the converse piezoelectric effect. *See Polarization of dielectrics*.

Piezoelectric materials are used extensively in transducers for converting a mechanical strain into an electrical signal. Such devices include microphones, phonograph pickups, vibration-sensing elements, and the like. The converse effect, in which a mechanical output is derived from an electrical signal input, is also widely used in such devices as sonic and ultrasonic transducers, headphones, loudspeakers, and cutting heads for disk recording. Both the direct and converse effects are employed in devices in which the mechanical resonance frequency of the crystal is of importance. Such divices include electric wave filters and frequency-control elements in electronic oscillator circuits. *SEE DISK RECORDING; MICROPHONE; PIEZOELECTRIC CRYSTAL.*

**Necessary condition.** The necessary condition for the piezoelectric effect is the absence of a center of symmetry in the crystal structure. Of the 32 crystal classes, 21 lack a center of symmetry, and with the exception of one class, all of these are piezoelectric. In the crystal class of lowest symmetry, and type of stress generates an electric polarization, whereas in crystals of higher symmetry, only particular types of stress can produce a pieozoelectric polarization. For a given crystal, the axis of polarization depends upon the type of the stress. There is no crystal class in which the piezoelectric polarization is confined to a single axis. In several crystal classes, however, it is confined to a plane. Hydrostatic pressure produces a piezoelectric polarization in the crystals of those 10 classes that show pyroelectricity in addition to piezoelectricity. The pyroelectric axis is then the axis of polarization.

The converse piezoelectric effect is a thermodynamic consequence of the direct piezoelectric effect. When a polarization $P$ is induced in a piezoelectric crystal by an externally applied electric field $E$, the crystal suffers a small strain $S$ which is proportional to the polarization $P$. In crystals with a normal dielectric behavior, the polarization $P$ is proportional to the electric field $E$, and hence the strain is proportional to this field $E$. Superposed upon the piezoelectric strain $S$ is a much smaller strain which is proportional to $P^2$ (or $E^2$). This strain is called the electrostrictive strain. It is present in any dielectric. *SEE ELECTROSTRICTION.*

**Matrix formulation.** The relation of the six components $T_j$ of the stress tensor (three compressional components and three shear components) to the three components $P_i$ of the polarization vector can be described by a scheme (matrix) of 18 piezoelectric moduli $D_{ij}$. The same scheme ($d_{ij}$) also relates the three components $E_i$ of the electric field to the six components $S_j$ of the strain:

| | | Compression | | | Shear | | |
|---|---|---|---|---|---|---|---|
| | | $S_1$ $T_1$ | $S_2$ $T_2$ | $S_3$ $T_3$ | $S_4$ $T_4$ | $S_5$ $T_5$ | $S_6$ $T_6$ |
| $E_1$ | $P_1$ | $d_{11}$ | $d_{12}$ | $d_{13}$ | $d_{14}$ | $d_{15}$ | $d_{16}$ |
| $E_2$ | $P_2$ | $d_{21}$ | $d_{22}$ | $d_{23}$ | $d_{24}$ | $d_{25}$ | $d_{26}$ |
| $E_3$ | $P_3$ | $d_{31}$ | $d_{32}$ | $d_{33}$ | $d_{34}$ | $d_{35}$ | $d_{36}$ |

The direct effect is obtained by reading this scheme in rows, as in Eq. (1). The converse effect is obtained by reading it in columns, as in Eq. (2).

$$P_i = -\sum_{j=1}^{6} d_{ij}T_j \qquad i = 1,2,3 \tag{1}$$

$$S_j = \sum_{i=1}^{3} d_{ij}E_i \qquad j = 1,2,\ldots,6 \tag{2}$$

An analogous matrix ($e_{ij}$) relates the strain to the polarization and the electric field to the stress, as in Eqs. (3).

$$\begin{aligned} P_i &= \sum_{j=1}^{6} e_{ij}S_j \qquad i = 1,2,3 \\ T_j &= -\sum_{i=1}^{3} e_{ij}E_j \qquad j = 1,2,\ldots,6 \end{aligned} \tag{3}$$

The matrices ($d_{ij}$) and ($e_{ij}$) are not independent, but are related by expressions involving the elasticity tensor $c_{jh}{}^E$ (for constant electric field $E$), as in Eq. (4).

$$e_{mh} = \sum_{j=1}^{6} d_{mj}c_{jh}^{E} \qquad m = 1,2,3 \quad h = 1,2,\ldots,6 \tag{4}$$

Alternative formulations can be made by introducing the dielectric displacement $D$ or visualizing the simultaneous action of electrical and mechanical stresses.

The number of independent matrix elements $d_{ij}$ or $e_{ij}$ depends upon the symmetry elements of the crystal. For the lowest symmetry, all 18 matrix elements are independent, whereas piezoelectric classes of higher symmetry can have as few as one independent element in the matrix ($d_{ij}$). The matrix takes its simplest form if the natural symmetry axes of the crystal are chosen for the coordinate system.

**Electromechanical coupling.** The direct piezoelectric effect makes a crystal a generator, and the converse effect makes it a motor. Consequently, a piezoelectric crystal has many properties in common with a motor-generator. For example, the electrical properties, such as the dielectric constant, depend upon the mechanical load; conversely, the mechanical properties, such as the elastic constants, depend upon the electric boundary conditions. The electromechanical coupling factor $k$ can be defined as follows. Suppose electrodes are attached to a piezoelectric crystal and connected to a battery. Then the ratio of the energy stored in mechanical form to the electrical energy delivered by the battery is equal to $k^2$. In general, $k$ ranges from below 1 to about 30%. In quartz, for example, the coupling is roughly 10%. In ferroelectric crystals, $k$ can approach unity in certain circumstances. *SEE FERROELECTRICS.*

In quartz, a stress of 1 newton/m applied along the diad axis produces a polarization of about $2 \times 10^{-12}$ coulomb/m$^2$ along the same axis. Conversely, an electric field of $10^4$ volts/m produces a strain of about $2 \times 10^{-8}$. In ferroelectric crystals, such as rochelle salt and potassium dihydrogen phosphate, and in certain antiferroelectrics, such as ammonium dihydrogen phosphate (ADP), these effects can be several orders of magnitude larger.

**Molecular theory.** Quantitative theories based on the detailed crystal structure are very involved. Qual-

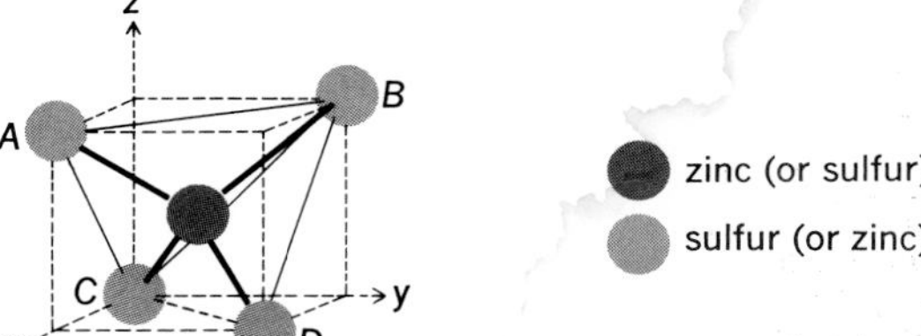


**Fig. 1. Tetrahedral structure of zincblende, ZnS. Only part of unit cell is shown. Size of circles has no relation to size of ions.**

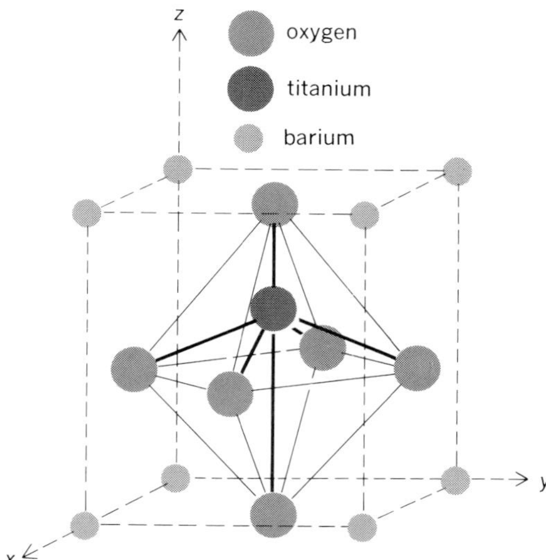


**Fig. 2. Unit cell of tetragonal barium titanate, $BaTiO_3$. Deviation from cubic symmetry is exaggerated. Size of the circles has no relation to the size of the ions.**

itatively, however, the piezoelectric effect is readily understood for simple crystal structures. **Figure 1** illustrates this for a particular cubic crystal, zincblende (ZnS). Every Zn ion is positively charged and is located in the center of a regular tetrahedron *ABCD*, the corners of which are the centers of sulfur ions, which are negatively charged. When this system is subjected to a shear stress in the *xy* plane, the edge *AB*, for example, is elongated, and the edge *CD* of the tetrahedron becomes shorter. Consequently, these edges are no longer equivalent, and the Zn ion will be displaced along the *z* axis, thus giving rise to an electric dipole moment. The dipole moments arising from different octahedrons sum up because they all have the same orientation with respect to the axes *x*, *y*, and *z*.

Another simple type of piezoelectric structure is encountered in barium titanate as shown in **Fig. 2**. The positive Ti ions are surrounded by an almost regular octahedron of negative oxygen ions. The Ti ions are not in the center of the octahedron, but somewhat displaced along the *z* axis. This structure already has a dipole moment or spontaneous polarization in the absence of externally applied stresses. It is clear from Fig. 2 that the Ti ion is pushed more off center when the crystal is mechanically compressed in the *xy* plane or elongated along *z*. The additional polarization associated with this deformation is the piezoelectric polarization. *See Barium titanate*.

**Piezoelectric ceramics.** Barium titanate and a few related compounds have the remarkable property that, by means of a sufficiently strong electric field, the direction of the spontaneous polarization can be switched to any one of the *x*, *y*, or *z* axes. This makes it possible to produce polycrystalline samples (ceramics) which are piezoelectric. The electromechanical coupling factors of such ceramics can reach about 50%.

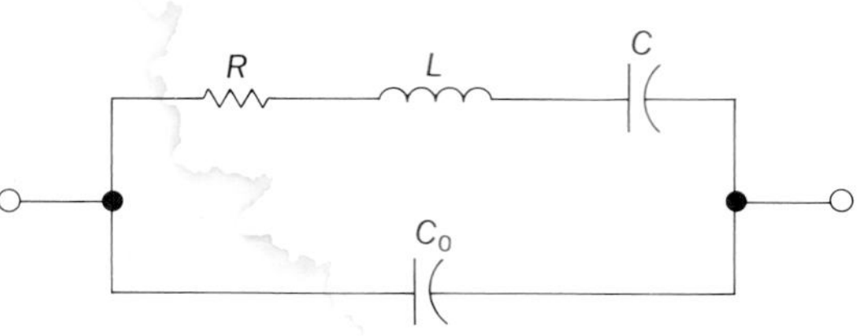


**Fig. 3. Network equivalent to a piezoelectric resonator near and at a resonance frequency.**

**Piezoelectric resonator.** The piezoelectric strains that can be induced by a static electric field are very small, except in certain ferroelectrics. Larger strains can be obtained when a piezoelectric crystal is driven by an alternating voltage, the frequency of which is equal to a mechanical resonance frequency of the crystal. The vibrating crystal reacts back on the circuit through the direct piezoelectric effect. In the range of a mechanical resonance, this reaction is equivalent to the response of the network shown in **Fig. 3**, provided that the series reasonance frequency of the network is equal to a mechanical resonance frequency of the crystal, as in Eq. (5). An important

$$f_R = 1/(2\pi\sqrt{LC}) \quad (5)$$

difference between the network of Fig. 3 and the piezoelectric resonator is that the latter has many discrete modes of vibration, whereas the network has only one resonance frequency.

***Network elements.*** The elements $L$, $C$, and $C_0$ of the equivalent network can be calculated from the physical constants of the crystal. Consider, for example, the simple resonator shown in **Fig. 4**. A rectangular

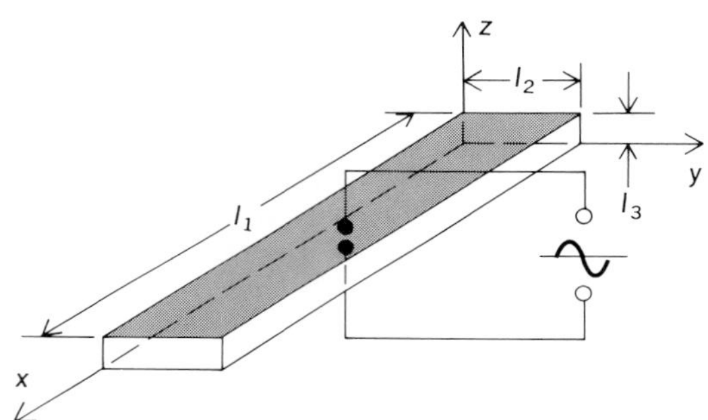


**Fig. 4. Simple piezoelectric resonator. A voltage applied to the electrodes shortens or lengthens the bar, thus exciting longitudinal vibrations.**

crystal bar with the dimensions $l_1 \gg l_2 \gg l_3$ is excited to compressional lengthwise vibrations. The *xy* faces have adherent electrodes, and the bar is oriented with respect to the natural crystal axes so that an electric field $E_3$ along $z$ causes a strain $S_1$ along the bar according to the equation $S_{1(\text{piezoel})} = d_{31}E_3$. A mechanical stress $T_1$ along the bar causes a strain $S_{1(\text{mech})} = s_{11}^E T_1$, where $s_{11}{}^E$ is the elastic compliance measured at constant electric field $E_3$. The resonance frequency for the fundamental lengthwise compressional mode is then given by Eq. (6), where $\rho$ is the

$$f_R = 1/(2l_1\sqrt{\rho s_{11}^E})\ \text{Hz} \quad (6)$$

density of the crystal. The parallel capacitance $C_0$ is the static capacitance of the crystal, as in Eq. (7).

$$C_0 = 8.85\epsilon l_1 l_2 / l_3\ \text{picofarad} \quad (7)$$

Here $\epsilon$ is the relative dielectric constant along $z$. For $C$ and $L$, the analysis yields Eqs. (8) and (9). (All

$$C = \frac{70.8 d_{31}{}^2 \int_1 \int_2}{\pi^2 S_{11} E \int_3}\ \text{picofarad} \quad (8)$$

$$L = \frac{\rho(S_{11}{}^E)^2 \ell_1 \ell_3}{8 d_{31}{}^2 \ell_2} \text{ henry} \tag{9}$$

physical constants are in mks units.) For the $n$th overtone, $C_0$ and $L$ remain the same, whereas $C$ must be divided by $n^2$. The losses (damping) represented by the resistance $R$ in Fig. 3 arise, for example, from ultrasonic radiation, friction in the crystal mount, internal friction in the crystal originating in various imperfections, and dielectric relaxation.

At the mechanical resonance frequency $f_R$, the alternating current is maximum and is determined by $R$. At the antiresonant frequency, given by Eq. (10), the

$$f_A = \sqrt{(C_0 + C)/LCC_0} \tag{10}$$

current is minimum. The difference $\Delta f = f_A - f_R$ increases with increasing electromechanical coupling according to relation (11).

$$\Delta f \approx 4k^2/\pi^2 \tag{11}$$

The reactance depends upon frequency, as shown in **Fig. 5**. For a typical piezoelectric crystal such as quartz, resonating at about $10^5$ Hz, the orders of magnitude given by relations (12) are typical for the ele-

$$L \approx 10^2 \text{ henry}$$
$$C \approx 0.02 \text{ picofarad} \tag{12}$$
$$C_0 \approx 5 \text{ picofarad}$$

ments of the equivalent network. The damping resistance $R$ varies from about $10^2$ to $10^4$ ohms; that is, the $Q$ factors, given by Eq. (13), are in the range

$$Q = \frac{1}{R}\sqrt{\frac{L}{C}} \tag{13}$$

between $10^6$ and $10^4$, and the resonances are very sharp. These characteristics cannot be achieved with conventional coils and condensers as circuit elements.

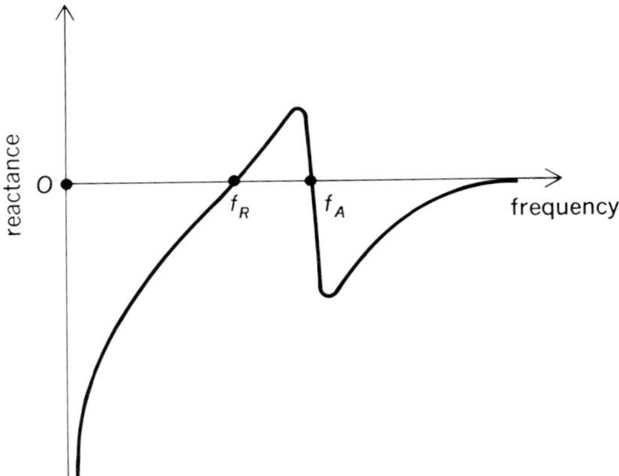


**Fig. 5. Diagram showing reactance versus frequency for a piezoelectric resonator.**

***Vibration modes.*** With piezoelectric resonators of various types, the range from audio frequencies to many megahertz can be covered. The vibration modes frequently used are, in order of increasing frequency: (1) flexural vibrations of bars and plates, (2) longitudinal vibrations of bars and plates, (3) face shear vibrations of plates, and (4) thickness shear vibrations and compressional vibrations of plates. **Figure 6** il-

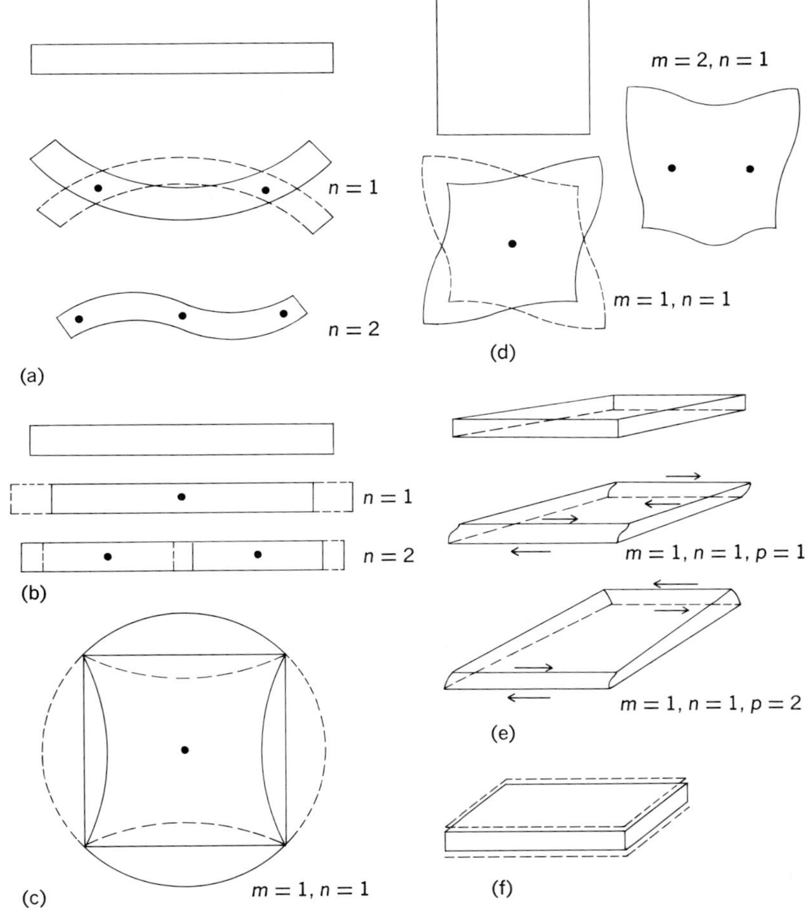


**Fig. 6. Diagrammatic representation of examples of vibration modes of bars and plates. (*a*) Flexural vibrations of a bar. (*b*) Longitudinal vibrations of a bar. (*c*) Longitudinal vibration of a plate. (*d*) Face shear vibrations of a plate. (e) Thickness shear vibrations of a plate. (*f*) Thickness vibration of a plate.**

lustrates some of these modes. The excitation of particular vibration modes can be achieved by proper orientation of the resonator with respect to the natural crystal axes, by proper positioning of the electrodes, and by proper mounting. A simple example is illustrated by **Fig. 7**. A bar is oriented so that an electric field along $x$ causes an expansion or contraction along $y$. The electrodes are split and cross-connected so that the bar flexes in the $yz$ plane when a voltage is applied. The fundamental flexure mode is easily excited with this arrangement; however, excitation of higher

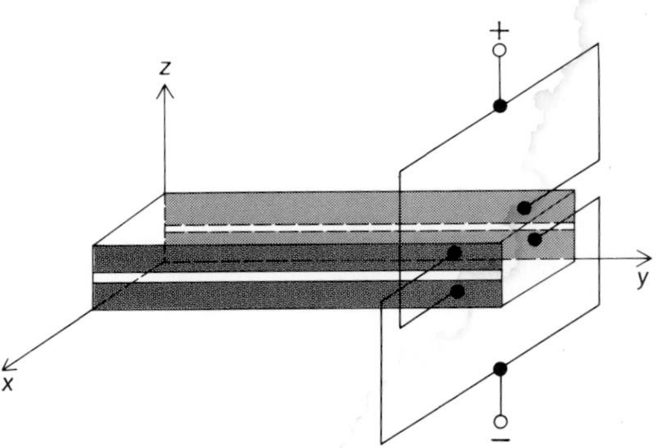


**Fig. 7. Excitation of flexure mode by split electrodes.**

even-numbered flexural modes is also possible. Interesting resonators are possible with piezoelectric ceramics (barium titanate type) because different parts of the resonator can be polarized in different directions.

**Common applications.** The sharp resonance curve of a piezoelectric resonator makes it useful in the stabilization of the frequency of radio oscillators. Quartz crystals are used almost exclusively in this application. The main advantages of quartz are high *Q* factor, stability with respect to aging, and the possibility of orienting the resonator with respect to the natural crystal axes so that the temperature coefficient of the resonance frequency vanishes near the operating temperature. **Figure 8** illustrates the orientation of commonly used cuts.

In vacuum-tube oscillators, the crystal generally is part of the feedback circuit. In the circuit proposed by G. W. Pierce, the conditions for oscillation are not satisfied unless the crystal reactance is positive. Hence, the oscillation frequency is between the resonant and antiresonant frequency of the crystal (Fig. 5). Circuits of this type hold the frequency within a few parts per million. Much greater stability can be achieved with the bridge circuit of L. A. Meacham. Here the oscillation conditions are fulfilled by zero phase shift in the feedback circuit, that is, at the exact series resonance frequency of the crystal. Long-term frequency stability of about one part in $10^8$ and short-term stability of one part in $10^9$ can be achieved with such oscillators; for an example of this SEE QUARTZ CLOCK. For detailed information on the Pierce and Meacham circuits SEE OSCILLATOR.

Selective band-pass filters with low losses can be built by using piezoelectric resonators as circuit elements. With a simple network consisting of resonating crystals only, a passband of twice the difference between resonant and antiresonant frequency can be obtained. For quartz resonators, this passband is about 0.8%. At relatively low operating frequencies, this band is too narrow, and combinations of crystal resonators with coils and condensors are generally

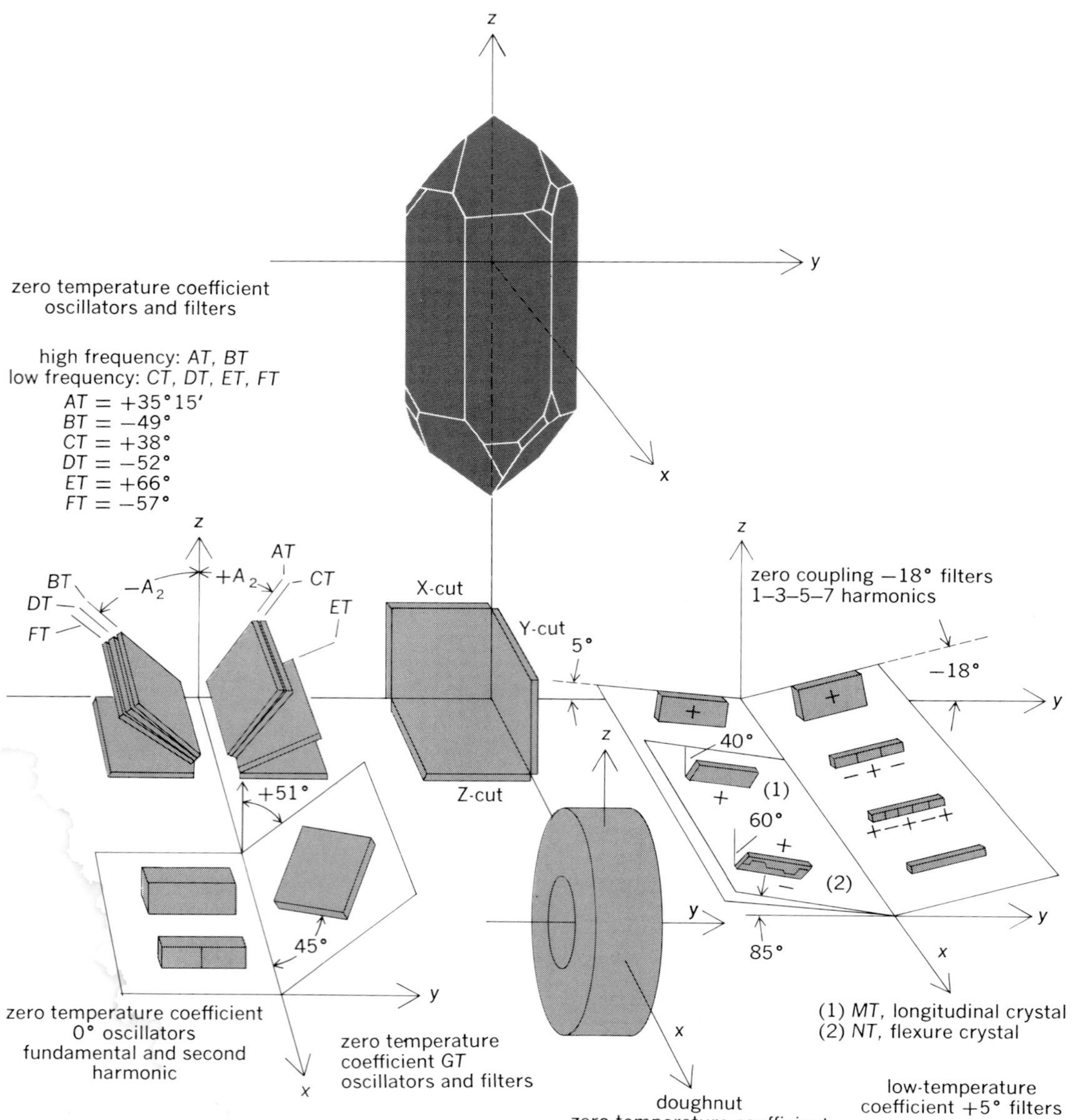


**Fig. 8. Orientation with respect to the natural crystal axes of some of the more commonly used special cuts of quartz. (*After W. P. Mason, Piezoelectric Crystals and Their Application to Ultrasonics, Van Nostrand, 1950*)**

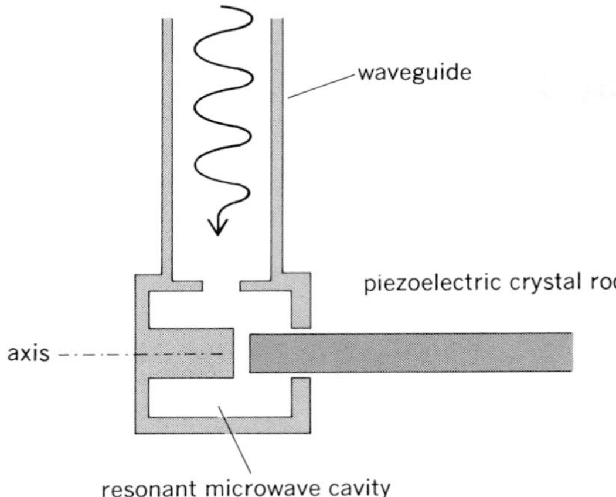


**Fig. 9. Diagram showing experimental arrangement for generation of ultrasound at microwave frequencies by means of a piezoelectric crystal.**

used. A synthetic piezoelectric crystal which is often substituted for quartz in this application is ethylene diamine tartrate.

Piezoelectric crystals provide the most convenient means for generation and detection of vibrations in gases, liquids, and solids at frequencies above $10^4$ Hz. Quartz, ammonium dihydrogen phosphate, rochelle salt, and barium titanate are frequently used in sonic and ultrasonic transducers. The mechanical impedances of liquids and solids are generally close enough to the mechanical impedance of the piezoelectric crystal so that efficient energy transfer is possible. The intensity of ultrasonic radiation that can be achieved is mainly limited by the mechanical strength of the piezoelectric crystal. The maximum ultrasonic intensity theoretically obtainable in water by means of quartz or ammonium dihydrogen phosphate is of the order 2000 watts/cm$^2$ and 200 watts/cm$^2$, respectively. For gases, the mechanical impedance match is so poor that the corresponding values are about 4000 times smaller. However, the mechanical impedance match can be greatly improved by using piezoelectric devices consisting of two differently oriented crystal cuts cemented together in such a way that a voltage applied to the electrodes causes the elements to deform in opposite directions, and a twisting or bending action results. Assemblies of this type (bimorphs) with barium titanate ceramics or rochelle salt are widely used in such devices as microphones, earphones, and phonograph pickup cartridges.

Ultrasonic waves at microwave frequencies up to $2.4 \times 10^{10}$ Hz have been generated by means of the piezoelectric effect. The arrangement is shown in **Fig. 9**. The end surface of a piezoelectric crystal rod is exposed to a strong microwave electric field in a resonant reentrant cavity. The ultrasonic waves travel through the crystal rod in a guided wave mode. The attenuation is low only at very low temperatures.

*H. Granicher*

***Bibliography.*** W. G. Cady, *Piezoelectricity*, 1964; W. P. Mason, *Crystal Physics of Interaction Processes*, 1966; J. J. Gagnepain and T. R. Meeker (eds.), *Piezoelectricity*, 1982; W. P. Mason (ed.), *Physical Acoustics*, vol. 1, pt. A, 1964; J. F. Nye, *Physical Properties of Crystals: Their Representation by Tensors and Matrices*, 1957.

## Point-contact diode

A semiconductor rectifier using the barrier formed between a specially prepared semiconductor surface and a metal point to produce the rectifying action. The contact is usually maintained by mechanical pressure, but in some instances it may be welded or bonded. The rectifying action implies that the resistance of the contact is significantly greater for one direction of applied voltage (reverse direction) than for the other (forward direction). *See Semiconductor rectifier.*

Point-contact diodes have been widely used in radio and television, and most notably in computers, microwave detectors, and ultrahigh-frequency mixers. Today their use is very small, having been usurped by junction diodes and Schottky barrier diodes.

Whenever a metal-semiconductor contact is made, an electrical barrier generally exists between the two. Only specially prepared ohmic contacts show no barrier. This barrier impedes the flow of majority carriers. For a definition of majority carriers and a discussion of conductivity type *see Semiconductor.*

In an *n*-type semiconductor the majority electrons are immobilized by the barrier, and a bias, which renders the semiconductor positive with respect to the metal, repels the positive holes (electron vacancies) in the metal. Very little current flows under this condition and the resistance is high. If the *n*-type semiconductor is negative with respect to the metal, most of the electrons are still immobilized by the barrier. However, holes can now enter from the metal and a relatively large current flows, that is, low resistance is present. For a *p*-type semiconductor the barrier impedes holes, and the bias polarities are reversed for the high- and low-resistance conditions.

The small physical size of the point contact forces a high current density in the neighborhood of the point. The current distribution in the semiconductor gives rise to a spreading resistance in series with the barrier. The forward current is limited by this resistance while the reverse current is limited by the barrier. The spreading resistance steadily decreases with increasing forward current because of heating and the injection of minority carriers. *See Transistor.*

In the reverse direction there is a breakdown phenomenon at relatively high voltages due either to heating or avalanching of the minority carriers passing through the high field barrier region.

*Lloyd P. Hunter*

## Point-contact transistor

A transistor in which the emitter and collector consist of metal point contacts closely spaced on the surface of a block of semiconductor. The usual configuration is with both points on the same surface and about 2 mils (50 micrometers) apart (see **illus.**), although good devices have also been made with the points on opposite sides of a thin wafer of semiconductor.

This type of transistor was the first transistorlike device invented. The most common type uses *n*-type semiconductor material, beryllium-copper emitter-point material, and phosphor-bronze collector-point material. In fabrication the surface of the semiconductor is carefully lapped and etched. The sharp points are mechanically assembled with some spring pressure against the surface. The collector point is

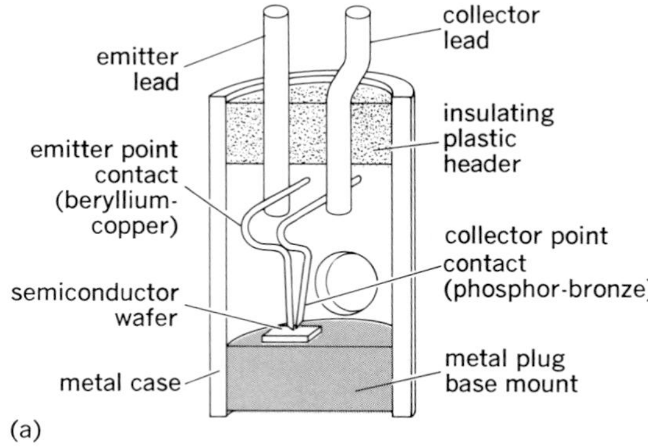


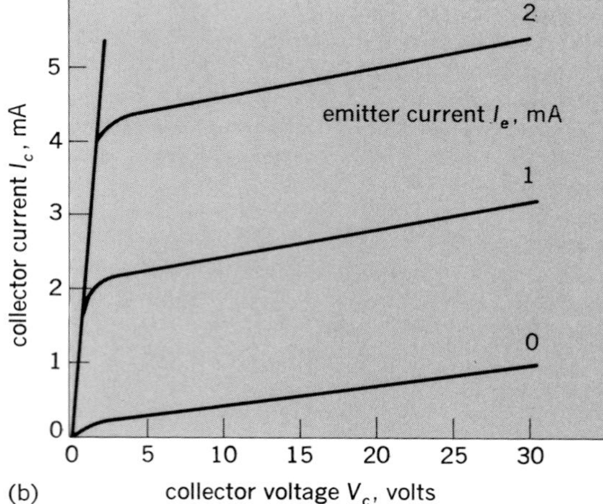


**Point-contact transistor. (*a*) Cutaway view. (*b*) A graph of the characteristics.**

electrically pulsed in the reverse-bias direction with sufficient voltage and total energy to cause electrical breakdown. The point of contact is heated nearly to the melting point of the semiconductor. The pulse duration is a millisecond or less. The result of this electric forming procedure is to increase the current multiplication factor $\alpha^*$ of the collector point from something much less than unity to the order of 10.0. The injection efficiency $\gamma$ of the point emitter is about 0.3 and the transfer efficiency is about 1.0 so that the overall current gain $\alpha$ of the device is 3.0. *See* SEMICONDUCTOR; TRANSISTOR.

The electrical forming process, besides increasing $\alpha^*$, also increases the collector barrier leakage current $I_{co}$ so that, at a collector voltage of 10 volts, a typical point-contact device will draw 1 milliampere in the absence of emitter current. This compares to 1 microampere for a junction transistor under the same condition. *See* JUNCTION TRANSISTOR.

Point-contact transistors can be made with frequency ranges up to 100 MHz and power ratings of 200 milliwatts. They can be used quite conveniently for oscillators and flip-flops, because their $\alpha > 1.0$ causes them to show a negative resistance characteristic when the base is used as an input. They have not achieved widespread acceptance because of the variability of their characteristics and because of their relatively high $I_{co}$. Today point-contact transistors are almost unknown in practical use, having been replaced by junction transistors, which are more reliable.

*Lloyd P. Hunter*

**Bibliography.** L. P. Hunter (ed.), *Handbook of Semiconductor Electronics*, 3d ed., 1970; W. Schockley, *Electrons and Holes in Semiconductors*, 1950, reprint 1976.

## Potentiometer (variable resistor)

A variable-resistance device with three terminals used in electric circuits. As shown schematically in **Fig. 1**, the three terminals are the two ends of a resistor (or series combination of resistors) and a movable connection, which allows adjustment of the resistance between this movable connection and either end connection. The movable connection often consists of a sliding contact which moves along the actual resistor element. The size or rating or a potentiometer is specified by giving its total resistance in ohms and the permissible losses in watts. By using only the movable and one fixed connection, a potentiometer may be used as a rheostat. *See* RESISTOR.

The term potentiometer is also applied to a precision instrument used to measure or compare electrical voltages. For this device which depends on the same type of resistor arrangement *see* POTENTIOMETER (VOLTAGE METER).

**Use.** A potentiometer is used to adjust and control the electric potential difference (voltage) applied to some device or part of a circuit. The output voltage may be varied from zero to the value of the input voltage. Examples of its use are as a field-current control on an electric generator and as a volume control on a radio. Since the resistance between the input terminals is fixed (assuming the load device takes little current), potentiometers with precision resistors are used as range selector switches on vacuum-tube voltmeters and other precision electronic measuring equipment. Other uses are to divide a voltage into two parts, to compare two voltages, and to divide the total resistance between two parts of a circuit. The ratio between output and input voltage, as shown in **Fig. 2**, is given by the equation below.

$$\frac{e_{\text{out}}}{e_{\text{in}}} = \frac{r_2}{r_1 + r_2}$$

**Construction.** A potentiometer may be linear or nonlinear. In the linear case the resistor is uniform, and the voltage distribution along the resistor is the same for any fixed fraction of its total length. Therefore, the output voltage (Fig. 1) is proportional to the slider position. In a nonlinear potentiometer the resistance per unit length varies, and the output voltage varies as some function (such as the logarithm, the square, or the sine) of the slider position. Nonlinear potentiometers are often called tapered potentiome-

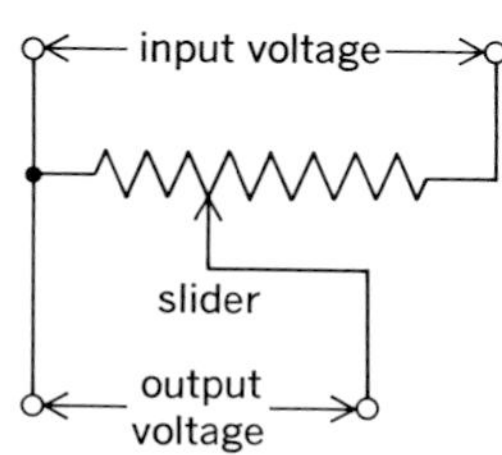


**Fig. 1. Schematic of potentiometer.**

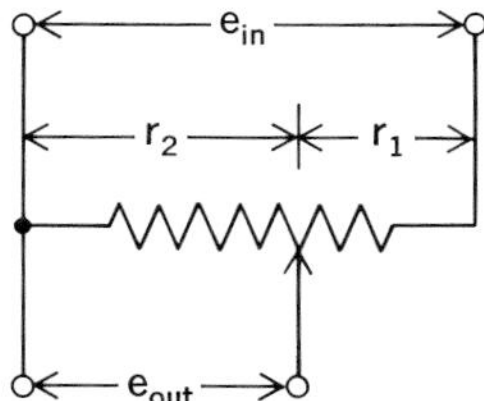


**Fig. 2.** Schematic of voltage divider.

ters. In some cases the current-carrying capacity of various parts of the potentiometer may be different.

A slide-wire potentiometer employs a movable sliding connection on a length of resistance wire.

A wire-wound potentiometer is similar to a slide-wire one, except that the resistance wire is wound on a form and contact is made by a slider which moves along an edge from turn to turn. The form may be straight or bent into a part of a circle, in which case the slider is mounted on an arm which is rotated by a knob. The form may be made of a ceramic material for heat resistance or a good grade of stiff paper or plastic (known as a card).

A carbon potentiometer uses a thin layer of carbon or graphite in place of a resistance wire.

A button-type potentiometer uses fixed contact points which are touched by the slider. Fixed resistors are then connected between the buttons.

***Multiturn potentiometers.*** Sold under various trade names, these have the resistance material, usually coiled resistance wire, placed in the form of a cylindrical helix. A slider is moved down the helix by a lead-screw arrangement. This arrangement permits a long length of potentiometer in a small volume and gives more accurate adjustment than is possible with a single-turn potentiometer.

***Trimmer potentiometer.*** This is a potentiometer used to provide a small percentage adjustment and is often used with a course control.

*Clarence F. Goodheart*

## Potentiometer (voltage meter)

An instrument that precisely measures an electromotive force (emf) or a voltage by opposing to it a known potential drop established by passing a definite current through a resistor of known characteristics. There are two ways of accomplishing this balance: (1) the current $I$ may be held at a fixed value and the resistance $R$ across which the $IR$ drop is opposed to the unknown may be varied; (2) current may be varied across a fixed resistance to achieve the needed $IR$ drop. SEE IR DROP.

**Constant-current potentiometer.** The essential features of a general-purpose constant-current instrument are shown schematically in **Fig. 1**. The value of the current is first fixed to match an $IR$ drop to the emf of a reference standard cell. With the standard-cell dial set to read the emf of the reference cell, and the galvanometer (balance detector) in position $G_1$, the resistance of the supply branch of the circuit is adjusted until the $IR$ drop in 10 steps of the coarse dial plus the set portion of the standard-cell dial balances the known reference emf, indicated by a null reading of the galvanometer. This adjustment permits the potentiometer to be read directly in volts. Then, with the galvanometer in position $G_2$, the coarse, intermediate, and slide-wire dials are adjusted until the galvanometer again reads null. If the potentiometer current has not changed, the emf of the unknown can be read directly from the dial settings. There is usually a switching arrangement so that the galvanometer can be quickly shifted between positions 1 and 2 to check that the current has not drifted from its set value. SEE ELECTROMOTIVE FORCE (CELLS).

The switch contacts in the coarse-dial and slide-wire elements are in the galvanometer branch of the circuit and, since at balance they carry no current, their resistance does not affect the measurement. However, there can be only two noncontributing contact resistances in the circuit. The switch for adjusting the intermediate dial does carry current at balance, and its resistance does affect the measurement, so care is taken in its construction to ensure low and repeatable resistance; and often (as in Fig. 1) the circuit is arranged so that only a fraction of the current goes through these current-carrying contacts, and the contribution of their $IR$ drop is correspondingly reduced.

Also illustrated is the availability of reduced ranges. Resistances of range shunts are such that at the 0.1 (or 0.01) position of the range-selector switch, only a tenth (or a hundredth) of the reference current goes through the measuring branch of the circuit, and its range is correspondingly reduced.

In addition to accuracy limits imposed by contact resistances in the measuring circuit, there are thermal emf's generated at circuit junctions. These limiting factors are increasingly important as range is reduced. Thus, in low-range potentiometers (especially where

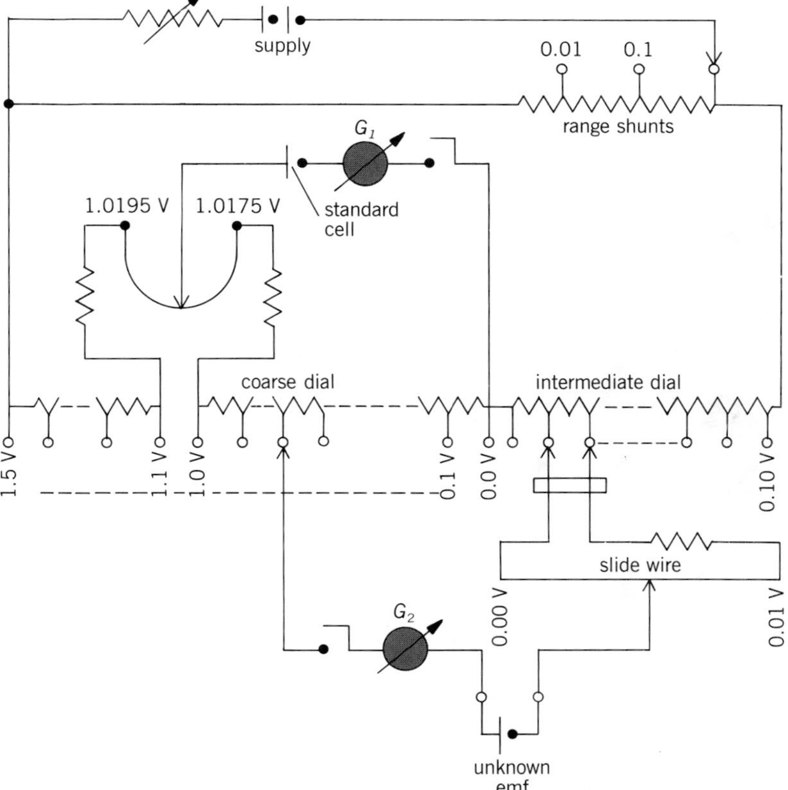


**Fig. 1.** Circuit diagram of a general-purpose constant-current potentiometer, showing essential features.

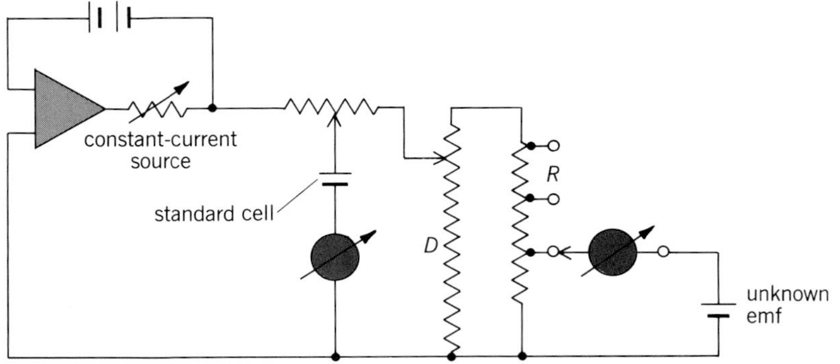


Fig. 2. Simplified circuit diagram of a typical constant-resistance potentiometer.

the measurement of microvolts is involved) care must be taken to keep circuit junctions and contact resistances out of the measuring circuit as much as possible, to use thermal shielding, to arrange the circuit and galvanometer switches to minimize temperature differences between junction points in the measuring circuit, and to use alloys in switches which will minimize thermal emf's. In microvolt potentiometers, the galvanometer is usually connected to the circuit through a special thermo-free reversing switch so that the thermal emfs in the galvanometer may be eliminated, the balance point being that for which there is no change in galvanometer deflection on reversal.

**Brooks deflection potentiometer.** This potentiometer is a modification of the constant-current type, in which a low-range millivoltmeter is substituted for a null-reading balance detector; and its reading is added to or subtracted from a dial reading whose individual steps are such that intermediate (unbalance) values are read on the millivoltmeter. Thus, the slower process of obtaining an exact balance is avoided. This instrument has limited accuracy (0.05%), but has found wide use in instrument testing. *See Voltmeter.*

**Constant-resistance potentiometer.** A typical constant-resistance potentiometer (**Fig. 2**) consists of a constant-current source, a resistive divider *D* (used in the current divider mode), and a fixed resistor *R* in which the current and *IR* drop are determined by the divider setting at balance. The output of the current source is adjusted by equating the emf of a standard cell to an *IR* drop in the circuit, making the instrument direct-reading. Multirange operation is accomplished through tap points on the resistor *R*. Accuracy depends on divider uniformity, resistor stability, and stability of the current source.

Another type of constant-resistance potentiometer (**Fig. 3**) operates from a current comparator which senses and corrects inequality of ampere-turns in two windings on a magnetic core. Two matched toroidal cores, wound with an identical number of turns, are excited by a fixed-frequency oscillator. The fluxes induced in the cores are equal and oppositely directed so that they cancel with respect to a winding which links both cores. In the absence of any additional magnetomotive force (mmf), there is no signal in the detector winding which links both cores. If, in another winding *A* linking both cores, a direct current is injected, its mmf adds to the flux in one core and subtracts from the other at any instant. The resulting net flux in the detector winding induces a voltage in it. This signal is used to control direct current in another winding *B* that also links both cores. Its mmf is opposed to that of *A* and when they are equal, there is no signal in the detector winding. Thus a constant current in an adjustable number of turns in winding *A* is matched to a variable current in a fixed number of turns in winding B; that is, their ampere-turns are equal and opposed. The voltage drop $I_BR$ is used to oppose the emf to be measured. The potentiometer is made direct-reading in volts in terms of the turns-ratio *B*/*A*, by adjusting the constant-current source, using a standard-cell circuit (omitted to simplify the figure). An advantage of this potentiometer over those whose long-term accuracy depends on the stability of a resistance ratio is that the ratio here is the turns-ratio of windings on a common magnetic core, dependent solely on conductor position and therefore not subject to drift with time.

**Volt box.** Volt boxes, used to extend the range of potentiometers (in some instances to 1500 V), are resistive voltage dividers having a limited number of fixed-position taps (**Fig. 4**). Depending on its anticipated value, the unknown voltage is connected across appropriate input terminals (say 0–150 V), and the potentiometer is connected to the 0–1.5 V output terminals. The potentiometer is balanced in the usual way, and its reading is multiplied by the factor cor-

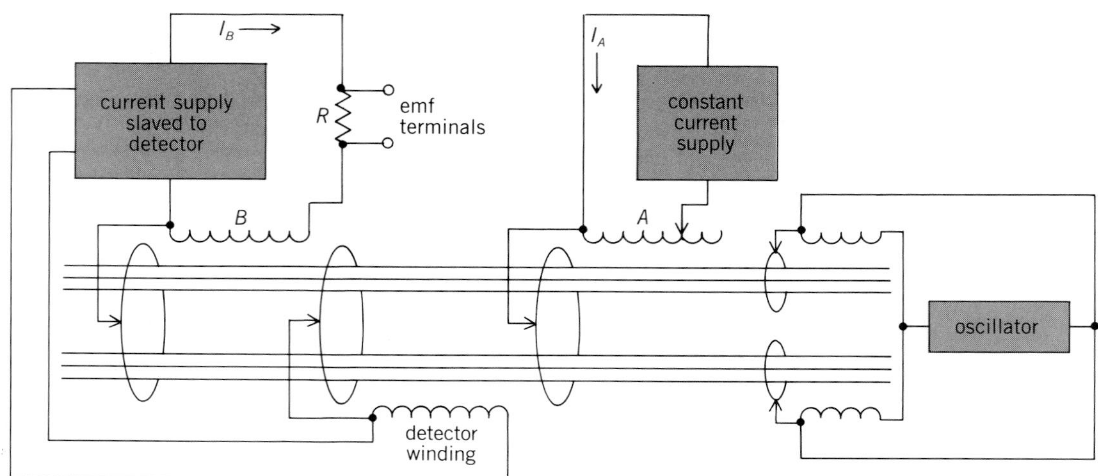


Fig. 3. Circuit diagram of a current-comparator potentiometer, a type of constant-resistance potentiometer.

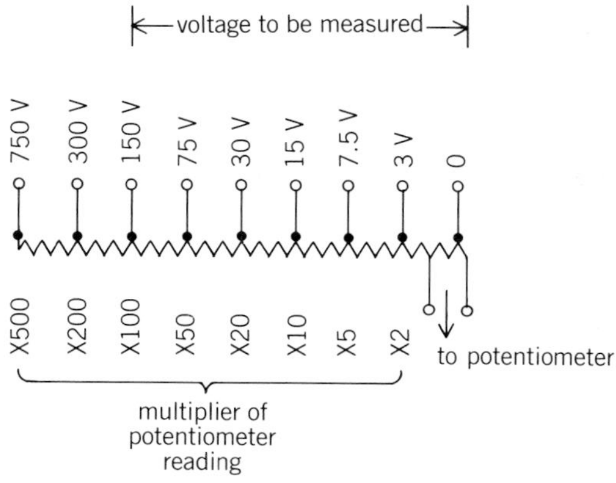


**Fig. 4. Configuration of fixed-position taps in a volt box.**

responding to the tap point used. While no current is taken by the potentiometer at balance, current is supplied to the volt box by the source, and it is the voltage drop in the divider resistance which is measured, not the open-circuit emf of the source. For a given voltage, power consumption and internal heating are greater in a low than in a high-resistance circuit, with consequent greater change in resistance ratio. Thus a higher ohms-per-volt design is desirable. However, the quality of insulation becomes more critical in high-resistance designs, since the insulating structures that support the resistance elements are themselves high-resistance leakage paths. As a compromise, the resistance of working volt boxes ranges between 200 and 750 ohms/V. High-accuracy standard volt boxes (1000 ohms/V) have a guard circuit which maintains shields at appropriate potentials along the insulating structure.

**Current measurements.** Potentiometer techniques may also be used for current measurement, the unknown current being sent through a known resistance and the $IR$ drop opposed by balancing it at the voltage terminals of the potentiometer. Here, of course, internal heating and consequent resistance change of the current-carrying resistor (shunt) may be a critical factor in measurement accuracy; and the shunt design may require attention to dissipation of heat resulting from its $I^2R$ power consumption. SEE CURRENT MEASUREMENT; JOULE'S LAW.

**Alternating-voltage measurements.** Potentiometer techniques have been extended to alternating-voltage measurements, but generally at a reduced accuracy level (usually 0.1% or so). Current is set on an ammeter which must have the same response on ac as on dc, where it may be calibrated with a potentiometer and shunt combination. Balance in opposing an unknown voltage is achieved in one of two ways; (1) a slide-wire and phase-adjustable supply; (2) separate in-phase and quadrature adjustments on slide-wires supplied from sources that have a 90° phase differences. Such potentiometers have limited use in magnetic testing. SEE ALTERNATING CURRENT; ELECTRICAL MEASUREMENTS; VOLTAGE MEASUREMENT.

*Forest K. Harris*

***Bibliography.*** F. K. Harris, *Electrical Measurements,* 1953; L. Julie, A constant resistance potentiometer, *Trans. IEEE,* IM-16:187–191, 1967; N. L. Kusters and M. P. McMartin, A current-comparator potentiometer, *Trans. IEEE,* IM-15:212–220, 1966; D. S. Luppold, *Precise DC Measurements,* 1969.

## Power amplifier

The final stage in multistage amplifiers, such as audio amplifiers and radio transmitters, designed to deliver appreciable power to the load.

Power amplifiers may be called upon to supply power ranging from a few watts in an audio amplifier to many thousands of watts in a radio transmitter. In audio amplifiers the load is usually the dynamic impedance presented to the amplifier by a loudspeaker, and the problem is to maximize the power delivered to the load over a wide range of frequencies. The power amplifier in a radio transmitter operates over a relatively narrow band of frequencies with the load essentially a constant impedance.

The mode of operation of power amplifiers is denoted by class A, AB, B, and C. Class C operation is limited to radio frequencies with a tuned load. The other classes may be used for audio and high-frequency operation. For discussion of the modes of operation SEE AMPLIFIER.

**Class A.** Class A operation is used when the amount of power transferred to the load is relatively small, say, less than 10 W. The amount of harmonic distortion introduced into the load voltage can be kept small by operating transistors or tubes within the nearly linear region of their characteristics. Class A operation has relatively little use because the conversion efficiency (the efficiency of a power amplifier) is low. The maximum possible efficiency is 50%. However, for the usual operating conditions the efficiency is on the order of 10%. If the power amplifier were required to deliver 10 W with 10% efficiency, the tube or transistor would have to be capable of dissipating an average power of 100 W. Furthermore, the power supply must be capable of supplying the power dissipated as heat plus the useful power delivered to the load. This poses an unnecessary burden upon the power supply. Other classes of operation have a higher conversion efficiency and are therefore used for higher-power applications.

**Class AB.** An improvement in the conversion efficiency can be had by using class AB operation. However, while a class A amplifier can be operated single-ended (one output transistor or tube), a class AB amplifier must be operated push-pull. In class AB operation the transistor or tube current does not flow for the complete cycle of the input voltage. In a single-ended circuit this would introduce excessive distortion. SEE PUSH-PULL AMPLIFIER.

**Class B.** This class is often used for the power amplifier in an audio amplifier. The amplifier in this class must be a push-pull circuit. Theoretically, with ideal transistors or tubes, the class B amplifier can have a conversion efficiency of 78.5%; practically, the efficiency is on the order of 50%, an appreciable improvement over that of class A operation.

The load is usually transformer-coupled to the two transistors or tubes operating in push-pull. For maximum power transfer the dynamic load impedance presented to the amplifier is determined by the amount of harmonic distortion that can be tolerated.

Use of more sophisticated circuitry than that considered in an elementary presentation of a push-pull amplifier operating in class B can produce nearly distortionless power amplification. This is of prime importance in the final amplifier stages of a high-fidelity audio amplifier.

Vacuum-tube power amplifiers can operate in class

$B_2$ with an appreciable amount of grid current flowing for a small portion of the cycle of an input sinusoidal signal. This imposes additional requirements upon the driving stage of the amplifier. If the equivalent circuit of the driver has too large an equivalent output impedance, the flow of grid current through this impedance will cause a distortion of the grid waveform. This class of operation is usually encountered in driver circuits for class B amplifiers operating in the radio-frequency region where high-$Q$ circuits counteract effects of grid current. Audio operation is usually restricted to class $B_1$ operation, because the usual form of phase-inverter circuitry has a large output impedance. In radio-frequency operation the transformer phase inverter can be used with tuned circuitry and air-core or powdered-iron slug coils, because the operation is essentially at one frequency.

**Class C.** Because the collector or plate current flows for less than one-half cycle of the input sinusoidal signal, this class of operation is restricted to radio-frequency operation where a tuned load is employed. The load is usually the input impedance of an antenna or of an antenna matching network. The load voltage will be nearly sinusoidal, even though the current in the tube flows in pulses, because of the relatively sharp tuning of the load. This phenomenon allows the amplification of large amounts of power at conversion efficiencies as high as 80%. This is extremely important for applications requiring delivery of large amounts of power to the load.

The driving source must usually be called upon to deliver power to the base circuit or grid circuit of the power amplifier, in many cases as much as 10% of the power delivered to the load. This requirement is not excessive. A class B power amplifier can be used in the grid-driving circuit to obtain an efficient combination of driver and final amplifiers.

*Harold F. Klock*

**Bibliography.** C. H. Evans, *Electronic Amplifiers: Theory, Design and Use*, 1979; D. G. Fink and D. Christiansen, *Electronics Engineers' Handbook*, 2d ed., 1982; C. A. Holt, *Electronic Circuits, Digital and Analog*, 1978; J. Millman, *Micro-Electronics*, 1979; D. L. Schilling and C. Belove, *Electronic Circuits, Discrete and Integrated*, 2d ed., 1979.

## Preamplifier

A voltage amplifier suitable for operation with a low-level input signal. It is intended to be connected to another amplifier with a higher input level. Preamplifiers are necessary when an audio amplifier is to be used with low-output transducers such as magnetic phonograph pickups. A preamplifier may incorporate frequency-correcting networks to compensate for the frequency characteristics of a given input transducer and to make the frequency response of the preamplifier-amplifier combination uniform. SEE VOLTAGE AMPLIFIER.

The design of preamplifiers is critical because the input signal level is low and the amplification is high. The hum introduced by tubes and the noise voltages from resistors and vacuum tubes must be closely controlled. Furthermore, the preamplifier must be shielded from external magnetic fields that would otherwise induce stray voltages in the circuit. For a discussion of these undesirable conditions SEE AMPLIFIER.

*Harold F. Klock*

## Printed circuit

A generic term applied to circuits fabricated by any of several graphic art processes. Printed circuits greatly simplify mass production and increase equipment reliability. Their most important contribution, however, is the tremendous reduction achieved in size and weight of electronic devices. Printed circuits are used in practically all types of electronic equipment, radio and television sets, telephone systems units, electrical wiring behind automobile dashboards, guided-missile and airborne electronic equipment, computers, and industrial control equipment.

Advances in electronic equipment since World War II could not have been achieved without the sophisticated manufacturing processes made possible by graphic technology. Fabrication of very lightweight, extremely small equipment containing such devices as transistors, diodes, and integrated circuits depends upon the high precision attainable only through applied graphics. The rapid adoption of graphic art processes by industry is a demonstration of the effectiveness of those processes in achieving significant cost reduction and equipment miniaturization. SEE JUNCTION DIODE; SEMICONDUCTOR DIODE; TRANSISTOR.

Printed circuits are of interest to industry because:

1. They are the common denominator for almost all approaches to mechanized fabrication of electronic equipment.
2. Their use has greatly reduced the labor required for the wiring of an electronic circuit. This reduction is especially significant for small units used in computer and guided-missile requipment.
3. They can be manufactured uniformly because graphic art processes provide repeatable results.
4. Their uniformity improves the product through simplification of quality control.
5. Printed circuitry has helped to minimize unskilled labor and to greatly reduce one major cause of unreliability in electronic equipment (individually soldered connections) by permitting the use of dip-soldering rather than hand-soldering processes. (In dip soldering, connections between the electronic component and the conductor are exposed to molten solder and joined in one precisely controlled operation.)
6. Precision capabilities of graphic art processes (particularly in integrated circuits) have resulted in significant size and weight reductions, which are especially important in electronic equipment for such applications as medical instrumentation and space exploration.

### Technology

Printed circuit technology may be divided into three basic parts: engineering, photography, and manufacturing.

**Engineering.** The configuration in which circuit elements are located and the routing of conductor paths establish the precise circuit pattern. Using this pattern, an artwork master normally several times larger than the final size of the printed circuit is prepared. Scale depends on the type of circuit that is to be fabricated. Masters are prepared by applying matte-finished black or red tapes to a clear, stable-based material or by the cut-and-strip method, in which a photographically opaque coating on a stable base is cut and stripped away as necessary. The automation of the design for optimum location of circuit elements and of the preparation of masters using com-

**Fig. 1. In response to input commands from punched paper tape, this automatic photographic plotter accurately plots circuit patterns directly on a photographic glass plate, completing a typical 4 × 6 in. (10 × 15 cm) circuit pattern in 20–45 min. (*TRW Inc.*)**

puter programs for conductor routing and the use of automated photopolotting equipment (**Fig. 1**) have become essential as a result of increased circuit complexity and the need for greater accuracy.

**Photography.** Enlarged masters are photographically reduced to the required size within the allowable tolerance, thereby reducing any dimensional inaccuracies which have occurred in the master. When a number of circuits are to be fabricated simultaneously, precision step-and-repeat equipment provides a composite master, with each circuit precisely positioned relative to key indexing locations, and all identical.

A typical camera used for thin-film reductions, glass plate tooling, and first- and second-stage reductions of integrated circuit patterns requires that the three important vertical planes, the copyboard, lens, and plane of the film, maintain alignment within 5 seconds of arc; therefore, rigid construction is essential. Precision adjustment of the location of the copyboard relative to the lens must be provided so that reduction ratios can be very accurately controlled. Precision measuring equipment, such as optical vernier and comparator systems, permits the positioning and measurement of an image on the film or glass plate within ±0.0001 in. (±2.5 micrometers).

**Manufacturing.** The circuit pattern masters are used to fabricate the screens and masks for the application of photoresistive materials in the actual formation of the required patterns on the finished parts. The masters are also used in the preparation of numerous types of tooling, for example, drill templates, tapes for operation of numerical-tape-controlled drilling equipment (especially common where high precision is required), routing templates and dicing fixtures for trimming printed circuits to final configuration, and laminating and holding fixtures. Numerous processes (described later), including etching, screening, plating, laminating, vacuum deposition, diffusion, and application of protective coatings, are used in combination to produce various types of printed circuits. Completed printed circuits are inspected visually and dimensionally, using such techniques as microsectioning and infrared photospectrometer measurements in determining thicknesses of critical materials; in addition, they may be x-rayed and electrically tested to assure conformance to requirements. *See Printing.*

## Applications

Printed circuits can be divided, in terms of applications, into (1) printed wiring, (2) thick and thin films, (3) hybrid circuits, and (4) integrated circuits.

**Printed wiring.** Printed wiring is undoubtedly the most common type of printed circuit. The printed wiring board is a copper-clad dielectric material with conductors etched on one or both sides (**Fig. 2**). Single-sided boards are commonly used in such commercial applications as automotive equipment, radio and television sets, and, occasionally, in military electronic ground-support equipment in which space and weight are not critical.

Two-sided boards may use plated-through holes or eyelets to provide electrical continuity between the sides. They are used in those applications in which the maximum number of interconnections (conductors) in a given area are required for minimum cost. Typically such applications include airborne, shipboard, and a large percentage of missile and spacecraft equipment.

***Multilayer boards.*** Multilayer printed wiring boards capitalize on the reduced size of miniaturized and microelectronic parts and accommodate the increasing complexity of communication satellites which has caused increased density of circuitry. The surface area required for mounting of these subminiature parts and integrated circuit packages has decreased significantly while the number of interconnections has increased many-fold. Formerly, a part that occupied a given mounting areas had only two or three leads; today a part that occupies the same area may have 20 or more leads. In a multilayer board, conductors are located on several insulated internal layers. Common multilayer circuits consist of a number of two-sided etched copper foil boards, separated by an insulating layer (the prepreg) and laminated together under controlled temperature, pressure, and time. Feed-through and connection holes are drilled, and the cylindrical surface is plated by a chemical deposition process, then electroplated to form the interconnections between circuit layers or for the mounting of electronic parts (**Fig. 3***a*). The monolithic (or plated-up) approach to multilayer printed wiring boards (Fig. 3*b*) is also used, but to a much lesser degree due to higher costs and more difficult production processes.

Responding to the demand for greater miniaturization by reducing the circuit board size, conductor line widths as narrow as 0.02 in. (0.5 mm) and minimum spacing between conductors of 0.015 in. (0.4 mm) with up to eight layers (16 conductor surfaces) are common in space applications. The fabrication of a multilayer printed circuit is a precision manufacturing process requiring tight control of tolerances for both the conductor pattern and the indexing of each layer of the circuit board. Thus, only dimensionally stable glass-cloth-based plastic laminates are used. Due to their much lower cost, phenolic paper laminates are used as the base material on single- or two-sided printed circuits for consumer products and on some commercial equipment. The use of higher radio frequencies (1-GHz range) or more rapid response digital circuitry has required other than the 1-oz (28-g) or 2-oz (57-g) copper on an epoxy glass laminate, standard printed circuit board material. In the gigahertz range, polytrifluoromonochlorethylene (Teflon) glass is used as the laminate base for the copper foil. At still higher frequencies (above 3 GHz) a ceramic base material (substrate) such as alumina is used, and the conductors or circuit elements such as inductance and transmission lines are fabricated by a vacuum deposition process. In the 10-GHz range, synthetic sapphire is sometimes used on account of its superior

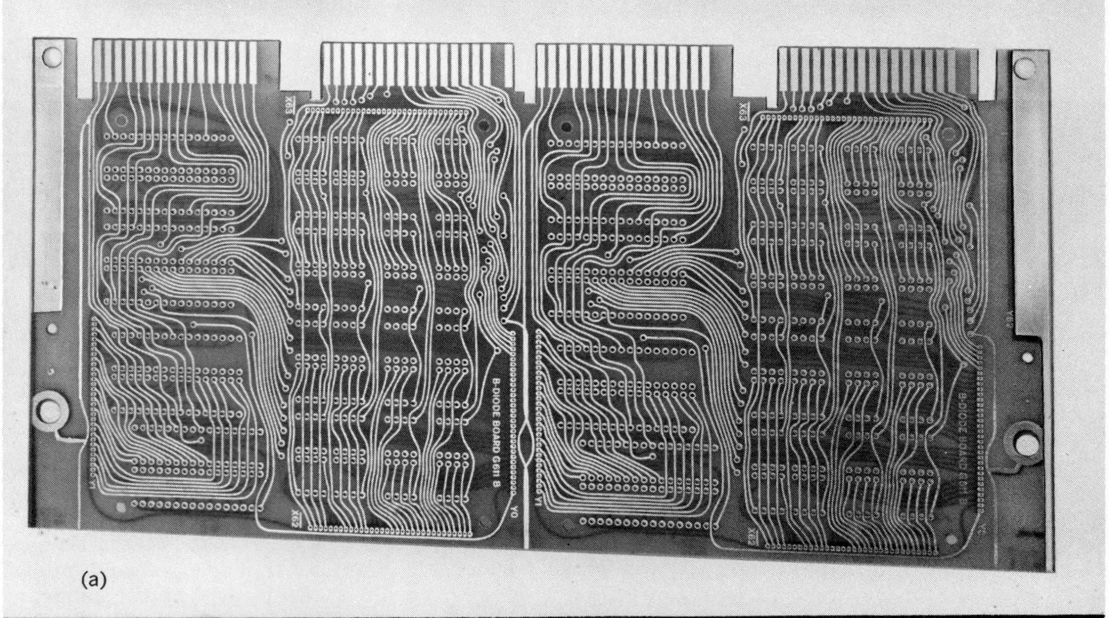

Fig. 2. Both sides of a printed circuit board after the etching and plating processes. (*a*) Component side. (*b*) Side that components are soldered to. (*Digital Equipment Corp., Maynard, Massachusetts*)

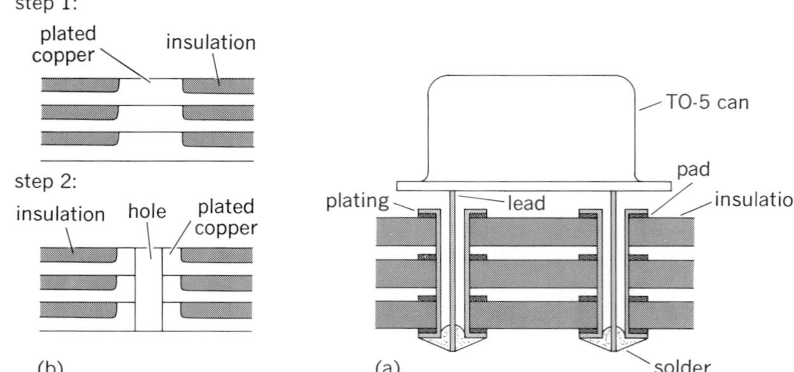


Fig. 3. Cross-sectional detail of multilayer printed wiring board. (*a*) TO-5 can is attached by its leads to a plated-through multilayer circuit. (*b*) Two steps in the fabrication of a hole in a plated monolithic multilayer circuit. (*TRW Inc.*)

dielectric properties, although high cost has limited its use. Polyimide glass is sometimes used to replace epoxy glass as the laminate base, especially when very narrow line widths are used. The polyimide material is stronger mechanically, but, even more important, it can withstand the high temperatures used for soldering components to the circuit board. This characteristic is especially useful when conductor widths are at a minimum 0.02 in. (0.5 mm).

***Heat dissipation.*** Heat-dissipating sinks for heat-generating components may be provided by leaving most of the copper clading intact on the surface on which the electronic parts are mounted; conductors are then routed on the opposite side or on internal layers of multilayer board. A metal sheet coated with a thermally conductive dielectric, such as hard-anodize thermal conductive aluminum oxide, with the circuit pattern bonded on the dielectric coating, may be used where large quantities of heat must be dissipated.

***Protective finish.*** The copper pattern on both single- and double-sided board and exposed layers of multilayer boards are normally given a protective finish, commonly either gold or tin-lead alloy to improve solderability. Tin-lead is used more often, when the assembly is to be dip-soldered.

***Flexible printed wiring.*** Flexible printed wiring (**Fig. 4**) is another form which reduces assembly line time significantly when used to interconnect subassemblies. Several layers of etched conductors may be sandwiched between thin, flexible, dielectric materials to form wiring between units in consoles and cabinets of ground-support equipment. This method of interconnection has the added feature of rigidly fixing the position of each conductor, thus controlling the electromagnetic and electrostatic coupling between circuits, and is especially advantageous at high frequencies.

***Connections.*** Methods most often used to attach parts to printed wiring boards are: soldering leads in terminal holds to surrounding pads which are part of the conductive pattern and lap soldering or thermocompression bonding of flat leads to pads on the surface of the board (**Fig. 5**).

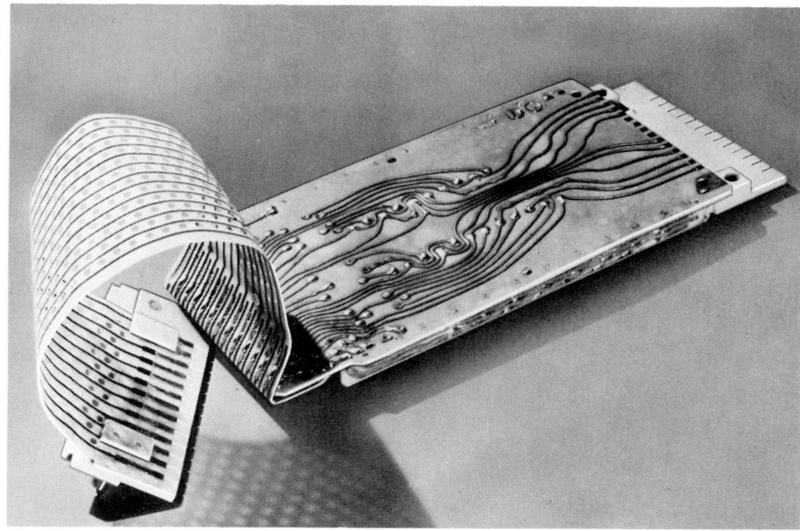

**Fig. 4. Flexible printed wiring, used to interconnect subassemblies. (*Technical Liaison Co., Inglewood, California, and Flexible Circuits Inc., Warrington, Pennsylvania*)**

## Thick-film circuits.

Thick-film circuits (**Fig. 6**) consist of such passive elements as resistors, capacitors, and inductors deposited on wafers or substrates of such dielectric materials as ceramic, glass, porcelain-coated metal, and the like. They are used commercially for mass fabrication of passive networks for use in linear microcircuits and large-signal digital modules. A large-scale electronic computer may contain millions of these circuits. Thick-film design and manufacture are usually based on film thickness of approximately 0.001 in. (25 μm).

Each type of circuit element requires: (1) a master pattern defining the configuration of the specific element or portion of the element; this pattern is commonly 5–25 times actual size; (2) a precision photographic reduction within ±0.005 in. (±125 μm) of actual size and within ±0.002 in. (±50 μm) of the other patterns in a set; (3) a photolithographically prepared stainless steel stencil of the pattern; (4) deposition of the appropriate ink through the stencil; (5) air-drying of the film; and (6) firing at an elevated temperature.

***Resistor networks.*** Typically, a printed resistor network consists of a pattern using resistive inks and a conductor. The inks are high-viscosity mixtures of precious metals or precious metal oxides and a vitreous binder suspended in an organic vehicle. After being printed in the designed pattern on the dielectric, these inks are fired at a temperature of approximately 1380°F (750°C), and a conductor pattern of silver or gold inks is then printed in registration and fired at temperatures ranging from 1560 to 1830°F (850 to 1000°C). Printed resistances range from 10 to $10^6$ ohms and are determined by varying the type of ink used, the aspect ratio (the ratio of length to width) of the rectangular pattern, and, to some extent, the thickness of the film.

Through careful process control and minimized master and photographic tolerances, resistive values within ± 5% can be produced. When tighter tolerances are required, the resistive value may be adjusted by abrading the surface or one edge of the pattern. Thus the resistive element is formed with a value below that required and then adjusted upward to fall within design tolerance limits. The stability of the resistance depends primarily upon the type of ink used. In general, resins or glass binders cured at higher temperatures provide the more stable resistances; therefore, an epoxy or silicone binder provides a more stable resistance than that obtained with a phenolic binder. Stability can be improved by aging at high temperatures.

Carbon inks fired at temperatures between 150 and 600°F (65 and 315°C) are frequently used in the manufacture of printed resistors in such consumer products as radios or television sets which the tolerance requirements and operating environment are not too severe. *See* RESISTOR.

***Capacitances.*** Printed capacitive elements are formed by first depositing a base electrode of the same material as that of the conductor patterns, then depositing a dielectric film (barium titanate, titanium dioxide, and borosilicate glass frit being among those commonly used) fired at approximately 1440°F (775°C), and finally, depositing the counter electrode and connection to the conductor pattern. Capacitors fabricated in this manner generally range in value from 10 to $10^8$ picofarads, depending n the area used (3000–8000 picofarads/cm$^2$/mil of dielectric thickness or 75,000–200,000 picofarads/cm$^2$/μm) and the type of dielectric material. Capacitances can be adjusted after fabrication by: (1) providing several small parallel trimming capacitances integral with the basic capacitance; (2) fabricating the capacitor on the high side of the desired value; (3) severing the trimming capacitances as required to reduce the total value to

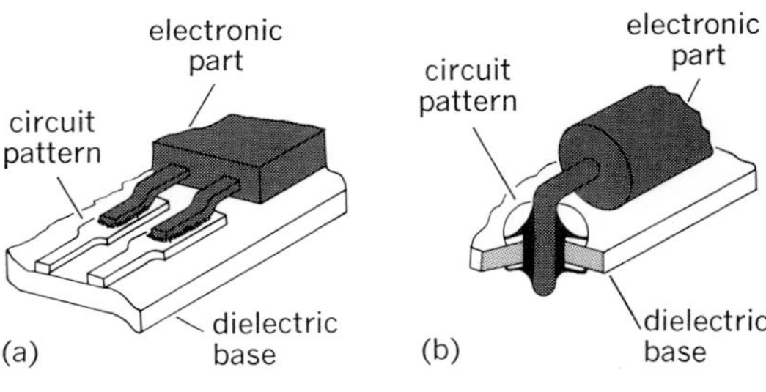


**Fig. 5. Methods for attaching parts to printed wiring boards. (*a*) Swaged or welded connections. (*b*) Soldered connections. (*TRW Inc.*)**

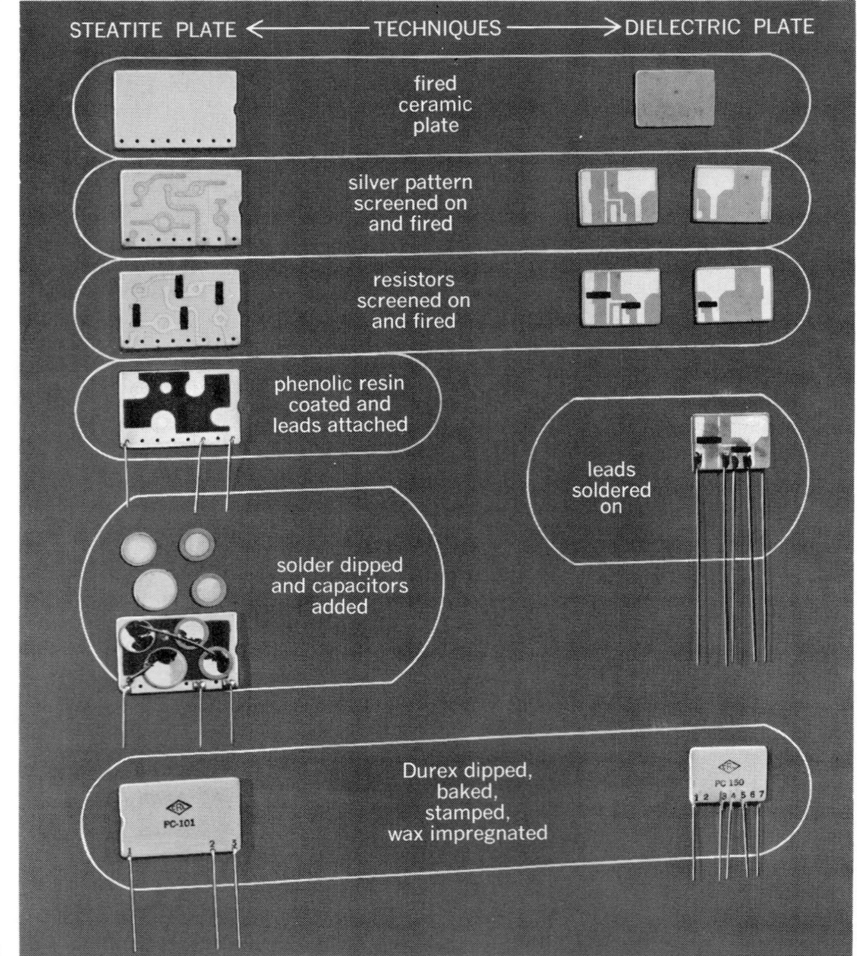

(a)

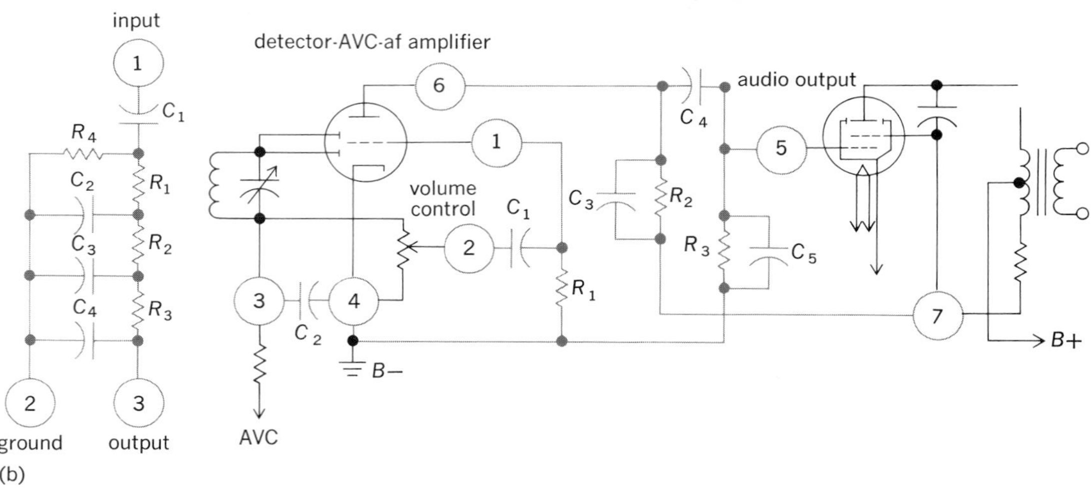

(b)

**Fig. 6. A printed circuit on ceramic-base materials. (*a*) Circuits in left column screened on a steatite ceramic with barium titanate ceramic capacitors soldered to base. Circuits on right column screened on a high-electric-constant ceramic. The base plate is used as the dielectric for the capacitor formed by screening a conductive area on opposite sides of the plate. (*b*) Schematics of circuits in *a* (color). Circuit on right in representative situation. AVC = automatic volume control; af = audio frequency. (*Centralab Div., Globe Union, Inc.*)**

within ±1% of the nominal capacitance. *See* Capacitance.

Printed capacitors are also fabricated by screening the electrodes on opposite sides of a ceramic wafer with a high dielectric constant, such as one of the titanates. The dielectric constant of the titanates, however, varies widely with temperature; thus these capacitors are temperature-sensitive and are limited to circuits that can accommodate wide circuit tolerances.

***Inductors.*** Inductors in the form of printed spiral patterns of conductive inks are sometimes used. Inductances ranging from 1 to 900 microhenries are attainable. Use of ferrite coupling increases these values fivefold; however, the increased surface area required for printed inductors at frequencies lower than 10 MHz generally makes the use of other types of inductors desirable. SEE INDUCTOR.

***Protective coatings.*** Resistive and capacitive elements are commonly coated with glass or nonhygroscopic resins to protect the elements from environmental effects and from other processing operations, such as solder coating or electroplating, which may be applied to conductor and inductor patterns in order to improve conductivity and solderability.

**Thin-film circuits.** The deposition of thin films was the first application of printed circuit technology to microelectronics. Like thick-film circuits, thin-film circuits consist primarily of passive elements; however, such active elements as field-effect transistors and diode devices are becoming available. The most important operational difference between thick- and thin-film circuits is that thin films have greater precision and stability. Some important characteristics of thin-film circuits are: (1) Films with a uniform thickness in the range from $5 \times 10^{-6}$ to $5 \times 10^{-3}$ mm can be vacuum-deposited and controlled by measuring the resistance across a test pattern during deposition to ensure that final thicknesses are within design limits; (2) patterns formed during deposition or by selective etching afterward are much more precisely controlled than those which are stenciled, as in thick-film circuits; and (3) more stable thin-film resistive materials can be used than those in thick-film circuits. Because of this precision and stability, thin-film circuits are frequently used in such aerospace and industrial electronics as differential amplifiers, ladder networks, and dc-to-ac signal converters.

**Fig. 7. Using a coordinatograph, designers prepare artwork for a thin-film circuit pattern. (*TRW Inc.*)**

Master artwork for the circuit pattern is prepared at 25 times actual size using cut-and-strip material. The pattern is cut on a coordinatograph (**Fig. 7**) which is dimensionally accurate within ±0.0015 in. (±40 μm). Temperature, humidity, and dust control of the area in which the masters are prepared and photoprocessed is essential.

***Resistor networks.*** Resistor networks (**Fig. 8**) are generally formed in one of two ways: The resistor pattern is formed on a substrate by vacuum-depositing resistive material on the substrate through a metal mask (**Fig. 9**), and the conductor pattern (frequently gold over nichrome) is added in a subsequent vacuum deposition cycle; or patterns are photoetched directly on a substrate on which the resistive and conductive materials have been previously deposited. The latter technique has proved to be more practical for complex networks; however, use of standard metal masks in automatic processing equipment is less expensive. The most commonly used resistive material is nichrome (80% nickel, 20% chromium alloy), which is used to form resistive elements ranging from 100 to 75,000 ohms—current state of the art permits a maximum of approximately 6 to 8 megohms total per square inch (0.9 to 1.2 megohms/cm$^2$). Resistances are established and adjusted in basically the same manner as thick films by varying material, aspect ratio of the pattern, and film thickness; however, trimming is normally accomplished by providing in parallel several small resistive elements which may be disconnected from the primary resistive element by etching or diamond scribing as necessary to increase the total resistance. This trimming technique can be used to reduce the +5% as-fabricated tolerance to within ±1%. Because of the high stability and durability of nichrome, resistor networks of this type have been utilized in aircraft servomechanisms since World War II.

A second type of resistive material is a ceramic-metallic film commonly called cermet, which is formed by the simultaneous evaporation of chromium and silicone monoxide (or similar materials). Cermet has a much higher resistivity than nichrome and therefore requires less space for equivalent resistances. Cermet resistors are not as stable as those of

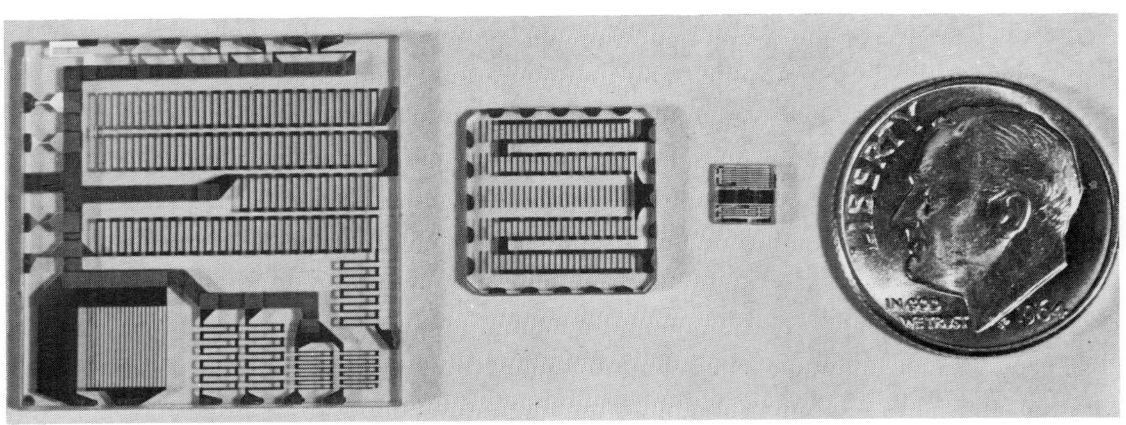


**Fig. 8. Three thin-film resistor networks, with 10-cent coin for size comparison. (*TRW Inc.*)**

nichrome. For these reasons, their use is generally limited to integrated circuits in which space is critical and subsequent processing of the circuit improves stability.

***Capacitances.*** Thin-film capacitors are vacuum-deposited using masks similar to those shown in Fig. 9. The method of fabricating and adjusting values of thin-film capacitors is basically identical to that used for thick-film capacitors (by deposition of a base electrode, dielectric, and counterelectrode, with provision for trimming capacitances, and so on). Some dielectric materials that have been used include silicon monoxide, silicon dioxide, magnesium fluoride, zinc sulfide, and tantalum pentoxide. Typical capacitances range 0.025–0.032 microfarad/in.$^2$ (3.9 to 5.0 nanofarad/cm$^2$) with voltage ratings of 25–50 V per micrometer of dielectric thickness.

***Post-deposition treatments.*** To accelerate stabilization by oxidation of the surfaces, complete circuits are frequently coated or encapsulated in resins following attachment of leads to provide both mechanical support and environmental protection.

**Hybrid circuits.** Thick thin-film hybrid circuits (**Fig. 10**) consist of one or more substrates upon which the passive elements of the circuit (resistor networks and inductances) have been deposited and to which discrete components (such as diodes, transistors, integrated circuits, capacitors, and inductors) have been attached by split-tip series resistance welding or by thermocompression bonding, or by soldering (thick-film hybrids only). After components and external leads are attached, the circuit is normally encapsulated in a resin compound. Hybrid circuits allow advantageous use of thick- and thin-film fabrication techniques for such applications as complex switching circuits and differential amplifiers in the form of functional electronic building blocks.

At microwave frequencies (above 1 GHz) the spatial configuration of the circuit elements and the dielectric constant and dielectric losses of the base or substrate material become important; thus, hybrid circuits used at these frequencies are constructed on alumina (aluminum dioxide) ceramic or synthetic sapphire as the substrate. Conductors, inductances, and transmission lines are formed by vacuum deposition, etching, and electroplating using a photographic process very similar to that for the etched circuit board. Other circuit elements and active devices are then soldered to the conductor pattern.

**Integrated circuits.** An integrated circuit is a semiconductor device with both active and passive elements diffused into a silicon wafer to form a functional circuit. Because of the tremendous size reduction and long life, many applications are found in aerospace equipment besides consumer and industrial uses. Many of the fabrication processes for integrated circuits such as photomasking, selective etching, and photoreduction are similar to those used in the manufacture of printed circuits. SEE INTEGRATED CIRCUITS.

## MANUFACTURING PROCESSES

Commonly used printed-circuit manufacturing processes may be divided roughly into three main groups listed in the order of greatest acceptance: (1) material removal, (2) film deposition, and (3) mold and die.

**Material removal.** Of the material-removal processes, photoetching and stencil etching are probably the most widely used techniques. They are used primarily in the fabrication of printed wiring.

***Photoetching.*** In photoetching, the etchant-resist (conductor) pattern is formed photographically. The copper foil is coated with a photosensitive emulsion. A photographic negative of the circuit pattern is su-

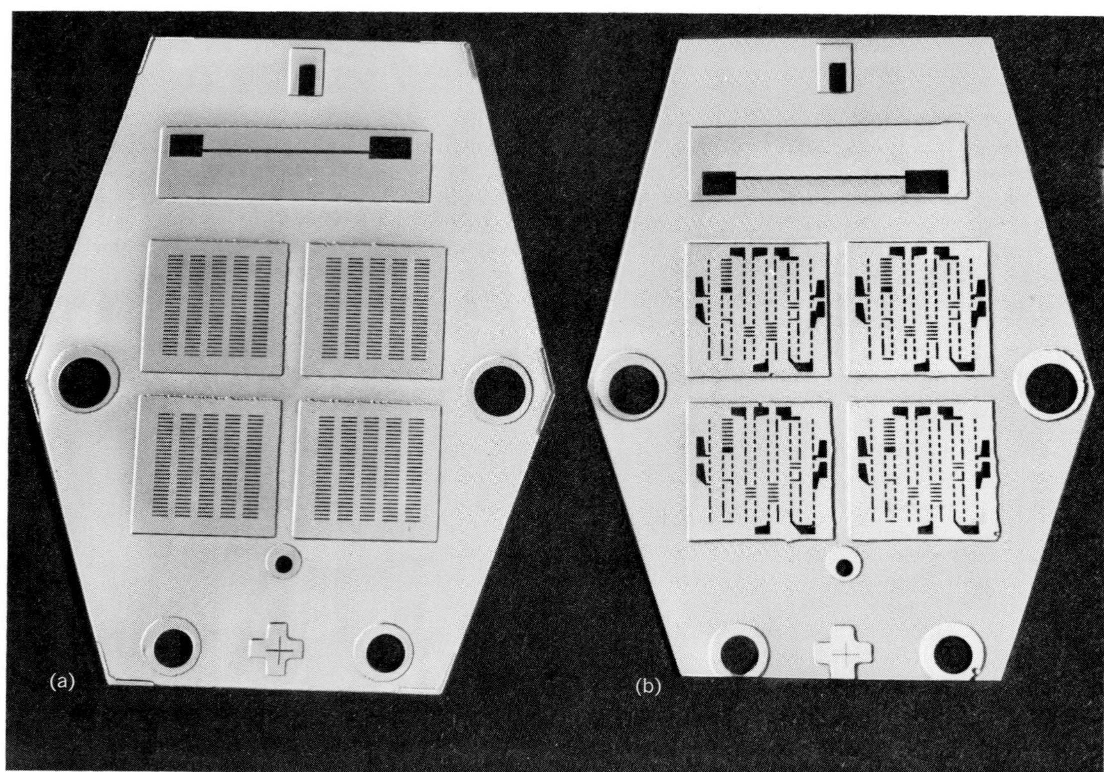


**Fig. 9. Metal masks for vacuum deposition of thin-film resistors. (*a*) Pattern for resistive elements. (*b*) Pattern for interconnection circuits. Conductor pattern is added in subsequent cycle. (*TRW Inc.*)**

**Fig. 10. Hybrid circuit that combines lumped-constant components and printed-circuit techniques. It forms part of the receiver shown above it. (*TRW Inc.*)**

perimposed on the emulsion and exposed to ultraviolet light. This method is similar to that for the production of a photographic positive. During exposure the photoemulsion hardens. The plate is then placed in alcohol to dissolve the unexposed emulsion from the copper foil. The exposed areas are left covered by the hardened emulsion, which serves to protect the copper foil during the subsequent etching process. The uncovered copper is next dissolved in an acid or ferric chloride etchant bath. Finally, the hardened emulsion is dissolved from the exposed areas, leaving the copper conductor pattern.

An alternate method, which is as commonly used, exposes the emulsion by using a positive of the circuit pattern. The unexposed emulsion is removed; the final plating (gold or tin-lead) for the board is electroplated on the exposed circuit pattern; the emulsion is removed; and the board is etched using the gold or tin-lead plating for the etchant resist.

***Stencil etching.*** In stencil etching, the protective film that forms the circuit pattern is applied by a printing process such as silk screening. The protective film, usually an enamel, is dried, and the exposed copper is etched as previously described. This method is not as precise as the photoetching technique; however, it is a more rapid and less expensive method of applying the etchant resist.

**Film deposition.** Stencil screening and electroplating are the processes most often used for deposition of materials to form resistances or capacitances. Photoelectrostatic techniques have also been developed, primarily for the fabrication of conductive elements.

***Screening.*** Commonly used screens consist of a photosensitive film over a finely woven stainless steel screen. The stencil is usually formed by a photographic process similar to that used for the photoetching process mentioned above. Films are applied in the same manner as in silk screening.

***Vacuum deposition.*** For vacuum deposition, films are deposited on the substrate by evaporating material (ultimately the film) in a vacuum of $10^{-5}$ torr ($10^{-3}$ pascal) or lower (**Fig. 11**). At these pressures, the mean free path of the evaporated molecules or atoms exceeds the chamber dimensions sufficiently so that they travel in an essentially straight line between the source and the substrate. Source temperatures high enough to reach vapor pressures of $10^{-1}$ to $10^{-3}$ torr (10 to $10^{-1}$ Pa) for the source material are usually

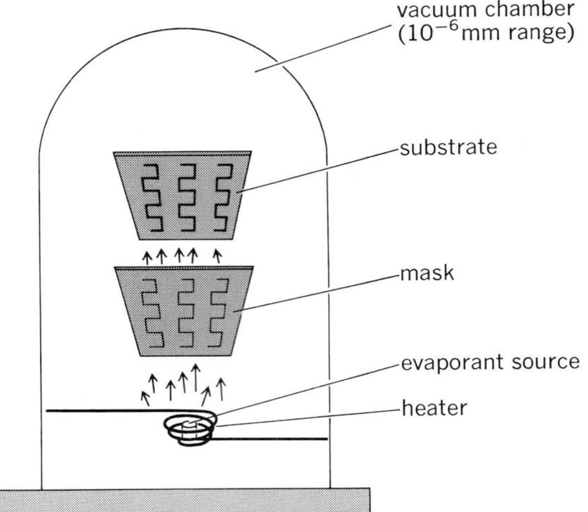


**Fig. 11. Schematic representation of basic thin-film vacuum deposition. (*TRW Inc.*)**

sufficient; such temperatures are in the 1500–2800°F (1100–1800 K) range. Metal masks may be used within the vacuum to deposit specific patterns, or the entire surface of the substrates may be covered.

***Plating.*** A plastic laminate, such as paper-base phenolic or epoxy-glass, is first coated with a material that conducts electricity. This may be done by depositing a thin (0.0001 in. or 2.5 μm) silver coating on the surface of the laminate in much the same way that mirrors are silvered. The silver film is then coated with a plating resist, usually an enamel, by stenciling, leaving exposed the area that will form the circuit pattern. The plating process is similar to that for the plating of decorative metals. After sufficient thickness (usually 0.001–0.005 in. or 25–135 μm) of copper is deposited, the plating resist is removed by a solvent. The exposed silver film is removed by acid etching, leaving the much thicker copper plating to form the circuit pattern on the plastic sheet. The bond strength between the conductor pattern and the base material resulting from this process is, however, relatively poor.

For electronic circuits that may be subjected to high humidity and continuous application of voltages (such that conditions for silver migration exist), the chemical reduction of copper instead of silver is used to form the plating electrode. All the subsequent processes are as described above. This approach is commonly used in the formation of plated-through holes in double-sided and multilayer printed wiring boards for the purpose of connecting one layer to another.

**Mold and die processes.** Of the mold and die processes, embossing and stamping are the most popular (**Fig. 12**). In general, these two processes are used for the fabrication of conductors or inductances. Usually copper foil is embossed on a phenolic laminate base plate, or powdered silver is stamped on a plastic sheet. Because of the relatively high cost of tooling and the limitations in circuit fabrication, these processes have not gained wide use.

*L. K. Lee*

**Fig. 12. Mold and die process. Closeup of machine embossing a copper foil circuit pattern onto a phenolic-paper laminate. The copper foil, feeding into the machine from left to right, has a temperature-sensitive adhesive on the undersurface. During the embossing operation a hot die cuts the circuit pattern, embeds the edges of the conductors into the phenolic, and temperature-cures the adhesive so that it forms a bond with the base plate. (*Courtesy of A. W. Franklin*)**

***Bibliography.*** C. J. Baer and J. R. Ottaway, *Electrical and Electronics Drawings*, 4th ed., 1980; C. Coombs, Jr., *Printed Circuits Handbook*, 2d ed., 1979; W. S. DeForest, *Photoresist: Materials and Processes*, 1975; J. Goldberg, *How to Make Printed Circuit Boards*, 1980; Institute of Electrical and Electronics Engineers, *Transactions on Components, Hybrids and Manufacturing Technology* (journal); W. S. Kinowitz, *Designing and Creating Printed Circuits*, 1981; D. Lindsey, *The Design and Drafting of Printed Circuit Boards*, 2d ed., 1983; P. Lund, *Generation of Precision Artwork for Printed Circuit Boards*, 1978.

## Privacy systems (scrambling)

Hardware devices or software methods for ensuring the security and integrity of voice, data, and video transmissions. Various techniques that are commonly utilized to perform such scrambling are discussed in this article.

**Voice.** The most simple method involves splitting the voice frequency spectrum in half by using filters and then shifting and reversing the halves for transmission; the reverse process takes place at the receiving end. This process is called simple inversion. *See* Electric filter.

A similar but more complex and more secure method involves dividing the voice frequency spectrum into five or six narrow bands, also using filters. These bands may then be selectively interchanged on a periodic basis via switches (for example, hourly, daily, weekly) or every few seconds automatically.

The most secure method is digital voice scrambling. This involves first converting the speech to binary digital form, which results in a data stream typically between 16,000 and 64,000 bits per second. Devices that do this are called analog-to-digital converters. The digital data are then scrambled, as discussed below. The scrambled data are either converted back to analog form or they are transmitted digitally, depending on the transmission medium; the reverse process takes place at the receiving end. *See* Analog-to-digital converter; Digital-to-analog converter.

**Data.** Scrambling data involves breaking up the data stream into fixed-length blocks and then performing a binary addition of a cipher word to each block. These ciphers may be of varying lengths from one form of code to another.

In addition, a feature that makes data-scrambling methods such as the Data Encryption Standard (DES) most secure is one which allows the cipher word to be periodically varied, based on a software algorithm and starting with a key word. Thus, high-quality privacy systems involve two levels of scrambling. *See Cryptography.*

**Video.** Video signals may be scrambled by a number of different methods. Fundamental to the understanding of three of these methods is the knowledge that a video picture consists of either 525 or 625 lines, and each such line is an analog signal consisting of synchronization, audio, luminance (black and white), and chrominance (color) information. *See Television.*

In the most simple scrambling method, the synchronization signal at the beginning of each transmitted video line is inverted; this prohibits a television receiver from properly displaying the received video information. In a second, similar method, the entire synchronization signal is removed or suppressed from each line of the picture. This approach virtually assures that a television receiver will not be able to acquire or "lock-on" to the transmitted image. However, since the video lines are transmitted in their proper sequence, an unauthorized receiver can sometimes get an idea of the picture content. Television cable systems sometimes utilize one of these two techniques. *See Closed-circuit television.*

To make unauthorized reception even more difficult, an approach known as line scrambling is utilized. That is, the lines making up the video image are transmitted out of sequence, as defined by a pseudorandom code which changes periodically. Since the synchronization signal is still present, the receiver can "lock-on" to the picture, but due to the scrambling method the displayed image is completely indecipherable.

The final scrambling method used for video is to convert the analog video information to digital form (data) and then to scramble it as described above. This technique is quite costly due to the requirements of digitizing a video signal.

*John J. Bleiweis*

***Bibliography.*** A. M. McCalmont, Achieving secure communications, *Defense Sys. Rev.*, pp. 30–35, January 1985; D. MacMillan, Single chip encrypts data at 14 MB/s, *Electronics*, 54(12):161–165, June 16, 1981; J. M. Nye, Data communication: To encrypt or not to encrypt, *Ind. Res. Dev.*, 24(5):122–126, March 1982; J. M. Nye, Satellite communications and vulnerability, *Computerworld*, 16(17):57–66, April 26, 1982.

## Programming languages

Notations with which people can communicate algorithms to computers and to one another. To accomplish this, programmers specify a sequence of operations to be applied to data objects. *See Algorithm.*

Computers process a rather low-level machine language, which has simple instructions (load, add, and so forth) and data (for example, words or partial words including those containing instructions). Example (1) shows machine code that assigns the absolute value of B − C to A.

| *Location* | *Machine code* | *Meaning* | |
|---|---|---|---|
| 040003 | 100020040001 | load B into register A1 | |
| 040004 | 250320040002 | subtract C from register A1 | |
| 040005 | 741020040007 | GOTO 040007 if A1 positive | (1) |
| 040006 | 110020000000 | negate A1 | |
| 040007 | 010020040000 | store contents of A1 into A | |

Writing in machine code places a tremendous burden on the programmers. They must write in an unusual number base (for example, eight), and transfer data from memory to registers in order to perform operations. They must know the machine's operation codes for the operations. [These appear in the first two digits of the machine code in example (1). Thus, load is 10; branch is 74; store is 01.] Finally, they must know the addresses of the operands (both registers and data words) and instructions (to be able to skip some operations with branches). In example (1) the last five digits give the address of one operand. Thus A is at 40000, B at 40001, C at 40002, and the target of the branch instruction at location 40005 is the instruction at 40007.

The introduction of assembler languages eased communication between programmers and machines by permitting symbolic rather than numeric or positional references for operation codes (opcodes) and addresses. Additional data and instructions could therefore be added to a program without changes to existing instructions. Thus, in example (2), which shows assembler code that assigns the absolute value of B − C to A, instructions could be added between the branch positive, BP, and its destination.

| *Label* | *Op-code* | *Operands* | *Comments* | |
|---|---|---|---|---|
| | L | A1, B | | |
| | AN | A1, C | ·A1 := B − C | (2) |
| | BP | A1, NEXT | | |
| | N | A1 | ·A1 := − A1 | |
| | S | NEXT A1, A | · A := \|B − C\| | |

Unfortunately, assembler language does not go very far in improving programmers' ability to communicate algorithms. A programmer must still be concerned with expressing algorithms in a form suitable to particular machines. For instance, if an expression requires more registers than are available, the programmer must create temporary variables to hold partial results of expressions. High-level languages allow programmers to communicate more easily with one another by providing structures that hide the architecture of the machine. Expressions in high-level languages can be written almost as they are in algebra so that the programmer need not worry about which register contains a particular computation or which registers are available. Higher-level control structures like the IF statement make it easier to see the overall structure of a program than do low-level branch instructions. High-level language code for assigning the absolute value of B − C to A is shown in example (3).

```
A := B−C;
IF A < 0                (3)
  THEN
    A := −A
```

*See* DIGITAL COMPUTER PROGRAMMING; DIGITAL COMPUTERS.

### Structure of Programming Languages

The components of a program and their relationships are shown in **Fig. 1**. The basic executable unit of a programming language is a program. Programs contain declarations of data and procedures, and a sequence of statements to be executed.

**Objects, variables, and identifiers.** Programming languages manipulate objects or values like integers or files. Objects are referred to by their names, called identifiers. Constant objects, such as the number 2 (one of whose names is the literal "2"), do not change. Variable objects may contain either other objects or the names of other objects. The same identifier may denote different objects at different places in the program or at different times during execution. Also, a single object may have several names, or aliases. Variable and constant identifiers are introduced by data declarations. Declarations (4) introduce the constant KilometersPerMile (whose value is 0.6) and the variables Miles, Hours, and MilesPerHour. Notice that in this example the object 0.6 has two names.

```
CONST
  KilometersPerMile = 0.6;
                                      (4)
VAR
  Miles, Hours, MilesPerHour;
```

**Expressions.** Expressions combine objects and operators to yield new objects. They may be written in one of several forms. Infix operators appear between their operands, as in expression (5); prefix operators precede their operands, as in expression (6); and postfix operators follow their operands, as in expression (7). Most languages adopt infix notation for binary operators and prefix notation for unary operators. However, LISP uses only prefix operators and FORTH uses only postfix operators.

```
B * B − 4 * A * C                     (5)
(− (* B B)(* (* 4 A) C))              (6)
((B B *)((4 A *) C *) −)              (7)
```

Two ideas govern the order in which infix operators are applied to their operands in expressions: precedence and associativity. Operators of higher precedence are evaluated before those of lower precedence. A typical operator precedence hierarchy is shown in (8). Operators with equal precedence are usually left associative, that is, they are evaluated from left to right.

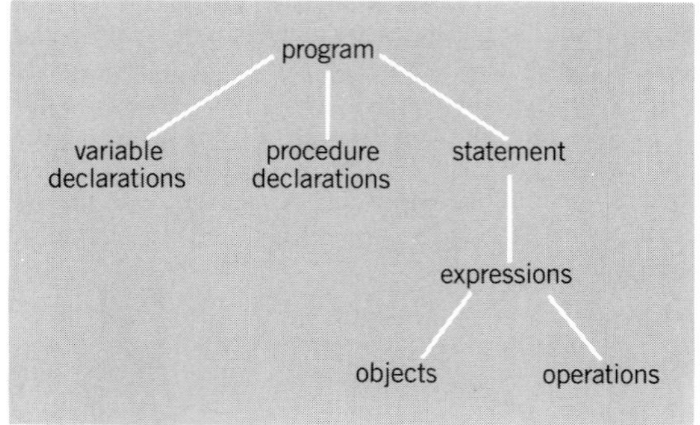


Fig. 1. Components of a high-level language.

```
Highest precedence   *(multiply)/(divide)
        |            +(add) − (subtract)
        |            < <= = <> > >=
        |              (relationals)          (8)
        |            NOT
        ↓            AND
Lowest precedence    OR
```

Not all languages using infix notation have the same operator precedence or associativity. PASCAL has fewer levels in its precedence hierarchy: NOT has the highest precedence, AND has the same precedence as *, and OR has the same precedence as +. APL has no precedence among its operators, which are right associative. Thus 5 − 4 + 3 has the value −2 in APL.

**Statements.** Important types of statements include assignment statements, compound statements, conditional statements, repetitive statements, and GOTO statements.

***Assignment statements.*** Assignment statements assign values to variables. In an assignment of form (9), the value in the object denoted by B is assigned to the object denoted by A. The order of evaluation of the two sides of an assignment statement differs among languages—some insist on left-to-right evaluation, while others leave the order of evaluation undefined. Some languages permit the same value to be assigned to several variables in a single statement; for example, the value of C can be assigned to both A and B by using statements (10). Other languages, like C (which uses the symbol = for assignment), treat assignment just like any other operator in an expression. Thus statement (11) assigns C + 2 to B and C + 5 to A.

```
A := B                                (9)
A, B := C        {PL/1}               (10)
A := B := C      {ALGOL 60}
A = (B = C + 2) + 3                   (11)
```

***Compound statements.*** A compound statement (12) groups a sequence of statements into a single statement. Execution of statements within a sequence of statements is in the order in which the statements appear in the sequence.

```
BEGIN stmt1; stmt2; . . . stmtn END   (12)
```

***Conditional statements.*** The IF statement (13) allows a programmer to indicate that a statement is to be executed if a stated condition is true. If the expression is true, the statement following the THEN is executed followed by the statement after the IF statement. If the expression is false, the statement is skipped. Many languages permit execution of one of two alternate statements with the form of IF statement (14). If the expression is true, statement 1 is executed; otherwise statement 2 is executed. In either case, execution continues with the statement after the IF.

```
IF expression THEN statement                        (13)
IF expression THEN statement1 ELSE statement2       (14)
```

***Repetitive statements.*** One of the advantages offered by computers is performing the same operations repetitively. Two statements in programming languages support this kind of execution: FOR and WHILE. The FOR statement (15) is generally used when a programmer knows how many times a statement is to be executed. The statement is executed a number of times given by (16), where expression1 and expression2 are the first and second expressions in statement (15). For example, statement (17) will write "hello" three times (2 − 0 + 1 = 3). If the first expression is greater than the second, the statement is not executed. While the statement is executed, the variable identifier (called the control variable) takes on successive values from the list (18).

```
FOR variable-identifier :=
  expression TO expression DO statement   (15)
```

```
expression2 − expression1 + 1   (16)
```

```
FOR i:= 0 to 2 DO   (17)
  write ("hello")
```

```
<expression1, expression1 + 1,
        . . . , expression2>   (18)
```

Usually the control variable may not be assigned to within the loop, and its value is usually considered to be undefined at the end of execution of the FOR statement. The two expressions are evaluated once at the start of execution of the FOR statement rather than each time the statement is executed. Thus, changing the values of the variables in these expressions has no effect on the number of times the statement is executed, as is illustrated in example (19). The statement is executed five times, even though the values of First and Last are changed during execution. The results printed by this statement are shown in (20).

```
First := 1;
Last := 5;
FOR Index := First TO Last DO
  BEGIN                                  (19)
    First := First + 1;
    Last := Last − 1;
    write (Index, First, Last)
  END
```

| Index | First | Last |
|---|---|---|
| 1 | 2 | 4 |
| 2 | 3 | 3 |
| 3 | 4 | 2 |
| 4 | 5 | 1 |
| 5 | 6 | 0 |

(20)

The WHILE statement (21) is used when continued execution depends on a condition that is true for an unknown number of repetitions. The statement is executed as long as the expression is true. When the expression becomes false, execution continues with the statement after the WHILE. The code fragment (22) can be used to approximate the square root of N by successive approximation.

```
WHILE expression DO statement   (21)
```

```
WHILE abs (X − N/X) > 0.1 DO   (22)
  X := 0.5 * (X+ N/X)
```

While the two approximations of the square root, X and N/X, differ by more than 0.1 (that is, the absolute value of their difference is greater than 0.1), new approximations are computed. After some unknown number of iterations, the difference between the two approximations is small enough and execution of the WHILE statement ceases.

***GOTO statements.*** The lowest-level control statement in most languages is the GOTO statement (23). This statement provides for the direct transfer of control to a statement labeled with the identifier that is the argument of the GOTO statement.

```
GOTO identifier   (23)
```

Any of the previous conditional or repetitive statements can be simulated with GOTO statements. For example, the previous WHILE statement would appear as (24).

```
Test: IF abs (X − N/X) < 0.1 THEN GOTO Done;
      X := 0.5 * (X + N/X);                  (24)
      GOTO Test;
Done: . . .
```

Many programming languages have eliminated the GOTO statement because it widens the gap between the textual structure and execution-time behavior of a program's source text. Control can transfer to a label from almost any GOTO statement in a program, and GOTO statements can be either forward or backward jumps. In addition, GOTO statements can affect storage allocation in many languages.

**Procedures.** As problems grow more complex, they must be divided into subproblems that can be solved independently. This approach to problem solving is supported by procedure declations, which group sequences of statements together and associate identifiers with the statements. A procedure identifier abstracts the details of the computation carried out by the statements of the procedure by encapsulating them. Procedures also help reduce the size of a program by permitting similar code to be written only once.

Procedure declarations, whose form is shown in (25), look just like programs, except they start with the word PROCEDURE instead of "program." In some languages each procedure has its own local data and procedure declarations. Since execution begins with the first statement of a program, the sequence of statements of a procedure can be executed only if they are explicitly invoked by a procedure-call statement containing the name of the procedure.

```
PROCEDURE ProcedureName;
  {data declarations}
  {procedure declarations}          (25)
  BEGIN {ProcedureName}
    {Sequence of statements}
  END {ProcedureName}
```

When the name of a procedure appears in a sequence of statements the procedure is called; that is, execution of the current sequence is suspended and the statement sequence associated with the procedure name in its declaration is executed. When execution of this sequence is completed, execution resumes in the previous sequence right after the procedure statement.

The designers of ALGOL 60 defined the effect of a procedure statement in terms of textual substitution. Their definition has come to be known as the copy rule. Essentially, the copy rule states that each procedure statement can be replaced by a compound statement containing the text of the procedure.

A procedure declaration is called recursive if it contains a procedure-call statement that invokes the procedure being defined. The WHILE statement that approximates the square root of N could be replaced by program fragment (26). If the approximation was not close enough, a new estimate would be assigned to X, execution of the current sequence of statements would be suspended, and control would be transferred to the first statement of a new copy of Approximate.

```
PROCEDURE Approximate;
  BEGIN {Approximate}
    IF abs(X − N/X) > 0.1
      THEN
        BEGIN
          X := 0.5 * (X + N/X);
          Approximate                          (26)
        END
  END; {Approximate}
BEGIN
    . . .;
    Approximate;
    . . .
END
```

When the approximation is close, the current copy of the procedure terminates and control is returned to the statement following the last procedure invocation. Since there are no more statements in this copy of the procedure, it also returns to a previous copy, which returns to a previous copy, and so forth. Eventually control returns to the statement after the first call of Approximate (indicated by ellipses). As this example demonstrates, recursion is not always the most efficient technique to use in problem solving. However, it can be a valuable tool in divide-and-conquer approaches to problem solving. With the exception of FORTRAN and COBOL, most programming languages support this feature.

## DATA TYPES

Data types are sets of values and the operations that can be performed on them. Data types offer programmers two principal advantages: abstraction and authentication. Data types hide representational details from programmers so they do not have to be concerned whether characters are represented by ASCII or EBCDIC codes, or whether they are left-aligned and blank-filled or right-aligned and zero-filled in machine words. The concept of data type also provides useful redundancy. The appearance of a variable as an operand in an expression implies a particular type for the variable (for example, A + B implies that A and B are either integer or real) that may be checked against the type of its current value.

**Scalar types.** Scalars are indivisible units of data; they are treated as single complete entities. Most languages contain several scalar types. The most common are integer, real, boolean, and character.

***Integer.*** Integer constants are positive and negative whole numbers and zero. Since machines have finite word lengths, only a subset of the integers are provided, as in (27), where MAXINT is a constant identifier corresponding to the largest integer value that can be represented on a particular machine. The usual arithmetic and relational operators are defined for integer values.

$$\{-\text{MAXINT}, \ldots, -2, -1, 0, 1, 2, \ldots, \text{MAXINT}\} \quad (27)$$

***Boolean.*** The boolean type consists of the constant values false and true, and the operators NOT, AND, OR. NOT is a unary prefix operator, taking a boolean argument and returning a boolean result. AND and OR are binary infix operators that each take two boolean values and produce a single boolean result. *SEE BOOLEAN ALGEBRA.*

***Character.*** The character constants are the uppercase and lowercase alphabetic characters, digits, and other punctuation symbols. Character constants are usually indicated by enclosing them in single quotation marks (for example, 'a', '7', or '?'). To represent the character constant, which is itself a single quote, a special notation is used (for example, doubling the internal quote "" or using a special escape character '\" in the C language). Almost all languages allow character comparison; however, the result of comparisons may differ across languages. In some languages, expression (28) is true, while in others it is false. However, languages generally define the relational operators on character values so that expressions (29) are valid.

$$'a' < 'A' \quad (28)$$

$$\begin{matrix} 'A' < 'B' < 'C' \ldots < 'Y' < 'Z' \\ 'a' < 'b' < 'c' \ldots < 'y' < 'z' \\ '0' < '1' < '2' \ldots < '8' < '9' \end{matrix} \quad (29)$$

***Real.*** Real numbers may be represented either as decimal fractions (for example, 1234.56) or in scientific notation (for example, 1.23456E3). The operators are the same as for type integer. Care must be exercised in the use of the equality and inequality operators, = and <>, on real values because the finite-word length restrictions on real machines can lead to problems of round-off and truncation so that, for example, expression (30) can occur.

$$1.0 <> (1.0/3.0 * 3.0) \quad (30)$$

***Enumerated types.*** New types can be defined by listing (enumerating) the constants of the type. The only operators that may be applied to operands with enumerated types are the relational operators. The enumerated type (31) defines a new type whose constants are the identifiers Jan, Feb, and so forth. The order of appearance of the identifiers in the type declaration defines their relative values (that is, the constant identifier with the smallest value appears first). Thus, relational operators can be applied to those objects, as in expression (32).

(Jan, Feb, Mar, Apr, May, June, July, Aug, Sept, Oct, Nov, Dec) (31)

Jan < July (32)

Constant identifiers declared in an enumerated type often replace mappings of integers to concepts in programs. For example, programmers who declare the enumerated type (31) and use its constants in their programs would not have to remember if 1 or 0 was used to represent January.

**References.** While variables usually hold values of objects, they may also hold the name of some object. Variables that can hold such values are called references or pointers. Reference constants are object names and a special value "nil" (which points to no variable). The operations defined for reference values are equality and dereferencing. Dereferencing is a unary operation that maps a pointer to the object it references. Dereferencing an object containing a reference (for example, by appending ^ to the object as in X^) yields the object referenced. An example of dereferencing is statement (33), in which X contains a reference to Y and Y contains the value 2. The result of dereferencing nil is undefined.

write (X^, Y) {prints 2 2} (33)

Languages also have operations that create reference values. For example, statement (34) creates an

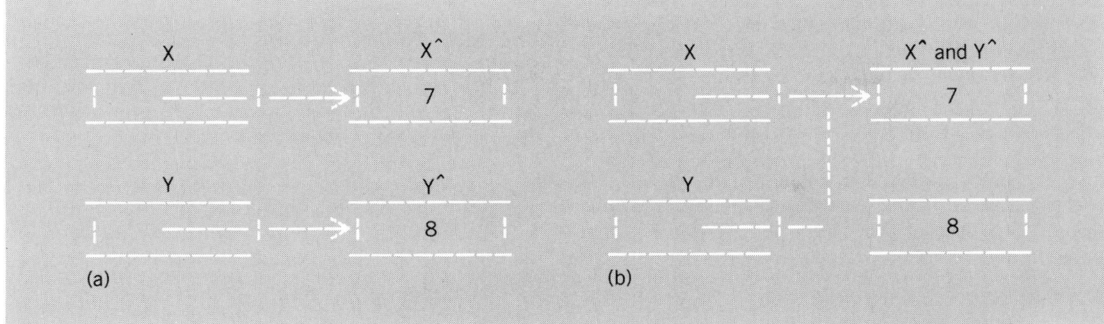


**Fig. 2. Effect of the assignment Y: = X. (*a*) Before Y: = X. (*b*) After Y: = X.**

object of type integer (with no initial value) and makes X point at the object.

$$X := \text{NEW (integer)} \qquad (34)$$

Since reference variables hold object names, an assignment between two reference variables X and Y results in X and Y pointing at the same object (**Fig. 2**). Thus X = Y and X^ = Y^. If X and Y are both dereferenced before the assignment (**Fig. 3**), the objects, X^ and Y^, will contain the same values, but could still be distinct objects. Thus X <> Y, but X^ = Y^.

**Aggregate types.** Collections of related values can be represented by aggregate types. Aggregate types can be characterized by the types of the objects that are their elements and the manner in which the elements are accessed. Elements of a collection can have homogeneous or heterogeneous types, and can be selected by their position in a collection or by a name associated with them.

***Arrays.*** An array is a mapping from a domain specified by a sequence of values to a range whose members are the values of the elements of the array. In statement (35), the array A is declared to have the domain {−3, −2, . . ., 4, 5}.

VAR A: ARRAY [−3 . . 5] (35)

In ALGOL, PL/1, PASCAL, and ADA, all the elements of an array must have the same type, but this restriction does not apply in SNOBOL, LISP, and APL.

Very few operations are defined for array objects. The access operation is called subscription and is usually indicated by enclosing an expression indicating the position of the desired element in brackets or parentheses. Thus, if A is an array, expression (36) selects its I + Jth element. Arrays often have multiple dimensions, each of which has its own range of values as subscripts. A chess board could be represented as an 8 × 8 array, as in statement (37).

A(I + J) or A[I + J] (36)

VAR B: ARRAY [1 . . 8, 1 . . 8] (37)

The diagonal elements of the board B are given by (38). Some languages (for example, ALGOL 68 and ADA) permit parts of arrays to be referenced by using trimming or slicing operations. Thus, expression (39) selects the first two rows of the board.

B[1, 1] B[2, 2] B[3, 3] B[4, 4]
B[5, 5] B[6, 6] B[7, 7] B[8, 8] (38)

B[1:2, 1:8] (39)

Most languages permit an array object to be assigned to an array variable; the values of the object are copied to the corresponding locations in the variables. PL/1 permits the assignment of a single value to every element in an array. The assignment (40) is equivalent to (41).

A := 0 (40)

A[1] := 0; A[2] := 0; . . . (41)

APL and ADA have array literals; the assignment (42) is equivalent to (43).

Odds := (1, 3, 5, 7, 9) (42)

Odds[1] := 1; Odds[2] := 3;
. . .; Odds[5] := 9 (43)

APL has the richest collection of array operators, having extended many of its operators which take scalar operands to work on array operands as well.

***Records.*** Records have components of different types (called fields), which are explicitly accessed by

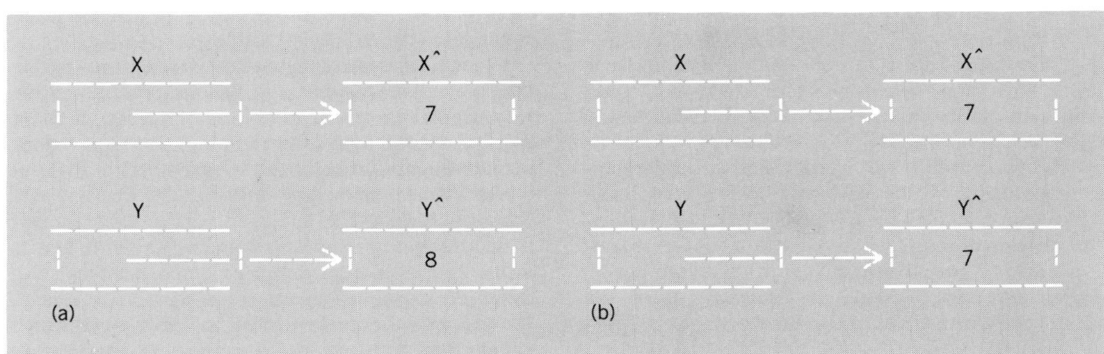


**Fig. 3. Effect of the assignment Y^: = X^. (*a*) Before Y^: = X^. (*b*) After Y^: = X^.**

identifiers (called selectors). For instance, in PL/1, X. Name is a qualified name that selects record component Name from record X. If X is a record object of the type given in (44), the names of the components are: X. Name, X. Address, X. Address. StNumber, X. Address. StName, X. Address. City, X. Address. State, X. Address. ZipCode, X. Age, and X. Salary. Some components of the record are scalar variables, some are arrays, and one (X. Address) is a record. The term record comes from COBOL and business data processing.

```
RECORD
  Name: ARRAY[1 . . 20];
  Address: RECORD
             StNumber;
             StName: ARRAY[1 . . 10];
             City: ARRAY[1 . . 10];            (44)
             State: ARRAY[1 . . 2];
             ZipCode
           END;
  Age;
  Salary
END
```

### Binding Attributes to Variables

Both constant and variable objects have values and attributes. Among the most important attributes of an object are its type, scope, and extent.

**Scope.** In most programming languages, the same identifier can name distinct objects in different parts of a program. The scope of an identifier is that part of a program in which the identifier has the same meaning. Generally that section of program is called a scope unit and corresponds to a procedure or compound statement. The set of objects that can be referenced in a scope unit is called the environment.

Identifiers are either declared locally (that is, in the immediately enclosing scope unit) or nonlocally (that is, in some other scope unit). Locally declared identifiers are like bound variables in formulas—their meaning does not change no matter where the procedure or compound statement containing their declaration is placed in a program, and is not available outside the scope unit. Nonlocally declared identifiers are like free variables—their meaning can depend on the placement of the text in which they are referenced or the execution sequence of the program.

In the program (45), the scope units are the program P and the procedures Q and R. The identifier I names distinct locally declared variables in P and R, and J names another variable in Q. The scope of each local identifier is marked to the right of the program. With the exception of the reference to I in Q, all identifier references are to locally declared variables.

There are three ways to resolve references to nonlocal variables:

1. Consider the use of nonlocal variables to be illegal. This scope rule is associated with both older languages like FORTRAN and modern languages like EUCLID.

2. Bind the reference to a declaration for the identifier occurring in the innermost lexically enclosing scope (for example, I is declared in P and P encloses Q). This method is called a static scope rule because it is based on the program text which does not change during execution. Among the languages using this scope rule are ALGOL, PL/1, PASCAL, C, and ADA.

```
PROGRAM P;              P's I   Q's J   R's I
  VAR I;                  |
  PROCEDURE Q;            |       |
    VAR J;                |       |
    BEGIN{Q}              |       |
      J := 0;             |       |
      I := I + 1          |       |
    END; {Q}              |       |
  PROCEDURE R;
    VAR I;                                 |
    BEGIN{R}                               |
      I := 1                               |      (45)
      Q;                                   |
      write(I)                             |
    END; {R}                               |
  BEGIN {P}               |
    read(I);              |
    IF I > 0              |
      THEN R              |
      ELSE Q;             |
    write(I)              |
  END{P}                  |
```

3. Bind the reference to a declaration in the procedure which has been most recently called, but has not yet completed execution. [In example (45), if the value read into I were greater than 0, the reference to I in Q would be bound to the declaration for I in R. Otherwise the reference would be bound to the declaration of I in P.] This association method is called a dynamic scope rule because nonlocal references can be bound to different variables depending on the sequence of statements executed. SNOBOL, LISP, and APL have dynamic scope rules.

**Data type.** Data types may be associated with objects statically via declarations or dynamically via assignment statements. In statically typed languages, the type associated with an object remains the same throughout the scope of the object. Declaration (46) binds the type INTEGER to I and CHARACTER to Ch. In dynamically typed languages, the type of an object is usually determined by the type of its value. Assigning a new value to a variable can change the type of the variable. Thus, in example (47), X initially has type integer and subsequently has type character.

```
VAR
  I: INTEGER;                          (46)
  Ch: CHARACTER;
```

```
X := 5;
write (X − 3);      {print: 2}         (47)
X := 'h';
write (X)     {print: h}
```

ALGOL, PL/1, PASCAL, C, and ADA are statically typed languages; SNOBOL, LISP, and APL are dynamically typed.

In statically typed languages the type of a variable may not be known when it is declared, or the variable may need to be bound to objects of several different types during the course of the program. Type unions permit variables to be bound to objects with different types. Two kinds of type unions exist: free and discriminated. In a free union, the programmer is permitted to treat a variable as being of any of the types in the union. In a discriminated union, another field, called the tag field, identifies the type of the object. Unions are often represented as records in which enumerated types are used to select alternatives. In example (48), a record type is defined that contains a single field whose name is either Ival or Cval. The number of the constant identifiers in the CASE portion of the record determines the number of alternate fields.

```
RECORD
  CASE (Int, Chr) OF
    Int: (Ival: INTEGER);                 (48)
    Chr: (Cval: CHARACTER)
END
```

In example (49), X is treated as though its type were a free union of the types INTEGER and CHARACTER.

```
IF Y = 0
  THEN X. Ival := 12                      (49)
  ELSE X. Cval := 'c';
X. Ival := X. Ival + 1
```

All the assignment statements in example (49) are legal. However, the final assignment adds one to the numeric representation for the character 'c' if the statement following the ELSE is executed.

The free union in example (49) could be converted to a discriminated union by adding a field named Tag whose value is either Int or Chr, depending on the value contained in the second field, as in (50).

```
RECORD
  Tag: (Int, Chr);
  CASE (Int, Chr) OF                      (50)
    Int: (Ival: INTEGER);
    Chr: (Cval: CHARACTER)
END
```

**Extent.** The extent or lifetime of a variable is the period of program execution during which the storage is allocated. Static storage is created at the beginning of the program execution and not deallocated until program termination. Local storage for variables is created on entry to the block or procedure containing the variable's declaration and destroyed on exit. Dynamic storage is created and destroyed by execution of special statements in the programming language.

Consider procedure (51). In a language like FORTRAN, the same storage location can be used for X no matter how many times P is invoked. The value of X is preserved between calls to P. However, in languages like ALGOL, PL/1, PASCAL, C, and ADA, local storage for X is allocated on each entry to the procedure and freed on each exit, so that the value of X is lost between executions of P. Local storage allocation permits two procedures to share storage locations if the procedures do not call one another. In example (52), the arrays A and B can share the same storage locations.

```
PROCEDURE P;
  VAR X;
  BEGIN                                   (51)
    {sequence of statements}
  END
```

```
PROGRAM Prog;
  PROCEDURE P;
    VAR A: ARRAY [1 . . 100];
    BEGIN {P}
      {sequence of statements not containing
        a call of Q}
    END; {P}
  PROCEDURE Q;
    VAR B: ARRAY[1 . . 75];                       (52)
    BEGIN {Q}
      {sequence of statements not
        containing a call of P}
    END; {Q}
  BEGIN
    P;
    Q
  END
```

Storage can be created dynamically through the execution of a statement like (53).

Ptr := new ( ) (53)

Such storage is independent of the structure of the source code of the program and remains allocated until a corresponding statement (54) is executed.

dispose(Ptr) (54)

Care must be taken that all dynamically allocated storage can be referenced through a pointer or the storage becomes garbage. The sequence of statements (55) results in the execution sequence shown in **Fig. 4**, in which the storage formerly referenced by X becomes garbage because there is no way to reference it. Dangling references are created when storage referenced by several pointers is freed. In the sequence of statements (56), Y contains a dangling reference to the storage formerly referenced by X. X may also contain a dangling reference if its contents are not set to nil by dispose, as in **Fig. 5**.

X := new (INTEGER); X^ := 7; X := nil (55)

new(X); X^ := 7; Y := X; dispose(X) (56)

## PARAMETERS

Parameters communicate information between the calling environment and the environment of the called procedure. Although this can be accomplished by referencing nonlocal variables, communicating with parameters permits a procedure to work on different variables each time it is called. Formal parameters are identifiers that are locally declared in a procedure definition; actual parameters are expressions in a procedure call statement. In the program fragment (57),

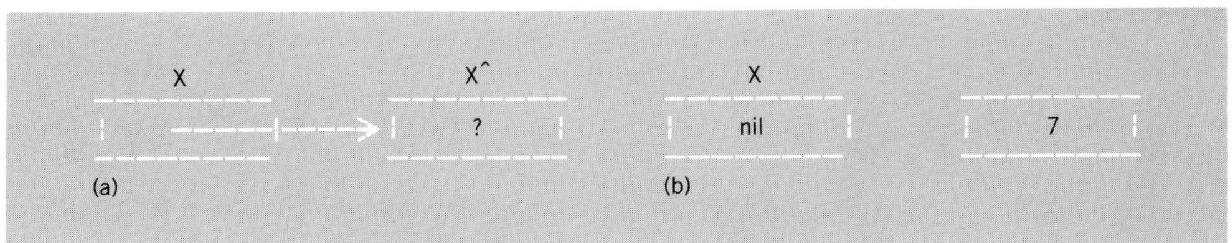


**Fig. 4. Execution sequence resulting in garbage. (*a*) After new (X). (*b*) After X: = nil.**

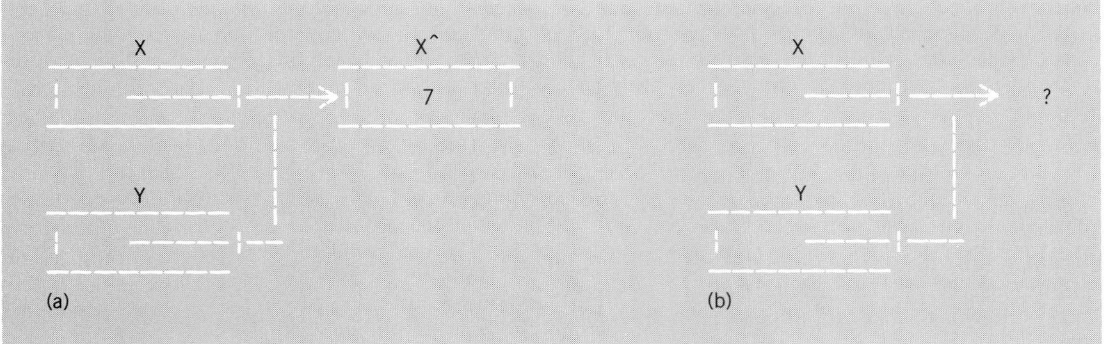


**Fig. 5. Execution sequence resulting in dangling reference. (*a*) After Y: = X. (*b*) After dispose (X).**

which shows two versions of a procedure named Max, X and Y are formal parameters and A, B, A + 2, and B − 3 are actual parameters. The nonlocal version of Max is slightly longer than the parameter version because the calling environment must initialize the nonlocal references before Max is called. This requires the calling environment to know the implementation details of Max, thereby losing some of the advantages of abstraction gained by making Max a procedure.

```
PROCEDURE Max (X, Y);         PROCEDURE Max;
  BEGIN {Max}                   BEGIN {Max}
    IF X > Y                      IF X > Y
      THEN                          THEN
        write (X)                     write (X)
      ELSE                          ELSE
        write (Y)                     write (Y)
  END; {Max}                    END; {Max}
BEGIN                         BEGIN
  . . .                         . . .
  Max(A, B);                    X := A;            (57)
  Max(A + 2, B − 3);            Y := B;
  . . .                         Max;
END                             X := A + 2;
                                Y := B − 3;
                                Max;
                                . . .
                              END
Parameter version             Nonlocal version
```

The correspondence between the formal and actual parameters is positional—the first actual parameter is bound to the first formal parameter, and so forth. Several different kinds of parameter binding occur in programming languages: reference, value, result, and name. The key issues in binding are when the binding takes place (usually when the procedure is called, but possibly each time a formal parameter is referenced in the procedure body), and what is bound (the value or address of the actual, or perhaps a procedure that computes the address of the actual).

**Reference binding.** When an actual parameter is bound by reference to a formal parameter, an alias is set up between the name of the actual parameter and the name of the formal parameter. The word alias is used because both names identify the same object. The object identified by the actual is evaluated at the point of call. Each time a value is assigned to a formal reference parameter, the value of the corresponding actual parameter is also altered. Thus reference parameters can be used to supply input values to procedures and to return values computed by the procedure.

**Value binding.** Many arguments to procedures are used as inputs only; no value is returned through these parameters. Input parameters are bound by value to formal parameters. In value binding, the value of the actual parameter at the point of call is assigned to a new object which is bound to the formal parameter, but no alias is established between the formal and the actual parameters. Thus, any assignment to a formal value parameter changes the value of the formal but not that of the actual parameter.

**Result binding.** A procedure called to compute an output can use result binding to assign the value to a result parameter. At the point of call, the actual parameter is bound by reference to its corresponding formal parameter. However, during execution of a procedure, assignments to a result parameter alter a local copy of the variable, but not the actual parameter. When the procedure completes execution, the result is transmitted by assigning the value of the formal parameter to the actual parameter.

**Name binding.** In name binding, actual parameters are passed unevaluated to formal parameters and are evaluated only when necessary. Actually, a procedure that computes the object represented by the actual parameter (called a thunk) is bound to the formal parameter. Each time the formal parameter is referenced, its corresponding thunk is called to deliver the actual object. This method of parameter transmission occurs only in ALGOL 60.

**Examples of different bindings.** Program (58) illustrates the differences in parameter binding mechanisms.

```
PROGRAM Bindings;
  VAR
    A: ARRAY[1 . . 2];
    I;
  PROCEDURE P (X, Y);
    BEGIN {P}
      Y := I + 1;
      X := Y + 3;                    (58)
      A[1] := A[1] + 20
    END; {P}
  BEGIN
    A[1] := 1;
    A[2] := 1;
    I := 1;
    P(A[I], I);
    write (I, A[1], A[2])
  END
```

The results printed for the different binding mechanisms are summarized in table (59).

| Bindings | I | A[1] | A[2] |
|---|---|---|---|
| Value | 1 | 21 | 1 |
| Reference | 2 | 25 | 1 |
| Result | 2 | 5 | 1 |
| Name | 2 | 21 | 5 |

(59)

In value binding, only the assignment to A[1] causes a change in the variables in the calling environment. X is aliased to A[1] and Y is aliased to I in reference binding. Thus the change to Y is reflected in I, and the changes to both X and A[1] affect the value of the latter. While the result mechanism yields the same bindings as the reference mechanism, the values of the result parameters (Y = 2 and X = 5) are not assigned to the actuals until P finishes execution. Thus the result of adding 20 to the value of A[1] is lost. As long as no local identifiers of P have the same name as any of the actual name parameters, name binding can be simulated by rewriting P's text with the text of the actuals replacing that of the formals, as in (60).

```
I := I + 1;
A[I] := Y + 3;                  (60)
A[1] := A[1] + 20
```

Since I is incremented from 1 to 2 by the first assignment statement, A[2] rather than A[1] is altered by the second assignment.

### Functions

Function declarations are similar to procedure declarations. But unlike a procedure, which communicates its results by assigning values to its parameters, a function communicates a distinguished value known as the result of the function. This result of the function is often indicated by assigning a value to the name of the function. The declaration of the function Max2 is given by (61).

```
FUNCTION Max2 (X, Y);
  {<Max2 := if X > Y then X else Y>}
  BEGIN {Max2}
    IF X > Y
      THEN                              (61)
        Max2 := X
      ELSE
        Max2 := Y
  END; {Max2}
```

Function calls look like procedure calls; the name of the function is followed by a list of actual parameters. However, there is an important difference between function and procedure calls. Since functions deliver values, function calls are expressions which may appear either within larger expressions or alone wherever an expression could appear in a program. Procedure calls, which do not deliver values, are statements.

To find the maximum of three values, Max3 could be declared, as in (62). The expression in the assignment statement would be evaluated by first calling Max(Y, Z) to obtain the maximum of Y and Z, and then calling Max2 again with X and the result of the earlier call.

```
FUNCTION Max3 (X, Y, Z);
  {<Max3> := <the largest value in [X, Y, Z]>}
  BEGIN {Max3}
    Max3 := Max2(X, Max2(Y, Z))         (62)
  END; {Max3}
```

**Side effects.** When a statement in a procedure or function alters the value of a nonlocal variable or reference or name parameter, the procedure is said to have a side effect. It may not be quite accurate to call such assignments in procedures side effects, because procedures must include such statements in order to communicate their results. Therefore, they are really main effects of procedures. Side effects in functions are less desirable because they make the results of expression evaluation unpredictable. While languages specify the order in which operators are applied, they do not always define the order in which operands are fetched in expressions. For example, if Identity returned the value of its actual parameter, but increased the value of its reference parameter and the nonlocal variable N1, as in (63), then expression (64) might have any of the values in (65).

```
FUNCTION Identity (Parm);
  BEGIN {Identity}
    Identity := Parm;                   (63)
    Parm := Parm + 1;
    N1 := N1 + 3
  END; {Identity}

N1 + Identity(In) + In                  (64)
```

```
N1 + In + In + 1    {if the operands are fetched
                      left to right
                      T1 := N1;
                      T2 := Identity(In);
                      T3 := In;
                      Result := T1 + T2 + T3}
N1 + 3 + In + In    {if the operands are fetched
                      right to left
                      T1 := In;
                      T2 := Identity(In);
                      T3 := N1;
                      Result := T3 + T2 + T1}
N1 + In + In        {if both operands are
                      fetched before the call
                      T1 := N1;
                      T2 := In;                 (65)
                      T3 := Identity(In);
                      Result := T1 + T3 + T2}
N1 + 3 + In + In    {if both operands are fetched
  + 1                 after the call
                      T1 := Identity(In);
                      T2 := N1;
                      T3 := In;
                      Result := T2 + T1 + T3}
```

Thus, it is good programming practice to avoid side effects in functions and to use procedures instead when side effects are desired.

**Procedure and function parameters.** When procedures and functions are passed as parameters, they are bound like name parameters. Actual procedure parameters are passed unevaluated to procedures and evaluated each time they appear in procedure call statements.

Procedure parameters may contain references to nonlocal identifiers that must be bound to variables. Deep binding associates a procedure parameter's nonlocal identifiers with variables in the environment in which the procedure was created. Shallow binding associates these identifiers with variables in the environment when the procedure is invoked.

In example (66), P contains a nonlocal reference to A, and Q is a function that returns a procedure that is subsequently invoked in R.

```
PROGRAM Main;
  VAR A, B;
  PROCEDURE P;
    BEGIN {P}
      A := A + 10;
      write(A)
    END; {P}
  FUNCTION Q(Proc);
    VAR A;
    BEGIN {Q}
      A := 2;
      Q := Proc
    END; {Q}                                  (66)
  PROCEDURE R(Proc);
    VAR A;
    BEGIN {R}
      A := 3;
      Proc; {really invokes P}
      write(A)
    END; {R}
  BEGIN {Main}
    A := 1;
    B := Q(P);
    B ( );
    write(A)
  END {Main}
```

In ALGOL-like languages, nonlocal references are associated with the variables in the environment in which the procedure is declared. This deep binding associates the references to A in P with the A declared in Main. Thus the output of the program is: 11 3 11.

In LISP, either deep or shallow binding can be specified by applying one of the functions FUNCTION and QUOTE to the value returned by Q, as in (67).

```
FUNCTION Q(Proc);        FUNCTION Q(Proc);
  VAR A;                   VAR A;
  BEGIN {Q}                BEGIN {Q}
    A := 2;                  A := 2;
    Q := FUNCTION            Q := QUOTE           (67)
      (Proc)                   (Proc)
  END; {Q}                 END; {Q}
    Deep binding             Shallow binding
```

The use of FUNCTION in Q binds P's A to the variable declared in Q, the most recently declared version of A since LISP has a dynamic scope rule. Thus the program output is: 12 3 1.

The use of QUOTE in Q delays the binding of P's A until P is invoked as Proc in R. At this time, P's A is bound to the most recent declaration of A, which occurs in R. Thus the program output is: 13 13 1.

While the ability to pass procedure and function parameters may seem too exotic to include in a programming language, it does facilitate construction of generic software. The alternative to passing a function parameter to a procedure is to embed the source for the function in the procedure. Thus the procedure can only operate with one specific function rather than with any function passed to it.

### Applicative and Object-Oriented Languages

Most programming languages are imperative languages, because their programs largely consist of a series of commands to assign values to objects. Examples of imperative languages are ALGOL, PL/1, FORTRAN, ADA, COBOL, and PASCAL. Two other types of languages exist: applicative and object-oriented. No commonly used language is purely imperative, applicative, or object-oriented, so every language has some characteristics of each type of language.

**Applicative languages.** A purely applicative language would be one in which there are no statements, only expressions without side effects. The name applicative refers to the repeated application of functions to the results of other functions to specify an algorithm. LISP, APL, and VAL are three languages in which programs are largely applicative.

LISP has a well-defined applicative subset known as pure LISP. Programs in LISP consist of a sequence of expressions known as S-expressions. If functions with side effects are excluded from these expressions, then the language becomes pure LISP. Pure LISP excludes such functions as SET, which assigns a value to a variable, and DEF (or DEFUN), which declares that a variable is a procedure with a certain body.

A program to find the absolute value of B − C would be written in pure LISP as in (68). COND is a function that takes a list of ordered pairs of expressions and returns the value of the second member of a pair whose first member evaluates true. The expression pairs in this example are given by (69). LISP uses prefix notation for operators, so the first member of the first pair is given by (70). The first member of the second pair, "t," or true, ensures that COND always delivers some result.

```
(COND ((> (−B C) 0) (−B C))
      (t (−C B)))                        (68)
```

((> (−B C) 0) (−B C)) and (t (−C B))     (69)

$$B - C > 0 \quad (70)$$

The main advantage of applicative over imperative programming is mathematical elegance. An applicative description of an algorithm has the form of a mathematical function definition, and so all the accumulated power of mathematical analysis can be used to understand it. This is especially useful in proving programs correct.

**Object-oriented languages.** Programs written in object-oriented languages consist of sequences of commands directed at objects. An object receiving a command invokes an internal procedure to respond to the command. Assignment statements are replaced by commands to objects requesting that they change their values.

SMALLTALK, ACTORS, and LISP are three languages that encourage object-oriented programming. As with applicative languages, there is an object-oriented subset of LISP, called FLAVORS. Since the only way to do something in an object-oriented language is to direct a command at an object, object-oriented programming means passing messages to objects. For instance, the way to add two integers in SMALLTALK is to pass a message to the first integer requesting that it add itself to the second integer.

A program to compute the absolute value of B − C might be written in object-oriented form as in (71). This program is read: send a message to the integer object asking it to make a new integer called A, send A an assign message with message body B, send A a subtract message with message body C, and finally send A a message requesting that it take the absolute value of itself.

```
(send INTEGER ''new'' ''A'')
(send A ''assign'' B)                    (71)
(send A ''–'' C)
(send A ''absolute'')
```

One advantage of object-oriented programming is the encapsulation of responses to commands within each object. For instance, when adding two numbers the programmer need not be concerned with whether the numbers are integer or real. The number receiving the ''add-yourself-to'' message is responsible for knowing how to add itself to any reasonable other number, and for complaining if it cannot. This effect can also be achieved in imperative languages such as ADA by using encapsulated data types.

A second advantage of object-oriented programming is the power of mixing types of objects. If the programmer defined a type of object which could respond to messages to add itself to things, and another type of object which could respond to messages to print itself, then by mixing types a new kind of object would be created which could do both. In LISP FLAVORS the ''vanilla flavor'' is the set of messages to which all objects respond; more complex objects are created by mixing other flavors in with vanilla.

### Defining New Data Types

Procedure and function declarations define new operations that operate on existing objects. Type declarations add new objects and operations to a programming language. Designing programs with user-defined types allows solutions to be stated in problem-oriented rather than machine-oriented terms. ALGOL 68- and PASCAL-type declarations allow programmers to define the representation of new objects of the data types, and ALGOL 68 permits the definition of operations. For example, declaration (72) defines a new type named Rational.

```
TYPE Rational = RECORD
                  Numerator,
                    Denominator:    (72)
                    INTEGER
                END
```

Once this definition is made, PASCAL programmers can declare variables and parameters with type Rational, but cannot add rational numbers without manipulating implementation directly (73). Dealing with the fields of the representation negates many advantages of abstraction.

```
VAR Op1, Op2, Result: Rational;
BEGIN
  . . .
  {Result: = Op1 – Op2}
  Result. Denominator :=                    (73)
    Op1. Denominator * Op2. Denominator;
  Result. Numerator :=
    Op1. Numerator * Op2. Denominator
    + Op1. Denominator * Op2. Numerator
END
```

Procedures and functions can be defined in PASCAL and operators in ALGOL 68 to encapsulate these sequences of operations, hiding the details of how functions are computed. However, these definitions are independent of the type definitions, that is, programmers can still directly manipulate the representation of objects. SIMULA 67 introduced the class concept to bind the definition of the representation and operations together, but still did not prohibit programmers from accessing the representation directly. By limiting access to objects with user-defined types to procedures defining operations, programmers can deal with data abstractly (that is, without caring how the data are represented). This enables programmers to change the representation of objects (for example, to improve the efficiency of their programs by changing the representation of rationals from a pair of integers to a single real) without changing any part of the program except the type definition and the procedures and functions implementing the operations. CLU, EUCLID, and ADA all have data abstraction functions that limit access to objects' representations. In example (74), written in ADA, the type Rational and the addition operator for rational numbers is made available through a package specification. However, the appearance of the word PRIVATE in the definition of Rational prevents programmers from accessing the fields of the record used to represent a rational number.

```
PACKAGE Rat IS
  TYPE Rational IS PRIVATE;
  FUNCTION ''+'' (Op1, Op2: Rational)
    RETURN Rational;
  . . .
PRIVATE
  TYPE Rational IS RECORD
        Numerator, Denominator: INTEGER;
        END RECORD;                         (74)
END; —Package Rat
PACKAGE BODY Rat IS
. . .
  FUNCTION ''+'' (Op1, Op2: Rational)
    RETURN Rational IS
  . . .
  END ''+'';
END Rat;
```

### Particular Languages

The more widely used languages include FORTRAN, ALGOL, COBOL, BASIC, PL/1, APL, SNOBOL, LISP, PASCAL, C, and ADA.

**FORTRAN.** FORTRAN was designed in the mid-1950s by a group at IBM headed by John Backus for efficient scientific applications. To achieve this goal, the data and control components of the language are very simple, providing programmers with low-level hardware operations.

FORTRAN control structures are particularly primitive; neither compound statements nor unbound repetitive statements are part of the language. Two conditional statements (arithmetic and logical IF's) and a bounded iteration statement (DO) provide the only relief from GOTO's and labels. An arithmetic IF, statement (75), provides a three-way branch depending on whether its expression is negative, zero, or positive. A logical IF, statement (76), permits execution of a single statement, which cannot be a DO or an IF, if its expression is true. The absence of nested statements causes heavy use of GOTO's and labels, as shown in example (77).

```
IF (expression) MinusLabel, ZeroLabel,
                          Plus Label    (75)

        IF (expression) statement       (76)
```

```
  IF (X GE 0) GOTO 1   IF X > = 0
  GOTO2                  THEN
1 A = B - C                A := B - C
  GOTO 3                 ELSE                (77)
2 A = C - B                A := C - B
3 CONTINUE
 FORTRAN version       ALGOL version
```

A revision of the FORTRAN language, FORTRAN-77, adopted many of ALGOL's control constructs.

Scaler data types include logical, integer, real, double-precision real, and complex. Arrays with homogeneous elements provide the only aggregate types. Types are associated with variables statically through declarations.

Procedures may not be nested in FORTRAN, so references are either global or local. The global variables are partitioned into named common blocks, which must be mentioned in a procedure if the procedure contains nonlocal references. Storage for both global and local variables is statically allocated before program execution, so local variables retain values between invocations of the procedures in which they are declared.

FORTRAN has both procedures and functions, but neither can be recursive. Parameter transmission is by reference, and procedures can be transmitted. Functions may only return scalar results.

**ALGOL 60.** ALGOL was designed by an international committee in the late 1950s and early 1960s as a language for scientific computation. The elegance of ALGOL's structure has made it the basis for several subsequent language design efforts, most notably ALGOL 68 and PASCAL, and its control structures have even been adopted by PL/1 and later versions of FORTRAN. ALGOL was also the first language whose syntax was defined with a formal grammar (called Backus-Naur Form or BNF after two of the principal designers of ALGOL). The concise definition of the language has made it an object of study in the computer science community for many years.

ALGOL control statements are very much like statements (12)–(15). However, all repetitive statements are variants of the FOR statement, and compound statements are units of scope that may contain declarations of their own local variables.

ALGOL has integer, real, and boolean scalar types; aggregate types are restricted to arrays with homogeneous elements. ALGOL has static rules for both scope- and data-type association. Unless they are declared as OWN, variables in ALGOL programs are locally allocated, coming into existence in the block or procedure in which they are declared and being deleted when that program unit finishes execution. The lack of user-defined data types and dynamic storage allocation limits the applications of ALGOL.

Procedures and functions can be recursive and accept parameters which have the standard data types as well as labels and procedures. Parameter binding can be either by name (the default) or by value.

**COBOL.** COBOL was designed in 1959 and 1960 as a language to support business applications on computers. As was the case with FORTRAN, efficiency was a primary concern. Because of its intended application area, COBOL has relatively poor features for specifying computations (such as expressions, functions, and parameters), but strong features for data description and input/output.

Two of the most noticeable features of COBOL programs are the English-like syntax and the division of programs into four parts. Either English-language syntax or algebraic notation can be used in expressions, as in (78).

```
ADD B, C, GIVING A
COMPUTE A = B + C          (78)
```

The identification division provides documentation, the procedure division describes algorithms, the data division contains descriptions of the files and working storage used in the procedure division, and the environment division collects machine-dependent information.

Statements in procedure divisions are grouped into labeled paragraphs. COBOL contains the usual IF and GOTO statements, but has unusual repetitive and procedure statements. The tasks of these last two statements are accomplished by the PERFORM statement (79) that executes a sequence of paragraphs before control is returned to the statement following the PERFORM. Bounded and unbounded repetition are also specified using PERFORMS, as in (80).

```
PERFORM label 1 THRU label N          (79)

PERFORM label 1 THRU label N expression TIMES
PERFORM label 1 THRU label N UNTIL condition     (80)
```

Numbers and character strings are the basic data types of COBOL. Data structuring is provided with arrays and records. Level numbers on declarations describe the hierarchical relationship of the data (with the exception of some special level numbers). Types are specified by picture clauses that specify how many characters are needed to represent the values to be assigned to the variables.

Procedures with parameters and local data are optional COBOL features. No functions are provided and procedures may not be recursive. Unless a version of COBOL contains these optional features, all variables in the data division are global and statically allocated. Like FORTRAN, the values of all variables (even those declared in local data divisions) are retained between calls.

**BASIC.** T. E. Kurtz and J. G. Kemeny developed BASIC at Darmouth College in the early 1960s. The goal of their design was to provide nonscience majors with a simple, interactive language.

BASIC supports real and string data as well as one- or two-dimensional arrays of one of these primitive types. Dimension statements permit string lengths and array subscripts to be specified. Variable names are restricted to single letters, followed by an optional digit if the variable is numeric or $ if the variable is a string. Thus, types are statically associated with variables.

Statements in BASIC programs are numbered, and control passes through them sequentially unless altered by a GOTO or conditional branch statement, such as statement (81). Repeated execution can be specified by a FOR statement.

```
IF expression THEN statement-number     (81)
```

There are no procedure declarations in BASIC; any sequence of statements can be considered to be a procedure. Procedure calls are indicated by the appearance of a GOSUB statement (82) that transfers control to the indicated statement number. The procedure is executed until a RETURN statement is encountered.

The lack of procedure declarations means that the notions of parameters and scope rules are foreign to BASIC.

```
GOSUB statement-number                    (82)
```

**PL/1.** PL/1 was designed by a committee organized by the IBM Corporation in the mid-1960s. The language was designed to meet the needs of a broad range of applications: scientific, business applications, and systems. PL/1 combines and extends many of the features of FORTRAN (parameter binding and formated input/output), ALGOL (scope rules, variable extents, recursive procedures, and control structures), and COBOL (record structures and picture data types). By providing redundant features from different languages, the designers have made the language difficult to learn and encouraged users to stay in one of the FORTRAN, COBOL, or ALGOL subsets of PL/1.

The control structures of PL/1 are like those of ALGOL, except that repetitive statements are introduced by DO instead of FOR.

Numeric types in PL/1 permit the programmer to specify four attributes: mode (real or complex), scale (fixed or floating point), base (decimal or binary), and precision (the number of digits). Since most programmers do not want to provide such detail in declarations (and it may hinder transportability to machines with different word lengths), PL/1 compilers provide many defaults. (There are actually more attributes describing the variable's lifetime and initial value.) PL/1 also provides bit and character strings with lengths that are either fixed or varying up to a maximum, as well as a reference type called POINTER. Both arrays and COBOL records called structures are provided.

PL/1 has static scope rules and type association. The extent of a variable may be either static (ALGOL's own), automatic (ALGOL's local), based, or controlled. The last two extent attributes provide dynamic storage allocation using the predefined procedures ALLOCATE and FREE. The based attribute can be used to provide free unions because pointer variables may reference data of any type. Example (83) illus-

```
DECLARE Int FIXED BASED;
DECLARE Chr CHARACTER(4) BASED;
DECLARE P POINTER;                        (83)
ALLOCATE Int SET P;
P->Int = 64;
PUT LIST(P->Chr);
```

trates this facility. The declaration of based variables does not cause storage to be reserved, but rather defines a template. The ALLOCATE statement reserves enough storage for an integer object and binds a reference to the object to P. The assignment statement dereferences P and treats the resulting object as an integer in order to assign the value 64 to the object. The PUT (or write) statement dereferences P and treats the resulting object as a character. Controlled storage must also be explicitly allocated and freed by the programmer, but unlike based storage only the last object allocated may be referenced. Thus, the language provides programmer-defined stack operations.

PL/1 may have recursive procedures and functions. Parameter transmission is by reference as in FORTRAN, but labels, procedures, and functions can also be transmitted as in ALGOL. PL/1 also provides primitives for parallel execution of procedures and for handling interrupts.

**APL.** APL was designed by Kenneth Iverson during the mid-1950s to the mid-1960s. It is an interactive language whose operators accept and produce arrays with homogeneous elements of type number or character. The only control construct is a GOTO statement, but this is inconsequential since many APL programs have a strong applicative flavor. Although they often consist of an imperative sequence of assignments, APL programs generally operate on array objects to produce new array objects. Thus repetitive constructs are not needed as frequently as they are in ALGOL-like languages.

There is really no such thing as an APL program because functions are defined independently and invoked either interactively by the programmer or by another function. A function definition for IN, which finds the positions at which one word appears in another, is shown in (84). IN would require at least one loop if it were written in an ALGOL-like language.

```
     ∇  Z ← A IN B; J
[1]     J ← (A[1] = B)/ιρB
[2]     J ← (J ≤ 1 + (ρB) − ρA)/J                (84)
[3]     Z ← (B[J° + ¯1 + ιρA]^ = A)/J
     ∇
```

APL functions consist of sequentially numbered statements, which may have control transferred to them via GOTO statements. A and B are formal parameters (only two are allowed but they can be arrays), J is a local variable, and Z is a special identifier that is assigned the result of any function. Parameters are passed by value and nonlocal references are resolved dynamically. Types are associated with variables and storage is allocated for variables dynamically. For example, if IN is invoked with the sequence of commands (85), then X and Y are dynamically allocated and assigned values of type vector of characters.

```
X<-'THE'
Y<-'THE MEN THEN                          (85)
  WENT HOME'
X IN Y
```

The assignment statements in function (84) have the following effects. A[1] = B returns a vector whose length is the same as B's length, and whose values are either 1 where A[1] = B[k] for 1 < = k < = Length (B) or 0 otherwise. The rho operator (ρ) gives the length of B, and the iota operator (ι) generates a vector of length B whose values are 1, 2, . . . , ρB. The first vector is used to compress the second by selecting those values from the second vector for which the corresponding value in the first vector is one. Thus J is assigned a vector with values (1 9 17). The second statement checks that a word with the same length as A could really start at these positions (without running past the end of the vector). The final statement subscripts B with a matrix of positions of words that could match A to obtain a matrix of characters, as in (86). The rows of this matrix are compared to the vector A, yielding a matrix (87) containing 1's where the values of the corresponding elements are equal and 0's otherwise. The elements of the rows are "anded" to form a vector of 0's and 1's (1 1 0) that is used to compress J.

$$B\begin{vmatrix} 1 & 2 & 3 \\ 9 & 10 & 11 \\ 17 & 18 & 19 \end{vmatrix} = \begin{vmatrix} \text{THE} \\ \text{THE} \\ \text{T H} \end{vmatrix} \qquad (86)$$

$$\begin{vmatrix} 1 & 1 & 1 \\ 1 & 1 & 1 \\ 1 & 0 & 0 \end{vmatrix} \qquad (87)$$

**SNOBOL.** During the 1960s, SNOBOL was developed by Ralph Griswold at Bell Laboratories as a string processing language. It went through several forms, only one of which is still in use: SNOBOL 4. SNOBOL has no real control constructs. Instead, every statement either "succeeds" or "fails" and may optionally GOTO a new statement depending on success or failure. SNOBOL statements provide extremely powerful operators for string manipulation. For instance, SNOBOL statement (88) will assign the value a to X and the value b to Y. The operators used here are the blank before a which means pattern match; the "." which means assign, and "arb" which matches an arbitrary string.

"This is a, this is b" "a" . X ARB "b" . Y (88)

Data types are dynamically declared and converted in SNOBOL, so that the same variable can at one instance contain an integer and the next instant contain a procedure. User-defined types permit the use of records. An interesting aggregate type is the "table," which is an array addressed by content. Variables are dynamically scoped.

SNOBOL has both procedures and functions, which may be recursive. Parameter transmission is by value, and procedures can be transmitted. Functions may return any type, including type NAME which can be used as the target of an assignment statement.

SNOBOL is used for string processing applications, such as editors, compilers, and data bases. It executes rather slowly, so once a program has been coded and debugged in SNOBOL it is often recorded in a more efficient language, such as PASCAL.

**LISP.** LISP was invented by John McCarthy while at MIT in the late 1950s. It is a very widely used language in the artificial intelligence community, which has never agreed on what version of LISP should be standard. The two most widely used forms are INTERLISP and MACLISP. *SEE ARTIFICIAL INTELLIGENCE*.

The basic type in LISP is the list, usually denoted by a sequence of items in parentheses. LISP programs also take the form of lists, thus LISP programs can manipulate themselves or other LISP codes. The only syntax in LISP is the matching of parentheses, thus LISP is easy to extend by adding additional functions.

Procedures and functions are recursive in LISP, and parameters are transmitted by value. The power of LISP comes from the representation of everything by lists, which leads to very powerful environments of tools and extensions to LISP. LISP is a good language to write experimental programs, since its flexibility is useful for dealing with the unexpected. However, it executes slowly and uses a lot of memory.

**PASCAL.** PASCAL was developed by Niklaus Wirth in 1969 to obtain a language which would be suitable to teach programming as a systematic activity with constructs that could be implemented reliably and efficiently. The control structures of PASCAL are similar to statements (12)–(15) and (21). However, a CASE statement (whose design had been proposed in a language called ALGOLX designed by Wirth and C. A. R. Hoare) was added as an additional selection statement. This statement permits execution of one alternative among several statements based on the value of a selection expression. The alternative selections are labeled and selection is performed by name rather than by position to minimize the chance for errors resulting from rearranged or omitted statements. Statement (89) is a sample CASE statement. If this expression has the value Disk, statement2 is executed and control skips to the statement following the CASE statement.

```
CASE expression OF
   Reader: statement1;
   Disk, Tape: statement2;          (89)
   Printer: statement3
END
```

PASCAL scalar types include integer, real, character, and boolean. PL/1's POINTER type is improved by adding information about the type of data referenced. Thus the PASCAL types "reference to type1" and "reference to type2" are not compatible, so assignments cannot take place between variables of one of these types and values of the other. Pascal extends ALGOL 60's data-structuring facilities by adding sets, records, files, and user-defined types. Type unions can be obtained through use of variant records.

Like ALGOL, PASCAL has a mandatory declaration of variables, static scope rules, and static association of types with variables. Except for those accessed through other reference variables, variables are locally allocated on procedure entry and deleted on procedure exit. Variables accessed via reference variables are dynamically allocated and freed by using NEW and DISPOSE, respectively.

Both procedures and functions can be recursive in PASCAL. Variables of any type can be bound by value (the default) or by reference to formal parameters. Procedures and functions can also be passed as parameters. Functions are limited to returning scalar or reference values as their results.

**C language.** C was designed and implemented in 1972 by Dennis Ritchie to implement the Unix operating system. Similar to PASCAL in many ways, C has enumerated types, records (called structures), the case statement, and reference variables. The main difference between programming in C and other languages is the extensive use of reference variables, which are defined to be equivalent to arrays. For instance, program (90) declares an integer array named array and a pointer to array named pointer. The first assignment statement sets the fourth element of the array to 1, and the second assignment sets it to zero. The dereferencing operator in C is represented by *. Reference variables allow the programmer to specify algorithms which are particularly efficient to execute on the underlying machine, at the expense of writing code which is difficult to read.

```
int array [10], *pointer = array;
array (3) = 1;                        (90)
*(pointer + 3) = 0;
```

C is usually used within the Unix operating system which is entirely written in C. Unix extends C to have storage allocation, multitasking and interrupt handling, and very flexible input/output facilities. *SEE OPERATING SYSTEM*.

**ADA.** ADA was designed by a group from Cii-Honeywell Bull headed by Jean Ichbiah in the mid-1970s. This group won a competition sponsored by the Department of Defense to design a new language to support development of embedded systems. ADA was designed using PASCAL as a base, to meet the reliability and efficiency requirements imposed by these applications.

Design decisions to include static scope rules and static association of types and variables were made in the name of reliability. ADA's most important contribution is to extend PASCAL's user-defined type to include packages; these permit users to define new operations and encapsulate the representations of their new types. While reliability required that types be statically associated with variables in ADA, efficiency required that controlled escapes from these associations be possible by specifying a target type for an expression. In example (91), a ten-element slice [similar to expression (39)] of B is assigned to A. Decile coerces the expression B(11 . . 20) to the same type as A, making the assignment possible.

```
TYPE Seq IS ARRAY (Integer RANGE <>) OF Integer;
SUBTYPE Decile IS Seq(1 . . 10);
A: Decile;                                        (91)
B: ARRAY (1 . . 100) OF Integer;
A := Decile(B(11 . . 20));
```

Like PL/1, ADA contains an exception-handling code so that code designed to handle exceptional situations can be separated from that for normal processing. For example, if a compound statement contained division operations and none of the divisors should be zero, the ADA structure (92) might be

```
BEGIN
  . . . statements containing
    divisions
EXCEPTION
  WHEN Numeric_Error=>
  . . . statements to inform user of     (92)
    error situation
  WHEN OTHERS =>
  . . . all other errors besides
    numeric errors
END;
```

used. If a division by zero occurs in the body of the compound statement, control is transferred to the statements in the exception handler labeled Numeric_Error. After these statements are executed, control returns to the caller. All other errors raised in the compound statement are handled by the OTHERS exception handler. If no exception handlers are specified, exceptions are propagated to the caller. Exceptions can also be declared and raised by users to handle the exceptional conditions of their applications (for example, stack overflow or singular matrix).

Efficiency considerations make it possible for programmers to describe interfaces to programs written in other languages and to access machine-level components (for example, instructions and particular memory locations).

Because many embedded systems are real-time applications, ADA provides tasks that can be concurrently executed, but communicate in very controlled ways. The ADA fragment (93) shows a task named Buffer with two entry points, Put and Get, defined by ACCEPT statements. Other concurrently executing tasks call Buffer through one of its two entry points, for example, Buffer Put(12). Each time the SELECT statement is executed, all the expressions guarding the operations (that is, those expressions after the

```
TASK BODY Buffer IS
  . . . local declarations
BEGIN
  LOOP
    SELECT
      WHEN QLength < Max =>
        ACCEPT Put(N: IN
          Integer) DO
          . . . statement list
        END;
        . . . statement list                (93)
    OR
      WHEN QLength > 0=>
        ACCEPT Get(Result: OUT
          Integer) DO
          . . . statement list
        END;
        . . . statement list
    END SELECT;
  END LOOP;
END Buffer;
```

WHEN's) are evaluated. From those entries whose expressions evaluate to true, one is arbitrarily chosen for execution. The task whose call was chosen and the Buffer task rendezvous until the statements between ACCEPT and END are executed. Then each task is free to proceed with its own execution.

*J. D. Gannon; M. D. Weiser*

**Bibliography.** C. Ghezzi and M. Jazayeri, *Programming Language Concepts*, 1982; E. Horowitz, *Fundamentals of Programming Languages*, 1983; H. Ledgard and M. Marcotty, *The Programming Language Landscape*, 1981; E. I. Organick, A. I. Forsythe, and R. P. Plummer, *Programming Language Structures*, 1978; T. W. Pratt, *Programming Languages: Design and Implementation*, 1975.

## Pulse generator

An electronic circuit capable of producing a waveform that rises abruptly, maintains a relatively flat top for an extremely short interval, and then rapidly falls to zero. A relaxation oscillator, such as a multivibrator, may be adjusted to generate a rectangular waveform having an extremely short duration, and as such it is referred to as a pulse generator. However, there is a class of circuits whose exclusive function is generating short-duration, rectangular waveforms. These circuits are usually specifically identified as pulse generators. An example of such a pulse generator is the triggered blocking oscillator, which is a single relaxation oscillator having transformer-coupled feedback from output to input. *See* Blocking oscillator; Multivibrator; Relaxation oscillator.

Pulse generators sometimes include, but are usually distinguished from, trigger circuits. Trigger circuits, by means of *RC* (resistance-capacitance) differentiating, gated *RLC* (resistance-inductance-capacitance) peaking circuits, or blocking oscillators, generate a short-duration, fast-rising waveform for initiating or triggering an event or a series of events in other circuits, such as monostable or bistable multivibrators. In the pulse generator, the pulse duration and shape are of equal importance to the rise and fall times. In this sense the blocking oscillator is a circuit which can be made to perform well in both respects. *See* Trigger circuit.

**Digitally controlled pulse generator.** The term pulse generator is often applied not only to an electronic circuit generating prescribed pulse sequences but to an electronic instrument designed to generate sequences of pulses with variable delays, pulse widths, and pulse train combinations, programmable in a predetermined manner, often microprocessor-controlled.

For example, in the circuit shown in **Fig. 1**, the basic pulse generator is a bistable *R-S* or *J-K* flip-flop under control of a sequence of clock pulses with a digital logic block to determine the appropriate combinations of set (*S*), reset (*R*), and clock pulses. An output pulse can be programmed to start with the next clock pulse following $R = (1)$ and stop with the clock pulse following $S = (1)$. Thus, the pulse width which can be programmed is $nT_c$, where $T_c$ is the clock pulse interval and $n$ is any number equal to or greater than unity.

**Pulse-forming networks.** A network, formed in such a way as to simulate the delay characteristics of a lossless transmission line, and appropriate switching elements to control the duration of a pulse form the basis for a variety of types of pulse generators. SEE DELAY LINE.

A lossless transmission line has a characteristic impedance, given by Eq. (1), where $L$ is the series

$$R_0 = \sqrt{\frac{L}{C}} \tag{1}$$

inductance and $C$ the shunt capacitance per unit length. Such a line may be approximated by a network consisting of a number $n$ of cascaded $LC$ elements. A pulse applied to the input of such a line reaching the output offers a time delay $T_d$, given by Eq. (2).

$$T_d = n\sqrt{LC} \tag{2}$$

An idealized circuit showing how such a network is used in a pulse generator is shown in **Fig. 2**. A source is connected by a switch to a simulated, unterminated transmission line in series with a resistance $R_0$ equal to the characteristic impedance of the line. As the time voltage is applied, and until all the capacitors in the line become fully charged, the input impedance of the line is equal to $R_0$, and the current $I$ is given by Eq. (3). The step function progresses

$$I = \frac{V_i}{2R_0} \tag{3}$$

along the line, charging each $C$ in succession. When it reaches the end, it is reflected back with no change in phase and returns to the source in a time $T$, in Eq. (4).

$$T = 2n\sqrt{LC} \tag{4}$$

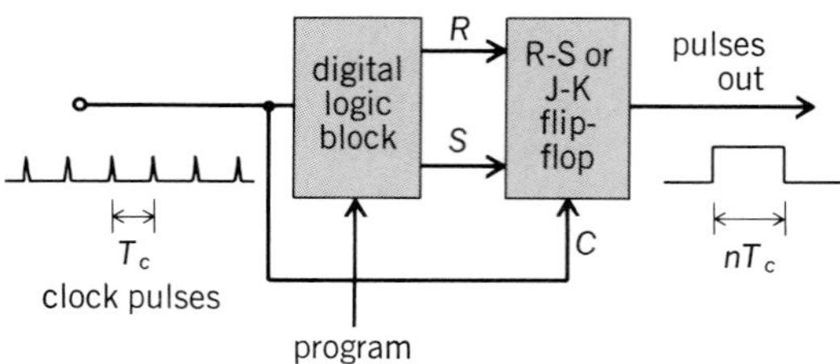


**Fig. 1. Digitally controlled pulse generator.**

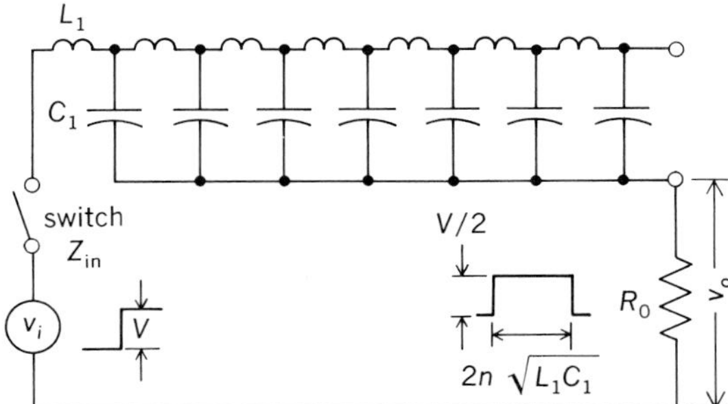


**Fig. 2. Principle of line-controlled pulse generator.**

At this time the line is fully charged, the impedance becomes infinite, and current ceases to flow. The pulse appearing across $R_0$ is suddenly terminated as shown. For discussion of switching circuits suitable for supplying the line-charging current SEE CLAMPING CIRCUIT; GATE CIRCUIT.

Similar results can be obtained from the use of a current generator as a source and a short-circuited line as the controlling circuit element.

Various forms of delay-line-controlled pulse generators can be found, and some are capable of generating pulses containing considerable amounts of power for such applications as modulators in radar transmitters. For an example of this type pulse generators SEE BLOCKING OSCILLATOR; WAVE-SHAPING CIRCUITS.

*Glenn M. Glasford*

***Bibliography.*** D. A. Bell, *Solid State Pulse Circuits*, 1976; R. L. Castellucis, *Pulse and Logic Circuits*, 1976; L. Strauss, *Wave Generation and Shaping*, 2d ed., 1970; R. J. Tocci, *Fundamentals of Pulse and Digital Circuits*, 3d ed., 1983; H. C. Veatch, *Pulse and Switching Circuit Action*, 1971.

## Pulse modulation

A system of modulation in which the amplitude, duration, position, or mere presence of discrete pulses may be so controlled as to represent the message to be communicated. These several forms of pulse modulation are commonly called, respectively, pulse-amplitude modulation (PAM), pulse-duration modulation (PDM), pulse-position modulation (PPM), and pulse-code modulation (PCM). For basic concepts, technical terms, and supplementary information SEE AMPLITUDE MODULATION; FREQUENCY MODULATION; MODULATION; PHASE MODULATION.

Of all the forms of pulse modulation, PCM is the most outstanding. With PCM, transmission circuits are simplified; overall transmission losses are avoided; crosstalk, interference, and distortion are virtually eliminated; signals may be repeated again and again without accumulating significant distortion; patterns of on-or-off pulses constitute the only type of signals that are propagated, regardless of the type of message to be communicated; in the interest of reliability, no on-or-off pulse can be lost (wrongly identified); and in the interests of efficiency and economy, little time is wasted.

### Principles of Operation

All forms of pulse modulation transmit message information intermittently rather than continuously.

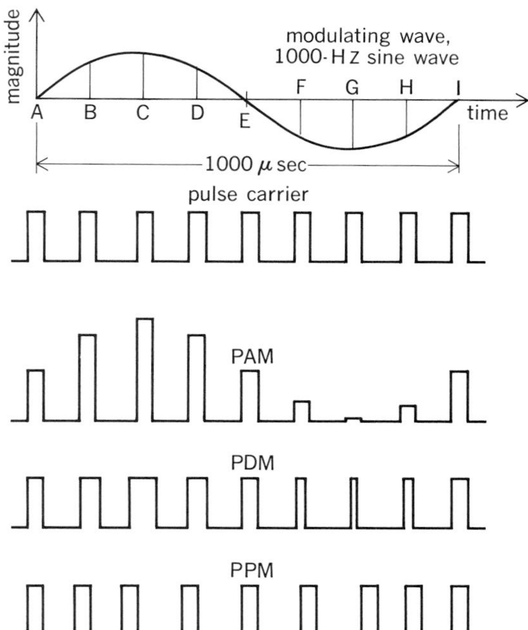


**Fig. 1. Examples of pulse modulation. (*After H. S. Black, Modulation Theory, Van Nostrand, 1953*)**

Therefore, unless the message information to be transmitted happens to be a time sequence of discrete values, it must be reduced to this form before transmission. Sampling (a process for obtaining a sequence of instantaneous values of a wave) accomplishes this by unambiguously representing a continuously varying wave by a series of distinct values (samples). Each message is momentarily sampled at regular intervals at a rate that is in excess of twice the highest message frequency to be communicated. In a PAM, PDM or PPM system (**Fig. 1**) a single pulse is used to specify the value of each sample.

Ease of multiplexing channels by time division is one of the important economic advantages of all forms of pulse modulation. Circuits for accomplishing this are simple and low in cost, and because this low cost is shared by a number of channels, the cost per channel is even lower. When pulse modulation is applied to long-distance communications, these time-division techniques also permit substantial simplification at way stations and branching points. Because each information-bearing pulse keeps its individuality in journeying from the first transmitter to the last receiver, it is comparatively easy to drop and add message channels at various intermediate points along the way.

**Basic concepts.** All forms of pulse modulation may be defined in terms of pulse carrier, and all involve sampling; in addition, PCM implies quantization and coding.

***Pulse carrier.*** This is a carrier (Fig. 1) consisting of a series of regularly recurrent pulses. In general, the power associated with each pulse differs essentially from zero only during a limited interval of time, which is the pulse width.

***Sampling.*** Sampling is a process of extracting successive portions of predetermined duration taken at regular intervals from a continuously varying magnitude-time wave. By sampling at a fast enough rate, namely, in excess of twice the highest significant frequency composing the sampled wave, the samples will unambiguously define the wave. And, conversely, given the samples, the wave can be reconstructed in all its detail. *SEE INFORMATION THEORY.*

For example, suppose the highest significant frequency in a voice wave is less than 4000 Hz. Then all the information necessary for its distortionless reconstruction is given by short samples of the voice wave taken at regular intervals at the rate of 8000 samples per second, that is, by samples taken every 125 microseconds. This complete process, including recovery of the voice wave, is illustrated in **Fig. 2**.

A voice wave passes through a low-pass filter (Fig. 2*a*) which cuts out all frequencies above less than one-half the sampling frequency. After filtering, the wave is designated $V$ (Fig. 2*b*).

The unit sampling function, designated $U$ (Fig. 2*c*), is used to sample the voice. To accomplish this, (Fig. 2*d*), $U$ is multiplied by $V$. Because $U$ is either unity or zero, the product $UV$ is a mathematical process for sampling the voice. The result is a series of positive and negative pulses. When $U$ is unity, the product is $V$. At all other times, the product is zero.

Physically, $UV$ is an array of amplitude-modulated pulses. Consequently, an attenuated replica of $V$ is obtained merely by passing $UV$ through a low-pass filter (Fig. 2*e*). This may be demonstrated by performing the indicated multiplication $UV$. Amplification restores the reconstructed wave to its original value.

Mathematically (Fig. 2*f*), $U$ is equal to dc component $k$ plus components at the sampling frequency $f_c$ and its harmonics. The interval between pulses is $1/f_c$, and $k$ is the ratio of pulse duration $t_0$ to the interval between pulses $T$.

A spectrum analysis of $V$, and also $UV$, is depicted by Fig. 2*g*. The top diagram is the spectrum of $V$. The spectrum of $UV$ is the spectrum of $V$, small but exact, plus upper and lower side bands about $f_c$ and about harmonics of $f_c$. This illustrates, in terms of the familiar concepts of amplitude modulation, that passing $UV$ through a low-pass filter gives an attenuated replica of the sampled wave.

**Pulse-amplitude modulation (PAM).** Pulse-amplitude modulation is amplitude modulation of a pulse carrier. The modulated wave (Fig. 1) is linearly proportional to equally spaced samples of the modulating wave. Another illustration is given in Fig. 2*d*.

Chief interest in PAM lies in its application to time-division multiplexing. Ordinarily, the bandwidth occupancy of PAM appreciably exceeds the theoretical minimum; that is, it appreciably exceeds the sum of the individual message bands. Yet, like other forms of amplitude modulation, PAM is not helped by wider bands; unlike FM and unlike other forms of pulse modulation, PAM connot trade extra bandwidth for noise reduction. *SEE ELECTRICAL NOISE.*

**Pulse-duration modulation (PDM).** Pulse-duration modulation is modulation of a pulse carrier wherein the value of each instantaneous sample of a modulating wave produces a pulse of proportional duration (**Fig. 3**) by varying the leading, trailing, or both edges of the pulse. PDM is also termed pulse-length modulation or pulse-width modulation (PWM).

In contrast to PAM, PDM, which was invented by R. A. Heising in 1924, is able to trade extra bandwidth for noise reduction. This noise advantage of PDM over PAM makes multiplexing by PDM even easier than multiplexing by PAM inasmuch as certain

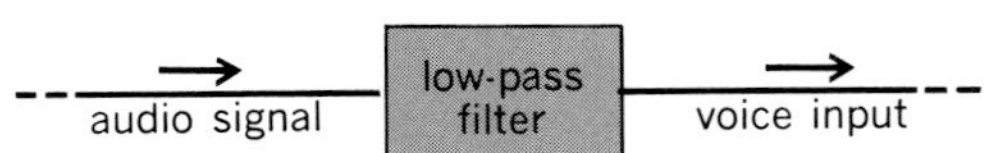


(a) source of voice input

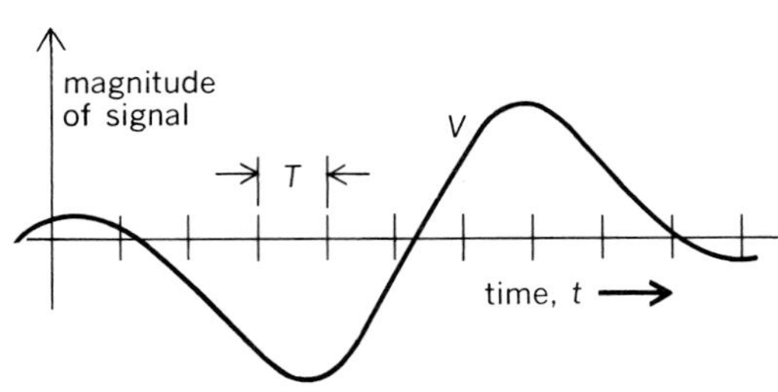


(b) typical voice input

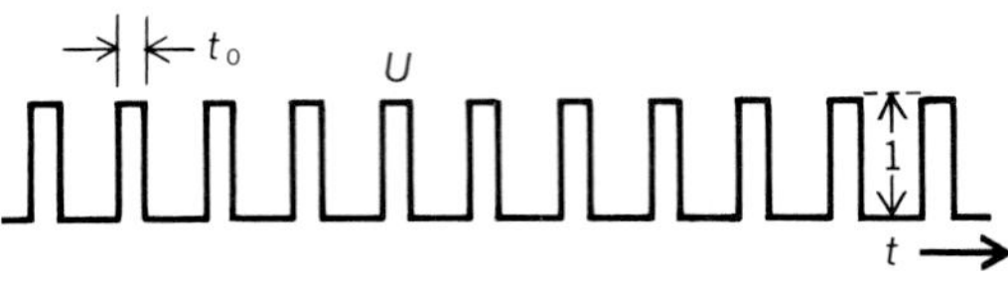


(c) diagram of $U$

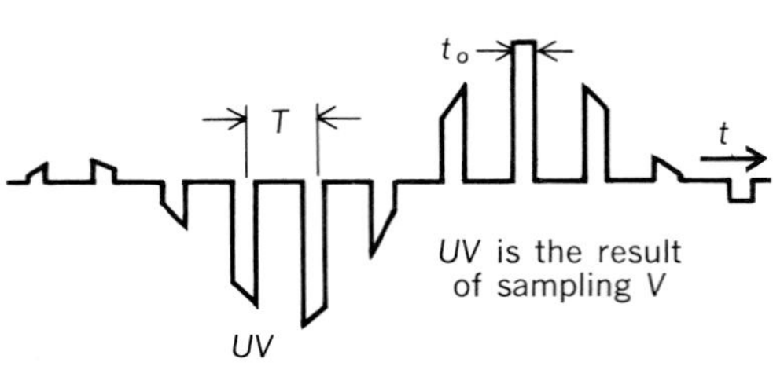


(d) diagram of $UV$

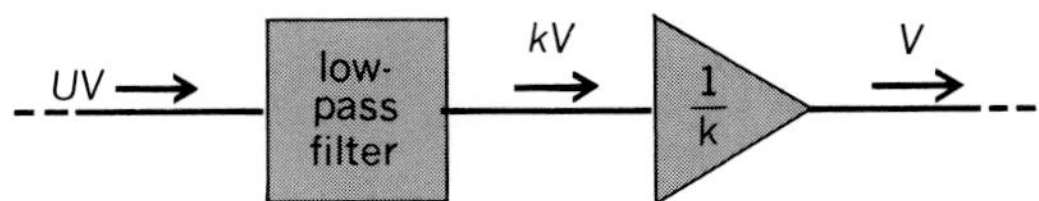


(e) passing $UV$ through a low-pass filter and amplifier to obtain $V$

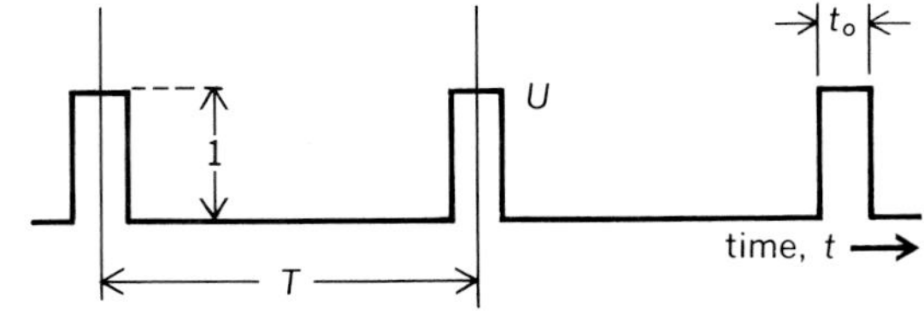


$$U = k + 2k \sum_{m=1}^{\infty} A_m \cos mCt$$

$$k = \frac{t_0}{T} = \text{duty cycle}$$

$$f_c = \frac{C}{2\pi}$$

$$\frac{1}{f_c} = T$$

$$A_m = \frac{\sin mk\pi}{mk\pi}$$

(f) enlarged diagram of $U$, unit sampling function

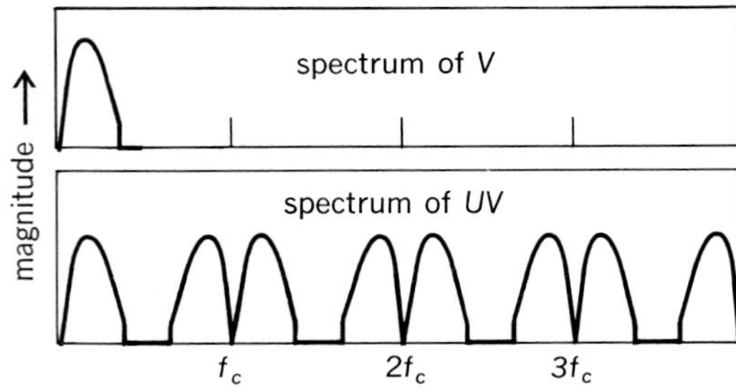


(g) spectrum analysis of $V$ and $UV$

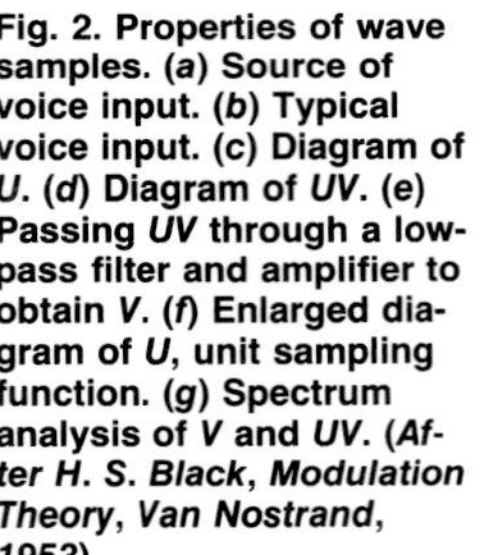
**Fig. 2. Properties of wave samples. (*a*) Source of voice input. (*b*) Typical voice input. (*c*) Diagram of *U*. (*d*) Diagram of *UV*. (*e*) Passing *UV* through a low-pass filter and amplifier to obtain *V*. (*f*) Enlarged diagram of *U*, unit sampling function. (*g*) Spectrum analysis of *V* and *UV*. (After H. S. Black, *Modulation Theory*, Van Nostrand, 1953)**

tolerances for controlling interchannel interference may be eased by an amount corresponding to the noise advantage. However, in order to achieve this important advantage, the instantaneous values of interference must not be permitted to exceed the so-called improvement threshold often enough to be disturbing.

Only the position of the modulated edge or edges conveys information, and the part of each PDM pulse that conveys no information represents wasted pulse power. When this wasted power is subtracted from PDM the result is PPM, which was invented by R. D. Kell in 1934. This power saving is the theoretical advantage of PPM over PDM.

**Pulse-position modulation (PPM).** Pulse-position modulation is modulation of a pulse carrier wherein the value of each instantaneous sample of a modulating wave varies the position in time of a pulse relative to its unmodulated time of occurrence.

**Figure 4** illustrates the sinusoidal modulation of the channel 2 pulse. Successive diagrams indicate the change in the relative position in time of the channel 2 pulses from sample to sample for nine successive samples. When a particular channel is idle, that channel pulse recurs every 125 μs in this example. When a channel is busy, its pulse comes earlier or later depending upon the polarity of the sample. The exact displacement of the pulse from its unmodulated position is proportional to the magnitude of the sample to be communicated. All channel pulses are of constant magnitude and constant duration.

Channel pulses, one for each channel, are transmitted in turn and are preceded by a synchronizing pulse called a marker. This array of marker-plus-channel pulses repeats itself every 125 μs and is called a frame. In Fig. 4 the synchronizing pulse is identified by its longer time duration. Its function is to control the timing of the receiver with high accuracy.

In practical applications, even though PPM is more efficient than PDM, both are highly inefficient when used for certain purposes, for example, when used for multiplexing ordinary telephone channels. Conse-

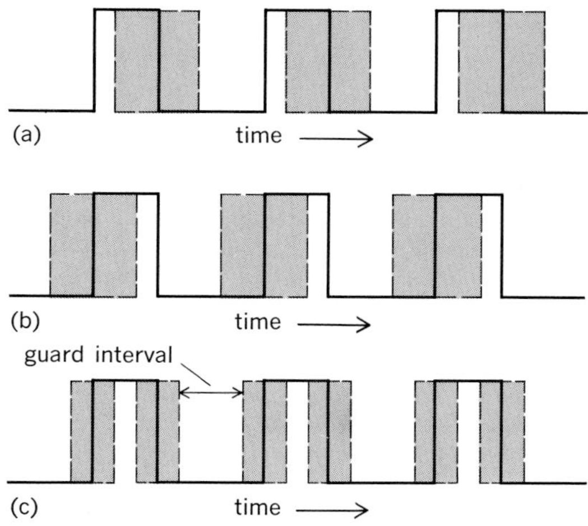


Fig. 3. Types of pulse-duration modulation. (*a*) Trailing edge modulated, leading edge fixed. (*b*) Leading edge modulated, trailing edge fixed. (c) Both edges modulated. Solid lines indicate duration of unmodulated pulses, shaded areas limits of maximum modulation. (*After H. S. Black, Modulation Theory, Van Nostrand, 1953*)

quently, PCM, which not only is more efficient but also possesses many other very important advantages, has been widely adopted.

**Pulse-code modulation (PCM).** Pulse-code modulation, invented by H. A. Reeves in 1939, is a method of transmitting continuously varying message waves in which (1) the message wave is sampled, (2) the value of each sample is replaced by the closest one of a finite set of permitted values, and (3) these permitted values are then each unambiguously represented by some one of the possible patterns of *N* on-or-off pulses. These three operations are known as sampling, quantizing, and coding, respectively.

***Sampling.*** Modern PCM is based upon the recognition that quantized samples may approximate an exact specification of a continuously varying wave as closely as desired. Assume for purposes of illustration that a 7-pulse code is to be used. This is a binary system whose capacity is $2^7$ permitted or quantized values. Each sample, after being coded, would be represented by some one of the 128 possible patterns of 7 on-or-off pulses.

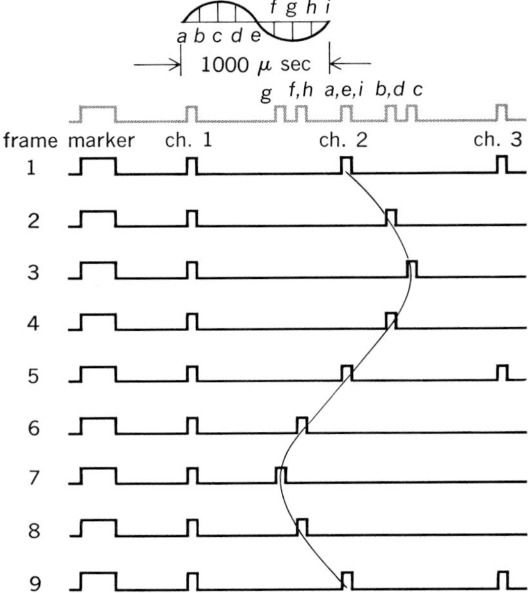


Fig. 4. Pulse-position modulation, modulation of channel 2 by a sine wave. (*After H. S. Black, Modulation Theory, Van Nostrand, 1953*)

***Quantization.*** Quantization changes a continuously varying signal to a stepped signal. Graphically quantization means that the straight line representing the relationship between input and output has been replaced by a stair-step function. Clearly, by using small enough steps, errors may be cut to an arbitrary minimum (**Fig. 5**), at the expense of increased communications channel bandwidths.

When speech samples are quantized, the steps are tapered as shown in Fig. 5*b*. By tapering most of the steps logarithmically, nearly uniform percentage precision is obtained over most of the range, and far fewer steps are required. To reproduce telephonic speech to a high degree of fidelity, 128 logarithmic steps will suffice.

***Coding and multiplexing.*** In PCM these 128 values are represented by a 7-pulse code. Each voice sample is represented with adequate accuracy by some one of the possible patterns of 7 on-or-off pulses (**Fig. 6**). Channels are multiplexed by time division.

Similarly, other forms of communication may also be represented by on-or-off pulses. In practice, a single PCM system may process many kinds of communications and may provide many channels of each kind.

Ordinarily, PCM systems are called upon to transmit large numbers of on-or-off pulses per second. For example, for each telephone conversation, PCM transmits 56,000 on-or-off pulses per second in each direction of transmission. This means that each one-way speech channel provided by PCM makes available a phenomenally fast one-way data channel, fast enough to operate simultaneously more than 1000 conventional teletypewriters. In general, the number of on-or-off pulses per second per message will depend upon the kind of message. A one-way television signal might, for example, be represented by 70,000,000 on-or-off pulses per second.

***Repeatering.*** By having to make only on-or-off distinctions, PCM is able to deliver a high-quality signal even when noise and interference are so bad that it is barely possible to recognize the pulses. At each regenerative repeater, just so long as incoming pulses are correctly identified, a new pulse generator may be caused to generate new pulses of correct magnitude, waveform, and timing.

### Applications of PCM

PCM systems are widely used in many ways and for many purposes by all branches of the military, Comsat, Intelsat, NASA, and private and public communications companies in virtually every country. Moreover, PCM systems transmitting secret information are used to protect many military and public services.

In 1979, Communications Satellite Corporation (COMSAT) installed a new type of high-speed (60,000,000 digital pulses per second) communications system on 250 seagoing ships, thereby linking each ship to every ship-to-shore receiver in the world via COMSAT's existing geostationary three-satellite system which utilizes PCM to transmit speech, teletypewriter, and facsimile messages. This means that

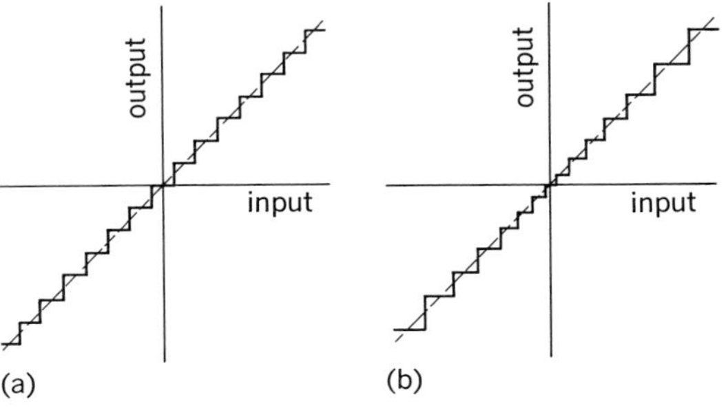


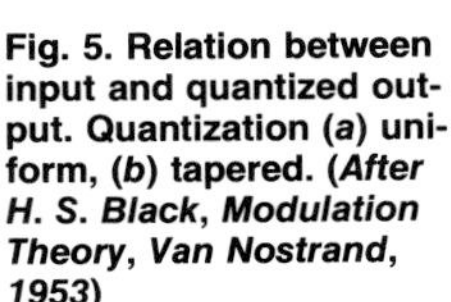

**Fig. 5. Relation between input and quantized output. Quantization (*a*) uniform, (*b*) tapered. (*After H. S. Black, Modulation Theory, Van Nostrand, 1953*)**

anyone with access to a telephone can talk via satellite to someone out to sea at all times. The system was subsequently expanded and is now operated by Inmarsat.

The telephone system uses PCM in the loop plant connecting customer premises and central offices, in the exchange plant between central offices, on microwave radio systems, on coaxial cable systems, and on optical fibers. Synchronized timing is required in every branch of each system in order to achieve superior performance and maximum economy.

Originally each one-way PCM channel used a seven-pulse code and transmitted 56 kilobits per second (kbps). An eight-pulse code has been developed (the extra pulse being used for both information and control) and is used to transmit 64 kbps. While 64 kbps occupies four times the bandwidth occupied by a one-way analog voice channel, pulse transmission provides lower cost and better performance, because it is only necessary to recognize the presence or absence of each pulse in order to reconstruct the original voice wave at the receiving end.

**Radio set AN/TRC.** AN/TRC (Army-Navy transportable radio transmitting and receiving communications equipment) was the first American-built microwave two-way multichannel PCM radio relay system to be used throughout the world. With many repeaters in tandem, its eight voice channels were outstanding for their high quality and remarkable stability. AN/TRC was the forerunner of microwave radio relay systems and was the first implementation of PCM. *See Microwave.*

**Telephone PCM systems.** The economic importance of using PCM for voice circuits on existing voice pairs in congested metropolitan ducts was recognized as early as 1945. In 1962, after 6 years of exploratory development, the T1 system went into operation. Its low-cost channel banks provide 24 one-way voice circuits which are unambiguously represented by patterns of 1,544,000 on-or-off pulses per second propagated over a twisted pair using regenerative repeaters spaced at 6000 ft (1.8 km). Millions of these systems are now in operation.

With the growing web of T1 systems in each part of an extended metropolitan area, the payoff for intercity and express-route digital lines to interconnect these T1 webs becomes attractive. This calls for the interleaving of many nonsynchronous T1 bitstreams to form a single high-bit-rate system. Bell Telephone Laboratories' engineers developed the technique of "pulse stuffing" in the 1960s to make this kind of interleaving possible.

In 1978 digital systems began to be used in customer loops, enabling 80 single-party lines in a rural district to be served over a digital line using T1 repeaters. Subsequently, a system serving 96 customers was introduced for more general application in the loop plant. Other extensions in loop plant services made possible by pulse modulation include amplification of voice signals as well as ringing and dialing pulses.

Nine pulse modulation systems have been developed, all of which provide the important advantage of pulse modulation and regenerative repeatering. These systems are: T1B4, T2, 1A, T1C, TCAS, DR18, DUV, WRT, and WT4. Some of the systems are designed for operation over relatively short distances and others over distances as long as 4000 mi (6400 km). They are employed on all the transmission media in current use: wire pair, coaxial cable, microwave radio, optical fibers and satellites.

These pulse modulation systems are being augmented by long-life, highly reliable optical fiber systems which will provide nationwide digital transmission. Existing microwave radio relay systems which carry over half of the telephone system's long-distance messages are also being augmented by high-capacity optical fiber transmission systems.

The L5 coaxial carrier transmission system is a long-haul, high-quality analog system designed to carry high-quality two-way telephone conversations. L5 systems carry over a quarter of the telephone system's long-distance messages, and similarly are being

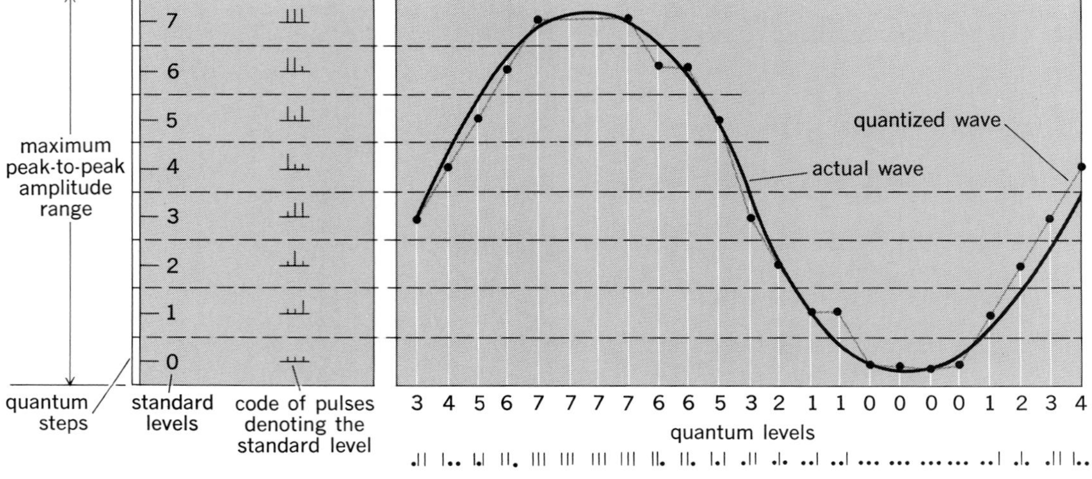


**Fig. 6. Pulse-code modulation. (*a*) Quantizing of amplitude level and level designation by a code of pulses; 3-pulse code in this example permits $2^3 = 8$ levels. (*b*) Representation of a wave by a succession of coded pulse groups. (*After F. E. Terman, Electronic and Radio Engineering, McGraw-Hill, 4th ed., 1955*)**

replaced by high-capacity optical fiber transmission systems. SEE COMMUNICATIONS CABLE.

**Synchronization.** For any digital system to deliver correct information, no bit can be lost. Moreover, the connection of a transmitting channel to its proper receiving channel requires that the transmitting and receiving terminals be synchronized. This means that the timing operations at the receiver, except for the time lost in propagating and repeatering, must follow closely the timing operations at the transmitting end. To accomplish this amounts to getting a local clock to keep the same time as a distant standard clock, except that the local clock is slow corresponding to the time required to transmit the signals. Once this objective is accomplished, every in-band frequency going into the network comes out unchanged at the distant end.

The most promising solution to this difficult problem is to provide one master oscillator for the entire network of the many different kinds of systems operating throughout the United States and then to provide and control a plurality of slave oscillators from the one master oscillator. To put this idea into practice requires three identical master standard oscillators. If one standard malfunctions, its reading will not match the readings of the other two. Were there only two standards, it would be impossible to determine which was faulty when the two readings failed to match. Each of the three standard reference frequencies is measured every 2.5 min to an accuracy of 1 part in $10^{12}$, and the three frequencies are simultaneously compared with each other. Should one be wrong, the integrity of the reference is guaranteed by unique fast-acting automatic switching circuits. The three standards, put into service in 1973, are based on cesium-beam atomic clocks and are buried deep underground at Hillsboro, Missouri.

The Hillsboro facility transmits a reference frequency of 20.48 MHz accurate to 1 part in $10^{11}$ to each slave oscillator, which in turn is required to deliver 20.48 MHz accurate to 1 part in $10^{10}$. Three slave oscillators are required for the same reason that three master oscillators are used. The heart of a slave oscillator is a 39A digitally controlled crystal oscillator accurate to almost 1 part in $10^{11}$. Of course, the incoming 20.48 MHz might be completely lost due to transmission difficulties or suffer short-time impairments due to excessive noise, switching transients, and so forth. The 39A oscillator is loosely coupled to the incoming reference signal in order to automatically correct any slow change in oscillator frequency due to aging, assuming that the reference signal is unimpaired. When the reference signal is impaired, the 39A oscillator automatically disconnects itself from the line and can operate continuously for weeks, delivering 20.48 MHz accurate to 1 part in $10^{10}$.

*Harold S. Black*

**Electronic switching.** Electronic switching generally refers to telecommunications systems developed for local and toll switching purposes. The No. 1 ESS (trademark of AT&T) switch, introduced in 1965, was developed for large metropolitan areas. It was followed by the No. 2 ESS switch for use in suburban areas and the No. 3 ESS switch for use in rural areas. The Nos. 1, 2, and 3 ESS switches are primarily local exchange switches, with the No. 4 ESS switch providing interexchange toll capabilities. The 5ESS (trademark of AT&T) switch offers both local and toll features, with modular capabilities to serve small, medium, and large communities.

All ESS switches are computer-based systems utilizing stored program control. Millions of program instructions and data words control the various stages of call processing. From digit reception of the dialed number to ringing the distant telephone, each step of the call progress is monitored and controlled by special-purpose digital computers. The calling capacity of ESS switches is much greater than that of electromechanical predecessors. The No. 4 ESS switch, for example, can switch 670,000 calls per hour to more than 100,000 telephone circuits.

The No. 4 ESS and 5ESS switches provide digital switching capabilities, connecting directly to digital T1 lines. PCM data is passed through the ESS switch without analog conversion. Data and voice signals can be switched between digital facilities, allowing precise digital transmission. Noise and transmission loss characteristics inherent with analog transmission facilities are eliminated. SEE SWITCHING SYSTEMS (COMMUNICATIONS).

*William L. Zarbock*

**Optical-fiber transmission systems.** A typical all-digital optical waveguide is an optical fiber consisting of a central core of only 0.002 in. (50 micrometers) in diameter with a surrounding cladding with an outer diameter of 0.005 in. (125 micrometers). The attenuation of the 5-mil fiber is essentially constant over a frequency band wide enough to transmit 300,000,000 on-or-off light pulses per second. The fiber loss is also essentially constant over the ambient temperature ranges encountered in practice (−40 to 212°F; −40 to 100°C). There exists no significant crosstalk between optical waveguides even when bundles of one hundred are so bunched that each waveguide is in contact with others and when as many as half may transmit signals in opposite directions. Many simpler and highly useful optical waveguide systems do not possess or need most of these advantages.

Low-loss, low-dispersion, high-silica-content fibers are produced by a process called chemical vapor deposition (CVD) which controls fiber manufacture with great precision. In this technique, silica and other glass-forming oxides are deposited at high temperatures on the inner wall of a fused silica tube. Once the CVD process is completed, the tube is collapsed and drawn at a high temperature into a fiber of the desired diameter. The fiber is drawn from specially prepared glass rod (preform) at typical speeds of 3 ft/s (1 m/s) with less than 1% deviation in diameter. This is accomplished by a monitoring system that measures the fiber 1000 times a second, automatically adjusting drawing speed to keep the diameter constant. An improved process for the production of these optical glass fibers, called modified chemical vapor deposition (MCVD), is a major contribution to fiber optics communications and is used by most of the major companies in the field.

An optical-fiber transmission system requires a reliable long-life light source. Semiconductor lasers are expected to operate unfailingly over a period in excess of 11 years. Light-emitting diodes (LEDs) are less-expensive sources of light but, unfortunately, provide less optical power coupled into the fiber. Both types of source can be directly modulated, which means that they can be turned on and off simply by turning the drive current from a semiconductor driver on and off. SEE LASER; LIGHT-EMITTING DIODE.

Light detection at the receiving end requires evaluation of the intensity of the incoming light pulses. This can be done with a photodiode which converts light pulses into weak electric pulses which are amplified by an amplifier of appropriate bandwidth. The photodiode may be of the *pin* type or the more sensitive, expensive avalanche type. *See Photodiode*.

There is a very large number of possible applications of optical-fiber transmission systems. Many important on-premise applications exist where fibers run from only a few feet to several hundred feet, so that the system requirements are not stringent. In the exchange plant hundreds of individual calls could be woven together into single-pulse streams at rates up to about 2,000,000 pulses per second for transmission from one central office to another through optical-fiber cables in underground conduits and, in heavily populated areas, the offices are so close together that repeaters may not be needed. Eventually, optical-fiber transmission systems, because of their freedom from interference, immunity to ground-loop problems, flexibility of system growth, large information capacity, and potential, will span the continent, adding significantly to the digitization of the network. *See Optical communications*.

*Harold S. Black*

**Nationwide digital transmission.** Nationwide digital transmission means the use of digital transmission over all of the transmission and switching facilities connecting every residential and business telephone in the United States. There exists an extensive hierarchy of switching offices and interconnecting paths over which calls using digital transmission are routed automatically and efficiently. The use of digital technology for electronic switching and transmission has increased at a rapid rate in the telephone network. For example, digital radio, coaxial cable systems, and optical fiber systems are expected to provide digital transmission over thousands of miles, thereby supplying the long-haul digital links between the rapidly expanding digital exchange network and the time division digital No. 4 ESS toll switching system. Digital switching is inherently a four-wire operation.

Interwoven with, and an important part of, the nationwide digital transmission network are special services (such as data transmission, facsimile, teletypewriter, microwave radio broadcasting, television programs, and other special network or enhanced services) offered to or requested by particular customers or stations.

To expedite nationwide digital transmission, thousands of miles of long-haul digital facilities have been under construction, linking the national telephone network. Over 10,000 miles (16,000 km) of light-wave, digital coaxial and digital radio transmission systems are already in service. One of the earliest light-wave systems serving the United States' Northeast Corridor (including Boston, New York, Philadelphia, and Washington) can carry up to 80,000 digitalized simultaneous telephone conversations along hair-thin optical fibers. This system links many all-digital high-capacity electronic switching offices. Optical-fiber light-wave technology has advanced very rapidly. Repeater spacings have increased manyfold, and bit rates and carrying capacities have increased to the point where tens of thousands of two-way conversations per pair of fibers will be realizable in the network.

*Judith Kagle Ferguson*

**Global digital transmission.** The availability of long-wavelength devices, single-mode filters, integrated optical repeaters, and single-mode optical fiber transmission systems will make it practical to plan to apply fiber optics to submarine cable systems transmitting $10^9$ digital pulses per second. Optical fiber systems are expected to be used in most applications where existing wire, waveguide, and microwave systems are employed.

**Other uses involving fiber optics.** The application of fiber optics to existing types of copiers promises a 40% price reduction, accompanied by smaller and more reliable machines requiring less maintenance.

Integrated circuits designed for use in a high-speed optical fiber scanner are being developed by the U.S. Postal Services for use on a system of electronic mail transmission. *See Electronic mail*.

During 1980 Bell Telephone Laboratories fabricated a high-speed integrated circuit called the digital speech processor (DSP) which is to make a wide range of new telephone services possible. This DSP chip contains over 45,000 transistors in an area smaller than 1 $cm^2$, and utilizes digital transmission to perform a million additions and multiplications in a second. Chips with 150,000 components are routinely manufactured. Smaller chips containing over 10,000,000 components are envisioned. *See Integrated circuits*.

**Digital filters.** The use of digitalized techniques has been applied to the numerous components of many different types of systems. Digital filters are a good example. Many signals are no longer represented by undulatory currents, but by sequences of numbers in digital form that represent periodic snapshots or samples of the original, continuously varying quantity. The tasks once performed by conventional filters composed of capacitors, inductors, and resistors are now accomplished by numerical operations on these samples. Each sample is represented by a number, and numerical operations on these numbers are carried out by miniaturized high-speed computers built from even smaller integrated solid-state circuits. These extremely small digital filters bear no relation to the bulky ladder and lattice structures of the 1920s and 1930s. *See Data communications; Digital computer; Electric filter; Electrical communications*.

*Harold S. Black*

**Bibliography.** T. A. Abelle, D. A. Alsberg, and P. T. Hutchison, A high-capacity digital communication system using $TE_{01}$ transmission circular waveguide, *IEEE Trans. Microwave Theory Tech.*, MTT-23(4):326–333, 1975; M. Barnoski (ed.), *Fundamentals of Optical Communications*, 1976; *Bell Syst. Tech J.*, 43(5):1831–2605, special issue, September 1964; H. S. Black, *Modulation Theory*, 1953; J. H. Bobsin and L. F. Forman, The T2 digital line: Extending the digital network, *Bell Lab. Rec.*, 51(8):239–243, 1973; R. G. Buus, D. L. Rechtenbaugh, and R. B. Whipp, T-carrier administration system speeds service restoration, *Bell Lab. Rec.*, 53(5):216–255, 1975; H. Feistel, W. A. Notz, and J. Lynn Smith, Some cryptographic techniques for machine-to-machine data communications, *Proc. IEEE*, 63(11):1547–1554, 1975; J. F. Graczyk, E. T. Mackey, and W. J. Maybach, T1C carrier: The T1 doubler, *Bell Lab. Rec.*, 53(6):256–263, 1975; J. C. Hancock, *An Introduction to the Principles of Communication Theory*, 1961; L5 coaxial cable transmission system, *Bell Syst. Tech. J.*, 53(10):1897–2269, special issue, 1974; E. T. Mackey, W. J. Maybach, and S. B. Pfeiffer, Mixing data and voice on the T1 line, *Bell Lab. Rec.*, 53(2):136–142, 1975; L. Marton (ed.), *Advances in Electronics (and Electron Physics)*, 2d ed., vol. 3, 1951; S. E. Miller, E. A. J. Marcatili, and T. Li, Research toward optical-fiber transmission systems, *Proc. IEEE*, 61(12):1703–1751, 1973; New digital radio transmission system, *Bell Lab. Rec.*, 52(11):362, 1974; J. F. Oberst, Keeping Bell System frequencies on the beam, *Bell Lab. Rec.*, 52(3):84–89, 1974; R. C. Prime and L. L. Sheets, The 1A radio digital system makes "data under voice" a reality, *Bell Lab. Rec.*, 51(11):334–339, 1973; J. G. Proakis, *Digital Communications*, 1983; J. M. Sipress, T4M: New superhighway for metropolitan communications, *Bell Lab. Rec.*, 53(9):352–359, 1975.

## Pulse modulator

A device for the pulse modulation of a radio-frequency carrier signal. In pulse modulation, information is transmitted by generating a train of discrete pulses whose amplitude, duration, position, or mere presence is controlled in accordance with the signal. There are several forms of pulse modualtion: pulse-amplitude modulation (PAM), pulse-width modulation (PWM) or pulse-duration modulation (PDM), pulse-position modulation (PPM), and pulse-code modulation (PCM). In each case, modulation is achieved by converting the continuous signal wave into a series of pulses which are transmitted to a point of reception where a demodulator is employed to reproduce the analog waveform. For a discussion of this form of modulation SEE *PULSE MODULATION*.

**Pulse-amplitude modulation.** In pulse-amplitude modulation the desired signal to be transmitted is sampled periodically (**Fig. 1**). PAM may be accomplished by the use of a multiplier circuit. The signal that contains the intelligence to be transmitted is applied to one of the multiplier inputs, and the train of pulses known as the sampling signal is applied to the other multiplier input. If this train of pulses has an amplitude of one during the pulse and zero elsewhere, the multiplier output will consist of a train of pulses, each having an amplitude equal to the signal amplitude at the time of sampling (Fig. 1). The main reason for using PAM is that several signals may be transmitted over a single communication channel by a technique known as multiplexing.

**Commutation.** The most simple technique for multiplexing several signals onto a single channel is to use a rotating multipole switch known as a commutator (**Fig. 2**). In fact, the commutator may serve as the sampler, or modulator, as well as the multiplexer. Although electronic commutators are used in modern technology, a rotating mechanical switch is shown in Fig. 2 for the sake of simplicity. A commutator must be used on the receiving end as well as the transmitting end of the multiplexed channel in order to unscramble the signals. These commutators must be synchronized so that each message is sent to its proper destination at the receiving end. For example, several telephone conversations might be sampled and multiplexed onto a single telephone line. An easily identifiable synchronizing signal must also be sent to synchronize the commutators at the two ends of the system. A low-pass filter is used in each message line at the receiving end to pass only the desired message frequencies and remove the higher frequencies of the pulses. SEE *ELECTRIC FILTER*.

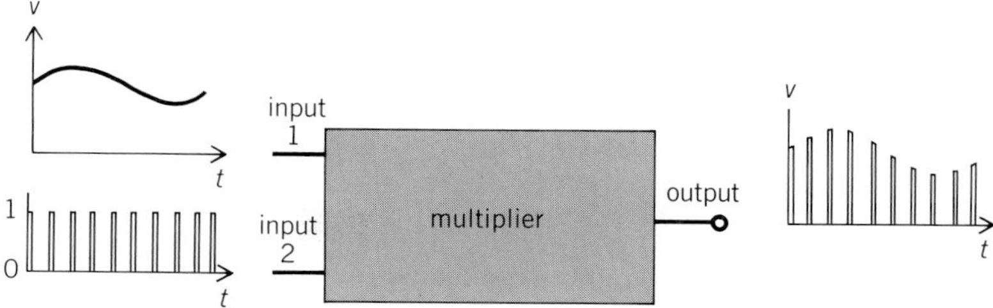


**Fig. 1. Pulse-amplitude modulation by means of a multiplier circuit.**

The number of messages that may be multiplexed onto a communication channel depends upon the frequency spectrum of the messages and the bandwidth of the channel. H. Nyquist showed that the frequency $f_s$ of the sampling pulses must be at least twice as high as the highest frequency component $f_m$ in the signal or message to be sampled. Then the slowest speed the commutator could have is $f_s = 2f_m$ revolutions, or cycles, per second. However, if there are $n$ equally spaced message contacts around the circumference of the commutator, the maximum time $\tau$ that the rotor could be in contact with any one message segment is $\tau = 1/nf_s = 1/2nf_m$ seconds. Then the minimum channel bandwidth is given by Eq. (1). It follows

$$B_c\ (\mathrm{min}) = \frac{1}{\tau} = 2nf_m \qquad (1)$$

from this equation that if the channel bandwidth is $B_c$ and the highest message frequency is $f_m$, then the number $n$ of messages, including synchronization, that may be multiplexed on the channel is given by Eq. (2), where $B_c$ is in hertz and $n$ must be rounded

$$n = \frac{B_c}{2f_m} \qquad (2)$$

to the next-lower integer value. The number of actual messages, excluding synchronization, is $n - 1$.

As an example of multiplexing, assume that a given communications channel will carry signals with frequencies up to 100 kHz but the telephone voice signals have an upper frequency limit of 3.2 kHz. Then the number of messages that may be multiplexed is (100 kHz/6.4 kHz) − 1 = 14.

**Pulse-width and pulse-position modulation.** PAM is a satisfactory method of communication when transmission distances are short enough to maintain high signal-to-noise ratios. However, when transmission distances become long, such as many miles, the atmospheric noise from lightning and other electrical sources that is induced into either a hard-wire line or a radio antenna may degrade the signal-to-noise ratio

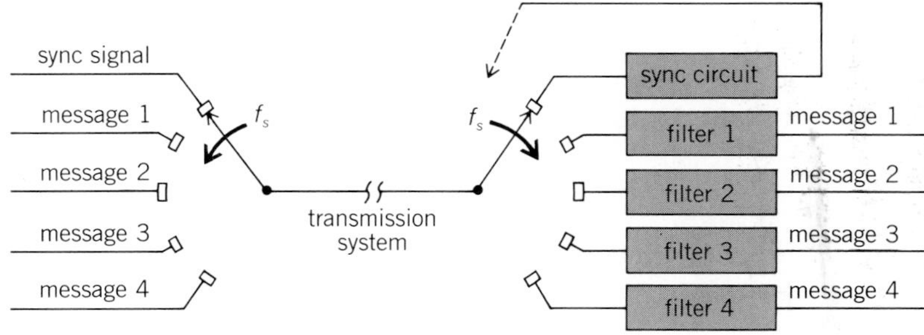


**Fig. 2. Commutators used to multiplex four PAM messages.**

sufficiently to at least cause annoyance and at worst render the message unintelligible. Both pulse-width modulation and pulse-position modulation have been used in the past with the hope of improving the signal-to-noise ratio. *See* ELECTRICAL NOISE; SIGNAL-TO-NOISE RATIO.

PWM may be obtained from the PAM pulse by charging a small capacitor to the peak voltage of each pulse as it comes along, and then discharging the capacitor through a constant current source before the next pulse arrives. Then the capacitor voltage decreases linearly to zero during a time that is proportional to the pulse amplitude. These triangular pulses may then be passed through a Schmitt trigger circuit to square them up and provide constant amplitude pulses of varying width.

PPM may then be obtained by differentiating the PWM signals to produce narrow pulses at both the leading and trailing edges of the PWM pulses. The leading-edge pulse is used as the reference pulse, and the time difference between it and the trailing-edge pulse represents the modulation amplitude. These sharp PPM pulses may be squared up by the use of either a Schmitt trigger circuit or a one-shot multivibrator. Both the PWM and PPM signals are subject to noise modulation so their use may or may not improve the signal-to-noise ratio in comparison with a PAM system. *See* MULTIVIBRATOR.

**Pulse code modulation.** A signal transmission system of any type may become essentially immune to atmospheric and other induced noise when pulse-code modulation is used. In this type of modulation, the modulating signal is first sampled (**Fig.** 3*a*). The resulting PAM signals are then quantized by a circuit that compares each pulse amplitude with a set of predetermined levels and produces a stepwise-varying replica of the original signal having only the predetermined voltage levels. In Fig. 3*b*, eight equally spaced levels were chosen to represent signals limited to the range from approximately 0 to 7 V peak amplitude. Thus the quantizing levels are separated by 1 V. Each quantized level is then represented by a sequence of pulses known as a code. Any of many different coding systems may be used, but the binary code is basic and is very commonly used (Fig. 3*c*). Analog-to-digital converters are available in integrated-circuit form. *See* ANALOG-TO-DIGITAL CONVERTER; INTEGRATED CIRCUITS.

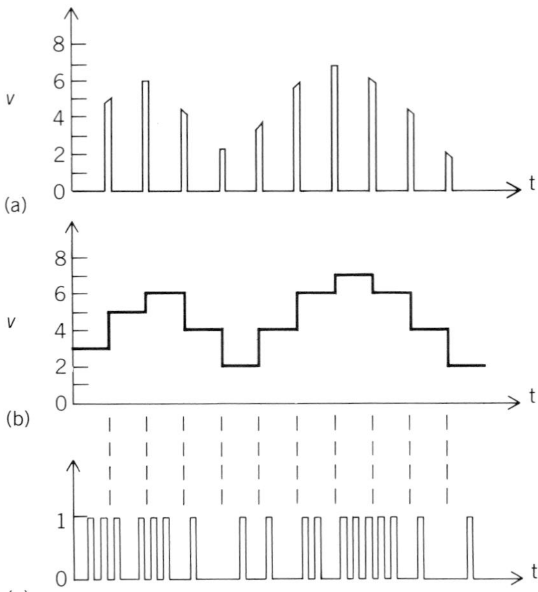


Fig. 3. Pulse-code modulation. (*a*) Signal sampling. (*b*) Quantization. (*c*) Binary pulse coding.

**Representation of eight levels by a pulse code**

| A | B | C | Level number |
|---|---|---|---|
| 0 | 0 | 0 | 0 |
| 0 | 0 | 1 | 1 |
| 0 | 1 | 0 | 2 |
| 0 | 1 | 1 | 3 |
| 1 | 0 | 0 | 4 |
| 1 | 0 | 1 | 5 |
| 1 | 1 | 0 | 6 |
| 1 | 1 | 1 | 7 |

In binary code, the number of bits or pulses, $n$, needed to represent each of the $m$ quantized levels is given by Eq. (3). Thus, since $m = 8$ in the above

$$m = 2^n \tag{3}$$

example, the number of pulses, $n$, needed to represent any of these eight levels is 3. If these pulses are labeled A, B, and C, any of which may have only values of either 0 or 1, the relationship may be written as in Eq. (4), where A is known as the most signifi-

$$\text{Decimal number} = A2^2 + B2^1 + C2^0 \tag{4}$$

cant bit (MSB) and C is known as the least significant bit (LSB). Then all of the eight levels may be represented by the pulse code shown in the **table**. *See* INFORMATION THEORY.

A few examples of representing a voltage level by a three-bit code are given in Fig. 3. When these coded pulses are transmitted through a communications channel, the quantized original signal may be almost perfectly reproduced, providing the amplitude of the pulses representing level 1 are larger than the induced noise. Then the noise can be removed from the signal by clipping circuits and the original modulating signal recovered by the use of a digital-to-analog converter. *See* DIGITAL-TO-ANALOG CONVERTER.

If the transmission path is very long, one or more repeater stations may be needed at intermediate points. These repeaters receive the signal while it is still larger than the noise, remove the noise, amplify the signal, and retransmit it along the channel. In fact, PCM signals that are weaker than the noise may be received and the noise rejected if a phase-locked loop is used as the demodulator in the receiver. *See* PHASE-LOCKED LOOPS.

Since $n$ pulses are required in PCM to transmit the amplitude information of a single PAM pulse, each PCM pulse may be only $1/n$ times as long as a PAM pulse. Thus, the bandwidth of the channel must be $n$ times as wide as a PAM channel when PCM is used for a given signal.

***Quantization noise.*** Although PCM may be immune to atmospheric and induced noise, a predictable and controllable type of noise known as quantization noise remains. This noise results from the uncertainty of the amplitude of the original signal after its quantization. For example, in the eight-level quantization of Fig. 3, the quantized level of 4 V could have resulted from any signal level greater than 3.5 V but less than 4.5 V. This 1-V peak-to-peak uncertainty produces the same effect as a 1-V peak-to-peak atmospheric or induced noise in an AM or PAM signal because this noise produces the same uncertainty in the signal amplitude. The quantization signal-to-noise ratio is easy to predict if it is assumed that all signal levels are equally likely. Then, since the peak-to-peak signal level is from 0 to $V_p$ and the peak-to-peak quantization noise voltage is $V_p/m$, the ratio of signal voltage to noise voltage is approximately equal to $m$. But the signal-to-noise ratio is a power ratio which is proportional to the square of the voltage ratio, and is therefore approximately $m^2$. Therefore, the signal-to-noise ratio of the eight-level quantization is $8^2 = 64 = 18$ dB. Although this signal-to-noise ratio may be acceptable for some voice communication or scientific instrumentation, the quantization noise, known as cackle, may be annoying and the $\pm 6\%$ accuracy would be inadequate for most instrumentation needs. The signal-to-noise ratio may be increased by 6 dB and the instrumentation error reduced by a factor of 2 for each additional binary digit added to the code group or word. However, either the channel bandwidth must be increased or the number of messages decreased as the number of bits $n$ is increased. A typical message bit number used for good-quality voice communication is $n = 7$, which provides a signal-to-noise ratio of 42 dB. The addition of a synchronizing bit would require an eight-bit word length.

**Signal compression and expansion.** The signal-to-noise ratio of PCM voice communication decreases if the signal level decreases significantly from its maximum permissible value because some of the quantization levels are then not used. In order to overcome this problem, signal compression is used prior to modulation. This compression is accomplished by amplifying the weak signals more than the strong ones so the variation in signal level is greatly reduced. In order to restore the original relative signal levels at the receiving end of the system after demodulation, a circuit known as an expander is used to amplify the stronger signals more than the weak ones. A circuit that will serve as either a compressor or expander is known as a compander.

*Charles L. Alley*

**Bibliography.** S. Haykin, *Communications Systems*, 2d ed., 1983; R. Kellejian, *Applied Electronic Communications: Circuits, Systems, Transmission*, 1980; M. Schwartz, *Information Transmission, Modulation and Noise*, 3d ed., 1980.

## Pulse transformers

Iron-cored devices which are used in the transmission and shaping of low-power pulses whose widths range from a fraction of a microsecond to about 25 μs. Among the extensive applications of pulse transformers are the following: (1) to couple between the stages of pulse amplifiers; (2) to invert the polarity of a pulse; (3) to change the amplitude and impedance level of a pulse; (4) to differentiate a pulse; (5) to effect "dc isolation" between a source and a load; (6) to act as coupling element in certain pulse-generating circuits.

In many cases the functions listed above can be accomplished as well or better with transistor circuits. However, the pulse transformer, being a passive element, has none of the instability associated with active circuits.

The **illustration** gives a schematic diagram of a pulse transformer. The primary inductance is $L_p$, the secondary inductance is $L_s$, and the mutual inductance is $M$. In a more accurate description of the pulse transformer it is necessary to take into account the primary and secondary resistances, all capacitances, the core loss, and the nonlinearity of the magnetic circuit. The coefficient of coupling $K$ between primary and secondary is defined by $K = M/\sqrt{L_pL_s}$. An ideal transformer is one for which $K = 1$ and $L_p$ is infinite. In this case, the output $e_o$ is an exact replica of the input $e_i$. For an ideal pulse transformer this relationship is expressed by the equation below,

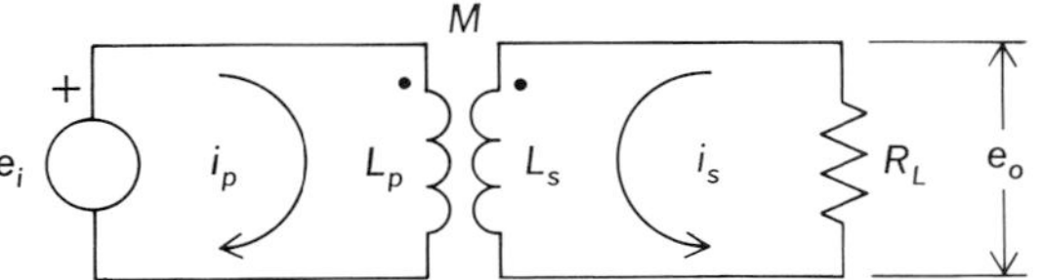


Schematic diagram of a pulse transformer.

$$n = \frac{e_o}{e_i} = \frac{i_p}{i_s} = \sqrt{\frac{L_s}{L_p}} = \frac{N_s}{N_p}$$

where $N_p$ is the primary number of turns and $N_s$ is the secondary number of turns. SEE TRANSFORMER.

A pulse transformer behaves as a reasonable approximation to a perfect transformer when used in connection with the fast waveforms it is intended to handle. The core of a pulse transformer is usually molded from a magnetic ceramic such as sintered manganese-zinc ferrite. The maximum permeability of this material is not very great, but its resistivity is at least 10,000,000 times that of Hipersil or Permalloy. This high resistivity means that the skin effect due to eddy currents is very small, and an effective permeability of the order of 1000 is attained. The windings of the pulse transformer are placed on a circular nylon or paper bobbin, which is then inserted in the core.

*Christos C. Halkias*

**Bibliography.** J. Millman and H. Taub, *Pulse, Digital and Switching Waveforms*, 1965; R. J. Tocci, *Fundamentals of Pulse and Digital Circuits*, 3d ed., 1983.

## Push-pull amplifier

A two-transistor or two-tube amplifier circuit often used as the power-output stage of a multistage amplifier. The power-output stage in an audio amplifier is normally expected to furnish from 5 to 50 W or more. Use of one active device in this stage is not feasible, because the transistor or tube would have to operate class A with a low conversion efficiency, on the order of 10%. Use of two or more active devices in parallel does not improve efficiency. However, with two active devices operating in push-pull, it is possible to supply the required amount of power with conversion efficiency on the order of 50%. This higher efficiency means that the amplifier does not require as much power from the power supply, because less power is dissipated as heat by the power amplifier active devices. SEE POWER AMPLIFIER.

**Operation.** A simplified circuit for a push-pull amplifier is shown in the **illustration**. The input signals must be of equal magnitude but 180° out of phase. The collector current in the transistor with the positive

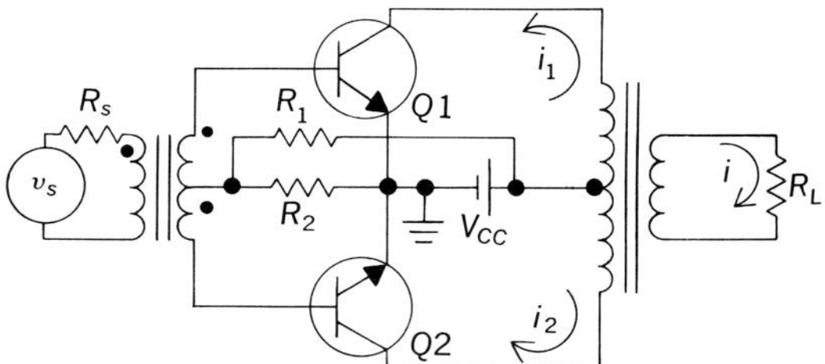


Two transistors in a push-pull arrangement.

signal is increasing while the transistor current in the other transistor is decreasing. This relation between the collector currents gave rise to the name push-pull. Because of their phase relationship, the two currents flowing in the two halves of the primary winding of the transformer produce an output similar to that of a single source connected to the transformer.

Although the active devices are indicated as junction transistors in the illustration, other devices such as triodes, beam power tubes, or field-effect transistors (FET) can also be used in this push-pull arrangement. The discussion to follow applies equally well regardless of the particular power device employed.

A push-pull amplifier may be operated class A, class AB, or class B. The greatest conversion efficiency occurs when the operation is class B. Therefore, if large amounts of power are required, the amplifier is designed for class B operation. An additional merit of class B operation is that the quiescent current is zero. Another advantage of push-pull operation is that the average currents of the two transistors or tubes flow in opposite directions through the primary winding of the output transformer, resulting in no average magnetization of the core. This allows the use of smaller cores with savings in size and weight.

If the two transistors have identical characteristics and the transformer is considered ideal, the even harmonic components of distortion are absent in the output signal. A high-power class B push-pull amplifier can be designed with little harmonic distortion. *See Amplifier; Distortion (electronic circuits).*

The circuit shown in the illustration indicates the basic push-pull amplifier. The interest in high-fidelity audio amplifiers has led to the development of more complicated circuits.

**Driver stages.** The input circuit shown in the illustration employs a transformer to produce the necessary phase inversion. Because of the limited frequency response of the transformer and also the size of transformer required, a transformer is rarely used. Instead, a transistor phase inverter is employed. Because some phase-inverter circuits have a gain considerably greater than unity, the overall gain of the amplifier can be increased more than it could be if a transformer with a step-up turns ratio were used. *See Phase inverter.*

A push-pull circuit using transistors having complementary symmetry has been used which requires neither an output nor an input transformer.

*Harold F. Klock*

**Bibliography.** J. J. Brophy, *Basic Electronics for Scientists*, 4th ed., 1983; C. H. Evans, *Electronic Amplifiers: Theory, Design, and Use*, 1979; C. A. Holt, *Electronic Circuits, Digital and Analog*, 1978; J. Millman, *Microelectronics*, 1979; D. L. Schilling and C. Belove, *Electronic Circuits, Discrete and Integrated*, 2d ed., 1979.

## Q (electricity)

Often called the quality factor of a circuit, $Q$ is defined in various ways, depending upon the particular application. In the simple $RL$ and $RC$ series circuits, $Q$ is the ratio of reactance to resistance, as in Eqs. (1), where $X_L$ is the inductive reactance, $X_C$ is the

$$Q = X_L/R \quad Q = X_C/R \quad \text{(a numerical value)} \qquad (1)$$

capacitive reactance, and $R$ is the resistance. An important application lies in the dissipation factor or loss angle when the constants of a coil or capacitor are measured by means of the alternating-current bridge.

$Q$ has greater practical significance with respect to the resonant circuit, and a basic definition is given by Eq. (2), where $Q_0$ means evaluation at resonance. For

$$Q_0 = 2\pi \frac{\text{max stored energy per cycle}}{\text{energy lost per cycle}} \qquad (2)$$

certain circuits, such as cavity resonators, this is the only meaning $Q$ can have.

For the $RLC$ series resonant circuit with resonant frequency $f_0$, Eq. (3) holds, where $R$ is the total cir-

$$Q_0 = 2\pi f_0 L/R = 1/2\pi f_0 CR \qquad (3)$$

cuit resistance, $L$ is the inductance, and $C$ is the capacitance. $Q_0$ is the $Q$ of the coil if it contains practically the total resistance $R$. The greater the value of $Q_0$, the sharper will be the resonance peak.

The practical case of a coil of high $Q_0$ in parallel with a capacitor also leads to $Q_0 = 2\pi f_0 L/R$. $R$ is the total series resistance of the loop, although the capacitor branch usually has negligible resistance.

In terms of the resonance curve, Eq. (4) holds,

$$Q_0 = f_0/(f_2 - f_1) \qquad (4)$$

where $f_0$ is the frequency at resonance, and $f_1$ and $f_2$ are the frequencies at the half-power points. *See Resonance (alternating-current circuits).*

*Burtis L. Robertson*

## Q meter

A direct-reading instrument widely used for measuring the $Q$ of an electric circuit at radio frequencies. Originally designed to measure the $Q$ of coils, the Q meter has been developed into a flexible, general-purpose instrument for determining many other quantities such as (1) the distributed capacity, effective inductance, and self-resonant frequency of coils; (2) the capacitance, $Q$ or power factor, and self-resonant frequency of capacitors; (3) the effective resistance, inductance or capacitance, and the $Q$ of resistors; (4) characteristics of intermediate- and radio-frequency transformers; and (5) the dielectric constant, dissipation factor, and power factor of insulating materials. *See Q (electricity).*

The **illustration** shows in simplified form the measurement circuit of a Q meter. The coil $L_x$ being measured is connected into the circuit by means of the external terminals HI and LO. The coil is brought into resonance by tuning the calibrated capacitor $C_c$. A controlled and measured input voltage $e$ is introduced into the circuit by means of an rf oscillator. A thermocouple voltmeter measures the input voltage $e$, and a vacuum-tube voltmeter (VTVM) measures the voltage $V$ across the calibrated capacitor. With the circuit

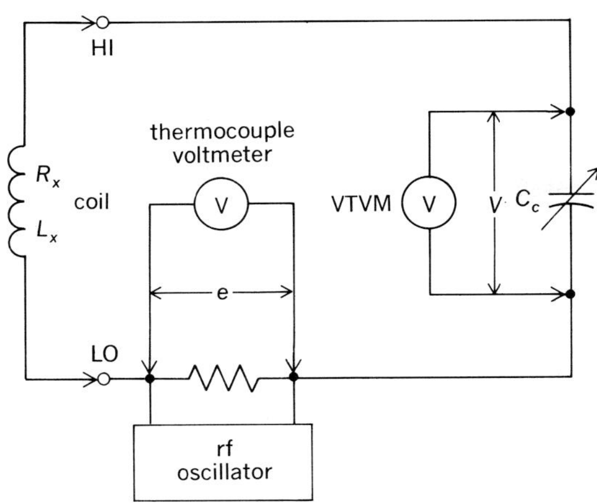


**Simplified measurement circuit of a Q meter.**

tuned to resonance, Eqs. (1) and (2) hold, where $R_x$ is the resistance of the coil. Since $Q = \omega L/R$, Eq. (3) is valid.

$$\omega L_x = 1/\omega C_c \quad (1)$$

$$\frac{V}{e} = \frac{(R_x^2 + \omega L_x^2)^{1/2}}{[R_x^2 + (\omega L_x - 1/\omega C_c)^2]^{1/2}} = (1 + \omega^2 L_x^2/R_x^2)^{1/2} \quad (2)$$

$$\frac{V}{e} = (1 + Q^2)^{1/2} \quad (3)$$

When $Q$ is large, the equation may be simplified to this basic equation of the Q meter, Eq. (4). The ther-

$$Q = \frac{V}{e} \quad (4)$$

mocouple voltmeter and the VTVM are calibrated in such a way that the product of their readings gives the $Q$ of the coil directly.

The many quantities enumerated above are determined by inserting suitable circuit elements in series with the coil or in parallel with the capacitor and measuring the effect on the circuit $Q$. Simple calculations based on the preceding equations are required to determine the desired quantity from the measured values of $Q$. SEE ELECTRICAL MEASUREMENTS; RADIO-FREQUENCY IMPEDANCE MEASUREMENTS.

*Isaac F. Kinnard; Edward C. Stevenson*

**Bibliography.** S. Geczy, *Basic Electrical Measurements*, 1984; B. A. Gregory, *An Introduction to Electrical Instrumentation and Measurement Systems*, 2d ed., 1981; R. L. Heiserman, *Electrical and Electronic Measuring Instruments*, 1983.

## Quantum electronics

A loosely defined field concerned with the interaction of radiation and matter, particularly those interactions involving quantum energy levels and resonance phenomena, and especially those involving lasers and masers. Quantum electronics encompasses useful devices such as lasers and masers and their practical applications; related phenomena and techniques, such as nonlinear optics and light modulation and detection; and related scientific problems and applications, such as quantum noise processes, laser spectroscopy, picosecond spectroscopy, and laser-induced optical breakdown.

In one sense any electronic device, even one as thoroughly classical in nature as a vacuum tube, may be considered a quantum electronic device, even one as thoroughly classical in nature as a vacuum tube, may be considered a quantum electronic device, since quantum theory is presently accepted to be the basic theory underlying all physical devices. In practice, however, quantum electronics is usually understood to refer to only those devices such as lasers and atomic clocks in which stimulated transitions between discrete quantum energy levels are important, together with related devices and physical phenomena which are excited or explored using lasers. Other devices such as transistors or superconducting devices which may be equally quantum-mechanical in nature are not usually included in the domain of quantum electronics.

**Stimulated emission and amplification.** Quantum electronics thus centers on stimulated-emission devices, primarily lasers and masers. Atoms, molecules, and other small isolated quantum systems typically have discrete, well-resolved quantum-mechanical energy levels. In a collection of a large number of identical such atoms or molecules, one can speak of the number of atoms, or the population, residing in each such energy level. Under normal thermal equilibrium conditions, lower energy levels always have larger populations. One may apply electromagnetic radiation (radio waves or light waves, as appropriate) to such a collection of atoms at a frequency (or wavelength) corresponding through Planck's law to the quantum-mechanical transition frequency between any two levels. This radiation will then be absorbed by the atoms, and some of the atoms will be correspondingly lifted from the lower energy level to the upper. Measurement of the strength of this absorption versus the probing frequency or wavelength provides a powerful way of studying the quantum energy levels, and provides the basic approach of spectroscopy or of resonance physics.

Under suitable conditions it is also possible, in a wide variety of atomic systems, to create a condition of population inversion, in which more atoms are temporarily placed in some upper energy level than in a lower energy level. Population inversion is created by "pumping" the atomic system, by using a wide variety of techniques. Application of a signal at the appropriate transition frequency then produces coherent amplification rather than absorption of the applied signal, with the amplification energy being supplied by a net flow of atoms from the upper to the lower energy level through stimulated transitions. The addition of electromagnetic feedback to the atomic system by means of lumped electrical circuitry, microwave circuity, or optical mirrors, as appropriate to the frequency range involved, can convert this amplification into coherent oscillation at the atomic transition frequency. While this type of stimulated emission and amplification has found useful but limited application at ordinary radio-wave and microwave frequencies (primarily in ultrastable atomic clocks and very lownoise microwave maser amplifiers), its overwhelming importance is at optical frequencies, where it makes possible for the first time the coherent amplification and oscillation of optical signals in laser devices.

**Nonlinear optical phenomena.** Soon after the invention of the laser, it was discovered that a wide assortment of interesting and useful nonlinear optical phenomena could be produced using coherent beams from lasers because of their unprecedentedly high power and coherence. By using nonlinear optical phenomena such as harmonic generation, subharmonic generation, parametric amplification and oscillation, as well as stimulated Raman and Brillouin scattering, it becomes possible to produce a wide range of new infrared, optical, and ultraviolet wavelengths, some of them widely tunable, in addition to obtaining important basic physical information about the nonlinear materials involved. Although the elementary description of these nonlinear optical devices is thoroughly classical in nature, they have become a major portion of the field of quantum electronics.

**Applications of lasers.** Lasers have found an enormous variety of important practical applications in engineering, technology, and medicine, ranging from highway surveying and supermarket checkout counters to automobile production lines and retinal surgery. As these applications have become established as routine techniques, they have generally moved out of the domain of quantum electronics considered as a scientific discipline. At the same time, the laser has been applied as the primary tool for many fundamental as well as exotic measurement techniques in science, including particularly high-resolution spectroscopy, such as saturated-absorption, tunable-laser, and picosecond spectroscopy. Many of these more complex techniques have been retained within the domain of quantum electronics, along with certain exotic engineering applications such as laser isotope separation and the study of laser interactions with plasmas, particularly for laser-induced fusion. *See Laser; Maser; Optical detectors; Optical modulators.*

*A. E. Siegman*

***Bibliography.*** F. T. Arecchi and E. O. Schulz-DuBois (eds.), *Laser Handbook*, 1972; D. Marcuse, *Principles of Quantum Electronics*, 1980; A. E. Siegman, *An Introduction to Masers and Lasers*, 1971; A. E. Siegman, *Lasers*, 1983; A. Yariv, *Quantum Electronics*, 1975.

## Quartz clock

A clock that makes use of the piezoelectric property of a quartz crystal. When a quartz crystal vibrates, a difference of electric potential is produced between two of its faces. The crystal has a natural frequency of vibration that depends on its size and shape. If it is placed in an oscillating electric circuit having nearly the same frequency as the crystal, it is caused to vibrate at its natural frequency, and the frequency of the entire circuit becomes the same as the natural frequency of the crystal. *See Oscillator; Piezoelectric crystal; Piezoelectricity.*

In the quartz oscillator, this natural frequency may be used to produce such other frequencies as 1 or 5 MHz. A clock displaying the time of day can also be driven by using one of these frequencies.

The natural frequency of a quartz crystal is nearly constant if precautions are taken when it is cut and polished and it is maintained at nearly constant temperature and pressure. After a crystal has been placed in operation, its frequency usually varies slowly as a result of physical changes. If allowance is made for changes, laboratory quartz-crystal clocks may run for a year with accumulated errors of less than a few thousandths of a second. However, quartz crystals typically used in watches may accumulate errors of several tens of seconds in one year.

For comparison, clocks using rubidium as a frequency standard might be expected to have accumulated errors of less than a few ten-thousandths of a second, while those using cesium might be expected to have accumulated errors better than a few millionths of a second.

The advantage of quartz clocks is that they are relatively inexpensive and easy to use in various applications such as computers and microprocessors. Thus, despite their inaccuracy relative to some other types of clocks, they enjoy wide popularity, particularly in applications requiring accurate timekeeping over a relatively short time span. In these applications, the rates and epochs of the quartz clocks may be readjusted periodically to account for possible accumulated errors. *See Computer; Microprocessor.*

*Dennis D. McCarthy*

## Radar

An acronym for radio detection and ranging, the original and still principal application of radar. The name is applied to both the technique and the equipment used.

Radar is a sensor; its purpose is to provide estimates of certain characteristics of its surroundings of interest to a user, most commonly the presence, position, and motion of such objects as aircraft, ships, or other vehicles in its vicinity. In other uses, radars provide information about the Earth's surface (or that of other astronomical bodies) or about meteorological conditions. To provide the user with a full range of sensor capability, radars are often used in combinations or with other elements of more complete systems.

Radar operates by transmitting electromagnetic energy into the surroundings and detecting energy reflected by objects. If a narrow beam of this energy is transmitted by the directive antenna, the direction from which reflections come and hence the bearing of the object may be estimated. The distance to the reflecting object is estimated by measuring the period between the transmission of the radar pulse and reception of the echo. In most radar applications this period will be very short since electromagnetic energy travels with the velocity of light.

Many different kinds of radar have been developed for a wide range of purposes, but they all use electromagnetic radiation (radio waves) to detect and measure certain characteristics of objects (or targets) in their vicinity.

**Historical development.** The fact that radio waves produce echoes was known before 1920. During the 1930s researchers in the United States, England, France, and Germany pointed out that ships and airplanes produced radio echoes which could be used to deduce their locations. Experiments and refinement continued independently in these countries for some time; the increase of secrecy as war preparations increased contributed to this independence. In the mid-1930s the British Air Ministry, responding to the findings and recommendations of Robert Watson-Watt authorized immediate development and subsequent installation of some 20 radar stations on the east and southeast coasts of England to provide surveillance of these air approaches. As World War II began, a continuous radar watch was maintained over the principal air and sea approaches to Britain. The radar network was so effective in locating German bombers and directing fighters against them that it is generally credited with making it possible for the severely outnumbered Royal Air Force to defeat the Luftwaffe in the Battle of Britain. When the Germans resorted to night bombing to reduce the losses suffered in daylight encounters, airborne radar aboard British fighters enabled them to train their guns on the enemy in the dark with devastating results.

During the war, American and British scientists cooperated to develop radars for such diverse applications as surveillance of large regions and early warning of approaching ships, aircraft, and missiles; fire control for automatically directing gunfire against air or surface targets; directing gunfire at enemy aircraft from aboard radar-equipped interceptor aircraft; radar bombsights; and detection of submarines from aircraft.

Many nonmilitary applications resulted from military developments; today civil and military applications are numerous. Development has turned to improvements in radar performance resulting from applications of the computer, integrated circuits in the apparatus, and more precise design to meet the specific needs of the user. *SEE COMPUTER; INTEGRATED CIRCUITS.*

**Kinds of radar.** Radar has so many valuable applications that the physical nature of radars varies greatly. Several radars are available for use on small boats as a safety and navigation aid, some so small as to be carried by an operator, others a little larger in which the transmitter, antenna, and receiver are all contained in a mast-mounted weatherproof unit which feeds a small inboard display. Another familiar small radar, also seen in a hand-held form, is that used by police to measure the speed of automobiles.

Perhaps the largest radars are those covering acres of land, long arrays of antennas all operating together to monitor the flight of space vehicles or astronomical bodies. Other very large radars are designed to monitor flight activity at substantial distances around the world. These are large mainly because they must use longer-than-usual radio wavelengths associated with longer-than-usual radio wavelengths associated with ionospheric containment of the signal for over-the-horizon operations; these longer wavelengths require very large antennas to form the narrow beams useful in the measurement of target positions.

More common in size are those radars seen at airports, those with rotating antennas 10–30 ft (3–9 m) wide, equipment housings the size of a small shed, and operator consoles the size of a small desk. Radars intended for mobile use, particularly airborne radars, are quite compact, usually very modular in construction and very well adapted to fit into the vehicle.

Radars intended principally to determine the presence and position of reflecting targets in a region around the radar are called search radars. Other radars examine further the targets detected: examples are height finders with antennas that scan vertically in the direction of an assigned target, and tracking radars that are aimed continuously at an assigned target to obtain great accuracy in estimating target motion. In some modern radars, these search and track functions are combined, usually with some computer control. Surveillance radar connotes operation of this sort, somewhat more than just search alone. There are also very complex and versatile radars with considerable computer control, with which many functions are performed and which are therefore called multifunction radars. Very accurate tracking radars intended for use at missile test sites or similar test ranges are called instrumentation radars. Radars designed to detect clouds and precipitation are called meteorological or weather radars. Certain radars, generally airborne, can be moved over great distances while operating in a special way to extract much detail from the region being examined (an area of the Earth's surface, for example); because of the very large "antenna" formed by the path of the vehicle carrying the radar during the operation, these are called synthetic aperture radars.

Some radars have separate transmit and receive antennas sometimes located kilometers apart. These are called bistatic radars, the more conventional single-antenna radar being monostatic. Some useful systems have no transmitter at all and are equipped to measure, for radarlike purposes, signals from the targets themselves. Such systems are often called passive radars, but the terms radiometers or signal intercept systems are generally more appropriate. Some genuine radars may, of course, occasionally be operated in passive modes. *SEE PASSIVE RADAR.*

The terms primary and secondary are used to describe, respectively, radars in which the signal received is reflected by the target and radars in which the transmission causes a transponder (transmitter-responder) carried aboard the target to transmit a signal back to the radar. The Identification Friend or Foe (IFF) system in both military and civil use is a secondary radar.

**Fundamentals of operation.** It is convenient to consider radars composed of four principal parts: the transmitter, antenna, receiver, and display. Each is discussed more fully below.

The transmitter provides the rf signal in sufficient strength (power) for the radar sensitivity desired and sends it to the antenna, which causes the signal to be radiated into space in a desired direction. The signal propagates (radiates) in space, and some of it is intercepted by reflecting bodies. These reflections, in part at least, are radiated back to the antenna. The antenna collects them and routes all such received signals to the receiver, where they are amplified and detected. The presence of an echo of the transmitted signal in the received signal reveals the presence of a target. The echo is indicated by a sudden rise in the output of the detector, which produces a voltage (video) proportional to the sum of the rf signals being received and the rf noise inherent in the receiver itself. The time between the transmission and the receipt of the echo discloses the range to the target through Eq. (1),

$$R = 1/2c\Delta T \qquad (1)$$

where $R$ is the range to the target, $c$ is the speed of electromagnetic propagation ($3 \times 10^8$ m/s), and $\Delta T$ is the time between the transmission and the receipt of the echo. The direction or bearing of the target is disclosed by the direction the antenna is pointing when an echo is received.

A pulse radar uses pulsed transmissions to perform a search function. The transmitter shown in **Fig. 1** is of the master oscillator, power amplifier (MOPA) type, discussed more completely below. The principal

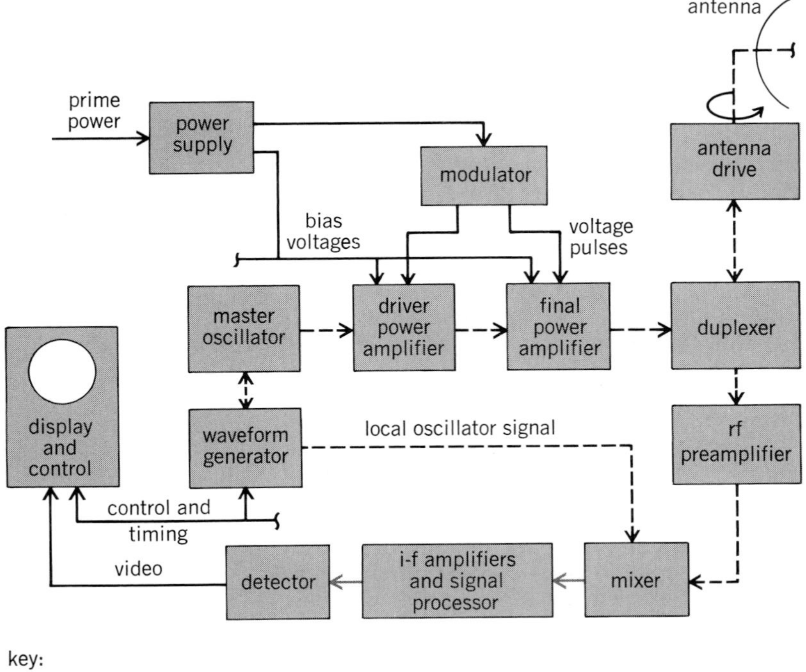


**Fig. 1. Block diagram of a pulse radar.**

conversion of electrical power to transmitted signal power comes in the final power amplifier stage under the control of the modulator forming the radar pulse. In some simpler radars, the amplifier used may itself be an oscillator, and hence its modulator (or pulser) constitutes the waveform generator, and there are no successive stages of amplification. *See* AMPLIFIER; MODULATOR; OSCILLATOR; RADIO TRANSMITTER.

The duplexer permits the same antenna to be used on both transmit and receive, and is equipped with protective devices to block the very strong transmit signal from going to the sensitive receiver and damaging it. The antenna forms a beam, usually quite directive, and, in the search example, rotates throughout the region to be searched. *See* ANTENNA.

The radar reflections are among the signals received by the antenna in the period between transmissions. Most search radars have a pulse repetition frequency (prf), antenna beamwidth, and rotation rate such that several pulses are transmitted (perhaps 20 to 40) while the antenna scans past a target. This allows a buildup of the echo being received. Some radars are equipped with low-noise rf preamplifiers to improve sensitivity. Almost all radars use some form of mixing of the received signal with a local oscillator signal to produce an intermediate frequency (i-f) signal, commonly at 30 or 60 MHz, more conveniently amplified and processed. The local oscillator signal, offset from the transmitted rf by precisely the i-f, can be supplied by the waveform generator as shown. The mixer is sometimes called the first detector. The i-f signal is then fed to the detector (sometimes called the second detector) which produces a video signal, a voltage proportional to the strength of the i-f at its input. This video may be amplified and used in the cathode-ray tube (CRT) of the radar display to cause a bright spot to be formed on the face of the tube when an echo is received, in a manner indicating the range and bearing of the target. *See* CATHODE-RAY TUBE; DETECTOR; ELECTRONIC DISPLAY; MIXER; RADIO RECEIVER.

**Figure 2** shows a reasonable waveform of an elementary search radar. Duty factors (the ratio of pulse width $\tau$, or transmit "on" time, to total time) in such radars are typically 0.1 to 1.0%. With modern signal processing, much more complicated waveforms are often used, and with the advent of transistors and other solid-state amplifiers, radar systems have been developed with duty factors of 10 to 50%.

**Radar range equation.** The equations which relate radar characteristics and performance can be derived from consideration of the echo power received, $S_r$. This signal results from a transmitter of peak power $P_t$ sending its signal into space through an antenna of directive gain $G_t$. The spatial power density decreases with range as though an effective transmitted signal of power $P_tG_t$ were radiated isotropically, with the power density (in, for example, watts per square meter) decreasing as the spherical surface $4\pi R^2$ ($R$ being the range in meters) increases. An object of a radar cross section $\sigma$ (in square meters) in the beam intercepts the incident power and reradiates it, again as if isotropically with $4\pi R^2$ decrease in power density. The reflection is intercepted by the receiving antenna of an effective aperture $A_e$ (given, again, in square meters). At the antenna terminals, then, this received signal strength is given by Eq. (2), where the factors

$$S_r = \frac{P_tG_tL_t}{4\pi R^2} \cdot \sigma \cdot \frac{1}{4\pi R^2} \cdot A_eL_r = \frac{P_tG_tL_t\sigma A_eL_r}{(4\pi)^2R^4} \qquad (2)$$

$L$ ($0<L<1$) account for various losses in signal power in the transmitting and receiving processes. Also, the ranges from transmitter to target and from target to receiver are treated identically in this monostatic radar case.

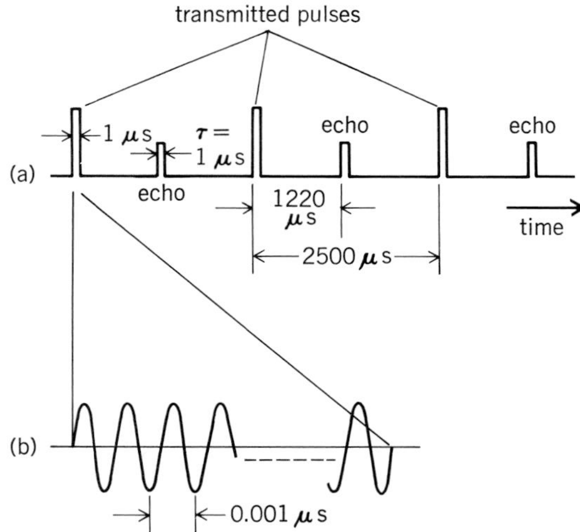


**Fig. 2. Waveform of a simple pulse radar. (*a*) Portion of transmitted pulse train and echoes (exaggerated). Echo corresponds to a target at 100 nautical miles (183 km). Pulse period corresponds to a pulse repetition frequency of 400 pulses per second. Example pulse width is 1 μs. (*b*) Single transmitted pulse showing carrier cycles for an L-band (1000-MHz) radar.**

Successful detection requires that $S_r$ meet some strength criterion, often that it exceed the level of signal produced by the receiver alone by a wide margin (a ratio, $W$, of 20:1, say). The receiver's noise production can be stated as $kTB_n$, where $k$ is Boltzmann's constant ($1.38 \times 10^{-23}$ joule per kelvin), $T$ is an effective noise temperature (Kelvin scale) representing the type of receiver and other conditions, and $B_n$ is the noise bandwidth of the receiver. The effective temperature shown here is not just ambient temperature; it represents thermal conditions and the receiver's noise factor (a measure of its noise-producing characteristics), and for convenience may include the effects of receive losses, requiring therefore an adjustment in the cited $L_r$. The noise bandwidth for many receivers is proportional to the i-f passband, $B_{i\text{-}f}$. This passband is generally designed to accommodate the transmitted pulse; ideally, this means setting $B_{i\text{-}f}$ equal to $1/\tau$, but in practice $B_{i\text{-}f}$ is only approximated by that value. SEE ELECTRICAL NOISE.

Detection occurs, then, when $S_r$ meets this criterion of Eq. (3). Solving Eq. (3) for $R$ produces a familiar

$$S_r = \frac{P_t G_t L_t \sigma A_e L_r}{(4\pi)^2 R^4} = WkTB_n \tag{3}$$

form of the radar range equation (4). Since antenna

$$R = \left(\frac{P_t G_t L_t \sigma A_e L_r}{(4\pi)^2 WkTB_n}\right)^{1/4} \tag{4}$$

performance is represented in this expression by both gain and aperture, it is sometimes convenient to use Eq. (5), relating the two to the carrier wavelength $\lambda$ giving Eq. (6).

$$G = \frac{4\pi A_e}{\lambda^2} \tag{5}$$

$$R = \left(\frac{P_t G^2 \lambda^2 \sigma L_t L_r}{(4\pi)^3 WkTB_n}\right)^{1/4} \tag{6}$$

The formulation to this point assumes that detection is based on a single pulse. If many pulses are "integrated" (as in the phosphor of a display), the factors $n$ for the number of pulses so integrated and $E(n)$ for the efficiency of integration can be included to give Eq. (7).

$$R = \left(\frac{P_t G^2 n E(n) \lambda^2 \sigma L_t L_r}{(4\pi)^3 WkTB_n}\right)^{1/4} \tag{7}$$

It is not always receiver noise with which the echo competes for detection. Other useful forms of this equation can be derived by substituting, for the receiver noise power $kTB_n$ considered here, expressions for signals received from jammers or strong clutter reflections.

**Radar carrier-frequency bands.** Radar carrier frequencies are broadly identified by a nomenclature that originated in wartime secrecy and has since been found very convenient and widely accepted. The spectrum is divided into bands, the frequencies and wavelengths of which are given in the **table**.

**Propagation.** The above presentation of the radar range equation includes no account of the medium; propagation in free space is assumed. Actually, the Earth's surroundings have many noteworthy properties. The charged layers of the ionosphere present a highly refractive shell at radio frequencies well below the microwave frequencies of most radars. Consequently, over-the-horizon radars have been built in the 10-MHz area to exploit this skip path. The Earth's surface represents such a distinct medium interface that microwave reflections take place. A multipath phenomenon results, causing the lobed interference structure seen in field strength graphs of microwave antennas (**Fig. 3**). The lobes in the plane normal to the reflecting surface are caused by the successive phase relationships in the direct and reflected signals due to the path lengths involved. When terrain is not so reflective, the lobe structure is less pronounced. A complete account of the reflection must include the nature (conductivity) of the surface, the diffusion (due to surface roughness), and the divergence of the reflection due to the spherical shape of the Earth.

The atmosphere also acts as a lens since its dielectric constant decreases with increasing altitude. Consequently, microwave rays are bent downward slightly and the radar horizon is somewhat beyond the visual. Under certain conditions defined as standard, the effect is such that if one were to draw the Earth with a radius 4⁄3 its actual value, the refracted rays would be bent back to straight lines. A simple expression, Eq. (8), results for the tangent line distances,

$$R_{\tan} = \sqrt{2h_1} + \sqrt{2h_2} \tag{8}$$

relating radar and target heights in feet (1 ft = 0.3 m), $h_1$ and $h_2$, to the tangent range $R_{\tan}$ (**Fig. 4**) in statute miles (1 mi = 1.6 km).

Frequently, an atmospheric condition involving a pronounced departure from the smoothly varying dielectric constant with altitude occurs, and a superrefractive or ducting condition results with low-altitude

**Radar carrier-frequency bands**

| Band designation | Nominal frequency range | Representative wavelength |
|---|---|---|
| HF | 3–20 MHz | 30 m at 10 mHz |
| VHF | 30–300 MHz | 3 m at 100 MHz |
| UHF | 300–1000 MHz | 1 m at 300 MHz |
| L | 1000–2000 MHz | 30 cm at 1000 MHz |
| S | 2000–4000 MHz | 10 cm at 3000 MHz |
| C | 4000–8000 MHz | 5 cm at 6000 MHz |
| X | 8000–12,000 MHz | 3 cm at 10,000 MHz |
| $K_u$ | 12.0–18 GHz | 2 cm at 15 GHz |
| K | 18–27 GHz | 1.5 cm at 20 GHz |
| $K_a$ | 27–40 GHz | 1 cm at 30 GHz |
| mm | 40–300 GHz | 0.3 cm at 100 GHz |

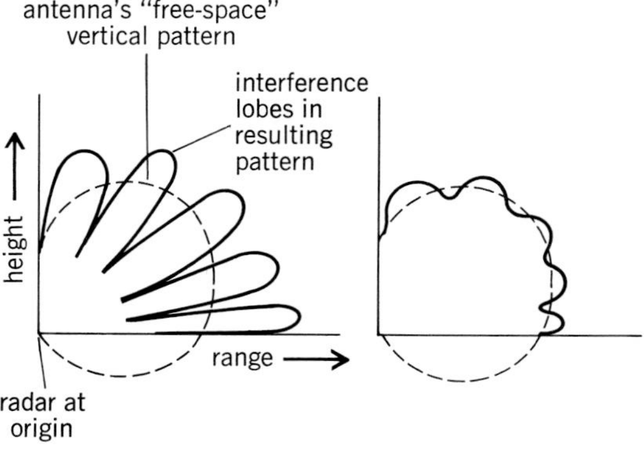


**Fig. 3. Effect of a reflecting earth surface on the radiation pattern of an antenna. (*a*) Reflection nearly perfect. (*b*) Reflection much reduced.**

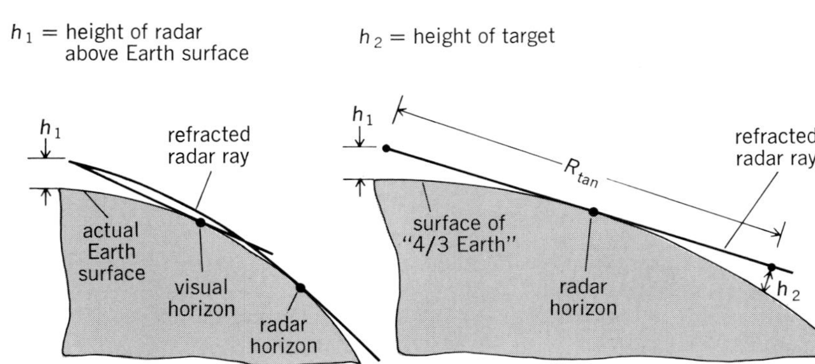


**Fig. 4. Atmospheric refraction and the "4/3 Earth." (*a*) Actual geometry. (*b*) Geometry with 4/3 Earth.**

targets detected well beyond 4/3-Earth predictions. The variation in such conditions over time of day, season, geographic location, and local weather makes reliable exploitation of the phenomenon difficult.

Attenuation of radar signals, also not accounted for in the above radar equations, is also encountered in the Earth's atmosphere. Attenuation is due to both molecular absorption by resonant excitation of uncondensed gases and scattering by particles such as dust or water droplets in fog and clouds. The attenuation due to water vapor and to oxygen molecules is shown in **Fig. 5** and is seen to be negligible below the L-band and tolerable through the X-band. The resonance peaks for these molecules cause much more concern in choosing frequencies in the millimeter region for special-purpose radars.

**Target characteristics.** In the radar equations, the target is represented by a single term, its radar cross section $\sigma$. The discussion here assumes that the target is a vehicle such as an aircraft, a truck, or a spacecraft, rather than coastlines or terrain features which are less frequently targets of interest.

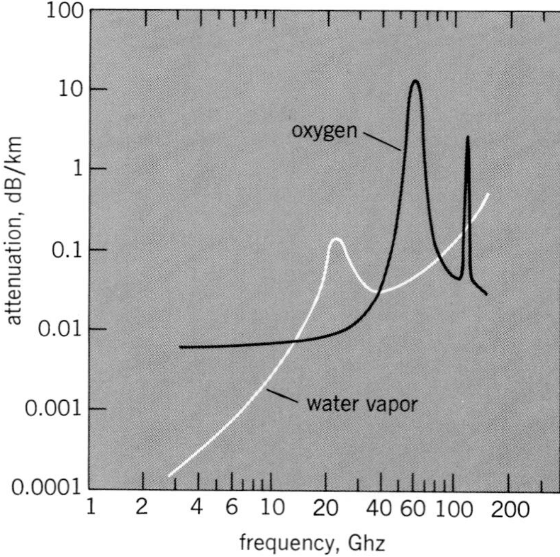


**Fig. 5. Attenuation of electromagnetic energy by atmospheric gases at 1 atm ($10^2$ kPa) pressure. Absorption due to water vapor is for an atmosphere containing 1% water vapor molecules (7.5 g water/m$^3$). (*After M. I. Skolnik, Introduction to Radar Systems, 2d ed., McGraw-Hill, 1980*)**

The amount of radar signal reflected by such targets is clearly a random variable, not a constant. Such targets are composed of many scatterers or reflecting surfaces, all of which contribute to the whole reflection. The individual reflections add coherently (that is, with both constructive and destructive phase interference, depending on the many path lengths involved) in composing the total reflection. Consequently over successive observations, the reflections will differ in magnitude if even the slightest repositioning of the scatterers occurs, or if a different carrier frequency is employed.

Such targets have been categorized by the degree to which their composition encourages independent values of reflected signal strength. Targets are described as Swerling models I through IV after P. Swerling. It is still convenient, however, to use single average values of cross section in radar computations to represent even these fluctuating targets. This is made possible by adjusting the $W$ factor of the range equation so that the same probabilities of detection and false alarm are maintained regardless of the fluctuations. **Figure 6** shows such adjustments for the single-pulse case. Similar curves for the multiple-pulse case should be used to complete the adjustment.

Some targets may be deliberately designed to increase the concentration of the signal reflected to the radar. For safety reasons, small ships, even life rafts, or small aircraft are often equipped with corner reflectors, reflective planes intersecting in a right trihedral, so that very nearly all the incident signal is bounced back in the direction from which it came regardless of the orientation of the device. The radar return, then, is far larger and more visible to a searching radar than if just random scattering from the vehicle alone were depended upon. Such reflectors range from a fraction of a meter to several meters in size. These reflectors and arrangements of reflecting antenna elements are known as retrodirective arrays and are said to enhance the radar cross section of the target on which they are installed.

**Noise.** The detectability of a radar echo is determined by its strength relative to various competing signals also causing a detector output. Among the sources of such signals is the receiver itself. The receiver produces rf and i-f signals as a result of thermal conditions (molecular agitation in the components) and of the mixing process (unintended constituents of the local oscillator signal, for example).

A measure of the receiver's noise production is called its noise factor. In general terms, the noise factor is the ratio of noise power at the output of a network to the noise power that would have resulted from the network simply acting on the noise power at the input (that power being $kT_0B_n$, $T_0$ = 290 K as a standard ambient). The added noise of the network itself causes a degradation in the signal-to-noise ratio from input to output. It can be seen, then, that a sensitive radar receiver might to good advantage use a first stage of low noise factor but of considerable gain, so that subsequent stages are provided with a relatively strong signal (and noise) at their inputs, their own noise production further degrading the now-amplified signal-to-noise ratio very little.

Noise factor when expressed in decibels is more commonly called noise figure. Such conditions as network terminations and test-signal bandwidth must be better specified in actual measurement procedures than is possible here.

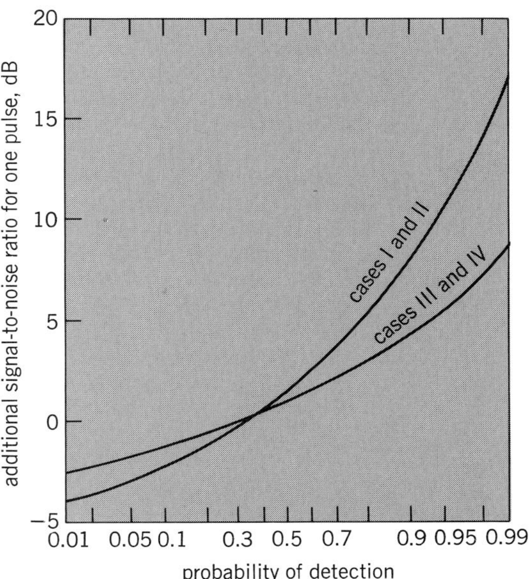


**Fig. 6. Additional signal-to-noise ratio required for detecting fluctuating targets, for the single-pulse case ($n$ = 1). (*After M. I. Skolnik, Introduction to Radar Systems, 2d ed., McGraw-Hill, 1980*)**

Other noise sources can be external to the radar. They include the Sun (in many radars, a sun strobe can be used as a bearing alignment check), other cosmic sources, electromagnetic interference as from urban areas, and deliberately energized sources intended to reduce the radar's sensitivity (jamming).

The minimum test-signal strength that can be fed into a receiver and reliably detected is called the radar's minimum discernible signal (MDS). Typical values are in the region of 90 to 120 dB below a milliwatt.

**Clutter.** While some radars are designed to examine land features and others weather phenomena, generally such radar returns are considered a nuisance, hindering the detection of targets of greater interest (such as aircraft) and producing false alarms. It is possible to state elementary formulas for the power of such returns and to use them in the radar range equation, as was done for receiver noise [Eq. (3)], but in general the simple expressions fail to account sufficiently for the statistical distribution of clutter backscatter encountered in practice.

In such approximations, backscatter statistics associated with different types of clutter are used. Surface clutter includes scattering from the sea surface (for various wave or sea-state conditions) and from land surface (for various terrain types). Volume clutter includes fog, clouds, rain, snow, and chaff (metallic threads deliberately sown in a region as a radar countermeasure). Birds and insects have been described in such computations, as have such phenomena as clear-air turbulence and thermal inversions, the returns from which are often called angels by radar users.

In the radar bands, clutter backscatter generally increases with increasing frequencies—in a given amount of rain, the clutter power will be worse for an X-band radar than for an L-band one. Radars using frequencies below L-band are called all-weather radars. Radars at S-band and higher may use high resolution (narrow beams, very short pulses) in part to reduce the amount of clutter competing with a target at any one time.

Not only the amount of backscatter but also the spread in frequency of the return, due to Doppler shift resulting from turbulence among the scatterers, are of concern in radar design, since some signal-processing techniques intended to suppress returns from stationary clutter are made less effective by this spectral spread.

**Detection process.** Detecting a target in many radars means that an operator correctly judges that a bright spot on a display discloses the existence of a target and not just a spurious impulse of noise. To improve judgment, careful receiver and display adjustments are made so that the background of noise on the display is only faintly visible; this minimizes the probability that a target will be declared to exist when in fact none does (a noise-induced false alarm), and allows recognition of even slight intensifications of the display due to weaker echoes. Turning these adjustments down too far (reducing the false alarm probability to nearly zero) unfortunately increases the probability of missing a genuine target. Proper detection balances these two probabilities, the probability of detection, $P_D$, and the probability of false alarm, $P_{FA}$.

The graph of **Fig. 7** represents the possible range of voltage values at the detector output for two cases: $N$, only noise exists; and $S + N$, a desired signal exists with the noise. The figure shows that a bright spot on a display fed properly by this voltage is possible but not likely when only noise is present. If a threshold in voltage, $v_t$, is imagined, the $P_{FA}$ is given by the proportion of the area under the $N$ curve to the right of $v_t$ to the whole area under the $N$ curve. The figure also shows that for such a threshold it is always possible that a true target will be missed because the output $S + N$ can indeed be less than threshold value. This probability of miss $(1 - P_D)$ is similarly given by the area under the $S + N$ curve to the left of $v_t$. The threshold is shown here for a $P_{FA}$ of, say, 0.1 and a $P_D$ approximately 0.5. In practice, adjustments are made so that $P_{FA}$ is in the $10^{-4}$ to $10^{-8}$ region.

In operator (or manual) detection, $v_t$ depends on operator judgment of display brightness. In some modern radars, the detector output voltage is treated very precisely by computers and $v_t$ is a specific part of the programming. Such operation is called automatic detection. Usually the design must be some-

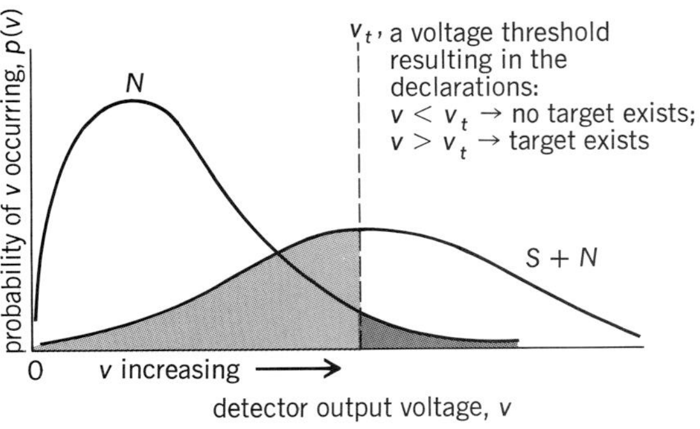


areas represent error probabilities:

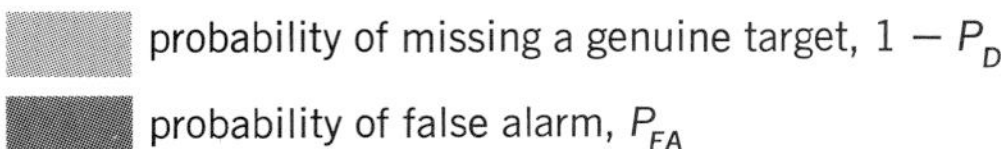


**Fig. 7. Detection based on the output of a detector in the presence of noise.**

Fig. 8. AN/FPS-16 tracking radar, a very accurate monopulse radar, operating in the C-band, installed at more than 50 sites around the world. (*RCA Corp.*)

what more conservative (less sensitive for a given false alarm rate than a good operator making manual detections), but the advantage of automatic detection is that very consistent performance and the handling of greater target densities are achieved.

Since receiver noise is not always the competing signal, an experienced operator learns to recognize clutter regions and tempers the declaring of targets; similarly an automatic detector must recognize abrupt changes of background statistics and adjust $v_t$ to maintain a constant false alarm rate. Such techniques have been developed and are called CFAR (constant false alarm rate) techniques.

The $W$ factor [the signal-to-noise ratio considered needed in Eq. (3) to assure reliable detection] can be seen in Fig. 7 to be related to the average values of the $N$ and $S + N$ curves, the latter accruing from a given target size $\sigma$ at a given range $R$. The error probabilities described above express the reliability of the detection.

**Tracking.** Many processes are used in radar systems to associate successive detections of a target, thereby providing an estimate of its motion or track. In a radar in which the antenna rotates regularly, a sequence of detections, in each of which the range and bearing of the target are estimated, may be manually plotted with a grease pencil or other implement on either the display face or a plotting board. The individual estimates of location are called contacts or plots, the sequence a track. In modern systems a computer can be programmed to accept contacts from an operator-activated marking device built into the display, or from an automatic detector, and to create an estimate of the target's present position and velocity, using various track-filtering algorithms to diminish the impact of measurement errors in the individual contacts, that is, to smooth the track. Such a com-

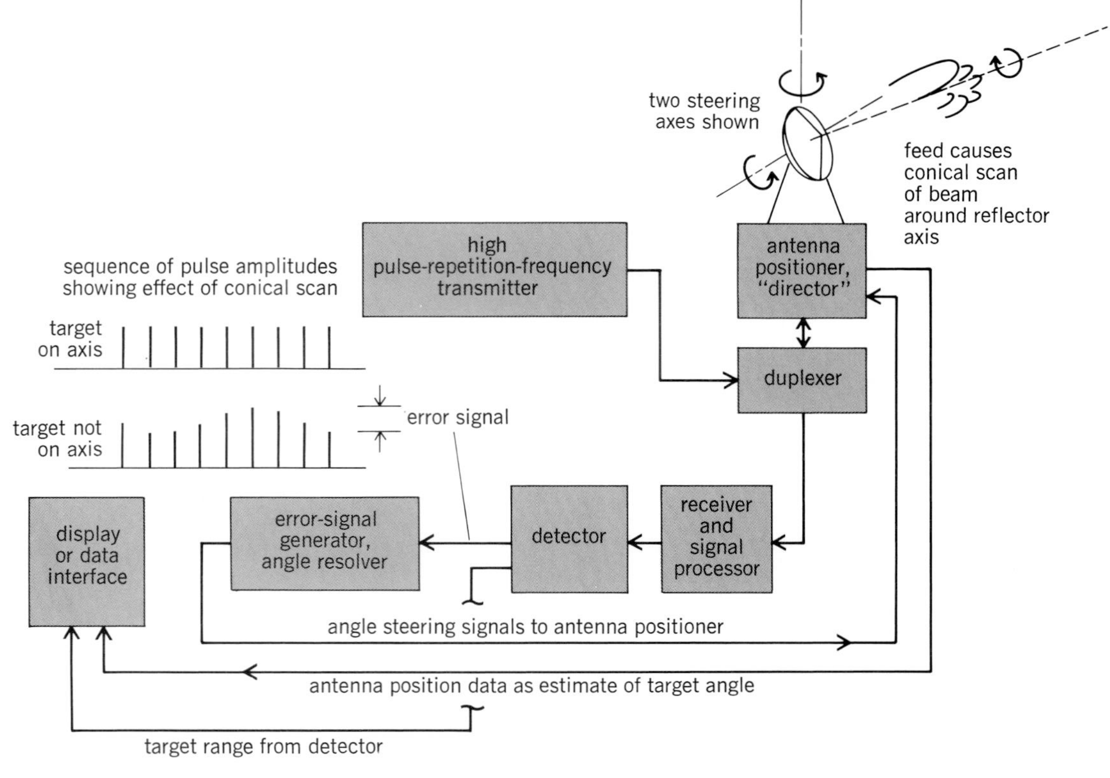


Fig. 9. Tracking radar using con-scan technique.

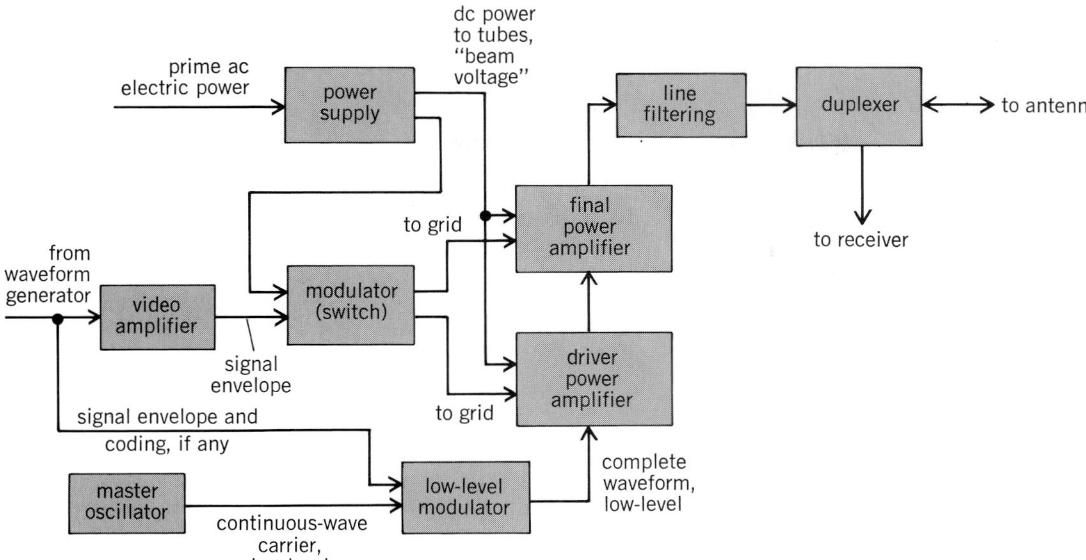


**Fig. 10. Transmitter of MOPA (master oscillator, power amplifier) type.**

puter operation is called automatic tracking. Some computers are programmed to accept contacts from more than one search radar with common fields of view and to combine them into single track estimates; such a process is called integrated automatic tracking. Whenever the radar supplying the contacts is of rotating search type, the tracking is called a track-while-scan (TWS) process.

Radars have been built that are dedicated to tracking just one target but to do so very accurately (**Fig. 8**). In these radars a dish antenna is steered to the direction of a known target. Such a designation may have come from a search radar, and the tracking radar may have to perform a small local search in order to acquire the target. After acquisition, a continuous stream of contacts results and is used to keep the antenna steered to the target. The dish antenna produces a beam narrow in both horizontal and vertical angles (a pencil beam). If this beam is scanned in a very small cone around the target's presumed direction, the amplitude and phasing of the resulting modulations of the returns (**Fig. 9**) can be detected and used to drive the motors that control the position of the antenna.

In con-scan trackers, usually only the feedhorn in front of the dish is caused to nutate; the whole dish and feed assembly is repositioned by the director. The final estimate of the target's angle is made by sensing the director's position; the inertia due to its mass acts as a smoothing filter in the track estimate.

Another technique used in such tracking radars is monopulse angle measurement, in which squinted simultaneous beams (or an equivalent) are generated by a cluster of feedhorns (usually in horizontal and vertical pairs). Then, with a single radar transmission, the error signals due to the target's not being precisely on axis can be generated from the proportion of signals in each beam (separate receivers are required) and used to reposition the antenna. Such radars are used to control the pointing of guns or to provide accurate data needed in missile guidance; they are also used in flight-test facilities as instrumentation radars to provide a measurement basis for experiments.

Another kind of tracking is that performed by radars equipped with phased-array antennas in which beams may be positioned in angle under computer control and at pulse-to-pulse rates. Such electronic beam steering permits sampling rates adapted to the track dynamics being experienced on each of hundreds of tracks at a time. This process is called sampled-data tracking.

**Composition of radar systems.** It is convenient to discuss radar systems in terms of four principal subsystems, namely the transmitter, the antenna, the receiver and signal processor, and the display and control apparatus.

***Transmitter.*** The transmitter converts electrical power (as from a motor-generator set or a utility system) to electromagnetic power at the carrier frequency and in the waveform desired. **Figure 10** shows a block diagram of a transmitter of the MOPA type. The waveform may actually be generated digitally in the receiver, then sent to the transmitter which in low-level equipment transfers the waveform to the output of an rf oscillator (a frequency synthesizer in frequency-agile radars). This signal is sent to the amplifier chain. Typical amplifiers are traveling-wave tubes in which the applied electrical power is converted to kinetic energy in an electron beam and the beam made to interact with the signal's electromagnetic

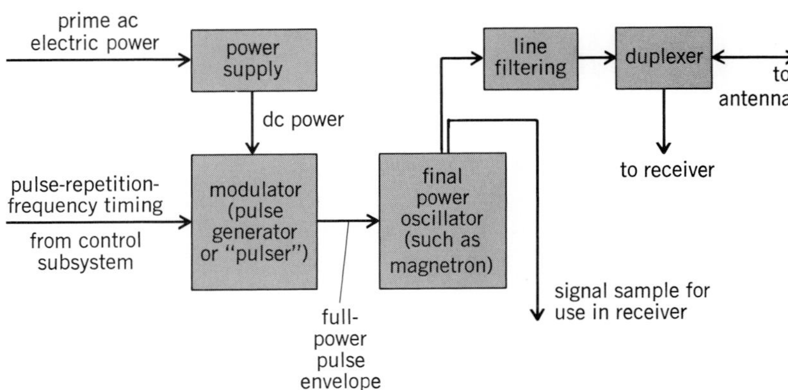


**Fig. 11. Radar transmitter of the final-power-oscillator type.**

Fig. 12. AN/SPS-49 search radar antenna, which forms a vertical fan beam for the two-dimensional L-band radar widely used in the U.S. Navy. (*Raytheon Co.*)

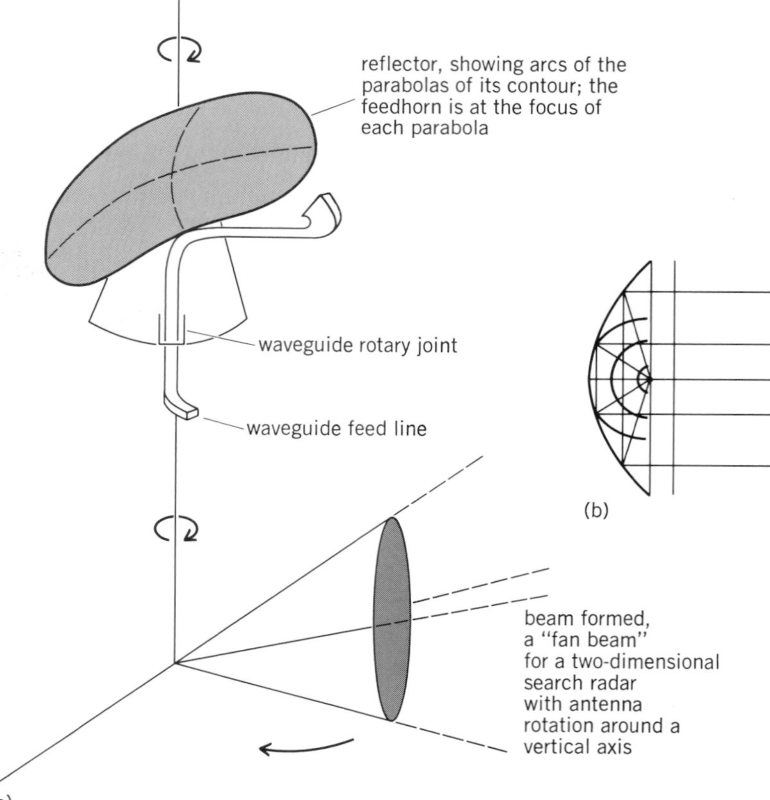


Fig. 13. Antenna forming a vertical fan beam. (*a*) Antenna configuration. (*b*) Principle of parabolic reflection, showing spherical wavefronts converted to planar fronts.

fields, amplifying them. Figure 10 shows modulation by a grid to turn the beam on and off, not always the case. *SEE TRAVELING-WAVE TUBE.*

Other useful amplifiers are klystrons, in which the rf fields in resonant cavities interact similarly with the electron beam; still others are crossed-field amplifiers, in which clouds of electrons, pulled from a cathode surface by the electric field applied by the power supply, are formed into periodically dense structures by the rf signal and similarly interact with that signal to amplify it. *SEE KLYSTRON; MICROWAVE TUBE.*

Continued refinement of semiconductor materials, junction designs, and related circuit technologies has permitted some microwave amplifiers to be composed entirely of combined modules of transistors or of diodes of various types, depending generally on the radar waveform intended. Radars would have in most cases such solid-state transmitters in the form of a central transmitter, but the same technology can be used at each element of array-type antennas as well.

The power supply includes rectification and filtering to convert alternating-current prime power to very well regulated direct-current power with absolutely no ripple in the bias voltages supplied the amplifiers. The modulator must supply a very faithful replica of the pulse to the modulating grid of the amplifiers. Some amplifiers require that the bias voltage itself be modulated with the signal envelope, there being no lower-power-capable modulation grid; in this case the final stage of the modulator must handle the entire pulse energy from the power supply. Modulators generally include a switch tube of a vacuum or gas-filled sort (thyratrons, for example), but since the late 1970s more stages have been built with solid-state (semiconductor) devices. *SEE ELECTRIC FILTER; GAS TUBE; MICROWAVE SOLID-STATE DEVICES; VACUUM TUBE.*

Line filtering is included to eliminate undesired spectral components from the output signal. Included as well is the receiver-protecting duplexer, an assembly permitting the single antenna to be used for both transmitting, receiving, and routing the signals correctly. New designs of power supplies and modulators use modular solid-state circuits far more than the vacuum-tube circuitry of older radars. Designers stress fail-safe characteristics by these modular and fault-tolerant approaches. Amplifiers are sometimes designed with integral power supplies to achieve greater total reliability as well.

Much simpler radar transmitters are also in wide use, those in which an oscillator (such as a magnetron) is used rather than an amplifier chain. In such a case (**Fig. 11**), the modulator supplies a cathode-to-anode voltage pulse which causes an rf signal to be generated. *SEE MAGNETRON.*

The transmitter subsystem must also include many safety features because of the lethal level of voltages and dangerous radiation present. Transmitters also require very involved cooling systems, since the efficiencies in the energy conversion processes are usually in the 15 to 40% region and much damaging heat is generated.

***Antenna.*** In a typical antenna the signal from the transmitter is carried by waveguide (usually rectangular metal piping) through a rotary joint and to a feedhorn at the focus of a parabolic reflector. Such an antenna is pictured in **Fig. 12**; the operation is shown in **Fig. 13**. *SEE WAVEGUIDE.*

The optical properties of antennas are such that the beam formed has a width inversely proportional to the dimension of the illuminated aperture—the wider (in units of wavelengths) the antenna, the narrower the beam in that direction. The beam shown in Fig. 13 is called a fan beam and is suitable for a two-dimensional (2D) search radar making target position estimates in just range and azimuth angle. Another parabolic antenna, the height finder (**Fig. 14**), forms a horizontal fan beam which can be nodded in the vertical to ascertain the elevation angle of targets to which the antenna has been directed in azimuth. Three-dimensional (3D) radars have been developed that measure azimuth, elevation, and range as they rotate in azimuth. **Figure 15** illustrates two such antennas, one in which a stack of beams (requiring separate receivers) is used to measure elevation, and one in which a single pencil beam is caused to scan rapidly in elevation while the antenna rotates in azimuth only one beam width.

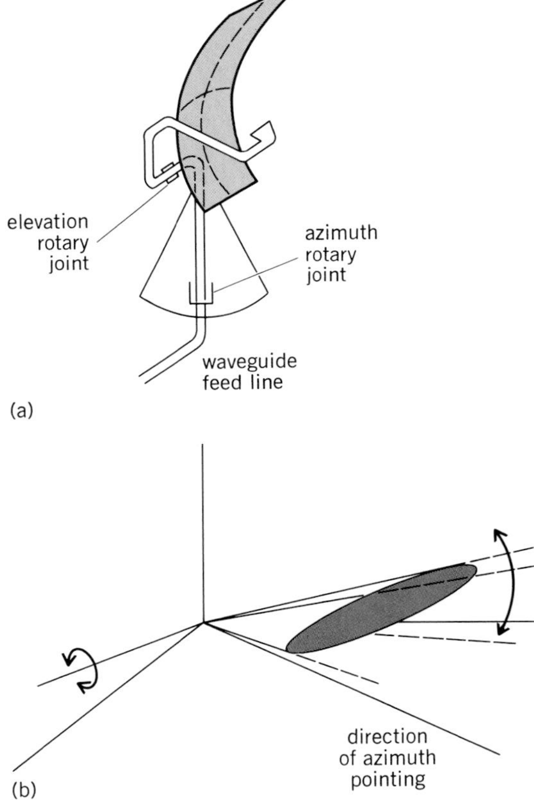


**Fig. 14. Antenna of a height-finder radar. (*a*) Antenna configuration. (*b*) Horizontal fan beam formed.**

Many tracking radars use dish antennas with some sort of multiple-beam feed complex to permit very accurate angle measurement. In **Fig. 16** are diagrammed two squinted-beam monopulse feed approaches (illustrated in one plane of measurement only), one with the feedhorns at the focus and the other of a Cassegrain type, wherein a hyperbolic subreflector is used and the feedhorn assembly can be located in the area of the parabolic reflector. When this optical scheme is combined with certain polarization rotation techniques in the two reflecting surfaces, the subreflector appears reflective to the signals from the feed but transparent after reflection from the parabola. Consequently the amount of aperture blockage (with detrimental effects in accuracy) is greatly reduced.

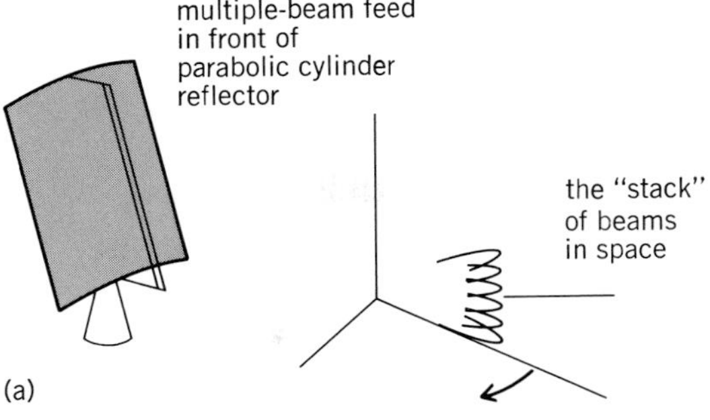


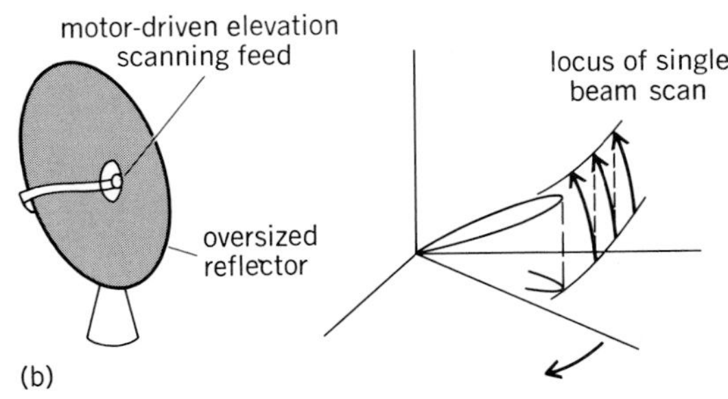


**Fig. 15. Two three-dimensional (3D) radar antennas. (*a*) Multiple simultaneous beams from a stacked-beam antenna. (*b*) Single-beam scanner.**

Several radars have been developed that use phased-array antennas, in which the transmitter power is divided among many radiating elements (possibly thousands) and in which the phase of each element is controlled by a computer. In such a fixed-aperture antenna, the beam can be steered in only microseconds from one position to another many beam widths away. Consequently a wide variety of dwell routines can be implemented that are not at all constrained by

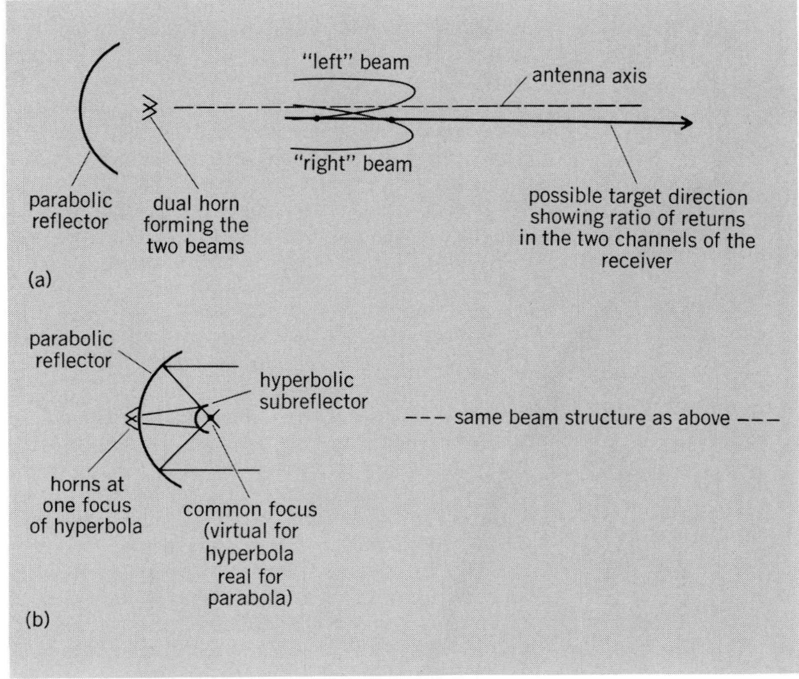


**Fig. 16. Monopulse antennas for tracking. (*a*) Single reflector. (*b*) Cassegrain feed.**

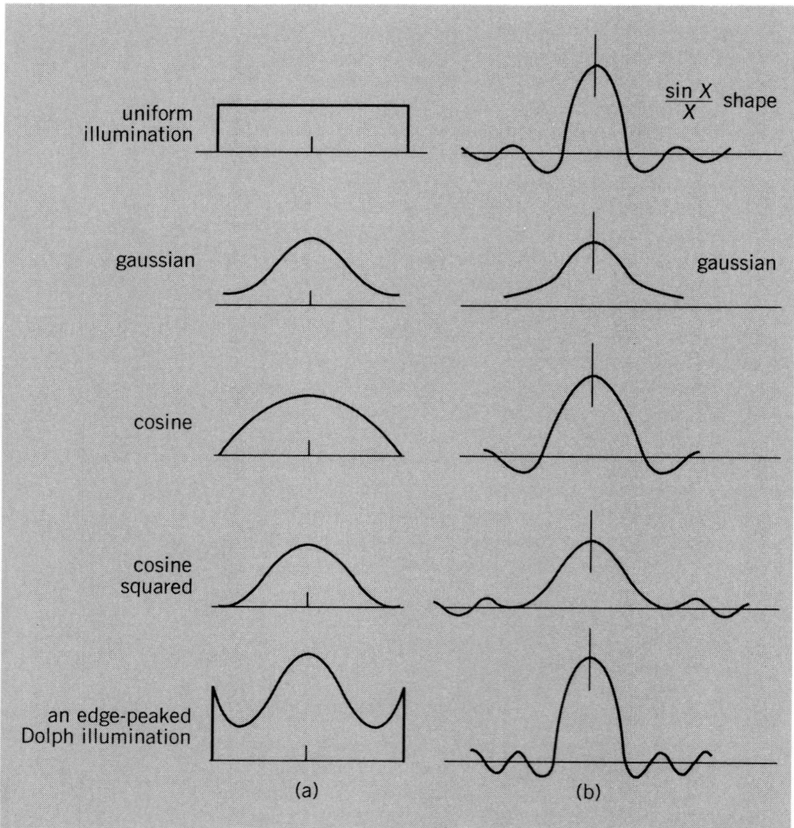


**Fig. 17. Antenna excitation functions and patterns. (*a*) Excitation functions. (*b*) Resulting patterns.**

mechanical rotation. Phased-array antennas are quite complex and expensive; they are used, therefore, only where great demand for very versatile operation exists.

In all antennas, the microwave optics involved results in formation of side lobes in the radiation pattern or gain function. The shape of the pattern is determined by the excitation function at the antenna. In **Fig. 17** are sketched some common excitation functions and the resulting patterns. High side lobes are very undesirable in radar because they permit unwanted signals to enter the receiver. Simple antennas usually have modest side-lobe levels. More severely weighted excitation functions can be generated for more desirable (low side-lobe level) patterns, but only at the expense of complicating the feed. *SEE MICROWAVE OPTICS*.

***Synthetic aperture radar.*** Since radar angular resolution is related to antenna beam width which is inversely related to the size of the antenna, it has occurred to radar designers to build very large antennas where possible. One way to "build" a large antenna is to move (as in an aircraft) a smaller antenna over a great distance and, in the signal processing, to "remember" all the characteristics of the signals received. With modern digital processing, it is then possible to reconstruct the radar scene as though the antenna had been as large as the path traversed. A radar using such a technique is called a synthetic aperture radar (SAR); these are used in the Earth-monitoring fields (**Fig. 18**).

Coherent signal processing, discussed below, involves using both the amplitude and phase of the signals reflected so that more information can be extracted about the target. In synthetic aperture radar operation, a radar of fairly high range-resolution (as achieved with broadband or very narrow pulses) can achieve a comparable lateral or cross-range resolution if the return phase of each pulse is remembered as the radar's position is changed relative to the target area, that is, as the aircraft carrying the radar moves along the path shown in Fig. 18*a*. The cross-range resolution achieved in the eventual imaging (from processing the stored signals) is greater the longer the synthetic aperture path. There are two limits upon that path length: First, the target distance $d$ changes as shown in Fig. 18*b*, and the detailed target imaging is limited by the signal-path-length phase excursion shown; a change of $\lambda/8$ in the signal path length, where $\lambda$ is the radar wavelength, causes a 90° phase change in signals, jeopardizing the image processing. Second, the aperture path is limited simply by the beamwidth of the actual antenna being used; after a while the side-looking antenna fixed in the aircraft no longer illuminates the target area. Generally the former limit is reached long before the latter limit. To overcome the former limit, a process of compensating for the path-length phase progression called focusing is used. This results, however, in the remarkably detailed imaging being confined to just a range strip

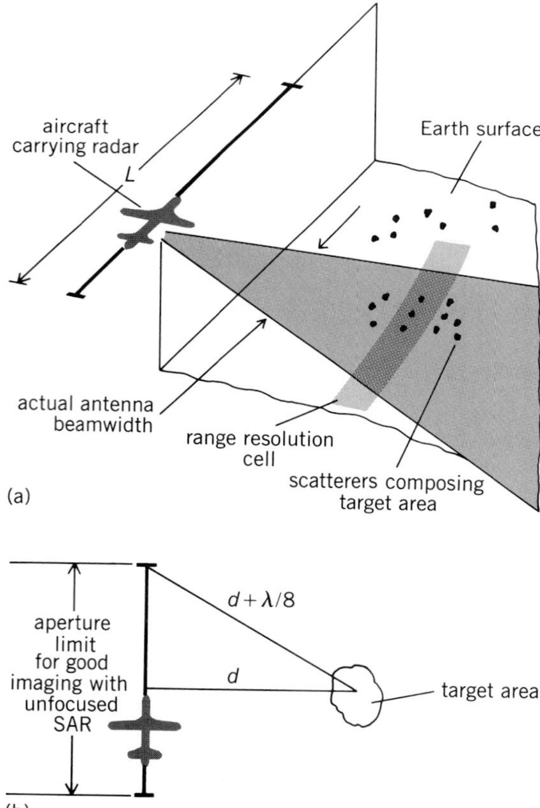


**Fig. 18. Operation of synthetic aperture radar (SAR). (*a*) Configuration. *L* = aircraft path during period of coherent processing—the synthetic aperture. Successive changes in phase structure as viewing angle changes permit image processing to achieve cross-range resolution. (*b*) Geometry of aperture limit imposed by change in signal path length.**

around a chosen range; several such swaths, then, may be required for a detailed picture of a very large area.

***Receiver and signal processor.*** The signals collected by the antenna are amplified in some radars (those with rf preamplifiers), then converted to the i-f for further amplification and processing. There may be several parallel channels of receiver necessary, depending on the type of radar (for the several beams in a stacked-beam radar or for the angle error channels in a monopulse tracker, for example), each requiring all the processing described here.

Many radars require a long pulse for the requisite energy on each transmission (product of pulse width and peak power, which can be limited in many transmitters), yet require the range resolution (the ability to discern two closely spaced targets) of a short pulse. The effect in range resolution of a very short pulse can be achieved by modulating the long pulse with either frequency or phase modulation so that it has the same bandwidth as the very short pulse desired. Then, on receive, the waveform generator supplies a replica of the modulation on the transmitted pulse to the receiver so that a matched-filter action takes place in circuitry called the pulse compressor. The result is that the high energy for detection sensitivity and the resolution effects of a short pulse have both been obtained (**Fig. 19**).

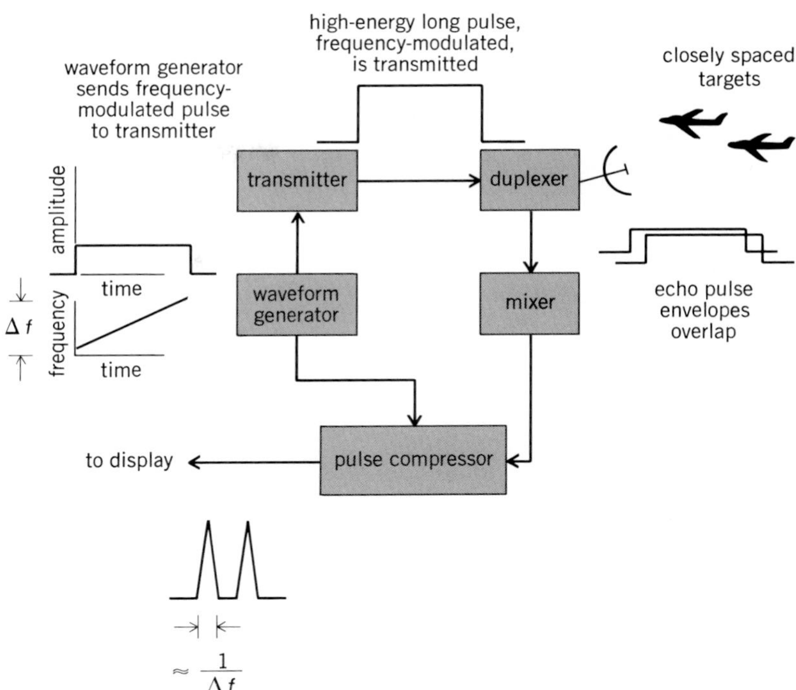


**Fig. 19. Pulse compression. The pulse compressor, using knowledge of the modulation in the transmitted pulse, acts as a matched filter producing maximum amplitude narrow responses, thus resolving the closely spaced targets.**

In many radar applications it is desired to determine if returns are Doppler-shifted, that is, if certain returns are coming from moving targets rather than from stationary clutter. Even the simplest radars can be equipped with moving target indication (MTI), wherein successive echoes are examined for a progressive phase change (indicative of slight round-trip path change between pulses), the Doppler shift in frequency being too slight to filter out on a single pulse. All MTIs require, then, a phase reference in the receiver. This reference can range from reflections from clutter (assumed fixed) in the vicinity of targets and simply a part of the total return, to a local oscillator signal in the receiver, carefully phase-locked to the transmitted signal with each transmission. In low-pulse repetition frequency radars, the returns may be compared on an each-succeeding-pair basis in an appropriate canceller. In high-pulse repetition frequency pulse-Doppler radars, the process results in actually measuring Doppler shift (hence the radial component of target velocity) and not just in estimating that such a shift exists, as in the simpler cancellation schemes. *SEE DOPPLER RADAR; MOVING-TARGET INDICATION.*

The pulse compression and Doppler processing schemes are regarded as coherent signal processing insofar as both the phase and amplitude of the signals are involved. Further stages of the whole signal processor may be noncoherent; that is, a signal detector may now act on the amplitude of the signal resulting from the coherent processing, producing video signals with no carrier to convey phase relationships. These video signals (detector output voltages described above) may be displayed for operator observation and detection judgment; in more sophisticated radars they may be processed further in an automatic detector with constant-false-alarm-rate features in the noncoherent units of the signal processor. In such units, various comparisons among the sum and difference (angle error) channels (carried in parallel to this point) may be made to refine the position estimate, or other comparisons may be made to reduce the false alarm effects of antenna side lobes or interference signals.

The object of all coherent and noncoherent signal processing is to increase the probability that correct estimates and accurate measurements are made at the user's end of the radar and that effects of undesired signals seen by the antenna are greatly reduced.

In newer radars, signal-processing equipment consists of a cabinet (or several) of printed circuit boards with tiny integrated circuit units on them, and extensive back-plane wiring to interconnect properly the many circuit boards. Both coherent and noncoherent processing can be done with digital computerlike equipment to a large degree.

***Display and control.*** In simple radars, the operator may observe the output of an elementary video-producing detector on one of several formats on a cathode-ray-tube display. The most common format is the PPI (plan position indication), in which a radial trace (the path of the cathode-ray-tube electron beam exciting the phosphor) is synchronized to the pulse repetition frequency, resulting in radar range being displayed radially from the center, and in which this trace is moved around the display, linked electronically to the antenna rotation. The detector output is applied to the intensity grid of the cathode-ray tube so that a bright spot results when a strong video voltage is produced by the detector. The display circuitry may also superimpose upon the radar video certain calibration pulses (range marks and bearing lines, for example), maps of the local terrain, or other symbols of importance in the entire sysrem of which the radar is a part.

The PPI format and several other useful formats for video display are shown in **Fig. 20**. Similar displays are produced not always with actual video signals but often with computer-generated ''synthetic'' video conveying the same information more clearly.

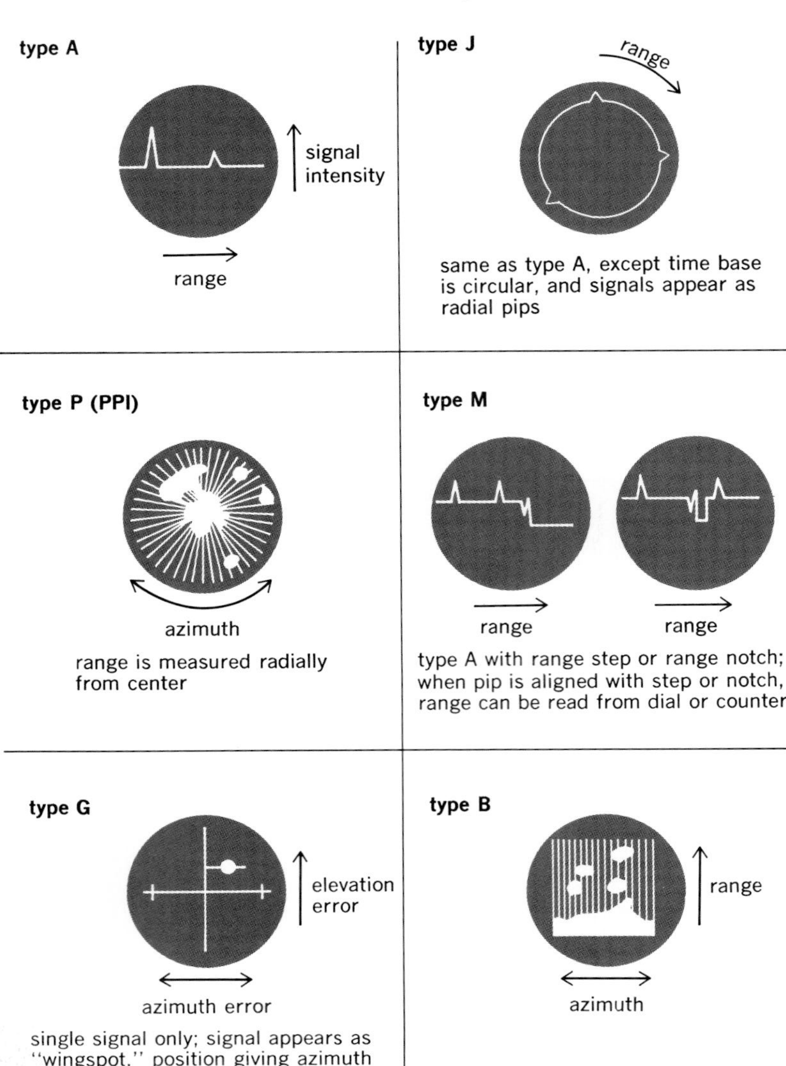


**Fig. 20. Cathode-ray-tube display formats.**

In a radar equipped with still more automation, the operator may play a more managerial role, and a suitable display would show numerous symbols and alphanumeric notation about the targets and traffic activities rather than merely displaying the radar video itself. Such information would permit the operator either to instruct the radar (as in establishing boundaries for special modes of operation) or to alert the rest of the overall system of which the radar is a part to any unusual situation observed. In such a radar, the specific data on individual targets may well be passed from the report-formatting computers of the radar to other user computers or displays without any particular judgment or action by the operator. SEE CONTINUOUS-WAVE RADAR; MONOPULSE RADAR.

*Robert T. Hill*

***Bibliography.*** D. K. Barton, *Radar System Analysis*, 1964 ed., reprint 1976; E. Brookner (ed.), *Radar Technology*, 1977; F. E. Nathanson, *Radar Design Principles*, 1969; A. W. Rihaczek, *Principles of High-Resolution Radar*, 1969; M. I. Skolnik, *Introduction to Radar Systems*, 2d ed., 1980; M. I. Skolnik (ed.), *Radar Handbook*, 1970.

## Radar-absorbing materials

Materials that are designed to reduce the reflection of electromagnetic radiation by a conducting surface in the frequency range from approximately 100 MHz to 100 GHz. The level of reduction achieved varies from a few decibels to greater than 50 dB, in percentage terms reducing the reflected energy by up to 99.999%.

**Theory.** The performance of any material as a microwave absorber can be calculated from Maxwell's equations if the electrical and magnetic properties are known. However, in the most simple terms, two conditions are necessary to produce absorption. First the characteristic impedance of the material must match the characteristic impedance of free space so that the electromagnetic energy may enter the material. Second, the material must then attenuate the electromagnetic radiation, which means that it must exhibit either dielectric or magnetic loss (or both).

Consider a material with a characteristic impedance $Z_i$ which is given by Eq. (1), where $\mu_i$ is the magnetic

$$Z_i = \sqrt{\frac{\mu_i}{\epsilon_i}} \qquad (1)$$

permeability of the material and $\epsilon_i$ is the permittivity. Both $\mu$ and $\epsilon$ may be expressed as complex numbers, in which case the imaginary part represents the magnetic loss or dielectric loss, respectively. For electromagnetic radiation incident on this lossy material at normal incidence, the energy reflection coefficient is given by expression (2), where $Z_0$ is the characteristic

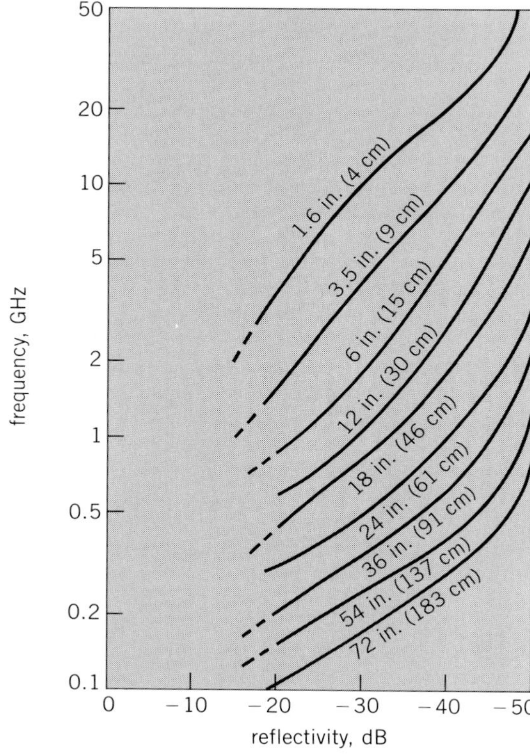


**Fig. 1. Absorption of thick, profiled lossy layers at normal incidence as a function of frequency, for several different absorber thicknesses. The height of the pyramids is given for each material.**

$$\left(\frac{1 - Z_i/Z_0}{1 + Z_i/Z_0}\right)^2 \tag{2}$$

impedance of free space. SEE ELECTRICAL IMPEDANCE.

Zero reflection will occur in the case where $Z_i$ is equal to $Z_0$, which also implies that Eq. (3) is satis-

$$\frac{\mu_i}{\epsilon_i} = \frac{\mu_0}{\epsilon_0} \tag{3}$$

fied. This condition must be met for $\mu_i$ and $\epsilon_i$ as complex numbers. Since either $\mu_i$ or $\epsilon_i$ must contain an imaginary component in order to attenuate the radiation, it necessarily follows that in this case both $\mu_i$ and $\epsilon_i$ must be complex numbers with both the real parts and imaginary parts in the same ratio as the ratio of $\mu_0$ to $\epsilon_0$.

**Design methods.** In theory, this simple solution offers the possibility of a perfect absorber. In practice, materials have not been found which will give such a good impedance match over an appreciable frequency range. It is therefore necessary to adopt specific design methods to manufacture practical absorbing materials.

Two methods have been widely adopted in order to produce such absorbers. The first is to avoid a discrete change of impedance at the material surface by gradually varying the impedance, for example by the use of a thick profiled lossy layer. The removal of the discrete discontinuity at the surface allows the microwave energy to be transmitted into the absorbing medium without reflection. Tapered carbon-loaded pyramids which are used for the lining of anechoic chambers are typical of this type of absorber. To produce such absorbers, it is necessary in practice to taper the material over distances which are large compared with the wavelength, in the material, of the frequencies to be absorbed. Therefore, practical absorbers of this type giving greater than 20 dB absorption vary in thickness from about 0.8 in. (2 cm) at 10 GHz and above to 6 ft (2 m) at 100 MHz and above. **Figure 1** shows approximately the level of absorption as a function of frequency at normal incidence for several different absorber thicknesses. While this type of absorber is capable of producing a very high degree of absorption over a broad bandwidth, it is at the same time a relatively thick material.

The second method of absorber design has been developed to give much thinner absorbing layers which are capable of producing good absorption (≥25 dB) with restricted bandwidths. These materials consist of lossy layers where the absorption is produced by a destructive interference at the frequency for which the material is electrically a quarter wavelength (**Fig. 2**).

The typical performance of these materials as a function of frequency is illustrated in **Fig. 3**. It is possible to tune these materials to any desired center frequency over most of the range from 100 MHz to 100 GHz. While this type of material intrinsically provides a relatively narrow bandwidth frequency performance, it is also possible to broaden the effective bandwidth by various techniques such as multiple layer absorbers. With two layers of material it is possible to tune one absorber to two different frequencies. By placing these two frequencies appropriately, for example within one octave of each other, a broadband absorber is obtained in practice.

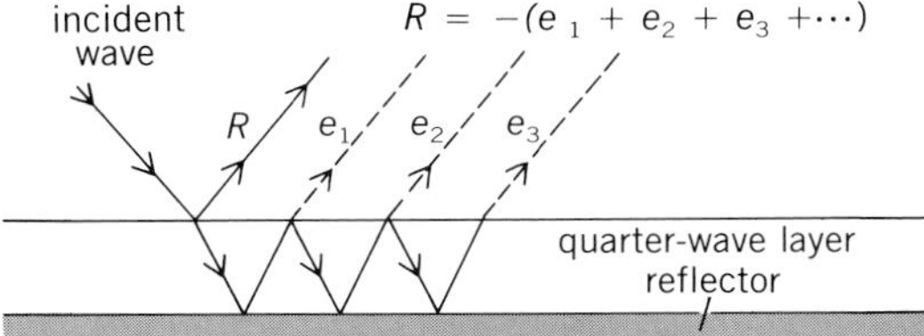


**Fig. 2. Mode of operation of a lossy quarter-wave layer. There is a mutual cancellation of the reflected wave *R* and the emergent waves $e_1$, $e_2$, $e_3$, and so forth.**

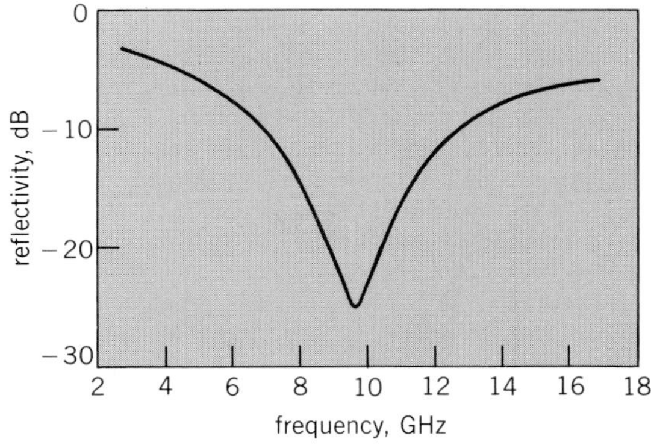


**Fig. 3. Performance of a typical lossy quarter-wave layer as a function of frequency.**

**Uses.** Microwave-absorbing materials are widely used both within the electronics industry and for defense purposes. Their uses can be classified into three major areas: (1) for test purposes so that accurate measurements can be made on microwave equipment unaffected by spurious reflected signals (the most common example is the anechoic chamber); (2) to improve the performance of any practical microwave system by removing unwanted reflections which can occur if there is any conducting material in the radiation path; and (3) to camouflage a military target by reducing the reflected radar signal. SEE MICROWAVE; MICROWAVE MEASUREMENTS.

*R. J. Lowin*

## Radio

Communication between two or more points, employing electromagnetic waves as the transmission medium.

**Technical history.** In 1840 two separate events began the long history of radio. Joseph Henry first produced high-frequency oscillations, and at roughly the same time, Samuel F. B. Morse was demonstrating the telegraph in Washington, D.C. In 1873 James Clerk Maxwell first tied together the theories of Henry and Morse to explain the theory of propagation of energy from wires. He also showed, at least mathematically, that these generated waves would travel at the speed of light.

Heinrich Hertz was able to demonstrate practically Maxwell's theory in 1888, by passing a rapidly alternating current through a wire, creating what were to become known as Hertzian waves. Guglielmo Marconi made practical application of Hertz's work. He experimented with an antenna and ground setup from 1895 on, and broadcast the first paid radiogram from the Isle of Wight in 1898.

Hundreds and thousands of other inventions and

discoveries were to follow, but the basis of radio had been established. The same formula is in use today. **Figure 1** shows the audio pulse and the carrier pulse being blended into a modulated carrier wave, which is then amplified and fed into the antenna. The receiving antenna and tuner catch the weak signal, amplify it, sort the audio pulse from the carrier, and play a now reamplified audio pulse through the speaker at home.

The first significant radio applications employed frequencies of about 500 kHz for ship communications. Their value was demonstrated dramatically in 1909 and 1912, when assistance was obtained by the sinking passenger ships *Republic* and *Titanic*, and hundreds of lives were saved.

Roughly 10 years later, the first real overseas radio complex was established, upon discovery that frequencies of 3000–30,000 kHz traveled over great distances by reflection from the ionosphere. Today, although cable and ionosphere reflection signals are still used to a great extent, satellite relay has almost completely taken over transmission of broadcast-station quality. In later years, many other services, such as television, FM broadcasting, radar, and microwave relaying were developed as the unique properties of much higher frequencies were discovered and exploited.

**Methods of information transmission.** Radio waves transmitted continuously, with each cycle an exact duplicate of all others, indicate only that a carrier is present. The message must cause changes in the carrier which can be detected at a distant receiver. The method used for the transmission of the information is determined by the nature of the information which is to be transmitted as well as by the purpose of the communication system **(Fig. 2)**.

***Code telegraphy.*** The carrier is keyed on and off to form dots and dashes. The technique, often used in ship-to-shore and amateur communications, has been largely superseded in many other point-to-point services by more efficient methods.

***Frequency-shift transmission.*** The carrier frequency is shifted a fixed amount to correspond with telegraphic dots and dashes or with combinations of pulse signals identified with the characters on a typewriter. This technique is widely used in handling the large volume of public message traffic on long circuits, principally by the use of teletypewriters. SEE TELETYPEWRITER.

***Amplitude modulation.*** The amplitude of the carrier is made to fluctuate, to conform to the fluctuations of a sound wave. This technique is used in AM broadcasting, television picture transmission, and many other services. SEE AMPLITUDE MODULATION; AMPLITUDE-MODULATION DETECTOR; AMPLITUDE-MODULATION RADIO; AMPLITUDE MODULATOR.

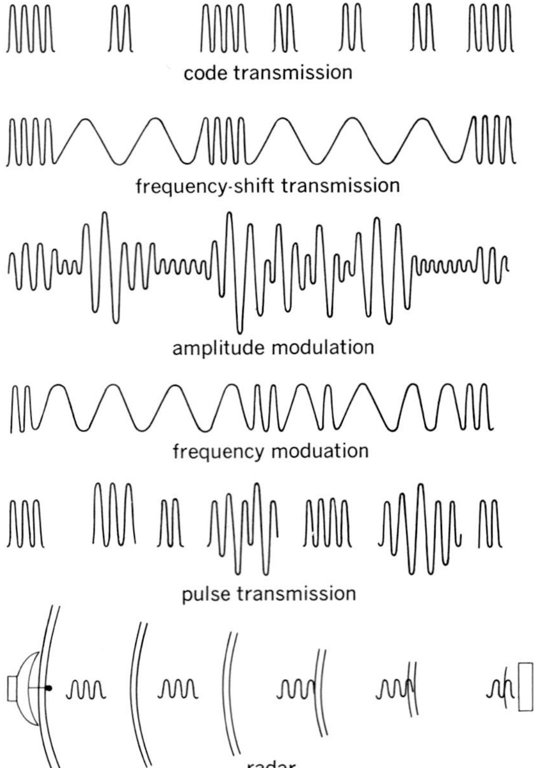


**Fig. 2. Methods for transmission of information.**

***Frequency modulation.*** The frequency of the carrier is made to fluctuate around an average axis, to correspond to the fluctuations of the modulating wave. This technique is used in FM broadcasting, television sound transmission, and microwave relaying. SEE FREQUENCY MODULATION; FREQUENCY-MODULATION DETECTOR; FREQUENCY-MODULATION RADIO; FREQUENCY MODULATOR.

***Pulse transmission.*** The carrier is transmitted in short pulses, which change in repetition rate, width, or amplitude, or in complex groups of pulses which vary from group to succeeding group in accordance with the message information. These forms of pulse transmission are identified as pulse-code, pulse-time, pulse-position, pulse-amplitude, pulse-width, or pulse-frequency modulation. These complex techniques are employed principally in microwave relay systems. SEE PULSE MODULATION; PULSE MODULATOR.

***Radar.*** The carrier is normally transmitted as short pulses in a narrow beam, similar to that of a searchlight. When a wave pulse strikes an object, such as an aircraft, energy is reflected to the station, which measures the round-trip time and converts it to distance. A radar can display varying reflections in a maplike presentation on a cathode-ray tube. SEE RADAR.

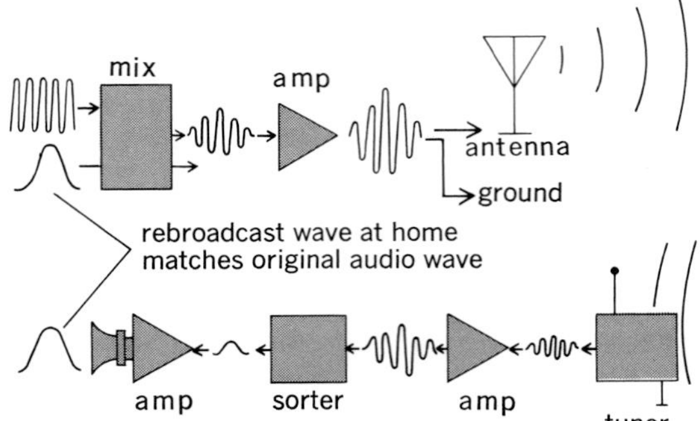


**Fig. 1. Transmission of audio information by radio.**

**Uses of radio.** The first practical application of radio, in the 1900s between ships and shore stations, was followed quickly by overseas communication and communication between other widely separated fixed points. Subsequently, the applications have become widely diversified. Some of the important uses are listed below.

1. Public safety: marine and aviation communications, police and fire protection, forestry conservation, and highway traffic control.

2. Industrial: power utilities, pipelines, relay services, news systems, agriculture, and petroleum processing.

3. Land transportation: railroads, motor carriers, taxicabs, and automobile emergency needs.

4. Broadcasting: television, FM broadcasting, AM broadcasting, and shortwave broadcasting.

5. Military and space: radar, communications, navigation, telemetering, missile tracking, satellite photographic surveys, and missile guidance.

6. Fixed point-to-point: long-distance message and picture transmission.

7. Relaying: television, sound, picture, and public message relaying over long distances. Most recently, and soon to be a major part of the relaying function of radio, communications satellites have handled a great deal of overseas communications. These satellites supply not one but many services, including several thousand narrow channels for telephone, telegraph, and teletype, with wide channels for television and other video transmission. With the exception of military satellites, all United States communications satellites are privately owned, by Federal decree, by the Communications Satellite Corp. *SEE TELEVISION.*

8. Telemetering: remote indication of water levels in reservoirs and rivers, performance of experimental aircraft, missiles, and satellites.

9. Weather reporting: early warning and location of hurricanes and other storms, trends of weather for industrial and public information.

**Frequency separation.** Hundreds of thousands of radio transmitters exist, each requiring a carrier at some radio frequency. To prevent interference, different carrier frequencies are used for stations whose service areas overlap and receivers are built to select only the carrier signal of the desired station. Resonant electric circuits in the receiver are adjusted, or tuned, to accept one frequency and reject others.

Each station operates within a specific radiofrequency (rf) channel. All other stations within a geographical area are excluded from using this channel. Each channel must be wide enough to accommodate the message information, provide tolerance for small carrier frequency drift, perhaps provide a guard band, and allow for imperfect receiver selectivity capabilities. The minimum usable channel widths (or bandwidths) vary from service to service, depending upon the amount of information a channel must accommodate. In television it is 6000 kHz (kc in former terminology) because of the large amount of essential picture information. In FM broadcasting it is 200 kHz and in AM broadcasting 10 kHz. The great demand for authorizations requires efficient channel utilization. In the mobile transportation service in the United States, the Federal Communications Commission was compelled to reduce channel widths 50% when technical developments made it feasible.

**Federal Communications Commission.** All nations have a sovereign right to use freely any or all parts of the radio spectrum. But a growing list of international agreements and treaties divides the spectrum and specifies sharing among nations for their mutual benefit and protection.

Each nation designates its own regulatory agency. Functioning within the international agreements, it issues authorizations; assigns frequencies; polices operations; creates technical standards, rules, and practices; and safeguards and protects the public interest.

In the United States all nongovernmental radio communications are regulated by the Federal Communications Commission (FCC), according to the provision of the Communications Act of 1934, as amended. Creation of a radio station or service requires authorization by the FCC. Upon completion of an authorized facility, a license to operate is issued. Radio stations are inspected regularly by engineers attached to FCC field offices. Stations must comply with the terms of their authorization regarding carrier-frequency tolerance, power limitations, permissible communications, calls signals, and control by properly licensed personnel. *SEE AMATEUR RADIO.*

*John D. Singleton*

**Bibliography.** American Radio Relay League, *Radio Amateur's Handbook*, rev. ed., 1984; E. Barnouw, *A History of Broadcasting in the United States*, 3 vols., 1966, 1968, 1970; G. Kennedy, *Electronic Communication Systems*, 3d ed., 1985; Howard W. Sams Engineering Staff, *Reference Data for Radio Engineers*, 6th ed., 1975; R. L. Shrader, *Electronic Communication*, 5th ed., 1985.

## Radio-frequency amplifier

A tuned amplifier that amplifies the high-frequency signals commonly used in radio communications. The frequency at which maximum gain occurs in a radio-frequency (rf) amplifier is made variable by changing either the capacitance or the inductance of the tuned circuit. A typical application is the amplification of the signal received from an antenna before it is mixed with a local oscillator signal in the first detector of a radio receiver. The amplifier that follows the first detector is a special type of rf amplifier known as an intermediate-frequency (i-f) amplifier. *SEE AMPLIFIER; INTERMEDIATE-FREQUENCY AMPLIFIER.*

An rf amplifier is distinguished by its ability to tune over the desired range of input frequencies. The shunt capacitance, which adversely affects the gain of a resistance-capacitance coupled amplifier, becomes a part of the tuning capacitance in the rf amplifier, thus permitting high gain at radio frequencies. The power gain of an rf amplifier is always limited at high radio frequencies, however, for reasons which will be discussed.

**Basic circuit.** Two typical rf amplifier circuits are shown in **Fig. 1**. The conventional bipolar transistor amplifier of Fig. 1*a* uses tapped coils in the tuned circuits to provide optimum gain-bandwidth characteristics consistent with the desirable value of tuning capacitance. Inductive coupling provides the desired impedance transformation in the input and output circuits. The tuning capacitors are usually ganged so as to rotate on a single shaft, providing tuning by a single control knob. Sometimes varactor diodes are used to tune the circuits, in which case the tuning control is a potentiometer that controls the diode voltage. Automatic gain control (AGC) is frequently used on the rf amplifier, as shown. AGC voltage controls the bias and hence the transconductance of the amplifier. In the field-effect transistor (FET), circuit (Fig. 1*b*)

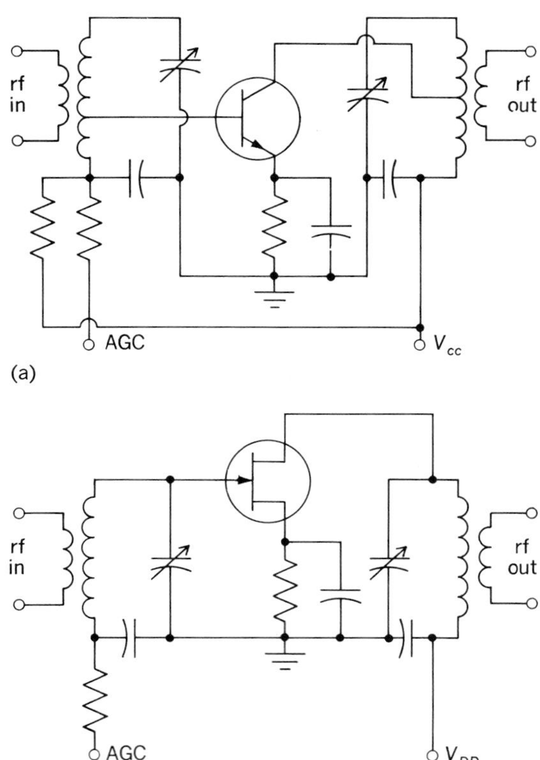


**Fig. 1. Typical rf amplifiers. Circuits with (*a*) bipolar transistor and (*b*) field-effect transistor.**

tapped coils are not required because of the very high input and output resistances of the FET. Characteristics of the FET are similar to those of a pentode tube except for the lower drain voltage and higher capacitance between the input and the output. Thus the FET circuit is similar to a pentode circuit except that it is much simpler because it has no heater, screen grid, or suppressor grid equivalents. *SEE AUTOMATIC GAIN CONTROL (AGC); SEMICONDUCTOR; TRANSISTOR.*

**High-frequency limit.** The power gain of a bipolar transistor is strongly dependent upon the forward current transfer ratio $\beta$, or $h_{fe}$, as well as on the transconductance $g_m$. However, the current transfer ratio (or current amplification factor) $\beta$ decreases as the frequency increases because of the base region diffusion capacitance resulting from the finite time required for the charge carriers to traverse the base region. A graph of $\beta$ as a function of frequency for a typical transistor is given in **Fig. 2**. The current transfer ratio $\beta$ remains essentially constant at the low-frequency value $\beta_0$ (200 for the transistor of Fig. 2) below the frequency known as the beta cutoff frequency $f_\beta$, at which $\beta = 0.707\beta_0$. As the frequency increases above $f_\beta$, $\beta$ decreases and is essentially inversely proportional to frequency. The frequency at which $\beta$ decreases to 1 is known as the transitional frequency $f_T$, which is 300 MHz for the transistor of Fig. 2.

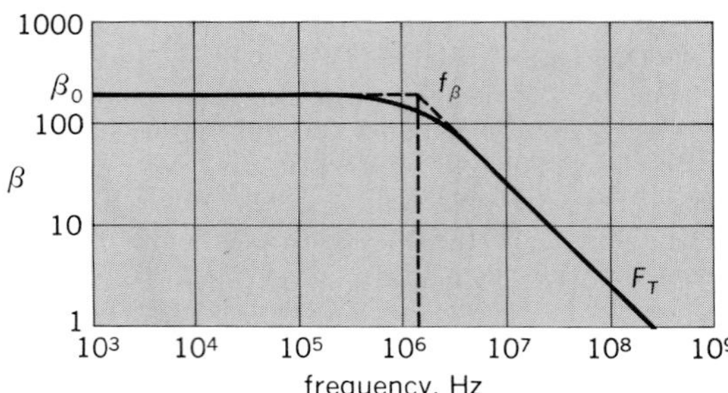


**Fig. 2. Variation of current transfer ratio as a function of frequency for typical transistor.**

Because of the linear relationship between $\beta$ and the frequency, $\beta_0 f_\beta = f_T$ and $\beta f = f_T$ for frequencies above $f_\beta$. Therefore, $\beta$ can be determined for any desired frequency, provided $\beta_0$, or $h_{fe}$, and $f_T$ are given by the manufacturer. For example, if $f_T$ = 300 MHz and $\beta_0 = 200$ for the transistor of Fig. 2, then $f_\beta$ = 300 MHz/200 = 1.5 MHz. Also, at 30 MHz the value of $\beta = f_T/f$ = 300 MHz/30 MHz = 10. Therefore, the available current gain of a common emitter transistor is approximately equal to the ratio $f_T/f$, where $f$ is the desired operating frequency, provided $f$ is above $f_\beta$. Transistors are available with very high values of $f_T$, in the neighborhood of $2.5 \times 10^9$ Hz. The transistor type must be carefully chosen for high-frequency rf amplifiers. The parameter $f_{fb}$ or $f_\alpha$ which is approximately equal to $f_T$, is sometimes given for transistors. Field-effect transistors and vacuum tubes have similar frequency limitations imposed by the carrier transit time between source and drain or cathode and plate. Special amplifying devices such as traveling-wave tubes or parametric amplifiers are used as rf amplifiers in the microwave region, or for frequencies above $10^9$ Hz. *SEE MICROWAVE TUBE.*

**Capacitive feedback.** Careful design is required in rf amplifiers to avoid oscillation or instability. The inherent instability results from the capacitive coupling between output and input circuits; this coupling permits feedback in the amplifier, which can be regenerative when inductive loads or tuned circuits are used in the amplifier output. The coupling capacitance is primarily the collector junction capacitance in a bipolar transistor, the gate-drain function capacitance in an FET, or the grid-plate capacitance in a vacuum tube. The tetrode and pentode tubes were developed primarily to reduce this capacitance and were popular as rf amplifiers until transistors with good high-frequency characteristics were developed. However, pentode tubes generate more noise than triodes or transistors and therefore are not well suited for amplifying very weak signals.

Transistor or triode amplifiers can be stabilized by either of two methods. The first method, known as neutralization, cancels the effect of the capacitive feedback in the device by providing equal feedback current of opposite polarity from the amplifier output to the input. This feedback current is usually obtained by connecting a capacitor, known as a neutralizing capacitor, between the input and an output-circuit point that has opposite polarity to the collector (drain or plate). This opposite polarity voltage is available either at the secondary of a coupling transformer or opposite the collector end of a tapped coil in the output circuit. The neutralizing capacitance is adjusted until the neutralizing current is equal to the feedback current through the amplifier. Some transistors require a resistor in series with the neutralizing capacitor to provide the 180° phase difference.

The second method is to limit the voltage gain of the amplifier stage to a value at which the feedback current will be insufficient to produce oscillations or other undesirable characteristics. This method requires more stages to produce a total specified amplifier gain but eliminates the need to neutralize each

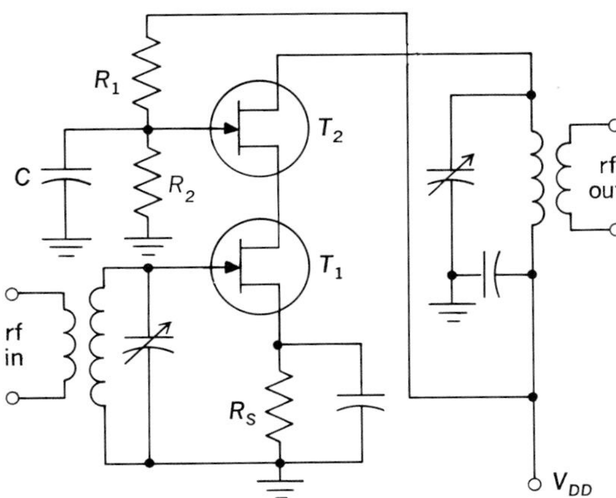


**Fig. 3. Cascode amplifier for low-noise rf application.**

stage. The criterion for stability is given by notation (1), where $R_i'$ and $R_0'$ are the effective shunt resis-

$$R_i' \; R_0' > 2/\omega_0 C_c g_m \qquad (1)$$

tances in the input and output circuits respectively, $\omega_0$ is the resonant frequency, $C_c$ is the coupling capacitance, and $g_m$ the transconductance. SEE FEEDBACK CIRCUIT.

**Cascode circuit.** A technique commonly used to provide stable low-noise amplification at radio frequencies is illustrated in **Fig. 3**. This amplifier is known as a cascode amplifier. Two transistors are connected in series so that the source input resistance of the second transistor $T_2$ is the load for input transistor $T_1$. Because the resistance looking into the source terminal is approximately $1/g_m$ and the voltage gain of the FET is approximately $g_m R_L$, the voltage gain across transistor $T_1$ is only unity. Since the gate of transistor $T_2$ is maintained at signal ground potential by capacitor $C$ and the drain signal voltage of transistor $T_1$ is applied between the source and gate of transistor $T_2$, the tuned load in the drain circuit of transistor $T_2$ therefore provides the normally large voltage gain for this transistor.

The primary advantage of the cascode connection results from the fact that the gate of transistor $T_2$ is maintained at signal ground potential. Therefore, the current which flows through the gate-drain capacitance of $T_2$ flows through capacitor $C$ to ground and not into the signal input of the amplifier. Thus the effectively grounded gate of transistor $T_2$ essentially eliminates the capacitance between the drain of $T_2$ and the gate of $T_1$, thereby avoiding feedback. Capacitance still exists between the drain of transistor $T_1$ and its input gate, but because the voltage gain across this transistor is only unity, the amplifier is unconditionally stable. The proper drain-source voltage $V_{DS}$ for transistor $T_1$ is obtained from Eq. (2). Resistor $R_S$ in

$$V_{DS} = V_{DD} R_2 / R_1 + R_2 \qquad (2)$$

the source of transistor $T_1$ provides the desired gate-source bias voltage $V_{GS}$ for both transistors.

Bipolar transistors or triode tubes can be used in the cascode connection with slight bias circuit modifications as compared with Fig. 3. The cascode connection eliminates another problem, which results from capacitance between the input and output of an amplifier. This capacitance has an effective value, when viewed from the input of the amplifier, which is proportional to the voltage gain of the amplifier. This effect is known as the Miller effect and causes detuning of the resonant input circuit whenever the gain of the amplifier is changed, as with AGC.

*Charles L. Alley*


**Bibliography.** C. L. Alley and K. W. Atwood, *Electronic Engineering*, 3d ed., 1973; J. J. Brophy, *Basic Electronics for Scientists*, 4th ed., 1983; C. A. Holt, *Electronic Circuits: Digital and Analog*, 1978; J. Millman, *Microelectronics*, 1979.


## Radio-frequency impedance measurements

Measurements of electrical impedance at frequencies ranging from a few tens of kilohertz to about 1 gigahertz. This broad radio-frequency (rf) range encompasses frequencies from the extra-low-frequency band, through the long-, medium-, and short-wave ranges, and then through the very high-frequency (VHF) and the ultrahigh-frequency (UHF) bands. In the electrical context, impedance is defined as the ratio of voltage to current (or electrical field strength to magnetic field strength), and it is measured in units of ohms (Ω). SEE ELECTRICAL IMPEDANCE.

At zero frequency, that is, when the current involved is a direct current, both voltage and current are expressible as real numbers. Their ratio, the resistance, is a scalar (real) number. However, at nonzero frequencies, the voltage is not necessarily in phase with the current, and both are represented by vectors, and therefore are conveniently described by using complex numbers. To distinguish between the scalar quantity of resistance at zero frequency and the vectorial quantity at nonzero frequencies, the word impedance is used for the complex ratio of voltage to current. The real part $R$ of the complex impedance, $Z = R + jX$, is the (series-equivalent) resistance, and the imaginary part, the reactance $X$, is the reactive impedance of the (series-equivalent) inductance or capacitance (for positive or negative signs, respectively). Admittance $Y$ is defined as the inverse of impedance, $Y = 1/Z$, and some instruments measure admittance directly, in units of siemens (S). Network theory states that at a given frequency the impedance of any two-terminal linear (that is, level independent) circuit may be represented either as a series or a parallel connection of a resistance and a reactance. SEE

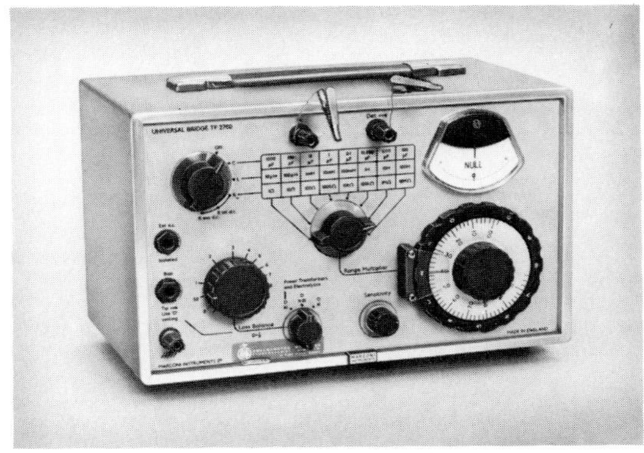

**Fig. 1. Universal *LCR* (inductance-capacitance-resistance) bridge. The bridge circuit is reconfigured when measuring resistors, inductors, or capacitors. (*Marconi Instruments Ltd.*)**

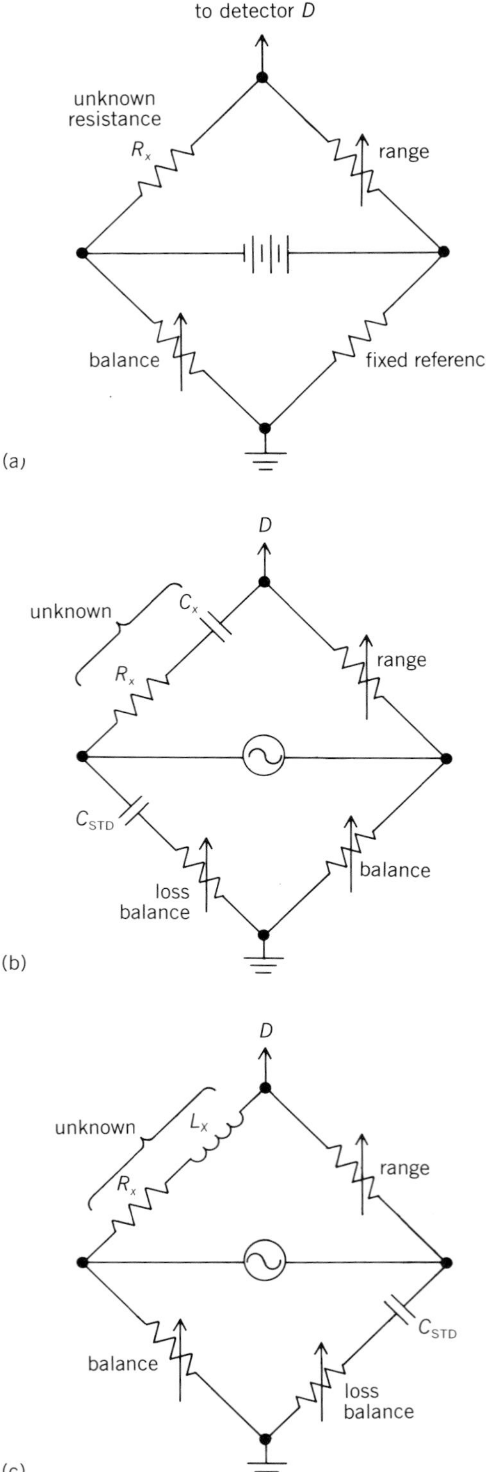


**Fig. 2. Three internal bridge circuits used in the *LCR* bridge of Fig. 1. (*a*) Wheatsone bridge. (*b*) Series-resistance-capacitance bridge for capacitance measurements. (c) Maxwell bridge for the measurement of inductances.**

*ALTERNATING-CURRENT CIRCUIT THEORY; DIRECT CURRENT; ELECTRICAL RESISTANCE; NETWORK THEORY.*

The measurement of impedance at radio frequencies cannot always be performed directly by measuring an rf voltage and dividing it by the corresponding rf current, for the following reasons: (1) it may be difficult to measure rf voltages and currents without loading the circuit by the sensing probes; (2) the distributed parasitic reactances (stray capacitances to neighboring objects, and lead inductances) may be altered by the sensing probes; and (3) the spatial voltage and current distributions may prevent unambiguous measurements (in waveguides, for instance).

Impedance measurements may be classified according to the principle used, be they resonance methods, bridge methods, or reflectometers, or may be classified according to the physical nature of the conductors, such as two-terminal, three-terminal, coaxial line, stripline, or waveguide. For a discussion of resonance methods *SEE Q METER.*

**Bridge methods.** At low frequencies, impedance measurements are often carried out by measuring separately the resistive and reactive parts, using either Q-meter instruments (for resonance methods), or reconfigurable bridges, which are sometimes called universal LCR (inductance-capacitance-resistance) bridges. In one such bridge (**Fig. 1**) the resistive part of the impedance is measured at dc with a Wheatstone bridge (**Fig. 2*a***). Capacitive reactance is measured with a series-resistance-capacitance bridge (Fig. 2*b*), and inductive reactance is measured with a Maxwell bridge (Fig. 2*c*), using alternating-current (ac) excitation and a standard capacitance $C_{STD}$. If the impedances of open structures or remote components have to be measured, lead capacitances may significantly alter the impedance sought. In such cases, a quasi-three-terminal measurement may be performed by making connections to the measurand via shielded (coaxial) cables, in which case the bridge senses primarily the impedance between the inner conductors. The outer conductors of the cables are grounded (**Fig. 3**). Cable capacitance $C_1$ is across the detector, and therefore has no effect, and for accurate measurements $C_2$ may be measured and subtracted from the value of $C_{STD}$. *SEE WHEATSTONE BRIDGE.*

***Transformer bridge.*** Transformer bridges (**Fig. 4*a***), are capable of operating up to 100 MHz. The use of

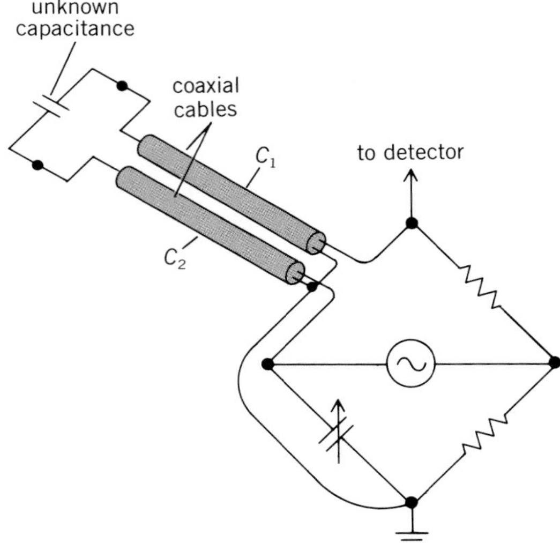


**Fig. 3. Three-terminal measurement of impedance. This connection permits the remote measurement of impedance, since the measurement is between the inner conductors of the connecting coaxial cables, and lead capacitances are shielded from each other.**

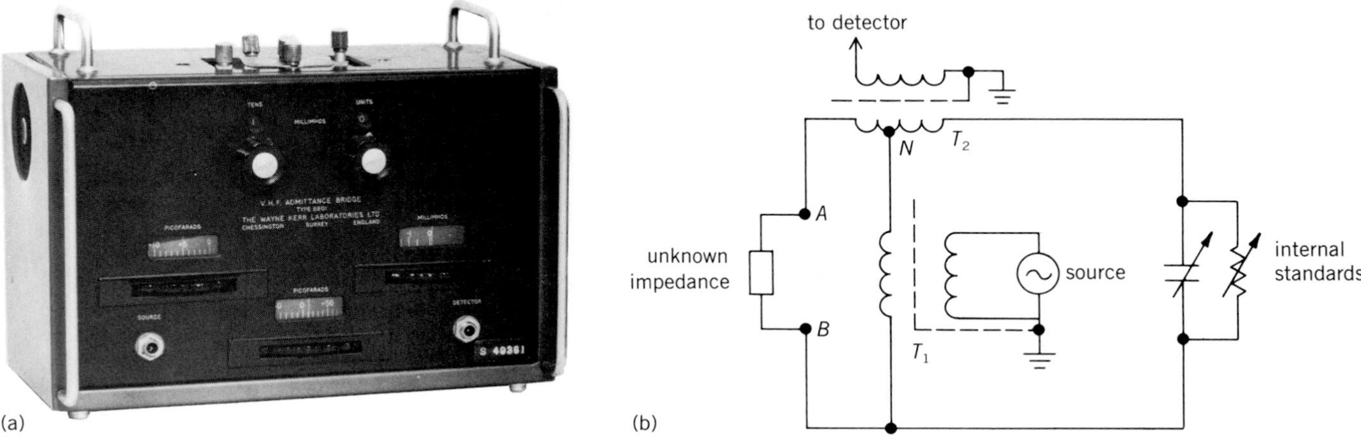


**Fig. 4. Transformer bridge usable up to 100 MHz. (*a*) Instrument (*Wayne Kerr Laboratories Ltd.*). (*b*) Basic circuit diagram. Point *N* (neutral) is for the connection of the ground terminal of three-terminal measurements.**

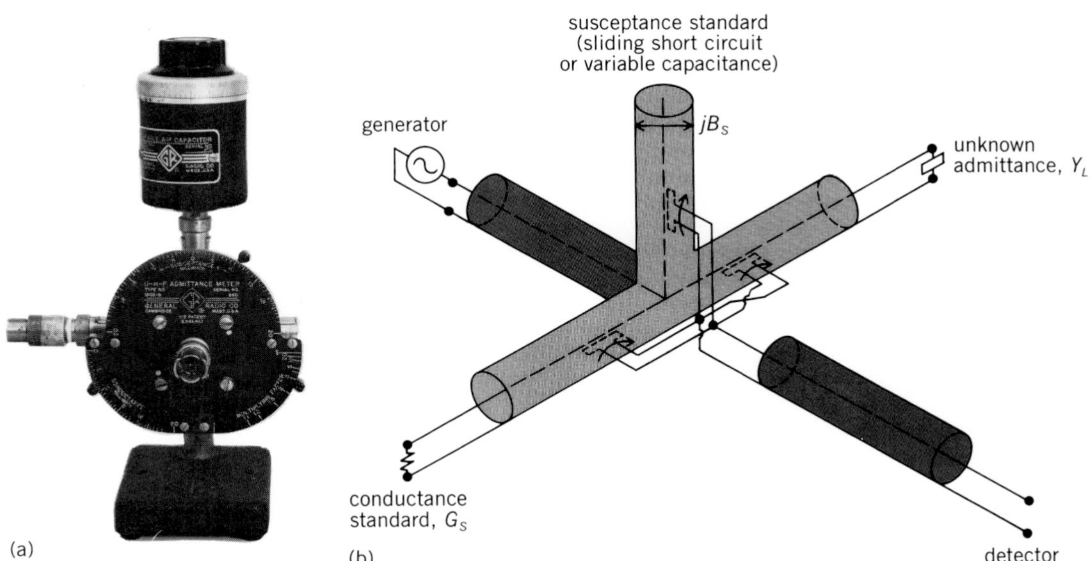


**Fig. 5. Admittance bridge. (*a*) Instrument (*General Radio Co.*). (*b*) Circuit.**

transformers (Fig. 4*b*) offers the following advantages: (1) only two bridge arms are needed: the standard, and the unknown arms. Phase opposition between them (necessary for a bridge null) is provided by transformer $T_2$, driven at a tap on the winding; and (2) both the detector and the source may be grounded at one of their terminals, minimizing ground-loop problems and leakage. The point *N* (neutral) on Fig. 4*b* may be regarded as an rf virtual ground point, and for three-terminal measurements is used for the connection of the coaxial cable outer conductors, because capacitances between *A-N* and *B-N* effectively shunt the transformers and have negligible effect on the balance. *See* Transformer.

***Coaxial line admittance bridge.*** A coaxial line admittance bridge (**Fig. 5**) is usable from 20 MHz to 1.5 GHz. The currents flowing in three coaxial branch lines are driven from a common junction, and are sampled by three independently rotatable, electrostatically shielded loops, whose outputs are connected in parallel. Two of the branch lines are terminated by conductance and susceptance (inverse of reactance) standards, and the third by the unknown admittance. The currents in the conductance and susceptance arms are in quadrature, and by rotating the loops the correct proportions of these two currents are found to balance the current in the unknown arm. Scales beneath the arms which rotate the loops can be read directly in units of admittance. (The third rotatable loop in the unknown arm provides a common scaling factor to the real and imaginary parts of the admit-

**Fig. 6. Resistive VSWR bridge, operable from 50 kHz to 32 MHz. (*Wiltron Co.*)**

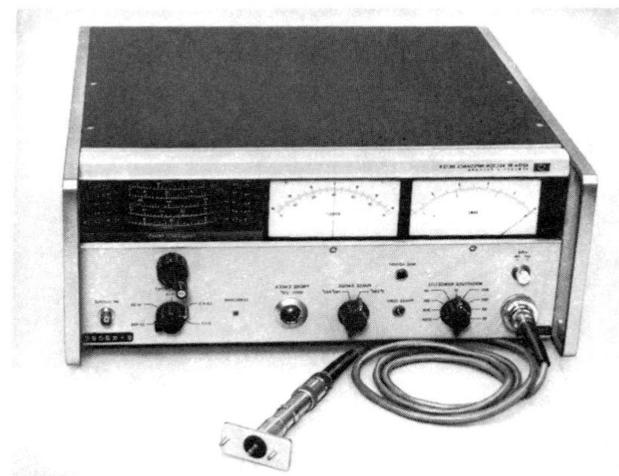

**Fig. 7. Radio-frequency vector impedance meter. (*Hewlett-Packard*)**

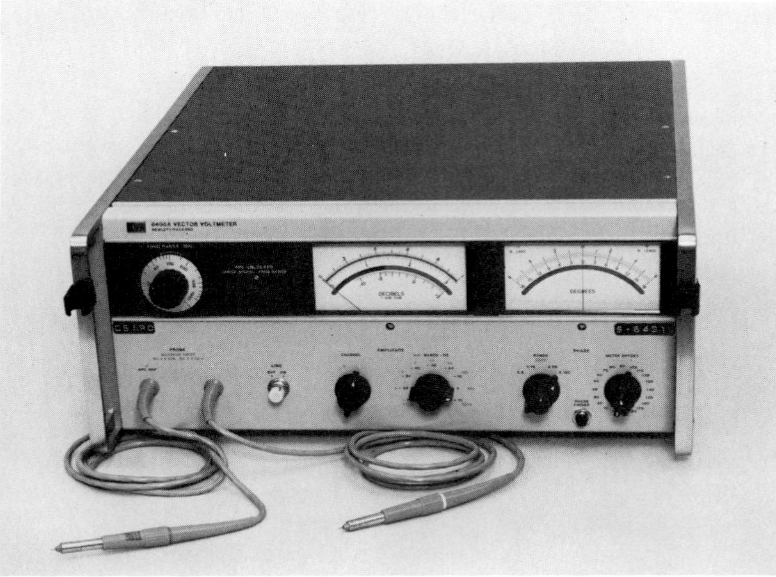

(a)

vector voltmeter
magnitude (*A* or *B*)
phase
probe *A*
splitter
probe *B*
$\Gamma_x$ (unknown)
50-Ω termination
*d*
attenuators (matched pads)
$\Gamma_{oc}$ = 1 (open circuit)
generator

(b)

**Fig. 8. Vector voltmeter. (*a*) Instrument. (*b*) A possible connection for the measurement of impedance. (*Hewlett-Packard*)**

tance.) The attainable accuracy of this instrument is between 3 and 5%, depending on frequency.

***Reflection coefficient.*** A quantity related to impedance is the complex (voltage) reflection coefficient, defined as the ratio of the reflected voltage to the incident voltage, when waves propagate along a uniform transmission line in both directions. Usually, uppercase gamma (Γ) or lowercase rho (ρ) is used to represent the reflection coefficient. When a transmission line of characteristic impedance $Z_0$ is terminated in impedance $Z_T$, the reflection coefficient at the load is given by Eq. (1), and the voltage standing-wave

$$\Gamma = \frac{Z_T - Z_0}{Z_T + Z_0} \tag{1}$$

ratio (VSWR) is related to the magnitude of Γ by Eq. (2).

$$\text{VSWR} = \frac{1 + |\Gamma|}{1 - |\Gamma|} \tag{2}$$

SEE TRANSMISSION LINE.

***Resistive bridge.*** When it is sufficient to measure only the voltage standing-wave ratio (VSWR), resistive bridges may be used. Resistive bridges employed as reflectometers (**Fig. 6**) use a matched source and detector, and therefore differ from the Wheatstone bridge (Fig. 2*a*), which aims to use a zero-impedance voltage source and an infinite-impedance detector. When the bridge is driven by a matched generator and uses a matched rf detector (that is, with impedances $Z_G = Z_D = Z_0$), the detected output is proportional to $|\Gamma|$. If a square-law detector (power meter or diode detector at low levels) is used, the output is proportional to $|\Gamma|^2$, from which the VSWR may be calculated by using Eq. (2). Such a bridge is first calibrated by connecting a known termination, such as an open or a short circuit (with reflection coefficients +1 or −1, respectively). The advantages of the VSWR bridge are low cost and potentially wideband operation. Without adopting special techniques to reduce measurement uncertainty, $|\Gamma|$ may be measured with an uncertainty of ±0.01.

**Voltage-current method.** Some specialized electronic instruments make use of the basic definition of impedance, and effectively measure voltage and current. One such instrument is called an rf vector impedance meter (**Fig. 7**). Instead of measuring both the voltage and the current, it drives a constant current into the unknown impedance, and the resultant voltage is measured. With a constant driving current, the rf voltage across the unknown is proportional to the magnitude of its impedance, $|Z|$. The phase difference between the current and the voltage is measured with a discrete phase-measuring circuit. The unknown impedance is thus obtained in magnitude and phase. The instrument linearly downconverts the measuring frequency (0.5 to 108 MHz) to a 5-kHz intermediate frequency (if), where the amplitude and phase measurements are performed.

**Vector voltmeter method.** Vector voltmeters (VVM) are instruments with two (high-impedance) voltmeter probes, which display the voltages at either probe (relative to ground) as well as the phase difference between them. One type (**Fig. 8***a*) operates from 1 MHz to 1 GHz, and linearly converts to a 20-kHz intermediate frequency by sampling. When connected as shown in Fig. 8*b*, it may be used to measure impedance. The signal is split and sent toward a matched termination (50 Ω) and toward the unknown impedance. The reference probe $A$ senses the voltage in the matched transmission line while, in the unknown arm, probe $B$ measures the voltage at a position equidistant from the junction. Attenuators may be inserted in both arms to minimize interaction. The measurement is normalized by connecting a (shielded) open circuit in the plane of the unknown, and the complex voltage at probe $B$ is noted as $V_{oc}$. The unknown is connected and the indication of probe $B$ is noted as $V_x$. Then the unknown reflection coefficient is calculated from Eq. (3), where $\phi$ is the electrical

$$\Gamma_x = e^{j2\phi}\left[\frac{V_x}{V_{oc}}(1 + e^{-j2\phi}) - 1\right] \qquad (3)$$

angle ($2\pi d/\lambda$, where $\lambda$ is the wavelength) between probe $B$ and the unknown. Because the substitution is on the same arm, the lack of symmetry of the splitter, the lack of equality of the attenuators, and the lack of equality of the two voltmeter channels $A$ and $B$ do not cause errors.

Since the probe responds to the sum of the incident and reflected waves, the resolution becomes poorer as the reflection coefficient magnitude approaches zero. This method is therefore not suitable for measuring impedances near the characteristic impedance of the transmission line (50 Ω in this case). For the accurate measurement of such impedances, directional couplers are used. *See* Directional coupler.

At radio frequencies the realization of directional couplers is quite different from microwave realizations because the component is much shorter than the wavelengths encountered. For this reason, lumped-element directional couplers may be constructed. A 20-dB directional coupler operable from 2 to 500 MHz is shown in **Fig. 9***a*, with its approximate circuit diagram shown in Fig. 9*b*. Equal electric and magnetic coupling results in directional behavior so that

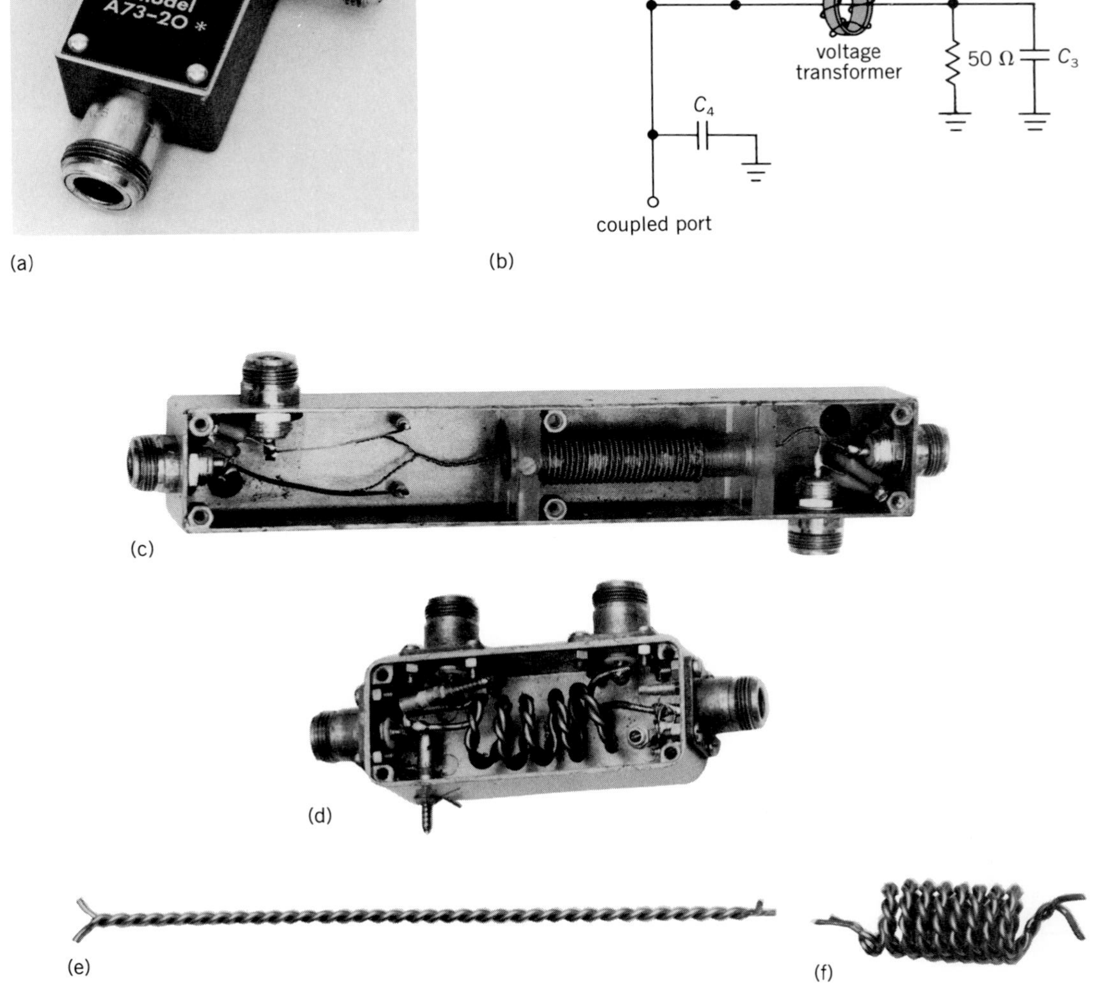


**Fig. 9. Radio-frequency directional couplers. (*a*) 20-dB coupler operable from 2 to 500 MHz (*Wideband Engineering Co.*). (*b*) Its internal circuit. (c) High-directivity twisted-wire couplers for 1 MHz and (*d*) 30 MHz, with (*e*) twisted pair of insulated wires and (*f*) the coil formed from it, for the 30-MHz coupler.**

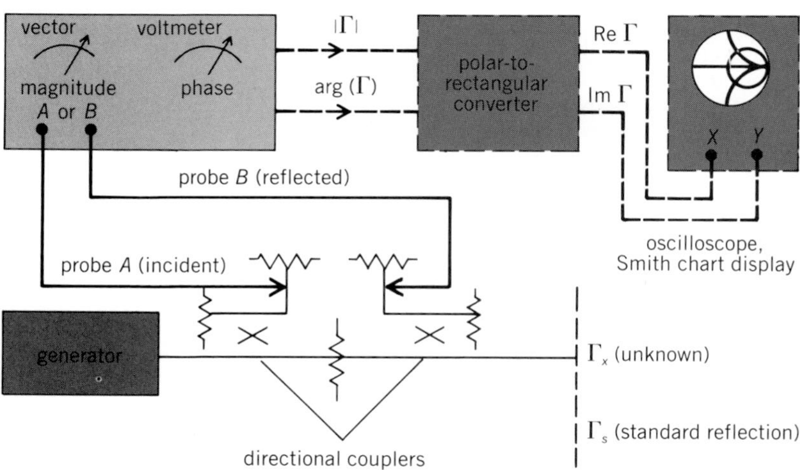


**Fig. 10. Circuit of a vector voltmeter–directional coupler type of impedance meter. With the addition of a polar-to-rectangular converter and an oscilloscope, a direct display on the Smith chart is obtained.**

the coupled output responds (ideally) only to signals traveling in one direction in the main line. In Fig. 9*b* the electric and magnetic couplings are provided by voltage and current transformers, whose signals are summed. Distributed-circuit directional couplers may also be constructed by twisting a pair of insulated copper wires together (Fig. 9*c*) to provide mainly capacitive coupling between them. Then the twisted pair is formed into a coil to provide additional inductive coupling. By stretching the coil, the magnetic coupling may be varied, and adjusted to equal the capacitive coupling. Such directional couplers have been constructed from 1 to 300 MHz and, if equipped with small trimmer capacitors near the terminals, can achieve directivities in excess of 50 dB at selected frequencies.

A coaxial-line, rf impedance-measuring circuit using a vector voltmeter and directional couplers is shown in **Fig. 10**. Probe *A* serves as a phase reference only. Probe *B* samples the reflected signal, and therefore the vector voltmeter indication is proportional to the reflection coefficient. The readings are normalized by first connecting a reflection standard, which may be a short or an open circuit, or a mismatched resistor. In measuring small reflection coefficients (impedances near 50 Ω), the sensitivity of the vector voltmeter may be increased in 10-dB steps, offering high resolution. If the analog magnitude and phase outputs are converted into their rectangular form, these voltages may be connected to the *X* and *Y* deflection inputs of an oscilloscope to give a display of the impedance on the circle diagram (Smith chart). By controlling the frequency and the calibration sequence with a computer, the VVM-coupler method may be automated, and this forms the basis of automatic network analyzers (ANA). *See* MICROWAVE IMPEDANCE MEASUREMENT; MICROWAVE TRANSMISSION LINES.

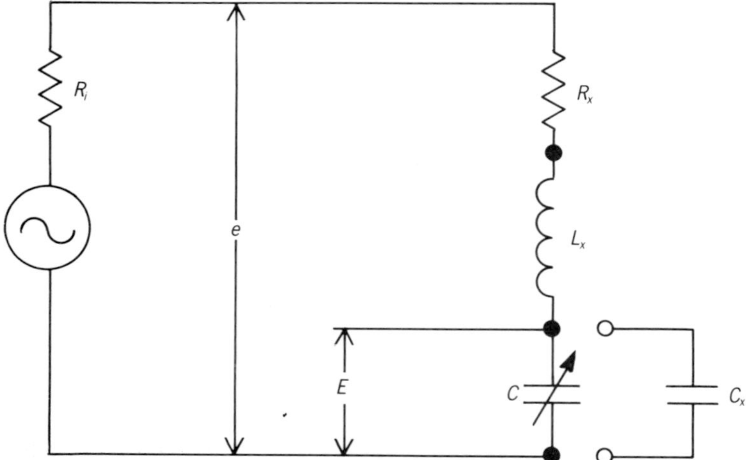


**Fig. 11. Circuit of a Q meter.**

**Resonance method.** When the magnitude of the reactive part of the impedance is much greater than the resistive part at a given frequency *f*, resonance methods may be employed to measure impedance. The most commonly used instrument for this purpose is the Q meter. The *Q* (quality-factor) of an impedance is defined as $2\pi$ times the ratio of energy stored to energy lost per cycle. Numerically, *Q* is equal to $\omega L/R$ or $1/R\omega C$ for the series combination of a resistor *R* and inductor *L* or a resistor and capacitor *C* respectively, where $\omega = 2\pi f$.

A Q-meter-type measurement requires a radio-frequency source of frequency *f*, which drives a current through a current-limiting injection resistor $R_i$ into the circuit shown in **Fig. 11**. The ratio of the magnitude of the voltage *E* developed across the calibrated capacitor *C* to the voltage *e* across the combination of capacitor, inductor, and resistor is indicated with a high-impedance rf voltmeter, and has a maximum value of $Q_{ind}$ when *C* is set to maximize this reading.

To measure low-loss capacitors, the circuit is first resonated (with a suitably chosen inductor of high *Q*) to find $Q_{ind}$. The capacitor setting at resonance is noted. Then the unknown capacitor is paralleled with *C*, and the reduction in *C* needed to restore resonance is the value of $C_x$.

A low-loss inductor is measured by resonating it with *C* and substituting into Eq. (4). Since the magnitude of *E*/*e* is given by Eq. (5), the *Q* factor of the inductor is given by Eq. (6), which, for high-*Q* circuits, approximates to $Q = Q_{ind}$. The series resistance is given by Eq. (7), and the inductance is given by Eq. (8), which, for $Q_{ind} \gg 1$ reduces to Eq. (4).

$$L_x \simeq 1/(\omega^2 C) \tag{4}$$

$$|E/e| = [(\omega^2 L_x + (\omega R_x C)^2]^{-1/2} \tag{5}$$

$$Q = (Q_{ind}^2 - 1)^{1/2} \tag{6}$$

$$R_x = \frac{(Q_{ind}^2 - 1)^{1/2}}{Q_{ind}^2 \omega C} \tag{7}$$

$$L_x = \frac{Q_{ind}^2 - 1}{Q_{ind}^2 \omega^2 C} \tag{8}$$

**Slotted lines and six-port methods.** At the upper end of the rf range, microwave methods of impedance measurement may also be used, employing slotted lines and six-port junctions. For completeness, these methods will be briefly discussed.

A slotted line is a transmission line, with an axial slot cut in the outer conductor, permitting a traveling probe to sample the electric field. When an unknown impedance is connected to one end and a generator to the other, the ratio of the maximum to minimum sig-

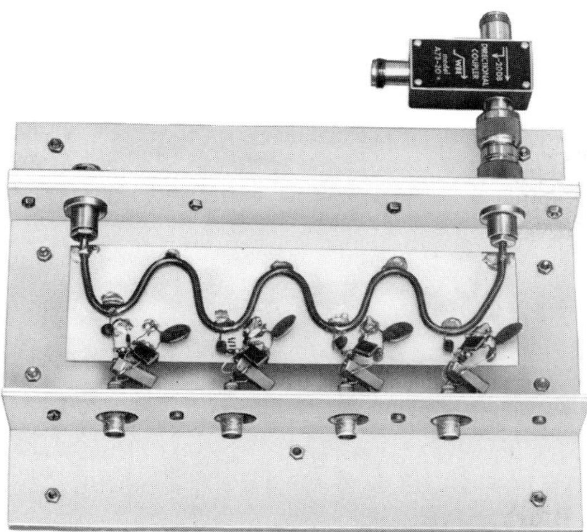

**Fig. 12. Simple six-port junction for operation near 300 MHz.**

nals as the probe is sliding is the voltage standing-wave ratio, and is related to the reflection coefficient by Eq. (2). The phase of Γ is found from Eq. (9),

$$\phi_x = \pi[1 - 4\,(d_{sc} - d_x)/\lambda] \qquad (9)$$

relating the positions of the minima when the unknown is connected and when a short circuit is connected, where $d_{sc}$ and $d_x$ are the probe positions for the minima for the short circuit and the unknown connected, and λ is the wavelength.

According to the theory of six-port junctions (**Fig. 12**), an unknown impedance may be uniquely determined from four power-meter readings (if the six-port junction is such that the power meters are sufficiently independent of each other). In Fig. 12, diode detectors sample the power along a coaxial line at intervals of λ/8. The differences between the outputs of alternate pairs of detectors yield a Smith chart display directly, and the outputs of three of the four detectors together with a sample of the incident power are used for six-port operations. Six-port junctions are calibrated by connecting a number of impedance standards in place of the unknown.

*Peter I. Somlo*

***Bibliography.*** Howard W. Sams Engineering Staff, *Reference Data for Radio Engineers*, 6th ed., 1975; P. I. Somlo and J. D. Hunter, *Microwave Impedance Measurements*, 1985; M. Sucher and J. Fox, *Handbook of Microwave Measurements*, 1963.

## Radio paging systems

Systems, consisting of three basic elements—a personal paging receiver, radio transmitter, and an encoding device—whose primary purpose is to alert an individual, or group of individuals, and deliver a short message of a temporary or perishable nature. Characteristics that are used to define a specific paging system include distance covered, radio frequency, modulation type, paging code format, and message type.

On-site systems cover a single building or a small complex of buildings typically utilizing one low-power transmitter. Wide-area systems can cover an entire city or country and usually use multiple transmitters which simulcast the paging signals. Most paging systems now utilize the very high-frequency (VHF) or ultrahigh-frequency (UHF) radio spectrum using frequency modulation (FM). There are systems which use a special subcarrier on an FM broadcast transmitter, and others which use the citizens-band (CB) channels. The latter is often used for "auto-theft" pagers and small on-site systems using amplitude modulation (AM). *See* Amplitude modulation; Frequency modulation.

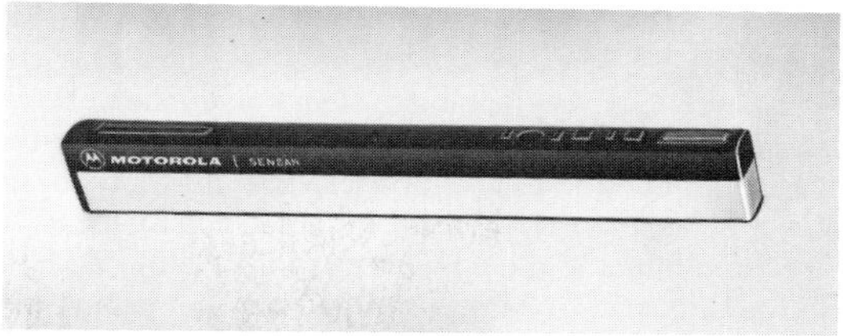


**Fig. 1. Pen-sized tone alert personal pager. (*Motorola Inc.*)**

**Paging formats.** Each individual paging receiver is alerted by transmitting its unique address code or codes. Many paging formats are available and they fall into two categories—analog and binary digital. Analog codes use audible, or subaudible, tones. The most common analog formats are two-tone sequential and five/six-tone decimal digital. Two-tone typically provides for several thousand individual codes, while five/six-tone allows 1-million unique codes and is used in many wide-area systems. Binary digital paging formats are composed of binary patterns and can support tens of millions of codes. Moreover, binary digital codes are particularly well suited for encoding numeric and alphanumeric messages. Two of the most common binary digital formats are known as the POCSAG and GOLAY codes.

**Paging receivers.** Paging receivers fall into four basic categories: tone alert, tone and voice, numeric, and alphanumeric. Tone pagers (**Fig. 1**) emit a "beep" when they are signaled. Some models silently alert the user with a vibration in place of a beep; other models use differing staccato beeps to provide the user with several alert messages. Tone and voice pagers allow the initiator of the page to transmit a simple voice message which will follow a pager's beep alert. Numeric pagers, sometimes called digital pagers, allow the initiator to convey numerical information. These messages are typically composed by using a tone telephone key pad. Alphanumeric pagers (**Fig. 2**) allow the initiator to send a complete textual message to the pager user. These messages are composed on word processors, personal computers,

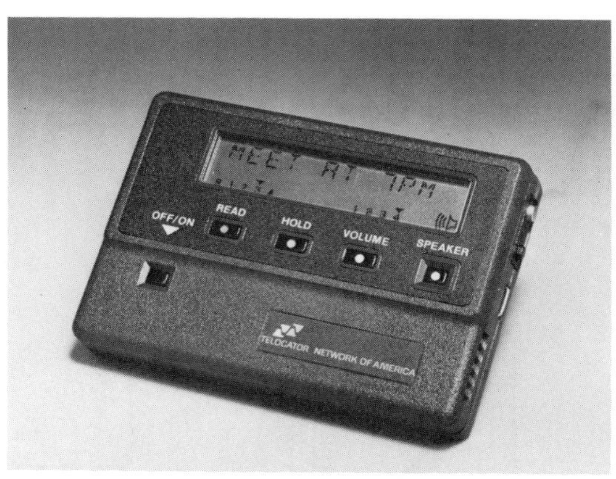


**Fig. 2. Alphanumeric personal message center pager. (*Telocator Network of America*)**

or dedicated terminals which can connect to a paging terminal. *See Microcomputer; Word processing.*

**Encoders.** Every paging system contains an encoding device which provides the interface between the page initiator and the pager user. The encoder's basic function is to receive a pager number and message from the initiator and convert this information into the correct format to be transmitted to the paging receiver. The output from the encoder is connected directly to the system's radio transmitter. Encoders range from simple manual desktop models to large telephone interconnected central offices. Manual encoders are used to initiate pages from a single location such as a dispatcher or switchboard operator. In many large on-site or area-wide systems, it is desirable to initiate pages from the standard telephone network. These systems use an interconnected automatic paging terminal. In addition to generating the correct pager code and message format, terminals develop page/message queues, store system usage statistics, and even store short voice messages in solid-state recorders.

*James A. Wright*

## Radio receiver

The part of a radio communications system responsible for extracting information from radio-frequency (rf) signals. While some circuits and functions are common to all receivers, other functions and subsystems are unique to particular types of receivers. The specialized circuits are needed because there are several commonly used techniques for modulating radio-frequency signals with information. *See Radio.*

The tasks of a radio receiver can be broadly categorized as selection, amplification, and detection. These tasks may be performed by different circuits on the receiver, or a single circuit may accomplish more than one task. **Figure 1** is a diagram of a crude receiver for amplitude-modulation (AM) radio signals. Only basic receiver functions are performed by the circuits in this receiver. *See Amplitude modulation.*

**Selection.** Many signals are delivered to a receiver by its antenna, but the goal of the receiver is to extract information from only one radio-frequency signal. The receiver must be able to select the desired signal. In Fig. 1, selection is performed by a tuned circuit at the input of the receiver. This circuit consists of an inductor with inductance $L$ and a variable capacitor with capacitance $C$, and is tuned to a frequency $F$ determined by Eq. (1).

$$F = \frac{1}{2\pi\sqrt{LC}} \tag{1}$$

*See Capacitor; Inductor.*

Modern radios use several filters and tuned amplifiers at various points in the receiver. These circuits can select between radio-frequency signals that are as little as several hundred hertz apart. Such receivers are said to have good selectivity, and selectivity is one of the measures of receiver performance. *See Electric filter.*

**Detection.** The detector is the circuit that recovers information from the radio-frequency signal. If the information is voice or music, the input to the detector is a radio-frequency signal, and its output (information) is an audio signal. Each form of modulation of the radio-frequency signal requires a different detector circuit. A detector for amplitude-modulated signals must recover information from the amplitude variation of the incoming radio-frequency signal. A detector for frequency-modulated signals must recover information from the frequency variation of these signals. Figure 1 includes a simple amplitude-modulation detector. It first rectifies the radio-frequency signal and then filters out the rapid radio-frequency fluctuations, leaving only the relatively slowly changing audio-frequency (af) information. *See Amplitude-modulation detector; Detector; Frequency modulation; Modulation.*

**Amplification.** Amplification allows very weak radio signals to produce information signals that are strong enough to be useful. The radio-frequency signals delivered by an antenna to a receiver are often

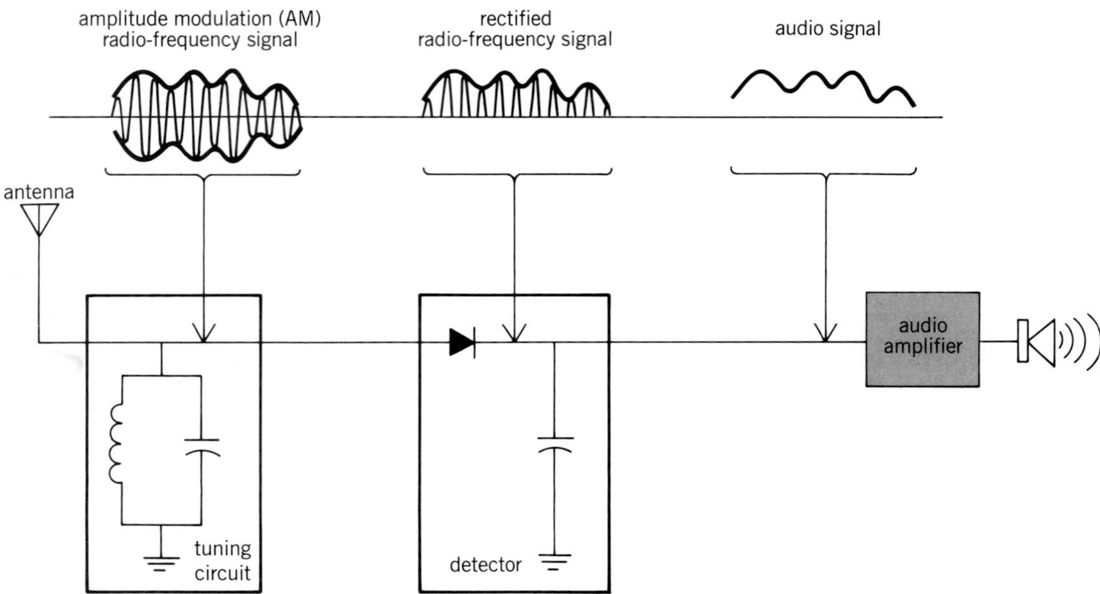


**Fig. 1. Simplified diagram of an amplitude-modulation (AM) receiver with one radio-frequency tuning circuit.**

only microvolts in amplitude. For aural reception, a signal on the order of 0.1 V should be delivered to the speaker. Thus, an overall signal amplification of the order of $10^5$ is necessary. This amplification can be provided before or after detection. Thus, modern receivers have both radio-frequency and audio-frequency amplifiers. The ability of a receiver to detect weak signals is called sensitivity. *SEE AMPLIFIER.*

**Noise.** Simply increasing the amplification in a receiver will not necessarily increase its sensitivity. Each amplifier in the receiver adds some noise to the signal. Although noise can be reduced through proper circuit design, it can never be eliminated. The noise generated in a receiver can mask weak signals. An important measure of receiver sensitivity is the weakest signal from the antenna that will override noise generated in the receiver. *SEE ELECTRICAL NOISE.*

**Conversion methods.** Radio receivers are now much more complex than the receiver in Fig. 1. The additional circuits are generally aimed at providing increased sensitivity and selectivity. In receivers like that in Fig. 1, the input to the detector is at the desired radio frequency; to receive a station at 10 MHz, the filter is tuned to 10 MHz, and the desired signal is applied to the detector. Because all tuning of such receivers is done at the radio frequency of interest, they are called tuned radio-frequency (TRF) receivers. Unfortunately, one filter or one tuned amplifier does not provide much selectivity. To increase the selectivity of a tuned radio-frequency receiver, several amplifiers tuned to the desired frequency are placed before the detector. These amplifiers are usually tuned by individual variable capacitors ganged to a common tuning dial. Tuned radio-frequency receivers are useful only below a few hundred kilohertz, because the higher in frequency the desired radio-frequency signal, the harder it is to build a practical, selective tuning filter or tuned amplifier.

One method previously used to increase receiver selectivity was regeneration. The amplifiers in regenerative receivers employed positive feedback at the desired frequency of the radio-frequency signal. This feedback increased the gain of the amplifiers at that frequency and resulted in some added selectivity. Unfortunately, the feedback caused oscillations at the radio frequency, and the oscillations were radiated by the receiver. These unwanted transmissions caused unreasonable interference, and the regenerative receiver has disappeared from use.

**Heterodyning.** The technique used to increase the selectivity of modern radio receivers is called heterodyning. Heterodyning is the process of combining two signals at frequencies $f_1$ and $f_2$ to produce signals at frequencies of $f_1$, $f_2$, $f_1 - f_2$, and $f_1 + f_2$. If, for instance, a modulated radio-frequency signal at 10 MHz is mixed with an unmodulated signal at 9.5 MHz, the resulting heterodynes or mixing products would be reproductions of the modulated signal at 0.5 and 19.5 MHz. Because it is easier to produce highly selective tuned circuits at lower frequencies than at higher frequencies, the results of heterodyning can be used to build very selective receivers. The desired radio-frequency signal is heterodyned down to a low frequency and passed through selective filters and amplifiers. Receivers employing this technique are called superheterodyne receivers.

Single-conversion superheterodyne receivers (**Fig. 2**) employ one mixing stage, resulting in one frequency conversion. The receiver in Fig. 2 is designed to receive a radio-frequency signal at 14 MHz. The tuned amplifier works at a frequency called the intermediate frequency (i-f), and is called the intermediate-frequency amplifier. The intermediate frequency in the example is 455 kHz, a commonly used value. The local oscillator (LO) produces the signal that is heterodyned with the incoming radio frequency to produce a signal at the intermediate frequency. In this case, the local oscillator must be at either 13.545 MHz, as in Eq. (2), or at 14.455 MHz, as in Eq. (3).

$$\begin{aligned} \text{rf} - \text{LO} &= 14 \text{ MHz} - 13.545 \text{ MHz} \\ &= 0.455 \text{ MHz} \end{aligned} \tag{2}$$

$$\begin{aligned} \text{LO} - \text{rf} &= 14.455 \text{ MHz} - 14 \text{ MHz} \\ &= 0.455 \text{ MHz} \end{aligned} \tag{3}$$

A 13.545-MHz local oscillator was chosen for Fig. 2. When the local-oscillator and radio-frequency signals are introduced to the mixer, the resulting products are a signal at the radio frequency minus the local-oscillator frequency (455 kHz, which is the desired intermediate frequency) and the radio frequency plus the local oscillator frequency (27.545 MHz). The intermediate-frequency amplifier is selective, and it rejects the higher signal, amplifying only

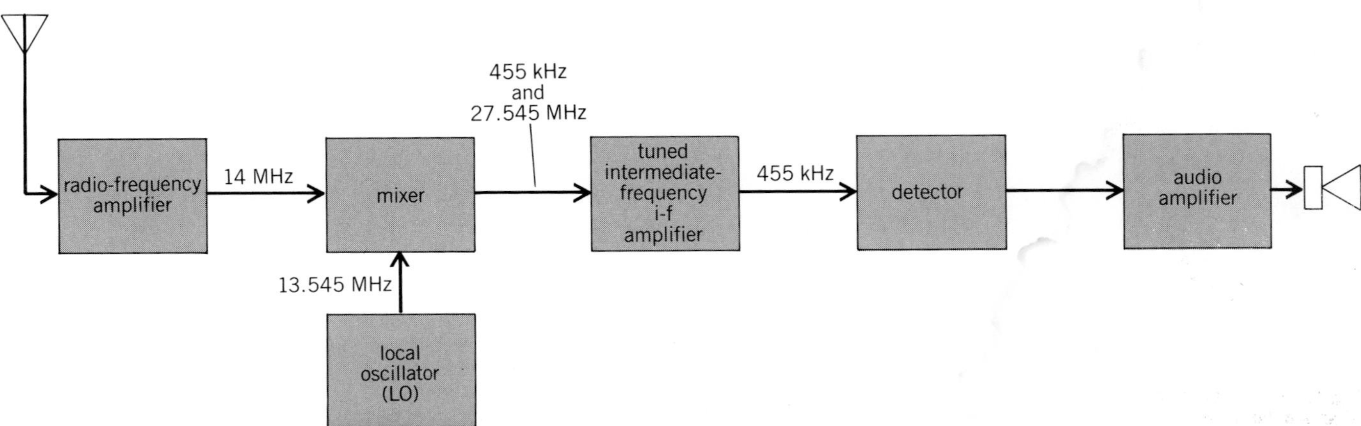


**Fig. 2. Block diagram of a single-conversion superheterodyne receiver. The local oscillator (LO) is set to 13.545 MHz, so that a 14-MHz radio-frequency signal is converted to the 455-kHz intermediate frequency.**

the desired signal, which is now at 455 kHz. After amplification and filtering, the signal is sent to the detector. The selectivity that is gained by conversion to a low intermediate frequency is well worth the complexity of the superheterodyne receiver. SEE OSCILLATOR.

**Image signals.** There are two radio-frequency signals ($f_1$ and $f_2$) that, when mixed with a given local oscillator, will result in the desired intermediate frequency. One of these signals satisfies Eq. (4) and the other Eq. (5). Equation (6) shows that these signals

$$f_1 - \text{LO} = \text{i-f} \quad (4)$$

$$\text{LO} - f_2 = \text{i-f} \quad (5)$$

$$f_1 - f_2 = 2 \text{ i-f} \quad (6)$$

are separated by twice the intermediate frequency. One of them is the desired radio-frequency signal, and the other, unwanted signal is called the image. If the image signal is mixed with the local oscillator and converted to the intermediate frequency, there is no way to separate it from the desired signal. Filters must be provided before the mixer to assure that the image does not mix with the local oscillator and enter the intermediate-frequency amplifiers. These filters must be radio-frequency filters, and it is hard to make them selective enough to provide good image rejection. To place the image signal far from the desired signal, the intermediate frequency should be at a high frequency. It was shown above, however, that the intermediate frequency should be a low frequency so that its amplifiers and filters can be more selective. Thus, conflicting demands of image rejection and selectivity affect the choice of an intermediate frequency.

**Double-conversion receivers.** These receivers resolve the conflict between image rejection and selectivity. A double conversion receiver (**Fig. 3**) has two mixers, two local oscillators, and two intermediate frequencies. The first intermediate frequency is at a high frequency, providing great separation between a signal and its image. The second intermediate frequency is at a low frequency, allowing practical construction of selective filters and amplifiers. The 8-MHz first intermediate frequency in the example results in 16 MHz between the desired signal and the image signal; radio-frequency filters can easily select between two such widely separated signals. The second intermediate frequency is at 455 kHz and can be very selective. Virtually all modern receivers have at least two intermediate-frequency sections, and some have more.

**Tuning.** It is usually desirable to have a receiver that can be tuned to receive on more than one frequency. In a tuned radio-frequency receiver, variable capacitors in the radio-frequency filter and amplifier circuits allow the frequency of the receiver to be varied. The frequency of a superheterodyne receiver is changed by varying one of the local-oscillator frequencies. If the local oscillator in Fig. 2 is changed from 13.545 to 13 MHz, the radio-frequency signal converted to the 455-kHz intermediate frequency will be 13.455 MHz rather than 14 MHz. Thus, a tunable local oscillator or variable-frequency oscillator (VFO) can change receiver frequency. The frequency of a variable-frequency oscillator, like that of a tuned amplifier or filter, is determined by a combination of capacitance and inductance. Varying the capacitor or inductor will change the frequency of the variable-frequency oscillator. Although variable inductors are used in some designs, variable capacitors are found in most variable-frequency oscillators.

There are practical limits on the tuning range of a variable-frequency oscillator. A variable-frequency oscillator stable enough for a receiver may have a tuning range of only 1 or 2 MHz. To make such a variable-frequency oscillator produce a wider range of local-oscillator frequencies, the variable-frequency oscillator signal is heterodyned with a signal from a stable fixed-frequency oscillator. **Figure 4** shows how a variable-frequency oscsillator tuning from 2 to 3 MHz can be mixed with a selected crystal-oscillator frequency to produce a wide range of local-oscillator signals. Instead of a crystal oscillator, many advanced receivers mix the variable-frequency oscillator signal with the output of a phase-locked loop (PLL). To make large changes in frequency (band changes), the phase-locked loop frequency is changed. To tune within a band, the frequency of the variable-frequency oscillator is varied. The output from the phase-locked loop provides a stable signal for heterodyning, but is tuned more easily than a crystal oscillator. Such variable-frequency oscillator/phase-locked loop combinations are usually hybrids of digital and analog circuit techniques. The phase-locked loop is a digital circuit constructed of one or more integrated circuits and controlled by digital inputs. The variable-frequency oscillator is analog, and it is controlled by a variable conductor or capacitor. SEE INTEGRATED CIRCUITS.

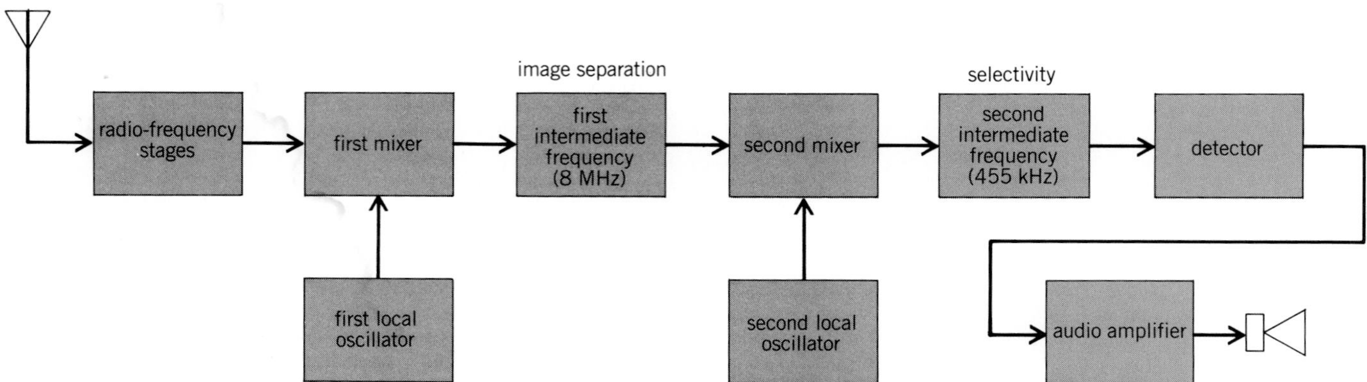


**Fig. 3. Block diagram of a double-conversion superheterodyne receiver. The first intermediate frequency is at 8 MHz, to provide wide image separation. The second intermediate frequency is a standard 455-kHz, highly selective circuit.**

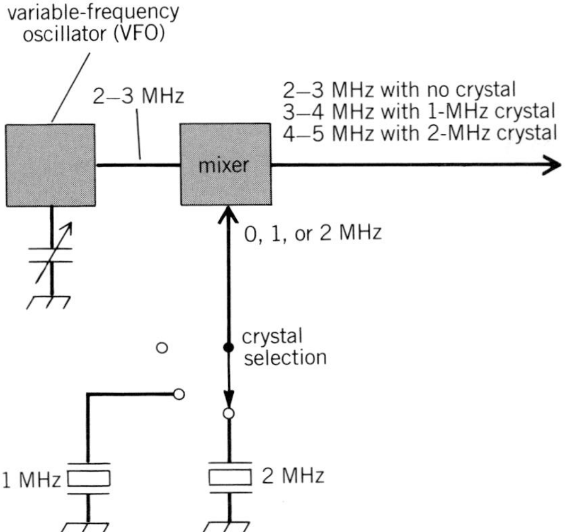


**Fig. 4. Two crystals and a 2- to 3-MHz variable-frequency oscillator (VFO) configured to provide output from 2 to 5 MHz.**

**Synthesized receivers.** Advances in digital circuitry have made possible digital synthesizers capable of generating a wide range of local-oscillator frequencies without any variable capacitors or inductors. In digitally synthesized receivers, the local-oscillator frequency is generated and controlled by one or more phase-locked loops. These phase-locked loops are built by using temperature-stable digital integrated circuits referenced to a quartz crystal–controlled clock. They do not suffer from the drift and inaccuracy that affect even well-designed analog variable-frequency oscillators. Digital control allows the receiver to be controlled by internal microprocessors. Modern computerized receivers often cover all frequencies between 3 and 30 MHz, have several digital memories for storing frequencies of specific interest, and employ sophisticated digital techniques for changing the characteristics of filter circuits. Phase-locked loop circuits employ digital frequency counters, so synthesized receivers usually have highly accurate digital frequency readouts. These readouts reflect the exact frequency of the local oscillator, rather than merely indicating the physical position of a tuning capacitor or inductor as older analog dial or "slide-rule" displays did. In fact, the tuning knob on a digitally synthesized receiver does not mechanically tune the receiver; as the knob is turned, its motion is digitally encoded and used to vary the synthesized frequency.

While digitally synthesized receivers are stable and versatile and have accurate frequency displays, they do have some disadvantages. Digital circuits generate radio-frequency noise, and this digital circuit noise sometimes interferes with the reception of desired signals. Phase-locked loop synthesizers, unless they are very carefully designed, generate low-level spurious signals near their operating frequency. This "synthesizer noise" mixes with strong, nearby radio-frequency signals, and the resulting heterodynes degrade the weak-signal performance of the receiver. These disadvantages of digital receiver tuning can be minimized in good designs, and are overshadowed by the increased accuracy and flexibility of synthesized receivers.

**Size.** Advanced receivers use integrated circuits and miniaturized components in many circuits. There are two important results of this miniaturization. First, a large receiver can be extremely complex. A sophisticated, computer-controlled, general-coverage receiver can be placed in a package the size of a simple broadcast receiver from the 1950s. Second, if needed, an extremely small receiver can be built. An entire AM broadcast receiver (except the tuning and volume controls) has been manufactured in a single integrated circuit. Receivers built using these integrated circuits are much smaller than the speakers or headphones used with them. Advances in technology will continue, increasing the capabilities that can be placed in a fixed-size receiver and decreasing the size of miniature receivers.

**Frequency-modulation (FM) receivers.** While AM radio transmissions carry information in the amplitude of a radio-frequency signal, FM transmissions carry information in the frequency of this signal. Because of this difference, FM receivers differ from AM receivers in some respects. Most important, the detector in an FM receiver must respond to variations in frequency, rather than variations in amplitude. An FM detector is called a discriminator, and frequency variations at the discriminator intermediate-frequency input result in amplitude changes in its audio output. Since the frequency of an FM signal varies, while the frequency of an AM signal is constant, the intermediate-frequency filters in an FM receiver must be wider than those in an AM receiver. Amplitude variations on an FM signal are noise, not information, and most FM receivers include a limiter that removes am-

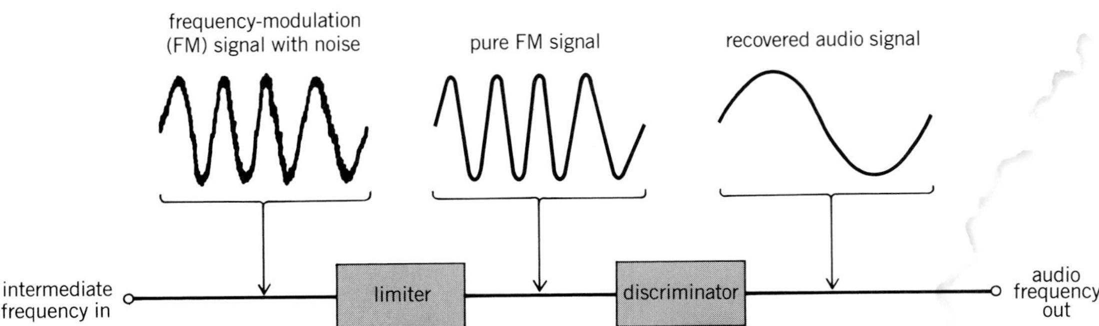


**Fig. 5. Block diagram showing the unique subsections found in an FM receiver. The limiter removes all amplitude noise from the signal. The discriminator converts the frequency variations of the intermediate-frequency signal to amplitude variations of an audio signal.**

plitude noise from incoming signals. The ease with which such noise can be removed from an FM signal is one of the greatest advantages of FM over AM for high-fidelity reception. While the limiter and discriminator are unique to an FM receiver (**Fig. 5**), conversion, amplification, and tuning methods used in FM receivers are the same as those in AM receivers. *See* *Frequency-modulation detector; Limiter circuit.*

**Single-sideband (SSB) receivers.** Single-sideband communication is superior to both FM and standard AM in conservation of radio-frequency spectrum and transmitter power. The most common single-sideband signals are single-sideband suppressed carrier signals, from which all energy at the transmission carrier frequency has been removed. For proper detection of such signals, energy at the carrier frequency or the equivalent intermediate frequency must be mixed with the incoming signal. This signal is generated in the receiver by a beat-frequency oscillator (BFO). When the proper beat-frequency oscillator signal is mixed with the single-sideband intermediate-frequency signal, the transmitted information is correctly recovered. Single-sideband signals are narrower than conventional AM signals, and intermediate-frequency filters for single-sideband use are narrower than those for AM. *See Single sideband.*

*Jeffrey Ward*

***Bibliography.*** American Radio Relay League, *The ARRL Handbook for the Radio Amateur*, 1986; J. J. Carr, *The Complete Handbook of Radio Receivers*, 1980; W. I. Orr, *Radio Handbook*, 1981; R. L. Shrader, *Electronic Communication*, 1980.

## Radio transmitter

A generator of high-frequency electric current whose characteristics of amplitude, frequency, or phase angle may be altered, or modulated, in accordance with the intelligence to be transmitted. A radio transmitter consists of several distinct major components to accomplish the objectives of a particular design for a particular requirement.

The power a transmitter delivers to the antenna may vary from a fraction of a watt to 1,000,000 W. Lower powers are used mainly for portable or mobile services, while higher powers are required for broadcasting over large areas and in point-to-point communications.

Transmitters may be classified by the type of modulation used. Amplitude-modulation (AM) transmitters are employed for broadcast purposes at medium frequencies. Frequency modulation (FM) and phase modulation require much larger bandwidths in broadcast service, and are used mainly at very high frequencies for broadcast purposes. Frequency and phase modulation provide greater signal-to-noise ratio than amplitude modulation for the same antenna input power. There is also an advantage in operating at very high frequencies, where noise is considerably less than at the lower or medium frequency band. Single sideband (SSB) or independent-sideband (ISB) transmitters are used for the transmission of single or independent adjacent sidebands. The carrier is suppressed or reduced to an amount which is negligible in comparison to the total power of the transmitter. The modulation of the transmitter in this mode is both amplitude and angular. The principal application of single-sideband transmission is for point-to-point long-distance telephone and telegraph circuits. A particular type of SSB transmission called compatible single-sideband may be utilized for broadcast program transmission since it can be received by the usual AM broadcast receiver. *See Amplitude modulation; Frequency modulation; Phase modulation; Single sideband.*

**Amplitude-modulation transmitters.** AM transmitters (**Fig. 1**) have two principal design types, either low-level modulated or high-level-modulated. The low-level modulated transmitter is modulated at its low power stages, requiring little modulation power. The high-level modulated transmitter, which usually accomplishes modulation at the anode of the output power amplifier, requires modulation power to be equal to about 50% of the carrier's power.

In order to amplify faithfully and reproduce the modulation at low levels, the power amplifiers must be linear. These are usually class B linear amplifiers, which are much less efficient than the class C amplifiers employed in high-level modulated carrier amplifiers. Because it operates over a large band of frequencies, the high-power modulator must have linear power amplification to achieve low distortion. *See Amplifier.*

***Typical equipment.*** A low-power radio-frequency oscillator, whose frequency is very accurately controlled (since it determines the final carrier frequency), is the exciter for the transmitter. The exciter is followed by several stages of power amplification, which are required to drive the final power output stage. In low-level modulated transmitters, all the amplifiers following the modulated stage are tuned to the same frequency. Those ahead of the modulated stage may be used to double or triple the frequency of the exciter. In a high-level modulated transmitter the power amplifier stages are seldom tuned to the

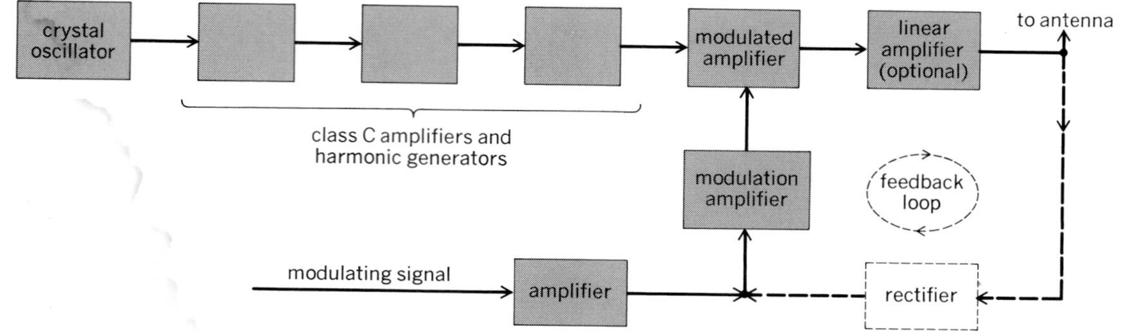


**Fig. 1. AM radiotelephone transmitter. (*After F. E. Terman, Electronic and Radio Engineering, 4th ed., McGraw-Hill, 1955*)**

same frequency, except for the input and output tank circuits of the power amplifier which feeds the antenna.

The modulator of a high-level transmitter derives its input from a microphone or other source of audio signal and amplifies the signal, with low distortion of the order of 1%, to a level which is usually half that of the carrier power.

Most high-power modulators utilize push-pull in either class A or linear class B to reduce distortion by balancing even harmonics and to balance out some hum and noise components. Negative feedback is also used for this purpose. SEE AMPLITUDE MODULATOR.

***Antennas.*** Antennas used with transmitters transform the power generated to an electromagnetic field. They are designed to have a high ratio of radiation to total resistance, which determines the efficiency. Other factors in the design are a sufficient bandwidth to accommodate the frequency band transmitted, directivity, and the restriction of the solid angle of radiation. With certain types of antennas, it is possible to suppress radiation of harmonic frequencies which may cause interference for other services. Usually, harmonic traps are used to couple the antenna to the transmitter. SEE ANTENNA.

***Protection.*** This important design objective in transmitters assures continuity of operation and protection of personnel. The power supply and high-voltage system design are probably the major problems for any new transmitter type. Safety interlocks, circuit breakers, and warning lights are employed extensively. Automatic discharge of capacitors for the protection of personnel is important. For the protection of equipment, the temperature of the cooling water or air draft must be maintained low enough for efficient operation or the equipment is shut down automatically.

***Monitoring.*** The operation of a transmitter must be monitored at all times to keep the operating personnel informed of the condition of transmission. Meters, in important parts of the circuit, oscilloscopes, and aural monitoring are all used.

**Frequency-modulation transmitters.** The transmitting frequency in an FM transmitter is varied above and below the median by an amount according to the amplitude of the modulating signal, and at a rate determined by the modulating signal. The amplitude of the transmitted radio frequency is constant; therefore the entire FM system is arranged to be insensitive to amplitude disturbances.

FM transmitters are basically similar to AM transmitters, except that the AM modulation amplifying system is dispensed with and the exciter must be a variable frequency source. One method of modulating the frequency at the exciter utilizes a reactance in the frequency-determining section of the oscillator in the exciter (**Fig. 2**). The reactance value is changed electronically or electrically in accordance with the low-frequency modulating signal. The remainder of the transmitter, as in AM transmitters, is made up of frequency doubling and tripling stages of power amplification and a power output stage.

***Carrier stabilization.*** For FM transmitters, this is a more difficult problem than for AM transmitters. Many schemes have been used, including those used for carrier automatic frequency control in receivers. Another means of frequency stabilization involves heterodyning a high-frequency, crystal-generated wave with a lower-frequency, well-stabilized, tank-circuit oscillator, modulated by push-pull reactance tubes. SEE AUTOMATIC FREQUENCY CONTROL (AFC); FREQUENCY MODULATOR.

***Protection.*** Protection of FM transmitters is similar to that of AM transmitters, except that there are fewer components involved and the system is therefore not as extensive.

***Monitoring.*** FM transmitter monitoring differs from that in the AM transmitter, because the means of detecting frequency modulation are different from the means of detecting amplitude modulation. A frequency discriminator tuned to the relevant frequency must be used to reconstitute the modulation at the transmitter monitoring position.

**Single sideband/independent sideband.** The use of SSB/ISB transmission for communications has become very popular because of several peculiar system characteristics. Its ability to transmit intelligence occupying only half the bandwidth, as compared to AM and FM modes, and its adaptability for modulation by many low-frequency subcarriers are principal advantages. The decreased band occupancy and reduced carrier effectively concentrate all the intelligence in half the bandwidth, greatly increasing the effective power in voice or broadcast. Decreased bandwidth required for transmission doubles the number of services which can use any portion of the frequency spectrum.

Without SSB/ISB means for transmission, radiotelegraph and radiotelephone circuits are difficult to operate on closely spaced frequency assignments. Maintaining precision and stability at high radio frequencies is much more exacting than at the subcarrier modulation frequencies in the low audio spectrum.

Typical equipment arrangement for SSB transmission comprises an SSB generator (exciter), which makes the SSB or ISB signal (using a system of balanced modulators usually) and filters to separate out the carrier for reinsertion in the desired amount, select the desired sideband, and reject the undesired sideband. The output, at low levels of several watts, is

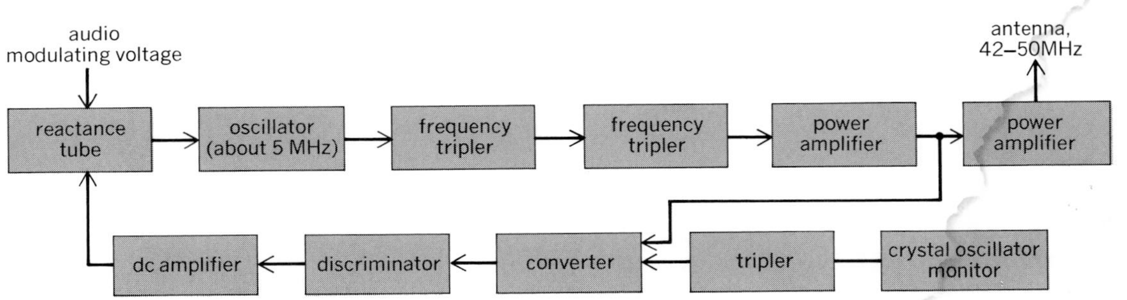


**Fig. 2. FM reactance tube transmitter. (*After F. E. Terman, Radio Engineers' Handbook, McGraw-Hill, 1943*)**

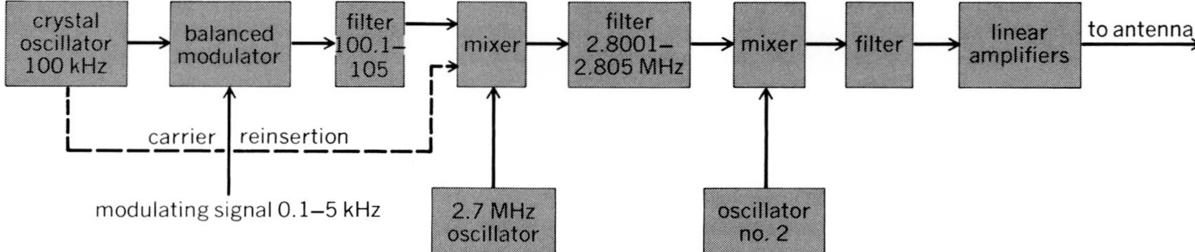


**Fig. 3. SSB transmitter. (*After F. E. Terman, Electronic and Radio Engineering, 4th ed., McGraw-Hill, 1955*)**

then amplified without frequency changing in linear class B amplifiers to the final power output for coupling to the antenna. This method (**Fig. 3**) is commonly referred to as linear SSB transmission. A principal design objective is the maximizing of power output in order to minimize spurious radiation.

A more complex transmission system employs an AM modulated transmitter of normal design, an exciter or adaptor which splits the SSB signal into its two components of amplitude and phase modulation, the normal transmitter stages (which may employ frequency multiplication and class C power amplifiers for amplifying the phase component), and a rectifier for rectifying the AM component for insertion into the modulator as an ordinary AM signal. These two components are then recombined, after phase and amplitude equalization, at the highest power level. This method is called envelope elimination and restoration single sideband. The major design objective here is the reduction of spurious radiation, which is independent of the power output.

A so-called compatible single-sideband system, utilizing the techniques of the last paragraph, modifies the amplitude envelope by using product detection for the AM component and full instead of reduced carrier. Compatibility is effected because the amplitude envelope of this SSB wave is similar to that of a normal AM wave and can be received by the usual AM receiver. *See Radio*.

*Walter Lyons*

**Bibliography.** G. W. Bartlett (ed.), *NAB Engineering Handbook*, 6th ed., 1975; J. J. Carr, *The Complete Handbook of Radio Transmitters*, 1980; Howard W. Sams Engineering Staff, *Reference Data for Radio Engineers*, 6th ed., 1975; E. M. Noll, *Radio Transmitter Principles and Projects*, 1973; G. Woodward (ed.), *Radio Amateur's Handbook*, rev. ed., 1983.

## Radome

A strong, but electrically transparent, thin shell used to house a radar antenna, or a space-communications antenna of similar structure. The shell must be large enough not to interfere with the scanning motion of the antenna. In airborne radar the radome prevents the antenna from upsetting the aerodynamic characteristics of the airplane or missile and protects the antenna against aerodynamic forces. Shipboard radars frequently require radomes to protect them against wind and water damage and blast pressures from nearby guns. Large land-based radars are usually shielded by radomes, especially in severe climatic conditions.

None of the materials available for radomes possesses a dielectric constant equal to that of the atmosphere. The resulting impedance mismatch causes reflections at the inner and outer faces of the shell. In particular, if the shell thickness is a substantial fraction of the carrier wavelength, the reflections from the inner and outer faces may reinforce, causing a standing wave between the radome and the antenna. This affects the antenna impedance in a variable manner as it scans and may change the load on the transmitter sufficiently to seriously degrade the performance. The standing wave may also distort the antenna pattern, producing undesirable side lobes and changing the orientation of the main beam. Also, the reflected power is not transmitted; therefore effective power output is reduced. *See Electromagnetic wave transmission*.

Several means are employed to prevent reflections. If the shell is very thin compared to the carrier wavelength, the reflections from the inner and outer faces are almost a half cycle out of phase and cancel each other. This condition can be obtained easily at frequencies below and including L-band or in the uncommon situations in which a very thin, weak radome can be employed. Alternatively, if the shell thickness is an integral number of half wavelengths, the reflections from the inner and outer faces cancel each other; this arrangement is frequently employed. Numerous multilayer and sandwich-type radomes have been developed in the reasonably successful attempt to combine the properties needed for cancellation of reflections with mechanical strength, stiffness, and lightness.

An additional requirement is that the radome material not cause so much loss as to subtract substantial power from the waves passing through it. A number of available materials satisfy this requirement and also possess chemical and mechanical properties for ease of forming and production. Most of these are organic high polymers, such as resins, rubbers, and fibrous material. Fine glass yarn is also employed. Since the usual production run is small and specialized, radomes are produced either by drawing large flat sheets to the desired shape, in the case of single-layer radomes, or by low-pressure molding and bonding in the case of multilayer and sandwich types. *See Antenna; Radar*.

*Robert I. Bernstein*

## Reactance

The imaginary part of the impedance of an alternating-current circuit.

The impedance $Z$ of an alternating current circuit is a complex number given by Eq. (1). The imaginary

$$Z = R + jX \tag{1}$$

part $X$ is the reactance. The units of reactance, like those of impedance, are ohms. Reactance may be positive or negative. For example, the impedance of an inductor $L$ at frequency $\omega$ is given by Eq. (2), so

$$Z = jL\omega = jX \quad (2)$$

$X$ is positive. The impedance of a capacitor $C$ is given by Eq. (3), so $X$ is negative.

$$Z = -j/C\omega = jX \quad (3)$$

The reactance of a circuit may depend on both the resistors and the inductors or capacitors in the circuit. For example, the circuit in the **illustration** has admittance given by Eq. (4) and impedance given by Eq. (5), so that the reactance, given by Eq. (6), depends

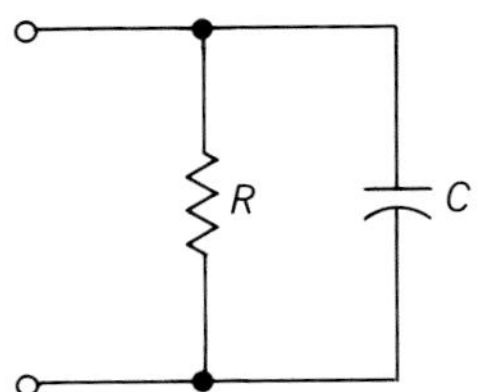


**Circuit with a resistor and capacitor in parallel.**

$$Y = \frac{1}{R} + jC\omega \quad (4)$$

$$Z = \frac{R}{1 + jRC\omega} \quad (5)$$

$$X = -\frac{R^2C\omega}{1 + R^2C^2\omega^2} \quad (6)$$

on both the capacitor $C$ and the resistor $R$. SEE ADMITTANCE; ALTERNATING-CURRENT CIRCUIT THEORY; ELECTRICAL IMPEDANCE.

*J. O. Scanlan*

## Real-time systems

Computer systems in which the computer is required to perform its tasks within the time restraints of some process or simultaneously with the system it is assisting. Usually the computer must operate faster than the system assisted in order to be ready to intervene appropriately.

**Types of systems.** Real-time computer systems and applications span a number of different types.

***Real-time control and real-time process control.*** In these applications the computer is required to process systems data (inputs) from sensors for the purpose of monitoring and computing system control parameters (outputs) required for the correct operation of a system or process. The type of monitoring and control functions provided by the computer for subsystem units ranges over a wide variety of tasks, such as turn-on and turn-off signals to switches; feedback signals to controllers (such as motors, servos, and potentiometers) to provide adjustments or corrections; steering signals; alarms; monitoring, evaluation, supervision, and management calculations; error detection, and out-of-tolerance and critical parameter detection operations; and processing of displays and outputs.

***Real-time assistance.*** Here the computer is required to do its work fast enough to keep up with a person interacting with it (usually at a computer terminal device of some sort, for example, a screen and keyboard). These are people-amplifier-type real-time computer systems. The computer supports the person or persons interacting with it and provides access, retrieval, and storage functions, usually through some sort of data-base management system, as well as data processing and computational power. System access allows the individual to intervene (control, adjust, supply parameters, direct, and so forth) in the system's operation. The real-time computer also often provides monitoring or display information, or both. SEE DATA-BASE MANAGEMENT SYSTEMS; MULTIACCESS COMPUTER.

***Real-time robotics.*** In this case the computer is a part of a robotic or self-contained machine. Often the computer is embedded in the machine, which then becomes a smart machine. If the smart machine also has access to, or has embedded within it, artificial intelligence functions (for example, a knowledge base and knowledge processing in an expert system fashion), it becomes an intelligent machine. SEE ARTIFICIAL INTELLIGENCE; EMBEDDED SYSTEMS; EXPERT SYSTEMS; ROBOTICS.

**Evolution.** Real-time computer systems have been evolving constantly since the interrupt function, which allowed the computer to be synchronized with the external world, was invented. There are five primary paths along which real-time systems continue to advance:

First-generation real-time control systems comprise process control (for example, an oil refinery); guidance and control (for example, antiballistic missile and intercontinental ballistic missile systems); numerical control (for example, factory machine operations); dedicated (mini) computer systems; and store-and-forward message switching. SEE DATA COMMUNICATIONS.

Second-generation real-time computer systems comprise time-shared and multiprocessor computing; interactive computing; smart and intelligent terminals; and computer networks (distributed computers, distributed smart machines, and distributed intelligent machines). SEE MULTIPROCESSING.

Third-generation real-time assistance systems comprise operating systems; CAD (computer-aided design), CAM (computer-aided manufacturing), CAI (computer-assisted instruction), MIS (management information systems), and DSS (decision support systems); personal computers; word processing and work stations; and artificial intelligence expert systems. SEE COMPUTER-AIDED DESIGN AND MANUFACTURING; MICROCOMPUTER; OPERATING SYSTEM; WORD PROCESSING.

Fourth-generation real-time machines comprise smart machines with embedded computers; intelligent machines; and robots (dumb, smart, and intelligent).

Fifth-generation real-time integrated systems comprise the factory-of-the-future (totally automated factories); just-in-time (JIT) systems (in the factory and in distribution); computer utilities and knowledge utilities; and knowledge inference processing systems.

**Artificial intelligence and experts systems.** A new technology, artificial intelligence (AI), is rapidly advancing beyond the research stage into practical use by scientists, management, and many other areas of business and society. One branch is directed toward the development of real-time expert systems. Thus, widespread use of artificial intelligence, knowledge bases, expert systems, and people-amplifiers is expected to develop, and decision making will be amplified with real-time and intelligent computer systems. SEE ARTIFICIAL INTELLIGENCE; EXPERT SYSTEMS.

**Real-time simulation.** The real-time computer can serve as a tool allowing simulation of models of the real world. By coupling this tool with artificial-intelligence knowledge-base expertise, scientific experimentation becomes possible without cumbersome laboratory equipment and procedures. Scientists can play serious real-time experimental and mathematical games with the object of their research without first needing to learn sophisticated laboratory techniques or mathematics. The detailed mathematical and discipline-oriented experimental skills and procedures are embedded within the computerized model. Such robot simulators allow the scientist to concentrate upon the investigation, rather than the scientist becoming buried within the relevant mathematics and discipline crafts. However, the scientist must first learn his or her field plus the computer simulation/modeling language. Thus, robot simulator assistants increasingly do for the scientist what the calculator does for the average person: they remove the need to perform bulky, precise, and rote skill functions, allowing the researcher to get more quickly and easily to the core of scientific investigation.

With robot simulators the researcher can ask questions of a computer modeling system, and have simulated experiments performed that are otherwise nearly impossible or too time-consuming and costly. For example, the researcher can ask "What happens if . . .?" After performing the simulated experiment, the computer gives an answer, while the experimenter views the progress of the computerized experiment and intervenes when desired. Then the experimenter can ask "What happens if something else is done instead?" to arrive at a different comparable answer from the robot simulator. Through such real-time interactive simulations the researcher becomes directly involved in the experiment as a surrogate participant.

Future robot simulators are expected to take the form of advanced hand-held calculators with voice dialog and artificial intelligence capabilities, and to contain specialized expert knowledge making them capable of general decision making. Such smart robot simulators will be used as people-amplifiers or electronic assistants by managers, programmers, doctors, politicians, voters, and others. SEE COMPUTER; DIGITAL COMPUTER; SIMULATION.

*Earl C. Joseph*

**Bibliography.** S. T. Allworth, *Introduction to Real-time Software Design*, 1981; C. C. Foster, *Real-time Programming*, 1981; H. J. Hindin, Minicomputer operating systems, *Comput. Des.*, 23(9):161–228, August 1984; H. J. Hindin and W. B. Rauch-Hindin, Real-time systems, *Systems & Software*, 2 (1):89–113, January 1983; E. L. Keller, Real-time systems, *Systems & Software*, vol. 4, no. 2, February 1985; J. Martin, *Design of Real-time Computer Systems*, 1967; D. A. Mellichamp, *Real-time Computing*, 1983.

## Reciprocity principle

In the scientific sense, a theory that expresses various reciprocal relations for the behavior of some physical systems. Reciprocity applies to a physical system whose input and output can be interchanged without altering the response of the system to a given excitation. Optical, acoustical, electrical, and mechanical devices that operate equally well in either direction are reciprocal systems, whereas unidirectional devices violate reciprocity. The theory of reciprocity facilitates the evaluation of the performance of a physical system. If a system must operate equally well in two directions, there is no need to consider any nonreciprocal components when designing it.

**Examples of reciprocal systems.** Some systems that obey the reciprocity principle are any electrical network composed of resistances, inductances, capacitances, and ideal transformers; systems of antennas, with restrictions according to Eq. (2); mechanical gear systems; and light sources, lenses, and reflectors.

Devices that violate the theory of reciprocity are transistors, vacuum tubes, gyrators, and gyroscopic couplers. Any system that contains the above devices as components must also violate the reciprocity theory. The gyrator differs from the transistor and vacuum tube in that it is linear and passive, as opposed to the active and nonlinear character of the other two devices.

**Rayleigh's theorem of reciprocity.** Reciprocity is concisely expressed by a theorem originally proposed by Lord Rayleigh for acoustic systems and later generalized by J. R. Carson to include electromagnetic systems. Both mathematical expressions of the theory of reciprocity are closely related to the mathematical theorem known as Green's theorem. The acoustical reciprocity theorem of Lord Rayleigh is as follows: In an acoustic system consisting of a fluid medium having boundary surfaces $s_1, s_2, \ldots, s_k$ and subject to no impressed body forces, surface integral (1) holds.

$$\int_s (p_1 v_{2n} - p_2 v_{1n})\, ds = 0 \qquad (1)$$

Here $p_1$ and $p_2$ are the pressure fields produced respectively by the components of the fluid velocities $v_{1n}$ and $v_{2n}$ normal to the boundary surfaces $s_1, s_2, \ldots, s_k$. The integral is evaluated over all boundary surfaces.

For a region containing only one simple source H. L. F. Helmholtz has shown that the theorem can be expressed as follows: A simple source at A produces the same sound pressure at B as would have been produced at A had the source been located at B. In other words, the response of a human ear at B due to a vibrating tuning fork at A is the same as the response of the ear at A due to the same tuning fork when located at B. The human ear, the tuning fork,

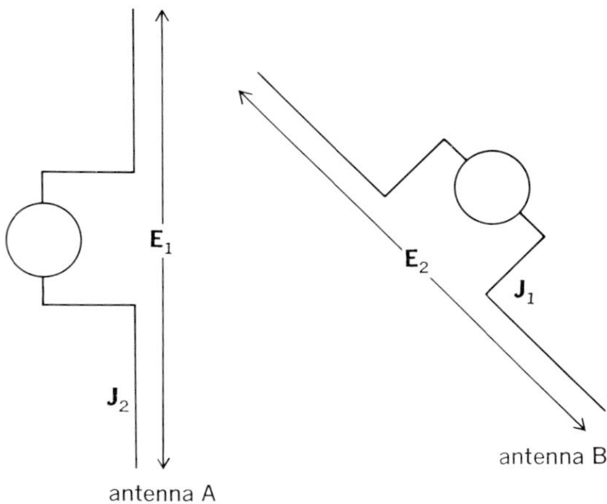


**Fig. 1. Antenna system.**

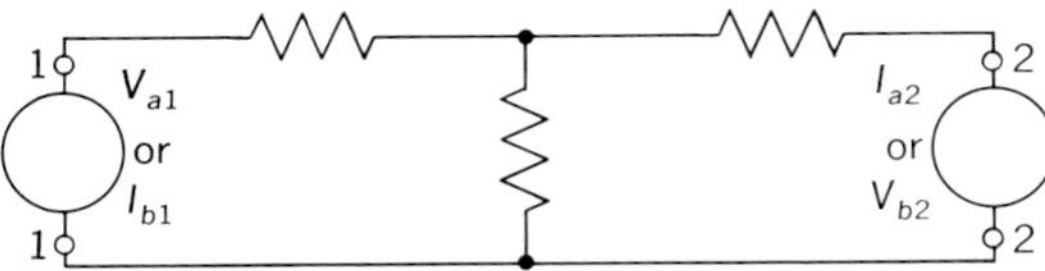


**Fig. 2. Two-mesh network.**

and the intervening acoustical media constitute a physical system that obeys the theory of reciprocity.

**Electromagnetic systems.** The generalization of Lord Rayleigh's theorem to electromagnetic systems can be mathematically expressed by volume integral (2), where $\mathbf{E}_1$ and $\mathbf{H}_1$ are the electric and magnetic

$$\int_v \nabla \cdot (\mathbf{E}_1 \times \mathbf{H}_2 - \mathbf{E}_2 \times \mathbf{H}_1)\, dv = 0 \qquad (2)$$

field vectors describing a state due to one electromagnetic sound and $\mathbf{E}_2$ and $\mathbf{H}_2$ describe another state due to a second source. The above relation is valid as long as the medium is isotropic and the field vectors are finite and continuous, and vary according to a linear law (thus excluding ferromagnetic materials, electronic space charges, and ionized gas phenomena).

By means of Maxwell's equations, relation (2) can be expressed in another form when restricted to systems of conduction current only where $\mathbf{J}_1$ and $\mathbf{J}_2$ are the conduction current densities in an electromagnetic system due to the action of the external electric fields $\mathbf{E}_1$ and $\mathbf{E}_2$, respectively.

Equation (3) is readily applied to antennas and ra-

$$\int_v (\mathbf{E}_1 \cdot \mathbf{J}_2 - \mathbf{E}_2 \cdot \mathbf{J}_1)\, dv = 0 \qquad (3)$$

diation. If, in **Fig. 1**, $\mathbf{J}_1$ is the resulting current density in antenna B due to an electric field $\mathbf{E}_1$ established by antenna A, and $\mathbf{J}_2$ is the current density in antenna A due to electric field $\mathbf{E}_2$ established by antenna B, then $\mathbf{J}_1 = \mathbf{J}_2$, provided $\mathbf{E}_1 = \mathbf{E}_2$. The two emfs need not be applied at the same instant of time. The integral in Eq. (3) over all space reduces to an integral over the two antennas since $\mathbf{J}_1$ and $\mathbf{J}_2$ are zero elsewhere. From this particular application of the reciprocity theorem it is seen that the transmitting and receiving patterns of an antenna are the same.

Equation (3), when evaluated over an $N$-mesh electrical network, reduces to Eq. (4), where $a$ and $b$ are

$$\sum_{j=1}^{N} V_{aj} i_{bj} = \sum_{j=1}^{N} V_{bj} i_{aj} \qquad (4)$$

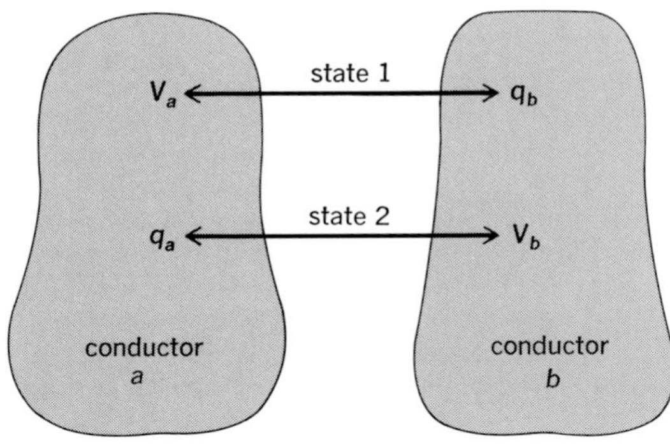


**Fig. 3. Charged conducting bodies.**

two different states of the network and the $j$ subscript denotes in which of the $N$ meshes the voltage and current are measured. For the two-mesh network in **Fig. 2**, Eq. (4) gives Eq. (5). Expressed in words: If

$$V_{a1} i_{b1} = V_{b2} i_{a2} \qquad (5)$$

an emf source of magnitude $V$ and zero internal impedance, when applied to terminals 1–1, produces a current $I$ at terminals 2–2, then the same current $I$ will be measured at terminals 1–1 when the emf $V$ is applied to terminals 2–2. This statement, that is, Eq. (5), is probably the most familiar form of the theorem of reciprocity.

**Electrostatic systems.** The statement of reciprocity for electrostatics is given by Eq. (6), where $V_1$ and $V_2$

$$\int_v \rho_1 V_2 dv = \int_v \rho_2 V_1 dv \qquad (6)$$

are the electric potentials produced at some arbitrary point due to the volume charge distributions $\rho_1$ and $\rho_2$, respectively. When the integral expression in Eq. (6) is applied to the electrostatic system of two charged conductors in **Fig. 3**, it becomes Eq. (7).

$$V_a q_a = V_b q_b \qquad (7)$$

Here $V_a$ is the potential on conductor $a$ due to charge $q_b$ on conductor $b$; the remaining quantities are similarly defined. In other words, if a charge $q_b$ on conductor $b$ raises the potential of conductor $a$ to $V$, then the same charge on conductor $a$ raises the potential of conductor $b$ to $V$.

**Electrical networks.** A somewhat different approach to reciprocity is the so-called black box, or two-terminal pair, method illustrated in **Fig. 4**. The

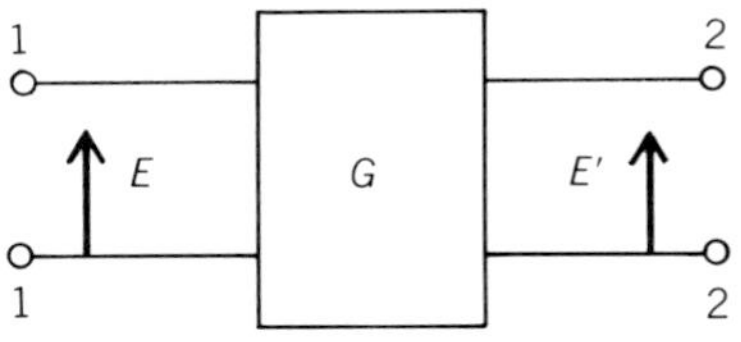


**Fig. 4. Four-terminal, black-box network.**

box might contain a mechanical, acoustical, optical, or electrical system. The applied excitation or cause is $E$ and the response or effect is $E'$. The ratio of $E/E'$ (or $E'/E$) is the transfer function $G$ for the system within the black box. Using the subscript notation of $G_{12}$ when $E$ is impressed at terminals 1–1 and $E'$ is measured at terminals 2–2, then $G_{21}$ represents a response measured at 1–1 for an excitation at 2–2. Mathematically the general behavior of the box to excitations at both sets of terminals can be expressed by Eqs. (8), as long as the response bears a linear rela-

$$\begin{aligned} E_1 &= G_{11}E'_1 + G_{12}E'_2 \\ E_2 &= G_{21}E'_1 + G_{22}E'_2 \end{aligned} \qquad (8)$$

tion to the excitation.

If, in addition to its linear characteristic, the system satisfies Eq. (9), the principle of reciprocity is

$$G_{12} = G_{21} \qquad (9)$$

obeyed, and the device will operate equally in either direction. Whenever $G_{12} \neq G_{21}$, the system violates the theory of reciprocity, with the result that the response in one direction is different from that obtained in the other direction. SEE NETWORK THEORY.

*Hugh S. Landes*

**Bibliography.** B. Bleaney and B. I. Bleaney, *Electricity and Magnetism*, 3d ed., 1976; D. E. Gray (ed.), *American Institute of Physics Handbook*, 3d ed., 1972; Howard W. Sams Engineering Staff, *Reference Data for Radio Engineers*, 6th ed., 1975; J. D. Kraus, *Antennas*, 1950; J. D. Kraus and K. R. Carver, *Electromagnetics*, 3d ed., 1984; J. A. Stratton, *Electromagnetic Theory*, 1941.

## Rectifier

A nonlinear circuit component that allows more current to flow in one direction than in the other. An ideal rectifier is one that allows current to flow in one (forward) direction unimpeded but allows no current to flow in the other (reverse) direction. Thus, ideal rectification might be thought of as a switching action, with the switch closed for current in one direction and open for current in the other direction. Rectifiers are used primarily for the conversion of alternating current (ac) to direct current (dc). SEE ELECTRONIC POWER SUPPLY.

A variety of rectifier elements are in use. The vacuum-tube rectifier can efficiently provide moderate power. Its resistance to current flow in the reverse direction is essentially infinite because the tube does not conduct when its plate is negative with respect to its cathode. In the forward direction, its resistance is small and almost constant. Gas tubes, used primarily for higher power requirements, also have a high resistance in the reverse direction. The semiconductor rectifier has the advantage of not requiring a filament or heater supply. This type of rectifier has approximately constant forward and reverse resistances, with the forward resistance being much smaller. Mechanical rectifiers can also be used. The most common is the vibrator, but other devices are also used. SEE GAS TUBE; SEMICONDUCTOR RECTIFIER.

A rectifying element can be illustrated by assuming a device having a forward resistance $R_1$ and a reverse resistance $R_2$, which is much greater than $R_1$. A sinusoidal alternating voltage $E_m \sin 2\pi ft$ is applied to the rectifier, where $E_m$ is the maximum value of the applied voltage, $f$ is the frequency of the voltage wave, and $t$ is time. The magnitude of the current in the forward direction is $(E_m/R_1) \sin 2\pi ft$. This current flows from $t$ equals 0 to $1/(2f)$, or for one-half the cycle of the alternating voltage wave. The forward current, averaged over one cycle, is $E_m/(\pi R_1)$. The reverse current has the magnitude $(E_m/R_2) \sin 2\pi ft$ and flows from $t$ equals $1/(2f)$ to $1/f$, or for the other half-cycle. The reverse current, averaged over one cycle, is $E_m/(\pi R_2)$. The net forward average current is $E_m(R_2 - R_1)/(\pi R_1 R_2)$.

If reverse resistance $R_2$ is extremely large compared to $R_1$, the average current approaches $E_m/(\pi R_1)$. If the average current is subtracted from the current flowing in the rectifier, an alternating current results. This ripple current flowing through a load produces a ripple voltage which is often undesirable. Filter and regulator circuits are used to reduce it to as low a value as is required. SEE ELECTRIC FILTER; VOLTAGE REGULATOR.

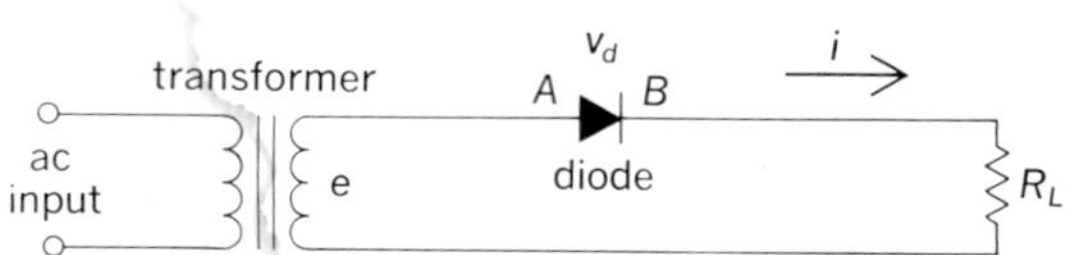

Fig. 1. Half-wave diode rectifier.

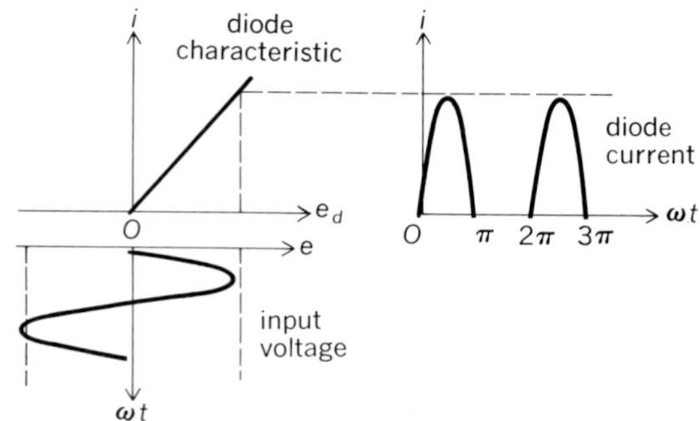

Fig. 2. Rectifying action of half-wave diode rectifier.

**Half-wave rectifier circuit.** A half-wave rectifier circuit is shown in **Fig. 1**. The rectifier is a diode, which allows current to flow in the forward direction from $A$ to $B$ but allows practically no current to flow in the reverse direction from $B$ to $A$. The ac input is applied to the primary of the transformer; secondary voltage $e$ supplies the rectifier and load resistor $R_L$.

The rectifying action of the diode is shown in **Fig. 2**, in which the current $i$ of the rectifier is plotted against the voltage $e_d$ across the diode. The applied sinusoidal voltage from the transformer secondary is shown under the voltage axis; the resulting current $i$ flowing through the diode is shown at the right to be half-sine loops. Averaging the value of these half-sine loops gives the direct current flowing; the ripple current is the variation of load current about the average value.

**Full-wave rectifier circuit.** A full-wave rectifier circuit is shown in **Fig. 3**. This circuit uses two separate diodes, $D_1$ and $D_2$. The center tap of the transformer is connected through the load resistance $R_L$ to the $B$ sides of both diodes. During one-half cycle of the ac input the $A$ terminal of diode $D_1$ is positive with respect to the $B$ terminal, and $D_1$ conducts current from $A$ to $B$. This current passes through the load resistor $R_L$ in the direction shown by $i$. During this time diode $D_2$ is not conducting because terminal $A$ is negative with respect to $B$. When the ac potential goes through zero, $A$ of diode $D_1$ becomes negative and the diode stops conducting. The potential on $A$ of $D_2$ then becomes positive, and $D_2$ starts to conduct. The resulting current wave shape is shown in **Fig. 4**.

The effect of using two diodes instead of one is to produce a more continuous flow of direct current through load $R_L$ because the first diode conducts for the positive half-cycle and the second diode conducts for the negative half-cycle, as shown in Fig. 4. Com-

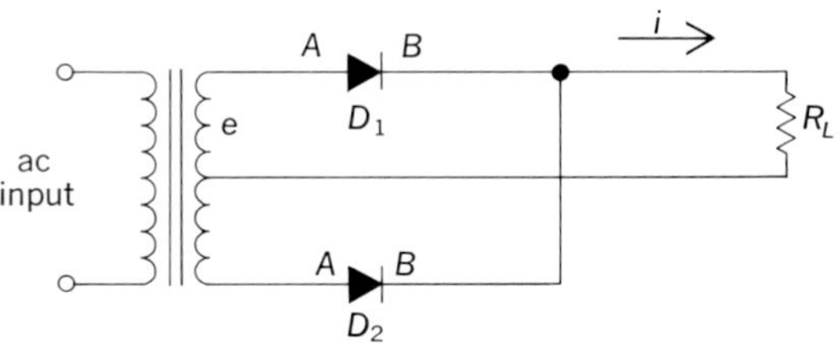

Fig. 3. Full-wave diode rectifier.

parison of Figs. 2 and 4 indicates that a full-wave circuit will produce a more nearly uniform output than will the half-wave circuit.

**Polyphase rectifier circuits.** When high dc power is required by an electronic circuit, a polyphase rectifier circuit may be used. It is also desirable when expensive filters must be used. This is particularly true of power supplies for the final radio-frequency and audio-frequency stages of large radio and television transmitters. The rectifier employed in polyphase circuits generally is a gas tube that has a low voltage drop in the forward direction and thus has a high efficiency. Semiconductor diodes are also used. The number of phases used in these circuits is most often 3, but 2, 4, 6, and 12 phases are used occasionally.

The simplest polyphase circuit is the three-phase half-wave circuit of **Fig. 5**. The primaries of the transformers are connected in delta to the three-phase ac line, and the secondaries are connected in wye with the common connection going to one end of the load resistor. The other end of the load resistor is attached to the *B* terminals of the three rectifier diodes required in the circuit. The *A* terminals are connected to the separate ends of the three transformer secondaries.

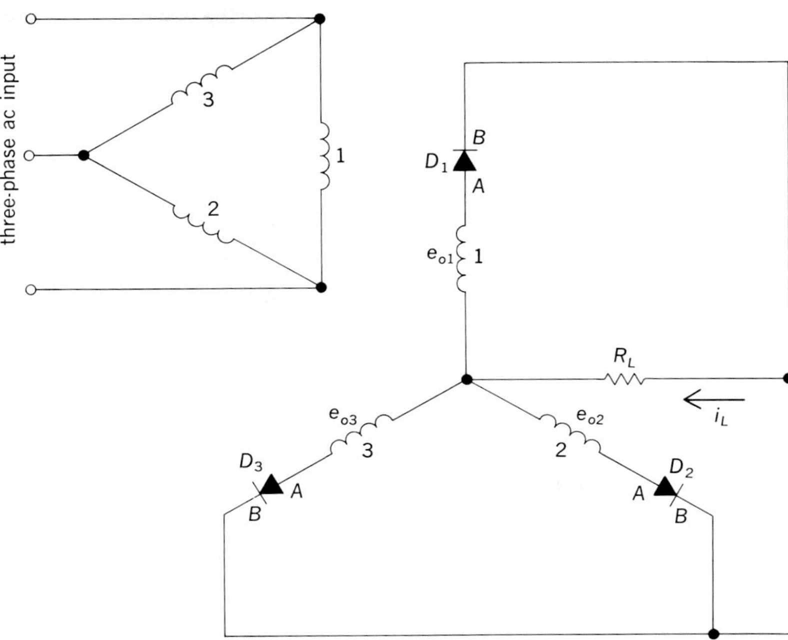


**Fig. 5. Three-phase half-wave rectifier.**

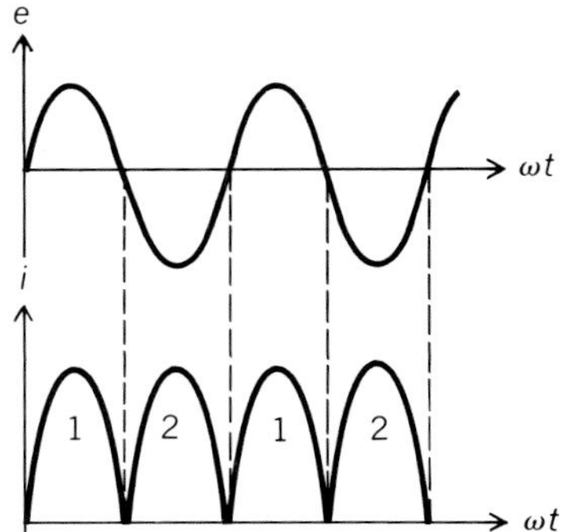


**Fig. 4. Applied voltage and output current of full-wave rectifier.**

Operation of the circuit is such that diode $D_1$, connected to the first secondary, conducts for 120° of the ac cycle. As soon as the voltage on secondary 2 equals that of secondary 1, diode $D_2$ starts to conduct and diode $D_1$ stops conducting. Secondary voltages $e_{o1}$, $e_{o2}$, and $e_{o3}$ are shown in **Fig. 6**, and diode currents are indicated as $i_1$, $i_2$, and $i_3$. The resulting load current $i_L$ is also shown in Fig. 6. This current is much closer to a true direct current than is that for the single-phase circuits of Figs. 1 and 3. Ripple voltage is much lower, and less elaborate filter circuits are needed to smooth the output wave. The diodes in Fig. 5 could be replaced by gas rectifier tubes or ignitrons if higher load currents were required.

Another common polyphase rectifier circuit is the three-phase full-wave or six-phase half-wave circuit in **Fig. 7**. In this circuit the tubes conduct for 60° instead of 120°, as in the circuit of Fig. 5. The ripple voltage for the full-wave circuit is much smaller.

Many other polyphase rectifier circuits are possible.

**Bridge rectifier circuits.** Bridge rectifier circuits are useful in both single-phase and polyphase applications in which a transformer must be used whose secondary has no center tap or in which dc voltages approximately equal to the total secondary voltage of the transformer must be obtained. Another use of the bridge circuit is in ac rectifier-type meters. The bridge circuit is shown in **Fig. 8**. Four separate half-wave rectifier diodes are used. When the left-hand side of the transformer secondary is positive, current flows through diode $D_1$, the load resistor $R_L$, and diode $D_3$. When the secondary voltage reverses, the current flows through diodes $D_2$ and $D_4$, passing through resistor $R_L$ in the same direction as during the first half cycle.

**Parallel rectifiers.** If greater current is desired, two or more rectifiers can be connected in parallel. In such an arrangement small resistors or inductors are put in series with the rectifiers before they are connected in parallel.

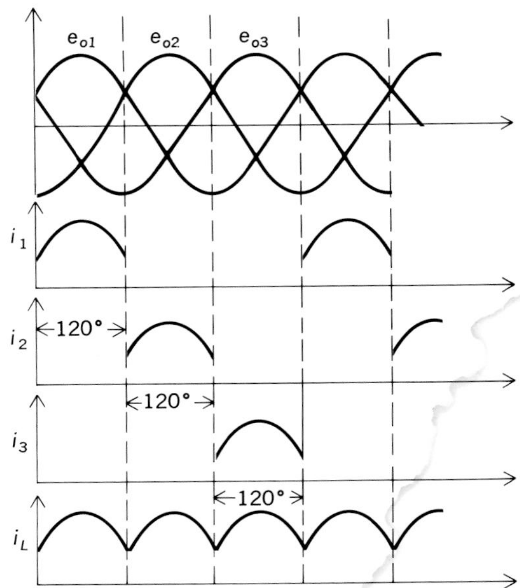


**Fig. 6. Transformer voltages, diode currents, and load current in a three-phase half-wave rectifier.**

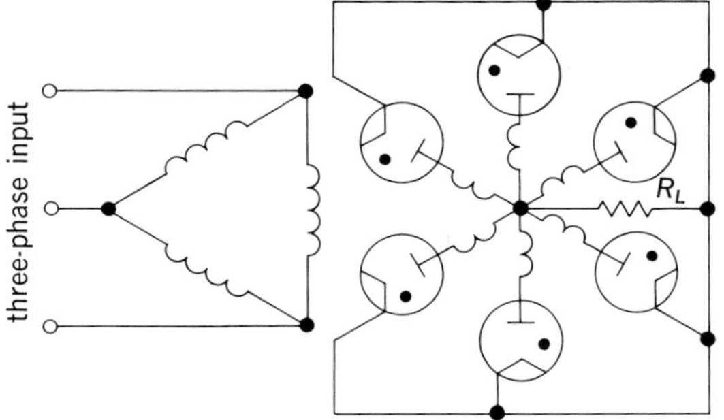


**Fig. 7.** Three-phase full-wave or six-phase half-wave rectifier, as example of polyphase rectifier circuit.

**Controlled rectifiers.** Controlling the current delivered by a rectifier can be accomplished by varying the primary voltage of the power transformer or by changing a resistance in series with the load resistor. The first technique has the disadvantage of being expensive; the second leads to poor efficiency. A more convenient and less expensive method is to control the angle at which the rectifier tube starts to conduct. Special gas tubes that accomplish this control are thyratrons and ignitrons. Silicon controlled rectifiers (SCR) may also be used for this purpose. Thyratrons are hot-cathode gas tubes with a large grid structure that prevents the arc from being ignited until the correct voltage is applied to the grid. An ignitron is a cold-cathode pool-type tube with an igniter grid actuated by an electrical pulse. The igniter of the ignitron requires a substantial amount of power, which is usually supplied by an auxiliary thyratron in the control circuit. The SCR is a silicon semiconductor device which conducts when the trigger gate electrode is raised to the triggering potential. *See* Controlled rectifier; Semiconductor rectifier.

One circuit for an SCR is shown in **Fig. 9**, with control of the triggering point of the SCR possible over a full-half-cycle of 180 electrical degrees. When the upper terminal of the ac input is positive, capacitor $C$ will charge to the triggering voltage of the SCR in a time determined by the $RC$ time constant and the voltage across the SCR. Current then flows through load resistor $R_L$ until the ac input voltage starts to reverse. When the lower terminal of the ac input is positive, capacitor $C$ charges negatively through the diode $D_2$, and the cycle of conduction repeats. Diode $D_1$ prevents the negative peak voltage from appearing on the gate of the SCR. By varying the resistor $R$, the triggering point can be varied from zero degrees when the SCR will conduct the maximum current and to 180° when the SCR conducts zero current. Hence a continuous control from zero to maximum current is achieved. Other control circuits can also be used.

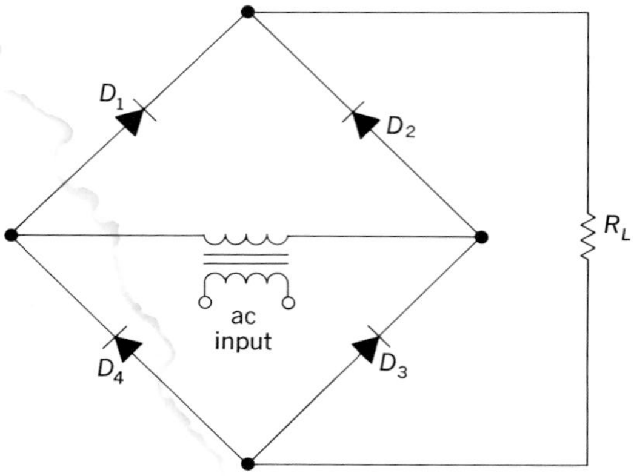

**Inverse voltage.** The inverse voltage of a rectifier is the voltage that the rectifier must withstand when it is not conducting or when it is conducting slightly in the reverse direction. As an example, in the full-wave rectifier circuit of Fig. 3, when diode $D_2$ is conducting, diode $D_1$ has impressed upon it the total secondary voltage of the power transformer minus the voltage drop in $D_2$. For a well-designed power supply the maximum value of the inverse voltage should not exceed the rated value of the rectifier specified by the manufacturer.

**Current ratings.** Another important rating for a rectifier is the average current through it. The average rectifier current of a half-wave single-phase rectifier is the same as the average load current. For a full-wave single-phase rectifier the average rectifier current is one-half the average load current. The maximum value of instantaneous current through the rectifier should not exceed the peak current rating of the rectifier. This is particularly true when capacitor-input filters are employed, because these filters generally produce high peak-to-average current ratios in the rectifier. For information on electronic circuits in general *see* Circuit (electronics).

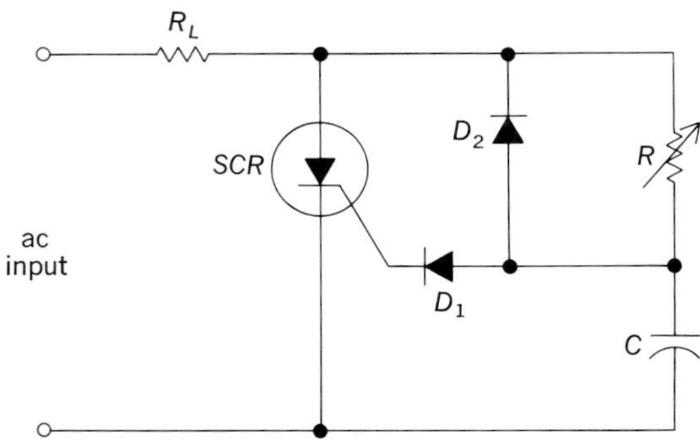


**Fig. 9.** One circuit for a silicon-controlled rectifier with phase control triggering network.

*Donald L. Waidelich*

***Bibliography.*** J. J. Brophy, *Basic Electronics for Scientists*, 4th ed., 1983; A. H. Lytel, *Solid-State Power Supplies and Converters*, 1965; J. Millman, *Microelectronics*, 1979; G. Scoles, *Handbook of Rectifier Circuits*, 1980.

## Regeneration

The process of feeding back a portion of the output signal of an amplifier to its input in such a way that the input signal is reinforced. The result is greatly increased amplification. The feedback must be positive; that is, the two signals must be in phase, and it must be limited in magnitude to prevent the circuit from going into oscillation. *See* Feedback circuit.

In storage devices for computers, regeneration involves the restoration of deteriorating electrostatic, magnetic, or other conditions to their original state. This is particularly essential in charge-storage cathode-ray tubes to overcome natural decay effects, as well as loss of charge by reading out the information stored. *See* Storage tube.

**Fig. 8.** Single-phase full-wave bridge circuit.

In the nuclear power field, regeneration involves the purification of contaminated nuclear fuel for reuse.

*John Markus*

## Regulation

The process of maintaining a quantity or condition essentially constant despite variations in such factors as line voltage and load. In an industrial process-control system, the speed, temperature, voltage, or position of a critical element can be kept constant by measuring the condition being regulated and feeding back into the system a signal representing the difference between the actual and the desired quantities. For example, if the temperature of a mixture of chemicals is too low, a sensing element feeds back to the controller a signal that results in the application of more heat.

The term regulation is also used in the opposite sense to indicate the difference between the maximum and minimum voltages at the terminals of a tube, transformer, generator, or other device over the range of normal operating conditions. When used in this manner, regulation $R$ in percent is computed from the equation below, where $E_{max}$ and $E_{min}$ are, respectively, maximum and minimum voltages (or other property whose regulation is being computed) in the region of interest. SEE VOLTAGE REGULATOR.

$$R = \frac{E_{max} - E_{min}}{0.5(E_{max} + E_{min})}100$$

*Frank H. Rockett*

## Relaxation oscillator

An electronic circuit which has two stable states, resulting in two distinct output levels, and which switches between the two states at a rate determined by the rate of rise or decay of voltage across the storage element in an *RC* (resistance-capacitance) or *RL* (resistance-inductance) circuit. The output waveform is usually nonsinusoidal and may be approximately a square wave, a sawtooth wave, or a series of short repeating pulses. SEE WAVE-SHAPING CIRCUITS.

One of the most widely used forms of relaxation oscillator is the astable multivibrator, which generates a rectangular or square wave. In this circuit two devices are connected so that they are alternately ON and OFF. Connected together by a positive feedback path, they are driven rapidly from one state to the other. SEE MULTIVIBRATOR.

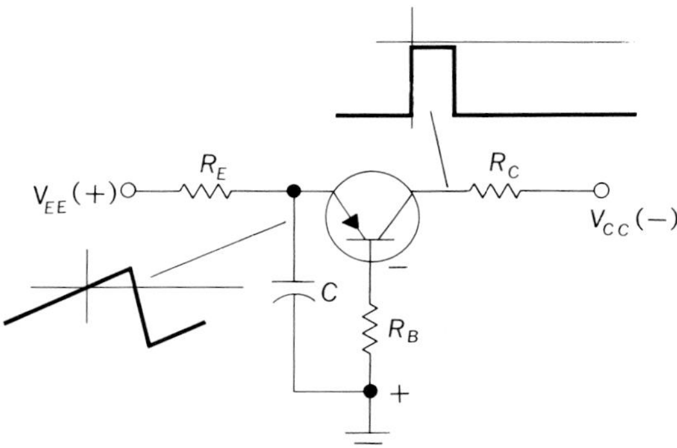

**Fig. 1. Point-contact transistor relaxation oscillator.**

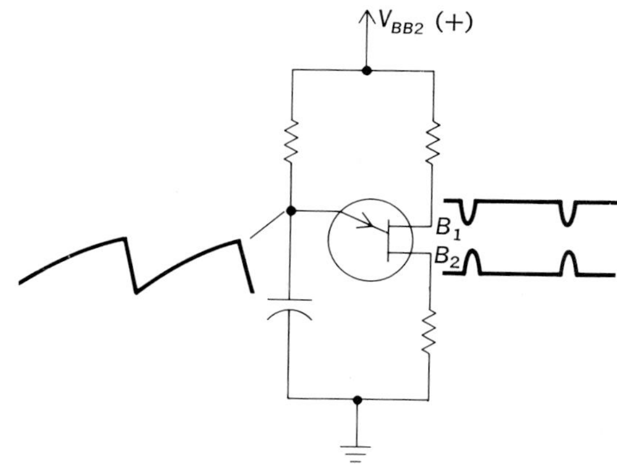

**Fig. 2. Unijunction transistor as relaxation oscillator.**

There is also a class of circuits in which a single device has two stable conditions, either ON-OFF or ON with two distinct states or levels. Switching between the two states usually involves an *RC* time constant. The blocking oscillator is representative of such a circuit, which also includes a positive feedback path. SEE BLOCKING OSCILLATOR.

There are other relaxation oscillators using single transistors or transistorlike devices with a current gain greater than unity, such as the point-contact transistor, which can be arranged as a relaxation oscillator as shown in **Fig. 1**. During the ON period a large collector current flows through $R_B$ and $R_C$, making the base slightly negative, and the capacitance $C$ charges toward a negative potential through the emitter circuit. It finally reaches a point at which the current gain drops to less than unity. The voltage drop across $R_B$ suddenly decreases, and the emitter circuit becomes reverse biased. The emitter will remain reverse-biased until $C$ can again charge to the conduction level through $R_E$. The circuit is suitable for the generation of short pulses, such as those needed for trigger circuits.

As shown in **Fig. 2**, a unijunction transistor, sometimes called a double-base diode, may be used as a simple relaxation-oscillator trigger generator. Negative-resistance devices such as tunnel diodes can be used as a relaxation oscillator. SEE NEGATIVE-RESISTANCE CIRCUITS; TUNNEL DIODE.

*Glenn M. Glasford*

***Bibliography.*** J. J. Brophy, *Basic Electronics for Scientists*, 4th ed., 1983; J. Millman and H. Taub, *Pulse, Digital, and Switching Waveforms*, 1965.

## Reluctance

A property of a magnetic circuit analogous to resistance in an electric circuit.

Every line of magnetic flux is a closed path. Whenever the flux is largely confined to a well-defined closed path, there is a magnetic circuit. That part of the flux that departs from the path is called flux leakage.

For any closed path of length $l$ in a magnetic field $H$, the line integral of $H \cos \alpha \, dl$ around the path is the magnetomotive force (mmf) of the path, as in Eq. (1), where $\alpha$ is the angle between $H$ and the path. If

$$\text{mmf} = \oint H \cos \alpha \, dl \quad (1)$$

the path encloses $N$ conductors, each with current $I$, Eq. (2) holds.

$$\text{mmf} = \oint H \cos \alpha \, dl = NI \quad (2)$$

Consider the closely wound toroid shown in the **illustration**. For this arrangement of currents, the magnetic field is almost entirely within the toroidal coil, and there the flux density or magnetic induction $B$ is given by Eq. (3), where $l$ is the mean circumference

$$B = \mu \frac{NI}{l} \quad (3)$$

of the toroid and $\mu$ is the permeability. The flux $\phi$ within the toroid of cross-sectional area $A$ is given by either form of Eqs. (4), which is similar in form to

$$\Phi = BA = \frac{\mu A}{l} NI$$
$$\Phi = \frac{NI}{l/\mu A} = \frac{\text{mmf}}{l/\mu A} = \frac{\text{mmf}}{\mathcal{R}} \quad (4)$$

the equation for the electric circuit, although nothing actually flows in the magnetic circuit. The factor $l/\mu A$ is called the reluctance $\mathcal{R}$ of the magnetic circuit. The reluctance is not constant because the permeability $\mu$ varies with changing flux density. From the defining equation for reluctance, it is seen that when the mmf is in ampere-turns and the flux is in webers, the unit of reluctance is the ampere-turn/weber.

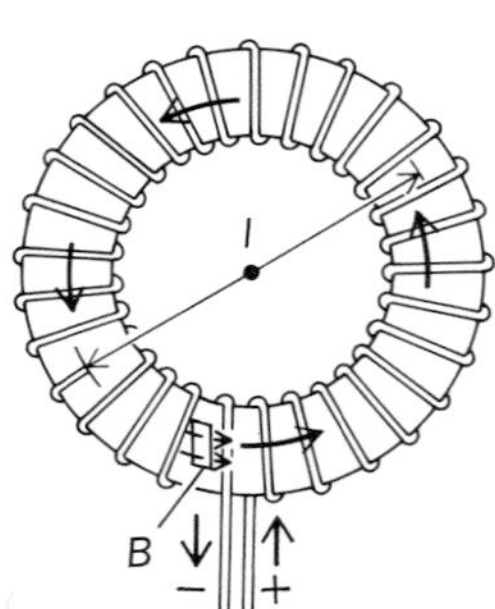


A toroidal coil.

**Reluctances in series.** For the simple toroid, all parts of the magnetic circuit have the same $\mu$ and the same $A$. More complicated circuits may include parts that differ in permeability, in cross section, or in both. Suppose a small gap were cut in the core of the toroid. The flux would fringe out at the gap, but as a rough approximation, the area of the gap may be considered the same as that of the core.

The magnetic path then has two parts, the core of length $l_1$ and reluctance $l_1/\mu_1 A$, and the air gap of length $l_2$ and reluctance $l_2/\mu_2 A$. Since the same flux is in both core and gap, this is considered a series circuit and Eq. (5) holds. Since the relative permeability of

$$\mathcal{R} = \mathcal{R}_1 + \mathcal{R}_2 = \frac{l_1}{\mu_1 A} + \frac{l_2}{\mu_2 A} \quad (5)$$

the ferromagnetic core is several hundred or even several thousand times that of air, the reluctance of the short gap may be much greater than that of the much longer core. For any combination of paths in series, $\mathcal{R} = \Sigma l/\mu A$. Then Eq. (6) holds.

$$\Phi = \frac{\text{mmf}}{\Sigma \mathcal{R}} = \frac{\text{mmf}}{\Sigma l/\mu A} \quad (6)$$

**Reluctances in parallel.** If the flux divides in part of the circuit, there is a parallel magnetic circuit and the reluctance of the circuit has the same relation to the reluctances of the parts as has the analogous electric resistance. For the parallel circuit Eq. (7) is valid.

$$\frac{1}{\mathcal{R}} = \frac{1}{\mathcal{R}_1} + \frac{1}{\mathcal{R}_2} + \cdots \quad (7)$$

*Kenneth V. Manning*

## Resistance measurement

The quantitative determination of that property of an electrically conductive material, component, or circuit called electrical resistance. The ohm, which is the SI unit of resistance, is defined through the application of Ohm's law as the electric resistance between two points of a conductor when a constant potential difference of 1 volt applied to these points produces in the conductor a current of 1 ampere. Ohm's law can thus be taken to define resistance $R$ as the ratio of dc voltage $V$ to current $I$; that is, Eq. (1) holds.

$$R = \frac{V}{I} \quad (1)$$

For bulk metallic conductors, for example, bars, sheets, wires, and foils, this ratio is constant. For most other substances, such as semiconductors, ceramics, and composite materials, it may vary with voltage, and very many electronic devices depend on this fact. The resistance of any conductor is given by the integral

$$\int_0^l \frac{\rho dl}{A}$$

where $l$ is the length, $A$ the cross-sectional area, and $\rho$ the resistivity. SEE ELECTRICAL RESISTANCE; OHM'S LAW; SEMICONDUCTOR.

**Realization of the ohm.** The above definition of the ohm may be experimentally realized through either the calculable capacitor or measurement of quantized Hall resistance.

***Calculable capacitor.*** Neither the volt nor the ampere can at present be realized experimentally as accurately as is needed. However, it is possible to realize the ohm quite independently of the volt and the ampere. The dielectric constant of free space $\epsilon_0$ is given by Eq. (2), where $\mu_0 = 4\pi \times 10^{-7}$ henry per meter (a

$$\epsilon_0 = \frac{1}{c^2 \mu_0} \quad (2)$$

consequence of the definition of the ampere), and $c$ is the velocity of light, which has been declared by the International Committee for Weights and Measures (CIPM) to be 299,792,458 m/s. Given this value, the capacitance in farads of any assembly of conductors can be calculated through the use of electromagnetic theory. The Thomson-Lampard theorem in electrostatics gives the result that the capacitance per unit length between the opposite members of cylinders ar-

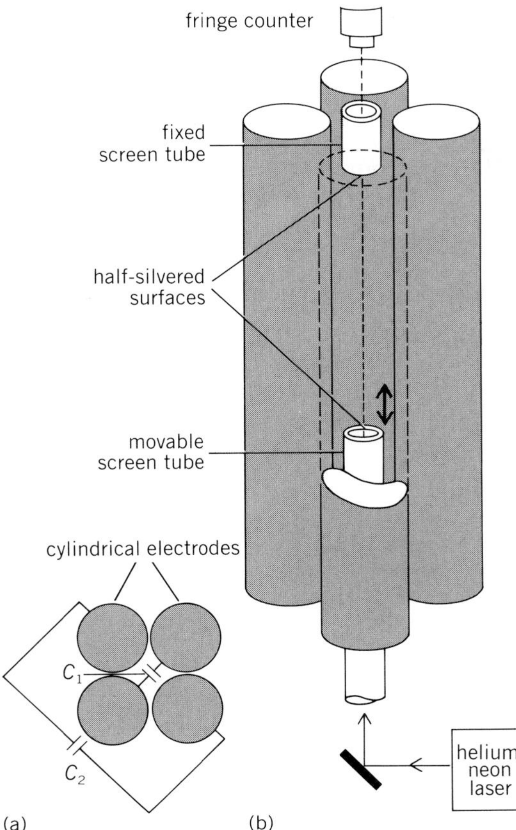


**Fig. 1. Thompson-Lampard calculable capacitor. (*a*) Cross section of electrodes. (*b*) Arrangement of components.**

ranged in a symmetrical quadrupole (**Fig. 1***a*) is given by Eq. (3), a result which is independent of the dimensions of the apparatus.

$$C = \frac{\epsilon_0}{\pi} \log_e 2 \ F/\mathrm{m} \qquad (3)$$

This is made use of to construct a calculable capacitor, in which the active length is defined by two central screen tubes, one of which can be moved along the axis. The change in the capacitance between either of the opposite pairs of conducting cylinders is then given by the Eq. (3). The change in effective length is measured by arranging a Fabry-Perot interferometer between the faces of the screen tubes (Fig. 1*b*).

Several such instruments exist, and produce a change in capacitance of about 0.4 picofarad with an uncertainty of about 1 part in $10^7$. Through the use of accurate transformer bridges, this change in capacitance is used to establish the value of a 1-nanofarad capacitor, and the reactance of this at a frequency of 1592 Hz (10,000 radians/s) is then used to establish the resistance value of 100 kilohms (kΩ) at the same frequency. Again using transformer bridges, the value of 1000 Ω is obtained, and this in turn is used to establish a 1000-Ω dc value by using a coaxial resistor having a single thin-wire element which permits accurate calculation of the difference between the resistance values at 1592 Hz and dc. The final step from 1000 Ω to 1 Ω is made by dc comparison techniques, for example, through the use of a series-parallel network of 32 × 32 Ω resistors, discussed below. The added uncertainties of all these intermediate stages are sufficiently small so that the absolute or SI value of the national standards of the ohm of the United States and United Kingdom have been compared with each other and with the standards of International Bureau of Weights and Measures (BIPM) and are known with 3-standard-deviation uncertainties of about 3 in $10^7$. SEE CAPACITANCE MEASUREMENT; RADIO-FREQUENCY IMPEDANCE MEASUREMENTS; RESISTOR.

***Quantized Hall resistance.*** This approach depends on the macroscopic quantum behavior exhibited by extremely thin conducting films at temperatures near absolute zero in the presence of a large transverse magnetic flux of about 10 teslas (100 kilogauss). One experimental arrangement (**Fig. 2**) consists of a MOSFET gate to which four additional electrodes have been added. In use, either of the two pairs *AA* or *BB* permit measurement of the Hall voltage, while *A* and *B* permit measurement of the voltage in the direction of current flow. When these two qualities are measured as the gate voltage is varied, curves such as shown in **Fig. 3** are obtained. This shows a series of regions in which the axial voltage falls to zero, and in which the Hall voltage is constant. This behavior permits identification of the density of energy states in the film, and theory then predicts that in these regions the resistance, defined by Eq. (4), is

$$R_H = \frac{\text{Hall voltage}}{\text{source/drain current}} \qquad (4)$$

given by Eq. (5), where $e$ is the electron charge, $h$ is

$$R_H = \frac{1}{n}\frac{e^2}{h} \qquad (5)$$

Planck's constant, and $n$ = successively 1, 2, 3, 4, etc.

This is of interest to physicists in providing an experimental value of $e^2/h$, but it is also of more immediate value to electrical metrology in giving the possibility of a resistance value dependent only on fundamental constants. Using the $n = 4$ region gives a value of 6.453 kΩ. Because of the small levels of current and voltage to be measured, under cryogenic conditions the measurement is not easy, and the best

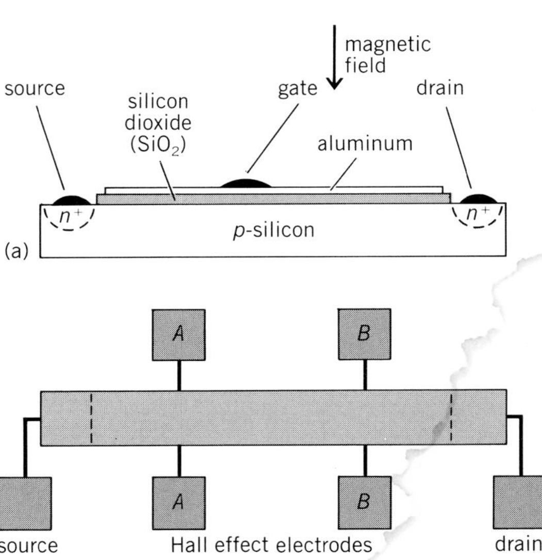


**Fig. 2. MOSFET gate modified for measurement of quantized Hall resistance. (*a*) Cross section. (*b*) Top view.**

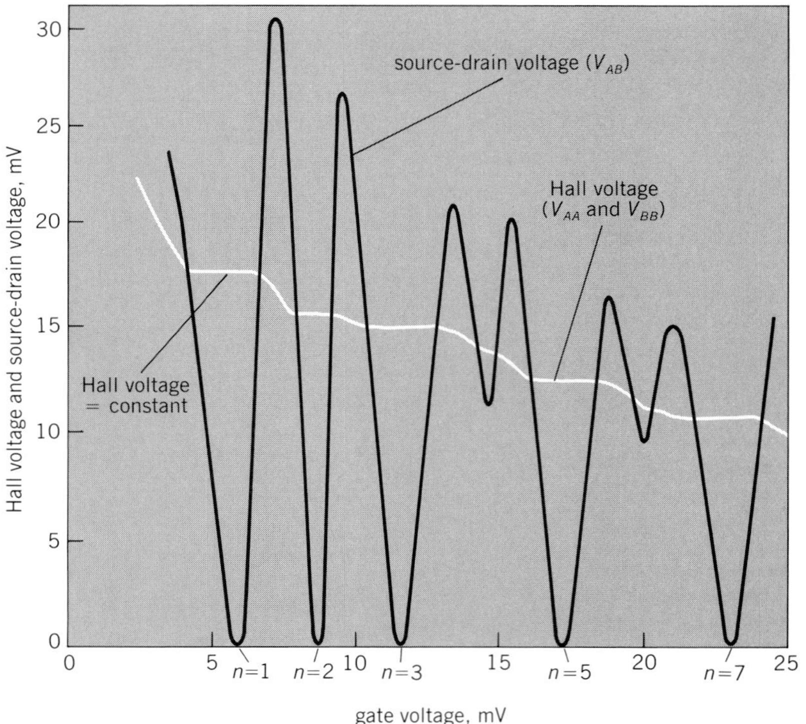


**Fig. 3. Quantized Hall voltage in silicon MOSFET device.**

uncertainties have been in the region of 1 part per million (ppm). *SEE HALL EFFECT.*

**Resistance standards.** Various resistance standards are in common use.

***Wire-wound standard resistors.*** The day-to-day primary reference standards of national laboratories are 1-Ω resistors wound either from a quaternary alloy, which is a nickel-chrome alloy with small amounts of other metals added to produce better stability and reduced variation with temperature, or of manganin, which is a copper-nickel-manganese alloy. Both materials have temperature coefficients of zero at some temperature close to 68°F (20°C). The wire is best wound and located in a strain-free manner, and is immersed in oil to assist temperature uniformity. In use, the power dissipated is normally kept below a few milliwatts. The best resistors of this type have been found to change by less than 1 part in $10^7$ per year. Basically similar construction is used for standard resistors at decade values from 1 mΩ to at least 100 kΩ, and at 25 Ω, a value at which a standard is needed as the basis for platinum resistance thermometry. These are all four-terminal resistors (**Fig. 4**); the ends of the resistive element are connected by pairs of leads, one of which is used to conduct the current, while the other carries only the much smaller current needed by the detector.

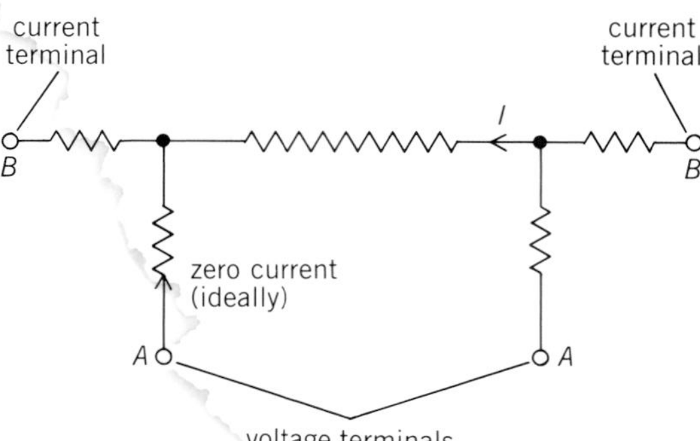


**Fig. 4. Four-terminal resistor. Resistance = $V_{AA}/I$.**

The resistive elements are often wound in a bifilar or hairpin fashion to reduce the self-inductance. All resistors necessarily have some inductance and capacitance, and can be simply represented by the circuit of **Fig. 5**. To first order, the impedance $Z$ is given by Eq. (6), where $C$ is the stray capacitance, $L$ is the

$$Z = R(1 - \omega^2 C^2 R^2) + j\omega(L - R^2 C) \qquad (6)$$

stray inductance, and ω is the angular frequency. For resistors below about 300 Ω the inductive effect predominates, while resistors of more than this value are essentially capacitative. *SEE ALTERNATING-CURRENT CIRCUIT THEORY.*

Standard resistors below 100 kΩ in value are usually measured in thermostatic oil baths, permitting temperature stability to within a few millidegrees, and under these conditions it is possible to achieve repeatability of a few parts in $10^8$. Higher values of resistance, above 1 MΩ, cannot be oil-immersed because the conductance of the oil becomes significant. These are usually loosely wound on bobbins, and are two-terminal resistors. They may be fitted with a guard, which can be used to reduce the effects of leakage or stray conductance. Such resistors extend as far as $10^7$ Ω. Beyond that level they become prohibitively large and expensive because of the quantity of wire involved.

***Thick-film resistors.*** These resistors, which are of comparatively recent origin, consist of elements of di-

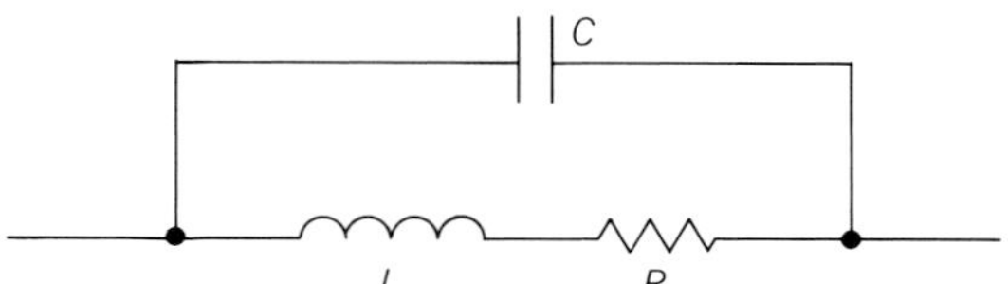


**Fig. 5. Equivalent circuit of two-terminal resistor. The capacitor represents the stray capacitance *C* of the resistor, and the inductor represents its stray inductance *L*.**

mensions of only a fraction of an inch (a few millimeters), in which thick nichrome films are deposited on glass or ceramic substrates. These provide good stability with temperature by acting as compensated strain gages, in which the increase of resistivity due to change in temperature is compensated by the effect of strain produced by the differential expansion between the metal and the substrate. The chips are made and adjusted by printed-circuit techniques, and assemblies of very good overall performance can be obtained by selection of suitable elements. They have zero voltage coefficients, and overall temperature coefficients which may be as good as a few ppm/°C. Their stability with time is also in the ppm range. Because of their size, they have low inductance and capacitance, and so can be used over a wider range of frequency than wire-wound resistors. Resistors of similar form, printed onto a single substrate, are widely used in measuring instruments where accurate and constant ratios are required, since the maintenance of the ratio will normally be much better than the actual stability of the resistance.

***Very high resistances.*** Above $10^9$ Ω, the best available resistors are of protected thin-metal films, often completely encapsulated in glass. At these low conductances any stray conductance due to moisture or dirt becomes increasingly important. These resistances must therefore be kept clean and dry. Their resistance value is voltage-dependent to some extent, and so the voltage at which measurements are made must be specified.

***Current-carrying resistors.*** These are needed for the calibration of resistive shunts which are used for measurement of direct current in the range from 10 to 10,000 A or higher. They are four-terminal resistors made from rods or strips of manganin, using several elements in parallel for the lower-resistance high-current values. They are mounted in oil-filled containers, fitted with some means of continuously stirring the oil. The range of resistance is from about 0.01 mΩ to 0.01Ω, and in those intended for the larger currents the case is fitted with a water-cooled jacket. Because of the less well-defined thermal conditions, the accuracy obtainable is limited to 0.01% at the low current values and degrades to about 0.1% for high current values.

***Decade resistors.*** These are switched assemblies of resistors, usually wire-wound, to provide variable resistances for laboratory work. They are necessarily two-terminal instruments, and hence have inbuilt errors due to lead resistances and variation of switch contacts. As in most switched decade resistance elements, each dial includes a 10 position in addition to the values from 0 to 9. This permits a ready self-calibration procedure to check linearity.

***Kelvin-Varley dividers.*** These are used as variable voltage dividers for potentiometric work, for example, for the calibration of digital voltmeters from a fixed voltage standard. They consist (**Fig. 6**) of a series of sets of equal resistors connected by switches. In each set there are 11 resistors, 2 of which are spanned by the resistors of the next decade. This arrangement maintains an input resistance which is independent of the setting, and a low output resistance. SEE DIGITAL VOLTMETER; POTENTIOMETER (VOLTAGE METER).

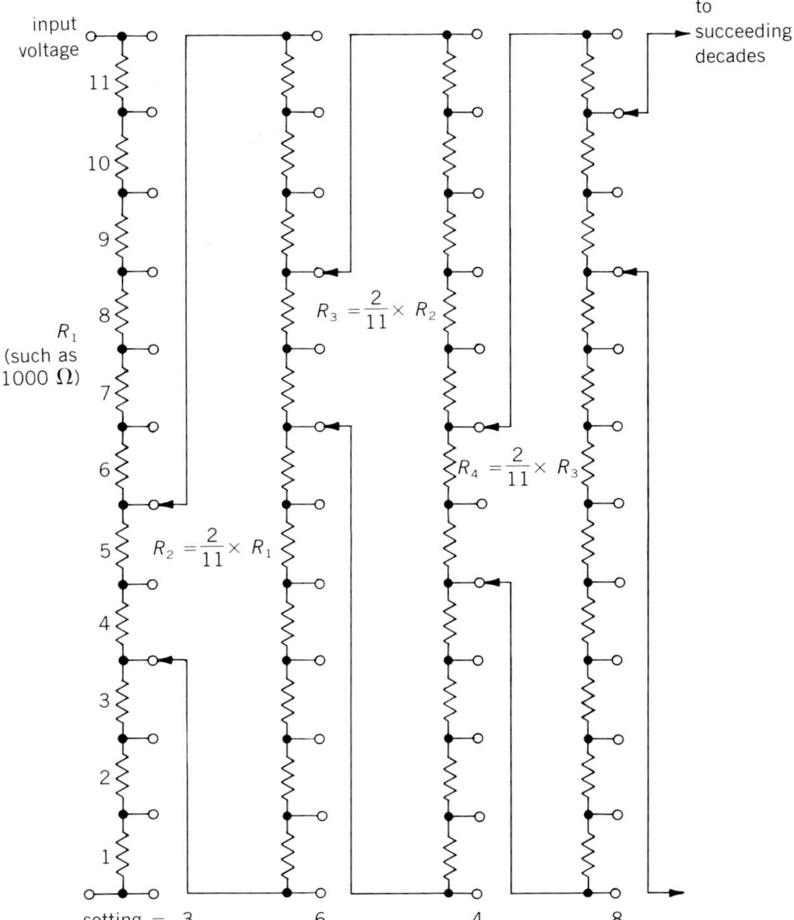


**Fig. 6. Kelvin-Varley divider. Setting of divider with taps in the positions shown is 0.3648.**

**Comparison methods.** The value of an unknown resistance $R_x$ is determined by comparison with a standard resistor $R_s$.

***Wheatstone bridge.*** This bridge (**Fig. 7**) is perhaps the most basic and widely used resistance- or impedance-comparing device. Its principal advantage is that its operation and balance are independent of variations in the supply. At balance, Eq. (7) is satisfied.

$$R_x = R_S \times \frac{R_1}{R_2} \tag{7}$$

The greatest sensitivity is obtained when all resistances are similar in value, and the comparison of standard resistors can then be made with a repeatability of about 3 parts in $10^8$, the limit arising from thermal noise in the resistors. In use, the direction of supply is reversed periodically to eliminate effects of thermal or contact emf's. The bridge is normally arranged for two-terminal measurements, and so is not suitable for the most accurate measurement at values below about 100 Ω, although still very convenient for lower resistances if the loss of accuracy does not matter.

Typically a bridge will have two decade-ratio arms, for example, of 1, 10, 100, 1000, and 10,000 Ω, and a variable switched decade arm of 1–100,000 Ω, although many variations are encountered. For the measurement of resistors of values close to the decade values, a considerable increase in accuracy can be obtained by substitution measurement, in which the bridge is used only as an indicating instrument. The resistors being compared can be brought to the same value by connecting a much higher variable resistance across the larger of them, and the accuracy of this high-resistance shunt can be much less than that of

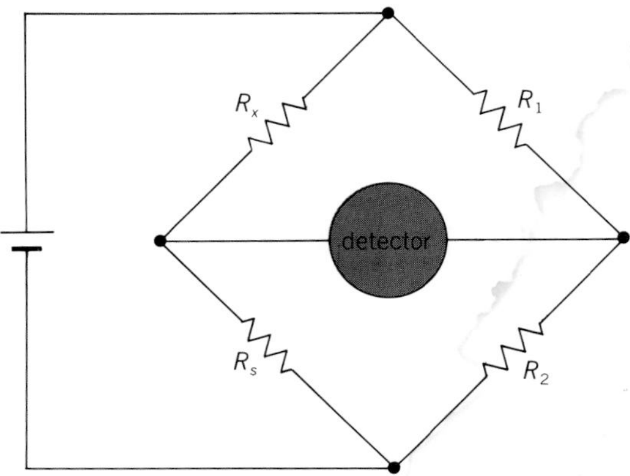


**Fig. 7. Wheatstone bridge. At balance, $R_1/R_2 = R_x/R_s$.**

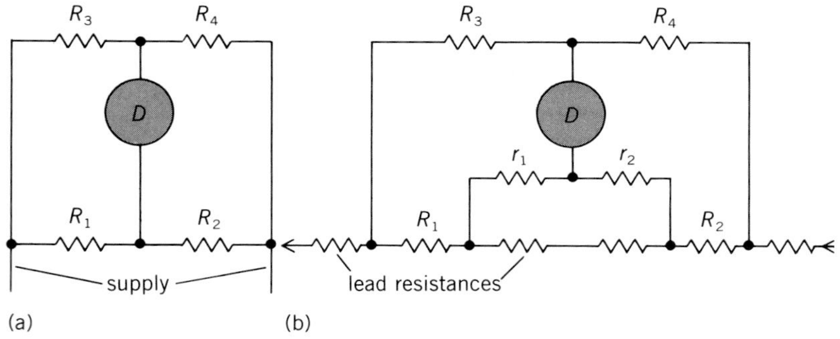


**Fig. 8. Comparison of bridge circuits. (*a*) Wheatstone bridge. At balance, $R_1/R_2 = R_3/R_4$. (*b*) Kelvin double bridge. At balance, $R_1/R_2 = R_3/R_4 = r_1/r_2$.**

the resistance being compared. *See* WHEATSTONE BRIDGE.

***Kelvin double bridge.*** This is a double bridge (**Fig. 8**) designed for four-terminal measurements, and so can be used for very low resistances. The double condition for balance is given by Eq. (8). In addition to

$$\frac{R_3}{R_4} = \frac{R_1}{R_2} = \frac{r_1}{r_2} \qquad (8)$$

its use for accurate laboratory measurement of resistances below 100 Ω, it is very valuable for finding the resistance of conducting rods or bars, or for the calibration in the field of air-cooled resistors used for measurement of large currents. *See* KELVIN BRIDGE.

**High-resistance measurements** Measurements of resistances from 10 MΩ to 1 TΩ ($10^{12}$ Ω) or even higher with a Wheatstone bridge present additional problems. The resistance to be measured will usually be voltage-dependent, so the measurement voltage must be specified. The resistors in the ratio arms must be sufficiently high in value so that they are not overloaded. If a guard electrode is fitted, it is necessary to eliminate any current flowing to the guard from the measurement circuit. As an example, for measurement of 1 TΩ at 100 V, the ratio arms could be as shown in **Fig. 9**. The power dissipated in the 1-MΩ resistor is then 10 mW, and the bridge ratio is $10^6$. The guard is connected to a subsidiary divider of the same ratio, so that any current flowing to it does not pass through the detector.

***DC current comparator bridge.*** This is a very effective instrument, which offers simple four-terminal measurements of resistors up to a value of 100 kΩ (or to 1 MΩ by modification). The essential feature of the comparator (**Fig. 10**) is that the ratio of the currents in the two circuits is measured by means of balancing the fluxes they produce in a high-permeability toroidal comparator, a device like a transformer but connected so that the dc fluxes due to each winding are in opposition. The balance condition of zero flux is sensitively detected by a third winding. This balance condition is then maintained by a servo circuit controlling one of the power supplies, and is obtained when the ampere-turns products of the two windings are equal. The resistors to be compared are connected to the two circuits, and the turns' ratio adjusted by rotary switches until the emf's across the resistors balance.

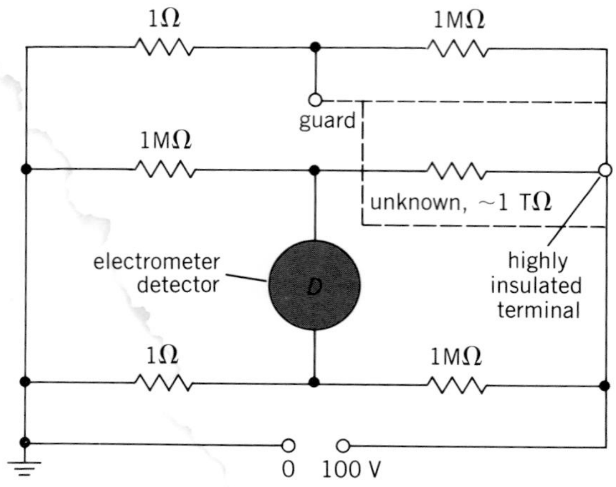


**Fig. 9. Wheatstone bridge for high-resistance measurement.**

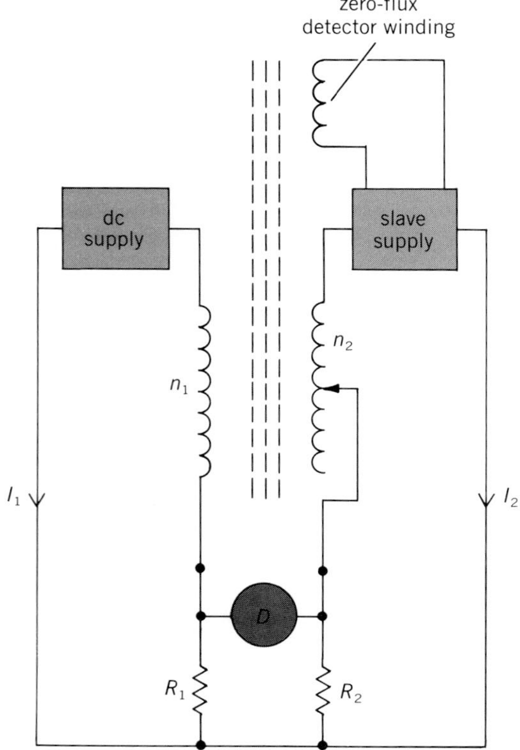


**Fig. 10. DC current comparator bridge. $I_1/I_2 = n_2/n_1$; $R_1/R_2 = n_1/n_2$.**

As with the Wheatstone bridge, a quick check can be made by reversing the positions of the two resistors being compared. An important merit of the system is that the ratio measured depends only on numbers of turns on the comparator, and not on ratio resistors which will inevitably drift to some extent.

***Series-parallel resistance networks.*** The values of standard resistors at decade values are usually established from the 1Ω level by means of build-up boxes. If $n$ similar resistors are connected first in parallel and then in series, they provide the ratio $n^2$ between the series and parallel values. It can readily be shown that if each resistor is different from the mean by no more than some small amount δ (for example, 1 in $10^4$), the ratio is achieved with an accuracy no worse than $\delta^2$ (in this case, 1 in $10^8$). This readily provides ratios of 100:1. A 10:1 ratio can be provided by connecting 10 resistors first in series, and then in three groups of

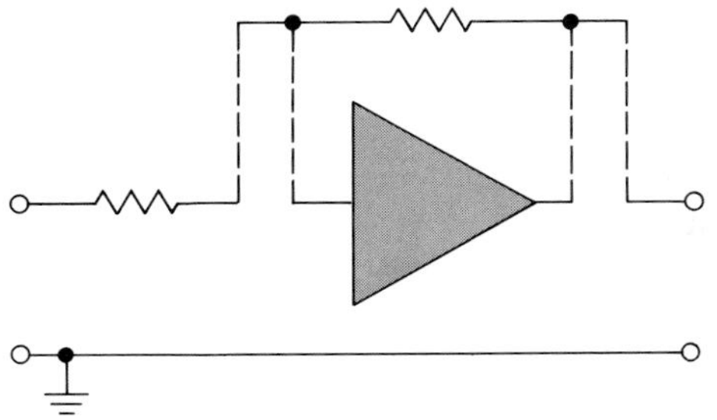

Fig. 11. Constant current resistance measurement circuit.

3 resistors in parallel connected in series with the remaining resistor, although this does not give as good accuracy as does the 100:1 arrangement. In order to connect four-terminal resistors so that only the resistive elements are truly in series, it is necessary to use special symmetrical four-terminal junctions, which are made so that the transresistance defined by the ratio of the voltage across any two connections to the current passing between the other two connections is less than $10^{-9}$ Ω. Resistance networks made in this way, for use below 1000 Ω, are called Hamon resistors after their inventor. The nano-ohm junctions are made from solid copper, usually of cylindrical or cubic form, with the connecting wires brazed symmetrically into them.

***Voltage and current measurement.*** An obvious and direct way of measuring resistance is by the simultaneous measurement of voltage and current, and this is usual in very many indicating ohm-meters and multirange meters. In most digital instruments, which are usually also digital voltage meters, the resistor is supplied from a constant current circuit and the voltage across it is measured by the digital voltage meter. This is a convenient arrangement for a four-terminal measurement, so that long leads can be used from the instrument to the resistor without introducing errors (**Fig. 11**). The simplest systems, used in passive pointer instruments, measure directly the current through the meter which is adjusted to give full-scale deflection by an additional resistor in series with the battery. This gives a nonlinear scale of limited accuracy, but sufficient for many practical applications. *SEE CURRENT MEASUREMENT; VOLTAGE MEASUREMENT.*

***AC resistance measurements.*** The use of inductive voltage dividers makes it possible to create simple ac resistance bridges in which the ratio arms of the bridge are composed of the two parts of the inductive voltage divider. Inductive voltage dividers are inherently very accurate and stable devices, and so do not need the extensive regular recalibration needed by resistive bridges. The simple bridge shown in **Fig. 12** is principally suitable for the comparison of resistors when their reactance (due to their stray inductance or capacitance) is negligible in comparison with the resistance, for example, at low frequencies. An important field of application is for platinum resistance thermometry, in which the resistance to be measured is usually in the range 1–1000 Ω.

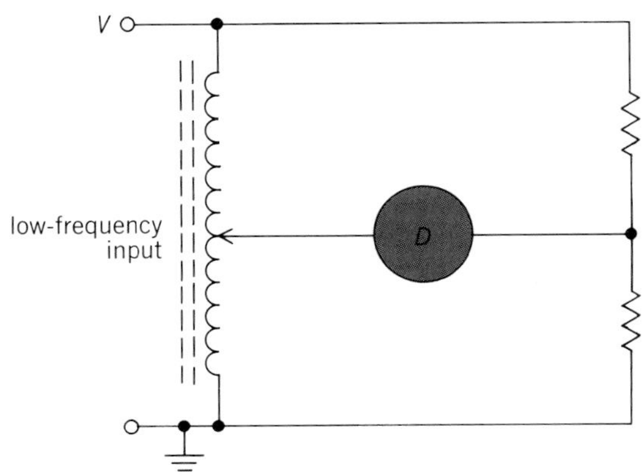


Fig. 12. Inductive divider resistance bridge.

At high frequencies two effects occur which change the measured value of resistance. The stray shunt capacitance $C$ reduces the measured value of resistance by a factor $1/(1 + \omega^2C^2R^2)$ in addition to introducing resistance, and the resistance is increased due to the fact that the current flows only in the surface of the conductor. At radio and microwave frequencies, resistance becomes of importance principally in limiting the resolution or $Q$ factor of circuits, and its measurement is often made by the measurement of this factor. *SEE Q (ELECTRICITY).*

Radio-frequency resistance is also used to evaluate the state of annealing of metals used in aircraft construction, and for this purpose it is measured by the coupled resistance induced in an inductor placed close to the metal. *SEE EDDY CURRENT.*

*Cyril H. Dix*

***Bibliography.*** C. H. Dix and A. E. Bailey, Electrical standards of measurement, *Proc. IEE*, vol. 122, no. 1OR, October 1975; S. Geczy, *Basic Electrical Measurements*, 1984; B. A. Gregory, *An Introduction to Electrical Instrumentation and Measurement Systems*, 2d ed., 1981; B. V. Hamon, A 1–100 Ω build-up resistor for the calibration of standard resistors, *J. Sci. Instrum.*, 31:450–453, 1964; F. K. Harris, *Electrical Measurements*, 1952, reprint 1975; R. L. Heiserman, *Electrical and Electronic Measuring Instruments*, 1983; J. J. Hill, Calibration of d.c. resistance standards and voltage ratio boxes by an a.c. method, *Proc. IEE*, pt. 1, 112:112, 1963.

## Resistor

One of the three basic components of an electric circuit that displays a voltage drop across its terminals and produces heat when an electric current passes through it. The electrical resistance, measured in ohms, is equal to the ratio of the voltage drop across the resistor terminals divided by the current measured in amperes. *SEE OHM'S LAW.*

Resistors are described by stating their total resistance in ohms along with their safe power-dissipating ability in watts. A more detailed description would specify the residual inductance and stray shunt capacitance of the resistor. *SEE ELECTRICAL RESISTANCE.*

**Classification by use.** Resistors may be classified according to the general field of engineering in which they are used.

***Integrated circuit resistors.*** Large-scale integrated (LSI) circuits employed inside the chips that constitute computer component boards require the use of resistors that can be fabricated along with the many transistors that occupy a single chip. *SEE INTEGRATED CIRCUITS.*

***Power resistors.*** Such resistors range in size from about 5 W to many kilowatts and may be cooled by air convection, air blast, or water. The smaller sizes, up to several hundred watts, are used in both the power and electronics fields of engineering.

***Instrument resistors.*** Direct-current (dc) ammeters employ resistors as meter shunts to bypass the major portion of the current around the low-current elements. These high-accuracy, four-terminal resistors are commonly designed to provide a voltage drop of 50 mV when a stated current passes through the resistor.

Voltmeters of both the dc and the ac types employ scale-multiplying resistors designed for accuracy and stability. The arc-over voltage rating of these resistors is of importance in the case of high-voltage voltmeters.

***Resistors for electronic circuits.*** By far the greatest number of resistors manufactured are intended for use in the electronics field. The majority of these resistors are intended for use in frequency-selective circuits involving potentials up to several hundred volts but currents seldom over 10–100 mA. Their power-dissipating ability is small, as is their physical size.

**Classification by construction.** Resistors are also classified according to their construction, which may be composition, film-type, or wire-wound. Further classification may be made according to whether the resistor has a fixed or adjustable resistance. Adjustable resistors may be further classified as adjustable-slide, rheostat, and potentiometer types.

***Composition resistor.*** This resistor is by far the most widely manufactured type because of its low cost, reliability, and small size. Basically it is a mixture of resistive materials, usually carbon, and a suitable binder molded into a cylinder. Copper wire leads are attached to the ends of the cylinder, and the entire resistor is molded into a plastic or ceramic jacket. The overall length of the jacketed resistor excluding the leads is ½–1⅓ in. (13–34 mm) for resistors varying in power rating from 0.25 to 2 W. After manufacture the resistors are automatically zoned according to their individual resistance values, which are indicated on the jacket of the resistor by means of a color code.

Composition resistors are commonly used in the range from several ohms to 10–20 megohms, and are available with tolerances of 20, 10, or 5%. Higher values of resistance are available but are not normally used in communication equipment or most electronic instruments. For very high resistance values, above about 100 megohms, special jacketing is often required to prevent the leakage resistance over the surface of the jacket from altering the overall resistance of the resistor.

All resistors possess a finite shunt capacitance across their terminals. This capacitance is a function of the geometry and physical size of the resistor and is essentially independent of the value of the resistor. The result is that at higher frequencies each resistor is effectively paralleled by a capacitive reactance which decreases in magnitude with increasing frequency. At approximately 100 kHz the overall impedance of a 1-megohm resistor begins to decrease with an increase of frequency. A 1000-ohm resistor will not display this effect until a frequency of about 100 MHz is reached.

The wattage rating of resistors is normally based upon the amount of thermal drift in resistance that can be tolerated. If greater thermal stability is required, the designer should use resistors with a higher power rating. Composition resistors are easily damaged permanently by overheating. Because of this, care must be exercised when soldering a resistor into a circuit.

***Film-type resistor.*** This resistor is rapidly replacing the composition resistor in applications in which greater stability of resistance with voltage, temperature, and humidity is demanded. The design of the film resistor further lends itself to the controlled manufacture of precision resistors of any desired value. Basically this resistor consists of a conducting film of carbon, metal, or metal oxide deposited upon a ceramic cylinder. The value of the resistance is controlled by controlling the thickness and length of the film. The length of the film is often controlled by cutting a spiral groove around the resistor, the groove passing through the film to the insulating cylinder. This spiral groove increases the effective length of the resistor and thereby determines its ohmic value. By accurately controlling the pitch of the spiral the manufacturer can make a resistor of any value and can maintain close manufacturing tolerances.

The film resistor is often finished by coating it with an insulating varnish. Often a plastic sleeve is slipped over the resistor to provide mechanical protection. The spiral-cut resistor displays a small inductive effect at the higher frequencies.

***Integrated circuit resistor.*** These resistors must be capable of fabrication on a silicon integrated circuit chip along with transistors and capacitors. There are two major types; thin-film resistors and diffused resistors.

Thin-film resistors are formed by vacuum deposition or sputtering of nichrome, tantalum, or Cermet (Cr-SiO). Such resistors are stable, and the resistance may be adjusted to close tolerances by trimming the film. Typical resistor values lie in the range from 100 ohms to 10 kilohms with a matching tolerance of ±0.2% and a temperature coefficient of resistance (TCR) of ±10 to ±200 ppm/°C.

Diffused resistors are based upon the same fabrication geometry and techniques used to produce the active transistors on the silicon chip or die. A diffused base, emitter, or epitaxial layer may be formed as a bar with contacts at its extremities. The resistance of such a semiconductor resistor depends upon the impurity doping and the length and cross section of the resistor region. In the case of the base-diffused resistor, the emitter and collector regions may be formed so as to pinch the base region to a very small cross-sectional area, thereby appreciably increasing the resistance. Because of the relatively large impurity carrier concentration in *n*- and *p*-type regions, there is a limit to the maximum resistance values attainable for an acceptable resistor size. Resistor values between 100 ohms and 10 kilohms are common with a matching tolerance lower than ±2% but with a temperature coefficient of resistance approaching 2000 ppm/°C. The epitaxial layer resistor has a much lower impurity carrier concentration and offers resistance values up to 50 kilohms but with a higher temperature coefficient of resistance of 3000 ppm/°C and a matching tolerance of about ±6%.

***Wire-wound resistors.*** Wire remains the most stable form of resistance material available; therefore all high-precision instruments rely upon wire-wound resistors. Wire-wound resistors are available in resistance ratings from a fraction of an ohm to several hundred thousand ohms, at power ratings from less than 1 W to several thousand watts, and at tolerances from 10 to 0.1%. Because mechanical manufacturing problems limit the smallest wire size that can be used, these resistors are usually limited to values below about 100 kilohms. Both inductive and noninductive types of resistor are manufactured.

The inductive design is the common construction and consists of a spiral winding of wire about a cylindrical ceramic form. After winding, the entire resistor is covered with a vitreous material. The spiral winding introduces a considerable amount of inductance into the circuit, which may become objectionable at the higher audio frequencies and all radio frequencies.

The noninductive design includes several winding methods. One of the simplest and most satisfactory is to reduce the cross-sectional area of the coil by winding the wire around a thin, flat card.

**Adjustable resistors.** The deposited-film and wire-wound resistors lend themselves to the design of adjustable resistors or rheostats and potentiometers. Adjustable-slider power resistors are constructed in the same manner as any wire-wound resistor on a cylindrical form except that when the vitreous outer coating is applied an uncovered strip is provided. The resistance wire is exposed along this strip and a suitable slider contact can be used to adjust the overall resistance, or the slider can be used as the top on a potentiometer. SEE POTENTIOMETER (VARIABLE RESISTOR).

Where continuous adjustment of the resistor is intended, a ring-shaped form is generally used. For power resistors the ring is wound with resistance wire. For compact 0.5- and 1-W resistors, the ring is coated on one surface with a resistance film. Each type possesses all the advantages and disadvantages described above under fixed-value resistors of its type. In addition, adjustable resistors have the problem of maintaining a good, noise-free, electrical contact at the wiper, which is mounted on a shaft concentric with the ring.

For discussion of nonlinear resistors SEE VARISTOR.

*Robert L. Ramey*

***Bibliography.*** D. G. Fink and D. Christiansen (eds.), *Electronic Engineers' Handbook*, 2d ed., 1982; A. B. Glaser and G. E. Subak-Sharpe, *Integrated Circuit Engineering*, 1977; P. R. Gray and R. G. Meyer, *Analysis and Design of Analog Integrated Circuits*, 1977; C. A. Harper, *Handbook of Components for Electronics*, 1977; Howard W. Sams Engineering Staff, *Reference Data for Radio Engineers*, 6th ed., 1975.

## Resonance (alternating-current circuits)

A condition in a circuit characterized by relatively unimpeded oscillation of energy from a potential to a kinetic form. In an electrical network there is oscillation between the potential energy of current in inductance. This is analogous to the mechanical resonance seen in a pendulum.

Three kinds of resonant frequency in circuits are officially defined. Phase resonance is the frequency at which the phase angle between sinusoidal current entering a circuit and sinusoidal voltage applied to the terminals of the circuit is zero. Amplitude resonance is the frequency at which a given sinusoidal excitation (voltage of current) produces the maximum oscillation of electric charge in the resonant circuit. Natural resonance is the natural frequency of oscillation of the resonant circuit in the absence of any forcing excitation. These three frequencies are so nearly equal in low-loss circuits that they do not often have to be distinguished.

Phase resonance is perhaps the most useful in many practical situations, as well as being slightly simpler mathematically. The following discussion considers phase resonance in passive, linear, two-terminal networks.

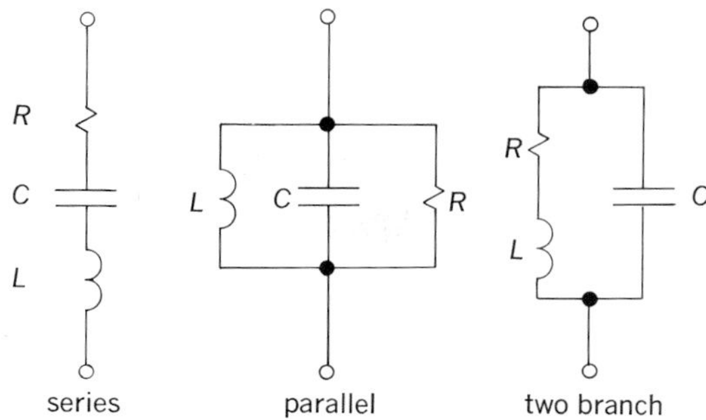

**Fig. 1. Resonant circuits.**

Resonance can appear in two-terminal networks of any degree of complication, but the three circuits shown in **Fig. 1** are simple and typical. The first illustrates series resonance and the second, parallel resonance; the third is a series-parallel resonant circuit of two branches (sometimes referred to as antiresonance). Series resonance is highly practical for providing low impedance at the resonant frequency. Parallel resonance is the dual of series resonance, but it is not practical because it assumes an inductive element with no resistance. The third example, however, shows an eminently practical means of providing the typical characteristic of parallel resonance, which is high impedance at the resonant frequency.

**Use.** Resonance is of great importance in communications, permitting certain frequencies to be passed and others to be rejected. Thus a pair of telephone wires can carry many messages at the same time, each modulating a different carrier frequency, and each being separated from the others at the receiving end of the line by an appropriate arrangement of resonant filters. A radio or television receiver uses much the same principle to accept a desired signal and to reject all the undesired signals that arrive concurrently at its antenna; tuning a receiver means adjusting a circuit to be resonant at a desired frequency.

Many frequency-sensitive circuits are not truly resonant, and oscillations of a certain frequency can be produced or enhanced by networks that do not involve inductance. It is difficult and expensive to provide inductance with integrated circuits, but frequency selection can be provided by the use of capacitance and resistance, a large amount of amplification being obtained from the semiconductor material employed.

**Series resonance. Figure 2** shows a phasor diagram of the voltage, resulting from a given current (steady alternating current) in a series-resonant cir-

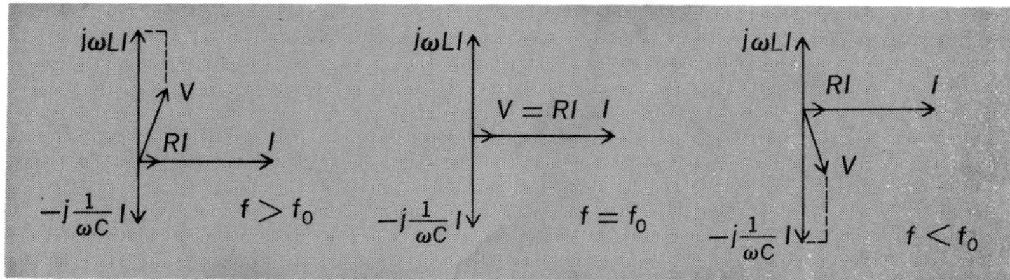

**Fig. 2. Phasor diagrams at frequencies near resonance ($Q$ = 5).**

cuit, such as shown in Fig. 1. The component voltages across the three circuit elements add to give the total applied voltage $V$, as shown for a frequency slightly above resonance, for the resonant frequency, and for the frequency below resonance. It is of course possible in low-loss (high $Q$) circuits for the voltage across the capacitance and the voltage across the inductance each to be many times greater than the applied voltage.

Analytically, the impedance of the series-resonant circuit is given by Eq. (1). The resonant frequency $f_0$

$$Z = R + j\omega L + \frac{1}{j\omega C} = R + j\left(\omega L - \frac{1}{\omega C}\right) \quad (1)$$

is the frequency at which $Z$ is purely real (phase resonance), so $\omega_0 L = 1/\omega_0 C$, or $2\pi f_0 L = 1/2\pi f_0 C$, from which Eq. (2) obtains.

$$f_0 = \frac{1}{2\pi\sqrt{LC}} \quad (2)$$

A more convenient notation is expressed by Eq. (3).

$$Z = R_0\left(\frac{R}{R_0} + jQ_0\delta\frac{2+\delta}{1+\delta}\right) \quad (3)$$

In Eqs. (1)–(3):

$Z$ = impedance at the terminals of the series-resonant circuit
$R, L, C$ = the three circuit parameters
$R_0$ = resistance (effective) at resonant frequency
$Q_0 = \omega_0 L/R_0$
$\delta = (\omega - \omega_0)/\omega_0$
$\omega = 2\pi f$, where $f$ is frequency (hertz)
$\omega_0 = 2\pi f_0$, where $f_0$ is resonant frequency

Equation (3) is true for all series-resonant circuits, but interest is mainly in circuits for which $Q_0$, the quality factor at the resonant frequency, is high (20 or more) and for which $\delta$, the fractional detuning, is low (perhaps less than 0.1). Assuming high $Q_0$ and low $\delta$, which means a low-loss circuit and a frequency near resonance, Eq. (4) is very nearly the relative admittance of the series-resonant circuit.

$$\frac{Y}{Y_0} = \frac{Z_0}{Z} = \frac{1}{1 + j2Q_0\delta} \quad (4)$$

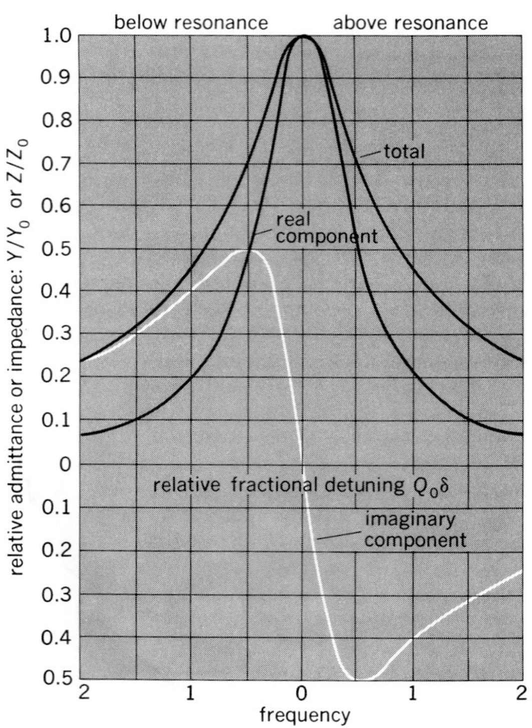


**Fig. 3. Universal resonance curve. (*After H. H. Skilling, Electrical Engineering Circuits, 2d ed., John Wiley and Sons, 1955*)**

**Universal resonance curve.** The magnitude and the real and imaginary components of Eq. (4) are usefully plotted in the universal resonance curve of **Fig. 3**. Since $Y/Y_0$ is plotted as a function of $Q_0\delta$, this curve can be applied to all series-resonant circuits. (If $Q_0$ = 20, the error in Y barely exceeds 1% of $Y_0$ for any $\delta$, and is less for small $\delta$.)

Moreover, because of the duality of the network, the curve can also be applied to any parallel-resonant circuit (Fig. 1) provided $Q_0$ is now interpreted as $Q_0 = R_0/\omega_0 L$. When used for a parallel-resonant circuit, the curve of Fig. 3 gives not $Y/Y_0$ but the relative input impedance $Z/Z_0$.

Finally, the universal resonance curve of Fig. 3 can also be applied (with the same slight approximations) to the two-branch resonant circuit of Fig. 1. For this purpose the curve shows $Z/Z_0$ (as for the three-branch parallel-resonant circuit), but the value of Q to be used is $Q_0 = \omega_0 L/R_0$, exactly as with the series-resonant circuit. Note that $Z_0$ for this circuit is given by Eq. (5) (instead of being equal to $R_0$ as it is in the other two circuits of Fig. 1).

$$Z_0 = (\omega_0 L)Q_0 = R_0 Q_0^2 \quad (5)$$

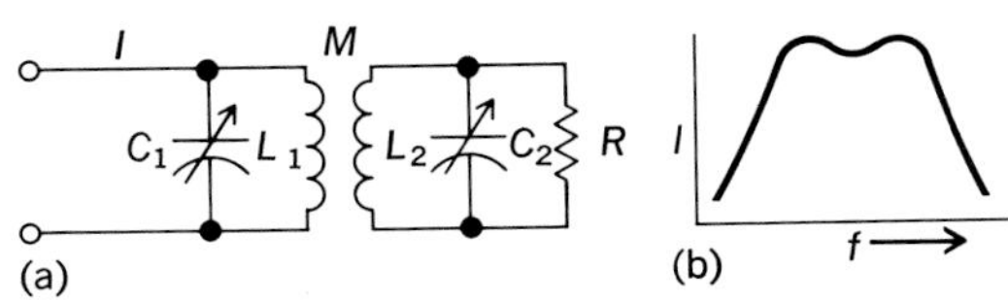


**Fig. 4. Multiple resonance. (*a*) Double-tuned network. (*b*) Current in *R* as function of frequency.**

**Multiple resonance.** If two or more coupled circuits are resonant at slightly different frequencies, many valuable characteristics can be obtained. **Figure 4** shows a double-tuned network and a typical curve of current in $R$, the load, as a function of frequency. SEE ALTERNATING-CURRENT CIRCUIT THEORY; NETWORK THEORY.

*Hugh Hildreth Skilling*

**Bibliography.** D. Bell, *Fundamentals of Electric Circuits*, 2d ed., 1981; J. R. Duff and M. Kauffman, *Alternating Current Fundamentals*, 1980; Institute of Electrical and Electronics Engineers, *IEEE Standard Dictionary of Electrical and Electronics Terms*, 2d ed., 1977.

## Response

A quantitative expression of the manner in which a microphone, amplifier, loudspeaker, or other component or system performs its intended function. A linear response means that the output signal is exactly proportional to the input signal for the entire range of frequencies over which the device is intended to operate. A logarithmic response means that the output signal is a logarithmic function of the input signal. The response of a device is often presented as a curve on a graph, indicating deviation over the frequency range from the response at some selected frequency, such as 1000 Hz. An example is the frequency-response curve of an amplifier. *See* Amplifier; Characteristic curve.

*John Markus*

## Ripple voltage

The total voltage across the load resistor of a rectifier minus the average voltage across the same resistor. The ripple can be expressed as a Fourier series. The fundamental frequency of the ripple voltage of single-phase half-wave circuits is the same as that of the alternating-current (ac) input. For a single-phase full-wave circuit the fundamental frequency is twice that of the ac input voltage, while for a three-phase half-wave the fundamental frequency is three times that of the ac supply. To reduce the ripple voltage, a low-pass filter is usually placed between the rectifier and the load. The filter is more efficient in reducing the ripple voltage if the fundamental frequency of the ripple voltage is high. *See* Electric filter; Rectifier.

*Donald L. Waidelich*

## Robotics

The study of problems associated with the design and application of robots and their control and sensory systems. The term robot has been loosely used historically, and has been applied to almost any feedback-controlled mechanical system. While the exact usage of "robot" is a matter of preference, the computer-controlled mechanical arm used in industrial applications probably represents a reasonable middle ground for definition by example (**Fig. 1**). Most of the concerns of practitioners of robotics can be present in such devices, and in turn much of the current work in robotics relates directly to them.

Robotics is also a broadly interpreted term; it is generally considered as covering research and engineering activities related to the design and construction of robots, but persons engaged in planning robot manufacturing or in studying the economic impact of robots might also consider themselves to be engaged in robotics. Much of this breadth of usage arises from the fact that robotics is a highly interdisciplinary field, involving mechanical engineering, computer science, artificial intelligence, biomechanics, control theory, cybernetics, and electrical engineering, to name only a few. *See* Artificial intelligence; Computer.

The emergence of robotics as a separate discipline has been given impetus by the developing complexity of robot systems. This has emphasized the fact that the design of the mechanical, electronic, and computational aspects of robots are interdependent. Previously it was possible for mechanical engineers to view a robot as just another numerically controlled machine tool, and for computer scientists to regard it as just another peripheral device. Although this viewpoint is possible for many simpler forms of robot, it is no longer a workable approach for current, complex, hierarchically controlled, sensory-interactive robots. In typical robotics research laboratories, specialists in many different areas work cooperatively on an integrated robot system.

**Mechanical design.** Almost all robots produce some sort of mechanical motion which, in most cases, has the purpose of manipulation or locomotion. For example, robot arms manipulate tools and parts to perform jobs such as welding, painting, and assembly; robot carts are used to transport materials. The design of the mechanical structures of robots is thus of great importance in robotics. Areas of concern in the mechanics of robots include degrees of freedom of movement, size and shape of the operating space, stiffness and strength of the structure, lifting capacity, velocity, and acceleration under load. In addition, good mechanical design is a factor in other performance measures such as accuracy and repeatability of positioning, and freedom from oscillation and vibration.

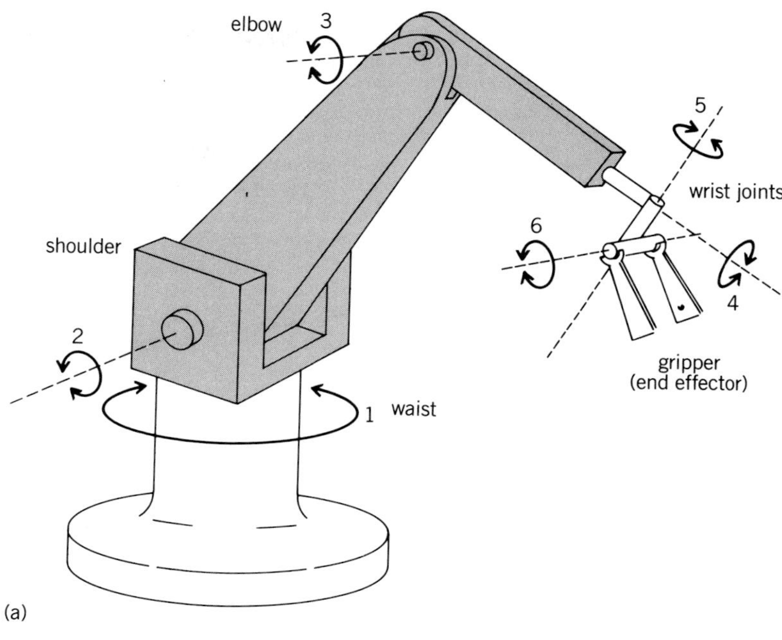


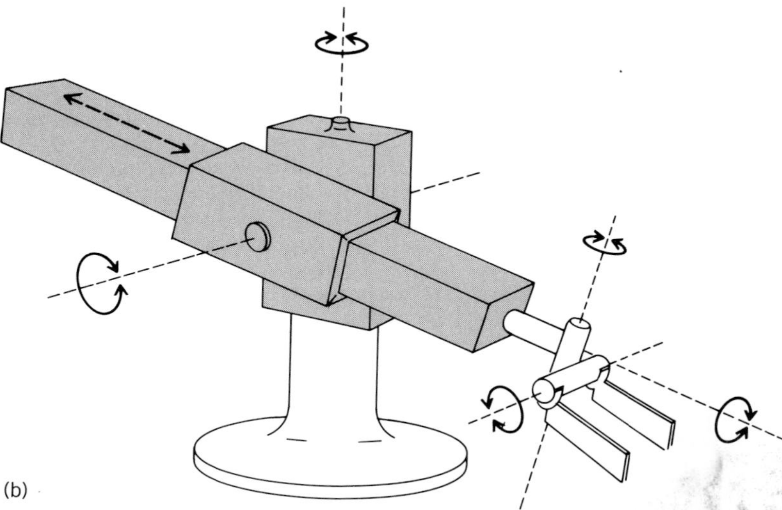


**Fig. 1. Six-degree-of-freedom robot arms. (*a*) Arm with all rotational joints (numbered 1 to 6). (*b*) Arm with one sliding joint.**

***Degrees of freedom.*** Some robots have very simple mechanical designs involving only a few degrees of freedom of movement. However, the design of robot manipulators can also be quite complex; in a typical industrial robot arm, six degrees of freedom of movement (exclusive of gripper closure) are required to en-

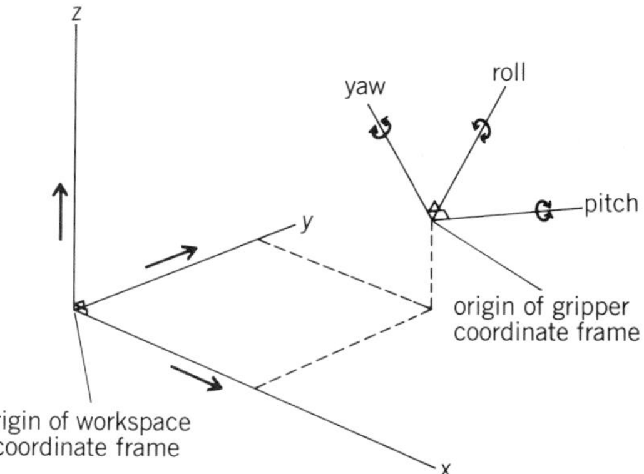


**Fig. 2. Coordinate relations for a six-degree-of-freedom robot.**

able the gripper to approach an object from any orientation. This is usually accomplished with three arm joints, which can position the "wrist" at any *x*, *y*, *z* coordinate in the working volume. The complex three-axis wrist joints can then orient the gripper attached to it by three independent motions (roll, pitch, yaw) around the *x*, *y*, *z* location of the wrist (**Fig. 2**). In effect, the wrist represents the origin of a three-axis coordinate system fixed to the gripper. Moving the first three joints of the arm translates this origin to any point in a three-axis coordinate system fixed to the working volume; motion of the final three joints (in the wrist) orients the gripper coordinate system in rotation about an origin at the wrist point. For clarity, the robots in these figures have wrist-joint axes which do not all intersect at a single point. Some robots are constructed this way, but the mathematics of robot motion (kinematics) is considerably simplified if these axes do intersect at a single point. A wrist of this type is referred to as spherical, and the mechanical complexity of many robot wrists is due to this requirement.

***Types of joints.*** Both sliding joints and rotational joints may be included in the robot's articulation (joint structure). Many robots use only rotational joints (as does the human arm), but only limited actions can be produced by using sliding joints alone (Fig. 1). Robot mobility usually involves adaptations of traditional devices such as wheels and treads, but walking robots, usually in some stable configuration such as a six-legged hexapod, have also been developed. The mechanical design problems of articulated legs are similar to those of robot arms. *See* Mechanism.

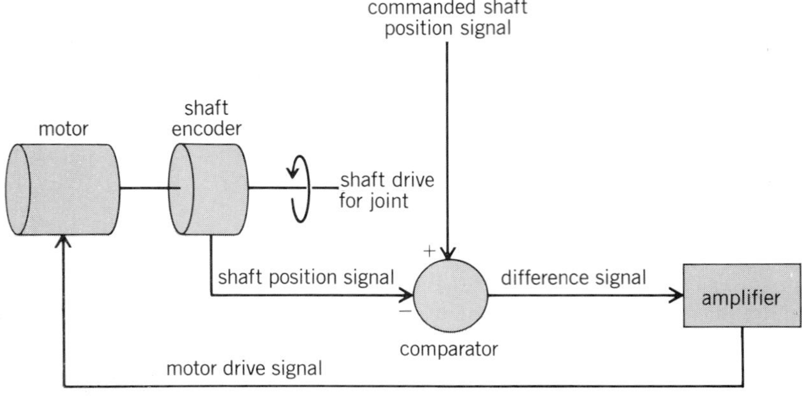


**Fig. 3. Servo control for a single robot joint.**

***Powering joints.*** The problem of powering the robot's joints is made difficult by the complex mechanical articulation. One approach is to place a prime mover (electrical, hydraulic, or pneumatic) at the joint itself. Power for these can be brought with relative ease through the joints and members of the arm. However, the weight and bulk of such motors and their associated gearing place constraints on the performance and mechanical design of the arm, particularly for joints in the wrist. A second approach is to place the prime movers in the immobile base of the robot and to transmit motion to the joints through mechanical linkages such as shafts, belts and cables, or gearing. This overcomes many of the problems associated with the first approach, but introduces a new set of problems in designing intricate backlash-free mechanical linkages which can transmit power effectively through the complex articulations of the arm in all of its positions. No one approach has clearly dominated the field.

***End effectors.*** The purpose of the elaborate mechanical arm is to position an end effector (frequently a gripper) where it can perform some useful function. End effectors may be highly specialized for particular applications, or may be simple general-purpose pincers. Some robots change their own end effectors to suit the job at hand from a selection of special-purpose attachments. The development of more elaborate and dexterous general-purpose end effectors, including hands with humanlike fingers, is an area of intense study. The mechanical and control problems associated with such effectors are, however, exceedingly complex.

**Control systems.** A robot control system is the apparatus (usually electronic) which directs the activities of the mechanical parts. This may consist only of a sequencing device and a set of mechanical stops so that the mechanism moves in a repetitive pattern between selected positions, but more sophisticated systems employ servo-controlled positioning of the joints.

***Servo systems.*** In this case, a measure of the actual joint position is obtained from a transducer such as an optical shaft encoder, and this is compared with the position specified for the joint. If the desired position and the measured position differ, the circuitry applies a correcting drive signal to the joint motor (**Fig. 3**). Such servo systems may be digital or analog, and in addition to position they may control joint velocity.

Servo devices allow the robot to be moved through any selected sequence of positions on command, without the necessity to preset mechanical stops. If the appropriate sequence of commands is generated, servo-controlled joints may be driven through continuous, smoothly varying paths. The sequence of positions defining the robot's trajectory may be preprogrammed by numerically specifying positions in the robot's coordinate frame, or they may be "taught" to the system by moving the robot to the desired point and recording the outputs of the joint position transducers. Such teaching methods allow a human to direct a complex action once, and to have the robot repeat it indefinitely thereafter. *See* Tranducer.

***Computer control.*** More sophisticated systems generate the robot's trajectory automatically by computer; such computations may be made on the basis of mathematical descriptions of work objects or tasks contained in the computer's data base. The computer may also generate trajectories for the robot which are are not fixed but vary with the state of the external world as reported by the robot's sensory system. This sensory-interactive type of control permits the robot to act appropriately in relation to conditions, rather than relying on assumptions about the world. For example, without expensive fixturing and timing of the work, the actual location of a part may vary from one instance to the next; without sensory-interactive control in such cases, the robot could proceed blindly through a set of actions at preprogrammed but incorrect positions. SEE DIGITAL CONTROL.

***Hierarchial control.*** The most advanced robot control systems make use of hierarchical control. In such systems each level of a hierarchy of control stages accepts, from its superior level, a statement of a goal to be achieved. The complexity of this goal will depend on the position of the level in the hierarchy; the lowest level is the joint position servo, where the goal is simply the next position commanded for that joint. Each higher level attempts to achieve its own current goal by issuing sequences of commands (subgoals) to its subordinate level. In selecting these subgoals, each level takes into account its own current goal, the current state of the external world as described by its sensory input, and the current status of its subordinate level. Thus, each level of the hierarchy acts as a servo control on the actions of the next lower level, giving it commands appropriate to reducing the difference between the current state of events and the state of events defined by its own goal (**Fig. 4**). Such systems are sensory-interactive, and constitute a task-decomposition hierarchy similar to that of many functions in the human nervous system. They allow the robot to be instructed with very general commands which define the goal at the highest level.

**Sensory systems.** The purpose of a robot sensory system is to gather specific information needed by the control system and, in more advanced systems, to maintain an internal model of the environment which has predictive power. The joint position transducers used in feedback control are in fact a minimal sensory system, but other sensors are usually included to gather data about the external environment. Visual, proximity, tactile, acoustic, and force-torque senses are all used.

***Tactile sensors.*** Tactile (touch) sensors may be mounted in the robot gripper to detect contact with objects. These may take the form of simple switches, or may be analog transducers indicating degree and direction of pressure. Arrays of such transducers may be used to give a sense of patterned pressure which enables the robot to discriminate types and orientations of objects. Force and torque sensors, frequently mounted in the robot's wrist or fingers, are used to sense the degree and direction of resistance encountered by the gripper. These resistive forces may be due to the weight of the object being manipulated, or to contact with other objects or surfaces. Such sensors are used to adjust gripping pressure, to avoid applying destructive forces, and to guide proper mating of surfaces and parts. In combination, these senses allow a robot to feel the proper fit of work parts much as a human worker does.

***Visual sensors.*** The most commonly used means of sensing objects at a distance is some form of visual sense. Usually this is done by computer analysis of an image from a television camera. Two important approaches are ambient light systems and structured light systems. Ambient light systems rely on normal sources of scene illumination, while structured light systems provide special patterns of illumination

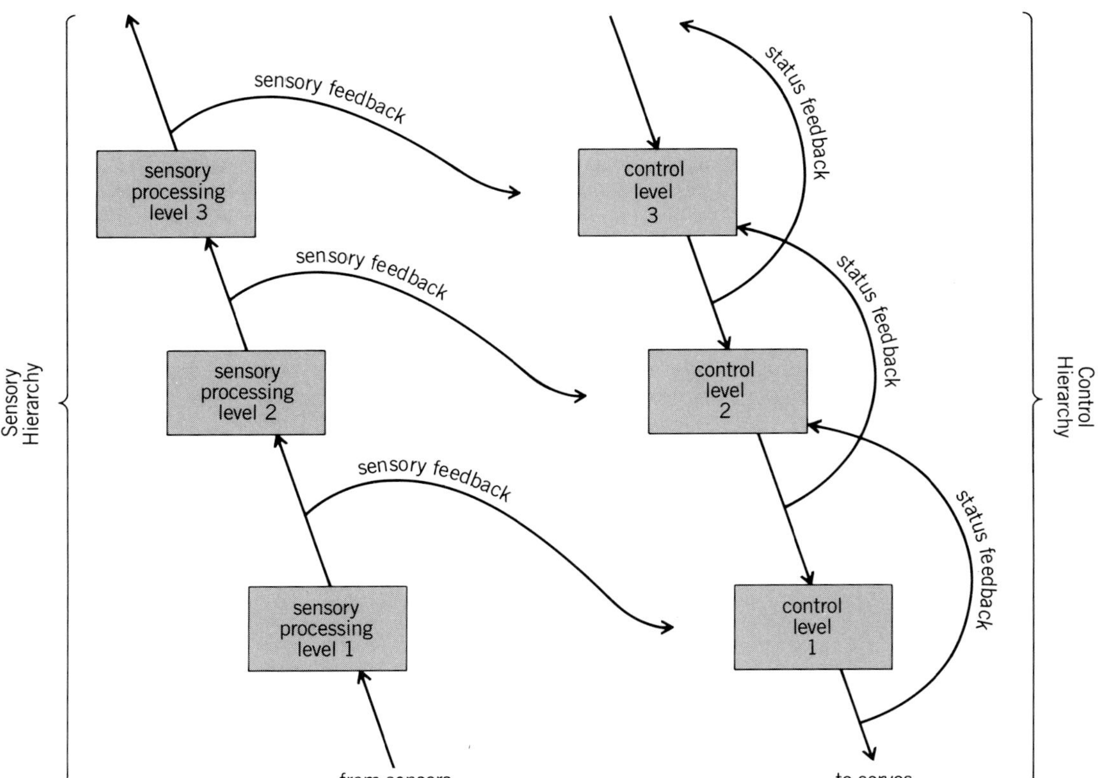


**Fig. 4. Complex, hierarchical, sensory-interactive robot control system.**

whose shape and orientation are known to the sensory system. The advantage of structured light is that the special patterns of illumination may be chosen to simplify and speed up the processing required to interpret the image. Procedures for determining depth in images rely fundamentally on triangulation, but in structured light systems the triangulation is between the camera and the light projector; in ambient light systems corresponding points in two images taken from different viewing positions must be triangulated, and this is much more difficult. Speed is important in robot vision because visual information is used by the control system to correct the robot's movements in real time, a process called visual servoing. SEE COMPUTER VISION.

Whatever the system of illumination used, the techniques of computer image processing are similar. At low levels, they include algorithms to do thresholding, and to find lines, edges, corners, and connected regions; these low-level vision processes are sufficient to perform many fundamental visual servoing operations. More complex systems include subsequent image-understanding operations which allow the robot to identify objects and to determine their orientation; this requires the robot to have some sort of previous knowledge about the kinds of objects in its environment. Such a knowledge base is used, together with the sensory data from vision (perhaps combined with other senses), to generate a world model describing the state of the environment.

***Multimodal systems.*** The robot's world model can be continually updated, on the basis of new sensory input, and can also generate expectations about how the view will transform under movements in progress. The world model's hypotheses in turn aid in the interpretation of incoming sensory data. The most advanced robot sensory systems are multimodal (based on several senses), and are also hierarchically structured to generate successive levels of description, at increasing degrees of complexity and decreasing rates, suited to use by the successive levels of a hierarchical control system (Fig. 4).

**Applications and forms of robots.** The majority of robots are of the six-axis, jointed-arm variety, such as those depicted in Fig. 1. However, this basic type has been produced in a very large variety of sizes, shapes, and capacities which have been applied to a wide variety of tasks.

The initial impetus for robotics was to replace humans in heavy, repetitive labor, and to replace hard-automation (fixed-function) machinery with more flexible equipment which could be reprogrammed. Also, because of their initial limited sensory abilities, robots were best suited to those tasks with clearly prescribed paths of motion. Thus, the earliest applications of robots were found in tasks such as lifting parts to and from pallets and conveyors, loading automated machinery, and welding and spray-painting items traveling down assembly lines. By virtue of their earlier start, these applications numerically dominate the field of robotics.

The robots employed for these purposes range from small models with lifting capacities of several pounds to very large types which can lift many hundreds of pounds. In many lifting and placing tasks, less than six degrees of freedom are required, and many industrial robots have three, four, or five degrees of freedom. Designs also vary according to the size and shape of the work-volume required by the task; for example, many robots are designed to reach a full circle around themselves, because this enables them to achieve high productivity by tending several machines simultaneously.

With later developments in robotics, new industrial applications exploited the robot's speed and precision in such tasks as drilling and other light machining, gluing and fastening, simple assembly, packing and sealing, and testing and measuring. The machines developed for these tasks may have a repeatability of movement of better than 0.001 in. (25 micrometers), yet be able to move at high rates from one position to another; usually they are not adapted to heavy payloads. These robots are often fitted with highly specialized, changeable end-effectors which are actually automated tools in their own right. Robots of this sort are almost invariably of the continuous-path type because of the frequent necessity of following complex trajectories. Their control systems are correspondingly more elaborate, and frequently include sensory capability. Devices of this sort may, for example, place components into printed circuit boards, with very small clearances, after visually locating positioning marks on the circuit board.

***Assembly tasks.*** Complex assembly tasks are prominent among the robot applications which have emerged with the more sophisticated sensory capabilities of robots. Such robots must be capable of locating and positioning complex three-dimensional parts, mating them to high tolerances, and then performing a variety of complex joining operations, such as screwing in bolts. Robot manipulators for assembly often have more than six degrees of freedom; this allows them to reach a given position and orientation in more than one way (for example, to avoid hitting an obstructing part). They are usually equipped with force-torque sensors or tactile sensors of some sort to enable them to feel, and adaptively respond to, insertion forces that would result in sticking and jamming of parts during positioning and mating. Since assembly usually implies a variety of parts present in the workspace, vision is often included to enable the robot to identify and locate parts for assembly; the alternative is complex or inflexible parts-presentation machinery. Vision capabilities required for assembly range in practice from simple to very complex. In many cases, parts have only a few stable positions in which they rest, and recognition and location of two-dimensional outlines is sufficient to acquire and orient them, particularly if they are separated. The most complex tasks involve picking jumbled, mixed parts from bins, and this capability is not yet found in commercial robots.

***Mobile robots.*** Simple mobile robots have long been employed for materials movement in factories, mail delivery within office buildings, and similar tasks requiring intelligent choice of path and a limited ability to avoid obstacles. Mobile robots for the home are available, although they have, as yet, little function other than novelty and entertainment. Developments in robot control and sensing, combined with advances in mechanisms for robot locomotion, promise to generate a significant expansion of applications for mobile robots. Among those applications are robots for guard and sentry duty and for commerical cleaning and vacuuming. Research and development has been undertaken on robots for agriculture, construction, mining, fire fighting, rescue, handling of hazardous materials, and undersea exploration. In some cases this involves the provision of sensory, world-modeling, and control devices for existing machines which already possess mobility and actuators, such as earth-moving equipment. In other cases, wholly new devices have been designed.

One of the principal problems in mobile robotics is the enhanced sensory requirement imposed by navigation in an unpredictable environment. For this reason, a truly autonomous mobile robot is not yet in sight for most outdoor uses. In many applications, however, semiautonomous robots can be employed to advantage. An interesting concept is robot ships which will have the capacity to deal with ordinary problems of ship operation, but which will be employed in convoys following a lead ship with a crew aboard. Similar concepts in land vehicles have also been considered.

***Robot factory.*** Among the most complex applications of robotics is the robot factory. This is not a factory in which robots are used, even to the exclusion of human workers, but rather a factory which is itself a robot. That is, it is a collection of production machines, robot manipulators, materials handling systems, and other devices, all of which usually have their own local intelligence, but all of which are connected with, and coordinated and organized by a central control system which plans the operations and scheduling of production, and employs its resources in a flexible manner to accomplish its goals. Some commercial manufacturing systems are in place which trend strongly in this direction, without yet being fully self-sufficient. Experimental robotic factory systems, such as the Automated Manufacturing Research Facility at the U.S. National Bureau of Standards, are already fully automatic, although limited to simple machining. Research is expected to give such systems the ability to handle all phases of manufacturing, including process planning, scheduling, and production operations, when supplied with specifications for the desired product. *SEE COMPUTER-INTEGRATED MANUFACTURING.*

**Emerging areas.** As robots become more complex, they quickly exhaust the capacity of traditional computers. Computer science in robotics is focusing on the design of parallel multicomputer systems, and ultimately may evolve entirely special-purpose hardware for robot "brains." The robot factory presages the development of other robotic systems composed of multiple individual machines. The growth of robotic technology is also producing new disciplines concerned with the utilization, economics, and societal impact of robots. As robotics matures, these concerns can be expected to assume a major role in the field. *SEE CONCURRENT PROCESSING; INTELLIGENT MACHINE; MULTIPROCESSING.*

*Ernest W. Kent*

***Bibliography.*** M. Brady et al. (eds.), *Robot Motion*, 1982; W. B. Gevarter, *An Overview of Artificial Intelligence and Robotics*, vol. 2: *Robotics*, NBSIR 82–2479, U.S. Department of Commerce, March 1982; R. P. Paul, *Robot Manipulators: Mathematics, Programming, and Control*, 1981; W. E. Snyder, *Industrial Robots: Computer Interfacing and Control*, 1985.

## Rochelle salt

The sodium potassium salt of the *d*-tartaric acid $NaKC_4H_4O_6 \cdot 4H_2O$, also called Seignette salt, the first crystalline solid discovered to possess the properties of ferroelectricity. Such crystals are grown easily and have been widely used, for example, in microphones and phonograph pickup cartridges, because of their large piezoelectric effect. *SEE PIEZOELECTRICITY.*

The crystal structure has orthorhombic symmetry (point group 222) above 75°F (24°C) and below 0°F (−18°C). Between these Curie temperatures the crystal is ferroelectric, having a spontaneous polarization along the **a** axis and a spontaneous shear deformation $y_z$ in the (100) plane. This reduces the symmetry to monoclinic. In general, the crystal consists of ferroelectric domains of opposite polarization direction. By applying an electric field along the **a** axis or a shear stress $Y_z$ the spontaneous polarization can be aligned and reversed (hysteresis). Its highest value of $2.5 \times 10^{-3}$ coulomb/m$^2$ ($2.3 \times 10^{-4}$ coulomb/ft$^2$) is reached at about 37°F (3°C). The dielectric constant shows peak values of several thousand at the Curie points. It drops, according to the Curie-Weiss law, on both sides of the ferroelectric temperature range. *SEE FERROELECTRICS.*

For technical applications the anomalously large effects are impaired by the narrow temperature range of ferroelectric behavior and by the limited stability of the crystals with respect to temperature and humidity.

*H. Granicher*

***Bibliography.*** W. G. Cady, *Piezoelectricity*, 1964; J. M. Herbert, *Ferroelectric Transducers and Sensors*, 1982; M. E. Lines and A. M. Glass, *Principles and Applications of Ferroelectrics and Related Materials*, 1977; T. Mitsui, *An Introduction to the Physics of Ferroelectrics*, 1976.

## Sampling voltmeter

A special class of voltmeter that uses sampling techniques and is particularly effective in measuring high-frequency signals or signals mixed with noise. High-frequency sampling instruments can operate on signals with frequencies as high as 12 GHz and amplitudes as small as 1 mV. Measurements are generally of average-absolute or root-mean-square voltage with accuracies of 5–10%. Sampling voltmeters, as conventional voltmeters, may use scale and pointer meters, graphic recorders, cathode-ray tubes, or digital-type indicators for readout of measured quantities. *SEE VOLTAGE MEASUREMENT.*

**Sampling technique.** The sampling technique detects the instantaneous value of an input signal at prescribed times by means of an electronic switch connecting the signal to a memory capacitor. Waveforms of the input signal and the sampled signal that appears across the memory capacitor are shown in simplified form in **Fig. 1**. At the points in time indicated by the heavy dots on the input signal voltage waveform, the switch is closed for a very short interval and the memory capacitor is thereby briefly connected to the signal. The connection generates a sample; that is, the capacitor charges to a voltage proportional to the input voltage at the instant of sampling. After a sample the capacitor voltage remains constant until the next sample is taken. The sampled voltage from this type of sample-and-hold circuit is an approximate replica of the signal waveform assembled bit by bit and therefore at a much lower frequency. The input signal frequency $F_1$, the output sampled voltage frequency $F_0$, and the frequency of sampling $F_S$ are related by $F_1 - NF_S = F_0$, where $N$ is a whole number closest to the number of cycles of input signal between sam-

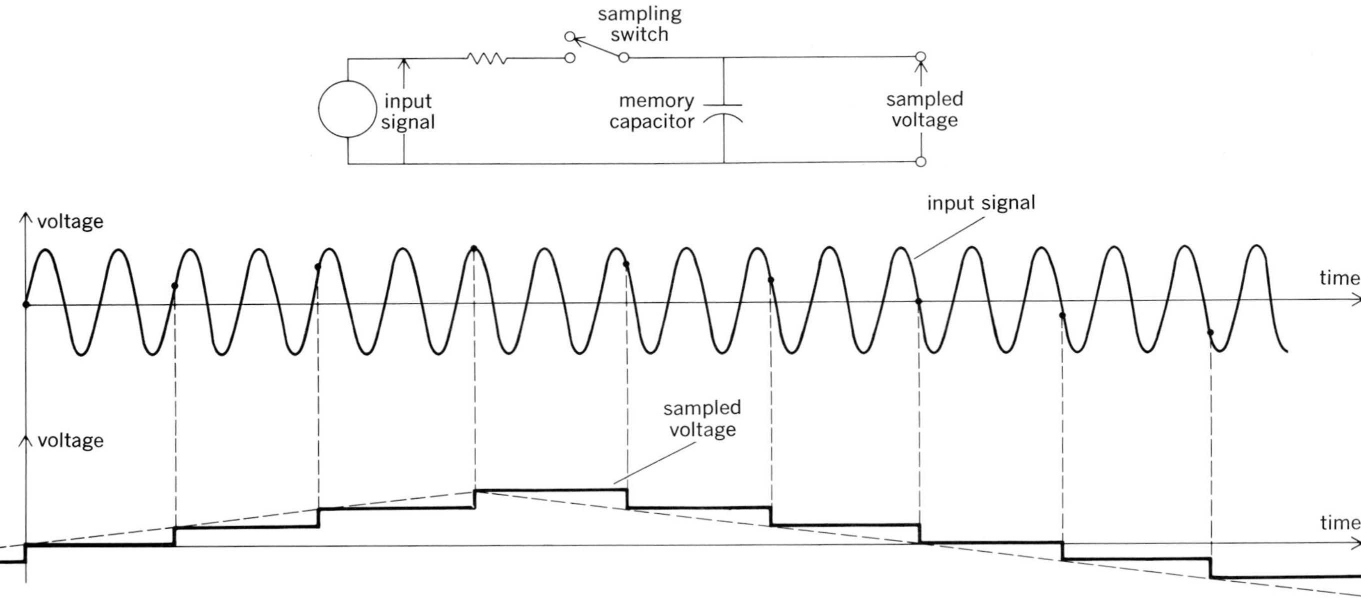


**Fig. 1. Simplified sampling circuit and waveforms.**

ples (two in the waveforms above). By proper adjustment of frequencies and by filtering, the sampled signal waveform may be made to be an extremely exact waveform replica of the input signal. Since the reproduced waveform is on a different time scale than the original, the type of sampling described above is sometimes called equivalent-time sampling. Equivalent-time sampling is analogous to the apparent slowing of motion of rotating machinery when viewed with stroboscopic light. In that case the eye is briefly exposed to the high-frequency rotating object by the flash of light that illuminates the object approximately every $N$ rotations. The after-image characteristic of the eye serves to hold the brief image or sample until the next sample is produced. If the flashing rate is made exactly equal to a subharmonic of the rotation rate ($NF_S = F_1$), motion of the object appears to be stopped. In the electrical case this corresponds to sampling the input signal at the same point in its cycle, with every sample producing a constant (dc) output sampled voltage. If $NF_S$ is made greater than $F_1$, the rotating object appears to move backward and an electrical sampled voltage waveform will also appear reversed in time. SEE CAPACITOR.

For instrumentation purposes the principal advantage of equivalent-time sampling is that the low-frequency sampled output voltage is a replica of the high-frequency input and it can be measured by means that, because of economic or technological limitations, cannot be extended in frequency response to directly measure the input signal.

**High-frequency sampling voltmeter.** High-frequency voltmeters consist of the sample-and-hold circuits described in principle above, conventional voltmeter circuits, and synchronizing circuitry to adjust the sampling frequency to a value that maintains the sampled signal frequency within the proper range for the voltmeter circuits. The vector voltmeter described below synchronizes the sampling frequency by sweeping it until the sampled output is at the proper frequency. The sampling rate is then maintained at the correct value by means of a phase-lock servomechanism or feedback system that compares the output signal phase to the phase of a reference signal and uses the phase error to maintain the proper sampling rate. SEE VOLTMETER.

The sampling gate must be extremely fast to measure high-frequency signals. It must connect the input signal and the memory capacitor for a time interval that is short compared to the minimum period of the input signal. Highly specialized techniques are used to generate gate durations as short as 30 picoseconds. Light, which can travel to the Moon in about 1.5 s, moves only 0.9 cm in 30 ps.

**Vector voltmeter.** The vector-type voltmeter is a two-channel high-frequency sampling voltmeter that measures phase as well as voltage of two input signals of the same frequency. The two signals are sampled at the same instant of time to produce corresponding sampled waveforms that have the same phase relationship as do the input signals. Since both input signals must have the same frequency to make phase measurements meaningful, only one phase-lock synchronizing circuit is needed.

**Random-sampling voltmeter.** This class of sampling voltmeter takes advantage of random sampling to simplify or eliminate the synchronizing portions of the instrument. If samples of an input signal are taken at random times instead of at a controlled constant rate, the result is loss of waveform information in the output. However, the amplitude statistics are pre-

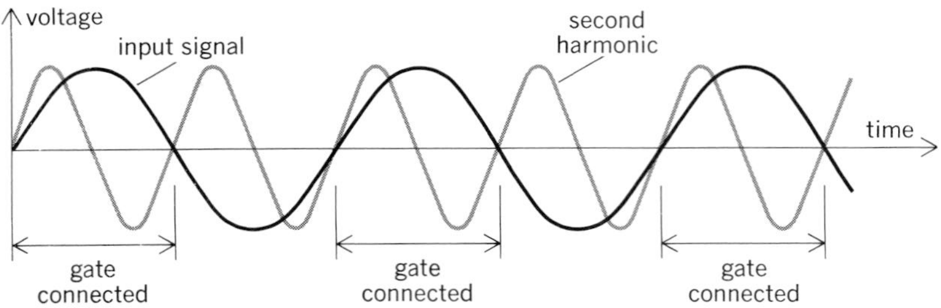


**Fig. 2. Waveforms and timing for synchronous rectifier.**

served; that is, the average, peak, root-mean-square, and other values of a random-sampled signal are the same as those of the input signal. The effect is as though the individual samples of a regularly sampled signal were stored and then replayed in random time order. The randomness in time of sampling does not have to be exact to preserve amplitude statistics. Simple variations such as low-frequency modulation of the sampling rate are satisfactory in most cases. Random sampling requires no information on input or sampled signal frequency, and synchronizing circuits are therefore not required.

**Noise reduction techniques.** Conventional sampling techniques are limited to operation only on periodic input signals. Techniques that recognize this periodicity and thereby reduce the effects of noise upon a signal may be employed in voltage measurement. Instruments that use signal enhancement techniques generally operate at requencies of less than 1 MHz and have relatively long gate durations. The sampling circuits may operate with sampling gate alternately connected to the input signal for one-half cycle and then disconnected for one-half cycle as shown in **Fig. 2**. During the connected intervals the input signal is integrated or, more properly, averaged. When gate and signal are related as shown, operation is similar to that of a half-wave rectifier circuit, and a large average results. Odd harmonics of the signal produce an average whose amplitude diminishes inversely as the harmonic number. Even harmonics such as the second harmonic shown have an average value of zero during the gate duration and therefore ideally produce no response. Most noise signals, including white noise, which has a symmetrical gaussian amplitude distribution, produce an average near zero for long averaging times. Signals that are not of the same basic frequency as the gating frequency also tend to produce small average values. The synchronous rectifier thus responds to a signal of the proper frequency and its odd harmonics, but rejects even harmonics and most noise. This narrow-band property improves small-signal capabilities of synchronous-rectifier instruments. A synchronous-rectifier type voltmeter may measure signals in the microvolt amplitude range with 3–10% accuracies even when these signals are accompanied by noise with an amplitude up to 10 times the signal amplitude. Extensive synchronizing circuits such as those described for high-frequency sampling voltmeters are used to capture and lock the sampling rate to the signal frequency.

A variety of sampling systems are available for signal enhancement; some systems with other than half-wave gating are capable of full waveform recovery.

*James K. Skilling*

**Bibliography.** A. B. Carlson, *Communication Systems*, 2d ed., 1974; B. P. Lathi, *Signals, Systems and Controls*, 1974; M. Schwartz, *Information Transmission Modulation and Noise*, 3d ed., 1980.

## Saturation

The condition in which, after a sufficient increase in a causal force, further increase in the force produces no additional increase in the resultant effect. Many natural phenomena display saturation. For example, after a magnetizing force becomes sufficiently strong, further increase in the force produces no additional magnetization in a magnetic circuit; all the magnetic domains have been aligned, and the magnetic material is saturated.

After a sponge has absorbed all the liquid it can hold, it is saturated. In thermionic vacuum tubes thermal saturation is reached when further increase in cathode temperature produces no (or negligible) increase in cathode current: anode saturation is reached when further increase in plate voltage produces substantially no increase in anode current. SEE DISTORTION (ELECTRONIC CIRCUITS); VACUUM TUBE.

In an *npn* transistor when the collector voltage becomes more negative than the base voltage, the base-to-collector diode becomes forward-biased: the collector then emits and the transistor is saturated. Current flow is controlled by a stored charge of carriers in the base region. SEE SEMICONDUCTOR; TRANSISTOR.

In colorimetry the purer a color is, the higher its saturation. Radiation from a color of low saturation contains frequencies throughout much of the visible spectrum.

In an induced nuclear reaction, saturation exists when the decay rate of a given radionuclide is equal to its rate of production. In an ionization chamber, saturation exists when the applied voltage is high enough to collect all the ions formed by radiation but not high enough to produce ionization by collision. When addition of the dissolved species produces no further increase in the concentration of a solution at a certain temperature and pressure, the solution is said to be saturated.

*Frank H. Rockett*

## Saturation current

A term having a variety of specific applications but generally meaning the maximum current which can be obtained under certain conditions.

In a simple two-element vacuum tube, it refers to either the space-charge-limited current on one hand or the temperature-limited current on the other. In the first case, further increase in filament temperature produces no significant increase in anode current, whereas in the latter a further increase in voltage produces only a relatively small increase in current. SEE VACUUM TUBE.

In a gaseous-discharge device, the saturation current is the maximum current which can be obtained for a given mode of discharge. Attempts to increase the current result in a different type of discharge. Such a case would be the transition from a glow discharge to an arc discharge. SEE ELECTRICAL CONDUCTION IN GASES.

A third case is that of a semiconductor. Here again the saturation current is that maximum current which just precedes a change in conduction mode. SEE SEMICONDUCTOR.

*Glenn H. Miller*

## Sawtooth-wave generator

A device which generates a current or voltage waveform whose magnitude is a continuously increasing function of time for a fixed interval, and then repeats the sequence periodically. The most widely used sawtooth waveform is ideally a linear function of time during the forward or rising interval and appears as

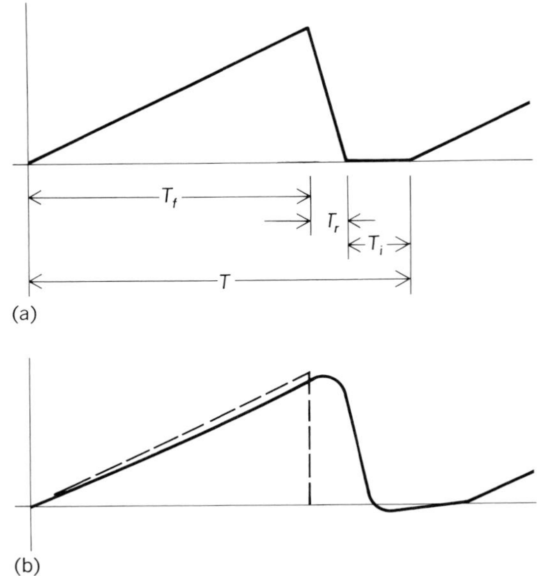

**Fig. 1. Sawtooth wave. (*a*) An ideal linear sawtooth. (*b*) Approximate sawtooth generated by actual circuits.**

shown in **Fig. 1***a*, with the total period $T$ made up of the active forward interval $T_f$, a retrace interval $T_r$, and an inactive interval $T_i$. Often it is desirable to make the two intervals $T_r$ and $T_i$ as small as possible, with $T_i$ often being zero.

Mathematically the sawtooth wave may be expressed in terms of a Fourier series of harmonically related components with the fundamental having a period equal to the total period $T$ of the sawtooth. If a sufficient number of harmonics having the proper amplitude and phase relationships is included, the mathematical representation will be an accurate approximation of the waveform.

Electronic circuits can generate only an approximation of the idealized waveform which, as a result, tends to have deviations which are often of the type shown in Fig. 1*b*. Generally the delayed start (with respect to the ideal) and the extended retrace time are caused by high-frequency deficiencies (inadequate generation or transmission of the higher-order harmonics), whereas the inability to maintain a constant slope for large values of $T_f$ is a low-frequency deficiency in the generation or transmission of components near the fundamental frequency.

Sawtooth waveforms are used as time-base elements or sweep generators and in time-delay and time-measuring equipment. SEE SWEEP GENERATOR.

**Sawtooth voltage generation.** The complexity of electronic circuitry required to generate linear sawtooth voltage waves depends upon the accuracy to which such generation is specified. An approximate linear sawtooth may be generated by a dc voltage source, a series *RC* circuit, and a switch which has a small but nonzero resistance when closed. This elementary sawtooth generator is shown schematically in **Fig. 2**.

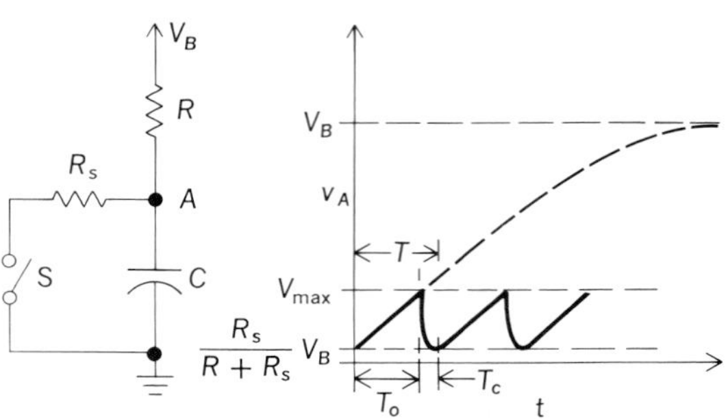

**Fig. 2. Elements of sawtooth sweep circuit.**

If the switch S in the illustration is suddenly opened, the voltage at point A will rise from an initial value of $V_B R_s/(R + R_s)$ toward $V_B$ according to exponential equation as shown by the dashed curve in Fig. 2. Now if the switch is closed after a time $T_o$, the rise will be interrupted at a value $V_{max}$ obtained from the solution for $v_A$ in Eq. (1) for $t = T_o$. While

$$v_A = \frac{R_s}{R + R_s} V_B + V_B \left(1 - \frac{R_s}{R + R_s}\right)(1 - \epsilon^{-(t/RC)}) \quad (1)$$

the switch is closed during the period $T_c$ the potential will fall in accordance with Eq. (2).

$$v_A = \frac{R_s}{R + R_s} V_B + \left(V_{max} - \frac{R_s}{R + R_s} V_B\right) \epsilon^{-(t/R_sC)} \quad (2)$$

If $R_s$ is very small, the waveform will essentially have recovered to its initial value in a short retrace interval $T_r$ less than $T_o$. This complete cycle will repeat itself for alternate opening and closing of the switch. If the time $T_c$ during which the switch is closed is less than the time $T_r$ required for complete recovery, the minimum value for the waveform will be higher than $V_B R_s/(R + R_s)$. The maximum and minimum excursions of the waveform can then be found by simultaneous solution of Eqs. (1) and (2) for the appropriate periods, $T_0$ and $T_c$.

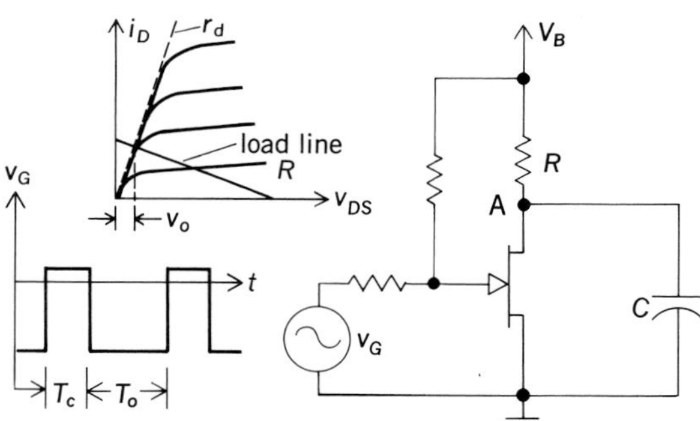

**Fig. 3. Pulsed triode sawtooth generator.**

A periodic sawtooth waveform can be generated by using an astable relaxation oscillator as a switch in the above circuit. When used as switches in sawtooth generators, relaxation oscillators may be synchronized with external pulses to maintain an accurately controlled period. SEE RELAXATION OSCILLATOR.

If the switch of Fig. 2 is the switch in a synchronous or keyed clamp each interval of the total period of the waveform may be controlled directly from an external source of pulses. A simple triode unidirectional clamp using an *n*-channel junction field-effect transistor (FET) is shown in **Fig. 3**. During the time $T_c$ that the switch is closed, the gate is held at a

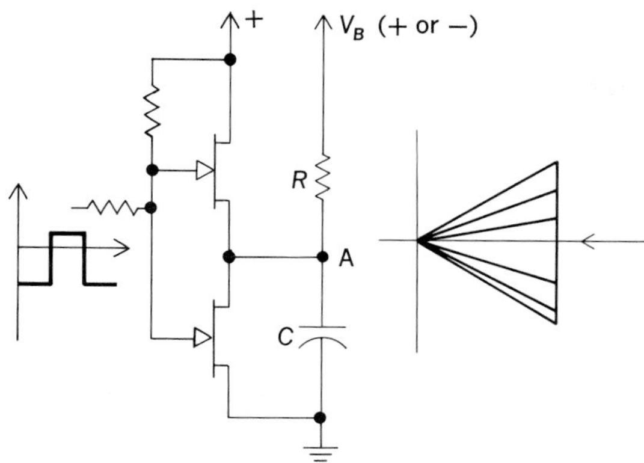


**Fig. 4. Sweep generator using bidirectional clamp.**

slightly positive value by limiting, and the drain resistance $r_d$ is low. During the open time, the gate voltage is sufficiently negative that no drain current will flow and the switch is open.

The use of a *p*-channel FET together with a negative value for $V_B$ and negative control pulses would produce a negative-going sawtooth. *See* Clamping circuit.

Either a positive-going or a negative-going sawtooth may be generated by making $V_B$ either positive or negative and replacing the clamp with a bidirectional clamp as shown in **Fig. 4**. If the potential $V_B$ is variable at a rate which is slow compared to the periodicity of the waveform, a succession of sawtooth waveforms of varying amplitude will be generated. One particular application of such a circuit would be to generate one of the components of the rotating radial sweep if $V_B$ were to be made to vary sinusoidally with the desired angular modulation.

***Improvement of linearity.*** A linearly increasing voltage $v_c$, given by Eq. (3), will appear across the terminals of a capacitor $C$ if a constant current $I_c$ is flowing, since Eq. (4) applies. Therefore, improvement of

$$v_c = (I_c/C)t \tag{3}$$

$$v_c = (1/C) \int I_c dt \tag{4}$$

linearity of the simple *RC* sawtooth generators basically depends upon keeping the current through the capacitor more constant. For a specified sawtooth amplitude this may be done by increasing the supply voltage $V_B$. This is a practical solution only within narrow limits. Another method in effect replaces $R$ with an active device, such as the output circuit of a transistor, which has a relatively low absolute resistance but an extremely high ac or incremental resistance over the limits of the desired amplitude range. In the circuit of **Fig. 5**, when point A is not clamped to the ground and the base-emitter bias voltage, as determined by the diode operating in the Zener breakdown region, is such that the transistor is in its normal range, the collector current will be relatively independent of collector voltage.

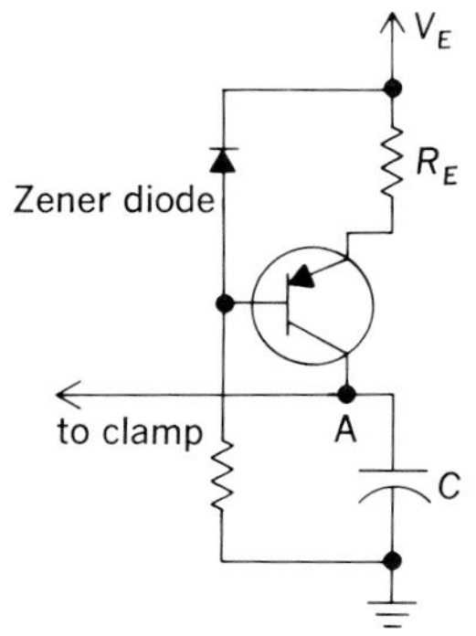

**Fig. 5. Constant-current sawtooth generator.**

The circuit of **Fig. 6** often referred to as the bootstrap sawtooth generator. When the clamp is closed, point $A$ is at ground potential, point B is at $V_B$ minus the small diode voltage drop, and point C is approximately at the potential of A if the amplifier is direct-coupled and noninverting with near unity gain and has high input and low output impedance. In other words, the amplifier is an emitter follower. When the clamp is opened, capacitor $C$ starts to charge toward $V_B$ through $R$ and the diode resistance. Point C follows closely since the amplifier gain is close to unity. If capacitor $C_f$ is very large compared to capacitor $C$, point B will rise the same amount. This causes the diode to stop conducting. Capacitor $C$ will continue to charge through $R$ and $C_f$. If sufficiently large, $C_f$ functions as a constant-voltage source, and to the extent that it does, and if the gain of the amplifier is near but less than unity, the charging current will be nearly constant and a nearly linear sawtooth of a magnitude approaching the supply voltage can be gener-

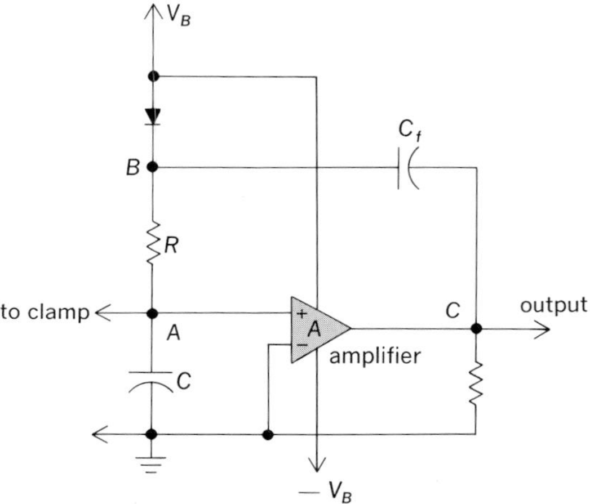


**Fig. 6. Bootstrap sawtooth generator.**

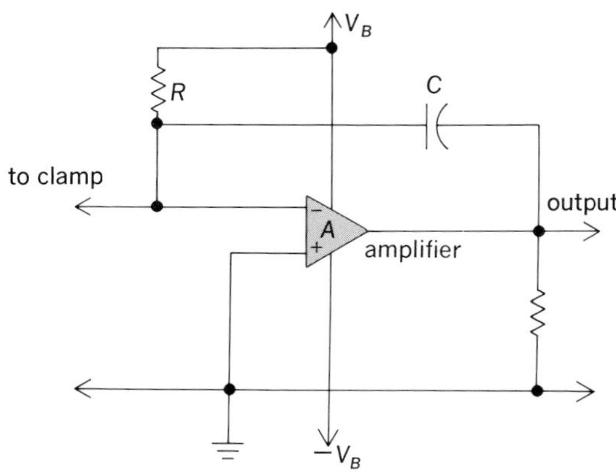


**Fig. 7. Basic Miller integrator.**

ated. To a good approximation, the voltage at point C can be expressed by Eq. (5), where $A$ is the voltage

$$v_C(t) = AV_B \frac{C_f}{C + C_f(1 - A)} (1 - \epsilon^{-[C + C_f(1-A)/RCC_f]t}) \quad (5)$$

gain of the amplifier. If $C_f$ is much larger than $C$, this is an exponential charging curve with an effective supply voltage of $(A/1 - A)\ V_B$. If $A$ is near unity, this represents a great increase in effective supply voltage and a corresponding increase in linearity for a required amplitude. It can be shown that with an amplifier gain slightly greater than unity, a condition for an exactly linearly rising voltage can be established.

A circuit in which an integrating amplifier is used in addition to the clamp and $RC$ time constant is sometimes referred to as the Miller integrating circuit (**Fig. 7**). If the input impedance of the amplifier is high, the output impedance low, and the gain high, the output approximates the integral of the suddenly impressed constant-amplitude supply voltage $V_B$. The approximate equation of the output waveform is given by Eq. (6), where $A$ is the magnitude of the gain of

$$v_O = -AV_B (1 - \epsilon^{-(t/ARC)}) \quad (6)$$

the amplifier. The result will be a negative-going sawtooth, the first part of an exponential charging toward the effective supply voltage $-AV_B$. Thus the linearity is increased by the same amount that a charging voltage $V_B$ multiplied by a factor $A$ would increase it.

***Hyperbolic and other waveforms.*** A sawtooth waveform other than linear may be generated by using $RC$ circuits more complicated in form than the simple ones which have been described. For example, the bootstrap generator shown in **Fig. 8** generates an approximate hyperbola.

**Sawtooth current generation.** Often a sawtooth current waveform must be applied to a circuit having an inductive component, such as the deflection coil of a magnetically deflected cathode-ray device. If the coil can be represented by an inductance and resistance in series as shown in **Fig. 9**, the voltage appearing across the terminals of the coil will be given by Eq. (7), and if the current $i(t)$ is specified as a

$$v = Ri(t) + L\frac{di(t)}{dt} \quad (7)$$

linear sawtooth, $i(t) = kt$, then the voltage will be given by Eq. (8). This voltage is a step added to a

$$v = Rkt + Lk \quad (8)$$

linear sawtooth as shown. Such a voltage waveform, required for a linear sawtooth of current, may be generated by using any of the previous circuits with an additional circuit element $R_2$ as shown in **Fig. 10**. Initially, since the voltage across $C$ cannot change instantaneously when the clamp is opened, the total voltage $V_B$ will divide between $R$ and $R_2$, making the potential at point A suddenly rise to $V_BR_2/(R + R_2)$.

A more common method of generating a current waveform is to generate a voltage waveform of the same form and apply it to a negative feedback amplifier with a large amount of current feedback, which forces the current in the coil to be approximately the form of the generated voltage. Such a system is shown in block form in **Fig. 11**. Such current feedback makes the output impedance of the amplifier high and thus approximates a current source which is a replica of the applied voltage.

If dc levels do not have to be preserved, the deflection coils may be transformer-coupled to the output device as shown in **Fig. 12**.

**High-frequency limitations.** Any actual deflection coil can be represented as a series inductance and re-

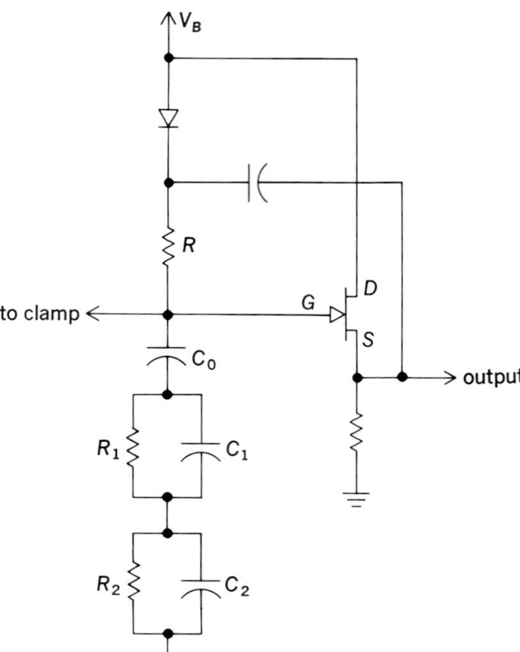

**Fig. 8. Hyperbolic sweep generator.**

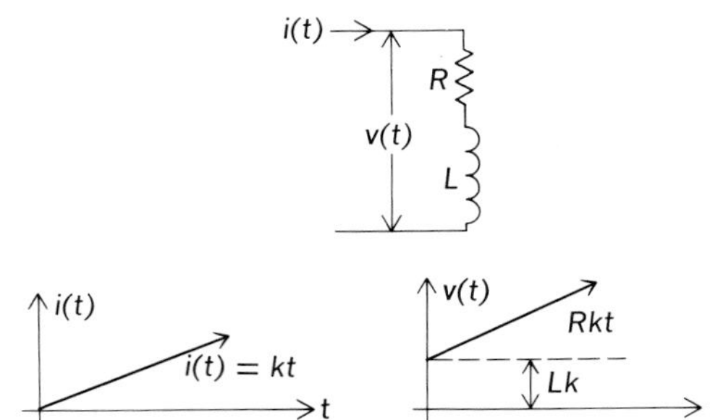

**Fig. 9. Linear current in inductive circuit.**

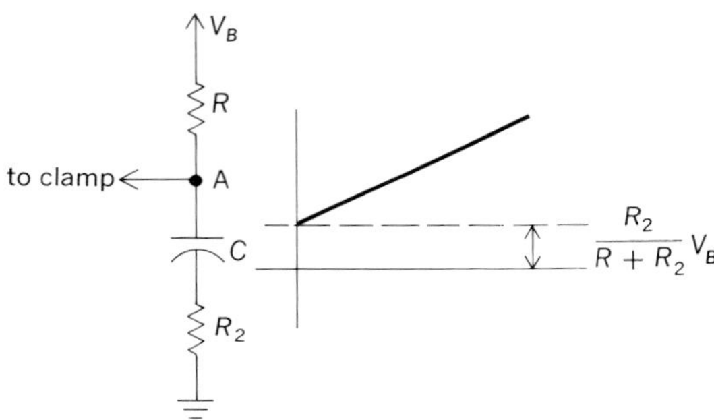

**Fig. 10. Trapezoid voltage generator.**

sistance only at relatively low frequencies. It also has distributed capacitance, which can be represented crudely by a shunt capacitance as in **Fig. 13**. This capacitance accounts principally for the delay in the start of the sweep and for the minimum retrace time $T_r$ necessary for recovery. The best conditions occur when the oscillatory circuit is critically damped by the addition of the shunt resistance $R$. Typical sweep waveforms for critical damping and departures from it are shown.

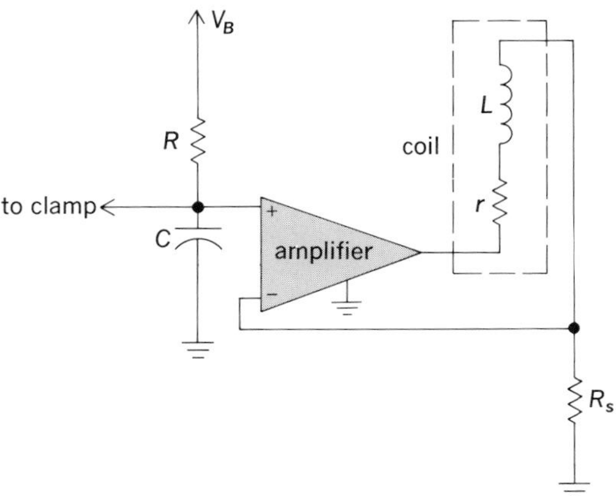


**Fig. 11. Current feedback sweep generator.**

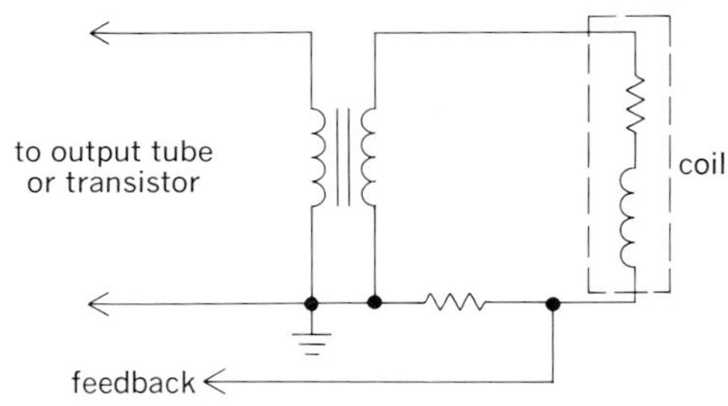


**Fig. 12. Transformer-coupled deflection coil.**

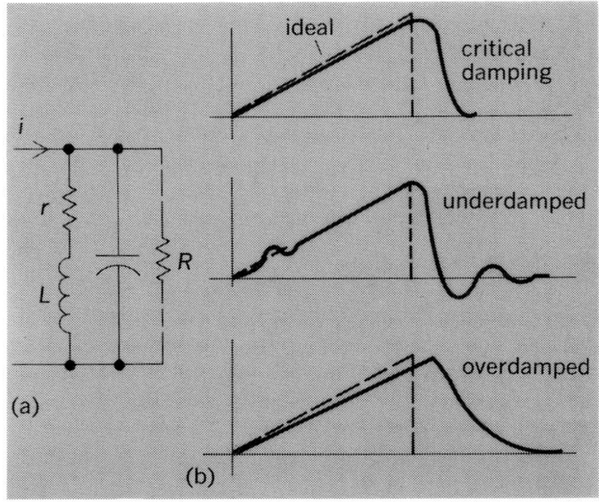


**Fig. 13. Effect of shunt capacitance on deflection system. (*a*) Circuit diagram. (*b*) Typical waveforms.**

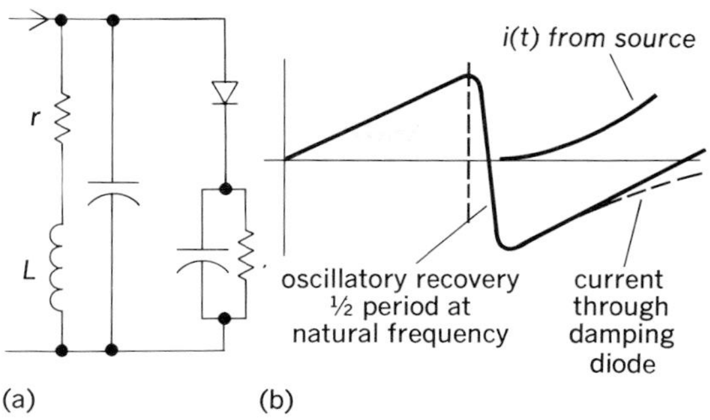


**Fig. 14. Deflection system with diode damping. (*a*) Circuit diagram. (*b*) Typical waveform.**

The horizontal deflection circuit of the television system represents a special case where the circuit is underdamped, or allowed to be oscillatory, for half a period with the beginning of the sweep waveform controlled by special diode circuits as shown in **Fig. 14**. For other types of waves *SEE WAVE-SHAPING CIRCUITS*.

*Glenn M. Glasford*

***Bibliography***. J. J. Brophy, *Basic Electronics for Scientists*, 4th ed., 1983; G. M. Glasford, *Fundamentals of Television Engineering*, 1955; J. Millman, *Microelectronics*, 1979; J. Millman and H. Taub, *Pulse, Digital, and Switching Waveforms*, 1965; L. Strauss, *Wave Generation and Shaping*, 2d ed., 1970.

## Schottky effect

The enhancement of the thermionic emission of a conductor resulting from an electric field at the conductor surface. Since the thermionic emission current is given by the Richardson formula, an increase in the current at a given temperature implies a reduction in the work function $\phi$ of the emitter. *SEE WORK FUNCTION (ELECTRONICS); THERMIONIC EMISSION*.

With reference to **Fig. 1**, let the vacuum level represent the energy of an electron at rest in free space and let *CD* be the energy of a conduction electron at rest in a metal. If an electron approaches the metal surface from infinity, its potential energy *V* relative to the vacuum level is given by the well-known image potential $V(x) = -e^2/4x$, where $x$ is the distance from the surface, and $e = 1.6 \times 10^{-19}$ coulomb is the electron's charge. The image potential is valid only for $x > x_0$, where $x_0$ is of the order of the distance between neighboring atoms in the metal; that is, $x_0$ is a few angstroms. In the absence of an applied field, *CAB* then represents the potential energy of an electron as a function of $x$. *AB* corresponds to the image potential; the exact shape of the curve between *C* and *A* is uncertain.

Suppose now a constant field $F$ is applied externally between the surface of the emitting cathode and an anode; this produces a potential energy of an electron of $-eFx$ (line *PQ* in Fig. 1), and hence the total potential energy of an electron for $x > x_0$ is given by Eq. (1), indicated by the dashed line *CAQ* in Fig. 1.

$$V(x) = \frac{e^2}{4x} - eFx \qquad (1)$$

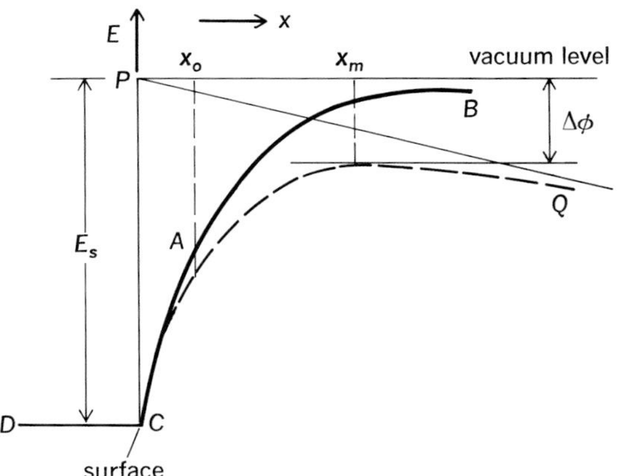


Fig. 1. Surface potential barrier and Schottky effect; the lowering of the work function $\Delta\phi$ is highly exaggerated.

This function has a maximum value given by Eq. (2).

$$x = x_m = {}^1\!/_2 \left(\frac{e}{F}\right)^{1/2} \quad (2)$$

The maximum lies below the vacuum level by an amount $\Delta\phi$, given in Eq. (3), which represents the

$$\Delta\Phi = V(x_m) = -e(eF)^{1/2} \quad (3)$$

reduction in the work function of the metal. For $F$ = 1000 volt/cm, $x_m \cong 10^{-5}$ cm and $\Delta\phi \cong 10^{-2}$ eV; the actual change in the work function is thus small. If a field is present, the work function $\phi$ in the Richardson formula should be replaced by $(\phi - \Delta\phi)$. Hence, the current increases by the factor given by notation (4).

$$\exp\,[(e/kT)\,(eF)^{1/2}] \quad (4)$$

According to this interpretation, a plot of the logarithm of the current versus the square root of the anode voltage should yield a straight line. An example is given in **Fig. 2** for tungsten; the deviation from the straight line for low anode voltages is due to space-charge effects. *See Space charge.*

The straight portion of the line (the Schottky line) confirms the interpretation; the true saturation current for zero field is obtained by extrapolation of the Schottky line as indicated. Detailed studies have shown extremely small periodic deviations with reference to the Schottky line; these deviations are interpreted on the basis of the wave-mechanical theory describing the motion of electrons across the image potential barrier shown in Fig. 1.

*Adrianus J. Dekker*

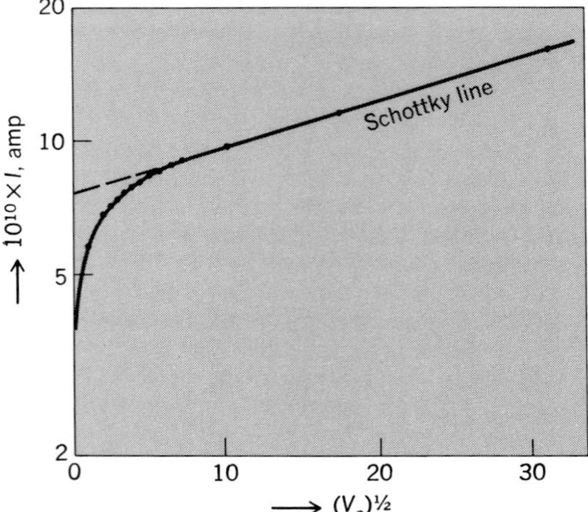


Fig. 2. Logarithm of thermionic emission current $I$ of tungsten as function of square root of anode voltage $V_a$. (After W. B. Nottingham, Phys. Rev., 58:927-928, 1940)

## Secondary emission

The emission of electrons from the surface of a solid into vacuum caused by bombardment with charged particles, in particular, with electrons. The mechanism of secondary emission under ion bombardment is quite different from that under electron bombardment; the discussion here is limited to the latter case because it is in this sense that the term secondary emission is generally used.

The bombarding electrons and the emitted electrons are referred to, respectively, as primaries and secondaries. Secondary emission has important practical applications because the secondary yield, that is, the number of secondaries emitted per incident primary, may exceed unity. Thus, secondary emitters are used in electron multipliers, especially in photomultipliers, and in other electronic devices such as television pickup tubes, storage tubes for electronic computers, and so on.

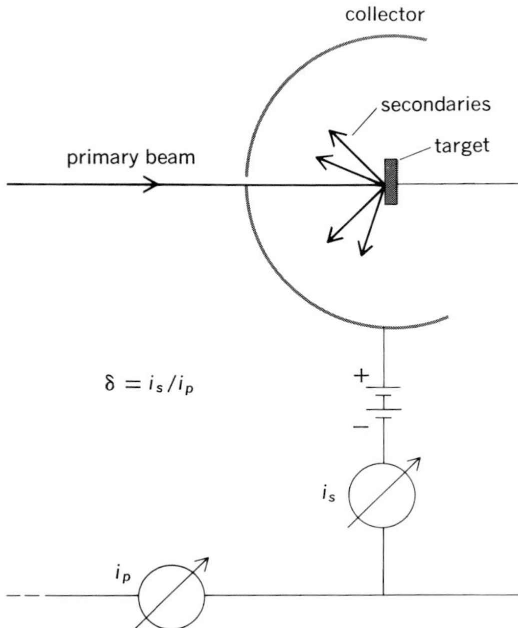


Fig. 1. Schematic circuit for measuring secondary yield; $i_p$ and $i_s$ represent the primary and secondary currents.

**Secondary yield.** The most thoroughly investigated property of secondary emission is the yield as a function of the energy of the primaries. The yield may be measured by means of the circuit shown schematically in **Fig. 1**. A beam of primary electrons strikes a target with an energy determined by the potential difference between the target and the cathode. The primary beam passes through a hole in the collector, which has been made positive with respect to the target. The secondaries emitted by the target then flow to the collector, and the yield is obtained as the ratio of the secondary current $i_s$ to the primary current $i_p$.

**Mechanism of the process.** The emission of secondary electrons can be described as the result of three processes: (1) excitation of electrons in the solid into high-energy states by the impact of high-energy primary electrons, (2) transport of these secondary electrons to the solid-vacuum interface, and (3) escape of the electrons over the surface barrier into the vacuum. The efficiency of each of these three processes, and hence the magnitude of the secondary emission yield δ, varies greatly for different materials.

Taking into account the material characteristics that, in addition to the value of the primary energy $E_p$ determine the yield δ, one arrives at the equation below for the dependence of δ upon $E_p$, where $\epsilon$ is the

$$\delta = \frac{B_1 B_2 E_p}{\epsilon R}(1 - e^{-R/L})$$

energy required to produce a secondary electron; $R$ is the range of primary electrons; $B_1$ is the coefficient, taking into account that only a fraction of the excited electrons diffuse toward the surface; $L$ is the mean free path of the secondary electron; and $B_2$ is the probability that an electron reaching the solid-vacuum interface can escape over the surface barrier. Here $\epsilon$ and $R$ are associated with process 1 above, $B_1$ and $L$ with process 2, and $B_2$ with process 3. Without giving a detailed derivation of the equation above, it is qualitatively plausible that δ increases with increasing $B_1$, $B_2$, $E_p$, and $L$ and decreases with increasing $\epsilon$ and $R$.

On the basis of the equation, a universal curve can be derived (**Fig. 2**) in which $\delta/\delta_{max}$ is plotted versus $E_p/E_{pmax}$, where $\delta_{max}$ is the maximum yield and $E_{pmax}$ is the corresponding primary energy. Whereas curves for the absolute values of δ versus $E_p$ vary over a wide range for different materials, experiments have generally confirmed the validity of the curve in Fig. 2. The peak in the curve can be interpreted as follows: With increasing $E_p$, the number of secondaries produced within the solid increases, but at the same time the primaries penetrate to a greater depth in the material. Because of energy loss processes, the "escape depth" of the secondaries has a finite value which is determined by some of the parameters entering the equation above. Thus the peak of the curve represents the point beyond which the number of secondaries produced at a depth greater than the escape depth exceeds the number of additional secondaries produced due to the higher primary energy. Because the escape depth is predominantly determined by $L$ and $B_2$ in the equation, the variations in these two parameters are the main reasons why the δ values for different materials vary over such a wide range.

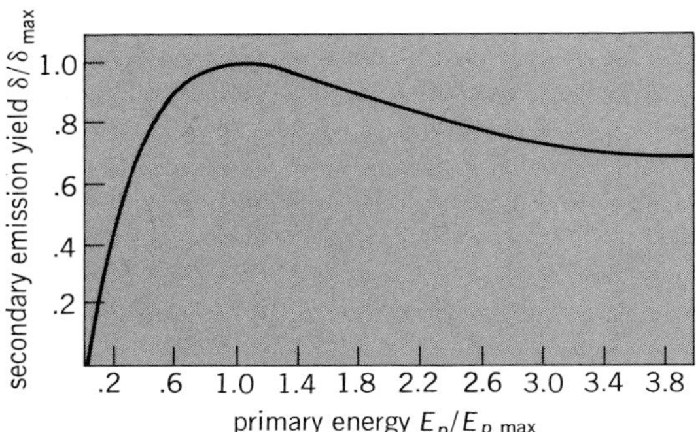


**Fig. 2. Theoretical curve of secondary emission yield as a function of primary energy in normalized coordinates.**

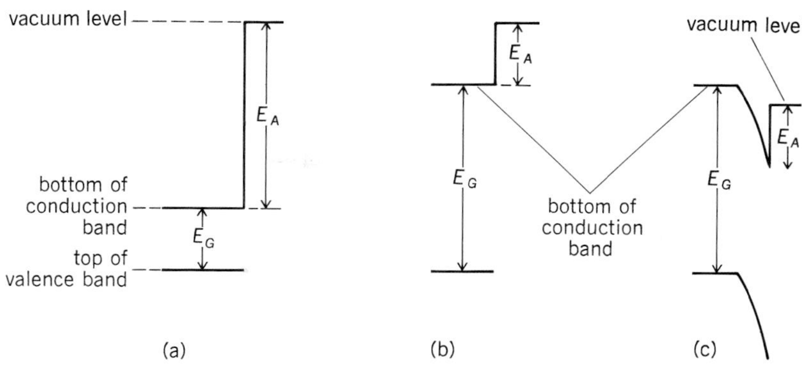


**Fig. 3. Typical energy band models for semiconductors (or insulators). (a) $E_G \ll E_A$. (b) $E_G \gg E_A$. (c) Negative electron affinity.**

**Experimental yield curves.** In a discussion of measured δ and $E_p$ curves, it is useful to consider metals and semiconductors (or insulators) separately. In metals the secondaries lose their energy rapidly by electron-electron scattering. As a result, $L$ and $B_2$ in the equation are small, and the escape depth is of the order of, at most, nanometers. Hence, $\delta_{max}$, and consequently $E_{pmax}$, have low values, typically well below 2.

For semiconductors and insulators, the situation is more complicated and is best understood in terms of energy-band models. Referring to **Fig. 3**, the highest δ values that can be obtained depend on the relative position of the top of the valence band (where the secondary electrons originate), the bottom of the conduction band, and the vacuum level. Three typical band models are shown in Fig. 3. The model shown in Fig. 3*a* is characterized by a small ratio of band-gap energy $E_G$ to electron affinity $E_A$. In the model shown in Fig. 3*b* the $E_G$ to $E_A$ ratio is large. In the model shown in Fig. 3*c* the bands are bent downward to such an extent that the vacuum level lies below the bottom of the conduction band in the bulk. A material with this characteristic is said to have negative effective electron affinity. This concept is also of great importance in photoelectric emission. The differences in secondary emission yields associated with each of the three band models can be qualitatively summarized as follows. *See* Photoemission.

***$E_G \ll E_A$ model.*** Secondary electrons excited from the valence band to levels above the vacuum level tend to lose their energy by exciting additional electrons from the valence band into the conduction band and thus to arrive at the solid-vacuum interface with insufficient energy to overcome the surface barrier. In other words, the escape depth is very small, and the maximum δ values are below 2, similar to those of metals. Examples of this model are germanium and silicon.

***$E_G \gg E_A$ model.*** Whereas secondary electrons excited from the valence band gradually lose energy by phonon-phonon scattering, an appreciable number of secondaries reach the solid-vacuum interface with sufficient energy to overcome the surface barrier. In other words, the escape depth is larger than in the case where $E_G \ll E_A$, of the order of tens of nanometers, and maximum δ values in the 8–15 range are typically obtained. Most of the materials used in practical devices fall into this category. Examples are MgO (see **Fig. 4**). BeO, $Cs_3Sb$ (cesium antimonide), and KCl.

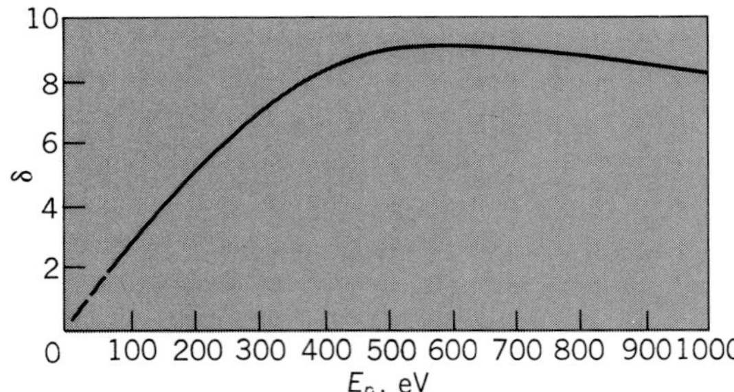


**Fig. 4. Secondary emission yield versus primary energy for MgO.**

***Negative effective electron affinity.*** Here the vacuum level is below the bottom of the conduction band. This case differs drastically from that shown in Fig. 3*b* because electrons that have dropped to the bottom of the conduction band as a result of phonon-phonon scattering still have enough energy to escape into the vacuum. Because the lifetime of electrons in the bottom of the conduction band is orders of magnitude longer than in states above this level, the escape depth of the secondaries is orders of magnitude greater than in the case represented in Fig. 3*b*. The most important material in this category is cesium-activated gallium phosphide, GaP(Cs). **Figure 5** shows the δ versus $E_p$ curve for GaP(Cs) by comparison with MgO. Because of the much greater escape depth, δ values exceeding 100 are readily obtained. The curve for GaP(Cs) still follows quite closely the universal curve (Fig. 2), but the $E_{p\max}$ value is now in the 5–10-kV region compared with several hundred volts for materials represented in Fig. 3*a* or *b*.

Materials of the GaP(Cs) type represent a major breakthrough in the use of secondary emission for practical devices. In photomultipliers, for example, GaP(Cs) is superior to the conventional materials represented in Fig. 3*b* for a number of reasons, the greatest advantage being the improved signal-to-noise ratio. Negative effective electron affinity materials are not in universal use because of the more complex activation procedure and the associated higher cost. SEE BAND THEORY OF SOLIDS; SEMICONDUCTOR.

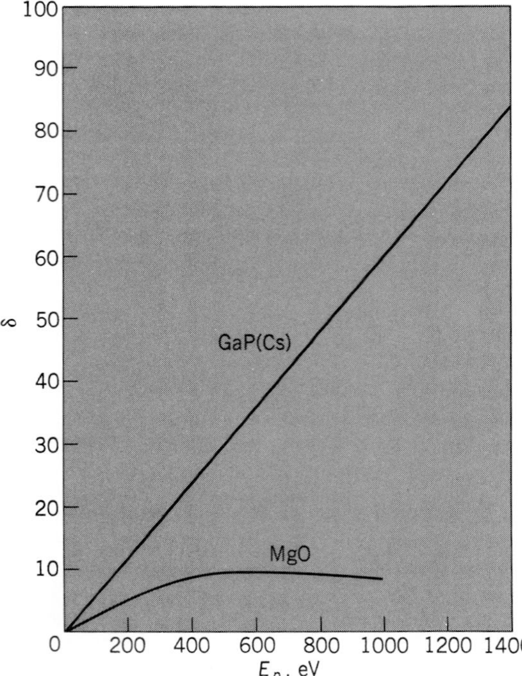


**Fig. 5. Secondary emission yield versus primary energy for GaP(Cs). The curve for MgO is shown for comparison.**

**Dependence on angle of primary beam.** The secondary yield for a given primary energy increases as the angle θ between the primary beam and the normal to the surface increases; the secondaries are then produced closer to the surface and consequently have a larger escape probability. At the same time, the energy for which the yield reaches its maximum value increases with increasing θ.

**Secondary energies.** A typical energy distribution of secondary electrons emitted by a silver target bombarded with primaries of 160-eV energy is given in **Fig. 6**. Note that most of the secondaries have relatively low energies. A small fraction of the emitted electrons have the same energy as the incident primaries and are called reflected primaries.

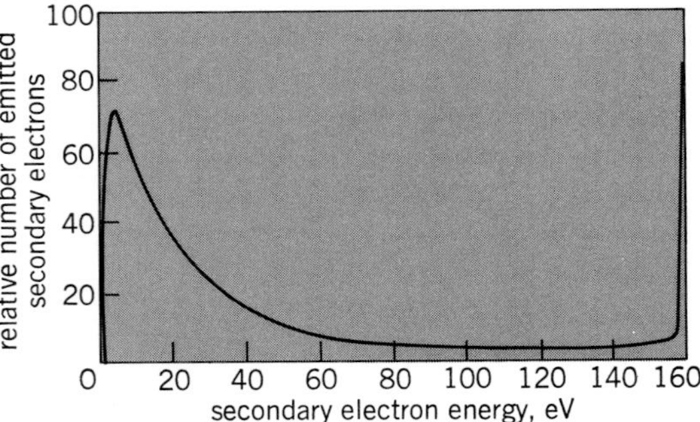


**Fig. 6. Relative number of secondary electrons as a function of secondary energy for $E_P$ = 160 V.**

*Alfred H. Sommer*

***Bibliography.*** R. L. Bell, *Negative Electron Affinity Devices*, 1973; A. J. Dekker, Secondary electron emission, in *Solid State Physics*, vol. 6, p. 251, 1958; R. U. Martinelli and D. G. Fisher, Application of semiconductors with negative electron affinity surfaces to electron emission devices, *Proc. IEEE*, 62:1339–1360, 1974; R. E. Simon and B. F. Williams, Secondary-electron emission, *IEEE Trans. Nucl. Sci.*, NS-15:167–170, 1968.

## Selectivity

The ability of a radio receiver to separate a desired signal frequency from other signal frequencies some of which may differ only slightly from the desired value. Selectivity is achieved by using tuned circuits that are sharply peaked and by increasing the number of tuned circuits. With a sharply peaked circuit, the output voltage falls off rapidly for frequencies lower or higher than that to which the circuit is tuned. SEE Q (ELECTRICITY); RADIO RECEIVER; RESONANCE (ALTERNATING-CURRENT CIRCUITS).

*John Markus*

## Semiconductor

A solid crystalline material whose electrical conductivity is intermediate between that of a metal and an insulator. Semiconductors exhibit conduction properties that may be temperature-dependent, permitting their use as thermistors (temperature-dependent resistors), or voltage-dependent, as in varistors. By making suitable contacts to a semiconductor or by making the material suitably inhomogeneous, electrical rectification and amplification can be obtained. Semiconductor devices, rectifiers, and transistors have replaced vacuum tubes almost completely in low-power electronics, making it possible to save volume and power consumption by orders of magnitude. In the form of integrated circuits, they are vital for complicated systems. The optical properties of a semiconductor are important for the understanding and the application of the material. Photodiodes, photoconductive detectors of radiation, injection lasers, light-emitting diodes, solar-energy conversion cells, and so forth are examples of the wide variety of optoelectronic devices. *See* INTEGRATED CIRCUITS; LASER; LIGHT-EMITTING DIODE; PHOTODIODE; PHOTOELECTRIC DEVICES; SEMICONDUCTOR DIODE; SEMICONDUCTOR RECTIFIER; TRANSISTOR; VARISTOR.

### Conduction in Semiconductors

The electrical conductivity of semiconductors ranges from about $10^3$ to $10^{-9}$ ohm$^{-1}$ cm$^{-1}$, as compared with a maximum conductivity of $10^7$ for good conductors and a minimum conductivity of $10^{-17}$ ohm$^{-1}$ cm$^{-1}$ for good insulators. *See* ELECTRIC INSULATOR; ELECTRICAL CONDUCTIVITY OF METALS.

The electric current is usually due only to the motion of electrons, although under some conditions, such as very high temperatures, the motion of ions may be important. The basic distinction between conduction in metals and in semiconductors is made by considering the energy bands occupied by the conduction electrons.

A crystalline solid consists of a large number of atoms brought together into a regular array called a crystal lattice. The electrons of an atom can each have certain energies, so-called energy levels, as predicted by quantum theory. Because the atoms of the crystal are in close proximity, the electron orbits around different atoms overlap to some extent, and the electrons interact with each other; consequently the sharp, well-separated energy levels of the individual electrons actually spread out into energy bands. Each energy band is a quasicontinuous group of closely spaced energy levels. *See* BAND THEORY OF SOLIDS.

At absolute zero temperature, the electrons occupy the lowest possible energy levels, with the restriction that at most two electrons may be in the same energy level. In semiconductors and insulators, there are just enough electrons to fill completely a number of energy bands, leaving the rest of the energy bands empty. The highest filled energy band is called the valence band. The next higher band, which is empty at absolute zero temperature, is called the conduction band. The conduction band is separated from the valence band by an energy gap which is an important characteristic of the semiconductor. In metals, the highest energy band that is occupied by the electrons is only partially filled. This condition exists either because the number of electrons is not just right to fill an integral number of energy bands or because the highest occupied energy band overlaps the next higher band without an intervening energy gap. The electrons in a partially filled band may acquire a small amount of energy from an applied electric field by going to the higher levels in the same band. The electrons are accelerated in a direction opposite to the field and thereby constitute an electric current. In semiconductors and insulators, the electrons are found only in completely filled bands, at low temperatures. In order to increase the energy of the electrons, it is necessary to raise electrons from the valence band to the conduction band across the energy gap. The electric fields normally encountered are not large enough to accomplish this with appreciable probability. At sufficiently high temperatures, depending on the magnitude of the energy gap, a significant number of valence electrons gain enough energy thermally to be raised to the conduction band. These electrons in an unfilled band can easily participate in conduction. Furthermore, there is now a corresponding number of vacancies in the electron population of the valence band. These vacancies, or holes as they are called, have the effect of carriers of positive charge, by means of which the valence band makes a contribution to the conduction of the crystal. *See* HOLES IN SOLIDS.

The type of charge carrier, electron or hole, that is in largest concentration in a material is sometimes called the majority carrier and the type in smallest concentration the minority carrier. The majority carriers are primarily responsible for the conduction properties of the material. Although the minority carriers play a minor role in electrical conductivity, they can be important in rectification and transistor actions in a semiconductor.

**Electron distribution.** The probability $f$ for an energy level $E$ to be occupied by an electron is given by the Fermi-Dirac distribution function, Eq. (1),

$$f = \left[1 + \exp\left(\frac{E - W}{kT}\right)\right]^{-1} \quad (1)$$

where $k$ is the Boltzmann constant and $T$ is the absolute temperature. The parameter $W$ is the Fermi energy level; an energy level at $W$ has a probability of 1/2 to be occupied by an electron. The Fermi level is determined by the distribution of energy levels and the total number of electrons.

In a semiconductor, the number of conduction electrons is normally small compared with the number of energy levels in the conduction band, and the probability for any energy level to be occupied is small. Under such a condition, the concentration of conduction electrons is given by Eq. (2), where $h$ is Planck's

$$N_n = \frac{2}{h^3}(2\pi m_n kT)^{3/2} \exp\left[\frac{(W - E_c)}{kT}\right] \quad (2)$$

constant, $E_c$ is the lowest energy of the conduction band, and $m_n$ is called the effective mass of conduction electrons. The effective mass is used in place of the actual mass to correct the coefficient in the equation and to bring the results in line with experimental observations. This correction is necessary because the theory leading to these equations is based upon electrons moving in a field free space, which is not the exact picture. The electrostatic Coulomb potential throughout the crystal is varying in a periodic manner, the variation being due to the electric fields around the atomic centers. The concentration of holes in the valence band is given by Eq. (3), where $m_p$ is

$$N_p = \frac{2}{h^3}(2\pi m_p kT)^{3/2} \exp\left[\frac{(E_v - W)}{kT}\right] \quad (3)$$

the effective mass of a hole and $E_v$ is the highest energy of the valence band.

**Mobility of carriers.** The velocity acquired by charge carriers per unit strength of applied electric field is called the mobility of the carriers. The velocity in question is the so-called drift velocity in the direction of the force exerted on the carriers by the applied field. It is added to the random thermal velocity. In semiconductors the carrier mobility normally ranges from $10^2$ to $10^5$ cm$^2$/(s)(V). A material's conductivity is the product of the charge, the mobility, and the carrier concentration.

Electrons in a perfectly periodic potential field can be accelerated freely. Impurities, physical defects in the structure, and thermal vibrations of the atoms disturb the periodicity of the potential field in the crystal, thereby scattering the moving carriers. It is the resistance produced by this scattering that limits the carriers to only a drift velocity under the steady force of an applied field.

**Intrinsic semiconductors.** A semiconductor in which the concentration of charge carriers is characteristic of the material itself rather than of the content of impurities and structural defects of the crystal is called an intrinsic semiconductor. Electrons in the conduction band and holes in the valence band are created by thermal excitation of electrons from the valence to the conduction band. Thus an intrinsic semiconductor has equal concentrations of electrons and holes. The intrinsic carrier concentration $N_i$ is determined by Eq. (4), where $E_g$ is the energy gap. The

$$N_i = \frac{2}{h^3} (2\pi kT)^{3/2} (m_n m_p)^{3/4} \exp\left(-\frac{E_g}{2kT}\right) \quad (4)$$

carrier concentration, and hence the conductivity, is very sensitive to temperature and depends strongly on the energy gap. The energy gap ranges from a fraction of 1 eV to several electron volts. A material must have a large energy gap to be an insulator.

**Impurity semiconductors.** Typical semiconductor crystals such as germanium and silicon are formed by an ordered bonding of the individual atoms to form the crystal structure. The bonding is attributed to the valence electrons which pair up with valence electrons of adjacent atoms to form so-called shared pair or covalent bonds. These materials are all of the quadrivalent type; that is, each atom contains four valence electrons, all of which are used in forming the crystal bonds.

Atoms having a valence of +3 or +5 can be added to a pure or intrinsic semiconductor material with the result that the +3 atoms will give rise to an unsatisfied bond with one of the valence electrons of the semiconductor atoms, and +5 atoms will result in an extra or free electron that is not required in the bond structure. Electrically, the +3 impurities add holes and the +5 impurities add electrons. They are called acceptor and donor impurities, respectively. Typical valence +3 impurities used are boron, aluminum, indium, and gallium. Valence +5 impurities used are arsenic, antimony, and phosphorus.

Semiconductor material "doped" or "poisoned" by valence +3 acceptor impurities is termed *p*-type, whereas material doped by valence +5 donor material is termed *n*-type. The names are derived from the fact that the holes introduced are considered to carry positive charges and the electrons negative charges. The number of electrons in the energy bands of the crystal is increased by the presence of donor impurities and decreased by the presence of acceptor impurities. Let $N$ be the concentration of electrons in the conduction band and let $P$ be the hole concentration in the valence band. For a given semiconductor, the relation $NP = N_i^2$ holds, independent of the presence of impurities. The effect of donor impurities tends to make $N$ larger than $P$, since the extra electrons given by the donors will be found in the conduction band even in the absence of any holes in the valence band. Acceptor impurities have the opposite effect, making $P$ larger than $N$. SEE ACCEPTOR ATOM; DONOR ATOM.

At sufficiently high temperatures, the intrinsic carrier concentration becomes so large that the effect of a fixed amount of impurity atoms in the crystal is comparatively small and the semiconductor becomes intrinsic. When the carrier concentration is predominantly determined by the impurity content, the conduction of the material is said to be extrinsic. There may be a range of temperature within which the impurity atoms in the material are practically all ionized; that is, they supply a maximum number of carriers. Within this temperature range, the so-called exhaustion range, the carrier concentration remains nearly constant. At sufficiently low temperatures, the electrons or holes that are supplied by the impurities become bound to the impurity atoms. The concentration of conduction carriers will then decrease rapidly with decreasing temperature, according to either exp $(-E_i/kT)$ or exp $(-E_i/2kT)$, where $E_i$ is the ionization energy of the dominant impurity.

Physical defects in the crystal structure may have similar effects as donor or acceptor impurities. They can also give rise to extrinsic conductivity.

An isoelectronic impurity, that is, an atom which has the same number of valence electrons as the host atom, does not bind individual carriers as strongly as a donor or an acceptor impurity. However, an isoelectronic impurity may show an appreciable binding for electron hole pairs, excitons, and thereby have important effects on the properties. An example is nitrogen substituting for phosphorus in gallium phosphide; the impurity affects the luminescence of the material.

**Hall effect.** Whether a given sample of semiconductor material is *n*- or *p*-type can be determined by observing the Hall effect. If an electric current is caused to flow through a sample of semiconductor material and a magnetic field is applied in a direction perpendicular to the current, the charge carriers are crowded to one side of the sample, giving rise to an electric field perpendicular to both the current and the magnetic field. This development of a transverse electric field is known as the Hall effect. The field is directed in one or the opposite direction depending on the sign of the charge of the carrier. SEE HALL EFFECT.

The magnitude of the Hall effect gives an estimate of the carrier concentration. The ratio of the transverse electric field strength to the product of the current and the magnetic field strength is called the Hall coefficient, and its magnitude is inversely proportional to the carrier concentration. The coefficient of proportionally involves a factor which depends on the energy distribution of the carriers and the way in which the carriers are scattered in their motion. However, the value of this factor normally does not differ from unity by more than a factor of two. The situation is more complicated when more than one type of carrier is important for the conduction. The Hall coefficient then depends on the concentrations of the various types of carriers and their relative mobilities.

The product of the Hall coefficient and the conductivity is proportional to the mobility of the carriers when one type of carrier is dominant. The proportionality involves the same factor which is contained in the relationship between the Hall coefficient and the carrier concentration. The value obtained by taking this factor to be unity is referred to as the Hall mobility.

### MATERIALS AND THEIR PREPARATION

The group of chemical elements which are semiconductors includes germanium, silicon, gray (crystalline) tin, selenium, tellurium, and boron.

**Elemental semiconductors.** Germanium, silicon, and gray tin belong to group IV of the of the periodic table and have crystal structures similar to that of diamond. Germanium and silicon are two of the best-known semiconductors. They are used extensively in devices such as rectifiers and transistors. Gray tin is a form of tin which is stable below 13°C (55°F). White tin, which is stable at higher temperatures, is metallic. Gray tin has a small energy gap and a rather large intrinsic conductivity, about $5 \times 10^3$ $ohm^{-1}$ $cm^{-1}$ at room temperature. The *n*-type and *p*-type gray tins can be obtained by adding aluminum and antimony, respectively.

Selenium and tellurium both have a similar structure, consisting of spiral chains located at the corners and centers of hexagons. The structure gives rise to anisotropy of the properties of single crystals; for example, the electrical resistivity of tellurium along the direction of the chains is about one-half the resistivity perpendicular to this direction. Selenium has been widely used in the manufacture of rectifiers and photocells.

**Semiconducting compounds.** A large number of compounds are known to be semiconductors. Copper(I) oxide ($Cu_2O$) and mercury(II) indium telluride ($HgIn_2Te_4$) are examples of binary and ternary compounds. The series zinc sulfide (ZnS), zinc selenide (ZnSe), zinc telluride (ZnTe), and the series zinc selenide (ZnSe), cadmium selenide (CdSe), and mercury(II) selenide (HgSe) are examples of binary compounds consisting of a given element in combinations with various elements of another column in the periodic table. The series magnesium antimonide ($Mg_2Sb_2$), magnesium telluride (MgTe), and magnesium iodide ($MgI_2$) is an example of compounds formed by a given element with elements of various other columns in the periodic table.

A group of semiconducting compounds of the simple type AB consists of elements from columns symmetrically placed with respect to column IV of the periodic table. Indium antimonide (InSb), cadmium telluride (CdTe), and silver iodide (AgI) are examples of III–V, II–IV, and I–VI compounds, respectively. The various III–V compounds are being studied extensively, and many practical applications have been found for these materials. Some of these compounds have the highest carrier mobilities known for semiconductors. The compounds have zincblende crystal structure which is geometrically similar to the diamond structure possessed by the elemental semiconductors, germanium and silicon, of column IV, except that the four nearest neighbors of each atom are atoms of the other kind. The II–VI compounds, zinc sulfide (ZnS) and cadmium sulfide (CdS), are used in photoconductive devices. Zinc sulfide is also used as a luminescent material. *SEE PHOTOCONDUCTIVITY.*

Binary compounds of the group lead sulfide (PbS), lead selenide (PbSe), and lead telluride (PbTe) are sensitive in photoconducivity and are used as detectors of infrared radiation. The compounds, bismuth telluride ($Bi_2Te_3$) and bismuth selenide ($Bi_2Se_3$), consisting of heavy atoms, are found to be good materials for thermocouples used for refrigeration or for conversion of heat to electrical energy.

The metal oxides usually have large energy gaps. Thus pure oxides are usually insulators of high resistivity. However, it may be possible to introduce into some of the oxides impurities of low ionization energies and thus obtain relatively good extrinsic conduction. Copper(I) oxide ($Cu_2O$) was one of the first semiconductors used for rectifiers and photocells: extrinsic *p*-type conduction is obtained by producing an excess of oxygen over the stoichiometric composition, that is, the 2-to-1 ratio of copper atoms to oxygen atoms. A number of oxide semiconductors can be obtained by replacing some of the normal metal atoms with metal atoms of one more or less valency. The method is called controlled valence. An example of such a semiconductor is nickel oxide containing lithium.

Some compounds with rare-earth or transition-metal ions in their composition, such as EuTe and $NiS_2$, are semiconductors with magnetic properties. Another interesting type of semiconductor is characterized by layered structures. The interaction within a layer is significantly stronger than that between layers. A number of semiconductors of this type are known, such as $PbI_2$, GaSe, and various transition-metal dichalcogenides such as $SnSe_2$ and $MoS_2$.

**Preparation of materials.** The properties of semiconductors are extremely sensitive to the presence of impurities. It is therefore desirable to start with the purest available materials and to introduce a controlled amount of the desired impurity. The zone refining method is often used for further purification of obtainable materials. The floating zone technique can be used, if feasible, to prevent any contamination of molten material by contact with crucible.

For basic studies as well as for many practical applications, it is desirable to use single crystals. Various methods are used for growing crystals of different materials. For many semiconductors, including germanium, silicon, and the III–V compounds, the Czochralski method is commonly used. The method of condensation from the vapor phase is used to grow crystals of a number of semiconductors, for instance, selenium and zinc sulfide. For materials of high melting points, such as various metal oxides, the flame fusion or Vernonil method may be used.

The introduction of impurities, or doping, can be accomplished by simply adding the desired quantity to the melt from which the crystal is grown. Normally, the impurity has a small segregation coefficient, which is the ratio of equilibrium concentrations in the solid and the liquid phases of the material. In order to obtain a desired impurity content in the crystal, the amount added to the melt must give an appropriately larger concentration in the liquid. When the amount to be added is very small, a preliminary ingot is often made with a larger content of the doping agent; a small slice of the ingot is then used to dope the next melt accurately. Impurities which have large diffusion constants in the material can be introduced directly by holding the solid material at an elevated temperature while this material is in contact with the doping agent in the solid or the vapor phase.

A doping technique, ion implantation, has been developed and used extensively. The impurity is introduced into a layer of semiconductor by causing a controlled dose of highly accelerated impurity ions to impinge on the semiconductor. SEE ION IMPLANTATION.

An important subject of scientific and technological interest is amorphous semiconductors. In an amorphous substance the atomic arrangement has some short-range but no long-range order. The representative amorphous semiconductors are selenium, germanium, and silicon in their amorphous states, and arsenic and germanium chalcogenides, including such ternary systems as Ge-As-Te. Some amorphous semiconductors can be prepared by a suitable quenching procedure from the melt. Amorphous films can be obtained by vapor deposition.

## Rectification in Semiconductors

In semiconductors, narrow layers can by produced which have abnormally high resistances. The resistance of such a layer is nonohmic; it may depend on the direction of current, thus giving rise to rectification. Rectification can also be obtained by putting a thin layer of semiconductor or insulator material between two conductors of different material.

**Barrier layer.** A narrow region in a semiconductor which has an abnormally high resistance is called a barrier layer. A barrier may exist at the contact of the semiconductor with another material, at a crystal boundary in the semiconductor, or at a free surface of the semiconductor. In the bulk of a semiconductor, even in a single crystal, barriers may be found as the result of a nonuniform distribution of impurities. The thickness of a barrier layer is small, usually $10^{-3}$ to $10^{-5}$ cm.

A barrier is usually associated with the existence of a space charge. In an intrinsic semiconductor, a region is electrically neutral if the concentration $n$ of conduction electrons is equal to the concentration $p$ of holes. Any deviation in the balance gives a space charge equal to $e(p - n)$, where $e$ is the charge on an electron. In an extrinsic semiconductor, ionized donor atoms give a positive space charge and ionized acceptor atoms give a negative space charge. Let $N_d$ and $N_a$ be the concentrations of ionized donors and acceptors, respectively. The space charge is equal to $e(p - n + N_d - N_a)$.

A space charge is associated with a variation of potential. A drop in potential $-\Delta V$ increases the potential energy of an electron by $e\Delta V$; consequently every electronic energy level in the semiconductor is shifted by this amount. With a variation of potential, the electron concentration varies proportionately to $\exp(eV/kT)$ and the hole concentration varies as $\exp(-eV/kT)$. A space charge is obtained if the carriers, mainly the majority carriers, fail to balance the charge of the ionized impurities.

A conduction electron in a region where the potential is higher by $\Delta V$ must have an excess energy of $e\Delta V$ in order for it to have the minimum energy on reaching the low potential region. Electrons with less energy cannot pass over to the low potential region. Thus a potential variation presents a barrier to the flow of electrons from high to low potential regions. It also presents a barrier to the flow of holes from low to high potential regions.

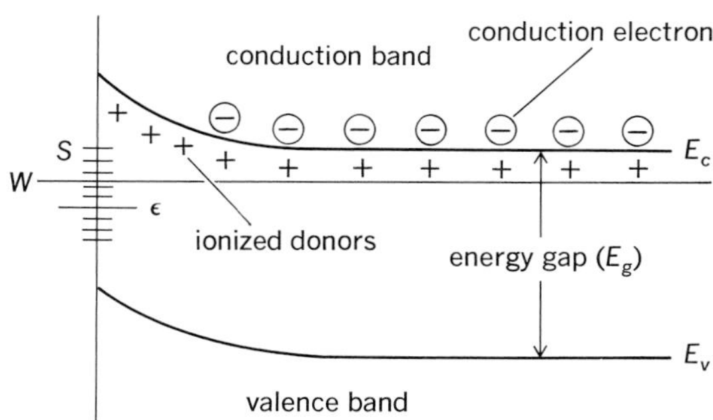


**Fig. 1.** Energy diagram of a surface barrier as employed in an *n*-type semiconductor.

**Surface barrier.** A thin layer of space charge and a resulting variation of potential may be produced at the surface of a semiconductor by the presence of surface states. Electrons in the surface states are bound to the vicinity of the surface, and the energy levels of surface states may lie within the energy gap. Surface states may arise from the adsorption of foreign atoms. Even a clean surface may introduce states which do not exist in the bulk material, simply by virtue of being the boundary of the crystal.

The surface is electrically neutral when the surface states are filled with electrons up to a certain energy level $\epsilon$ in the energy gap $E_g$, which is the energy difference between the bottom of the conduction band $E_c$ and the top of the valence band $E_v$. If the Fermi level $W$ in the bulk semiconductor lies higher in the energy gap, more surface states would be filled, giving the surface a negative charge. As a result the potential drops near the surface and the energy bands are raised for $n$-type material (**Fig. 1**). With the rise of the conduction band, the electron concentration is reduced and a positive space charge due to ionized donors is obtained. The amount of positive space charge is equal to the negative surface charge given by the electrons in the surface states between $\epsilon$ and the Fermi level.

**Contact barrier.** The difference between the potential energy $E_o$ of an electron outside a material and the Fermi level in the material is called the work function of the material. **Figure 2** shows the energy diagram for a metal and a semiconductor, the work functions of which differ by $eV$. Upon connecting the two bodies electrically, charge is transferred between them so that the potential of the semiconductor is raised relative to that of the metal; that is, the electron energy levels in the semiconductor are lowered. Equilibrium is established when the Fermi level is the same in the two bodies. In this case, the metal is charged negatively and the semiconductor is charged positively. The negative charge on the metal is concentrated close to the surface, as is expected in good conductors. The positive charge on the semiconductor is divided between the increase of space charge in an extension of the barrier and the depopulation of some of the surface states. The charging of the semiconductor is brought about by a change of $eV_2$ in the barrier height $\phi$. The sum of $eV_2$ and the potential energy variation $eV_1$ in the space between the two bodies is equal to the original difference $eV$ between the work functions.

With decreasing separation between the two bodies, the division of $eV$ will be in favor of $eV_2$. However, if there is a very large density of states, a small $eV_2$ gives a large surface charge on the semiconductor due to the depopulation of surface states.

It is possible that $eV_2$ is limited to a small value even at the smallest separation, of the order of an interatomic distance in solids. In such cases, the barrier height remains nearly equal to the value $\phi$ of the free surface, irrespective of the body in contact. This situation has been found in germanium and silicon rectifiers. Before the explanation was given by J. Bardeen, who postulated the existence of surface states, it had been assumed that the height of a contact barrier was equal to the difference of the work functions. SEE WORK FUNCTION (ELECTRONICS).

The understanding and the application of metal-semiconductor contacts have been extended to various kinds of contacts, such as that between different semiconductors, heterojunctions, and metal oxide semiconductor (MOS) junctions.

**Single-carrier theory.** The phenomenon of rectification at a crystal barrier can be described according to the role played by the carriers. Where the conduction property of the rectifying barrier is determined primarily by the majority carriers, the single-carrier theory is employed. Such cases are likely to be found in semiconductors with large energy gaps, for instance, oxide semiconductors. **Figure 3** shows the energy diagrams of metal-semiconductor contact rectifiers under conditions of equilibrium. The potential variation in the semiconductor is such as to reduce the majority carrier concentration near the contact. If the energy bands were to fall in the case of an *n*-type semiconductor or to rise in the case of a *p*-type semiconductor, the majority carrier concentration would be enhanced near the contact, and the contact would not present a large and rectifying resistance. It is clear that in the cases shown in Fig. 3, the minority carrier concentration increases near the contact. However, if the energy gap is large, the minority carrier concentration is normally very small, and the role of minority carriers may be still negligible even if the concentration is increased.

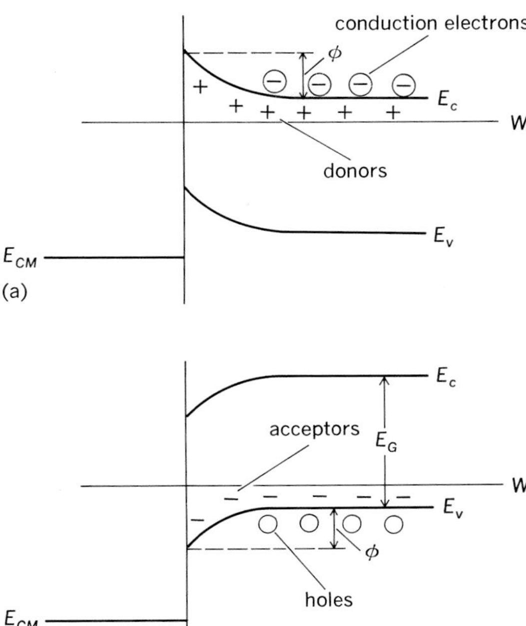


**Fig. 3. Energy diagrams of a rectifying contact between a metal and a semiconductor: (*a*) *n*-type semiconductor; (*b*) *p*-type semiconductor.**

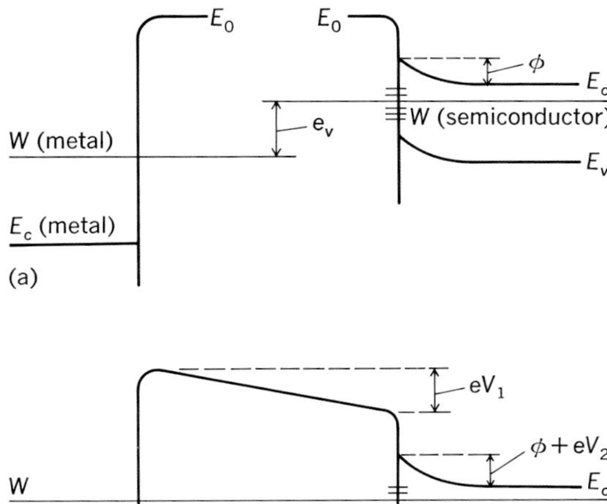


**Fig. 2. Energy diagram for a metal (left) and an *n*-type semiconductor (right). $E_0$ is the potential energy of an electron outside the material, $E_c$ is the energy at the bottom of the conduction band, and $E_v$ is the energy at the top of the valence band. (a) Semiconductor and metal isolated. (*b*) Semiconductor and metal in electrical contact, $eV_1 + eV_2 = eV$.**

Under equilibrium conditions, the number of carriers passing from one body to the other is balanced by the number of carriers crossing the contact in the opposite direction, and there is no net current. The carriers crossing the contact in either direction must have sufficient energies to pass over the peak of the barrier. The situations under applied voltages are shown in **Fig. 4** for the case of an *n*-type semiconductor. When the semiconductor is made positive, its energy bands are depressed and the height of the potential barrier is increased, as shown in Fig. 4*a*. Fewer electrons in the semiconductor will be able to cross over into the metal, whereas the flow of electrons across the contact from the metal side remains unchanged. Consequently, there is a net flow of electrons from the metal to the semiconductor. The flow of electrons from the metal side is the maximum net flow obtainable. With increasing voltage, the current saturates and the resistance becomes very high. Figure 4*b* shows the situation when the semiconductor is negative under the applied voltage. The energy bands in the semiconductor are raised. The flow of electrons from the semiconductor to the metal is increased, since electrons of lower energy are able to go over the peak of the barrier. The result is a net flow of electrons from the semiconductor to the metal. There is no limit to the flow in this case. In fact, the electron current increases faster than the applied voltage because there are increasingly more electrons at lower energies. The resistance decreases, therefore, with increasing voltage. The direction of current for which the resistance is low is called the forward direction, while the opposite direction is called the reverse or blocking direction. A general expression for the current can be written in the form of Eq. (5), where $j$ is

$$j = enC\left(\exp\frac{-\phi}{kT}\right)\left[\exp\left(\frac{eV}{kT}\right) - 1\right] \quad (5)$$

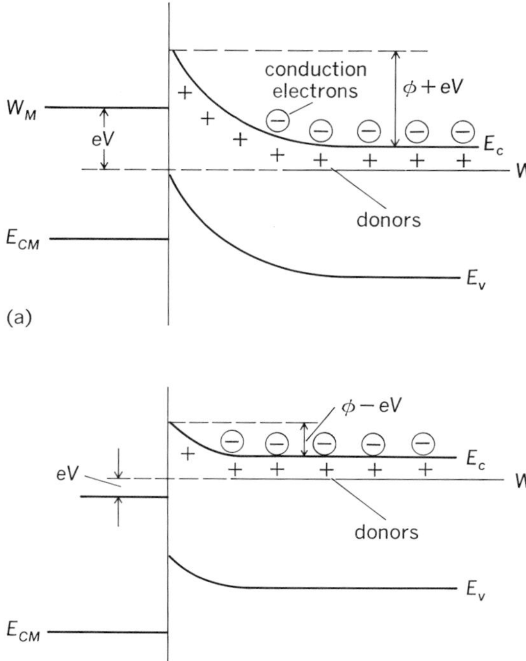


**Fig. 4. Energy diagrams of a rectifying contact between a metal and an *n*-type semiconductor under an applied voltage *V*. (*a*) Positive semiconductor. There is a net flow of electrons from metal to semiconductor. (*b*) Negative semiconductor. There is a net flow of electrons from semiconductor to metal.**

the current density, $n$ is the carrier concentration in the bulk of the semiconductor, $\phi$ is the barrier height, and $V$ is the applied voltage taken as positive in the forward direction. The factor $C$ depends on the theory appropriate for the particular case.

***Diffusion theory.*** When there is a variation of carrier concentration, a motion of the carriers is produced by diffusion in addition to the drift determined by the mobility and the electric field. The transport of carriers by diffusion is proportional to the carrier concentration gradient and the diffusion constant. The diffusion constant is related to the mobility, and both are determined by the scattering suffered by moving carriers. The average distance traveled by a carrier in its random thermal motion between collisions is called the mean free path. If barrier thickness is large compared to mean free path of carriers, motion of carriers in the barrier can be treated as drift and diffusion. This viewpoint is the basis of the diffusion theory of rectification. According to this theory, the factor $C$ in Eq. (5) depends on the mobility and the electric field in the barrier.

***Diode theory.*** When the barrier thickness is comparable to or smaller than the mean free path of the carriers, then the carriers cross the barrier without being scattered, much as in a vacuum tube diode.

According to this theory, the factor $C$ in the rectifier equation is $v/4$, where $v$ is the average thermal velocity of the carriers.

***Tunneling theory.*** Instead of surmounting a potential barrier, carriers have a probability of penetrating through the barrier. The effect, called tunneling, becomes dominant if the barrier thickness is sufficiently small. This effect is important in many applications. SEE TUNNELING IN SOLIDS.

***Two-carrier theory.*** Often the conduction through a rectifying barrier depends on both electron and hole carriers. An important case is the *pn* junction between *p*- and *n*-sections of a semiconductor material. Also, in metal-semiconductor rectifiers, the barrier presents an obstacle for the flow of majority carriers but not for the flow of minority carriers, and the latter may become equally or more important.

***Rectification at pn junctions.*** A *pn* junction is the boundary between a *p*-type region and an *n*-type region of a semiconductor. When the impurity content varies, there is a variation of electron and hole concentrations. A variation of carrier concentrations is related to a shift of the energy bands relative to the constant Fermi level. This is brought about by a variation of the electrostatic potential which requires the existence of a space charge. If the impurity content changes greatly within a short distance, a large space charge is obtained within a narrow region. Such is the situation existing in a rectifying *pn* junction.

When a voltage is applied to make the *n*-region negative relative to the *p*-region, electrons flow from the *n*-region, where they are abundant, into the *p*-region. At the same time, holes flow from the *p*-region, where holes are abundant, into the *n*-region. The resistance is therefore relatively low. The direction of current in this case is forward. Clearly, the resistance will be high for current in the reverse direction.

With a current in the forward direction, electrons in the *n*-region and holes in the *p*-region flow toward the junction and there must be continuous hole-electron recombination in the neighborhood of the junction. The minority carrier concentration in each region is increased near the junction because of the influx of the carriers from the other region. This phenomenon is known as carrier injection. When there is a current in the reverse direction, there must be a continuous generation of holes and electrons in the neighborhood of the junction, from which electrons flow out into the junction, from which electrons flow out into the *n*-region and holes flow out into the *p*-region. Thus current through a *pn* junction is controlled by the hole-electron recombination or generation in the vicinity of the junction.

The transistor consists of two closely spaced *pn* junctions in a semiconductor with an order *pnp* or *npn*.

***Contact rectification.*** If the height of a rectifying contact barrier is high, only a very small fraction of majority carriers can pass over the barrier. The fraction may be so small as to be comparable with the concentration of the minority carriers, provided the energy gap is not too large. The current due to the minority carriers becomes appreciable if the barrier height above the Fermi level approaches the energy difference between the Fermi level and the top of the valence band (Fig. 3).

The concentration of minority carriers is higher at the contact than in the interior of the semiconductor. With a sufficiently high barrier, it is possible to obtain at the contact a minority carrier concentration higher than that of the majority carriers. The small region where this condition occurs is called the inversion layer.

As in the case of a *pn* junction, a forward current produces injection of minority carriers. With the presence of an inversion layer, the injection can be so strong as to increase appreciably the conductivity in the vicinity of the contact. Ordinarily, contact rectifiers consist of a semiconductor in contact with a metal whisker. For large forward currents, the barrier resistance is small, and the resistance of the rectifier is determined by the spreading resistance of the semiconductor for a contact of small area. By increasing the conductivity in the vicinity of the contact where the spreading resistance is concentrated, carrier-injection may reduct considerably the forward resistance of the rectifier.

**Surface electronics.** The surface of a semiconductor plays an important role technologically, for example, in field-effect transistors and charge-coupled devices. Also, it presents an interesting case of two-dimensional systems where the electric field in the surface layer is strong enough to produce a potential wall which is narrower than the wavelengths of charge carriers. In such a case, the electronic energy levels are grouped into subbands, each of which corresponds to a quantized motion normal to the surface, with a continuum for motion parallel to the surface. Consequently, various properties cannot be trivially deduced from those of the bulk semiconductor. *See* Charge-coupled devices; Surface physics.

*H. Y. Fan*

**Bibliography.** B. L. Crowder (ed.), *Ion Implantation in Semiconductors and Other Materials*, 1973; N. B. Hannay and U. Colombo (eds.), *Electronic Materials*, 1973; *Nuovo Cimento*, vol. 38B, no. 2, 1977; Proceedings of the 8th (1976 International) Conferences on Solid State Devices, *Jap. J. Appl. Phys.*, suppl. 16–1, 1977; F. Seitz and D. Turnbull (eds.), *Solid State Physics*, vol. 1, 1955; W. Shockley, *Electrons and Holes in Semiconductors*, 1950; S. Sze, *Physics of Semiconductor Devices*, 2d ed., 1981; R. K. Willardson and A. C. Beer (eds.), *Semiconductors and Semimetals*, vols. 1–22, 1966–1985.

## Semiconductor diode

A two-terminal electronic device that utilizes the properties of the semiconductor from which it is constructed. In a semiconductor diode without a *pn* junction, the bulk properties of the semiconductor itself are used to make a device whose characteristics may be sensitive to light, temperature, or electric field. In a diode with a *pn* junction, the properties of the *pn* junction are used. The most important property of a *pn* junction is that, under ordinary conditions, it will allow electric current to flow in only one direction. Under the proper circumstances, however, a *pn* junction may also be used as a voltage-variable capacitance, a switch, a light source, a voltage regulator, or a means to convert light into electrical power. *See* Semiconductor.

Silicon and germanium are the semiconductors most often used in diodes. However, other materials may be used for special purposes: cadmium sulfide and cadmium selenide in photoconductors; gallium phosphide, gallium arsenide–phosphide, and silicon carbide in light-emitting diodes; and gallium arsenide in microwave generators.

**Diodes without pn junctions.** The band structure of each semiconductor contains a forbidden energy gap. That is, there is a range of energies, $\Delta E$, in which there are no quantum states that electrons may occupy. When the semiconductor is in thermal equilibrium, its electrons are distributed among the allowed quantum states according to Fermi statistics: The free electrons tend to reside near the minimum in the conduction band, and the unoccupied states in the valence band, called free holes, tend to be concentrated near the maximum in the valence band. **Figure 1** shows a schematic of the band structure in gallium arsenide, GaAs. According to Fermi statistics, the holes are located mainly at $E = 0$, $p = 0$; and the electrons are concentrated near $E = E_1$, $p = 0$.

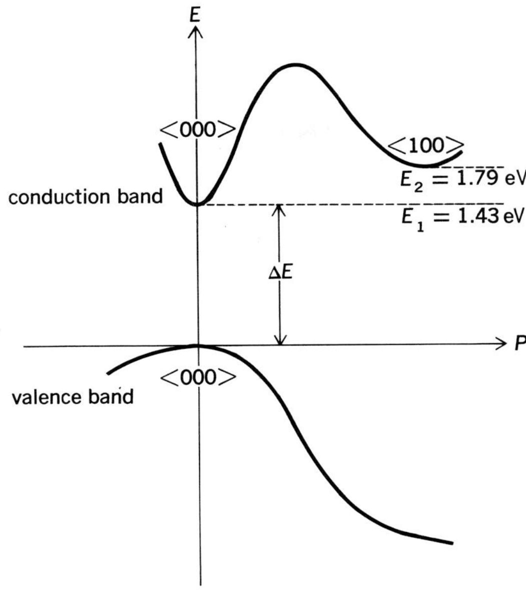


**Fig. 1. Band structure of gallium arsenide; $E$ = electron energy, $P$ = momentum.**

The conductivity of a semiconductor is proportional to the number of electrical carriers (electrons and holes) it contains. In a temperature-compensating diode, or thermistor, the number of carriers changes with temperature. For example, in an intrinsic diode the number of carriers and the conductivity are proportional to $e^{-\Delta E/kT}$. As Temperature $T$ increases, the conductivity increases. This effect may be used to cancel out other conductivity changes in an electrical circuit so that the net change is zero.

In a photoconductor the semiconductor is packaged so that it may be exposed to light. Light photons whose energies are greater than $\Delta E$ can excite electrons from the valence band to the conduction band, increasing the number of electrical carriers in the

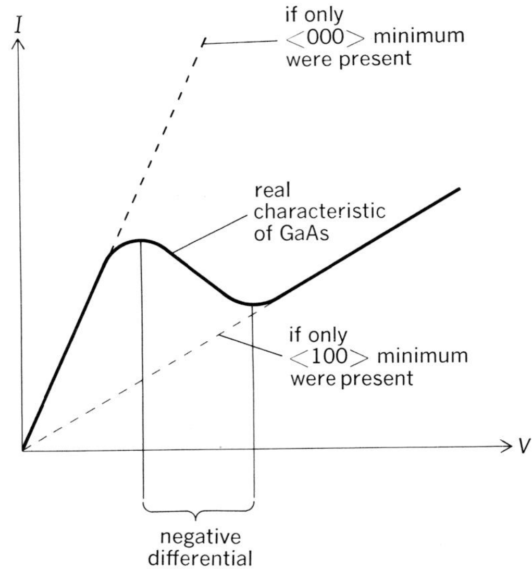


**Fig. 2. Current-voltage characteristic bulk of GaAs.**

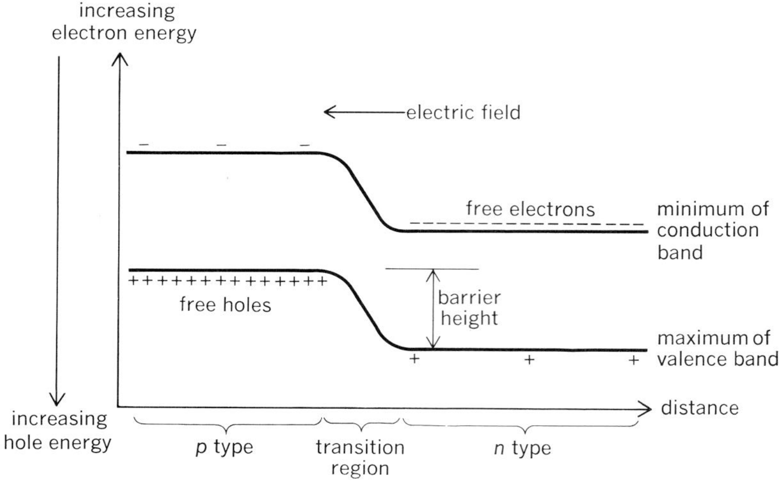


**Fig. 3. Energy bands at the potential barrier for *pn* junction of a diode.**

semiconductor. Thus the conductivity of a semiconductor is a measure of the light intensity striking the semiconductor. *See* PHOTOCONDUCTIVITY.

In some semiconductors the conduction band has more than one minimum. An example is gallium arsenide, as shown in Fig. 1. Here the <000> minimum is located 1.43 eV above the valence band, and the <100> minimum is located 0.36 eV above the <000> minimum. When an electric field is applied to GaAs, the electrons start out in the <000> minimum and the current-voltage relationship initially follows Ohm's law, as shown in **Fig. 2**. In this and other figures, *I* represents current and *V* represents voltage. When the field approaches 3200 V/cm, a significant number of electrons are scattered into the <100> minimum. Since carriers in the <100> minimum have lower mobilities than those in <000>, the conductivity must decrease. This results in a region of negative differential conductivity, and a device operated in this region is unstable. The current pulsates at microwave frequencies, and the device, a Gunn diode, may be used as a microwave power source. *See* MICROWAVE SOLID-STATE DEVICES.

**Diodes with pn junctions.** A rectifying junction is formed whenever two materials of different conductivity types are brought into contact. Most commonly, the two materials are an *n*-type and a *p*-type semiconductor, and the device is called a junction diode. However, rectifying action also occurs at a boundary between a metal and a semiconductor of either type. If the metal contacts a large area of semiconductor, the device is known as a Schottky barrier diode; if the contact is a metal point, a point-contact diode is formed. *See* POINT-CONTACT DIODE; SCHOTTKY EFFECT.

The contact potential between the two materials in a diode creates a potential barrier which tends to keep electrons on the *n* side of the junction and holes on the *p* side. This barrier is shown in the energy band diagram of **Fig. 3**. When the *p* side is made positive with respect to the *n* side by an applied field, the barrier height is lowered and the diode is forward biased. Majority electrons from the *n* side may flow easily to the *p* side, and majority holes from the *p* side may flow easily to the *n* side. When the *p* side is made negative, the barrier height is increased and the diode is reverse-biased. Then, only a small leakage current flows: Minority electrons from the *p* side flow into the *n* side, and minority holes from the *n* side flow into the *p* side. The current-voltage characteristic of a typical diode is shown in **Fig. 4**. Rectifying diodes can be made in a variety of sizes, and much practical use can be made of the fact that such a diode allows current to flow in essentially one direction only. At one extreme, single devices may be used to handle thousands of watts of power in changing alternating current to direct current. At the other extreme, a small diode may be used to detect an amplitude-modulated (AM) radio signal that has only microwatts of power.

The potential barrier at a *pn* junction consists of an electric dipole made up of charged impurity atoms, positively charged on the *n* side and negatively charged on the *p* side. Because the ends of the dipole are separated by a small distance, the junction acts like a capacitor. Moreover, the capacitance is voltage-variable since the barrier height is voltage-dependent. A diode which is specifically designed to utilize this capacitance characteristic is called a varactor.

When light photons with energies greater than $\Delta E$ strike a semiconductor near a *pn* junction, the potential barrier will sweep the conduction electrons that were generated by the light into the *n* side of the diode, and the newly created holes into the *p* side. If the diode, now called a solar cell, is connected to an

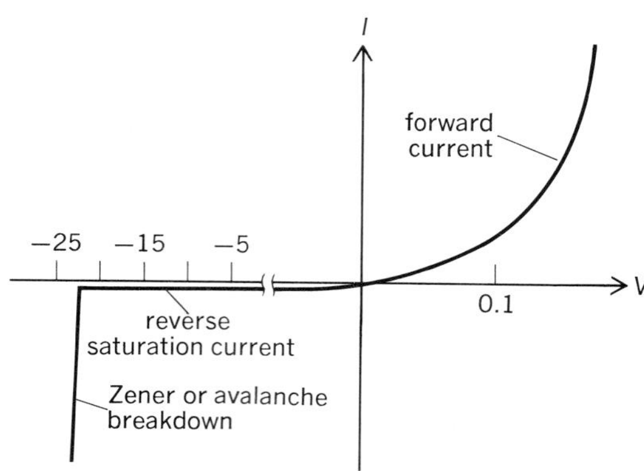


**Fig. 4. Current-voltage characteristic of a *pn* junction.**

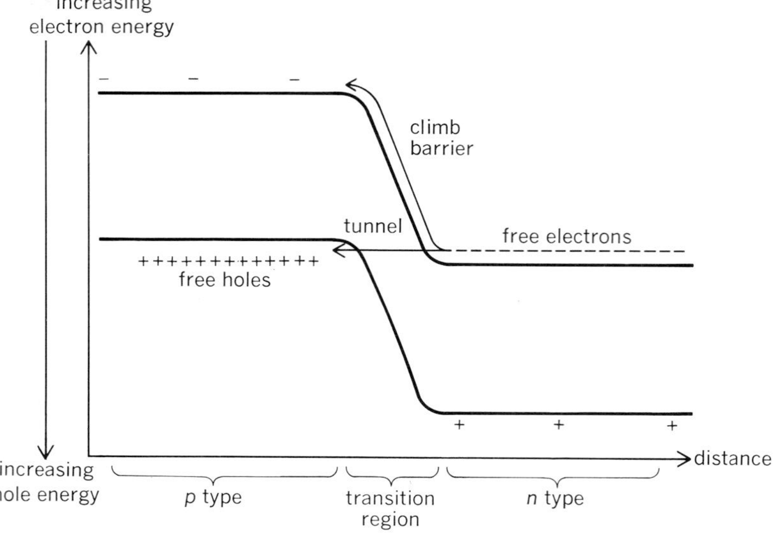


**Fig. 5. Energy bands at *pn* junction in a tunnel diode.**

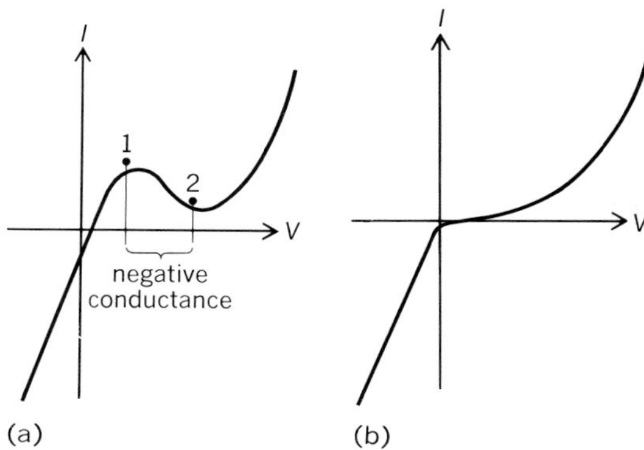


**Fig. 6. Current-voltage characteristic of (*a*) a tunnel diode and (*b*) a backward diode.**

external circuit, the diode will supply electrical power to the circuit as long as light strikes the *pn* junction. If, on the other hand, the diode is reverse-biased, the magnitude of the reverse saturation current can be used to measure light intensity. In this configuration the diode is called a photodiode. *See* Solar cell.

When a junction diode is forward-biased, the number of electrons on the *p* side and the number of holes on the *n* side are increased far above their equilibrium values. This makes the recombination of electrons with holes highly probably, and the recombination energy may be released as photons of light.

In some materials, notably GaP for red or green light and GaAs for infrared light, the conversion of electrical energy directly to light can be made quite efficient. And in materials like GaAs, where the valence band maximum and the conduction band minimum are at the same value of crystal momentum, laser action may be achieved.

An Esaki tunnel diode is formed when both the *n* and *p* sides of a junction diode are very heavily doped. In this case, as shown in **Fig. 5**, an electron may move from the *n* side to the *p* side under forward bias in either of two ways: It may climb over the barrier, as in an ordinary diode; or it may quantum-mechanically tunnel through the barrier, since there are some available states on the *p* side that are at the same energy as states on the *n* side. Tunneling is highly probably at low and medium reverse voltages and at low forward voltages. As shown in **Fig. 6*a***, a tunnel diode has an unstable negative-resistance region. The diode may be operated either at point 1 or point 2, but may not be operated in between. This feature may be used to advantage in logic circuits, where the diode is made to switch from one point to the other. *See* Tunnel diode.

A backward diode is similar to a tunnel diode except that it has no forward tunnel current (Fig. 6*b*). It is useful as a low-voltage rectifier.

Although simple diode theory predicts a constant reverse saturation current no matter how high the reverse voltage, all real diodes eventually break down either by tunneling or by avalanche (Fig. 4).

Avalanching occurs when the electrons or the holes gather so much energy that they can create new hole-electron pairs by collision. This process is cumulative and can result in a rapid buildup of current carriers. A diode that has a sharp breakdown provides a virtually constant voltage over a wide range of current. Popularly known as a Zener diode, this device may be used to provide a reference voltage or to regulate the voltage at some point in a circuit.

*Stephen Nygren*

***Bibliography.*** J. Millman, *Microelectronics*, 1979; S. M. Sze, *Physics of Semiconductor Devices*, 2d ed., 1981; E. S. Yang, *Fundamentals of Semiconductor Devices*, 1978.

## Semiconductor heterostructures

Structures consisting of two different semiconductor materials in junction contact, with unique electrical or electrooptical characteristics. A heterojunction is a junction in a single crystal between two dissimilar semiconductors. The most important differences between the two semiconductors are generally in the energy gap and the refractive index. In semiconductor heterostructures, differences in energy gap permit spatial confinement of injected electrons and holes, while the differences in refractive index can be used to form optical waveguides. Semiconductor heterostructures have been used for diode lasers, light-emitting diodes, optical detector diodes, and solar cells. In fact, heterostructures must be used to obtain continuous operation of diode lasers at room temperature. Heterostructures also exhibit other interesting properties such as the quantization of confined carrier motion in ultrathin heterostructures and enhanced carrier mobility in modulation-doped heterostructures. Structures of current interest utilize III–V and IV–VI compounds having similar crystal structures and closely matched lattice constants. *See* Band theory of solids; Laser; Light-emitting diode; Optical detectors; Solar cell.

**Carrier and optical field confinement.** The most intensively studied and thoroughly documented materials for heterostructures are gallium arsenide (GaAs) and aluminum gallium arsenide ($Al_xGa_{1-x}As$). Several other III–V and IV–VI systems also are used for semiconductor heterostructures. The variation of the energy gap $E_g$ and the refractive index $\bar{n}$ with aluminum arsenide (AlAs) mole fraction $x$ are shown in **Fig. 1**. The lattice constant $a_0$ is also noted in Fig. 1 to emphasize that $a_0$ for GaAs and AlAs differs, but by an amount less than 0.14%. A close lattice match is necessary in heterostructures in order to obtain high-quality crystal layers by epitaxial growth and thereby to prevent excessive carrier recombination at the heterojunction interface.

A GaAs-$Al_{0.3}Ga_{0.7}As$ double heterostructure is illustrated in **Fig. 2**. The energy gap $E_g$ versus $x$ given in Fig. 1*a* shows that $E_g$ for $Al_{0.3}Ga_{0.7}As$ is 0.37 eV greater than for GaAs. When a positive potential is connected to the *p*-type $Al_{0.3}Ga_{0.7}As$, electrons are injected into the GaAs layer from the wider-energy-gap *n*-type $Al_{0.3}Ga_{0.7}As$, and holes are injected into the GaAs from the wider-energy-gap *p*-type $Al_{0.3}Ga_{0.7}As$. The wider energy gap $Al_{0.3}Ga_{0.7}As$ layers also confine the injected electrons and holes to the GaAs layer, where they can recombine radiatively. This confinement is illustrated in Fig. 2*a*.

Figure 1*b* shows that the refractive index for the $Al_{0.3}Ga_{0.7}As$ layers will be less than for the GaAs layer. This refractive index step is shown in Fig. 2*b*. Solution of the reduced wave equation shows that the optical field will be confined to the larger-refractive-index GaAs layer. The resulting optical field distribution is shown in Fig. 2*c*. When this heterostructure

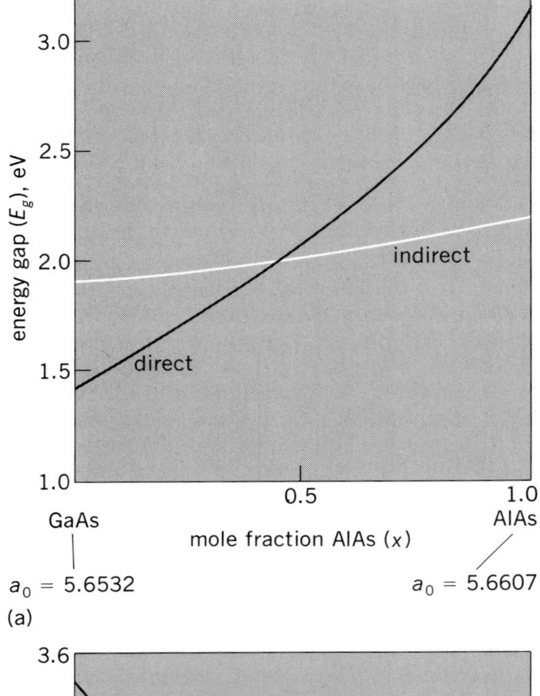


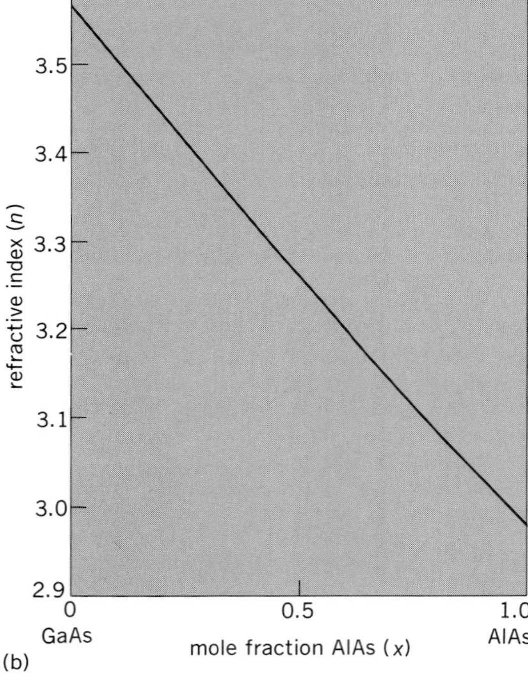


**Fig. 1. Compositional dependence in $Al_xGa_{1-x}As$ of (*a*) the energy gap and (*b*) the refractive index at a photon energy of 1.38 eV. In both cases, temperature = 297 K (75°F). (*After S. E. Millet and A. G. Chynoweth, eds., Optical Fiber Telecommunications, Academic Press, 1979*)**

is formed as a rectangular bar with parallel reflecting surfaces, it can become a diode laser at current densities near $2 \times 10^3$ A/cm$^2$ at a forward voltage of 1.6 V.

**Quantum well effects.** When the narrow energy gap layer in heterostructures becomes a few tens of nanometers or less in thickness, new effects that are associated with the quantization of confined carriers are observed. These ultrathin heterostructures are referred to as superlattices, artificially layered structures, or quantum well structures, and they consist of alternating layers of GaAs and $Al_xGa_{1-x}As$ (**Fig. 3***a*). These structures are generally prepared by molecular-beam epitaxy. Each layer has a thickness in the range of 5 to 40 nanometers. The energy band diagram for the quantum well structure is shown in Fig. 3*b*. The abrupt steps in the energy gaps form potential wells in the conduction and valence bands. SEE ARTIFICIALLY LAYERED STRUCTURES.

In the GaAs layers, the motion of the carriers is restricted in the direction perpendicular to the heterojunction interfaces, while they are free to move in the other two directions. The carriers can therefore be considered as a two-dimensional gas. The Schrödinger wave equation shows that the carriers moving in the confining direction can have only discrete bound states. As the thickness of the quantum wells gets large, a continuum of states then results. The discrete states in the undoped GaAs quantum wells are illustrated in Fig. 3*b* and are accurately predicted by the well-known quantum-mechanical problem of the particle-in-a-box.

The presence of the discrete quantum states may readily be observed by low-temperature optical absorption measurements. The observation wavelength is from 0.6 to 0.9 micrometer. These measurements are generally made at liquid helium temperatures with 20 or more GaAs quantum wells separated by $Al_xGa_{1-x}As$ layers. The absorption of photons takes place in the GaAs quantum wells by the transition of electrons in quantized states of the valence band to the quantized states of the conduction band. Sharp peaks in the absorption spectrum occur at the energies that separate the quantized states in the valence and

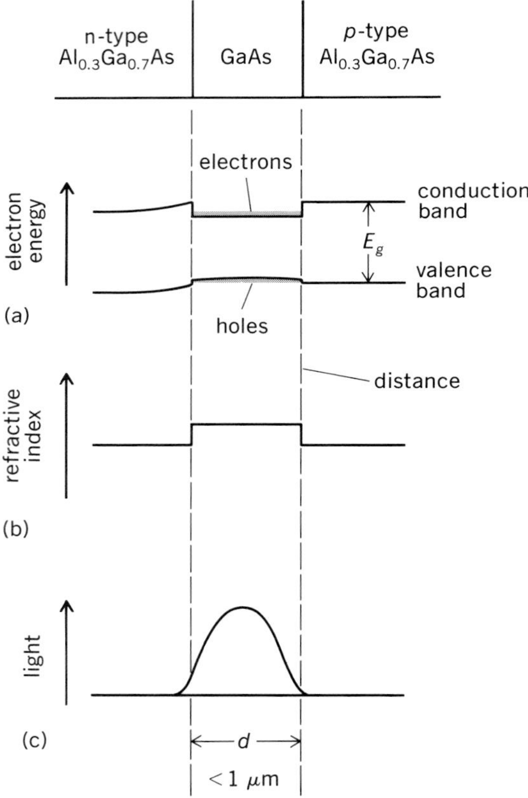


**Fig. 2. Schematic representation of an $Al_{0.3}Ga_{0.7}As$-GaAs-$Al_{0.3}Ga_{0.7}As$ double heterostructure laser showing (*a*) energy band diagram at high forward bias, (*b*) refractive index profile, and (c) optical field distribution. (*After H. C. Casey, Jr., and M. B. Panish, Heterostructure Lasers, part A, Fundamental Principles, Academic Press, 1978*)**

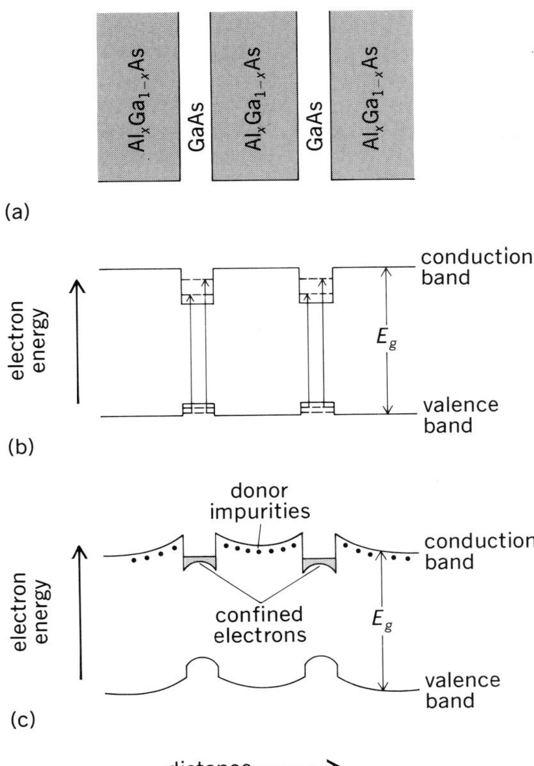


**Fig. 3.** **GaAs-$Al_{0.3}Ga_{0.7}$As superlattice. (*a*) Schematic representation. (*b*) Quantum wells, with the discrete conduction and valence band states for undoped GaAs. (c) Quantum wells with modulation doping.**

conduction bands, and the photon energies of these absorption peaks vary with the thickness of the GaAs layer as predicted.

**Modulation doping.** Another property of semiconductor heterostructures is illustrated by a modulation doping technique that spatially separates conduction electrons and their parent donor impurity atoms. As illustrated in Fig. 3*c*, the donor impurities are incorporated in the wider energy gap $Al_xGa_{1-x}As$ layer but not in the GaAs layer. The GaAs conduction band edge is lower in energy than the donor states in the $Al_xGa_{1-x}As$, and therefore electrons from the donor impurities will move into the GaAs layers.

The useful feature of modulation doping is that the mobile carriers are the electrons in the GaAs layers and that these mobile carriers are spatially separated from their parent donor impurities in the $Al_xGa_{1-x}As$ layers. Since the carrier mobility in semiconductors is decreased by the presence of ionized and neutral impurities, the carrier mobility in the modulation-doped GaAs is larger than for a GaAs layer doped with impurities to give the same free electron concentration. Higher carrier mobilities should permit preparation of devices that operate at higher frequencies than are possible with doped layers.

**Heteroepitaxy.** In order to prepare optical sources and detectors that operate at a desired wavelength or to achieve high-mobility semiconductors, often it is necessary to use quaternary solid solutions. To obtain high-quality layers, the epitaxial layers must be grown on binary substrates that have the same lattice constant as the solid solutions. An example of considerable interest is the growth of $Ga_xIn_{1-x}P_yAs_{1-y}$ layers lattice-matched to InP. In this case, the heterojunction is used to obtain a similar lattice constant for dissimilar semiconductors at a desired bandgap. The heteroepitaxial growth techniques are chemical-vapor deposition, liquid-phase epitaxy, and molecular-beam epitaxy.

*H. C. Casey, Jr.*

**Chemistry.** The III–V and II–VI compounds and alloys commonly used in heterostructures are usually formed either by direct synthesis from the elements or by vapor-phase decomposition reactions using compounds containing hydrogen, halogen, or organic radicals. Substrates used for the growth of heterostructures are usually gotten from single-crystal boules synthesized directly from the elements. Most heterostructure materials can be doped either *n* or *p* type. However, in some cases one conductivity type can be difficult to obtain due to a "self-compensation" mechanism in which the formation of one type of vacancy is energetically favorable and compensates the opposite doping type. For example, the *p*-type beryllium (Be) doping of aluminum nitride (AlN) is compensated by the formation of *n*-type nitrogen vacancies. In general, variations in stoichiometry will greatly affect electrical and optical properties. Also, the properties of heterostructures greatly depend on the lattice constant match and chemical abruptness of the interface. A lattice mismatch of greater than 0.5% usually results in an interface with a significant density of both electron and hole traps. The chemical rule that determines the allowable alloy compositions is that the sum of the atom fraction of the group III (or group II) elements must equal the sum of the atom fractions of group V (or group VI) elements in the crystal, for example, $Ga_{1-x}Al_xAs$, $0 \leq x \leq 1$.

**Fabrication.** Semiconductor heterostructures are usually fabricated as single-crystal structures using thin-film epitaxial crystal growth techniques such as liquid-phase epitaxy (LPE), chemical vapor deposition (CVD), and molecular-beam epitaxy (MBE).

***Liquid-phase epitaxy.*** The liquid-phase epitaxy method has been the most widely used technique for fabricating heterostructures. The principal advantage is the ease of fabrication of high-purity heterostructures with good electrical, optical, and interface prop-

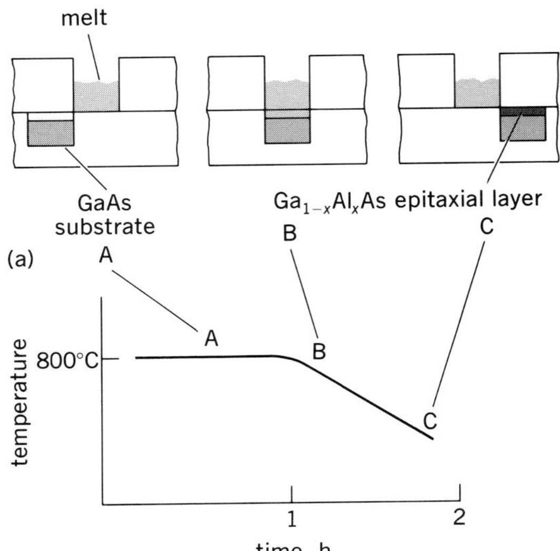


**Fig. 4. Liquid-phase epitaxy method for GaAs-$Ga_{1-x}Al_xAs$ heterostructures. (*a*) Simplified diagrams of successive stages of the process. (*b*) Variation of temperature during the process. 800°C = 1500°F. (*After J. M. Woodall, III-V compounds and alloys: An update, Science, 208:908–915, 1980*)**

erties as a result of impurity segregation from the growing layer into the melt during growth. The main disadvantage is the poor control of layer thickness and interface morphology and abruptness. Epitaxial growth by the liquid-phase epitaxy method occurs when a melt or solvent becomes supersaturated, usually by supercooling, with respect to a solid phase in presence of a single-crystal substrate. For the growth of III–V materials, the melt usually has a large concentration of one of the group III components in epitaxial layer. For example, epitaxial growth of $Ga_{1-x}Al_xAs$ for $0 \leq x \leq 1$ can be obtained from melts containing about 90% Ga and 10% Al plus As. A "typical" schedule for the liquid-phase epitaxy growth of a $Ga_{1-x}Al_xAs$ layer on GaAs is shown in **Fig. 4**. The important features are a "bottomless" bin to contain the melt and a fixture with a slightly recessed substrate which can be moved with respect to the melt bin. The first step is to thermally equilibrate the melt prior to contact with the substrate (A in Fig. 4). This means that the melt is either at solid-liquid equilibrium or slightly undersaturated. Next, the melt is cooled, usually at constant rate, while the substrate is in contact with it (B of Fig. 4). The desired layer thickness is obtained by programming either a change in temperature or elapsed time and then removing the substrate from the melt (C of Fig. 4). The growth of heterostructures can also be accomplished by using multimelt fixtures, moving the substrate between the various melts during cooling. The term liquid-phase epitaxy originally referred to growth from supercooled melts. The technique now includes growth from melts supersaturated by other techniques such as electroepitaxy, in which the solid-liquid interface region becomes supersaturated due to the flow of electric current across the interface and isothermal melt mixing techniques in which solid-liquid equilibrium melts of different compositions are mixed together and become supersaturated.

***Chemical vapor deposition.*** The chemical vapor deposition method refers to the formation of thin solid films as the result of thermochemical vapor-phase reactions. When the films are epitaxial, the method is sometimes called vapor phase epitaxy (VPE). For III–V materials two different chemistries have been widely studied: the group III and group V halogen compounds and group V hydrogen compounds; and

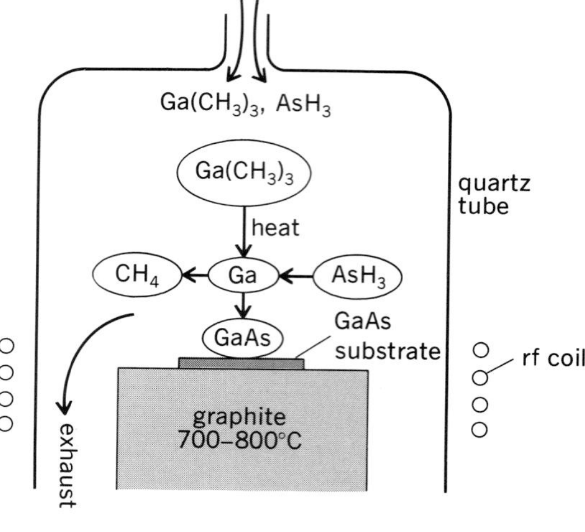


**Fig. 5. Simplified diagram of the metal-organic method for chemical vapor deposition. 700–800°C = 1300–1500°F.**

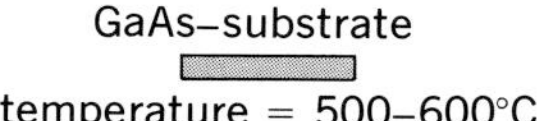


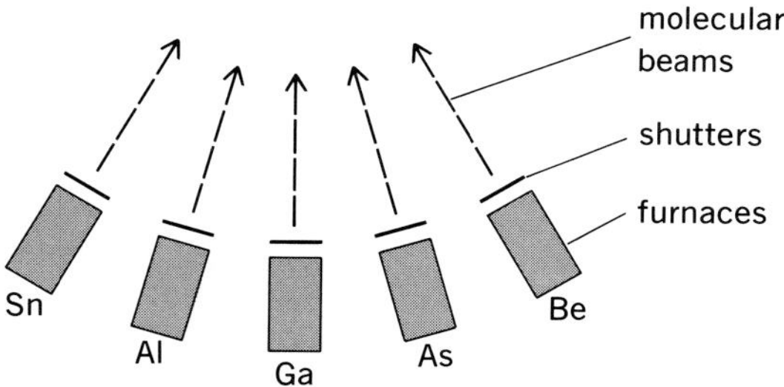


**Fig. 6. Schematic illustration of a system configuration for growth of doped $Ga_{1-x}Al_xAs$ by molecular-beam epitaxy. 500–600°C = 900–1100°F. (*After P. E. Luscher, Crystal growth by molecular beam epitaxy, Solid State Technol., 20(12):43–52, 1977*)**

the group III metal-organic compounds and V-hydrogen compounds such as $Ga(CH_3)_3$ and $AsH_3$. The halogen transport reactions are of the "hot" to "cold" type in which the III-halogen is produced in a high-temperature zone by the reaction of the III element with HCl. The III-halogen then diffuses to the low-temperature zone, where it combines with the V species to form an epitaxial layer of III–V material. Vapor-phase epitaxy using metal-organic compounds (metal-organic chemical vapor deposition; MOCVD) occurs when the organic radical R of the III-R compound is "cracked" or pyrolyzed away at a "hot wall" or hot substrate in the presence of the $V\text{-}H_3$ compound. A schematic illustration of the metal-organic chemical vapor deposition technique applied to GaAs is shown in **Fig. 5**. Both the halogen and metal-organic chemistries have been successfully used to fabricate heterostructures. It is thought that the metal-organic chemical vapor deposition method may have long-term advantages such as better purity, composition, and thickness control and the ability to produce a wide range of III–V compounds and alloys.

***Molecular-beam epitaxy.*** The molecular-beam epitaxy technique is relatively new compared with liquid-phase epitaxy and chemical vapor deposition. For heterostructure fabrication, it is capable of a layer thickness and interface abruptness control on a monoatomic scale. This represents almost two orders of magnitude improvement in structural resolution in the growth direction compared to liquid-phase epitaxy and chemical vapor deposition. The molecular-beam epitaxy technique is similar to evaporation techniques used to deposit thin metal films. The key features of the molecular-beam epitaxy method are the use of an ultrahigh-vacuum environment and epitaxial growth by the reaction of multiple molecular beams of differing flux and chemistry with a heated single-crystal substrate. A schematic illustration of molecular-beam epitaxy applied to doped $Ga_{1-x}Al_xAs$ is shown in **Fig. 6**. Each furnace heats a crucible which is charged with one of the constituent elements or compounds of the desired film. Tin (Sn) functions as an $n$-type dopant, and beryllium (Be) functions as a $p$-type dopant. The furnace temperature is chosen so that the vapor pressure is sufficient to produce the desired beam flux at the substrate surface. The furnaces are arranged so that the flux from each is maximum at the substrate position. The quality and composition of the epitaxial film are determined by the quality of the ultrahigh-vacuum system, the substrate temperature, and the furnace temperature. The shutters interposed between each furnace and the substrate allow the beams to be modulated. This feature, coupled with typical growth rates of a few tenths of a nanometer per second, facilitates the fabrication of very thin and very abrupt heterostructures. SEE SEMICONDUCTOR.

*Jerry M. Woodall*

**Bibliography.** H. C. Casey, Jr., and M. B. Panish, *Heterostructures Lasers*, A: *Fundamental Principles*, and B: *Materials and Operating Characteristics*, 1978; R. Dingle, in H. J. Queiser (ed.), *Festkörperprobleme*, Advances in Solid State Physics, vol. 15, pp. 21–48, 1975; R. Dingle et al., Electron mobilities in modulation-doped semiconductor heterojunction superlattices, *Appl. Phys. Lett.*, 33:665–667, October 1, 1978; J. W. Matthews (ed.), *Epitaxial Growth*, Materials Science and Technology Series, 1975; A. G. Milnes and D. L. Feucht, *Heterojunctions and Metal-Semiconductor Junctions*, 1972; M. B. Panish, Molecular beam epitaxy, *Science*, 208:916–922, 1980; J. M. Woodall, III–V compounds and alloys: An update, *Science*, 208:908–915, 1980.

## Semiconductor memories

Devices for storing digital information that are fabricated by using integrated circuit technology. Semiconductor memories are widely used to store programs and data in almost every digital system. Initially developed as a replacement for magnetic core memories, which were used as the main computer storage memory, semiconductor memories started to appear in the early 1970s and have almost totally replaced core memories as the main computer memory elements.

Many different types of semiconductor memories are used in computer systems to perform various functions—bulk data storage, program storage, temporary storage, and cache (or intermediate) storage. Almost all of the memories are a form of random-access memory (RAM), where any storage location can be accessed in the same amount of time. However, there are many different types of RAMs, the most frequently used of which is the writable and readable memory that is simply referred to as a RAM.

**Read/write RAMs.** Although the RAM acronym indicates the random-access capability, it is a misnomer since almost all semiconductor memories except for a few specialty types can be randomly accessed. A more appropriate name for the memory would be a read/write RAM to indicate that data can be written into the memory as well as be read out of it.

***Dynamic and static types.*** Even within this one class of memory, there are finer subdivisions. Basically there are two different types of read/write RAMs—dynamic and static. The RAM type refers to the structure of the actual storage circuit used to hold each data bit (the cell structure) within the memory chip. A dynamic memory uses a storage cell based on a transistor and capacitor combination, in which the digital information is represented by a charge stored on each of the capacitors in the memory array. The memory gets the name "dynamic" from the fact that the capacitors are imperfect and will lose their charge unless the charge is repeatedly replenished (refreshed) on a regular basis (every few milliseconds). If refreshed, the information will remain until intentionally changed or the power to the memory is shut off. Static memories, in contrast, do not use a charge-storage technique; instead, they use either four or six transistors to form a flip-flop for each cell in the array. Once data are loaded into the flip-flop storage elements, the flip-flop will indefinitely remain in that state until the information is intentionally changed or the power to the memory circuit is shut off.

In addition to static and dynamic RAMs, there is an attempt to combine both technologies, thus merging the high storage density of dynamic memory cells with the simplicity of use of static RAMs. Referred to as pseudostatic or pseudodynamic RAMs, these memories include circuits on the chip to automatically provide the refresh signals needed by the dynamic cells in the memory array. Since the signals do not have to be supplied by the external system, the memory appears to function like a static RAM.

***Redundancy.*** As memory chips increase in storage capacity, manufacturing defects can often cause several storage cells to fail and thus render the chip useless. To counter that problem and thus improve production yield, many manufacturers have incorporated redundant storage cells that can be swapped into the memory array during unpackaged chip testing via the blowing of electrical fuses or the use of a laser to burn away microscopic fuses. Most static and dynamic RAMs now incorporate some degree of redundancy, and all memory types except the read-only memories can include a small number of redundant cells as a hedge against defects.

***Capacity.*** In the early 1970s, dynamic memories with a capacity (density) of 1024 bits per chip were introduced. Improvements in semiconductor processing and circuit design have made practical an increase in density, first to 4096 bits on a chip, then to 16,384 bits, and in 1980 to 65,536 bits (often rounded off to 64 kbits). Dynamic RAMs with 262,144 bits (the 256k dynamic RAM) first appeared in 1982 and went into mass production in 1984. The first samples of 1-megabit dynamic RAMs (1,048,576 bits) were announced in 1984, and these memories went into limited production in 1985, thus yielding an increase in memory capacity of three orders of magnitude in about 15 years.

Until 1983, all dynamic RAMs were organized with word widths of 1 bit and depths of 1024, 4096, 16,384, and 65,536 words (often expressed as 1-k × 1, 4-k × 1, and so forth). However, 1983 saw new directions develop as dynamic RAMs with 4- and 8-bit-wide word widths were introduced at densities of 64 kbits. Application-specific memories that offer features such as special memory-access modes, multiple ports, and shift registers to improve memory performance in such systems as high-speed video displays also appeared. The diversification of architecture has continued with the announcement of 1-, 4-, and 8-bit-wide versions of 256-kbit and 1-megabit dynamic memories. Additionally, unique functions such as on-chip parity generation and checking for 8-k × 9 and 32-k × 9 chips were introduced in 1986.

Static memories require more complex structures for each cell, and thus cannot pack as many cells on a chip. They have typically lagged behind dynamic memories in density by a factor of four. For example, at the time the 1024-bit dynamic memory was introduced, static memories had densities of 256 bits per chip. In 1980, when the 64-kbit dynamic RAM was introduced, static densities were just reaching 16,384 bits on a chip. And, in 1983, as samples of the 256k dynamic RAM appeared, 64-kbit static RAMs were in limited production. The first 256-kbit static RAMs were announced in 1984, and went into limited production in 1985.

Additionally, static RAMs are starting to include special features to improve their versatility in various applications. One such feature is a reset capability that returns all bits to a "zero" state, while another is a "shadow" register that can be used during system diagnostics to aid in troubleshooting.

**Nonvolatile memories.** There are many other forms of semiconductor memories in use—mask-programmable read-only memories (ROMs), fuse-programmable read-only memories (PROMs), ultraviolet-erasable programmable read-only memories (UV EPROMs), electrically alterable read-only memories (EAROMs) electrically erasable programmable read-only memories (EEPROMs), and nonvolatile static RAMs (NV RAMs). All of these memory types are also randomly accessible, but their main distinguishing feature is that once information has been loaded into the storage cells, the information stays there even if the power is shut off.

***ROM.*** The first of these memory types, the ROM, is programmed by the memory manufacturer during the actual device fabrication. Here, though, there are two types of ROMs; one is called last-mask or contact-mask programmable, and the other is often called a ground-up design. In the last-mask type of ROM, the final mask used in the fabrication process determines the connections to the internal transistors. The connections, in turn, determine the data pattern that will be read out when the cell is accessed. The ground-up type of ROM is designed from the bottom up—all fabrication masks used in the multiple mask process are custom-generated.

Last-mask ROMs are theoretically less area-efficient (the final chip size is larger than for a ground-up design), and thus tend to cost slightly more since chip area is directly related to price. However, they offer a rapid turnaround time (the time it takes for a user to obtain finished and programmed devices from the manufacturer from the time the code pattern was provided to the manufacturer by the user), since all circuits can be premanufactured up to the next-to-last mask step. Typically, ground-up designs offer lower cost and slightly higher performance, since they are more area-efficient. However, ROMs require that the user make a commitment to a specific code pattern or place an order for a large number of devices to obtain the low unit cost.

ROMs can be had with capacities of up to 1 megabit, with almost all chips available with 8-bit word widths, which, at the largest size, results in a 128-k × 8 structure. The increased use of 16- and 32-bit microprocessors, however, has moved ROMs toward 16-bit-wide word organizations, and chips with such structures have been sampled at the 1-megabit level. Additionally, at that density the cost of manufacturing the chip and the manufacturing losses due to imperfections that destroy stored data bits require that some method to correct bad bits be used. Thus, ROMs with built-in error detection and correction circuits have been put into limited production. One design even goes so far as to provide 100% redundancy: for every bit there are two memory cells, each storing the same data. If one cell fails, the other cell takes over. However, this makes the size of the chip extremely large and is not a very economical or practical approach. SEE MICROPROCESSOR.

***Fuse PROM.*** As an alternative to the mask-programmable memories, semiconductor manufacturers developed all the other programmable memory types to permit the users to program the memories themselves and order as few as they want, even a single device. The first of the user-programmable devices was the fuse PROM. Offered in standard sizes ranging from a few hundred bits to over 64,000 bits, the fuse-programmable memories are one-time programmable memories—once the information is programmed in, it cannot be altered. There are basically two types of fuse-programmable memories; one type uses microscopic fuse links that are blown open to define a logic one or zero for each cell in the memory array; the other type of fuse programming causes metal to short out base-emitter transistor junctions to program the ones or zeros into the memory.

***Reprogrammable memories.*** The birth of the microprocessor in the early 1970s brought with it new memory types that offered a feature never before available—reusability. Information stored in the memory could be erased—in the case of the UV EPROM, by an ultraviolet light, and in the case of the EAROM, EEPROM, or NV RAM, by an electrical signal—and then the circuit could be reprogrammed with new information that could be retained indefinitely. All of these memory types are starting to approach the ideal memory element for the computer, an element that combines the flexibility of the RAM with the permanence of the ROM when power is removed. At the present time there are still some limiting factors in the various memory types that must be overcome before that ideal goal can be attained.

The ideal memory circuit should allow unlimited read and write operations without any unusual voltage levels or extra circuitry. At present, UV EPROMs require an external ultraviolet lamp to erase the stored information and a programming voltage of about 21 V (for old-generation UV EPROMs) and about 12.5 V for the newer versions. To operate in their read-only mode, the UV EPROMs just require a 5-V supply. The older EAROMs and EEPROMs (pre-1983) also required storage-control voltages of several times the read-mode supply voltage, and in many cases the EAROMs and EEPROMs also required external support logic to minimize the amount of control time that the host processor in a system had to devote to storing data into the memory. However, some of the newer EAROMs and EEPROMs have been able to place circuitry on the same chip to boost the standard 5-V supply voltage up to the level necessary to program or erase the cell, as well as provide the other necessary support functions. Coming closest to the ideal specification is the NV RAM, a memory that combines a static RAM with a nonvolatile memory array, so that for every stored bit there are two memory cells, one of which is volatile and the other nonvolatile. During normal system operation, the NV RAM uses the volatile memory array, but when it receives a special store signal, information held in the RAM area is transferred into the nonvolatile section. Thus the RAM section provides unlimited read and write operations, while the nonvolatile section provides back-up when power is removed.

However, the EAROM, EEPROM, and NV RAM suffer one common failing that keeps them from reaching the ideal—they wear out. The electrical process used to store information in the nonvolatile array causes a steady deterioration in the ability of the memory to retain data for a guaranteed time period. Currently available capabilities range from about 10,000 to over 1,000,000 write cycles, but many times that number are needed for general-purpose use.

To overcome the limited number of storage cycles possible with the true nonvolatile memory technologies, ultralow-power-consumption static RAMs (with a standby current of just 1 microampere or less) have been combined with some power control circuitry and a button-type long-life battery in a single package. When built into a system, this form of NV RAM operates with the characteristics of a static RAM when the system supplies power—fast access times and unlimited reads and writes. However, when the power supply line drops below a preset level, the control circuitry in the memory package detects the drop, disables the memory's ability to store new data, and then switches over to the built-in battery to keep the stored data alive until main power returns.

**Semiconductor technology.** The semiconductor technology used to fabricate all the different memory types spans the entire range of available commercial processes, as summarized in the **table**. The dynamic memory, originally introduced in a *p*-channel MOS process (PMOS), has been upgraded through the use of higher performing *n*-channel MOS (NMOS) and, subsequently complementary MOS (CMOS) processes. The use of CMOS memory structures (the combination of both *p*- and *n*-channel devices to form the memory cells and supporting logic on the memory chip) permits a reduction of orders of magnitude in the standby power consumption, and often a reduction by a factor of two to five in the active power requirements of a memory chip, as compared to its NMOS equivalent. Typical dynamic RAMs provide access times that range from well under 100 nanoseconds per word for the fastest standard versions, while special operating modes such as page, serial nibble, and static column modes provide access to data at speeds as fast as 10 ns/bit. Speed selections with access times as slow as 300 ns are also available.

The NMOS static RAM has given way to CMOS at densities above 16 kbits, and in many cases even at densities below 16 kbits. Commercial devices with access times as fast as 15 ns have appeared in CMOS at capacities of 1024 bits. Prototype 256-kbit CMOS static RAMs have attained sub-50-ns access times. RAM organizations with word widths of 1, 4, and 8 bits are commonly available at most density levels. Slower versions of these memories, with access times stretching out to 400 ns, are also available.

For even faster access times, bipolar technologies such as emitter coupled logic (ECL) and forms of Schottky transistor-transistor logic (STTL) permit RAMs with access times of 3 to 5 ns to be fabricated. However, bipolar technologies consume the most power, and the speed is thus obtained at the expense of power—many of the bipolar RAMs consume two to three times the power of the NMOS memories. Another technology that has been applied to semiconductor memories is gallium arsenide. The nature of the material permits faster electron movement, and thus faster access times; several 1024-bit memories with access times of 1 to 2 ns have been realized.

A move toward CMOS technology for most other

**Summary of memory types and technologies**

| Memory type | Maximum capacity[a] commercially available 1985–1986 | Relative access speed[b] | Programmability | Technology |
|---|---|---|---|---|
| Dynamic RAM | 1 Mbit | Fast/medium | Read/write, volatile | CMOS or NMOS |
| | 1 Mbit | Fastest[c] | Read/write, volatile | CMOS or NMOS |
| Static RAM | 256 kbit | Fast | Read/write, volatile | CMOS |
| | 64 kbit | Fastest | Read/write, volatile | Bipolar, ECL |
| | 4 kbit | Fast | Read/write, volatile | Bipolar, TTL |
| | 16 kbit | Fast | Read/write, volatile | NMOS |
| | 1 kbit | Fastest | Read/write, volatile | Gallium arsenide |
| ROM | 1 Mbit | Fast/medium | Factory mask | CMOS or NMOS |
| PROM | 4 kbit | Fastest | Fuse, one-time electrical | Bipolar ECL |
| | 64 kbit | Fast | Fuse, one-time electrical | Bipolar TTL |
| | 16 kbit | Medium | Fuse, one-time electrical | CMOS |
| | 32 kbit | Fast | UV EPROM cell, one-time electrical | CMOS (floating gate) |
| UV EPROM | 1 Mbit | Fast | Ultraviolet erasable, electrical programmability | CMOS or NMOS (floating gate) |
| | 512 kbit | Fast | Ultraviolet erasable, electrical programmability | NMOS (floating gate) |
| EEPROM (and EAROM) | 256 kbit | Fast | Electrically erasable | CMOS or NMOS (electron tunneling) |
| | 64 kbit | Fast | Electrically erasable | MNOS (electron tunneling) |
| NV RAM | 4 kbit | Fast | Read/write nonvolatile | NMOS (electron tunneling) |
| | 64 kbit | Fast | Read/write nonvolatile[e] | CMOS (battery backup) |

[a]1 kbit = 1024 bits, 1 Mbit = 1,048, 576 bits.
[b]Fastest ≤ 35 ns; 36 ns ≤ fast ≤ 150 ns; 151 ns ≤ medium ≤ 350 ns.
[c]Special static column or rapid serial-access mode.
[d]Limited life read/write capability.
[e]Unlimited read/write but limited nonvolatile storage capability.
[f]Built-in lithium battery allows unlimited storage and read/write operations.

memory types has also taken place. UV EPROMs, ROMs, PROMS, and the various EAROMs, EEPROMs, and NV RAMs are available in NMOS and CMOS processes at various density levels. Access times for the various nonvolatile memories range from less than 100 ns in their read modes to about 10 ms when data are stored. Most of the ROMs and UV EPROMs are available only with 8-bit word widths, while PROMs are commonly offered in 4- and 8-bit-wide organizations. The various electrically alterable memories, however, offer a diverse choice of capacities and architectures that include devices with serial access modes to reduce the number of package pins. *SEE COMPUTER STORAGE TECHNOLOGY; INTEGRATED CIRCUITS; LOGIC CIRCUITS.*

*David Bursky*

**Bibliography.** C. Brown, Memories: More bits and more smarts, *Electr. Eng. Times*, no. 317, pp. 1, 16, February 18, 1985; D. Bursky, ISCCC: Digital circuits, *Electr. Des.*, 33(4):121–136, February 21, 1985; D. Bursky, Nonvolatile memories en route to higher density, speed and reliability, *Electr. Des.*, 32(17):123–144, August 23, 1984; B. C. Cole, Memories dominate ISCCC, *Electr. Week*, 58(6):51–60, February 11, 1985; T. Costlow, Fast static memories, *Electr. Des.*, 33(22):223–230, September 19, 1985; R. Sommers, Variety, versatility make nonvolatile memory difficult to forget, *Electr. Des.*, 33(13):78–96, June 6, 1985.

## Semiconductor rectifier

An electrical component which conducts current preferentially in one direction and inhibits the flow of current in the other direction by utilizing the properties of a semiconductor material such as silicon. A major use of the semiconductor rectifier is as a component in electrical equipment designed to convert electrical power from alternating current (ac) to direct current (dc). Such total equipment, consisting of not only the semiconductor components but also circuit breakers, bus work, fuses, sharing reactors, control circuits, and so forth, is often referred to as a semiconductor rectifier equipment. *SEE CONTROLLED RECTIFIER; RECTIFIER; SEMICONDUCTOR; SEMICONDUCTOR DIODE.*

Early rectifier components, utilizing the semiconductor properties of such polycrystalline materials as selenium and copper oxide, were called metallic rectifiers. Selenium rectifiers were introduced commercially around 1930 in Germany. In the early 1950s, following the invention of the transistor at Bell Laboratories, monocrystalline semiconductor rectifiers found commercial application—first germanium, then silicon in about 1954. Since then the silicon semiconductor rectifier diode has completely taken over the field in applications ranging from small electronic power supplies for radio and television to very large power-rectifier installations in the electrochemical and aluminum industries, which convert many millions of amperes from ac to dc for plating, refining, and reduction of aluminum oxide ore (bauxite) to pure aluminum. In doing so, the silicon rectifier has also technologically displaced the mercury-arc rectifier.

In 1957 the first commercial silicon-controlled rectifier (SCR) was developed and introduced by General Electric in the United States. This electrical semiconductor component has, besides the anode and cathode of the rectifier diode, a third control electrode, or gate, which allows initiating conduction through the device by means of a small trigger pulse signal from a suitable control circuit. Functionally the SCR is a semiconductor version of the thyratron (gas) tube. By the late 1960s the SCR had become the dominant power-control component. It displaced the technologies of the thyratron tube, the controlled mercury-arc rectifier (ignitron), and by the 1970s the rotating motor-generator set type of power conversion device. Its application ranges from adjustable speed control of fractional horsepower motors, to lighting and heating controls, to control of the largest dc motors.

**Silicon rectifier diodes.** Rectifier diodes are usually distinguished from other types of semiconductor diodes by the nature of their application as power-rectifying devices. While this function can take place at power conversion frequencies of from 50 Hz to 50 kHz, other diodes are used in information-processing areas such as computers, and are called computer diodes and tunnel, or Esaki, diodes. Zener diodes are employed as voltage-regulating or voltage reference devices and may be used at signal or power levels. Still another class of diodes is used in microwave-frequency applications, extending beyond the X and Ku bands, to 20 GHz. These diodes are known as Impatt, PIN, and step-recovery diodes. They are used in both signal and power applications in microwave transmitters and receivers to generate, control, and switch microwave frequencies. They are also used in high-speed instrumentation equipment, such as oscilloscopes and counters. In the rectifier diode, the important properties are current- and voltage-handling capability, recovery time (a measure of speed), efficiency, and favorable heat transfer characteristics. The information-processing and microwave-frequency type of diodes are usually very small and of lower voltage capability, and are optimized for operation at frequencies very much greater than the power-frequency (50 Hz–50 kHz) range of operation associated with rectifier diodes. *SEE MICROWAVE SOLID-STATE DEVICES; TUNNEL DIODE; ZENER DIODE.*

The electrical heart of the rectifier diode is the junction between a *p*-type region and an *n*-type region of conductivity within a monocrystalline slice of silicon semiconductor material called the pellet or the chip. The processing required to form such a *pn* junction is accomplished in commercially available silicon devices by either a diffusion or an alloying process. For a discussion of conductivity types and doping of semiconductors *SEE SEMICONDUCTOR.*

In the diffusion process, a chemically very pure slice of silicon is exposed to the hot vapor of a dopant material. Three-valence elements, such as gallium or boron, accept electrons and form a *p*-type region; 5-valence elements, such as phosphorus, donate electrons and form an *n*-type region of conductivity. If, for example, an *n*-type slice of silicon is exposed to an acceptor material, a *p*-type region will be formed at the surfaces. If subsequently one of these regions is removed, a *pn* junction will remain.

In the alloy process, a similar result is accomplished by placing a die of suitable dopant material in physical contact with the silicon slice under the proper conditions.

Once the *pn* junction is formed, it exhibits its rectifying characteristic by allowing current to flow in the conventional sense from anode (*p*-type) to cathode (*n*-type) under a very small forward bias voltage; when the voltage polarity is reversed, the *pn* junction blocks the flow of current and only a very small reverse blocking or leakage current will flow under high-reverse-voltage bias.

**Figure 1** shows the volt-ampere characteristic of a typical 250-A silicon rectifier diode. Quadrant I shows the conducting characteristic (high current, low forward voltage drop); quadrant III shows the reverse blocking characteristic (high blocking voltage, low reverse blocking current). Note the difference in scale factor. The respective voltage polarities are shown on the circuit symbol of the diode in each quadrant. An ideal diode would have zero forward drop and zero reverse blocking current. Practical silicon power diodes have forward voltage drops of the order of 1 V at rated forward current, and reverse blocking current of the order of milliamperes for large diodes at their maximum rated operating temperature (usually about 150–200°C or 300–400°F). With decreasing temperature, reverse blocking current likewise decreases, but the forward voltage drop increases, displaying the negative temperature coefficient at normal rated current densities characteristic of all silicon *pn* semiconductor junction devices.

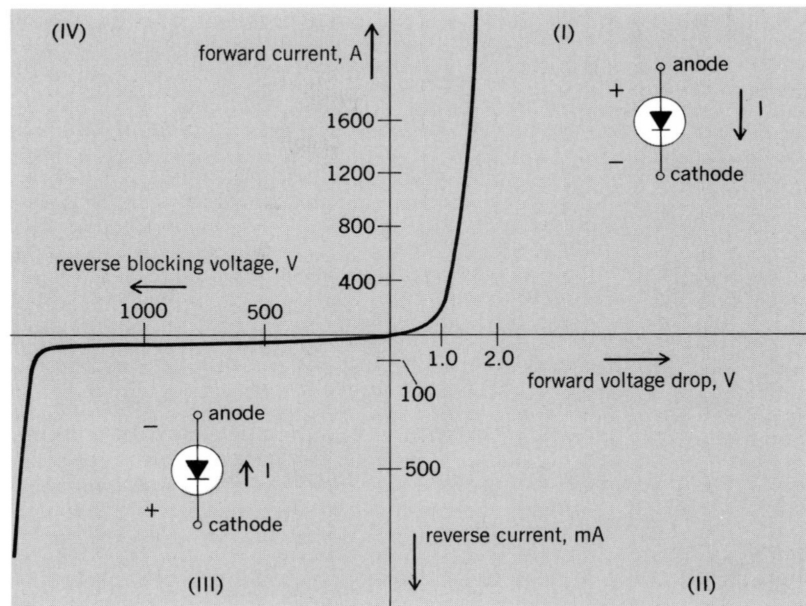


**Fig. 1. Volt-ampere characteristic of a typical 250-A silicon rectifier diode.**

The maximum value of forward current that a silicon diode can carry is limited by the power dissipation (the characteristic 1-V forward voltage drop times the current) capability of the diode housing and any external heat-sink system. In some types of construction it is limited by the internal joints between the silicon and the other parts necessary to mount the brittle silicon pellet (or chip) to the housing (usually copper).

The typical thickness of the rectifier diode pellet is of the order of 0.35 mm, with a diameter of up to 100 mm for some of the larger devices rated in thousands of amperes. The pellet must be mounted in a suitable protective housing which allows the heat to be dissipated to the external cooling ambient and which allows for proper electrical contact. Usually, housing or packages are lead-mounted for currents up to a few amperes, stud-mounted and flat-base-mounted for currents up to several hundred amperes, and external-pressure-mounted for the largest devices (**Fig. 2**). The lead-mounted package dissipates the losses directly into the ambient air, whereas all other packages are mounted on heat sinks suitable for either air or water cooling.

**Figure 3** shows the external and internal views of a typical silicon pellet subassembly enclosed by a hermetically sealed package. An SCR assembly is shown; the diode assembly is similar but does not have the small auxiliary gate and cathode leads.

Single-pellet silicon diodes are commercially available in current ratings from under 1 A to the order of 5000 A. Diodes may be connected in parallel for greater current capability when suitable means are employed to provide for current sharing between individual diodes.

The maximum value of reverse voltage blocking capability of a silicon diode is limited by the inherent semiconductor properties of the blocking *pn* junction, by the surface characteristics of the silicon pellet, particularly where the blocking junction meets the surface, and to a lesser degree by the housing. If the reverse blocking voltage is limited by the inherent or bulk semiconductor properties of the pellet, the volt-ampere characteristic will show a certain voltage beyond which the current increases very rapidly (Fig. 1, quadrant III). This is referred to as avalanche breakdown, usually a nondestructive phenomenon if the resulting power dissipation is limited to a safe value. If, on the other hand, the voltage capability of a silicon diode is limited by the surface properties of the pellet, the resulting breakdown following an excessive voltage stress is usually destructive.

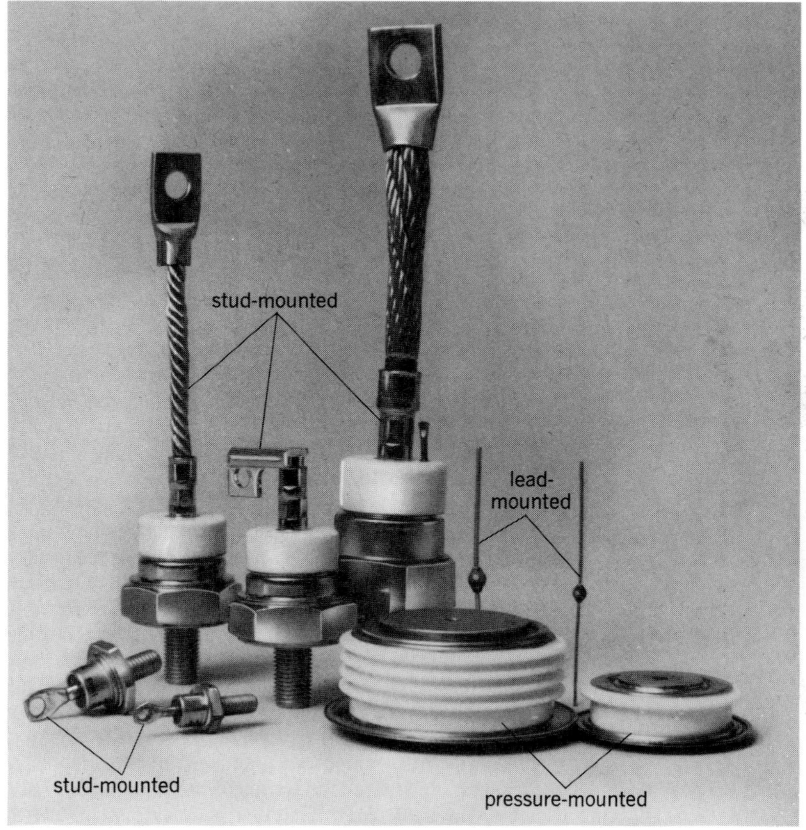


**Fig. 2. Typical rectifier diode packages which allow heat dissipation and proper electrical contact. (*General Electric Co.*)**

(a)

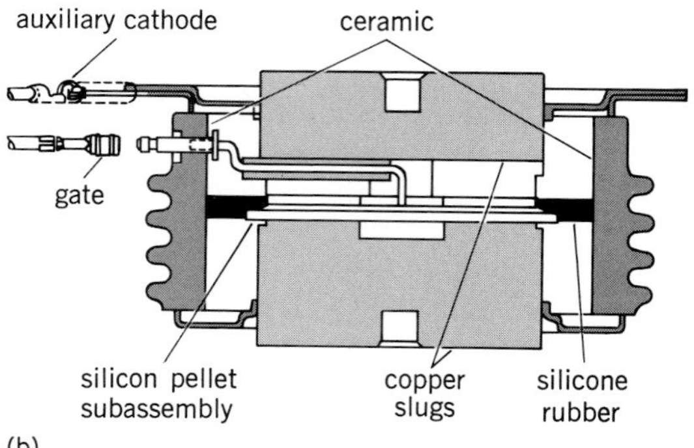


(b)

**Fig. 3. High-current SCR in a pressure-mounted package. (*a*) External view. (*b*) Cross section. (*General Electric Co.*)**

Voltage ratings of single-pellet silicon rectifier diodes commercially available cover a range from 50 to over 5000 V. Whenever a single diode has insufficient voltage capability to meet the requirements of an application, individual diodes can be connected in series for greater voltage capability. In addition to connecting individual diodes in series, diodes can be obtained prepackaged in series strings for high-voltage applications. There are commercially available single packages containing multiple diodes with voltage ratings in excess of 100 kV and current ratings in the range of 200 mA to 2 A. Lower-voltage, multiple-diode packages can be purchased with voltage ratings in the 10–20-kV range and current ratings up to 10 A.

**Schottky silicon rectifier diodes.** Unlike the *pn* junction of a regular silicon rectifier diode, the Schottky diode makes use of the rectification effect of a metal-to-silicon barrier. The Schottky diode, sometimes called Schottky barrier diode, overcomes a major limitation of the *pn* junction diode; being a majority-carrier device, it has both higher forward conductivity (lower forward voltage drop) and faster switching speeds than its minority-carrier *pn* junction counterpart. However, other factors confine its use to low-voltage power supply applications—chiefly its limited reverse blocking voltage, typically 45 V. Secondary shortcomings are high reverse blocking current and restricted temperature of operation, with commercial devices providing a maximum of 175°C (347°F), compared with 200°C (392°F) for *pn* junction diodes. **Figure 4** compares the forward and reverse electrical characteristics of the two types of devices.

Integrated circuits used in computer and instrument systems commonly require voltages less than 15 V and frequently as low as 5 V. Thus, the advantage of low forward voltage drop and faster switching favors the Schottky rectifier diode, due to its inherent efficiency. This is particularly true for the high-frequency-switching regulator supply applications where power at switching frequencies of 20–50 kHz has to be rectified. The higher reverse blocking current of the Schottky diode is more than compensated for by the Schottky's superior switching speeds. However, its cooling is more critical because of its high reverse blocking current temperature coefficient and lower maximum operating temperature. Thermal runaway and consequent destruction is more likely to occur with the Schottky diode than its *pn* junction counterpart. This occurs when a diode's power dissipation reaches a level that exceeds the ability of the cooling system to maintain the diode's temperature in equilibrium. It can be thought of as analogous to that of a sailboat which, when tipped beyond a certain angle, can no longer maintain equilibrium and will capsize. Sailboats with ballasted keels have increased stability over unballasted boats. Likewise, *pn* junctions have increased thermal stability over Schottky diodes.

**Rectifier circuits.** The greatest usage of rectifier diodes is in the conversion of electrical power from ac to dc by means of employing the diodes in a suitable electric circuit. **Figure 5** shows some basic rectifier circuits.

In Fig. 5*a* a single diode supplies power to the load only on the positive (or on half of the available) cycles of the ac supply. The load current is unidirectional and has an average value; hence, the supply current has been rectified.

Figure 5*b* shows a popular circuit for rectification of both of the available half-cycles of the supply. In both cases the waveform of the output current departs from a pure dc current which could be supplied by a battery. A measure for the quality of the output of a rectifier circuit relative to the direct current that a battery could supply is called the ripple voltage. The output ripple voltage of the full-wave circuit is less than that of the half-wave circuit. When the load requirements call for less ripple, polyphase rectifier circuits are used in high-power applications. In lower-power applications from a few watts to a few tens of kilowatts, such as are used in computers and television receivers, it is common either to use a switching regulator to generate high-frequency ac power (10–50 kHz) from the high-ripple rectified 50–60-Hz ac power supply commonly available from the local utility, or to add a relatively bulky and expensive filter to the output of the 50–60-Hz rectifier circuit. The advantage of the switching regulator approach stems from the ease of filtering high-frequency ripple resulting from rectifying high-frequency ac as opposed to filtering low-frequency ripple.

**Silicon-controlled rectifier.** The SCR is a triode reverse-blocking thyristor. Whereas diodes use two alternate layers of *pn*-type semiconductor material and transistors use three such layers, thyristor devices utilize four layers forming three or more junctions within a slice of silicon semiconductor material. Thyristor devices exhibit regenerative, or latching-type, switching action in one or two quadrants of their volt-ampere characteristic. They can be switched into the ON state (conducting condition) but must usually be restored to their OFF state (voltage-blocking condition) by circuit action. **Figure 6** shows a family of thyristor devices.

The most widely used of all thyristor devices for power control is the SCR. For specialized ac-switching power control, such as in lamp dimmers and heating controls, the bidirectional triode thyristor, popularly called the triac, has also come into widespread usage. Other types of thyristors are discussed below.

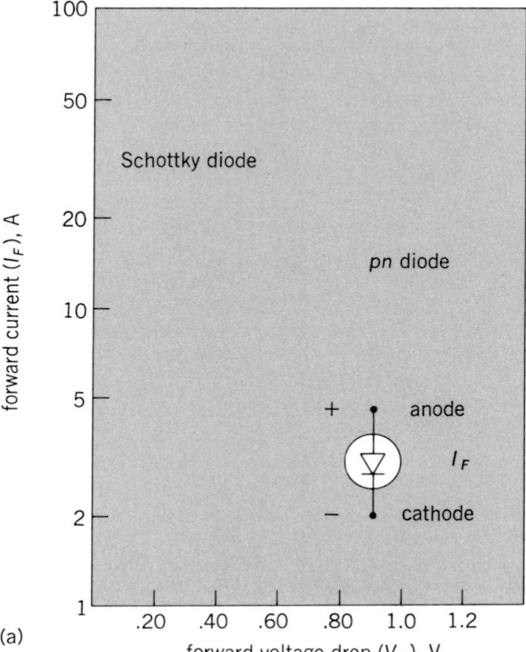


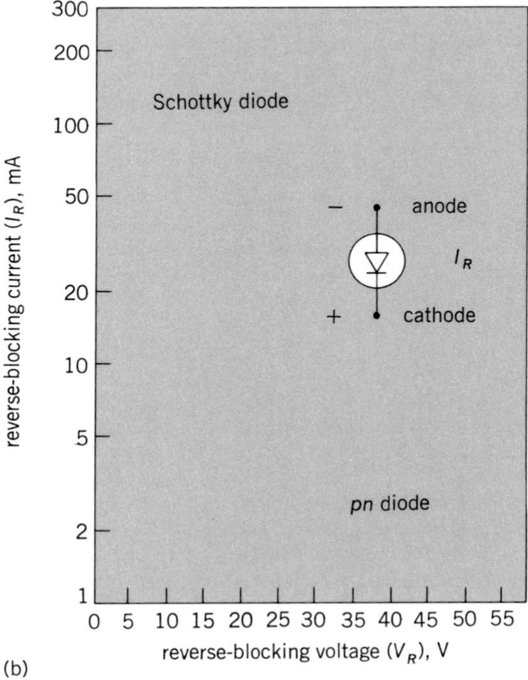


**Fig. 4. Comparison of electrical characteristics of a Schottky diode with a *pn* diode of similar ratings. (*a*) Forward characteristics. (*b*) Typical reverse characteristics. Schottky diode is operated at 45 V, 30 A, with junction at 125°C (257°F) in *a*, 150°C (302°F) in *b*. The *pn* diode is operated at 50 V, 30 A, with junction at 200°C (392°F).**

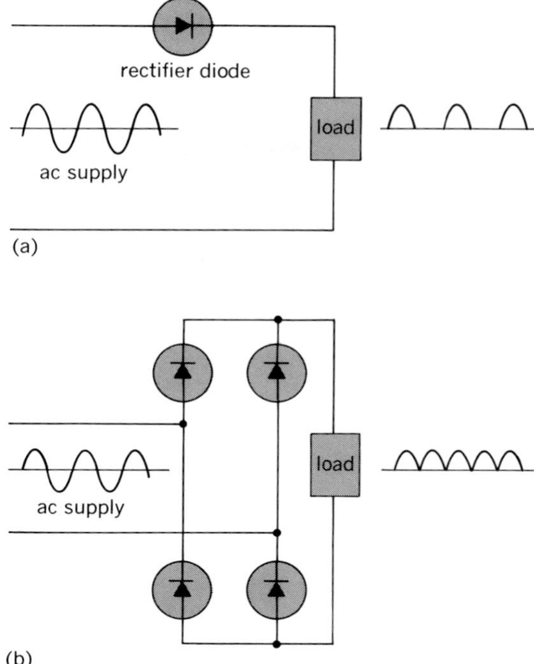


**Fig. 5. Some basic rectifier circuits. (*a*) Half-wave rectifier circuit. (*b*) Full-wave bridge rectifier circuit.**

**Figure 7** shows a typical arrange of alternate *p* and *n* layers in an SCR structure. The thickness is exaggerated in proportion for clarity of illustration. With positive voltage on its cathode with respect to its anode, the SCR blocks the flow of reverse current in a manner similar to that of a conventional silicon rectifier diode. When the voltage is reversed, the SCR blocks forward current flow until a low-power trigger signal is applied beteween the gate terminal and the cathode, whereupon the SCR switches into a highly conductive state with a voltage drop of approximately 1 V between anode and cathode similar to that of the rectifier diode. Once in conduction, the SCR continues to conduct even after the gate signal is removed, provided the anode (or load) current remains above the holding current level, typically in the order of milliamperes. If anode current momentarily drops below the holding current level or if the anode voltage is momentarily reversed, the SCR reverts to its blocking state and the gate terminal regains control. Typical SCRs turn on in about 1–5 microseconds and require 10–100 microseconds of momentary reverse voltage on the anode to regain their forward-blocking ability. The details of the ON and OFF switching characteristics of SCRs vary with different types made for varying applications.

Anode voltage applied to the SCR significantly in excess of the voltage rating of the SCR can trigger the device into conduction even in the absence of a gate signal. Excess reverse voltage, however, can permanently damage the SCR much as in the case of the silicon rectifier diode. SCRs, like the silicon diode and all power semiconductors, have a failure mechanism called thermal fatigue. Thermal fatigue failure is due to the thermal stresses induced during repetitive

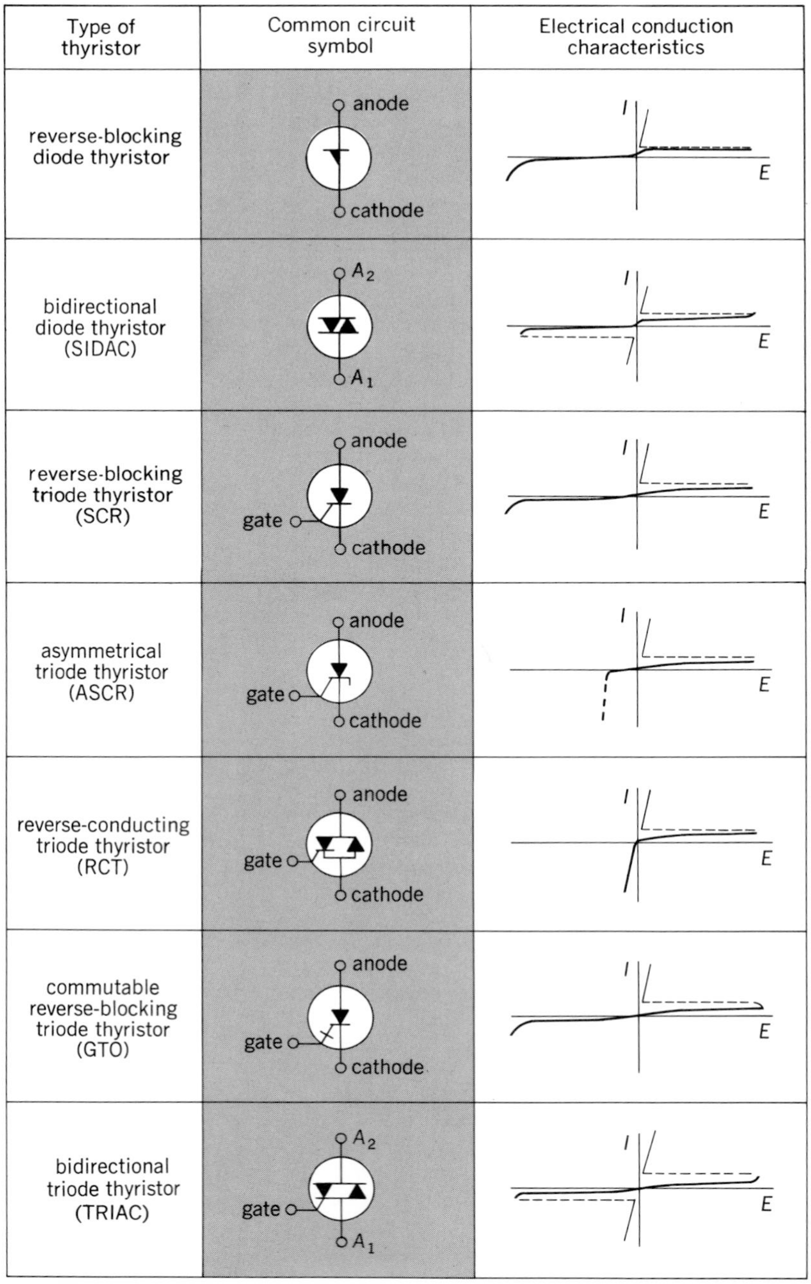

| Type of thyristor | Common circuit symbol | Electrical conduction characteristics |
|---|---|---|
| reverse-blocking diode thyristor | anode, cathode | I, E |
| bidirectional diode thyristor (SIDAC) | $A_2$, $A_1$ | I, E |
| reverse-blocking triode thyristor (SCR) | anode, gate, cathode | I, E |
| asymmetrical triode thyristor (ASCR) | anode, gate, cathode | I, E |
| reverse-conducting triode thyristor (RCT) | anode, gate, cathode | I, E |
| commutable reverse-blocking triode thyristor (GTO) | anode, gate, cathode | I, E |
| bidirectional triode thyristor (TRIAC) | $A_2$, gate, $A_1$ | I, E |

**Fig. 6. Family of thyristor devices.**

temperature changes occurring in the normal operation of the device. These stresses are inherent in all devices undergoing substantial temperature changes which contain dissimilar metals. When power semiconductors, such as rectifier diodes and SCRs, are properly applied to take into account their thermal fatigue limitations, they can be expected to perform their function faultlessly for the life of the equipment in which they are used.

Current ratings of SCRs range from under 1 to 5000 A. Blocking voltage capability of commercially available devices extends to 4400 V for the higher-power types, with voltages up to 6 kV having been demonstrated in the laboratory.

Like most semiconductor devices, SCRs are dependent on temperature in some of their characteristics. Usual operating junction temperatures are 125°C (257°F), and some devices are available up to 150°C (302°F).

The mounting considerations for SCRs are similar to those for diodes. Small devices are lead-mounted, and above 2 and 4 A SCRs are generally mounted to radiating fins or some type of heat sink for adequate cooling of the semiconductor junction. **Figures 8** and **9** show two typical SCRs: a small 2-A plastic-encapsulated SCR for use in consumer applications, and a 100-A 1400-V SCR water-cooled assembly used in glass-melting applications.

Processing techniques used in SCRs are similar to and extensions of the processing used for silicon diodes. In addition to alloy and diffusion processing technology, epitaxial processing is sometimes used. In small devices, similar to the one shown in Fig. 8, a planar structure such as that developed for signal transistors and monolithic integrated circuits is used. Higher-power SCR structures are of a mesa type of construction, with the edges of the pellet often shaped in a manner to reduce the surface field across the blocking junction for higher voltage-blocking capability.

SCR applications fall into two general categories. In one category the devices are used from an ac supply, much as the silicon rectifier diode is used. However, unlike the rectifier diode, which conducts load current as soon as the anode voltage assumes a positive value, the SCR will not conduct load current until it is triggered into conduction. If, when applied in rectifier circuits of the type shown in Fig. 5, conduction through the SCR is delayed from the point of the natural zero crossing of the forward anode-to-cathode voltage, the power delivered to the load can be varied. This mode of control is referred to as ac phase control. It is used extensively in ac to variable-voltage dc output types of applications, such as the adjustable-speed dc motor drives in the circuits similar to those shown in Fig. 5*a* and *b*, in which the diodes have been replaced by SCRs and suitable control circuitry is provided to drive the gates. The circuit of **Fig. 10** is the parallel-inverse, or ac-switch, circuit which can supply variable voltage to ac loads. It is used extensively in lighting and heating control (see Fig. 9).

Turnoff of the SCR in ac circuits is accomplished by the reversal in voltage polarity of the AC supply line. Since the SCR, like the diode, blocks the flow of reverse current, there is no flow of load current during the half-cycle of applied line voltage which places reverse bias across the SCR.

The other basic category of application for SCRs from a circuit point of view is operation from a dc supply. The major distinguishing feature of dc operation from ac operation is that there is no reversal of

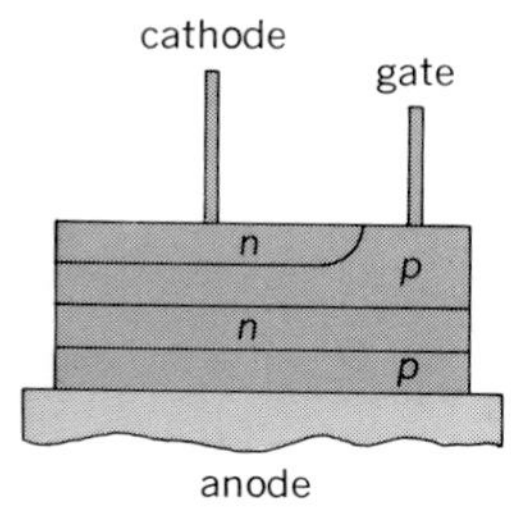


**Fig. 7. Diagrammatic view of typical SCR structure.**

Fig. 8. Small plastic-encapsulated SCR. (*General Electric Co.*)

supply voltage polarity for turnoff of the SCR, which would allow the gate electrode to regain control of the device. Therefore, auxiliary circuit means must be employed to effect turnoff of the SCR. One common way to accomplish this is to switch a previously charged capacitor across the load-carrying SCR in such a manner that the voltage on the capacitor reverse-biases the SCR sufficiently to reduce the load current through the SCR to zero, and then to allow the device a short time (about 10–50 μs) before reapplying forward blocking voltage to the anode of the SCR.

**ASCRs, RCTs, and GTOs.** These devices are all in the thyristor family and are mainly used in place of SCRs in power circuits requiring operation from a dc source. The ASCR, asymmetrical silicon-controlled rectifier, and RCT, reverse-conducting thyristor, have the advantage of faster turnoff time than the SCR, that is, 5–25 μs, and thus require a less costly auxiliary circuit to effect turnoff. The RCT has an added circuit advantage, as it has a built-in reverse rectifier diode in parallel with the device. (The RCT is the integrated equivalent of a discrete ASCR in parallel with a discrete rectifier diode.) Along with faster turnoff times, the ASCR and RCT devices have lower forward-voltage drops for comparable forward-blocking voltage ratings and silicon area, thus increasing the device's efficiency.

The GTO, gate turnoff device, is also a thyristor. Like the SCR, it is a symmetrical reverse-blocking triode thyristor (unlike the ASCR and RCT, which cannot block reverse voltages), but it has the added advantage of being able to turn off current when a negative signal is applied to the gate. (Voltage and current characteristics are given in Fig. 6.) Thus the GTO does not require an auxiliary circuit to commutate it off as do the SCR, ASCR, and RCT devices. The added complexity of gate turnoff makes the GTO higher priced than similarly rated SCRs.

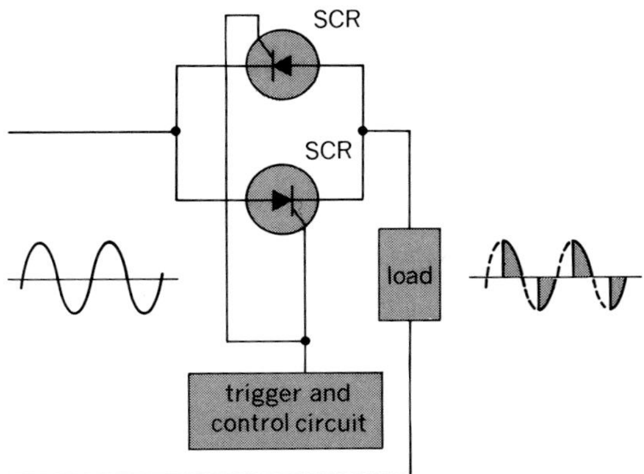


Fig. 10. Phase-controlled SCR ac switch circuit.

Fig. 9. High-current water-cooled SCR ac switch for glass-melting applications. (*General Electric Co.*)

The GTO, ASCR, and RCT all came into commercial usage during the latter half of the 1970s, primarily at voltage levels greater than 800 V and currents exceeding 25 A. It is expected that they will soon be manufactured in all current and voltage ratings that are presently available in SCRs above the lower values stated. It is projected that the greatest utilization will be of voltage ratings exceeding 1400 V and currents exceeding 100 A. **Figure 11** shows a rating comparison of rectifier diodes, thyristors, and Schottky barrier diodes.

It is necessary to operate thyristors from a dc supply in order to achieve power conversion from the dc (battery or rectified ac line) supply to a load requiring an alternating supply (dc to ac inversion) or to a load requiring a variable-voltage dc supply (dc to dc conversion). Since the rate of switching the thyristors in dc circuits can be varied by the control circuit, a thyristor inverter circuit can supply an ac load with a variable frequency. An important application of this mode of operation is for adjustable speed operation of ac synchronous and induction motors in industrial processing.

A battery source can be converted to a variable-voltage dc source for a dc motor by "chopping" the dc source voltage either at a variable rate at constant pulse width (frequency power modulation) or by operating the chopper circuit at a constant frequency and varying the pulse width (pulse-width power modulation). An important application of chopper circuits is

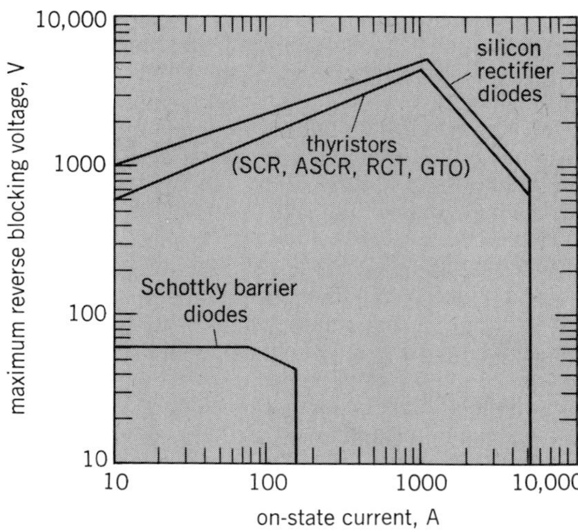


**Fig. 11. Rating comparison of SCRs, rectifier diodes, and Schottky barrier diodes commercially available with single silicon discrete devices. The horizontal scale gives rms current for SCRs, average current for rectifier diodes.**

tion). An important application of chopper circuits is in battery-operated vehicles, such as forklift trucks and mining locomotives. SEE CHOPPER; MULTIVIBRATOR.

*F. B. Golden*

**Bibliography.** S. K. Ghandhi, *Semiconductor Power Devices: Physics of Operation and Fabrication Technology*, 1977; F. B. Golden and D. R. Grafham, *SCR Manual*, 6th ed., 1979; *Power Semiconductor D.A.T.A. Book*, 13th ed., vol. 25, book 23, 1980; J. Schaefer, *Rectifier Circuits: Theory and Design*, 1968.

## Sensitivity

The ability of the output of a device or system to respond to an input stimulus. Mathematically, sensitivity is expressed as the ratio of the response or change induced in the output to a stimulus or change in the input. If the sensitivity varies with the level of the input signal, then sensitivity is usually expressed in terms of the derivative of the output with respect to the input at a specified input level.

The reciprocal of sensitivity is called the scale factor or figure of merit, and it represents the conversion factor by which the output indicator or scale reading must be multiplied to obtain the magnitude of the input. Occasionally the scale factor is called the sensitivity through loose usage.

Sensitivity is closely related to noise. Quite often the limiting factor in increasing the sensitivity of devices or systems is the inherent noise level. For instance, the noise level for an electric galvanometer or a gravitational weight balance arises from the random or brownian movement of the air molecules surrounding the apparatus. In electrical circuits, the noise level arises from the random movement of electrons in resistors. SEE ELECTRICAL NOISE.

Examples of sensitivity are visual contrast sensitivity, which is the ability of the eye to distinguish between the luminances of adjacent areas; galvanometer sensitivity, expressed as the ratio of the scale deflection in millimeters per microampere input; and radio receiver sensitivity, which is actually expressed in terms of reciprocal sensitivity in the form of antenna voltage in microvolts necessary to cause a specified output.

The sensitivity of a radio receiver is a measure of its ability to reproduce weak broadcast signals with satisfactory output volume. The sensitivity of a television camera tube determines its ability to deliver a usable picture signal under poor lighting conditions.

*John Markus*

## Series circuit

An electric circuit in which the principal circuit elements have their terminals joined in sequence so that a common current flows through all the elements.

The circuit may consist of any number of passive and active elements, such as resistors, inductors, capacitors, electron tubes, and transistors.

The algebraic sum of the voltage drops across each of the circuit elements of the series circuit must equal the algebraic sum of the applied voltages. This rule is known as Kirchhoff's second law and is of fundamental importance in electric circuit theory. SEE KIRCHHOFF'S LAWS OF ELECTRIC CIRCUITS.

When time-varying voltages and currents are involved, it is necessary to employ differential or integral equations to express the summation of voltages about a series circuit. If the voltages and currents vary sinusoidally with time, functions of a complex variable are used in place of the calculus. SEE ALTERNATING-CURRENT CIRCUIT THEORY; CIRCUIT (ELECTRICITY); DIRECT-CURRENT CIRCUIT THEORY.

*Robert Lee Ramey*

## Shunting

The act of connecting one device to the terminals of another so that the current is divided between the two devices in proportion to their respective admittances. Shunting is widely used in ammeters, galvanometers, and other current-measuring instruments to bypass part of the current around the instrument so as to change the measuring range. Resistors are frequently shunted across tuned circuits to broaden the tuning characteristics.

Shunting is equivalent to connecting in parallel. Shunting one resistor with another gives a lower resistance for the combination, whereas shunting one capacitor with another gives a total capacitance equal to the sum of the individual values. SEE ALTERNATING-CURRENT CIRCUIT THEORY; DIRECT-CURRENT CIRCUIT THEORY.

*John Markus*

## Sideband

The frequency band located either above or below the carrier frequency within which fall the frequency components of the wave produced by the process of modulation. The term sideband is most commonly used in conjunction with a linear modulation format such as amplitude modulation (AM), double sideband (DSB) or single sideband (SSB). For an AM signal, the spectrum consists of a carrier component plus the spectrum of the modulating waveform shifted from being centered at dc (zero frequency) to being centered at the carrier frequency. Those frequency components which are higher than the carrier frequency are referred to as the upper sideband, while those frequency component having values less than the carrier frequency are referred to as the lower sideband. These sidebands have conjugate symmetry, meaning the value of the spectrum at a frequency $\Delta f$ Hz above the carrier frequency is the complex conjugate of the value of the spectrum located $\Delta f$ Hz below the carrier frequency. *See* Amplitude modulation; Carrier; Single sideband.

Because the carrier component conveys no information, it can be suppressed, and the resulting waveform, known as double sideband, contains only the two sidebands. Furthermore, because of the conjugate symmetry of the sidebands, either sideband by itself contains all the information in the modulating signal, and hence only the upper or the lower sideband has to be transmitted. This gives rise to a single-sideband signal.

For angle modulation formats the spectrum of the resulting waveform is much more difficult to determine, but for certain special cases the spectrum is known and the idea of sidebands is again meaningful. For example, a sinusoidal signal frequency modulating a radio-frequency carrier gives rise to a spectrum consisting of an infinite number of harmonics, each displaced from its adjacent neighbors by the frequency of the modulation. An even-order harmonic above the carrier component is equal to the corresponding harmonic below the carrier frequency, but an odd-order harmonic above the carrier is equal to the negative of the corresponding component below the carrier frequency. *See* Angle modulation.

For digital modulation systems, the spectrum is determined by the statistics of the modulating signal as well as the type of modulation being used. If a random sequence of constant-amplitude bipolar pulses having constant time duration is used to represent the information to be transmitted (this is commonly referred to as a random binary sequence), and if this pulse sequence phase-modulates a carrier, thus forming a phase-shift keyed (PSK) signal, the shape of the spectrum will have the form of the function shown below, with the zeroes falling at multiples of the bit

$$\left(\frac{\sin x}{x}\right)^2$$

rate. It is again possible to envision the frequencies above the carrier frequency forming the upper sideband and those below the carrier forming the lower sideband.

*Laurence B. Milstein*

**Bibliography.** S. Haykin, *Communication Systems*, 1983; B. P. Lathi, *Modern Digital and Analog Communication Systems*, 1983; R. E. Ziemer and W. H. Tranter, *Principles of Communications*, 1976.

## Signal generator

A piece of electronic test equipment that delivers a sinusoidal output of accurately calibrated frequency. The frequency may be anywhere from audio to microwave, depending upon the intended use of the instrument. The frequency and the amplitude are adjustable over a wide range. The oscillator must have excellent frequency stability, and its amplitude must remain constant over the tuning range.

The Wien-bridge oscillator is commonly used for frequencies up to about 200 kHz. For a radio-frequency signal generator up to about 200 MHz, a resonant circuit oscillator is used (such as a tuned-plate tuned-grid, Hartley, or Colpitts). Beyond this range vhf and microwave oscillators are used.

Many signal generators contain circuitry that allows the output to be either amplitude- or frequency-modulated. The most common forms of amplitude modulation are sinusoidal, square-wave, or pulse. The frequency is either kept constant, is sinusoidal-modulated, or is swept linearly across a band of frequencies. For example, for testing broadcast receivers, it is important to sweep the generator frequency over a range of ±10 kHz at a low rate, say 60 times a second. *See* Oscillator; Pulse generator; Wave-shaping circuits.

*Jacob Millman*

**Bibliography.** B. A. Gregory, *An Introduction to Electrical Instrumentation and Measurement Systems*, 2d ed., 1981; R. L. Heiserman, *Electrical and Electronic Measuring Instruments*, 1983; J. Markus, *Modern Electronic Circuits Reference Manual*, 1980.

## Signal-to-noise ratio

The ratio of the signal power to the noise power at the point of measurement, abbreviated S/N or SNR. It is a most important measure of the quality of a signal, for example, a radio or television signal. Signal-to-noise (power) ratios for good-quality telephony, radio, or television must equal or exceed 10,000 (40 dB). At the first amplifier in a receiving system, the signal power is minimum; this power, the noise power received with it, and the noise power generated in the amplifier determine the final receiver signal-to-noise ratio. Because the noise power generated in the amplifier often dominates, specially designed low-noise amplifiers generally are used to maximize the signal-to-noise ratio. *See* Amplifier; Radio receiver.

All matter emits electromagnetic radiation in the form of noise, the amount of the noise being proportional to the absolute temperature of the source. An effective noise temperature $T$ can be assigned to any noise source corresponding to the amount of noise radiating from it. This concept is used to describe the sources of noise in microwave satellite systems, with each noise source assigned an effective temperature value proportional to its noise power contributed to the output. The effective temperature may be much more and (sometimes) less than the actual temperature of the device. Noise sources include background radiation from outer space, rain, the Earth, and the receiver itself. Receiver noise temperatures range from near absolute zero to several thousand kelvins. The overall system noise temperature is the result of noise contributions from many sources in an electronic system. The signal-to-noise ratio can be determined by using the noise temperature. A higher noise temperature results in a lower signal-to-noise ratio. *See* Electrical noise.

*Clyde L. Ruthroff*

## Simulation

The development and use of computer models for the study of actual or postulated dynamic systems. This definition, based on the current meaning of the word to the technological community, requires some interpretation.

The essential characteristic of simulation is the use of models for study and experimentation rather than the actual system modeled. In practice, it has come to mean the use of computer models because modern electronic computers are so much superior for most kinds of simulation that computer modeling dominates the field. "Systems," as used in the definition, refers to an interrelated set of elements, components, or subsystems. "Dynamic systems" are specified because the study of static systems seldom justifies the sophistication inherent in computer simulation. *See* Analog computer; Computer; Digital computer.

"Postulated" systems as well as "actual" ones are included in the definition because of the importance of simulation for testing hypotheses, as well as designs of systems not yet in existence. The "development" as well as "use" of models is included because, in the empirical approach to system simulation, a simplified simulation of a hypothesized model is used to check educated guesses, and thus to develop a more sophisticated and more realistic simulation of the simuland. The simuland is that which is simulated, whether real or postulated.

The impracticality of developing intercontinental ballistic missiles and spacecraft by actual flight testing gave simulation its big impetus just after World War II. Since then the equipment and the techniques have been adopted by workers in other fields where the simuland does not exist or is intractable to experimental manipulation, or where experiments with the actual system would entail high cost, danger to the system or the experimenter, or both. Among these nonaerospace systems which have been simulated, in addition to those that are considered later, are chemical and other industrial processes; structural dynamics; physiological and biological systems; automobile, ship, and submarine dynamics; social, ecological, political, and economic systems; electrical, electronic, optical, and acoustic systems; and learning, thinking, and problem-solving systems. *See* Optimization.

Simulations may be classified according to (1) the kind of computer used (analog, digital, hybrid); (2) the nature of the simuland (spacecraft, chemical plant, economic system); (3) the signal flow in the simuland (continuous, discrete or mixed); or (4) the temporal relation of events in the simuland (faster-than-real-time, real-time, slower-than-real-time, with real-time being clock or simuland time). Thus, for example, one may have a continuous real-time analog spacecraft simulation, or a sampled-data (discrete) faster-than-real-time digital economic system simulation, though such complete classification is seldom spelled out.

**Mathematical modeling.** Mathematical modeling is a recognized and valuable adjunct, and usually a precursor, of computer simulation. In practice the mathematical equations describing the interrelation of components of the simuland are written in a form suitable for the computer. In true simulation the computer is programmed to retain an identifiable correspondence between computer functions and the dynamics of the simuland. If mathematical manipulations or computer characteristics obscure this relationship, the computer may be processing information relative to the simuland, but it cannot properly be said to be simulating it.

Mathematical modeling does not necessarily precede simulation, however; sometimes the simuland is not well enough understood to permit rigorous mathematical description. In such cases it is often possible to postulate a functional relationship of the elements of the simuland without specifying mathematically what that relationship is. This is the building-block approach, for which analog computers are particularly well suited. Parameters related to the function of the blocks can be adjusted intuitively, systematically, or according to some established technique for system identification until some functional criteria are met. Thus the mathematical model can be developed as the result of, rather than as a requirement for, simulation.

**Analog simulation.** Simulation, as defined here, has been developed since World War II. Analog computers, in which signals are continuous and are processed in parallel, were originally the most popular for simulation. Their modular design made it natural to retain the simulation-simuland correspondence, and their parallel operation gave them the speed required for real-time operation. The result was unsurpassed human-machine rapport.

**Digital simulation.** However, block-oriented digital simulation languages (such as MIDAS, CSMP, and their successors) were developed which allow a pseudo–simulation-simuland correspondence, and digital computer speeds have increased to a degree that allows real-time simulation of all but very fast or very complex systems. Inadequate input/output facilities degrade human-machine interaction in all but the most sophisticated digital systems which embody expensive input/output equipment; nevertheless, digital computers are better than analog for simulating certain kinds of systems, particularly those requiring high precision or extremely wide dynamic ranges. *See* Data-processing systems; Digital computer programming; Programming languages.

**Hybrid simulation.** Hybrid simulation, in which both continuous and discrete signals are processed, both in parallel and serially, is the result of a desire to combine the speed and human-machine rapport of the analog computer with the precision, logic capability, and memory capacity of the digital computer. After years during which the weak points of each kind of computer seemed to combine more readily than their strengths, hybrid simulation now makes possible the simulation of a new array of systems which require combinations of computer characteristics unavailable in either all-analog or all-digital computers.

In the past, most hybrid simulation systems were engineered by connecting a general-purpose digital computer to one or more general-purpose analog computers through interface equipment consisting largely of digital-to-analog and analog-to-digital signal converters (**Fig. 1**). However, the practice of hybridizing analog computers by the addition of a complement of digital logic and the development of specialized digital hardware was followed by the development of powerful hybrid systems specifically designed for the simulation of large complicated simulands. The relatively high cost of such systems is more than justified for some types of problems, primarily by the speed derived from the parallel operation of the analog elements, particularly the integrators, which are so prominent in any computer simulation program. Such speed pays dividends when the simulation involves high frequencies or when many iterations of an experiment are required—for instance, when it is necessary to get a statistically significant number of simulation runs of a stochastic process. In such systems the digital processer can select and program analog elements and the interface equipment, and check out the simulation. *See* ANALOG-TO-DIGITAL CONVERTER; DIGITAL-TO-ANALOG CONVERTER.

As the digital computer is capable of determining which parts of the model are simulated in the central processor and which in the remote terminal, the operator need not know what parts of the simuland are being simulated digitally and what parts by analog components.

**Trends.** With the advent of still more powerful digital computers, indications were that large computation centers would be designed around extremely fast time-shared digital central processors, accessed through many different special-purpose remote terminals (**Fig. 2**), and this has indeed been the case in many instances. Terminals for business data-processing and purely mathematical computation by such systems can consist of digital alphanumeric input/output devices, sophisticated successors to the teletypewriter. Terminals for engineering design, however, usually have graphic input and output, and use programs to facilitate interactive human-machine discourse. Either of the above kinds of terminals may be used for computer-assisted instruction, but still more sophisticated special-purpose terminals, designed specifically for educational purposes such as those used with the PLATO system, are coming into use. *See* COMPUTER-AIDED DESIGN AND MANUFACTURING; COMPUTER-AIDED ENGINEERING; COMPUTER GRAPHICS; MULTIACCESS COMPUTER.

Some special-purpose remote terminals which are particularly well suited for simulation are functionally similar to a small- to medium-sized hybrid computer. These "intelligent terminals" contain elements to facilitate human-machine interaction and have a limited capability for independent computation under local control. Typically, however, these terminals are used for communication with a central processor.

As the computing capacity of the remote terminals increases, they take on more of the character of satellite computers, and the overall system that of a computer network. The effect of such networks on simulation will be to provide access to more powerful simulation programs and to make more powerful equipment more widely and economically available. It should also discourage the practice of individuals who wish to simulate building their own model; ready-made models of many kinds can be accessed through the network.

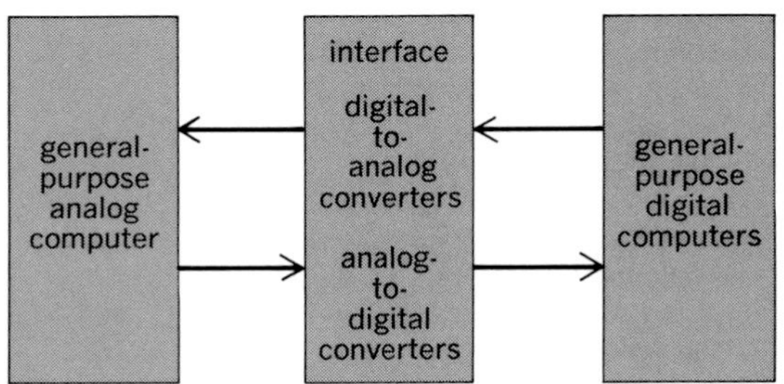

**Fig. 1. Hybrid simulation system.**

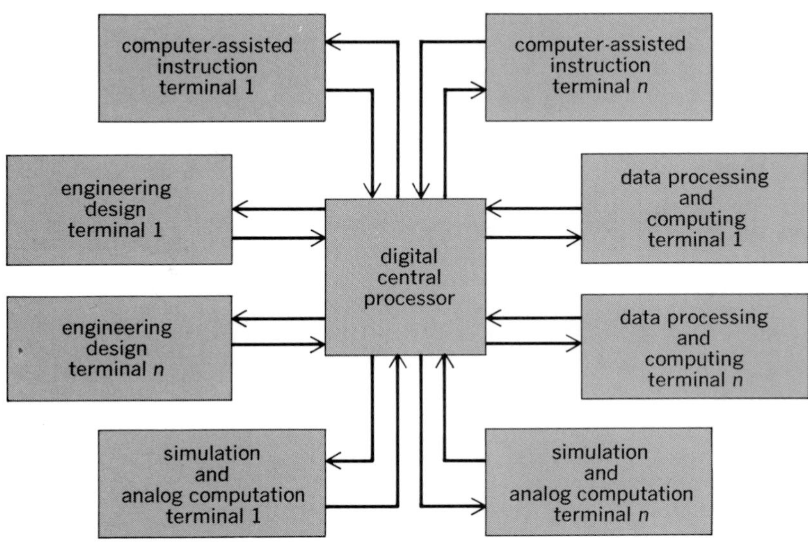

**Fig. 2. Time-shared digital central processor with multiple inputs.**

The foregoing is a trend toward bigness; however, there is a countertrend. Started by the minicomputers and now getting a boost of unpredictable importance by the microcomputers, the current trend is such that it may not be long before all users can have as much computing power as they need in their own facility—if not at their own desk—so that the need to go to a network will be diminished if not eliminated. The exception may be the need for access to a large data bank, which becomes a communication, not a simulation problem. *See* MICROCOMPUTER.

**Applications.** Some simulationists have claimed that any system which can be adequately described in a natural language can be modeled on a computer, and thus simulated. Admittedly this seems to be an extremely broad statement, but it becomes credible if the meaning of "adequately" in this context is examined. A simulation study does not require that the simuland be completely described (an impractical if not impossible task in the case of many complicated systems). The simuland is adequately modeled when those factors—the parameters and the variables and their interrelationships which will significantly influence the results of a simulation experiment—are modeled and described with an accuracy commensurate with the accuracy required of the results.

The above is a qualitative description of adequacy as it applies to computer modeling for simulation. But computer modeling is completely quantitative; everything—parameters, variables, relationships, and even external influences—must be described by numbers. To do this, the modeler must be thoroughly familiar with the simuland and, having obtained the data required to assign the necessary numbers, must be able to program a computer to relate these factors. The modeler must also know the accuracy required of the results. Therefore most simulations of complicated systems are done by teams—an expert in the field of the simuland (economics, for example), a mathematician, a computer programmer, and an analyst working together to produce results useful to a decision maker (a business executive or a politician, for example).

Because simulation is a methodology for improving insight relative to complex issues in general, rather than in just certain fields, it has been used to investigate problems of all kinds. Only a few will be mentioned here.

Mental models of an economy have always been a tool of economic research. Three applications of simulation in economics are: (1) forecasting the effects on the economy (employment, production, consumption expenditure, inflation, balance of payments) of various policy changes (changes in government expenditure, tax rates, interest-rate ceilings, or the treatment of depreciation); (2) examining the behavior of the individual units in the economy (such as households, business firms, laborers); and (3) improving statistical tools used in estimating relationships among economic variables.

Management cannot be divorced from economics, and neither can be studied without regard to the social impacts involved. This is reflected in the computer simulation techniques that have been adopted by corporations in the advanced industrial countries. But with the increasing availability of low-cost microcomputers, simulation is also a tool for the management of small businesses. Their needs and problems are very similar to those of larger firms.

Traffic and transportation systems as well as business organizations require management, and effective management requires an understanding of the system of concern and, if possible, a means of studying the impact of alternative methods of controlling that system. Simulation fulfills these requirements.

Energy, however, has become the subject of the most intense simulation activity. Hundreds of models to support simulation studies of the generation, distribution, and use of electrical energy, triggered by the oil embargo of 1973, have been developed. The study of electrical energy systems has not been the only use of simulation to study energy-related problems. Another important application has been to study tradeoffs among the many existing and proposed sources of energy.

Computer simulation has become an indispensible tool in the study of complex biological processes ranging from intracellular chemical reactions, through the behavior of various organ systems, to the evolution of entire ecosystems. For example, computer simulation is uniquely suited to the study of plant disease epidemics, complex biological phenomena in which growth and interaction of the pathogen and host are affected by environmental factors; and the crop manager, when intervening by means such as chemical treatment, can become a third interactive component. The simulation of ecosystems via numerical models is essential in studying the way in which these ecosystems operate normally, how resistant this operation is to the short- or long-term effects of perturbation, and how such effects can be predicted; all these questions are important in current ecological research as the pressures of human economic growth threaten to impair or even destroy the function of many natural ecosystems.

*John H. McLeod, Jr.*

***Bibliography.*** P. Bratley et al., *A Guide to Simulation,* 1983; P. W. House and J. McLeod, *Large-Scale Models for Policy Evaluation,* 1977; A. M. Law and D. Kelton, *Simulation Modelling and Analysis,* 1982; J. McLeod (ed.), *Simulation in the Service of Society,* monthly; J. A. Payne, *Introduction to Simulation,* 1982; *Proceedings of the Annual Summer Computer Simulation Conference; Proceedings of the International Scientific Forum on an Acceptable World Energy Future,* Cambridge, Massachusetts, 1979; *Proceedings of the National Computer Conference; Proceedings of the Pittsburgh Modeling and Simulation Conference; Proceedings of the Simulation Symposium; Proceedings of the Winter Simulation Conference;* N. Roberts and D. Andersen, *Introduction to Computer Simulation: The System Dynamics Approach,* 1983; *Simulation Councils Proceedings Series,* semiannual; Society for Computer Simulation, *Simulation,* monthly.

## Single sideband

An electronic signal-processing technique in which a spectrum of intelligence is translated from a zero reference frequency to a higher frequency without a change of frequency relationships within the translated spectrum. Single-sideband (SSB) signals have no appreciable carrier. After translation, only the single-sideband energy remains. This form of intelligence transmission requires distortion-free amplification of the SSB signal prior to transmission and occupies only the spectrum bandwidth of that intelligence. These advantages allow SSB to be selected for communication of voice and digital data wherever there is a premium on having a minimum of transmitted power and available frequency spectrum.

Amplitude-modulated (AM) signals have identical upper and lower sidebands symmetrically located on each side of the translation frequency, which is often called the carrier. The SSB spectrum differs from the AM spectrum in having little or no carrier and only one sideband. (A double-sideband signal is one in which only the carrier is suppressed, leaving both sidebands. This technique is not commonly used.) *See Amplitude modulation.*

**Generation.** In the SSB signal-processing action, the intelligence spectrum to be translated is applied to the signal input port of a balanced modulator. A higher-frequency sinusoidal signal, often called a carrier, is applied to the other input port of this circuit. Its function is to translate the zero reference spectrum to the carrier frequency and to produce the upper and lower sidebands, which are symmetrically located on each side of the carrier. The carrier frequency power is suppressed to a negligible value by the balanced operation of the modulator and does not appear at the output. Generally, the balanced modulator operates at an intermediate frequency which is lower than the frequency of transmission. Following the balanced modulator is a sideband filter which is designed to remove the unwanted sideband signal power and to allow only the desired intelligence spectrum to pass. A block diagram and drawings of the signal characteristics at each major circuit interface are shown in the **illustration**. *See Amplitude modulator; Modulator.*

The outputs of several sideband filters having adjacent frequency passbands may be added to produce a succession of intelligence channel groups, each with differing information content. These may be translated to higher frequency and amplified for transmission; amplified and transmitted directly; or used as an input to a frequency, phase, or pulse code modulation system. *See Frequency modulation; Multiplexing; Phase modulation; Pulse modulation.*

The SSB signal-handling processes are carefully designed to avoid distortion of the frequency relationships within the sideband spectrum. Amplifier circuits and components are chosen to provide a highly linear signal-handling capability. Linearity is measured by determining the level of the third-order tone and the fifth-order tone produced when two tones ($f_1$, $f_2$) occupy the intelligence channel. Typically linearity requirements allow a third-order tone level less than 1/1000 (30 decibels below) the desired tone's power level and a fifth tone almost 1/1,000,000 (60 decibels below) the desired tone's power level. Filters are designed for equal amplitude response and uniform time delay of the frequency components in the signal passband.

A technique is under development and in early commercial use which compresses both the frequency range and the amplitude range of the intelligence spectrum before translation. This technique is referred to as amplitude compandered sideband (ACSB). ACSB processing improves the signal-to-noise performance for a given transmitted power and furthermore decreases the required transmission bandwidth.

**Reception.** Reception of SSB signals is essentially a reverse process from signal generation. The signal energy derived from the antenna is selected for a desired frequency range by radio-frequency filtering, is amplified to a desired level, and is translated down to an intermediate frequency. The signal-processing circuitry required to derive the desired intelligence channel spectrum from the intermediate frequency requires a demodulator which is similar to the modulator of the SSB generator. ACSB reception requires an inverse signal processing of the intelligence spectrum to that used in transmission in which the original frequency and amplitude range are precisely restored.

**Frequency stability requirements.** Frequency stability of a high order is required of the signal generators that provide the translation frequencies in both SSB generation and reception. In the precise recovery of the intelligence spectrum there is a direct dependence upon total system frequency accuracy in returning the received intelligence sideband to zero reference frequency. Voice communication intelligibility suffers little with a system frequency error of up to 50 Hz, although digital data may be disrupted severely with only a few hertz error. Many SSB systems use a frequency synthesizer which makes all translation frequencies dependent upon a single piezoelectric frequency generator which can be designed for frequency accuracy on the order of 1 part in $10^9$ under severe environmental conditions. Atomic standards for frequency generation can provide reference frequency accuracy on the order of 1 part in $10^{12}$.

The Doppler shift, caused by motion of high-velocity vehicles carrying SSB equipment, for example, supersonic aircraft or satellites, necessitates transmitting some reference frequency power (suppressed carrier) to provide at the receiver a source for frequency or phase locking of the frequency standard. In ACSB transmission and reception there is need for a high relative stability of the reference (carrier) frequency. Thus a pilot tone is transmitted, and upon reception it provides a stable frequency reference to which the translator frequency is phase-locked. SEE AUTOMATIC FREQUENCY CONTROL (AFC).

**Communications.** There are many advantages in the use of SSB techniques for communication systems. The two primary advantages are the reduction of transmission bandwidth and transmission power. The bandwidth required is not greater than the intelligence bandwidth and is one-half that used by amplitude modulation. The output power required to give equal energy in the intelligence bandwidth is one-sixth that of amplitude modulation.

Propagation of radio energy via ionospheric refraction and when the transmitted signal energy is reflected from terrain objects or from buildings (as in land mobile communications) provides the possibility for multiple paths of differing path length which cause a selective cancellation of frequency components at regular frequency spacings. This produces in amplitude modulation (AM) a severe distortion of the intelligence because of the critically dependent carrier-to-sideband amplitude and phase relationships. Frequency-modulated (FM) multipath signals in conjunction with the motion of a vehicular receiver cause a rapid fading to occur so that when the median received signal is near the required noise quieting threshold level the receiver will emit bursts of noise.

SSB is much less affected under these conditions. SSB does not have an abrupt noise quieting threshold as does FM, since with SSB there is a nearly linear increase of noise as the signal level decreases. SSB has proved to be a highly satisfactory communication signaling method where signal-to-noise ratio levels of under 10:1 are present, and SSB can produce intelligible voice communication at less than unity signal-to-noise ratio.

SSB and its close relative ACSB are inherently less affected by interference than are either AM or FM due to the narrow bandwidth occupied by SSB/ACSB, and since the reference frequency is adjusted for clarity of the desired signal, the undesired signal appears noiselike. Thus in SSB the signal-to-noise ratio of the desired signal is reduced by interference. In FM the interfering signal either can capture the demodulator when the interference is stronger than the desired signal or can severely distort the desired signal when the interference is less than the desired signal. In AM a weaker interfering signal will appear as an intelligible signal at a lower level than the desired signal. SSB techniques are finding wide use in wire line, coaxial cable, long-range high-frequency communications, microwave multiplex, ground-to-air—air-to-ground voice communication and land mobile (ASCB) communications, and are being used in experimental satellite-to-Earth channels.

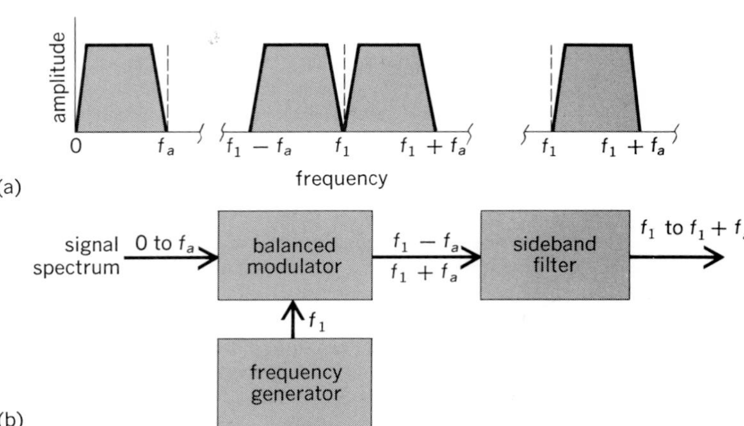


**Generation of a single-sideband signal. (*a*) Spectrum. (*b*) Block diagram.**

High-channel-density microwave systems which formerly employed FM multiplex techniques are now being installed using SSB-modulation techniques to achieve more than twice the number of channels in the same spectrum bandwidth. SSB microwave has equal or improved performance when compared to that of FM multiplexed microwave.

**History.** The discovery of SSB can be credited to John R. Carson in 1915. He found from the mathematical equations that there was a preservation of the premodulation spectrum in the remaining sideband after the removal of the lower sideband and the carrier of an AM signal. He experimentally proved this by using the filtering capability of a frequency-selective antenna. His Patent No. 1,449,382, filed in 1915 and granted in 1923, recognized this. Transoceanic experiments were also in progress by 1923, and were soon followed by commercial radio telephone channels. Wider utility followed developments in stable frequency generators and improved filter technology and amplifier components.

*David M. Hodgin*

***Bibliography.*** American Radio Relay League, *Radio Amateur's Handbook*, revised periodically; American Radio Relay League, *Single Sideband for the Radio Amateur*, revised periodically; G. W. Bartlett (ed.), *NAB Engineering Handbook*, 6th ed., 1975; F. R. Connor, *Modulation*, 1973; W. C. Y. Lee, *Mobile Communications Engineering*, 1982.

## Slide rule

A mechanical analog computing aid which is used for multiplication and division and, to a lesser degree, for looking up functions. In its most common form a slide rule consists of a body formed from two parallel members rigidly fastened together, a slide which can be moved left or right between the body members, and a transparent indicator which carries a hairline and can be moved left or right over the face of the body and the slide. Scales are provided on the body and the slide as shown in the **illustration**.

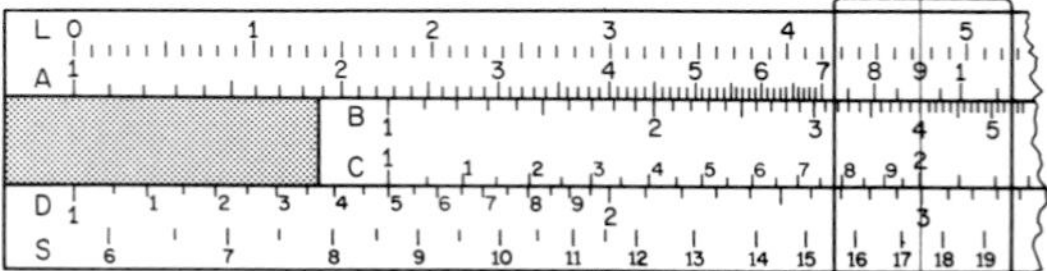


Left of slide rule, showing multiplication of 1.5 by 2.

The C and D scales, used for multiplication and division, are graduated from 1 on the left to 10 on the right, with intermediate numbers distributed logarithmically. Multiplication on a slide rule is based upon the fact that the product of two numbers can be obtained by adding the logarithms of the two numbers and then taking the antilogarithm. To perform multiplication, the index on the slider is aligned with the graduation on the body that represents the multiplicand, and the indicator hairline is placed over the position on the slider that represents the multiplier. The product appears under the hairline on the body. The illustration shows the positions of the body, slider, and indicator for performing the multiplication of 1.5 by 2.

Division, which is accomplished by subtraction of the logarithm of the divisor from that of the dividend, is performed in reverse sequence to multiplication. Thus, in the illustration the indicator would be set over the dividend 3 as read on the D scale, and then the slider would be moved until the divisor 2 as read on the C scale also appeared under the hairline. The quotient 1.5 then appears on the D scale opposite the index on the slider.

Numbers for which graduations do not exist must be estimated by eye, and a rough mental calculation must be performed to determine the position of the decimal point in the result obtained.

Many slide rules also carry scales from which sines, cosines, tangents, natural logarithms, logarithms to the base 10, squares, and cubes can be read. The S scale on the body of the rule illustrated is calibrated from approximately 6 to 90°, with the angles placed opposite the corresponding sines as read on the D scale. Thus the sine of 17.5° is 0.3. Logarithms to the base 10 can be read using the L and D scales.

The most common rule has a 10-in. scale, but larger and smaller straight rules and circular rules are used. Circular rules offer a convenience in multiplication. For example, multiplication of 2 by 6 using the left-hand C index is not possible with a straight rule. Instead, one must reverse ends and use the right-hand C index. With a circular rule this problem does not arise, because the scale is continuous.

In addition to the usual type of slide rule, many special rules have been devised to mechanize particular computations. Examples include slide rules for carrying out Ohm's law calculations and for finding the reactance of a given inductance or capacitance at a prescribed frequency. These may be thought of as mechanized nomographs.

*William W. Seifert*

## Soft fails

Noise bursts in microelectronic circuits, caused by cosmic-ray particles, that result in spontaneous changes in the information stored in computer memories. These changes are called soft fails. This sensitivity to cosmic rays is one of the unanticipated results of the ever-decreasing size of the components of integrated microelectronic circuits, and it presents new considerations in the development of very large-scale integrated circuits. The problem is not necessarily catastrophic, since modern computers are usually made to continue to work properly, despite errors, by internal correction of electronic mistakes. However, the creation of soft fails adds an additional load to any internal corrections scheme.

**Microelectronics.** The transistor, invented in 1948, was initially utilized as a separate component with which to build electronic circuits by using the same methods as had been developed for vacuum tube circuits. There was one obvious difference between vacuum tubes and transistors, however: transistors are inherently much smaller. This led to the realization that one can build integrated circuits, that is, electronic devices, with transistors, resistors, capacitors, and so forth, all made at the same time on one chip of silicon by using photolithographic techniques.

Since the first integrated circuit in 1958 (**Fig. 1**), the size of components in integrated circuits has decreased at a remarkable rate—almost a factor of 2 for every year. Now integrated circuits are available

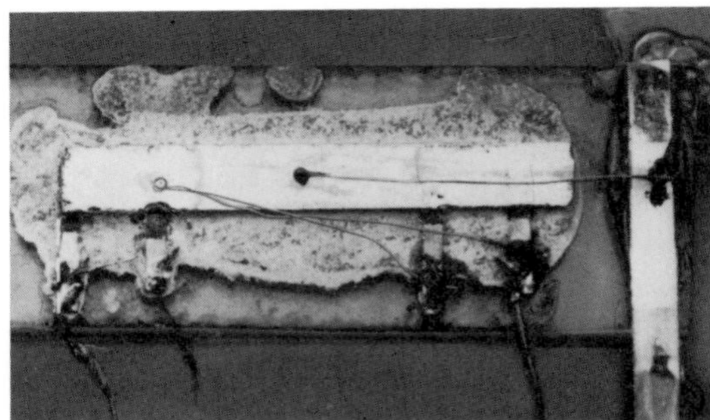

**Fig. 1. One of the first integrated circuits, made in 1958. *(Texas Instruments)***

which have hundreds of thousands of components built on a single chip only a few millimeters across (**Fig. 2**). A typical state-of-the-art example is a 64K (1K = 1024 bits) dynamic random-access computer memory (d-RAM) where binary information may be stored by charging (or not charging) a small capacitor. This capacitor stores approximately 1,500,000 electrons when charged, and is made of a thin film of conducting metal with an area of about 100 $\mu m^2$ on a thin insulator on a single-crystal silicon substrate. It is the very small amount of stored charge, along with the design of the capacitor, which makes such devices susceptible to the loss of bits of information by ionizing particles penetrating the underlying silicon. SEE INTEGRATED CIRCUITS; TRANSISTOR.

**Ionization-induced soft fails.** The spontaneous flipping of a bit stored in a computer memory is referred to as a soft fail, as distinguished from a hard fail in which a circuit component is permanently damaged and must be replaced. Integrated-circuit storage memories are normally extraordinarily reliable. The usual industry reliability unit is in failures per million hours per chip with nominal reliability being one fail per million hours. That means that if a chip stores 64,000 bits of binary information, the mean time to fail for each bit is 7,500,000 years!

In 1978 a new and unexpected source of soft fails became apparent to the microelectronics industry. Memory circuits which had been designed based on seemingly reasonable extrapolations of previous devices had measured soft-fail rates far above expectation. The source of these unexpected upsets was traced to α-particles (helium nuclei) being emitted by naturally occurring radionuclides which had been inadvertently introduced as part of a ceramic support for

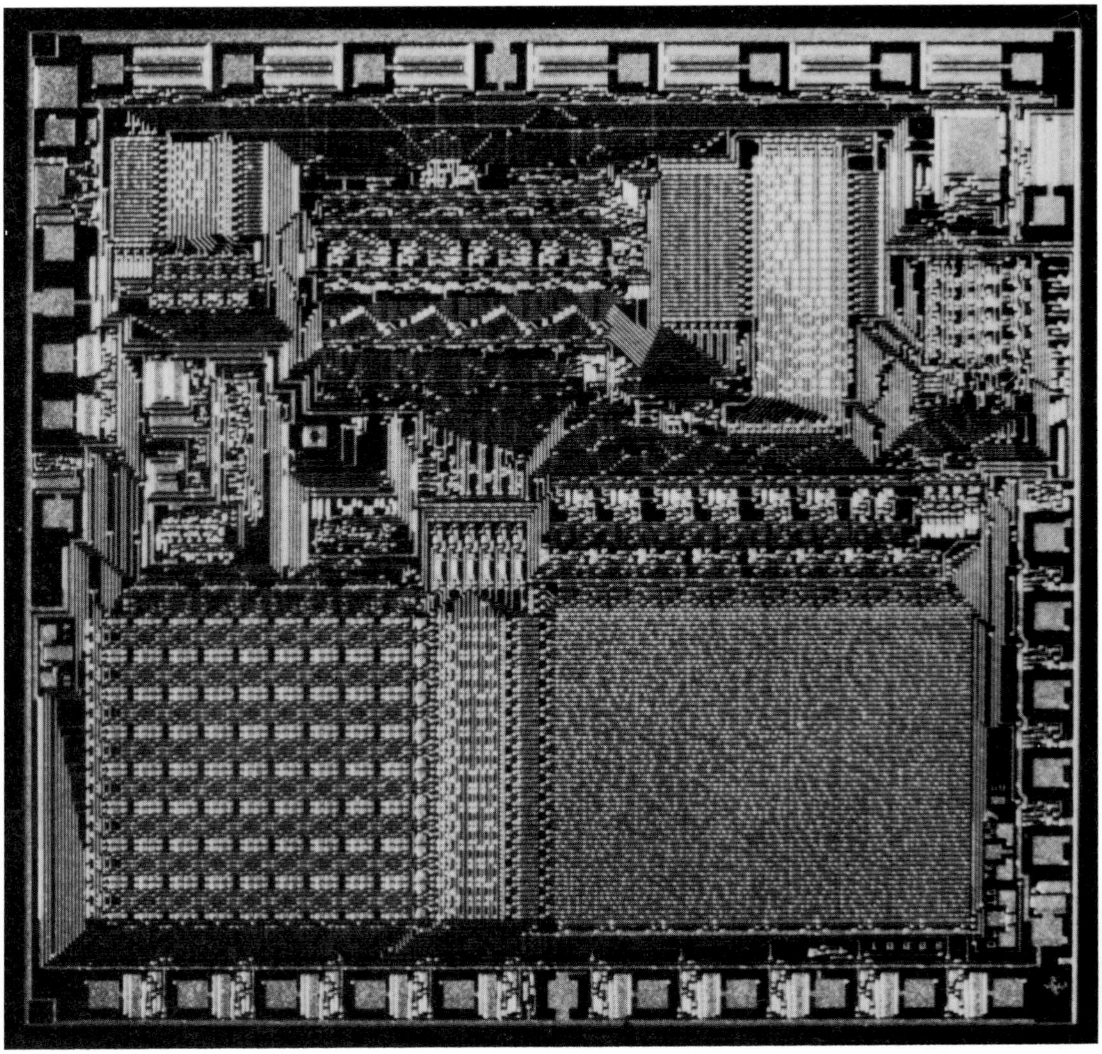

**Fig. 2. Complete microcomputer built on one chip a few millimeters across. *(Texas Instruments)***

the memory. The dramatic effect of α-particles on electronic memories is shown by the experimental array in **Fig. 3**. The charge-coupled device (CCD) memory matrix was filled with 1's, and then an α-particle from a radioactive source hit the memory at an angle of 20°. An array of hits spontaneously flipped to zeros in the pattern shown. This α-particle problem rapidly led to a study of the sources of the α-emitting contaminations and to the introduction of low background techniques in the semiconductor industry. *SEE CHARGE-COUPLED DEVICES*.

The discovery that α-particles from naturally occurring radionuclides could cause soft fails of computer memories led to the consideration of possible effects of another well-known source of naturally occurring radiation, cosmic rays. The average fluxes of various types of cosmic-ray particles at sea level are shown in **Fig. 4**. Investigations have demonstrated that sea-level cosmic rays have important effects which limit the reliability of memory devices.

The mechanism which causes these soft fails is familiar to all nuclear scientists because it is the basis for one of the most common types of radiation detectors, the solid-state ionization detector. While the detailed geometry, voltages, and so forth, vary considerably with memory circuit design, the underlying principle used to store information in integrated-circuit computer memories is always the same. Binary information is stored by the presence of charge on some element of the integrated circuit. In the case of d-RAM memories, the charge is on a capacitor.

In the case of charge-coupled devices, the charge is stored in a potential well at the interface between crystal silicon and a covering insulator such as silicon dioxide ($SiO_2$). This charge then migrates in a "racetrack" and stores information by the sequence of charges stored in this racetrack. In all such devices, the stored charges have to be periodically refreshed because of the slow but continual leakage of charge through the semiconducting silicon substrate.

The presence of charge results in an electric field in the silicon so that any electrons or holes created in this biased region are rapidly collected at the "anodes" and "cathodes," respectively. These are just the conditions needed to create a solid-state ionization chamber used as a particle detector. In the detector case, the charge pulse of electron-hole pairs created by ionizing radiation passing through the biased region of the silicon is used as a signal to measure the amount of ionization created by the particle. In the integrated-circuit memory case, the charge pulse of electron-hole pairs created by ionizing radiation decreases the stored charge (for example, on the capacitor in a d-RAM) and may result in the loss of the bit of information represented by this stored charge.

**Ionization density thresholds.** As the size of microelectronic circuits has decreased, the amount of charge used to store a bit of information has also decreased. For example, a 64K d-RAM may have a stored charge of order 1,500,000 electrons, and a 64K CCD has a stored charge an order of magnitude smaller. **Table 1** lists some typical dimensions and charges for such devices. If this charge is decreased by an amount called $Q_{\text{critical}}$, the bit will be misread and a soft fail occurs. $Q_{\text{critical}}$ is of order 0.2 times the stored charge for most devices. While $Q_{\text{critical}}$ decreases with the size of the device, it also becomes progressively more difficult to deposit charge in the smaller active volume as dimensions decrease. For example, suppose $Q_{\text{critical}}$ is 500,000 electrons, and the active volume of the device has a mean diameter of order 10 μm. An ionizing particle must deposit charge within the sensitive volume at a rate of at least 500,000 electron-hole pairs per 10 μm = 50,000 electron-hole pairs per micrometer. Such a device would be insensitive to the ionization wakes of protons, muons, or electrons, because the maximum ionization density of any charge-one particle is 37,000 electron-hole pairs per micrometer. On the other hand, α-particles (which have charge number $Z = 2$)

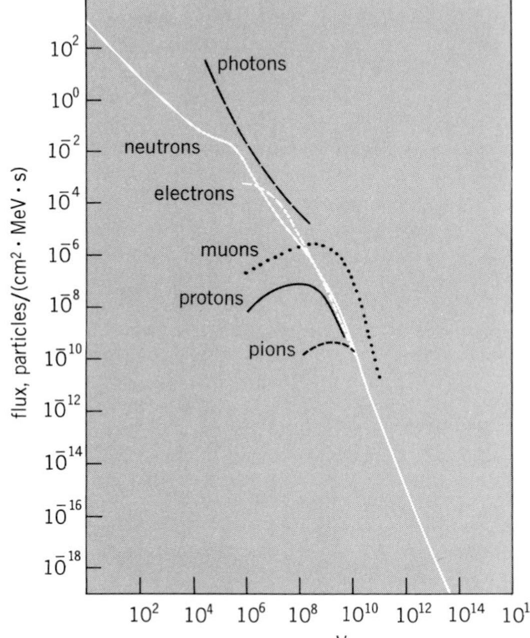


**Fig. 4. Flux of cosmic-ray particles at sea level and geomagnetic latitude 45°N. These curves are average values, and large fluctuations exist, attributed to magnetic latitude, time of day, season, solar cycle, angle of incidence, and so forth. (*After J. Ziegler and W. A. Lanford, Effects of cosmic rays on computer memories, Science, 206:776–788, 1979*)**

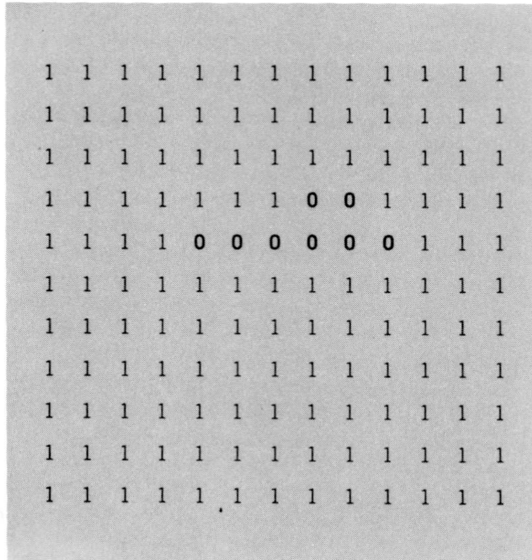


**Fig. 3. Effect of α-particle ionization on a CCD memory matrix. (*Institute of Electrical and Electronics Engineers*)**

**Table 1. Device parameters for model computer memories**

| Parameter | 64K d-RAM | 64K CCD |
|---|---|---|
| Active area, $\mu m^2$ | 100 | 200 |
| Stored charge, $e^-$ | 1,500,000 | 180,000 |
| $Q_{critical}$, $e^-$ | 300,000 | 36,000 |
| Mean collection diameter, $\mu m$ | 12 | 16 |
| Bits per chip | 65,536 | 65,536 |

have a maximum ionization density of 100,000 electron-hole pairs per micrometer and, hence, could cause soft fails in such a device. The ionization wake density of electron-hole pairs in silicon following the passage of various charged particles is shown in **Fig. 5**.

While there are many more detailed considerations, the concept of thresholds in ionization density is central to understanding when soft fails may occur. When, as a consequence of minimization, devices were made with $Q_{critical}$ below the threshold of maximum α-particle ionization density, the α-particle soft-fail problem became important. Most early devices had $Q_{critical}$ so large that even α-particles could not deposit enough charge in the sensitive column to cause a soft fail. Such devices may, however, be susceptible to heavy-ion cosmic rays, which, while not present at sea level, are present above the Earth's atmosphere. Indeed, such heavy-ion-induced upsets were discovered in satellite computers.

**Soft-fail rates for typical devices.** Calculations for some model devices have been carried out by assuming the characterizations given in Table 1. The results for the estimated fail rates for the mechanisms considered are shown in **Table 2**. For the 64K d-RAM, the single most important cause of soft fails is the production of α-particles by the interaction of cosmic-ray neutrons with silicon nuclei. The 64K CCD has such a low $Q_{critical}$ that it is sensitive to the primary ionization wake of cosmic-ray muons.

As can be seen in Table 2, both these model devices have fail rates larger than the traditional reliability standard of 1 fail per million hours with the 64K CCD memory orders of magnitude above this rate. These results are representative in the sense that,

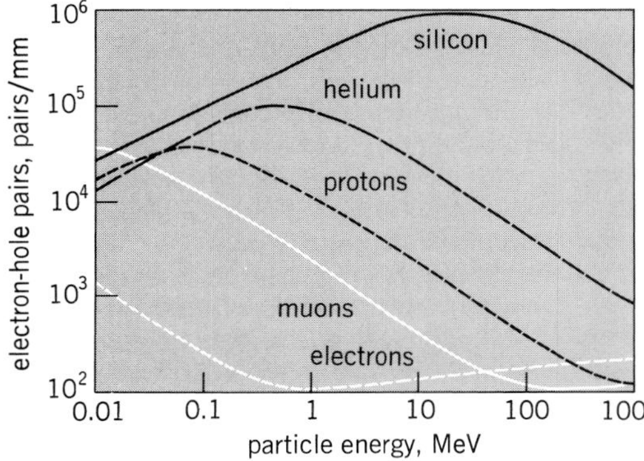


**Fig. 5. Ionization wake density of electron-hole pairs in silicon following the passage of various charged particles. *(After J. F. Ziegler and W. A. Landford, Effects of cosmic rays on computer memories, Science, 206:776–788, 1979)***

as $Q_{critical}$ falls below about 100,000 electrons for a device with dimension about 10 μm, it becomes sensitive to the ionization wake of $Z = 1$ particles and, consequently, has a rather large soft-fail rate. Because muons are so penetrating, it is impractical to avoid this problem by shielding, and if high reliability is needed, either the device design has to be changed or error-correcting codes must be used to detect and correct soft fails as they occur.

There is another area where integrated-circuit technology is employed and where cosmic rays are causing serious concern. As indicated above, the conditions in a single memory cell are very similar to those in solid-state ionization detectors. This fact has led to the development of large-area imaging detectors consisting of arrays of CCD memory cells. Such CCD cameras have the potential of becoming important low-level light detectors for use in astronomy. However, the importance of cosmic-ray-induced "background" events in CCD cameras has been demonstrated.

**Table 2. Cosmic-ray-induced soft fails of model computer memories chip fails per million hours**

| Mechanism | 64K d-RAM | 64K CCD |
|---|---|---|
| Electron ionizatin wake | 0 | 0 |
| Proton ionization wake | 0 | 140 |
| Muon ionization wake | 0 | 330 |
| Si (silicon) recoils from electron scattering | 0 | <1 |
| Si recoils from proton scattering | <1 | <1 |
| Si recoils from neutron scattering | 1 | 100 |
| Si recoils from muon scattering | <1 | 3 |
| Proton + Si → α-particles | <1 | <1 |
| Neutron + Si → α-particles | 6 | 22 |
| Muon capture → nuclear disintegration | ≤1 | 7 |
| TOTAL | ~7 | ~600 |

In summary, it has become clear that cosmic-ray-induced soft fails present a new unanticipated problem to the future minimization of microelectronic circuits. However, the microelectronics industry has faced several seemingly more difficult problems in the past which it has successfully solved, and it is anticipated that suitable solutions will be found to the problem of cosmic-ray soft fails.

*William Lanford; James Ziegler*

**Bibliography.** J. F. Ziegler and W. A. Lanford, *IEEE Elec. Dev. Trans.*, 1980; J. F. Ziegler and W. A. Lanford, *IEEE 1980 International Solid State Circuits Conference Proc.*, pp. 70–80, 1980; J. F. Ziegler and W. A. Lanford, *Science*, 206:776–788, 1979.

## Software engineering

The process of engineering software, that is, not only the programs that run on a computer, but also the requirements of definition, functional specification, design description, program implementation, and test methods that lead to this code. Engineering implies the systematic application of scientific and technological knowledge through the medium of sound engineering principles to reach a practical goal. This goal becomes practical through the process of trading off performance, reliability, cost, and other characteristics of the resulting product in the light of the funds and time available for development. In short, software engineering is based on fundamental engineering principles and guided by economic considerations.

## Motivation

In the early years of computer development, as computer generations succeeded one another, the hardware performance-price ratio kept climbing at an average rate of about 25% a year; it was still advancing rapidly in the early 1980s. Programming productivity, on the other hand, while hard to measure, gained at a much slower rate—something like 7–9% per year. The continuing hardware improvement created a series of computer systems on which it was economically feasible to run ever larger programs, but the slower rate of improvement in programming led to progressively larger programming organizations requiring more levels of management. Some software systems approached a million instructions and absorbed 5000 worker-years of development time. By the mid-1960s the fact that program development almost defied effective management control was becoming evident.

Programs of this era were not only extremely large, but frequently lacked clarity as well. They were typically all in one piece, that is, not modularized. The sequence of program execution from one instruction to the next in line would jump instead to an instruction that was pages away in the program listing. A reader could track one or two of these jumps or branches, but scores of them made the program logic hard to grasp.

Since the product being developed was something of a mystery, it was nearly impossible for managers to find out enough about it to supervise the work of the programmers, to coordinate them with other groups, or to estimate how much time such poorly defined tasks would take or how many programmers were needed. It was under these circumstances that the NATO Software Engineering Conference (1968) pointed out the direction in which solutions to the "software crisis" should be sought.

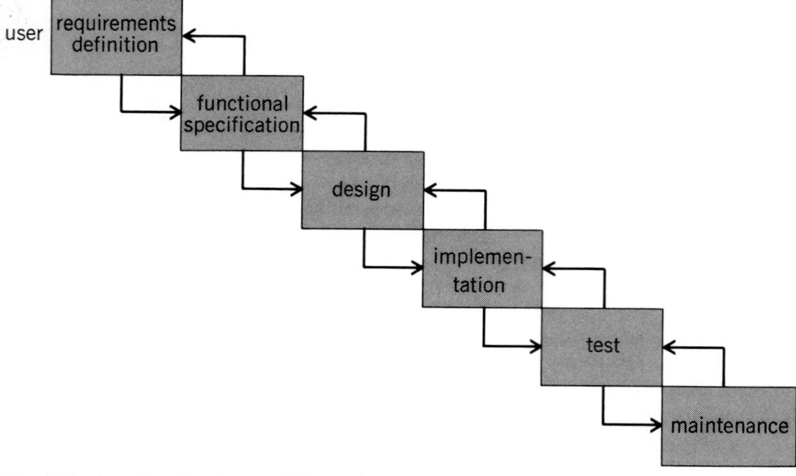


**Fig. 1. Engineering development life cycle.**

Several aspects of software engineering may be distinguished. From one vantage point it appears as a process taking place over time, a process that is divided into perhaps a half dozen principal stages. Each stage can be examined more closely, and the various methods employed can be identified. Finally, from a broader point of view, the software development process must be managed.

## Development Stages

A programmer tends to program, that is, to write a series of instructions in a programming language, and to give less thought to other stages of what is really, considered as a whole, a design process. On the other hand, in terms of software engineering, the problem-solving steps that have been learned in the other branches of engineering may be applied also here.

In general, these steps include formulating the problem, searching for and developing solutions, evaluating the solutions in terms of the goals, and refining and verifying the solution selected. In each branch of engineering these general steps have been adapted to the needs of the branch. In software engineering there is now considerable agreement on the six stages shown in **Fig. 1**. As work proceeds through this series of stages, the findings of later stages flow back to influence earlier stages.

**Requirements definition.** In the first stage, requirements definition, the basic question is what exactly the user expects the software to do. This problem-oriented definition provides the guide to later development stages and a checklist upon which the using and the development organizations can achieve agreement on what must be done. It provides a base against which the resulting software can eventually be compared for acceptance by the user.

If the using organization is unfamiliar with what computing systems can do and the development organization is inexperienced in the user's application area, defining the requirements becomes a learning process for both. Even if both organizations have some experience, the definition of requirements will still involve learning. In addition, this learning continues into later stages as the problem becomes better understood. Consequently the requirements definition must be revised periodically to match what has been learned.

**Functional specification.** At the functional specification stage, the user requirements are converted into a specification of the functions to be performed by the proposed system. While the requirements definition may have set values for some performance objectives that were closely related to the problem circumstances, the functional specification carries the goal-setting process further. Under constraints set by the current capabilities of computer technology and the user's resources, the specification sets target numbers for performance, reliability, compatability, and other product objectives.

This specification should serve at least three purposes. It should fulfill the needs expressed by the requirements definition and at the same time characterize the system to be built. It should lead into the design stage, and it can do this more effectively if the specification mirrors the structure of the problem. Finally, its clear expression of the functions and objectives should establish the criteria against which the completed system will be functionally tested.

**Design.** Software design is the process of going from what a system is to do to how it is to do it. In

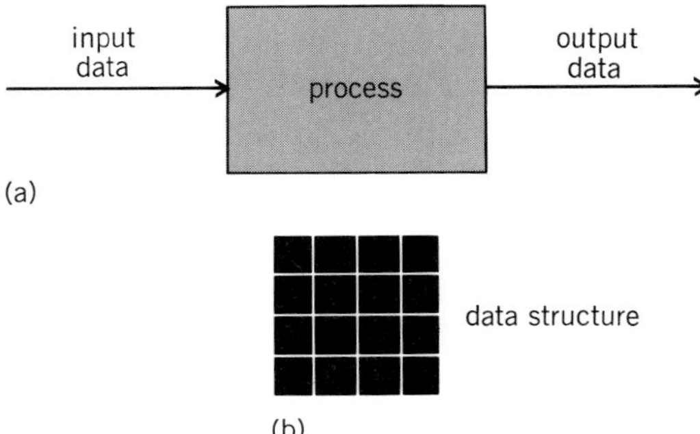


**Fig. 2. Data considered from two points of view: (*a*) their processing and (*b*) their structure.**

this stage the designer transforms the functional specification into a form from which the programmer can more easily code the problem represented by the specification into a list of programming instructions. While small, simple problems can sometimes be coded directly by a programmer, experience shows that most real problems cannot be coded directly and that an intervening design step is needed.

Design includes the task of partitioning (or decomposing) the entire problem area into subsystems, routines, subroutines, modules, and so forth, which individually become easier to understand than the whole. Together these elements may be thought of as a hierarchy, like an organization chart, or alternatively, a flow diagram, like a strip road map. In either case, a key task of the design process is determining the manner in which these elements relate to one another—their interconnections. Developing the best possible arrangement—best in terms of the constraints imposed by the product specified and development resources—makes design an engineering activity.

The nature of design is suggested by **Fig. 2**. Input data go in, and undergo some processing; and output data come out (Fig. 2*a*). The data have some kind of structure, suggested by Fig. 2*b*. During the process of detailed design, this diagram is expanded by using a variety of methods described later.

**Implementation.** In its essentials the implementation stage transforms the output documents of the design stage into program instructions. These instructions are converted by a software support program called a compiler or an interpreter into machine code, that is, the binary digits that constitute the internal language of a computer.

In practice, however, if the program is of more than trivial size, the probability of making errors in programming is high. One of the most effective ways of finding these errors is the program review, conducted before the program is compiled. In a formal review the full weight of the organization is put behind the effort. The errors found are formally recorded and analyzed to provide corrective feedback to the entire programming organization. Unfortunately the reliance on the formal organization may discourage the willing cooperation of the psychologically less secure programmers.

To overcome this drawback, the structured walk-through was conceived. The programmer arranges the meeting and invites his or her peers. Management is not included, and no formal record of the errors found is filed. The term walk-through is derived from the practice of assigning sample values to the data and walking these numbers through the program steps one by one. This less threatening atmosphere is believed to make it easier for a programmer to cooperate in finding errors and later correcting them. The point of view of the structured walk-through is that programming is known to be difficult and the peer group is there to help.

Errors can occur in the earlier stages, too. In fact, studies of the development process indicate that errors tend to be more frequent in the early stages than in the later ones, and more expensive to correct in later stages than in earlier ones. Thus it is important to review the results at each stage and to eliminate errors as early as possible.

**Testing.** After the program is compiled, it is tested, that is, a set of values is assigned to the inputs, the program is run, and the program outputs are compared to the correct outputs. Since the test is being done by computer, a large number of input sets may be run. Moreover, the task of comparing the test output with the known correct output can also be performed by computer. When this match fails, the circumstances are reported back to the programmer to find and correct the errors.

While the above outlined testing task is simple in concept, it becomes difficult in execution. The reasons are that each input may have a large number of values, combinations of these numbers become larger still, and the number of different paths through a processing network of more than trivial size is enormous. Even at computer speeds, the test of all combinations and paths might run up into years of test time. So it becomes the task of test personnel to devise test procedures that exercise the program adequately in a reasonable time and at affordable cost.

**Maintenance.** The term maintenance, adopted from hardware terminology, has a different meaning in software. Software maintenance takes place in response to finding a previously unknown error, or to a change in the environment in which the system functions, or to an opportunity to improve performance. The ''repair'' does not return the software to its original state, as hardware repair does. It advances the system to a new and sometimes poorly understood state. One result is often the introduction of further errors, leading to the need for further maintenance as soon as they are discovered, and so on.

Software has been considered, perhaps unwisely, to be easily changeable. It followed, then, that it could be adapted to new circumstances simply by changing it, unlike hardware, which has to be redesigned and manufactured as a new model. Experience has demonstrated, however, that unstructured software is rather difficult to change successfully. As a result of the ensuing errors and complications, such software tends to deteriorate over time as changes are implemented.

## METHODS

The stages of the life cycle provide a framework for spreading a number of activities over the time dimension, and consequently limiting the number which must be dealt with at any one time. Still, in each stage of a large system under development there remains too much complexity to deal with all at once. Psychological research has revealed that the human mind can only cope with about five to nine entities at a time. Above this limit people lose track of some of the factors and make errors.

Although the physical computer is a very complex machine, the software interfaces not only to this complex machine, but also to the great complexity of all the rest of the natural and human-made world, at least potentially. The development of large software systems is probably the most complex analytical task that the human race has ever encountered.

Thus one of the tasks of software engineering is to acquire from computer scientists or to develop for itself methods for partitioning a problem area into pieces small enough to be dealt with by the limited human brain. Concomitant with this task is that of finding satisfactory ways to represent this process of analysis and synthesis, both to bolster the capability of the analyst and to communicate the results of the work to others.

**Structured design.** At the beginning of the design stage, the designer knows that there are inputs and outputs, joined by a process, as diagrammed in Fig. 2. The methods of design are used to break out further detail. One way is by means of the flow of data, as shown in **Fig. 3**. The transformation of the data, symbolized by the circles, may be further refined in a series of steps into a greater number of individually simpler operations. Another way is to show the flow or movement of program control from one process or decision point to another, as the flow chart does (**Fig. 4**).

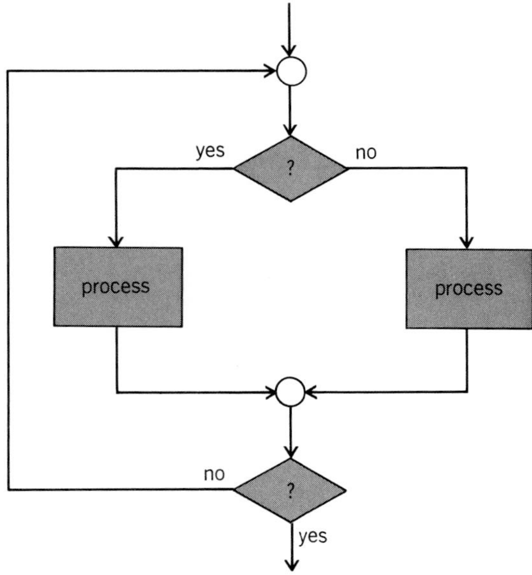

**Fig. 4. Flow chart.**

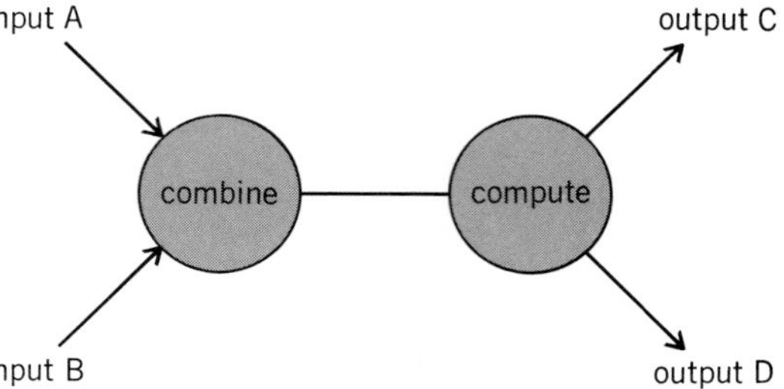

**Fig. 3. Data flow diagram. Data inputs are transformed by the operations specified in each circle.**

Thus, the problem, as defined by the requirements and specification, is decomposed into smaller pieces and these, in turn, into still smaller pieces until a minimal size, called the software module, is reached.

If the decomposition process begins at the top and works downward, it is called top-down design. If it begins with other machines with which the program is to interface, it sorts out first the functions needed to manage these interfaces, then builds a structure up from there, and is called bottom-up design. The several levels of program modules form a hierarchy.

This hierarchy may be thought of as a series of levels of abstraction (**Fig. 5**). Each level is composed of a number of modules (**Fig. 6**). The levels-of-abstraction concept is comparable to the working levels of an organization chart. Modules on the bottom level handle details, such as physical files of data. Modules on higher levels deal with broader matters. Only such information is abstracted from a lower-level module as is necessary for a higher-level module to perform its duties. The rest is "hidden," easing the comprehension task of programmers of higher-level modules. Similarly, all the programmer of a lower-level module need know about higher-level modules is that they may call this lower-level module in some prescribed form.

Levels and modules compose a structure. However, the fact of "structure" is not inherent in either the problem or the ultimate program. At the beginning, the problem looks like a "big buzzing confusion." At the other end of the development process, the program is a large linear list which may be complicated by branch or jump instructions that can move the sequence of execution up or down the list at any time, sometimes pages away (**Fig. 7**). It may have no more perceptible structure than a long string tangled by a kitten. Modularization has not been an obvious approach, and in fact most programs before the 1970s were not modularized.

The business of design is to introduce order. The purpose of modularization is to reduce the number of entities with which the designer and later the programmer have to work at a given time. Also, a program with structure is easier to maintain and modify.

In a modular program there are two sets of entities. One set consists of the function or functions that the module is to perform internally. The other comprises the interrelationships it is to have with other modules. Complexity is reduced if the module is "cohesive," that is, performs only one function or a few closely related functions. Complexity is also reduced if the "coupling" between modules is limited and clearly

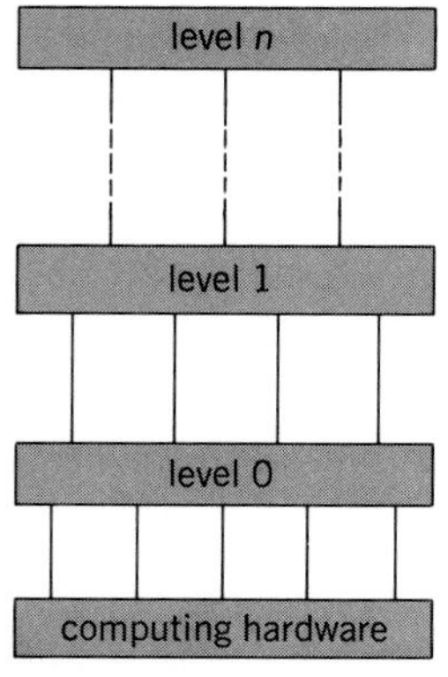

**Fig. 5. Levels of abstraction. Building on the hardware, each level retreats further from detail.**

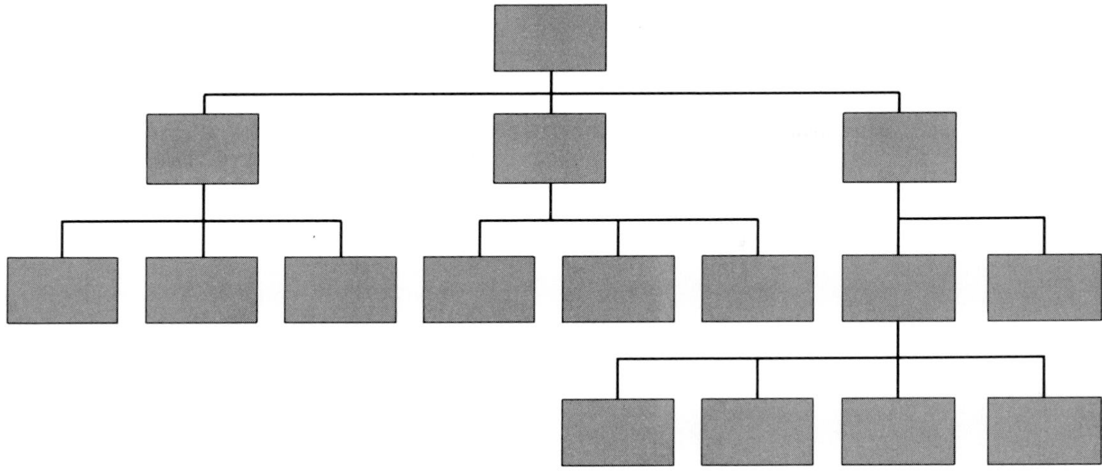

**Fig. 6. Module hierarchy. Software modules are arranged in a structure, with defined relationships between the modules.**

defined. Under these circumstances a designer has only a few functions and a few relationships to keep in mind at one time.

Software engineers have conceived these and other ways of helping themselves think through the complexities of software design. In contrast to the earlier methods, modern practices emphasize structure, both in methodology and the result, and have come to be called structured design.

**Design data representation.** One achievement of other branches of engineering has been to draw systems so as to convey the intent of the designer to the manufacturer and others. Software designers, too, need methods of documenting their design data for its many users. The prime use is to convey the design to the programmers. However, the design data representation also serves as a source for test engineers, software maintenance programmers, and documentation specialists.

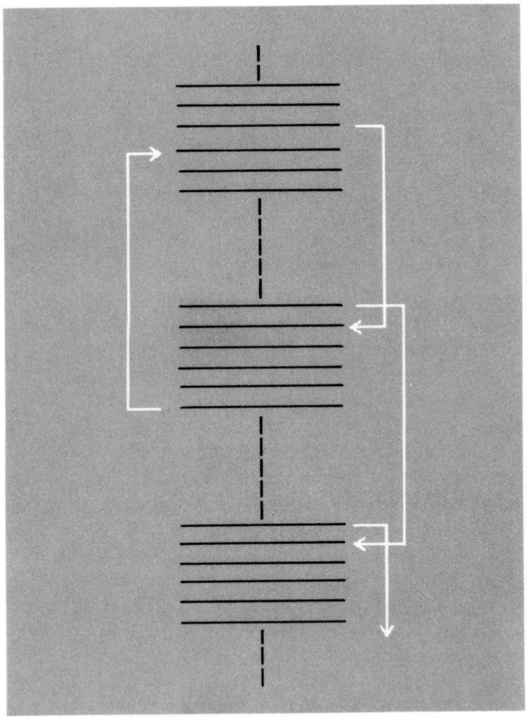

**Fig. 7. Part of a sequential list of instructions containing branches or jumps that move the sequence of execution up or down the list.**

Software design took over the flow chart (Fig. 4) from other branches of engineering and still uses it widely. However, it has drawbacks. For one thing flow charts are not naturally structured. Hence several other forms of design data representation have been developed and gained adherents, and new methods are still being developed.

In a broad sense these representation techniques can be divided into three classes: diagrammatic, decision tables, and pseudocode. The diagrammatic techniques, of which the flow chart is one, represent module functions and relationships in some kind of visual form. Some examples are data flow diagrams, structure charts, HIPO (hierarchy plus input-process-output) charts, Nassi-Shneiderman charts, SDAT (structured design analysis technique), and data-structure charts (Warnier-Orr and Jackson method).

The decision table is a tabular method of sorting out the logic of a problem (**Fig. 8**). It has the advantage over the diagram methods of considerably compressing the amount of space needed for analysis.

Pseudocode is a combination of logical structures, the flow of control, and a language (**Fig. 9**). The logical structures are such constructs as:

*Do* first operation *then* second operation
*If* condition *then* action *else* other action
*While* condition *do* action

Mathematically, all logical operations can be reduced to just these three. However, other logical operations exist, and it is often shorter and more convenient to make use of them.

The flow of control proceeds from one line of pseudocode to the next. Digressions to distant parts of the list of operations are not inherent in this method.

The language is normally English, or the user's natural language. Hence pseudocode is not a high-level programming language, since such languages are, by definition, compilable. (A compiler is a computer program that recognizes only the words permitted by the high-level programming language with which it works; it is not set up to recognize all the words of a natural language.) On the other hand, if the logical constructs available in a particular pro-

| CONDITIONS | | | | |
|---|---|---|---|---|
| newcomer to field | Y | N | | |
| want more information on topic | | | Y | N |
| **ACTIONS** | | | | |
| read this article carefully | X | | | |
| scan article quickly | | X | | |
| read referenced encyclopedia article | | | X | |
| no action | | | | X |

**Fig. 8. Decision table. The user lists conditions at the top which have binary answers, yes or no. At the bottom are the actions that result from each state of the conditions.**

gramming language are used in a pseudocode analysis and the blanks in the logical operations are filled in with terms belonging to that language (and, hence, recognizable by its compiler), then one has, in effect, moved to the implementation stage and programmed the design.

Through the use of pseudocode it is possible to start with a very broad version of the initial problem, since there is no limit to the concepts that may be employed. As the problem is gradually worked through, the pseudocode is refined in a stepwise manner to solve in more detail smaller pieces of the big problem. Ultimately a level of refinement is reached at which the conversion to programming language is deemed to be feasible without problems.

**Structured programming.** Contemporary programming languages incorporate the basic control structures (logic operations) in their instruction sets. In consequence, the final refinement of the design stage is simply converted to the corresponding logic structure of the language and is then compilable. However, the earlier programming languages, such as Fortran, were not based on these structures, and as a result the control structures from the design stage have no direct counterparts in the programming language. To overcome this deficiency, versions of these languages have been developed which do contain the control structures. However, these versions have to be first processed by a preprocessor (a computer operation) into the standard language, which is then compiled in the normal manner. *See* PROGRAMMING LANGUAGES.

In a structured program there is ideally one entry point to the module and one exit point. Branch or Go-To instructions are used to signify its structure and enhance its readability. In general, each module of the design turns into only a page or two of code listing, short enough to be readily comprehensible by persons other than the programmer. Understandability is further enhanced by preceding the actual code with a module description in natural language. The pseudocode design may also be included. Particular lines are further explained by comments. Such a program is said to be machine-documented. In this form it is more readily updated and accessible to later users.

## Software Management

The methods of software engineering find application in business, industry, and government. The problems are often very large. The resulting projects employ many people and substantial resources over long time periods. Personnel, money, and time are the factors with which management works, so that software development becomes subject to the methods of management: planning, organizing, scheduling, directing, monitoring, controlling, and so on. But because software engineering is relatively new, experienced managers lack working experience in it, and software engineers have not had time to grow into management. Even when some of them do, the pace of oncoming technology may outmode them.

If management could confine itself to management and engineers to engineering, the problems would be fewer and less severe. In software, however, there is reason to believe that management decisions, that is, decisions properly within the management sphere, can influence design matters, and vice versa.

It is well established, for example, that large software projects consume more development resources per unit of accomplishment than smaller projects, largely because of the increased burden of training, coordination, and communication. Mealy's "law" states: There is an incremental person who, when added to a project, consumes more energy (resources) than he or she makes available. Thus, beyond a certain point, adding resources (people) slows progress, in addition to increasing the cost.

One solution to this problem is to break large projects into small components. But management cannot

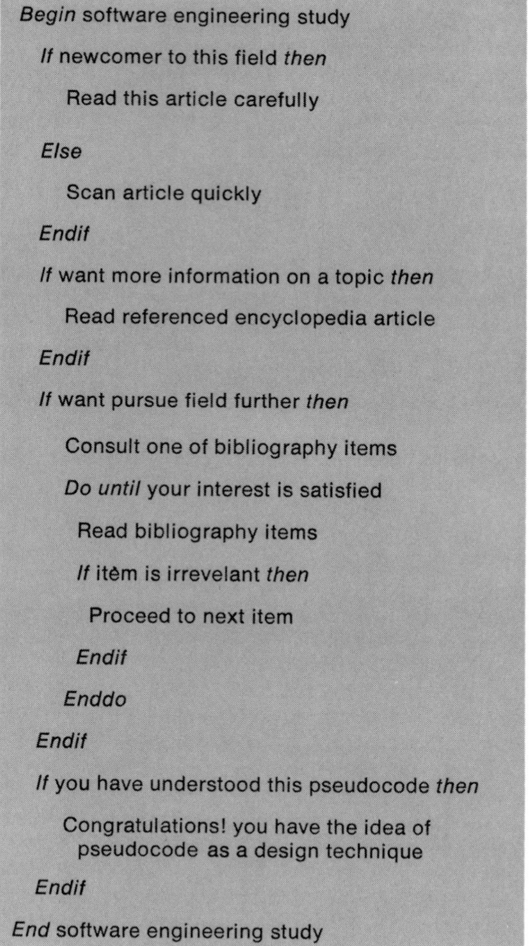


**Fig. 9. Example of pseudocode, a software design data representation technique.**

make independent small projects simply by ordering them. If the small projects are all aspects of one large problem area, then there are relationships between them. In that case, coordinating relationships between projects takes just as much time as coordinating the same relationships within one large project; the technical relationships are there in both cases.

Of course, a large system can be partitioned into subsystems and eventually modules and the work divided, but this task—maximizing cohesiveness and minimizing coupling—is highly technical. The extent to which a system can be decomposed into independent systems is an engineering question, not a matter of managerial prerogative.

To take another example, the assignment of personnel is a common management responsibility. At the beginning of a project a manager might wish to assign to it right away the number of people that the project is planned to average over its lifetime, to get it off to a good start. Unfortunately, only a few highly skilled people can be usefully employed in the first design steps. More than these few just get in the way. One experienced software manager recommends sending the extra ones off to pertinent training programs. As the few sort out the problems and begin to structure the design, they create new elements to which more talent can be applied. This process repeats itself, and the staff gradually expands. It appears that the proper timing of additional personnel is largely dependent on the rate of technical progress. Again, management has the authority, but should be guided in its exercise by technical considerations.

According to Frederick P. Brooks, Jr., adding worker-power to a software project that is running behind schedule only slows it down further. In other words, under the circumstances that Brooks described, the managerial prerogatives of setting schedules and monitoring them appear to be hollow rights. There seem to be factors at work, technical in nature, more powerful than adding more people can offset.

### Effectiveness

The very success of computer systems led to the software predicament: software became too costly, too error-prone, too complex, too hard to maintain, too people-heavy. In fact, these problems threaten to delay the spread of computers into new fields.

It is now clear that the methods of software engineering, while not easy to apply, do help overcome the software predicament. Formal studies of the before-and-after type show improvements in the 25–75% range in cost, error reduction, and productivity. Executives with before-and-after experience have reached similar conclusions.

### Software Portability

Portability refers to the ease with a program can be moved from one computer environment to another. If there were just one programming language, translated to just one type of computer by one compiler, then all application programs would be portable. However, with the many different types of computers and application domains and the hundreds of programming languages and compilers available, a particular program is generally not transportable between different types of computers, domains, or languages.

It follows, then, that a large number of programmers are needed, and this number would have to increase as rapidly as the number of different installations. The discrepancy between the rate at which hardware can be manufactured (very fast) and the rate at which programmers can be found and trained (very slow) is called the software crisis. One way to ameliorate this crisis is to improve the portability of software. Portability could be enhanced if the computer community were willing to settle on a limited number of languages, standardize them, and adhere to the standards. In practice, most implementations of languages have deviated to some degree from the language standard, thus restricting portability. In the past some manufacturers may have tacitly accepted incompatability as a means to lock up a captive market, but this attitude seems to be declining as the software crisis becomes more evident.

Another approach is to accept at least some variety in computers and languages as a given, and develop exchange methods. Several companies translate a number of languages into a common intermediate code, variously called *p*-code or *q*-code, and then translate that into the native assembly language of each of many processors.

### Software Piracy

Piracy refers to the process of copying commercial software without the permission of the originator. It is the dark side of portability—without portability piracy could not exist. Piracy is found among amateurs, who copy programs for friends without direct pecuniary gain, and professionals, who copy programs in quantity for sale at low prices to amateurs.

The amateurs seem to have need for more software, little money, and the feeling that just a few copies among friends will not make any difference. However, surveys reveal that thousands of amateurs are pirating software for their friends. All together they do make a difference; in fact, some suppliers have abandoned the amateur marketplace. In any case others' work is being appropriated by amateurs without recompense.

The professional pirates have a need to make money. They are not likely to be deterred by the fact that moralists consider copying to be unethical; it would have to be illegal to have an effect on them. There are three approaches in law to protecting intellectual effort: patents, copyrights, and trade secrets.

Algorithms—and thus commercial software—are unpatentable. Source programs can be copyrighted, but object code cannot, because it is not intended to be read by a human being, thus making it legal (perhaps) to copy the 0 and 1 code of a read-only memory.

Several courts have ruled in different ways on this question and it remains unclear. As for the trade secrets approach, a for-sale program can be kept secret only to the extent that it can be coded to prevent copying. Code protection is being used, leading to an escalating contest between the code writers and the code breakers. Some feel that Congress should take up the Supreme Court's invitation, repeated several times, to draft a law suited to the peculiarities of software. Others hope that the courts will eventually sort out the inconsistencies. *See Digital computer; Digital computer programming.*

*Ware Myers*

**Bibliography.** F. P. Brooks, Jr., *The Mythical Man-Month: Essays on Software Engineering*, 1975; P. Freeman and A. I. Wasserman, *Tutorial: Software Design Techniques*, 1980; R. W. Jensen and C. C.

Tonies, *Software Engineering*, 1979; C. Jones, Alternatives to programming, in C. Jones (ed.), *Tutorial: Programming Productivity: Issues for the Eighties*, IEEE Computer Society, pp. 377–381, 1981; R. H. Stern and J. L. Squires, Can we stop software theft?, *IEEE Micro*, 2(1) 12–25, February 1982; R. C. Tausworthe, *Standardized Development of Computer Software*, 1977; E. Yourdon and L. L. Constantine, *Structured Design: Fundamentals of a Discipline of Computer Program and System Design*, 1979.

## Solar cell

A semiconductor electrical junction device which directly and efficiently absorbs the radiant energy of sunlight and converts it into electrical energy. Solar cells may be used individually as light detectors, for example in cameras, or connected in series and parallel to obtain the required values of current and voltage for electric power generation.

Most solar cells are made from single-crystal silicon and have been very expensive for generating electricity, but have found application in space satellites and remote areas where low-cost conventional power sources have been unavailable. Research has emphasized lowering solar cell cost by improving performance and by reducing materials and manufacturing costs. One approach is to use optical concentrators such as mirrors or Fresnel lenses to focus the sunlight onto smaller-area solar cells. Other approaches replace the high-cost single-crystal silicon with thin films of amorphous or polycrystalline silicon, gallium arsenide, cadmium sulfide, or other compounds.

**Solar radiation.** The intensity and quality of sunlight are dramatically different outside the Earth's atmosphere from that on the surface of the Earth, as shown in **Fig. 1**. The number of photons at each energy is reduced upon entering the Earth's atmosphere

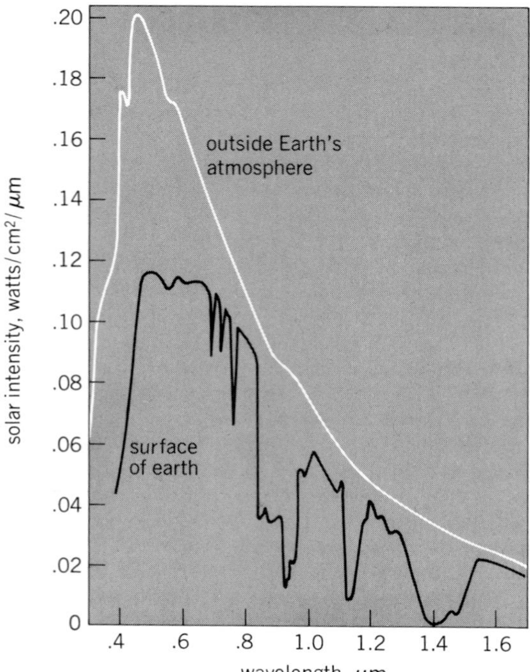


**Fig. 1. Variation of solar intensity with wavelength of photons for sunlight outside the Earth's atmosphere and for a typical spectrum on the surface of the Earth.**

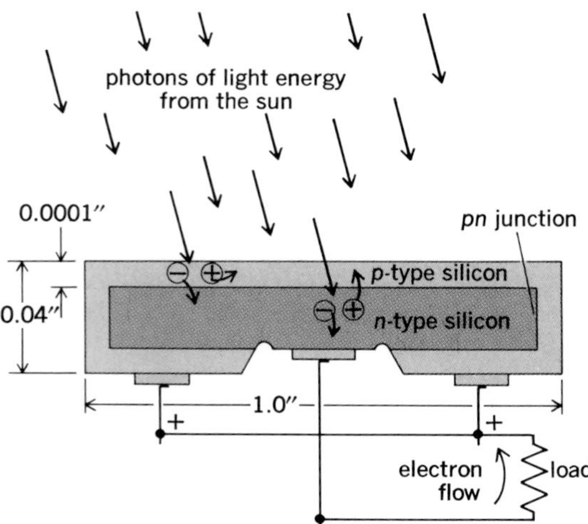


**Fig. 2. Cross-sectional view of a silicon *pn* junction solar cell, illustrating the creation of electron pairs by photons of light energy from the Sun. 0.0001″ = 2.5 μm; 0.04″ = 1 mm; 1.0″ = 25 mm.**

due to reflection, to scattering, or to absorption by water vapor and other gases. Thus, while the solar energy at normal incidence outside the Earth's atmosphere is 1.36 $kW/m^2$ (the solar constant), on the surface of the Earth at noontime on a clear day the intensity is about 1 $kW/m^2$.

On clear days the direct radiation is about 10 times greater than the diffuse radiation, but on overcast days the sunshine is entirely diffuse. The mean annual solar energy falling on the Earth's surface varies greatly from one location to another. The sunniest regions of the globe receive about 2500 $kWh/m^2$ per year of total sunshine on a horizontal surface. The Earth receives about $10^{18}$ kWh of solar energy each year. The worldwide annual energy consumption is about $80 \times 10^{12}$ kWh, so that from a purely technical viewpoint, the world energy consumption corresponds to the sunlight received on about 0.008% of the surface of the Earth.

**Principles of operation.** The conversion of sunlight into electrical energy in a solar cell involves three major processes: absorption of the sunlight in the semiconductor material; generation and separation of free positive and negative charges to different regions of the solar cell, creating a voltage in the solar cell; and transfer of these separated charges through electrical terminals to the outside application in the form of electric current.

In the first step the absorption of sunlight by a solar cell depends on the intensity and quality of the sunlight, the amount of light reflected from the front surface of the solar cell, the semiconductor bandgap energy which is the minimum light (photon) energy the material absorbs, and the layer thickness. Some materials such as silicon require tens of micrometers' thickness to absorb most of the sunlight, while others such as gallium arsenide, cadmium telluride, and copper sulfide require only a few micrometers.

When light is absorbed in the semiconductor, a negatively charged electron and positively charged hole are created. The heart of the solar cell is the electrical junction which separates these electrons and holes from one another after they are created by the light. An electrical junction may be formed by the contact of: a metal to a semiconductor (this junction

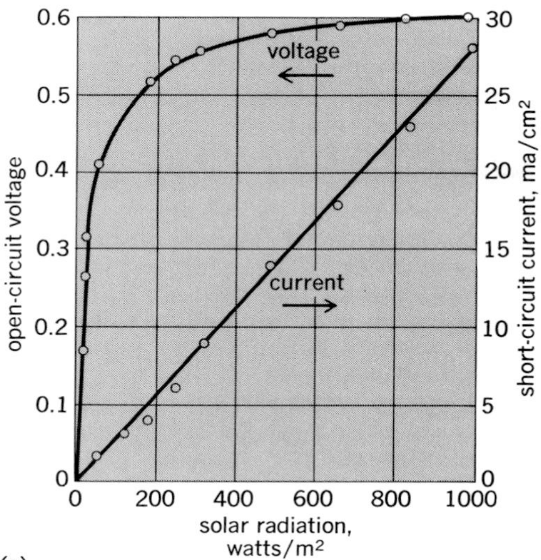


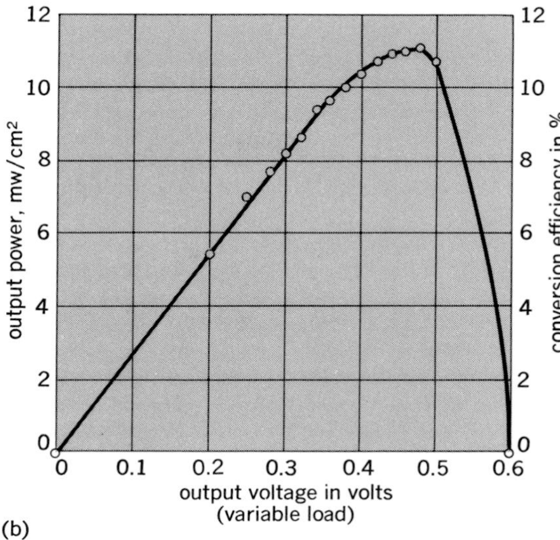


**Fig. 3.** Electrical characteristics of silicon *pn* junction solar cell, at operating temperature of 63°F (17°C). (*a*) Variation of open-circuit voltage and short-circuit current with light intensity. (*b*) Variation in power output as load is varied from short to open circuit.

is called a Schottky barrier); a liquid to a semiconductor to form a photoelectrochemical cell; or two semiconductor regions (called a *pn* junction).

The fundamental principles of the electrical junction can be illustrated with the silicon *pn* junction. Pure silicon to which a trace amount of a fifth-column element such as phosphorus has been added is an *n*-type semiconductor, where electric current is carried by free electrons. Each phosphorus atom contributes one free electron, leaving behind the phosphorus atom bound to the crystal structure with a unit positive charge. Similarly, pure silicon to which a trace amount of a column-three element such as boron has been added is a *p*-type semiconductor, where the electric current is carried by free holes. Each boron atom contributes one hole, leaving behind the boron atom with a unit negative charge. The interface between the *p*- and *n*-type silicon is called the *pn* junction. The fixed charges at the interface due to the bound boron and phosphorus atoms create a permanent dipole charge layer with a high electric field. When photons of light energy from the Sun produce electron-hole pairs near the junction, the built-in electric field forces the holes to the *p* side and the electrons to the *n* side (**Fig. 2**). This displacement of free charges results in a voltage difference between the two regions of the crystal, the *p* region being plus and the *n* region minus. When a load is connected at the terminals, electron current flows in the direction of the arrow, and electrical power is available at the load. *See* Semiconductor; Semiconductor diode.

**Characteristics.** The electrical characteristics of a typical silicon *pn*-junction solar cell are shown in **Fig. 3**. Figure 3*a* shows open-circuit voltage and short-circuit current as a function of light intensity from total darkness to full sunlight (1000 W/m$^2$). The short-circuit current is directly proportional to light intensity and amounts to 28 mA/cm$^2$ at full sunlight. The open-circuit voltage rises sharply under weak light and saturates at about 0.6 V for radiation between 200 and 1000 W/m$^2$. The variation in power output from the solar cell irradiated by full sunlight as its load is varied from short circuit to open circuit is shown in Fig. 3*b*. The maximum power output is about 11 mW/cm$^2$ at an output voltage of 0.45 V.

Under these operating conditions the overall conversion efficiency from solar to electrical energy is 11%. The output power as well as the output current is of course proportional to the irradiated surface area, whereas the output voltage can be increased by connecting cells in series just as in an ordinary chemical storage battery. Experimental samples of silicon solar cells have been produced which operate at efficiencies up to 18%, but commercial cell efficiency is around 10–12% under normal operating conditions.

Using optical concentration to intensify the light incident on the solar cell, efficiencies above 20% have been achieved with silicon cells and above 25% with gallium arsenide cells. The concept of splitting the solar spectrum and illuminating two optimized solar cells of different bandgaps has been used to achieve efficiencies above 28%, with expected efficiencies of 35%. Thin-film solar cells have achieved between 4 and 9% efficiency and are expected in low-cost arrays to be above 10%.

*K. W. Mitchell*

**Arrays.** Individual silicon solar cells are limited in size to about 40 cm$^2$ (6.2 in.$^2$) of surface area. At a 15% conversion efficiency, such a cell can deliver about 0.6 W at 0.5 V when in full sunlight. To obtain higher power and higher voltage, a number of cells must be assembled in panels or arrays (**Fig. 4**). Cells may be connected in series to multiply their output voltage and in parallel to multiply their output current. Cells operated in series must be closely matched in short-circuit current since the overall performance of a solar cell array is limited by the cells having the lowest current.

**Applications.** Although the photovoltaic effect was discovered by A. C. Becquerel in 1839, practical solar cells made of silicon crystals were not developed until 1955. Beginning with *Vanguard 1*, launched in 1958, silicon solar cell arrays have become the almost exclusive power source for satellites. *Skylab*, launched in 1973, had a 20-kW solar cell array.

Terrestrial applications of solar cells increased rapidly after 1970. Solar cell arrays have been used primarily to power small remote electrical loads that would otherwise be impractical or uneconomical to power by conventional means such as storage batteries or motor-generator sets. Solar cell arrays are sold worldwide to power such equipment as remote radio

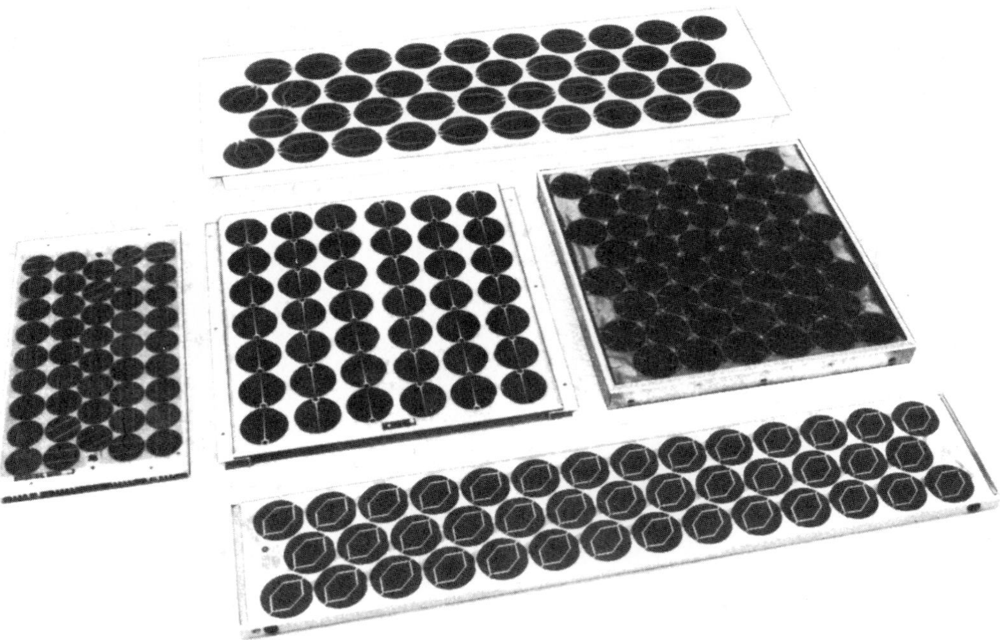

**Fig. 4.** Silicon solar cells assembled into panels and arrays to obtain higher voltage and power output. Peak power of modules is at 140°F (60°C) and 15.8 V. (*U.S. Department of Energy*)

repeaters, navigational aids, consumer products, railroad signals, cathodic protection devices, and water pumps. **Figure 5** shows a remote solar cell–powered communication link. Since most of the aforementioned uses require power to the load at times even when the Sun is not shining, electrical storage batteries are typically used in conjunction with solar cell arrays to provide reliable, continuous power availability.

Although extended terrestrial uses await cheaper solar arrays, a number of experiments have been undertaken to explore the use of solar cell arrays in larger agricultural, residential, commercial, and industrial applications (**Fig. 6**). When powering loads which require ac voltage, a static inverter is used to convert the dc voltage from the solar cell array into usable ac power.

**Future prospects.** The growing worldwide demand for energy, its increasing cost, and the depletion of nonrenewable energy reserves make solar cell power

**Fig. 5.** A 3-kW solar cell–powered communication link in southern California. (*Spectrolab, Inc., Sylmar, California*)

**Fig. 6. A 25-kW photovoltaic array which is operating in an agricultural irrigation experiment located at Mead, Nebraska. (*U.S. Department of Energy and MIT Lincoln Laboratory*)**

systems an attractive alternative for supplying electricity for a wide range of uses. Despite significant progress in this technology, the cost of solar cells must be significantly reduced before they can economically supply a substantial amount of electricity. Research has been undertaken to develop new approaches lowering the cost of solar cell materials and manufacturing processes.

*Donald G. Schueler*

**Bibliography.** J. A. Merrigan, *Sunlight to Electricity: Prospects for Solar Energy Conversion by Photovoltaics*, 1975; W. Palz, *Solar Electricity: An Economic Approach to Solar Energy*, 1978; D. L. Pulfrey, *Photovoltaic Power Generation*, 1978.

## Space charge

The net electric charge within a given volume. If both positive and negative charges are present, the space charge represents the excess of the total positive charge diffused through the volume in question over the total negative charge. Since electric field lines end on electric charge, the space-charge density $\rho$ may also be defined in terms of the divergence of the electric field **E** or the laplacian of the electric potential $V$ by Eq. (1) (Poisson's equation). Here $\epsilon$ is the dielec-

$$-\frac{4\pi\rho}{\epsilon} = -\operatorname{div} \mathbf{E} = \nabla^2 V = \frac{\partial^2 V}{\partial x^2} + \frac{\partial^2 V}{\partial y^2} + \frac{\partial^2 V}{\partial z^2} \quad (1)$$

tric constant of the medium and $x$, $y$, and $z$ are rectangular coordinates defining the position of a point in space. If, under the influence of an applied field, the charge carriers acquire a drift velocity $v$, the space charge becomes $j/v$, where $j$ is the current density. For current carried by both positive and negative carriers, such as positive ions and electrons, the space charge density is given by Eq. (2). Here the sub-

$$\rho = \frac{j_+}{v_+} - \frac{j_-}{v_-} \quad (2)$$

scripts + and − indicate the current density and drift velocity for the positive and negative carriers, respectively. Thus a relatively small current of slow-moving positive ions can neutralize the space charge of a much larger current of high-velocity electrons. SEE LANGMUIR-CHILD LAW.

*Edward G. Ramberg*

## Spark gap

The region between two electrodes in which a disruptive electrical spark may take place. The gap should be taken to mean the electrodes as well as the intervening space. Such devices may have many uses. The ignition system in a gasoline engine furnishes a very important example. Another important case is the use of a spark gap as a protective device in electrical equipment. Here, surges in potential may be made to break down such a gap so that expensive equipment will not be damaged. The dependence of spark-gap operation on such factors as pressure, length, electrode characteristics, and time dependence of potential is quite complicated. SEE BREAKDOWN POTENTIAL; ELECTRIC SPARK.

*Glenn H. Miller*

## Spectrum analyzer

A measuring instrument for the analysis of audio-frequency, radio-frequency, and microwave signals, and complex waveforms. It is a special type of harmonic analyzer. For a description of frequency domain analysis and a general introduction SEE HARMONIC ANALYZER.

**Operation.** A cathode-ray-tube screen with a calibrated graticule displays the components of the input signal. The vertical scale displays the amplitude of each component, and the chosen frequency band is displayed horizontally. Components of the signal being analyzed are displayed as vertical lines whose height is proportional to amplitude and whose horizontal displacement equates to frequency. SEE CATHODE-RAY TUBE.

The method of operation is illustrated in **Fig. 1**. The spectrum analyzer is essentially a swept heterodyne analyzer. The ramp generator simultaneously increases the frequency of the local oscillator and moves the spot across the display. When the ramp

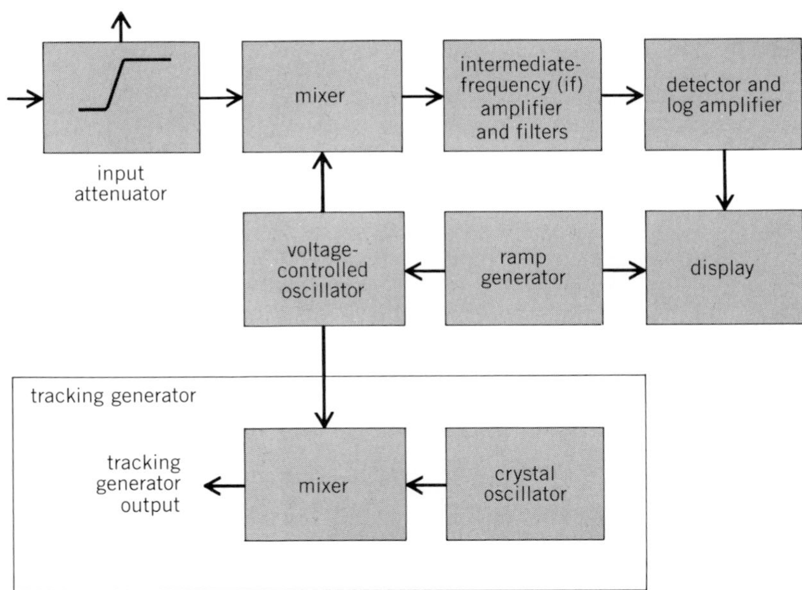


**Fig. 1. Simplified block diagram of a spectrum analyzer with a tracking generator.**

**Fig. 2. Typical modern spectrum analyzer. (*Marconi Instruments*)**

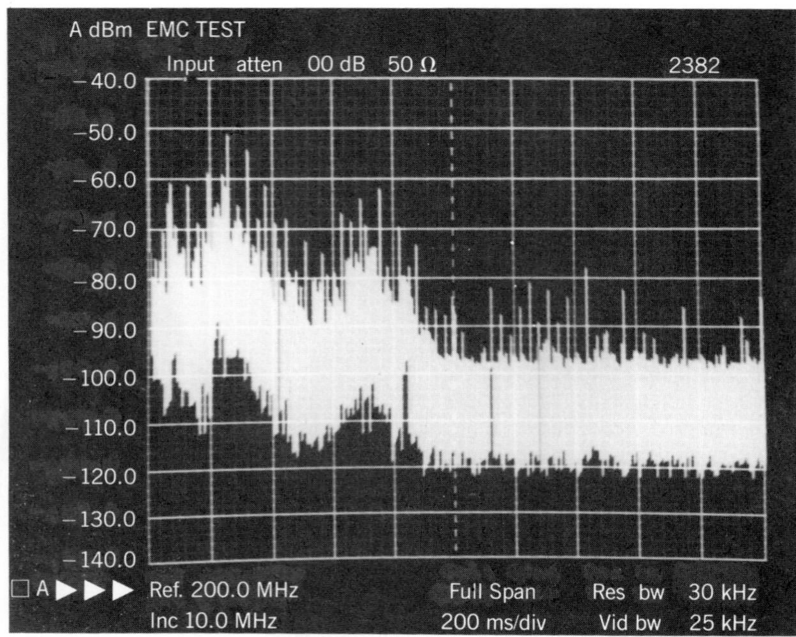


**Fig. 3. Spectrum analyzer display showing spurious radio-frequency interference.**

voltage is zero, the spot will be on the left side of the display and the local oscillator will be at a low frequency. Any signal at the input, at a frequency such that the difference between its frequency and the local oscillator is within the intermediate-frequency (i-f) filter bandwidth, will be detected and will vertically deflect the spot on the display by an amount proportional to the amplitude of input signal. As the ramp voltage increases, the spot moves across the display and the analyzer tunes to increasingly higher-frequency signals. Each component of a complex waveform is thus isolated and displayed.

Modern spectrum analyzers (**Fig. 2**) incorporate sophisticated microprocessor control to make the instrument more versatile, easier to use, and more accurate than earlier types. An additional benefit of newer types is that they can be remotely programmed so that a computer can control all functions. *See Microprocessor.*

The operator normally has four basic groups of controls to operate: frequency, horizontal-scale, vertical-scale, and markers. Digital keypads or rotary controls are generally provided. The frequency controls determine the center or reference frequency of the display. The horizontal-scale controls determine the portion of the spectrum that can be viewed; this can be a scan from, say, 100 Hz up to 20 GHz or beyond. Separate controls are used to determine the vertical scale (typically from 10 to 1 dB per division and a voltage scale) and the sensitivity. Steerable markers are available on modern instruments so that discrete spectral lines can be isolated and their absolute and relative frequencies and levels accurately measured.

Further controls are provided so that the operator can optimize operation for different conditions, For example, the i-f bandwidth can be changed to alter the resolution.

A major innovation in spectrum analyzers has been the use of digital storage. In order to obtain high resolution over a relatively wide band of frequencies, it is necessary to sweep the spectrum slowly; sometimes a single sweep may take up to 100 s. Digital storage gives the effect of a constant display even though a very slow sweep may have been used to acquire the displayed data.

**Applications.** Early spectrum analyzers were developed to measure the performance of microwave radar transmitters. The bandwidth of the transmitted pulse-modulated signals could be measured and spurious output signals identified. Another early application, this time in the high-frequency (hf) radio band (3 to 30 MHz), was the analysis of signals from single sideband (SSB) transmitters, intermodulation and modulation performance being the main parameters measured. *See Radar; Single sideband.*

Although these early uses are still relevant, the introduction of more advanced and comprehensive instruments has led to a dramatic increase in the number of applications and uses. A typical use is the measurement of spurious radiation from electrical machinery and circuits, known as radio-frequency interference (RFI; **Fig. 3**). Other uses include monitoring and surveillance, since unauthorized or unintended transmissions can be detected and intercepted; this use includes the civil monitoring of broadcast and communication channels as well as military applications, including detection of electronic warfare signals. A further common application is the analysis of radio communication transmitters and receivers including those used in radio and television broadcasting, satellite systems, and mobile radio communication.

Spectrum analyzers also fulfill a variety of general-purpose uses in research, development, manufacture, and maintenance of all types of electrical and electronic equipment. For certain applications they are used instead of an oscilloscope, since the spectrum analysis display of a complex waveform can provide more information than an oscilloscope display. Another major limitation of an oscilloscope is the limited frequency range; 300 MHz is a typical upper limit for a sophisticated oscilloscope, while spectrum analyzers can measure microwave radio signals up to at least 300 GHz. *See Oscilloscope.*

**Tracking generator.** The tracking generator (Fig. 1) is an enhancement on modern spectrum analyzers. The tracking generator output delivers a swept signal whose instantaneous frequency is always equal to the input tuned frequency of the analyzer. The swept signal is used to measure the frequency response of circuits such as filters and amplifiers over a wide dynamic range which would not be possible using a broadband nonselective measurement method.

*S. J. Gledhill*

***Bibliography.*** J. Browne, Spectrum analyzers: Windows on an RF world, *Microw. RF*, pp. 71–153, April 1984; C. F. Coombs, Jr., *Basic Electronic Instrument Handbook,* 1972; M. Engleson and F. Telewski, *Spectrum Analyzer Theory and Applications,* 1974; B. M. Oliver and J. M. Cage, *Electronic Measurements and Instrumentation,* 1971; T. Peccolo, The spectrum analyzer comes of age, *Microw. J.*, pp. 125–132, April 1983; A. M. Rudkin, *Electronic Test Equipment*, 1981.

## Speech recognition

The process of analyzing an acoustic speech signal to identify the linguistic message that was intended, so that a machine can correctly respond to spoken commands. Procedures must be incorporated for distinguishing linguistic contrasts from irrelevant acoustic changes that are due to variabilities among speakers and environmental conditions.

**Motivation.** Speaking commands to a computer is the ultimate in natural human-to-machine communications. Natural, spontaneous interactions are possible, with little or no user training, permitting direct access by the physically handicapped or those who cannot type well. The user can communicate in the dark or blinding light, around obstacles, and while walking about in an area, without direct contact with a computer console or need for large data-input devices. Telephones and radios can become low-cost computer input terminals, and there is interest in voice control of toys, appliances, wristwatch calculators, and other consumer products.

Speech allows rapid data entry and frees the user's hands and eyes for other tasks. Experiments show that complex tasks can be accomplished in half the time if speech is allowed as one mode of interaction. Even when one of the communicators is replaced by a restricted machine that can recognize only single words or phrases, preceded and followed by pauses, the speed and accuracy of complex data entry are still better for speech than for keyboard or graphical pen.

Speech recognizers have been advocated, sold, and used for various hands-busy applications such as: quality control and inspection; package sorting for automatic conveyor systems; control of machine tools; entry of topographical data in mapmaking facilities; and cockpit controls. Voice-actuated wheelchairs, hospital room environmental controls, and recognizer-resynthesizer translators for pathological speech are of public interest. Telephone banking, voice authorization of credit card transactions, and catalog ordering are other applications, which introduce difficulties related to telephone bandwidth, noise, and distortions.

**Difficulty.** Fluent conversation with a machine is difficult to achieve because of intrinsic variabilities and complexities of speech, as well as limitations in current practical capabilities. Recognition difficulty increases with vocabulary size, confusability of words, reduced frequency bandwidth, noise, frequency distortions, the population of speakers that must be understood, and the form of speech to be processed. To limit the problem, speech recognizers have been primarily confined to small vocabularies of words with large differences in sound structure, and isolated words, with pauses before and after each word. As illustrated in **Fig. 1**, word boundaries are then relatively easy to find, as transitions into and out of silences. Contextual influences of surrounding words on the pronunciation of each word are minimized by pausing. In contrast, the continuous flow of natural speech can make it difficult to tell when one word ends and the next word begins. Coarticulatory degenerations from ideal dictionary pronunciations (for example, "dija" for "did you," or "lisum" for "list some") can be avoided with strict constraints (formats) on allowable word sequences, and can be practically eliminated by pausing between words, but at some loss in naturalness and speed of data entry.

Isolated word recognizers are thus the easiest to develop, followed in turn by recognizers of digit strings and strictly formatted word sequences. Sometimes the identification of every spoken word is not necessary, and detecting key words in context is enough to determine the topic of a conversation. Such a word-spotting system usually deals only with the important words, which are stressed and well articulated, easing the recognition, despite arbitrary contexts. Full understanding of the total sentence meaning and intended machine response involves cooperative use of many "knowledge sources" like acoustics, phonetics, prosodics, restricted syntax, semantics, and task-dictated discourse constraints. The term speech-understanding system is frequently used to describe such a sentence-understanding device. An even more ambitious system goal would involve accurately identifying all the words in any possible utterance, yielding what is variously called a phonetic typewriter, an automatic transcription facility, a speech-to-text machine, or a task-independent continuous-speech recognizer.

**Accuracy.** The difficulty of recognition is closely correlated with required recognition accuracy, defined as the percentage of all received utterances that are correctly identified (that is, for which the machine response is as intended). Substitutions of the wrong response are usually considered more serious than machine rejections of the utterance as being too similar to other possible utterances to be reliably categorized. Studies are needed regarding necessary accuracy in various practical situations, although most field tests suggest that 4% error rates are not acceptable to serious users. Error rates alone are not necessarily the best total measures of the effectiveness of recognizers. Usually it is the total cost of interactions (errorful or not) that determines the merit of a vocal (or manual) input facility, and users need to examine the distribution of errors among various vocabulary items, and the likelihoods of falsely rejecting an acceptable vocabulary word or falsely accepting an extraneous noise or background conversation, and so forth, along with the total consequences of each such error.

One of the most important areas in speech recognition technology is the human factors aspect, concerned with determining what specific tasks warrant voice input, what accuracies are needed, and how to balance the trade-offs between versatility and cost, criticality of errors and technical feasibility, and exploitation of task constraints versus flexible enhancement for use on new tasks.

**Operation of speech recognizers.** Speech recognition requires the transformation of the continuous-speech signal into discrete representations which may be assigned proper meanings, and which, when comprehended, may be used to effect responsive behavior. Only some of the information in the speech signal is related to selecting the correct machine response, so that a critical task is to extract all, and only, those parts that convey the message. Recognizers primarily differ on how they reduce the data to message-distinguishing features, and how they classify utterances from that reduced data.

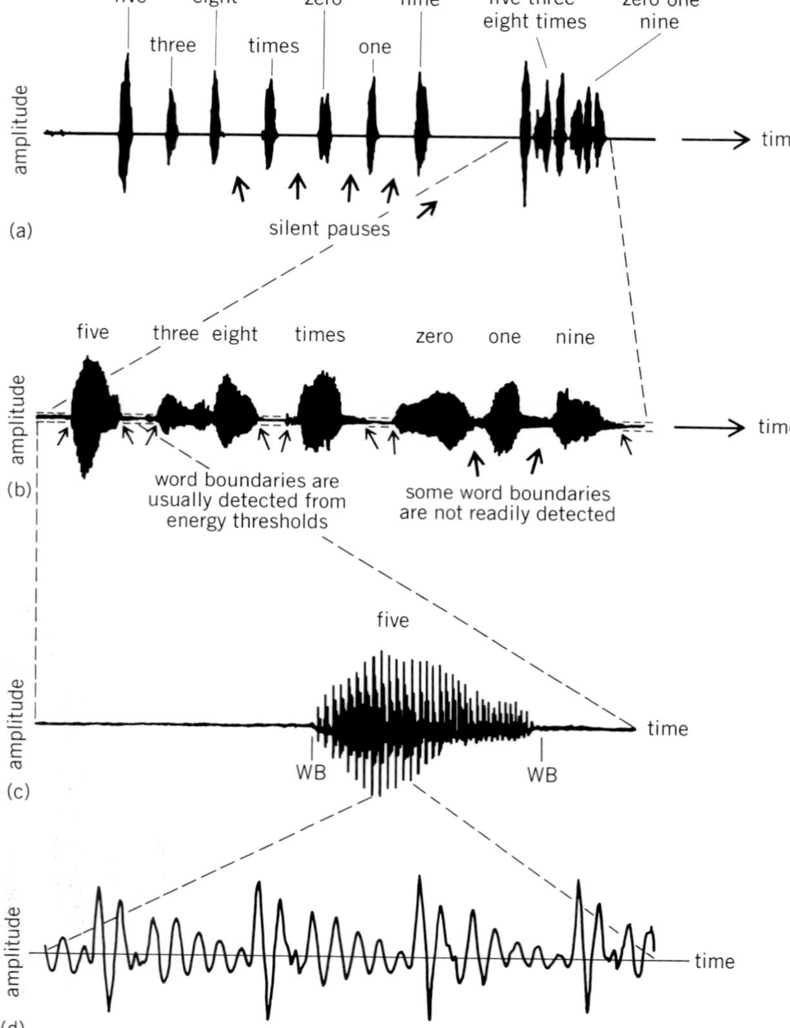


**Fig. 1. Series of progressively more detailed views of an acoustic waveform, showing how a recognizer can detect utterance boundaries and identify words and messages. (*a*) Words isolated from each other by silent pauses, followed by a continuously spoken version of a calculator command. (*b*) Waveform of the continuous-speech portion of *a*, showing how some, but not all, word boundaries can be detected from energy thresholds. (*c*) Further expansion of the time scale of part of the waveform of *b*, so that the constantly changing sound structure within the word "five" is evident, and word boundaries (WB) are illustrated. (*d*) Local resonant structure of the diphthongal transition from /a/ to /1/ in the "five" of diagram *c*.**

**Figure 2** illustrates one general structure for how a machine acquires knowledge of expected pronunciations and compares input data with those expectations. Since most devices must be trained to the specific pronunciation of each talker, a precompiling stage involves the user speaking sample pronunciations for each allowable utterance (word, phrase, or sentence), while identifying each with its typewritten form or a vocabulary item number. Later, when an unknown utterance is spoken, it is compared with all the lexicon of expected pronunciations to find which training sample it most closely resembles. For complex utterances, other linguistic and situational information can be used to help guide and confirm hypothesized word sequences. Figures 1, 3, 4, and 5 detail some of the processes needed in the system components diagrammed in Fig. 2.

***Word boundary detection.*** Figure 1 illustrates the initial process of detecting word boundaries, for word sequences with or without deliberate pauses between words. Silent pauses (Fig. 1*a*) permit easy detection of word onsets at transitions from no signal to high energy (above some threshold amount), and word offsets as energy dips below the threshold. In continuous speech, pauses normally occur only at boundaries between sentences or clauses, or at thoughtful hesitations just before important words. Even the rapidly spoken calculator command shown in Figure 1*b* shows more prominent energy dips, and very brief pauses, between words than is usual in conversationally flowing speech. Word boundary confusions can occur, however, when short silences (usually less than 100 ms in duration) during stop consonants (/p, t, k/) may look like intended pauses. Thus, a word such as ''transportation'' could appear to divide into three ''words'': ''transp,'' ''ort,'' and ''ation.'' Recognizers looking for pauses between words must thus measure the duration of the pause, to distinguish short consonantal silences from longer deliberate pauses.

***Feature extraction.*** Once a word or other utterance unit has been delimited, its identity can be determined from the details of its pronunciation. Figures 1*c* and *d* show that the sound structure in a word is constantly changing, with frequent alternations (and transitions) between vowellike damped resonant structures and weak or noiselike consonantal sounds such as /p, t, k, f, s/. Not all aspects of the pronunciation of a word will be consistent from time to time, from one talker to another, or from one context to another. Hence, important information-carrying features are usually sought in the acoustic data to detect contrasts of linguistic significance and to detect segments such as vowels and consonants.

**Figure 3** shows a few typical acoustic parameters used in recognizers. From the acoustic waveform, one can extract local peak values, such as at 1 in Fig. 3*a*, as an amplitude measure. Also, the sum of the squares of all waveform values over a time window can provide a measure of the energy in that window of speech data. The number of times the signal passes

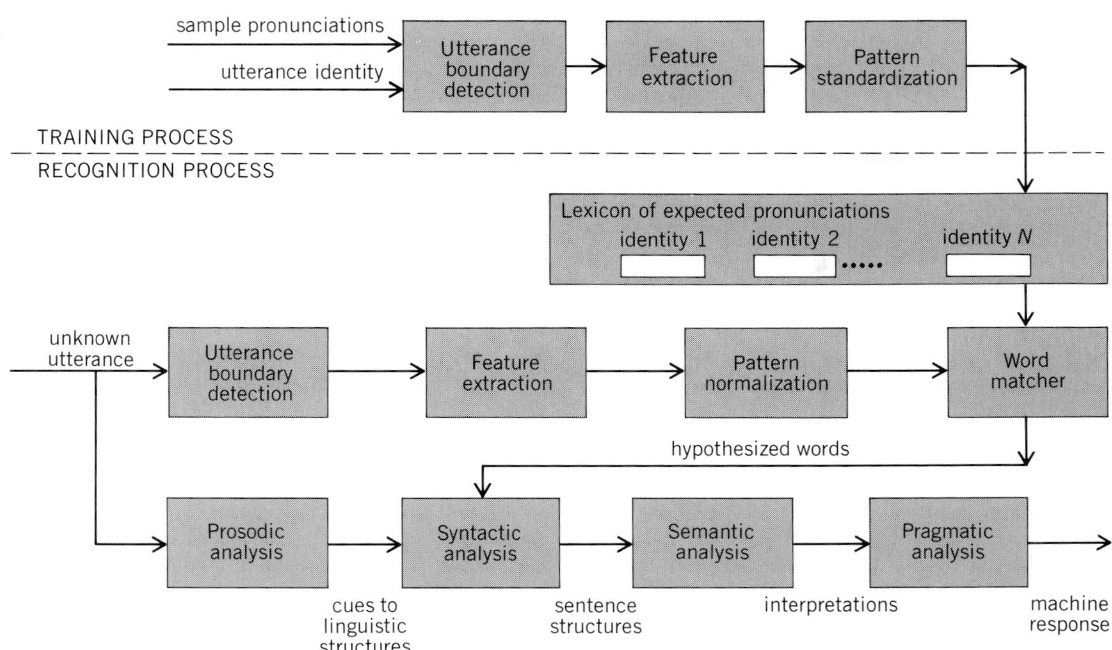


**Fig. 2. Typical structure for a trainable speech recognizer that could recognize words, phrases, or sentences.**

through a value of zero (zero crossings) can be used as a cue to vowellike smooth waveforms (with few crossings per unit time) versus noiselike fricative segments (with many crossings per unit time). The time between the prominent peaks at onsets of pitch cycles can be used to determine the pitch period $T_0$, or its inverse, the rate of vibration of the vocal cords, called fundamental frequency or $F_0$. Resonant frequencies are evident from the number of peaks per pitch period. For example, the third pitch period in Fig. 3*a* shows seven local peaks, indicating a ringing resonance of about seven times the fundamental frequency. This resonance is the first formant or vocal tract resonance of the /a/-like vowel, and is one of the best cues to the vowel identity.

Figure 3*b* shows the superimposed results of two methods for analyzing the frequency content of the short sample of speech in Fig. 3*a*. The computer can achieve rapid determination of the total jagged Fourier frequency spectrum, with its peaks at harmonics of the fundamental frequency, using a fast Fourier transform (FFT). However, to extract the exact positions of major spectral peaks at the formants of the speech, an advanced method called linear predictive coding (LPC) can yield the smoothed-linear predictive coding spectrum shown passing through the middles of the vertical jumps of the FFT spectrum. The peaks in such a spectrum then indicate the basic resonant frequencies of the speaker's vocal tract, and can be tracked versus time, as in Fig. 3*c*, to indicate the nature of the vowel being articulated. Another common spectral analyzer is a filter bank, with narrow band-pass filters spaced across the frequency spectrum, to monitor the amount of energy in each frequency range versus time. SEE HARMONIC ANALYZER.

***Pattern standardization and normalization.*** **Figure 4** shows why a recognizer needs pattern standardization and pattern normalization components. The word "five" spoken on two successive occasions in Fig. 4*a* has different amplitudes (A1 and A2). A recognizer must neglect (normalize for) such amplitude variations that have nothing to do with intended linguistic contrasts. Also, as a comparison of Fig. 4*b* and *c* illustrates, the timing of speech events may not be the same for two repetitions of the same utterance. With identical time scales, the /w/ in 4*b* lines up with the timing of the /ʌ/ in *c*. A recognizer must realign the data, so that the proper portions of an unknown utterance are aligned with corresponding portions of the templates. This normally requires nonuniform time

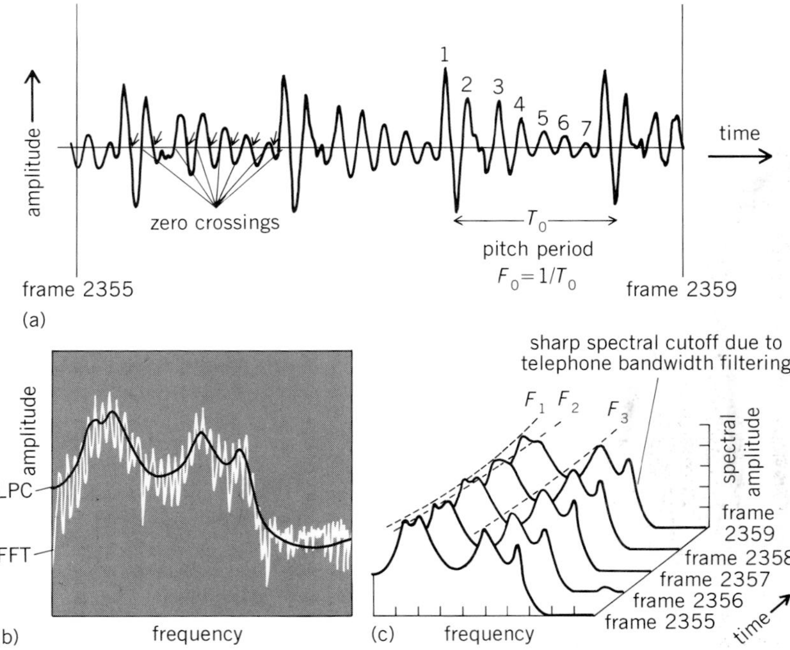


**Fig. 3. Typical acoustic parameters used in speech recognizers. (*a*) Time waveform of Fig. 1c, showing parameters that can be extracted. (*b*) Frequency spectrum of the waveform of *a*, with the detailed frequency spectrum derived from a fast Fourier transform (FFT) being smoothed by linear predictive coding (LPC) to yield a smooth spectrum from which formats can be found as the spectral peaks. (c) Smoothed LPC spectra for five successive short time segments (frames, each 6.4 ms long), with formants $F_1$, $F_2$, and $F_3$ tracked as the spectral peaks.**

normalization, as suggested by the different phonemic durations in Fig. 4. Dynamic programming is a method for trying all reasonable alignments, and picking the one that yields the closest match to each template. Another possible pattern normalization might be speaker normalization, such as moving one speaker's formants in a pattern such as Fig. 3*c* up or down the frequency axis to match those of a "standard" speaker, for whom the machine has been trained. Channel normalization is another need; if training data were collected under broadband conditions, but unknown utterances come over the band-limited telephone, the sharp cutoff due to telephone filtering may have to be introduced into the training data before spectral comparisons. During training, the speaker's data for amplitudes, timing, and spectral content can be set to standard values, or calibrated, so that unknowns can later be warped (normalized) to match those standard values.

***Word matching.*** From such feature extraction, standardization, and normalization processes, an array of feature values versus time can be obtained. During training, this array can be stored as a template of expected pronunciation; during recognition, a new array can be compared with all stored arrays, to see which word is closest to it. This involves a distance measure that weights all the features and time slices in some manner, and accumulates a total difference in structure from one array to another.

Ambiguities in possible wording result from errors and uncertainties in detecting the expected sound structure of an utterance. Some "robust" segments like vowels and strong consonants may be evident, but a variety of words could usually correspond with a detected sound structure. To prevent catastrophic errors in word identifications, recognizers will often give a complete list of possible words, in decreasing order of agreement with the data (that is, increasing distance from the input pattern). For each time period of the unknown utterance, the word matcher of Fig. 2 then hypothesizes many words that are to varying degrees close to the sound structure of the incoming speech in that region. As shown in **Fig. 5**, the first word might look like "five," based on the correspondence between the detected vowel AY and the expected vowel AY, and the matching of initial and final consonants "f" and "v" also. The first word is also similar to "nine" and "times" in a small vocabulary of calculator terms. Later in the utterance, words such as "zero," "seven," "clear," and "one" might compete as candidates for the same region of speech. One reason for such potential confusions is that a practical recognizer may mislabel segments, fail to detect certain segments, or insert segments that are not actually in the utterance. Figure 5 shows only the more robust detected segments, such as vowels and some consonants, around which the remainder of the sound structure must be carefully (but less reliably) matched.

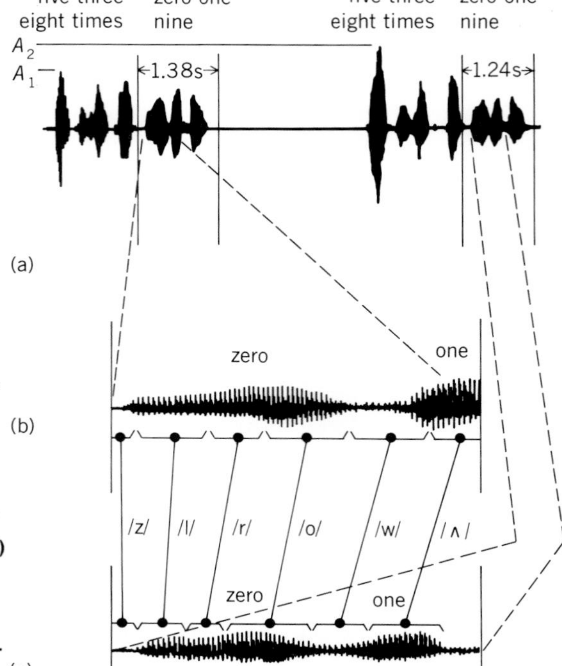


**Fig. 4.** Two successive utterances of the same phrase, showing need for amplitude and time normalization processes in speech recognizers. (*a*) Utterances in succession, showing differences in amplitudes $A_1$ and $A_2$. (*b,c*) Expansion of portions of the utterances, showing how rate of speaking can cause misalignment of data, so that time normalization is needed.

***Higher-level linguistic components.*** A challenge for speech recognizers is how to keep down the combinatorial explosion of alternative word sequences to consider. That is the primary purpose for higher-level linguistic components such as prosodics, syntax, semantics, and pragmatics. Prosodic information such as intonation can help distinguish questions from commands, and can divide utterances into phrases and rule out word sequences with incorrect syllabic prominences or stress patterns. A syntactic rule may be written into the computer to disallow consideration of ungrammatical sequences like two operators in a row, so that "plus divide," "multiply clear plus," and so forth, are ruled out from hypothesized word sequences. A collection of such word-sequence constraints forms a grammar. Most practical recognizers use a simple grammar type called a finite-state grammar that determines the allowable next words based on the immediately preceding word. A semantic constraint might disallow meaningless but grammatical sequences such as "zero divide by zero." A pragmatic constraint might eliminate unlikely or impractical sequences such as the useless initial "zero" in "zero one nine" of Fig. 1. In a chessplaying task, to take another example, syntactic rules limit word sequences to those for acceptable statements of movements of pieces, such as "pawn to queen four"; semantic rules then would rule out illegal or meaningless moves; pragmatic rules would discount the likelihood of ridiculous or counterproductive moves, such as moves that were just made in the immediately previous step. Some sophisticated recognizers have included all these sources of knowledge to help correctly identify an utterance. Isolated word recognizers usually use finite-state grammars, if any higher-level linguistics is used at all.

It is also possible to restructure the recognizer components shown in successive steps in Fig. 2. One promising structure avoids the propagation of errors through successive stages of a recognizer by having all the components intercommunicate directly through a "blackboard" or central control component that, for example, might allow syntax or semantics to affect feature-extraction or word-matching processes, or vice versa.

**Practical implementations.** **Figure 6** illustrates the variety of available hardware and software implementations of speech recognizers. A primary distinguishing specification of speech recognizers is the type of speech handled, whether it be "isolated words" sep-

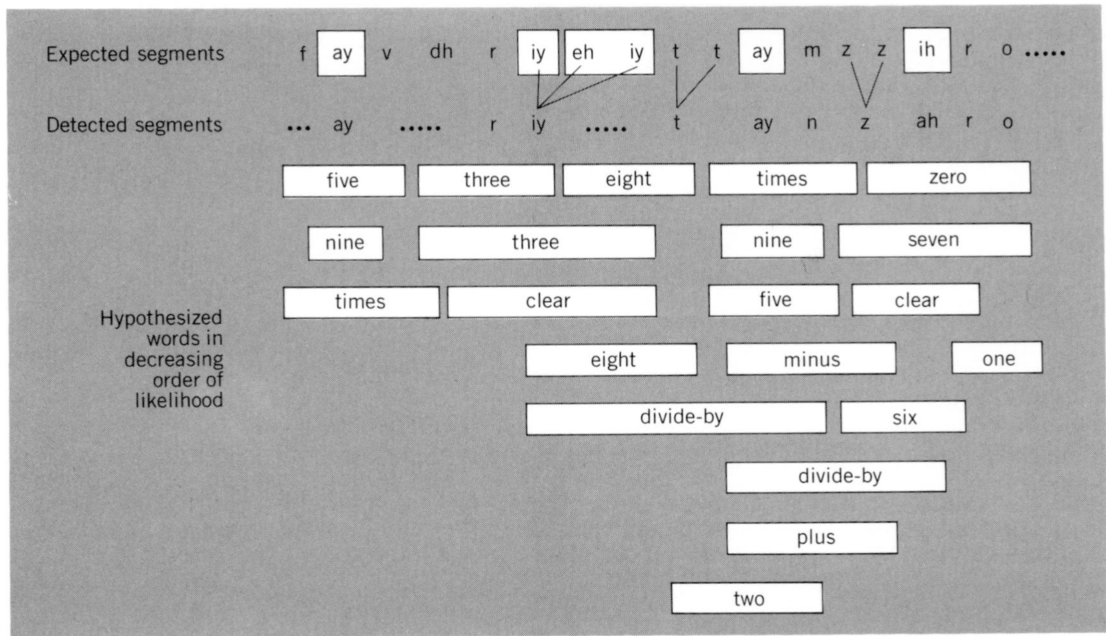


Fig. 5. Process of word matching.

arated by pauses, or "connected word sequences" (digits, or other words from some small vocabulary, spoken in rapid succession but with strict syntactic formats), or "continuous speech" within entire natural sentences. Another important distinction is whether the recognizer must be trained to the speaker's voice ("dependent") or can work with essentially any voice without prior training ("independent"). The solid blocks in Fig. 6 indicate many attempts at achieving the type of recognizer represented by the coordinates of that position, while open boxes suggest that few attempts were made at that particular type of capability.

***Types of recognizer.*** Each type of recognizer begins from a foundation of research systems (typically implemented on general-purpose computers). In the 1970s, expensive full commercial systems were first offered that stood alone and provided a recognizer box, a microphone or headset, an alphanumeric display to show recognizer decisions, and facilities for using recognition results to affect machinery responses. However, with the expanding availability of computers to perform the display and control processes, the late 1970s saw the emergence of "voice terminals" that were compatible with (and could look to the computer just like) manual interfaces such as keyboards. These voice terminals were recognition circuit boards embedded in a box that provided necessary power and interfacing to other equipment.

The 1980s began with the popularity of a simpler recognition device, a single circuit board, with the special recognition algorithms implemented on microprocessors, read-only memories, random-access memories, and related analog or hybrid hardware. A few manufacturers have offered integrated-circuit chip sets, or single chips, that can be incorporated into users' boards or systems as the simplest form of recognition hardware. This trend toward reduced hardware intrinsically yields a dramatic trend toward lower costs, so that systems that once cost tens of thousands of dollars may be priced at only a few dollars per chip, in large quantities as used by original equipment manufacturers. *See* *Integrated circuits; Microprocessor; Semiconductor memories.*

The widespread trend toward flexible software has penetrated the speech recognition industry, so that in the mid-1980s some companies began offering licensable software for speech recognition, rather than providing specific special-purpose hardware. *See* *Microcomputer.*

The focus in the speech recognition industry has been on the easiest problem of speaker-dependent isolated-word recognition, but clear trends are toward limited forms of connected speech and speaker independence in commercial devices, especially for telecommunications applications. Research on the challenges of continuously spoken sentences forms an integral part of the international effort toward intelligent fifth-generation computers. *See* *Artificial intelligence; Digital computer.*

***Circuit-board implementation.*** **Figure** 7*a* schematically illustrates a typical circuit-board implementation

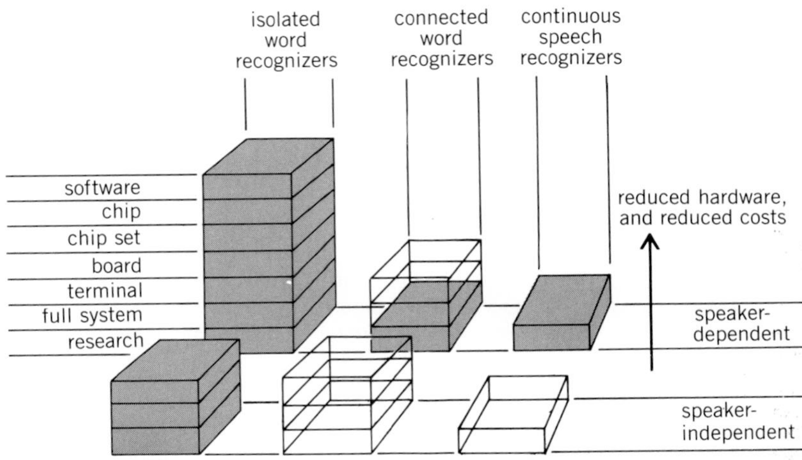


**Fig. 6. Types of hardware and software configurations for speech recognition under various application conditions. Shaded boxes represent many attempts at that type of recognizer, while open boxes indicate only a few attempts at that type of device.**

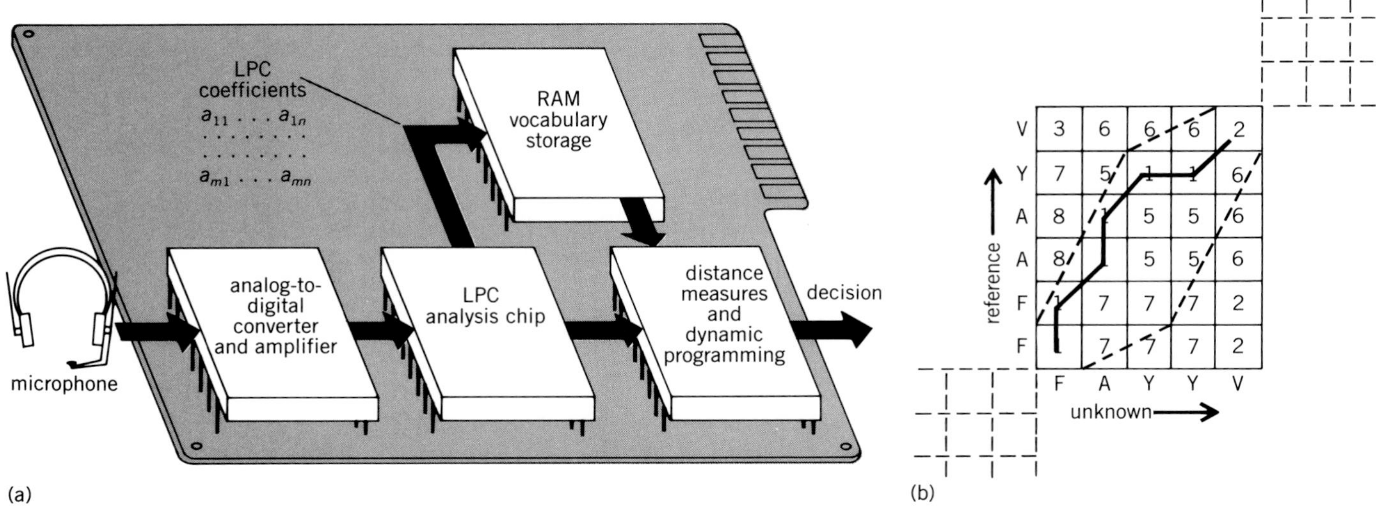


**Fig. 7. Practical speech recognizer based on linear predictive coding (LPC) analysis and dynamic programming. (*a*) Major components of a circuit-board speech recognizer using LPC analysis. (*b*) Matrix of speech sound differences between reference words and word portions of unknown inputs. Alternative alignments are allowed within the parallelogram, and the path with least accumulated distance (heavy line) is chosen for best alignment of reference and input words.**

of a popular method of word (or word-sequence) recognition using linear predictive coding for spectral data representation, and dynamic programming for time alignment and word matching. The microphone or telephone handset signal is amplified, digitized through a general-purpose 12-bit analog-to-digital converter chip, and subjected to an acoustic analysis procedure on either a special-purpose linear predictive coding chip or a general-purpose digital signal processor chip. Linear prediction is a method of separating the speech signal into an ''excitation'' component due to the human vocal cords (or a vocal-tract noise source) and a vocal-tract transfer function or filter that shapes the excitation to the form of multiple-resonance structure produced by the varying-cross-section human vocal tract. The smooth frequency spectra of Fig. 3 illustrate the prominant peaks that correspond to the acoustic resonances of the vocal tract. A linear predictive analysis involves determining the necessary coefficients (usually 10–15 in number) for specifying an inverse filter that separates such smooth resonance structure from the harmonically rich pulses produced by the vocal cords (or the noisy spectum of a frication noise source in the vocal tract). *See* Analog-to-digital converter.

A matrix of such linear predictive coding coefficients versus time thus represents the articulatory structure of a word. Word matching can be based on comparing such coefficients with those found throughout each word of the vocabulary with which the recognizer is trained. In a practical speech recognizer, a distance measure is developed to determine how different two sets of linear predictive coding coefficients are, and such distances are calculated for every analysis frame of the input word compared to every analysis frame of training samples. As Fig. 7*b* illustrates, the analysis frames of the input can be distributed along one (horizontal) axis, while those of a candidate reference word from the training data can be aligned along the other (vertical) axis, and the distances between the respective frames of the input and reference words can be entered into the corresponding intersection cells in the matrix. To decide if the reference word occurred, the distances along the best possible (lowest-accumulated-distance) alignment of input and reference data are accumulated. If that distance is less than the distance for any other reference word inserted in place of the illustrated reference word, then that reference word is accepted as the identity of the input.

Since words spoken at different times may vary in duration and detailed timing, nonuniform alignment may be necessary. Dynamic programming is a method for picking that path through all the successive distance increments that produces the lowest accumulated distance. As shown by the heavy line in Fig. 7*b*, a couple of frames of ''f''-like sound of the reference word may be identified with a single ''f''-like frame of the input, or two input frames of ''y''-like sound may be associated with one such frame in the reference. Dynamic programming restricts alignments to local paths of specific shape, such as horizontal steps, vertical steps, or diagonal steps, but not negative-slope steps, and so forth. Indeed, it usually is found computationally efficient and realistic to restrict alignment paths to lie within a parallelogram such as the illustrated one of slopes between ½ and 2.

As indicated by the matrices of broken lines extending each way from the basic single-word matrix, it is possible to apply dynamic programming to word sequences, looking for beginning and end points of each word, and matching with reference words by best paths between such end points. The same procedure can be applied with larger (or smaller) units, in successive steps, to yield ''multiple-level'' dynamic programming, which is used in some commercial recognition devices. *See* Voice response.

*Wayne A. Lea*

**Bibliography.** J. L. Flanagan, Synthesis and recognition of speech: Teaching computers to listen, *Bell Lab. Rec.*, pp. 146–151, May–June 1981; W. A. Lea, *Computer Recognition of Speech*, 1986; W. A. Lea, *Selecting, Designing, and Using Speech Recognizers*, 1986; W. A. Lea, *Towards Robustness in Speech Recognition*, 1986; W. A. Lea, *Trends in Speech Recognition*, 1980, reprint 1986; L. Rabiner and R. Shafer, *Digital Processing of Speech Signals*, 1979; S. E. Levinson and M. Y. Liberman, Speech recognition by computers, *Sci. Amer.*, 244(4):64–76, April 1981.

## Spread spectrum communication

A means of communicating by purposely spreading the spectrum (frequency extent or bandwidth) of the communication signal well beyond the bandwidth of the unspread signal. Spread spectrum signals are typically transmitted by electromagnetic waves in free space with usage in both nonmilitary and military systems.

Motivation for using spread spectrum signals is based on the following facts: (1) These systems have the ability to reject intentional and unintentional jamming by interfering signals so that information can be communicated. (2) Spread spectrum signals have a low probability of being intercepted or detected since the power in the transmitted wave is "spread" over a large bandwith or frequency extent. (3) Since these signals cannot be readily demodulated without knowing the code and its precise timing, message privacy is obtained. (4) The wide bandwidth of the spread spectrum signals provides tolerance to multipath (reflected waves that take longer to arrive at the receiver than the direct, desired signal). (5) A high degree of precision in ranging (distance measuring) can be obtained by using one type of spread spectrum signal, with applications to navigation. (6) Multiple access, or the ability to send many independent signals over the same frequency band, is an important feature in spread spectrum signals.

Systems employing spread spectrum methods to communicate in a secure manner include the space shuttle, the Tracking and Data Relay Satellite System (TDRSS), Milstar and Navstar (Global Positioning System or GPS). Indeed, if secure communications are required, spread spectrum principles will be utilized. SEE BANDWIDTH REQUIREMENTS; PRIVACY SYSTEMS (SCRAMBLING).

There are four generic types of spread spectrum signals: direct sequence (DS) or pseudonoise (PN), frequency hopping (FH), time hopping (TH), and linear frequency modulation (chirp). The latter two types are not of as much interest as the first two types; frequency hopping systems are the most commonly used.

**Chirp modulation.** Chirp modulation is an older spread spectrum method which was developed for radar use. The basic idea is to transmit a long rectangular pulse whose carrier frequency is linearly increased from frequency $f_1$ to, say, $f_2$ ($f_2 > f_1$). The frequency-modulated signal returned from the target passes through a filter in the receiver at a velocity of propagation proportional to frequency. The result is a pulse that is much shorter in time duration than the transmitted pulse with a larger peak power content. Unchirped pulses such as interference or jamming pulses do not "compress" at the receiver, so that this method yields a processing gain or advantage for the chirped signal. SEE RADAR.

**Time hopping.** Time hopping, which is not normally used alone, is a method in which the transmitted pulse occurs in a manner determined by a pseudorandom code which places the pulse in one of, say, $n$ possible positions per frame. If $n$ is sufficiently large, then the pulse is on only $1/n$ of the time, and again the transmitted pulse has a processing gain against a full frame jamming pulse of equal energy.

**Direct sequence systems.** Direct sequence systems were once the most prevalent method of communicating in spread spectrum communications. Direct sequence modulation is characterized by phase-modulating a sine wave by an unending string of pseudonoise code chips (symbols of much smaller duration than a bit). This unending string is typically based on pseudonoise code that generates an apparently random sequence of code chips that repeats only after the pseudonoise code period. The pseudonoise code–modulated signal that is transmitted can be characterized by the equation below, where $P$ is the

$$s(t) = \sqrt{2P}\, PN(t)d(t) \cos(\omega_0 t + \theta)$$

transmitted power; $PN(t)$ represents the unit-amplitude pseudonoise code chips (the spectrum spreading code); $d(t)$ is the data sequence, which is inherently random or at least unknown to the receiver and contains the information to be communicated bit by bit; $\omega_0$ is the radian frequency; and $\theta$ is the phase. Both the data and the pseudonoise code are multiplied by the carrier, $\cos(\omega_0 t + \theta)$. This modulation method is called phase shift keying. If $T_b$ is the duration of a bit expressed in seconds, then typically the duration of a pseudonoise code chip, $T_c$, would be much smaller than $T_b$ so that many chips would occur during one bit (of the order of hundreds). Both the data and the pseudonoise code phase-modulate the carrier by 0° or 180° according to whether $PN(t)d(t)$ is $+1$ or $-1$.

**Figure 1** illustrates a basic biphase pseudonoise-encoded spread spectrum system transmitter and receiver of the type discussed. Digital data representing the information to be transmitted is biphase-modulated onto the carrier, and then the pseudonoise code generator biphase-modulates the carrier, the result of which can be represented mathematically by the equation above. SEE PHASE MODULATION; PULSE MODULATION.

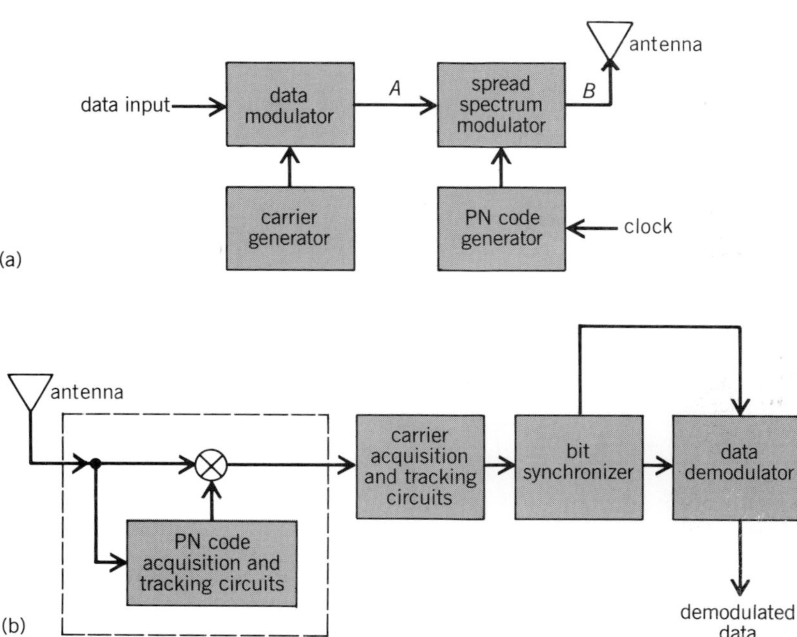


**Fig. 1.** Basic direct sequence system, pseudonoise-encoded spread spectrum equipment for (*a*) transmitter and (*b*) receiver.

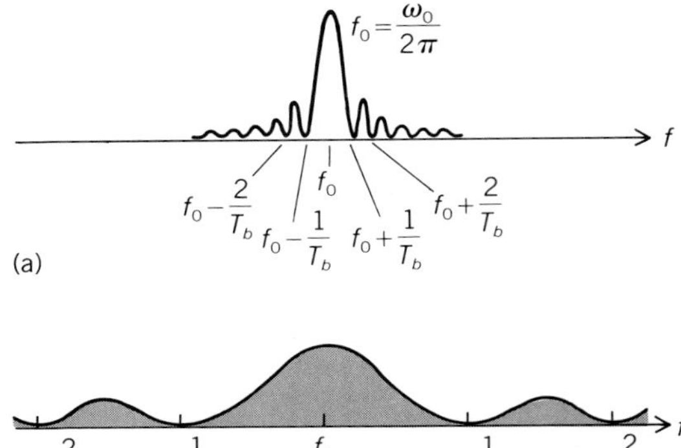


**Fig. 2. Spectra of (*a*) data-modulated carrier at point A of Fig. 1*a*, and (*b*) spread spectrum signal at point B of part *a*.**

***Spectra.*** The spectra of both the data-modulated carrier at point $A$ and the spread spectrum signal at point $B$ in Fig. 1*a* are illustrated in **Fig. 2**. The bandwidth of the signals can be taken as the null-to-null frequency width. Thus, the data modulation has a bandwidth $BW_d = 2/T_b$, whereas the spread spectrum signal has bandwidth $BW_{PN} = 2/T_c$. Since $T_b$ is much larger than $T_c$, it follows that $BW_{PN}$ is much larger than $BW_d$; that is, the pseudonoise-encoded signal has much greater bandwidth than the data-modulated signal. Furthermore, it follows that the spectral height is much lower in the spread case (since the power is conserved); hence it is much harder to detect in the presence of the ever-present receiver noise. *SEE ELECTRICAL NOISE.*

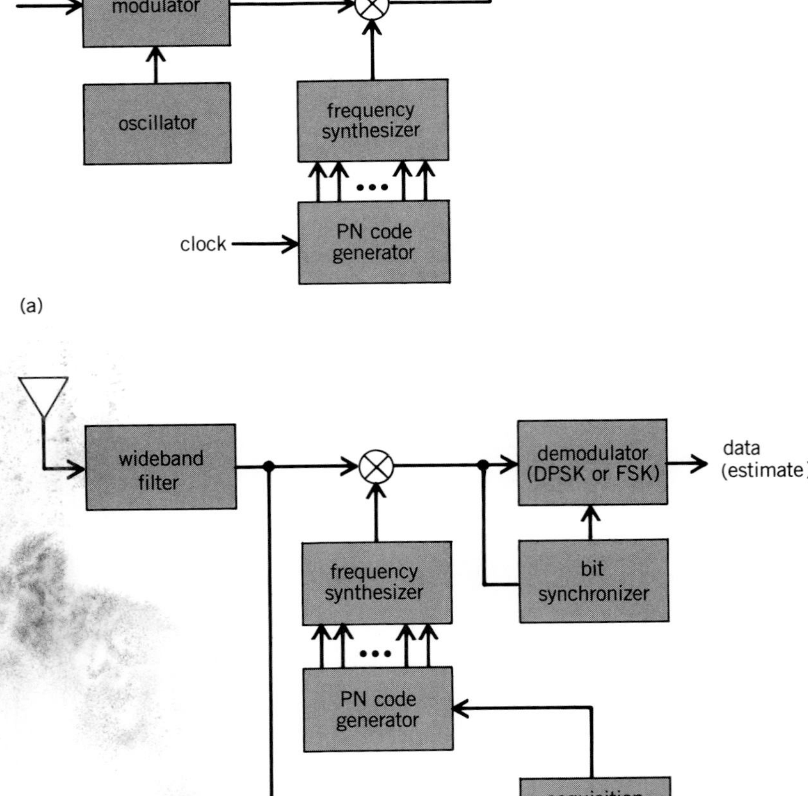


**Fig. 3. Frequency-hopping equipment for (*a*) transmitter and (*b*) receiver.**

***Receiver.*** For the receiver to function, it must first align the receiver pseudonoise code generator timing with the received pseudonoise code timing. This is accomplished in two distinct steps, acquisition and tracking. Acquisition is the searching phase where time shifts of the locally generated code are correlated with received signal plus receiver noise. When code alignment is close, the correlator output becomes large and the tracking circuit is engaged. The received signal is then said to be despread.

The tracking circuit, which is called a code tracking loop, tracks the code (keeps the local receiver code aligned with the received code) once it has been acquired. Once the received code is being tracked, it can be multiplied by the locally generated pseudonoise code [$PN(t)$ in the equation above] which then removes the code on the received signal since $[PN(t)]^2 = 1$.

At this point a biphase-modulated signal is left to be demodulated. In order to do this, a carrier tracking loop must be utilized, such as a Costas loop or a squaring loop. Their function is to track the carrier $\cos(\omega_0 t + \theta)$ and thereby allow phase-coherent demodulation of the data $d(t)$, that is, multiplication by a signal exactly in phase with the received carrier. Demodulation of the data can be described mathematically by multiplying the equation given above by $\sqrt{2}\cos(\omega_0 t + \theta_0)$, leaving just the data $d(t)$ (plus an unimportant term at twice the carrier frequency).

A bit synchronizer then tracks (provides bit timing for) the data bit sequence, and a data demodulator integrates over a bit period and electronically dumps (resets to zero), thereby determining whether a positive unit pulse (bit) or a negative unit pulse was transmitted. This bit sequence determines the message being sent.

The above discussion has been oversimplified. For example, the reconstructed pseudonoise code is never perfectly aligned with the received code, and the locally generated carrier likewise is not exactly in phase with the received carrier. Degradations therefore occur to the system as compared to an idealized system.

***Attributes.*** The six attributes of spread spectrum systems that were discussed above apply in this direct-sequence, pseudonoise spread spectrum system. Suppose an unmodulated tone at the carrier frequency is present at the receiver along with the spread signal of the above equation. Then in the pseudonoise code despreading process [multiplication by $PN(t)$], the undesired tone is spread or multiplied by the local pseudonoise code, thereby spreading its spectrum to a bandwidth $2/T_c$. However, the received signal is collapsed to a bandwidth of $2/T_b$ ($T_b \gg T_c$) so that the data detector only "sees" a small fraction, $T_c/T_b$, of the original tone energy. The processing gain, the ratio $T_b/T_c$ ($\gg 1$), is used to determine the efficiency of a spread spectrum system in rejecting unwanted interference. Low probability of intercept is achieved by virtue of the fact that the spread signal is very wideband and has low spectral height, and therefore cannot be easily detected in a noise background. Message privacy is assured if the actual pseudonoise code sequence used by the transmitter and receiver is unknown to unwanted listeners. Multipath tolerance is achieved by searching first with minimum delay and then expanding the search to larger delays. The desired signal will have less delay than the multipath signal and will be acquired first. Additional processing can be used to greatly minimize the multipath problems. If a set of essentially orthogonal codes such as Gold codes (modified pseudonoise codes) are used, many users can occupy the same bandwidth and only transmitter-receiver pairs with the same code can communicate. Since the pseudonoise chips are very short in time, ranging can be made accurate to a small fraction (5%) of a chip time.

**Frequency-hopped systems.** In a direct sequence system, the phase of the carrier changes pseudorandomly with the pseudonoise code. In a frequency-hopping system, the frequency of the carrier changes according to a pseudonoise code with a consecutive group of pseudonoise code chips defining a particular frequency. Typically either multiple frequency shift keying (MFSK) or differential phase-shift keying (DPSK) is used. Multiple frequency shift keying is a modulation scheme in which one of a number of tones (2, 4, 8, and so forth) are transmitted at a given time according to a group of consecutive data bits ($n$ bits produce $2^n$ tones). In conjunction with frequency hopping, multiple frequency shift keying would imply, at each instant of time, a given carrier frequency that depends on the hop-pseudonoise code sequence and the consecutive group of the most recent $n$ bits. Differential phase-shift keying is similar to phase shift keying except that only the differences of the phases are encoded and noncoherent techniques (involving no carrier loop) can be employed at the receiver. *SEE FREQUENCY MODULATION.*

Frequency-hopped systems can be classified as fast or slow. Slow hopping occurs if two or more data symbols are transmitted in the time interval of one hop. Fast hopping occurs if one or more hops occur per data symbol. Although fast hopping is more complex to implement, it offers greater jammer protection.

The actual frequency selection is achieved by a device called a frequency synthesizer. For example, a 12-bit segment of the pseudonoise code may correspond to a particular frequency, so that every 12 bits a new frequency is produced in the frequency synthesizer. Synthesizers are used for both the transmitter and the receiver (**Fig. 3**). The transmitter modulates the data by typically using either multiple frequency shift keying or differential phase-shift keying modulation, which in turn is frequency-hopped by the frequency synthesizer. At the receiver, an acquisition process is utilized to synchronize the receiver frequency synthesizer with the received hopping signal, and then a tracking system maintains synchronism. Finally a bit synchronizer provides timing for the data demodulator which estimates the original, transmitted data bits. Of course, as in all systems, some errors are made due to noise or jamming.

**Hybrid systems.** Besides the four basic systems discussed above, hybrid schemes combining one or more of these systems have been used, including pseudonoise–frequency hopping, pseudonoise–time hopping, and pseudonoise–frequency hopping–time hopping. *SEE MODULATION.*

*Jack K. Holmes*

***Bibliography.*** C. E. Cook and H. S. Marsh, An introduction to spread spectrum, *IEEE Commun. Mag.*, March 1983; R. C. Dixon, *Spread Spectrum Systems,* 1976; J. K. Holmes, *Coherent Spread Spectrum Systems,* 1982; D. J. Torrieri, *Principles of Military Communication Systems,* 1981.

## Sputtering

The ejection of material from a solid or liquid surface following the impact of energetic ions, atoms, or molecules. Sputtering was first noted in 1853 by W. R. Grove and in 1854 by M. Faraday as the occurrence of a metallic coating on the glass walls of a discharge tube. E. Goldstein in 1902 showed that the sputtering effect was caused by positive ions of the discharge striking the cathode and ejecting cathode material. Sputtering now is the basis of a large variety of methods for the synthesis and analysis of materials.

**Classification.** Sputtering can be classified according to the mode of energy loss of the incident (primary) particle. Nuclear stopping involves billiard ball–like atomic collisions in which a significant momentum transfer occurs; it dominates for incident ion energies below about 1–2 keV per nucleon. Electronic stopping involves collisions in which little momentum is transferred, but significant electronic excitation is caused in the target; it dominates for energies above about 10 keV per nucleon.

Sputtering has also been classified into physical and chemical sputtering. Physical sputtering involves a transfer of kinetic energy from the incident particle to the surface atoms leading to ejection, while chemical sputtering occurs when the incident species react chemically with the target surface leading to the formation of a volatile reaction product which evaporates thermally from the surface.

The main models for physical sputtering are the thermal sputtering and the collision cascade models. The thermal sputtering model suggests that the ion impact instantaneously heats a small region of the surface to a temperature well above the boiling point of the material, so that a small amount of material can evaporate before the heat is dissipated to the surrounding solid. The collision cascade model suggests that the impinging ion collides with surface atoms, transferring kinetic energy to these atoms which then collide with their neighbors, and so on. Atoms at or near the surface which are set in motion out of the surface with a kinetic energy great enough to overcome the chemical binding to their neighbors are sputtered. There is little evidence that thermal sputtering is important for most materials; in contrast, the collison cascade model accounts for the vast majority of observed sputtering phenomena. In particular, sputtering of single crystals leads to ejection in certain preferred directions correlated with the crystal lattice, which clearly would not occur in a random disordered hot zone.

**Yields.** In the nuclear stopping regime, sputtering yields, $Y$, can be expressed as in the equation below,

$$Y \propto S_n/U \quad \text{atom/ion}$$

where $S_n$ is the nuclear stopping coefficient (energy deposited in the solid per unit distance traversed) and $U$ is the surface binding energy of the target material (assumed equal to the heat of sublimation per atom). Sputtering threshold energies—the incident ion energy at which sputtering is just detectable—are on the order of 10 times the sublimation energy, or some tens of electronvolts, for most elements. Sputtering yields are a maximum for incident ion energies around 200–300 eV per nucleon, where the nuclear stopping coefficient is a maximum. For argon ions (atomic mass 40) this corresponds to energies around 10 keV, at which energy sputtering yields for most materials under argon ion bombardment are in the range 1–10 atoms sputtered per incident ion. For incident ion energies below about 10 keV, a major fraction (80–90%) of the sputtered atoms come from the outermost surface atom layer, most of the remainder from the second layer, while essentially all the sputtered atoms come from no deeper than about four atomic layers; this is the basis of the use of sputtering in surface analysis.

Sputtering yields in the electronic stopping regime cannot be expressed simply, as mechanisms are still obscure. Hard, "billiard-ball" collisions are rare at high energies, because the incident ion travels through the solid as a bare nucleus, or certainly with many of its electrons stripped away, and is thus extremely small. However, highly energetic particles can deposit up to several thousand electronvolts per nanometer into electronic excitation and ionization in the substrate. Mechanisms suggested for coupling of this electronic excitation to the nuclear motion necessary for sputtering include Coulomb repulsion of ionized atoms from one another along the particle track, or excitation to antibonding (repulsive) electronic states.

**Complex materials.** Sputtering of complex materials—metal alloys, inorganic and organic compounds and polymers, and minerals—can produce complex results. The relative efficiencies with which different elemental species are ejected following ion impact can differ, giving rise to preferential sputtering. When preferential sputtering occurs, the species sputtered with the lower efficiency accumulates to a higher concentration at the surface. Subsurface collisions of the incident ion, which penetrates several nanometers into the solid at keV energies, cause atomic motion leading to ion beam–induced atomic mixing of surface and subsurface layers over the ion penetration depth. Chemical bonds can be broken, and sometimes new bonds can be formed. Sputtering of solids which have multiple phases, or which are polycrystalline, leads to the development of surface roughness due to the differences in sputtering yields between different regions. *SEE ION BEAM MIXING.*

**Semiconductor devices.** Sputtering is widely used in the manufacture of semiconductor devices; sputter deposition is used to deposit thin films with a high degree of control by sputtering material from a target onto a substrate; sputter etching is used to remove unwanted films in a reversal of this process. Most removal and deposition systems generate the energetic sputtering ions in radio-frequency (rf) or direct current (dc) glow discharges in argon gas. Reactive ion etching is a chemical sputtering process in which chemically active sputtering species form volatile compounds with the target material leading to significantly higher etch rates and great selectivity. For example, fluorine-containing compounds etch silicon rapidly by forming volatile silicon tetrafluoride ($SiF_4$) but do not etch aluminum or other metals used to make electrical interconnections between devices on a semiconductor chip because the metal fluorides are involatile. Sputter etching and reactive ion etching have the useful advantage of being anisotropic—that is, they etch only in one direction (usually normal to the surface) so that very fine surface features can be delineated. *SEE GLOW DISCHARGE; INTEGRATED CIRCUITS.*

**Materials characterization.** In materials characterization, sputtering is used to remove surface material controllably, allowing in-depth concentration profiles of chemical composition to be determined with a surface-sensitive sampling technique such as Auger electron spectroscopy, x-ray photoelectron spectroscopy, secondary ion mass spectrometry, or ion scattering spectrometry. Sputtering ejects not only atomic but also molecular species from surfaces, and a fraction of these ejected species are ionized as a result of the energetic collisions leading to ejection. Analysis of these secondary ions forms the basis of secondary ion mass spectrometry. Inorganic materials can be analyzed by identification of atomic secondary ions; organic materials can give characteristic molecular ions. Degradation of organic materials by the ion beam irradiation is reduced by dispersal in a liquid matrix or by operation at very low irradiation rates. Projectile energies both in the nuclear stopping and in electronic stopping regimes result in ejection of very large molecular ions up to 5000 atomic mass units for nuclear stopping and over 15,000 atomic mass units for electronic stopping, allowing analysis of very large biomolecules by mass spectrometry. *SEE SURFACE PHYSICS.*

*Peter Williams*

***Bibliography.*** R. Berisch (ed.), *Sputtering by Particle Bombardment I: Physics and Applications*, 1981.

## SQUID

A device which, in its original form, consists of two Josephson tunnel junctions connected in parallel on a superconduction loop (**Fig. 1**). The term is an acronym for superconducting quantum interference device. A small applied current $I$ flows through the junctions as a supercurrent, without developing a voltage, by means of Cooper pairs tunneling through the barriers. However, when the applied current exceeds a certain critical value $I_c$, a voltage $V$ is generated. As shown in **Fig. 2**, the value of $I_c$ is an oscillatory function of the magnetic flux $\Phi$ threading the loop, with a period of one flux quantum, $\Phi_0 = h/2e \approx 2.07 \times 10^{-15}$ weber. The oscillations arise from the interference of the two waves describing the Cooper pairs at the two junctions, in a way that is closely analogous to the interference between two co-

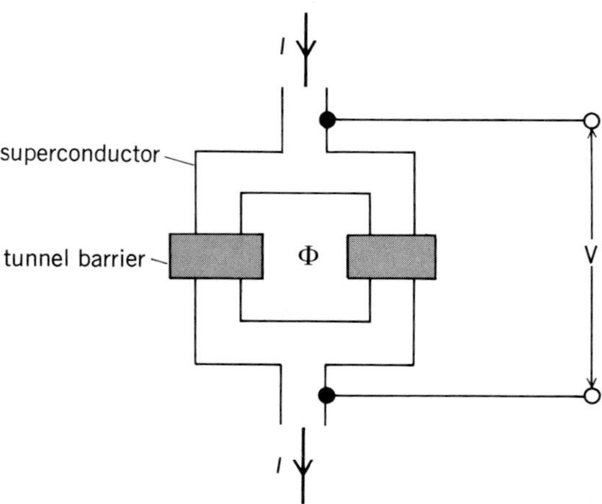


**Fig. 1. Direct-current SQUID with enclosed magnetic flux Φ.**

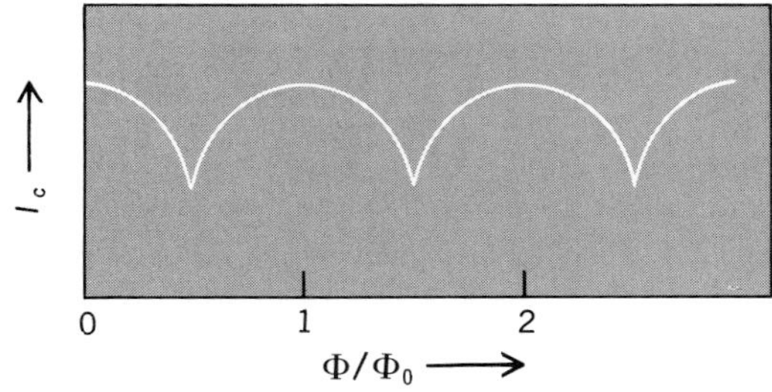


**Fig. 2. Maximum supercurrent $I_c$ vs. $\Phi/\Phi_0$ for a dc SQUID.**

herent electromagnetic waves. Thus the SQUID is often also called an interferometer. *See Josephson effect; Superconductivity.*

The SQUID has important device applications. When each Josephson tunnel junction is shunted with an external resistance to eliminate hysteresis on the current-voltage characteristic and the SQUID is biased with a constant current greater than the critical value $I_c$, the voltage across the SQUID is also an oscillatory function of $\Phi$. If one measures the change in voltage produced by the application of a flux equivalent to a small fraction of one flux quantum, one has a very sensitive magnetometer. Since the device in this mode operates with a constant bias current, it is usually referred to as the dc SQUID. Another important potential application is as a logic element or memory cell in high-speed computers. When an unshunted (hysteretic) SQUID is appropriately current-biased, the application of a flux pulse switches it from the zero-voltage to the nonzero-voltage state, a function that can be used to perform logic; three-junction SQUIDs are also used for this purpose. The SQUID can be used as a dissipation-free memory cell to store a 1 or 0 as a clockwise or anticlockwise circulating persistent supercurrent. *See Computer storage technology; Logic circuits.*

The rf SQUID consists of a single junction interrupting a superconducting loop. It can be operated as a magnetometer by coupling it to the inductor of an LC-tank circuit excited at its resonant frequency by a rf current. The rf voltage across the tank circuit oscillates as a function of the magnetic flux in the loop, again with a period $\Phi$. The rf SQUID is in fact misnamed, since no interference takes place. *See Superconducting devices.*

*John Clarke*

**Bibliography.** A. Barone and G. Paterno, *Physics and Applications of Josephson Effect*, 1982; R. C. Jaklevic et al., Quantum interference effects in Josephson tunneling, *Phys. Rev. Lett.*, 12:159–160, 1964; B. D. Josephson, Possible new effects in superconductive tunneling, *Phys. Lett.*, 1:251–253, 1962; T. Van Duzer and C. W. Turner, *Principles of Superconductive Devices and Circuits*, 1981.

## Standing-wave detector

An electric indicating instrument used for detecting standing waves along a transmission line or in a waveguide and measuring the resulting standing-wave ratio. It can also be used to measure the wavelength and hence the frequency of an electromagnetic wave in a line. The detecting device is usually a bolometer, thermocouple, or crystal, connected to an indicating meter directly or through an amplifier. The detecting device is moved along the line while observing the meter indication; the positions along the line at which maximum and minimum readings are obtained correspond to the nodes and antinodes of the standing wave that is produced by transmitted and reflected waves of equal frequency moving in opposite directions. The reflected wave is generated at a discontinuity in the transmission line or waveguide. *See Microwave impedance measurement; Wavelength measurement; Wavemeter.*

*John Markus*

## Storage tube

An electron tube into which information can be introduced and then extracted at a later time; also called a memory tube. *See Electron tube.*

**Operation.** The process of introducing information into a storage tube is known as writing, and that of extracting useful information is called reading. The deliberate removal of information from the storage surface is called erasing. In some tubes, reading automatically effects erasing; in others, a separate operation is required. A charge storage tube is one in which information is retained on a surface in the form of electric charges.

The characteristics of a storage tube are largely governed by the nature of the storage surface. This surface is usually a deposit or sheet of insulating or semiconducting material. The point-by-point potential of this surface is varied, in a controlled way, by the dielectric charging processes associated with electron bombardment of an insulator. The low conductivity of the storage-surface material ensures that the charge (or potential) pattern will not be dissipated before the reading operation is initiated and completed.

In the reading operation, the potential pattern established by writing controls: (1) the percentage of the primary beam that is able to pass through the openings of a fine-mesh screen on which the storage surface may be deposited, or (2) the percentage of the primary beam which impinges on a phosphor screen, or (3) the magnitude of the secondary-electron current which results when the primary beam strikes the storage surface. In any case, the current collected by the output electrode is modulated in accordance with the stored charge pattern.

Storage tubes utilize electron guns to address the storage surface and effect the operations of reading, writing, and erasing. The electron gun will produce a fine pencil beam of electrons which may be deflected, as in a cathode-ray tube, to any desired location on the storage surface, or it will produce a flood beam which uniformly and simultaneously floods the entire storage surface with electrons. Because the use of the pencil-beam electron gun is related to its use in the cathode-ray tube, these tubes are often termed cathode-ray charge storage tubes. *See Cathode-ray tube.*

Storage tubes may be classified according to the general nature of the input and output signals associated with them. Thus there are visual-electrical, electrical-electrical, and electrical-visual storage tubes. For visual-electrical storage tubes, known as camera tubes, *see Television camera tube.*

**Electrical storage tubes.** Several different types of electrical-electrical storage tubes have been of commercial importance. These include the Radechon, recording storage tube, Graphechon, and silicon target storage tube. Each of these cathode-ray charge-storage tubes requires an electrical input signal and provides an electrical output signal. They have found use as devices for computer storage, signal time delay, signal comparison service, systems for the conversion of signal time bases, and scan conversion.

The widespread availability of low-cost solid-state memory devices and integrated circuits which will perform many of the same functions as electrical storage tubes has led to a general decline in the use of these tubes in new equipment designs.

**Direct-view storage tubes.** This group consists of cathode-ray charge storage tubes which require an electrical input and provide a visual output. Among those of commercial importance are the display tube and the phosphor storage tube.

***Display storage tube.*** The display storage tube employs a pencil beam of electrons, scanned across an insulating material coated on one side of a fine-mesh screen, to effect the writing process. This writing beam establishes a dielectric charge pattern on the insulating surface corresponding to the written information.

Erasing and reading processes in the display storage tube are accomplished through the use of a continuous low-velocity flood beam having a cross-sectional area equal to that of the fine-mesh-screen storage surface. The flood beam is switched between the erasing and reading modes by a change of a few volts in the beam-accelerating voltage. The flood beam in the reading mode passes through the fine-mesh storage screen, modulated point by point by the written charge pattern, and strikes a phosphor screen, producing a visible display of the pattern. Because of the action of the storage screen, these tubes are frequently termed transmission-control storage tubes.

Display storage tubes provide a bright display, including halftones, and have controlled persistence. They are used in radar displays and in oscillography. Growth in the use of display storage tubes has been restricted by the increasing availability of solid-state devices which will perform many similar storage functions when used in conjunction with conventional cathode-ray tubes.

***Phosphor storage tube.*** The phosphor storage tube is closely akin to the display storage tube. An important difference in construction is that the phosphor screen, which is an insulator, itself serves as the storage surface, eliminating the need for a separate fine-mesh screen.

The phosphor storage tube operates in a bistable mode, that is, without halftones. Its availability in sizes up to a screen diagonal of 19 in. (48 cm) has led to its widespread use in computer graphics displays. *See Computer graphics; Electronic display.*

*Norman W. Patrick*

***Bibliography.*** C. Curtin, Recent advances in direct view storage tubes, in Society for Information Display, *1977 SID Symposium: Digest of Technical Papers*, pp. 132–133, 1977; B. Kazan and M. Knoll, *Electronic Image Storage*, 1968.

## Supercomputer

A computer which, among existing computers at any given time, is superlative, often in several senses: highest computation rate, largest memory, or highest cost. Predominantly, the term refers to the fastest "number crunchers," that is, machines designed to perform numerical calculations at the highest speed that the latest electronic device technology and the state of the art of computer architecture allows.

As of 1984, the fastest supercomputers built in the United States (**Fig. 1**) were capable of peak speeds of about 400 megaflops (million floating point operations per second). Japanese manufacture of supercomputers began in 1984: these machines were rated from 500 megaflops to 1.3 gigaflops (billion floating point operations per second). [The term floating point refers to a particular method of representing numerical values in a digital computer. A floating point number consists of an exponent and a mantissa, and is similar to the written form of numbers called scientific notation. A floating point operation is one of the common arithmetic operations, such as add, subtract, multiply, or divide, performed on floating point numbers.]

In the 1980s the term supercomputer also began to be applied to predicted future machines designed to perform symbolic, or artificial intelligence–oriented, computations. In 1984 the Department of Defense's Defense Advanced Research Projects Agency (DARPA) initiated its Strategic Computing Program, a five-year research and development program aimed at producing very high-speed, parallel computers especially for artificial intelligence applications. In Japan there are two government-funded research and development activities with goals of producing supercomputers: the National Superspeed Computer Project, oriented toward numerical computation; and the Fifth-Generation Computer System Project, aimed at producing a high-speed, artificial intelligence–oriented computer by the early 1990s. *See Artificial intelligence.*

**Scientific applications.** The demand for the ability to execute arithmetic operations at the highest possible rate originated in computer applications areas collectively referred to as scientific computing. Researchers in fields such as physics, structural mechanics, meteorology, and aerodynamics often need to do large-scale numerical simulations of physical processes. A technique common to several of these disciplines is to compute an approximate numerical solution to a set of partial differential equations which mathematically describe the physical process of interest, but are too complex to be solved by formal mathematical methods. The approximate numerical solution is obtained by first superimposing a grid on a region of space, with a set of numerical values attached to each grid point. Each of these values represents a physical quantity hypothetically measurable at that point in space, such as temperature, pressure, or velocity. Then, the physical process is computationally "simulated" by repetitively updating the values at each grid point according to a system of algebraic equations, derived from the defining partial differential equations, which specify the relationships between the values. Each repeated step might represent a span of time; that is, the simulated time is divided into a series of discrete steps, just as space is divided into a set of grid points. A more accurate solution requires a finer spatial grid and shorter time intervals. Large-scale scientific computations of this type often require hundreds of thousands of grid points with 10 or more values attached to each point, with 10 to 500 arithmetic operations necessary to compute each updated value, and hundreds of thousands of time steps over which the computation must be repeated before a steady-state solution is reached.

Large problems in computational physics and aerodynamics sometimes require 100 h of computer time on current supercomputers. *See* *Numerical analysis; Simulation*.

There is no foreseeable end to the demand for increased speed of numerical computation. Additional speed can always be exploited in two ways: first, problems which previously took hours can be executed in minutes, enhancing the user's ability to rely on the computer for assistance in an interactive manner; and second, new, larger problems can be attempted which were computationally infeasible on slower machines. An example of both kinds of opportunities is the effect of a 1000-times-faster supercomputer on the applications area of aerodynamics: First, an aeronautical engineer might repeatedly modify an aircraft design on a supercomputer-based design system, and be able to determine the aerodynamic implications of each design refinement in a few minutes, instead of 100 h. Second, such an increase in computational speed over current supercomputers would allow three-dimensional airflow simulations of a complete airplane design, whereas simulations of two-dimensional cross sections of parts of the aircraft (wing, engine nacelle) are now the rule.

There are two lines of technological advancement which have significantly contributed to what roughly amounts to a doubling of the fastest computers' speeds every year since the early 1950s—the steady improvement in electronic device technology and the accumulation of improvements in the architectural designs of digital computers.

**Advances in electronics technology.** The successive advancements in device technology are commonly summarized by the list of generations into which electronic digital computers of the past and present are categorized. The first-generation computers were constructed in the 1940s and early 1950s by using electromechanical relays and later vacuum tubes as switching devices. Second-generation computers of the early 1950s through the early 1960s employed transistors as switching devices and were the first to incorporate magnetic core memories. Third-generation computers were built from the early 1960s to the mid-1970s. They are characterized electronically by the use of small-scale integrated (SSI) and medium-scale integrated (MSI) circuits. Solid-state memories began replacing magnetic cores. Today's computers belong to the fourth generation. They incorporate large-scale integrated (LSI) circuits with tens of thousands of transistors per silicon chip for both logic and memory components.

Supercomputers generally employ a variant of silicon-based integrated circuitry known as emitter-coupled logic (ECL). It is less dense than other types of integrated circuits, offering at most a few thousand transistors per chip, but providing switching speeds in the range of a few nanoseconds. The next generation of supercomputers is expected to employ faster versions of emitter-coupled logic, complementary metallic oxide semiconductors (CMOS), or switching devices which are based on gallium arsenide (GaAs) semiconductor technologies instead of the silicon-based materials currently employed. *See* *Computer storage technology; Integrated circuits; Logic circuits; Semiconductor memories*.

**Advances in computer architecture.** Increases in computing speed which are purely due to the architectural structure of a computer can largely be attributed to the introduction of some form of parallelism into the machine's design: two or more operations which were performed one after the other in previous computers can now be performed simultaneously. An explanation of techniques to increase parallelism requires the introduction of a few basic terms of computer architecture. A simple, general view of a digital computer divides it into two major components: the central processing unit (CPU) and the memory. Both data and programs are stored in the memory. The central processing unit contains the logic circuitry for repeatedly fetching program instructions, decoding them, fetching from memory the data items the instructions call to be operated upon, performing the arithmetic or logical operations required by each instruction, and returning the resultant data to the memory. *See* *Computer systems architecture*.

**Fig. 1.** Two-processor Cray X-MP, which is capable of as many as 400 million arithmetic operations per second. (*Cray Research, Inc.*)

***Pipelining.*** This is a technique which allows several operations to be in progress in the central processing

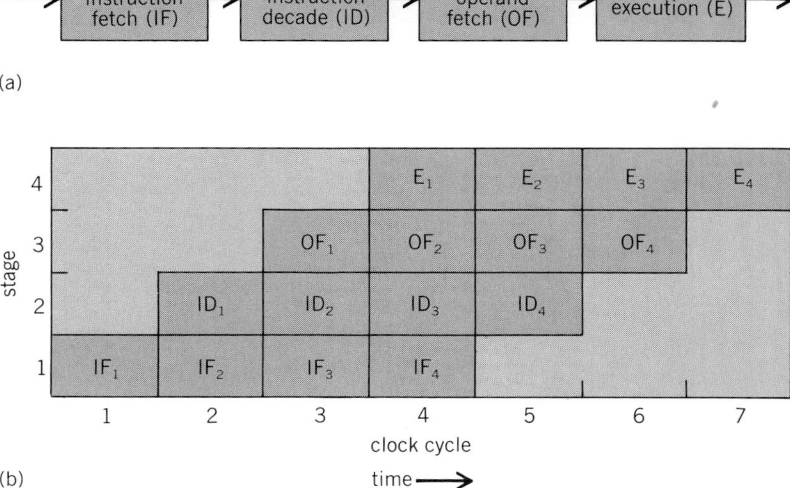


**Fig. 2.** Instruction pipeline. (*a*) Instruction processing stages. (*b*) Chart illustrating the overlapping of stages for four consecutive instructions.

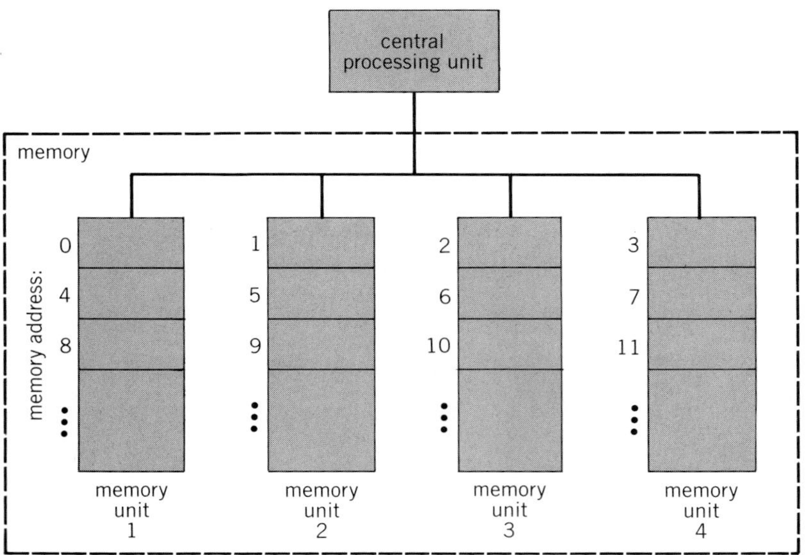


**Fig. 3. Simplified diagram of memory interleaving. In this example, the memory is four-way interleaved, that is, the central processing unit can initiate the fetching of data values from four consecutive memory locations before having to wait for a memory unit to become idle.**

unit at once. It is analogous to an assembly line, in the sense that operations which take several steps pass through a sequence of stages, each stage represents one step closer to completion of the entire operation, and already-passed stages can be simultaneously active, performing their respective steps of the operation on separate sets of operands.

The first form of pipelining used was instruction pipelining. Since each instruction must have the same basic sequence of steps performed, namely instruction fetch, instruction decode, operand fetch, and execution, it is feasible to construct an instruction pipeline, where each of these steps happens at a separate stage of the pipeline (**Fig. 2**). The efficiency of the instruction pipeline depends on the likelihood that the program being executed allows a steady stream of instructions to be fetched from contiguous locations in memory. If one instruction is a branch, that is, it orders the central processing unit to begin fetching instructions starting at a different memory location, then the instructions in the pipeline stages behind the branch instruction are no longer valid. They must be removed from the pipeline without being executed (flushed). Thus, each branch instruction causes a decrease in instruction execution speed until the pipeline is refilled with instructions from the new location. Variations of this problem are common to all pipelined architectures. The IBM STRETCH computer, built in the late 1950s, was the first computer to incorporate a pipelined architecture for the central processing unit.

***Interleaved memory.*** The central processing unit nearly always has a much faster cycle time than the memory. This implies that the central processing unit is capable of processing data items faster than a memory unit can provide them. Interleaved memory is an organization of memory units which at least partially relieves this problem. Consecutive memory addresses are located in different memory units, allowing the central processing unit to initiate fetches from several units in sequence whenever the instructions of a program call for the fetching of the contents of each successive word from a contiguous block of memory words (**Fig. 3**). This happens often with the processing of matrices and vectors in scientific computations. The first computers to employ memory interleaving were the IBM STRETCH and the Illiac II, built in the late 1950s.

***Circuitry.*** Parallelism within arithmetic and logical circuitry has been introduced in several ways. Adders, multipliers, and dividers now operate in bit-parallel mode, while the earliest machines performed bit-serial arithmetic. The Control Data Corporation 6600, designed in 1964, incorporated a higher level of parallelism: it had 10 independently operating parallel functional units within the central processing unit, each of which could perform an arithmetic operation such as add, multiply, or shift. The CDC 6600 and its follow-on, the 7600, were the highest-speed supercomputers of the 1960s and early 1970s.

***Array processing.*** This is a form of parallelism in which the instruction execution portion of a central processing unit is replicated several times and connected to its own memory device as well as to a common instruction interpretation and control unit. In this way, a single instruction can be executed at the same time on each of several execution units, each on a different set of operands (**Fig. 4**). This kind of architecture is often referred to as single-instruction-stream, multiple-data stream (SIMD). The Illiac IV was the first array processor supercomputer. It contained an array of 64 processing units, which could be operated in the "lockstep" manner described above. The Illiac IV (only one was built) was operated from 1973 until 1982, and was the fastest supercomputer of its time on certain classes of problems.

***Vector processing.*** This is the term applied to a form of pipelined arithmetic units which are specialized for performing arithmetic operations on vectors, which are uniform, linear arrays of data values. It can be thought of as a type of SIMD processing, since a single instruction invokes the execution of the same operation on every element of the array. The Cray-1 (1976) was the first supercomputer to contain vector pipelines, and the leading supercomputers are now vector processors. This necessitates that the programs

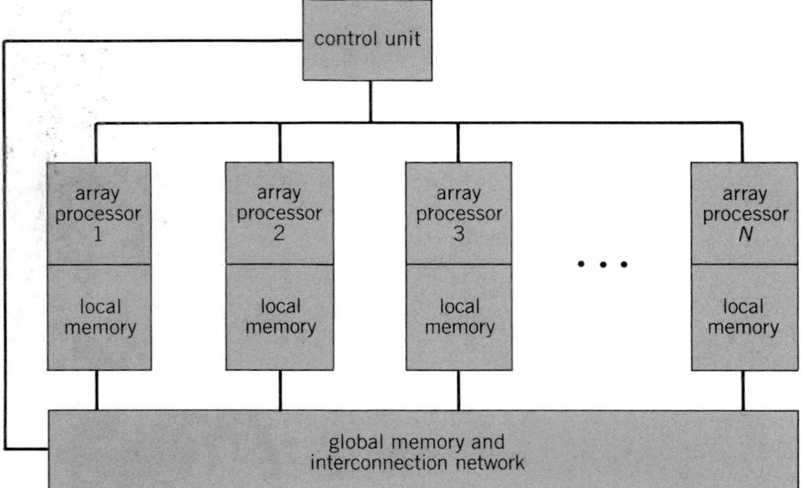


**Fig. 4. Conceptual diagram of an array processor. The array processors simultaneously perform the same operation on separate sets of data stored in their local memories, as directed by the control unit.**

they execute be heavily oriented toward vector operations, in order that the vector pipelines are kept full, and the maximum efficiency of the machine is realized.

It has been often pointed out that a supercomputer's speed should not be judged simply on its peak performance rating, that is, its highest possible instruction execution rate, assuming that the pipelines are full and all potential parallelism is completely exploited, but rather a means should be found for predicting the usable-instruction-throughput rate on certain classes of computer programs. The Livermore Loops are a well-known set of 14 programs designed by supercomputer users at Lawrence Livermore National Laboratory, which are intended to provide a uniform basis for comparison of supercomputer performance on a variety of different possible program structures.

One of the most important software components of a contemporary supercomputer is a compiler (an automatic translator of programs written in a high-level language, usually FORTRAN, into the supercomputer's low-level machine operation codes) which contains sophisticated techniques for vectorizing programs. That is, the compiler must detect as many instances as possible of segments of a program that can be expressed as vector operations, and translate them accordingly for machine execution. *See Digital computer programming; Programming languages.*

***Multiprocessing.*** This is a form of parallelism that has complete central processing units operating in parallel, each fetching and executing instructions independently from the others. This type of computer organization is called multiple-instruction, multiple-data (MIMD) stream. The Cray X-MP is a MIMD supercomputer with two processors and a shared memory.

As in the case of vector processing, the advent of multiprocessing raises software-oriented issues of how to effectively utilize this type of parallelism. One approach calls for compilers to contain parallelization techniques analogous to the vectorization techniques now in use; that is, they will detect inherent parallelism in the input programming language and produce parallel code for the machine. Another approach argues that automatic detection of parallism will be found insufficient and that multiprocessors will be used efficiently only if they are programmed in languages which contain high-level, parallel constructs which a programmer can explicitly invoke. *See Concurrent processing; Data flow systems; Digital computer; Multiprocessing.*

*David W. Mizell*

***Bibliography.*** K. Hwang and A. F. Briggs, *Computer Architecture and Parallel Processing*, 1984; R. D. Levine, Supercomputers, *Sci. Amer.*, 246(1): 118–134, January 1982; W. D. Marbach et al., The race to build a supercomputer, *Newsweek*, 102(1):58–64, July 4, 1983; R. Mendez and S. Orszag, The Japanese supercomputer challenge, *Datamation*, 30(7): 113–119, May 15, 1984; D. P. Siewiorek, G. Bell, and A. Newell, *Computer Structures: Principles and Examples*, 1982.

## Superconducting computers

High-performance computers whose circuits employ superconductivity and the Josephson effect to reduce cycle time.

**Computer performance.** A stored-program digital computer generally consists of a central processing unit (CPU) memory, and input/output (I/O) system. All problems that have to be solved on the computer are reduced to a series of elementary instructions (stored in memory) that govern the various operations to be performed on the data, such as add, multiply, and compare. The instructions are interpreted and the execution is controlled by the CPU, containing the arithmetic-logical unit (ALU) which performs the operations on the data; the CPU also has registers which store intermediate results. Ultimately the operating performance of the computer is governed by how the machine is organized to deal with the various problems and how fast the circuits used in the computer operate. Presently, high-performance, synchronous digital computers have operating cycle times in the range of 12 to 60 nanoseconds, and it normally takes from 1 to 10 cycles to execute an elementary instruction. High-performance computers are usually measured in terms of how many million instructions per second (MIPS) they can execute. This figure typically runs from a few to over 100 MIPS, depending on the machine, its technology, its organization (architecture), and the problem set (specific or general-purpose). *See Computer systems architecture; Digital computer; Supercomputer.*

Josephson technology and superconductivity are being explored as ways of reducing the cycle time further; initially the goal is to reduce the cycle time below 4 ns, and ultimately it is thought that a subnanosecond cycle time will be possible. The reasons that a change from the well-established silicon technology may be needed to enter the subnanosecond region have to do with the nature of the limitations on the computer's cycle time.

**Limitations on cycle time.** There are principally two components to the cycle time of a computer: the circuit delay and the package delay. The circuit delay, reflecting the time required to perform the logical operations, is a strong function of the chosen technology (CMOS, NMOS, bipolar, or Josephson), the power dissipated per circuit, and the level of integration (100 circuits per chip, 1000 circuits per chip, and so forth). Usually, for a given technology, higher circuit speed can be obained by increasing dissipation or reducing circuit dimensions. The reduction in device size, paced by available lithographic tools, is also very desirable from the point of view of reliability and cost. However, there are two principal limitations to available circuit speed, both of which are related to power requirements. *See Integrated circuits.*

The first is associated with the wasted power: the power dissipated in the form of heat. This has to be removed by a cooling medium, and the level of heat removal from circuit chips is limited on the one hand by the cost and complexity of the heat removal structures, and on the other hand by the allowable rise in temperature that the circuits can sustain while still operating correctly. Heat removal structures usually also limit the volumetric efficiency of packing circuit chips.

The second limitation to the power comes from the circuit engineers' ability to provide regulated power to the circuit chips. A large fraction of the chip input/output connections is devoted to power input—to carry the current, but even more importantly to reduce the power voltage swings caused by varying current drain on the chip as the circuits change their binary-encoded state under program control. This inductive variation of chip voltage (sometimes called the $\Delta i$ noise problem) becomes an increasingly difficult problem to solve as the circuit chip performance is improved. Of the two principal power limitations to circuit performance, this one appears the most demanding and severe.

The package delay component of the cycle time depends on the way the integrated circuit chips are arranged. A high-performance supercomputer usually consists of a large number of high-speed logic and memory chips that are required to be able to communicate with one another within a single cycle time. Signals propagate at typically one-third to three-fourths of the velocity of light in high-performance machines, and yet the total path length can easily become the principal limit to how small a cycle time can be realized. The chips must be packed closer and closer together—not only in a two-dimensional arrangement but most effectively in a three-dimensional arrangement. Put another way, the ultimate goal of high-performance computer packaging schemes is to achieve the highest possible density of circuits in a given volume, and this not only means high circuit density on each chip, but also high-density packing of chips. It is necessary to approach as closely as possible the ideal of a three-dimensional arrangement, and a good approximation is the card-on-board package (**Fig. 1**), where chips are attached to both sides of the card. The cards in turn are plugged closely together in to the board.

**Advantages of Josephson technology.** The Josephson effect, predicted in 1962 and observed very soon thereafter, was quickly identified as being the basis of very promising computer technology. Initially, the very high switching speed and low power dissipation of this device were the main attractions, but it soon developed that many other aspects of the physics and engineering were very favorably inclined toward superconducting computer technology. Principal among these was the essentially lossless-transmission-line characteristics of all superconducting circuit interconnection lines. Intercircuit and interchip signals could be transmitted on matched lossless lines, allowing communication in a single pass with no reflections and with a speed of approximately one-third that of light. The characteristic wave impedances of such lines suitable from both fabrication and circuit criteria are sufficiently low (for example, 10 ohms) that interline crosstalk and disturbs are very small and, for all practical purposes, negligible. The interconnection lines have very small cross section; they are nearly lossless, and so there is no concern with respect to series resistance losses which significantly lower the projected and actual limits on the conductor cross-sectional area that semiconductor technology can employ. Furthermore, the very serious limit of electromigration is also absent in superconducting lines. SEE JOSEPHSON EFFECT.

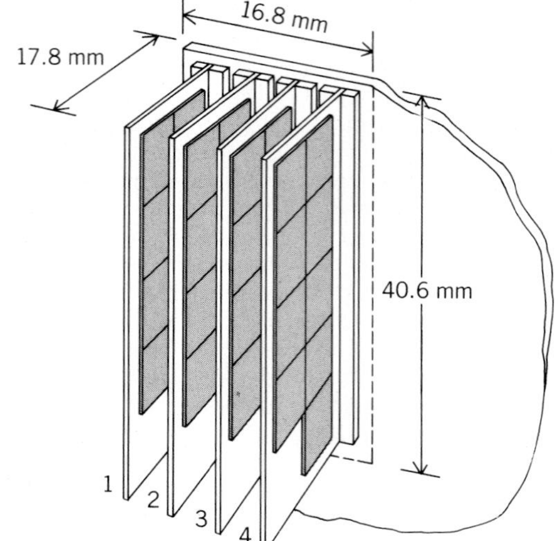


Fig. 1. Card-on-board package for high-density packing of chips. Typical dimensions expected for a small computer are indicated. (*After F. F. Tsui, JSP: A research signal processor in Josephson technology, IBM J. Res. Develop., 24:243–252, 1980*)

It soon became apparent that circuits with such low power dissipation would not, for a very long time in the development of this technology, be concerned about fundamental cooling limits; the power removal problem was no longer a concern. This has enabled particularly attractive and novel techniques to be applied to power supply and regulation concerns faced by the circuit designer; active power supply and regulation circuits can be incorporated into the on-chip design, thereby removing the $\Delta i$ problem.

These advantages naturally accrue from the basic physics of the superconducting state and the Josephson effect. The energy gap that characterizes these devices has shrunk from the hundreds of meV of the semiconductor electronic devices to just a few meV with the superconducting Josephson devices.

The next significant advantage that Josephson technology realized was in the techniques and technologies that are available to the circuit package engineer. With little or no cooling constraint, simple attachment of high-performance chips to the package is feasible; there are no heat removal structures required, and the package can be fabricated in a high-density three-dimensional card-on-board arrangement such as that shown in Fig. 1, where the total power dissipation is estimated at only 400 mW. Josephson technology also makes possible the high-density superconducting interconnection lines and the ability, for the first time, to make a monolithic package in the sense that the package components are all made from the same substrate material: silicon. This has significant importance in that it allows the engineer to work with little concern for differential thermal expansion in the package design. The use of silicon, not for its electrical properites but for its crystal perfection and machining properties, as well as mechanical strength and thermal properties, opens up a new door to micromachine fabrication techniques that can be applied to this novel package.

As package dimensions are shrunk and chip densities increase, it becomes increasingly difficult to provide an adequate number of very small, high-speed, pluggable connectors for each card. The techniques presently being explored consist of the use of very small solder joints to take signals around corners, and of platinum micropins that plug into extremely small sockets each containing a captured mercury drop, 200 μm in diameter. The pins are only 80 μm in diameter and 200 μm long, and they are arranged in a square array of a thousand or more pins with 300 μm between centers (**Fig. 2**).

Finally, there is a significant anticipation that one of the advantages in Josephson technology will be the low-temperature operation. Most of the failure-inducing mechanisms that plague present room-temperature computers will be frozen out and will not affect an operating computer at 4.2 K (−452°F); thus, com-

**Fig. 2. Scanning electron micrograph of high-speed pluggable connections: array of platinum micropins, line of right-angle solder joints from mid-left to top right, and larger guidepin in foreground. (*From M. B. Ketchen et al., A Josephson technology system level experiment, IEEE Electr. Device Lett., EDL-2(10):262–265, 1981*).**

puter operation at this temperature holds the promise of high reliability.

**Disadvantages of Josephson technology.** The significant optimism generated by the attractions of Josephson technology and superconductivity is tempered by the fact that a lot of detailed engineering and materials work remains to be done before a superconducting computer becomes a reality. Josephson devices are not simple extensions of transistor circuits. They involve a much more significant break with the past than there was in going from the triode vacuum tube to the transistor. The change involves much more than reducing power supply voltage and reducing impedances. Current and magnetic flux become of prime importance, rather than potentials and charge. Duality has been helpful only at providing physicists and engineers with hints of what must be done.

The biggest challenge is perhaps the sheer magnitude of the tasks involved in introducing a fundamentally new technology: chip technology, circuit design, package technology, design techniques, testing, and so forth. Good control over the prime circuit parameters has to be shown on a scale that allows superconducting computers to be contemplated. In this respect the control of the device threshold current presents a significant challenge. The superconducting-pair tunneling current depends exponentially on the barrier thickness to such an extent that average oxide thickness control to an accuracy of better than 0.1 nm is required to control the tunneling current to better than 10 or 20%. Also, the methods needed to ensure sufficient device isolation and power gain for reliable logic-circuit and memory design are still evolving.

There are obvious difficulties associated with the use of liquid helium. Cooling the computer from 300 to 4.2 K (80 to −452°F) will undoubtedly produce stresses. These have to be understood and taken care of; they affect the choice of materials both for the devices and for the package. The choice of more familiar but relatively ductile lead-alloy Josephson devices has to be weighed against the more robust refractory-based devices, such as niobium. More is known with respect to lead-alloy processes and device design, and this technology also provides a faster device since the device capacitance represented by lead-oxide (PbO) is approximately one-third that of niobium oxide ($Nb_2O_5$). However, sufficient progress has been made with the refractory-based devices that they have begun to challenge the position held in the 1970s by lead alloy, particularly with respect to low capacitance and low device leakage in the nonzero voltage state.

Perhaps the most obvious disadvantage of a superconducting computer, that of the liquid helium environment, is in fact not a particularly significant one. Admittedly, small liquid helium refrigerators are inefficient at converting kilowatts of electrical energy to only a few watts of cooling power at 4.2 K; however, this is not the bottleneck in the conventional cooling problem. That bottleneck, which is in the transistor technology of getting the heat away from the circuit without affecting correct operation and impacting packaging efficiency, has been broken with the direct cooling of Josephson chips in liquid helium.

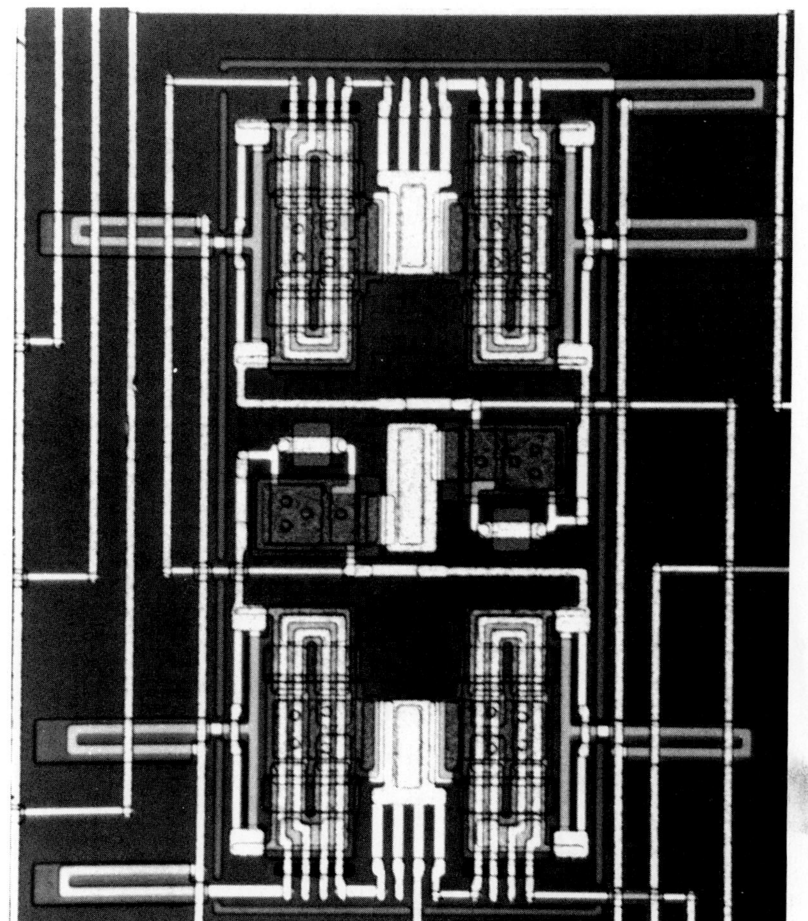

**Fig. 3. Josephson chip circuit consisting of six Josephson devices configured into two logical AND gates. (*IBM*)**

**Progress and prospects.** Logic and memory test vehicles have received very active attention at a number of locations. **Figure 3** shows an example of Josephson chip technology: six Josephson devices configured into two logical AND gates. This circuit was designed and fabricated by using a 2.5-μm design rule. **Figure 4** is a portion of a Josephson logic chip with a regular array of logic gates, such as those shown in Fig. 3, connected together by wires running in wiring channels configured in a rectangular array. Across the center of the figure runs a utility line in the form of the on-chip power regulation and distribution system.

In 1981 some results associated with a cross-section model of a prototype machine were announced. This experiment, which attempted to explore all of the fundamental aspects of the packaging and circuit technologies, was designed to reveal potential problems associated with the fabrication of this card-on-board design. A representative path through the package was exercised with a minimum cycle time of 3.7 ns.

There is still much to be done before a superconducting supercomputer will be involved in calculations on weather forecasting, hydrodynamics, and so forth, but the direction of development appears to have been set. Fundamental considerations involving information processing and thermal noise argue that ultimately 4.2 K operation will be used for computers. *See Superconducting devices*.

*Dennis J. Herrell*

***Bibliography.*** W. Anacker, Computing at 4 degrees Kelvin, *IEEE Spectrum*, 16(5):26–37, May 1979; *IBM J. Res. Develop.*, vol. 24, no. 2, March 1980 (issue devoted entirely to Josephson computer technology); M. B. Ketchen et al., A Josephson technology system level experiment, *IEEE Electr. Device Lett.*, EDL-2(10):262–265, October 1981; J. Matisoo, The superconducting computer. *Sci. Amer.*, 242(5):50–65, May 1980.

Fig. 4. Portion of Josephson logic chips showing regular array of logic gates. (IBM)

## Superconducting devices

Devices that perform functions in the superconducting state that would be difficult or impossible to perform at room temperature, or that contain components which perform such functions. The superconducting state involves a loss of electrical resistance and occurs in many metals and alloys at temperatures near absolute zero. Superconducting devices may be conveniently divided into two categories: small-scale, electronic devices used in measuring instruments and computers, most of which involve Josephson tunneling; and large-scale devices which employ zero-resistance superconducting windings made of type II superconducting materials, and whose applications include high-energy physics research, power generation and transport, motors for marine propulsion, and levitated trains. *See Superconductivity*.

The unique properties of superconductors have led to the development of tiny measuring and computing devices that are superior in performance to their nonsuperconducting counterparts. Most of the devices operate at or below 4.2 K (−452°F), the temperature of liquid helium boiling under standard atmospheric pressure, and involve Josephson tunneling. The initial development of these devices took place in the second half of the 1960s. Fabrication of the devices has increasingly involved photolithography and electron-beam lithography, and superconducting junctions and circuits are now at the forefront of electronic ultraminiaturization. This section describes five areas of interest: SQUID magnetometers, digital computers, signal-processing devices, physical measurement standards, and detectors of high-frequency electromagnetic radiation.

**SQUID magnetometers.** There are two types of superconducting quantum interference device (SQUID) for detecting changes in magnetic flux: the dc SQUID and the rf SQUID. The dc SQUID, which operates with a dc bias current, consists of two Josephson junctions incorporated into a superconducting loop (**Fig. 1***a*). The maximum dc supercurrent, known as the critical current, and the current-voltage (*I-V*) characteristic of the SQUID, shown in Fig. 1*b*, oscillate as a function of the magnetic flux $\Phi$ threading the ring, with a period of one flux quantum, $\Phi_0 = h/2e \approx 2.07 \times 10^{-15}$ weber, where $h$ is Planck's constant and $e$ is the magnitude of the charge of the electron. Thus, when the SQUID is biased with a constant current, the voltage is periodic in the flux (Fig. 1*c*). The SQUID is almost invariably operated in the flux-locked loop shown in Fig. 1*d*. A change in the applied flux gives rise to a corresponding current in the coil that produces an equal and opposite flux in the

SQUID. The SQUID is thus the null detector in a feedback circuit, and the output voltage $V_0$ is linearly proportional to the applied flux. Modern dc SQUIDs are fabricated from thin films, and usually involve Josephson tunnel junctions, resistively shunted to eliminate hysteresis in the $I$-$V$ characteristics. **Figure 2** shows a typical example, a planar dc SQUID overlaid with a 50-turn superconducting spiral coil. A current applied to the coil induces a magnetic flux in the SQUID, and is thereby measured. Devices of this type have a magnetic flux sensitivity of a few microflux quanta in a unit bandwidth. DC SQUIDs with very small loop inductances can approach the sensitivity limit set by quantum mechanics. It appears that the dc SQUID is an ideal, quantum-limited amplifier, although much work remains to be done to exploit this property fully. *SEE JOSEPHSON EFFECT.*

The rf SQUID (**Fig. 3***a*) consists of a single Josephson junction incorporated into a superconducting loop and operates with a rf bias. The SQUID is coupled to the inductor of an *LC*-resonant circuit excited at its resonant frequency, typically 30 MHz, although frequencies as high as 10 GHz have been used successfully. The rf voltage across the tank circuit versus the rf current is shown in Fig. 3*b*. When the amplitude of the rf current is properly adjusted, the amplitude of the rf voltage across the tank circuit oscillates as a function of applied flux (Fig. 3*c*), with a period $\Phi_0$. The rf SQUID is also usually operated in a feedback mode (Fig. 3*d*). Most rf SQUIDs are made from machined niobium components with a point contact junction. Although they have been used more widely than dc SQUIDs, their sensitivity is now considerably lower, and it seems unlikely that their performance will be able to match that of the dc SQUID.

Most SQUIDs are used in conjunction with input circuits. Figure 1*d* shows a voltmeter, the sensitivity of which is usually limited by Johnson noise in the resistor to typically $10^{-15}$ to $10^{-12}$ V $Hz^{-1/2}$. Figure 3*d* shows a magnetic field gradiometer, in which two balanced superconducting pick-up loops are connected in series with a superconducting coil coupled to the SQUID. If a uniform magnetic field is applied, no flux is linked to the SQUID, while the application of a field gradient $\partial H_z/\partial z$ induces a flux in the SQUID proportional to the difference of the flux in the two loops. Sensitivities of $10^{-13}$ tesla $m^{-1}$ $Hz^{-1/2}$ are typical. A gradiometer can be adapted to measure the paramagnetic susceptibility of tiny samples: one inserts the sample into one of the loops in the presence of a constant magnetic field, and measures the resulting change in flux. A system with a single pick-up loop is a magnetometer, with a typical sensitivity of $10^{-14}$ T $Hz^{-1/2}$; however, substantially higher sensitivities have been achieved. *SEE VOLTMETER.*

SQUIDs have been widely used in low-temperature research. One application is to measure tiny voltages arising, for example, from Hall effects or thermoelectric effects. Another major application has been the measurement of magnetic susceptibility over a temperature range from 1 to 300 K (−458 to +80°F). The use of SQUIDs in nuclear magnetic resonance has grown rapidly. In addition to their uses in low-temperature research, however, SQUIDs are essential tools for a wide range of noncryogenic applications. One area of major importance is biomagnetism—for example, magnetocardiology; the study of spontaneous or evoked brain activity; the detection and location of magnetic particles in the human body; the determination of eye movements; and even the detection of a signal propagating in a single frog nerve. In most of these measurements, the magnetic signals are detected by a second-derivative magnetic gradiometer that responds to $(\partial^2 H_z/\partial x^2)$ [**Fig. 4**]. This device gives sufficient rejection of magnetic noise from external sources that the measurements can be performed in an unshielded environment. SQUIDs are also used in geophysical studies, in which it is often necessary to operate cryostats under adverse conditions in remote areas. Applications include magnetotellurics, a technique to determine the electrical resistivity of the ground; gravity gradiometry; rock magnetism; paleomagnetism; piezomagnetism; tectonomagnetism; and the observation of internal ocean waves. Finally, a quite different realm of sensitive measurement is in various tests of fundamental physical theories, for example, gravitational wave antennas, magnetic monopole detectors, and an orbiting gyroscope test of general relativity. *SEE HALL EFFECT; SQUID.*

**Digital computer elements.** Typical high-speed digital mainframe computers, using large-scale integration of semiconductor devices, have cycle times of 30–50 nanoseconds, although the fastest machines have cycle times as short as about 10 ns. It is to be expected that the next generation of computers will have substantially shorter cycle times. To reduce the cycle time to below, say, 1 ns, both the switching time of the individual circuit elements and the time required to transmit a signal between different parts of the computer must be less than 1 ns. Because the signal propagation speed is typically $10^8$ $ms^{-1}$, the second requirement implies that the largest dimension of the computer must not exceed 0.1 m. Although semiconducting devices with switching times substantially less than 1 ns are certainly available, they dissipate considerable amounts of power. Because of the difficulty in extracting this power from a small vol-

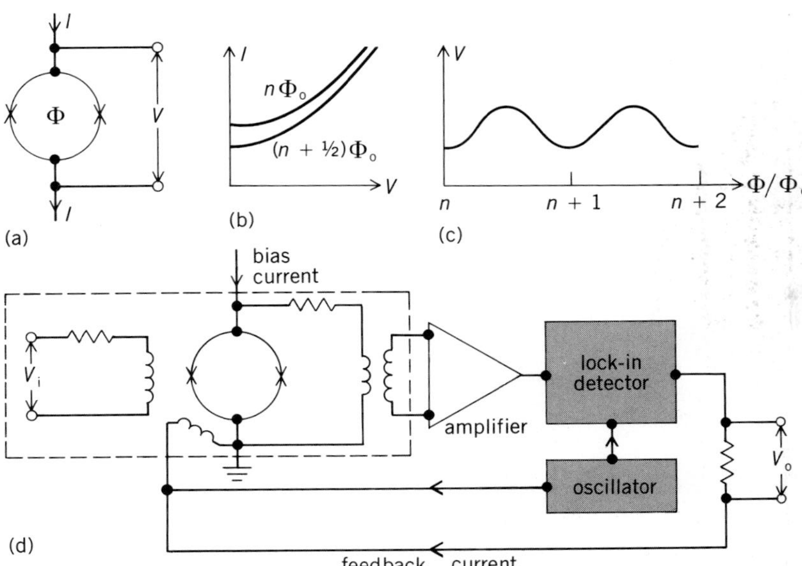


Fig. 1. The dc SQUID. (*a*) Schematic diagram. The symbol × denotes a Josephson junction. (*b*) Current-voltage (*I-V*) characteristic with applied flux $\Phi = n\Phi_0$ and $\Phi = (n + ½)\Phi_0$, where *n* is an integer. (c) Graph of voltage *V* versus $\Phi/\Phi_0$. (*d*) Block diagram of device in feedback loop with input circuit for measuring voltage. The broken line encloses cryogenic components.

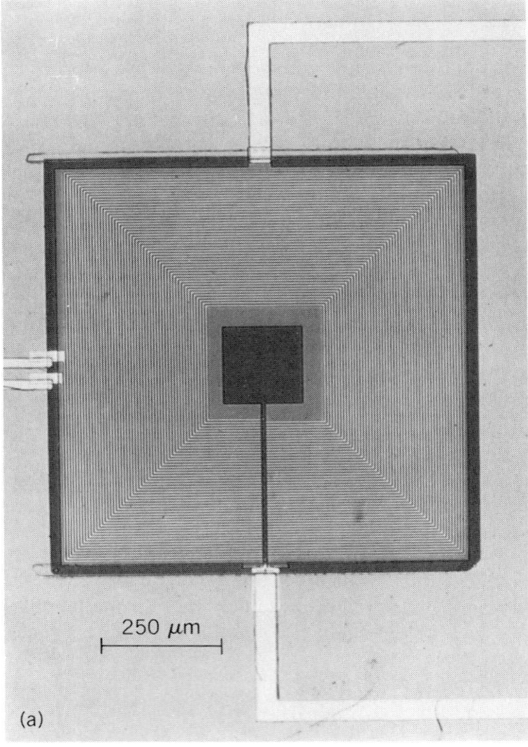


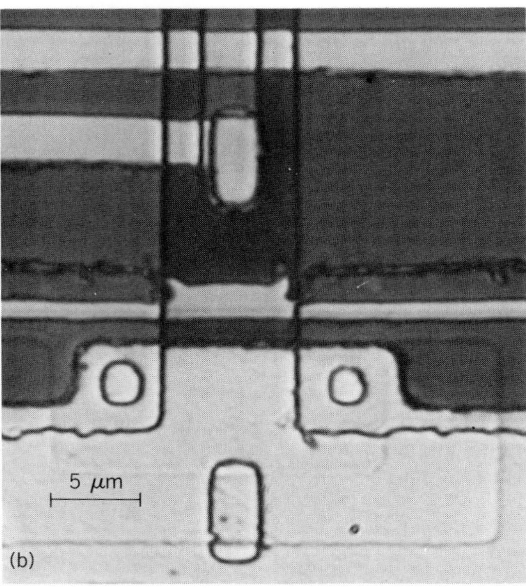


**Fig. 2.** Planar dc SQUID. (*a*) Entire device with 50-turn superconducting input coil. The leads at top and bottom are current and voltage leads to the SQUID, while the two leads to the left are the input leads to the spiral coil. (*b*) Enlarged view of bottom center part of the SQUID, showing the two Josephson tunnel junctions. (*Lawrence Berkeley Laboratory*)

ume, there are difficulties in reducing the dimensions of a mainframe computer sufficiently to achieve a subnanosecond cycle time. On the other hand, preliminary studies of Josephson junction computer elements in the latter half of the 1960s established that these devices had the combined requirements of very high switching speed and very low dissipation. Thus, such devices appeared to be attractive candidates for a new generation of ultrafast computer, and the level of research and development in the United States grew steadily through the 1970s. During the early 1980s, several Japanese companies entered the field. However, the effort in the United States was greatly reduced in 1983, so that the field became dominated by Japan. SEE INTEGRATED CIRCUITS.

The two essential elements of a computer are logic circuits and memory cells. As an example of a logic device, **Fig. 5*a*** shows an OR gate involving a three-junction SQUID. Initially the device is biased in the zero voltage state by a current below the critical current. A current pulse in either of the control lines couples a magnetic flux into the device that lowers the critical current and induces a transition into the nonzero voltage state. The output from the gate thus represents A or B. The fastest switching times that have been measured are less than 10 picoseconds. SEE LOGIC CIRCUITS.

There are two types of cryogenic memory, a very fast cache memory that is coupled directly to the logic circuits, and a larger but slower main memory. One design for the cache memory (Fig. 5*b*) consists of an interferometer incorporated into a superconducting loop. A "1," represented by a persistent supercurrent, or a "0," represented by zero supercurrent, can be written into the memory by the application of appropriate current pulses on the column line and the control lines. The contents of the cell can be read nondestructively by applying pulses to the column line and the sense line. The cell is designed for operation in an array, in which individual cells can be addressed. The main memory loop is more compact, and consists of two-junction interferometers that are read destructively. Both types of memory dissipate power during writing or reading, but not during storage. SEE COMPUTER STORAGE TECHNOLOGY.

Much of the early development work was per-

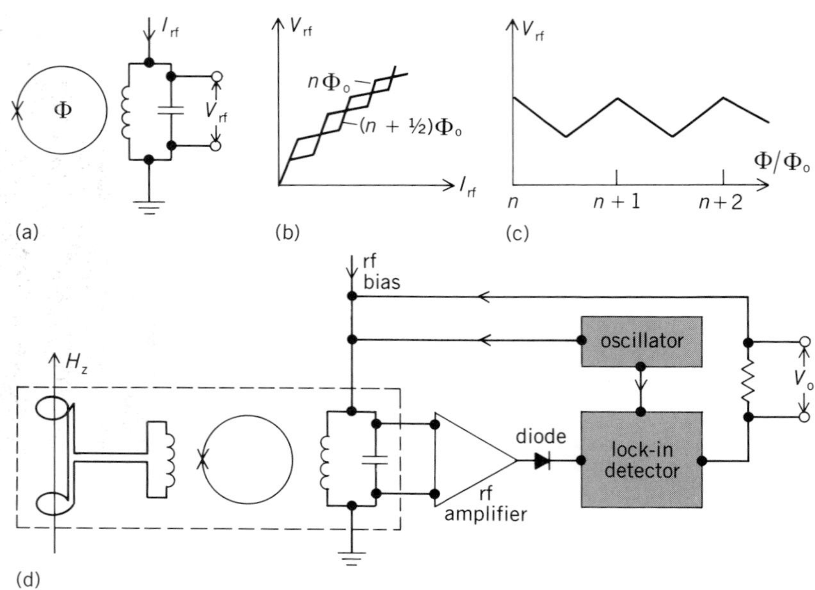


**Fig. 3.** Radio-frequency (rf) SQUID. (*a*) Schematic diagram of device coupled to *LC*-resonant circuit. (*b*) Graph of rf voltage $V_{rf}$ versus rf current $I_{rf}$ with applied flux $\Phi = n\Phi_0$ and $\Phi = (n + ½)\Phi_0$. (*c*) Graph of $V_{rf}$ versus $\Phi/\Phi_0$. (*d*) Block diagram of device in feedback loop with input circuit for measuring magnetic field gradients. The broken line encloses cryogenic components.

formed on circuits fabricated photolithographically on silicon chips by using a lead alloy technology. Subsequently, the Japanese, in particular, successfully produced circuits based on niobium and niobium alloys that are both reproducible and extremely durable. All of the necessary components for a computer have been constructed and successfully tested, but much remains to be done in regard to large-scale integration and packaging of individual chips. Whether or not this technology can be carried through to the production of a mainframe computer remains an open question. *SEE DIGITAL COMPUTER; SUPERCOMPUTER.*

**Signal-processing devices.** A relatively new class of superconducting devices is concerned with fast signal processing. Although most of these devices have not yet reached their full potential, they show considerable promise for future development. One type of device is the analog-to-digital (A/D) converter; **Fig. 6** shows a 6-bit converter. The device involves a set of six comparators, each of which consists of two 2-junction SQUIDs. The conversion time of the analog-to-digital converter is about 100 ps, and the maximum signal frequency is about 100 MHz. It is projected that signal bandwidths of 300 MHz with 6-bit accuracy and of 1 GHz with 4-bit accuracy should be feasible; these performances are several times better than those of existing semiconductor devices. One application of these fast, superconducting analog-to-digital converters is in conjunction with a superconducting convolver, a device that performs the convolution function of two electromagnetic signals. Prototype convolvers operating at 3 GHZ have been successfully tested, and operation at frequencies up to 10 GHz seems feasible. Other superconducting devices in this family include correlators and programmable filters. *SEE ANALOG-TO-DIGITAL CONVERTER.*

Another type of signal-processing device is the Josephson sampler. This device is used to sample very fast repetitive signals, and thus to reconstruct their waveforms. Resolutions of about 2 ps have been reported.

**Standards.** The Josephson effects have an established role in standards laboratories. The most important applications are the measurement of the fundamental constant ratio $e/h$, and maintaining the standard volt. When a Josephson junction is irradiated with microwaves of frequency $f$, constant-voltage steps are induced on the $I$–$V$ characteristic at voltages $nhf/2e$, where $n$ is an integer. Precise measurements of the voltages at which the steps are induced by a known frequency have led to the most accurate determination available of $e/h$. Furthermore, the standard volt at the United States National Bureau of Standards and at a number of other national laboratories is now maintained (but not defined) by these voltage steps, which may be compared periodically with the conventional standard cells. Since frequency can be measured very accurately, it is a relatively simple procedure for widely spaced laboratories to compare their voltage standard. *SEE ELECTRICAL MEASUREMENTS.*

Josephson devices have been used in two ways as noise thermometers for temperatures down to the millikelvin range. In the first, a junction shunted with an external resistance is biased with a stable current. The Johnson noise voltage generated by the resistance, which is proportional to the absolute temperature $T$, induces fluctuations in the frequency of the Josephson radiation emitted by the junction. By measuring the bandwidth of these fluctuations, one can determine $T$. In the second method, a SQUID voltmeter (Fig. 1*d*)

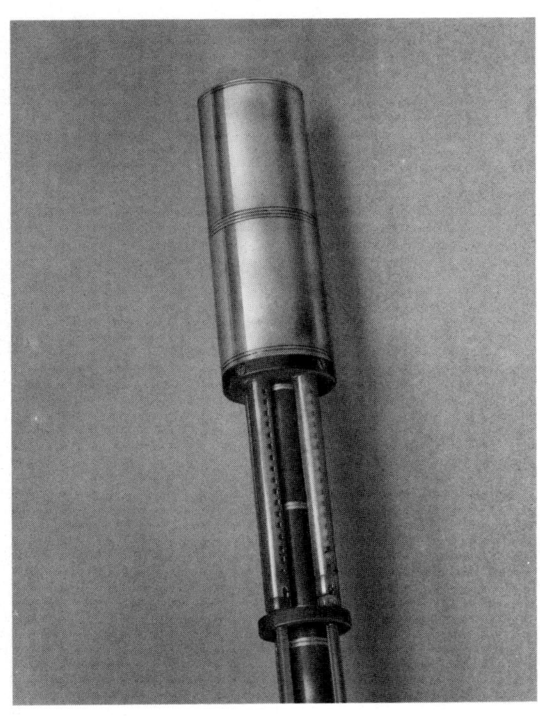

Fig. 4. Second-derivative magnetic field gradiometer used for biomagnetic measurements. (*S. H. E. Corp.*)

is used to measure the Johnson noise voltage generated by a resistor.

Other applications of SQUIDs to standards include the comparisons of static voltages or currents to high precision, and the measurement of rf power levels. Josephson junction mixers can be used to synthesize frequencies up to 1 THz or more from microwave sources. Fixed-point thermometers that rely on the reproducibility of the superconducting transition temperature of a series of metals are available for the temperature range 0.015 K or 0.027°F above absolute zero (tungsten) to 7.2 K or 13.0°F above absolute zero (lead).

**Electromagnetic radiation detectors.** There has been extensive investigation of Josephson junctions as sensitive detectors of microwave, millimeter, and submillimeter electromagnetic radiation. Various modes of operation have been investigated, including square law detectors, mixers, and parametric amplifiers. Of these, only the version of the parametric amplifier that involves a Josephson junction shunted with an inductance shows much promise: in the microwave-frequency range, the sensitivity of this device is second only to that of the master. *SEE PARAMETRIC AMPLIFIER.*

However, a superconducting device that does not involve Josephson tunneling has been developed, the superconductor-insulator-superconductor (SIS) quasiparticle mixer. The device consists of a small-area

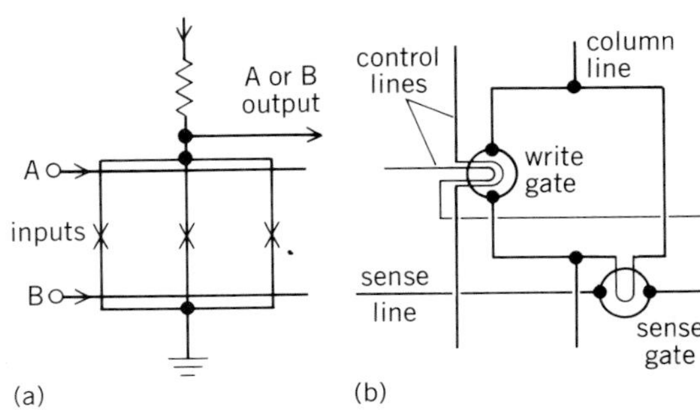


Fig. 5. Schematic diagrams of Josephson junction computer elements. (*a*) Three-junction interferometer OR gate. (*b*) High-speed memory cell.

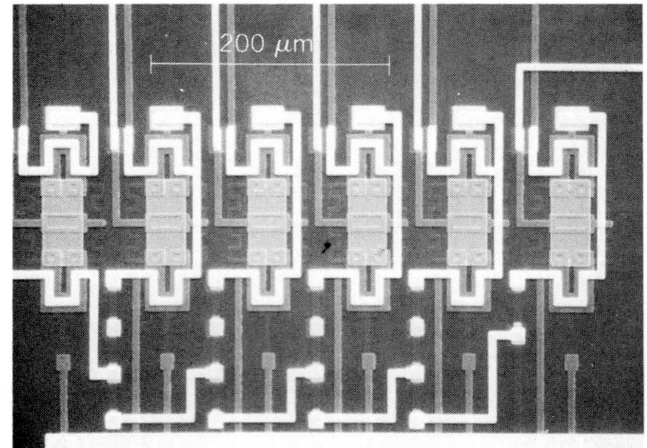


**Fig. 6. Scanning electron microscope picture of 6-bit analog-to-digital converter using comparators. (*National Bureau of Standards, Boulder, Colorado*)**

tunnel junction, fabricated from lead alloys, with the *I-V* characteristic shown in **Fig. 7**. The mixer is operated near the sharp onset in the current, where the characteristics are highly nonlinear. The nonlinearity is used to mix the signal frequency $f_S$ with the local oscillator frequency $f_{IF} = |f_S - f_{LO}|$ that is coupled out of the junction into a low-noise preamplifier. At 36 GHz the detector has achieved the quantum limit, that is, it can detect single photons, and exhibits conversion gain. Mixers operating near 100 GHz have not yet achieved quantum-limited performance, but have the lowest available noise temperature. Work has been done to extend the application of these devices into the submillimeter range. Series arrays of

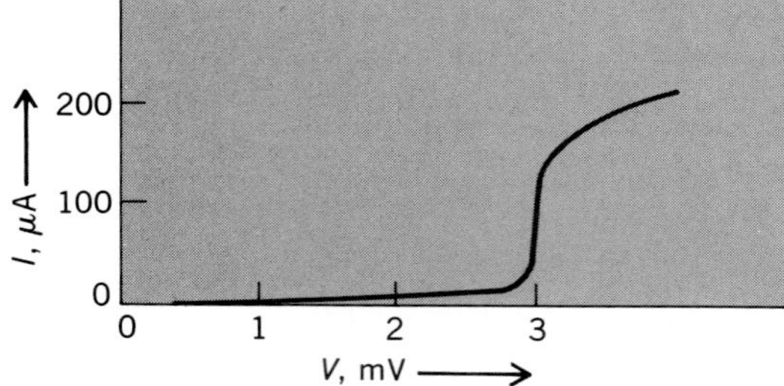


**Fig. 7. Current-voltage (*I–V*) characteristic of superconductor-insulator-superconductor (SIS) quasiparticle junction.**

junctions have been shown to be capable of exhibiting the same gain and noise temperature as single devices, with a greatly extended dynamic range that scales as the square of the number of junctions. Wide use of such arrays is likely. Mixers operating in the frequency range 90 to 115 GHz, where there is a window in the absorption by atmospheric water vapor, are in operation on several radio telescopes. This device is also likely to be of major importance in astronomical measurements made from aircraft, balloons, and satellites, as well as in communications.

*John Clarke*

***Bibliography.*** A. Barone and G. Paterno, *Physics and Applications of Josephson Effect*, 1982; P. G. de Gennes, *Superconductivity of Metals and Alloys*, 1966; S. Foner and B. B. Schwartz (eds.), *Superconducting Machines and Devices: Large-Scale Systems Applications*, 1974; J. Matisoo, The superconducting computer, *Sci. Amer.*, 242(5):50–65, May 1980; Proceedings of the Applied Superconductivity Conference, 1980, 1982, and 1984, *IEEE Trans. Magnet.*, vol. 17, no. 1, January 1981, vol. 19, no. 3, May 1983, and vol. 21, no. 2, March 1985; B. B. Schwartz and S. Foner (eds.), *Superconductor Applications: SQUIDS and Machines*, 1977; Special issue on Josephson computer technology, *IBM J. Res. Develop.*, 24(2):107–252, 1980; Special issue on superconducting devices, *IEEE Trans. Elec. Devices*, ED-27(10):1855–2042, 1980; T. Van Duzer and C. W. Turner, *Principles of Superconductive Devices and Circuits*, 1981.

## Superconductivity

A phenomenon occurring at very low temperatures in many electrical conductors, in which the electrons responsible for conduction undergo a collective transition to an ordered state with many unique and remarkable properties. These include the vanishing of resistance to the flow of electric current, the appearance of a large diamagnetism and other unusual magnetic effects, substantial alteration of many thermal properties, and the occurrence of quantum effects otherwise observable only at the atomic and subatomic level.

Superconductivity was discovered by H. Kamerlingh Onnes in Leiden in 1911, while studying the variation with temperature of the electrical resistance of mercury within a few degrees of absolute zero. He observed that the resistance dropped sharply to an unmeasurably small value at a temperature of 4.2 K (−452°F). Kamerlingh Onnes's original data are shown in **Fig. 1**. The temperature at which the transition occurs is called the transition or critical temperature, $T_c$. The vanishingly small resistance (very high conductivity) below $T_c$ suggested the name given the phenomenon.

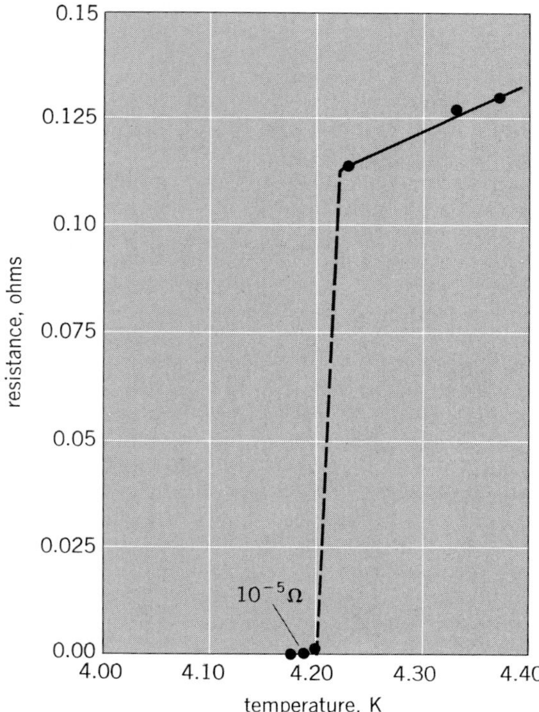


**Fig. 1. Resistance in ohms of a specimen of mercury versus absolute temperature. °F = (K × 1.8) −459.67. (*After H. Kamerlingh Onnes, Akad. van Wetenschappen, Amsterdam, 14:113, 818, 1911*)**

In 1933 W. Meissner and R. Ochsenfeld discovered that a metal cooled into the superconducting state in a not-too-large magnetic field expels the field from its interior. This discovery demonstrated that superconductivity involves more than simply very high or infinite electrical conductivity, remarkable as that alone is.

Superconductivity remained a much studied but puzzling phenomenon for nearly half a century after its discovery. A great deal of experimental information was amassed on its occurrence and its properties, and several useful phenomenological theories were developed. Then, in 1957, J. Bardeen, L. N. Cooper, and J. R. Schrieffer reported the first successful microscopic theory of superconductivity. It describes how and why the electrons in a conductor may form an ordered superconducting state, and makes predictions about many properties of superconductors which are in good agreement with experimental information.

Since the appearance of the Bardeen-Cooper-Schrieffer (BCS) theory, theoretical and experimental understanding of superconductivity has continued to expand. New superconducting materials and effects have continued to be discovered. Practical applications of the phenomenon are becoming common, ranging from powerful electromagnets and machinery to ultrasensitive electronic instruments and computer elements. *SEE SUPERCONDUCTING DEVICES.*

## BASIC EXPERIMENTAL PROPERTIES

Soon after its discovery in mercury, superconductivity was found to occur also in such common metals as lead and tin. Initially, the number of known superconductors was quite small. This was so in part because experiments were then confined to temperatures above about 1 K (−450°F), the minimum temperature readily available using liquid helium ($^4He$) as a refrigerant, so that only superconductors with transition temperatures above 1 K could be discovered. It was therefore thought that superconductivity might be a relatively rare phenomenon. Scientists now know that it is not, but in fact occurs quite generally. Advances in the technology for achieving low temperatures have pushed the minimum available temperature down to about 0.001 K, and progress in the preparation of materials has greatly expanded the number and variety of materials which have been tested for superconductivity. Some 26 of the metallic elements are known to be superconductors in their normal forms, and another 10 become superconducting under pressure or when prepared in the form of highly disordered thin films (**Fig. 2**). The number of known superconducting compounds and alloys runs into the thousands. Superconductivity is thus a rather common characteristic of metallic conductors, so much so that its absence is often more unusual and striking than its presence.

Despite the existence of a successful microscopic theory of superconductivity, there are no completely reliable rules for predicting whether a metal will be a superconductor. Certain trends and correlations are apparent among the known superconductors, however—some with obvious bases in the theory—and these provide empirical guidelines in the search for new superconductors. Superconductors with relatively high transition temperatures tend to be rather poor conductors in the normal state. For many years, no superconductors were known among the noble metals,

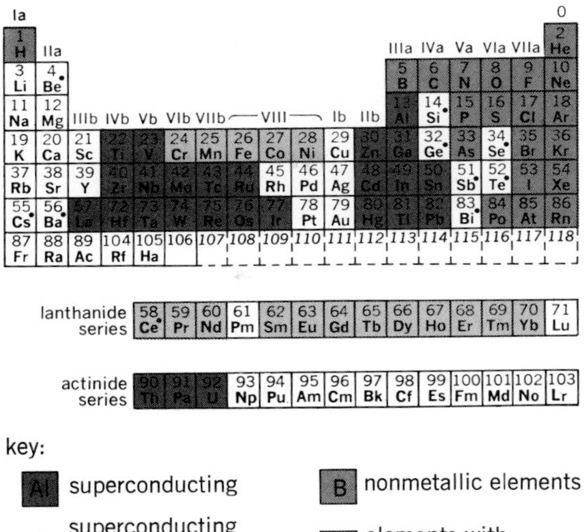


**Fig. 2. Superconducting elements in the periodic table. (*After N. W. Ashcroft and N. D. Mermin, Solid State Physics, Holt, Rinehart and Winston, 1976*)**

the alkali metals, and the alkaline earth metals. However, cesium, beryllium, and barium have been found to be superconducting under high pressure or in disordered films, and there is some evidence that at least one of the noble metals may be superconducting at extremely low temperatures.

The ordered superconducting state appears to be incompatible with any long-range-ordered magnetic state: None of the ferromagnetic or antiferromagnetic metals are also superconducting. (Cerium displays antiferromagnetic order but is not superconducting in the phase which exists at ordinary pressures; it is superconducting but not magnetically ordered in a different phase which occurs at pressures above about 5 gigapascals or 7 × $10^5$ lb/in.$^2$) This distaste of superconductors for magnetism extends to the effects of impurities. The presence of nonmagnetic impurities in a superconductor usually has very little effect on the superconductivity, but the presence of impurity atoms which have localized magnetic moments can markedly depress the transition temperature even in concentrations as low as a few parts per million.

Some semiconductors with very high densities of charge carriers are superconducting, and others such as silicon and germanium have high-pressure metallic phases which are superconducting. Many elements which are not themselves superconducting form compounds which are. Examples are copper sulfide (CuS) and a polymeric form of tin. Although nearly all the classes of crystal structure are represented among superconductors, certain structures appear to be especially conducive to superconductivity. An example is the so-called A15 structure shared by a series of intermetallic compounds based on niobium, for example, niobium tin ($Nb_3Sn$) with $T_c$ = 18.1 K (−427°F). High values of transition temperature occur most frequently in elements, compounds, or alloys having three, five, or seven valence electrons per atom.

The highest transition temperature observed is 23 K (−418°F) for a specially prepared alloy of niobium, aluminum, and germanium. There is no widely accepted theoretical proof that superconductivity is necessarily restricted to low temperatures. Encouraged by this and motivated by visions of the immense practical and fundamental implications of a "high-temperature" superconductor, many investigators have searched for materials with higher transition temperatures.

**Electrical resistance.** It is, of course, not possible to establish that the dc (zero-frequency) electrical resistance of a superconductor is identically zero, but a rather stringent upper limit on the resistance can be established by inducing an electrical current in a superconducting loop or coil and observing whether it dies away in time. The decay time of such a current in a nonsuperconducting coil at low temperatures is on the order of 1 s or less. Induced currents have been observed to persist in superconducting loops for several years. Very precise measurements of the magnetic field produced by a persistent current, using nuclear magnetic resonance over shorter periods of time, have established that the supercurrent decay time is at least 100,000 years. This implies that the resistance in the superconducting state is at least $10^{12}$ times less than in the normal state.

It can be shown theoretically that the persistent current state is not really absolutely stable, but only metastable. In superconducting materials such as those used to build superconducting magnets, finite persistent current decay times are often observed, due to processes which cause irreversible redistribution of magnetic flux in the material. But under many conditions the lifetime of the metastable persistent current state is so long that it is not unreasonable to say that the lifetime is infinite, and the electrical resistance is zero.

**Magnetic properties.** The existence of the Meissner-Ochsenfeld effect, the exclusion of a magnetic field from the interior of a superconductor, is direct evidence that the superconducting state is not simply one of infinite electrical conductivity. If this were so, a superconductor cooled in a magnetic field through its transition temperature would trap the field in its interior. If the external source of the field were subsequently removed, persistent eddy currents would be induced in the superconductor which would preserve the interior field even in the absence of the external source. Instead, the Meissner-Ochsenfeld effect implies that the superconducting state is a true thermodynamic equilibrium state, a new phase which has lower free energy than the normal state at temperatures below the transition temperature and which somehow requires the absence of magnetic flux.

The exclusion of magnetic flux by a superconductor costs some magnetic energy. So long as this cost is less than the condensation energy gained by going from the normal to the superconducting phase, the superconductor will remain completely superconducting in an applied magnetic field. If the applied field becomes too large, the cost in magnetic energy will outweigh the gain in condensation energy, and the superconductor will become partially or totally normal. The manner in which this occurs depends on the geometry and the material of the superconductor. Consider first the simplest geometry, a very long cylinder with field applied parallel to its axis. Two distinct types of behavior may then occur, depending on the type of superconductor.

***Type I superconductors.*** Below a "critical field" $H_c$ which increases as the temperature decreases below $T_c$, the magnetic flux is excluded from a type I superconductor, which is said to be perfectly diamagnetic. If the applied field is increased above $H_c$, the entire superconductor reverts to the normal state and the field penetrates completely. The curve of $H_c$ versus temperature $T$ in **Fig. 3** is thus a phase boundary in the magnetic field-temperature plan separating a region where the superconducting phase is thermodynamically stable from the region where the normal phase is stable. The curve of $H_c$ versus $T$ for any type I superconductor is approximately parabolic: To within a few percent, $H_c = H_0[1 - (T/T_c)^2]$, where $H_0$ is the value of $H_c$ at absolute zero. Values of $T_c$ and $H_0$ for some typical superconductors are given in the **table**. All of the known elemental superconductors except niobium are of type I.

***Type II superconductors.*** For a type II superconductor, there are two critical fields, the lower critical field $H_{c1}$ and the upper critical field $H_{c2}$. In applied fields less than $H_{c1}$, the superconductor completely excludes the field, just as a type I superconductor does below $H_c$. At fields just above $H_{c1}$, however, flux begins to penetrate the superconductor in microscopic filaments called fluxoids or vortices. Each fluxoid consists of a normal core in which the magnetic field is large, surrounded by a superconducting region in which flows a vortex of persistent supercurrent which maintains the field in the core. The total magnetic flux in each fluxoid is exactly equal to a fundamental quantum of magnetic flux, $\phi_\Phi = 2.07 \times 10^{-7}$ gauss cm$^2$ = $2.07 \times 10^{-15}$ Wb. The diameter of the fluxoid is typically $10^{-7}$ m. In a sufficiently pure and defect-free type II superconductor, the fluxoids tend to arrange them-

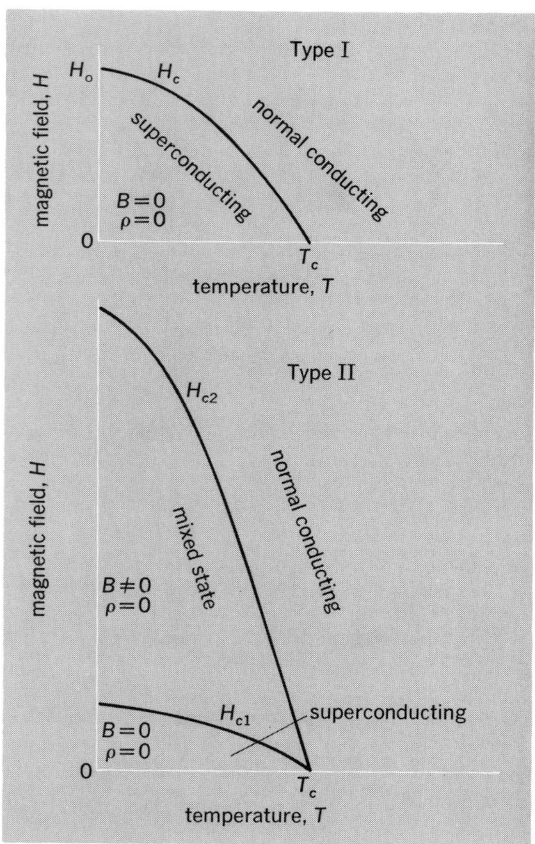


**Fig. 3. Superconductive state in the magnetic-field temperature plane.**

**Values of $T_c$ and $H_0$ for the superconducting elements***

| Element | Phase | $T_c$, K | $H_0$, oersteds† |
|---|---|---|---|
| Al | | 1.196 | 99 |
| Cd | | 0.56 | 30 |
| Ga | | 1.091 | 51 |
| Hf | | 0.09 | — |
| Hg | α(rhomb) | 4.15 | 411 |
| | β | 3.95 | 339 |
| In | | 3.40 | 293 |
| Ir | | 0.14 | 19 |
| La | α(hcp) | 4.9 | 798 |
| | β(fcc) | 6.06 | 1096 |
| Mo | | 0.92 | 98 |
| Nb | | 9.26 | 1980‡ |
| Os | | 0.655 | 65 |
| Pa | | 1.4 | — |
| Pb | | 7.19 | 803 |
| Re | | 1.698 | 198 |
| Ru | | 0.49 | 66 |
| Sn | | 3.72 | 305 |
| Ta | | 4.48 | 830 |
| Tc | | 7.77 | 1410 |
| Th | | 1.368 | 162 |
| Ti | | 0.39 | 100 |
| Tl | | 2.39 | 171 |
| U | α | 0.68 | — |
| | λ | 1.80 | — |
| V | | 5.30 | 1020 |
| W | | 0.012 | 1 |
| Zn | | 0.875 | 53 |
| Ar | | 0.65 | 47 |

*After N. W. Ashcroft and N. D. Mermin, *Solid State Physics*, Holt, Rinehart, and Winston, 1976.

†At $T = 0$ K. 1 Oe = 76.9 A/m.

‡For Nb, a type II superconductor, the zero-temperature critical field quoted is obtained from an equal-area construction: The low-field ($H < H_{c1}$) magnetization is extrapolated linearly to a field $H_c$ chosen to give an enclosed area equal to the area under the actual magnetization curve.

selves in a regular lattice. This vortex state of the superconductor is known as the mixed state. It exists for applied fields between $H_{c1}$ and $H_{c2}$. At $H_{c2}$, the superconductor becomes normal, and the field penetrates completely. (Actually, a superconducting surface sheath may persist up to an even higher critical field $H_{c3}$, which is approximately 1.5 $H_{c2}$.)

In contrast to critical fields in type I superconductors, which tend to be less than 1000 oersteds (1 Oe = 79.6 A/m), $H_{c2}$ for type II superconductors may be several hundred thousand oersteds or more. (The maximum known $H_{c2}$ is about 600,000 Oe). Since a zero-resistance supercurrent can flow in the mixed state in the superconducting regions surrounding the fluxoids, a type II superconductor can carry a lossless current even in the presence of a very large magnetic field. Such superconductors are therefore of considerable practical importance in high-field magnets.

A type II superconductor in the mixed state is not necessarily completely lossless, however. The presence of an electric current creates a force on the fluxoids. They therefore tend to move. Moving magnetic flux creates voltages by electromagnetic induction, and the presence of nonzero voltages together with the current implies power dissipation. This loss mechanism can often be suppressed by introducing defects into the crystal structure of the superconductor which tend to pin down the fluxoids and prevent them from moving.

***Penetration depth.*** The way in which a superconductor excludes from its anterior an applied magnetic field smaller than $H_c$ (type I) or $H_{c1}$ (type II) is by establishing a persistent supercurrent on its surface which exactly cancels the applied field inside the superconductor. This surface current flows in a very thin layer of thickness λ, which is called the penetration depth. The external field also actually penetrates the superconductor within the penetration depth. Lambda depends on the material and on the temperature, the latter variation being given approximately by $\lambda = \lambda_0[1 - (T/T_c)^4]^{-1}$ ($\lambda_0$ is the penetration depth at zero temperature for the particular material, and is typically of order $5 \times 10^{-8}$ m).

***Intermediate state.*** Another kind of magnetic effect occurs in type I superconductors for all but the simplest geometries. The exclusion of magnetic flux by the superconductor distorts the field in its vicinity. As a result, the magnetic field may reach $H_c$ at some points on the surface of the superconductor while remaining below $H_c$ elsewhere. The superconductor near the points of highest field will tend to go normal. The magnetic flux then begins to penetrate the superconductor in nonsuperconducting lamellae separated by regions where superconductivity remains. If the applied field is further increased, the fraction of the specimen occupied by the normal lamellae increases, while the fraction occupied by the intervening superconducting regions decreases. With increasing applied field, this continues until the specimen becomes completely normal and the field penetrates everywhere. A type I superconductor with such alternating superconducting and normal lamellae is in the intermediate state.

There are superficial similarities between the intermediate state in a type I superconductor and the mixed state in a type II superconductor, but the two states are really quite different. In the intermediate state, the lamellae are of macroscopic size, sometimes an appreciable fraction of a millimeter. This size is determined by two energies, a magnetic energy which increases as the size of the lamellae increases, and a positive surface energy associated with the interface between the superconducting and normal regions, rather like the surface energy associated with the surface tension at a liquid-gas interface. This surface energy increases with the supernormal interface area and hence with the number of lamellae, that is, it decreases as the size of the lamellae increases. The magnetic energy favors small lamellae, and the surface energy favors large lamellae. The equilibrium lamellar structure is determined by a compromise between the two and is rather sensitive to the geometry and degree of perfection of the specimen. In type II superconductors, on the other hand, the supernormal interface energy turns out to be negative. It is therefore energetically favorable for the regions of flux penetration to be as small as possible. Their minimum size is limited only by a fundamental quantum constraint on the nature of the superconducting state itself. It is this which sets the level of magnetic flux contained within a fluxoid at the flux quantum mentioned above and determines the microscopic scale of the fluxoid structure in the mixed state.

***Critical current.*** The existence of the critical field leads to another property of superconductors which is of some practical importance. In his Nobel prize lecture, Kamerlingh Onnes referred to the possibility of constructing powerful electromagnets which would consume no electrical power, using superconductors. However, a supercurrent flowing in a superconducting wire will itself create a magnetic field, and this field will drive the superconductor normal at some critical value of the current (the Silsbee critical current). Unfortunately, the critical currents which accompany typical critical fields for type I superconducting wires of macroscopic size are so small that Kamerlingh Onnes's dream remained unrealized until the exploitation of type II superconductors nearly 40 years later.

**Thermal properties.** The appearance of the superconducting state is accompanied by quite drastic changes in both the thermodynamic equilibrium and thermal transport properties of a superconductor.

***Heat capacity.*** **Figure 4** shows the heat capacity of an aluminum specimen in both the normal and superconducting states. In the normal state (produced at temperatures below the transition temperature by applying a magnetic field greater than the critical field), the heat capacity is determined primarily by the normal electrons (with a small contribution from the thermal vibrations of the crystal lattice) and is nearly proportional to the temperature. In zero applied magnetic field, there appears a discontinuity in the heat capacity at the transition temperature. At temperatures just below the transition temperature, the heat capacity is larger than in the normal state. It decreases more rapidly with decreasing temperature, however, and at temperatures well below the transition temperature varies exponentially as $e^{-\Delta/kT}$, where $\Delta$ is a constant and $k$ is Boltzmann's constant. Such an exponential temperature dependence is a hallmark of a system with a gap $\Delta$ in the spectrum of allowed energy states. Heat capacity measurements provided the first indications of such a gap in superconductors, and one of the key features of the macroscopic BCS theory is its prediction of just such a gap.

***Thermal conductivity.*** Ordinarily a large electrical conductivity is accompanied by a large thermal conductivity, as in the case of copper, used in electrical wiring and cooking pans. However, the thermal conductivity of a pure superconductor is less in the superconducting state than in the normal state, and at very low temperatures approaches zero. This property is applied in "heat switches" for use at low temperatures, in which the thermal contact between two bodies connected by a superconducting wire can be switched on and off simply by application of a magnetic field which switches the superconductivity on and off. Crudely speaking, the explanation for the association of infinite electrical conductivity with vanishing thermal conductivity is that the transport of heat requires the transport of disorder (entropy). The superconducting state is one of perfect order (zero entropy), and so there is no disorder to transport and therefore no thermal conductivity. *SEE ENTROPY; THERMAL CONDUCTION IN SOLIDS.*

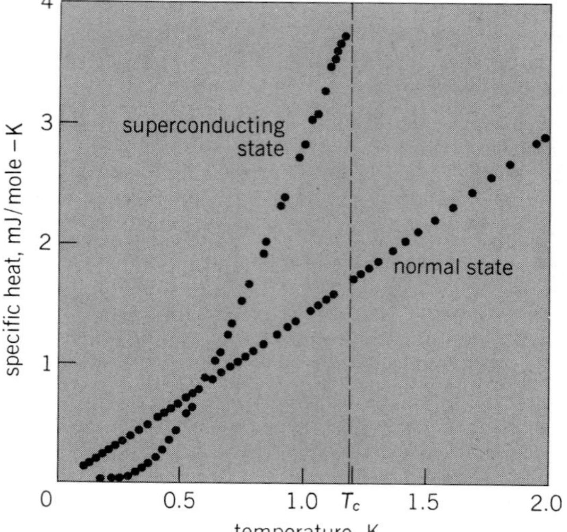


**Fig. 4. Low-temperature specific heat of normal and superconducting aluminum. °F = (K × 1.8) − 459.67. (*After N. E. Phillips, Heat capacity of aluminum between 0.1 K and 4 K, Phys. Rev., 114:676–685, 1959*)**

***Thermoelectric properties.*** A combined thermal and electrical effect of interest and practical importance is the Peltier effect, which is the basis of operation of thermocouples used for temperature measurement. If the two junction regions of a loop made of two different metals are maintained at different temperatures, an electrical current is driven around the loop. A greatly weakened form of this current occurs in the superconducting state, because some "normal" electrons remain at any non-zero temperature. However, the presence of superconductivity "shorts out" the usual thermoelectric voltage.

**High-frequency electromagnetic properties.** The electrical and magnetic behavior of superconductors at high frequencies differs from the zero frequency behavior described above. In the radio-frequency (up to about $10^8$ Hz) and microwave-frequency (from $10^8$ to about $10^{11}$ Hz) regions of the electromagnetic spectrum, it is found that superconductors do not have zero resistance to the flow of current. The resistance and the accompanying electrical energy loss are still much smaller than in the normal state, but they are not zero, and they increase with increasing frequency. On the other hand, in the optical region of the spectrum (about $10^{15}$ Hz), the electromagnetic response in the superconducting state is indistinguishable from that in the normal state. This may be confirmed simply by looking at a superconductor as it transforms from the normal state to the superconducting state; there is no change in its appearance. Clearly something interesting happens somewhere between $10^{11}$ and $10^{15}$ Hz. It is found that in the region of $10^{11}$ to $10^{12}$ Hz, depending on the material, the absorption of electromagnetic radiation by a superconductor rises quite sharply from a small value to the value characteristic of the normal state. This behavior provides another clear indication of the presence of a gap in the electronic energy spectrum of a superconductor, rather like the gaps which occur in semiconductors. (In semiconductors, however, gaps tend to be on the order of 1 eV, whereas the gaps in superconductors are typically a thousand times smaller.) The sharp rise in electromagnetic absorption occurs at the frequency for which the energy of a single photon (equal to Planck's constant times the frequency) becomes just sufficient to produce an excitation of some sort (consisting, in fact, of two "electrons") out of the superconducting state across the gap. *SEE SEMICONDUCTOR.*

**Isotope effect.** The availability of substantial quantities of separated isotopes of the elements after World War II made it possible to test whether the superconducting state depended in some way on atomic mass. The result provided a crucial key to the development of the BCS microscopic theory of superconductivity. It was found that the superconducting transition temperature for a given element was proportional to $M^{-1/2}$, where $M$ is the isotopic mass. The vibration frequency of a mass $M$ on a spring is proportional to $M^{-1/2}$, and the same relation holds for the characteristic vibrational frequencies of the atoms in a crystal lattice. Thus, the existence of the isotope effect indicated that, although superconductivity is an electronic phenomenon, it nevertheless depends in an important way on the vibrations of the crystal lattice in which the electrons move. Fortunately, not until after the development of the BCS theory was it discovered that the situation is more complicated than it had appeared. For some superconductors, the exponent of $M$ is not $-\frac{1}{2}$, but near zero, and for at least one it is positive.

**Absence of effects.** While most of the electronic properties of a superconductor are profoundly affected by the transition to the superconducting state, many other properties are changed very little if at all. These include the mechanical and elastic properties, tensile strength, sound velocity, and density, among others.

## THEORY

The principal theories which have been constructed to explain the basic experimental properties of superconductors are discussed in this section. Those which preceded the BCS microscopic theory are no less useful for being phenomenological and incomplete. The original BCS theory was based on an idealized model, but nevertheless has been broadly successful in explaining the properties of real superconductors. It has been extended and elaborated to cover ever more complex and realistic situations.

**Two-fluid model.** C. J. Gorter and H. B. G. Casimir introduced in 1934 a phenomenological theory of superconductivity based on the assumption that in the superconducting state there are two components of the conduction electron "fluid" (hence the name given this theory, the "two-fluid model"). One, called the superfluid component, is an ordered condensed state with zero entropy, hence is incapable of transporting heat. It does not interact with the background crystal lattice, its imperfections, or the other conduction electron component and exhibits no resistance to flow. The other component, the normal component, is composed of electrons which behave exactly as they do in the normal state. It is further assumed that the superconducting transition is a reversible thermodynamic phase transition between two thermodynamically stable phases, the normal state and the superconducting state, similar to the transition between the liquid and vapor phases of any substance. The validity of this assumption is strongly supported by the existence of the Meissner-Ochsenfeld effect and by other experimental evidence. This assumption permits the application of all the powerful and general machinery of the theory of equilibrium thermodynamics. The results tie together the observed thermodynamic properties of superconductors in a very satisfying way.

***Thermodynamic relations.*** From a thermodynamic point of view, the superconducting phase appears below the transition temperature because the free energy of the superconducting phase becomes less than the free energy of the normal phase for all temperatures below $T_c$. The exclusion of magnetic flux by the superconductor in an applied field $H$ increases the free energy per unit volume of superconductor by $\mu_0 H^2/2$ (in SI units); it costs energy to push the flux lines out of the superconducting region. When this increase in free energy becomes equal to the decrease in free energy associated with the normal-to-superconducting transition, it no longer pays the superconductor to remain superconducting, and the superconductor goes normal. Hence, the superconducting condensation energy must equal $\mu_0 H_c^2/2$. This can be verified experimentally by comparing the results of critical field measurements with direct measurements of the heat capacity in the normal and superconducting states.

The zero-field heat capacity in Fig. 4 shows a finite discontinuity at the transition temperature, not an infinite singularity. This means that there is no latent heat at the transition, that is, the transition is "second-order," and therefore the entropy is the same in the superconducting and normal states at the transition temperature. At all but the lowest temperatures, the electronic heat capacity in the superconducting state is nearly proportional to $T^3$. In the normal state, it is proportional to $T$, $C_n = \gamma T$, where $\gamma$ is a constant. All of these facts may be combined to yield the results that the heat capacity in the superconducting state $C_s = 3\gamma T^3/T_c^2$ and that the entropy in the superconducting state is less than that in the normal state for all temperatures below the transition temperature, that is, the superconducting phase is more ordered than the normal state. Further, consideration of the free energy yields the results $\gamma T_c^2 = 2\mu_0 H_0^2$, where $H_0$ is the critical field at $T = 0$ K (in SI units), and $H_c = (\gamma/2\mu_0)^{1/2} T_c[1 - (T/T_c)^2]$. There is thus a direct thermodynamic connection between the $T^3$ heat capacity and the parabolic critical field curve; one implies the other. SEE PHASE TRANSITIONS.

More general thermodynamic relations exist between the superconducting parameters $H_c$ and $T_c$ and the normal state heat capacity constant $\gamma$, which do not depend on any assumption about the temperature dependence of the heat capacity in the superconducting state or the form of the critical field curve. The good agreement of these relations with experimental data is the basis of the conviction that the superconducting state is indeed a thermodynamic equilibrium phase.

Another result of the two-fluid model is that the normal fluid forms a fraction $x = (T/T_c)^4$ of the total electron fluid. The superfluid fraction $1 - x = 1 - (T/T_c)^4$ therefore rises rapidly from 0 to 1 as $T$ falls below $T_c$.

***London equation.*** In order to understand the electromagnetic behavior of superconductors within the two-fluid model, it is necessary to postulate something about how the superfluid responds to electric and magnetic fields. This was done by the brothers F. London and H. London in 1935. It is natural to suppose that any electric field in a superconductor will give rise to a force on the superfluid electrons and hence will accelerate the superfluid. Since the supercurrent $\mathbf{J}_s$ is proportional to the superfluid velocity, this implies a rate of change with time of $\mathbf{J}_s$ which is proportional to the electric field. This is simply equivalent to an assumption that the superfluid has infinite conductivity. Straightforward combination of this assumption with the classical Maxwell equations relating the electric and magnetic fields yields a relation between the supercurrent and the magnetic field which does not lead to the Meissner-Ochsenfeld effect. (This indicates that the Meissner effect is not simply a consequence of infinite conductivity.) The Londons therefore postulated a modification of this relation, now called the London equation, which in one simple form is $\mathbf{J}_s = -K\mathbf{A}$. Here $\mathbf{A}$ is the so-called vector potential from which the magnetic field can be derived, and $K$ is a constant which contains the density of superfluid electrons. This equation does lead to the Meissner effect.

With the addition of the London equation to describe the electrodynamics, the two-fluid model predicts magnetic-field penetration depths and finite conductivity at nonzero frequencies in reasonable accord with experiment. The source of the latter is qualitatively apparent: At zero frequency all of the current will be carried by the superfluid, which will "short out" the normal fluid. At nonzero frequencies, however, the electromagnetic fields induced in the surface of the superconductor will tend to drive the normal fluid as well as the superfluid, and this will cause some dissipation.

**Nonlocal theory.** In the course of experiments on the electromagnetic response of superconductors at very high frequencies, A. B. Pippard in 1952 observed significant discrepancies between his results and the predictions of London electrodynamics. He traced these to a failure of the London equation $\mathbf{J}_s = -K\mathbf{A}$. This equation is a "local" one, relating as it does the supercurrent at a given point in the superconductor to the vector potential at that point. Pippard found that the correct relation is nonlocal; the supercurrent at a point actually depends on the vector potential throughout a region around the point of size $\xi$. The parameter $\xi$ is called the coherence length and may be as large as $10^{-6}$ m. Nonlocality turns out to be a very fundamental feature of the superconducting state, and $\xi$ is a fundamental length of great importance in a variety of superconducting phenomena. For example, the distinction between type I and type II superconductors depends entirely on the relative sizes of the penetration depth and the coherence length: If $\lambda$ is greater than $\xi$, the surface energy is negative and the superconductor is type II. The coherence length can be decreased from its value in a pure superconductor by adding impurities which scatter electrons, and this can change a superconductor from type I to type II.

**Ginzburg-Landau theory.** V. I. Ginzburg and L. D. Landau proposed in 1950 a highly innovative phenomenological theory of superconductivity which now bears their names. Their objective was to understand the situation of supernormal interfaces like those which occur in the intermediate state of type I superconductors. Since the superconducting state varies from something to nothing at such an interface, they needed a theory which describes a spatial variation of the superconducting state. They began by supposing that the "strength" of the superconducting state can be described by an "order parameter" $\psi$ which may be spatially varying. In the normal state, $\psi$ is zero. Then they assumed that sufficiently near $T_c$, where superconductivity is weak and $\psi$ is small, the free energy of a superconductor can be expressed as a sum of a series of terms in increasing powers of $|\psi|^2$; $|\psi|^2$ is interpreted as proportional to the superfluid density. The absolute value is used here because $\psi$ is allowed to be a complex number with an amplitude $\psi_0$ and a phase $\varphi, \psi = \psi_0 e^{i\varphi}$. This is a crucial if initially inexplicable feature of the order parameter. Thus $\psi$ has something of the character of a quantum-mechanical wave function. This similarity is reinforced by the addition to the free-energy sum of a term involving the spatial gradient of $\psi$ and the magnetic vector potential. This term has the same form as the standard representation of the kinetic energy in the Schrödinger wave equation of quantum mechanics, and here represents the kinetic energy of the superfluid electrons. The equilibrium form of $\psi$ is then assumed to be that which minimizes the free energy. This leads to a rather complicated nonlinear differential equation for $\psi$. Together with an electrodynamic equation which relates the supercurrent $\mathbf{J}_s$ to $\psi$, this equation forms a pair of simultaneous differential equations called the Ginzburg-Landau equations.

Obtaining solutions of the Ginzburg-Landau equations is in general rather difficult. Nevertheless, they have been a remarkably powerful tool in superconductivity. They are intrinsically nonlocal because of the presence of the spatial gradient of $\psi$ in the original free-energy equation. This has the consequence that a local disturbance (such as a sharp boundary between a normal and a superconducting metal) causes $\psi$ to vary on the scale of a characteristic length which can be identified with the coherence length $\xi$. The other characteristic length in superconductivity, the penetration depth $\lambda$, also appears in a natural way. In 1957 A. A. Abrikosov reported a solution of the Ginzburg-Landau equations for the case $\lambda > \xi$ which constituted the first theoretical explanation of the mixed state in type II superconductors. Although the Ginzburg-Landau equations have many limitations, they continue to provide the basis for most understanding of the spatially varying superconducting state.

**Microscopic (BCS) theory.** The key to the basic interaction between electrons which gives rise to superconductivity was provided by the isotope effect. It is an interaction mediated by the background crystal lattice and can crudely be pictured as follows: An electron tends to create a slight distortion of the elastic lattice as it moves, because of the Coulomb attraction between the negatively charged electron and the positively charged lattice. If the distortion persists for a brief time (the lattice may ring like a struck bell), a second passing electron will see the distortion and be affected by it. Under certain circumstances, this can give rise to a weak indirect attractive interaction between the two electrons which may more than compensate their Coulomb repulsion.

H. Frölich recognized in 1950 that such an interaction might be responsible for superconductivity. However, all initial attempts to develop a theory based on the interaction failed. The average energy per electron associated with the superconducting condensation is tiny compared with typical electron kinetic or Coulomb interaction energies. It was natural to try to exploit this by trying to arrive at the quantum-mechanical description of electrons in the superconducting state by small pertubations of the description in the normal state. In retrospect, it is clear why this approach failed. The superconducting quantum wave function is qualitatively different from any normal state wave function.

The first forward step was taken by Cooper in 1956, when he showed that two electrons with an attractive interaction can bind together to form a "bound pair" (often called a Cooper pair) if they are in the presence of a high-density fluid of other electrons, no matter how weak the interaction is. The two partners of a Cooper pair have opposite momenta and spin angular momenta. Then, in 1957, Bardeen, Cooper, and Schrieffer showed how to construct a wave function in which all of the electrons (at least, all of the important ones) are paired. Once this wave function is adjusted to minimize the free energy, it can be used as the basis for a complete microscopic theory of superconductivity.

With the discovery of the BCS superconducting-ground-state wave function, the fundamental reason for the remarkable properties of the superconducting state became clear. An analogy is useful in understanding it. Consider an enormous ballroom packed with dancers, shoulder to shoulder. Suppose each dancer is vigorously doing his or her own individual dance. The dancers will collide with each other and with any other objects which may be scattered about the dance floor. If there is some pressure on the whole group to move toward one side of the ballroom, dancing all the while, the collective motion will be random and chaotic, and a lot of energy will be lost in collisions. This situation represents the electrons in a normal metal, colliding with each other and with irregularities or impurities in the crystal lattice. If an electric field is applied and a current induced, collisions will dissipate energy and cause a finite conductivity.

Now suppose the dancers are paired in couples, each pair dancing together. This represents Cooper pairs, but now an important feature of the pairs enters. The pairing interaction is so weak that the two members of a pair are separated on the average by a distance which turns out to be just the coherence length. The average distance between two paired electrons not involved in the same pair, however, is about a hundred times smaller. The partners comprising each couple are not dancing cheek to cheek, but are separated by a hundred other dancers. Consequently, if every couple is going to dance together, it is clear that everybody must dance together. The result is a single coherent motion, with order extending all the way across the ballroom. The superconducting state is something like that. A localized pertubation which might deflect a single electron in the normal state, and thus give rise to some resistance, cannot do so in the superconducting state without affecting all the electrons participating in the superconducting ground state at once. That is not impossible, but extremely unlikely, so that a collective drift of the coherent superconducting electrons, corresponding to a current, will be dissipationless.

The successes of the BCS theory and its subsequent elaborations are manifold. One of its key features is the prediction of an energy gap. Excitations called quasiparticles (which are something like normal electrons) can be created out of the superconducting ground state by breaking up pairs, but only at the expense of a minimum energy of $\Delta$ per excitation; $\Delta$ is called the gap parameter. The original BCS theory predicted that $\Delta$ is related to $T_c$ by $\Delta = 1.76\ kT_c$ at $T = 0$ for all superconductors. This turns out to be nearly true, and where deviations occur they are understood in terms of modifications of the BCS theory. The manifestations of the energy gap in the low-temperature heat capacity and in electromagnetic absorption provide strong confirmation of the theory. The theory accounts for all the thermodynamic properties of superconductors, including such details as deviations from parabolicity of the critical field curve. The theory is intrinsically nonlocal. The Ginzburg-Landau theory and the Pippard nonlocal electrodynamics can be derived from it. The Ginzburg-Landau order parameter $\psi$ can be associated with the BCS ground-state wave function, and the coherence length with the size or range of a Cooper pair.

### Further Experimental Properties

Some experiments which illustrate some special features of the superconducting wave function are developed in the modern theory of superconductivity discussed in this section.

**Flux quantization.** Consider the complex order parameter or wave function $\psi$ for a superconductor in the form of a hollow cylinder. If $\psi$ is to be a well-defined object, its phase $\varphi$ must change by an integral multiple of $2\pi$ along any closed path which lies entirely within the superconductor, including any path which surrounds the hole in the cylinder. There is a fundamental relation between the spatial gradient of $\psi$, hence of its phase, and the magnetic vector potential $\mathbf{A}$. A consequence of this relation and the constraint on the phase change around a closed path is that the hole in the cylinder cannot contain an arbitrary amount of magnetic flux, but only integral multiples of a fundamental quantum of flux, $\Phi_0 = h/2e = 2.07 \times 10^{-15}$Wb in SI units, or $\Phi_0 = hc/2e = 2.07 \times 10^{-7}$ gauss cm$^2$ in cgs units; $h$ is Planck's constant, $c$ is the velocity of light, and $e$ is the electron charge. This is the reason for the quantization of flux in fluxoids in type II superconductors. There the hole in the cylinder is the normal core of the fluxoid. Flux quantization has been observed in macroscopic hollow cylinders. The factor of 2 in the flux quantum is related to the two electrons of a Cooper pair, so that observation of the expected magnitude of the flux quantum may be interpreted as experimental evidence for electron pairing in the superconducting state.

**Quasiparticle tunneling.** The phenomenon of tunneling is a direct consequence of the wave nature of material particles and was recognized very early in the development of quantum or wave mechanics. A particle, such as an electron, can pass into a region which classically would be forbidden to it and, if the region is not infinitely thick, can pass (tunnel) through it. Consider, for example, two metals separated by an insulating barrier which prevents electrons from passing between the metals. The resulting structure, called a junction, will be nonconducting. However, if the barrier is thin enough ($10^{-9}$ to $10^{-8}$ m), electrons can tunnel from one metal to the other and this "tunnel junction" will become conducting. In 1960 I. Giaever discovered that if one or both of the metals in such a junction are superconducting, the dependence of the current on the voltage across the junction becomes highly nonlinear. The lower curve in **Fig. 5** shows an example for a junction composed of two thin films of tin separated by a tin oxide barrier. The junction passes very little current until the voltage reaches a value of about 1.2 mV, where it rises sharply. This behavior is a direct consequence of the existence of the superconducting energy gap. The voltage $V_g$ at which the current rises is related to the gap parameter by the simple relation $eV_g = 2\Delta$. Giaever's discovery made it possible to measure the gap parameter with nothing much more than an ammeter and a voltmeter. Previous determinations of the gap had come from much more difficult very low-temperature heat capacity experiments or far-infrared absorption experiments. The tunnel junction has become the single most valuable tool for the study of the superconducting state. For example, the current-

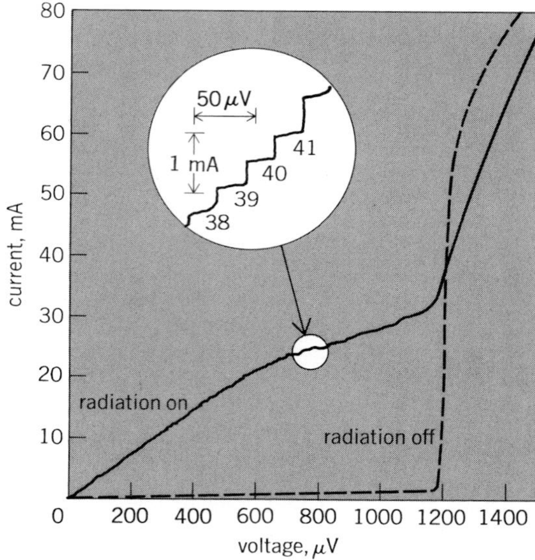


**Fig. 5. Current-voltage curves of a Sn-Sn tunnel junction at 1.2 K (−457.5°F) displaying radiation-induced current steps. (*After W. H. Parker et al., Determination of e/h, using macroscopic quantum phase coherence in superconductors, I, Phys. Rev., 177: 639–664, 1969*)**

voltage characteristic at voltages above the gap voltage contains small structures which can be unraveled to yield the complete energy dependence of the electron-lattice interaction function responsible for the superconductivity. SEE TUNNELING IN SOLIDS.

**Pair tunneling.** In 1962 B. D. Josephson made a remarkable theoretical discovery: Not only can quasiparticles ("normal electrons") tunnel through an insulating barrier between two superconductors, but so can Cooper pairs. This implies a coupling between the superconducting wave functions of the two superconductors which leads to the existence of a tunnel supercurrent which depends on the difference between the phases of the two wave functions. Josephson's predictions were soon verified experimentally. They include the following: It is possible for a lossless supercurrrent to pass through the insulating barrier; this is called the dc Josephson effect. If a voltage $V$ is applied between the two superconductors, an oscillating supercurrent with frequency $2\,eV/h$ exists in the junction; this is the ac Josephson effect. The factor of 2 again comes from the pairing. The upper curve in Fig. 5 shows one way to detect the ac supercurrent. A microwave field of frequency $\nu$ is applied to the junction. This field frequency modulates the ac supercurrent, producing zero-frequency increments in the supercurrent when the frequency of the ac supercurrent is equal to an integer multiple of the microwave frequency. These appear as steps in the current-voltage characteristic of the junction at voltage intervals of $h\nu/2e$. This effect provides by far the most accurate way to measure the fundamental physical constant $h/e$, as well as the basis for the United States national standard of voltage.

A Josephson tunnel junction can be thought of as a quantum phase meter. The Josephson effects have been used to confirm experimentally that the superconducting order parameter has all the quantum-phase coherence characteristics of an atomic wave function, but on a scale $10^{10}$ times larger. The fundamental connection between the quantum phase and the magnetic vector potential makes the Josephson effects incredibly sensitive to magnetic fields. Josephson junctions have been used to detect fields $10^{10}$ times smaller than the Earth's magnetic field and the tiny magnetic fields produced by neural currents in the human brain. SEE JOSEPHSON EFFECT; SQUID.

### FURTHER RESEARCH

Research on superconductivity has continued actively on a variety of fronts. New superconducting materials have been sought, with higher transition temperatures and more favorable properties for practical applications. There have been theoretical conjectures that much higher transition temperatures, perhaps higher than room temperature, might be achieved with exotic materials in which conduction occurs in one- or two-dimensional molecular structures, or through the exploitation of some electron-electron attractive interaction mechanism which is stronger than the electron-lattice interaction which acts in all known superconductors. These possibilities have been pursued. Superconductivity may have a cosmic role, for the interiors of neutron stars and of the planet Jupiter may be superconducting. There has been much interest in fluctuations in the properties of superconductors near the superconducting phase transition, and in the behavior of superconductors forced into states far from thermal equilibrium. An enormous range of practical applications have been investigated, from superconducting electric power transmission lines to superconducting computers.

*D. N. Langenberg*

***Bibliography.*** A. C. Rose-Innes and E. H. Roderick, *Introduction to Superconductivity*, 2d ed., 1977; D. R. Tilley and J. Tilley, *Superfluidity and Superconductivity*, 1975; M. Tinkham, *Introduction to Superconductivity*, 1975, reprint 1980.

## Superheterodyne receiver

A receiver that uses the heterodyne principle to convert the incoming modulated radio-frequency signal to a predetermined lower carrier frequency, the intermediate-frequency (i-f) value. This is done by using a local oscillator tuned simultaneously with the input stage of the receiver, so that the oscillator frequency always differs from that of the incoming carrier by the i-f value.

With a fixed and favorably chosen i-f value, the i-f amplifier can efficiently provide the major portion of the amplification and selectivity required by the receiver. After amplification, the i-f signal is demodulated by the second detector to obtain the desired audio output signal. A similar circuit arrangement is used in television and radar receivers to obtain the desired video output signal. For amplitude-modulated (AM) radio broadcast receivers the i-f value is usually 455 kHz. For frequency-modulated (FM) radio receivers the standard i-f value is 10.7 MHz. For modern television receivers the usual i-f values are about 45 MHz for video and 4.5 MHz for sound.

In a double superheterodyne receiver, the incoming carrier signal is changed to one i-f value for preliminary amplification and filtering, then changed to the final i-f value by beating with another oscillator frequency in a second mixer. This gives higher gain without instability, improves adjacent-channel selectivity, and provides greater suppression of undesired signal frequencies. SEE HETERODYNE PRINCIPLE; RADIO RECEIVER.

*John Markus*

## Superposition theorem (electric networks)

Essentially, that it is permissible, if there are two or more sources of electromotive force in a linear electrical network, to compute at any element of the network the response of voltage or of current that results from one source alone, and then the response resulting from another source alone, and so on for all sources, and finally to compute the total response to all sources acting together by adding these individual responses.

Thus, if a load of constant resistance is supplied with electrical energy from a linear network containing two batteries, two generators, or one battery and one generator, it would be correct to find the current that would be supplied to the load by one source (the other being reduced to zero), then to find the current that would be supplied to the load by the second source (the first source now being reduced to zero), and finally to add the two currents so computed to find the total current that would be produced in the load by the two sources acting simultaneously.

Note that while any one source is being considered all other independent sources are reduced to zero. An independent-voltage source is reduced to zero by making the voltage between its terminals equal zero (short circuit), or an independent-current source is reduced to zero by making current through it equal zero (open circuit).

By means of the principle of superposition, effects are added instead of causes. This principle seems so intuitively valid that there is far greater danger of applying superposition where it is incorrect than of failing to apply it where it is correct. It must be recognized that for superposition to be correct the relation between cause and effect must be linear.

In an electrical network, linearity implies that the parameters of resistance, inductance, and capacitance must be constant (with respect to current or voltage) and that the voltage or current of sources must be independent of, or directly proportional to, other voltages and currents (or their derivatives) in the network. Sources or parameters may vary as functions of some other independent variable such as time, however; an example of this is a source of sinusoidal or other time-varying voltage.

The constant resistance of a metal wire is an example of a linear relation. There is no linear relation between voltage and current in many crystalline materials, however, including those classed as diodes or transistors. In such a nonlinear conductor, the resistance $R$ is not independent of the current $i$. The inductance of a coil is not independent of current if the coil has an iron core; this phenomenon of nonlinearity is termed saturation. The capacitance of certain capacitors is not independent of applied voltage, thus making the current-voltage relation nonlinear. SEE SATURATION.

Linearity requires a proportionality of cause and effect. Thus the relation of current to voltage may be linear, but the relation of current to power ($p = i^2R$) is nonlinear. If a load of constant resistance (as considered above) is supplied from two sources, it would be wrong to attempt to find the total power to the load by adding the two values of power supplied by each of the two sources acting individually.

**Mathematical definition.** Linearity is defined mathematically as follows: If a disturbance $x_1(t)$gives a response $y_1(t)$and a disturbance $x_2(t)$ gives a response $y_2(t)$, then if a disturbance $Ax_1(t)+Bx_2(t)$, in which $A$ and $B$ are constants, gives a response $Ay_1(t) + By_2(t)$, the disturbed system is linear.

Linearity implies homogeneity and additivity. If $x_1(t)$ gives $y_1(t)$ and $x_2(t)$ gives $y_2(t)$, then if $Ax_1(t)$ gives $Ay_1(t)$, the relation is said to be homogeneous. If $x_1(t) + x_2(t)$ gives $y_1(t) + y_2(t)$, the relation is said to be additive.

For example, let current and voltage be related by Eq. (1).

$$v = Ri + \frac{d(Li)}{dt} \tag{1}$$

With a disturbance $i_1$, the response is given by Eq (2).

$$v_1 = R_1 i_1 + \frac{d(L_1 i_1)}{dt} \tag{2}$$

With a different disturbance $i_2$, the response is given by Eq (3).

$$v_2 = R_2 i_2 + \frac{d(L_2 i_2)}{dt} \tag{3}$$

If the disturbance is $Ai_1 + Bi_2$, the response is given by Eq. (4).

$$\begin{aligned} v_3 &= R_3(Ai_1 + Bi_2) + \frac{d[L_3(Ai_1 + Bi_2)]}{dt} \\ &= A\left[R_3 i_1 + \frac{d(L_3 i_1)}{dt}\right] + B\left[R_3 i_2 + \frac{d(L_3 i_2)}{dt}\right] \end{aligned} \tag{4}$$

If $R$ and $L$ are constant, so that $R_1 = R_2 = R_3$ and $L_1 = L_2 = L_3$, then $v_3 = Av_1 + Bv_2$, and hence Eq.(1) is linear. But if $R$ or $L$ changes with the value of current carried, Eq (1) is not linear.

It is hardly necessary to show $p = i_2R$ is not a linear relation between current and power. Current $i_1$ gives $p_1 = i_1^2R$ and $i_2$ gives $p_2 = i_2^2R$, but a current of $i_1 + i_2$ gives $p_3 = (i_1 + i_2)^2R$, which is not $(i_1^2 + i_2^2)R$.

**Uses.** The principle of superposition is possibly the most useful relation in physical theory. In electrical networks it is used in deriving both loop and node equations from branch equations and in many network theorems.

In numerical solutions, superposition provides a means of finding currents and voltages resulting from multiple sources in a network. This is helpful if the method of solution used does not take into account more than one source. Also, it is helpful if two sources do not add to give a convenient function, as, for example, in finding current produced by an alternating-current generator and a direct-current generator in the same network.

Perhaps most important, the concept of fundamental and harmonic frequencies each producing its own response is dependent on the principle of superposition. Thus the principle of superposition underlies network analysis by means of Fourier series, or by

Fourier transformation or Laplace transformation. SEE NETWORK THEORY.

*Hugh H. Skilling*

**Bibliography.** H. H. Skilling, *Electric Networks,* 1974.

## Suppression

The process or technique of reducing electrical interference to acceptable levels or to situations having no adverse effect. Suppression techniques may be applied to the interference source, the intervening path, the victim or receptor, or any combination. Normal strategy for interference control is to first suppress the source, if possible, since it may disturb many victims.

For intentional transmitters, suppressing interference may include reducing or eliminating harmonic radiations, restricting the bandwidth, or restricting levels of unnecessary or excessive modulation sidebands. These are usually accomplished by radio frequency filters. SEE ELECTRIC FILTER.

For many devices involving incidental radiators, such as brush-type motors and fluorescent lights, interference suppression may require both filtering and shielding. Electrical filtering may take the form of transient surge suppressors, feed-through capacitors, electromagnetic interference (EMI) filters, ferrite absorbers, isolation transformers, or Faraday shielded isolation transformers.

Shielding to control radiation involves using metal boxes, cases, cabinet housings, or metalized plastic versions thereof. Since the interconnecting cables between equipment offer the greatest threat as an "antenna farm," the dominant suppression technique is to shield the cables, wires, or harnesses. For the best protection from electromagnetic interference, the cable shield should be designed as an extension of the box or equipment shield. Other forms of interference hardening of cables include twisting parallel wire pairs, multiple-layer shields, and absorbing jackets. Where possible, best electromagnetic compatibility performance is obtained by replacing the signal cables with fiber-optic links. SEE ELECTRICAL SHIELDING.

From a system point of view, the radiated emission propensity or pickup susceptibility of interconnected equipment is proportional to the maximum length or dimension and frequency until this length corresponds to an electrical length of about one-half wavelength. Thus, to help suppress electromagnetic interference, the corresponding frequency should not fall within the passband of victims or receptors. SEE ELECTROMAGNETIC COMPATIBILITY.

*Donald R. J. White*

## Surface acoustic-wave devices

Devices which employ surface acoustic waves (SAW) in the analog processing of electronic signals with frequencies in the range $10^7$–$10^9$ Hz.

**Background.** Surface acoustic waves which contain both compressional and shear components in phase quadrature, propagating nondispersively along and bound to solid surfaces, were discovered by Lord Rayleigh in the 1880s. As an example, earthquakes furnish sources for propagating these waves on the Earth's surface. It is of importance for electronic applications that if the solid is a piezoelectric material, the surface acoustic energy is complemented by a small amount of electric energy. This electric energy provides the physical mechanism for the coupling between conventional electromagnetic signals and propagating surface acoustic waves. The coupling is attained by means of interdigital transducers (IDT). Surface acoustic-wave devices have led to a versatile microminiature technology for analog signal processing in the frequency range $10^7$–$10^9$ Hz. Notable devices include bandpass filters, resonators, oscillators, pulse compression filters, and fast Fourier transform processors. Application areas include the color television consumer market, radar, sonar, communication systems, and nondestructive testing. SEE PIEZOELECTRIC CRYSTAL; PIEZOELECTRICITY.

**Transduction.** The basic arrangement is shown in **Fig. 1**. A piezoelectric substrate, often crystalline quartz, has a polished upper surface on which two transducers, denoted $T$, with terminals $A$ and $A'$, and $B$ and $B'$, are deposited. The left-hand input transducer is connected, via fine bonded leads, to the electric source through an electrical matching network. The right-hand output transducer drives the load $R_L$, usually 50 ohms, through another electrical matching network. $R_g$ and $E_g$ represent the resistance and voltage of the generator. Because these transducers are bidirectional, they lead to devices with at least 6 dB loss even in the passband. The unwanted acoustic waves are absorbed by terminations at the ends of the piezoelectric substrate. At the symmetry plane $C$-$C'$ a metal baffle serves to isolate electromagnetically the two transducers.

The transducers originally demonstrated in 1966 consist of a set of metal interdigital electrodes, each a few hundred nanometers thick, fed from two busbars (**Fig. 2***a*). For this transducer arrangement the period $p$ of the interdigital electrode structure is constant and equals one surface acoustic wavelength $\lambda_0$ at the center of frequency $f_0$ of the response. The width of the metal electrodes is typically $p/4$, being 100 micrometers at $10^7$ Hz and 1 micrometer at $10^9$ Hz. The electrode overlap distance $w$ is also constant and defines the acoustic beam width, which is typically 40 wavelengths. SEE TRANSDUCER.

The 100-μm electrodes are readily fabricated by using techniques standard to the semiconductor integrated circuit industry of metallization: phototoresist, masking, and chemical etching. Important piezoelectric substrates are ST-cut, X-propagating quartz for temperature stability; Y-cut, Z-propagating lithium niobate, because of its high piezoelectric coupling; and bismuth silicon oxide, which has found application in color television filters. SEE INTEGRATED CIRCUITS.

The acoustic response at frequency $f$ for this simplest surface acoustic-wave structure can be calculated approximately by regarding each $N$-period transducer as an end-fire array antenna. For the pair of transducers the acoustic response is proportional to $[(\sin x)/x]^2$, where $x = N\pi(f - f_0)/f_0$, giving a bandpass filter characteristic. The electrical matching networks are normally arranged to minimize filter loss without overriding the acoustic response. The optimum number of periods, $N$, is inversely proportional to the piezoelectric coupling as is the filter bandpass width. SEE ANTENNA.

Delay $T$ is an important parameter in surface acoustic-wave signal processing devices. Here, $T$ is proportional to the center-to-center path separation of the transducer pair and is typically 3 microseconds per centimeter (μs/cm) of piezoelectric substrate length.

**Bandpass filters.** A disadvantage of constant-$p$, constant-$w$ transducers is that the minimum out-of-band rejection is only 26 dB. However, the filter designer can control the characteristics of the filter by varying the overlap between adjacent transducer electrodes, a technique termed apodization (Fig. 2*b*), or by grading the periodicity (Fig. 2*c*). In contrast to conventional *LC* (inductive) filters, surface acoustic-wave filters are members of a class of nonminimum phase networks having the property that linear phase response can be achieved independently of the amplitude response. Further, surface acoustic-wave filters are transversal filters in which the signal is repetitively delayed and added to itself, as in antenna arrays and digital filters. The optimization procedures of digital filters have been applied in the synthesis of surface acoustic-wave filters with equiripple bandpass response. Another basic design procedure is to compute the inverse Fourier transform of the prescribed filter response, giving the impulse response, which is the spatial image desired of the electrodes in the transducer. Due to finite piezoelectric substrate lengths, the infinitely long time-duration impulse response is not realizable. This has necessitated the use of weighting functions to multiply and truncate the impulse response.

A vital factor in surface acoustic-wave filters is amplitude weighting, that is, alteration of the amplitude-frequency response, in order to improve the filter's selectivity. A popular method of achieving this, due to ease of design and relative insensitivity to fabrication errors, has been apodization of the input transducer. However, an apodized transducer generates a spatially nonuniform surface-acoustic wave. This necessitates an output transducer of constant electrode overlap and a few electrodes to reproduce faithfully the apodized transducer response. Undesirable consequences are high loss and poor selectivity for the filter.

One solution to this problem embodies a multistrip coupler (MSC). This device has the property of converting the spatially nonuniform surface acoustic wave generated by one apodized transducer into a spatially uniform wave received by an identical apodized transducer. The apodized transducers incorporate special electrodes to reduce surface acoustic wave impedance mismatch between the unloaded and metallized substrate surface. An alternative approach obtains amplitude weighting by selective withdrawal of electrodes from identical and constant-overlap transducers arranged in nondispersive combination. In this arrangement, the electrodes at the right end of each interdigital transducer are spaced by a large amount (that is, low frequencies are excited), whereas those to the left of both transducers are spaced by a small amount (that is, high frequencies are excited; Fig. 2*c*). Thus, both low- and high-frequency components of the excitation travel exactly the same distance before being received, so that the nondispersive characteristics of the surface acoustic wave are preserved.

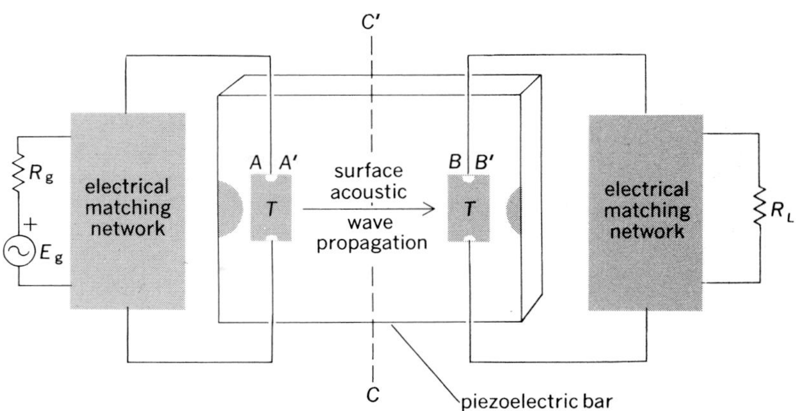


Fig. 1. Basic arrangement of surface acoustic-wave bandpass filter.

Normal and projected performance of surface acoustic-wave bandpass filters are shown in the **table**. Sidelobe rejection specifies the magnitude of the loss of sidelobes, that is, unwanted but naturally occurring responses close to but outside the bandpass, with respect to magnitude of the loss at the center of the bandpass. Ultimate rejection specifies the greatest magnitude of the loss at frequencies far removed from the bandpass region with respect to that at the center of the bandpass. Linear phase deviation expresses the undesired deviation in the response of the filter from a linear phase change with frequency. The majority of the data in the table are not obtainable simultaneously.

The minimum loss of 6 dB assumes a three-transducer configuration in which the outer transducers are connected electrically in parallel. This removes half the 6-dB bidirectionality loss. The remaining 3 dB is composed of resistive losses in the transducers and matching networks; propagation, beam steering, and

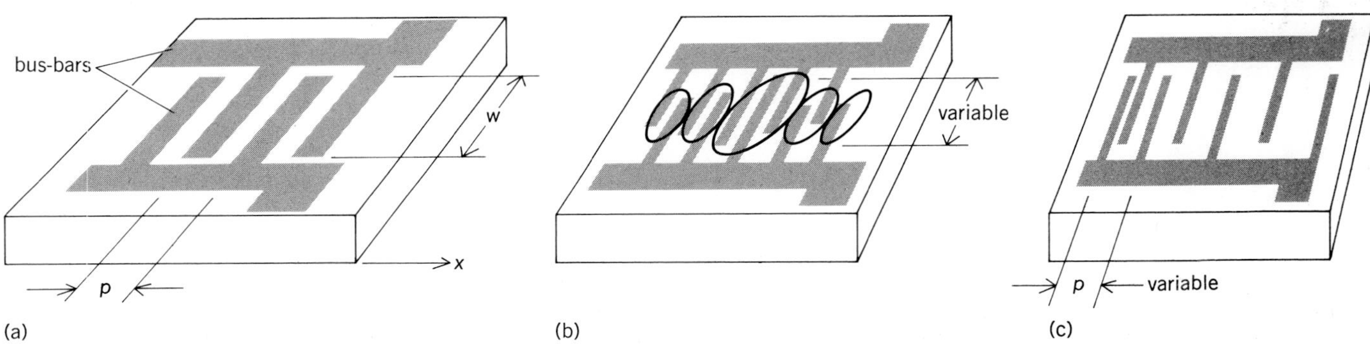


Fig. 2. Transducers. (*a*) Interdigital construction. (*b*) Apodization technique. (c) Graded periodicity technique.

diffraction losses on the piezoelectric; and losses associated with apodization. The projected minimum insertion loss is dependent on the development of better unidirectional transducers.

The minimum transition bandwidth data given in the table are an important indicator of the maximum selectivity inherent in surface acoustic-wave filters. The transition bandwidth must exceed the inverse of the impulse response length of the transducer. Hence, a minimum transition bandwidth is equally applicable to narrow- and wide-band filters. This implies that low shape factors cannot be achieved for filters with extremely narrow bandpass widths, and this has led to the development of the surface acoustic-wave resonator. **Figure 3** shows both the impulse response in the time domain and the bandpass response of a surface acoustic-wave filter having $3.06 \times 10^8$ Hz center frequency and a sidelobe rejection of 60 dB.

The smallest surface acoustic-wave filters are 0.02 in.$^3$ (0.3 cm$^3$) in volume. Unfortunately, high performance as indicated in the table demands complex surface acoustic-wave structures, thus increasing both substrate size and cost. This dilemma presents a considerable challenge for applications in the consumer market. *See* ELECTRIC FILTER.

**Surface acoustic-wave bandpass filter capabilities**

| Parameter | Current | Projected |
|---|---|---|
| Center frequency, $f_0$ (Hz) | $10^7 - 10^9$ | $10^6 - 2 \times 10^9$ |
| 3-dB bandwidth (Hz) | $5 \times 10^4 - 0.4\, f_0$ | $2 \times 10^4 - 0.8\, f_0$ |
| Minimum loss (dB) | 6 | 1.5 |
| Minimum shape factor (ratio of bandpass width at 3 dB and 40 dB) | 1.2 | 1.2 |
| Minimum transition width from bandpass to bandstop (Hz) | $5 \times 10^4$ | $2 \times 10^4$ |
| Sidelobe rejection (dB) | 55 | 65 |
| Ultimate rejection (dB) | 65 | 80 |
| Amplitude of bandpass ripple (dB) | 0.5 | 0.2 |
| Linear phase deviation (degrees) | 5 | 2 |

**Resonators.** The surface acoustic-wave resonator comprises two thin metallic strip arrays, similar to those of the multistrip coupler, each normal to the surface acoustic-wave beams with an interdigital transducer interposed symmetrically for coupling the electromagnetic energy in and out. The metallic strips and the gaps between are arranged to be each $\lambda_0/4$ wide. Cumulative reflection is obtained from each metallic strip array due to the slight surface acoustic-wave impedance discontinuity between each metallic strip and each gap. For Y-cut, Z-propagating lithium niobate, which has an impedance discontinuity of 1.2%, 200 metallic strips are required in the array for a reflection coefficient of 98%. Both resonant and antiresonant behavior can be obtained, depending on whether the spacing between the arrays is an integral number of half-wavelengths of the surface acoustic wave or there is an additional $\lambda_0/4$. The maximum Q and operating frequency achieved with surface acoustic-wave resonators is $10^4$ and $4 \times 10^8$ Hz, respectively, although a Q of $10^5$ seems realizable. Features of the surface acoustic-wave resonator not shared by its bulk-wave counterpart are the ability to control the resonator coupling precisely by the interdigital transducer and a rugged structure. Applications are envisaged as multipole narrow-band filters and in single superheterodyne radio-frequency receivers.

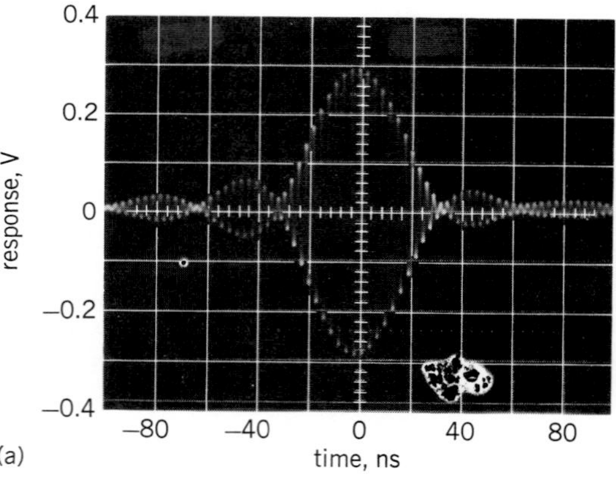


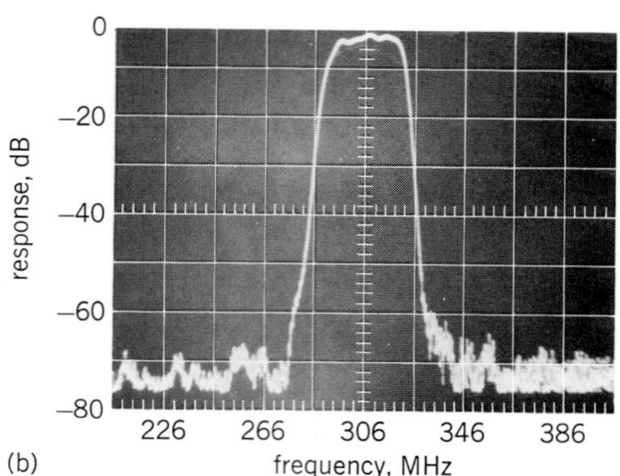


**Fig. 3. Surface acoustic-wave bandpass filter performance, showing oscillograms of (*a*) impulse response and (*b*) bandpass response. (*Texas Instruments*)**

**Oscillators.** Two classes of oscillators are in common use, the quartz crystal oscillator and the *LC* oscillator, including the resonant cavity type. The quartz crystal oscillator is highly stable ($Q > 10^4$) but suffers from a number of disadvantages, including mechanical fragility, low fundamental frequency operation ($< 3 \times 10^7$ Hz), and limited frequency modulation (FM) capability (500 parts per million, or ppm). In contrast, the LC oscillator is much less stable ($Q \ll 10^4$) but has superior FM performance. The surface acoustic-wave oscillator has demonstrated an intermediate stability and modulation capability, with practical advantages over both. The basic surface acoustic-wave oscillator comprises a surface acoustic-wave quartz delay line with a transistor amplifier as the feedback element arranged to give unity gain with an integral number of $2\pi$ phase shifts around the loop.

The frequency of operation is determined by the interdigital transducer pattern and not by a dimension of the quartz crystal. Hence, the crystal is rugged and can be firmly bonded to the encapsulating package. This good thermal contact allows output powers up to

1 W. Performance of the surface acoustic-wave oscillator is strongly determined by the interaction between the amplifier characteristics and the delay line Q. Typical figures are: frequency deviation up to 2%; short-term stability of <1 in $10^9$ for 1 s; medium-term stability of 100 ppm for a temperature excursion of ±72°F (±40°C); and single-sideband FM noise of −138 dB/Hz, 10 kHz away from the carrier. Limits to the long-term stability are not resolved. A level of ±1 ppm per month is achievable following a burn-in period of a month. *See Oscillator.*

**Pulse compression filters.** The goal in pulse compression filters is to output an energy pulse of narrow time duration, with minimal spurious response, when the input of the filter is fed with a coded wave train having a substantially longer time duration. The ratio of the time duration of the input wave train to that of the output pulse is defined as the processing gain, which is equivalent to the improvement in signal-to-noise ratio. Pulse compression filters find application in high-resolution radar systems where the transmitter radiates energy pulses of duration $\Delta T$ which are linearly frequency-modulated over $\Delta f$. The pulse compression filter is employed in the receiver and has a processing gain of $\Delta T \times \Delta f$. Surface acoustic-wave versions of pulse compression filters have found significant engineering application in upgrading the resolution capabilities of airborne radars. Processing gains up to 5000 and spurious responses below 40 dB have been achieved.

Two distinct techniques have been developed for surface acoustic-wave pulse compression filters. The first uses the interdigital transducer of Fig. 2*c* on quartz to yield a quadratic phase-frequency response, or equivalently, a time delay which is a linear function of frequency. Apodization is used to ensure low spurious responses. The acoustic energy is received on the transducer of Fig. 2*a* arranged to have *N* small so that the waveform is undistorted. The second technique involves passing the surface acoustic wave under an array of suitably angled reflective slots. The spacing of these slots determines the frequency selectivity, and the depth of these slots determines the amplitude weighting. The first array of reflective slots is matched by a second group to reform the surface acoustic-wave beam, parallel to but displaced from the incident beam. Thereby, the required pulse compression characteristics are obtained. Dimensionally the slots must have a depth in the region of one-thousandth of an acoustic wavelength, be approximately one-half wavelength wide, and be spaced by one wave-length between centers. Slot depths are typically 3 nanometers at $10^9$ Hz, necessitating controlled ion-beam etching of the lithium niobate substrate. Results for a high-resolution radar module deploying the first technique for realizing an amplitude-weighted surface acoustic-wave pulse compression filter with a processing gain of 80 are shown in **Fig. 4**.

*J. H. Collins*

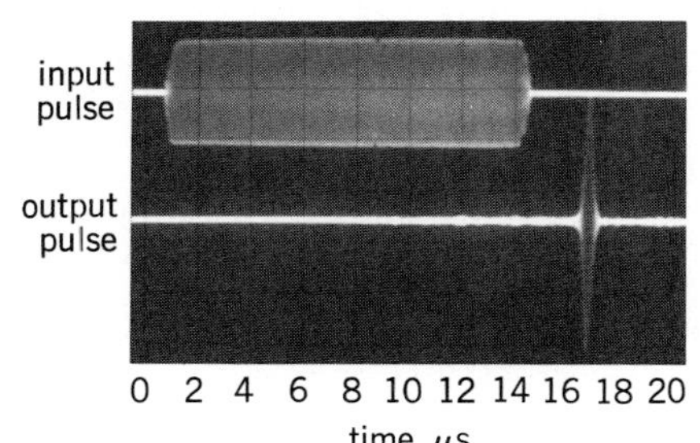


(a)

(b)

**Fig. 4. SAW pulse compression filter for high-resolution radar. (*a*) Oscillograms showing input rectangular pulse centered at 75 MHz and the output compressed pulse, whose sidelobes are below 35 dB. (*b*) Module deploying filter complete with all peripheral electronics. (*Results courtesy of MESL, Scotland*)**

**Bibliography.** *IEEE Trans. Microwave Theory Tech.*, Special Issue on Microwave Acoustics, MTT-21(4), April 1973; *1974 Ultrasonics Symposium Proceedings*, IEEE Cat. 74; W. R. Smith et al., Analysis of interdigital surface wave transducers by use of an equivalent circuit model, *IEEE Trans. Microwave Theory Tech.*, MTT-17(11):856–864, November 1969; R. H. Tancrell, Analytic design of surface wave band pass filters. *IEEE Trans. Sonics Ultrasonics,* SU-21(1):12–22, January 1974.

## Surface-mount technology

A revolutionary packaging technology in which through-hole mounted components are replaced by surface-mounted components. The conventional methods of assembling electronic components onto printed wiring boards, in which wire leads are inserted through holes in the boards, have essentially reached their limits with respect to cost, weight, volume and reliability. For increased board density, the current trend is toward the use of surface-mount technology (SMT), in which usually smaller components are mounted on the surfaces of the boards. This technology makes it possible to produce more reliable assemblies at reduced weight, volume, and cost. The weight of the printed wiring assemblies using surface-mounted components can weigh up to 10 times less than their conventional counterparts and can occupy about one-half to one-third as much space on the printed wiring board surface. *See Printed circuit.*

The assembly is soldered by reflow (vapor phase, infrared) or wave soldering processes, depending upon the mix of surface-mounted and through-hole-mounted components. Examples of surface-mounted active components include small outline integrated circuits (SOIC) and plastic leaded chip carriers (PLCC). The smaller size of surface-mounted components, compared with their conventional equiva-

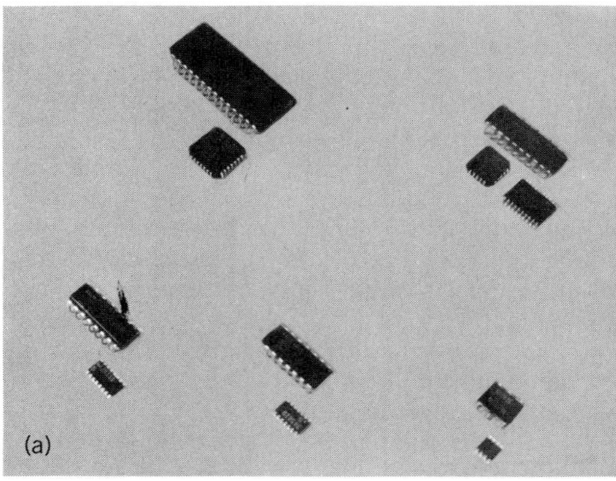

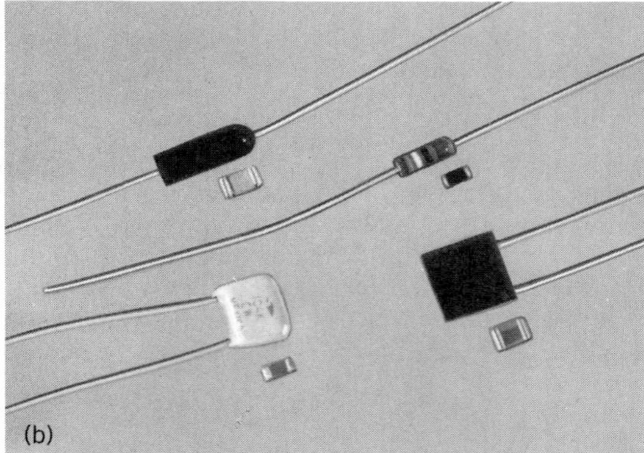

**Fig. 1. Surface-mounted components and their conventional equivalents. (*a*) Active components, (*b*) Passive components.**

lents (**Fig. 1**), and the option of mounting them on either or both sides of the printed wiring board can reduce board area from 20 to 80%. The surface-mounted components, actives and passives, when attached to printed wiring boards, form three major types of surface-mount technology assemblies, commonly referred to as type I, type II, and type III (**Fig. 2**). Type I assemblies consist entirely of surface-mounted components, on either one or both sides of the board. Type II and type III assemblies have both surface-mounted and leaded components; in type II assemblies the surface-mounted components are on both sides of the board, while in type III assemblies they are only on the bottom of the board.



**Fig. 2. Configuration of components in conventional and surface-mounted (types I, II, and III) assemblies, and the soldering processes required for each type.**

**Component identification.** Surface-mounted components, especially resistors and capacitors, are very small, making it very difficult to provide part markings on them. This requires a system of part handling and control to prevent part mixing. If parts do get mixed, they must be either positively identified or discarded. In most cases, discarding such parts is the cheaper alternative. For this reason, it is of critical importance to use surface-mounted chip resistors and capacitors only on tapes and reels that not only provide positive part markings (on the reel cover) but also prevent loss of part solderability of the component terminations during handling.

**Component placement.** The requirements for accuracy in component placement make it almost mandatory to use autoplacement machines to place surface-mounted components on the board. Selection of the appropriate autoplacement machine is dictated by the types of components to be placed and their volume. There are basically four types of autoplacement machines available: in-line placement equipment, simultaneous placement equipment, sequential placement equipment, and sequential/simultaneous placement equipment.

There are many autoplacement equipment machines available in each of the four categories. Guidelines must be established for the selection of a machine specifying, for example, what kind of parts are to be handled; whether they come in bulk, magazine, or on a tape; and whether the machine can accommodate future changes in tape sizes. Selection and evaluation of tapes from various vendors for compatibility with the selected machine is very important. Special features, such as adhesive application, component testing, board handling, and reserve capability for further expansion in a machine, may be of special interest for many applications. Reliability, accuracy of placement, and easy maintenance are important to all users.

**Soldering.** Like the selection of autoplacement machines, the soldering process selection depends upon the type of components to be soldered and whether or not they will be used in combination with leaded parts. There is no one best method of soldering, and the sequence and process of soldering depend upon the type of surface-mounted assembly (Fig. 2). For example, if all components are of surface-mounted types, the reflow method (vapor phase, infrared) may be desirable. However, for type III surface-mount technology, wave soldering is most desirable. No matter which soldering method is chosen, some process issues will require resolution.

***Wave soldering.*** In wave soldering, adhesive is used to glue the passive surface-mounted components onto the bottom of the board, and the whole assembly is wave-soldered in one operation. The surface-mounted components go through the wave.

Outgassing and solder skips are two main concerns in wave soldering. The outgassing or gas evolution occurs on the trailing terminations of chip resistors and capacitors. It is believed to be caused by insufficient drying of flux, and can be corrected by raising the printed wiring assembly preheat temperature. The other concern, solder skips, is caused by the shadow effect of the part body on the trailing terminations. Orienting the part in such a way that both termina-

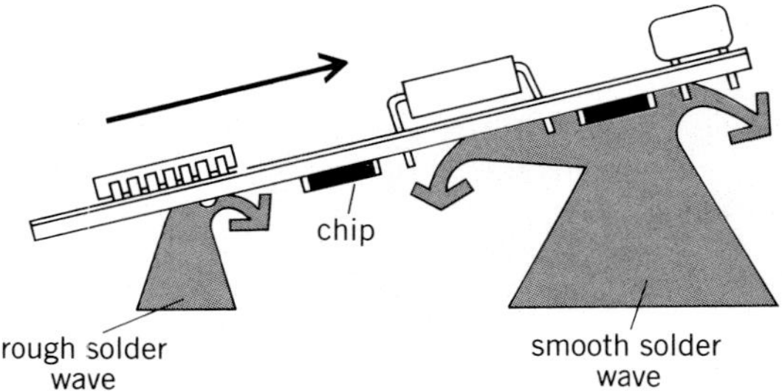


**Fig. 3. Dual-wave soldering system for surface-mounted assembiles.**

tions are soldered simultaneously solves shadow effect problems.

The most common method of solving both outgassing and shadow effect problems is to use the dual-wave system, where the first wave is a rough wave and the second wave is smooth (**Fig. 3**).

***Adhesive application.*** In wave soldering, selection and application of adhesive plays the most critical role. With too much adhesive, no fillets or poor solder fillets may result if adhesive gets on pads. Too little adhesive will fail to accomplish its objective of holding parts through the solder wave. A good adhesive should form a single part, be colored, have a long shelf life, be easy to apply, and have an adequate bond strength with short cure time. In addition, after curing and soldering, the adhesive should remain moisture-resistant, nonconductive, noncorrosive, and be reworkable.

***Vapor-phase soldering.*** Vapor-phase soldering is used for type II and type I assemblies (Fig. 2). Also known as condensation soldering, it uses the latent heat of vaporization of an inert liquid. Solder paste is screened on the board, the part is placed by an autoplacement machine, and the whole assembly is soldered in the vapor of the inert liquid at 419°F (204°C). The vapor is used only as a heating medium. A secondary vapor and cooling coils (**Fig. 4**) are used to minimize the vapor loss of the primary fluid, which is fairly expensive. The main concerns in vapor-phase soldering are part movement and formation of solder balls which can short conductors or component leads. Such problems can be avoided by proper selection of solder paste, pad design, and process control. Both solder joint defects and reliability depend to a great degree on component footprint design (pad size and orientation).

***Infrared reflow soldering.*** In infrared reflow soldering, radiant or convective energy is used to heat the assembly. There are basically two types of infrared reflow processes: focused (radiant) and nonfocused (convective). The latter has proven more desirable for surface-mount technology. The focused infrared process radiates heat directly on the parts and may unevenly heat assemblies. The heat input on the part may also be color-dependent. In the nonfocused or diffused infrared process, the heating medium can be air or an inert gas or simply the convection energy. A gradual heating of the assembly is necessary to drive off volatiles from the solder paste. After an appropriate time in preheat, the assembly is raised to the reflow temperature for soldering and then cooled.

**Cleaning.** Cleaning of surface-mount technology assemblies, in general, is harder than that of conventional assemblies because of smaller gaps between surface-mounted components and the printed wiring board surface. The smaller gap may entrap flux which may cause potential reliability problems if the printed wiring assembly is not properly cleaned. Hence, the cleaning process to be used is dependent upon the flux used for wave soldering. Most companies use rosin-based fluxes generally known as rosin-activated (RA) or rosin-mildly-activated (RMA). For rosin-activated fluxes both solvent and aqueous cleaning are required, whereas for rosin-mildly-activated flux, solvent cleaning alone is sufficient.

**Repair and rework.** Due to the absence of plated through-holes, surface-mounted components are easier to remove and the possibility of thermal damage

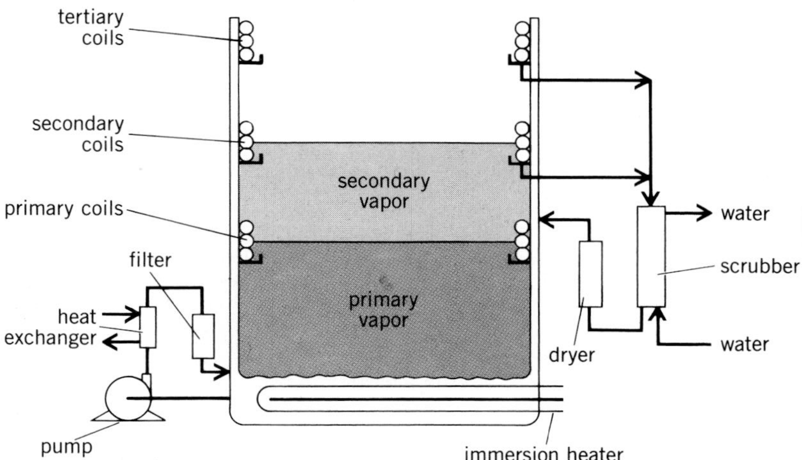


**Fig. 4. Vapor-phase soldering system for surface-mounted assemblies.**

is nonexistent. There are various tools available for removing components. One of the most common is a forklike tip attachment made for the conventional soldering iron to fit the part being removed (**Fig. 5**). Heat is provided by the soldering iron, and the part is removed by twisting the tool. Hot air equipment is also used to remove components. One of the main concerns when this equipment is being used is preventing damage to adjacent components.

**Testability.** Most companies use ''bed-of-nails'' in-circuit testing for conventional assemblies. Use of surface-mounted components does not impact testability if the rule for testability of assemblies is not violated. The rule that must be followed is to provide through-hole passages or test pads to allow electrical access to each test node during in-circuit testing. If

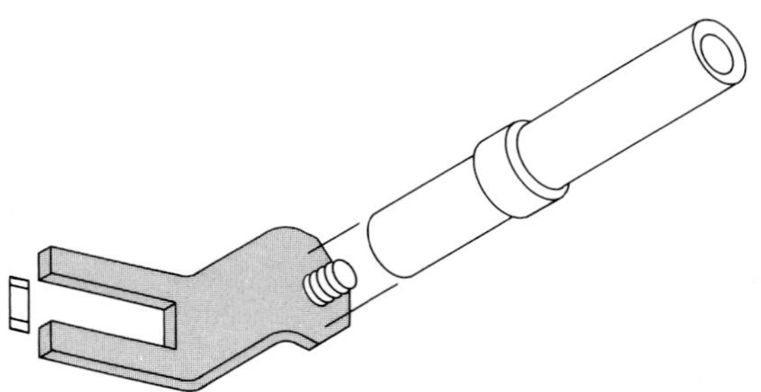

**Fig. 5. Soldering iron tip attachment for removing surface-mounted components.**

possible, this electrical access should be provided both at top and bottom of the wiring board, but the bottom access is a necessity.

*Ray Prasad*

**Bibliography.** C. Capillo, How to design reliability into surface mount assemblies, *Electr. Pack. Prod.*, 25(7):74–80, July 1985; H. W. Marstein (ed.), Automation thrives as companies strive for SMT capability, *Electr. Pack. Prod.*, 25(5):68–74, May 1985; T. Ormond (ed.), Surface mount technology: A special report, *EDN*, 9:104–124, April 18, 1985; R. P. Prasad, Critical issues in implementation of SMD technology, *IPC-Tech. Rev.*, 24(10):15–18, December 1983.

## Surface physics

The study of the structure and dynamics of atoms and their associated electron clouds in the vicinity of a surface, usually at the boundary between a solid and a low-density gas. Surface physics is a branch of solid-state physics which deals with those regions of large and rapid variations of atomic and electron density that occur in the vicinity of an interface between the two "bulk" components of a two-phase system. In conventional usage, surface physics is distinguished from interface physics by the restriction of the scope of the former to interfaces between a solid (or liquid) and a low-density gas, often at ultrahigh-vacuum pressures $p = 10^{-10}$ torr ($1.33 \times 10^{-8}$ newton/m$^2$ or $10^{-13}$ atm).

More specifically, surface physics is concerned with two separate but complementary areas of investigation into the properties of such solid-"vacuum" interfaces. Interest centers on the experimental determination and theoretical prediction of surface composition and structure (that is, the masses, charges, and positions of surface species), of the dynamics of surface atoms (such as surface diffusion and vibrational motion), and of the energetics and dynamics of electrons in the vicinity of a surface (such as electron density profiles and localized electronic surface states). As a practical matter, however, the nature and dynamics of surface species must be determined experimentally by scattering and emission measurements involving particles or electromagnetic fields (or both) external to the surface itself. Thus, a second major interest in surface physics is the study of the interaction of external entities (that is, atoms, ions, electrons, and electromagnetic fields) with solids at their vacuum interfaces. It is this aspect of surface physics which most clearly distinguishes it from conventional solid-state physics, because quite different scattering and emission experiments are utilized to examine surface as opposed to bulk properties of a given sample.

**Physical principles of measurements.** Since the mid-1960s, surface physics has enjoyed a renaissance by virtue of the development of a host of techniques for characterizing the solid-vacuum interface. All of these techniques are based on one of two simple physical mechanisms for achieving surface sensitivity. The first, which is the basis for field-emission and field-ionization microscopy, is the achievement of surface sensitivity by utilizing electron tunneling through the potential-energy barrier at a surface. This concept has been utilized for the direct determinations of the energies of individual electronic orbitals of adsorbed complexes via the measurement of the energy distributions either of emitted electrons or of Auger electrons emitted in the process of neutralizing a slow (energy $E \sim 10$ eV) external ion. It also provided the basis for the recent development of a scanning tunneling microscope to examine directly the atomic structure of surfaces. SEE FIELD EMISSION MICROSCOPY.

The second mechanism for achieving surface sensitivity is the examination of the elastic scattering or emission of particles which interact strongly with the constituents of matter, for example, "low-energy" ($E \lesssim 10^3$ eV) electrons, thermal atoms and molecules, or "slow" (300 eV $\lesssim E \lesssim 10^3$ eV) ions. Since such entities lose appreciable ($\Delta E \sim 10$ eV) energy in distances of the order of tenths of nanometers, typical electron analyzers with resolutions of tenths of an electron volt are readily capable of identifying scattering and emission processes which occur in the upper few atomic layers of a solid. This second mechanism is responsible for the surface sensitivity of photoemission, Auger-electron, electron-characteristic-loss, low-energy-electron-diffraction (LEED), and ion-scattering-spectroscopy techniques. The strong particle-solid interaction criterion which renders these measurements surface-sensitive is precisely the opposite of that used in selecting bulk solid-state spectroscopies. In this case, weak particle-solid interactions (that is, penetrating radiations) are desired in order to sample the bulk of the speciman via, for example, x-rays, thermal neutrons, or fast ($E \gtrsim 10^4$ eV) electrons. SEE PHOTOEMISSION.

**Surface preparation.** An atomically flat surface, labeled by $M(hkl)$, may be visualized as being obtained by cutting an otherwise ideal, single-crystal solid M along a lattice plane specified by the Miller indices ($hkl$), and removing all atoms whose centers lie on one side of this plane. On such a surface the formation of a "selvedge" layer can also be envisaged. Such a layer might be created, for example, by the adsorption of atoms from a contiguous gas phase. It is characterized by the fact that its atomic geometry differs from that of the periodic bulk "substrate." From the perspective of atomic structure, this selvedge layer constitutes the "surface" of a solid. In principle, its thickness is a thermodynamic variable determined from the equations of state of the solid and of the contiguous gas phase. In practice, almost all solid surfaces are far from equilibrium, containing extensive regions (micrometers thick) of surface material damaged by sample processing and handling.

Another reason for the renaissance in surface physics is the capacity to generate in a vacuum chamber special surfaces which approximate the ideal of being atomically flat. These surfaces may be prepared by cycles of fast-ion bombardment, thermal outgassing, and thermal annealing for bulk samples (for example, platelets with sizes of the order of 1 cm × 1 cm × 1 mm) or field evaporation of etched tips for field-ion microscopes. Alternatively, the sample may be cleaved in a vacuum chamber. In such a fashion, reasonable facsimiles of uncontaminated, atomically flat solid-vacuum interfaces of many metals and semiconductors have been prepared and subsequently have been characterized by various spectroscopic techniques. Such characterizations must be carried out in an ultrahigh vacuum ($p \lesssim 10^{-8}$ N/m$^2$), however, so that the surface composition and structure are not altered by gas adsorption during the course of the measurements.

**Experimental apparatus.** Modern experimental surface physics is devoted to the determination of the chemical composition, atomic geometry, and electronic structure of surfaces. Since different measurements are required to assess each of these three aspects of a surface, the typical surface-characterization instrument consists of equipment for carrying out a combination of several measurements in a single ultrahigh-vacuum chamber. Two types of sample geometry are common. Platelet samples are studied using scattering and emission experiments. A typical modern apparatus, such as that shown in **Fig. 1**, contains an electron gun, an ion gun, an electron energy analyzer, a source of ultraviolet or x-ray electromagnetic radiation, and a sample holder permitting precise control of both its orientation and temperature. Occasionally other features (such as a mass spectrometer) also are incorporated for special purposes. For specific applications in which less than a complete characterization of the surface is required, commercial instruments designed to embody only one or two measurements often are available. Such instruments commonly are utilized to determine the chemical composition of surfaces by, for example, ion scattering, secondary ion mass spectrometry, x-ray photoemission, or Auger-electron emission. Obviously, the utility of such instruments is not limited to atomically flat or even crystalline surfaces, so that they find widespread applications in metallurgy and polymer science. Analogous measurements also are commonly utilized for the in-situ characterization of materials made by vacuum deposition techniques, such as sputtering or molecular beam epitaxy.

The second common sample geometry is an etched tip, about a hundred nanometers in radius. Such specimens are studied by field emission and ionization experiments, which provide a direct magnified image of the surface structure in contrast to the statistical description of platelet surfaces afforded by instruments like that shown in Fig. 1.

**Data acquisition, analysis, and theory.** Given the ability to perform surface-sensitive spectroscopic measurements, questions naturally arise concerning analysis of the raw spectra to extract parameters characterizing the structure of a given surface and the synthesis of such data to form a coherent picture of the behavior of electrons and atomic species at surfaces. Thus, surface physics may be divided into three types of activity: the acquisition of surface-sensitive spectroscopic data, the analysis of these data using physical models of the appropriate scattering or emission spectroscopy, and the construction of broad theoretical models of surface structure and properties to be tested via critical comparison of their predictions with the results of such data analyses.

***Ground- and excited-state properties.*** Theoretical models have been proposed for the description of two distinct types of surface properties. The stability of surface structures is examined by calculations of ground-state properties, such as surface energies or effective potential-energy diagrams for adsorbed species. These quantities are difficult to measure experimentally, although they are the most direct manifestations of the intrinsic behavior of an undisturbed surface. The interactions of external projectiles or fields with a solid create excited states of the electrons or atoms within the solid. Consequently, the associated scattering and emission spectra indicate the nature and energies of these excited states (called excitations) rather than of the ground state. Two kinds of excitations occur. Electronic excitations are generated when a disturbing force causes the electrons in the solid to alter their quantum states, whereas atomistic excitations are associated with the vibration or diffusion of atomic species (such as adsorbed atoms or molecules). It is important to distinguish between ground-state properties, electronic excitations, and atomistic excitations because different models are used to describe each of these three types of phenomena.

***Quantum theory of surfaces.*** The theory of the properties of solid surfaces does not differ in any fundamental way from the quantum theory of bulk solids. Specifically, the conventional quantum theory of interacting electron systems is thought to be applicable, although technical refinements are required because of the loss of translational symmetry and the presence of large electron density gradients normal to the surface.

***Macroscopic models.*** It is premature to speak of an embracing theory of surface phenomena. Rather, a diverse array of specific models have been proposed for the description of various properties. In the case of macroscopic models, the presence of a surface is treated as a boundary condition on an otherwise continuum theory of bulk behavior. Such models have found widespread use in semiconductor and insulator physics because the penetration depth of electrostatic fields associated with surface charges usually is large ($\lambda_e \sim 10^4 - 10^5$ nm) relative to the spatial extend of the charges themselves ($d \lesssim 1$ nm). To describe the atomistic and electronic properties associated with the upper few atomic layers at a surface, however, one must make use of a description of surfaces at the atomistic or electronic level. *See Semiconductor.*

***Microscopic models.*** Four major classes of microscopic models of surface properties have been explored. The simplest of these consists of models in which consideration of the electronic motion is suppressed entirely, and the solid is visualized as composed of atomic species interacting via two-body forces. While such models may suffice to describe the vibrational motion of atoms near a surface, they are inadequate to describe ground-state properties such as adsorbate potential-energy curves. The next more sophisticated models are empirical quantum chemical models (such as ''tight-binding'''' or ''empirical pseudopotential'' models in solid-state terminology), in which electronic motions are considered explicitly but electron-electron interactions are incorporated either phenomenologically or not at all. Such models have proved useful in solid-state physics, although their value for surface physics is more limited because the large charge rearrangements (relative to the bulk) which occur at surfaces require an accurate, self-consistent treatment of both electron-electron and electron-ion interactions. The simplest model in which electron-electron interactions are treated explicitly is the ''jellium'' model of metals, in which the positive charge associated with the ion cores immersed in the sea of conduction electrons is replaced by a uniform positive ''background'' charge terminating along a plane. This model permits an informative but approximate treatment of electron-electron interactions at the expense of losing the effects of atomic lattice structure because of the uniform-positive-background hypothesis. Electronic computers have permitted, however, the construction of more realistic pseudopotential, local-density, and quantum-chemical mod-

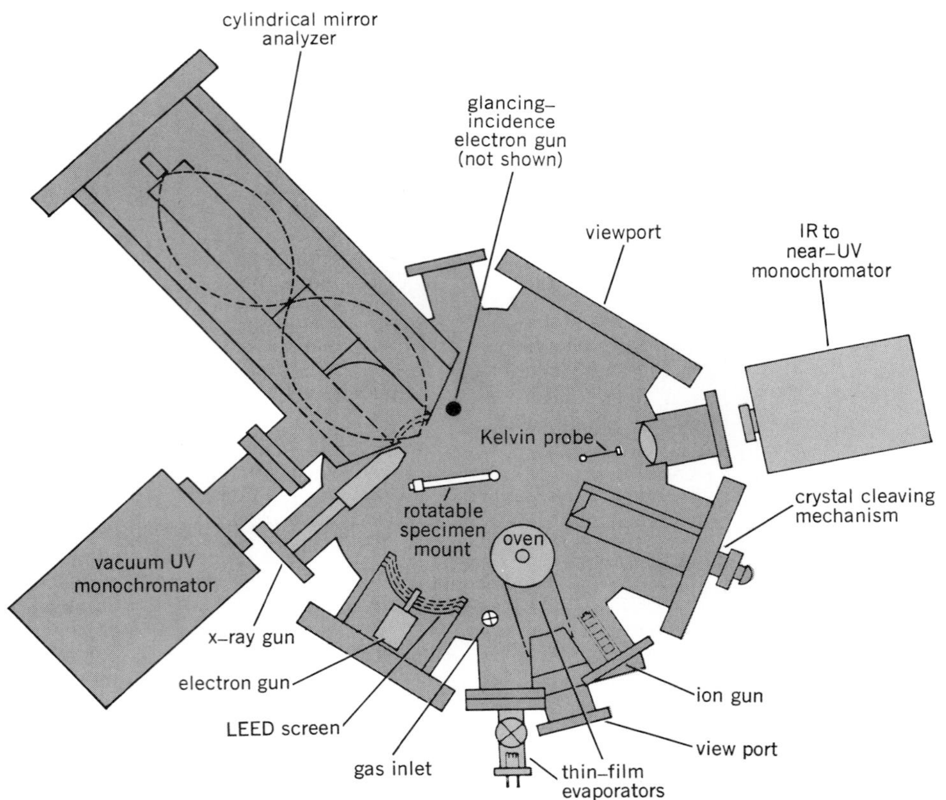


**Fig. 1. Photograph and schematic diagram of modern multiple-technique ultra-high-vacuum surface characterization instrument for study of insulator surfaces. (*L. J. Brillson, Xerox Corporation*)**

els in which both the electron-electron and electron-ion interactions can be treated in a self-consistent, if approximate, fashion. Such models have been applied to examine ground-state electronic charge densities and localized electronic surface states at the surfaces of simple (that is, *s-p* bonded) and transition metals, as well as semiconductors. The major tests of their adequacy arise from comparisons of their predictions with measured work functions, photoemission spectra, and characteristic electron-loss spectra. Quite detailed calculations of the work functions, surface-state eigenvalue spectra, and surface geometries are now available for a variety of metal and semiconductor surfaces. Indeed, the geometries of both metal and semiconductor surfaces can be predicted semiquantitatively by energy-minimization techniques.

***Theoretical models for data analysis.*** Another distinct but important group of theoretical models in surface physics consists of those utilized to analyze observed scattering and emission spectra in order to extract therefrom quantitative assessments of the atomic and electronic structure of surfaces. These models differ substantially from their bulk counterparts because of the necessity of strong particle-solid interactions to achieve surface-sensitive spectroscopies. Consequently, the fundamental assumption underlying the linear-response theory of bulk solid-state spectroscopies—that is, the appropriate particle-solid interaction is weak and hence can be treated by low-order (usually first) perturbation theory—is invalid. This fact results in collision theories of surface-sensitive particle-solid scattering exhibiting a considerably more complicated analytical structure in order to accommodate the strong elastic as well as inelastic scattering of the particle by the various constituents of the solid.

***Applications to LEED and photoemission.*** While the above considerations are quite general, the special case in which they have been developed in most detail is the coherent scattering (that is, diffraction) of low-energy electrons from the surfaces of crystalline solids. This is an important case because elastic low-energy electron diffraction (ELEED) is the analog of x-ray diffraction for surfaces—that is, it is the major vehicle for the achievement of a quantitative surface crystallography. Since 1968 quite complete quantum-field-theory models of the ELEED process have been developed, tested, and reduced to computational algorithms suitable for the routine analysis of ELEED intensity data. From such analyses the surface atomic geometries of the low-index faces of a host of metals and semiconductors have been determined, as have the geometries of a wide variety of overlayer structures. Similar quantitative analyses of inelastic low-energy electron diffraction (ILEED) intensities have yielded the energy-momentum relations of collective surface electronic excitations (surface plasmons). Using the techniques developed in the theory of LEED, analogous models of the diffraction of photogenerated electrons have been developed and applied to determine the atomic geometry of adsorbate systems via the analysis of photoemission spectra.

***Data acquisition.*** It is the development of a host of novel surface-sensitive spectroscopic techniques, however, which has provided the foundation for the renaissance in surface physics. Having recognized that low-energy electrons, thermal atoms, and slow ions all constitute surface-sensitive incoming or exit entities in a particle-solid collision experiment, one can envisage a wide variety of surface spectroscopies based on these plus quanta of electromagnetic radiation (photons) as possible incident or detected species. Most of these possibilities have been realized in some form. The selection of which technique to use in a particular application depends both upon what one wishes to learn about a surface and upon the relative convenience and destructiveness of the various measurements.

Typically, one wishes to determine the composition of a surface region, and often to ascertain its atomic geometry and electronic structure as well. For planar surfaces of crystalline solids, measurement of the rms surface-atom displacements is an ancillary to that of the atomic geometry because the values of these displacements emerge from an examination of the temperature dependence of the same ELEED intensities whose analysis yields the atomic structure of the surface. In the measurement of any of these quantities, however, important issues are the spatial and depth resolution of the possible techniques. Typically the depth resolution is determined by the particle–solid force law of the incident and exit particles, higher resolution being associated with stronger inelastic collision processes. The lateral spatial resolution depends on the ability to focus the incident beam. It is of the order of 1 $cm^2$ for photon beams, $10^{-8}$ to $10^{-12}$ $cm^2$ for electron beams, and $10^{-8}$ $cm^2$ for ion beams. Thus, scanning microscopies are both feasible and common with electron and ion beams but not with photon beams. A scanning microscope based on tunneling from a mobile mounted field-emission tip has been developed. Depth resolution is a single monolayer for thermal-atom and slow-ion scattering, and a few monolayers for slow-electron scattering. It can become 1000 atomic layers or more, however, for fast (MeV) ions and (10 keV) electrons.

***Surface composition.*** The elemental composition of surfaces is specified by measuring the masses or atomic numbers, or both, of resident species. Their masses may be ascertained either by the elastic backscattering of slow incident ions (ion scattering spectrometry, or ISS) or by using such ions to erode the surface, detecting the ejected surface species in a mass spectrometer (secondary ion mass spectrometry, or SIMS).

The atomic numbers of surface species are determined by measuring the energy of tightly bound "core" electrons. A schematic diagram illustrating the nature and labeling of the various physical processes which can be utilized to accomplish this task is shown in **Fig. 2**. An electron, photon, or chemical species incident on a surface excites a low-energy core electron. The binding energy of this electron commonly is determined directly by measuring the energy loss of the incident electron (characteristic loss spectroscopy, or CLS), the energy of the core electron ejected by an incident x-ray photon (x-ray photoelectron spectroscopy, or XPS, sometimes referred to as electron spectroscopy for chemical analysis, or ESCA), or the threshold energy of an incident particle necessary to generate a threshold in the secondary x-ray yield (soft-x-ray appearance potential spectroscopy, or SXAPS). Alternatively, the binding energy of the core electron may be ascertained by "secondary" processes in which an initially empty core state (generated by a direct process) is filled by an electron in a higher energy state. If the filling process is radiative recombination, then the energy of the emitted x-ray yields the binding energy (soft x-ray emission spectroscopy). If this process is radiationless, however, then the energy of the electron excited by the

Auger process indicates the binding energy of the initially empty core state (Auger electron spectroscopy, or AES).

These techniques operate on the dictionary premise; that is, calibration spectra are obtained on surfaces of independently known composition, with elemental analysis on unknown samples being performed by comparison of their spectra with the reference calibration spectra. Consequently, although the detailed interpretation of observed line shapes often has eluded surface physicists, the use of these spectroscopies for elemental analysis has proved both practical and eminently useful. Difficulties in interpretation usually preclude the use of these techniques for quantitative chemical analysis (for example, the determination of whether C and O are adsorbed on aluminum as CO, $CO_2$, or C on $Al_2O_3$, and so on). Progress has been made, however, in developing this aspect of the core-electron spectroscopies.

***Surface atomic geometry.*** The atomic geometry of planar surfaces of crystalline solids usually is obtained by electron diffraction, although in certain cases slow-ion backscattering, MeV ion channeling, photoelectron diffraction, surface-sensitive extended x-ray absorption fine structure, or valence-electron photoemission spectroscopy also may be employed. Two experimental configurations commonly are used, as indicated in **Fig. 3**. The reflection high-energy electron diffraction (RHEED) configuration embodies glancing incidence electrons at keV energies. It yields primarily the space-group symmetry of the surface, and is quite sensitive to surface topography. The ELEED experiment consists of measuring the backscattering intensities of electrons in the energy range 50 eV $\lesssim E \lesssim$ 500 eV. The configuration of diffracted beams reveals the space group symmetry of the surface structure, whereas analysis of their intensities permits determination of their atomic geomtry. In the case of tip sample geometries, field-ion microscopy permits the direct imaging of atoms on the tip surface.

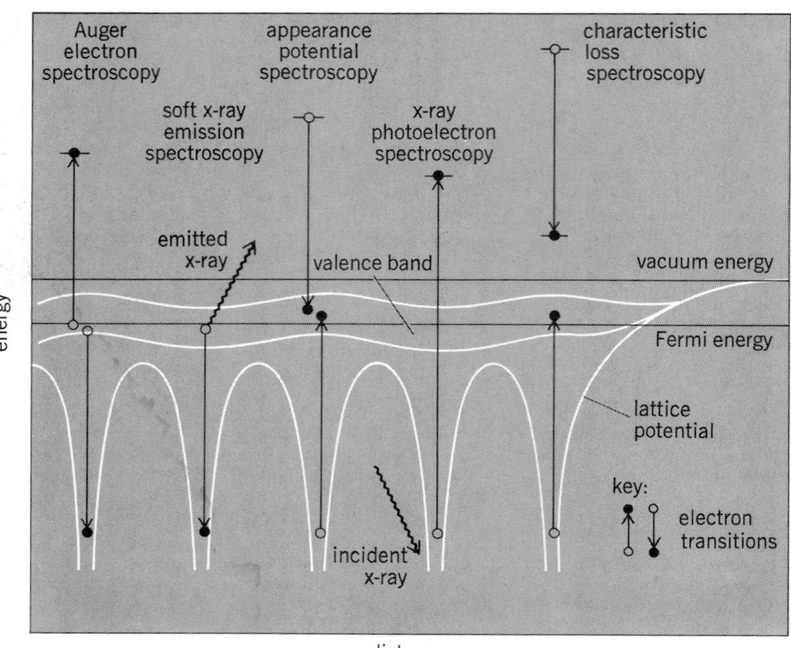


**Fig. 2. Schematic diagram of the core-electron transitions utilized to ascertain the atomic number of surface species. (*After R. L. Park, Inner-shell spectroscopy, Phys. Today, 28(4):52–59, April 1975*)**

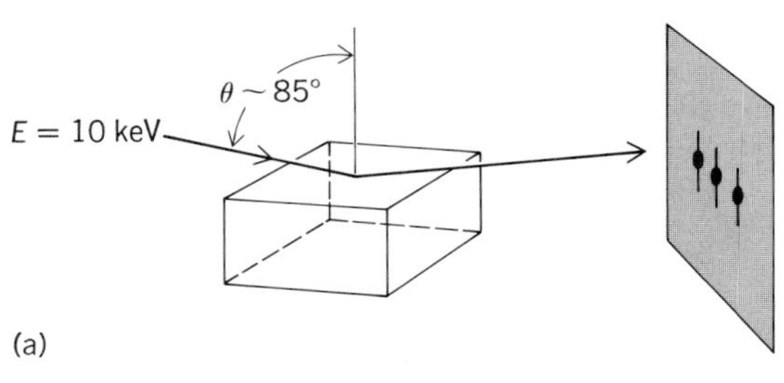


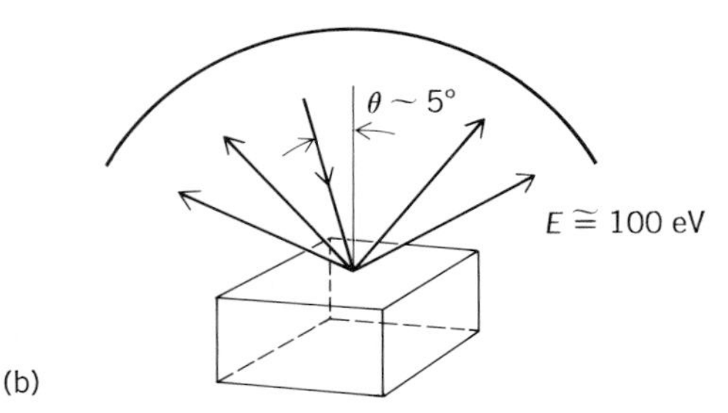


**Fig. 3. Schematic diagram of the two electron diffraction techniques used to determine the geometry of single-crystal surface. (*a*) Reflection high-energy electron diffraction (RHEED). (*b*) Elastic low-energy electron diffraction (ELEED). (*After I. Prigogine and S. A. Rice, eds., Adv. Chem. Phys., 27(1):1–209, 1974*)**

***Surface atomic motion.*** The vibrational motion of surface species may be examined either by analysis of the temperature dependence of ELEED intensities or by direct observation of small ($\Delta E \sim 0.01$ eV) electron energy losses caused by the excitation of a normal mode of vibration. The first approach provides the rms vibrational amplitudes of surface species, whereas the second yields the frequencies of localized ''surface'' normal modes of vibration. Nonstandard equipment is required in both cases: an ultrahigh-vacuum goniometer embodying precise temperature control in the former, and a high resolution ($\Delta E \lesssim 0.01$ eV) electron spectrometer in the latter. Both high-resolution electron energy-loss spectroscopy (HREELS: $\Delta E \sim 0.01$ eV) and infrared reflection and transmission spectroscopy have become popular techniques for the measurement of the vibrational spectra of adsorbed species.

***Surface electronic structure.*** The electronic structure of a solid-vacuum interface is studied by measuring the emission of valence electrons (induced by external fields, electrons, ions, or photons) or the inelastic scattering of an incident electron. A special situation arises when an emitted Auger electron is a valance electron. In this case, the initially empty core state is highly localized in space. Consequently, the emission line shape is a measure of the local electronic structure in the vicinity of this core state. The shifts in energy of core-level photoemission and Auger transitions (called chemical shifts) caused by the nearby electronic charge densities also yield an indication of the local electronic structure around a particular kind of surface atom.

In contrast to these emission processes involving localized core electrons, the photoemission, field-emission, ion-neutralization, and characteristic-loss spectroscopies of valence electrons provide measures of their average behavior in the vicinity of a surface. Indeed, for precisely this reason such spectra from clean surfaces may be difficult to interpret because the distinction between ''bulk'' and ''surface'' features is often vague. Thus, their major use has occurred in the arena of chemisorption, in which case the changes in spectra upon adsorption can be monitored, and qualitative features of the electronic structure of the chemisorbed complexes inferred therefrom. A proper theoretical analysis of these valence electron emission processes is needed to convert the observed spectra into quantitative indicators of surface structure. Such analyses are not yet routine, although they have been given for a few exemplary materials like clean Ni and GaAs surfaces and a few chemisorption systems. The advent of synchrotron radiation has provided a major incentive for the development of computer programs to perform such analyses.

*C. B. Duke*

**Bibliography.** C. R. Brundle and H. Morawitz (eds.), Vibrations at surfaces, *J. Electron Spect. Rel. Phenom.*, vols. 29 and 30, 1983; L. A. Casper and C. J. Powell (eds.), *Industrial Applications of Surface Analysis*, 1982; H. L. Davis (ed.), Surface physics, *Phys. Today*, special issue, 28(4):23–71, April 1975; H. L. Davis (ed.), Vacuum: A special report, *Phys. Today*, 25(8):23–58, August 1972; J. W. Gadzuk (ed.), Solid films and surfaces, *Appl. Surf. Sci.*, vols. 11 and 12, 1982; F. Garcia-Moliner and F. Flores, *Introduction to the Theory of Solid Surfaces*, 1979; F. O. Goodman (ed.), *Dynamic Aspects of Surface Physics: Proceedings of the International School of Physics 'Enrico Fermi,'* course 58, 1975; K. Heinz et al., *Structural Studies of Surfaces*, 1982; F. J. Himpsel and R. W. Klaffky (eds.), *Science with Soft X-Rays*, 1984; H. Ibach (ed.), *Electron Spectroscopy for Surface Analysis*, 1977; T. S. Jayadevaiah and R. Vanslow (eds.), Surface science: Recent progress and perspectives, *Crit. Rev. Solid State Mater. Sci.*, vol. 7, no. 2–4, vol. 8, no. 1–2, 1978, vol. 10, no. 2–4, 1982; S. R. Morrison, *The Chemical Physics of Surfaces*, 1977; I. Prigogine and S. A. Rice (eds.), Aspects of the study of surfaces, *Adv. Chem. Phys.*, vol. 27, 1974; Proceedings of the Annual Surface Science Symposia of the American Vacuum Society, *J. Vacuum Sci. Tech.*, January and February 1976–1986, M. Prutton, *Surface Physics*, 1975; G. A. Somorjai and M. A. Van Hove, *Adsorbed Monolayers on Solid Surfaces*, 1979.

## Surging

A sudden and momentary change of voltage or current in a circuit. It can be due to a sudden change in the applied input signal, a sudden change in the load placed on the circuit, or the action of a relay, switch, or other device that changes operating conditions within the circuit. The resulting surges or transients are often called pulses or impulses when they have only one polarity. An oscillatory surge includes both positive and negative polarity values. Surging in electric circuits corresponds to overshooting. Cathode-ray oscilloscopes are frequently used to obtain visual patterns of the transient voltages due to surging. SEE ELECTRIC TRANSIENT.

*John Markus*

## Susceptance

The imaginary part of the admittance of an alternating-current circuit.

The admittance, $Y$, of an alternating current circuit is a complex number given by Eq. (1). The imaginary

$$Y = G + jB \quad (1)$$

part, $B$, is the susceptance. The units of susceptance like those of admittance are called siemens or mhos. Susceptance may be either positive or negative. For example, the admittance of a capacitor $C$ at frequency $\omega$ is given by Eq. (2), and so $B$ is positive. For an

$$Y = jC\omega = jB \quad (2)$$

inductor $L$, the admittance is given by Eq. (3), and so

$$Y = -j/L\omega = jB \quad (3)$$

$B$ is negative.

In general, the susceptance of a circuit may depend on the resistors as well as the capacitors and inductors. For example, the circuit in the **illustration** has

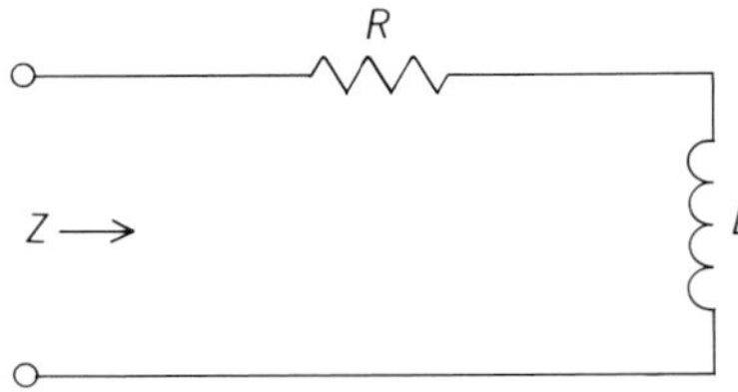


**Circuit with a resistor and inductor in series.**

impedance given by Eq. (4) and admittance given by

$$Z = R + jL\omega \quad (4)$$

Eq. (5), so that the susceptance, given by Eq. (6),

$$Y = \frac{1}{R + jL\omega} \quad (5)$$

$$B = \frac{-L\omega}{R^2 + L^2\omega^2} \quad (6)$$

depends on the resistor $R$ as well as the inductor $L$. SEE ADMITTANCE; ALTERNATING-CURRENT CIRCUIT THEORY; ELECTRICAL IMPEDANCE.

*J. O. Scanlan*

## Sweep generator

An electronic circuit that generates a voltage or current, usually recurrent, as a prescribed function of time. The resulting waveform is used as a time base to be applied to the deflection system of an electron-beam device, such as a cathode-ray tube. Sweep generators are classified as linear, circular, rotating radial, or hyperbolic.

**Linear sweep generation.** A linear sweep generator provides a current or voltage that is a linear function of time. The waveform is usually recurrent at uniform periods of time (**Fig. 1**). The deflection of the electron beam in a cathode-ray tube of the type normally used in the cathode-ray oscilloscope may be expressed by Eq. (1), where $k$ is a constant which is

$$d = kv_d \quad (1)$$

inversely proportional to the beam-accelerating potential, and $v_d$ is the potential applied between the deflection plates. Thus, if the sweep waveform applied to the plates has the form $v_d = k_2t$ at repeating intervals, the deflection of the beam between the plates will be a linear function of time, recurrent at the same rate. SEE SAWTOOTH-WAVE GENERATOR.

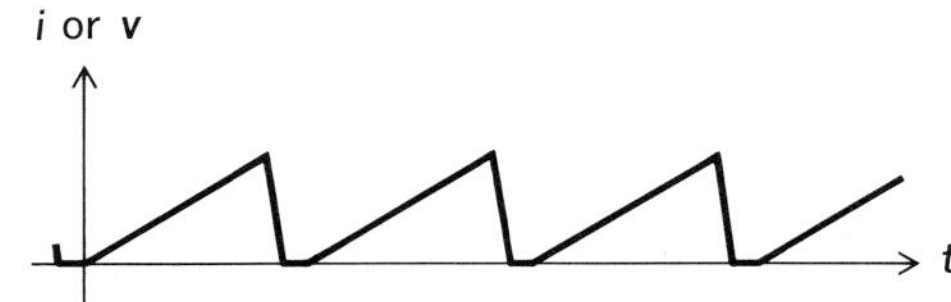


**Fig. 1. Sawtooth wave.**

If the deflection system in a cathode-ray device is electromagnetic, the deflection of the beam is proportional to the transverse magnetic flux density in the deflection region. In this case, the deflection is approximately proportional to the current in the deflection coils, external to the tube, which produce the magnetic field. The sweep waveform is a waveform of current rather than voltage. SEE OSCILLOSCOPE.

The well-known raster scan of the television system is produced if simultaneously linear recurrent sweep waveforms are applied to the horizontal and vertical deflection systems of the cathode-ray device, and the vertical period is many times longer than the horizontal period (**Fig. 2**). Thus a number of equally spaced, nearly horizontal scans are produced, the number being the ratio of the horizontal sweep period to the vertical sweep period. In the cathode-ray oscilloscope, a desired time-varying function may be visually presented by applying a linear voltage sweep waveform to the horizontal deflection system and the function to be plotted to the vertical system. Where

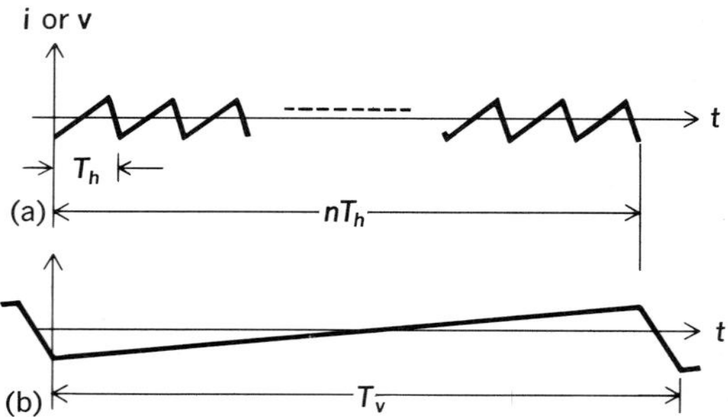


**Fig. 2. Waveforms producing the raster scan. (*a*) Horizontal sweep. (*b*) Vertical sweep.**

the raster scan is used, as in the television receiver, the information to be plotted usually appears on the viewing screen as intensity variations produced by modulation of the current in the cathode-ray tube beam. SEE TELEVISION SCANNING.

**Circular sweep generation.** A circular sweep is generated by applying a constant-frequency sinusoid to the horizontal component of a deflection system and another of the same frequency but shifted in phase by 90° to the vertical component. If the horizontal component of deflection $d_x$ is $A \cos \omega t$, and the vertical component $d_y$ is $A \sin \omega t$, the total deflection $d$ is the vector sum $\sqrt{d_x^2 + d_y^2}$, which equals $A$. The deflection path is circular at a constant radius $A$. The angular position $\theta$, with respect to the horizontal, is given by $\tan \theta = \tan \omega t$. The angular rate of change of the deflected beam is constant.

A spiral scan is generated if, in addition to the sinusoidal $x$ and $y$ components, a linear sawtooth waveform ($v = kt$) is used to modulate equally both the horizontal and voltage deflection waveform (**Fig. 3**). Thus the deflection is given by Eq. (2), which reduces

$$d = \sqrt{A^2k^2t^2 \cos^2 \omega t + A^2k^2t^2 \sin^2 \omega t} \qquad (2)$$

to Eq. (3). If the active period of the sawtooth is $n$

$$d = Akt \qquad (3)$$

times the period of the sinusoid, the spiral will have $n$ revolutions for each period of the sawtooth. Circular and spiral sweeps are useful in special forms of oscilloscopes where a long time base is desirable.

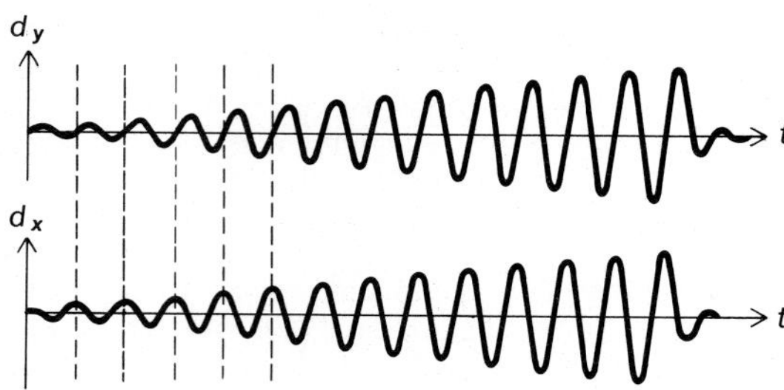


**Fig. 3. Waveforms producing spiral scan.**

**Rotating radial sweep generation.** A rotating radial sweep may be generated by applying a linear sawtooth of current to the deflection system of a magnetically deflected cathode-ray device and rotating the deflection coil producing the magnetic field at a constant angular velocity. Such a sweep may also be generated by using a fixed position deflection system having separate $x$ and $y$ components of deflection. The same combination of linear and sinusoidal modulation as that of the spiral sweep may be used, except that the period of the linear modulation component to the $x$-$y$ deflection system must be short compared to the period of the angular deflection. As indicated in **Fig. 4**, such a combination of sweeps produces one complete radial line for a negligible change in angle. The rotating radial sweep is most widely used in radar display systems, where the angle of rotation is made synchronous with the scan angle of a radar antenna. The linear radial sweep is proportional to radar range. Thus intensity modulation on a display cathode-ray tube having such sweeps will present a true position of individual radar returns. SEE RADAR.

**Hyperbolic sweep generation.** There are applications, particularly in airborne radar systems, where hyperbolic sawtooth sweeps are preferred to linear sawtooth sweeps. Such a hyperbolic sweep, shown in **Fig. 5**, may be given by Eq. (4). Such a sweep is

$$d = k\sqrt{t^2 - T_0^2} \qquad (4)$$

asymptotic to a linear sweep for large values of $t$, but

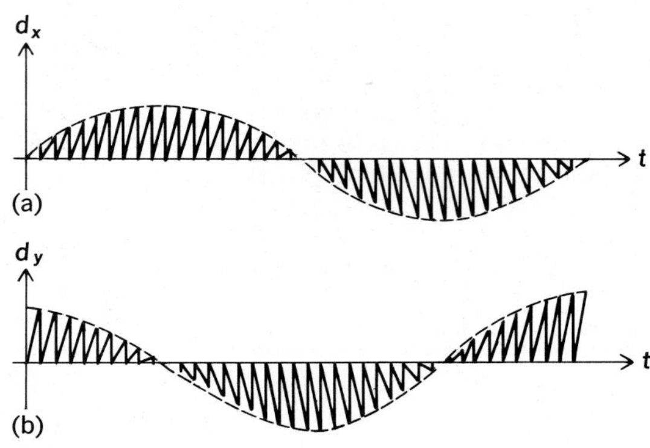


**Fig. 4. Components of rotating radial sweep. (*a*) Horizontal sweep. (*b*) Vertical sweep.**

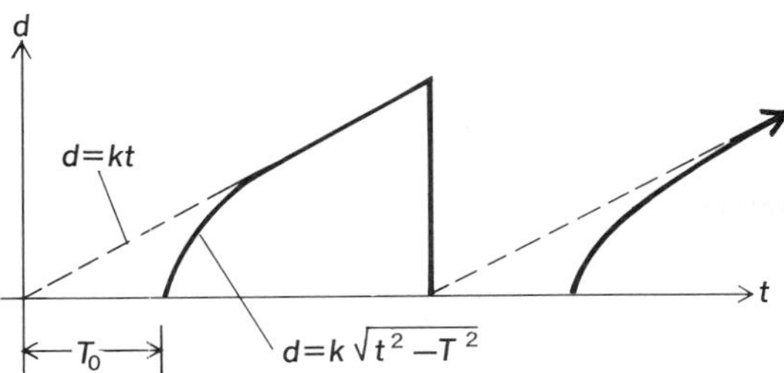


Fig. 5. Hyperbolic sweep.

is delayed with respect to the beginning of it by a time, $T_0$. Such a hyperbolic sweep used in a rotating radial sweep system provides for true ground range radar mapping in an airborne system. Here the time $T_0$ is made equal to $h/c$, where $h$ is the height of the aircraft, $c$ is the velocity of propagation of electromagnetic energy. The factor $k$ is a constant which represents the scale factor of the display.

Hyperbolic sweeps may be generated as a modification of the type of circuitry used in the generation of sawtooth sweep waveforms.

*Glenn M. Glasford*

**Bibliography.** D. G. Fink and D. Christiansen, *Electronics Engineers' Handbook*, 2d ed., 1982; J. Millman, *Microelectronics*, 1979; J. Millman and H. Taub, *Pulse, Digital and Switching Waveforms*, 1965; L. Strauss, *Wave Generation and Shaping*, 2d ed., 1970.

## Switched capacitor

A module consisting of a capacitor with two metal oxide semiconductor (MOS) switches connected as shown in **Fig. 1***a*. These elements in the module are easily realized as an integrated circuit on a silicon chip by using MOS technology. The switched capacitor module is approximately equivalent to a resistor, as shown in Fig. 1*b*. The fact that resistors are relatively difficult to implement gives the switched capacitor a great advantage in integrated-circuit applications requiring resistors. Some of the advantages are that the cost is significantly reduced, the chip area needed is reduced, and precision is increased. Although the switched capacitor can be used for any analog circuit realization such as analog-to-digital or digital-to-analog converters, the most notable application has been to voice-frequency filtering. SEE ANALOG-TO-DIGITAL CONVERTER; DIGITAL-TO-ANALOG CONVERTER.

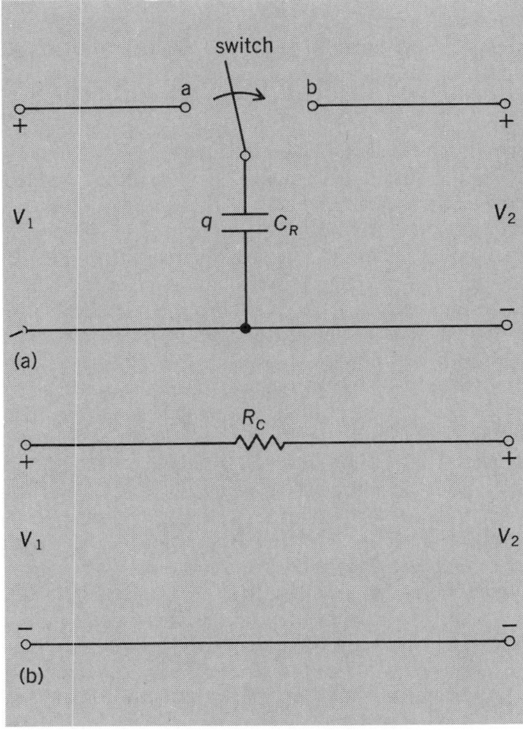


Fig. 1. Switched capacitor. (*a*) Basic circuit. (*b*) Equivalent resistive circuit.

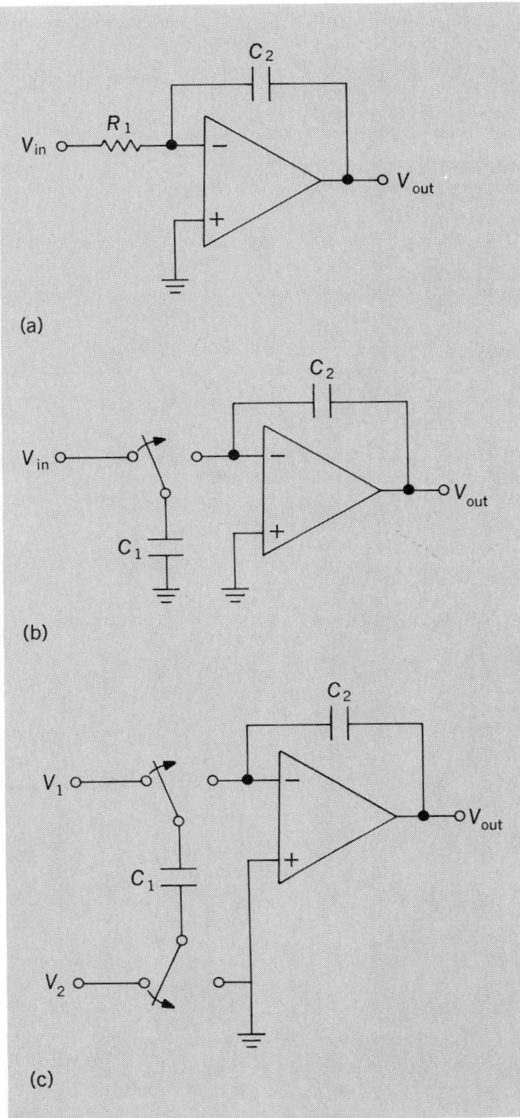


Fig. 2. Integrator circuits. (*a*) Conventional *RC* integrator circuit. (*b*) Single-input switched-capacitor integrator. (*c*) Switched-capacitor differential integrator circuit.

Although a switch has long been used as an element in circuits and systems, it was not until the late 1970s that its potential and practicality in integrated-circuit design was realized.

**Integrator circuits.** A conventional *RC* (resistance-capacitance) integrator circuit is shown in **Fig. 2***a*.

The output voltage is given by Eq. (1), where $1/s$

$$V_{\text{out}} = \frac{1}{R_1 C_2} \frac{1}{s} V_{\text{in}} \tag{1}$$

indicates the operation of integration ($s$ is the differential operator), showing that integrator performance depends on $R_1$. In MOS integrated circuits, the value of $R_1$ cannot be controlled better than 20% by using standard fabrication techniques. In addition, considerable chip space is required to realize resistors in the megohm range. In contrast, the switched capacitor realizations shown in Fig. 2*b* and *c* depend on the ratio of capacitors which can be controlled with great accuracy. For example, the output voltage of the differential integrator shown in Fig. 2*c* is given by Eq. (2),

$$V_{\text{out}} = \frac{C_1 f_c}{C_2 s} (V_2 - V_1) \tag{2}$$

where $f_c$ is the clock frequency. With $C_1$ and $C_2$ in the range of 1 picofarad and $f_c$ at 100 kHz, this circuit has an equivalent resistance of 10 megohms, and the gain of the circuit is about $10^4$. The silicon chip area required to implement the capacitors is about 0.01 $\text{mm}^2$. If a resistor is used in place of the switched capacitors, an area at least 100 times larger would be required.

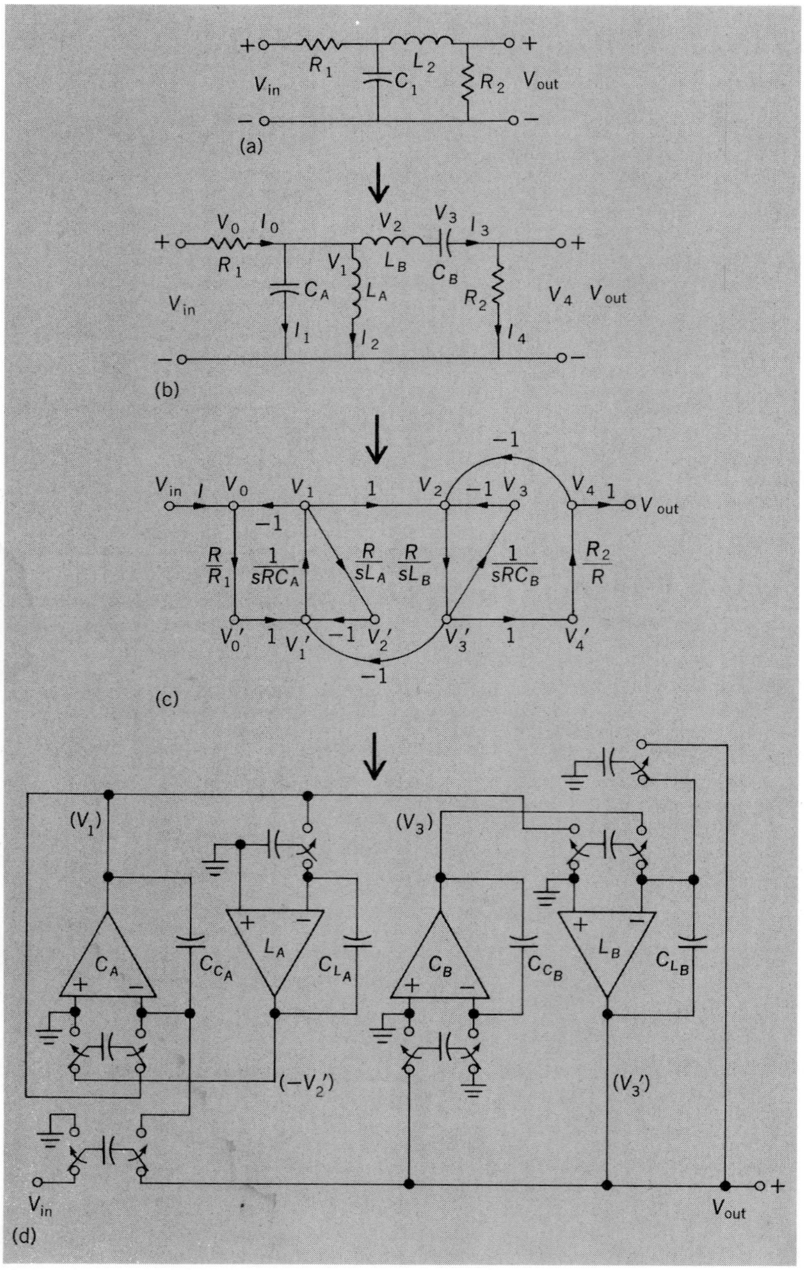

**Equivalent resistance.** Returning to the switched-capacitor circuit of Fig. 1*a*, the operation may be visualized as follows. With the switch in position *a*, the capacitor $C_R$ is charged to the voltage $V_1$. The switch is then thrown to position *b*, and the capacitor discharged at voltage $V_2$. The amount of charge transferred is then $q = C(V_2 - V_1)$. If the switch is thrown back and forth at a clock frequency $f_c$, the average current will be $C(V_2 - V_1) f_c$. The size of an equivalent resistor to give the same value of current is given by Eq. (3). From this equation, it is seen

$$R_C = \frac{1}{Cf_c} \tag{3}$$

that with $C = 1$ pF and $f_c = 100$ kHz, the value of 10 megohms used previously is obtained.

The accuracy of the equivalence between the switched capacitor and the resistor depends on the relative size of the clock frequency $f_c$ and the frequencies in the signal being processed. If the switching frequency is much larger than the signal frequencies of interest, the equivalence is excellent and the time sampling of the signal can be ignored in a first-order analysis, such that the switched capacitor is a direct replacement for a conventional resistor. If this is not the case, then sampled-data techniques in terms of a *z*-transform variable must be used for accuracy.

**Analog operations.** The switch that has been used in describing the switched capacitor is actually realized by an MOS transistor to which a pulse of voltage at the clock frequency is applied to produce the off and on conditions of the switch. This periodically operating switch is used for a number of analog operations, such as addition, subtraction, inversion, and integration. These operations are essential in the construction of analog filters, as well as in other applications of switched capacitors. These operations may be explained in terms of the circuits of Fig. 2. In Fig. 2*a* and *b* the analog operation of integration is accomplished. In addition, these circuits are of the inverting type, meaning that a sign reversal is accomplished in addition to integration. The sign reversal of a voltage can be accomplished directly by using switches and a capacitor, as seen in Fig. 2*c*. Assume that $V_1$ is grounded or $V_1 = 0$. The operation of the switches is such that the voltage applied to the MOS operational amplifier is the negative of $V_2$. With the switch operating from left to right, $V_2$ with respect to ground is reversed. With $V_1$ not grounded, the circuit of Fig. 2*c* is a differential integrator, meaning that the output voltage is a function of the voltage difference, $V_2 - V_1$. In conventional active-filter design, these analog operations are accomplished by means of additional stages incorporating operational amplifiers. In switched-capacitor design, these analog operations are implemented with switches. SEE AMPLIFIER; ANALOG COMPUTER; TRANSISTOR.

**Fig. 3. Steps in the realization of a switched-capacitor filter. (*a*) Low-pass prototype filter. (*b*) Corresponding band-pass filter. (c) Signal flow graph representation of the circuit of *b*. (*d*) Final switched-capacitor band-pass filter.**

**Filter design.** Although there are many strategies for filter design, the discussion will be restricted to the case of filters based on the passive *LC* (inductance-capacitance) ladder with resistive terminations at both ends. Extensive tables are available giving element values to achieve various forms of frequency response, such as Butterworth, Chebyshev, and Cauer (elliptic). All tables are given in terms of a normalized termination of 1 ohm, and a normalized frequency of $\omega_o = 1$ rad/s and for the low-pass case. It is standard procedure to make use of frequency transformations to realize high-pass, band-pass, band-elimination, and similar kinds of responses, and to use frequency and magnitude scaling to give practical element values. The passive ladder structure with double terminations is chosen because it has low sensitivity of changes in transmission with changes in element sizes.

Starting with the low-sensitivity, low-pass ladder structure, a frequency transformation is first accomplished. From these steps, a structural simulation is then carried out by replacing the actual filter by its signal flow graph representation. The flow graph is chosen so that most of the operations required are integration. The elements in the flow graph are then simulated by circuits like that shown in Fig. 2*c*.

An example of filter design is shown in **Fig. 3**. The ladder network shown in Fig. 3*a* is known as the low-pass prototype. In the usual case, $R_1 = R_2 = 1$ ohm. The elements $C_1$ and $L_2$ are determined from tables, depending on the form of frequency response required. Going from Fig. 3*a* to *b* accomplishes a low-pass to band-pass transformation in which all element values are determined from those in Fig. 3*a*, and the specification of the center frequency and bandwidth of the band-pass case. In Fig. 3*c* the filter of Fig. 3*b* is represented by its flow graph, in which the lines and arcs with arrows indicate the structure of the circuit of Fig. 3*b*, and the associated symbols represent the impedance or admittance. To this structural simulation of the ladder filter, an element simulation is next applied. All elements of a form such as $1/RC_AS$ are realized by using the integrator of Fig. 2*c* with differences of voltages accomplished by the switched capacitors. The final result, shown in Fig. 3*d*, is then implemented as an integrated circuit containing only switched capacitors, ordinary capacitors, and operational amplifiers. The chip area required to realize a filter of modest order might be 100 mils (2.5 mm) on each side. SEE ELECTRIC FILTER; INTEGRATED CIRCUITS.

*M. E. Van Valkenburg*

***Bibliography.*** G. M. Jacobs et al., Touch-tone decoder mates analog filters with digital logic, *Electronics*, 52(4):105–112, February 15, 1979; G. M. Jacobs et al., *IEEE Trans. CAS*, 25:1014–1020, December 1978.

## Switching circuit

A constituent electric circuit of a switching or digital data-processing system which receives, stores, or manipulates information in coded form to accomplish the specified objectives of the system. Examples include digital computers, dial telephone systems, and automatic accounting and inventory systems. SEE DIGITAL COMPUTER; SWITCHING SYSTEMS (COMMUNICATIONS); SWITCHING THEORY.

Physically, switching circuits consist of conducting paths interconnecting discrete-valued electrical devices. The most generally used switching circuit devices are two-valued or binary, such as switches and relays in which manual or electromagnetic actuation opens and closes electric contacts; vacuum and gas-filled electronic tubes, and semiconductor rectifiers and transistors, which do or do not conduct current; and magnetic structures, which can be saturated in either of two directions.

The electrical conditions controlling these switching circuit devices are also generally two-valued or binary, such as open versus closed path, full voltage versus no voltage, large current versus small current, and high resistance versus low resistance. Such two-valued electrical conditions, as applied to the input of a switching circuit, represent either (1) a combination of events or situations which exist or do not exist; (2) a sequence of events or situations which occur in a certain order; or (3) both combinations and sequences of events or situations. The switching circuit responds to such inputs by delivering at its output, also in two-valued terms, new information which is functionally related to the input information.

Electronic switching circuits are characterized by these functional relationships between input and output information, as well as by such attributes as response time, power consumption, packaging densities, and other performance parameters.

**Functional characteristics.** Functional characteristics of switching circuits are defined by the logical operation and memory capabilities of the discrete devices from which they are assembled, as well as by the means used to interconnect the devices.

For example, switching circuits embody such logical relationships as output X is to exist only if input A and B occur simultaneously; and output Y is to exist if either input A or input B occurs. The factor of memory, in turn, enables a switching circuit to hold or retain a given state after the condition that produced the state has passed.

Even in large and complex switching systems, the majority of circuit requirements can be met by a relatively small number of types of circuits, each of which performs one or a limited number of somewhat distinct functions. These functional circuits, some examples of which are described below, are the basic building blocks of a switching system.

***Basic combinational circuits.*** A combinational switching circuit is one in which a particular set of input conditions always establishes the same output, irrespective of the history of the circuit. An example involving a simple combinational circuit is the con-

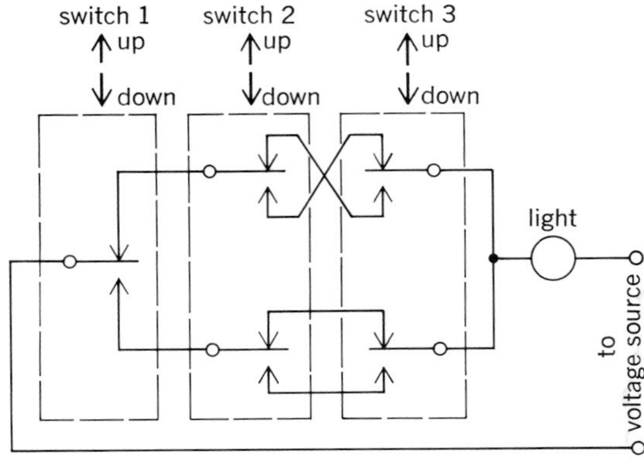


**Fig. 1. Elementary combinational switching circuit.**

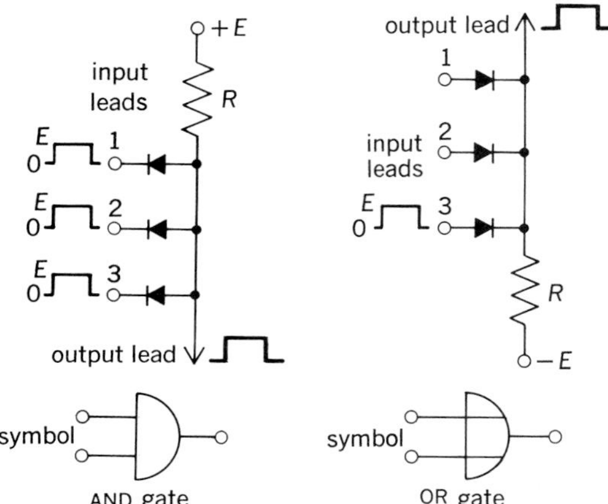


**Fig. 2. Typical switching gates using crystal diodes.**

trolling of the entrance-hall light of a residence by three up-down wall switches located in three different rooms. Analysis of this problem shows that the circuit must meet the following simple requirements. If any one or all three wall switches are down, the hall lamp must light; if any one or all three switches are up, the lamp must be dark. An obvious (but not the most efficient) circuit meeting these requirements is shown in **Fig. 1**. In this problem the circuit inputs are, of course, the manual switch settings, and the circuit output is the control of the light.

In electronic switching circuits, so-called gates are used to perform logical functions equivalent to these series-parallel networks of switch contacts. In this sense, an electronic gate is an elementary combinational circuit. Gates do not function by physically inserting or removing metallic conduction paths between contacts of manually operated switches or remotely controlled relays. Instead, they function by control of voltage or current levels at their output.

The most commonly encountered gates are the AND and the OR gates. The AND gate produces an output only if all its inputs are concurrently present; an OR gate produces an output if any one or any combination of its inputs is present. **Figure 2** shows both an AND gate and an OR gate, using rectifier or diode elements. *SEE LOGIC CIRCUITS.*

In the AND gate the rectifiers are so oriented that current from a positive voltage source $E$ passes through the relatively large resistance $R$ and then through the low forward resistance of any one of the rectifiers to ground in the circuits controlling the gate.

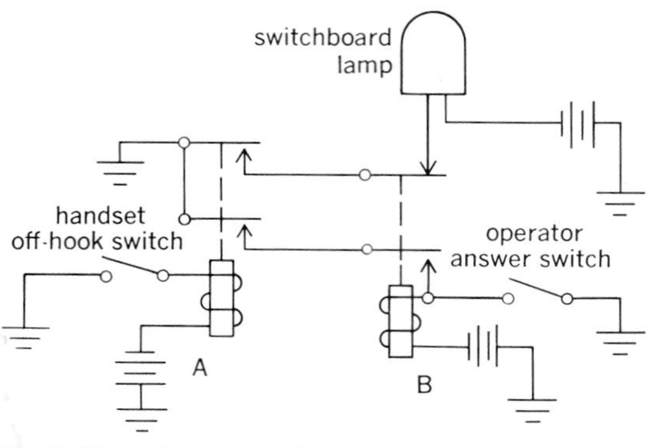


**Fig. 3. Elementary sequential relay switching circuit.**

Thus, in the inactive state of the gate, the output lead is at or near ground potential. If all three input leads of this gate concurrently receive a positive voltage pulse of magnitude $E$, the rectifiers approach open circuit, and the output lead will be raised from near ground to a positive potential for the duration of the input pulse. In other words, input leads 1 and 2 and 3 must all receive the positive pulse to obtain the positive output voltage.

In the OR gate the rectifiers are reversed so that current flows from ground in the input circuits through the low forward resistance of any rectifier and then through the relatively large resistance $R$ to the negative voltage source $-E$. Thus, in the inactive state of the gate the output lead is at or near ground potential. If, however, a relatively high positive voltage pulse is applied to input leads 1 or 2 or 3, the remaining two diodes are cut off and the output is raised to a positive potential for the duration of the input pulse.

Gates may, of course, be constructed with other electronic devices, such as tubes, transistors, and magnetic cores.

***Basic sequential circuits.*** A sequential switching circuit is one whose output depends not only upon the

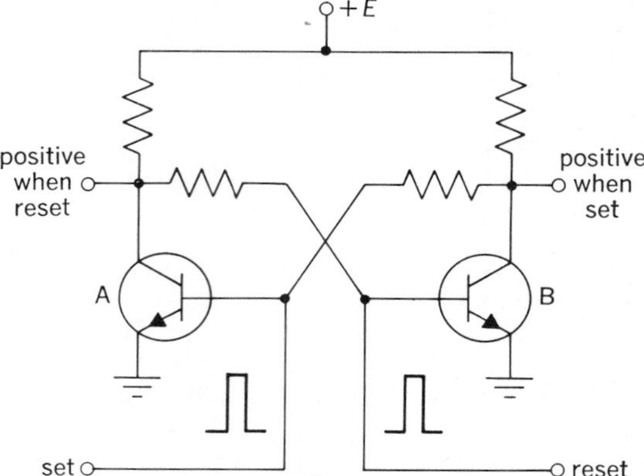


**Fig. 4. Transistor switching memory element (flip-flop).**

present state of its input, but also on what its input conditions have been in the past. Sequential circuits, therefore, require memory elements.

By way of illustration, consider the following simple sequential circuit problem. When a telephone customer lifts the handset, a lamp is to light in front of a switchboard operator. When an operator answers, the light should go out to avoid other operators also answering. After satisfying the customer's request for a connection, the operator withdraws. The light, however, should not relight now, even though the conditions existing at this time are seemingly identical with those at the start; that is, the customer has the handset lifted and no operator is on the line. A sequential relay circuit meeting these simple requirements is shown in **Fig. 3**. In this circuit, when the hand is lifted, the handset off-hook switch connects a ground input to relay A which operates and lights the switchboard lamp. When the operator answers, another ground input operates relay B and this relay puts out the light. A holding circuit on relay B keeps relay B operated until the handset off-hook switch is again opened and relay A is deenergized. Relay B "remembers" that the operator has answered and prevents the relighting of the lamp when the operator withdraws.

It is, therefore, the memory element of the circuit.

A typical electronic memory element used in sequential circuits is a simple circuit called a flip-flop. A flip-flop consists of two amplifiers connected so that the output of one amplifier is the input of the other. A voltage pulse will set the flip-flop into one of two states, and that state remains until another voltage pulse resets the flip-flop or returns it to its original state. It can therefore be used to remember that an event has taken place.

**Figure 4** is an *npn*-transistor flip-flop. When set, transistor A is conducting and transistor B is cut off. When reset, transistor B is conducting and transistor A is cut off. A positive output voltage with respect to ground may be obtained from either transistor to indicate the condition of the flip-flop. *See* Transistor.

Relays, flip-flops, and similar memory elements provide static, or fixed, memory; they hold the stored information indefinitely, or until they are told to "forget," commonly called "resetting." In contrast, a delay line provides transient memory. A delay line has the property that an electrical signal applied to its input is delayed on its way to the output.

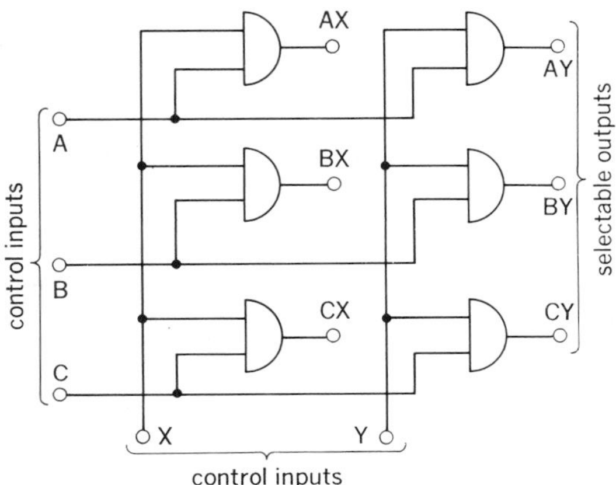


**Fig. 5. Matrix selecting circuit using AND gates.**

***Selecting circuits.*** A selecting circuit receives the identity (called the address) of a particular item and selects that item from among a number of similar ones. The selectable items are often represented by terminals or leads. Selection usually involves marking the specified terminal or lead by applying to it some electrical condition, such as a voltage or current pulse, or a steady-state dc signal. By means of this electrical condition, the selected circuit is alerted, sized, or controlled.

An electronic selecting circuit using AND gates is the matrix type (**Fig. 5**). In this type of circuit an input signal appears on one of the horizontal input leads and concurrently on one of the vertical input leads. The selected output is at the cross point of these two leads.

***Connecting circuits.*** A switching system is an aggregate of functional circuit units, some of which must sometimes be directly coupled to each other to interchange information. **Figure 6** shows a simple electronic connecting circuit using AND and OR gates. In this arrangement a communication path is provided over a single link from any one of the three functional circuits A, B, C, to either the X or Y circuit by an external control circuit activating the appropriate pair of AND gates. To provide a multilead link, or to provide for other simultaneous interconnections, additional AND gates would, of course, be required. The OR gate maintains separation of the inputs at the common junction point.

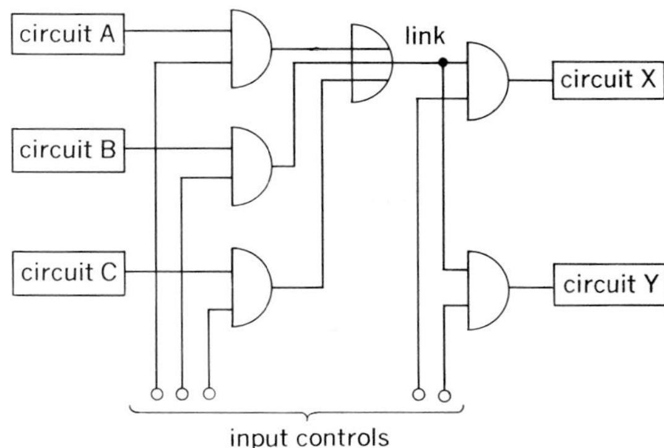


**Fig. 6. Connecting circuit using AND and OR gates.**

***Lockout circuits.*** In switching systems, situations often arise where several similar circuit units are ready at the same instant to request collaboration with another type of functional circuit. Mutual interference among the requesting circuits is prevented by the lockout circuit (sometimes referred to as hunting or finding circuits). In response to concurrent inputs from a number of external circuits, a lockout circuit provides an output indication corresponding to one, and only one, of these circuits at any time.

**Figure 7** shows a typical electronic lockout circuit using cold-cathode gas-filled tubes. The external circuits furnish positive potential on the input leads to the control gaps of the tubes as indications of service requests. The operation of the circuit is based on the dynamic negative-resistance characteristics of gas tubes. If such tubes are provided with a common impedance in their conduction paths (the cathode

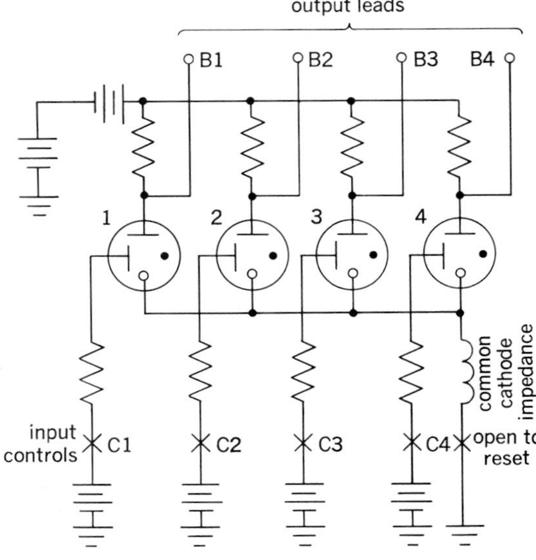


**Fig. 7. Lockout circuit using cold-cathode gas tubes.**

impedance in this circuit), simultaneous input signals will result in the ionization of only one tube. Once the control gap of a tube is ionized, conduction current starts flowing in its main gap and this current through the common impedance instantaneously reduces the voltage across all the other tubes below the value needed to ionize them. This reduced voltage is, however, adequate to keep the single ionized tube in the conducting state until its conduction path is opened. The identity of the particular ionized tube is derived from the anode resistance individual to each tube; the output lead whose potential has been lowered by this resistance represents the circuit whose request has been granted.

***Translating circuits.*** Switching systems process information in coded form; the information is generally in the form of numbers. Numerical codes are many and varied, each with its own characteristics and more or less distinct advantages for different switching circuit situations. Therefore, one of the common functional circuits in switching systems is the translating circuit, which translates information received in one code into the same information expressed in another code. These translating circuits are combinational circuits; a given input signal combination representing a code to be translated always produces the same output signals, which represent the desired code.

**Figure 8** is an example of a magnetic-core translating circuit that translates from binary code (1,2,4) to a one out of eight code (0,1,2, . . .,6,7). The circuit has three flip-flops which are set or reset (not set) according to the binary input code combination. The translating elements are eight magnetic cores, each with five windings, and are represented in Fig. 8 by a heavy vertical line. Each short, slanting line segment represents a separate winding on a core. These short slanting lines also symbolize a mirror action; an input current pulse coming from a flip-flop sets a core if it is reflected upward by the mirror, and prevents setting or resets the core if reflected downward. Once set, the subsequent resetting of a core induces a current which flows upward in the vertical line (in a direction opposite to the resetting current) and is reflected to the left or to the right by each mirror symbol.

With this explanation of the symbolism, the circuit works as follows. The input is binary; that is, it consists of a positive voltage pulse to each of the three flip-flops either on its set or on its reset input lead, according to the **table**. (By adding the numerical designations to those flip-flops which are set in a particular combination, the value of the output digit is determined.)

While the flip-flops are being set, their output current is prevented from flowing into the core windings by the transistor set-gate which is normally nonconducting. Shortly after the binary input combination is recorded in the flip-flops, this set-gate is pulsed for a moment into its conducting state. During this moment, output current will flow from each flip-flop in its "1" output lead (if the flip-flop has been set) or in its "0" output lead (if the flip-flop has been reset). As Fig. 8 shows, the output current of flip-flop 4 is always used to set the cores; that is, the current in the "0" output lead of this flip-flop is used to magnetize the first four cores in the set direction, or the current in its "1" output lead is used to magnetize the last four cores in the set direction. In contrast, the output currents from flip-flops 2 and 1 are always used to magnetize the cores in the opposite or reset direction. Initially, all cores are in the reset condition, and cores that receive both set and reset currents simultaneously will not change this initial condition. An analysis of Fig. 8 will therefore show that, for any desired digit, one and only one of the eight cores will be set by the flip-flops in combination. For instance, if output 3 is desired, the current from flip-flop 4 tends to set cores 0, 1, 2, and 3, but cores 0, 1, and 2 are prevented from being set by the output current from either or both flip-flops 2 and 1. When the translated code is needed, the current pulse on the advance lead resets the single previously set core, and consequently an induced output current pulse appears on the appropriate output lead. (The rectifiers in the input and output portions of the circuit prevent unwanted reverse current.)

***Register circuits.*** Information received by a switching system is not always used immediately. It must be stored in register circuits for future use.

In a register circuit the coded information to be stored is applied as input and retained by memory elements of the circuit, and when needed, the registered information is taken as output in the same code or in a different code. Figure 8 embodies a register function as well as a translating function. Register circuits are devised with a great variety of memory elements and have capacities to store from a few to millions of information bits.

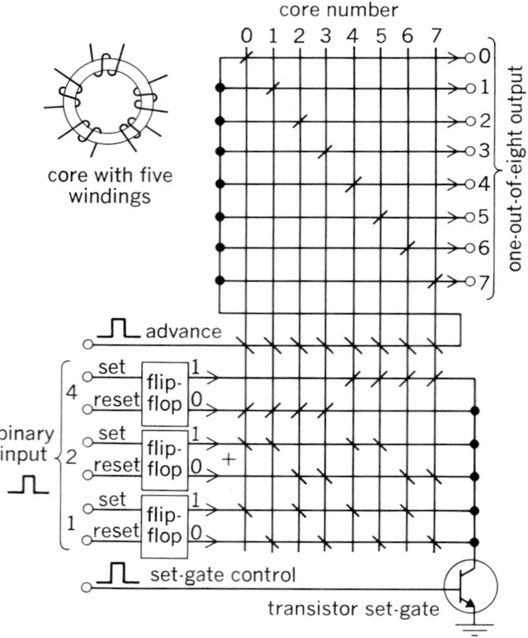


| Output digit desired | Flip-flop 4 | | Flip-flop 2 | | Flip-flop 1 | |
|---|---|---|---|---|---|---|
| | Set | Reset | Set | Reset | Set | Reset |
| 0 | | x | | x | | x |
| 1 | | x | | x | x | |
| 2 | | x | x | | | x |
| 3 | | x | x | | x | |
| 4 | x | | | x | | x |
| 5 | x | | | x | x | |
| 6 | x | | x | | | x |
| 7 | x | | x | | x | |

**Fig. 8. Code register and translating circuit using magnetic cores, each of which has five windings.**

**Digital integrated circuit families**

| Logic type | Gate delay ($t_d$), ns | Power dissipation ($P_D$), mW/gate | Density, gates/mm² (gates/in.²) |
|---|---|---|---|
| I. Bipolar—use bipolar junction transistors as basic switching elements | | | |
| A. Transistor-transistor logic (TTL) | | | |
| 1. Standard small-scale integration/medium-scale-integration (SSI/MSI) TTL | 5–10 | 10 | 20–80 (13,000–50,000) |
| 2. Low-power Schottky (LPS) | 5–10 | 2 | 20–80 (13,000–50,000) |
| 3. Advanced LPS for large-scale integration (LSI)* | 1–2 | 1–2 | 200–600 (130,000–400,000) |
| B. Emitter-coupled logic (ECL) | | | |
| 1. Standard SSI/MSI ECL | 0.5–1 | 25 | 20–50 (13,000–32,000) |
| 2. Advanced ECL for LSI* | 0.7–1 | 10 | 100–200 (65,000–130,000) |
| 3. Current-mode logic (CML)† | 0.5–1 | 0.2–1 | 200–300 (130,000–200,000) |
| C. Integrated injection logic ($I^2L$) | | | |
| 1. Standard LSI $I^2L$* | 2–5 | 0.05 | 200–400 (130,000–250,000) |
| 2. Integrated Schottky logic (ISL)† | 2 | 0.3 | 500–1000 (320,000–650,000) |
| 3. Schottky transistor logic (STL)† | 2 | 0.3 | 500–1000 (320,000–650,000) |
| 4. Implanted advanced composed technology (impact)† | 1–2 | 0.1 | 800 (500,000) |
| II. Metal oxide semiconductor (MOS)—use MOS field-effect transistors (MOSFETs) as basic switching elements | | | |
| A. *P*-channel MOS (PMOS) | | | |
| Standard LSI PMOS | 50 | 1 | 100–200 (65,000–130,000) |
| B. *N*-channel MOS (NMOS) | | | |
| 1. Standard LSI NMOS | 10–20 | 1–2 | 200–400 (130,000–250,000) |
| 2. Very large-scale-integration (VLSI) NMOS† | 0.5–1 | 0.5 | 1500–3000 (1,000,000–2,000,000) |
| 3. Exotic structures | | | |
| a. Vertical channel (VMOS) | 0.5–1 | 0.5 | 500–1000 (320,000–650,000) |
| b. Double-diffused (DMOS) | 0.5–1 | 0.5 | 500–1000 (320,000–650,000) |
| C. Complementary MOS (CMOS) | | | |
| 1. Standard SSI/MSI CMOS | 20–50 | 0.01–0.1 | 50–100 (32,000–65,000) |
| 2. LSI*/VLSI† CMOS | 0.5–1 | 0.01–0.5 | 500–2000 (320,000–1,300,000) |
| 3. Silicon-on-sapphire (CMOS/SOS) | 0.5–1 | 0.01–0.5 | 750–2500 (500,000–1,600,000) |

*Uses advanced fabrication technology with feature sizes below 5 μm.
†Feature sizes of 2.5 μm or smaller.

A frequently encountered form of register circuit is the shift register. This type of register has the ability to shift its stored digital information internally to positions representing higher or lower numerical values in the code employed. For example, in decimal code registration a digit may be shifted from the units to the tens position. An obvious use of such registers is in digital computers when, for example, partial multiplication products have to be lined up for addition.

***Counting circuits.*** One of the most frequently encountered circuits in switching systems is the counting circuit whose function, in general, is to detect and count repeated current or voltage pulses which represent incoming information.

**Performance characteristics.** In theory, functionally equivalent switching circuits can be designed by using any available switching technology; that is, mechanical manual or relay-operated switches, or a number of electronic devices including a wide variety of semiconductors, and vacuum or gas-filled tubes. The selection of a particular technology for use in computer systems is often determined by the time required to perform logical operations. The maximum number of logical operations per second which a computer switching circuit can execute is determined by both the time required by the switching device to change state (gate delay, $t_d$) and the time it takes signals to propagate between switching circuits, the latter being proportional to the distance between the circuits. Device gate delay is dependent upon the active element's principle of operation, and is normally inversely proportional to gate power dissipation ($P_D$) since larger current supplied to the switching devices reduces the effects of junction storage time, capacitance, and parasitic elements. The product of $t_d$ and $P_D$ is a popular figure of merit for comparing different device technologies.

***Circuit density.*** One of the objectives of large-scale integrated-circuit (LSI) and very large-scale integrated-circuit (VLSI) design is to incorporate fast device technologies into compact packages which reduce, to the greatest extent possible, propagation delay between circuits. Thus, circuit density, in terms of the number of gates per square millimeter, is another important parameter affecting overall logic speed. Thin-film fabrication techniques for both active and passive components result in dense packaging with higher reliability, finer adjustment of component values, and simpler manufacturing processes. The table lists the major semiconductor switching circuit technologies, along with their acronyms and important performance characteristics. SEE INTEGRATED CIRCUITS.

***Josephson junctions.*** Since semiconductors produce heat, dense circuit packaging is hampered by the need to remove heat. The Josephson junction avoids this problem by using superconducting circuits, that is, circuits cooled to near absolute zero where the electrical resistance that generates heat virtually vanishes. Josephson found that a superconducting current between two wires separated by an ultrathin insulating film can be controlled by a magnetic field applied to the insulator. While the heat dissipated is very small (5 nanowatts per gate), gate delays of less than 0.01 nanosecond in miniaturized devices a few micrometers in length and width can be achieved. Implementation problems, including the need to provide cryostats for low operating temperatures, have thus far precluded commercially viable products. *See* Jospehson effect; Superconducting devices.

***Magnetic bubble memory.*** Another advanced technology is based on the fact that the polarization of tiny cylindrical magnetized areas, contained in a thin film of magnetic material, can be used to represent data 1's or 0's. Such devices are called magnetic bubble memories, and when used for data storage, the principal advantages are extremely high storage density (7000 bits/mm$^2$ or $4.5 \times 10^6$ bits/in.$^2$) and the fact that they are nonvolatile (data are not lost when power is shut off). The memory access time of 10 milliseconds is faster than a disk drive but slower than semiconductor memories. Power consumption is extremely low, being 10 microwatts per bit during reading or writing operations. *See* Magnetic bubble memory.

*Joseph A. Pecar*

***Bibliography.*** W. Anacker et al., Special issue on Josephson technologies, *IBM J. Res. Develop.*, vol. 24, no. 2, March 1980; K. L. Chopra and I. Kaur, *Thin Film Device Application*, 1983; A. Friedman and P. R. Memon, *Theory and Design of Switching Circuits*, 1975; F. Judd and D. Wiggert, *Techniques for Mass Storage, with Applications II: Bubble Memories*, National Telecommunications Conference, 1979; M. P. Mitchell, *Switching Circuits for Engineers*, 3d ed., 1975.

## Switching systems (communications)

The assemblies of switching and control devices provided so that any station in a communications system may be connected as desired with any other station. A telecommunications network consists of transmission systems, switching systems, and stations. Transmission systems carry messages from an originating station to one or more distant stations. They are engineered and installed in sufficient quantities to provide a quality of service commensurate with the cost and expected benefits. To enable the transmission facilities to be shared, stations are connected to and reached through switching system nodes that are part of most telecommunications networks. Switching systems act under built-in control to direct messages toward their ultimate destination or address.

Most switching systems, known as central or end offices in the public network and as private branch exchanges (PBXs) when applied to business needs, are used to serve stations. These switching systems are at nodes that are economically and centrally located with respect to the community of interest of the served stations. With improvements in technology, it has become practical to distribute switching nodes closer to stations. In some cases to serve stations within a premise, switching is distributed to take place at the stations themselves. A smaller number of systems serve as tandem (intermediate) switching offices for large urban areas or toll (long-distance) offices for interurban switching. These end and intermediate office functions are sometimes combined in the same switching system.

There are many types of telecommunication services. The principal ones are voice, data (record), picture (still), and video (motion pictures). For each service there is a different balance between the relative investment in transmission, switching, and station (terminal) facilities. When several of the services are offered in the same network and the network is growing, it is difficult to make general conclusions concerning the economic balance between switching and transmission. Also, as new technologies are introduced into any portion of the network, new economic balances among the elements may materialize. This article deals primarily with systems for the switching of voice. Some data services use the voice network. Since separate networks for data services are available, a brief discussion will be given of switching exclusively for voice and data services.

Public telecommunications have grown over a long period, principally for the telephone and teletypewriter (Telex), and large investments have been made. As new technology becomes available, it is usually first used for growth of the network. When a detailed cost analysis shows that the cost of continued use of old equipment exceeds the cost of providing new equipment, new technology replaces older equipment. Since telecommunications is a mature discipline in industrialized nations, and particularly in the United States, the processes of growth and replacement are much in evidence. At the same time, new technology is appearing and being adapted for replacement at an increasing rate.

### Switching System Fundamentals

Telecommunications switching systems generally perform three basic functions: they transmit signals over the connection or over separate channels to convey the identity of the called (and sometimes the calling) address (for example, the telephone number), and alert (ring) the called station; they establish connections through a switching network for conversational use during the entire call; and they process the signal information to control and supervise the establishment and disconnection of the switching network connection.

In some data or message switching when real-time communication is not needed, the switching network is replaced by a temporary memory for the storage of messages. This type of switching is known as store-and-forward switching.

**Signaling and control.** The control of switching systems is accomplished remotely by a specific form of data communications known as signaling. Switching systems are connected with one another by telecommunication channels known as trunks. They are connected with the served stations or terminals by lines. Until recently most signals were sent by direct- or alternating-current pulses over the lines and trunks. Starting in 1976, a new form of signaling was introduced between many toll offices in the United States, and may eventually be used between end offices. Known as common channel signaling (CCS), it comprises a network of separate data communication paths used for transmitting all signaling information between offices.

In some switching systems the signals for a call directly control the switching devices through which the transmission path is established. This direct control was the earliest, and is still the most prevalent, form of automatic switching around the world. The

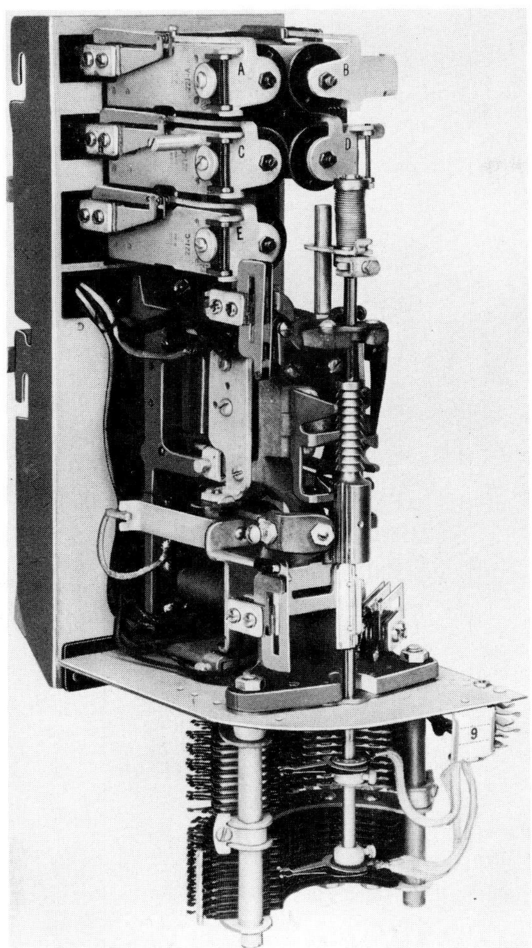


Fig. 1. Step-by-step switch.

step-by-step system described below is the foremost example of direct control. It employs a switch (**Fig. 1**) in which metallic wipers are moved up and around by electromagnetic actions to contact one out of 100 sets of fixed terminals.

For most modern switching systems the signals for identifying or addressing the called station are received by a central control that processes calls on a time-shared basis. Central controls receive and interpret signals, select and establish communication paths, and prepare signals for transmission. These signals include addresses for use at succeeding nodes or for alerting (ringing) the called station.

Until the introduction of electronics into switching, the central controls employed complex relay logic circuits often known as markers. Most electronic controls are now designed to process calls not only by complex logic but also by logic tables or a program of instructions stored in bulk electronic memory. The tabular technique is known as action translator (AT). The electronic memory is now the most accepted technique and is known as stored program control (SPC). Either type of control may be distributed among the switching devices rather than residing centrally. Microprocessors on integrated circuit chips are a popular form of distributed stored program control. *See* Computer storage technology; Integrated circuits; Microprocessor.

Common channel signaling became practical as a result of processor control. To reduce the number of data channels between all switching nodes, a signaling network of signal switching nodes is introduced. The switching nodes, known as signal transfer points (STPs), are fully interconnected with each other and the switching offices they serve. All links and signal transfer points are duplicated to ensure reliable operation. Each stored-program-control toll switching system connects to the two signal transfer points in its region.

**Numbering plan.** In an automatic telephone system, a numbering plan provides for uniquely identifying every main telephone station so that calls may be directed to it. The North American system is based upon decimal digits. (When letters are on the dial, the telephone system actually recognizes the numerals associated with the letters.)

A telecommunications central office customarily has the nominal maximum capacity to serve 10,000 main stations, using the number series 0000–9999. When there are more than 10,000 main stations, more than one central office is provided, sometimes in more than one building or wire center. Each office is given a separate three-digit designation or code. The minimum requirement is for an adequate number of digits or characters in each number to address each main station in the dialing area. When a call reaches the called office, the called telephone station is determined from the last four numerals (the main station code).

A seven-digit numbering plan has adequate capacity for only a small portion of the telephones in North America. Hence, a geographical area, such as a state or a Canadian province, is selected as a numbering plan area (NPA), within which there are no duplications of seven-digit numbers. The more populous states, which have large numbers of central office codes, are divided into two or more numbering plan areas.

Each numbering plan area is given a three-digit NPA code, the middle digit of which is a 1 or 0. Examples are 803 for the state of South Carolina and 415 for the portion of California that includes San Francisco (**Fig. 2**). In dialing the number of a subscriber outside the local or home numbering plan area, the area code is dialed ahead of the seven-digit number. For example, a subscriber or operator in Asbury Park, New Jersey, wishing to dial 421-9000 in San Francisco would first dial area code 415 followed by 421-9000. From any other numbering plan area, the dialing would be identical to reach 421-9000, except from within the 415 area, where only the seven digits of the telephone number need be dialed. With this plan the equipment uses, first, the NPA code to determine which area is desired; second, the central office code to select the office in that area; and third, the main telephone number to determine the particular telephone being called. To enable the reuse of area codes as central office codes, a 1 is dialed ahead of each 10-digit number.

In addition to central office and area codes, code numbers for special services, such as 411 for directory assistance and 911 for emergency calls, are used.

**Switching connectives.** Space and time division are the two basic techniques used in establishing connections. When an individual conductor path is established through a switch for the duration of a call, the system is known as space division. When the trans-

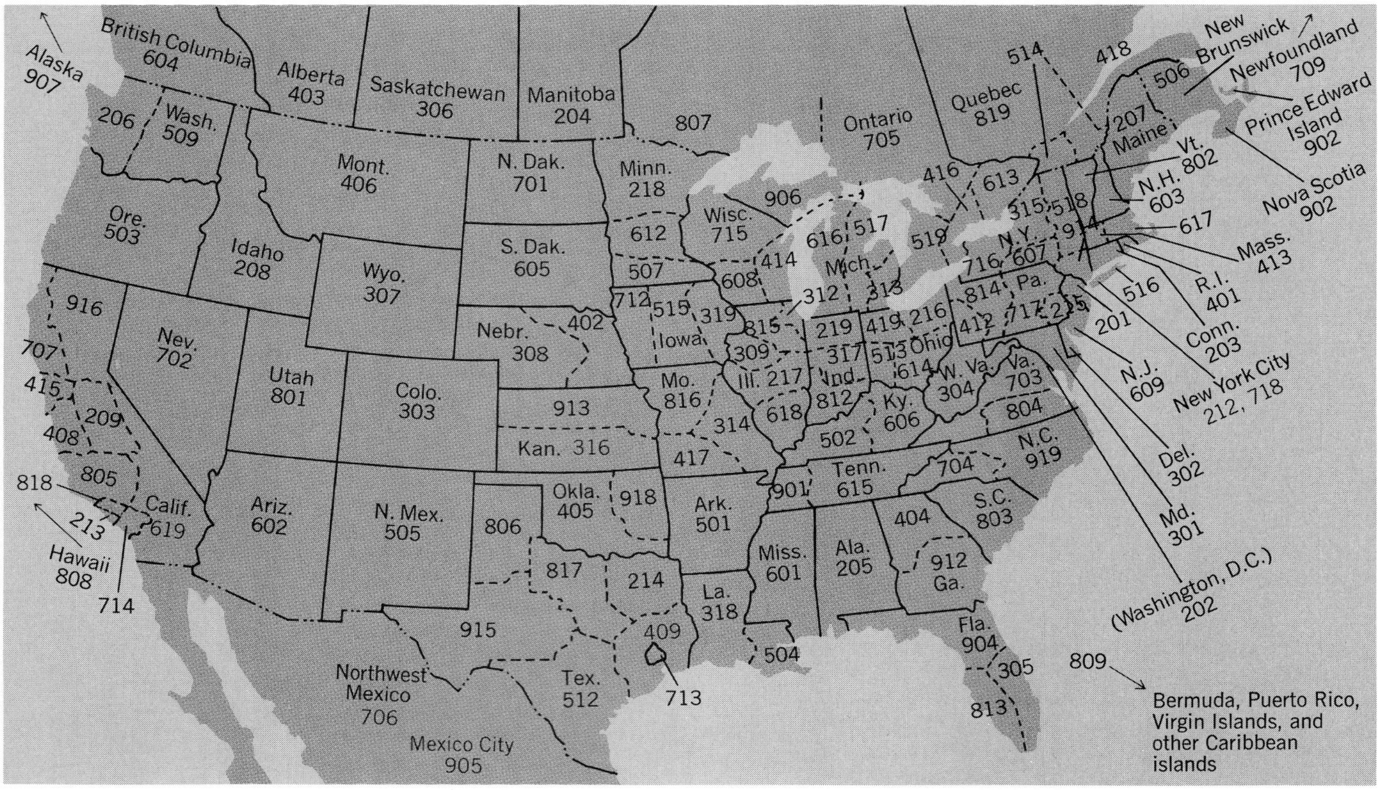

Fig. 2. Numbering plan areas with codes.

mitted speech signals are sampled and the samples multiplexed in time so that high-speed electronic devices may be used simultaneously by several calls, the switch is known as time division. Space-division switching has been employed since the early manual switchboards in which the connectives were cords, plugs, and jacks.

Most switching is now automatic. Operators are required only for ancillary functions that cannot yet be economically automated. Such systems use the most modern techniques. In the United States, cord, plug, and jack switchboards have almost disappeared, having been replaced by cordless consoles in which calls are distributed automatically to operators who are provided only with keys and lamps to permit them to serve calls. **Figure 3** shows a cordless traffic service position (TSP) used for completion of person-to-person, credit card, and some coin toll calls. The positions may be located many miles from the stored-program-control system through which the connection is established or processed.

Fig. 3. Traffic service position.

### Electromechanical Switches

Formerly, most switching systems placed in service were space division and employed some form of electromechanical switch. These switching systems, unless controlled electronically (for example, stored program control) are referred to by the name of the electromechanical device (for example, a step-by-step, panel, crossbar, EMD, codebar, XY, or rotary system). These gross motion devices are connected together in successive stages to concentrate, distribute, and select idle paths as required to establish the required connections. The simplest arrangement is one in which, as each digit is received, the call progresses from one stage to the next by making a selection and finding an idle link at each stage until the selection process is completed.

**Direct control.** In direct control systems such as the step-by-step, XY, and EMD systems, the switches are arranged in stages that are accessed progressively. While very few new offices of this type of system are now being installed, present systems serve about 42% of the world's telephones (with about 22% in the

United States). The switches are of three main types following the basic connective functions, with the names line finders (for concentration), selectors, and connectors (for distribution and selection). The line finder acts on its own to reach a line requesting service. The selector acts under control of the dial (1-out-of-10 selections) and then seeks (hunts for) an idle path to the next stage (also usually a 1-out-of-10 selection). Each selector and connector switch also has a third capability to home or restore the switch to normal. Signaling and control relays are generally mounted with each switch (shown above the mechanism in Fig. 1). The connector is arranged to make two selections under direct control of dial, thereby selecting one of 100 lines for completing the connection.

**Figure 4** shows such a switching system with an arrangement of switches to respond to a seven-digit number such as 595-5465. All available terminals in such a system may not always be needed. To avoid the expense of completely equipping unneeded selector stages, these selectors may be arranged to absorb specific received digits without any connection being made through the switch. By so doing, the seven-digit number plan may be preserved without providing selectors for the codes not in use.

**Indirect control.** Some electromechanical switching devices are not amenable to direct dial control since they are not based on the decimal system. Furthermore, with the introduction of pushbutton (Touch-Tone) dialing, the switches are not fast enough to keep up with the pulsing of a digit at a time. As a result, a number of systems have been developed that use indirect control. With indirect control the line finder connection is extended through another stage of concentration to a signaling circuit known as a register-sender. The progressive control of the switches then takes place after the dialed digits are partially or completely received (registered). The register sends (pulses) the same or substituted digits forward to operate switches. Different types of pulsing may be used. The routing plan is thereby divorced from the numbering plan. To secure more economical trunking, a call may then be routed through an intermediate or tandem office.

The register-sender may be used to provide a number of other features in addition to tandem routing, such as different routings for certain classes of lines (such as coin calls). The step-by-step system with registers is used in some large British cities, where they are known as directors. The register arrangement also lends itself to the provision for the automatic recording of call billing information known as automatic ticketing or automatic message accounting (AMA). This permits subscribers to dial their toll calls without the necessity of employing operators to record billing information. The provision of this feature also requires identifying the calling line number. Automatic number identification (ANI) equipment is often used. For local calls, so-called message units are increasingly being employed to measure service usage. These units are accumulated for each station, and the sum is reported periodically for purposes of determining the charges.

**Systems using coordinate switches.** In systems with a common or central system control, the connective elements or crosspoints are usually assembled in matrices. These matrices can be made up of individual metallic or nonmetallic crosspoints in a coordinate array such as sealed contact relays or *PnPn* diodes (where *P* stands for heavy positive doping and *n* stands for negative doping) of an integrated circuit, or with common row and column operating elements to select a crosspoint as in the crossbar switch. About 35% of the nonelectronic systems of the world, as well as many electronic systems, use some form of coordinate switch. A crosspoint in each row and column may be operated so that, unlike the other electromechanical switches, such coordinate switches may be used by several calls at the same time. This is made possible by use of the common control.

**Crossbar switch.** A crossbar switch (**Fig. 5**) consists of 100 or 200 contact sets, or crosspoints. Each crosspoint may have from three to six pairs of contacts. The individual crosspoints are operated by interposing a flexible select finger, moved by the rotation of a horizontal bar, between the contact set and the armature of a vertical-hold magnet. The horizontal bar with a butterfly-shaped armature is located between two contact sets and is rotated through a small arc either upward or downward by energizing either of two electromagnets. Once the horizontal bar and fingers move into position, the vertical-hold magnet is energized to close the crosspoint contacts. The flex-

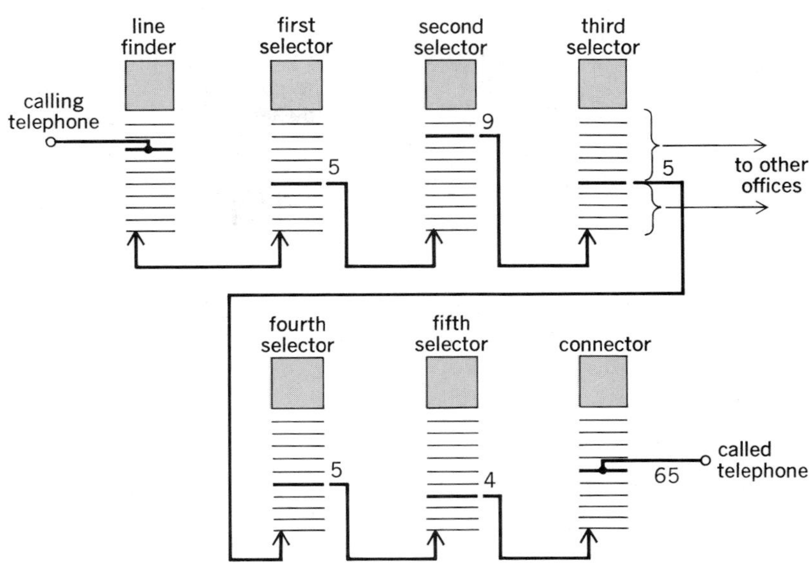

**Fig. 4. Diagram of seven-digit step-by-step system.**

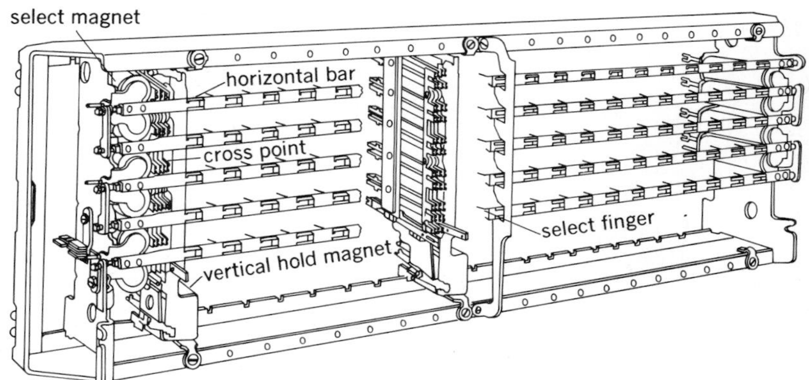

**Fig. 5. Crossbar switch, showing configuration of cross points, select fingers, and horizontal bars and magnets.**

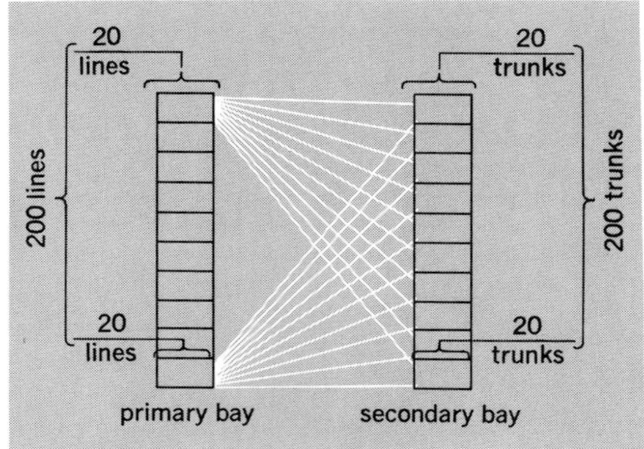


**Fig. 6. Primary-secondary link arrangement.**

ible finger is held interposed between the operated vertical armature and contacts when the horizontal magnet is deenergized. Contact sets associated with other vertical magnets may then be actuated. The matrices are formed by wiring or multiplying the contact pairs horizontally and vertically.

The size of the matrices is generally limited due to the relatively high cost of the crosspoints. Typically sizes are 8 × 8, 10 × 10, 20 × 10, 16 × 16, and 14 × 25. To obtain greater access, the matrices are linked in stages; in a well-known two-stage linking arrangement (**Fig. 6**) the stages are called primary and secondary. Each input to the first stage of 20 × 10 switches can then be connected to each of the 200 outputs of the second stage of 20 × 10 switches. While access to a particular output may be blocked by a link being busy on another call, networks of successive frames of two-stage arrays may provide very low probability of blocking for connections between any two terminals.

While there are many crossbar switching systems in use, only the two most prominent in the United States, the No. 5 and the No. 4A crossbar systems, are described below. Variants of the No. 5 crossbar system are manufactured and used in Canada, Japan, Greece, and elsewhere.

Connections in a crossbar system are controlled by a relay marker. The time required to set up a connection is short, and consequently a small number of markers and other associated common control equipment is sufficient to handle most offered calls.

Most crossbar systems differ from progressive electromechanical switching systems. When a call is originated in a crossbar office, the location of the calling line in the switches is noted. The location of the called line or outgoing trunk to another office is marked. The marker then selects an idle talking channel through the crossbar switches to interconnect the marked points and causes all contacts in this channel to be closed simultaneously. The channel is held busy for the duration of the call.

Also, unlike other electromechanical systems, the marker of crossbar systems is arranged to look at alternate routes to the called office in case all trunks of the first-choice route are busy. The crossbar circuits are designed so that the marker can detect certain trouble conditions in the office and make a second trial using other circuits to complete the calls. A record of the trouble and its probable location is made for subsequent analysis by maintenance people.

**No. 5 crossbar switching system.** This system has been the most popular form of crossbar equipment for local central office use. Although local switching is its primary use, it has been adapted for toll, tandem, private line, private branch exchange, Telex, and video switching.

The switching network of this system comprises two primary-secondary arrangements: first, the line link (LL) frames on which the telephone lines appear and, second, the trunk link (TL) frames on which the trunks appear. A switching entity may grow to a maximum of 60 line link and 30 trunk link frames. Each line link frame is interconnected with every trunk link frame by a network of links called junctors. Each line link frame has a basic capacity for 290 telephone lines and may be supplemented in 50-line increments to a maximum of 590 lines. The size used in a particular office depends upon the calling rate and holding time of the assigned lines.

**Figure 7** is a block diagram of a No. 5 crossbar office. When a call is originated, the dial-tone marker causes the calling telephone to be connected through the line link and trunk link frames to an idle originating register. The register then places a dial tone on the line as an indication for the customer to begin dialing. When the complete called number is dialed, a completing marker is chosen to establish a connection. The completing marker examines the first three or six digits (area code plus central office code) to determine if the call is to be completed within the office, to another local office, or to a toll office. If the call is destined for the same office, the called number, together with the line link frame location of the calling telephone, is transferred to the completing marker. The completing marker consults a number group to find the line link frame location of the called number. An idle intraoffice trunk and channels through the trunk link and line link frames are chosen to interconnect these two locations. Crosspoints are closed and the called telephone is rung. The connection to the originating register is released in the process.

If the call is to a telephone in another switching entity (local or toll), the completing marker selects an outgoing trunk to the called office. The called number is transferred through the completing marker into the outgoing sender. The outgoing sender pulses forward the called number to the terminating point and releases.

The No. 5 crossbar system is able to interconnect with all types of switching systems. It is arranged to send out and receive different types of signals—multifrequency pulses between No. 5 crossbar offices, dial pulses to and from offices using step-by-step equipment, and other forms of pulsing to operate with electromechanical switches that operate only on an indirect basis.

A call originating in some other office for a number in the crossbar office reaches the office over an incoming trunk to which an incoming register is temporarily connected. The called number is pulsed from the originating office into the register. The register associates itself with a completing marker which, with the help of the number group, selects and closes the channels through the trunk link and line link frames to the called telephone. By using the number group, the line terminations need not appear on the line link frames in numerical order.

The system uses automatic message accounting (AMA) to make call records for billing purposes. Originally AMA consisted of perforating the data on a 3-in.-wide (7.5-cm) paper tape. Other developments use minicomputers located in the office or reached over data links to record the AMA data on magnetic tape. On calls within the local area where a message-unit basis of charging applies, frequently only the calling telephone and the number of message units are recorded. For toll calls, the calling and called numbers, answering and disconnect times (from which the length of conversation is computed), and other data are recorded. Automatic data processors at accounting centers convert the recorded information into a form for printing the bill statement.

Centralized automatic message accounting (CAMA) has been applied to the offices used for tandem or toll switching functions. The CAMA equipment may be similar to the local office AMA equipment. The calling station is identified automatically in the local office, and this number is pulsed over the trunk to the tandem office. Where local offices are not so arranged, an operator is momentarily connected to ask the calling party for his or her number and to key it into the register.

The No. 5 crossbar system has been extended to provide switching services such as Touch-Tone, Centrex, private line, and call distribution to large groups of operators.

**Toll calling.** Local service in the United States is provided geographically in local access transport areas (LATAs). Service between LATAs is now provided by many interLATA carriers (IXC). There are several methods by which calls are extended to these carriers. A popular arrangement for serving these toll calls, both inward and outward, is known as equal access. Interconnection between the interLATA carriers and the local companies is usually through an access tandem (**Fig. 8**). The call is switched to the interLATA carrier of the caller's choice either by presubscription or by dialing the prefix 10XXX, where XXX represents identification of the desired carrier. The calling line identification number is then forwarded through the tandem to the interLATA carrier. The called number is then forwarded from the originating office to the interLATA carrier. Both numbers are sent by using alternating-current trunk signaling. In some cases the IXC has trunks directly to or from end offices.

The No. 4A crossbar and the No. 4 ESS described below are the most commonly used systems for the switching of most interLATA toll calls, as well as for some intraLATA calls. Figure 8 shows the paths for toll calls between distant cities A and B. It illustrates at the originating point two methods of placing calls from the calling telephones. In one, the call is routed from a local office through an access tandem to the nearest toll office. Generally a 1 is dialed ahead of the area code on such calls. In the other, a call is routed from the local office through an operator system, such as the traffic service position system (TSPS) when a customer dials 0 before the called number or makes a long-distance call from a public telephone.

**No. 4A crossbar switching system.** The 4A crossbar system also has two main primary-secondary switching frames. Incoming trunks from originating points appear on the incoming link frame, and the outgoing trunks leave from the outgoing link frames. Using an initial set of 10 × 20 crossbar switches, a particular entity may have a maximum of 40 frames of each type, serving as many as 8000 incoming trunk terminations and 12,000 outgoing trunk terminations. The number of terminations may be increased. There is a full flexibility for any incoming trunk to be connected to any outgoing trunk.

A call arriving at the No. 4A crossbar office in city A appears at the incoming trunk and is connected to an incoming sender, into which the called telephone number (7 or 10 digits) is pulsed. The electronic stored program control processor determines the routing of the call from this number and connects to an idle marker, passing the routing information to it. The marker closes through the channel to interconnect the incoming trunk with the outgoing trunk, which in Fig. 8 is a No. 4 ESS (discussed below) in city B.

The signaling for the call may be sent to city B either over the trunk by pulsing seven digits from the sender A to the sender B or, since each office includes a stored-program-control processor, it may be connected to the common-channel-signaling network. In the latter case the identify of the selected outgoing trunk, the called number, and perhaps other information about the call, will be sent at high speed (4800 bits per second) over a link to a regional signal transfer point serving city A. The signal transfer point will transfer the information to a signal transfer point serving city B. This signal transfer point will then contact the No. 4 ESS office at which the trunk terminates. The stored program control in the office at B determines the routing and completes the connection to the local office, which in turn sets up the connection to the called telephone. The common-channel-signaling process includes a check that the transmission path selected for the call is suitable.

An important feature of crossbar systems is their ability to pick an alternate route if the first choice route between cities A and B has no idle toll lines. For example, a route from city A to city C to city B may be selected if no direct trunk to city B is available. Several such alternate routes may be examined, and a call may be routed through several switching points before reaching the terminating toll center. The use of this plan ensures good service and economical trunking since, if one route is either busy momentarily or out of service due to an equipment or cable

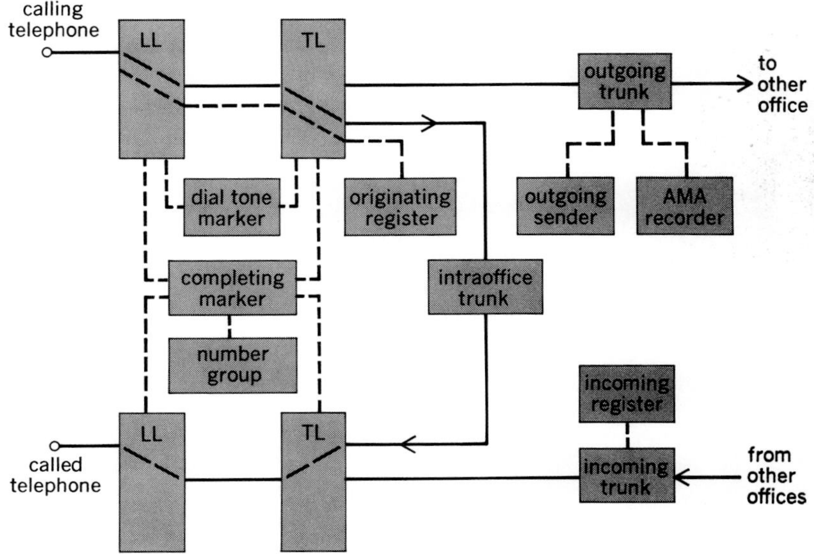


**Fig. 7. Block diagram of the No. 5 crossbar system.**

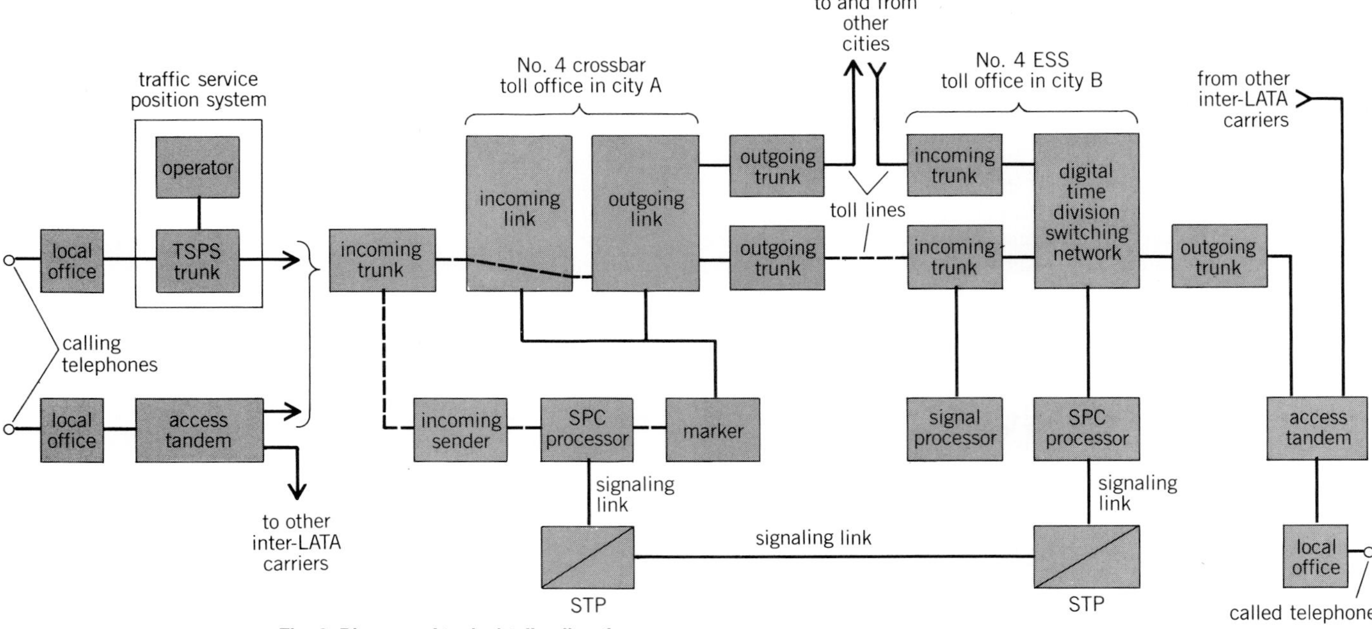


**Fig. 8. Diagram of typical toll-call path.**

failure, the network is engineered to ensure that there is a good possibility that a toll line in some other route is available. The switching systems in complex networks employing alternate routing must be capable of sending pulses of the required type to operate the switches in the various switching centers. They can also delete digits or add digits to the called telephone number as required to operate the various switches.

As contrasted with most electromechanical switching systems, all No. 4A and some installations of the No. 5 crossbar systems are arranged for four-wire switching. In these systems, to facilitate connection with carrier transmission systems and to ensure good transmission quality, the voice is carried over one pair of wires in one direction, and over another pair of wires in the opposite direction.

### Electronic Switching

The invention of the transistor spurred the introduction of electronics and semiconductor technology into switching system design. Many experiments were conducted in the decade 1954–1964. The first commercially produced stored-program-control electronic switching system was placed in service in 1963 in the United States. Since that time 3000 local and 450 toll stored-program-control switching systems have been placed in service there, involving more than 60,000,000 lines (as of 1984). Stored program control has become the principal type of control for all types of new switching systems throughout the world, including toll, private branch, data, and Telex systems. About 1500 small systems were earlier placed in service in Canada, Great Britain, and France using action translator electronic logic and memory controls.

**Service features.** New service and administrative features which are made more economic by the use of stored program techniques and bulk memories are among the most important aspects of electronic switching systems. Two types of data are stored in the memories of electronic switching systems.

One type is the data associated with the progress of the call, such as the dialed address of the called line. Another type, known as the translation data, contains infrequently changing information, such as the type of service subscribed to by the calling line and the information required for routing calls to called numbers. These translation data, like the program, are stored in a memory which is easily read but protected to avoid accidental erasure. This information may be readily changed, however, to meet service needs. The flexibility of a stored program also aids in the administration and maintenance of the service so that system faults may be located quickly.

The availability of large memories and the ease of changing the program residing in them has led to the development and deployment in most stored-program-control systems of many new and optional services such as abbreviated dialing, call waiting, call forwarding, and three-way calling. The wide introduction of common-channel signaling into the network broadens the range of stored-program-control service offerings. These services take advantage of the rapid exchange of information about calls between the originating, intermediate, and terminating offices before connections are established. As a result, calls may be directed within the entire network to suit the individual users and subscribers whose needs are likely to be nationwide rather than residing in a single central office or private branch exchange.

One of the most impressive results of employing electronics in switching is the space savings. Even though the early systems that were installed used mostly discrete semiconductor components, the space savings were as high as 60% when compared with electromechanical switching. Additional space savings have been achieved as integrated circuits are applied.

**No. 1A electronic switching system.** The high speed of electronics enables the systems to be designed so that all calls in progress are processed and supervised by the same control equipment. **Figure 9**

is a block diagram of the No. 1A electronic switching system widely used in the United States for large local and small toll offices. This system has a capacity as high as 450,000 local calls per hour and may serve as many as 125,000 lines. High-speed peripheral buses connect the store-program-control processor to the peripheral circuits of the system that access lines, trunks, and the switching network control.

The stored program control comprises a general-purpose assemblage of semiconductor circuits that are structured to interpret the instructions used in programs for the processing of the calls and for the maintenance of the system. These instructions are stored in a memory subsystem as coded programs that are read in sequences that determine actions to be taken.

Portions of the call-processing functions are used repetitively for each call. The programs are relatively fixed and remain in the system memory while the call information is stored for relatively short periods. The No. 1A ESS is provided with integrated circuit (IC) memory for call data, translation, and program storage. Integrated circuit chips of 64,000 bits are used in a random-access storage. A typical program requires more than 500,000 words of 32 bits each. All control circuits are duplicated to ensure service continuity should a component fail, or to enable the system to grow while in service. Memory redundancy is also provided. Copies of the call processing as well as additional, less frequently used maintenance, administrative, and operations (MAO) programs are stored on magnetic disks. The periphery includes data links to centralized MAO facilities and for common-channel signaling, as well as local maintenance consoles and tape drive units.

**Space-division switching networks.** Initially, most stored-program-control systems employed space-division networks. As indicated above, many unique matrix arrays of devices, both metallic and nonmetallic, have been developed and used in commercial electronic switching systems. These arrays are used in the same topology of primary-secondary link arrangements and line and trunk link frames as in crossbar systems.

For some electronically controlled switching systems, metallic contacts are used in the space-division network. Many of these contacts are magnetic reeds sealed in glass with an inert gas. They latch magnetically when activated by a short pulse of one polarity and release with a pulse of opposite polarity. When the contacts are made of hard magnetic material, such as those employed in the No. 1A ESS, they are known as remreeds. Other switching systems use miniature crossbar or similar coordinate switches. In all of these space-division networks, the switching device is slow in comparison to the speed of the electronic controls. The network controller provides the buffering between high-speed stored program or action translator controls and the slower space division networks.

Electronics in the form of semiconductor or integrated circuit devices are used as crosspoints or gates in the electronic switching networks. Generally their use has been confined to smaller systems or PBXs (less than 2000 terminals) or in combination with metallic crosspoints for larger systems.

Semiconductor crosspoints may be used in network configurations in the same manner as reed switches. They are designed to be bistable and held actuated over the established speech path. Therefore, these devices combine both transmission and control characteristics. Each crosspoint may use a pair of bistable devices as the two conductors of the connection, or a single device with one wire and a ground return. Some modern semiconductor crosspoint devices are

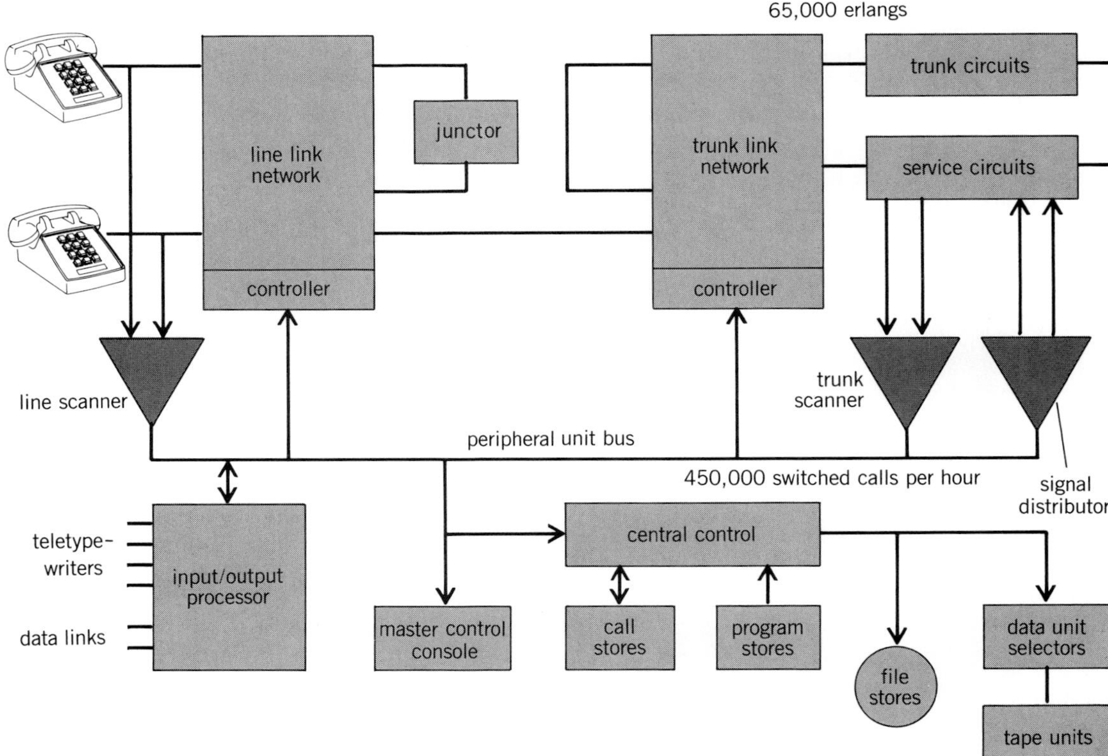


**Fig. 9. Block diagram of No. 1A electronic switching system. Junctor is an intraoffice trunk circuit.**

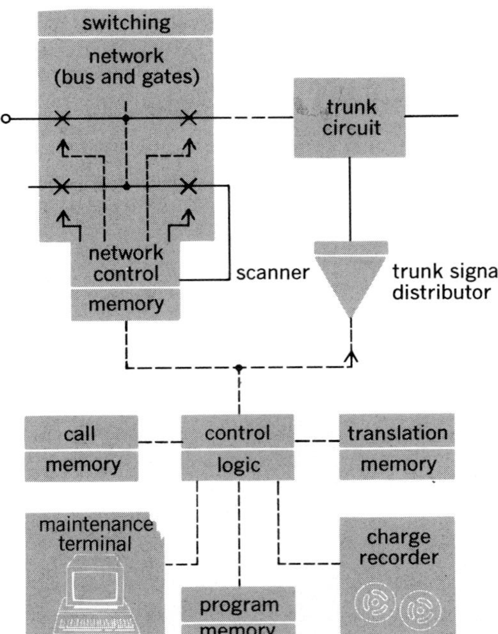


Fig. 10. Block diagram of time-division stored-program-control system.

designed to function in the same high-energy environment as metallic devices.

**Time-division switching networks.** Time-division switching is practical only with high-speed electronic techniques. It is used in switching networks as well as in the control portions of systems. For time division, transmitted signals are sampled at a rate at least twice the highest frequency to be transmitted. Typically for voice this is 8000 times per second.

***Pulse modulation.*** In a switching system the samples may be pulses of varying amplitude that are analogs to the electrical signals representing the voice. This is known as pulse-amplitude modulation (PAM).

The first commercial electronic switching system (1963) used pulse-amplitude-modulation time-division techniques, since digital coding techniques were not then economical. The input signals on lines and trunks are sampled periodically (**Fig. 10**). Each active input is associated with the desired output for a specific time slot. This type of time-division network utilizes semiconductor gate elements which, during each time slot, connect together on a common bus the terminals associated with a particular call. These associations for each call are read from a cyclically arranged memory which, together with the gates and bus, constitutes the network control. The number of simultaneous conversation paths which may be established through these networks is limited by the speed of the semiconductor devices and the associated circuitry that must accurately transfer the representation of the electrical amplitude of the sample with sufficient power. The sampling rate must be high enough to permit the faithful reproduction of the signal when passed through a low-pass filter. Generally, networks of the time-division type have been applied where there are less than 500 time slots.

More robust forms of pulse modulation use digital or on-off signals that can be readily encoded from the amplitude pulse, sent over a transmission medium, and periodically reformed to eliminate most of the impairments of transmission and switching. These types of digitally sampled transmission are known by the form of coding employed; the most popular is referred to as pulse-code modulation (PCM). In one type of pulse-code modulation, each sample is coded into one of approximately 256 amplitudes and represented by eight binary (on-off) pulses. The eight pulses representing each speech channel may be placed in sequence or time-multiplexed into groups, typically of 24 or 32 channels, so that the line and repeaters may be used more efficiently. SEE PULSE MODULATION.

***Switching techniques.*** Time-multiplexed coded-voice signals reaching a switching system are switched by using two techniques. Assuming signals arrive at the switching network on different multiplexed lines, they first need to be synchronized with respect to multiplex channel identification. This usually requires some form of time delay or buffering. This establishes uniform channel periods or time slots. Within the switch there may be more time slots than in the lines delivering the signals.

One necessary switching network function uses further time buffering by placing successive digitized channel samples in a memory in one order and removing them as indicated by the switching selection requirements of each call. This function is known as time slot interchange (TSI).

The other switching network function provides for interchanging channels between time-multiplexed lines. Generally this function is carried out by using a high-speed space-division network of one or more stages. The space-division network control acts to change the actuated crosspoints between time slots so that the successive channels of input lines may be switched to corresponding channels in the same or other lines. Space-division stages operating at time slot rates are time-multiplexed switches (TMS).

Time-division switching networks are based upon the use of successive time slot interchanges, called T (for time) stages, and time-multiplexed switches, called S (for space) stages. Typical systems are said to employ T-S-T or S-T-S types of networks. Lines or trunks not reaching the switching system by time-multiplexed facilities must first be multiplexed with

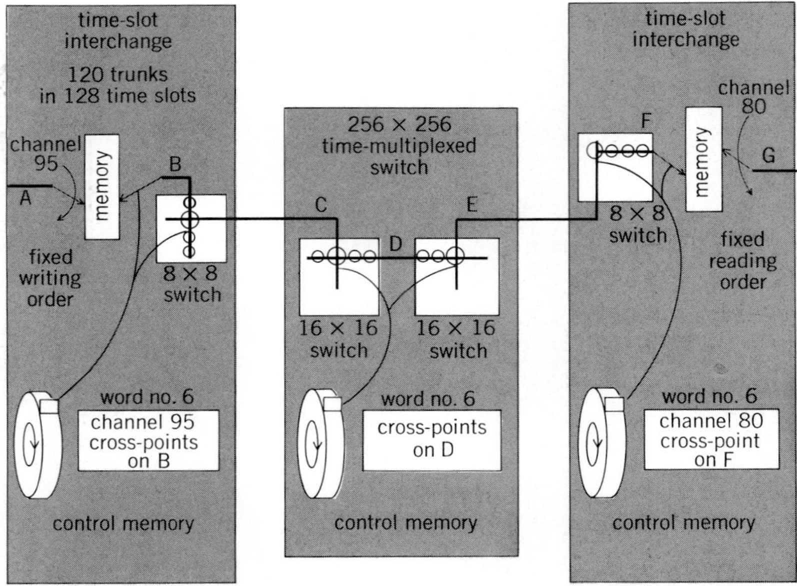


Fig. 11. Diagram of digital time-division switching network showing a typical connection. The network has 128 time slots throughout, and the sample shown is in time slot number 6 throughout the network.

similar inputs as part of the time-division switching-network function.

Since the coded signals represent only one direction of transmission, the switching-network function in a circuit switch is duplicated by reciprocity to provide for the other direction of transmission. Also, since the elements of the network are active and may be used for hundreds of simultaneous calls, redundancy of the network and its controls, similar to that used in the call-processing portions of the system, is usually part of the system design.

***Digital (PCM) toll systems.*** Time-division switching is a natural adjunct to digital time-division transmission where the coding is performed for purposes of multiplexing. Pulse-code-modulation transmission was initially economical on interoffice trunk routes from 10 to 50 mi (16 to 80 km). This made time-division digital switching initially attractive where such facilities were found, namely, for tandem and toll applications.

The No. 4 stored-program central time-division digital switching system was developed for this application and is the largest switching system. It has a capacity of 100,000 trunks, and its stored program control is capable of switching 670,000 calls per hour.

The switching network for the No. 4 ESS consists of both time-slot-interchange and time-multiplex-switching stages: the latter is reconfigured at the rate of 1,024,000 times per second (128 time slots for each frame of 8000 samples per second). **Figure 11** illustrates how a sample progresses through both the memory (time-slot-interchange) and four-space-division time-multiplexed switch stages for one direction of a typical time-slot connection, with the network control memory being read out cyclically at a rate of 8000 times per second.

As shown in the block diagram (**Fig. 12**), the No. 4 ESS serves three types of transmission channels: analog metallic, analog multiplex carrier, and digital multiplex carriers. The digital time-division switching network routes digital signals from incoming trunks to the desired outgoing trunks. The audio signals on the analog channels are converted by the LT-2 connectors or D4 channel banks into pulse-code-modulation digital samples. The digital interface frame (DIF) processes the digital signals into the format required for the switching network and removes the signaling information. For analog and digital channels, signaling information is detected by the equivalent of trunk circuits in the digital interface frame except where common channel signaling is now being used. Echo suppression on a digital basis is inserted ahead of the switching network.

All operations are directed and supervised by the stored-program-control processor and are aided in routine tasks by the signal processors built into the digital interface frames. The signal processors provide the scanner and distributor functions for a portion of the trunks and, in turn, pass the significant information content in a more compact form to the central control. The use of peripheral or distributed processors enables the central processor to devote its attention to the more critical decisions in the processing of calls, thereby providing for greater call-attempt ca-

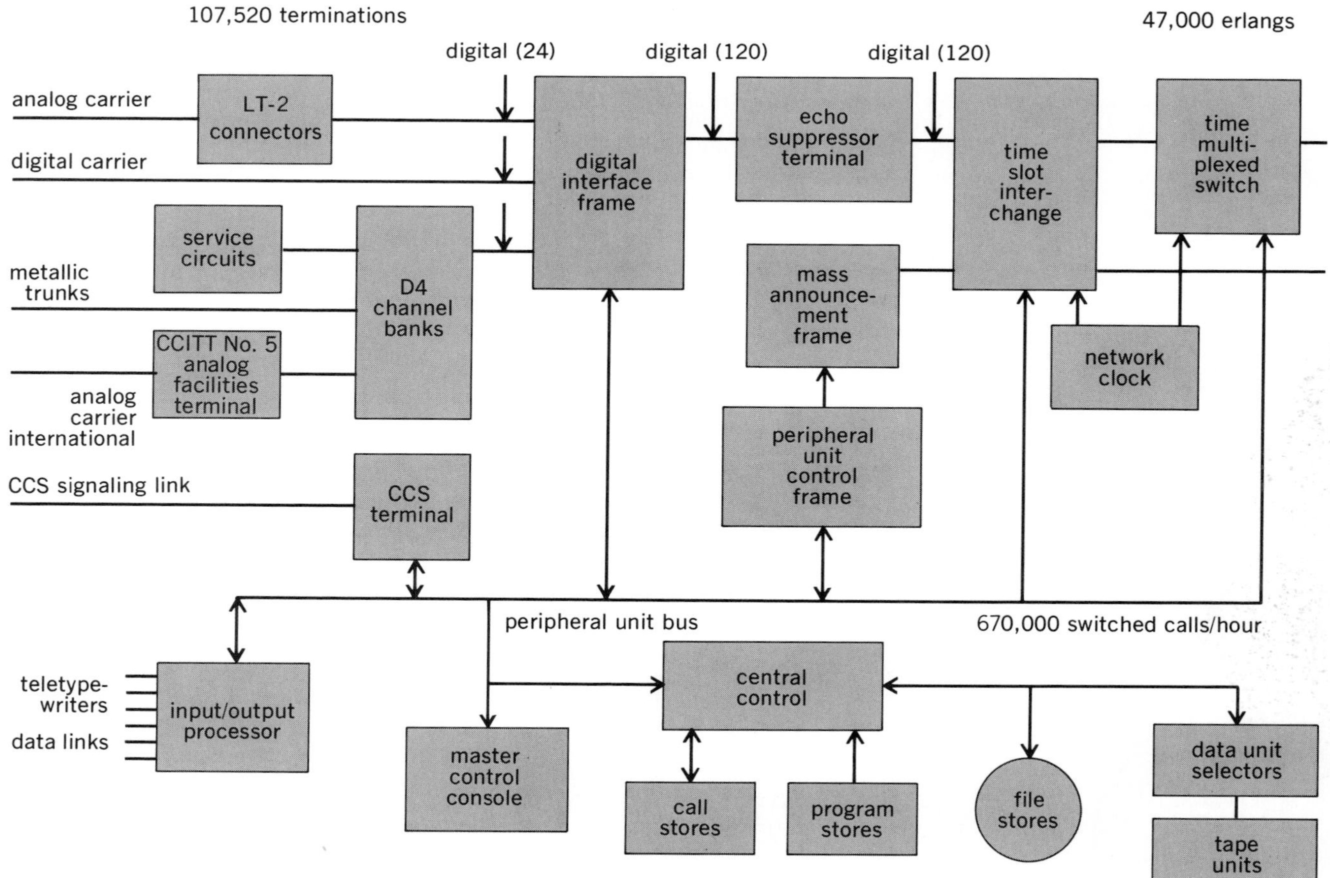


**Fig. 12. Block diagram of No. 4 electronic switching system. CCITT = Comité Consultatif International des Téléphonique et Télégraphique.**

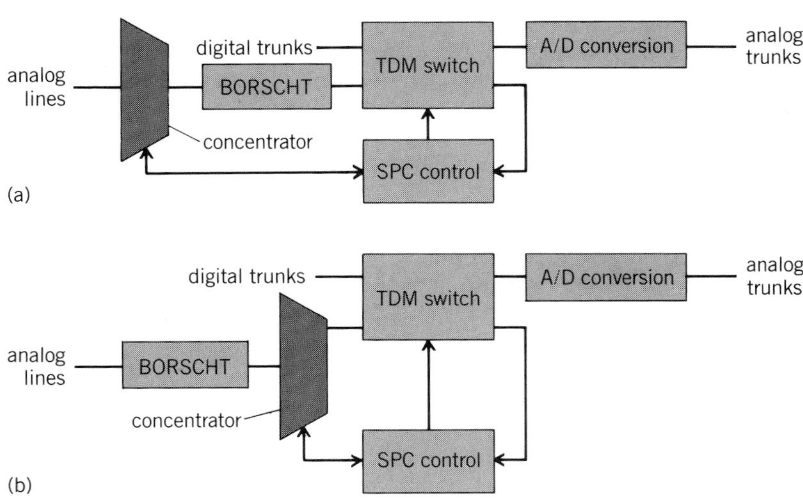


**Fig. 13. First-generation local time-division digital switching system. (*a*) System without interface (BORSCHT) circuitry on each line. (*b*) System with interface (BORSCHT) circuitry on each line.**

pacity. System units synchronize their operations under the control of a system clock.

***Digital (PCM) local systems.*** Initially, most time-division-multiplex (TDM) switching systems were used to switch calls between trunks to and from intermediate offices or between trunks and internal links. In the first-generation local offices, the conversion of signals from analog to digital (A/D), and vice versa, took place in trunk or link interface circuitry. As the cost of interface circuitry has decreased, newer systems have been designed to terminate ordinary telephone lines carrying analog voice signals directly on analog-to-digital conversion circuits. To use time-division-multiplex switching, voice signals are digitized, assigned time slots, and then multiplexed. The line interface circuit, colloquially known as BORSCHT, provides the system with these capabilities, as well as those normally expected within local space-division switching systems. BORSCHT is an acronym for Battery (to feed the analog telephone transmitter), Overvoltage protection, Ringing, Supervision, digital Coding, Hybrid to separate directions of transmission (a requirement for digital time-division-multiplex systems), and Test access (to reach both the in-office and outside plants).

Most early time-division-multiplex local switching systems (**Fig. 13*a***) employed space-division concentrators using metallic crosspoints, such as crossbar or sealed reed switches between the lines and the interface circuits. These were located in the links so that their cost could be spread over more lines. The first-generation switches of this type were pioneered by the French in 1970. Semiconductor crosspoint concentrators are in use, and in the United States include a variety that has electrical characteristics much like metallic devices, in that they can carry the high energy required by analog telephone lines for talking and ringing.

In anticipation of the rapidly decreasing cost of integrated circuits and the prospects for including much of the interface in them, some first-generation local systems introduced into North America were designed with a BORSCHT circuit on each line (Fig. 13*b*). Local time-division digital systems are also suitable for application where there is considerable growth of lines and where digital multiplex transmission facilities are the economic choice. Since much local trunking employs digital time-division multiplex, the use of time-division-multiplex digital switching for intermediate offices (tandem, toll, and transit) has also been popular.

To provide large call-attempt capacity, particularly for toll system applications, additional control processors are used, usually by providing several identical processors that share the load. These are called multiprocessor systems. Also, microprocessors are being associated with the periphery of systems to distribute some of the stored-program-control functions. For smaller systems, some basic control functions are built into logic circuits rather than being stored as programs in the processor memory. These are action translator systems with call sequences determined by the use of memory on a look-up-table basis.

**Table 1** lists central-office stored-program-control time-division digital switching systems, both toll and local.

***Distributed-control TDM systems.*** In more advanced local digital switching systems, not only is the interface circuit highly integrated, but line and trunk terminations are grouped into modules that permit the application of distributed control techniques. Some or all of the routine call-processing functions are performed by programs stored in microprocessors associated with the modules. In addition, the first switching stage, usually a time stage, is included in the module. The module therefore includes all of the

**Table 1. Central stored-program-control time-division-multiplex switching systems**

| Country of origin | Code | Manufacturer | First service | Type | Size (1K = 1000) |
|---|---|---|---|---|---|
| United States | No. 4 ESS | AT&T—Technologies | 1976 | Toll | 107K trunks |
| United States | ITS 4/5* | TRW-VIDAR | 1976 | Local/toll | 7K lines |
| Canada | DMS 10* | Northern Telecom | 1977 | Local | 7K lines |
| United States | DCO† | Stromberg-Carlson | 1977 | Local | 32K lines |
| United States | 1210* | ITT-North | 1978 | Local/toll | 26K lines |
| Sweden | AXE‡ | L. M. Ericsson | 1978 | Local/toll | 64K lines |
| United States | No. 3 EAX | GTE-Auto Electric | 1978 | Toll | 60K trunks |
| Japan | NEAX-61 | Nippon Electric | 1979 | Local/toll | 100K lines |
| Canada | DMS 100/200* | Northern Telecom | 1979 | Local/toll | 100K lines |

*Local systems have a BORSCHT circuit on each line.
†1977 design had a BORSCHT circuit on each line.
‡1982 design had a BORSCHT circuit on each line.

**Table 2. Distributed stored-program-control time-division-multiplex switching systems**

| Country of origin | Code | Manufacturer | First service | Type |
|---|---|---|---|---|
| West Germany | EWS-D | Siemens | 1980 | Local/toll |
| United Kingdom | System X | Plessey/GEC | 1981 | Local/toll |
| Italy | UT10/3 | Italtel | 1981 | Local |
| Belgium | 1240 | ITT-BTM-SEL | 1982 | Local/toll |
| United States | No. 5 ESS | AT&T—Technologies | 1982 | Local/toll |
| United States | No. 5 EAX | GTE-Auto Electric | 1982 | Local/toll |
| France | MT20/25* | Alcatel-Thompson | 1982 | Local/toll |
| France | E10S/E20-5 | CIT-Alcatel | 1983 | Local |
| Netherlands | 5-ESS/PRXD | AT&T International Philips | 1985 | Local/toll |

*Local systems have a BORSCHT circuit on each line.

basic switching functions of the network, interface, and control (**Fig. 14**). Systems with varying degrees of distributed control and network are known as distributed switching systems. The close association of these functions in a unit leads to further opportunities for the use of very large-scale integrated (VLSI) circuits.

Distributed switching has also renewed interest in separating the modules from the time-multiplex-switching and central control system core, that together are sometimes called the host. The modules may be located away from the system core, closer to the customers. Not only are line facilities saved, but they use digital transmission to connect these modules to the host. Typically these remote units serve from a hundred to several hundred lines. For the larger units, the microprocessor controls used in the switch module are sufficiently autonomous to enable them to function on intralocal calls should the trunk linking the module with the host be disrupted. When remote units provide for some operation independent of the host central office, they are known as remote switching modules, units, or systems.

Changes in the system core have also begun to appear as a result of the application of distributed switching and large-scale circuit integration (LSI). These changes affect both the network and the control. The network employs both time-multiplex switching and time-slot interchange techniques, interchanging channel information between multiplexed links to and from the modules and between time slots. Large-scale integrated circuit chips can be designed with sufficient intelligence that the modules themselves may control the establishment of paths through the switching network. This technique is known as self-selection since the switching actions in the chip are controlled by signals arriving over the links.

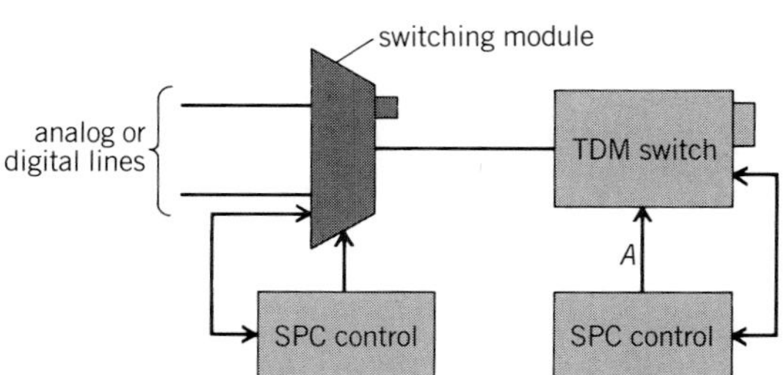


**Fig. 14. Second-generation local time-division digital switching system. If the TDM switch is self-directing, the path labeled A is omitted.**

**Table 2** lists the distributed time-division switching systems that have been deployed in many countries.

**Alternative switching techniques.** In the past, switching utilized technology that was unique, such as step-by-step and crossbar switches. In the immediate past, technology from computer and digital transmission was used in local time-division digital systems. Switching is currently gaining its own technology with integrated circuits that include complete time slot interchange, line interface (BORSCHT) and other circuits. As a result, many different system architectures and devices are being introduced around the world. Most new systems are of the stored-program type with high-capacity random-access memory chips, such as those with 256,000 and $10^6$ bits.

New technology, as well as services, first appears in small switching systems, such as private branch exchanges, in advance of the general trend in central office switching. This trend also applies to the combining of digital data and digitized voice switching for integrated digital services. In such systems, the signaling from station terminals also employs new digital subscriber line protocols.

Increasingly, maintenance and administrative functions have been centralized in computer that serve several central offices. Communication with these centers is two-way, with some information for special calls being stored at the central location.

The time-division digital switching technique is being used in newly installed systems as it becomes economically competitive with space division. Distributed switching is applicable to space division as well as time division. These applications may also use powerful low-cost microprocessors for call processing in switching modules remote from the host. A remote switch employing a nonmetallic switching network has been deployed in the United States.

Another technique for the switching of digital signals is the use of existing metallic space-division switching systems. Most modern switching systems will pass 64,000 bit/s digitized voice signals, highlighting the fact that a digital switching system may employ time or space division. But there is interfacing synergy between time-division-multiplex transmission and time-division switching systems. Furthermore, a time-division system provides an opportunity to transmit digital signals from nonvoice sources, such as computers and terminals. This capability gives rise to the concept of networks integrating digital multiplex transmission, switching, and services.

**Message switching systems.** The types of electronic switching systems described so far provide

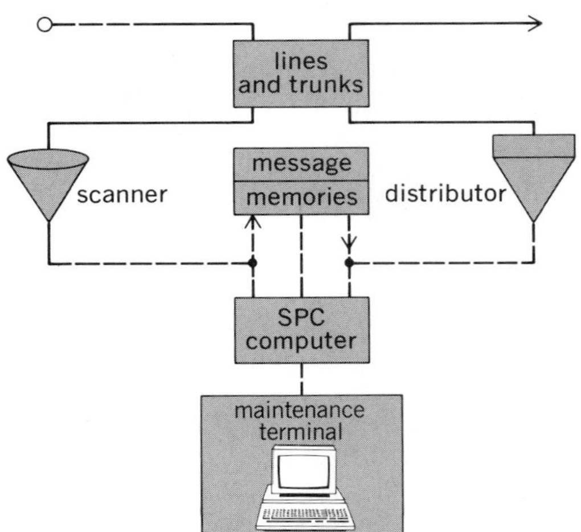


**Fig. 15. Block diagram of a store-and-forward switching system.**

two-way communication circuit paths (or their equivalent for voice) in real time. The systems of this type are known as circuit or line switching systems. They are used for voice and data service where instant two-way message exchange is required. Another type of system (**Fig. 15**) known as a message or store-and-forward switching system is used to process and deliver messages or data, which may be stored temporarily in a memory awaiting the availability of outgoing trunk or line facilities. Depending upon the form of messages and the engineered delay time, message switching systems may provide several different capacities and access times. Sometimes short messages are stored at stations and transmitted to the switch in segments as determined (poled) by the switch. One such system in which the message is divided into uniform segments with an address placed on each segment is known as packet switching. The switch intermixes the packets from all sources and may route individual packets of the same message over different routes. Many message switching systems employ stored program control supplied by commercial digital computers.

New systems are being developed that will service lines that carry both the voice and data needed by subscribers. The voice and data are digitized. Fully end-to-end digital network facilities with common channel signaling serve calls from station terminals. The concept is known as integrated services digital network (ISDN). *See Data communications; Packet switching; Telephone.*

*Amos E. Joel, Jr.*

**Bibliography.** A. E. Joel, Jr., *Electronic Switching: Digital Central Offices of the World*, 1982; J. C. McDonald, *Fundamentals of Digital Switching*, 1983; *Proceedings of the International Switching Symposium*, Montreal, September 1981, IEEE Publ. CH 1736-8, 1981; *Proceedings of the International Switching Symposium*, Florence, Italy, May 1984, AEI Publication, Milan, 1984.

## Switching theory

The theory of circuits made up of ideal digital devices. Included are the theory of circuits and networks for telephone switching, digital computing, digital control, and data processing.

Switching theory generally is concerned with circuits made of devices or elements that can be in two or more discrete conditions or states. Examples of such devices are switches or relay contacts, which can be opened or closed, rectifying diodes, which can be either forward- or back-biased, solid-state elements (such as transistors), which can be saturated or cut off, and magnetic elements which can be magnetized to saturation in either of two directions. Switching theory establishes an ideal representation of the digital circuit, examines the properties of the representation, then interprets these as properties of the circuit. Switching theory is not concerned with the physical phenomena of action or stability in a particular condition or with the details of transition from one state to another. It takes these as established and proceeds to examine more or less complex combinations of digital devices whose properties are assumed to be ideal.

The bulk of switching theory is concerned with circuits that are made of binary (two-valued) devices, since these are most common. Switching theory can be based in part on mathematical logic. *See Boolean algebra.*

A switching circuit whose outputs are determined only by the concurrent inputs is called a combinational circuit (or logic circuit). A circuit in which outputs at one time may be affected by inputs at a previous time is called a sequential circuit.

**Combinational circuits.** A rule by which the outputs of a combinational circuit can be determined from its inputs is called a switching function. Since the variables are discrete, a switching function may be expressed in tabular form as a truth table, or may be indicated by a diagram or geometric pattern. If the function and variables are binary, the symbols of 1 and 0 are commonly used to represent the two values. The function may then be represented by a boolean algebraic expression. The two values of a switching function can represent closed and open circuits, as for switches or relay contacts, or high and low or plus and minus voltages, as in electronic circuits.

The simplest combinational switching functions are the NOT function, the AND function, and the OR function. The NOT function is designated by the prime in boolean algebra; $Y = X'$ means that $Y$ is closed (high, plus) when $X$ is open (low, minus), and vice versa. The AND function is designated by the boolean product; $Z = X \cdot Y$ means that $Z$ is closed (high, plus) only if both $X$ and $Y$ are closed. The OR function is designated by the boolean sum; $Z = X + Y$ means that $Z$ is closed if either $X$ or $Y$ or both are closed. All other combinational switching functions can be made by combining these elementary building blocks.

For example, **Fig. 1** shows a switching circuit with three switches, or contacts, $X$, $Y$, and $Z'$, each of which can be either open or closed. These can be thought of as input variables. The circuit as a whole will be open or closed depending upon the individual positions of $X$, $Y$, and $Z'$. Its condition can be designated by $W$, an output variable. Let 0 represent the open condition, and 1 the closed condition. The table in Fig. 1 represents the switching function of the circuit. The boolean expression for this function is $W = Z'(X + Y)$. To interpret this expression the rules of simple boolean algebra must be used:

$$\begin{array}{lll} 0+0=0 & 0\cdot 0=0 & 0'=1 \\ 0+1=1 & 0\cdot 1=0 & 1'=0 \\ 1+0=1 & 1\cdot 0=0 & \\ 1+1=1 & 1\cdot 1=1 & \end{array}$$

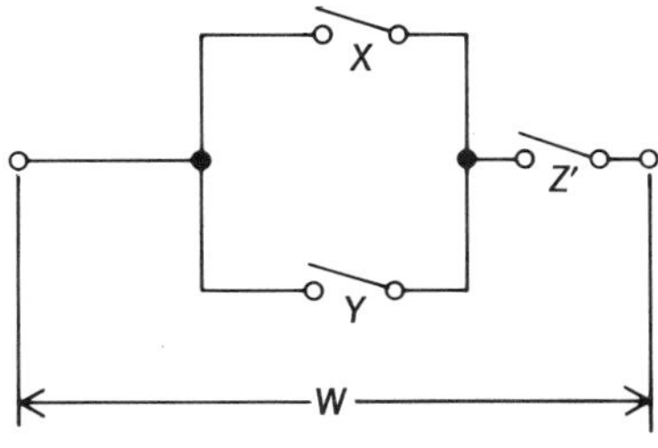


| X | Y | Z′ | W |
|---|---|---|---|
| 0 | 0 | 1 | 0 |
| 0 | 0 | 0 | 0 |
| 0 | 1 | 1 | 1 |
| 0 | 1 | 0 | 0 |
| 1 | 0 | 1 | 1 |
| 1 | 0 | 0 | 0 |
| 1 | 1 | 1 | 1 |
| 1 | 1 | 0 | 0 |

**Fig. 1. Combinational circuit. $W = Z'(X + Y)$. $X$ and $Y$ are normally open contacts. $Z'$ is a normally closed contact.**

Switching theory establishes a number of methods for analysis and synthesis of combinational circuits. A significant problem is minimization, that is, given a switching function, to synthesize the simplest circuit which will realize it. A problem of some theoretical difficulty is that of realizability, that is, given a statement of specifications, to determine whether a switching circuit exists which satisfies them.

Analysis of a series-parallel combination of switches or relay contacts can be carried out by a direct application of boolean algebra. Variables or terms corresponding to contacts, or combinations in parallel, are added, and those in series are multiplied. The values are interpreted according to the rules of boolean algebra. Similar methods can be applied to combinational circuits which employ various solid state switching elements, such as transistors. Circuits that are not series-parallel can be dealt with by an extension of the boolean method, by the use of matrices with discrete-valued elements, or by a number of special methods.

A switching function can be simply synthesized as a series-parallel combination of contacts by giving boolean symbols circuit interpretations explained previously. Electronic logic circuits can be synthesized in a similar fashion. This approach will lead to a method for embodying any switching function expressed in boolean terms. The boolean expression of a function given in tabular or diagrammatic form is easily obtained.

Synthesizing the minimal circuit, or minimization, is more difficult since for every switching function there are many possible circuits. Where the number of variables is small, the minimization problem can often be reduced to one that has already been solved. Tables of minimal or nearly minimal solutions for relay circuits and solid-state circuits are available for circuits with one output and as many as four inputs. Harvard chart methods and Karnaugh map methods utilize geometrical relationships to explore systematically functions with one output and as many as six inputs.

As the number of variables increases, the possible number of functions rapidly becomes large. For example, there are more than $10^{19}$ different functions of six binary variables. No completely general and practical design methods have been discovered. However, a growing array of special methods for synthesis and minimization is available.

**Sequential circuits.** Since the outputs of sequential circuits depend on past, as well as present, inputs, they must contain means for remembering or storing the effect of past inputs, such as locking relays, flip-flops, delay lines, or solid-state memories. A device with two stable states can remember one binary digit, or bit. The amount of memory in a circuit can be measured either in bits or in internal states. An internal state of a circuit is a particular configuration of its internal memory devices. The number of internal states is equal to $2^n$, where $n$ represents its number of bits. Binary counters and shift registers are examples of sequential circuits.

It is possible to represent a sequential circuit as a combinational circuit with feedback. Thus, the combinational circuit of **Fig. 2** becomes a sequential circuit with two bits of memory if two of its outputs are connected to two of its inputs. Any such closed loop must contain gain and some delay; sometimes additional delay is inserted.

If the combinational circuit and the delays in Fig. 2 are completely specified, the internal description of the circuit is known and its behavior can be analyzed. If the switching function of the combinational circuit is such that $m_1 = M_1$ and $m_2 = M_2$ for a given set of inputs, no change can occur as a result of the action of the memory loops and the circuit is stable; otherwise, it is unstable. If it is unstable, the inputs must cause a transition to a new state, which in turn may be stable or unstable. If no stable state is reached, the circuit is said to buzz. If the state to which a circuit may pass depends on which of two or more memory loops acts first, the circuit is said to have a race condition, and its performance may be ambiguous. This difficulty does not occur in circuits in which changes are caused or timed by repetitive clock pulses. Such circuits are called synchronous. Circuits which make transitions at the natural internal rate are known as asynchronous, and these asyn-

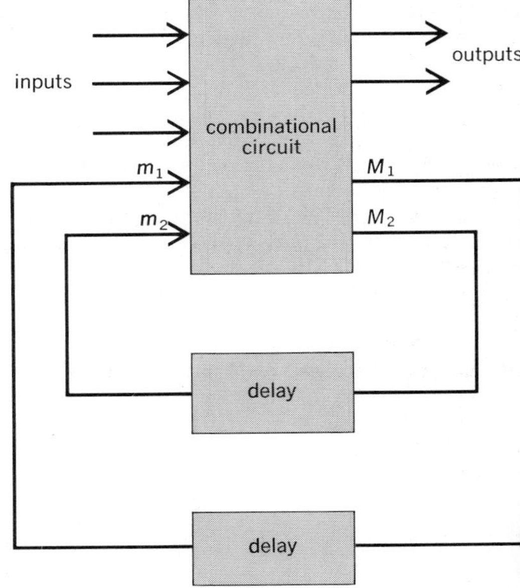


**Fig. 2. Sequential circuit with two memory loops.**

chronous circuits must be designed with greater care.

To proceed from external circuit requirements to an internal description of a sequential circuit requires art and skill, as well as knowledge of switching theory. *See* DATA-PROCESSING SYSTEMS; DIGITAL COMPUTER; LOGIC CIRCUITS; SWITCHING CIRCUIT; SWITCHING SYSTEMS (COMMUNICATIONS).

*Willard D. Lewis*

**Bibliography.** N. U. Biswas, *Introduction to Logic and Switching Theory*, 1975; F. J. Hill and G. R. Peterson, *Introduction to Switching Theory and Logical Design*, 1981; Z. Kohavi, *Switching and Finite Automata Theory*, 2d ed., 1974; S. C. Lee, *Modern Switching Theory and Digital Design*, 1978; R. Miller, *Switching Theory*, 1965, reprint 1979.

## Symbolic mathematical computation

The manipulation of symbols, representing variables, functions, and other mathematical objects, and combinations of those symbols, representing formulas, equations, and expressions, according to mathematical rules (for example, the rules of algebra or calculus). It is distinct from numerical computation, in which operations can be carried out only on numbers. Symbolic mathematics is used in all fields of science and engineering to solve problems exactly when possible, to generate approximate solutions, and to perform or check tedious manipulations too large (perhaps thousands of pages long) to compute with certainty by hand. Often, a single small formula may result whose meaning is much easier to understand than a large table of numerical values of some approximation to it.

There exist several general-purpose computer programs for symbolic mathematics that are running and undergoing active development on a variety of computers. The examples in this article were generated by using SMP. Programs begun earlier include MACSYMA, REDUCE, SCRATCHPAD, and muMATH, while a newer program is MAPLE. A number of special-purpose programs have also been written.

```
# I [1] : : D [Sin[1/(x+1)],x]

                   1
           -Cos [-----]
                  1+x
# O [1] :  --------------
                     2
             (1 + x)

# I [2] : : Graph [Sin [ 1/ (x+1) ],x, - .99, -.97]

# O [2] :
```

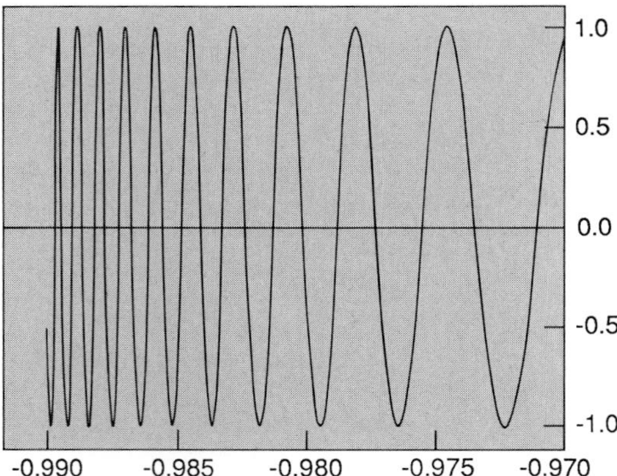


```
# I [3] : : N [S [#0 [1], x -> -.98], 12]

# O [3] : : -2412.41507123

# I [4] : : Sol [{0=x y - c y - d x+ c d,0=x y - 3 y+7 x-21},{x,y}]

# O [4] : : {{x -> 3,y -> d},{y -> -7,x -> c}}

# I [5] : : fib [1] : fib [2] : 1 ; fib [$n_= Natp [$n]] : fib [$n-1]+fib [$n-2] ;

# I [6] : : Tan [a] : 2-z ; fib [3+2z+2Tan [a]]

# O [6] : 13
```

**Transcript of session with the SMP computer program for symbolic mathematics.**

**Examples.** The **illustration** is a transcript of an SMP session. SMP asks for the first input expression with the prompt **#I[1]::**. Whatever the user types will be the first element in a list of input expressions that can be referred to later, and whatever SMP calculates from the input will be the first element of a list of output expressions named **#O**. In this case, a trigonometric expression, **Sin[1/(x + 1)]**, is differentiated with respect to $x$, producing the result **−Cos[1/(1 + x)]/(1 + x)²**. The function **D** performs differentiation of its first argument with respect to the second, the arguments being delimited by square brackets and separated by commas. The function treated here is highly oscillatory near **x = −1**; this behavior is shown by the graph produced by SMP in response to input line 2, where the user has passed an expression, the variable, and the lower and upper limits of its range to the **Graph** function. An attempt to numerically differentiate the function at **x = −.98** by constructing the slope between two nearby points, say **x = −.985** and **x = −.975**, gives grossly inaccurate results. Evaluating the symbolic formula for the derivative at some value of $x$ can be easily done to arbitrary accuracy as shown in line 3 of the session, in which −.98 is substituted (using the function **S**) for **x** in the result of the first calculation, and the result is numerically evaluated (using the function **N**) to 12 places.

At the fourth input prompt, the user types **Sol** [{**0 = x y − c y − d x + c d,0 = x y − 3y + 7x − 21**},{**x,y**}] to direct SMP to solve a set of simultaneous nonlinear equations for **x** and **y**, producing two families of solutions, not obtainable numerically. (Since symbols and variables can have multiletter names, the terms of a product must be separated by a space or asterisk.)

Input line 5, **fib**[**1**] **:** **fib**[**2**] **: 1;fib**[**$n__ = Natp** [**$n**]] **: fib**[**$n − 1**] **+ fib**[**$n − 2**], defines the terms of the Fibonacci series: the first two terms are unity, any other term is the sum of the two previous terms. The last part of the definition restricts it to arguments that are natural numbers ("__=" can be read as "such that"). This requirement ensures that any use of this recursive (self-invoking) definition will always terminate by reaching one of the forms **fib**[**2**] or **fib**[**1**]. Given only this definition, SMP would return exactly the user's input if asked for **fib**[**5.7**], but if SMP is now told that the tangent of **a** has a particular value, **2 − z**, and **fib** [**3 + 2z + 2Tan**[**a**]] is then requested, the result is 13, the value of **fib**[**7**]. The quantity **fib**[**7**] is defined in terms of **fib**[**6**] and **fib**[**5**], and so on, down to **fib**[**1**] and **fib**[**2**].

This result, and all others, is obtained by a general process called simplification, which consists of replacing parts of the input expression by their values. The values can be obtained by internal algorithms (for example, the sum of the terms after replacing **Tan**[**a**] above), by values assigned to symbols or expressions by the user, or by general or specific transformation rules defined by the user (or found in libraries of routines written by the program's developers and other users). Usually, the arguments to a function such as **fib** are simplified before the function definition is used; that is why the definition of **fib** for natural number arguments can be used. None of the examples can be performed by numerical programs.

Most general-symbolic mathematics programs contain facilities to evaluate expressions to specified numerical precision. Many also have graphical capabilities, and the capability, after performing desired transformations of symbolic expressions, of translating them into programs in a numerical programming language such as FORTRAN.

**Nature of systems.** The ideal of designers of symbolic mathematics systems is to provide a program that can carry out any mathematical operation, including one unknown to the designer or not yet invented, preferably in a notation similar to that used by a mathematical practitioner. All existing systems imperfectly realize that goal, falling short in different ways and degrees.

***Operational systems.*** Existing designs of symbolic mathematics systems fill a spectrum between two distinct design philosophies. The first is mechanistic, or operational. The language provided by the symbolic mathematics program allows the user to define a transformation rule which takes combinations of symbols satisfying a given set of conditions as input and then produces the desired new combination of symbols as output. If the language is rich enough to describe any possible transformation of symbols by some sequence or combination of its primitives, if the program can recognize any given expression or combination of symbols that satisfies the necessary conditions, and if the language allows facilities that control where the rule should be used, any mathematical operation can be carried out. SMP is a language designed mainly in accordance with this approach, but all the languages contain access to some pure symbol manipulation primitives, perhaps by direct use of the lower-level language used to implement the program. SMP's pattern recognizer is perhaps the most deeply embedded of those available.

***SCRATCHPAD program.*** The SCRATCHPAD program goes farthest toward the other extreme of design philosophy, using deep mathematical knowledge more heavily than unconstrained symbol manipulation. An operation in SCRATCHPAD is not fully specified until the algebraic domains from which its operands are drawn are specified. In different parts of a computation, a single expression may be viewed as an element of several different domains. (For example, the number 3 may be treated as an integer, a real or complex number, polynomial in $x$ of degree 0, and so forth.)

The allowed operations of each domain are fully specified, and the program can perform legal conversions between domains and proper manipulations of expressions that belong to composite domains of great complexity, using knowledge of the hierarchical relations between domains. New domains can be added by the user, or built up from already included ones, to implement new areas of mathematics. These new domains inherit much machinery from their components.

For example, if two matrices are multiplied, SCRATCHPAD automatically checks that the elements of the matrices are from consistent domains (which can be coerced into a common domain), and forms the elements of the product matrix by using appropriate multiplication and addition rules for the elements. For example, to multiply a matrix of complex numbers by a matrix of polynomials in the variable $z$ with integer coefficients, SCRATCHPAD will determine that the elements of both matrices are from consistent domains; in particular, they can be regarded to be members of the domain of, and be coerced automatically into SCRATCHPAD's internal representation for, polynomials in $z$ with complex coefficients. The multiplication and addition operations for that common domain are used to carry out the matrix multiplication. Thus, any operations defined properly are guaranteed to produce mathematically correct results for any inputs upon which they are allowed to work.

***Comparison of systems.*** The user of SMP employs ingenuity to specify a mechanism for producing the answer, while a SCRATCHPAD user often employs ingenuity to find a set of known operations and domains in which the answer is automatically derived. It is easy to find problems in which one approach or the other leads most conveniently to the desired result. For this reason the implementation of each system is not as radical as its design approach; each adopts features of the other for the convenience of users. In particular, SCRATCHPAD contains facilities for using rewrite rules such as SMP's and SMP contains some ability to implement algebraic domains and hierarchies. A result can usually be more directly justified rigorously by reviewing the transcript of a SCRATCHPAD session than an SMP session.

A user approximating **p**, a polynomial of many terms in **x**, for $x$ near zero, may decide to ignore (as small and inconsequential) terms with high powers of $x$. Before further manipulations occurred, a person doing the problem with pencil and paper would probably cross out all such terms. Similarly, a user of SMP can type **S[p,x^($n_ =$n>5) − >0]**, meaning "Everywhere $x$ is raised to some power greater than 5 in the expression $p$, substitute zero." A user of SCRATCHPAD would more likely tell the system to regard $p$ as a power series in $x$ truncated at fifth order. (SMP can also produce the result in this way.)

In a slightly more complicated problem, each term of the polynomial $p$ may be multiplied by an unknown function $f(x)$. The user may be intending to eventually integrate this expression over all real values of $x$, and may know enough about the physical laws governing the behavior of whatever physical system the expression models to know that integrals of terms with odd powers of $x$ multiplying $f(x)$ vanish, and that integrals of terms with large powers of $x$ (greater than 5) are small and can be ignored. An SMP user could type **S[p,x^($n_ = ($n>5| Oddp[$n])) − >0]** to substitute 0 for powers of $x$ that are either odd or greater than fifth power before the integral is carried out. The SCRATCHPAD user would probably take a similarly nonrigorous approach to avoid a more cumbersome sequence of commands needed to achieve the same result by setting up an appropriate domain for the problem.

***Use of advanced algorithms.*** In principle, all standard mathematical operations could be built out of symbol manipulation primitives. In practice, however, all of these systems provide the standard operations of algebra and calculus, including highly sophisticated recent algorithms for polynomial factorization, exact solution of algebraic equations, and indefinite integration, much more powerful and efficient than the methods known by most users. The developers of many of the programs heavily emphasize these components of the systems and refer to their products as computer algebra systems, or algebra engines.

**Research.** Research continues in more powerful and complete algebraic algorithms. Development of graphical user interfaces to symbolic mathematics programs is beginning to make them easier to use, at least on high-resolution bitmap terminals. Study of the important engineering problem of improving the performance of automatically generated programs using symbolic transformations of the mathematical expressions those programs represent is in progress. SEE DIGITAL COMPUTER PROGRAMINING; PROGRAMMING LANGUAGES.

*Jeffrey M. Greif*

***Bibliography.*** B. Caviness (ed.), *Eurocal '85: European Conference on Computer Algebra*, vols. 1 and 2, 1985; B. Char (ed.), *SYMSAC '86: Proceedings of ACM Symposium on Symbolic and Algebraic Computation*, Association for Computing Machinery, 1986; C. Cole and S. Wolfram, SMP: A symbolic manipulation program, in P. S. Wang (ed.), *Proceedings of SYMSAC '81*, Association for Computing Machinery, pp. 20–22, 1981; R. D. Jenks, A primer: 11 keys to new Scratchpad, in J. Fitch (ed.), *Proceedings of EUROSAM '84*, pp. 123–147, 1984; D. Stoutemeyer and D. Y. Y. Yun, Symbolic mathematical computation, in *Encyclopedia of Computer Science and Technology*, vol. 15, pp. 235–310, 1980

## Synchronization

The process of maintaining one operation in step with another. The commonest example is the electric clock, whose motor rotates at some integral multiple or submultiple of the speed of the alternator in the power station. In television, synchronization is essential in order that the electron beams of receiver picture tubes are at exactly the same spot on the screen at each instant as is the beam in the television camera tube at the transmitter. Synchronism in television is achieved by transmitting a synchronizing pulse at the end of each scanning line, to make all receivers move simultaneously to the start of the next line. A similar vertical synchronizing pulse is transmitted when the camera beam reaches the bottom of the picture, to make all beams go back to the top for the start of the next field. SEE OSCILLOSCOPE; TELEVISION.

*John Markus*

## Synchroscope

An instrument used for indicating whether two alternating-current (ac) generators or other ac voltage sources are synchronized in time phase with each other. In one type, for example, the position of a continuously rotatable pointer indicates the instantaneous phase difference between the two sources at each instant; the speed of rotation of the pointer corresponds to the frequency difference between the sources, while the direction of rotation indicates which source is higher in frequency. In more modern synchroscopes, a cathode-ray tube serves as the indicating means.

The term synchroscope is also applied to a special type of cathode-ray oscilloscope designed for observing extremely short pulses, using fast sweeps synchronized with the signal to be observed. SEE OSCILLOSCOPE.

*John Markus*

## Tank circuit

An inductor and capacitor in parallel. The term is quite often used to denote the parallel resonant circuit in the output stage of a radio transmitter, but it has been applied to any parallel resonant circuit. In many cases the inductance in the tank circuit is one winding of a two-winding, air-core transformer. The secondary is connected to some load, such as an antenna. Power is delivered from the source to the load through the tank circuit, with an effort usually made to adjust the parameters for maximum power transfer. SEE IMPEDANCE MATCHING; RESONANCE (ALTERNATING-CURRENT CIRCUITS); TRANSFORMER.

Since the tank circuit is a parallel resonant circuit, the parameters can be chosen so that at a desired frequency the voltage across the tank circuit will be a maximum. In radio transmitters this is done by varying the capacitance, but in other situations, such as oscillators, the inductance may be varied by means of a tuning slug in the coil. SEE OSCILLATOR.

Tank circuits have an important role as a plate load in class C amplifiers, in which the plate current flows for only a small fraction of a cycle. If the damping in the circuit is small and the circuit is excited at its resonant frequency, the plate-current impulses produce a sustained sinusoidal voltage across the tank. If a load is transformer-coupled to the tank, the voltage across the load is sinusoidal. SEE AMPLIFIER.

*Harold F. Klock*

## Teleconferencing

Broadly, the various ways and means by which people communicate with one another over some distance. In a narrow sense, a teleconference is a two-way, interactive meeting, between relatively small groups of people (approximately 1 to 10 at each end), who usually use permanent teleconferencing facilities. A teleconference involves audio communication between the locations, but may also involve video, graphics, or facsimile.

**Teleseminar.** A teleseminar is utilized for educational purposes; it is primarily one-way communication to many destinations from one source. A teleseminar almost always uses audio communication, and may also use video and some form of graphics. The source location usually has just lecturers, and the destination locations are usually classrooms or meeting rooms with no more than 20–30 people in each location. There are typically 2–10 receiving locations. A means is provided for the receiving locations to ask questions of the instructor via microphones or telephone handsets. The facilities are usually built or converted especially for teleseminars.

**Telemeeting.** A telemeeting is often called an ad hoc teleconference, with the ad hoc referring to places, times, participants, and purpose. A telemeeting is similar to a teleseminar in that it is primarily a one-way communication, usually staged or prepared by video program professionals. It is set up to order, using temporary equipment or circuits, and typically utilizing hotel facilities. Events include stockholders' meetings, new product introductions, sales meetings, promotions, and press conferences, and thus involve large numbers of people at all locations. Audio and video are almost exclusively used to communicate and, as with a teleseminar, a means is usually provided at the receiving locations for questions to be asked of those at the transmitting location.

**Computer conferencing.** Computer conferencing is a method for people to communicate by using computers. The medium is quite flexible, as it can be used between just two people, between one and many people, or among many people. Basically, it involves typing a message on a computer terminal and transmitting it to one or more destinations electronically.

Sophisticated networks are required to accomplish computer conferencing in real time between many users, or a simple data modem and telephone circuit can allow two people at a time to conference. The network arrangements also allows non-real-time conferencing to occur, which is like an electronic mailbox whereby, for example, a paper could be distributed to certain people via computer with a request for comments; each person could transmit comments via computer to the originator. Computer conferencing is not widely used at present, but it is expected to become widespread as offices become more automated. *See* Data communications; Wide-area networks.

**Audio communication.** As a minimum, teleconferencing audio systems utilize a device such as a speakerphone to allow hands-free operation. More typically, microphones are either clipped to people or attached to a table or ceiling, and loudspeakers are mounted in a wall, cabinet, or ceiling. Depending on the circuits utilized, the audio performance can vary greatly in quality with corresponding variations in cost and complexity. Scrambling is used in some systems to assure communications privacy. *See* Loudspeaker; Microphone; Privacy systems (scrambling); Telephone.

**Video and videographic communication.** Video systems use one or more cameras as image sources, and television receivers, monitors, or large-screen projectors as a means of display. Cameras may be used to view people, objects, chalkboards or easels, slides, transparencies, or text on paper; video tape players are also used as sources. Again, as a function of the communications equipment and circuits used, the nature and quality of the video images may range from that of broadcast television to that of slow scan or freeze frame. Slow scan paints a new picture on the screen in 10 to 60 s, but nevertheless succeeds in providing a perception of presence of people and good-quality videographics. High-speed digital compression codecs are also used to transmit images, which are near full motion, over telephone trunks. Audio and graphic information may also be sent through these codecs, thus allowing one circuit to be used for all forms of communication. *See* Magnetic recording; Television; Television camera; Television receiver; Video telephone.

**Graphic communications.** Numerous devices are available that allow nonvideo graphics to be used in conferencing. These include electronic blackboards and writing tablets which digitize, transmit, and reproduce an exact replica of the source at the destination. Computers are also used to generate graphic material for conferences. The material can be created before a meeting, and with the computer connected into the communications system, the material can be transmitted to a similar computer and displayed at the distant end. *See* Computer graphics.

**Facsimile communications.** Equipment of this type basically consists of office facsimile units that are used in teleconferences to send standard-size pages of textual material between sites, either over telephone circuits or through codecs over high-speed circuits. There are more elaborate versions of the equipment available which also allow the transmitted page to be displayed via a monitor or projector at both the transmitting and receiving locations. *See* Facsimile.

*John J. Bleiweis*

***Bibliography.*** T. B. Cross, Teleconferencing can reduce need to travel, *The Office*, pp. 100 and 115, April 1982; R. Gatty, So far and yet so near, *Nation's Bus.*, pp. 62–67, March 1983; E. M. Gold, Wideband conferencing: The other side of teleconference systems, *Telespan Newslett.*, pp. 15–17, August 2, 1982; A. L. Harvey, Why offices will never be the same, *The Washingtonian*, pp. 247–251, September 1982.

## Telephone

An instrument containing a transmitter for converting the acoustic signals of a person's voice to electrical signals, a receiver for reconverting electrical signals to acoustic signals, and associated signaling devices for communicating with other persons using similar instruments connected to a network. The term telephone also refers to the complicated system of transmission paths and switching points that are connected to this instrument. This article discusses the instrument.

Telephone design has undergone a steady evolution from the first instruments of A. G. Bell and T. A. Edison, and many basic physical principles have been exploited in subtle ways. Developments in digital electronic circuits are heavily exploited in new designs, both to provide new features and to replace older components. The basis of Bell's original invention, the creation of an electrical analog to the acoustic signal of a person's voice, is still the basis for the speech-related circuitry of most telephones. Digital techniques, now used almost exclusively for nonspeech features, will in time also be used to provide some of the speech-related functions.

A telephone set contains seven basic parts: a transmitter, a receiver, an anti-sidetone network, a dial, a ringer, a switchhook, and a chassis. Added to these may be other feature-oriented hardware (and computer programs) such as electronic memory (for dialing of preprogrammed numbers), loudspeakers and microphones (for hands-free use), a voice synthesis unit, or a video screen (for displaying text, graphs, or animated cartoons). The set's complexity, depending on its intended usage, can approach that of a small computer. The telephone's original function, that of permitting voice communication with another person, may therefore be enhanced to permit communication with computers, automatic reporting of emergencies, and the use of written or graphic information.

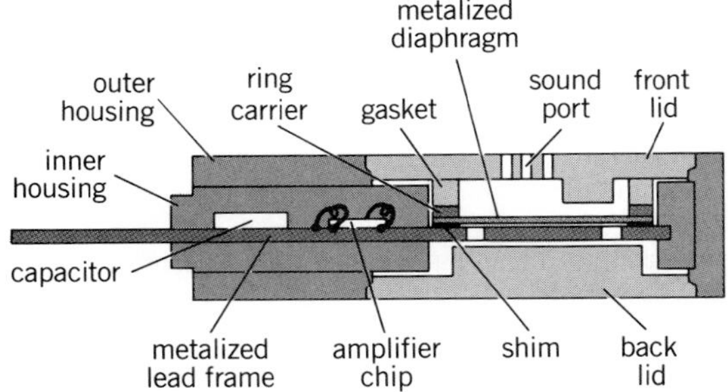


**Fig. 1. Cross section of electret transmitter.**

**Transmitter.** The transmitter is a transducer that converts acoustic energy into electric energy. E. Berliner's invention of the carbon transmitter was the key to practical telephony. This transmitter is still the least costly and is preferred for noisy locations as it tends to suppress background noise; however, it has high signal distortion. It is gradually being replaced by designs based on the charged electret (a condenser microphone) or on electrodynamic principles. Both the electret and electrodynamic transmitters use transistors to provide needed power gain; they introduce less distortion than the carbon transmitter. *See Electret transducer; Microphone; Transducer; Transistor.*

Transmitters have a frequency-response range from 250 to 5000 Hz. Some of the extremes of this range are lost by other components in the telephone system. The frequency response rises uniformly to a broad maximum in the region of 2500 Hz. Even though normal human hearing has a much broader frequency response, speech heard on the telephone resembles closely that of direct mouth-to-ear speech as heard by a listener a few feet from the person speaking. Confusion is possible between "f" and "s" sounds, but the listener usually subconsciously resolves this by the context of the speech.

The heart of an electret transmitter (**Fig. 1**) is an electrical capacitor formed by the metal on the diaphragm, a conductive coating on top of the metalized lead frame, and the plastic and air between the metal layers. The diaphragm is made of a special plastic which can be given a permanent electrostatic charge (analogous to the magnetization of a permanent magnet). As sound waves entering the sound port cause pressure changes, the diaphragm moves closer to and farther away from the metalized lead frame. This changes the value of capacitance and produces a varying electric voltage which is the analog of the impinging sound-pressure wave. The power of this signal is amplified by the internal amplifier chip to a level which is suitable for transmission on the telephone network.

In the carbon transmitter, sound pressure on the diaphragm varies the pressure on the carbon. Changes in pressure on the carbon granules vary the resistance of the transmitter, causing the magnitude of the current supplied by the central office to change in proportion to the sound, a process called modulation. *See Modulation.*

**Receiver.** The receiver transducer operates on the relatively low power used in the telephone circuit; it converts electric energy back into acoustic energy. Unlike a loudspeaker, the telephone receiver is designed for close coupling to the ear. As in the transmitter, careful design of the relationship of the acoustical and electrical elements produces a desired response-frequency characteristic.

There are two common types of receiver units with fixed coil windings, the ring armature receiver and the bipolar receiver. Moving-coil designs, which are similar to loudspeakers, are also used in some instances.

Fixed-coil receivers are designed to have low acoustic impedance and high available power response over the frequency range 350–3500 Hz. Careful control of both the acoustic and electric design parameters is necessary to achieve the desired response and to avoid undesirable resonances. In a ring armature receiver (**Fig. 2**), sound is produced by the piston action of a thin, nonmagnetic, lightweight diaphragm, which is attached at its periphery to a ring-shaped armature of magnetic material. A ring-shaped coil that is associated with a permanent magnet and pole piece constitute the stationary parts of the design. The diaphragm contains a small hole that introduces a low-frequency cutoff. This is desirable to reduce interference picked up from electric power circuits.

The diaphragm, magnet, and coil are encased in a ferrule grid attached to a molded terminal plate. A membrane between the ferrule grid and diaphragm protects the diaphragm from dirt and mechanical damage. Because of its mechanical impedance, the membrane acts as one of the controls over the diaphragm to help achieve the desired frequency response.

The acoustic chamber between the membrane and diaphragm is connected to a chamber molded in the terminal plate behind the diaphragm, called the back chamber. These chambers are connected by passageways having acoustic mass and resistance. The back chamber exhausts into the handset through acoustic fabric. All of these controls are designed to extend the frequency range of the receiver and to reduce undesirable diaphragm resonance. A click-reducing varistor is mounted on the back of the receiver. *See Varistor.*

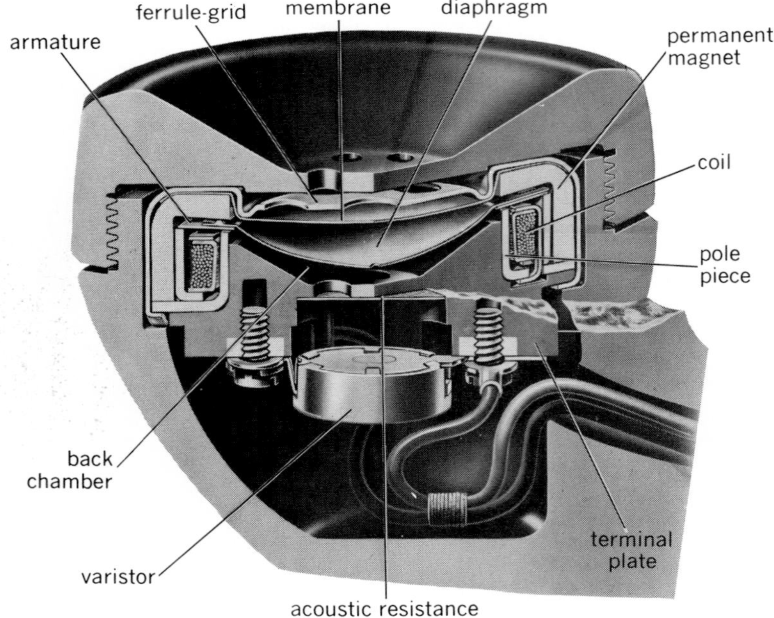


**Fig. 2. Cutaway view of ring armature telephone receiver.**

**Anti-sidetone network.** The anti-sidetone network has two basic functions: to reduce sidetone (explained below), and to provide equalization (reduce the variation in loudness that is caused by varying lengths of cable between the central office and different subscribers). This network may also provide more efficient coupling of the transducers to the telephone line if it incorporates a transformer.

Sidetone is the sound of the speaker's voice reaching his or her own ear. Normally this occurs through the air. However, when one is using a telephone handset, the acoustic sidetone path to one ear is replaced by an electric sidetone path through the telephone's transmitter, network, and receiver. Since the transmitter amplifies power impinging on its diaphragm, this may result in a louder sound in the ear coupled to the receiver than would exist if the receiver were not being used. This is unpleasant and can also cause the telephone user to talk more softly, thereby making it harder for the person at the far end to understand the conversation. Anti-sidetone networks may consist entirely of passive electric components such as transformers, capacitors, and resistors; or may include active components such as transistors embedded in integrated circuits. *See Electric filter; Integrated circuits.*

Passive networks achieve equalization by introducing power loss on short loops between the subscriber and the central office and so must be used with transmitters having internal gain. Active networks supply loss or gain as needed, for example, for use with a loudspeaker or with a low-efficiency transmitter.

**Dial.** The dial was originally designed to permit selection of a particular "far-end" station by operation of switches in the central office. In its simplest form, a rotary dial contains a pair of electric contacts which periodically interrupt the power flowing from the central office. The resulting direct-current pulses are generated at the rate of 10 per second and operate specially designed relay circuits in the central office to choose the desired far-end station.

Dual-tone multifrequency (DTMF) codes, decoded by electronic circuits at the central office, are used for the same purpose in most newer telephones. In this system, two audio tones are used to represent each digit. The tones are selected from a $3 \times 4$ matrix of pushbuttons which replace the dial. Each time a button is pushed, the two tones are sent simultaneously. The tone pairs are selected so that they are unlikely to occur in natural speech, thereby avoiding the inadvertent simulation of digits by speech during the normal dialing interval. These tones have an advantage over the direct-current pulses in that they can be transmitted over the transmission network to the far-end station (as is the electrical analog of the voice signal), whereas direct-current pulses normally will not carry beyond the local central office. Used this way, the multifrequency tone signals can convey information to a computer at the far end of the connection.

**Ringer.** The ringer, which normally is powered by a 20-Hz, 88-V, alternating current, serves to alert the subscriber to an incoming call. Mechanical ringers consist of a clapper that periodically strikes a gong, the bell. This device is complicated, as both the electrical circuit that powers the clapper and the mechanical elements of the clapper are made resonant at the right frequencies to maximize sound output and minimize sensitivity to signals of other frequencies. A nonlinear magnetic circuit serves to present a higher impedance to speech signals on the telephone line than to the ringing signal. Electronic (or tone) ringers are powered by the same alternating-current signal from the central office and make use of electrical oscillator design techniques to produce their sound. A ringer must be designed to prevent ringing when dial pulse or noise signals, which might simulate the normal ringing signal, are present on the telephone line.

**Switchhook.** The switchhook contains a set of electrical contacts that interrupt the flow of current from the central office whenever the set is "on hook." The closing of these contacts when the handset is lifted signals the central office that the set's user wants to initiate or answer a call.

**Chassis.** The chassis provides a mechanical support to hold all the other parts together. This chassis must be capable of withstanding considerable abuse as telephones are often inadvertently dropped. The chassis must also present the components in a way that is convenient for the user of the telephone. The dial in desk sets, for example, should be mounted at an angle easy to use.

**Special features.** Many attempts were made in early telephones to add memory to the telephone dial. This feature was never very popular, however, until digital circuits were used instead of mechanical devices to store telephone numbers. A display, included in some sets, allows the user to see what telephone number has been stored. This same display can also give the time and date when not showing telephone numbers. The dramatic reductions in cost and space that digital integrated circuits provided in this application have led to advanced telephone products. *See Microprocessor.*

***Communication with machines.*** Applications of telephony in which one of the two parties communicating is a machine have become common. One example is the ECS–Smoke/Fire (registered trademark) automatic alarm calling equipment. Such equipment can detect emergency events such as a fire, provide notification at the local telephone set via voice-synthesis circuitry to allow aborting of false alarms, and then dial an alarm bureau or other emergency number. The same voice-synthesis hardware allows inexpensive and reliable transmission of the alarm message. As end-to-end acknowledgment of emergency notification is desirable, dual-tone multifrequency signaling back to the alarm reporting station may be employed. This feature only requires the location receiving the alarm to have a dual-tone multifrequency telephone and the sending station to have a simple single-digit, integrated-circuit, dual-tone multifrequency receiver. *See Voice response.*

***Features for hard-of-hearing users.*** Special features are provided for hard-of-hearing users. These include small amplifiers for either the transmitter or the receiver built into the handset, devices analogous to ringers which provide visual signals, and receivers having a leaky magnetic field which can be picked up by specially equipped hearing aids. For the totally deaf, a teletype machine may be used in place of an acoustic instrument.

***Cordless telephones.*** Cordless telephones use a two-way radio link to replace the cord between the handset and a base unit, which in turn is connected by normal wire to the central office. Typically, the dial and switchhook functions are built into the handset, providing full calling and answering capability on a portable basis within a radius of several hundred feet of the base unit. The base unit normally requires a connection to alternating-current power, as well as to the telephone network, while the handset uses batteries which are recharged when the handset is replaced on the base unit. Units of this type operate on a small number of duplex (two-way) frequency-modulation (FM) radio channels. All signaling information (such as dialing or paging) must flow over the same channels, so typically audio tones just outside the band reproduced by the telephone are used to convey signaling information. Interference with other users is a concern because of the limited number of channels assigned and the fact that these channels are shared with other services besides telephony such as radio-controlled toys. As a consequence, allowable radio power between the handset and the base unit is severely limited by law, resulting in a telephone suitable for use around a residence but not suitable for any longer distances. *See Radio spectrum allocations.*

The cellular radio system, an advanced form of mobile radio telephony, serves the need for a telephone which can operate several miles from a base station. Through the use of many base stations in such a system, the user can move through a large geographical area while making a call. *See Mobile radio.*

*Richard M. Rickert*

**Business terminals.** Modern business telephones designed for use on a customer's premises may connect to an on-premises switching system known as a private branch exchange (PBX), or a central office switch. These telephones are characterized by the electronic nature of their control circuits as compared to the electromechanical control circuits employed in previous generations. The control circuit capabilities in these terminals range from transducers of user input and network control signaling in simpler terminals to substantial local processing in more powerful terminals. These telephones offer users a wide range of functionality that is derived from local processing in the telephone, in the private branch exchange, or from a centralized computer. For example, some of these telephones offer the ability to display the calling party identity and to retrieve messages left by calling parties when the user is busy or unavailable. They may also offer the ability to support multiline appearances without requiring more than a single port on the switch. Multiline appearances provide the ability to receive or originate additional voice or data calls at the terminal while still being engaged in a primary voice call, and the ability to bring additional parties onto a primary call (forming a conference call) or to transfer the primary call to a second party. *See Teleconferencing.*

**Fig. 3. Digital terminal with capability of multiline appearances, simultaneous voice-data transmission over a single pair of wires, and an integrated data module capable of connecting to data terminals at up to 19.2 kilobits per second. (*American Telephone and Telegraph Co.*)**

**Fig. 4. Digital terminal with capability of multiline appearances, an optional built-in data module, and an 80-character liquid-crystal alphanumeric display. (*American Telephone and Telegraph Co.*)**

Many advanced business telephones, alternately called business terminals, provide the ability to transmit the users' voice and data and switch control information simultaneously between the terminal and the switch. In the most advanced business terminals, these voice, data, and control signals are multiplexed into a single digital bit stream in each direction to and from the switch. **Figure 3** illustrates a digital terminal capable of connecting to data terminals at up to 19.2 kilobits per second. **Figure 4** shows a digital terminal with an optional built-in data module and an 80-character alphanumeric display. The telephone, data, and display capabilities may also be integrated with a touch-sensitive cathode-ray tube and keyboard to provide user-friendly simultaneous voice and data terminal capabilities (**Fig. 5**). *See Data communications; Electronic display.*

*Kelly B. Morgan; Peter S. Warwick*

**Digital transmission.** Digital transmission of speech is used in long-distance telephony because digital signals can be precisely regenerated and thus are much less subject to degradation as a function of increasing transmission distance than are analog signals. However, the cost of converting the analog signal back and forth from the digital format usually makes this mode of operation uneconomic for local loops (those within a single central office). When a major part of the information flow from a set to a central point is already in digital format, as in the business terminals discussed above, it is often more economical to digitize the speech at the set. In this

**Fig. 5. Digital terminal with cathode-ray-tube display to provide simultaneous voice and data terminal capabilities. (*American Telephone and Telegraph Co.*)**

arrangement, all the information flowing from the instrument (including the voice signals) is converted to the form of binary digits before leaving the set. In this case the local loop and serving central office or private branch exchange must also be digital. A gradual conversion, extending over several decades, to an all-digital telephone plant known as the Integrated Services Digital Network (ISDN) appears likely. Since an all-digital set cannot communicate directly with standard analog instruments, equipment is needed at some central point in the transmission system to convert the digital bit stream to an analog signal, and vice versa, until the conversion is complete. *SEE PULSE MODULATION; SWITCHING SYSTEMS (COMMUNICATIONS).*

*Richard M. Rickert*

***Bibliography.*** R. W. Berry, P. Miller, and R. M. Rickert, A tone generating integrated circuit, *Bell Lab. Rec.*, 44:318–324, 1966; D. G. Fink and D. Christiansen, *Electronics Engineers' Handbook*, 2d ed., 1982; C. L. Krumreich and W. Mosing, The evolution of a telephone, *Bell Lab. Rec.*, 44:8–14, 1966; W. H. Martin, Seventy-five years of the telephone: An evolution in technology, *Bell Sys. Tech. J.*, 30:215–238, 1951.

## Teleprocessing

A form of information handling in which a data-processing system utilizes communication facilities. The chief example of this mode of computing is computer time-sharing, which requires communication support facilities, both hardware and software. Communications support facilities will be considered in terms of the logical communications support required by the user, and the hardware or software which are required to implement communications support functions.

**Logical communications support.** It is important to consider any computer or communications requirement first in terms of the logical process which the user wants to perform independent of the actual physical (that is, hardware and software) means of implementation. Logical process refers to functions, operations, the sequence of operations, and characteristics of the data to be manipulated by the operations. For example, the user may require an information retrieval function consisting of systematic inquiry-response operations in which each inquiry triggers a response which may consist of one line of data presented on a terminal screen. This scenario immediately suggests a logical half-duplex operation: data can flow in both directions between terminal and computer but in only one direction at a time. This will be the case even if the hardware and software used to implement the support function are capable of full duplex operation, transmitting data in both directions simultaneously. By understanding the logic of their requirements, users are able to specify a functional requirement which will constrain the implementation to essential capabilities, thus making the installation cost-effective.

One of the major user considerations in specifying time-sharing communications support is the choice between asynchronous and synchronous communication. The contrast between the two types of communication has both logical and physical aspects. From the logical standpoint, asynchronous communication is characterized by sporadic transmissions of data from terminal to computer—independent bursts in time and content, as in inquiries made for a particular purpose. This mode can be compared to synchronous communication in which data transmissions are neither time- nor content-independent, as during file transfers between a microcomputer and a mainframe machine. This consideration has major implications concerning the nature of the hardware-software solution, as discussed below. *SEE DATA COMMUNICATIONS.*

**Hardware.** The major pieces of communications hardware which are required to support timesharing are a terminal, a modem and communication facility, and a communication controller at the mainframe computer site.

***Terminal.*** The terminal may have line or full-screen editing capability. Line editing refers to an editing or data manipulation capability which is limited to adding or changing only one line of text with each terminal entry action, usually the carriage return. Line editing is also associated with the use of typed commands for editing lines of text. In contrast, a full-screen editing capability provides cursor-controlled editing over an entire screen of text or an entire file by scrolling to position various pages of text on the screen. By moving the cursor to various positions on the screen, numerous changes can be made prior to an entry action resulting from an Enter or Return key depression. Because of the relatively low data transmission rate and the sporadic data entry pattern, line editing terminals are typically asynchronous, whereas the block transmission format of a full-screen editing terminal demands high-speed, clock-controlled transmission as in synchronous communication. Because of the low cost of asynchronous-communication line editing, so-called dumb terminals are ubiquitous. They are designed for dial-up communication on telephone channel facilities and usually support the ASCII data code. The pervasiveness of this type of communication generates the demand for other hardware components: modems and communication facilities and controllers.

***Modem and communication facility.*** A modem is required to convert the digital signals of the terminal to the analog signals of the telephone network and back again to the digital signals of the computer. Important modem characteristics involve choices between asynchronous or synchronous communication; half-duplex or full-duplex operation; the use of an acoustic coupler or a direct connect; and dial-up, leased line, or limited distance communication. An acoustic coupler is a type of modem which converts two frequency tones (one for binary one and one for binary zero) to the analog signal used on a telephone line, and vice versa. A direct connect, on the other hand, is a pair of wires which directly connects a terminal to a computer without going through the telephone network. In a dial-up communication service, users dial a computer service through their modems, whereas in leased-line communication a line is leased from the telephone company for guaranteed access to the computer. A limited-distance modem is used within a building for improving the quality of the signal in the case where there is a long distance between the terminal and the computer. This type of modem is not used for external communication (outside a building) on the telephone network.

The great majority of requirements are satisfied by an asynchronous, half-duplex, direct-connect, dial-up modem. Exceptions to this will occur when (1) the mainframe computer hardware requires a synchronous full-duplex protocol, (2) the terminal must be portable (requiring an acoustic coupler), (3) a leased line is used because guaranteed access is required, or (4) a limited-distance modem is installed, with telephone cable but without telephone company service, to improve communication quality. If, as in the typical case, a full-screen edit terminal is hardwired to the mainframe computer with coaxial cable, no modem is required.

***Communication controller.*** In the planning of teleprocessing requirements, the characteristics of equipment in the mainframe computer room with which the terminal communicates are frequently overlooked. This may be a controller, front-end processor, or mainframe. The terminal and modem must be compatible with the protocol used by the mainframe or its subordinate unit, such as the controller. For example, IBM protocols are often half-duplex; ARPANET protocols are full-duplex. Communications capabilities acquired by the user must be compatible with the way that data are handled by the remote computer. Since there is a great variety of protocols, it is desirable to have communications parameters (for example, half-duplex) established and changed by menu-driven communications software, which operates in concert with the modem. However, even with this flexibility, there are some fundamental physical parameters, such as control signal frequencies, bandwidth, and modulation technique, which software cannot control. Therefore, to guarantee compatibility it is necessary that a modem conform to modem standards that were developed by the Bell System.

**Software.** As indicated above, an important addition to teleprocessing communications support is software for providing communications parameter management, menu-selectable commands for invoking a variety of communication protocols, and some constraints on terminal-to-mainframe file transfer. Usually these capabilities are furnished by a microcomputer which takes the place of the terminal with disk storage, an asynchronous communication adapter board installed in the microcomputer, asynchronous communications software operating in the microcomputer and compatible with its operating system, and a modem which is compatible with both the communications software and adapter. *See Microcomputer.*

Once the communication program is loaded into memory, under control of the operating system, communication parameter files may be created, modified, or invoked. After a communication file has been created, it can be invoked by entering its name at the proper place in the menu, with the result that the mainframe computer is automatically dialed, connection is established, and the modem is set to the correct communication parameters. The creation of a series of communication parameter files allows various time-sharing computer services to be contacted without any need for physical adjustments, such as changing modem switch settings. Most communication software packages provide linkages to various information retrieval services. In addition, a limited file-transfer capability is usually provided. As data are scrolled to the screen by the mainframe computer, it can be recorded in a microcomputer disk file or listed on its printer. Conversely, data from a microcomputer disk file can be recorded in a file of a mainframe computer if that file has been opened by that computer's editor and the editor is set to the insert mode, allowing the file to receive new data. *See Digital computer; Multiaccess computer; Operating system.*

*Norman F. Schneidewind*

***Bibliography.*** J. E. McNamara, *Technical Aspects of Data Communication*, 2d ed., 1982; W. Stallings, *Data and Computer Communications*, 1985; A. Tanenbaum, *Computer Networks*, 1981.

## Teleterminal

An instrument that combines the functions of a computer terminal with those of a telephone. The communications and computing disciplines are merging. This confluence is most apparent in the corporate and regulatory events in the industries that have grown so rapidly around each discipline. The electronic revolution is driving the confluence because the systems in each discipline are made from the same components. Since the respective systems are virtually indistinguishable in their appearance, technology, and operational features, their convolution is beginning to carry into the services they provide to their respective users. Research in integrated services and instruments began only about 1979, and commercial products, both hardware and software, are just becoming available. The convolution of services is more than a simple union of two sets because of attempts to present the services to the user in a unified fashion. But it is also more than integration of services because they combine synergistically and new services are possible.

Consider two services: (1) Computers provide a means for a user at a conventional terminal to retrieve a record of information from a file by typing in one field of the desired record. If the file is the English dictionary and the input is an English word, the output would be the meaning of the word. (2) Some modern telephones or telephone adjuncts allow their users to store telephone numbers and assign them to extra buttons on the instrument. Some telephone systems allow the subscriber to simulate this service from a regular telephone. The user perceives that one of these special calls may be placed without having to dial the entire telephone number.

In the synergy of these services, the user accesses a telephone directory as a computer file and types in the name of the desired party. Instead of a telephone number appearing on a terminal screen, however, the call is placed automatically. Such a service is logical to the naive user who does not know that it is half computer discipline and half communications discipline, and it is now feasible in the convolved superdiscipline. The missing ingredient is the integrated instrument that delivers the services. A teleterminal is such an instrument.

**User interface.** **Figure 1** shows a research prototype of a teleterminal. It has the handset, ringer, modular connection, and size of a telephone. It has a keyboard and video screen like a conventional computer terminal, but in miniature. Since the terminal features conform to the size of a telephone, the user perceives the instrument as a telephone that doubles as a terminal. The services provided through the instrument are consistent with this perception. The user would perceive an instrument that is the size and shape of a conventional terminal, but with a handset on the side, as a terminal that doubles as a telephone.

In the software interface to the user, services are chosen by menu selection. The user need not know all the available services and need not have previously memorized the detailed name of a desired service. On the teleterminal of Fig. 1, function buttons mounted adjacent to each side of the video screen provide the user with a mechanism for pointing that further simplifies the selection of a service from the menu. The program dynamically labels the buttons.

Since the list of services is larger than the number of buttons, a means of partitioning the list is required. Scrolling and paging are useful, but organizing the list into a tree structure has proven to be friendlier, that is, easier for the user to handle. All services are assigned as leaves in a tree. Starting from the base, the user climbs the tree by selecting appropriate branches at successive nodes. The video screen displays only the labels of those branches and leaves attached to the current node of the tree. Because there are only 12 buttons, the teleterminal never confronts the user with more than 12 choices. After selecting a branch, the user perceives the traversal by a new display of button labels. When the user reaches the node containing the desired leaf, the corresponding service is selected. The tree is customized for each user and, even, by the user.

**Figure 2** shows a typical base of such a tree structure. ''Personal Assistant'' is a branch leading to the node in **Fig. 3*a*** that contains access to electronic mail and calendar services. ''General Directories'' is a branch leading to a node that contains access to white-page, yellow-page, and organization-chart directories. ''Personal Directory'' is a branch leading to a node that allows access to a special personal directory service. From this node the user makes new entries in the personal directory or retrieves existing entries by traditional alphabetic sort or by matches on key words. ''New Services'' is a branch leading to a node that is the repository for newly created or improved services. The user tries one at his leisure and then discards it or moves it to a more appropriate place in the tree. ''Operating System'' is a leaf providing direct access into the host computer's command interpreter. When the user pushes this button, the video screen is cleared and the user perceives the teleterminal as a regular computer terminal. When the user pushes the ''—explain—'' button, its text is capitalized to ''—EXPLAIN—'' and the next button push is explained on the video screen instead of executed. ''Special Dialing'' is a branch leading to a node that contains translation services from mnemonics into area codes, tie-line codes, and dialing sequences for services like transfer and call forwarding. The next three buttons are leaves that cause telephone calls to be placed to the respective parties. These are three parties that the owner of this tree apparently calls frequently because the owner placed these leaves directly on the base of the tree to reduce the access time. The user installed 10 other parties that are called almost as frequently in the node reached by the button labeled ''Top 10'' (more precisely, the last 10 of the top 13). The button marked ''—quit—'' is the means for the user to shut off the software.

Fig. 1. Prototype teleterminal.

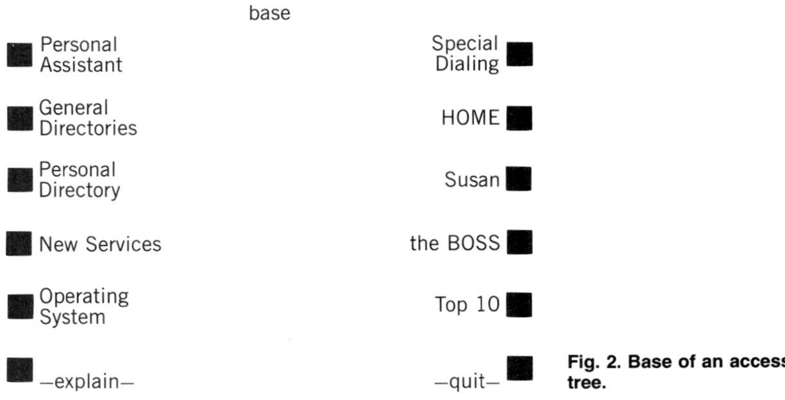


**Fig. 2. Base of an access tree.**

**Service example.** Suppose Moe tried to call someone while the callee was away from the telephone. Assume that either someone else answered the phone and left a message by electronic mail or Moe sent the mail directly because no one answered the phone. The callee returns to find the teleterminal screen as in Fig. 2 except that the bottom line of the video screen has the message: ''You have new mail.'' By pressing the ''Personal Assistant'' button, the ''Personal Assistant'' node (Fig. 3*a*) can be reached. In similar fashion, the buttons ''Read New Mail,'' ''Moe,'' ''—proc message—,'' and ''Telephone Call'' can be pressed in succession to reach, in succession, the nodes ''New Mail'' (Fig. 3*b*), ''Message 3'' (Fig. 3*c*), ''Message Actions'' (Fig 3*d*), and ''Telephone Call'' (Fig. 3*e*). After the callee presses ''—place the call—'' and lifts the receiver, Moe's telephone number is called and the screen returns to Moe's message

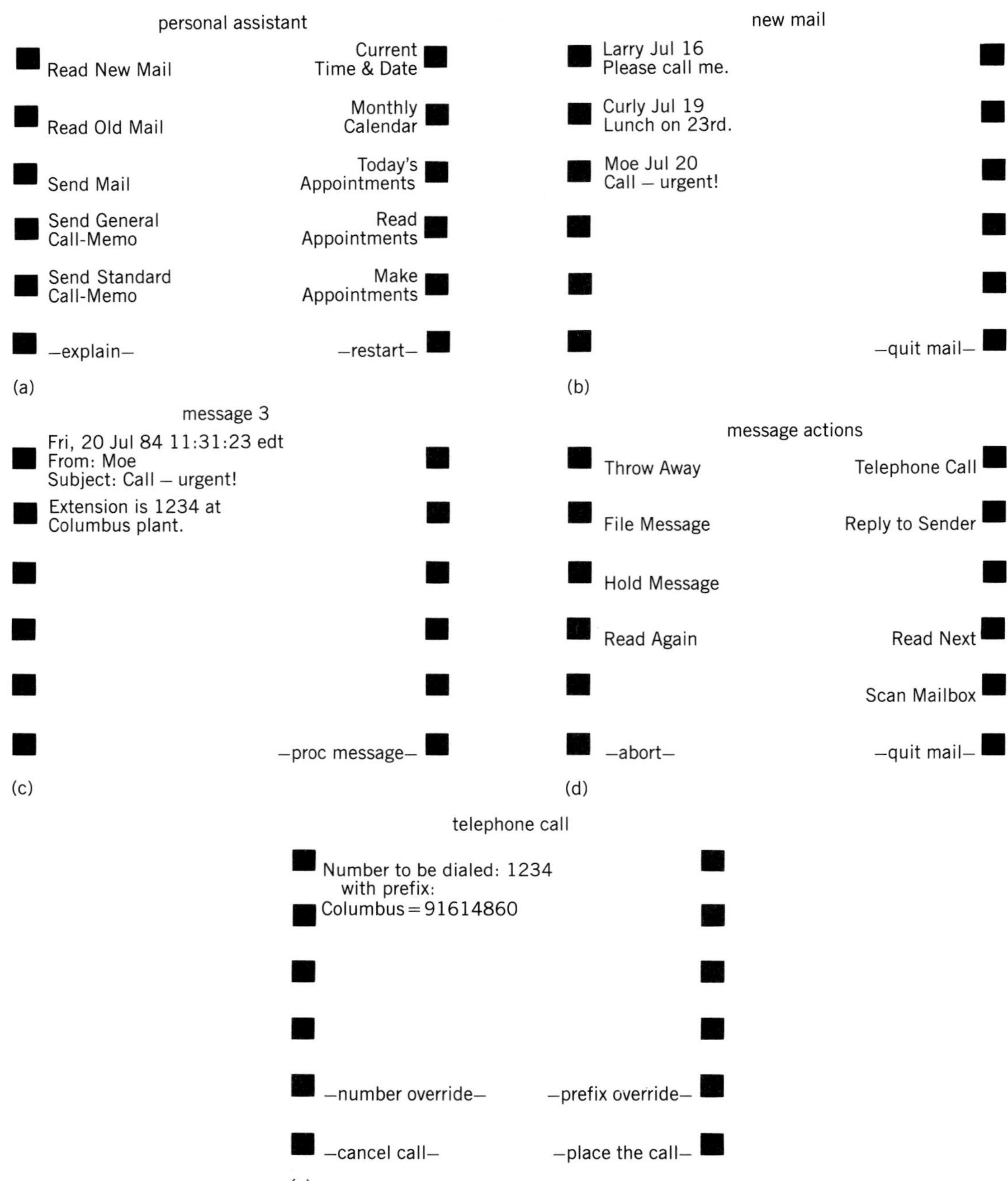


**Fig. 3. Successive nodes in an access tree. (*a*) "Personal Assistant" node. (*b*) "New Mail" node. (c) "Message 3" node. (*d*) "Message Actions" node. (e) "Telephone Call" node.**

(Fig. 3*c*). If Moe answers, while speaking with him the callee would probably press "—proc message—" to get message actions, and then "Throw Away" and "—quit mail—" to return to the "Personal Assistant" node.

**Implementation.** The particular teleterminal described here was initially designed for a research environment. The research objective is to investigate synergistic services and the user interface. The teleterminals are deliberately provided with little local intelligence and must be permanently connected to a host computer during operation. They have two independent communications ports, one for connection to the telephone network and one for connection like a terminal to the computer. Each user executes the same program in the time-shared host. The user perceives customization because the program reads an access tree file that each user owns and maintains.

For a real market a different environment might be logical. More local computing power in the teleterminal might be practical to reduce the data communications requirements. Access through the tree file and some of the services, like calendars and directories, are provided well by the teleterminal directly. Other services, like centralized directories and mail, are best implemented in a centralized computer. These price-performance issues will be resolved in the marketplace as teleterminals become commercially available.

As voice communications become increasingly digital, voice and data will use the same communications media. The need for two separate ports will be removed, and the distinction between remote and local computing will become more blurred. In the more distant future, as photonics provides extremely high bandwidth, this exercise will be repeated because of a convolution with the video discipline. The instrument will then be a synergy of the telephone, the computer terminal, and the television set. SEE ELECTRONIC MAIL; MULTIACCESS COMPUTER; TELEPHONE; VIDEOTELEPHONE.

*Richard A. Thompson*

**Bibliography.** D. W. Hagelbarger and R. A. Thompson, Experiments in teleterminal design, *IEEE Spectrum*, 20(10):40–45, October 1983.

**Fig. 1. Keyboard send-receive (KSR) teletypewriter. (*AT&T Teletype Corp.*)**

## Teletypewriter

An electronic-mechanical device, also called a teleprinter, for preparing, storing, transmitting, and receiving messages over a telegraph or data communication circuit. The term teletypewriter was used first for teleprinters utilized in teletypewriter exchange (TWX) service in the early 1930s. It was later applied to terminals used in other services, and became interchangeable with the terms teleprinter and printing telegraph terminal. A generic term, it should be used instead of Teletype, which is a registered trademark of the AT&T Teletype Corporation. Teletypewriters were invented by several individuals in the early 1900s, initially being adaptations of the commercial typewriters of the day. Relays, magnets, and solenoids were added to provide telegraph signal generation from the operation of the typewriter keyboards, and caused the typebaskets or typewheels to print automatically on sheets of paper.

When greater ruggedness was required, the inventors devised more sturdy mechanisms. Unreliable machinery and open-wire telegraph circuits caused many errors to occur, necessitating repetition of an errored message to get good printed copies. The use of punched tape helped somewhat, with operators fixing their perceived keyboarding errors before transmission, and expedited the repetition process by allowing reruns of the punched tape. The next generation of teletypewriters printed on narrow paper tape that was gummed on the back. Each line of a message was moistened from a sponge or wick, cut off, and pasted onto a telegram form, with errors being corrected by pasteovers (a repetition of the error portion of the message, in correct form). Although this was labor-intensive, with low wage scales the tape printers were commercially successful. Later, the increasing cost of labor led to the return to page printers exclusively.

**Components.** The keyboard of a send-receive set (**Fig. 1**) controls the generation of coded electrical signals that are sent to another set, near or distant, or to a computer. The associated printer converts sent and received signals into a typed-page message. A receive-only set has only the printer.

An automatic send-receive set includes a memory or storage medium facility (electronic buffer, paper tape punch and reader, or a magnetic tape or magnetic disk recorder/reader) for preparing messages prior to transmission, providing off-line correction of operator keyboarding errors, thereby allowing most economic ultimate use of on-line communication circuit time.

A cathode-ray-tube (CRT) display set (**Fig. 2**) is an adjunct to the teletypewriter that provides transient soft copy when communicating with other terminals or a computer. If equipped with a buffer memory, it also serves as an automatic send-receive set for preparation and transmission of messages. Permanent hard copy for such a set can then be obtained via use of an auxiliary receive-only printer. SEE DATA COMMUNICATIONS; ELECTRONIC DISPLAY.

Modern teletypewriter sets use integrated electronic circuitry in place of the older motor-powered mechanisms. Very large-scale integration (VLSI) and incorporation of microprocessors are common. Personal computers, when supplied with the proper software and equipped with modems (modulators/demodulators) to interface with the communication circuit, are used as teletypewriters in many instances. SEE MICROCOMPUTER.

***Keyboard.*** An integral part of earlier send-receive sets, automatic send-receive sets, or CRT display sets, the keyboard has become a separate unit that plugs into the teletypewriter control circuits and can be positioned for the convenience of the typist. The so-called QWERTY key arrangement matches that of most office typewriters. Each key controls a contact, capacitor, or Hall-effect device; alternatively, touch-sensitive-membrane printed circuitry may be supplied under a flat or embossed surface. Key legends are usually molded-in plastic and resist fingernail wear. Keytops, if present, are usually interchangeable so different languages or symbol arrangements can be accommodated. Tactile feedback is usually provided,

**Fig. 2. Cathode-ray-tube (CRT) display set. (*AT&T Teletype Corp.*)**

or a click or beep may be heard whenever a key is depressed. Some keyboard arrangements include numeric pads (like calculator arrangements); control keys, some of which may include signal lamps; or programmable keys that generate predetermined fixed messages such as answer-back identifications, names and addresses, commonly used phrases and paragraphs, or even telephone numbers for automatic dialing if the set includes a modem and is to be used on the public telephone network.

A universal synchronous-asynchronous receiver-transmitter (USART) circuit provides the generation of the transmitted serial signals to be sent to a telegraph or data circuit. The USART is programmable as to speed, for example, 45, 50, 75, 100, or 110 bauds (bits-per-second) on older Telex or TWX networks, or 300, 1200, 2400, 4800, 9600 bands, or even 19.2 kilobits on more recent voice channel or digital networks; number of code and stop bits, for example, five code bits plus one start and one or one and one-half stop bits for Baudot code, seven code bits and a parity bit plus one start bit and one or two stop bits for ASCII (American Standard Code for Information Interchange) or EBCDIC (Extended Binary Coded Decimal Interchange Code); and so on. The inclusion of microprocessors also permits the operator to select directly from a wide range of other options included as software in the keyboard circuitry. *See Microprocessor*.

***Printer.*** The printer typically utilizes friction-fed paper from a roll 8½ in. (21.6 cm) wide that is torn off into separate variable length messages after being printed. Alternately, fan-folded continuous-web paper may be used, the latter being transversely perforated at fixed page-length intervals which may be preprinted as business forms. This paper has holes punched at ½-in. (1.27-cm) intervals in removable borders, for positive feeding by pin or tractor feed mechanisms. Form widths may be as narrow as 3 in. (7.5 cm) or as wide as 15 in. (38 cm), most feeding devices being adjustable to accommodate a selected width.

Impact-type printing is most common, providing multiple carbon copies at speeds up to 55 or more characters per second (cps) from a daisy wheel or thimble (cup) printing mechanism which provides typewriterlike copy. Daisy wheels (and thimbles) are readily interchangeable, and available in a variety of standard typefaces. Speeds of up to 300 cps are attained from dot matrix mechanisms where lower print quality can be tolerated. These may give a grainy appearance, from the separate dots, considered acceptable for data copy and rough drafts of memoranda. A compromise style, called near-letter-quality printing, can be obtained through use of smaller printing pins, through more pins per head, or through making multiple printing passes per line printed, thereby causing overlapping of dots so that the characters seem to be more like solid type. This applies a penalty in speed and cost to the overall set. The basic dot matrix character has four or five dots horizontally and seven vertically, plus one or two dots for descenders on five lowercase letters where reasonably good readability is required. Placing dots at half-dot positions horizontally improves the appearance of characters with diagonal and rounded vertical lines. Using two columns of printing pins increases the speed, each column printing alternate dots on the horizontal lines, in leapfrog fashion for basic matrix characters, or printing alternate overlapping lines of dots for near-letter-quality characters.

A stepping-motor-driven print head moves transversely across the paper web, a print hammer driving the selected raised type leaf on daisy wheel and thimble printers against an inking ribbon and the paper, printing the character. In matrix printers, pin-driving magnets are selected at the proper instants for printing the dots. In both cases printing is done on-the-fly as the print head moves. Ribbons are usually enclosed in cartridges, and some contain porous reinking rollers that apply a constant amount of ink to the ribbon, greatly extending the period of high-quality dense printing. Multicolor printing is sometimes provided through use of ribbons with separate longitudinal colored areas. Thus red typing can denote transmitted messages, and black can show received messages, or vice versa. A wide ribbon can have several primary color areas, thereby permitting printing of full-color graphs or pictures.

Nonimpact printers use a liquid ink jet or thermal printing process, the latter requiring special, more expensive paper. Both provide only a single copy. Print heads on ink jet printers have one or more jets. The output of single jets may be swept across the page in a raster pattern and sychronously modulated to print each character, or a column of jets may each print one horizontal row of dots across the page. Jets may also have different colored inks for colored copy printing. Thermal printers have multiple electrodes at each character printing position, with no moving print head; these are the quietest, only the paper movement being audible.

Software associated with microprocessors permits operator selection of numerous options, such as characters-per-inch spacing of 6, 10, 12, 15, 16.5, and so on (2.36, 3.94, 4.72, 5.91, 6.5 characters per centimeter); or lines-per-inch spacing of 2, 3, 4, 6, 8, and so on (0.79, 1.18, 1.57, 2.36, 3.15 lines per centimeter). On-line enablement of many printing functions through reception of various signal codes and patterns is frequently featured. These include utilization of special characters and symbols needed for various languages, or the conversion of a dot matrix printer into a graphics machine so that pictures and line drawings can be intermixed in a report, or captions can be printed thereon.

***Display.*** The simple CRT set usually consists of a keyboard and a cathode-ray-tube monitor unit on which a set of 1920 characters, in a format of 24 lines of 80 characters each, is shown. Such a display matches the hard copy capability of an 80-column printer recording on 8½-in.-wide (21-cm) paper at 10 characters per inch (3.94 characters per centimeter). Some CRTs also provide 132 character lines, for a total of 3168 characters, matching the output of a wide-platen printer at the same character spacing, or of a narrow-platen printer recording at 16.5 characters per inch (6.5 characters per centimeter). This would be used for spreadsheet purposes for statistical and financial reports. A refresh memory renews the display in a flicker-free manner some 60 times per second. A cursor consisting of a light rectangle or a blinking underline symbol designates the character area to be recorded next. This marker moves from space to space as entries are made from the keyboard, just like the printing on a typewriter. Some displays start at the top line and move to the right and down as the message is entered, ending on the bottom line, and then the message scrolls upward as new lines are added at the bottom. Others allow the cursor to move only to right and left at the center of the display, with scrolling of the copy as mentioned above. This duplicates carriage and paper motion in typewriters. In addition to normal typing functions such as backspace, carriage return, and line feed (or new line), the cursor may be moved over recorded information without modifying it through use of cursor positioning keys marked with horizontal or vertical arrows. Overtyping with a new character from a regular key can then be accomplished, correcting errors or inserting additional characters or words. Keys for inserting or deleting entire words or lines, and for similar editing functions, are frequently also included. *See Word processing.*

Displayed characters consist of dot patterns in 5 × 7 or 7 × 9 matrices, similar to the printed characters from matrix printers. No dot overlapping is allowed, but the use of more and smaller dots can improve the readability. More sophisticated displays provide true descenders on lowercase letters, and underlining below those letters. Colors may be white on black background, green on black, or amber on black. Black-on-white or multicolored displays may also be featured. Some displays show additional control information beneath the text display area, such as the number of the line or column that is being recorded, or the functions available from the special programmable keys on the associated keyboard.

A simple CRT set has no buffer storage, and must rely on an associated computer memory for message-composing capability. It usually communicates one line at a time with the computer, which accepts a line of data upon reception of a NEW LINE character (sometimes called ENTER), or of one of the control characters, such as the ASCII X-OFF. *See Computer storage technology.*

A buffered CRT usually provides three complete 1920 (or 3168) character fields of displayed data, with nondestructive scrolling occurring until the memory is filled. Separate scrolling keys are supplied on the keyboard that permit searching quickly through the recorded data for a particular entry. A high-speed packet transmission protocol is usually used with such sets, the data being accumulated and transmitted in blocks of 200–300 characters.

**Teletypewriters for the deaf.** Commercially obsolete machines can be used by deaf persons who cannot use regular telephones. Several thousand teletypewriters have been equipped with modems or acoustic couplers for attachment to telephone handsets or lines. A visible alarm lamp is provided to signal the deaf person whenever a call is being received. Many of the sets are equipped with automatic answering facilities, including an answer-back message transmitter that identifies the terminal, so that messages can be received in the owner's absence. If a regular telephone happens to connect to one of these terminals, the person making the call will hear a whistle as the station answers. An improved instrument for deaf people is a portable teletypewriter with a built-in modem which can couple acoustically to any standard telephone handset, allowing use anywhere. These teletypewriters have compact keyboards, and some are equipped with a display that shows one line of characters, allowing conversational visible communication. Others may have a very compact printing mechanism that uses a narrow roll of paper, similar to that used in some calculators; other designs feature a small CRT display.

*Ransom D. Slayton*

**Bibliography.** Datapro Research Corp., *All about Teleprinter Terminals*, pp. 21a–21mm, 1980; N. Rosenberg, Impact matrix printers reach for daisy quality, *Mini-Micro Sys.*, 16(1):145–156, January 1983; M. Stiefel, Low cost display terminals gain in capability, *Mini-Micro Sys.*, 16(11):141–158, November 1983; C. E. Vidales, Design considerations on word processing printers, *IEEE Global Telecommun. Conf. Rec.*, pp. 1380–1383, 1982; L. Yencharis, Wire-matrix advances fuel rise of impact printers, *Electr. Des.*, 28(17):75–86, August 16, 1980.

## Television

The electrical transmission and reception of transient visual images. Like motion pictures, television consists of a series of successive images, which are registered on the brain as a continuous picture because of the persistence of vision. Each visual image impressed on the eye persists for a fraction of a second. In television in the United States, 30 complete pictures are transmitted each second, which with the use of interlaced scanning is fast enough to avoid evident flicker.

At the television transmitter, minute portions of a scene are sampled individually for brightness (and color for color television), and the information for each portion is transmitted consecutively. At the receiver, each portion is synchronized and reproduced in its proper position and with correct brightness (and color) to reproduce the original scene.

The scene is focused through a lens on a photoelectric screen of a camera tube. Each portion of the screen is changed by the photoelectrons to a degree depending upon the brightness of the particular portion of the scene. The screen is scanned by an electron beam just as a reader scans a page of printed type, character by character, line by line. When so scanned, an electric current flows with an instantaneous magnitude proportional to the brightness of the portion scanned. *See Television camera; Television camera tube.*

Variations in the current are transmitted to the receiver, where the process is reversed. An electron beam in the picture tube is varied in intensity (modulated) by the incoming signals as it scans the picture-tube screen in synchronism with the scanning at the transmitter. The photoelectric surface of the picture tube produces light in proportion to the intensity of the electron beam which strikes it. In this way the minute portions of the original scene are re-created in their proper positions, brightness, and (for color transmission) color values. The elements of a color television system are shown in **Fig. 1**. *See Color television; Picture tube; Television receiver; Television transmitter.*

**Scanning.** In the United States an individual picture (frame) is considered to be made up of 525 lines, each line containing several hundred picture elements. All these lines are scanned and the light values are sent to the receiver so that each second 30 pictures are received. These figures vary from nation to na-

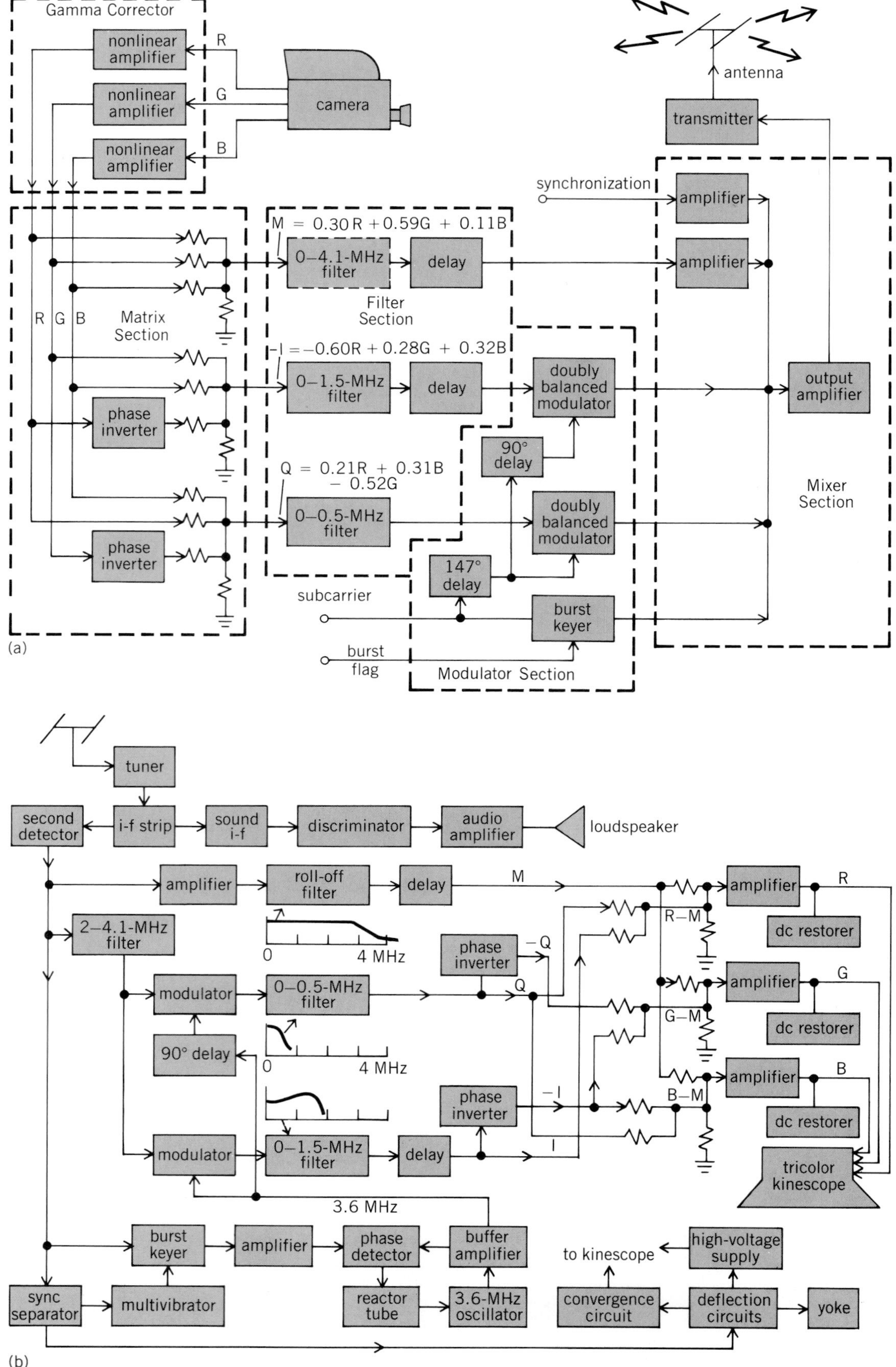


**Fig. 1. Elements of (*a*) color-transmitting system and (*b*) color-receiving system. (*After G. W. Bartlett, ed., NAB Engineering Handbook, 6th ed., National Association of Broadcasters, 1975*)**

tion. The picture is blanked out at the end of each line while the scanning beam is directed to the next line. During these short intervals, synchronizing signals are transmitted to keep the scanning process at the receiver in step with that at the transmitter.

To take full advantage of the persistence of vision, each frame is scanned twice, alternate lines being scanned in turn. This technique is called interlaced scanning.

Since 525 horizontal lines are scanned in 1/30 s, the horizontal scanning rate is 15,750 times per second. Since two vertical fields are scanned in 1/30 s, the vertical scanning rate is 60 times per second. *See Television scanning.*

**Bandwidth.** The bandwidth required for any information transmission system is a function of the number of bits of information, or the detail, to be transmitted per second. For a television picture, the greatest detail would be required if the picture consisted of a checkerboard pattern of the smallest squares the system must handle to provide acceptable resolution. The standard of 525 lines sets the vertical detail. The standard aspect ratio (picture width to height) of 4:3 requires 700 horizontal picture elements for equal horizontal and vertical resolution, or 350 sets of alternate black-and-white squares. The picture is reproduced 30 times a second, for a total of 525 × 350 × 30 or 5,512,500 complete cycles per second. Less detail than this is actually transmitted and received; the highest video frequency actually transmitted is 4.2 MHz. *See Bandwidth requirements.*

**Frequency.** The band of frequencies assigned to a television station for the transmission of synchronized picture and sound signals is called a television channel. In the United States a television channel is 6 MHz wide, with the visual carrier frequency 1.25 MHz above the lower edge of the band and the aural carrier 0.25 MHz below the upper edge of the band.

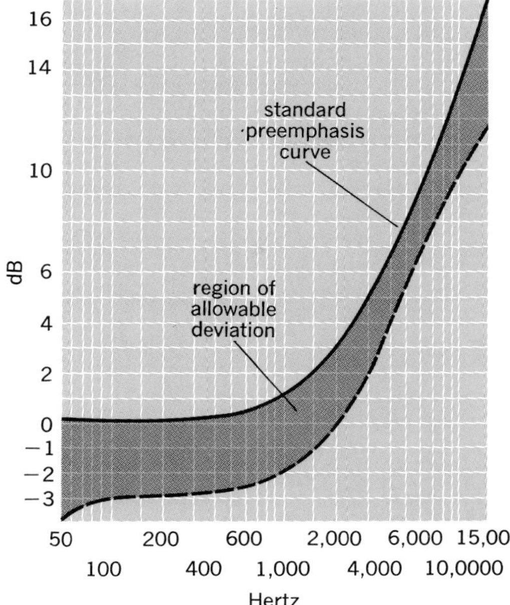


**Fig. 2.** Standard preemphasis curve, showing extent of allowable deviation.

Television channels in the United States are identified by numbers, starting with channel 2. The frequency assigned to channel 1 was later reassigned to other uses. The **table** shows that these channels are in three frequency bands. Channels 2–6 occupy the region from 54 to 88 MHz, channels 7–13 are from 174 to 216 MHz, and channels 14–69 are from 470 to 806 MHz. The first two groups of channels fall in the very-high-frequency (vhf) band; the channels in the last group are in the ultra-high-frequency (uhf) band.

**Sound transmission.** In the United States the sound portion of the program is transmitted by frequency modulation at a carrier frequency 4.5 MHz above the picture carrier. Maximum frequency deviation (bandwidth) of the sound signals is 25 kHz. *See Frequency modulation.*

The normal frequency response is altered in the transmitter to emphasize the higher audio frequencies with respect to the lower frequencies. Called preemphasis, this is accomplished by a circuit that causes the audio response to increase with frequency. A corresponding circuit is used in the receiver to produce an equal and opposite decrease of response to higher audio frequencies. By so doing, noise produced in the receiver is attenuated without the overall audio-frequency response being affected. The Federal Communications Commission (FCC) requires that the response of the aural transmitting system must not exceed the limits shown in **Fig. 2**.

The harmonic distortion of the audio-frequency signals must not exceed the following rms values when the harmonics are measured out to 30 kHz:

| *Frequency range, Hz* | *% Distortion* |
|---|---|
| 50–100 | 3.5 |
| 100–7500 | 2.5 |
| 7500–15,000 | 3.0 |

**Television channels in the United States**

| Channel no. | Frequency band, MHz | Channel no. | Frequency band, MHz |
|---|---|---|---|
| 2 | 54–60 | 36 | 602–608 |
| 3 | 60–66 | 37 | 608–614 |
| 4 | 66–72 | 38 | 614–620 |
| 5 | 76–82 | 39 | 620–626 |
| 6 | 82–88 | 40 | 626–632 |
| 7 | 174–180 | 41 | 632–638 |
| 8 | 180–186 | 42 | 638–644 |
| 9 | 186–192 | 43 | 644–650 |
| 10 | 192–198 | 44 | 650–656 |
| 11 | 198–204 | 45 | 656–662 |
| 12 | 204–210 | 46 | 662–668 |
| 13 | 210–216 | 47 | 668–674 |
| 14 | 470–476 | 48 | 674–680 |
| 15 | 476–482 | 49 | 680–686 |
| 16 | 482–488 | 50 | 686–692 |
| 17 | 488–494 | 51 | 692–698 |
| 18 | 494–500 | 52 | 698–704 |
| 19 | 500–506 | 53 | 704–710 |
| 20 | 506–512 | 54 | 710–716 |
| 21 | 512–518 | 55 | 716–722 |
| 22 | 518–524 | 56 | 722–728 |
| 23 | 524–530 | 57 | 728–734 |
| 24 | 530–536 | 58 | 734–740 |
| 25 | 536–542 | 59 | 740–746 |
| 26 | 542–548 | 60 | 746–752 |
| 27 | 548–554 | 61 | 752–758 |
| 28 | 554–560 | 62 | 758–764 |
| 29 | 560–566 | 63 | 764–770 |
| 30 | 566–572 | 64 | 770–776 |
| 31 | 572–578 | 65 | 776–782 |
| 32 | 578–584 | 66 | 782–788 |
| 33 | 584–590 | 67 | 788–794 |
| 34 | 590–596 | 68 | 794–800 |
| 35 | 596–602 | 69 | 800–806 |

**Picture transmission.** The visual signals are transmitted at a carrier frequency 1.25 MHz above the lower limit of the channel, using amplitude modulation and vestigial sideband transmission. The upper sideband is fully transmitted, but the lower sideband is attenuated beginning at 0.5 MHz below the carrier. Attenuation is virtually complete at 1.25 MHz below the carrier. This method of transmission reduces the required bandwidth of the channel and allows more channels to use the available space in the radio spectrum. **Figure 3** shows how the 6-MHz band of a television channel is used for picture and sound transmission. *SEE AMPLITUDE MODULATION.*

Negative modulation for picture transmission is used in the United States to minimize the effects of noise during synchronizing signal reception. In negative modulation an increase in brightness causes a decrease in transmitted power. Some foreign systems use positive modulation.

***Ghost image.*** Radio waves from a transmitter to a receiver normally follow a straight path. However, it is possible for such waves to follow a long or short path to the receiver. Reflections from large objects, such as mountains or buildings, follow a long path. The reflected waves in this instance arrive later than the direct waves, so that a second picture is reproduced from a fraction of an inch to several inches to the right, depending on the length of the indirect path. The second picture is called a ghost image. There may be several such ghosts when reflecting objects are in an area. Short-path ghosts may actually be picked up by the antenna lead in wires or the actual input of the receiver and thus produce what is known as a leading ghost.

***Snow (noise).*** All electronic circuitry produces some voltages or currents that are not related to the signal. Such voltages or currents are referred to as noise. Generally speaking, noise has its most deleterious effect on reception quality when it occurs in the input circuitry of the receiver, since this is usually where the basic signal-to-noise ratio is established. The generation of noise in this area is principally caused by thermal agitation in resistive input components. When the incoming signal is too weak to override this noise, a visual effect is displayed on the picture tube that is commonly referred to as snow. Although there are other types of noise that produce different visual effects, snow is the most common visual effect.

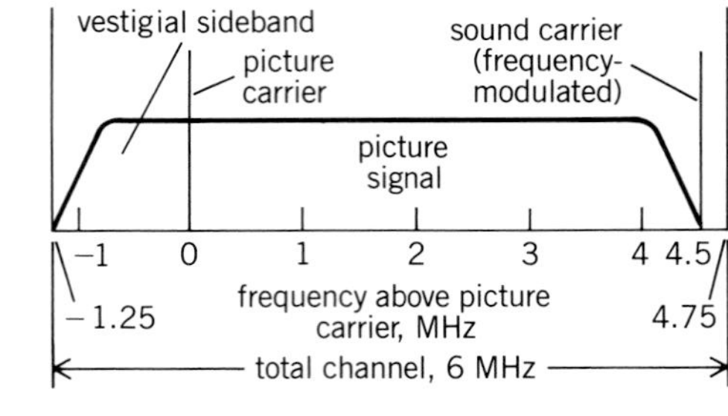


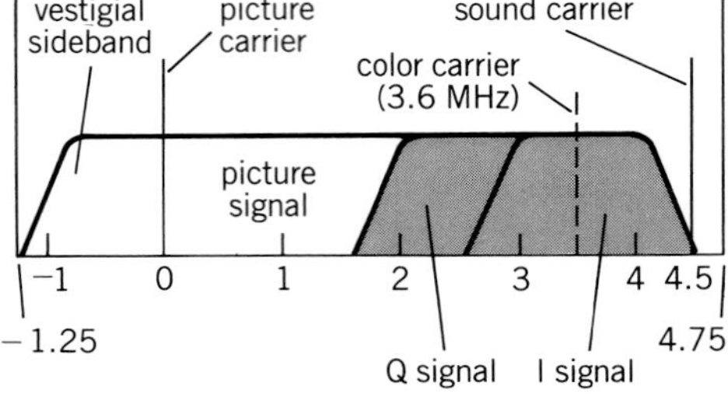


**Fig. 3. Television channels, showing portions occupied by various signal components. (*a*) Monochrome channel. (*b*) Color channel. (*After G. W. Bartlett, ed., NAB Engineering Handbook, 6th ed., National Association of Broadcasters, 1975*)**

**Scrambling of television signals.** Scrambling devices were developed for pay television, generally called pay TV (PTV), to prevent reception by anyone but a subscriber. If the synchronizing signals are caused to vary at random but predetermined rates, the signal is unusable in conventional receivers. Special receivers may contain unscrambling devices which, by a specially transmitted signal or a built-in keyer, cause the receiver to synchronize and produce normal pictures. *SEE CLOSED-CIRCUIT TELEVISION.*

**Recording television programs.** Television programs are recorded for rebroadcast at a later time and for many other reasons. The principal method is video tape recording (VTR) in which television sound and pictures are recorded on magnetic tape. Electrical signals constituting the sound and picture pass through magnetic recording heads. As the tape is drawn across these heads, the signal currents produce magnetization of finely powdered iron in the tape emulsion. The signals are recovered when the magnetized tape is drawn across a reproducing head and the magnetic fields intercept a pickup coil. There are two basic types of video tape recording. One type is known as quadruplex, most commonly used in television broadcasting. The second type of video tape recording is known as helical scan (commonly called helical) and initially was principally used for closed-circuit applications, but is now commonly used in broadcast applications.

Video tape recording has the great advantage that it can be used immediately without further processing, and that the tape can be erased by demagnetization and reused. It is of unique value for prerecording programs, reruns, special events coverage, test programs, and delayed program transmission for different network station time zones.

***Quadruplex.*** Quadruplex tape consists of a coated plastic base 2 in. (50.8 mm) wide. A 12½-in. (317.5-mm) reel provides 64 min of program time. Prior to recording, the video signal frequency modulates a carrier and produces a deviation of 4.25–6.8 MHz in low-band monochrome recording; for high-band color the deviation is 7.06 to 10.00 MHz. A vestigial sideband signal is recorded on transverse tracks 0.010 in. (0.254 mm) wide by means of four magnetic heads equally displaced on the circumference of a 2-in. (50.8-mm) wheel rotating 14,400 times per second. About 18.4 scanning lines are recorded on each transverse track. One picture frame (525 lines) comprises 32 transverse tracks or ½ in. (12.7 mm) of tape length. The accompanying sound and control signals are recorded on separate longitudinal tracks by means of separate recording heads. In reproduction the FM signal is recovered from the tape and demodulated.

***Helical scan.*** Helical recorders use tape widths of ½, ¾, 1, and 2 in. (12.7, 17.7, 25.4, and 50.8 mm). A 1-in. (25.4-mm) C-type format, a high-performance nonsegmented helical-scan recorder, is widely used for broadcast applications. A 10½-in. (266.7-mm) reel of 1-in. (25.4-mm) tape will record 96 min, and a 9-in. (228.6-mm) reel will record 64 min. Tape speed is 9.6 in./s (24.4 cm/s), and writing speed is 83.96 ft/s (25.59 m/s).

C-format video tape recorders contain three audio channels which allow for easy stereo recording, with the third audio channel usually assigned to record time code. These machines utilize two rotary video heads. One head records and plays the video information, and the other records and plays the vertical interval. This configuration allows for continuous recording without any dropout time and is not subject to color banding. SEE MAGNETIC RECORDING.

**Grades of television service.** The FCC has established by definition two grades of television service for the United States. Grade A service provides relatively high freedom from interference from other television stations and also good freedom from artificial and receiver noise. It specifies that picture quality acceptable to the average observer is expected to be available at least 90% of the time at the best 70% of all receiver locations at the outer geographical limits of this service. Grade B service recognizes that service is provided but may be more vulnerable to interference and noise. It specifies that service equal to that of grade A is available, but to only 50% of all receiver locations at the limiting distance.

**Teletext and videotext.** Teletext is the general term that describes the transmission of alphanumeric characters as part of the television signal. This telecommunications service can deliver textual information and simple graphics at low cost to a wide range of users. The television receiver acts as a display terminal which converts digital information into text and graphics on the television screen. This information is inserted in digital form onto unused lines which are hidden on top of the screen, commonly known as the vertical interval portion of the television picture. This form of telecommunications can deliver information such as weather, program guides, store prices, and stock market reports.

The teletext system originates with a data base that is able to compose pages, store them until needed, code them into digital pulses, and insert this data stream into the vertical interval of the normal program information. A decoder retrieves this information at the television receiver by detecting the digital pulses, removes them from the vertical interval, and composes the digital information into pages of text which are then stored in a minicomputer after being decoded into letters, numbers, and graphics. After the information has been decoded, it is fed into a memory where it is retained until the viewer recalls the various pages desired by pressing a special button on the remote-control key pad located in the viewer's home. After viewing the index, another combination of selector buttons allows the selection to appear on the screen in detail.

Videotext is the generic term applied to those services that provide transmission using an interactive system, generally via telephone, between the television receiver and a computer. SEE DATA COMMUNICATIONS; MULTIACCESS COMPUTER; VIDEOTEXT AND TELETEXT.

For other aspects of television SEE VIDEO TELEPHONE.

*Steve de Satnick*

***Bibliography.*** A. Abramson, *Electronic Motion Pictures*, 1955, reprint 1974; G. W. Bartlett (ed.), *NAB Engineering Handbook*, 6th ed., 1975; K. B. Benson (ed.), *Television Engineering Handbook*, 1986; B. Grob, *Basic Television and Video Systems*, 5th ed., 1984; B. Hartman, *Fundamentals of Television: Theory and Service*, 1975; K. Henney (ed.), *Radio Engineering Handbook*, 5th ed., 1959; M. S. Kiver and M. Kaufman, *Television Electronics: Theory and Service*, 8th ed., 1983.

## Television camera

An electrooptical system used to pick up and convert a visual image or scene into an electrical signal called video. The video may be transmitted by cable or wireless means to a suitable receiver or monitor some distance from the actual scene.

A television camera may fall within one of several categories: studio, portable, or telecine (**Fig. 1**). It may also be one of several highly specialized cameras used for remote viewing of inaccessible places, such as the ocean bottom or inside nuclear power reactors. The camera may be capable of producing color or monochrome (black and white) pictures. Modern cameras are entirely solid-state, except for the actual pickup tube. Even the pickup tube may be replaced by solid-state semiconductors called charge-coupled devices.

A television camera may be one-piece, with all components contained in one assembly, or it may consist of a head and a camera control unit (CCU) connected by a multiple-conductor cable, and be called a camera chain. The head unit comprises the optical system with lens, the picture pickup tubes, and a minimum of electronics necessary to generate and amplify the minute signals from the pickup tubes. The CCU (**Fig. 2**) may contain electronics and controls which allow a skilled operator to adjust brightness (luminance), color (balance, saturation, and hue), and certain correction circuits (registration, gamma, and aperture) which improve the picture. A specially calibrated oscilloscope, called a waveform monitor, is generally provided to the CCU operator so that accurate voltage levels may be set. Modern cameras provide for automatic as well as manual setup of some or all of the above adjustments. Some cameras have a built-in microprocessor which enables complete setup of all parameters by simply pushing one button. Triax cameras are those which utilize a small-diameter triaxial cable (three concentric conductors) to connect the camera head to the CCU, instead of the heavier, multiple-conductor cable known as TV-81, which has 81 conductors. Triax can be used because all of the normal signals are multiplexed onto the three wires. SEE MICROPROCESSOR.

**Essential elements.** Every camera shares certain essential elements: an optical system, one or more picture pickup devices, preamplifiers, scanning circuits, blanking and synchronizing circuits, and video processing circuits and control circuits. Color cameras also include some kind of color-encoding circuit.

***Optical system.*** The optical system consists minimally of a fixed-focal-length lens placed directly in front of a pickup device. Provision must be made to focus the image on the focal plane of the pickup device. Usually the pickup device, complete with its mounting and scanning components, is adjusted with respect to the lens, while the lens is set at the distant extreme of its focusing range. This establishes the correct back-focus so that a sharp image can be obtained by adjusting only the lens-focusing ring as camera-to-subject distances vary. More elaborate systems provide for insertion of various filters into the optical path, and usually replace the fixed-focal-length lens with a zoom type which allows smooth, continuous transition from wide-angle to telephoto focal lengths while the image remains focused. Color cameras with multiple pickup devices must split the incoming light into suitable primary colors. This is

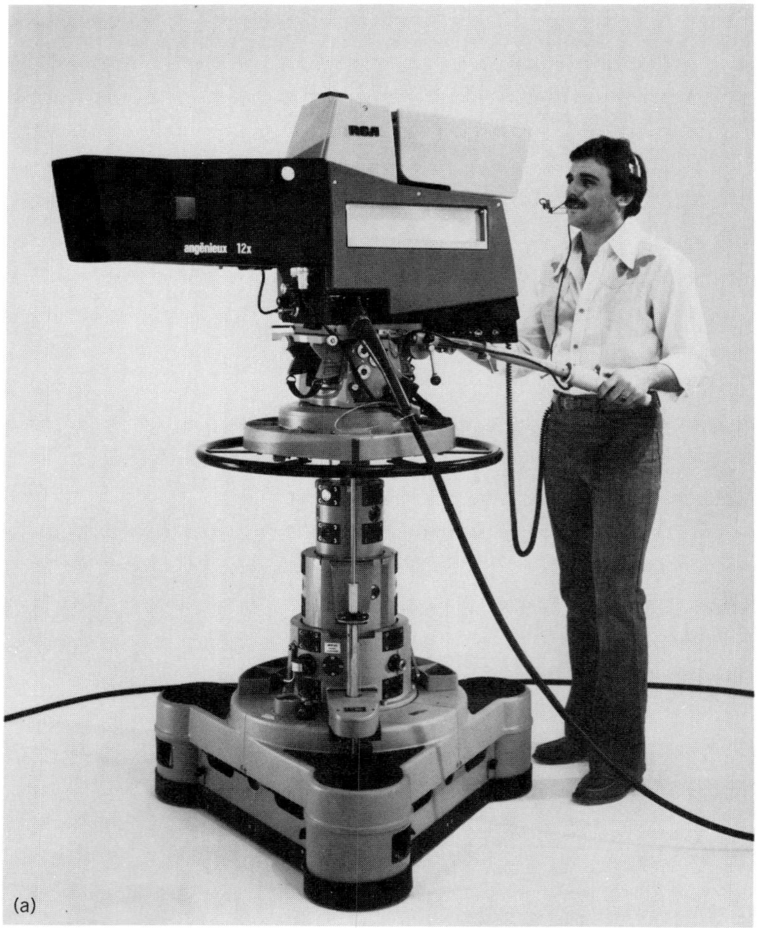

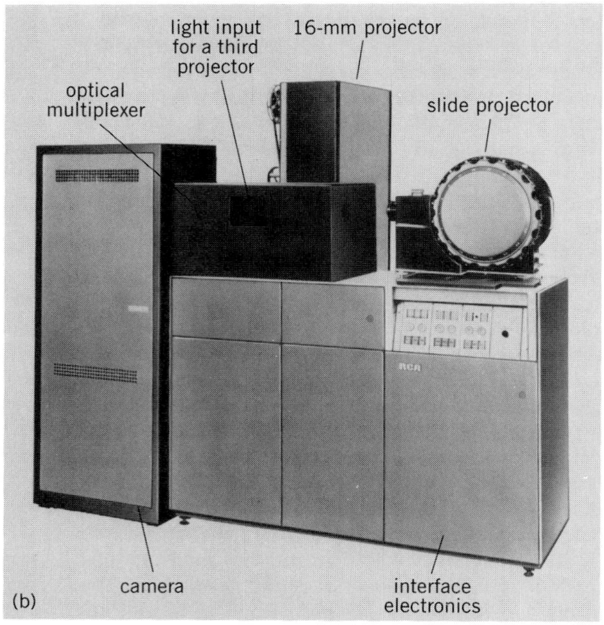

Fig. 1. Television cameras. (*a*) Studio camera. (*b*) Telecine camera. (c) Portable camera. (*RCA Corp.*)

usually done by means of a relay lens and dichroic mirror system placed between the objective lens and the pickup devices (**Fig. 3***a*). Dichroic mirrors reflect light of one color, while passing all others; that is, a red dichroic mirror reflects red and passes all other colors. An improvement on the mirror system utilizes prisms with dichroic materials coated onto the glass (Fig. 3*b*). The advantages of the prism system include ruggedness and, most importantly, the elimination of air-to-glass surfaces except at the entry and exit points. This reduces image deterioration due to misalignment of the mirrors and dust accumulation on the surfaces.

Fig. 2. Modern camera control unit for an automatic camera. (*RCA Corp.*)

***Pickup device.*** The picture pickup device used in most cameras is a photosensitive vacuum tube. The tube is oriented so that the image from the lens is focused on a light-sensitive target within the tube. The target is scanned by an electron beam, which results in an output voltage from the tube that varies in proportion to the amount of light striking each point on the target. Monochrome cameras and less-sophisticated color cameras utilize vidicon pickup tubes. High-quality broadcast cameras may use Plumbicons, Leddicons, Saticons, or other proprietary tubes. Monochrome cameras invariably have only one pickup tube; color cameras may have one, two, or three pickup tubes. Those color cameras which have only one or two pickup tubes employ a color-stripe filter in front of the photosensitive target effectively dividing the target into red, blue, or green areas. As the electron beam scans the target, it sequentially represents the red, blue, or green light levels. Electronic circuits within the camera separate the three colors. Such systems are not used in the highest-quality cameras because of the inherent loss of resolution and sensitivity which results from the stripe filter and the smaller effective area of the pickup tube. Modern broadcast color cameras employ three tubes, one for each of three primary colors used to derive the full-color spectrum. Red, green, and blue are used in additive color systems, while subtractive color systems have been devised which use white (full-spectrum luminance), red, and blue. Most color cameras use the additive scheme. Each pickup tube is scanned in synchronism so that separate red, blue, and green representations of the scene being picked up are always being generated. SEE TELEVISION CAMERA TUBE.

A few cameras have appeared which utilize charge-coupled device arrays in lieu of pickup tubes. These solid-state devices essentially consist of a large number of photodiodes aligned in a matrix so that each diode's output voltage can be related to a particular point in the picture which is focused on the array (**Fig. 4**). The amount of light falling on each diode determines its output level. Charge-coupled device pickups are very resistant to shock, have precise image geometry, and should have nearly indefinite life. They also offer freedom from microphonic noise and image burn-in commonly found in pickup tubes. SEE CHARGE-COUPLED DEVICES.

***Preamplifier.*** The pickup device's output is fed to a preamplifier, which helps to maintain a high signal-to-noise ratio and also provides a level sufficient to operate an electronic viewfinder at the camera. SEE PREAMPLIFIER.

***Scanning circuits.*** The electron beam which scans the pickup tube's photosensitive target is caused to sweep through the action of magnetic fields impressed on the tube by means of deflection coils. These coils are assembled into an integrated yoke assembly. Yokes must be made with great precision and are often computer-matched so that all pickup tubes in a multiple-tube camera scan with precisely the same geometry. Horizontal and vertical drive circuits cause the deflection yoke to deflect the electron beam so that it scans the photosensitive target in the pickup tube according to a definite pattern, called a raster. These drive circuits are synchronized by pulses from a synchronizing generator, which also provides horizontal and vertical blanking pulses to suppress the pickup tube output during the retrace interval. If not suppressed, there would be objectionable lines through the camera's picture output. Charge-coupled device cameras, on the other hand, do not require complicated deflection or blanking circuits. By their very nature, they are scanned by using computer-type addressing techniques. Pulse counters, divider chains, and memory provide the correct sequential readout of the charge-coupled device array so that a picture is recovered from the individual photodiode outputs. SEE TELEVISION SCANNING.

***Blanking and synchronizing, and video processing and control circuits.*** Before the camera output can be viewed on a conventional video monitor, horizontal and vertical synchronizing and blanking pulses must be added. In two-piece cameras this is ordinarily done in the CCU. Other functions which are necessary to obtain high-quality pictures include gamma correction, aperture correction, registration, and color balance. Gamma correction is required because the pickup tubes do not respond linearly to increasing light levels. It allows the CCU operator to capture detail in the dark areas of high-contrast scenes, essentially by "stretching" the video levels in those areas. Aperture correction provides several benefits mainly

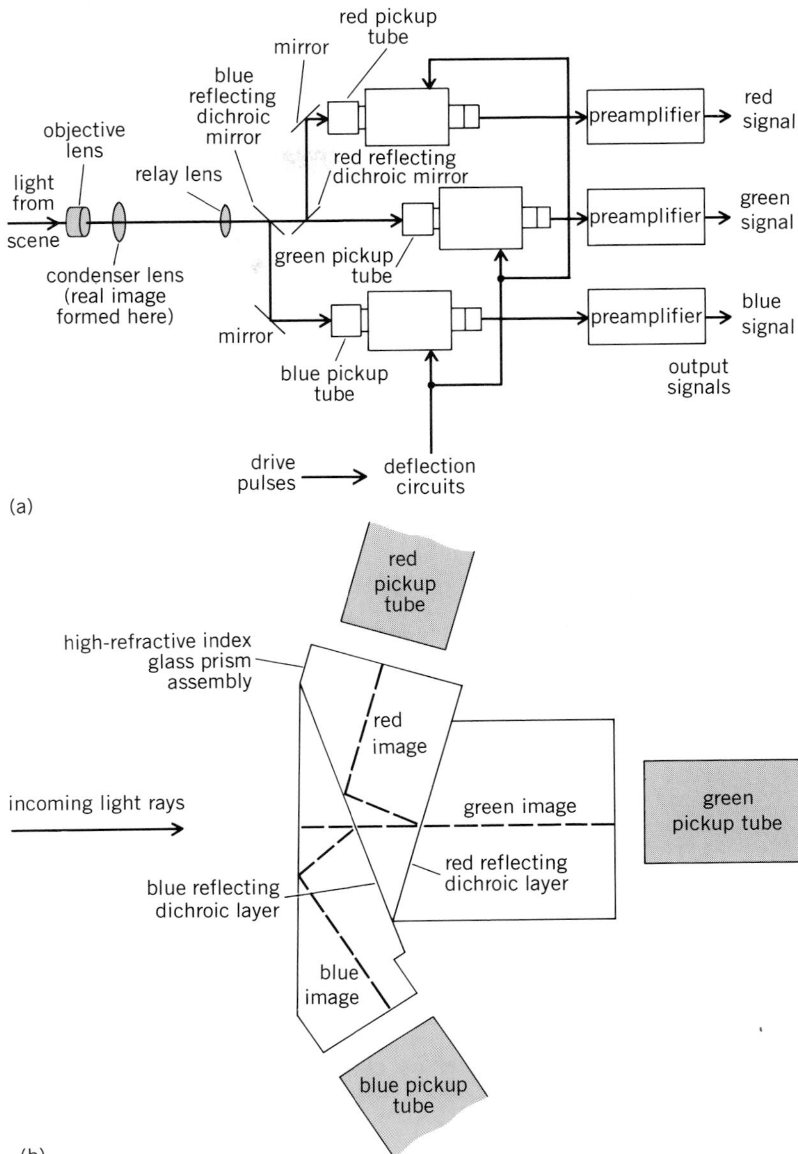


**Fig. 3. Color television camera optical systems. (*a*) Dichroic mirror system (*after G. W. Bartlett, ed., NAB Engineering Handbook, 6th ed., National Association of Broadcasters, 1975*). (*b*) Prism optical beam splitter.**

related to an even overall response to scenes with more or less detail. It also helps to improve the signal-to-noise ratio of the camera's output video. Registration must be adjusted on multiple-tube cameras to ensure that the separate red, blue, and green images are precisely aligned on one another. Color balance must be properly set on color cameras and must be consistent from dark scenes to bright scenes, or there will be an objectionable "tint" to the camera output. This is referred to as black balance and white balance. The former is set up with all light blocked from the camera's lens, while the latter is set up by using a "white card" under the actual lighting conditions of the scene. Color balance is frequently an automatic push-button feature on modern cameras.

Color cameras also have a color encoder which combines the three primary colors into a composite signal that must conform to one of several standards used in various countries. In the additive color NTSC (National Television Systems Committee) system

Fig. 4. Charge-coupled device (CCD) array. (*Fairchild Camera and Instrument*)

used in the United States, the red (R), blue (B), and green (G) signals are matrixed by a combining network and amplified to provide three new signals, M, I, and Q. The M signal contains luminance information, while I and Q contain the color, or chrominance, information from the televised screen. Component M consists of 30% red plus 59% green plus 11% blue. The I signal consists of 60% red minus 28% green minus 32% blue. Component Q is made up of 21% red minus 52% green plus 31% blue (**Fig. 5**). It is possible to subtract voltage levels by inverting the phase and summing, and this is exactly what is done in the color encoder. I and Q then modulate a 3.58-MHz carrier in a two-phase balanced modulation system, and the resulting amplitude-modulated sidebands, 90° out of phase, are added to the M signal along with the synchronizing and blanking signals already mentioned. A short reference burst of 3.58-MHz carrier is also added before the start of each television line. The resultant signal, known as composite NTSC video, contains all necessary information to recreate the original color scene on a color monitor or receiver. The M signal is used by black and white monitors or receivers, which are insensitive to I and Q, to create an image in shades of gray. Color monitors and receivers have special circuits to process the I and Q signals back into the primary colors. In a monochrome scene the red, green, and blue signals are equal, and therefore I and Q become zero and a black and white picture is produced on both monochrome and color television monitors. SEE COLOR TELEVISION.

**Typical configurations.** Live studio cameras (Fig. 1*a*) are equipped with several ancillary systems to enhance their operation. An electronic viewfinder, actually a small television monitor, shows the camera operator what the camera is seeing, making it possible to frame and focus the picture. The tally system consists of one or more red lights which illuminate when the camera's picture is "on the line" so that production and on-camera personnel know which camera is active. Generally an intercom system is built into the camera so that the director can communicate with the camera operator. The camera itself may be mounted upon a tripod, but more often it is on a dolly and pedestal, which allows the camera to be moved around on the studio floor and raised or lowered as desired. A pan head permits the camera to be rotated to the left or right and furnishes the actual mounting plate for the camera. The lens zoom and focus controls are mounted on a panning handle convenient to the operator. A common accessory on studio cameras is the videoprompter. This is a television monitor on which the program script may be displayed and read by the on-camera personnel.

Telecine cameras (Fig. 1*b*) are used in conjunction with film or slide projectors to televise motion pictures and still images. They generally employ vidicon tubes, one for monochrome or three for color, and many of the usual controls are automatic so as to require less operator attention. The film projectors used in television may use either a constant-rate pulldown or 3-2 intermittent mechanism to translate the motion picture's 24 frames per second to the 30 frame-per-second television frame rate. The constant-rate pulldown has a shutter which is closed before the film is rapidly pulled down. The shutter opens 120 times per second so that the camera sees each film frame in a 5:4 ratio. The 3-2 pulldown moves the film intermittently, so that one film frame is held in the film gate for two television fields (2/60 s) and the next film frame is held for three television fields (3/60 s). Hence two film frames are displayed in 5/60 s, and 24 film frames are shown in 1 s (30 television frames).

One telecine camera serves several projectors through the use of an optical multiplexer. The optical multiplexer may use stationary, half-silvered mirrors or movable, front-silvered mirrors to direct the image from each projector into the camera. Movable mirrors offer superior light-transmission efficiency and are preferable in color systems due to the light losses inherent in the pickup tube dichroic mirror splitter.

Portable cameras (Fig. 1*c*) usually combine all of the basic elements into one package and may be used for a multitude of purposes. They have found their way into electronic news gathering for broadcast tele-

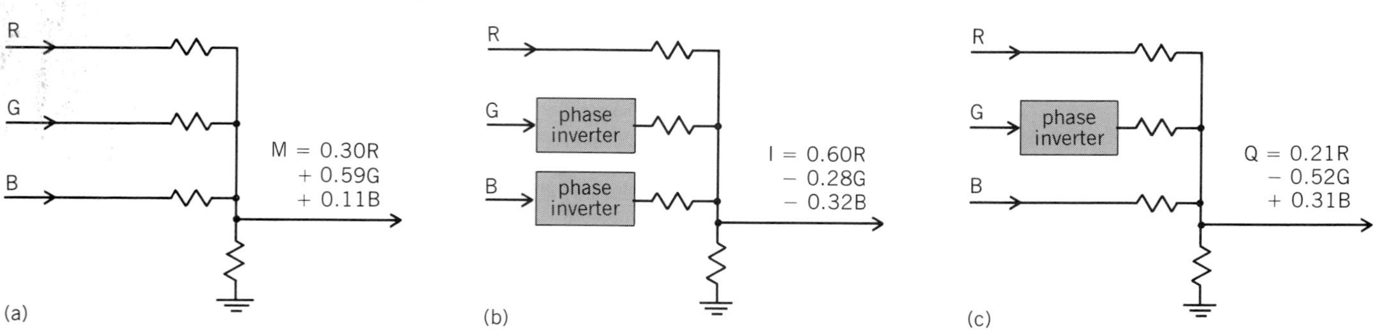


Fig. 5. Resistor matrices showing derivation of (*a*) M, (*b*) I, and (*c*) Q signals. (*After G. W. Bartlett, ed., NAB Engineering Handbook, 6th ed., National Association of Broadcasters, 1975*)

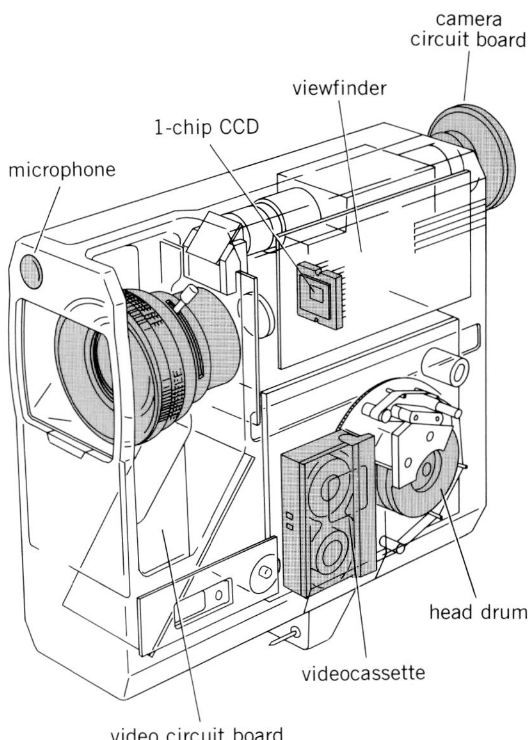


**Fig. 6. Prototype portable charge-coupled device (CCD) camera with built-in videotape recorder. (*Sony Corp.*)**

vision, and into electronic field production, where they can be used for production of broadcast programs, commercials, and educational programs. The units are lightweight, often have built-in microphones for sound pickup, and can be handled by one person. Used in conjunction with modern battery-powered portable videocassette recorders, an entire video and audio pickup system can be carried and operated by one or two people. Low-cost color cameras have become popular with home video enthusiasts and may someday supplant film-based home movie cameras (**Fig. 6**). *See Television; Television receiver; Television transmitter.*

*Earl F. Arbuckle III*

***Bibliography.*** B. Astle et al., Automatic set up system for a broadcast color camera, *121st Technical Conference of the Society of Motion Picture and Television Engineers*, October 21–26, 1979; G. W. Bartlett (ed.), *NAB Engineering Handbook*, 6th ed., 1975; CCD cameras: Coupled with the future, *Broadcast Manag./Eng.*, 16(9):47–50, September 1980; K. B. Benson, *Television Engineering Handbook*, 1986; M. Hermann and J. Wolber, The P-squared CCD 500B linear imager, *Electr. Components Appl.*, 1(3):183–190, May 1979.

## Television camera tube

An electron tube having a light-sensitive receptor that converts an optical image into an electrical television video signal. The tube is used in a television camera to generate a train of electrical pulses representing the light intensities present in an optical image focused on the tube. Each point of this image is interrogated in its proper turn by the tube, and an electrical impulse corresponding to the amount of light at that point of the optical image is generated by the tube. This signal represents the video or picture portion of a television signal. Television camera tubes are designed for broadcast television to pick up live programs, indoors or outdoors, as well as to reproduce motion pictures and other filmed material. *See Television camera.*

The tubes are also used extensively in closed-circuit cameras for surveillance, and in training studios, schools, video tape recorder cameras, and military special-purpose cameras. Special versions are designed to work with intensifier tubes which increase the effective sensitivity so that the cameras can operate at very low light levels. These are used for nighttime surveillance work, television astronomy, and viewing low-intensity x-ray fluoroscope images in medical x-rays and in baggage inspection units in airports. In general, three tubes are used in color television cameras. A class of tubes has built-in stripe color filters which allow a single tube to develop a complete color picture, although with somewhat reduced fidelity compared to the multitube cameras. Although the television camera tube is sensitive primarily to visible light, special tubes are sensitive to radiant energy in the infrared and the ultraviolet regions.

Charge-coupled devices are a new generation of solid-state electronic image sensors which can produce a television signal from an optical image. These can operate independently or can be incorporated into an intensifier-type vacuum tube to achieve enhanced sensitivity. **Figure 1** shows contemporary television camera tubes. *See Charge-coupled devices.*

**Image orthicon.** The image orthicon made broadcast television practical. It was used for more than 20 years as the primary studio and field camera tube for black and white and color television programming because of its high sensitivity and its ability to handle a wide range of scene contrast and to operate at very low light levels. It is one of the most complicated camera tubes. It is an outgrowth of the earlier multiplier orthicon and image iconoscope, and was made possible by the invention of the "two-sided" storage target. The image orthicon is divided into an image section, a scanning section, and a multiplier section (**Fig. 2**), within a single vacuum envelope.

***Image section.*** A light image is focused on the photoemissive layer, which is a continuous film inside the tube faceplate. Electrons absorb the energy and leave the surface in numbers proportional to the intensity of the illumination at each point. These photoelectrons flow in essentially parallel streams through the image section. The magnetic field focuses each to a sharp focus at the target plane. *See Photoemission.*

The two-sided target consists of a fine wire mesh screen placed several thousandths of an inch from a glass membrane less than 0.0002 in. (5.0 micrometers) thick. Most of the photoelectrons pass through the target mesh and hit the front surface of the target glass. Each photoelectron knocks several additional electrons from the target glass surface, producing a positive charge at the impact point. The secondary electrons are collected by the target mesh, which is held at a slightly more positive voltage. *See Secondary emission.*

***Scanning section.*** The positive charge pattern is stored on the front side of the target glass. A beam of low-velocity electrons generated by an electron gun is made to scan the rear surface of the glass by varying magnetic fields produced by the deflecting coils. As

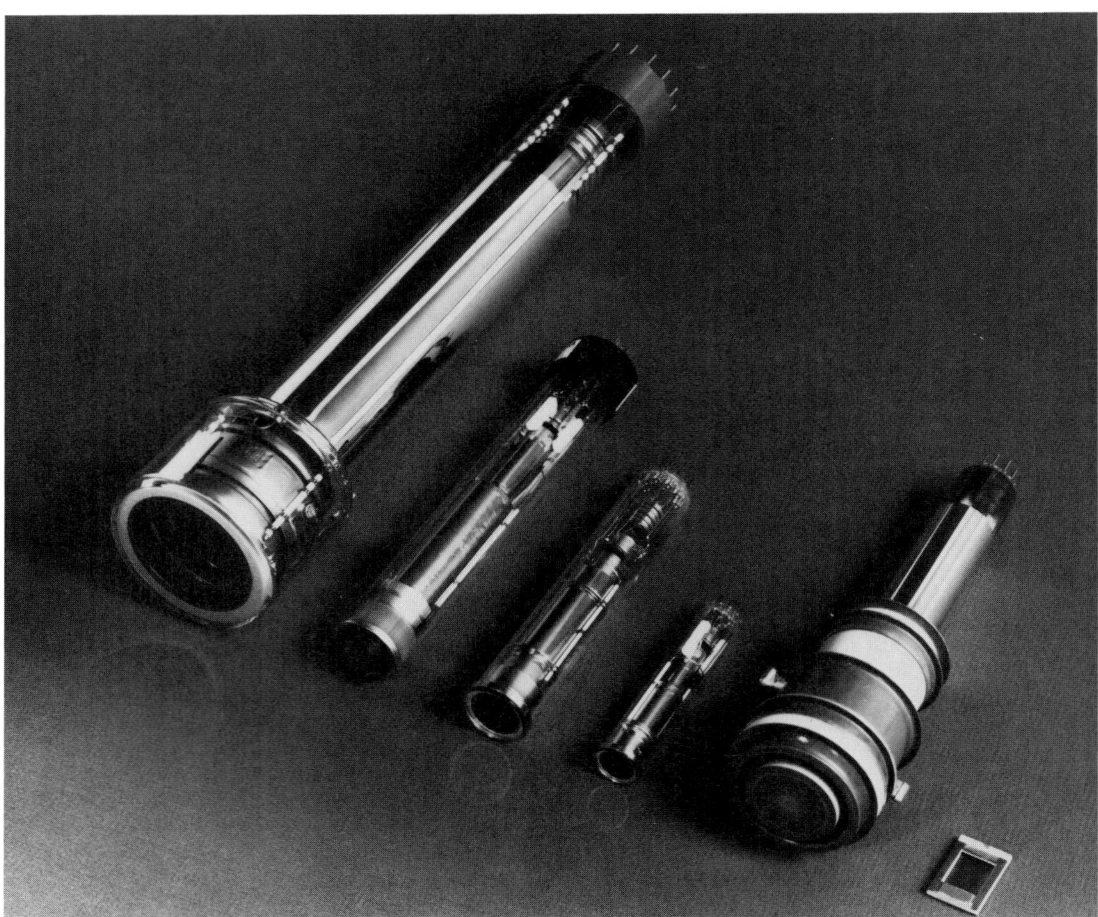

**Fig. 1. Typical television tubes in modern use. From left to right: image orthicon, lead oxide vidicon, industrial-type vidicon, miniature vidicon, silicon intensifier vidicon, and charge-coupled device. (*RCA Corp.*)**

the beam moves across the glass, it deposits electrons wherever positive charges are built up on the image side. The glass resistance is controlled so that charges can move from one face to the other before the scanning beam returns to the same spot; yet the glass is of high enough resistance to inhibit lateral movement of the charges. When the scanning beam has deposited enough electrons at each point to neutralize the charge on the glass and reduce it to the voltage of the electron gun cathode, the remaining electrons return toward the electron gun. When the beam scans an uncharged (dark) area, the full beam is returned. When the beam scans a highly charged (bright) area, most of the beam is deposited and little returns. The variations in the return beam current constitute the television picture information, at low intensity. The return beam is amplified about 1000 times in the electron multiplier section of the tube and then is taken out at the anode of the multiplier as a video signal current. SEE CATHODE-RAY TUBE.

***Multiplier section.*** The electron multiplier is of unique construction, although it operates like the multiplier used in a multiplier phototube. It consists of a flat first-dynode structure and a series of pinwheel multipliers. When the return beam strikes the first dynode, a shower of secondary electrons cascades through the pinwheels, which are maintained at progressively higher voltages, where repeated secondary emission multiplies their number. The final group of electrons is collected by the anode and forms the video signal current. SEE PHOTOMULTIPLIER.

**Image isocon.** The image isocon is a further development of the image orthicon. The excess primary electrons in the scanning beam of the image isocon are returned from the target in two components: the scattered electrons and those that are reflected (**Fig. 4**). The image isocon works on the principle of separating out these two components of the return scanning beam and utilizing the scattered electron component, which has the highest signal compared to the random noise in the beam current. The separation section (**Fig. 3**) directs only the scattered beam into the electron multiplier. This improves the signal-to-noise ratio of the output signal and allows the camera utilizing the image isocon to operate at very low light levels in such fields as astronomy and intensification of x-ray fluoroscopic images.



**Fig. 2. Image orthicon and its associated deflecting and focusing coils. (*After D. G. Fink, ed., Television Engineering Handbook, McGraw-Hill, 1957*)**

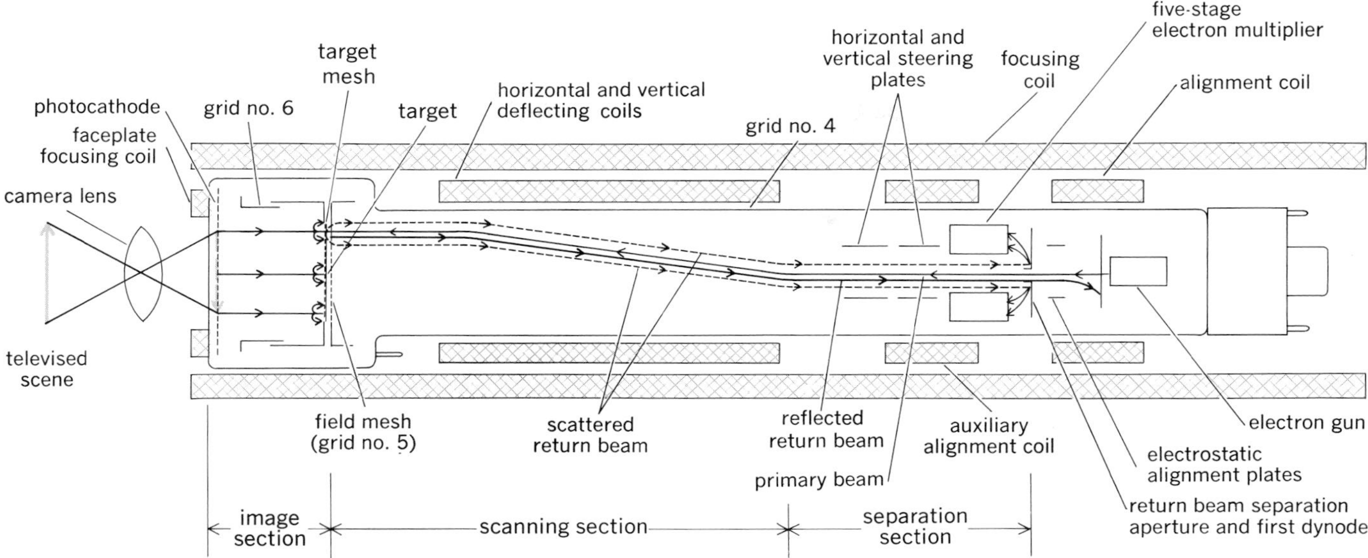


**Fig. 3. Image isocon and 175 associated deflectron and focusing components. The separation section isolates the scattered and reflected return beam components. (*RCA Corp.*)**

**Photoconductive tubes.** These types have a photoconductor as the light-sensitive portion. A photoconductor is a material that absorbs light and transfers the energy of the photons of light to electrons in the material. This frees some of the electrons and allows them to move through the material, and thereby changes the electrical conductivity of the material where the light is absorbed. The electron tube is designed to detect this change in electrical conductivity and develop a television signal. SEE PHOTOCONDUCTIVITY.

scattered electrons
primary electrons
conduction electrons
reflected electrons

**Fig. 4. Formation of the two components in the return beam of the image isocon: the scattered and the reflected electrons.**

The name vidicon was applied to the first photoconductive camera tube developed by RCA. It is loosely applied to all photoconductive camera tubes, although some manufacturers adopt their own brand names to identify the manufacturer or the type of photoconductive material used.

The vidicon tube is a small tube that was first developed as a closed-circuit or industrial surveillance television camera tube. The development of new photoconductors has improved its performance to the point where it is now utilized in one form or another in most television cameras. Its small size and simplicity of operation make the vidicon tube well suited for use in systems to be operated by relatively unskilled people.

The vidicon is a simply constructed storage type of camera tube (**Fig. 5**). The signal output is developed directly from the target of the tube and is generated by a low-velocity scanning beam from an electron gun. The target generally consists of a transparent signal electrode deposited on the faceplate of the tube and a thin layer of photoconductive material, which is deposited over the electrode. The photoconductive layer serves two purposes. It is the light-sensitive element, and it forms the storage surface for the electrical charge pattern that corresponds to the light image falling on the signal electrode.

The photoconductor has a fairly high resistance when in the dark. Light falling on the material excites additional electrons into a conducting state, lowering the resistance of the photoconductive material at the point of illumination. A positive voltage is applied to one side of the photoconductive layer by means of the signal electrode. On the other side, the scanning beam deposits sufficient electrons at low velocity to establish a zero voltage. In the interval between successive

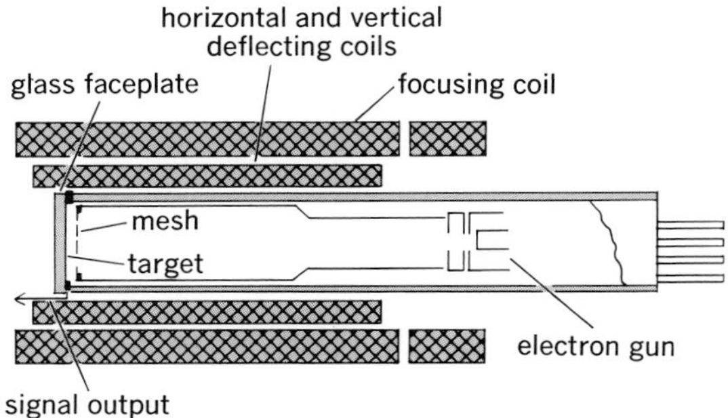


**Fig. 5. Cross section of a vidicon tube and its associated deflection and focusing coils.**

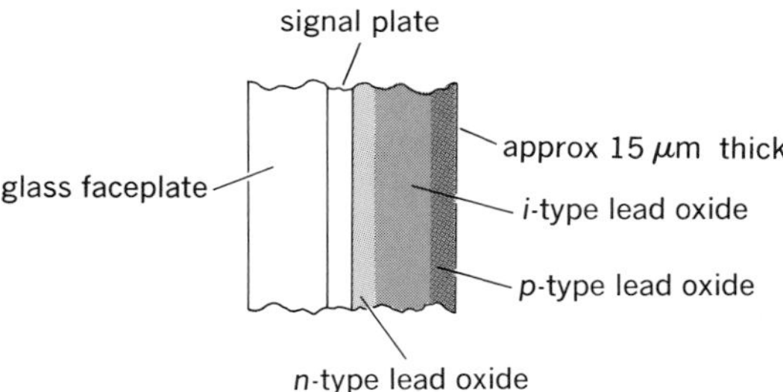


**Fig. 6. Cross-sectional view of lead oxide barrier-layer type of photoconductor.**

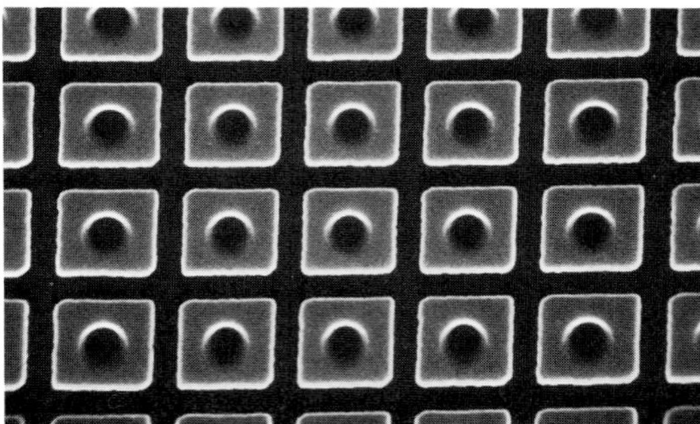

**Fig. 7. Small section of the scanned side of a silicon diode target. Diodes are circles, and beam landing pads are squares. (*RCA Corp.*)**

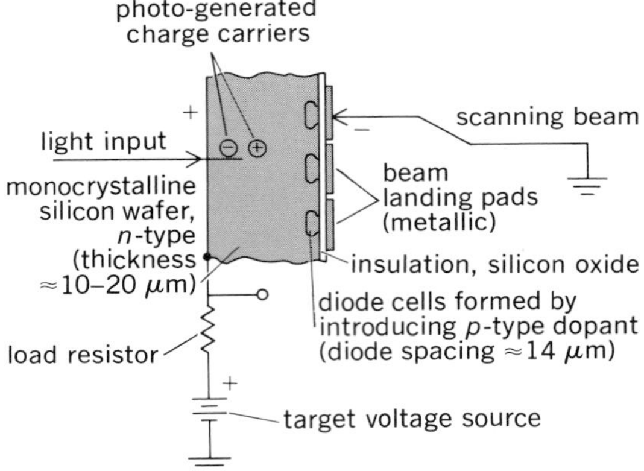


**Fig. 8. Cross section of silicon diode target.**

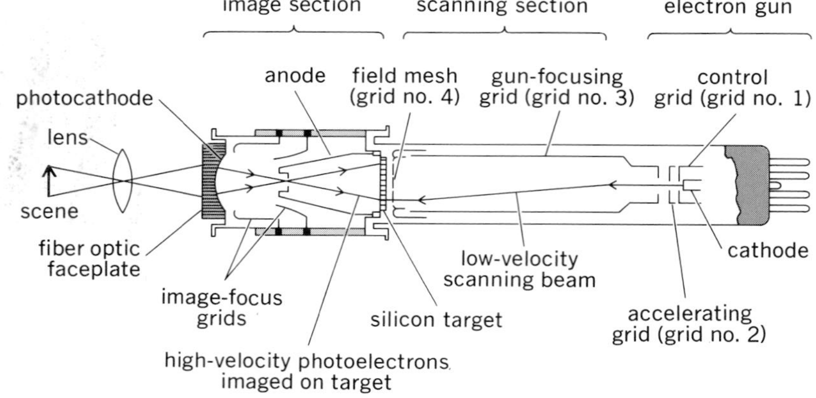


**Fig. 9. Silicon intensifier vidicon. (*RCA Corp.*)**

scans of a particular spot, the light lowers the resistance in relation to its intensity. Current then flows through the surface at this point, and the back surface builds up a positive voltage until the beam returns to scan the point. The signal output current is generated when the beam deposits electrons on these positively charged areas. An equal number of electrons flow out of the signal electrode and through a load resistor, developing a signal voltage that is fed directly to a low-noise video signal amplifier.

A fine-mesh screen stretched across the tube near the target causes the electron scanning beam to decelerate uniformly at all points and approach the target in a perpendicular manner. The beam is brought to a sharp focus on the target by the longitudinal magnetic field of the focusing coil and the proper voltage for the focusing electrode. The beam scans the target under the influence of the varying magnetic fields of the deflecting coils.

Photoconductor properties determine to a large extent the performance of the different types of vidicon tubes. The first and still widely used photoconductor is porous antimony trisulfide. The latest photoconductors are the lead oxide, selenium-arsenic-tellurium, cadmium selenide, zinc-cadmium telluride, and silicon diode arrays. All of these either improve the sensitivity or the speed of response (ability to capture motion without "smearing") or both. The first two are barrier-layer types that operate like large-area reversed-bias junctions. **Figure 6** illustrates the configuration of the barrier-layer or reversed-bias junction photoconductors; *n* refers to good electron conductivity, *i* refers to good electron and hole conductivity, and *p* refers to good hole conductivity. A positive voltage is applied to the *n* side through the signal plate, and a negative voltage is applied to the *p* side by the scanning beam electrons. This reverse-biases the junctions between the *i* and *p* and the *i* and *n* sections. This produces low dark current in the absence of light, a very desirable characteristic. Light is absorbed in the bulk of the material, where it produces charge carriers that provide a positive charge image on the side opposite the faceplate. The silicon diode tube is also a reversed-biased junction type, but consists of an array of hundreds of thousands of individual diodes on a wafer of silicon (**Fig. 7**). The photocarriers are generated in the silicon wafer, but are collected and stored on the diode cells (**Fig. 8**). *See Semiconductor*.

Most color television cameras utilize the lead oxide or selenium-arsenic-tellurium tubes. Industrial and scientific-industrial cameras utilize the other types.

**Silicon intensifier.** The silicon intensifier camera tube utilizes a silicon diode target, but bombards it with a focused image of high-velocity electrons. These electrons are emitted by a photoemitter on the inside of the window on the front of the image section (**Fig. 9**). A fiber-optics window is utilized so that the emitting surface can be curved to produce good uniformity of focus of the high-energy electrons on the silicon diode target. Each high-energy electron can free thousands of electron carriers in the silicon wafer (compared to one carrier per photon of light on a silicon diode vidicon). This high amplification allows the camera to operate at light levels below that of the dark-adapted eye. With such a camera tube, it is possible to "see" the individual photons of light that compose a low-level optical image. The silicon intensifier tube is utilized for nighttime surveillance and other extremely low-light-level television uses in industrial, scientific, and military applications. It can be operated over a very wide range of light levels by varying the image section voltage. This changes the amplification over a range of more than 1000 to 1.

**Solid-state imagers.** These are solid-state devices in which the optical image is projected onto a large-scale integrated-circuit device which detects the light image and develops a television picture signal. Typical of these is the charge-coupled-device imager. The term charge-coupled device refers to the action of the device which detects, stores, and then reads out an accumulated electrical charge representing the light on each portion of the image. The charge-coupled device transfers the individual charges to the output in the proper television scanning sequence to constitute a television video signal. The device detects light by absorbing it in a photoconductive substrate, such as silicon. The charge carriers generated by the light are accumulated in isolated wells on the surface of the silicon that are formed by voltages applied to an array of electrodes on top of an oxide insulator formed on the surface of the silicon. These wells are actually small MOS (metal-oxide-semiconductor) capacitors (**Fig. 10***a*). Charges are transferred through the structure by varying the voltages on the metal electrodes. For example, if electrodes A and B are made more negative and C is made positive, the charges will move laterally from point 1 to point 2 (Fig. 10*b*). *SEE INTEGRATED CIRCUITS*.

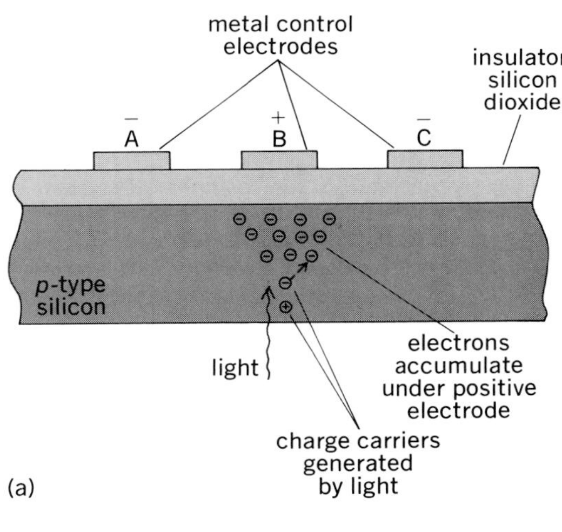


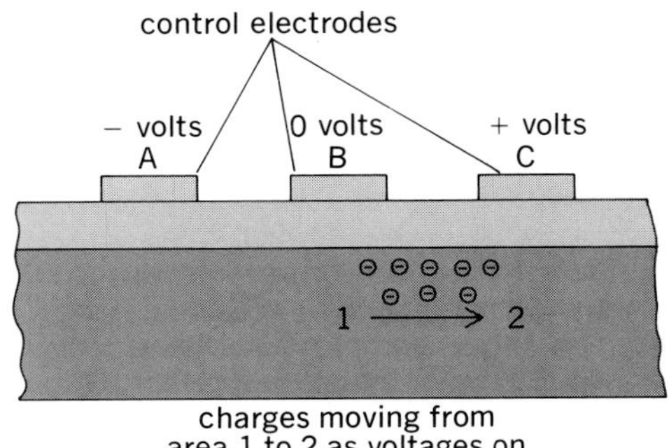


**Fig. 10. Charge-coupled device. (*a*) Accumulation of an electron charge in a pixel element. (*b*) Movement of accumulated charge through the silicon by changing the voltages on the electrodes A, B, and C.**

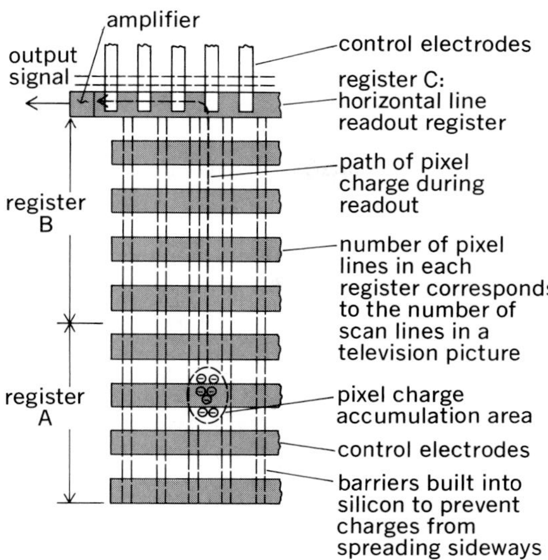


**Fig. 11. One type of charge-coupled-device imager. Register A accumulates the pixel charges produced by photoconductivity generated by the light image. The B register stores the lines of pixel charges and transfers each line in turn into register C. Register C reads out the charges laterally as shown into the amplifier.**

A practical charge-coupled-device imager employing these principles consists of a structure that forms several hundred thousand individual wells or pixels, and transfers the charges accumulated in these pixel wells out to an output amplifier in the proper sequence.

An example is shown in **Fig. 11**. Here the charges are accumulated by light exposure for the time it takes to complete a single television picture, or approximately $1/60$ s. Then all of the charges are rapidly transferred line by line upward into the storage register. In the storage area all charges are then moved upward one scan line at the end of each television line interval. The upper line of charges is moved into the horizontal readout register. Then the pixel charges are moved to the left through the horizontal readout register to the output amplifier. During this readout period of the lines in the storage area, a new group of image charges are being accumulated in the imaging area, and the complete sequence is repeated every $1/60$ s.

Investigation has been undertaken of many versions of solid-state imagers employing different light-sensitive materials and charge storage and readout methods.

A charge-coupled-device imager has been incorporated in an image intensifier tube. In this device the charge carriers are generated by a focused image of high-energy electrons in the charge-coupled-device imager in the same manner as in the silicon intensifier tube. This greatly enhances the sensitivity of the device and allows it to operate at very low light levels. *SEE LIGHT AMPLIFIER*.

*Robert G. Neuhauser*

***Bibliography.*** K. B. Benson (ed.), *Television Engineering Handbook*, 1986; B. Kazan (ed.), *Advances in Image Pickup and Display*, 1983; R. Kingslake (ed.), *Applied Optics and Optical Engineering*, vol. 2, 1965; R. G. Neuhauser, The silicon target vidicon, *J. SMPTE*, 86(6):414–418, June 1977; G. A. Robinson, The silicon intensifier target tube, *J. SMPTE*,

86(6):408–414, June 1977; H. V. Soule, *Electrooptical Photography at Low Illumination Levels*, 1968; V. K. Zworykin and G. A. Morton, *Television*, 2d ed., 1954.

## Television receiver

The equipment used to receive the transmitted modulated radio-frequency signals and produce synchronized visual images and sound for entertainment or educational purposes. The radio-frequency portion operates on the superheterodyne principle. *See* MODULATION; RADIO RECEIVER.

The first television receivers to be mass-produced were monochrome; that is, they provided pictures in black and white only. Later, color receivers, which produce pictures in full color as well as black-and-white, became available. Some television receivers are being introduced which can receive stereophonic sound or alternate language in accordance with multichannel television sound standards. For basic discussion of a television system *see* TELEVISION.

Early television receivers used vacuum-tube technology. Present-day receivers use solid-state technology with many functions integrated on a few chips. The only function still primarily implemented by using vacuum-tube technology is the display by the cathode-ray tube (CRT). *See* CATHODE-RAY TUBE; INTEGRATED CIRCUITS; VACUUM TUBE.

**Monochrome receivers.** **Figure 1** shows a block diagram of a conventional monochrome television receiver.

***Antenna and transmission line.*** Since most broadcast television transmissions in the United States are horizontally polarized (some are circularly polarized), the most basic type of television-receiving antenna is the horizontally mounted half-wave dipole. Because the stations serving a given area may operate on widely different frequencies, however, the dipole dimensions must be a compromise that permits reasonable performance on all the desired channels. More complex antennas combine several dipole elements of various lengths, and passive reflectors may be used to achieve some degree of horizontal directivity, which increases the amplitude of the receiver signal and reduces interference from other stations. Highly directive antennas are frequently mounted on remotely controlled rotators so that they can be pointed in the direction providing the best reception of the desired signal. The most common types of transmission line between the antenna and receiver are 300-ohm "twin-lead," employing polyethylene as a dielectric spacer between two uniformly spaced, unshielded wires. Also 75-ohm coaxial cable is used. *See* ANTENNA; COAXIAL CABLE; POLARIZATION OF WAVES; TRANSMISSION LINES; YAGI-UDA ANTENNA.

***Tuner.*** The tuner of a television receiver selects the desired channel and converts the frequencies received to lower frequencies within the passband of the intermediate-frequency amplifier. For very high-frequency (VHF) reception older tuners have 12 discrete switch positions, corresponding to channels 2–13. For ultra-high-frequency (UHF) reception, continuous tuning is employed in older tuners. Most receivers now use a frequency synthesizer circuit for generating the local oscillator frequency, and may be stabilized with an automatic frequency control. Nearly all VHF tuners employ a radio-frequency (rf) amplifier, a mixer, and local-oscillator circuits arranged as shown in Fig. 1. Some receivers are provided with additional channel-tuning capability for use with a community antenna television (CATV) system. *See* AMPLIFIER; AUTOMATIC FREQUENCY CONTROL (AFC); CLOSED-CIRCUIT TELEVISION; OSCILLATOR; RADIO-FREQUENCY AMPLIFIER.

The received signal and the local oscillator signal are applied to the mixer. Difference frequencies, representing the picture and sound carriers, are produced

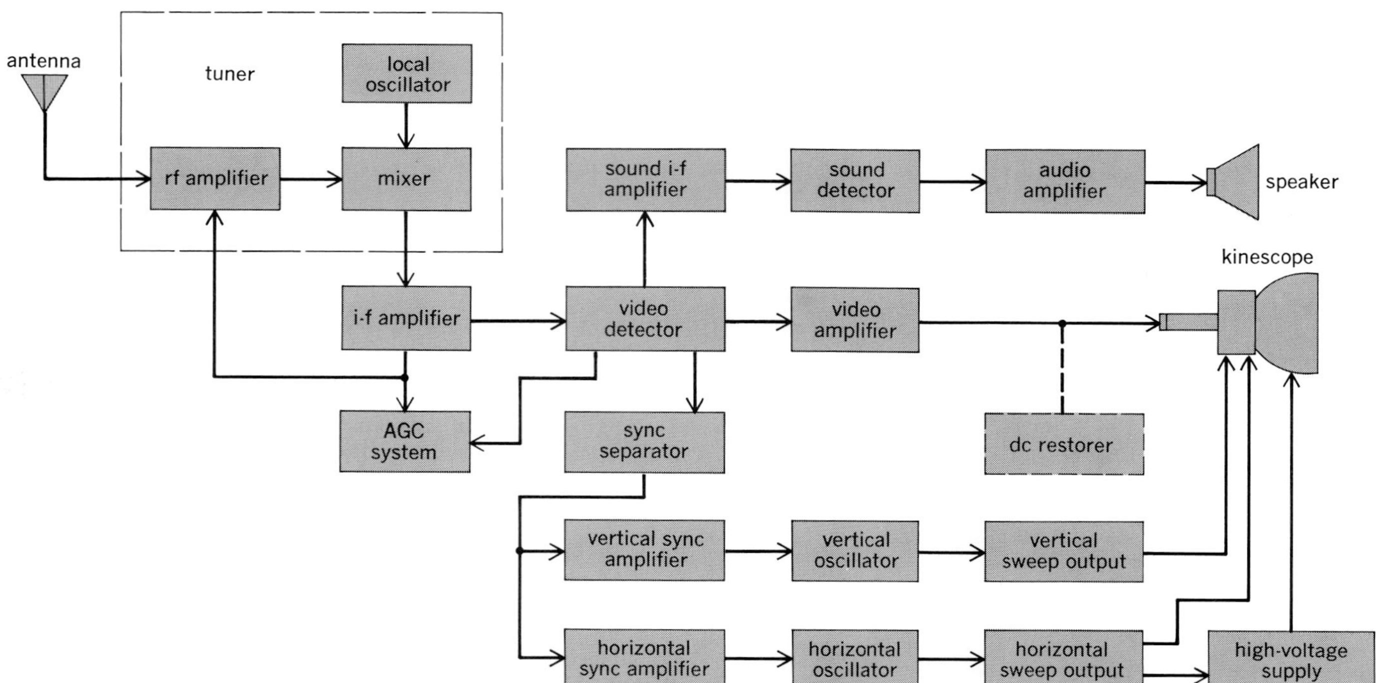

**Fig. 1. Block diagram of a typical monochrome television receiver.**

and remain essentially constant as the radio-frequency amplifier, mixer, and oscillator circuits are tuned to the different channels. Known as intermediate frequencies (41.25 MHz for sound and 45.75 MHz for picture), they are available for further amplification.

Such performance characteristics as noise factor, gain, bandwidth, and oscillator radiation must be optimized in the design of the tuner.

***Intermediate-frequency amplifier.*** The output from the tuner is applied to the intermediate-frequency (i-f) amplifier. The gain of this amplifier is essentially constant from 43 to 45 MHz. Above 45 MHz the response decreases such that at 45.75 MHz, the picture carrier frequency, it is 50%. This slope is required to compensate for the vestigial sideband transmitted signal.

Below 43 MHz the response decreases until at 41.25 MHz, the sound carrier frequency, it is 5–10% of the flat response. This minimizes cross modulation between picture and sound carriers. Fixed tuned trap circuits are used to produce sharp cutoffs at the lower and upper limits of the intermediate-frequency passband. Sufficient selectivity is provided to minimize interference from signals originating in adjacent television channels.

***Separation of video and audio.*** The output of the intermediate-frequency amplifier consists of two modulated radio-frequency signals. One of these, which is amplitude-modulated, provides a varying signal corresponding to the black-and-white portions of the picture, a blanking signal to render the return trace invisible on the picture tube, horizontal sync pulses to initiate the retrace of the beam at the end of each line, and vertical sync pulses to initiate the retrace of the beam at the end of each picture field. The other signal is frequency-modulated and contains the transmitted sound information. *See Amplitude modulation; Frequency modulation.*

There are two types of detector which may be used for video modulation detection: the envelope detector and the synchronous detector. In the envelope detector the two radio-frequency signals are applied to a diode which produces a rectified output that follows the instantaneous peak value of the amplitude-modulated picture carrier. *See Amplitude-modulation detector; Diode.*

The synchronous detector is a highly linear device and is used in the better television receivers where high-quality results are desired for color, teletext, alphanumeric and graphical data digital signals, and multichannel sound. The band-pass filter characteristic has much less attenuation for the sound carrier and upper video-frequency components. The synchronous detector is basically an analog multiplier.

The polarity of the video detector output depends upon the design of the video amplifier and method of picture-tube drive. Usually, maximum picture carrier (sync-pulse modulation) produces a negative output voltage.

Coincidentally a 4.5-MHz signal results from the heterodyne beat of the picture and sound carriers. This signal contains the frequency-modulated sound information, which can be further amplified and detected in the sound channel. This is known as the intercarrier sound (ICS) system.

Following the detector is a video amplifier. An output level of about 100 volts is ordinarily sufficient to assure full drive of the picture tube over its modulation range. A 4.5 MHz trap is included in the video amplifier circuit to prevent the appearance of the intercarrier sound signal on the picture tube. The sound reproduction system is discussed below. *See Video amplifier.*

***Automatic gain control.*** Since television receivers, like radio receivers, may be subjected to widely varying incoming signal strengths, some form of automatic gain control (AGC) is necessary. Circuits for this function provide a nearly constant carrier signal level to the video detector. *See Automatic gain control (AGC).*

***Sync separator circuits.*** Picture synchronizing information is obtained from the video signal by means of sync separation circuits. In addition, these circuits must separate this information from noise and interference during the reception of weak signals, particularly if impulse noise is present. In general, sync separation circuits perform the following functions: (1) separation, by means of amplitude clipping, of the sync information from the picture information; (2) separation of the desired horizontal and vertical timing information by means of frequency selection; and (3) rejection of noise signals that are higher in amplitude than sync pulses by amplitude limiting or gating (noise suicide) circuits. *See Clipping circuit; Electrical noise.*

***Sweep systems.*** Two independent systems are employed in the vertical and horizontal sweep circuits. Each employs a timing generator, generally of the oscillatory type, controlled by the synchronizing information obtained from the sync separators. The oscillators are followed by drive and waveform-shaping circuits. These are followed by power amplifier stages capable of providing the currents required by the deflection coils of the yoke for picture-tube beam deflection. Substantially different techniques are required for vertical and horizontal scanning.

***Vertical deflection.*** Generally the vertical oscillator is of the relaxation type operating at approximately 60 Hz. Its frequency is accurately controlled by a signal obtained from the sync separator. The output waveform of the sync separator consists of a train of pulses representing the horizontal and vertical synchronizing pulses. When these are passed through a low-pass filter or integrating circuit, a sawtooth-shaped voltage wave representing vertical sync is obtained. This is used to synchronize the vertical oscillator. A frequency control in the vertical oscillator circuit is so adjusted that its free-running frequency is slightly lower than the synchronizing signal frequency. For good interlace it is necessary that no horizontal frequency components be included in the vertical synchronizing voltage. *See Electric filter; Relaxation oscillator; Sawtooth-wave generator; Television scanning.*

The vertical output stage is generally operated as a class A amplifier. The yoke is transformer-coupled to the plate of the output tube to match the yoke impedance to the output tube impedance. Since the yoke impedance is partly resistive and partly inductive, the voltage waveform across it is the sum of a sawtooth and a rectangular pulse. The current through the yoke has essentially a sawtooth waveform, but each sawtooth has a symmetrical S shape to take care of picture-tube faceplate geometry and result in a linear scan. *See Power amplifier; Transformer.*

***Horizontal deflection.*** A more complex system is required for horizontal scanning. There are several basic reasons for this: (1) Horizontal sync pulses are of much shorter duration than are vertical sync pulses; (2) some form of automatic frequency control (AFC) of the horizontal oscillator is required to average the incoming horizontal sync information and retain accurate phase; and (3) considerably greater power output is required to generate the deflecting yoke fields as well as the high voltage, of 10–20 kV, for the picture tube. SEE AUTOMATIC FREQUENCY CONTROL (AFC).

The horizontal oscillator is generally of the Hartley or Colpitts type. The frequency of oscillation is determined both by a time-constant control and by a bias voltage derived from an AFC circuit. The AFC circuit may be a phase comparator, in which the pulses from the sync separator are compared to the oscillator output signal. The output of the comparator is a voltage proportional to the phase departure of the two signals. Many receivers lock the horizontal and vertical scanning waveforms together with a countdown circuit thus eliminating the vertical oscillator. In this case the countdown begins at a harmonic of the horizontal scan rate.

The desired current waveform in the horizontal windings of the deflection yoke is a line-frequency sawtooth, possibly modified by the addition of a small amount of S curvature to compensate for picture-tube face geometry. Energy from the horizontal drive, or output tube, is normally supplied to the yoke (through the horizontal output transformer) only during approximately the last half of each sawtooth period. At the conclusion of the sawtooth period, the horizontal driver is cut off, and the energy stored in the form of current through the yoke causes an oscillation in the self-resonant circuit consisting of the yoke, horizontal output transformer, and the associated capacitances. This oscillation is permitted to continue for only one half-cycle, during which time the current through the yoke reverses in polarity and attains a negative value almost equal to the original positive value. The self-resonant frequency of the horizontal output circuit must be high enough to permit the full current reversal to be accomplished within the horizontal blanking interval. The oscillation is stopped after the first half-cycle by the action of a damper (normally a diode), which controls the release of the energy stored in the yoke in such a way that the current follows the desired sawtooth waveform. In approximately the middle of the sawtooth period, the damper becomes nonconductive, and the horizontal driver takes over the task of supplying the energy required for the next cycle.

***High-voltage supply.*** Since the impedance of the yoke at horizontal scan frequency is primarily inductive, the voltage across the horizontal deflection windings is essentially constant during active scan. During the retrace period, however, the high rate of current change causes the generation of a high-voltage pulse having a shape similar to that of a half sine wave and a duration equal to the retrace period. It is common practice to employ a stepup winding on the horizontal output transformer to raise this so-called kickback pulse up to a still higher voltage level, commonly about 18 kV for black-and-white displays, and to pass it through a simple rectifier and filter to serve as the high-voltage supply for the cathode-ray tube.

***Picture tubes.*** The display device for a monochrome television receiver is a cathode-ray tube, consisting of an evacuated bulb containing an electron gun and a phosphor screen, which emits light when excited by an electron beam. The intensity of the electron beam is controlled by the video signal, which is applied either to the grid or the cathode of the electron gun. The position of the electron beam is controlled by electromagnetic fields produced by the deflection yoke placed around the neck of the tube. SEE PICTURE TUBE.

***Controls.*** Certain controls are available to the user for adjustment of the receiver. These are the audio volume, channel selector, brightness and contrast controls. In some receivers fine tuning, horizontal hold, and vertical hold controls are also available. Other controls, normally mounted on the rear of the chassis or under a removable panel, may include height, width, and linearity controls.

The ON-OFF switch for the receiver is frequently mounted on the same shaft as the audio volume control, which controls the gain of the audio channel. The channel selector adjusts the tuner's selective circuits for optimum performance at the desired channel, and fine tuning is a vernier control for the frequency of the local oscillator. Brightness is usually a manual adjustment of the bias on the electron gun in the picture tube. The contrast control adjusts the level of the video signal by some means such as a potentiometer in one of the video amplifier stages.

The horizontal and vertical hold controls adjust the free-running frequencies of the horizontal and vertical oscillators to achieve the most reliable synchronization with the incoming signal. In some cases, the controls may actually consist of variable resistors in the circuits of the respective oscillators.

Vertical linearity is generally controlled by a variable resistance in the circuit of the vertical output stage, and picture height may be controlled by a variable resistor in the circuit of the vertical oscillator. Horizontal linearity may be controlled by a variable inductor placed between the damper and the source of voltage.

**Color receivers.** Television receivers designed to produce images in full color are necessarily more complex than those designed to produce monochrome images only, because additional information must be handled to produce color. In monochrome systems, the video signal controls only the luminance of the various areas of the image. In color systems, it is necessary to control both the luminance and chrominance of the picture elements.

The chrominance of a color refers to those attributes which cause it to differ from a neutral (white or gray) color of the same luminance. While chrominance can be expressed in a great variety of ways, it is always necessary to employ at least two variables to express the full range of chrominance that can be perceived by the human eye. In qualitative terms, chrominance may be regarded as those properties of a color that control the psychological sensations of hue and saturation. For color television purposes, chrominance is most frequently expressed quantitatively in terms of the amounts of two hypothetical, zero-luminance primary colors (usually designated $I$ and $Q$), which must be added to or subtracted from a neutral color of a given luminance to produce the color in question.

As a practical matter, color television receivers produce full-color images as additive combinations of red, green, and blue primary-color images, and it is necessary to process the luminance and chrominance information in a color signal in such a way as to make it usable by a practical reproducing device.

***Color signal.*** Color television broadcasts in the United States employ signal specifications that are fully compatible with those used for monochrome, making it possible for color programs to be received on monochrome receivers and monochrome programs to be received on color receivers. (Color pictures are produced, of course, only when color programs are viewed through color receivers—in all other cases, the images are in black and white only.) Compatibility is achieved by encoding the color information at the transmitting end of a color television system in such a way that the transmitted signal consists essentially of a normal monochrome signal (conveying luminance information) supplemented by an additional modulated wave conveying chrominance information. **Figure 2** shows the major components of a color television signal. Although it is added directly to the monochrome signal component before transmission, the color subcarrier signal does not cause objectionable interference, because of the use of the frequency interlace technique. Because the chrominance information involves two variables, the modulated subcarrier signal varies in both amplitude and phase, and it is necessary to employ synchronous detectors to recover the two variables. A phase reference for the special local oscillator, which provides the synchronized carriers in each color receiver, is transmitted in the form of so-called color synchronizing bursts. These are short samples of unmodulated subcarrier transmitted during the horizontal blanking periods after the horizontal sync pulses.

***Performance standards and requirements.*** A simplified block diagram for a color television receiver is shown in **Fig. 3**. Many of the circuits in a color receiver are the same in principle as the corresponding circuits in a monochrome receiver, but all circuits handling the complete color signal must be designed for high performance standards. Because the chrominance information is received in the form of sidebands occupying the upper portion of the video spectrum (centered on approximately 3.6 MHz), it is necessary that the antenna, tuner, intermediate-frequency amplifier, and video detector be designed to handle the full 4-MHz bandwidth provided in the broadcast transmission standards if degradation of the color information is to be avoided. Because the color subcarrier signal is simply added to the normal monochrome signal before transmission, it is necessary that all stages handling the complete signal be linear, so as to avoid intermodulation or distortion of the various signal components. The deflection circuits for a color receiver are similar in principle to those used in monochrome receivers, although the output stages are normally designed for a higher power level because of the greater deflection requirements for color cathode-ray tubes. Color displays use 22 to 30 kV for the high-voltage supply.

***Color decoding circuits.*** Special decoding circuits are necessary in a color receiver to process the luminance and chrominance information in a color signal so that it can be used for the control of a practical color cathode-ray tube utilizing red, green, and blue primary colors. The major features of the most common approach to the color decoding circuits are shown within the broken lines in Fig. 3.

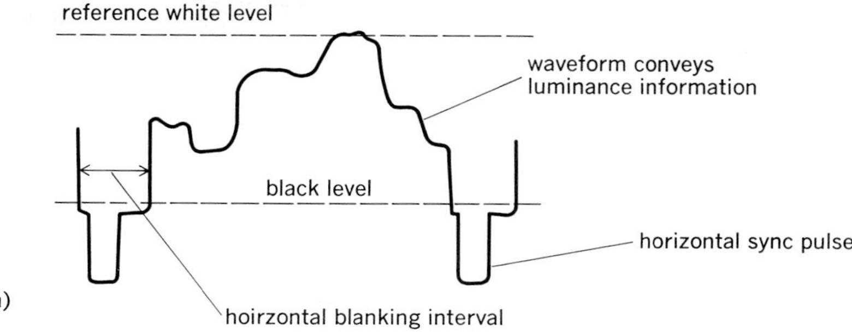


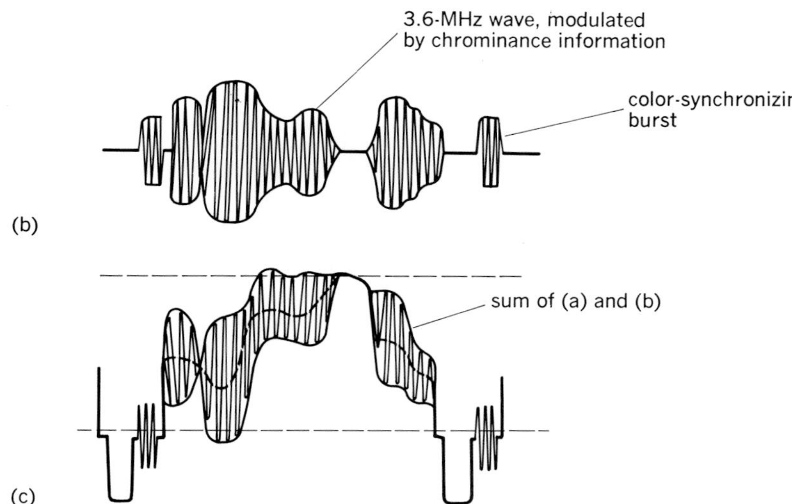


**Fig. 2. Waveform sketches of major components of color television signal. (*a*) Normal monochrome signal. (*b*) Color subcarrier signal. (*c*) Complete color signal.**

The video amplifier shown at the bottom handles the monochrome portion of the signal and is designed to provide attenuation in the vicinity of 3.6 MHz to block the passage of chrominance information. The chrominance information is recovered from the modulated subcarrier signal through a band-pass filter (centered at 3.6 MHz) and a pair of synchronous demodulators, in which the modulated wave is heterodyned against fixed carriers of two different phases but of the same frequency. In the most rigorous type of color decoding circuit, the chrominance components recovered from the modulated subcarrier signal are the same $I$ and $Q$ originally used to produce the modulated wave, but it is possible to use almost any two phase positions (not necessarily 90° apart) to recover any two independent combinations of the original $I$ and $Q$ signals. The bandwidths of the signals produced by the demodulators are normally adjusted somewhere between 0.5 and 1.5 MHz, and delay compensation may be required to keep all three signal components in time coincidence. The matrix circuit is essentially a linear cross-mixing network for combining the $M$, $I$, and $Q$ signals in the proper proportions to produce red, green, and blue signals. If signals other than $I$ and $Q$ are produced by the chrominance demodulators, it is necessary only to design the matrix circuit with slightly different mixing constants.

The synchronous carriers required for the demodulation of the chrominance information are provided by a subcarrier regenerator, which is usually a burst-controlled oscillator operating at the subcarrier fre-

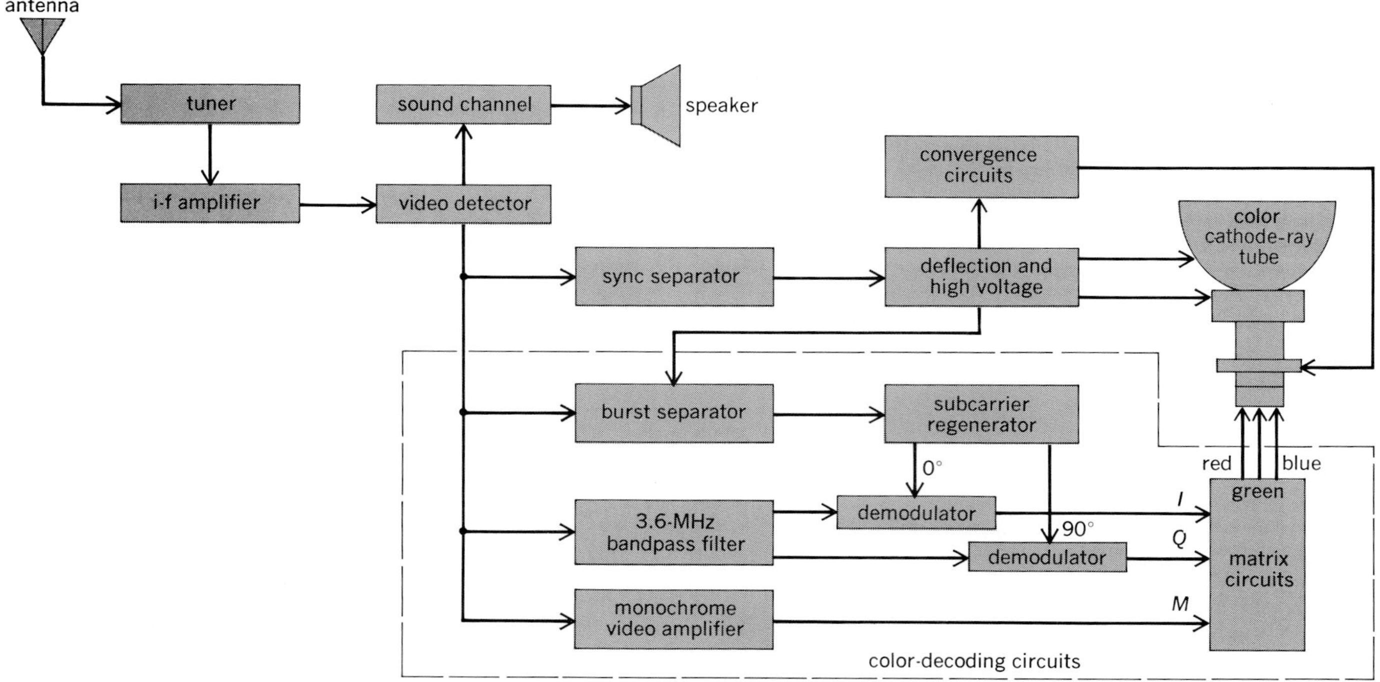


**Fig. 3. Simplified block diagram of a color television receiver.**

quency. Control information for the subcarrier regenerator is obtained from a burst separator, which is a gate circuit turned on only during the horizontal blanking periods by pulses derived from the horizontal deflection system. The separated bursts are compared with the output of the local subcarrier oscillator in a phase detector. If an error exists, a correction voltage is developed, which may be applied to restore the subcarrier oscillator to the proper frequency and phase. For good noise immunity, a time constant is normally provided so that control information is averaged over at least several line periods.

***Color cathode-ray tube and convergence circuits.*** The great majority of color television receivers employ the shadow-mask color cathode-ray tube in which color images are produced in the form of closely intermingled red, green, and blue dots. The primary-color phosphor dots are excited by three separate electron beams, which are prevented from striking dots of the wrong color by the shadowing effect of an aperture mask located about ½ in. (1.25 cm) behind the special phosphor screen. The beams in such a cathode-ray tube are deflected simultaneously by the fields produced by a single deflection yoke placed conventionally around the neck of the tube. New cathode-ray-tube designs and deflection yokes are self-converging and do not require auxiliary convergence deflection.

***Color controls.*** In addition to the same controls required for monochrome receivers, color receivers normally have controls for convergence, hue, and saturation. The convergence controls, considered servicing adjustments only, adjust the relative amplitudes and phases of the signal components that are added together to form the proper waveforms for the convergence yoke. The hue control usually adjusts the phase of the burst-controlled oscillator and alters all the colors in the image in a systematic manner comparable to the effect achieved when a color circle diagram is rotated in one direction or the other. The proper setting for the hue control is normally determined by observing skin tones on actors and actresses. The saturation control, frequently labeled chroma or simply color, adjusts the gain of the chrominance circuits relative to the monochrome channel and controls the saturation or vividness of the reproduced colors. When this control is set too low, the colors are all pale or pastel, and when it is reduced to zero, the picture is seen in black and white only. SEE COLOR TELEVISION.

**Sound reproduction.** The typical circuit for recovery of the sound from the aural transmitter consists of a band-pass filter to extract the frequency-modulated 4.5-MHz carrier from the video detector, amplification and amplitude limiting, frequency-modulation detection with a frequency discriminator, deemphasis with a resistance-capacitance (*RC*) low-pass filter having a time constant of 75 microseconds, followed by volume control, a power amplifier, and a loudspeaker. The result is single-channel monophonic sound. SEE LOUDSPEAKER.

***Multichannel television sound.*** Standards have been adopted for the broadcasting of multichannel television sound (MTS) consisting of a monophonic service, a stereophonic service, and a simultaneous sec-

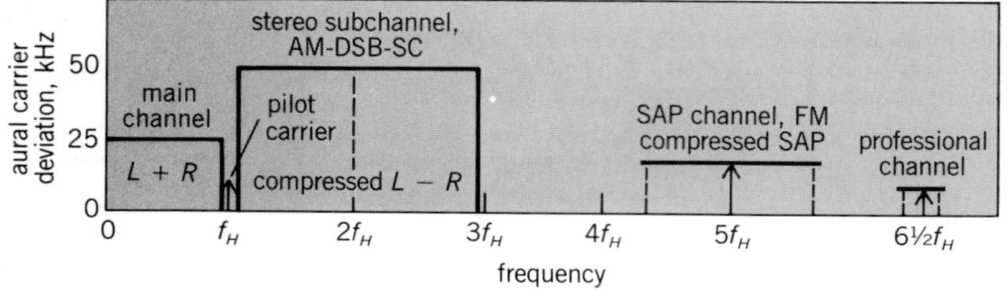


**Fig. 4. Composite multichannel television sound signal baseband frequency spectrum. $f_H$ is the horizontal scanning frequency, 15.734 kHz.**

ond-audio-program (SAP) service. A frequency spectrum plot of the multichannel sound modulation impressed upon the aural frequency-modulation transmitter is shown in **Fig. 4**. The main channel signal consists of the normal audio-frequency components up to 15 kHz, and in the case of stereophonic transmissions is made up of the arithmetic sum of the left and right audio signals ($L+R$), thus making for a compatible result for the monophonic listener. Stereophonic audio information in the form of the arithmetic difference between the left and right audio signals ($L-R$) is amplitude-compressed in accordance with a specific algorithm and impressed as double-sideband, suppressed-carrier, amplitude modulation (AM-DSB-SC) on a carrier at twice the picture horizontal scanning frequency (31.47 kHz). A pilot carrier is sent at the picture horizontal scanning frequency (15.73 kHz) to synchronize the receiver stereo demodulator. Additionally, a second audio program (SAP; a second language, for example) is frequency-modulated on a carrier centered at five times the picture horizontal scanning frequency (78.67 kHz). The SAP audio is monophonic and is compressed with the same algorithm as the stereophonic difference ($L-R$) audio. A professional channel centered at a frequency of about 6.5 times the horizontal scanning frequency may be present and is reserved for use by the broadcaster. The sum of all the components using defined ratios is the composite multichannel baseband signal which frequency-modulates the aural carrier.

***Multichannel sound receiver.*** The MTS receiver design is still evolving, but many receivers make direct use of the 4.5-MHz frequency-modulation intercarrier available at the video detector to feed a tuned amplifier which has a wider bandwidth than that used in the monophonic receiver, a limiter, and a wideband discriminator (much wider than the monophonic equivalent) to reproduce the MTS composite baseband signal as described above. The main channel is deemphasized as in the monophonic case to recover $L+R$ audio. The stereophonic subcarrier at 31.47 kHz is synchronously demodulated with a reference carrier derived from the second harmonic of the pilot at 15.73 kHz to recover the compressed $L-R$ audio. A complementary expander using the inverse of the compression algorithm provides the correct $L-R$ audio signal which is matrixed with the $L+R$ audio to make the original left ($L$) and right ($R$) audio signals. A stereophonic amplifier and tone, balance, and volume controls complete the system together with appropriate loud speakers. The SAP channel requires a separate FM subcarrier demodulator centered at 78.67 kHz to recover the compressed SAP audio. When the SAP audio is chosen for listening, a switch routes the compressed SAP audio to the $L-R$ expander, and disconnects both $L+R$ and $L-R$ audio signals. The compression-expansion (companding) scheme provides an effective way to reduce noise and other interferences encountered in the transmission path between transmitter and receiver, such as when the received signal is weak. The main monophonic channel noise performance is adequate without a companding scheme. *See Volume control systems.*

*Carl G. Eilers*

***Bibliography.*** C. G. Eilers, TV multichannel sound: The BTSC system, *IEEE Trans. Consumer Electr.*, CE-31:1-7, 1985; B. Grob, *Basic Television and Video Systems*, 5th ed., 1984; B. Hartman, *Fundamentals of Television: Theory and Service*, 1975; M. S. Kiver, *Television Electronics: Theory and Servicing*, 8th ed., 1983; L. B. Tyler, M. F. Davis, and W. A. Allen, A companding system for multichannel TV sound, *IEEE Trans. Consumer Electr.*, CE-30:633-640, 1984.

## Television scanning

The process of scrutinizing the brightness of each element of detail contained in the image of a scene to be transmitted by television. In monochrome television, the process is instrumental in converting the brightness of each individual element so scrutinized into a unique voltage-time response suitable for transmission. In color television, the brightness of variations of each scene are first separated by red, green, and blue filters, after which the conversion from brightness to voltage on a time basis occurs separately for each of the three colors. Scanning also takes place in the receiver in exact synchronism with the camera-tube scanning, and synchronizing signals are transmitted for that purpose. *See Television; Television camera tube; Television receiver.*

**Interlaced scanning.** An image is analyzed by scanning it according to a fine structure of parallel, nearly horizontal lines called a scanning raster. The complete raster is rectangular in shape. Scanning may be done conventionally by starting at the upper left-hand corner along line 1 and moving toward the right at constant speed. At the end of line 1 a quick return is made to the left-hand side to start the scanning of line 2, again moving toward the right. When all lines have been scanned in this way, from top to bottom, the process is repeated by returning quickly to the upper left-hand corner to line 1. If all the lines are scanned in sequence, the process is called sequential scanning.

A variation of this kind of scanning, called interlaced scanning, is used to conserve bandwidth in the transmission system without introducing intolerable flicker. Flicker is a function of the frequency of repetition of coverage of the raster. With interlaced scanning, alternate (odd-numbered) lines are scanned first, and the remaining (even-numbered) lines are scanned next. The entire raster area is covered or scanned twice. Therefore, the picture repetition rate for interlaced scanning is twice that of sequential scanning, which is at the same velocity along each line, and a corresponding reduction in the sensation of flicker is obtained. This is called double interlacing and is standard in all broadcast television systems. The entire raster is covered 30 times per second; therefore, the picture area is scanned 60 times a second.

**Lines and frequency of scanning.** The United States standards require that 15,750 lines be scanned per second. With a vertical scanning rate of 30 times a second, there are 525 lines allocated to each frame and 262.5 lines to each field. Each line is 63.49 microseconds in duration. A finite period of time is required to return the scanning beam of electrons in the camera or picture tube to the left edge of the scene for the next line. This period, blanking or retrace time, requires 16–18% of the total line time, or 10.16–11.43 μs. Similarly, 7.5–8% of the vertical field period, or 1250–1333 μs, is required for the scanning beam to return to the top of the picture. This is the equivalent of about 21 scanning lines. Blanking circuits prevent the transmission of brightness variations during both the horizontal and vertical retrace intervals.

The scanning process is shown in the **illustration**. Line 1 begins at the top center of the image. The beam proceeds for half a line to the right edge. Retrace to the left occurs, and line 3 follows. At the right end of line 3, 1½ lines have been scanned. Line 5 and successive odd-numbered lines are scanned, for a total of 241.5 lines, ending at the lower right corner. Twenty-one lines elapse during the vertical retrace interval while the scanning beam is moved to the upper left corner, placing it in position to start scanning line 2. This completes one full field. Then, 241.5 successive even-numbered lines are scanned, ending at the middle bottom of the scene. Again 21 lines elapse for vertical retrace, during which time the scanning beam is returned to the top center of the scene. This completes the second field and a full frame. The sequence then repeats.

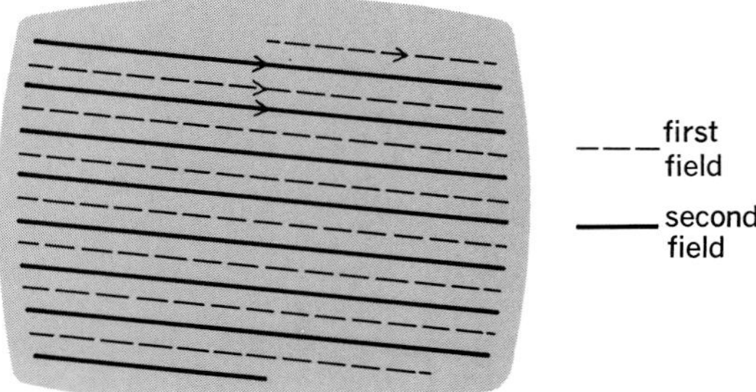


**Scanning sequence for interlaced scanning. Spacing between lines is greatly exaggerated. (*After F. E. Terman, Electronic and Radio Engineering, McGraw-Hill, 1955*)**

**Resolution.** The resolution of a television system is a measure of its ability to reproduce fine detail. It is measured in terms of the number of lines appearing in the reproduced image of a test pattern at the output of a system. The diameter of the electron scanning beam in the camera tube limits the resolution. The smaller the spot, the higher is the resolution. With the 525-line system, the bandwidth $f$ limits resolution according to the equation $f = 0.0125n$, where $n$ is the number of lines and $f$ is in megahertz. The resolution is 320 lines when the bandwidth is 4.0 MHz. A camera tube may have a resolution of 800 lines, but bandwidth limitations imposed by the television channel reduce that figure to about 300. *SEE TELEVISION STANDARDS.*

**Color coding.** A color television camera has separate tubes for red, green, and blue, each of which scans in the same manner as for monochrome. The three camera signals are combined in a colorplexer into a single signal containing both luminance and chrominance information. *SEE COLOR TELEVISION.*

*Donald G. Fink*

## Television transmitter

An electronic device that converts audio and video signals into modulated radio-frequency (rf) energy which can be radiated from an antenna and received on a television receiver. The term can also refer to the entire television transmitting plant, consisting of the transmitter proper, associated visual and aural input and monitoring equipment, transmission line, the antenna with its tower or other support structure, and the building in which the equipment is housed.

A television transmitter is really two separate transmitters integrated into a common cabinet (**Fig. 1**). Video information is transmitted via a visual transmitter, while audio information is transmitted via an aural transmitter. Because video and audio have different characteristics, the two transmitters differ in terms of bandwidth, modulation technique, and output power level. Nevertheless, a common transmitting antenna is generally used, and the two transmitters feed this antenna via an rf diplexer or combiner.

Television stations are licensed to operate on a particular channel, but since it takes a very wide bandwidth to transmit a television picture, these channels are allocated over a broad range of frequencies. Channels 2 through 6 are low-band very-high-frequency (VHF) channels, while channels 7 through 13 are high-band VHF channels. Channels 14 through 83 are ultrahigh-frequency (UHF) channels. Each channel is 6 MHz wide. Because of the wide range of frequencies, television transmitters are designed to work in only one of the foregoing groups, and employ specific circuits which are most efficient for the channels involved. Nevertheless, every television transmitter, regardless of operating frequency, transmits a standard television signal in conformity with the regulations of the country in which it is operated.

**Signal characteristics.** In the United States the Federal Communications Commission (FCC) specifies the standard television signal in *FCC Rules and Regulations*, vol. 3, pt. 73. This specification enables receiver manufacturers to market receivers that are compatible with all television transmitters.

The FCC requires that a visual transmitter produce an amplitude-modulated (AM) carrier with an upper sideband extending to 4.2 MHz above the carrier and a lower sideband extending to only 0.75 MHz below the carrier. The lower sideband is restricted to this narrow bandwidth in order to conserve valuable frequency spectrum. Since both sidebands contain the same information, only one is required to transmit a picture. This is known as vestigial sideband transmission (**Fig. 2**). *SEE AMPLITUDE MODULATION; SINGLE SIDEBAND.*

FCC rules provide that the aural transmitter be fre-

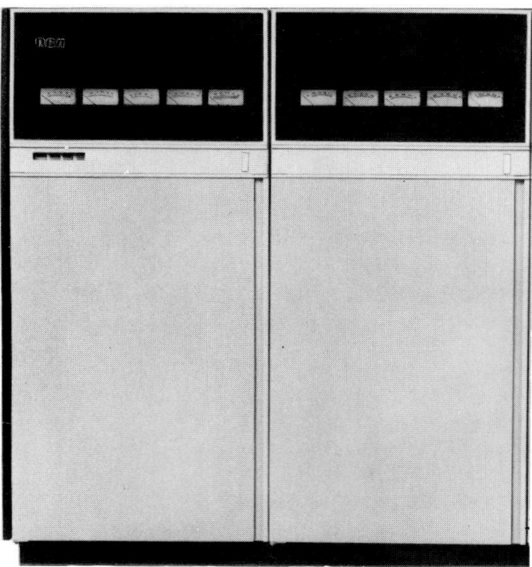

**Fig. 1. Modern television transmitter. (*RCA Corp.*)**

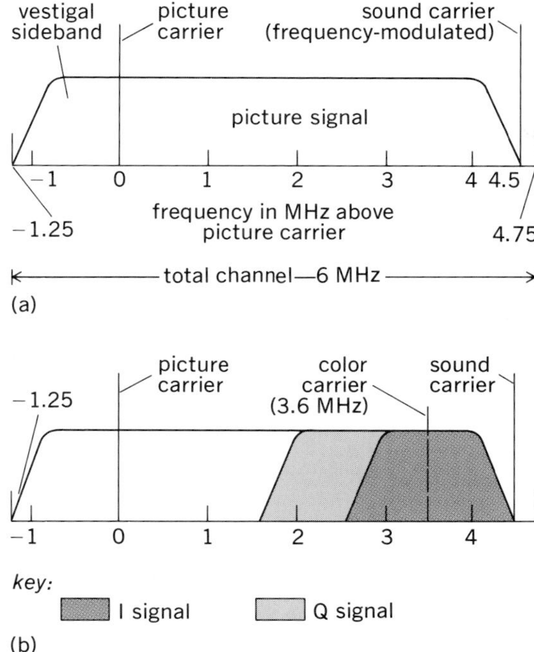


**Fig. 2.** **Diagram of television channel showing portions occupied by color and monochrome signal components. (*a*) Monochrome television channel. (*b*) Color television channel. (*After G. W. Bartlett, ed., NAB Engineering Handbook, 6th ed., National Association of Broadcasters, 1975*)**

quency-modulated (FM) and that its carrier frequency must be 4.5 MHz above the visual carrier. This standard spacing between carriers allows use of a simplified sound receiver in most television sets. In the aural transmitter 100% modulation is defined as equal to 25 kilohertz deviation, and the transmitter must be capable of faithfully passing audio-modulating frequencies from at least 50 Hz to 15 kHz. SEE FREQUENCY MODULATION.

**Transmitter power.** Television broadcast stations are limited to a specific effective radiated power (ERP) by the FCC. ERP is defined as the transmitter output power multiplied by transmitting antenna gain and an efficiency factor (less than 100%) due to the losses of the tranmission line components between the transmitter and antenna.

To provide a consistent signal strength at the receiver, the FCC allows UHF stations to operate with more power (5 MW maximum visual ERP) then high-band VHR stations, and high-band VHR stations may operate with greater power (316 kW maximum) than low-band VHF stations (100 kW maximum). The maximum power that any station may utilize is reduced proportionately if its antenna height exceeds 1000 ft (305 m) above average terrain. Furthermore, due to its narrower bandwidth and other factors, the aural FM signal tends to carry better than the visual signal, so it is restricted to between 10 and 20% of the visual power by the FCC.

Because transmitting antennas usually have a power gain greater than unity, television transmitters need only provide a fraction of the ERP. Modern transmitters are rated at 10 W to 30 kW for the low-band VHF, and 10 W to 75 kW for high-band VHF; UHF transmitters are manufactured with outputs ranging from 100 W to 165 kW.

The lowest-power transmitters are generally configured as television translators, which are used to relay the signal of a high-power primary station into areas where geography or other factors prevent viewers from being able to receive the primary station. The translator accepts the input on the primary channel and shifts its output to another channel so that one does not interfere with the other.

**Transmitting antennas.** Antenna gain is a function of design and the number of sections employed. Gain

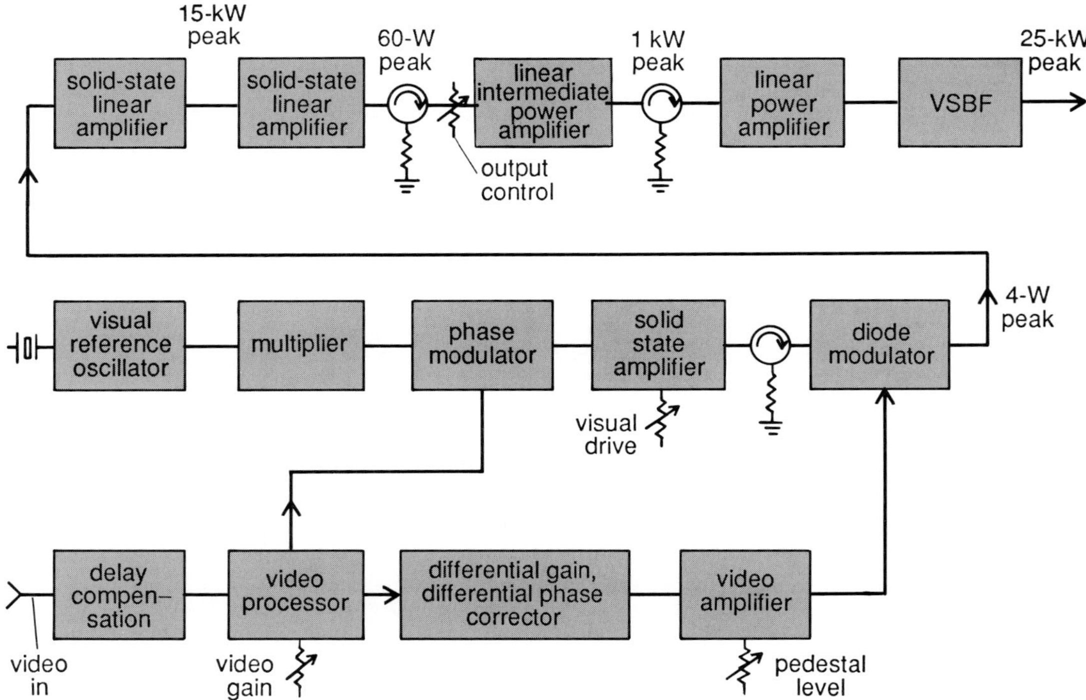


**Fig. 3.** **Visual transmitter with modulation and vestigial-sideband filter (VSBF) at final frequency. (*After G. W. Bartlett, ed., NAB Engineering Handbook, 6th ed., National Association of Broadcasters, 1975*)**

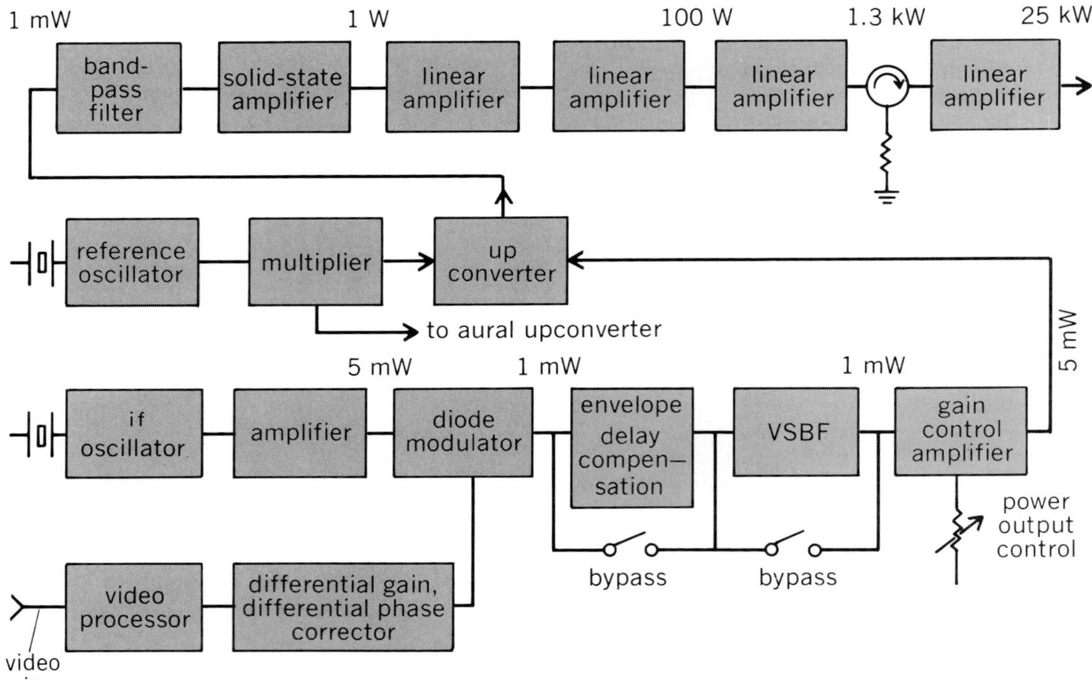


**Fig. 4. Visual transmitter with modulation and vestigial-sideband filter (VSBF) at intermediate frequency. (*After G. W. Bartlett, ed., NAB Engineering Handbook, 6th ed., National Association of Broadcasters, 1975*)**

usually increases with physical size, due to increased radiating area, and may be increased further by stacking identical elements vertically; VHF stations usually operate with antenna gains of less than 5, while UHF stations commonly use gains of up to 50 in order to generate the much greater effective radiated power allowed by the FCC.

The horizontal radiation pattern of most television transmitting antennas is circular, providing equal radiated signal strength to all points of the compass. Higher-gain antennas achieve greater power in the direction of the horizon by reducing the power radiated at vertical angles above and below the horizon. Since this could result in weaker signals at some receivers close to the transmitter, beam tilt and null fill are often used to lower the angle of maximum radiated power.

Until about 1978, all television stations employed horizontally polarized antennas so that their signals would suffer less interference from impulse noise sources, such as automobile ignition systems, which tend to be vertically polarized. Some broadcasters then began utilizing circularly polarized antennas in the belief that television sets with ''rabbit-ear'' receiving antennas will obtain a better signal.

Because television signals travel in a ''line of sight,'' transmitting antennas are usually placed as high as possible above ground with respect to the surrounding service area. Such locations minimize signal blockage or ghosting due to tall buildings and hills. It

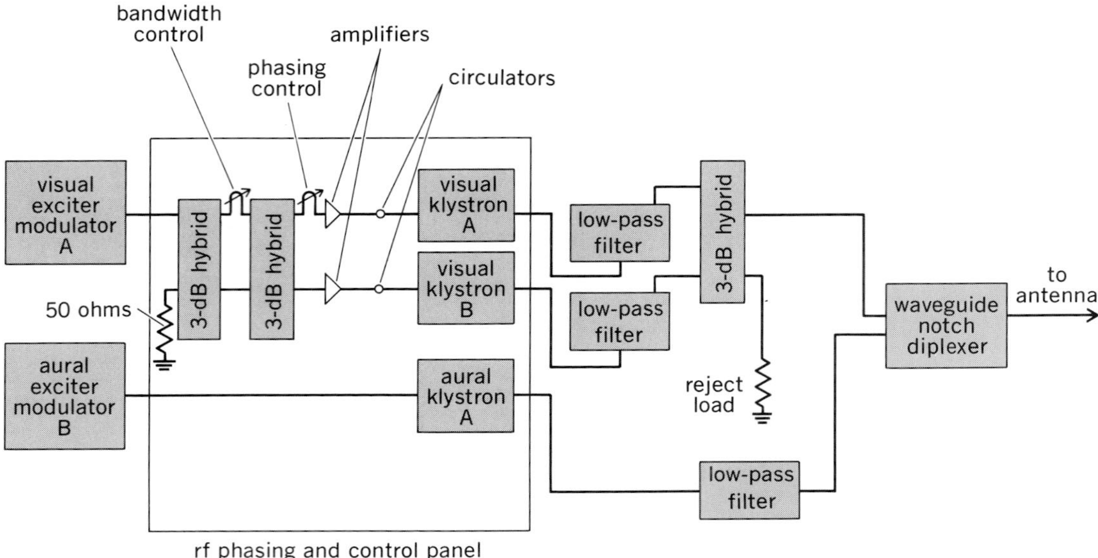


**Fig. 5. Typical UHF transmitter block diagram.**

is also desirable to locate all of the transmitting antennas serving a given locality in the same place. This allows viewers to orient their receiving antennas in one direction for the best reception from all of the stations. In Los Angeles, for example, advantage is taken of a 5700-ft (1740-m) summit, Mount Wilson, to locate most of the transmitting antennas on individual 200- to 500-ft (60- to 150-m) towers. In New York City all of the transmitting antennas are mounted on a common 365-ft (111-m) mast atop the 1366-ft (416-m) World Trade Center. In areas with neither mountains nor tall buildings, extremely tall towers have been erected, some of which exceed 2000 ft (600 m). *SEE ANTENNA (ELECTROMAGNETISM).*

**Transmitter designs.** There are two broad classes of VHF visual television transmitter design philosophy. The classical approach modulates the carrier at a moderate power level, amplifies the carrier to rated output power by means of linear amplifiers, and then filters this high-power carrier to obtain the required vestigial-sideband signal (**Fig. 3**). The more contemporary approach, used by nearly all transmitter manufacturers, employs modulation at a very low power level of an intermediate-frequency (i-f) signal. The required vestigial-sideband filtering is imposed on this low-level signal, generally by means of a highly stable surface acoustic-wave filter, whereupon the signal is upconverted to the carrier frequency and amplified by linear amplifiers to rated output power (**Fig. 4**). *SEE AMPLIFIER; SURFACE ACOUSTIC-WAVE DEVICES.*

Generally, UHF transmitters employ very large tubes, called klystrons, to produce the large amounts of rf carrier power required. **Figure 5** shows a block diagram of a typical UHF transmitter. *SEE KLYSTRON; MICROWAVE TUBE.*

Every transmitter contains a visual and aural exciter. This element determines the operating frequency of the visual and aural carriers and must be extremely stable, since the FCC requires that they be kept within 1 kHz of the assigned frequencies. The aural exciter produces the required frequency modulation by varying the frequency of the rf carrier oscillator at an audio rate (**Fig. 6**).

Regardless of the visual modulation approach taken, certain parameters must be kept within FCC tolerances. Nonlinearity of the rf power amplifier stages must be compensated by suitable circuits. Certain time delays, within the transmitter, called envelope delays, must be the complement of those found in the home television receiver, so that colors in the picture are properly superimposed. Flat frequency response over adequate bandwidth is necessary to ensure that the picture has good detail and accurate color rendition. Excessively wide response is not permitted by the FCC, however, so that a low-pass filter which attenuates video above 4.75 MHz by at least 20 dB is commonly inserted in the video input circuit. *SEE ELECTRIC FILTER.*

Transmission of color requires that the color subcarrier (3.58 MHz above the visual carrier) not be affected by changes in the luminance level of the picture. A change in color saturation (chrominance level) brought about by a change in luminance level is termed differential gain. A change in color hue (subcarrier phase) brought about by a change in luminance level is termed differential phase. Both parameters are to be minimized. *SEE COLOR TELEVISION.*

The radiated rf carrier is also strictly regulated by the FCC. Harmonics, or multiples, of the carrier frequency must be attenuated at least 60 dB below the peak power level. Harmonic filters are placed on the output of both the visual and aural transmitters, ahead of any aural–visual diplexers, to ensure compliance.

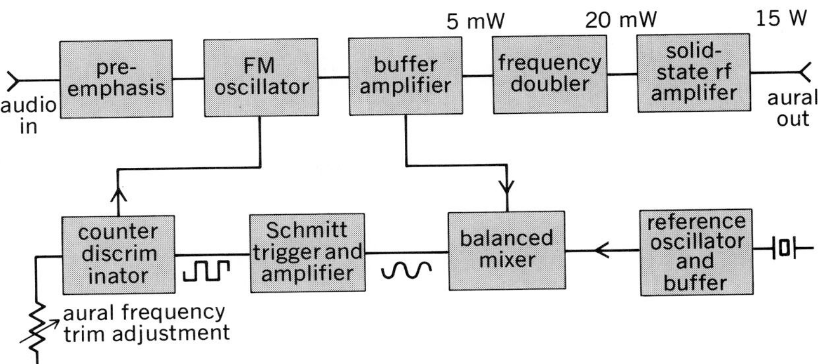


**Fig. 6. Typical aural exciter.** (*After G. W. Bartlett, ed., NAB Engineering Handbook, 6th ed., National Association of Broadcasters, 1975*)

In those transmitters which employ high-level vestigial-sideband filtering, a device known as a filterplexer often combines the functions of sideband filtering and aural–visual diplexing.

Modern transmitters are essentially all solid-state, with the exception of the final power amplifier stages. One manufacturer has employed semiconductor amplifiers to the 1600-W level. Beyond this point, large metal and ceramic vacuum tubes are used to generate rated output in both aural and visual transmitter sections. *SEE TELEVISION; TELEVISION CAMERA; TELEVISION CAMERA TUBE; TELEVISION RECEIVER; TELEVISION SCANNING.*

*Earl F. Arbuckle, III*

**Bibliography.** G. W. Bartlett (ed.), *NAB Engineering Handbook*, 6th ed., 1975; K. B. Benson (ed.), *Television Engineering Handbook*, 1986; A. H. Bott, *SAW Filter Application in a TV Transmitter*, 1977; Progress report: Circularly polarized antennas for TV, *Broadcast Manage./Eng.*, 14(10):48–57, October 1978; D. G. Fink and D. Christiansen (eds.), *Electronics Engineers' Handbook*, 2d ed., 1982; E. M. Noll, *Broadcast Radio and TV Handbook*, 6th ed., 1982.

## Thermal converters

Devices consisting of a conductor heated by an electric current, with one or more hot junctions of a thermocouple attached to it, so that the output emf responds to the temperature rise, and hence the current. Thermal converters are used with external resistors for alternating-current (ac) and voltage measurements over wide ranges.

**Basic form.** In the most common form, the conductor is a thin straight wire less than 0.4 in. (1 cm) long, in an evacuated glass bulb, with a single thermocouple junction fastened to the midpoint by a tiny electrically insulating bead. Thermal inertia keeps the temperature of the heater wire constant at frequencies above a few hertz, so that the constant output emf is a true measure of the root-mean-square (rms) heating value of the current. The reactance of the short wire is so small that the emf can be independent of frequency up to 10 MHz or more. An emf of 10 mV can be obtained at a rated current less than 5 mA, so that resistors of reasonable power dissipation, in series or in shunt with the heater, can provide voltage ranges up to 1000 V and current ranges up to 20 A. However, the flow of heat energy cannot be controlled precisely, so the temperature, and hence the emf, generally changes with time and other factors. Thus an ordinary thermocouple instrument, consisting of a thermal converter and a millivoltmeter to measure the emf, is accurate only to about 1–3%. SEE VOLTMETER.

**AC-DC transfer instrument.** To overcome this, a thermal converter can be used as an ac-dc transfer instrument (ac-dc comparator) to measure an unknown alternating current or voltage by comparison with a known nearly equal dc quantity (see **illus.**). By

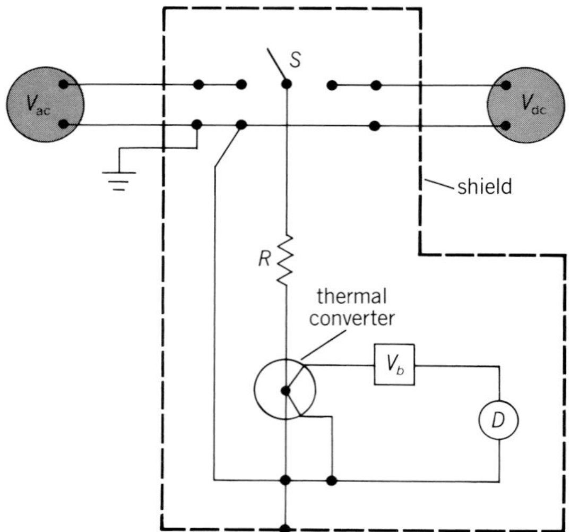


Basic circuit for ac-dc transfer measurements of ac voltages.

replacing the millivoltmeter with an adjustable, stable, opposing voltage $V_b$ in series with a microvoltmeter $D$, very small changes in emf can be detected. The switch $S$ is connected to the unknown ac voltage $V_{ac}$, and $V_b$ is adjusted for a null (zero) reading of $D$. Then $S$ is immediately connected to the dc voltage $V_{dc}$, which is adjusted to give a null again, without changing $V_b$. Thus $V_{ac} = V_{dc}\,(1 + d)$, where $d$ is the ac-dc difference of the transfer instrument.

In many commercial instruments, all of the components are conveniently packaged in the shield, shown with a broken line, and several ranges are available by taps on $R$. Accuracies of 0.005% are attainable at audio frequencies. For the highest accuracy, the average of the two directions of $V_{dc}$ should be taken as the reference, because of slight imperfections of the thermal converter, and the ac measurement should be repeated, to guard against small drifts. The resistances of the two pairs of leads from $V_{ac}$ and $V_{dc}$ to $S$ should be equal, and the leads should be shielded.

The values of $d$ (which depend on range and frequency) are best determined by comparison with ac-dc transfer instruments of known characteristics. These, in turn, are evaluated in metrology laboratories, such as the National Bureau of Standards in the United States, where ac-dc differences have been studied very carefully, because the ultimate accuracy of almost all alternating-current and voltage measurements depends upon thermal converters. SEE ELECTRICAL MEASUREMENTS.

*F. L. Hermach*

**Bibliography.** F. L. Hermach, AC-DC comparators for audio-frequency current and voltage measurements of high accuracy, *IEEE Trans. Instrum. Meas.*, IM-25:489–494, 1976; E. S. Williams, *The Practical Uses of AC-DC Transfer Instruments*, NBS Tech. Note 1166, 1982.

## Thermionic emission

The emission of electrons into vacuum by a heated electronic conductor. In its broadest meaning, thermionic emission includes the emission of ions, but since this process is quite different from that normally understood by the term, it will not be discussed here. Thermionic emitters are used as cathodes in electron tubes and hence are of great technical and scientific importance. Although in principle all conductors are thermionic emitters, only a few materials satisfy the requirements set by practical applications. Of the metals, tungsten is an important practical thermionic emitter; in most electron tubes, however, the oxide-coated cathode is used to great advantage. For a detailed discussion of practical thermionic emitters SEE VACUUM TUBE.

**Richardson equation.** The thermionic emission of a material may be measured by using the material as the cathode in a vacuum tube and collecting the emitted electrons on a positive anode. If the anode is sufficiently positive relative to the cathode, space charge (a concentration of electrons near the cathode) can be avoided and all electrons emitted can be collected; the saturation thermionic current is then measured. Actually, the emission current increases slightly with increasing field strength at the cathode, and in order to obtain the true saturation current it is necessary to extrapolate to zero applied field. SEE SCHOTTKY EFFECT.

The emission current density $J$ increases rapidly

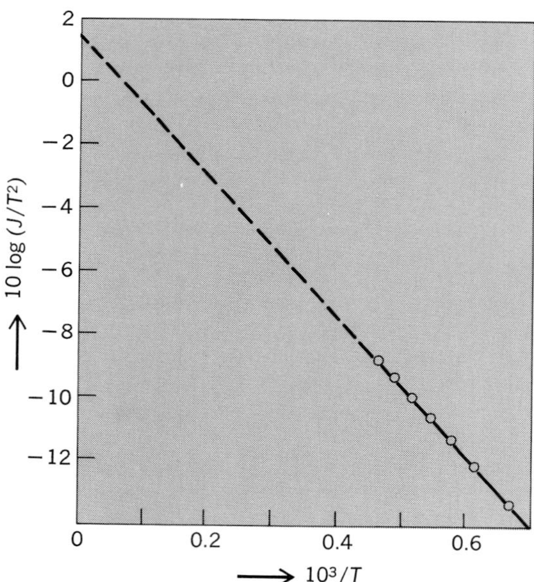


**Fig. 1.** Richardson plot for tungsten, an important thermionic emitter. (*After G. Herrmann and S. Wagener, The Oxide-Coated Cathode, vol. 2, Chapman and Hall, 1951*)

with increasing temperature; this is illustrated by the following approximate values for tungsten:

| $T$ (K) | 1000 | 2000 | 2500 | 3000 |
|---|---|---|---|---|
| $J$ (A/cm$^2$) | $10^{-15}$ | $10^{-3}$ | 0.3 | 15 |

The temperature dependence of $J$ is given by Eq. (1),

$$J = AT^2e^{-(\phi/kT)} \tag{1}$$

the Richardson (or Dushman-Richardson) equation. Here $A$ is a constant, $k$ is Boltzmann's constant ($= 1.38 \times 10^{-23}$ joule per degree), and $\phi$ is the work function of the emitter. The work function has the dimensions of energy and is a few electronvolts for thermionic emitters. For a table of values for metals *SEE WORK FUNCTION (ELECTRONICS)*.

The temperature dependence of $J$ is essentially determined by the exponential factor, since its temperature dependence predominates strongly over that of the factor $T^2$. Both $A$ and $\phi$ may be obtained experimentally by plotting the logarithm of $J/T^2$ versus $1/T$, as for tungsten in **Fig. 1**. The Richardson formula can be derived for metals and semiconductors on the basis of relatively simple physical models.

**Metals.** According to quantum theory the electrons in a free atom occupy a set of discrete energy levels. When atoms are brought together to form a solid, these energy levels broaden into energy bands; the broadening is a result of the perturbing fields produced by neighboring atoms on the electrons and is most pronounced for the outer or valence electrons. In a metal, the perturbing influence on the valence electrons is so strong that they can no longer be associated with particular atoms but must be considered as moving freely throughout the crystal. These so-called free, or conduction, electrons are responsible for the high electrical and thermal conductivity of metals and also for the thermionic emission. *SEE BAND THEORY OF SOLIDS*.

The free electrons may be assumed to move in an approximately constant potential as indicated in **Fig. 2**. The bottom of the box corresponds to the energy of a conduction electron at rest in the metal; the "vacuum" level represents the energy of an electron at rest in free space. According to quantum mechanics, the electrons in this model can assume only particular states of motion which correspond to a set of very closely spaced energy levels. The probability for a given state to be occupied depends on the energy $E$ of the state and on the absolute temperature $T$ in accordance with Eq. (2), the so-called Fermi-Dirac distribution function.

$$F(E) = \frac{1}{1 + \exp[(E - E_F)/kT]} \tag{2}$$

tribution function. The quantity $E_F$ is called the Fermi energy; it is determined by the number of electrons per unit volume in the metal and is of the order of a few electronvolts. Since $kT$ at room temperature ($T = 300$ K) is only about 0.025 eV, $E_F \ll kT$ for all temperatures below the melting point of metals. Note that for $T = 0$, $F(E) = 1$ for $E < E_F$, and $F(E) = 0$ for $E > E_F$. Hence, at absolute zero all energy levels up to $E_F$ are occupied by electrons, whereas those above $E_F$ are empty. For temperature different from zero, some electrons have energies larger than $E_F$ and the thermionic emission is due to those electrons in the "tail" of the Fermi distribution for which the energy lies above the vacuum level in Fig. 1. Note that when $E = E_F$, $F(E) = 0.5$; that is, the Fermi energy corresponds to those states for which the probability of being occupied is equal to 0.5.

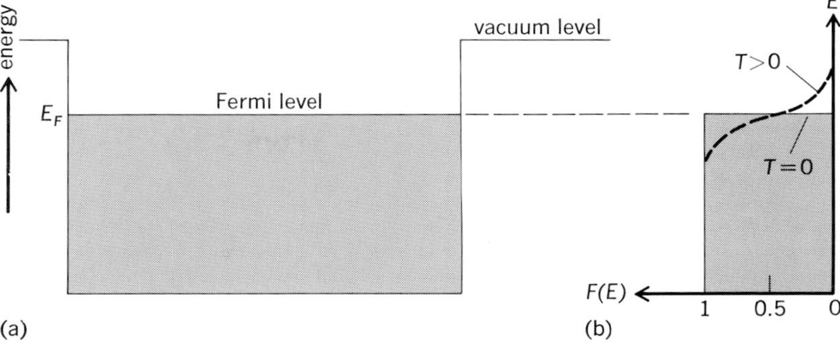


**Fig. 2. Free electrons are assumed to move in approximately constant potential. (*a*) Occupation of electron states between the bottom of the conduction band and the Fermi level of a metal is indicated for $T = 0$ by the shaded area. (*b*) Fermi distribution function is represented schematically for $T = 0$ and for $T > 0$.**

When these ideas are put in a quantitative form, one arrives at the Richardson equation with the specific value $A = 120$ A/cm$^2$ (if one takes into account reflection of electrons against the surface potential barrier, the theoretical value of $A$ is $< 120$ A/cm$^2$).

Experiments by M. N. Nichols in 1940 and by G. F. Smith in 1954 on single crystals of tungsten have shown that experimental values for $A$ and $\phi$ depend on the crystallographic plane from which the emission is measured; values for $A$ (in A/cm$^2$) and $\phi$ (in electronvolts) for two crystallographic directions are given in the **table**. For polycrystalline metals, the experimental values for $A$ and $\phi$ are thus average values for the particular specimen.

**Semiconductors.** For semiconductors, the thermionic emission is also due to the escape of electrons which have energies above the vacuum level. The theory leads to the Richardson formula, as it does for metals. The work function measures again the difference between the Fermi level of the semiconductor and the vacuum level. *SEE SEMICONDUCTOR*.

*A. J. Dekker*

**Experimental values for single crystals of tungsten**

| | Nichols | | Smith | |
|---|---|---|---|---|
| Direction | $A$ | $\phi$ | $A$ | $\phi$ |
| (111) | 35 | 4.39 | 52 | 4.38 |
| (100) | 117 | 4.56 | 105 | 4.52 |

## Thermionic tube

An electron tube that relies upon thermally emitted electrons from a heated cathode for tube current. Thermionic emission of electrons means emission by heat. In practical form an electrode, called the cathode because it forms the negative electrode of the tube, is heated until it emits electrons. The cathode may be either a directly heated filament or an indirectly heated surface. With a filamentary cathode, heating current is passed through the wire, which ei-

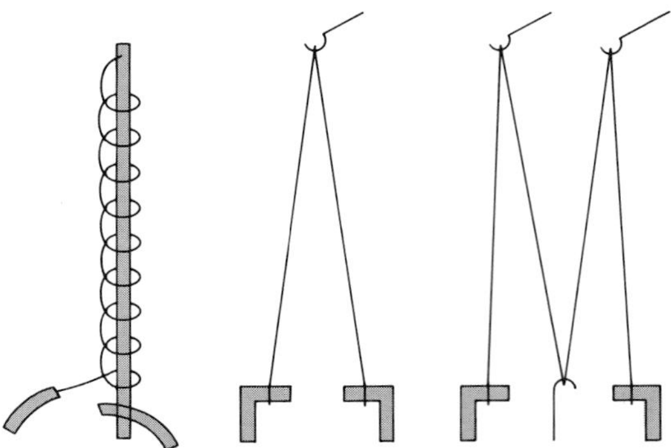

Fig. 1. Typical filament structures.

ther emits electrons directly or is covered with a material that readily emits electrons. Some typical filament structures are shown in **Fig. 1**. Filaments of tungsten or thoriated-tungsten are commonly used in high-power transmitting tubes where their ruggedness and ability to withstand high voltages are essential. Oxide-coated filaments are used in a few small high-voltage rectifier tubes.

Indirectly heated cathodes have a filament, commonly called the heater, located within the cathode electrode to bring the surface of the cathode to emitting temperature. Some common forms are shown in **Fig. 2**. They are usually coated with barium-strontium oxide, on the periphery in receiving tubes and on the end in kinescopes. Because the emitting surface carries no heating current, there is no voltage drop along the surface. Hence such cathodes are usually known as equipotential cathodes. The high emission capability, the equipotential surface, and the favorable geometry of these cathodes make possible the close-spaced tube structures that lead to the high transconductances required in modern applications. Hence, oxide-coated equipotential cathodes are used in almost all receiving and medium-power transmitting tubes. They are also used in some high-power pulsed transmitting tubes, where the remarkable ability of the oxide cathode to emit very high current densities (tens of amperes per square centimeter, for microsecond periods at low repetition rates) is exploited. The majority of all vacuum tubes are thermionic tubes. It is possible to make so-called cold-cathode tubes, but they tend to be unstable in vacuum and find their main application in gas tubes, not vacuum tubes. SEE ELECTRON TUBE; GAS TUBE; THERMIONIC EMISSION; VACUUM TUBE.

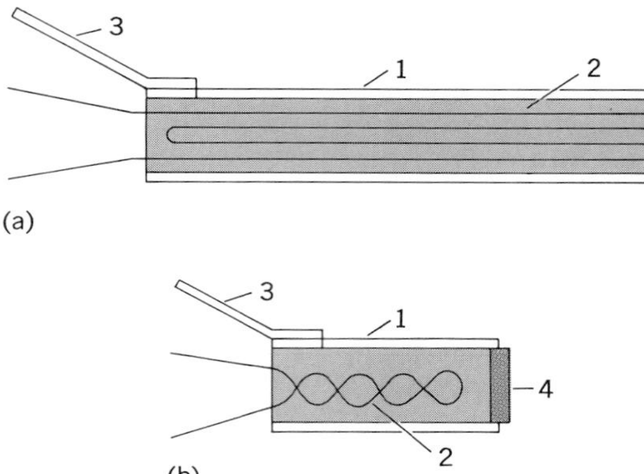


Fig. 2. Cathodes. (*a*) Receiving-tube cathode; 1, cathode sleeve, oxide-coated on exterior; 2, folded heater, insulated with refractory oxide; 3, cathode tab, for electrical connection. (*b*) Kinescope cathode: 1, cathode sleeve; 2, heater, insulated with refractory oxide; 3, cathode tab, for electrical connection; 4, emitting "button," oxide-coated on right surface.

*Leon S. Nergaard*

## Thévenin's theorem (electric networks)

A theorem from electric circuit theory. It is also known as the Helmholtz or Helmholtz-Thévenin theorem, since H. Helmholtz stated it in an earlier form prior to M. L. Thévenin. Closely related is the Norton theorem, which will also be discussed. Laplace transform notation will be used.

Thévenin's theorem states that at a pair of terminals a network composed of lumped, linear circuit elements may, for purposes of analysis of external circuit or terminal behavior, be replaced by a voltage source $V(s)$ in series with a single impedance $Z(s)$. The source $V(s)$ is the Laplace transform of the voltage across the pair of terminals when they are open-circuited; $Z(s)$ is the transform impedance at the two terminals with all independent sources set to zero (**Fig. 1**). The Thévenin equivalent may also be found experimentally.

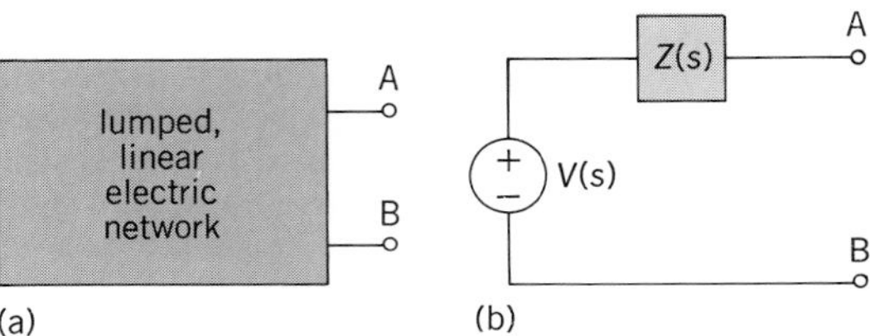


Fig. 1. Network and its Thévenin equivalent. (*a*) Original network. (*b*) Thévenin equivalent circuit.

Norton's theorem states that a second equivalent network consists of a current source $I(s)$ in parallel with an impedance $Z(s)$. The impedance $Z(s)$ is identical with the Thévenin impedance, and $I(s)$ is the Laplace transform of the current between the two terminals when they are short-circuited (**Fig. 2**).

Thévenin's and Norton's equivalent networks are related by the equation $V(s) = Z(s) \cdot I(s)$. This may be seen by comparing Figs. 1*b* and 2*b*. In Fig. 1*b*, if terminals A and B are short-circuited, a current $I(s) = V(s)/Z(s)$ will flow; this is also true in Fig. 2*b*. Similarly the open-circuit voltage in Fig. 2*b* is $V(s) = Z(s) \cdot I(s)$. SEE ALTERNATING-CURRENT CIRCUIT THEORY.

These theorems are useful for the study of the behavior of a load connected to a (possibly complex) system that is supplying electric power to that load. The system may be a power distribution system, such as in a home or office, in which case the load may be lights or appliances. The system may be an electronic amplifier, in which case the load may be a loudspeaker. However, the theorem is of no value in studying the internal system behavior, because the behavior of the equivalent network is very different from that of the original.

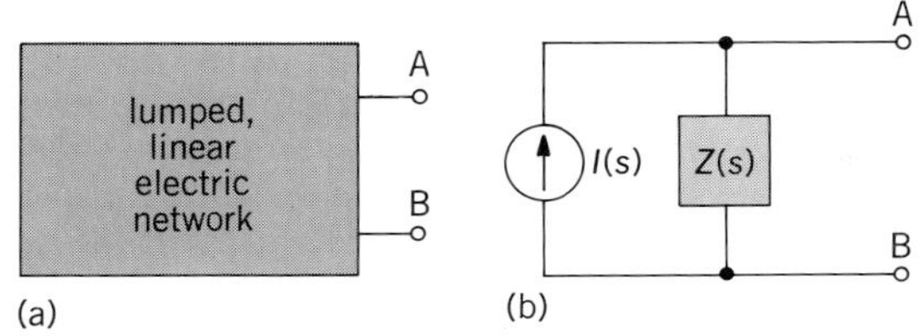


**Fig. 2. Network and its Norton equivalent. (*a*) Original network. (*b*) Norton equivalent circuit.**

**Examples.** Two examples will be used to show how Thévenin and Norton equivalent networks may be calculated from the original network and then used for some typical calculations.

***Power distribution circuit.*** Suppose a simplified power distribution circuit contains the elements shown in **Fig. 3*a***. Sinusoidal steady-state operation is assumed. In this circuit the voltage across A, B is given by Eq. (1), and with the source set to zero, the

$$V_{AB} = \frac{Z_3}{Z_1 + Z_2 + Z_3} \cdot V_s = \frac{-j122.6}{0.55 + j3.5 - j122.6} \cdot 240\underline{/0^\circ} = 247.1\ \underline{/-0.26^\circ}\ V \qquad (1)$$

impedance at A, B is given by Eq. (2). Thus the

$$Z_{TH} = Z_4 + \frac{Z_3(Z_1 + Z_2)}{Z_1 + Z_2 + Z_3} = 0.35 + \frac{(-j122.6)\ (0.55 + j3.5)}{0.55 + j3.5 - j122.6} = 3.72\ \underline{/75.47^\circ}\ \text{ohms} \qquad (2)$$

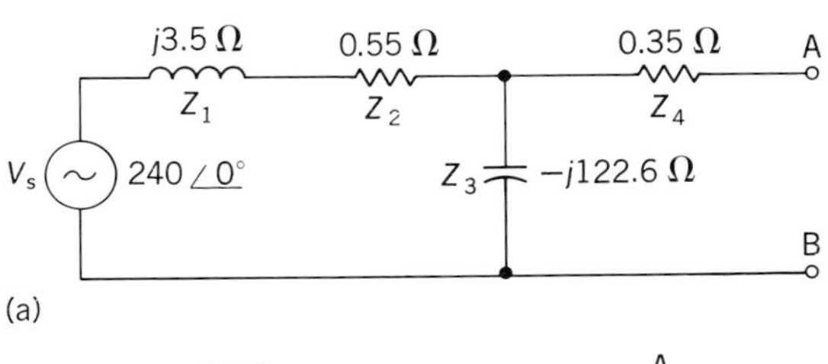


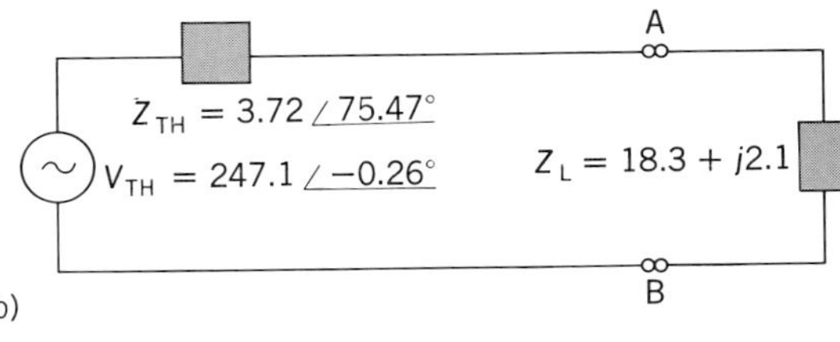


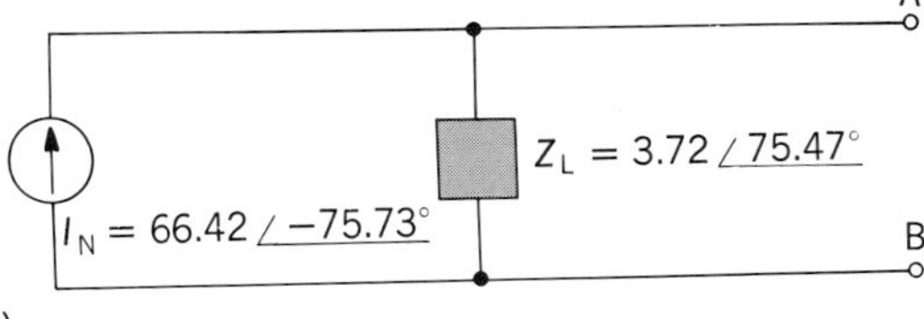


**Fig. 3. Power distribution circuit and its Thévenin and Norton equivalents. (*a*) Original circuit. (*b*) Thévenin equivalent circuit with its load $Z_L$ connected. (*c*) Norton equivalent circuit.**

Thévenin equivalent is given in Fig. 3*b*, and the Norton equivalent in Fig. 3*c*.

When a load $Z_L = 18.3 + j2.1 = 18.42\underline{/6.55^\circ}$ is connected, at A, B, the current through the load is given by Eq. (3), and the power delivered to the load

$$I_L = \frac{V_{TH}}{Z_{TH} + Z_L} = \frac{247.1\underline{/-0.26^\circ}}{3.72\underline{/75.47^\circ} + 18.42\underline{/6.55^\circ}} = 12.32)^2\underline{/-16.77^\circ} \qquad (3)$$

is $(12.32)^2(18.3) = 2.776$ kW. Other loads are handled in a similar fashion.

***Amplifier.*** As a second example, suppose that the circuit of **Fig. 4*a*** is a simplified model of an electronic amplifier, and that a load (loudspeaker) is to be connected at A, B. The circuit is driven by a current source $I(s)$. For analysis, the voltages $V_1(s)$ and $V_2(s)$

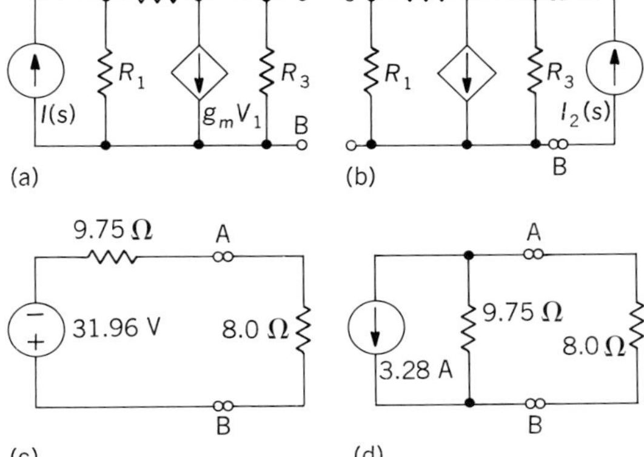


**Fig. 4. Amplifier and its Thévenin and Norton equivalents. Numerical values are given in the text. (*a*) Original circuit. (*b*) Circuit constructed to find Thévenin impedance. (*c*) Thévenin equivalent circuit. (*d*) Norton equivalent circuit.**

are the transforms of the voltages on their respective nodes, and become the dependent variables in the analysis. The dependent or controlled source ($g_m V_1$) models the amplification. Two Kirchhoff current law equations, (4) and (5), may be used to find the Thévenin voltage, which is also $V_2$. Solution of this pair of equations gives Eq. (6).

$$I(s) = V_1\left(\frac{1}{R_1} + \frac{1}{R_2}\right) - V_2\left(\frac{1}{R_2}\right) \qquad (4)$$

$$-g_m V_1 = -V_1\left(\frac{1}{R_2}\right) + V_2\left(\frac{1}{R_2} + \frac{1}{R_3}\right) \qquad (5)$$

$$V_2(s) = \frac{(-g_m + 1/R_2) \cdot I(s)}{\dfrac{1}{R_1R_2} + \dfrac{1}{R_1R_3} + \dfrac{1}{R_2R_3} + \dfrac{g_m}{R_2}} \qquad (6)$$

SEE KIRCHHOFF'S LAWS OF ELECTRIC CIRCUITS.

To find the Thévenin impedance, $I(s)$ must be set to zero, which leaves an infinite impedance in the branch, and an auxiliary current source $I_2(s)$ must be added between A and B (Fig. 4*b*). A new set of equations, (7) and (8), is written, and solved for the ratio

$$0 = V_1\left(\frac{1}{R_1} + \frac{1}{R_2}\right) - V_2\left(\frac{1}{R_2}\right) \qquad (7)$$

$$-g_m V_1 + I_2(s) = -V_1\left(\frac{1}{R_2}\right) + V_2\left(\frac{1}{R_2} + \frac{1}{R_3}\right) \qquad (8)$$

$V_2(s)/I_2(s)$, which is the desired Thévenin impedance: the controlled source must not be set to zero.

Solution of Eqs. (7) and (8) gives, after simplification, Eq. (9).

$$Z_{TH}(s) = \frac{V_2(s)}{I_2(s)} = \frac{R_3(R_1 + R_2)}{R_1 + R_2 + R_3 + g_m R_1 R_3} \quad (9)$$

To make a numerical example in a purely resistive circuit, let $R_1 = 2.0\ k\Omega$, $R_2 = 8.2\ k\Omega$, $R_3 = 400\ \Omega$, $g_m = 510 \times 10^3$ S (siemens), and $I = 4.0$ mA. Substitution of these into the equations gives a Thévenin voltage $V_{TH} = -31.96$ V, and a Thévenin impedance $Z_{TH} = 9.75\ \Omega$. This is shown in Fig. 4*c*, and the corresponding Norton equivalent is shown in Fig. 4*d*, where $I_N = -31.96/9.75 = -3.28$ A. In both cases the negative signs lead to a polarity reversal, which is reflected in Fig. 4*c* and *d*.

Suppose an 8.0-ohm speaker is connected at A, B. A current of $31.96/(8.0 + 9.75) = 1.80$ A will flow, giving a power of $(1.80)^2(8.0) = 25.95$ W.

**Proof.** To prove this theorem, consider a general network with two accessible terminals, as in Figs. 1*a* and 2*a*, to which an auxiliary voltage source $V$ and an impedance $Z_L(s)$ have been added (**Fig. 5**). Let this

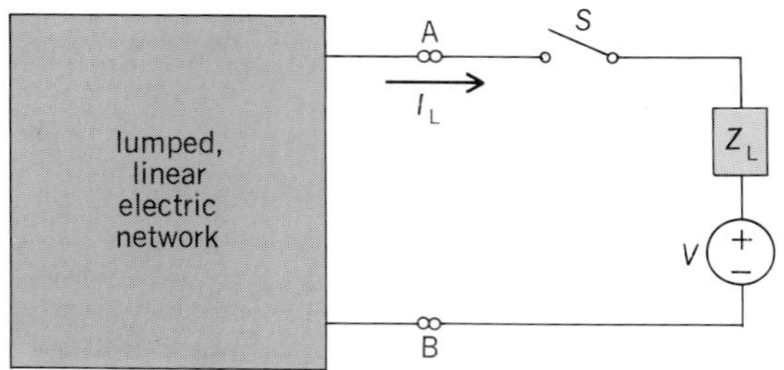


Fig. 5. Circuit constructed to demonstrate Thévenin's theorem.

source be such as to cause $I_L = 0$ when switch $S$ is closed. By superposition, Eq. (10) is valid. This

$$I_L = 0 = \frac{V_{TH}}{Z_{TH} + Z_L} - \frac{V}{Z_{TH} + Z_L} \quad (10)$$

shows that $V_{TH} = V$, and that the current that flows when $V$ is removed is given by Eq. (11).

$$I_L = \frac{V_{TH}}{Z_{TH} + Z_L} \quad (11)$$

*See* Network theory; Superposition theorem (electric networks).

*Edwin C. Jones, Jr.*

**Bibliography.** V. K. Aatre, *Network Theory and Filter Design*, 1982; J. Choma, *Electrical Networks: Theory and Analysis*, 1985; M. E. Van Valkenburg, *Network Analysis*, 3d ed., 1974.

## Time constant

The time required for a physical quantity to change its initial (zero-time) magnitude by the factor $[1 - (1/\epsilon)]$ when the physical quantity is varying as a function of time, $f(t)$, according to the decreasing exponential function as in Eq. (1), or the increasing ex-

$$f(t) = \epsilon^{-kt} \quad (1)$$

ponential function as in Eq. (2) [see **illus.**].

$$f(t) = 1 - \epsilon^{-kt} \quad (2)$$

The number $\epsilon$ has the value 2.71828. Therefore, the change in magnitude of $[1 - (1/\epsilon)]$ has the frac-

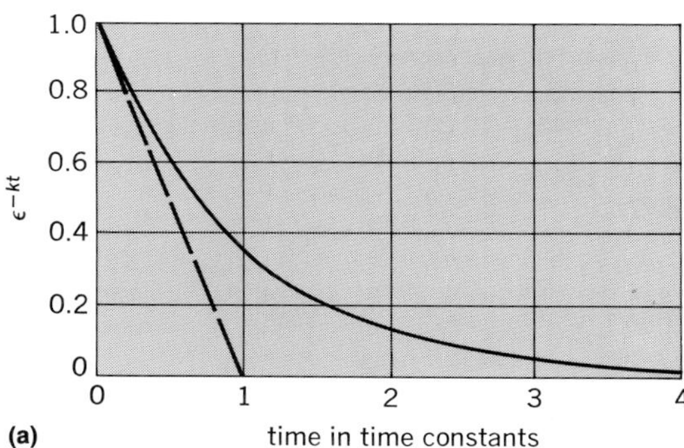


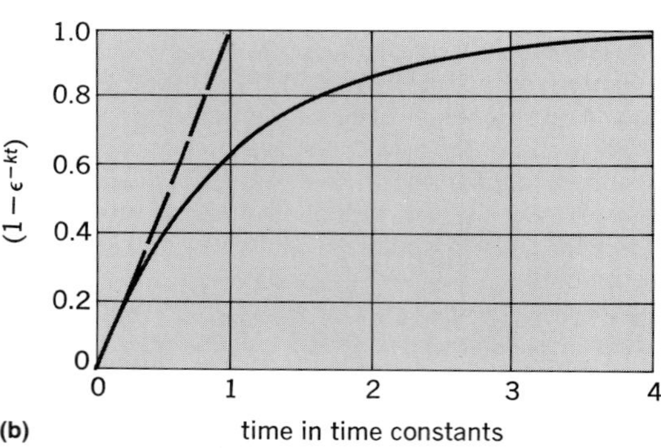


Universal time-constant curve indicated (*a*) for the decreasing function and (*b*) for the increasing function.

tional value 0.632121. Thus, after a time lapse of one time constant, starting at zero time, the magnitude of the physical quantity will have changed 63.2%.

When time $t$ is zero, Eq. (1) has the magnitude 1, and when time $t$ is $1/k$, the magnitude is $\epsilon^{-1}$, or $1/\epsilon$. The corresponding change in magnitude is $[1 - (1/\epsilon)]$. The specific time required to accomplish this change is shown in Eq. (3), where $T$ is called the time constant and is usually expressed in seconds. The

$$t = 1/k = T \quad (3)$$

same results are obtained for Eq. (2).

The initial rate of change of both the increasing and decreasing functions is equal to the maximum amplitude of the function divided by the time constant. Parts *a* and *b* of the illustration are universal in that the plotted function is of unit height and the time scale is given in terms of time constants. To use these curves for a specific problem, the values in the ordinate axis are multiplied by the maximum amplitude of the quantity occurring in the problem, and the values in the abscissa axis are multiplied by the numerical value of the corresponding time constant.

The concept of time constant is useful when evaluating the presence of transient phenomena. The relative amplitude of a transient after an elapsed time of a certain number of time constants is readily computed:

| *Elapsed time, time constants* | *Transient completed, %* |
|---|---|
| 1 | 63.2 |
| 2 | 86.5 |
| 3 | 95.0 |
| 4 | 98.2 |
| 5 | 99.3 |
| 10 | 99.996 |

Usually a transient can be considered as being over after a period of 4–5 time constants.

For electric circuits, the coefficient $k$ and thus the time constant $T$ is determined from the parameters of the circuit. For a circuit containing resistance $R$ and capacitance $C$, the time constant $T$ is the product $RC$. When the circuit consists of inductance $L$ and resistance $R$, the time constant is $L/R$. SEE ELECTRIC TRANSIENT.

The concept of time constant can be applied to the transient envelope of an ac signal; however, it is more common to describe the change in amplitude in terms of logarithmic decrement.

*Robert L. Ramey*

## Townsend discharge

A particular part of the voltage-current characteristic curve for a gaseous discharge device named for J. S. Townsend, who studied it about 1900. It is that part for low current where the discharge cannot be maintained by the field alone. Thus, if the agents producing the initial ionization were removed, conduction would cease.

In the lower end of this region, conduction is accomplished only by charges produced by external agents. As the electric field is increased, secondary ionization and more efficient collection of the primary ionization cause an increase in the current. After further increase in the field, the end of the Townsend region is reached. Any additional increase in the field causes a transition into a region where the discharge may be maintained by the field alone, whether it be glow, brush, or arc. SEE DARK CURRENT; ELECTRICAL CONDUCTION IN GASES; GLOW DISCHARGE.

*Glenn H. Miller*

## Transducer

A device which converts energy or information carried by one physical quantity into corresponding values of another quantity. A simple example is a mercury-in-glass thermometer which converts the temperature of the surroundings into the length of a column of mercury. A transducer is to be distinguished from a transformer, which converts one level of a quantity into another level of the same quantity, as in an electrical transformer or a mechanical lever. SEE TRANSFORMER.

**Sensors and actuators.** Transducers are widely used in measurement and control systems. In this context they are conveniently divided into two classes: sensors and actuators. Sensors are used to measure some property and to convert the measured value into a signal, often electrical, for recording or for processing and use in a control system. A good sensor usually should have high sensitivity and cause little disturbance to the system being measured, or extract a minimum amount of energy. An actuator responds to a command signal and controls the value of some quantity, such as linear or angular position, rate of fluid flow, or rate of generation of heat. Sensitivity is not usually of great importance, but it is often necessary to operate at high power levels.

A familiar example of the use of sensors and actuators is provided by a domestic hot-water system (**Fig. 1**). The sensor consists of a temperature-sensitive element in the hot-water tank which opens or closes a switch when the water temperature is above or below a preset level. The switch controls the supply of electricity to a remote water heater. In this case the signal is the presence or absence of a voltage on the line, and the actuator consists of an electromagnetically operated valve that controls the supply of gas or oil fuel to the heater. By this simple on-off arrangement the temperature of the water in the tank is maintained more or less constant.

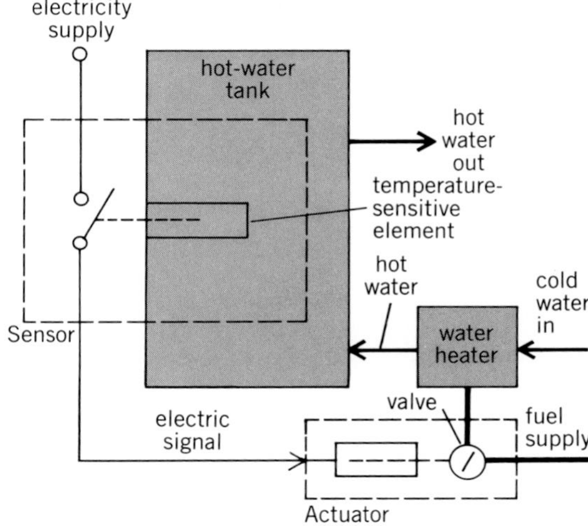


**Fig. 1. Domestic water heating system with remote water heater, illustrating use of sensor and actuator.**

Many industrial applications, and indeed many modern domestic systems, are of course much more complex than this. Instead of being on-off devices, sensors are required to measure a variety of quantities with high accuracy over a range of values. In a large chemical plant, for example, a number of sensors may be used to measure temperature, composition, and flow rate at a number of points; their outputs may all be fed into a central computer for sophisticated processing, with command signals being sent to a number of actuators.

Although sensors and actuators are convenient conceptual categories, their use is not always consistent, and the terms transducer and sensor are sometimes used interchangeably. Furthermore, the functions of sensors and actuators are not always clearly separate in practice. In a hot-water system using an electric immersion heater (**Fig. 2**), the sensor directly controls the electricity supply to the heater and thus also functions as an actuator.

**Development.** Some of the simplest and earliest transducers effectively expanded the scale of an instrument to enable reading with better precision. Two examples are the micrometer, in which a linear movement is changed into a rotation, and the optical lever, used in sensitive galvanometers, in which a beam of light is reflected from a mirror on the shaft whose angle of rotation is to be measured onto a long circular scale. The next stage, largely the result of the development of sensors with electrical outputs, was the introduction of remote-reading instruments in which the display was separated from the sensor; examples are automobile instruments and the vast arrays of instruments on modern aircraft. Recording instruments using transducers with mechanical outputs were in isolated use at least as early as the eighteenth century, but sensors with electrical outputs in conjunction with, for example, self-balancing potentiometers

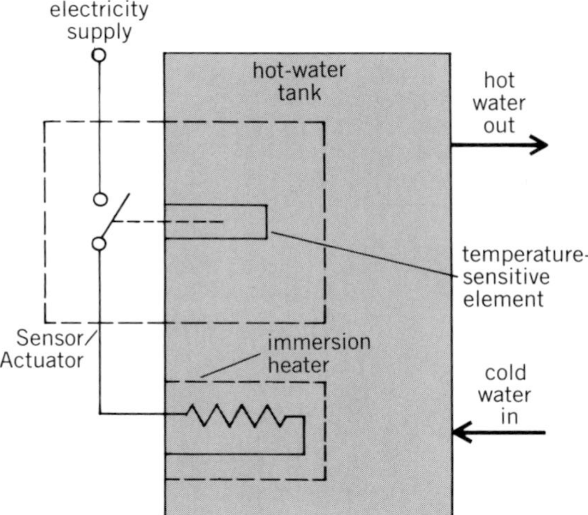


**Fig. 2. Domestic water heating system with immersion heater.**

driving chart-recorder pens made remote recording comparatively simple.

A major step forward was the use of transducers in closed-loop automatic control systems. Although pneumatic, hydraulic, and other means of transmission are sometimes encountered, as in a servo-assisted hydraulic brake, electrical systems are again the most usual and most versatile. The simple domestic heating system discussed above is one example; others can be found in almost every aspect of modern life, literally at the press of a button. More recently, the development of transducers using digital signaling has opened the way to even more versatile systems incorporating computer processing of the control data.

Any sensor with an electrical output can be used in conjunction with an analog-to-digital converter to provide a digital output. *SEE ANALOG-TO-DIGITAL CONVERTER.*

Sometimes a digital output can be provided directly, as in the case of the optical shaft encoder in which a glass disk with concentric rings of alternating black and white segments rotates between a light source and an array of photocells. The angular spacing of the segments in each ring is half that of the adjacent inner ring. The outputs of the photocells taken in sequence give a binary representation of the angle of rotation of the disk (**Fig. 3**). In order to avoid difficulties with a number of digits changing simultaneously as the disk rotates, a modified form of binary coding, known as the Gray code, is normally used. With this code the transitions between successive digits are staggered and the output is converted into digital form by a simple circuit.

**Types of transducer.** Transducers for the measurement and control of physical, chemical, and biological systems are available in a great variety of types differing in complexity and precision. Only a few of the principles and applications can be discussed here.

***Measurement of linear and angular movement.*** Many types of transducer are available for the measurement of linear or angular motion. Either one can be readily converted into the other by means of a rack and pinion or lead screw.

Direct measurement of distance can be carried out by means of a linear potentiometer to give an electrical output with moderate accuracy. Interferometric methods at optical, infrared, or microwave wavelengths can give greater accuracy but are more difficult to use. Ultrasonic waves are often employed to measure thickness of biological and other materials, and the absorption of emissions from radioactive sources is used to measure the thickness of steel emerging from a rolling mill. *SEE POTENTIOMETER (VARIABLE RESISTOR).*

A widely used type of transducer for the accurate measurement of small changes in distance is the capacitance gage. The principle of the method is that the capacitance between two parallel plates of area $A$ separated by a distance $d$ is given by the equation below, where $\epsilon_0$ is the permittivity of free space,

$$C = \frac{\epsilon\epsilon_0 A}{d}$$

8.8 picofarads per meter, and $\epsilon$ is the relative permittivity of the medium between the plates, roughly 1 for air. The capacitance between two plates of area 1 $cm^2$, 1 mm apart in air, is thus roughly 1 pF. Changes of capacitance of about $10^{-5}$ pF can be measured electrically; thus transducers can be made to gage changes of distance down to a fraction of a nanometer. *SEE CAPACITANCE; CAPACITANCE MEASUREMENT.*

Circular potentiometers and rotating capacitors can be used to give a measure of angle, but one of the most widely used types of transducer for angular rotation is the synchro (**Fig. 4**). This is a three-phase variable transformer. The primary coil rotates and carries an alternating current. The voltages induced in the secondary coils, which are set 120° apart, depend on the angle of the primary. These voltages can be carried by wire from the transmitter synchro to a re-

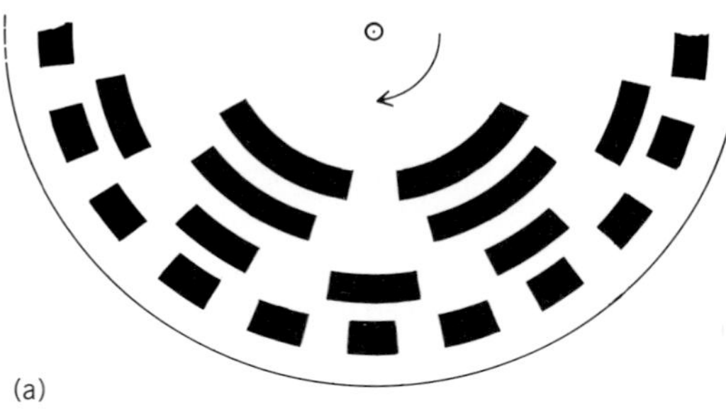


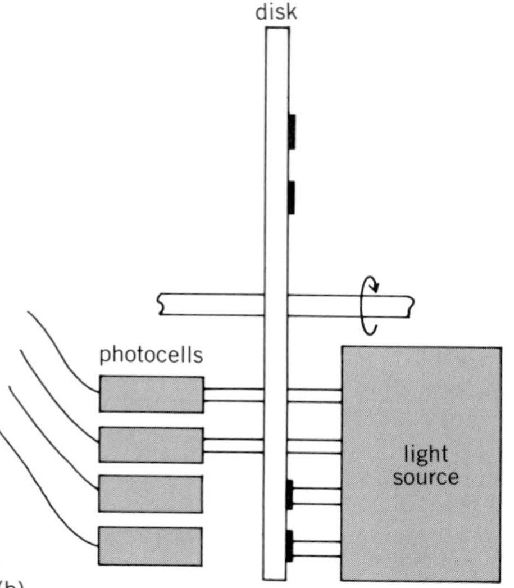


**Fig. 3. Optical shaft encoder with digital disk. (*a*) White and black segments on disk. (*b*) Arrangement of disk, light source, and photocells.**

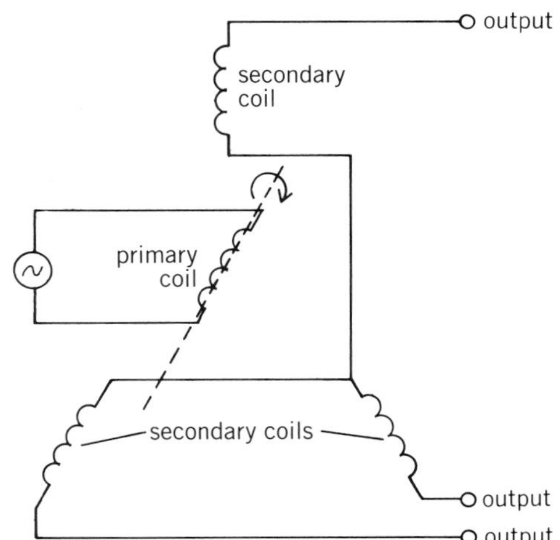

Fig. 4. Schematic diagram of synchro system.

mote receiver of similar design in which the rotating coil fed with alternating current from the same supply will duplicate the angle of the primary coil in the transmitter. Synchros can thus be used both as sensors and as actuators. Angle sensors with digital outputs use the principle of the optical shaft encoder illustrated in Fig. 3.

Other types of actuators include varieties of electric motors, solenoids for electrically generated linear movement, and pneumatic and hydraulic actuators, some of which are capable of exerting very large forces. For accurate control of rotation or, through gearing, of linear motion, the stepping motor has found increasing use. This device can operate directly from a digital input signal.

***Force, pressure, and flow measurement.*** Many force and pressure transducers rely on known, or calibrated, deformation characteristics of springs or other mechanical devices. A measurement of the mechanical displacement by any of the means already described then gives a measure of the force or pressure. Capacitance gages are often used, with the variation of capacitance changing the frequency of an oscillator so that a digital output may be derived by counting. A piezoelectric transducer can be used to give a direct electrical output from the application of a force. *See Oscillator.*

Strain gages are extensively used in mechanical and aeronautical engineering to determine the distortion of structures in response to applied forces. They usually depend for their action on the change of resistance of a wire or semiconductor under stress when fixed rigidly to the structure to be studied. *See Strain gage.*

The measurement of gas or liquid flow is of great technological importance, particularly in chemical engineering. Sensors using a variety of principles have been developed for different circumstances. These include pitot-tube, orifice-plate, small-turbine, Doppler, and ultrasonic designs.

***Temperature transducers.*** Liquid-in-glass thermometers are simple devices that provide a visual indication of temperature. They may have high accuracy but are not suitable for remote measurement or for use in automatic control systems. Almost any property of a material which changes with temperature can in principle be used as the basis of a temperature transducer. In practice the majority of devices rely on thermal expansion, change of electrical resistance, or the generation of electromotive force.

Bimetallic strips, which are two strips of different metals with different expansion coefficients, can be used to convert temperature changes into mechanical movement to operate an on-off switch or to give a continuously varying electrical output from a potentiometer. For greater accuracy, transducers giving direct electrical outputs are used. In a platinum resistance thermometer the change of resistance with temperature is measured by a form of Wheatstone bridge. A similar arrangement is used with a thermistor, which is a semiconductor with a large temperature coefficient of resistance and is smaller and easier to use than a platinum thermometer, although not quite so accurate. Another widely used device is a thermocouple, in which a voltage difference is generated between two junctions of dissimilar metals at different temperatures as a result of the Seebeck effect. *See Wheatstone bridge.*

***Acoustic and ultrasonic transducers.*** Another class of transducers, not used solely for measurement purposes, includes microphones, loudspeakers, and ultrasonic transducers. These convert pressure waves in air, water, or other media into electrical signals or vice versa.

The requirements for acoustic transducers are usually that they should handle without distortion signals of sufficient bandwidth to reproduce speech or music with acceptable quality, roughly 3 kHz for telephony or 15 kHz for high-fidelity music. Microphones based on a variety of physical principles are available, including electromagnetic, electrostatic, and variable-resistance microphones. An example of the last is the carbon-granule telephone microphone. Telephone receivers and most loudspeakers use an electromagnetic method to drive a diaphragm which generates sound pressure waves in the air; construction details, however, are quite different in the two cases because of the widely different power levels and bandwidths required. *See Loudspeaker; Microphone; Telephone.*

Important applications of ultrasonics are in sonar, nondestructive testing, and medicine. At comparatively low frequencies magnetostrictive transducers are available, but in the majority of cases piezoelectric crystals are used both for transmission and for reception. Application of an oscillating electric field between the two faces of a thin slice of crystal sets up longitudinal oscillations in the crystal which are transmitted as pressure waves into the medium with which the crystal is in contact. The reverse process takes place on reception, converting the ultrasonic waves into electrical signals. *See Piezoelectric crystal; Piezoelectricity.*

***Chemical and biological sensors.*** Some information for the control of chemical and biological systems can be gained by using sensors to measure their physical characteristics, such as temperature or viscosity. More specific information can be obtained in suitable circumstances by spectrographic means, but complex and expensive equipment is involved. Piezoelectric, electrochemical, and chemical field-effect transistor (CHEMFET) sensors have been developed to respond to particular molecular species. These advances may lead to new fields of transducer applications.

**Optical fiber transmission.** The use of electrical conductors to carry signals from sensors to processors causes problems in some cases, for example, in high-voltage electrical transmission systems or in the human body. The development of optical fibers for information transmission and of sensors capable of feeding information directly into such fibers has made possible new areas of instrumentation.

*A. Earle Bailey*

**Bibliography.** R. G. Seippel, *Transducers, Sensors, and Detectors*; 1983; Special issue on sensors and their applications, *J. Phys. E, Sci. Instrum.*, vol. 18, no. 9, September 1985; P. H. Sydenham; *Transducers in Measurement and Control*, 3d ed., 1985.

## Transformer

An electrical component used to transfer electric energy from one alternating-current (ac) circuit to another by magnetic coupling. Essentially it consists of two or more multiturn coils of insulated conducting material, so arranged that any magnetic flux linking one coil will link the others also. That is to say, mutual inductance exists between the coils. The mutual magnetic field acts to transfer energy from one input coil or primary winding to the other coils, which are called secondary windings. Under steady-state conditions, only one winding can serve as a primary. *See Coupled circuits; Inductance.*

The transformer accomplishes one or more of the following effects between two circuits: (1) a developed voltage of different magnitude, (2) a developed current of different magnitude, (3) a difference in phase angle, (4) a difference in impedance level, and (5) a difference in voltage insulation level, either between the two circuits or to ground.

Transformers are used to meet a wide range of requirements. Pole-type distribution transformers supply relatively small amounts of power to residences. Power transformers are used at generating stations to step up the generated voltage to high levels for transmission. The transmission voltages are then stepped down by transformers at the substations for local distribution. Instrument transformers are used to measure voltages and currents accurately. Audio- and video-frequency transformers must function over a broad band of frequencies. Radio-frequency transformers transfer energy in narrow frequency bands from one circuit to another.

Transformers are often classified according to the frequency for which they are designed. Power transformers are for power-frequency circuits, audio transformers for audio-frequency circuits, and so forth. Of course, many of the basic principles of operation apply to all.

### Power Transformers

Systems for the transmission and distribution of alternating-current electrical energy would be impractical without transformers. Transformers are capable of stepping alternating voltages up or down with very little loss of power in the process. They thus allow engineers to design different parts of a power system to operate at different voltage levels. Electric generators may then be designed for voltages which make possible the most economical use of materials. These generators are connected through transformers to transmission lines operating at the much higher voltages required for high transmission efficiency. Transformers again step the voltage down to levels which permit the energy to be used safely by the ultimate consumer. Large ac generators, called alternators, are designed to operate at 20 to 25 kV. Power transmission voltages in the United States range from 115 to 750 kV, and utilization voltages range from 115/230 V for home use to 13,200 V in large industrial equipment. *See Transmission lines.*

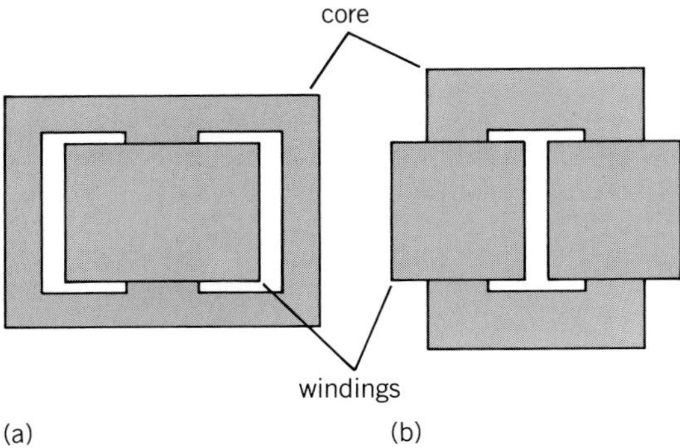


**Fig. 1. Location of windings in single-phase cores. (*a*) Shell form. (*b*) Core form.**

Power transformers, as a class, may be defined as those designed to operate at power-system frequencies: 60 Hz in the United States and Canada, and 50 Hz in much of the rest of the world. The largest power transformers connect generators to the power grid. Since a generator, together with its driving turbine and prime energy source, is called a generating unit, such transformers are called unit transformers. The classification "distribution transformers" refers to those supplying power to the ultimate consumers. They are designed for lower power and output-voltage ratings than the other transformers in the system.

**Configuration.** Any magnetic flux which arises from a current in one winding of a transformer, but is not mutual to the other windings, is called the leakage flux of that winding. General-purpose power transformers are designed to maximize the mutual component of the flux of each winding by providing an iron-alloy core which links all windings. This core acts as a high-permeance path for the mutual magnetic flux. Practically speaking, all of the mutual flux flows in this core.

Typical configurations for single-phase transformers are shown in **Fig. 1**. The arrangement in Fig. 1*a* is called a shell-form transformer, while that in Fig. 1*b* is called a core-form transformer. Each of the rectangles labeled "windings" in this figure represents at least two coils. The coils may be concentric, or interleaved (**Fig. 2**). In the shell form, all of the windings are on the center leg. In the core form, half of the turns of the primary and half of those of the secondary are on each leg. The two halves of a given winding may be connected in series or in par-

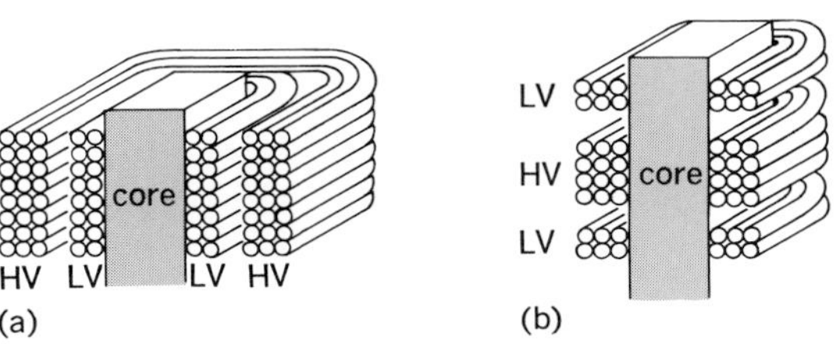


**Fig. 2. Winding arrangements. (*a*) Concentric. (*b*) Interleaved.**

allel. In the concentric arrangement, the low-voltage winding is closer to the core, so that less insulating material is required in the construction of the transformer.

**Principles of operation.** Power transformers operate on the basis of two fundamental physical laws: Faraday's voltage law and Ampère's law. Faraday's law states that the voltage induced in a winding by a magnetic flux linking that winding is proportional to the number of turns and the time rate of change of the flux; that is, Eq. (1) holds, where $e_i$ is the voltage

$$e_i = N_i \frac{d\phi_i}{dt} \qquad \text{volts} \tag{1}$$

induced in a coil of $N_i$ turns which is threaded by a flux of $\phi_i$ webers changing at a rate of $d\phi_i/dt$ webers per second. The ratio of the voltages induced in two windings of a transformer by the core flux is, then, given by Eq. (2). In other words, the voltages in-

$$\frac{e_1}{e_2} = \frac{N_1\, d\phi_{\text{core}}/dt}{N_2\, d\phi_{\text{core}}/dt} = \frac{N_1}{N_2} \tag{2}$$

duced in the windings are proportional to the numbers of turns in the windings. This is the basic law of the transformer. A high-voltage winding will have many turns, and a low-voltage winding only a few. The $N_1/N_2$ ratio is usually called the turns ratio or transformation ratio and is designated by the symbol $a$, so that Eq. (3) holds.

$$\frac{e_1}{e_2} = a \tag{3}$$

*SEE FARADAY'S LAW OF INDUCTION.*

Since the flux must change to induce a voltage, steady-state voltages can be obtained only by a cyclically varying flux. This means that alternating voltages and fluxes are required for normal transformer operation, and that is the fundamental reason for ac operation of power systems. Devices operated on ac have fewer losses when the voltages and fluxes are sinusoidal in form, and sinusoidal fluxes and terminal voltages will be assumed in this discussion. *SEE ALTERNATING-CURRENT CIRCUIT THEORY.*

***Core excitation.*** **Figure 3** shows the elements of a two-winding, shell-form transformer. The center leg of the core carries the full mutual flux, and each of the outside legs carries half of it. Thus the cross-sectional area of each outside leg is half of that of the center leg.

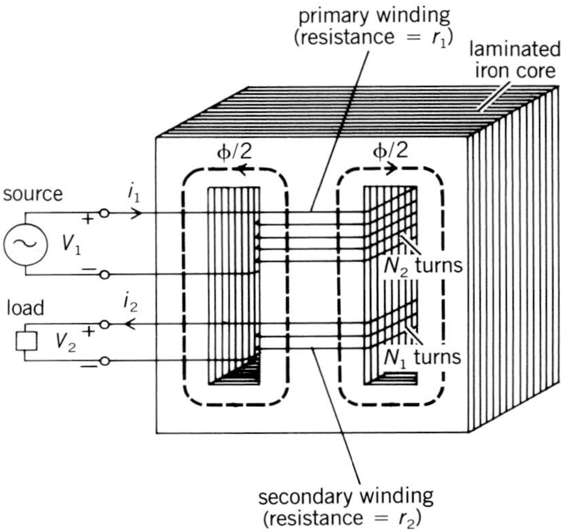


**Fig. 3. Elements of a transformer.**

The core is laminated; that is, it is made up of a stack of iron-alloy sheets. The laminations are insulated from each other by iron oxide or by some other coating. If this were not the case, the core would act like a closed, single-turn winding, and the voltage induced in it by the core flux would cause large circulating currents in the core, called eddy currents. These currents would cause excessive core heating, and result in a severe reduction in the efficiency of the transformer. There is some eddy-current loss even in laminated cores. *SEE EDDY CURRENT.*

The thickness chosen for the laminations is determined by the operating frequency. For 60 Hz, the thickness is usually 0.014 in. (0.36 mm). Lamination makes the core mechanically weak, so arrangements must be provided for its support. Cores for distribution transformers are often wound from iron-alloy strip, and the possibility of using magnetic glass in power transformer cores is being investigated.

The constant reorientation of the magnetic domains in the core iron as the flux alternates in direction results in hysteresis loss. The sum of the hysteresis and eddy-current losses is called the core loss.

The concept of exciting current may be defined by considering the situation in which the secondary winding in Fig. 3 is open (the load is disconnected) and a sinusoidal voltage is applied to the terminals of the primary winding, given by Eq. (4). In this equa-

$$v_1 = \sqrt{2}\, V_1 \cos 2\pi f t \qquad \text{volts} \tag{4}$$

tion $V_1$ is the effective or root-mean-square (rms) voltage, the peak voltage is $\sqrt{2}\, V_1$, $f$ is the frequency in hertz, and $2\pi f$ is the angular frequency $\omega$ in radians per second. An alternating flux is set up in the core and a voltage $e_1$ is induced in the $N_1$ turns in the primary which is almost equal to $v_1$ and opposed to it. The small difference between $v_1$ and $e_1$ is due to the leakage flux and to the winding resistance. This difference is enough to allow a small current to flow, sufficient to set up the core flux and to supply the hysteresis and eddy-current losses of the core. This small current (1–5% of rated primary current) is called the exciting current, $i_{ex}$. Its root-mean-square phasor $I_{ex}$ may be considered to be made up of two components, as in Eq. (5), where $I_\phi$ is the magnetiz-

$$I_{ex} = I_\phi + I_{cl} \qquad \text{amperes} \tag{5}$$

ing component, which lags the applied voltage by 90°; and $I_{cl}$ is the core-loss component, which is in phase with the voltage. Even though the applied voltage and core flux are sinusoidal, the nonlinearity of the iron causes the exciting current to be nonsinusoidal; it contains a large third-harmonic component. (The concept of the phasor $I_{ex}$ is actually an approximation; it represents a sinusoid having the same root-mean-square value as the actual nonsinusoidal waveform.)

The applied voltage $v_1$ and the voltage induced by the core flux are so nearly equal that Eq. (6) follows

$$\sqrt{2}\, V_1 \cos 2\pi f t = N_1 \frac{d\phi_{\text{core}}}{dt} \tag{6}$$

from Eqs. (1) and (4). Integrating Eq. (6) gives Eq. (7), where $\phi_K$, the constant of integration, is a tran-

$$\phi_{core} = \frac{V_1}{N_1}\frac{\sqrt{2}}{2\pi f}\sin 2\pi ft + \phi_K \quad \text{webers} \quad (7)$$

sient flux which dies out after a few cycles, due to effects not included in Eq. (6). This transient is responsible for the phenomenon of current inrush. The peak value of the core flux is, in the steady state, given by Eq. (8), and is seen to be proportional to the

$$\phi_{max} = \frac{V_1}{N_1 f}\frac{\sqrt{2}}{2\pi} \quad (8)$$

volts per turn of the primary winding. Since the core flux density (teslas, or webers/m$^2$) is limited by saturation, the designer's choice of volts per turn of the windings will determine the cross-sectional area of the core, or vice versa.

***Transformation of the secondary load.*** When an electrical load is connected to the terminals of the secondary winding, current flows through that winding and the load as a result of the voltage $e_2$ induced in the secondary by the alternating core flux. In Fig. 3, source current flows into the positive terminal of the primary, but out of the positive terminal of the secondary. Application of the right-hand rule to the two windings shows that the load current in the secondary results in a magnetomotive-force (MMF) field, which is opposed to the magnetomotive-force field of the primary. Now, Ampère's law in circuital form states that the magnetomotive force applied to a closed path is simply equal to the net current enclosed by that path. In Fig. 3, Ampère's law may be applied to either of the two $\phi/2$ paths. In either case, the net current enclosed is $N_1 i_1 - N_2 i_2$, and the magnetomotive force applied to the core around either path is given by Eq. (9).

$$F_{core} = N_1 i_1 - N_2 i_2 \quad \text{amperes} \quad (9)$$

Now the core flux is also given by the core permeance $P$ times the applied magnetomotive force, Eq. (10). Combining Eqs. (9) and (10) gives Eq. (11),

$$\frac{\phi_{core}}{2} = \frac{P}{2}F_{core} \quad \text{webers} \quad (10)$$

$$\frac{\phi}{P} = N_1 i_1 - N_2 i_2 \quad \text{amperes} \quad (11)$$

and solving Eq. (11) for $i_1$ gives Eq. (12). The term

$$i_1 = \frac{N_2}{N_1} i_2 + \frac{\phi_{core}}{PN_1} \quad \text{amperes} \quad (12)$$

$\phi_{core}/PN_1$ is the instantaneous value of the exciting current of Eq. (5). The large permeance of the core makes this term very small. Equation (12) may be rewritten as Eq. (13). Thus, with a load on the sec-

$$i_1 = \frac{i_2}{a} + i_{ex} \quad \text{amperes} \quad (13)$$

ondary, the primary current is equal to the secondary current transformed by the inverse of the turns ratio, plus the current required to excite the core.

**Ideal transformer.** An ideal transformer would require no exciting current. In other words, its core would have infinite permeance, and the primary current would be given by Eq. (14). The windings of an

$$i_1 = \frac{i_2}{a} \quad \text{amperes (ideal)} \quad (14)$$

ideal transformer would have zero resistance, and would be wound so as to have no leakage flux (a physical impossibility). Then the induced voltages would exactly equal the terminal voltages, and Eq. (15) follows from Eqs. (3) and (14). Thus in an ideal

$$v_1 i_1 = v_2 i_2 \quad \text{volt-amperes} \quad (15)$$

transformer, the instantaneous input apparent power equals the instantaneous output apparent power. There are no internal losses, and the ideal transformer has an efficiency of 100%.

In terms of root-mean-square phasors, the voltages and currents are related by Eqs. (16). The complex

$$V_1 = aV_2 \qquad I_1 = \frac{I_2}{a} \quad (16)$$

load impedance, in ohms, is given by Eq. (17), but

$$Z_{L2} = \frac{V_2}{I_2} \quad (17)$$

the impedance seen by the generator connected to the primary is given by Eq. (18). Thus impedances are

$$Z_{in1} = \frac{V_1}{I_1} = \frac{aV_2}{I_2/a} = a^2 Z_{L2} \quad (18)$$

transformed by the square of the turns ratio. Similarly, if a load were applied to the number 1 winding, the impedance appearing at the number 2 terminals would be given by Eq. (19). Most power transformers

$$Z_{in2} = \frac{Z_{L1}}{a^2} \quad (19)$$

are so nearly ideal that, for many engineering purposes, Eqs. (16), (18), and (19) may be used to obtain satisfactory numerical values with real transformers. *See* Electrical impedance.

**Circuit model.** When the detailed performance of a transformer must be accounted for in a power system calculation, a circuit which models the performance of the actual transformer is included in the system circuit (**Fig. 4***a*). To simplify the problem solution, the primary and secondary series impedances are nearly always combined into one equivalent impedance. This is accomplished through the impedance-transforming property of the ideal transformer. If the secondary winding resistance and leakage reactance are transferred to the primary by the factor $a^2$, and are then added to the primary series impedance, the result is called the equivalent impedance referred to the primary, given in Eq. (20) and diagrammed in Fig. 4*b*,

$$\begin{aligned} Z_{eq1} &= R_{eq1} + jX_{eq1} \\ &= r_1 + a^2 r_2 + j(x_1 + a^2 x_2) \end{aligned} \quad (20)$$

where $r_1$ and $r_2$ are the resistances of the primary and secondary windings, and $x_1$ and $x_2$ are the reactances due to leakage fluxes. When the primary impedance is transferred and combined with the secondary impedance, the equivalent impedance referred to the secondary results, given in Eq. (21) and diagrammed

$$\begin{aligned} Z_{eq2} &= R_{eq2} + jX_{eq2} = \frac{r_1}{a^2} + r_2 + j\left(\frac{x_1}{a^2} + x_2\right) \\ &= \frac{Z_{eq1}}{a^2} \end{aligned} \quad (21)$$

in Fig. 4c. The operator $j$ in these expressions indicates that the voltages across the reactive elements of these impedances leads the voltages across the resistive elements by 90°. All voltages and currents in Fig. 4 are to be treated as ac phasor quantities. SEE REACTANCE.

The model makes it easy to calculate the primary voltage required to have rated secondary voltage at a given volt-ampere load and power factor. If the phase of the secondary voltage is set equal to 0°, as in Eq. (22), and if the power factor is cos θ, then the sec-

$$V_2 = V_{2\text{rated}} \angle 0° \quad (22)$$

ondary current is given by Eq. (23), and from Fig.

$$I_2 = \frac{kVA \cdot 1000}{|V_{2\text{rated}}|} \angle\theta = |I_2| \angle\theta \quad (23)$$

4c, the primary voltage is given by Eq. (24). The sign

$$V_1 = a[V_2 + |I_2|(\cos\theta \pm J \sin\theta) \cdot Z_{eq2}] \quad (24)$$

on the $j$ sin θ term is positive for leading and negative for lagging power factor, and $Z_{eq2}$ is a complex number.

The model allows easy comparison between realistic and ideal transformers, as follows:

| *Realistic* | *Ideal* |
|---|---|
| $V_1 = a(V_2 + I_2 Z_{eq2})$ | $V_1 = aV_2$ |
| $I_1 = \frac{I_2}{a} + I_{ex}$ | $I_1 = \frac{I_2}{a}$ |

The ratio of rated primary to secondary voltages shown on the transformer nameplate gives the actual turns ratio. This means that, if the secondary voltage is at rated value, the primary voltage will differ a little from its rated value.

**Percent impedance.** The equivalent series impedance of a transformer is nearly always expressed as a fraction of the load impedance which would draw rated current at the rated voltage. This full-load impedance for a given winding is called the base impedance of that winding, Eq. (25). The "percent"

$$Z_{\text{base}2} = \frac{V_{2\text{rated}}}{I_{2\text{rated}}} \quad (25)$$

impedance of a transformer is given by Eq. (26). The

$$Z\% = \frac{Z_{eq2}}{Z_{\text{base}2}} \cdot 100\% = R\% + jX\% \quad (26)$$

$R\%$ is considerably smaller than $X\%$, so usually only the $X\%$ is shown on the transformer nameplate. Typical values of $R\%$ range from 0.3% in very large transformers to 1.0% in distribution transformers. It can be shown that $R\%$ is equal to the internal ohmic ($I^2R$) loss of the transformer at full load, expressed as a percent of the rated volt-amperes of the device.

The value of $X\%$ depends on the amount of leakage flux. High-voltage windings require more insulating material, and this results in more space between windings for leakage fluxes. Consequently a transformer with a very high-voltage winding will have a large value of $X\%$. Typical values range from 1.5% in distribution transformers to 15% in transformers with, say, a 345-kV winding.

**Transforming three-phase power.** Three-phase power may be transformed from one voltage level to another by sets of three single-phase transformers or

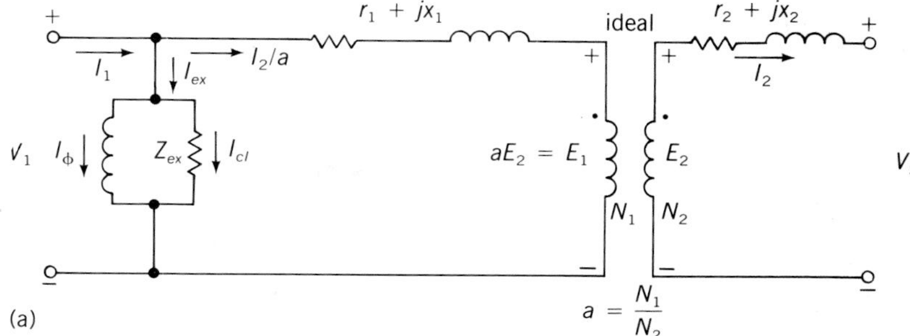


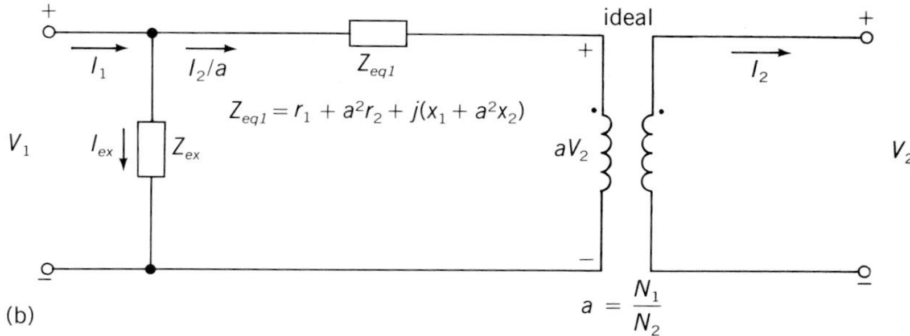


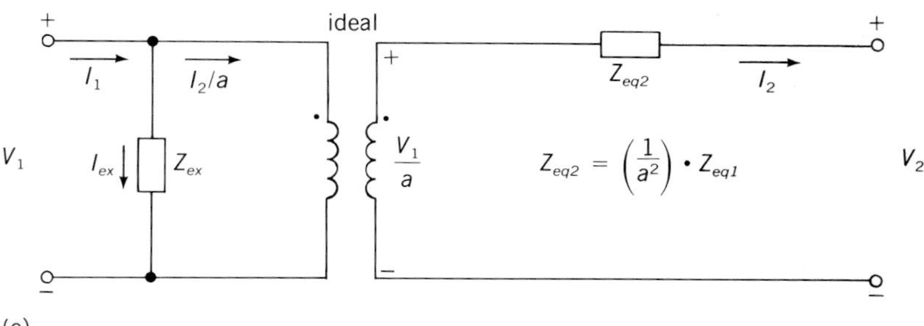


**Fig. 4. Circuit models for performance calculations. (*a*) Transformer model showing separate primary and secondary impedances. $r_1$ and $r_2$ are resistances of primary and secondary windings, and $x_1$ and $x_2$ are reactances due to their leakage fluxes. (*b*) Secondary impedances transformed by ideal transformer and combined with primary impedance to form $Z_{eq1}$. (*c*) Transformer model in terms of the equivalent impedance referred to the secondary, $Z_{eq2}$.**

by three-phase transformers. Three-phase transformers have three primary/secondary sets of windings on a single core. The arrangements for core and shell-form three-phase transformers are shown in **Fig. 5. Figure 6** shows a core-form, three-phase transformer removed from its tank.

When the core-form, three-phase transformer is operating with balanced voltages, the alternating fluxes of the three phases are equal in magnitude and 120° out of phase with each other. They thus add to zero at the center junctions of the core. When it is anticipated that the transformer will operate under unbalanced conditions, additional core legs are added at one or both ends of the core, to form "four-limbed"

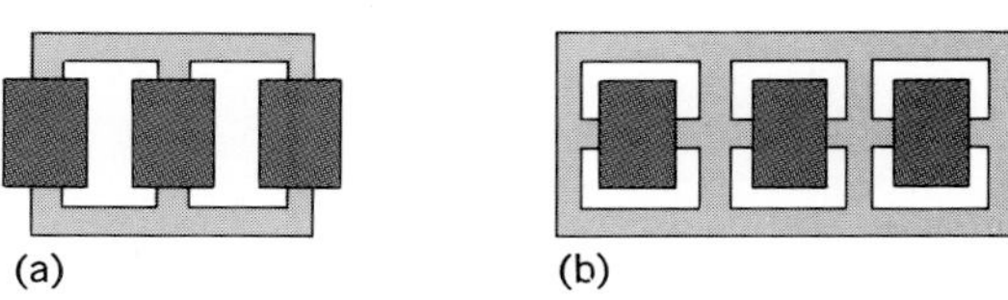


**Fig. 5. Typical three-phase cores showing location of windings. (*a*) Core form. (*b*) Shell form.**

Fig. 6. Three-phase core and coils, rated at 50,000 kVA, 115,000 V.

or "five-limbed" cores. These added legs carry the net flux resulting from the unbalance, which could otherwise flow in the steel transformer tank and cause overheating.

Three-phase transformers may be connected with their primary windings in wye or delta and their secondary windings in wye or delta, providing a great deal of flexibility. A wye-delta connection is illustrated in **Fig. 7**, having wye-connected windings with high-voltage line terminals $a_1$, $b_1$, and $c_1$, and delta-connected windings with low-voltage terminals $a_2$, $b_2$, and $c_2$. In wye-delta or delta-wye, there is always a 30° phase shift between the primary and secondary line voltages. It is standard practice in the United States to connect the windings in such a way that the voltages on low-voltage side (such as $V_{a2b2}$, the phasor voltage drop from line $a_2$ to line $b_2$ in Fig. 7) lag those on the high-voltage side (such as $V_{a1b1}$, the drop from line $a_1$ to line $b_1$) by 30°. There is some advantage in connecting the high-voltage windings in wye, because the neutral (with terminal $N$ in Fig. 7) may be grounded, making the insulation requirements less severe. (In Fig. 7, $V_{a1}N$, the line $a_1$ to neutral phasor voltage on the high-voltage side, is the primary voltage of the transformer element whose secondary voltage is $V_{a2b2}$; thus $V_{a2b2}$ is in phase with $V_{a1N}$.) It is desirable to have one set of windings in delta, because a delta tends to maintain balanced phase voltages and serves as a solution to certain third-harmonic problems associated with the wye connection. When a wye-wye connection is essential, a set of delta-connected "tertiary" windings is often provided, whose terminals may or may not be made accessible outside the transformer. Three-phase power transformation may also be accomplished by means of sets of two transformers, connected in T, open-delta, or open-wye-open-delta. These arrangements are usually used as distribution transformers, involving relatively small ratings, say, up to 500 kVA.

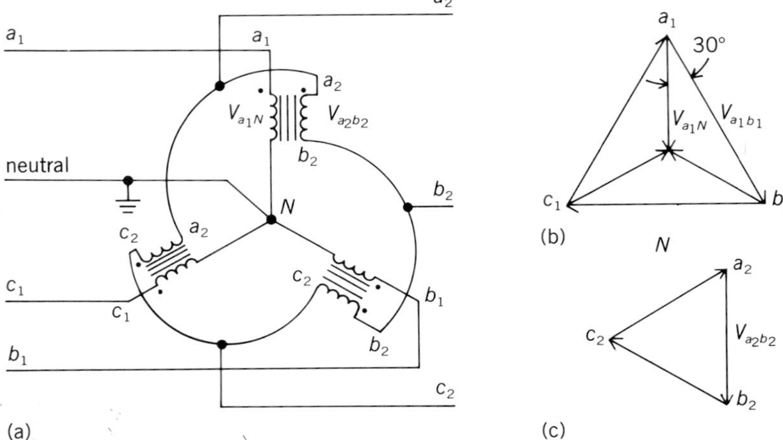


Fig. 7. Wye-delta connection of a three-phase transformer. (a) Wiring diagram. (*b*) Voltage-phasor diagram for the high-voltage (wye) side. (c) Voltage-phasor diagram for the low-voltage (delta) side.

**Efficiency.** Efficiency is defined by Eq. (27). The

$$\eta = \frac{\text{output power}}{\text{input power}} \tag{27}$$

output power is equal to the input power, less the internal losses of the transformer. These losses include the ohmic ($I^2R$) loss in the windings, called copper loss, given by Eq. (28), and the core loss,

$$\begin{aligned} \text{Copper loss} &= |I_2|^2 R_{eq2} \text{ (single-phase)} \\ &= 3\,|I_2|^2 R_{eq2} \text{ (three-phase)} \quad \text{watts} \end{aligned} \tag{28}$$

called the no load loss. The input power is thus the sum of the output power and the copper and core losses. Typical efficiency for a 20,000 kVA power transformer at full load is 99.4%, while that of a 5-kVA transformer is 94%

**Cooling.** Transformer losses in the windings and core generate heat, which must be removed to prevent deterioration of the insulation and the magnetic properties of the core. Most power transformers are contained in a tank of oil. The oil is especially formulated to provide good electrical insulation, and also serves to carry heat away from the core and windings by convection. In smaller transformers, the hot oil is cooled by flowing along the inside of the tank wall. Larger transformers have ribbed walls or are provided with fins or radiators to cool the oil. Very large transformers have pumps to circulate the oil through external radiators, which may be provided with fans. Transformers which are designed to operate in air are called "dry-type" transformers.

**Bushings.** Leads from the transformer windings are brought out of the tank through bushings inserted in openings in the tank wall or lid. When high voltages are involved, these bushings may be quite complex, consisting of concentric capacitors enclosed in a ceramic case filled with oil. The capacitors form a voltage divider which distributes the electric field between the transformer lead and the case in such a way

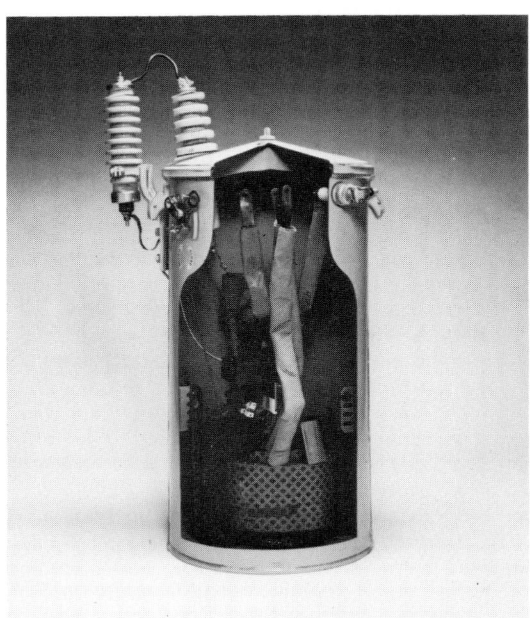

**Fig. 8. Cutaway of single-phase, pole-type, completely self-protected (CSP) distribution transformer. (*Westinghouse Electric Corp.*)**

as to minimize the probability of breakdown of the insulation. SEE CAPACITOR.

**Figure 8** shows a cutaway 20-kVA, single-phase, shell-form, distribution transformer, designed for mounting on a utility pole. The tank is normally three-quarters filled with insulating, cooling oil. The transformer has one high-voltage bushing; the other terminal of the high-voltage winding is connected to the steel tank. A spark gap connects the high-voltage terminal to a lightning arrester, which protects the transformer insulation from overvoltage. Immediately above the core, inside the tank, is an overcurrent circuit breaker. Such a transformer is said to be completely self-protected (CSP). *George McPherson, Jr.*

### AUDIO- AND RADIO-FREQUENCY TRANSFORMERS

A second important application for transformers is in signal processing. Transformers are used to deliver a waveform of some kind from one circuit to a second (for example, the output of one transistor or integrated circuit to the input of another). Energy is delivered to the second circuit, and the manner of utilization of the energy is extremely important.

With signal processing, it is vital that the waveform of the signal be controlled. For this to be possible, the signal energy must be delivered to a load that is usually linear; often it should also be resistive. If the transformer is unloaded, the signal energy is used to induce magnetization in the transformer core, leading to harmonic and intermodulation distortion due to magnetic hysteresis, and frequency distortion due to the variation of the input reactance of the transformer primary. The resistive load must be placed on the secondary output to minimize the adverse effects of the nonlinear magnetizing current. In addition, the load impedance must be chosen so that it swamps out the magnetizing reactance effect and introduces the desired load impedance characteristics. It can be chosen to reduce the effects of variation of the impedance as a function of signal voltage developed on the secondary, since these variations can also introduce both harmonic and intermodulation distortion. As discussed below, the load may also be selected in a way that will limit the magnitude of the phase distortion introduced by a following amplifier and will assure stable operation. (This distortion often is called departure from the minimum-phase condition, and is a result of parasitic feedback paths in a circuit.) SEE DISTORTION (ELECTRONIC CIRCUITS).

Audio or video (broad-frequency band) transformers are used to transfer complex signals containing energy at a large number of frequencies from one circuit to another. Radio-frequency (rf) and intermediate-frequency (i-f) transformers are used to transfer energy in narrow frequency bands from one circuit to another. Audio and video transformers are required to respond uniformly to signal voltages over a frequency range three to five or more decades wide (for example, from 10 to 100,000 Hz), and consequently must be designed so that very nearly all of the magnetic flux threading through one coil also passes through the other. These units are designed to have a coupling coefficient $k$, given in Eq. (29), nearly equal to 1.

$$k = \frac{M}{\sqrt{L_1 L_2}} \tag{29}$$

Here $L_1$ and $L_2$ are the primary and secondary inductances, respectively, and $M$ is the mutual inductance (**Fig. 9**). The high coupling coefficient is obtained by the use of interleaved windings and a high-permeability iron core, which concentrates the flux. Typical values of $k$ for highest-quality video transformers may be as high as 0.9998; that for power transformers need not be greater than 0.98.

Radio-frequency and intermediate-frequency transformers are built from individual inductors whose magnetic fields are loosely coupled together, $k < 0.30$; one or more inductors are resonated with a capacitor to make efficient energy transfer possible near the resonant frequency. The structure of audio- and radio-frequency transformers is shown in **Fig. 10**. SEE RESONANCE (ALTERNATING-CURRENT CIRCUITS).

**Audio and video transformers.** Audio and video transformers have two resonances (caused by existing stray and circuit capacitances) just as many tuned transformers do. One resonance point is near the low-signal-frequency limit; the other is near the high limit. As the coefficient of coupling in a transformer is reduced appreciably below unity by removal of core material and separation of the windings, tuning capacitors are added to provide efficient transfer of energy. The two resonant frequencies combine to one when the coupling is reduced to the value known as critical coupling, then stay relatively fixed as the coupling is further reduced. It is possible for a single-tuned coupled circuit to be overcoupled, leading to a

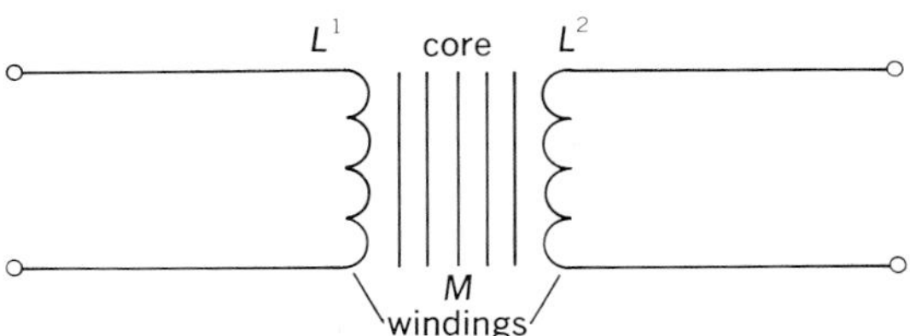


**Fig. 9. Schematic of a transformer with symbols explained in the text.**

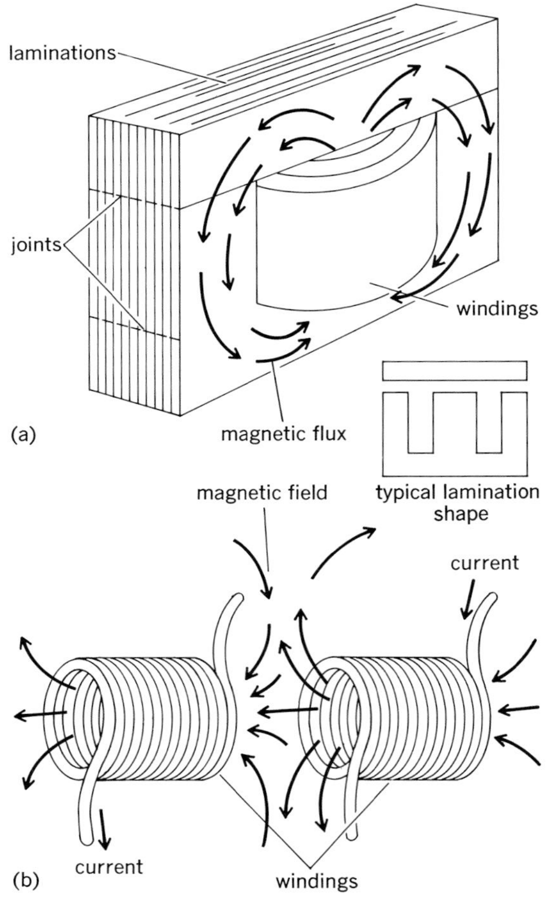


Fig. 10. Audio- and radio-frequency transformers. (a) Iron-core audio transformer. (b) Air-core radio-frequency transformer.

broad-tuned coupled circuit. This factor necessitates resistive loading on audio and video transformers. Overcoupling is also observed in the input coupled circuits commonly used in television receivers, and causes the susceptibility to spurious signals often noted in such receivers.

All transformers are devices for transferring energy from one circuit to another. The energy transferred is absorbed either in the circuits themselves or in an external load circuit. For this reason, proper termination is essential for achieving optimum behavior in circuits containing transformers.

Audio and video transformers have a minimum operating frequency at which the open-circuit reactance of the primary is approximately twice its effective loaded impedance. As with wide-band resistance-capacitance (*RC*) amplifiers, gain may be traded for bandwidth with transformer-coupled amplifiers. The reduction of the terminating resistance across the secondary of the transformer reduces the minimum operating frequency $f_{min}$ and, in the presence of output capacitance, raises the maximum frequency $f_{max}$. The approximate values of the minimum and maximum frequencies and the resonant frequency $f_r$ are given by Eqs. (30), where $L_{22} = L_2 - (M^2/L_1) = L_2(1 - k^2)$. This $L_{22}$ is the secondary inductance with the primary short-circuited; $C_2$ is the output capacitance, both external and internal, on the transformer; and $R_c$ is the load resistance (**Fig. 11**). The resonant frequency $f_r$ should be larger than $f_{max}$ for best performance. SEE AMPLIFIER.

$$f_{min} = \frac{R_c(N_1/N_2)^2}{\pi L_1}$$

$$f_{max} = \frac{1}{2\pi R_c C_2} \qquad (30)$$

$$f_r = \frac{1}{2\pi\sqrt{L_{22}C_2}}$$

A transformer used to activate terminating circuitry is called an output transformer; one to activate an input circuit is an input transformer; and others are called interstage transformers.

**Distortion.** The distortion introduced into the amplified signal by a transformer is caused primarily by its hysteresis loss. This loss effect may be minimized by proper loading on the secondary. The load component of current then is large compared to the magnetizing current. In addition, a resistive load keeps the amplification uniform as a function of frequency, and keeps the phase distortion to a minimum.

The magnetic core in an audio or video transformer is subject to two kinds of saturation, that due to applied direct current in the windings, and that due to excessively large signal currents. The direct current in the windings may make the hysteresis loop of the iron core nonsymmetrical, necessitating the use of a larger core having a built-in air gap. Both large signal amplitudes and low frequencies can cause signal saturation to occur in the core. SEE DISTORTION (ELECTRONIC CIRCUITS).

The development of ultracompact radios and other consumer electronics has caused critical problems for component designers. The problems are particularly difficult for units that employ bipolar transistors. The total volume of iron and copper severely influences the impedance and the coupling coefficient as well as the signal amplitude and the saturation characteristics of a transformer. The overall result is limitation of signal amplitude, frequency response, and power-handling capability.

**RF and i-f transformers.** These use two or more inductors, loosely coupled together, to limit the band of operating frequencies. Efficient transfer of energy is obtained by resonating one or more of the inductors. By using higher than critical coupling, a wider bandwidth than that from the individual tuned circuits is obtained, while the attenuation of side frequencies is as rapid as with the individual circuits isolated from one another.

The tuning of the primary, the secondary, or both may be accomplished either by the variation of the tuning capacitor or by an adjustable magnetic or conducting slug that varies the inductance of the inductor (**Fig. 12**).

***Impedance.*** The operating impedance of a tuned circuit of a radio frequency transformer is a function of its $Q$ and its tuning capacitance. (Its $Q$ measures the rate of dissipation of stored energy in a tuned circuit as it decays from a starting pulse.) In general, high-power circuits require a high capacitance for energy

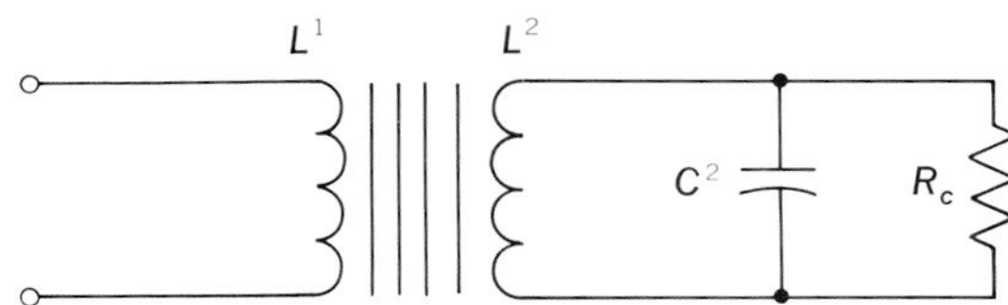


Fig. 11. Circuit of loaded transformer.

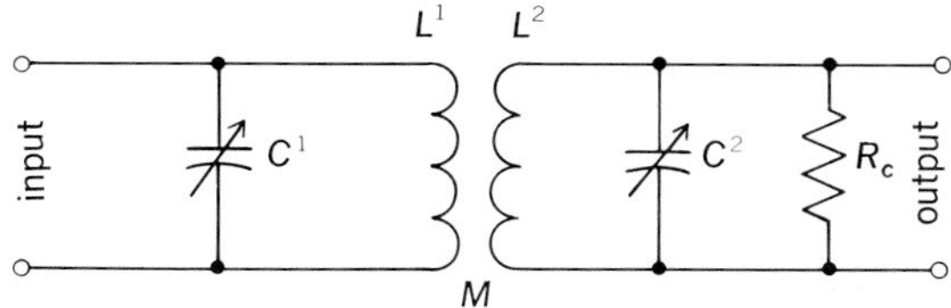


**Fig. 12. Tuned radio-frequency transformer.**

storage, and therefore have low values of impedance. In any application, the impedance level must be kept sufficiently small to prevent instability and oscillation. *See* Q (*electricity*).

***Transformer-coupled amplifiers.*** Control of voltage gain of transformer-coupled amplifiers is a crucial requirement for effective, stable, radio-frequency and intermediate-frequency amplifiers, both low-power and high-power types. Voltage gain is a function of tuned impedance and the transconductance of the active device, whether tube or transistor.

The tuned impedance $Z_t$ of a tuned circuit depends on both the operating $Q$ of the tuned circuit and its inductance-to-capacitance ratio. (Its operating frequency is a function of the product of inductance $L$ and capacitance $C$.) Impedance of a capacitor is an inverse function of capacitance and frequency, according to Eq. (31).

$$Z_t \text{ (tuned)} = L/CR = \text{function of } (L/C)^{1/2} \quad (31)$$

The voltage gain takes the form of the product of the transconductance and the tuned impedance, $g_m Z_t$. The transconductance can be expressed in terms of Eq. (32), where kappa κ is the transconductance-per-

$$g_m = \kappa\left(\frac{q}{kT}\right)I_c \quad (32)$$

unit-current efficiency, $q$ is the electron charge, $k$ is Boltzmann's constant, $T$ is absolute temperature, and $I_c$ is the instantaneous value of the output current for the device. The kappa for a bipolar transistor is approximately unity; for field-effect transistors and electron tubes, it normally is less than 0.02. The value of $q/kT$ is approximately 39 siemens per ampere. A load impedance that gives an overall stage voltage gain of 10 or less in a circuit will usually operate in the proper mode and can be stabilized. Should the load impedance determined in this way prove to be too large, a radio-frequency transformer may be used to reduce the impedance level. The critical issue is that the input circuit to the amplifier look into a voltage source so that input loading will not degrade the operation of the previous amplifier. *See* Circuit (*electronics*); Radio-frequency amplifier.

*Keats A. Pullen*

***Bibliography.*** Army Material Command, *Reliable Electronic Circuits*, AMCP 706–124 (NTIS 008–020–00602–5), 1976; R. Feinberg, *Modern Power Transformer Practice*, 1979; A. Franklin and D. Franklin, *J&P Transformer Book*, 11th ed., 1983; Institute of Electrical and Electronics Engineers, *Application of Distribution and Power Transformers*, IEEE Publ. 76 Ch1159–3–PWR, 1976; R. Lawrence and H. Richards, *Principles of Alternating Current Machinery*, 4th ed. 1953; G. McPherson, *An Introduction to Electrical Machines and Transformers*, 1981; K. A. Pullen, *Design of Transistor Circuits, with Experiments*, 1979.

## Transistor

An active component of an electronic circuit which may be used as an amplifier, detector, or switch. A transistor consists of a small block of semiconducting material to which at least three electrical contacts are made. Transistors are of two general types, bipolar and field-effect. The bipolar type involves excess minority current carrier injection. The field-effect type involves only majority current carriers. Historically the bipolar type was developed before the field-effect type. Today both are widely used. The unmodified term transistor usually refers to the bipolar type.

In a bipolar transistor, at least one contact is ohmic (nonrectifying), and at least one contact is rectifying. Usually there are two closely spaced rectifying contacts and one ohmic contact. For a discussion of rectifying contacts *see* Junction diode; Point-contact diode; Semiconductor rectifier.

The operation of a simple transistor consists of the control of the current flowing in the high-resistance direction through one rectifying contact (called the collector) by the current flowing in the low-resistance direction in the other rectifying contact (called the emitter). The third contact, which is ohmic, is called the base contact.

These contacts usually consist of two or more regions. The regions in which the actual rectification processes take place are called the emitter barrier and collector barrier. The region between these two barriers is called the base region, or simply the base. The regions outside of these barriers are called the emitter and collector regions.

Transistors are used in radio receivers, in electronic computers, in electronic instrumentation and control equipment, and in almost any electronic circuit where vacuum tubes are useful and the required voltages are not too high. Transistors have the advantages over their vacuum-tube counterparts of being much smaller, consuming less power, and having no filament to burn out. They are at a disadvantage in that they do not yet operate at as high voltages as some vacuum tubes and their action is degraded at high temperatures.

**Classification of transistors.** Transistors are classified chiefly by four criteria: (1) by the type and number of structural regions of the semiconductor crystal; (2) by the technology used in fabrication; (3) by the semiconductor material used; and (4) by the intended use of the device. A typical designation following this scheme would be *npn* double-diffused silicon switching transistor. It is not necessary to include all of the above criteria in a single designation nor to rigidly follow this order.

A modern transistor type is the *npn* double-diffused silicon planar passivated transistor (**Fig. 1**). The term double-diffused refers to the fabrication technique in which the base region is formed by diffusion through a mask into the body of the silicon wafer which forms the collector region.

In turn, the emitter region is formed by diffusion through a second mask into the previously formed base region. The term planar refers to the fact that all three electrical connections are found on a single surface of the device. The term passivated means that the surface to which all junctions return is protected by a layer of naturally grown silicon oxide which, together with an overcoating of glass or other inert material, passivates the surface, electrically minimizing leakage currents. The double-diffusion process allows very close control of narrow base widths. The base diffusion provides a resistivity gradient in the base region which has an associated electric field. In this field charge transport is by drift. Such transistors have been called drift transistors to distinguish them from most other transistors in which the charge transport is by a diffusion process. Silicon planar transistors have power ratings in the 100 mW to 50 W range with characteristic frequencies between 50 and 2000 MHz, usually of the *npn* type. The designation *npn* stands for the conductivity type of the emitter, base, and collector regions, respectively. The *n* stands for negative since the charge on an electron is negative and electrons carry most of the current in a region of *n*-type conductivity. In a region of *p*-type conductivity most of the current is carried by electron vacancies, called holes, which behave as if they were positively charged. For a discussion of conductivity type SEE SEMICONDUCTOR.

A historically important type was the *pnp* alloy-junction germanium transistor. This type was very widely used in the first decade of the solid-state electronics era. The term alloy-junction in this transistor designation refers to the fabrication method. The emitter and collector regions were produced by recrystallization from an alloy of some suitable metal doped with a *p*-type impurity. The alloy had previously been fused in contact with the opposite surfaces of the original *n*-type semiconductor body and had dissolved some of the semiconductor material. Fused-junction is equivalent terminology. This type of transistor was made in power ratings from 50 mW to 200 W, and in frequency ranges up to about 20 MHz.

For further classification of transistors SEE JUNCTION TRANSISTOR; POINT-CONTACT TRANSISTOR. See also the sections of this article on special devices and transistor manufacture.

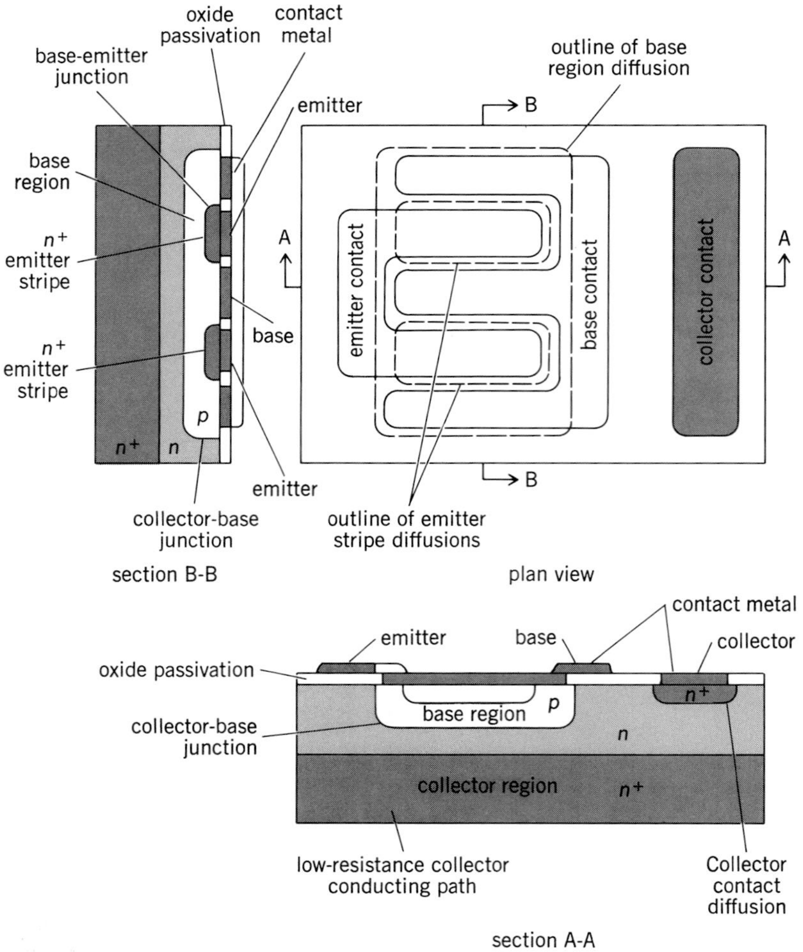

**Transistor action.** To explain transistor action in more detail, some of the basic properties of a semiconductor material are first presented. An *n*-type semiconductor contains electrons, and a *p*-type semiconductor contains holes. These are called the majority carriers of the two types. Actually there are always present a small number of holes in an *n*-type semiconductor and a small number of electrons in a *p*-type semiconductor. These are called the minority carriers of the two types. At a given temperature with a given material the product of the densities of the majority and minority carriers is a constant. This means that if there is present a very high density of majority carriers (low-resistivity material), there will be a correspondingly low density of minority carriers.

The emitter current controls the collector current in a simple transistor. To understand this, first consider the magnitude of the collector current in the absence of emitter current. In normal operation the collector barrier is biased in the high-resistance (reverse) direction. Under this condition of bias the majority carriers are stopped by the barrier, and only the minority carriers are free to flow. If the collector barrier is a silicon *pn* junction, the minority-carrier diffusion current is negligible and the reverse-bias leakage current will consist of thermally generated carriers and be in the nanoampere range. If emitter current is present, the portion consisting of carriers entering the base will continue across the collector barrier and thus control the collector current.

***Injection.*** The emitter controls the density of minority carriers by injecting extra minority carriers into the base region when the emitter is biased in the low-resistance (forward) direction. This is the fundamental process of simple transistor action. Whenever a rectifying barrier is forward-biased, extra minority carriers are added to the semiconductor near the barrier. Since the source of these minority carriers is the majority-carrier density on the other side of the barrier, it is clear that the largest part of the forward current will be carried by those carriers which come from the largest majority density. A *pn* junction will have a high injection efficiency for electrons if the *n* region has a much larger density of carriers (lower resistivity) than the *p* region. Therefore, in a *npn* transistor the emitter *n* region should have a low resistivity compared to the *p*-type base region. The phenomenon of minority-carrier injection is observed also in rectifying metal-semiconductor contacts, and such contacts may be used as emitters as well as *pn* junctions.

***Current gain.*** The current gain $\alpha$ of a simple transistor may be expressed as the product of three factors: the fraction $\gamma$ of the emitter current carried by the injected carriers, and fraction $\beta$ of the injected carriers which arrive at the collector barrier, and the current multiplication factor $\alpha*$ of the collector. For a double-diffused transistor, typical values of these factors are $\gamma = 0.985$, $\beta = 0.999$, and $\alpha* = 1.000$, giving $\alpha = 0.984$. From this it can be seen that most of the current which flows into the emitter flows right



**Fig. 1. Plan and sections of a planar *npn* double-diffused silicon transistor.**

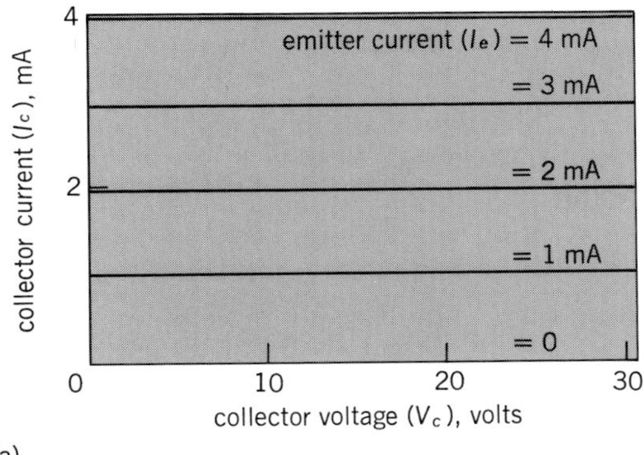


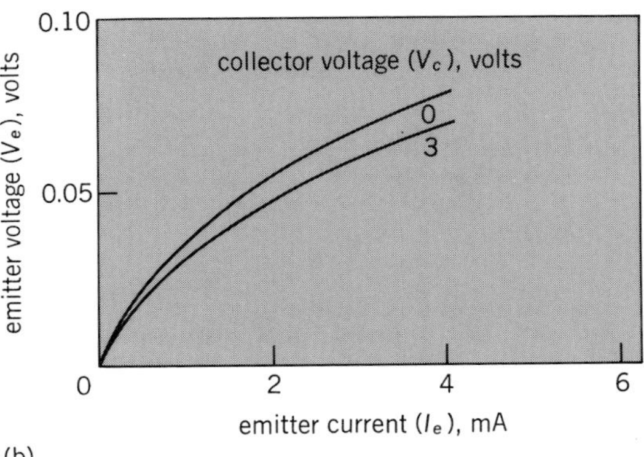


**Fig. 2. Typical transistor dc characteristics. (*a*) Collector characteristics. (*b*) Emitter characteristics.**

on through the base region and out the collector, while only a small fraction (here 0.016) flows out the base connection.

For a fixed value of emitter current $I_e$ there is a fixed value of collector current $\alpha I_e$ added to the collector-barrier leakage current $I_{co}$, giving a total collector current, $I_c = I_{co} + \alpha I_e$. This means that the slope of the dc characteristics should be the same as the slope of the collector-barrier leakage current curve for $I_e = 0$. The typical characteristics in **Fig. 2** illustrate this. The slope of the collector leakage curve is very low since the collector voltage does not influence the relatively fixed number of minority carriers carrying the current. For a discussion of transistor characteristics SEE TRANSISTOR CONNECTION.

***High-frequency effects.*** These originate in three distinct properties of transistors: the transit time of injected carriers across the base region, the charging time of the collector- or emitter-barrier capacitance through the base region and collector-region resistance in series, and the time required to build up the proper density of injected carriers in the base region (called storage-capacity effect). In alloy-junction transistors with a base region of uniform resistivity, the transport of injected carriers across the base is usually the limiting factor. Of course, base transit time alone introduces only a phase shift between the emitter and collector signals, but this time also gives a chance for injected carriers, bunched by the emitter signal, to diffuse apart and therefore degrade the signal (**Fig. 3**).

In double-diffused (drift) transistors the base transit time is usually negligible compared to the charging time of the collector or emitter capacitance, and in some units the storage capacity (often called diffusion capacity) seems to be an appreciable limitation.

Storage capacity also shows up in another way in transistors used as switches. Here it introduces a time delay both in turning on and in turning off the transistor. The turn-off delay is usually longer than the turn-on delay, because the density of injected carriers in the base region has had time to build up to large values during the time the transistor was on, and therefore takes a long time to subside to the level where the transistor can turn off. These delays are only slightly related to the actual time of rise or fall of the collector level, which is determined primarily by the collector-capacitance–base-resistance time constant.

A fabrication technique, called epitaxial growth, is used to minimize the storage capacity effects in high-speed transistors. In this process a transistor structure is formed entirely in a very thin skin of good semiconductor material grown upon the surface of a wafer of heavily doped material. The heavily doped material has very low lifetime for excess carriers and, therefore, a very low storage effect, as well as a low series resistance. The collector junction of such a transistor is close to this low-lifetime material but is formed in the high-quality, epitaxially grown skin so that its properties are not degraded by the heavily doped material. Such transistors are called epitaxial transistors.

Close control of the injection ratio $\gamma$, defined above, is afforded by the fabrication technique of ion implantation. In this technique a beam of ions composed of the desired dopant material is accelerated to a specific kinetic energy and caused to strike the surface of the region to be doped. The ions penetrate the surface and remain embedded in the semiconductor material. By controlling the ion-beam current and the time of bombardment, a very accurate control of the total number of dopant ions in the region is achieved. After heating the semiconductor to diffusion temper-

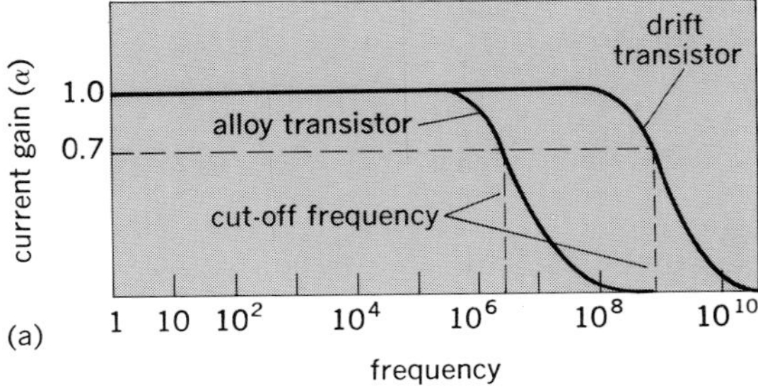


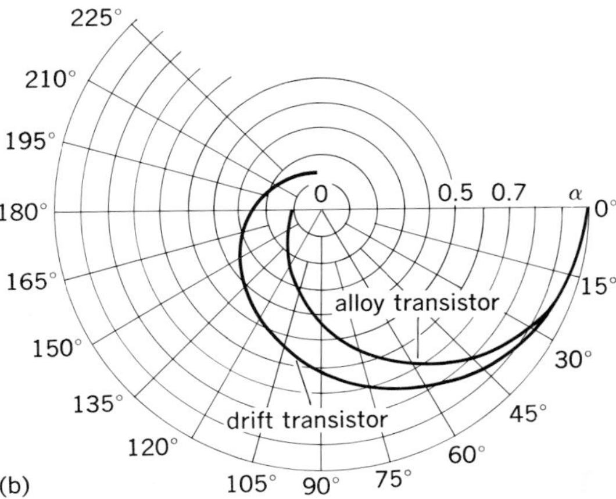


**Fig. 3. Typical transistor frequency characteristics. (*a*) Frequency dependence of $\alpha$. (*b*) Phase of collector current $I_c$ versus emitter current $I_e$.**

ature, the ions move on into the material, creating the emitter and base regions of the double-diffused structure. These regions now have precisely controlled doping and hence show a γ-factor within ±1% of the design value. SEE ION IMPLANTATION.

***Transistor noise.*** Noise is quite low if a low source impedance is used. With source impedances of about 1000 ohms, a good junction transistor will have a noise factor of about 4 dB. The noise factor is independent of the connection but rises with source impedances above 10,000 ohms and with frequencies below 1000 Hz.

***Temperature effects.*** These are most marked in connection with the collector-barrier leakage current with no emitter current flowing $I_{co}$. This current increases exponentially with temperature and leads to a phenomenon called thermal runaway. If a transistor is operated at a given ambient temperature and a given initial power dissipation, this power will soon raise the temperature of the collector barrier, which then draws more current and in turn increases the dissipation. The process is cumulative, and precautions must be taken to stabilize against it. Current gain increases slightly with increased temperature in most *npn* transistors, but this is a small effect unless the current gain is unusually close to unity.

**Power switching.** There are several transistor structures which are used for power switching and make use of current gains greater than unity to achieve a thyraton-like characteristic. These devices are often called four-layer devices since they usually contain four regions of alternating *n*- and *p*-type semiconductor material. Connections are made to the end regions and to one of the interior regions. The end regions are oppositely biased so that the center junction is reverse-biased. The connection to the interior region is then the control and is usually called the gate. When the gate is biased to cause injection of excess carriers across the junction between it and the nearest end connection, the device is triggered on and a saturation current is drawn between the two end connections normally called anode and cathode. Such devices are normally classified as rectifiers but in reality are a form of transistor. SEE CONTROLLED RECTIFIER; SEMICONDUCTOR RECTIFIER.

**Field-effect transistor (FET).** There are two major types of field-effect transistors, the junction-gate FET (JFET) and the insulated-gate FET (IGFET). The IGFET is commonly called MOSFET or MOS transistor. The acronym MOS stands for metal-oxide-semiconductor which describes, in order, the structure of the device from the gate toward the channel. The JFET was developed first, since it involved no technology beyond that of the planar bipolar silicon transistor. The development of the MOSFET was delayed while the technology was extended to stable control of silicon surface potential. The MOSFET is very widely applied in large-scale integration, particularly in implementing large random-access high-speed memories for computers. SEE COMPUTER STORAGE TECHNOLOGY; INTEGRATED CIRCUITS; SEMICONDUCTOR MEMORIES.

***JFET.*** **Figure 4*a*** shows a section of a JFET. The channel consists of relatively low-conductivity semiconductor material sandwiched between two regions of high-conductivity material of opposite type. When these junctions are reverse-biased, the junction depletion regions encroach upon the channel and finally, at a high reverse bias, pinch it off entirely. The thickness of the channel, and hence its conductivity, is controlled by the voltage on the two gates. This device is therefore normally on and may be switched off. It is called a depletion-mode FET. In practice this FET has an input impedance several orders of magnitude greater than that of a silicon bipolar transistor. JFETs are made in both *n*-channel and *p*-channel types. They are used in amplifiers, oscillators, mixers, and switches. The general performance limits are about 500 MHz, 1 W, 100 V, and 100 mA (saturation drain current). They also find application in integrated circuits employing bipolar transistors since their technology is compatible.

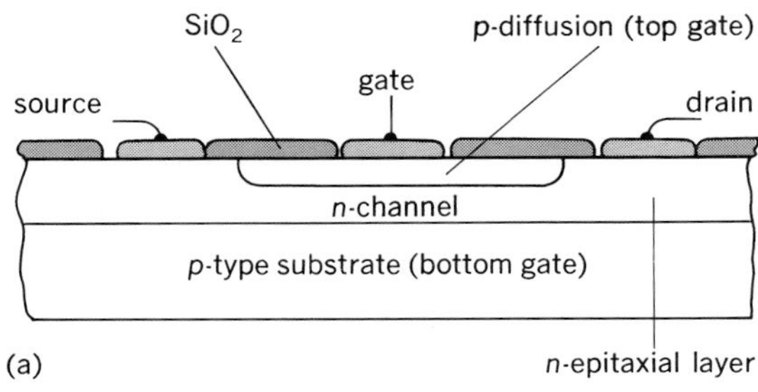


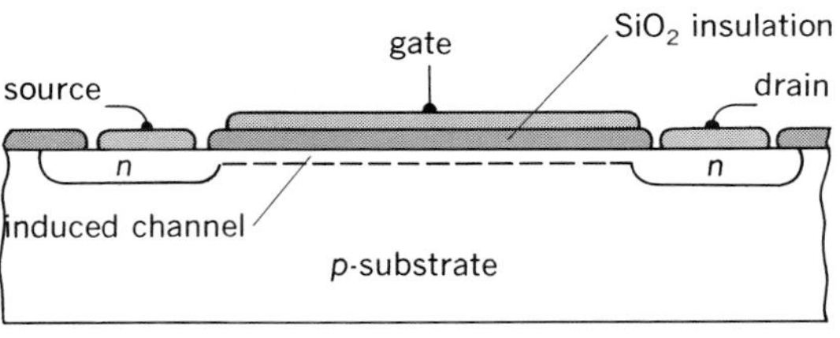


**Fig. 4. Field-effect transistors. (*a*) Junction-gate FET (JFET). (*b*) Insulated-gate FET (IGFET or MOSFET).**

***MOSFET.*** Figure 4*b* shows a section of a MOSFET. Here the source and drain regions consist of *n* diffusion in a *p*-type substrate. The gate is a metal film evaporated on a thin silicon dioxide ($SiO_2$) insulator spanning the separation between the source and drain. With no voltage on the gate, the source and drain are insulated from each other by their surrounding junctions. When a positive voltage is applied to the gate, electrons are induced to move to the surface of the *p*-type substrate immediately beneath the gate, producing a thin surface of induced *n*-type material which now forms a channel connecting the source and drain. Such a surface layer is called an inversion layer since it is of opposite conductivity type to the substrate. The number of induced electrons is directly proportional to the gate voltage, so that the conductivity of the channel increases with gate voltage. This device is called an *n*-channel enhancement-mode MOSFET. It is normally off at zero gate voltage.

Because of the quality of the silicon dioxide gate insulator, the input impedance of a MOSFET is several orders of magnitude greater than that of a JFET. Typical MOSFET dc characteristics are shown in **Fig. 5**. The low-drain voltage channel resistance is inversely proportional to $(V_{gs} - V_{th})$, where $V_{gs}$ is the gate-source voltage and $V_{th}$ is the threshold voltage, and the saturation drain current is proportional to $(V_{gs} - V_{th})^2$.

MOSFET devices are fabricated in both *p*-channel and *n*-channel types, as well as for both depletion (normally on) and enhancement (normally off) modes

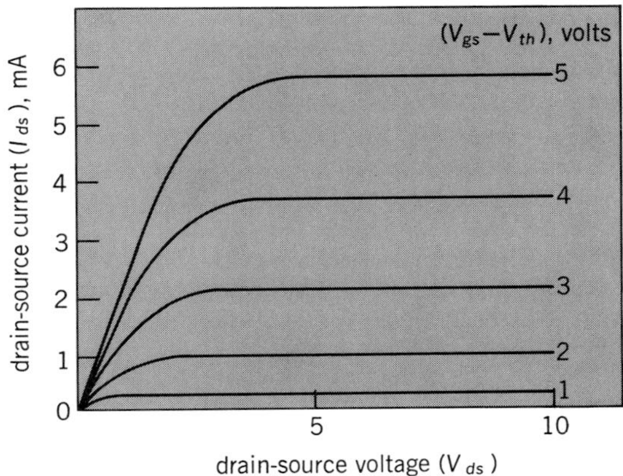


**Fig. 5. Typical MOSFET drain characteristics.**

of operation. In a MOSFET the mode of operation is determined by a threshold voltage of the gate at which the device changes from off to on, or vice versa. In modern technology this threshold voltage can be set for a wide range of values by the use of ion implantation through the gate oxide.

MOSFET discrete devices are used for ultrahigh-input impedance amplifiers such as electrometers where the input leakage current is less than $10^{-14}$ A. Dual-gate depletion types can be used as mixers up to 1000 MHz, and power-switching types (the VMOS discussed below) are good to 25 W, 2 A, or 100 V. Most integrated circuits using MOSFETs are called CMOS integrated circuits, where the C stands for complementary. These circuits use $n$-channel and $p$-channel types together to achieve digital logic. Typical propagation delay times through small-scale integrated building-block circuits such as three-input NAND or NOR gates is about 20 nanoseconds for a 20-picofarad load. At a 10-MHz clock rate, the power dissipation for such a gate is about 10 mW. For large-scale integration, a typical 16 kilobit random-access memory has an access time of 200 ns, an active power of 500 mW, and a standby power of 20 mW.

***VMOS and SOS.*** There are a number of variations of the MOS technology. Two of particular interest are VMOS (V for vertical) and SOS (silicon on sapphire). The VMOS device is fabricated by etching a notch down through a planar double-diffused structure similar to that of an *npn* bipolar transistor. The surface of the notch is first oxidized and then covered with the gate metallization. The source contact bridges the $n^+$-$p$ junction near the surface, and the drain connection corresponds to the collector contact of the bipolar structure. The channel length is now determined by the thickness of the $p$ region. This allows controlled short channels and gives both high current and high voltage capability.

The SOS device is fabricated in a very small silicon body grown epitaxially on a sapphire substrate. An experimental MOS/SOS 1000-bit memory has shown a standby power of only 1 microwatt.

**Double-base diode.** Also called a unijunction transistor, this consists of a single rectifying contact situated approximately midway along a semiconductor bar which carries two ohmic contacts at its ends. If a steady bias is applied between the ends of the bar, a negative-resistance diode characteristic is observed between the rectifying contact and one end of the bar. This device is used primarily for switching.

**Transistor manufacture.** The manufacture of transistors has required a whole new field of exacting technology. Good semiconductor material requires the maintenance of chemical purities far beyond the spectroscopic range. A purity of 1 part in $10^8$ is not unusual. Most devices must be made from oriented single crystals of semiconductor material which can have only very low densities of structural defects.

Physical tolerances of the high-frequency transistor structures are microscopic; the separation of emitter and collector junctions must be of the order of a few micrometers in these units.

To solve these problems new techniques have appeared. Purity is achieved by melting a small zone of a bar, or ingot, and gradually passing this molten zone from one end of the bar to the other. Impurities in the material remain in the liquid phase and are carried along with the molten zone, leaving high-purity material behind.

Tolerances are achieved by a collection of new techniques, such as epitaxial growth, solid-state diffusion, ion implantation, and the photolithographic delineation of diffusion masks.

*Lloyd P. Hunter*

***Bibliography.*** J. Millman, *Microelectronics*, 1979; S. M. Sze, *Physics of Semiconductor Devices*, 1981; E. S. Yang, *Fundamentals of Semiconductor Devices*, 1978.

## Transistor connection

The method of connecting a transistor into a circuit. Bipolar transistor connections and field-effect transistor (FET) connections will be discussed.

**Bipolar transistor connection.** The common-emitter, common-base, and common-collector connections are the most frequently used connections of bipolar transistors, and of these the common-emitter connection is by far the most popular for transistors with current gain $\alpha < 1.0$. To compare these connections, the following should be examined: small-signal current gain, voltage gain, input resistance with shorted output, and output resistance with open-circuited input. Shorted output means an ac short; the dc bias voltage is still present. Open-circuited input means a constant dc current bias. These quantities are easily measured and are useful in calculating the performance of a transistor in a circuit connection.

***Common-emitter connection.*** This connection (**Fig. 1**) has a base-to-emitter input and a collector-to-emitter output connection. The slope of the illustrated $I_c$ versus $V_c$ characteristics gives a commonly used conductance $h_{cc}$, which is the reciprocal of the output resistance with open-circuited ($I_b$ = constant) input.

The current gain $h_{cb}$ (equal to $\partial I_c/\partial I_b$, with $V_c$ = constant) is related to the current gain $\alpha$ by $h_{cb} = \alpha/(1 - \alpha)$. The input resistance $h_{bb}$, with a short-circuited ($V_c$ = constant) output, is given by the slope of the $V_b$ versus $I_b$ characteristics. Finally the voltage gain $1/h_{bc}$ (equal to $\partial V_c/\partial V_b$, with $I_b$ = constant) can be obtained from the separation of these curves. Typical values of these small signal parameters are $h_{bb} = 1800$ ohms; $1/h_{bc} = 1600$; $h_{cb} = 50$; and $1/h_{cc} = 0.05 \times 10^6$ ohms.

***Common-base connection.*** This has an emitter-to-base input and a collector-to-base output connection. As with the common-emitter connection, the output resistance $1/h_{cc}$ is found from the slope $h_{cc}$ of the $I_c$

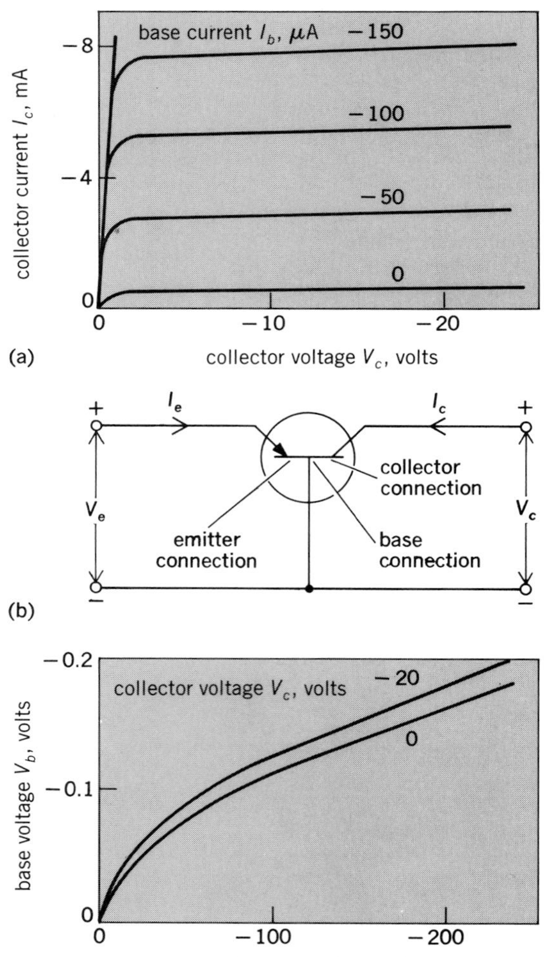


**Fig. 1. Common-emitter connection of an alloy-junction transistor. (*a*) Collector characteristics. (*b*) Schematic diagram. (*c*) Base characteristics.**

versus $V_c$ characteristics. The current gain $h_{ce}$ equals $\partial I_c/\partial I_e$ ($h_{ce} = -\alpha$ because of the assigned polarity of the currents; **Fig. 2**). The input resistance $h_{ee}$ is found from the slope of the $V_e$ versus $I_e$ characteristics. The voltage gain $1/h_{ec}$ equals $\partial V_e/\partial V_c$. Typical values of the common-base parameters are $h_{ee} = 36$ ohms; $1/h_{ec} = 1500$; $h_{ce} = -0.98$; and $1/h_{cc} = 2.5 \times 10^6$ ohms.

***Common-collector connection.*** This connection, as shown in **Fig. 3**, has a base-to-collector input and an emitter-to-collector output connection. Again the output resistance $1/h_{ee}$ is found from the slope $h_{ee}$ of the $I_e$ versus $V_e$ characteristics. The current gain $h_{eb}$ equals $\partial I_e/\partial I_b$. The input resistance $h_{bb}$ is found from the slope of the $V_b$ versus $I_b$ characteristics. The voltage gain $1/h_{bc}$ equals $\partial V_c/\partial V_b$. Typical values of the common-collector parameters are $h_{bb} = 1800$ ohms; $1/h_{be} = 1$; $h_{eb} = -50$; and $1/h_{ee} = 0.05 \times 10^6$ ohms.

***Selection of bipolar transistor connections.*** From the foregoing definitions, it is possible to compare these connections for use in amplifiers. The power gain of the common-emitter connection (current gain times voltage gain) is the highest. This is the reason that this connection is used most frequently. The common-base connection shows the lowest input resistance and the highest output resistance. Its most useful characteristic is its linearity, which gives low distortion when driven by a current source. Accordingly, it is often used with a driver transformer. The common-collector connection shows the highest input resistance and the lowest output resistance. It is somewhat analogous to a cathode follower.

Switching circuits or pulse circuits can be monostable, bistable, or astable. The input characteristic must have a negative-resistance region to be useful in such circuits. Such a characteristic may be achieved by a single transistor if it has a current gain $\alpha > 1.0$. Four-region transistors have such an $\alpha$ and show a negative-resistance region in the base $I_b$ versus $V_b$ characteristic directly, or in the emitter $I_e$ versus $V_e$ characteristic if there is a sufficiently high resistance to the base circuit. It is customary to use more than one transistor to achieve a negative-resistance characteristic, with the exception of the controlled rectifier device used in power switching. The operation of the circuit is monostable if the load line intersects this characteristic in only one point on one of the positive-resistance branches of the curve, bistable if the load line intersects the curve in two such points, and astable if it intersects the curve in only one point and that in the negative-resistance region. The bistable circuit finds wide application in counters and computers. If transistors are used which have $\alpha < 1.0$, two transistors are required for each bistable switching circuit.

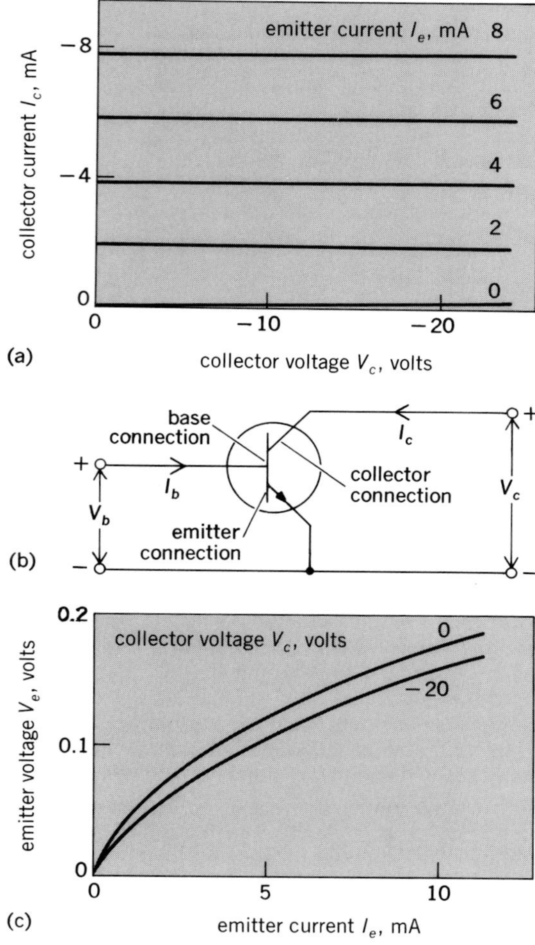


**Fig. 2. Common-base connection of an alloy-junction transistor. (*a*) Collector characteristics. (*b*) Schematic diagram. (*c*) Emitter characteristics.**

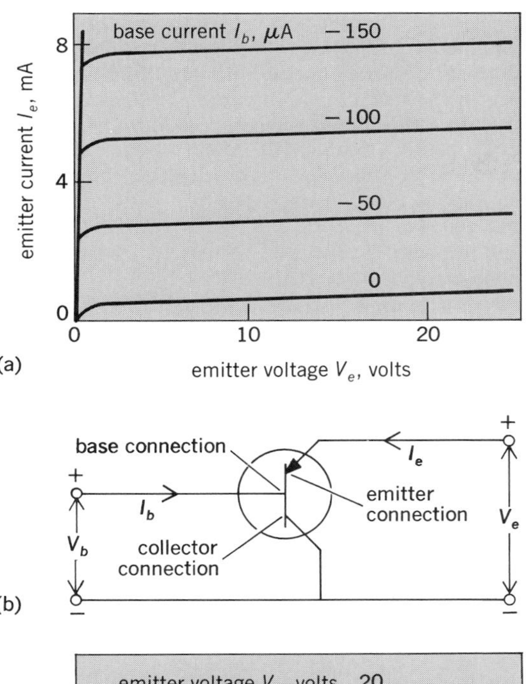


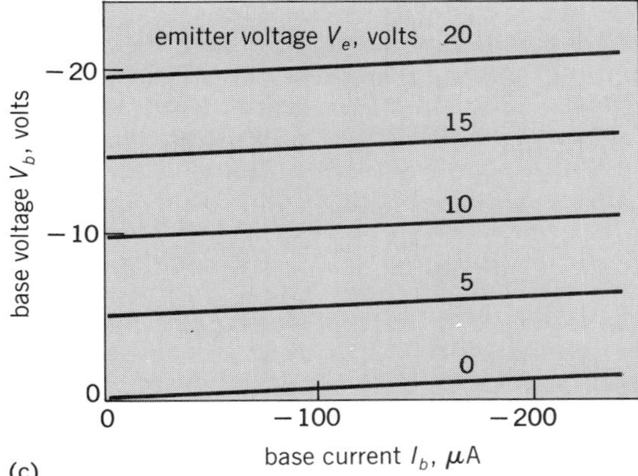


emitter voltage $V_e$, volts 20
15
10
5
0
−20
−10
0
base voltage $V_b$, volts
0
−100
−200
base current $I_b$, μA
(c)

**Fig. 3. Common-collector connection of an alloy-junction transistor. (*a*) Emitter characteristics. (*b*) Schematic diagram. (c) Base characteristics.**

Complementary symmetry is the use of both *pnp* and *npn* transistors together to take full advantage of their opposite bias and signal polarities. For example, an emitter-follower circuit with base input and grounded collector provides a positive drive to a load for a negative base signal in the case of a *pnp* transistor and for a positive base signal in the case of an *npn* transistor. If the two are connected in parallel, they give a positive drive to a load with either polarity of input signal.

**FET connections.** By far the largest use of field-effect transistors (FET) today is in the large-scale integration of computer memory and logic circuits. In particular the *n*-channel MOSFET technology (NMOS) prevails. The basic circuit most used in this technology is the inverter circuit in **Fig. 4*a***. In this circuit a depletion-mode MOSFET is used to load an enhancement-mode MOSFET switching device. The switching device is designated $Q$ and is shown at the bottom of Fig. 4*a*. The load device is designated $L$ and is shown at the top of Fig. 4*a*. The grounded arrows indicate that the substrates of both devices are grounded. The two states of the inverter are given in Fig. 4*b* and are shown in the loaded drain characteristic diagram in Fig. 4*c*.

The nature of an inverter circuit is that if the input voltage goes up the output voltage goes down, and vice versa. Figure 4*b* illustrates this. Considering the circuit of the inverter (Fig. 4*a*), it can be seen that $Q$ and $L$ are in series between the supply voltage $V_{DD}$ and ground. The load device is always conducting because it is a depletion-mode device and because its gate is permanently connected to its source. The switching device may be either conducting or nonconducting, depending on the input signal $V_i$ on its gate terminal. When $V_i$ is positive, electrons are collected in the channel of $Q$ and it is conducting. When conducting, the channel resistance of $Q$ is very much lower than that of $L$. This means that the output voltage $V_0$ is held just above ground. When $V_i$ is nearly zero, the switching device is not conducting and the conducting channel of $L$ holds $V_0$ just below the positive supply voltage $V_{DD}$. The circuit thus fulfills the criterion for inverter action. This behavior is illustrated in Fig. 4*c*. Here the drain characteristic of the load device is drawn as a nonlinear load line on the drain characteristic curves of the switching device. This load line is marked $L$ device. The intersection of the load line with the operating characteristic of the $Q$ device determines the quiescent point of the circuit. SEE LOAD LINE.

For a switching inverter there are two quiescent points. One, where the Q device is not conducting, is

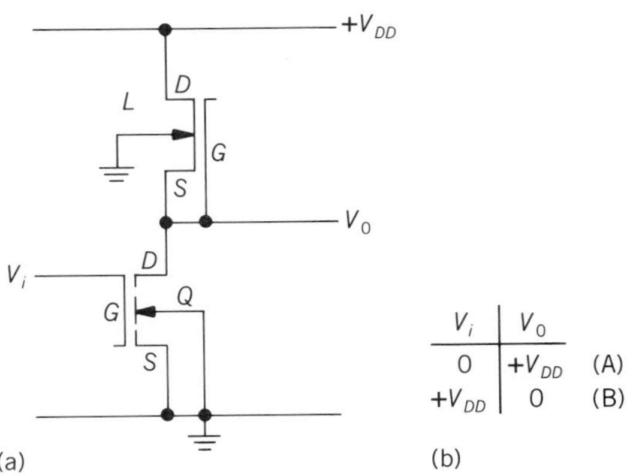


| $V_i$ | $V_0$ | |
|---|---|---|
| 0 | $+V_{DD}$ | (A) |
| $+V_{DD}$ | 0 | (B) |

(b)

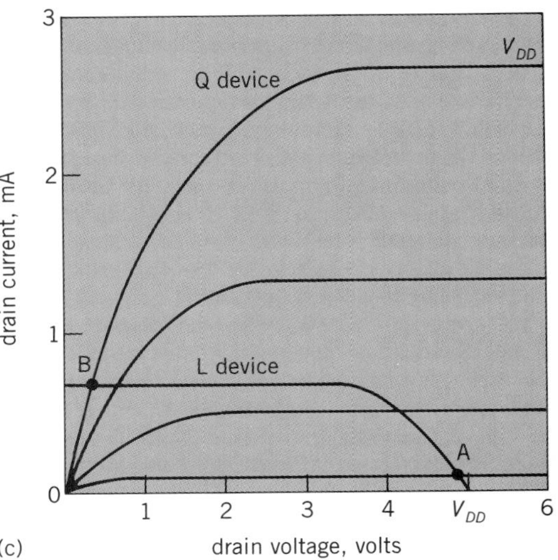


**Fig. 4. Typical *n*-channel MOSFET inverter. (*a*) Circuit; *S* = source, *D* = drain, *G* = gate; *Q* = enhancement-mode switching device; *L* = depletion-mode load device. (*b*) Truth table for the circuit. (c) Loaded drain characteristics.**

designated A in Fig 4$c$ and is called the off-state. The second, where the $Q$ device is conducting, is designated B in Fig. 4$c$ and is called the on-state. There is a single load line while there are several curves in the family of the switching characteristics. The reason for this is that the gate of the load device is connected to its source and cannot change its voltage relative to the source whereas the gate of the switching device can take on any value of input (gate-source) voltage. In the circuit shown, however, the Q device gate voltage moves between the limits of zero and $+V_{DD}$. Some intermediate gate voltage curves are shown as a reminder that there are a multiplicity of states of the inverter between the off-state and the on-state and that considerable power may be dissipated during the switching process. The off-state (A) has negligible standby power drain. The on-state (B) dissipates typically about 0.1 mW. The switching time ratio (pull-up time to pull-down time) is about 4 to 1, and the total switching delay time of a pair of inverters is of the order of 20 nanoseconds.

In small-scale integrated circuit chip components, it is customary to use complementary MOSFET devices (CMOS). In such circuits both $n$-channel and $p$-channel devices are used together, one as the load of the other. The use of complementary devices this way greatly reduces standby power to about 10 nanowatts. *See* COMPUTER STORAGE TECHNOLOGY; INTEGRATED CIRCUITS; LOGIC CIRCUITS; SEMICONDUCTOR; TRANSISTOR.

*Lloyd P. Hunter*

**Bibliography.** J. J. Brophy, *Basic Electronics for Scientists*, 4th ed., 1983; L. P. Hunter (ed.), *Handbook of Semiconductor Electronics*, 3d ed., 1970; J. Millman, *Microelectronics*, 1979.

## Transmission lines

A system of conductors suitable for conducting electric power or signals between two or more termini. For example, commercial-frequency electric power transmission lines connect electric generating plants, substations, and their loads. Telephone transmission lines interconnect telephone subscribers and telephone exchanges. Radio-frequency transmission lines transmit high-frequency electric signals between antennas and transmitters or receivers. In this article the theory of transmission lines is considered first, followed by its application to power transmission lines.

Although only a short cord is needed to connect an electric lamp to a wall outlet, the cord is, properly speaking, a transmission line. However, in the electrical industry the term transmission line is applied only when both voltage and current at one line terminus may differ appreciably from those at another terminus. Transmission lines are described either as electrically short if the difference between terminal conditions is attributable simply to the effects of conductor series resistance and inductance, or to the effects of a shunt leakage resistance and capacitance, or to both; or as electrically long when the properties of the line result from traveling-wave phenomena.

Depending on the configuration and number of conductors and the electric and magnetic fields about the conductors, transmission lines are described as open-wire transmission lines, coaxial transmission lines, cables, or waveguide transmission lines.

**Open-wire transmission lines.** Open-wire lines may comprise a single wire with an earth (ground) return or two or more conductors. The conductors are supported at more or less evenly spaced points along the line by insulators, with the spacing between conductors maintained as nearly uniform as feasible, except in special-purpose tapered transmission lines, discussed later in this section.

Open-wire construction is used for communication or power transmission whenever practical and permitted, as in open country and where not prohibited by ordinances.

Open-wire lines are economical to construct and maintain and have relatively low losses at low and medium frequencies. Difficulties arise from electromagnetic radiation losses at very high frequencies and from inductive interference, or crosstalk, resulting from the electric and magnetic field coupling between adjacent lines accompanying the characteristic field configuration (**Fig. 1**).

**Coaxial transmission lines.** A coaxial transmission line comprises a conducting cylindrical shell, solid tape, or braided conductor surrounding an isolated, concentric, inner conductor which is solid, stranded, or (in certain video cables and delay cables) helically wound on a plastic or ferrite core. The inner conductor is supported by ceramic or plastic beads or washers in air- or gas-dielectric lines, or by a solid polyethylene or polystyrene dielectric.

The purpose of this construction is to have the shell prevent radiation losses and interference from external sources. The electric and magnetic fields shown in

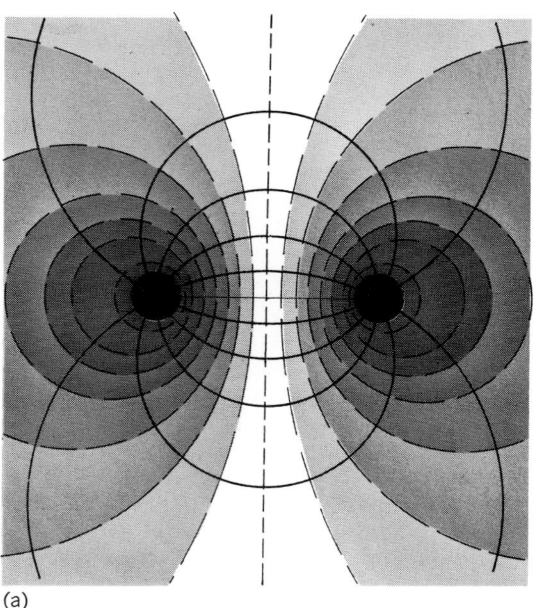
(a)

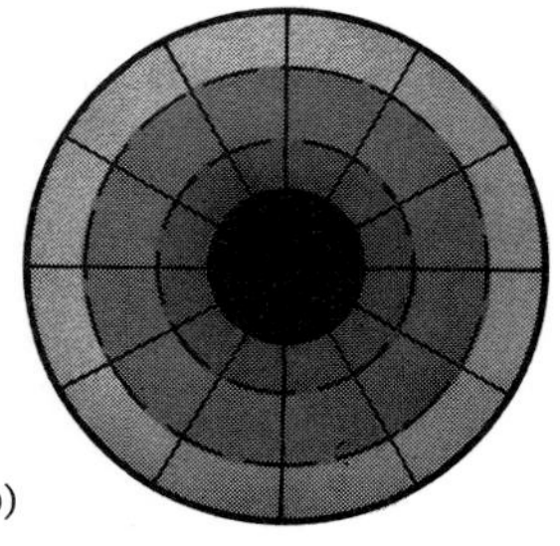
(b)

**Fig. 1. Electric (solid lines) and magnetic (broken lines) fields about two-conductor (*a*) open-wire and (*b*) coaxial transmission lines in a plane normal to the conductors, for continuous and low-frequency currents.**

Fig. 1*b* are nominally confined to the space inside the outer conductor. Some external fields exist, but may be reduced by a second outer sheath.

Coaxial lines are widely used in radio, radar, television, and similar applications.

**Sheathed cables.** Also termed shielded cables, these comprise two or more conductors surrounded by a conducting cylindrical sheath, commonly supported by a continuous solid dielectric. The sheath provides both shielding and mechanical protection.

Coaxial lines, sheathed cables, or shielded cables are often termed simply cables. For cable assemblies of coaxial lines and other circuits SEE COAXIAL CABLE.

**Traveling waves.** When electric power is applied at a terminus of a transmission line, electromagnetic waves are launched and guided along the line. The steady-state and transient electrical properties of transmission lines result from the superposition of such waves, termed direct waves, and the reflected waves which may appear at line discontinuities or at load terminals.

**Principal mode.** When the electric and magnetic field vectors are perpendicular to one another and transverse to the direction of the transmission line, this condition is called the principal mode or the transverse electromagnetic (TEM) mode. The principal-mode electric- and magnetic-field configurations about the conductors are essentially those of Fig. 1. Modes other than the principal mode may exist at any frequency for which conductor spacing exceeds one-half of the wavelength of an electromagnetic wave in the medium separating the conductors. Such high-frequency modes are called waveguide transmission modes. SEE WAVEGUIDE.

In a uniform (nontapered) transmission line, the voltage or current applied at a sending terminal determines the shape of the initial voltage or current wave. In a line with negligible losses the transmitted shape remains unchanged. When losses are present, the shape, unless sinusoidal, is altered, because the phase velocity and attenuation vary with frequency.

If a wave shape is sinusoidal, the voltage and current decay exponentially as a wave progresses. The voltage or current, at a distance $x$ from the sending end, is decreased in magnitude by a factor of $\epsilon^{-\alpha x}$, where $\epsilon$ is the napierian base (2.718), and $\alpha$ is called the attenuation constant. The voltage or current at that point lags behind the voltage or current at the sending end by the phase angle $\beta x$, where $\beta$ is called the phase constant.

The attenuation constant $\alpha$ and the phase constant $\beta$ depend on the distributed parameters of the transmission line, which are (1) resistance per unit length $r$, the series resistance of a unit length of both going and returning conductors; (2) conductance per unit length $g$, the leakage conductance of the insulators, conductance due to dielectric losses, or both; (3) inductance per unit length $l$, determined as flux linkages per unit length of a line of infinite extent carrying a constant direct current; and (4) capacitance per unit length $c$, determined from charge per unit length of a line of infinite extent with constant voltage applied.

The values of $\alpha$ and $\beta$ may be found from complex equation (1), where $j$ is the notation for the imaginary

$$\alpha + j\beta = \sqrt{(r + j2\pi fl)\,(g + j2\pi fc)} \qquad (1)$$

number $\sqrt{-1}$, and $f$ is the frequency of the alternating voltage and current. The complex quantity $\alpha + j\beta$ is often called the propagation constant $\gamma$. Since $r + 2\pi fl$ is the impedance $z$ per unit length of line, and $g + 2\,\pi fc$ is the admittance $y$ per unit length of line, the equation for the propagation constant is often written in the form of Eq. (2). The velocity at which

$$\gamma = \sqrt{zy} \qquad (2)$$

a point of constant phase is propagated is called the phase velocity $v$, and is equal to $2\pi f/\beta$. For negligible losses in the line (when $r$ and $g$ are approximately zero) the phase velocity is $1/\sqrt{lc}$, which is also the velocity of electromagnetic waves in the medium surrounding the transmission-line conductors.

The distributed inductance and resistance of the lines may be modified from their dc values because of skin effect in the conductors. This skin effect, which increases with frequency and conductor size, is usually, but not always, negligible at power frequencies.

**Characteristic impedance.** The ratio of the voltage to the current in either the forward or the reflected wave is the complex quantity $Z_0$, called the characteristic impedance.

When line losses are relatively low, that is, when relationships (3) apply, the characteristic impedance

$$r \ll 2\pi fl \qquad g \ll 2\pi fc \qquad (3)$$

is given by Eq. (4), and is a quantity nearly indepen-

$$Z_0 = \sqrt{l/c} \qquad (4)$$

dent of frequency (but not exactly so since both $l$ and $c$ may be somewhat frequency-dependent). The magnitude of $Z_0$ is used widely, at high frequencies, to identify a type of transmission line such as 50-ohm line, 200-ohm line, and the popular 300-ohm antenna lead-in line used with television antennas. SEE ELECTRICAL IMPEDANCE.

**Distortionless line.** Transmission lines used for communications purposes should be as free as possible of signal waveshape distortion. Two types of distortion occur. One is a form of amplitude distortion due to line attenuation, which varies with the signal frequency. The other, delay distortion, occurs when the component frequencies of a signal arrive at the receiving end at different instants of time. This occurs because the velocity of propagation along the line is a function of the frequency.

Theoretically, a distortionless line can be devised if the line parameters are adjusted so that $r/g = l/c$. In practice this is approached by employing loading circuits. Under these conditions the propagation constant is given by Eq. (5).

$$\gamma = \alpha + j\beta = \sqrt{r/g}(g + j2\pi fc) \qquad (5)$$

The attenuation constant $\alpha$ is $\sqrt{rg}$, which is independent of frequency $f$. Therefore, there will be no frequency distortion.

The phase constant $\beta$ is $2\pi f\sqrt{lc}$, which depends upon frequency. The velocity of propagation along any transmission line is $2\pi f/\beta$, and for the distortionless lines this becomes $1/\sqrt{lc}$. Thus the velocity of propagation is independent of frequency, and there will be no delay distortion.

**Transmission-line equations.** The principal-mode properties of the transmission-line equations are described by Eqs. (6) and (7), in which $e$ and $i$ are in-

$$\frac{\partial e}{\partial x} = -\left(ri + l\frac{\partial i}{\partial t}\right) \quad (6)$$

$$\frac{\partial i}{\partial x} = -\left(ge + c\frac{\partial e}{\partial t}\right) \quad (7)$$

stantaneous values of voltage and current, respectively, $x$ is distance from the sending terminals, and $t$ is time.

For steady-state sinusoidal conditions, the solutions of these equations are given by Eqs. (8) and (9)

$$E = E_s \cosh \gamma x - I_s Z_0 \sinh \gamma x \quad (8)$$

$$I = I_s \cosh \gamma x - \frac{E_s}{Z_0} \sinh \gamma x \quad (9)$$

for voltage $E$ and current $I$ at a distance $x$ from the sending end in terms of voltage $E_s$ and current $I_s$ at the sending end. In Eqs. (8) and (9) $Z_0 = \sqrt{(r + j2\pi fc)/(g + j2\pi fc)}$. All values of current and voltage in these and the following equations are complex.

In terms of receiving-end voltage $E_r$ and current $I_r$, these solutions are given by Eqs. (10) and (11), where

$$E = E_r \cosh \gamma x + I_r Z_0 \sinh \gamma x \quad (10)$$

$$I = I_r \cosh \gamma x + \frac{E_r}{Z_0} \sinh \gamma x \quad (11)$$

$x$ is now the distance from the receiving end.

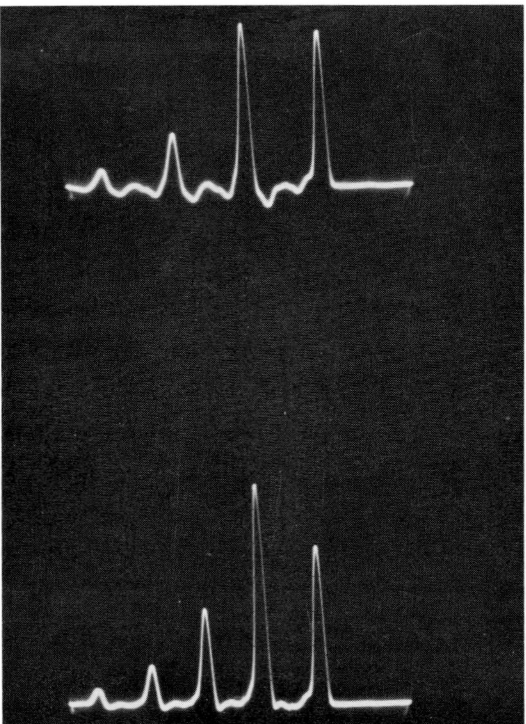

**Fig. 2. Typical transient phenomena in a transmission line. These are oscillographic recordings of voltage as a function of time at the sending end of a 300-m transmission line with the receiving end open-circuited. Time increases from right to left; the first (right-hand) pulse is delivered by a generator, equivalent to an open circuit, so that a new forward wave results from each reflected wave arriving at the sending end. At the end of each 2-μs interval, an echo arrives from the receiving end. In the upper trace, minor discontinuities in the line at intermediate points result in intermediate echos. Intermediate discontinuities are minimized in the lower trace.**

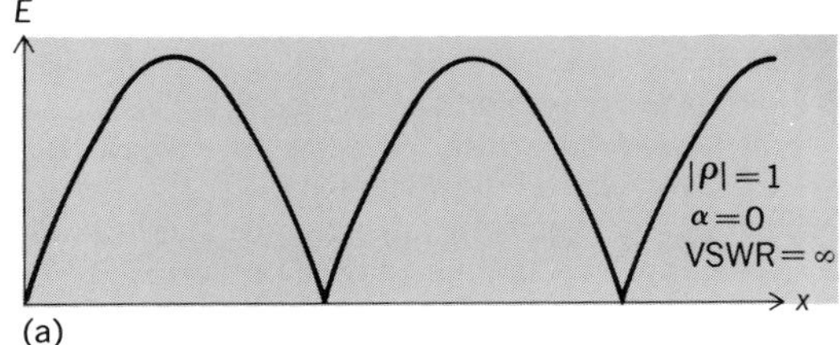


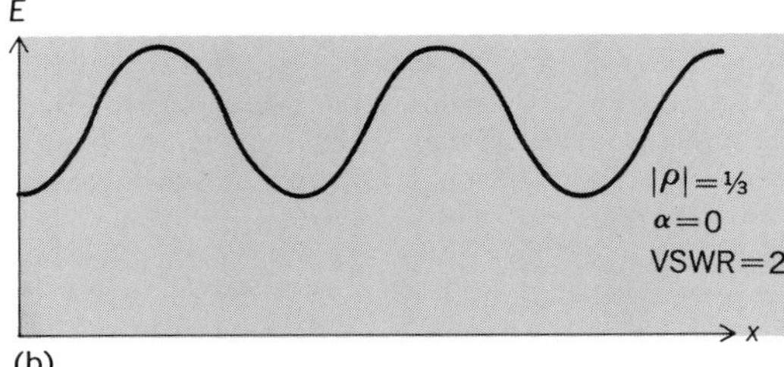


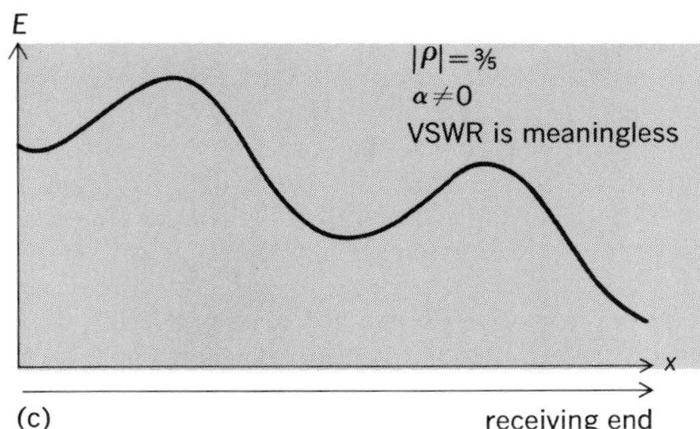


**Fig. 3. Voltage distribution under sinusoidal steady-state conditions on a section of transmission line, illustrating three standing-wave conditions: (*a*) line with negligible losses, reflection coefficient of unity, (*b*) line with negligible losses, reflection coefficient of one-third, and (c) line with finite losses, reflection coefficient of three-fifths. Position of the voltage wave in each case is dependent on angle of phasor value of reflection coefficient. In each case a current maximum (not shown) appears at a voltage minimum in the wavelength.**

**Reflection coefficient.** If the load at the receiving end has an impedance $Z_r$, the ratio of reflected voltage to direct voltage, known as the reflection coefficient $\rho$, is given by Eq. (12).

$$\rho = \frac{Z_r - Z_0}{Z_r + Z_0} \quad (12)$$

When the load impedance is equal to $Z_0$, the reflection coefficient is zero. Under this condition the line is said to be matched.

**Pulse transients.** The transient solutions of Eqs. (6) and (7) are dependent on the particular problem involved. Typical physical phenomena with pulse transients are shown in **Fig. 2**. The characteristic time delay in transmission is often advantageously employed in radar and other pulse-signal systems. For examples *SEE DELAY LINE*.

**Standing waves.** The superposition of direct and reflected waves under sinusoidal conditions in an unmatched line results in standing waves (**Fig. 3**).

***Voltage standing-wave ratio.*** When losses are negligible, successive maxima are approximately equal; under this condition a quantity, the voltage standing-wave ratio, abbreviated VSWR, is defined by Eq. (13).

$$\text{VSWR} = \frac{V_{max}}{V_{min}} \qquad (13)$$

***Power standing-wave ratio.*** This quantity, abbreviated PSWR, is equal to $(\text{VSWR})^2$. Measurements of voltage magnitude and distribution on a line of known characteristic impedance $Z_0$ can be used to determine the magnitude and phase angle of an unknown impedance connected at its receiving end. Lines adapted for such impedance measurements, known as standing-wave lines, are widely used.

**Transmission-line circuit elements.** The impedance $Z_s$ at the sending end of a loss-free section of transmission line that has a length $d$, in terms of its receiving-end impedance $Z_r$, is given by Eq. (14).

$$Z_s = \frac{Z_r \cos \beta d + jZ_0 \sin \beta d}{\cos \beta d + j(Z_r/Z_0) \sin \beta d} \qquad (14)$$

This equation describes the property of a length of line which transforms an impedance $Z_r$ to a new impedance $Z_s$. In the simple cases, in which $Z_r$ is a short circuit or open circuit, $Z_s$ is a reactance. Various lengths of line may be used to replace more conventional capacitors or inductors. These properties are widely applied at high frequencies, where suitable values of $\beta x$ require only physically short lengths of line.

**Tapered transmission lines.** Transmission lines with progressively increasing or decreasing spacing are used as impedance transformers at very high frequencies and as pulse transformers for pulses of millimicrosecond duration. Although tapers designed to produce exponential-varying parameters, as in the exponential line, are most common, a number of other tapers are useful. *SEE MICROWAVE TRANSMISSION LINES.*

*Everard M. Williams*

***Bibliography.*** American Radio Relay League, *ARRL Antenna Book*, revised periodically; L. N. Dworsky, *Modern Transmission Line Theory and Applications*, 1979; J. R. Eaton and E. Cohen, *Electric Power Transmission Systems*, 2d ed., 1983; D. G. Fink and H. W. Beaty (eds.), *Standard Handbook for Electrical Engineers*, 12th ed., 1987; P. Graneau, *Underground Power Transmission*, 1979; E. W. Kimbark, *Direct Current Transmission*, vol. 1, 1971; S. Y. King and N. A. Halfter, *Underground Power Cables*, 1982; W. D. Stevenson, Jr., *Elements of Power System Analysis*, 4th ed., 1982; E. Uhlmann, *Power Transmission by Direct Current*, 1975; B. M. Weedy, *Electric Power Systems*, 3d ed., 1979.

## Traveling-wave tube

A microwave electronic tube in which a beam of electrons interacts continuously with a wave that travels along a circuit, the interaction extending over an appreciable distance measured in wavelengths. Traveling-wave tubes are normally used in amplifiers with exceedingly wide bandwidths. Typical bandwidths are 10–100% of the center frequency, with gains of 20–60 dB. Such traveling-wave amplifiers serve at the inputs to sensitive radars or communication receivers. High-power traveling-wave amplifiers operated as the final stages of radars or scatter communication transmitters deliver pulsed powers exceeding a megawatt. For use in satellite transmitters, lightweight traveling-wave amplifiers develop 35 W continuously at 45% overall efficiency.

In a traveling-wave tube amplifier (**Fig. 1**), a thermionic cathode produces the electron beam. An electron gun initially focuses the beam, and additional focusing means retain the electron stream as a beam throughout the length of the tube until the beam strikes the collector electrode. Microwave energy enters the tube near the electron gun and propagates along a slow-wave circuit. The tube delivers amplified microwave energy into a matched load connected near the collector end. The slow-wave circuit serves to propagate the microwave energy along the tube at approximately the same velocity as that of the electron beam. Interaction between beam and wave is continuous along the tube with contributions adding in phase.

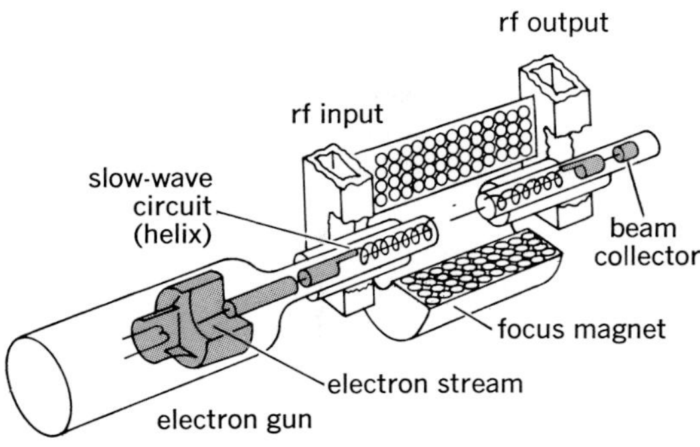


**Fig. 1. Traveling-wave tube.**

In principle, operation in a traveling-wave tube is similar to that in a klystron: Velocity modulation of the electrons results in current modulation of the beam because of the nonzero transit time. However, unlike a klystron, the traveling-wave tube provides for the process to take place continuously along the slow-wave circuit. Thus, at one point along the circuit, the microwave field accelerates the electrons axially. As these electrons proceed along the tube, they bunch with those ahead. At the same point along the circuit, but a half-cycle later in time, the microwave field decelerates electrons; these electrons bunch with those behind. Because average velocity of the electrons is made to be slightly faster than the velocity of the energy on the slow-wave circuit, the electron bunches that form drift into a decelerating microwave field, thereby delivering energy to the field. In this manner the original energy in the electron beam is converted into microwave energy and delivered to the slow-wave circuit. Because of the continuous distributed interaction, the circuit wave grows exponentially as it travels along the tube.

Among the particular design features of a traveling-wave tube are the electron gun, means for focusing the beam, the slow-wave circuit, and the collector.

**Electron gun.** The usual electron gun for a traveling-wave tube is a cylindrical cathode with a plane face followed by a focusing electrode and an anode (**Fig. 2*a***). The face of the cathode is the active emit-

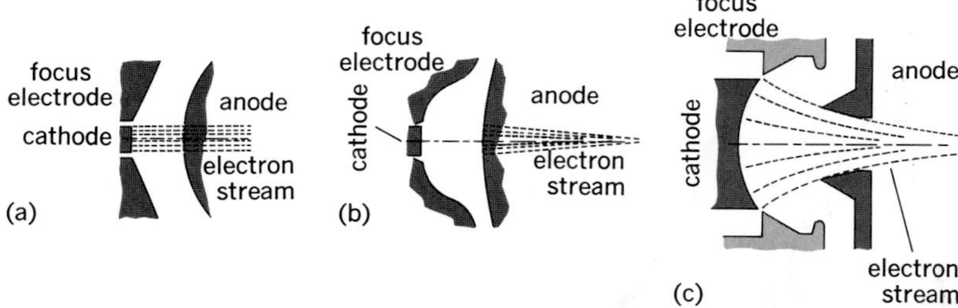


**Fig. 2. Electron guns for traveling-wave tubes. (*a*) Pierce gun. (*b*) Pierce gun with converging flow. (*c*) High-perveance gun.**

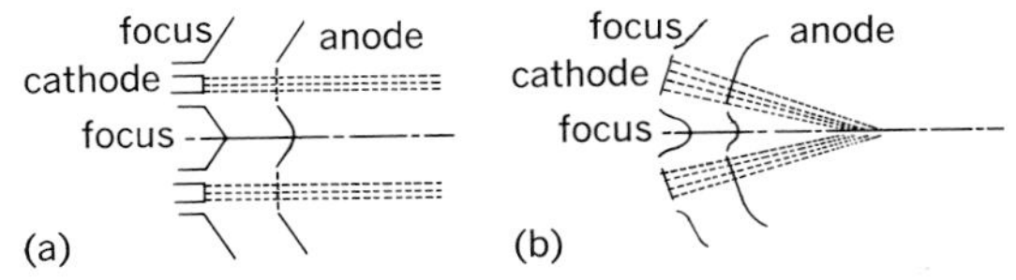


Fig. 3. Hollow-beam electron guns. (a) Parallel flow. (b) Converging flow.

ting surface. The focusing electrode (or beam-forming electrode) is biased close to cathode potential, producing a repelling force on the electrons to counteract the beam-spreading space-charge forces within the beam. Thus, the beam leaves the gun with electron trajectories straight and parallel. Because of this beam configuration, current density is limited to that available from the cathode. For an oxide-coated cathode this density is a fraction of an ampere per square centimeter of oxide-coated cathode. To make the perveance of such a gun much above $1 \times 10^{-6}$ is difficult; perveance is defined by Eq. (1).

$$\text{Perveance} = \frac{\text{dc current}}{(\text{dc beam voltage})^{3/2}} \qquad (1)$$

If higher current densities are required than those obtainable directly from the cathode surface, converging guns are designed (Fig. 2*b*). Spherical electrodes produce radial electron flow to concentrate the beam. For perveances above $1 \times 10^{-6}$, the anode aperture becomes so large that the focusing field for simple electrode geometries is distorted. More controlled shapes of focus electrode and anode (Fig. 2*c*) result in perveances as high as $5 \times 10^{-6}$. Some high-perveance guns are constructed with spherical control grids close to the spherical cathode; this construction permits pulsing of the electron beam from a low-voltage source.

For higher-perveance guns in power tubes or in backward-wave tubes, hollow electron beams may be desirable. Gun design for a hollow beam is similar to that for a solid beam, except that focusing electrodes are placed inside the beam as well as outside it (**Fig. 3*a***). Convergent flow guns for hollow beams, although more difficult to design than those for solid beams, can be made using a similar structure (Fig. 3*b*).

For low-noise guns, additional noise-reducing electrodes are introduced to modify the space-charge waves produced by the statistical fluctuation of current and velocity of the electrons as they emerge from the cathode. Without such noise-reducing means, the noise figure of a traveling-wave tube amplifier is in the range of 15–30 dB; with low-noise guns that have a series of electrodes each at different dc potentials, noise figures as low as 3.5 dB are possible. The dc potential profile along the beam is adjusted for optimum noise reduction by means of these electrodes (**Fig. 4**).

**Focusing methods for the beam.** To hold the beam in focus throughout the interaction region of the tube, beam focusing is normally required to overcome the space-charge spreading forces of the relatively high-density beams in these tubes. The simplest focusing method is a longitudinal fixed magnetic field along the length of the tube (**Fig. 5*a***). This method is called confined flow. In confined flow, any tendency of an electron to move radially outward is converted by the magnetic field to a tight spiraling motion. The required magnetic field is typically from a few hundred to a few thousand gauss. Although such a field strength can be obtained from permanent magnets or electromagnets, the structure may be undesirably heavy. However, this focusing scheme is usually used for low-noise tubes, the magnetic field in the critical gun region often being higher than that in the interaction region.

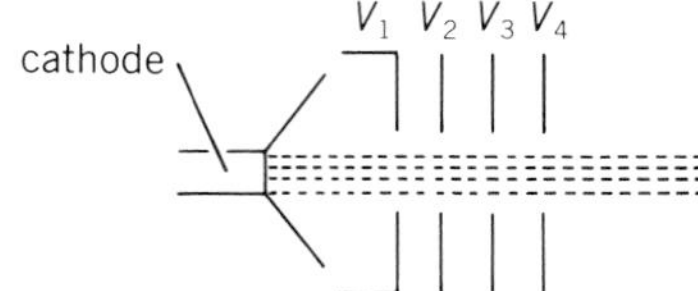


Fig. 4. Low-noise disk-type gun with graded acceleration.

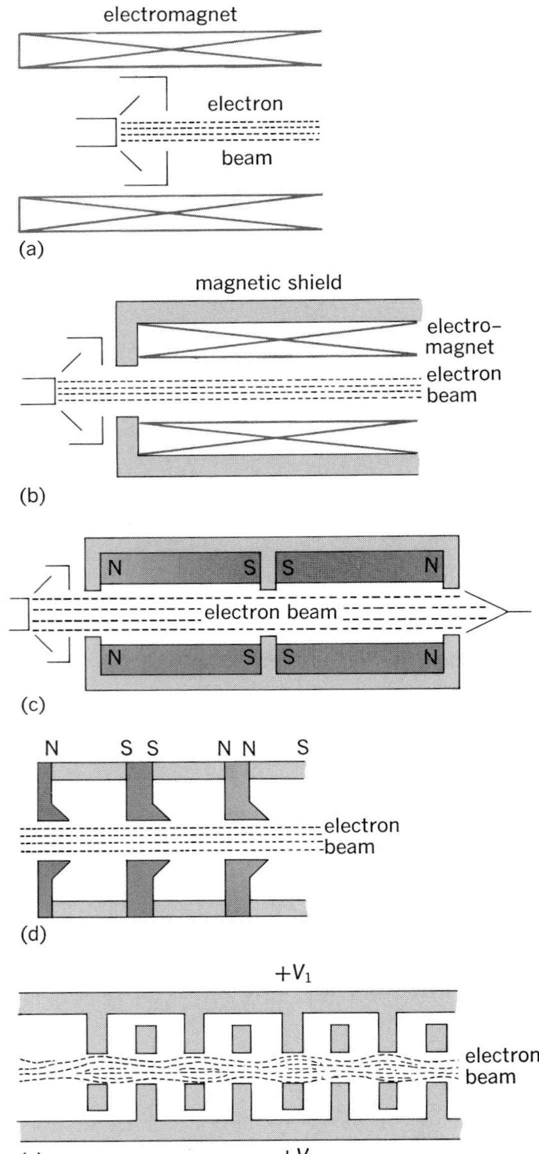


Fig. 5. Beam-confining methods. (a) Confined flow. (b) Brillouin flow. (c) Single-reversal focusing. (d) Periodic magnetic lens focusing. (e) Electrostatic lens focusing.

A similar method of focusing is called space-charge balanced flow. For this method, the magnetic field in the gun region is lower than the field strength in the interaction region. At the transition between the two

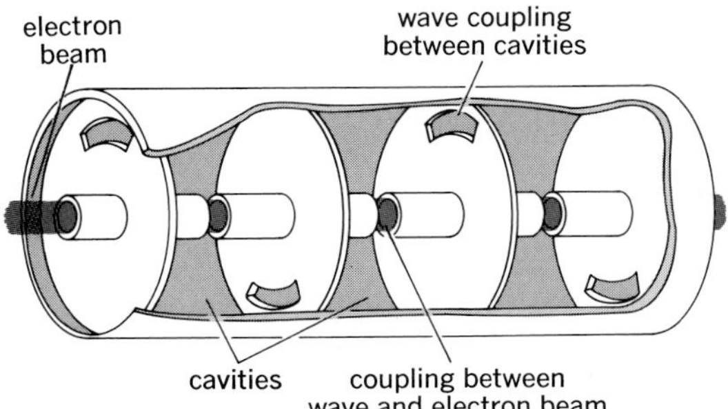


**Fig. 6. Coupled-cavity slow-wave circuit for a high-power traveling-wave tube.**

values of magnetic field strength the beam is given a rotation with a direction to produce an inward force as the beam proceeds along the axial magnetic field in the interaction region. This inward force counterbalances the outward forces from space charge and from the centrifugal force set up by the rotation. A special type of space-charge balanced flow is called Brillouin flow; there is no magnetic field at the cathode (Fig. 5*b*).

In some tubes with permanent-magnet focusing, two bar magnets with like poles adjacent produce a reversal of the magnetic field (Fig. 5*c*). Such single-reversal focusing results in considerable saving in magnet weight.

Magnetic or electrostatic lenses for focusing have been developed for many traveling-wave tubes, with considerable saving in weight. A system of magnetic lenses requires a periodic magnetic field, which is usually produced by permanent magnets (Fig. 5*d*). A system of electrostatic lenses is attractive because of its further reduction in weight, but it is limited in application, being easy to apply only with slow-wave circuits that have natural separations for the application of different dc potentials, such as folded-line circuits (Fig. 5*e*). Periodic magnetic focusing has so far proved the more practical and is widely used.

**Slow-wave circuit.** In order that the electromagnetic signal wave will travel along the tube at a velocity approximately equal to the beam velocity, the signal is guided by a slow-wave circuit. Beam velocity is typically 2–10% of the velocity of a free-space electromagnetic wave. The signal must be slowed down to this velocity at all wavelengths within the bandwidth of the tube. The electric field produced by the slow-wave circuit at the beam for a given power on the circuit is also of interest. This relation, termed the interaction impedance, is given by Eq. (2) in

$$K = \frac{(\text{ac electric field at beam})^2}{2(\text{average power flow on circuit})\beta^2} \quad (2)$$

which β, which is another important characteristic, is the phase constant.

A helix is one of the simplest and best slow-wave circuits; it is used in most traveling-wave tubes (Fig. 1). The electromagnetic signal wave travels along the wire at about the free-space velocity. Consequently the signal phase velocity along the tube axis is given by Eq. (3). As this approximation shows, since phase

$$v_p \approx \text{free-space velocity} \left(\frac{\text{pitch}}{\text{circumference}}\right) \quad (3)$$

velocity is independent of wavelength, wide-band amplifiers are possible. A helix also has good interaction impedance.

Helix tubes have delivered up to 250 W of continuous output power at frequencies as high as 18 GHz. For higher power outputs, coupled-cavity slow-wave circuits are generally used (**Fig. 6**). This circuit has a narrower bandwidth than does a helix, 10% of center frequency being typical.

Other design features of the circuit are the coupling in and out and the providing of attenuation so that reflected waves do not cause the tube to oscillate. The couplings must be matched over the desired operating band to eliminate reflections. This requirement necessitates careful design. Attenuation is provided relatively easily in low-power tubes by lossy material sprayed onto the circuit or onto its dielectric supports near the center of the tube. In high-power coupled-cavity circuits, loss-impregnated ceramics are placed in selected cavities. When the lossy cavities are separated by sections of lossless circuit with 20 dB of gain, stability is good with only negligible degradation of efficiency.

**Beam collector.** The collector electrode and the slow-wave circuit are often connected to the same dc potential for simplicity. The interaction between electrons and signal wave has, however, produced a spread in electron velocities. If the collector potential is made low enough to collect the slowest-moving electron, overall efficiency is improved. The technique is used extensively in satellite applications.

For the backward-wave class of traveling-wave tubes *SEE* BACKWARD-WAVE TUBE. For other microwave tubes *SEE* KLYSTRON; MAGNETRON; MICROWAVE TUBE.

*James W. Gewartowski*

***Bibliography.*** C. H. Dix and W. H. Aldous, *Microwave Valves*, 1966; J. W. Gewartowski and H. A. Watson, *Principles of Electron Tubes*, 1965; S. Liao, *Microwave Devices and Circuits*, 1980.

## Trigger circuit

An electronic circuit that generates or modifies an existing waveform to produce a pulse of short time duration with a fast-rising leading edge. This waveform, or trigger, is normally used to initiate a change

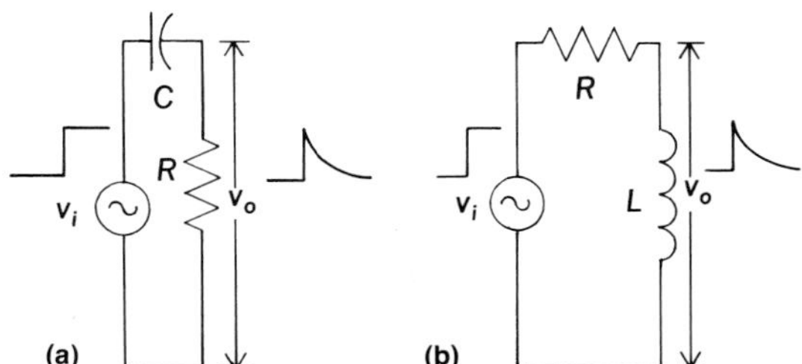


**Fig. 1. Simple peaking circuits: (a) resistance-capacitance network; (b) resistance-inductance network.**

of state of some relaxation device, such as a multivibrator. The most important characteristic of the waveform generated by a trigger circuit is usually the fast leading edge. The exact shape of the falling portion of the waveform often is of secondary importance, although it is important that the total duration time is not too great. A pulse generator such as a blocking oscillator may also be used and identified as a trigger

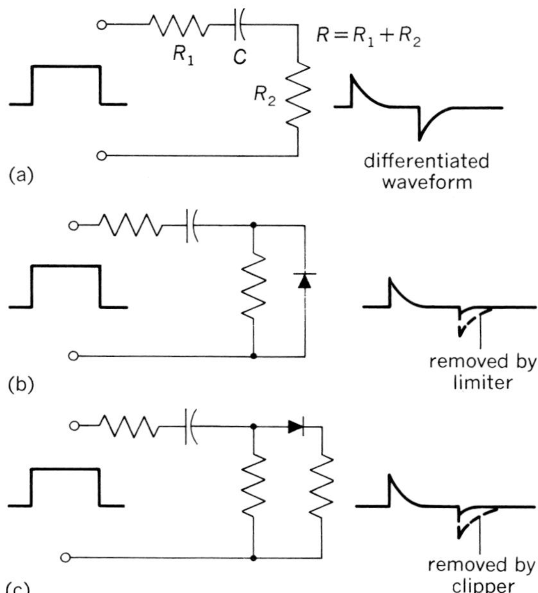


**Fig. 2.** **Differentiated pulses. (*a*) Basic circuit. (*b*) Limiting unwanted portion. (c) Clipping unwanted portion.**

circuit if it generates sufficiently short pulses. SEE BLOCKING OSCILLATOR; PULSE GENERATOR.

**Peaking (differentiating) circuits.** These circuits, which accent the higher-frequency components of a pulse waveform, cause sharp leading and trailing edges and are therefore used as trigger circuits. The simplest form of peaking circuits are the simple *RC* (resistance-capacitance) and *RL* (resistance-inductance) networks shown in **Fig. 1**. If a steep wavefront of amplitude $V$ is applied to either of these circuits, the output will be a sudden rise followed by an exponential decay according to the equation $v_0 = V\epsilon^{-kt}$, where $k = 1/RC$ or $R/L$.

These circuits are often called differentiating circuits because the outputs are rough approximations of the derivative of the input waveforms, if the *RC* or *R/L* time constant is sufficiently small.

If the pulse is applied to the differentiating circuits, the resultant waveform shown in **Fig. 2** may be used as a trigger. It is sometimes necessary, however, to remove by limiting or clipping the undesired portion of the waveform to prevent circuits from responding to it.

The *RL* circuit of Fig. 1 cannot be considered in its simplest form when extremely fast rise times are required because of the distributed capacitance and small series resistance associated with the inductance. A more accurate representation of the circuit is that in **Fig. 3**. The response is limited as shown for a fixed value of $L$ and $C$. The value for $k = 1$ is referred to as critical damping. A value of $k$ slightly less than unity provides a pulse that is a suitable trigger for many applications.

**Ringing circuits.** A circuit of the form shown in Fig. 3 that is highly underdamped, or oscillatory ($k \gg 1$), and is supplied with a step or pulse input is often referred to as a ringing circuit. When used in the output of a field-effect or bipolar transistor as in **Fig. 4**, this circuit can be used as a trigger circuit. When the input pulse is applied, current in the output circuit is immediately cut off. Since the current in $L$ cannot change instantaneously, it flows in the $LC$ circuit in an oscillatory manner, gradually decaying because of the resistance in the circuit. However, if the diode is in the circuit, the circuit will be highly overdamped for the negative portion of the oscillatory waveform, and the oscillations will be damped out as shown.

If a transistor is used as the current source and operated near saturation, damping will take place when the transistor goes into saturation as shown in **Fig. 5**.

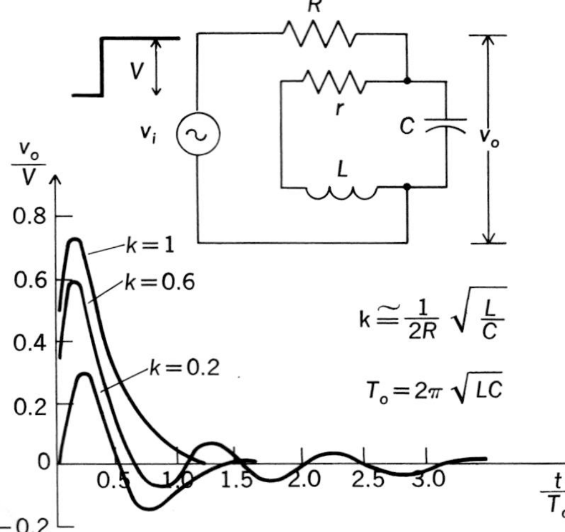


**Fig. 3. Resistance-inductance-capacitance peaking circuit.**

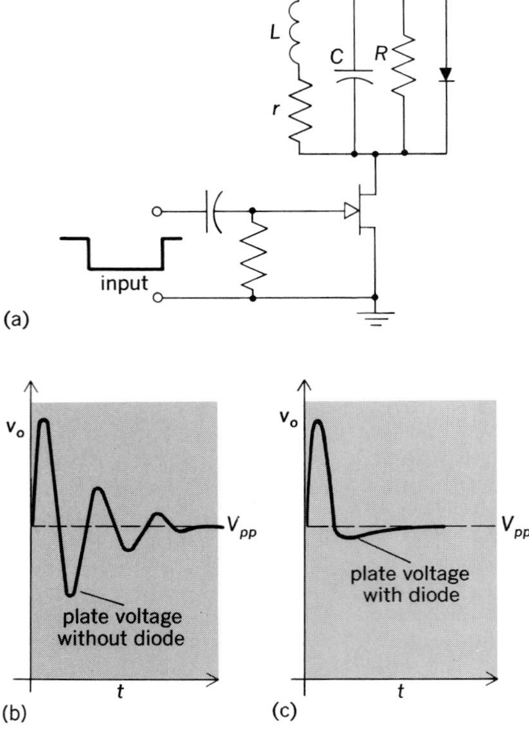


**Fig. 4. Ringing circuit as trigger source. (*a*) Circuit diagram. (*b*) Plate-voltage waveform without diode limiter. (c) Plate-voltage waveform with diode limiter.**

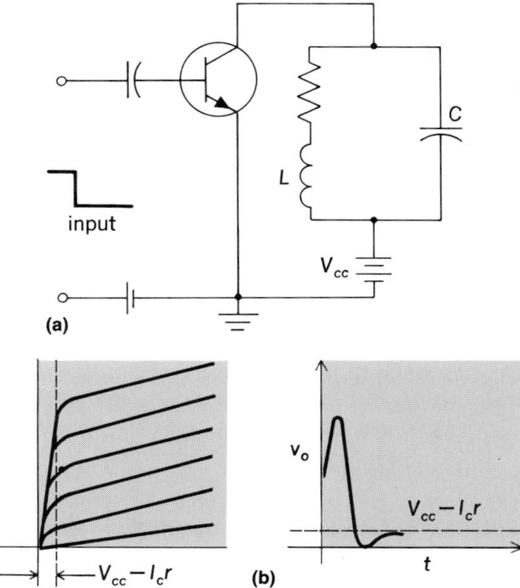


**Fig. 5. Ringing circuit with transistor saturation damping: (*a*) circuit diagram; (*b*) waveforms.**

The diode is not required. For other waveforms SEE WAVE-SHAPING CIRCUITS.

*Glenn M. Glasford*

**Bibliography.** D. G. Fink and D. Christiansen, *Electronics Engineers' Handbook*, 2d ed., 1982; J. Millman and H. Taub, *Pulse, Digital and Switching Waveforms*, 1965; S. Seely, *Electronic Circuits*, 1968; U. Tietze and C. Schenk, *Advanced Electronic Circuits*, 1978.

## Tuning

The process of adjusting the frequency of a vibrating system to obtain a desired result. The term is applicable to a wide variety of such systems, but is most commonly used in connection with musical instruments, electronic circuits, and machinery.

**Musical instruments.** The frequency (pitch) of stringed instruments is determined by the length, mass, and tension of vibrating strings. In members of the violin family, for example, tuning is accomplished by adjusting the tension of each string individually. In keyboard instruments, the process of tension adjustment must achieve a tempered scale in each octave throughout the range of the keyboard. The pitch of wind instruments depends on the volume and shape of a vibrating column of air. Tuning is accomplished by adjusting the shape of the column, usually its length.

**Electronic circuits.** In electronic circuits, there are a variety of frequency-determining elements. The most widely used is a combination of an inductance $L$ (which stores energy in a magnetic field) and a capacitance $C$ (which stores it in an electric field). The frequency of oscillation is determined by the rate of exchange of the energy between the two fields, and is inversely proportional to $\sqrt{LC}$. Tuning is accomplished by adjusting the capacitor or the inductor until the desired frequency is reached. The desired frequency may be one that matches (resonates with) another frequency. This occurs when a piano tuner adjusts a string's tension until its vibration agrees with that of a tuning fork, and when a radio receiver is tuned to a desired station. Another purpose of tuning may be to match a frequency standard, as when setting an electronic watch to keep accurate time. The frequency-determining element in such watches, as well as in radio transmitters, digital computers, and other equipment requiring precise frequency adjustment, is a vibrating quartz crystal. The frequency of vibration of such crystals can be changed over a narrow range by adjusting a capacitor connected to it. SEE QUARTZ CLOCK; RADIO RECEIVER; RESONANCE.

At extremely high radio frequencies (in the range above a gigahertz, or $10^9$ vibrations per second), the inductance and capacitance are not discrete elements, but are distributed over the surface of the apparatus to be tuned. An example is the microwave cavity, in which electromagnetic waves are trapped and reflected. The cavity is tuned by a plunger or other movable element that changes the volume of the cavity. SEE CAVITY RESONATOR; MICROWAVE.

Another function of tuning in electronics is the elimination of undesired signals. Filters for this purpose employ inductors and capacitors, or crystals. The filter is tuned to the frequency of the undesired vibration, causing it to be absorbed elsewhere in the circuit. SEE ELECTRIC FILTER.

Automatic tuning by electrical control is accomplished by a varactor diode. This is a capacitor whose capacitance depends on the direct-current (dc) voltage applied to it. The varactor serves as a portion of the capacitance of the tuned circuit. Its capacitance is controlled by a dc voltage applied to it by an associated circuit, the voltage and its polarity depending on the extent and direction of the mismatch between the desired frequency and the actual frequency. SEE VARACTOR.

The extremely high-frequency electromagnetic waves associated with visible, infrared, and ultraviolet radiation could not be tuned in the manner of the longer radio waves until the advent of the laser. The very narrow spectrum regions of radiation produced by lasers can be tuned by various means, such as temperature control or the insertion of prisms or gratings in the laser cavity. SEE LASER.

**Machinery.** Tuning is a technique also applied to the vibrations of machinery. The vibrating elements are typically weights associated with springs, or their equivalent inertial mass and restoring force. Suppression of undesired vibration is the usual aim of mechanical tuning, by the mechanical equivalent of an electrical filter. SEE RESONANCE (ACOUSTICS AND MECHANICS).

*Donald G. Fink*

## Tunnel diode

A two-terminal semiconductor junction device (also called the Esaki diode) which does not show rectification in the usual sense, but exhibits a negative resistance region at very low voltage in the forward-bias characteristic and a short circuit in the negative-bias direction.

The short-circuit condition exists because both the $p$ and $n$ regions of the device are doped with such high concentrations of the appropriate impurities that

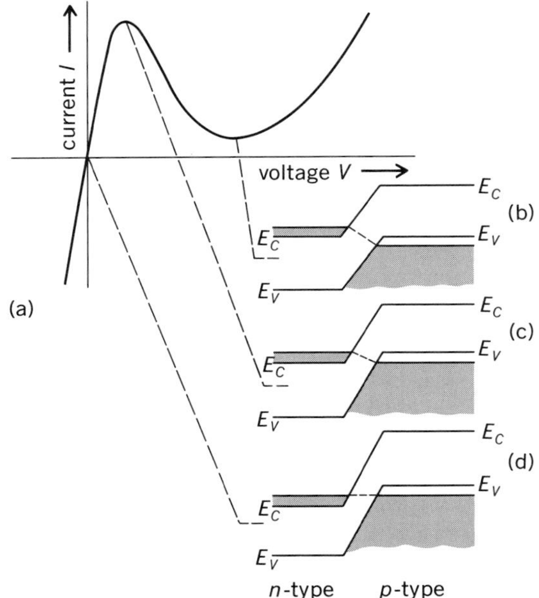


**Tunnel diode characteristic. (a) Forward-bias voltage-current plot. (b) Band-potential diagram for the current minimum. (c) Band-potential diagram for the current maximum. (d) Band-potential diagram for zero bias.**

the normal barrier is rendered sufficiently thin to allow the free passage of current at zero and all negative-bias conditions. The forward-bias characteristic (**illus.** *a*) shows a maximum and a minimum in the current with a negative-resistance region between. Band-potential diagrams show the internal electronic situation existing at the current minimum (illus. *b*), the current maximum (illus. *c*), and zero bias (illus. *d*). The top of the shaded regions of the band-potential diagrams shows the level to which electrons fill the available energy levels in the valence and conduction bands of the materials forming the *pn* junction. The bottom of the conduction band is designated $E_c$ and the top of the valence band $E_v$. No electrons can penetrate the forbidden energy gap between $E_c$ and $E_v$ except in the barrier region, where it is thin enough to allow electron transit by tunneling.

The observed characteristic may be accounted for as follows. In illus. *d* the electron level is the same on both sides of the junction (zero bias). No net current flows because there is no difference in electronic energy across the junction. As forward bias is applied, tunneling current will flow since now the electrons in the *n*-type material on the left will rise to a level above those on the right (illus. *c*). As long as these electrons are still below the top of the valence band $E_v$ on the right, current will increase. When the top of the elevated electron distribution exceeds the level of $E_v$, current will begin to decrease and the diode has entered the negative-resistance region. In illus. *c* the top of the electron distribution on the left is even with $E_v$ on the right, and any further increase in bias will reduce the number of electrons available for the tunneling current. Therefore, illus. *c* corresponds to the current maximum. As bias continues to increase, the point is reached where the bottom of the conduction band $E_c$ on the left is even with $E_v$ on the right, and the entire electron distribution, being above $E_v$, is removed from the tunneling process. At this point, only normal forward-bias diffusion current flows. This current is composed of energetic electrons diffusing over the top of the barrier while remaining in the conduction band. Illustration *b* shows the point at which tunneling is no longer possible and thus corresponds to the current minimum at the end of the negative-resistance region. For further discussion of the properties of junction diodes SEE JUNCTION DIODE; SEMICONDUCTOR; ZENER DIODE.

*Lloyd P. Hunter*

**Bibliography.** J. J. Brophy, *Basic Electronics for Scientists*, 1983; S. M. Sze, *Physics of Semiconductor Devices*, 2d ed., 1981; E. S. Yang, *Fundamentals of Semiconductor Devices*, 1978.

## Tunneling in solids

A quantum-mechanical process which permits electrons to penetrate from one side to the other through an extremely thin potential barrier to electron flow. The barrier would be a forbidden region if the electron were treated as a classical particle. A two-terminal electronic device in which such a barrier exists and primarily governs the transport characteristic (that is, current-voltage curve) is called a tunnel junction.

During the infancy of the quantum theory, L. de Broglie introduced the fundamental hypothesis that matter may be endowed with a dualistic nature—particles such as electrons, particles, and so on, may also have the characteristics of waves. This hypothesis found expression in the definite form now known as the Schrödinger wave equation, whereby an electron or an alpha particle is represented by a solution to this equation. The nature of such solutions implies an ability to penetrate classically forbidden regions of negative kinetic energy and a probability of tunneling from one classically allowed region to another. The concept of tunneling, indeed, arises from this quantum-mechanical result. The subsequent experimental manifestations of this concept, such as high-field electron emission from cold metals, alpha decay, and so on, in the 1920s, can be regarded as one of the early triumphs of the quantum theory. SEE FIELD EMISSION.

In the 1930s, attempts were made to understand the mechanism of electrical transport in resistive contacts between metals and rectifying metal-semiconductor contacts in terms of electron tunneling in solids. In the latter case, since a proposed theoretical model did not properly represent the actual situation, the theory predicted the wrong direction of rectification. In many cases, however, conclusive experimental evidence of tunneling was lacking, primarily because of the rudimentary stage of material science.

**Tunnel diode.** The invention of the transistor in 1947 spurred the progress of semiconductor technology. By the 1950s, materials technology for semiconductors such as Ge and Si was sufficiently advanced to permit the construction of well-defined semiconductor structures. The tunel diode (also called the Esaki diode) was discovered in 1957 by L. Esaki. This discovery demonstrated the first convincing evidence of electron tunneling in solids, a phenomenon which had been clouded by questions for decades. This device is a version of the semiconductor *pn* junction diode which is made of a *p*-type semiconductor, containing mobile positive charges called holes (which correspond to the vacant electron sites), and an *n*-type semiconductor, containing mobile electrons (the electron has a negative charge). Esaki succeeded in making the densities of holes and electrons in the respective regions extremely high by doping a large amount of the appropriate impurities with an abrupt transition from one region to the other. Now, in semiconductors, the conduction band for mobile electrons is separated from the valence band for mobile holes by an energy gap, which corresponds to a forbidden region. Therefore, a narrow transition layer from *n*-type to *p*-type, 5 to 15 nm thick, consisting of the borbidden region of the energy gap, provided a tunneling barrier. Since the tunnel diode exhibits a negative incremental resistance with a rapid response, it is capable of serving as an active element for amplification, oscillation, and switching in electronic circuits at high frequencies. The discovery of the diode, however, is probably more significant from the scientific aspect because it has opened up a new field of research—tunneling in solids. *See* BAND THEORY OF SOLIDS; CIRCUIT (ELECTRONICS); HOLES IN SOLIDS; JUNCTION DIODE; NEGATIVE-RESISTANCE CIRCUITS; SEMICONDUCTOR; SEMICONDUCTOR DIODE; TUNNEL DIODE.

Esaki and colleagues have explored negative resistance phenomena in semiconductors which can be observed in novel tunnel structures. One obvious question is: What would happen if two tunnel barriers are placed close together, or if a periodic barrier structure—a series of equally spaced potential barriers—is made in solids? It has been known that there is a phenomenon called the resonant transmission. Historically, resonant transmission was first demonstrated in the scattering of electrons by atoms of noble gases and is known as the Ramsauer effect. In the abovementioned tunnel structures, it is clear that the resonant tunneling should be observed. In preparing double tunnel barriers and periodic structures with a combination of semiconductors, the resonant tunneling was experimentally demonstrated and negative resistance effects were observed. *See* SEMICONDUCTOR HETEROSTRUCTURES.

**Tunnel junctions between metals.** As discussed above, tunneling had been considered to be a possible electron transport mechanism between metal electrodes separated by either a narrow vacuum or a thin insulating film usually made of metal oxides. In 1960, I. Giaever demonstrated for the first time that, if one or both of the metals were in a superconducting state, the current-voltage curve in such metal tunnel junctions revealed many details of that state. At the time of Giaever's work, the first satisfactory microscopic theory of superconductivity had just been developed by J. Bardeen, L. N. Cooper, and J. R. Schrieffer (BCS theory). Giaever's technique was sensitive enough to measure the most important feature of the BCS theory—the energy gap which forms when the electrons condense into correlated, bound pairs (called Cooper pairs).

The tunneling phenomenon has been exploited in many fields. For example, small-area tunnel junctions are used for mixing and synthesis of frequencies ranging from dc to the infrared region of the spectrum. This leads to absolute frequency measurement in the infrared and provides the most accurate determination of the speed of light. *See* PARAMETRIC AMPLIFIER.

To study nonequilibrium superconducting properties, two tunnel junctions, one on top of the other sharing the middle electrode, are used. One junction seems to inject quasi-particles, while the other detects their effects on the important parameters. Tunnel junctions are also used as a spectroscopic tool to study the phonon and plasmon spectra of the metals and the vibrational spectra of complex organic molecules introduced inside the insulating barriers (tunneling spectroscopy). *See* SUPERCONDUCTIVITY.

**Josephson effects.** Giaever's work opened the door to more detailed experimental investigations—it pioneered a new spectroscopy of high accuracy to study the superconducting state. In 1962, B. Josephson made a penetrating theoretical analysis of tunneling between two superconductors by treating the two superconductors and the coupling process as a single system, which would be valid if the insulating oxide were sufficiently thin, say 2 nanometers. His theory predicted, in addition to the Giaever current, the existence of a supercurrent, arising from tunneling of the bound electron pairs.

This led to two startling conclusions: the dc and ac Josephson effects. The dc effect implies that a supercurrent may flow even if no voltage is applied to the junction. The ac effect implies that, at finite voltage $V$, there is an alternating component of the supercurrent which oscillates at a frequency of 483.6 MHz per microvolt of voltage across the junction, and is typically in the microwave range. The dc Josephson effect was soon identified among existing experimental results, while the direct observation of the ac effect eluded experimentalists for a few years. The effects are indeed quantum phenomena on a macroscopic scale. Extraordinary sensitivity of the supercurrents to applied electric and magnetic fields has led to the development of a rich variety of devices with application in wide areas of science and technology. Superconducting quantum interference devices (SQUIDs) are made of one or more Josephson junctions connected to form one or more closed superconducting loops. Owing to their unprecedented sensitivity, SQUIDs are the main building blocks of many sensitive instruments such as magnetometers, power meters, voltmeters, gradiometers, and low-temperature thermometers. These are finding wide-range application in the fields of solid-state physics, medicine, mineral exploration, oceanography, geophysics, and electronics. Josephson junction and SQUIDs are used as switches for digital applications. They are the basic elements found in the picosecond-resolution sampling oscilloscope, as well as memory and logic circuits featuring high switching speed and ultralow power dissipation, in the order of 1 microwatt. In the communication field, they are used in analog applications, such as high-frequency local oscillators, detectors, mixers, and parametric amplifiers. Furthermore, the ac Josephson effect is now used to define the volt in terms of frequency in standards laboratories, eliminating the antiquated standard cell. *See* JOSEPHSON EFFECT; SQUID; SUPERCONDUCTING DEVICES.

*Leo Esaki*

***Bibliography.*** L. Esaki, Long journey into tunneling, *Science*, 183:1149–1155, 1974; I. Giaever, Electron tunneling and superconductivity, *Science*, 183:1253–1258, 1974; B. D. Josephson, The discovery of tunneling supercurrents, *Science*, 184:527–530, 1974.

## Vacuum tube

An electron tube evacuated to such a degree that its electrical characteristics are essentially unaffected by any residual gas or vapor.

**Classification.** According to function, vacuum tubes are classified as receiving tubes, transmitting tubes, phototubes, and cathode-ray tubes, microwave tubes, and storage tubes. Structurally, they are classified according to number of electrodes as diodes, triodes, tetrodes, pentodes, and so on, as discussed in later sections of this article.

Prior to the advent of semiconductor devices, hundreds of types of vacuum tubes were developed, many differing only in minor respects. With a few exceptions, most of these have been replaced by semiconductor devices or are used only as replacements in older equipment designed for vacuum tubes. Important exceptions include cathode-ray tubes, microwave tubes, high-power transmitting tubes, and x-ray tubes. In spite of the obsolescence of many types of vacuum tubes, they are still of considerable interest because the principles that underlie their operation and design have wide application in the field of electronics. *SEE SEMICONDUCTOR.*

Receiving tubes are low-voltage and low-power tubes designed for use in radio receivers, computers, and sensitive control and measuring equipment. Phototubes are two-electrode electron tubes in which the current is controlled by light flux incident upon one of the electrodes. They are used in sound-film equipment, in light-controlled switches, and in many industrial and scientific applications. Cathode-ray tubes function by virtue of an electron beam that can be focused to a small cross section on a screen and varied in position and intensity by means of electrical signals. They include oscilloscope tubes, television picture tubes, and camera tubes. Oscilloscope tubes make possible the visual examination of electrical signals. Picture tubes transform television signals into pictures upon a luminescent screen. Conversely, camera tubes convert light images into electrical output or, as image converters or intensifiers, produce a visible picture from incident infrared light or from x-rays.

Microwave tubes are designed for operation at frequencies of the order of 3 GHz and above. They are used in such diverse applications as radar equipment, space communication and control channels, scientific research, and radio-frequency ovens. Storage tubes, which are electron tubes designed so that information can be introduced and then extracted after a required storage interval, were developed for use in computers. *SEE BACKWARD-WAVE TUBE; CATHODE-RAY TUBE; KLYSTRON; MAGNETRON; MICROWAVE TUBE; PHOTOTUBE; PICTURE TUBE; STORAGE TUBE; TELEVISION CAMERA TUBE; TRAVELING-WAVE TUBE.*

**Basic operation.** Vacuum tubes depend upon two basic physical phenomena for their operation. The first is the emission of electrons by certain elements and compounds when the energy of the surface atoms is raised by the addition of heat (thermionic emission), by incident light photons (photoelectric emission), by kinetic energy of bombarding particles (secondary emission), or by potential energy (field emission). The second phenomenon is the control of the movement of electrons within an evacuated enclosure by forces exerted upon them by electric and magnetic fields. *SEE ELECTRON EMISSION; ELECTRON MOTION IN VACUUM.*

Vacuum tubes consist of an electrode capable of electron emission and one or more electrodes for collecting the emitted electrons and for establishing variable electric fields in order to control the movement of the electrons between the emitting electrode and the collecting electrode or electrodes. Where magnetic fields are required, they are produced by permanent magnets or by electromagnets, usually external to the evacuated space of the tube. This article deals almost entirely with thermionic vacuum tubes, in which the primary source of electrons is thermionic emission, and in which control is by electric fields. The emitting electrode is called the cathode, or filament when it is filamentary in form, and the collecting electrodes are called anodes. The principal anode is usually called the plate. Control electrodes are termed grids.

Thermionic vacuum tubes are all basically unilateral circuit elements; that is, the net flow of electrons can normally take place only from cathode to anode. In other words, conventional current, which is opposite in direction to the movement of electrons, is observed only from a positive electrode to the cathode.

**Structure and fabrication.** The mechanical structure of vacuum tubes is exemplified by the glass pentode receiving tube of **Fig. 1**. It consists of an assemblage of electrodes, made of nickel in low-power tubes, mounted on a base through which electrical connections are brought out, and enclosed in an evacuated glass or metal envelope.

After the electrode assembly has been mounted within the envelope, the tube is partially evacuated by a mechanical pump, capable of reducing the gas pressure to $10^{-3}$ mm of mercury, or one-millionth of atmospheric pressure (0.1 pascal). During this process, the envelope and electrodes must be heated by gas flames, or by high-frequency currents induced in metal parts by electromagnetic fields, in order to remove absorbed or adsorbed gases. The tube is then sealed off by closing the gas passage between envelope and pumping system.

When the tube has been sealed off, the vacuum must be improved; that is, the pressure must be further reduced. This is accomplished by flashing (evaporating) a "getter" material contained in a small

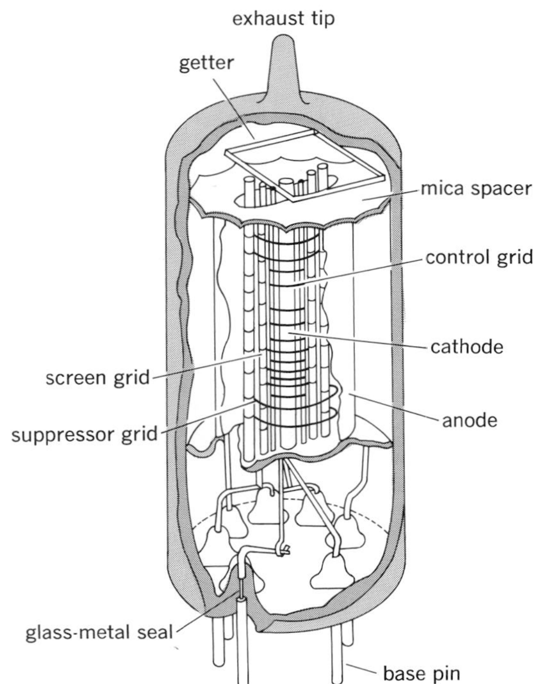


**Fig. 1. Miniature glass receiving tube.**

nickel container previously mounted within the envelope. The getter vapor condenses upon the inner surface of the envelope in the form of a thin film. When gas molecules come into contact with this film, they combine with it to form stable compounds, with the result that the vacuum becomes progressively better with time until the pressure reaches a value of about one-billionth of atmospheric pressure ($10^{-4}$ Pa). While the getter is being flashed, the emitter material of the cathode is heated by passing current through the heater winding or through the cathode itself. Gas released by the emitter material when it is heated is captured by the getter. Barium is the most extensively used getter material, although magnesium, calcium, sodium, and phosphorus have been used.

**Cathode materials.** Thermionic emission is negligible at room temperature. The cathode must therefore be heated either directly by an electric current through it or indirectly by an electrical heater within the cathode structure. A satisfactory thermionic emitter must produce the required electron emission with as little heating power as possible, must have long life both in operation and in storage, must not be adversely affected by small amounts of residual gas within the envelope, and must have high resistance to mechanical shock. In addition, it should be cheap and readily fabricated.

The thermionic emission current density from an emitter surface is given by Eq. (1), in which $A$ and $k$

$$J = AT^2\epsilon^{q_e w/kT} \qquad (1)$$

are physical constants, $T$ is absolute temperature, $q_e$ is the magnitude of charge of an electron, and $w$ is the work function of the emitting material, which is defined as the energy required to remove an electron through the surface of the material. The work function depends upon the emitting material and the condition of its surface. A low work function ensures large electron emission at temperatures well below the vaporization temperature of the emitter and a high ratio of emission current to heating power. Commonly used emitters are of three types: pure metals, thin films of one metal upon the surface of another metal, and coatings of rare-earth oxides upon metals. *See* Thermionic emission.

Pure-metal cathodes are usually made of tungsten or tantalum and are filamentary in form. Although tungsten and tantalum have values of work function high in comparison with values of thin-film or oxide emitters, and must therefore be operated at relatively high temperature, these metals have the advantage of high resistance to the deleterious effects of residual gases. This feature is particularly important in tubes operated at high voltages, where bombardment of the cathode surface by ionized gas molecules accelerated in the high electric fields can cause severe damage or destruction of the cathode. For this reason, pure-metal cathodes are used in high-power tubes. Tantalum has a slightly lower work function than tungsten, but is less rugged. It is more readily worked than tungsten in the manufacture of cathodes.

A thorium film of atomic thickness, formed upon the surface of tungsten, lowers the work function considerably below the value for pure tungsten and thus makes possible emitter operation at much lower temperatures. Thoriated tungsten emitters have the serious disadvantage, however, that the thorium film may be partially or completely removed as the result of bombardment by ionized residual gas molecules or operation at too high a temperature. Formation of the film involves a number of steps and therefore complicates manufacture of tubes having this type of cathode.

Oxide-coated emitters usually consist of a mixture of barium and strontium oxides upon a nickel base. Although the manufacture of this type of emitter also involves a number of steps that must be carefully controlled, the work function of oxide-coated emitters is less than half that of thoriated tungsten emitters, and they are therefore capable of providing high emission at relatively low values of heating power and at temperatures well below that at which vaporization may damage the emitting surface. Oxide-coated emitters are capable of long life when they are properly operated. However, like thoriated tungsten emitters, they are susceptible to damage or destruction from bombardment by ionized gas molecules or excessive temperature. For this reason, they are not used in high-voltage transmitting tubes.

An instructive comparison of the efficiencies of emitters is afforded by **Fig. 2**, in which emission current density and emission in milliamperes per watt of heating power are shown as functions of operating temperature and of heating power.

**Electrode configurations.** Because characteristics and functions of vacuum tubes are determined by the number and configurations of the electrodes that the tubes incorporate, one of the most useful classifications of vacuum tubes is by number of electrodes.

***Diode.*** The simplest tube is the diode; it has only two electrodes: the cathode, which emits electrons,

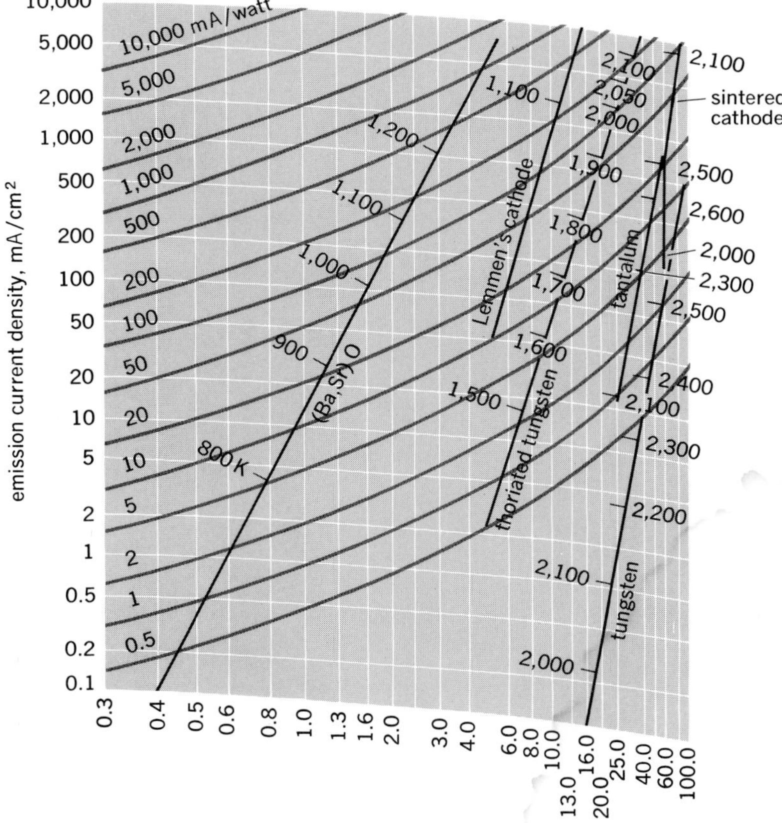

**Fig. 2. Curves showing the relative emission efficiencies of various emitters.**

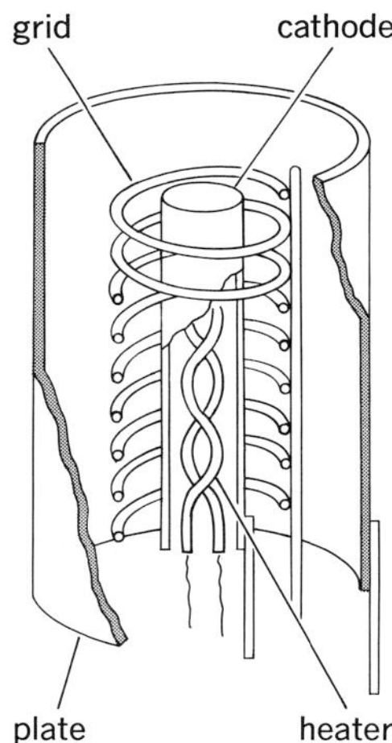


**Fig. 3. Basic electrode structure of a cylindrical triode.**

and the anode or plate, which collects the electrons. In most diodes, electrodes have the form of concentric cylinders, although plane structures are also used. Utility of the diode rests mainly in the fact that conduction between plate and cathode occurs only when the plate is positive with respect to the cathode; when the plate is negative, electrons emitted by the cathode are prevented from reaching the plate.

The current-voltage characteristic of a vacuum diode with an indirectly heated cathode, which is a unipotential surface, closely approximates the relation given in Eq. (2), in which $i$ is the current, $A$ is a

$$i = Av^{3/2} \qquad (2)$$

constant that depends upon electrode size and configuration and upon cathode emission capability, and $v$ is the voltage (positive) of the plate relative to the cathode. In diodes with filamentary cathodes, in which heating current flows directly through the cathode, the voltage drop along the filament causes the current-voltage characteristic to follow more nearly a 5/2-power law. The unidirectional-conduction (rectification) property of the vacuum diode is used in the conversion of alternating current into direct current in power supplies. This property is also useful in the detection of modulated voltages and in other circuit functions. *See* Demodulator; Detector; Diode; Limiter circuit; Rectifier.

***Triode.*** A three-electrode tube, called a triode, is formed by the addition of a grid between the cathode and the plate of a diode. Electrons, in moving from the cathode to the plate, can pass through openings in the grid. The principal value of this third electrode is that large plate current and plate-circuit power can be controlled by small variations of grid voltage and with the expenditure of little power in the grid circuit. A commonly used triode electrode configuration is shown in basic form in **Fig. 3**. Although the control electrode in vacuum tubes is usually a helix (Fig. 3) rather than a grid, the term grid is used for any electrode having one or more apertures through which electrons or ions can pass.

The grid of a triode functions by changing the electric field near the surface of the cathode and thus the number of electrons that leave the cathode and arrive at the plate. If the grid voltage relative to the cathode is zero, a large fraction of the electric field produced by the positive plate voltage terminates on the surface of the cathode and accelerates emitted electrons toward the plate. A few of these electrons strike the

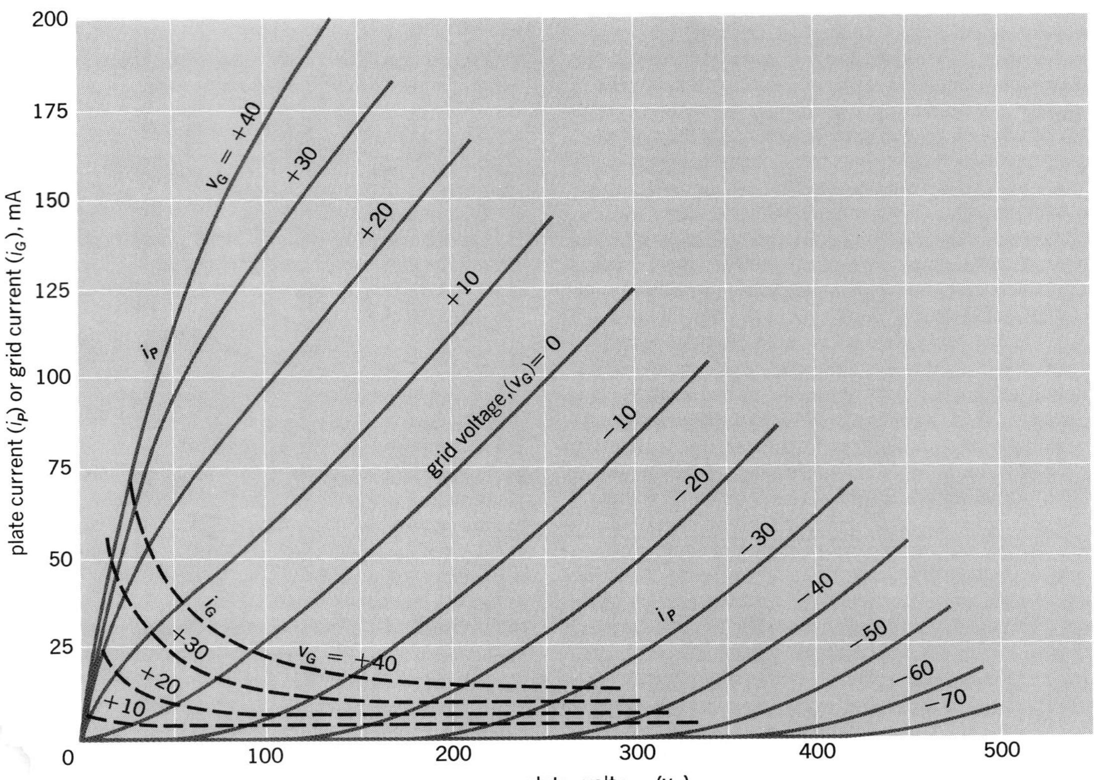


**Fig. 4. Typical plate characteristics and grid-plate transfer characteristics of a triode.**

grid and thus cause a small grid current, but most of them reach the plate. If the grid is positive relative to the cathode, the accelerating field at the cathode surface is increased. This causes an increase in the number of electrons reaching the plate. However, the positive potential of the grid causes more electrons to strike the grid. The resulting increase of grid current is undesirable in many applications of the triode, especially because it causes power to be drawn from the source of grid voltage.

On the other hand, if the grid is negative relative to the cathode, the accelerating field at the cathode is reduced and fewer electrons reach the plate. Because electrons are repelled by the grid if it is at a negative potential, the grid current is negligible when the grid voltage is negative by more than one-half to three-quarters of a volt. This fact accounts for the ability of the grid to control plate current and plate-circuit power without the expenditure of appreciable power from the source of controlling voltage. If the grid voltage is more negative than a value called the cutoff grid voltage, essentially all electrons, including those that leave the cathode with a finite initial velocity of emission, are returned to the cathode, and the plate current is zero.

Typical curves relating the electrode voltages and currents of a triode are shown in **Figs. 4** and **5**. The

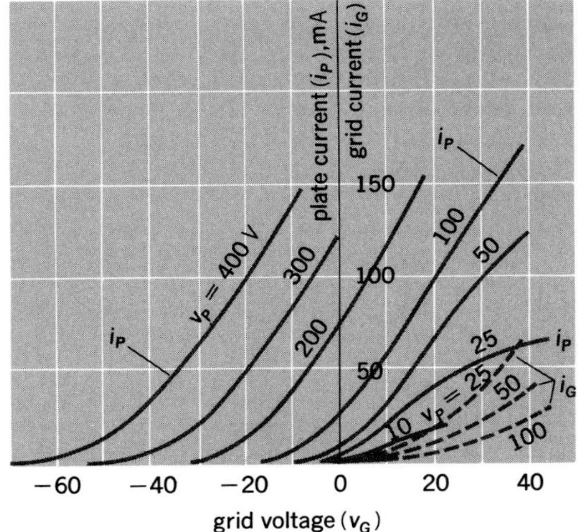


**Fig. 5. Typical grid-plate transfer characteristics and grid characteristics of a triode.**

curves relating plate current $i_P$ with plate voltage $v_P$ at constant grid voltage $v_G$, which are called plate characteristic curves, or simply plate characteristics, are shown by the solid lines in Fig. 4. The dashed lines are curves of grid current $i_G$ as a function of plate voltage $v_P$ at constant grid voltage $v_G$, and are called the plate-grid transfer characteristics. The solid curves of Fig. 5 relate plate current $i_P$ to grid voltage $v_G$ at constant plate voltage $v_P$; they are called the grid-plate transfer characteristics. The broken-line curves, showing changes of grid current $i_G$ with grid voltage $v_G$ at constant plate voltage $v_P$, are called grid characteristics. Figure 5 shows clearly that the plate current can be varied over a wide range without grid conduction if the grid voltage is maintained negative. This range is used in all low-power voltage, current, and power amplifiers. The positive-grid-voltage range

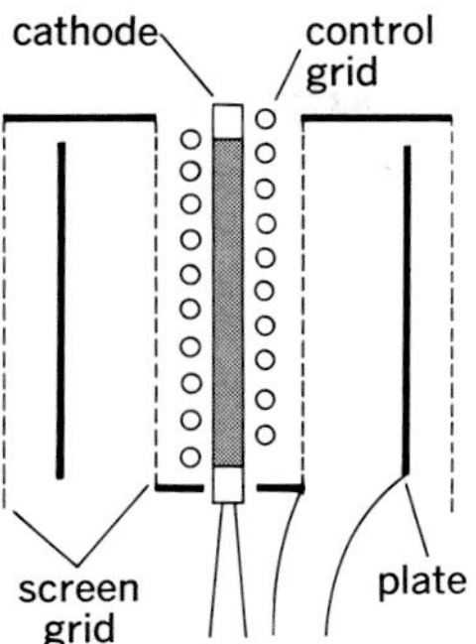


**Fig. 6. Typical electrode structure of a low-power tetrode.**

is used in some types of power amplifiers. SEE AMPLIFIER; OSCILLATOR.

***Tetrode.*** In the use of vacuum triodes in very high-frequency amplifiers, undesirable oscillation may result from the feedback of plate-circuit power to the grid circuit through the capacitance between plate and grid. Although this difficulty can be avoided by making circuit modifications, a much more desirable solution is the reduction of the grid-plate capacitance. This can be accomplished by placing between grid and plate a fourth electrode, which functions as an electrostatic shield. The name of this electrode, screen grid, is descriptive both of its function and of its physical structure. The first grid, which is used to control the plate current, is called the control grid. Such a four-electrode tube is called a tetrode. A typical low-power voltage-amplifier tetrode is shown in **Fig. 6**. In this tube, the capacitance between the control grid and the plate is reduced to a low value by the use of a screen grid that encloses the plate almost completely and thus effectively shields the control grid from the plate field.

To permit most of the electrons to pass through to the plate, the screen grid of a tetrode must be operated at a positive potential. If the plate voltage falls below the screen-grid voltage, secondary electrons emitted from the plate as the result of bombardment of the plate surface by electrons from the cathode are attracted to the screen grid. Because the movement of electrons away from the plate constitutes a negative component of plate current, the plate current falls markedly as the plate voltage is reduced below the screen-grid voltage. This is apparent in **Fig. 7**, in which the value of the screen-grid voltage is indicated by the vertical line at 90 V. The rise in plate current as the plate voltage is reduced below about 70 V is caused by the decrease of secondary emission from

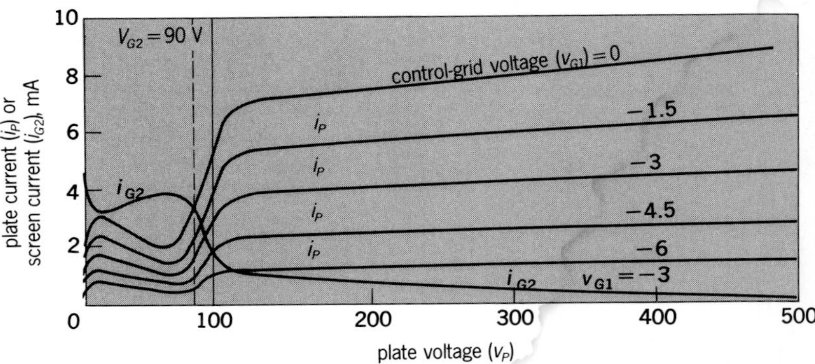


**Fig. 7. Typical plate characteristics of a low-power tetrode.**

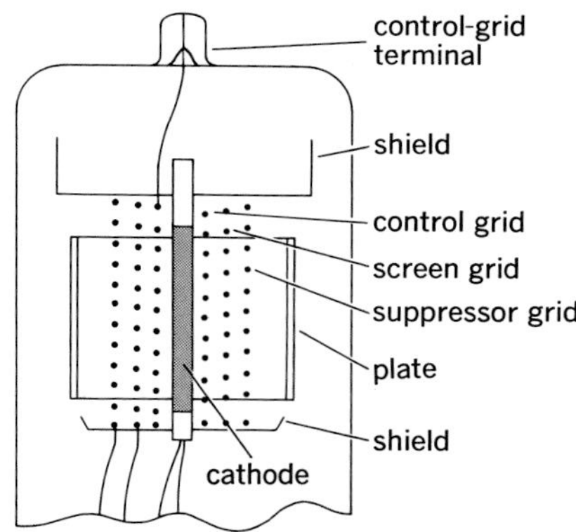


Fig. 8. Electrode structure of low-power pentode.

the plate as the reduction of accelerating voltage reduces the velocity with which the primary electrons strike the plate.

***Pentode.*** The negative-slope region of the tetrode plate characteristics, which is undesirable in most applications, can be eliminated by the addition of a third grid located between the screen grid and the plate. If the potential of this grid relative to the cathode is zero or negative, the field between it and the plate is of the proper polarity to return to the plate secondary electrons emitted from the plate. The name of this grid, suppressor grid, is indicative of its function in suppressing secondary-electron plate current. The structure of a typical type of five-electrode tube, called a pentode, is shown in Fig. 1 and **Fig. 8**.

To minimize interception of electrons by the grids, the wires of the three grids are usually aligned. The presence of the suppressor grid reduces the capacitance between plate and control grid to an even lower value than that of the tetrode. Typical plate characteristics of a low-power voltage-amplifier pentode are shown in **Fig. 9**. The absence of the negative-slope region present in the tetrode at low plate voltages is apparent. It is of interest that the pentode plate characteristic curves resemble the collector characteristic curves of junction and field-effect transistors. *See Junction transistor*.

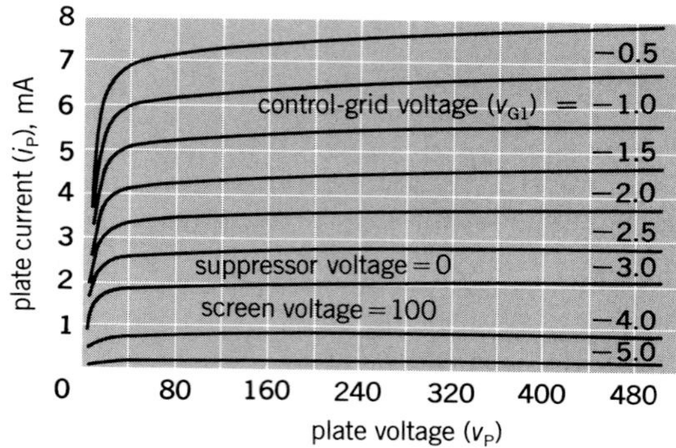


Fig. 9. Typical plate characteristics shown graphically for a low-power pentode.

***Beam tetrode.*** Use of a suppressor grid is not the only way to prevent the undesirable effects of secondary emission from the plate. In a type of tube called the beam power tetrode, suppression is accomplished by the use of beam-forming electrodes that focus the electron stream from the cathode into dense beams in the vicinity of the plate. The high density of electrons produces a retarding field between screen grid and plate that returns to the plate secondary electrons emitted from it. Because of the relatively low electron density in tubes designed for voltage amplification, this method of suppressing secondary-electron current is limited to tubes designed for power amplification, as the term beam power tetrode suggests. The electrode structure of a beam power tetrode is illustrated in **Fig. 10**, and a typical family of plate characteristics for such a tube is shown in **Fig. 11**.

***Other multielectrode tubes.*** Special tubes containing four, five, or six grids were developed for special applications. The additional grids may serve as a means of impressing additional control voltages, or they may serve as shields between other electrodes. If two control voltages of different frequencies are impressed upon different control grids, the nonlinear properties of the tube cause the generation of new frequencies equal to the sums and the differences of the impressed frequencies (and their multiples). This process, called frequency conversion, is essential to the operation of certain types of radio receivers. Tubes used for this purpose are called mixer tubes or mixers. In another type of multigrid tube, called a frequency converter, some of the electrodes are used in conjunction with an oscillator circuit to generate a high-frequency alternating voltage while the remaining electrodes serve as a mixer or as shields. The nonlinear properties of the tube result in the generation of new signals of frequencies equal to the sum of and the difference between the oscillator frequency and the frequency of an impressed signal. According to the number of electrodes that they incorporate, mixers and frequency converters are called hexodes, heptodes, and octodes. *See Mixer; Superheterodyne receiver*.

In another class of vacuum tubes, two or more complete electrode assemblies are incorporated within a single envelope, sometimes with a common cathode. Useful combinations include two diodes, two triodes, a diode and a triode or pentode, and a triode and a pentode. The circuit symbols for the more commonly used types of vacuum tubes are shown in **Fig. 12**.

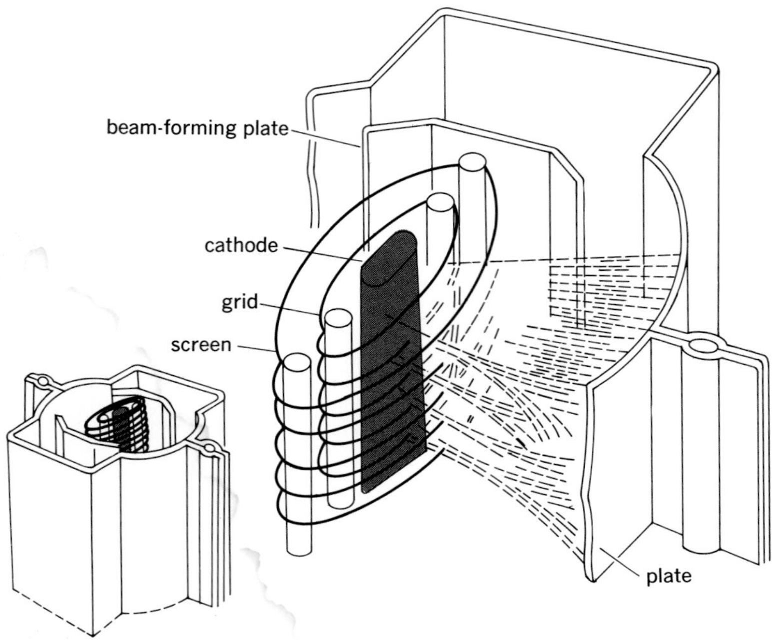


Fig. 10. Electrode structure of a beam power tetrode.

**Tube factors.** Electrical behavior of vacuum tubes in specific circuits can be predicted from a knowledge of the circuit parameters, the tube interelectrode capacitances, and several important tube factors, including the amplification factor, the plate resistance, and the transconductance. The amplification factor $\mu$, which is a measure of the voltage amplification of which the tube is capable, is defined as the negative ratio of an infinitesimal change of plate voltage $v_P$ to the corresponding increment of control grid voltage $v_G$ necessary to maintain the plate current constant. Mathematically the amplification factor is expressed by Eq. (3). The amplification factor at any combination of electrode voltages and currents is the negative of the slope of a curve of plate voltage as a function of control-grid voltage at constant plate current at the point corresponding to the selected values of current and voltage. This factor is a measure of the effectiveness of the control grid, relative to that of the plate, in controlling the plate current.

$$\mu = -\frac{\partial v_P}{\partial v_G}\bigg|_{i_P} = \text{constant} \qquad (3)$$

The amplification factor is relatively independent of the electrode voltages except in the vicinity of plate-current cutoff (zero plate current), where its value decreases. Its value depends upon electrode geometry and increases with increase of grid-wire diameter, decrease of grid-wire spacing, and increase of grid-plate spacing. Geometrically similar tubes of different size have the same amplification factor. Typical magnitudes of triode amplification factor range from 10 to 100. Values for voltage-amplifier pentodes are higher.

The dynamic ac plate resistance $r_P$ is defined as the quotient of an incremental change in plate voltage $v_P$ by the corresponding increment of plate current $i_P$ when the control grid voltage and all other electrode voltages are maintained constant. Usually the term dynamic plate resistance is simplified to plate resistance $r_P$, because the static plate resistance (quotient of the direct plate voltage by the direct plate current) is ordinarily of no interest.

Mathematically, the plate resistance is expressed by Eq. (4). At any combination of values of electrode voltages, the plate resistance is the slope of the corresponding plate characteristic curve at these values. It is essentially the resistance offered to an alternating plate current of small magnitude between the plate and the cathode when all electrode voltages except that of the plate are constant. The characteristic curves of Figs. 4, 7, 9, and 11 show that the plate resistance varies greatly with electrode voltages and is higher in tetrodes and pentodes than in triodes.

$$r_P = \frac{\partial v_P}{\partial i_P}\bigg|_{v_G} = \text{constant} \qquad (4)$$

The transconductance (mutual conductance) $g_m$ is defined as the quotient of an incremental change in plate current by the corresponding increment of grid voltage that causes it, when the plate voltage and all other electrode voltages are maintained constant. Mathematically, the transconductance is defined by Eq. (5). Thus transconductance of the triode whose grid-plate characteristics are shown in Fig. 5 is the slope of the characteristic at the chosen values of plate voltage and grid voltage. The term transconductance is also generalized to apply to the relation between the current to any electrode and the voltage of any other electrode, the term then being preceded by an adjective denoting the electrodes, such as suppressor-plate tranconductance.

$$g_m = \frac{\partial i_P}{\partial v_G}\bigg|_{v_P} = \text{constant} \qquad (5)$$

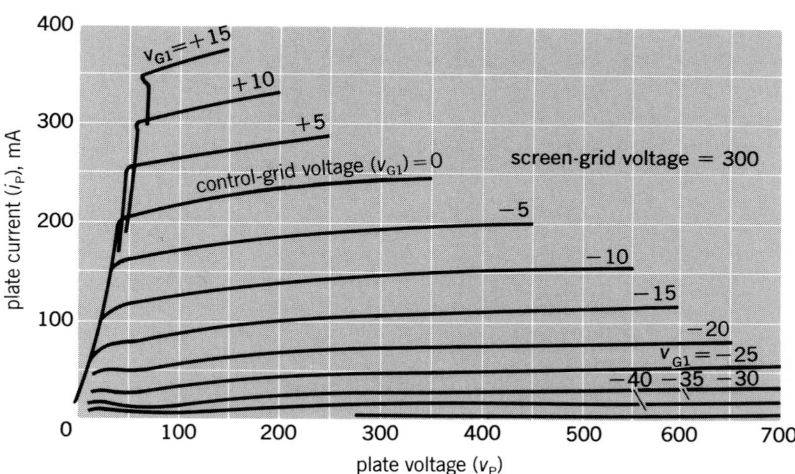


Fig. 11. Plate characteristics of a beam power tetrode.

Grid-plate transconductance can be shown to be equal to the amplification factor divided by the plate resistance. Because the amplification factor varies little with electrode voltages, whereas plate resistance depends greatly upon electrode voltages, the grid-plate transconductance is also greatly dependent upon electrode voltages. This is also shown by the triode grid-plate characteristics of Fig. 5 and by the transfer characteristics of tetrodes and pentodes.

The voltage amplification or gain of a triode increases with the amplification factor and with the ratio of the external-plate-circuit resistance to the plate resistance. That of pentodes is approximately equal to

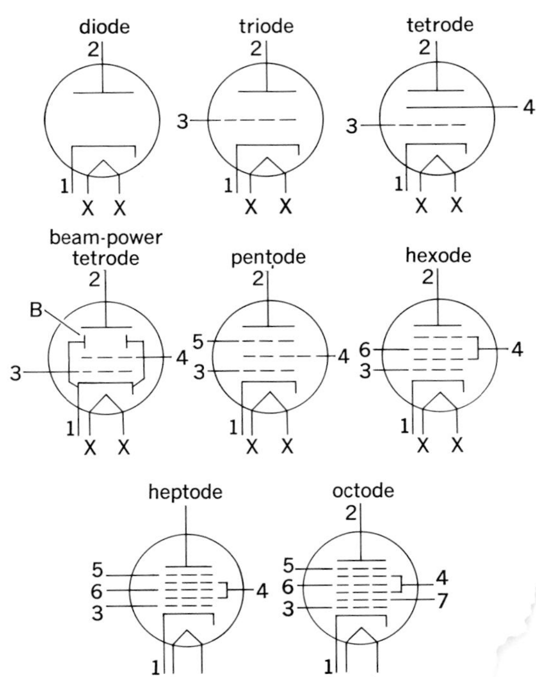


Fig. 12. Circuit symbols for common tubes.

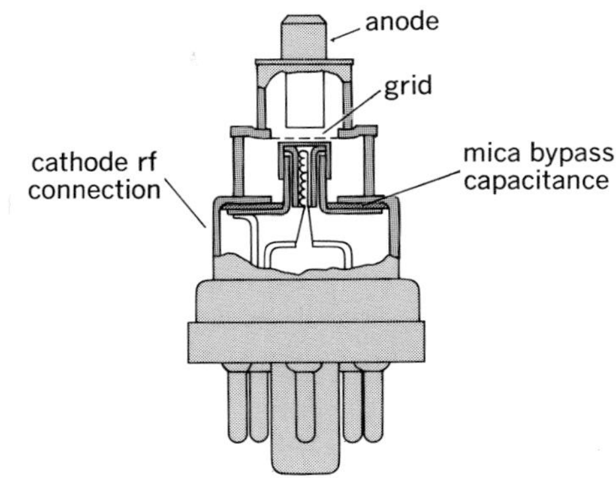


Fig. 13. Structure of a disk-seal tube.

the product of the transconductance and the external plate-circuit resistance. Transconductance is also important in many other applications of vacuum tubes, including power amplification, oscillation, and control.

**Interelectrode capacitance.** The performance of vacuum tubes in various types of circuits depends greatly upon, and may be limited by, capacitances that are invariably present between electrodes. The most important capacitances are the capacitance $C_{gk}$ between control grid and cathode, the capacitance $C_{pk}$ between plate and cathode, and the capacitance $C_{gp}$ between control grid and plate. The effective input and output capacitances $C_i$ and $C_o$ of a vacuum tube used in an amplifier are not merely $C_{gk}$ and $C_{pk}$, but include a component that is caused by the grid-plate capacitance in conjunction with the tube amplification. The value of this component of the input capacitance may approximate the product $AC_{gp}$, where $A$ is the voltage amplification of the tube, if the magnitude of amplification is high. For this reason small grid-plate capacitance is essential in many applications of vacuum tubes. Shielding provided by the screen and suppressor grids of a pentode reduces the capacitance between the control grid and the plate to a low value and thus results in a low value of effective input capacitance, even though the voltage gain of pentodes may be high.

**Frequency and gain limitations.** The maximum frequency at which vacuum tubes can be used effectively as amplifiers or oscillators is limited by interelectrode capacitances, by inductances of the leads connecting the electrodes with the external circuits, and by transit time of the electrons between the electrodes.

At high frequencies, the input capacitance of the tube tends to short-circuit the control grid to the cathode; this reduces the alternating grid-to-cathode voltage and, consequently, the alternating output voltage. Undesirable resonances may also occur between tube capacitances and the lead or circuit inductances. It can be shown that circuit modifications to increase the voltage gain in general also reduce the bandwidth over which the gain is essentially constant and give a gain-bandwidth product that is, therefore, approximately constant. The gain-bandwidth figure of merit for a vacuum tube is the ratio $g_m/(C_i + C_o)$, which is the ratio of the transconductance to the sum of the effective input and output capacitances. It follows that pentodes, which have low input and output capacitances and relatively high transconductance, are particularly suitable for use in amplifiers having high gain over a wide frequency band. The gain-bandwidth figure of merit $g_m/(C_i + C_o)$ is also indicative of the maximum frequency of oscillation obtainable when a tube is used in an oscillator circuit and of the maximum attainable switching speed when a tube is used in a bistable circuit. SEE NEGATIVE-RESISTANCE CIRCUITS.

Lead inductance is undesirable at high frequencies because it introduces high reactance between the electrode and the external circuit. This reactance reduces the alternating voltage of the electrode and shifts the phase of the electrode voltage. In the cathode lead, it provides a feedback path between input and output circuits that may cause considerable reduction in gain and, in conjuction with tube and circuit capacitances, may lead to undesired oscillation.

Transit time of electrons between electrodes of a vacuum tube causes the alternating component of plate current to be out of phase with the alternating control-grid voltage that produces it. Consequently, the low-frequency transconductance $g_m$ is replaced by an admittance $y_m$ having an inductive susceptive component. Of greater importance is a reduction of the magnitude of $y_m$ and of the conductive component $g_m$ of $y_m$ to a value below the low-frequency value of $g_m$. The reduction is the result of differences of transit time of individual electrons caused by differences of acceleration or deceleration of the electrons in the varying grid-cathode electric field. The reduction of magnitude of $y_m$ with increase of frequency reduces the gain in amplifiers and the maximum attainable frequency of oscillation in oscillators.

Although the gain of amplifiers can be made as high as desired, in practice useful gain is limited by noise generated by undesired fluctuations of voltage and current within the amplifying device and associated circuits. In vacuum tubes, noise results from random emission of electrons from the cathode and from the random partition of electron flow to two or more electrodes in multielectrode tubes such as the tetrode and the pentode. Circuit noise is mainly the result of the random motion of electrons among the thermally agitated molecules of the conductors. The magnitude of the noise generated in a circuit element having resistance is proportional to the square root of the product of the resistance, the absolute temperature, and the frequency bandwidth over which the noise is measured. The noise voltage generated in a tube is inversely proportional to the square root of the transconductance and is greater in pentodes than in triodes.

**Lighthouse tube.** At frequencies in the microwave range, the open-wire leads and lumped capacitances, inductances, and resistances that are used at low frequencies must be replaced by enclosed transmission

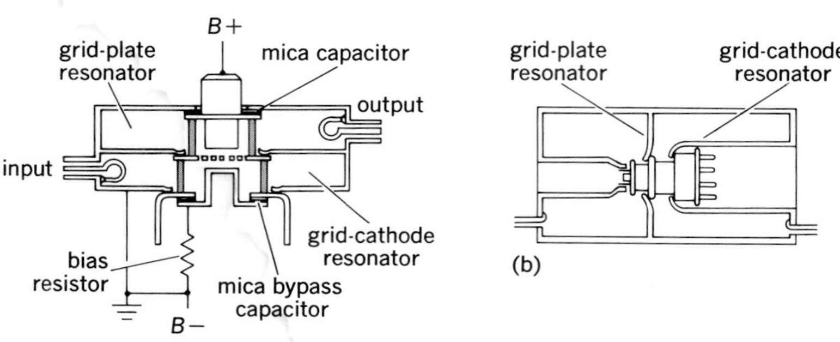


Fig. 14. Use of disk-seal tube with (*a*) cavity and (*b*) coaxial resonators.

lines and enclosed cavity resonators. In such circuits, the undesirable effects of electrode capacitances and lead inductances can be greatly reduced by the use of electrode and lead configurations that allow them to form portions of the conducting surfaces for lines and resonators. A structure that makes this possible is the disk-seal (lighthouse) tube, one form of which is shown in **Fig. 13**. In this tube, the grid lead and other electrode leads have the form of disks. The manner in which a disk-seal tube can be incorporated into an amplifier or oscillator with completely enclosed cavity resonators is shown in **Fig. 14**.

The disk-seal structure also allows the use of small spacing between the electrodes and thus greatly increases the frequency above which transit-time effects limit the performance of amplifiers and oscillators. At low frequencies, the disk-seal structure does not afford significant advantages over the conventional electrode structure because the required size of the cavity resonators increases inversely with decrease of wavelength and becomes prohibitive at frequencies below a few hundred megahertz.

**Field-emission tubes.** It is possible to obtain cold emission from a sharp point in a vacuum when the voltage gradient is large enough to pull electrons out of the metal without heating it. This usually requires a point with a radius of curvature of the order of one-millionth of an inch. With such a point it is possible to produce electric fields of the order of millions of volts per inch in the immediate vicinity of the point.

Field-emission tubes must be much more highly evacuated than ordinary vacuum tubes; otherwise the emitting point will become contaminated and fail to emit satisfactorily. Tremendous current densities can be obtained by this means, although the total currents are of the order of fractions of an ampere. Field emission has been used in high-voltage rectifier and x-ray tubes.

*Herbert J. Reich*

**Bibliography.** D. G. Fink and D. Christiansen (eds.), *Electronics Engineer's Handbook*, 2d ed., 1982; Y. Kano, *Electron Tubes*, 1972; *RCA Receiving Tube Manual*, RC-30, 1978; H. J. Reich, J. G. Skalnik, and H. L. Krauss, *Theory and Applications of Active Devices*, 1966; G. F. Tyne, *Saga of the Vacuum Tube*, 1977.

## Vacuum-tube voltmeter

Any of several types of instruments in which vacuum tubes, acting as amplifiers or rectifiers, are used in circuits for the measurement of the dc voltages. The introduction of the vacuum-tube voltmeter (VTVM; **Fig. 1**) marked the start of the dramatic changes which electronic circuits brought to electrical measurements. The use of active devices meant that the energy required to deflect the indicator no longer had to be drawn from the signal circuit. It became possible to provide considerable gain, while efficient rectification permitted ac measurements to be achieved over a wide bandwidth. The use of negative feedback gave great improvements in accuracy.

**Measurement of dc voltages.** The dc measurement circuit of **Fig. 2** demonstrates many of the essential principles. The signal is applied to an input having a very high input impedance, a vacuum-tube grid. The indicator $M$, usually a standard d'Arsonval movement (moving coil) of modest sensitivity, is connected between the plates of the two tubes, and therefore receives a very much larger current than is drawn from the signal. Two tubes are used in a symmetrical arrangement to minimize the effects of drift as the devices warm up. Provision is made for adjusting the zero. Another possible mode of use is to calibrate the zero control and carry out the measurement by first finding the deflection given by zero input, then applying the signal to be measured and sliding back the control until the indicator is restored to its original position. In this mode, the instrument is called a slide-back voltmeter. Further improvements in sensitivity can be provided by using several similar stages of amplification. Accuracies of a few percent can be achieved by using these techniques.

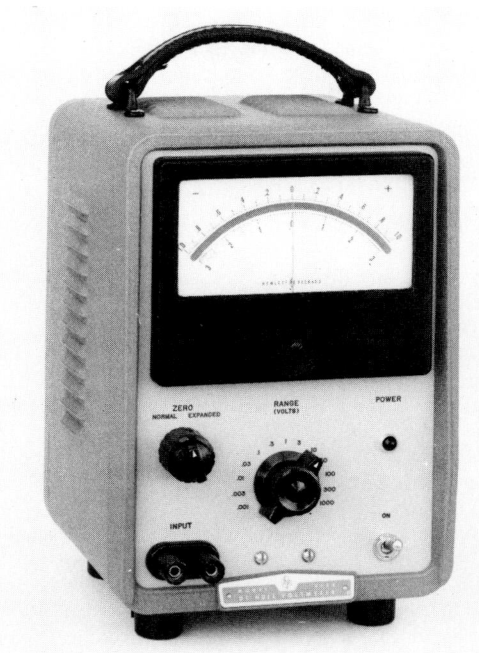


**Fig. 1. Direct-current null vacuum-tube voltmeter. Instrument has floating, high-impedance input (10 megohms on the most sensitive scale, 200 megohms on 300-mV range and above), 13 zero-centered ranges running from 1 mV to 1000 V, and expanded zero feature allowing pointer to be set to either end-scale position to measure voltages up to twice end-scale values.**

**Measurement of ac voltages.** Alternating-current measurements involve the use of some form of rectification. Although other methods have been used, the

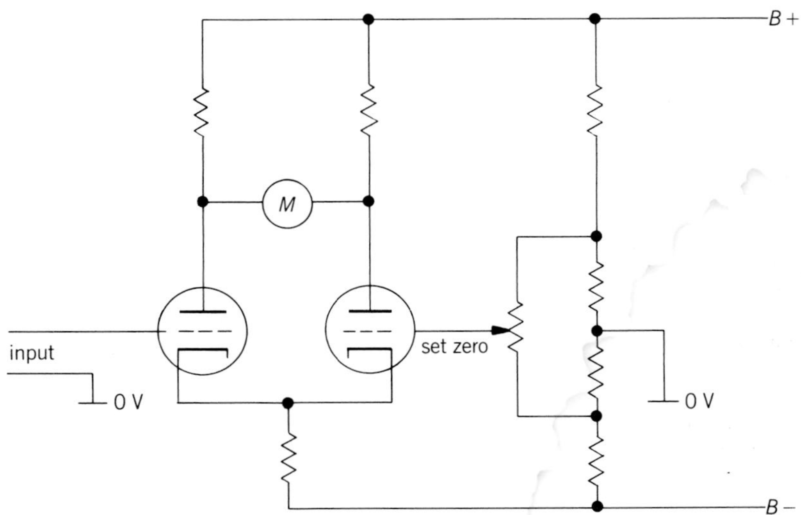


**Fig. 2. Direct-current vacuum-tube voltmeter. $B^+$ and $B^-$ are the positive and negative supplies which drive the circuit.**

most satisfactory device is the diode. However, all diodes, and especially the thermionic type, have a significantly nonlinear relationship between the applied voltage and the resulting current. In the simplest instruments the indicator can be provided with an appropriately drawn scale, but it is difficult to provide better sensitivity than about 1 V for full-scale deflection.

One method of overcoming the problem is to use two matched rectifier systems. The outputs are compared, and any difference is used to control the voltage output from an internal oscillator which runs at a convenient frequency. One diode rectifies the unknown signal, while the other rectifies a known fraction of the signal from the oscillator. In this way, feedback is used to ensure that the oscillator amplitude is accurately related to that of the signal and hence can itself be used to indicate the voltage of the input. This arrangement considerably improves sensitivity and has an additional advantage. Since few components are involved in the signal rectification and these can be of very small size, it is possible to build this part of the circuit in a small probe unit which is separate from the main instrument. Hence the signal connections can be short, making it possible to operate at high frequencies. Useful performance at 500 MHz is not uncommon. *SEE DIODE; FEEDBACK CIRCUIT; OSCILLATOR; RECTIFIER*.

Another application of feedback is shown in the ac voltmeter in **Fig. 3**. In this example the rectifiers are within the feedback loop and matching of devices is not critical. The first two stages, $V_1$ and $V_2$, provide high gain. The third stage, a cathode follower, delivers the output current which drives the indicator $M$. This current passes through the cathode resistor of $V_1$, giving heavy negative current feedback. In this way the current is very accurately related to the input signal. The bridge of diodes ensures that both half-cycles of the ac signal pass through the meter movement in the same direction. The varying and nonlinear voltages which appear across the diodes do not affect the results significantly, as the feedback causes the current to be the controlled parameter. This arrangement of three vacuum tubes, sometimes called a ring of three, is very effective in these instruments. Further voltage gain can be obtained by using additional similar stages in which the rectifier bridge and indicator are replaced by a suitable (large) value of resistor. Instruments of this type may have a full-scale deflection of 1 mV, or even less, a working frequency range of 10 Hz to several MHz, and errors of about 1%. *SEE BRIDGE CIRCUIT*.

Depending on the particular requirements, variations of the above general principles have been used to design a wide range of instruments. Simplicity and low cost, great sensitivity, or wide bandwidth each make their own demands on the designer. Developments in theoretical understanding of negative feedback brought designs to the point where the major error contribution lay in the d'Arsonval movement itself.

**Replacement by solid-state devices.** Following the discovery of the transistor and the increasing availability of semiconductor devices of ever improving performance, more and more of the features offered by vacuum-tube voltmeters have become available from instruments based upon solid-state components. First, thermionic diodes were replaced by germanium or silicon devices which require no heater, are physically smaller, and have lower capacitances and less voltage drop. Then amplifiers began to be replaced by discrete transistor designs, now themselves often superseded by integrated circuit amplifiers. Most recently the field-effect transistor, and especially the metal oxide semiconductor field-effect transistor (MOSFET), has arrived to provide input devices having inherently high input impedances. *SEE AMPLIFIER; INTEGRATED CIRCUITS; TRANSISTOR*.

The remaining limitation of the conventional vacuum-tube voltmeter had to be overcome by the replacement of the d'Arsonval movement by an alternative, higher-resolution indicator. This became a

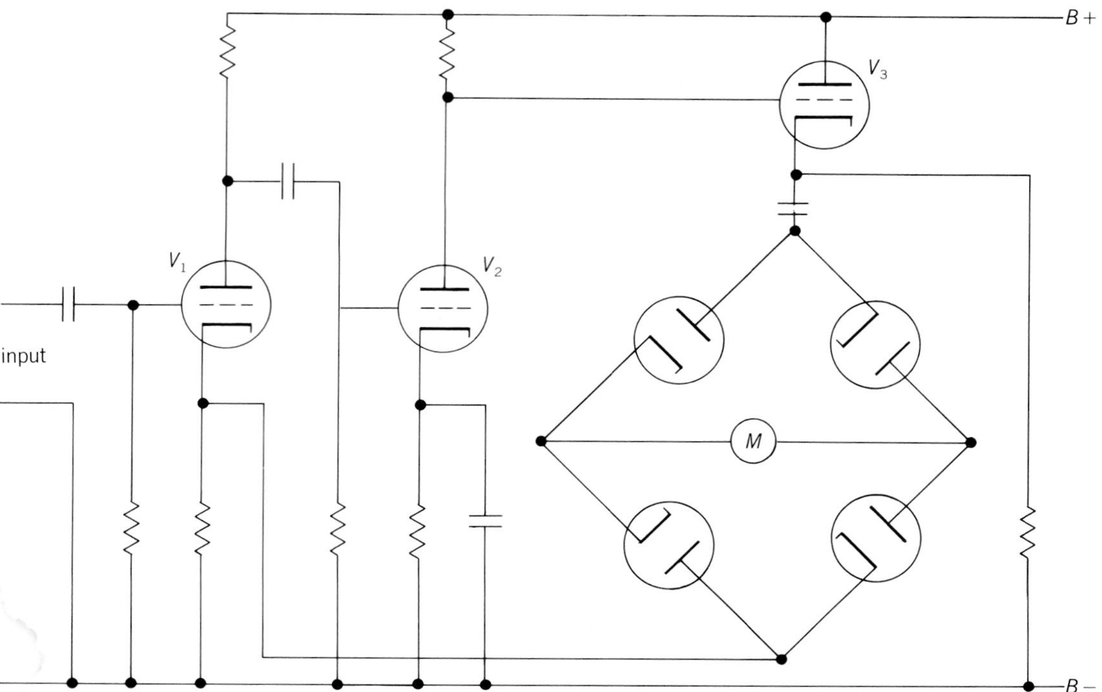


**Fig. 3. Alternating-current vacuum-tube voltmeter.**

practical possibilty with the development of digital displays. At first the interface between the (analog) signal and the display was a serious problem. Using vacuum tubes was too bulky and too expensive for most applications. However, ciruits and techniques were developed for this purpose which, in conjunction with the contemporaneous advances in semiconductor technology, were well suited to manufacture in large quantities. Digital indicators based on large-scale integrated circuits are now readily available and have low manufacturing cost. *See Digital voltmeter; Electronic display.*

As a result of these developments, vacuum-tube voltmeters have disappeared from the market, and the majority of measurements which, in the past, might have been made by using them are now the province of digital voltmeters or digital multimeters, which are invariably solid-state designs throughout. Radio-frequency instruments, for which the market is relatively small and the achievable accuracy modest, can be expected to be the last available with other than digital display. *See Voltage measurement; Voltmeter.*

*R. B. D. Knight*

## Valence band

The highest electronic energy band in a semiconductor or insulator which can be filled with electrons. The electrons in the valence band correspond to the valence electrons of the constituent atoms. In a semiconductor or insulator, at sufficiently low temperatures, the valence band is completely filled, and the conduction band is empty of electrons. Some of the high energy levels in the valence band may become vacant as a result of thermal excitation of electrons to higher energy bands or as a result of the presence of impurities. When some electrons are missing, the remaining ones may be redistributed among the energy levels within the valence band under an applied electric field, giving rise to an electric current. The net effect of the valence band is then equivalent to that of a few particles which are equal in number and similar in motion to the missing electrons but each of which carries a positive electronic charge. These "particles" are referred to as holes. *See Band theory of solids; Conduction band; Holes in solids; Semiconductor.*

*H. Y. Fan*

## Varactor

A semiconductor diode designed to maximize the variation of its capacitance with applied reverse bias voltage. Such diodes are also often called variable capacitance diodes. Today they are almost exclusively junction diodes. The free-charge depletion region of any *pn* junction in a semiconductor widens with the application of reverse bias. Since the surfaces of this free-charge depletion region represent the effective plates of the capacitance of the junction, the application of increasing reverse bias voltage will cause a decrease in the capacitance. The design and fabrication of varactors then reduces to the art of doping the two sides of the junction in such a way that the desired voltage variation of depletion region width (and hence capacitance) is obtained.

It is easily shown that, with an abrupt junction in which the doping level on the *n*-side and the *p*-side is uniform right up to the plane of the junction, the capacitance varies as $V^{-1/2}$, where $V$ represents the reverse bias voltage. For junctions with suitable doping profiles, the power of the voltage dependence of the capacitance can be designed in the range from $-1/3$ to $-1.0$.

Since varactor diodes are primarily used in parametric amplifiers and subharmonic generators, it has become customary to rate varactors by a so-called cutoff frequency. This is defined as the frequency at which the $Q$ of the diode, under the condition of zero dc bias, drops to unity. This frequency may be expressed as Eq. (1), where $C_0$ is the zero bias capacitance and $R_S$ is the series resistance of the diode structure.

$$f_{\text{cutoff}} = \frac{1}{2\pi C_0 R_S} \qquad (1)$$

Above this frequency the diode is predominantly resistive and will not oscillate. For an abrupt junction with the *n*-region doped lightly enough and made thin enough so that the free-charge depletion region just fills the *n*-region at the breakdown voltage, the cutoff frequency can be given in terms of the conductivity $\sigma_n$ of the *n*-region and the diode capacitance at breakdown $C_B$, as in Eq. (2), where $\epsilon$ is the dielectric constant of the semiconductor material.

$$f_{\text{cutoff}} = \frac{\sigma_n C_B}{2\pi\epsilon(C_0 - C_B)} \qquad (2)$$

From this it is seen that there is a trade-off between cutoff frequency and breakdown voltage. *See Junction diode; Q (electricity); Semiconductor; Semiconductor diode.*

*Lloyd P. Hunter*

**Bibliography.** D. G. Fink and D. Christiansen, *Electronics Engineers' Handbook*, 2d ed., 1982; J. Millman, *Microelectronics*, 1979; S. M. Sze, *Physics of Semiconductor Devices*, 2d ed., 1981; E. S. Yang, *Fundamentals of Semiconductor Devices*, 1978.

## Varistor

Any two-terminal solid-state device in which the electric current $I$ increases considerably faster than the voltage $V$. This nonlinear effect may occur over all, or only part, of the current-voltage characteristic. It is generally specified as $I \propto V^n$, where $n$ is a number ranging from 3 to 35 depending on the type of varistor. The main use of varistors is to protect electrical and electronic equipment against high-voltage surges by shunting them to ground.

One type of varistor comprises a sintered compact of silicon carbide particles with electrical terminals at each end. It has symmetrical characteristics (the same for either polarity of voltage) with $n$ ranging from 3 to 7. These devices are capable of application to very high power levels, for example, lightning arresters.

Another symmetrical device, the metal-oxide varis-

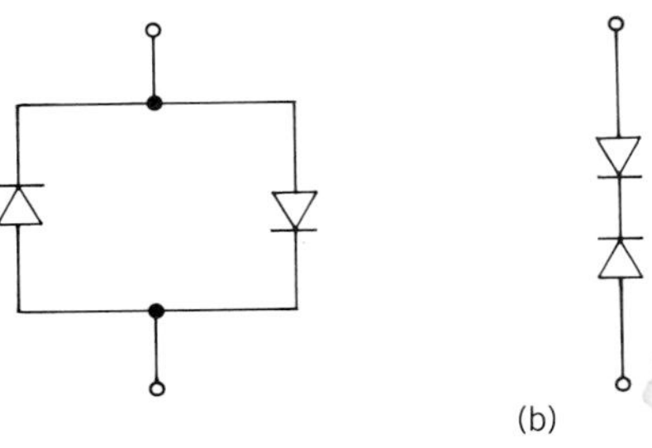


**Fig. 1. Symmetrical rectifier varistors. (a) Low voltage. (b) High voltage.**

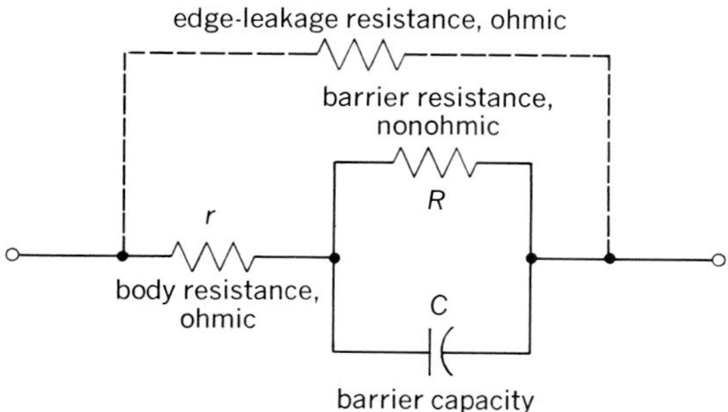


**Fig. 2. Equivalent circuit of a single-rectifier varistor.**

tor, is made of a ceramiclike material comprising zinc oxide grains and a complex amorphous intergranular material. It has a high resistance (about $10^9$ ohms) at low voltage due to the high resistance of the intergranular phase, which becomes nonlinearly conducting in its control range (100–1000 V) with $n > 25$.

Semiconductor rectifiers, of either the *pn*-junction or Schottky barrier (hot carrier) types, are commonly utilized for varistors. A single rectifier has a nonsymmetrical characteristic which makes it useful as a low-voltage varistor when biased in the low-resistance (forward) polarity, and as a high-voltage varistor when biased in the high-resistance (reverse) polarity. Symmetrical rectifier varistors are made by utilizing two rectifiers connected with opposing polarity, in parallel (**Fig. 1***a*) for low-voltage operation and in series (Fig. 1*b*) for high-voltage use. For the high-voltage semiconductor varistor, *n* is approximately 35 in its control range, which can be designed to be anywhere from a few volts to several hundred. *See* SEMICONDUCTOR RECTIFIER.

Silicon rectifiers are fabricated mostly by solid-state diffusion techniques similar to those utilized for transistors and integrated circuits. A thin plate of *n*-type silicon is exposed to a gaseous atmosphere containing a dilute *p*-type impurity at a high temperature (about 2200°F or 1200°C). Some atoms of the *p*-type impurity diffuse into the silicon surface by displacing silicon atoms, forming a *pn* junction within about 0.001 in. (0.025 mm) of the surface. Metal electrodes are applied to *p*- and *n*-type regions by plating or evaporation. *See* INTEGRATED CIRCUITS; JUNCTION DIODE; TRANSISTOR.

The equivalent circuit of a *pn*-junction varsitor is shown in **Fig. 2**. The capacitance is high, limiting high-frequency performance.

*I. A. Lesk*

**Bibliography.** E. Bleuler and R. O. Haxby (eds.), *Methods of Experimental Physics*, vol. 2, pt. A, 1975; J. D. Harnden, Jr., et al., Metal-oxide varistor: A new way to suppress transients, *Electronics*, 45(21):91–95, October 9, 1972; J. R. O'Connor and J. Smiltens (eds.), *Silicon Carbide*, 1960.

## Video amplifier

A low-pass amplifier having a bandwidth in the range from 2 to 100 MHz. Typical applications are in television receivers, cathode-ray-tube computer terminals, and pulse amplifiers. The function of a video amplifier is to amplify a signal containing high-frequency components without introducing distortion.

In a single stage of an *RC* (resistance-capacitance) coupled amplifier the high-frequency half-power limit is determined essentially by the load resistance, the internal transistor capacitances, and the shunt capacitance in the circuit. To extend the bandwidth of an *RC*-coupled amplifier, it is necessary to overcome the effects of these capacitances. In the past, this was often done by adding an inductance *L*, as shown in the **illustration**, employing shunt peaking. The principal design requirement is to choose a value for the inductance that will extend the frequency response without introducing an undesirable hump in the gain characteristic for frequencies near the upper half-power frequency.

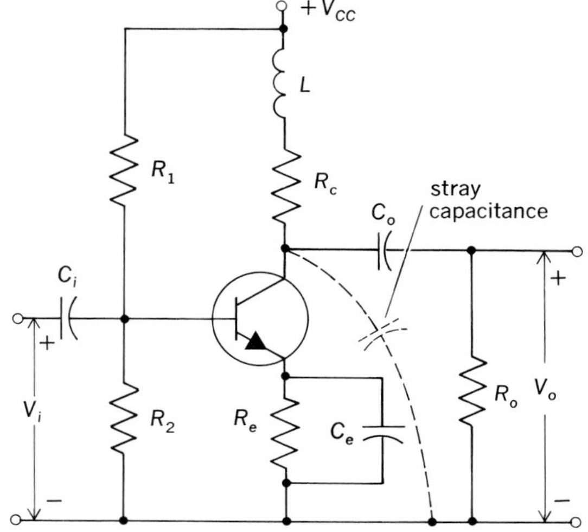


**Shunt-compensated amplifier, in which effect of capacitances is overcome by adding inductance *L*.**

Modern video amplifiers use specially designed integrated circuits. With one chip and an external resistor to control the voltage gain, it is possible to make a video amplifier with a bandwidth between 50 and 100 MHz having voltage gains ranging from 20 to 500. The use of integrated video amplifiers minimizes cost and space. These amplifiers also eliminate the need for the shunt-peaking inductor shown in the illustration. *See* AMPLIFIER; INTEGRATED CIRCUITS.

*Harold F. Klock*

**Bibliography.** C. H. Evans, *Electronic Amplifiers: Theory, Design and Use*, 1979; D. G. Fink and D. Christiansen (eds.), *Electronics Engineers' Handbook*, 2d ed., 1982; C. A. Holt, *Electronic Circuits, Digital and Analog*, 1978, reprint 1985; J. Millman, *Microelectronics*, 1979.

## Video disk recording

A disk system used to reproduce television pictures and sound. The reproduction system consists of three parts: disk, disk player, and television receiver. The disk player rotates the disk, whose information density is several hundred times that of conventional audio long-playing records, at high speed and reads the recorded signal by a sensor. The signal can be seen on the picture tube or heard from the loudspeaker of the television receiver. The recording of television signals is not yet possible in the home; the system operates only for reproduction. Although the video

**Comparison of video disk reproduction systems**

| Characteristics | VHD | VLP | | SV-Disk |
|---|---|---|---|---|
| Disk diameter (mm) | 260 | 301.6 | | 300 |
| Disk groove | Without | Without | | With |
| Sensor | Capacitive sensor (sapphire stylus) | Optical sensor (laser) | | Capacitive sensor (diamond stylus) |
| Reproduction time | 60 min × 2 | 30 min × 2 | 60 min × 2 | 60 min × 2 |
| Special effects (stop, slow, and quick motion); random access | Possible | Possible | Impossible | Impossible |
| Number of audio channels | 2 | 2 | | 1 |
| Disk life | 50,000 h in normal motion (>1 h in stop motion) | — | | 500 plays |
| Stylus life | >2000 h | — | | 300 h |

tape recorder (VTR) can record and reproduce the television signal at home, the tape is expensive. A video disk can be mass-produced and is relatively inexpensive. Further, the degradation of recorded signal with elapsed time is far less than that of magnetic tapes. *See Television receiver.*

The various types of video disk systems, which have been investigated since the early 1960s, have been reduced to three major types, whose developers are RCA, Philips-MCA, and the Victor Company of Japan. Unfortunately, these systems are technically quite different from each other and have no compatibility. For example, a video disk of the RCA type cannot play on the Philips disk player. This problem is one of the great barriers to the popularization of video disks. The **table** compares the main features of these systems.

**SV-Disk.** In the recording of the Selectavision Video Disk, input electrical signals are transformed into the corresponding modulated groove in an original disk record. Because the bandwidth of video signals is so wide that the high-frequency components of the signal cannot be recorded directly, a time-stretched signal, 25 times as slow as the real-time signal, is used as the input signal of the disk recorder. The cutting of the original disk is carried out in a similar manner as in the case of an audio disk. The processes for mass production of this type of video disk are also the same as those of conventional long-playing records. *See Disk recording.*

In reproduction, the disk is rotated on a disk player at a speed 25 times as fast as that at the recording stage. The diamond stylus follows the groove, and an electrostatic sensor picks up the recorded signal.

This type of disk is a simple technical extension of conventional audio disk recording technology, and existing production facilities are largely available. Therefore the commercial price of disk and disk player is expected to be the lowest among the three types. However, slow motion, stop motion, quick motion, and random access of images in reproduction are impossible because the stylus must constantly move along the groove. Further, this type is not suitable for stereophonic sound reproduction and cannot provide bilingual services because the number of audio channels is limited to one.

**VHD.** The Video High Density Disk System is a grooveless, capacitive pickup system. It can provide random access and special effects such as still (stop), slow, and quick motion in reproduction, and has two audio channels.

The recording system (**Fig. 1**) employs a smooth,

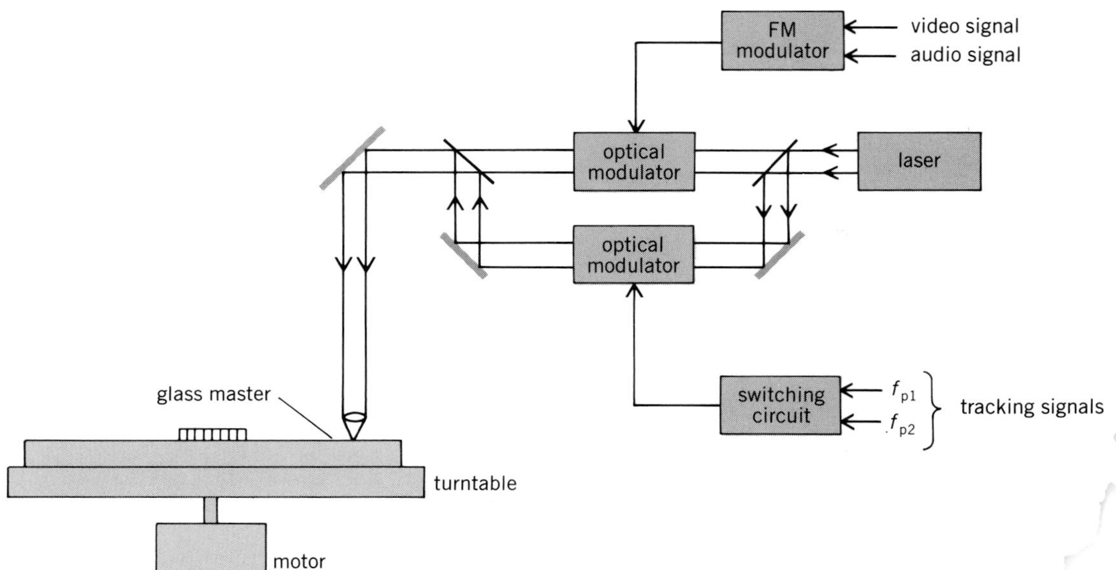


**Fig. 1. Recording system of VHD. (*Victor Company of Japan*)**

Fig. 2. Microscopic photograph of pit pattern in VHD. (*Victor Company of Japan*)

flat glass disk coated with ordinary photosensitive material. Minute laser beams irradiate the disk while it rotates at a speed of 900 revolutions per minute. The source of beams is moved radially at a constant speed. A laser beam is first split in two, one half for modulation of video and audio signals, the other for modulation of tracking signals. Fine pits are recorded spirally on the glass disk (**Fig. 2**). A metallic master disk is produced from the original glass disk. Mother disks, which have indented pits, are made from the metallic master. Then stamper disks are produced from each mother. Each stamper, with its extended pits, produces approximately the same number of final disks as the typical audio stamper. Mass production of VHD disks is similar to that of the SV type. *See Laser*.

In reproduction, a five-sided stylus, which is far broader than that of a stylus-in-groove system, is used for signal pickup (**Fig. 3**). This broader construction of stylus and electrode, which runs the height of the stylus, makes long life of the stylus possible. The electrode on the stylus simultaneously picks up the video-audio and tracking signals electronically as capacitance variations between the disk surface and the electrode on the stylus. In Fig. 3, the schematic view of the pit structure is shown. The two tracking signals are indicated as $f_{p1}$ and $f_{p2}$. The cantilever arm which holds the stylus is servocontrolled to track the virtual grooves on the disk and to correct for the time base error (jitter) of the rotating disk by means of an electrotracking system.

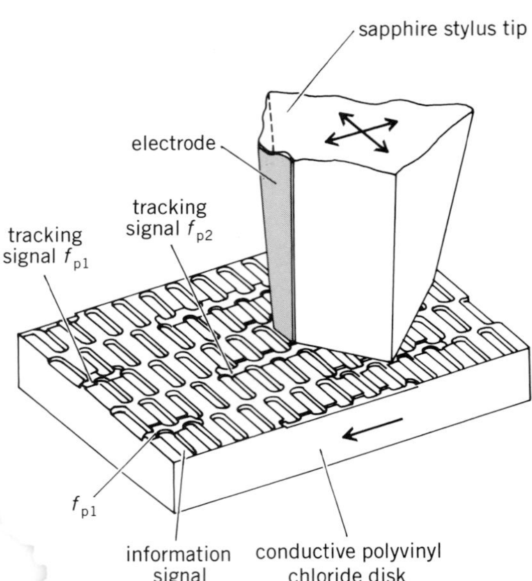


Fig. 3. Signal pickup mechanism in VHD. (*Victor Company of Japan*)

There are no actual mechanical grooves on the disk's surface to guide the stylus; instead, the stylus merely slides along the surface and is guided electronically to pick up the recorded signals. This feature enables the pickup arm to move freely over the entire surface of the disk, and permits special effects such as still, slow, and quick motion, quick search, and random access to be achieved. **Fig. 4** shows the loci of the stylus for various special effects in reproduction. The third pilot signal $f_{p3}$, which corresponds to the vertical blanking interval of a television signal, is inserted four times per revolution. The transistion to the next virtual groove is carried out during the interval where $f_{p3}$ is detected. The picked-up signal which contains video and audio information is applied to the television receiver after electronic processing.

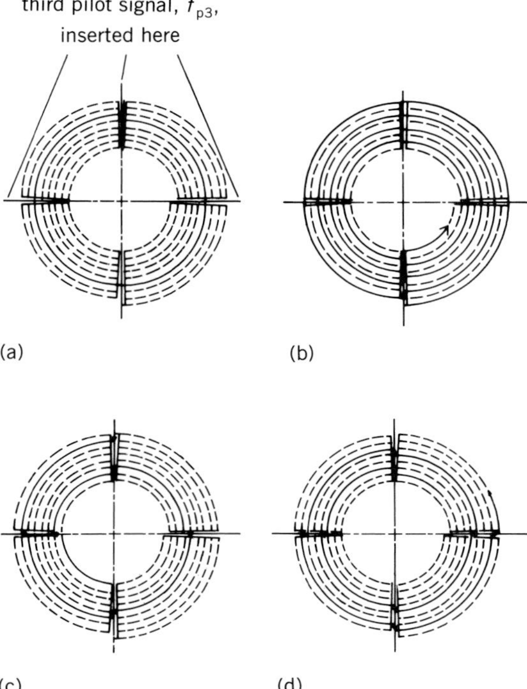


Fig. 4. Locus of stylus for various special effects in VHD reproduction: (*a*) still-picture reproduction, (*b*) fast reproduction (double speed), (c) fast reproduction (quintuple speed), (*d*) fast backward reproduction (treble speed). (*Victor Company of Japan*)

The VHD system is fully equal to the VLP system in performance for home use and is expected to be cheaper than the VLP and more expensive than the SV-Disk system.

**VLP.** Quite different from the above two systems, the Video Long Play System is essentially an optical system using lasers for both recording and reproduction. This system is grooveless, has no stylus, has special features such as still, slow, and quick motion and random access, and provides two audio channels. It is thus quite equal in performance to the VHD system. The optical technology used in VLP is highly advanced and promising, and is expected to become widely available in various aspects of future optical

Fig. 5. Microscopic photograph of pit pattern in VLP. (*Pioneer Co. Ltd., Tokyo*)

communications. But the VLP disk player is the most expensive of the three systems. *SEE OPTICAL COMMUNICATIONS.*

The signal-processing scheme for video and audio signals prior to recording is quite similar to that of the VHD system except that no special tracking signals are used in this case. The microscopic photograph of the pits pattern thus obtained is shown in **Fig. 5**. The depth of pits is equal to a quarter wavelength of helium-neon laser light, that is, 0.15 micrometer. The width of the pits is 0.8 μm and the separation width of tracks is 1.6 μm. The length of each pit along a track represents the information of recorded radio-frequency signals containing one video and two audio channels.

Replication processes are similar to but slightly more complex than those of the VHD and SV-Disk systems. **Figure 6** shows the optical system of the VLP player. The complete pickup unit can move backward and forward on a carriage or rails underneath the record disk to follow the track. The player has excellent servomechanisms. The light beam from the laser is focused automatically at the record by the objectives controlled by a focusing servo. Other automatic control systems act on the pivoting mirror, thus keeping the spot centered on the track. A prism ensures that light reflected by the record falls on the detector. The detected electrical signal is separated into three parts by filters and FM-demodulated into a video and two audio signals. The production of special effects is very similar to that of the VHD case.

**Reproduction of audio signals.** Pulse-code modulated (PCM) sound has very superior quality to any existing high-fidelity audio systems, but it requires a very wide frequency range. Video disks have enough bandwidth to record PCM audio signals. Both VHD and VLP systems provide a PCM decoder as an option to the disk player, and super-high-fidelity reproduction of audio signals can be heard at home. *SEE PULSE MODULATION.*

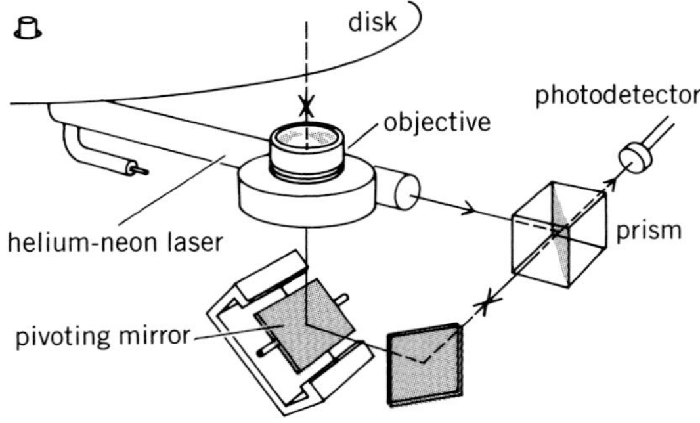


Fig. 6. Optical system of the VLP player. (*Philips*)

*H. Date*

**Bibliography.** K. Compaan and P. Kramer, The Philips VLP system, *Philips Tech. Rev.*, 33(3):178–189, 1973; T. Inoue, T. Hidaka, and V. Roberts, VHD videodisc system, *SMPTE J.*, 91:1071–1076, 1982; J. Isailovic, *Videodisc and Optical Memory Technologies*, 1985; E. Sigel et al., *Video Discs: The Technology, the Applications and the Future*, 1980; Special issue on RCA's Selecta Vision, *RCA Rev.*, vol. 39, no. 1, March 1978; Special issue on video long play systems, *Appl. Opt.*, 17:1993–2000, 1978; Victor Company of Japan, *New Technology, Video Audio High-Density Disc System, VHD/AHD*, 1980.

## Video telephone

A communications system used for two-way communication of audio and video. A complete system uses a television camera and display with a hands-free speakerphone at each terminal, and shares in the use of an electrical transmission and switching system for interconnection. Graphical (sketch pad) and logic (computer) equipment and a wide variety of signal-processing apparatus may also be involved. The same equipment may be arranged for closed-circuit television, surveillance, and other purposes. *SEE CLOSED-CIRCUIT TELEVISION; IMAGE PROCESSING; TELEPHONE; TELEVISION; VIDEOTEXT AND TELETEXT.*

Experiments in transmitting images along with voice date from 1927, and since 1960 most major communication agencies throughout the world have been exploring the subjective, technical, and economic feasibility of video telephony. However, major impediment to the introduction of a person-to-person communication service using video telephones is that the service is of little value to a customer until the majority of people in an integrated community also are connected. The more successful video communication operations have been within limited communities such as law enforcement services, business or manufacturing operations, and hospital communities. If person-to-person video telephony is to become popular, it will probably grow from interconnecting such communities, from the interactive use of computerized graphical work stations with camera facilities, or from the growth of intercom and surveillance systems. Most systems now use television broadcast scanning standards for display and thus are compatible with much commercial station equipment.

**Video transmission.** The wide bandwidth required to transmit a video signal substantially adds to system cost, and much effort and ingenuity have gone into schemes intended to reduce the transmission rate needed for the signal. A differential pulse-code modulation (DPCM) system operating at 6.132 megabits per second was used in experiments in the early 1970s and was compatible with the evolving digital hierarchy of the telephone plant, allowing the mixing of video telephone and other signals on long-distance transmission facilities. Efforts to reduce the transmission rate requirement while allowing improved display standards have centered on taking advantage of the redundancy inherent in a video signal and sacrificing a degree of temporal and spatial resolution.

Wider-bandwidth, more expensive systems have attempted to maintain ''full-motion'' rendition and the high picture quality of full-bandwidth systems by removing signal redundancy more effectively than is accomplished with DPCM. Three basic method have contributed to success. One method transforms and codes segments of the picture, sending areas of low detail digitally with fewer bits and the high detail parts, such as edges, with more bits. Other methods digitally store the picture signal at both transmitter and receiver. Only information needed to convey differences in the picture are transmitted to the receiving store, which can then display the new pictures, using adjacent picture element values for prediction of changes. To reduce the redundancy still further, the detailed motion of elements in the picture is tracked, and elements in new frames are predicted accordingly. With these techniques, substantially full motion and good (monochrome) detail in presentation for conference or person-to-person transmission are realized at transmission rates of 384 kilobits per second (10 to 20 megabits per second for broadcast quality, including color and camera panning). Considerable effort has gone into making the transmission rates and channel coding compatible with standardized digital facilities, operating at 56 kilobits, 384 kilobits, or 1.5 megabits per second, but picture source coding generally is incompatible between different systems.

Most of these systems use a digital buffer store at each end of the transmission path to provide a uniform rate of transmission of rapidly fluctuating picture content. The time delay may be a significant fraction of a second and can be as large as several seconds. When combined with the 0.6-s delay inherent in satellite circuits, the additional delay in the buffer circuits can hinder two-way person-to-person communication.

Several improved slow scan or freeze-frame systems that transmit digital video signals at a rate of 56 kilobits per second and lower have been developed. The more successful of the systems that operate with a low transmission rate have used a progressive or hierarchical picture refreshment so that an excellent picture is presented when there is minimal motion. As object motion increases, there is a progressive degradation in spatial resolution and motion rendition.

**Video conferencing.** By the early 1970s group video conferencing had been introduced by public carriers in several countries. As domestic satellite and optical fiber circuits have provided more economical transmission, and as bandwidth reduction systems have become more affordable, conference television, independent of public carriers, has grown apace. Numerous companies offer conference services, and many large corporations have their own multiterminal teleconferencing systems. *See* COMMUNICATIONS SATELLITE; OPTICAL COMMUNICATIONS.

Frequently, the broadband transmission is one-way, with answer-back by narrowband, perhaps freeze-frame, or merely audio and graphical transmission. Conferencing systems frequently combine several operations, devoting the circuits preferentially to the busiest of several cameras and associated displays, to graphical attachments, or to recorded material. Voice switching with a manual override generally is used, but the systems vary in format. *See* TELECONFERENCING.

*C. Chapin Cutler*

***Bibliography.*** *GLOBECOM Conference Proceedings*, 1985; W. R. Iverson, Picture phones get a new image, *Electronics*, 58(33):30–32, August 19, 1985; S. Millman (ed.), *A History of Science and Engineering in the Bell System*, AT&T Bell Laboratories Technical Staff, 1984; Special issue on visual communication systems, *Proc. IEEE*, vol. 73, no. 4, April 1985; Telecoms, *Teleconf. News Lett.*, vol. 8, no. 6, June 1985.

## Videotext and teletext

Computer communications services that take advantage of standard television receivers and use them as display terminals to retrieve information from data bases. A ''black box'' is placed between the television set and the signal carrier. The signal carrier may be a telephone network, a data communications network, a television cable, or a broadcast signal. The black box receives data from the signal carrier. It formats that data into a signal suitable for display on the television set. The user interacts with the black box to determine what information is actually displayed on the screen of the television set.

Both videotext and teletext use the same display technology. The difference between them is that videotext is a two-way, or interactive, service, which allows the user to interact with the service in selecting information to be displayed, while teletext is a broadcast service. In the teletext service, preprogrammed sequences of frames of data are broadcast cyclically. The user interacts with the black box to ''grab'' the frames of relevant information. The textual and graphic information in teletext is inserted into the ''blanking period'' in television signals. While select frames of information can be viewed in the teletext service, the user cannot interact with the data base.

In videotext, the black box is actually a limited computer terminal which uses the television screen for display. Both videotext and teletext provide the user with a numeric keypad for interacting with the black box. Some videotext terminals also provide, as an option, a full alphanumeric keyboard for interacting with videotext services.

In both videotext and teletext the user will normally make selections from a series of menus to select the desired information. In videotext the user may then continue to interact with the service selected.

**Display alternatives.** Alphamosaic, alphageometric, and alphaphotographic are three different display technologies that may be used with videotext and teletext services.

Alphamosaic, the first to be introduced, is the kind of display technology used in many video games. The screen is divided into a series of rectangular mosaic elements. The picture to be displayed is transmitted as a series of rasters, line by line, similar to the way that a basic television signal is transmitted. Both alphanumeric characters and pictures are built up from these elements, a line at a time.

Alphageometric technology is more closely related to conventional computer graphics. The alphageometric format is the basis for the Canadian Telidon technology, which has heavily influenced the American

Telephone and Telegraph videotext standard for North America. This technology stores and transmits commands to draw graphic objects on the display screen. For example, the command to draw an arc will consist of a series of instructions giving the location of the center of the circle, the radius of the circle, the starting point of the arc (in degrees), and the end point of the arc. Each object to be drawn on the screen is transmitted as a series of commands. *See Computer graphics*.

The alphageometric display technology gives higher-resolution images and requires lower bandwidths for data transmission than alphamosaic. However, the black box which acts as a computer terminal is more complex. It translates graphics commands into the actual display on the television screen. The alphageometric display black box does more processing than the alphamosaic black box.

Alphaphotographic display technology provides the highest resolution of the three alternatives, making it possible to incorporate full-color photographs into the data. The display quality is similar to a normal, good-quality television frame. Conceptually, there is little difference between alphaphotographic and alphamosaic. However, in alphaphotographic the size of the displayed mosaic element is reduced to the minimum displayable picture element on the television tube. In practice, alphamosaic videotext systems are designed to operate at much lower bandwidths, while alphaphotographic systems require relatively high bandwidths to the videotext terminal.

The data which make up frames of information are different for each of the three display technologies. Some work has been done to allow conversion from one format to another, but one cannot generally retrieve information stored in one format and display it on a terminal equipped for a different format.

**Implementations.** The United Kingdom led the world with the first operational teletext services (Ceefax and Oracle) and videotext service (Prestel). Both of these use alphamosaic format displays. The German Bildschirmtext is a compatible alphamosaic format service. The French Teletel is another alphamosaic format videotext service, but it uses the French Antiope technology, which is a different approach from Prestel in the way it does character coding. Many other European countries have begun operating videotext and teletext services based on alphamosaic technology that is compatible with either Antiope or Prestel.

One of the first major North American videotext trial systems was Bell-Canada's VISTA service, and the Trans Canada Telephone System (TCTS) trial Intelligent Network (iNET) continues to provide access across Canada to alphageometric videotext data bases. There are numerous other trial systems in Canada. All employ the Canadian Department of Communication's Telidon protocol with an alphageometric format.

Numerous technical trials, market tests, and full commercial services are now available or starting up in the United States. Some use alphageometric formats, while others use alphamosaic. Three major but incompatible trial systems in the United States include Knight-Ridder's and American Telephone and Telegraph's Viewtron in Florida, Cox Cable's Indax in San Diego, and Times-Mirror's service in southern California.

Most North American trial systems follow American Telephone and Telegraph Standard 709E, which is compatible with the Canadian Telidon standard. There is not yet a single internationally agreed-upon standard; however, there is considerable effort among international standards committees to reach agreement. Alphaphotographic formats are not being used in any current trial system.

**Services.** A variety of information has been made available on videotext and teletext, with varying degrees of acceptance. A few examples follow.

Data-base retrieval forms a major class of videotext and teletext services. Examples include restaurant guides, hotel information, stock market information, and travel information. These are suitable for both the broadcast mode of teletext and the interactive mode of videotext.

Typically, a user might start with a menu listing categories for hotels or restaurants. Upon selecting one of the categories, the user is given a screen with more information, such as a list of four-star hotels or a list of Chinese restaurants. The user can continue a tree-structured search until the desired information is obtained.

Another major class of services is interactive, and therefore is suitable only for videotext. Examples include calculation services, electronic mail, teleshopping, and financial services. Calculation services prompt the user for inputs to a program which does the calculation and displays the result. Electronic mail generally requires a full keyboard to input the text of a message to be sent from one user to another. Teleshopping displays items a user might want to purchase, and accepts orders, like a catalog store, when the user chooses to purchase an item. A variety of financial services, such as transferring funds from one account to another, are possible. *See Electronic mail*.

Because of its inherent one-way broadcast nature, teletext service can be offered only on a subscription basis. However, videotext services can be charged on the basis of individual requests. This offers a real potential for stimulation of the information marketplace. *See Data-base management systems; Data communications; Electronic mail; Multiaccess computer; Television receiver*.

*Ronald P. Uhlig*

***Bibliography.*** H. B. Thomas and M. Tyler, Videotext and Teletext: Computing and communication for the mass market, *Proceedings of the Fifth International Conference on Computer Communications*, p. 490, 1980; J. Tydeman et al., *Teletext and Videotext in the United States: Market Potential, Technology, Public Policy Issues*, 1982; *Videotext '81 Proceedings* and *'82 Proceedings*, On-Line Publications Ltd.

## Voice response

The process of generating an acoustic speech signal that communicates an intended message so that a machine can respond to a request for information by talking to the human user. Communication of speech from the machine to the human requires abilities to convert machine information into a desired word sequence, with the pronunciations of all desired words carefully sequenced and inflected to produce the natural flow of continuous speech waves.

Talking machines permit natural interactions that can be valuable for announcing warnings, reporting machine status, or otherwise informing the computer user, especially when the user cannot view displays, due to concurrent visual tasks, visual handicap, or remote telephone links. The many advantages of voice interactions with machines and the expanding uses of computers in offices, factories, schools, and homes have encouraged the development, sales, and use of voice response systems as voice warning devices, cockpit advisory systems, automated telephone-directory assistance systems, time-of-day services, bank-by-phone facilities, talking clocks and appliances, toys that speak, and automatic readers of printed texts for the blind. Low-cost synthesizers on circuit boards or in microminiaturized integrated circuit chips are rapidly giving machines the ability to speak.

**Reproduction of stored speech.** For simple tasks involving small vocabularies, machine production of speech is not difficult to achieve. Human speech can be stored and reproduced later on demand, using techniques similar to those in familiar devices like audio tape recorders, phonograph records, and other analog or digital magnetic media. Simple machine control of the position of the pickup device on an audio recorder can determine the sequence of words or phrases. The earliest commercial voice response devices were simple machine-accessed analog recordings on tape loops and magnetic drums.

**Word concatenation systems.** It is only a small conceptual step from such recorders to the simplest form of modern voice response system, called a word concatenation system (**Fig. 1**). Acting like automated tape recorders, word concatenation systems can retrieve previously spoken versions of words or phrases and carefully concatenate them without pauses to approximate normally spoken word sequences.

The processes involved in word concatenation begin off-line, when a trained speaker (for example, a radio announcer) in a quiet booth speaks words or phrases from a selected vocabulary, and this high-quality speech is digitized and placed in a temporary signal store. The speech is edited (automatically or with human help) to adjust sound levels, to locate the beginning and ending of each word, to assess the naturalness and clarity of the pronunciation, and to check the inflection of the voice. If necessary, words may be spoken again until good examples are obtained. Some systems store two versions of certain words: one with flat intonation for nonfinal positions in word sequences, and another with the characteristic falling intonation of terminal parts of declarations and commands. The result is a pronunciation dictionary, or permanent store of human utterances of desired words or phrases, as illustrated on the left in **Fig. 2**. It is not uncommon for some vocabulary items to be long phrases like "voice response system" or "at the tone the time will be," spoken as a unit.

Voice response from the machine is accomplished later by input instructions dictating to the "synthesis program" or utterance composer that (for the example shown at the top of Fig. 2) the first word to be spoken will be some vocabulary item $I_{68}$, then comes item $I_{82}$, then $I_5$, then $I_9$, and then $I_{47}$. The composer produces $I_{68}I_{82}I_5I_9I_{47}$, heard as "The voice response system concatenates human speech," as a juxtaposing of the stored signals for each of the vocabulary items. Such juxtaposing will usually be guided by internal rules that select nonterminal versus terminal versions of words, like $I_{46}$ versus $I_{47}$ in Fig. 2. Rules may also correct for anomalies or bad transitions at junctures between words. The concatenated word sequence then is converted into a continuous signal that drives a loudspeaker. Figure 2 shows another utterance being generated in the same fashion, but with a different word sequence.

There are problems with such a simple head-to-tail composition of word sequences. The speech may sound choppy, with unnatural intonations and timing, and with noticeable breaks at word boundaries. Also, the storage of a high-quality digitized waveform may require as much as 64,000 bits per second of speech, so that large computer disk packs can store perhaps at most 1200 seconds of speech, and microcomputer memories might be able to store only hundreds, or perhaps only a few tens, of words. Low-cost concatenation systems are thus restricted to small vocabularies. *See* Computer storage technology.

**Parameterized voice response systems.** A spectrum of alternative solutions to the storage problem for voice response is illustrated in **Fig. 3**. There is a general tradeoff between storage requirements and the complexity of coding and decoding of the speech. Storage requirements can be reduced substantially by first extracting informative parameters from the original human speech and later reconstructing speech from such stored parameters. Parameterized voice response systems typically use signal-processing methods like delta modulation, adaptive differential pulse-code modulation, spectral filtering through a bank of band-pass filters (channel encoding), linear predictive coding (LPC), or tracking of important speech features like natural resonant frequencies (formants) of the speaker's vocal tract and fundamental frequency (pitch) of the voice. Such parameterized approaches assume that not all the information in the original signal is important to conveying the message. Informative parameters totaling about 16,000 bits/s to as low as 600 bits/s can be stored as simplified instructions for controlling reconstitution of the waveform.

**Figure 4** illustrates a parameterized voice response system based on extensive evidence that the resonant

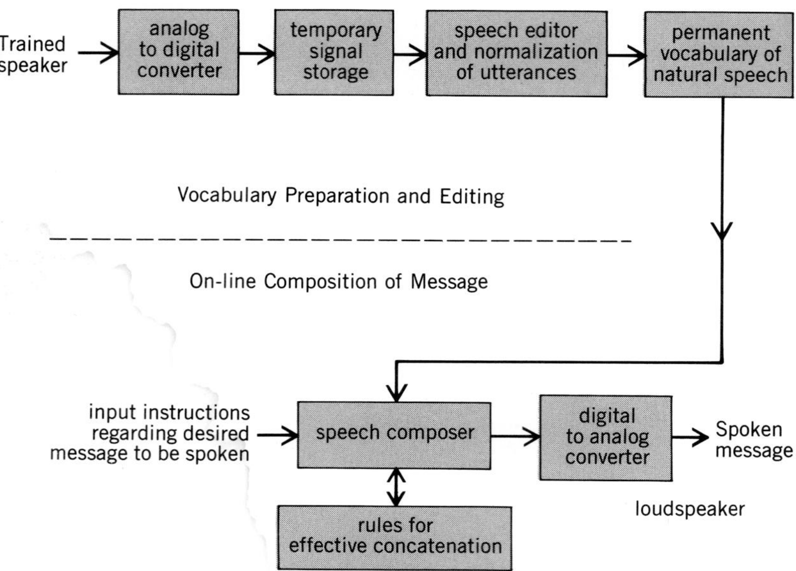


**Fig. 1. Voice response system which is based upon concatenation of words spoken by a human.**

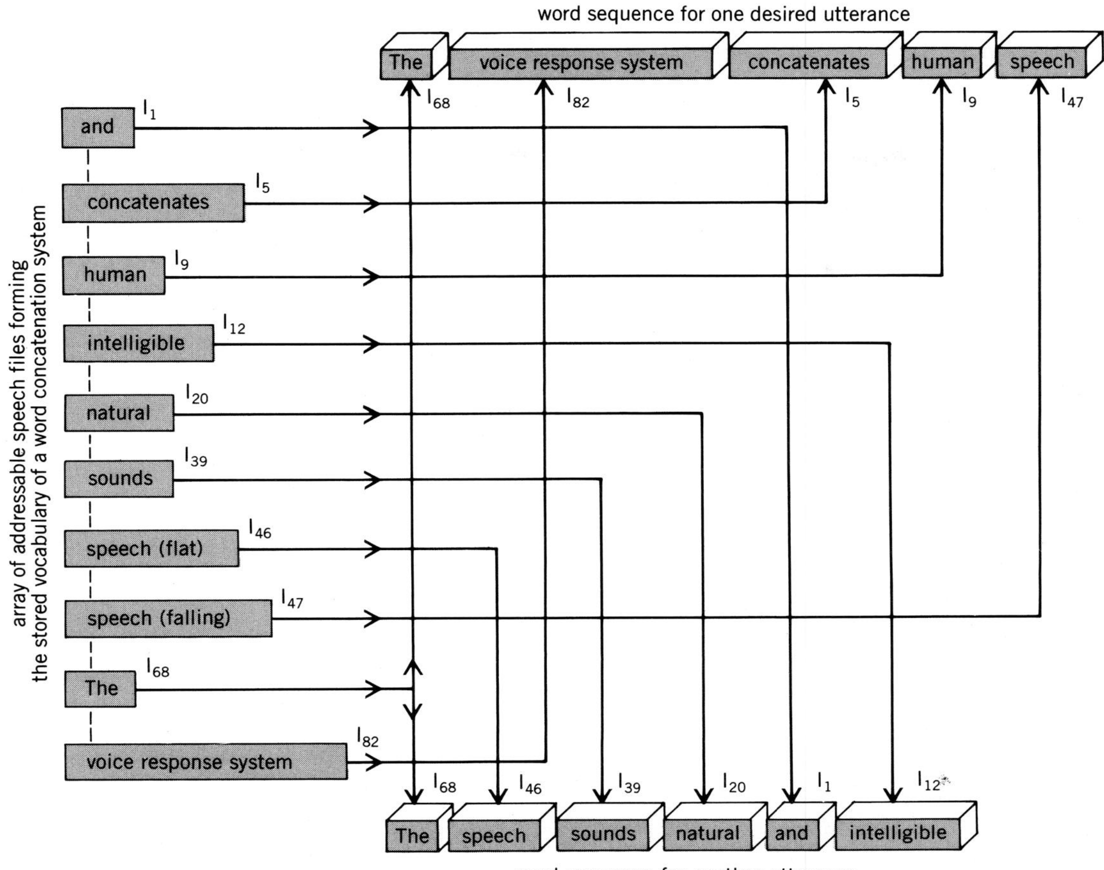


**Fig. 2. Waveforms of words or phrases from the dictionary are connected end to end to achieve connected voice output from a word concatenation system.**

peaks (formants) of the voice are important cues to the identities of vowels and other vowellike sounds. Words or phrases spoken by a human are analyzed in off-line mode to extract time variations of the frequencies ($F_1$, $F_2$, $F_3$) and amplitudes ($A_1$, $A_2$, $A_3$) of the formants, as well as the variations of the rate of vibration (fundamental frequency $F_0$, or pitch) and amplitude $A_0$ of the vocal cords versus time. The system notices "unvoiced" periods when the vocal cords are not vibrating, so that the signal is an aperiodic noise of amplitude $A_N$. All these parameters may require less than 1000 bits/s for vocabulary storage.

Later, upon input of a command specifying the desired message, the formant synthesizer reconstructs the overall acoustic character of the speech by using the stored parameters to control signal generation processes in the random number generator (for unvoiced speech), the pitch pulse or glottal wave generator (for controlling fundamental frequency), and the bank of resonating digital filters (controlled by formant amplitudes and frequencies). For fricative sounds, the formant resonances are replaced by broad spectral peaks (of frequency $F_P$ and bandwidth $B_P$) and antiresonances (frequency $F_Z$ and bandwidth $B_Z$). A separate path for the nasal tract also has its own resonances (frequency $F_{NP}$ and bandwidth $B_{NP}$) and antiresonances (frequency $F_{NZ}$ and bandwidth $B_{NZ}$). The combination of these processes produces a signal resembling the resonating or noiselike character of each portion of the original speech.

One advantage of the parameterized voice response system is the possibility of altering the parameters to have them differ from the original speech. For example, formant trajectories, or prosodic characteristics like pitch, durations of certain parameter configurations, and intensity of the speech, can be computer-controlled to achieve smooth transitions at

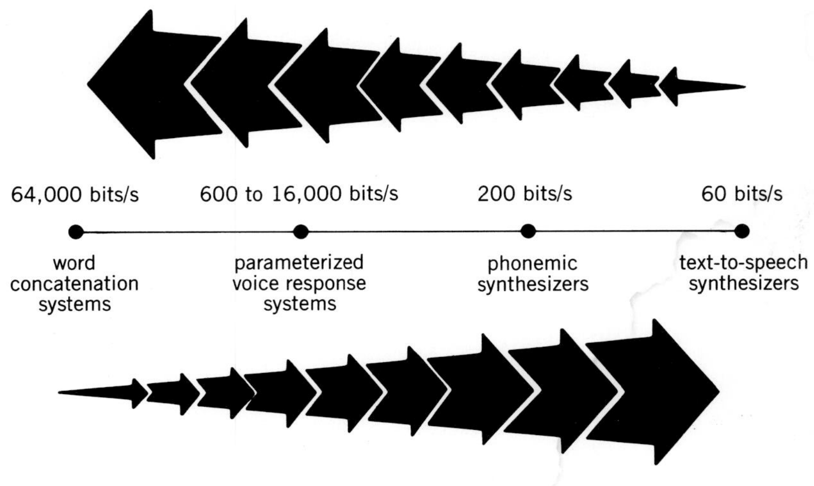


**Fig. 3. Spectrum of alternative types of voice response systems.**

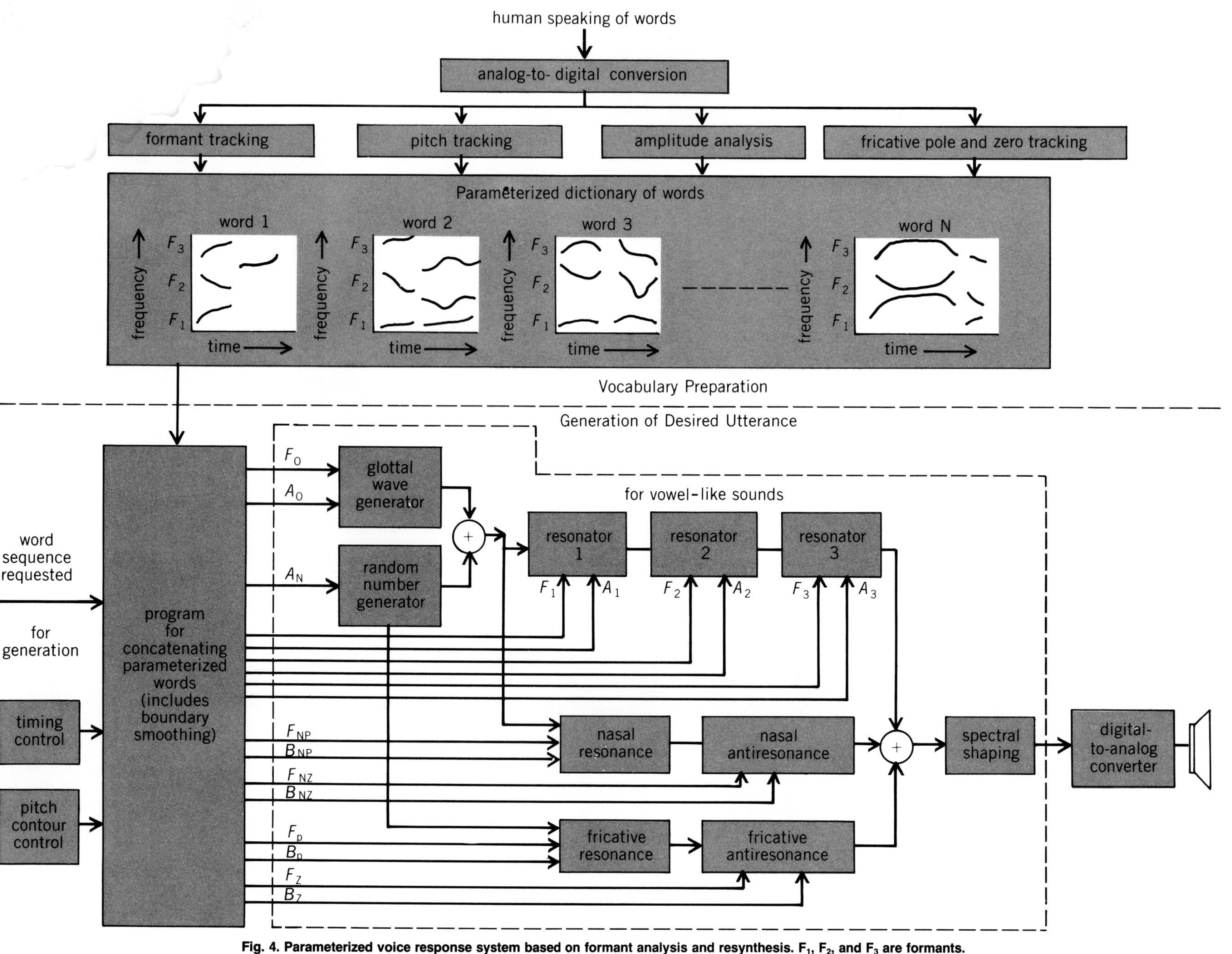


**Fig. 4.** Parameterized voice response system based on formant analysis and resynthesis. $F_1$, $F_2$, and $F_3$ are formants.

word boundaries. Words spoken with flat pitch contours can be analyzed and resynthesized with the terminal intonation fall of a command or the terminal rise of a yes-no question. Such parameterized synthetic speech can thus be valuable in testing the perceptual consequences of various acoustic parameter patterns.

**Phonemic synthesizers.** Another type of speech generation system listed in Fig. 3 is a phonemic synthesizer. Human speech is not the direct basis for stored representation of words or phrases in this type of system. Rather, each word is abstractly represented as a sequence of expected vowels and consonants (phonemes, or phones if more detailed articulatory contrasts are included). Speech is composed or synthesized by juxtaposing the expected phonemic sequence for each word with the sequences for preceding and following words. Each phonemic unit is used as a set of instructions for the form of acoustic data to be produced at the appropriate times during the utterance. For example, the phonemic sequence /fa̲ɪr/ could dictate that a formant synthesizer will first produce a period of weak unvoiced noise like an /f/, followed by an /a̲/-like vowel period of voiced, resonant sound, with formant frequencies placed appropriately for the phoneme /a̲/, followed by an /ɪ/-like vowel period of voiced, resonant sound, with formant frequencies of an /ɪ/, followed by an /r/-like resonant period. Transitions into and out of each expected target configuration of formant data will be necessary, and must be derived either by computer rules or by human judgment. Similarly, the durations and intensities of each phoneme must be specified, as must the pitch of the voice during each voiced period. Such a synthesizer system thus requires extensive rule-governed modeling of the steady-state sound structures of phonemes, and predictions of the forms of transitions. Also, prosodic features must be specified by rules. Commercially available phonemic synthesizers have typically not provided comprehensive sets of such rules, so that uses of phonemic synthesizers have normally required extensive linguistics expertise or outstanding patience in trying out alternative phonemic sequences, until the resulting speech sounds somewhat natural and intelligible.

**Text-to-speech synthesizers.** Problems with the extensive hand-tailoring required for phonemic synthesis have prompted the development of complex rule sets for predicting the needed phonemic states directly from the input message and dictionary pronunciations. Such synthesis-by-rule permits virtually unlimited-vocabulary voice response. By providing automatic means to take a specification of any English text at the input and to generate a natural and intelligible acoustic speech signal at the output, a text-to-speech synthesizer represents the most ambitious form of voice response system listed in Fig. 3. Without the need for intervening human sequence selection such as a phonemic synthesizer needs, and with less storage requirement than other synthesizers, the text-to-speech synthesizer is probably the primary choice for large-vocabulary speech generation.

**Figure 5** illustrates a typical structure for a text-to-speech synthesizer suitable for use in automatically reading books to the blind. An optical character recognizer can read typewritten characters and produce a computer-readable specification of the spellings of words in the text. Next, words must be identified, and extensive text-to-sound rules must be used to provide the basic phonetic and prosodic instructions for controlling a speech synthesizer. Each common word is stored in a pronouncing dictionary, with its phonetic

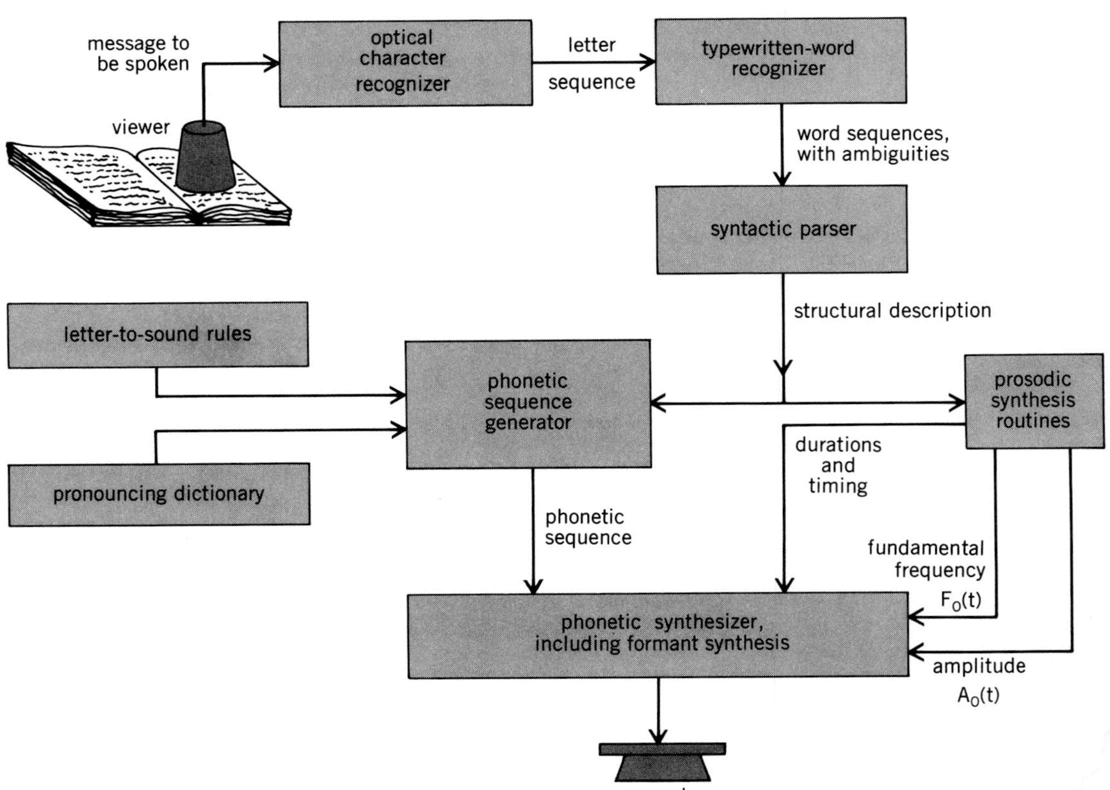


**Fig. 5. Text-to-speech system for generating complex sentences with large vocabularies.**

form, word stress pattern, and rudimentary syntax information such as whether it is a verb or noun. Unusual words like surnames can be generated by letter-to-sound rules. The parser examines the spelled input to determine the structural role of each word in the sentence, so that word ambiguities like the noun "*con*vict" versus the verb "con*vict*," or "average" as an adjective versus "average" as a verb, can be resolved. Also, homographs like "lead" (a metal) versus "lead" (to guide) can be distinguished by studying the syntactic structures in which they appear.

Parsing can also control the prosody of the synthesized speech, so that sound intensity, phonemic and syllabic durations, and pitch contours throughout utterances are determined by the phonemic sequence, the lexical stress pattern, the syntactic bracketing into phrases, the placement in sentence intonation and rhythm patterns, and so forth. Indeed, rule-governed control of prosody is one of the primary aspects of text-to-speech synthesis, since prosodies are the primary acoustic correlates of linguistic structures, and prosodies are critical to the achievement of natural flow, emphasis, and inflection in synthesized speech.

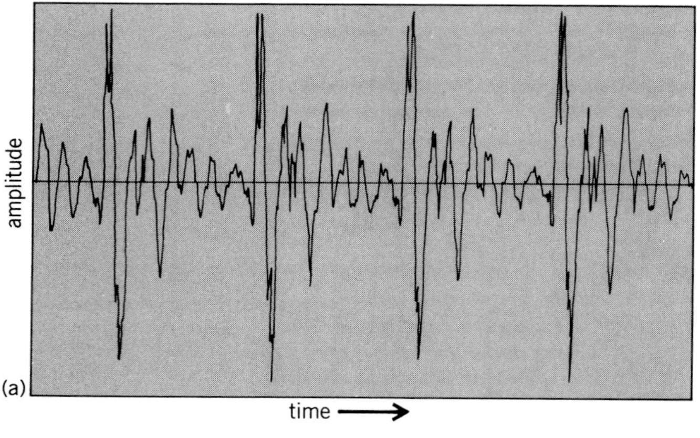


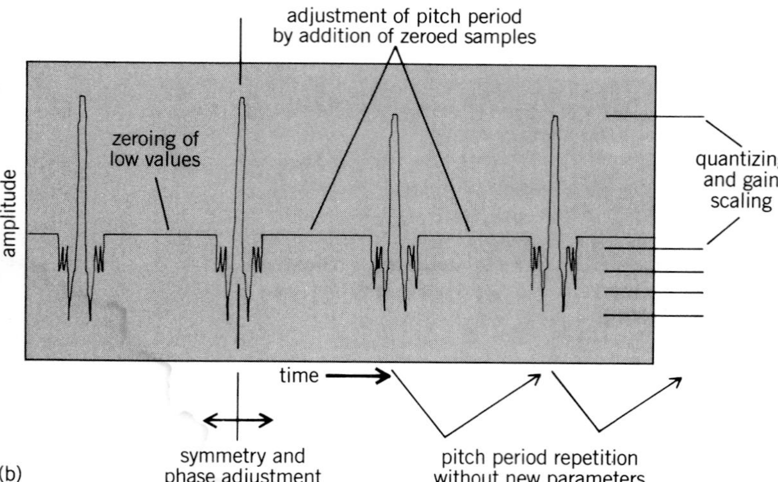


**Fig. 6. Mozer methods of efficient time-domain coding for speech resynthesis. Complex speech waveforms are replaced with synthetic waveforms, whose phases and amplitude are adjusted for simplification while the amplitude frequency spectrum of the original speech is preserved. (*a*) A portion of vowellike human speech whose amplitude frequency spectrum must be preserved to assure human perception of the intended message. (*b*) A simplified waveform with a short-time frequency spectrum similar to that for *a*, but with several forms of data reduction before storage for resynthesis.**

Text-to-speech synthesizers must also adjust word pronunciations to take into account effects of neighboring words on expected forms of word-initial or word-final phonemes. Extensive research and rule testing are needed before text-to-speech synthesizers will be able to produce arbitrary English sentences without flaw in phonetic or prosodic details. *SEE CHARACTER RECOGNITION.*

**Low-cost implementations.** Speech output from machines has become much more commonplace since the development of single-chip microprocessors, digital signal processing chips, and a variety of fabrication technologies and integrated circuit architectures. The choices in voice output devices include: single-chip synthesizers (with a choice of algorithms); small circuit boards (offered as single evaluation boards or low-cost boards for incorporation into other manufacturers' products); stand-alone voice-generating boxes; and development systems that permit users to adapt voice response capabilities to specific applications with distinctive vocabularies. *SEE INTEGRATED CIRCUITS; MICROPROCESSOR.*

***Time-domain methods.*** Generally, synthesis algorithms and the system architecture are more critical to the quality of the output speech than are hardware concerns such as speed and density of components on the chips or boards. Memory requirements are reduced with efficient speech encoding methods such as the Mozer time-domain methods (**Fig. 6**). Rather than performing complex spectral transforms involving digital filters and spectral feature selections, speech can be divided into short analysis periods, and the perceptually important features of the waveform within each period can be determined and stored as minimal representations of the sound to be produced. The complex speech waveform can be replaced by synthetic waveforms which do not even resemble the waveforms of actual speech in appearance, but which sound the same when heard by the phase-insensitive and linguistically categorical human ear.

Mozer time-domain methods replace each analysis period of human speech by time-symmetric waveforms, whose frequency spectrum is similar to that of speech, but whose phases are selected so that only a small number of bits are needed to represent the waveform. Characteristic of such synthetic waveforms are long silent portions, the need for only a small number of discrete (quantized) amplitude levels, and methods for repeating previous parameter patterns for successive analysis periods until the spectral changes are severe enough to warrant a new pattern. The synthetic waveform may be set equal to zero for half of the analysis period by neglect of low-amplitude portions of the speech waveform, and the pitch of the voice can be controlled by inserting different periods of silence between successive analysis frames. These synthetic waveforms are derived through complex speech analysis procedures at the manufacturer, and synthesis within the purchased device then consists of merely reading such stored data to produce a proper sequence of synthetic waveforms that sound like the desired speech.

Other time-domain methods use idealized speech segments which are stored and read out in fixed-rate or variable-rate controlled sequences during synthesis. For example, one single-chip sound-synthesis microcomputer has a read-only memory (ROM) containing the software synthesis program, the detailed parameter patterns for selected speech segments, parameters

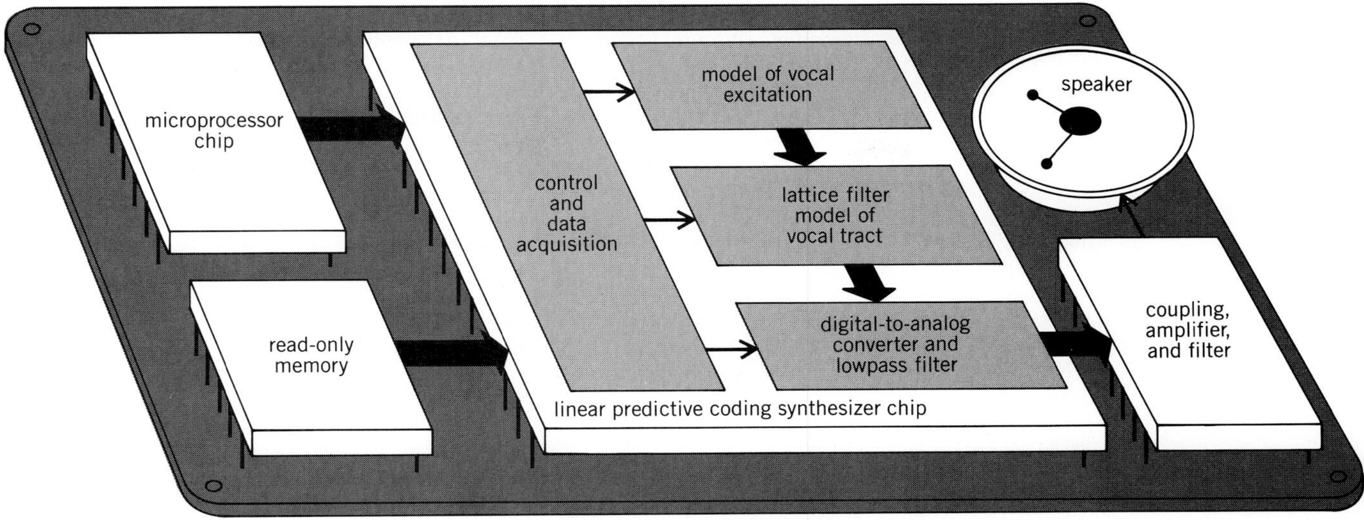


**Fig. 7. Basic components of a single-circuit-board speech synthesizer, based on the linear predictive coding (LPC) method for modeling human vocal production processes.**

for representing the amplitude envelope of the speech, pitch data, and instructions for sequencing through segments to produce utterances. The chip includes a processing unit that multiplies envelope and segment data, with pitch control of sampling rate. An on-chip digital-to-analog converter completes the production of speech through a speaker. A low-pass filter and amplifier may be needed in the speech production process.

***System components.*** Speech output from a microcomputer can be achieved with a synthesizer, a digital-to-analog converter, a low-pass filter, and a speaker. Some synthesizer chips include the digital-to-analog converter and the filter, along with synthesis algorithms and read-only memory to store data for vocabularies to be synthesized. General-purpose digital signal processing chips can be used instead of synthesizer chips, to allow the synthesis algorithm to be readily changed, and otherwise permit flexibility in operation, but at slightly higher costs and usually with additional external circuitry such as that for digital-to-analog conversion, interfacing, and vocabulary-storing in read-only memory. Digital signal processors are particularly well suited to the prototyping of new synthesizers or new configurations for new applications.

***Linear predictive coding.*** One of the most widely used low-cost speech synthesis methods is the linear predictive coding (LPC) method (**Fig. 7**). A single-chip microcomputer provides interfacing with keyboard inputs and other peripherals, and control of synthesis processes, while a read-only memory stores linear predictive coding data for the chosen vocabulary. The heart of the synthesizer is the dedicated large-scale integration (LSI) chip which has logic blocks for modeling the speech production processes of vocal-source excitation and acoustic-tube filtering, plus digital-to-analog processing, all supervised by a control and data acquisition interface. A typical filtering process involves a so-called two-multiply lattice which models successive short sections of an acoustic tube of varying cross-sectional area. Chips have been developed that can, through pipelining processes, perform the necessary hundreds of thousands of multiplications per second that are needed, and also can provide digital-to-analog conversion and filtering to produce outputs for coupling to the speaker.

***Text-to-speech devices.*** The time-domain and linear predictive coding methods described above are among the parameterized voice response methods. More complex single-board speech synthesizers provide text-to-speech capabilities, which include text processing, dictionary look-up, letter-to-phoneme rules, stress and syntactic assignment, allophonic sequences, prosodic variables, generation of parameter patterns, and final synthesis of the speech. Some compromising of naturalness and intelligibility of speech results from low-cost text-to-speech devices, but the flexibility in producing any desired word sequences is very attractive for general-purpose applications.

Trends have developed toward low-power CMOS (complementary metal-oxide-semiconductor) fabrication, more memory and less demand for sophisticated algorithms, and improvement of the quality of voice output. Manufacturers offer services for the custom design, recording, and storage of a vocabulary for specific applications. However, many users desire the ability to develop their own vocabularies, so special vocabulary development systems have been devised. Improved performance can be achieved with software enhancements offered by speech service groups.

**Assessment of systems.** Parameterized voice response systems and text-to-speech synthesizers are expected to dominate most applications, since one provides high-quality speech in a reliable manner while the other permits unlimited vocabulary and fully automatic production of arbitrary English utterances. Critical to the assessment of any speech generator are the intelligibility and the quality (or naturalness) of the generated speech. Methods are needed for accurate measurement of the intelligibility of continuous speech and the subjective assessment of adequacies of machine-quality speech. In some applications, such as for cockput warnings, the machine-generated speech should sound robotic or distinctive to attract attention and be heard above noises, while in other situations, such as with bank-by-phone or consumer products, naturalness and good quality will be essential.

Since the cost of storage is decreasing rapidly, larger-vocabulary concatenation systems (with or without parameterization) are likely to be increasingly used, but the flexibility in sound construction and the unrestricted vocabulary and discourses permitted by text-to-speech systems will promote further work on them as well. As techniques advance, and the markets and uses expand, there will be a growing interest in methods for systematically evaluating the performances of all aspects of voice response systems. Standard tests for intelligibility and quality assessment will allow side-by-side comparisons of devices. Further research in phonetics, prosodics, syntax, and application of synthesized speech will contribute improved voice response capabilities, and those capabilities will provide informative assessment of abilities to model processes of human speech production. SEE SPEECH RECOGNITION.

*Wayne A. Lea*

***Bibliography.*** G. Bristow, *Electronic Speech Synthesis*, 1984; J. L. Flanagan, *Speech Analysis, Synthesis and Perception*, 2d ed., 1972; J. L. Flanagan and L. R. Rabiner (eds.), *Speech Synthesis*, 1973.

## Volt-ohm-milliammeter

A self-contained test instrument for measuring a wide range of voltages (both ac and dc), resistances, and currents (usually dc only), particularly in radio, television, and electronic servicing.

All readings are obtained on a single multiscale indicating instrument. The selection of the correct ranges and function is accomplished either by means of one or two rotary switches, by multiple pin jacks, or by a combination of both.

Instrument sensitivity for dc-voltage measurements is usually 20,000 ohms per volt, although the figure ranges from 1000 to 100,000; for ac-voltage measurements the sensitivity ranges from 1000 to 20,000 ohms per volt. Accuracy is usually about 3% for dc, and 5% for ac measurements.

The terms multimeter and analyzer (or circuit analyzer) are quite commonly used as synonyms for volt-ohm-milliammeter. SEE AMMETER; OHMMETER; VOLTMETER.

*Isaac F. Kinnard*

## Voltage amplifier

An electronic amplifier that produces, with minimum distortion, an output voltage greater in magnitude than the input voltage. For a general discussion of amplifiers SEE AMPLIFIER.

Voltage amplifiers are built to amplify signals with frequency components in the range from zero hertz to thousands of megahertz. To cover this frequency range, several different types of amplifiers are required. An amplifier which cannot amplify voltage signals with zero frequency (direct-current) components is called *RC* (resistance-capacitance) coupled. If zero frequency (dc) components are amplified, the amplifier is known as dc or direct-coupled. In the range from a few hertz to 30 kHz, amplifiers are classified as audio. In the frequency range up to 10 MHz for use in television, pulse circuits, and electronic instruments, amplifiers are known as video. For the radio-frequency range from a few hundred kilohertz to hundreds of megahertz, tuned amplifiers are normally used. At ultrahigh frequencies, amplifiers designed around special tubes are employed. SEE KLYSTRON; MAGNETRON; TRAVELING-WAVE TUBE.

**RC-coupled amplifier.** The *RC*-coupled amplifier is employed in the frequency range from a few hertz to about 10 MHz. However, operation at the higher frequencies in this range is obtained only by employing frequency-compensation networks. The term *RC*-coupled amplifier generally refers to any set of amplifier stages that are coupled by a resistance-capacitance network. **Figure 1*a*** illustrates a grounded-source circuit. The coupling capacitor $C_b$ is required to block the dc voltage at the drain of the first field-effect transistor (FET) from appearing at the gate of the following FET. This capacitor limits the lower frequency for which the amplifier will have a usable gain because the reactance $1/2\pi f C_b$ of the capacitor is inversely proportional to frequency $f$. Therefore, as the frequency decreases, the amplified signal voltage at the drain of the FET will be attenuated by the voltage divider formed by this reactance and the gate resistor.

A similar condition occurs when two transistor stages are *RC*-coupled as in Fig. 1*b*. Here, two common-emitter stages are coupled by means of capacitor $C_b$, and the same problem of reduced gain at lower frequencies exists.

The high-frequency limit of usable amplification is determined by the shunt capacitance and the effective drain load resistance of a FET, or output load resistance of a transistor. The shunt capacitance is composed of the input capacitance of the following FET or transistor, the drain-to-source capacitance of the FET or output capacitance of the transistor in the stage, and the stray wiring capacitance. SEE VIDEO AMPLIFIER.

The input capacitance to a FET in a grounded-source amplifier stage is composed of the capacitance formed from the gate-to-source and from the drain-to-gate capacitance multiplied by 1 minus the gain of the stage. Similarly, the input capacitance of a transistor in the grounded-emitter configuration is the sum of the emitter-junction capacitance and the collector-junction capacitance multiplied by 1 minus the gain of the stage. The gain is negative in the midband region, permitting the input capacitance to be large, on the order of 30–50 picofarads.

If the upper and lower half-power (or cutoff) frequencies are, respectively, high and low, compared with the frequency spectrum of the signal to be amplified, then the gain is essentially uniform with frequency.

***Midfrequency gain.*** In the case of the FET amplifier the midfrequency gain is shown by Eq. (1), where $g_m$

$$A_v = -g_m R_{\text{eq}} \quad (1)$$

is the transconductance of the FET, the minus sign indicates a 180° phase reversal between the input gate signal and the output signal, and the equivalent load resistance $R_{eq}$ is the parallel combination of the dynamic drain resistance $r_d$ of the FET, the gate resistance $R_g$, and the load or coupling resistance $R_d$.

For the transistor amplifier the computation of gain is more involved, because of the relatively lower input and output impedances of the transistors. The midfrequency voltage gain is shown by Eq. (2). The input

$$A_v = A_i \frac{R_L}{R_{\text{in}}} \quad (2)$$

resistance of this stage is given by Eq. (3). $R_L$, the

$$R_{\text{in}} = \frac{\Delta^h R_L + h_{ie}}{h_{oe} R_L + 1} \tag{3}$$

total load resistance seen by this transistor, includes the parallel combination of the collector resistor $R_c$, the bias network $R_B$ where $R_B = R_1R_2/(R_1 + R_2)$, and the input resistance $R_{\text{in}}$ of the next stage. The $h_{ie}$ is the input impedance and $h_{oe}$ the output admittance of the transistor; $h_{re}$ is the voltage-feedback ratio and $h_{fe}$ is the forward-current ratio, and the quantity $\Delta^h$ is $h_{ie}h_{oe} - h_{re}h_{fe}$. Because of the dependence of the gain on the $R_{\text{in}}$ of the next stage, it is necessary to compute the gain per stage in a transistor amplifier by starting with the last stage and working backward toward the input. The current gain is given by Eq. (4).

$$-A_i = \frac{h_{fe}}{1 + h_{oe}R_L} \tag{4}$$

***High-frequency gain.*** The upper half-power frequency is that frequency for which the reactance of the effective shunt capacitance is equal to the equivalent load resistance.

For the FET amplifier the equivalent load resistance $R_{eq}$ is the parallel combination of $r_d$, $R_d$, and $R_g$, the gate resistance in Fig. 1*a*. The upper half-power frequency is shown by Eq. (5).

$$f_2 = \frac{1}{2\pi R_{\text{eq}} C_{\text{shunt}}} \tag{5}$$

For the transistor amplifier the equivalent resistance is the parallel combination of $R_c$, $R_B$, the input resistance of the next stage $R_{\text{in}}$, and the output resistance of the transistor $R_o$. The upper half-power frequency is formed from the same equation as given for the FET, provided there is a long chain of stages.

***Low-frequency gain.*** The lower half-power frequency is that frequency for which the reactance of the coupling capacitator $C_b$ equals the effective resistance $R$ appearing in parallel with the coupling capacitator. For the FET amplifier at low frequencies, the effective resistance is the dynamic drain resistance $r_d$ and the coupling resistance $R_d$ in parallel, and this combination in series with the gate resistor $R_g$ of the next stage. Therefore, the lower half-power frequency is shown by Eq. (6).

$$f_1 = \frac{1}{2\pi RC} \tag{6}$$

In the case of the transistor amplifier, the resistors appearing across $C_b$ are the output resistance $R_o$, in parallel with the collector resistor $R_c$, and this combination in series with the parallel combination of the bias resistor $R_B$ and the input resistance $R_{\text{in}}$ of the next stage. The same expression for $f_1$ is applicable.

***Passband.*** At the half-power frequencies the gain is equal to the midband gain divided by the square root of 2. For either the FET or transistor *RC*-coupled amplifier the gain at any low frequency $f$ can be expressed in terms of the midfrequency gain, as shown in Eq. (7). At high frequencies, gain is shown by Eq.

$$A_{\text{low}} = \frac{A_{\text{mid}}}{1 - j(f_1/f)} \tag{7}$$

(8). This simple relationship permits drawing a uni-

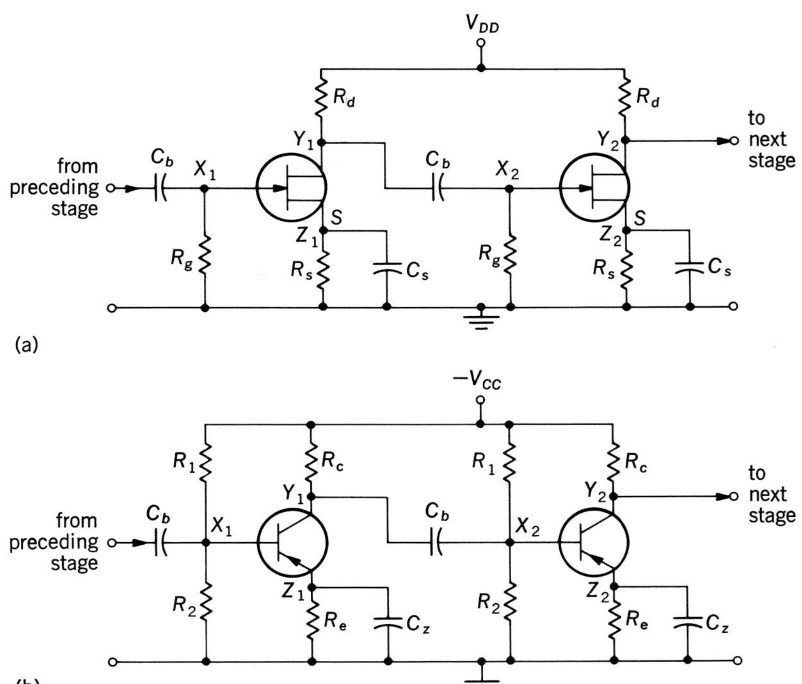


**Fig. 1. Cascade of (*a*) common-source (CS) depletion-type, or JFET, stages; (*b*) common-emitter (CE) transistor stages.**

$$A_{\text{high}} = \frac{A_{\text{mid}}}{1 + j(f/f_2)} \tag{8}$$

versal frequency-response curve A, **Fig. 2**, applicable to any single stage of either a FET or transistor amplifier. The graph is made universal by plotting relative gain as a function of the ratio of the signal frequency to the half-power-point frequencies. The slope of the curve approaches −6 dB per octave for a single stage of amplification. One octave is a change in frequency by a factor of 2. The frequency range $f_2 - f_1$ is called the bandwidth $B$ of the stage.

The gain of a multistage amplifier is equal to the product of the gain of each of the individual stages. Curve B of Fig. 2 is for three identical stages. For this specific case the slope of the curve is −18 dB per octave, which is the sum of the −6 dB per octave slope inherent in each of the three stages. When stages are cascaded, the half-power (70.7%, or −3 dB) points are moved in toward the midfrequencies.

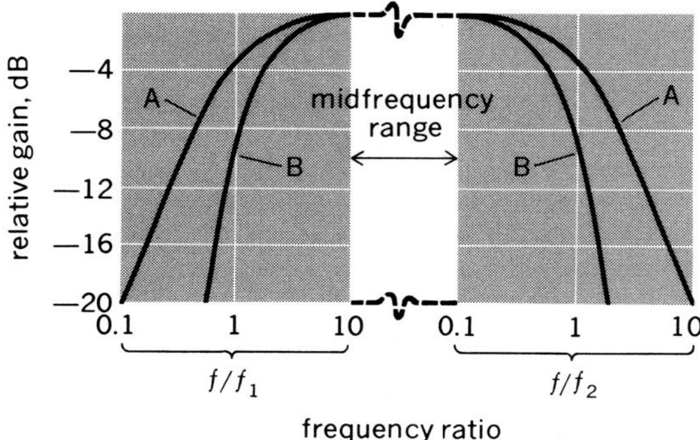


**Fig. 2. Universal frequency-resonse curve for *RC*-coupled amplifiers. Curve A is for any single stage of amplification. Curve B is for three identical stages.**

Therefore, the cascading of stages decreases the frequency passband between the half-power points.

For reasons of economy, amplifiers used for entertainment purposes and similar applications sometimes make use of the frequency regions beyond the flat midfrequency region. Amplifiers employed in calibrated instruments, such as electronic voltmeters and cathode-ray oscilloscopes, are limited to the midfrequency range.

***Interstage transfer function.*** One important distinction arises between the FET and the transistor amplifier. The FET is inherently a voltage amplifier, and a voltage appearing across the gate resistor $R_g$ in Fig. 1*a* also appears from gate to source in the next FET and is amplified. The situation is considerably different with transistors. A signal current leaving the first transistor collector follows two paths, each of which shunts a portion of this current to ground. This reduces the current gain and must be accounted for in computing the overall amplifier current gain and hence the voltage gain.

The interstage transfer function is given by the ratio of the current flowing into the input resistance $R_{in}$ of the next stage, divided by the current from the preceding transistor. In terms of the parameters of the circuit, the transfer function is shown by Eq. (9),

$$a = \frac{R_c R_B}{R_c R_B + R_{in}(R_c + R_B)} \quad (9)$$

where $R_B$ is as given before. For well-designed, broadband amplifiers, transfer function $a$ is in the neighborhood of 0.7.

The overall voltage gain of a multistage FET amplifier is shown by Eq. (10) where $A_{v1}$, $A_{v2}$, $A_{v3}$, is

$$A_{total} = A_{v1} \cdot A_{v2} \cdot A_{v3} \cdots \quad (10)$$

the voltage gain of each stage. For a transistor amplifier the overall voltage gain is shown in Eqs. (2) and (11). $A_1$, $A_2$, . . . are the current gains per stage, and

$$A_i = a_1 \cdot A_1 \cdot a_2 \cdot A_2 \cdot a_3 \cdot A_3 \cdots \quad (11)$$

$a_1$, $a_2$, . . . represent the interstage transfer functions.

**Tuned amplifier.** A tuned amplifier amplifies voltage signals in a selected narrow frequency band and suppresses signals outside the desired band. A tuned amplifier is thus a bandpass amplifier with the additional constraint that its bandwidth can be a small fraction of the center frequency. Such amplifiers are commonly used as radio-frequency (rf) or intermediate-frequency (i-f) amplifiers for superheterodyne radio receivers. In the case of rf amplifiers it is required that the center frequency be tunable or variable and that, in addition, over the tuning range the overall selectivity should remain constant. Constant selectivity means that the bandwidth should remain constant. In order to obtain the necessary selectivity and high voltage gain, *LC* tank or resonant circuits are used as loads with transistor or FET amplifiers as shown in **Fig. 3**.

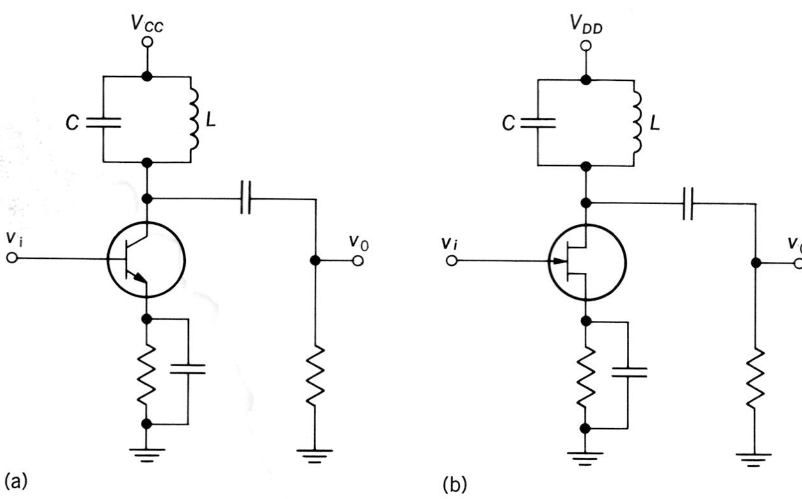


**Fig. 3. Single-tuned amplifier: (*a*) transistor; (*b*) field-effect transistor.**

The important characteristics of a tune amplifier are the voltage gain at resonance, the variation of voltage gain with frequency near the resonant frequency, and, if the center frequency is to be varied, the way in which the voltage gain changes.

***Single-tuned amplifier.*** The circuits of Fig. 3 show single-tuned amplifiers. Resonance occurs when the capacitive and inductive reactances are equal, that is, when $\omega_0 L = 1/\omega_0 C$, where $\omega_0 = 2\pi f_0$, or Eq. (12)

$$f_0 = \frac{1}{2\pi\sqrt{LC}} \quad (12)$$

is satisfied.

The quality of the inductor in any tuned circuit can be described in terms of the quality factor $Q$ as given in Eq. (13), where $L$ is the inductance in henries, $R$

$$Q = \frac{\omega L}{R} \quad (13)$$

is the series resistance of the coil in ohms, and $\omega$ equals $2\pi$ times the frequency at which $Q$ is evaluated.

The impedance at resonance of the tank circuit is given by Eq. (14).

$$Z = \frac{L}{RC} = \omega_0 L Q \quad (14)$$

The maximum voltage gain at resonance for the FET amplifier of Fig. 3*b* is given by Eq. (15), where

$$A_v = -g_m Z \quad (15)$$

$g_m$ is the transconductance of the FET. A similar expression holds for the transistor-tuned amplifier.

The bandwidth of the parallel-tuned (or single-tuned) amplifier is given by Eq. (16).

$$B = \frac{f_0}{Q} \quad (16)$$

***Double-tuned amplifier.*** Double-tuned amplifiers are used where the pass band is centered on a fixed frequency, as is the case for i-f radio amplifiers. The two circuits may be coupled inductively or compacitively or a combination of both. Usually one circuit is known as the primary circuit and the other as the secondary circuit, as is the case with a transformer-coupled amplifier. The transformer primary and secondary are both tuned with suitable capacitors. Often the transformer has either air or powdered metal cores. The core slug is about as long as the length of the coil form for the windings. Tuning in this case may be accomplished by moving the core slug partially in and out of the coil. SEE TRANSFORMER.

For the double-tuned transformer-coupled FET amplifier, the gain at the resonant frequency $f_0$ is given by Eq. (17). The subscripts indicate primary and sec-

$$A = g_m k \frac{\omega_0 \sqrt{L_p L_s}}{k^2 + 1/Q_p Q_s} \qquad (17)$$

ondary inductances and $Q$s. The transconductance of the FET is $g_m$, $\omega_0 = 2\pi f_0$, and $k$ is the coefficient of coupling between the coils.

For critical coupling ($k = 1/\sqrt{Q_p Q_s}$), nearly identical primary $L_p$ and secondary $L_s$ coils ($Q_p = Q_s = Q$), and large $Q$s, the voltage gain at resonance is a maximum and is shown by Eq. (18). The associated

$$A = g_m \omega_0 L Q/2 \qquad (18)$$

bandwidth between half-power points is given by Eq. (19), when the coupling is critical and $B$ and $f_0$ are in the same units.

$$B = \frac{\sqrt{2} f_0}{Q} \qquad (19)$$

When transistors are employed, the possibility of obtaining considerable voltage gain from the tuned transformer, as is possible with FETs, becomes more difficult because of the relatively low input and output impedances of transistors. The tuned transformer functions more as an impedance-matching device. Taps or auxiliary windings are often provided on rf and i-f transformers for use with transistors to provide means for impedance matching.

**Source and emitter-follower stages.** If the drain of the FET is connected directly to the power-supply source and the output is taken from the source, the resulting circuit has special properties which are useful. Such a circuit is called a source-follower. Similarly, if collector is connected directly to the power supply, the circuit is called an emitter follower and the same overall results are obtained. Simple versions are illustrated in **Fig. 4**. Voltage gain of these circuits

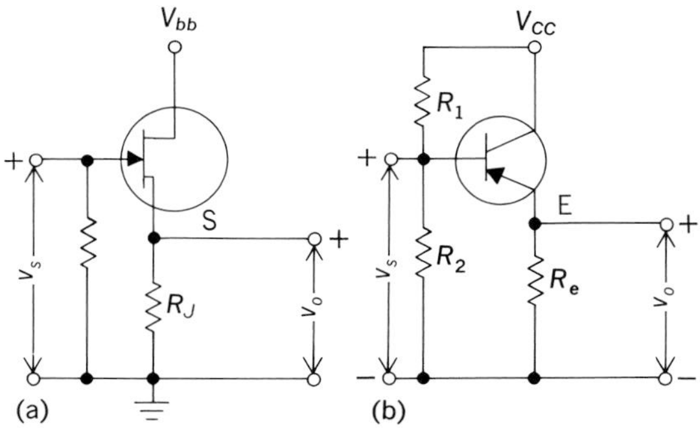


**Fig. 4. Amplifiers in which the FET or transistor is connected directly to the power source. (*a*) Source-follower amplifier. (*b*) Grounded-collector amplifier. The drain supply voltage is $V_{bb}$ and the collector supply voltage is $V_{CC}$.**

is less than unity, typical values ranging from 0.90 to 0.99. Input and output voltages are in phase. The principal properties of interest are the relatively high input impedance and the low output impedance. The amplifier is often used as an impedance-matching device. In such application an emitter follower can be inserted between a source and a load with only slight decrease in voltage gain. Current and power gain may be quite high if desired.

The input capacitance of a source-follower stage is low, because gain is nearly equal to unity and is positive. Therefore, the input capacitance is essentially

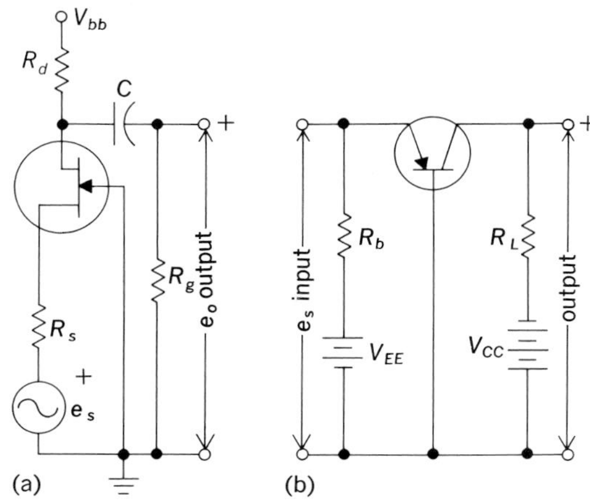


**Fig. 5. Amplifiers in which the gate or base is grounded. (*a*) Grounded-gate amplifier. (*b*) Grounded-base amplifier. $V_{bb}$ is the drain supply voltage, $V_{EE}$ the emitter supply voltage, and $V_{CC}$ the collector supply voltage.**

the gate-to-drain capacitance, which is of the order of 2 pf. Thus the source follower is ideally suited for use in the interstage coupling of a broad-band amplifier.

The midfrequency gain of a source-follower circuit is given by Eq. (20). The symbol $\mu$ represents the

$$A_v = \frac{\mu R_s}{r_d + (\mu + 1) R_s} \qquad (20)$$

amplification factor, $r_d$ is the dynamic drain resistance, and $R_s$ is the source load resistor. The output impedance that the source follower presents to its output circuit is of interest and is given by Eq. (21),

$$Z_{\text{out}} = \frac{R_s}{1 + g_m R_s + R_s/r_d} \qquad (21)$$

where $g_m$ is the transductance. By proper selection of FET and source load resistor $R_s$, a wide range of output impedances may be obtained.

If transistors are used at midfrequency, the voltage gain is approximated by Eq. (22).

$$A_v = \frac{v_0}{v_s} = -\frac{(1 + h_{fe}) R_e}{h_{ie} + (1 + h_{fe}) R_e} \qquad (22)$$

The input resistance is shown by Eq. (23). The two vertical lines in Eq. (23) mean the parallel combina-

$$R_i = R_1 \| R_2 \| [h_{ie} + (1 + h_{fe}) R_e] \qquad (23)$$

tion of the corresponding resistors. $R_1$ and $R_2$ represent the bias resistors of the transistor input.

The output admittance of the emitter follower is given by Eq. (24), where zero source resistance is assumed.

$$Y_{\text{out}} = \frac{1}{R_e} + h_{oe} + \frac{1 + h_{fe}}{h_{ie}} \qquad (24)$$

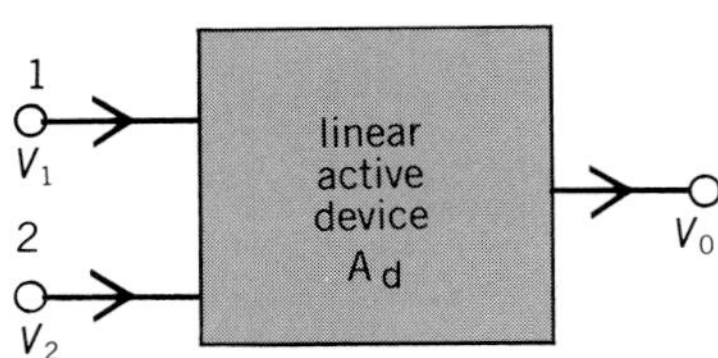


**Fig. 6. The output is a linear function of $v_1$ and $v_2$. For an ideal differential amplifier, $v_0 = A_d(v_1 - v_2)$.**

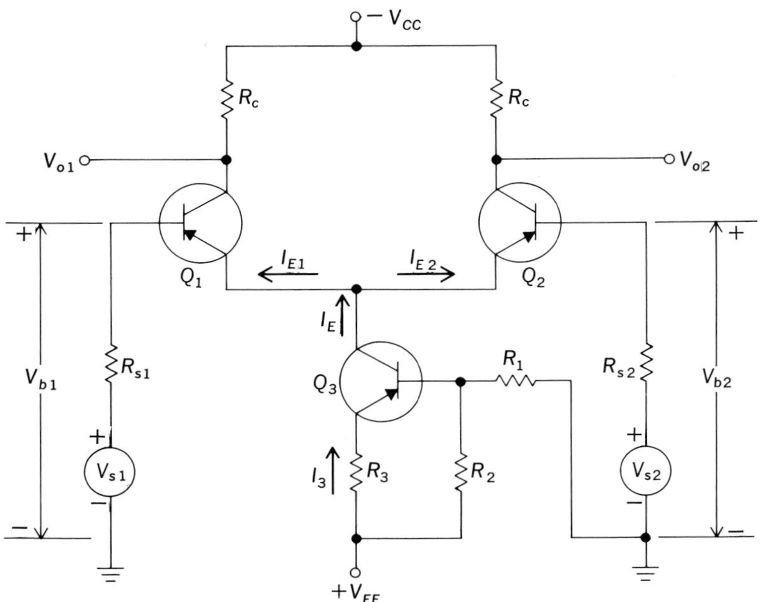


**Fig. 7.** Emitter-coupled difference amplifier, with a constant-current stage in the emitter circuit. Nominally, $R_{s1} = R_{s2}$.

**Grounded-gate (base) amplifier.** If the gate (or base) is grounded and the input signal is applied to the source (or emitter) with the output taken from the drain (or collector), the circuit is called a grounded-gate (or grounded-base) amplifier (**Fig. 5**). This circuit features a low input impedance and a high output impedance. Because of the low input impedance, the amplifier will draw power from the source and must, therefore, be used with a low-impedance source. It has found its chief application in rf amplifiers operating at very high frequencies, such as the tuner in a television receiver; at these frequencies it gives a high signal-to-noise ratio with low input-output capacitance. It does so at the expense of rf selectivity. This excludes it from use in a narrow-band receiver application.

***Grounded-gate amplifier.*** Voltage gain of the grounded-gate amplifier is given by Eq. (25). $R_s$ is the

$$A = \frac{(\mu + 1)\, Z_L}{r_d + (\mu + 1)\, R_s + Z_L} \tag{25}$$

internal resistance of the signal source, $\mu$ and $r_d$ are the amplification factor and dynamic drain resistance, respectively, of the FET, and $Z_L$ is the load impedance. For the midfrequency gain in an *RC*-coupled amplifier $Z_L$ is the parallel combination of the coupling resistor $R_d$ and the gate resistor of the next stage $R_g$.

The input impedance of the stage is shown by Eq. (26). The stage can be used to match low-impedance

$$Z_{\text{in}} = \frac{r_d + Z_L}{\mu + 1} \tag{26}$$

circuits to high-impedance circuits.

***Grounded-base amplifier.*** Voltage gain of the grounded-base amplifier is given approximately by Eq. (27), where $h_{fe}$ and $h_{ie}$ are the short-circuit current

$$A = h_{fe}\frac{R_L}{h_{ie}} = \frac{v_o}{v_2} \tag{27}$$

gain and input resistance for the common-emitter connection.

The input and output resistances are approximated by Eqs. (28) and (29).

$$R_i = \frac{h_{ie}}{1 + h_{fe}} \tag{28}$$

$$R_o = R_L \tag{29}$$

**Direct-coupled amplifier.** When the coupling between successive stages of an amplifier is such that direct current may flow from the output of one stage to the input of the following stage, the amplifier is said to be direct-coupled. *See* DIRECT-COUPLED AMPLIFIER.

**Difference amplifiers.** The function of a difference, or differential, amplifier is, in general, to amplify the difference between two signals. The need for differential amplifiers arises in many physical measurements, in medical electronics, in analog computers, and in direct-coupled amplifier applications.

**Figure 6** represents a linear active device with two input signals $v_1$, $v_2$, and one output signal $v_o$, each measured with respect to ground. In an ideal differential amplifier the output signal $v_o$ should be given by Eq. (30), where $A_d$ is the gain of the differential

$$v_o = A_d(v_1 - v_2) \tag{30}$$

amplifier. Thus it is seen that any signal, such as noise, which is common to both inputs will have no effect on the output voltage. However, a practical differential amplifier cannot be described by Eq. (30) because, in general, the output depends not only upon the difference signal $v_d$ of the two signals, but also upon the average level, called the common-mode signal $v_c$. The values of $v_d$ and $v_c$ are given by Eqs. (31) and (32). It can be seen that if, for example, one sig-

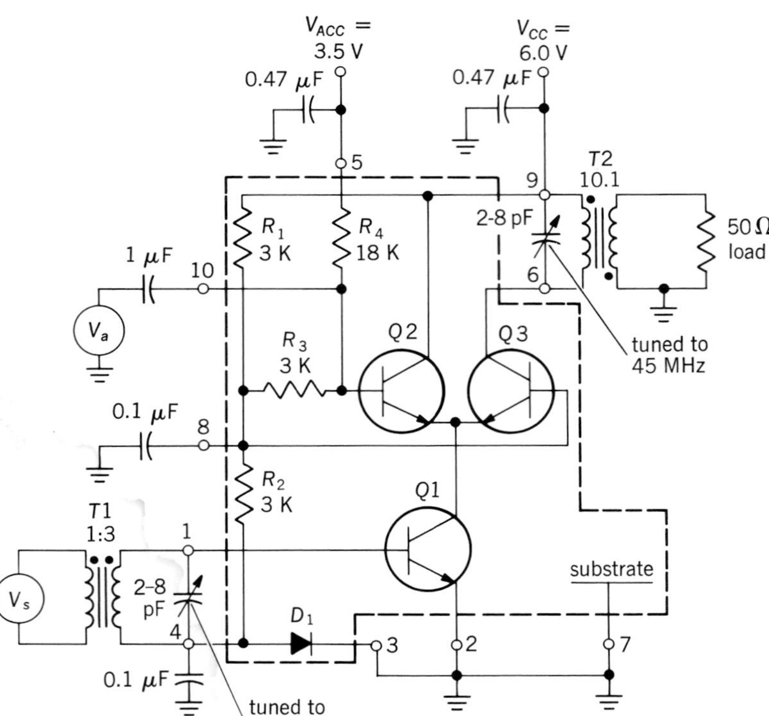


**Fig. 8.** A practical 45-MHz tuned amplifier (with $V_a = 0$), or an rf modulator if $V_a \neq 0$. (*Motorola Semiconductor, Inc.*)

$$v_d \equiv v_1 - v_2 \quad (31)$$

$$v_c \equiv 1/2\,(v_1 + v_2) \quad (32)$$

nal is $+50\ \mu v$ and the second is $-50\ \mu v$, the output will not be exactly the same as if $v_1 = 1050\ \mu v$ and $v_2 = 950\ \mu v$, even though the difference $v_d = 100\ \mu v$ is the same in the two cases.

In general, the output of the difference amplifier is given by Eq. (33), where ρ is a quantity called the

$$v_o = A_d v_d \left(1 + \frac{1}{\rho}\frac{v_c}{v_d}\right) \quad (33)$$

common-mode rejection ratio. An emitter-coupled difference amplifier is shown in **Fig. 7**. This circuit can also be used as a single-signal amplifier by grounding one base and taking the output at either $v_{o1}$ or $v_{o2}$. The noise voltage still is present at each base and cancels in the output, making possible low-noise amplification of the signal $v_{s1}$.

**Integrated amplifier.** Integrated circuit amplifiers are dc amplifiers commonly referred to as operational amplifiers. The basic building block of an integrated tuned amplifier is the emitter-coupled different amplifier of Fig. 7. Such a circuit is shown in **Fig. 8**. The block enclosed by a dashed line is an integrated circuit; all other components are discrete elements added externally. The input signal is applied through the tuned transformer *T*1 to the base of *Q*1. The load $R_L$ is applied across the tuned transformer *T*2 in the collector circuit of *Q*3. The amplification is performed by the transistors *Q*1 and *Q*3, whereas the magnitude of the gain is controlled by *Q*2. The combination *Q*1–*Q*3 acts a common-emitter common-base pair, known as cascode combination. *SEE INTEGRATED CIRCUITS.*

*Christos C. Halkias*

***Bibliography.*** C. H. Evans, *Electronic Amplifiers: Theory, Design and Use*, 1979; C. A. Holt, *Electronic Circuits*, 1978; J. Millman, *Microelectronics*, 1979.

## Voltage measurement

Determination of the difference in electrostatic potential between two points. The unit of voltage in the International System of Units (SI) is the volt, defined as the potential difference between two points of a conducting wire carrying a constant current of 1 ampere when the power dissipated between these two points is equal to 1 watt.

Accurate realization of this unit involves exceedingly difficult measurements, which have not led to an agreed value of the SI volt or ampere with an uncertainty at three-standard-deviation limits of less than about 1 part in $10^5$. However, new methods promise to greatly improve the accuracy.

**Voltage standards.** These comprise standard cells, Josephson junction standards, and electronic standards.

***Standard cells.*** The saturated Weston cell, which consists of electrodes of mercury and mercury-cadmium amalgam in an electrolyte of saturated cadmium sulfate solution, has been in use since the latter part of the nineteenth century as a portable room-temperature voltage standard.

By means of a relatively simple potentiometer, standard-cell voltages can be compared to within 1 part in $10^7$, and by comparing the voltage of each cell against the mean of a group it is possible to detect and eliminate less stable cells, and thus to maintain a voltage standard of high stability. Saturated standard cells are very sensitive to environmental conditions and to the passage of any current through them, and are therefore rather unsatisfactory and inconvenient devices for use as reference standards and even more so as transfer standards. Unfortunately there is as yet no other device which approaches the stability of good cells, which may vary by less than 100 nanovolts per year. *SEE POTENTIOMETER (VOLTAGE METER).*

The precision of such voltage measurements is considerably better than that of the actual realization of the volt. Room-temperature measurements are limited only by thermal (Johnson) noise in the cells themselves and in null detectors to a resolution of a few nanovolts, whereas the true (SI) value of the volt is not known to better than about 1 in $10^5$.

***Josephson junction standards.*** The need for some international agreement at a higher level of accuracy was resolved in 1972, following the introduction of the Josephson junction as a frequency-voltage converter. A Josephson junction consists of two superconductors separated by a thin insulating or poorly conducting barrier, across which conduction can occur by the tunneling process. Frequently this is effected by evaporating a film of tin or niobium on the surface of a similar film which has been coated with the desired insulating film by controlled oxidation. The dimensions of the junction are considerably less than 1 mm (0.04 in.).

When such a junction is irradiated by radio-frequency energy, usually in the frequency range 10–40 GHz, its voltage-current characteristic becomes broken into a "staircase" form (**Fig. 1**). The height *V* of

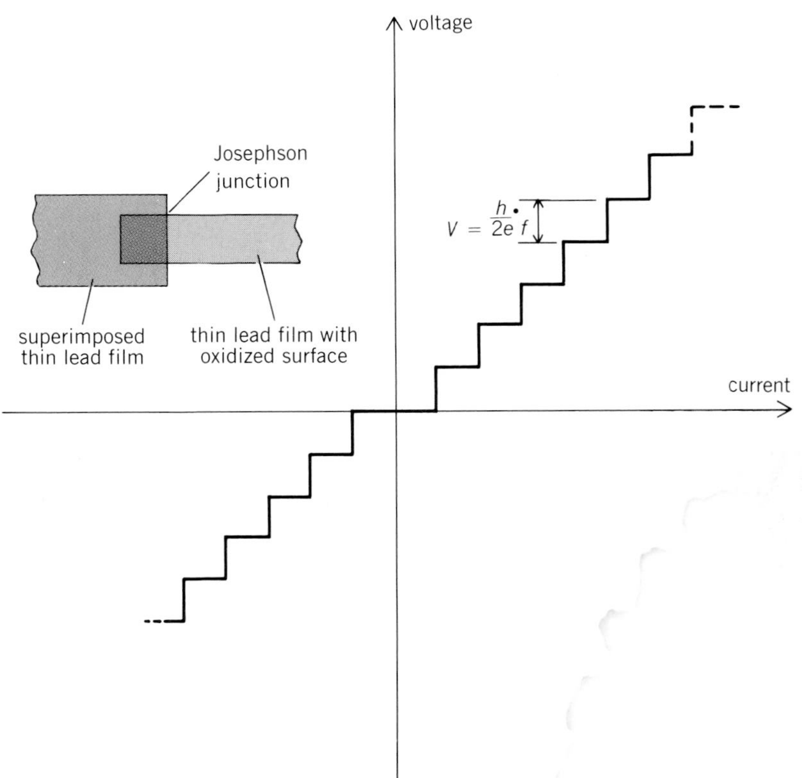


**Fig. 1. Ideal Josephson junction voltage-current characteristic. Inset shows configuration of Josephson junction.**

each voltage step is given by Eq. (1), where $f$ is the

$$hf = 2eV \quad (1)$$

irradiating frequency, $h$ is Planck's constant, and $e$ is the electron charge. The measurement of this voltage is made by a system such as shown in **Fig. 2**, and since the junction must be immersed in a helium cryostat at a temperature of a few kelvins in order to produce the superconducting effect, it is convenient to include a large part of the system in the cryostat. It is also possible to use another Josephson junction as a null detector, and hence to compare the step voltage of a few tens of microvolts with that of a room-temperature standard cell to within less than 1 part in $10^8$. *SEE SQUID.*

In 1972 the International Bureau of Weights and Measures (BIPM) issued a declaration recognizing the value 483,594.0 GHz/V for the frequency/voltage ratio of a Josephson junction. This is to some extent an arbitrary value; however, it makes it possible to have international standards of adequate precision, and Josephson junctions for this purpose are now used in the national laboratories of all technologically advanced countries. (The great majority of countries use the value recognized by the BIPM declaration, but for various reasons some use slightly different values.) *SEE JOSEPHSON EFFECT; SUPERCONDUCTING DEVICES.*

***Electronic voltage standards.*** Diodes used for voltage regulation (Zener diodes) pass a current that increases rapidly when the voltage rises above some critical value, and hence tend to act as constant-voltage devices. If such diodes are fed from a well-stabilized source, for example, if they are controlled by another Zener diode, they can provide voltage references which may have a stability as good as 1 in $10^6$, at least for short periods. Since they are much less sensitive to environmental conditions and to overloads than standard cells, they are much more suitable for use as transfer standards for all except the most accurate purposes, and are also in almost universal use as voltage references in electronic measuring instruments. *SEE ZENER DIODE.*

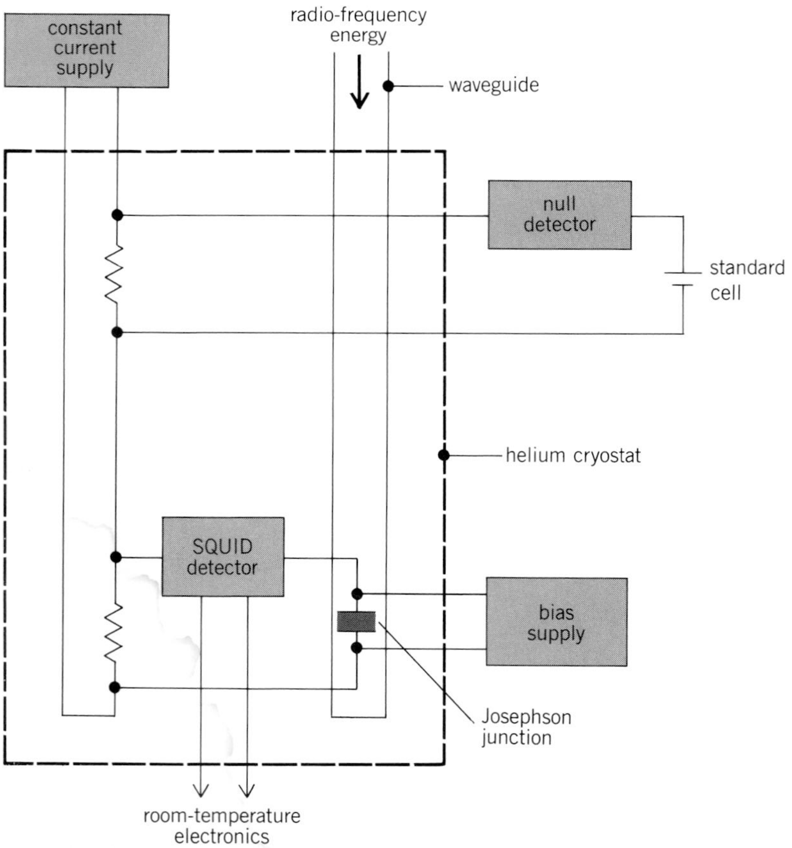

**Fig. 2. Simplified Josephson junction measuring system.**

**Direct-current voltage measurements.** The chief types of instruments for measuring direct-current (constant) voltage are potentiometers, resistive voltage dividers, electronic voltmeters, and pointer instruments.

***Potentiometer measurements.*** The most fundamental dc voltage measurements from 0 to 2 V at the highest achievable accuracy are still made by the use of precision potentiometers, using photocoupled galvanometer amplifiers as low-impedance null detectors. Potentiometers are capable of self-calibration, since only linearity is important, and can give accurate measurements down to a few nanovolts. This level can now also be achieved by the use of a very few electronic amplifiers, and it may often be more convenient to use one of these to measure small residual imbalance voltages when a potentiometric circuit is approximately balanced rather than to seek an exact balance. *SEE AMPLIFIER.*

In all dc low-voltage measurements, care is necessary to avoid thermal emf's. All wiring must be of pure copper, which may be plated with gold but not tin or nickel, and any movement of conductors must be avoided. It is necessary to wait several seconds after any switch operation to allow thermal emf's which are generated to die away.

***Resistive voltage dividers.*** The most accurate dc measurements of voltages above 2 V are made by using resistive dividers, which are tapped chains of wire-wound resistors, often immersed in oil, which can be self-calibrated for linearity by using a build-up method. Instruments for use up to 1 kV, with tappings typically in a binary or binary-coded decimal series from 1 V, are known as volt ratio boxes, and provide uncertainties of only a few parts per million.

Higher voltages can be measured by extending such chains, but as the voltage increases above about 15 kV, increasing attention must be paid to avoid any sharp edges or corners which could give rise to corona discharges or breakdown. High-voltage dividers for use up to 100 kV with an uncertainty of about 1 in $10^5$, and to 500 kV with an uncertainty of about 1 in $10^4$, have been made. *SEE CORONA DISCHARGE; ELECTRICAL BREAKDOWN.*

***Electronic voltmeters.*** These instruments, also known as digital voltmeters (DVMs), are now in widespread use, and are rapidly becoming the principal means used for voltage measurement at all levels of accuracy up to a few parts in $10^6$, and at all voltages up to about 1 kV. Essentially they consist of a power supply, which may be supplied by either mains or batteries; a voltage reference, usually provided by a Zener diode; an analog-to-digital converter; and a digital display system. This provides measurement over a basic range from zero to a few volts. Additional lower ranges may be provided by amplifiers, whose gain is stabilized by precision resistors; and, for instruments offering the greatest sensitivity, down to 1 nanovolt, the input is normally converted into an ac signal by a solid-state chopper to avoid drift. The amplified signal is then synchronously rectified. The limits of sensitivity on the lowest range then arise principally from noise in the chopper and from the noise performance of the amplifier, and figures as low as 1 nV in a 1-Hz bandwidth are available from the best of such instruments. The accuracy on the basic range, which is the best the instrument can offer, is limited to that of the analog-to-digital converter. *SEE ANALOG-TO-DIGITAL CONVERTER*.

In this type of digital voltmeter, analog-to-digital conversion is by a successive approximation converter, in which the input is compared successively against the voltages on a binary resistive divider connected to the reference voltage, taking the bits in decreasing order of sensitivity. Any errors in this type of analog-to-digital converter arise principally in the resistor chain, and are therefore relatively stable and can be determined and applied as corrections. It is unusual to find analog-to-digital converters of more than 16 bits (1 in 65,536), and interpolation may then be provided to give a resulting display to six decimal digits.

Microprocessors are extensively used in these instruments to provide automatic error correction, using errors established by a previous calibration, or to carry out the calibration, using only the calibrated value of the voltage reference. They are also widely used to provide digital instruments with computer interfaces, so that the instruments can be operated under computer network control. *SEE MICROPROCESSOR*.

In simpler instruments an analog-to-digital conversion may be effected by a voltage-controlled oscillator, that is, an oscillator whose frequency is proportional to the voltage, and the digital output is then obtained by measuring the frequency or period of the oscillation. More frequently used is the dual-ramp converter, in which the signal is applied to a capacitor through a switched gate for a fixed time. The capacitor is then discharged at a constant rate until its voltage crosses zero, and the time taken for this to happen is measured by counting the cycles of a reference oscillator. This time is then a direct measure of the voltage. *SEE OSCILLATOR*.

The input resistance of digital voltmeters, which is usually very high (for example, greater than 50 megohms) when operating, may fall to a much lower value if the power is removed.

The best technique for accurate dc voltage measurement is, if necessary, to reduce the voltage to be measured to a few volts by means of a calibrated resistive divider, and to measure the small difference between this voltage and that of an available standard, for example, a calibrated Zener diode standard, by means of a suitable digital voltmeter. This is usually referred to as an injection or backing-off technique. *SEE DIGITAL VOLTMETER*.

***DC pointer instruments.*** For most of the twentieth century the principal dc indicating voltmeters have been moving-coil milliommeters, usually giving full-scale deflection with a current in the region of 1 mA, and provided with a suitable series resistor. Many of these will certainly continue to be used for many years, giving an uncertainty of about 1% of full-scale deflection. Since about 1950 it has become increasingly common to drive such instruments through solid-state amplifiers. This reduces the possibility of mechanical damage through overload, and may also give an increase in sensitivity and in impedance. In laboratory work, such instruments, which may offer full-scale deflection far less than 1 microvolt, are now widely used as null detectors, and more widely in place of the previous multirange passive multimeters.

**Alternating-current voltage measurements.** The mean voltage of a number of complete cycles of any symmetrical waveform is always zero. It is therefore necessary to define what is being measured in alternating voltage measurements. The value of greatest interest is the root-mean-square (rms) value, since this is a direct measure of energy content.

In a sinusoidal waveform the peak and root-mean-square values are related by Eq. (2). DC instruments

$$V_{\text{rms}} = \frac{1}{\sqrt{2}} V_{\text{peak}} \qquad (2)$$

fitted with rectifiers usually respond to the mean of the modulus of the signal, often (incorrectly) referred to as the mean. This "mean" voltage is thus $2/\pi \cdot V_{\text{peak}}$. A periodic voltage is rarely purely sinusoidal, and departure from a sinusoidal waveform is usually specified by harmonic content. *SEE NONSINUSOIDAL WAVEFORM; WAVEFORM*.

***Thermal transfer.*** The most accurate measurement of voltages at frequencies from about 10 Hz to about 1 MHz is through the use of thermal converters. The multijunction type of converter has calculated dc/ac differences well below 1 part per million over its restricted frequency range of about 10 Hz to 10 kHz, and agreement between these devices is usually of that order. They can then be used to select single-junction converters, which are considerably more durable and extend up to at least 1 MHz, of similar performance.

Single-junction converters consist of a thin wire, usually of nickel-chrome alloy, which is heated by the incoming signal to produce a rise in temperature of roughly 180°F (100°C). The temperature rise is detected by a single thermocouple junction fixed in a glass bead near the center of the wire. The whole device is enclosed in an evacuated glass envelope. The heating current is usually 5, 10, or 20 mA. The device is calibrated by comparison with similar devices whose performance has already been established, by the sequential application of dc, ac, reversed dc, and ac signals, and the measurement results are processed to eliminate drift errors. By this means the dc-ac differences can be certified at a level of about 10 parts

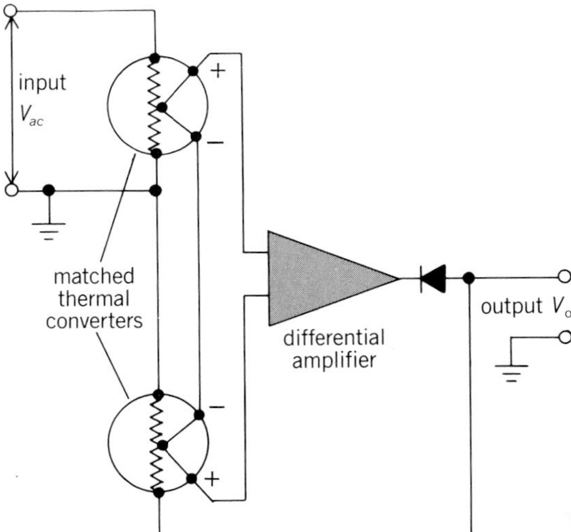


**Fig. 3. Root-mean-square voltmeter using matched thermal converters.**

per million at low frequencies, falling to about 0.01% at 100 kHz. The single-junction converters are used in thermal transfer instruments, in which they are mounted with switched series resistors of special design to give voltage ranges from 1 V to about 1 kV. The measurement at the highest level of accuracy of an alternating voltage is thus made by establishing a dc voltage equivalent to the root-mean-square ac voltage through the use of such an instrument. *See Thermal converters.*

***Voltage ratio devices.*** Two voltage ratio devices are important and widely used at power and audio frequencies, namely, voltage transformers and inductive voltage dividers.

Voltage transformers have the secondary circuit very lightly loaded, and usually use high-permeability cores run at a flux density sufficiently low to give adequate linearity. The primary/secondary voltage ratio then closely approaches the turns ratio, and phase errors are also very small. Ratio and phase errors can be measured by bridge techniques using inductive or capacitative dividers, and once measured are normally stable through the life of the transformer. Voltage transformers are used chiefly at power frequencies at voltages up to 100 kV for accurate measurement, and at higher voltages for protection purposes. *See Transformer.*

In essence, inductive voltage dividers are self-inductors, usually toroidal in form, in which a tapped primary winding is wound on a core of very high permeability, usually of supermumetal. To achieve exact equality of division between windings, the winding consists of a rope of 10 (for a decade divider) insulated similar strands of wire, which are then connected end to end to give the successive sections. This construction provides an equality of division to better than 1 part per million. In a two-stage divider, a second winding of the same number of turns and threading only part of the core is connected across the first. This winding then carries most of the magnetizing current, and the equality of division of the measurement winding is improved to better than 1 in $10^8$. Such dividers can be connected in a decade arrangement to give variable ratios and provide perhaps the most important variable device for measurement or generation of alternating voltage ratios.

***Digital voltmeters.*** As in the dc case, digital voltmeters are now probably the instruments in widest use for ac voltage measurement, and frequently cover both ac and dc regimes and offer resistance measurement ranges as well. Many systems are in use for this purpose. The simplest use diode rectification of the ac to provide a dc signal, which is then amplified and displayed as in dc instruments. This provides a signal proportional to the mean. However, if an array of successively biased diodes is used, the output can be made to approximate to a square law. To obtain a true root-mean-square value, one method in use is to apply the signal, reduced in amplitude if necessary by resistive or inductive dividers using solid-state switches, to the input of one of a pair of matched thermal converters. The second converter is fed from the output of a differential amplifier whose input is fed with the difference voltage between the converters' dc outputs (**Fig. 3**). This results in a dc output voltage which reproduces the law of the thermal converter, which is usually close to a mean-square law.

Another very successful analog approach uses the surprisingly accurate logarithmic relation of Eq. (3)

$$V_{eb} = k \log I_c \tag{3}$$

between the base-emitter voltage $V_{eb}$ and the collector current $I_c$ of a planar transistor, where $k$ is a constant. In the circuit of **Fig. 4** the current through $T_1$ and $T_2$ is proportional to the input voltage $V$; hence the sum of their base-emitter voltages, which is applied to the base-emitter junction of $T_3$, is proportional to $\log V^2$. The base-emitter voltage of $T_3$, which is included to provide compensation, is proportional to $\log V_{ref}$, and so the total base-emitter voltage of $T_3$ is proportional to $(\log V^2 - V_{ref})$, and this will be proportional to $\log V_0$; hence the smoothed value of $V_0$ is proportional to $V^2$. The best instruments using this principle provide ac voltage measurement with uncertainties of about 0.02%. *See Transistor.*

Sampling digital voltmeters are also used, in which the applied voltage is switched for a time very short compared with the period of the signal into a sample-and-hold circuit, of which the essential element is a small capacitor. The voltage developed can then be held and transferred to another device at greater leisure. At low frequencies this approach offers high accuracy and great versatility, since the voltages can be put into digital form and processed or analyzed as desired. At higher frequencies, for example, in the microwave region, it makes possible the direct presentation of voltage waveforms on an oscilloscope. *See Oscilloscope; Sampling voltmeter.*

***AC pointer instruments.*** The analog methods mentioned above produce dc output voltages which are proportional to the ac values, and hence at lower levels of accuracy can be used to drive dc pointer instruments. However, most pointer ac voltmeters are either of the rectifier type, indicating "mean" voltage, or of the moving-iron type which provide a square-law scale. Electrostatic voltmeters, which also produce a square-law scale, are sometimes used for voltages in the range 1 to 10 kV.

**Frequencies above 1 MHz.** Voltage measurements at radio frequencies are mostly made by the use of rectifier instruments up to a few hundred megahertz, although there are some instruments using single-junction converters which cover frequencies up to 500 MHz, or use matched bolometers or calorimeters. At these higher frequencies the use of voltage at a point must be linked to information regarding the transmission system in which it is measured, and most measuring instruments effectively measure the power in a

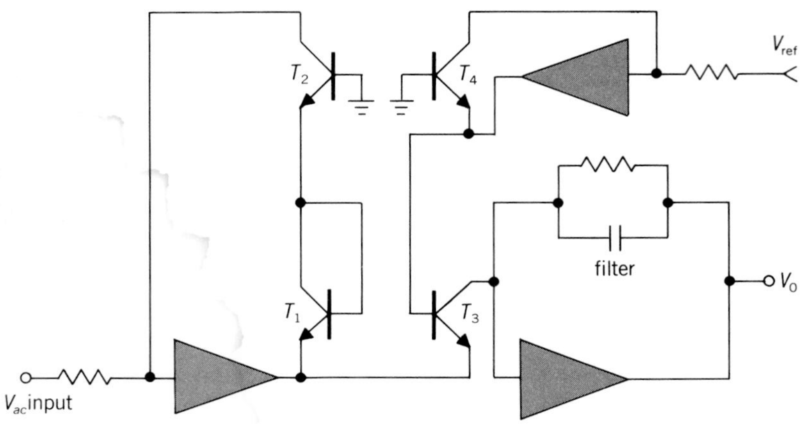


**Fig. 4. Root-mean-square voltmeter using the relation $V_{eb} = k \log I_c$ of a planar transistor.**

matched transmission line, usually of 50 ohms characteristic impedance, and deduce the voltage from it. *SEE MICROWAVE MEASUREMENTS; TRANSMISSION LINES.*

**Pulse measurements.** Pulse voltage measurements are most simply made by transferring the pulse waveform to an oscilloscope, the deflection sensitivity of which can be directly calibrated. If the voltage is too high for direct application to the oscilloscope, it may be reduced by the use of a resistive voltage divider. Two precautions are necessary: (1) the voltage across each resistor, which will be of the film or bulk conductor type, must be kept low in order to preserve voltage linearity; and (2) the divider output must be connected to the oscillograph through a matched line which will effectively be part of the terminating resistance of the divider. *SEE ELECTRICAL MEASUREMENTS.*

*Cyril H. Dix*

**Bibliography.** C. H. Dix and A. E. Bailey, Electrical standards of measurement, *Proc. IEE*, vol. 122, no. 10R, October 1975; S. Geczy, *Basic Electrical Measurements*, 1984; B. A. Gregory, *An Introduction to Electrical Instrumentation and Measurement Systems*, 2d ed., 1981; F. K. Harris, *Electrical Measurements*, 1952, reprint 1975; R. L. Heiserman, *Electrical and Electronic Measuring Instruments*, 1983; H. W. Hellwig (ed.), Conference of precision electromagnetic measurements, *IEEE Trans. Instrum. Meas.*, vol. 32, no. 1, March 1983; *International System of Units (SI)*, NBS Spec. Publ. 330, 1981.

## Voltage-multiplier circuit

A rectifier circuit capable of supplying a dc output voltage that is two or more times the peak value of the ac input voltage. Such circuits are especially useful for high-voltage, low-current supplies. These supplies are usually lighter in weight, smaller in size, and less expensive than the more usual half-wave and full-wave rectifier supplies. They require either no power transformer or a much smaller transformer, but they have the disadvantage of requiring more rectifiers and capacitors. If, for safety or other reasons, input and output must be isolated, a transformer may be required at the input even thought the voltage-multiplier circuit does not need it for operation. Common configurations are the half-wave and full-wave voltage-doubling circuits, but tripling and higher orders of multiplication are used.

A full-wave voltage-doubling rectifier circuit is shown in **Fig. 1**. When the ac input voltage is positive at terminal $A$, diode $D_1$ conducts, producing voltage $V_1$ across capacitor $C_1$. On the other half-cycle,

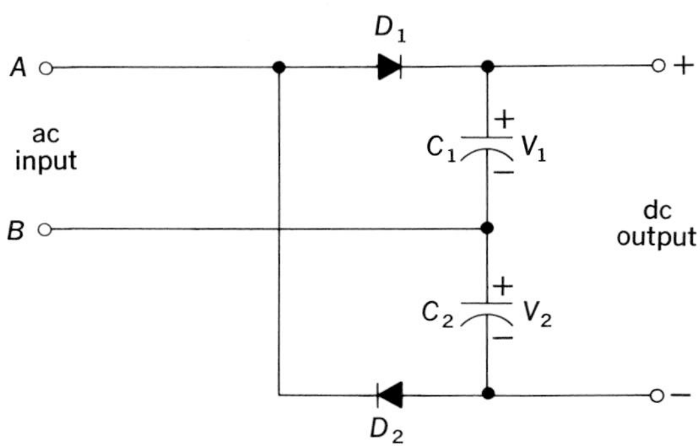


**Fig. 1. Full-wave voltage doubler.**

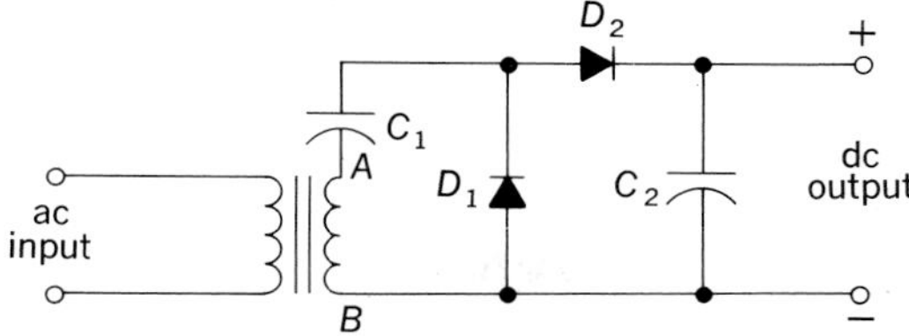


**Fig. 2. Half-wave voltage doubler.**

diode $D_2$ conducts producing the voltage $V_2$ across capacitor $C_2$. Both $V_1$ and $V_2$ will have a magnitude approaching the maximum value of the ac input voltage, so the output voltage approaches twice the maximum value of the ac input voltage. Because the output voltage receives one pulse every half-cycle, ripple voltage is similar to that of a single-phase full-wave rectifying circuit. *SEE RECTIFIER.*

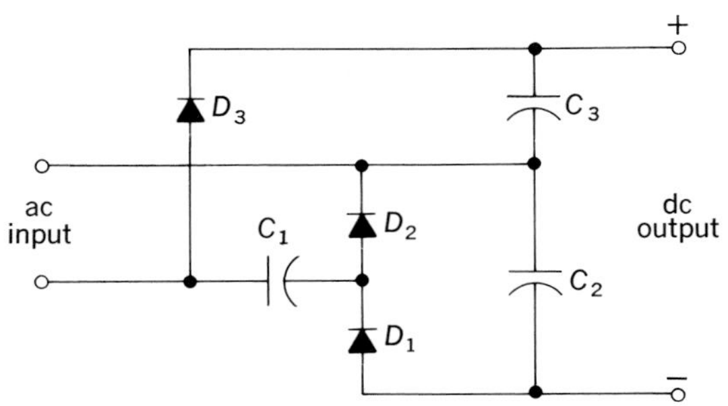


**Fig. 3. Voltage-tripler circuit, a voltage doubler in series with a half-wave rectifier.**

A half-wave voltage-doubling rectifying circuit is shown in **Fig. 2**. When top terminal $A$ of the transformer secondary is positive, current flows through diode $D_1$, charging capacitor $C_1$ with its lower terminal positive in potential. When bottom terminal $B$ of

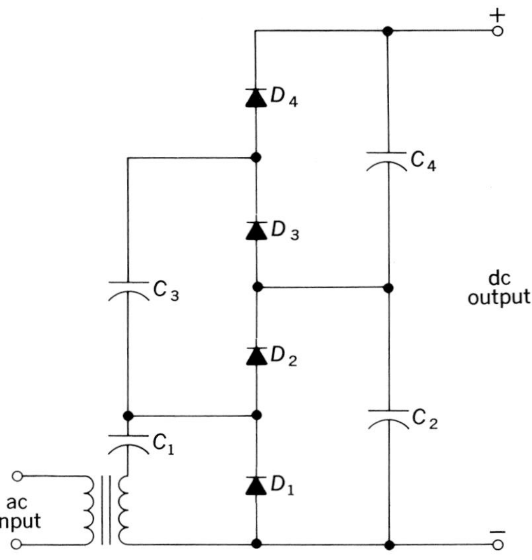


**Fig. 4. A half-wave voltage-quadrupling circuit.**

the transformer secondary is positive, current flows through diode $D_2$, charging capacitor $C_2$ to nearly twice the maximum value of the secondary voltage. Only one pulse per cycle is received by capacitor $C_2$, so the ripple voltage is similar to that of a single-phase half-wave rectifying circuit. The full-wave doubler has the advantage over a half-wave doubler of better voltage regulation and smaller ripple voltage: the half-wave doubler has the advantage of having a common ground.

A voltage-tripling rectifier circuit is shown in **Fig. 3**, and a half-wave voltage-quadrupling rectifier circuit is shown in **Fig. 4**. Comparison of Figs. 2 and 4 shows that a half-wave doubler can be transformed into a half-wave quadrupler by adding two capacitors and two diodes. Theoretically, this may be continued indefinitely to achieve as high a multiplication as is desired. In practice, each stage added contributes slightly less to the output voltage than the preceding stage, so that a point is finally reached where an additional stage does not contribute enough to make it worthwhile. *See Electronic power supply.*

*Donald L. Waidelich*

**Bibliography.** B. M. Bird and K. G. King, *Power Electronics*, 1983; A. H. Lytel, *Solid-State Power Supplies and Converters*, 1965; C. A. Schuler, *Electronics: Principles and Applications*, 2d ed., 1984; G. Scoles, *Handbook of Rectifier Circuits*, 1980.

## Voltage regulator

A device or circuit that maintains a load voltage nearly constant over a range of variations of input voltage and load current. Voltage regulators are used wherever the unregulated voltage would vary more than can be tolerated by the electrical equipment using that voltage. Alternating-current distribution feeders use regulators to keep the voltage supplied to the user within a prescribed range. Electronic equipment often has voltage regulators in dc power supplies.

### Electronic Voltage Regulators

In much electronic equipment the dc power supply voltage must remain constant in spite of input ac line voltage variations and output load variations. To perform this function, two types of voltage-regulator circuits are used in electronic power supplies. The first uses a nearly constant voltage device, such as a Zener diode or a gas tube, as the voltage regulator; the second uses the variable-resistance properties of a transistor or a vacuum tube. Because of the rapid response of these devices, either type regulator serves not only to compensate for irregular changes in input or output but also to counteract ripple voltage. Thus an electronic regulator makes possible the use of simpler filters. The voltage regulator circuit may also augment the filtering action of the power-supply filters, and it may also raise or lower the internal impedance of the power supply as seen from the load. The trade off for the regulator action is a considerable power loss in the regulator circuit. Most of the power is lost either in a regulator resistor or in the regulator diodes or tubes. *See Rectifier; Ripple voltage.*

**Diode regulator circuit.** A Zener-diode regulator circuit is shown in **Fig. 1**. The Zener diode is characterized by an almost constant voltage over its specified range of current, as shown in **Fig. 2**. The constant voltage depends upon the particular diode employed and may be from about 2 to 200 V.

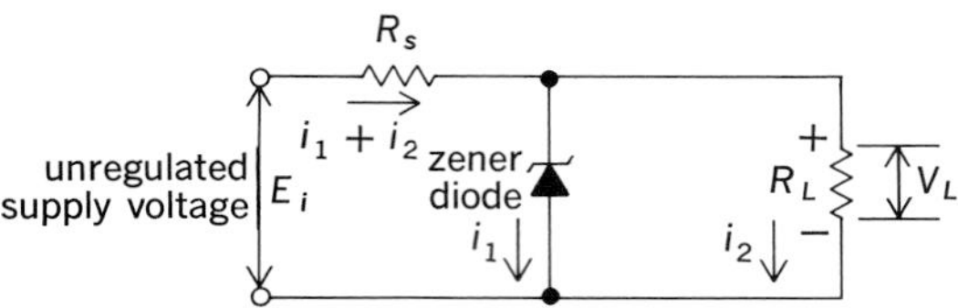

Fig. 1. Zener diode voltage regulator.

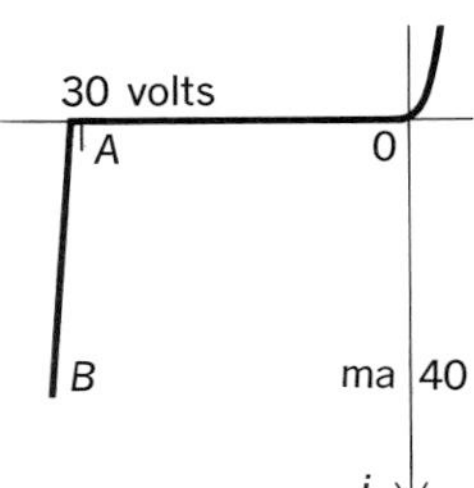

Fig. 2. Typical Zener diode characteristic.

The circuit of Fig. 1 depends on two conditions: (1) Input voltage $E_i$ is always the sum of voltage drop $V_s$ across series resistor $R_s$ and output load voltage $V_L$ which is maintained constant by the Zener diode; and (2) the current through series resistor $R_s$ is always the sum of load current $i_2$ and diode current $i_1$.

Because the voltage drop across the series resistor is constant for a given input voltage, the current through the resistor must also be constant. Therefore a change in load current must be accompanied by an equal, but opposite, change in current through the diode.

If the input voltage varies, $V_s$ must also vary if $V_L$ is to remain constant. This variation in $V_s$ must be produced by a change in diode current if load current $i_2$ is to remain constant. The substantially constant voltage drop for a wide range of current, characteristic of a Zener diode in the region $A$ to $B$ of Fig. 2, provides the required change in $i_2$ to maintain $V_L$ nearly constant over wide changes of input voltage $E_i$ and of load current $i_2$.

**Transistor regulator circuits.** A single transistor regulator circuit is the shunt regulator using a transistor and a Zener diode as shown in **Fig. 3**. Resistor $R$ is chosen so that the Zener diode has a current approximately in the middle of its operating range. If voltage $E_o$ across the load increases, the base of the transistor rises in potential, increasing the collector current and, in consequence, the voltage across $R_s$. This action tends to return the load voltage to where it was initially. In this manner the circuit compensates for load voltage variations.

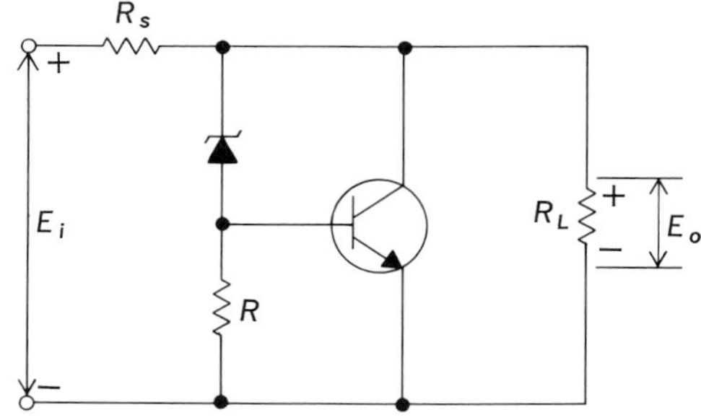

Fig. 3. Transistor shunt regulator.

If input voltage $E_i$ increases, again the base of the transistor rises in potential, so that, as before, the voltage across $R_s$ increases. This increase largely overcomes the increase in the input voltage, so that the output voltage increases very little. Thus the circuit also compensates for input voltage variations.

The regulator is not perfect; a small change in output voltage does occur in the presence of a much larger change in input voltage. This change in output voltage can be reduced even more by adding one or more transistor amplifier stages.

A series transistor regulator circuit is shown in **Fig. 4**. Resistor $R$ is chosen so that the Zener diode is approximately in the middle of its operating range. The transistor must be capable of carrying all of the load current and withstanding a voltage equal to the difference of the input and output voltages. An increase in the output voltage $E_o$ increases the voltage from emitter to base, in effect increasing the voltage across the transistor. Voltage $E_o$ is thus reduced, approaching its original value. Conversely, if input voltage $E_i$ increases, the emitter-to-base voltage increases and the transistor voltage rises to overcome most of the increase. Again, an amplifier would make the circuit more responsive to very small changes.

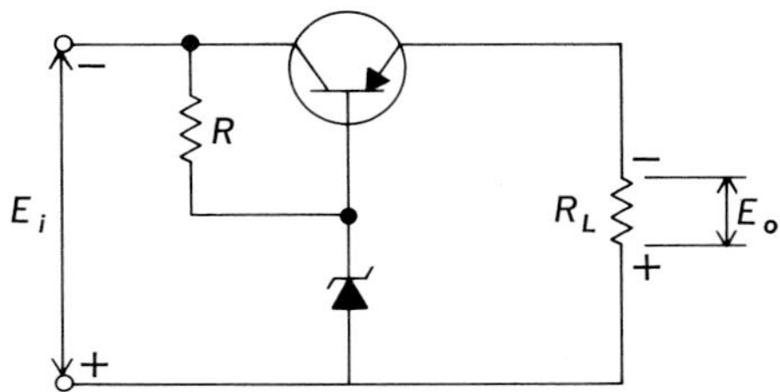


**Fig. 4. Series transistor regulator.**

A simplified circuit incorporating an amplifier is shown in **Fig. 5.** Transistor $Q_1$ is the series regulating device, while the transistor $Q_2$ is the amplifier. If output voltage $E_o$ increases for some reason, the emitter-to-base voltage on $Q_2$ increases. This change in turn increases the base current and the potential drop across $Q_1$ in such a manner as to oppose the original increase in $E_o$. The net effect is to keep the output voltage nearly constant and to compensate for load variations. In a similar fashion, if the unregulated supply potential increases, voltage $E_o$ across the output tends to increase. The sequence of events enumerated above again occurs, tending to increase the voltage across $Q_1$ and again keeping the load voltage practically constant. If the amplifier $Q_2$ had sufficient gain, the voltage regulation would be nearly perfect. If the current taken by the load is too high for one transistor $Q_1$, two or more may be connected in parallel.

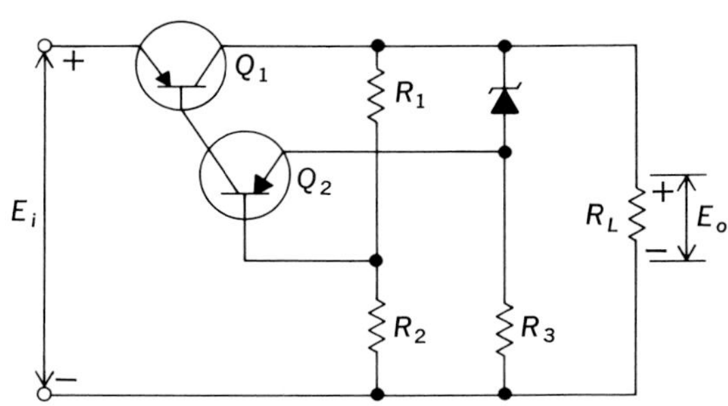


**Fig. 5. Basic electronic series regulator circuit.**

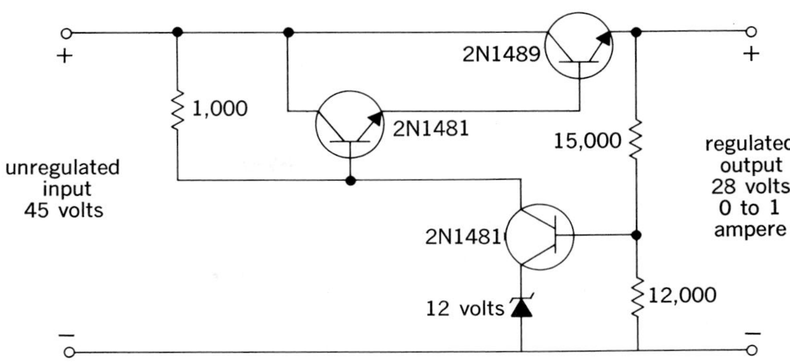


**Fig. 6. Electronically regulated power supply. All resistances in ohms.**

An actual voltage regulator circuit using these principles is shown in **Fig. 6**. The voltage of the 12-V reference diode is compared to a portion of the output voltage through a 2N1481 transistor. The difference voltage is amplified by another 2N1481 transistor and is then applied to the 2N1489 transistor, which acts as the series regulating device. To improve the response to fast changes such as those caused by pulses, square waves, high-frequency sine waves, and so forth, a capacitor of about 1 microfarad can be connected across the 12,-000-ohm resistor. Such a regulator is used in an electronic power supply, as shown in **Fig. 7**, to provide constant output voltage to load

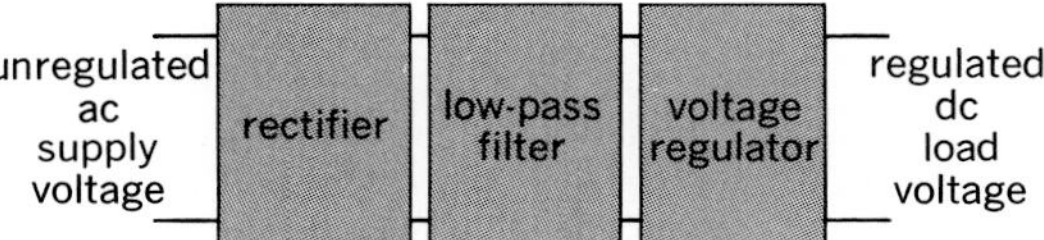


**Fig. 7. If a voltage regulator is used in an electronic power supply, the rectifier circuit may be required to handle higher voltage than without the regulator, but the filter may be simpler than without the regulator.**

circuits and to produce a low impedance so that several load circuits cannot interact on each other through their common power supply. SEE ELECTRONIC POWER SUPPLY.

*Donald L. Waidelich*

## Power-system Voltage Regulators

Voltage regulators are used on distribution feeders to maintain voltage constant, irrespective of changes in either load current or supply voltage. Voltage variations must be minimized for the efficient operation of industrial equipment and for the satisfactory functioning of domestic appliances, television in particular. Voltage is controlled at the system generators, but this alone is inadequate because each generator supplies many feeders of diverse impedance and load characteristics. Regulators are applied either in substations to control voltage on a bus or individual feeder or on the line to reregulate the outlying portions of the system. These regulators are variable autotransformers with the primary connected across the line. The secondary, in which an adjustable voltage is induced, is connected in series with the line to boost or buck the voltage.

A control and drive provide automatic operation. A

voltage-regulating relay senses output voltage. When the voltage is either above or below the band of acceptable voltage maintained by the regulator, this relay causes the motor to operate and change the regulator position to raise or lower the voltage as required to bring it back within the control band. It is desirable to maintain constant voltage at the average load center out on the feeder rather than at the regulator terminals. Hence the control circuit includes a line-drop compensator with resistance and reactance elements that can be adjusted to represent line impedance. These impedances carry current proportional to circuit load, thereby simulating the voltage drop between the regulator and the load center, and modify the voltage sensed by the voltage-regulating relay.

Two principal types of feeder regulators are used: the step regulator, which provides increments or steps of voltage change, and the induction regulator, which provides continuous voltage adjustment.

**Step voltage regulator.** The transformation ratio of the autotransformer in this regulator is adjusted by a voltage selector switch which changes the secondary winding tap connected to the line. **Figure 8** shows the most commonly used circuit.

Switching is performed without interrupting load current by means of the two switch fingers in the selector switch. When the switch moves from the full-tap position shown in Fig. 8, one finger contacts the next tap before the other finger leaves the first tap; this constitutes a tap-bridging position. Switching reactors limit the current circulating between the bridged taps. Most regulators are designed to operate continuously in these bridging positions (as well as the full-tap positions) to provide voltages midway between the voltages of adjacent taps. Thus the voltage step between adjacent positions is half-tap voltage, and the number of winding taps required is half the number of operating positions in the boosting range. The automatic reversing switch changes the polarity of the secondary relative to the primary, thus providing a bucking range equal to the boosting range. Single- and three-phase designs are available with a range of ±10% in 16 or 32 steps. Other design variations may employ single-finger switching and operate continuously only in full-tap positions.

Load tap-changing transformers are often used to provide both regulation and transformation from one voltage level to another. They are similar to step voltage regulators, except that they have separate high- and low-voltage windings.

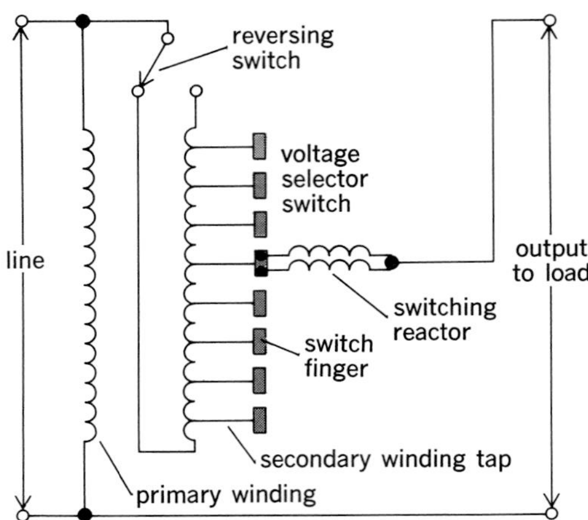


Fig. 8. Step voltage regulator circuit.

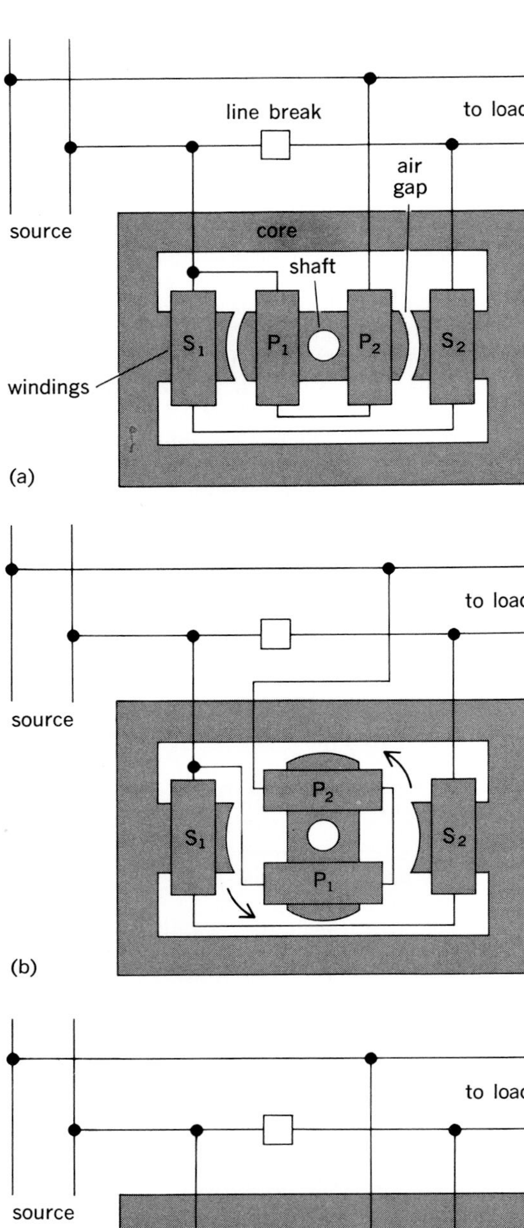


Fig. 9. Induction voltage regulator. (*a*) Full boost position. (*b*) Neutral position. (c) Full buck position of rotor. *P* coils are rotor primary coils, *S* coils are stationary secondary coils. (*B. G. A. Skrotski, ed., Electric Transmission and Distribution*, McGraw-Hill, 1954)

**Induction voltage regulator.** This is similar in structure to a wound-rotor induction motor with rotor restrained so that it moves only to adjust voltage. The primary winding on the rotor is magnetically coupled with the series secondary winding on the stator.

The principle of a two-pole single-phase regulator is illustrated in **Fig. 9**. Secondary voltage is continuously adjusted from full buck to full boost by changing the relative angular position of these windings through 180 electrical degrees.

Single-phase regulators require an additional permanently short-circuited rotor winding that is in space quadrature to the primary winding. Without this winding, the reactance of the regulator to the line current flowing in the secondary would be excessive in the neutral region between buck and boost. Three-phase induction regulators, if built on a three-phase core, do not require a short-circuited winding. Such induction regulators inherently introduce phase shift between primary and secondary voltages and are no longer supplied for feeder regulation.

**Other regulators.** Other types of regulators are also used outside the United States. One construction is a transformer structure with moving coils to change coupling; another has contacts moving over the exposed conductors to provide a large number of small, discrete steps.

Line voltage may be increased by drawing leading-power-factor current through the line reactance. Static capacitors, shunt-connected in fixed or automatically switched banks, are often applied near the loads to raise voltage. The increase in voltage is not limited solely to the vicinity of the capacitor. They also help compensate for the usual system condition of lagging power factor. The application of series capacitors on fluctuating loads is increasing.

Infrequently, synchronous machines called synchronous condensers, overexcited to draw leading current, are connected to lines. Their use has decreased with the availability of low-cost reliable static capacitors.

Conditions may exist where the inherent static capacity of the circuit is excessive. The line voltage may rise on cable systems or lightly loaded lines; shunt reactors may be used to neutralize the capacity of such systems.

*Donnell D. MacCarthy*

***Bibliography.*** B. M. Bird and K. G. King, *Power Electronics*, 1983; J. J. Brophy, *Basic Electronics for Scientists*, 4th ed., 1983; A. H. Lytel, *Solid-State Power Supplies and Converters*, 1965; J. Millman, *Microelectronics*, 1979; A. I. Pressman, *Switching and Linear Power Supply, Power Converter Design*, 1977; J. D. Spencer and D. E. Pippenger, *The Voltage Regulator Handbook for Design Engineers*, 1977.

## Voltmeter

An instrument for the measurement in volts of potential difference between two points. Derivatives of the voltmeter are the microvoltmeter, millivoltmeter, and kilovoltmeter, for measurement of voltages with a measurement span of 1,000,000,000:1. Voltmeters are connected between points of a circuit, between which the potential difference is to be measured. The accuracy rating is usually stated in terms of the full-scale reading. SEE VOLTAGE MEASUREMENT.

**Classifications.** Voltmeters are classified in respect to the kind of voltage to be measured and the kind of mechanism used, as follows: (1) for measurement of direct voltage, (*a*) the moving-coil permanent-magnet voltmeter, (*b*) the fixed-coil moving-magnet voltmeter, and (*c*) the electrostatic voltmeter; (2) for measurement of alternating voltage, (*a*) the fixed-coil moving-magnet voltmeter, (*b*) the fixed-coil moving-iron voltmeter, (*c*) the thermovoltmeter consisting of a thermal converter and dc millivoltmeter, and (*d*) rectifier and vacuum-tube voltmeters.

Voltmeters, in general, are secondary instruments consisting of voltage-to-current transducers and mechanisms which respond to milliamperes or microamperes. In the simpler forms, the transducer consists of a resistor of constant value, which may have taps for several voltage ranges. Since by Ohm's law the current is proportional to the potential difference, calibration of the combination using a primary standard, such as the potentiometer and standard cell, is valid. In the more specialized forms, the transducer consists of a thermal converter (ac to dc), rectifier, or amplifier. The electrostatic instrument is the only voltmeter which measures potential difference directly.

**Moving-coil voltmeter.** This voltmeter consists of a permanent magnet, moving coils pivoted in jewel bearings, control springs, and a pointer (**Fig. 1**). The current $I$ is passed through the moving coil of $N$ turns via the two control springs which apply a restraining torque $T_r$ equal to $K_s\theta$, where $K_s$ is the spring constant and $\theta$ is the angle of deflection. The deflecting torque $T_e$ is equal to the product of the magnetic moment of the coil and the field intensity $B$, as in Eq. (1), where

$$T_e = NIwlB \qquad (1)$$

$w$ and $l$ are coil width and length, respectively. The deflection $\theta$ resulting from the current $I$ is given by Eq. (2). Since the magnetic field is usually uniform,

$$\theta = BNIwl/K_s \quad \text{radians} \qquad (2)$$

the voltmeter scale is usually calibrated in uniform intervals.

The moving system must be damped to eliminate unwanted oscillations of the pointer. This is accomplished electromagnetically by a damping shell, usually aluminum, on which the moving coil is wound. As the coil moves, the shell moves in the magnetic field. A voltage and current are induced in the shell in the direction of the winding. This current reacts with the magnetic field to produce a braking action proportional to the angular velocity of the moving system. The amount of damping is controlled by the cross section and conductivity of the shell. It is customary to damp voltmeters so that a small but definite overshoot will result if full voltage is suddenly applied. In some instances, the shell is replaced by an equivalent coil and in others the instrument may be

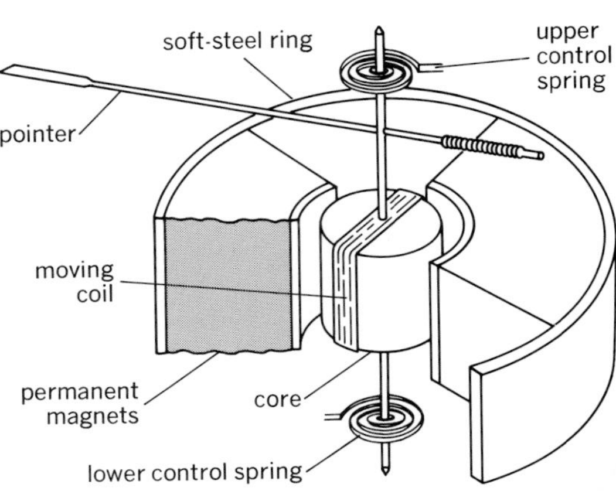


**Fig. 1. Direct-current permanent-magnet moving-coil voltmeter. (*General Electric Co.*)**

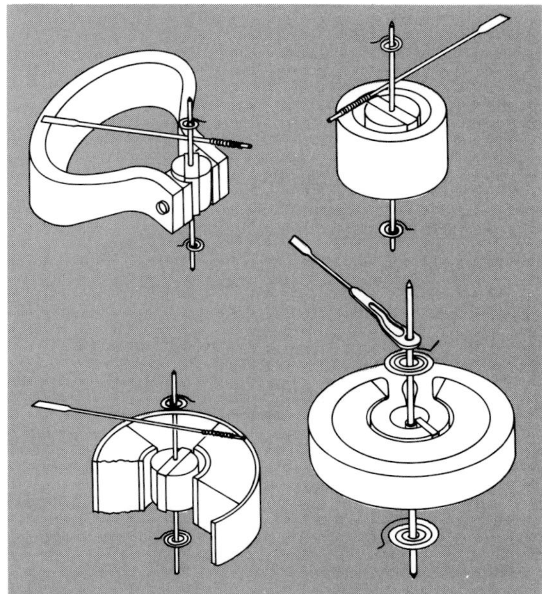

**Fig. 2. Four forms of dc moving-coil mechanisms. (*After I. F. Kinnard, Applied Electrical Measurements, John Wiley and Sons, 1956*)**

damped by the action of the driving coil itself. The latter condition is achievable only when the loop circuit resistance is low.

Permanent-magnet moving-coil instruments are made in several forms; four common ones are illustrated in **Fig. 2**.

The first three figures illustrate the evolution of the magnet structure, beginning with the expanded U-shaped magnet constructed to chrome or tungsten steels, and extending to the internal cylindrical magnet made with Alnico material of high-energy content. These mechanisms have scale lengths of about 90°. The fourth shows an annular magnet and offset coil with a scale length of 240°.

Voltmeters and their various derivatives are available in ranges of 10 mV to 750 V, with resistances of 100–10,000 ohms/volt. Maximum errors range from 0.1% of full scale for secondary standards to 2.0% of full scale for panel-type instruments.

**Moving-magnet voltmeter.** This voltmeter (**Fig. 3**) has the magnet attached to the pivoted shaft which carries the pointer. The magnet is surrounded by the field coil and aligned by a control magnet which supplies the restoring torque. A fixed copper frame damps the movement electromagnetically, and the magnetic shield minimizes the effect of external fields, as well as providing a path for the internal fluxes. As current is applied to the field coil, the coil and restoring-magnet fields produce a resultant field. The rotor aligns itself with this resultant field and indicates the magnitude of the current and thus the potential difference. The construction shown is used in commercial 2½- and 3½-in.-diameter (6.2- and 8.7-cm) panel instruments of 2% accuracy rating (maximum error 2%).

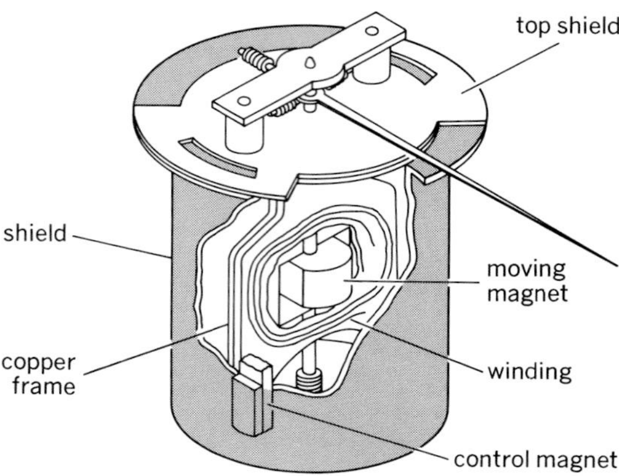


**Fig. 3. Moving-magnet dc voltmeter. (*General Electric Co.*)**

**Electrostatic voltmeter.** The electrostatic voltmeter action is based on the force of attraction or repulsion between two charged conductors, such as the plates of a variable air capacitor. The moving plate, when charged, tends to move so as to increase the capacitance between it and the fixed plate. If this capacitance is $C$ farads, the voltage is $E$ volts and the spacing is $s$ meters, the energy $W$ in joules of the capacitor is expressed by Eq. (3). If the upper plate

$$W = \tfrac{1}{2}CE^2 \qquad (3)$$

is moved vertically a distance $ds$ while the voltage is held constant, an energy change $dW$ takes place, numerically equal to the work done in moving the plate. The resultant force $F$ is given by Eq. (4). Thus, the

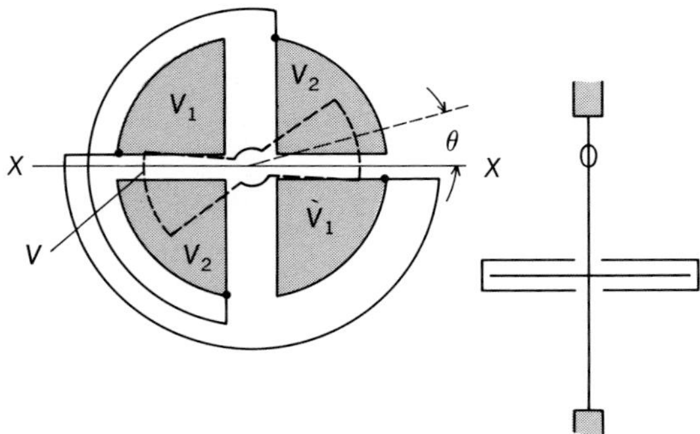


**Fig. 4. Schematic of quadrant electrometer. (*After I. F. Kinnard, Applied Electrical Measurements, John Wiley and Sons, 1956*)**

$$F = dW/ds = (E^2/2)\, dC/ds \qquad (4)$$

force acting on the upper plate is proportional to $E^2$ times the space rate of capacitance change. For a rotatable system the corresponding torque is given by Eq. (5).

$$T = (E^2/2)\, dC/d\theta \quad \text{radians} \qquad (5)$$

The quadrant electrometer, **Fig. 4**, is a useful embodiment of this principle. The four quadrants compose the fixed capacitor plates and surround the movable vane suspended by a conducting torsion fiber at the center of the system. Opposite quadrants are electrically connected and potentials $V_1$ and $V_2$ are applied. In the heterostatic method, the vane is independently energized to potential $V_3$. The capacitance effect causes the vane to turn out of one pair of quadrants and into the other. This movement actuates the indicating needle and the deflection of the needle is directly proportional to the voltage difference $(V_1 - V_2)$ between the two sets of quadrants.

In the idiostatic method, the vane is connected to quadrant 1. This method has the advantage of dispensing with the auxiliary voltage, and the deflection is proportional to the square of the voltage difference.

The Lindemann electrometer, **Fig. 5**, is a variant of the quadrant electrometer, designed for portability and insensitivity to changes in position. The quadrants 1 and 2 are two sets of plates about 6 mm apart

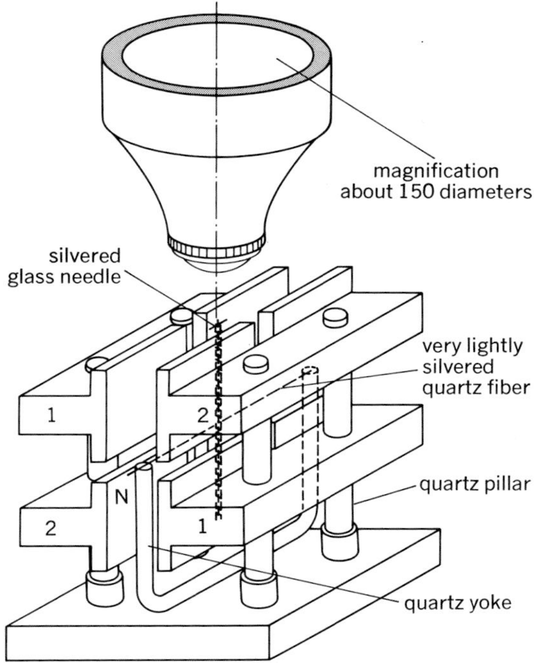


**Fig. 5. Lindemann electrometer. (*After F.A. Laws, Electrical Measurements, 2d ed., McGraw-Hill, 1938*)**

and mounted on insulating quartz pillars. A taut silvered quartz suspension fixes the center of rotation of the moving system. When voltage is applied to the needle, the needle rotates toward the oppositely charged plates. This movement is observed through a microscope. This electrometer has a low capacitance of about 1 picofarad, and currents of the order of $10^{-15}$ A can be observed with it.

**Electrodynamic ac voltmeter.** This voltmeter has two coils connected in series through a resistor to the source, the potential of which is to be measured (**Fig. 6**). The fixed coil provides the field in which the moving coil, supported by a pivoted shaft, operates. The deflection of the moving system is restrained by a control spring. When the circuit is closed, the current which flows through the coils produces a deflecting torque which moves the indicating needle. This current $I$ produces a deflecting torque $T_e$ defined by Eq. (6), where $M$ is that portion of the total field flux

$$T_e = K_1 I^2 \, dM/d\theta \tag{6}$$

which links the moving system, $K_1$ is a constant of proportionality, and $\theta$ is the angle between moving coil and fixed coil. Since the control spring produces a restoring torque $T_r$ at deflection $\alpha$, Eq. (7) holds,

$$T_r = K_S \alpha \tag{7}$$

where $K_S$ is the constant of the spring. The moving system will come to rest at an angle where deflecting

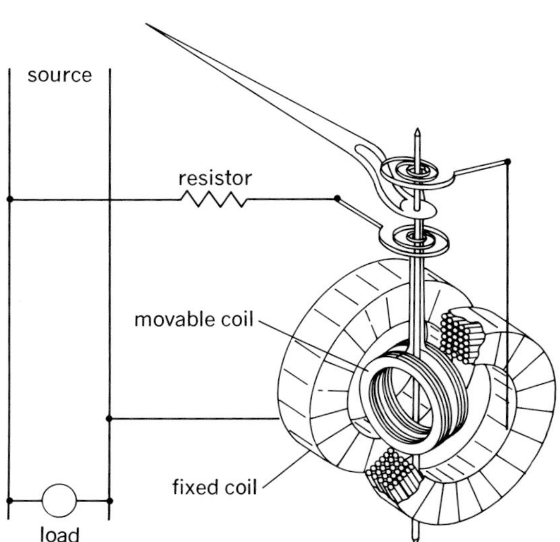


**Fig. 6. Electrodynamic mechanism used as voltmeter. (*General Electric Co.*)**

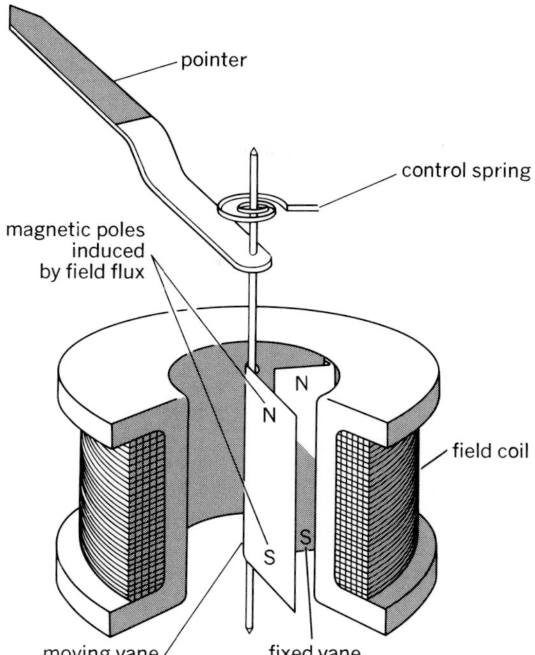


**Fig. 7. Moving-iron radial-vane ac repulsion voltmeter. (*General Electric Co.*)**

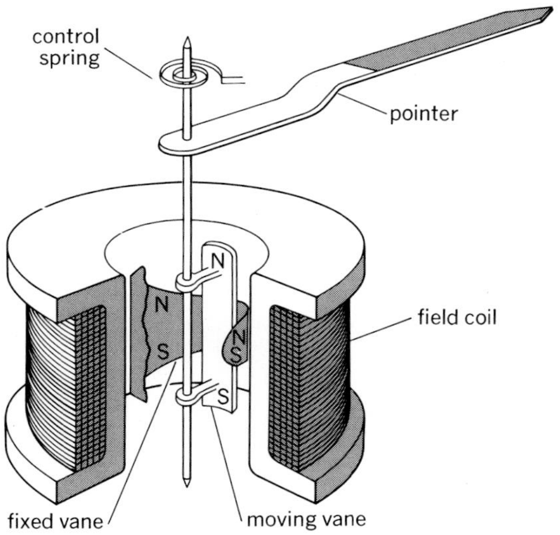


**Fig. 8. Concentric-vane ac repulsion voltmeter. (*General Electric Co.*)**

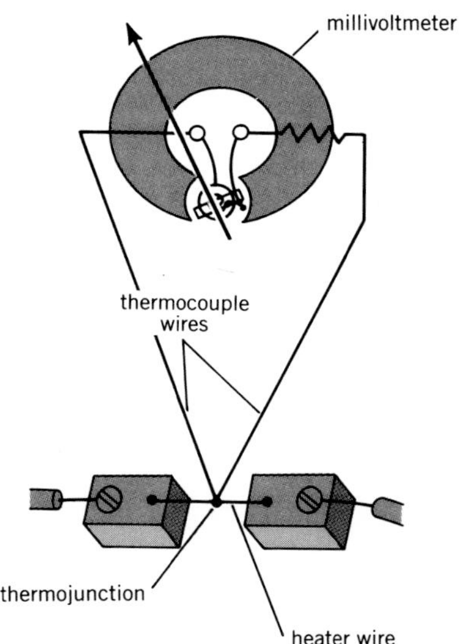


Fig. 9. Elementary thermo-voltmeter circuit. (*General Electric Co.*)

and restoring torques are equal, and the indication is given by Eq. (8). The scale distributions of electro-

$$\alpha = \left(\frac{K_1}{K_S}\right)\left(\frac{I^2 dM}{d\theta}\right) \quad (8)$$

dynamic voltmeters are in general contracted at low voltages and expanded at higher voltages. This is due in part to the necessary square-law response and in part to designing for scale legibility over the upper half of the scale. The inherent accuracy of the electrodynamic voltmeter is excellent, and this construction is used in secondary standards of 0.1% error rating as

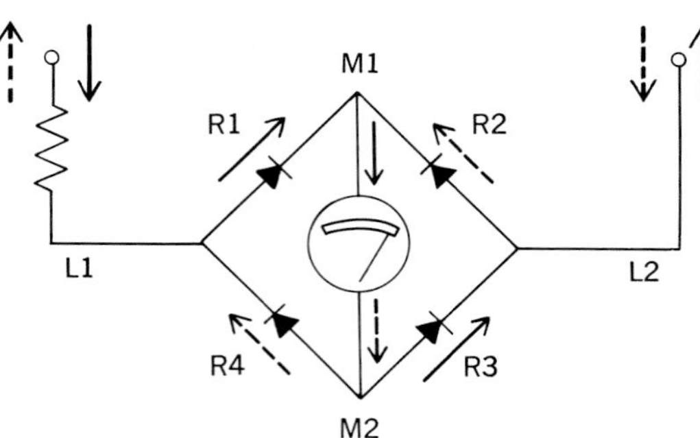


Fig. 10. Operating principle of the bridge-type rectifier voltmeter. The solid arrows show direction of current during the positive half-cycle of ac input; the broken-line arrows show direction of current during the negative half-cycle. (*General Electric Co.*)

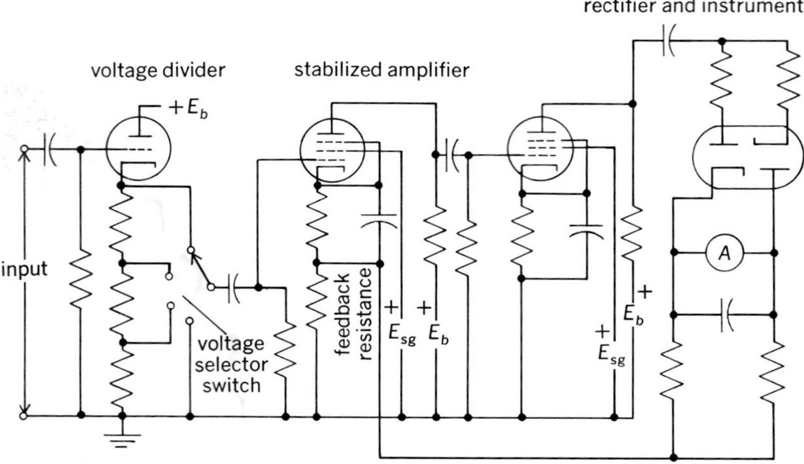


Fig. 11. Circuit for amplifier-rectifier electronic voltmeter. (*After I. F. Kinnard, Applied Electrical Measurements, John Wiley and Sons, 1956*)

well as in portable voltmeters of 0.25 or 0.50% error rating. Voltage ranges of 10–750 V are available in commercial instruments. Refinements in design include magnetic shielding, damping of the moving system, and compensation for temperature and frequency errors.

**Moving-iron voltmeter.** There are many forms of this voltmeter. **Figure 7** is representative. Here, the field coil is connected to the line through a series resistor (not shown). Inside the field coil are two rectangular vanes, one fixed and the other attached to the shaft which carries the pointer. When a current traverses the coil, the vanes are similarly magnetized, and the moving vane is repelled from the fixed vane, deflecting the pointer in a clockwise direction. The deflecting torque $T_e$ is given by Eq. (9), where $I$ is the

$$T_e = K\frac{I^2}{2}\frac{dL}{d\theta} \quad (9)$$

current traversing the coil, $L$ is the inductance of the field coil, and $\theta$ the angle between the vanes. Since the coil inductance is a maximum when the vanes are at maximum separation, the moving vane will, unless restrained, move 180° away from the fixed vane. The control spring exerts a restraining torque defined by Eq. (10) or the deflection given by Eq. (11).

$$T_r = K_S\alpha \quad (10)$$

$$\alpha = \frac{K}{K_S}\frac{V^2}{2}\frac{dL}{d\theta} \quad (11)$$

The moving-iron instrument, like the electrodynamic voltmeter, when properly calibrated indicates true root-mean-square (rms) volts. The scale length and distribution can be controlled over wide limits by suitable configuration of the fixed iron. Figure 7 illustrates an arrangement for scale lengths of 90–100°. **Figure 8** illustrates a circumferential fixed-vane design used in long-scale (250°) switchboard voltmeters. Moving-iron voltmeters with magnetic damping are available in commercial 2½- and 3½-in. (6.2- and 8.7-cm) panel instruments (2% error), 4- and 6-in. (10- and 15-cm) switchboard instruments (1% error), and portable instruments of ¼ or ½% error. Scale ranges vary from 0–10 to 0–750 V. Instruments of 1% accuracy and higher are magnetically shielded. Power consumption varies from 1.5 to 10 W, depending on size, range, and the specific design.

**Thermovoltmeter.** This unit utilizes a thermojunction and dc millivoltmeter (**Fig. 9**). A current from the voltage source is passed through a resistor (not shown) and a fine vacuum-enclosed platinum heater wire. A thermocouple, attached to the midpoint of the heater, generates millivolts proportional to the temperature. *See Thermocouple.*

The thermovoltmeter is a true rms instrument, in which the squaring, integration, and averaging are accomplished thermally rather than electromagnetically. The inductance of the heater wire is negligible, and the thermovoltmeter is especially suitable for measurement at high frequencies. Its sensitivity, while greater than that of electromagnetic instruments, is limited by the current necessary to heat the wire, usually several milliamps.

**Rectifier voltmeter.** This voltmeter consists of a dc milliammeter calibrated in volts and connected to the voltage source through a rectifier bridge (**Fig. 10**). The individual rectifiers are connected so that the current through the milliammeter is always in the same direction. This meter measures the average value of the current. While not an rms instrument, the rectifier voltmeter may be calibrated in rms volts for sine waves and will measure sine-wave voltages accurately. Harmonics in the voltage wave cause appreciable errors, but this circuit has the advantage of low power consumption. Commercial forms of rectifier voltmeters having resistance of 1000 Ω/V and ratings of 10–750 V are available.

**Electronic ac voltmeter.** This voltmeter consists of a dc milliammeter calibrated in volts and connected to an amplifier-rectifier circuit, of which **Fig. 11** is typical. The input voltage is connected to the grid of the first triode. A voltage-range selector switch is connected to the tapped cathode resistor. The two stages of amplification are resistance-coupled to cover a wide frequency range. The amplifier output is applied to a rectifier section consisting of two diodes, milliammeter, and feedback resistor. *See* Digital voltmeter; Sampling voltmeter; Vacuum-tube voltmeter.

By use of adequate feedback, errors due to changes in power-supply voltage and tube characteristics are minimized. Electronic voltmeters usually respond to average voltage but are calibrated in rms values for sine waves. The addition of the amplifier greatly increases the sensitivity and range of measurement, 0.001–300 V at frequencies of 20 Hz to 2 MHz and with input impedances of several megohms.

*Almon J. Corson*

**Bibliography.** J. Cunningham, *Understanding and Using the VOM and EVM*, 1973; S. Geczy, *Basic Electrical Measurements*, 1984; B. A. Gregory, *An Introduction to Electrical Instrumentation and Measurement Systems*, 2d ed., 1981; R. L. Heiserman, *Electrical and Electronic Measuring Instruments*, 1983.

## Volume control systems

Electronic systems that regulate the signal amplification or limit the output of circuits. Examples are volume compressors, limiters, and expanders. A volume compressor is an electronic system that reduces the amplification of an amplifier when the signal being amplified is large and increases the amplification when the signal is small. Compressors are used to reduce the volume range in sound motion picture and phonograph recording, sound broadcasting, public address and sound reinforcing systems, and so forth.

A volume limiter is an electronic system in which the relationship between the input and output signals is constant up to a certain level, but beyond this point the output remains constant regardless of the input. The limiter is useful for protection against sudden overloads, as for example, in the audio input to a radio or television transmitter.

A volume expander is an electronic system that increases the amplification of an amplifier when the signal is large and decreases the amplification when the signal is small. In reproduction, a volume expander is used to counteract or complement the effect of the compressor in recording or the transmission of an audio signal.

Volume compressors, limiters, and expanders are electronic amplifiers in which the amplification varies as a function of the average level of the signal. Compressor, limiter, and expander systems and their input-output characteristics are shown schematically in the **illustration**.

In all the systems, the input signal to the control circuits is rectified and applied to a capacitor-resistance network. The direct-current (dc) voltage across the capacitor is used to vary the amplification of a vacuum tube or transistor amplifier operating in a variable gain mode. In the case of a vacuum tube amplifier, the dc voltage is used to vary the bias on the control grid and as a consequence the amplification of a push-pull amplifier with variable transconductance. In the case of the transistor amplifier, the dc voltage is used to vary the bias of a field effect transistor which results in a change in the gain of the amplification of the transistor. *See* Transistor; Vacuum tube.

In the compressor characteristic shown in the illustration, there is a gradual reduction in gain with the

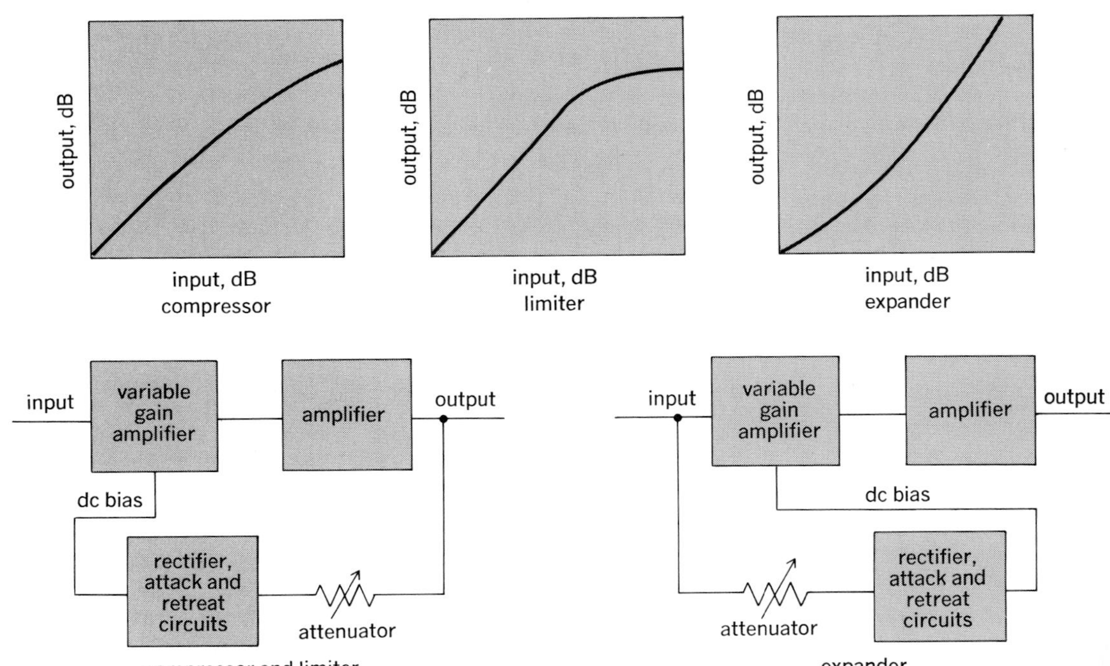


**Schematic block diagrams, with input-output characteristics above, for electronic compressors, limiters, and expanders.**

increase of the input. This characteristic may be varied over very wide limits. A reduction in the volume range in radio and phonograph sound reproduction makes it possible to reproduce a wide range of orchestral music in the home without excessive top levels. The compressor may also be used to increase the signal-to-noise ratio in an audio signal. Use of a compressor improves the intelligibility of speech and enhances music reproduction when the ambient noise is high, for example, in sound motion picture reproduction and sound reinforcing applications.

The main application for the limiter characteristic shown in the illustration is to protect equipment against overload. Below the overload point, the limiter does not alter the signal.

In the expander characteristic shown in the illustration, there is gradual increase in gain with increase of input. The combination of a compressor and expander system, in which the two characteristics are complementary, may be used to reproduce a wide amplitude range by means of a much smaller recorded or transmitted amplitude range.

The attack time for a gain reduction of 10 dB in compressors and limiters is of the order of a millisecond. The retreat to normal is of the order of a second. *See Amplifier; Automatic gain control (AGC).*

*Harry F. Olson*

**Bibliography.** H. F. Olson, *Modern Sound Reproduction*, 1972, reprint 1978.

## Wave-shaping circuits

Electronic circuits used to create or modify a specified time-varying electrical quantity, usually voltage or current, using combinations of electronic devices, such as vacuum tubes or transistors, and circuit elements including resistors, capacitors, and inductors.

One such waveform is the square wave, in which a quantity such as voltage alternately assumes two discrete values during repeating periods of time. Where each period is composed of two equal intervals, the wave can be obtained by amplifying a sinusoidal time-varying voltage and removing all but the section near the zero-voltage axis. Also, square waves of either equal or unequal intervals, sometimes referred to as rectangular waves, can be generated by multivibrators or various other forms of vacuum-tube or transistor switching or gating circuits. *See Clipping circuit; Limiter circuit; Multivibrator; Relaxation oscillator.*

Other wave shapes of particular interest in electronics are the linearly increasing function of time or ramp function (which if recurring at equally spaced periods is usually called the linear sawtooth waveform), the hyperbolic waveform, and the rectified sine wave. Such recurrent waveforms are shaped by the combination of electronic switches or gating circuits, resistance-capacitance time constants, and linear feedback amplifiers. *See Clamping circuit; Coincidence amplifier; Electronic display; Electronic switch; Pulse generator; Rectifier; Sweep generator; Trigger circuit.*

*Glenn M. Glasford*

## Waveform

The pictorial representation of the form or shape of a wave, obtained by plotting the amplitude of the wave with respect to time. There are an infinite number of possible waveforms. Some of the more common electrical waveforms are shown in the **illustration**. These diagrams are plots of voltage against time. It is equally possible to show current waveforms.

It is possible to represent any periodic waveform mathematically as a Fourier series of sine and cosine terms at harmonic frequencies. Any nonsinusoidal wave is composed of a constant or dc term, plus a series of harmonic terms in which the frequencies are

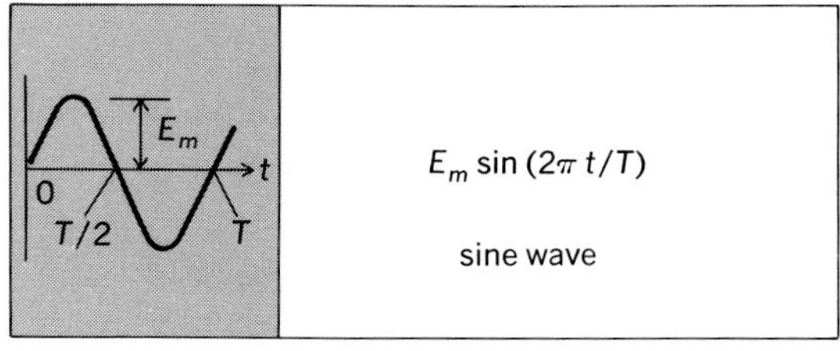


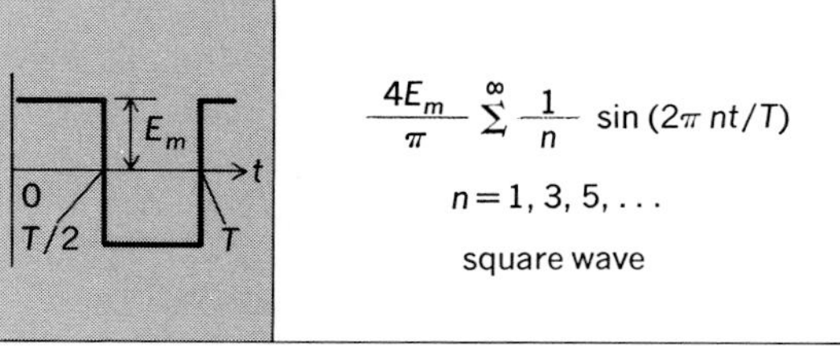


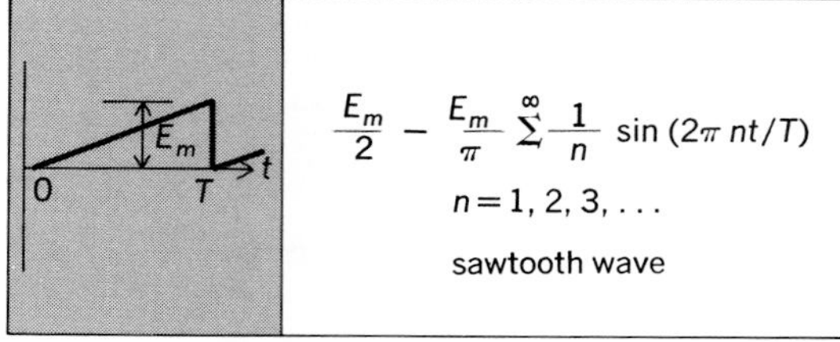


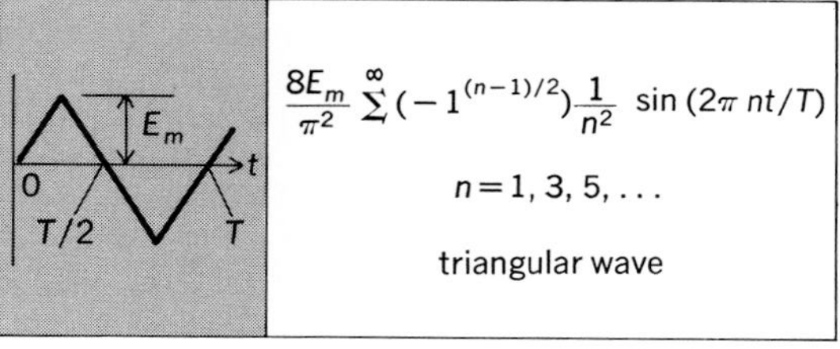


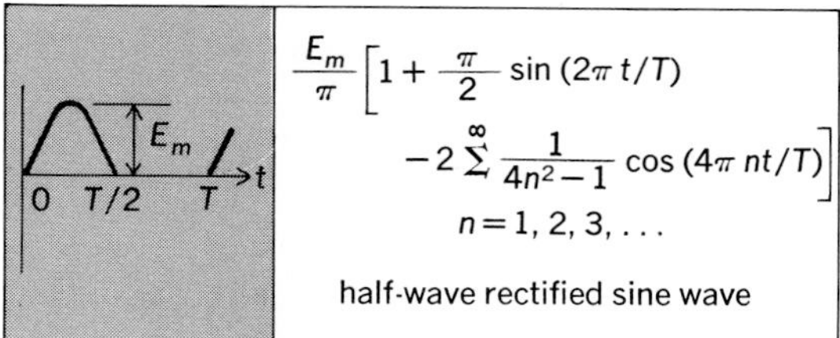


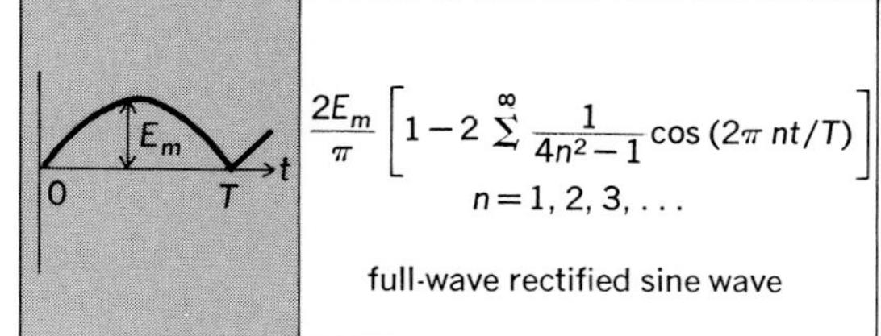


**Common electrical waveforms.**

integral multiples of the fundamental frequency. The Fourier series for each waveform is given beside each figure as functions of time $t$, where $E_m$ is the maximum value of the wave and $T$ is the period. SEE NONSINUSOIDAL WAVEFORM.

Sine waves are obtained from sine-wave generators and $LC$, $RC$, and beat-frequency oscillators. SEE OSCILLATOR.

Square waves are obtained from square-wave generator circuits, such as multivibrators and clippers. SEE MULTIVIBRATOR.

Sawtooth waves are obtained from gas-tube relaxation oscillators and thyratron, transistor, and vacuum-tube sweep circuits. SEE RELAXATION OSCILLATOR; SAWTOOTH-WAVE GENERATOR; SWEEP GENERATOR.

Triangular waves are obtained from integrated square waves.

The output wave shape of a half-wave rectifier with resistance load is as illustrated. SEE RECTIFIER.

The output wave shape of a full-wave rectifier with resistance load is as illustrated.

*Donald L. Waidelich*

## Waveform determination

The defining of a curve, or waveform, that represents the variation of the magnitude of a quantity with time. Waveform is determined either with oscillographs that display and record the waveform directly, or with wave analyzers that indicate the numerical values of amplitude, frequency, and sometimes phase angle of the harmonic components of a complex wave.

The measurement and control of waveform is of real concern to the electrical industry's engineers, because the transformers, motors, lighting circuits, and other equipment are designed to operate at maximum efficiency when the voltage waveform is a sine wave with a predetermined crest voltage. Departures from the specified waveform cause losses in efficiency. In radio communication systems the carrier waveform is sinusoidal, and deviations from the sine wave introduce noise that interferes with the intelligence being transmitted.

Waveforms are of two basic types: (1) periodic or continuous waves, and (2) aperiodic or transient waves. For periodic waves SEE NONSINUSOIDAL WAVEFORM; WAVEFORM. For aperiodic waves SEE ELECTRIC TRANSIENT.

Two general classes of measurement devices are used to determine waveforms. The harmonic analyzer is widely used and is the most accurate for determining the waveform of a continuous wave. Any continuous wave can be defined by a Fourier series of sine waves, including a wave at fundamental frequency and waves at harmonics of this fundamental frequency. The harmonic analyzer indicates numerical values of the amplitude, frequency, and phase of the fundamental and each of the harmonics of the waveform under study. When required, the complete waveform may be constructed by graphically superimposing the component waves.

The second type of measurement device, the oscillograph, is used to determine transient waveforms. The oscillograph may also be used to determine the waveform of continuous waves but with considerably less accuracy than that provided by the harmonic analyzer. SEE ELECTRICAL MEASUREMENTS; HARMONIC ANALYZER; OSCILLOSCOPE.

*Isaac F. Kinnard/Edward C. Stevenson*

## Waveguide

A device which constrains or guides the propagation of electromagnetic waves along a path defined by the physical construction of the guide. In a broad sense, devices such as a pair of parallel wires and a coaxial cable can certainly be called waveguides. When used in a more restricted sense, however, the term waveguide usually means a metallic tube which can confine and guide the propagation of electromagnetic waves in the hollow space along the lengthwise direction of the tube. For reasons which will become clear in the following discussion, hollow waveguides of convenient sizes are best adapted to the transmission of microwaves.

The concept that hollow waveguides can transmit electromagnetic waves may seem strange to people who lean heavily on experiences with low-frequency waves. It will not appear so strange, however, if one thinks in terms of an analogy with sound waves going through pipes (for example, pipe organs). Because a sound wave can transmit through a pipe only when its wavelength is comparable to or smaller than the size of the pipe, one would expect that a similar requirement should hold true for electromagnetic waves. Indeed, if the frequency of an electromagnetic wave is high enough that the wavelength is comparable to or smaller than the waveguide dimension, then wave transmission through the hollow waveguide becomes possible.

Although hollow waveguides and coaxial cables are the commonest in application, some other types of waveguides are also occasionally used. A single conductor (called a G-string) is sometimes used as a waveguide. Another waveguide takes the form of a flat conducting strip having a certain spacing from a ground plane, known as a microwave strip. Still another example is found in a dielectric rod.

**Maxwell's equations.** The most basic approach to the understanding and analysis of the behavior of electromagnetic waves in any waveguide is obtained by the application of Maxwell's equations to a given physical situation. These are a set of partial differential equations relating the quantities electric intensity $\mathbf{E}$, electric induction $\mathbf{D}$, magnetic intensity $\mathbf{H}$, and magnetic induction $\mathbf{B}$. Each quantity is regarded as a vector, having a direction as well as a magnitude which is a function of space coordinates and time. In the ordinary case of a homogeneous isotropic medium, electric induction is proportional to electric intensity. The constant of proportionality is known as the dielectric constant $\epsilon$. Similarly, magnetic induction is related to magnetic intensity by a constant known as the permeability $\mu$.

A general solution of Maxwell's equations leads to a wave equation which points definitely to the possible existence of electromagnetic waves in the medium. Thus, for a dielectric medium of infinite extent, all solutions of the wave equation are equally admissible. One common characteristic for all these waves is that there is a velocity of propagation which is completely determined by the dielectric and permeability constants of the medium. SEE WAVE EQUATION.

Any particular solution for a realizable guided wave must obey certain boundary conditions imposed by the physical situation. The walls of a hollow waveguide are almost always made of a highly conducting metal like copper, brass, or aluminum. The electrical conductivity of such materials, while always finite, is so high that it can be considered to be infinite for the present considerations. It is well known that no electric intensity can exist inside a perfect conductor. On the basis of this fact and the application of Maxwell's equations, the boundary conditions for the electric and magnetic intensities at the interface between a perfect conductor and a dielectric (usually air) in a hollow waveguide turn out to be that both the tangential component of **E** and the normal component of **H** are zero at the boundary.

**Transmission modes.** Consider a hollow waveguide with a given cross section which is uniform throughout its entire length. As a result of the application of these boundary conditions to the wave equation, it can be shown that only certain unique patterns for the distribution of **E** and **H** (taken together) can exist in the waveguide. Each unique pattern of the field distribution is called a mode. There are two types of mode possible in a hollow waveguide. One type is called the transverse electric (TE) mode, in which **E** has only a component transverse (that is, perpendicular) to the direction of propagation, whereas the magnetic intensity **H** has both transversal and longitudinal components. The other type is called the transverse magnetic (TM) mode, in which the magnetic intensity has only a transverse component and the electric intensity has both components. Each type (TE or TM) of mode has an infinite number of submodes which have the common characteristics of the type to which they belong, but differ among themselves in the details of field distribution. Since it is known that the transverse electric and magnetic (TEM) mode is not possible in a hollow waveguide, any arbitrary electromagnetic wave inside such a waveguide can be considered as a linear superposition of all possible modes of both the TE and TM types.

**Rectangular waveguides.** The type of waveguide with a rectangular cross section is not only the commonest in use but also the simplest in theoretical analysis. It is used here as a concrete example to illustrate various common properties of a waveguide. Consider a rectangular waveguide as shown in **Fig. 1**. The wave propagates along the $z$ axis. The simplest and also the most commonly used mode is called the $TE_{01}$ wave; its electric and magnetic intensities can be described by the expressions satisfying the boundary conditions of Eqs. (1), where $A$ = arbitrary constant

$$\begin{aligned} E_x &= A \sin\left(\frac{\pi}{b} y\right) \sin \omega\left(t - \frac{z}{v}\right) \\ H_y &= \frac{1}{\mu v} A \sin\left(\frac{\pi}{b} y\right) \sin \omega\left(t - \frac{z}{v}\right) \\ H_z &= -\frac{\pi}{\mu\omega b} A \cos\left(\frac{\pi}{b} y\right) \cos \omega\left(t - \frac{z}{v}\right) \\ H_x &= E_y = E_z = 0 \end{aligned} \tag{1}$$

depending upon the strength of wave excitation, $\omega = 2\pi \times$ frequency, $t$ = time, $v$ = velocity of propagation of the wave, and $\mu$ = permeability of the dielectric filling the waveguide. It is particularly important to note that the velocity of propagation $v$ in a waveguide is different from that in an infinite space filled with the same dielectric material $v_0$. These two quantities are related for the $TE_{01}$ wave by the Eq. (2), in which $f$ = frequency. By applying the simple

$$v = \frac{v_0}{\sqrt{1 - (v_0/2fb)^2}} \tag{2}$$

formula $v = f\lambda$, it is seen that the wavelength in the waveguide is similarly related to the corresponding quantity (for the $TE_{01}$ wave) in an infinite dielectric ($\lambda_0$) as in Eq. (3).

$$\lambda = \frac{\lambda_0}{\sqrt{1 - (\lambda_0/2b)^2}} \tag{3}$$

The expressions in Eq. (1) reveal the wave nature of the field quantities through the sinusoidal functions of $\omega(t - z/v)$, which are a description of wave motion with velocity $v$ along the $z$ axis. On any cross section (constant $z$), these sinusoidal functions depend simply on time. Hence, each of the field quantities oscillates at the common frequency $f$ and with an amplitude which varies with the field point ($y$ in this particular case).

***Phase velocity.*** Equation (2) represents the phase velocity of the guided wave because the quantity $v$ is contained in $\omega(t - z/v)$, which is called the phase of wave propagation. If $\lambda_0 < 2b$, the phase velocity in a waveguide is larger than that in an open space filled with the same dielectric material. Correspondingly, the wavelength in a waveguide is longer than that in an infinite dielectric medium, as indicated by Eq. (3). All waves with $\lambda_0 < 2b$ belong to the transmission region of the waveguide because only the waves in this region are allowed to pass through. When $\lambda_0 = 2b$, both $v$ and $\lambda$ are infinite, and when $\lambda_0 > 2b$, they are imaginary. It can be shown that waves are not allowed to propagate in a waveguide when $\lambda_0 \geqslant 2b$. The critical value of $\lambda_c = 2b$ is known as the cutoff, or critical, wavelength.

***Generalization to other TE waves.*** The preceding discussion can be carried through in a parallel fashion for the general case of any TE wave designated as $TE_{nm}$, where $n$ and $m$ are integers. Each $TE_{nm}$ wave has its characteristic field distribution, velocity, and wavelength. The expression for the wavelength in the waveguide, for example, is given by Eq. (4). The

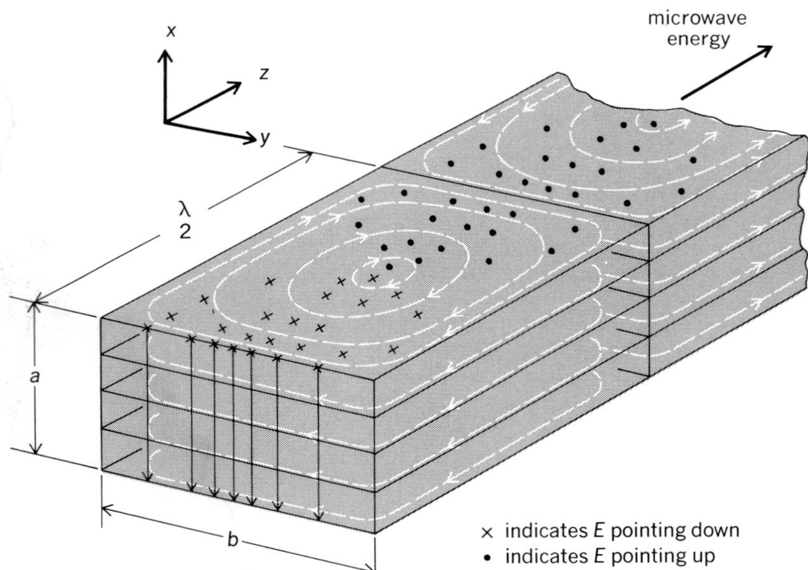


**Fig. 1. Instantaneous field pattern for the $TE_{01}$ wave in a rectangular waveguide. Solid lines indicate the electric intensity E, and broken lines the magnetic intensity H.** (*After MIT Radar School Staff, Principles of Radar, 1952*)

$$\lambda = \frac{\lambda_0}{\sqrt{1 - \left(\frac{n\lambda_0}{2a}\right)^2 - \left(\frac{m\lambda_0}{2b}\right)^2}} \quad (4)$$

corresponding cutoff wavelength is given by Eq. (5),

$$\lambda_c = \frac{2}{\sqrt{\left(\frac{n}{a}\right)^2 + \left(\frac{m}{b}\right)^2}} \quad (5)$$

which reduces to $\lambda_c = 2b$ for the special case of $TE_{01}$, where $n = 0$ and $m = 1$. A $TE_{00}$ wave ($n = 0$ and $m = 0$) would have an infinite cutoff wavelength which is characteristic of a principal mode, if such were possible. Actually, the solution of the field equation shows that the principal mode cannot exist in a hollow metallic waveguide. Equation (5) further shows that any other values of $n$ and $m$ in $TE_{nm}$ would lead to a cutoff wavelength shorter than that of $TE_{01}$, which is called the dominant mode for this reason.

***TM waves.*** The TM waves can be treated in almost exactly the same manner as the TE waves. Although the field distributions in the two cases are completely different, the wavelengths (similarly, the velocities of propagation) in the guide for both cases obey Eqs. (4) and (5), except that neither $n$ nor $m$ can become zero for a $TM_{nm}$ wave.

***Designation of rectangular waveguides.*** It is highly desirable and customary for practical use to excite only the dominant mode ($TE_{01}$) in a rectangular waveguide. This means that a waveguide of a given size is useful for this one-mode operation only for a certain range of free-space wavelengths (or frequencies). Four waveguides of certain dimensions and their corresponding wavelength bands have been conventionally designated by the letters S, C, X, and K, as shown in the **table**.

**Band designation for rectangular waveguides**

| Band | Dimension, $cm^2$ | $\lambda_0$, cm |
|---|---|---|
| S | 7.62 × 2.54 | 8.9–10.5 |
| C | 3.48 × 1.58 | 3.7– 5.1 |
| X | 2.54 × 1.27 | 3.0– 3.5 |
| K | 1.06 × 0.43 | 1.2– 1.5 |

## Joints, bends, and junctions.

To achieve certain effects, waveguides are frequently joined together, bent or twisted, or formed into networks known as junctions.

***Joints.*** Waveguides are often joined together under various conditions. Identical waveguide terminals may be connected from end to end for extension or for inserting circuit elements. This can be done by providing a flange at each end of the waveguide and then butting the two flat surfaces of the flanges together so that the waveguide ends form a contact joint smoothly. Sometimes, to alleviate the difficulty of making good contact, a choke joint is operated. This is based on the principle that an artificially created current nodal line at the joint will make the physical contact of the waveguide ends unnecessary.

Another type of waveguide joint is required when a coaxial cable is to be joined to a hollow waveguide. Here, a transformation of the wave is to take place between the coaxial mode and, for instance, the $TE_{01}$ mode of a rectangular waveguide. In this case the coaxial cable is usually led into the blocked end (or into a tunable short-circuiting plunger) of the regular waveguide, and the center conductor is extended to touch the opposite face so that the extended wire will act as an antenna for the excitation of the wave in the rectangular guide (**Fig. 2**).

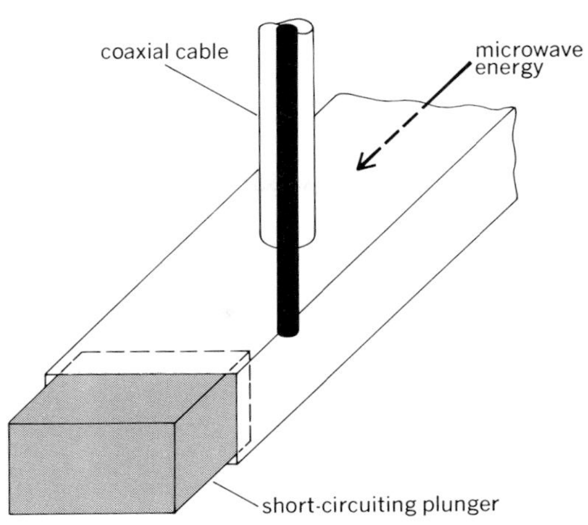


**Fig. 2. Coupling between waveguide and coaxial cable.**

***Bends and twists.*** Waveguide bends are often used to change the direction of the waveguide by a desired angle. There are two types of 90° bend—one in the **H** plane and the other in the **E** plane. A 90° bend in the **H** plane is shown in **Fig. 3**. Twists are used to change the plane of polarization by a desired angle while maintaining the direction of the waveguide. A 90° twist is shown in **Fig. 4**.

***Junctions.*** The term junction is used to denote a network of waveguides joined in a specified manner to give certain desired properties to the whole network. Common examples are a T junction, a directional coupler, and a magic-tee junction.

A T junction is a network with three waveguide terminals arranged in the form of the letter T. In rectangular waveguides, there are two ways of arranging a symmetrical T junction: Either all three broad sides are in one plane or two broad sides are in one plane and the third in a perpendicular plane; the latter arrangement is shown in **Fig. 5**. In any case, when a microwave is incident to one waveguide terminal, the incoming power is divided equally between the remaining two waveguides, and the two branch waves go along their separate directions.

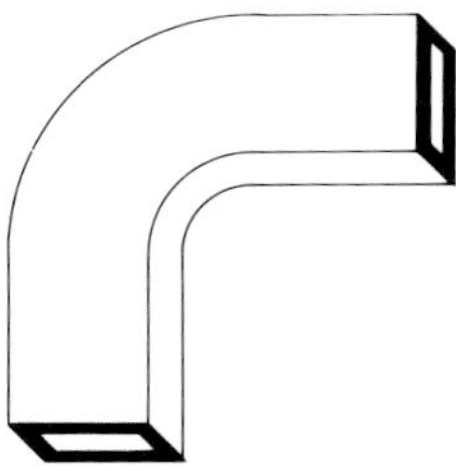

**Fig. 3. H-plane 90° bend for a rectangular waveguide.**

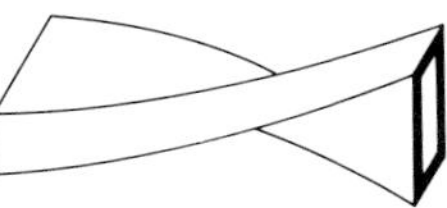

**Fig. 4. A 90° twist for a rectangular waveguide.**

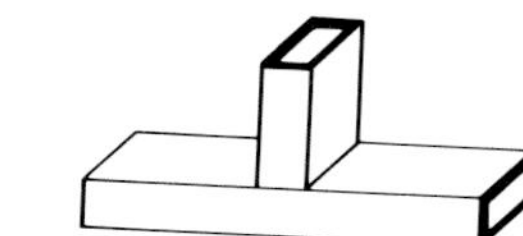

Fig. 5. T junction.

A directional coupler is a network of four waveguide terminals. When suitably arranged, it has the property that for each terminal there is another with which it does not interact in any way. A special directional coupler known as the magic tee is described here. For a discussion of the two-hole interference type of directional coupler SEE DIRECTIONAL COUPLER.

A magic-tee junction is shown in **Fig. 6**. This network has a plane of symmetry as indicated. Consider only the dominant mode $TE_{01}$ for all the waveguides. The mode in waveguide A is always symmetrical to the plane of symmetry, while the mode in waveguide C is always antisymmetrical. The symmetrical mode in A can excite symmetric modes in B and D but not in C. The antisymmetric mode in C can excite antisymmetric modes in B and D but not in A. A superposition of simultaneous excitations in A and C of equal strength must necessarily cause the intensity in either B or D to vanish because, if it is exactly in phase for one of them, it must be exactly out of phase for the other. Hence, in addition to the isolation between A and C, there is an isolation between B and D. These rather intricate properties are used in microwave circuits in a variety of ways, including the direct measurement of both incident and reflected intensities.

**Waveguide shapes.** Next to the rectangular type, metallic waveguides with circular cross sections are most frequently used. Because of its circular cylindrical symmetry, this type of waveguide can sustain waves of all kinds of field polarization (linear, circular, and elliptic) in many ways which are not possible with the rectangular type. However, the general notions of transmission modes, propagation velocities, cutoff wavelengths, and so on are just as applicable to circular waveguides as they are to rectangular waveguides, except that the mathematics used for circular shapes is somewhat more involved. Waveguides of elliptical cross section are almost never used on purpose, but they may represent results of deformation from the original circular waveguides. Detailed descriptions of wave behavior in elliptical waveguides are available in the literature.

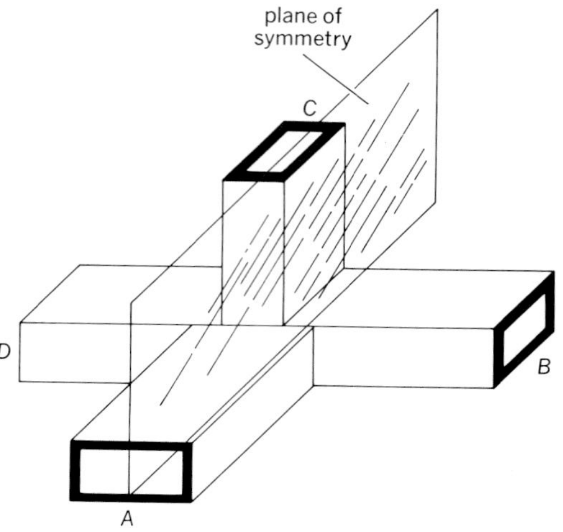


Fig. 6. Magic-tee junction.

**Attenuation of hollow waveguides.** In the preceding discussion, there has been an implicit assumption that the attenuation of a wave by the waveguide is negligible. Although this assumption is quite justifiable for interpretive purposes, the effect of attenuation should be considered for all quantitative evaluations. As a wave passes through a waveguide (say in the $z$ direction), its power becomes reduced exponentially according to Eq. (6), where $P_0$ is the power at $z =$

$$P_z = P_0 e^{-\alpha z} \tag{6}$$

0, $P_z$ is the power at a distance, $z$, and $\alpha$ is called the attenuation constant of the waveguide. The quantity $\alpha$ is a measure of the lossy character of the waveguide in absorbing the wave energy because of the currents set up on the inner walls of the waveguide and because of dielectric losses, if any. The same quantity is a function of the electrical conductivity of the waveguide walls, geometric dimensions, mode of propagation, and frequency of the wave. Other things being equal, $\alpha$ becomes smaller with a larger conductivity or a greater volume-to-surface ratio. For practical reasons, hollow waveguides are usually made of copper or brass, but on rare occasions they are also made of silver (or coated inside with silver) for higher conductivity.

The dominant mode ($TE_{01}$) of a rectangular copper waveguide in the X-band has an attenuation constant of the order of 0.1 dB/m. The overall attenuation may be regarded as small for a short guide length, but it would become undesirably large as the length increased. Consequently, rectangular waveguides are not considered suitable for long-distance microwave transmission.

In contradistinction to the rectangular waveguide, a circular waveguide operated at the $TE_{01}$ mode has the unusual characteristic that its attenuation constant decreases indefinitely with increasing frequency. It is thus possible to choose a frequency sufficiently high to keep the attenuation constant satisfactorily low, even with small waveguide dimensions. For example, at a frequency corresponding to a free-space wavelength of 6 mm, the attenuation constant for the $TE_{01}$ mode in a circular waveguide can be almost 100 times smaller than that in a corresponding rectangular waveguide. However, for the realization of long-distance transmission with circular waveguide, it is necessary to prevent the degradation of the low-attenuation property resulting from interconversion between the degenerate modes $TE_{01}$ and $TM_{11}$, the interconversion being caused by manufacturing and laying (chiefly bending imperfections). Some preventive measures have been devised and demonstrated.

**Coaxial cable.** A coaxial cable consists of a hollow cylindrical conductor coaxially placed with respect to an inner cylindrical conductor. It is very extensively used as a waveguide, though seldom so called, for very high as well as very low frequencies. The adaptability of a coaxial cable to a wide range of frequencies (including zero) is due to the existence of a principal mode, which is in fact a TEM wave. The analysis of the wave propagation in a coaxial cable is simple and is analogous to that of two parallel wires or plane plates. The velocity of propagation in such systems is the same as in infinite space filled with the same dielectric material. In common with a hollow waveguide, coaxial cable has the advantage that the outside conductor acts as a shield against external electrical interference. However, it does not have the ability possessed by hollow waveguides of filtering low frequencies, when such filtering is desired. Also, for very high frequencies, the attenuation of a coaxial cable is apt to be higher than that of a comparable hollow waveguide because of higher losses due to either the dielectric medium or the supports. SEE COAXIAL CABLE.

**Other special waveguides.** A single conductor, often thinly coated with a dielectric substance, can act as a waveguide under the nickname of G-string. A wave, usually of the TM mode, is guided along the surface of the conductor. The transmission characteristics are quite favorable in the frequency range of 80 to 300 MHz.

A special waveguide adaptable to microwave circuit wiring has been developed under the name of a microwave strip. It consists of a flat conducting strip separated from the ground plane by a dielectric layer. Its chief advantage is convenience of fabrication by printed circuit techniques.

Dielectric rods not involving any conductor can guide very high-frequency (vhf) waves quite successfully. The propagating wave is partly inside the dielectric and partly outside. Such dielectric waveguides can be used for short-distance transmission. SEE ELECTROMAGNETIC WAVE TRANSMISSION; MICROWAVE; MICROWAVE TRANSMISSION LINES; TRANSMISSION LINES.

*C. K. Jen*

## Wavelength measurement

Determination of the distance between successive wavefronts of equal phase of a wave. The wavelength of an oscillating electromagnetic wave depends upon the frequency of the oscillation and the velocity of propagation in the medium or in the transmission system in which the wave is propagating. This article discusses wavelength measurement of electromagnetic waves in the radio and microwave regions.

The speed of electric waves in free space is, by definition, exactly 299,792.458 km/s (186,282.397 mi/s), or approximately $3 \times 10^8$ m/s. The presence of any dielectric material (such as air) or any magnetic matter with permeability greater than unity will cause the wave to travel at a lower velocity. Also, the presence of various types of transmission lines and waveguides will affect the velocity. In general the group velocity, or velocity of propagation of the wavefront of a suddenly applied signal, is less than that in free space, but it is possible for the phase velocity to be greater than the value for free space. In particular, the phase velocity in a waveguide operated with waves near the cutoff frequency is greater than the phase velocity in free space. SEE ELECTROMAGNETIC WAVE TRANSMISSION; TRANSMISSION LINES; WAVEGUIDE.

**Wavelength by frequency measurement.** In order to specify the wavelength of an electromagnetic wave, it is essential to know the medium or device through which the wave is propagating. However, unless otherwise specified, it is general practice to quote the wavelength of an oscillatory electric wave as that in air, or free space. When this convention is used, all that is necessary is a frequency measurement in order to apply Eq. (1), where $c$ is the velocity of

$$\lambda_0 = c/f \tag{1}$$

light, $\lambda_0$ is the free-space wavelength, and $f$ is frequency.

**Standing-wave method.** In view of the direct relationship between frequency and wavelength, the earliest method used for specifying the tuning point of a given radio wave was the wavelength of the wave. Early experimenters found that standing-waves existed in space wherever reflections occurred. In a standing-wave field, interference occurs between forward-propugating and reverse-propagating or reflected waves. A distance equal to one-half wavelength exists between successive minima or maxima in the standing-wave pattern. Thus, the wavelength can be determined by measuring the distance between two maxima, or two minima of a standing-wave field with a meter stick or measuring tape, the location of the field maxima being observed by moving a suitable detector unit to various points in the field. SEE STANDING-WAVE DETECTOR; WAVEMETER.

**Interferometer methods.** The standing-wave method of measurement is somewhat similar to the interferometer measurements used in optics. With shorter-wavelength radio waves it is possible to apply optically derived interferometer techniques directly to the measurement of wavelength.

An example of an interferometer used in the millimeter wavelength range is shown in **Fig. 1**. Essentially, a microwave beam is directed at a beam splitter, which splits the beam into two parts, $A$ and $B$, by partial reflection. The $A$ beam is reflected to a movable reflector and reflected again as $A'$. The beam splitter transmits part of this as $A''$. The transmitted part $B$ of the original beam is reflected by a fixed microwave reflector as $B'$. This is partially reflected by the beam splitter as $B''$. The beams $A''$ and $B''$ combine to form standing waves, which are then detected. Movement of the movable reflector causes the position of the standing wave to move, which causes the detected signal to pass through successive points of maximum and minimum amplitude. The distance between points of successive maxima or minima is one-half wavelength. This distance may be determined from the motion of the movable reflector.

**Lecher wires.** A more convenient, if less precise, measurement method for the determination of wavelength is the Lecher wire wavemeter (**Fig. 2**). With this simple device, wavelength is measured by sliding the short circuit along the line from a first to a second

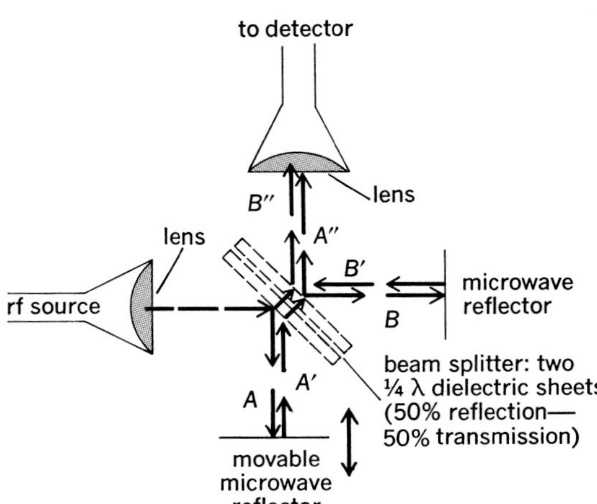


**Fig. 1. Wavelength measurement by the Michelson interferometer used at millimeter wavelengths.**

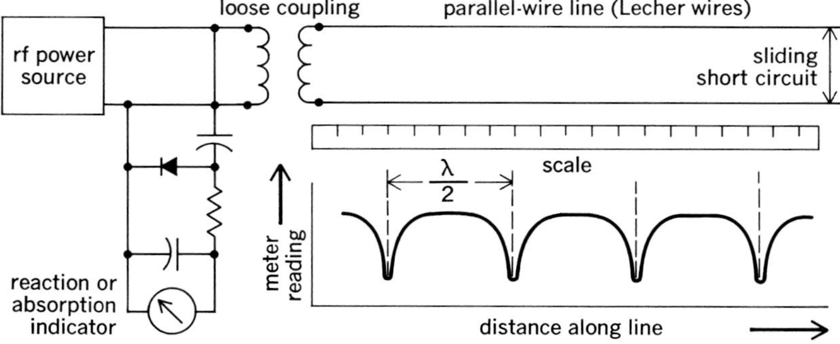


Fig. 2. Lecher-wire (resonant-line) wavemeter.

point of equal amplitude of effect, as indicated by absorption of signal being detected by an external detector, the variation in input power to oscillator or amplifier being checked, or by some similar method, such as the dc grid current of a negative-grid triode oscillator. The distance between two successive absorption maxima is one-half wavelength ($\lambda/2$); thus, by this length measurement, the wavelength is measured directly.

**Tuned circuits.** At lower frequencies, inductance-capacitance resonant circuits may serve similar functions as absorption devices. With calibrated values of inductance $L$ and capacitance $C$, it is possible to provide a scale calibrated in wavelength or frequency. For low-loss circuits the resonant frequency is $1/(2\pi\sqrt{LC})$. **Figure 3** shows a schematic diagram of a simple absorption-type wavemeter. Wavemeters of this type, often constructed with the principal inductance $L_1$ as a plug-in coil, are used for frequency or wavelength measurement up to frequencies of approximately 1000 MHz. *See* Resonance (alternating-current circuits).

A variation of the absorption wavemeter, known as a grid-dip meter or grid-dip oscillator, provides in one instrument an absorption wavemeter and a calibrated oscillator, which may be used to determine the resonant frequency (or wavelength) of a passive network, such as an antenna system or an $LC$ tuned circuit, by observing the dip in grid current of the oscillator as the oscillator frequency is tuned to the network resonant frequency.

Microwave wavemeters make use of resonant coaxial-line sections or cavities as tuned elements. The two general types of microwave wavemeters are the absorption, or reaction, type and the transmission type. Wavemeters of low or medium selectivity are frequently used as coarse measuring devices to establish the general range of frequency of operation of a system before applying more refined and complex methods for accurate frequency checking. *See* Cavity resonator; Coaxial cable.

A modern resonant-cavity microwave wavemeter is shown in **Fig. 4**. The dimensions of the cavity determine the resonant frequency of the wavemeter. A signal is fed in from either a coaxial line or waveguide, and energy is fed out to a suitable detector by a second coaxial line. The cavity is tuned by means of a micrometer-driven plunger, which may be calibrated in terms of wavelength. *See* Microwave.

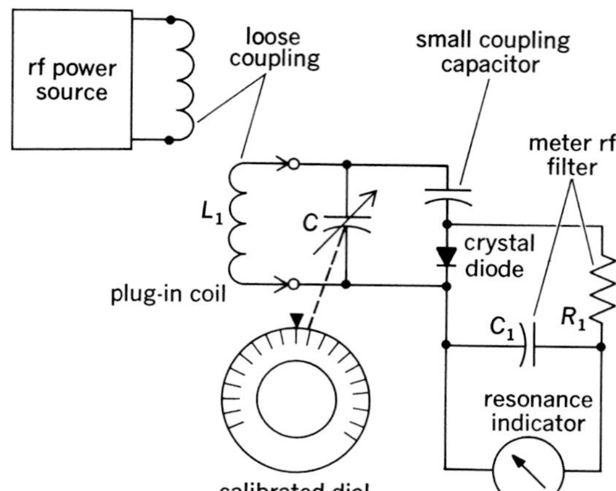


Fig. 3. Schematic diagram of inductance-capacitance type of absorption wavemeter (for frequencies between approximately 50 kHz and 1000 MHz).

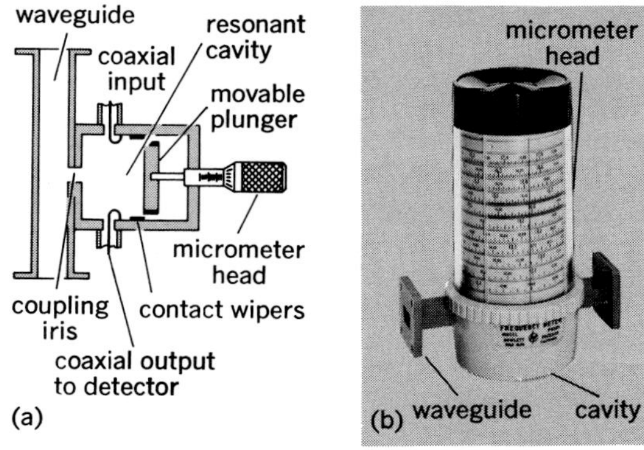


Fig. 4. Resonant-cavity wavemeter. (a) Typical construction providing either coaxial or waveguide inputs. (b) Commercial model. (*Hewlett-Packard Co.*)

Frank D. Lewis

**Bibliography.** A. H. Cook, *Interference of Electromagnetic Waves*, 1971; K. C. Gupta, *Microwaves*, 1980; F. A. Jenkins and H. E. White, *Fundamentals of Optics*, 1976; T. S. Laverghetta, *Microwave Measurements and Techniques*, 1976; R. A. Sawyer, *Experimental Spectroscopy*, 2d ed., 1951; J. J. Snyder, Laser wavelength meters, *Laser Focus*, 18(5):55–61, 1982; B. N. Taylor and W. D. Phillips, *Precision Measurements and Fundamental Constants II*, Nat. Bur. Stand. Spec. Publ. 617, 1984.

## Wavemeter

A device for measuring the geometrical spacing between successive surfaces of equal phase along an electromagnetic wave. To avoid instrument calibration problems due to the dependence of the phase velocity upon the particular transmission system under measurement, it is common procedure to calibrate wavemeters in terms of free-space wavelength, which is the ratio of the velocity of light (299,792,458 m/s) divided by the frequency of the signal in hertz.

At frequencies up to about 100 MHz, wavemeters consist basically of a tuned $LC$ circuit and a suitable resonance indicator not noticeably different from that originally used by H. Hertz. The choice of a detector depends upon the power level of the signal and the desired accuracy. For power levels greater than several watts and for moderate accuracy, a miniature lamp bulb in series with the inductor $L$ serves as a resonance indicator by glowing brightly when the induced current is a maximum. For low power levels or for higher accuracy the loading effect of the bulb cannot be tolerated. Therefore a suitable electronic voltmeter is used to measure the capacitor voltage, which is a maximum at resonance. The capacitor is variable and calibrated in units of wavelength or frequency.

At higher frequencies it is necessary to employ well-defined transmission systems such as open-wire or coaxial lines and waveguides. Any open-circuited or short-circuited section of transmission system can be adjusted in physical size to cause it to resonate at a give wavelength. From a construction standpoint short-circuited sections are preferred and may take the form of Lecher wires, coaxial wavemeters, and cavity resonators. Suitable electronic standing-wave detectors are employed to indicate when the wavemeter is tuned to resonance. *SEE CAVITY RESONATOR; STANDING-WAVE DETECTOR; WAVELENGTH MEASUREMENT.*

*Robert L. Ramey*

## Wheatstone bridge

A device used to measure the electrical resistance of an unknown resistor by comparing it with a known standard resistance. This method was first described by S. H. Christie in 1833, only 7 years after Georg S. Ohm discovered the relationship between voltage and current. Since 1843 when Charles Wheatstone called attention to Christie's work, Wheatstone's name has been associated with this network. *SEE RESISTANCE MEASUREMENT.*

The Wheatstone bridge network consists of four resistors $R_{AB}$, $R_{BC}$, $R_{CD}$, and $R_{AD}$ interconnected as shown in **Fig. 1** to form the bridge. A detector G, having an internal resistance $R_G$, is connected between the B and D bridge points; and a power supply, having an open-circuit voltage $E$ and internal resistance $R_B$, is connected between the A and C bridge points. *SEE BRIDGE CIRCUIT.*

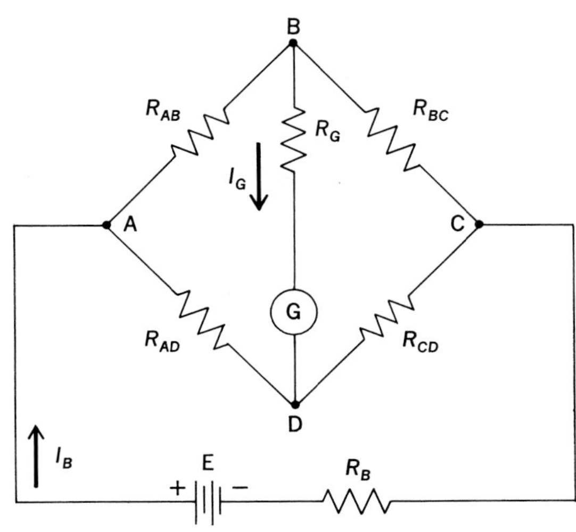


Fig. 1. Wheatstone bridge circuit.

Application of Ohm's and Kirchhoff's laws to this network results in the equation

$$I_G = \frac{I_B(R_{BC}R_{AD} - R_{AB}R_{CD})}{\left[\begin{array}{l} R_G(R_{AB} + R_{BC} + R_{CD} + R_{AD}) \\ + (R_{BC} + R_{CD})(R_{AB} + R_{AD}) \end{array}\right]} \quad (1)$$

for the detector current. In this expression,

$$I_B \approx \frac{E}{R_B + \dfrac{(R_{AB} + R_{BC})(R_{AD} + R_{CD})}{R_{AB} + R_{BC} + R_{CD} + R_{AD}}} \quad (2)$$

It is apparent, from Eq. (1), that if the network is adjusted so that

$$R_{BC}R_{AD} - R_{AB}R_{CD} = 0 \quad (3)$$

the detector current will be zero and this adjustment will be independent of the supply voltage, the supply resistance, and the detector resistance. Thus, when the bridge is balanced,

$$R_{BC}R_{AD} = R_{AB}R_{CD} \quad (4)$$

and, if it is assumed that the unknown resistance is the one in the CD arm of the bridge, then

$$R_{CD} = \left(\frac{R_{BC}}{R_{AB}}\right) \times R_{AD} \quad (5)$$

Three methods of adjustment to achieve this condition are possible when the circuit is used as a ratio arm bridge: (1) use of a fixed ratio $R_{BC}/R_{AB}$ and a continuously adjustable standard $R_{AD}$, (2) use of a continuously adjustable ratio and a fixed standard, and (3) a combination of the foregoing with the ratio usually adjustable in discrete steps of decade values. The first method provides a linear calibration of unknown versus standard resistance but is limited in resistance range to the adjustable range of the standard. The second method provides a wide range, since the ratio is easily adjustable from zero to infinity, but results in a nonlinear scale, highly expanded for low resistances and greatly compressed for high resistances. The third method, using a ratio adjustable in several decade steps and a resistance standard of three to five decades, provides a wide range and linear calibration and is the most practical of the combinations for the general use with reasonable accuracy.

If the circuit is considered as a product arm bridge, it is seen that conductance $G_{CD}$ of unknown resistance

$$R_{CD} = \frac{R_{BC}R_{AD}}{R_{AB}} \quad (6)$$

is measured directly in terms of the adjustable standard $R_{AB}$ since

$$G_{CD} = \frac{1}{R_{CD}} = \frac{R_{AB}}{R_{BC}R_{AD}} \quad (7)$$

**Sensitivity.** The sensitivity of the bridge assembly (battery, bridge, and detector) is of interest for two purposes: (1) to determine the required detector sensitivity for a given deviation in the unknown resistance, or (2) to determine the change in resistance which can be measured using a detector of a stated sensitivity. The precision balance is affected by the detector sensitivity, the detector resistance, the ohmic value of the bridge resistors, the bridge supply voltage, and the bridge supply resistance, which except for special cases can be neglected.

If the detector circuit BD (Fig. 1) is opened, the open-circuit voltage between points B and D is

$$e = E_{BC} - E_{CD}$$

or

$$e = E\left(\frac{R_{BC}}{R_{AB} + R_{BC}} - \frac{R_{CD} - \Delta R_{CD}}{R_{CD} - \Delta R_{CD} + R_{AD}}\right) \quad (8)$$

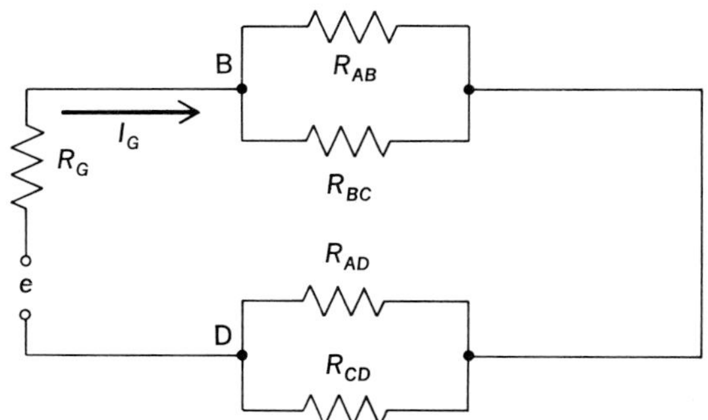


Fig. 2. Equivalent circuit of unbalanced bridge.

where $\Delta R_{CD}$ is a small, incremental change in the unknown resistance $R_{CD}$. To a close approximation, this open-circuit voltage due to a small bridge unbalance can be expressed in terms of the bridge ratio, the fractional change in the unknown resistance, and the applied voltage as follows:

$$e = E \frac{r}{(r+1)^2}\left(\frac{\Delta R_{CD}}{R_{CD}}\right) \tag{9}$$

where $r = R_{BC}/R_{AB}$.

Sensitivity can also be expressed in terms of the unbalance voltage per volt applied to the bridge

$$e' = \frac{e}{E} = \frac{r}{(r+1)^2}\left(\frac{\Delta R_{CD}}{R_{CD}}\right) \tag{10}$$

If the detector circuit is closed, a current flows through the detector. Neglecting the battery resistance, this current can be calculated from Thévenin's theorem and **Fig. 2** as

$$I_G = \frac{e}{R_G + \dfrac{R_{AB}R_{BC}}{R_{AB} + R_{BC}} + \dfrac{R_{AD}R_{CD}}{R_{AD} + R_{CD}}} \tag{11}$$

or

$$I_G = \frac{E\left(\dfrac{\Delta R_{CD}}{R_{CD}}\right)}{\dfrac{R_G}{r/(r+1)^2} + R_{AB} + R_{BC} + R_{CD} + R_{AD}} \tag{12}$$

and in terms of unbalance current per volt applied to the bridge

$$I_G' = \frac{I_G}{E} = \frac{\left(\dfrac{\Delta R_{CD}}{R_{CD}}\right)}{\dfrac{R_G}{r/(r+1)^2} + R_{AB} + R_{BC} + R_{CD} + R_{AD}} \tag{13}$$

The unbalance current can thus be expressed in terms of (1) the fractional change in unknown resistance, (2) an "effective" detector resistance which depends upon the bridge ratio in use, (3) the sum of all of the bridge resistors, and (4) the applied voltage.

**Accuracy.** The errors in a Wheatstone bridge measurement are caused by (1) the value of unknown resistance and the conditions of measurement, (2) the ability to balance the bridge to the required precision, (3) the available bridge sensitivity, (4) the errors of the comparison resistors, ratios, or both, and (5) an accumulation of small errors resulting from practical circuit and construction problems.

Once the allowable errors of measurement have been determined, the bridge components and the detector should be selected so that the allowable limit of error, the ability to physically adjust the bridge, and the detector sensitivity are in the proportions 1:½:¼. For an allowable error of ±0.1%, the equipment should be adjustable to at least ±0.05%, and the detector should be sufficiently sensitive to detect at least ±0.025% deviation in the measurement.

If the ratio resistors have been adjusted to their individual limits of error, the error in the ratio will probably be larger than the error of each resistor. For this reason, bridge ratio arms are often adjusted for a specified error in ratio, maintaining only a nominal resistance value.

*Charles E. Applegate*

## Wide-area networks

Systems consisting of sets of nodes that are interconnected by sets of links. The nodes and links cover a relatively large geographic area, usually on the order of hundreds of miles. This very general definition provides a framework for describing any one of a large number of network configurations, each of which may differ in application, hardware, software and other features. For example, the nodes may be used for switching and routing messages in a communications network; the nodes in another network may be host computers which do application processing. The links in one network may be land-line cables; in another network, they may be satellite channels. In contemporary networks, it is common to find a variety of nodes and links; each type is allocated to tasks which it can do effectively. *See* Communications cable; Digital computer; Switching systems (communications).

**Purposes.** There are many reasons for developing and using wide-area networks (WANs), including message communication, resource sharing, remote computing, file transfer, integrated networking, application performance improvement, and combinations of some or all of these functions.

***Message communication.*** With computer-based communication, it is possible to provide very flexible and high-speed mail systems. Messages can be sent, received, examined, forwarded, answered, stored, recalled, and deleted. Message examination may be performed by using a variety of criteria, including sender, subject, date, old, new, answered, unanswered, and key words. Sophisticated distribution lists can be composed. Users may subscribe to bulletin board services which allow them to automatically receive messages about specified subjects. *See* Electronic mail.

***Resource sharing.*** A major advantage of networks is that a variety of hardware, operating systems, and software packages can be made available to a large community of users at reasonable cost. Economical operation is achieved because resources are shared by the users, who pay for services on a pro rata basis. *See* Digital computer programming; Operating system.

***Remote computing.*** In many situations the computer hardware and software needed to do a job are not available on the user's premises. It may be possible for the user to access resources through a computer network. A key idea in networking is to make computing independent of distance. That is, except for possible differences in performance (for example, response time), it should be as convenient for a user to access a computer which is 3000 mi (4800 km) away as to access a personal computer in the user's office. Related to this idea is the objective of eliminating distance as a constraint to computing and opening up many more opportunities to satisfy computing needs than are provided by locally available resources. SEE MULTIACCESS COMPUTER.

***File transfer.*** A frequent need of computer users is to transfer a file which is stored on one computer to another computer. The file may consist of a program, data, or both. The transfer may be from a remote computer to the user's local computer, or vice versa. There can be many reasons for doing a file transfer, including the following: (1) the program or data are needed at a particular computer in order to execute a program; (2) the user wants faster or more economical access (reduced communication line charges) to the file from his or her local computer; (3) the file may be a public-domain file which the user wants to transfer into his or her account; (4) the file may consist of operating-system software which can be used on a particular computer more effectively because of that computer's greater storage capacity or speed; or (5) the user receives a request to transfer a file to another user.

***Integrated networking.*** Networks are frequently developed or extended to tie together a conglomerate of networks whose purpose is to provide resource sharing and communication across a variety of diverse networks. This is an extremely important activity in networking—integrating wide-area networks and local-area networks (LANs) which were built with different technologies; connecting networks to allow flow of data between nations; and extending the geographic span of networks to provide greater user accessibility. SEE LOCAL-AREA NETWORKS.

***Application performance improvement.*** A user who has access to more and better software packages and hardware via a network ought to be able to improve the functional performance of his or her applications. This is the motivation for much of networking. The advantage of greater accessibility to resources must be weighed against possibly slower response time and lower reliability caused by the use of communication facilities.

***Multiple applications.*** Seldom is a network built for a single application (for example, electronic mail). Since networks are built from general-purpose computers, it is possible to provide for a variety of applications in a single network and to extend this concept further by internetting (that is, tieing multiple networks together). Thus the user can integrate the applications of, for example, data-base management, scientific computing, electronic mail, and word processing. SEE DATA-BASE MANAGEMENT SYSTEMS; WORD PROCESSING.

**Architectures.** Modern networks are designed according to standards which have been developed by international standards organizations. Standards were developed to facilitate compatibility between networks and to allow for a mix of vendor equipments in a network. The most common standard is the International Standards Organization (ISO) layered model. A layer is a partition of a network which has responsibility for a major function (for example, switching and routing). The layered concept provides the following advantages: (1) manufacturers can design their networks to implement the specifications of specific layers, thereby achieving compatibility with the standard; (2) the complicated architecture is partitioned into understandable and maintainable pieces; and (3) a hierarchical design approach is implemented, whereby a given layer $N$ uses its functions and the services of the layer below it, $N-1$, to provide a service for the layer above it, $N+1$, analogous to the way in which human activities are organized.

***ISO model.*** The ISO seven-layer model was developed to achieve compatibility among diverse networks developed by various vendors and nations. The model specifies what is to be accomplished by each layer; it does not specify how it is to be accomplished. Each layer specifies requirements for protocols, which are sets of rules and procedures for the exchange of information in a network. The primary functions of each layer are as follows:

1. Physical layer: Physical transmission of data between two nodes.
2. Data link layer: Reliable transmission of data between two nodes.
3. Network layer: Switching and routing across all switching nodes in the network.
4. Transport layer: End-to-end control of communication between processes, where a process is a program in execution.
5. Session layer: Opens, closes, coordinates, and monitors sessions between communicating processes. (A session consists of the activities which take place when a user processes a transaction in a computer network.)
6. Presentation layer: Formats user input data for presentation to the system and formats system data for presentation to the user.
7. Application layer: Processes user application functions.

***Types of services.*** There are two major services offered by networks which are related to network architecture: datagram and virtual circuit.

Datagram service provides best-effort type of message delivery and is used in noninteractive applications (for example electronic mail and transaction processing where no interaction with the user is necessary). Loosely speaking, this type of service may be considered one-way transmission. Each datagram (a type of message) is transmitted independently of other datagrams. There is no relationship between datagrams; hence, there is no need to sequence them. In addition, since this is a fast, low-cost service, extensive error checking is not performed on the received data. Only the physical, data link, and network layers are needed to implement datagram service.

In contrast, virtual circuit service is for interactive processing, where sequenced, error-checked message delivery is essential for correct transmission and response of interactive commands (for example, text editing). In addition to the layers used in datagram service, virtual circuit service requires the functions of the transport layer to sequence, acknowledge, and error-check the datagrams so that the user's interactive session is executed correctly. Some networks (for example, the Defense Data Network of the Department of Defense) provide both a datagram service and a virtual circuit service, where datagram service can be used either alone or to support virtual circuit service. *See* Data communications.

*Norman F. Schneidewind*

**Bibliography.** D. W. Davies et al., *Computer Networks and Their Protocols*, 1980; P. E. Green, Jr., *Computer Network Architectures and Protocols*, 1982; K. Sherman, *Data Communications: A User's Guide*, 1985; W. Stallings, *Data and Computer Communications*, 1985; A. S. Tanenbaum, *Computer Networks*, 1981; E. A. Yakubaitis, *Network Architectures for Distributed Computing*, 1983.

## Word processing

Writing and editing text by using computers or computerlike equipment. It may be thought of as writing with a typewriter that has some of the capabilities of a computer, and in most cases word processing uses a computer and a word processing program. It has become the preferred way to create text wherever large quantities of writing, rewriting, and editing are done. *See* Digital computer; Digital computer programming.

A typewriterlike keyboard is used (**Fig. 1**). The typed text is not immediately printed on paper but is displayed on a screen and simultaneously stored electronically. The displayed and stored text may be changed or corrected while it is being typed or after it is stored. At any time a copy of the text may be printed out on paper without destroying what is stored. *See* Cathode-ray tube.

Thus the essential interconnected parts of a word processor are a keyboard, a display screen, a printer, and a computer or computerlike device both to electronically store what has been typed and to control the whole system (**Fig. 2**). These parts are available in many forms and different capabilities. Word processors are essentially personal computers that use word processing programs. They range in size from a desktop full of equipment to a unit that will fit in a briefcase and can be held on the lap (**Fig. 3**).

Word processing has two major advantages over typewriting: it simplifies the tasks of typing and editing, and it makes it possible to go from the first typed draft to the final copy without ever retyping, except for new material, corrections, and additions. The word processor continuously and automatically maintains a clean copy in its electronic storage ready to be printed.

**Development.** The designers and users of the first computers recognized in the late 1940s that they could manipulate text as well as numbers, but the machines were so large and expensive that it was inconceivable to use them as typewriters. By the late 1950s some text manipulation experiments were being made, chiefly in the academic world, using smaller computers and time-sharing arrangements. Over a period of about 15 years, these experiments devised and tested most of the techniques and features of today's word processing systems. The early configurations of hardware were usually called text editing systems. They performed so-called text processing to convey the notion of processing letters and words the way that electronic data processing handles numbers.

As technological advances increased the capability of electronic computing and storage equipment, two developments made obsolete the early word processing systems, involving magnetic storage typewriters and centralized typing centers. The first development was the stand-alone dedicated word processor, which combined in a fairly large desk-top unit the essential parts of keyboard, video display, high-speed printer, and electronic storage. The other development was an arrangement in which each typist had his or her own desk-top keyboard and video display unit. The separated units were connected by wires to a central point where the document printer, the magnetic storage facility, and the large controlling computer were shared by the separated users. *See* Multiaccess computer.

By the late 1970s technological developments had allowed the word processing function to go far beyond the simple preparation and printing of text to advanced levels of document editing, formatting, filing, and the electronic transmission of information. The next step was taken in the 1980s with the introduction of personal computers and word processing programs. *See* Microcomputer.

**Functions.** Word processing consists of five functions: writing, editing, formatting, printing, and sending and saving. Since the many word processing programs and systems are all different from each other, the following description is confined to the most common functions shared by most programs.

***Writing.*** Writing is basically similar to typing ex-

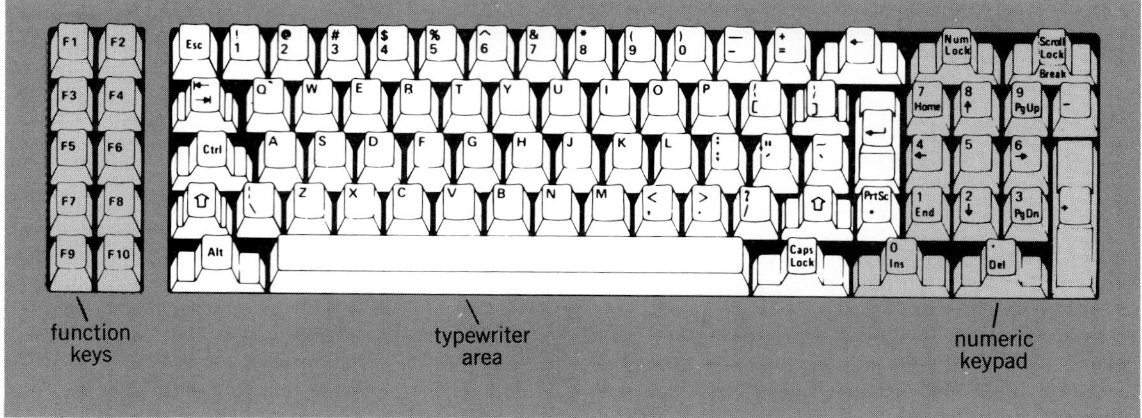


**Fig. 1. Typical word processing keyboard. (*IBM*)**

cept that nothing is printed on paper immediately. Pressing the keys on the keyboard causes letters, numbers, spaces, punctuation, and other common symbols to appear in lines on a display screen. Most displays show about 26 lines on a screen, each line being 80 characters long.

As typing proceeds, a cursor, which is a small blinking box or underline bar, moves across the screen and marks the place where the next letter will appear (**Fig. 4**). The processor automatically ends each line when it is full, and starts the next line with the next complete word, never breaking a word (automatic word wrap.) When the screen is full, the processor makes room for the next line by moving all the lines on the screen up (scrolling.) If the keys are depressed faster than the processor can put the letters on the screen, the letters are temporarily stored and the processor catches up at the typist's next pause, so that nothing is lost and type-bar jams are not possible.

***Editing.*** Editing consists of making corrections and changes in the text by deleting, changing, moving, or inserting characters. To edit, the cursor is moved to the place on the screen where the change is to be made. Usually the cursor movement is controlled by pressing one of a set of four keys (up, right, down, left; Fig. 4), but with some processors it can be controlled with a "mouse" or by touching the display screen at the desired location. The contents of the screen itself can be scrolled up or down by a single line, a screenful, or more, and the cursor can be moved to get to any part of the document.

The text at the cursor-marked spot may be changed by deleting or inserting. A block of text may be moved from one place in the document to another, even between parts of the document that are not visible at the same time on the screen, and from a previously stored document to the one being worked on. For insertions, deletions, or block moves, the processor automatically moves the text to make room or to take up any vacant space created, wrapping words as needed to make the lines correct.

***Formatting.*** Formatting gives the finished document its desired appearance, and includes specifying the margins and the space between lines; making the right margin even (justification); adding headings and footings to each page; having the pages automatically counted and their numbers printed; and putting footnotes on the proper pages. Some word processors have formatting capabilities that allow printing with several different kinds of typefaces (**Fig. 5**). All of this is done by adding to the text various symbols or specially marked words which will not be printed out on the final copy.

Ideally, the display screen should show exactly what will be printed out and should look exactly like the printed page. Unfortunately there will always be some differences. For example, some of the formatting symbols and words should be displayed on the screen so that they can be checked, but of course they should not show on the printed page. Often a way is provided to "print preview" or "print to screen" to check on how the printed document will look.

***Printing.*** When the document has been written, edited, and formatted, it may be printed out. With some programs the word processor can be used to work on another document while the printing is going on. The

**Fig. 2. Essential parts of a personal computer word processor: keyboard, computer, display screen, and printer. (*IBM*)**

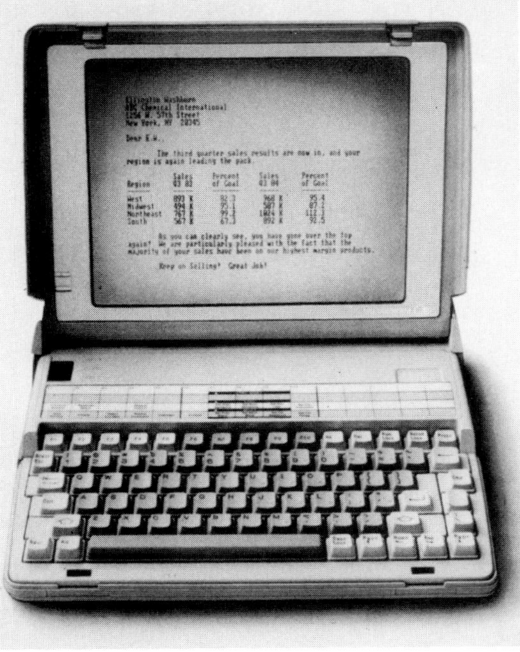

**Fig. 3. Lap-size computer. (*Data General Corp.*)**

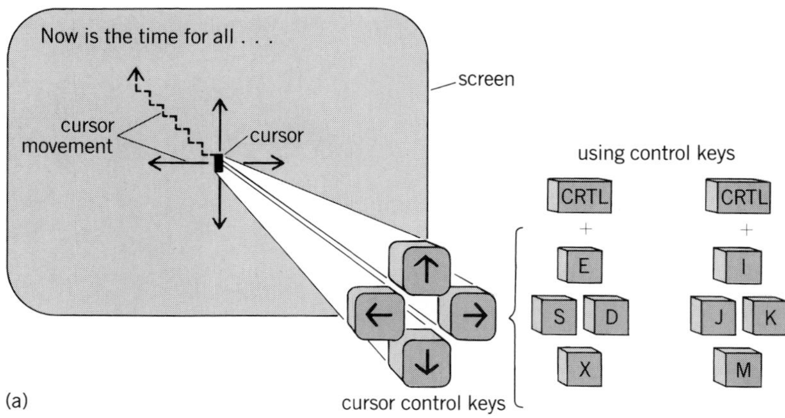


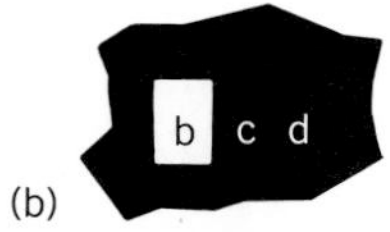


**Fig. 4. Cursor. (*a*) Movement is usually controlled by pressing one of a set of four keys. On keyboards without cursor control keys, the cursor may be moved by pressing a control (CRTL) key along with various letter keys. (*b*) In the example shown, normal characters are white on black and, with the cursor over a character, the character becomes black on white. (On some screens, the cursor is an underline bar.) (*After M. Waite and J. Arca, Word Processing Primer, BYTE/McGraw-Hill, 1982*)**

quality of the printed product, some of the things that can be done in terms of formatting, and particularly the speed with which the document is printed, depend chiefly on the quality of the printer.

***Sending and saving.*** These are the final steps in word processing and are the equivalent of sending out the finished document and filing a copy. If the document is to be sent electronically rather than as a paper copy, the word processor must be connected through a modem to a telephone line. After making this connection, the typist uses the keyboard to indicate the document's destination. On command, the word processor makes the call and, when the recipient's modem responds, transmits the document electronically over the telephone lines. The recipient may choose to have the document printed out as received or have it stored in his or her word processor, to be read later on the display screen. The sender may easily transmit the same document to many addresses or may send it to an electronic bulletin board, a central computer with which others may communicate. *See* DATA COMMUNICATIONS; ELECTRONIC MAIL.

In its most elementary form, saving is done by printing out an extra paper copy. However, with word processing, while the text is being typed it is also being temporarily saved electronically in the word processor. This copy is destroyed and lost when the processor is turned off or if there is an interruption in power. However, the typist can direct the word processor to save a copy of what is being written onto a disk. Some word processors save copies automatically.

Magnetic storage of text has advantages over paper files. For example, by using special programs, magnetic files can be sequenced in alphabetical order, added to, referred to, and retrieved from with little effort. They are far more compact; a 5¼-in. (133-mm) disk, for example, can store the equivalent of 50 to 100 typed pages. Most important, a magnetically stored copy need never be retyped, and can be used, in whole or in part, as the basis for creating other documents without any manual copying. *See* COMPUTER STORAGE TECHNOLOGY.

***Advanced features.*** Some word processing programs can be used to check a document for spelling, punctuation, and simple grammatical errors. Others will automatically create indexes and tables of contents.

DATA PROCESSING

ABCDEFGHIJKLMNOPQRSTUVWXYZ@[\]^_0123456789:;<=> abcdefghijklmnopqrstuvwxyz{|}~?`!"#$%&'()*+,-./
ABCDEFGHIJKLMNOPQRSTUVWXYZ@[\]^_0123456789:;<=>
abcdefghijklmnopqrstuvwxyz{|}~?`!"#$%&'()*+,-./

ENHANCED QUALITY

ABCDEFGHIJKLMNOPQRSTUVWXYZ@[\]^_0123456789:;<=> abcdefghijklmnopqrstuvwxyz{|}~?`!"#$%&'()*+,-./
ABCDEFGHIJKLMNOPQRSTUVWXYZ@[\]^_0123456789:;<=>
abcdefghijklmnopqrstuvwxyz{|}~?`!"#$%&'()*+,-./

CORRESPONDENCE QUALITY

ABCDEFGHIJKLMNOPQRSTUVWXYZ@[\]^_0123456789:;<=> abcdefghijklmnopqrstuvwxyz{|}~?`!"#$%&'()*+,-./
ABCDEFGHIJKLMNOPQRSTUVWXYZ@[\]^_0123456789:;<=>
abcdefghijklmnopqrstuvwxyz{|}~?`!"#$%&'()*+,-./

**Fig. 5. Various kinds of typefaces, produced by a multimode dot-matrix printer. (*From W. Hession and M. Rubel, Performance Guide to Word Processing Software, McGraw-Hill, 1985*)**

Almost all will count the number of words in a document.

*Eric A. Weiss*

**Bibliography.** S. Brand (ed.), *Whole Earth Software Catalog*, 1985; P. A. McWilliams, *The Word Processing Book: A Short Course in Computer Literacy*, 1982; M. Waite and J. Arca, *Word Processing Primer*, 1982; W. Zinsser, *Writing with a Word Processor*, 1983.

## Work function (electronics)

A quantity with the dimensions of energy which determines the thermionic emission of a solid at a given temperature. The thermionic electron current density $J$ emitted by the surface of a hot conductor at a temperature $T$ is given by the Richardson formula, $J = AT^2e^{-\phi/kT}$, where $A$ is a constant, $k$ is Boltzmann's constant ($= 1.38 \times 10^{-23}$ joule per degree Celsius) and $\phi$ is the work function; the last may be determined from a plot of log $(J/T^2)$ versus $1/T$. For metals, $\phi$ may also be determined by measuring the photoemission as a function of the frequency of the incident electromagnetic radiation; $\phi$ is then equal to the minimum (threshold) frequency for which electron emission is observed times Planck's constant $h$ ($= 6.63 \times 10^{-34}$ joule second). The work function of a solid is usually expressed in electronvolts (1 eV is the energy gained by an electron as it passes through a potential difference of 1 V, and is equal to $1.60 \times 10^{-19}$ J). This table lists average values of work functions (in electronvolts) for metals.

**Average values of work functions for metals, in eV**

| Metal | Value | Metal | Value | Metal | Value |
|---|---|---|---|---|---|
| Al | 4.20 | Cs | 1.93 | Na | 2.28 |
| Ag | 4.46 | Cu | 4.45 | Ni | 4.96 |
| Au | 4.89 | Fe | 4.44 | Pd | 4.98 |
| Ba | 2.51 | K | 2.22 | Pt | 5.36 |
| Cd | 4.10 | Li | 2.48 | Ta | 4.13 |
| Co | 4.41 | Mg | 3.67 | W | 4.54 |
| Cr | 4.60 | Mo | 4.24 | Zn | 4.29 |

The work function of metals varies from one crystal plane to another and also varies slightly with temperature (approximately $10^{-4}$ eV/degree). For a metal, the work function has a simple interpretation. At absolute zero, the energy of the most energetic electrons in a metal is referred to as the Fermi energy; the work function of a metal is then equal to the energy required to raise an electron with the Fermi energy to the energy level corresponding to an electron at rest in vacuum. The work function of a semiconductor or an insulator has the same interpretation, but in these materials the Fermi level is in general not occupied by electrons and thus has a more abstract meaning. SEE FIELD EMISSION; PHOTOEMISSION; THERMIONIC EMISSION.

*Adrianus J. Dekker*

## Y-delta transformations

Electrically equivalent networks with three terminals, one connected internally by a Y configuration and the other connected internally by a Δ configuration.

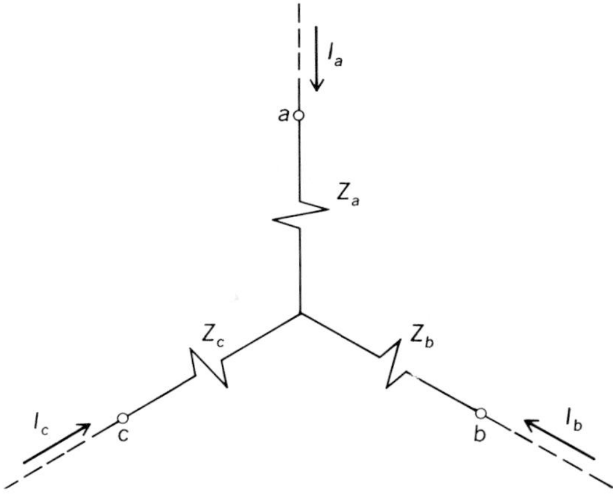


Fig. 1. Three-terminal star, or Y.

Before considering these networks, consider the simpler two-terminal network. If the path consists of a network, however complicated, of passive linear elements, the input impedance is the ratio of the transform or phasor of input voltage to the transform or phasor of entering current. It is usually not difficult to find the input impedance of any passive, linear, two-terminal network, commonly by series and parallel combination of impedances. The input impedance will in general be a function of frequency. At one particular frequency it is possible to design a single element to have the same impedance, and this element can be said to be equivalent to the given network at that frequency, in the sense that the terminal relations of voltage and current will be the same (at that frequency) for either. In certain particular networks the equivalence is valid at all frequencies.

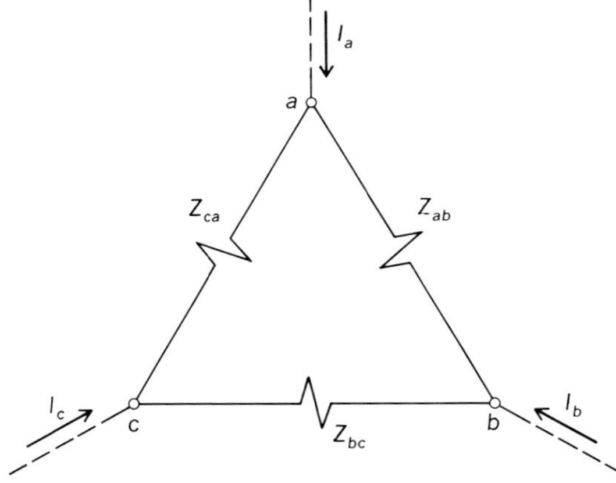


Fig. 2. Three-terminal mesh, or Δ.

If a network connects three terminals with one an-

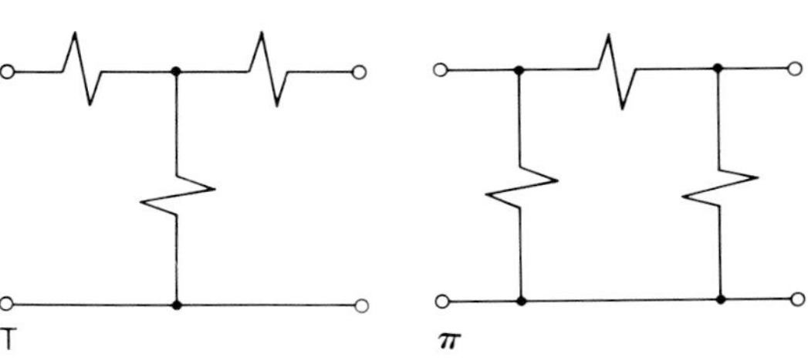


Fig. 3. Three-terminal star and mesh drawn as T and π.

other, it is called a three-terminal network. The simplest configurations of three-terminal networks are the Y or star (**Fig. 1**) and the Δ or mesh (**Fig. 2**). [The star of three elements may also be called a T, and the mesh of three elements a π (**Fig. 3**).]

If a given three-terminal network, passive and linear, has a Y configuration, it is possible to design an equivalent Δ network that could be substituted for the Y without changing the relations of voltage and current at the network terminals, or elsewhere external to the network. Similarly, if a Δ network is given, an equivalent Y network can be found. Impedances of equivalent networks are usually functions of frequency, and realization of these impedances by use of physically possible elements is usually limited to a single frequency.

**Derivation.** If terminal-to-terminal voltages $V_{ab}$, $V_{bc}$, and $V_{ca}$ are taken to be equal in the Y and Δ of Figs. 1 and 2, then the terminal currents $I_a$, $I_b$, and $I_c$ are equal in the two networks if and only if the impedance relations in Eqs. (1)–(3) are satisfied.

$$Z_a = \frac{Z_{ab}Z_{ca}}{Z_{ab} + Z_{bc} + Z_{ca}} \qquad (1)$$

$$Z_b = \frac{Z_{bc}Z_{ab}}{Z_{ab} + Z_{bc} + Z_{ca}} \qquad (2)$$

$$Z_c = \frac{Z_{ca}Z_{bc}}{Z_{ab} + Z_{bc} + Z_{ca}} \qquad (3)$$

These are derived by expressing the three currents of each configuration in terms of the three voltages, equating, and solving simultaneously. Only one of these three equations is needed, for the subscripts $a$, $b$, and $c$ are arbitrary (**Fig. 4**).

The same equivalence can be expressed in admittances instead of impedances by Eq. (4). Again, only

$$Y_a = \frac{Y_{ab}Y_{bc} + Y_{bc}Y_{ca} + Y_{ca}Y_{ab}}{Y_{bc}} \qquad (4)$$

one equation is needed, for the subscripts are arbitrary.

To change Y to Δ, a simultaneous solution of Eqs. (1), (2), and (3) gives a set of relationships, Eqs. (5)–(7), to be used if the impedances or admittances of a Y are known and those of an equivalent Δ are wanted.

$$Z_{ab} = \frac{Z_aZ_b + Z_bZ_c + Z_cZ_a}{Z_c} \qquad (5)$$

For admittances, the equivalence is expressed by Eq. (6).

$$Y_{ab} = \frac{Y_aY_b}{Y_a + Y_b + Y_c} \qquad (6)$$

**Example.** The following example, though rather artificial, shows several interesting aspects of equivalence. Given the Δ (**Fig. 5**), with two sides purely resistive and the other side purely inductive, to find an equivalent Y. Given values are 20 ohms in each of two sides, and $L = 5$ henrys or $Z = j\omega5$ ohms in the third side. From Eq. (1), relation (7) can be written.

$$Z_a = \frac{(20)\,(20)}{20 + 20 + j\omega5} = \frac{400}{40 + j\omega5} \text{ ohms} \qquad (7)$$

Similarly, from Eq. (2), relation (8) can be written.

$$Z_b = \frac{(20)\,(j\omega5)}{20 + 20 + j\omega5} = \frac{j\omega100}{40 + j\omega5} \text{ ohms} \qquad (8)$$

In this example $Z_c = Z_b$.

The impedances of the equivalent Y can be computed at any particular frequency; for example, at 60 cycles per second, or 60 Hz, $\omega = 377$. At low frequency, $Z_a$ approaches 10 ohms of resistance, but for all finite frequencies it is somewhat less than 10 ohms and is more or less capacitive. $Z_b$ and $Z_c$ are equal because of symmetry in the original Δ network; at low frequency they have low inductive values, approaching zero, whereas at high frequencies each approaches 20 ohms of resistance.

At any particular frequency, each of the Y impedances can be physically realized as resistance in series with either a capacitance or an inductance, but physical realization is not simple over any range of frequencies.

Difficulty with physical realization, however, does not invalidate the mathematical equivalence, and the Y network that has here been determined can be substituted for the given Δ network for all analytical or computational purposes. SEE ALTERNATING-CURRENT CIRCUIT THEORY; NETWORK THEORY.

*Hugh H. Skilling*

***Bibliography.*** J. Choma, *Electrical Networks: Theory and Analysis*, 1985; H. H. Skilling, *Electric Networks*, 1974.

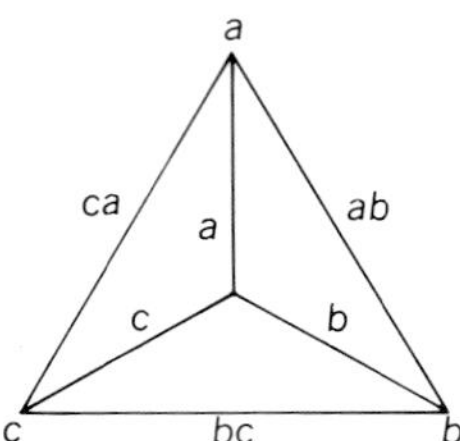


**Fig. 4.** Diagram to show the pattern of subscripts used in equations.

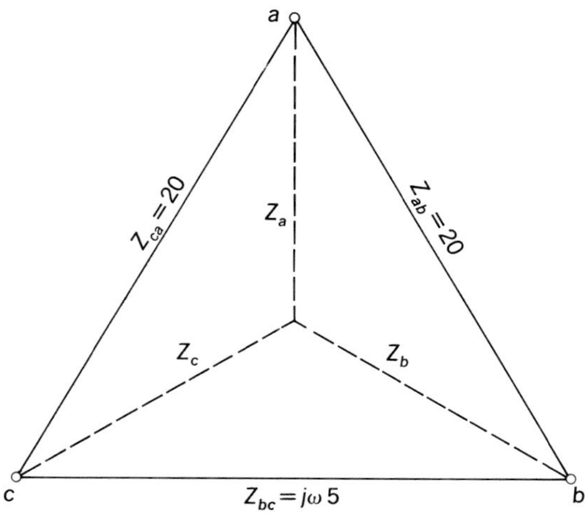

**Fig. 5.** Example of a Y that is equivalent to a given Δ.

## Yagi-Uda antenna

A combination of a single driven antenna and a closely coupled parasitic element which may function either as a reflector as a result of inductive reactance,

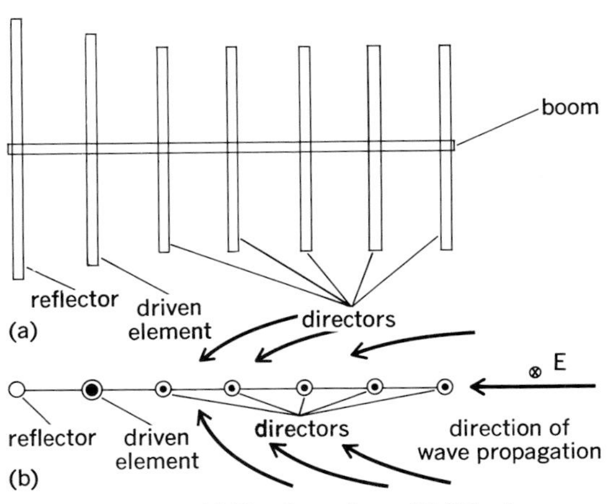


**Yagi-Uda antenna. (*a*) View from above. (*b*) Side view; arrow shows energy flow close to parasitic elements.**

or as a director as a result of capacitive reactance, depending on both the length and spacing of the parasitic element; also called the Yagi antenna (see **illus.**). Such structures are not only feasible but have a rather important place in antenna practice and concept, particularly in very high-frequency and ultrahigh-frequency ranges. Since wave propagation velocity from one element to the next is somewhat less than the velocity characteristic of free space, the power flow of the Poynting vector tends to fall toward the array in the receiving case (illus. *b*).

Wide-band characteristics can be obtained by adding reactance, using thick elements, or using proper coupling to transmission line. The gain over a half-wave dipole of a Yagi-Uda antenna is shown in the **table**.

**Gain of Yagi-Uda antenna over a half-wave dipole**

| Antenna type | Gain, dB |
|---|---|
| Two-element | 3 - 4.5 |
| Three-element | 6 - 8 |
| Four-element | 7 - 10 |
| Five-element | 9 - 11 |

An array antenna of this kind was invented by H. Yagi and S. Uda at Tohoku Imperial University (now called Tohoku University) in Japan in 1926 and was reported first in Japanese in 1926 and 1927 by Uda. In 1928 it was described in English, by Yagi. SEE ANTENNA.

*Kunitaka Arimura*

## Zener diode

A two-terminal semiconductor junction device with a very sharp voltage breakdown in the reverse-bias region. This device is used principally in voltage regulator circuits to provide a voltage reference. It is named after C. Zener, who first proposed electronic tunneling as the mechanism of electrical breakdown in insulators. SEE SEMICONDUCTOR; VOLTAGE REGULATOR.

Most semiconductor diode applications make use of the normal *pn*-junction rectification characteristic for the functions of rectification, switching, or mixing. In the Zener diode, the normal rectifying characteristic of the junction is of no interest. The electrical breakdown in the normally blocking polarity of the junction is the critical characteristic. This breakdown must be sharp enough and sufficiently temperature-insensitive to provide a good reference voltage for voltage regulator circuits to be of use. For silicon diodes with breakdown voltages of 6 V or less, the Zener mechanism of breakdown is operative and provides excellent voltage reference diodes. Above about 6 V, the breakdown mechanism involves avalanching instead of tunneling, and the breakdown characteristic begins to show more temperature sensitivity and becomes less sharp. Up to about 15 V, the characteristic is still reasonably suitable for voltage reference use, and all such diodes today are called Zener diodes regardless of the actual mechanism of breakdown. SEE JUNCTION DIODE; TUNNELING IN SOLIDS.

*Lloyd P. Hunter*

**Bibliography.** J. J. Brophy, *Basic Electronics for Scientists*, 4th ed., 1983; J. Millman, *Microelectronics*, 1979; S. M. Sze, *Physics of Semiconductor Devices*, 2d ed., 1981; E. S. Yang, *Fundamentals of Semiconductor Devices*, 1978.

# INDEX

# Index

*Asterisks indicate page references to article titles.*

## A


Abacus 1–2*
Abakanowicz, A. 47
Abrikosov, A.A. 868
Abstract data types 2–4*
  classification 2
  data structures 2
  files and data bases 3–4
  motivation 2
  primitive 2–3
  queues, lists, and stacks 3
  relation to algorithms 4
  sets 3
  trees and graphs 3
ac *see* Alternating current
Acceptor atom 4*
A/D converter *see* Analog-to-digital converter
ADA programming language 366, 724–725
Adjustable capacitor 107
Adjustable resistor 783
Adleman, L. 210
Admittance 4*
  conductance 194*
  susceptance 883*
ADT *see* Abstract data types
af *see* Audio-frequency
AFC *see* Automatic frequency control
AGC *see* Automatic gain control
Air capacitor 107
ALGOL 722
Algorithm 5*
  cryptographic 205–206
  digital control algorithms 259–260
  hardware implementation 5
  properties 5
  public-key 210
  relation to abstract data types 4
Alternating current 5–8*
  advantages 5–6
  circuits *see* Alternating-current circuit theory
  current measurement 318
  measurement of quantities 6
  phase difference 6–7
  power and information 8
  power factor 7
  sinusoidal form 6
  three-phase system 7–8
  voltage measurement 318, 1003–1004
Alternating-current circuit theory 8–19*
  active circuits 18–19
  admittance 4*
  circuit analysis 13–16
  circuit elements 11–13
  circuits 129
  complex representation 10–11
  conductance 194*
  electric transient 307–308
  electrical impedance 316*
  immittance 437*
  microwave circuits 18
  network *see* Network theory
  nonsinusoidal waveforms 19
  numerical examples 17–18
  phasor diagrams 9–10
  practical circuit elements 18
  reactance 768–769*
  resonance 783–784*
  resonant circuit 16–17
  susceptance 883*
  waveforms 9
AM *see* Amplitude modulation
Amateur radio 19–20*
  associations 20
  privileges 19–20
  regulations 20
  requirements 19
  technical developments 20
Ammeter 20–23*
  electrodynamic type 22
  permanent-magnet movable-coil type 20–21
  polarized-vane type 21–22
  soft-iron type 22
  taut-band type 21
  thermal type 22–23
Amorphous semiconductor 23–25
  electronic structure 24
  glassy chalcogenides 24
  tetrahedrally bound solids 24–25
Amorphous solid 23–25*
  glass switch materials 412
  preparation 23
  semiconductors 23–25
  types 23
  uses 23
Ampère, A.M. 213
Amplifier 25–35*
  audio amplifier 81*
  audio-frequency amplifier 31
  automatic gain control 84–85*
  backward-wave amplifier 86
  cascade amplifier 31
  cascode amplifier 109*, 755
Amplifier (*cont.*):
  classification by application 31
  classification by coupling methods 30
  classification by operating mode 30–31
  classification by selectivity 30
  coincidence amplifier 144–145*
  degeneration 32
  differential amplifier 32–33
  direct-coupled *see* Direct-coupled amplifier
  distortion 32
  electrical instability 316*
  feedback 375
  field-effect transistor *see* Field-effect transistor
  frequency multiplier 403
  gain 405*
  high-frequency compensation 31
  intermediate-frequency amplifier 31, 467*
  klystron 483–485
  light amplifier 494–495*
  lock-in amplifier 506–507*
  low-frequency compensation 31–32
  microwave 548–549
  noise 32
  operational amplifier *see* Operational amplifier
  oscilloscope vertical amplifier 653–654
  parametric amplifier 659–660*
  paraphase 667
  power amplifier 701–702*
  preamplifier 702*
  pulse rise time 32
  push-pull amplifier 735–736*
  radio-frequency amplifier 31, 753–755*
  RC-coupled amplifier 30
  regeneration 32
  response 784–785*
  signal response 31–32
  summing amplifier 34
  transformer-coupled amplifier 30
  transistor *see* Transistor amplifier
  tuned *see* Tuned amplifier
  undesirable conditions 32
  untuned amplifier 30
  vacuum-tube type 29–30
  video amplifier 984*
  voltage *see* Voltage amplifier
Amplitude (wave motion) 35*
Amplitude modulation 35–38*, 577
  demodulator *see* Amplitude-modulation detector
  detector *see* Amplitude-modulation detector
  modulator *see* Amplitude modulator
  radio transmitter 766–767
  single sideband *see* Single sideband
  use in multiplexing 36–38
  vestigial sideband 34
Amplitude-modulation detector 38–41*, 242
  diode detectors 38–40
  regenerative detectors 40–41
  square-law detectors 40
  synchronous detectors 41
Amplitude-modulation radio 41–43
  aviation and navigation aids 42–43
  high frequency 42
  low frequency 41
  medium frequency 41–42
  single-sideband hf telephony 42
  telephony and telegraphy 42
  television broadcasting 43
Amplitude modulator 38, 43–46*, 579
  basic requirements 43
  high-level modulation 43–45
  low-level modulation 45–46
  multiplier modulators 46
Analog computer 46–60*, 156
  applications 49
  components 49–53
  description and uses 48–49
  digital equivalents 46–47
  digital multiprocessor analog system 47
  history 47–48
  hybrid computers 58–60
  inverse operations in programming 55–56
  linear computing units 49–52
  multipliers 53
  nonlinear computing elements 52–53
  operation 58
  programming 53–58
  programming for use as simulator 57–58
  programming for use with calculus 56–57
  programming symbols 55
  programming to solve algebraic equations 56

Analog computer (*cont.*):
representation of variables in programming 55
switched capacitor 886
types 46–47
unique features 49
Analog-to-digital converter 60–63*
concepts and structure 60–61
physical electronics 62–63
techniques 61–62
Anderson, P.W. 472
Angle modulation 63*, 577–578*
frequency modulation *see* Frequency modulation
phase modulation *see* Phase modulation
Antenna 63–72*
arrays 71–72
bandwidth 67–68
corner reflector antenna 198–199*
direct-aperture 69–70
efficiency 65–66
electrically small 68
electromagnetic wave transmission 330–331
frequency-independent 69
gain 405*
impedance 66–67
mechanism of radiation 63–64
microwave 547–548
nonresonant 68–69
pattern shape 64–65
polarization 66
radar 746–748
radome 768*
reflector 70–71
resonant 68
television transmitting 939–941
two-reflector 71
Yagi-Uda antenna 1028–1029*
Antiresonance 72*
APL programming language 723–724
Appel, K. 418
Arc discharge 72–74*
arc production 73
regions of an arc 73–74
Artificial intelligence 74–77*
examples 75–76
expert systems *see* Expert systems
foundations 74–75
games 75
natural language processing 592–595*
perception *see* Speech recognition
real-time systems 769–770
scope and implications 76–77
Artificially layered structures 77–78
applications 78
physical properties 77–78
preparation 77
structure of 77
ASCR *see* Asymmetrical silicon-controlled rectifier
Asymmetrical silicon-controlled rectifier 819
Asynchronous data transmission 225
Attenuation (electricity) 78–81*
characteristic impedance 78
decibel 78–79
definition 79
insertion loss 79
measurement 80–81
neper 78–79, 599–600*
types of attenuators 79–80
Audio amplifier 81*
Audio-frequency amplifier 31
Audio magnetic recording 523–525
Audion 81–82*, 362
Automata theory 82–84*
finite-state machines 83–84
Turing machines and intermediate automata 82–83
Automatic frequency control 84*
Automatic gain control 84–85*
Automatic volume control *see* Automatic gain control
Automaton *see* Automata theory
Avalanche diode 568–569
AVC (automatic volume control) *see* Automatic gain control

# B

Backward diode 807
Backward-wave tube 85–86*
backward-wave amplifier 86
M-type backward-wave oscillator 86
O-type backward-wave oscillator 85–86
Bain, A. 355
Band theory of solids 86–89*
allowed and forbidden bands 86–87
conduction band 195*
density of states 88
effective mass 87
energy band calculation 87–88
experimental information 88–89
transitions between states 87
valence band 983*
Bandpass filter: surface acoustic-wave 873–874
Bandwidth requirements (communications) 89–90*
broadbanding 89–90
Shannon's equation 89
signal processing 89
Bardeen, J. 362, 973
Bardeen-Cooper-Schrieffer theory 473, 863, 867, 868–869, 973
Barium titanate 90*
BASIC programming language 722–723
Becquerel, A.C. 837
Bell, A.G. 629, 674, 909
Berge, C. 419
Bias of transistors 90–92*
bipolar transistors 90–91
FET and MOSFET 91–92
Binary number system 612–613
Bipolar integrated circuits 448–450
fabrication 456–457
linear circuits 449
semiconductor devices 449–450
Bipolar transistor: biasing 90–91
connection 961–963
logic circuits 511–512
multivibrator circuits 589
silicon bipolar transistors 566–567
Bistable optical devices 628–629
Bit 92–93*
data compression 225–228*
digital computer codes 247
microcomputer registers 535
Bit-sliced microprocessor 544–545
Block cipher 210–211
Blocking oscillator 93–94*
free-running astable type 93
synchronized type 93–94
Boole, G. 94
Boolean algebra 94–95*
abstract relationships 94
forms 95
infinite relationships 94
set-theoretic interpretation 94
Boys, C.V. 47
Brattain, W. 362
Braun, K.F. 343
Breadboarding 95*
Breakdown potential 95–96*
applications 96
increasing 96
Bridge circuit 96*
capacitance measurement 101–103
Kelvin bridge *see* Kelvin bridge
oscillator 650–651
radio-frequency impedance measurements 756–758
Wheatstone bridge *see* Wheatstone bridge
Broadbanding (communications) 89–90
Brooks deflection potentiometer 700
Brush discharge 96–97*
Bubble memory *see* Magnetic bubble memory

# C

C programming language 724
Cable television 141–142
Cache memory 178–179
CAD *see* Computer-aided design
CAE *see* Computer-aided engineering
Calculators 97–99*
electronic 97–98
mechanical 97
programmable 98–99
special-purpose 99
Calibration 99*
CAM (computer-aided manufacturing) *see* Computer-aided design and manufacturing
Capacitance 99–100*
alternating-current circuits 12
alternating-current transients 307–308
capacitor *see* Capacitor
capacitor guard ring 100
direct-current transients 305–307
human body 100
Capacitance measurement 100–107*
bridge methods 101–103
calibration of a fixed capacitor 104–105
calibration of standard capacitors 105
distributed capacitance 103–104
properties of standard capacitors 105–107
resonance method 101
susceptance variation 101
Thompson-Lampard capacitor 104
time-constant methods 103
Capacitor 107–109*
air, gas, and vacuum types 107
capacitance *see* Capacitance
classification 107
Capacitor (*cont.*):
guard ring 100
properties 99–100
solid-dielectric types 107–108
switched capacitor 885–887*
thick-film types 109
thin-film types 109
Thompson-Lampard capacitor 104
Capacitor diode 265
Carbon microphone 541
Carrier 109*
Carrier amplifier 266
Carson, J.R. 770, 826
Cascade amplifier 31
Cascode amplifier 109*, 755
Casimir, H.B.G. 869
CAT *see* Computer-aided testing
Cathode-ray tube 110–118*
basic elements 110–111
cathodoluminescence 118–119*
color television picture tube 147–148
design considerations 111
development 110
electron gun 110–111, 112–115
electronic display 344
envelope 110, 112
nonstorage oscilloscope 653
performance 111–112
phosphor screen 111, 115–116
picture tube 689–691*
storage oscilloscope 655
varieties of tubes 117–118
Cathode rays 118*
Cathodoluminescence 118–119*
Cavity resonator 119–121*
coupling 119–120
microwave-resonant cavities 119
optical 120–121
quality factor 120
sound-resonant pipes 119
Cayley, A. 418
CCD *see* Charge-coupled devices
Cellular mobile radio 576
Ceramic capacitor 108
Character recognition 121–125*
optical *see* Optical character recognition
pattern recognition 121
Characteristic curve 125*
Charge-coupled devices 125–128*
applications 127–128
control of charge motion 125–126
input and output ports 127
lifetime 127
transfer efficiency 126–127
CHDL *see* Computer hardware description languages
Chemical laser 490
Choke (electricity) 128*
Chopper 128*
Chopper-stabilized amplifier 266
Chopping 128*
CIM *see* Computer-integrated manufacturing
Circuit (electricity) 128–130*
alternating current *see* Alternating-current circuit theory
bridge circuit 96*
coupled *see* Coupled circuits
direct current *see* Direct-current circuit theory
electric network 129–130
electric transient 129, 303–308*

Circuit (electricity) (*cont.*):
- electrical instability 316*
- electronic circuit *see* Circuit (electronics)
- equivalent circuit 367*
- inductance 438–439*
- integrated *see* Integrated circuits
- IR drop 472*
- Kelvin bridge *see* Kelvin bridge
- Kirchhoff's laws of electric circuits 482–483*
- magnetic circuits 129
- negative resistance *see* Negative-resistance circuits
- nonsinusoidal waveforms 129
- Ohm's law 619*
- open *see* Open circuit
- parallel *see* Parallel circuit
- printed *see* Printed circuit
- Q (electricity) 736*
- series *see* Series circuit
- series-parallel 129
- short *see* Short circuit
- switching circuit 887–892*
- tank circuit 908*
- theory 129
- voltage-multiplier circuit 1005–1006*

Circuit (electronics) 130–137*
- audio amplifier 81*
- breadboarding 95*
- clamping circuit 137–139*
- clipping circuit 139–141*
- comparator circuit 154–155*
- component specifications 133–137
- design 132–133
- detector 246*
- distortion 281–282*
- electronic components 130–132
- electronic power supply 359–360*
- emitter follower 366–367*
- equivalent circuit 367*
- feedback circuit 374–376*
- frequency divider 387*
- frequency modulator 402–403*
- frequency multiplier 403–404*
- gate circuit 408–409*
- integrated *see* Integrated circuits
- limiter circuit 498–499*
- logic circuit *see* Logic circuits
- oscillator *see* Oscillator
- phase inverter 666–667*
- phase modulator 672–674*
- phase-locked loops *see* Phase-locked loops
- printed *see* Printed circuit
- pulse generator 725–726*
- rectifier 772–774*
- relaxation oscillator 775*
- resistors for 782
- soft fails 826–829*
- sweep generator 883–885*
- trigger circuit 969–971*
- tuning 971
- wave-shaping *see* Wave-shaping circuits

Circuit analyzer *see* Multimeter

Clamping circuit 137–139*
- DC restorer 138–139
- keyed (synchronous) clamp 138
- triode clamp 139
- voltage-amplitude-controlled clamp 137–138

Clipping circuit 139–141*
- diode 139–140

Clipping circuit (*cont.*):
- triode clipper 140–141

Closed-circuit television 141–142*
- applications 141–142
- technical considerations 142

CMOS *see* Complementary metal-oxide semiconductor

Coaxial cable 142–144*
- communications systems 150–152
- flexible 143
- materials 143
- microwave transmission lines 570
- semirigid 143
- terrestrial 144
- undersea 143
- waveguide 1018–1019
- radio-frequency impedance measurements 757–758

COBOL 722

Code-division multiplexing 586

Coil 144*

Coincidence amplifier 144–145*

Color television 145–148*
- cameras 145–146
- encoding and decoding 146–147
- picture tube 147–148, 691
- receivers 934–936
- use of primary colors 145

Communications: bandwidth requirements 89–90*
- cable *see* Communications cable
- crosstalk 204–205*
- data *see* Data communications
- electrical *see* Electrical communications
- frequency-response equalization 404*
- information theory 442–445*
- local-area networks 505–506*
- microwave 550
- optical *see* Optical communications
- packet switching 657–658*
- privacy systems (scrambling) 710–711*
- pulse-code modulation 729–732
- radio paging systems 761–762*
- single sideband 825–826
- switching systems *see* Switching systems (communications)
- voice response 989–996*
- wide-area networks 1022–1024*

Communications cable 148–154*
- coaxial cable systems 150–152
- multipair cables 152–153
- optical 149–150
- shielding 324

Comparator circuit 154–155*
- applications 155
- digital comparator 155
- integrated circuit comparators 154–155
- linear comparator 154
- regenerative comparator 154

Complementary metal-oxide semiconductor 179
- integrated circuit fabrication 457–458
- integrated circuits 451

Computer 156–157*
- abstract data types 2–4*
- algorithm *see* Algorithm
- analog *see* Analog computer
- architecture *see* Computer systems architecture

Computer (*cont.*):
- artificial intelligence *see* Artificial intelligence
- bit 92–93*
- cathode-ray tube display 117
- character recognition *see* Character recognition
- concurrent processing 193–194*
- conferencing 909
- cryotron 205*
- data-base management systems 216–222*
- data-processing management 230–231*
- data-processing systems 231–237*
- digital *see* Digital computer
- electronic mail 355
- embedded systems 365–366*
- expert systems *see* Expert systems
- fault-tolerant systems 373–374*
- graphics *see* Computer graphics
- hardware description languages *see* Computer hardware description languages
- intelligent machine 465–467*
- local-area networks 505–506*
- magnetic recorders 525–526
- memory *see* Computer storage technology
- microcomputer *see* Microcomputer
- multiaccess computer 584–586*
- multiprocessing 586–588*
- natural language processing 592–594*
- networks *see* Computer networking
- operating system 619–620*
- optical computing 634
- personal computer displays 348
- programming languages *see* Programming languages
- real-time systems 769–770*
- security *see* Computer security
- soft fails 826–829*
- software engineering 829–836*
- speech recognition 841–847*
- supercomputer 852–855*
- superconducting computers 855–858*
- teleprocessing 913–914*
- teleterminal 914–917*
- vision *see* Computer vision
- wide-area networks 1022–1024*
- word processing 1024–1027*

Computer-aided design and manufacturing 157–158
- integrated 158
- robotics 158

Computer-aided engineering 157, 158–162*
- computer graphics and modeling 160
- computer hardware trends 161
- computer software trends 161–162
- data acquisitions and control 161
- data base and communications technology 159–160
- simulations and analysis 160–161

Computer-aided testing 157

Computer graphics 162–166*
- applications 166
- computer-aided engineering 160
- graphical input 164–165
- graphical output 162–164
- graphics in conferencing 909

Computer graphics (*cont.*):
- interactive input/output arrangements 165–166

Computer hardware description languages 166–168*
- evolution of 166–167
- hierarchies of levels of detail 166
- VLSI synthesis 167

Computer-integrated manufacturing 168–172*

Computer networking 172–174*
- development 172–173
- principles 173–174
- prospects 174

Computer networking *see also* Local-area networks; Wide-area networks

Computer security 174–177*
- cryptographic controls 176
- cryptography *see* Cryptography
- inference controls 175–176
- information flow controls 175
- logical access controls 175
- physical and logical 174–175
- security kernels 175

Computer storage technology 177–186*
- bubble memory *see* Magnetic bubble memory
- cache memory 178–179
- EEPROMs 180
- ferrite devices 377
- half-inch magnetic tapes 184–185
- intelligent disk controller memory 179
- magnetic disk storage 181–183
- magnetic tape units 184–185
- main semiconductor memory 179–180
- memory hierarchy 177
- memory organization 177–179
- microcomputer 535
- optical recording 183
- ovonic memory switch 412
- RAM chips, 256K-bit 179
- RAM chips, types and technologies 179–180
- ROMs, PROMs, and EPROMs 180
- secondary memory 180–184
- semiconductor memories *see* Semiconductor memories
- storage architecture 186–188
- mass storage tape systems 185–186

Computer systems architecture 186–189*
- auxiliary memory 187
- main memory 186–187
- memory mapping 187–188
- microcomputer 535
- microprogramming 186
- parallelism 186–187
- peripherals and communication 189
- processing 188–189
- registers 186
- storage 186–188

Computer vision 189–193*
- description 191
- intelligent machine 467
- interpretation and models 191–193
- recognition 191
- segmentation 190–191
- visual sensing 189–190

Concurrent processing 193–194*
advantages and disadvantages 193
communication and synchronization 193–194
computer architecture 188–189
specifying concurrency 193
Condenser microphone 538–539
Conductance 194*
Conduction (electricity) 194–195*
Conduction band 195*
Constant-current potentiometer 699–700
Constant-resistance potentiometer 700
Constant-voltage diode 265
Contact potential difference 195*
Continuous-wave radar 195–198*
applications 196–197
design objectives 196
digital control 256–260*
Controlled rectifier 198*
Cooper, L.N. 863, 973
Cooper pair: Josephson effect 472–475*
microscopic superconductivity theory 868–869
Corner reflector antenna 198–199*
Corona discharge 199*, 407
brush discharge 96–97*
Counter: digital *see* Digital counter
frequency counter 385–387*
Coupled circuits 130, 199–202*
coefficient of coupling 201
core loss 202
equality of mutual inductance 201
equivalent circuits 201–202
ideal transformers 201
polarity 200
steady-state equations 200–201
transformation of impedance 202
transformers 202
voltage equations 200
CPM *see* Critical path method
Critical path method 202–204*
Crosstalk 204–205*
harm 205
mitigation 205
multiplexing methods 204–205
Cryotron 205*
Cryptography 205–213*
algorithms 205–206
block ciphers 210–211
cipher feedback 212–213
computational complexity 206–208
computer security 176
Data Encryption Standard 208–210
data scrambling 710–711
digital signatures 208
privacy and authentication 208
stream ciphers 211–212
strong algorithms 206
unbreakable ciphers 206
Crystal oscillator 651
Current *see* Electric current
Current-carrying resistor 779
Current measurement 213–215*
alternating current 318
ammeter 20–23*
current at high frequencies 214–215
direct and low-frequency currents 214
direct current 318
potentiometer techniques 701
very small currents 214
Cyclotron resonance experiments 215*
Cyclotron resonance maser *see* Gyratron


# D


D/A converter *see* Digital-to-analog converter
DAC *see* Digital-to-analog converter
Dantzig, G.B. 499
Dark current 215–216*
Data-base management systems 216–222*
architecture 217–218
cost of information systems 216
data administration 219
data-base administrator 218–219
data dictionary 219
design and implementation 219–221
management control of data 216–217
modeling data 218
rapid prototyping 219
three-scheme data-base methodology 221–222
Data communications 222–225*
communications processing 224
media conversion 223–224
PCM digital transmission 732
teletypewriter 917–919*
transmission 224–225
types of applications 223
Data compression 225–228*
arithmetic coding 227–228
dictionary encoding 226–227
Huffman's method 226
special-purpose techniques 228
Ziv-Lempel compression 227
Data Encryption Standard 176, 208–210
Data flow systems 228–230*
advantages and limitations 230
basic concepts 228–229
comparison of conventional systems 229–230
Data-processing management 230–231*
Data-processing systems 231–237*
character recognition *see* Character recognition
data-processing functions 231–232
distributed systems 283–285*
electronic 232–236
punched-card systems 232
switching theory 904–906*
teleprocessing 913–914*
Data reduction 237*
dc *see* Direct current
Decade resistor 779
Decimal number system 611–612
Decision theory 237–241*
DeForest, L. 81, 343, 361
Delay line 241–242*
Demodulator 242–243*
AM type *see* Amplitude-modulation detector
FM type *see* Frequency-modulation detector
modems 242
optical *see* Optical detector
Depletion-mode high-electron-mobility transistor 429
DES *see* Data Encryption Standard
Desorption 243–246*
stimulated 243–244
thermal 244–246
Destriau, G. 325
Detector 246*
*see also* Demodulator
Dicke, R.H. 550
Dielectric capacitor 107–108
barium titanate 90*
Difference (differential) amplifier 32–33, 1000–1001
Digital comparator 155
Digital computer 156–157, 246–254*
applications 156–157
codes 246–247
computer efficiency 250–251
digital control 256–260*
digital system fundamentals 246–248
distributed systems 283–285*
electronic versus mechanical 156
evolution of capabilities 250–254
fifth-generation computer 253–254
first-generation computer 251
fourth-generation computer 253
industry growth 254
instructions for stored-program type 249–250
logical circuit elements 247–248
physical components 248
programming *see* Digital computer programming
second-generation computer 251–252
stored-program computer 248–250
stored-program computer characteristics 250
stored-program operation 156
superconducting devices 859–860
switching circuit 887–892*
switching theory 904–906*
system building blocks 248
third-generation computer 252–253
visual sensing technology *see* Computer vision
Digital computer programming 254–256*
binary operation 254
flow-charting 255–256
instruction format 254–255
notation 254
number operations 254
programming 255
programming languages 256
Digital control 256–260*
computer/process interface 257–258
control algorithms 259–260
programming considerations 258–259
real-time computing 256
Digital counter 260–262*
applications 261–262
frequency counter 385–387*
specifications 262
types 260–261
Digital disk recording 281
Digital filter 301–302
Digital magnetic recording 523
Digital modulation 578
Digital storage oscilloscope 655–656
Digital-to-analog converter 262–264*
circuitry 262–263
construction 263–264
uses 262
Digital voltmeter 264*
analog-to-digital conversion 264
data processing 264
Dijkstrain, E. 419
Diode 264–265*
avalanche 568–569
capacitor diodes 265
clipping action 139–140
constant-voltage diodes 265
IMPATT 568–569
junction *see* Junction diode
light-emitting *see* Light-emitting diode
light-sensitive diodes 265
negative-resistance diodes 265
PIN 569
point-contact *see* Point-contact diode
rectifier diodes 264, 814–816
Schottky-barrier 569
TRAPATT 568–569
tunnel *see* Tunnel diode
varactor *see* Varactor
Zener *see* Zener diode
Diode detector 38–40
conditions for high efficiency 39
requirements for linearity 39–40
special features 39
Direct-aperture antenna 69–70
Direct-coupled amplifier 30, 265–266*, 1000
carrier amplifier 266
chopper-stabilized amplifier 266
differential type 265
Direct current 266–267*
circuits *see* Direct-current circuit theory
current measurement 318
direct-coupled amplifier 265–266*
electronic power supply 359–360
resistance measurement 317
voltage measurement 317–318, 1002–1003
Direct-current circuit theory 267–269*
circuit response 268–269
circuits 129
classification of circuits 267
current sources 268
electric transient 305–307
physical laws of circuit analysis 267–268
power 268
series-parallel circuits 268
Directional coupler 269–270*
applications 270
microwave reflectometer
multipath and slot 269–270
open waveguides 270
relation of output to input 270
two-hole 269
Discriminator 271*
Disk recording 271–281*
commercial disk records 275
digital recording 281
distortion in reproduction 275–276
frequency-response equalization 404*
monophonic system 271–275
quadraphonic system 279–280
stereophonic system 276–279

Disk recording (*cont.*):
surface noise 276
video *see* Video disk recording
Display storage tube 852
Distortion (electronic circuits) 281–282*
amplifier condition 32
amplitude distortion 281–282
cross modulation 282
frequency distortion 282
phase distortion 282
reduction by feedback 282
Distributed data processing *see* Distributed systems
Distributed systems 283–285*
advantages 285
characteristics 283
evolution 283
forms of processing 283–284
hierarchical systems 283
horizontal systems 284
hybrid systems 284
Donor atom 286*
Doppler radar: airborne vehicular systems 286–287
meteorological systems 287–288
Double-base diode *see* Unijunction transistor
Double-sideband modulation 36
DSB *see* Double sideband
Dynamic earphones 289
Dynamic-electrostatic earphones 289
Dynamic microphone 540–541


# E


Earphones 288–291*
dynamic 289
dynamic-electrostatic 289
electret headphones 295
electrostatic 289
magnetic 288–289
miniature magnetic 289
piezoelectric 289–290
realistic simulation 290–291
real-ear response 290
stereophonic headphones 431–432
ECD *see* Electrochromic display
Echo box 291*
Eddy current 291–293*
braking and damping 292–293
causes 291
laminations of conductor 291
testing 291–292
Edison, T.A. 81, 343, 361, 909
EDP *see* Electronic data processing
EEPROM *see* Electrically erasable programmable read-only memory
Einstein, A. 680
Einstein photoelectric law 680
E-JFET *see* Enhancement-mode junction field-effect transistor
Electret 293–294*
applications 293–294
dipolar-charge 293
real-charge 293
Electret transducer 294–296*
applications 296
electret headphones 295
electret microphones 294–295
foil electret 294
Electric charge 296–297*
electric current 297*
Electric circuit *see* Circuit (electricity)
Electric current 297*
alternating *see* Alternating current
ammeter 20–23*
conduction current 297
conduction in semiconductors 799–801
direct *see* Direct current
displacement current 297
eddy current 291–293*
electrical breakdown 310–311*
glass switch 410–412*
Kirchhoff's current law 483
measurement *see* Current measurement
sawtooth current generation 794
Electric filter 297–302*
applications 298
crystal and ceramic filters 301
design 299–301
digital filters 301–302
distributed RC filters 301
electromagnetic compatibility 327
ferrite devices 377
matched filters 301
mechanical filters 301
microwave filter 301, 547
optimum filters 301
switched capacitor 887
switched filters 301
types 297–298
Electric spark 302–303*
mechanisms 302–303
theory 303
Electric transient 129, 303–308*
alternating-current circuits 307–308
direct-current circuits 305–307
introduction 304–305
resistance and capacitance in ac series 308
resistance and capacitance in dc series 305–306
resistance and inductance in ac series 308
resistance and inductance in dc series 305
resistance, inductance, and capacitance in ac series 307–308
resistance, inductance, and capacitance in dc series 306–307
Electric uninterruptible power system 308–310*
Electrical breakdown 310–311*
in gases and solids 310–311
laser-induced breakdown in gases 311
Electrical communications 312–313*
crosstalk 204–205*
data communications *see* Data communications
frequency division multiplex 312–313
information theory 312
modulation *see* Modulation
multilink channels 312
multiplexing *see* Multiplexing
network configurations 312
radar *see* Radar
radio *see* Radio
sources 312
teleconferencing 908–909*
telephone *see* Telephone
teleprocessing 913–914*
Electrical communications (*cont.*):
teleterminal 914–917*
teletypewriter 917–919*
television *see* Television
time division multiplexing 313
transducers 312
transmission media 312
video telephone 987–988*
Electrical conduction in gases 313–316*
arc discharge *see* Arc discharge
basic effects 314–315
corona discharge 199*
dark current 215–216*
gas discharge *see* Gas discharge
mechanism 315–316
saturation current 791
Townsend discharge 947*
Electrical impedance 316*
immittance 437*
impedance matching 437–438*
microwave impedance measurement 553–558*
radio-frequency impedance measurements 755–761*
reactance 768–769*
Electrical instability 316*
Electrical loading 316–317*
Electrical measurements 317–319*
alternating-current measurements 6, 318
ammeter 20–23*
audio-frequency measurements 319
current *see* Current measurement
direct-current measurements 317–318
electrical noise generator 322–323*
inductance *see* Inductance measurement
microwave *see* Microwave measurements
phase-angle measurement 664–666*
power and energy measurements 318–319
power frequency measurements 318–319
Q meter 736–737*
radio-frequency impedance measurements 755–761*
radio-frequency measurements 319
resistance *see* Resistance measurement
voltage *see* Voltage measurement
Electrical noise 319–322*
amplifier condition 32
crosstalk 205
generator 322–323
mathematical analysis 320
measurement 322
microwave noise measurement 560
noise figure and noise temperature 320–321
in optical detectors 321–322
parasitic oscillation 660*
radar noise 742–743
shielding *see* Electrical shielding
shot noise 321
signal-to-noise ratio 821*
sources 319–320
thermal noise 321
Electrical noise generator 322–323*
Electrical resistance 323*
alternating-current circuits 11–12
Electrical resistance (*cont.*):
alternating-current transients 307–308
direct-current transients 305–307
measurement *see* Resistance measurement
Ohm's law 619*
superconductivity 864
Electrical shielding 323–324*
cable shields 324
effectiveness 323
electromagnetic compatibility 327
grounding and shielding practices 352–354
leaky apertures 323
metal shields 323
shielded rooms 323–324
semiconductor devices 812–813
Electrically erasable programmable read-only memory 180
Electrochromic displays 324–325*
optical materials 581–582
tungsten trioxide displays 325
viologen displays 325
Electrodynamic ammeter 22
Electrodynamic voltmeter 1011–1012
Electroluminescence 325–326*
Destriau effect 325
injection 325–326
light panel 497*
miscellaneous effects 326
Electrolytic capacitor 108
Electromagnetic compatibility 326–327*
filters 327
grounds and bonds 326–327
interference coupling 326
mathematical models 327
mutual effects 327
shields 327
sources of interference 326
standards 327
Electromagnetic pulse 327–329*
characteristics for high-altitude nuclear burst 328
coupling 329
discovery 327
generation in high-altitude nuclear burst 328
generation in surface nuclear burst 328
initial nuclear radiation 327–328
internal 329
Electromagnetic wave transmission 329–334*
features of electromagnetic waves 329–330
hollow waveguides 331–332
propagation over the Earth 331
radiation from an antenna 330–331
two-conductor transmission lines 332–334
Electromotive force 334*
Faraday's law of induction 373*
inductance 438–439*
open circuits 334
potentiometer (voltage meter) 699–701*
types 334
Electron emission 334–335*
cathode rays 118*
field emission 382–383*
photoemission 680–683*
secondary emission 796–798*
thermionic emission 942–943*

Electron-hole recombination 335–337*
 nonradiative recombination 336–337
 *pn* junctions 335
 radiative recombination 335–336
Electron lens 337*
Electron motion in vacuum 337–342*
 combined fields with axial symmetry 339
 effect of space charge 341–342
 electron tube 343*
 magnetic fields 338–339
 quadrupole fields 339–341
 static electric fields 337–338
 time-varying fields 342
Electron optics 342–343*
 image-intensifier tubes 494–495
Electron tube 343*
 application 343
 audion 81–82*
 cathode-ray tube *see* Cathode-ray tube
 characteristics 343
 gas tube *see* Gas tube
 history 343
 klystron 483–487*
 numerical indicator tube 617–618*
 phototube 687–688*
 storage tube 851–852*
 thermionic tube 943–944*
 traveling-wave tube 967–969*
 vacuum tube *see* Vacuum tube
Electronic calculator 97–98
 display 97–08
 entry notation 98
 operand range 98
 speed 98
 storage registers 98
Electronic circuit *see* Circuit (electronics)
Electronic data-processing systems 232–236
Electronic display 343–349*
 calculators 97–98
 categories 345
 cathode-ray tube 344
 color 346
 display electronic addressing 347
 electrochromic displays 324–325*
 flat-panel display 344–345
 font 347
 light-emitting diode *see* Light-emitting diode
 liquid crystals 503–504
 special-purpose 345–346
 technique 346–347
Electronic equipment grounding 349–354*
 data transmission 354
 ground gradients 351–352
 importance of low-noise environment 352
 need for 349
 noise coupling into signal circuit 349–351
 optical isolator 354
 shielding practices 352–354
Electronic listening devices 354–355*
Electronic mail 355–356*
 facsimile 355–356
 office automation systems 356
 small computers 355
 specially designed services 356
 telegraphy 356
Electronic packaging 356–359*
 advanced packages 357–358
 current technology 356–357
 future materials 358
 new processes 358
Electronic power supply 359–360*
 battery 360
 choke (electricity) 128*
 direct current 359–360
 filament or heater power supply 359
 high voltage 360
 power-supply filters 360
Electronic switch 360–361*
Electronic voltmeter 1013
Electronics 361–363*
 applications 362–363
 high-temperature electronics 432–434*
 history 361–362
 industry growth 362
 molecular electronics 579–582*
 quantum electronics 737–738*
Electrooptics: optical modulators 636–637
 television camera 923–927*
Electrostatic earphones 289
Electrostatic lens 363–365*
 axially symmetric lenses 363–365
 lenses of plane symmetry 365
Electrostatic microphone 538–539
Electrostatic voltmeter 1010–1011
Electrostriction 365*
Embedded systems 365–366*
 Ada programming language 366
 VHSIC program 365–366
emf *see* Electromotive force
Emitter follower 366–367*
 impedance matching 437–438
EMP *see* Electromagnetic pulse
ENFET *see* Enhancement-mode field-effect transistor
Enhancement-mode field-effect transistor 461
Enhancement-mode high-electron-mobility transistor 429
Enhancement-mode junction field-effect transistor 461
EPROM *see* Erasable programmable read-only memory
Equivalent circuit 367*
Erasable programmable read-only memory 180, 812
Erdös, P. 419
Esaki, L. 569, 972
Etalon devices 605–606, 628
Euler, L. 417
Excitation 367*
Excitation potential 367–368*
Expert systems 76, 368–371*
 accomplishments 369
 components 369–371
 distinguishing characteristics 368
 importance of expert knowledge 368
 intelligent machine 467
 real-time systems 769–770
 types 369
External photoelectric effect *see* Photoemission

# F

Fabry-Perot etalon 605, 628
Fabry-Perot interferometer 628
Facsimile 355–356, 371–373*
 FM transmission 402
 recording 371
 scanning 371
 systems 372–373
 transmission 371–372
 use in teleconferencing 909
FAMOS *see* Floating-gate metal-oxide semiconductor
Faraday, M. 849
Faraday's law of induction 373*
Fault-tolerant systems 373–374*
 fault prevention and tolerance 374
 fault tolerance techniques 374
 faults and errors 374
Federal Communications Commission: radio regulation 753
Feedback circuit 374–376*
 amplifier feedback 375
 distortion reduction 282
 input and output impedances 375
 oscillator feedback 375
 positive and negative feedback 375
 servomechanism feedback 375–376
Feibelman, P.J. 243
Ferrite devices 376–378*
Ferroelectrics 378–382*
 antiferroelectric crystals 381
 applications 381–382
 classification 378
 crystal structure 380–381
 dielectric properties 379
 ferroelectric domains 378–379
 photoferroelectric imaging 683–685*
 piezoelectric properties 379–380
 Rochelle salt 789*
FET *see* Field-effect transistor
Fidelity 382*
Field-effect transistor 960–961
 amplifiers 26–29
 biasing 91–92
 connection 963–964
 gallium arsenide 460
 high-electron-mobility transistor 428–430*
 junction *see* Junction field-effect transistor
 microwave gallium arsenide type 567
 MOS type *see* Metal-oxide-semiconductor field-effect transistor
Filter, electric *see* Electric filter
Field emission 382–383*
Finite automaton 83–84
Fixed capacitor 107
Flat-panel electronic display 344–345
Fleming, J.A. 81, 343, 361
Floating-gate metal-oxide semiconductor 180
Floppy disk 182, 526
Flying-spot scanner 117–118
FM *see* Frequency modulation
Ford, G. 418
FORTRAN 721–722
Foster-Seely discriminator 397–398
Fourth-generation languages 383–384*
 characteristics 384
 DMS 384
 motivation 383
Fourth-generation languages (*cont.*):
 program generators 383–384
 prototyping 384
 using the languages 383
Free-electron laser 490
Frequency (wave motion) 384–385*
Frequency counter 385–387*
 audio-frequency measurement 392
Frequency divider 387*
 digital division 387
 subharmonic triggering 387
Frequency-division multiplexing 586
 crosstalk 204
 electrical communications 312–313
Frequency-independent antenna 69
Frequency measurement 387–394*
 audio-frequency meters 388–392
 laser frequencies 394
 primary frequency standard 388
 radio frequency 392–394
 secondary frequency standard 388
 standards of time and frequency 387–388
Frequency modulation 394–397*, 578
 advantages 395
 demodulation *see* Frequency-modulation detector
 instantaneous frequency 394
 magnetic recording 523
 modulator *see* Frequency modulator
 noise advantage 395–396
 principles 394–395
 production and detection 396–397
 radio receiver 765–766
 radio transmitter 767
 spectrum 395
Frequency-modulation detector 242, 396, 397–399*
 discriminator 397–398
 integrating detector 398–399
 locked-oscillator detector 399
 modification for phase-modulated waves 671
Frequency-modulation radio 399–402*
 broadcasting 399–400
 facsimile 402
 mobile transmission 400–401
 quadraphonic sound 400
 radio relaying 401–402
 stereophonic broadcasting 400
 telegraphy 402
 telemetry 402
Frequency modulator 402–403*
 linearity and bandwidth 403
 varactor modulator 402–403
 voltage-controlled oscillators 403
Frequency multiplier 403–404*
 nonlinear amplifier 403
 nonlinear coupler 403–404
Frequency-response equalization 404*
Frequency-shift keying 63
 demodulation 672
Frolich, H. 868
Frucht, R. 418
FSK *see* Frequency-shift keying
Fulkerson, D. 419
Function generator 404–405*
Fuse-programmable read-only memory 812

# G

Gain 405*
Gallium arsenide: integrated circuits 460–462
Gallium arsenide field-effect transistor: microwave devices 567
Gas capacitor 107
Gas discharge 405–407*
  corona discharge *see* Corona discharge
  gas breakdown 406
  glow discharge *see* Glow discharge
  glow-to-arc transition 406
  sources of electrons 405
  Townsend discharge *see* Townsend discharge
Gas-discharge laser 489
Gas-dynamic laser 490
Gas tube 407–408*
  applications 407
  choice of gas 407
  thermionic cathode 407
  types 407–408
  voltage and current characteristics 407
Gate circuit 408–409*
  switching gate 409
  transmission gate 408–409
Gate turnoff device 819
GERT 409–410*
  applications 410
  GERTE 409
  Q-GERT 409–410
Giaever, I. 973
Ginzburg, V.I. 868
Ginzburg-Landau theory (superconductivity) 868
Glass switch 410–412*
  amorphous switch materials 412
  applications 412
  device characteristics 411–412
Glassy chalcogenides 24
Glow discharge 406, 412–414*
  aspects 414
  regions of discharge 413–414
Goldstein, E. 849
Gorter C.J. 867
Grain boundaries 414–417*
  applications 416–417
  effects on macroscopic properties 414–415
  electronic properties of semiconductors 415–416
  microscopic structure 414
  transport of charge in semiconductors 416
Graph theory 417–419*
  applications 418–419
  definitions 417–418
  map coloring problem 418
  origin of 417
  planarity 418
  variations 418
Grounded-gate amplifier 1000
Grounding *see* Electronic equipment grounding
Grove, W.R. 849
GTO *see* Gate turnoff device
Gunn, J.B. 567
Gunn diode 567–568, 599
Gyrator 419–423*, 548
  practical 420–423
Gyrator (*cont.*):
  reciprocity 420
  theoretical 420
Gyratron 423–424*
  basic characteristics 423
  capabilities 424

# H

Haken, W. 418
Hall, E.H. 424
Hall effect 424–426*
  anomalous quantum Hall effect 426
  magnetic materials 425
  quantization of Hall resistance 425–426
  semiconductors 425, 800–801
  theory 424–425
Hard magnetic disk storage 181–182
Harmonic analyzer 426–427*
  applications 427
  distortion factor meter 427
  fast Fourier transform analyzer 427
  heterodyne analyzer 426–427
  parallel filter analyzer 427
  spectrum analyzer *see* Spectrum analyzer
  stepped filter analyzer 426
  time compression analyzer 427
  tunable filter analyzer 426
Hartley, R.V.L. 312, 442
Heawood, P.J. 418
Heising, R.A. 727
Helmholtz, H. 944
Helmholtz theorem *see* Thévenin's theorem (electric networks)
HEMT *see* High-electron-mobility transistor
Henley, A. 323
Henry, J. 751
Hertz, H. 343, 751
Heterodyne frequency meter 394
Heterodyne oscillator 652
Heterodyne principle 427–428*
  microwave measurements 560
High-electron-mobility transistor 428–430*
  applications 429–430
  performance characteristics 429
  structure and operating principles 428–429
High-polymer transducer 430–432*
  applications 432
  direct radiator loudspeakers 431
  electromechanical transducers 432
  microphones 432
  piezoelectric high polymers 430–431
  stereophonic headphones 431–432
High-power, short-pulse laser 490–491
High-temperature devices: integrated thermionic circuits 433–434
High-temperature electronics 432–434*
  amorphous metal films 434
  compound semiconductor devices 433
  silicon devices 433
Hoff, M.E. 362
Hogan, C.L. 422
Holes in solids 434–435*
  electron-hole recombination 335–337*
Hopcroft, J. 418
Horn radiator 69
Huffman, D. 226
Huffman data compression method 226
Hull, A.W. 343

# I

Ideal transformer 201
i-f *see* Intermediate frequency
IGFET *see* Insulated-gate field-effect transistor
Image processing 435–437*
  applications 436
  compression 436
  digitization 435
  enhancement 435
  restoration 435–436
Immittance 437*
Impact avalanche and transit time diode 567–568
IMPATT diode *see* Impact avalanche and transit time diode
Impedance *see* Electrical impedance
Impedance matching 437–438*
  emitter follower 437–438
  microwave transmission lines 572
  network 437
  transformers 437
Inductance 438–439*
  alternating-current transients 307–308
  direct-current transients 305, 306
  electrical loading 316–317*
  inductor 441–442*
  mutual inductance 438–439
  mutual inductance in alternating-current circuits 12–13
  self-inductance 438
  self-inductance in alternating-current circuits 12
Inductance measurement 439–441*
  mutual inductance 440–441
  phase defect 439
  precautions 439
  self-inductance 439–440
  shielding of capacitive currents 441
Inductor 441–442*
  adjustable 441
  coil 144*
  ferrite devices 377
  fixed 441
  inductance 438–439*
  variable 442
Information theory 442–445*
  algebraic codes 444–445
  bit 93
  channel capacity 444
  communication systems 442
  electrical communications 312
  encoding and decoding 442–443
  information content of message 443–444
  Shannon's equation 89
Infrared imaging devices 445–448*
  display 447
  scanning systems 446–447
Injection electroluminescence 325–326
Insulated-gate field-effect transistor: multivibrator 589
Insulator: property changes by ion implantation 470
  valence band 983*
Integrated circuits 130, 448–462*
  amplifier 1001
  bipolar 448–450
  comparators 154–155
  electronic packaging 356–359*
  fabrication 453–460
  gallium arsenide circuit device technologies 461
  gallium arsenide circuits 460–462
  gallium arsenide FET 460
  gallium arsenide FET switching speed 460–461
  history 362
  logic gate configurations 461–462
  microcomputers 453
  microprocessor 543–545*
  monolithic microwave circuits 549
  MOS 450–452
  optical devices *see* Integrated optics
  printed circuit 708
  resistors 781, 782
  silicon on insulator 493–494
  switching circuit 891
  thermionic circuits 433–434
  types 448–452
  VLSI design with computer hardware description languages 167
Integrated optics 462–465*
  coupling of external light beams 463–464
  directional coupler 269–270*
  guided waves 463
  lasers and distributed feedback 464
  materials and fabrication of waveguides 463
  optical devices 452
  spectrum analyzer 464
  switches and modulators 464
Integrating FM detector 398–399
Intelligent machine 465–467*
  computer vision 467
  control hierarchy 466–467
  expert systems 467
  intelligent control 465
  intelligent robots 465–466
  interconnection of machines 467
Intermediate frequency: automatic frequency control 84*
Intermediate-frequency amplifier 31, 467*
Ion beam mixing 467–469*
  applications 469
  mixing mechanisms 468
  stable- and metastable-phase formation 468–469
Ion implantation 469–471*
  applications 470
  insulator property changes 470
  laser annealing of layers 492–493
  metals 470–471
  process 469–470
  prospects 471
  semiconductor doping 470
Ionization 471*
Ionization potential 471–472*
IR drop 472*
Iron vane ammeter 22

# J

JFET *see* Junction field-effect transistor
Jobst, G. 343
Josephson, B.D. 472, 870
Josephson effect 472–475*
  advantage for superconducting computers 856
  applications 475
  cryotron 205*
  disadvantage for superconducting computers 857
  Josephson junction voltage standards 1001–1002
  Josephson junctions 474–475
  nature of 472
  superconductivity 870
  theory of 472–474
  tunneling in solids 973
Joule, J.P. 323, 475
Joule's law 475–476*
Junction diode 476–478*
  characteristics 478
  fabrication methods 476–477
  junction rectification 477
  optical properties 477–478
  PIN diode 569
  tunnel diode 971–972*
  Zener diode *see* Zener diode
Junction field-effect transistor 26–27, 960
  multivibrator circuits 588–589
Junction transistor 478–481*
  alloy-junction transistors 479
  growth-junction transistors 479–480
  mesa transistors 481
  planar diffused epitaxial transistors 480–481
  power transistor 481
  unijunction transistor

# K

Kell, R.D. 728
Kelvin bridge 481–482*
  errors 482
  resistance measurement 780
  sensitivity 482
Kerr effect: optical modulators 636
Kinescope *see* Picture tube
Kirchhoff, G. 419
Kirchhoff's laws of electric circuits 482–483*
  current law 483
  voltage law 482–483
Klystron 483–487*
  amplifier 483–485
  reflex oscillator 485–487
Knotek, M.L. 243
Kompfner, R. 343
Konigsberg bridge 417
Kuhn, H. 419
Kuratowski, K. 418

Lampard, D.G. 104
Landau, L.D. 868
Langmuir-Blodgett film 581
Langmuir-Child law 487*
Laser 487–491*
  applications 491, 738
  chemical 490
  comparison with other light sources 487–488
  free-electron 490
  frequency measurements 394
  gas-discharge 489
  gas-dynamic 490
  high-power, short-pulse 490–491
  laser-induced gas breakdown 311
  nuclear 490
  optically pumped 488–489
  photodissociation 490
  pulsed gas 489–490
  semiconductor 490
  stimulated emission and amplification 737
Laser-solid interactions 491–494*
  annealing of ion-implanted layers 492–493
  laser-induced-damage gettering 494
  photon-electron-phonon interactions 492
  silicon on insulator 493–494
LED *see* Light-emitting diode
Lempel, A. 227
Light amplification by stimulated emission of radiation *see* Laser
Light amplifier 494–495*
  image-intensifier tubes 494–495
  solid-state image intensifiers 495
Light-emitting diode 265, 495–497*
  applications 496–497
  fabrication methods 495–496
  optical isolator 635
Light panel 497*
Light-sensitive diode 265
Limiter circuit 498–499*
  diode limiters 498–499
  limiting by saturation 499
  triode limiters 499
  use of both limits 499
Linear comparator 154
Linear programming 499–501*
  applications 500–501
  general theory 500
  methods of calculation 500
Linearity 501*
Liquid crystals 501–504*
  applications 503–504
  classification and structure 501–503
Liquid-phase epitaxy: semiconductor heterostructure fabrication 809–810
Load line 504–505*
Local-area networks 505–506*
  architectures 505–506
  purposes 505
Lock-in amplifier 506–507*
  applications 507
  dynamic range 507
  heterodyne 507
  operating principles 507
Locked-oscillator FM detector 309
Loeb, L.B. 303
Logic circuits 507–512*
  combinational and sequential logic 508–509
  digital comparator 155
  digital computer elements 247–248
  embodiment 509–510
Logic circuits (*cont.*):
  integrated circuit configurations 461–462
  multivibrators 591–592
  operation 508
  switching circuit 887–888
  switching gate 409
  technology 510–512
  types of logic functions 508
London, F. 869
London, H. 869
Lord Kelvin 47
Lord Rayleigh 421, 872
  reciprocity theorem 770–771
Loudspeaker 512–518*
  crossover network 516–517
  diaphragm material 516
  enclosure 517–518
  equivalent electrical circuit 513–514
  high-polymer transducer 431
  physical performance characteristics 515–516
  radiation impedance 514–515
  response 784–785*
  types 512–513
Lovell, C.A. 48
Luminescence: cathode-ray tube phosphor screen 115–116
  cathodoluminescence 118–119*
  electroluminescence 325–326*
Luneberg lens 69–70

M-type backward-wave oscillator 86
Magnetic bubble memory 518–520*
  magnetic thin films 527*
  principles of operation 518–519
  storage devices 183–184
  switching circuit 892
  technology status 519–520
Magnetic disk computer storage 181–183
Magnetic earphones 288–289
Magnetic lens 520–521*
Magnetic microphone 541
Magnetic recording 521–527*
  audio recorders 523–525
  digital 523
  frequency modulation 523
  frequency-response equalization 404*
  high-frequency bias 522–523
  instrumentation recorders 526
  magnetic heads 522
  magnetic thin films 527*
  noise and wavelength limitations 523
  playback process 522
  principles of operation 521–523
  recorders for computers 525–526
  recording medium 521–522
  recording process 522
  tape duplication 526–527
  television programs 922–923
  types of recording systems 523–527
  video recorders 525
Magnetic tape: cartridges for computer storage 185
  cassettes for computer storage 185
  computer storage units 184–185
Magnetic tape (*cont.*):
  half-inch tapes 184–185
  magnetic recording 521–527*
Magnetic thin films 527*
  coercivity 527
  domain structure 527
  fabrication 527
  magnetic anisotropy 527
  magnetic order 527
Magnetron 527–531*
  coaxial cavity magnetron 530
  configuration 528
  crossed-field tubes 530–531
  electron bunching 528–529
  microwave circuit 529–530
  microwave generation 528
Marconi, G. 751
Maser 531–534*
  circuits 533–534
  gas masers 531–532
  infrared masers 532–533
  optical masers 532–533
  solid-state masers 532
  stimulated emission and amplification 737
Mask-programmable read-only memory 812
Maxwell, J.C. 546, 680, 751
Mealy machine 260
Mechanical calculator 97
Memory tube *see* Storage tube
Menger, K. 419
Metal-nitride-oxide semiconductor 180
Metal-oxide semiconductor: integrated circuits 450–452
  logic circuits 510–511
  RAM chips 179–180
  switched capacitor 885–887*
Metal-oxide-semiconductor field-effect transistor 27–28, 960–961
  biasing 91–92
Metallic-disk rectifier 534*
Mica capacitor 108
Microcomputer 534–537*
  applications 537
  development system 537–538
  hardware 534–535
  integrated circuits 453
  local-area networks 505–506*
  operating system 620
  software 536
Microphone 538–543*
  carbon 541
  dimensional scheme 542
  directional characteristics 541–543
  dynamic 540–541
  electret microphones 294–295
  electrostatic (condenser) 538–539
  gradient scheme 541–542
  high-polymer transducer 432
  magnetic 541
  piezoelectric 539–540
  response 784–785*
  sensitivity calibration 542–543
  types 538–541
Microprocessor 543–545*
  applications 545
  architecture and instruction set 543
  bit-sliced 544–545
  digital system design 545
  fundamentals and operations 543–544
Microprogramming 188

Microwave 545–551*
amplifier 548–549
antenna 547–548
applications 549–551
attenuator 547
cavity resonator 119
circuit elements 546–549
circuits 18
detector 547
development of knowledge 546
ferrite devices 377
filter 547
free-field standards 551–553
frequency measurement 393
generation 546
gyrator *see* Gyrator
measurements *see* Microwave measurements
monolithic integrated circuits 549
noise standards 560–562
optics 562–564
phase shifter 547
propagation 549
radar *see* Radar
radar-absorbing materials 750–751*
receiver 549
reflectometer 566
solid-state devices *see* Microwave solid-state devices
stripline 547
transmitter 549
varactor *see* Varactor
waveguide 546–547
Microwave amplification by stimulated emission of radiation *see* Maser
Microwave free-field standards 551–553*
calibration of measuring devices 552–553
free-field measuring sites 551–552
measurements on antennas 552
near and far fields 551
standard antennas 551
Microwave impedance measurement 553–558*
comparison reflectometer 557–558
locating reflectometer 557
microwave reflectometer 566*
network analyzer 556
reflectometer 555–556
scattering parameters 554–555
six-port network analyzer 556–557
slotted line 555
swept-frequency reflectometry 557
time-domain reflectometer 557
Microwave measurements 558–560
attenuation 559–560
frequency measurements 319
heterodyne principle 560
impedance *see* Microwave impedance measurement
microwave free-field standards 551–553*
microwave sources, detection, and automation 560
noise 560
power *see* Microwave power measurement
scattering coefficients 559
Microwave noise standards 560–562*
blackbody radiator 560–561
radiometers 561–562
temperature 561
Microwave optics 562–564*
diffraction 562–563
Faraday effect 563–564
polarization 563
rectilinear propagation 562
reflection and refraction 562
Microwave oscillator 652
Microwave power measurement 558–559, 564–566*
power sensors 565
standards 565–566
terminating power meters 564
two-port power monitor 564–565
Microwave reflectometer 566*
Microwave solid-state devices 566–570*
active 566–569
avalanche diodes 568–569
gallium arsenide field-effect transistor 567
optically controlled 570
passive 569–570
PIN diodes 569
point-contact diode *see* Point-contact diode
Schottky-barrier diode 569
silicon bipolar transistors 566–567
transferred-electron (Gunn) devices 567–568
tunnel diode *see* Tunnel diode
varactor diodes *see* Varactor
Microwave strip line 570–571
Microwave transmission lines 546–547, 570–572*
coaxial 570
impedance measurement 553–558
matching techniques 572
phase and group velocity 571
propagation impedance 571
reflections and standing waves 571–572
strip 570–571
waveguides 571
Microwave tube 572–573*
alternative designs 573
backward-wave tube 85–86*
effect of transit time 573
effect of tube geometry 572–573
gyratron 423–424*
magnetron 527–531*
traveling-wave tube 967–969*
Mixer 573*
MNOS *see* Metal-nitride-oxide semiconductor
Mobile radio 573–577*
cellular 576
development 575–576
dispatch systems 574
FM transmission 400–401
public-correspondence systems 574–575
radio paging *see* Radio paging systems
SMR service 574
types of system 574–575
uses 573–574
Modulation 577–579*
amplitude *see* Amplitude modulation
angle *see* Angle modulation
carrier 109*
demodulator 242*
digital 578
frequency *see* Frequency modulation
Modulation (*cont.*):
modulator *see* Modulator
multiple 578
phase *see* Phase modulation
pulse *see* Pulse modulation
Modulator 579*
*see also* Amplitude modulator; Frequency modulator; Optical modulators; Phase modulator; Pulse modulator
Molecular-beam epitaxy: semiconductor heterostructure fabrication 810–811
Molecular electronics 579–582*
high-polymer transducer 430–432*
Langmuir-Blodgett films 581
optical materials 581–582
polymers 580–581
Monophonic disk recording: compatibility with quadraphonic system 280
compatibility with stereophonic system 279
recording system 271–273
reproducing system 273–275
Monopulse radar 582–583*
Moore machine 260
Morse, S.F.B. 751
MOSFET *see* Metal-oxide semiconductor field-effect transistor
Motorboating 583*
Moving-coil voltmeter 1009–1010
Moving-iron voltmeter 1012
Moving-magnet voltmeter 1010
Moving-target indication 583–584*
measures of merit 584
principles of operation 583–584
use of charge-transfer devices 584
Multiaccess computer: software capabilities 585–586
system components 584–585
system operating requirements 585
Multimeter 586*
Multiple modulation 578
Multiplexing 586*
choice of technique 586
code division 586
crosstalk 204–205
Day's system 38
frequency division *see* Frequency-division multiplexing
phase-discrimination 37–38
time division *see* Time-division multiplexing
use of amplitude modulation 36–38
Multiprocessing 586–588*
classification 587
high-availability 587
response-oriented 587–588
throughput-oriented 587
Multivibrator 588–592*
astable 590
logic gate 591–592
monostable 590
symmetrical bistable multivibrator 588–589
triggering 590–591
unsymmetrical bistable circuits 589–590
Munkres, J. 419
Mutual inductance 438–439
alternating-current circuits 12–13
measurement 440–441


# N


*n*-channel metal-oxide semiconductor 179
Natural language processing 592–595*
contextual analysis 594–595
language generation 595
overall organization 595
parsing 593
semantic analysis 593–594
Negative-resistance circuits 595–599*
astable circuits 598
basic circuits: 595–596
bistable circuits 597–598
monostable circuits 598
negative-resistance devices 599
sine-wave oscillators 598–599
typical circuits 596–597
Negative-resistance diode 265
*see also* Gunn diode; Tunnel diode
Neper 599–600*
Network theory 600–604*
branch equation 600–601
elements 600
Kirchhoff's laws of electric circuits 482–483*
loop equation 601–602
node equations 602–604
reciprocity principle 771
superposition theorem 871–872*
Thévenin's theorem 604, 944–946*
Y-delta transformations 1027–1028*
NMOS *see* *n*-channel metal-oxide semiconductor
Noise *see* Electrical noise
Nonlinear optical devices 604–607*
for frequency generation 605
for optical signal processing 605–606
Nonlinear optics: quantum phenomena 738
Nonlinear programming 607–608*
application 607
computational methods 607–608
general theory 607
Nonsinusoidal waveform 608–610*
effect of even harmonics 609
effect of odd harmonics 609
even and odd functions 610
example of nonsinusoidal waves 610
Fourier series representation 608–609
power 610
power factor 610
rms value of nonsinusoidal wave 610
symmetry 609–610
Nonvolatile static random-access memory 812–813
Norton's theorem (electric networks) 604
Nuclear laser 490
Number systems 610–614*
binary system 612–613
bit 92–93*
decimal system 611–612
digital computer system codes 246–247
octal system 613–614, 618

Numerical analysis 614–617*
differential equations 616–617
solution of linear systems 615–616
interpolation and approximation 614–615
Numerical indicator tube 617–618*
NV RAM *see* Nonvolatile static random-access memory
Nyquist, H. 442

# O

O-type backward-wave oscillator 85–86
OCR *see* Optical character recognition
Octal number system 613–614, 618*
Ohm, G. 419
Ohmmeter 618–619*
Ohm's law 619*
OMS *see* Ovonic memory switch
Op amp *see* Operational amplifier
Open circuit 130, 619*
Operating system 619–620*
control programs 619–620
microcomputer systems 620
processing programs 620
time-sharing operation 620
Operational amplifier 33–35
function in analog computer 50–51
integrator 34–35
summing amplifier 34
voltage amplifier 34
Operations research 620–627*
Optical bistability 627–629*
all-optical systems 627–628
bistable optical devices 628–629
fundamental studies 629
Optical cavity resonator 120–121
Optical character recognition: applications 123–125
cursive writing 124
different alphabets 124–125
element design 123
feature extraction and classification 123
functional systems 121–123
hand-printed characters 124
postal address readers 123–124
preprocessing 122–123
scanning 122
stylized font characters 123
typewritten and typeset characters 124
Optical communications 629–632*
atmospheric 630
communications cable 149–150
directional coupler 269–270*
free-space communications 630
light-emitting diodes for transmission 497
optical fiber communications 630–631
optical fiber PCM systems 731–732
optical materials 581–582
receivers 632
transmitters 631–632
Optical computing 634
nonlinear optical devices 605–606
Optical detectors 424, 632–633*
optical isolators 635–636
Optical devices, nonlinear 604–607
Optical fiber: communications 630–631
communications cable 149
Optical information systems 633–635*
image processing 633
optical computing 634
Optical isolator 354, 635–636*
optical detectors 635–363
optical emitters 635
Optical modulators 636–638*
acoustooptic modulation and deflection 637
electrooptic effect 636
electrooptic intensity modulation 637
integrated optical circuitry 464
optical waveguide devices 637–638
Optical noise 321–322
Optical parametric oscillator 605
Optical recording 638–643*
computer storage technology 183
laser-beam film recording 641–642
optical film system 639–641
PCM optical sound disk player 642–643
Optically pumped laser 488–489
Optimization 643–648*
Oscillator 648–652*
backward-wave tube 85–86*
basic principles 648
blocking *see* Blocking oscillator
bridge 650–651
crystal 651
feedback 375
general form of circuit 649–650
heterodyne 652
integrated 651–652
klystron 485–487
magnetron 527–531*
microwave 652
phase-locked loops 667–670*
phase-shift 648–649
quartz clock 738*
relaxation *see* Relaxation oscillator
very high frequency 650
voltage-controlled 403
Oscilloscope 652–657*
cathode-ray tube 117
CRT storage oscilloscope 655
digital storage oscilloscope 655–656
equivalent-time nonstorage oscilloscope 655
nonstorage types 653–655
phase-angle measurement 665
photography of waveforms 656
plug-in types 656
real-time nonstorage oscilloscope 653–655
selection 656–657
signal acquisition 657
storage types 655–656
OTS *see* Ovonic threshold switch
Ovonic memory switch 411–412
Ovonic threshold switch 411–412

# P

Packet switching 657–658*
applications 658
packet format 658
Packet switching (*cont.*):
packet networks 658
switching techniques 657–658
PAM *see* Pulse-amplitude modulation
Paper capacitor 108
Parallel circuit 129, 659*
direct current 267
Parametric amplifier 659–660*
advantages 660
effects 659–660
Paraphase amplifier 667
Parasitic oscillation 660*
Parkinson, D.B. 48
Pascal 724
Paschen, F. 302
Passive radar 661*
PCM *see* Pulse-code modulation
PDM *see* Pulse-duration modulation
Permanent-magnet movable-coil ammeter 20–21
Personal computer: electronic displays 348
PERT 661–664*
Phase 662*
Phase-angle measurement 664–666*
electronic phase-angle meter 664–665
electronic switch 665
oscilloscope methods 665
phase-order indicators 665–666
phase-relation indicators 666
synchronizer or synchroscope 666
three-voltmeter method 664
Phase-discrimination multiplexing 37–38
Day's system 38
Phase inverter 666–667*
paraphase amplifiers 667
transformer inverter 667
Phase-locked loops 667–670*
basic operation 668
phase detectors 668–669
use of 669–670
voltage-controlled oscillators 668
Phase modulation 578, 670*
advantages 670
applications 670
fundamental properties 670
noise response 670
Phase-modulation detector 671–672*
demodulation of frequency-shift keying 672
demodulation of phase-shift keying 671–672
modification of FM detector 671
multiplier circuit 671
Phase modulator 579, 672–674*
phase-shift keying 673–674
types 672–673
Phase-shift discriminator 397
Phase-shift keying 63
demodulation of 671–672
phase modulator 673–674
Phase-shift oscillator 648–649
Philbrick, G.A. 48
Phosphor storage tube 852
Photoacoustic spectroscopy 674–677*
Photoconductive cell 677*
Photoconductivity 677–679*
device forms 679
photosensitivity 678
spectral response 678
speed of response 678–678
television camera tubes 929–930
Photodetector: noise in 321–322
Photodiode 679*, 806–807
Photodissociation 490
Photoelectric devices 679–680*
Photoelectricity 680*
Photoemission 680–683*
alkali halides 682–683
Einstein photoelectric law 680
metals 680–681
miscellaneous compounds 683
semiconductors 681–682
Photoferroelectric effect: photosensitivity enhancement 684
Photoferroelectric imaging 683–685*
imaging devices 683
intrinsic photoferroelectric effect 684
Photomultiplier 685–687*
applications 686
detection limits 686
dynode materials 685–686
operation and design 685
photocathode materials 686
Photorecording tube 117
Phototransistor 687*
Phototube 687–688*
applications 688
characteristics 687
photocathodes 687–688
Photovoltaic cell 688*
Photovoltaic effect 688–689*
alternative materials 689
multiple-layered devices 689
power generation 689
principles 688–689
Picture tube 689–691*
color 691
construction 690–691
Piezoelectric crystal 691–692*
applications 692
characteristics and manufacture 691–692
crystal oscillators 651
piezoelectric materials 691
quartz clock 738*
Piezoelectric earphones 289–290
Piezoelectric microphone 539–540
Piezoelectricity 692–697*
applications 696–697
electromechanical coupling 693
high polymers 430–431
matrix formulation 693
molecular theory 693–694
necessary conditions 693
piezoelectric ceramics 694
piezoelectric resonator 694–696
properties of ferroelectrics 379–380
surface acoustic-wave devices 872
PIN diode 569
PL/1 programming language 723
Plastic-film capacitor 108
PLL *see* Phase-locked loops
Plug-in oscilloscope 656
Point-contact diode 569, 697*
Point-contact transistor 697–698*
Polarized-vane ammeter 21–22
Pólya, G. 418
Potentiometer (variable resistor) 698–699*
construction 698–699
use 698
Potentiometer (voltage meter) 699–701*
alternating-voltage measurements 701

Potentiometer (voltage meter) (*cont.*):
Brooks deflection potentiometer 700
constant-current 699–700
constant-resistance 700
current measurements 701
volt box 700–701
Poulsen, V. 521
Power amplifier 701–702*
push-pull amplifier 735–736*
Power factor: alternating current 7
Power resistor 781–782
Power supply, electronic 359–360
Power transformer 950–955
bushings 954–955
circuit model 952–953
configuration 950–951
cooling 954
efficiency 954
percent impedance 953
principles of operation 951–952
transforming three-phase power 953–954
PPM *see* Pulse-position modulation
Preamplifier 702*
Printed circuit 702–710*
applications 703–708
hybrid circuits 708
integrated circuits 708
manufacturing processes 708–710
printed wiring 703–705
technology 702–703
thick-film circuits 705–707
thin-film circuits 707–708
Privacy systems (scrambling) 710–711*
data 710–711
television signal scrambling 922
video 711
voice 710
Programmable calculator 98–99
Programmable read-only memory 180
semiconductor devices 812
Programming languages 711–725*
Ada 724–725
aggregate data types 715–716
ALGOL 722
APL 723–724
applicative 720
BASIC 722–723
binding attributes to variables 716–717
C language 724
COBOL 722
comparison with data flow systems 229–230
data types 714–716
defining new data types 721
digital computer programming 256
expressions 712
FORTRAN 721–722
fourth-generation languages 383–384*
functions 719–721
object-oriented 720–721
objects, variables, and identifiers 712
parameters 717–719
Pascal 724
PL/1 723
procedures 713–714
references 714–714
scalar data types 714
SNOBOL 724
statements 712–713
Programming languages (*cont.*):
structure of 712–714
PROM *see* Programmable read-only memory
PSK *see* Phase-shift keying
Public-key encryption 176
algorithm 210
Pulse amplifier: video amplifier 984*
Pulse-amplitude modulation 727
pulse modulator 733
time-division switching networks 900
Pulse-code modulation 729
applications 729–732
digital filters 732
digital transmission 732
electronic switching 731
optical-fiber transmission systems 731–732
optical sound disk player 642–643
pulse modulator 734–735
radio set AN/TRC 730
synchronization of transmitter and receiver 731
telephone systems 730–731
time-division switching networks 900–902
Pulse-duration modulation 727–728
pulse modulator 733–734
Pulse generator 725–726*
blocking oscillator 93–94*
digitally controlled 726
pulse-forming networks 726
Pulse modulation 578, 726–733*
applications of pulse-code modulation 729–732
basic concepts 727
modulator *see* Pulse modulator
principles of operation 726–729
pulse-amplitude modulation *see* Pulse-amplitude modulation
pulse-code modulation *see* Pulse-code modulation
pulse-duration modulation *see* Pulse-duration modulation
pulse-position modulation *see* Pulse-position modulation
Pulse modulator 733–735*
commutation 733
pulse-amplitude modulation 733
pulse-code modulation 734–735
pulse-position modulation 733–734
pulse-width modulation 733–734
Pulse-position modulation 728–729
pulse modulator 733–734
Pulse transformers 735*
Pulse-width modulation *see* Pulse-duration modulation
Pulsed gas laser 489–490
Push-pull amplifier 735–736*
driver stage 736
operation 735–736
phase inverter 666–667*

Q (electricity) 736*
Q meter 736–737*
coding and matrixing system 279–280
compatibility with monophonic and stereophonic systems 280
discrete system 280
Quantum electronics 737–738*
applications of lasers 738
nonlinear optical phenomena 738
stimulated emission and amplification 737
Quartz clock 738*

Radar 738–750*
antenna 746–748
automatic frequency control 84*
carrier-frequency bands 741
cathode-ray tube 117
clutter 743
composition of systems 745–750
continuous-wave radar 195–198*
detection process 743–744
display and control 749–750
Doppler *see* Doppler radar
echo box 291*
fundamentals of operation 739–740
historical development 738–739
kinds 739
microwaves 549–550
monopulse radar 582–583*
moving-target indication 583–584*
noise 742–743
passive radar 661*
propagation 741–742
radar range equation 740–741
radome 768*
receiver and signal processor 749
synthetic aperture radar 748–749
target characteristics 742
tracking 744–745
transmitter 745–746
Radar-absorbing materials 750–751*
Radio 751–753*
amateur radio 19–20*
amplitude modulation *see* Amplitude-modulation radio
antenna *see* Antenna
diode detectors 38
Federal Communications Commission 753
frequency-modulation *see* Frequency-modulation radio
frequency separation 753
methods of information transmission 752
mobile *see* Mobile radio
receiver *see* Radio receiver
technical history 751–752
transmitter *see* Radio transmitter
uses 752–753
Radio-frequency amplifier 31, 753–755*
basic circuit 753–754
capacitive feedback 754–755
cascode circuit 755
high-frequency limit 754
Radio-frequency impedance measurements 319, 755–761*
bridge methods 756–758
resonance methods 760
slotted lines and six-port methods 760–761
vector voltmeter method 758–760
voltage-current method 758
Radio-frequency measurement 392–394
heterodyne frequency meters 394
Radio-frequency measurement (*cont.*):
microwave measurements 393
spectrum analyzer 839–841*
transfer oscillator methods 394
Radio-frequency meter 388–392
audio-frequency bridge methods 391
direct-comparison methods 391–392
frequency counter 392
moving-coil type 389–390
moving-iron meter 390–391
reed type 389
Radio paging systems 575, 761–762*
encoders 762
FM transmission 401
paging formats 761
paging receivers 761–762
Radio receiver 762–766*
amplification 762–763
automatic frequency control 84*
automatic gain control 84–85*
conversion methods 763
detection 762
detector 246*
double-conversion 764
frequency modulation 765–766
heterodyning 763–764
image signals 764
mixer 573*
noise 763
selection 762
selectivity 798*
single sideband 766
size 765
superheterodyne receiver 763–764, 870–871*
synthesized 765
tuning 764
Radio transmitter 766–768*
amplitude modulation 766–767
frequency modulation 767
single sideband/independent sideband 767–768
Radiometry: microwave noise standards 561–562
microwaves 550
Radome 768*
Ragazzini, J.R. 48
RAM *see* Random-access memory
Randall, R.H. 48
Random-access memory: chip types and technologies 179–180
semiconductor read/write RAMs 811–812
256K-bit chips 179
RC-coupled amplifier 30, 996–998
RCT *see* Reverse-conducting thyristor
Reactance 768–769*
Read, W.T. 567
Read-only memory 180
ovonic memory switch 412
semiconductor devices 812
Real-time systems 769–770*
artificial intelligence and expert systems 769–770
evolution 769
real-time simulation 770
types 769
Reciprocity principle 770–772*
antenna 63
electrical networks 771
electrostatic systems 771

Reciprocity principle (*cont.*):
examples of reciprocal systems 770
Rayleigh's theorem 770–771
Rectifier 772–774*
bridge rectifier circuits 773
controlled rectifier 198*, 774
current ratings 774
full-wave rectifier circuits 772–773
half-wave rectifier circuit 772
inverse voltage 774
parallel rectifiers 773
polyphase rectifier circuits 773
ripple voltage 785*
semiconductor *see* Semiconductor rectifier
Rectifier diode 264
Schottky silicon 816–817
silicon 814–816
Rectifier voltmeter 1012–1013
Reeves, H.A. 729
Reflector antenna 70–71
Regeneration 774–775*
Regenerative comparator 154
Regenerative detector 40–41
Regulation 775*
Relaxation oscillator 775*
blocking oscillator 93–94*
multivibrator *see* Multivibrator
Reluctance 775–776*
in parallel 776
in series 776
Repulsion-vane ammeter 22
Resistance *see* Electrical resistance
Resistance measurement 776–781*
comparison methods 779–780
direct current 317
high-resistance measurements 780–781
ohmmeter 618–619*
realization of the ohm 776–778
resistance standards 778–779
Wheatstone bridge *see* Wheatstone bridge
Resistive bridge: radio-frequency impedance measurements 758
Resistor 781–783*
adjustable resistors 783
classification by construction 772–773
classification by use 781–782
current-carrying 779
decade 779
integrated circuit resistors 781, 782
potentiometer (variable resistor) 698–699*
power resistor 781–782
wire-wound 782–783
wire-wound standard resistors 778
Resonance (alternating-current circuits) 783–784*
cavity resonator 119–121*
multiple resonance 784
resonant circuit 16–17
series resonance 783–784
tank circuit 908*
universal resonance curve 784
Response 784–785*
Reverse-conducting thyristor 819
rf *see* Radio frequency
rf SQUID 858–859
Ringel, G. 418
Ripple voltage 785*
Rivest, R.L 210
Robotics 785–789*
computer-aided manufacturing 158
intelligent machine 465–467*
Rochelle-electrics *see* Ferroelectrics
Rochelle salt 789*
Roentgen, W.C. 110, 343
ROM *see* Read-only memory
Round, H.J. 325
Rowell, J.M. 472
Russell, F.A. 48
Russell, J.B. 48

# S

Sampling gate *see* Transmission gate
Sampling voltmeter 789–791*
high-frequency 790
noise reduction techniques 791
random-sampling 790–791
sampling technique 789–790
vector 790
Saturation 791*
Saturation current 791*
Sawtooth-wave generator 791–795*
high-frequency limitations 794–795
sawtooth current generation 794
sawtooth voltage generation 792–794
Schering bridge: capacitance measurement 102
Schottky, W. 343
Schottky-barrier diode 569
Schottky diode: silicon rectifier diodes 816–817
Schottky effect 795–796*
Schrieffer, J.R. 863, 973
SCR *see* Silicon-controlled rectifier
Second-harmonic generation 605
Secondary emission 796–798*
Seignette-electrics *see* Ferroelectrics
Seignette salt *see* Rochelle salt
Selectivity 798*
Self-inductance 438
alternating-current circuits 12
measurement 439–440
Semiconductor 798–805*
acceptor atom 4*
amorphous 23–25
barrier layer 802
charge transport at grain boundaries 416
charge-coupled device *see* Charge coupled devices
conduction band 195*
conduction in 799–801
contact barrier 802–803
diode *see* Semiconductor diode
donor atom 286*
electron distribution 799–800
electron-hole recombination 335–337*
elemental semiconductors 801
field emission 382–383*
grain boundaries and electronic properties 415–416
Hall effect 425, 800–801
heterostructures *see* Semiconductor heterostructures
high-temperature devices 433
holes in solids 434–435*
impurity semiconductors 800
injection electroluminescence 325–326
Semiconductor (*cont.*):
integrated circuits *see* Integrated circuits
intrinsic semiconductors 800
ion implantation doping 470
junction diode 476–478*
light-emitting diode 495–497*
materials and their preparation 801–802
memory *see* Semiconductor memories
mobility of carriers 800
photoemission 681–682
preparation of materials 801–802
rectification in 802–805
saturation current 791
semiconducting compounds 801
single-carrier theory 803–804
sputtering 850
surface barrier 802
surface electronics 805
thermionic emission 943
two-carrier theory 804–805
valence band 983*
Semiconductor diode 805–807*
limiter circuit 498–499
photodiode 679*
with *pn* junctions 806–807
without *pn* junctions 805–806
varactor *see* Varactor
Semiconductor heterostructures 807–811*
carrier and optical field confinement 807–808
chemistry 809
fabrication 809–811
heteroepitaxy 809
modulation doping 809
quantum well effects 808–809
Semiconductor laser 490
Semiconductor memories 811–814*
microcomputer 535
nonvolatile memories 812–813
read/write RAMs 811–812
semiconductor technology 813–814
Semiconductor rectifier 814–820*
ASCRs, RCTs, and GTOS 819–820
controlled rectifier 198*
metallic-disk rectifier 534*
point-contact diode 697*
rectifier circuits 817
Schottky silicon rectifier diodes 816–817
silicon-controlled rectifier 817–819
silicon rectifier diodes 814–816
Sensitivity 820*
Series circuit 129, 820*
alternating-current transients 307–308
direct current 267, 268
direct-current transients 305–307
Shamir, A. 210
Shannon, C.E. 89, 312, 442
Shannon's equation (communications bandwidth) 89
Shapiro, S. 472
Shockley, W. 362
Short circuit 130
Shunting 820*
Sideband 820–821*
single *see* Single sideband
Signal generator 821*
Signal-to-noise ratio 821*
Silicon: amorphous 24–25
Silicon-controlled rectifier 814, 817–819
Silicon rectifier diode 814–816
Simulation 822–824*
automata theory 82–84*
Single sideband 824–826*
communications 825–826
frequency stabilization requirements 825
generation 824–825
hf telephony 42
modulation 36
radio receiver 766
radio transmitter 767–768
reception 825
Slide rule 47, 826*
S/N *see* Signal-to-noise ratio
SNOBOL 724
SNR *see* Signal-to-noise ratio
Soft fails 826–829*
ionization density thresholds 828–829
ionization-induced 827–828
microelectronics 826–827
rates for typical devices 829
Software engineering 829–836*
maintenance 831
design data representation 833–834
design of software 830–831
development stages 830–831
functional specification 830
implementation stage 831
methods 831–834
microcomputer 536
requirements definition 830
software management 834–835
software piracy 835
software portability 835
structured design 832–833
structured programming 834
testing the program 831
Sohon, H. 665
Solar cell 836–839*
applications 837–838
arrays 837
characteristics 837
principles of operation 836–837
solar radiation 836
Space charge 839*
crosstalk 204
Spark gap 839*
Spectrum analyzer 839–841*
applications 840–841
integrated optical circuitry 464
operation 839–840
tracking generator 841
Speech recognition 75, 841–847*
Spread spectrum communication 847–849*
chirp modulation 847
direct sequence systems 847–849
frequency-hopped system 849
hybrid systems 849
time hopping 847
Sputtering 849–850*
classification 849
complex materials 850
materials characterization 850
semiconductor devices 850
yields 849–850
Square-law detector 40
SQUID 850–851*, 973
magnetometers 858–859
SRAM *see* Static random-access memory

SSB *see* Single sideband
Standing-wave detector 851*
Static random-access memory 180
Stereophonic disk recording:
compatibility with monophonic system 279
compatibility with quadraphonic system 280
recording system 277
reproducing system 277–278
side thrust 279
surface noise 279
tracing distortion 278–279
vertical tracking angle 279
Stereophonic FM radio broadcasting 400
Stereophonic headphones 431–432
Storage tube 851–852*
direct-view 852
electrical 851–852
operation 851
Stored-program digital computer 248–250
Stream cipher 211–212
Submarine cable: coaxial cable 143
coaxial cable communications system 151–152
Summing amplifier 34
Supercomputer 852–855*
array processing 854
circuitry 854
interleaved memory 854
multiprocessing 855
vector processing 854–855
Superconducting computers 855–858*
advantages of Josephson technology 856–857
disadvantages of Josephson technology 857
limitations on cycle time 855–856
performance 855
progress and prospects 858
Superconducting devices 858–862*
cryotron 205*
digital computer elements 859–860
electromagnetic radiation detectors 861–862
signal processing devices 860–861
SQUID *see* SQUID
standards 861
switching circuit 891–892
Superconducting quantum interference device *see* SQUID
Superconductivity 862–870*
basic experimental properties 863–864
electrical resistance 864
flux quantization 869
Ginzburg-Landau theory 868
high-frequency electromagnetic properties 866
isotope effect 866–867
Josephson effect 472–475*
magnetic properties 864–866
microscopic (BCS) theory 868–869
nonlocal theory 868
pair tunneling 870
quasiparticle tunneling 869–870
theory 867–869
thermal properties 866
two-fluid model 867–868
Superheterodyne receiver 763–764, 870–871*
heterodyne principle 427–428*
Superposition theorem (electric networks) 871–872*
mathematical definition 871
uses 871–872
Suppression 872*
Surface acoustic-wave devices 872–875*
background 872
bandpass filters 873–874
oscillators 874–875
pulse compression filters 875
resonators 874
transduction 872–873
Surface-mount technology 875–878*
cleaning 877
component identification 876
component placement 876
repair and rework 877
soldering 876–877
testability 877–878
Surface physics 878–883*
desorption 243–246*
Surging 883*
Susceptance 883*
Sweep generator 883–885*
circular sweep generation 884
hyperbolic sweep generation 884–885
linear sweep generation 883–884
rotating radial sweep generation 884
Switched capacitor 885–887*
analog operations 886
equivalent resistance 886
filter design 887
integrator circuits 885–886
Switching circuit 887–892*
basic combinational circuits 887–888
basic sequential circuits 888–889
connecting circuits 889
counting circuits 891
functional characteristics 887–891
lockout circuits 889–890
performance characteristics 891–892
register circuits 890–891
selecting circuits 889
translating circuits 890
Switching gate 409
Switching systems (communications) 892–904*
alternative switching techniques 903
crossbar switch 895–896
data communications 225
direct control systems 894–895
electromechanical switches 894–898
electronic switches 898–904
indirect control systems 895
message switching systems 903–904
No.1A electronic system 898–899
No.4A crossbar system 898
No.5 system 896–897
numbering plan 893
packet switching 657–658*
PCM electronic switching 731
signaling and control 892–893
space-division switching networks 899–900
switching circuit 887–892*
switching connectives 893–894
system fundamentals 892–894
Switching systems (communcations) (*cont.*):
time-division switching networks 900–903
toll calling 897–898
use of coordinate switches 895
Switching theory 904–906*
combinational circuits 904–905
sequential circuits 905–906
Symbolic mathematical computation 906–908*
Synchronization 908*
Synchronous data transmission 225
Synchronous detector 41
Synchroscope 908*
Synthetic aperture radar 748–749


# T


Tank circuit 908*
Tarjan, R. 418
Taut-band ammeter 21
TED *see* Transferred electron device
Teleconferencing 908–909*
audio communication 909
computer conferencing 909
facsimile communications 909
graphic communications 909
telemeeting 908–909
teleseminar 908
teletext and videotext 988–989*
video and videographic communication 909
video telephone conferencing 988
Telegraphy 356
amplitude-modulation telegraphy 42
FM signaling 402
teletypewriter 917–919*
Telephone 909–913*
amplitude-modulation telephony 42
anti-sidetone network 911
business terminals 912
chassis 911
data communications network 224–225
dial 911
digital transmission 912–913
pulse-code modulation systems 730–731
receiver 910
ringer 911
single-sideband hf telephony 42
special features 911–912
switchhook 911
switching systems (communications) 892–904*
switching theory 904–906*
teleconferencing 909
teleterminal 914–917*
transmitter 910
video telephone 987–988*
Teleprocessing 913–914*
hardware 913–914
logical communications support 913
software 914
Teleterminal 914–917*
implementation 916–917
service example 915–916
user interface 915
Teletypewriter 917–919*
components 917–919
Teletypewriter (*cont.*):
for the deaf 919
Television 919–923*
bandwidth 921
broadcasting 43
cable television 141–142
camera *see* Television camera
camera tube *see* Television camera tube
cathode-ray tube 110–118*
closed-circuit television 141–142*
color *see* Color television
frequency 921
grades of service 923
picture tube 689–691*
portable TV displays 348–349
receiver *see* Television receiver
recording programs 922–923
scanning 919–921, 937–938
signal scrambling 711, 922
sound transmission 921–922
teleconferencing 909
teletext and videotext 923
transmitter *see* Television transmitter
Television camera 923–927*
color television 145–146
essential elements 923–926
typical configurations 926–927
Television camera tube 927–932*
image isocon 928
image orthicon 927–928
photoconductive tubes 929–930
silicon intensifier 930–931
solid-state imager 931
Television receiver 932–937*
automatic frequency control 84*
cascode amplifier 109*
color receivers 934–936
monochrome receivers 932–934
sound reproduction 936–937
video amplifier 984*
Television scanning 937–938*
color coding 938
interlaced scanning 937
lines and frequency of scanning 937–938
resolution 938
Television transmitter 938–941*
designs 941
power 939
signal characteristics 938–939
transmitting antennas 939–941
Tellegen, B.D.H. 343, 420, 548
Thermal ammeter 22–23
Thermal converters 941–942*
ac-dc transfer instrument 942
basic form 941–942
Thermionic emission 942–943*
metals 943
Richardson equation 942–943
semiconductors 943
Schottky effect 795–796*
thermionic tube 943–944*
work function (electronics) 1027*
Thermionic tube 943–944*
Thermoammeter *see* Thermal ammeter
Thermovoltmeter 1012
Thévenin, M.L. 944
Thévenin's theorem (electric networks) 604, 944–946*
Thompson, A.M. 104
Thompson, J.J. 81, 110, 343
Thompson-Lampard capacitor 104

Thomson, W. *see* Lord Kelvin
Thyristor *see* Controlled rectifier
Time constant 946–947*
  capacitance measurement 103
Time-division multiplexing 37, 586
  crosstalk 204–205
  electrical communications 313
  switching systems 902–903
Townsend, J.S. 302, 947
Townsend discharge 216, 406, 947*
Transducer 947–950*
  development 947–948
  electret *see* Electret transducer
  high-polymer transducer 430–432*
  loudspeaker *see* Loudspeaker
  microphone 538–543*
  optical fiber transmission 949–950
  sensors and actuators 947
  types 948–949
Transferred-electron device 567–568
Transformer 950–957*
  audio and video 955–956
  audio- and radio-frequency 955–957
  bridge method for radio-frequency impedance measurement 756–757
  coupled circuits 202
  distortion in audio- and radio-frequency transformers 956
  ferrite devices 377
  ideal transformer 201
  impedance matching 437
  phase inverter 667
  power *see* Power transformer
  pulse transformers 735*
  rf and i-f 956–957
Transformer-coupled amplifier 30
Transistor 957–961*
  action 958–960
  biasing *see* Bias of transistors
  bipolar *see* Bipolar transistor
  classification 957–958
  connection 961–964
  field-effect *see* Field-effect transistor
  high-electron-mobility transistor 428–430*
  history 362
  junction *see* Junction transistor
  limiter circuit 499
  manufacture 961
  negative-resistance devices 599
  ovonic threshold switch 412
  phototransistor 687*
  point-contact *see* Point-contact transistor
  power switching 960
  soft fails 826–827
  voltage regulator 1006–1007
Transistor amplifier 25–26
  basic principles 25
  cascode amplifier 109*
  potential distribution 25–26
Transistor connection 961–964*
  bipolar transistor 961–963
  field-effect transistor 963–964
Transmission gate 408–409
Transmission lines 964–967*
  characteristic impedance 965
  circuit elements 967
  coaxial 964–965
  coaxial cable 142–144*
  delay line 241–242*
  distortionless line 965
Transmission lines (*cont.*);
  electrical loading 316–317*
  electromagnetic wave transmission 332–334
  microwave *see* Microwave transmission lines
  neper 599–600*
  open-wire 964
  principal mode 965
  pulse transients 966
  reflection coefficient 966
  sheathed cables 965
  standing waves 966–967
  tapered 967
  transmission-line equations 965–966
  traveling waves 965
TRAPATT diode *see* Trapped-plasma avalanche-triggered transit diode
Trapped-plasma avalanche-triggered transit diode 568–569
Traveling-wave tube 967–969*
  backward-wave tube 85–86*
  beam collector 969
  electron gun 967–968
  focusing methods for the beam 968–969
  slow-wave circuit 969
Trigger circuit 969–971*
  oscillator trigger generator 655
  peaking (differentiating) circuits 970
  ringing circuits 970–971
Triode:
  clamping circuit 139
  clipping action 140–141
Tuned amplifier 30, 998–999
  intermediate-frequency amplifier 467*
Tuning 971*
  tuned amplifier 30
Tunnel diode 569, 599, 807, 971–972*, 973
Tunneling cryotron 205
Tunneling in solids 972–973*
  Josephson effect 472, 973
  tunnel diode *see* Tunnel diode
  tunnel junctions between metals 973
Turan, P. 419
Turing, A.M. 82
Turing machine 82–83
Tutte, W. 419
Two-reflector antenna 71

U

Uhlenbeck, G. 418
Ultraviolet erasable programmable read-only memory 180
Unijunction transistor 961
Untuned amplifier 30
UVPROM *see* Ultraviolet erasable programmable read-only memory

Vacuum capacitor 107
Vacuum tube 973–981*
  amplifiers 29–30
Vacuum tube (*cont.*):
  basic operation 974
  cathode materials 975
  classification 973–974
  electrode configuration 975–978
  field-emission tubes 981
  frequency and gain limitations 980
  history 361–362
  interelectrode capacitance 980
  lighthouse tube 980–981
  microwave *see* Microwave tube
  saturation current 791
  structure and fabrication 974–975
Vacuum-tube voltmeter 981–983*
  measurement of ac voltages 981–982
  measurement of dc voltages 981
  replacement by solid-state devices 982–983
Valence band 983*
Vapor-phase epitaxy: semiconductor heterostructure fabrication 810
Varactor 548, 983*
  frequency modulator 402–403
  frequency multiplier 403–404
  microwave 569–570
  parametric amplifier component 659
  voltage-controlled oscillator 668
Variable capacitor 107
Varian, S. 343
Varian, W. 343
Varistor 983–984*
Vertical metal-oxide semiconductor 961
Vestigial-sideband modulation 34
Video amplifier 984*
Video disk recording 984–988*
Video magnetic recording 525
Video telephone 987–988*
  video conferencing 988
  video transmission 987–988
Videotext and teletext 923, 988–989*
VMOS *see* Vertical metal-oxide semiconductor
Voice response 989–996*
  assessment of systems 995–996
  low-cost implementations 994–995
  parameterized systems 990–993
  phonemic synthesizers 993
  reproduction of stored speech 990
  text-to-speech synthesizers 993–994
  word concatenation systems 990
Volt-ohm-milliammeter 996*
  multimeter 586*
Voltage: Kirchhoff's voltage law 482–483
  ripple voltage 785*
  sawtooth voltage generation 792–794
Voltage amplifier 34, 996–1001*
  difference amplifiers 1000–1001
  direct-coupled amplifier 1000
  grounded-gate amplifier 1000
  integrated amplifier 1001
  preamplifier 702*
  RC-coupled amplifier 996–998
  source and emitter-follower stages 999
  tuned amplifier 998–999
Voltage-controlled oscillator 668
Voltage measurement 1001–1005*
  alternating current 318, 1003–1004
Voltage measurement (*cont.*):
  digital voltmeter 264*
  direct current 317–318, 1002–1003
  frequencies above 1MHz 1004–1005
  potentiometer (voltage meter) 699–701*
  pulse measurements 1005
  sampling voltmeter 789–791*
  vacuum-tube voltmeter 981–983*
  volt-ohm-milliammeter 996*
  voltage standards 1001–1002
  voltmeter *see* Voltmeter
Voltage-multiplier circuit 1005–1006*
Voltage regulator 1006–1009*
  diode regulator circuit 1006
  electronic 1006–1007
  induction 1008–1009
  power-system 1007–1009
  step 1008
  transistor regulator circuits 1006–1007
  Zener diode 1029*
Voltmeter 1009–1013*
  classifications 1009
  digital voltmeter 264*
  electrodynamic 1011–1012
  electronic 1013
  electrostatic 1010–1011
  moving-coil 1009–1010
  moving-iron 1012
  moving-magnet 1010
  rectifier 1012–1013
  sampling voltmeter 789–791*
  thermovoltmeter 1012
  vacuum-tube voltmeter 981–983*
  volt-ohn-milliammeter 996*
Volume control systems 1013–1014*
VSB *see* Vestigial sideband

Wave-shaping circuits 1014*
  function generator 404–405*
  pulse generator 725–726*
  relaxation oscillator 775*
  sawtooth-wave generator 791–795*
  trigger circuit 969–971*
Waveform 1014–1015*
Waveform determination 1015*
Waveguide 1015–1019*
  attenuation of hollow waveguides 1018
  coaxial 1018–1019
  directional coupler 269–270*
  electromagnetic wave transmission in hollow waveguides 331–332
  integrated optics 462–465*
  Maxwell's equations 1015–1016
  microwave transmission lines 571
  microwaves 546–547
  optical 606
  optical modulators 637–638
  rectangular 1016–1918
  shapes 1018
  transmission modes 1016
Wavelength measurement 1019–1020*
  by frequency measurement 1019
  interferometer methods 1019
  Lecher wires 1019–1020

Wavelength measurment (*cont.*):
  standing-wave detector 851*
  standing-wave method 1019
  tuned circuits 1020
Wavemeter 1020–1021*
Wheatstone bridge 1021–1022*
  accuracy 1022
  capacitance measurement 101–102
  Kelvin bridge 481–482*
  radio-frequency impedance
    measurements 756
Wheastsone bridge (*cont.*):
  resistance measurement 779–
    780
  sensitivity 1021–1022
Whitney, H. 419
Wide-area networks 1022–1024*
  architectures 1023
  computer conferencing 909
  purposes 1022–1023
Wiener, N. 312
Wire-wound resistor 778, 782–783
Word processing 1024–1027*
Work function (electronics) 1027*

Y-delta transformations 1027–
  1028*
Yagi-Uda antenna 1028–1029*
Youngs, J.W.T. 418

# Z

Zener, C. 1029
Zener diode 807, 1029*
  direct-coupled amplifier 165
  voltage regulator 1006
Ziv, J. 227
Ziv-Lempel data compression method
  227
Zworykin, V.K. 110